12 $\frac{ов}{3/o}$

Harvard Dictionary of Music

Harvard Dictionary
of Music

Second Edition, Revised and Enlarged

Willi Apel

The Belknap Press of Harvard University Press

Cambridge, Massachusetts

Twelfth Printing, 1979

Library of Congress Catalog Card Number 68-21970
ISBN 0-674-37501-7

Burton L. Stratton, Typographer

Composed on the Intertype Fotosetter by Graphic Services, Inc.

Printed & Bound by Halliday Lithograph Corporation

Printed in the United States of America

Preface to the Revised Edition

In the twenty-five years of its existence, the *Harvard Dictionary of Music* has become a standard book of music literature. Contrary to my assumption —stated in the initial sentence of the original Preface—that it was "predestined to be read without leisure and to be consulted (somewhat like a dentist) in the case of an emergency only," many people have read it extensively, and not a few from cover to cover.

The interest aroused by the book has been reflected by the extraordinarily great number of comments made by colleagues, students, professional musicians, and amateurs, who have expressed approval or disapproval, indicated mistakes, questioned statements, or suggested emendations of various kinds. Moreover, a large amount of research published in books and periodicals has been taken into consideration. All this material has been incorporated in the Second Edition. In addition, the editorial staff of the Harvard University Press has eliminated a great many errors.

In the years since the original publication of this dictionary, the field of musicology has grown enormously, so that it has become virtually impossible for a single individual to be conversant with all the specialized branches of the field. This new and greatly enlarged edition of the dictionary includes the efforts of many persons who gave generously of their time and talents to contribute new articles and revise old ones. Many are eminent scholars, as a glance at the list of contributors will reveal. In numerous instances, contributors assisted with the preparation of articles other than their own. Without the painstaking research and careful checking of all those involved, this edition would be considerably less complete and less accurate.

Since the publications consulted in preparing this revision number in the thousands, it is impossible to cite them in detail. For spellings of composers' names and dates of birth and death, I have relied largely on *Baker's Biographical Dictionary of Musicians,* Fifth Edition, except in the article Editions, for which the sources themselves were followed exactly. Some of the illustrations of instruments are based on N. Bessaraboff's *Ancient European Musical Instruments,* for which grateful acknowledgment is made to the Harvard University Press.

In addition to those whose names appear as contributors, I am especially grateful to the following for their valuable assistance in the preparation of the Second Edition; Luciano Berio, Juilliard School of Music; David Burrows, New York University; Hans Busch and Ralph T. Daniel, Indiana University; Phyllis A. Cooper, Cambridge, Massachusetts; Alice P. Davison, Lincoln, Massachusetts; Hans Eppstein, Stocksund, Sweden; Paul Hooreman, Lausanne, Switzerland; David G. Hughes, Nino Pirrotta, and John M. Ward, Harvard University; Janet Knapp, Brown University; R. B. Lenaerts, Louvain, Belgium; Mary Lou Little, Loeb Music Library, Harvard University; Caroline Lockwood Busch, Bloomington, Indiana; William S. Newman, University of North Carolina; Mary Rasmussen, Durham, New Hampshire; David Stone, Temple University; James Reginald Wilson, Rutgers University; illustrator Carmela Ciampa; research editor Camilla H. Conley; and researchers Henry Gibbons, James Hinchliff, Kathleen Kohl, Keith Larsen, Joel Lazar, Beth Petrow, Margaret Radin, Carl Schmidt, Elizabeth Kady Schmidt, and Paul van Sickle.

Willi Apel

Bloomington, Indiana

Note to the Sixth Printing: It is hardly possible that a publication consisting of specific and detailed information on several thousands of subjects and terms should be free of errors. The *Harvard Dictionary of Music,* Second Edition, is no exception to this rule. In the present printing, many—I would not dare say all—of these errors have been corrected.

W.A.

Contributors

A.B.   André Boucourechliev, Paris (Aleatory music; Atonality; Electronic music; Expressionism; *Musique concrète*).

A.E.   Alfred Einstein, Smith College (Madrigal comedy).

A.G.   Anne Gombosi, All-Newton Music School, West Newton, Mass. (rev. Switzerland).

A.T.D.   Archibald T. Davison, Harvard University (Glee; Hymn, English; Psalter).

A.T.M.   A. Tillman Merritt, Harvard University (Harmonic analysis).

A.W.   Allen Winold, Indiana University (Music therapy).

B.J.O.   Barbara J. Owen, Organ Historical Society (Fuge tune; Organ XII; *Rückpositif;* rev. Tremulant; add. to Vocabulary; *Zymbelstern*).

B.N.   Bruno Nettl, University of Illinois (rev. American Indian music I).

B.S.   Bence Szabolcsi, Bartók Archivium, Budapest (Hungary).

C.B.F.   Charles B. Fisk, Gloucester, Mass. (Organ and related articles).

C.G.R.   Clare G. Rayner, California State College, Long Beach (add. to Dictionaries).

C.T.   Caldwell Titcomb, Brandeis University (rev. Orchestration, various percussion instruments).

D.D.   Dorothea Doig, Athens, Greece (Tests and measurements in music).

D.J.G.   Donald J. Grout, Cornell University (Ballet in opera; Comic opera; Opera and related articles).

D.M.   David Morton, University of California, Los Angeles (Thailand).

D.P.McA.   David P. McAllester, Wesleyan University (American Indian music II).

D.S.   Donald Sur, Seoul, Korea (Korea).

E.A.L.   Edward A. Lippman, Columbia University (Sociology of music).

E.B.H.   Everett B. Helm, *Musical America* (Degrees; Profession of music; Scholarships; Societies).

E.C.G.   Eunice Crocker Gilmore, Wellesley Hills, Mass. (Canzona).

E.C.K.   Ernst C. Krohn, Webster Groves, Mo. (Dulcimer 2).

E.M.R.   Edwin M. Ripin, Forest Hills, N.Y. (Clavichord; Electronic instruments; rev. Piano).

E.R.   Eduard Reeser, Instituut voor Muziekwetenschap, Utrecht (rev. Netherlands).

E.S.	Ezra Sims, Cambridge, Mass. (Microtone and related articles).
E.V.	Edith Vogl, Brookline, Mass. (Czechoslovakia).
E.W.F.	Edward W. Flint, Lincoln, Mass. (Organ I–XI).
E.Z.	Ella Zonis, University of Chicago. (Persia).
F.A.K.	Fritz A. Kuttner, New York, N.Y. (Stroboconn).
F.B.Z.	Franklin B. Zimmerman, University of Pennsylvania (rev. England, Ireland, and related articles).
F.H.	Frank Hubbard, Waltham, Mass. (Harpsichord; Pedal harpsichord; Spinet 1).
F.N.	Frederick Neumann, University of Richmond (*Inégales*).
F.W.S.	Frederick W. Sternfeld, Oxford University (Film music).
G.C.	Grosvenor Cooper, University of Chicago (Accent 1; rev. Meter, Rhythm, and related articles).
G.W.W.	G. Wallace Woodworth, Harvard University (Music appreciation; Symphony).
H.C.S.	H. Colin Slim, University of California, Irvine (rev. Ricercar).
H.G.M.	Henry G. Mishkin, Amherst College (Academy).
H-J.H.	Hans-Jörgen Holman, Andrews University (Norway).
H.K.	Helmut Kallmann, Canadian Broadcasting Corporation (Canada).
H.L.	Hugo Leichtentritt, Harvard University (Music criticism).
H.N.	Hugo Norden, Boston University (Bowing).
H.P.	Henri Pousseur, Malmédy, Belgium (Period; Serial music).
I.B.	Ingrid Brainard, West Newton, Mass. (rev. Ballet; Dance music and related articles).
I.H.	Isobel Henderson, Oxford University (Greece I–III; Pyknon).
J.F.	John Ferris, Memorial Church, Harvard University (Organ I–XI).
J.F.O.	John F. Ohl, Northwestern University (Recorder).
J.H.	John Horton, Brentwood, Essex, England (rev. Denmark, Finland, Sweden).
J.LaR.	Jan La Rue, New York University (Computer; Plate numbers; Style analysis).
J.M.	José Maceda, University of the Philippines (Philippines).
J.O-S.	Juan Orrego-Salas, Indiana University (Latin American music articles).
J.R.W.	John Reeves White, Pro Musica Antiqua, New York, N.Y. (Aleatory music; *Klangfarbenmelodie;* rev. Music criticism).
J.S.	Joel Sheveloff, Boston University (Mazurka; rev. Poland).
J.T.H.	John Tasker Howard (Negro music; American Indian music I).
J.W.	James Walker, Harvard University (Band; Brass band; Military music; Symphonic band).

J.W.W.   John Wesley Work, Fisk University (add. to Negro music; Jazz and related articles).

K.L.   Kenneth Levy, Princeton University (rev. Russia I).

K.N.   Kalman Novak, South End Music Center, Boston (rev. Sight-reading).

L.B.S.   Lincoln B. Spiess, Washington University (Tune book).

L.E.   The Rev. Leonard Ellinwood, Washington, D.C. (Anglican chant; Anglican church music and related articles).

L.G.   Lawrence Gushee, University of Wisconsin (rev. Tonus, Trope 1, 3).

L.G.R.   Leonard G. Ratner, Stanford University (Development).

L.H.   Lloyd Hibberd, West Texas State University (Blues; Dictionaries).

L.H.M.   Lawrence H. Moe, University of California, Berkeley (Passamezzo, Romanesca, and related dances).

M.H.   Mantle Hood, University of California, Los Angeles (Bali; Ethnomusicology; Java).

M.K.   Masakata Kanazawa, Tokyo (Japan and related articles).

M.V.   Milos Velimirović, Yale University (Bulgaria; Gusle; Yugoslavia).

N.P.   Norman Phelps, Ohio State University (Theory).

N.S.   Nicolas Slonimsky, University of California, Los Angeles (Russia II).

O.A.   Olga Averino, Longy School of Music, Cambridge, Mass. (rev. Voice).

O.W.   Owen Wright, University of London (Arab music).

P.A.   Putnam Aldrich, Stanford University (Ornamentation and related articles).

P.L.M.   Philip Lieson Miller, New York Public Library (Phonograph).

R.A.   Ross Allen, Indiana University (Radio and television broadcasting).

R.A.R.   Robert A. Rosevear, University of Toronto (Music education).

R.B.   Rose Brandel, Hunter College of the City University of New York (Africa).

R.C.P.   Rulan C. Pian, Harvard University (China and related articles).

S.B.   Steven Barwick, Southern Illinois University at Carbondale (rev. Spain and related articles).

S.K.   Sylvia Kenney, Smith College (rev. Descant; Discant).

T.J.Y.   T. J. Young, Wellington, New Zealand (Australia II).

T.V.K.   Trân Van Khê, Centre National de Recherche Scientifique, Paris (Vietnam).

V.H.D.   Vincent H. Duckles, University of California, Berkeley (rev. Libraries).

V.P.D.   Vernon Perdue Davis, Courtland, Virginia (Liturgical books III; Response; Suffrages).

V.Y.	Victor Yellin, New York University (United States).
V.Z.	Victor Zuckerkandl, St. John's College, Annapolis (Schenker system).
W.C.	William Christ, Indiana University (add. to Degrees).
W.D.D.	William D. Denny, University of California, Berkeley (Böhm system; Orchestration; various instruments).
W.H.C.	William H. Cavness, WGBH, Boston (rev. Radio and television broadcasting).
W.K.	Walter Kaufmann, Indiana University (India).
W.P.	Walter Piston, Harvard University (Harmonic rhythm).

Abbreviations

Abbreviations used in this dictionary are grouped in the following sections below: Periodicals; Books; Collective Publications; Signs and Symbols.

Periodicals

Reference is usually made by annual volume numbers (i, ii, iii), if a list of contents is given with the volume. Otherwise, copy or page numbers are added. Special methods of reference (e.g., when volume numbering is inconsistently used) are indicated below. When the title of an article is essentially identical with that of the subject under consideration, this title is usually omitted. "Editions" refers to the article on Editions, historical, in the body of the book.

AM	*Acta musicologica,* 1928–; the first two volumes were published as *Mitteilungen der internationalen Gesellschaft für Musikwissenschaft.*
AMF	*Archiv für Musikforschung,* 1936–43.
AMW	*Archiv für Musikwissenschaft,* 1918–27; 1952–.
AnM	*Anuario musical,* 1946–.
AnnM	*Annales musicologiques,* 1953–.
BAMS	*Bulletin of the American Musicological Society,* 1936–48.
BJ	*Bach Jahrbuch,* 1904–.
BSIM	Abbreviation for a monthly publication that appeared from 1905 to 1914 under five different titles, as follows: i–iii, *Le Mercure musical;* iv–v, *Bulletin français de la Société internationale de musique;* vi–vii, *S.I.M. revue musicale mensuelle;* viii–ix, *Revue musicale S.I.M.;* x, *La Revue musicale S.I.M.* See also *RMC.*
BUM	*Bulletin de la société "Union musicologique,"* 1921–26.
DM	*Die Musik,* 1901–15 in 24 copies per year, numbered i.1–i.24 to xiv.1–xiv.24; 1922–42 in 12 copies per year, numbered xv.1–xv.12, etc.
GSJ	*The Galpin Society Journal,* 1948–.
JAMS	*Journal of the American Musicological Society,* 1948–.
JMP	*Jahrbücher der Musikbibliothek Peters,* 1894–1940.
JMT	*Journal of Music Theory,* 1957–.
JMW	*Jahrbücher für musikalische Wissenschaft,* 2 vols., 1863, 1867.
KJ	*Kirchenmusikalisches Jahrbuch,* 1886–1938, 1950–; preceded by *Cäcilien Kalender,* 1876–85.
LRM	*La Rassegna musicale,* 1928–.
MA	*The Musical Antiquary,* 1909–13.
MD	*Musica disciplina,* 1948–; the first volume was published as *Journal of Renaissance and Baroque Music,* 1946–47.
MF	*Die Musikforschung,* 1948–.
MfM	*Monatshefte für Musik-Geschichte,* 1869–1905.
ML	*Music and Letters,* 1920–.
MM	*Modern Music,* 1924–46.
MQ	*The Musical Quarterly,* 1915–.
MR	*The Music Review,* 1940–.
Notes	*Notes for the Music Library Association,* Series One, nos. 1–15, July 1934–December 1942; Second Series i, 1, December 1943.

PAMS	*Papers Read by Members of the American Musicological Society,* 1936–41; this periodical appeared under various similar titles.
PMA	*Proceedings of the [Royal] Musical Association,* 1874–; the designation *Royal* was added beginning with vol. lxxi.
RBM	*Revue belge de musicologie,* 1946–.
RCG	*Revue du chant grégorien,* 1892–1939.
RdM	*Revue de musicologie,* 1922–; preceded by *Bulletin de la Société française de musicologie,* 1917–21. Three volumes (1942–44) appeared under the title *Société française de musicologie, rapports et communications.* References are made by year and page. The volume numbering is inconsistent.
RG	*Revue grégorienne,* 1911–; there was an English language edition for the years 1954–58.
RM	*La Revue musicale,* 1920–. References are made to year (1920, etc.) and number.
RMC	*La Revue musicale,* ed. J. Combarieu, 1901–10; the first volume was called *Revue d'histoire et de critique musicales;* in 1911 it was merged with *BSIM.*
RMI	*Rivista musicale italiana,* 1894–1955.
SIM	*Sammelbände der internationalen Musikgesellschaft,* 1899–1914.
SJ	*Schweizerisches Jahrbuch für Musikwissenschaft,* 1924–38.
StM	*Studien zur Musikwissenschaft* (Beihefte der *Denkmäler der Tonkunst in Österreich*), 1913–34, 1955–.
TG	*La Tribune de Saint-Gervais,* 1895–1929.
TV	*Tijdschrift der Vereeniging voor Noord-nederlands Muziekgeschiedenis,* 1882–. Vols. xviiff entitled *Tijdschrift voor Muziekwetenschap.*
VMW	*Vierteljahrsschrift für Musikwissenschaft,* 1885–94.
ZIM	*Zeitschrift der internationalen Musikgesellschaft,* 1899–1914.
ZMW	*Zeitschrift für Musikwissenschaft,* 1918–35.

Books

AdHM	G. Adler, *Handbuch der Musikgeschichte,* 2 vols., 1930.
ApGC	W. Apel, *Gregorian Chant,* 1958.
ApMZ	W. Apel, *Musik aus früher Zeit für Klavier,* 2 vols., 1934.
ApNPM	W. Apel, *The Notation of Polyphonic Music 900–1600,* 5th ed., 1961.
AR	*Antiphonale sacrosanctae Romanae ecclesiae,* 1949 (no. 820A, edition in neumatic signs).
BeMMR	H. Besseler, *Die Musik des Mittelalters und der Renaissance,* 1931 (part of *BüHM*).
BG	Bach-Gesellschaft, *Johann Sebastian Bachs Werke,* 46 vols., (1851–1900).
BüHM	E. Bücken, ed., *Handbuch der Musikwissenschaft,* 13 vols., 1927–31.
BuMBE	M. F. Bukofzer, *Music in the Baroque Era,* 1947.
BWV	W. Schmieder, ed., *Bach-Werke-Verzeichnis,* 1950–61.
CS	C.-E.-H. de Coussemaker, *Scriptorum de musica medii aevi novam seriem a Gerbertina alteram collegit nuncque primum edidit E. de Coussemaker,* 4 vols., 1864–76; fac. ed., 1931, 1963.
DdT	*Denkmäler deutscher Tonkunst,* 65 vols., 1892–1931 (see Editions XIII).
DTB	*Denkmäler der Tonkunst in Bayern,* 36 vols., 1900–31 (see Editions XIV).
DTO	*Denkmäler der Tonkunst in Österreich,* 115 vols., 1894– (see Editions XV).
EiBM	A. Einstein, *Beispielsammlung zur Musikgeschichte,* 1930 (incorporated in his *A Short History of Music,* 2nd ed., 1938).
GD	G. Grove, *Grove's Dictionary of Music and Musicians,* 4th ed. (H. C. Colles), 5 vols., 1940.
GDB	G. Grove, *Grove's Dictionary of Music and Musicians,* 5th ed. (E. Blom), 9 vols., 1954.

GéHM	T. Gérold, *Histoire de la musique des origines à la fin du XIV ͤ siècle,* 1963.
GR	*Graduale sacrosanctae Romanum ecclesiae,* 1961 (no. 696, edition in neumatic signs).
GrHWM	D. J. Grout, *A History of Western Music,* 1960.
GS	M. Gerbert, *Scriptores ecclesiastici de musica sacra potissimum,* 3 vols., 1784; fac. ed., 1931, 1963.
HAM	*Historical Anthology of Music,* ed. A. T. Davison and W. Apel, 2 vols., rev. ed., 1949, 1950.
LavE	A. Lavignac, *Encyclopédie de la musique,* 1913–31; *Histoire:* i.1–5; *Technique:* ii.1–6.
LBCM	P. Lang and N. Broder, ed., *Contemporary Music in Europe,* 1965 (also in *MQ* li).
LU	*Liber usualis missae et officii,* 1961 (no. 801, edition in neumatic signs).
MaMI	S. Marcuse, *Musical Instruments: A Comprehensive Dictionary,* 1964.
MGG	*Die Musik in Geschichte und Gegenwart,* ed. F. Blume, 13 vols. to date, 1949–.
NBA	*Neue Ausgabe Sämtlicher Werke* [J. S. Bach], 1954; 8 ser. (projected *c.* 84 vols.); each vol. has a summary (Kritischer Bericht) in a separate vol.
NOH	*New Oxford History of Music,* vols. i–iii, 1954–60.
OH	*The Oxford History of Music,* vols. i–vi, 1901–05; mainly vol. i.
ReMMA	G. Reese, *Music in the Middle Ages,* 1940.
ReMR	G. Reese, *Music in the Renaissance,* rev. ed., 1959.
RiHM	H. Riemann, *Handbuch der Musikgeschichte,* 5 vols., 1904–13.
RiMB	H. Riemann, ed., *Musikgeschichte in Beispielen,* 1912.
RISM	*Répertoire international des sources musicales,* 1960–.
SaHMI	C. Sachs, *The History of Musical Instruments,* 1940.
SaRM	C. Sachs, *Real-Lexikon der Musikinstrumente,* 1913.
SchGMB	A. Schering, ed., *Geschichte der Musik in Beispielen,* 1931.
SSR	O. Strunk, ed., *Source Readings in Music History from Classical Antiquity through the Romantic Era,* 1952.
TaAM	G. Tagliapietra, ed., *Antologia di musica . . . per pianoforte,* 18 vols., 1931–32.
WoGM	J. Wolf, *Geschichte der Mensural-Notation von 1250–1460,* 3 vols., 1904.
WoHN	J. Wolf, *Handbuch der Notationskunde,* 2 vols., 1913–19.

Collective Publications

The abbreviation *CP* is used for the following collective publications (reports of congresses, and *Festschriften*):

CP 1900	*Congrès international d'histoire de la musique tenu à Paris . . . 1900* (1901).
CP 1906	*Bericht über den zweiten Kongress der internationalen Musikgesellschaft zu Basel . . . 1906* (1907).
CP 1909	*Haydn-Zentenarfeier: III. Kongress der internationalen Musikgesellschaft, Wien . . . 1909* (1909).
CP 1911	*Report of the Fourth Congress of the International Musical Society, London . . . 1911* (1912).
CP 1924	*Bericht über den musikwissenschaftlichen Kongress in Basel . . . 1924* (1925).
CP 1925	*Bericht über den I. musikwissenschaftlichen Kongress der deutschen Musikgesellschaft in Leipzig . . . 1925* (1926).
CP 1927	*Beethoven-Zentenarfeier Wien . . . 1927: Internationaler musikhistorischer Kongress* (1927).
CP 1930	*Société internationale de musicologie, premier congrès, Liége 1930* (1931).
CP 1939	*Papers Read at the International Congress of Musicology . . . New York . . . 1939* (1944).

CP 1949   Société internationale de musicologie, quatrième congrès, Bâle . . . 1949 (n.d.).
CP 1950   Atti del congresso internazionale di musica sacra . . . Roma . . . 1950 (1952).
CP 1950a Kongress-Bericht Gesellschaft für Musikforschung Lüneburg 1950 (n.d.).
CP 1952   Société internationale de musicologie, cinquième congrès, Utrecht . . . 1952 (1953).
CP 1953   Bericht über den internationalen musikwissenschaftlichen Kongress Bamberg 1953 (1954).
CP 1955   Les Colloques de Wégimont: II–1955: L'Ars nova (1959).
CP 1956   Bericht über den internationalen musikwissenschaftlichen Kongress Wien Mozartjahr 1956 (1958).
CP 1956a Bericht über den internationalen musikwissenschaftlichen Kongress Hamburg 1956 (1957).
CP 1958   Bericht über den siebenten internationalen musikwissenschaftlichen Kongress Köln 1958 (1959).
CP 1961   International Musicological Society: Report of the Eighth Congress New York 1961, vol. i (1961).
CP 1962   Bericht über den internationalen musikwissenschaftlichen Kongress Kassel 1962 (1963).
CP Abert   Gedenkschrift für Hermann Abert (1928).
CP Adler   Studien zur Musikgeschichte: Festschrift für Guido Adler (1930).
CP Anglés   Miscelánea en homenaje a Monseñor Higinio Anglés, 2 vols. (1958, '61).
CP Apel   Essays in Musicology: A Birthday Present for Willi Apel (1967).
CP Bartók   Studia memoriae Belae Bartók sacra (1956).
CP Besseler   Festschrift Heinrich Besseler zum sechzigsten Geburtstag (1961).
CP Blume   Friedrich Blume Festschrift (1963).
CP Borren   Hommage à Charles van den Borren (1945).
CP Borren, 1964   Liber amicorum Charles van den Borren (1964).
CP Closson   Mélanges Ernest Closson (1948).
CP Davison   Essays on Music in Honor of Archibald Thompson Davison (1957).
CP Fellerer   Festschrift Karl Gustav Fellerer zum sechzigsten Geburtstag (1962).
CP Kretzschmar   Festschrift Hermann Kretzschmar (1918).
CP Kroyer   Theodor Kroyer-Festschrift (1933).
CP Laurencie   Mélanges de musicologie offerts à M. Lionel de la Laurencie (1933).
CP Liliencron   Festschrift . . . Rochus Freiherrn von Liliencron (1910).
CP Masson   Mélanges . . . offerts à Paul-Marie Masson, 2 vols. (1955).
CP Nef   Festschrift Karl Nef (1933).
CP Orel   Festschrift Alfred Orel (1960).
CP Osthoff   Festschrift Helmuth Osthoff zum 65. Geburtstage (1961).
CP Reese   Aspects of Medieval and Renaissance Music: A Birthday Offering to Gustave Reese (1966).
CP Riemann   Riemann-Festschrift (1909).
CP Sachs   The Commonwealth of Music in Honor of Curt Sachs (1965).
CP Sandberger   Festschrift . . . Adolf Sandberger (1918).
CP Schering   Festschrift Arnold Schering (1937).
CP Scheurleer   Gedenkboek aangeboden an Dr. D. F. Scheurleer (1925).
CP Schmidt-Görg   Festschrift Joseph Schmidt-Görg (1957).
CP Schneider   Festschrift Max Schneider zum 60. Geburtstag (1935).
CP Schneider, 1955   Festschrift Max Schneider zum achtzigsten Geburtstage (1955).
CP Seiffert   Musik und Bild: Festschrift Max Seiffert (1938).
CP Waesberghe   Organicae Voces: Festschrift Joseph Smits van Waesberghe (1963).
CP Wagner   Festschrift Peter Wagner (1926).
CP Wolf   Musikwissenschaftliche Beiträge: Festschrift für Johannes Wolf (1929).

Signs and Symbols

For the method employed to indicate octaves, see under Pitch names.

* indicates that this subject is covered in a separate article (whose exact title sometimes differs slightly from the starred word, e.g., * Greek music is covered under Greece, * intermezzi under Intermezzo, etc.)

‡ indicates publication consisting mainly or exclusively of music

abbr.	abbreviation, abbreviated	Hung.	Hungarian
		Icel.	Icelandic
add.	addition	ill.	illustration
app.	appendix	It.	Italian
Arab.	Arabic	Jap.	Japanese
bibl.	bibliography	L.	Latin
Bibl.	Bibliothèque, Biblioteca, etc.	lit.	literally, literature
		movt.	movement
Brit.	British	opp.	opposite, facing
Brit. Mus.	British Museum	pl.	plural
c.	circa	Pol.	Polish
Cat.	Catalan	Port.	Portuguese
cent.	century, centuries	Prov.	Provençal
ch.	chapter(s)	Ps.	Psalm
comp., compl.	complete	pub.	published
comp. ed.	complete edition	rev.	revised
Cz.	Czech	rev. ed.	revised edition
Dan.	Danish	repr.	reprinted, reproduced
diss.	dissertation	Rus.	Russian
E., Eng.	English	ser.	series
ed.	editor, edited, edition	Sp.	Spanish
		sup.	supplement
ex.	example	suppl.	supplementary
F.	French	Swed.	Swedish
fac.	facsimile	trans.	translated (by)
fac. ed.	facsimile edition	transcr.	transcribed
G.	German	unpub.	unpublished
Gael.	Gaelic	vol(s).	volume(s)
Gr.	Greek		

Harvard Dictionary of Music

If you want to understand the invisible,
look carefully at the visible.

The *Talmud*

Harvard Dictionary of Music

A

A. (1) See Pitch names; Letter notation; Hexachord; Pitch. (2) On the title page of *partbooks of the 16th century *A* stands for *altus*. In liturgical books it stands for antiphon. (3) *A; à* [It.; F.], to, at, with; e.g., **a piacere; a 2, a 3 voci,* etc.

Ab [G.]. Off, with reference to organ stops or mutes.

Abandonné [F.], **con abbandono** [It.]. Unrestrained, free.

A battuta [It.]. See *Battuta*.

Abbellimenti [It.]. Embellishments, *ornaments.

Abbreviations. The most important abbreviations used in musical notation are indicated in the accompanying illustration.

Abbreviations

Abdämpfen [G.]. To mute, especially kettledrums.

Abduction from the Seraglio. See *Entführung aus dem Serail, Die*.

Abegg Variations. R. Schumann's Variations for piano op. 1, dedicated to his friend Meta Abegg. The first five notes of the theme, a′b′♭ e″g″g″, read, in German pitch names, A-B-E-G-G.

Abendmusik [G.]. Evening musical performances, usually of a religious or contemplative nature. The term applies particularly to the famous concerts started in 1673 by Dietrich Buxtehude in the Marienkirche of Lübeck in North Germany. These took place annually on the five Sundays before Christmas, following the afternoon service, and consisted of organ music and concerted pieces of sacred music for orchestra and chorus [see *DdT* 14]. They continued until 1810. In 1705 J. S. Bach walked 200 miles from Arnstadt to Lübeck to hear the *Abendmusik*.

Lit.: C. Stiehl, *Die Organisten an der St. Marienkirche und die Abendmusiken zu Lübeck* (1885); W. Stahl, *Die Lübecker Abendmusiken* (1937); W. Maxton, in *ZMW* x.

A bene placito [It.]. Same as *a piacere*.

Abgesang [G.]. See *Bar* form.

Abnehmend [G.]. Diminuendo.

Abschieds-Symphonie [G., Farewell Symphony]. Popular name for Haydn's Symphony no. 45 in F-sharp minor, composed in 1772. It refers to the last movement, whose closing section is so designed that the players can leave one by one, the last measures being played by only two violins. This charming jest was meant to inform the Prince of Esterháza, whom Haydn served as a conductor, of the orchestra's desire to leave his summer palace in the country and return to Vienna.

Abschnitt [G.]. Section.

Absetzen [G.]. (1) To separate, either notes [*détaché;* see Bowing (b)] or phrases. (2) In 16th-century terminology, *absetzen in die Tabulatur* means to transcribe (vocal music) into *tablature.

Absolute music. Music that is free from extramusical implications. The term is used most frequently in contradistinction to *program music, in which pictorial or poetic ideas are portrayed. It usually excludes vocal music, especially the type in which the text clearly influences the musical language and structure (e.g., a song by Schubert). Occasionally the term is employed in a stricter sense, excluding not only program and vocal music but also music of a definite emotional character (romantic music), so that Bach and, to some extent, Mozart are considered composers of absolute music.

Absolute pitch [G. *absolute Tonhöhe*]. Properly, "the position of a tone in reference to the whole range of pitch . . . , conceived as independently determined by its rate of vibration" (Webster). Usually, however, the term is used for what might more accurately be called "absolute judgment of (absolute) pitch," i.e., the capacity of a person to identify a musical sound immediately by name, without reference to a previously sounded note of different pitch [see Relative pitch]. This faculty, called in German *absolutes Gehör,* is a tonal memory that is sometimes innate but can also be acquired by training, as recent experiments have shown. The faculty, whether innate or acquired, is found chiefly in persons possessing some degree of musical experience or aptitude but can by no means be considered a yardstick of musical talent. Many instrumentalists have absolute pitch (probably acquired through years of training), but among outstanding composers and performers it is probably as often lacking as not. While Mozart had an extremely acute sense of absolute pitch, Wagner and Schumann are reputed to have lacked it.

Absolute pitch is in various respects a valuable asset to a musician, particularly to a conductor, but it may prove a real inconvenience when music must be transposed in performance to another key, as often happens in vocal music to accommodate the range of the singer. Whether it is an advantage or a disadvantage to hear a composition "all wrong" simply because it is a half-tone higher or lower is indeed questionable. All the discussions about the "true pitch" of Beethoven's C-minor Symphony, for example, are entirely pointless unless the standard pitch of Beethoven's day is taken into account. Since

standard pitch has gradually changed (greatly in the case of Bach), usually to become higher, it could be said that, from the standpoint of absolute pitch, all present-day performances of music written prior to the general acceptance of the modern concert pitch [see Pitch (2)] are "wrong." If a musician with absolute pitch who lived one hundred years ago were alive today, he would be horrified to hear Beethoven's Fifth Symphony played in what would be to him C-sharp minor.

Lit.: C. H. Wedell, *The Nature of the Absolute Judgment of Pitch* (1934); L. A. Petrau, *An Experimental Study of Pitch Recognition* (1932); A. Wellek, *Das absolute Gehör und seine Typen* (1938), bibl.; C. E. Seashore, *The Measurement of Musical Memory* (1917); O. Abraham, in *SIM* iii, viii; F. Auerbach, in *SIM* viii; H. Riemann, in *ZIM* xiii; J. Kobelt, in *AMW* ii, bibl.; G. Révész, "Über die beiden Arten des absoluten Gehörs" (*ZIM* xiv); N. Slonimsky, in *American Mercury* xxi; W. K. Sumner, "A History of Musical Pitch" (*Hinrichsen's Musical Year Book* vii); E. B. Hartman, "The Influence of Practice . . . on the Absolute Identification of Pitch" (*The American Journal of Psychology* lxvii).

Absonia [L.]. See under *Musica ficta* II.

Abstossen [G.]. (1) In violin playing, same as *abgestossen,* i.e., *détaché* [see Bowing (b)]. (2) In organ playing, to take off a stop [see *Ab*].

Abstract music. Same as *absolute music.

Abstrich [G.]. Down-bow.

Abzug [G.]. *Scordatura. Also, older term for *appoggiatura.

Academic Festival Overture. See *Akademische Festouvertüre.*

Academy. A term used for scholarly or artistic societies and musical organizations of various types. The rediscovery, in the late 15th century, of Greek antiquity and Greek literature led to the foundation in 1470 of an Accademia di Platone at the court of Lorenzo de' Medici in Florence, in direct imitation of Plato's Academy. In the 16th century a number of academies were established in France, among them Baïf's Académie de Poésie et Musique (1567), which played a role in the development of the *vers mesurés. With the beginning of the 17th century, the movement spread enormously in Italy; every place of some repute had its *accademia,* and larger cities had numbers of them. They were of two types: (a) Learned societies founded for the promotion of science, literature, and the arts, part of whose activity was the encouragement and cultivation of music. The most famous of these was the A. dei Arcadi of Rome (founded 1692), which included among its members the musicians Marcello, Corelli, A. Scarlatti, and Gluck. Handel attended many meetings but as a foreigner was not eligible for membership. Other institutions of the same type existed in Florence: A. della Crusca (1588), A. dei Filarmonici; in Bologna: A. dei Gelati (1588), A. dei Concordi (1615), A. dei Filomusi (1622); in Venice: A. Pellegrina (1550), A. degli Olimpici; in Verona: A. Filarmonica (1543), probably the earliest musical academy; and elsewhere. (b) Organizations of professional and amateur musicians whose sole purpose was the cultivation of music. The activities of these groups were varied; they gave public and private concerts, carried on research in the history of music and in the science of sound, founded music schools, and even launched operatic enterprises. The most important of these was the A. dei Filarmonici of Bologna, founded in 1666 by Count Vincenzo Carrati, which included among its members such distinguished figures as Bassani (c. 1657–1716), Corelli (1653–1713), Torelli (1658–1709), Domenico Gabrielli (c. 1650–90), Padre Martini (1706–84), Mozart (1756–91), Rossini (1792–1868), and Busoni (1866–1924).

Today there are many similar institutions (some no longer using the name "academy"), which can be divided into three categories: (a) Learned associations, part of whose activity is the promotion of musical studies. They usually have a membership limited to those of demonstrable ability, hold periodic discussions and proceedings that often are published, and generally offer honors, medals, or prizes for achievement in composition or research. Many of these are state-supported: Paris, Institut de France, division Académie des Beaux Arts; Berlin, Akademie der Künste; Brussels, Académie Royale; others in Stockholm and Moscow. (b) Organizations for the presentation of operas and concerts: Paris, Théâtre national de l'Opéra (formerly Académie nationale de Musique); London, Royal Academy of Music and Academy of Ancient Music; Munich, Akademie der Tonkunst; New York, Metropolitan Opera Association (formerly the Academy of Music); Brooklyn, Academy of Music (founded 1861), etc. [see Opera houses]. (c) Institutions of musical education: London, Royal Academy of

Music; Berlin, Staatliche Akademie für Kirchen- und Schulmusik; Munich, Königliche Akademie der Tonkunst (founded 1846); Philadelphia, Academy of Music (1870); New York, Academy of Allied Arts (School of Music, 1928). For a medieval institution of a similar nature, see *Puy*. See also Societies.

Lit.: M. Maylender, *Storia delle accademie d'Italia*, 5 vols. (1926ff); F. A. Yates, *The French Academies of the Sixteenth Century* (1947); N. Morini, *La Reale Accademia filarmonica di Bologna* (1930); G. Turrini, *Riordino della biblioteca . . . della società L'Accademia Filarmonica di Verona . . . 1543–1600* (1933); A. Einstein, in *BAMS* vii, 22; H. Burton, in *RdM* 1955, p. 122 (France, 18th century); *id.*, in *ML* xxxvii.

H.G.M. and W.A.

Acalanto [Port.]. A Brazilian cradle song, also known as *cantigas de ninar*. These have developed within a great variety of folk traditions, including some originating in northeastern Indian cultures that still retain pure Portuguese influences.   J.O-S.

A cappella [It.]. Designation for choral music without instrumental accompaniment. Originally the name referred to unaccompanied church music like that written by Palestrina. Today it is used for all unaccompanied choral music, whether sacred or secular. Historians of the 19th century believed that all "early music" —i.e., music before 1600—was *a cappella*. Recent investigations, however, have clearly shown that instruments played a prominent role in the performance of medieval music, at least as an *ad libitum* addition to or substitution for one voice-part or another [see Performance practice]. Probably it was not until 1450 (motets and Masses of Ockeghem) that purely choral performance became generally accepted and universally practiced in the field of sacred music. Often the term *a cappella* has the connotation of a specific style, namely that of Palestrina.

Lit.: J. Handschin, "Die Grundlagen des a cappella-Stils," in *Hans Häusermann und der Häusermannsche Privatchor* (1929), p. 109; T. Kroyer, "Acappella [sic] oder Conserto?" (*CP Kretzschmar*); *id.*, in *AMW* ii; *id.*, in *AM* vi.

Acathistus. *Akathistos.

Accacciatura. Erroneous spelling for *acciaccatura.

Accelerando [It.]. Becoming faster.

Accent (1) Emphasis on one note or chord. In this sense, the term is equivocal, because the emphasis may be physically discernible, or it may lie solely in the way the listener perceives musical movement. Physically, a note or chord may be louder than its surroundings (dynamic accent), or it may be higher (*tonic accent), or of longer duration (*agogic accent). See Ex. 1. On the other hand, since the listener perceives music as sound in motion, an upbeat (or a more extended anacrusis) is felt as leading somewhere, and the note or chord to which it leads is thus emphasized (accented) in the mind, even if the goal of motion should be softer, lower, or shorter than its surroundings; in like manner, a feminine rhythm is perceived as an accent followed by a movement away from it.

In measure-music [see Measure], both physical and mental accents normally fall on the downbeat, with secondary accents occurring in the middle of the measure in compound meters, e.g., on the third beat in 4/4 time. Frequently, however, irregular accents are found on weak beats [see Syncopation]. Irregular dynamic accent is usually indicated by signs such as *sf*, >, —. Ex. 2 (Mozart, Symphony in G minor no. 40) shows an irregular dynamic accent that is at the same time tonic and agogic. The emphasis on the weak beat is often enhanced by means of striking dissonances, as in Ex. 3. The tonic accent has played a role in the discussions on Gregorian chant and other types of medieval monophonic music.

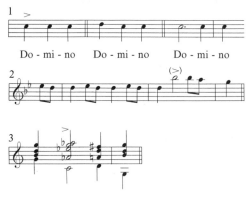

1

Do - mi - no   Do - mi - no   Do - mi - no

2

3

See G. W. Cooper and L. B. Meyer, *The Rhythmic Structure of Music* [1960], *passim;* V. d'Indy, *Cours de composition musicale,* 2 vols. in 3 pts. [1902?–10], vol. i, pp. 29–46.

(2) [F.]. In French music of the 17th and 18th centuries, an ornament belonging to the class of *Nachschläge. In Bach's table of ornaments (*Klavierbüchlein für Wilhelm Friedemann Bach*), a long appoggiatura.

(3) Signs used in ancient Greek writing to indicate a change of pitch of the voice in recitation: *accentus acutus* ´, for a rise; *a. gravis* `, for a lowering; *a. circumflexus* ^, for an inflection (rise, followed by lowering) of the voice. These signs are now thought to be the origin of the (accent) neumes [see Neumes II] and certain other related systems of notation, called *ecphonetic notation.

(4) The notational signs used in Jewish chant [see Jewish music II].   (1) by G.C.

Accentualists. See under Gregorian chant VI.

Accentuation. The proper placement of accents, especially in music set to a text. See Text and music.

Accentus, concentus. Terms introduced (?) by Ornithoparchus (in his *Musicae activae micrologus,* 1517) for two opposite types of plainsong: the simple recitations, such as lesson tones, psalm tones (*accentus*); and the chants having distinctive melodic contours, such as antiphons, responsories, hymns, Mass chants, etc. (*concentus*). The terms also imply a distinction between two kinds of performer: the *accentus* is sung by the priest; the *concentus* by the trained musicians (*schola,* with soloists and choir). See P. Wagner, *Einführung in die Gregorianischen Melodien,* iii (1921), 4.

Acciaccatura. Italian name for an ornament of keyboard (harpsichord) music (*c.* 1675–1725) that calls for the playing, together with the normal note, of its neighboring tone (usually the lower second), which is to be released immediately "as if the key were hot" (Geminiani). This ornament usually occurs in connection with chords, the chords often including two and occasionally even three *acciaccatura* tones. The tones are written as ordinary notes, so that the chord takes on the appearance of an extremely dissonant *tone cluster [Ex. 1]. Such formations occur in several compositions by A. Scarlatti [*Editions X, 13, p. 90] and figure prominently in a sonata by D. Scarlatti [Ex. 2; see *HAM,* no. 274]. A simpler example occurs in the Scherzo of Bach's Partita no. 3 [Ex. 3]. The French counterpart is the *arpègement figuré,* in which the dissonant tone (usually only one) is indicated by a diagonal dash, and which, as the name implies, is performed as an arpeggio [Ex. 4]. A sonata by Blasco de Nebra (*c.* 1750–84) contains similar

forms, in which, however, the dissonant note is obviously intended to be held [Ex. 5; see *HAM*, no. 308].

For an erroneous usage, common in modern writings, of the term *acciaccatura* (often misspelled *accacciatura*), see Appoggiatura III.

Accidentals. I. *General*. The signs used in musical notation to indicate chromatic alterations or to cancel them. The alterations valid for the entire composition are contained in the *key signature, while the term "accidentals" refers specifically to those alterations introduced for single notes. The signs for chromatic alteration, together with their names in English, French, German, Italian, and Spanish, are given in the following table:

	♯	♭	✕
E.	sharp	flat	double sharp
F.	dièse	bémol	double dièse
G.	Kreuz	Be	Doppelkreuz
It.	diesis	bemolle	doppio diesis
Sp.	sostenido	bemol	doble sostenido

	♭♭		♮
E.	double flat		natural
F.	double bémol		bécarre
G.	Doppel-Be		Auflösungszeichen, Quadrat
It.	doppio bemolle		bequadro
Sp.	doble bemol		becuadro

The sharp raises the pitch one semitone, the flat lowers it one semitone; the double sharp and double flat raise and lower two semitones respectively; the natural cancels any of the other signs. The use of the compound signs ♮♯, ♮♭, ♮♮ to cancel partly or entirely a previous ✕ or ♭♭ is quite common but unnecessary. The simple

signs ♯, ♭, ♮ answer the purpose [Ex. 1]. In modern practice a sign affects the note immediately following and is valid for all the notes of the same pitch (but not in different octaves) within the same measure. Modern composers frequently add bracketed accidentals to those demanded by this rule in order to clarify complicated passages or chords.

II. *History*. All the signs used for chromatic alteration developed from the same sign, namely, the letter b, which indicates the whole tone above a. The fact that in the diatonic scale no perfect fourth above f is available necessitated, as early as the 10th century, the introduction of another b, a semitone lower than the diatonic b [see Hexachord]. These two b's were distinguished by their shape, the higher one being written in a square form and called *b quadratum* (also *b durum;* L. *durus,* hard, angular), the lower in a rounded form and called *b rotundum* (also *b molle;* L. *mollis,* soft, round). It is from these designations that the German names *Dur* and *Moll* for major and minor mode are derived.

$$♮ = b \; quadratum$$
$$♭ = b \; rotundum$$

When in the ensuing period the introduction of other chromatic tones became necessary, the square b (*b durum*) and its later modifications (♮, ♯) were used to indicate the higher of two semitones, and the rounded b (*b molle*) or ♭ the lower one. Thus, in early music, ♮f is not f natural but f-sharp; likewise, ♭f is not f-flat, but f (in contradistinction to a previous f-sharp; see Ex. 2, from Frescobaldi's *Canzone,* 1628). Bach

continued to use the sign ♭ for the cancellation of a previous f♯. In Germany, during the 15th century, the square b for *b durum* was erroneously interpreted as the letter h, to which it bears some visual resemblance. Hence, in German terminology h denotes the b natural, and b the b-flat.

In the printed books of the 16th century the sharp sign usually occurs in a diagonal position. The double sharp (used as early as 1615 in G. M. Trabaci's *Il Secondo Libro de ricercare*) originally appeared as a sharp with doubled lines, in either a straight or a diagonal position. The present sign is a simplification of the latter.

In music prior to 1700 (probably even later) an accidental is not valid for the entire measure but only for the next note and immediate repetitions of the same note [see Ex. 3]. This practice

was still observed by Bach, as seen in Ex. 3, reproduced from his autograph of the *Fantasia super Komm heiliger Geist* (fac. ed. by P. Wackernagel, 1950; alto of meas. 6). Note that Bach did not write a flat for the E at the beginning of meas. 7, although it is separated from the preceding E-flat by a bar line.

For the problem of accidentals in music of the 13th to 16th centuries, see *Musica ficta*. See F. Niecks, "The Flat, Sharp, and Natural" (*PMA* xvi).

Acclamation. A type of Byzantine poetry and music that served as a salutation for the emperor (also the empress and the Patriarch) in the ceremonial of the Byzantine court of the 9th and 10th centuries. The acclamations are practically the only type of nonliturgical Byzantine music known today. Acclamations are still used in Russia and the Balkans for welcoming high church dignitaries. Those beginning with the traditional phrase "Many be the years" were called *polychronia*. [See the examples in *ReMMA*, p. 77, and in *MQ* xxiii, 207.]

Lit.: *AdHM* i, 128; E. Wellesz, *A History of Byzantine Music and Hymnography*, rev. ed. (1961), *passim;* H. Tillyard, in *Annual of the British School of Athens* xviii.

Accolade [F.]. *Brace.

Accompagnato [It.]. See Recitative II (c).

Accompaniment. I. The musical background provided for a principal part. For instance, in piano music the left hand often plays chords that are an accompaniment for the melody played by the right hand. Similarly, a solo singer or instrumentalist may be accompanied by a pianist or an orchestra. The auxiliary role of the accompaniment frequently leads to underestimation, by the soloist as well as the audience, of its musical and artistic importance. Vocalists especially are inclined to demand undue subordination of their accompanists, condemning them to complete slavery in questions of interpretation, tempo, dynamics, etc.

The modern church organist, as well as the leader of a choir, is frequently confronted with the problem of providing suitable accompaniment, either improvised or written out, for the singing of the congregation or the chorus. Following are a number of books on this subject: J. F. Bridge, *Organ Accompaniment of the Choral Service* [1885]; D. Buck, *Illustrations in Choir Accompaniment* (1877); W. Hickin, *Pianoforte Accompaniment* (1923); A. H. Lindo, *The Art of Accompanying* (1916); C. W. Pearce, *The Organist's Directory to the Accompaniment of Divine Service* (1908); A. M. Richardson, *Modern Organ Accompaniment* (1907); E. Evans, *How to Accompany at the Piano* [1917]; J. R. Tobin, *How to Improvise Piano Accompaniments* (1956). See also Vamp.

In Roman Catholic services Gregorian chant, although properly monophonic, is usually considered to need organ accompaniment, frequently in the style of 19th-century harmony. Attempts have been made to replace this style with modal harmonies, e.g., H. Potiron, *Practical Instruction in Plainsong Accompaniment* (1949); J. H. Arnold, *Plainsong Accompaniment* [1927]; E. Evans, *The Modal Accompaniment of Plain Chant* [1911] or with even more archaic idioms, such as *quartal harmonies or parallel organum [see Bernard Jones, *An Ambrosian Mass* (1962)].

II. There are many references to instrumental accompaniment of songs in the Bible (accompaniment on some stringed instrument is suggested by the term "Neginoth" in the heading of Ps. 6 in the King James Version; see also Pss. 91 [92] and 143 [144]) and in the writings of the ancient Greeks. Pictorial reproductions and literary documents of the Middle Ages show the use of harps, fiddles, bells, small drums, trumpets, etc., in connection with the monophonic songs of the troubadours and minnesingers, and in conjunction with dance music. In neither ancient nor medieval music was this improvised type of accompaniment ever of a harmonic nature; it was merely a unison (or octave) doubling of the voice-part, with occasional heterophonic elements [see Heterophony]. The same type of accompaniment is to be found in the East, especially China, India, and Arabia. While the texture of polyphonic music of the 9th to 13th centuries (organa, motets) does not permit its separation into parts of greater or less importance, such separation does occur in the French secular compositions of the 14th and early 15th centuries (ballades, virelais by G. de Machaut and his successors [see Ars nova]; chansons of Dufay and his contemporaries [see Burgundian school]). It disappears again with the rise of Flemish sacred music and Flemish counterpoint (Ockeghem, Obrecht), which are essentially opposed to any distinction between principal and auxiliary parts. The instrumental doubling of vocal parts that was occasionally practiced in this period can scarcely be considered an accompaniment. In the 16th century the renewed emphasis on the secular immediately led to a revival of accompanied melody, e.g., in the lute songs of the German Schlick (1512), of the Spanish Valderrabano (1547), and of the English Dowland (1597).

III. A new era of accompaniment began with the period of thoroughbass (baroque period, 1600–1750), which called for a harmonic accompaniment to be improvised upon the notes of the bass. Moreover, the growing interest in florid and singable melody brought about a gradually increasing separation of the musical substance into a predominant melody with subordinate accompaniment (e.g., in the aria). While throughout the baroque period the written-out accompaniment (and consequently also the improvised one) shows many traits of contrapuntal and harmonic interest, it degenerated in the second half of the 18th century into a stereotyped pattern of plain chords, arpeggios, *Alberti-bass figures, etc. As a curiosity it may be mentioned that, about 1760, sonatas were frequently written for the "pianoforte with the accompaniment of a violin or flute" (Mondonville, 1734, see Editions XLIX, 9; Schobert, see DdT 34; Edelmann, see HAM, no. 304), that is, with the violin or flute merely duplicating the upper part of the piano. Thus Samuel Wesley speaks of J. S. Bach's violin sonatas as "six sonatas for harpsichord with an obbligato violin accompaniment."

IV. About 1780 Haydn and Mozart evolved a new type of accompaniment known as accom-panimento obbligato, characterized by a greater individuality of the lower parts, by the occasional introduction of fugal elements, by the occasional shift of the melody from the higher part into a lower part, etc. This style is particularly evident in the quartets written in this period. Because of these efforts Beethoven was able to say of himself: "Ich bin mit einem obligaten Accompaniment auf die Welt gekommen" (I was born with an obbligato accompaniment). What Haydn and Mozart did in the field of instrumental music, Schubert achieved in the field of song, freeing the piano accompaniment from the slavery of mere chord-filling and making it an independent (sometimes the most interesting) part of the composition. Composers such as Schumann, Brahms, and H. Wolf adopted his method, whereas others (e.g., Tchaikovsky) rarely went beyond a chordal accompaniment in lush harmonies of rather ephemeral interest. Other composers (Mahler, Strauss) have repeatedly used the whole orchestra as an instrumental background for a solo singer.

V. The extraordinary growth of accompanied melody in the songs of the 19th century had a deplorable effect upon the minds of musical scholars and editors engaged in the study and publication of early monophonic music (Greek music, exotic melodies, Gregorian chant, the songs of the trouvères, minnesingers, etc.). Numerous volumes have been published in which the melodies of the pre-Christian era or the Middle Ages are coupled with cheap accompaniments in the style of Schumann, Brahms, or Debussy. Even well-known scholars have not withstood this temptation [see O. Fleischer, Reste der altgriechischen Tonkunst (1899) or J. Ribera's edition of the *cantigas]. For literature on the 17th-century accompaniment see Thoroughbass. See also Additional accompaniment.

Accord [F.]. (1) Chord. (2) Manner of tuning, especially of such instruments as the lute, for which various systems of tuning were in use during the 17th century [see WoHN ii, 91; ApNPM, p. 71f]. See Scordatura.

Accordare [It.], **accorder** [F.]. To tune.

Accordatura [It.]. See Accord (2).

Accordion. A portable musical instrument consisting of two rectangular headboards connected by a folding bellows. Inside the headboards are metal tongues that act as free-beating reeds. The instrument has pushed-out and drawn-in reeds, the former sounding when the headboards are moved outward (expiration), the latter when they are moved inward (inspiration). The modern accordion has a keyboard on the right side for playing melody notes, while buttons on the left side operate bass notes and full chords. See ill. under Wind instruments. The earliest instruments of this type were made by Buschmann (1822), Buffet (1827), and Damian (1829).

A similar instrument, preferred in England, is the concertina, invented by Wheatstone in 1829. It is hexagonal in shape and has a number of studs on each side. It possesses a full chromatic scale and produces the same note whether the bellows are pressed or drawn. Artistically, this instrument is superior to the accordion and has occasionally been used in the orchestra (Tchaikovsky, Orchestral Suite op. 53). Much solo music has been written for it by such virtuosos as G. Regondi, W. B. Molique, G. A. Macfarren, and E. Silas. The *bandoneon* is an Argentine variety of accordion with buttons on each side, for single tones only.

Accordo [It.]. Chord.

Accusé [F.]. With emphasis.

Achromatic. *Diatonic.

Achtel, Achtelnote; Achtelpause [G.]. Eighth note; eighth rest. See Notes.

Achtfuss [G.]. Eight-foot (stop). See Foot (2).

Acis and Galatea. A dramatic cantata composed by Handel (about 1720) for the Duke of Chandos. Originally designated as masque, pastorale (pastoral play), or *serenata*, it was intended to be sung in costume but without action. Based on the Greek legend, the work includes some selections for a chorus, which plays the role of commentator as does the chorus in ancient Greek drama.

Acoustic bass (also called resultant bass). On organs, a 32-foot stop that is obtained as a differential tone of a 16-foot stop and a 10⅔-foot stop. According to the acoustic phenomenon of the differential tones [see Combination tones], the simultaneous sounding of C (produced by the 16-foot) and of G (produced by the 10⅔-foot) produces the tone C_1 (32-foot). The acoustic bass is frequently used where the great expense of the large 32-foot pipes is prohibitive.

Acoustics. The science that treats of sounds and therefore describes the physical basis of music. For the musician the most important problems of acoustics are: (1) the nature of musical sound; (2) intervals; (3) consonance and dissonance; (4) resonance; (5) architectural acoustics. Only the first subject will be treated here; for the others, see the respective entries. [For the method of indicating the different octaves, see Pitch names II.]

I. *Vibration.* The generation of sound is invariably bound up with the vibration of an elastic body, i.e., a body that, when displaced from its normal position, develops internal forces that tend to restore the body to its original position. (The body may be a solid, like a violin string, or a gas, like the air in an organ pipe.) When the body has returned to its rest position, it is still moving and its momentum carries it past its rest position so that a new contrary displacement results. This leads to a repetition of the whole movement in the reverse direction and, in fact, to a succession of movements back and forth that would continue indefinitely were it not for friction, which causes the successive displacements to diminish and finally to stop. A tongue of steel fastened at one end may serve as an example [Ex. 1].

The movement A–B–A (or A–C–A or B–A–C) is called a "single vibration" (half vibration); the movement A–B–A–C–A (or B–A–C–A–B) is called a "double vibration" or simply a "vibration" or "cycle" (in modern writings usually the double vibration is used as the unit of measure). The distance A–C [Ex. 1] is called the *amplitude*. The number of double vibrations or cycles made in one second is called the *frequency*.

Ex. 2 represents a vibration of three cycles per second. In order to understand the relation of this graph to the vibration it is meant to represent, one may imagine the lowest point of the tongue, A, to be made luminous and then photographed. If during the exposure the film is moved rapidly downward, the picture will show a wavy curve [Ex. 3] of the same shape as that of Ex. 2.

If the same tongue is plucked with different degrees of force, the initial displacements will be different. Then the vibrations will have different amplitudes and the sounds heard by the ear will have different loudnesses [see Bel]; *the greater the amplitude of the vibration, the louder the sound.* As the amplitude diminishes [Ex. 4] the sound fades away.

If the photographic experiment described above is repeated with a shorter tongue, the vibrations will be more rapid—of higher frequency— so that (if the speed of the moving film is the same) the waves of the curve will be closer

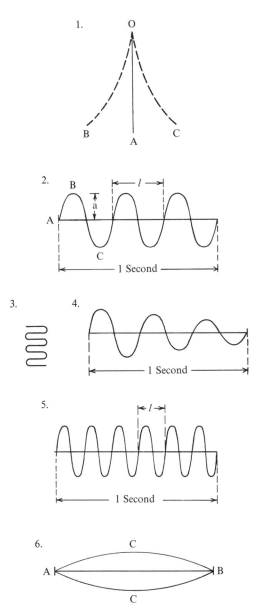

1. Elastic tongue fixed at O; A, rest position; B, position after initial displacement; C, position after first half-cycle of vibration.   2. Vibration of three cycles per second; a = amplitude; l = one wavelength, i.e., a distance corresponding to one cycle. 3. Photograph of tip of vibrating tongue on moving film.   4. Fading sound: reduction in amplitude without change in frequency.   5. Vibration of six cycles per second.   6. Vibrating string; A, B, fastened ends of string; C, point of plucking.

together [Ex. 5] and the pitch of the corresponding sound will be higher. In fact, *the pitch of a sound depends only on the frequency of the vibration that produces it.*

A sound of sufficient loudness is audible if its frequency is between approximately 16 and 20,000 cycles per second; the tones of the piano vary from about 30 to 4,000, those of the violin from about 200 to 3,000 cycles per second. The frequency of middle a (a′) at concert pitch is 440 cycles per second.

In the italicized statement above, the word *only* is of particular importance. As every musician knows, the pitch of a vibrating string is not altered by altering the force with which the string is set into vibration. In other words, the pitch does not depend upon the amplitude. The piano player obtains a tone of the same pitch regardless of whether he uses a pianissimo or fortissimo touch. Similarly, the pitch of a sound does not change as the loudness decreases and the sound dies away.

II. *Vibrating strings.* If a violin string is plucked or bowed, each single point of the string will make a back-and-forth vibration comparable to that made by the lowest point of the steel tongue previously described. All these vibrations have the same frequency but differ in amplitude. For the purpose of our explanation, we can fix our attention on the point of the string that has the largest amplitude, i.e., the point at which the string is plucked. If this is the middle point of the string, the resulting phenomenon can be roughly illustrated by Ex. 6.

III. *Frequency, vibrating length, and pitch.* The pitch of the sound produced by a vibrating string depends upon its weight per unit length (i.e., its material and its diameter), its tension, and its length. For the present purpose it is sufficient to consider only the last factor, the others being regarded as constant. These conditions are realized in the case of a single string whose vibrating length can be changed by stopping (violin) or by means of a movable bridge (*monochord). The following fundamental law results: *The frequency of vibration of a string is inversely proportional to the vibrating length.* This means that if a string one yard long gives a sound of the frequency 600 cycles per second, a string one-half yard long gives a sound of the frequency 1200 cycles per second, while a string two-thirds of a yard long produces a frequency of $600 \times \frac{3}{2} = 900$ cycles per second, and so on. The results have a more general application, however, if they are expressed in terms of frequency rather than in terms of vibrating lengths. Thus expressed, they remain unchanged regardless of whether the sound is produced by a vibrating string or by a vibrating air column in a pipe, and they do not depend upon additional factors, such as the tension, thickness, or material of the string.

The fundamental principle is: *If the frequency of a tone is n, that of its octave is 2n, that of the fifth is 3/2n, and that of the major third is 5/4n.* From these tones, all the others of the diatonic scale can be derived [see Intervals, calculation of, II]. The result is as follows:

	c	d	e	f	g	a	b	c′
Frequency ($n = 1$):	1	9/8	5/4	4/3	3/2	5/3	15/8	2
Frequency ($n = 24$):	24	27	30	32	36	40	45	48
Vibrating length:	1	8/9	4/5	3/4	2/3	3/5	8/15	1/2

The illustration [Ex. 7] shows a number of frequencies calculated for the tone f′ = 360 (the correct frequency for f′ is 352). It must be noted that these frequencies give the tones of *just intonation, not of equal temperament [see Temperament].

IV. *Harmonics, overtones.* A string or other elastic body vibrating in the manner described above would produce what is called a pure tone, consisting of a single frequency. However, practically no vibrating body produces a pure tone. All musical instruments produce composite tones, consisting of many pure tones, called

7

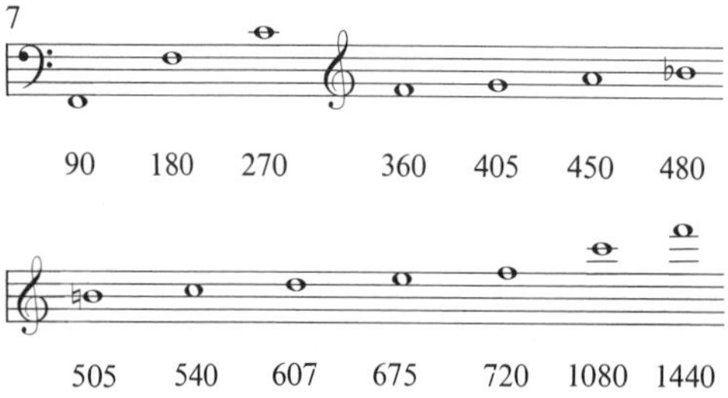

8

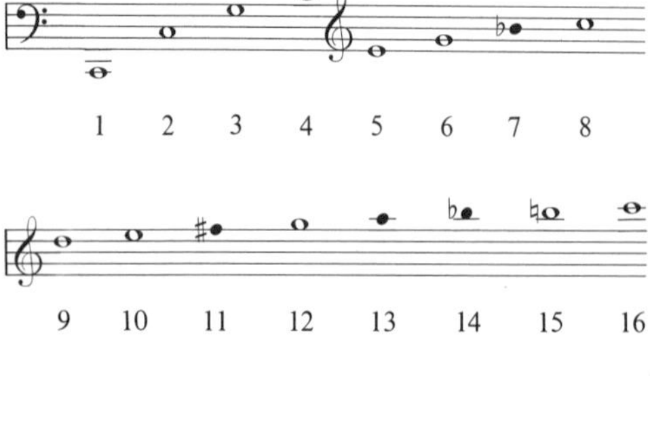

9

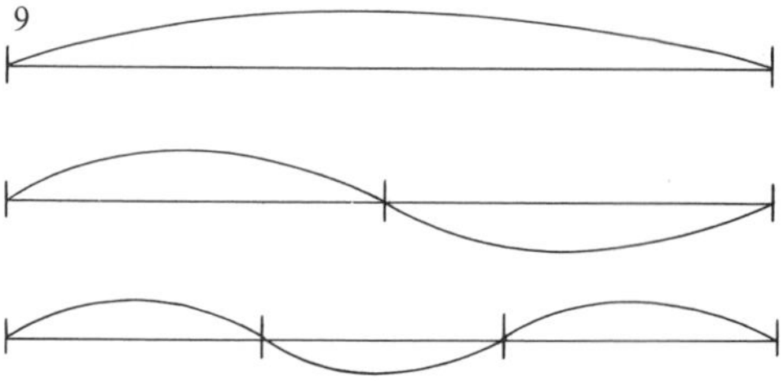

harmonics, produced simultaneously. The harmonic of lowest frequency is called the fundamental, and because it is louder than the others it determines the pitch of the composite tone. The frequencies of the other harmonics are exact multiples of the frequency of the fundamental; thus if the frequency of the fundamental is *n*, the other harmonics have frequencies of 2*n*, 3*n*, . . . , 20*n* or more. The illustration [Ex. 8] shows the first 16 harmonics of the tone C.

The harmonics above the fundamental are also called overtones. If the terms are properly used, the first overtone is the second harmonic, the second overtone is the third harmonic, and so on. Another term for the harmonics is partial tones, or partials. Although the terms harmonics and partials are frequently used as if interchangeable, the latter term has, in scientific studies, a wider significance, since it also includes nonharmonic overtones like those that occur in bells and in the complex sounds called noises. With the exception of the octaves (2, 4, 8), no harmonics are tones of equal temperament. Those that result from the factors 3 and 5 (3, 5, 6, 9, 10, 12, etc.) are tones of just intonation (see the table of frequencies above), whereas the harmonics 7, 11, 13, and 14 (indicated by black notes) can be only approximately identified with tones available in our system of tuning and notation. As can easily be seen, the 7th harmonic, which is 7 = 63/9, is lower than the b-flat of just intonation, which is 16/9 × 4 = 64/9; this, in turn, is slightly lower than the b-flat of equal temperament (the three tones form intervals, from c, of 969, 996, and 1000 *cents respectively). Similarly, the 11th harmonic, which is 11 = 44/4, is lower than the f-sharp of just intonation (15/2 × 3/2 = 45/4) and, in fact, is as close to the f as to the f-sharp of equal temperament (f = 500, 11th harmonic = 551, f-sharp = 600 cents). Finally, the 13th harmonic is 13 = 39/3, whereas the a of just intonation is 5/3 × 8 = 40/3. Thus the 13th harmonic is actually closer to the g-sharp than to the a of equal temperament (g-sharp = 800, 13th harmonic = 840, a = 900 cents).

The physical cause of the harmonics is that a vibrating body, such as a string, vibrates simultaneously as a whole and in sections of one-half, one-third, one-fourth, etc., of its entire length [Ex. 9]. The secondary vibrations, however, have a much smaller amplitude, approximately one-fifth to one-fiftieth of that of the fundamental, and the tones they produce are correspondingly less loud. Points on the string, such as the fixed ends, where the displacement is always zero, are called nodes; points midway between adjacent nodes, where the amplitude of vibration is greatest, are called antinodes or loops. The distance from one node to the next is one-half wavelength [cf. Ex. 2].

The existence of these additional tones in what the ear believes to be a single sound was shown first by Helmholtz (1821–94), who used *resonators of various sizes that reinforce one frequency and eliminate all the others. The harmonics can be easily demonstrated by the following simple experiment on the piano: depress the key for C without producing the sound, i.e., merely raise the damper of the string for C; then strike forcibly the key for C_1 and release it at once; the higher C, corresponding to the tone of the depressed key, will be clearly heard. The experiment can be repeated by depressing the keys for G, c, e, g, etc., and striking each time the key for C_1. In every case, the tone corresponding to the depressed key will be heard. The explanation of this phenomenon is that the harmonics C, G, c, ... produced by the fundamental tone C_1 generate, by way of resonance, sympathetic vibrations in the shorter strings corresponding to these tones.

The harmonics are the cause of three important musical phenomena, namely, *timbre, the natural tones of *wind instruments, and the *harmonics of the violin.

V. *Pipes.* In pipes (organ pipes, and all wind instruments) an enclosed air column is caused to vibrate. The molecules of air vibrate (in directions parallel to the length of the pipe) in such a way that the density of the air at any point in the pipe changes regularly from a highest to a lowest value and back again. In an open pipe (i.e., one open at both ends) the changes in density of the air are greatest; these points correspond to antinodes. Between them is a place where the density does not change; this is a node (N). The wavelength of the fundamental tone of an open pipe is therefore twice the length of the pipe (l = 2AB). In a stopped pipe (i.e., closed at one end and open at the other) there is a loop (L) at the open end and a node (N) at the closed end. The wavelength of the fundamental is therefore four times the length of the pipe (l = 4AB). Since wavelength is inversely proportional to frequency, the open pipe has a fundamental an octave above that of a closed pipe of the same length. An open pipe sounding C measures approximately eight feet [see Foot (2)].

Like a vibrating string, an air column vibrates not only as a whole but also in parts (½, ⅓, ¼, ⅕, etc., of its length), thus producing harmonics. While an open pipe produces all the harmonics (as does a string), a stopped pipe segments so as to give out only the odd-numbered harmonics, 1, 3, 5, etc. The reason is that an even harmonic (e.g., 2) would call for an antinode at both ends of the pipe, while in a stopped pipe there must

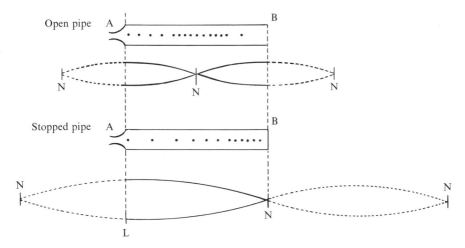

always be a node at the closed end [see Wind instruments III; Organ IX].

VI. *Interference.* This is the technical term (not a very apt one) for the numerous phenomena resulting from the superposition of two or more air vibrations. The general principles of this very complex phenomenon can be grasped from the drawing [Ex. A], showing two original vibrations (I, II) of the same frequency as well as one possible result of their superposition (III = I + II). More important is the interference of vibrations of different frequencies, e.g., of 2 and 3 cycles per second, or of 12 and 14 cycles per second [Ex. B]. The example illustrates the manner in which *beats are produced, in the present case 2 (14 − 12) per second. For a more complicated phenomenon of interference, see Combination tone.

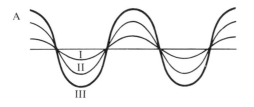

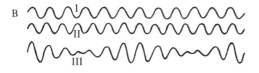

Related articles: Architectural acoustics; Beats; Bel; Cents; Combination tone; Comma; Consonance, dissonance; Intervals, calculation of; Just intonation; Pitch; Pythagorean scale; Resonance; Savart; Temperament; Timbre.

Lit.: W. T. Bartholomew, *Acoustics of Music* (1942), bibl.; P. C. Buck, *Acoustics for Musicians* (1918); H. Lowery, *A Guide to Musical Acoustics* [1956]; A. Wood, *The Physics of Music,* rev. ed. by J. M. Bowsher [1947]; E. G. Richardson, *The Acoustics of Orchestral Instruments and of the Organ* (1929); J. Jeans, *Science and Music* (1937); D. C. Miller, *Science of Musical Sounds* (1916); J. Redfield, *Music: A Science and an Art* (1928); S. S. Stevens and H. Davis, *Hearing* (1938); A. H. Davis, *Modern Acoustics* (1934); N. W. McLachlan, *The New Acoustics* (1936); H. F. Olson and F. Massa, *Applied Acoustics* (1934); C. A. Culver,

Musical Acoustics (1941); H. Lowery, *The Background of Music* (1952), bibl.; H. Simbriger, *Handbuch der musikalischen Akustik* (1951); H. Burris-Meyer, "The Place of Acoustics in the Future of Music" (*Journal of the Acoustical Society of America,* July 1947, p. 532); A. Small, "The Partnership between Music and Modern Acoustics" (*JAMS* ii). See also under Architectural acoustics; Electronic instruments. Additional bibliography in D. H. Daugherty, *A Bibliography of Periodical Literature in Musicology* (1940), pp. 117ff.

Action. Any kind of mechanism used in instruments as a means of transmitting the motion of the fingers (or feet) to the sound-producing parts; in other words, a sort of artificial extension of the fingers (or feet). On keyboard instruments, the action forms an essential, even the characteristic, part of the instrument [see Piano I; Organ II]. The term is applied to the key mechanism of woodwind instruments, which enables the player to control holes that are beyond the hand's reach (e.g., the *Böhm system for the flute). The action of the harp is the mechanism, controlled by the player's feet upon the pedals, by which a transposition of a semitone or a whole tone can be effected [see Harp].

Act tune. See Entr'acte.

Actus tragicus [L.]. An early cantata (no. 106) by Bach, composed in Weimar (1708–17) for an occasion of mourning. The German title is *Gottes Zeit ist die allerbeste Zeit* (God's Time Is Best).

Adagietto [It.]. (1) A tempo somewhat faster than adagio. (2) A short composition in slow speed.

Adagio [It.]. (1) Designation for slow tempo, between andante and largo. See Tempo marks. (2) A composition in slow tempo, especially the second (slow) movement of a sonata, symphony, etc.

Adagissimo. Extremely slow.

Adaptation. *Arrangement.

Added sixth. The sixth added to a triad, or the entire chord thus obtained; e.g., c–e–g–a. In classical harmony, the chord of the added sixth occurs preferably on the fourth degree, i.e., with a subdominant function (f–a–c'–d' in C major; also f–a♭–c'–d'). It is usually explained as the first inversion of the seventh chord on the second degree (d–f–a–c'). Although according to strict rules the chord must be resolved into the dominant or the tonic, it is used in some works (*impressionism) as a color modification of the triad that does not call for resolution. Jazz musicians have abundantly availed themselves of this cloying effect, especially for the final chord of a piece.

Additional accompaniment. Designation for 19th-century revisions or enlargements of earlier orchestral scores, especially of the 17th and 18th centuries. With the ever increasing size of the 19th-century orchestra and concert hall, the need was felt for expanded instrumentation; but with the ever diminishing understanding of true baroque style, many stylistic incongruities were perpetrated. Thus, not only were admissible and sometimes necessary changes made (replacement of obsolete instruments by newer ones, doubling of certain parts, etc.), but the voice leading was changed, the writing was "improved," new parts were added, and in many instances the original intention of the composer was thoroughly misunderstood or disregarded. The composers whose works were most frequently subjected to arrangement were Handel and Bach. The *Messiah* of Handel has been particularly unfortunate in this regard. Mozart was among the first to make a more modern arrangement of it; subsequently various other musicians made further arrangements of Mozart's arrangement. Many other works of Handel's have fared similarly, e.g., at the hands of Mendelssohn, who later expressed regret for having published his arrangements. Bach's cantatas suffered mistreatment by Robert Franz. Wagner made arrangements of Beethoven's Ninth Symphony, Gluck's *Iphigénie en Aulide*, etc. The 20th century has witnessed a growing understanding of the baroque style and a consequent demand for authentic, unarranged performances. See Performance practice. See N. Kilburn, "Additional Arrangements to Handel's *Acis*" (*SIM* iii); A. Hutchings, "A Note on the 'Additional Accompaniments'" (*MR* vii, 161).

Adelaide. A famous song by Beethoven (op. 46), composed in 1795 or 1796 to words by F. von Matthisson.

Adélaïde Concerto. A violin concerto attributed to Mozart and edited by Marius Casadesus from a violin part dedicated to the French Princess Adélaïde. The orchestral accompaniment was added by Casadesus. Although it is known that Mozart did write such a piece for the Princess, it is almost certain that this is not the work.

Adeste, Fideles [L.]. A Latin hymn usually sung today in the English translation, beginning "O come, all ye faithful." The words and music are attributed to John F. Wade, and it was published in 1750 for use in the English Roman Catholic College in Lisbon; hence, the tune name "Portuguese Hymn."

À deux [F.]. See *A due.*

Adieux, Les [F.]. Beethoven's Sonata for piano op. 81a, in E-flat (1809), entitled (in full) *Les Adieux, l'absence, et le retour* (Farewell, Absence, and Return). Also known as the Farewell Sonata, it was inspired by the Archduke Rudolf's departure from Vienna.

Ad libitum [L.]. An indication that gives the performer liberty to: (1) vary from strict tempo (contrast *a *battuta*); (2) include or omit the part of some voice or instrument (contrast *obbligato); (3) include a *cadenza according to his own invention.

Adoración. See under *Aguinaldo.*

Adriana Lecouvreur. Opera in four acts by F. Cilèa (libretto after E. Scribe and Legouvé), produced in Milan, 1902. Setting: Paris, 1739.

A due [It.]. Direction in orchestral parts indicating that two instruments notated on one staff (e.g., Flute 1 and 2) should play in unison (*All'unisono*) [see Unison]. However, the term is also used in the almost opposite meaning, synonymous with *divisi. The same ambiguity exists with the French term *à deux. A due corde,* see *Due corde. A due mani,* for two hands; *a due voci* (*cori, stromenti,* etc.), for two voices (choirs, instruments, etc.).

Aeolian, aeolian mode. See under Church modes; Modality.

Aeolian harp. A sound-producing contrivance consisting of a long narrow box with six or more gut strings stretched inside over two bridges. The strings are tuned in unison but vary in thickness and, therefore, tension. If the box is placed in a free current of air (preferably in an open window), the strings vibrate differently, according to their different tensions, and thus produce a large variety of harmonics over the same fundamental (cf. the "singing" of telephone wires). The sound varies considerably with the changing force of the wind and produces a romantic, mysterious effect. The instrument was known in ancient China and India, and in Europe during the Middle Ages. It enjoyed special popularity in the romantic period about 1800. Its intimate charm is beautifully described in Eduard Mörike's poem "Die Aeolsharfe" with musical settings by Brahms and (especially) Hugo Wolf.

Various attempts have been made to harness this elusive sound to a keyboard, with an artificial jet of wind provided by foot bellows (J.-J. Schnell's *Anémocorde* or *Aeroclavichord*, 1789; H. Herz's *Piano éolien*, 1851). See *SaRM*, p. 16; J. G. Kastner, *La Harpe d'Éole* (1856).

Aeoline. Old name for mouth organ [see Harmonica]. Also, an early type of *harmonium (*aeolodicon*).

Aeolopantalon. An instrument invented in 1825 by Jozé Dlugosz, Warsaw; it was a combination of a harmonium-like instrumnet (*aeolomelodikon*, with brass tubes affixed to the reeds) and a piano, so that both instruments could be used in alternation. It is remembered largely because the young Chopin played on it in various recitals.

Aequalstimmen [G.]. (1) The eight-foot pipes of the organ. (2) *Equal voices.

Aer. See under Aria II.

Aerophon. See Aerophor.

Aerophones. See under Instruments III.

Aerophor. A device invented by B. Samuel in 1912 that provides the player of a wind instrument with additional air from a small bellows operated by the foot. By means of a tube with a mouthpiece, air can be supplied to the player's mouth whenever his breath is not sufficient for long-held tones or long melodies in full legato. R. Strauss has written passages requiring this device, as in his *Alpensinfonie* (where it is incorrectly called "aerophon").

Aesthetics of music. I. Aesthetics is generally defined as the philosophy or study of the beautiful. Musical aesthetics, therefore, should be the study of the beautiful in music, the ultimate goal of such a study being the establishment of criteria that would allow us to say whether or not a particular composition is beautiful, or why one is beautiful while another is not. The main objection to such a point of view is that beauty is by no means the only (and possibly not even the foremost) criterion of what may be roughly described as "merit" or "artistic worth." Music, like other works of art, may be aesthetically satisfying without necessarily being "beautiful." Therefore a definition such as the following provides a much better basis for the study in

question: *Musical aesthetics is the study of the relationship of music to the human senses and intellect.* This definition corresponds to the original meaning of the Greek word *aisthesis,* i.e., feeling, sensation. The following words by Robert Schumann (*Gesammelte Schriften über Musik und Musiker,* rev. ed., 1914, i, 44) adequately describe the peculiar problem of musical aesthetics [trans. by W. A.]: "In no other field is the proof of the fundamentals as difficult as it is in music. Science uses mathematics and logic; to poetry belongs the decisive, golden word; other arts have taken nature, whose forms they borrow, as their arbiter. Music, however, is a poor orphan whose father and mother no one can name. But, perhaps, it is precisely this mystery of her origin which accounts for the charm of her beauty."

II. For more than two thousand years philosophers have tried to solve the mystery of music. Among them we find Pythagoras (550 B.C.), who explained music as the expression of that universal harmony which is also realized in arithmetic and astronomy; Plato (400 B.C.), to whom, like Confucius, music seemed the most appropriate means of social and political education; Plotinus (d. 270), who interpreted music as a mystic and occult power; Boethius (d. 524), who divided music into three fields, *musica mundana* (the Pythagorean harmony of the universe), *musica humana* (the harmony of the human soul and body), and *musica instrumentalis* (music as actual sound), a classification that prevailed in musical theory for more than ten centuries; J. Kepler (*Harmonices mundi libri v,* 1619), who erected a great edifice of ideas in which he correlated musical tones and intervals with the movements of the planets and their astrological functions; G. W. Leibnitz (1646–1716), who paved the way for the psychological system of musical aesthetics by interpreting music as an "unconscious exercise in arithmetic"; A. Schopenhauer (*Die Welt als Wille und Vorstellung,* 1819), who considered music the purest incarnation of the "absolute will" and the expression of human feelings (love, joy, horror) in their abstract interpretation as metaphysical ideas; G. T. Fechner (1801–87), called the founder of experimental aesthetics, who insisted that music is the expression of "general mood" rather than specific "feelings"; and finally C. Stumpf (*Tonpsychologie,* 2 vols., 1883, '90), who inaugurated the scientific study of musical psychology on the basis of experiments and statistics, especially with regard to the problem of consonance and dissonance. Stumpf's procedure has been the point of departure for many investigations along similar lines, especially in America, e.g., C. E. Seashore, *Psychology of Music* (1938); M. Schoen, ed., *The Effects of Music* (1927), and others [see Tests]. For a criticism of these methods, see C. C. Pratt, *The Meaning of Music* (1931), pp. 131ff.

Not until the advent of the 19th century did these theories of music begin to accord with the present-day interpretation of musical aesthetics as defined above. This statement should not be construed as deprecating the much broader and, in a sense, more profound views—cosmic, political, or theological—held by the philosophers of antiquity and the Middle Ages. Whereas in those periods justification for music was considered to have its origin in the state, in the universe, or in God, today music has lost these transcendental affiliations but has gained instead a secure place in everyday life.

III. Musicologists, as might be expected, aim at a more technically detailed penetration into the subject of musical aesthetics, usually being concerned with the study of specific techniques or compositions rather than with music in the abstract. Their various theories of aesthetics can be divided into two groups, according to whether they consider music (1) as a heteronomous art, i.e., as the expression of extramusical elements, or (2) as an autonomous art, i.e., as the realization of intrinsic principles and ideas (F. Gatz).

(a) In the former class are the *Affektenlehre* (doctrine of *affections), according to which music in its various manifestations is the expression of human temperaments, passions, moods, etc. In the 17th century, music was frequently treated as an oratorical art (*Figurenlehre,* doctrine of *figures), its structural and stylistic elements (such as *repetitio, fuga, climax*) being related to corresponding rhetorical devices. In the romantic period the interpretation of musical compositions was largely based upon programmatic and allegorical concepts. Music was thought of as a sort of psychological drama and explained in terms such as "desperate struggle," "the knocking of Fate," "threatening fortissimo," or "gloomy minor." An early exponent of this school of thought was A. B. Marx, in his *Ludwig van Beethoven* (1859). A more intelligent use of this approach was attempted by H. Kretzschmar, the inventor of *musikalische Hermeneutik* [see Hermeneutics]. He considered music a *Sprachkunst,* i.e., a language, of less clarity but with finer shades and deeper effects than ordinary speech. He harked back to the "affects" of the 18th century, which, according to him, should be based upon the study of musical elements (themes, intervals, rhythm, etc.). He also related the composer's music to his life (Beethoven's "period of happiness," etc.). The last point was emphasized by H. Riemann, who maintained that the written composition as well as the actual performance is nothing but a means of transferring an experience (*Erlebnis*) from the fancy of the composer to that of the listener. Kretzschmar's method has been elaborated by A. Schering. An American book, E. Sorantin's *The Problem of Musical Expression* (1932), represents an example of 20th-century *Affektenlehre.*

(b) In strong contrast to all these theories is the more recent school of thought that rejects the allegorical, emotional, programmatic, poetical foundation of musical aesthetics and explains music as a purely musical phenomenon, as an autochthonous and autonomous creation that can be understood only in its own terms. An early "autonomist" was M. de Chabanon, who in 1785 published a book entitled *De la Musique considérée en elle-même.* The main representative of musical autonomy has been E. Hanslick, who, in his *Vom Musikalisch-Schönen* (1854), formulated the sentence: "Musik ist tönend bewegte Form"—"music is form in tonal motion" (trans. by D. Ferguson; the term *form, naturally, must be taken in its broadest sense, including all structural and stylistic elements of music). He admits the use of designations such as "powerful," "graceful," "tender," "passionate," but only in order to illustrate the musical character of the passage, not to suggest a definite feeling on the part of composer or listener. Still further in this direction went A. Halm (*Von zwei Kulturen der Musik,* 1913), one of the most outstanding writers on musical aesthetics. The following quotation from the Talmud, given at the beginning of his book, is a very apt expression of the central thought of musical autonomy: "If you want to understand the invisible, look carefully at the visible." Halm, as well as his successors, E. Kurth, H. Mersmann, F. Jöde, and others, advocated the separation of the musical work from the emotional worlds of both composer and listener and the emancipation of musical thought from "sensuous intoxication and hallucination."

See also Affections; Figures; Hermeneutics; *Musica reservata;* Psychology of music.

Lit.: H. H. Britan, *The Philosophy of Music* (1911); H. Scherchen, *The Nature of Music*

(1950); V. Zuckerkandl, *Sound and Symbol* (1956); *id., The Sense of Music* (1959); D. Ferguson, *Music as Metaphor* (1960); L. Meyer, *Emotion and Meaning in Music* (1956); S. K. Langer, *Feeling and Form* (1953); R. W. Lundin, *An Objective Psychology of Music* [1953]; D. Cooke, *The Language of Music* (1959); F. M. Gatz, ed., *Musik-Ästhetik in ihren Hauptrichtungen* (1929); R. Schäfke, *Geschichte der Musikästhetik* (1934); E. G. Wolff, *Grundlagen einer autonomen Musikästhetik,* 2 vols. (1934, '38); H. Pfrogner, *Musik: Geschichte ihrer Deutung* (1954); H. J. Moser, *Musikästhetik* (1953); C. Lalo, *Éléments d'une esthétique musicale scientifique,* rev. ed. (1939); G. Brelet, *Esthétique et création musicale* (1947); *id., Le Temps musical: Essai d'une esthétique nouvelle de la musique,* 2 vols. (1949); H. Besseler, "Grundfragen der Musikästhetik" (*JMP* xxxiii); A. Einstein, "Musical Aesthetics and Musicology," in *Music in the Romantic Era* (1947), pp. 337–55; R. Tischler, "The Aesthetic Experience" (*MR* xvii, 189). For additional bibl. see "Musik-Ästhetik" in *MGG*.

Aevia. An artificial word, consisting of the vowels of *alleluia (u = v). It is occasionally used as an abbreviation in manuscripts of Gregorian chant. See *Euouae.*

Affabile [It.]. Gentle, pleasing.

Affannato, affannoso [It.]. Excited, hurried, agitated.

Affections, doctrine of [also doctrine of affects; G. *Affektenlehre*]. An aesthetic theory of the late baroque period, formulated by A. Werckmeister (*Harmonologia musica,* 1702), J. D. Heinichen (1711), J. Mattheson (1739), J. J. Quantz (1752), F. W. Marpurg (*Kritische Briefe,* vol. ii, 1763), and other 18th-century writers. It was treated in greatest detail by Mattheson (*Der vollkommene Capellmeister,* 1739), who enumerates more than twenty affections and describes how they should be expressed in music, e.g.: "Sorrow should be expressed with a slow-moving, languid and drowsy melody, broken with many sighs," and "Hate is represented by repulsive and rough harmony and a similar melody." He also describes the affections (characteristic emotions) of numerous dances, saying that the gigue expresses "heat and eagerness," the courante, "sweet hope and courage." These rather trite explanations reveal the difficulty involved in any attempt to formulate the doctrine of affections. There can be no doubt, however, that musicians of the late baroque, particularly in Germany,

were fully familiar with this aesthetic approach and often incorporated its tenets in their compositions. A basic aspect of the doctrine of affections is the principle that each composition (or, in the case of composite forms, each movement) should embody only one affection.

Although the term *Affektenlehre* is associated with the 18th century, the close relationship between music and the human affections has often been recognized and emphasized not only in Western music (Plato, Aristotle, Isidore of Seville, Ramos de Pareja, Glareanus, Monteverdi, Descartes) but also in that of the Orient, especially in the Hindu conception of the *ragas* [see India I]. Also see Aesthetics of music III(a); *Musica reservata.*

Lit.: H. Goldschmidt, *Die Musikästhetik des 18. Jahrhunderts* (1915); W. Serauky, *Die musikalische Nachahmungsästhetik im Zeitraum von 1700 bis 1850* (1929); E. Katz, *Die musikalischen Stilbegriffe des 17. Jahrhunderts* (1926); F. T. Wessel, "The Affektenlehre in the Eighteenth Century" (diss. Indiana Univ., 1955); M. Kramer, "Beiträge zu einer Geschichte des Affektbegriffs in der Musik von 1550–1700" (diss. Halle, 1924); H. Abert, in *AMW* v; H. Kretzschmar, in *JMP* xviii, xix; F. Stege, in *ZMW* x; A. Schering, in *JMP* xlv; H. Lenneberg, in *JMT* ii (Mattheson); R. Schäfke, in *AMW* vi (Quantz); G. Frotscher, in *CP 1925* (Bach).

Affektenlehre [G.]. See Affections, doctrine of.

Affetti [It.]. The term appears in the title of various publications of the late 16th and early 17th centuries [*Dolci Affetti,* 1582; S. Bonini, *Affetti spirituali . . . in istile di Firenze o recitativo,* 1615; B. Marini, *Affetti musicali,* op. 1, 1617; G. Stefani, *Affetti amorosi,* 1621, see Editions V, 3], probably to emphasize the affective character of the music. It is also used in early violin sonatas to designate a certain type of ornament, either tremolo or arpeggio [see *SchGMB,* no. 183; *RiHM* ii, 2, 120].

Affettuoso [It.]. Tender.

Affinales [L., sing. *affinalis*]. In medieval theory of the church modes, name for the pitches a, b, and c', which occur as the finals of transposed chants [see *Speculum musicae; CS* ii, 248a]. In a *Tonale* ascribed to Bernard of Clairvaux (1091–1153), it is stated that the first *maneria has the finals d and a, the second e and b, the third f and c', the fourth only g [see *GS* ii, 266a]. Many of the Ambrosian chants close on the *affinales,* including the d'. See Transposition II.

Affrettando [It.]. Hurrying.

Africa. The musical cultures of Africa may be very broadly classified as North African (essentially Islamic; see Arab music) and sub-Saharan. The latter is considered here in its traditional aspects.

I. *Background.* The interpenetration of sub-Saharan tribal Africa with Western and Eastern civilization has resulted in a vivid cultural dualism, reflected in a fast-diminishing body of traditional, tribal music on the one hand and a slowly emerging nucleus of art and "city" music on the other. Unfortunately, a historic view of the tribal music remains vastly limited, owing to the relative sparsity, prior to *c.* 1950, of notated examples, and the fact that recorded evidence, such as that supplied to E. M. von Hornbostel by the Czekanowski Central African Expedition of 1907–08, begins only with the 20th century. However, some of the history may be reconstructed by tracing the musical legacies of past contacts with other cultures. Preliminary observations concerning possible legacies of the Malayo-Polynesian migrations (*c.* 2000 B.C.– *c.* A.D. 500) to Malagasy (Madagascar) and the African mainland, for example, include the following: (1) C. Sachs shows that several instruments of Malagasy, including an idiochordic tube zither tuned in thirds (*valíha*) and a free-log thigh-supported xylophone, are of Malayan origin (the xylophone especially is known from Celebes to the Molucca islands). He also relates the resonated xylophones of the African mainland to those of Indonesia. (2) Certain African xylophone tunings, as pointed out by J. Kunst (*PMA* lxii) and others, strongly resemble (but may not necessarily derive from) some "ideal" (theoretic) isotonic tunings of the Far East, notably the five-step Indonesian *sléndro* and the seven-step isotonic scale of Thailand [see III C below]. (3) The use of double xylophone beaters in one hand, held or fastened at an angle, has been noted among some African peoples, e.g., the Azande of the Congo-Kinshasa (Democratic Republic of the Congo) and the Venda of South Africa, and also in Indonesia.

Musical ties, particularly rhythmic, with the Middle East and India may be even stronger than those with the Far East. Such ties may have been gradually defined through early migrations, invasions of ancient Egypt south of the Sudan, the South Indian trade on the East African coast during the third or second centuries B.C., and, of course, throughout the period of Islamic spread in Africa.

Sub-Saharan Africa includes a large variety of tribes and languages. While anthropologists and linguists have been able to map important culture and language areas (which, incidentally, are generally not congruent—e.g., Bantu languages cut across both cattle and agricultural areas), a similar delineation of musical style areas has thus far not proved practicable. For example, although there is, at first glance, a preponderance of polyphony in parallel fourths and fifths in the eastern and southern regions and in parallel thirds in the central and western regions, further study reveals greater intermingling of intervals than hitherto believed.

II. *Social function and professionalism.* Music and dance permeate nearly all phases of African tribal life. They are vital to the many rituals, such as those concerned with birth, puberty and secret-society initiation, marriage, etc., and rituals of "livelihood," e.g., hunting, farming, etc. Ceremonial music, costumes, masks, and instruments usually attain an aura of sacredness. Each of the Watutsi (Watusi) royal drums, for example, has been thought to possess a "soul," represented by a large pebble inside the drum, that can do away with evil spirits.

Music may also serve in legal, political, and historical capacities. Thus, there are public litigation ceremonies, such as those of the Bambala (Congo-Kinshasa), in which the litigants present portions of their legal briefs in song; there are songs of criticism, or of praise, directed at chiefs, employers, governments, etc.; and there are songs narrating historical or current events, such as the warrior epics of the Watutsi of Rwanda.

There is also a great deal of music and dance for entertainment. This ranges from the highly informal to a more "theatrical," prepared type, such as the *chikona,* the leading ceremonial and social dance of the Venda (South Africa), which features a circle of men playing vertical flutes of reed in hocket and dancing counterclockwise around drummers, most of whom are women.

Various levels of musical professionalism, engaged in mostly by men but also by women, have long been apparent in African tribal life, in addition to communal music-making. Thus, there are trained instrumentalists, dancers, master instrument builders, and tuning specialists (composing is usually subsumed under the performer's craft), some attached to a chief's or king's court, others traveling as paid performers, as well as the skilled leaders of a singing or dancing community group, who are perhaps also official or semiofficial religious leaders. Training, which may be long and involved, is generally informal and based on rote learning, often with such mnemonic aids as the singing of nonsense or stylized syllables (especially for drum patterns). Such aids recall similar methods in Hindu drumming and Japanese *gagaku.

III. *Style.* Although diversity of style is evident, there are certain elements that represent a reasonably common musical denominator.

A. *Rhythm and tempo.* Probably the most outstanding feature of much African music is the complexity of rhythmic structure, a complexity no doubt well comprehended by musicians trained in unequal-beat styles (Sachs' "additive" category), such as those of the Middle East and India and of the Western Renaissance and 20th century. The essence of what the present writer has termed the "African hemiola style" lies in the contrast of two unequal "conductor" beats in a 2:3 length-ratio, e.g., ♩♩. or ♪♪, both horizontally and vertically. Horizontally, the 2:3 contrast may be texturally (1) concentrated, i.e., the two unequal conductor beats appear close to each other within a short space, as in a pattern of 6/8 + 3/4 (the European hemiola; see Ex. 4, line 2) or in measures (appearing individually or in any combination) such as 5/8, 7/8, 8/8 (e.g., the *dochmiac* ♩♩♩), 12/8 (e.g., ♩♩♩♩.; see Ex. 4, top line and Ex. 2, line 2), etc.; or the 2:3 contrast may be (2) wide-paced and sectional, involving change from the short to the long beat (or vice versa) by sections, one section (several measures) perhaps featuring the ♩ in 3/4 time and another the ♩. in 6/8 ; or (3) the 2:3 contrast may be entirely absent in an individual line, so that equal-beat rhythm prevails, as in the steady reiteration of the dotted-quarter beat in 3/8 figures (e.g., Ex. 1, line 1; Ex. 2, lines 3, 4). Furthermore, whatever the type of beat contrast, a line often features one distinctive rhythmic pattern constantly repeated [see Ex. 1, line 1; Ex. 2, lines 2–4; Ex. 4, lines 1, 2], somewhat like the Hindu *tāla* patterning. However, patterns are open to variation, especially in vocal music (owing to text requirements) and in certain "leader" parts, such as that of the master drummer.

Vertical realization of the hemiola style is a direct concomitant of the strong African propensity for "orchestral," polyphonic music. The contrast of the two unequal conductor beats in their multipart setting may then take on the greatest intricacy, an intricacy deriving from true vertical *polyrhythm. In such polyrhythm each line maintains a certain degree of rhythmic independence, especially with respect to the organization of the conductor beats. Specifically, in African polyrhythm [see Ex. 1-4] each line may carry its own distinctive beat pattern (in Hindu music all parts are controlled by one common beat pattern). This means that beats may not coincide vertically: the two unequal beats obviously cannot coincide, because one beat is one and one-half times as long as the other, and equal beats may not coincide because each line pattern may enter at a different point (Ex. 2, lines 3 and 4). In other words, there may be vertical overlapping of entire patterns and of their internal beats. Clearly, this is not syncopation, in which all lines are subsumed under one underlying regular beat and in which any kind of line-independence is considered to derive from "off-beat" stress of the one equal-beat base.

1. Watutsi royal drums excerpt (Rwanda) [R. Brandel]. 2. Yoruba song with dùndún drums of Ògún, war god (Nigeria) [A. King].

3. = c. 96 Right hand forefinger_____thumb

Left hand (thumb only)

4. = c. 177 = c. 118

Boat-shaped
iron idiophone

up (against palm)

Gourd rattle

down (against thigh)
Right foot

Feet (knee lift
on eighth-note,
step on quarter)

Left foot

Shoulders forward (with stomach
contraction)

Shoulders (with
elbows bent)

Shoulders back (with stomach
release)

3. Lemba deze, i.e., sanza (South Africa) [P. R. Kirby]. 4. Ewe dance figure with portion of ensemble (Ghana) [R. Brandel].

The vertical tug between the two unequal beats and between the simultaneous independent patterns in which they are set is further complicated by the appearance of a subtle rhythmic Gestalt, the "over-all perception" pattern, or composite, of all (or some) of the lines. Mainly through timbre and pitch accents, especially vivid in tuned drum ensembles, this composite pattern is ever fluid and changing, sometimes resulting from the variation techniques of the master drummer, sometimes from changing orchestral density and texture, and also from other factors. The performer, particularly, must to some extent be aware of such an over-all pattern for the sake of ensemble coordination (or else each part would theoretically require its own conductor). But no doubt there are various Gestalt perceptions, depending on the type of participation (dancer's, singer's, etc.), the skill of the performer, and the kind of material he executes (variations, unchanging ostinatos, one or two lines at a time—in the last case, as singer-player, dancer-player, player of "harmonic" instrument, etc.). An ensemble usually pays

special attention to the part of the master drummer, which may give rhythmic signals for changes in dance steps, changes in tempo, type of section to be performed, etc., and frequently to the part of some over-all tempo-setter, such as the *adawuraa*, the boat-shaped iron idiophone of the Akan (Ghana), which may perhaps also act as a central "rhythmic post" for the entire ensemble. Dance rhythms may also play an important "governing" role.

Tempo, as judged from the speed of the basic units, such as the ever-present "running eighths" from which the and . beats are constructed, tends on the whole toward the very rapid (in distinct contrast with music of the Middle East and India). The eighth-note units may average roughly from = c. 240 to c. 450, thus giving conductor beats of = c. 120 to c. 225, and . = c. 80 to c. 150.

B. *Polyphony.* Another distinguishing characteristic of African music is a strong tendency toward polyphony, both vertical ("harmonic") and horizontal ("contrapuntal"). The codevelopment of polyrhythm and some degree of harmony in this music is an interesting contrast with the nonharmonic but rhythmically complex music of the Middle East and India. A further comparison may be made with the polyrhythmic emphasis of the Western Renaissance and its gradual movement toward harmonic and equal-beat emphasis.

The principal African polyphonic types are parallel intervals (mainly thirds, fourths, fifths), overlapping choral antiphony and solo-choral response (particularly the latter), ostinato and drone-ostinato (but not the Hindu continuous drone), and, less frequently, polymelody (mainly double). The types may often intermingle within one piece and may appear in any vocal and instrumental combination. The characteristic orchestral attitude frequently results in the piling up of parts, so that vertical densities of three and four different pitches are not uncommon, whether achieved through parallel block motion or through contrapuntal techniques [see Ex. 6]. Such densities are in constant flux, however, even in parallel motion, so that continuous triads throughout an entire piece, for example, are rare. "Spot" or intermittent fullness resulting from sudden choral *divisi* or solo interjection of variational segments, often at strategic cadential or phrase points, is a favored practice.

Parallel thirds, which frequently move diatonically, are found in numerous areas [see I, above]. Ex. 5 illustrates parallel fourths and fifths, together with responsorial technique. Whether overlapping or not, the responsorial or antiphonal section in African music may be a repetition of the first phrase (Ex. 5), which may result in canonic imitation, or the section may contain new melodic material, such as a brief punctuating refrain, a completion of the first phrase, or a distinctly contrasting melody.

The African ostinato, usually quite small in length and pitch range, may be continuous or intermittent, vocal or instrumental, and may appear above or below the main line. Frequently there is a multi-ostinato, two or more ostinatos moving contrapuntally, with or without a longer melodic line. The African propensity for *hocket (especially favored by the Mambuti Pygmies) is often allied to multi-ostinato. In Ex. 6, five ivory horns (part of a professional band), playing one note (pitch) each, execute melodic and harmonic hocket (largely through sustaining notes) in two ostinato lines, the top line being a kind of forecast of the vocal melody.

Although complex polymelody (simultaneous independent melodies of some length and inner organization) is not common, there are many simple varieties, involving phrases longer than those of the multi-ostinato. Also, there are certain types of heterophonic variations on a theme, which often achieve a distinctness of line movement approaching genuine polymelody.

There are hints of some functioning "chordal" relationships in African polyphony, although these are not the Western major-minor system, nor are they formally and verbally articulated. The type of functioning, involving concepts of tension-relaxation, dissonance-consonance (which are by no means fixed universals), cannot as yet be gauged. It is clear, however, that there are varieties of "chord" clusters (as there are varieties of scales), and that some level of harmonic patterning may be aimed at through oral tradition. A few samples, resulting either from parallel or contrapuntal motion, follow (all hyphenated notes are to be read vertically). It should be noted that interval sizes are not those of equal temperament: (1) a repeated tritonic (augmented fourth) "chord" in a minor seventh or larger span, e.g., a–c′–e♭′–f′–g′–a′ of Ex. 6 (cents given in the next section below), popular among the Mambuti Pygmies and in many parts of Central Africa, and also appearing elsewhere; (2) a cadential sequence resting on parallel major thirds, with roots a major second apart, e.g., Gangele (Angola), c′–e′–g′, b♭–d′–f′, c′–e′–g′, and Baduma (Congo-

Brazzaville), b♭–d′, c′–e′; (3) another cadence-like sequence of the Baduma (bracketed notes are the most important), e′–g′, a–d′–f♯′, a–c′–e′–g′; (4) "plagal" motion with roots (or focal notes) a fourth apart, e.g., Babinga Pygmies (Congo-Brazzaville), b♭–e♭′–f′–a′–c″, c′–e♭′–g′–a′, and a related (reversed and inverted) form of the Venda (South Africa), g′–c″–e♭″, f′–a′–c″–e♭″. See also the patterning of Ex. 5, e.g., (meas. 6), g′–c″, e♭′–b♭′, c′–g′.

5. *Wasukuma wedding song (Tanzania)* [R. Brandel].
6. *Kukuya ivory horns (Congo-Brazzaville)* [R. Brandel].

C. *Scale and melody.* Among the large variety of African scales there is no one scale that is more idiomatic than the others. However, scales and melodies of very small range, two or three notes spanning the interval of a second or a third, appear somewhat infrequently (other than in ostinato accompaniments, which are usually part of pieces with larger scale gamuts). Tetrachordal and pentachordal spans are common, while scales and melodies of even larger range are quite prevalent. (A ladder of thirds spanning a ninth, F–A–C–E–G, may be found in a Batwa Pygmy song of Rwanda.) Furthermore, scales and melodies may be chasmatonic (gapped) or diatonic, within any span. Thus, there are chasmatonic five-note octaves, e.g., C–D–E♭–G–B♭–C of Ex. 5, and A–C–E♭–F–G–A of Ex. 6 with its tritonic melodic and harmonic emphasis (the diatonic upper tritone tends to descend, as in Ex. 6 and among the Mambuti Pygmies; see also the vocal line of a Chopi piece in Kirby, p. 65); chasmatonic five-note hexachords, e.g., C–D–E–G–A, often featuring triadic tunes; diatonic octaves, e.g., C–D–E–F(F♯)–G–A–B(B♭)–C; diatonic hexachords, e.g., G–A–B–C–D–E, etc. In addition, there appear to be some equal-stepped or isotonic scales, e.g., some Uganda harps with a four-step octave (among the Bagwere) or with a five-step octave (among the Baganda), and some xylophones with a five-step octave (parts of both Congos, Uganda) or with a seven-step octave (among the Chopi of Mozambique). Scales and melodies are frequently constructed in a "plagal" manner, featuring a central pivot note with a lower fourth and an upper fifth, e.g., G–C–G.

Interval sizes vary greatly, pointing up a variety of scale temperaments, especially evident in the tuning of instruments. (Ex. 6 horn intervals in cents reveal two small "minor" thirds and a large and a small "major" second: 279, 283, 227, 191.) Temperament norms, however, are not always easy to gauge.

The influence of the tonal languages (Bantu, etc.) on melody is marked but not rigid. Although high-pitched and low-pitched speech syllables (pitch height governs meaning and grammar) tend to be set to correspondingly pitched melodic notes [see Ex. 2], melodic flow is often controlled by purely musical considerations. Over-all melody shapes are varied, octave tunes often curving downward and tunes sometimes zigzagging through interlocking thirds.

D. *Form.* The most prevalent form is the litany type, i.e., immediate (but not necessarily exact) repetition of a musical idea throughout a piece. The length of melodic phrases, however, will vary from the very brief (one or two measures) to long-lined melodies of several measures. Frequently the length and inner organization are such that a two- or three-sectional "sentence" with contrasting phrases is apparent, often executed in the popular antiphony or response. There is also evidence of some verse forms, such as those found in various Akan songs of Ghana. A sense of larger sectional formation and contrast is often achieved through the repetition of two or more melodies, e.g., A...B...A...C...etc. (the form of the complete piece of Ex. 5). Such sectional contrast is heightened by some abrupt shifts in tonality in a Mangbetu choral piece (Brandel, *The Music of Central Africa,* p. 111). Lengthy ceremonies may provide even broader formal contrast through a series of musical "acts," each consisting of a piece repeated numerous times. Variation is common, but developmental techniques are rare.

E. *Performance style.* Density and motion are perhaps the best clues to over-all performance texture, both vocal and instrumental: masses of sound tend to pile up "orchestrally," timbres—often pungent and staccato—are contrasted, *tessiture* are juxtaposed, dynamic levels are usually high, and motion is constant, hurried, and complex as melodies, musical rhythms, and rhythms of dancers' and players' muscles converge with as much "action" as possible within a short span of time. This is, of course, a broad generalization. The qualities of speed and concentration are not always present. An evening story-singer, a private session on the musical bow or on the *sanza* may be quite different.

Vocal styles often point up emphatic, full-voice singing, at times punctuated by shouts and screams. Timbres are often tense-hoarse, somewhat guttural, and tenorlike for the men, owing to a predominant use of the arytenoid vocal muscles at great intensities and at high pitch ranges, as well as to some laryngeal constriction by neck muscles. Women's voices frequently are strident, owing to a predominant use of the thyroid group of vocal muscles at great intensities and at generally lower pitch ranges. Special effects may include glissando (especially at phrase endings); excessive nasality (perhaps for disguise or spirit imitation); excessive breathiness (often as a timbre accent); *Sprechstimme;* among some peoples, yodeling (e.g., Babinga Pygmies and N'Gundi of Congo-Brazzaville, and Bushmen) and humming (as in some Watutsi bard songs), and a variety of animal imitations. Most singing is highly syllabic (nonmelismatic), vibratoless, and nonornamented, except where Arab influence is evident (e.g., in some Watutsi bard songs).

Hocket is a favorite instrumental and vocal device, and, in its achievement of rapid timbre contrast, decidedly contributes to the over-all performance texture. Dance styles include broad, outflowing motions, often part of depictive dances, and self-contained, sometimes convulsive movement, usually set within abstract or symbolic contexts.

IV. *Instruments.* Orchestral emphasis is an important feature of African music. An ensemble consisting of hand-clapping singers, several different instruments, often including a set of one type, and usually dancers (or dancer-singers, dancer-players) is very common. *A cappella* as well as purely instrumental performance is also prevalent. In addition, certain instruments, notably the *sanza* and instruments of the chordophone family, are frequently used in a solo, nonensemble capacity, particularly to accompany a singer (who may be his own instrumentalist). Ensemble instruments center about idiophones (especially rattles, xylophones, bells) and membranophones, although aerophone bands are also popular. Many instruments (mainly slit drums, but also membrane drums, bells, horns, flutes, etc.) are used also for the purpose of telegraphy, which usually consists of duplication of actual speech tones and rhythms, particularly of stylized proverbs.

Idiophones include a variety of rattles, single or strung, manually operated or tied to the body, made of gourd, woven fibers, skin, etc. Percussion sticks and pounded bamboos occasionally occur in "tuned" sets (as in Southeast Asia). Iron bells are of many sizes and forms and are usually clapperless and struck; two-toned double bells, joined by an arch or a common handle, are found mainly in western, central, and south central regions. West Africa (and also parts of Ethiopia and Egypt) features a double bell, such as the *nnawuta* of Ghana, with two unequal components, pitched perhaps a fifth or more apart. There is also a type of folded, flattened iron, sometimes bell-like (Uganda, Congo-Kinshasa) and sometimes reminiscent of the slit drum and somewhat banana- or boat-shaped (e.g., the *kende* of the Kissi of Liberia; it is also found in West Central Africa and has been excavated in Rhodesia). Kunst has noted the same split-banana shape in the metal *kemanak* of Java and considers a common origin in the East Mediterranean or the Caucasus. The metal disk of the Far East, the gong, seems to be entirely absent from Africa.

The idiophonous slit drum, important in signaling, is made of wood and is stick-beaten; it may be cylinder-shaped, wedge-shaped, or footed and animal-shaped. The edges of the slit are usually of different thickness to produce two pitches. The trapeze-shaped *lukumbi* of the Batetela (Congo-Kinshasa) can emit six different pitches, three on each side of the drum.

Xylophones are quite widespread and are frequently played in ensembles, both small and large. Chopi *timbila* bands, popular in mining camps, may contain 20 to 30 xylophones in three or four different sizes, ranging from "soprano," with *c.* 15 slabs, to "bass," with *c.* 4 slabs. There are two main types of xylophone: (a) The rudimentary loose-key xylophone, without resonators, resting on tree trunks, is found in both Congos, Uganda, Central African Republic,

Cameroon, etc. A root name in the northern Congo-Kinshasa is *padingbwa;* (b) the fixed-key xylophone, sometimes suspended from the shoulders, usually has resonators and is found in most areas. A root name in the southern Congo-Kinshasa is *malimba* or *madimba.* The wooden slabs are fixed to a frame, and beneath each slab is an acoustically matched resonator, usually of calabash, which may be round (e.g., Mandingo people, Liberia; Chopi, Mozambique) or long (e.g., Yaswa, Congo-Brazzaville; Venda, South Africa). The latter recalls the vertical resonance tubes of the Indonesian *gendèr.* Buzzing timbres are often produced by fixing spider-webbing over a small lower-end hole in the calabash. The xylophone is frequently played by two or more persons, and one or two mallets may be used in each hand. The number of keys may exceed 20, and tunings, some of which appear to be isotonic, vary considerably in different areas [see III C above].

Indigenous to Africa is the *sanza* (Central Africa, Mozambique, etc.), *mbira* (Southeast Africa), *kembe* (Central Africa), or *limba* (East Central and Southeast Africa), a relatively small plucked idiophone with a set of flexible iron (sometimes bamboo) tongues fixed across a board or box; underneath, a calabash resonator may be attached or may loosely enclose the board. Tuning is accomplished by shifting the tongues, thereby altering their vibrating lengths. The number of tongues varies greatly (*c.* 5 to 25 or more), as do the tunings; unlike the xylophone, the lowest-pitched tongues not infrequently are set in the center of the board and the upper ones to either side, or tongues may be intermingled in various ways. Thumbs, and at times other fingers, produce a delicately metallic, hocketlike pizzicato [see Ex. 3], sometimes enlarged by the rattling or buzzing of attached devices. The sanza may be played singly or in sets of two or three.

Membranophone drums, usually used melodically as well as rhythmically, are of numerous sizes and shapes; single- and double-headed; with laced, nailed, or glued skins; hand-beaten (fingers, palms, base, fist), stick-beaten, and rubbed; and are commonly played in tuned sets of various numbers. Pitch (and timbre) contrast may also be obtained on a single drum by utilizing different striking points or by altering membrane tension (pressing on the skin or its fastenings). The long, conelike single-headed drum, such as the *ndungu* of the Babembe (Congo-Brazzaville), is one of the most popular. Others

22

include the kettledrum, e.g., the hemispherical, stick-beaten *ngoma* of the Venda (South Africa), and the West African hourglass "pressure" drum (also found in ancient and modern India and in the Far East), e.g., the professional shoulder-suspended *dùndún* types (Ex. 2) of the Yoruba (Nigeria), which are played with a hooked stick and are capable of variable pitch via elbow or hand manipulation of the thongs connecting the two skins. (In Ex. 2 this method is used only for the master drum.) There are also barrel and goblet drums; footed, stool-like drums with open lower ends, e.g., the *igbin* of the Yoruba and the *ganda* of the Digo (Kenya); clay-pot drums, e.g., the *bompili,* a women's drum of the Mbole (Congo-Brazzaville); frame drums, of Arab origin, e.g., the *mantshomane* of the Thonga (South Africa); and many others. Drums are among the major ceremonial instruments, although they are also used for secular purposes, and skilled drummers (especially the master drummer) may be trained from childhood.

Aerophones include vertical wooden or bamboo flutes (often without finger holes); whistles; mirlitons; the typically African transverse trumpets and horns of ivory (frequently with raised embouchures), e.g., the *bompate* of the Nkundo (Congo-Kinshasa), or of animal horn, wood, or gourd; and ocarinas. Ensembles of *c.* 5 or more horns (Ex. 6) or flutes (with or without other instruments), often playing in hocket, are common in many areas. Winds also include flutes with finger holes, e.g., the 4-holed notched *endere* of the Baganda (Uganda), panpipes, transverse flutes, end-blown trumpets, occasionally nose flutes, and the free aerophone, the bullroarer, often associated with circumcision rites.

Chordophones are important solo and song-accompanying instruments. One of the most common is the musical bow, frequently appearing with attached resonator at one end or at a midpoint where the string is divided in two; the mouth often acts as resonator. Partials above the fundamental may be emphasized, melodically and harmonically, through fingering or changing mouth resonance. Related to the bow and especially prevalent in Central Africa is the multiple-bow lute (Sachs: *Bogenlaute*), which consists of 5 to 8 one-stringed bows attached at one end (the strings above, the bows below) to a resonance case. Mainly playing with a vine plectrum rolled around the thumb, a professional *longombe* player of the Nkundo (Congo-Kinshasa) used to be carried around the village on a plat-

form, singing and playing for an all-night celebration. Zithers, frequently with resonators, exist in stick, board, raft, trough, and frame forms (e.g., the 6-stringed triangular frame zither of the Bassa of Liberia, which recalls the Persian *chank*). The trough is especially characteristic of Central East Africa (e.g., the *inanga* of Rwanda). Harps (usually arched) and lyres, possibly based on Egyptian models, are generally not common below the Equator. Rudimentary one-stringed fiddles are in many instances derived from Arab sources. As for Western instruments, the guitar, frequently used in nightclub ensembles (e.g., "high life"), has become one of the most popular. Modern trends in art music include use of traditional material in Western symphonic, operatic, church, and other forms.

Lit. (selected and generally recent; for other works and bibl., see Brandel, Gaskin, Thieme, Wolff): R. Brandel, *The Music of Central Africa* (1961; music, bibl.); L. J. P. Gaskin, *A Select Bibliography of Music in Africa* (1965); W. V. Brelsford, *African Dances of Northern Rhodesia* (Rhodes-Livingstone Museum Papers 2, 1959); E. M. von Hornbostel, *African Negro Music* (1928); A. King, *Yoruba Sacred Music from Ekiti* (1961); P. R. Kirby, *The Musical Instruments of the Native Races of South Africa,* rev. ed. (1965); D. L. Thieme, *African Music; a Briefly Annotated Bibliography* (1964); K. M. Trowell and K. P. Wachsmann, *Tribal Crafts of Uganda* (1953; instr.); C. Sachs, *Les Instruments de musique de Madagascar* (1938); B. Söderberg, *Les Instruments de musique au Bas-Congo et dans les régions avoisinantes* (1956); R. Günther, *Musik in Rwanda* (1964); J. H. K. Nketia, ‡*Folk Songs of Ghana* (1963); J. Blacking, "Problems of Pitch, Pattern and Harmony in the Ocarina Music of the Venda" (*African Music* ii, no. 2); R. Brandel, "The African Hemiola Style" (*Ethnomusicology* iii); *id.,* "Types of Melodic Movement in Central Africa" (*ibid.* vi); *id.,* "Polyphony in African Music," in *CP Sachs;* J. Kunst, "The Origin of the Kemanak (*Bijdragen tot de Taal-, Land- en Volkenkunde* 116, 1960); *id.,* "A Musicological Argument for Cultural Relationship between Indonesia . . . and Central Africa" (*PMA* lxii); G. Rouget, "Un Chromatisme africain" (*L'Homme* i, no. 3, 1963); K. P. Wachsmann, "An Equal Stepped Tuning in a Ganda Harp" (*Nature* clxv); *id.,* "A Study of Norms in the Tribal Music of Uganda" (*Ethnomusicology* i, pt. 11); H. C. Wolff, "Die Musik Afrikas" (*Deutsches Jahrbuch der Musikwissenschaft* ix

[1964]). See also "Current Bibliography, Africa," in all issues of *Ethnomusicology*.

Disc.: Publishers (1) Folkways Record Corp., N.Y.; (2) International Library of African Music, Roodepoort, Transvaal, South Africa; (3) Musée de l'Homme, Dept. d'Ethnomusicologie, Paris; and (4) UNESCO-Collection: An Anthology of African Music; see also *An International Catalogue of Published Records of Folk Music* ("Africa," pp. 1–13), ed. K. P. Wachsmann (International Folk Music Council, 1960).   R.B.

Africaine, L' [F., The African Woman]. Opera in five acts by G. Meyerbeer (libretto by E. Scribe), produced in Paris, 1865. Setting: Lisbon and Madagascar, end of 15th century.

Afternoon of a Faun, The. See *Aprés-midi d'un faune, L'*.

Agende [G.]. The German Protestant counterpart of the Roman Catholic liturgy or the Anglican rites, i.e., the entire ritual of the service of the German Protestant Church. See R. von Liliencron, *Liturgisch-musikalische Geschichte der evangelischen Gottesdienste vom 1523 bis 1700* (1893); F. Smend, *Neue Beiträge zur Reform unserer Agenden* (1913).

Agevole [It.]. Easy, smooth.

Agiatamente [It.]. With ease.

Agilmente [It.]. Nimbly, with agility.

Agitato [It.]. Excited.

Agnus Dei. The last item (except for the "Ite, missa est") of the Ordinary of the Mass [see Mass A and B III]; therefore, the final movement in Mass compositions. It consists of three invocations: "Agnus Dei, qui tollis peccata mundi: miserere nobis. Agnus Dei, . . . miserere nobis. Agnus Dei, . . . dona nobis pacem." It was introduced into the Roman Mass by the Greek Pope Sergius I (687–701). There exist about 300 melodies, 20 of which are in present-day use. The most common structure of the music is a a a or a b a. See *ApGC*, p. 418.

The Agnus Dei was retained in the first English Prayer Book (1549) but was suppressed in the second (1552). It is now commonly used in the Anglican service.

In the polyphonic Masses of the 16th century, the third invocation is often composed in a more involved style, using special contrapuntal devices, particularly canons. Examples are found in *L'Homme armé* Masses of Josquin and La Rue (triple, quadruple mensuration canon; see

HAM, no. 89; *ApNPM*, p. 181) and in many of the Masses of Palestrina.

Agogic. An accent is said to be agogic if it is effected not by dynamic stress or by higher pitch but by longer duration of the note [see Accent]. The German term *Agogik* (translated "agogics") is used to denote all the subtleties of performance achieved by modification of tempo, as distinct from *Dynamik* (dynamics), i.e., gradations that involve variety of intensity. Thus, the use of rallentando and accelerando, of tempo rubato, the dwelling on certain notes, as well as rests, breathing signs, fermatas, etc., all fall under *Agogik*. The term was introduced by H. Riemann (*Musikalische Dynamik und Agogik,* 1884) to describe those deviations from strict tempo and rhythm that are necessary for an intelligent rendering of the musical phrase.

Agréments [F.]. The ornaments introduced in French music of the 17th century, which were finally adopted into all European music and were generally indicated by stenographic signs or notes in small type. The *agréments* are characterized by a definitely stereotyped melodic contour, a close relationship with a single note of the melody to be ornamented, and a small melodic range. See Ornamentation II.   P.A.

Aguinaldo [Sp.]. Religious folksong of Spanish origin based on texts praising Jesus, the saints, or the angels, sung throughout Latin America. Prevailingly modal, it has a simple melodic structure and follows the conventional pattern of refrain (*estribillo*)–stanza (*copla*)–refrain (*estribillo*). Also called *alabanza, adoración,* and **villancico.*   J.O-S.

Aïda. Opera in four acts by Verdi (libretto by A. Ghislanzoni), commissioned by the Khedive of Egypt for the celebration of the opening of the Suez Canal and produced in Cairo, 1871. Setting: Egypt under the Pharaohs. Although reputedly making use of a few Egyptian musical themes, the general style is that of Italian grand opera. Striking features are the brief atmospheric prelude (in place of a conventional operatic overture) and the use of a few **leitmotivs.*

Air. (1) French 17th- and 18th-century term for song in general [see under Chanson]. *Air à boire,* drinking song. (2) In French opera and ballet of the 17th–18th centuries, an instrumental or vocal piece designed to accompany dancing but not cast in one of the standard dance patterns such as the minuet, gavotte, etc. Sometimes the composer (e.g., Rameau) qualifies it as *air tendre, air gracieux,* etc. (3) In the suites written about and after 1700, a movement, found in the optional group, of a melodic rather than dancelike character—in a way, a "song without words" [cf. Bach's Partitas nos. 4 and 6]. Early examples occur in the suites of Locke and Purcell. (4) See Ayre.

Air de cour [F.]. A type of short strophic song, sometimes with a refrain, for one or more voices with lute or harpsichord accompaniment, which was cultivated in France in the late 16th and in the 17th centuries, and which appears for the first time in Le Roy and Ballard's *Livre d'airs de cour* (1571). The songs are in simple syllabic style and binary form. The texts are chiefly love poems in affected *précieux* language, some of them in *vers mesuré.* The repetition of each of the two sections was frequently ornamented at will by the singer. Principal composers are Pierre Guédron (*c.* 1565–1625), Antoine Boësset (*c.* 1585–1646), Jean de Cambefort (d. 1661), and Michel Lambert (1610–96).

Lit.: T. Gérold, *L'Art du chant en France au XVIIe siècle* (1921); L. de La Laurencie, A. Mairy, and G. Thibault, *Chansons au luth et airs de cour français du XVIe siècle* (1934); ‡*Editions V, 7; D. P. Walker, "The Influence of *Musique mesurée . . .* on the *Airs de cour*" (*MD* ii, 141ff); J. Dodge, "Les Airs de cour d'Adrien Le Roy" (*BSIM* 1907, p. 1132); O. Chilesotti, "Gli 'Airs de court' . . . di J. B. Besard" (*Atti del congresso internazionale di scienze storiche* viii [1905], 131); A. Arnheim, in *SIM* x.   D.J.G.

Aire [Sp.]. Dance-song form cultivated in Argentina and Chile between 1830 and 1860 and almost extinct today. It consisted of two sections. The first, called *relación* or *estrofa,* was always sung to a kind of pantomime in which men and women dancers approached each other from opposite corners but never actually touched. The second section, much livelier and purely instrumental, accompanied a sort of tapping dance, which usually ended with shouts of "Aire!" when the man, kneeling on the floor, looked at his partner circling around him. Most of the examples preserved are bimodal, and only a few use the major mode.   J.O-S.

Ais, aisis [G.]. A-sharp, a-double-sharp; see Pitch names.

Akademie [G.]. *Academy. About 1800 the term was also used for concerts or recitals. Beethoven in one of his letters says: "Heute keine Akademie," i.e., "No concert tonight."

Akademische Festouvertüre [G., Academic Festival Overture]. Orchestral composition by Brahms, op. 80, written for the University of Breslau in appreciation for the degree of doctor of philosophy conferred on him in 1879. It includes several German student songs, skillfully arranged and connected.

Akathistos [Gr.]. A famous hymn of the Byzantine Church in honor of the Virgin, originally sung on the Feast of the Annunciation (March 25), now sung in part during certain Matins of Lent and in its entirety during the vigil of the fifth Saturday of Lent. According to one of several legends, it was written by the Patriarch Sergios in 626 on the occasion of the deliverance of Constantinople from the Persians and was sung by the choir and congregation standing throughout a nightlong service of thanksgiving [Gr. *Akathistos,* not seated]. The Akathistos belongs to the general species of Byzantine poetry known as *kontakion* [see Byzantine chant II] and consists of a prologue and 24 stanzas whose initial letters comprise the Greek alphabet (acrostic). It is the only *kontakion* that has remained intact, the rest having been reduced to the prologue and first stanza. The authorship of the Akathistos has not been settled, although some indications point to Romanos (*fl.* 500–555), one of the greatest Byzantine hymnographers, who joined the clergy of the Theotokos Church in Constantinople at the time of Anastasius I (491–518).

Lit.: E. Wellesz, *A History of Byzantine Music and Hymnography,* rev. ed. (1961), pp. 191ff and *passim; id.,* ‡*The Akathistos Hymn* (1957); *Editions XXIX, C, 9; G. G. Meerssemann, *Der Hymnos Akathistos im Abendland,* 2 vols. (1958, '60); E. Wellesz, in *MF* vi, xi, xiv, *id.,* in *Dumbarton Oaks Papers* ix, x.

Akkord [G.]. Chord.

Akoluthia [Gr.]. The order of service of the Byzantine Church, particularly that of the Office, thus usually not including the Mass (which was called *leiturgeia,* "liturgy"). The term was also used for the sequence of eight odes that form the *kanon* [see Byzantine chant II]. The theory advanced by W. Christ (*Anthologia Graeca carminum Christianorum,* 1871, p. lvii) that the medieval term "sequence" was the Latin translation of akoluthia is without foundation.

Akzent [G.]. Accent.

Akzentneumen [G.]. Accent neumes. See Neumes II.

Al [It.], **à la** [F.]. To the, at the; see, e.g., *Al fine*.

A la. See *Al; Alla.*

Alabado [Sp.]. Originally, a Spanish hymn in praise of the Eucharist, brought to the New World by the Franciscans, probably during the 17th century. It became a hymn in praise of Jesus, the Virgin Mary, and other saints. Some forms of *alabado* (occasionally called *alabanza*) have survived in numerous Roman Catholic communities of Mexico, New Mexico, etc., especially in the unusual rites of the Penitent Brothers. See J. B. Rael, *The New Mexico Alabado* (1951); A. B. McGill, "Old Mission Music" (*MQ* xxiv); L. T. Shaver, "Spanish Mission Music" (*Proceedings of the MTNA* [1919]).

Alabanza [Sp.]. See under *Aguinaldo; Alabado.*

Alalá. A type of folksong from northwest Spain (Galicia) expressing passion and longing. Older examples use syllables such as "la-la" or "ai-le-lo-la" and are interesting because of the preservation of plainsong-like elements. See F. Pedrell, ‡*Cancionero musical popular español* (1918–22), ii, 127ff.

A la mi re, alamire. See under Hexachord III.

Alba [Prov.]. In the repertory of the troubadours, a poem dealing with the lover's departure in the early morning. It is usually cast in the form of a dialogue between the lover and a watchman (*gaite de la tore*, guard of the tower), who warns him of approaching danger. The oldest known prototype is an 11th-century Latin poem, "Phebi claro nondum orto." Three Provençal *albas* are preserved with music: Guiraut de Bornelh's "Reis glorios" [*HAM*, no. 18c], Cadenet's "S'anc fui belha," and an anonymous "Gaite de la tor" [see *ReMMA*, p. 214f]. The minnesinger counterpart of the *alba* is the *Tagelied* [G., day song] or *Wächterlied* (guard song), which Wagner revived in the second act of *Tristan und Isolde* (Brangäne's warning call). Many examples of the *Tagelied*, however, are of a more devotional nature, serving as a sort of morning prayer [see, e.g., "Ein ander tagwyss (Tageweise) graff Peters von Arberg," in P. Runge, ‡*Die Sangesweisen der Colmarer Handschrift* (1896), p. 173]. See also *Alborada; Aubade.*

Albert Herring. Comic opera in three acts by B. Britten (libretto by E. Crozier after "Le Rosier de Madame Husson" by De Maupassant), produced in Glyndebourne, 1947. Setting: England, late 19th century.

Alberti bass. Stereotyped figures of accompaniment for the pianist's left hand, consisting of broken chords [see also Murky]. They are named

for Domenico Alberti (1710–40?), who used them extensively. Similar broken-chord patterns occur in the works of the virginalists (*c.* 1600) and in various keyboard compositions of the 17th century, e.g., the fourth variation of the G-minor aria in Pachelbel's *Hexachordum Apollinis* of 1699 [see *DTB* 2; *TaAM* ix, 46]. They are still common in the works of Haydn, Mozart, and the early Beethoven. See G. A. Marco, "The Alberti Bass Before Alberti" (*MR* xx).

Albisiphone. See under Flute I (d).

Alborada [Sp.]. A type of Spanish (Galician, particularly) music, played on the *dulzaína* (rustic oboe) and *tamboril* (small drum), originally a morning song [see G. Chase, *The Music of Spain*, 1941, p. 237]. Ravel's *Alborada del gracioso* (The Jester's Morning Song; 1905) derives certain features from the Spanish *alborada*. See also *Alba; Aubade.*

Albumblatt [G., album leaf]. A fanciful name for a short piece of 19th-century music, such as might be inscribed in an autograph album.

Alceste. Opera in three acts by Gluck (Italian libretto by R. di Calzabigi, based on Euripides' tragedy), produced in Vienna, probably 1767. Rev. French version produced in Paris, 1776. Setting: Thessaly, in legendary times. Written in simple, nonvirtuoso style, *Alceste* was one of the first of Gluck's "reform" operas, embodying his theories about the proper relation of drama and music. Its French version touched off the famous quarrel between the "Gluckists" and the "Piccinnists" (supporters of Niccolò Piccinni), who favored traditional Italian operatic style.

Aleatory music. Music in which the composer introduces elements of chance or unpredictability with regard to either the composition or its performance. The terms *aleatoric, chance* *music, music of indeterminacy* have been applied to many works created since 1945 by composers who differ widely as to the concepts, methods, and rigor with which they employ procedures of random selection. Chance may be involved in the process of composition, in performance, or in both. In the composition process, pitches, durations, degrees of intensity, etc., and/or their distribution in time may be chosen by dice throwing, interpretations of abstract designs (Cage), etc., or according to certain mathematical laws of chance (Xenakis). In performance, chance is allowed to operate by leaving some elements and/or their order of appearance to the performer's discretion (Boulez, Stockhausen, Pousseur, *et al.*), thus introducing the idea of *choice*. Most of these procedures are derived from and motivated by new general concepts of music, according to which form and structure are no longer regarded as definitely fixed and final but as subject to partial or total transformations from one performance to another (open forms, mobile forms). The composers adhering to such ideas are part of a general movement—in science and philosophy as well as in the arts—that tends to consider, and therefore to express, the world in terms of possibility rather than necessity.

"Dice music" was well known in the 18th century. The most famous example is a *Musikalisches Würfelspiel* of unknown authorship but attributed by several publishers to Mozart (K. Anh. C 30.01). It appeared in London in 1806 with the description: "Mozarts Musical Game, fitted in an elegant box, showing by an easy system to compose an unlimited number of Waltzes, Rondos, Hornpipes, and Reels." It consists of a set of first measures, second measures, etc., from each of which a measure is selected by a throw of the dice. J. P. Kirnberger contributed to this entertainment in his *Der allezeit fertige Polonaisen- und Menuettenkomponist* of 1757. A number of similar publications followed, among them ones ascribed to Haydn, one to K. P. E. Bach, and the *Würfelspiel* mentioned above. See P. Löwenstein, "Mozart-Kuriosa" (*ZMW* xii, 342); O. E. Deutsch, *ibid.,* p. 595; H. Gerigk, in *ZMW* xvi, 350; A. Laszló, *The Dice Composer* (1941).

The first well-known example of 20th-century aleatory composition was John Cage's *Music of Changes* for piano (1951). In this work the pitches or pitch aggregates are precisely notated, while their duration and frequency of occurrence are dictated by the *I-Ching* (Book of Changes),

an ancient Chinese prescription for arriving at random numbers by throwing coins or sticks. In other compositions Cage has employed templates (*Music for Carillon*) and incidental imperfections of the music paper (*Music for Piano 21–52*) to determine compositional elements. Cage's *Concert* for piano and orchestra (1958) is a prime example of indeterminacy in performance. Its 63-page piano part contains 84 different sound-aggregates to be played in whole or in part and in any sequence. The wind and string parts are of a similar nature, and the *Concert* includes an "Aria" for soprano that may or may not be sung simultaneously.

Considerably less license is given in some scores involving alternatives from which the performer may—indeed, must—choose, preferably at the moment of performance. Karlheinz Stockhausen's *Klavierstück XI* (1956) has nineteen sections to be played in any order, and the pianist may choose from six different tempos, dynamics, and kinds of touch (legato, staccato, etc.). His *Zyklus* (1959) for one percussion player is a spiral-bound score that may be read from any point clockwise or counterclockwise and even upside down. The work ends when the player returns to his starting point. Perhaps the ultimate in indeterminacy of performance is reached in Mauricio Kagel's *Sonant* for guitar, harp, and percussion, where one is told, "the player may mimic his part or rebel against it entirely."

The use of mathematical laws of chance, such as theory of probability, games theory, etc., is represented by the Greek composer Yannis Xenakis, most of whose works belong to this general category, which he calls *stochastic* music. In such works as *ST/10-1,080262* and *Stratégie* (both 1962), he also uses the assistance of computers.

Lit.: U. Eco, *Opera aperta* [1962]; J. Cage, *Silence; Lectures and Writings* [1961]; W. Mellers, *Music in a New Found Land* [1964], pp. 177–93; *Die Reihe* (German ed. [1955—], English ed. [1958—], *passim; Incontri musicali* nos. 1–4 (1956–60), *passim; Perspectives of New Music* [1962—], *passim;* J. Cage, "To Describe the Process of Composition Used in 'Music for Piano 21–52' " (*Die Reihe,* Eng. ed., iii, 41ff); P. Boulez, "Sonate, que me veux-tu?" (*Perspectives of New Music* i, 32); *id.,* "Alea" (*Incontri musicali* iii, 3); Y. Xenakis, "Musiques Formelles" (*RM* nos. 253–4, 1963).   J.R.W. and A.B.

Al fine [It., to the end]. Indication to repeat a composition from the beginning (*da capo*) or from the sign § (*dal segno*) to the place marked *fine*.

Aliquot strings, aliquot scaling. *Sympathetic strings added by some piano makers (first by Blüthner) above the strings of the upper register in order to produce a fuller sound through resonance.

Alla, all' [It.], **à la, à l'** [F.]. In the manner of; e.g., *alla *turca, alla *zingarese,* etc.; *à l'espagnol,* in the Spanish manner.

Alla breve [It.]. A tempo mark (₵) indicating quick duple time, i.e., with the half note rather than the quarter note as the beat; in other words, 2/2 instead of 4/4. Both the name and the sign are a vestige of *mensural notation and of the *proportions (*tempus imperfectum diminutum*). Originally (and properly) *alla breve* meant that the unit of musical time (*tactus*) was represented by the *brevis* (corresponding to our double whole note), not, as was usual, by the *semibrevis* (corresponding to our whole note). Today it means that the half note should be regarded as the unit of time, instead of, as is usual, the quarter note. It should be noted, however, that at least in earlier practice this unit could be fairly slow. An example in point is the overture to *Don Giovanni,* marked andante and ₵. Mozart obviously wanted the music to be interpreted in a more animated tempo but, at the same time, in much broader terms than is customarily done by modern conductors, who play it largo and often employ eight beats to the measure instead of two.

Allargando [It.]. Slowing down, usually accompanied by a crescendo at a climax.

Allegretto [It.]. (1) A tempo between andante and allegro; see Tempo marks. (2) A short piece in fast (allegro) tempo.

Allegro [It.]. (1) General indication for fast speed [see Tempo marks]. Originally the term was employed primarily as an expression mark [It., cheerful, joyful], as appears from designations such as "allegro e presto" (M. Cazzati, *Il Secondo Libro delle sonate,* op. 8, 1648) or "andante allegro" (first movement, Handel's Organ Concerto no. 6, op. 4). (2) A composition in fast tempo, especially the first and last movements of a sonata, symphony, etc.

Alleluia [L.]. An exclamation of praise to God (from the Hebrew *hallelujah,* praise ye the Lord), which occurs at the beginning or end of Psalms 110–118 (111–113, 115–117). It is men-

tioned by Tertullian, St. Jerome, and particularly St. Augustine, who describes and extols it as an "old tradition of the Church." Jerome says it was sung at festive meals and also by the plowmen in the fields. Sidonius Apollinaris (born *c.* 430) says that it was sung by the boatmen on the Loire, and Bede reports that the Britons used it as a battle cry in 448. In liturgical use it occurs as an expression of rejoicing added to antiphons, introits, offertories, communions, etc., during Eastertide and on Christmas Day, Corpus Christi, and other feast days. A special type of chant is the alleluiatic antiphon, consisting of the word "alleluia" repeated three or more times [e.g., *LU,* p. 776kk].

More specifically, Alleluia refers to an elaborate chant sung as the third item of the Proper of the Mass. (Concerning its alleged introduction by Pope Damasus I, reigned 366–84, see *ApGC,* p. 376f.) There is evidence that about 450 it was sung in Rome only once during the year, on the first day of Easter; that before St. Gregory (reigned 590–604) it was sung during the period from Easter to Pentecost (Paschaltide), and that Gregory extended its use, probably from Advent to the last Sunday after Epiphany. Finally it was introduced into all Masses except during Lent, for which the original *tract was preserved. During Paschaltide (more correctly, from Saturday after Easter to Friday after Pentecost) the Mass includes two Alleluias, one in place of the Gradual.

The Alleluia of the Mass consists of the word "alleluia" followed by a brief sentence referring to the occasion, the so-called verse (*versus alleluiaticus,* abbr. ℣), e.g.: "Alleluia. ℣ Surrexit Dominus de sepulcro" [see *LU,* p. 790; also *HAM,* no. 13]. The music for the word "alleluia" closes with a long vocalization on the final "a," the so-called *jubilus [see also Neuma]. In nearly all Alleluias the music of the jubilus (often that of alleluia plus jubilus) recurs at the end of the verse [see Rhyme]. The jubilus melodies and also the melismas found within the verses frequently show repeat structures such as a a b, a a b b c, etc. [see *ApGC* pp. 386ff]. Many Alleluia melodies reveal their relatively late date (10th, 11th cent.) by their use of extended scale formations, usually in descending motion. See also Gregorian chant III; Psalmody II; Sequence II.

Allemande [F.]. A dance in moderate duple time that first appeared in the early 16th century. Early examples occur in T. Susato's *Het derde musyck Boexken* (Third Music Book) of 1551; in

C. Gervaise's *Troisième Livre de danceries* (1556; see *HAM*, no. 137); in B. Schmid, *Zwey Bücher einer neuen kunstlichen Tabulatur* (1577; see W. Merian, *Der Tanz in den deutschen Tabulaturbüchern,* 1927, p. 111); and in the *Fitzwilliam Virginal Book* (c. 1620), where the name "Alman," "Almayne," is used. Arbeau, in his *Orchésographie* (1589), considers the dance already outmoded [see Dance music II]. The 16th-century allemande shows a plain, essentially homophonic style. The dance steps were simple, as appears from the following description by T. Morley (*A Plaine and Easie Introduction to Practicall Musicke,* 1597, p. 181): "The *Alman* is a more heavie daunce then this [i.e., the galliard] (fitlie representing the nature of the people [German], whose name it carieth) so that no extraordinarie motions are used in dauncing of it." Like the pavane and passamezzo, the allemande was frequently followed by a jumping

dance in triple meter (called *tripla, Proportz*) or, in the 17th century, by the courante. In the 17th century the allemande became a stylized dance type that was regularly used as the first movement of the *suite. These allemandes are in very moderate 4/4 time, with a short upbeat, and frequently make use of short running figures that are passed through the various voices of a pseudocontrapuntal fabric. The examples here (1. Ammerbach, 1571; 2. Purcell, c. 1660; 3. J. K. F. Fischer, c. 1690) illustrate the stylistic development of the dance [examples in *HAM*, nos. 216, 232, 250, 253].

In the late 18th century the name Allemande was used in South Germany as an equivalent for *deutscher Tanz,* a quick waltzlike dance in 3/4 or 3/8 time. Cf. Beethoven's "à l'Allemande" in his *Bagatellen* op. 119, and his *Zwölf deutsche Tänze* (1795) for orchestra. See Dance music III.

Lit.: E. Mohr, *Die Allemande* (1932); A. Anders, "Untersuchungen über die Allemande als Volksliedtyp des 16. Jahrhunderts" (diss. Frankfurt, 1940).

Allentando [It.]. Slowing down.

Alliteration. A characteristic feature of ancient North European poetry (*Beowulf, Edda*), consisting of the use of words with the same initial letter. This principle was adopted by Wagner in *Ring des Nibelungen,* e.g., "Nach Welten-Wonne mein Wunsch verlangte aus wild webendem Bangen."

All' ongarese. See *Ongarese.*

All' ottava [It.]. See *Ottava.*

All' unisono [It.]. See Unison.

Alman, almayne. A 16th-century English corruption of *allemande.

Alma Redemptoris Mater [L.]. One of the Marian antiphons; see Antiphon 2. Dunstable, Dufay [see *HAM*, no. 65], Ockeghem, Obrecht, Josquin, and others composed polyphonic settings. Leonel's *Missa Alma Redemptoris Mater* is the earliest known *cantus firmus* Mass.

Almérie [F.]. A variety of lute invented c. 1650 by Jean Lemaire (not c. 1750 by Louis Lemaire). The name is an anagram on the inventor's name. See M. Brenet, *Les Concerts en France sous l'ancien régime* (1900), p. 54.

Alpensinfonie, Eine [G., An Alpine Symphony]. A long symphonic poem in one movement by R. Strauss, op. 64 (1911–15), describing a day of

Alpine climbing. Particularly noteworthy for its time is the extreme dissonance and daring use of instruments in the section entitled "Erscheinung."

Alphabet (in music). See Pitch names; Letter notation; Tablature.

Alphorn, alpine horn. A primitive wind instrument, still used by herdsmen in the Alps for signaling over a great distance and for simple melodies. Made of wooden staves bound with strips of birch bark, it is 3 to 10 feet long and appears in various shapes, straight or bent. The tones produced are the harmonics [see Acoustics IV], somewhat modified by the material and the irregular width of the inner tube. In particular, the fourth (11th harmonic) is halfway between f and f-sharp (Alphorn fa) [see *Ranz des vaches*]. Similar instruments are found in Scandinavia, Poland, Rumania, and among the South American Indians. See *SaRM*, p. 7; H. Szadrowsky, in *Jahrbuch des schweizer Alpenclub* iv; K. Nef, in *De Muziek* v. See ill. under Brass instruments.

Alpine Symphony, An. See *Alpensinfonie, Eine.*

Al segno. See *Segno.*

Also sprach Zarathustra [G., *Thus Spake Zarathustra*]. *Symphonic poem by R. Strauss, op. 30, completed in 1896. It is based on Nietzsche's work of the same name.

Alt. (1) Term for the tones of the octave above the treble staff (g″ to f‴), which are said to be "in alt." The tones of the next higher octave are called "in altissimo." (2) In German, the lower of the two female voices, i.e., the contralto [see Alto]. In connection with instruments, the term denotes the second highest member of the family (*Altklarinette,* alto clarinet; *Altsaxophon,* alto saxophone). See the various instruments. *Altgeige* is the viola alta [see Violin family (d)], rarely the ordinary viola.

Alta [It., Sp.]. The *alta,* or *alta danza,* is a dance of the 15th century, which, according to the Italian theorist A. Cornazano ("Libro dell' arte del danzare," 1455?), was the Spanish equivalent of the Italian saltarello, the French *pas de Brabant* (It., *passo brabante*). Each of the numerous *basse danse* melodies could also be used for the *alta* [see *Basse danse*]. An *Alta* by Francesco de la Torre (for three instruments; *HAM*, no. 102a) is based on the *basse danse* melody *Il Re di Spagna* [see *Spagna*].

The term also occurs in the phrase *alta musica*

(Tinctoris, *c.* 1435–1511) as a designation for an ensemble of loud instruments, such as trombone, shawm, bombarde.

Alteration. (1) See Mensural notation III. (2) The raising or lowering of a note by means of a sharp or flat, also called chromatic alteration. See Accidentals; Chromaticism; Harmonic analysis V.

Altered chord. See Harmonic analysis V.

Alternation (alternatim). A term used with reference to early liturgical compositions (12th–16th cent.), primarily to indicate the alternation of polyphony and plainsong, a method that developed from a similar practice in Gregorian chant of alternation between the soloists (*cantores*) and choir (*schola*) [see Responsorial singing; Psalmody II]. Polyphonic composition of such chants (Graduals, responsories, Alleluias) was restricted to their solo sections, which therefore alternated with sections sung in plainsong by the choir. Among the earliest examples is an "Alleluia Angelus Domini" from *c.* 1100 [Chartres, MS 109; see *HAM*, no. 26]. Consistent application of this principle occurs in the organa of the school of Notre Dame [see Organum V]. In the 15th and 16th centuries the *alternatim* method was used particularly in psalms and the *Magnificat but also for sequences and hymns. An interesting example of a relatively late date is Tallis' setting of the responsory "Audivi vocem" [*HAM*, no. 127].

The practice of alternation is even more important in liturgical organ music. Here not only the psalms, the Magnificat, the *Salve Regina, and the hymns consisted of organ music alternating with plainsong, but also the various items of the Mass [see Organ Mass]. The normal scheme for the Kyrie was as follows (organ music in italics): Kyrie *Kyrie* Kyrie Christe *Christe* Christe *Kyrie* Kyrie *Kyrie.*

Alternativo [It.]. **alternativement** [F.]. Indication for one section to alternate with another, as in an A B A structure (ternary form; see Binary and ternary form). In the suites of Bach, an indication such as "Bourrée I, alternativement—Bourrée II" calls for repeat of section A (first *bourrée*) after section B (second *bourrée*). Schumann occasionally used the term *alternativo* as a designation for an internal section.

Altgeige [G.] See under Alt (2).

Althorn. See under Brass instruments III (f).

Altissimo [It.]. See Alt.

Altistin [G.]. A contralto singer.

Alto [It.]. (1) A female voice of low range, also called contralto. See Voices, range of. (2) Originally the alto was a high male voice [It. high], which through use of *falsetto nearly reached the range of the female voice (contralto). This type of voice, also known as *countertenor, was cultivated especially in England, where the church music of the 16th and 17th centuries definitely implies its use. [For an explanation of the term, see Contratenor.] (3) The second highest part of the normal four-part chorus; L. *altus*. (4) In French and Italian, the second highest instrument of the violin family, i.e., the viola. (5) Applied to clarinet, flute, saxophone, etc., the term refers to the third or fourth highest member of the family.

Lit.: G. E. Stubbs, *The Adult Male Alto or Counter-Tenor Voice* (1908); A. H. D. Prendergast, "The Man's Alto in English Music" (*ZIM* i); W. J. Hough, "The Historical Significance of the Countertenor" (*PMA* lxiv).

Alto clef. See Clef.

Alto Rhapsody. See *Rhapsodie aus Goethe's 'Harzreise im Winter.'*

Altra volta [It.]. Encore.

Altschlüssel [G.]. Alto clef.

Altus [L.]. See under Alto (3).

Alzati [It.]. Indication to remove the mutes.

Amabile [It.]. Amiable, with love.

Amahl and the Night Visitors. Opera in one act by Gian Carlo Menotti (to his own libretto), produced in New York by N.B.C.-TV Opera Theater on Christmas Eve, 1951, the first opera commissioned specifically for television. Stage premiere, Indiana University, 1952. Setting: near Bethlehem, birth of Jesus.

Ambitus [L.]. The range of the melodies of Gregorian chant, varying from a fourth (in some of the simple antiphons) to an octave or more (Graduals, Alleluias, etc.). In the Graduals the ambitus of the verse is often one or two tones higher than that of the respond, e.g., in "Universi" [*LU*, p. 320]. The same is true of the Offertories and their verses (no longer used). The largest ambitus is found in the Offertory "Tollite portas" and its two verses, namely two octaves (from F to f′). In the theory of the church modes

the ambitus is the chief mark of distinction between an authentic and a plagal mode. [See Gregorian chant V (b); Church modes.] See F. Krasuski, *Über den Ambitus der gregorianischen Messgesänge* (1903); *ApGC*, pp. 133ff, 144ff.

Amboss [G.]. *Anvil.

Ambrosian chant. A repertory of liturgical chant named after St. Ambrose (340?–397), Bishop of Milan, and still in use today in the cathedral of that city; therefore also called Milanese chant. It constitutes one of the four (or five) branches of Western Christian chant [see Chant]. Its connection with St. Ambrose is even more nominal than that of Gregorian chant with St. Gregory, modern investigations having made it seem probable that most of its melodies are even later than those of the Gregorian repertory, perhaps belonging to the 10th and 11th centuries [see *ApGC*, p. 508f]. Like the Gregorian Mass, the Ambrosian includes ten musical items, only three of which, however, belong to the Ordinary, there being no Kyrie or Agnus (the Credo is called *Symbolum*). The seven items of the Ambrosian Proper are shown here together with the corresponding items of the Gregorian:

Ambrosian	*Gregorian*
Ingressa	Introit
Psalmellus	Gradual
Hallelujah (Cantus)	Alleluia (Tract)
Post Evangelium	—
Offertorium	Offertory
*Confractorium	—
Transitorium	Communion

Among the Ambrosian offices, that of Vespers is noteworthy for its elaborate structure, including (in addition to the Gregorian items) the *lucernarium, responsorium* (two), *psallenda* (two), and *completorium* (four), as well as a threefold Kyrie.

The Ambrosian psalm tones lack the mediation [see Psalm tones] but are much more diversified and flexible than the Gregorian in the selection of the reciting tone and termination (clausula), both of which are determined in a rather intricate manner by the antiphon. They contain no reference to the eight-mode or eight-tone system of Gregorian chant, and neither antiphons nor any other chants are ever assigned to a mode. A considerable number of chants close on the *affinales, that is, a, b, c′, d′. In contrast to the Gregorian repertory there is very little uniformity of style within a given category of chant. Thus, some of the *ingressae* are very simple and short and others quite long and highly melismatic. In many other details as well, the Ambrosian repertory lacks the thorough organization of the Gregorian (or, from another point of view, shows greater freedom from strict rule and system).

Selective quotation has done much to spread the misconception that Ambrosian chant in general is prolix and ornate in the extreme, whereas in fact most of its melodies are comparable to those of the Gregorian repertory. Occasionally, however, one encounters extraordinarily long melismas (up to 200 or more notes), particularly in the responsories of Matins. A number of Ambrosian chants have Gregorian counterparts, and in these cases the Ambrosian version is always much more elaborate than the Gregorian [see *HAM*, no. 10; *SchGMB*, no. 2; *BeMMR*, p. 58; *LavE* i.1, 561; O. Ursprung, *Die katholische Kirchenmusik*, 1931, p. 20; A. Gastoué, *Cours ... de chant grégorien*, 1917, pp. 67, 128, 149]. Possibly these chants represent a later stage characterized by a tendency toward amplification and paralleling the period of troping in Gregorian chant. See Ambrosian hymns.

Lit.: *ApGC*, pp. 465ff; M. Huglo, *Fonti e paleografia del canto ambrosiano* (1956); R. Jesson, "Ambrosian Chant: The Music of the Mass" (diss. Indiana Univ., 1955); R. G. Weakland, in *CP Reese;* K. Ott, "L'Antifonia ambrosiana," in *Rassegna gregoriana* v (1906), and similar articles in v–viii, x (1906–11); ‡*Editions XLII, A, 5, 6; ‡*Antiphonale missarum ... sanctae ecclesiae Mediolanensis* (1935); ‡*Liber vesperalis ... sanctae ecclesiae Mediolanensis* (1939).

Ambrosian hymns. The hymns of the Roman and Milanese (Ambrosian) rites written by St. Ambrose (340?–397), or others of the same type written later.

I. *Text.* Formerly nearly all the hymns (*c.* 120) of the *antiphonarium* were ascribed to Ambrose, under the generic name *hymni Ambrosiani.* Actually the number of true Ambrosian hymns is much smaller, hardly more than a dozen. With four of them Ambrose's authorship is placed beyond doubt by the testimony of St. Augustine; these are "Aeterne rerum conditor," "Deus Creator omnium," "Jam surgit hora tertia," and "Veni Redemptor gentium." [See J. P. Migne, *Patrologiae cursus completus,* Latin series, 221 vols. (1844–64), xxxii, col. 618; xxxii, col. 777; xliv, col. 284; xxxix, cols. 1662–63]. Two others,

"Illuxit orbi" and "Bis ternas horas," are mentioned by Cassiodorus (d. *c.* 583). The scheme of all the Ambrosian hymns is simple, consisting of eight stanzas of four lines each, in iambic tetrameter, e.g.:

> Vĕnī Rĕdēmptŏr gēntĭūm
> Ŏstēndĕ pārtūm vīrgīnīs
> Mīrētūr ōmnĕ sēcŭlūm
> Tālīs dĕcēt părtūs dĕūm.

[For the early history of hymnody, see Hymn I, II.]

II. *Music.* The earliest source for an Ambrosian hymn is the *"Musica enchiriadis" of *c.* 900, which contains, in *daseian notation, a melody for "Aeterna Christi munera" [see *GS* i, 154; *HAM*, no. 9b]. In these circumstances the question of whether this or other melodies are compositions of Ambrose, "early Christian folksongs" (as has been surmised), or products of a later period remains entirely open. Scholars who believe that they date from the 4th century have reconstructed an "original form," i.e., strictly syllabic (the melodies as preserved often contain groups of two or three notes over a

syllable) and in triple meter. The accompanying example shows a melody (a) in its 9th-century form and (b) in its hypothetical reconstruction [see also *HAM*, no. 9]. The rhythmic interpretation rests on a passage in Augustine's *De musica,* which defines an iambic foot as "a short and a long, of three beats" (*brevis et longa, tria temporum*). Since Augustine's work is a treatise not on music but on poetic versification, this evidence is of rather doubtful validity [see *ApGC*, p. 428f].

The term "Ambrosian hymn" [G. *Ambrosi-*

anischer Lobgesang] is erroneously used for the *Te Deum.

Lit.: L. Biraghi, *Inni sinceri . . . di S. Ambrogio* (1862); E. Garbagnati, *Gli Inni del breviario ambrosiano* (1897); G. M. Dreves, *Aurelius Ambrosius* (1893); G. Bas, in *Musica divina* xvii; J. Jeannin, in *TG* xxvi, 115.

Ambrosian modes. See under Church modes II.

Âme [F.]. The sound post of the violin.

Amelia al ballo [It., Amelia Goes to the Ball]. Opera in one act by Menotti (to his own libretto), produced (in English) in Philadelphia, 1937. Setting: Milan, 1910.

Amen. A Hebrew word, meaning "so be it," which occurs in the Scriptures as an affirmative expression (e.g., in Numbers 5:22 and at the end of Ps. 40 [41]) and is widely used in Christian rites. It is usually spoken by the congregation (or recited by the choir) as a confirming answer to the lection or the prayer of the priest [see *AR*, p. 35*]. In Gregorian chant it occurs at the end of the lesser *doxology (" in saecula saeculorum. Amen.") and in the Mass at the end of the Gloria ("in gloria Dei Patris. Amen.") as well as of the Credo ("Et vitam venturi saeculi. Amen."). In the polyphonic Masses of the 17th and 18th centuries the confirming character of the Amen led to the writing of extensive closing sections in fugal style, called Amen fugue or Amen chorus, in which the word is repeated over and over. This practice began with Antonio Bertali (1605–69; see *AdHM* i, 516) and continued throughout the periods of Handel (Amen chorus in *Messiah*), Bach, Mozart, Beethoven, etc. In Cherubini's D-minor Mass, at the end of the Credo the soprano alone repeats the word 107 times. Also noteworthy is the parodistic Amen chorus in Berlioz' *Damnation de Faust* (Part II). For Amen cadence, see Plagal cadence.

Amener [F.]. A 17th-century dance in moderate triple time with phrases of six measures (three plus three or four plus two) as a characteristic feature. It occurs in the suites of Heinrich Biber, J. K. F. Fischer, Alessandro Poglietti, in the instrumental suites edited by Écorcheville (*Vingt Suites d'orchestre*, 1906), etc. The derivation of the *amener* from the *basse danse,* given in most reference books, is very questionable. More likely, it is one of the numerous species of *branle, a branle à mener,* i.e., a *branle* in which one couple led while the others followed. See also Minuet.

American Guild of Organists. See Societies, musical, I (1).

American Indian music. I. *North America.* Although the collection and scientific study of North American Indian music did not commence until the late 19th century, numerous earlier references to it are found, beginning shortly after the coming of the English colonists.

In the 18th century, F. W. Marpurg, the German music historian, published *Remarks on Three Songs of the Iroquois* (Berlin, 1760), and an early attempt at adaptation of an actual Indian melody, called *Alknomook* or *Alkmoonok* ("The death song of the Cherokee Indians"), was first published in London in 1784. In America, James Hewitt included *Alkmoonok* in the score he arranged and composed for the ballad opera *Tammany* (1794).

The first serious study of Indian music was undertaken by Theodore Baker, a German-American student at the University of Leipzig, who chose as the subject for his doctoral thesis the music of the North American Indians. In his *Über die Musik der nordamerikanischen Wilden* (Leipzig, 1882), he analyzed some forty songs, discussing their poetry, systems of notation, vocalization, scales, melodic progressions, and rhythms. A little later, Alice C. Fletcher visited the Omaha and Pawnee tribes. She was assisted by John C. Fillmore of Harvard University, who provided piano accompaniments for the melodies she transcribed. Miss Fletcher's findings were published at intervals from 1883 to 1911 by the Peabody Museum of American Archaeology and Ethnology at Harvard University and by the U. S. Bureau of American Ethnology. B. I. Gilman and J. W. Fewkes were pioneers in applying the scientific method to the analysis of Indian melodies. Gilman, who joined the Hemenway Southwestern Expedition, measured the interval structure of Zuñi and Hopi melodies by a mechanical device. Fewkes was one of the first to use the phonograph to record Indian singing (1890). Further studies of Pueblo songs were made by Natalie Curtis Burlin, and music of the Ojibways in Minnesota and Wisconsin was transcribed by Frederick R. Burton.

In 1911, the United States Government first undertook the perpetuation of Indian tribal melodies by appointing trained investigators to make phonograph recordings of the melodies with annotations for the Smithsonian Institution. Reports on research have been issued by the Bureau of American Ethnology. The most prominent worker under these auspices was Frances Densmore, who studied the music and customs of the Chippewa, Teton Sioux, Northern Ute, Mandan, Hidatsa, Cheyenne, Arapaho, Nootka, Menominee, and other tribes. Among later students of this field are Helen H. Roberts, George Herzog, David P. McAllester, Bruno Nettl, Alan P. Merriam, and Gertrude P. Kurath.

It is inaccurate to refer to American Indian music as though it were a unified body of material with a single style. The Indians of North America comprised more than fifty basic linguistic stocks and some six or eight distinct culture areas. However, a number of traits are common to the musical culture of all or most tribes. Music is rarely performed for its own sake; generally, songs are associated with some specific activity or with the performance of some tribal custom or religious rite. There are ceremonial songs, songs for treating the sick, for bringing success in battle, for singing at the time of death, to accompany passage from one age-grade group to another. There are game and gambling songs, songs learned in dreams or visions, children's songs, and songs of courtship. Common to some tribes was the idea of regarding a song as the property of its composer. Some tribes regarded all songs as having supernatural origin; others accepted the idea that songs could be performed by human beings, or "found" in dreams, or learned from other tribes. Some regarded accuracy in performance essential, others considered it possible to make coincidental and intentional changes.

Although there are important regional differences, the following traits characterize most North American Indian music: Most of the music by far is vocal. There is hardly any melodic instrumental music except for flute pieces, many of which may also be sung. Most singing is accompanied by drum or rattle but is monophonic. Men have the leading role in singing, which has a relatively tense, harsh, strident character. Scales are often (but not always) pentatonic, hexatonic, or tetratonic (in order of frequency). Most tribes also have a group of simple two- or three-tone melodies used for children's and gambling songs. The most prestigious instruments in many tribes are the drums, beaten with sticks, but rattles exceed them in number and variety. In some tribes, each ceremony has its own type of rattle.

The regional styles coincide to some extent with the culture areas, but not with the language families. Six main musical areas have been identified north of Mexico: (1) the Eskimo-Northwest Coast style, whose chief characteristics are complex rhythm, especially in the drumming, and relatively small intervals such as minor seconds; (2) the California-Yuman area, which includes most of California and the Yuman-speaking tribes of the Southwest, characterized by a type of form in which a short, sometimes repeated section alternates with one at higher pitch; (3) the Great Basin area (Nevada, Utah, northern California), characterized by a form in which each phrase is repeated, e.g., a a b b; (4) the Athabascan area, comprising the Navaho and Apache, characterized by the use of simple rhythms with only two note values, e.g., eighths and quarters, and occasional use of a clear falsetto voice; (5) the Plains-Pueblo area, which combines the complex songs of the Pueblo Indians of New Mexico and Arizona with the simpler ones of the Great Plains, and which is characterized by harsh, tense, pulsating vocal technique, descending, terrace-like melodic movement, and forms in which the stanza consists of two sections that are identical except that the second is an incomplete repetition of the first; and (6) the East, in many ways similar to (5) but distinguished by the occasional use of responsorial singing, by more regular rhythmic units, and some isorhythmic structure. The areas of greatest complexity are the Pueblo, the Northwest Coast, and the area adjoining the Gulf of Mexico. Little is known about aboriginal Mexican Indian music. Presumably the Aztecs and Mayans had a very advanced musical culture that greatly influenced the North American Indians. South American Indian music is in many respects similar to that of North America, but more variety of style and many more instruments seem to have been developed in South America. [See II below.]

There is evidence that the various tribal styles have changed greatly in the last several hundred years, partly because of the impact of Western civilization. The fact that there is some variety in each of many tribal repertories indicates that change also occurred in earlier times, and indeed one cannot assume that Indian music was static for thousands of years. Western civilization has affected Indian music mainly in an indirect fashion, causing different tribes to be thrown into intimate contact and giving rise to new religious movements. The most important of the latter, the Peyote cult, is known to many tribes and is accompanied by a special musical style that uses a more complex version of the Plains form together with Athabascan rhythm, a rapid accompaniment of drum and rattle, and a high, whining singing style. Also of recent origin is a pan-Indian movement that mixes tribal traditions and uses a musical style similar to that of the Plains for many tribes, who evidently feel that Indian culture can best be preserved by the merging of tribal differences.

Considering the fact that there were never more than about one million Indians in North America, their large musical repertories and the fullness of their musical lives are truly amazing. Certainly music played a great role in even the simplest Indian cultures.

Indian music has had some impact on art music in the United States. Edward MacDowell used Indian melodies in his Second Orchestral ("Indian") Suite of 1896, C. S. Skilton in his *Two Indian Dances* and *Suite Primeval,* C. W. Cadman in *Thunderbird Suite* and other works, Frederick Jacobi in his *Indian Dances,* C. T. Griffes in *Two Sketches on Indian Themes,* and Victor Herbert in the opera *Natoma;* H. W. Loomis, Arthur Farwell, Thurlow Lieurance, Carlos Troyer, Henry F. Gilbert, and others have made many settings of tribal material. Among European composers, Dvořák with his symphony "From the New World" and F. B. Busoni with his *Indianisches Tagebuch* may be mentioned.

II. *Central and South America.* Native American music south of the United States border is more difficult to distinguish. For one thing, the native city-states of Central and South America, with their populations in the millions, had a far different history from the relatively isolated tribes of North America.

The Spanish conquest was followed by 400 years of ready mingling of races and cultures. Conquistadors married into royal native families, and patents of nobility were granted by Spain to Indians who had helped the adventurers assume control.

Today, in the cities, composers who may be of Indian or European descent, or both, write symphonies and cantatas drawing on a combination of European and Indian sources. In the villages as well as in cities, the violin and harp may play dance tunes of 16th-century Spain, or one may hear guitars accompanying *huapangos,* fast fiesta songs that are thought to derive from Andalusia during the early colonial period. At church festivals in Mexico the *danza del arco* is accompanied by the fiddle, but also by rattles and a percussion instrument sounded by snapping the

string of a small bow, and feather headdresses (traditionally Indian) are part of the costume.

European influence tends to diminish in more rural areas. In relatively isolated Indian communities, celebrations like the Yaqui deer dance in northern Sonora, Mexico, are aboriginal in purpose and performance, including the music, but still they are performed under the aegis of the Church. Dances incorporating native features into Catholic ritual are common in Central and South America, particularly in Mexico and Guatemala.

The *Pascola* dances are performed at festivals, especially during Easter week. A man, wielding rattles and often wearing other rattles as part of his costume, like the strings of pebble-filled cocoons of the Yaquis, performs a high-stepping dance to the accompaniment of various combinations of flutes, harps, violins, and drums. The *Matachines,* also part of the Easter Week celebration, are danced in parades or in church; the figures are quadrille-like, and the music may be in responsorial sequences between two instruments, such as a pair of violins or a violin and a harp. In the Andes, the dance of the *Chunchus* and *Qollas* portrays incidents from the Conquest, as do the *Danza de la Conquista* and the *Moros y Christianos* of Mexico and the *Tecum Uman* of Guatemala. The *Chunchus* represent Spanish soldiers, led by the king, and the *Qollas* are Indians betrayed by the white man. The *Chunguinada* is fiesta music to accompany processions in which images of the saints are carried, and it also serves as dance music. The harp provides a base in old church chord progressions against flutes carrying characteristic Peruvian melodies in parallel minor thirds.

In Andean music a major role is played by the flute and drums, which may be played simultaneously by one man, and by batteries of panpipes in ensembles of up to 50 or 60 performers.

The chief differences between North and Latin American Indian music are the urban quality of all the latter as well as the profusion and manner of use of musical instruments. Early Spanish accounts of religious observances and state occasions mention processions of instrumentalists. The orchestra with the addition of European instruments has continued to be a feature of Central and South American Indian musical life. The list of musical instruments depicted in inscriptions and recovered from archaeologic excavations, numbering into the hundreds, includes trumpets of shell, pottery, and bamboo, whistles and panpipes, and many kinds of drum, flute, rattle, and bell. Many of these are in use today in recognizable forms. Musical instruments, used solo or in orchestral combinations, are found even in the hinterlands of the Amazon jungle and the Mato Grosso, where the social organization is tribal and vocal music is often somewhat similar to that of the North American Indians.

At many cultural levels, then, a wide spectrum of musical forms has to be recognized as "Indian." However unclear it may be for definition, there is no doubt as to its vitality and its many-faceted appeal.

Lit. *For I:* F. R. Burton, *American Primitive Music* (1909); N. Curtis (Burlin), ed., *The Indians' Book* (1907); F. Densmore, *Chippewa Music,* 2 vols. (1910, '13), and many other books published by the Bureau of American Ethnology; B. Nettl, *North American Indian Musical Styles* (1954); *id., Music in Primitive Culture* (1956); A. P. Merriam, *The Anthropology of Music* (1964); K. G. Izikowitz, *Musical and Other Sound Instruments of the South American Indians* (1935); G. Herzog, "African Influences in North American Indian Music" (*CP 1939*) and many articles; D. P. McAllester, *Peyote Music* (1949); H. H. Roberts, *Musical Areas in Aboriginal North America* (1936). Extensive bibliographies in G. Herzog, *Research in Primitive and Folk Music in the U. S.* (1936); J. Kunst, *Ethno-Musicology,* rev. ed. (1958); C. Haywood, *A Bibliography of North American Folklore and Folksong,* vol. ii (1961). Authentic recordings in large numbers have been issued by the Library of Congress Archive of Folksong and by Ethnic Folkways Library.

For II: R. and M. D'Harcourt, *La Musique des Incas et ses survivances* (1925); A. Genin, "Notes on the Dances, Music and Songs of the Ancient and Modern Mexicans," *Smithsonian Annual Report* (1920); K. G. Izikowitz, *Musical and Other Sound Instruments of the South American Indians,* in *Göteborgs Kungl. Vetenskaps- och Vitterhets-Samhälles Handlingar,* 5 földjen, ser. A, band 5, no. 1 (1935); S. Martí, *Canto, danza y música precortesianos* [1961]; N. Slonimsky, *Music of Latin America* [1945]; J. E. Núñez, "Música precolombina" (*Boletín Bibliografico* xxvi, 70–81); L. F. Ramon y Rivera, "Musica indígena de Venezuela," *Boletín del Instituto de Folklore* (1960); G. Chase, *A Guide to the Music of Latin America,* rev. ed. (1962).

I by J.T.H., rev. B.N.;
II by D.P.MCA.

American in Paris, An. See under Symphonic poem IV.

American Musicological Society. See under Societies I (2).

American Negro music. See Negro music.

American organ. See under Harmonium.

Amfiparnaso, L'. See under Madrigal comedy.

Am Frosch [G.]. Indication to use the portion of the violin bow nearest the right hand.

Am Griffbrett [G.]. In violin playing, bowing near the fingerboard (**sul tasto*). See Bowing (l).

Amor brujo, El [Sp., Love the Sorcerer]. Ballet by Manuel de Falla, produced in Madrid, 1915. The music includes numerous dance pieces inspired by folk dances, the best known being the "Ritual Fire Dance." A unique feature is the inclusion of two songs for the ballerina.

Amorevole, con amore [It.]. Amiable, with love.

Amorschall [G.]. See under Horn II.

Amour des trois Oranges, L'. See *Love for Three Oranges.*

Amphibrach [Gr.]. See under Poetic meter I.

Amplitude. See under Acoustics I.

Am Steg [G.]. In violin playing, bowing near the bridge (**sul ponticello*). See Bowing (k).

Anabole [Gr.]. Humanist (16th-century) name for prelude.

Anacrusis. Upbeat.

Analysis. With reference to music, the study of a composition with regard to form, structure, thematic material, harmony, melody, phrasing, orchestration, style, technique, etc. Analysis of composition plays a predominant part in musical instruction (as a practical application of technical studies in harmony, counterpoint, orchestration) and in writings on music. Analysis is of little value if it is mere enumeration of statistics; such methods, frequently encountered in modern writings, overlook the synthetic element and the functional significance of the musical detail. Another drawback is the one-sided application of only one point of view, for instance, that of form (D. F. Tovey, *A Companion to Beethoven's Pianoforte Sonatas,* 1931) or of phrasing (H. Riemann, *L. van Beethovens sämtliche Klavier-Solosonaten,* 3 vols., 1919–20). In present-day education special emphasis is placed on analysis of harmony and of form; melodic analysis, however, perhaps the most important and most informative of all, is all too often neglected [see Melody]. Also see Style analysis.

Lit.: A. J. Goodrich, *Complete Musical Analysis* (1889); J. Chailley, *Traité historique d'analyse musicale* (1951); M. McMullin, "The Symbolic Analysis of Music" (*MR* viii); K. Westphal, in *DM* xxiv; A. Halm, in *DM* xxi; W. Karthaus, in *DM* xxi; I. Krohn, in *CP 1911*, p. 250.

Anapest, anapaest. See under Poetic meter I.

Anche [F.]. *Reed. *Anche battante,* beating reed; *anche double,* double reed; *anche libre,* free reed. Also *anches,* reed stops of the organ; *trio d'anches,* trio for reed instruments.

Ancia [It.]. *Reed. *Ancia battente, doppia,* etc., as under *anche.

Ancora [It.]. Once more (repeat). *Ancora più forte,* still louder.

Ancus. See under Neumes I (table).

Andächtig, mit Andacht [G.]. With devotion.

Andamento [It.]. In 18th-century writings: (1) *Sequence. (2) A special type of fugal subject [see *Soggetto*]. (3) In more recent writings the term is used (preferably) to denote fugal episodes.

Andante [It.]. Tempo mark indicating very moderate walking speed, between allegretto and adagio [see Tempo marks]. To the present day there is no agreement among musicians as to whether andante belongs to the quick or the slow tempo. While this question as such would seem to be rather irrelevant, it becomes important in the case of terms such as *più andante, meno andante, molto andante, andantino.* According to the former interpretation, which is supported by the literal meaning of the word, *più andante* and *molto andante* indicate a tempo quicker than the normal andante, while *meno andante* indicates a slower speed. Brahms was undoubtedly aware of this meaning of the term when, at the end of his Andante from the Piano Sonata op. 5, he wrote "andante molto"; the tempo of this closing section is, of course, quicker than that of the preceding *andante espressivo.* However, other composers (perhaps the majority) use *molto andante* to mean a tempo still slower than andante. See Andantino.

Andante con mòto. See *Mòto.*

Andantino. Diminutive of andante, used mainly to characterize a short piece of andante tempo or character. If used as a tempo mark, it means a slight modification of andante, whose direction is, unfortunately, a matter of divergent opinion [see Andante]. Beethoven was puzzled by the question of whether andantino was to be understood as meaning faster or slower than andante, as appears from a letter he wrote to George Thomson [see *Thayer's Life of Beethoven,* ed. E. Forbes, 2 vols. (1964), i, 555]. Most modern musicians apparently use the term to indicate a tempo quicker than andante.

An die ferne Geliebte [G., To the Distant Beloved]. Song cycle by Beethoven, op. 98 (1816), consisting of six songs to poems by A. Jeitteles.

Andrea Chénier. Opera in four acts by Umberto Giordano (libretto by Luigi Illica), produced in Milan, 1896. Setting: Paris, French Revolution.

Anemochord. See under Aeolian harp; Sostenente piano.

Anenaiki. The term refers to an abuse of Russian chant [see Znamenny chant], practiced chiefly in the 16th and 17th centuries, in which long coloraturas were sung to meaningless syllables such as *a-ne-na.* This method was also known as *chomonie,* a term referring to the replacement of the Slavic half vowels by the full vowel *o,* resulting in syllables such as *chom* or *chomo* [see O. von Riesemann, in *CP Riemann,* p. 196f]. A similar method used in the Byzantine chant of the same period is known as *teretism,* owing to the use of such syllables as *te-re-rem* for the same purpose. The Russian syllables are probably related to the early Byzantine *enechamata* [see *Echos*]. They appear in a manuscript as early as the 12th century [see *ReMMA,* p. 99, n. 17]. See also *Noeane.*

Anfang [G.]. Beginning; *vom Anfang,* same as *da capo.

Angelica [L.], **angélique** [F.]. See under Lute III.

Angelito [Sp.]. A kind of Latin American funeral song performed for the death of a child. Also called *cantos de velorio,* they originated in the idea that a dead child goes to heaven and becomes a guardian angel to his living relatives. The songs, monotonous and repetitive in rhythm, vaguely follow certain liturgical modes. In the Barvolento region in Venezuela, they are known among Negroes as *mampulorios* and accompany a strange funeral game in which a member of the audience tries to blow out a candle held in front of the dead child's face while naming various objects being dropped into a hat on his lap. Among Colombian Negroes these songs are known as *chigualos*. J.O-S.

Angklung. See under Java.

Anglaise [F.]. A 17th- and 18th-century dance in fast duple time, obviously derived from the *country dance. It occurs in J. S. Bach's French Suite no. 3 and, under the name "balet anglois" or "air anglois," in J. K. F. Fischer's *Musicalischer Parnassus* of *c.* 1690. The name was also used for other dances of English origin or character, e.g., the (syncopated) hornpipe and, *c.* 1800, the country dance and the *écossaise*. See Dance music III.

Anglican chant. The harmonized singing of prose psalms and *canticles, so called because it is extensively used in the Church of England. Extended four-part settings by Tallis, Byrd, and Gibbons, which had the Gregorian psalm tone in the tenor and which were referred to as "festival psalms," were published in John Barnard's *The First Book of Selected Church Musick* (1641). These correspond to the *falsobordone* settings of Josquin des Prés, Victoria, and others on the Continent.

The modern abbreviated form was first published in 1644 in the second edition of James Clifford's *The Divine Services*. The psalm tone remained in the tenor part until the 18th century, when all memory of plainsong singing had passed and melodies were shifted to the treble or soprano part. The following example is "Christ Church Tune," psalm tone I_4, as printed in William Boyce's *Cathedral Music* (1760):

O come, let us sing un-to the Lord:

This is a "single chant," designed for use with a single verse of the psalm at a time. "Double chants" are twice as long and take two verses at a time. [Ex. also in P. Scholes, *The Oxford Companion to Music* (1955), p. 32.]

The prose texts to be sung with these chants are "pointed" to indicate the manner in which the words fit the music. The actual method of pointing varies somewhat among Psalters, but

the following will give an example to fit the tune above. (The strokes coincide with the bar lines. The dot following the word "unto" indicates that those two syllables have to be sung to a single note, preferably by singing that measure as if it contained a triplet of three half-notes. The bold-face type on the syllable "va" indicates that it must be extended over two notes, i.e., a full measure of the chant.)

O Come let us sing | unto . the | Lord; ‖
 let us heartily rejoice in the strength of | our
 sal | **va** | tion.‖

When sung in speech rhythm by well-trained choirs, Anglican chant can be as aesthetically satisfying as Gregorian chant. Unfortunately, it is most often judged on the basis of untrained congregational singing, where there is a tendency to hurry the initial reciting tones, putting a heavy "Anglican thump" on the last syllable before the bar line, and to stress unduly the final syllable of each line.

Until the 20th-century revival of the use of Gregorian plainsong, Anglican chant was used by churches of many denominations, including Roman Catholic churches. With the return to unison hymn singing among many Protestant congregations, there has been a corresponding trend toward Gregorian chanting in the vernacular, using the editions of Winfred Douglas, Francis Burgess, and others.

Lit.: I. M. McWilliam, *Steps toward Good Chanting* (1938); A. Ramsbotham, in *ML* i, 208–17; R. Bridges, in *MA* ii, 125–41, iii, 74–86; L. Ellinwood, "From Plainsong to Anglican Chant," in *Essays on Church Music in Honor of Walter E. Buszin*, ed. J. Riedel (1966); introduction to *American Psalter* (1929), etc. L.E.

Anglican church music. The music of the churches in various countries that derive from the Church of England (e.g., the Protestant Episcopal Church in the U. S. A.), known collectively as the Anglican Communion. For the liturgy of the various services, each national church uses its own Book of Common Prayer, which is closely patterned on the original 1549 Book of Common Prayer of the Church of England, in turn basically an abridgment of the Roman Catholic Breviary and Missal.

In most parish church services, music consists largely of congregational hymn singing and the *chanting of certain Psalms and *canticles [see Anglican chant]. Organ compositions are played as "preludes" and "postludes" before and after services. Until the late 19th century, it was customary to play an organ "voluntary" after the Psalms at Morning and Evening Prayer; this was often an improvisation.

Cathedrals and the larger urban churches employ professional organist-choirmasters and trained singers. In these churches, *anthems are sung during the collection of alms, and varying amounts of *service music are used. When the *Preces, Psalms, *Suffrages, and *Collects are chanted in Morning Prayer, the service is frequently called Matins, while that of Evening Prayer is called Evensong. In a fully choral Eucharist (the service of Holy Communion) the proper Collect, Epistle, Gospel, and Sursum Corda are intoned by the celebrant, while the *Decalogue or *Kyrie, *Sanctus, *Benedictus qui venit, *Agnus Dei, and *Gloria are sung by the choir. On some occasions a choral setting of the Creed will be sung by the choir. At other times, it and the Lord's Prayer may be intoned by the entire congregation.

Most of the chanting is done as *Anglican chant, but since c. 1850 there has been considerable use of plainsong (the medieval Gregorian *psalm tones and other melodies) adapted to English texts. Service music is always sung with English or other vernacular texts. While the works of Anglican composers are favored, anthems, cantatas, motets, etc., by other composers (Palestrina, Bach, Franck, Tchaikovsky, etc.) also are used. These are sometimes sung in the original language, with translations provided for the congregation to follow.

Mixed choirs of men and women are commonly found in parish churches. Most cathedrals and some larger city churches continue to use the traditional choir of men and boys. Although at the end of the 16th century Byrd and Gibbons extended the tonal range of choral music somewhat, that of the modern Anglican choir of men and boys dates only from the Restoration, when the Chapel Royal choir was revived under Captain Henry Cooke (c. 1616–72). In addition to the bass and tenor parts, men are used for the alto parts, singing either in falsetto or natural countertenor. Boys sing only the treble or soprano parts, with a clear, extremely flexible head tone and a range up to c'''. The boys' voices, blended with the men's voices, give a purity of choral tone that can be matched by no other ensemble.

Important early collections of Anglican church music are *Certaine Notes . . . to be Sung at the Communion, and Evening Praier,* 2nd ed.

(1565); John Barnard, *The First Book of Selected Church Musick* (10 partbooks; 1641); William Boyce, *Cathedral Music,* 3 vols. (1760–73; 2nd ed. 1788; 3rd ed. enlarged and ed. by Joseph Warren, 1849); Samuel Arnold, *Cathedral Music,* 4 vols. (1790; 2nd ed. 1847 by E. Rimbault). For a list of leading composers, see under Service and Anthem.

Lit.: J. S. Bumpus, *A History of English Cathedral Music, 1549–1889,* 2 vols. [1908]; E. H. Fellowes, *English Cathedral Music from Edward VI to Edward VII,* rev. ed. (1945); W. Douglas, *Church Music in History and Practice,* ed. by L. Ellinwood (1962); E. Walker, *A History of Music in England,* rev. ed. (1952); G. L. H. Gardner and S. H. Nicholson, *A Manual of English Church Music,* rev. ed. (1936); *Papers of the Church Music Society* (1913—). Also see under Church music.   L.E.

Angoscioso [It.]. Sorrowful, grieved.

Anhemitonic. An anhemitonic scale (also called tonal scale) possesses no semitones, e.g., one of the four pentatonic scales (c–d–f–g–a–c') or the whole-tone scale.

Anmutig [G.]. Graceful.

Années de pèlerinage [F., Years of Pilgrimage]. Collective title for three volumes of piano music by Liszt. Each volume contains several pieces with descriptive titles.

Anonymous. Of unknown authorship. The medieval Latin word *Anonymus* (abbr. *Anon.*) stands for certain unknown writers of medieval treatises in the collections of Gerbert and Coussemaker [see *Scriptores*], in which they are referred to as Anon. I, Anon. II, etc. It should be noted, however, that the same numbering begins anew in each of the several volumes edited by Coussemaker and Gerbert. Therefore, to prevent possible confusion with another Anonymous IV, the famous treatise known as Coussemaker's *Anon. IV* [see Theory II, 11] should be more precisely referred to as *Anon. IV* of Coussemaker i (*CS* i).

Anreissen [G.]. Forceful attack in string playing.

Ansatz [G.] (1) In singing, the proper adjustment of the vocal apparatus. (2) In playing wind instruments, proper adjustment of the lips [see Embouchure (2)]. (3) Crook or shank of brass instruments [see Wind instruments IV (b)]. (4) In violin playing, *attack.

Anschlag [G.]. (1) In piano playing, touch. (2) An ornament explained by K. P. E. Bach [see Appoggiatura, double, III].

Anschwellend [G.]. Crescendo.

Answer. In fugal writing, the answer is the second (or fourth) statement of the subject, so called because of its relationship to the first (or third) statement. Hence, the succession of statements is subject—answer—subject—answer. See M. Zulauf, in *ZMW* vi. See Fugue; Tonal and real; Antecedent and consequent.

Antar. Symphonic suite (op. 9) composed in 1868 (rev. 1875, '97) by Rimsky-Korsakov. In four movements, it is a descriptive piece based on the legend of Antar, an Arabian hero of the 6th century.

Antara. Quechuan name for a Peruvian panpipe of Nazca origin made of three to fifteen reeds or clay tubes that are tied or cemented together. In Peru the instrument is also known by the Spanish name *zampoña,* while in Ecuador it is called *rondador,* in Colombia *capador,* and in Bolivia *sico.*   J.O-S.

Antecedent and consequent. The terms are usually applied to melodic phrases that stand in the relationship of question and answer or statement and confirmation, as in the accompanying example (Beethoven, String Quartet op. 18, no. 2).

Cello   Violin

Here, as in other examples, the dialogue character of the melody is emphasized by its distribution between two instruments [see *Durchbrochene Arbeit*]. The terms are also used as synonymous with subject and answer in fugues and canons [see Answer].

Ante-Communion. The initial portion of the Anglican Holy Communion, usually ending with the Creed or the Prayer for the Whole State of Christ's Church. It is used as a separate service, similar to the Roman Catholic Mass of the Catechumens.

Anthem. A choral composition in English, with words from the Bible or some other religious text, performed during the worship service of Protestant churches, where it holds a position similar to that of the motet in the Roman Catholic rites. An anthem may be unaccompanied or accompanied by the organ or orchestra.

The anthem dates from the Reformation and the consequent establishment of English as the liturgical language of Great Britain. Although the anthem developed from the Latin motet, the first anthems, written by Christopher Tye (*c.* 1500–*c.* 1573), Thomas Tallis (*c.* 1505–85), and Robert White (*c.* 1530–74), are markedly different in style from previous and contemporary motets. They are rhythmically square, more harmonically conceived, more syllabic, and in shorter phrases, all features resulting from the greater consideration given to text and pronunciation. However, a few anthems are merely motets with texts translated into English (e.g., Tallis' "I call and cry" from *O sacrum convivium;* Byrd's "Bow thine ear" from *Civitas sancti tui*). Toward the end of the 16th century a new form, the verse anthem, was introduced by William Byrd (regarding an isolated earlier example, by Richard Farrant, see G. E. P. Arkwright, in *MA* i, 65n) and developed by Thomas Tomkins (1572–1656) and Orlando Gibbons (1583–1625) [see *HAM*, nos. 151, 169, 172]. This form, in which sections for full chorus alternate with sections for one or more solo voices, was preferred throughout the 17th century, with the full (i.e., completely choral) anthem returning to prominence in the subsequent period. Whereas in the Elizabethan verse anthem the parts are contrapuntally conceived, with the solo part accompanied by instruments, about 1630 a new declamatory arioso style of Italian origin [see Monody] was introduced in the anthems of Monteverdi's pupil Walter Porter (*c.* 1595–1659; see Arkwright, in *MA* iv, 246f), Thomas Tomkins (1572–1656), and, particularly, William Child (1606–97; see the list of his anthems in *GD* i, 623; *GDB* ii, 210; ex. in *OH* iii, 206). The Restoration anthem is represented by Henry Cooke (*c.* 1616–72), Matthew Locke (*c.* 1630–71), Henry Aldrich (1647–1710), Pelham Humphrey (1647–74; *HAM*, no. 242), Michael Wise (*c.* 1648–87), John Blow (1648/9–1708; see *GD* i, 396; *GDB* i, 772ff), Henry Purcell (*c.* 1659–95), and Jeremiah Clarke (*c.* 1673–1707). Blow and Purcell introduced instrumental interludes into the anthem, an innovation whereby it came to resemble the cantata. Another characteristic feature of the Restoration anthem, adopted in numerous later works, is a concluding hallelujah chorus, often in fugal style. The use of two choruses, called "dec(ani)" and "can(toris)," prevails in the anthem as well as in service music [see Polychoral style].

The baroque anthem reached its high point in the grandiose anthems of Handel, nearly all of which were written for special festive occasions where an unusual display was possible and appropriate (Chandos anthems, 1716–18; coronation anthems, 1727; Dettingen Te Deum, 1743). Other composers of this period were William Croft (1678–1727; *HAM*, no. 268), John Weldon (1676–1736), and Maurice Greene (1695–1755; *HAM*, no. 279). Their anthems, as well as those of William Boyce (1710–79; see *GD* i, 441; *GDB* i, 864), are modeled after the somewhat simpler style of Purcell.

The outstanding figure of the 19th century was S. S. Wesley (1810–76), whose two volumes of anthems, published in 1853, contain such standard works as "Blessed by the God and Father."

In America from 1762 until the mid-19th century, one or more simple anthems was included in most of the tune books that were used in churches and singing schools. Until the advent of octavo-size sheet music, they were almost the sole outlet for anthems by both native-born and foreign composers. Prolific but mostly inferior composers were John Goss (1800–80), Joseph Barnby (1838–96), John Stainer (1840–1901), George M. Garrett (1834–97), Arthur Sullivan (1842–1900), Charles Lee Williams (1853–1935), George C. Martin (1844–1916), and the Americans Dudley Buck (1839–1909), Harry Rowe Shelley (1858–1947), and James Hotchkiss Rogers (1857–1940).

Early 20th-century composers of distinction who moved away from the insipid harmonies of the Victorians were Charles Villiers Stanford (1852–1924), Charles Wood (1866–1926), Edward Elgar (1857–1934), Edward Bairstow (1874–1946), Henry Walford Davies (1869–1941), John Ireland (1879–1962), and, most important throughout his long life, Ralph Vaughan Williams (1872–1958). Across the Atlantic, there are the Canadian Healey Willan (b. 1880) and the Americans H. Everett Titcomb (b. 1884), David M. Williams (b. 1887), Joseph W. Clokey (1890–1960), and Philip James (b. 1890).

Among the more important later composers of anthems in England are Herbert Howells (b. 1892), Edmund Rubbra (b. 1901), Michael Tippett (b. 1905), and Benjamin Britten (b. 1913); in America, Randall Thompson (b. 1899), Samuel Barber (b. 1910), and Vincent Persichetti (b. 1915).

Lit.: E. H. Fellowes, *English Cathedral Music from Edward VI to Edward VII*, rev. ed. (1945); M. B. Foster, *Anthems and Anthem Composers* (1901); E. A. Wienandt, *Choral Music of the Church* (1965); R. T. Daniel, "The Anthem in New England before 1800" (diss. Harvard Univ., 1955); W. J. King, "The English Anthem from the Early Tudor Period through the Restoration Era" (diss. Boston Univ., 1962); G. E. P. Arkwright, "Purcell's Church Music" (*MA* i, 63, 234); H. W. Shaw, in *ML* xix, 429ff (Blow); L. A. Gill, in *MD* xi (Tomkins); R. T. Daniel, in *JAMS* xii, 49ff; W. Palmer, in *ML* xxxv, 107. For anthologies, see under Anglican church music.

rev. L.E.

Anticipation. See under Nonharmonic tones I; also Nachschlag.

Antienne [F.]. (1) *Antiphon. (2) *Anthem.

Antimasque. See Masque.

Antiphon. A term denoting various categories of Gregorian chant, all of which are remnants of the early method of antiphonal psalmody [see under (3) below].

(1) Short texts from the Scriptures or elsewhere, set to music in a simple syllabic style and sung before and after a psalm or canticle. On greater feasts the entire antiphon is sung both before and after the psalm; at other times only the first word or so is sung before, and the whole after [for more details, see under Psalm tones]. The repertory of Gregorian chant includes more than 1,000 such antiphons. The melodies are not all different and can be classified into about 40 (according to Gevaert, 47) groups of chants related to each other through an identical beginning and sometimes through additional common material. [See F. A. Gevaert, *La Mélopée antique dans le chant de l'église latine*, 1895, pp. 225ff; W. H. Frere, *Antiphonale Sarisburiense*, 4 vols., 1901–25, i, 64ff; P. Ferretti, *Esthétique grégorienne*, 1938, pp. 112ff; *ApGC*, pp. 394ff.] The antiphons for the canticles, particularly the Magnificat, are somewhat more elaborate textually as well as musically than the psalm antiphons [see *LU*, pp. 326, 333, etc.; see also O antiphons].

(2) The name "antiphon" is also used for two other types of chant that are not strictly antiphons, since they do not as a rule embrace a psalm or canticle but are independent songs of considerable length and elaboration. The first of these types includes the antiphons that are sung at certain feasts (Palm Sunday, Purification)

during processions (processional antiphons). They are usually of a narrative character, containing verses from the New Testament referring to the occasion, e.g., for Palm Sunday: "Occurrunt turbae cum floribus et palmis" [*LU*, p. 584]. Comprising the second class of pseudo-antiphons are the four antiphons *B.M.V.* (*Beatae Mariae Virginis*) or B.V.M. (Blessed Virgin Mary): *"Alma Redemptoris Mater," *"Ave Regina caelorum," *"Regina caeli laetare," and *"Salve Regina" [see *LU*, pp. 273–76]. Each of these chants, also known as Marian antiphons, is sung during one of the four seasons of the year, at the end of Compline (said at the end of each other Office hour). Although of a relatively late date (11th, 12th centuries), they are justly famous for their beauty. In the 15th and 16th centuries they were frequently composed polyphonically, for voices or for organ [see *HAM*, nos. 65, 100, 139].

(3) While the chants mentioned above are the only ones called antiphons in present-day liturgical books, in historical studies the name is also applied to certain chants of the Mass Proper, namely, the Introit (Introit antiphon, *antiphona ad introitum*), the Offertory (*antiphona ad offerendum*), and the Communion (Communion antiphon, *antiphona ad communionem*). The justification for this terminology is that these chants originally sprang from the same method of antiphonal psalmody that also survives, in a different form, in the antiphons embracing a psalm or a canticle [see Psalmody III].

History. In Greek theory, *antiphonia* (literally, countersound) means the octave, in contradistinction to *symphonia,* the unison, and *paraphonia,* the fifth. In the early Christian rites, *antiphonia* came to denote the singing of successive verses of a psalm by alternating choruses. This meaning of the term probably originated in the fact that the second chorus consisted at first of women or boys who repeated the melody at the higher octave. In the 4th century antiphonal psalm singing was enriched by the addition of a short sentence sung by the whole choir and repeated after each verse or pair of verses as a refrain. It was this additional text and melody that finally came to be known as antiphon. For a survey of the various forms that sprang from antiphonal psalmody, see Psalmody III; also Gregorian chant IV (c).

Antiphonal, antiphonary, antiphoner [L. *antiphonale, antiphonarium*]. A liturgical book containing all the chants for the Office as opposed to

a gradual, which contains all the chants for the Mass. Originally, *antiphonale* (*liber antiphonarius*) was a general designation for books containing the texts (and later texts and music) of the musical items of the Roman rite, as opposed to those containing the spoken texts (lectionaries, evangeliaries—readings from the Scriptures, the Gospels). Books consisting of the musical items for the Office or for the Mass were distinguished respectively as *antiphonale officii* (= antiphonal) and *antiphonale missarum* (= gradual). See Gradual (2); Liturgical books I (4).

Antiphonal singing. Singing in alternating choruses. Originally and properly the term should be applied to plainsong [see Antiphon, under *History*]. Regarding the present-day use of antiphonal singing in Gregorian chant, see Responsorial. The term is also used with reference to polyphonic music composed for two or more alternating groups (polychoral).

Antiphonarium Mediceum. A name formerly applied to a famous MS of the Medicean library at Florence (Bibl. Laur., *plut. 29.i*). Actually, it is not a book of plainsong but the most extensive collection of polyphonic music of the school of Notre Dame. See Sources, no. 3.

Antiphonia. In Greek theory, the octave. See Antiphon, under *History*.

Antony and Cleopatra. Opera in three acts by S. Barber (libretto by F. Zeffirelli), produced in New York, 1966. Setting: Alexandria and Rome, 1st century B.C.

Antwort [G.]. Answer, in fugues.

Anvil. Small steel bars struck with a hard wooden or metal mallet that have sometimes been used as a percussion instrument in operas, usually as a stage property (Auber, *Le Maçon,* 1825; Verdi, *Il Trovatore;* Wagner, *Das Rheingold*).

À peine entendu. See *Peine entendu.*

Aperto [It.]. Open. (1) In horn playing, the opposite of *chiuso.* (2) In 14th-century music, see *Ouvert.*

A piacere [It.]. Indication for the performer to use his discretion, particularly as to tempo and rhythm.

Apollo Club. A name given to American male singing organizations, generally amateur, corresponding to the French *Orphéon and the German *Männergesangverein. Remarkable for their high ambitions are the Apollo clubs of Boston (founded in 1871), Brooklyn (1878), Chicago (1872; see L. Edlund, *The Apollo Musical Club of Chicago,* 1946), Cincinnati (1882), and St. Louis (1893). Some of the clubs were expanded into mixed choruses.

Apollonicon. See under Mechanical instruments III.

Apollon Musagète [Apollo, Leader of the Muses]. Ballet for string orchestra by Stravinsky, produced in Washington, D.C., 1928 (rev. 1947). It consists of a prologue depicting the birth of Apollo, a group of allegorical dances in neo-classical ballet style, and a final apotheosis in which Apollo leads Terpsichore and the Muses to their eternal home on Mt. Parnassus.

Apostropha. See under Neumes I.

Apothéose. See under Lament (2).

Apotome. See under Pythagorean scale.

Appalachian Spring. See under Ballet III.

Apparebit repentina dies [L., Suddenly shall the day appear]. Cantata for full chorus and brass instruments by Hindemith, commissioned in 1947 for the Harvard Symposium on Music Criticism. The text is a medieval Latin poem describing the day of judgment [see *The Oxford Book of Medieval Latin Verse,* ed. Stephen Gaselee (1928)]. The music is in a series of neo-classic forms and includes a lengthy recitative for the entire bass section of the chorus.

Appassionata, Sonata appassionata [It.]. Name customarily given to Beethoven's Piano Sonata op. 57, in F minor. The title was not his but was added by a publisher. The original title is "Grande Sonate pour Piano" (1805). It may be said to form the "dark" companion piece to the *Waldstein Sonata composed two years earlier. Strikingly contrasted in character, the sonatas are similar in structure: each consists of three movements, the first and the last very long, the second forming a lyrical interlude leading directly into the final movement.

Applicatur. An 18th-century German term for fingering.

Appoggiando [It.]. "Leaning," i.e., emphasized; also, full legato.

Appoggiatura [It.]. (1) In modern parlance, a rhythmically strong dissonant note occurring in place of a harmonic note [see Nonharmonic

tones II]. (2) Originally, appoggiatura [F. *port de voix;* E. forefall, backfall, half-fall; G. *Vorschlag;* Sp. *apoyadura*] was an ornamental note, usually the lower second, that was melodically connected with the main note that followed it (i.e., the appoggiatura was sung in the same breath or played with the same stroke of the bow or articulation of the tongue or, in the case of keyboard instruments, slurred to the following note). It was indicated by means of a small note or special sign but was also frequently introduced extemporaneously in performance. The interpretation of the appoggiatura has varied considerably since the 17th century, when it first became a conventional ornament.

I. In the baroque period the appoggiatura was exceedingly flexible as regards both notation and rhythmic execution. Ex. 1A shows the various ways of indicating the appoggiatura and Ex. 1B the methods of performance that were prevalent around 1700. The choice among these interpre-

tations was left to the discretion of the performer—a "discretion," however, that was not haphazard but was governed by rules (based upon the conduct of the melody and other parts, the tempo and phrasing of the passage in question, and the expression of the accompanying text) that were formulated in textbooks (e.g., B. Bacilly, *Remarques curieuses sur l'art de bien chanter,* 1668) and taught to every student of performance. With the exception of a and b [Ex. 1B], which are exclusively French, these interpretations were taken over by musicians of all nationalities, and they are valid for the per-

formance of music by J. S. Bach, Handel, Purcell, D. Scarlatti, etc. Ex. 2 illustrates the application of these principles to the music of J. S. Bach (a: Little C-minor Fugue; b: Goldberg Variations, aria; c: St. Matthew Passion, bass aria no. 66; d: Sinfonia no. 3). See also *Appuy; Port de voix*.

II. After 1750 the performance of the appoggiatura was systematized by the German teachers and writers K. P. E. Bach, Leopold Mozart, F. W. Marpurg, and D. G. Türk. The ornament was then divided into two types: the long, or variable, appoggiatura (*veränderlicher Vorschlag*), and the short appoggiatura (*kurzer Vorschlag*), both to be performed upon the beat. The duration of the long appoggiatura was proportionate to that of the main note with which it was connected, according to the following rules: (a) if the main note can be divided into two equal parts the appoggiatura takes half its value; (b) an appoggiatura to a dotted note takes two-thirds of its value; (c) in 6/8 or 6/4 meter an appoggiatura to a dotted note tied to another note takes the whole value of the dotted note; (d) if the main note is followed by a rest, the appoggiatura takes the whole value of the main note, the latter is played in the time of the rest, and the rest ceases to exist. In Ex. 3 these four rules are illustrated by quotations from the works of Mozart and Beethoven (a: Mozart, Piano Sonata K. 311; Beethoven, Piano Sonata op. 2, no. 1, Minuet; b: Mozart, Piano Sonata K. 332; c: Mozart, Piano Sonata K. 332; d: Beethoven, "Adelaide").

The short appoggiatura was to be performed as a short note, regardless of the duration of the main note. It was to be used only in the following circumstances: (a) when the main note is itself an appoggiatura (i.e., a nonharmonic note occurring on the beat); (b) when the main note accompanies a suspension or syncopation; (c) when the appoggiatura fills up the intervals in a series of descending thirds; (d) when the main note is a short note that is followed by more notes of the same value; (e) when the main note is one of a series of reiterated notes (see Ex. 4—a: K. P. E. Bach; Beethoven, Piano Sonata op. 2, no. 3; b: K. P. E. Bach; c: Mozart, Rondo in D, K. 485; d: Beethoven, Piano Sonata op. 22, Minuet; e: Mozart, Piano Sonata K. 547a).

The notation of the appoggiatura in this period had no definite relationship to its performance. A few composers wrote the long appoggiatura as a small note of the exact value in which it should be performed and distinguished the short appoggiatura from it by means of a single stroke across the stem (for a 16th note) or a double stroke (for a 32nd note), but this practice was by no means consistently carried out. In music by K. P. E. Bach, Gluck, Haydn, Mozart, and Beethoven, the rules given above constitute a far surer guide to performance than does the physical appearance of the ornament, even in the most reliable editions. For an 18th-century practice of improvised appoggiatura, see Ornamentation I.

III. The 19th century brought still further changes in the treatment of the appoggiatura. The long appoggiatura became absorbed in the ordinary notation, and the short appoggiatura was invariably indicated by a small note with a single stroke across its stem, called a grace note or (erroneously) an *acciaccatura. The question then arises whether this grace note should be performed on the beat or in anticipation of the beat. The latter possibility had already been admitted

In der spiegelnden Flut

by some late 18th-century authorities (who referred to it as a *durchgehender Vorschlag,* distinct from both the *langer* and the *kurzer Vorschlag*) for certain exceptional circumstances. After 1800 this execution became decidedly more popular; it seems to be indicated for most of the grace notes in the works of Chopin, Schumann, Brahms, etc. (Schumann often prescribes it by placing the grace note before the bar line), but lack of material evidence leaves the matter open to controversy in many cases. In modern music it is customary to snap the grace note sharply onto the following note, so that it slightly anticipates the beat and imparts a decided accent to the main note. See Ornamentation. P.A.

Appoggiatura, double. The term "double appoggiatura" has been applied to each of the three distinct ways in which two appoggiaturas can be used: first, two appoggiaturas performed simultaneously, at the interval of a third or sixth; second, two conjunct appoggiaturas approaching the main note from the interval of a third above

or below it; and third, two disjunct appoggiaturas, one being placed below the main note, the other above it.

I. Little need be said of the simultaneous double appoggiatura save that each of its components is performed as though the other were not present, as in Ex. 1 (Bach, Suite in E♭, Sarabande; *BG* xxxvi, 10).

II. The conjunct double appoggiatura, or slide, was a common *agrément* in the 17th and 18th centuries. The 17th-century English lutenists and viol players referred to the ascending slide as an elevation or whole fall and called the descending slide a double backfall. The signs and execution of these ornaments are illustrated in Ex. 2 and 3. Their German equivalent is the *Schleifer,* which is indicated in the music of the baroque period by either a *direct (custos)* or two grace notes [Ex. 4]. It should always be played on the beat.

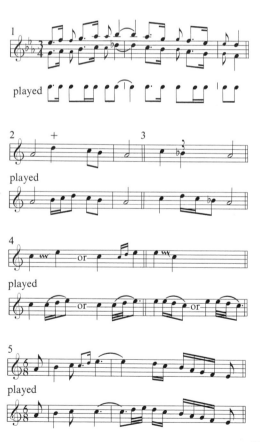

The *punctierte Schleifer,* or dotted slide, is a complicated ornament very popular with rococo composers between 1750 and 1780. Its performance is shown in Ex. 5 (by K. P. E. Bach). Another special form of slide, peculiar to keyboard music, is that in which the first note is held throughout. Introduced by the French clavecinists, who called it *coulé sur une tierce* or *tierce coulé,* this *agrément* is indicated and performed as shown in Ex. 6. It was adopted by Purcell and other English composers, who used the same notation but called it a slur. In romantic and modern music this execution of the slide is indicated with a tie, as in Ex. 7 (Schubert, *Moments musicaux* op. 94, no. 3). The performance of the slide in general has changed very little since the 18th century; it is still begun on the beat, as in Ex. 8 (Beethoven, *Bagatellen* op. 119, no. 5).

III. The disjunct double appoggiatura was written in ordinary notes until the last half of the 18th century, when K. P. E. Bach gave it the name *Anschlag* and introduced the two tiny grace notes that have since been used to represent it [Ex. 9]. The first of the two notes that make up the *Anschlag* may be at any distance from the main note, but the second is only one degree removed from it. The ornàment should always begin on the beat, as in Ex. 10 (Chopin, Rondo op. 16) and Ex. 11 (Chopin, Polonaise op. 44).   P.A.

Appreciation of music. See Music appreciation.

Apprenti sorcier, L' [F., The Sorcerer's Apprentice]. Symphonic poem by Paul Dukas, composed 1897, based on Goethe's ballad, "Der Zauberlehrling."

Appuy [F.]. An 18th-century term for a note having the quality of an appoggiatura. It usually refers to the appoggiatura that constitutes the first note of the *tremblement* or *cadence* [see Trill].   P.A.

Appuyé [F.]. With emphasis.

Après-midi d'un faune, L' [F., The Afternoon of a Faun]. Symphonic poem by Debussy, composed 1894, a musical interpretation of a poem by Mallarmé. It portrays a faun dozing in the warm sunshine of the Apennines, his dreams interrupted by a vision of fleeing nymphs. The complete title, *Prélude à l'après-midi d'un faune,* has given rise to the theory that Debussy planned additional sections. The work, in which the sensuous atmosphere of the poem is captured with consummate skill, is one of the first and most convincing realizations of musical *impressionism.

Apsidenchöre [G.]. The two choirs of a *coro spezzato,* so called because they were placed in the two apses of the church [see *Cori spezzati*].

Aquitanian neumes. The neumatic script from southern France (Aquitaine). See Neumes II (table, col. III).

Arabella. Opera in three acts by Richard Strauss (libretto by H. von Hofmannsthal, after his short novel *Lucidor*), produced in Dresden, 1933. Setting: Vienna, 1860.

Arabesque [F.; G. *Arabeske*]. A fanciful title used by Schumann, Debussy, and others for pieces of a more or less casual nature. The term is also used in the sense of figuration, ornamentation of a melody.

Arab music. The music of the Arab nations and tribes of Arabia, North Africa, and the Near East.

Our knowledge of the history of this music is derived chiefly from theoretical treatises since there are very few examples of notated compositions, and none prior to the 13th century. Among the most important treatises are those of Al-Kindī (*c.* 796–*c.* 873), Al-Fārābī (872–950), Ibn Sīnā (Avicenna, 980–1037), Ṣafī al-Dīn (d. 1294), and 'Abd al-Qādir (d. 1435). The *Kitāb al-mūsīqā al-kabīr* of Al-Fārābī in particular [trans. D'Erlanger, *La Musique arabe* i and ii] contains a detailed presentation of theory (going beyond its Greek models), information on practice, and an exemplary account of the main instruments. Material on musicians and the social background may be found in works of a more general nature, notably the *Kitāb al-aghānī*. There is also a considerable literature on the legal status of music, much of it hostile.

Most theorists discuss intervals and tetrachord species at great length, often presenting them through various frettings on the *'ūd,* a short-necked lute with four (later five) strings, which is the ancestor of the European lute. In the 8th and 9th centuries, according to Ibn al-Munajjim, its fretting was:

open string	g (0)	c'	f'	b♭'
first finger	a (204)	d' (702)	g' (1200=0)	c'' (498)
second finger	b♭' (294)	e♭' (792)	a♭' (90)	d♭'' (588)
third finger		e' (906)	a' (204)	d'' (702)
fourth finger	c' (498)	f' (996)	b♭'' (294)	e♭'' (792)
				e'' (906)

The notes f'–e'' formed a normative series from which eight diatonic modes were derived, the second and third finger notes being mutually exclusive. Al-Fārābī also gives a quite different fretting on another instrument (the *ṭunbūr baghdādī*, a long-necked lute with 2 strings) producing a series of approximate quarter tones within a range of little more than a minor third. He attributes this problematical fretting to the pre-Islamic period (6th and early 7th centuries), but it can hardly have represented the dominant tradition of that time.

During the 9th and 10th centuries Persian influence again made itself felt. There arose rival schools of musicians, those led by Ibrāhīm ibn al-Mahdī welcoming change and artistic freedom, while Isḥāq al-Mawṣilī (d. 850) and his followers adhered to the classical style. The most far-reaching innovation was the introduction into court music of a neutral third (perhaps of indigenous origin), which led to the disruption of the diatonic modal system. By the 11th century the notes found within the tetrachord (i.e., on any one string of the 'ūd) were g a♭ a♭̄ a b♭ b♭̄ b c' (♭̄ is halfway between ♭ and ♮). Various empirical formulas were given for locating frets for the neutral intervals. In the 13th century these were, however, integrated into the Pythagorean system by Ṣafī al-Dīn, being placed one comma below the diatonic intervals so that the tetrachord becomes in theory g (0), a♭ (90), a⁻ᶜ (180), a (204), b♭ (294), b⁻ᶜ (384), b (408), c' (498). In practice the neutral intervals of course remained, and Ṣafī al-Dīn's notation of the twelve main modes (*shudūd*, later *maqāmāt*, sing. *maqām*) may be amended to (f♯ is halfway between ♮ and ♯):

g a b c' d' e' f' g'	*'Ushshāq*
g a b♭ c' d' e♭' f' g'	*Nawā*
g a♭ b♭ c' d♭' e♭' f' g'	*Būsalīk*
g a b♭̄ c' d' e♭̄' f' g'	*Rāst*
g a♭̄ b♭̄ c' d♭' e♭̄' f' f♯' g'	*'Irāq*
g a b♭̄ c' d' e♭̄' f' f♯' g'	*Iṣfahān*
g a♭̄ b♭ c' d♭' e♭' e♭̄' f♯' g'	*Zīrāfkand*
g a♭̄ b c' c♯' d' e' f♯' g'	*Buzurg*
g a b♭̄ c' d♭̄' e' f' g'	*Zangūla*
g a♭̄ b c' d♭̄' e♭' f' g'	*Rāhawī*
g a♭̄ b♭ c' d♭̄' e♭' f' g'	*Ḥusaynī*
g a♭̄ b♭ c' d♭̄' e' f' g'	*Ḥijāzī*

The b in *Buzurg* and *Rāhawī*, and e' in *Zangūla* and *Ḥijāzī*, are notated as b⁻ᶜ and e'⁻ᶜ respectively.

These octave scales are to a certain extent artificial since the melody was articulated essentially in terms of tetrachords and/or pentachords, one being developed after another. By the beginning of the 16th century about forty modes were in use, and many were in fact notated in the form of melodic matrices [see D'Erlanger, iv, 429–52]. The rhythmic modes, characterized by the distribution of strong and weak beats as well as by the number of time units within the cycle, had also evolved throughout this period, increasing in number from eight (9th century) to more than twenty (16th century). From our sources it would appear that from the 13th to the 16th centuries most of these melodic and rhythmic modes were common to Persia and the eastern Arab world [see Persia].

The 16th to 19th centuries were a time of cultural stagnation and political decline for the Arabs, and the few extant treatises of this period are somewhat uninformative. They attach especial importance to the doctrine of *ta'thīr* (ethos) first mentioned by Al-Kindī, whereby music is integrated through complex series of associations (e.g., the twelve *maqāmāt* with the zodiac, the four strings of the 'ūd with the humors, elements, etc.) into the macrocosmic scheme [see Farmer, *The Influence of Music: from Arabian Sources*]. A similar attitude is evident in Sufi writings on music.

Arab music has not remained static since the 16th century; nevertheless the remarks above on the structure of the melodic and rhythmic modes are also valid for the present-day classical idiom (although not necessarily for folk music).

1. The beginning of a composition notated c. 1300 and ascribed to Ṣafī al-Dīn (d. 1294). The mode is Muḥayyir ḥusaynī, the rhythm Khafif. 2. The beginning of an improvisation in the mode Bayātī (recorded c. 1930?).

Ex. 1 and 2 develop just one pentachord and tetrachord respectively. The modern *maqām* may be made up of a considerable number of these, arranged in a fixed sequence, and may in addition be characterized by the position of prominent notes and by certain melodic features. In the eastern Arab world solo improvisation is generally unmeasured (*taqsīm*), but may be in a rhythmic cycle of 8 units (*taqsīm 'alā al-waḥda*). A rondo form, *bashraf,* is also important. In North Africa the most characteristic form is the *nawba,* comparable in the set order of its movements to the 18th-century suites of European classical music.

The most important instruments today are the *'ūd* and the *qānūn* (*kanun), followed by: the *rabāb,* a boat-shaped fiddle (but a spike fiddle in the eastern regions); the *nāy,* a vertical flute; the *kamānja,* a violin or viola; the *darbukka,* a vase-shaped drum; and the *duff* (or *riqq*), a tambourine.

Translations of treatises are: (French) Al-Fārābī, Ibn Sīnā (Avicenna), Ṣafī al-Dīn, and others in R. d'Erlanger, *La Musique arabe,* 6 vols. (1930–59); (German) Al-Kindī in R. Lachmann and Mahmud el-Hefni, *Ja'qūb ibn Ishāq al-Kindī* (1931); (English) Al-Fārābī in H. G. Farmer, *Al-Fārābī's Arabic-Latin Writings on Music.*

Lit.: J. B. de La Borde, *Essai sur la musique ancienne et moderne* (1780); G. A. Villoteau, in *Description de l'Égypte* xiii, xiv (1823, '26); E. W. Lane, *The Manners and Customs of the Modern Egyptians,* rev. ed. (1954; orig. pub. 1836); A. Chottin, *Tableau de la musique marocaine* [1939]; H. G. Farmer, *A History of Arabian Music to the XIIIth Century* (1929; repr. 1967), bibl.; *id., The Arabian Influence on Musical Theory* (1925); *id., Historical Facts for the Arabian Musical Influence* (1930); *id., Sa'adyah Gaon on the Influence of Music* (1943); *id., An Old Moorish Lute Tutor* (1933); *id., The Sources of Arabian Music* (1940); *id., The Influence of Music: from Arabic Sources* (1926; also in *PMA* lii); *id.,* "Ghinā'" and "Mūsīkī" in *The Encyclopaedia of Islām,* ed. M. T. Houtsma *et al.,* 4 vols. (1913–38); M. al-Ḥifnī (also El-Hefni), *Ibn Sina's Musiklehre* [1931]; H. G. Farmer, in *NOH* i, 421ff; J. Rouanet, in *LavE* i.5, 2676ff; A. Berner, *Studien zur arabischen Musik auf Grund der gegenwärtigen Theorie und Praxis in Ägypten* (1937); K. Schlesinger, *Is European Musical Theory Indebted to the Arabs?* (1925); X. Collangettes, "Étude sur la musique arabe" (*Journal Asiatique,* ser. 10, no. 4 [1904], no. 8 [1906]); A. Z. Idelsohn,

"Die Maqamen der arabischen Musik" (*SIM* xv); R. Lachmann, in *CP Wolf; id.,* in *AMW* v; O. Ursprung, in *ZMW* xvi; M. Schneider, in *CP 1953; id.,* in *AM* i and ix; B. Bartók, in *ZMW* ii; J. Rouanet, in *RM* v; J. B. Thibaut, in *BSIM* (1911) vii, 24.   O.W.

Arada drums. Set of three drums, one about 48 inches high, the others 26 and 20 inches high, made of hollow logs with cowhide skins held in place by hardwood pegs. They are used in Haiti primarily in connection with *voodoo religious dances and are played with special sticks, either straight or hooked.   J.O-S.

Aragonaise [F.], **aragonesa** [Sp.]. See under *Jota.*

Arcata [It.]. See under Bowing (a); *arcato,* bowed.

Archet [F.], **archetto** [It.]. Bow (of the violin).

Architectural acoustics. The study of the acoustic properties of a room or building (particularly of concert halls, opera houses, broadcasting studios), concerning resonance, reflection, echo, etc. Recent investigations have raised this field of study from the former stage of experimentation to an important branch of science.

Lit.: L. L. Beranek, *Music, Acoustics & Architecture* (1962); H. Bagenal and A. Wood, *Planning for Good Acoustics* (1931); A. H. Davis and G. W. C. Kaye, *The Acoustics of Buildings* (1927); P. R. Heyl, *Architectural Acoustics* (1930); V. O. Knudsen, *Architectural Acoustics* (1932); P. E. Sabine, *Acoustics and Architecture* (1932); F. R. Watson, *Acoustics of Buildings* (1923); H. H. Statham, in *PMA* xxxviii; A. Elson, in *MQ* vii.

Archives des maîtres de l'orgue. See Editions I.

Archivium musices metropolitanum mediolanense. See Editions II.

Archlute [F. *archiluth;* G. *Erzlaute;* It. *arciliuto;* Sp. *archilaúd*]. A lute with two pegboxes, one for the fingered strings, the other for the bass courses (theorbo, chitarrone). See Lute III.

Arcicembalo, arciorgano [It.]. Microtonic instruments of the 16th century, described by N. Vicentino in his *L'Antica Musica* (1555) and *Descrizione dell' arciorgano* (1561). Each had six manuals containing 31 keys to the octave, and these gave all the tones of the diatonic, chromatic, and enharmonic genera of ancient Greek theory. A simplified instrument of greater practical importance was built by the Belgian Charles Luython (1556–1620); it had 18 keys in each octave, namely—in addition to the diatonic tones—c♯ and d♭, d♯ and e♭, f♯ and g♭, g♯ and a♭, b♭, e♯, and b♯. This instrument, called "clavicymbalum universale" (M. Praetorius, in his *Syntagma musicum,* vol. ii [1618], praises it as "instrumentum perfectum, si non perfectissimum"), permitted enharmonic change and modulation in all the keys, without the compromise of equal temperament. Compositions such as John Bull's fantasia on the hexachord "Ut, re, mi, fa, sol, la" (*Fitzwilliam Virginal Book,* i, 183; see Hexachord IV) are evidently written for this instrument. In the preface to his *Correnti, Gagliarde e Balletti . . . libro quarto* (1645), Martino Pesenti mentions two other instruments, one built by Domenico de Pesaro in 1548, the other by Vido Trasentino in 1601, the former with 24, the latter with 28 keys in the octave.

Lit.: A. Koczirz, in *SIM* ix; Shohé Tanaka, in *VMW* vi, 66ff; W. Dupont, *Geschichte der musikalischen Temperatur* (1935), pp. 51ff.

Arco [It.]. Bow (of violins, etc.). See *Col arco.*

Arditamente [It.]. Boldly.

Ardore, con [It.]. With warmth.

A re, are. See under Hexachord III.

Areito. A dance of the West Indies. The music consists of alternating solo and group singing accompanied by percussion instruments. It is also known as *batoco,* and in Mexico as *mitote.*
                                                                    J.O-S.

Argentina. The beginnings of musical activity in Argentina are associated with a number of *ministriles* (Martin Nino, Juan Andrés Mendoza, Juan Jara, Rodrigo Melgarejo, and others) who joined Spanish expeditions to the New World. The *ministriles* were servants trained in the art of singing and playing certain instruments, such as the vihuela, lute, organ, and clavichord. Most of them lived in Asunción but were sent for short periods to Buenos Aires, then a small village.

Argentine musical life first began to have some continuity with the establishment of Jesuit missions in the Paraná River region and the arrival of trained musicians who joined these missions at the time Father Pedro Comental (1595–1665) founded the first school of music in this area. Accordingly, the earliest accomplishments in professional music education are linked with the names of Belgian-born Father Juan Vasseau (Vaseo or Vaiseau, 1584–1623) and to that of the French Father Luis Berger (1588–1639). Berger's activities extended throughout Argentina and Paraguay, and even to Chile. In

1691, the Austrian-born Father Antonio Sepp (1655–1733), who had participated for many years in the imperial court choir in Vienna, arrived in Buenos Aires. He was assigned to the Mission of Yapeyú, which he made one of the most important music centers by the end of the 17th century. The most distinguished musician to be assigned to the missions was the Italian composer and organist Domenico Zipoli (1688–1726), who arrived in Buenos Aires in 1717. He was stationed in Córdoba and became the organist of the Jesuit chapel there. References to "30 motets by Brother Zipoli" have been found in the National Archives, but so far only the manuscript of a Mass for four voices and continuo has been discovered. During the remainder of the 18th century Jesuit priests such as Martin Schmid (1694–1773), Juan Mesner (1703–68) and Florián Paucke (1719–80) played a role in Argentina's musical development.

In the 19th century a number of native composers were strongly influenced by Italian opera, especially by Bellini and Rossini. Among these were Amancio Alcorta (1805–62), Juan Pedro Esnaola (1808–78), and Juan Bautista Alberdi (1810–84). Alcorta, an economist and politician, became active as a composer after 1822, writing largely songs, piano pieces, chamber and church music. Esnaola, a native of Buenos Aires, founded the Academia de Música y Canto and composed a number of piano pieces, songs, hymns, church music, and two symphonies. Alberdi was a prominent writer who composed a number of songs and piano pieces on the side. He also wrote an essay, "The Spirit of Music," and in 1832 published a piano method for amateurs.

Between 1850 and 1880 a considerable number of composers of semiprofessional status, most of them living in Buenos Aires, produced salon music and a few orchestral and stage works. The most representative members of this group were Saturnino F. Berón (1847–98), author of a *Treatise of Modern Music* (1859); Luis José Bernasconi (1845–85); Juan Gutiérrez (1840–1906), founder and first director of the Conservatorio Nacional de Música (1880); Francisco A. Hargreaves (1849–1900), the first native Argentine composer of operas (*La Gatta Bianca,* 1875; *Los Estudiantes de Bologna,* 1897; *L'Assedio* and *Psyche,* unpub.); and Zenón Rolón (1856–1902), who also wrote operas (*Solané, Le Prove, Fides*) as well as a number of operettas and **zarzuelas.*

By 1880 a new generation of composers had emerged in Argentina, most of them professional and winning recognition abroad. All of them cultivated the major symphonic forms as well as chamber music and opera. Herman Bemberg (1861–1931) composed an opera, *Elaine,* that was performed in London (1892) and New York (1894); Justin Clérice's (1863–1908) opera *Figarello* was introduced with great success in Paris (1889), Antonio Restano's (1860–1928) *Un milioncino* in Turin (1885), and Eduardo Garcia Mansilla's (1866–1930) *Ivan* was staged in Russia (1905). The most important composer of this generation was Alberto Williams (1862–1952), closely followed in prestige by Arturo Berutti (1862–1938), Ettore Panizza (b. 1875), and Constantino Gaito (1878–1945). Williams, a grandson of Alcorta, studied in Paris for seven years. In 1889 he returned to Buenos Aires, where he devoted his time to teaching, giving piano concerts, conducting, and writing some 136 compositions, including nine symphonies, several symphonic poems, orchestral suites, chamber music, choral and piano works, and songs.

Julián Aguirre (1868–1924) is the most important of the immediate followers of Williams' early nationalist trends. The desire to create styles relatively free from European influences was shared by a group of composers active at the turn of the century, among them Carlos López-Buchardo (1881–1948), Gilardo Gilardi (1889–1963), and Athos Palma (1891–1951).

The development of opera in Argentina was particularly stimulated by the Teatro Colón (founded 1908) in Buenos Aires. Pascual de Rogatis (b. 1881), Raul H. Espolle (b. 1888), Enrique M. Casella (1891–1948) and Felipe Boero (b. 1884), the last-named the composer of *El Matrero,* which describes life in the Argentine pampas, are some of the outstanding figures of 1900–30 who produced operas strongly influenced by Italian verismo.

Nationalism remained an active force in Argentine symphonic and chamber music throughout the first half of the 20th century. It influenced not only those composers who still support the use of folk material in art music but also a number of those who, after 1950, gradually withdrew. Juan Carlos Paz (b. 1897) was among the first to lose interest in nationalism. By 1930 he was a strong supporter of serial techniques. As founder of the *Grupo Renovacion,* he attracted many younger followers and his influence remains strong in Argentina.

Juan José Castro (1895–1968) and his brothers José Maria Castro (1892–1964) and Wáshington Castro (b. 1909) represent a stream of composition that moved from the nationalism of the early 20th century toward greater universalism. This group also includes Floro M. Ugarte (b. 1884), Jacobo Ficher (b. 1896), Honorio M. Siccardi (b. 1897), Luis Gianneo (b. 1897), Carlos Suffern (b. 1905), Roberto Garcia Morillo (b. 1911), Carlos Guastavino (b. 1914), Guillermo Graetzer (b. 1914), the Spanish-born Julian Bautista (1901–60), and Alberto Ginastera (b. 1916), the last-named becoming one of the leading creative forces in Latin American music. From Ginastera's earliest nationalist compositions, such as his ballets *Panambí* (1937) and *Estancia* (1941), to the neoclassical approach of his Sonata for Piano (1952), *Variaciones Concertantes* (1953), and his two String Quartets (1948, '58), and thence to his more recent interest in atonal and serial techniques (*Cantata para América Mágica,* 1960; Concerto for piano, 1961; Concerto for violin, 1963; the opera *Don Rodrigo,* 1964), his work showed a considerable and important evolution. As head of the Center for Advanced Musical Studies established in Buenos Aires in 1962, Ginastera has helped train many of Latin America's most talented young composers.

Today a large group of outstanding musicians is continuing Argentina's musical development through the paths of the most advanced compositional techniques. Representative of this group are Roberto Casamaño (b. 1923); Antonio Tauriello (b. 1928); Mario Davidowsky (b. 1934), a composer of electronic music; Alcides Lanza (b. 1929); Mauricio Kagel (b. 1931), a native of Argentina and developer of electronic and aleatory techniques who has worked in Germany since 1960; Carlos Tuxen-Bang (b. 1932); Gerardo Gandini (b. 1936); and Armando Krieger (b. 1925).

The folksongs and dances of Argentina are linked to three chief traditions: the indigenous music of Andean origin, exemplified by the *huaiño* and *carnavalito* from the province of Jujuy and the *baguala* and *vidala* of the northeast; the Creole tradition, which developed mainly in the north, exemplified by such types as the *triste,* *gato,* *zamba,* and *estilo;* and the European tradition, exemplified by the *alabanza,* [see Aguinaldo], *villancico, polca* (polka), and *vals* (waltz). The modern *tango,* which took on its present form at the turn of the century, is more an expression of popular music from urban Buenos Aires than of folk music.

Lit.: A. T. Luper, *The Music of Argentina* [1953]; J. Subirá, *Historia de la música española e hispanoamericana* [1953]; V. Gesualdo, *Historia de la música en la Argentina,* 2 vols. [1961]; I. Aretz, *El Folklore musical argentino* [1952]; G. Furlong, *Músicos Argentinos durante la dominación hispánica* [1944]; C. Vega, *Panorama de la Música Popular Argentina* [1944]. Also see under Latin America.   J.O-S.

Aria. I. An elaborate composition for solo voice (occasionally for two solo voices; see Duet) with instrumental accompaniment. The aria figures prominently in the cantatas and oratorios of the 17th and 18th centuries and in opera up to the end of the 19th century except for the Wagnerian type. It is distinguished from the air, song, or lied by (a) generally greater length; (b) nonstrophic form (except for its earliest development; see II); and (c) emphasis on purely musical design and expression, often at the expense of the text. In fact, the small regard that many aria composers have shown for the text has evoked serious criticism of the form and, in some instances, has led writers of operas to banish the aria from the stage. By and large such criticism cannot be justified. Although at certain periods the aria style has been characterized by conventionalism and exaggeration, the great majority of arias represent a treasure of great musical value. Moreover, in opera the aria has a definite and important function, in representing lyric episodes that temporarily relieve the dramatic tension of the action.

II. The word "aria" is derived from Gr.-L. *aer* (air), a term that came to mean mode or manner, scheme, model, etc. [see Ayre (3)]. In O. Petrucci's *Strambotti, ode, frottole, sonetti . . . libro quarto* (1505) a composition is called "Aer de versi latini," and one in his *Frottole libro nono* (1508) is marked "Aer de capitoli." Each represents a model melody to be used for a variety of texts having the same poetic structure. M. A. Ingegneri's *Il Secondo Libro de' madrigali . . . a quattro voci* (1579) includes two "Arie di canzon francese per sonare" (for four instruments); M. Facoli's *Il Secondo Libro d'intavolatura di balli* (1588) has twelve *arie* for harpsichord, among them one "da cantar terza rima"; and G. M. Nanino's *Il Primo Libro delle canzonette* (1593) has an "Aria di cantar sonetti" and an "Aria da cantar in ottava rima." Designations such as "Aria di Ruggiero" and "Aria di Firenze" probably refer to strophic songs, in which the same melody was used for the different stanzas of the poem. This meaning is clearly present in G. Caccini's *Le Nuove Musiche* (1601), where the term "aria" is used for short mo-

nodic melodies to be repeated with a number of stanzas [see K. Jeppesen, *La Flora,* vols. i, iii], whereas the longer, more elaborate, and through-composed monodies are called madrigals. Caccini's type of aria was cultivated by such German composers as Johann Staden (1581–1634; see *DTB* 12 and 14), Heinrich Albert (1604–51; see *DdT* 12/13; *HAM,* no. 205; *SchGMB,* no. 193), Adam Krieger (1634–66; see *DdT* 19; *HAM,* no. 228; *SchGMB,* no. 209), and J. Philipp Krieger (1649–1725; see *DdT* 53/54). Those of A. Krieger [see Ritornello (2)] especially are important forerunners of the German strophic lied of the 18th and 19th centuries [see *RiHM* ii.2, 331ff].

III. One of Caccini's arias, "Ard' il mio petto," consists of three stanzas having the same bass but varied melodies [*SchGMB,* no. 172]. This is the earliest known example of the *strophic-bass aria, which became the most important type in the period up to *c.* 1630. The strophic-bass aria occurs in: Jacopo Peri, *Le Varie Musiche* (1609); Alessandro Grandi, *Cantade et arie a voce sola* (1620; see *RiHM* ii.2, 39f); Stefano Landi, *Arie a una voce* (1620); Girolamo Frescobaldi, *Primo Libro d'arie musicali* (1630; see Jeppesen, *La Flora,* vol. iii, no. 35); and other collections of arias. To the same type belongs the Prologue of Monteverdi's *Orfeo* (1609; *La Flora,* vol. ii, no. 1), in which each varied stanza is followed by an instrumental ritornello.

Shortly after 1630 a new type appeared in the ostinato aria, which is through-composed over a short *basso ostinato,* usually in descending motion. Among the earliest examples is an aria, "Io son pur giovinetta," in Benedetto Ferrari's *Musiche varie* of 1633, based entirely on an ostinato that descends through an octave. Many other examples are found in his *Musiche [e poesie] varie* (1637, 1641; see *RiHM* ii.2, 55ff, 64ff). Monteverdi employed this type in the final duet of *L'Incoronazione di Poppea* (1642; see *SchGMB,* no. 178), which at the same time is an early example of a tripartite *da capo* aria. The ostinato type, actually a "vocal passacaglia" [see Chaconne and passacaglia], continued to be used frequently by Italian, English, and French composers of the second half of the 17th century, among them Carissimi, Stradella, Provenzale [*HAM,* no. 222], Purcell, and F. Couperin [see also the Crucifixus of Bach's B-minor Mass].

IV. The next stage (*c.* 1650–1750) is characterized by the establishment of the *da capo* aria as the preferred form. It consists of two sections followed by a repetition of the first, resulting in

```
           A                        B                       A
  ┌───────────────┐        ┌──────────────┐        ┌──────────────┐
  a′  a″  a ─ ─ ─ ─ ─      b ─ ─ ─ ─ ─ ─ ─      (a′  a″)  a ─ ─ ─ ─
  T   T   D   T            R   D_R   R            T        T   D   T
```

Scheme of the da capo aria: T = tonic; D = dominant; R = relative key.

a tripartite structure A B A. An early example is the above-mentioned duet from Monteverdi's *L'Incoronazione.* Numerous others occur in the cantatas of Luigi Rossi (1598–1653; see *HAM,* no. 203), Giacomo Carissimi (1605–74; see Jeppesen, *La Flora,* vol. i), or in the operas of Pietro Francesco Cavalli (1602–76), Marc' Antonio Cesti (1623–69), Agostino Steffani (1653–1728; see *HAM,* no. 244), and others. These arias are usually of small dimension (brief *da capo* aria) and in triple meter, sometimes suggestive of dance rhythms. A special feature, introduced *c.* 1660 by Cesti and Legrenzi, was the use of a so-called motto [G. *Devise*], that is, two introductory announcements of the beginning of the melody, first by the singer (a′), then by the instruments (a″), after which the full melody (a) is sung [see Motto (b)]. The early 18th century saw the rise of the grand *da capo,* characterized by considerably larger dimensions, virtuoso style of singing, and the use of a three-part modulatory scheme in the over-all form (B usually in the relative key, R) as well as in each section. The material of B is generally different from that of A but not of a strongly contrasting character. This type was developed by Alessandro Scarlatti (1660–1725; see *HAM,* no. 258) and universally adopted by other late baroque composers, including Bach and Handel.

The grand *da capo* aria became the basic ingredient of the so-called Neapolitan opera [see Opera VIII], which usually consisted of some twenty arias of a highly virtuoso character, connected by *secco* recitatives. In keeping with the strict conventions of 18th-century Italian opera, the arias were codified and classified according to typical situations of the plot, e.g.: *aria di bravura* (quick, deliberately difficult, sung to express passion, vengeance, rejoicing, triumph); *aria di mezzo carattere* (moderate tempo, expression of gentle feelings); *aria cantabile* (slow, expression of grief or longing); *aria parlante* (emphasis on the text, often with only one note to the syllable). The desire of great singers to show their ability in various musical styles led, about 1750, to the double aria, a form consisting of two separate arias of contrasting character, the first usually dramatic, the second lyrical.

V. After 1750 the conventionalized *da capo* aria was gradually replaced by arias written in a variety of forms and showing more individual expression. This tendency probably received its first impulse from the *opera buffa,* which by its very nature had no use for the aria types of the *opera seria.* An early example of the new kind of aria is the *cavatina "Godi l'amabile" from K. H. Graun's *Montezuma* (1755). Many others are found in the operas of Jommelli, Traetta, and, of course, Gluck and Mozart. The aria remained in favor with operatic composers throughout the first half of the 19th century (Beethoven, Auber, Rossini). While Wagner discarded it (except in his earliest operas, *Rienzi, Der fliegende Holländer, Tannhäuser,* which still contain a few well-defined arias), Verdi continued to make full use of it except in his last two operas (*Otello,* 1886; *Falstaff,* 1893).

The term "aria" was also used for short instrumental pieces of a songlike character, e.g., movements of a suite [Muffat, Handel; see Air (3)] or a theme for variations (*aria con variazioni;* see Bach's "Goldberg" Variations, Pachelbel's *Aria Sebaldina*).

Lit.: K. Jeppesen, ‡*La Flora: arie &c. antiche italiane,* 3 vols. (1949); L. Landshoff, ‡*Alte Meister des Bel Canto,* 5 vols. [1912–27]; H. Riemann, ‡*Kantaten Frühling,* 4 vols. [19—]; M. Zanon, ‡*Venti Arie ... di Fr. Cavalli* [n.d.]; L. Walther, *Die Ostinatotechnik in den Chaconne- und Arienformen des 17. und 18. Jahrhunderts* (1940); I. Schreiber, *Dichtung und Musik der deutschen Opernarien, 1680–1700* (1934); B. Hjelmborg, in *CP Jeppesen;* B. Flögel, "Studien zur Arientechnik ... Händels" (*Händel-Jahrbuch,* 1929); L. Torchi, "Canzoni ed arie ... nel secolo xvii" (*RMI* i, 581); J. Godefroy, "Some Aspects of the Aria" (*ML* xvii, 200). See also under Cantata; Opera.

Ariadne auf Naxos. Opera in one act and a prologue by R. Strauss (libretto by H. von Hofmannsthal), originally produced in Stuttgart in 1912 as an entr'acte for Molière's play *Le Bourgeois Gentilhomme,* for which Strauss also wrote the incidental music. Setting: Vienna, 18th century, and Naxos, ancient Greece. In 1916 it was produced in Vienna as an independent work, with the addition of an introductory scene representing the stage rehearsal of the work.

Aribú. An Afro-Brazilian dance song of rural origin, performed during harvest celebrations to the accompaniment of guitars and castanets. It is also called *lundú*. See bibl. under Brazil.   J.O-S.

Arietta [It.], **ariette** [F.]. (1) A small aria, usually in binary form and lacking the musical elaboration of the aria; thus rather a song or a *cavatina*. (2) In French operas before 1750, an aria to Italian words, usually in brilliant coloratura style. (3) In the *opéra comique* of the second half of the 18th century, a solo song (aria) in French, preceded and followed by spoken dialogue, the work being known as a *comédie mêlée d'ariettes*.
                                                              D.J.G.

Arioso [It.]. Properly, *recitativo arioso*, that is, a recitative of a lyrical and expressive quality, not, as usual, narrative and speechlike. The arioso style, therefore, is midway between that of a recitative and an aria. A good example showing the difference among these three styles is a can-

Be - reu - e   dei - ne   Schuld

(Arioso)

mit   Schmerz   daß   Chri - sti

Geist mit dir sich fest ver-bin - - - de daß

tata by Marc'Antonio Cesti (*c.* 1650), reproduced in *AdHM*, pp. 439ff. Historically, the arioso came earlier than the speechlike recitative. All the composers of the Florentine opera (Peri, Caccini, Monteverdi) employed the *recitativo arioso*, the expressive and quasimelodic recitative. Bach often uses the arioso for the concluding section of a recitative in order to give it a particular expression of assurance or confidence [see *Cavata*]. The accompanying example is taken from his cantata *Ein' feste Burg*. Beethoven, in the final movement of his Piano Sonata op. 110, uses the term for an accompanied recitative played on the piano.

Arithmetic and harmonic mean. The arithmetic mean a of two numbers m and n is determined by the equation $m - a = a - n$, and the harmonic mean h by the same relationship between the reciprocals: $\dfrac{1}{m} - \dfrac{1}{h} = \dfrac{1}{h} - \dfrac{1}{n}$. Hence, $a = \dfrac{1}{2}(m + n)$, and $h = \dfrac{2mn}{m + n}$. The musical significance of these two means was recognized by Boethius, who pointed out that the arithmetic mean (L. *medietas*) of the octave (frequencies 1 and 2) is the fifth: $\dfrac{1 + 2}{2} = \dfrac{3}{2}$, while its harmonic mean is the fourth: $\dfrac{2 \times 1 \times 2}{1 + 2} = \dfrac{4}{3}$. Of even greater importance was the discovery, made by Zarlino, that the two corresponding divisions of the fifth $\left(m = 1; n = \dfrac{3}{2}\right)$ lead respectively to the major and minor thirds: $a = \dfrac{\left(1 + \dfrac{3}{2}\right)}{2} = \dfrac{5}{4}$; $h = \dfrac{\left(2 \times 1 \times \dfrac{3}{2}\right)}{\left(1 + \dfrac{3}{2}\right)} = \dfrac{6}{5}$. The major triad is represented by the arithmetic progression $1 : \dfrac{5}{4} : \dfrac{3}{2} = 40 : 50 : 60$; the minor triad by the harmonic progression $1 : \dfrac{6}{5} : \dfrac{3}{2} = 40 : 48 : 60$. It may be noted that the above measurements are in frequencies (octave $= 2$), and that the opposite correspondences are correct if the tones are determined by lengths of strings. Therefore Zarlino (who, of course, knew nothing about frequencies) quite properly calls the major triad c–e–g *harmonica* and the minor triad d–f–a *arithmetica*.

53

Arlésienne, L' [F., The Woman of Arles]. Incidental music by Georges Bizet (1838–75) to Alphonse Daudet's play *L'Arlésienne*. It is usually played in the form of two orchestral suites [see Suite V], the first arranged by Bizet in 1872 and the second by E. Guirand after Bizet's death.

Armenia. Since Armenia was the first country officially to adopt the Christian faith (A.D. 303), the history of Armenian sacred literature and music has attracted much attention. The Armenian liturgy, like that of Byzantium, consists chiefly of hymns. The oldest of the hymns were in prose. Later, versified hymns became prominent, especially through the activity of the great poet Nerses Schnorhali (11th cent.). The official book of hymns, called *sharakan*, contains 1,166 songs. The earliest preserved liturgical manuscripts containing musical signs date from the 14th century. The notation is a highly developed system of neumes (Armenian neumes), which certainly was the result of a long evolution [examples in *LavE* i.1, 552; J. Thibaut, *Origine byzantine de la notation neumatique de l'église latine,* 1907, pl. 4], but the lack of treatises explaining this notation renders the Armenian neumes undecipherable. In the early 19th century a new system of musical notation, similar to that of present-day Greek church music, was introduced, and it is still in use. Whether the present-day melodies are identical or similar to those of the early books cannot be ascertained, but the fact that the modern chants are grouped according to an *oktoechos* [see *Echos*] suggests an ancient origin for the melodies. The continuity of tradition is more doubtful so far as the rhythmic interpretation of Armenian chant is concerned. The melodies of the present liturgy are based upon strict time, with the temporal unit (*kèt,* i.e., beat) divided into an elaborate system of rhythmic formations of smaller values, including 32nd and 64th notes. Whereas scholars such as R. P. Dechevrens and J. C. Jeannin have considered this rhythm of great antiquity and have used it as an argument in favor of strictly rhythmical interpretation of Gregorian chant, P. Aubry considers it a fairly recent innovation due to Turkish influence (15th century). The purest source of Armenian church music is undoubtedly the music in use at Echmiadzin, which is also used at Tiflis and Erivan. The collections issued by European and American communities differ widely from the traditional forms, chiefly owing to the use of cheap modern harmonizations.

Lit.: A. K. Torossian, ed., *The Divine Liturgy ... According to the Rites of the Holy Apostolic Church of Armenians* (1933); P. Bianchini, *Les Chants liturgiques de l'église arménienne* (1877); M. Ekmalian, *Les Chants de la sainte liturgie* (1896); A. Apcar, *Melodies of the Holy Apostolic Church of Armenia* (Calcutta, 1897); Nerses Ter-Mikaelian, *Das armenische Hymnarium* (1905); P. Aubry, *Le Rhythme tonique* (1903); A. Gastoué, in *LavE* i.1, 541ff; P. Aubry, in *TG* vii, viii, ix; E. Wellesz, in *AdHM* i, 139; *id.,* in *JMP* xxvii; K. Keworkian, in *SIM* i; A. Gastoué, in *RdM* (Aug. 1929), p. 194; G. Kaftangian, in *CP 1950;* L. Dayan, *ibid.*

Secular music: K. H. Aiguni, *Songs of Armenia* (1924); K. Keworkian (Komitas), *Musique populaire arménienne,* 5 vols. (1925–30); F. Macler, *La Musique en Arménie* (1917); G. H. Paelian, *The Music of Armenia* (1939), bibl.; R. Pesce, *La Musica armena* (1935); S. Poladian, *Armenian Folk Songs* (1942). See "Bibliography of Asiatic Musics, Fifth Installment" (*Notes* vi, 122).

Armonica. See Glass harmonica.

Armure [F.]. Key signature.

Arpa [It., Sp.]. Harp. See also under Psaltery.

Arpègement [F.]. Older term for *arpège* (arpeggio). For *arpègement figuré,* see *Acciaccatura;* Arpeggio.

Arpeggio [It.; F. *arpège;* Sp. *arpegio*]. The notes of a chord played one after another instead of simultaneously. In modern music the arpeggio is indicated by one of the signs given in Ex. 1. Its execution always starts with the lowest note, and as a rule it should begin at the moment when the chord is due (i.e., on the beat), whether indicated by sign or by tiny notes [Ex. 2, Mozart, Sonata in C major, K. 309 (K. Einstein 284b); Ex. 3, Chopin, Nocturne op. 62, no. 1]. There are cases, however, in which the melody carried by the top note of the arpeggio will not bear the delay caused by this execution, so that the last note of the arpeggio must then be made to coincide with the beat [Ex. 4, Mendelssohn, *Songs without Words,* no. 30]. The latter performance is generally to be recommended in piano music whenever the arpeggio occurs in the left hand alone, as in Ex. 5 (Chopin, Mazurka op. 7, no. 3). A distinction should be made between an arpeggio played simultaneously with both hands. [Ex. 6] and a long arpeggio in which the right hand succeeds the left [Ex. 7]. The latter is (or should be) indicated by a long arpeggio sign, joining

the two staves. For the violin arpeggio, see Bowing (i).

In the music of the 17th and 18th centuries the execution of the arpeggio varied considerably (often at the discretion of the individual performer) in respect to direction and number of notes. The French clavecinists used the signs shown in Ex. 8 to indicate the *arpègement en montant* (ascending arpeggio) and those in Ex. 9 for the *arpègement en descendant* (descending arpeggio). Other special signs were used to indicate various kinds of *arpègement figuré,* or arpeggios in which unwritten notes are introduced [see Ex. 10, 11, 12]. In performance of these *arpègements figurés* all the notes are held except those that are foreign to the chord, which are immediately released [see *Acciaccatura*]. An appoggiatura to an arpeggio chord is incorporated in the arpeggio, occasioning a delay of the particular note to which it belongs, as in Ex. 13. A combination of *arpègements figurés* and an appoggiatura is shown in Ex. 14, from Bach's Partita in E minor.

In music of the time of Bach and Handel the word "arpeggio" is sometimes found written at

the beginning of a sequence of chords. In this case, the player is at liberty to break the chords up and down several times, to extend them, and to interpolate extraneous notes as he sees fit [see Handel's own notation of the last four bars of the Prelude to his keyboard Suite in D minor]. The note values, and even the tempo of such passages, are left entirely to the player's discretion. These chords (e.g., those in Bach's Chromatic Fantasia) are written in measured time only to facilitate reading, the style of performance being derived from the unmeasured preludes of the lutenists and early French clavecinists (Louis Couperin, D'Anglebert, etc.; see Prelude II).   P.A.

Arpeggione (also called guitar violoncello, *guitare d'amour*). A stringed instrument the size of a cello but with a guitarlike body and six strings tuned E, A, d, g, b, e′, invented in 1823 by G. Staufer. It is played with a bow. Franz Schubert wrote the only existing composition for it, a sonata for arpeggione and piano (1824; see *Franz Schuberts Werke,* 1888–97, ser. viii).

Arpicordo. Italian 16th-century name for a harpsichord that differed in some unknown detail from the clavicembalo [see Harpsichord II]. Note the title of a publication of 1551: *Intabolatura nova di varie sorte de balli da sonare per* *arpichordi, claviciembali, spinette et manachordi;* also G. Picchi, *Intavolatura di balli d'arpicordo* (1620; *Editions V, 2). See "Arpichordum" in *SaRM*. Perhaps it is identical to the *Arpichordum* as described by M. Praetorius (*Syntagma musicum,* 1619, ii, ch. 43), "a jack-action instrument or virginal on which a harplike sound is produced by means of a special stop which governs brass hooks under the strings." S. Virdung in his discussion of the *Claviciterium* in *Musica getutscht* (1511), J. Adlung (*Anleitung zu der musikalischen Gelahrtheit,* 1758, note r to Par. 246), and P. N. Sprengel (*Handwerk und Künste in Tabelen,* Berlin, 1773, xi, 265) all mention versions of the device. It seems to have produced a buzzing tone sometimes considered to be harplike and sometimes compared to the reed stops of the organ (*Schnarrwerk*). Metal pins or hooks were moved close to the strings so as to jar against them.   add. by F.H.

Arpitarrone. Name given by Adriano Banchieri to an instrument (made for him by Michel de Hodes) with the form of a harpsichord and the sound of a *chitarrone. See his *L'Organo suonarino* (1611), p. 57.

Arraché [F.]. Forceful pizzicato.

Arrangement. The adaptation of a composition for a medium different from that for which it was originally written, so made that the musical substance remains essentially unchanged. From the early 14th to the end of the 16th century, we have evidence of an ever increasing practice of arranging vocal music (motets, Mass items, madrigals, chansons, etc.) for a keyboard instrument or for lute in order to make such compositions available for domestic performance and enjoyment [see Intabulation]. In the baroque era this practice largely disappeared, no doubt because of the greatly reduced importance of vocal music. It is interesting to note that the greatest creative genius of this period, Bach, was almost the only one to take considerable interest in the recreative activity of arranging compositions of his own or others. Well-known examples are his arrangements for the harpsichord and organ of violin concertos by Vivaldi and others, and his transcription of the Fugue from his solo Violin Sonata in G minor for the organ (D minor; *BG* xv, 148). This last is of interest as being one of the earliest instances of an arrangement from a limited medium to one of ampler resources. To this category also belong Rameau's arrangements of his harpsichord pieces for an instru-

mental ensemble (*Pièces de clavecin en concerts,* 1741, for harpsichord, flute, and viol). Other noteworthy examples are Haydn's *Die Sieben Letzten Worte . . . am Kreuze* [see Seven (Last) Words], Liszt's concert arrangements of operatic scenes and of Schubert's songs, Brahms' transcription for two pianos of his orchestral *Variations on a Theme by Haydn,* etc.

In a different category are the customary piano arrangements of operas, symphonies, string quartets, etc., which are primarily designed for study purposes. The first such arrangements of symphonies by Haydn, Mozart, and Beethoven were made by F. Mockwitz (1785–1849).

Since about 1910 there has been an extraordinary amount of activity in transcribing Bach's organ works for the piano and the orchestra. Although this must be welcomed as a token of the ever growing interest in the work of the great master, the development has taken on forms that have recently led to a sharp reaction against the "business of arrangement." This opposition, however, is justifiable only with regard to certain methods of transcription. Several transcribers (e.g., Respighi), impelled by the richness of modern orchestration or piano technique, have tried—and certainly with success—to give Bach's organ pieces an impressionist lushness or a romantic emotionalism that is inconsistent with the intrinsic clarity of his style.

Lit.: K. Grunsky, *Die Technik des Klavierauszugs* (1911); E. Friedländer, *Wagner, Liszt und die Kunst der Klavierbearbeitung* (1922); M. Hansemann, *Der Klavier-Auszug von den Anfängen bis Weber* (1943); H. Hering, "Bachs Klavierübertragungen" (*Bach-Jahrbuch,* 1958); id., "Übertragung und Umformung" (*MF* xii); E. Howard-Jones, in *ML* xvi, 305.

Arrescu [Sp.]. See *Aurresku.*

Ars antiqua [L.]. I. The term *ars antiqua* (*ars veterum*) was used by writers of the early 14th century (e.g., "Speculum musicae" *c.* 1325; see *CS* ii, 429) to distinguish the late 13th-century school (Franco, *c.* 1260; Petrus de Cruce, *c.* 1290) from that of their own day, which was called *ars nova (or *ars modernorum*). Today, both terms are usually employed in a wider sense, denoting music of the 13th and 14th centuries respectively. The *ars antiqua,* then, includes the school of *Notre Dame with its two masters, Leoninus (second half of 12th cent.) and Perotinus (*c.* 1160–1220), and the ensuing period, which, for want of other names, may be divided into the period of Franco (middle 13th cent.) and that of Petrus de Cruce (late 13th cent.). The school of Notre Dame was preceded by the school of *St. Martial (*c.* 1100–50).

Leoninus, called "optimus organista" by the English Anon. IV [*CS* i, 342]—i.e., "greatest composer of organa," not, as some modern writers believe, "very able organist"—was the creator of the *"Magnus liber organi," which in its final form represents a complete cycle of two-part organa (*organa dupla*) for the ecclesiastical year, about 90 in all.

Perotinus, "optimus discantor" (i.e., greatest composer of *discantus*), enlarged this repertory by composing organa in three and occasionally four parts (*organum triplum* and *organum quadruplum;* see *AdHM* i, 226, 228–32). He and his collaborators also added a large number of short compositions, mostly in two parts, the so-called clausulae, which were designed to be used as substitutes for corresponding sections in Leoninus' organa. These clausulae constitute the link with the following period, since they were frequently transformed into motets. The motet is the representative form of the middle and second half of the 13th century, when it was cultivated almost to the exclusion of any other type of music. The propensity of the 13th-century musicians (practically all anonymous) for this form would be difficult to understand were it not for the fact that the motet, which originally was a strictly liturgical form (a clausula provided with a full text in the upper part), soon underwent secular influence, partly from the tradition of the trouvères, which brought with it fresh impulses and even various heterogeneous elements (mixture of Latin and French, of liturgical tenors and love lyrics). The repertory of the school of Notre Dame also includes a large number of *conductus, i.e., Latin songs in one to four parts, mostly to devotional texts, but without plainsong *cantus firmus,* such as occurs with all the organa, clausulae, and motets.

II. The 13th-century technique of composition may be described as "successive counterpoint." The composer starts out with one complete voice, the tenor, which is either a pre-existent plainsong melody (this is the case with organa, clausulae, and practically all motets) or one written by the composer himself (this is the case with conductus). To this fundamental part the others are added successively, first the *duplum* (called *motetus* in a motet), then the *triplum.* [Regarding the principles of consonance and dissonance, see Harmony II A.]

The most important contribution of the *ars*

antiqua lies in the field of rhythm. While the organa of the school of St. Martial employ for their upper part melismas in free, unmeasured rhythm, the period around 1180 marks the establishment of strict rhythm, based on the rhythmic modes [see Rhythm III (b), (c)]. This new rhythm presents itself clearly in the discant sections of Leoninus' organa, whereas the organum sections are written in a transitional style whose rhythmic interpretation is still a matter of controversy [see Organum]. With Perotinus, modal rhythm (usually reproduced in modern editions as $2 \times 3/8 = 6/8$ meter) was universally adopted for the entire organa and their derivative types. For the most important sources of 13th-century polyphony, see Sources, nos. 3–7. For more complete lists see F. Ludwig, in *AMW* v; also *ApNPM*, p. 201f, sections II, III.

Related articles: *Cantiga;* Clausula; Conductus; Discant; *Estampie;* Hocket; *Lauda;* Minnesinger; Modes, rhythmic; Motet A, I, II; Organum; Square notation; "Sumer is icumen in"; Troubadour; Trouvère.

Lit.: F. Ludwig, *Repertorium organorum recentioris et motetorum vetustissimi stili* (1910); G. D. Sasse, *Die Mehrstimmigkeit der Ars antiqua in Theorie und Praxis* (1940); *OH,* vol. i (preferably the edition of 1901); *ReMMA,* pp. 272–330 (bibl. pp. 445–56); *AdHM* i, 214–65 (bibl. p. 294); *BeMMR,* pp. 112–35 (bibl. p. 180); *ApNPM,* pp. 215–337; *GrHWM,* pp. 68–105 (bibl. pp. 671–72); ‡*HAM,* nos. 28–42; ‡*SchGMB,* nos. 16–20; H. Gleason, ‡*Examples of Music before 1400* (1942), pp. 36–76; W. G. Waite, ‡*The Rhythm of Twelfth-Century Polyphony* (1954); J. H. Baxter, ‡*An Old St. Andrews Music Book* (1931); fac. ed. of MS Wolfenbüttel 677); L. Dittmer, ‡*Facsimile Reproduction of the Manuscript Madrid 20486, with an Introduction* (1957); id., ‡*Facsimile Reproduction of the Manuscript Wolfenbüttel 1099 (1206)* [1960]; E. Thurston, ‡*The Music in the St. Victor Manuscript Paris lat. 15139* (1959); J. Handschin, "Zur Geschichte von Notre Dame" (*AM* iv); H. Schmidt, "Zur Melodiebildung Leonins und Perotins" (*ZMW* xiv); M. Schneider, "Zur Satztechnik der Notre-Dame Schule" (*ZMW* xiv); W. Apel, "From St. Martial to Notre Dame" (*JAMS* ii); W. G. Waite, "Discantus, Copula, Organum" (*JAMS* v); R. Ficker, "Polyphonic Music of the Gothic Period" (*MQ* xv); E. H. Sanders, "Peripheral Polyphony of the 13th Century" (*JAMS* xvii).

Arsis and thesis [Gr.]. Arsis means "lifting" [G. *Hebung*] and thesis means "lowering" [G.

Senkung]. In Greek poetry, these terms were used in the sense of bodily movement, such as the lifting and lowering of the foot (as in dancing) or the hand (in conducting). Consequently, thesis meant the long syllable, or upbeat, of a simple metrical foot (e.g., dactyl: ⁻ ˘ ˘), while the remainder of the foot was regarded as the arsis. Unfortunately, Roman and medieval writers reversed the meaning of the terms, interpreting them as referring to the raising and lowering of the voice, not the foot. Since with a pair of tones the higher one is usually accented more than the lower, the term arsis (high) was identified with accent, and thesis (low) with lack of accent:

a t a t a t

‒ ˘ ‒ ˘ ‒ ˘

It is in this sense that the terms are usually employed in French writings on meter and metrical music. The usage also persists in German terminology, in which *Hebung* (arsis) means strong beat, *Senkung* (thesis), weak beat [see *Vierhebigkeit*]. Modern English writers have returned to the original and proper meaning of arsis and thesis [see, e.g., *Webster's Collegiate Dictionary*]. This usage is observed in this book. See Poetic meter.

To 16th- and 17th-century theorists (G. Zarlino, C. Butler, T. Morley), the phrase *per arsin et thesin* meant "by contrary motion," i.e., by inversion. The same phrase was used later by F. W. Marpurg (*Abhandlung von der Fuge,* 1753–54) to designate a fugue in which the answer is in contrary rhythm, i.e., what had been on a strong beat in the subject was now on a weak beat.

Ars nova [L.]. I. *General.* Generic name for the music of the 14th century, in contradistinction to the *ars antiqua*, i.e., music of the 13th century. Properly, the name should be restricted, as it originally was, to French music of the first half of the 14th century, represented by the most recent compositions in the "Roman de Fauvel" [see Sources, no. 8] and by the works of Philippe de Vitry (1291–1361). Indeed, compositions of the late 14th century, especially French ones, show features of intellectual refinement, affectation, and even decadence that are scarcely compatible with the term [L., new art]. In the early 14th century, however, the *ars nova* began as a novel movement whose chief champion was Philippe de Vitry. About 1325, he employed the term *ars nova* as the title of a treatise, which unfortunately deals primarily with the notational rather than the musical innovations of the period [*CS* iii, 13; trans. by P. Bohn, in *MFM* xxii]. More illuminating from a general point of view are the discussions in the "Speculum musicae," whose author, Jacques de Liège [see Theory B, no. 13], gives extremely interesting information regarding the stylistic contrast between the *ars antiqua* and the *ars nova,* although he speaks from a decidedly antimodernist point of view, always extolling the *ars veterum* (Franco of Cologne and Petrus de Cruce) over the "unnatural" innovations of the *moderni* [Book VII, ch. 43–46: "Collatio veteris artis . . . ad novam"; see *CS* ii, 383, 427–32]. On the other hand, Johannes de Muris, who was formerly thought to have written the "Speculum musicae," actually was another leader of the new movement, as was the contemporary Italian writer Marchetto da Padua, who in his "Pomerium in arte musicae mensuratae" contrasts the Italian and the French notation of the 14th century and decides in favor of the latter. In the field of musical composition the 14th century saw continued activity in France and the rise of a new school of polyphonic music in Italy. There are also a limited number of English compositions of the 14th century whose main interest lies in their extended use of *voice exchange and in their early employment of *sixth-chord style [see England III; Worcester, school of].

II. *The French ars nova.* The main achievement of the *ars nova* (and at the same time the point of attack by its adversaries) was the conquest of new territory in the field of rhythm and meter. While the music of the late 13th century was dominated by the principle of triple division (*modus perfectus* and *tempus perfectum;* modern equivalent 3/4 time with eighth-note triplets), the binary divisions were now admitted, so that the composer could choose from a variety of meters—2/4, 3/4, 6/8, and 9/8. Another important difference is the replacement of the rhythmic formula ♪♩ by its inversion, ♩♪. Jacobus strongly defended the former, saying that it "conforms

Typical rhythms of (a) ars antiqua; (b) ars nova.

with nature, which is always stronger at the end than at the beginning," but it is the latter that prevails in the motets of Vitry and of the greatest French composer of the 14th century, Guillaume de Machaut (c. 1300–77). Still another important aspect of the motets of this period is the use of isorhythm, regularly in the tenor and occasionally in the upper parts as well. Even more radically new is the style of Machaut's secular works, the polyphonic *ballades,* rondeaux, and virelais, most of which are probably of a later date than his motets. These secular pieces show free contrapuntal texture, supple rhythms, and expressive melodies, and generally bear the stamp of high refinement, delicacy, individuality, spontaneous creation, and even personal feeling, so that one is almost tempted to speak of a "14th-century romanticism." Toward the end of the 14th century there flourished in southern France (papal court of Avignon; secular courts of Orléans, Navarre, Berry) and also in northern Spain (court of Aragon) a group of French and Italian composers (Solage, Senleches or Selesses, Grimace, Cordier, Matteo da Perugia, Antonello da Caserta, and others) who constitute the "mannerist school," so called because of its tendency toward exaggeration and overrefinement. They cultivated a style characterized by almost unbelievable rhythmic complexities (cross rhythms, extended syncopations, written-out rubatos), equally complex methods of notation [see ch. ix, "Mannered Notation," in *ApNPM*], extravagant harmonies, bold dissonances, etc., resulting in "a musical texture . . . as disintegrated as . . . Webern's" [*GDB*, s.v. "Ars nova"]. An entirely different segment of French music of the late 14th century is represented by the Codex Apt [see Sources, no. 19], which includes liturgical compositions written in a simple style, among them historically important settings of hymns.

The harmonic style of the *ars nova* shows some advance over that of the *ars antiqua* insofar as thirds are introduced more frequently. Of special interest is the treatment of dissonances, which frequently reminds one of the dissonant counterpoint of modern composers (e.g., Hindemith). The polyphonic texture stands, as it were, under the influence of "points of magnetic attraction," at which the parts start and converge in perfect consonances, mainly octaves, fourths, and fifths, while in between the lines move with a remarkable degree of individuality and independence from harmonic considerations.

III. *The Italian ars nova.* In the tradition of

Italian 14th-century music two schools can be distinguished, the earlier of which is represented by Magister Piero, Giovanni da Cascia (or Johannes de Florentia), and Jacopo da Bologna, and the later by Francesco Landini (1325–97), Paolo Tenorista, Ghirardello da Firenze, and others. Musical as well as notational features indicate that Italian polyphonic music branched off from the French tradition of the late 13th century, particularly from the style of Petrus de Cruce. However, in the half-century 1275–1325 it developed special traits that led to a decidedly national repertory and style. The forms of the earlier school are the madrigal and the *caccia,* while in the later school the *ballata* (the French virelai) prevails. The style of the earlier compositions may be described as an "ornamented conductus style." The voices, usually two and having the same text, move simultaneously, the lower part in longer note values, the upper frequently in quick figurations that remind one of the coloraturas of the 17th and 18th centuries. With Landini much of the elaborate texture and rhythmic refinement of French music (Machaut) appears in Italy. He largely abandoned the madrigal in favor of the *ballata* and often added an instrumental contratenor to the vocal duet formed by the discant and the tenor. Combining French subtlety and spirituality with Italian fullness and warmth, he created works that foreshadow the transparent beauty of early 15th-century music (Dunstable, Dufay). Paolo Tenorista is noteworthy for his fairly extensive use of imitation. At the end of the 14th century there appeared in Italy a Flemish composer, Johannes Ciconia (c. 1335–1411), who figures prominently in the development leading to the 15th century. In general, Italian music of the 14th century is much simpler than the French. Syncopations are rare or, if present, take place within the confines of a measure. Dissonances are much less pronounced and the feeling for tonality is considerably more developed, particularly through the frequent use of well-defined cadences.

Related articles: *Ballata; Ballade* [F.]; *Caccia; Estampie;* Isorhythmic; Madrigal I; Rondeau (1); Syncopation; Virelai. See also Sources, nos. 8–19.

Lit. *General: GrHWM,* pp. 106–29, bibl.; *ReMMA,* pp. 331–86, bibl.; *AdHM* i, 265–94, bibl.; *BeMMR,* pp. 136–80, bibl.; *ApNPM,* pp. 338–435; M. Schneider, *Die Ars nova . . . in Frankreich und Italien* [1930]; *HAM,* nos. 43–55; *SchGMB,* nos. 22–28; *WoGM* iii, nos. 13–62; F. Ludwig, "Die mehrstimmige Musik des 14.

Jahrhunderts" (*SIM* iv); V. Günther, "Das Ende der Ars nova" (*MF* xvi); F. J. Smith, "Ars nova—a Re-definition?" (*MD* xviii).

France: E. Dannemann, *Die spätgotische Musiktradition in Frankreich und Burgund* (1936); F. Ludwig, ed., ‡*Guillaume de Machaut, musikalische Werke,* 4 vols., i–iii (1926–29); vol. iv, ed. H. Besseler (1943; 1954); L. Schrade, ed., ‡*Polyphonic Music of the Fourteenth Century,* 4 vols. to date: vol. i (1956, *Roman de Fauvel,* Vitry), vols. ii and iii (1956, Machaut), vol. iv (1958, Landini); W. Apel, ed., ‡*French Secular Music of the Late Fourteenth Century* (1950); A. Gastoué, ed., ‡*Le Manuscrit de musique du trésor d'Apt* (1936); M. Johnson, ed., ‡"The Motets of the Codex Ivrea" (diss. Indiana Univ., 1955); H. Besseler, "Studien zur Musik des Mittelalters" (*AMW* vii, viii); G. Perle, "Integrative Devices in the Music of Machaut" (*MQ* xxxiv); W. Apel, "The French Secular Music of the Late Fourteenth Century" (*AM* xviii/xix).

Italy: K. von Fischer, *Studien zur italienischen Musik des Trecento und frühen Quattrocento* (1956); M. L. Martinez, *Die Musik des frühen Trecento* (1963); N. Pirrotta, ed., ‡*The Music of Fourteenth-Century Italy,* 4 vols. to date (1954–63); L. Ellinwood, ed., ‡*The Works of Francesco Landini* (1939); J. R. White, ed., ‡"The Music of the Early Italian Ars Nova" (diss. Indiana Univ., 1952); W. T. Marrocco, ed., ‡*The Music of Jacopo da Bologna* (1954); G. de Van, ed., ‡*Les Monuments de l'ars nova,* i [1939?, Italian liturgical pieces]; J. Wolf, *Der Squarcialupi-Codex* (1955); *id.,* "Italian Trecento Music" (*PMA* lviii); L. Ellinwood, "Origins of the Italian Ars Nova" (*PAMS,* 1937); *id.,* "The Fourteenth Century in Italy" (*NOH* iii, 31ff); F. Ghisi, in *MD* i (Codex Lucca); *id.,* in *MD* ii (Siena Fragment); N. Pirrotta and E. Li Gotti, in *MD* iii (Codex Lucca); N. Pirrotta, "'Dulcedo' e 'subtilitas' . . . al principio del '400" (*RBM* ii); various articles in *CP 1955;* K. von Fischer, "On the Technique, Origin and Evolution of Italian Trecento Music" (*MQ* xlvii).

Art ballad. See *Ballade* [G.].

Arte musicale in Italia, L'. See Editions III.

Articulation. A term used to denote (or demand) clarity and distinct rendition in musical performance, whether vocal or instrumental. Correct breathing, phrasing, attack, legato, and staccato are some of the aspects involved. See Phrasing and articulation.

Art of Fugue, The [G. *Die Kunst der Fuge*]. The last work of J. S. Bach, written in 1749 and published posthumously, in a rather careless manner, by his sons in 1750. It contains some 20 fugues and canons, called *contrapuncti,* all based on the same theme [Ex. 1], in which the various devices of imitative counterpoint, such as inversion, stretto, augmentation, diminution, canon, double fugue, triple fugue, etc. are exploited in the most elaborate and ingenious manner. The number of pieces varies in the different editions, some of which combine two related pieces under one number. Formerly *The Art of Fugue* was considered chiefly a magnificent manual of advanced counterpoint, but it is now universally recognized as one of the greatest musical creations. The turning point was the first public

performance, promoted by W. Graeser (1906–28) in Leipzig in 1927. This event was the beginning of a sensational revival that has since spread over the entire musical world.

The inaccuracy of the first printed edition has given rise to a century or so of controversy concerning the proper order of the *contrapuncti,* a controversy in which historical, paleographic, and artistic arguments as well as metaphysical speculations and mathematical abstractions have been advanced without yielding a final answer [see Lit., Hauptmann, Rust, Graeser,

David, Tovey, Apel]. A special problem is presented by the last (unfinished) fugue, which has frequently been considered extraneous to the work, since none of its three subjects (the last of which is *B–A–C–H) is the principal subject of *The Art of Fugue* [see A. Schweitzer, *J. S. Bach,* 2 vols. (1911), i, 424]. G. Nottebohm (1817–82), however, showed that this subject can be contrapuntally combined with those of the last fugue [Ex. 2]. This is sufficient reason for assuming that the unfinished "triple fugue" was planned as a gigantic quadruple fugue, a fitting climax to the whole work. The chorale "Wenn wir in höchsten Nöten sein," which was added by the editors "as a recompense for the incomplete fugue," does not belong to the work; yet, if played after the abrupt breaking off of the preceding fugue, it takes on a symbolic significance that may outweigh historical scruples. According to Mizler (1754), Bach planned to write still another quadruple fugue that could be reversed (crab motion) in all its parts [see *GD,* Sup. Vol., p. 10].

Another problem of *The Art of Fugue* is that of medium and performance—the question as to whether it is keyboard, orchestral, or chamber music. The lack of instrumental specifications in either the autograph or the first edition, together with the use of the scholarly *contrapunctus* as a designation for the various pieces, characterizes *The Art of Fugue* as a work that is not dependent upon specified medium or sound. Therefore any kind of performance that conforms to the austere spirit of the composition must be considered justifiable. On the other hand, it should not be overlooked that all the pieces, with the exception of the mirror fugues (nos. XII and XIII of the Peters ed.), are within reach of the hands of a keyboard player. Evidently, in composing the work, Bach was thinking of keyboard performance, if only for instructive purposes. F. Busoni, in his *Fantasia contrappuntistica* (1910), has offered a congenial modern version, fantastically expanded, of Bach's last fugue.

Lit.: *BG* xxv; other editions by Czerny, W. Graeser, H. T. David, D. F. Tovey (with completion of the unfinished fugue), Roy Harris (for string quartet), E. Schwebsch (for 2 pianos); M. Hauptmann, *Erläuterungen zu Joh. Sebastian Bachs Kunst der Fuge* (1841); D. F. Tovey, *A Companion to "The Art of Fugue"* (1931); B. Martin, *Untersuchungen zur Struktur der 'Kunst der Fuge'* (1941); G. M. Leonhardt, *The Art of Fugue, Bach's Last Harpsichord Work* (1952); C. S. Terry, in *MQ* xix; H. David, in *JMP* xxxiv; W. Apel, in *DM* xxii.4; H. Husmann, in *BJ* xxxv;

J. A. Burns, "L'Impiego della partitura e l'Arte della Fuga di J. S. Bach" (*L'Organo* ii, 163ff.).

Art song. A song of serious artistic intent written by a trained composer, as distinct from a folksong. See Song; Song cycle.

As, ases [G.]. A-flat, a-double-flat; see Pitch names.

ASCAP. American Society of Composers, Authors, and Publishers, a society founded in 1914 by Victor Herbert mainly to protect copyrights and performing rights. About 10,000 composers, authors and publishing firms belong to it.

Asia. See Mesopotamia; China; Japan; etc. See R. A. Waterman, *et.al.,* "Bibliography of Asiatic Musics" (*Notes* v–viii; 15 installments).

Aspiration [F.]. See under Nachschlag.

Assai [It.]. Much, e.g., *allegro assai,* quite fast.

Assassinio nella Cattedrale [It., Murder in the Cathedral]. Opera in two acts and an intermezzo by I. Pizzetti (libretto by A. Castelli after T. S. Eliot's play), produced in Milan, 1958. Setting: Canterbury Cathedral.

Assez [F.]. Enough, e.g., *assez vite,* fairly quick.

Assyria. See under Mesopotamia.

Atabal. Name for a set of three single-headed drums found in rural districts of the Dominican Republic. Also known as *palos,* the set consists of a *palo mayor* (large drum) about 48 inches high and 22 inches in diameter, a *palo segundo* (middle-sized drum) 42 inches high and 16 inches in diameter, and a *palo auxiliar* (small drum) 36 inches high and 12 inches in diameter. The drums are placed upright, the larger two being beaten with the palms and fingers and the smallest with a pair of *palitos* (drumsticks).

J.O-S.

Atabaqués. Set of three single-headed upright barrel drums used mainly in the *candomble* ritual dances in Bahía, Brazil. All three are beaten with the palm and fingers. They also are known as *tabaqués.* J.O-S.

Atem [G.]. Breath. *Atempause* (breathing pause), a very short rest used in instrumental performance for the sake of articulation or phrasing, is sometimes indicated by an apostrophe: '.

A tempo [It.]. Indicates return to normal tempo after deviations such as *ritenuto, più lento, ad libitum,* etc.

Atonality. Literally, absence of tonality. Tonality is a particular expression of the general principle of relaxation of tension, tension being a particular state that implies its "resolution," i.e., a return to relaxation, a stable state. Harmonically, the fundamental expression of tonality is the dominant-tonic relationship. When the harmonic relationships of a composition can be considered to derive from this fundamental relationship—remotely or closely, for a long or a short time—the music is said to be tonal.

In the history of Western music, tonality dominates a period of about two centuries, from the end of the 17th to the end of the 19th century. More precise limits cannot be set, since the development is a continuous one. The works of J. S. Bach represent a peak of this development. It is in the works of Wagner, Debussy, and many of their contemporaries that a progressive breakdown of tonality begins to appear: constant modulations denying, in the long run, any possible reference to a tonal center; harmonic structures that are less and less reducible to a cadential scheme; piling up of chords without polarity, i.e., without definite tension toward a resolution, like the chords of a diminished seventh, ninth, etc. Tonality was used less and less by Wagner's successors, notably Schoenberg, and thereafter the evolution from tonality to atonality continued. It might be said that the harmonic framework of *Tristan*—a fortiori that of Schoenberg's *Verklärte Nacht*—is already atonal, insofar as the tonal centers are no longer clearly evident to the listener. Nevertheless, the term *atonal* is generally (and preferably) confined to music that totally banishes tonality. Thus atonality, both as a concept and as a descriptive term, although at first challenged by Schoenberg himself, begins with the works he composed after 1909 (*Pierrot lunaire,* etc.).

The conscious suspension of tonality did not, however, at once bring a single substitute for it. It was only years later that Schoenberg proposed a new principle of organization [see under Serial music]. It is significant that *c.* 1900 the American composer Charles Ives, working quite independently of Schoenberg, wrote sections in certain chamber compositions in which tonality is practically suspended.

Lit.: R. Reti, *Tonality, Atonality, Pantonality* [1958]; G. Perle, *Serial Composition and Atonality* (1962); R. Leibowitz, *Schoenberg, et son école* [1947]; K. H. Ehrenforth, *Ausdruck und Form, Schönbergs Durchbruch zur Atonalität* (1963); H. Eimert, *Atonale Musiklehre* (1924);

L. Rognoni, *La Scuola musicale di Vienna* [1966]; T. W. Adorno, *Philosophie der neuen Musik* (1949); P. Boulez, *Relevés d'apprenti* (1965); *id., Penser la musique aujourd'hui* [1964]; *Incontri musicali,* nos. 1–4 (1956–60), *passim; Die Reihe* (German ed., 1955—, English ed., 1958—), *passim; Perspectives of New Music* [1962—], *passim;* D. Milhaud, "Polytonalité et atonalité" (*RM* 1923, no. 4); A. Machabey, "Dissonance, polytonalité, atonalité" (*RM* 1931, no. 116). See also under Tonality; Serial music.   A.B.

Attacca, attacca subito [It.]. Attack suddenly, an indication at the end of a movement that the next movement should follow without break.

Attacco. See under *Soggetto.*

Attack [F. *attaque*]. Promptness and decision in beginning a phrase, especially in forte passages. In orchestral parlance, attack means precise entry of the instruments. In French orchestras, the concertmaster is called *chef d'attaque.*

Aubade [F.; Sp. *alborada*]. Morning music, as distinct from *serenade, evening music. In the 17th and 18th centuries *aubades* were played in honor of royal or princely personages, at levees. The term has been used by various composers (e.g., Bizet, Rimsky-Korsakov) to denote a sort of idyllic overture. The beginning of Beethoven's "Pastoral" Symphony and Wagner's *Siegfried Idyll* may be considered idealized *aubades.* See *Alba.*

Auctoralis [L.]. Same as authentic (*church modes).

Audition. (1) A hearing given to a performer; a performance (particularly by students). (2) Faculty of hearing.

Aufforderung zum Tanz [G., Invitation to the Dance]. Piano composition by C. M. von Weber, op. 65 (1819), in the form of a waltz, preceded by an introduction (the "invitation") and concluded with an epilogue. It is the first example of a true waltz in art music.

Aufführungspraxis [G.]. See Performance practice.

Aufgeregt [G.]. Excited.

Auflösung [G.]. (1) Resolution (of a dissonance). (2) Cancellation (of an accidental). *Auflösungszeichen,* the natural sign, ♮.

Aufsatz [G.]. Tube of an organ reed pipe.

Aufschnitt [G.]. The mouth of an organ pipe.

Aufstrich [G.]. Up-bow.

Auftakt [G.]. Upbeat. For *Auftaktigkeit,* see under Phrasing and articulation.

Auftritt [G.]. Scene of an opera.

Aufzug [G.]. Act of an opera.

Augenmusik [G.]. See Eye music.

Augmentation and diminution. The presentation of a subject in doubled values (augmentation) or in halved values (diminution), so that, e.g., the quarter note becomes a half note (augmentation) or an eighth note (diminution). The note values may also be augmented (or diminished) in higher ratios, such as 1 : 3 (triple augmentation) or 1 : 4 (quadruple augmentation). These devices provide an important element of variety in fugal writing. They are usually introduced toward the end of the fugue; thus used, diminution bestows a character of *stretto, augmentation one of grandeur. Examples are: Bach, *The Well-Tempered Clavier* i, no. 8 (augmentation), *The Well-Tempered Clavier* ii, no. 9 (diminution), *The Art of Fugue,* nos. 6 and 7 (simultaneous appearance of the normal form, diminution, augmentation, and double augmentation); Beethoven, Piano Sonata op. 110, last movement (similar combinations; see Ex.). Augmentation and diminution are also used in the development sections of symphonies, particularly by Brahms and Bruckner.

Diminution (or augmentation) occurs first in a number of two-voice clausulae of the Perotinus period, in which a plainsong melody is used twice in succession, first in *duplex longae* (dotted half notes in modern transcription), then in plain *longae* (dotted quarter notes) [see *ApNPM,* p. 246]. In the 14th century, diminution is explained

in detail by theoretical writers (J. de Muris, Prosdocimus de Beldemandis) and is used almost regularly in the motets of G. de Machaut, the tenor having the *cantus firmus* twice, the second time in halved values [see Isorhythmic]. With the beginning of the 15th century, augmentation and diminution become notational devices, since the change of note values is no longer indicated by longer or shorter notes but by proportional signs [see Proportions] or by verbal instructions, such as *per augmentationem* or *per medium.* A last example of this method appears in Bach's *Musikalisches Opfer.* Many 16th-century ricercars use augmentation or diminution, e.g., A. Gabrieli's *Ricercare del primo tono* for organ [repr. in *Editions III, 3], in which each voice states the subject once in quadruple augmentation—exactly as in the *contrapunctus* 7 of Bach's *The Art of Fugue.* Augmentation and diminution are of basic importance in the fantasias of Sweelinck, which usually consist of three sections, with the theme (1) in normal values, (2) in augmentation, (3) in diminution.

Augmented intervals. See Interval. Augmented sixth chord, triad, see Sixth chord, Triad.

Aulos. The most important wind instrument of the ancient Greeks. It is not a flute (as has frequently been stated) but an oboe with double reed and a number of holes, ranging from four in the oldest instruments to fifteen in later specimens. The numerous pictures of aulos players show that the aulos usually consisted of two pipes; probably the larger pipe provided a drone or a few tones that were missing on the other. Many pictures show the player wearing a leather band over his mouth and tied at the back of his head. This probably served to increase the resistance of the cheeks, which acted as bellows, and enabled the player to build up considerable air pressure, thus producing a sound that occasionally must have been as shrill as that of a modern bagpipe.

The aulos originally was an Oriental instrument. According to legend, it was introduced into Greece about 900 B.C. by Olympos, who was later glorified as the "inventor of music." Throughout the history of Greek music the aulos has retained its Asiatic character. It was adopted for the orgiastic music symbolized by Dionysus, whereas the *kithara represented the restrained character of autochthonous Greek music, symbolized by Apollo. Aulos music was rapid, rhythmic, exciting. The slight modifications of pitch that could be obtained by half covering the holes of the aulos probably led to the enharmonic genus of Greek music. See also *Chroai.* See ill. under Oboe family.

Lit.: K. Schlesinger, *The Greek Aulos* (1939); *SaHMI*, pp. 138ff; A. Howard, "The [Aulos] or Tibia" (*Harvard Studies in Classical Philology,* iv); *id.,* "The Mouth-piece of the [*Aulos*]" (*ibid.,* x).

Aurresku, arrescu, auresca. An ancient ceremonial dance of the Basque regions (northern Spain), executed with a large variety of vigorous steps and gestures symbolizing courtship and other customs. It consists of several sections in varying meters (triple, quadruple, quintuple) and in different speeds. In its most complete modern form the *aurresku* consists of eight sections: *entra, atzescu, *zortziko, pasamano, desafio, *fandango, arin-arin, galop.* It is danced to the accompaniment of the chistu (a type of flute) and tamboril [see Pipe]. See V. Alford, in *MQ* xviii; F. Gascue, in *BSIM* 1912, viii, 41; *LavE* i.4, 2355ff.

Ausdrucksvoll, mit Ausdruck [G.]. With expression.

Aushalten [G.]. To sustain a note.

Aus Italien. See under Symphonic poem III.

Auslösung [G.]. The repeating mechanism (escapement) of the piano.

Australia and New Zealand. I. Organized musical activity in Australia may be said to begin with William Vincent Wallace (1812–65) and Isaac Nathan (1792–1864). Wallace, an Irish composer and violinist, visited Australia and New Zealand, giving a concert in Sydney in 1836. Nathan, an English singer and composer, settled permanently in Australia, arriving in Melbourne in 1841 and moving to Sydney, where he organized concerts and music societies, activities that later (1886) led to the establishment of the Philharmonic Society, and in 1890 to the building of a large organ in Sydney Town Hall. A conservatory of music was founded in 1916, and a symphony orchestra somewhat later. Melbourne has a University Conservatorium, established in 1894. Today each state capital has a symphony orchestra. Of great importance for the musical life of Australia was the establishment, in 1932, of the Australian Broadcasting Commission (A.B.C.). Chamber music has thrived under the auspices of the Musica Viva Society, and opera under the Australian Elizabethan Theatre Trust.

Composers of Australian (or New Zealand) descent include Alfred Hill (1870–1961), Percy Grainger (1882–1961; became a U.S. citizen), Frank Hutchens (b. 1892), Roy Agnew (1893–1944), Margaret Sutherland (b. 1897), Clive Douglas (b. 1903), John Antill (b. 1904), Dorian Le Gallienne (b. 1915), Donald Banks (b. 1923), and Malcolm Williamson (b. 1931). The Australian opera singers Nellie Melba (1859–1931) and Joan Sutherland (b. 1926) won world-wide recognition.

One of Australia's most outstanding contributions to music was made by Louise B. M. Dyer through the foundation of the Lyrebird Press (Les Éditions de l'Oiseau-Lyre). The magnificent publications of this press include, among others, the complete edition of the Montpellier Codex [see Sources, no. 4], the series *Polyphonic Music of the Fourteenth Century* (ed. L. Schrade), the 13-volume set of Attaingnant's motets (ed. A. Smijers and A. T. Merritt), and the complete works of François Couperin.

II. The early settlers of New Zealand found a Polynesian people, the Maoris, who themselves had settled there much earlier. The resulting impact of Western culture on Maori music was virtually annihilating.

In the early decades of New Zealand's colonization (from *c.* 1840) the new immigrants retained their English musical heritage, mainly Anglican church music, a strong choral tradition, and an emphasis on brass-band playing. In Christchurch particularly the Anglican pattern survived, and a choir school established there in 1881 still provides treble voices for the all-male cathedral choir. Christchurch secular choirs have sung in Adelaide, the United States, and England in recent years. While amateur orchestral societies maintained high standards, it was not until 1946 that the New Zealand Broadcasting Corporation established a fully professional orchestra. There is a flourishing National Youth Orchestra, and a strong Federation of Chamber Music Societies that encourages distinguished groups from abroad to visit New Zealand. Music education in the schools is under the direction of a national music adviser assisted by regional supervisors. The universities award degrees toward a Mus. B. according to the English system and recently have introduced courses in performance at the four main centers, Auckland, Wellington, Christchurch, and Dunedin. Courses in musicology are offered at the University of Otago, Dunedin. The first New Zealand-born composer to become outstanding is Douglas Lilburn (b. 1915; three symphonies, chamber music, songs).

Lit.: W. A. Orchard, *Music in Australia* (1952); E. I. Moresby, *Australia Makes Music* [1948]; A. P. Elkin and T. A. Jones, *Arnhem Land Music (North Australia)* [195?]; J. C. Andersen, *Maori Music, with Its Polynesian Background* (1934); M. Levine, in *Pierre Key's Music Year Book 1926–27,* p. 178 (Australia and New Zealand); T. Waters, *ibid.* (1928), p. 185; Dai-keong Lee, in *MM* xxii, no. 4; C. Carey, in *The Sackbut* ix, no. 1; V. A. Rucroft, "A Survey of Music in New Zealand" (*PMA* 1943, p. 56); C. H. Grattan, "The Australian Bush Songs" (*MQ* xv). There are numerous studies of the music of the Australian indigenes; s.v. "Australien und Austronesien," in *MGG.* See also the record and accompanying 19-page pamphlet (background, pictures, musical notations), *Songs of Aboriginal Australia and Torres Strait* (Ethnic Folkways Library), ed. G. List (Indiana Univ. Archives of Folk and Primitive Music). II by T.J.Y.

Austria. The development of music in Austria is included under Germany, as is customary and almost inevitable because of the close bonds—political, cultural, and musical—between the two countries. Not a few of the most outstanding "Austrian" composers were born in Germany (e.g., T. Stoltzer, Froberger, Beethoven, Brahms), while on the other hand many of the great "German" masters were actually Austrian by birth. Following is a survey of the development of music in Austria, excluding the numerous Flemish and Italian composers who were active in Vienna and other cities (composers born in Germany are marked G.).

The first Austrian composers known to us are the minnesingers Walther von der Vogelweide (*c.* 1170–*c.* 1230) and Neidhardt von Reuenthal (G.? 12th and 13th centuries). The development of "German" polyphony started in Austria with Hermann von Salzburg (14th century) and Oswald von Wolkenstein (1377–1445). The polyphonic lied was cultivated by Heinrich Finck (G., 1444–1527), P. Hofhaimer (1459–1537), T. Stoltzer (G., *c.* 1475–1526), and Arnold von Bruck (b. in Bruges, *c.* 1470–1554), and lute music by H. Judenkünig (G., *c.* 1450–1526).

In the 17th century, P. Peuerl (*c.* 1570–*c.* 1624), J. H. Schmelzer (*c.* 1623–80), Heinrich Biber (1644–1704), and Georg Muffat (b. in France, 1653–1704) made important contributions in the field of instrumental music, while keyboard music was cultivated by W. Ebner (G., 1612–65), J. J. Froberger (G., 1616–67), F. M. Techelmann (*c.* 1649–1714), Georg Muffat, and G. von

Reutter (1656–1738). J. J. Fux (1660–1741), famous for his treatise *Gradus ad Parnassum* (1725), wrote orchestral suites, Masses, and motets, as well as operas, thereby interrupting the Italian domination of opera in Austria that had begun with Cesti and ended only with Mozart.

In the 18th century, G. C. Wagenseil (1715–77) and G. M. Monn (1717–50) contributed to the early development of the symphony [see Mannheim school] and helped lay the foundation for the work of the "Viennese classics," Haydn (1732–1809), Mozart (1756–91), Beethoven (G., 1770–1827), and Schubert (1797–1828), who were followed by Bruckner (1824–96), Brahms (G., 1833–97), and Mahler (1860–1911). F. Schubert, the great master of the romantic lied, found a worthy successor in H. Wolf (1860–1903). J. Bittner (1874–1939) and E. W. Korngold (1897–1957) composed in a late romantic idiom.

The revolutionary trends of 20th-century music started in Vienna with A. Schoenberg (1874–1951) and J. M. Hauer (1883–1959), to be continued by Schoenberg's disciples A. Berg (1885–1935) and A. von Webern (1883–1945). Among the next generation of Austrian composers are E. Wellesz (b. 1885), also famous for his studies of Byzantine music, J. N. David (b. 1895), E. Krenek (b. 1900), H. E. Apostel (G., b. 1901), and H. Jelinek (b. 1901).

Lit.: E. Schenk, *950 Jahre Musik in Österreich* [n.d., 1946?]; H. J. Moser, *Die Musik im frühevangelischen Österreich* [1954]; R. F. Brauner, *Osterreichs neue Musik* [1948]; R. Klein, "Contemporary Music in Austria" (*LBCM*; also *MQ* li); G. Adler, "Musik in Österreich" (*StM* xvi); *Editions XV.

Ausweichung [G.]. Modulation, especially passing modulation.

Auszug [G.]. Arrangement, usually for piano [*Klavier-auszug*] of an opera, oratorio, etc.

Authentic cadence. See under Cadence I.

Authentic modes. See under Church modes I.

Auto [Sp.]. Spanish and Portuguese dramatic play of a religious or contemplative character, frequently with incidental music [see Liturgical drama]. Such plays were written by Juan del Encina (fl. 1500), Gil Vicente (1492–1557), Lope de Vega (1562–1635), Calderón (1600–81), and others. See G. Chase, in *MQ* xxv; A. Salazar, in *PAMS* 1938.

These religious plays were introduced into Latin America by missionaries as early as the 16th century and soon became very popular throughout the Spanish and Portuguese colonies. In 1672, *El Arca de Noé*, a sacred play in *música recitativa*, was presented in Lima, and the same year Tomás de Torrejón y Velasco (1644–1728) is mentioned as the composer of music for the productions of a *breve coloquio de música recitativa* and a *coloquio en forma de Auto Sacramental*. Reports on the productions of these plays in Brazil, starting in the late 16th century, occur in the Jesuits' chronicles. An *auto hierático* entitled *O Misterio de Jesus* was produced about 1583. Later, two others, an *Auto do Misterio das Onze Mil Virgens* and an *auto* of the *Martirio de Sao Sebastiao*, were produced. All these *autos* were complemented by vocal and instrumental episodes in the manner of the 16th- and 17th-century mystery plays and moralities in Europe.

add. by J.O-S.

Autographs, musical. The oldest extant autographs of compositions are by Heinrich Isaac (St. Bibl. Berlin *Mus. MS. 40021;* fac. in J. Wolf, *Musikalische Schrifttafeln*, no. 49). From the 16th century we have a few autograph pages by Senfl and Lassus. From the 17th century Monteverdi's *L'Incoronazione di Poppea* as well as the keyboard works of Tomkins, Froberger, and Pasquini have survived in autographs. For the autographs of Handel, Bach, Mozart, Beethoven, Chopin, and others, the reader is referred to special studies [see Lit.]. Autographs of a number of famous compositions, by Bach, Beethoven, Mozart, and others, have been published in facsimile editions. Anthony van Hoboken founded in 1927 an *Archiv für Photogramme musikalischer Meisterhandschriften* (archive for photographic reproductions of master autographs), a most valuable collection (Vienna, Nationalbibliothek) that includes a number of items whose originals were lost during World War II.

Lit.: E. Winternitz, *Musical Autographs from Monteverdi to Hindemith*, 2 vols. (1955); W. Gerstenberg, *Musikerhandschriften von Palestrina bis Beethoven* [1960]; id., *Musikerhandschriften von Schubert bis Strawinsky* [1961]; W. Schmieder, *Musikerhandschriften in drei Jahrhunderten* (1939); G. Schünemann, *Musikerhandschriften von Bach bis Schumann* (1936); L. M. Vauzanges, *L'Écriture des musiciens célèbres* (1913); G. Schünemann, *Ludwig van Beethovens Konversationshefte*, 3 vols. (1941–43); O. E. Albrecht, *A Census of Autograph Music Manuscripts of European Composers in American Libraries* (1953).

Autoharp. Trademark for an instrument of the *zither family, on which simple chords are produced by strumming the strings (with fingers, pick, or plectrum), while button-controlled damper bars damp all the strings except those required for the chord. It is intended chiefly as an accompanying instrument (for folk singers, etc.).

Automelon [Gr.]. See under *Idiomelon*.

Auxiliary tone. See under Nonharmonic tones I.

Ave Maria [L., Hail, Mary]. (1) A prayer of the Roman Catholic Church; see text and plainsong in *LU*, p. 1861. In a shortened form it is used as an *antiphon for the Feast of the Annunciation [*LU*, p. 1416]. There are polyphonic settings, most of them based on the plainsong melody, by Ockeghem, Josquin, Willaert, Victoria, and others; also a *Missa Ave Maria,* by Pierre de La Rue, Morales, Palestrina, and others. (2) The same title was used for a lachrymose piece by Schubert (based on a song from Sir Walter Scott's *Lady of the Lake*), and a lamentable piece by Gounod in which Bach's C-major Prelude from *The Well-Tempered Clavier* (vol. i) is misused as a harmonic background for a highly sentimental melody.

Ave maris stella [L.]. A hymn of the Roman Catholic Church, sung to various melodies in different modes [see *LU*, pp. 1259ff]. There are polyphonic settings (anon. in Codex Apt; Dufay), Masses (Josquin, Morales, Victoria), and organ compositions (Girolamo Cavazzoni, Cabezón, Titelouze), most of them based on the first melody in *LU*.

Ave Regina caelorum [L.]. One of the four Marian antiphons; see Antiphon (2). Particularly famous is a setting by Dufay [repr. in H. Besseler, *Capella*, vol. i], which is mentioned in his will and was probably performed at his funeral. Dufay also wrote a *Missa Ave Regina caelorum* (others by Arcadelt, Palestrina, Victoria).

Ayre. (1) A late 16th- and early 17th-century type of English song, which is derived from the French *air de cour* and, like it, was primarily a solo song accompanied by the lute (orpharion, theorbo, occasionally also virginal), often with the lowest part doubled by a bass viol (viola da gamba; see *HAM*, no. 162). In many cases the composers provided for an alternative (or additional?) vocal accompaniment, printed separately on the opposite page so that the parts could be read simultaneously by three singers seated, for example, north, south, and east at a table. The ayres range from serious songs, often through-composed, to light and gay tunes, usually strophic. The earliest publication was Dowland's *The first Booke of Songs or Ayres* of 1597 [see Editions XVII, which includes reprints of many collections]. Later publications are *Select Musicall Ayres and Dialogues* (1652) and *New Ayres and Dialogues* (1678), which include songs with the accompaniment of lute, theorbo, bass viol, by H. Lawes, W. Webb, Blow, Purcell, and others. See *ReMR*, pp. 835–41; A. Dolmetsch, *Select English Songs and Dialogues of the 16th and 17th Centuries*, 2 vols. (1898, 1912); P. Warlock, *The English Ayre* (1926); U. Olshausen, *Das lautenbegleitete Sololied in England um 1600*

(1963); P. Warlock and P. Wilson, ‡*English Ayres, Elizabethan and Jacobean.* 6 vols. (1927–31); H. J. Sleeper, ‡*John Jenkins, Fancies and Ayres* (1950).

(2) In the 17th century, a movement of a suite [see Air (3)]. For instance, each of the suites in M. Locke's *Consort of Ffoure Parts* consists of a fantasia, courante, ayre, and saraband [see *HAM*, no. 230, Commentary].

(3) English writers of the 17th century use the term ayre (aire) in the sense of key or mode, e.g., T. Morley: "these aires (which the antiquity termed *Modi*)," in *A Plaine and Easie Introduction to Practicall Musicke* (1597), p. 147; or T. Mace: "*Every Shake*, is to be made in the *Aire*," in *Musick's Monument* (1676), p. 104; also C. Butler, *The Principles of Musik* (1636), pp. 72, 80, 82; C. Simpson, *A Compendium of Practical Musick*, 5th ed. (1714), p. 36. See also under Fancy.

B

B. See (1) Pitch names; Letter notation; Hexachord; also Accidentals II. In German, b stands for b-flat. (2) In partbooks of the 16th century, *B* stands for *bassus* (bass).

Babacué. See *Macumba.*

Baborak. A Bohemian national dance, which has alternating sections in duple and in triple time.

Babylonia. See Mesopotamia.

Bacchetta [It.]. Drumstick; *b. di legno,* wooden; *b. di spugna,* spongeheaded.

B-A-C-H. The letters forming Bach's name, each of which denotes a tone (if the German terminology is used, in which *h* is b natural while *b* is b-flat; see Pitch names). The resulting theme, b♭ a c b, has been repeatedly used in compositions, first by Bach himself in his *Art of Fugue (in the last, unfinished fugue). Another fugue on the same subject that is often ascribed to him [see Peters ed. xv, 42] is definitely spurious. Various later composers have used the famous motif in fugues or fantasias, e.g., J. G. Albrechtsberger [see *Editions XV, 33]; Schumann (*Sechs*

Fugen über den Namen Bach, op. 60); Liszt (*Fantasia and Fugue on . . . B A C H* for piano and *Prelude and Fugue on B A C H* for organ); M. Reger (op. 46); W. Piston (*Chromatic Study on the Name of Bach*); A. Casella (*Due Ricercari sul nome Bach*). It also plays an important role in Busoni's *Fantasia contrappuntistica* [see under *Art of Fugue*].

Bach-Gesellschaft. See Societies, II 2.

Bachiana [Port.]. Title employed by Heitor Villa-Lobos [see Brazil] for some of his compositions, which he claimed were the product of applying Bach's contrapuntal techniques to Brazilian folk music. He wrote nine such works, for solo piano, full orchestra, or voice and smaller ensembles, following the general plan of a suite.   J.O-S.

Bach trumpet. See Clarino (2).

Backfall, forefall. English 17th-century names for an *appoggiatura, the former from above, the latter from below. It is indicated and performed as follows:

Badinage, badinerie [F.]. A dancelike piece of jocose character that occurs as a movement in the optional group of 18th-century suites, e.g., in Bach's Suite for orchestra in B minor.

Bagatelle [F.]. A short piece, usually for piano. The name was used by F. Couperin ("Les Bagatelles"; see his *Pièces de Clavecin,* ordre 10) and, in particular, by Beethoven, whose *Bagatellen* (op. 33, op. 119, op. 126) mark the beginning of the extensive literature of 19th-century *character pieces.

Bagpipe [F. *musette;* G. *Dudelsack, Sackpfeife;* It. *piva, zampogna;* Sp. *gaita*]. Generic name for a number of instruments having one or (usually) several reed pipes (single or double reeds) attached to a windbag that provides the air for the pipes; also, specifically, the name for the Irish and Scottish varieties of this family. [See ill. under Wind instruments.] One or two of the pipes, called "chanter" (chaunter), are provided with sound holes and are used for the melody, while the others, called "drones," produce only one tone each and are used for the accompaniment.

In the earlier, Eastern specimens, both chanter and drones are clarinets (i.e., have single reeds), while in the modern types either they are both oboes (i.e., with double reeds), as in Italy and some parts of France, or the drones are clarinets while the chanter is an oboe, as in Scotland, Ireland, and Brittany. In some bagpipes the wind in the bag is supplied from the mouth through an additional blowing pipe, while in others it is provided by a small pair of bellows placed under and operated by the arm. To the former type belong the *Old Irish bagpipe, Highland bagpipe* (Scotland), *biniou* (Brittany), *cornemuse* (France), *Dudelsack* or *Sackpfeife* (Germany), and *zampogna* and *piva* (Italy); to the latter, the *Northumbrian bagpipe* (England), modern *Irish bagpipe, gaita* (Galicia), and *musette* (France). A more primitive instrument was the *bladder pipe,* a single or double clarinet with a bladder used as a bag [illustrated in *GD,* pl. LX; *GDB,* pl. II].

Nothing certain is known about the origin of the bagpipe, although there is virtually no doubt that it developed in the Orient [see Sumponyah]. It is first attested in Rome under the name *tibia utricularis* (Suetonius). Nero is reported to have played on it. In the Middle Ages it is frequently mentioned under different names (*musa, chorus, symphonia, chevrette*). The famous illuminations of the 13th-century Spanish MS *Escorial j b 2* [see *Cantiga*] show players of bagpipes [see *GD* iv, 184; *ReMMA,* p. 222]. In the British Isles the bagpipes have been prominent for many centuries in folk and military music. Their Continental history is less interesting, except for a late 17th-century movement in France that for a short time raised the instrument's standing in society and in art music [see Musette]. See also Pibroch.

Lit.: W. H. Grattan Flood, *The Story of the Bagpipe* (1911); W. L. Manson, *The Highland Bagpipe* (1901); A. Baines, *Bagpipes* (1960); G. Askew, *A Bibliography of the Bag-pipe* (1932).

Baguala. Argentine folksong with a melody of triadic design and a rhythmic pattern of a quarter note followed by two eighth notes. These songs are usually accompanied by a *caja* (drum). Most ethnomusicologists consider the *baguala* indigenous to the Andean regions.　　　　J.O-S.

Baguette [F.]. Drumstick; *b. de bois,* wooden drumstick; *b. d'éponge,* spongeheaded drumstick. Also, the baton of the conductor and the stick of the violin bow.

Bailecito [Sp.]. Argentine folk dance-song in 6/8 meter, consisting of two contrasting sections. The first section is in lively tempo and is sung to the first four lines of the lyrics; the second is slower and sung to the remaining four lines of the text. There follows a repetition of the first section, but now sung to nonsense syllables. Owing to its northern Argentine origin the form is also known as *boliviana.*　　　　J.O-S.

Baile de palos. Elaborate ritual dance performed in the rural districts of the Dominican Republic, in which the set of indigenous drums known as *palos* or *atabal* is used with amazing rhythmical virtuosity. Also called *baile de atabales.*　　J.O-S.

Baisser [F.]. To lower a string.

Balalaika. A popular Russian instrument of the guitar family, characterized by a triangular body, long fretted neck, and (usually) three gut strings tuned in fourths. It is played with a plectrum and is made in six sizes that together constitute a balalaika band. [See ill. under Guitar family.] The forerunner of the balalaika was the *domra. See A. S. Rose, in *PMA* xxvii; W. von Kwetzinsky, in *DM* xxii.12.

Balancement [F.]. An 18th-century name for tremolo. Sometimes used synonymously with *Bebung.

Balg [G.]. Bellows of an organ.

Bali. I. *History* [also see Java]. The first important though short-lived cultural contacts between Java and Bali occurred in the reign of Airlangga in the first half of the 11th century. In the 14th century, under the rule of Gadjah Mada, the establishment of a permanent Javanese colony in Bali assured a continuous influence from East Java until late in the 18th century. The rich treasury of poetic literature that developed from the 10th to 16th centuries in East Java would have been lost but for the keen interest of the Javanese colonists and the Balinese aristocracy, who adopted this literature as the language and models for the literati. It is probably safe to assume that some of the musical forms associated with the literature of this period have also survived. For example, in contemporary Bali, one can hear 15th-century Javanese spoken in the course of the dance dramas known as *wajang wong* accompanied by the ancient seven-tone pélog *gamelan gambuh.* A number of musical instruments depicted in the bas-reliefs of early Hindu-Javanese monuments have survived in Bali but are no longer known in Java. Today Balinese Hinduism is practiced as a way of life by a communal society in which the former royal patronage of the arts has been largely replaced by that of the village community. Endless temple festivals and rites of passage demand the fullest participation by musicians, dancers, sculptors, and those responsible for decorative festoons, beautifully arranged offerings of food, flowers, etc. In the context of this form of religious worship, cultivation of the arts is as important as the cultivation of rice.

II. *Tunings and orchestras.* Like the ensembles of Java, no two Balinese gamelan are tuned precisely the same. More than a dozen different genres, some active survivors of ancient ensembles, can be related to either the sléndro or pélog system, better known in Bali as *saih lima* (series of five) and *saih pitu* (series of seven) respectively. The tunings of different ensembles include: four-tone sléndro and deviants of this type, five-tone sléndro, four-tone pélog, five-tone pélog and deviants of this type, six-tone pélog, and seven-tone pélog [see Lit., C. McPhee, *Music in Bali,* ch. vii]. As in Java, there is a tendency to stretch and compress octaves; the question of "tuning pattern" is yet to be studied [see under Java]. In Bali, throughout the compass of the orchestra the bronze instruments are tuned in pairs, designated as *pengumbang* (low) and *pengisep* (high), with a difference of several cycles per second between corresponding keys of the

two instruments. The number of musical beats produced by this method of paired tuning varies with taste from one gamelan to another [see M. Hood, "Sléndro and Pélog Redefined," *Selected Reports* (Institute of Ethnomusicology, Univ. of California at Los Angeles, 1966)].

The five-tone pélog tuning of the large ensemble known as *gamelan gong,* as well as its modern counterpart, *gong kebyar,* is derived from one of several possible scales found on the seven-tone pélog *gambuh.* Four of these large end-blown flutes are combined with the rebab (a spike fiddle), several gongs, a pair of *kemanak,* cymbals, and a pair of drums to form the ensemble known as *gamelan gambuh* mentioned above. The melodies of this ancient repertory are also performed by a five-, six-, or seven-tone pélog ensemble of metallophones known as *gamelan semar pegulingan,* formerly found in the royal courts. Although this ensemble has practically disappeared, the derivative five-tone *gamelan légong,* having an enlarged instrumentation that permits greater flexibility, is a popular orchestra that transforms the same music into a dramatic sound of suddenly shifting dynamics and tempo and sparkling ornamental figuration in the high register of the gamelan. It includes two small end-blown flutes and a rebab and is used to accompany a large repertory of dance dramas taken from the *gambuh* theater and Hindu mythology. A smaller ensemble, modeled after *gamelan légong* but made up entirely of bamboo instruments, is known as *gamelan jogèd* and provides an animated staccato accompaniment for the popular village dance called *jogèd.* Four-tone pélog is known only in the *gamelan bonang,* a group of individual gongs of different size played in processions. Five-tone sléndro is reserved for a special quartet of metallophones known as *gendèr wajang,* used to accompany the shadow plays, an indispensable part of cremation festivities, weddings, and other rites of passage. Four-tone sléndro is the tuning of *gamelan angklung,* a small group of bronze instruments that formerly included the *angklung,* a bamboo instrument now rarely used. This ensemble, heard in connection with temple anniversaries and village festivals, in smaller villages often replaces the heavier sound of the *gamelan gong* on ceremonial occasions. It is always used in connection with village cremation rites. [For a complete description of these and other ensembles, see Lit., C. McPhee, *Music in Bali.*]

III. *Musical practice.* Three elements are common to most of the various ensembles found in

Bali: a melody; a colotomy, or punctuating strata; and animated drumming. Melodies vary in character from long lyrical lines to short, rapid ostinato figures, and the music is usually marked by sudden contrasts in tempo and dynamics. Singing is almost unknown in gamelan performance and is largely reserved for certain forms of plays (e.g., *Ardja*) and temple rituals (e.g., *kekawin* for solo voice). The full *gamelan gong kebyar,* requiring about thirty instrumentalists, has the following musical organization: (1) a nuclear melody in relatively long note values, played by a pair of the single-octave *tjalon,* a low-pitched member of the *gangsa* family of metallophones resonated by bamboo; (2) an abstraction of the nuclear melody (usually every fourth tone), played by a pair of *djublag* tuned an octave lower than the *tjalon;* (3) the expansion of the nuclear melody to a full melody, performed by a pair of multioctave *gendèr;* (4) doubling or paraphrasing or ornamentation of the melody, played by two quartets of instruments having the same range as the *gendèr* but voiced one octave higher in the *panjatjah* and two octaves higher in the *kantilan;* (5) further ornamentation (*kotekan*) of the melody, supplied by the *réjong,* an instrument consisting of twelve inverted bronze kettles played by four musicians; (6) the colotomy that determines musical form, played by the large gong, the *kempur* (a medium-sized gong), the *klèntong* (a small gong), the *kempli* or *kadjar* (an inverted kettle); (7) the interlocking rhythms of a pair of drums or *kendang,* underscored by one or two pairs of hand cymbals or *tjèngtjèng.* Except for a slight freedom in solo passages there is no improvisation in Balinese gamelan. Two pairs of players in each of the paraphrasing or ornamenting quartets (*panjatjah, kantilan, réjong*) execute extremely rapid interlocking or "shared" parts that permit no deviation and demand meticulous rehearsal.

Lit.: C. McPhee, *Music in Bali* (1966); *id., A House in Bali* [1946]; *id., A Club of Small Men* (1948); D. A. Lentz, *The Gamelan Music of Java and Bali* [1965]; J. Kunst and C. J. A. Kunst-van Wely, *De Toonkunst van Bali,* 2 vols. (1925); J. R. Brandon, *Theatre in Southeast Asia* (1967); C. McPhee, "The Balinese Wajang Koelit and Its Music" (*Djawa* xvi, 322–66); *id.,* "Children and Music in Bali," in *Childhood in Contemporary Cultures,* ed. Margaret Mead and Martha Wolfenstein [1955]; *id.,* "The Five-Tone Gamelan Music of Bali" (*MQ* xxxv, 250–81); *id.,* "The 'Absolute' Music of Bali" (*Modern Music* xii,

163–69); E. Schlager, "Bali," in *MGG* i, 1109–15; W. Spies, "Bericht über den Zustand von Tanz und Musik in der Negara Gianjar" (*Djawa* xvi, 51–9); *id.,* "De Gamelan-wedstrijd te Gianjar . . . December 1938" (*Djawa* xix, 197–207); *id.,* and R. Goris, "Overzicht van Dans en Tooneel in Bali" (*Djawa* xvii, 205–27).   M.H.

Ballabile. A name given occasionally to dance-like pieces (ballets) in 19th-century operas.

Ballad. The term derives from medieval words such as *chanson balladée, *ballade* [F.], *ballata,* all of which originally denoted dancing songs [L. *ballare,* to dance] but lost their dance connotation as early as the 14th century and became stylized forms of solo song. In England this process of change went still further, and eventually (16th century) "ballad" came to mean a simple tale told in simple verse. There may have been a transitional period during which the recitation of the poems was still accompanied by some sort of dancing. Most ballads are narrative, and many deal with fabulous, miraculous, or gruesome deeds. Ballad singers made a living by singing their newest productions in the streets and at country fairs, and by selling the printed sheets, which usually gave a direction: "to be sung to the tune of . . . ," e.g., "Greensleeves." In its more recent (19th-century) meaning, a ballad is a popular song usually combining narrative and romantic elements, frequently with an admixture of the gruesome. These ballads are mostly written in common meter (8.6.8.6; see Poetic meter II). Today the term "ballad" is loosely applied to any kind of popular song. For art ballad, see *Ballade* [G.].

The word "ballad" is also used as an anglicized form of *ballade* [F.], *ballata* [It.], or *Ballade* [G.]. Such usage, however, is misleading in view of the fact that these terms denote entirely different things.

Lit.: J. W. Hendren, *A Study of Ballad Rhythm* (1936); M. E. Henry, *A Bibliography for the Study of American Folk-Songs* [n.d.; *c.* 1937]; C. Sandburg, *The American Songbag* [1927]; R. Smith, ed., ‡*South Carolina Ballads* (1928); A. K. Davis, ed., ‡*Traditional Ballads of Virginia* (1929): C. J. Sharp, ed., ‡*English Folk Songs from the Southern Appalachians,* 2 vols. (1932); S. Foster Damon, ed., ‡*Series of Old American Songs* (1936); J. A. Lomax and A. Lomax, ed., ‡*Our Singing Country* (1941); A. K. Davis, ed., ‡*More Traditional Ballads of Virginia* [1960]; F. B. Gummere, *The Popular Ballad* [1959]; A. Lomax, *The Folk Songs of North America* [1960]; B. H. Bronson, ed.,

‡*The Traditional Tunes of the Child Ballads*, 2 vols. (1959, '62); L. Shepard, *The Broadside Ballad* [1962]; H. H. Flanders, ed., ‡*Ancient Ballads Traditionally Sung in New England*, 4 vols. (1960–65); C. M. Simpson, *The British Broadside Ballad and Its Music* (1966); C. A. Smith, "Ballads Surviving in the United States" (*MQ* ii); R. Lamson, "English Broadside Ballad Tunes of the 16th and 17th Centuries" (*PAMS* 1939); B. Nettl, "The Musical Style of English Ballads Collected in Indiana" (*AM* xxvii).

Ballade [F.]. One of the three **formes fixes* of 14th-century French poetry and music. (Note the separate article on the German *Ballade* below.) The poem usually has three stanzas, each of seven or eight lines, the last one or two of which are identical in all the stanzas, thus forming a **refrain*. The form of the stanza is: a b a b c d E or a b a b c d E F (capital letters indicate the refrain), a scheme that, so far as the music is concerned, can be simplified as follows: A A B (A = ab; B = the remaining lines). Some *ballades* are in the form A A B B, the music for lines 5 and 6 being used also for lines 7 and 8.

The *ballade* plays a prominent role in the work of Machaut, who treated it as a polyphonic composition of great refinement and subtlety. His example was followed by the French and Italian composers of the late 14th century (mannerist school: Solage, Trébor, Selesses, Matteo da Perugia, and others; see *Ars nova*), with whom the polyphonic *ballade* became the most representative type of music, treated with great elaboration and affectation. The form continued to be cultivated, though much more sparingly, during the first half of the 15th century, by Cordier, Césaris, Arnold de Lantins, Dufay, and Binchois. An exceptionally late example is Josquin's "Bergerette savoyene" (*Harmonice Musices Odhecaton A*, 1501, no. 10).

Monophonic songs with the form A A B are common in the repertory of the **troubadours* and even more so in that of the **trouvères*. Although most of these differ from the *forme fixe* in some details of versification (absence of refrain, more than three stanzas, etc.), they may well be regarded as early *ballades*. The troubadour *ballades* have, without good reason, been designated as **canzo*. The *ballade* form, without refrain, was adopted by the minnesingers under the name *Bar* [see *Bar* form].

Several scholars have used the term *ballade* for the Italian 14th-century **ballata.* a usage bound to lead to confusion since the *ballata* is an en-tirely different form. For example, the piece by Enrique reproduced in *RiMB*, no. 12, is a *ballata* (or **villancico*), not a *ballade.*

Lit.: F. Brosch, "Die Balladen im Kodex von Turin" (diss. Vienna, 1931). See also under *Formes fixes.*

Ballade [G.]. In German usage *Ballade* denotes a type of poem derived from the English ballads but having greater artistic elaboration and poetic refinement. (Note the separate article on the French *ballade* above.) They usually deal with medieval subjects, either historical or legendary (e.g., Goethe's "Ballade vom vertriebenen und zurückkehrenden Grafen"), or with romantic tales (e.g., Goethe's "Erlkönig"). Such *Balladen* were frequently set to music, usually as through-composed songs of great length. Probably the earliest examples are the interesting settings of Gellert's moralizing and dry *Fabeln* by A. B. V. Herbing (1759; *DdT* 42), written in a continuous recitative with a highly dramatic accompaniment. Later examples are in the form of cantatas, i.e., in various movements of contrasting character (J. André, 1741–99; J. Zumsteeg, 1766–1802). A *Fantasie* op. 109 by Beethoven's pupil Ferdinand Ries (1784–1838) for piano alone, written to Schiller's poem "Resignation," is an interesting example of what might be called a "Ballade ohne Worte" [repr. in *TaAM* xiv]. The classical master of the vocal *Ballade* (sometimes referred to as "art ballad") is Karl Loewe (1796–1869), whose seventeen volumes of *Balladen* [compl. ed. by M. Runze] include a number of truly great songs ("Archibald Douglas," "Erlkönig," "Der Pilgrim vor St. Just," etc.). Loewe's form is a free combination of the strophic and through-composed types. Schubert's songs include a number of *Balladen*, e.g., "Erlkönig." In the late 19th century *Balladen* were composed for solo or chorus with orchestral accompaniment, e.g., H. Wolf's "Der Feuerreiter." Chopin and Brahms used the term for piano pieces written in the ternary A B A form frequently found in the 19th-century **character piece*. Here the highly dramatic character of A and the lyrical character of B would seem to portray heroic deeds and knightly love, thus justifying the title *Ballade.*

Lit.: A. B. Bach, *The Art Ballad* (1890); P. Spitta, "Ballade" (*Musikgeschichtliche Aufsätze*, 1894); H. J. Moser, ‡*Die Ballade* (H. Martens, ‡*Musikalische Formen in historischen Reihen* iii [1930]); R. Batka, *Martin Plüddemann und seine Balladen* (1896); A. König, *Die Ballade in der Musik* (1904, no. 9 in *Musikalisches Magazin*); S. Northcote, *The Ballad in Music* (1942).

Ballade style. A term referring to the typical texture of the 14th-century French **ballade* (Machaut), that is, in three parts, the top part vocal and the two lower parts (tenor, contratenor) instrumental. It is a somewhat misleading designation, since the same style was used for rondeaux and virelais as well. This style was occasionally employed for Mass compositions of the late 14th century, which have been (rather incongruously) termed *Balladenmesse*. The terms **cantilena* style and treble-dominated style have been suggested as substitutes for *ballade* style.

Ballad meter. The most usual poetic meter of English and American ballads, also known as common meter [see Ballad; Poetic meter II].

Ballad of Baby Doe, The. Opera in two acts by D. Moore (libretto by J. Latouche), produced in Central City, Colo., 1956. Setting: Colorado and Washington, D.C., 1880–99.

Ballad opera. A popular form of 18th-century stage entertainment in England, consisting of spoken dialogue alternating with musical numbers taken from ballad tunes, folksongs, or famous melodies by earlier or contemporary composers. The ballad opera, though it developed quite independently, resembled the contemporary French *opéra comique en vaudevilles* in its use of popular melodies and its occasional satire or parody of serious opera. It flourished in London from 1728 to after the middle of the century, when it was gradually replaced by a somewhat similar form of entertainment, with romantic or sentimental plots and mainly using original music (e.g., T. A. Arne's *Love in a Village*, 1762). *The Beggar's Opera* (1728) by John Gay, with music arranged by J. Pepusch (1667–1752), the first important example of this type, was also the most successful. Two ballad operas (or farces) by Charles Coffey, *The Devil to Pay* (1731) and *The Merry Cobbler* (1735), played a decisive role in the development of the German **Singspiel*. The music of the ballad operas included songs and arias by Locke, Purcell, Handel, Geminiani, Corelli, Scarlatti, and others; Playford's *The (English) Dancing Master* (numerous editions from 1650 to 1738) and similar collections of vocal and instrumental melodies were the chief sources for popular tunes. The style of the ballad opera has been imitated in Vaughan Williams' *Hugh the Drover* (1924) and in Kurt Weill's *Die Dreigroschenoper* (1928; *The Three-*

penny Opera, 1933), the latter a highly successful imitation of Gay's *Beggar's Opera.*

Lit.: E. M. Gagey, *Ballad Opera* (1937); F. Kidson, *The Beggar's Opera: Its Predecessors and Successors* (1922); W. E. Schultz, *Gay's "Beggar's Opera"* (1923); [Hinrichsen's] *Ninth Music Book containing John Gay and the Ballad Opera* [1959]; G. Calmus, "Die Beggar's Opera von Gay und Pepusch" (*SIM* viii, 286); W. Barclay Squire, "An Index of Tunes in the Ballad-Operas" (*MA* ii); G. Tufts, "Ballad Operas" (*MA* iv); W. J. Lawrence, "Early Irish Ballad Opera" (*MQ* viii); A. Berger, "*The Beggar's Opera,* the Burlesque, and Italian Opera" (*ML* xvii); W. H. Rubsamen, "The Ballad Burlesques and Extravaganzas" (*MQ* xxxvi); *id.,* "Mr. Seedo, Ballad Opera, and the Singspiel" (*CP Anglés* ii).

Ballata [It.]. The chief form of Italian 14th-century music [see *Ars nova*]. It is not related to the French *ballade* but is practically identical with the **virelai,* which was also called *chanson balladée.* As a poem, the *ballata* consists of a refrain (called *ripresa*) and, normally, three stanzas that alternate with the refrain: R S$_1$ R S$_2$ R S$_3$ R. The shorter form R S$_1$ S$_2$ S$_3$ R may also have been used. The stanza consists of two so-called *piedi* (feet) of identical versification and a *volta* (turn) having the same structure as the *ripresa.* In some cases the *ripresa* and (one) *piede* consist of two lines each, in others the *ripresa* of three and the *piede* of two, etc. Music is composed only for the *ripresa* and the first *piede,* and is repeated for the rest of the poem as follows:

ripresa	stanza		ripresa etc.
	piedi	*volta*	
A	bb	a	A etc.

In modern transcriptions the resulting form, A b b a A, is usually represented in the following manner:

‖:A   :‖:B   :‖

1. 5.   2.
4.   3.

with the text for 1. 5. printed in italics. In the original sources only the texts for 1. and 2. are given with the music, those of 3., 4., and 5. being written separately. In contrast to the virelai, *ballate* rarely have an **ouvert* and *clos* (for section B).

Because of its name [L. *ballare*, to dance], it is generally assumed that the *ballata* originally was a song accompanying round dances, although no definite evidence for this conclusion has been found. Anyhow, none of the surviving examples shows any traces of dancelike rhythm or style. Monophonic songs with the *ballata* structure are found in the religious *laude* [see *Lauda*] of the thirteenth century. In the fourteenth century the form was treated polyphonically, especially by F. Landini; in all, 91 two-voice and 49 three-voice *ballate* by Landini survive (mostly with only one stanza). The form of the *ballata* recurs, with modifications, in the **frottole* of the early 16th century. See also the general remarks under Virelai II. See W. T. Marrocco, "The Ballata—A Metamorphic Form" (*AM* ҳxxi).

Ballet. I. Ballet is a theatrical performance by a dancing group, usually with costumes and scenery, to the accompaniment of music but customarily without singing or spoken words. The origins of modern ballet date from the 15th century, when dance performances were introduced at the French, Burgundian, and Italian courts for weddings, receptions of foreign sovereigns, and similar festive occasions. In their early stages these performances consisted of loose sequences of dances, based on the steps of the conventional courtly repertory but performed in sumptuous costumes and oriented toward representing the over-all theme of the occasion (e.g., dances of the European nations paying homage to a visiting prince, dances of the Four Continents in honor of a newborn royal baby, etc.). In the course of time elaborate decorations were added, a story or plot provided dramatic interest and unity, and the music, originally played by small instrumental ensembles specializing in dance accompaniment, began to be performed by the full court orchestra (or even orchestras), often together with vocal soloists and ensembles.

When, in the early 16th century, the traditions of the Italian *intermedii* and *trionfi* on the one hand and the "horse ballets" (*balletti a cavallo, carrousels, danses equestres*) on the other merged with the art of ballroom dancing, the *ballet de cour* was born. Of Italian origin, this multifaceted form of courtly entertainment was brought to France in 1533 at the marriage of Catherine de'Medici and King Henry II. After a period of adjustment, the first short *mascarades* and *boutades* with dances, verse, and music grew into full-scale dramatic entertainments. One of

the most sumptuous of these was the *Balet comique de la Royne,* a choreographic invention of the ballet master Baldassare de Belgioioso (de Beaujoyeulx), performed for the marriage of Margaret of Lorraine-Vaudémont to the Duke of Joyeuse in the Salle du Bourbon in the fall of 1581 [fac. ed. by G. A. Caula, Turin, 1962]. It is the earliest *ballet de cour* for which the music has been preserved and is especially noteworthy for its inclusion of two monodic songs [see Editions VII; also *AdHM* ii, 642ff; L. Celler, *Les Origines de l'Opéra et le ballet de la Reine,* 1868]. Throughout the 17th century the *ballet de cour,* which was the French counterpart of the English court "masque," remained the undisputed favorite at the royal court and in the palaces of the French nobility. Among the first composers who contributed (often collectively) to these entertainments were Pierre Guédron (1565–1621), Antoine Boësset (c. 1585–1643), and Étienne Moulinié (d. after 1669), but little of the music that accompanied these presentations has been preserved (although some of it may survive in the **Philidor Collection).

The golden age of ballet came under Louis XIV (reigned 1643–1715), who himself liked to dance and was fond of appearing in ballets. With the ballet master C. L. Beauchamps and the musicians Cambefort (1605–61) and Lully (1632–87), the French ballet attained great cultural importance as well as musical significance. It became the origin of a large number of new courtly dances, such as the gavotte, passepied, bourrée, and rigaudon, which were later used in the optional movements of suites. Of particular importance among these was the minuet. Lully's activity in the ballet of the French court (*ballet de cour*) began in 1653 with the *Ballet de la Nuit* (together with Cambefort). In subsequent years he wrote about 28 ballets, the last being *Le Temple de la paix* (1685). In 1664 he and Molière jointly created the *comédie-ballet,* a unification of stage play and ballet. The first work of this type was *Le Mariage forcé* (1664), and the most famous *L'Impromptu de Versailles* (1663). [See Entr'acte.] Lully also introduced the ballet into French opera. His successors, Campra and Rameau, went further in this direction by establishing the *opéra ballet,* in which dramatic content was reduced to a minimum in favor of dancing [see Ballet in opera]. In the second half of the 17th century Vienna was a center of elaborate presentations, especially of equestrian ballets (*Rossballett*), among them *La Contesa dell'aria e dell'acqua* (1667), for which F. Sbarra wrote the libretto and J. H. Schmelzer and A. Bertali the music. [See *DTO* 56; *StM* viii, 47.]

Soon after 1700 the imperial court of Vienna, always in stiff competition with Versailles, became one of the foremost centers of professional ballet in Europe. During the reigns of Charles VI and Maria Theresa, almost all the leading dancers and choreographers of the time came to Vienna, either as dancing masters at the court or as guests or permanent members of the two main theaters in the city. Among them was Alexandre Phillebois, who early in the 18th century was named court ballet master (*Hofballettmeister*). One of his 13 *ballerini di corte* was Franz Hilverding van Weven (1710–68), who in 1742 became first ballet master at the Kärntnertor-Theater. Under his inspired guidance Viennese ballet began to turn from the merely spectacular to the dramatic; many of Hilverding's pantomimic ballets were based on plots from the works of Racine, Voltaire, Crebillon, and other renowned writers [see S. Arteaga, *Le Rivoluzioni del Teatro musicale italiano*, 3 vols., 1783–88].

II. From 1750 to 1850 the history of the ballet includes a galaxy of famous dancers, such as Marie Camargo (1710–70), J.-G. Noverre (1727–1810), the brothers Angiolo Maria Vestris (1730–1809) and Gaetano Apollino Vestris (1729–1808), Maria Taglioni (1804–84), Fanny Elssler (1810–51), and others. Unfortunately, little of the music used in their presentations has survived. Noverre, the great reformer of the ballet, found musical collaborators in Stuttgart (Florian Deller, 1729–73; Jean J. Rudolphe, 1730–1812; see *DdT* 43/44) as well as in Vienna (Ignaz Holzbauer, 1711–83; Gluck, 1714–87; Josef Starzer, 1726–87; and Mozart, 1756–91). Gluck's *Don Juan* (1761), Mozart's *Les Petits Riens* (1778), and Beethoven's *Die Geschöpfe des Prometheus* (1801) are the best-known ballets from this period. All three were produced in Vienna, the last-named for the Italian dancer Salvatore Vigano (1769–1821). Hilverding (from Vienna), following an invitation from Empress Elizabeth of Russia, completely reorganized the Russian ballet at St. Petersburg from 1758 to 1764. He worked with many of the leading dancers of his day, to the music of such composers as Holzbauer, J. A. Hasse, Starzer, and Gluck. During Hilverding's stay in Russia, the ballet productions at Vienna's Burgtheater were capably guided by Gasparo Angiolini (1723–96 or 1731–1803), while Bernardi reigned at the Kärntnertor. Angiolini became particularly

famous through his association with Gluck and the composer's operatic reform, as well as his ballet controversy with Jean-Georges Noverre (1727–1810), who succeeded Hilverding in 1768.

Public interest in ballet was so strong that as many as three new ballets were staged each month and no opera or drama could be performed without at least one major divertissement or pantomime. Ballet in Vienna remained on a high level until the death of Maria Theresa in 1780, after which the theaters were closed for a long time. When they reopened, after the French Revolution, the emphasis in ballet had shifted from feudal elegance to patriotic fervor, drama, and frank burlesque, which in turn were followed by the advent of romanticism and the emergence of its great representatives, Maria Taglioni (1804–84), Fanny Elssler (1810–51), and others. Some outstanding roles in the romantic ballet, with its emphasis on idyllic or supernatural rather than heroic or tragic subjects, were created by Taglioni (*La Sylphide*), Carlotta Grisi, and Elssler (**cachucha*). Of the numerous ballets of this period one has survived to the present day, *Giselle*, produced in Paris in 1841 with Grisi as *prima ballerina*, choreography by Jean Coralli, and music by Adolphe-Charles Adam.

III. In the second half of the 19th century ballet was cultivated particularly in Denmark and Russia. Danish ballets based on Nordic myths were written by J. P. E. Hartmann (*Valkyrien*, 1861; *Thrymskviden*, 1868) and his son, E. Hartmann (*Fjeldstuen*, 1859). These are still very popular in Denmark. The Russian center of greatest vitality was St. Petersburg (Leningrad), where Marius Petipa (1822–1910) paved the way for the modern ballet. Tchaikovsky's *Swan Lake* (1876; perf. 1877), *The Sleeping Beauty* (1889; perf. 1890), and *The Nutcracker* (1891; perf. 1892) represent the culmination of this activity. Two other important ballets of this period are *Coppélia* (1870) and *Sylvia* (1876) with music by Delibes.

The great flowering of modern ballet began in 1909 when a touring company of Russian dancers under director Sergei P. Diaghilev and dancer-choreographer Michel Fokine began to perform in Paris. Diaghilev not only changed the Russian troupe to conform to his ideals of ballet but also succeeded in transplanting the Russian tradition, particularly to France, England, and America. Diaghilev's Ballet Russe attracted composers, artists, and writers to create music, posters and scenery, and plots for their performances. Léon Bakst and Picasso created decorative and exotic backdrops. Debussy, Ravel, Stravinsky, Milhaud, Satie, and Honegger were among those commissioned to compose new works and make arrangements from other forms.

The 1909 Ballet Russe performance presented *Dances from Prince Igor* to the "Polovetsian Dances" from Borodin's opera *Prince Igor*. The group's outstanding musical collaborator was Igor Stravinsky, who wrote the scores for *L'Oiseau de feu* (*The Firebird*, 1910), *Petrushka* (1911), *Le Sacre du printemps* (*The Rite of Spring*, 1913), and others. Ravel contributed the music for *Daphnis et Chloé* (1912), Richard Strauss for *Josephslegende* (1914), De Falla for *Le Tricorne* (*The Three-Cornered Hat,* 1919, with décor by Picasso), and Milhaud for *La Création du monde* (1923). Debussy's ballet *Jeux* (1913), choreographed by Vaslav Nijinsky, leading male dancer of the troupe, was not well received. Other outstanding works of this period were Stravinsky's *Les Noces* (1914–19; perf. 1923); Prokofiev's *Chout* (*The Buffoon*, 1915; perf. 1921); Satie's three ballets, *Parade* (1917), *Mercure* (1924, with Picasso décor), and *Relâche* (1924); and Poulenc's *Les Biches* (1923, perf. 1924). With Diaghilev's death in 1929 the company disbanded, and the dancers and choreographers either joined other companies or formed their own. Also performed in the 1920's were Hindemith's *Der Dämon* (1924) and Bartók's *The Wooden Prince* (1914–16, perf. 1917 and 1922) and *The Miraculous Mandarin* (1919, perf. 1926 in an altered version). Ida Rubinstein, a choreographer with the Diaghilev Ballet Russe, left the company in 1925 to form her own, for which she choreographed Ravel's *Boléro* (1928) and a new version of his *La Valse* (1929). In England Ninette de Valois, who had also left the Diaghilev company in 1925, founded a small company of dancers that became the Sadler's Wells Ballet, later the Royal Ballet. Notable works performed by this company were R. Vaughan Williams' *Job* (1931) and William Walton's *Façade* (1931) with choreography by F. Ashton.

Since 1920 ballet has become increasingly popular in the United States. About 1933 a distinctly national flavor and style developed that depart markedly from traditional positions, movements, and techniques. Stravinsky's *Perséphone* of 1934 (with text by A. Gide) was still in the European tradition. The Russian George Balanchine, who came to the United States in 1933, was the first choreographer with revolutionary ideas. Balanchine created *Jeu de cartes* (1937) to Stravinsky's music, and 20 years later

the two men collaborated to create *Agon.* Among the best-known American works are Copland's *Billy the Kid* (1938), *Rodeo* (1942), and *Appalachian Spring* (1944), and Bernstein's *Fancy Free* (1944). British choreographer Anthony Tudor, a pupil of Diaghilev, came to the United States in 1940. He created *Undertow* (the case history of a psychopathic murderer) to music by William Schuman; it was performed in New York in 1945.

There is much disagreement about the quality of the ballet in the Soviet Union. Unlike the rest of Europe, Russia escaped Diaghilev's influence, for his innovations were created in France. Although the traditional full-length ballet that lasts a whole evening is still popular, shorter modern ballets such as Shostakovitch's *The Golden Age* (1930) are also being produced there. Other Soviet composers, notably Boris Asafiev (*The Flames of Paris,* 1932, and *The Fountain of Bakhchisarai,* 1934), Aram Khatchaturian (*Gayne,* 1942), and Prokofiev (*Romeo and Juliet,* 1940, and *Cinderella,* 1945), have also produced ballet scores.

Ballet in France was continued after Diaghilev's death by ballet director Serge Lifar. Albert Roussel (*Bacchus et Ariane,* 1931), J. Ibert (*Les Amours de Jupiter,* 1946), and G. Auric (*La Chambre,* 1955) are among the better-known composers of ballets. *Musique concrète has also been used for ballets, e.g., Pierre Henry's *Orphée 53* (1953) as well as his *Arcane* (1955) and *Haut Voltage* (1957). In other countries ballet has been less popular. In Italy L. Dallapiccola and L. Nono, in Germany Werner Egk and Hans W. Henze, in Denmark Knudåge Riisager, in Sweden Karl-Birger Blomdahl, in Yugoslavia Fran Lhotka, and in Hungary Ferenc Farkas and László Lajtha have written ballet music, each in his own idiom.

Much of the music originally written for ballet has been arranged as orchestral or solo music, e.g., Ravel's *Boléro* and Stravinsky's *Firebird Suite.*

Lit.: H. Searle, *Ballet Music: An Introduction* [1958]; V. Arvey, *Choreographic Music: Music for the Dance* [1941]; C. W. Beaumont, *Complete Book of Ballets* (1937; sup. 1942); G. Goode, *The Book of Ballets* (1939); S. J. Cohen, U.S. ed., *Dictionary of Modern Ballet* [1959]; J. Gregor, *Kulturgeschichte des Ballets* (1944); F. Reyna, *Des Origines du ballet* (1955); BuMBE, p. 141ff (ballet de cour); M. M. McGowan, *L'Art du ballet de cour en France 1581–1643* (1963); H. Prunières, *Le Ballet de cour en France* (1914); id., in *BSIM* x (Louis XIII); F. Ghisi, in *MQ* xxxv

(Florence, 1608–25); R. Lach, in *ZMW* iii (*Prometheus*); J. Jersild, in *AM* xiv (Denmark, 18th cent.); "Le Ballet au XIXe siècle" (*RM* ii, special no.). See also under Dance music; Ballet in opera. rev. I.B.

Ballet in opera. Ballets appear in opera usually as interludes unessential to the plot, although connected with it by some more or less specious pretext. Thus their function is to offer a diversion from the purely vocal and dramatic portions, and they frequently involve large choral groups and spectacular stage effects as well as dancing. They are therefore most appropriate in large-scale, serious, formal opera, and historically they are found chiefly in operas of the French school or works written under the influence of French taste. Ballets in comic opera are simpler and less formal than those in serious works, as, for example, the dances in the finale of the first act of Mozart's *Don Giovanni*.

Although Lully is commonly credited with having introduced the ballet into opera, it was not unknown in operas before his time. Aside from the choral dances of Greek tragedy, the general dances that frequently took place at the end of the medieval mystery plays [see Liturgical drama], or the ballet portions of the 16th-century *intermezzi, there are closing dances in Peri's and Caccini's *Euridice* (both 1600), a *ballo* at the end of Gagliano's *Dafne* (1608), and a *moresca danced by the shepherds in the finale of Monteverdi's *Orfeo* (1607). There are also ballets, though on a relatively small scale, in other Italian operas of the early 17th century (e.g., Landi's *Il Sant'Alessio*, 1632; M. Rossi's *Erminia sul Giordano*, 1633). Later Italian operas made some use of the ballet, together with spectacular stage effects, especially in works designed for festival occasions, like Cesti's *Il Pomo d'oro* (Vienna, 1667), which has several ballets in each act and a grand triple ballet in the finale.

The importance of ballet in French opera is due to the long previous tradition of the *ballet de cour* in France and to the fact that Lully, in establishing the national operatic form, practically incorporated the entire apparatus of the ballet in this new type of entertainment. The very name of the opera company, "Académie royale de musique et de danse," shows the intimate connection that was thought to exist between opera and ballet, a connection that has been maintained throughout subsequent French opera. So strong was the French fondness for ballet that before the end of the 17th century a

new form, the *opéra ballet,* was created (Campra, *L'Europe galante,* 1697), in which the dramatic content was reduced to a minimum in order to make room for practically continuous dancing, choral, and scenic elements (Rameau, *Les Indes galantes,* 1735). The dances of Lully's and Rameau's operas and *opéras ballet* furnish some of the finest examples of French instrumental music of their period.

English opera likewise introduced ballet, partly from the native tradition of the *masque and partly under French influence. There are ballets in Blow's *Venus and Adonis* (c. 1684–85) and Purcell's *Dido and Aeneas* (1689), as well as in Purcell's other dramatic music (e.g., the chaconne in *King Arthur,* 1691).

In Germany ballet in opera was introduced by foreign composers (C. Pallavicino's *La Gerusalemme liberata,* Dresden, 1687) and, under French influence, by native composers as well (J. S. Kusser's *Erindo,* Hamburg, 1694). The ballets in the original version of Keiser's *Croesus* (first perf. date unknown; MS score 1710, libretto 1711) were omitted in the revival of 1730.

In early 18th-century Italian opera the ballet was of minor importance, with rare exceptions in festival works such as Fux's *Costanza e fortezza* (Prague, 1723). Toward the middle of the century, however, with the first movements toward reform of the older model, ballet scenes began to be revived. This is especially evident in the works that Jommelli wrote from 1753 to 1769 at Stuttgart, where the celebrated ballet master Jean-Georges Noverre was also in residence, and in the operas of Traetta at Parma (1758–65) and St. Petersburg (1768–74), which show the influence of Rameau. Gluck's "reform" operas are filled with ballet scenes, like their French prototypes, and the ballet remained a constant and important feature in the works of Gluck's disciples as well as in the "grand opera" of the 19th century (Auber's *La Muette de Portici,* 1828; Rossini's *Guillaume Tell,* 1829; Meyerbeer's *Robert le Diable,* 1831; Halévy's *La Juive,* 1835; Wagner's *Rienzi,* 1842; Berlioz' *Les Troyens,* composed 1856–58; Gounod's *Faust,* 1859, recitatives added 1860, ballet music 1869). All the above-named works except *Rienzi* were first performed (or intended to be performed) at Paris, where a ballet was still considered an indispensable part of any large operatic work. Wagner's addition of the "bacchanal" music for the Paris performance of *Tannhäuser* (1861) is striking evidence of the power of this French tradition. In his later works Wagner occasionally had recourse to the ballet (*Die Meistersinger, Parsifal*) as did Verdi in *Aida* (1871). There are also important ballet scenes in Borodin's *Prince Igor* (comp. 1871–87, perf. 1890). The relative decline of "grand opera" in the late 19th and early 20th centuries led to the decreasing importance of ballet in opera, accompanied by a steady rise of interest in ballet as a separate form [see Ballet]. Incidental dance scenes closely connected with the action are found in R. Strauss's *Salome* (1905) and Berg's *Wozzeck* (1925). Many operas since 1925 have reintroduced the earlier custom of incorporating large dance and choral scenes, notably Milhaud's *Christophe Colomb* (1930) and *David* (1954), Schoenberg's unfinished *Moses und Aron* (comp. Acts 1 and 2, sketches only for Act 3, 1932), and Hindemith's *Die Harmonie der Welt* (1957), which closes with an elaborate allegorical ballet quite in the tradition of Lully and Rameau.   D.J.G.

Ballet suite. Modern designation for baroque suites consisting entirely of dance types derived from the French ballet of the 17th century. See Suite V.

Ballett. German spelling for *ballet. Also, 16th- and 17th-century English or German for *balletto* or for *ballo*.

Balletto [It.]. (1) A vocal composition of *c.* 1600, dancelike in character, written in a simplified madrigal style and frequently provided with a *fa-la burden, which may occasionally have been danced. The first publication in this field was G. Gastoldi's *Balletti a cinque voci ... per cantare, sonare, & ballare* (1591; see *HAM,* no. 158). His example was imitated by T. Morley in *The First Books of Balletts to Five Voices* (1595; see *HAM,* no. 159), by H. L. Hassler in *Lustgarten neuer teutscher Gesäng, Balletti* (1601), and in similar publications until *c.* 1620. (2) A dance of the 17th century, usually in 4/4 meter, bipartite form, and in a simple, near-homophonic style (somewhat similar to the early allemande), mostly for ensembles. Such *balletti* appear frequently in the German suites of the early 17th century, e.g., J. H. Schein, *Banchetto musicale* (1617; comp. ed. by A. Prüfer, vol. i), Paul Peurl, Melchior Franck, and Valentin Haussmann, as well as in Italian publications, e.g., Maurizio Cazzati, *Correnti Balletti Galiarde* (1659), Andrea Grossi, *Balletti, Correnti, Sarabande, e Gighe* (1679), etc. Frescobaldi's *Il Secondo Libro di Toccate* (1627) contains an "Aria del balletto" for keyboard (8 variations). (3) A dramatic choreography described in Cornazano's "Libro dell'Arte da Danzare" (*c.* 1450), fol. 8/9. It used the conventional step repertory as found in the contemporary *ballo* and *bassadanza* but added mimic gestures and facial expressions to tell the story. See also *Ballo.*

Ballo [It.]. A term used in various ways since the 15th century: (1) as a generic designation for dances (e.g., F. Bendusi, *Opera nova de balli,* 1553); (2) for scenic representations, more or less in the character of a ballet (as in Monteverdi's *Il Ballo delle ingrate,* 1608), and also for operatic ballets (as in M. Gagliano's *Dafne,* 1608); (3) in the meaning of *balletto* (2) and (3), as a rare substitute for this term.

Ballo in maschera, Un [It., A Masked Ball]. Opera in three acts by Verdi (libretto by A. Somma, based on Scribe's *Gustave III, ou Le Bal masqué*), produced in Rome, 1859. The original play was based on historical fact; Gustavus III of Sweden was shot in the back at a masked ball in Stockholm in 1792. To avoid inciting violence against royalty during a period of political unrest, Verdi was forced by the authorities to change the scene of the opera from Sweden to colonial Boston. Some modern performances revert to the original Swedish setting, while others set the scene in Naples.

Balsa. Name used in Mexico as early as 1810 for a ballroom type of dance strongly reflecting the traditions of the European waltz and especially those of its French models. During the second half of the 19th century it became increasingly popular, and its influences are reflected in most of the art music produced by the composers of this period, such as Felipe Villanueva, Melesio Morales, Ricardo Castro, and others [see Mexico].   J.O-S.

Bamberg, Codex. See Sources, no. 5.

Bambuco [Sp.]. One of the most representative of Colombian traditional dance-songs, using alternation of 6/8 and 3/4 meter in moderately quick tempo. Small guitars (*tiples*) and lutes (*bandolas*) provide accompaniment for the voice.   J.O-S.

Band [It., Sp. *banda*]. An instrumental group composed principally of woodwind, brass, and percussion instruments. In earlier periods the name was used for any group of instruments, and particularly for highly distinguished groups, e.g., the "24 violons du roy" under Lully (*La Grande Bande*), or the 24 fiddlers of Charles II (The King's Private Band). Today, the term is also used for groups of unusual instrumental combinations, e.g., marimba band, accordion band, etc. Different types of wind band include the brass band, military band, symphonic band, wind ensemble, jazz or dance band, etc. The Italian word *banda* means the brass and percussion combination in the orchestra, a meaning carried over from the earlier cavalry bands, consisting of brass and percussion. Also see Brass band; Military music; Symphonic band.

J.W.

Bandola [Sp.]. Small guitar typical of Colombia, with a set of fifteen strings tuned three to each of the following notes: G-d-a-e'-b'. It is usually used together with a smaller twelve-string guitar known as *requinto*.

J.O-S.

Bandoneon [Sp.]. See under Accordion.

Bandora, pandora, pandore. A 16th-century stringed instrument of bass size [see ill. under Lute], with a characteristic scalloped body. It had seven (originally six) pairs of metal strings tuned G_1-C-D-G-c-e-a and as many as 15 frets. Pieces for bandora in the Cambridge University Library [Ms. *Dd.2.11*] as well as some pieces by Barley call for the additional bass course which was tuned to G_1. It was supposedly invented by John Rose of London in 1562 and was in use for about a hundred years. There are close to 100 compositions for the bandora. A smaller instrument of the same type was the *orpharion. See W. W. Newcomb, *Lute Music of Shakespeare's Time* (1966; new ed. of W. Barley's *A new Booke of Tabliture* of 1596); T. Dart, "Le Pandore" (in *Le Luth et sa musique*, 1958, ed. J. Jaquot); D. Gill, "The Orpharion and Bandora" (*GSJ* xiii).

Bandura. Instruments referred to by this or a similar name can only be identified with reference to specific countries of origin, e.g., the bandura being Russian, the *bandurria Spanish.

Bandurria. A Spanish instrument of the guitar family, still widely used in southern Spain. In its present-day form it has six double strings tuned in fourths from $g^{\sharp\prime}$ to a'' and is played with a plectrum. See ill. under Guitar family. In Latin America the name is used for a twelve-string guitar similar to the *bandola* but smaller, used mainly in Colombia. It is also known as *pandura*.

Banjo. A stringed instrument with a long neck and a body in the form of a shallow, one-headed drum spanned with parchment. Sometimes fretted, it may have four to nine strings. Often

it has five, the highest of which, called the thumb-string, is placed next to the lowest, in the following arrangement: d', b, g, c, g'. It is plucked with either the fingers or a plectrum. The banjo was the typical instrument of the American Negro and has been frequently used in jazz. It was imported by slaves from West Africa (Senegambia), where it existed under the name "bania." In all probability it is not an aboriginal African instrument but a modification of the Arabian or European guitar [see ill. under Guitar family].

Bar. (1) In English, bar line or, more usually, measure (included between two bar lines). (2) In German, see *Bar* form.

Barber of Seville, The. See *Barbiere di Siviglia*.

Barbershop harmony. Colloquial term for a type of banal harmony used in popular American part singing such as was formerly practiced in barbershops [see Ex.]. Diminished seventh chords, dominant seventh chords, augmented

sixth chords, and triads with added sixths prevail, usually in close position. See S. Spaeth, *Barber Shop Ballads* (1940).

Barbiere di Siviglia, Il [It., The Barber of Seville]. (1) Opera in two acts by Rossini (libretto by C. Sterbini, originally entitled *Almaviva o sia L'Inutile Precauzione,* based on Beaumarchais' *Le Barbier de Seville*), produced in Rome, 1816. Setting: Seville, 18th century. It is one of the last examples of 18th-century Italian comic opera and, in particular, the last to use the *secco* *recitative. Figaro's aria "Largo al factotum" is one of the outstanding examples of *buffo* aria in rapid declamation. The plot of Mozart's *Nozze di Figaro* is based on Beaumarchais' sequel to *Le Barbier de Seville*. (2) Opera in two acts (4 parts) by G. Paisiello (libretto by G. Petrosellini, based on Beaumarchais). Produced in St. Petersburg, 1782. Setting: Seville, 18th century.

Barbitos. An instrument mentioned by various Greek and Latin writers, from the 6th century B.C. (Anacreon) to the 3rd century A.D. (Athenaeus). Anacreon likens it to the lyre and Theocritus says that it had many strings.

Barcarole [F. *barcarolle;* It. *barcarola*]. A boat song of the Venetian gondoliers [It. *barca,* boat], or an instrumental or vocal composition in imitation thereof. Well-known examples for the piano are found in Mendelssohn's "Songs without Words" (op. 19, no. 6; op. 30, no. 6; op. 62, no. 5); others were written by Chopin (op. 60) and Fauré. Vocal barcaroles occur in various operas with Italian settings, e.g., in Hérold's *Zampa* (1831), Auber's *Fra Diavolo* (1830), Offenbach's *Tales of Hoffmann* (1881); see also Schubert's song, "Auf dem Wasser zu singen." Barcaroles are always in moderate 6/8 or 12/8 time and use a monotonous accompaniment suggestive of the movement of the waves and the boat.

Bard. The pre-Christian and medieval poet-musician (minstrel) of the Celts, especially the Irish and the Welsh. In the early Middle Ages bards exercised great political power, serving as historians, heralds, ambassadors, officers of the king's household, and, in brief, constituting the highest intellectual class. Their activities are documented as early as the pre-Christian era by Greek writers such as Diodorus Siculus (1st cent. B.C.), who refers to the *crwth, the traditional instrument of the bards. Privileges of the Welsh bards were fixed by King Howel Dha in 940 and revised by Gryffyd ap Cynan in 1040. Their earliest persecutions (on political grounds) occurred after the conquest of Wales by Edward I in 1284. The bards continued to be active, (though at a level far below their former high station) in Ireland until 1690 (battle of the Boyne) and in Scotland until 1748. Annual congregations of the Welsh bards, called *Eisteddfod,* were revived as a regular practice in the early 19th century after an interruption of about 150 years. Their standards, extremely low, have recently been raised considerably. [Also see Pennillion.]

The music of the Welsh bards has been the subject of much discussion and controversy. Many exaggerated claims have been made, chiefly on the basis of certain music manuscripts, one of which, called *Musica neu Beroriaeth* (Penllyn MS; fac. ed. *Musica, Brit. Mus. Add. MS 14905,* University of Wales, Cardiff, 1936), bears the inscription, made by an 18th-century owner: "The following manuscript is the Music of Britains as settled by a Congress, or Meeting of Masters of Music, by order of Gryffydd ap Cynan, Prince of Wales, about A.D. 1100, with some of the most antient pieces of the Britains supposed to have been handed down to us from the British Druids." Actually, this manuscript dates from the 17th century and does not substantiate this supposition or support other extravagant claims voiced by modern advocates of the "medieval bardic music" movement (e.g., A. Dolmetsch). The notation is but a modification of the German organ tablature of the late 16th century [see *WoHN* ii, 294]. The transcriptions given by Dolmetsch (who succeeded in clarifying certain peculiarities of this notation) still further discredit the fantastic legends so frequently told. The style of these pieces seems to indicate that they may be end-products of "debasement through seepage," a process frequently noticeable in folk traditions [see Folk music II]. It is scarcely tenable, therefore, to state that "from internal evidence such music could not have been made later than the sixth century, and was probably much earlier" (A. Dolmetsch, in *The Consort,* no. 4, p. 14). The accompanying example, transcribed from

WoHN ii, 298, shows written out figurations in the style of the 17th-century *arpègement figuré* [see Arpeggio]. Only the beginning and the end of the piece are given here, but the intermediate measures can easily be found from the formula 11110000101011110000 1011 given in the original, which indicates the scheme of alternation for the two chords used in this piece, each being indicated by the figure 1 or 0, a method commonly used in 17th-century guitar tablatures [see *WoHN* ii, 171ff].

Lit.: J. C. Walker, *Historical Memoirs of the Irish Bards* (1786); E. Jones, *Musical and Poetical Relicks of the Welsh Bards* (1784); *id., The Bardic Museum* (1802); C. de la Borde, *Essai sur les Bardes,* 3 vols. (1840); G. Borrow, *Celtic*

Bards, Chiefs and Kings (1928); W. Evans, *The Bards of the Isle of Britain* [1930]; A. Dolmetsch, ‡*Translations from the Pennlynn Manuscript of Ancient Harp Music* (1937); id., in *The Consort*, no. 3; P. Crossley-Holland, "Secular Homophonic Music in Wales in the Middle Ages" (*ML* xxiii, 135).

Bar form [G.]. I. A term used frequently in modern studies for an old, very important musical form, schematically designated a a b. The name is derived from the medieval German term *Bar*, a poem consisting of three or more *Gesätze* (i.e., stanzas), each of which is divided into two *Stollen* (section a) and an *Abgesang* (section b). See the accurate description in Wagner's *Die Meistersinger*, Act I, 3, where Kothner says: "Ein jedes Meistergesanges Bar" consists of "unterschiedlichen Gesätzen" (different stanzas); "ein Gesätz" consists of "zweenen [two] Stollen" and "Abgesang." It appears that the form a a b should properly be called *Gesätz* form (form of the stanza), but the term *Bar* form has been generally accepted.

The aesthetic principle of the *Bar* form is adumbrated in the ancient Greek ode, which consists of *strophe* (a), *antistrophe* (a), and *epode* (b). In Gregorian chant, repeat structures of the a a b type occur particularly in the *jubili* and verse melismas of the Alleluias [e.g., "Timebunt gentes," *LU*, p. 1056], as well as in the verse melismas of the Offertories [see *ApGC*, p. 368f]. It is also clearly recognizable in some of the long Alleluia melismas of Mozarabic chant [e.g., *Antifonario . . . de Leon,* fac. ed. 1953, f. 187]. The *Bar* form also occurs in a few hymn melodies [e.g., "Iste confessor," *LU*, p. 1178] that have identical music for the first and second lines of the stanza (a a b c). From here it found its way into the repertory of the troubadours and particularly of the trouvères, where it is known as **ballade,* and ultimately into that of the minnesingers and Meistersinger, who called it *Bar* and used it for nearly all their lyrical songs [Ex. in *EiBM*, no. 8; *HAM*, nos. 20, 24; *SchGMB*, nos. 12, 21]. It is equally common in the German polyphonic songs of the 15th and 16th centuries (Locheimer Liederbuch, Glogauer Liederbuch, Hofhaimer, Stoltzer, etc.), as well as in the Lutheran chorales and the various compositions based on them (organ chorales, chorale cantatas, etc.).

An interesting modification found in the French and, particularly, in the German songs is the use of identical endings for the *Stollen*

and the *Abgesang,* resulting in the form ‖: a + x :‖ b + x, as, e.g., in W. von der Vogelweide's "Palestine Song" [see Ex. 1], in Hans Sachs' "Silberweise" [*SchGMB*, no. 78], and in many chorales of the 16th century, e.g., "Wachet auf, ruft uns die Stimme" [cf. Bach's chorale prelude and the first movement of the cantata]. It could

1
1. Al - ler - erst le - be ich mir   werde
3. Daz hêre lant und ouch die   er - de

2. Sit   min   sün - dic   ou - ge   siht.
4. Dem man   vil   der   ê - ren   giht.
7. Da   got   men - nisch - li - chen   trat.

5. Mirst ge - schehn   des   ich   ie   bat:

6. Ich bin kom - men   an   die stat (7, see above).

2   1   2
1. A - les   di - e - i   nun - ti - us
2. Lu - cem   pro - pin - quam   prae - ci - net.
4. Jam Chri - stus ad   vi - tam vo - cat.

3. Nos ex - ci - ta - tor men - ti - um (4, see above).

be designated as rhymed *Bar* form. Another subspecies is the "doubled *Bar*" ‖: a :‖: b :‖ c, which occurs in the melismas of some Alleluias (e.g., "Oportebat," *LU*, p. 822) and forms a connecting link with the **sequence;* yet another the "superposed *Bar*" (G. *potenzierter Bar*), in which the *Stollen* itself is a complete *Bar* [Ex. in F. L. Saran, *et al.,* ed., *Die Jenaer Liederhandschrift,* 2 vols. (1901), ii, 53, 57].

II. Of particular importance is the type of *Bar* in which the *Stollen* recurs complete at the end of the *Abgesang*, thus leading to the form a a b a or ‖: a :‖ b a. An appropriate designation for this is rounded *Bar* form (G. *Reprisenbar,* also *Rundkanzone*). Several hymn melodies show this form, e.g., "Jam sol" [*LU*, p. 312], "Lucis creator" [*LU*, p. 257], "Ales diei nuntius" [Ex. 2; see *AR*, p. 109]. Minnesinger songs showing this structure are quite numerous [see Neidhardt von Reuenthal, in *DTO* 71, p. 31; Saran (*op. cit.*), ii, 29; *HAM*, no. 20d; *ReMMA*, p. 235]. The special interest of the rounded *Bar* form lies in the fact that its scheme is identical with *sonata form, whose exposition (repeated), development, and recapitulation correspond to the *Stollen* (repeated), *Abgesang,* and restated *Stollen* of the rounded *Bar*. There is, of course, no historical relationship between the medieval *Bar* form and classical sonata form, which actually developed from the rounded binary form ‖: a :‖: b a :‖ in which both sections are repeated [see Binary and ternary form II]. However, the similarity is all the more noteworthy since the *Abgesang* of the medieval songs frequently takes on the function of a real development (higher range, motif continuation, greater intensity of the melodic line, etc.), e.g., in the "Palestine Song" and in Hans Sachs' "Morgenweise" [*EiBM*, no. 8]. The a a b a form is also the most common scheme of present-day popular songs (b is called the "bridge").

A. Lorenz has tried to show (with questionable success) that the *Bar* form is the main structural principle of Wagner's operas, particularly of *Die Meistersinger*. He interpreted them as consisting of numerous layers of superposed *Bars* (*Kleinbar, Mittelbar, Grossbar*), beginning with the smallest units of the musical line and culminating with the "gigantic" *Bar* of the three acts.

Lit.: A. Lorenz, *Das Geheimnis der Form bei Richard Wagner,* 4 vols. (1924–33); *id.,* "Das Relativitätsprinzip in den musikalischen Formen" (*CP Adler*); *id.,* "Homophone Grossrhythmik in Bachs Polyphonie" (*DM* xxii.4); H. A. Grunsky, in *ZMW* xvi.

Baricanor [L.]. See Baritonans.

Bariolage [F.]. A special effect in violin playing, obtained by quickly shifting back and forth between two or more strings, the lower strings being used to produce relatively higher tones. This technique may be employed for broken-chord passages [Ex. 1, Bach, Solo Partita in E major], for a "coloristic" tremolo [Ex. 2, Brahms, Symphony no. 4, last movt.], or for similar formations.

Baritonans, baricanor. Terms employed occasionally in the late 15th century (Busnois, La Rue) for bass parts.

Baritone or (rarely) **barytone.** (1) The male voice between the bass and the tenor; see Voices, range of. (2) Applied to instruments (oboe, horn, saxophone), any size above the bass size. (3) Abbr. for baritone horn; see Brass instruments III (c).

Baritone clef. See under Clef.

Baritone horn. See under Brass instruments III (c).

Bar line [F. *barre de mesure;* G. *Taktstrich;* It. *stanghetta;* Sp. *línea divisoria*]. A vertical line drawn through the staff to mark off measures. The general use of the bar line is relatively recent (17th century). Until 1600 bar lines were used only for keyboard and lute (vihuela) music, the earliest known being from the late 14th century (Codex Faenza). The use of bar lines in 16th-century compositions frequently differs from present-day practice, since they served primarily as a means of orientation, without implying a regular recurrent main beat. They are drawn at the distance of either a *brevis* or a *semibrevis* (two or one whole note), the choice depending to a certain extent on the absence or presence of small note values. In some compositions, mostly Spanish, the bar lines completely fail to indicate the musical meter because they mark off beats, three of which must be combined in order to produce a measure in the modern sense of the term (3/1, reduced to 3/2; see Narvaez's "Diferencias sobra O gloriosa Domina," *HAM*, no. 122). Particularly noteworthy is the fact that the marking-off began with the first note, even if it was an upbeat. See Ex. 1 (Pisador, "Pavana muy llana," *Libro de música de vihuela,* 1552), in which the original barring is given on the staff, the modern below the staff. The same usage occurs in Frescobaldi's *Partite sopra l'aria della Romanesca* [see *HAM*, no. 192].

In ensemble (vocal) music the bar line was not introduced until the latter part of the 16th century, when the notation in single parts gave way to notation in score arrangement. The arias of the 17th century frequently show the anomalous use of the bar line referred to above, i.e., the disregard of upbeat or of triple time [see the explanations and examples in *RiHM* ii.2, 12f].

Modern editors of polyphonic music of the 15th and 16th centuries have increasingly resented the "tyranny" of the bar line and have tried to make this indispensable device of modern notation less conspicuous by replacing it with apostrophes: ', punctuated lines: ⁝, or with the *Mensurstrich,* i.e., a line drawn between, not through, the staves [Ex. 2, from Josquin, *Ave Christe, immolate*]. However, the *Mensurstrich* is impracticable if different meters (mensurations) are used in different parts, e.g., 2/4 against 3/4, a practice not uncommon in the period of Obrecht and Josquin and still more common in the compositions of the late 14th century.

Lit.: W. H. Cummings, "Bar-lines" (*Musical Times,* 1904, p. 574); T. Wiehmayer, in *ZMW* vii; H. Keller, in *ZMW* vii; *WoHN* i, 427ff; *ApNPM, passim.*

Baroque music. The music of the period *c.* 1600–1750, following that of the Renaissance. It is also referred to as the "thoroughbass period." The term *baroque* (probably from Port. *barrôco,* irregularly shaped pearl; or from the painter F. Barocci, or Baroccio, d. 1612) was used formerly in a decidedly pejorative sense, to mean "grotesque," "in corrupt taste," overladen with scrollwork," etc. Its application to the fine arts was based on the opinion (Jacob Burckhardt) that 17th-century architecture and painting represented a debased Renaissance style. This opinion, however, was thoroughly revised about 1900 by Heinrich Wölfflin, who was the first to point out the positive contributions and great artistic qualities of baroque art and to vindicate the term "baroque" from any implication of inferiority.

Both the beginning and the end of the baroque period in music are rather clearly defined. Baroque music began about 1600, with the rise of monody, opera, oratorio, cantata, and recitative, and ended 150 years later, with the death of Bach and Handel. Preparatory phenomena were, on the one hand, the *balletto and *villanella, with their reaction against Flemish polyphony, and on the other hand, the style of the *Venetian school (G. Gabrieli), whose pomp and splendor exceed the limitations of true Renaissance art and foreshadow the aesthetic basis of baroque style. It may be noted that throughout the 17th century the tradition of Renaissance music persisted to some extent in the *Roman school, and that, on the other hand, a new period, the *rococo, had already begun when Bach and Handel were writing their greatest masterpieces, which represent the acme of baroque music.

Generally speaking, the baroque period is an era of ecstasy and exuberance, of dynamic tensions and sweeping gestures, an era of longing and self-denial, much in contrast to the assuredness and self-reliance of the Renaissance. It is a period when men liked to consider this life the "vale of tears," when the statues of the saints look rapturously toward heaven, when the clouds and the infinite landscape were discovered. Much of this attitude is reflected in the expressive melodies of the 17th century, in the long coloraturas, the pathetic recitative, the frequent use of chromaticism, the capricious rhythms. Early baroque music (prior to 1650) in particular shows, in its *canzonas and *toccatas, striking traits of capriciousness, exuberance, and irregularity, whereas later composers such as Carissimi and Corelli represent a trend toward greater restraint and regularity of style. On the other hand, the structural, or, as one might call it, the architectural element in baroque music must not be overlooked. More than any other period, the 17th century contributed toward the development and establishment of clearly defined types and forms, such as the ostinato forms, the variations, the suite, the sonata, the *da capo* aria, the rondo, the concerto, the opera, the oratorio, the cantata.

Stylistically, baroque music is characterized chiefly by the thoroughbass technique, leading to a texture of two principal contours, melody and bass, with the intervening space filled by improvised harmony. In Germany, however, the contrasting style of true polyphony not only persisted but reached, in Bach, the very acme of perfection. A third principle of baroque style is the *stile concertante,* that is, contrasting effects, a principle expressed in the abrupt changes of the early canzona as well as in the solo-tutti alternation of the *concerto grosso* and in the *echo effects of vocal and organ music. Other basic concepts of baroque music are *improvisation and *ornamentation. Finally, there is the definitive establishment of tonic and dominant as the principal chords of harmony and, *c.* 1650 (Carissimi), of four-measure phrases [see *Vierhebigkeit*].

At the beginning of the 17th century stand three great figures still rooted in the tradition of the Renaissance but inaugurating the novel trends of baroque music: Monteverdi, G. Gabrieli, and Sweelinck. They may be considered the sources of three mainstreams of baroque music, that is, vocal, instrumental, and organ music, with which, in turn, the three styles mentioned above can be roughly associated, namely, accompanied melody, concerto style, and contrapuntal style.

The first of these streams, starting in Florence (Caccini, Peri, later Monteverdi), produced the monodic style [see Monody] with the *recitative and *aria, and with the composite forms of the *cantata, *opera, and *oratorio (Passion). The second, "Venetian" stream found its realization in the instrumental canzona, the violin *sonata, the trio sonata in its two varieties, sonata da chiesa and *sonata da camera, and in the orchestral forms of the *concerto grosso [see also Concerto III], the French *overture, and the *sinfonia. The last stream, starting with Sweelinck and Frescobaldi but continuing chiefly in Germany (Scheidt, Froberger, Buxtehude, Pachelbel, Kuhnau, Muffat, Fischer, Bach), led to the *fugue, *organ chorale (chorale prelude), *toccata, and *suite (the latter also in France).

Lit.: *BuMBE; GrHWM,* pp. 266–410, bibl., pp. 681–86; P. H. Lang, *Music in Western Civilization* (1941), pp. 314–529; A. Milner, *The Musical Aesthetic of the Baroque* (1960); *AdHM* i, 411–700; *RiHM* ii.2–ii.3; A. Liess, *Wiener Barockmusik* (1946); E. Wellesz, *Der Beginn des musikalischen Barock und der Anfang der Oper in Wien* (1922); J. H. Mueller, "Baroque—Is it Datum, Hypothesis, or Tautology?" (*Journal of Aesthetics and Art Criticism* xii, 421ff); C. J. Friedrich, M. F. Bukofzer, H. Hatzfeld, J. R. Martin, W. Stechow (*ibid.* xiv, 143ff); "Le 'Baroque' musical" (*Les Congrès et Colloques de l'Université de Liège,* xxvii, 1964); E. Schenk, in *ZMW* xvii; E. Wellesz, in *ZIM* xi; C. Sachs, in *JMP* xxvi; A. Della Corte, in *LRM* vi, no. 5; *id.,* in *CP Laurencie;* G. Barblan, in *CP Anglés* i.

Baroque organ. See Organ XII.

Barpyknon. Same as *barypyknon.* See Pyknon.

Barré [F.]. In lute and guitar playing, term calling for the simultaneous shortening of the vibratory length of several or all strings by holding the forefinger across them. An artificial substitute is the *capotasto.

Barre de mesure [F.]. *Bar line.

Barrel organ. See under Mechanical instruments II.

Bartered Bride, The [Cz. *Prodaná Nevěstá*]. Opera in three acts by Bedřich Smetana (libretto by Karel Sabina), produced in Prague, 1866. Setting: A Bohemian village, 1850. It has been widely sung outside Czechoslovakia in the German translation (1893) as *Die verkaufte Braut.* Describing an episode from 19th-century Bohemian peasant life, *The Bartered Bride* is one of the first and most successful examples of national opera.

Baryton. (1) French and German spelling for *baritone (voice, size of instruments). (2) An instrument of the viol family. See Viol IV, 5. For ill. see Violin. See E. Fruchtman, "The Baryton: Its History and Its Music Re-examined" (*AM* xxxiv). *Barytonhorn,* i.e., euphonium [see Brass instruments III(d)].

Barytonans, barycanor. See Baritonans.

Barzelletta [It.]. A type of Italian poetry of about 1500, generally in the form of the *ballata* (*ripresa – piedi* [or *mutazione*] – *volta – ripresa*) or *bergerette* (*ballata* or *virelai* with one stanza). More than half of the *frottole* are *barzellette.* Indeed, the specific poetic-musical type generally known as *frottola* should perhaps be designated *barzelletta,* the term *frottola* being more a collective name for various types.

Base viol. Same as bass viol. See Viola da gamba.

Basilica. See under Diaphonia (3).

Basis [Gr.]. Humanist name for "bass" used by 15th- and 16th-century composers.

Bass. (1) The lowest of men's voices [see Voices, range of]. (2) German name (abbr. of *Kontrabass*) for the double bass. (3) Applied to instruments, the term indicates the lowest and consequently largest type of the family, e.g., bass clarinet. (4) In musical composition, the lowest of the parts. In the styles of the 18th and 19th centuries the bass has special significance as the determining factor of the harmonic structure [see Harmonic analysis]. The special role of the bass is particularly conspicuous in the practice and theory of *thoroughbass. For the origin of the bass, see Contratenor.

Bassa [It.]. Low. *Ottava bassa* (abbr. *8va bassa*), the lower octave of the written notes. *Con 8va bassa,* doubling of the written notes in the lower octave.

Bassadanza [It.]. See *Basse danse.*

Bass-bar. In violins, etc., a strip of wood glued inside the table, about 11 in. long and narrowing at both ends. Its function is to support the left foot of the bridge and to spread over the table the vibrations of the bridge produced by those strings.

Bass clef. See under Clef.

Bass-course. See Course.

Bass drum. See under Percussion instruments B 3.

Basse [F.]. *Basse chiffré* or *b. continue,* thoroughbass; *basse contrainte,* ground (basso ostinato); *basse profonde, chantante, taille,* see Voices, range of; *basse fondamentale,* fundamental bass; *basse-à-piston,* euphonium.

Basse danse [F.], **bassadanza** [It.]. One type of a "family of related dances" (*ReMR,* p. 37) of unknown origin cultivated at the courts of western Europe during the 15th century and, in a somewhat debased form, cultivated more generally during the early 16th century. The name (*bas,* low) probably refers to the gliding or walking movements of the feet, in contrast to the livelier steps of the *pas de Brabant* (It. *saltarello,* Sp. *alta* or *altadanza*), which often followed the *basse danse* proper. The earliest sources of information about the *bassadanza* include nine Italian MSS, of which the so-called "Trattato dell'arte del ballo di Guglielmo Ebreo" (*c.* 1463) and the "Libro dell'arte del danzare" of Antonio Cornazano (*c.* 1455) are the best known; three French sources, including the late 15th-century MS Brussels 9085, written (for Marie of Burgundy?) with gold and silver on black paper [see Lit., Closson], and *L'Art et instruction de bien dancer,* printed before 1496; and a single Spanish

source. The Italian treatises give prose descriptions of the choreographies and very little of the music; the French sources record the steps of each dance in a simple tablature notation (*s* = simple, *d* = double, *r* = reprise, *b* = branle, etc.) and give a monophonic tenor for each dance. Most of the dances have names such as "La crudele," "Triste plaisir," "Sans faire de vous departie," "La baixa de Castilla," etc. [see Ex. 1].

1

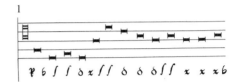

A few of the *basse danse* melodies have been identified as tenors of Burgundian chansons ("Triste plaisir" by Binchois; "Sans faire" by Fontaine). The three *bassadanza* tenors in Cornazano's treatise are written almost exclusively in white semibreves, whereas the 56 *basse danse* tenors included in the two French sources mentioned above are written almost exclusively in black breves. In both cases one note of the tenor corresponds to one step unit of the dance. However, the written notes do not constitute the dance melody but a tenor (in *cantus planus* style) above which one or two parts of a livelier character were improvised. (A typical *basse danse* band consisted of, e.g., two shawms and a slide-trumpet.) An instructive example of the use of a tenor is the *saltarello* in Perugia *MS.* 431 [M. Bukofzer, *Studies in Medieval and Renaissance Music* (1950), p. 199]; another, with the two upper parts moving in parallel fourths, is the *Spaniol Kochersperg* [W. Merian, *Der Tanz in den deutschen Tabulaturbüchern* (1927), p. 46]. According to Cornazano, the same tenor could be used for all dances of the *bassadanza* type—the *saltarello, quaternaria* (or *saltarello tedesco,* used by the Germans), *piva* (cacciata), and the *bassadanza* proper—the difference being in the number of beats allowed to each of the (tenor) written notes, 3 for the *saltarello,* 4 for the *quaternaria,* 2 (four half-beats) for the *piva,* and 6 for the *bassadanza.* A particularly interesting *basse danse* tenor is the *Spagna.*

In the 16th century the *basse danse* became a simpler, more stereotyped dance, its music no longer based on equal-note tenor melodies but on discant melodies, like the melody of Willaert's "Jouyssance vous donneray," the example given by Arbeau (*Orchésographie,* 1589) in his description of the *basse danse;* other examples are included in several of Attaingnant's publications, e.g., *Dixhuit Basses dances garnies de recoupes et tordions* (1530). The great majority of the *basses danses* are in slow triple meter (3/2), which, however, is sometimes obscured in modern editions by the use of bar lines separating beats rather than measures [see Bar line]. (Arbeau says that "it is always necessary to reduce into ternary meter the *basses danses* given by Attaingnant in binary meter.") The basic rhythm and a typical example of the later *basse danse* (*Beurre frais*) are shown in Ex. 2 and 3. However, Attaingnant's

2

3

publications also contain a few *basses danses* in duple meter. Sometimes the 16th-century *basse danse* is followed by a *recoupe* and a *tordion,* thus forming an early example of a suite.

Lit.: E. Closson, *Le Manuscrit dit des basses danses* (fac. ed., 1912); V. Scholderer, ed., *Lart et instruction de bien dancer* (fac. ed., 1936); *Trattato . . . di Guglielmo Ebreo,* in *Scelta di curiosità letterarie* cxxxi (1873); M. Bukofzer, *Studies in Medieval & Renaissance Music* (1950), pp. 190ff; F. Blume, *Studien zur Vorgeschichte der Orchestersuite* (1925); O. Kinkeldey, "A Jewish Dancing Master of the Renaissance (Guglielmo Ebreo)," in *Studies in Jewish Bibliography* (1929); *id.,* "Dance Tunes of the Fifteenth Century," in *Instrumental Music,* ed. D. G. Hughes (1959); J. L. Jackman, ed., ‡*Fifteenth Century Basse Dances* (The Wellesley Edition, no. 6, 1964); I. Brainard, "Die Choreographie der Hoftänze in Burgund, Frankreich und Italien" (diss. Göttingen, 1956); R. Meylan, in *AM* xxxviii; E. Southern, in *CP Reese;* O. Gombosi, "About Dance and Dance Music in the late Middle Ages" (*MQ* xxvii); W. Gurlitt, "Burgundische Chanson- und deutsche Lidekunst" (*CP 1924*); H. Riemann, in *SIM* xiv; E. Hertzmann, in *ZMW* xi, 401; C. Sachs, in *AM* iii; W. Apel, in *MD* i; E. Southern, in *AM* xxxv; D. Heartz, "The Basse Dance: Its Evolution

circa 1450 to 1550" (*AnnM* vi, 28ff); L. C. Maffai, "Il libro . . . di Antonio Cornazano" (*La Bibliofilia* xvii [1915–16], 1); D. Heartz, in *JAMS* xix; *id.,* in *CP Reese.* Ex. in *HAM,* nos. 102, 105, 137; *SchGMB,* no. 90.   rev. ED.

Basse d'harmonie [F.]. Ophicleide. See Brass instruments V (c).

Basse fondamentale [F.]. Fundamental bass.

Basset horn. See under Clarinet family III.

Bassetto, bassett, bassettl. Various 18th-century names for the *cello.

Bassflöte [G.]. (1) Bass flute. (2) An 18th-century name for bassoon.

Bass horn. See under Cornett. For ill. see under Brass instruments.

Bassist [G.], **bassista** [It.]. A bass singer.

Bass lute [G. *Basslaute*]. The chitarrone, or the theorbo. See Lute III.

Basso [It.]. Bass. *B. profondo, cantante,* see Voices, range of. *B. continuo,* see Thoroughbass.

Basson [F.]. Bassoon. *B. quinte,* a smaller bassoon, also called tenoroon. *B. russe,* *Russian bassoon.

Bassoon. See under Oboe family I, C.

Basso ostinato. See Ground; also under Ostinato.

Basso ripieno [It.]. In 18th-century orchestral works, a bass part for the tutti (*ripieno) passages only, i.e., not for the solo sections.

Basso seguente. An early type of thoroughbass, which merely duplicated (usually on the organ) whatever part of a vocal composition was the lowest at any given time. Thus, in a composition beginning with a downward imitation it would start with the soprano, then pick up the alto, tenor, and finally continue with the bass. The practice of adding such a part began in the late 16th century (G. Croce, *Motetti a otto voci,* 1594). After 1600 optional organ basses of the *seguente* type were added to madrigals, etc., in order to bring them in line with contemporary trends. An example is Monteverdi's fourth book of madrigals (1603), which was reprinted in 1615 with the addition of an organ part. See M. Schneider, *Die Anfänge des Basso continuo und seiner Bezifferung* (1918); *BuMBE,* pp. 26, 35.

Bassschlüssel [G.]. The F-clef.

Bass viol. Properly (17th century), the *viola da gamba [see also Viol II]. For ill. see Violin. Today, name for the double bass, a descendant of the old double-bass viol [see Viol IV, 1].

Bathyphone. See under Clarinet family III.

Battaglia [It.]. Name for a composition in which the fanfares, cries, drum rolls, and general commotion of a battle [It. *battaglia*] are imitated. This was a favorite subject of *program music from the 16th through the 18th centuries. Late 14th-century compositions such as Grimace's *Alarme, alarme* [W. Apel, *French Secular Music of the Late Fourteenth Century,* p. 122*] represent this genre in an incipient form. It appears fully developed in a 3-voice "Alla bataglia" (*c.* 1470?) in the Chansonnier Pixérécourt. Isaac's instrumental "A la bataglia" [*DTO* 32, p. 221] is probably an arrangement of a vocal composition. Particularly famous was Janequin's "La Guerre" (1529?), a highly realistic description of the battle of Marignano of 1515 [see Editions XXV, 7]. Hans Newsidler arranged it for the lute in 1544 [see *DTO* 37]. H. M. Werrekoren (Mathias Fiamengo) wrote "Die Schlacht vor Pavia" (1544; repr. 1549 as "La Bataglia taliana"), which portrays this important battle of 1525. The artistic culmination of the vocal *battaglia* is represented by Monteverdi's "Canti guerrieri" from his *Madrigali guerrieri et amorosi* (1638). Instrumental battle pieces were written by Byrd [*My Ladye Nevells Booke,* ed. H. Andrews, 1926], Banchieri [see *ApMZ* i], J. K. Kerll [*DTB* 3; also *TaAM* vii], J. Cabanilles [*Johannes Cabanilles... Opera omnia,* ed. H. Anglés, 4 vols., 1927–56, i, 130, 170; ii, 102, 109; one of these is almost identical with that of Kerll], and others. These pieces have rather limited artistic value, but even poorer are the numerous battle pieces (mostly English) of the 18th century, some of which prescribe actual gunfire at certain moments. Franz Kotzwara's *Battle of Prague* (1788?) is still known today. Beethoven contributed to the repertory with his "battle symphony," *Wellingtons Sieg oder die Schlacht bei Vittoria* (op. 91, 1813, pub. 1816). See R. Gläsel, "Zur Geschichte der Battaglia" (diss. Leipzig, 1931); E. Bienenfeld, in *ZIM* viii; K. G. Fellerer, in *DM* xxxii, no. 7.

Battement [F.]. French 17th-century term for any ornament consisting of an alternation of two adjacent tones, e.g., mordent, trill, vibrato. In modern parlance, *battements* are the acoustical beats.

Batterie [F.]. (1) The percussion group of the orchestra. (2) A drum roll. (3) An 18th-century name for arpeggio, broken-chord figures, Alberti basses, etc. (4) A manner of playing the guitar by striking the strings.

Battery. Old term for arpeggio; see *Batterie* (3).

Battle of the Huns, The. See *Hunnenschlacht, Die.*

Battle of Victoria. See *Wellingtons Sieg.*

Battle pieces. See *Battaglia.*

Battuta [It.]. Beat. *A battuta* indicates a return to strict time after some deviation (*ad libitum, a piacere,* etc.). In particular, *battuta* means the strong beat at the beginning of a measure; hence, Beethoven's indication "ritmo di tre [quattro] battute" (Scherzo, Ninth Symphony) means that three (or four) measures are to be grouped together, the tempo being so fast that there is only one beat to the measure.

Batuque [Port.]. Term for Brazilian dances of African origin, using marked syncopation and with the percussion standing out above the other instruments. The dancers usually form wide circles and clap their hands or strike together pieces of glass, wood, or iron. The *batuque* is also known as *batucada.* It is the ancestor of the *samba and *maxixe,* which represent its modern versions, modified by urban influences.

J.O-S.

Bauernkantate [G., Peasant Cantata]. A secular cantata by Bach, written to a text by Picander in Saxon dialect ("Mer hahn en neue Oberkeet," We Have a New Magistrate) and performed in 1742 to celebrate the installation of a new magistrate in a rural district of Saxony. The music includes several popular tunes of the day.

Baxa [Sp.]. A 16th-century term for *basse danse.*

Bay Psalm Book. A book of psalms, *The Whole Booke of Psalms Faithfully Translated into English Metre,* published in Cambridge, Mass., in 1640 (the first book printed in North America). It had numerous subsequent editions over more than a century. In 1698 music (in two parts) was added for thirteen tunes. See Psalter; United States I; I. Lowens, in *JAMS* viii, 22, and in his *Music and Musicians in Early America* (1964).

Bayreuth Festival. Annual festival held in the opera house of Bayreuth (Bavaria) for the performance of Wagner's operas. It originated in 1876 with the first complete performance of the *Ring des Nibelungen.*

Bayreuth tuba. Same as Wagner tuba; see under Tuba.

B B^b bass. See under Tuba (2).

B. c. Abbr. for *basso continuo.*

Be [G.]. The sign ♭.

Beak flute. *Recorder.

Bearbeitung [G.]. Arrangement, transcription.

Beat [F. *temps;* G. *Zählzeit, Schlag;* It. *battuta;* Sp. *tiempo*]. (1) The temporal unit of a composition, as indicated by the up-and-down movements, real or imagined, of a conductor's hand (upbeat, downbeat). In modern practice, the duration of such a beat varies from M.M. 50 to M.M. 140, with M.M. 80 being a middle speed. In moderate tempo, the 4/4 measure includes four beats, the first and third of which are strong, the others weak, while the 3/4 measure has three beats, only the first of which is strong. In quick tempo, there are only two beats, or even one, to the measure. In very slow tempo, the beats may be subdivided into two's or three's. In music prior to 1600, the beat was of much less variable duration [see Tactus; *Tempus*].

(2) A 17th-century English ornament that may be performed in two ways, depending on whether it is a *plain beat* (indicated by an ascending oblique line placed before or over the written note) or a *shaked beat* (indicated by a wavy line resembling the French sign for the trill). The plain beat is an inferior *appoggiatura performed on the beat and of flexible duration. The shaked beat consists of several rapid repetitions of the appoggiatura and its resolution, beginning with the former, so that it resembles an inverted trill. In the 18th century the term beat is often applied to the ornament commonly known as *mordent.

(3) See Beats,   (2) by P.A.

Béatitudes, Les [F., The Beatitudes]. Oratorio by Franck for solo voices, chorus, and orchestra, set to the well-known text from the Scriptures [Sermon on the Mount, *Matt.* 5 : 3–12]. It was completed in 1879.

Beats [F. *battements;* G. *Schwebungen;* It. *battimenti;* Sp. *batimientos*]. An acoustical phenomenon resulting from the interference [see Acoustics VI] of two sound waves of slightly different frequencies. It is heard as minute yet clearly audible intensifications of the sound at regular intervals. The number per second of these intensifications, or beats, is equal to the difference in frequency of the two tones. Thus, a tone of 440 cycles per second will make four beats per second with a tone of 444; three with a tone of 443; two with 442; one with 441; and the beats will disappear if the two strings are in perfect unison [see ill. of interference under Acoustics]. This phenomenon is therefore of fundamental importance in *tuning. Slow beats such as two to four to the second are not unpleasant to the ear. In certain organ stops (voix céleste, unda maris) beats are deliberately introduced, by using two pipes slightly out of tune, in order to give the combined tone an undulating quality. Beats of 5 or 6 per second produce a distinctly less agreeable result, and the unpleasantness of the effect increases until the number of beats is *c.* 30. From there on the unpleasantness diminishes because the beats rapidly become too quick to be distinguished. This phenomenon is the basis of Helmholtz's theory of *consonance and dissonance. See also Combination tone.

Bebization. See Solmization.

Be bop. See Bop.

Bebung [G.; F. *balancement*]. A *vibrato effect peculiar to the clavichord, whose action allows for a repeated pressure of the finger without releasing the key, a motion causing the tangent momentarily to increase the tension of the string and thus producing slight variations in pitch. K. P. E. Bach, in his *Versuch über die wahre Art das Clavier zu spielen,* 2 vols. (1753, '62), considers *Bebung* a great advantage of the clavichord over the harpsichord and piano, which both lack this effect. It is indicated by the sign shown:

[see various editions of K. P. E. Bach's 18 *Probestücke*]. *Bebung* is mentioned in the theoretical writings of W. K. Printz (1668), J. Mattheson (1735), F. W. Marpurg (1750), K. P. E. Bach, and many later authors. The sign, however, does not occur in the literature for the clavichord before Bach.

The reference in many music books to certain passages in Beethoven and Chopin as calling for *Bebung* is misleading. *Bebung* is a fluctuation of pitch, which cannot be produced on the piano. It is possible, however, that Beethoven, in writing such passages, tried to imitate on the piano the *Bebung* of the clavichord [see Tremolo, Ex. d].

Bec [F.]. The mouthpiece of the clarinet or recorder; see Mouthpiece (b), (d).

Bécarre [F.]. The natural sign [see Accidentals]. In the 17th century it also served to indicate the major mode, e.g., *mi bécarre,* E major.

Becken [G.]. Cymbals.

Bedächtig [G.]. Unhurried, deliberate.

Be fa, befa. See under Hexachord III.

Beggar's Opera, The. Ballad opera with music arranged by J. Pepusch (libretto by John Gay), produced in London, 1728. The plot is a satirical presentation of life among the lower classes in early 18th-century London, the characters being highwaymen, pickpockets, and harlots. The most successful of all *ballad operas, it has been revived several times (F. Austin, 1920; B. Britten, 1948), with fuller harmonization and orchestration. Another revival, with much the same plot but with new music, is Weill's *Dreigroschenoper.*

Begleitung [G.]. Accompaniment.

Behaglich [G.]. Comfortably, with ease.

Behende [G.] Nimbly, quickly.

Beisser [G.]. An 18th-century name for the *mordent.

Bel. A unit for measuring changes in the intensity of sound, i.e., loudness, named for Alexander Graham Bell. One bel is equal to an interval of intensity corresponding to a tenfold increase in sound energy. Thus, if the quietest sound audible to the human ear is generated by sound energy equal to E_0 and if $E_1/E_0 = 10$, the intensity corresponding to the energy E_1 (10 times greater than E_0) is 1 bel above zero. (Zero does not mean absence of sound but is an arbitrary point of reference; in this case it means the lowest audible sound.) Because 1 bel represents a considerable change in loudness, the more commonly used unit of measure is the decibel (db), equal to one-tenth of a bel. One db represents the smallest change in loudness that the average normal ear can detect, about 26 per cent. The ear's range between audibility and pain is about 12 bels. The intensity of sounds

used in practical music varies from *c.* 25 db (softest violin tone) to 100 db (fortissimo of full orchestra). See J. Mills, *A Fugue in Cycles and Bels* [1935]; S. S. Stevens and H. Davis, *Hearing: Its Psychology and Physiology* (1938), pp. 450ff.

Bel canto [It.]. The Italian vocal technique of the 18th century, with its emphasis on beauty of sound and brilliance of performance rather than dramatic expression or romantic emotion. In spite of repeated reactions against *bel canto* (or its abuses, such as display for its own sake; Gluck, Wagner) and the frequent exaggeration of its virtuoso element (coloratura), it must be considered a highly artistic technique and the only proper one for Italian opera and Mozart. Its early development is closely bound up with that of the Italian *opera seria* (A. Scarlatti, N. A. Porpora, N. Jommelli, J. A. Hasse, N. Piccinni). More recently the term *bel canto* has been associated with a mid-17th-century development represented by L. Rossi (1597–1653) and G. Carissimi (1605–74), who cultivated a simple, melodious vocal style of songlike quality, without virtuoso coloraturas [see *BuMBE,* esp. pp. 118ff].

Lit.: C. L. Reid, *Bel Canto. Principles and Practices* (1950); H. Klein, *The Bel Canto* (1923); A. Machabey, *Le Bel Canto* (1948); B. Ulrich, *Die altitalienische Gesangsmethode* (1933); L. Landshoff, ‡*Alte Meister des Bel Canto,* 5 vols. [1912–27]; G. Silva, "The Beginnings of the Art of 'Bel Canto'" (*MQ* viii).

Belebend, belebt [G.]. Brisk, animated.

Belgium. This article deals with the musical history of the southern portion of the Low Countries (Dutch, French, and mostly Roman Catholic), as distinguished from the northern part, the Netherlands (Dutch and mostly Protestant). The highly important role that Belgium played in the earlier history of music is obscured by the name "Netherlands school," widely used for a long line of 15th- and 16th-century composers, most of whom came from Belgium [see Flemish school]. This great period, during which Belgian musicians held leading positions everywhere in Europe, was followed, after 1600, by a long period of stagnation and decline. Only in the field of organ and harpsichord music did Belgium produce composers of some historical significance, e.g., Charles Luython (*c.* 1556–1620), Pieter Cornet (fl. 1600–25), Giovanni Macque (*c.* 1550–1614; see Neapolitan school II), Charles Guillet (d. 1654), Abraham van den

Kerckhoven (*c.* 1627– after 1673), Jean-Baptiste Loeillet (1680–1730), and Joseph-Hector Fiocco (1703–41) [see Editions XXVIII; the last two followed the trends of the French rococo (F. Couperin)]. At the Brussels court, Henri-Jacques de Croes (1705–86) and Pierre van Maldere (1729–68) were prominent choral and orchestral composers; Van Maldere contributed to the introduction of bithematism in the allegro of the early symphony. The next Belgian composer to be mentioned, François Gossec (1734–1829), was influenced by the *Mannheim group, and the slightly younger André Modeste Grétry (1741–1813) plays an important role in the history of French opera (*Richard Cœur de Lion,* 1784; see Leitmotiv). It should be noted that Belgium has an ancestral claim to one of the greatest composers, Beethoven, whose grandfather lived in Mecheln [see P. Bergmans, *Les Origines belges de Beethoven* (1927); E. Closson, *The Fleming in Beethoven* (1936)].

In the 19th-century music of Belgium, Henri Vieuxtemps (1820–81) is notable, though César Franck (1822–90) is by far the most important personality. Like Tchaikovsky, Franck adhered to the concept of music as an international language, whereas Peter Benoit (1834–1901) played a role comparable to that of Smetana, namely, that of the initiator of Flemish national music, freed from German as well as French influence. He is particularly noted for his oratorios and cantatas. Among his successors, Jan Blockx (1851–1912) and Edgar Tinel (1854–1912) deserve special mention. Paul Gilson (1865–1942) adopted some elements of Russian music and is particularly known for his symphonic poem *La Mer* (1892); Lodewijk Mortelmans (1868–1952) distinguished himself as a master of the late romantic lied. A composer who during his short life wrote several works of great promise was Guillaume Lekeu (1870–94). Joseph Jongen (1873–1953) is known mainly for symphonic and chamber music, and Paul de Maleingreau (1887–1956) wrote compositions in the neoclassical style. Among more recent composers, Jean Absil (b. 1893), Marcel Poot (b. 1901), and H. Pousseur (b. 1929) are worthy of mention.

Lit.: F. van der Mueren, *Vlaamsche Muziek en Componisten* [1931]; *id., Perspectief van de Vlaamse muziek sedert Benoit* [1961]; E. Closson, and C. van den Borren, ed., *La Musique en Belgique du moyen âge à nos jours* [1950]; R. Bragard, *Histoire de la musique belge,* 2 vols. (1946, '49); R. Vannes, *Dictionnaire des musiciens (compositeurs)* [belge] [1947]; A. van der Linden,

"Belgium from 1914 to 1964," in *LBCM; LavE* i.3, 1815ff; *AdHM* ii, 1074–77; C. van den Borren, "The General Trends in Contemporary Belgian Music" (*MQ* vii); *id.,* "Belgian Music and French Music" (*MQ* ix).

Bell. (1) The bell-shaped opening of wind instruments such as the horn or trumpet.

(2) A metal percussion instrument in the shape of a hollow vessel and sounded by a clapper, usually placed inside the bell. The best alloy for bells is 76 per cent pure copper and 24 per cent pure tin. Sometimes small amounts of zinc or lead are added. The tone of a well-tuned bell is characterized by a great number of partials, which in old bells (chiefly those of the Continent) are slightly out of tune; owing to the efforts of English bell-founders (especially Taylor of Loughborough), modern English bells have five prominent partials (including the minor, not the major, third) tuned with absolute accuracy. The pitch of a bell varies inversely with the cube root of its weight. Therefore, if a bell weighing 100 pounds sounds c''' (the actual tone is nearer b''), a bell of 800 pounds ($\sqrt[3]{8} = 2$) will be needed for the tone of the half frequency, c'', one of 6,400 pounds for c', 51,200 pounds for c, and 409,600 pounds for C. The largest bell ever founded was the Tsarina Kolokol (*kolokol* means "bell") of Moscow's Kremlin (cast in 1733, damaged by fire in 1737, excavated in 1836, and now displayed in the Kremlin), which according to the best estimate weighed *c.* 432,000 pounds and measured more than 22 feet in diameter. The largest bell in existence is the Trotzkoi, also in Moscow, weighing *c.* 383,000 pounds. Old French and German bells weigh from 20,000 to 40,000 pounds. Large modern bells usually weigh from 5,000 to 15,000 pounds.

The use of bells in churches can be traced back to the 6th century (Gregory of Tours, *c.* 560); the earliest record of large bells in England dates from the 10th century (Turketyl, Abbot of Croyland); the earliest preserved bells are to be found in Italy and in Germany (11th century).

There are three chief ways of sounding church bells: (a) chiming, in which a rope moves the bell just enough for the clapper to strike it; (b) ringing, in which the bell is swung round full circle, thus giving a more vigorous sound; (c) clocking, in which the clapper is moved instead of the bell—a method that should not be used since it is likely to cause the bell to crack. Whereas in Continental Europe church bells are sounded so as to produce a confused musical noise, in England bells are rung in succession according to certain elaborate systems so that a "melody" is produced. The latter method is known as *change ringing. See also Carillon; Campana.

Bells made of bronze, silver, or gold and dating from as early as 1000 B.C. have been found in China and Egypt. In many parts of the world bells were—and still are—used to accompany ritual dances, for religious ceremonies, and for numerous other purposes. It has long been customary to hang them around the necks of domestic animals such as camels (in Arabia) or cows (Europe, etc.).

The bell effect is frequently required in compositions, early examples being the "Anthonius motet" by Busnois (d. 1492) and Bach's solo cantata *Schlage doch, gewünschte Stunde* (two bells, probably an organ stop). In the modern orchestra real bells are not used (because of their lack of definite pitch), being replaced by "tubular bells" (*chimes; see also Bells), i.e., a number (7 to 10) of cylindrical metal tubes of different lengths, hung in a frame and struck with a hammer. Debussy's "La Cathédrale engloutie" and Busoni's *Sonatina in diem nativitatis Christi MCMXVII* contain bell effects produced on the piano. See Cymbalum.

Lit.: E. Morris, *Bells of All Nations* (1951); id., *Tintinnabula: Small Bells* (1959); G. S. Tyack, *A Book about Bells* [1898]; J. J. Raven, *The Bells of England* [1906]; S. N. Coleman, *Bells* [1928], condensed as *The Book of Bells* [1938], bibl.; G. Morrison, ed., *Bells: Their History and Romance* (1932); T. Ingram, *Bells in England* (1955); J. Smits van Waesberghe, *Cymbala (Bells in the Middle Ages)* (1951); A. Weissenbäck and J. Pfundner, *Tönendes Erz: Die abendländische Glocke als Toninstrument und die historischen Glocken in Österreich* (1916); W. W. Starmer, "Bells and Bell Tones" (*PMA* xxviii); H. Bewerunge, "On the Tuning of Bells" (*ZIM* vii); J. Biehle, "Die Analyse des Glockenklanges" (*AMW* i).

Belle Hélène, La [F., The Beautiful Helen]. Satirical comedy in three acts by Offenbach (libretto by H. Meilhac and L. Halévy), produced in Paris, 1864. Setting: ancient Greece.

Bell harp. A sort of psaltery invented *c.* 1700 by John Simcock. The name comes from the bell-shaped form of its frame. See *SaRM*, p. 44.

Bell-lyra. See under Glockenspiel.

Bell ringing. See Change ringing.

Bells. Recent name for the orchestral glockenspiel or the chimes [see Percussion instruments A, 2].

Belly. The upper plate of the resonant box of violins, lutes, etc. Also, the soundboard of the piano.

Be mi, bemi. See under Hexachord III.

Bémol [F.], **bemolle** [It.]. The flat sign [see Accidentals; also Pitch names]. In the 17th century it served also to indicate the minor mode, e.g., *mi bémol*, E minor.

Benedicamus Domino [L.]. A salutation of the Roman liturgy, with the response "Deo gratias." It is used, instead of the "Ite missa est," in Masses lacking the Gloria (e.g., during Lent; cf. *LU*, pp. 22, 28, etc., with pp. 62–63). It is also sung at the end of all Offices, for which purpose various melodies (*toni*) are provided [*LU*, p. 124]. It was frequently troped, in the form of long poems, often rhyming on -*o* or closing with words such as "Benedicamus socii Domino" [see Trope]. The "Benedicamus Domino" of the Office (especially Vespers) plays a very important role in the history of early polyphony (schools of St. Martial and Notre Dame) since its melodies, especially the first one given in the Antiphonarium, have been very frequently used as the tenor of organa in two or three parts as well as of clausulae and motets [see *HAM*, nos. 28a–*i*]. See H. Schmidt, ‡*Drei Benedicamus-Domino-Organa* (1933); *Editions XLVI, 11; ReMMA*, p. 266; *ApNPM*, p. 247 (fac.); *AdHM*, p. 179; *BeMMR*, p. 97*f.*

Benediction. An extraliturgical popular service of the Roman Catholic Church, usually following Vespers and including the blessing of the congregation with the Host. See *LU*, pp. 93ff.

Benedictus Dominus Deus Israel [L.] The *canticle of Zachary (Blessed be the Lord; Luke 1 : 68–79), sung at Lauds, in the monastic Offices, and in the Anglican Morning Prayer. Not to be confused with "Benedictus es, Domine Deus Israel," the canticle of David (I Chronicles 29 : 10–13). The term Benedictus alone nearly always refers to *"Benedictus qui venit."

Benedictus qui venit [L.]. The second part of the Sanctus of the Mass. In polyphonic compositions it is usually treated as a separate movement [see Mass III].

Beneventan neumes. The neumatic script from Benevento (southern Italy) [see Neumes II].

Bequadro [It.]. The natural sign. See Accidentals.

Berceuse [F.]. Lullaby. Usually the name refers to instrumental pieces (piano, orchestra) in moderate 6/8 time and with an accompaniment reminiscent of the rocking of a cradle. A famous example is Chopin's op. 57.

Bergamasca. (1) A generic term for dances, dance-songs, and popular poetry from the district of Bergamo in northern Italy. Early musical examples occur in G. Gorzanis' *Il Terzo Libro de intabolatura di liuto,* 1564 (no. 12, "Saltarello dito il Bergamasco") and in F. Azzaiolo's *Il Terzo Libro delle villotte del fiore alla padoana con alcune napolitane e bergamaschi,* 1569 (nos. 3 and 7, "Bergamasca"). Gorzanis' title suggests it is music for a Bergamascan dance; Azzaiolo's refer to the texts written in the Bergamascan dialect. The music is different in each of the three examples, and none is related to the harmonic pattern described below. Many compositions—even sophisticated ones—written in the 17th, 18th, and 19th centuries bear the title because of real or fancied relationship to Bergamo [see *MGG,* 1685–87]. Debussy wrote a *Suite bergamasque,* an example of a free composition based on impressions of the peasant life of Bergamo.

(2) Late in the 16th century, the term was attached to pieces composed on repetitions of a specific harmonic pattern: I–IV–V–I [cf. G. C. Barbetta, *Intavolatura de liuto,* 1585, p. 14, "Moresca quarta deta la Bergamasca" and J. Abondante, *Il Quinto Libro de tabolatura da liuto,* 1587, p. 58, "Bergamasca"]. In the 17th century, hundreds of compositions, largely for the guitar, were written on that pattern. Early in the 17th century a single discant began to be associated with it and in some cases supplanted the pattern itself [see Frescobaldi's "Bergamasca" in the *Fiori Musicali,* 1635]. It is worth noting that the melody "Kraut und Rüben" used by Bach in the final *quodlibet* of his Goldberg Variations is the same discant.

The I–IV–V–I pattern has a long history predating its association with the title bergamasca. Adumbrated forms occur in late 15th-

and early 16th-century sources such as the "Cancionero Musical de Palacio" and Italian MSS dating from the turn of the century. The earliest examples of variations on the pattern proper are found in G. A. Casteliono's *Intabolatura de leuto* [1536] (f. 24v), "Le riprese" of the "Saltarelo chiamato el Mazolo," and M. Barberiis' *Intabolatura di lauto* ix, 1549, no. 25, "Saltarello."   L.H.M.

Bergerette [F.]. (1) An 18th-century type of French lyric poetry with a pastoral or amorous subject [F. *berger,* shepherd]. See J.-B. Weckerlin, *Bergerettes* (Eng. ed. 1913). (2) In the 15th century, bergerette denoted a fixed form of French poetry and music, identical in structure with the *virelai* but having only one stanza. Early examples of this type (by Grenon, Binchois) may be virelais of which only one stanza has been preserved. After 1450, however, the one-stanza type was generally adopted (Ockeghem, Busnois, Chansonnier Laborde, Copenhagen Chansonnier, "Odhecaton," etc.). The story that Busnois invented the bergerette is generally discredited [see *ReMR,* p. 15, 69n]. See H. Hewitt, *Harmonice Musices Odehecaton A* (1942), pp. 49ff; R. W. Linker and G. S. McPeek, in *JAMS* vii. (3) In the 16th century, a title (rarely used) for instrumental dances in quick triple time, similar to the *saltarello.*

Berg(k)reyen [Old G.; G. *Bergreihen,* mountain dance]. Title of 16th- and 17th-century collections of popular poetry, mainly from the mountainous area of Silesia (*Erzgebirge*), having religious as well as various secular subjects, such as the work of miners. Only two of the numerous publications, Erasmus Rotenbucher's *Bergkreihen* (1551) and Melchior Franck's *Musicalischer Bergkreyen* (1602; *Editions VIII, 38), contain music. The exact meaning of such designations as "auf Bergkreyen Weis" (Johann Walter, *Geystlich Gesangk-Buchleyn,* 1524) or "Bergkraische Art" (Kaspar Othmayr, *Bicinia sacra,* 1547?) is not clear. Also see *MGG* i, 1696ff.

Bergomaska. Same as *bergamasca.

Berkshire Festival. See under Festivals.

Berlin school. Collective designation for a group of composers, also known as *Norddeutsche* (North German) *Schule,* who worked in Berlin during the second half of the 18th century. Most of them were connected with the court of Frederick the Great (1712–86), who with his numerous flute sonatas and other compositions himself contributed actively to the musical life of his court. The most important members of the group were: J. J. Quantz (1697–1773; flute sonatas, etc.); J. G. Graun (1703–71; symphonies, trio sonatas); K. H. Graun (1704–59; opera *Montezuma,* text by Frederick the Great [*DdT* 15], and oratorio *Der Tod Jesu*); F. Benda (1709–86; violin sonatas, concertos); K. P. E. Bach (1714–88); C. Nichelmann (1717–62; songs, harpsichord sonatas); F. W. Marpurg (1718–95; songs; editor of *Berlinische Oden und Lieder,* 3 vols. [1756–63]; numerous theoretical books); J. P. Kirnberger (1721–83; songs, harpsichord pieces, theoretical books); and J. F. Agricola (1720–74; operas, songs).

While these men, particularly K. P. E. Bach, made significant contributions in instrumental music, their activity in the field of the lied (*Berliner Liederschule*) was largely frustrated by the spirit of rationalism and the Enlightenment to which Frederick the Great, a close friend of Voltaire's, had given ready admittance. The situation changed when a younger generation, known as the *Zweite* (Second) *Berliner Liederschule,* turned from the dry moralism of Gellert to the inspiring poems of Klopstock and the young Goethe. J. A. P. Schulz (1747–1800), J. F. Reichardt (1752–1814), and C. F. Zelter (1758–1832) are the most important members of this group. See Lied IV; also Singspiel. The name *Berliner Schule* is sometimes restricted to this latter group.

Lit.: *AdHM* ii, 699ff; M. Friedländer, *Das deutsche Lied im 18. Jahrhundert,* 2 vols. (1902); M. Flueler, "Die norddeutsche Sinfonie" (diss. Berlin, 1908); H. Hoffmann, "Die norddeutsche Triosonate" (diss. Kiel, 1924); E. Stiltz, "Die Berliner Klaviersonate zur Zeit Friedrichs des Grossen" (diss. Berlin, 1930); A. Mayer-Reinach, "Carl Heinrich Graun als Opernkomponist" (*SIM* i).

Bersag horn. See under Brass instruments IV.

Beruhigt, beruhigend [G.]. Calm, quieting.

Bes [G.]. B-double-flat.

Beschleunigt [G.]. Accelerando.

Besetzung [G.]. A term denoting the instruments and/or voices employed in a composition, e.g., *Besetzung für Chor und kleines Orchester* (for chorus and small orchestra). There is no exact English equivalent for this, although "scored" and "setting" come close to it.

Bestimmt [G.]. With decision.

Betont [G.]. Stressed, emphasized.

Bewegt [G.]. Animated, with motion.

Bezifferter Bass [G.]. Figured bass, i.e., *thoroughbass.

B fa. See under Hexachord III.

BG. Abbr. for *Bach-Gesellschaft* [see under Societies II, 2].

B. & H. Abbr. for Breitkopf & Härtel, publishers of numerous complete editions.

Biann. Same as *pien.

Bible regal [G. *Bibelregal*]. See Regal.

Bibliography of music. Following is a list of the most important publications in the field of music bibliography, divided into three sections: I. Bibliographies of music (compositions); II. Bibliographies of books on music; III. History (bibliographies before 1850). For a very comprehensive bibliography, now in process of publication, see *RISM.*

I. *Bibliographies of music.* O. E. Albrecht, *A Census of Autograph Music Manuscripts of European Composers in American Libraries* (1953); American Society of Composers, Authors and Publishers, *ASCAP Symphonic Catalog* (1959); F. P. Berkowitz, *Popular Titles and Subtitles of Musical Compositions* (1962); A. Boll, *Répertoire analytique de la musique française des origines à nos jours* [1948]; H. Brown, *Instrumental Music Printed before 1600* (1965); A. Davidsson, *Catalogue critique et descriptif des imprimés de musique des XVIe et XVIIe siècles, conservés dans les bibliothèques suédoises, excepté la Bibliothèque de l'Université Royale d'Upsala* (1952); R. Eitner, *Biographisch-bibliographisches Quellen-Lexikon der Musiker und Musikgelehrten der christlichen Zeitrechnung bis zur Mitte des 19. Jahrhunderts,* 10 vols. (1900–04; rev. ed., 11 vols. in 6, 1959); *id., Verzeichnis neuer Ausgaben alter Musikwerke aus der frühesten Zeit bis zum Jahre 1800* (1871); *id.* and F. X. Haberl, *et al., Bibliographie der Musik-Sammelwerke des XVI. und XVII. Jahrhunderts* (1877; repr. 1963); W. H. Frere, *Bibliotheca Musico-Liturgica,* 2 vols. (1901–32); F. Gennrich, *Bibliographie der ältesten französischen und lateinischen Motetten* (1957); A. Hofmeister, ed., *C. F. Whistlings Handbuch der musikalischen Literatur oder allgemeines systematisch-geordnetes Verzeichnis . . . bis zum Anfang des Jahres 1844 ergänzte Auflage* (1845; 3 parts, bibl. to 1844 [1845]; vols. iv–vi, covering 1844–51 [1852–68]; vols. vii–xviii, ed. F. Hofmeister [1876–1934]); W. Lott, *Verzeichnis der Neudrucke alter Musik,* 7 vols. (1937–43); *Universal-Handbuch der Musikliteratur aller Zeiten und Völker,* 14 vols. (1904–10?); A. Taylor and F. H. Ellis, *A Bibliography of Meistergesang* (Indiana Univ. Studies, no. 113, 1936); E. Vogel, *Bibliothek der gedruckten weltlichen Vocalmusik Italiens aus den Jahren 1500–1700,* 2 vols. (1892).

See also the authors mentioned in the following articles: *Ars antiqua* (Ludwig); *Ars nova* (Von Fischer); Autographs (Winternitz); Cello (Nogué, Weigl); Chamber music (Altmann, Richter); Chorale (Wackernagel, Zahn); Church music (Bäumker, Schreiber); Clarinet family (Foster, Opperman); Conductus (Gröninger); Double bass (Grodner); Editions (Heyer); Flute (Girard, Pellerite); Hymn (Chevalier); Instrumental music (Altmann, Sartori); Lied (Friedländer); Meistersinger (Linker); Minnesinger (Linker); Motet (Gennrich, Ludwig); Opera (Altmann, Loewenberg); Organ (Weigel); Organum (Geering, Ludwig); Piano duet (Moldenhauer, Rowley); Piano music (Prosniz, Friskin, Parent, Teichmüller, Ruthardt); Quartet (Altmann); Quintet (Altmann); Recorder (Winterfeld); String quartet (Altmann); Trio (Altmann); Troubadour (Gennrich, Pillet); Trouvère (Raynaud); United States (Sonneck); Violin (Tottman); Violin music (Baudet-Maget); Vocal music (Kagen, Knapp); Wind instruments (Helm); Woodwinds (Houser).

II. *Bibliographies of books on music* (arr. alphabetically by author): A. Aber, *Handbuch der Musikliteratur in systematisch-chronologischer Anordnung* (1922); H. Alker, *Blockflöten-bibliographie* (1960); H. W. Azhderian, *Reference Works in Music and Music Literature in Five Libraries of Los Angeles County* (1953); A. P. Basart, *Serial Music, A Classified Bibliography of Writings on Twelve-Tone and Electronic Music* (1961); C. W. Beaumont, *A Bibliography of Dancing* (1929); *Bibliographie des Musikschriftums* (1936–64); *A Bibliography of Periodical Literature in Musicology,* 2 vols. (1940, '43); A. Davidsson, *Bibliographie der musiktheoretischen Drucke des 16. Jahrhunderts* (1962); *Deutsche Musikbibliographie* (Jahrgang 1 [1829—], supersedes *Handbuch der musikalischen Literatur* [1817–29]; Jahrgang 1–79: *Musikalisch-literarische Monatsbericht über neue Musikalien, musikalische Schriften und Abbildung;* Jahrgang 79–114: *Hofmeisters musikalisch-literarischer Monatsbericht*); R. Eitner, *Bücherverzeichnis der Musik-literatur aus*

den Jahren 1839 bis 1846 im Anschluss an Becker und Büchting (1885); H. M. Hewitt, *Doctoral Dissertations in Musicology,* rev. ed. (1960; new ed., 1965; additions appear in *JAMS*); *JMP* [see Abbreviations]; W. Kahl and W.-M. Luther, *Repertorium der Musikwissenschaft* (1953); E. C. Krohn, *The History of Music; An Index to the Literature Available in a Selected Group of Musicological Publications* (1952); E. B. Long and M. McKee, *A Bibliography of Music for the Dance* (1936); P. D. Magriel, *A Bibliography of Dancing* (1936); A. P. Merriam, *A Bibliography of Jazz* (1954); *The Music Index; The Key to Current Music Periodical Literature* (1949—); Music Teachers National Association, *Volume of Proceedings* (1906–50); R. G. Reisner, *The Literature of Jazz; A Selective Bibliography,* rev. ed. (1959); R. Schaal, *Verzeichnis deutschsprachiger musikwissenschaftlicher Dissertationen, 1861–1960* (1963; add. in *MF* xvii, 421ff).

See also the authors mentioned in the following articles: Africa (Thieme); Arab music (Farmer); Asia (Waterman); Brazil (Correia); Congresses (Briquet); Dictionaries of music (Coover); Ethnomusicology (Herzog); Flute (Miller); Folk music (Haywood, Henry, Lomax); Jazz (Merriam, Reisner); Jewish music (Sendrey); Latin America (Chase); Periodicals (Freystätter, Rohlfs); Printing of music (Steele); Publishing (Lesure and Thibault, Sartori, Smith, Stellfeld); Serial music (Basart); Sweden (Davidsson); Theory (Davidsson, Smits); Violin (Heron-Allen).

Additional bibliographical information is available in library catalogs [see Libraries], in current book lists of periodicals (*AM, MD, MQ, Notes, ZIM, ZMW*), and in the bibliographies of nearly all books on music history. For lists of records, see Phonograph (Lit.) and the current lists in *Notes.* For microfilm material, see *Union List of Microfilms* (Ann Arbor, 1951—; entries on music are marked M or ML) and *Deutsches Musikgeschichtliches Archiv Kassel, Katalog der Filmsammlung,* nos. 1–7 (1955–65; continued).

III. *History.* The earliest bibliographical material of interest consists of dealers' catalogs (*Messkataloge*) published for the annual book fairs (G. *Buchmesse*) at Frankfurt (*c.* 1560 and later) and Leipzig (*c.* 1600 and later). An important bibliographical publication of early date is Georg Draudius, *Bibliotheca librorum germanicorum classica* (1611, 1625), which includes a separate chapter of "Teutsche musicalische Bücher" in alphabetical arrangement: *Allmand, Balletten, Bergreyhen,* etc. (fac. ed. by K. Ameln,

1957). Sébastien de Brossard, author of the *Dictionaire de musique* (1703), worked for many years on a bibliographical work that he could not complete. L. Mizler, with his *Musikalische Bibliothek* (1735–54), J. Adlung, with his *Anleitung zu der musikalischen Gelahrtheit* (1758), and J. G. Walther, with his *Musicalisches Lexikon oder musicalische Bibliotec* (1732), paved the way for J. N. Forkel's monumental *Allgemeine Litteratur der Musik* (1792), which has retained considerable value to the present day (it includes about 3,000 titles). The last two volumes of P. Lichtenthal's *Dizionario e bibliografia della musica,* 4 vols. (1826), are an abridged translation of Forkel's work brought up to date. Somewhat later K. F. Becker published his *Systematisch-chronologische Darstellung der musikalischen Literatur,* 2 vols. (1836, '39). There followed, in 1870 and later, Eitner's work, which marks the beginning of modern musical bibliography.

Lit.: L. B. Spiess, *Historical Musicology* [1963]; V. Duckles, *Music Reference and Research Materials,* rev. ed. (1967); K. E. Mixter, *General Bibliography for Music Research* (1962); *id., An Introduction to Library Resources for Music Research* (1963); A. H. King, *Recent Work in Music Bibliography* (1945); O. E. Deutsch, *Music Bibliography and Catalogues* (1943); A. Göhler, *Verzeichnis der in den Frankfurter und Leipziger Messkatalogen der Jahre 1564 bis 1759 angezeigten Musikalien* (1902); L. R. McColvin and H. Reeves, *Music Libraries . . . with a Bibliography of Music and Musical Literature,* 2 vols. (1937, '38); M. Brenet, "Bibliographie des bibliographies musicales" (*L'Année musicale* iii, 1913); K. Meyer, in *CP Wolf;* G. Schulz, in *CP Sandberger;* H. Springer, in *CP 1925.* See under II, above, Kahl and Luther, *Repertorium,* pp. 2–8.

Biblioteca di rarità musicali. See Editions V.

Bicinium. A 16th-century name, used chiefly in Italy and Germany, for a composition (vocal or instrumental) in two parts. In contrast to the *duet, *bicinia* are without accompaniment. The Greek synonym *diphona* also has been used.

The *bicinia,* which form a delightful contrast to the rich texture of the late 16th-century motet, madrigal, etc., represent a little-known treasure of great artistic value and educational significance. The earliest known publication of this type is the *Musica di Eustachio Romano* of 1521 [see K. Jeppesen, *Die italienische Orgelmusik am Anfang des Cinquecento* (1943), p. 18]. A number of French and Italian compositions of a slightly

later date are reproduced in Editions XIX, 8. The most important German publications are: Georg Rhaw, *Bicinia Gallica Latina Germanica* (1545; partly repr. by K. Ameln, ed., 1950; H. Reichenbach, ed., 1961); Kaspar Othmayr, *Bicinia sacra* (1547; partly repr. by W. Lipphardt, ed., 1957); Erasmus Rotenbucher, *Diphona amoena et florida* (1549; repr., D. Degen, ed., 1951, as vol. lxxiv of *Hortus musicus*); Seth Calvisius, *Bicinia septuaginta ad sententias Evangelioram* (1599), *Biciniorum libri duo* (1612); Erhard Bodenschatz, *Bicinia XC. selectissima* (1615; see *SchGMB,* no. 163). Outstanding examples are found among the works of Ludwig Senfl (*DTB* 5, pp. 79ff) and Michael Praetorius (comp. ed., vol. ix and *passim;* see *HAM,* no. 167a). Italian publications of *bicinia* are Antonio Gardano, *Il primo libro a due voci de diversi autori* (1543, '53) and Pietro Vinci, *Il primo libro della musica a due voci* (1560). Vincenzo Galilei's *Contrapunti a due voci* of 1584 (see Editions XLVIII, 8) and about half the duets of Lasso (*Sämtliche Werke,* 1894–1926, vol. i) are without text, as are the numerous pieces in two parts that were published in Italy during the 17th century under the name *ricercare* [see Ricercar II (d); also Invention]. Such pieces were primarily instructive in purpose; see A. Einstein, "Vincenzo Galilei and the Instructive Duo" (*ML* xviii, 360; in It., *LRM* xi) and D. Kämper, "Das Lehr- und Instrumentalduo um 1500 in Italien" (*MF* xviii). S. Scheidt, in his *Tabulatura nova* (1624), uses the term *bicinium* for organ verses and variations in two voice-parts. Also see *Tricinium.*

Bien nourri. See *Nourri.*

Billy Budd. Opera in four acts by Benjamin Britten (libretto by E. M. Forster and E. Crozier, after the short novel by H. Melville), produced in London, 1951. Setting: aboard *H.M.S. Indomitable,* 1797. The music is somber, providing an effective background for the tragic events of the plot.

Bina. Same as vīṇa [see India VIII; Inst. IV].

Binary and ternary form. I. Two basic musical forms consisting of two and three main sections respectively. The binary form follows the scheme A B, with each section repeated; the ternary form (also called *song form) follows the scheme A B A. Examples of the former abound in the allemandes, gavottes, etc., of Bach's suites, while the latter is frequently found in the slow movements of sonatas (e.g., Beethoven, Piano Sonata op. 7; op. 10, no. 3), in the minuet or scherzo with trio, and in numerous *character pieces of the romantic composers, such as Schumann's novelettes, Chopin's nocturnes, Brahms' fantasias, etc.

The binary and ternary forms are not so similar as the nomenclature might suggest. In fact, to consider them analogous forms is quite misleading. The binary form is essentially a stylistic and structural entity, a unified whole that, like many phrases in music, falls into two parts, the second of which forms the logical and necessary completion of the first. The ternary form, on the other hand, is usually the sum of three single units, each complete in itself. This difference is clearly reflected in the harmonic scheme normally found in these forms: in the binary form each section is harmonically "open," the first leading from T to D, the second back from D to T; in the ternary form each section is harmonically "closed," beginning and ending in the same key but with a different key (dominant, relative key, parallel key) often used for the middle section. Stylistic considerations corroborate this fundamental difference: the binary form uses the same or similar material throughout, whereas the ternary form uses different, often contrasting material for the middle section. In brief, the binary form is a continuous form, the ternary a sectional form. The minuet (scherzo) with trio of the sonata combines the two forms, since the whole movement is in ternary form and each section is usually in binary form.

II. The historical development of the binary form is of particular interest, since it includes one of the most important developments of music history, namely, that leading to the sonata form of the classical sonata, symphony, etc. Owing to the fact that this form includes three main sections—the exposition, the development, and the recapitulation (= exposition)—it is frequently considered a ternary form. Such an interpretation, although perhaps admissible in program notes, is too much of an oversimplification for serious studies. Its main drawback is that it does not take into account the repetition of the exposition that is almost invariably prescribed in the works of the Viennese classical composers, including Brahms—an oversight for which the blame must be put on conductors and pianists who in performance consistently disregard a feature whose aesthetic importance was clearly recognized by the great masters of the sonata. Another objection is that in sonata form the middle section (development) is based on the thematic material of the first section (exposi-

tion),whereas in true ternary form it has different, contrasting material. Finally, the historical development of sonata form clearly shows its derivation from binary schemes, such as were used in the dance movements of the suite [see Sonata form II]. Three such schemes can be distinguished: (1) the *symmetrical binary form,* in which both sections are of equal length; (2) the *asymmetrical binary form,* in which the second section is longer than the first, owing to a "bulging-out" process at its beginning; (3) the *rounded binary form,* where the first section is repeated, in whole or in part, at the end of the second [see Ex.1–3]. The last is structurally

identical with the earlier type of sonata form (Haydn, Mozart) in which both sections are repeated. The same scheme is used in some dance movements and other pieces by J. S. Bach (e.g., in the Anglaise from his French Suite no. 3, in the C-minor Fantasy, and in the Prelude in D of *The Well-Tempered Clavier,* vol. ii, as well as in practically all the minuets (scherzos) and trios of the classical period. In fact, any of these pieces may well serve as a rudimentary example of sonata form. For a medieval type of binary form in which the first section only is repeated (as in the later examples of sonata form), see *Bar* form II.

III. The principle of ternary structure is present in various types of Gregorian chant, e.g., in the responsories and graduals, in which the respond is repeated after the verse: R V R [see Psalmody, Gregorian II]. Also tripartite are the *Agnus and *Kyrie. The ternary form of *"L'Homme armé" probably accounts to a large extent for its popularity as the basis of Mass compositions. Many of the chansons of the early 16th century are in the form A B A, e.g., Josquin's "Faulte d'argent" [*HAM*, no. 91]. The idea of a contrasting middle section is quite clearly expressed in the shepherd's solo of Monteverdi's *Orfeo*, 1607 [see also his famous duet "Pur ti miro" from *L'Incoronazione di Poppea*, 1642; *SchGMB*, no. 178]. Ternary form with a continuing rather than contrasting middle section became established in the *da capo* aria, c. 1700. Another manifestation of the ternary principle is the alternation of two dances, the first being repeated after the second [see *Alternativo*]. In 19th-century music, the ternary form was frequently broadened into a five-part scheme: A B A B A or A B A C A, particularly in slow movements of symphonies, e.g., in Bruckner's Symphony no. 7. See Forms, musical; Rondo. See E. J. Dent, "Binary and Ternary Form" (*ML* xvii, 309).

Bind. Same as *tie.

Biniou. See under Bagpipe.

Bird song. The song of birds, being practically the only case of "music in nature," has been the subject of numerous studies. Interesting facts are that only small birds sing, that the best singers (nightingale, lark, thrush, blackbird, finches) are unobtrusively colored, that they prefer to sing in solitude rather than in flocks, that only male birds have loud musical voices, and that good singers are found mainly in moderate climates.

Much attention has been given to the relationship between bird song and man-made music. Certainly no biological relationship exists, since most animals do not sing. Whether or not man's music developed in imitation of bird song, as has been frequently maintained, is a matter of speculation. Although bird song does have many features in common with some primitive folksong (irregularity, wavering of pitch, microtonic deviations from the Western scale, improvisation), this type of folksong exists chiefly in the non-Western countries (Africa, Asia) where there are few singing birds. Concerning

the imitation of bird song in art music, see Program music III.

Lit.: S. P. Cheney, *Wood Notes Wild* (1892); F. S. Mathews, *Fieldbook of Wild Birds and Their Music* (1904); W. Garstang, *Songs of the Birds* (1922); A. R. Brand, *More Songs of Wild Birds* (1936; with records); E. M. Nicholson and L. Koch, *Songs of Wild Birds* (1936; with records); A. A. Saunders, *A Guide to Bird Songs . . . of Northwestern United States* (1935); W. B. Hoffmann, *Kunst und Vogelgesang* (1908); H. Tiessen, *Musik der Natur* [1953]; J. Graf, *Vogelstimmen in Natur und Kunst* [1962]; W. B. Olds, in *MQ* viii.

Bis [L.]. (1) In French and Italian, request for *encore. (2) Indication that notes or passages should be repeated.

Bisbigliando [It.]. A special effect of harp playing, obtained by a quickly reiterated motion of the finger and resulting in a soft tremolo.

Biscroma [It.]. Thirty-second-note. See Notes.

Bisdiapason [L.]. The interval or range of two octaves.

Bistropha. Same as *distropha*. See Neumes I (table).

Bitonality, polytonality. The simultaneous use of two (occasionally three or four) different keys in different parts of the musical fabric, e.g., B-flat minor in the left hand against F-sharp minor in the right hand of a piano piece [Ex. 1, from Prokofiev's *Sarcasmes*, op. 17, no. 3, 1912–14]. This device has been used considerably by 20th-century composers seeking new effects within the general framework of tonality. The combination of C against F-sharp or, in terms of the piano

keyboard, of "white against black," has become known as the "Petrushka chord" because it occurs in Stravinsky's *Petrushka,* composed in 1911 [Ex. 2]. This device has been exploited, somewhat facetiously, by numerous other composers, often in pieces they consider suitable for children (A. Casella, *11 Pezzi infantili,* 1920). The main champion of bitonal music has been Darius Milhaud, who also occasionally used three or four keys simultaneously.

Prior to *c.* 1900 bitonality was occasionally used for satirical purposes, e.g., by Hans Newsidler in his lute piece *Der Juden Tantz* (The Jew's Dance) of 1544 [see *HAM,* no. 105b] and by Mozart in his *Ein musikalischer Spass* (A Musical Joke), composed in 1787 (K. 522). Bitonality was generally accepted about 1910, but earlier examples occur in Ravel's *Jeux d'eau* (1901; C and F major) and in the works of Charles Ives, whose *Variations on "America"* for organ (1891) has two Interludes (added before 1894), the second written in F major against A-flat major. It is interesting to note that Ives, as if afraid of his boldness, marks one of the conflicting keys *ppp,* the other, *ff.*

Lit.: J. Deroux, "La Musique polytonale" (*RM* 1921, no. 11; 1923, no. 4); A. Machabey, "Dissonance, polytonalité, atonalité" (*RM* 1931, no. 116).

Biwa. The Japanese lute. See Pyiba. For ill. see Lute.

Bkl. [G.]. Abbr. for *Bassklarinette,* bass clarinet.

Blackening. Same as coloration [see Mensural notation V].

Bladder pipe [G. *Platerspiel*]. See under Bagpipe.

Blanche [F.]. Half note. See Notes.

Blasinstrument [G.]. Wind instrument. *Blasmusik,* music for wind instruments.

Blasquinte [G.]. See Blown fifth.

Blatt [G.]. Sheet; also, reed (**Rohrblatt*). *Blattspiel,* sight reading.

Blech [G.]. Brass, used as a collective designation for *Blechinstrumente,* i.e., brass instruments. *Blechmusik,* music for brass bands.

Blind musicians. Many blind persons are musically gifted and have become expert performers, particularly on the organ. Some of them have achieved great fame as composers or theorists,

e.g., Francesco Landini, Conrad Paumann, Arnolt Schlick (perhaps blind only late in life, like Bach), Antonio de Cabezón, Francisco de Salinas, Antonio Valente (?), Martino Pesenti (*cieco a nativitate*), Pablo Bruna (*Ciego de Daroca*), and Pablo Nassarre. Also see Braille music notation. See H. J. Moser, *Blinde Musiker aus Sieben Jahrhunderten* [1956].

Blind octaves. A trick device of piano virtuosity. Both hands alternate rapidly with octaves, the passage (usually a trill or a scale) being played with the thumbs and doubled by the little fingers alternately in the higher and lower octave.

Blockflöte [G.]. Block flute, i.e., recorder. See also under Whistle flute.

Block harmony. Term for a succession of identical or similar chords, e.g., parallel triads or seventh chords, a characteristic trait of Debussy's piano style. See Parallel chords.

Blown fifth [G. *Blasquinte*]. A term introduced by E. von Hornbostel for a fifth of 678 cents, i.e., ⅛ of a whole tone lower than the Pythagorean (pure) and tempered fifth (of 702 and 700 cents respectively). From this interval, which results if a stopped pipe (bamboo) is overblown, Hornbostel derived a circle of blown fifths (*Blasquintenzirkel*) similar to that of the ordinary *circle of fifths and based on the absolute pitch of the Chinese *hwangjong* (*huang chung*) [see China II]. He was able to show that these tones recur in many musical cultures of the Far East and South America, most clearly in the Javanese *pélog* scale [see Java]. Recent studies have shown, however, that the blown fifth is without physical foundation. Hornbostel's theory has been attacked by Bukofzer and Lloyd, and defended by Kunst.

Lit.: E. M. von Hornbostel, "Die Massnorm als kulturgeschichtliches Forschungsmittel" (*Festschrift . . . P. W. Schmidt,* 1928); id., "Musikalische Tonsysteme," in H. Geiger and K. Scheel, *Handbuch der Physik,* vol. viii (1927); M. F. Bukofzer, in *Zeitschrift für Physik,* vol. 99

(1936); *id.*, in *Anthropos* xxxii (1937); *id.*, in *CP 1939;* L. Lloyd, in *Monthly Musical Record* lxxvi; J. Kunst, "Around von Hornbostel's Theory of the Cycle of Blown Fifths (*Mededeling* no. 81, *Afdeeling volkenkunde* no. 30, Koninlijk Vereeniging Indisch Instituut, 1948). Also s.v. "Blasquinte" in *MGG.*

Bluebeard's Castle [Hung. *A Kékszakállú Herceg Vára*]. Opera in one act by Bartók (libretto by B. Balázs after Maeterlinck), produced in Budapest, 1918. Setting: hall in Bluebeard's castle.

Blue notes. See Blues.

Blues. A type of American popular music, both vocal and instrumental, introduced in the first decade of the 20th century. Despite evidence of earlier examples ("Mamie's Blues," *c.* 1900), its traceable history begins with the "Jelly Roll Blues," written by Jelly Roll Morton in 1905 (© 1915) and W. C. Handy (pub. "Memphis Blues" in 1912). The principal sources of the blues appear to be Negro work songs and spirituals. Although the blues evolved in part from spirituals, there are numerous differences between the two genres. The spirituals are sung by groups of worshipers, whereas the blues are solo utterances. Prior to 1920, spirituals were sung without instrumental accompaniment, whereas the accompaniment is a vital part of a blues performance. The tempo of many spirituals is fast and the dynamic level is usually very high, whereas the blues are generally in slow tempo and sung on a medium dynamic level.

The blues are distinguished from the earlier *ragtime by several features: (1) groups of 12 measures rather than of 8 or 16; (2) more frequent harmonization with seventh chords, especially with those on the subdominant side of the key (I^{b7}, IV^{b7}), as well as with those in rapid succession, producing *barbershop harmonies; (3) a melody in the tradition of the work songs and spirituals, making the early blues more singable than ragtime; (4) usually the presence of special melodic features (also found in spirituals) such as (a) certain "blue" notes, i.e., notes (in particular the III and VII degrees, later also the V) whose intonation is unstable and lies between the normal major and minor pitches, (b) the use of portamento, and (c) cadential formulas that avoid the VII degree in favor of II or VI as penultimate tone of the melody; (5) a trend toward declamatory style with a steady pulsating accompaniment, and a smoother, less percussive, and less staccato rhythm as well as a slower

tempo in the blues of New Orleans and St. Louis (as contrasted with the fast blues of Texas); (6) frequent use of habanera and tango rhythms; (7) use of the "break," a brief improvised instrumental cadenza (usually about two measures) characterized by many syncopations. See W. C. Handy, ed., ‡*A Treasury of the Blues* (1949); Carl Gregor Herzog zu Mecklenburg and W. Scheck, *Die Theorie des Blues in modernen Jazz* (1963); O. Gombosi, "The Pedigree of the Blues" (*Proceedings of the Music Teachers National Association,* 1946, p. 382). Also see Jazz I.

L.H.; rev. J.W.W.

Blumen [G.]. Name for the coloraturas of the Meistersinger.

B mi. See under Hexachord III.

B-minor Mass. A great Mass by Bach, for soloists, chorus, and orchestra, composed 1733–38 to the (Latin) text of the Roman Catholic *Mass. The five items of the Mass are subdivided into many sections treated as choruses, arias, duets, etc. Several of these are rewritten from earlier cantatas, among them the famous *Crucifixus* (from Cantata no. 12, *Weinen, Klagen*). The fact that the foremost Protestant composer wrote a Catholic Mass has long been a matter of special interest and controversy. Undoubtedly some opportunism was involved when, in 1733, Bach sent the Kyrie and Gloria to the Catholic King of Saxony, requesting the title of court composer. Whatever the motives, we can only be grateful that denominational considerations are set aside in this magnificent work.

B moll [G.]. B-flat minor.

B. M. V. See under Antiphon (2).

Bobization. See under Solmization III.

Bocal [F.]. Mouthpiece of a brass instrument.

Bocca chiusa [It.]. Same as *bouche fermée. Bocca ridente* (laughing mouth) indicates, in singing, a smiling position of the lips.

Bocedization. See under Solmization III.

Bockstriller [G.]. See Goat's trill.

Boehm. See Böhm system.

Boethian notation. See under Letter notation.

Bogen [G.]. (1) The bow of a violin, etc. (2) The *tie. *Bogenform,* see Forms, musical (after I, A). *Bogenführung,* bowing. *Bogenklavier, Bogenflügel,* see Sostenente piano.

Bohème, La. Opera in four acts by Puccini (libretto by G. Giacosa and L. Illica, based on H. Mürger's novel *Scènes de la vie de Bohème*), produced in Turin, 1896. Setting: Latin Quarter, Paris, 1830. One of the best-known examples of *verismo, the opera is, with its light texture, orchestral clarity, and lyricism, closer to the French than to the typically Italian (Verdi) opera. Interesting are the *parallel chords in the opening to the second act. Leoncavallo wrote an unsuccessful opera on the same subject (produced in Venice, 1897), without knowledge of Puccini's score.

Bohemian music. See Czechoslovakia.

Böhm clarinet (flute). See Böhm system; Clarinet family I; Flute I.

Böhm system. A system of keying a woodwind instrument that allows the holes to be cut in the proper acoustical position and size and yet be within the spread of the average hand. It was invented about 1830 by the flutist Theobald Böhm (1794–1881) of Munich to supersede earlier methods of keying, in which the holes were not placed exactly from the acoustical point of view but in a sort of compromise position, with greater regard for the hand than for the ear. In spite of its complicated mechanism and the fact that it detracts slightly from the tonal quality of the instrument, it has been universally adopted in the manufacture of flutes, and has also been applied to oboes, clarinets, and (to a lesser extent) bassoons. Duplicate fingerings are used that facilitate passages previously impossible, and the system has the advantage of keeping different keys on more or less the same level of difficulty. The pre-Böhm types of flute and oboe are now obsolete, but clarinets with the older system are still used.

Lit.: T. Böhm, *An Essay on the Construction of Flutes* (1882); H. C. Wysham, *The Evolution of the Boehm Flute* [1898]; C. Welch, *History of the Boehm Flute*, rev. ed. (1896). W.D.D.

Bois [F.]. The woodwinds.

Boite à musique [F.]. Music box; see Mechanical instruments III. Also, title of pieces imitating the high notes and mechanical motion of a music box.

Bolero. A Spanish dance said to have been invented by Sebastián Cerezo, a celebrated dancer of Cádiz, about 1780. Danced by one dancer or a couple, it includes many brilliant and intricate steps, quick movements such as the *entrechat* of

classical ballet, and a sudden stop in a characteristic position with one arm held arched over the head (*bien parado*). The music is in moderate triple time, with accompaniment of the castanets and rhythms such as those in the accompanying figure. Probably the earliest extant example is a "Bolero a solo" by Beethoven [see W. Hess, in *DM* xxx.12]. Operatic boleros occur in Auber's *La Muette de Portici* and *Le Domino noir* and Weber's *Preciosa*. Particularly famous are Chopin's *Boléro* op. 19 for piano and Ravel's *Boléro* for orchestra (1927).

The Cuban bolero is in 2/4 meter. It consists of a short introduction followed by two highly syncopated *allegretto* sections of sixteen to thirty-two measures each. The most characteristic rhythmic pattern of the *Cuban bolero* is:

Today the bolero is also very popular in Puerto Rico, where it tends to have a more sentimental character. add. by J.O-S.

Bolivia. Three main streams can be traced in Bolivia's traditional music: that of the Indian tribes of the Amazon region, which preserves its primitive quality; a second, centered in the Andean highlands (Altiplano), a development of Aymara and Quechua origins; and a third developed in the lowlands and valleys, where Spanish influence prevails.

In the Altiplano, a pentatonic scale or a mixture of the pentatonic and European diatonic scales prevails. The music is melancholy. Typical examples are all of the songs generically known as *Aire Indio*, such as the *llaquiaru*, very similar to the *Yaraví*, sung in Bolivia as well as in Peru and Ecuador. Music from the valleys is gayer, more rhythmic and sensual, and closely related to that of Argentina and Chile. The *bailecito* and *cueca are good examples of this group. Other Bolivian traditional and regional songs and dances are the *huaiño, *cacharpaya, *pasacalle, *triste, and *zamba.

Art music in Bolivia dates from the time of the Viceroyalty of Peru, which included present-day Bolivia. In 1568 two musicians, Hernan Garcia and Juan de la Peña, opened a school in the capital city of La Plata (today Sucre) to teach the Indians singing, dancing, and various instruments. In 1597 Gutierre Fernandez Hidalgo (c. 1553–1618) was appointed musical director of the Cathedral of La Plata. Previously he had been active in *Colombia.

The most distinguished of the 17th-century La Plata composers was Juan de Araujo (1646–1714), a native of Spain who came to America at an early age and became the musical director of the Cathedral in 1680. Approximately two hundred of his compositions, including Latin psalms, *villancicos,* and part songs, are preserved in the (Sucre) Cathedral archives, and a few others are stored in Cuzco. The most prolific musician of the 18th century was Manuel Mesa y Carrizo, a noted psalmodist and also composer of *jácaras* and *juguetes,* gay secular songs for voice and instruments.

After the colonial period art music in Bolivia developed rather slowly. Not until 1940 was the first symphonic organization established, the National Orchestra under the leadership of the composer and conductor José María Velasco Maidana (b. 1899). He is the foremost Bolivian composer of his day, author of a ballet *Amerindia* (1938) and several other programmatic works for orchestra. His contemporaries and most of the composers belonging to the immediately succeeding generation share a strong nationalist stand. This is true of Eduardo Caba (b. 1890), author of a ballet, *Kollana,* based on Indian motifs; Antonio González Bravo (b. 1885), also a prominent educator; and Humberto Viscarra Monje (b. 1898).

Jaime Mendoza-Navas (b. 1925) has worked with the pentatonic native music of the Altiplano, exploring its tonal possibilities and using its characteristic rhythms. He has written piano pieces, three symphonic poems (*Don Alvaro, Antawara, Pachamama*), a concerto for piano and orchestra, and *Estampas y Estampillas* for an orchestra of cellos. Also noteworthy is Alberto Villalfando, whose works include *Estructuras,* for piano and percussion, a composition free from nationalist implications.

Lit.: M. d'Harcourt, *Mélodies populaires indiennes; Équateur, Pérou, Bolivie* (1923); R. M. Stevenson, *The Music of Peru* (1960). Also see under Latin America.   J.O-S.

Bologna school. A group of 17th-century instrumental composers who were active in Bologna. Among its members are M. Cazzati (1620–77),

G. B. Vitali (1644?–92), P. degli Antonii (1648–1720), G. B. Bassani (c. 1657–1716), D. Gabrielli (c. 1650–90), G. B. Borri (?), G. Torelli (1658–1709), T. A. Vitali (1665–1747), and G. Aldrovandini (1665–1707). See History of music V.

The Bologna school was important in the formal development of the trio sonata (Cazzati, Bassani, G. B. Vitali), solo violin sonata (degli Antonii, Aldrovandini), solo cello sonata (Gabrielli), concerto grosso (Torelli, Gabrielli), and violin concerto (Torelli). The stylistic contributions of these men were in the direction of balanced structure, elegance of expression, and a pervasive lyricism. These characteristics, combined with deliberate avoidance of virtuosity, are in contrast to the technical exuberance of the string composers of the early baroque, Biagio Marini, Carlo Farina, Marco Uccellini (and their German successors Rosenmüller, Walther, and Biber), who early developed such special idioms of violin playing as *col legno, scordatura, sul ponticello,* double and triple stops, and higher positions (5th and 6th). The Bologna school thus constitutes an interlude between the virtuoso experimentation of the early baroque and the bravura style of the later baroque (Vivaldi, Tartini, Handel).

The most illustrious proponent of the Bologna style was Arcangelo Corelli (1653–1713), who studied and worked at Bologna from 1666 until 1671, becoming a member of the famous *Accademia Filarmonica* [see Academy] in 1670. His identification with the Bologna school is evident from the restrained classicism of his style, as well as from the designation "detto il bolognese" that appears in his op. 1 (1681) and op. 2 (1685).

Much of the activity of the Bologna school centered around the chapel of San Petronio, which was organized by Cazzati in 1657. The reorganization of this institution in 1701 to conform with the new Neapolitan taste and retrenchments owing to financial strictures were factors in the decline of the Bologna school.

Lit.: G. Gaspari, *Dei musicisti bolognesi nel secolo XVII°* (1878); id., in *Atti e memorie della Regia Deputazione di Storia patria per le provincie della Romagna,* ser. 1, vii–ix (1868–70), ser. 2, i, ii (1875, '76) and *Atti e memorie . . . dell' Emilia,* new ser., i–v (1877–80); F. Vatielli, *Arte e vita musicale a Bologna* (1927); id., ‡*Antichi maestri Bolognesi,* ii; L. Frati, in *RMI* xxi, xxiv, xxvi, xxxii; H. G. Mishkin, "The Solo Violin Sonata of the Bologna School" (*MQ* xxix). Musical examples in *SchGMB,* nos. 228, 241, 257; *HAM,* nos. 219, 245, 246, 252, 253, 263; Torchi, *L'Arte musicale in Italia,* vii; J. W. Wasielewski, *Die Violine im XVII. Jahrhundert* (*Instrumentalsätze,* 1905).   H.G.M.

Bombarde [F.], **bombarda** [It.]. (1) Names for the shawm, particularly the bass size of this instrument. In Germany, such corruptions as *Bomhart, Pomhart, Pumhart,* and *Pommer* were used. See Oboe family III. (2) Same as bombardon [see Brass instruments III (e)]. (3) An organ stop of the solo-reed type [see Organ X].

Bombardon. See under Brass instruments III (e).

Bombo [It.]. See under Tremolo I.

Bomhart [G.]. See Bombarde (1).

Bonang. See under Java.

Bonne chanson, La [F., The Good Song]. Song cycle by Fauré (1892), based on eight poems from Verlaine's collection of the same title.

Boogie-woogie. Originally, a special type of piano *blues, first heard in Chicago in the early 1920's. It was revived about 1935, becoming very popular for a number of years. This type of playing is characterized by an ostinato bass figure, usually sharply rhythmic, against which the right hand rhapsodizes freely, the sections usually comprising twelve measures and the treatment often being contrapuntal (sometimes in only two widely spaced parts), with repeated tones, broken-octave tremolos, and short figures reiterated in great rhythmic variety (*riff* technique).

Bop (also rebop, bebop). A term coined about 1945 to describe jazz characterized by improvised solo performances in a dissonant idiom with complex rhythmic patterns and continuous, highly florid melodic lines. Sometimes nonsense syllables are sung, a practice from which the name is thought to have originated. It became popular after World War II under the leadership of trumpeters Dizzy Gillespie and Miles Davis and alto saxophonist Charlie ("Bird") Parker. Its later development is characterized by the adoption of Latin American or Afro-Cuban rhythms. Bop evolved into "modern" jazz, the latter softening the harmonic and rhythmic innovations of the "boppers." See Jazz IV.
                                    J.W.W.

Bordun [G.], **bordone** [It.]. See Bourdon.

Borea [L., It.]. **boree, borre, borry** [O. Eng.]. See Bourrée.

Boris Godunov. Opera in four acts by Mussorgsky (libretto by Mussorgsky after Pushkin's play and Karamzin's *History of the Russian State*), rev. produced in St. Petersburg, 1874; rev. by Rimsky-Korsakov, 1896, 1908. Setting: Russia and Poland, 1598–1605. *Boris Godunov* is the masterpiece of Russian national opera. Its musical style is remarkably advanced for its time, and although its bold unconventionality aroused resentment, many innovations of a more recent date have been traced to this work, e.g., the use of *parallel chords and *modality. Striking is the prominence of the chorus, standing for the Russian people, who, it has been said, represent the real hero of the opera rather than Boris himself.

Boston, valse Boston. A term hardly known in America but widely used in Europe (particularly Germany) during the period after World War I for the hesitation waltz, a slow waltz with a sophisticated rhythm, characterized by the frequent suppression of single beats or entire measures in the accompaniment. In postwar Germany it acquired a prominent position as an American importation and was imbued with jazzlike elements. Numerous composers of note have written Bostons, e.g., Hindemith (1st String Quartet; *1922 Suite für Klavier*); Erwin Schulhoff (*Esquisses de Jazz,* 1927; *Partita,* 1925); Louis Gruenberg (*Jazzberries,* 1925); Conrad Beck (*Zwei Tanzstücke,* 1929).

Bouché [F.]. See under Horn I.

Bouche fermée [F.], **bocca chiusa** [It.]. Singing without words and with closed mouth or, at least, closed teeth. This is a special effect used occasionally in choral music in order to obtain variety of color. Examples occur in Verdi's *Rigoletto,* last act, and Debussy's *Sirènes.*

Bouffons [F.]. In the 15th and 16th centuries, costumed dancers performing the *moresca or *matasin. For *Querelle* (*Guerre*) *des bouffons,* see War of the Buffoons.

Boulevard Solitude. Opera in seven acts by H. W. Henze (libretto by G. Weil), produced in Hanover, 1952. Setting: Paris, 1950.

Bourdon [F.]. Generally, a low note of long duration, i.e., a drone or pedal point. As early as *c.* 1280 the medieval Latin term *burdo* was used for the sustained tenor tones of the organum duplum [see H. Sowa, *Ein anonymer glossierter Mensuraltraktat 1279* (1930), p. 53]. The term was also applied to instrumental devices producing such tones, e.g., to the low-pitched bass-courses of the *vielle and *hurdy-gurdy, which could be sounded continuously against a melody played on the higher strings [see Petrus Picardus, *CS* i, 153], to the large pipes of the organ, or to the drones of the bagpipe. In French 17th-century music, the name *"bourdon"* is given to uniform bass accompaniments similar to that of the drones of a bagpipe, e.g., C-g-c-g C-g-c-g [see F Couperin's "Les Viéleux et les gueux" in his *Pièces de Clavecin,* Book 2, ed. Augener, ii, 209].

H. Besseler has advanced the theory (in *Bourdon und Fauxbourdon,* 1950) that sometime about 1400 the term *bourdon* was used for a low instrumental contratenor, in a wide range and with the function of a harmonic bass, as occurs in some motets by Ciconia. This surmise (for which there is no documentary evidence) represents one of various attempts to explain the term *fauxbourdon (replacement of the hypothetical bourdon by a pseudobass of an entirely different character, namely a middle part in parallel motion with the discant).

The often alleged relationship between *bourdon* and *burden is very doubtful.

Bourrée [F.]. A French 17th-century dance, probably from Auvergne, usually in quick duple meter with a single upbeat [Ex. from Bach's French Suite, no. 6]. The dance is mentioned by M. Praetorius (*Syntagma musicum,* 1615) but does not appear in musical composition before c. 1660 [see J. Écorcheville, ed., ‡*Vingt Suites d'orchestre,* 2 vols. (1906), nos. 1, 5, 6, 7, 14, 16].

Lully used it in his ballets (*Les Amours déguisés,* 1664) and operas, whence it was transferred to the suites of the late 17th and early 18th centuries (Pachelbel, J. K. F. Fischer, J. S. Bach). In Italy the *borea* appears in the suites of Tomaso Motta (*Armonia capricciosa di suonate musicali da camera,* 1681). See Dance music III.

Boutade [F.]. A dance or ballet in a capricious style. The name is also used for 18th-century instrumental pieces of a similar nature.

Bow [F. *archet;* G. *Bogen;* It. *archetto;* Sp. *arco*]. This implement of violin playing takes its name (in all languages) from the fact that it originally was shaped like the bow used in archery. Chinese

and Arabian fiddles are still played with almost semicircular bows, as were stringed instruments in Europe until about the 15th century. During the 16th and 17th centuries various shapes of bow were used, some of which are reproduced here. Ex. 3 shows Corelli's bow, which was short

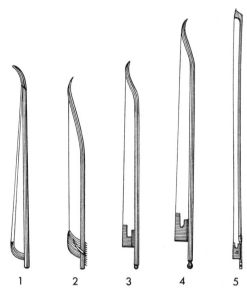

1. *Mersenne (1620).*   2. *Bassani (1680).*
3. *Corelli (1700).*   4. *Tartini (1740).*   5. *Tourte (c. 1820).*

and of hard inelastic wood, while Tartini's bow [Ex. 4] was longer and more elastic. In Germany players used bows with a slightly outward curving stick, which may have facilitated the playing of the polyphonic violin music cultivated there (Biber, Bach). It has been frequently stated that on these bows it was possible to loosen the tension of the hair by releasing the pressure of the thumb and thus play chords without arpeggio. Although there is no evidence for this supposition, the greater distance between stick and hair was of some advantage.

The nut (frog) originally was a small piece of wood fastened to the stick, around which the hair was tightly wrapped. The horn-shaped nut shown in Ex. 1 is reminiscent of this early shape. Ex. 2 shows a device that was used temporarily before 1700 in order to allow for an adjustment of the tension of the bow, namely, a wire loop that could hook into a series of teeth (dentated bow). About 1700 this device was replaced by a screw mechanism like the one still used today [Ex. 3–5].

The bow was given its classical and final form by François Tourte (1747–1835). The most important characteristics of his bow [Ex. 5] are the long, tapering, and slightly inward curving stick, the use of metal or ivory plates for the tip, of Pernambuco wood for the stick, the exact measurements for perfect balance, and probably also the metal ferrule of the frog through which the hair passes evenly spread (this last invention has also been attributed to Tourte's contemporary, John Dodd).

The bows used for the viola, cello, and double bass are designed like the violin bow but are successively heavier and, for the two last-named instruments, shorter.

Lit.: W. C. Retford, *Bows and Bow Makers* (1964); J. Roda, *Bows for Musical Instruments of the Violin Family* (1959); H. Balfour, *The Natural History of the Musical Bow* (1899); H. Saint-George, *The Bow*, rev. ed. (1922); F. Wunderlich, *Der Geigenbogen* (1936); *LavE* ii.3, 1744ff; H.-H. Dräger, "Die Entwicklung des Streichbogens" (diss. Berlin, 1937). See also the literature under Violin. For the 18th-century bow (and bowing) see S. Babitz, "Differences between 18th Century and Modern Violin Bowing" (*The Score*, 1957); D. Boyden, in *MQ* xxxvi; C. Dolmetsch, in *The Consort*, no. 12 (July 1955); A. Schering, in *BJ* 1904; K. Gerhartz, in *ZMW* vii.

Bowed harp. Modern name for the *crwth and similar instruments of northern Europe. See O. Andersson, *The Bowed-Harp* (1930).

Bowing. The technique of using the bow on stringed instruments (violins, etc.). The mastery of the bow includes a considerable number of different manners of bowing, the most important of which are briefly described below. It should be noted that these terms, except for the most common ones, like *détaché, sautillé, spiccato, staccato,* are not much used by players, and that the various effects frequently are not indicated exactly with the proper notation although they are clearly suggested to the player by the character of the music.

(a) *Plain bowing (legato).* This consists of two basic strokes: down-bow [F. *tiré;* G. *Abstrich, Herabstrich, Herstrich, Herunterstrich, Niederstrich;* It. *arcata in giù;* Sp. *arco abajo*] and up-bow [F. *poussé;* G. *Aufstrich, Heraufstrich, Hinstrich;* It. *arcata in su;* Sp. *arco arriba*]. In

down-bow, indicated by a sign [Ex. 1], the arm is moved away from the body, and in up-bow [Ex. 2] the arm moves toward the body. The slur [Ex. 3] indicates the number of notes to be taken in a single stroke.

(b) *Détaché* [F.]. A broad, vigorous stroke in which the notes of equal time value are bowed singly with a slight articulation owing to the rapid change of bow. This stroke is much used for loud passages of not very great speed. Sometimes it is indicated by lines under (or above)

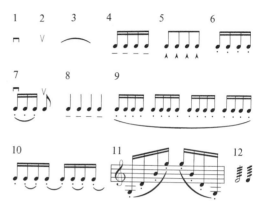

the notes [Ex. 4]. An exceptionally long stroke is called *le grand détaché.*

(c) *Martelé* [F.; It. *martellato*]. Literally, a "hammered" stroke, an effect obtained by releasing each stroke forcefully and suddenly. It can be played in any section of the bow and is indicated by an arrowhead [Ex. 5].

(d) *Sautillé* [F.; It. *saltando;* G. *Springbogen;* Sp. *saltillo*]. A short stroke played in rapid tempo in the middle of the bow so that the bow bounces slightly off the string. It is a most brilliant effect and can be done from very soft to quite loud. It is indicated by dots [Ex. 6]. The same indication is used for the *spiccato* [It., detached], in which the bow is dropped on the string and is lifted again after each note.

(e) *Jeté* [F.; also known as *ricochet*]. This is done by "throwing" the bow on the string in the upper third of the bow so that it will bounce a series of rapid notes on the down-bow. Notation as in Ex. 7. Usually from two to six notes are taken in one stroke, but up to ten or eleven can be played.

(f) *Louré* [F.] or *portato* [It.]. A stroke useful in slow tempo to separate slightly each of several notes taken in a slur. It is indicated as in Ex. 8. It is used in passages of a *cantabile* character.

(g) *Staccato* [It.]. This is a solo effect and theoretically consists of a number of *martelé* notes taken in the same stroke. It can be executed with dazzling brilliance either up-bow or down-bow, but the latter is more difficult. When the bow is allowed to spring slightly from the string it is known as *staccato volante* (flying staccato). Notation as in Ex. 9.

(h) *Viotti-stroke*. This is attributed to Giovanni Battista Viotti (1755–1824) and consists of two detached and strongly marked notes, the first of which is unaccented and given very little bow, while the second comes on the accent and takes much more bow. Its use is practically limited to the works of Viotti, Kreutzer, and Rohde. Notation as in Ex. 10.

(i) *Arpeggio, arpeggiando* [It.]. A bouncing stroke played on broken chords so that each bounce is on a different string. Indicated as in Ex. 11.

(j) *Tremolo* [It.]. This is primarily an orchestral effect and is produced by moving the bow back and forth, in short and extremely rapid strokes, on one note [Ex. 12]. See Tremolo.

(k) *Sul ponticello* [It.; F. *au chevalet;* G. *am Steg;* Sp. *sobre el puentecillo*]. A nasal, brittle effect produced by bowing very close to the bridge.

(l) *Sul tasto, sulla tastiera* [It.; F. *sur la touche;* G. *am Griffbrett*]. A flutelike effect (also called *flautando*), produced by bowing very slightly over the fingerboard.

(m) *Col legno* [It.]. This is done by striking the string with the stick instead of the hair. A purely orchestral effect.

(n) *Ondulé* [F.; It. *ondeggiando*]. An obsolete form of tremolo ("undulating tremolo") in which several notes are taken in the same bow [see Tremolo I].

Recent investigations have shown that 18th-century bowing was quite different from that of the present day. See the studies mentioned at the end of the article on Bow.   H.N.

Brabançonne, La. See under National anthems.

Braccio [It.] In the baroque period, the members of the violin family (*viola da braccio*) that were held at arm level [*braccio*, arm], as distinguished from the viols (simply called *viola*), which were held downward, resting on the knees, or from the larger *viola da gamba* [*gamba*, leg], which was held resting between the player's legs. Later, after the name "violin" had become established, only the second smallest size of the family retained the name *viola da braccio*. The first half

of the name survives in the English term "viola" and the second in the German *Bratsche*.

Brace [F. *accolade*]. The bracket connecting two or more staves of a score; also, the group of staves thus connected.

Braille music notation. The method of writing music according to the principles of the Braille system for the blind. In this system, raised dots are used in various configurations, all of which are derived from an elementary configuration of six dots: ∷ Following are the signs for the C-major scale and a few other symbols.

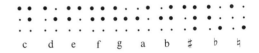

The rhythmic value of the note signs is an eighth note, unless a dot is added underneath to the right or to the left. In the former case, the

Example of Braille notation.

value is ¼ or ¹⁄₆₄, in the latter ½ or ¹⁄₃₂. If both dots are added, the value is ¹⁄₁ or ¹⁄₁₆. [See Ex.] The octave position is indicated by special signs that normally appear at the beginning of each measure. Other signs indicate rests, time signatures, etc. For more details, see A. Reuss, *Development and Problems of Musical Notation for the Blind* (1935); *WoHN* ii, 449ff; *LavE* ii.6, 3836ff.

Brande [Old G.]. *Branle.

Brandenburg Concertos. Six concertos written 1718–21 by J. S. Bach (who called them *Concerts a plusiers instruments*) and dedicated to Christian Ludwig, Margrave of Brandenburg. They represent the artistic peak of the baroque concerto. Each consists of three movements, fast–slow–fast, except for the first, which has a Minuet and a Polonaise added at the end. Three of them, nos. 2, 4, and 5, are *concerti grossi*, employing a group of solo instruments against the string orchestra. See N. Carrell, *Bach's Brandenburg Concertos* (1963).

Brando [It.], **brangill** [Old E.]. *Branle.

Branle [F.]. In the 15th century, one of the various dancing steps of the *basse danse,* indicated in the dance notation by the letter *b*. In the 16th century, the branle was an independent popular dance. There were a large number of local varieties (Arbeau's *Orchésographie* enumerates more than 20), many of which were of the follow-the-leader type, similar to the farandole, the hay, and the cotillon. It was accompanied by singing and apparently included some swaying movements of the body or hands. The *branle double* and *branle simple* were in duple meter (the former with phrases of four, the latter, of three measures), whereas the *branle gay* was in triple meter. The *branle à mener* survived in the *amener* of the 17th century and, very likely, in the *minuet. In England the dance was known as "brangill" or "brawl" [see Shakespeare, *Love's Labour's Lost,* Act III, Sc. I]. An early example of the Italian branle (*brand*) is found in Carlo Farina's *Libro delle pavanne* (1626). See Dance music II.

Brass band. A group of brass instruments. Today, the term "brass band" refers to a fairly standardized combination of 24 or 25 players, consisting of 1 E^b soprano cornet, 8 B^b cornets, 1 B^b *Flügelhorn,* 3 E^b tenor horns, 2 B^b baritone horns, 2 B^b euphoniums, 2 B^b tenor trombones, 1 B^b bass trombone, 2 E^b basses, and 2 BB^b basses.

The brass band dates from the time when valves began to be used in brass instruments in the reorganization of Prussian cavalry bands, beginning about 1830 [see Brass instruments]. The increased versatility of these brass groups prompted the creation of civilian brass bands, the first being founded in 1833. Such bands were vastly popular. In fact, until "Gilmore's Grand Boston Band" was formed in 1859, most bands in America were brass bands. Since then, their popularity in America has declined. In England, however, they continued to flourish, becoming an integral part of recreational and educational programs offered by industry, religious groups, and schools. Regularly scheduled "festivals" and "contests," plus a standard instrumentation, has led some outstanding French and English composers to contribute to the repertory.

Lit.: H. C. Hind, *The Brass Band,* rev. ed. (1952); J. F. Russell and J. H. Elliot, *The Brass Band Movement* (1936); D. Wright, *The Brass Band Conductor* (1948); R. F. Goldman, *The Concert Band* (1946); *id., The Wind Band: Its Literature and Technique* (1961). J.W.

Brass instruments [F. *instruments de cuivre;* G. *Blechinstrumente;* It. *stromenti d'ottone;* Sp. *instrumentos de metal*].

I. *General.* The section of the orchestra consisting of the instruments made of brass or other metal, such as trumpets, horns, trombones, tubas, as distinguished from those made of wood [see Wind instruments; also Orchestra]. This feature, however, has only superficial significance, since the material from which a wind instrument is made has almost no effect on its tone quality and other properties. Moreover, various instruments of the "brass family" were formerly made of wood [see V], while the "woodwind family" includes instruments made of metal, e.g., the flute and saxophone. A more characteristic feature of the brasses is their mouthpiece, which is nearly always cup-shaped; hence the name "cupped-mouthpiece family" might be a more accurate designation. If this definition is rejected—on the ground that in certain obsolete or Oriental instruments the mouthpiece is not cup-shaped—the instruments in question must be defined as lip-vibrated aerophones, i.e., wind instruments in which the player's lips serve as a reed.

The so-called "brass instruments" form an extremely large group, including not only numerous ancient instruments but also many later ones that were invented in the 18th and 19th centuries for military purposes, for bands, and as improvements on older orchestral types. The subsequent grouping is intended to place the various instruments in certain general categories that show their historical or other position, a grouping that, needless to say, involves some overlapping. [For the general acoustical properties of the brass instruments, see under Wind instruments.]

II. *Orchestral instruments.* The brass section of the modern orchestra consists mainly of the French *horn, *trumpet, *trombone, and *tuba. The tuba is related to the horn, both having a pipe whose diameter increases throughout the greater part of its length (conical pipe), whereas in the trumpet and trombone the pipe is to a great extent (about two-thirds) cylindrical and widens only at the end into a relatively small bell. The mouthpieces also are different, being more cup-shaped in the trumpet and trombone than in the horn and tuba, which have funnel-shaped mouthpieces. For more details on these instruments, see the separate entries. Other instruments that have occasionally been used in the modern orchestra are the Wagner tubas [see

Tuba (2)], cornet, and several types discussed below under III.

III. *Band instruments.* In this category are all the brass instruments that are used chiefly in the brass band and in other bands, primarily for open-air performance of marches and other popular music. Some of them, however, have occasionally been called for in orchestral scores, particularly the cornet. Most of these instruments can be considered hybrid horns or trumpets since they combine features of the horn (e.g., conical bore) with features of the trumpet (e.g., cup-shaped mouthpiece). A methodical survey of these instruments is extremely difficult, owing to the large variety of types and sizes as well as the utterly confusing terminology. The subsequent survey of the most important types follows in principle the description given in N. Bessaraboff, *Ancient European Musical Instruments* (1941), pp. 150ff.

(a) Cornet [F. *cornet à pistons;* G. *Kornett;* It. *cornetta;* Sp. *cornetín*]. An instrument similar in shape to the trumpet but shorter and with a relatively longer conical portion and cupped mouthpiece. It is pitched in B^b (sometimes in A), and has a written range from f♯ to c'''', sounding a whole tone (or three semitones) lower. The cornet's timbre is similar to that of the trumpet. Owing to its shorter tube it has considerably more agility. It has been used a good deal by French and Italian composers (Berlioz, Bizet, Rossini). Its tone has been described as coarse and vulgar and has been compared unfavorably with the brilliant tone of the trumpet. This difference, however, is largely due to an inferior style of playing and to the music commonly associated with the instrument.

(b) Flügelhorn [G.; F. *bugle;* It. *flicorno;* Sp. *fiscorno*]. An instrument similar in design and size to the cornet (sometimes to a tuba or helicon) but with a wider conical bore, usually with three valves. It is usually built in B^b, more rarely in C. Its sound is somewhat similar to that of the horn but lacks the latter's mellowness. The instruments named below are larger sizes constructed on the principles of the Flügelhorn. They might be regarded as forming a family for which the generic name "bugles" is often used. The largest members of the family are the *tubas, which are the only ones used in the orchestra. See also below, under (f).

(c) Baritone [F. *bugle ténor;* G. *Tenorhorn;* It. *flicorno tenore;* Sp. *fiscorno tenor*]. This is a larger instrument in C or B^b and built in one of two shapes, either in the oblong shape of the trum-

pets, with the bell pointing directly upward, or oval, with the bell at an angle. The range is from E to b$^{b'}$.

(d) Euphonium [F. *basse à pistons;* G. *Baryton;* Sp. *eufonio*]. Its shape, pitch, and range are the same as those of the baritone. A larger bore, however, gives it a broader, mellower timbre and favors the lower notes. French and other composers have used it in place of the tuba, e.g., Stravinsky in *Petrushka.*

(e) Helicon. This name is used for bass and contrabass tubas in a circular shape (similar to that of the horn) instead of the upright shape of the tubas. The circle is wide enough to allow the player to carry the instrument over his shoulder. An American variety, characterized by a specially designed bell, is the *sousaphone* (named after John Philip Sousa, who suggested it). In Germany a similar instrument is called *Bombardon.*

(f) Saxhorn. A family of instruments invented by Adolphe Sax and designed on a uniform model. Their bore is somewhat narrower than that of the instruments described above, resulting in a more brilliant timbre. They all are upright, with the pipe starting horizontally from the funnel-shaped mouthpiece (as in the tubas, etc.) and the pistons on top of the upper horizontal part of the tube. It should be noted that the saxhorns made today frequently differ in details (width of bore, etc.) from Sax's original design and therefore are closer to the Flügelhorn. Indeed, most authorities maintain that it is practically impossible to make a clear distinction between the saxhorns and Flügelhorns. Usually, the latter term is restricted to the one size described under (b). All agree that there is a hopeless confusion of nomenclature in this group. For example: (1) in E^b or F (sopranino saxhorn, soprano saxhorn, Soprano Flügelhorn, etc.); (2) in B^b or C (soprano saxhorn, alto saxhorn, Alt Flügelhorn); (3) in low E^b or F (alto saxhorn, saxhorn, Althorn, tenor saxhorn, etc.); (4) in low B^b or C (baritone saxhorn, Althorn, tenor horn, etc.); (5) in EE^b or FF (saxtuba).

The *saxtromba* is a modification of the saxhorn that has a less conical bore, approaching that of the trumpet (tromba). It is little used today.

IV. *Military instruments.* Under this heading brief mention may be made of instruments used for signaling. They all are natural instruments, restricted to the tones 2 to 6 of the harmonic series, e.g., g d' g' b' d'' for an instrument built in G. The most common of them is the *bugle*

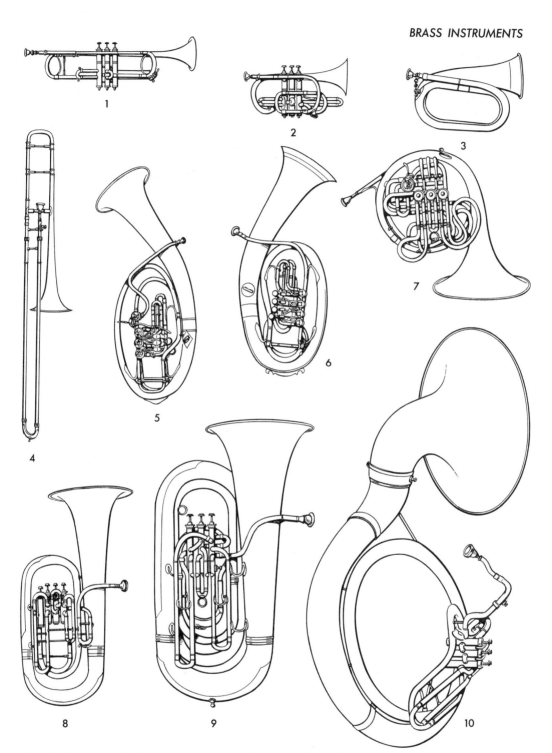

Brass instruments: 1. Trumpet. 2. Cornet. 3. Bugle. 4. Trombone. 5. Wagner tuba. 6. Double B-flat baritone. 7. French horn. 8. B-flat euphonium. 9. Double B-flat tuba. 10. Sousaphone.

BRASS INSTRUMENTS

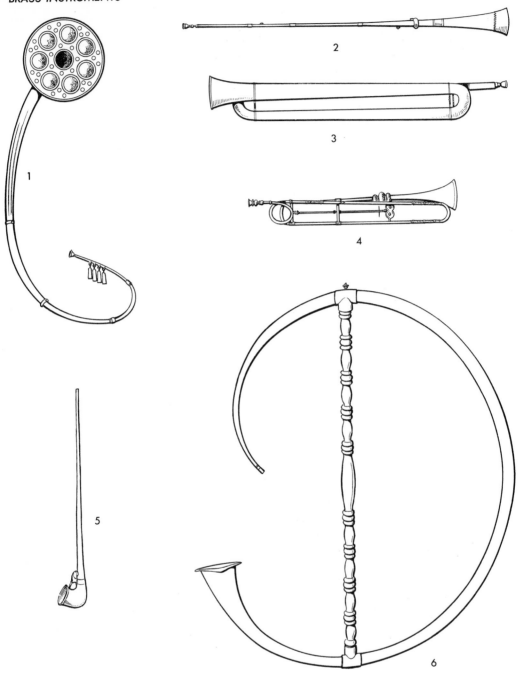

Old brass instruments: 1. Lur.   2. Buisine.   3. Alphorn.   4. Slide trumpet.   5. Lituus.   6. Buccina.

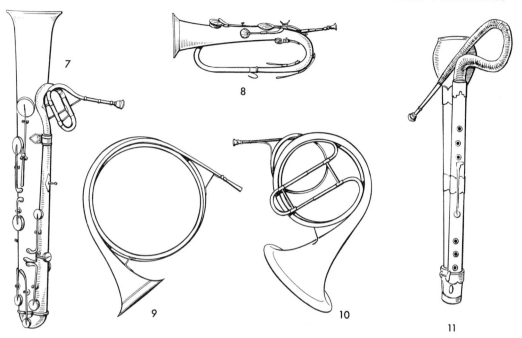

Old brass instruments: 7. Ophicleide. 8. Key bugle. 9. Natural horn. 10. Hand horn. 11. Bass horn.

[F. *clairon;* G. *Signalhorn;* It. *cornetta segnale;* Sp. *cuerno de caza, bocina, clarín, corneta*], built in G or B♭ and occasionally in F. Bugles that have been furnished with a single valve lowering the pitch a fourth are known as *Bersag horn.*

V. *History.* (a) Trumpets and horns, though used in many ancient cultures, were very late in acquiring properties that made them useful as proper musical instruments. Only a few tones of the harmonic series were available on the primitive instruments (made from animal horns, seashells or snails, bark, etc.), a fact that restricted their use to the purpose of signaling, either in religious ceremonies or in military service. Moreover, the trumpets and horns of the Greeks, Romans, Jews, etc., possessed a sound that was far from agreeable but was rather startling, as are to the present day the trumpets of China, Tibet, and India. Plutarch likens the sound of the Egyptian trumpet to the bray of an ass, and the Jewish ceremonial horn, the *shofar, even today fills the congregation with awe. The Jews also had a long straight trumpet made of silver, the *hasosra* [see Jewish music]. The Greek straight trumpet, called *salpinx,* was taken over from the Orient. The same shape occurs in the Roman *tuba,* a straight instrument made of bronze, about four feet in length. The Romans

also had a trumpet that curved up at the end in the shape of a J, called *lituus,* whereas their *buccina* was entirely curved, in the shape of a G, and had a wooden crossbar by which it was carried over the shoulder. Among the most interesting examples of ancient trumpets is the Nordic *lur type, which shows a high degree of perfection in bronze founding.

Horns were originally made from animals' horns as, e.g., the alphorn, the shofar or the Roman *cornu,* made from a ram's-horn or ox-horn, which, we are informed, was covered with gold and studded with precious stones. Metal horns, S-shaped and widening like the animal's horn, are much rarer in ancient cultures than the more cylindrical trumpets, probably owing to the greater difficulty of founding them. They are also relatively rare among the Oriental nations.

(b) In Europe the *oliphant, a signaling horn made from an elephant's tusk, appeared in the 10th century, imported from Byzantium. The Roman armies brought their trumpets all over Europe. After A.D. 1000 the straight *tuba* acquired the shape of a long slim pipe with a rather large, funnel-shaped bell. This instrument was called *buisine* (from L. *buccina,* which, however, was circular), while smaller sizes were called *trombetta.* From the early part of the 15th century comes the first evidence of a folded trumpet. The same principle was also applied to the larger *buisine,* which by the 15th century had acquired the distinguishing feature of the modern trombone, i.e., the slides [see Trombone II; for slide trumpet, see Trumpet]. In the 15th and 16th centuries trumpets became associated with heraldry [see Trumpet II], and the wooden *cornett [G. *Zink*] acquired a prominent place in 16th-century chamber music. Its bass size had an odd, serpentine shape and therefore was called *serpent.* All these instruments had side-holes covered by the fingers [see Wind instruments IV (d)]. Later a few keys were added in order to facilitate playing, particularly in the large serpent, which in an improved form doubled up on itself like the bassoon and became known as the *Russian bassoon* or its metal counterpart, the *bass horn* [see under Cornett].

(c) About 1650 began the development of the modern horn and trumpet, which is briefly described under Horn II and Trumpet II. [For hand horn and natural horn, see under Horn.] Here it will suffice to mention a group of instruments that were developed about 1800 and are characterized by the use of side-holes (as in the much older cornetts) operated by keys. This principle was applied not only to horns and trumpets but also to bugles [see IV above], in which it proved more successful (Joseph Halliday, 1810). The *key bugle* or *Kent bugle* (*Kent horn*), named in honor of the Duke of Kent [F. *bugle à clés,* G. *Klappenhorn*], remained in use until the second half of the 19th century. Later a larger size was constructed; called *ophicleide,* it had the doubled-up shape of the Russian bassoon. Spontini prescribed it in his opera *Olympie* (1819) and Mendelssohn in his overture to *A Midsummer Night's Dream* (1826). Although soon replaced by the tuba in the orchestra, the ophicleide was used in Italian, French, Spanish, and South American bands up to this century.

Lit.: H. Bahnert, T. Herzberg and H. Schramm, *Metallblasinstrumente* (1958); A. Carse, *Musical Wind Instruments* (1939); L. G. Langwill, *An Index of Musical Wind-Instrument Makers,* rev. ed. [1962]; A. Baines, *European and American Musical Instruments* [1966]; M. Rasmussen, *A Teacher's Guide to the Literature of Brass Instruments* [1964]; P. Farkas, *The Art of Brass Playing* [1962]; H. Hofmann, *Über den Ansatz der Blechbläser* [1956]; *GSJ passim.* For detailed bibliography see "Brass Bibliography," *Brass Quarterly* i–vii. See also under Woodwinds; Turmsonaten.

Bratsche [G.]. *Viola. *Bratschist,* viola player.

Brautlied [G.]. Bridal song.

Brawl. English term for *branle.

Brazil. Primitive Indian music in its original form had relatively little influence on the development of Brazilian music. Most of the Indians living in the coastal areas at the time of the European conquest moved inland to the jungles of western Brazil. Consequently, the only important sources in the development of native Brazilian music are African and Iberian. African immigration to the country had begun by the middle of the 16th century. From that period dates a continuous development of Afro-Brazilian styles of music, which today represent a powerful force of folk expression bearing only slight resemblance to their original African models. The Portuguese contribution has been at least as important. Art music in Brazil dates from the early 17th century, when the Jesuits established large plantations in Santa Cruz, near Rio de Janeiro, and set up a small organization for the musical instruction of their slaves, later called Conservatorio dos Negros. Among the first composers whose names are known (though their works are not) are Father Manoel de Silva Reis, Friar de Santa Eulalia, and Friar Santa Clara.

The earliest composers whose works have been traced—and some of them even published—emerged during the last decades of the 18th century. One of them, Father José Mauricio Nuñez Garcia (1767–1830), born in Rio de Janeiro, became choir director of the cathedral of his native city (1798) and director of music of the Royal Chapel (1808–21) during the reign of King John VI in Brazil. He wrote several Masses, among them a *Missa de Requiem* that was sung at the funeral service of Queen Dona Maria I (1811). Other church composers of the same period were José Joaquim Emérico Lobo de Mesquita, Marcos Coelho Netto (*c.* 1763), Francisco Gomes da Rocha, Ignacio Parreira Neves (*c.* 1790), and Jerónimo José Ferreira.

During the first half of the 19th century, Rio de Janeiro became one of the most brilliant music centers in South America. The Portuguese-born composer Marcos Antonio da Fonseca Portugal (1762–1830), whose operas were well received in Europe, came to this city in 1811 to become general director of music and helped found the Teatro São João, which from 1813 until the end of the Empire (1889) produced grand opera on a large scale. An important composer of this period was Francesco Manoel da Silva (1795–1865), composer of the Brazilian national anthem (1834), sacred compositions, and *modinhas. In 1841 he founded the Conservatory of Rio de Janeiro, today the National School of Music of the University of Brazil. Da Silva's immediate successor was Henrique Alves de Mesquita (1830–1906), composer of operas and operettas (*La Nuit au chateau, O Vagabundo, Ali Babá*) with French, Portuguese, and Italian librettos. His contemporary, Antonio Carlos Gomes (1836–96), became Latin America's foremost composer of operas modeled on Italian styles. He was trained in Italy and several of his works, including *Il Guaraní* (1870), were acclaimed at La Scala in Milan. In 1861 his first opera with a Portuguese libretto, *A Noite do Castelo*, was presented. Other operas by Gomes are *Salvador Rosa* (1874), *O Escravo* (1889), and *Condor* (1891); he also wrote an oratorio, *Colombo* (1892), for the World's Columbian Exposition in Chicago.

In opposition to the facile Italian style of Carlos Gomes and his followers, Leopoldo Américo Miguez (1850–1902) composed symphonic music and operas (*Os Saldunes,* 1896) in a Wagnerian idiom, while Herique Oswald (1852–1931), wrote orchestral and chamber music in the French manner. Alberto Nepomuceno (1864–1920), took the first steps toward the development of a national style. With techniques borrowed from Wagner, Puccini, and Debussy, he wrote songs, piano pieces, and a *Serie Brasileira* for orchestra of a definite Brazilian spirit. Alexandre Lévy (1864–92) also followed the stream of romantic nationalism, exemplified in his *Suite Brasileira* and a symphonic poem, *Comala*. Francisco Braga (1868–1945) was less concerned with nationalism, instead being attracted to French impressionism. He wrote two operas, *Jupira* and *Anita Garibaldi*, as well as several symphonic poems, songs, and church music.

During the first decades of the 20th century Brazilian music won international recognition through an outstanding group of composers sharing a keen perception of both the national spirit and the latest trends of European composition. The most prominent in this group was Heitor Villa-Lobos (1887–1959), one of the most powerful creative forces that Latin America has produced. He was an amazingly prolific composer (more than 1,000 works) for every conceivable medium, sometimes weak from the viewpoint of musical form or overexuberant in his musical textures but always original and imaginative. Especially notable are his 14 *Choros,* single-movement compositions ranging from instrumental solos to large orchestral works; his piano music (*Guia Prático,* numerous suites and cycles); and his nine *Bachianas Brasileiras,* works in several movements for various instrumental and vocal media. Villa-Lobos also wrote twelve symphonies; a number of symphonic poems and suites; ten concertos; a considerable amount of chamber music, including sixteen string quartets; a large number of songs; choral compositions, including the *Canto Orfeónico;* five operas; etc.

Among Villa-Lobos' contemporaries, the most important are Luciano Gallet (1893–1931); Oscar Lorenzo Fernandez (1897–1948), composer of a successful opera, *Malazarte* (1941), and a number of symphonic and chamber works and songs; and Francisco Mignone (b. 1897), conductor, pianist, and also a prolific composer whose works reflect the restless spirit of an experimenter always seeking new modes of expression. The next generation includes Radamés Gnatalli (b. 1906), Luiz Cosme (b. 1908), and Camargo Guarnieri (b. 1907). The last-named, considered the foremost successor of Villa-Lobos in Brazil, is an extremely prolific composer of orchestral and chamber music, songs, piano compositions, and choral works. In general Guarnieri no longer draws his materials from folk music, yet his works sound utterly Brazilian and at the same time show a discipline of form and an economy of means that has led many critics to classify him as a neoclassicist.

The young generation is headed by C. Guerra Peixe (b. 1914); Claudio Santoro (b. 1919), a strong supporter of nationalism in his early works who turned next to atonal music; and German-born Hans Joachim Koellreutter (b. 1915), who moved to Brazil in 1937. Still younger composers are Edino Krieger (b. 1928), Marlos Nobre (b. 1939), and Osvaldo Lacerda (b. 1927). Another group of recent composers associated with the newer experimental streams and represented by the New Music Group established in São Paulo are Damiano Cozzella (b. 1929), Roger Duprat (b. 1932), Gilberto Mendes (b. 1922), Olivier Toni, Willy Correa de Oliveira, Luis Carlos Vinholes, and José Luiz Paes Nunes.

Present-day Brazilian folk music stems from two main sources: one of African origin, which developed into the so-called *Negra* music from Bahia, the second the *Nortista* or *Cabocla*, product of the ethnic stratification combining Iberian and native traditions. The most characteristic features of the former are its rigorous highly syncopated rhythm and its melodic formulas, originating in Portuguese song, found in such forms as the *batuque, congada* [see *Congo*], *maxixe,* and *samba.* The *Nortista* (*Cabocla*) is dominantly melodic. Traces of the old modes are seen in its preference for the minor keys. Rhythmically, this music follows the movements of the text rather than conforming to dance patterns. The *modinha, toada, chula,* and *cantilena* are among the many forms belonging to this group.

Lit.: A. T. Luper, *The Music of Brazil* (1943); L. H. Corrêa de Azevedo, *Brief History of Music in Brazil* (1948); R. Almeida, *História da Música Brasileira,* rev. ed. (1942); M. Andrade, *Ensaio sôbre a música brasileira* (1962); *id., Música do Brasil* (1941); Oneida Alvarenga, *A Influência negra na música brasileira* (1946); *id., Música popular brasileña* (1947); F. Curt Lange, *La Música en Minas Gerais* (1946); L. H. Correa de Azevedo, *Bibliografia musical brasileira, 1820–1950* (1952); V. Mariz, *A cançaõ brasileira* (1959). Also see under Latin America.   J.O-S.

Breit [G.]. Broad, largo. *Breit gestrichen,* broadly bowed.

Breve, brevis [L.]. An old note value that, as implied by the name [L. *brevis,* short], originally (early 13th century) was the shortest value then in use; see Notation III. Because of the subsequent introduction of six or more degrees of smaller value (*semibrevis, minima,* etc.; see Notation IV; also Mensural notation I), it became, in the late 16th century, the longest value. Today it is occasionally used as the equivalent of two whole notes, written ⊨ or |o|. See also *Alla breve.*

Breviary [L. *breviarium*]. See under Liturgical books I (2).

Bridge [F. *chevalet;* G. *Steg;* It. *ponticello;* Sp. *puente*]. (1) In stringed instruments, the wooden support resting on the table over which the strings are stretched. Its shape and size vary in the different instruments. The bridge of the double bass has "legs." Although they appear symmetrical, the two halves of the bridge serve somewhat different purposes. The right (treble) foot rests firmly on the table, very nearly above the sound post, while the other, having no such support, transmits the vibrations of the string to the body of the instrument. The present-day shape of the violin bridge was developed in the time of Antonio and Girolamo Amati (*c.* 1550–1630).

(2) Short for *bridge passage.

Bridge passage. In musical compositions, a passage of subordinate importance serving to connect two themes. It consists of figurations, sequences, or other subsidiary material. Frequently it effects a modulation of key, e.g., from the first to the second theme in *sonata form.

Brillenbass [G.]. Derogatory nickname for stereotyped accompanying figures in the manner of the *Alberti bass, whose abbreviated writing [see Abbreviations, Ex. h] suggests a pair of spectacles [G. *Brille*].

Brindisi [It.]. Drinking song, particularly in operas, e.g., in Verdi's *La Traviata* ("Libiamo"), Mascagni's *Cavalleria rusticana* ("Viva il vino").

Brio, con; brioso [It.]. With vigor and spirit.

Brisé [F.]. An 18th-century name for the turn. In modern terminology, indication for arpeggio playing, or for detached bowing. See also *Style brisé.*

Broadcasting. See Radio and television broadcasting.

Broderie [F.]. (1) French term for coloratura. Also used in German writings, more in the sense of "delicately embroidered melody," as in 15th-century music. (2) Same as auxiliary tone [see Nonharmonic tones I (5)].

Broken consort. See Consort.

Broken cord. Term for figurations consisting of the notes of a chord (triad, seventh chord, etc.), e.g., those of the C-major Prelude of *The Well-Tempered Clavier,* vol. i, or the stereotyped patterns known as *Alberti bass. The earliest examples are found in the works of the virginalists. Chopin's works contain many ingeniously devised broken-chord formations. The term "arpeggio" is often used as a synonym.

Broken octave. See under Short octave.

Browning. Designation for a body of 16th- and 17th-century English compositions based on the tune "The leaves be greene, the nuts be browne." Thomas Ravenscroft's *Deuteromelia* (1609) contains a vocal canon on the tune, with the text "Browning Madame." [See J. A. Fuller Maitland and W. Barclay Squire, ed., *The Fitzwilliam*

Virginal Book, 2 vols. (1899), ii, 381; W. Chappell, ed., *Old English Popular Music,* 2 vols. (1893), i, 154; *ReMR,* p. 845.] Most brownings are intricate variations for instrumental ensembles, e.g., Byrd's "Browning" in five parts [E. H. Fellowes, ed., *The Collected Works of William Byrd,* 20 vols. (1937–50), xvii, 30]. Other composers of brownings were E. Bevin, C. Woodcocke, R. Parsons, H. Stoninge, and J. Jenkins (?). See E. H. Meyer, *Die mehrstimmige Spielmusik des 17. Jahrhunderts in Nord- und Mitteleuropa* (1934); id., *English Chamber Music* (1946).

Brumeux [F.]. "Misty," veiled.

Brummeisen [G.]. *Jew's-harp.

Brummscheit [G.]. Corruption of *Trumscheit* [see Tromba marina].

Brummstimmen [G.]. See under *Bouche fermée.*

Brunette [F.]. A 17th- and 18th-century type of French popular song, with or without accompaniment, with idyllic, pastoral, or amorous subjects. It replaced the earlier bergerette and *vaudeville.* The name is probably derived from one famous example, "Le beau berger Tirsis," which has the refrain "Ah petite brunette, ah tu me fais mourir" [see *SchGMB,* no. 217]. C. Ballard published three collections of *Brunetes ou petits airs tendres* (1703, '04, '11). Some of these songs occur in the harpsichord pieces by Chambonnières and D'Anglebert, e.g., the *Sarabande Jeunes Zéphirs,* and the *Gavotte Où estes vous allées.* Others were used later in comic opera. See P.-M. Masson, in *SIM* xii; G. Cammaert, in *RBM* xi.

Brusque [F.]. A 17th-century dance known only through two examples, by Chambonnières, which have some characteristics of the gigue.

Bruststimme [G.]. Chest voice.

Brustwerk, Brustpositiv [G.]. A special group of smaller organ pipes placed in the middle of the front of the organ, between the large pedal pipes. The group has softer intonation than the *Hauptwerk* (great organ) and is usually played on the second manual.

Buccina [L.]. An ancient Roman brass instrument [see Brass instruments V (a)]. The name reappears in the medieval term *buysine,* in the German word *Posaune* (i.e., trombone), and in the French *buccin* (or *buccine*). The last was a pseudoantique variety of trombone with a bell

shaped like a dragon's head, which was used during the French Revolution for festive occasions. See *LavE* ii.3, 1449.

Buchstabenschrift [G.]. *Letter notation.

Buckwheat note. See under Fasola.

Buffet [F.]. Organ case.

Buffo [It.]. In Italian 18th-century opera, a comic character, usually a *basso buffo* (e.g., Leporello in Mozart's *Don Giovanni*). Hence, a singer for comic roles. See Comic opera.

Buffonistenstreit [G.]. *War of the Buffoons.

Bügelhorn [G.]. German term for the entire family sometimes referred to as *bugles. See *SaRM,* p. 62.

Bugle. A military instrument [see Brass instruments IV]. The term is also used generically for the entire group of brass instruments described under Brass instruments III (b)–(e). For the key bugle (Kent bugle), see Brass instruments V (c).

Bühne [G.]. Stage. *Bühnenfestspiel* (stage festival play) and *Bühnenweihfestspiel* (stage-consecrating festival play) are names used by Wagner, the former for his *Ring* cycle, the latter for *Parsifal. Bühnenmusik* means *incidental music for plays, or, in operas, music played on the stage itself, as in the final scene of Mozart's *Don Giovanni.*

Buisine. See *Buysine.* For ill. see under Brass instruments.

Bulgaria. Bulgarian folk music combines possibly Thracian folksongs and Byzantine and Near Eastern elements with its indigenous traditions. Its most distinct feature is the prominent use of asymmetrical rhythmic patterns (five, seven, and nine beats within one measure), which permeate both songs and dances. Although some such patterns also appear in Greek and Yugoslav folk music, it has become customary to refer to them as "Bulgarian rhythm." Folksongs are usually short but intensely melismatic, and they use both diatonic and chromatic modes. In some parts of Bulgaria one still finds examples of "primitive" polyphony (parallel fourths and fifths or parallel seconds). Folk dances are usually accompanied by singing, which is almost invariably accompanied by an instrument. The chief instruments are the *gaida* (bagpipe), *caval* (fife, related to flute), *gadulka* (two-stringed [or more] instrument played with a primitive bow, occasionally called *gusla*), and the *gusle* (a primitive bowed instrument with one string, sometimes two). The main publications of folk music are by Wassil Stoin (1880–1938) and Dobri Christov.

The liturgical music of the Bulgarian church developed from Byzantine chant and was strongly influenced by Russian church music from the 16th to 18th centuries. This influence is still evident despite the addition of folk elements and the acceptance, in more recent times, of certain forms of the Greek rite.

Art music, influenced at first by Russia, began to develop toward the end of the 19th century. The first composers to use Bulgarian folksong as the basis of composition were Emanuél Manolov (1860–1902), Dobri Christov (1875–1941), and Georgi Atanasov (1881–1931). Of all the Bulgarian composers, only Pantcho Vladigerov (b. 1899) has become internationally known. His contemporaries include Lubomir Pipkov (b. 1904), Wesselin Stojanov (b. 1902), and Marin Goleminov (b. 1908). Among the younger generation of Bulgarian composers is Constantin Iliev (b. 1924).

Lit.: W. Spassoff, *Volksmusik, Volksinstrumente und Tänze der Bulgaren* (1931); E. Pantscheff, *Die Entwicklung der Oper in Bulgarien von ihren Anfängen bis 1915* (1962); B. A. Kremenliev, *Bulgarian-Macedonian Folk Music* (1952); R. P. Verdeil, *La Musique byzantine chez les Bulgares et les Russes* [*Editions XXIX B 3]; P. Panóff, *Die altslavische Volks- und Kirchenmusik* (Bühm, 1930); C. Obreschkoff, *Das bulgarische Volkslied* (1937); V. Stoin, ‡*Narodni pesni ot zapadnite pokrainini* (Sofia, 1959); R. Katzarova *et al.*, ‡*Narodni Pesni ot Severoiztochna Bulgaria* (Sofia, 1962); P. Panóff, "Die Volksmusik der Bulgaren" (*Melos* iv, H. 1); L. Pichler, "Antichi canti liturgici bulgari e russi" (*CP 1950*); P. Panóff, in *ZIM* x; *AdHM,* p. 1169f; S. Braschowanov, "Bulgarische Musik," in *MGG* ii.   M.V.

Bund [G.; pl. *Bünde*]. Fret. *Bundfrei,* see under Clavichord.

Burden. Same as *refrain. The term is used particularly in connection with the 15th-century *carol.

Burdo [L.]. See Bourdon.

Burgundian cadence. See under Landini cadence.

Burgundian school. The leading Continental school of composers of the early 15th century, represented chiefly by Guillaume Dufay (*c.* 1400–74), and Gilles Binchois (*c.* 1400–60).

It forms the link between the *ars nova* (14th century) and the Flemish schools (1450–1600) [see History of music]. In older writings, the Burgundian school is called First Netherlands school [see Netherlands schools]. Today, the term "Burgundian school" is preferred because the musical activity of this period centered in the cultural sphere of the duchy of Burgundy, which, under Philip the Good (1419–67) and Charles the Bold (1467–77), included the whole of eastern France as well as Belgium and the Netherlands. Its court at Dijon was the leading center of culture for western Europe, a culture that manifested itself in the paintings of the brothers Van Eyck as well as in the fantastic fashion of peaked shoes, long cone-shaped hats, and extravagant colors that has survived in the "once-upon-a-time" setting of our fairy tales. Another important musical center of the period was Cambrai. Occasionally the term "Burgundian" has been challenged [see *ReMR.* p. 8] on the ground that none of the composers was born in Burgundy, but such reasoning is hardly valid.

The Burgundian school includes a number of composers who were connected with the Burgundian court. In approximately chronological order, they are: Jacques Vide (fl. 1423–33), Nicolas Grenon (fl. 1385–1449), Pierre Fontaine (fl. 1404–47), Gilles Binchois (*c.* 1400–60), Guillaume Dufay (*c.* 1400–74), Hayne van Ghizeghem (fl. 1457–72), and Robert Morton (*c.* 1440–75). Dufay was only temporarily connected with the Burgundian court, probably in the 1440's, but nevertheless held the title of *cantor illustrissimi ducis burgundie.* Ghizeghem was Flemish by birth and Morton English. Certain other composers whose musical production is closely related to that of the "Burgundians" may well be added to the group, notably Arnold and Hugo de Lantins.

The musical style of the Burgundian school stands in marked contrast to the complexity and mannerism of the late 14th century (Selesses, Solage, Matteo da Perugia) and the severe rigidity of the "early Parisians" (Tapissier, Carmen, and Césaris). Strongly influenced by the English school of Dunstable and his contemporaries, and possibly also by Italian models, Dufay and Binchois developed a musical language of translucent beauty and tenderness that has as much immediate appeal today as it must have had 500 years ago. Perhaps their most important contribution (probably derived from English tradition) was the establishment of the third as a principal melodic interval. Many of their melodies could well be considered "ornamented triads" [see Ex., Dufay, "Craindre vous vueil"]. No less important is the establishment

of a strongly consonant idiom based on triadic harmonies that often occur in dominant-tonic relationship. The major mode prevails to a much larger extent than in the subsequent period of Ockeghem and Josquin. An important innovation was *fauxbourdon. Except for Dufay, who wrote also Masses [see Mass II] and motets [see Motet IV], Burgundian composers concentrated on secular forms, especially the *rondeau. These, which are often referred to as polyphonic *formes fixes, are usually in three parts, in a high range, and in 3/4 meter (tempus perfectum). Not without justification has the music of this period been called a "celestial symphony," symbolized in contemporary paintings that show the various instruments of the period—viols, shawms, recorders, trombones, tromba marina—in the hands of angels. Examples in HAM, nos. 65–72. See also Basse danse.

Lit.: E. Dannemann, Die spätgotische Musiktradition in Frankreich und Burgund vor dem Auftreten Dufays (1936); J. Marix, Histoire de la musique et des musiciens de la cour de Bourgogne . . . 1420–1467 (1939); C. van den Borren, Études sur le quinzième siècle musical (1941); W. L. Bethel, "The Burgundian Chanson (1400–1477)" (diss. Univ. of Pennsylvania, 1950); W. Stephan, Die burgundisch-niederländische Motette zur Zeit Ockeghems (1937); F. van der Mueren, "École bourguignonne, école néerlandaise ou début de la renaissance?" (RBM xii); H. Besseler, "Von Dufay bis Josquin" (ZMW xi); W. Gurlitt, "Burgundische Chanson- und deutsche Liedkunst des 15. Jahrhunderts" (CP 1924); C. van den Borren, ‡Polyphonia sacra (1932); J. F. R. and C. Stainer, ‡Dufay and His Contemporaries (1898); K. Dèzes, ‡Messen- und Motettensätze des 15. Jahrhunderts (1927); *Editions VIII, 19, 22; J. Marix, ‡Les Musiciens de la cour de Bourgogne au XVe siècle (1420–1467) [1937]. See also under Chansonnier.

Burla, burlesca [It.]. A composition of a playful character. Bach's A-minor Partita includes a burlesca, Schumann's Albumblätter a burla. A modern example is R. Strauss's Burleske for piano and orchestra.

Burlesque, burletta. An English (and later, American) type of stage entertainment of the late 18th and 19th centuries, which may be considered the successor of the ballad opera. Like the latter, it was a "low-brow" entertainment consisting of comic dialogue and songs sung to borrowed melodies. Its beginning is indicated by Kane O'Hara's Midas, a "burlesque burletta" produced in Dublin in 1762. See W. Rubsamen, in MQ xxxvi.

Burrasca [It.]. A composition descriptive of a tempest or thunderstorm, e.g., the overture of Rossini's Guillaume Tell.

Butterfly. See Madama Butterfly.

Buxheimer Orgelbuch [G., Buxheim Organ Book]. A manuscript (formerly in the possession of the monastery of Buxheim near Munich; now Munich, Staatsbibl., Cim. 352b; olim mus. ms. 3725), written c. 1460–70 (in Munich?), that contains more than 250 organ compositions, notated in the so-called old German organ tablature system. Among these are c. 110 settings (or *intabulations) of German songs, more than 30 intabulations of French chansons (some by Dunstable, Dufay, Binchois), c. 40 liturgical compositions (Kyries, Introits, Marian antiphons, hymns), c. 20 preludes, a number of *basses danses, and 4 (5?) collections similar to Conrad Paumann's *Fundamentum organisandi, although much more extensive. A facsimile edition (by B. A. Wallner) was published in 1954. Transcription in *Editions XVIII, 37–39. See R. Eitner, "Das Buxheimer Orgelbuch" (Beilage of MfM xix/xx); E. Southern, The Buxheim Organ Book [1963]; R. Zöbeley, Die Musik des Buxheimer Orgelbuchs (1964); A. Schering, Studien zur Geschichte der Frührenaissance (1914); H. Schnoor, in ZMW iv; L. Schrade, "Die Messe in der Orgelmusik des 15. Jahrhunderts" (AMF i); E. Southern, "An Index to 'Das Buxheimer Orgelbuch'" (Notes xix); W. Schrammek, "Zur Numerierung im Buxheimer Orgelbuch" (MF ix).

Buysine, buzine, busine, buisine, buzanne [L. buccina]. A medieval straight trumpet. See Buccina; Brass instruments V; also Trombone II.

B.V.M. See under Antiphon (2).

BWV. Abbr. for Thematisch-Systematisches Verzeichnis der musikalischen Werke von Johann Sebastian Bach (1950), i.e., the thematic catalog of the works of J. S. Bach, edited by W. Schmieder. The initials stand for Bach-Werke-Verzeichnis.

Byzantine chant. I. The ecclesiastical chant of the Byzantine Empire (founded A.D. 330 by Constantine the Great; destroyed 1453, with the fall of Constantinople). With the exception of a few ceremonial songs, the *acclamations, no music other than liturgical chants has been preserved. Although the language of the Byzantine Church was Greek, it has become more and more apparent that Byzantine music was not a continuation of ancient Greek music (as long was assumed) but constituted a new tradition based to some extent on Oriental (Jewish, Syrian) models. The Byzantine system of modes (*echos, pl. echoi), for example, differs sharply from that of the so-called Greek modes (tonoi) but is quite similar to that of the Western Church [see Church modes].

II. Byzantine chant has many features in common with Gregorian chant, being monophonic, unaccompanied, chiefly diatonic, and devoid of strict meter. A fundamental difference between the two bodies of chant, however, is their textual basis. Whereas psalmodic and other scriptural texts prevail in Gregorian chant, the texts of Byzantine chant are mostly nonscriptural, although often modeled after psalms or the canticles. Most of them are hymns, written in metrical arrangements that often employ the isosyllabic principle. Another difference is that in the Eastern tradition the Offices are much more elaborate than the Mass.

The earliest hymns, the *troparia* (4th, 5th centuries), were intercalations sung originally between the verses of the psalms. The 6th century marks the beginning of a new era, that of the *kontakion,* with Romanos (*c.* 500) and Sergios (*c.* 600) the leading figures. A *kontakion* is a poem consisting of a short *proœmium* (introduction) and a number (20–30) of stanzas of uniform structure that end with a refrain (either a single word such as " . . . time" or a complete line) and whose initial letters form an acrostic. The most famous example of this kind is the *akathistos. Troparia* and *kontakia* were superseded about 700 by the *kanon* (Andrew of Crete, *c.* 650–720; John of Damascus; and Kosmas of Jerusalem, *c.* 750). The *kanons* are extremely long poems consisting of nine parts (called hymns, odes), each of which was supposed to contain allusions to one of the nine canticles (as a rule, the second ode was omitted on account of the somber nature of the second canticle; all the others are chants of praise and joy). The poetic activity came to an end in the 11th century.

III. The earliest Byzantine sources containing musical signs date from the 9th century and are written in *ecphonetic notation. According to recent interpretation [see C. Høeg, *La Notation ekphonétique* (1935)] these signs, which always occur in pairs (one at the beginning, the other at the end of a sentence), represent certain stereotyped formulas that were employed for frequently used phrases, such as: "And Jesus said." Beginning with the 10th century, sources show a more fully developed type of musical notation, indicating a continuous melody. As is the case in the notation of Gregorian chant, the early Byzantine "neumes" (*c.* 950–1200) cannot be deciphered. Only a few melodies from some of the latest MSS of this period, written in the so-called *Coislin system,* have been transcribed with the help of parallel versions existing in later sources that use the later *middle* (or *round) notation.* The latter system, which was in use *c.* 1100–1450, has been deciphered in all essential details, including the rhythmic significance of the neumatic signs, on the basis of information contained in certain theoretical manuals called *papadike.* The principal feature of this notation is that its signs do not indicate pitches (as do, more or less exactly, the Western neumes), but intervals to be taken from the tone reached previously. The starting note was indicated by a special sign (the *martyrion*), which signified the *echos* of the melody. Thus, in Byzantine notation, the melody d e g g a f g d would be notated as a succession of intervals according to the following scheme: (d) s t u s t– s f– (s = second, u = unison, t = third, f = fourth; descending intervals with a minus sign) [ex. in *GD* i, 520; *GDB* i, 1075].

IV. After about 1100 the traditional chant, which was largely syllabic, was enriched by the introduction of coloraturas that, owing to abuse and individual license, eventually led to the decadence of Byzantine chant. Kukuzeles, who flourished about 1300, seems to have been the first to codify these florid, "kalophonic" chants. In the 14th century the chants were occasionally provided with long coloraturas sung to syllables such as *te-re-rem,* a practice known as *teretism* [see Anenaiki]. At the beginning of the 19th century the Greek archimandrite Chrysanthos developed a notation that utilizes the principles and some of the details of the Byzantine notation and is still used today for the chants of the Greek Church.

So far as we know, the MSS of the 12th and 13th centuries represent the classical tradition of Byzantine chant. The following example [see

Ὑμ-νοῦ-μεν τὸν σω-τῆ-ρα, τὸν ἐκ τῆς παρ-θέ - νου

σαρ-κω - θέν-τα,＿＿＿＿ δι' ἡ - μᾶς γὰρ ἐ - σταυ -

ρω - θη καὶ τῇ τρί-τῃ ἡ - μέ-ρᾳ ἀν＿＿ ἔσ - τη,

δω-ρού - με-νος ἡ-μῖν τὸ μέ - γα ἔ - λε - ος.

First ode of a canon for Saturday in Holy Week.

MQ xxiii, 208] illustrates the syllabic or somewhat neumatic style that prevails in the chants of this period [see also *HAM*, no. 8]. However, there are Alleluias in a highly melismatic style.

In 1935 C. Høeg, H. J. W. Tillyard, and E. Wellesz began a scholarly edition of medieval Byzantine musical MSS entitled *Monumenta Musicae Byzantinae* [see Editions XXIX]. Also

see Acclamation; Akathistos; Akoluthia; *Echos, Ecphonetic notation; Idiomelon; Sticheron.*

Lit.: E. Wellesz, *A History of Byzantine Music and Hymnography*, rev. ed. 1961 (bibl.); *id.; Eastern Elements in Western Chant* (1947); *id., Byzantinische Musik* (1927); *id., ‡Trésor de Musique Byzantine* [1934]; *id., Die Hymnen der Ostkirche* (1962); *id.,* "Music of the Eastern Churches" (*NOH* ii, 14ff); H. J. W. Tillyard, *Byzantine Music and Hymnography* (1923); O. Tiby, *La Musica bizantina* (1938); L. Tardo, *L'antica melurgia bizantina* (1938); *ReMMA*, pp. 75ff; *AdHM* i, 126ff; O. Strunk, *Specimina notationum antiquiorum* (1965); K. Levy, "A Hymn for Thursday in Holy Week" (*JAMS* xvi); H. J. W. Tillyard, "Mediaeval Byzantine Music" (*MQ* xxiii); *id.,* "Byzantine Music" (*ML* iv, 269); *id.,* "Gegenwärtiger Stand der byzantinischen Musikforschung" (*MF* vii); *id.,* "Byzantine Music about A.D. 1100" (*MQ* xxxix); E. Wellesz, "Zum Stil der Melodien der Kontakia" (*CP Anglés* ii); *id.,* "Early Byzantine Neumes" (*MQ* xxxviii); O. Strunk, "The Antiphons of the Oktoechos" (*JAMS* xiii); *id.,* "The Notation of the Chartres Fragment" (*AnnM* iii); *id.,* "The Tonal System of Byzantine Music" (*MQ* xxviii). For additional bibl. see *ReMMA*, pp. 432ff, and O. Tiby, in *RMI* xli, xlii.

C

C. (1) See Letter notation; Pitch names; Hexachord. (2) As an abbreviation, *C* may stand for: *con* (*colla, coll'*), i.e., with [*c.a.; *c.b., *C.O.; *c.s.*]; *cantus* [*c.f.*]; *capo* [*D.C.*]. In modern part songs *C* means *contralto;* in 16th-century partbooks, *cantus*. (3) C clef, see Clef.

C.a. [It.]. Abbr. for *col arco* (with the bow).

Cabaletta [It.]. A short operatic song in popular style, characterized by a rather uniform rhythm in the vocal line and accompaniment. There are many *cabalette* in Rossini's operas. One of the earliest examples is "Le belle immagini" in Gluck's *Paride ed Elena* (1770). In later Italian opera (Verdi) the term was applied to the final stretto close of arias or duets, in which elaborate

treatment usually gives way to quick, uniform rhythm.

Cabocla. An archetype of Brazilian folk music. See under Brazil.

Caça [Sp.]. See *Chace.*

Caccia [It.]. A form of 14th-century Italian poetry and music. The text often deals with hunting and fishing scenes or with similar realistic subjects (a fire, cries of street vendors, etc.). The musical form is a strict canon in two parts, the second usually beginning six or more measures after the first, which is followed by a ritornello that sometimes is also canonic. The two "chasing" voices are usually supported by a tenor line in longer note values that does not imitate the canon melody. The importance of the *caccia* in the history of imitation has been somewhat exaggerated [see Imitation]. Of greater historical significance is the fact that the *caccia* marks the earliest appearance of a supporting lower part, obviously an addition to the duet of the upper parts [see Successive counterpoint]. Some 26 *cacce* survive, by Magister Piero, Giovanni da Cascia, Jacopo da Bologna, Landini, and others.

Although both of the above-mentioned characteristics—realistic text and canonic treatment—are usually present, in some cases a realistic text is composed as a madrigal and in others a madrigal text is composed as a *caccia*. The latter have occasionally been termed "canonic madrigals." It would seem, however, that the term *caccia* referred primarily not to the subject of hunting but to the musical "hunt," i.e., to canonic treatment. Thus, the canonic madrigals would also belong to the category of *caccia*. For a similar type of French music, see *Chace*.

Lit.: G. Carducci, *Cacce in rima* (1896; texts only); W. T. Marrocco, ‡*Fourteenth-Century Italian Cacce*, rev. ed. (1961); R. Fosse, ‡*Fourteenth-Century Canonic Madrigals* (1954); N. Pirrotta, in *RMI* xlviii, 305; A. Einstein, "Eine Caccia im Cinquecento" (*CP Liliencron*, p. 72); *WoGM* ii, iii, nos. 42, 56; *HAM*, no. 52; J. Wolf, *Sing- und Spielmusik aus älterer Zeit* (1926), no. 7; A. Main, "Lorenzo Masini's 'Deer Hunt'" (*CP Sachs*).

Caccia Mass, motet. Modern terms for Mass compositions (mainly Glorias) and motets from the period *c.* 1320–1420 that make use of canonic imitation, either at the beginning or throughout. The term "*caccia* style" is used in the same sense. In all such cases, the designation "canonic" is preferable, being more to the point. Examples of such motets are De Vitry's *Lugentium-Petre*, Ciconia's *O felix templum*, and Dufay's *O sancte Sebastiane;* examples of the Mass are Glorias by Arnold and Hugo de Lantins [see C. van den Borren, *Polyphonia Sacra* (1932), pp. 10ff, 118ff], Dufay's *Gloria ad modum tubae*, and several Glorias by English composers [see M. Bukofzer, *Studies in Medieval and Renaissance Music* (1950), pp. 53ff, 80ff]. See also W. Apel, "Imitation in the Thirteenth and Fourteenth Centuries" (*CP Davison*).

Cacharpaya. Name given either to a fast round of the Andean countries or to a dance performed at the end of carnival festivities. In the Quechuan language the word corresponds to the English "good-bye."   J.O-S.

Cachua. Term (also *cachina, kashwa, kjaswa*, etc.) in the Quechuan language meaning "round dance." Chronicles of the early 17th century indicate that the *cachua* was popular before the Spanish conquest and describe it as a dance in which men and women formed a circle "while around them wove the dancers." A report sent to Charles IV of Spain between 1788 and 1790 includes a collection of melodies from northern Peru, which is headed by two Christmas songs subtitled *cachua*. The present-day *cachua* is also a circle dance, performed by betrothed couples. The men tap their shoes while the women spin around. Various kinds of native flute and the *caja* (small drum) are used to accompany the song, which is in quick 2/4 meter and usually based on the following pattern:

J.O-S.

Cachucha. An Andalusian dance in triple time, similar to the bolero. It was introduced by the dancer Fanny Elssler in the ballet *Le Diable boiteux* (1836).

Cachullapi. Indian song from Ecuador consisting of a single theme in fast 6/8 meter, which is used in the vocal section as well as in the interludes played on a guitar. The melody is usually based on a descending pentatonic scale (c′–a–g–f–d).   J.O-S.

Cacophony. Harsh, discordant sound; dissonance. Richard Strauss' tone poems were decried as cacophony when they were first performed.

Cadence [G. *Kadenz;* F. *cadence;* It. *cadenza;* Sp. *cadencia*]. I. A melodic or harmonic formula that occurs at the end of a composition, a section, or a phrase, conveying the impression of a momentary or permanent conclusion. Each period of music history has a rather limited number of such formulas or, at least, a limited number of models of which all closing passages are but variations or modifications. The cadences in use during the 18th and 19th centuries have been studied in great detail. Unfortunately, the classification and terminology in this area lack uniformity and frequently also clarity. The following discussion is not intended to present a complete list of terms but to clarify the essential points [see the chapter on "Cadences" in W. Piston, *Harmony*, rev. ed. (1962)].

A cadence is called *perfect* (*final, full*) if it can

be satisfactorily and normally used as the close of a composition. According to the standards of classical harmony, the last chord must be the tonic triad (I) and must have the tonic note in the soprano. For the penultimate chord, there is

V   I   IV   I   IV   V   I   IV I^6_4 V   I

V   I V^6 I   V/V   V   IV/V   V   V/IV   IV
                   (I   V) (I   IV)

IV/IV   IV   V   VI   V VI^b V   III   V I^7

a choice between the dominant (V) and the subdominant (IV), both in root position. The combination V–I is called *authentic* cadence [Ex. 1], the progression IV–I, *plagal* cadence [Ex. 2]. The authentic cadence usually occurs in the fuller form IV–V–I (II⁶–V–I) [Ex. 3] or, still more complete, IV–I^6_4–V–I (II⁶–I^6_4–V–I) [Ex. 4]. The last four are sometimes called *mixed* cadences.

The remaining cadences fall into two classes, *imperfect* cadences and *deceptive* (or *interrupted*) cadences. The imperfect cadences are the same as the two elementary perfect cadences except that they have the tonic chord in another arrangement, e.g., with the third or fifth in the soprano [Ex. 5]; or they have the penultimate chord in inversion [Ex. 6]—these are called *inverted* or *medial* cadences, as opposed to a *radical* [L. *radix*, root] cadence—or occur in transposition to the dominant (or more rarely, the subdominant) [Ex. 7-10]. These "transposed" cadences occur almost regularly at the end of the first half of a musical phrase and are therefore termed *half-cadence* (authentic or plagal).

The deceptive cadence [F. *cadence rompue, c. évitée;* G. *Trugschluss;* It *.inganno;* Sp. *cadencia interrumpia*] is an authentic (or, sometimes, plagal) cadence whose tonic chord (I) is—deceptively—replaced by some other chord, most frequently by VI [Ex. 11]. Some other possibilities are indicated in Ex. 12-14. See also Masculine, feminine cadence.

II. The cadences of early music differ sharply from those described above, particularly prior to 1500, when progressions such as V–I and IV–I were very seldom used [see Harmony]. The history of these cadences is interesting, since the various formulas are characteristic of their period and may well serve as identifying marks. In Gregorian chant, by far the most frequent cadential motion is that of the descending second, II–I, with III–I being next in importance. Ascending motion is much rarer and is practically limited to the ascending second (VII–I). It appears more often in later chants, such as hymns of sequences, but almost never as a leading tone (e–f). Prior to 1450, practically all cadences of polyphonic music are based on the progression II–I in the lowest part (tenor). This cadence appears with various modifications [Ex. 15-19], among which that with two "leading tones," one before the octave and the other before the fifth, is particularly common before and after 1400 [Ex. 16-18; see Lydian; also Landini cadence]. After 1400 another modification of the II–I cadence appears, in which the contratenor jumps up an octave from the fourth below to the fifth above the tonic [Ex. 20]. This cadence is interesting because it foreshadows the authentic cadence, with its V–I movement in the lowest part [Ex. 21]. This, as well as the plagal cadence, was introduced about 1450 as a result of the addition of a true bass to musical texture (Ockeghem, Obrecht; see Flemish school). The earlier type (II–I) survived only in the so-called Phrygian cadence [Ex. 22; see Phrygian]. It should be noted that until 1500 the third is almost always omitted in the final chord of the authentic as well as the plagal cadence [see

Triad; Picardy third]. In the 16th century the "suspension" formula [Ex. 21] was universally accepted, while in the 17th century the "anticipation" formula [Ex. 23] is very common. Composers of the 17th century frequently used both formulas simultaneously in two parts (violins) in a strikingly dissonant combination known as *Corelli clash* [Ex. 24; for an early instance, in Stefano Landi's *Il Sant' Alessio* (1634), see H. Goldschmidt, *Studien zur Geschichte der italienischen Oper*, 2 vols. (1901, '04), i, 212].

III. The cadences of the classical and romantic periods are of little historical interest since they usually conform to the standard types outlined in I. Toward the end of the 19th century, however, the amplification of the harmonic vocabulary brought with it numerous novelties in the writing of cadences, such as the use of modal cadences [Ex. 25; Mussorgsky, *Boris Godunov*, 1869], the use of a dissonant final chord [Ex. 26; Ravel, *Les Grands Vents*, 1906], polytonal formations [Ex. 27; Busoni, *Sonatina Seconda*, 1912], and, later, the return to a "contrapuntal" type of cadence reminiscent of medieval cadences in the steplike motion of the bass and in their "plagal" feeling [Ex. 28; Hindemith, *Sonate für Klavier*, 1936].

Lit.: A. Casella, *The Evolution of Music, throughout the History of the Perfect Cadence*

(1924): F. W. Homan, "Final and Internal Cadential Patterns in Gregorian Chant" (*JAMS* xvii); R. W. Wienpahl, "The Evolutionary Significance of 15th-Century Cadential Formulae" (*JMT* iv); J. A. Westrup, in *CP Jeppesen;* E. M. Lee, "Cadences and Closes" (*PMA* xxxi); G. Haydon, "The Cadence" (*Proceedings of the Music Teachers National Association* xxix); A. Shepherd, "The Cadence in the Music of J. S. Bach" (*ibid.*); G. S. Dickinson, "A View of Cadence with Reference to Modern Contratonal Systems" (*ibid.*); H. J. Moser, "Das Schicksal der Penultima" (*JMP* xli); *id.,* "Die harmonischen Funktionen in der tonalen Kadenz" (*ZMW* i); M. E. Brockhoff, "Die Kadenz bei Josquin" (*CP 1952*); C. Artom, "Cadenze e pseudocadenze" (*RMI* xxxiv); R. Tenschert, "Die Kadenzbehandlung bei Richard Strauss" (*ZMW* viii); A. Schmitz, "Die Kadenz als Ornamentum musicae" (*CP 1953*).

Cadence [F.] A 17th-century name for the trill.

Cadent. See under Nachschlag.

Cadenza. A passage or section of varying length in a style of brilliant improvisation, usually inserted near the end of a composition, where it serves as a retarding element, giving the performer a chance to exhibit his technical mastery. Its traditional place is in the concerto, between the six-four chord (marked with a *fermata*) and the dominant chord of the final cadence [see Ex.]. Such cadenzas make ample use of highly virtuoso passage work but also draw from the thematic substance of the movement, presenting its subjects in artfully devised modifications or combinations. They usually close with an extended trill on the dominant chord.

In most of the earlier concertos (Haydn; Mozart; Beethoven, Piano Concertos nos. 1–4) the cadenzas are not included in the composition but were supposed to be provided by the performer. In the 19th century, cadenzas to the famous concertos were written by the outstanding virtuosos (Hummel, Thalberg, Moscheles, Reinecke, Joachim), frequently without proper regard to style, so that it is not unusual to hear a Mozart concerto with a cadenza full of the lush harmonies and heavy texture of late romanticism. Beethoven was the first to write his own cadenzas as an integral part of the work, in his last Piano Concerto, op. 73 (Emperor Concerto). This precedent was followed by most of his successors (Schumann, Brahms), who wanted to guard their works against the poor taste and stylistic incongruities of the "pianist-composers." There exist authentic cadenzas (written by the composers themselves) for all of Beethoven's concertos and for a number of Mozart's concertos. Although not entirely satisfactory, they should be consulted by anyone confronted with the necessity of choosing (or writing) a cadenza. Judicious artists will probably find them preferable to any of those in current use, with the sole exception of the excellent cadenzas to Mozart's piano concertos written by Busoni. In the piano compositions of Chopin and Liszt, ample use is made of another type of cadenza, consisting of relatively short portions of glittering passage work, written in small notes and inserted where a momentary retardation or a display of pianistic brilliancy was desired.

Cadenzas in the form of running passages following (rather than preceding) the final chord of a cadence occur in early keyboard and guitar music ("Praeambulum super D," in *Editions XVIII, 39, p. 318f; Milán, Libro de musica de vihuela da mano, 1535). Early examples of the modern cadenza, on I_4^6, are found in Corelli and Vivaldi (c. 1700). Throughout the 18th century improvised cadenzas of a highly virtuoso type were an established feature of the solo arias in the Neapolitan operas and provided the inspiration for the cadenzas written into contemporary concertos (Mozart).

Lit.: R. Stockhammer, "Die Kadenzen zu den Klavierkonzerten der Wiener Klassiker" (diss. Vienna, 1936); H. Knödt, "Zur Entwicklungsgeschichte der Kadenzen im Instrumentalkonzert" (SIM xv); A. Schering, "Die freie Kadenz im Instrumentalkonzert des 18. Jahrhunderts" (CP 1906).

Cadenzato [It.]. Rhythmical.

Caecilianismus [G.]. See Cecilian movement.

Caisse [F.]. Drum. See Percussion instruments B, 1–3.

Calando [It.]. Gradually diminishing.

Calascione [It.]. Same as colascione [see Lute II].

Calata [It.]. An Italian dance of the early 16th century known only (?) through thirteen examples in Petrucci's Intavolatura de lauto Libro quarto (1508). Ten of them—including one for two lutes—are in 3/2 time (notated in three measures of 2/4), thus resembling the bassadanza [see Basse danse]. The others are in 6/8 time, similar to the *pivas of the same publication. See J. W. Wasielewski, Geschichte der Instrumentalmusik im xvi. Jahrhundert (1878), Suppl.

Calenda [Sp.]. An early dance form, very popular in Santo Domingo, that supposedly originated on Africa's Guinea coast and then spread throughout South America. It is the precursor of the Chilean zamacueca. During the 16th century it was so popular that it was performed in religious processions and even inside churches on Christmas Eve.   J.O-S.

Callino casturame. Title of a piece in the Fitzwilliam Virginal Book. It is probably a corruption of the Irish "Cailinog a stuir me" (Young girl, my treasure).

Calliope. An instrument invented in America in the 1880's and named after the Muse of Eloquence, probably because its inventor expected it to have divine powers of persuasion. It consists of a number of steam-blown whistles played from a keyboard. It can be heard at a great distance and is still occasionally used at fairs and circuses.

Callithump. Same as *charivari.

Calmando, calmato [It.]. Quieting, quieted.

Calm Sea and Prosperous Voyage. See Meerestille und glückliche Fahrt.

Calore, con; caloroso [It.]. With warmth.

Calypso. A regional type of ballad sung in Trinidad that employs a peculiar mixture of French, English, and even African words. Its origin has been traced to the late 18th century when, on the island's plantations, popular singers known as shatwel sang satirical songs about unpopular members of the community. Later these songs were mingled with the kalinda (Sp. calenda) and became part of carnival festivities. From the kalenda derive most of the devices of calypso musical accompaniments, the drum rhythms, and also the use of the shakshak (maraca) and the bottle-and-spoon.

In Trinidad today there is a community of professional calypso singers who usually compose both the words and music of their songs or rework a popular calypso melody of the past. Special emphasis is put on the invention of new words, on stressing of local events, and on use of a colloquial idiom full of slang and artificially accented words. The music, however, continues to use a limited number of melodic patterns. Always strident, it is based on breathless tunes, highly syncopated and repetitious.   J.O-S.

Cambia, cambiano [It.]. Direction in orchestral scores to change instruments or tuning [see under Muta].

Cambiata [It., Sp.; F. *note de rechange;* G. *Wechselnote*]. A term used, rather confusingly, for a variety of formations that belong to the general category of nonharmonic notes. All the various interpretations of the term go back to the *Gradus ad Parnassum* (1725) of J. J. Fux, who explains the *cambiata* as the formation shown in Ex. a. This presents an exception from the general rule that a dissonant note (the second of the four quarter notes) should be resolved in conjunct motion. K. Jeppesen [*The Style of Palestrina and the Dissonance,* rev. ed. (1946), p. 213; *Counterpoint* (1939), p. 125] has broadened the meaning of the term, applying it to somewhat similar but shorter formations that occur in 15th- and 16th-century music, one (Ex. b) consisting of three notes, the other (Ex. c, common in Palestrina) of four. The term has also been used for formations such as shown in Ex. d and e. All these have in common a dissonant note followed by the inter-

val of a third, not, as the strict rules would require, a (descending) second. For yet another meaning of the term, see Nonharmonic tones. See C. Dahlhaus, "Die 'Nota Cambiata'" (*KJ* xlvii).

Cambodia. See under Thailand.

Camera [It.]. In baroque music (1600–1750), *da camera* indicates music for use outside the church, as distinguished from *da chiesa,* music to be performed in the church [see *Chiesa*]. This dichotomy was applied to sonatas, cantatas, duettos, etc. In the first case especially it entailed a distinct difference of form that is discussed under *Sonata da camera, da chiesa.* In modern Italian usage, *musica da camera* means chamber music.

Camerata [It.]. In the 16th century, a name for small academies. Specifically, a group of literary men, musicians, and amateurs who, about 1580, began to gather in the palace of Count Giovanni Bardi at Florence to discuss the possibilities of a new musical style in imitation of the music of the ancient Greek drama [see Nuove musiche; Opera]. Members of this "charmed circle" were the poet Ottavio Rinuccini and the musicians Vincenzo Galilei, Giulio Caccini, and Jacopo Peri. In 1592, when Bardi went to Rome, Jacopo Corsi became the leader of the group.

Lit.: C. Palisca, *Letters on Ancient and Modern Music to Vincenzo Galilei and Giovanni Bardi* (1960); *id.,* "The Beginnings of Baroque Music" (diss. Harvard Univ., 1954); H. Martin, "La 'Camerata' du Comte Bardi et la musique florentine du xvie siècle" (*RdM* 1932, pp. 63, 152, 227; 1933, pp. 92, 141); G. Gilli, *Una Corte alla fine del '500* (1928); R. Paoli, "Difesa del primo melodramma" (*LRM* 1950, p. 93).

Camminando [It.]. "Walking," pushing on.

Campana [It.]. Bell. Campanology is the art of bell-founding and bell-ringing. *Campanella* (little bell) is the *glockenspiel; also, the title of a violin piece by Paganini and an etude by F. Liszt (a piano adaptation of the former) in which the sound of small bells is imitated.

Campanello di Notte, Il [It., The Night Bell]. Opera in one act by Donizetti (to his own libretto), produced in Naples, 1836. Setting: a suburb of Naples, early 19th century.

Can. Abbr. for *cantoris;* see *Decani* and *cantoris.*

Canada. For the music of the original inhabitants of Canada, see American Indian music and Eskimo music.

In the earliest time of permanent French settlement (Quebec, 1608) music was employed in attempts to convert Indians to the Roman Catholic faith. Although plainsong was taught to French boys as early as 1635 and an organ is mentioned in Quebec in 1661 (the first in North America), church music, unlike religious art, did not receive systematic encouragement. A liturgical composition by Abbé Charles Amador Martin (1648–1711) has been preserved. Secular art music seems to have been restricted to the parties and balls of a few members of the ruling classes. Far more widespread was French folksong, much of which has been preserved through oral tradition and which, together with variants and new songs, such as those of the *voyageurs,* forms a literature of many thousands of items. A similar process took place with the English and Gaelic songs of the Atlantic provinces.

The establishment of British rule (1760) and the growth of urban centers encouraged theater, opera, and subscription concerts. Chamber and orchestral music by Gyrowetz, Haydn, Mozart, and Pleyel was imported and performed. The Frenchman Joseph Quesnel (1749–1809; arrived 1779) became a pioneer of the theater in Montreal and wrote plays, poetry, and music, including a tuneful *comédie mêlée d'ariettes* entitled *Colas et Colinette* (Montreal, 1790). Church music was aided by the importation of organs, printing of music (1800), and, in Protestant communities, "singing schools."

In the second half of the 19th century the apparatus of modern musical life was established, with its societies (usually choirs with *ad hoc* orchestras), visits by virtuoso performers, private, conservatory and elementary-school teaching, piano and organ manufacturing, and sheet-music publishing. But most enterprises were short-lived. Taste was shallow; concerts were dominated by vocal renditions or instrumental fantasias of operatic and national airs and bravura pieces. Nevertheless, individual musicians did succeed in introducing the great oratorios (*Messiah,* Toronto, 1857) and orchestral works (Beethoven, Ninth Symphony, Montreal, 1897) and in raising the level of church music. By the beginning of the 20th century Canada excelled in choral singing. German immigrants were active in teaching and in the music trade, whereas British organist-choirmasters wielded the dominant influence in music education and church music from Confederation (1867) until World War II.

French-speaking Canada was the first region to depend largely on its own musicians. Outstanding among them were Calixa Lavallée (1842–91), composer of the national song "O Canada" (1880) and also of operettas and band music; the Montreal organist-teacher-composers Romain Octave Pelletier (1844–1927), Guillaume Couture (1851–1915), and Alexis Contant (1858–1918); and the Quebec folksong collector Ernest Gagnon (1834–1915) and bandmaster Joseph Vézina (1849–1924). The soprano Emma Lajeunesse (1847–1930) achieved world fame as Mme. Albani. The earliest Anglo-Canadian composers included Wesley Octavius Forsyth (1859–1937), Clarence Lucas (1866–1947), and British-born Charles A. E. Harriss (1862–1929; arrived 1882). By World War I a fair number of respectable choral-orchestral works (cantatas, oratorios, Masses), light operas, and piano pieces had been produced, but almost nothing in the larger instrumental forms. About 1925 folksong collectors, led by Marius Barbeau (b. 1885), began to publish material that was seized upon by composers like Alfred Laliberté (1882–1952), Claude Champagne (1891–1965), and Ernest MacMillan (b. 1893; knighted 1935), the last-named Canada's leading conductor and musical statesman. Paris-trained musicians such as Léo-Pol Morin (1892–1941) and Rodolphe Mathieu (1896–1962) brought impressionist and other contemporary techniques to Canada. But it was a younger generation whose determination and talent made a place in Canada for the professional composer. These composers include Barbara Pentland (b. 1912), John Weinzweig (b. 1913), Alexander Brott (b. 1915), Jean Vallerand (b. 1915), Jean Papineau-Couture (b. 1916) and Godfrey Ridout (b. 1918). Aided by the Canadian Broadcasting Corporation, these composers employ various media of composition. Those born in the 1920's and later became the first to receive training in contemporary techniques at home as well as abroad. Harry Somers (b. 1925) and Pierre Mercure (1927–1966) are typical of this generation. A wide range from conservative to avant-garde is also apparent among the immigrants, including Healey Willan (1880–1968), known for his organ and choral music, Arnold Walter (b. 1902), Otto Joachim (b. 1910), Oskar Morawetz (b. 1917), Istvan Anhalt (b. 1919), and Udo Kasemets (b. 1919).

Lit.: H. Kallmann, *A History of Music in Canada 1534–1914* (1960); E. MacMillan, ed., *Music in Canada* (1955); H. Kallmann, ed., *Catalogue of Canadian Composers* (1952); Sœurs de Sainte-Anne, *Dictionnaire biographique des musiciens canadiens* (1935); M. Dwyer, ed., *A Bio-bibliographical Finding List of Canadian Musicians* (1961); A. Lasalle-Leduc, *La Vie musicale au Canada français* (1964); E. Gagnon, *Chansons populaires du Canada,* rev. ed. (1956); E. Fowke and R. Johnston, ‡*Folk Songs of Canada* (1954); E. Fowke, A. Mills, and H. Blume, ‡*Canada's Story in Song* (1960); H. Creighton, ‡*Maritime Folk Songs* (1962); K. Peacock, ‡*Songs of the Newfoundland Outports,* 3 vols. (1965); M. and R.

d'Harcourt, ‡*Chansons folkloriques françaises au Canada* (1956); M. Barbeau, ‡*Le Rossignol y chante* (1962); M. Barbeau, "Folksongs of French Canada" (*ML* xiii, 169).   H.K.

Canarie, canario. A French dance of the 17th century, obviously designed as an imitation of the "sauvages des îles Canaries," the natives of the Canary Islands, who represented an exotic element in the European culture of the 16th and 17th centuries. Arbeau, in his *Orchésographie (1589), says that it originated in the *mascarade* (masked dance) and gives a melody in the rhythmic pattern |♩♪♪|. The known examples, dating from the 17th century, are all (?) in quick 3/8 or 6/8 time, usually with a dotted note on each strong beat. The earliest *canario* occurs in a "Balletto con gagliarda, saltarello e canario" in M. F. Caroso's *Nobilità di Dame* (1600), where it forms a short conclusion of eight measures. More fully developed examples are found in the harpsichord suites of Chambonnières (*c.* 1602–72) and Louis Couperin (*c.* 1626–61). Others occur in the operas of Lully, Purcell (*Dioclesian*, 1690), in J. K. F. Fischer's *Les Pièces de Clavessin* (1696), in G. Muffat's *Florilegium primum* (1695), etc. Examples in *TaAM* vii, 43. See P. Nettl, in *StM* viii. Also see Dance music III.

Cancan. A French dance of the late 19th century that developed from the quadrille and became world famous for its vulgarity and lasciviousness. J. Offenbach introduced it into his *Orphée aux enfers* (1874).

Cancel. Same as natural (sign).

Canción [Sp.]. Song. Specifically, a 15th-century type of poetry, differing from the contemporary *villancico* through its association with the aristocracy, its regularity of verse structure, and complete agreement between the metrical and musical schemes. See under Virelai. See I. Pope, in *AnnM* ii, 198.

Cancionero [Sp.]. (1) Collection of Spanish folksongs. Publications of this type have been issued by F. Pedrell and by E. M. Torner. (2) Collections of Spanish (Portuguese) polyphonic art songs of the 15th and 16th centuries, identical in scope with the French **chansonniers.* The earliest and most important ones are the *Cancionero of Seville* (bibl. Colombina MS 7-1-28; see R. C. Lawes, "The Seville Cancionero: Transcription and Commentary" [diss. North Texas College, 1960]) and the *Cancionero de Palacio* [see Editions XXXII, 5, 10; Sources,

no. 27], which together contain more than 500 secular songs (*canciones, villancicos,* etc.) of the 15th and early 16th centuries. Other collections are: *Cancionero de Juan del Encina, 1496* (fac. ed. by Real Academia Española, 1928); *Cancioneiro of Elvas* (Portuguese; pub. in M. Joaquim, *O Cancioneiro . . . da Biblioteca Públia Hortênsia,* 1940); *Cancionero de Upsala* (Venice, 1556; new ed. R. Mitjana, J. Bal y Gay, and I. Pope, Mexico, 1944); *Cancionero musical de la Casa de Medinaceli* [see Editions XXXII, 8, 9]; *Cancionero de Sablonara* (Munich, Staatsbibl. *Mus. E 200;* pub. in D. J. Aroca, *Cancionero . . . del siglo XVII recogido por Claudio de la Sablonara,* 1918). For their contents, see *ReMR,* pp. 582ff, 611ff.

Cancrizans. In crabwise motion; see Retrograde.

Canntaireachd. See under Pibroch.

Canon. (1) A contrapuntal device whereby an extended melody, stated in one part, is imitated strictly and in its entirety in one or more other parts. Usually the imitating part follows at a short distance (one measure), as in the accompanying example by Schubert (Piano Trio op. 100, Scherzo). Thus, in a canon the normal contrapuntal texture of horizontal (melodic) and vertical (harmonic) relationships is "reinforced" by diagonal threads that consistently connect the places of imitation [see Texture]. It is this added dimension that accounts for the special

artistic charm of the canon. Any phrase heard in the leading voice (*dux,* antecedent) will soon be heard in the following voice or voices (*comes,* consequent); in the meantime, however, the *dux* has proceeded to another motif that sounds against the first and that will, in turn, soon occur in the *comes.*

I. *Types.* The following types of canon are commonly distinguished. (a) According to the temporal distance between the parts: canon of one, two, etc., measures. In earlier terminology: *canon ad minimam, ad semibrevem, ad brevem* (or *ad tempus*), i.e., in the distance of a minim, etc. (b) According to the interval of imitation: canon in unison, at the fifth, fourth, etc. Earlier terms are: *canon ad unisonum, ad subdiapente* (the *comes* begins at the lower fifth), *ad diatessaron* (the *comes* begins at the higher fourth), etc. According to special devices: (c) canon by augmentation or diminution (the *comes* has the melody in doubled or in halved values); (d) canon by inversion (the *comes* has the inverted melody; also called *per motu contrario*); (e) retrograde canon, crab canon, or *canon cancrizans* (the *comes* imitates the *dux* in retrograde motion; see Retrograde); (f) *canon al contrario riverso* (the *comes* is the retrograde inversion of the *dux;* such a canon can be executed by two players reading the same melody simultaneously from opposite sides of the page); (g) *group canon* (the *dux* and, consequently, the *comes* consist of two or more parts each; a famous example of this type is Byrd's motet "Diliges Dominum"; most of the many-voiced canons of the 17th century —for 12, 16, or even 48 voices—belong to this group); (h) *circle canon* or perpetual canon (i.e., one that leads back to the beginning and that therefore may be repeated several times; most of the popular canons called *rounds belong to this type); (i) *spiral canon* or *canon per tonos* (here the melody ends one tone higher than it started; thus the canon must be played six times, first in C, then in D, E, F-sharp, etc.; an example is found in Bach's *Musikalisches Opfer* under the title: "Ascendenteque modulatione ascendat gloria regis," i.e., "May the glory of the king rise as the modulation ascends"). A canon is called *mixed* if parts are added (usually in the bass) that do not participate in the imitation (e.g., the canons in Bach's *Goldberg Variations*). The term "canon" is also used for what is more properly called (fugal) *stretto.

II. *History.* The technique of canonic imitation, that is, of canon in the present-day sense, was first used in the 13th century. Several motets include long passages in canonic imitation, a particularly striking example being the motet "S'on me regarde" (Codex Montpellier, no. 325). *Sumer is icumen in* is the earliest composition consisting exclusively of a canon. Also in this category are the *caccia and *chace of the 14th century. A number of 14th- and 15th-

1. Canon by augmentation (Vaqueiras, Missa L'Homme armé). 2. Canon by inversion (Mouton; see SchGMB, no. 66). 3. Canon by inversion (Bach, Kanonische Veränderungen über das Weinachtslied). 4. Retrograde canon. 5. Retrograde-inverted canon.

century motets and Mass compositions open with a section in canonic imitation [see *Caccia* Mass]. Of particular interest are the various canonic treatments of the *L'Homme armé* melody in the 15th-century Masses based on the *cantus firmus* [see Lit., Apel]. A landmark of canonic art, comparable to the canons in Bach's *Goldberg Variations,* is Ockeghem's *Missa prolationum,* each movement of which consists of a double mensuration canon [see *ReMR,* pp. 133ff]. Prominent in late 15th- and early 16th-century music (Josquin and others) is the canonic chanson, in which two voices form a canon [see *HAM,* no. 91; see Lit., Rubsamen]. Palestrina often used canons in the last Agnus Dei of his Masses. Of special interest is the technique of writing a two-part canon to a *cantus firmus*. Introduced by Zarlino (*Le Istitutioni harmoniche*, 1558, Part 3, ch. 63), it was used by Nanino [see *HAM*, no. 152; *ReMR*, p. 482f], Titelouze, Scheidt, and Bach [**Musikalisches Opfer*], *as well* as in a collection of 16th-century English keyboard pieces by Thomas Woodson [see H. Miller, in *JAMS* viii]. A group canon in 40 (4 × 10) parts occurs in Venegas' *Libro de cifra nueva* (1557; see Editions XXXII, 2, p. 163), and a group canon for two lutes in V. Galilei's *Il Fronimo* (1568; see Editions XXIII, 4, p. 12). Both are called "fuga."

In the 17th century, canons were frequently devised so as to admit a number of solutions. A well-known example is a "Non nobis domine" (attributed, probably wrongly, to W. Byrd), which admits six or seven solutions depending on the number of parts, the intervals, and the distance of the imitating parts [see *GD* iii, 642; *GDB* vi, 99, 100]. Pier Francesco Valentini (*c.* 1570–1654) wrote a canon that boasts of more than two thousand solutions. At the same time, the English provided a great number of popular canons in their *catches. It was chiefly through Bach that the canon again won an important position in music, a position it has maintained to the present day. Particularly noteworthy are Bach's *Kanonische Veränderungen über das Weihnachtslied* and the canons in his **Goldberg Variations*. Haydn, Mozart, and Beethoven contributed many charming examples to the popular repertory and also used canon technique in their sonatas (mostly in the minuets) and variations. A well-known later example is the last movement of Franck's Violin Sonata (1886), which, however, employs a rather facile technique, whereas Brahms made more ingenious use of the canon. e.g., in his *13 Canons* (for women's voices), op. 113.

The 20th-century development has brought with it a remarkable revival of canonic writing. Schoenberg has written canons as birthday greetings for G. B. Shaw, T. Mann, and Carl Engel. The last-named piece is a triple mensuration canon like Josquin's "Fuga trium vocum" (see under III). Bartók used canonic writing, particularly in his string quartets, and his *Music for Strings, Percussion and Celesta* has a mirror canon in the first movement. Berg's Violin Concerto has much canonic writing in the second movement, including a four-part canon for solo violin. L. Dallapiccola's *Tartiniana* has a crab canon in the third movement. Serial composers have made extensive use of canons.

III. *Early meaning of the term.* In early music, the present-day type of canon occurs under such names as *caccia, chace* (14th century) or *fuga* (16th century), while the term canon means any kind of inscription ("rule") giving a clue for the execution of a composition that is intentionally notated incompletely or obscurely (*riddle canon*). Such canons appear first in the works of Machaut, among them a motet "Trop plus est belle" [see F. Ludwig, *G. de Machaut, Musikalische Werke* ii, 71; J. Wolf, *Musikalische Schrift-Tafeln* (1930), p. 23], whose tenor is to be sung "ad modum rondelli" (*rondellus* here means not "round" but *rondeau), i.e., as follows: a b a a a b a b, although only a b is notated. Examples of much greater complexity occur in the French MSS of the late *ars nova* [see, e.g., the "Canon balade" in *WoHN* i, 375]. In the Flemish era (*c.* 1450–1550) the canonic inscriptions grew more and more enigmatic so that Tinctoris, in his *Diffinitorium* (*c.* 1475), aptly defines the canon as "a rule which shows the intention of the composer in an obscure way" [*CS* iv, 179]. Among the simpler examples of riddle canon are the various inscriptions indicating *inversion and *retrograde motion. More complicated is the inscription given with the Agnus Dei of Dufay's *Missa L'Homme armé*: "Cancer eat plenus et redeat medius" (the crab proceed full and return half). This means that the tenor should be read first backwards (a crab "proceeds" backwards) in the full note values, then forward from the beginning, but in halved note values [see *HAM*, no. 66c]. Even more oracular are inscriptions such as "Ne recorderis" (lit., Don't remember), which must be read "Ne re corderis," i.e., "Don't remember *re*," "Don't sing *re*," "Omit all the notes *re*," i.e., "*d*." Particularly complicated riddle canons occur in the English 15th-century *Missa O quam suavis* [new ed. by H. B. Collins (1927)]. For more details see W. Ambros, *Geschichte der Musik*, iii, 62ff; *WoHN* i, 427; *GD* ii, 713 ("Inscriptions"); *RiHM* ii.1, 83–95; *ApNPM*, pp. 179ff.

Less obscure are the so-called *mensuration canons* of the 15th and 16th centuries. Here, a single written part must be read simultaneously in different mensurations or proportions. In such a canon the voices start simultaneously but proceed differently, owing to the different value of the longer notes (*longa, brevis*) under the various signs of mensuration. The accompanying example shows a portion of a "Fuga trium vocum" by Josquin des Prez [see *ApNPM*, p. 181; *HAM*, no. 89].

Lit.: S. Jadassohn, *Canon and Fugue* (1899); C. H. Kitson, *Invertible Counterpoint and Canon* (1927); E. Prout, *Double Counterpoint and Canon* [1891]; B. Ziehn, *Canonical Studies* (1912); L. Feininger, *Die Frühgeschichte des Kanons bis Josquin* (1937); W. R. Rubsamen, ‡*Canonic Chansons and Motets of the Early 16th Century* (1954); F. Jöde, ‡*Der Kanon* (1926); W. Apel, "Imitation Canons on L'Homme armé" (*Speculum* xxv); A. Schering, "Ein Rätseltenor Okeghems" (*CP Kretzschmar*); A. Ghislanzoni, "La Genesi storica della fuga" (*RMI* li, lii, liii); P. Mies, "Der Kanon im mehrsätzigen klassischen Werk" (*ZMW* viii); O. E. Deutsch, "Haydns Kanons" (*ZMW* xv).

(2) In ancient Greek music, canon (*kanón*) is the name of the monochord that served to demonstrate the "laws" of acoustics. See *Kanun.*

(3) In Byzantine chant, a special type of poetry, more correctly spelled *kanon;* see Byzantine chant II.

(4) In the Roman liturgy, the Canon is the central and most solemn part of the Mass, said by the officiating priest after the Sanctus. It begins with the words "Te igitur" [see LU, p. 4].

Canonical hours. See under Office.

Canonic treatment, style. Term for short passages written as a more or less free canon and forming part of a larger composition such as a sonata (frequently in the development section).

Canso. See *Canzo.*

Cantabile [It.]. Singable, singing.

Cantata. A composite vocal form of the baroque period, consisting usually of a number of movements, such as arias, recitatives, duets, and choruses, which are based on a continuous narrative text that is lyrical, dramatic, or religious. Owing to the activity of J. S. Bach, the church cantata, i.e., a cantata with devotional subject matter, is particularly well known and clearly defined. However, the secular cantata was not only the earlier but also the more common type throughout the 17th century, especially in Italy.

I. The cantata appeared shortly after 1600 as an offspring of the monodic style. In its early, experimental stage (before 1630) it occurs under different names and in a great variety of forms and styles. Certain pieces in Caccini's *Nuove musiche* (1602) and in Peri's *Varie musiche* (1609), written in the form of strophic arias with the same bass used for every stanza but with different melodies for the voice [see Strophic bass], may be considered the point of departure. As a matter of fact, Alessandro Grandi's cantatas (*Cantade et arie a voce sola,* repr. 1620; first use of the name) as well as the majority of cantatas written before 1650 follow the same scheme as the "strophic-bass cantata" [see *RiHM* ii.2, 20, 31; *AdHM* i, 437; *BuMBE,* p. 32]. On the other hand, a piece such as Peri's "Se tu parti" more clearly foreshadows the later cantata, since its three stanzas (written to the same bass) contain contrasting sections, arioso and recitativo, separated by instrumental ritornellos, and thus anticipate to some extent the composite structure of the developed cantata. This structure becomes more clearly evident in the cantatas of Francesco Rasi (*Dialoghi rappresentativi,* 1620; see *RiHM,* p. 299), G. Pietro Berti (*Cantate ed arie,* 1624), G. F. Sances (*Cantade,* 4 vols., 1633–40), and Benedetto Ferrari (*Musiche varie,* 1637). The free composite cantata—in a way, the vocal counterpart of the contemporary *canzona da sonare*—reached a peak in Luigi Rossi (1597–1653; see *RiHM,* pp. 371ff), Giacomo Carissimi (1605–74; see *RiHM,* p. 383f), and Marc'-Antonio Cesti (1623–69; see *AdHM* ii, 439). This form was taken over by F. Provenzale and A. Scarlatti. After 1700, the form of the cantata became standardized as a sequence of two, or sometimes three, *da capo* arias connected by a recitative. It is interesting to note that an almost identical process of standardization took place simultaneously in the instrumental field, leading from the canzona to the *sonata da chiesa* and *sonata da camera.* A. Stradella wrote more than 190 cantatas and A. Scarlatti more than 600, mostly of the type described above, which was almost exclusively adopted in the 18th century as a convenient and conventional scheme for virtuoso display and sentimentality (G. F. Handel, L. Leo, L. Vinci, N. Jommelli, J. A. Hasse).

II. In France the cantata was not cultivated

until the 18th century, the only exceptions being two cantatas by Marc-Antoine Charpentier (1634–1704), a pupil of Carissimi. A large number of cantatas, mostly to French secular texts, appeared between 1705 and 1730, written by A. Campra (1660–1744), N. Bernier (1664–1734), M. Montéclair (1667–1737), J.-B. Morin (1677–1745), L. N. Clérambault (1676–1749), J. J. Mouret (1682–1738), and Rameau (1683–1764). Rameau's cantatas (compl. ed., vol. iii) are mostly for one voice and usually consist of three recitatives, each followed by an aria. See *LavE* i.3, 1557ff.

III. The development of the cantata in Germany, although strongly influenced by the Italians, was entirely different, chiefly on account of the emphasis on the church cantata (Kaspar Kittel's *Arien und Kantaten* of 1638 are practically the only German secular cantatas of the 17th century; see *RiHM*, p. 349). Schütz's *Symphoniae sacrae* (1629) contain several compositions that, although based on Latin texts, must be regarded as cantatas, being similar in form and style to those of Grandi or Rossi. However, the cantatas of F. Tunder (1614–67), M. Weckmann (1619–74; *DdT* 6), J. R. Ahle (1625–73; *DdT* 5), Buxtehude (*c.* 1637–1707; *DdT* 14), and J. S. Bach's uncle Johann Christoph Bach (1642–1703) already show a distinctly German character, being more serious, more genuinely dramatic, and more elaborate musically than the contemporary Italian cantata, owing chiefly to the inclusion of orchestral and choral participation. An especially interesting type is the *chorale cantata, which was cultivated by Tunder, Johann P. Krieger (*DdT* 53/54), Kuhnau (*DdT* 58/59), and others, while most of Buxtehude's numerous cantatas are based on free poetic texts and are, in a way, more "Italian" than those of the other German composers. The changeover from the chorale to free texts (and, as a consequence, from *cantus firmus* pieces to entirely free composition) was spurred about 1700 when Pastor E. Neumeister began publishing annual sets of his own cantata texts, mostly poetic paraphrases of scriptural passages appropriate for the various feasts of the church year. Some of these sets were written expressly for particular composers, e.g., for Krieger (Set i, 1704), P. Erlebach (Set ii, 1708), and Telemann (Sets iii, iv, 1711, 1714). However, many other musicians also were eager to seize upon these extremely timely and popular texts, particularly J. S. Bach, who, through the artistic greatness and religious dignity of his music, sanctioned

Neumeister's "theatrical" poetry as well as the "operatic" form of the *da capo* aria. Bach's cantatas (195 are preserved out of a total of probably close to 300) usually open with a chorus in fugal style that sometimes assumes great proportions, continue with a number of recitatives and arias, one for each of the two or three soloists, and close with a harmonized chorale. See Chorale cantata.

IV. After Bach, the cantata merged with the oratorio, of which it represents a shorter and more casual type. Most such cantatas were written for special occasions, e.g., Haydn's *Birthday Cantata* for Prince Nikolaus Eszterházy (1763), Mozart's cantata *Die Maurerfreude* (The Joy of the Masons, 1785), Beethoven's *Der glorreiche Augenblick* (The Glorious Moment, op. 136, 1814). Numerous later composers (Schubert, Spohr, Weber, Schumann, Mendelssohn, Liszt, Brahms, D'Indy, Saint-Saëns, Bennett, Stanford, Parry, Sullivan, Vaughan Williams) have made contributions to the repertory, but none of lasting importance. American composers of cantatas include John K. Paine and Dudley Buck (*The Voyage of Columbus*).

In the 20th century a considerable number of cantatas were written, some designated as such, others not but nevertheless belonging to the same category. Examples are Hindemith, *Plöner Musiktag* (1923), *Ite, angeli veloces* [1955]; Milhaud, *Cantata of Peace* (1937), *Cantata of War* (1940); Bartók, *Cantata Profana* (1930); Honegger, *Cantate de Noël* (1953); Webern, 2 Cantatas, op. 29, op. 31; Stravinsky, *Cantata on Old English Texts* (1952), *Threni* (1958), *Canticum Sacrum* (1955); W. Schuman, *A Free Song* (1942); Britten, *Saint Nicholas* [1948]. Debussy's *L'Enfant prodigue* (1884) is one of the numerous cantatas written according to the stipulations of the *Prix de Rome*.

Lit.: E. Schmitz, *Geschichte der weltlichen Solokantate* (1914); M. Lange, "Die Anfänge der Kantate" (diss. Leipzig, 1938); K. F. Rieber, "Entwicklung der geistlichen Solokantate im 17. Jahrhundert" (diss. Freiburg, 1925); W. S. Hannam, *Notes on the Church Cantatas of J. S. Bach* (1928); W. G. Whittacker, *Fugitive Notes on Church Cantatas and Motets of J. S. Bach* (1923); E. J. Dent, "Italian Chamber Cantatas" (*MA* ii); D. L. Burrows, "Antonio Cesti on Music" (*MQ* li, 518–29); H. Prunières, "The Italian Cantata of the 17th Century" (*ML* vii, 120); *id.*, in *Encyclopédie de la musique et dictionnaire du conservatoire*, pt. v, 3390ff; E. Schmitz, "Zur Geschichte des italienischen Kammerduetts im 17. Jahrhundert" (*JMP* xxiii); E. B. Helm, in *BAMS* vi; H. Goldschmidt, in *ZMW* ii; H. Riemann, in *SIM* xiii; A. Heuss, in *ZIM* x; F. Treiber, in *AMF* ii.

Musical publications: DdT 3 (Tunder); *DdT* 6 (Bernhard, Weckmann); *DdT* 14 (Buxtehude); *DdT* 21/22 (Zachow); *DdT* 51/52 (Graupner); *DdT* 53/54 (J. P. Krieger); *DdT* 58/59 (Kuhnau, Schelle); *DTB* 10 (Nuremberg masters); cantatas by Buxtehude (ed. by W. Gurlitt), Georg Böhm (ed. by J. Wolgast), Nikolaus Bruhns (ed. by F. Stein); H. Riemann, *Kantatenfrühling*, 4 vols.; F. A. Gevaert, *Les Gloires de l'Italie*, 2 vols. (1869); L. Landshoff, *Alte Meister des Belcanto*, 5 vols. (1912–27); K. Jeppesen, *La Flora*, 3 vols. (1949); L. Torchi, *L'Arte musicale in Italia*, vol. v; D. L. Burrows, *The Italian Cantata* (The Wellesley Edition, no. 5, 1963); *Editions IX, 17 (Marcello), 30 (Scarlatti); *Editions X, 2 (Marcello).

Cantatory [L. *cantatorium*]. See under Liturgical books I (ii); also Gradual (2).

Cante flamenco, cante hondo, cante jondo. See under Flamenco.

Canti carnascialeschi [It.]. Late 15th- and early 16th-century part songs designed for the elaborate carnival festivities that took place in Florence under the Medicis, particularly Lorenzo de' Medici (ruled 1469–92), who himself wrote a number of the poems. H. Isaac composed carnival songs during his stay at Lorenzo's court (*c.* 1480). Unfortunately these have been lost. Numerous compositions in three and four parts, by A. Coppinus, Jacopo da Bientina, and others, exist in several Italian MSS of the early 16th century. In style as well as form, the *canti carnascialeschi* are very similar to the *frottole*. In many cases the music has the form a b b c (b b = *piedi*), repeated for a number of stanzas. Particularly interesting are the songs of the various guilds, the *Canto de' sartori* (tailors), *de' profumieri* (perfumers), *de' scrittori* (scribes; see *HAM*, no. 96), etc. The texts often contain double meanings of a satirical or obscene nature.

Lit.: F. Ghisi, *I canti carnascialeschi* (1937); id., ‡*Feste musicali della Firenze Medicea* (1939); id., in *MQ* xxv and in *RBM* ii; *ReMR*, pp. 167ff; P. M. Masson, ‡*Chants de carnaval florentins* (1913); K. Westphal, ‡*Karnevalslieder der Renaissance* (*Editions VIII, 43).

Canticle [L. *canticum*]. In the Roman and Anglican liturgies, a scriptural text similar to a psalm but occurring elsewhere than in the Book of Psalms. Canticles are classified as (a) *cantica majora* (greater or Gospel canticles), i.e., from the New Testament, e.g., "Magnificat anima mea Dominum" (*canticum Mariae, canticum B. M. V.;* see Magnificat); "Benedictus Dominus Deus Israel" (*c. Zachariae*); "Nunc dimittis" (*c. Simeonis*). In the Roman Catholic rite they form the climax of Vespers, Lauds, and Compline respectively. In Anglican churches they occur in the Morning and Evening Prayers. (b) *Cantica minora* (lesser canticles), fourteen in number, are from the Old Testament. In the Roman rite they all belong to Lauds, where they function as one of the five psalms. Two of them are assigned to each day of the week, one for normal use, the other for the period of Lent. Among them are "Cantemus Domino" (*c. Moysi I*), "Audite caeli" (*c. Moysi II*), "Audite verbum" (*c. Jeremiae*), and "Benedicite omnia opera" (*c. trium Puerorum*, or canticle of Daniel). In Anglican churches they occur in the Morning Prayer. See *ApGC*, p. 20. See also Byzantine chant II.

Canticum canticorum is the Song of Solomon, selections from which have been frequently used for motets (e.g., "Quam pulchra es," by Dunstable; see *SchGMB*, no. 34), most completely by Palestrina (29 motets; see comp. ed., vol. iv).

Cantiga. A Spanish monophonic song of the 13th century, mostly in honor of the Virgin Mary (*c. de Santa María*). A large number of *cantigas* (more than 400) are preserved in four MSS in the Bibl. Nacionale in Madrid and in the monastery library of El Escorial. They were collected for Alfonso X (*el Sabio*, the Wise; 1221–84), King of Castile and Leon, who was a great lover of poetry and music and who probably contributed a good part of the contents. The pictorial reproductions of medieval instruments and players in the MSS are of the greatest importance [see *GD* ii, opp. 482; iii, opp. 260; iv, opp. 184; *GDB* iii, opp. 848; iv, opp. 496, 500; v, frontis.]. The chief form of the *cantiga* is that of the virelai [see Virelai II; also *Villancico*]. An earlier type of great interest is the *cantiga d'amigo* of *c.* 1200, the song of a girl in love [see Lit., Pope].

The *cantigas* were first published by J. Ribera, who believed they were of Arab origin and transcribed them in what he thought were "Arab rhythms," providing some of them with a 19th-century dance accompaniment. According to recent investigations (Anglés), their rhythm is part modal, part nonmodal (even meter), and part mixed. Ex. in *HAM*, no. 22.

Lit.: H. Anglés, *Las Cantigas* (1927); id., ‡*La*

Música de las cantigas de Santa Maria [*Editions IV, 15, 18, 19]; J. Ribera, ‡*La Música de las cantigas* (1922; superseded by Anglés); G. Sunyol, *Cantigues de Montserrat* (Publicaciones del Monasterio de Montserrat); P. Aubry, *Iter hispanicum* (1908), pp. 37ff (fac.); *ReMMA*, p. 245 (bibl. p. 450); H. Anglés, in *CP 1949*, p. 45; I. Pope, "The 13th-Century Galician Lyric" (*Speculum* ix).

Cantilena. (1) A vocal melody of a lyrical rather than a dramatic or virtuoso nature; also, an instrumental passage of the same kind. (2) In medieval writings the term is loosely used for the secular vocal compositions, homophonic as well as polyphonic (*ballades,* rondeaux, etc.; see *ReMMA*, pp. 294, 322; also *ReMR*, p. 764). The term "cantilena style" has been suggested (by Handschin) and widely adopted in place of *"ballade* style" (Ludwig, Besseler) to describe 14th- and 15th-century compositions with a vocal upper part and two instrumental accompanying parts. This style is found not only in the *ballades* but also in the virelais, rondeaux, and some Mass compositions and motets of the period of Machaut and Dufay. Another term is "treble-dominated style" (*ReMR*, p. 16f). (3) *Cantilena romana* means Roman (i.e., Gregorian) chant.

Cantillation. Religious chanting in recitative style, especially that of the Jewish service. See S. Rosowsky, *The Cantillation of the Bible* (1957); S. Corbin, "La Cantillation des rituels chrétiens" (*RdM* xlvii, 3ff); A. Machabey, "La Cantillation Manichéenne" (*RM* 1955, no. 227).

Cantino [It.; F. *chanterelle*]. The highest string of lutes, viols, etc. A 16th-century German equivalent is *Sangsaite.*

Cantionale [L.]. Title of several publications containing simple, homophonic settings of chorales, etc. for the German Protestant service, e.g., A. Raselius, *Cantionale oder Kirchengesenge* (1588); J. H. Schein, *Cantional oder Gesangbuch* (1627). In modern writings the term is used as a generic designation for publications containing such music, for instance, L. Osiander's *Funffzig geistliche Lieder und Psalmen* (1586). Hence the designation "cantional style" [G. *Kantionalstil*], used for chorale settings in a homophonic style, with the melody in the topmost voice.

Cantio sacra [L.]. Motet. Many collections of motets bear the title *Cantiones Sacrae* (Tallis,

Byrd, G. Gabrieli, Schütz). An Italian synonym is *Canzoni spirituali.*

Cantique [F.]. Canticle. Also, a religious song. See A. Gastoué, *Le Cantique populaire en France* (1924).

Canto [It.]. Song; melody; soprano. *C. carnascialesco,* see *Canti carnascialeschi; c. fermo,* *cantus firmus; c. piano* [Sp. *canto llano*], plainsong.

Canto de órgano [Sp.]. Spanish term for polyphony (as opposed to *canto llano,* plainsong) in the Renaissance and baroque eras. Ramos de Pareia [see under Theory, no. 18] says that *cantus figuratus* is usually called *organi cantus,* and in Juan Bermudo's *Declaración de instrumentos musicales* (1555) the chapter dealing with polyphonic music is entitled "Comiença el arte de canto de organo" (f. 48 verse).

Cantor. In the Roman Catholic liturgy, the soloist (usually two *cantores*) who sings the solo portions of the chants (incipits and verses), as opposed to the *schola* (chorus). In Protestant churches, the director of music (e.g., Bach in Leipzig). In the Jewish service, the solo singer, also called *chazzan.*

Cantus [L.]. In 12th-century polyphony, name for the original voice part, generally lower than the added one, called *discantus.* In 15th- and 16th-century polyphony, designation for the topmost part (abbr. C). The term was also used for entire vocal compositions, chiefly secular, as, in the three volumes of the *Odhecaton,* entitled Canti A, Canti B, Canti C. *Cantus figuratus* (*figuralis*), *cantus fractus,* and *cantus mensuratus* all refer to the use of exactly measured (*mensuratus*) note values (*figurae*) of different lengths such as result from the breaking up (*fractus*) of a long note value into smaller parts. Hence, they designate polyphonic music as opposed to plainsong (*cantus choralis, cantus planus*) with its notes of (supposedly) equal duration. In the Ambrosian Mass [see Ambrosian chant] *cantus* is the name for the chant corresponding to the Tract.

Cantus firmus [L., pl. *cantus* (or *canti*) *firmi;* It. *canto fermo*]. An existing melody that becomes the basis of a polyphonic composition through the addition of contrapuntal voices. In terms of their origin, the *cantus firmi* can be divided into four groups: (a) plainsong melodies; (b) Protestant chorales; (c) secular melodies; (d) abstract subjects. To group (a), which is by far the largest, belong all the organa and clausulae, practically all the motets of the 13th and 14th centuries, some motets and numerous Masses of the 15th and 16th centuries [see Mass C II a, b], the organ Magnificats, and the organ hymns of the 16th century. The latter lead to group (b), which includes the organ chorales (chorale preludes) of Buxtehude, Pachelbel, Bach, Brahms, *et al.*, as well as the chorale choruses in cantatas and Passions (e.g., the first chorus of Bach's St. Matthew Passion). Group (c) includes some motets of the 13th to 14th centuries (e.g., Machaut's motet on "Pour quoy me bat mon mari") and many Masses of the 15th century,

such as Ockeghem's Masses *L'Homme armé, Fors seulement,* and *De plus en plus.* In these the *cantus firmus* is usually taken from the tenor or *superius* of a chanson by the same or another composer (e.g., Binchois' rondeau *De plus en plus*). To the last group belong the various compositions based on the hexachord (e.g., Sweelinck, "Fantasia super ut re mi fa sol la") or those based on a *soggetto cavato.*

The *cantus firmus* appears most frequently in the tenor, usually in long notes that contrast with the more florid design of the other parts. In the 13th century, its rhythmic structure was determined by the system of the rhythmic *modes, in the 14th by the principle of *isorhythm. In the 15th century and later the *cantus firmus* often occurred in long notes of equal value [see *Cantus planus* style; see Ex. 1, Cabezón, *Ave maris*

stella]. In the organ chorales of the 17th and 18th centuries these often form the bass, being played on the pedal (Pachelbel, Bach). The opposite method is that of the *discant cantus firmus,* in which the *cantus firmus* appears in the topmost part, often paraphrased or ornamented. Early examples are in the Codex Apt [see Sources, no. 19] and in the hymns of Dunstable and Dufay [Ex. 2, Dufay, *Ave maris stella*], in which the plainsong is skillfully changed into a graceful melody in triple meter. Essentially the same method is employed in the melody chorales or ornamented chorales of the baroque period (Buxtehude, Bach). English composers of the 14th and 15th centuries often used a *migrant cantus firmus,* which changed its position from one part to another [see M. F. Bukofzer, in *MQ* xxxiv, 522ff]. Some scholars have maintained that seemingly free upper parts of 15th-century Masses are actually extremely complex elaborations of a *cantus firmus;* see Discant Mass.

The term *cantus firmus* was used very rarely before 1500. It occurs only in the "Discantus positio vulgaris" of *c.* 1225 ("Motetus est super determinatas notas firmi cantus . . . multiplex consonans" (A motet is a multiple consonant song based on the fixed notes of a *cantus firmus;* see *CS* i, 96) and in Guilelmus Monachus' "De preceptis artis musice," *c.* 1470, referring to the English practice ("debet assumi supranum cantum firmum" (A *cantus firmus* must be taken for the upper part; *CS* iii, 292b). The term is not mentioned in Tinctoris' *Diffinitorium* (*c.* 1475). Zarlino, in his *Istitutioni harmoniche* of 1558, speaks of "canto fermo et figurato," thus indicating that for him (as well as for the earlier writers) *cantus firmus* meant a "plain" Gregorian melody, without figuration. Bach, however, employed the term *canto fermo* for both plain and ornamented chorale melodies. See Felix namque; In nomine; In seculum; *L'Homme armé.*

Lit.: P. Aubry, *Recherches sur les "tenors" français dans les motets du treizième siècle* and *Recherches . . . "tenors" latins . . . .* (both 1907; also in *TG* xiii); E. H. Sparks, *Cantus firmus in Mass and Motet, 1420–1520* (1963); J. Mattfeld, "*Cantus firmus* in the Liturgical Motets of Josquin des Prez" (diss. Yale Univ., 1959); id., "Some Relationships between Texts and Cantus firmi in the Liturgical Motets of Josquin des Pres" (*JAMS* xiv); F. H. Sawyer, "The Use . . . of Canto Fermo by the Netherlands School" (*PMA* lxiii); A. Krings, "Die Bearbeitung der gregorianischen Melodien in der Messkomposition von Ockeghem bis Josquin" (*KJ* xxxv); G. Schmidt, "Zur Frage des Cantus firmus im 14. und beginnenden 15. Jahrhundert" (*AMW* xv).

Cantus lateralis [L.]. A 16th-century term for the notation in which the parts of a polyphonic composition were written "side by side" on the double page of a large choirbook, in contrast to the *partbook.

Cantus planus [L.]. Plainsong, Gregorian chant. The term was not used until the 13th century, earlier names being *cantus choralis, cantilena Romana,* etc. The word *planus* (even, level) is usually thought to refer to the fact that in this period the original tradition of Gregorian rhythm was lost and the chant began to be interpreted in uniform values of rather long duration (a *brevis* each), an interpretation that was probably a concomitant of its adoption as a *cantus firmus* for polyphonic compositions. The original meaning of *cantus planus,* however, was a melody in a relatively low range, as opposed to *cantus acutus* (Odo of Cluny; see *ReMMA,* p. 121).

Cantus planus style. Term recommended (by W. Apel) for the presentation of a *cantus firmus* in long notes of equal value, usually one to the measure, in distinction from other presentations, e.g., isorhythmic, ornamented, or paraphrased. The term is the equivalent of the German *Pfundnoten.

Cantus prius factus [L.]. Same as *cantus firmus.

Cantus visibilis [L.]. A misleading translation by John Hothby (d. 1487) of the English term *sight.

Canun. See *Kanun.*

Canzo, canso [Prov.; F. *chanson*]. This term (or similar ones, such as *canzone, Kanzone, chanson,* as well as the derivative *Rundkanzone,* round-chanson) has been used for a type of troubadour song characterized by initial repeat, a a b [see *Bar* form; *Ballade* (F.)], as opposed to the through-composed song, called *vers.* The use of these terms in this sense is, however, arbitrary. We know nothing about their original meaning except for some vague references to poetical content (*canzo* = love song; *vers* = more learned?), and that "what formerly was called *vers* is now called *canzo.*" See W. Apel, in *JAMS* vii, 124; R. H. Perrin, in *JAMS* viii, 77, ix, 14.

Canzona, canzone [It., pl. *canzone, canzoni*]. (1) In Italian poetry of the 13th through 17th centuries, a serious lyrical poem, usually in four or five stanzas of eight lines each. (2) In 18th- and 19th-century music, a lyrical song (e.g., the *canzone* "Voi che sapete" in Mozart's *Le Nozze di Figaro*) or an instrumental piece of a similar character (e.g., the slow movement of Tchaikovsky's Symphony no. 4, designated "in modo di canzone"). (3) See *Canzo.*

(4) A designation of 16th-century Italian secular vocal music, including: (a) certain members of the *frottola* family, set to free poems (called *canzoni*) of Petrarch and others, which because of their high literary quality and relatively free form must be regarded as the most important predecessors of the early madrigal (examples in *Canzoni sonetti strambotti et frottole,* 1513; 1517 ed. repr. in *Editions XLVIII, 4; see also A. Einstein, *The Italian Madrigal,* iii, no. 12); (b) later popular forms of the *villanella* type, called *canzoni villanesche* (anon. ed. of 1537; Nola, 1541; Cimello, 1545) and *canzoni alla napolitana* (Ferretti, 1568; Conversi, 1572). In the later decades of the century, the *canzonetta* became popular (Orazio Vecchi, 1580 and later; Hassler, 1590).

Lit.: A. Einstein, *The Italian Madrigal,* 3 vols. (1949): W. Rubsamen, *Literary Sources of Secular Music in Italy (c. 1500)* (1943); E. Hertzmann, *Adrian Willaert in der weltlichen Vokalmusik seiner Zeit* (1931); E. Helm, "The Beginnings of the Italian Madrigal" (diss. Harvard Univ., 1939).

(5) An important type of instrumental music of the 16th and 17th centuries that developed from the Franco-Flemish chansons of Josquin, Janequin, Crécquillon, Sermisy, and others [see Chanson (2)]. The immense popularity of these chansons is reflected in the numerous arrangements found in nearly all 16th-century sources of lute and keyboard music, French as well as Spanish, German, and Italian. In Italy, where the French chanson was called *canzona francese* (or *c. alla francese*), composers went even further, writing original compositions in the style and form of the French models, either for organ (*canzona d'organo*) or for instrumental ensembles (*canzona da sonar*). This procedure marks the beginning of a long and interesting development, which in the instrumental field eventually led to the sonata of the 17th century and in keyboard music paved the way for the fugue. Like their vocal models, the instrumental canzonas were characterized by clarity of texture, sectional

structure often involving repetition (in schemes such as a b a, a b b, a a b c, etc.), and variety of treatment (imitative versus homophonic style, duple versus triple meter). They differed from the contemporary ricercar in their tendency toward a harmonically conditioned counterpoint, in the absence of the various devices of "learned counterpoint," in their more lively rhythm, moving in quarter and eighth notes, and in their frequent use of themes starting with reiteration of the same pitch [see Ex.]. During the 17th century, however, the keyboard can-

zona showed a tendency toward stylistic unification and structural concentration, whereas in the ensemble canzonas increasing emphasis was placed on variety and contrast.

I. *Keyboard canzona*. The earliest known organ canzonas, found in Marco Antonio Cavazzoni's *Recerchari motetti canzoni, Libro I* (1523; repr. in K. Jeppesen, *Die italienische Orgelmusik am Anfang des Cinquecento*, rev. ed., 1960; also in *Editions X, 1) are probably arrangements of vocal chansons. The first steps in the development of independent canzonas were taken by his son, Girolamo Cavazzoni (*Intavolatura cioè ricercari, canzoni*, 1542; repr. in *Editions IX, 6), in pieces such as his "Canzone sopra Falt d'argent," which uses the thematic material of Josquin's famous chanson "Faulte d'argent" but differs from it in the contrapuntal elaboration of the themes [see *HAM*, nos. 91, 118]. Andrea Gabrieli's canzonas (two books of *Canzoni alla francese per sonar sopra istromenti da tasti*, 1605) are mostly arrangements of vocal chansons. Claudio Merulo's three books of *Canzoni d'intavolatura d'organo* (1592, 1606, 1611) contain, besides 5 arrangements, 18 canzonas of his own, which, however, seem to belong primarily to the category of ensemble canzona. Original organ canzonas were published by Pellegrini (1599), Mayone (1603, '09), Cima (1606), Trabaci (1603, '15), Cifra (1619), and many others. Among the canzonas of Trabaci [see Neapolitan school II] are the earliest known examples of a new type that became predominant in the 17th century, the so-called *variation canzona*, in which the various sections are based not on different themes but on free rhythmic and melodic variants of a single theme [see *HAM*, no. 191]. Frescobaldi used this procedure in

many of his canzonas (publications of 1615, '28, '35, '45). His example was followed by Froberger, Kerll, Poglietti, and other German composers, including Bach (*BG* xxxviii, no. 20). Although throughout its development the organ canzona retained a sectional form that distinguishes it from the fugue, it influenced the development of the fugue, mainly through the lively character and individual design of its thematic material, in contrast to the ricercar. In Germany the term *Fuge* was occasionally used as synonymous with canzona [B. Schmid, *Tabulatur Buch*, 1607: "Fugen, oder wie es die Italiener nennen, canzoni alla francese"; F. X. A. Murschhauser, "Fuga sive Canzon"; see Editions XIV, 30, pp. 159–61.].

II. *Ensemble (instrumental) canzona*. As early as *c.* 1490–1500 Obrecht and Isaac wrote compositions that in every respect can be regarded as instrumental canzonas. A particularly interesting example is Obrecht's *Tsaat een meskin* [*HAM*, no. 78], with its strongly contrasting sections: first, a contrapuntal elaboration of the Dutch folk tune; second, a more homophonic section based on short motifs. Similar traits are present in some of the *carmina* of the period [see *Carmen* (2)]. In spite of these early precedents, it was not until the 1570's that the ensemble canzona became established, under the name *canzon da sonar* [see Editions XXIII, 2, for description and reprints of these works]. Flourishing chiefly in Lombardy and Venice, such canzonas were published by Merulo (see under I), Maschera (1584; see *HAM*, no. 175), G. Gabrieli (1597, 1615), Canale (1600), Mortaro (1600, '10), Rognioni (1605), Soderini (1608), Banchieri (1596, 1603, etc.), and many others. They fall into three categories. Some works, generally in four parts and closely modeled on the chanson in style and form, were primarily contrapuntal (they always began with an imitative exposition) and had little stylistic contrast among their various sections. Canzonas of this rather conservative type continued to be written throughout the early 17th century. A second type, allied in principle to the ricercar, occasionally manifested tendencies toward thematic unity (Canale) of the sort found in the variation canzonas for keyboard written by Frescobaldi [see above]. A third type, represented by the brilliant polychoric canzonas of Giovanni Gabrieli and his followers (1597, Raverii collection 1608, '15), was freer in structure, consisting of an alternation between sections in lively imitation and 4/4 time, and homophonic sections in triple time. Occasionally these sections were very short and fragmentary [see Quilt canzona].

The free, multisectional type of canzona reached a climax in the ensemble works of Frescobaldi (four editions, 1623–34). These canzonas, marked in the later editions by systematic changes of tempo ("allegro" for the imitative sections in canzona style, "adagio" for the homophonic sections in slower rhythms), may well be considered a turning point leading to the *sonata da chiesa*. At the same time, vestiges of the old canzona, such as the a b a structure typical of the original chanson and the lengthy introductory fugal section, were retained for a long time. These characteristics are present in certain canzonas (*sonate*) of Marini (1626), Buonamente (1636), Merula (1615, '37, '39, '51; see *HAM*, no. 210), Neri (1644, '51), and Cazzati (1642, '48, and later). By *c.* 1650 the terms *canzona* and *sonata* were synonymous and the former was in general replaced by the latter (Legrenzi, Vitali), although the older term continued to be used by some composers. Long associated by theorists and composers with the "allegro" style and also with the fugal style of writing, canzona (or canzone) came to mean the principal fugal movement of the sonata (Young, 1653; Purcell, 1683, '97; Baldacini [1699], 1720; see also Brossard, *Dictionnaire*, 1703). It also occasionally figures in the operatic *overture (e.g., in S. Landi's *Il Sant' Alessio*, 1634; see *HAM,* no. 208). See Sonata B, I.

Lit.: A. Schlossberg, *Die italienische Sonata für mehrere Instrumente im 17. Jahrhundert* (1932); *RiHM* ii.2, *passim;* Bu*MBE, passim;* Gr*HWM*, pp. 252ff, 297ff; A. Sutkowski and A. Ostowicz-Sutkowska, ed., ‡*The Peplin Tablature: A Thematic Catalogue* (1963); A. Einstein, ed., ‡*G. Gabrieli: Canzoni per sonar a quattro* [1933]; S. Kunze, ed., ‡*Die Instrumentalmusik Giovanni Gabrielis,* 2 vols. (1963); A. Biales, "Sonatas and Canzonas for Larger Ensembles in Seventeenth Century Austria" (diss. U.C.L.A., 1962); J. M. Knapp, "The Canzone francese and Its Vocal Models" (master's thesis, Columbia Univ., 1941); E. Crocker (Gilmore), "An Introductory Study of the Italian Canzona for Instrumental Ensembles" (diss. Radcliffe College, 1943); B. Disertori, in *RMI* xlvi (Merulo); A. Heuss, in *SIM* iv (canzona and sonata).

E.C.G.

Canzona francese. See under Canzona (5).

Canzonet, canzonetta [It.]. In the late 16th and throughout the 17th century, a short vocal piece in a light vein, much in the character of a dance song [see *Balletto*]. The term was used by (among others) Quagliati (1588), Vecchi (various publications between 1580 and 1600), Monteverdi (1584, 1619), H. L. Hassler (1590; see *DTB* 9), several of the English madrigalists [see Editions XVI, 1, 3, 20, 28], and even later by Cazzati (1660's). The later *canzonette* usually had instrumental accompaniment.

The name was also used for short instrumental pieces (Vecchi, *Selva di varia ricreatione*, 1590), as well as for short organ canzonas (Buxtehude).

Caoine [pronounced Keen]. An Irish dirge of ancient tradition. See the articles in *GD, GDB*. See also Coronach.

Capelle, Capellmeister [G.]. Old spelling for *Kapelle, Kapellmeister.*

Capitolo [It.]. One of the various subspecies of the *frottola,* consisting of a number of three-line stanzas (rhyme scheme aba bcb cdc) sung to the same music. Sometimes the final stanza consisted of four lines, the last of which was sung to a different melody, a sort of coda.

Capotasto [It., corrupted forms are *capodastro, capotaster;* G. *Kapodaster;* F. *barré*]. A mechanical contrivance used with guitars, lutes, etc., to shorten the vibrating length of all the strings simultaneously. It consists of a small piece of hardwood or metal that can be fixed across the fingerboard. By setting the capotasto across, e.g., the first fret, a piece in C-sharp can be played with the same fingering as if it were in C. See Barré.

Cappella [It.]. In the Middle Ages, a small place of worship (chapel). In the 14th century the name was used for groups of clerical singers (*cappellani*), superseding the earlier designation *schola cantorum* and eventually coming to mean church choir [see A *cappella*]. After 1600 *cappella* meant any large group of musicians—vocal, instrumental, or mixed. Also see *Kapelle.*

Capriccio [It.; F. *caprice*]. (1) A title used by various 19th-century composers, among them Mendelssohn and Brahms, for short piano pieces of a humorous or capricious character. They are usually in ternary form. It also appears as a title of *potpourris* or fantasias (e.g., Saint-Saëns, "Caprice sur les airs de ballet d'Alceste de Gluck"). (2) In the 17th century, capriccio is one of the four important prefugal forms [see Ricercar; Canzona (5); Fantasia]. The capriccio, as the name suggests, is less restrained than the others and frequently involves certain peculiarities, such as the use of special themes. This is especially true in the case of Frescobaldi (*Capriccio sopra il cucu; Capriccio sopra ut re mi fa sol la; Capriccio sopra la bergamasca*). Froberger's 18 capriccios are scarcely different from his canzonas, both being based on Frescobaldi's variation-canzona. Earlier fugal capriccios for instruments (I) or for keyboard (K) were written by V. Ruffo (1564; I), F. Stivori (1599; I), G. de Macque (*c.* 1590; K), G. M. Trabaci (1603; K), and others. Later pieces, such as J. K. Kerll's *Capriccio sopra il cucco* (*c.* 1680) and Bach's *Capriccio sopra la lontananza del suo fratello dilettissimo* (1704), are like free fantasias, the latter being a piece of program music about "the departure of his beloved brother." (3) The term also occurs as a noncommittal title of 16th- and 17th-century publications, often vocal; e.g., Jachet Berchem, *Capricci* (1561); Ascanio Mayone, *Primo Libro di diversi capricci per sonare* (1603).

Capriccio. Opera in one act by R. Strauss (libretto by C. Krauss), produced in Munich, 1942. Setting: near Paris, 1775.

Capriccio Espagnol. A symphonic suite, op. 34, by Rimsky-Korsakov, composed in 1887. A masterpiece of brilliant orchestration, the work is in five sections. Native dance rhythms and melodic figures evoke a Spanish atmosphere.

Capriccio Italien. A symphonic poem by Tchaikovsky, op. 45, written in 1880 while the composer was visiting Italy. Italian folksongs provide most of the thematic material.

Capricorn Concerto. A concerto for small orchestra, op. 21, composed by Samuel Barber in 1944 and named for his house, "Capricorn," in Mt. Kisco, N.Y. The instruments are treated in the manner of the baroque *concerto grosso,* with the flute, oboe, and trumpet set off both as a group and as individual soloists against the string orchestra.

Caramba. A musical bow found in El Salvador, Honduras, and Guatemala. Also known as *carimba* and *zambumbia.*   J.O-S.

Carcelera [Sp.]. A type of *cante hondo* describing prison scenes. See *Flamenco.*

Card Game, The. See *Jeu de cartes.*

Cardillac. Opera in three acts by P. Hindemith (libretto by F. Lion, after E. T. A. Hoffmann),

produced in Dresden, 1926; new version in Zurich, 1952. Setting: Paris, 17th century.

Caricature. See Satire.

Carillon [F.]. A set of bells (originally four) hung in the tower of a church and played by means of a keyboard or a clockwork mechanism. As early as the 13th century sets of bells were operated mechanically. The use of a keyboard for playing bells can be traced to the early 16th century (Audenarde, 1510). Carillons became extremely popular and achieved a high degree of perfection in the Netherlands, Belgium, and northern France from the 15th through 18th centuries. In the 19th century they spread to England and thence to America. A modern carillon consists of 30 to 50 bells with a clapper inside, tuned chromatically from C or G through three or four octaves. The clappers are connected by wires to long wooden keys, arranged like those of a manual and a pedal of an organ. The manual keys are struck with the closed hand, which is protected by a glove. The largest carillons are those at the University of Chicago Chapel and at the Riverside Church of New York. Other carillons with extensive recital series are the Bok Tower in Lake Wales (Florida), the Luray Tower in Virginia, and the Princeton Carillon. The Curtis Institute, Philadelphia, offers instruction in carillon playing. Modern carillon players make ample use of tremolos, full chords, rapid passages, and other effective devices. In certain circles, however, there is a tendency toward a more reserved style of playing that is certainly worthy of support.

Early composers of carillon music were Matthias van den Gheyn (1721–85) and Potthoff (b. 1726). Old keyboard arrangements called "carillon" are found in O. Chilesotti, *Musica del passato* (*Editions V, 8) and in Louis Couperin, *Oeuvres complètes* (ed. P. Brunold, 1936). Probably these were played by means of an organ glockenspiel such as that used in Bach's cantata "Schlage doch, gewünschte Stunde." For a lute piece, "Carillon d'Anvers," see *DTO* 50, p. 64. More recent composers of works for carillon are Josef Denijn, J. A. F. Wagenaar, Daniel Pinkham, and John Cage.

Lit.: W. G. Rice, *Carillon Music* (1926); F. P. Price, *The Carillon* (1933); A. L. Bigelow, *Carillon* (1948); id., *English Type Carillonic Bells* (1949); E. W. van Heuven, *Acoustical Measurements on Church-bells and Carillons* (1949); X. van Elewijck, ‡*Anciens Collection . . . d'clave-*

135

cinistes flamandes (1877; contains two pieces by Van den Gheyn); L. Rizzardi, *Les Carillons de Belgique* (1938); G. W. Rice, in *MQ* i; J. S. Archer, in *ML* xviii, 176; W. W. Starmer, in *PMA* xxxi; *id.*, in *ZIM* vi; E. Buhle, "Das Glockenspiel in den Miniaturen des frühen Mittelalters" (*CP Liliencron*).

Carimba. See *Caramba.*

Carmen [L., pl. *carmina*]. (1) A term used by 14th- and 15th-century writers for the upper part (*cantus*) of polyphonic compositions, or for entire compositions, specifically chansons. (2) About 1500, name for instrumental compositions of various types, some of them perhaps arrangements of vocal pieces. They could be considered early instrumental canzonas, *carmen* probably being humanist Latin for *chanson*. Examples exist in the Glogauer Liederbuch [see Editions XVIII A, 4, 8], Isaac (*DTO* 28), Hofhaimer, Senfl, Kotter's tablature of 1515, etc. See H. J. Moser and F. Piersig, ‡*Carmina* (*Nagels Musik-Archiv*, liii).

Carmen. Opera in four acts by Bizet (libretto by H. Meilhac and L. Halévy, after a story by Mérimée), produced in Paris, 1875. Setting: Seville and environs, 1820. Not only is *Carmen* one of the most popular operas ever written, but its music has more artistic quality than that of many more ambitious and more "serious" operas.

Carmina burana. See under Goliard songs. Carl Orff's *Carmina burana* (1937) is a scenic oratorio based on 25 Latin poems of the 13th century.

Carnaval des animaux, Le [F., The Carnival of the Animals]. A "Grand Zoological Fantasy" for orchestra and two pianos by Saint-Saëns, composed in 1886. In a series of brief pieces named for the different animals, the composer uses various instruments and sections of the orchestra in descriptive fashion. Best known from this work is the cello solo, "Le Cygne" ("The Swan").

Carnavalito [Sp.]. Early species of a gay dance in duple meter and with a pentatonic melody, still performed by many groups in the Bolivian *Altiplano*.   J.O-S.

Carnaval romain, Le [F., The Roman Carnival]. Concert overture by Berlioz, op. 9, composed 1843. The themes are taken from his unsuccessful opera, *Benvenuto Cellini,* after its failure in Paris (1838).

Carnival songs. See *Canti carnascialeschi.*

Carol [F. *noël;* G. *Weihnachtslied;* It. *canzone di Natale;* Sp. *villancico, cántico de Navidad*]. In present-day usage, a traditional song for the celebration of Christmas. Occasionally the term is used also for other devotional songs of a joyful character (Easter carol; May carol). The name is thought to be derived from the medieval French word *carole,* a round dance, the assumption being that this term was associated with early pagan dance-songs performed in celebration of the winter solstice, a ritual that was later merged with Christmas. It should be noted, however, that originally the carol was not necessarily associated with Christmas. The numerous examples in 15th-century sources [see Editions XXXIV, 4] show that the distinguishing characteristic of the carol was not its subject matter but its form, especially the presence of a *burden sung in alternation with a number of uniform stanzas called verses. Some of these medieval carols have a verse refrain as well as a burden, the refrain being the closing line of the burden: B–r V$_1$–r B–r V$_2$–r, etc. [see Editions XXXIV, 21]. In the 16th century the carol became more varied in form and style but more uniform in subject matter, the emphasis being on Christmas. Numerous carols of the 16th to 18th centuries have been published in collections that also include French and German Christmas songs. See Noël.

Lit.: R. L. Greene, *The Early English Carols* (1935); *id., A Selection of English Carols* (1962); *Editions XXXIV, 4 (J. Stevens, ‡*Mediæval Carols,* 1952); E. Routley, *The English Carol* [1958]; E. B. Reed, ‡*Christmas Carols Printed in the 16th Century* (1932; facsimiles); J. A. Fuller Maitland, ‡*English Carols of the Fifteenth Century* [1891, not wholly reliable]; P. Dearmer, R. Vaughan Williams, and M. Shaw, ‡*The Oxford Book of Carols* (1928); G. R. Woodward, ‡*The Cowley Carol Book* (1902); M. F. Bukofzer, *Studies in Medieval and Renaissance Music* (1950), ch. iv; E. Duncan, *The Story of the Carol* (1911); H. J. Massé, in *ML* ii, 67; C. K. Miller, in *Renaissance News* iii (1950); J. Stevens, in *PMA* lxxvii; Y. Lacroix-Novaro, in *RdM* 1935, p. 1; R. H. Robbins, "The Burden in Carols" (*Modern Language Notes* lvii, 16).

Carole [F.]. Medieval French name for round dances, danced in a closed circle. The name has been variously derived from *caraula* (late L. for jump, dance; Lacroix), from *corolla* (small *corona*, i.e., circle; Sachs), from *Kyrie eleison* (Sahlin); and from *chorea* (Gr., dance, dimin. *choreola, charola, carole;* see the explanation "chorea, gallice charole" given in the 13th-century "Dictionarius metricus" of J. de Garlandia [see Dictionaries of music III]). No specific music for such dances has survived. Possibly the virelai in its original monophonic form was sung with the *carole*. See M. Sahlin, *Étude sur la carole médiévale* (Uppsala, 1940); Y. Lacroix-Novaro, in *RdM* 1935, p. 1; C. Sachs, *World History of the Dance* (1937).

Carrée [F.]. The double whole note, or breve.

Carrure [F.]. The symmetrical construction of musical phrases in measures of 2, 4, 8, etc., found particularly in dances. See *Vierhebigkeit.*

Cascarda [It.]. A dance type of the late 16th century, known only (?) through eleven examples found in Fabrizio Caroso's *Nobiltà di dame* (2nd ed., 1605; see Editions V, 1), which also contains a detailed description of the dance. The dances are all in quick triple meter, very similar to a *gagliarda* (*galliard).

Cassa [It.]. Drum. See Percussion instruments B 2, 3.

Cassation. An instrumental form of the 18th century, designed for outdoor performance, that includes elements of the symphony as well as the suite; hence, practically identical with the divertimento and serenade. Among the few compositions so named is a *Cassatio* by Dittersdorf (for 2 horns, violin, viola, cello; *c.* 1769), another by Haydn (for 2 horns, 2 violins, viola, cello), and two works called *Cassation* by Mozart (K. 63, for 2 violins, 2 violas, cello, 2 oboes, 2 horns; K. 99, for 2 violins, viola, cello, 2 oboes, 2 horns), both in seven movements and opening with a march (instead of a sonata-form movement, as in his divertimenti).

Casse-noisette. See *Nutcracker Suite.*

Castanets [F. *castagnettes;* G. *Kastagnetten;* It. *nacchere, castagnette;* Sp. *castañuelas*]. A percussion instrument (clappers) consisting of two shell-shaped pieces of hardwood hinged together with a string that passes over the player's thumb and first finger. They are used by Spanish dancers as an accompaniment for the bolero, fandango, etc., usually in pairs (one set in each hand). Similar instruments were used in ancient

Rome and were pictured in medieval manuscripts [see under *Cantiga*]. The castanets of the modern orchestra (e.g., in Bizet's *Carmen*) have springs and handles (or a connecting stick) that greatly facilitate playing but detract from the finesse of true castanet playing. For ill. see under Percussion instruments.

Castrato. The castration of boy singers was frequently practiced in Italy from the 16th through 18th centuries to preserve the boyish character of the voice. The singing apparatus of the *castrato* (also called *evirato*) combined the larynx of a youth with the chest and lungs of an adult, resulting in an unusually wide range together with sound of great power and of a special timbre that hearers found fascinating. *Castrati* are first documented in the Papal Chapel in 1562. The most famous were F. Senesino (1680–*c.* 1750), G. Caffarelli (1710–83), and Carlo Farinelli (or Carlo Broschi, 1705–82).

Lit.: A. Heriot, *Castrati in Opera* (1956); F. Haböck, *Die Gesangskunst der Kastraten* (1927); id., ‡*Die Kunst des Cavaliere Carlo Broschi Farinelli* (1923); G. Monaldi, *Cantanti evirati celebri del teatro italiano* (1920); id., in *RMI* xxvi; F. Rogers, in *MQ* v; *AdHM*, p. 1221f.

Catalectic. In poetry, a line from which one (or even two syllables of the normal scheme are missing at the end, so that a line of, e.g., eight syllables is reduced to seven (or even six, as in the so-called common meter):

$$\text{normal:} \quad \times\,'\times\,'\times\,'\times\,' \ (8)$$

$$\text{catalectic:} \begin{cases} \times\,'\times\,'\times\,' \quad\ ' \ (7) \\ \times\,'\times\,'\times\,'\times \ \ (7) \\ \times\,'\times\,'\times\,' \quad\ (6) \end{cases}$$

Catch. An English *round of the 17th and 18th centuries. Morley, in his *A Plaine and Easie Intoduction to Practicall Musicke* (1597), mentions the catch as similar to the canon in construction. Today it is often defined as a circular canon, or round. The first publications were Thomas Ravenscroft's *Pammelia* (1609), *Deuteromelia* (1609), and *Melismata* (1611), the second of which contains "Three Blind Mice." These were followed by a long series of collections, among which John Hilton's *Catch that Catch can* (1652; the pun was used earlier as a subtitle for the *Deuteromelia*) is the most famous. Catches were most in vogue in the reign of Charles II, and it was mainly in this period that they acquired a bad reputation because of their indecent texts. Numerous catches of the Restoration, including some of Purcell's, are so un-bashedly obscene that their texts were bowdler-ized in late 19th- and early 20th-century editions. More recent editions, such as that of *The Catch Club* brought out by Da Capo Press (1965), pub-lish Restoration catches in their original state. Sometimes the canonic melody is so constructed that voices entering later fill in rests with melodic fragments set to words that, affixed to the origi-nal phrase, change its meaning or create a *double entendre* [see Ex., from *Pammelia;* also P. Scholes, *The Oxford Companion to Music,* s.v.

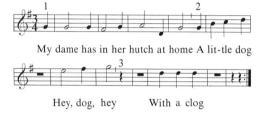

My dame has in her hutch at home A lit-tle dog

Hey, dog, hey   With a clog

"Catch"]. Frequently the change introduces a salacious note. A long list of publications con-taining catches is given in *GD* and *GDB*. Modern editions (with revised texts) are: E. F. Rimbault, *The Rounds, Catches, and Canons of England* (1864); P. Heseltine (P. Warlock), ed., *Thomas Ravenscroft: Pammelia and Other Rounds and Catches* [1928]; C. K. Scott, *The Euterpe Round Book* (1913); H. Purcell, *Complete Works* xxii. Ex. in *HAM,* no. 309b. Also see E. F. Hart, "The Restoration Catch" (*ML* xxxiv, 288ff).

Cathedral music. See Anglican church music.

Catholicon. A term (meaning "universal"), coined by Glareanus in his *Dodecachordon* (1547), for compositions so designed that they may be sung in more than one church mode. The two best-known examples are Ockeghem's *Missa cuiusvis toni* (Mass in any mode) and his *Prennez sur moy fuga,* a triple canon at the dis-tance of a fourth. Both are notated without clefs, and both have been the subject of much discus-sion. According to the most recent investigation (J. S. Levitan, "Ockeghem's Clefless Composi-tions," in *MQ* xxiii) the Mass can be performed in four positions, the canon in two.

Cat's Fugue. Popular name of a fugue by Do-menico Scarlatti, so called because the theme consists of wide and irregular skips in ascending motion, such as might be (and possibly were) produced by a cat walking on the keyboard.

Cauda [L.]. (1) In mensural notation, the vertical dash attached to certain notes (*maxima, longa, minima,* etc.) or to ligatures. With *ligatures, the presence or absence of the cauda determines the *proprietas,* i.e., the value of the initial note. In the

early 14th century numerous note forms, called *semibreves caudatae* (or *signatae*), were derived from the *semibrevis* by the addition of upward and downward dashes, with or without flags, etc. They form the basis of the Italian notation of the 14th century [see *ApNPM*, pp. 368ff].

(2) In the 13th century, name for passages without texts that are inserted in many con-ductus as extended vocalizations over the first and/or the last (or next-to-last) vowel of a line of the text, e.g., [*OH* i, 293]:

> *Salvatoris hodi-e------*
> *Sanguis pregus-ta------tur*
> *In quo Syon fili-e------*
> *Stola candi-da------tur*
> *Ec------ce nomen domi-ni------*
> *De longinquo venit,* etc.

Anon. IV (*CS* i, 360) distinguishes between the conductus with and without *cauda,* saying that the latter were preferred by the "minores can-tores" and thus implying that the former were superior. In numerous conductus the *caudae* (melismatic passages) far outweigh the syllabic passages in length and weight. They also intro-duce a stylistic contrast, that is, between true polyphony and homophony. Some of them in-clude very interesting examples of imitation, e.g., of *invertible counterpoint.

Cavalleria rusticana [It., Rustic Chivalry]. Opera in one act by P. Mascagni (libretto by G. Me-nasci and G. Targiono-Tozzetti, based on G. Verga's play), produced in Rome, 1890. Setting: Sicilian village, late 19th century. This opera, which was Mascagni's only success, owes its appeal to the concise and dramatic plot as well as to the realistic musical approach. Widely welcomed as a relief from the numerous imita-tions of Wagner, it inaugurated the musical movement known as *verismo and was respon-sible for a mushroom crop of one-act operas.

Cavata [It.]. An inscription or an epigram concisely expressing an important thought. In 18th-century music the term is used occasionally for short epigrammatic ariosos found at the end of a long recitative (*recitativo con cavata*). There are many examples in Bach's choral works, e.g., in the recitativo no. 3 of his cantata "Ein' feste Burg" [see Arioso]. The *cavate* in Traëtta's operas [see *DTB* 25] approach the * *cavatina.*

Cavatina [It.]. In 18th- and 19th-century operas and oratorios, a short solo song, simpler in style than the aria and without repetition of words or phrases. The proper form for the *cavatina* would seem to be in one section without repetition (except for a short instrumental anticipation of the beginning of the song), in other words, just a "sentence" set to music [see *Cavata*]. Examples of this type are the two *cavatine* in Haydn's *The Seasons,* and also the "Porgi amor" and "L'ho perduta" from Mozart's *Le Nozze di Figaro,* whereas the "Se vuol ballare" from the same opera shows an unusually developed type similar to an aria. Other examples are in Karl Heinrich Graun's *Montezuma* (1755; see *HAM,* no. 282), Rossini's *Il Barbiere di Siviglia* (1816), Weber's *Der Freischütz* (1820), and Gounod's *Faust* (1859). The name has also been applied to instrumental pieces of a songlike character, e.g., Beethoven, Quartet op. 130.

C.b. [It.]. Abbr. for *col basso* or *contrabasso.*

C.d. [It.]. Abbr. for *colla destra* (with the right hand).

Cebell. See Cibell.

Cecilian movement. A 19th-century movement for the reform of Roman Catholic church music, initiated by K. Proske (1794–1861) and named for St. Cecilia, the patron saint of music. The movement aimed at the reinstatement of Palestrina's *a cappella* music to replace the pompous and rather worldly church music for choir and instruments that had come into use during the 18th century (e.g., Haydn's and Mozart's Masses). It led, in 1867, to the foundation of the *Allgemeiner Deutscher Caecilienverein* (F. X. Witt, 1834–88), which was sanctioned by the Holy See in 1870. In the United States the movement is represented by the St. Cecilia Society, founded (1873) by John Singenberger. The term "Cecilianism" has come to stand for the puristic and rather reactionary tendencies of this society.

Cédez [F.]. Slow down.

Cefaut, ce fa ut. See Hexachord III.

Celere [It.]. Quick, swift.

Celesta. See Percussion instruments A, 4.

Cello (abbr. for *violoncello*). The bass size of the violin, tuned an octave and a fifth below it: C G d a. It is about twice the length of the violin (48½ in. as against 23½ in.) with the other measurements nearly in proportion, except for higher ribs (5 in. as against 1¼ in.). [For ill. see under Violin.] The cello came into existence along with the violin and viola. Two instruments by Andrea Amati, made between 1560 and 1570, are the earliest preserved specimens. Throughout the 17th century it was used only for accompaniment [see Thoroughbass II]. Domenico Gabrielli (1659–90) was one of the first to use it as a solo instrument. Particularly interesting are his pieces (called *ricercare) for cello without accompaniment (MS of 1689; see *SchGMB,* no. 228), which are in the same category as Bach's celebrated six suites for cello solo. Another composer of "ricercare" for the cello was G. B. degli Antonii (1687, '90).

Giuseppe M. Jacchini's *Concerti . . . con violoncello obligato,* op. 4 (1701) begin the repertory of the cello concerto, which was expanded during the 18th century by Antonio Vivaldi, E. F. dall'Abaco (in *Concerti a quattro da chiesa,* op. 2, 1712–14), Leonardo Leo (6 concertos, 1737–38), G. Tartini (properly for viola da gamba), Anton Filtz, Georg Matthias Monn, G. F. Wassmuth (d. 1766), K. P. E. Bach, and Haydn (8 concertos, 2 of which are preserved). Domenico della Bella wrote 12 sonatas "a 2 violini e violoncello" (1704), and G. Bononcini (1670–1747) a sonata for two cellos and other solo pieces. More important is Giacomo Bassevi (called Cervetto; c. 1682–1783), who brought the cello into favor in England and published *Twelve (Six) Solos for a Violoncello with a Thorough Bass for the Harpsichord (c. 1747, c. 1749), as well as pieces for two and three cellos. His son, Giacomo Cervetto (1747–1837), published *Six Solos* (c. 1775), *Six Duets* (c. 1792), etc. Italian cello music of the 18th century reached a peak with L. Boccherini (1743–1805), who composed numerous cello concertos and sonatas, as well as 113 quintets with two cellos. An important method was published in 1741 by Michel Corrette, who devoted a full chapter to the higher thumb positions. The classical school of cello playing is set forth in the *Essai sur le doigter du violoncelle* (1806–19) of Jean-Louis Duport (1749–1819), who also composed sonatas, duets, and other pieces for the instrument.

The 19th- and 20th-century repertory includes concertos by Schumann (op. 129; 1850), Dvořák (op. 104; 1895), Robert Volkmann (op. 33; *c.* 1860), Saint-Saëns (op. 33, 1873; op. 119, 1902), Lalo (1876), Elgar (op. 85; 1919), Prokofiev (op. 58; 1935–38), Shostakovitch (op. 107), Toch (chamber orchestra, op. 35), Hindemith (chamber orchestra, op. 36; 1925), Bloch (*Voice in the Wilderness,* 1936; *Schelomo, 1916*), A. Tcherepnin (*Rapsodie georgienne,* 1922), André Chaplet (*Epiphanie;* 1923), and Ibert (*Concerto;* 1925); sonatas by Beethoven (5), Brahms (op. 38, 1866; op. 99, 1867), Saint-Saëns (op. 32, 1873; op. 123, 1905), Fauré (2), R. Strauss (op. 6; 1883), Lalo (op. 16), Rachmaninoff (op. 19; 1901), Jean Huré (3; *c.* 1905), Ropartz (2; 1904, '19), Reger (4), Debussy (1915), Casella (1907, '27), Hindemith (op. 25, 1923; op. 11, A minor, 1922), Prokofiev (1), Tcherepnin (3), Britten (op. 65; 1961), and others. Pieces for solo cello have been written by Reger, Kodály, Wellesz, and Hindemith.

Lit.: E. van der Straeten, *History of the Violoncello, the Viol da gamba* (1915); M. Eisenberg, *Cello Playing of Today* (1957); A. Broadley, *The Violoncello* (1921); K. Schröder, *Handbuch des Violincellspiels,* rev. ed. (1920); D. Alexanian, *Theoretical and Practical Treatise of the Violoncello* (1922); W. J. von Wasielewski, *The Violoncello and Its History* (1894); M. Merseburger, *Das Violoncello und seine Literatur* (1920); B. Weigl, *Handbuch der Violoncell-Literatur* (1929); E. Nogué, *La Littérature du violoncelle* (1925); L. Forino, *Il Violoncello* (1905); K. Marx, *Die Entwicklung des Violoncells und seiner Spieltechnik bis J. L. Duport (1520–1820)* (1963); E. Rapp, "Beiträge zur Frühgeschichte des Violoncellkonzerts" (diss. Würzburg, 1934); H. Weber, "Das Violoncellkonzert des 18. und beginnenden 19. Jahrhunderts" (diss. Tübingen, 1932); F. Vatielli, "Les Origines de l'art du violoncelle" (*RM,* Feb. 1923, iv, no. 4); E. Albini, "Domenico Gabrielli" (*RMI* xli).

Cellone. See under Violin family (i).

Cembal d'amour. *Clavecin d'amour.

Cembalo [G.; It., abbr. of *clavicembalo*]. Harpsichord. According to C. Sachs (*SaRM,* p. 74f), the word is not derived from Gr. *kymbalon* (hollow vessel, bell; see Cymbal) but from *tym-* *panon* (same root as tip, zip, G. *zupfen,* to pluck). Therefore the name does not indicate that the instrument's sound resembles that of bells but refers to the plucking of the strings. For *cembalo d'amore,* see Clavecin d'amour.

Cenerentola, La [It., Cinderella]. Opera in two acts by Rossini (libretto by J. Ferretti), produced in Rome, 1817. Setting: Italy, 18th century (suggested).

Cent. See Cents.

Centitone. Unit for measuring intervals, exactly equal to ¹⁄₁₀₀ of a whole tone, hence equal to two *cents. See Intervals, calculation of, VI. See J. Yasser, "Decitones—Centitones—Millitones" (*Pro Musica,* March 1928, vi, no. 3, p. 12).

Cento [L.], **centon** [F.], **centone** [It., patchwork]. The term and its derivatives, "centonization" and "to centonize," refer to literary and musical works made up of selections from other works. Johannes Diaconus, in his *Vita S. Gregorii Magni* (*c.* 870), says that Pope Gregory I (reigned 590–604) compiled an "*antiphonarius cento,* which is of the greatest usefulness" [see *ApGC,* p. 246n]. This probably means that Gregory's work was a combination and revision of earlier books of a similar kind, i.e., books containing the texts (without music) for the sung items of the Mass. The term "cento" has been used for poems consisting only of refrains [see Refrain III], for *quodlibets,* and for 18th-century operas put together by several composers [see Pasticcio]. Melodies are said to be centonized if they are pieced together from pre-existing fragments. This procedure is of basic importance in the Tracts of Gregorian chant and to a certain extent also in the Graduals and Responsories, all of which make use of so-called migrant melismas (P. Wagner) or standard phrases (W. Apel).

Central America. See under Costa Rica, El Salvador, etc., and under Latin America.

Cents. The unit of a scientific and exact method of measuring musical intervals that was introduced by A. J. Ellis (1814–90) and has been widely adopted in acoustics as well as in ethnomusicology. The cent is equal to ¹⁄₁₀₀ of the semitone of the well-tempered scale; thus, the semitone equals 100 cents, and the octave contains 1200 cents. The tones of the well-tempered scale are represented by multiples of 100, as follows:

0	100	200	300	400	500	600
c	c♯	d	d♯	e	f	f♯

700	800	900	1000	1100	1200
g	g♯	a	a♯	b	c

This scale can be conveniently used for diagrams showing the exact position of other intervals, e.g., those of the Pythagorean scale, of just intonation, of non-Western scales, etc. [see Java]. Mathematically, cents are a logarithmic measurement; see Intervals, calculation of, IV.

Cephalicus. See under Neumes I (table).

Cercar la nota [It.]. In vocal technique, a slight anticipation of the following note, e.g., d–(c)–c. It may also occur in the form of a passing note, e.g., e–(d)–c.

Ceremony of Carols, A. A setting for treble voices and harp of nine medieval English carols, composed by Benjamin Britten in 1942. A Latin plainsong processional and recessional enframe the carols, which retain their Middle English texts.

Cervelas, cervelat [F.]. French name for the racket (sausage bassoon); see Oboe family III.

Ces, Ceses [G.]. C-flat, c-double-flat; see Pitch names.

Cesolfa(ut), ce sol fa (ut). See under Hexachord III.

Cetera, cetra [It.]. (1) Zither. (2) Cittern [see Guitar family].

C.f. Abbr. for *cantus firmus.*

Chacarera. [Sp.]. A rural dance originating in the province of Buenos Aires and now performed throughout Argentina. It consists of a seven-measure instrumental introduction in alternating 6/8 and 3/4 meter, followed by a seven-measure vocal section in 6/8 meter. After three repetitions of these two sections, a six-measure coda based on a new melody is added. Usually the solo instrumental parts, played by the guitar, are highly ornamented and the rhythm is often syncopated.   J.O-S.

Chace [F.]. A French composition of the early 14th century in the form of a strict canon at the unison. Unlike the contemporary Italian *caccia,* it does not have a free supporting tenor and is usually a triple canon. The Codex Ivrea [see Sources, no. 9] contains four *chaces,* one of which, "Talent m'est pris," is a circular canon

[see Handschin, in *MD* iii, 81]. Eighteen additional examples are in Machaut's *Le Lay de la fonteinne* and *Le Lay de confort* [see *Polyphonic Music of the Fourteenth Century,* ed. L. Schrade, (3 vols., 1956), ii, 39–51, 52–74], in which every other verse is a triple canon. To the same type belong three Spanish *caças* found in the *Llibre Vermell,* set to Latin religious texts. One of the Ivrea *chaces,* "Se je chant," is transcribed in *AMW* vii, 251f (by Besseler; the third imitation is missing).

Chaconne and passacaglia. I. Two closely related forms of baroque music, each a kind of continuous variation [see Variations I] in moderately slow triple meter and with a slow *harmonic rhythm,* changing generally with the measure. There have been many futile attempts to explain the derivation and original meaning of these terms, and just as many attempts, equally futile, to make a clear distinction between them. Actually, baroque composers used the terms indiscriminately. This does not mean that they could not be put to more apt use today, but unfortunately, modern writers have not succeeded in deciding on acceptable definitions and the literature is full of contradictory and frequently arbitrary statements about the difference between a chaconne and a passacaglia. The attempts at distinction made by later baroque writers such as Walther and Mattheson, e.g., on the basis of tempo (but contradicting each other; see J. Hedar, *Dietrich Buxtehudes Orgelwerke* [1951], pp. 60ff) are of no more than academic interest. The only distinction that is valid is that between continuous variations with or without a *basso ostinato* (*ground). To conform with the titles of the two most famous examples, those by Bach, the former type should be called passacaglia and the latter chaconne. A passacaglia, then, is a continuous variation based on a clearly distinguishable ostinato that normally appears in the bass but that may occasionally be transferred to an upper voice, as in Bach's passacaglia. A chaconne, on the other hand, is a continuous variation in which the "theme" is a scheme of harmonies (e.g., I–VI–IV–V) usually treated so that the first and last chords are fixed whereas the intervening ones can be replaced by substitutes. The difference between these two types is illustrated in the accompanying examples. Ex. 1 and 2 show a very usual ground, the descending tetrachord in its diatonic form and in its chromatic modification, which is used in many passacaglias; Ex. 3 shows the use of a (related)

nazione di Poppea [*SchGMB*, no. 178; see also Aria III]. To the class of chaconne belong Frescobaldi's "Cento partite sopra il passacaglio" [*TaAM* v, 11] and Georg Muffat's Passacaglia [see *HAM*, no. 240], as well as Bach's Chaconne.

It should be noted that French baroque composers usually employed the terms "chaconne" and "passecaille" for pieces in an entirely different form, i.e., for a rondeau, with reiterated refrain and several couplets [see Rondeau (2)]. Examples are a Chaconne by Chambonnières [*HAM*, no. 212], a Chaconne-rondeau by D'Anglebert [*TaAM* vii, 133; *HAM*, no. 232], and a Passacaille by F. Couperin [*Pièces de clavecin* ii].

A primitive stage of the development is probably represented by *passacalli* and *chiacone* in early 17th-century books for the Spanish guitar, which consist of a series of four-measure phrases such as shown here (from Caliginoso, *Intavolatura di chitarra spagnola*, 1629; see *WoHN* ii, 182).

scheme of harmonies, without ground (chaconne). The characteristic trait of the chaconne is, therefore, a regularly recurrent harmonic structure without a clearly recognizable ostinato. The frequently given interpretation of Bach's chaconne as an ostinato composition is hardly convincing. Although with a reiterated scheme of harmonies it is often possible to reconstruct to some extent an ostinato, such a procedure leads, in the case of Bach's chaconne, to a clearly derivative bass line, which Bach never would have chosen as a point of departure.

II. There is reason to believe that the chaconne originally was a wild and sensual Mexican dance that was imported into Spain during the 16th century. Surviving from 1599 is "An invitation to go to Tampico in Mexico and there dance the chacona." Quevedo calls it the "chacona mulata," and Cervantes the "Indiana amulatada" [see C. Sachs, *World History of the Dance* (1937)]. In Europe, it completely lost its unbridled character, as did the sarabande and, 300 years later, the tango. The passacaglia (probably from Sp. **pasacalle*) also originally was a dance or a march. As mentioned above, baroque composers made no clear distinction between passacaglia and chaconne. To the class of passacaglia (as defined in I) belong the Passacaglia of Bach (for organ) and that of Louis Couperin (for harpsichord; *Pièces de clavecin de Louis Couperin*, ed. P. Brunold, rev. ed. by T. Dart [1959], pp. 95ff), as well as "ciaconas" of Buxtehude (*Dietrich Buxtehude: Complete Organ Works*, ed. J. Hedar, 4 vols. [1952], vol. i) and J. K. Kerll [*TaAM* vii, 106], both for organ, and of Pachelbel (for harpsichord; *TaAM* ix, 59). To the same class belong numerous vocal compositions in 17th-century operas and cantatas, e.g., Monteverdi's famous duet "Pur ti miro" from *L'Incoro-*

After 1750 the chaconne and passacaglia became almost obsolete. Beethoven, although probably unfamiliar with the old forms, came very close to the chaconne in his C-minor Variations for piano (1806). The final movement of Brahms' Symphony no. 4, on the other hand, is a deliberate imitation of the baroque chaconne. The 20th-century, with its general interest in older forms and methods of composition, has seen a remarkable revival of the chaconne and even more of the passacaglia, which, because of its contrapuntal rather than harmonic structure, proved particularly attractive to composers such as Busoni (*Tocatta: Preludio, Fantasia, Ciacona*, 1921), Krenek (*Tocatta und Chaconne*, op. 13, 1922), Hindemith (in *Das Marienleben*, op. 27, 1922–23; *Nobilissima visione*, 1938), Berg (in *Wozzeck*, 1922), Piston (*Passacaglia* for piano, 1943), and many others.

Lit.: *BuMBE, passim;* A. Machabey, in *RdM* 1946, p. 1 (origins); K. von Fischer, in *RBM* xii; P. Mies, in *Händel Jahrbuch* ii, 113 (Handel);

L. Stein, in *ML* xl, 150 (20th century); T. Walker, in JAMS xxi. See also under Ostinato.

Chaldean chant. See P. C. Mousses, "La Musique liturgique chaldéenne" (*CP 1950*, p. 164).

Chalumeau [F.]. (1) A 17th-century name for (a) an early oboe (shawm), (b) an early clarinet. For ill. see under Clarinet family. The chalumeau in Gluck's *Orfeo ed Euridice* (1762) is probably a real clarinet (with keys). (2) The lowest register of the modern clarinet.

Chamade [F.] Same as **chiamata.*

Chamber music. I. *General.* Instrumental ensemble music performed by one player for each part, as opposed to orchestral music in which there are several players for each part. According to the number of players (or parts), chamber music is classified as follows: trio (three players), quartet (four), quintet (five), sextet (six), septet (seven), octet (eight). String trios (quartets, etc.) are for stringed instruments only; if one of the strings is replaced by another instrument, names such as piano trio (piano and two strings) or horn quintet (horn and four strings) are used. The violin (cello) sonata, for violin (cello) and piano, is sometimes not considered chamber music on account of the markedly solo character of the parts. In chamber music, emphasis lies on the ensemble, not on the individual player.

The present-day repertory of chamber music begins with the late string quartets (written after 1780) of Haydn and Mozart. These works established the basic principles of form and style to which practically all composers of chamber music have adhered: the form is that of the sonata in four movements; the style is characterized by individual treatment of the parts and exclusion of virtuoso-like elements. Naturally, in some cases these principles have not been observed, as in Beethoven's String Quartet in C-sharp minor, op. 131, with its extremely free form. Yet the fact remains that in chamber music composers have shown a greater respect for tradition than in other fields, the obvious reason being that the relatively limited and fixed resources of, e.g., a string quartet prohibited the introduction of novel features comparable to those of contemporary orchestral or piano music.

The chamber music works (chiefly string quartets) of Haydn, Mozart, Beethoven (opus numbers below 100), and Schubert represent the classical period of chamber music. In his late quartets (op. 127, 130–133, 135, written between 1824 and 1826) Beethoven created an entirely singular type of chamber music, a type too personal to be called "classic" yet too transcendental to be considered romantic. The romantic period of chamber music embraces Schumann, Brahms, Dvořák, and Franck (to name only the most important composers), with Brahms ranking first among them. While Debussy, Ravel, and others (e.g., Schoenberg, string sextet *Verklärte Nacht*, op. 4) tried to exploit the impressionist and colorist resources of chamber music, some later composers returned to a purer style, as a result of the contemporary revival of the contrapuntal approach to composition and of the adoption of a more objective and sober type of expression than prevailed in late romanticism and impressionism [see Neoclassicism]. Also see the entries for different kinds of chamber music, particularly String quartet.

II. *History.* Chamber music in its broadest sense already existed in the late Middle Ages. The "instrumental motets" of the Codex Bamberg (c. 1280; see In seculum), ensemble pieces such as occur in the Glogauer Liederbuch (c. 1480; see Liederbuch), or the *carmina* of Obrecht, Isaac, and Hofhaimer (c. 1500) bear all the hallmarks of true chamber music. So do the 16th-century ensemble **ricercars* of Adrian Willaert, Buus, and Padovano, as well as the instrumental canzonas [see Canzona (5), I] from the end of the century. (Regarding the claim that a canzona by Allegri was the "first string quartet," see under String quartet II.) Naturally, all these pieces were not written for, nor restricted to, specific instruments but were performed on whatever instruments were available—viols, recorders, cornettos, or mixed ensembles. The chief type of baroque chamber music is the trio sonata in its two varieties, the *sonata da chiesa* and the *sonata da camera* [see Sonata da camera]. It developed in Italy and spread, about 1675, to France, Germany, and England, where it replaced the earlier **fancy.* About 1750 there emerged a new type of chamber music, the string quartet, with its associates, the string quintet (Boccherini) and string trio (Haydn).

A long list of chamber music associations is found in *Pierre Key's Music Year Book.*

Lit.: *Cobbett's Cyclopedic Survey of Chamber Music,* ed. W. W. Cobbett, 2 vols. (1929; suppl., ed. C. Mason, 1963); H. Ulrich, *Chamber Music* (1948); T. F. Dunhill, *Chamber Music* (1913); N. Kilburn, *Chamber Music,* rev. by G. E. H. Abraham [1932]; G. Stratton and A. Frank, *The Playing of Chamber Music* (1935); H. S. Drinker,

The Chamber Music of Johannes Brahms (1932); R. H. Rowen, *Early Chamber Music* (1949); H. Mersmann, *Die Kammermusik*, 4 vols. (1930–33); W. Altmann, *Kammermusik-Katalog* [music pub. between 1841–1941], rev. ed. (1942); N. Ruet, *Musique de chambre* (1930); J. F. Richter, *Kammermusik-Katalog* (music pub. between 1944–1958; 1960); LavE ii.5, pp. 3144ff (repertory and bibliography); S. Laciar, "The Chamber-Music of Franz Schubert" (*MQ* xiv); H. Mersmann, "Beiträge zur Aufführungspraxis der vorklassischen Kammermusik in Deutschland" (*AMW* ii); L. de La Laurencie, "Les Débuts de la musique de chambre en France" (*RdM*, 1934, pp. 25ff, 86ff, 159ff, 204ff).

Chamber opera. An opera of small dimensions, of an intimate character, and for small orchestra (chamber orchestra). Sometimes produced in reaction against the great Wagnerian operas, such works include R. Strauss' *Ariadne auf Naxos* (second version, 1916), Hindemith's *Cardillac* (1926; rev. 1952), V. Thomson's *Four Saints in Three Acts* (1928), and Menotti's *The Old Maid and the Thief* (1939).

Chamber orchestra. A small orchestra of about 25 players. Before 1800 most orchestras were of this size, and recent composers have again written for such groups (chamber symphony). See Saltonstall and Smith, *Catalogue of Music for Small Orchestra* (1947); M. Pincherle, *L'Orchestre de chambre* [1948].

Chamber pitch [G. *Kammerton*]. See under Pitch.

Chamber sonata. The baroque *sonata da camera;* see *Sonata da camera;* Suite IV.

Chance music. See Aleatory music.

Chandos Anthems. Twelve anthems by Handel, composed 1716–18 for the Earl of Carnarvon, later Duke of Chandos, and performed at his palace. There also are a *Chandos Te Deum* and a *Chandos Jubilate.*

Change ringing. The ringing of a set (peal) of church bells by individual men and in a methodical order, the sequence being prescribed not by a melody but by certain schemes of arithmetic permutation. For instance, a set of five bells, 1, 2, 3, 4, 5, may be played in the order 4 5 2 3 1, 3 5 1 4 2, etc. In actual performance, usually a limited selection of such permutations is played in succession, the main principle being the exchange of two numbers. For instance, in a peal of five bells, the first "change" would be 1 2 3 4 5,

the second, 2 1 3 4 5, the third, 2 3 1 4 5, and so on. Certain standard selections are known under traditional names such as "Grandsire Triple," "Treble Bob," etc. The history of change ringing goes back to the 16th century. An important landmark was the publication of *Tintinnalogia* by F. Stedman (1688). Change ringing is still widely practiced in England.

Lit.: J. Trollope, *Standard Methods in the Art of Change-Ringing*, rev. ed. (1940); *id., Grandsire*, rev. ed. (1948); *id., Stedman . . . Incorporating the History of the Method (1938);* E. Morris, *The History and Art of Change Ringing* (1931); J. M. Turner, *The Art and Science of Hand Bell Ringing* [1950?]; R. H. Dove, *A Bellringer's Guide to the Church Bells of Britain*, rev. ed. (1956); J. Stainer, in *PMA* xlvi. See the article in *GDB.*

Changing note. See under Nonharmonic tones III.

Chanson [F.]. (1) The French word for song, hence the counterpart of the German *Lied.* However, while the lied has generally been cultivated by professional musicians, the chanson is usually of a more popular nature. Throughout the last two centuries there has been an enormous output of popular chansons, short strophic songs mostly of an amorous character, which are frequently written, set to music, sung on the streets, and sold by one and the same man. Not until the end of the 19th century was the chanson cultivated as an artistic form.

The virtual nonexistence of French art songs in the 18th and 19th centuries is in striking contrast to earlier periods. In fact, the early history of the chanson (i.e., of songs with French text) is more ancient, fertile, and musically important than that of any other nation's song literature. The earliest preserved example, a Provençal song, "Hora vos dic vera raizun" [see P. Aubry, *Les Plus Anciens Monuments de la musique française* (1905), pl. I], dates from the 11th century. The 12th and 13th centuries were the era of the troubadours and trouvères, whose melodies constitute an unparalleled treasure of early secular song. The 14th century saw the rise of accompanied songs under G. de Machaut and his successors. These songs are usually in three parts (one vocal and two instrumental) and invariably in one of the *formes fixes* (ballade, rondeau, virelai). Composers of the late 14th century (Solage, Senleches, also the Italians Matheus de Perusio and Antonellus de Caserta) developed a style of unparalleled rhythmic and contrapuntal complexity, which bears the earmarks of overrefinement and decadence. As an antithesis there developed in the Burgundian school of the 15th century (Dufay, Binchois, Lantins; also Ockeghem, Busnois) a new style of singular charm and beauty that may well be regarded as the artistic culmination of early French song. These composers cultivated mostly the *rondeau and *virelai (*bergerette), less frequently the *ballade. A large number of such songs exist in the various 15th-century *chansonniers.

The last quarter of the 15th century marked the beginning of a new development characterized by the abandonment of the *formes fixes,* a change from three- to four- and five-part writing, from triple to duple meter, and the adoption of imitative counterpoint as the basic principle of style. This is the type to which the term "chanson" specifically refers in historical studies. It prevailed throughout the 16th century [see below under (2)]. With the early 17th century and the rise of the monodic style, the polyphonic chanson disappeared and, strangely enough, the creative activity in the field of art song ceased abruptly. The interest turned to *vaudevilles, *pastourelles, *bergerettes, and *brunettes, i.e., to the more popular types that predominated throughout the 18th and 19th centuries [see also Air de cour]. Extensive collections of such chansons were published by Ballard, e.g., Recueil de chansons pour dancer et pour boire, 21 vols. (1627–62). For the development in the 19th and 20th centuries, see Song III.

(2) Specifically, the term "chanson" (polyphonic French chanson) is used for 15th- and 16th-century compositions that are not cast in one of the *formes fixes but either are throughcomposed or (later) employ other repeat forms. Early examples are Dufay's "La Belle se siet" [see J. and C. Stainer, Dufay and His Contemporaries, 1898, pp. 122ff] and Binchois' "Files à marier" [HAM, no. 70], the latter being exceptionally advanced both in style (rapid declamation) and form (A A B). These, however, seem to be isolated cases. Later composers, such as Hayne van Ghizeghem, J. Ockeghem, or A. Busnois, composed only rondeaux and virelais (or bergerettes). The continuous development of the free chanson began near the end of the 15th century. The *Odhecaton of 1501 contains about twelve such pieces, among them three by Louis Compère (nos. 26, 28, 41), and one each by Heinrich Isaac (no. 11), Pierre de La Rue (no. 15), and Jean Mouton (no. 36). Com-

père, La Rue, and Josquin (all born c. 1450) are the most prominent of the early chanson composers. With Clément Janequin (c. 1485–c. 1560), Claudin Sermisy (c. 1490–1562), Pierre Certon (c. 1510–72), and numerous later composers the chanson changed from Flemish to typically French, from reserved dignity to nimble elegance and frivolity. The popularity of this new chanson is evident from a vast number of contemporary publications as well as the many hundreds of arrangements that fill the German and Italian lute and keyboard books of the 16th century. Pierre Attaingnant alone printed 70 collections containing chansons between 1528 and 1549; at the same time Jacques Moderne published the eleven books of his Parangon des chansons (1538–43).

Many of the chansons are composed in the imitative style of the contemporary motet but with such modifications as were required by the different purpose and text, i.e., quicker and more pungent rhythm, a tendency toward homophonic texture, sectional construction in relatively short phrases ending simultaneously in all parts, and frequent repetition of a section for another line of the poem. Among the various repeat forms are A B A [Josquin's "Faulte d'argent": HAM, no. 91; also many chansons by Janequin], A A B (*Bar form), A A B C C, A B A' C A" (incipient *rondo form), etc. A characteristic feature of the chanson (as well as its derivative, the instrumental *canzona) is the use of repeated notes in the initial subject, as illustrated in the accompanying example (Jacotin's "Je suis déshéritée": see SchGMB, no. 117). A type of special interest, though of somewhat mediocre quality, is the program chanson of Janequin [see Program music]. See also Canzona (5).

Lit. For (1): See under Troubadours, Trouvères, Ars nova, Burgundian school, etc.; J. and C. Stainer, ‡Dufay and His Contemporaries

(1898); L. de la Laurencie, ‡*Chansons au luth et airs de cour français du xvie siècle* (1934); E. Olsson, "The French Chanson between 1400 and 1450" (*BAMS* 1948, p. 36f); G. Perle, "The Chansons of Antoine Busnois" (*MR* xi, pp. 89ff). See also under *Chansonnier*. For (2): J. Haar, ed., *Chanson and Madrigal, 1480–1530: Studies in Comparison and Contrast* (1964); H. M. Brown, ed., ‡*Theatrical Chansons of the Fifteenth and Early Sixteenth Centuries* (1963); C. L. W. Boer, *Chanson vormen op het einde van de XVIe eeuw* (1938); F. Lesure et al., ‡*Anthologie de la chanson parisienne au xvie siècle* [1952]; M. Cauchie, ‡*Quinze Chansons françaises du xvie siècle* (1926); *Editions XXV, XXXIII, various vols.; *Editions VIII, 3; F. Lesure and G. Thibault, "Bibliographie des éditions musicales publiées par Nicolas du Chemin (1549–76)" (*AnnM* i); E. Hertzmann, "Trends in the Development of the *Chanson* in the Early Sixteenth Century" (*PAMS* 1940); E. B. Helm, "The Sixteenth Century French Chanson" (*Proc. of the Music Teachers National Association* xxxvi, 236ff); L. Laloy, "La Chanson française au xvie siècle" (*RMC* i); J. Tiersot, "Ronsard et la musique de son temps" (*SIM* iv); D. Bartha, "Probleme der Chansongeschichte im 16. Jahrhundert" (*ZMW* xiii). Examples in *HAM*, nos. 91 (cf. no. 118), 107, 145; *SchGMB*, nos. 116–118.

Chanson balladée [F.]. Alternative (older?) name, used chiefly by Machaut, for the *virelai.

Chanson de geste [F.]. A French epic poem of the Middle Ages, such as the "Chanson de Roland" (11th century). Such poems were extremely long (more than 10,000 lines of nearly equal meter) and were divided into sections of various lengths (20 or 50 lines), each of which, called a *laisse*, contained one continuous "thought" of the poem. The question as to whether or how the *chansons de geste* were sung has been repeatedly studied without conclusive results. Perhaps they were sung to a short melodic formlua that was repeated for every line of a *laisse* except the last, for which a new formula with a more definite close was employed (a a a a . . . b). Two such melodies survive, one in the epic "Bataille d'Annezin" (see *GéHM*, p. 261f; also Chailley, in *RdM* 1948, p. 3), the other as a late quotation inserted in Adam de la Halle's play "Le Jeu de Robin et Marion" of c. 1280 [see *ReMMA*, p. 204].

Lit.: Italo Siciliano, *Les Origines des chansons de geste* (1951); F. Gennrich, *Der musikalische Vortrag der altfranzösischen Chansons de geste*

(1923); *GéHM*, pp. 258ff; J. Chailley, "Études musicales sur la chanson de geste et ses origines" (*RdM* 1948, pp. 1ff); J. Chailley, *Histoire musicale du moyen âge* (1950), p. 91.

Chanson de toile [F.]. A trouvère poem of the early 13th century dealing with the sufferings of a lovesick girl or an unhappy wife. Five of them survive with their melodies in the "Chansonnier de St. Germain." They consist of six or more stanzas with refrain, the stanza being sung to melodies having forms such as a b a b C ("Bele Doëtte"), a a b c B′ D ("Bele Yolanz"), a b a b c D A ("Oriolanz en haut solier"), etc. The alleged relationship between the musical structure of the *chansons de toile* and that of the much older *chansons de geste* (see F. Gennrich, *Grundriss einer Formenlehre des mittelalterlichen Liedes,* 1932, pp. 45ff) is, to say the least, very tenuous.

Chanson mesurée. See *Vers mesuré.*

Chansonnier. (1) A medieval (13th-century) MS containing the songs of the troubadours and trouvères. The most important ones are (Tb = troubadour; Tv = trouvère): Milan, Bibl. Ambr. *R. 71 sup.* (Ambrosiana Ch.; Tb; new ed. in U. Sesini, *Le Melodie trobadoriche nel canzoniere Provenzale della Biblioteca Ambrosiana,* 1942). Paris, Bibl. nat. *fr. 22543* (Tb, the central source). Paris, Bibl. nat. *fr. 20050* (Ch. de St.-Germain; Tb and Tv; fac. ed., G. Raynaud and P. Meyer, 1892). Paris, Bibl. nat. *fr. 844* (Ch. du Roi; Tv; fac. ed., J.-B. Beck, 1938). Paris, Bibl. nat. *fr. 846* (Ch. Cangé; Tv; new ed. J.-B. Beck, 1927). Paris, Bibl. nat. *fr. 12615* (Ch. Noailles; Tv). Paris, Bibl. de l'Arsenal *5198* (Arsenal Ch.; Tv; new ed., P. Aubry and A. Jeanroy, 1909–14). Arras, Bibl. de la Ville *657* (Ch. of Arras; Tv; fac. ed., A. Jeanroy, 1925). See G. Raynaud, *Bibliographie des chansonniers français des XIIIe et XIVe siècles,* 2 vols. (1884); J.-B. Beck, *Die Melodien der Troubadours* (1908), pp. 7ff.

(2) MS collections of 15th-century polyphonic chansons. Some of the most important ones are: Escorial *V.III.24* (fac. ed., W. Rehm, 1958; see P. Aubry, *Iter hispanicum* [1908], p. 19). Copenhagen, Kgl. Bibl. *Thott 2918* (new ed., K. Jeppesen, *Der Kopenhagener Chansonnier,* 1927). Dijon, Bibl. de la Ville *Ms. 517* (partly repr. in E. Droz, *Trois Chansonniers français du XVe siècle,* 1927). Seville, Bibl. Colombina *5-1-43* (fac. ed. of Colombina *5-1-43* and Paris N. A. *Fr. 4379,* D. Plamenac [1962]; see D. Plamenac, in *MQ* xxxvii, xxxviii). Escorial *IV.a.24* (see P. Au-

bry, *Iter hispanicum,* p. 30). Washington, Libr. of Congress *M.2.i L 25 Case* (Laborde Chansonnier; see H. E. Bush, in *PAMS* 1940, p. 56). New Haven, Conn., Yale Univ., Mellon Chansonnier (see M. F. Bukofzer, in *MQ* xxviii). Paris, Bibl. nat. Jean de Montchenu Chansonnier (Chansonnier cordiforme; see J. Porcher, in *Les Trésors des bibliothèques de France* v, 100). Paris, Bibl. nat. *fr. 15123* (Pixérécourt Chansonnier; E. J. Pease, "An Edition of the Pixérécourt Manuscript" [diss. Indiana Univ., 1960]). Paris, Bibl. nat. *fr. 1597* (see C. M. Shipp, "A Chansonnier of the Dukes of Lorraine" [diss. North Texas State College, 1960]).

There also exist two 15th-century MSS containing monophonic chansons; see *ReMR,* p. 205; G. Reese and T. Karp, in *JAMS* v.

Chant. General term for liturgical music similar to plainsong, i.e., monophonic and in free rhythm. Music of this type exists in many non-Western cultures. In particular, the term applies to the liturgical music of the Christian churches, which falls into two main divisions, Eastern chant and Western chant. To the former belong Armenian chant [see Armenia], and *Byzantine, *Coptic, and *Syrian chant; to the latter *Ambrosian, *Gallican, *Mozarabic, *Gregorian, and *Old Roman chant. Also see Anglican chant; Psalm tones.

Chanter. See under Bagpipe.

Chanterelle [F.]. See Cantino.

Chantey. See Shanty.

Chanting. The singing of the psalms and canticles in the daily offices of the Roman Catholic and, in particular, the Anglican Church. It is characterized by the use of a melody, called psalm tone, that is repeated with every verse of the psalm but that can be adapted to the different lengths of the verses by the iteration of the same tone, the recitation tone. The psalm tones of the Latin (Gregorian) rite are monophonic and in free rhythm. The Anglican chants are harmonized and the cadence is in strict meter. The Anglican Church, however, also makes frequent use of the Gregorian chant. See Psalm tones; Anglican chant.

Chanty. See Shanty.

Chapel [F. *chapelle;* G. *Kapelle;* It. *cappella;* Sp. *capilla*]. Derived from It. *cappa,* i.e., cape or cloak, the term originally meant a building where the cloaks or other revered relics of saints were housed. It was later extended to apply to private churches of sovereigns, Popes, and bishops, as well as the staff attached to these churches and, in particular, the musicians and singers employed there. The connotation of "private body of musicians" survives in the Chapel Royal of the English kings, an institution that played a valuable part in the development and cultivation of English music [see *GD* i, 607; *GDB* ii, 176ff; W. H. Grattan Flood, in *ML* V, 85]. See also *Kapelle.*

Characteristic note. Leading note.

Character notation. See Fasola.

Character piece [G. *Charakterstück*]. A convenient term for a large repertory of short 19th-century compositions, mostly for piano or piano and one solo instrument, designed to express a definite mood or programmatic idea. Often these pieces have titles that suggest briefness or casualness, e.g., Bagatelle, Impromptu, Moment musical. Many have programmatic titles, such as "Der Dichter spricht" (The Poet Speaks; Schumann) or *Jeux d'eau* (Water Games; Ravel). Although there is a considerable body of third-rate character pieces, most 19th-century masters also contributed to this field, beginning with Beethoven, who opens the repertory with his *Bagatelles.* Schubert followed with his *Impromptus* and *Moments musicals,* Mendelssohn with his *Lieder ohne Worte* (Songs without Words) and *Kinderstücke* (Children's Pieces), Chopin with his *Nocturnes, Préludes, Études, Impromptus,* etc. Whereas these composers usually included a number of pieces under one collective title, Schumann went a good deal further toward individualization and programmatic thought by choosing separate names for each piece, as in his *Kinderszenen* op. 15 or in his *Fantasiestücke* op. 12. New collective names introduced by him are *Novelletten, Nachtstücke* (Night Pieces), *Bunte Blätter* (Colored Leaves), and *Albumblätter* (album leaves). Brahms followed with *Balladen, Rhapsodien,* capriccios, and intermezzi, and Debussy with numerous impressionist character pieces, notably the two books of *Préludes pour piano.* Schumann also wrote long and difficult compositions consisting of a number of character pieces to be played in succession and representing a unified idea (character cycle), among them his *Papillons, Davidsbündlertänze, Kreisleriana,* and *Carnaval.* In sum, the character piece was the favorite and characteristic form of romantic piano music, serving as a vehicle for expressing every conceivable mood, thought, attitude, or emotion. Most of these pieces are written in the ternary form A B A, a form that proved especially suitable for depicting two contrasting moods, the first dramatic (A), the second lyrical (B), or vice versa.

Interesting precursors of the 19th-century character piece are found in the harpsichord suites of F. Couperin, who introduced an important technique of this genre, i.e., the use of a certain "pianistic figure" as the basic motif of the entire piece (e.g., "Les Barricades mystérieuses" from the *sixième ordre* of his *Pièces de Clavecin*). Many pieces by Rameau and Domenico Scarlatti are in the same category. See Editions XXXIX, 8; M. Vidor, "Zur Begriffsbestimmung des musikalischen Characterstückes" (diss. Leipzig, 1924); W. Kahl, in *AMW* iii; *id.*, in *ZMW* iii, 459–69; *id.*, in *Zeitschrift für Musik* lxxxix (1922), 177–82, 201–6.

Charango. A small guitar (approximately 25 inches long) used mainly in the Andean highlands by Indians and *mestizos* but known throughout South America. It is made of a dried armadillo or *tatú* shell. Most examples have ten strings tuned in pairs according to the following pattern:

Some *charangos* are also built of wood carved to resemble the animal shell used traditionally.
J.O-S.

Charivari. A French term of unknown origin that signifies a deliberately distorted and noisy performance, such as was given in provincial towns in front of the homes of unpopular or objectionable persons, or as a mock serenade for a newly married couple. An American corruption of the name is "shivaree," a German term is *Katzenmusik* (cat music), an Italian, *scampata*. There is even a book on the history of the charivari from its origins in the 4th century: G. Peignot, *Histoire morale, civile, politique et littéraire du charivari, depuis son origine vers le IVe siècle* (1833).

Charleston. A kind of *fox trot with a characteristic rhythm, probably named for the city in South Carolina. It was popular in the 1920's and was briefly revived in the 1950's (especially in musical comedies).

Chasse, La [F., The Hunt]. Title for pieces imitating the commotion of a hunt. Also, modernized spelling for the 14th-century *chace. Examples are the "Hunt" Quartet (Haydn, Mozart) and the "Hunt" Symphony (Haydn).

Chasseur maudit, Le [F., The Accursed Huntsman]. Symphonic poem by Franck (1882), based on a ballad by Gottfried Bürger (1747–94) entitled "Der wilde Jäger." It tells the story of a huntsman who goes hunting on Sunday instead of going to church, and who is therefore bewitched and pursued by demons.

Chaunter. See under Bagpipe.

Check. A part of the action of the piano.

Chefs-d'oeuvre [classiques] de l'opéra français. See Editions VII.

Chef d'orchestre [F.]. Conductor. *Chef d'attaque*, concertmaster.

Chegança [Port.]. A kind of traditional dramatic dance-song of Brazil, usually performed at Christmas and probably derived from a dance of the same name that was popular in Portugal during the 18th century. In Brazil the form developed into a short melodrama. Two different specimens became especially popular: the *Chegança dos Marujos* (Arrival of the Mariners) and the *Chegança dos Mouros* (Arrival of the Moors), the former a dramatization of a fight between sailors on board a ship, the latter a battle between Christians and Moors.
J.O-S.

Cheironomy. See Chironomy.

Chekker. See Echiquier.

Chelys [Gr.]. (1) Greek name for the *lyre, which was frequently made from the shell of a turtle. (2) A 16th-century humanist name for the lute. See Testudo.

Cheng. (1) See Jeng. (2) French spelling for sheng, the Chinese mouth organ.

Cherubic hymn. (1) In the Byzantine Mass, the *cherubikon (cheroubikon)*, sung by the choir at the "Great Entrance" (the symbolic entrance of Christ and the cherubim, i.e., angels). An Ordinary chant, it corresponds to the Proper Offertory of the Roman Mass. (2) Name for the Sanctus of the Mass or, more properly, for its Biblical source, the vision of Isaiah, who heard the angels crying unto each other: "Holy, holy, holy is the Lord of hosts" (Isaiah, 6 : 3).

Chest of viols. A set of six or more viols, usually including two trebles, two tenors, and two basses, which, in the 17th century, was kept in a chest with several partitions. See T. Mace's *Musick's Monument* (1676), p. 245. See Consort.

Chest voice. The lower register of a voice [see Register (2)].

Cheute [F.]. Old spelling for *chute.

Chevalet [F.]. Bridge of violins, etc. See Bowing (k).

Chevé system. A system of musical notation invented by a French physician, E. Chevé (1804–64), and much used in France for teaching purposes. It combines the principle of the movable do with the old idea of indicating notes by figures (Spanish keyboard tablature—see Tablature II; Jean Jacques Rousseau, 1742; Pierre Galin, 1817). The figures 1 to 7 represent the tones of the scale (in any given key); lower or higher octaves are indicated by a dot under or above the figures. A rest is indicated by o. See E. and N. Chevé, *Méthode élémentaire de musique vocale* (1844); *WoHN* ii, 403.

Cheville [F.]. Peg of stringed instruments. *Cheviller,* pegbox.

Chevrotement [F.]. Unsteadiness in singing, like the bleating of a goat [F. *chèvre*]. See Goat's trill.

Chiamata [It.; F. *chamade*]. In Venetian operas of the 17th century, pieces written in imitation of the "call" after the end of a hunt. See H. Kretzschmar, in *VMW* viii.

Chiaramente [It.]. Clearly, distinctly.

Chiarenzana. An occasional dance of the Renaissance. It was performed in Florence as early as 1459 at a festival in honor of Pope Pius II. Marcantonio de Pifaro includes fourteen examples in his *Intabolatura de lauto* (1546) that are indistinguishable from the common *pavane* or *passamezzo* of the day. An isolated example in F. Caroso's *Il Ballarino* of 1581 is in the 6/8 meter of a *saltarello* or galliard.   L.H.M.

Chiave [It.]. Clef.

Chiavette (sing. *chiavetta*), **chiavi trasportati** [It.]. A late 16th-century system of writing vocal music with all the clefs moved down or up a third from their normal position, so that, e.g., the F-clef would appear on line 3 (baritone clef) or on line 5 (subbass clef) rather than on line 4

(bass clef; see Clef, Ex. d, nos. 8, 9, 10). Examples of compositions notated in the lowered clefs are quite numerous (Palestrina, *Missa Papae Marcelli;* Taverner, motet "O splendor," see Editions LI, 3; Josquin, "De profundis," see Editions XLVII, 6), while the system with the raised clefs was much more rarely used.

The significance of the *chiavette* has raised considerable controversy among musicologists. Until recently it was generally thought that they indicated a transposition to the lower or upper third, the vocal analogue to transposing instruments of the orchestra. According to this theory, Ex. 1 meant to the singer c e g but was actually sung at the pitch suggested by the position of the notes in connection with the standard clef, i.e., A c♯ e, or perhaps A♭ c e♭. The implied change can be very easily effected: the notes remain in the same position on the staff, the clef is moved to its normal position, and the key signature of A or of A-flat (E or E-flat for the system of raised clefs) is added. Thus, Ex. 1 has the meaning of Ex. 2 or of Ex. 3. The over-all result of this interpretation is that a composition written in C would actually be in the key of A or A-flat. This interpretation was advanced by R. Kiesewetter (*Galerie der alter Contrapunctisten,* 1847) and H. Bellermann (*Der Contrapunct,* 1877) as a convenience to the modern musician, which indeed it is, and advocated as a historical fact by Riemann and Kroyer. The system with the lowered clefs has been (rather pointlessly) called "high" *chiavette,* because the notation (c e g) is higher than the sound (A c♯ e), and the other "low" *chiavette.*

Recent studies (Ehrmann, Mendel) have shown that this theory is without historical foundation. The clefs were moved mainly in order to avoid the use of ledger lines, so that the *chiavette* notation would simply mean a change of clef [Ex. 4]. Evidence has been found, however, that the high *chiavette* occasionally indicated transposition down a fourth or a fifth (Federhofer). In a way the whole question is futile, since it depends entirely on the absolute pitch of the 16th century, about which nothing is known, and which, for that matter, probably did not exist. At any rate, the importance of the *chiavette* has been greatly exaggerated in scholarly studies as well as in books for instruction.

Lit.: T. Kroyer, *Der vollkommene Partitur-spieler* (1931); *id.,* in *CP Adler; id.,* in *ZMW* xiii; A. Schering, in *ZMW* xiii; R. Ehrmann, in *StM* xi; A. Mendel, "Pitch in the 16th and 17th Centuries" (*MQ* xxxiv); H. Federhofer, "Hohe und tiefe Schlüsselung im 16. Jahrhundert" (*CP Blume*); S. Hermelinck, in *MF* xiv; *ReMR,* pp. 531ff.

Chiesa [It.]. In baroque music, *da chiesa* indicates instrumental pieces (sonatas) or vocal pieces with instrumental accompaniment (cantatas) designed for use in the church (*chiesa*), as opposed to similar pieces for secular use, designated *da *camera.* See *Sonata da camera, sonata da chiesa.*

Chifonie [F.]. Medieval (12th–15th cent.) corruption of *symphonia, i.e., *hurdy-gurdy.

Childhood of Christ, The. See *Enfance du Christ, L'.*

Children's Corner. Set of piano pieces (with English titles) by Debussy, composed 1906–08, including: 1. *Doctor Gradus ad Parnassum* (humorous allusion to Clementi's **Gradus ad Parnassum*); 2. *Jimbo's Lullaby;* 3. *Serenade for the Doll;* 4. *Snow is Dancing;* 5. *The Little Shepherd;* 6. *Golliwogg's Cakewalk.* They were written for Debussy's daughter, Claude-Emma, referred to as "Chou-chou" in the dedication.

Chile. Chilean music of the colonial period is known only through chronicles and histories since no compositions have as yet been found. During the 16th and 17th centuries music was used mainly for civic and religious purposes. In the 18th century, as French influences appeared, a type of salon music was developed for the *tertulias* (social gatherings). Works by such Spanish composers as Antonio Soler and José Pons were performed, and some examples of native music, mostly anonymous, have survived, among them *villancicos* such as *Coplas al Niño Dios, con violines, oboes, organo y continuo,* and *Venid festivos zagales, a 4 con clarinete, clarin y baxo continuo,* as well as some hymns to the Virgin and the saints.

The first composer and musical director of the Cathedral of Santiago was the Franciscan Father Cristobal Ajuría (*c.* 1750). Ajuría's popularity was overshadowed, however, by the arrival of a Spaniard, José Campderros, who became musical director of the Cathedral in 1793. Fifteen of his compositions, including two Masses, have been preserved. A contemporary of his, Antonio Aranaz, wrote a *Misa con todo instrumental* in 1793.

The first native composers in Chile appeared at the time of independence (1810), roughly coinciding with the advent of Italian opera's influence in the country. To this group belong Manuel Robles (1780–1837), composer of the original national anthem (1920); Isidora Zegers de Huneeus (1803–69), a noted singer and composer of several songs, minuets, and *contradanzas* for piano, founder of the *Sociedad filarmónica* (1862) and promoter of the founding of the *Conservatorio nacional de música* of Santiago (1849); José Zapiola (1802–85), composer of several hymns, including a highly popular patriotic song, "Himno de Yungay," and band music, as well as author of a book of reminiscences, *Recuerdos de treinta años,* containing valuable information on musical life in Chile from 1810 to 1840; Federico Guzman (1837–85), a noted pianist and composer of more than two hundred works for this instrument as well as for voice and chamber ensembles; Guillermo Frick (1813–96), born in Berlin but living in Chile from 1840 on; and Aquinas Ried (1810–69), a native of Bavaria who came to Chile in 1844, composer of a *Misa Solemne* (1844) and of the first opera written in the country, *La Telésfora* (1846), followed by *Il Granatiere* (1857).

Between 1850 and 1900, art music in Chile seldom rose above the amateur level. Most of the compositions from this period were short salon or virtuoso pieces strongly reflecting European influences. By the end of the century a few opera composers, influenced by Italy, became prominent. In 1895 *La Florista de Lugano* by Eleodoro Ortíz de Zarate (1865–1953) was introduced in Santiago, three years after the first performance in Milan of his *Juana la Loca* (1892). He also wrote *Lautaro* (1897), as well as two more operas, symphonic compositions, and chamber music. In 1902 Remigio Acevedo's (1863–1911) opera *Caupolican* was staged.

Not until a notable group of composers born in the 1880's and 1890's became active did Chile begin to take steps toward its present prominence in Latin American music. Most of these composers were strong supporters of musical nationalism, though they did not neglect abstract music altogether. Enrique Soro (1884–1954), composer of more than eighty works in the romantic tradition, was the first major Chilean composer of high professional competence. His contemporary, Pedro Humberto Allende Sarón (1885–1959), used impressionist techniques to exploit native rhythms, developing a highly individual style. Following similar paths at about the same time were Próspero Bisquertt (1881–1959), Carlos Lavin (1883–1961), Samuel Negrete (b. 1893), and Juan Casanova Vicuña (b. 1894).

Whereas Javier Rengifo (1884–1958) and Roberto Puelma (b. 1893) remained attached to the romantic tradition, more progressive tendencies appear in the works of Acario Cotapos (b. 1889), Alfonso Leng (b. 1884), Carmela Mackenna (b. 1879), and Carlos Isamitt (b. 1887), the last-named being the first Chilean supporter of serial techniques and the use of Araucanian Indian rhythms.

The most prominent member of the succeeding generation is Domingo Santa Cruz Wilson (b. 1899), internationally recognized as both a composer and an intellectual. He founded the *Sociedad Bach* (1922) and promoted the creation of a faculty of music for the University of Chile (1929), the *Asociación de Conciertos Sinfónicos* (1931), the *Asociación de Compositores* (1936), and the *Instituto de Extensión Musical* (1940), an organization established to operate the National Symphony Orchestra, the National Ballet, and several other ensembles. As a composer he tended to follow contemporary European trends. His efforts toward centralizing all musical activity under university control help account for Chile's prominent place on the musical scene and directly benefited such postimpressionist composers as Jorge Urrutia Blondel (b. 1905), René Amengual Astaburuaga (1911–54), and Alfonso Letelier Llona (b. 1912), as well as their successors.

Of the younger generation of Chilean composers, Juan Orrego-Salas (b. 1919) is known for his chamber music, three symphonies, two ballets, and an opera, *El Retablo del Rey Pobré*. His contemporaries include Guillermo Maturana (b. 1920), Carlos Botto (b. 1923), Carlos Riesco (b. 1925), Claudio Spies (b. 1925), Alfonso Montecino (b. 1925; also a noted pianist), Gustavo Becerra (b. 1925; an extremely talented modernist), Leon Schidlowsky (b. 1932), Roberto Falabella (1926–58), Darwin Vargas (b. 1925), Tomas Lefever (b. 1925), and Juan Lemann (b. 1928). Still younger composers include José Vicente Asuar (b. 1933), who has composed electronic music; Enrique Rivera (b. 1941), Miguel Letelier (b. 1939); and Fernando Garcia (b. 1930).

Folk music in Chile is largely Spanish in origin, indigenous influences being slight. Use of 3/4 and 6/8 meters predominate in songs and dances such as the *villancico, *esquinazo, *tonada, *cuando, *aire, and *cueca. The last-named, also known as *zamacueca,* is considered Chile's national dance.

Lit.: E. Pereira Salas, *Los Orígenes del Arte Musical en Chile* (1941); *id., Historia de la música en Chile* (1957); *id., Guia Bibliográfica para el estudio del folklore chileno* (1952); V. Salas Viu, *La Creación Musical en Chile, 1900–1951* [1951]; J. Orrego-Salas, *Pasado y Presente de la Música Chilena* (1960); D. Quiroga, "Aspectos de la ópera en Chile en el siglo XIX" (*Rev. mus. chil.* v); J. Urrutia Blondel, "Apuntes sobre Los Albores de la Historia musical chilena" (*Boletín latino-americano de música* iii). Also see under Latin America.   J.O-S.

Chimes. See under Percussion instruments A, 5. The term is also used for a set of real bells (*carillon), for the orchestral glockenspiel [see Percussion instruments A, 2], and for various Oriental instruments consisting of a series of tuned sonorous agents (gong chimes, stone chimes). See W. W. Starmer, in *PMA* xxxiv, xxxvi. Also see Cymbalum.

Chiming. See under Bell.

Ch'in. See Chyn.

China. I. *History and sources.* Yang Yinnliou (see Lit.) divides the music history of China into three major periods: (1) from prehistoric times through the Shang (*c.* 1700–*c.* 1100 B.C.) and Jou (Chou; *c.* 1100 B.C.–246 B.C.) dynasties; (2) the Chyn (Ch'in; 246–209 B.C.), Hann (Han; 209 B.C.–A.D. 220), the Three Kingdoms and the Northern and Southern States (220–605), Swei (605–618), and Tarng (T'ang) dynasties (618–906); (3) the Five Dynasties (906–960), Sonq (Sung; 960–1279), Yuan (1279–1368), Ming (1368–1644), and Ching (Ch'ing; 1644–1911) dynasties. This division is based on the rise, decline, and renascence of Confucian influence on musical thought in China.

Archaeologists have discovered well-preserved Shang dynasty chimes, bells, and ocarinas, and from the late Jou, fragments of zithers. As early as the 6th century B.C. the classical works of poetry, history, and philosophy mention folksongs, folk dances, court songs and dances, tribal music, and military and hunting music. Toward the end of this first period a systematized theory and practice of ceremonial music evolved, much of it presumably based on the Jou dynasty tradition. Such music was used by the emperor for rituals honoring gods and ancestors, for entertaining royal guests, and by the emperor and provincial officers for paying homage to the elderly and virtuous. Instruments from all of the "eight categories" (a division based on the material) are mentioned in the classics. There are bells (metal), chimes (stone), ocarinas (earth), drums (skin), zithers (silk), percussion blocks (wood), mouth organs (gourd), and flutes (bamboo).

During the second period (246 B.C.–A.D. 906) elements of foreign culture introduced through political expansion were readily absorbed. Already before the Hann, the old Jou tradition of ceremonial music had been interrupted by war and finally destroyed by the deliberate purge of Confucianism in the late 3rd century B.C. When the Hann rulers tried to revive the ancient ceremonies, they had to resort to folksongs, newly composed melodies, and even popular and foreign music for melodic materials. Music associated with Buddhist and Taoist rites also began to appear, but it was secular music that dominated the scene.

From central Asia came foreign musical instruments, musicians, and dancers. During the Swei and Tarng periods regular sections of the Music Bureau were in charge of foreign orchestras, which brought with them new musical forms, new modes, and new tunes. Bas-reliefs in the Hann tombs and wall paintings and sculpture in the Duenhwang Caves of northwest China show dancers and orchestras of the first millenium A.D. Further information is contained in the special sections on music often included in the histories compiled for every dynasty since the early Hann, which usually contain extensive citations from musical writings that are otherwise lost. In addition, many memoirs from this period supply anecdotes about famous singing girls, *pyiba players, and virtuoso drummers, and describe the establishment of musical conservatories under royal patronage. Music, musical performances, and musicians are favorite subjects for Tarng poets. These sources in sum give a vivid impression of the musical life of the times, but the only musical examples from this period that have been preserved are an isolated *chyn melody and a manuscript of twenty-five pieces written for the *pyiba found in Duenhwang. The gay entertainment music of Tarng, when introduced into Japan, became a solemn court music, *gagaku. Since Japanese musical traditions are

conservative, Tarng music may still be present in *gagaku*. Evidence can be found in the notation used for the *biwa and the mouth organ (shō), which is identical to the Duenhwang pyiba notation, as well as in the Chinese names of orchestral pieces and in the many instruments that are of Chinese origin.

With the Sonq dynasty (960–1279) began a nationalist era very different from the cosmopolitan past, a time of return to Confucian ideals. Previously imported music was Sinicized, foreign theories brought in line with Confucian cosmology, and reconstruction of Confucian ceremonial music occupied much of the scholars' attention. Throughout the Sonq, Yuan, Ming, and Ching dynasties, volumes of treatises were written advocating musical reform of one kind or another. However, the chronicles show that conservativism was not wholly dominant. Secular musicians hired for ceremonial performances continued to bring in popular idioms, and they ignored the pitches that had been meticulously calculated by the theorists. Nevertheless the theoretical writings are important sources for later historians. True to the spirit of neo-Confucianism, the theorists stressed detailed examination of concrete matters and wrote much more informatively than the writers from the previous period. With the advent of printing from the end of the Tarng dynasty (618–906), more books with musical notation are preserved. Beginning with the 12th century ritual songs recorded by the philosopher Ju Shi, sources of this kind of music, all written in an easily decipherable pitch notation, appear continuously through the 18th century.

In entertainment music, Tarng dynasty dances gave way to the more intimate Sonq dynasty songs. Leading poets provided new texts for old melodies. The 17 Poetic Songs of Jiang Kwei (12th century), written in a special kind of Sonq dynasty popular notation, are examples of this genre. Such poetic songs, gradually organized into regular sequences in a scheme of modes, together with the folk narratives already popular in early Sonq, were two important influences on the musical drama of the following centuries. More than 150 librettos of the (Mongol) Yuan dynasty (1260–1368) are still preserved. Although no music is given in these texts, the names of the individual tunes all are indicated. The same is true of the musical drama of the Ming dynasty. There is, however, a huge compilation of selections from musical dramas and independent songs published in the early 18th century (*Jeou Gong Dah Cherng*) that may contain pieces of much earlier date.

The *kuencheu,* often referred to as the classical Chinese opera, is a 16th-century development of the musical drama. Still heard fairly frequently today, it is characterized by a sophisticated singing style and prominent use of the dance, which is closely integrated with the song. The orchestra, which uses the flute as the melody instrument, is generally mellow. The *kuencheu* dominated the musical scene for nearly 400 years. Its literature, melodic materials, dance, and different staging techniques have greatly influenced the various regional theatricals, especially the Peking opera, which was established about 1850 and which today has taken its place in popularity.

Both the *kuencheu* and the Peking opera employ the technique of composing with *melody types, i.e., use of the same melodic fragments in different songs. However, the two forms differ in that the *kuencheu* also uses a great number of different melodies without repetition whereas the Peking opera relies chiefly on the repeated use of a very few melodies. These few melodies are divided into two groups, the so-called *shipyi* and *ellhwang* types, within which they are either related in melodic materials or by cadential formulas. However, the melodies contrast sharply in tempo and rhythm, and with the added resource of varied percussion figures to underline action and mood and to mark changes of scene, the Peking opera actually has a much wider range of dramatic possibilities than the *kuencheu* of today. The Peking opera has a short history (*c.* 100 years). Although the highly stylized singing and acting demands a cultivated taste, the Peking opera remains the most popular musical art form.

Instrumental music seems to have been written idiomatically only for the *chyn and *pyiba. The chyn repertory is quite large, with compilations dating from the early 15th century. The pyiba repertory, on the other hand, is very modest; collections of pyiba music begin with the early 19th century. Other instruments, such as the 16-stringed zither (jeng), horizontal flute (dyitz), two-stringed fiddle (ellhwu), three-stringed banjo (sanshyan), psaltery (yangchyn), oboe (suoonah), etc., are popular as solo instruments today. Little is known of their early music. What they play today seems to have been mostly borrowed from the chyn and pyiba, or consists of arrangements of traditional popular tunes. A few unusual 19th-century scores for

instrumental ensembles have been preserved, but the kind heard today has developed in South China since the 1920's. Originally such instrumental pieces were used in the musical drama, the melodic materials being based on traditional tunes from various parts of the country. Since the instrumental ensemble became an independent form, original pieces have been composed for it, with new idioms and instruments from other regions sometimes being added. At one time, these even included some elements of popular Western music.

After World War I the mainstream of musical development in China was once more dominated by foreign influences, from Europe, America, and modern Japan. Today, music, if taught in schools at all, is generally only of the Western variety. In musical composition, the rapid social and political changes in China since 1900 have generated a great demand for functional music —songs for political and educational purposes. There are countless organizational songs, propaganda and war songs, and songs commemorating special public and private occasions. Choral music seems to be enjoying great popularity. Cantatas and new-style musical drama constitute a good percentage of the total musical output today.

Many composers have a thorough training in Western music, and they work both in the purely Western idiom and in various combinations of Chinese and Western styles. Composers such as Heh Luhting (Rodin Ho), Hwang Tzyh (Tzu Huang), Jaw Yuanrenn (Y. R. Chao), Lii Weining (W. N. Lee), Liou Sheue'an, Maa Sytsong (Ma Sitson), and Shean Shinghae have written essentially in the style of the common practice period.

Attempts at a harmonic interpretation of Chinese melodies has met with varying degrees of success, because not all traditional melodies suggest a well-defined tonal orientation. Maa, for example, has made use of modal harmonies in folksongs, and Hwang is well-known for his treatment of pentatonic melodies with seventh chords. Although the concept of harmony has indeed opened new possibilities for composition, the more recent developments in Western music, tending away from traditional tonality, have already influenced such younger composers as Jou Wenjong (Chou Wenchung) and Sheu Charnghuey (Shu Tsang-houei) and may well become an equally important factor in the future development of Chinese music.

In traditional music, conscious efforts have

been made—often inspired by nationalism—to preserve and study folksongs, musical theatricals, folk narratives, and instrumental music, all of which have been rapidly disappearing. With the establishment of the Institute of National Music in Peking in 1954, the movement once more gained momentum, and now there are several specialized journals devoted to this field. In general the attitude has been that, technically, these arts need reform. Attempts have been made to adopt Western techniques of composition and performance, and to make changes in the construction of traditional instruments to alter the intonation and enlarge their range and volume. During the first half of the 20th century, except for the handful of compositions for the pyiba and the two-stringed ellhwu by Liou Tianhwa, there were not many widely known new compositions for traditional instruments. The Peking opera is one medium that has remained relatively creative, in spite of modern-minded critics who began to complain that the melodies were lacking in originality, the acting unrealistic, and the orchestra too loud. In the recent surge of Peking opera writing, however, up-to-date subject matter is still handled in the traditional style. It is too soon to say how successful these new operas will be, but the effort has at least spurred a deeper study and understanding of the genre.

II. *Theory*. A. *Tonal system*. An overworked aspect of Chinese music theory is the *hwangjong* (*huang chung*, yellow bell), a principal tone of absolute pitch represented by a bamboo pipe whose exact measurement was, for many centuries, both an important theoretical issue for the cosmologists and a practical concern for the government since it involved the metrical standards of length and weight. Time and again, attempts were made to find *the* correct measurement. Recent investigations (Yang Yinnliou) have shown that there were thirty-five pitch reforms, extending from the late Jou period to the Ching dynasty, during which the pitch for *hwangjong* varied between c$^{\sharp\prime}$ and a'. (Today writers who are not chiefly concerned with the issue of absolute pitch often equate *hwangjong* with middle c.) From the principal note *hwangjong* eleven additional pitches were derived by the *Pythagorean (circle-of-fifths) method. The earliest complete account of this method of calculation appears in *The Spring and Autumn of Leu* (3rd century B.C.), although a similar method used to produce a series of five notes already appeared in *Goan Tzyy* (4th century

B.C.) and more recent discoveries of very accurately tuned stone chimes (*chinq*) suggest that the system must have been known in the 2nd millennium B.C. The difficulty with this system is that by continuing the same procedure from the 12th note, the resulting *hwangjong* is a little higher than the original [see Comma]. For centuries, this worried the theorists, because—for the sake of cosmological implications—they wanted a closed circle that would make the 12 notes rotate their functions symmetrically. Various methods were attempted. The earliest was by pushing the circle of fifths further in the hope of finding the right note. This resulted in adding a considerable number of extra notes within the octave. Jing Farng (1st century B.C.) went as far as the magic number 60, and Chyan Yuehjy (A.D. 5th century) went on to 360. But in principle they still had not solved the problem. Tsay Yuandinq (12th century) compromised by stopping at 18, since he was content simply to produce an identical seven-note scale from each of the 12 pitches without rotating the functions of every note.

The tempered scale was first attempted by Her Cherngtian (A.D. 5th century), who arbitrarily shifted upward by increasing degrees each succeeding note after the first of the Pythagorean scale. Ju Tzayyuh (16th century) finally created the tempered scale of 12 notes by the method of successively dividing by the 12th root of 2. However, none of these mathematical calculations was put into practice. In fact, in many treatises there was no clear indication as to whether the calculation was based on the lengths of tubes or of strings. Nor was the diameter of the tubes always taken into account.

To what extent *just intonation is used on the seven-stringed chyn is still a moot question. Although the stopping positions are marked at the simple divisions of the strings [see Chyn] and the harmonics are certainly much used in chyn music, the chyn manuals since the 16th century have indicated certain adjustments that seem to bring the intonation closer to the Pythagorean or equal temperament. Some evenly divided minor thirds are indicated by the frets on the traditional model of the pyiba. The resulting 3/4-tone intervals that are clearly discernible in pyiba music can also be heard in other types of traditional instrumental and vocal music.

B. *Scales and modes*. The first seven notes produced by the circle-of-fifths method form a fa-scale that is the orthodox basic scale, *gong diaw*, as mentioned in all theoretical treatises. Their names are, in ascending order: *gong* (fa), *shang* (sol), *jyue* (la), *biann* [*pien*]-*jyy* (si), *jyy* (do), *yeu* (re), *biann-gong* (mi). The series of five notes that is mentioned in *Goan Tzyy* (4th cent. B.C.), given in numerical terms, is in the relationship of do-re-fa-sol-la. However, it was the series fa-sol-la-do-re, which first appeared in the 1st century B.C., that became the more common pentatonic scale. The heptatonic fa-scale was first described explicitly by a theorist of the 1st century B.C., although passages vaguely mentioning sets of six notes and seven notes had appeared in the classics long before.

The heptatonic do-scale, although not an orthodox scale, was evidently also used. In the 6th century there were complaints that the do-scale was confused with the fa-scale. In later centuries the modes of ceremonial music were always correctly named with reference to the fa-scale, but in 13th-century chyn music the do-scale was the basis for modal designations.

The Chinese system of modes in its fullest form consists of 84 combinations of scales and final notes. They are produced in the following manner: on the basic heptatonic fa-scale each note can be used as the final; the basic scale itself can begin on any of the 12 pitches. Since there is only a limited ambitus of one octave, the higher the pitch of fa, the greater the portion of the basic scale appears below the final; that is why the pitch of the basic scale at times can also be a relevant factor in characterizing a mode. Thus, with the constant ambitus of c to c', a so-called sol-of-c-mode has its basic scale beginning on c (the notes being c–d–e–f♯–g–a–b) and final on d; a re-of-b♭-mode has its basic scale beginning on b♭ (the notes being c–d–e–f–g–a–b♭) and final on g.

Some kind of modal concept may have existed in China before the wholesale importation of Central Asian modes in the middle of the 1st millenium A.D. But it was after this foreign impact, which had a lasting influence on Chinese musical theory, that writings about modes became more explicit. By the Sonq dynasty, the complete set of 84 modes, some still retaining their foreign names, was codified. In practice during the Sonq, however, some adjustments were made. For example, in both ceremonial and popular music, four additional semitones above the basic scale were also used; in at least one practical treatise some scales show pentatonic features. The Sonq performer must have been very familiar with the modal system of his day. The popular notational system of the time had ambiguous symbols, but given the modal

name of a piece, he would have to know immediately the true value of the notes. Tsay Yuandinq (12th century), a controversial figure of his time, had an entirely different concept of modes. He built the basic fa-scale from each of the 12 pitches upward; hence he extended the ambitus of the entire system to 2 octaves. However, it is doubtful that this was ever put into practice. He also reduced the total system to 60 modes by omitting the mi and si modes, but his most significant contribution was to initiate the use of the beginning and final notes of a melody as a criterion in determining its mode.

Not all of the 84 modes were used in musical composition. Even the so-called "28 modes for popular music" used in the Tarng and early Sonq periods (the fa-, sol-, la-, and re-modes on C, D♭, E♭, F, G, A♭, and B♭), which were probably the original nucleus of the 84, were only a theoretical list. Although some academic-minded composers in the Sonq dynasty still occasionally experimented with the less common modes, the list was reduced to 19, 18, or 17; in the Yuan to 12 and 9; and during the Ming to 8. Modes were used not only to organize melodies formally but also for the practical purpose of categorizing music. Gradually, as the meanings of the modes were forgotten, the same melodies were regrouped for nonmusical reasons and their modal labels were confused. The 18th-century *Anthology of Songs* is a case in point.

Even while academic musicians were concentrating on elaborate modal theories, some use seems to have been made of melody-types. At least in some of the Sonq dynasty examples preserved, pieces belonging to the same mode tend to have similar melodic fragments. In the present day Peking opera, melody-types are recognized as such and are given generic names while modes are no longer mentioned.

C. *Speech tones and music.* Tonal inflection of individual syllables is a phonemic element in Chinese speech. Some tones move up or down while others remain on a fairly even level. Some dialects also distinguish relative pitch and length of duration. The musical contour of the tone for the same word will change from one period to another and will vary from dialect to dialect. However, the change by entire tonal groups during the past 1,500 years is so regular that it is possible to establish the abstract tone class for the great majority of words without too much difficulty.

From very ancient times onward, tones were grouped into four classes—Even, Rising, Going and Entering—the last consisting of syllables ending abruptly in a voiceless stop consonant. In poetry and song, the four tones are grouped under Even on the one hand and Oblique on the other, the latter consisting of the other three tones. The existing Sonq dynasty songs show that there was indeed a certain amount of distinction in the treatment of the Even and Oblique Tones in music. In *kuencheu* the writers pay great attention to tonal adjustment. In the Peking opera, the relation between melody and word-tone is at times less strict, but there are also many places where the writer makes a special effort to bring out the word-tones for dramatic purposes. Since in these dramatic forms new texts are set to melody-types rather than to a fixed melody, there is much leeway in making adjustments to the tones. In performance, *kuencheu* singers even make some distinction within the three Oblique Tones. For example, there are rules for adding such ornaments as the *échappée* [see Nonharmonic tones I] or *cambiata to bring out more specifically the Going Tone.

The traditional practice is to give the Even Tones relatively longer notes or a slightly descending line, while the Oblique Tones are given quicker, up-and-down moving notes. Many present-day composers still more or less follow this traditional dichotomy of tones, but others adhere more closely to the actual values of modern Mandarin. Composers whose interest is purely in the music itself also compose without regard for the speech tones.

D. *Aesthetics.* The use of music as a medium for the social and political education of the people has been a serious concern of Chinese governments from the time of Confucius. Among the few who have protested against using music for such purposes were the early Taoists, who objected to all the arts on moral grounds, and the Moists, who disapproved of ceremonial music for reasons of economy. The power of music as a force for molding society is already mentioned in the early classics. In the 2nd century B.C., there were elaborate discourses on music in relation to the human spirit and on the use of music to inculcate moderation. About this time, seasonal, directional, and other cosmological connotations of the pitches became an integral part of Chinese musical thought. Men like Ji Kang, the 3rd-century chyn player who came close to a modern psychological explanation of music's influence on the human emotions, or Sheen Gua, a 10th-century intellectual who

observed acoustical phenomena with a scientific eye, were exceptions to the cosmological approach. We read discussions in allegorical terms of the hierarchy of the notes in the scale and anecdotes about the effect of melodies sung with certain notes. At times the do-mode was forbidden; the notes mi and si were regarded by some as unorthodox. In the 14th century, when modes were used to organize the acts in musical drama, their emotional connotations were listed. Even today the choice between the *Shipyi* and *ellhwang* melodies in the Peking opera is still sometimes based upon the emotion associated with each.

The enjoyment of music, instrumental or vocal, is usually assumed to be based on extramusical elements. Thus, with a few exceptions, all instrumental works, often including the smaller sections, have programmatic or allegorical titles.

In the midst of the Marxist movement for realism in the arts in mainland China, the authorities had on occasion also taken the position of defenders of the stylized tradition in the Peking opera. For example, to summarize a declaration by Ah Jea in *Shihcheu Yanjiou [Journal for the Study of the Musical Drama,* Peking, Jan., 1957]: The Peking opera presents life in an artistic language of its own that has been accepted by the people. It is effective because it selects the essence of reality, and, through condensation and heightening, presents a new kind of reality that is bigger than life.

Lit. *Bibl. of Western works: Notes* (1950) vii, no. 3, 4; J. Kunst, *Supplement to the Third Edition of Ethnomusicology* (1960).

Western works: J. H. Levis, *Foundations of Chinese Musical Art* (1936); L. Pickens, in *NOH* i, 83ff; R. Ally and E. Siao, *Peking Opera* (Peking, 1957); Y. R. Chao, "Tone, Intonation, Singsong, Chanting, Recitative, Tonal Composition and Atonal Composition in Chinese," in *For Roman Jakobson...* Compiled by Morris Halle, *et al.* (1956), pp. 52–59; S. Kishibe, *A Historical Study of the Music in the T'ang Dynasty* (1961); R. C. Pian, *Sonq Dynasty Musical Sources and Their Interpretation* (1967); E. H. Schafer, *The Golden Peaches of Samarkand* (1963); A. C. Scott, *Traditional Chinese Plays* (1967); W. P. Malm, *Music in Cultures of...Asia* (1967), pp. 107–29; K. Reinhard, *Chinesische Musik* (1956); Hsiao Ch'en, ‡*A Harp with a Thousand Strings: A Chinese Anthology* (1944); H. M. Stimson, in *Tsinghua Journal of Chinese Studies* i (1965), 86–106; F. A. Kuttner, in *Ethno-*

musicology viii, 121–27; Juang Beenlih, "Ch'ih: The Ancient Chinese Flute" (*Bulletin of the Institute of Ethnology,* Academia Sinica, Nankang, Taiwan, no. 19 [1965]); E. M. von Hornbostel, in *AMW* i (notation); R. W. Marks, in *MQ* xviii (instruments); L. Picken, in *CP Bartók* (Tarng melodies); *id.,* in *GSJ* viii, *MQ* xliii; A. Tcherepnin, in *MQ* xxi (modern music).

Bibl. of Chinese works: R. H. van Gulik, *The Lore of the Chinese Lute* (Tokyo, 1940), pp. 163–72; K. T. Bartlett-Wu, "Books on East Asiatic Music in the Lib. of Cong. compiled before 1800: Works on Chinese" (suppl. to H. Bartlett, *Lib. of Cong: Catalogue of Early Books on Music,* 1944, pp. 121–31); *Revue Bibliographique de Sinologie* (Paris, 1957–60), i–iv; *Jonggwo Guuday Inyueh Shumuh* (*Chu-gao*) ([Preliminary] List of Ancient Chinese Books on Music; Institute of National Music, Peking, 1961).

Standard works in Chinese: Wang Guangchyi, *Jonggwo Inyueh Shyy* (History of Chinese Music; repr. Taipei, 1956); Yang Yinnliou, *Jonggwo Inyueh Shyy Gang* (Outline History of Chinese Music; Chungking, 1944; Shanghai, 1952).

Journals on Chinese music: Tōyō Ongaku Kenkyū (Journal of the Society for Research in Asiatic Music; Tokyo, 1937–41, 1951—); *Renmin Inyueh* (People's Music; Peking, 1950, 1954—); *Inyueh Yanjiou* (Journal of Musicological Studies; Peking, 1958–60).   R.C.P.

Chinese block. A percussion instrument used in jazz bands that consists of a hollowed-out wooden block. Played with a drumstick, it produces a dry, hollow sound.

Chinese crescent. See Turkish crescent.

Chinese pavilion. See Turkish crescent.

Ching. Korean gong, corresponding to the Chinese *cheng (2).

Chironomy. A term for neumatic signs lacking clear indication of pitch, the inference being that such signs were interpreted to the choir by the conducting precentor, who moved his hands [Gr. *cheir*] in an appropriate and suggestive manner. The clearest information about this method is found in Byzantine sources, according to which it dates from the time of Kosmas and John Damascene (8th century). Motions of the right hand were used together with specific signs of a "finger language," fingers being raised, lowered, extended, contracted, put together, etc. Similar signs, no doubt, were used for interpretation of the chironomic neumes found in the

earliest MSS of Gregorian chant (10th century). See Neumes II. See E. Wellesz, *A History of Byzantine Music and Hymnography,* rev. ed. (1961), p. 287; M. Huglo, in *RdM* xlix, 155ff.

Chispa. A Colombian air similar to the *bambuco. It uses alternating groups of three and four beats, in moderately fast tempo, and usually is in the minor mode.   J.O-S.

Chitarra [It.]. *Guitar. The *chitarrina* is a smaller type, used in Naples.

Chitarra battente [It.]. See under Guitar family.

Chitarrone [It.]. See under Lute III.

Chiterna [It.]. Same as cittern, gittern; see Guitar family.

Chiuso [It.]. In horn playing, same as stopped; see Horn I. In 14th-century music, see Ouvert and clos.

Choir. A body of church singers, as opposed to a secular chorus. The name is also used for instrumental groups of the orchestra, e.g., brass choir, string choir, woodwind choir.

Choirbook [G. *Chorbuch*]. The large-sized manuscripts of 15th- and 16th-century polyphonic music that were placed on a stand and from which the whole choir (about 15 singers) sang. Examples are Cambrai, Bibl. de la ville, MS. 11 (*c.* 1430); Bologna, Bibl. univ., MS 2216 (*c.* 1430); Brussels, Bibl. royale, MS 6428 (*c.* 1500). See the pictures in *BeMMR*, pp. 234, 248. For choirbook arrangement [G. *Chorbuch-Anordnung*], see under Score II. See also *Cantus lateralis.*

Choir organ. Originally, a small organ used to accompany the choir. Today, the third manual of the normal organ, which is provided with stops useful for accompaniment purposes. See Organ III.

Choir pitch. See under Pitch (2).

Chomonie. See under *Anenaiki.*

Chor [G.]. A chorus or choir.

Choral [G.]. (1) The plainsong of the Roman Catholic Church, usually called *Gregorianischer Choral* [see Gregorian chant]. Derivatives are: *Choralnotation* (*monophonic notation); *Choralnote* (plainsong note); *Choralrhythmus* (plainsong rhythm). (2) The hymn tunes of the German Protestant Church [see Chorale]. Derivatives are: *Choralbearbeitung* (this term may also apply to the Gregorian *Choral*); *Choralfantasie* (chorale fantasia); *Choralkantate* (chorale cantata); *Choralpartita* (chorale partita); *Choralvorspiel* (chorale prelude).

Choral, chorale. In view of the different meanings and confusing usage of these terms, a few general explanations are needed. According to Webster, *cho'ral* (adj.) means of or belonging to a chorus or a choir, while *choral'* (noun) means a hymn tune, a sacred melody. For the latter meaning, the spelling "chorale" is preferred, and the same preference is used in this dictionary. Thus, a "choral fantasia" is a fantasia employing a chorus, whereas a "chorale fantasia" is a fantasia based on a hymn tune. Unfortunately, the situation is further complicated by the fact that the word "chorale" usually refers to the hymn tunes of the German Protestant Church, which in German are called *Choral* (accent on the last syllable), while, on the other hand, the equivalent of the English adjective "choral" is the German noun *Chor-* (united to the noun it precedes). Thus, we have the following equivalents: E. choral fantasia = G. *Chorfantasie;* E. chorale fantasia = G. *Choralfantasie.* Similarly: choral cantata = *Chorkantate;* chorale cantata = *Choralkantate.*

Choralbearbeitung [G.]. Generic term for any composition based on a *Choral* (chorale). The term refers chiefly to the various methods of composition used for Protestant chorales from 1600 to 1750 [see Chorale cantata; Chorale fantasia; Chorale prelude; Chorale variations; Organ chorale]. However, it has also been used by German musicologists (Handschin and others) for compositions based on Gregorian melodies, especially for the organa and clausulae of the 12th and 13th centuries. In its broadest sense, the term would also apply to numerous other types, e.g., 15th- and 16th-century settings of Gregorian hymns, of the Marian antiphons, the Magnificat, and even to Masses such as a *Missa Salve regina.*

Choral cantata [G. *Chorkantate*]. A cantata that employs a chorus (as most cantatas by Bach do), as opposed to a solo cantata (the usual type of the 17th-century Italian cantata). For the German term *Choralkantate,* see Chorale cantata.

Chorale [G. *Choral*]. A hymn tune of the German Protestant Church. The importance of the Protestant chorale lies in its central position in German baroque music as the basis of numerous

cantatas and of the whole tradition of the organ chorale.

Long before any other people, the Germans began to sing hymns in their native language [see Hymn IV]. This continuous tradition came to full flower under Martin Luther (1483–1546). An accomplished musician himself, Luther considered the chorale a pillar of his reform movement and played a very active part in building a repertory of texts and melodies suitable for this purpose. In conformity with his principle of congregational participation, he favored vernacular texts and simple, tuneful melodies. In his search for suitable texts Luther resorted chiefly to Roman Catholic hymns, many of which he (or his collaborators) translated into German, e.g.: "Num komm, der Heiden Heiland" ("Veni redemptor gentium"); "Herr Gott, dich loben wir" (*"Te deum laudamus"); "Der Tag, der ist so freudenreich" ("Dies est laetitiae"); "Wir glauben all' an einen Gott" ("Credo in unum deum patrem omnipotentem"), etc. The chief sources for his melodies were secular songs for which he or his collaborators provided new (sacred) texts ["geistliche Kontrafaktur"; see Parody]. Examples of chorale melodies borrowed from such songs are: "Durch Adams Fall ist ganz verderbt" (from the Pavia song: "Freut euch, freut euch in dieser Zeit"); "Von Gott will ich nicht lassen" (from a love song: "Einmal tat ich spazieren"); "Was mein Gott will, das g'scheh' allzeit" (from the chanson: "Il me suffit de tous mes maulx," published by Attaingnant, 1529); "Auf meinen lieben Gott" (from Regnart's "Venus du und dein Kind").

The earliest sources of Protestant chorales are two publications of 1524, the co-called "Achtliederbuch" (containing 8 poems to 4 melodies; original title: *Etlich Cristlich lider Lobgesang . . . in der Kirchen zu singen*) and the two-volume *Enchiridion oder eyn Handbüchlein* with 25 poems to 16 melodies. These books, as well as those published by Klug (Wittenberg, 1529, '35, '43), Blum (Leipzig, 1530), Schumann (Leipzig, 1530), and Babst (Leipzig, 1545, '53), give only melodies, which were sung by the congregation in unison. Many of the most beautiful chorales, still sung today, are found in these early books. It should be noted, however, that their original form shows a much less conventional and, for that matter, a much more impressive rhythmic form than that of the present day. Especially interesting is the irregularity of phrasing and meter [ex. in *AdHM* i, 448].

The year 1524 also marks the beginning of

musical composition based on the Protestant chorales. J. Walther's *Geystliches Gesangk Buchleyn* [see Editions XLVII, 7] contains 38 polyphonic settings (for three to six voices) of such melodies in the style of the Flemish motet, i.e., with the melody in the tenor and with occasional imitation in the contrapuntal voices [see *HAM*, no. 111; *AdHM* i, 449]. Similar publications are G. Rhau, *Newe deudsche geistliche Gesenge* (1544; *DdT* 34) and J. Spangenberg, *Cantiones ecclesiasticae latinae . . . Kirchengesenge deudtsch* (1545). The involved polyphonic texture of these pieces naturally excludes the possibility of congregational performance or even participation. A decisive step toward fuller realization of Luther's ideal was taken by Lucas Osiander (1534–1604) in his *Fünfftzig geistliche Lieder und Psalmen* (1586). Here the melody was placed in the discant and a simple homophonic style (cantional style; see *Cantionale*) was adopted for the accompanying parts. His example was followed by Sethus Calvisius (*Harmonia cantionum ecclesiasticarum*, 1597), H. L. Hassler (*Kirchengesänge, Psalmen und geistliche Lieder . . . simpliciter gesetzt*, 1608), and S. Scheidt (*Tabulatur-Buch Hundert geistlicher Lieder und Psalmen*, 1650).

The 17th century saw continued activity in the creation of chorale melodies (monophonic as well as polyphonic or with figured bass), although generally with inferior results. The tunes do not possess the originality and forcefulness of the earlier ones, becoming more sentimental and conventional. Nonetheless, composers such as J. Crüger (1598–1662), J. Schop (*c.* 1590–1667), J. G. Ebeling (1637–76), J. Hintze (1622–1702), and J. R. Ahle (1625–73) contributed many fine tunes to the texts of Paul Gerhardt, Johann Rist, and others. Particularly important is the repertory of compositions based on chorale melodies. The cantatas, oratorios, and Passions of the late 17th and early 18th centuries (especially those of Bach) contain numerous examples of vocal chorale composition in a simple homophonic style as well as in elaborate contrapuntal texture. Simultaneously, there developed the no less impressive repertory of the *organ chorale, or, as it is often called, chorale prelude.

To the present-day musician the chorales are best known through Bach's harmonized versions. It is interesting to compare Bach's settings with, e.g., those of S. Scheidt, his predecessor by 100 years (b. 1587). The accompanying example (*Jesus Christus unser Heiland;* a. Scheidt,

b. Bach) shows that all the elements of Bach's method are already present in Scheidt. Ex. in *HAM*, nos. 111, 167a, 190.

Lit.: J. Zahn, *Die Melodien der deutschen evangelischen Kirchenlieder*, 6 vols. (1889–93); P. Wackernagel, *Bibliographie zur Geschichte des deutschen Kirchenliedes im XVI. Jahrhundert* (1853; repr. 1961); Johann Westphal, *Das evangelische Kirchenlied in geschichtlicher Entwicklung* (1911); C. Böhm, *Das deutsche evangelische Kirchenlied* (1927); P. Gabriel, *Das deutsche evangelische Kirchenlied von Martin Luther bis zur Gegenwart* (1951); Archibald W. Wilson, *The Chorales; Their Origin and Influence* (1920). See also the books on Bach by Spitta, Schweitzer, and C. S. Terry; G. R. Woodward, "German Hymnody" (*PMA* xxxii).

Chorale cantata [G. *Choralkantate*]. A term applied, usually with reference to Bach's works, to cantatas in which chorale texts (and, as a rule, chorale melodies) are used for movements other than the final one, which is nearly always a harmonized chorale. The following types may be distinguished [see W. G. Whittaker, *Fugitive Notes on Certain Cantatas and the Motets of J. S. Bach* (1924)]: (a) those in which chorale texts are used for all the movements; (b) those in which some of the chorale verses are recast in free poetry in order to allow for aria-like treatment; (c) those in which chorale texts are used in some movements while the others are free recitatives or arias. The only example of (a) is Bach's early cantata, "Christ lag in Todesbanden." An example of (b) is, "Ach Gott vom Himmel," and of (c), "Wachet auf" and "Ein' feste Burg." C. S. Terry's book, *J. S. Bach, Cantata Texts* (1926), affords an excellent aid to such classification since the chorale texts are distinguished from the free texts by being printed in italics. Bach's predecessors in the use of chorale texts and melodies for cantatas were F. Tunder (1614–67; *DdT* 3), J. Kindermann (1616–55; *DTB* 24), J. Rosenmüller (*c.* 1620–84), W. Briegel (1626–1712), J. P. Krieger (1649–1725; *DdT* 53/54); J. Pachelbel (1653–1706; *DTB* 6), and J. Kuhnau (1660–1722; *DdT* 58/59).

Chorale fantasia. An organ composition in which a chorale melody is treated in the free manner of a fantasia, involving various techniques, such as ornamentation, fragmentation, echo effects, etc. S. Scheidt's *Fantasia super Ich ruf zu dir, Herr Jesus Christ* [*DdT* 1; also in K. Straube, *Alte Meister* (1904)], his greatest organ composition, is actually a *chorale motet. True chorale fantasias, all of large dimensions (150 to 400 measures), occur in the works of the North German composers. The earliest examples are two compositions by Johannes Stephani, preserved in the organ tablature of Celle, 1601 [*Editions XI, 17]. Others are by J. Praetorius (*Durch Adams Fall;* in G. Gerdes, *46 Choräle für Orgel* [1957]), H. Scheidemann (*Ein' feste Burg,* preserved in the Peplin tablature), N. Hasse (*Komm heiliger Geist;* in *Editions XI, 10), J. A. Reincken (*An Wasserflüssen Babylon;* in *Editions XI, 16), F. Tunder (*Komm Heiliger Geist; Was kann uns kommen an für Not;* repr. in R. Walter, ed., *Franz Tunder: Sämtliche Choralbearbeitungen für Orgel* [1958]), D. Buxtehude (*Nun freut euch, Gelobet seist du, Wie schön leuchtet*), V. Lübeck (*Ich ruf zu dir Herr Jesu Christ*), and G. Böhm (*Vater unser im Himmelreich;* repr. in J. Wolgast, *Georg Böhm: Sämtliche Werke* [1927–32]). To the same type belong some early compositions of Bach's (*Christ lag in Todesbanden, Ein' feste Burg*) that show the influence of Böhm, especially in the peculiar fragmentary treatment of the chorale melody.

Chorale fugue. A term often used as a synonym of *chorale motet but that might better be used for a different type of chorale composition, nearly always for organ, in which there is imitative treatment only of the initial line of the chorale melody, which thus becomes the theme of a real fugue. As a result of this restriction, the chorale fugue is much shorter as well as stylistically simpler than the chorale motet. This type was cultivated mainly by the Middle German composers. One of the earliest examples is

Erbarm dich mein by J. S. Bach's great-uncle, Heinrich Bach (1615–92; repr. in A. Ritter, *Zur Geschichte des Orgelspiels,* 2 vols. [1884], ii, no. 101). Many others were written by his sons, Johann Christoph (1642–1703) and Johann Michael (1648–94), and by Pachelbel. Those by J. S. Bach are often termed *fughetta.*

Chorale motet. A composition in which a chorale melody is treated in motet style [see Motet II], i.e., as a succession of fugal sections, each based on one of the successive lines of the chorale. Examples abound in vocal music from Josquin ("Veni sancte spiritus") to Bach (first movements of cantatas nos. 16, 27, 58, 60, 73, 95, etc.) as well as in organ music, where the chorale motet is one of the principal types of organ chorale. Perhaps the earliest example is H. Buchner's *Maria zart* (preserved in Kleber's tablature of 1524, where it is designated as *fuga optima*). A number of 16th-century organ hymns also belong to the same type, e.g., Cavazzoni's *Pange lingua* (see Editions IX, 6) and Cabezón's *Christe redemptor* (see Editions XX, 3, p. 54f). In the 17th century the chorale motet represents the most solemn and magnificent treatment of a chorale. M. Praetorius' *Christ unser Herr* (410 measures) and Scheidt's *Fantasia super Ich ruf zu dir,* for example, indicate the beginning of a development that culminated in such works as Bach's *Nun komm, der Heiden Heiland* and *Wenn wir in höchsten Nöten sein.* See W. Morgan, "The Chorale Motet between 1650 and 1750" (diss. Univ. of Southern California, 1956).

Chorale prelude [G. *Choralvorspiel*]. An organ composition based on a Protestant chorale and designed to be played before the chorale is sung by the congregation. Actually only simple and short settings belong to this category. For this reason, and because of the close historical connection between the Protestant chorale prelude and the earlier organ hymns of the Roman Catholic service, which cannot in any sense be considered "preludes," the whole subject is treated under Organ chorale.

Chorale variations. Variations on a chorale melody, nearly always for organ or harpsichord, occasionally for lute. In the late baroque period this form was often called a partita (Pachelbel, Bach). It was favored especially by the earliest composers of Protestant organ chorales. All the settings by Sweelinck and nearly all those by Scheidt consist of variations, called *versus.* There are many other examples in the works of

Scheidemann, Tunder, Buxtehude, Pachelbel, Böhm, Walther, and others. Bach contributed to this field three sets of his earlier period as well as one of his latest works, the *Fünf canonische Veränderungen über das Weihnachtslied.* The number of variations is sometimes the same as the number of stanzas of the chorale. Occasionally the textual meaning of a stanza is reflected in the musical treatment of the corresponding variation, e.g., by the use of a chromatic motif for a stanza expressing grief. Particularly remarkable for their dramatic pictorialism are Tunder's variations on "Jesus Christus unser Heiland" (repr. in K. Straube, *Choralvorspiele alter Meister* [1951], and in R. Walter, ed., *Franz Tunder: Sämtliche Choralbearbeitungen für Orgel* [1956]). A recent example of chorale variations are E. Krenek's (b. 1900) variations on "Ja ich glaub an Jesum Christum" (*Toccata und Chaconne,* op. 13), in which the chorale is treated as an allemande, sarabande, gavotte, waltz, fugue, and foxtrot (*sic!*). The impression of sacrilege is somewhat mitigated by the reference to what may have been Krenek's model, namely, Buxtehude's variations on "Auf meinen lieben Gott," which consist of an allemande, sarabande, courante, and gigue, thus forming one of the numerous examples of the 17th-century fusion of variation and suite [see Variations IV (2)].

Choralfuge [G.]. *Chorale fugue or *chorale motet.

Choralis Constantinus. A large cycle of liturgical compositions written by H. Isaac (*c.* 1450–1517) for the Cathedral of Constance, completed by his pupil, L. Senfl, and published posthumously by Formschneider (Nuremberg) in three volumes (1550–55). Similar to the *"Magnus liber organi," written more than 300 years earlier, it consists of settings of the Proper of the Mass but on a much more comprehensive scale. Book I contains the Mass Propers for all Sundays; Book II, those for the feasts of the Lord and the Saints; Book III, those for the Common of Saints and for the Virgin. Each Mass consists (normally) of Introit, Alleluia or Tract, Sequence, and Communion, the Graduals and Offertories being regularly omitted. Books I and II are reprinted in *DTO* 10 and 32, Book III in L. E. Cuyler, *Heinrich Isaac's Choralis Constantinus Book III* (1950).

Lit.: R. Wagner, "Die Choralverarbeitung in Heinrich Isaacs Offizienwerk 'Choralis Constantinus'" (diss. Munich, 1950); L. E. Cuyler,

in *JAMS* iii; O. zur Nedden, in *ZMW* xii, 449; P. Blaschke, in *KJ* xxvi.

Choralmotette [G.]. *Chorale motet.

Choral music. Music for a chorus or choir, i.e., vocal music for more than one singer to the part. The music may consist of a single part (monophonic) or of a number of parts (polyphonic, in the broadest sense), with or without instrumental accompaniment.

Choral groups were used in Biblical times as well as in the Greek drama [see Greece; Jewish music]. Their music, as well as that of Christian chant, was monophonic. Gregorian chant was performed either by two alternating choirs [see Antiphonal singing] or by a soloist alternating with a choir [see Responsorial singing]. The latter method was used in polyphonic responsorial chants (graduals, alleluias, responsories), such as the organa of the school of Notre Dame. Only the solo sections of the chant were composed and, accordingly, were sung by a small group of specially trained soloists, the other sections being performed by the choir in plainsong. Evidence of choral polyphony, i.e., polyphonic music performed by a choir, first appears in compositions from *c.* 1425, in which alternating sections are marked *unus* (or *duo*) and *chorus.* An example is a Credo by Guillaume Legrant [see *HAM,* no. 56], in which the solo sections are written in two-part polyphony and the choral sections in three-part homophony. The appearance, *c.* 1430, of large *choirbooks [see Lit., Bukofzer, in *PAMS,* p. 27] is an indication that choral performance became a more general practice. A famous miniature from *c.* 1470 [see *MGG* ix, opp. cols. 1839–40] shows Ockeghem leading a group of eight singers, obviously two to each part. The papal chapel of that time consisted of nine to twenty-four singers. Throughout the 16th century, Masses, motets, and other forms of sacred music were probably performed by groups of similar size, while solo performance, with one singer to each part, seems to have been the prevailing practice for secular music (chansons, madrigals, etc.).

In the mid-15th century the antiphonal method of Gregorian chant was applied to polyphonic music written for two alternating choruses, which, from *c.* 1520 on, were also used simultaneously [see Polychoral style]. A similar practice is represented by the *decani* and *cantoris* choirs used in Anglican churches. The essentially homophonic style of these compositions suggests that fairly large choirs were employed, especially in the magnificent compositions of the *Venetian school.

In the early 17th century, the chorus of ancient Greek tragedy was revived in opera, the earliest examples being in Peri's *Euridice* (1600) and Monteverdi's *La Favola d'Orfeo* (1607). The Roman opera particularly is distinguished by extensive use of the chorus [see Opera III]. About the same time, G. Carissimi gave the chorus a prominent role in the oratorio, and H. Schütz, F. Tunder, D. Buxtehude, and others introduced it into the German cantata [see Cantata III]. The long choral compositions in Handel's oratorios and in Bach's Passions and cantatas represent the climax of this development. Their choirs included no more than twenty to thirty singers. The subsequent history of choral music is closely connected with that of the oratorio (Haydn, Mendelssohn, Schumann, and others; see Oratorio IV) and 19th-century opera (Weber, Verdi, and others). A singular contribution to the literature is the last movement of Beethoven's Ninth Symphony [see Choral Symphony].

A significant aspect of 19th- and 20th-century choral music is the use of greatly enlarged choruses. Under the influence of democratic and nationalist ideas, choral groups consisting of many hundreds of middle-class amateurs, both men and women, were formed, first in England for performances of Handel's oratorios, later in Germany. Mendelssohn, in his performance of the St. Matthew Passion in 1829, employed a chorus of 300 singers, more than ten times the number used in Bach's day. Groups numbering into the thousands were not uncommon in some of the *festivals. Since about 1945 this trend has been partly reversed in performances of old choral compositions for which small groups of well-trained singers have been employed, with most successful results. See Performance practice.

Lit.: J. M. Knapp, *Selected List of Music for Men's Voices* (1952); A. W. Locke and C. K. Fassett, *Selected List of Choruses for Women's Voices,* rev. ed. (1964); E. Valentin, *Handbuch der Chormusik,* 2 vols. (1953, '58); G. Schünemann, *Führer durch die deutsche Chorliteratur,* 2 vols. (1935, '36; i, Männerchor, ii, Gemischter Chor); E. Wienandt, *Choral Music of the Church* (1965; bibl.); P. M. Young, *The Choral Tradition* (1962); A. T. Davison, *The Technique of Choral Composition* (1945); K. G. Fellerer, *The History of Catholic Church Music* (1961); E. Routley, *Twentieth-Century Church Music* (1964);

P. Huot-Pleuroux, *Histoire de la musique religieuse* (1957); M. F. Bukofzer, "The Beginnings of Polyphonic Choral Music" (*PAMS* 1940; also in his *Studies in Medieval and Renaissance Music,* 1950); H. C. Schmidt, "Problems of Choral Texture in the Twentieth Century" (*CP Davison*).

Choralnotation [G.]. Properly, the notation of Gregorian chant [G. *Gregorianischer Choral*]. Actually, the term is applied mainly to later repertories of monophonic music, such as hymns and sequences, or the songs of the troubadours, trouvères, minnesingers, etc. [see *WoHN* i, 146–197]. See Monophonic notation.

Choralpartita [G.]. *Chorale variations.

Choralrhythmus [G.]. The rhythmic interpretation of the "Gregorianische Choral," i.e., Gregorian chant; see Gregorian chant VI.

Choral Symphony. Popular name for Beethoven's Symphony no. 9 in D minor, op. 125 (1823–24), which in the last movement uses a chorus (and four soloists) in addition to the orchestra. The formal plan of the symphony is: I. Allegro; II. Scherzo with Trio; III. Adagio; IV. Introduction (with quotations of themes from the preceding movements), Allegro assai (with chorus on Schiller's poem, "Ode to Joy" [G. "Freude, schöner Götterfunken"]). The original title is: *Sinfonie mit Schlusschor über Schillers Ode: "An die Freude," für grosses Orchester, 4 Solo- und 4 Chorstimmen.*

Choralvorspiel [G.]. *Chorale prelude.

Chorbuch [G.]. *Choirbook.

Chord. The simultaneous sounding of three or more tones, two simultaneous tones usually being designated as an interval. Chords can be divided into two main classes, consonant and dissonant. To the former belong the major and minor *triad and their *inversions, i.e., the *sixth chord and the *six-four chord; to the latter all the others, e.g., the *seventh chord, the *ninth chord, the augmented sixth chord, and the numerous strongly dissonant formations of recent music, some of which are derived from the *fourth chord [see also Mystic chord], while others are completely unrestricted [see Pitch aggregate; Tone cluster]. The study of the chords, their relationships and functions, is an important field of music theory called *harmonic analysis. See also Consonance, dissonance II.

Chorda [Gr., L.]. In medieval treatises, term meaning note or pitch, each of which was thought to be represented by a string (of the kithara, etc.). Generally, fifteen *chordae* are postulated, each corresponding to one note of the Greek scale, from A to a'' (Boethius; Regino, in *GS* i, 240b; Adam of Fulda, in *GS* iii, 351a).

Chordal style. A composition or a passage is said to be in chordal style if its texture consists essentially of a series of chords. In strict chordal style there is a given number of parts, usually four (e.g., a hymn); in free chordal style there is no such restriction (e.g., Chopin's *Prélude* no. 20). See Homorhythmic.

Chordophone. See under Instruments IV.

Chorea [L.]. In medieval writings, a dancing song [Johannes de Grocheo, *c.* 1300; Robert de Handlo, 1326, see *CS* i, 402]. In 16th- and 17th-century lute books, *chorea* is a generic term for dance (e.g., in the MS lute book of W. Dlugoraj, 1619; see J. Dieckmann, *Die in deutscher Lautentabulatur überlieferten Tänze des 16. Jahrhunderts,* 1931, pp. 103ff), or for specific dances such as the *passamezzo* [B. de Drusina, *Tabulatura continens . . . fantasias . . . choreas . . .* (1556); see *ibid.,* p. 116] and the allemande [see J.-B. Besard, *Thesaurus harmonicus* (1603): "Chorea quas Allemande vocant germanico"].

Chorister. Boy singer in an English choir. See *GD* i, 641f; *GDB* ii, 123f.

Chorlied [G.]. Choral song, particularly without accompaniment (Schumann, Mendelssohn, and others).

Choro [Port.]. Originally, Brazilian term for an ensemble of serenaders, i.e., a kind of popular band consisting of small and large guitars, flutes, trumpets, and percussion instruments. The kind of music played by these groups in popular festivities was known as *músicas de chôro.* Today the term is very loosely used for many kinds of ensemble music in which one instrument dominates the others and is used for virtuoso improvisation. In form the *chôro* may resemble a waltz, a *maxixe,* or a *samba.* Villa-Lobos and many other Brazilian composers have used the *chôro* in art music.   J.O-S.

Chororgel [G.]. Choir organ.

Chorton [G.]. See under Pitch (2).

Chorus. (1) A large body of singers, not connected with a church [see Choir]. Also, music for such a body [see Choral music]. (2) Medieval

Latin name for the *crwth or the *bagpipe [see *SaRM,* p. 80]. (3) Same as burden, refrain.

Chorwerk, Das. See Editions VIII.

Christmas Concerto. Corelli's Concerto Grosso in G minor, op. 6, no. 8, entitled "Fatto per la Notte di Natale" (made for Christmas Night). The closing movement is a *pastorale.

Christmas Oratorio [G. *Weihnachtsoratorium*]. Bach's *Christmas Oratorio,* composed in 1734, consists of six church cantatas, intended to be performed on six different days between Christmas Day and Epiphany. The title *Oratorium,* though Bach's own, is somewhat inappropriate, since the work is not based on a continuous narrative. A number of the pieces in the oratorio are borrowed from earlier cantatas. An important forerunner of Bach's work is H. Schütz's Christmas oratorio, entitled *Historia der freuden- und gnadenreichen Geburth Gottes und Marien Sohnes, Jesu Christi* (1664). The edition by Spitta in vol. i of Schütz's complete works was completed (on the basis of newly discovered material) by A. Schering, who also edited a score for practical use.

Christ on the Mount of Olives. See *Christus am Ölberge.*

Christophe Colomb [F., Christopher Columbus]. Opera in two parts by D. Milhaud (libretto by P. Claudel), produced in Berlin, 1930. Setting: Spain, end of 15th century.

Christus. Oratorio by Liszt to words from the Scriptures and the Roman Catholic liturgy, composed 1855–66. Also, an unfinished oratorio by Mendelssohn.

Christus am Ölberge [G., Christ on the Mount of Olives]. Oratorio by Beethoven, op. 85 (libretto by F. X. Huber), produced in Vienna, 1803.

Chroai [Gr.]. In ancient Greek theory, the microtonic modifications of the two movable tones of the tetrachord. Aristoxenos mentions, in addition to the enharmonic tetrachord that divides the interval of the fourth (a to e downward) into the steps $2 + \frac{1}{4} + \frac{1}{4}$, divisions such as $1\frac{1}{4} + \frac{3}{4} + \frac{1}{2}$ (variant of the diatonic tetrachord $1 + 1 + \frac{1}{2}$) and $1\frac{5}{6} + \frac{1}{3} + \frac{1}{3}$ or $1\frac{3}{4} + \frac{3}{8} + \frac{3}{8}$ (variants of the chromatic tetrachord $1\frac{1}{2} + \frac{1}{2} + \frac{1}{2}$). These schemes probably represent attempts on the part of theorists to rationalize microtones such as occur in Oriental melodies, or in the playing of the *aulos. See C. Sachs, *The Rise of Music in the Ancient World* [1943]; *RiHM* i.1,

218; T. Reinach, *La Musique grecque* (1926), p. 20 ("Nuances").

Chromatic. The adjective is used in the following connections: (1) Chromatic scale [see Chromaticism]. (2) Chromatic tetrachord or genus [see Greece II]. (3) Chromatic instruments, i.e., instruments capable of producing all (or nearly all) the tones of the chromatic scale. Thus, chromatic horn is the name of the valve horn, as distinct from the natural horn. For chromatic harp, see Harp II. (4) In the 16th century the word *cromatico* occasionally refers to the use not of semitones but of the black notes, *semiminima, fusa* (or *croma*), *semifusa* (or *semicroma*), i.e., of the smallest values, corresponding to our modern eighth notes, sixteenth notes, etc. This usage occurs particularly in titles such as *Il Primo Libro de madregali cromatici a cinque* (C. de Rore, 1544), which means madrigals in shorter note values, hence in faster tempo than the earlier madrigals, written in a more sedate style. Another name for the same type was *madrigali a note nere* (in black notes; see J. Haar, "The *Note nere* Madrigal," in *JAMS* xviii).

Chromatic Fantasia and Fugue. A composition for harpsichord by J. S. Bach, which uses extended chromatic harmonies in the fantasy and a chromatic progression in the theme of the fugue. The fantasy is in the character of a free improvisation, alternating among brilliant passage work, quiet arpeggios, and highly expressive recitatives. It is a relatively early work of Bach's, displaying an exuberance and subjectivity absent in his later works.

Chromaticism. In the widest sense, the use of pitches not present in the diatonic scale but resulting from the subdivision of a diatonic whole tone into two semitonal intervals, e.g., of f–g into f–f♯ and f♯–g. The application of this principle to all five whole tones of the diatonic scale produces the chromatic scale, with twelve tones to the octave.

Chromaticism appeared first in the chromatic tetrachord of Greek music, in which the (descending) fourth is subdivided into a minor third and two semitones: a–f♯–f–e, e–c♯–c–B. One of the few remnants of Greek music, the First Delphic Hymn [*HAM*, no. 7a], includes truly chromatic progressions such as b–c'–c'♯–c'–b and a♯–b–c'–c'♯–c'–b. In Western music, certain semitonal degrees, b♭, e♭, f♯, occur as early as *c.* 900 in the "Musica enchiriadis" [see Theory, 3] and in Gregorian chant; in the latter, however,

the e♭ and f♯ were eventually eliminated by means of transposition [see *ApGC,* pp. 161ff]. In the early 14th century a full chromatic scale was not only discussed by theorists (Marchetto da Padua) but also found on keyboard instruments, at least in the middle octave. However, the "chromatic" tones were not used for chromaticism but for transposed diatonicism, the introduction of leading tones, etc. See *Musica ficta*.

True chromaticism, involving two successive semitones, appears in the 16th century, as the result of Vicentino's endeavors to revive the diatonic, chromatic, and enharmonic genera of ancient Greek music (*L'Antica Musica ridotta alla moderna prattica,* 1555). The role played by Willaert in this matter is uncertain. The earliest indisputable example of melodic chromaticism occurs in the madrigal "Calami sonum ferentes" (1561) by Willaert's pupil Cypriano de Rore, which starts with an imitative passage based on the subject B–c–c♯–d–d♯–e–f♯–g [see *ReMR*, p. 331]. Luca Marenzio (1553–99) and particularly Carlo Gesualdo (*c.* 1560–1613) exploited the new tonal material harmonically and melodically, by juxtaposing chords such as G major and E major, or A minor and F-sharp major [see *HAM,* no. 161; *SchGMB,* nos. 165, 167]. Highly expressive examples of chromaticism are found in the motets of Lassus' *Prophetiae sibyllarum,* written perhaps as early as 1560.

In vocal music of the baroque period, chromaticism occurs mainly in the form of motifs that accompany words expressing grief, e.g., in H. L. Hassler's motet "Ad Dominum cum tribularer" [see Editions VIII, 14]. Several composers wrote pieces requiring a full chromatic keyboard, e.g., John Bull in his "Ut re mi fa sol la" [see Hexachord VI], G. P. Cima in his *Partito de ricercari* (1606), which contains an appendix where a short example is transposed in all twelve keys, and M. A. Rossi (b. *c.* 1600), whose Toccata no. 7 closes with an ascending chromatic scale in major thirds [see Editions IX, 26]. An amusing example of chromatic pictorialism is found in the variation "Alter Weiber Conduct" (Old Hags' Procession) from Poglietti's *Aria allemagna* of *c.* 1670 [*DTO* 27; *TaAM* viii]. Also common is the use of chromatic progressions for fugal subjects (Sweelinck, Frescobaldi, Kerll, and others; *SchGMB, no. 158*), particularly for countersubjects (common in Bach: *The Well-Tempered Clavier* ii, no. 18; Harpsichord Fugue in A minor; the theme *B–A–C–H of the *Art of Fugue). An important innovation of the late 17th century is the use of chromatic chords, mainly the diminished seventh chord. The accompanying figure shows a passage from a toccata by A. Scarlatti [*Editions X, 13, p. 39]. The most famous example of this kind occurs in the closing passage of Bach's Chromatic Fantasy.

In the classical period of Haydn, Mozart, and the early Beethoven, chromaticism is comparatively rare, aside from the use of rapid chromatic scales in coloraturas, cadenzas, etc. It is not until Beethoven's latest works (e.g., the short slow movement of his Piano Sonata in A major, op. 101) that we find passages reminiscent of those from Bach's Chromatic Fantasy or from his Fantasy and Fugue in G minor for organ. After Beethoven, however, began a new era of chromaticism, characterized by the exploitation of chromatically altered harmony. To describe this phase of chromaticism would be tantamount to writing a study on romantic harmony. The examples given under harmony [see Harmony B (8)] show how greatly chromaticism changed music in the period from 1850 to 1900. After 1900 chromaticism lost its former connotation as a "color modification" of diatonicism and established itself as a tonal province in its own right, based on the equivalence of the twelve tones of the chromatic scale. This idea is clearly apparent in Debussy's *whole-tone scale and was brought to its extreme in Schoenberg's *atonality and twelve-tone technique, in which the twelve chromatic notes are treated as a material in their own right, without any pre-established relationships between them [see Serial music].

About 1920, there began a reaction against excessive chromaticism, whether romantic, impressionist, or atonal (expressionist). It found its most conspicuous manifestation in the *pandiatonicism of composers such as Stravinsky, Poulenc, and others.

Chromatic scale. See Chromaticism.

Chronos, chronos protos [Gr.]. The temporal or rhythmic unit of ancient Greek music. It is not divisible into smaller values and is usually represented in modern transcriptions by an eighth note. Values of double or triple duration (quarter note, dotted quarter note) can be derived from it. The *chronos protos* [F. *temps premier*] is also the basis of rhythm in many Eastern cultures, e.g., Arab, Syrian, Hindu, etc.

Chrotta. See under Crwth.

Church modes [L. *modus, tonus*]. I. The church modes (ecclesiastical modes) are a medieval system of eight scales, each consisting of the tones of the C-major scale (white keys) but starting and closing on d, e, f, or g and limited to the range of about an octave. For each of these four notes, called a final (*finalis*), there exist two modes distinguished by the different position of the octave range (ambitus) and called respectively authentic and plagal. In the *authentic modes* the ambitus extends from the final to the upper octave; in the *plagal modes,* from the fourth below the final to the fifth above it. The octave range or ambitus of either form of mode may be enlarged by the addition of the *subtonium,* i.e., the tone below its lower limit or by a tone (even two) above. This additional tone is of particular importance in the authentic modes, where it is used for cadences (c–d, d–e, etc.), and in these it is also called the subfinal (*subfinalis*). The eight scales just described are the tonal basis of Gregorian chant. Ex. 1 illustrates the two modes on d (the note in parentheses is the

subtonium). In the 16th century (H. Glareanus, *Dodecachordon,* 1547), the eight-mode system of Gregorian chant was enlarged to include the two scales on a and the two scales on c' (essentially our minor and major), thus bringing the number up to twelve.

The earliest designation (9th century) for the modes was derived from the names *protus, deuterus, tritus,* and *tetrardus* (corruptions of Gr., first, second, third, fourth) given to the four basic finals: *protus authenticus* (final d; range d–d'), *protus plagius* (d; A–a), *deuterus authenticus* (e; e–e'), *deuterus plagius* (e; B–b), etc. Slightly later we find the most common (and preferable) designation, in which the modes (originally called *tonus) are numbered in the same order: *primus tonus* (d; d–d'), *secundus tonus* (d; A–a),

			Fin.	Amb.	Dom.
I. *Protus auth.*	*Primus tonus*	Dorian	d	d–d′	a
II. 〃 *plag.*	*Secundus t.*	Hypodorian	d	A–a	f
III. *Deuterus auth.*	*Tertius t.*	Phrygian	e	e–e′	c′
IV. 〃 *plag.*	*Quartus t.*	Hypophrygian	e	B–b	a
V. *Tritus auth.*	*Quintus t.*	Lydian	f	f–f′	c′
VI. 〃 *plag.*	*Sextus t.*	Hypolydian	f	c–c′	a
VII. *Tetrardus auth.*	*Septimus t.*	Mixolydian	g	g–g′	d′
VIII. 〃 *plag.*	*Octavus t.*	Hypomixolydian	g	d–d′	c′
IX.	*Nonus t.*	Aeolian	a	a–a′	e′
X.	*Decimus t.*	Hypoaeolian	a	e–e′	c′
XI.	*Undecimus t.*	Ionian	c′	c′–c″	g′
XII.	*Duodecimus t.*	Hypoionian	c′	g–g′	e′

Church modes (Roman numerals refer to Ex. 2, below).

etc. Another terminology, rarely employed in the Middle Ages but commonly used today, borrows its names from ancient Greek theory: the four authentic modes are called Dorian, Phrygian, Lydian, and Mixolydian; the prefix hypo- is employed for the plagal modes (Hypodorian, etc.). To these names Glareanus added Aeolian (for a) and Ionian (for c′). See also Maneria.

II. In addition to the final and ambitus, each mode is usually said to have a third characteristic, called the dominant, somewhat in the nature of a secondary tonal center. As a rule, the dominant is a fifth above the final in the authentic modes, a third above it in the plagal modes. However, the tone b, which was not used as a final [see above], was also avoided as a dominant and was replaced by c′ (in modes III and VIII). Another change occurred in mode IV, where the dominant g was raised to a. Actually, these dominants are a characteristic less of the modes—they play only a minor or, at least, a very questionable role in the Gregorian melodies—than of a few special recitation formulas associated with the modes, that is, the eight psalm tones (also tones for the Magnificat, etc.), in which they are used as the pitch for the monotone recitation. Therefore, what is called dominant should properly be called recitation tone (*repercussio, tenor, tuba;* see Psalm tones). Other so-called "characteristics" of the modes—mediant, participant, modulation [see *GD* iii, 483; *GDB* v, 405]—are of very little or highly questionable importance. The above-explained characteristics and names are shown in the table above and in Ex. 2.

In modern writings the twelve-mode system is sometimes enlarged to one of fourteen by the

addition of the Locrian and Hypolocrian, based on the tone b as the final. These modes are mentioned by Glareanus (under the names Hyperaeolian and Hyperphrygian) but rejected because they involve a diminished fifth (b–f′) above the final, an obvious impossibility in the practice of his day. It is interesting to note, however, that "Locrian" passages are not uncommon in Gregorian melodies of mode III, which sometimes introduce a temporary b-flat.

III. To account for melodies that exceed the ambitus as prescribed in the eight-mode system, late medieval theorists (Marchetto da Padua; see *GS* iii, 101b) introduced, in addition to the terms *tonus perfectus* and *imperfectus* (normal and small range), *tonus plusquam perfectus* (upward extension of authentic, downward extension of plagal), *tonus mixtus,* also called *mixed mode* (downward extension of authentic, upward extension of plagal), and *tonus commixtus* (combination of an authentic with a different plagal). Tinctoris (*CS* iv, 28f) calls the last two formations *mixtio* and *commixtio.*

Zarlino, in his *Istitutioni harmoniche* of 1558, adopted Glareanus' system of twelve modes but placed the Ionian and Hypoionian first, so that the series began with the two modes on c—an early indication of the growing awareness of the importance of the "major mode." In the latter part of the 16th century, French musicians adopted a new terminology by applying Glareanus' names—from Dorian to Ionian—to Zarlino's series of tones, from c to a. This practice occurs for the first time in Claude Le Jeune's *Octonaires de la vanité . . . du monde (c.* 1606; see Editions XXXIII, 1, 8) and is fully explained in C. Guillet, *Vingt quatre Fantaisies . . . disposées selon l'ordre des douze modes* (1610; see Editions XXVIII, 4). It is also observed in Denis Gaultier's *La Rhétorique des dieux* (Editions XLIX, 6, 7; see O. Fleischer, in *VMW* ii).

IV. At one time it was customary to treat the church modes together with the "Greek modes," considering the former derivatives of the latter. This procedure is not to be recommended, since what are usually called "Greek modes" represent a phenomenon of such complexity and involving so many historical changes (many of which are still obscure) that summary statements are likely to be misleading rather than helpful [see Greece II]. The most striking (though by no means the essential) difference between the Greek and medieval systems is that in the former the names Dorian, Phrygian, Lydian, and Mixolydian (D, P, L, M) are associated with a descending series of tones, namely, e, d, c, B, whereas in the latter they occur in an ascending order (d, e, f, g). A (much simplified) explanation of this change is that the Greek octave-segments all had one and the same "tonic," i.e., the tone *a (mese)*, and that by transposing the descending segments into one and the same octave (e.g., a–a') these "tonics" appear in an ascending order, as shown below:

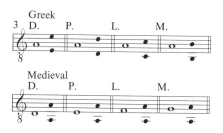

For a fuller discussion of this problem, see *ReMMA*, pp. 153ff.

The designation, still occasionally en-

countered, of the authentic modes as "Ambrosian" and of the plagal modes as "Gregorian" is entirely without historical foundation. Particularly discreditable is the frequently repeated story that Ambrose "invented" the authentic modes and that Gregory "added" the plagal modes. The implication that the establishment of the theoretical system preceded the actual writing of melodies contradicts the fundamental principles of musical development. Very likely the system of the modes did not originate until the 9th century (they are described for the first time in Aurelian's "Musica disciplina" of *c.* 850; see *GS* i, 27–63) as an attempt to codify the large repertory of chants that had accumulated, and there is reason to believe that numerous chants were modified to make them conform to the theoretical system.

V. The basic facts and the main problems of the relationship between the eight-mode system and the Gregorian melodies are outlined under Gregorian chant V. Concerning the use of the modes as the tonal basis of polyphonic composition, there is no evidence of methodical treatment prior to the latter part of the 15th century, when the *Flemish school renewed interest in the Gregorian tradition and in sacred music. The compositions of the 14th century particularly are remarkably free in their tonality, as is already evident from their liberal use of accidentals [see *Musica ficta* IV]. In this respect it is interesting to note that not until after 1500 did composers begin to write polyphonic settings of, e.g., the Magnificat in the various modes (*Magnificat primi toni*, etc.), and that designations such as "toccata primi toni" do not occur before *c.* 1550 (Andrea Gabrieli). Tinctoris, who seems to have been the first to consider the modes in connection with polyphonic compositions ("Liber de natura et proprietate tonorum," ch. 24; *CS* iv, 29), concludes that a mode is attributable not to the entire composition but only to the individual lines, of which the tenor is the most important. Similarly Glareanus, in his brilliant analyses of the compositions of Josquin and others (*Dodecachordon*), never investigates the mode of a polyphonic composition as such but only the modes of the different voice parts. Pietro Aaron (*Trattato della natura et cognitione di tutti gli tuoni di canto figurato,* 1525), on the other hand, made an attempt to assign a definite mode to a polyphonic composition, saying that the tenor is the determining element [for the difficulties inherent in this proposition and Aaron's attempt to resolve them, see *ReMR,* p. 182f]. Modern investigations of "modal usage" in music before 1600 naturally proceed from a different point of view, involving the consideration of harmonic progressions (II–I and III–I rather than IV–I and V–I), cadences, over-all tonality, etc. The omnipresence of the problem of *musica ficta* makes it very difficult to arrive at valid conclusions in this matter. For the role of the church modes in modern music, see Modality (also Mode). See also the entries under Dorian, Lydian, Mixolydian, and Phrygian.

Lit.: F. S. Andrews, "Mediaeval Modal Theory" (diss. Cornell Univ., 1935); W. Apel, *Gregorian Chant* (1958), pp. 133ff; H. Potiron, *L'Origine des modes grégoriens* (1948); H. Potiron, *La Composition des modes grégoriens* (1953); A. Auda, *Les Modes et les tons de la musique* (1930); E. Werner, "The Origin of the Eight Modes of Music" (*Hebrew Union College Annual* xxi); O. Gombosi, "Studien zur Tonartenlehre des frühen Mittelalters" (*AM* x, xi, xii); O. Ursprung, "Die antiken Transpositionsskalen und die Kirchentöne" (*AMF* v); K. W. Niemöller, "Zur Tonus-Lehre" (*KJ* xl).

For V: J. Chailley, *L'Imbroglio des modes* (1960); G. Reaney, "Modes in the Fourteenth Century" (*CP Waesberghe*); L. Balmer, "Tonsystem und Kirchentöne bei Johannes Tinctoris" (diss. Bern, 1935); H. E. Wooldridge, "Studies in the Technique of 16th-Century Music" (*MA* iii, iv); R. W. Wienpahl, "Modal Usage in Masses of the 15th Century" (*JAMS* v); M. Cauchie, "La Pureté des modes dans la musique vocale franco-belge du début du XVIe siècle" (*CP Kroyer*).

Church music. The music of the Christian churches consisted originally of *chant. In the Eastern Churches (Byzantine, Armenian, Coptic, Syrian) it did not essentially develop beyond monody, but the development in the Roman Catholic Church as early as the 9th century began to embrace polyphonic treatment, thus laying the foundation for the entire development of Western music. Following is a brief survey of the evolution of music of the Roman Catholic, Anglican, and German Protestant churches.

I. The music of the Roman Catholic Church is rooted in the tradition of the Jewish liturgy, as is already evident from the fact that the oldest portions of the Catholic service were the *psalms and the *canticles. Some Greek influence appears in the hymns of St. Ambrose [see Ambrosian hymns], which differ from the psalms and canticles in the strictly metrical structure of the text and in the syllabic rather than melismatic style of the music. During the ensuing centuries numerous other chants were added, a process that reached its final stage probably about 800 [see Gregorian chant VII]. About the same time came the first attempts to enlarge the Gregorian repertory with newly invented texts and melodies, an activity that is generally known as troping. This led to the monophonic *sequences, *tropes, and *liturgical dramas, as well as, about 900, to the "polyphonic tropes," the organa and their derivatives, the *clausulae and *motets of the 13th century. In the latter part of the 13th century the motet, though still retaining its Gregorian ancestry in the *cantus firmus* melody of the tenor, adopted secular (French) texts and occasionally even secular melodies [see *Enté*] for the upper parts, thus showing for the first time an influence of elements that, from the standpoint of the Church, was to be condemned. This and other abuses of a similar nature led to the decree of Pope John XXII, issued from Avignon in 1322, that not only the sacrilegious French motets but all kinds of polyphonic music, with the exception of the archaic organum in parallel fourths or fifths, were no longer to be used. This decree apparently had results that, although sympathetic to the aims of the Church, were detrimental to the development of church music. Indeed, the relative scarcity of sacred compositions in the French and Italian sources of the 14th century may well be explained by the restrictions resulting from the edict; even as late as 1408, polyphonic music (discant) was forbidden in the Cathedral of Notre Dame in Paris. Recent investigations have brought to light a number of Mass compositions, most of which, including the Mass of Machaut, probably were written before 1340 [see Mass C].

II. A new era of church music began about 1425. After a long period of secularization, the center of musical activity again shifted back to the Church. Masses and motets became the chief forms of composers such as the English Dunstable (d. 1453), the French Dufay (*c.* 1400–74), and the long series of *Flemish masters from Ockeghem (*c.* 1420–95) and Obrecht (*c.* 1450–1505) to Lasso (1532–94). Around 1550, Italian composers (Andrea Gabrieli, 1510–86; Palestrina, 1525–94) and Spanish composers (Morales, *c.* 1500–53; Vittoria, 1540–1611) appeared in successful competition with the Flemish masters, thus leading to an unparalleled flowering of Roman Catholic church music. There also began, about 1500, a remarkable development of ecclesiastical organ music, designed to supplant the choral performance of hymns, psalm verses [see Verset], the Ordinary of the Mass [see Organ Mass], and certain chants of special importance, particularly the *Magnificat and the *Antiphons *B.M.V.* [see *Salve Regina*]. Composers such as A. Schlick (*c.* 1450–1527), J. Redford (b. *c.* 1480), G. Cavazzoni (*c.* 1525–?), and A. de Cabezón (1510–66) made outstanding contributions in this field.

III. At the same time, however, came the Reformation, which by 1550 led to the establishment of new bodies of church music, chiefly in England [see Anglican church music] and Germany. While the English movement found artistic expression in the *anthem and the *service (Tallis, 1505–85; Byrd, 1543–1623; Purcell, 1658–95; Handel, 1685–1759), the German Reformation (Luther, 1483–1546) proved to be an event of the greatest musical importance, owing chiefly to the establishment of the Protestant *chorale as a source of musical creation and inspiration comparable to the Gregorian chant. The chorale not only gave rise to the great wealth of *organ chorales (Scheidt, 1587–1654; Tunder, b. 1614; Buxtehude, 1637–1707; Pachelbel, 1653–1706; Bach, 1685–1750) but had a lasting—though gradually decreasing—influence on the *cantata, the chief type of German church music in the baroque period [see also Chorale cantata]. Alongside the cantata grew the *oratorio and the *Passion, represented by a number of composers from Schütz (1585–1672) to Bach, as well as by Handel in England.

IV. In 17th-century Italy the tradition of Palestrina was continued by the *Roman school. More important than the activity of this conservative group was the establishment of the oratorio (Carissimi, 1605–74) and the development of instrumental church music, particularly the *sonata da chiesa* (Biagio Marini, 1597–1665; Legrenzi, 1626–90; Corelli, 1653–1713), which, about 1685, spread to England, Germany, and France [see under *Sonata da camera*]. In the 18th century, Italian composers known mostly for their operas (so-called *Neapolitan school) wrote a large body of church music for voices and instruments, which frequently shows the influence of the virtuoso operatic style. This group includes F. Durante (1684–1755), D. Terradellas (1713–51; *HAM,* no. 298), N. Jommelli (1714–74; *HAM,* no. 299), and G. B. Pergolesi (1710–36), whose *Stabat mater* is one of the few examples of Italian 18th-century church music generally known today.

V. In the period after 1750 the production of great church music became more scarce, and the ensuing history is a somewhat thinly spread succession of isolated masterworks rather than a continuous development. The oratorio, which found one of its greatest masters in Handel, is perhaps the only type of religious music that can boast of an almost uninterrupted line of composers, English as well as German. More and more, however, it became music for concert hall rather than church. Among the outstanding works of this period are Mozart's Requiem (1791), Beethoven's *Missa solemnis* (1823), Rossini's *Stabat mater* (1832), Berlioz' *Messe des Morts* (1837), Brahms' *Ein deutsches Requiem* (1868), Verdi's Requiem (1874), Bruckner's Masses (1864–67) and *Te Deum* (1881), and Horatio Parker's *Hora novissima* (1893).

Noteworthy 20th-century compositions are Elgar's *Dream of Gerontius* (1900); Holst's *Hymn of Jesus* (1917); Stravinsky's *Symphony of Psalms* (1930) and Mass (1948); Walton's *Belshazzar's Feast* (1931); Ernest Bloch's *Sacred Service* (1933); Poulenc's *Messe* (1937); Milhaud's *Service sacré;* Samuel Barber's *Prayers of Kierkegaard* (1954); Randall Thompson's *Passion according to St. Luke* (1963–65), *Mass of the Holy Spirit* (1956), and Requiem (1958); and Britten's *War Requiem* (1962). Significant contemporary composers of church music in England and America are listed under Anthem and Service.

Lit.: W. Douglas, *Church Music in History and Practice,* rev. L. Ellinwood (1962); E. A. Wienandt, *Choral Music of the Church* (1965); A. T. Davison, *Church Music* (1952); id., *Protestant Church Music in America* (1933); H. W. Davies and H. Grace, *Music and Christian Worship* (1934); G. Gardner and S. Nicholson, *A Manual of English Church Music* (1936); D. Stevens, *Tudor Church Music* [1955]; F. L. Harrison, ed., ‡*Early English Church Music,* 4 vols. [n.d.]; L. Ellinwood, *The History of American Church Music* (1953); K. Weinmann, *History of Church Music* (1910; Roman Catholic); O. Ursprung, *Die katholische Kirchenmusik* (1931; vol. of *BüHM*); R. Schlecht, *Geschichte der Kirchenmusik* (1871; Roman Catholic); K. G. Fellerer, *The History of Catholic Church Music* (1961; trans. from German ed. of 1949); A. Weissenbäck, *Sacra musica: Lexikon der katholischen Kirchenmusik* (1937); F. Blume, *Die evangelische Kirchenmusik* (1931; vol. of *BüHM*); H. J. Moser, *Die evangelische Kirchenmusik in*

Deutschland (1954); W. Blankenburg and K. F. Müller, *Die Musik des evangelischen Gottesdienstes* (1960); A. Gastoué, *La Vie musicale de l'Église* (1929); R. Aigrain, *Religious Music* (1931); W. Bäumker, *Das katholische deutsche Kirchenlied in seinen Singweisen,* 4 vols. (1883–1911); M. Schreiber, *Kirchenmusik von 1500–1600* (1932); *id., Kirchenmusik von 1600–1700* (1934); A. Hughes, in *ML* v, 145 (16th-century Service); H. B. Collins, in *ML* iv, 254 (Byrd); K. G. Fellerer, in *ZMW* xi (17th–18th centuries); A. Cœuroy, "Les Formes actuelles de la musique religieuse" (*RM* vi).

Church sonata. The *sonata da chiesa* of the baroque; see under *Sonata da camera.*

Chute [F.]. Name for ornamental tones similar to a passing tone (such as occur in the *arpègement figuré;* see Arpeggio) or to an anticipation (*Nachschlag).

Chyn, guuchyn (*ch'in, ku-ch'in*). A Chinese seven-stringed zither made of hollowed wood, about 4 feet long, 8 inches wide, and 3 inches thick [see ill. accompanying Zither]. The strings, made of silk, are stretched over the entire length of the board. The most common tuning is C–D–F–G–A–c–d. Instead of frets there are 13 studs along the outer edge of the instrument, indicating the following divisions of the strings: 7/8, 5/6, 4/5, 3/4, 2/3, 1/2, 2/5, 1/3, 1/4, 1/5, 1/6, 1/8. If one stops the C-string at these points the notes produced by plucking are D–E♭–E–F–G–A–c–e–g–c′–e′–g′–c″. Except for 7/8, all the divisions are those of *just intonation. However, various divisions between the studs are also used, e.g., a slight raising of the A and the E. A readjustment for the 7/8 stud, which is higher than the major second of the *Pythagorean scale (8/9), is so general a practice that a special symbol has been in use since the 13th century to tell the player to stop the string slightly to the left of the stud.

Chyn playing involves various ways of plucking (e.g., outward and inward), as well as the use of ornaments such as the portamento, vibrato, mordent, and glissando. The notation for the chyn, a tablature, consists of clusters of abbreviated symbols specifying the string number, stopping position, hand, finger, and direction of plucking. Tempo is usually indicated by terms such as "slow down" or "hurriedly." Some 20th-century chyn books also indicate the main beats.

The chyn enjoys great prestige because of its age and legendary association with the sages and philosophers. Throughout Chinese history it has been the instrument of the accomplished gentleman. Illustrations of the chyn and relics of chyn-like instruments date back to at least the 3rd century B.C. In the Tarng (T'ang) dynasty (618–906) the chyn was somewhat overshadowed by newly imported instruments but in the Sonq (Sung) (960–1279) it was revived. The chyn cult reached its height in the Ming dynasty (1368–1644), when numerous treatises and collections of chyn music were printed. The chyn continued to be played throughout the 18th and 19th centuries. Beginning with the 20th century, interest in the chyn sharply declined, and in recent years chyn players of professional quality have been very few. In all, they have managed to preserve an oral tradition of only about eighty pieces.

The earliest chyn melody, "Iou Lan" (The Melancholy Orchid), preserved in a Tarng manuscript, is ascribed to a composer of the 6th century. Seven chyn melodies from the 13th century are still found in present-day collections. The first printed chyn book, *Shern Chyi Mih Puu,* appeared in 1425 and was followed by numerous other collections, together comprising more than six hundred pieces. Practically all chyn pieces have programmatic titles, such as "Liehtzu Riding on the Wind," or "Dialogue of the Fisherman and the Woodman." A typical piece has several sections, each based on the thematic material more or less extended, reduced, or rearranged.

In present-day performances, the introductory and concluding sections and the interludes, which are mostly played in harmonics, are in free rhythm, while the other sections are in a more regular rhythm, duple, triple, quintuple, or at times irregular combinations of these.

Lit.: R. H. van Gulik, *The Lore of the Chinese Lute* (Tokyo, 1940); *id., Hsi Kang and His Poetical Essay on the Lute* (Tokyo, 1941); L. Picken, in *NOH* i, 111f, 117ff; Ja Fuhshi, ed., *Jiann Tzay Guuchyn Cheu Chwanpuu Jieetyi Hueybian Chugao* (Draft Compilation of the Names of All Existing Chyn Melodies in the Present Day with Bibliography of Sources and Annotation), 4 vols. (Peking, 1956); R. C. Pian, *Sonq Dynasty Musical Sources and Their Interpretation* (1967), ch. 3; *SaHMI,* pp. 187ff; ‡*Chyn Cheu Jyicherng* (A Collection of Chyn Books; Peking, 1963); Yang Yinnliou, *et al.,* ed., ‡*Guuchyn Cheu Hueybian* (A Repertory of Chyn Music; Peking, 1956); ‡*Guuchyn Cheu Jyi* (A Collection of Chyn Music), compiled by Institute of National Music (Peking, 1962); Li Chi, "Iou Lan Hersheng" (The Intervals Used in *Iou Lan; Tsinghua Jour-*

nal ii [1925] 2.573–8); Cha Fu-hsi (Ja Fuhshi), "Chin: The Chinese Lute" (*Eastern Horizon* [1960], no. 1); H. Trefzger, "Über das K'in" (*Schweizerische Musikzeitung* [1948], no. 3).

R.C.P.

Ciaccona [It.]. *Chaconne.

Cialamello [It.]. Shawm. See under Oboe family III.

Cibell, cebell. A 17th-century name for the gavotte, used by Purcell and others. The name is derived from a song in praise of the goddess Cybele, found in Lully's opera *Athys*. See T. Dart, in *RBM* vi.

Cim. Abbr. of *cimelium* [Gr.-L., jewel], librarian's term for a rare book.

Cimbalom. A large *dulcimer used by Hungarian Gypsies and also in dance bands. The peculiar effects of the cimbalom are imitated in Liszt's Hungarian Rhapsody no. 11 ("quasi Zimbalo"). See A. Hartmann, in *MQ* ii. For ill. see under Zither.

Cimbasso [It.]. A narrow-bore tuba in B♭.

Cinelli [It.]. Cymbals.

Cinfonie. See Hurdy-gurdy.

Cinque-pace [It. *cinque passi;* F. *cinq pas;* Eng. *sinkapass, sink pas, sink-a-pace, sinck a part,* etc.]. The basic five steps of the Renaissance *galliard and *saltarello, consisting of a forward thrust of alternate legs (L R L R) on the first four beats of the measure (coincidentally with each thrust the opposite foot executes a bounce), a leap on the fifth beat, and a resting stance (posture) on the sixth. All movements were gentle for the *saltarello* and pronounced for the galliard. The *cinque-pace* sequence was not used continuously; dancers improvised many variations of the simple steps for an indefinite number of measures and the *cinque-pace* sequence was reserved for strategic cadence measures. L.H.M.

Ciphering. In organ building, the continued sounding of a pipe, due to some defect of the mechanism.

Circle canon. See Canon (1), I (h).

Circle of fifths [G. *Quintenzirkel*]. The circular, clockwise arrangement of the twelve keys in an order of ascending fifths (C, G, d, a, etc.), showing that after twelve such steps the initial key is reached again. It presents the keys in their natural order, that is, increasing by one the num-

ber of sharps in the signature. If the circle is viewed counterclockwise (i.e., order of descending fifths: c′, f, B♭, etc.), the keys follow each other with one more flat in the signature. At one point of the circle the transition from the sharp keys to the flat keys must be made, for instance, at G-sharp = A-flat (*enharmonic change). The scheme of signatures might also serve for the minor keys, by starting from A instead of from C. The series of fifths "closes" only in well-

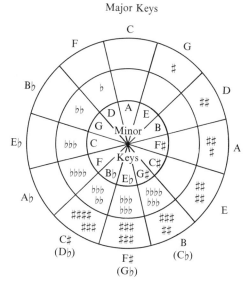

1. Circle of Fifths

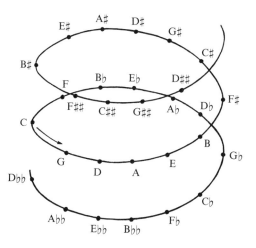

2. Spiral of Fifths

tempered tuning [Ex. 1]. If Pythagorean (pure) fifths are considered, the 12th of these fifths is higher by the Pythagorean comma (about one-eighth of a tone) than the starting tone. Here, a "spiral of fifths" would give a good picture of the unending series of ascending and descending fifths [Ex. 2].

The circle of fifths was first described by J. D. Heinichen, in his *Der General-Bass* (1728, pp. 837ff) and was illustrated (pp. 885ff) by a composition (beginning and ending in A minor) that modulates through 22 keys. (Only E major and F♯ minor are omitted.) A similar work, "Kleines harmonisches Labyrinth," tentatively ascribed to J. S. Bach (*BWV* 591; reprinted in Bach's *Orgelwerke*, ed. Peters, ix, 16), may also be by Heinichen.

Circular canon. See under Canon (1), I (h).

Cis, Cisis [G.]. C-sharp, C-double-sharp; see Pitch names.

Cister, cistre, cither, citole, cittern. See under Guitar family.

Cithara. Medieval spelling of *kithara.

Cl. Abbr. for clarinet.

Clair de lune [F.]. A very popular piano piece by Debussy, properly the third movement of his *Suite bergamasque*. Written 1890–95, it belongs to his early period, before he began to experiment with such characteristic devices of his later style as parallel chords, whole-tone scale, etc.

Clairon [F.]. Bugle. See under Brass instruments IV.

Claquebois [F.]. *Xylophone.

Clarinblasen [G.]. See Clarino (2).

Clarinet family. A large group of single-reed woodwind instruments [see Reed], in distinction to the oboe family, which includes the double-reed instruments.

I. *The clarinet.* The clarinet consists of a cylindrical pipe made of wood or ebonite (recently also of metal) with a bell-shaped opening at one end and a characteristic mouthpiece (beak) at the other. The beak looks as if it were pinched to form a sharp edge at the top and has a single reed (made from a thin piece of cane) fixed to its back. Played by means of holes and keys, the clarinet has the acoustical properties of a "stopped" pipe, thus overblowing at the twelfth, i.e., the second partial—the octave—

while the even-numbered partials in general cannot be obtained by overblowing, a fact that also affects its *timbre. From a distance the clarinet looks very much like an oboe, from which, however, it is easily distinguished by the mouthpiece. While the oboe produces a "pastoral," slightly quaint and nasal sound of fairly constant quality, the clarinet is not only fuller and "creamier" in timbre but also shows a distinct variation of timbre in its various ranges (registers). It lends itself to the expression of love and passion as well as fury and parody. On the whole, it is much more "modern" (and, in fact, a much more recent) instrument than the oboe.

Owing to the fact that only the odd-numbered partials can be obtained by overblowing (e.g., c–g′–e″), a number of holes and, consequently, a complicated key mechanism are necessary to obtain the tones in between. The *Böhm system is popular in America but has not been universally adopted. All clarinets have a written range as shown in Ex. 1, although the higher members of the family occasionally exceed its high point and the lower members become somewhat weak in the top octave. The least characteristic and most troublesome portion of their range is, to the average player, at the top of the first twelfth, the so-called "break" or throat register [see Ex. 2]. The register below the break is called *chalumeau* and that above it *clarion* or *clarino*. All clarinets are notated as *transposing instruments.

II. *Present forms.* The most common form is the *clarinet in B♭*, which sounds a whole tone lower than written. Next in importance is the *clarinet in A*, the part for which sounds a minor third lower than written. The former instrument is the more brilliant without sacrificing any perceptible fullness. The clarinet in A is sometimes preferred for parts in the sharp keys, which are, of course, easier to play on this instrument than on the other. The bass instrument of the clarinet family is the *bass clarinet in B♭*, whose range is an octave lower than that of the clarinet in B♭ plus an additional semitone provided by a low E♭ key, thereby enabling performance of music written for the now obsolete bass clarinet in A. To avoid too unwieldy a length, the lower

Clarinets: 1. Pibgorn. 2. Hornpipe (Basque). 3. Clarinette d'amour. 4. Chalumeau. 5. Heckel-clarina (Heckelphonklarinette). 6. Basset horn (old). 7. Basset horn (modern). 8. Bass clarinet. 9. Clarinet. 10. Tarogato. 11. Saxophone.

end of the instrument is curved upward and ends in a metal bell, while the upper end, likewise of metal, is curved downward to bring the mouthpiece within easier reach for the player. The bass clarinet has less marked differences of register than the higher instruments and its top register is relatively weak. Its lower tones are of remarkable richness and have the advantage, unlike the bassoon, of a very wide dynamic range.

Additional types are the *clarinet in E^b,* a small instrument pitched a perfect fourth above the clarinet in B^b; the *alto clarinet in E^b,* pitched a fifth below the clarinet in B^b; and the *contrabass clarinet in B^b* (pedal clarinet), pitched an octave below the bass clarinet. They are commonly found in bands and are occasionally called for in orchestral scores. Parts for the E^b clarinet are found in Strauss's *Ein Heldenleben,* in Stravinsky's *Sacre du printemps,* and in Ravel's *Daphnis et Chloé;* for the double-bass clarinet in D'Indy's *Fervaal,* in Strauss' *Josephs Legende,* and in Weingartner's *Orestes.* Three obscure modern instruments, related to the clarinet only in that they possess a single reed, have been invented for the sole purpose of playing the solo English horn part in Act III of *Tristan.* They are the *Heckel-clarina, Holztrompete,* and **tarogato.* The music in question is generally played by the English horn. Another single-reed instrument is the **saxophone.*

III. *Obsolete forms.* During the 19th century a great many other clarinets were built, e.g., the clarinet in C, the clarinet in D (called for in Liszt's *Mazeppa* and Strauss' *Till Eulenspiegel;* now replaced by the clarinet in E^b), the bass clarinet in C or A (Liszt, *Mazeppa*), the *bathyphone* (constructed by E. Skorra, 1839), etc. An older instrument is the *basset horn,* an alto clarinet with a narrower bore, thinner wall, and a range four semitones beyond the low E (which sounds A in the usual F pitch). Originally (*c.* 1770) it was crescent-shaped and in this form was called for by Mozart, singly or in pairs, in *La Clemenza di Tito, Die Zauberflöte, Die Entführung aus dem Serail,* the Requiem, and in various instrumental works (e.g., K. 411). About 1800 the crescent shape was replaced by a model that was sharply bent (almost forming a right angle) and, somewhat later, it was given the straight form in which it is constructed today. Beethoven used it only in *Prometheus,* and Mendelssohn wrote two concert pieces for clarinet and basset horn with piano (op. 113, 114). Rare later examples, generally played on the

alto clarinet in E^b, are to be found in R. Strauss' *Elektra,* in F. S. Converse's *Iolan or The Pipe of Desire,* and in R. Sessions' Concerto for violin and orchestra. Finally, there is the *clarinette d'amour,* a larger clarinet in G or A^b with the pear-shaped bell of the oboe d'amore.

IV. *History and repertory.* In early periods and in non-Western cultures single-reed instruments are much rarer than double-reed instruments (oboes). Double clarinets (in pairs) were known in ancient Egypt but scarcely at all in the Far East. To the present day a triple clarinet, called *launedda,* is used in Sardinia [see *SaHMI,* p. 31]. A primitive European instrument is the *pibgorn* (also called stockhorn, hornpipe), which was originally made of the shinbone of a sheep, with a part of a cow's horn attached as a bell [see *GD* iv, 172, v, 141; *GDB* vi, 752, viii, 90–93]. The forerunner proper of the clarinet is the *chalumeau* (the single-reed type; there was also a chalumeau with double reed, more properly called shawm), a small, usually keyless cylindrical pipe. In the 17th century there existed a number of strangely shaped instruments of this type, especially for the bass size [see W. Heinitz, *Instrumentenkunde,* in *BüHM,* p. 57]. The change from the chalumeau to the clarinet took place between *c.* 1690 and 1720, owing to the activity of Johann C. Denner and his son Johann Denner, who added finger keys and a speaker key [see *SaHMI,* p. 411f]. These early clarinets had the timbre of oboes rather than of the modern clarinet, owing chiefly to the use of small reeds. Thus, Johann Walther says in his *Musicalisches Lexicon* of 1732 (first mention of the name "clarinet"): "From a distance it sounds rather like a trumpet." This probably explains the name clarinet [see Clarino; Clairon].

Chalumeaux, whether in their primitive or improved form, were used in Reinhard Keiser's operas *Croesus* (1710) and *Serenata* (1716), and are still prescribed in Gluck's *Orfeo* (1762). Rameau, J. W. Stamitz, and Gossec are the composers associated particularly with the early use of the real clarinet in the orchestra. Stamitz also is the composer of one of the earliest clarinet concertos on record. Mozart used the clarinet in some of his later symphonies, notably that in E^b (1788; K. 543), in which prominent parts covering a wide range are given to two B^b clarinets. Since that time, two clarinets have been included in every normal orchestra. Berlioz was among the first to use various sizes of clarinet for their particular tonal quality, a practice continued by Liszt, Strauss, and Mahler. From the time of

Wagner the number of clarinets in the orchestra has often been increased, e.g., in Strauss' *Salome* and *Elektra*. Composers since Mozart have provided the instrument with a repertory that in quality and variety is equaled by no other wind instrument. Outstanding compositions are: clarinet concertos by Mozart, K. 622, Weber, op. 73, 74, Concertino, op. 26, Hindemith (1947), and Nielsen, op. 57; clarinet sonatas by Brahms, op. 120, nos. 1 and 2, Hindemith (1939), and Honegger (sonatina); clarinet quintets by Mozart (K. 581), Brahms, op. 115, Reger, op. 146; clarinet trios by Beethoven, op. 11, Brahms, op. 114; Schumann, *Fantasiestücke* for clarinet and piano, op. 73; Stravinsky, 3 *Pieces* for clarinet solo (1919); Berg, 4 *Stücke*, op. 5.

Lit.: F. G. Rendall, *The Clarinet*, rev. ed. [1957]; K. Opperman, *Handbook for Making and Adjusting Single Reeds* [1956]; K. Stein, *The Art of Clarinet Playing* (1958); K. Opperman, *Repertory of the Clarinet* [1960]; L. W. Foster, *A Directory of Clarinet Music* [1940]; T. Dart, "The Mock Trumpet" (*GSJ* vi); E. Halfpenny, "Early English Clarinets" (*GSJ* xviii).   I–III by W.D.D.

Clarino. (1) The high register of the clarinet [see Clarinet family I]. (2) In the 17th and 18th centuries, a virtuoso method of trumpet playing, practiced by trumpeters trained specially and exclusively in the art of producing the highest harmonics, i.e., from the third octave onward, where they form a continuous scale. It was this training that enabled the trumpeters of Bach's time to play (without valves!) those rapid passages in high position that have baffled the most outstanding trumpet virtuosos of modern times [see Ex., from Cantata 75; *BG* xviii, 183]. Clarino, therefore, is less a name for a special instrument (*clarin trumpet*) than a special manner of playing the natural long-tube trumpet of the baroque period. The modern *Bach trumpet*, a short, straight, three-valve instrument introduced by J. Kosleck in 1884 and designed for rendering clarino passages in Bach's cantatas, is a poor substitute owing to its unsatisfactory tone quality.

Lit.: J. E. Altenburg, *Versuch einer Anleitung zur heroisch-musikalischen Trompeter- und Pauker-Kunst* (1795; new ed. 1911); W. Menke, *History of the Trumpet of Bach and Handel* [1934]; N. Bessaraboff, *Ancient European Musical Instruments* (1941), pp. 192ff, 413n; W. F. H. Blandford, in *Monthly Musical Record*, July 1931, and March to June 1935; H. Eichborn, *Das alte Clarinblasen auf Trompeten* (1894); C. Sachs, in *AMW* ii; M. Rasmussen, in *Brass Quarterly* v, 37–40.

Clarin trumpet. See Clarino (2).

Clarion. An ancient English trumpet in round form [see *SaRM; MaMI*].

Clarone [It.]. (1) Bass clarinet. (2) Older name for the basset horn (Mozart); see Clarinet family II.

Clarsech, clairseach, clarseth. The Irish harp [see Harp III].

Classical Symphony. Prokofiev's First Symphony, op. 25, composed 1916–17, so called because it is written in a "modernized" Mozart-Haydn idiom, with harmonic dissonances, unexpected rhythmic turns, etc. It is scored for a typical classical orchestra of strings and pairs of each wind instrument. The work is one of the earliest examples of 20th-century *neoclassicism.

Classici della musica italiana, I. See Editions IX.

Classici musicali italiani, I. See Editions X.

Classicism. In ordinary usage, the term [see Webster] "denotes primarily the principles and characteristics of Greek and Roman literature and art; considered as embodying formal elegance, simplicity, dignity, and correctness of style, and just and lucid conception and order . . . . [It] is often used of the principles and qualities of other than Greek and Roman works, esp. when similar in spirit and established as a formal standard." In music the word is used in various ways. Most commonly it means the antithesis of romanticism and is, therefore, applied to periods prior to the romantic school, either to its immediate predecessors, Haydn, Mozart, and Beethoven (Viennese classic school), or to what amateurs sometimes consider "all music before romanticism," i.e., from Palestrina to Beethoven. To others, the word "classic" denotes music of established value and fame, as distinguished from ephemeral works that quickly disappear from the programs. For still others it means art music or "highbrow" music, as opposed to "popular" music or music for entertainment. The latter definitions, of course, do not deserve serious consideration. The term should be used in either of the following ways: (a) to denote only the "Viennese classic school," that is, Haydn, Mozart, Beethoven, and to some extent Schubert; (b) in a more general way, to denote any period that gives the impression of greater stability, repose, clarity, balance, self-reliance, objectivity, and traditionalism than that preceding or following it. If the latter meaning is adopted, the entire evolution of music might be seen as a recurring shift from the classical to the romantic, romanticism being associated with unrest, exaggeration, experimentation, ostentation, diffusion, subjectivism, etc. Typically classical periods in this sense are those of the 13th century (Perotinus, Franco), the Flemish era (1450–1600), the period of Bach and Handel, and that of the Viennese classic school, whereas the 14th century (Machaut and his successors) as well as the 17th (Frescobaldi, Froberger; see Lament, Courante) and the period of K. P. E. Bach show features more characteristic of romanticism.

The high Viennese classic school embraces the decades from 1770 to 1830 [see Germany V]. Its forms and style emerged from a very complex development that began about 1740 and to which various groups of composers in southwest Germany (Mannheim), Vienna, Paris, Italy, and Bohemia contributed. See Mannheim school; Sonata; Sonata form; String quartet; Symphony.

Lit.: E. Bücken, *Die Musik des Rokokos und der Klassik* [1927]; K. Westphal, *Der Begriff der musikalischen Form in der Wiener Klassik* (1935); A. Damerini, *Classicismo e romanticismo nella musica* (1942); F. Torrefranca, *Le Origini dello stile mozartiano* (1930; also in *RMI* xxvi, xxviii, xxxiii, xxxiv, xxxvi); G. Adler, "Haydn and the Viennese Classical School" (*MQ* xviii); *id.*, "Schubert and the Viennese Classic School" (*MQ* xiv); F. Corder, "The Classical Tradition" (*MQ* iii); H. Tischler, "Classicism, Romanticism and Music" (*MR* xiv); G. Becking, "Klassik und Romantik" (*CP 1925*); W. Fischer, "Zur Entwicklungsgeschichte des Wiener klassischen Stils" (*StM* iii).

Clausula [L.]. (1) Cadence, particularly the cadential formulas of 16th-century polyphonic music. Tinctoris (*Diffinitorium* [*c.* 1475; printed *c.* 1494]; see *CS* iv, 180) defined clausula as a "particle at the end of which there is a general pause or a perfection [perfect consonance?]" An elaborate system of classification and terminology (*clausula vera, plagalis, ficta, media, diminuta,* etc.) was worked out by 16th- and 17th-century theorists [see "Cadence" in *GD, GDB*]. See reference under Glosa. (2) In Ambrosian chant, name for the terminations (**differentiae*) of the psalm tones.

(3) The term is employed mainly for a large repertory of polyphonic compositions of the late 12th and early 13th centuries (school of Notre Dame) that are based on a short fragment of a Gregorian chant, in contrast to the organa, which are based on the entire chant (i.e., the entire solo section thereof; see Organum). This meaning of the term goes back to Anon. IV, who says that Perotinus "fecit clausulas sive puncta plurima meliora" (wrote many beautiful clausulae or puncta; *CS* i, 342). Very likely, the compositions referred to are those called "clausulae" today. They are relatively short compositions, invariably based on a melisma of a responsorial chant (Gradual, Alleluia, Responsory). Accordingly, there is no full text in the tenor of a clausula, but only one or two words or sometimes only a syllable [see Incipit] to indicate from which chant the tenor is borrowed. For instance, the clausula GO (of which there are a great number, with identical tenor but different upper parts) is taken from the Gradual *Benedicta es et venerabilis,* whose verse begins with the words: *Vir-go Dei genetrix.* Below is the beginning of this verse in plainsong [*LU*, p. 1265], together

with the beginning of a clausula GO. The parts of a clausula usually are to be sung in vocalization, in the present example to the vowel O.

Many such clausulae (well over 500; about a dozen in three parts, the others in two) are preserved in the sources of Notre Dame. They were probably intended to serve as substitutes [G. *Ersatzklausel*, substitute clausula] for the corresponding sections (in the case above, the section GO) in the organa of Leoninus, which form the *"Magnus liber organi." These organa consist, in alternation, of "organal" sections in a relatively free rhythm and of "discant" sections [see Discant] in strictly measured counterpoint. It is the latter sections for which Perotinus and his collaborators provided substitutes, often longer and in a more precise rhythm [see *HAM*, nos. 28 and 30]. Occasionally the original discant sections of the Leoninus organa are also spoken of as clausulae.

No less important than the connection of the clausulae with the older organum is another, pointing toward a later development, i.e., the motet. In fact, most of the early motets are directly derived from clausulae, retaining their music but underlaying a full text to the upper part. For the identification of a clausula (such as GO, *IN SECULUM, NOSTRUM, LATUS) the complete list given in F. Ludwig, *Repertorium organorum recentioris et motetorum vetustissimi stili* (1910), pp. 25–29 and, particularly, pp. 79–95, is indispensable. See F. Gennrich, *Sankt Victor Clausulae und ihre Motetten* (1953). See also F. Gennrich, ed., ‡*Aus der Frühzeit der Motette*, 2 vols. (1963); *ReMMA*, pp. 298ff; *AdHM*, pp. 218ff.

Clave. See Claves; also Percussion instruments B, 8.

Clavecin, clavessin [F.]. *Harpsichord.

Clavecin d'amour, cembal d'amour, cembalo d'amore. A clavichord (not a cembalo, i.e., harpsichord), built by G. Silbermann about 1721, in which the strings are twice the normal length and are struck in the middle. The instrument had no damping cloth woven between the strings, like that required in the ordinary clavichord to damp the shorter section of the string. Therefore both sections of the string would sound the same tone, with a highly desirable result of increased volume. In spite of its various advantages, the instrument did not become popular. It is described in Mattheson's *Critica musica,* 2 vols. (1722–25), ii, 243n, 380, and in Adlung's *Musica mechanica organoedi,* 2 vols. (1768), i, 212, ii, 123–26. See E. van der Straeten, in *Musical Times,* Jan. 1924.

Claves. Cylindrical hardwood blocks used in Cuba and throughout the Antilles. They are struck together, with the cupped palm of the hand providing resonance.   J.O-S.

Clavicembalo [It.]. Harpsichord.

Clavichord [F. *clavicorde;* G. *Klavichord, Clavier;* It. *clavicordo;* Sp. *clavicordio*]. A stringed keyboard instrument in use from the 15th through 18th centuries. The clavichord consists essentially of a rectangular case with a keyboard either projecting from or set into one of the longer sides. The part of the case to the right of the keyboard is occupied by the soundboard, and the strings run across the case from right to left. When the player depresses a key, its tangent (a brass blade driven into the back end of the key) strikes a pair of strings. The portion of the strings to the left of the tangent is damped by a strip of cloth (listing); the portion to the right (which passes over a bridge that transmits the strings' vibrations to the soundboard) is set into vibration by the blow of the tangent. When the key is released, the tangent falls away from the strings, which are then immediately silenced by the cloth damping. Since the point at which the tangent strikes the strings determines their vibrating length, one can produce several different pitches from a single pair of strings by causing a number of tangents to strike the strings at

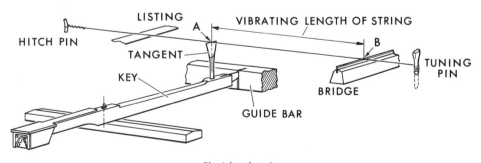

Clavichord action.

different points along their length. However, since a single pair of strings can produce only one pitch at a time, keys whose tangents strike the same pair of strings cannot be sounded simultaneously. For this reason, clavichord builders seem from the earliest times to have taken care that only notes forming dissonances with each other would be sounded from the same string. Clavichords in which pairs of strings are struck by more than one tangent are called fretted [G. *gebunden*]; those in which each key has its own pair of strings are called unfretted or fret-free [G. *bundfrei*].

The sound of the clavichord is very soft and is often disappointing at first hearing. However, after becoming accustomed to the small tone and the special touch required to make the instrument sound its best, the performer is usually won over by the extraordinary sensitivity and responsiveness of the instrument. Variations in the force with which the keys are struck produce variations in loudness in much the same way as they do on the piano, and the dynamic range of good instruments is quite wide. A special (and often overrated) effect unavailable on any other keyboard instrument is the *Bebung*, a kind of vibrato achieved by varying the pressure with which a key is held down.

History. The clavichord appears to have developed from the *monochord, as evidenced by the facts that the instrument was often called *monochordium* in the 15th century and that, until the third quarter of the century, its strings were all tuned in unison. The earliest record of the name "clavichord" is in the "Der Minne Regel" of Eberhard Cersne (1404). The mid-15th-century manuscript of Henri Arnaut de Zwolle shows a layout drawing of a three-octave instrument, and an intarsia of 1479–92 depicts an instrument with a range of four octaves. A somewhat smaller range of C–g″ or C–a″ with a *short octave in the bass seems to have been usual in the early part of the 16th century. By the middle of the century, however, the range of C–c‴ (still with a short octave) became standard. This range was only rarely exceeded in the 17th century, but by the middle of the 18th century builders were making clavichords with a five-octave compass FF–f‴.

The earliest surviving clavichords are all Italian and date from the middle of the 16th century. However, interest in the instrument appears to have died out in Italy by the end of the century, and the vast majority of the surviving 17th- and 18th-century examples are

German. In contrast to the Italian instruments, which had projecting keyboards and strings that ran parallel to the back of the case, the typical German clavichord has an inset keyboard and strings that run obliquely from the front right to the back left. Although instruments in which some strings were struck by as many as four tangents continued to be built in the 17th century, the larger instruments generally had no more than two tangents striking the same pair of strings. The only real limitation of these instruments lay in the fact that their tuning could not be changed when desired to permit playing pieces in remote keys (possible only when each pitch has its own pair of strings). Consequently, instruments of this kind continued to serve the needs of most musicians well into the 18th century and were built by makers of the first rank at least as late as the 1780's.

Unfretted clavichords, which required about half again as many strings as the instruments just described (and were, accordingly, more difficult to tune and maintain) appeared in the last years of the 17th century. The exact date of their introduction is difficult to establish. However, Johann Speth in the preface to his *Ars magna consoni ed dissoni* (1693) explicitly calls for a clavichord in which "each key has its own strings and not some [strings] touched by two, three, and even four keys." Large unfretted clavichords continued to be built in Germany and Scandinavia through the first decade of the 19th century, in most cases by makers who were building pianos during the same period.

The precise role of the clavichord in the history of keyboard music is difficult to establish. Although the word *Clavier* appears frequently on the title pages of German publications, the term means "keyboard instrument" as well as "clavichord," and such a collection as Bach's *Clavier-Übung* (4 pts., 1731–42) contains works explicitly designated for harpsichord and for organ. The clavichord was, however, the usual domestic instrument of the 16th, 17th, and 18th centuries in Germany, and its value as an instrument for teaching and practice had been emphasized from the early years of the 16th century. This popularity doubtless stemmed as much from musical considerations as the more mundane ones of cheapness and ease of maintenance and tuning. On the other hand, the clavichord seems to have been the preferred medium of performance only during the period of *Empfindsamkeit* [see *Empfindsamer Stil*] in the second half of the 18th century, a period that produced the instrument's most ardent partisans, including K. P. E. Bach. His *Versuch über die wahre Art das Clavier zu spielen* (2 pts., 1753–62; new ed. and trans. by W. J. Mitchell [1949]) is an eloquent appreciation of the clavichord as well as a thorough study of keyboard technique. His F-sharp minor fantasia "K. P. E. Bach's Empfindungen" and "Abscheid vom Silbermannschen Clavier" (new ed. by A. Kreutz [1950]), with their abrupt contrasts, crescendos, diminuendos, and explicitly indicated *Bebung,* are among the most idiomatic clavichord pieces ever written. See also Keyboard music.

Lit.: R. Russell, *The Harpsichord and Clavichord: An Introductory Study* (1959); H. Neupert, *The Clavichord* [1965]; D. H. Boalch, *Makers of the Harpsichord and Clavichord, 1440–1840* (1956); C. Auerbach, *Die deutsche Clavichordkunst des 18. Jahrhunderts,* rev. ed. (1953); F. A. Goehlinger, *Geschichte des Klavichords* (1910); M. F. Schneider, *Beiträge zu einer Anleitung Clavichord und Cembalo zu spielen* (1934); O. Kinkeldey, *Orgel und Klavier in der Musik des 16. Jahrhunderts* (1910); J. Adlung, *Musica mechanica organoedi* (1768; fac. ed. 1961); G. Le Cerf, *Instruments de musique du XVe siècle: Les Traités d'Henri-Arnaut de Zwolle et de divers anonymes* (1932); *MaMI;* E. M. Ripin, "The Early Clavichord" (*MQ* liii); M. S. Kastner, "Portugiesische und spanische Clavichorde des 18. Jahrhunderts" (*AM* xxiv).   E.M.R.

Clavicymbal. *Harpsichord.

Clavicytherium. A harpsichord with a vertical body like that of the upright piano [see Harpsichord II]. It was in use from the 16th through 18th centuries. An early record of it is a reproduction in Virdung's *Musica getutscht* (1511). See *SaRM,* p. 217; N. Bessaraboff, *Ancient European Musical Instruments* (1941), pp. 324ff.

Clavier. (1) French term for keyboard (pronounced klavi-é; in English usage klá-vi-er). (2) German term (pronounced kla-véer) used in the baroque period as a generic designation for keyboard instruments such as the harpsichord, clavichord, and organ [see *Clavier-Übung*]. Later it denoted mainly, if not exclusively, the clavichord (K. P. E. Bach). Johann Adam Hiller, in the preface to his *Lieder für Kinder* (1769), clearly refers to the clavichord when he says that the pieces should never be played on the "Flügel oder Spinet" but on a good "Clavier." In the 19th century the term was transferred to the piano (in modern German, *Klavier*).

Clavier Hans. See Keyboard III.

Clavier-Übung [G.]. A title (lit., keyboard study) used by J. S. Bach for four publications of keyboard music. *Clavier-Übung* i (1731) contains the six partitas; ii (1735), the *Italian Concerto and the French Overture; iii (1739), a number of organ chorales preceded by the Prelude in E♭ and ending with the Fugue in E♭ (*St. Anne's Fugue) and four duets; iv (1742), the *Goldberg Variations. The contents of vols. i, ii, and iv are specifically for the harpsichord, while that of vol. iii is specifically for the organ except for the duets, which could also be played on the harpsichord or clavichord. The title was adopted by Bach from earlier publications such as Kuhnau's *Neue Clavier-Übung* (1689, '92) and Johann Krieger's *Anmuthige Clavier-Übung* (1699).

Clavilux. An instrument invented by Thomas Wilfrid *c.* 1920 for the performance of color music [see Color organ].

Clavis [L., pl. *claves*]. Literally, a key to open a door. In medieval theory *clavis* was primarily the designation for the "clef" letters f, c' and (later) g' because these provide the "key" for the correct reading of the notes written on the staff. Thus, Marchetto da Padua says that there are two *claves,* f and c' (*F grave, c acutum*), that "open every *cantus*" [*GS* iii, 120]. Other writers use the term with a wider meaning, similar to that of the present-day key. Simon Tunsted says [*CS* iv, 207] that the seven Latin letters A, B . . . G are called *claves* because through them the melody of all music is opened. Tinctoris speaks [*CS* iv, 4] of twenty *claves,* one for each note from G to e″, as did Philippe de Vitry [*CS* iii, 36] and others. The *clavis* letters were often written on the keys of the instruments [see *CS* i, 214, 257], and this custom probably accounts for terms such as clavichord, clavicembalo, clavier, Klavier, etc.

Clef [F.; G. *Schlüssel;* It. *chiave;* Sp. *clave*]. A sign written at the beginning of the staff in order to indicate the pitch of the notes. There are three such signs [see Ex. a], which respectively represent the tones g', c', and f, hence the names G-clef, C-clef, and F-clef. The G-clef, also called violin clef, is used on the second line of the staff; it indicates that the note on the second line is g'. The F-clef, also called bass clef, is used on the fourth line; it indicates that the note written on the fourth line is f. The C-clef is used in two positions, on the third line (alto clef or viola clef) or on the fourth line (tenor clef); see Ex. b. The G-clef is used for the upper staff of piano music and for all high instruments (violin, flute); the F-clef is used for the lower staff of piano music and for all low instruments (cello, double bass). The alto clef is used for the viola and instruments of a similar range; the tenor clef for the high range of the cello, the bassoon, the tenor trombone, etc.

History. The clef signs evolved from the letters they stand for. Ex. c shows early shapes, illustrating the gradual corruption of the letters c, f, and g. In music prior to 1750 each of these signs occurs in various positions. See Ex. d, which also shows the position of middle C (c′)

a. *The G-clef; three forms of the C-clef; the F-clef.*
b. *Positions of the clefs on the staff.*
c. *Early forms of the clefs.*
d. *Position of each clef and middle C(c′) in music prior to 1750: 1. French violin clef. 2. Violin clef, also called G-clef or treble clef. 3. Soprano clef or descant clef. 4. Mezzo-soprano clef. 5. Alto clef or C-clef. 6. Tenor clef. 7. Baritone clef. 8. Baritone clef. 9. Bass clef or F-clef. 10. Subbass clef.*

in each clef. In the 17th century the G-clef on the first line was essentially French and that on the second line Italian. This distinction was so definite that Couperin resorted to it to differentiate the two styles in his *Apothéose de Lully.*

The great variety of clef positions encountered in old music results from the desire to avoid ledger lines. Whenever the range of a voice exceeded the five-line staff, the position of the clef was changed or another clef was introduced. In modern musicological publications of 15th- and 16th-century music the old clefs are largely retained, a method that, although justifiable

on historical and scholarly grounds, has been a practical drawback. It is gratifying to see that in most present-day publications only the F-clef and the G-clef are used, the latter also in a modification (with subscript 8) indicating transposition an octave below. As a matter of fact, this

clef is very well suited to replace the alto clef as well as the tenor clef since its range is practically the same as that of the other two [see Ex. e]. For reforms of clefs, see *WoHN* ii, 339ff. See *Chiavette.*

Clemenza di Tito, La [It., The Clemency of Titus]. Opera in two acts by Mozart (libretto by Metastasio, rev. by C. Mazzolà), produced in Prague, 1791, at the coronation of Emperor Leopold II as King of Bohemia, for which it had been commissioned. Setting: ancient Rome. While it contains much fine music, it cannot be compared with Mozart's masterpieces of the same period, *Le Nozze di Figaro, Don Giovanni,* and *Die Zauberflöte.*

Clerical dances. See under Dance music I; Religious dances.

Climacus. See under Neumes I (table).

Clivis. See under Neumes I (table).

Cloches [F.]. Bells, especially those of the orchestra.

Clocking. See under Bell.

Clock Symphony. Popular name for Haydn's Symphony no. 101 in D major, composed in 1794 in London. The name refers to the ticking motif in the Andante.

Clockwork instruments. See under Mechanical instruments I, III.

Clos [F.]. See Ouvert and clos.

Close. *Cadence.

Close harmony. Chords in close position, i.e., with all the four notes within an octave or a twelfth. See Spacing.

Clubs, musical. See Societies.

Clutsam keyboard. See under Keyboard III.

C.O., c.o. [It.]. Abbr. for *coll′ ottava; c.o.b., coll′ ottava bassa.* See *Coll′ ottava.*

Cobla [Cat.]. The popular dance band of Catalonia (northeast Spain, Barcelona). It consists of *pipe and tabor (*fluviol i tambori*), shawms, cornetts, horns, trombone, and double bass. The use of pipe and tabor (formerly also bagpipes) indicates a very ancient tradition. The main dance played by the *coblas* is the *sardana. See H. Besseler, "Katalanische Cobla und Alta-Tanzkapelle" (*CP 1949*).

Coda [It.]. A concluding section or passage, extraneous to the basic structure of the composition but added in order to confirm the impression of finality. Probably the earliest realization of the coda is found in compositions of the early Flemish masters (Ockeghem, Obrecht, Josquin), in which the final note of one or two voices frequently is sustained while the remaining parts continue for two or three measures [see, e.g., Hofhaimer's "Meins Traurens ist," in *HAM*, no. 93]. Fugues often close with a shorter or longer coda, usually based on a pedal point (e.g., Bach, *The Well-Tempered Clavier* i, C major). Bach's Organ Fugue in A minor closes with a coda in brilliant toccata style. Likewise in sonatas, symphonies, etc., a coda is found at the end of each movement. In slow movements it usually serves as an epilogue, whereas in fast movements it often leads to a final climax, frequently combined with quickening of tempo (*stretto). In movements in sonata form the coda frequently takes on considerable dimension, occasionally becoming a second development section [e.g., the first movement of Beethoven's Fifth Symphony]. A short coda is sometimes called *codetta*. However, this term more commonly means a closing passage at the end of an inner section, such as the exposition in sonata form or the first section (A) of a slow movement in ternary form A B A). Beethoven's Piano Sonata op. 2, no. 3 is recommended for a study of the coda in its various manifestations. Here even the Scherzo ends with a coda to be played after the repetition of the Scherzo ("Scherzo da capo e poi la coda").

Codetta. (1) See under Coda. (2) In the exposition of a fugue, any short transitional section between two entries of the subject (generally between the second and third).

Codex Bamberg, Burgos, etc. See under Sources.

Coffee Cantata. A secular cantata by Bach, "Schweigt stille, plaudert nicht" (Be quiet, don't prattle), for solo voices, chorus, and orchestra, composed *c.* 1732. It is a little dramatic scene between the father, Schlendrian, and his daughter, Lieschen, who, in spite of threat and persuasion, will not give up her beloved coffee until the father promises to get her a husband. In the end, however, she will have the coffee as well. The music is appropriate for this innocent jest to a degree hardly expected of Bach.

Col arco [It.]. With the bow (after *pizzicato*).

Colascione, colachon. See under Lute II.

Colinde. See Koleda.

Colla, coll' [It.]. "With the." *Colla destra, sinistra,* with the right, left hand. *Colla parte, colla voce* (with the part) is an indication directing the player of the accompaniment to "follow along" with the main part, which is to be performed in free rhythm. *Colla punta d'arco,* with the point of the bow. Also *col,* as in *col arco.

Collect. In the Roman Catholic rite, one of the prayers [L. *oratio*] offered by the priest at Mass (after the Gloria; see Mass, table), so called because it represents the collected prayers of all present. It is sung to special recitation tones called *toni orationum* [see *LU,* p. 98]. It is part of the Proper of the Mass, and normally two or three collects are used in one Mass.

In Anglican rites, the collect is a short prayer to be used for a particular day in liturgical services. It normally consists of four parts: the Address to the Deity, the Petition, the Oblation, and a final Doxology. When intoned by the officiant, this form is clearly brought out by the cadence at the end of the Address, a half-step inflection at the end of the Petition and again at the end of the Oblation, and another cadence on the Doxology. The following example is the proper Collect for Christmas Day from the Book of Common Prayer:

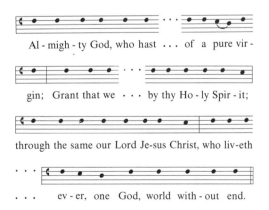

Al - migh - ty God, who hast ... of a pure vir-

gin; Grant that we ••• by thy Ho - ly Spir - it;

through the same our Lord Je-sus Christ, who liv-eth

••• ev - er, one God, world with - out end.

See *LU,* p. 98; *The Choral Service,* rev. ed. (1927), pp. xiii–xv.

Collegium musicum. Name for musical associations formed by amateurs for the performance of serious music. Nowadays the name is used for such associations connected with a university and devoted to the cultivation of old music. As early as 1616 a musical society in Prague was called *Collegium musicum.* In 1660 M. Weckmann (d. 1674) founded a *collegium musicum* at Hamburg. Particularly famous was that of the University of Leipzig, which flourished under Kuhnau (1688), Telemann, and Bach (1729–39). The movement was transferred to America in 1744 by the Moravians, who established such organizations at Bethlehem, Pa., Salem, N.C., and elsewhere in Pennsylvania, Maryland, and North Carolina. The first modern *collegium musicum* was founded by H. Riemann at the University of Leipzig, in 1909, as a revival of the old one. An important step was the introduction, at the University of Freiburg under W. Gurlitt (*c.* 1920), of old instruments such as recorders, viols, harpsichord, baroque organ, etc. Today most German and a number of American universities have a *collegium musicum.* See M. Gondolatsch, in *ZMW* iii; M. Seiffert, in *SIM* ii; D. McCorkle, "The Collegium Musicum Salem" (*JAMS* viii).

Col legno [It.]. In violin playing, striking the strings with the bow-stick instead of playing with the hair.

Coll' ottava [It.]. At the octave. An indication to duplicate the written notes at the upper octave. Similarly, *coll' ottava bassa* calls for duplication at the lower octave.

Colombia. Art music in Nueva Granada— present-day Colombia—dates from 1537, when Juan Perez Materano, expert in plainchant, organist, and author of the treatise *Canto de órgano y canto llano* (which, according to a Royal License of the time, was to have been published in 1554) arrived in Cartagena de Indias. The most important composer who came from Spain to the New World during the 16th century was Gutierre Fernandez Hidalgo (*c.* 1553–1618), who arrived in Bogotá in 1584. The following year he was appointed musical director of the Cathedral, a position to which Gonzalo Garcia Zorro (*d.* 1617), a *mestizo* priest and musician, had been appointed ten years before. Ten Psalms, three Salves, and nine Magnificats by Fernandez Hidalgo are preserved in the Cathe-dral archives. By the turn of the century the Cathedral of Bogotá had become an important center for church music. Its archives contained —and still contain—a large store of European polyphony and early baroque music. In 1650 José de Cascante (d. 1702) was appointed musical director. A dozen of his compositions, mainly *villancicos,* are preserved. His successor, Juan de Herrera y Chumacero (*c.* 1665–1738), a native of Bogotá, was one of the most prolific colonial composers of Nueva Granada. Thirty-three of his works survive, among them six Masses, polychoral Latin compositions, lamentations, psalms, and *villancicos.* Juan Ximenez, one of Herrera's eleven assistants, between 1709 and 1724 wrote a number of *villancicos* for voice and continuo that are preserved in the archives of the Bogotá Cathedral. The first composer to succeed Herrera as musical director of the Cathedral was Salvador Romero, whose *Lectio secunda a 12* (1762) is also preserved in Bogotá. The development of church and secular music in Bogotá at the end of the 18th century owed much to Archbishop Baltasar Martinez Compañon, one of the foremost intellectuals of the colonial period, who had taught plainchant in Peru before coming to Bogotá in 1791.

The first famous church composer following Colombia's independence was Juan de Dios Torres, who produced two extremely simple Masses (1827, '28) and a hymn (1844), preserved in the cathedral archives. Among his contemporaries were Nicolas Quevedo Rachadell (1803–74); Juan Antonio de Velasco (d. 1859), composer and conductor, the first to promote Haydn, Beethoven, and Mozart in Colombia; and Enrique Price (1819–63), who was born in England and about 1840 came to Bogotá, where he founded the *Sociédad Filarmónica* (1847). This institution served as the basis for the creation of the *Academia Nacional de Música,* established in 1882 by his son, Jorge W. Price (1853–1953), and transformed in 1909 into the *Conservatorio Nacionál.*

During the second half of the 19th century numerous Colombian composers followed the Italian operatic tradition of the time. Among them were Julio Quevedo Arévalo (1829–97), especially noted for his church music, and José Maria Ponce de León (1846–82), who composed the first operas written by a native Colombian, *Esther* (1874) and *Florinda* (1880), as well as a Requiem Mass (1880), *Apoteósis de Bolivar,* and *Sinfonia sobre temas colombianos* (1881), an early example of musical nationalism here.

During the first decades of the 20th century a group of composers known as the forerunners of modern nationalism in Colombia contributed to the generally inactive musical scene. The most important of them were Carlos Umaña Santa-Maria (1862–1917), Andrés Martinez Montoya (1869–1933), and Santos Cifuentes (1870–1932). Not until the 1930's did Colombian music regain some stature, largely owing to a distinguished group of composers that includes Antonio María Valencia (1902–52), founder of the Cali Conservatory, Jesús Bermudez Silva (b. 1884), Daniel Zamudio (1887–1952), Gonzalo Vidal Pacheco (1863–1933), and José Rozo Contreras (b. 1894). The most important figure of this generation is Guillermo Uribe-Holguín (b. 1880), a skillful composer and educator who has produced more than one hundred works, most of them nationalist in character.

In 1936, Guillermo Espinosa (b. 1905), a well-known conductor and promoter of Latin American music abroad, founded the National Symphony Orchestra. In 1953 he was appointed chief of the Music Division of the Pan-American Union in Washington, D.C.

The most important Colombian composers of the next generation are Carlos Posada-Amador (b. 1908); Adolfo Mejía (b. 1909); Roberto Pineda-Duque (b. 1910), who uses the twelve-tone technique; Fabio Gonzalez-Zuleta (b. 1920), an eclectic and skillful composer of symphonies, choral works, and chamber music; and Luis Antonio Escobar (b. 1925), a talented neoclassicist who has won international recognition. Still younger composers are Blas Emilio Atehortúa (b. 1933) Marco Aurelio Venegas, Alfredo Aragon Guerrero, and Jacquelin Nova (b. 1938).

The folk music of Colombia derives from various sources, of which the most important are Spanish and African. Some scholars would also mention Arab and Jewish influences. All these have mingled in varying proportions with indigenous elements. The *bambuco, the most characteristic of all dance-songs and the best known throughout Colombia, represents a combination of African, Spanish, and Indian traditions. The *pasillo reflects stronger Spanish influences, and the *torbellino and guabina are closer to indigenous music. Other native songs and dances are the porro, *galerón, *chispa, cañas, bundes, fandanguillos, and *mejorana, the last-named imported from Panama.

Lit.: R. M. Stevenson, La Música colonial en Colombia (1964); G. Espinosa, Colombian Music and Musicians (1962); A. Martínez Montoya, Reseña historica sobre la música en Colombia (1932); E. de Lima, Folklore Colombiano (1942); J. Perdomo-Escobar, Historia de la música en Colombia (1945); A. Pardo Tovar, "Los Problemas de la cultura musical en Colombia" (Rev. mus. chil. xiii); id., "Música Autoctonia Nacional" (Colombia, nos, 6, 7, June–July 1944). Also see under Latin America.   J.O-S.

Colophane, colophony. See under Rosin.

Color [L.]. (1) In 13th-century theory color signified various special devices of composition and performance, such as the repetition of a melodic phrase, its imitation (in Stimmtausch; see Stimm-), quotations from other sources [see Refrain III], or embellishments, especially the vocal *vibrato [see J. de Garlandia, CS i, 115f]. The first meaning survived in the color of the *isorhythmic motet; the last in the present-day term *coloratura. (2) For color temporis, color prolationis, see Mensural notation V.

Color and music. The physical and psychological relationships between colors and sounds have been the subject of numerous studies. Physically, both the pitches of the musical scale and the colors of the optical spectrum are vibrations of specific frequencies. The frequencies of audible sound range from about 16 to 40,000 cycles per second; those of visible light, from about 450 to 780 million million cycles per second. Since the latter two figures are nearly in the ratio 1:2, it would seem reasonable to compare the visible spectrum from red to violet not to the entire audible musical scale but only to an octave or, more nearly, to a seventh, e.g., to the tones 450 to 780 (approximately a' to g''). This analogy seems to be supported by the fact that both the colors in the spectrum and the diatonic tones are seven in number. However, there are various incongruities: (a) Newton's distinction of seven colors is arbitrary; in fact, his scheme was partly influenced by the preconceived analogy to the musical scale. (b) There are infinitely more colors in the spectrum than there are tones in the musical octave, since the former is a continuous and the latter a discrete multitude. (c) Most serious of all, the spectrum, unlike the musical octave, lacks the identity or, at least, similarity, of its lower and upper end. The chief studies in this field are those of Newton (1700), Goethe (1810), and Helmholtz (numerous essays, 1860–80).

Among musicians the psychological or synesthetic approach to the question of color and sound has been more popular than the physical. A number of musicians, particularly in Russia and England, have been inclined to associate particular sounds with particular colors. The various schemes of coordination differ widely, however. For instance, Rimsky-Korsakov interpreted the keys of C, D, A, F and F-sharp (all major) as white, yellow, rosy, green, and grayish-green, respectively, while Scriabin interpreted them as red, yellow, green, red, and bright blue. In Chinese music, certain tones are associated with specific colors. Colors have also been associated with entire works—e.g., *Tannhäuser,* blue; *The Flying Dutchman,* green (the "blue cave" of Venus and the "green sea"?)—and even with composers (Mozart, blue; Chopin, green; Beethoven, black). An example of a composition based on color impressions is Arthur Bliss' *Colour Symphony* (1922; rev. 1932), each movement of which represents the associations of a specific color (e.g., purple: royalty, pageantry, and death). Obviously the whole matter of color-sound synesthesia is largely subjective.

More important are the synesthetic analogies between the optical colors and the timbres (tone "colors," G. *Klangfarben*) of instruments. The terms "orchestral colors" and "orchestral palette" are widely used to signify a musical technique reminiscent of, and largely derived from, methods used in modern painting [see Impressionism]. However, these terms refer only to the general technique of modern orchestration, without implying any specific analogy between particular colors and instruments. In fact, any such specific coordination is no less subjective than color-key relationships. Color associations are common in Oriental music (China, India, Egypt, etc.), where, however, they are part of a cosmologic symbolism far removed from the subjective and psychological approach of Western music [see Lit., Wellek]. See Color organ.

Lit.: A. B. Klein, *Colour-music—The Art of Light* (1926), bibl.; O. Ortmann, *Theories of Synesthesia in the Light of a Case of Color-Hearing* [1933]; A. W. Rimington, *Colour-Music The Art of Mobile Colour* (1912); T. F. Karwoski and H. S. Odbert, *Color-Music* [1938]; A. Lange, *Arthur Lange's Spectrotone System of Orchestration* (1943); F. Suarez de Mendoza, *L'Audition colorée* (1899), bibl.; G. Anschütz, *Kurze Einführung in die Farbe-Ton-Forschung* (1927); *WoHN* ii, 460f; L. Sabaneyev, in *ML* x, 266; E. Whomes, in *PMA* xiii; A. Wellek, in *ZMW* xi.

Coloration. (1) The use of colored (originally red, later black) notes in early notation; see Mensural notation V. (2) The use of stereotyped written-out ornaments in music of the 15th and 16th centuries; see Ornamentation III; Colorists; Intabulation.

Coloratura [It.]. A rapid passage, run, trill, or similar virtuoso-like material, particularly in vocal melodies of 18th- and 19th-century operatic arias: *aria di coloratura, aria di bravura, Koloraturarie.* A famous example is the aria of the Queen of the Night in Mozart's *Zauberflöte.* The term is also used for the stereotyped ornamentation formulas of 16th-century keyboard and lute music [see Colorists].

Colorists [G. *Koloristen*]. A name introduced by A. G. Ritter [see Lit.] and widely adopted for a group of German organ composers of the late 16th century, including Elias Nicolaus Ammerbach (1530–97), Bernhard Schmid the older (c. 1520–90), Jacob Paix (1556–1617), B. Schmid the younger (b. 1548), and others, who used stereotyped ornamentation formulas (coloraturas) in their lute and keyboard compositions. Although the name serves as a convenient designation, it is rather misleading in both its literal interpretation as well as its pejorative implication. It is true that the musicians of this group made abundant use of coloraturas that now seem stereotyped and meaningless, particularly in their arrangements [see Intabulation] of motets and chansons. However, this method reflects contemporary performance practice and was used by many organists and lutenists throughout the 16th century; it occurs in the keyboard and lute books of Attaingnant (c. 1530) and the lute books of Hans and Melchior Newsidler (1536, '76), as well as in A. Gabrieli's keyboard arrangements of French chansons (c. 1550) and in those of the Fitzwilliam Virginal Book (c. 1600). Ritter's harsh judgment of the "colorists" is all the more unjust since these composers actually made outstanding contributions in another field, i.e., dance music. It should also be noted that B. Schmid the older in his publication of 1577 expressly says that he would prefer to leave the "art of the composer unchanged," and that his "modest" coloraturas are added only for the benefit of young and inexperienced players" [see Frotscher i, 154]. To include Johannes Woltz (tablature of 1617) in this group, as Ritter does, is not correct, since Woltz renounced the addition of coloraturas altogether. Even more misleading is the inclusion of Arnolt Schlick [see *AdHM* i, 385], who is not only much too early (died *c.* 1520) but also has much greater stature than the others.

Lit.: A. G. Ritter, *Zur Geschichte des Orgelspiels* (1884); G. Frotscher, *Geschichte des Orgelspiels und der Orgelkomposition* (1935); W. Apel, "Early German Keyboard Music" (*MQ* xxiii, 231f); W. Merian, *Der Tanz in den deutschen Tabulaturbüchern* (1927; transcriptions).

Color organ. The keyboard of the organ, harpsichord, and piano has been frequently used as a medium for coordinating sound and color [see Color and music]. In 1720 a Jesuit priest, L.-B. Castel (1688–1757), constructed a "Clavecin oculaire" in which the keys were mechanically connected to colored tapes; numerous similar contrivances were devised during the 18th and 19th centuries. These apparatuses were based on the idea of an exact correspondence between a single sound and a single color and were intended to provide an "optical translation" of a composition. More recently, the idea of a literal translation has been replaced by "general coordination" between musical and optical impressions, as in the color organ of Mrs. M. H. Greenwalt (exhibited in New York, 1921). Still further from the idea of strict sound-color analogy is the *clavilux* of T. Wilfred, which was exhibited in New York in 1922 and which, so far, has proved the most successful color organ, probably owing to the fact that it altogether renounces the coordination of sound and light and merely bestows upon optical phenomena the essential musical factors of time, rhythm, and changing combinations. It has no sound-producing apparatus and is designed only as a medium for a new art of color, in which optical phenomena (colored circles, squares, spirals, etc.) projected on a screen move rhythmically in "crescendo," "decrescendo," "accelerando," "ritardando," etc.

Among composers, Scriabin was the most outspoken protagonist of color music. In *Prometheus* (op. 60, 1910) he undertook to demonstrate the affinity, scientific and spiritual, that he believed existed between tone and color. He prescribed a special instrument for it, a "clavier à lumières" [It. *tastiera per luce*] invented by Rimington. The only recorded performance of the composition with color accompaniment took place in 1915 in Carnegie Hall, New York. For literature, see under Color and music.

Colpo d'arco [It.]. Stroke of the bow (of violins, etc.).

Combattimento di Tancredi e Clorinda, Il [It., The Duel between Tancred and Clorinda]. Opera (madrigal) in one act by Monteverdi (libretto based on Tasso's *Gerusalemme liberata*), produced in Venice, 1624. Setting: battlefield, 1099.

Combination pedal, stops. See under Organ IV.

Combination tone, resultant tone [F. *son résultant;* G. *Kombinationston;* It. *tono di combinazione;* Sp. *tono resultante*]. In musical acoustics, a tone of different pitch that is heard when two loud tones are sounded simultaneously. Its frequency is the difference (*differential tones*) or the sum (*summation tones*) of the frequencies of the two primary tones or of their multiples. For example, if the two primary tones have the frequencies 1200 and 700, the following differential tones (D) and summation tones (S) can be heard: D_1: $1200 - 700 = 500$; D_2: $2 \times 1200 - 700 = 1700$; D_3: $2 \times 700 - 1200 = 200$; S_1: $1200 + 700 = 1900$; S_2: $2 \times 1200 + 700 = 3100$; S_3: $2 \times 700 + 1200 = 2600$, etc. Although the combination tones are frequently referred to as an acoustical phenomenon, they actually are a physiological phenomenon. If the vibrations 1200 and 700 are produced, none of the vibrations 500, 1700, etc., actually exists; it is the inner ear (*cochlea*) that, owing to its "nonlinear" organization, produces the aural sensations corresponding to the greater or lesser frequencies. "Nonlinear" here means that the combination of two sounds with the intensities a and b is not a simple linear sum, a + b, but a more complicated formula, involving powers of a and b. The linear formula is valid only for small intensities; as a matter of fact, combination tones are heard only if the original tones are sufficiently loud.

The differential tones, which are more easily recognized than the summation tones, were discovered by G. Tartini in 1714 and described in his *Trattato di musica* of 1754 (an earlier description appeared in a book by G. A. Sorge, *Vorgemach der musicalischen Composition,* 1745–47). The tone known as Tartini's tone [It. *terzo suono,* "third tone"] is the first of the combination tones above, determined by the difference of the original frequencies. The accompanying table shows Tartini's tone for various intervals (c′ arbitrarily = 300).

Tartini's tone can easily be heard on the harmonium, organ, and violin. On the violin, it was recommended by Tartini and other violinists (Leopold Mozart) as a means of controlling the

correct intonation of double stops, since a slight inaccuracy results in a more recognizable change of the low-pitched differential tone. The name "beat-tones," formerly applied to differential tones, is misleading. It is derived from the theory advanced by T. Young (1773–1829) that the differential tones are quick *beats (more than 40 per second). This theory was refuted by Helmholtz, who discovered the summation tones by calculations based on the principle of "nonlinear superposition," thus paving the way for the modern theory. Modern research has shown that certain well-established musical sounds, e.g., that of the G-string of the violin, are physically nonexistent, being produced only aurally as the differential tones of their upper partials [see Tone color].

Practical application of the first differential tone is made in the *acoustic bass of organs. For literature, see under Acoustics; also E. Darmois, in *CP Masson.*

Come [It.]. As, like. *Come prima, come sopra,* as at first, as above; *come stà,* as it stands, i.e., without improvisations.

Comédie [F.]. Term occasionally used for operas in a light, slightly comical vein. For *comédie-ballet,* see under Ballet; also Entr'acte.

Comes [L.]. See *Dux, comes.*

Comic opera. I. *Definition.* General name for an opera or other dramatic work with a large admixture of music, on a light or sentimental subject, with a happy ending, and in which comic elements are present. The category thus includes a number of types, such as the operetta, vaudeville, *opéra bouffe,* musical comedy, etc., the distinctions among which are not always clearly marked. Until the middle of the 19th century comic operas (except for the Italian *opera buffa*) usually contained spoken dialogue; in more recent times this feature has tended to disappear, so that a distinction on this basis is no longer generally valid. Incidentally, it should be noted that not all operas with spoken dialogue are "comic," though in France the name *opéra comique* is traditionally applied to such works, even when they are serious or tragic,

e.g., Bizet's *Carmen.* The music of comic opera is almost always more "popular" in style than that of serious opera, generally easier both to perform and to comprehend, and appealing to less sophisticated audiences. Its function is relatively less important than in serious opera, and in some forms (e.g., musical comedy) it is usually confined to a series of "hit" songs or other musical specialties. The scenes and personages of comic opera are apt to be taken from everyday life, or if fantasy is present it is treated in a sentimental or amusing fashion. Frequently there is satire of manners, allusion to current topics, or parody of the serious opera style.

II. *History.* A. Comic scenes early made their way into serious opera, and the juxtaposition of serious and comic episodes is a general feature of 17th-century librettos. Examples may be found in S. Landi's *La Morte d'Orfeo* (1619) and *Il Sant' Alessio* (1632), in D. Mazzocchi's *La Catena d'Adone* (1626), and G. Cornachioli's *Diana schernita* (1629), all of the Roman school. L. Rossi's *L'Orfeo* (Paris, 1647) is another instance. The same practice may be observed in Monteverdi's *L'Incoronazione di Poppea* (1642), Cavalli's *Giasone* (1649), Cesti's *Il Pomo d'oro* (1666 or '67), and to an even greater degree in later Venetian works. The earliest independent comic operas are V. Mazzocchi's *Chi soffre speri* (1639) and A. Abbatini's *Dal male il bene* (1653), both in collaboration with M. Marazzoli and to librettos by Giulio Rospigliosi (later Pope Clement IX). The last-mentioned work is notable for its use of parlando recitative and for its ensemble finales, features that are prominent in the later comic-opera style. Another early example is J. Melani's *La Tancia* (Florence, 1656), which contains a parody of the famous incantation scene of Cavalli's *Giasone.* In the second half of the 17th century Venice was the center of a considerable school of comic opera that has not yet been fully studied [see H. C. Wolff, "Die venezianische Oper," in *ZMW* xvi].

B. With the abolition of comic episodes in the "reformed" opera librettos of Apostolo Zeno and Pietro Metastasio, the comic opera as a separate genre took on renewed importance. Comic opera of the 18th century shows well-defined national types. The Italian *opera buffa* began early in the century to evolve out of *in-termezzi performed between the acts of serious operas. The fully developed independent form, of which the most famous early example is Pergolesi's *La Serva padrona* (1733), retained traces of its origin in the designation "intermezzo" and in the customary division into two acts (as opposed to the three-act arrangement of the *opera seria*). The Italian buffo operas are remarkable for the liveliness and humor of their action, for the high development of comic characterization in their music, and for the use of ensemble finales. The leading composers were Logroscino, Galuppi, Pergolesi, Anfossi, P. A. Guglielmi, Piccinni, J. Haydn, Paisiello, Cimarosa, and Mozart. Toward the end of the century the Italian comic opera (like that of all other countries) tended to combine with the earlier farcical-intrigue plot some elements of the semiserious, sentimental drama; at the same time its music changed accordingly, becoming on occasion more expressive, lyric, and dignified. Examples of this later type are Piccinni's *La Buona Figliuola* (1760, libretto by Goldoni), Paisiello's *Nina* (1789), Mozart's *Le Nozze di Figaro* (1786), and Cimarosa's *Il Matrimonio segreto* (1792).

C. The French *opéra comique*, beginning before 1715 with popular farces and satires that mingled spoken dialogue with songs to familiar airs (*vaudevilles*), was given a new direction by the example of the Italian buffo opera [see War of the Buffoons] and developed a type known as *comédie mêlée d'ariettes*, i.e., a spoken "comedy mingled with [newly composed] songs," of which the chief composers were J.-J. Rousseau (*Le Devin du village*, 1752), Gluck (*La Rencontre imprévue*, Vienna, 1764), F.-A. Philidor (*Tom Jones*, 1765), Monsigny (*Le Déserteur*, 1769), and Grétry (*Zémire et Azor*, 1771; *Richard Cœur-de-Lion*, 1784). The romantic quality of the librettos of many of these works and the frequent comment on political and social problems show the influence of Rousseau and the Encyclopedists.

D. The typical English 18th-century form was the *ballad opera, which was succeeded by similar works using original music by such composers as Thomas Arne (*Love in a Village*, 1762), Charles Dibdin (*The Waterman*, 1774), William Shield (*Rosina*, 1782), and Stephen Storace (*The Haunted Tower*, 1789). With respect to subject matter and treatment, the course of English comic opera in this period parallels the French *opéra comique*.

The corresponding form for this period in Spain is the *tonadilla* [see also *Zarzuela; Sainete*].

E. In Germany the *Singspiel was cultivated at Leipzig by J. A. Hiller, using for the most part plays adapted from French *opéras comiques* by C. F. Weisse (*Die Jagd*, 1770, from Monsigny's

Le Roi et le fermier). Other North German composers were Georg Benda (*Der Dorfjahrmarkt*, 1775; in *DdT* 64), C. Neefe, and J. André. In Vienna a different type of Singspiel, strongly influenced by the Italian buffo style, developed. The chief composers were I. Umlauf (*Die Bergknappen*, 1778; in *DTO* 36), Mozart (*Die Entführung aus dem Serail*, 1782), Dittersdorf (*Doktor und Apotheker*, 1786), and J. Schenk (*Der Dorfbarbier*, 1796; in *DTO* 66).

F. In the 19th century comic opera lost some of its earlier distinctive character, approaching on the one hand the style, form, and subject matter of serious opera or on the other hand tending toward the light, purely "entertainment" types, such as *vaudeville, *operetta, *zarzuela, etc. In Italy the *opera buffa* was continued by Simon Mayr, F. Paër, Rossini, and Donizetti. The French *opéra comique* is represented by Boieldieu (*La Dame blanche*, 1825), Auber (*Fra Diavolo*, 1830), L. J. F. Herold (*Le Pré aux clercs*, 1832), Adam (*Le Postillon de Longjumeau*, 1836), and Victor Massé (*Les Noces de Jeannette*, 1853). A special type of comic opera is represented by the *opéras bouffes* of Offenbach (*Orphée aux enfers*, 1858, rev. 1874; *La Belle Hélène*, 1864; *La Vie parisienne*, 1866). English comic operas were composed by Sir Henry R. Bishop (works of 1804–40), but the best English works in the comic vein are those of W. S. Gilbert and Arthur Sullivan (*H.M.S. Pinafore*, 1878; *Iolanthe*, 1882; *The Mikado*, 1885). The best-known German comic operas of this period (known as *Spieloper*) are K. Kreutzer's *Das Nachtlager von Granada* (1834), Lortzing's *Czaar und Zimmermann* (1837) and *Der Wildschütz* (1842), O. Nicolai's *Die lustigen Weiber von Windsor* (1849), Flotow's *Martha* (1847), and P. Cornelius' *Der Barbier von Bagdad* (1858). Similar to these is H. Berlioz's *Béatrice et Bénédict* (1862). One of the most popular comic operas of the 19th century was Smetana's *The Bartered Bride* (1866). The Viennese operetta of the late 19th and early 20th centuries (J. Strauss the younger, *Die Fledermaus*, 1874, *Zigeunerbaron*, 1885; F. Lehár, *Die lustige Witwe*, 1905) inspired imitation in many countries.

Since the middle of the 19th century, comic opera of various sorts has been cultivated in all countries, chiefly by composers not distinguished in any other field. These works are very numerous but for the most part ephemeral. A few comic operas of lasting merit and on a large scale have been produced, of which three deserve particular mention: Wagner's *Meister-*

singer von Nürnberg (1868), Verdi's *Falstaff* (1893), and R. Strauss' *Rosenkavalier* (1911). An extremely clever and witty *opéra bouffe* is Poulenc's *Les Mamelles de Tirésias* (1947). Notable examples of modern comic opera in England include Holst's one-act *The Perfect Fool* (1923) and Vaughan Williams' *Sir John in Love* (1929).

Lit.: M. Cooper, *Opéra comique* (1949); A. della Corte, *L'Opera comica italiana nel 1700*, 2 vols. (1923); M. Scherillo, *L'Opera buffa napoletana durante il settecento*, rev. ed. [1917]; G. Cucuel, *Les Créateurs de l'opéra-comique français* (1914); G. Bonnet, *Philidor et l'évolution de la musique française au XVIIIe siècle* (1921); E. M. Gagey, *Ballad Opera* (1937); A. Williamson, *Gilbert & Sullivan Opera: A New Assessment* (1953); K. Lüthge, *Die deutsche Spieloper* (1924); G. Calmus, *Die ersten deutschen Singspiele von Standfuss und Hiller* (1908); J. Subirá, *La Tonadilla escénica*, 3 vols. (1928–30); R.-A. Mooser, *L'Opéra-comique français en Russie au XVIIIe siècle*, rev. ed., 2 vols. (1954); D. J. Grout, "The Origins of the Opéra-comique" (diss. Harvard Univ., 1939); R. L. Weaver, "Florentine Comic Operas of Seventeenth Century" (diss. Univ. of North Carolina, 1958); R. Vené, "The Origin of *Opera buffa*" (*MQ* xxi); N. D'Arienzo, "Le Origini dell' Opera comica" (*RMI* ii, iv, vi, vii); E. J. Dent, "Ensembles and Finales in 18th Century Italian Opera" (*SIM* xi, xii); F. Vatielli, "Le Opere comiche di G. B. Martini" (*RMI* xl); M. Cauchie, "The Highlights of French Opéra-Comique" (*MQ* xxv); *L'Opéra-comique au xixe siècle* (*RM* 1933, no. 140); L. Holzer, "Die komischen Opern Glucks" (*StM* xiii); H. Abert, "Paisiello's Buffokunst und ihre Beziehungen zu Mozart" (*AMW* i).   D.J.G.

Comma, schisma. Terms for minute differences in pitch that occur in the calculation of intervals if the same note is obtained through different combinations of octaves, perfect fifths, and pure major thirds. The *ditonic* (or *Pythagorean*) comma is the difference between twelve perfect fifths and seven octaves. Thus the *circle of fifths, if based on pure fifths, becomes a "spiral" of fifths. The *syntonic* (or *Didymic*) comma (named for Didymus, a Greek theorist, b. 65 B.C.) is the difference between four perfect fifths (C–G–d–a–e') and two octaves plus a major third (C–c–c'–e'). The *schisma* is the difference between eight perfect fifths plus one major third (C–g–d–a–e'–b'–f♯''–c♯'''–g♯''''–b♯''') and five octaves (C–c–c'–c''–c'''–c''''). The *diaschisma*

is the difference between three octaves (C–c–c'–c'') and four perfect fifths plus two major thirds (C–G–d–a–e'–g♯'–b♯'). The following table shows these differences expressed in various ways (*F* = fifth; *O* = octave; *T* = third; see Intervals, calculations of, II).

Ditonic comma 12 *F* − 7 *O*

$$= \left(\frac{3}{2}\right)^{12} \times \left(\frac{1}{2}\right)^{7} = \frac{3^{12}}{2^{19}} = \frac{531441}{524288}$$
$$= 23.5 \text{ cents}$$

Syntonic comma 4 *F* − 1 *T* − 2 *O*

$$= \left(\frac{3}{2}\right)^{4} \times \frac{4}{5} \times \left(\frac{1}{2}\right)^{2} = \frac{3^{4}}{2^{4} \times 5} = \frac{81}{80}$$
$$= 21.5 \text{ cents}$$

Diaschisma 3 *O* − 4 *F* − 2 *T*

$$= 2^{3} \times \left(\frac{2}{3}\right)^{4} \times \left(\frac{4}{5}\right)^{2} = \frac{2^{11}}{3^{4} \times 5^{2}} = \frac{2048}{2025}$$
$$= 20 \text{ cents}$$

Schisma 8 *F* + 1 *T* − 5 *O*

$$= \left(\frac{3}{2}\right)^{8} \times \frac{5}{4} \times \left(\frac{1}{2}\right)^{5} = \frac{3^{8} \times 5}{2^{15}} = \frac{32805}{32768}$$
$$= 2 \text{ cents}$$

The first three microintervals have approximately the value of one-fourth of a semitone (25 cents). A difference of six cents is discernible to very sensitive ears.

The ditonic comma is also the difference between the two semitones of the *Pythagorean scale, and the syntonic comma that between the two whole tones of *just intonation. The schisma is also the difference between the ditonic and syntonic comma, as well as that between the syntonic comma and diaschisma:

$$\frac{3^{12}}{2^{19}} \times \frac{5 \times 2^{4}}{3^{4}} = \frac{3^{8} \times 5}{2^{15}};$$

$$\frac{3^{4}}{2^{4} \times 5} \times \frac{3^{4} \times 5^{2}}{2^{11}} = \frac{3^{8} \times 5}{2^{15}}$$

The diaschisma is explained by medieval theorists (Boethius, Tinctoris), as one-half of the *semitonium minus* (*diesis*) of the Pythagorean scale. The schisma nearly equals the difference between the Pythagorean fifth (3⁄2 = 702 cents) and the fifth of equal temperament (700 cents). This difference is therefore also called schisma.

Commedia dell' arte [It.]. A type of comical stage presentation that developed in Italy about 1500. It had no music, but its traditional characters— the rich Venetian merchant, his unfaithful wife, the unscrupulous lawyer, the Bolognese doctor, the comic servant, etc.—have often been introduced into musical comedies, from O. Vecchi's *L'Amfiparnaso* (1597) and G. Pergolesi's *La Serva padrona* (1733) to Mozart's *Le Nozze di Figaro* (1786) and Stravinsky's *Pulcinella* (ballet, 1920). See W. Smith, *The Commedia Dell'Arte* (1964); N. Pirrotta, "Commedia dell'Arte and Opera" (*MQ* xli).

Commiato [It.]. See under Envoi.

Commixtio [L.]. See under Church modes III.

Common chord. Name for the major triad.

Common meter. See under Poetic meter II.

Common of the Mass. Term sometimes used instead of Ordinary of the Mass [see Ordinary and Proper].

Common of Saints [L. *Commune Sanctorum*]. See under Gregorian chant I.

Common time. Name for 4/4 meter.

Commune sanctorum [L.]. See under Gregorian chant I.

Communion [L. *communio*]. In the Roman Catholic service, the last of the five items of the Proper of the Mass, sung after (originally during) the distribution of the Host. Originally it was an antiphon with the psalm verse *Gustate et videte* (*Taste ye and see*) from Psalm 33 (32) or with other psalm verses [see Antiphon (3)]. However, these verses disappeared in the 12th century so that only an antiphon (*antiphona ad communionem*) remained. The Communion antiphons are moderately melismatic melodies (although many are neumatic), sung chorally with a soloistic *incipit*. They are particularly interesting from the point of view of Gregorian tonality [see *ApGC*, pp. 140ff]. In the Anglican rite, Communion often means the entire Mass. See Mass D.

Community music schools. Evolved during the late 19th century in the United States, these schools offer individual instrumental and vocal instruction to all ages. As either independent, nonprofit organizations or as Settlement departments these schools have placed the study of music within the reach of all. The National Guild of Community Music Schools was organized in 1937 to coordinate these schools across the country.

Comodo [It.]. Comfortable, easy.

Comparative musicology [G. *Vergleichende Musikwissenschaft*]. See under Ethnomusicology.

Compass. The range of notes obtainable from an instrument or voice.

Complement. The difference between the octave and any interval, therefore identical with inverted interval [see Inversion (1)]. For instance, the complement of the fifth is the fourth, and that of the sixth, the third.

Completorium [L.]. In Roman Catholic liturgy, Compline [see Office]. In the Milanese rites, a chant sung at Vespers [see Ambrosian chant].

Compline. See under Office.

Composition. I. The process of creating musical works; also, a musical work. Literally meaning "putting together," the term is particularly suitable for early polyphonic music, in which various voice-parts are indeed put together. In the more complex music of later periods, this meaning is less obvious, yet an opera by Wagner or a symphony by Tchaikovsky involves the "putting together" of numerous diversified elements just as much as voice-parts were "put together" in early music. Moreover, the term is highly appropriate for the twelve-tone technique and even more for more recent methods of creating music by putting together assorted sounds on a recording tape [*electronic music, *serial music].

It is well-nigh impossible to make general statements that would be valid for the whole field of musical creation. The composition of a Gregorian Tract or of a troubadour song has as little in common with that of a B-minor Mass as has Schumann's writing the *Kreisleriana* with Messiaen's *Mode de valeurs et d'intensités*. Only with reference to a given period is it possible to indicate to some degree what elements enter into the creative process. Thus, a symphony by Beethoven may be said to result from the coordination of traditional ingredients, such as tonality, harmony, rhythm, orchestration, and form, with others of a highly original and personal character, notably the gifts of melodic invention and dramatic development.

II. The term *componere* was used first in connection with the writing of melodies. Guido's "Micrologus" of *c.* 1030 includes a chapter, "De commoda vel componenda modulatione" (About the Appropriate Composition of a Melody), in which he points out certain principles (similarity, contrast, symmetry) that should be observed when small particles (neumes) are put together into a coherent whole. Johannes de Grocheo (*c.* 1290) was perhaps the first to apply the term to polyphonic music. He calls a two- or three-part piece *musica composita* and its author *compositor*. Writers of the 14th and 15th centuries emphasized the difference between written composition and improvised singing. Thus, Tinctoris in his "Liber de arte contrapuncti" (1477) speaks of "sive componere sive super librum canere" [see *Discantus supra librum*]. His definition, "compositor est alicuius novi cantus editor," is the first indication that originality was recognized as an essential attribute of a composer. Nicolaus Wollick (*Opus aureum,* 1501) again emphasized the contrast between *compositio* and **sortisatio.*

In subsequent centuries there appeared numerous books about composition. A few of these are mentioned here in order to illustrate the various elements that enter into the process in increasing number and diversity. D. Ortiz, in his *Trattado de glosas* (1553), deals with the art of diminution (figuration) for voices and instruments. G. Coperario's "Rules how to compose" (*c.* 1610) provide instruction in counterpoint, as does J. Fux's *Gradus ad Parnassum* (1725). A. Agazzari's *Del sonare sopra il basso con tutti li stromenti* (1607) is the first of a long series of treatises on thoroughbass. With J. Rameau's *Traité de l'harmonie* (1722) the harmonic aspect of music becomes the center of attention. Berlioz in his *Grand Traité d'instrumentation* (1844) laid the foundation for the art of orchestration. With D'Indy's *Cours de composition musicale,* 4 vols. (1903–50), we arrive at the first attempt to treat the subject from a historical point of view, beginning with Gregorian chant and closing with the forms and styles of late romanticism. To the present day, D'Indy's work has remained unique. Among the books dealing with 20th-century methods of composition, two written by eminent composers may be singled out: P. Hindemith's *The Craft of Musical Composition,* 2 vols. [1942] and E. Krenek's *Studies in Counterpoint Based on the Twelve-Tone Technique* [1941].

Composition pedals, stops. See under Organ IV.

Compostela, school of. A mid-12th-century school housed in the monastery of Santiago (St. James) at Compostela in the Pyrenees. A number of compositions, monophonic and polyphonic, for the Office of St. James are preserved in the Codex Calixtinus [see Sources, no. 2] The polyphonic style of this school is closely related to that of *St. Martial. Examples in *HAM,* nos. 27b, 28b. See Conductus; Organum (2) III.

Compound binary form. Name for *sonata form. It expresses the fact that the sonata form is originally and historically a binary form but of large dimensions and composite structure. See also Binary and ternary form.

Compound interval. See under Interval.

Compound meter, time. See under Meter.

Compound stop. Same as mixture stop. See Organ VI, IX (f).

Computer, musical applications of. The use of digital computers and other electronic data-processing devices for musicologic purposes began about 1948, notably in the folksong research of Bertrand Bronson. Computers have made significant contributions to music and musical research in at least five areas: (1) information retrieval, using input languages developed by Brook and Gould, Logemann, Kassler and Regener, Bauer-Mengelberg, and others, with applications such as H. Lincoln's thematic index of 16th-century Italian music, L. Bernstein's index of 16th-century chansons, K. Levy's comparative studies of Byzantine notation, and J. LaRue's concerto and symphony indexes; (2) *style analysis, such as L. Lockwood's study of Josquin's Masses, A. Forte's analysis of atonal structures, J. LaRue's studies on the formation of tonality and criteria for articulation, G. Mc-Peek's classification of 15th-century chansons, S. Jay's harmonic analysis of Mozart and Beethoven, G. Lefkoff's systematic analysis, and R. Jackson's harmonic analysis; (3) composition, as in Hiller and Isaacson's *Illiac Suite* (1956); (4) sound generation, as in the Bell Laboratories' Music IV system; and (5) acoustic analysis. New York University has undertaken a comprehensive project to develop a collection of programs and routines of general utility, including translators for a variety of input languages, event compilers, correlation of paired distributions, and specialized display formats. [Also see under Electronic music.]

An important development is the digital electronic computer, which by-passes the special electronic oscillators and wave-shaping circuits of the RCA instrument [see Synthesizer] and synthesizes musical sounds directly from mathematical functions supplied to the computer by the composer. The output of the computer is simply stored on magnetic tape and played back like an ordinary sound recording. The inherent versatility and precision of this method presents virtually unlimited possibilities.

Lit.: L. A. Hiller, Jr., and L. M. Isaacson, *Experimental Music; Composition with an Electronic Computer* (1959); B. Bronson, "Mechanical Help in the Study of Folk Song" (*Journal of American Folklore* lxii, 81–6); L. Meyer, "Meaning in Music and Information Theory" (*Journal of Aesthetics and Art Criticism* xv, 412–24); J. Cohen, "Information Theory and Music" (*Behavioral Science* vii); A. Forte, "A Theory of Set-Complexes for Music" (*Journal of Music Theory* viii); M. Babbitt, "Twelve-Tone Invariants as Compositional Determinants" (*MQ* xlvi, 246–59); L. A. Hiller, Jr. and R. A. Baker, "Automated Music Printing" (*Journal of Music Theory* ix); S. Bauer-Mengelberg and M. Ferentz, "On Eleven-Interval Twelve-Tone Rows" (*Perspectives of New Music* iii); J. C. Tenney, "Sound-Generation by means of a Digital Computer" (*Journal of Music Theory* vii); M. V. Mathews, "An Acoustic Compiler for Music and Psychological Stimuli" (*Bell Telephone System Technical Journal* xl); L. Bernstein, "Data Processing and the Thematic Index" (*Fontes Artis Musicae* xi); B. Brook and M. Gould, "Notating Music with Ordinary Typewriter Characters (A Plaine and Easie Code)" (*Fontes Artis Musicae* xi); M. Gould and G. Logemann, "Computer Input Languages for Music" (*Perspectives of New Music* iv); J. K. Randall, "A Report from Princeton" (*Perspectives of New Music* iii); J. LaRue, "Music and Computers" (*MQ* lii). For additional Lit. see Electronic instruments.

J.LaR.

Con [It.]. With; e.g., *con brio,* with vigor; *con moto,* with motion; *con ottava* (*con 8va*), with the higher octave; *con alcuna licenza,* with some license, specifically regarding tempo.

Con amore. See *Amorevole.*

Con ardore. See *Ardore.*

Con brio. See *Brio.*

Con calore. See *Calore.*

Concentus. See *Accentus, concentus.*

Concert. I. A public performance of music, especially one involving a group of musicians (a performance given by a soloist is called a recital). Concerts are a fairly recent institution. Through the end of the 17th century, musical performances took place in churches, in the homes of princes or wealthy persons who could afford a private orchestra, or in closed circles, such as *academies or *collegia musica.* Actually, the church was the only place where the common people could hear well-prepared performances of good music. The first step toward public performance was taken with the foundation of the Teatro San Cassiano in Venice in 1637 [see Opera houses]. The first concerts (nonoperatic) open to the public were organized by John Banister, a London violinist, in 1672. They continued for six years, with a daily afternoon program. They were followed, in 1678, by a long series of concerts arranged by a London coal merchant, T. Britton, which took place in a loft over his coal-house, continuing weekly for thirty-six years. Later came the Concerts of Ancient Music (1776–1848; after 1785 called "King's Concerts"), which were largely devoted to the works of Handel; the Salomon Concerts (1791–95), for which Haydn wrote his famous twelve symphonies (London Symphonies); and the Crystal Palace Concerts (1855–1901), conducted by August Manns every Saturday afternoon in the winter season.

II. In France, public concerts began with the foundation, by A. Philidor, of a series of concerts called *Concert spirituel,* which continued from 1725 until the French Revolution (1789). They took place only around Easter and were largely devoted to sacred music. They became the model for similar institutions in Leipzig, Berlin, Vienna, and Stockholm. Although revived in 1805, the *Concert spirituel* became less important with the establishment of the *Concerts du Conservatoire.* which were started by F.-A. Habeneck in 1828 and which still continue. These concerts greatly enhanced the 19th-century development of orchestral music and contributed much to the growing interest in the music of Beethoven, Berlioz, Schubert, *et al.* A more popular enterprise and of international fame are the *Concerts populaires,* conducted by J. Pasdeloup from 1861 till 1884 and revived in 1920, under the name *Concerts Pasdeloup,* by Rhené-Baton and A. Caplet.

III. The earliest German concert institutions are the *Gewandhaus Konzerte* of Leipzig, which started in 1781 under J. A. Hiller as a continuation of his *Liebhaberkonzerte* (1763–78) and other enterprises of passing importance. Until 1884 they took place in the *Alte Gewandhaus* (Old Cloth Hall), which was replaced in that year by a new concert hall, the *Neue Gewandhaus.* Famous conductors there were Mendelssohn (1835–43), under whom the concerts first attained international recognition, Arthur Nikisch, Wilhelm Furtwängler, and Bruno Walter.

For the development of concerts in America, see under United States. Also see Orchestras.

Lit.: K. Meyer, *Das Konzert* [1925]; G. Pinthus, *Die Entwicklung des Konzertwesens in Deutschland bis zum Beginn des 19. Jahrhunderts* (1932); E. Hanslick, *Geschichte des Concertwesens in Wien,* 2 vols. (1869, '70); A. Dörffel, *Geschichte der Gewandhauskonzerte* (1884); G. Dandelot, *Les Concerts du Conservatoire* (1897); M. Brenet, *Les Concerts en France sous l'ancien régime* (1900); A. Elwart, *Histoire de la Société des concerts du Conservatoire impérial de musique* (1860); id., *Histoire des concerts populaires de musique classique* (1864); E. Deldevez, *La Société des concerts, 1860 à 1885 (Conservatoire national de musique)* (1887); M. Tilmouth, "Some Early London Concerts and Music Clubs" (*PMA* lxxxiv).

Concertant [F.], **concertante** [It.]. An 18th-century name for symphonies (*symphonie concertante, sinfonia concertante*) with parts for one or more solo instruments, after the model of the earlier *concerto grosso but in the style and form of the Mannheim school. Such works were written by C. Cannabich, K. Stamitz, Haydn, and Mozart. See also B. Brook, *La Symphonie française dans la seconde moitié du XVIIIe siècle,* 3 vols. (1962), ii, pt. 2.

Concertante. See under Concerto III.

Concertato [It.]. A term used occasionally in the early 17th century in connection with various manifestations of the novel principle of "contrast" or "rivalry," e.g. in T. Merula's *Canzoni, overo sonate concertate* (1637). In 17th-century vocal works, *coro concertato* means a small body of singers, in contrast to the full chorus, the *coro ripieno* or the *cappella.* The term has been recommended as a generic designation for the numerous and varied forerunners of the true concerto [see *BuMBE,* p. 20 and *passim*].

Concertgebouw. See under Orchestras III.

Concert grand. The largest size of piano, built for concert performance. See Piano.

Concert halls. For the acoustical properties of concert halls, see bibl. under Architectural acoustics. See also *LavE* ii.6, 3860.

Concertina. See under Accordion.

Concertino. (1) In baroque music, the soloist group of the *concerto grosso. (2) A composition of the 19th–20th centuries in the style of a con-

certo but in free form, usually in a single movement with sections of varying speed and character. A German name for this type is *Konzertstück.* Examples are Weber, Concertino for Clarinet op. 26; Schumann, Introduction and Allegro appassionato op. 92 (piano and orchestra). Others are by Anton Rubinstein (piano, op. 113), Bruch (violin, op. 84), John Carpenter (piano, 1917), E. von Dohnányi (cello, op. 12), Leo Janáček (piano and chamber orchestra), Jean Françaix (piano, 1932), and W. Piston (piano and chamber orchestra, 1937).

Concertmaster [F. chef *d'attaque;* G. *Konzertmeister;* It. *violino primo;* Sp. *concertino*]. The first violinist of an orchestra. He is entrusted with violin solo passages, represents the orchestra in negotiations with the management and the conductor, and occasionally substitutes for the latter.

Concerto [F., It.; G. *Konzert;* Sp. *concierto, concerto*]. I. *General.* A concerto is a composition for orchestra and a solo instrument (most often piano or violin), formerly also for orchestra and a small group of solo instruments [see *Concerto grosso*]. An essential trait of the concerto is that the soloist(s) and the orchestra are not in a master-servant relationship (as in the case of orchestral accompaniment) but compete on equal terms. This meaning is implied by the name itself, which is usually thought to be derived from L. *concertare,* "to fight," "to contend." Recently another derivation has been suggested, from L. *conserere,* "to join together," "to unite" [see F. Giegling, in *CP 1949,* p. 129], mainly because the spelling *conserto* occasionally has been found (A. Agazzari, 1607 and 1613).

The development of the concerto from Mozart to the present day generally follows that of the *sonata, from which it borrowed its chief features of form and style. There are, however, the following differences: (a) the concerto practically always has only three movements, the scherzo being omitted (Brahms' Piano Concerto op. 83 is one of the few exceptions); (b) the first movement is written in a modified *sonata form in which the exposition, instead of being repeated in full, is written out twice, first in a preliminary and abbreviated form with the tonic as the main key throughout and for the orchestra only, then in its full form for the soloist and orchestra and with the proper modulation into the dominant, a form known as *concerto-sonata form;* (c) the last movement is usually in *rondo form, whose light character lends itself well to displays of brilliance and to a "happy ending"; (d) a soloist *cadenza appears regularly in the first movement, usually near the end of the re-capitulation but sometimes, less elaborately, in the other movements as well.

The solo part of a concerto is always written in a highly virtuoso style designed to show the equality, if not superiority, of the single player over the entire orchestra. Concertos are classified according to the solo instrument, as piano (violin, cello, etc.) concertos. A concerto in a free one-movement form is called a *concertino [G. *Konzertstück*].

II. *The present repertory.* The present-day repertory of the piano concerto begins with the latest concertos by Mozart, composed between 1785 and 1791 (K. 466 in D minor; K. 467 in C major; K. 482 in E-flat major; K. 488 in A major; K. 491 in C minor; K. 503 in C major; K 537 in D major (*Coronation Concerto); K. 595 in B-flat major). In these compositions Mozart established the classical form and style of the concerto. Beethoven's five piano concertos, especially the last two, in G major (op. 58, 1805–06) and in E-flat major (*Emperor Concerto, op. 73, 1809), represent the artistic high point of the literature. There followed Weber (op. 11, 1810; op. 32, 1812; *Konzertstück* op. 79, 1821), Mendelssohn (op. 25, 1831; op. 40, 1837), Chopin (op. 11, op. 21, both *c.* 1830), and Schumann with his beautiful Concerto in A minor (op. 54, 1841–45). Chopin's concertos suffer from an inferior treatment of the orchestra. Liszt's two concertos, in E-flat major (1849) and A major (1849–57), show a tendency toward technical display for its own sake that continues, particularly in the concertos of Russian composers such as Anton Rubinstein (five concertos, notably op. 70 in D minor and op. 94 in E-flat), Tchaikovsky (B-flat minor op. 23, 1875; G major op. 44, 1880; E-flat major op. 75, 1893), Rimsky-Korsakov (C-sharp minor, 1882–83), and many others. A conspicuous feature of the Russian concertos is the prevalence of octave-playing over other devices of piano technique. Grieg contributed an effective and very popular concerto in A minor (op. 16, 1868). A new peak of artistic perfection was reached by Brahms in his piano concertos in D minor (op. 15, 1854) and B-flat major (op. 83, 1878–81). There followed concertos by Franck (*Variations symphoniques,* 1885); MacDowell (D minor op. 23, 1884–85); Scriabin (F-sharp minor op. 20, 1898); Rachmaninoff (F-sharp minor op. 1, 1890–91,

rev. 1917; C minor op. 18, 1901, rev. 1942; D minor op. 30, 1909; G minor op. 40, 1927, rev. 1942); Reger (F minor op. 114, 1910); Prokofiev (D-flat major op. 10, 1911; G minor op. 16, 1912–13, rev. 1923; C major op. 26, 1917–21; B major op. 53, 1931, for the left hand alone; G major op. 55, 1932); Ravel (G major, 1930; D major, 1930, for the left hand alone); Bartók (1926, 1930–31, 1945); Stravinsky (for piano and wind instruments, 1922–24, rev. 1950); Hindemith (op. 36, one for piano and twelve solo instruments); Copland (1925); and Vaughan Williams (1926–30). Some of the 20th-century *neoclassical works approach the idiom of the baroque *concerto grosso* [see below for concertos for orchestra].

The repertory of violin concertos is somewhat smaller and, on the whole, less significant. It includes works by J. S. Bach (3, 1 for two violins), Haydn (9), Viotti (29), Mozart (7), Kreutzer (19, 2 for two violins), Beethoven (1), Paganini (4), Spohr (15), Mendelssohn (1), Schumann (1, recently discovered), Gade (1), Brahms (1), Wieniawski (2), Saint-Saëns (3), Bruch (3), Tchaikovsky (1), Dvořák (1), Elgar (1), Delius (1), R. Strauss (1), Glazunov (2), Sibelius (1), Pfitzner (1 for two violins), Reger (1), Schoenberg (1), Holst (1 for two violins), Respighi (1), Bloch (1), Bartók (2), Stravinsky (1), Syzmanowski (2), Casella (1), Bax (1), Berg (1), Prokofiev (2), Milhaud (3), Piston (2), Hindemith (1), Krenek (1), Walton (1), Khatchaturian (1), Shostakovitch (1), Barber (1), Menotti (1), and Britten (1).

Several modern composers have written compositions under the seemingly self-contradictory title "concerto for orchestra," i.e., without a solo instrument. This was an attempt by the neoclassicists of the 1920's to revive the baroque *concerto grosso,* in which the soloist role is much less important than in the modern concerto. These concertos resemble the old form in their use of a chamber orchestra, emphasis on "motoric" rather than emotional impulse, and linear design rather than massed sound or orchestral effects (Stravinsky, *Concerto en mi^b,* 1937–38). Some of them introduce the baroque *concertino,* i.e., a group of three or two solo instruments alternating with the full ensemble, e.g., H. Kaminski, *Concerto grosso* (1922); E. Bloch, *Concerto grosso* no. 1 (1924–25), no. 2 (1953); E. Krenek, *Concerto grosso* (2; 1921, '24); P. Hindemith, *Konzert für Orchester* op. 38 (1925); W. Piston, Concerto for orchestra (1933); B. Bartók, Concerto for Orchestra (1943);

S. Barber, *Capricorn Concerto* op. 21 (1944).

III. *History.* The term "concerto" was first used for vocal compositions supported by an instrumental (or organ) accompaniment, in order to distinguish such pieces from the then current style of unaccompanied *a capella* music. To this category belong the *Concerti ecclesiastici* (church concertos) of Andrea and Giovanni Gabrieli (1587; see *HAM,* no. 157) and Adriano Banchieri (1595), both for double chorus, as well as those by Ludovico Viadana (1602; see *HAM,* no. 185; *SchGMB,* no. 168) and Hortensio Naldi (1607; see *RiHM* ii.2, 313f), both for solo parts in the then novel monodic style. The use of the name "concerto" for accompanied vocal music persisted throughout the baroque period, e.g., in Schütz's *Kleine Geistliche Concerte* of 1636 and several cantatas by Bach that he called "Concerto."

In purely instrumental music the term came to mean contrasting performing bodies playing in alternation. This style, which some 17th-century writers called *stile moderno,* is one of the most typical traits of baroque music. On the basis of the definition above, the history of the concerto prior to Mozart can be divided into three periods: 1620–70; 1670–1750; 1750–80. It should be noted that, particularly in the first period, the presence or absence of the names *concerto* or *concertante* is not decisive, since various names, such as *canzona, sonata,* and *sinfonia,* were used without clear distinction for a variety of styles and types.

(*a*) *1620–70.* While Viadana's *Sinfonie musicali a otto voci* (1610) represents the instrumental application of G. Gabrieli's double-chorus style, the *Sonate concertate in stilo moderno* by D. Castello (1621, '29) mark the beginning of an important literature, that of the *canzona (a one-movement piece with a number of short sections of contrasting character) with solo passages, mostly for the violin. [For a slightly earlier example by Usper (Francesco Spongia), see A. Einstein, in *CP Kretzschmar.*] This *concerto canzona,* as it might be called, was further cultivated by G. B. Fontana (d. 1630; *Sonate a 1.2.3 per il Violino, o Cornetto,* 1641), T. Merula (*Canzoni, overo sonate concertate per chiesa, e camera,* 1637; also *Il quarto libro delle canzoni da suonare,* 1651), M. Neri (*Sonate et canzone a quatro,* 1644; *Sonate da sonarsi con varij stromenti,* 1651; see *RiHM* ii.2, 150ff; also J. Wasielewski, *Instrumentalsätze*), V. Albrici (*Sinfonia à 6,* 1654), and A. Bertali (MS sonatas, 1663).

(*b*) *1670–1750.* In this period the baroque concerto reached its peak. The main advance over the previous period is the replacement of the sectional canzona structure by a form in three or four different movements, and the adoption of a fuller, more homophonic style, with increasing melodic emphasis on the upper parts. Within the extensive literature of this period three types can be distinguished (according to A. Schering): the *concerto-sinfonia,* the *concerto grosso,* and the *solo concerto.* The first category, which is of passing importance, uses contrasting technique (sections in tutti character and others in a more brilliant style) rather than contrasting instrumental bodies. It preceded the other two and is important chiefly because it contributed to the development of a virtuoso violin style. It was cultivated first by the members of the *Bologna school, including Cazzati, G. M. Bononcini, Aldrovandini, and Torelli, and later by Albicastro (*Concerti, c.* 1703) and E. Dall'Abaco (*Concerti a quattro da chiesa, c.* 1712–14).

Closer to the mainstream of the concerto's development is the *concerto grosso,* which must be considered the classical type of baroque concerto. It is characterized by the use of a small group of solo players (*concertino*) in contrast to the full orchestra (*concerto*) [see *Concerto grosso*].

The solo concerto, i.e., the concerto for a single soloist and orchestra, is the latest of the three types. Although solo technique was extensively used in the concerto-canzonas, the first examples of this style applied to the baroque sonata are in the *Concerti a cinque* op. 2 (1700?) by Tomaso Albinoni. His concertos (also in his op. 5, 7, 9) are usually in three movements and contain short solo passages, mostly in the character of figural passage-work. Important progress was made by the great master Giuseppe Torelli (d. 1709), who holds a central position in the development of all the types of baroque concerto. In his op. 6 (*Concerti musicali a 4,* 1698) and still more in op. 8 (*Concerti grossi,* 1709; see *HAM,* no. 246; *SchGMB,* no. 257), the solo violin is of equal importance with the orchestra. He also established the standard form of the concerto, in three movements, allegro–adagio–allegro, with the first movement in *ritornello form. Torelli's idea was continued by Alessandro Scarlatti (1659–1725; see *HAM,* no. 260) and particularly by Vivaldi (*c.* 1680–1743), whose numerous violin concertos (*Estro armonico* op. 3, 4, 6, 7) soon became famous owing to the expanded role of the solo instrument and a new style of rhythmic vitality and precision.

Vivaldi's soon became the model of concerto style [see *HAM,* no. 270]. Bach (together with J. G. Walther) transcribed a number of Vivaldi's concertos for the organ (or harpsichord) alone, and Bach also made, in his famous Italian Concerto (1735), an original contribution to the somewhat self-contradictory type of concerto for a single player who in turn represents first the orchestra and then the soloist. It should be noted that pieces such as the introduction to his English Suites nos. 3 and 5 are also "Italian concertos" or at least first movements thereof.

Bach also wrote the first concertos for harpsichord and orchestra, starting with transcriptions of violin concertos (by himself, Vivaldi, and others). Of his 18 concertos for one to four harpsichords (with orchestra), only the one in C major for two harpsichords and the two for three harpsichords are original compositions. Handel's 18 organ concertos (pub. 1738, '40, '60) belong to the last examples of the baroque solo concerto. Here, as in his harpsichord suites, he mixed sonata movements with dancelike ones (minuet, musette, siciliano). In Italy the violin concerto remained the favored type, and violinists such as F. M. Veracini (1690–c. 1750), C. Tessarini (1690–c. 1765), P. Locatelli (1695–1764), and Tartini (1692–1770) gradually moved away from the true baroque style of the Vivaldi concerto toward a new type, characterized by more melodious though frequently sentimental themes, a clearly homophonic structure, and forms foreshadowing the classical concerto.

(c) *1750–80.* In this period of transition from the baroque concerto to the classical concerto the initiative was taken by German composers, mainly two sons of J. S. Bach's. K. P. E. Bach's concertos follow in their first movements a scheme that clearly shows three sections, exposition–development–recapitulation, with the exposition played twice, first by the orchestra, then by the soloist, and the recapitulation being shortened. While his exposition still lacks a second theme, this is generally found in the concertos of Johann Christian Bach (1735–82), which, more than any others, are the true predecessors of Mozart's piano concertos. Haydn's numerous concertos (17 for piano, 9 for violin, 6 for cello, and others) seldom rise above the mediocre, lacking the inspiration that pervades his quartets and symphonies. Only one piano concerto and one or two cello concertos by Haydn are of more than academic interest.

Lit.: *Editions XXXIX, 25; A. Veinus, *The Concerto,* rev. ed. (1964); J. Culshaw, *The Concerto* (1950); B. Swalin, *The Violin Concerto* (1941); F. H. Garvin, *The Beginnings of the Romantic Piano Concerto* (1952); A. J. B. Hutchings, *The Baroque Concerto* [1961]; *BuMBE, passim;* A. Schering, *Geschichte des Instrumentalkonzerts* (1905, '27); H. Daffner, *Die Entwicklung des Klavierkonzerts bis Mozart* (1906); Hans Weber, *Das Violoncell-konzerts des 18. . . . . Jahrhunderts* (1932); E. Rapp, *Beiträge zur Frühgeschichte des Violoncellkonzerts* (1932); H. Uldall, *Das Klavierkonzert der Berliner Schule* (1927); H. Engel, *Das Instrumentalkonzert* (1932); I. Amster, *Das Virtuosenkonzert in der 1. Hälfte des 19. Jahrhunderts* (1931); F. Giegling, *Giuseppe Torelli* (1949); H. Engel, *Die Entwicklung des deutschen Klavierkonzertes von Mozart bis Liszt* (1927); T. Stengel, *Die Entwicklung des Klavierkonzerts von Liszt bis zur Gegenwart* [1931]; C. M. Girdlestone, *Mozart's Piano Concertos* (1948); G. Piccioli, *Il "concerto" per Pianoforte e orchestra . . . da Mozart a Grieg* (1936); R. Erlebach, "Style in Pianoforte Concerto Writing" (*ML* xvii, 131); D. D. Boyden, "When Is A Concerto Not A Concerto?" (*MQ* xliii); H. Uldall, "Beiträge zur Frühgeschichte des Klavierkonzerts" (*ZMW* x); M. Brusotti, "Di alcuni inediti 'Klavierkonzerte' di J. Haydn" (*RMI* xxxviii). See also *Concerto grosso.*

Concerto form. Name for the form of the concerto (three movements) or, more commonly, for that employed in the first movements of the late baroque concertos (Torelli to Bach). See Ritornello form.

Concerto grosso. The most important type of baroque concerto [see Concerto III (b)], characterized by the use of a small group of solo instruments, called *concertino* or *principale,* against the full orchestra, called *concerto, tutti* or *ripieni.* The concertino usually consists of two violins and a thoroughbass (cello plus harpsichord), i.e., the same ensemble that constitutes the baroque *trio sonata.* The ripieni are a small string orchestra, later occasionally including wind instruments (trumpets, oboes, flutes, horns).

The earliest known examples of the *concerto grosso* principle occur in two *Sinfonie a più instrumenti* by A. Stradella (1644–82). Some *concerti grossi* by Corelli (1653–1713), although published much later, would seem to be of a date close to Stradella's, because they show the patchwork structure of the earlier canzona with quick changes of a considerable number of short "movements" (nos. 1, 2, 5, 7 of the 12 *Concerti grossi* op. 6, 1712). G. Muffat's (1645–1704) 6 *concerti grossi,* published 1701 [*DTO* 23], probably also belong to about 1680. They contain suitelike movements (e.g., sonata–corrente–grave–gavotta–rondeau) and show relatively little contrast between the concertino and the concerto. In Torelli's (1658–1709) *concerti grossi* (pub. 1709, written *c.* 1690) the two violins of the concertino are treated much more individually, so that the style approaches that of a concerto for two solo violins. These *concerti,* together with the later *concerti* of Corelli's op. 6, represent a high point of classical balance and dignity. F. Geminiani (1687–1762; op. 2, 1732; op. 3, 1733) carried on the tradition of Corelli but adopted the four-movement scheme of the *sonata da chiesa* as the standard form (most of Corelli's *concerti* have five or more movements).

A new trend in *concerto grosso* style was inaugurated by Vivaldi (1669?–1741), who consistently used the three-movement scheme allegro–adagio–allegro and largely discarded the contrapuntal treatment of the earlier masters in favor of a novel style of rhythmic precision and dynamic drive. The *concerti grossi* of P. Locatelli (1695–1764) are direct imitations of Vivaldi's, as are, on a much higher artistic level, Bach's *Brandenburg Concertos of 1721. Handel, in his Grand Concertos op. 6 (1740), although incorporating elements of Vivaldi's style, retained, like Corelli, the larger number of movements.

The neoclassical movement of the 20th century has brought about a remarkable revival of the *concerto grosso,* chiefly as a reaction against the virtuoso-like solo concerto of the 19th century. See Concerto II.

Lit.: *Editions XXXIX, 23; A. Hutchings, *The Baroque Concerto* [1961]; *BuMBE,* pp. 222ff; *LavE* ii. 4, 2446ff; W. Krüger, *Das Concerto grosso in Deutschland* (1932); A. Bonaccorsi, "Contributo alla storia del concerto grosso" (*RMI* xxxix). See also Concerto.

Concert pitch. See Pitch (2).

Concitato. [It.]. Excited, agitated. For *stile concitato,* see under Style.

Concord, discord. Concord is a combination of sounds that is pleasing to the ear (triads, seventh chords, and other "agreeable-sounding" chords), while discord consists of deliberately harsh and unpleasant combinations. The terms are used for aesthetic rather than technical descriptions.

Concordance, discordance. Terms introduced by C. Stumpf [G. *Konkordanz, Diskordanz*] to denote the subjective aspect of *consonance, dissonance. According to this terminology, the third, although a consonance, was a discordance in the Middle Ages but is now a concordance. Conversely, the fourth, always a consonance, was a concordance in the 9th century (organum of the fourth) and a discordance in the 16th.

Concord Sonata. The second of two piano sonatas by Charles Ives, composed 1909–15. Its complete title is "Concord, Mass., 1840–1860." Ives provided a guide to the content by adding titles to the four movements: *Emerson, Hawthorne, The Alcotts,* and *Thoreau.* Stylistically the sonata is representative of Ives' progressive techniques (extreme dissonance, complex rhythms, etc.), which mark him as a pioneer in 20th-century musical developments.

Concrete music. See *Musique concrète.*

Conducteur [F.]. An abridged orchestral score, usually a reduction for the piano, as distinct from the *grande partition,* or full score.

Conducting. I. *Technique.* Conducting means directing a performing group—orchestra, chorus, opera—in order to bring about complete coordination of all the players and singers. Its basic aspect is beating time, i.e., the clear indication of the metric pulse by the conductor's right hand, often with the help of a baton. A clear and decisive downstroke will fall on the first beat of each measure, while the last beat will be indicated by an upstroke. The intermediate motions of the hand depend upon the meter and tempo, and may require from two to six or more beats. The accompanying illustration shows the basic diagrams for 2, 3, 4, and 6 beats. In addition, the conductor indicates—mainly with the left hand—the entrances of instruments or voice-

parts, shadings of dynamics, and other details of performance. Suggestive motion of the whole body and facial expressions are used to indicate subtle changes of mood.

Many present-day conductors, especially the leaders of choral groups, discard the baton, preferring to use both hands in evocative gestures. Side by side with this there has been a tendency to neglect time-beating and to cultivate highly expressive (and, often, somewhat undisciplined) motions, which represent a supreme effort to impose the conductor's personality upon the orchestra but frequently are irritating to the audience. C. Munch's book, *I Am a Conductor* (1955), has provoked comments that indicate a reaction against the attitude of many present-day conductors: "It is not their hearts and souls that conductors need to cultivate, but their brains and tastes. . . . Just for a change, I would like to hear performances that are only correct" [see *Notes,* June 1955, p. 441]. The ideal, attained by only a few, is, no doubt, a combination of all these qualities.

Attempts have been made by orchestras to perform without a conductor, especially in the Soviet Union under the obvious influence of political considerations. They were soon abandoned because they required a disproportionate number of rehearsals and turned out to be rather ineffective. Indeed, their failure has enhanced rather than detracted from the stature of the modern conductor, who today is a dominating figure of musical life. Often his role is that of a star, and he is surrounded by admirers who consider all other conductors inferior and his "readings" alone authoritative. Many a concert-goer, it must be feared, is more interested in the attitudes and interpretations of his favorite conductor than in the music itself. Not since the days of the celebrated "songbirds" of the 18th century has there been such partisanship over the relative merits of performance. True enough, the temptation of the spectacular, with an occasional sacrifice of musical truth, is not always resisted. Nonetheless, discounting overpraise and occasional lapses from good taste, the modern orchestra and the command of its resources by a number of outstanding conductors is one of the great musical achievements of our time.

II. *History.* The earliest manifestation of conducting is *chironomy, i.e., the use of hand signs to indicate melodic motion. Egyptian and Sumerian reliefs dating from *c.* 2800 B.C. show "conductors" directing players of harps and flutes by means of such signs. The choric dances of Greek antiquity were led by a *choreutes* who indicated the main beat by an audible downward motion of the foot [see Arsis and thesis]. In Gregorian chant, hand signs were used in order to explain to the singers the melodic motion of the "chironomic" neumes. Early polyphonic music was performed by soloists and therefore—like the modern string quartet—did not require a conductor. This situation changed about the

middle of the 15th century, when performance of polyphonic music by small choirs became a common practice [see Choral music]. The basis of 15th- and 16th-century conducting was the *tactus, indicated by a downward and upward hand motion, each such motion representing the beat (temporal unit) somewhat as a "visible metronome." No attempts to distinguish between strong and weak beats entered into this practice, which is eminently suitable for music of this period and has indeed been revived in some present-day performances of compositions by Ockeghem, Josquin, Palestrina, and other early masters.

In the 17th century, the change from a polyphonic to an essentially homophonic texture, which often shows the influence of dance rhythms, together with the employment of larger ensembles consisting of voices and instruments, paved the way for the modern type of conducting, characterized by a visible distinction between strong and weak beats. The leader of the group—often the organist or harpsichordist—may have used his hand, a rolled-up sheet of paper, a wooden stick, or some other suitable implement. Occasionally, when the conductor's signs could not be seen by all the performers—as was often the case in churches—it was necessary to make them audible, e.g., by lightly knocking a key against the organ bench, as Daniel Speer recommended in 1687 (*Grund-richtiger, kurtz, leicht und nöthiger Unterricht der musicalischen Kunst*). By the end of the 17th century the violin had acquired so much authority that the first violinist replaced the organist as conductor. Lully may have been one of the first to assume this role and, at the same time, to introduce the traditional motions for beating time, which are explained by M. de Saint Lambert (*Les Principes du clavecin,* 1702) and M. P. de Montéclair (*Nouvelle Méthode pour apprendre la musique,* 1709). In Germany and in Italy, however, the older practice of repeated down- and up-motions was generally retained throughout the 17th century. Not infrequently there were two conductors, as during Haydn's visits to London in 1791 and 1794, when Haydn directed from the piano and Salomon from his violin. The last great violinist-conductor was F. Habeneck (1781–1849).

In the early part of the 19th century leadership became generally entrusted to an independent and authoritative conductor standing in front of the group and using a baton. Most of these were composers, e.g., Spontini, Spohr,

Weber, and Mendelssohn. The first professional conductor was O. Nicolai (1810–49) in Vienna, followed by Hans von Bülow (1830–94), Ernst von Schuch (1846–1914), Arthur Nikisch (1855–1922), Felix Weingartner (1863–1942), Bruno Walter (1876–1962), Wilhelm Furtwängler (1886–1954), and Fritz Busch (1890–1951). In France, Habeneck was followed by C. Lamoureux (1834–99), E. Colonne (1838–1910), Camille Chevillard (1859–1923), and Pierre Monteux (1875–1964). The most famous Italian conductor was Arturo Toscanini (1867–1957).

Lit.: B. Grosbayne, *A Bibliography of Works and Articles on Conductors* (1934); *id., Techniques of Modern Orchestral Conducting* (1956); D. E. Inghelbrecht, *The Conductor's World* [1954]; K. van Hoesen, *Handbook of Conducting* (1948); M. Rudolf, *The Grammar of Conducting* (1950); R. Wagner, *On Conducting* (trans.; 1919); F. Weingartner, *On Conducting* (trans.; 1906); A. Carse, *Orchestral Conducting, A Textbook* (1929); V. Bakaleinikoff, *Elementary Rules of Conducting* [1938]; H. Scherchen, *Handbook of Conducting* (1933); A. Boult, *A Handbook on the Technique of Conducting*, rev. ed. (1949); M. H. Holmes, *Conducting An Amateur Orchestra* (1951); A. T. Davison, *Choral Conducting* (1941); G. Schünemann, *Geschichte des Dirigierens* (1913); C. Munch, *I Am a Conductor,* trans. L. Burkat (1955); *AdHM* i, 1208ff; B. Grosbayne, "A Perspective on the Literature of Conducting" (*PMA* lxvii); G. Schünemann, "Zur Frage des Taktschlagens . . . in der Mensuralmusik" (*SIM* x); A. Chybiński, in *SIM* x; E. Vogel, in *JMP* v; R. Schwartz, in *JMP* xiv.

Conductor's part. An abbreviated score of orchestral works. It usually includes the leading part (chiefly first violin) with the other important instruments cued in.

Conductus [pl. *conductus* or *conducti*]. A term commonly used today as a generic designation for Latin strophic songs of the 12th and 13th centuries, a repertory that is the counterpart of the body of troubadour and trouvère songs of the same period. Originally conductus probably meant "introduction." The liturgy of St. James in the Codex Calixtinus of *c.* 1150 [see Compostela, school of] includes four "conductum S. Jacobi," each of which serves as an introduction to a lesson [ed. P. Wagner, pp. 39ff, 94ff]. In Beauvais' Daniel play of *c.* 1140 [see Liturgical drama] the term seems to mean "escorting" or "processional" song (*Conductus reginae venientis ad regem*). See also the *Conductus ad tabulam*

(known as "Song of the Ass") in *HAM*, no. 17a. Although these are the only known references in the 12th century, the term is now used in the much wider sense indicated above. Thus it includes poems with quite varied subject matter—religious, contemplative, lyrical, political, satirical, etc. A large repertory of such songs exists in the sources of *St. Martial (there called *versus*) and also in the Florentine Codex of the school of Notre Dame [see "Magnus liber organi"]. These songs all are monophonic, some of those in the latter being by Perotinus [*HAM*, no. 17c]. However, many of the polyphonic compositions (organa?) of St. Martial have also been considered conductus, particularly by H. Spanke [see St. Martial, Lit.].

Much better defined is the polyphonic conductus of the 13th century, which, according to the author of "Discantus positio vulgaris," Franco, Odington, and other theorists of the time, represents one of the chief types of 13th-century polyphony, side by side with organa,

Hac in an-ni ja-nu-a Hoc in ja-nu-a-ri-o

clausulae, and motets. However, the conductus are not based on liturgical chants but (with few exceptions) on freely invented melodies, to which one, two, or (rarely) three parts are added in note-against-note style [see Homorhythmic], a technique that sharply contrasts with the rhythmically differentiated style of the organa, clausulae, and motets. A special type of conductus that was considered superior was the *conductus habens caudam*, i.e., a conductus with cadential extensions over some vowels of the various lines of the poem [see *Cauda* (2)] and sometimes melismatic beginnings. There are a number of three-voice conductus (at least one, *Salvatoris hodie*, by Perotinus) that are remarkable for their great length, resulting from the insertion of numerous elaborate *caudae* that, in contrast to the syllabic sections, are in a style similar to that of the organa or clausulae [see *OH* i, 293ff]. Some conductus, found in the so-called MS of St. Victor (Paris, Bibl. nat., *lat.*

15139), have *caudae* making use of double counterpoint [see Y. Rokseth, "Le contrepoint double vers 1248," in *CP Laurencie*] and other very advanced devices. They mark the end of a production that, in sheer quantity, far outweighs the organa, clausulae, and even motets of the 13th century.

The rhythmic interpretation of the (simply syllabic) conductus is still controversial. Some scholars advocate interpretation in modal rhythm, e.g., $\frac{6}{4}$ | ♩♩♩♩ |, instead of $\frac{4}{4}$ | ♩♩♩♩ | [see Modal theory]. Others prefer the latter rendition, admitting modal rhythm only for the *caudae* that are written in the ligature system of *modal notation [see *ApNPM*, pp. 258ff]. Examples in *HAM*, nos. 38, 39; *SchGMB*, no. 16 (the "instrumental" opening and close is actually vocalization).

The term "conductus style" has been widely adopted by musicologists to denote note-against-note style, particularly with reference to English compositions of the 14th and 15th centuries and to early 14th-century Italian compositions (madrigals), which are written in what might be called "ornamented conductus style."

Lit.: E. Gröninger, *Repertoire-Untersuchungen zum mehrstimmigen Notre Dame-Conductus* (1939); A. Geering, *Die Organa und mehrstimmigen Conductus... des deutschen Sprachgebietes* (1952); J. E. Knapp, ‡*Thirty-five Conductus* (1965); id., "The Polyphonic *Conductus* in the Notre-Dame Epoch" (diss. Yale Univ., 1961); D. D. Colton, ‡"The Conducti of MS Madrid 20486" (thesis Indiana Univ., 1964); E. Thurston, "The Conductus Compositions in Manuscript Wolfenbüttel 1206" (diss. New York Univ., 1954); *OH* i, 245–318; *ReMMA*, pp. 307ff; J. Handschin, in *CP 1925*, *ZMW* vi, *AMW* ix; L. Ellinwood, in *MQ* xxvii. For the problem of rhythm, see B. Stäblein, in *CP Blume;* M. F. Bukofzer, in *BAMS* 1948 (p. 63), *CP 1952, JAMS* vi, *AnnM* i; H. Husmann, in *AMW* ix; L. Schrade, in *AnnM* i; G. Reaney, in *CP 1958.*

Conductus motet. See under Motet A II.

Confinalis [L.]. Same as *affinalis* [see *Affinales*].

Conflicting signatures. Another term for Partial signatures.

Confractorium [L.]. In *Ambrosian, *Gallican, and *Mozarabic chant, an item of the Proper of the Mass, corresponding liturgically to the Roman Communion.

Con fuoco. See *Fuoco.*

Conga. [Sp.]. Dance of African heritage, developed mainly in Cuba but popular in many other Latin American countries where carnival festivities take place. The music is in 2/4 meter based on a two-measure rhythmic pattern, always with a symmetrical first measure and a syncopated second: ♪ ⅞ ♪ ⅞ | ♫ ♪ ⅞ |. This pattern is the rhythmic backbone for constantly repeated short phrases of two to four measures. The dancers stand behind one another and form a chain that moves in circles or in a straight line. The texts of the *conga* often satirize current events.   J.O-S.

Congada. See *Congo.*

Con garbo. See *Garbato.*

Congo. A kind of symbolic play presented by Negro slaves in Brazil from the mid-17th century on, during religious celebrations honoring certain Negro saints. Most famous are the *congos* in honor of St. Balthazar and St. Benedict. The music for these plays was the *congada*, a markedly African dance in duple meter, based on the monotonous repetition of short, syncopated rhythmic patterns.   J.O-S.

Congoerá. Scraper made of human or animal bone used by the Guaraní Indians of Paraguay. It is similar in function to the Cuban *güiro* and the Brazilian *reco-reco.   J.O-S.

Con grandezza. See *Grandezza.*

Congresses. Among the numerous congresses held more or less regularly by the various music societies, those devoted to musicological topics deserve special mention. Most of them have been held under the auspices of the *Internationale Gesellschaft für Musikwissenschaft* and the *Internationale Musikgesellschaft* [see Societies III, 1, 2]. See R. S. Angell, "Congresses in Musicology" (*Notes* I, no. 2). The reports containing the papers read at these congresses are listed in the Abbreviations at the front of this book under *CP 1906*, etc. For more complete information, see W. Kahl and W.-M. Luther, *Repertorium der Musikwissenschaft* (1953), p. 43. See also M. Briquet, *La Musique dans les congrès internationaux, 1835–1939* (1961).

Con gusto. See *Gusto.*

Conjunct, disjunct. Notes are called "conjunct" if they are successive degrees of the scale, "disjunct" if they form intervals larger than a second. For conjunct, disjunct tetrachord, see Greece II.

Conjunctura [L.]. A symbol (ligature) of *square

notation, consisting of a *longa* followed by two or more rhombs (lozenges; the later *semibrevis*), always forming a descending scale passage. It developed from the neume *climacus* [see Ex. under Neumes]. For the rhythmic interpretation, see *ApNPM*, pp. 240ff.

Con lancio. See *Lancio*.

Consecutives. See under Parallel fifths, octaves.

Consequent. See Antecedent and consequent.

Conservatory [F. *conservatoire;* G. *Konservatorium;* It., Sp., *conservatorio*]. A school specializing in musical training. Originally, a *conservatorio* was a charitable institution for the education of orphans, but at an early time the main emphasis was placed on music. The oldest institutions of this type are the *ospedali* of Venice, so called because they were attached to hospitals, e.g., *Ospedale dei Mendicanti* (1262), *della Pietà* (1346), *San Salvadore degl' Incurabili* (1517), etc. The name *conservatorio* originated in Naples: *Conservatorio Santa Maria di Loreto* (1537), *Sant' Onofrio a Capua* (1576), *De' Poveri di Gesù Cristo* (1589), *Della Pietà dei Turchini* (1583). Nearly all the great Italian composers of the 17th and 18th centuries were pupils or teachers at these institutions. [See H. Hucke, in *CP Osthoff*.]

The most important of the present-day conservatories are:

Austria. Akademie für Musik und darstellende Kunst, Vienna (1817) and Salzburg (Mozarteum, 1880); Linz, Bruckner-Konservatorium (1823); Innsbruck, Städtische Musikschule (1818).

Belgium. Conservatoire Royal de Musique in Brussels (1813), Ghent (1812), Liège (1826).

British Isles. London, Royal College of Music (founded 1873 as National Training School of Music; present name assumed 1883) and Royal Academy of Music (1822); Birmingham, Birmingham and Midland Institute of Music (1866); Glasgow, Royal Scottish Academy of Music (1885); Dublin, Royal Irish Academy of Music (1848).

Canada. Toronto, Toronto Conservatory of Music (1886); Montreal, McGill University (1821), Faculty of Music; Halifax, Dalhousie University (1818), Conservatory of Music.

Finland. Helsinki, Sibelius-Akademie (1882).

France. Paris, Conservatoire National de Musique (1784) with branches in many other cities.

Germany. Berlin, Hochschule für Musik (1869), Städtisches (formerly Stern'sches) Kon-

servatorium (1850); other institutions, called Staatliche Hochschule für Musik, in Dresden (1856), Frankfurt (1878), Cologne (1850), Leipzig (1843), Munich (1846), Stuttgart (1856), Weimar (1872).

Italy. Bologna, Conservatorio di Musica G. B. Martini (1804); Florence, Cons. di Musica Luigi Cherubini (1811); Genoa, Liceo Musicale Pareggiato N. Paganini (1829); Milan, Cons. di Musica Giuseppe Verdi (1807); Naples, Cons. di Musica S. Pietro a Majella (1808); Rome, Cons. di Musica S. Cecilia (1877); Venice, Cons. Musicale Benedetto Marcello (1877).

Netherlands. Amsterdam, Amsterdamsch Conservatorium (1862); The Hague, Koninklijk Conservatorium voor Muziek (1826); Rotterdam, Muziekschool van de Maatschappij tot Bevordering der Toonkunst (1829).

Scandinavia. Copenhagen, Det Kongelige Danske Musik-konservatorium (1866); Stockholm, Kungliga Musikhögskolan (1771); Oslo, Musikk-Konservatoriet (1883).

Spain and Portugal. Barcelona, Conservatorio Nacional de música y Declamación (1838); Madrid, Real Conservatorio de Música y Declamación (1830); Lisbon, Colegio de Música y Arte (1835).

Switzerland. Basel, Musikschule und Konservatorium (1867); Geneva, Conservatoire de Musique (1835); Zurich, Konservatorium für Musik (1876).

United States. In the United States (as well as in Canada) most of the institutions specializing in musical training are connected with universities and colleges, nearly all of which have a department or a school of music. Of the independent conservatories, or those loosely affiliated with colleges or universities, the following may be mentioned: Baltimore, Peabody Conservatory of Music (founded 1857; opened 1866); Oberlin, Ohio, Oberlin Conservatory of Music (1865); Boston, New England Cons. of Music (1867); Cambridge, Longy School of Music (1915); Cleveland, Cleveland Institute of Music (1920); New York, Juilliard School of Music (1920; begun in 1905 as the Institute of Musical Art); Rochester, Eastman School of Music (1921); Philadelphia, Curtis Institute of Music (1924); St. Louis, St. Louis Institute of Music (1924); San Francisco, San Francisco Cons. of Music (1917).

U.S.S.R. Moscow, Gossudarstvĕnnaja Konsservatorija Imĕnĕm P. I. Tschaikovskovo (1886); Leningrad, G. K. Imĕnĕm N. A. Rimskovo-Korssakova (1862).

Con slancio. See *Slancio*.

Console. (1) The case that encloses the keyboard, stops, etc., of an organ. Formerly placed in front of the organ, it is now often detached, the sole connection being electric wiring. (2) See Piano III.

Consonance, dissonance. Terms used to describe the agreeable effect produced by certain intervals (consonant intervals, e.g., octave, third) compared to the disagreeable effect produced by others (dissonant intervals, e.g., second, seventh) or similar effects produced by chords.

Consonance and dissonance are the very foundation of harmonic music, in which the former represents the element of normalcy and repose, the latter the no less important element of disturbance and tension.

In spite of numerous efforts, no wholly satisfactory explanation and definition of consonance and dissonance have yet been found. The shortcoming of the definition above is not so much that it is based entirely on subjective impressions but that it fails to account for the consonant quality of the fourth and fifth. Indeed, from the point of view of musical composition of all eras, these two intervals must be regarded as consonances second only to the unison and octave; however, according to the definition above they would certainly rank after the third and sixth and might perhaps be termed dissonant (especially the fourth has a decidedly unpleasant effect for an unbiased listener). It is chiefly for this reason that the "pleasant-unpleasant" theory is unsatisfactory. Following are the most important theories of consonance and dissonance.

I. (a) According to the Pythagorean theory, the smaller the numbers that express the ratio of the frequencies of intervals (or of the lengths of the corresponding strings), the more consonant the intervals. This theory leads to an order of the intervals that conforms rather well to musical practice:

unis.	8ve	5th	4th	6th	3rd
c-c	c-c'	c-g	c-f	c-a	c-e
1:1	1:2	2:3	3:4	3:5	4:5

3rd	6th	2nd	7th	7th
c-e^b	c-a^b	c-d	c-b	c-b^b
5:6	5:8	8:9	8:15	9:16

The chief objection to this theory is that it fails to account for the fact that a minute modification of a consonant interval—too slight to be noticed by the ear—brings about highly complicated ratios of frequencies. For instance, the well-tempered fifth, which the ear cannot distinguish from the Pythagorean (pure) fifth, is represented by (approximately) the fraction $^{293}/_{439}$.

(b) According to Helmholtz' theory of beats [see Helmholtz-Ellis, *Sensations of Tone*, rev. ed. (1885), pp. 186ff], intervals are consonant if no disturbing *beats are produced by the two tones or by their harmonics; otherwise, they are dissonant (beats are most disturbing if they number 33 per second, least disturbing if they are less than 6 per second, or more than 120 per second). The chief disadvantage of this theory is that the dissonant or consonant character of an interval varies with the octave in which it lies, as appears from the following table:

c-e	33 beats	c-d	16 beats
c'-e'	66 beats	c'-d'	32 beats
c''-e''	132 beats	c''-d''	64 beats
		c'''-d'''	128 beats

It appears that the third c-e would be as "dissonant" as the second c'-d', and that the second c'''-d''' would be as "consonant" as the third c''-e''.

(c) According to Helmholtz' theory of *Klangverwandtschaft* (relationship of sounds), two tones are consonant if their harmonics (up to the eighth, but excluding the seventh) have one or more tones in common. From the accompanying example it appears that there are three such common tones in the case of the octave, two for the fifth and the fourth, and one for the third and the sixth, major as well as minor. No such common tones exist for the second and the seventh, which therefore are classed as dissonance. This definition is more satisfactory and useful than any other, since it establishes a clear

demarcation between consonant and dissonant intervals, a result that, from the musical point of view, is more desirable than the "gradual decline of consonance" implied by the other theories. Its only drawback is that the "dissonant" seventh harmonic must be eliminated (otherwise

D, with the seventh harmonic c″, would be consonant to C). One could, however, argue that the seventh harmonic of D is noticeably lower than c″ ($^6\%_4$ versus 1).

(d) C. Stumpf's theory of *Tonverschmelzung* (amalgamation of sounds) is a psychological explanation based on large-scale experimentation. The consonant nature of an interval is measured by the degree to which the sound produced by the two simultaneous tones evokes, in the mind of musically untrained listeners, the impression of a single sound instead of two different tones. Thus, the percentage of listeners judging (wrongly) in favor of "one tone" (*Verschmelzung*) gives a measurement of the degree of consonance or dissonance. Following is the result of Stumpf's experiment:

8ve	5th	4th	3rd	tritone	2nd
75%	50%	33%	25%	20%	10%

It should be noted that in this series the fifth and the fourth appear as better consonances than the third. The chief shortcoming of this theory is that consonance and dissonance are no longer contradictory or exclusive terms but represent gradations.

(e) After an examination of all these scientific theories, the practical musician will probably be satisfied with a very simple common-sense rule, in a way a practical condensation of Helmholtz' *Klangverwandtschaft: Every interval contained in the major (or minor) triad and its inversions is a consonance; all other intervals are dissonances.*

II. Chords can be classified as consonant or dissonant on the basis of the following definition: A consonant chord is one in which only consonant intervals (octave, perfect fifth, perfect fourth, third, sixth) are found; a dissonant chord is one that includes at least one dissonant interval (second, seventh, diminished fifth, etc.). This places the triads and their inversions (except for the diminished and augmented triad) in the former category, and all the other chords (seventh chords, ninth chords) in the latter, in full conformity with musical experience and practice.

III. *History.* Ideas about which intervals are consonant and which dissonant have changed considerably during the course of music history. In the earliest polyphony, *c.* 900, the fourth was the foremost consonant interval, with the fifth replacing it at a somewhat later date [see Organum (2), I]. Guido admitted four *concordiae—* fourth, whole tone, major third, and minor third

—but ruled out the fifth and the semitone ["Micrologus," ch. xiii]. In the 13th century the unison and octave were regarded as perfect consonances, the major and minor third as imperfect, the fourth and fifth as intermediate [Garlandia; *CS* i, 104]. Both major and minor sixths were considered dissonances. Tinctoris, in his *Diffinitorium* (*c.* 1475), distinguished between *concordantia perfecta,* which cannot be used in parallel motion, and *concordantia imperfecta,* which can. To the former category belong the unison and upper and lower fifth, to the latter, the major and minor third and sixth [*CS* iv, 180a]. The fourth, although theoretically a consonance, was admitted only with a third or fifth below it. These concepts remained basic until the end of the 19th century. Also see Third.

In 20th-century music the distinction between consonance and dissonance has become more or less obsolete, particularly in styles using atonality and serial techniques. Hindemith [*The Craft of Musical Composition,* 2 vols. (1941–45)], however, devised a system whereby the 12 tones are arranged in a definite order of consonance-degree derived from the combination tones: octave, fifth, fourth, major third, minor sixth, minor third, major sixth, major second, minor seventh, minor second, major seventh, and tritone (augmented fourth or diminished fifth).

Lit.: K. Jeppesen, *The Style of Palestrina and the Dissonance,* rev. ed. (1946); H. Husmann, *Vom Wesen der Konsonanz* (1953); E. Hartmann, "Konsonanz und Dissonanz" (diss. Marburg, 1923); K. Lenzen, *Geschichte des Konsonanzbegriffes im 19. Jahrhundert* (1933); S. Krehl, "Die Dissonanz als musikalisches Ausdrucksmittel" (*ZMW* i); A. Machabey, "Dissonance, polytonalité, atonalité" (*RM* 1931, no. 116).

Consort. A 17th-century English term for instrumental chamber ensembles or compositions written for them. A group including only instruments of the same family was called "whole consort" (consort of viols, recorders; see Chest of viols), whereas a group consisting of various kinds was called "broken consort." Thomas Morley's *First Booke of Consort Lessons* of 1599, written for treble lute, pandora, cittern, bass viol, flute, recorder, and treble viol, contains good examples of the broken consort. Later publications are: Philip Rosseter, *Lessons for the Consort* (1609); John Adson, *Courtly Masquing Ayres* (1611; repr. 1621); William Lawes (d. 1645), "The Royal Consort" and the "Great Consorte" (MSS; see *GD* iii, 118; *GDB* v, 94);

Matthew Locke, *Little Consort of Three Parts* (1656) and "Consort of Foure Parts" (MS; see *GD* iii, 224; *GDB* v, 353–55). The compositions in these collections vary from ricercar-like fantasias [see Fancy] in the earliest works to suite-like pieces in the latest. Locke's consorts [new ed., P. Warlock (1932)] are suites consisting of a Fantasia, Courante, Ayre, and Sarabande [see Suite III]; according to Roger North [*Memoires of Musick*, 1728] these were "the last of the kind that hath been made." A publication by William Leighton, *The Teares or Lamentacions of a Sorrowfull Soule* (1614), includes a number of "consort songs," i.e., four-part compositions (psalms, hymns) for voices reinforced by a broken consort.

Lit.: T. Dart, ‡*Jacobean Consort Music* (Editions XXXIV, 9); E. H. Meyer, *English Chamber Music* (1946); id., *Die mehrstimmige Spielmusik des 17. Jahrhunderts in Nord- und Mitteleuropa* (1934); T. Dart, in *PMA* lxxiv (Morley).

Consul, The. Opera in three acts by Gian Carlo Menotti (to his own libretto), produced in New York, 1950. Setting: a European country, the present. For the most part, the drama takes precedence over the music, which consists largely of accompanied recitative with occasional arias, numerous ensembles, and ballet scenes of considerable dramatic strength.

Contemporary music. See Twentieth-century music.

Contes d'Hoffmann, Les [F., The Tales of Hoffmann]. *Opéra fantastique* in three acts with prologue and epilogue by J. Offenbach (libretto by J. Barbier and M. Carré, based on stories by E. T. A. Hoffmann), produced in Paris, 1881. Setting: Germany and Italy, 19th century. Offenbach died before completing the work, which was orchestrated by E. Guiraud. In musical style the opera approximates the operetta form, which Offenbach had preferred in his earlier works. Within this class, however, it is among the most ambitious and successful examples.

Continuo. Abbr. for *basso continuo;* see Thoroughbass. In the scores of baroque composers (Bach, Handel), the bass part that was performed by the harpsichord or organ, together with a viola da gamba or cello.

Contra [It.]. (1) Abbr. for *contratenor. (2) As part of other terms, the word has one of two meanings: (a) "against," e.g., in *contrapunctus* [see Counterpoint] or *contratenor, from which

terms such as contralto, haut-contre, and basse-contre are derived; (b) the lower octave, a meaning probably derived from the 16th-century manner of indicating the tones below the great octave (C, D . . .) by a dash written underneath (C̲, D̲ . . .), i.e., in a position "contrary" to that used for the higher octaves (c̅, d̅ . . . or, c', d' . . .). This led to the term "contra-octave" for the octave below the great octave and, consequently, to names such as *contrabasso* [G. *Kontrabass*], contrabassoon, and contrabass-clarinet for instruments of the lowest range.

Contra(b)basso [It.]. *Double bass.

Contrabassoon. See under Oboe family I, D.

Contradanza [It.]. See Contredanse.

Contrafactum [L.]. A vocal composition in which the original text is replaced by a new one, particularly a secular text by a sacred one, or vice versa. The earliest known examples of this procedure (also called "adaptation") are in Gregorian chant in connection with feasts of a later date, such as that of the Trinity (9th century), whose Mass chants employ older melodies supplied with new texts referring to this feast [see *ApGC*, p. 69]. Numerous Alleluias, antiphons, hymns, and sequences are *contrafacta,* the same melody occurring with different texts, in one case more than eighty (antiphon *Apud Dominum;* Gevaert's *thème 29,* see *ApGC*, p. 399). In the 13th century, substitution of French for Latin texts (or vice versa?) was common. A famous example is the Provençal (troubadour) *Lai Markol,* for which there is a French as well as a Latin *contrafactum.* Even more common is the replacement of Latin by French texts in the upper parts of 13th-century motets [see *AdHM* i, 234f]. Oswald von Wolkenstein's "Der May" [see *HAM*, no. 60] is a *contrafactum* of J. Vaillant's "Par maintes foys" [see W. Apel, *French Secular Music of the Late Fourteenth Century* (1950), no. 69]. Numerous Protestant chorales employ pre-existent melodies for their new texts, and many of the melodies used for the Calvinist Psalter were borrowed from secular songs [see *Souterliedekens*]. Similar methods were employed in the *laude* of the 16th century, a particularly striking example being the use of the same music for the *lauda* "Jesu, Jesu" and the carnival song "Visin, visin" [see *ReMR*, p. 167].

In 17th- and 18-century French usage the transfer of texts was called *parodie,* e.g., in *Parodies bachiques sur les airs et symphonies des opéra* (pub. C. Ballard, 1695). These *parodies* were instrumental pieces (dances) to which a poetic text was added. The songs of Lully's operas especially were often provided with new texts, occasionally parodistic, i.e., caricaturing, a procedure frequently termed *parody rather than contrafactum by modern writers. Quite a few contrafacta are in the works of Bach (e.g., B-minor Mass) and Handel. J.-J. Rousseau, in his Dictionnaire de musique (1768), under "Parodie," made the remark that all the stanzas of a strophic song except the first are "parodies," i.e., contrafacta.

Lit.: F. Gennrich, Die Kontrafaktur im Liedschaffen des Mittelalters (1965); id., Lateinische Liedkontrafaktur (1956); K. Hennig, Die geistliche Kontrafactur im Jahrhundert der Reformation (1909); F. Gennrich, "Interationale mittelalterliche Melodien" (ZMW xi); K. von Fischer, "Kontrafakturen und Parodien italienischer Werke des Trecento und frühen Quattrocento" (AnnM v); J. Müller-Blattau, "Kontrafakturen im älteren geistlichen Volkslied" (CP Fellerer); D. J. Grout, "Seventeenth-Century Parodies of French Opera" (MQ xxvii); R. Haas, "Wiener deutsche Parodieopern um 1730" (ZMW viii); G. Cucuel, "Les Opéras de Gluck dans les parodies du XVIIIe siècle" (RM 1922, nos. 5, 6); R. T. Daniel, "Contrafacta and Polyglot Texts in the Early English Anthem" (CP Apel).

Contrafagotto [It.]. Double bassoon.

Contralto [It.]. (1) Same as *alto voice (female). (2) See Violin family (d).

Contra-octave. See under Pitch names.

Contrappunto [It.; L. contrapunctus]. Counterpoint. C. doppio, double counterpoint. C. alla mente, extemporized counterpoint [see Discantus supra librum].

Contrapunctus [L.]. See under Counterpoint II.

Contrapuntal. In the style of counterpoint.

Contrary motion. See under Motion.

Contratenor, abbr. contra. In compositions of the 14th and early 15th centuries, name for a third voice-part, added to the basic two-voice texture of discant (superius) and tenor. It has about the same range as the tenor, with which it frequently crosses, so that the lowest note may fall now to the tenor, now to the contra. Its contour is usually much less melodic than that of the other two parts, to which it was added for harmonic completeness. With the establishment, about 1450 (Ockeghem, Obrecht), of four-part

writing and the consequent separation of ranges, the contratenor split in two parts: the contratenor altus (high c.) or, simply, altus (alto), and the contratenor bassus (low c.) or, simply, bassus (bass). This process explains the name *alto (high) for a part that, from the modern point of view, can hardly be considered "high," as well as the use of the term countertenor for the male alto.

Contra-violin. See under Violin family (b).

Contrebasse [F.]. Double bass. Contrebasson, double bassoon.

Contredanse [F; G. Contratanz or Kontretanz; It., Sp. contradanza]. A dance that attained great popularity in France and elsewhere during the late 18th century. It was performed by two (or more) couples facing each other and executing a great variety of steps and motions. The music consists of a long series of eight-measure phrases that may be repeated over and over. It is now generally accepted that the contredanse developed and took its name from the English *country dance, which it resembles in various respects. As early as 1699 we find "Contredanses anglaises" in Ballard's Suite de danses. The contredanse developed later into the française and the *quadrille. Beethoven wrote 12 Contredanses for orchestra (1803), one of which (no. 7) he used in the final movement of the Eroica Symphony. See also Cotillon.

Con vaghezza. See Vaghezza.

Convertible counterpoint. Same as *invertible counterpoint.

Conzert [G.]. See Konzert.

Coperto [It.]. Covered. Timpani coperti, kettledrums muted by being covered with a cloth.

Copla [Sp.]. Couplet or stanza of Spanish songs such as the *cantiga or *villancico. See Couplet.

Coptic church music. The liturgical music of the Copts (a Christian sect in Egypt and other parts of northeast Africa). See GD, sup. vol., p. 178f; GDB ii, 867f; H. Hickmann, in CP 1950; R. Ménard, in RdM 1954, p. 21; id., in Études grégoriennes iii, 135.

Copula [L.]. A term pertaining to 13th-century polyphonic music, which is discussed by several theorists (J. de Garlandia, Franco, Odington; see CS i, 114, 116, 133, 247) but in such uncertain and contradictory terms that it is difficult to determine its meaning. Relatively clear (and in agreement with the etymological derivation from L. *copulare,* to connect, couple) is Garlandia's statement that "copula is midway between organum purum and discantus" (*CS* i, 114). To this he adds rather cryptic remarks seeming to indicate that quicker note values are used in the *copula.* Very likely the term denotes the short connecting passages that frequently appear in organa at the end of a section, connecting it with the next section. These often are written in smaller values (*fractio modi*). See W. G. Waite, "Discantus, Copula, Organum" (*JAMS* v).

Copyright, musical. The Constitution of the United States gives Congress the power to "promote the progress of science and useful arts by securing for limited times to authors and inventors the exclusive right to their respective writings and discoveries." [Art. I, Sec. 8.] The first Copyright Act of the United States was signed by President Washington in 1790, and thereafter several general revisions and numerous amendments were enacted. A copy of the copyright regulations presently in force may be obtained from the Copyright Office, The Library of Congress, Washington, D.C. 20540.

Copyright is applied for through the Copyright Office in Washington and may be secured for both published and unpublished musical and dramatic works. As soon as the formal requirements are fulfilled, the authorized person receives the exclusive right to print, reprint, publish, copy, and vend the work in question, or authorize someone else to do so; to arrange or adapt it if it is a musical work; and to perform or represent the work publicly for profit. The composer of a copyrighted work is protected against mechanical reproduction (phonograph records, tape recordings, etc.) as well as live performance. Moreover, judicial decisions in various cases have established precedents concerning performances of musical works in hotels and restaurants, motion-picture theaters, radio broadcasts, etc.

Owing to the proliferation of media since 1900, it has become increasingly difficult for the single author to protect his rights adequately in an individual capacity. As a result, collective musical organizations have been established in most countries. The leading American organization is the American Society of Composers, Authors and Publishers (ASCAP).

Since the need for legal protection of copyright passes national boundaries, several international conventions and treaties have been established. The most important of these are the International Copyright Union, established by the first Bern Convention (1886) and reinforced by three later conferences, and the Pan-American Copyright Conventions, a series of agreements entered into by the United States and various Latin American countries. Further, in the past international copyright could be secured by individual treaties between single countries. Even without a treaty, mutual protection of copyright (reciprocity) could be acknowledged by a proclamation of the President of the United States, and numerous such proclamations have been issued. Further details about such international agreements are found in the *United States Code,* Title 17, and in *Copyright Protection throughout the World,* published by the United States Department of Commerce.

Lit.: H. A. Howell, *The Copyright Law* (1942); A. Shafter, *Musical Copyright* (1939); S. Rothenberg, *Copyright and Public Performance of Music* (1954); H. Pohlmann, *Die Frühgeschichte des musikalischen Urheberrechts* (*ca.* 1400–1800) (1962); H. Kownatsky, "Copyright Law Revision" (*Notes,* March 1961).

Coq d'or, Le. See *Golden Cockerel, The.*

Cor [F.]. (French) horn. *Cor anglais,* English horn; *cor à pistons,* valve horn; *cor de basset,* basset horn; *cor de chasse,* hunting horn; *cor des Alpes,* alphorn; *cor d'harmonie,* valve horn; *cor naturel,* natural horn. Also see under Horn I, II.

Coranto [It.]. See Courante.

Corda [It.]; **corde** [F.]. String. In piano compositions, *una corda* (abbr. *u. c.*) calls for the use of the left pedal (soft pedal), whereby the entire keyboard is moved a little to the right so that the hammers strike only one string instead of two or three. This muting effect is canceled by *tutte le corde* (*t. c.*) or *tre corde.* In the slow movement of his Sonata op. 106 Beethoven demands the almost impossible finesse of *poco a poco due e poi tre corde* ("gradually two and then three strings"). *Corde à vide, corda vuota* mean open string (of the violin).

Corda vuota. See *Vuoto.*

Corelli clash. See under Cadence II [Ex. 24].

Coriolan Overture. Orchestral composition by Beethoven (op. 62, 1807), written as an overture to a play by H. J. von Collin about the same subject as Shakespeare's *Coriolanus*. It is one of Beethoven's most concisely dramatic and masterful compositions, similar in spirit to the Fifth Symphony.

Cori spezzati [It.]. Properly, *coro spezzato,* i.e., divided choir. See Polychoral style.

Corista [It.]. Orchestral pitch; tuning fork. *C. di camera,* chamber pitch.

Cornamusa [It.]. (1) A bagpipe used in the Abruzzi mountains of Italy. (2) A 16th-century reedcap instrument (described by Praetorius), probably similar to the dolzaina. See *MaMI.*

Cornemuse [F.]. Generic term for *bagpipe.

Cornet [F. *cornet à pistons;* G. *Kornett;* It. *cornetto;* Sp. *cornetín*]. See Brass instruments III and accompanying illustrations. Not to be confused with the *cornett. Also, name of an organ stop; see Organ IX (e).

Cornett [F. *cornet à bouquin;* G. *Zink;* It. *cornetto;* Sp. *corneta*]. A medieval instrument (the earliest known picture of it dates from the 13th century; see *Cantiga*) that, in one form or another, was used until the middle of the 19th century. It consists of a straight or slightly bent tube of wood (occasionally ivory, possibly originally goathorn), which is octagonal in cross section, usually with a cup-shaped mouthpiece. Although in some books this instrument is called a *cornet, leading to confusion with an entirely different 19th-century instrument, the two types usually are distinguished by the different spelling. The cornett had a very gentle sound that blended well with strings and with the human voice. It was widely used in church music, e.g., in eleven of Bach's cantatas, as a support for the chorale melody. In addition to the normal cornett (*Zink, cornetto*), pitched in a, there was a soprano size (*Kleiner Zink, cornettino*) pitched in e' and a tenor size (*Grosser Zink; cornone*) pitched in d. The above-mentioned instruments had a separate cup-shaped mouthpiece, but there was also a cornett, usually of straight shape, that had a small funnel-shaped opening carved out of the upper end of the tube. This was the *Gerader Zink* (*cornetto diritto*) or *Stiller Zink* (*cornetto muto*), so called on account of its softer sound. In the 16th century a bass size was added, which, in order to bring the finger holes within easy reach of the hands, was bent in a clumsy serpentine shape and therefore was called *serpent.* In spite of its appearance, which has been compared to a drainpipe suffering from an

intestinal disorder, it was a highly artistic instrument that was held in great esteem throughout the 16th century. It was particularly favored in French church music, hence the 19th-century name *serpent d'Église,* "church serpent." The serpent was still in favor with early 19th-century composers, such as Rossini (*Le Siège de Corinthe*), Mendelssohn (*Meeresstille und glückliche Fahrt; Paulus*), Wagner (*Rienzi*), and Verdi (*Les Vêpres siciliennes,* 1855). By this time, however, the instrument had a shape similar to the tuba's. Instead of the serpentine tube, in 1788 J. J. Regibo built one bent back on itself in the shape of a bassoon, and in this form it became known as *Russian bassoon.* An improved variety of this instrument was the metal *bass horn,* invented about 1800, also called *English bass horn* [F. *basse-cor*]. All these instruments retained the six finger holes of the old cornetts. [See Brass instruments V (b).] The addition of more finger holes operated by keys led to the *chromatic bass horn* and *ophicleide.* [See ill. under Brass instruments.] See G. Karstadt, in *AMF* ii; M. Rasmussen, in *Brass Quarterly* i.

Cornetta [It.]. *Cornet.

Cornetto [It.]. *Cornett or *cornet.

Cornett-ton [G.]. See under Pitch (2).

Corno [It.]. Horn. *Corno a mano,* natural horn; *corno a macchina* (*a pistoni, cromatico, ventile*), valve horn; *corno inglese,* English horn; *corno di bassetto,* basset horn; *corno da caccia,* hunting horn. In Bach's scores *corno* usually means the old *cornett [G. *Zink*]. For Bach's *corno da tirarsi* see under Trumpet II (slide trumpet). See also Horn I, II.

Cornopean. Older name for the *cornet.

Cornu [L.]. An ancient Roman horn; see Brass instruments V (a).

Coro [It.]. Choir, chorus. *Coro spezzato* (also *coro battente*), see under Polychoral style. In organ music, *gran coro* means full organ.

Corona [L., It.]. The pause, the sign for which resembles a crown.

Coronach, corronach. A funeral dirge of Scotland. It was chanted by the bard (*Seannachie*) on the death of a chief or other prominent personage of the clan. The verses described the virtues and deeds of the dead person. The music was rather wild and rude, frequently interrupted by the wails of women mourners. Similar songs and customs prevailed in Ireland (*caoine). Schubert wrote a "Coronach" for women's chorus (op. 52, no. 4) to a text from Sir Walter Scott's *The Lady of the Lake.*

Coronation Anthems. Four anthems by Handel, composed for the coronation of George II (1727), entitled: 1. "Zadok the Priest"; 2. "The King shall rejoice"; 3. "My heart is inditing"; 4. "Let thy hand be strengthened." Purcell also wrote a coronation anthem, "My heart is inditing," for the coronation of James II (1685).

Coronation Concerto. Mozart's Piano Concerto in D major (K. 537, 1788), so called because he played it (together with another concerto, K. 459) at the coronation of Emperor Leopold at Frankfurt in 1790. The latter is also called Coronation Concerto.

Coronation Mass. Mozart's Mass in C major (K. 317, 1779), composed for the annual coronation of the statue of the Virgin at the shrine of Maria Plain, near Salzburg, Austria.

Corrente [It.]. See Courante.

Corrido [Sp.]. A Mexican type of narrative folk ballad, derived from the Spanish *romanze* and sung also in various other Latin American countries. The texts concern either local events or historical and legendary subjects and are arranged in stanzas of eight-syllable lines. The music is secondary to the text. The melodies are repeated as many times as there are stanzas, and the only element of variation is found in the instrumental episodes interpolated between stanzas. The singing is usually accompanied by guitars and harps or by a full *mariachi* ensemble.   J.O-S.

Cortège [F.]. A composition in the character of a solemn procession or a triumphal march.

Cortholt, cortol. Same as curtall [see Oboe family III].

Cosa rara, una. See *Una Cosa rara.*

Così fan tutte, osia la scuola degli amanti [It., Thus Do All (Women), or The School of Lovers]. Comic opera in two acts by Mozart (libretto by L. da Ponte), produced in Vienna, 1790. Setting: Naples, 18th century.

Costa Rica. The traditional music of Costa Rica is strongly Spanish in character, indigenous and Negro influences being less obvious than in the music of other Latin American countries. The most typical native form is the *punto,* a gay and

lively dance associated especially with the province of Guanacaste. The *pasión* is a song in the Spanish tradition, and its cultivation in Costa Rica dates from the early colonial era.

The beginning of art music in Costa Rica coincides with the composition of the national anthem (1853) by a native amateur composer and band leader, Manuel María Gutiérrez (1829–87). His son, Carlos María Gutiérrez (1865–1934), is also well known in Costa Rica. A considerable number of 19th-century composers are listed by J. R. Araya [see Lit.]. Most of them wrote songs and instrumental pieces in the popular vein, and occasionally major forms. Among the most prominent are Rafael Chavez Torres (1839–1907); José Campadabal (1849–1905), and his son, Roberto Campadabal (1881–1931); Pedro Calderón Navarro (1864–1909), a native of Spain and composer of church music; and Alejandro Monestel (1865–1950), a noted organist and composer, a prolific composer of church music as well as works for band and orchestra based on folk materials.

To a later generation belong Julio Fonseca (1885–1950), who wrote a *Suite Tropical* based on folk materials, several Masses, and a romanticist *Cantata a la Música;* Julio Mata (b. 1899), a modernist, whose works include a *Suite Abstracta,* a light opera (*Toyupán*), and an operetta (*Rosas de Norgaría*); Cesar A. Nieto (b. 1892), composer of a ballet, *La Piedra de Toxil;* José Quesada (b. 1894), whose works include an orchestral poem, *El Son de la luna,* and band arrangements of Costa Rican dances; and J. Ismael Cardona (b. 1877), author of a *Suite Miniatura* for orchestra.

The younger generation of Costa Rican composers includes Bernal Flores (b. 1937), who has written a Symphony no. 1 for strings (1964) in traditional European style.

Lit.: A. Prado Quesada, *Apuntes sintéticos sobre la historia y producción musical en Costa Rica* [1941]; id., ed., *Costa Rica su música tipica y sus autores* (1962); J. R. Araya, "Vida musical de Costa Rica" (*Educación* xvi, nos. 96–97). See also under Latin America.   J.O-S.

Cotillon, cotillion. A popular dance of the 18th and 19th centuries, used especially at the close of an entertainment. It includes a large variety of steps and figures that are executed by a leading couple and imitated by all the others. The cotillon has no particular music; any dance music (waltz, polka, mazurka) can be played for it. The cotillon is mentioned, as a variety of the *contredanse,* in the 1752 edition of the *Diction-*

naire universel de Trévoux but not in the edition of 1743. See also Farandole.

Coulé [F.]. A French 18th-century *agrément* in the character of an appoggiatura. For *coulé sur une tierce,* see Appoggiatura, double II; Nachschlag.

Coulisse [F.]. The slide of a trombone or a slide trumpet.

Council of Laodicea. A church council (A.D. 367) that played an important part in the development of Byzantine church music. It abolished the use of instruments and congregational participation in the performance of the chant in order to prevent it from deteriorating.

Council of Trent. A council of the Roman Church, held at Trento (South Tyrol, now Italy) 1545–63, where important decisions regarding church music were made. The council abolished all the tropes and sequences with the exception of four [see Sequence II D]. The Cardinals' determination to restore the dignity of the service, after the growing corruption and secularization of the previous centuries, acutely endangered the continued development of polyphonic music because for a time they considered abolishing all music in the service other than plainsong. There is, however, no truth to the frequently repeated story that Palestrina "saved music" by composing his *Missa Papae Marcelli,* which, we are told, so greatly impressed the Cardinals that they desisted from their plan [see Marcellus Mass]. Actually, Palestrina's role in the council was rather inconspicuous and much slighter than that of Jacobus de Kerle and others. See also Mass C II e. See K. Weinmann, *Das Konzil von Trient und die Kirchenmusik* (1919); O. Ursprung, in the preface to *DTB* 26; H. Leichtentritt, in *MQ* xxx; K. G. Fellerer, in *MQ* xxxix; *ReMR*, pp. 448ff.

Counterexposition. A name sometimes given to the second exposition of a fugue.

Counterfugue [G. *Gegenfuge*]. A fugue in which the answer (*comes*) is the inverted form of the subject (*dux*), e.g., nos. 5, 6, 7 of Bach's *Art of Fugue.* This method was used as early as the 16th century, probably first by A. Gabrieli. See Inversion (2).

Counterpoint [G. *Kontrapunkt;* F. *contrepoint;* It. *contrappunto;* L. *contrapunctus;* Sp. *contrapunto*]. I. *Definition.* The term, derived from *punctus contra punctum,* i.e., "note against note" or,

by extension, "melody against melody," denotes music consisting of two or more lines that sound simultaneously. Counterpoint is practically synonymous with *polyphony except for differences of emphasis. The latter term is preferred for early music and the former for later periods (16th to 18th centuries). Also, the latter has the connotation of a broad stylistic and historical classification (polyphony vs. monophony and homophony), and the former that of systematic study for the purpose of instruction (Palestrina counterpoint, Bach counterpoint, strict and free counterpoint, etc.).

The individual melodies or strands of a contrapuntal composition constitute the horizontal element of its *texture, while the intervals occurring between them represent the vertical element. These two elements, distinct and yet inseparable, represent a generating and a controlling force respectively. The former is essential, the latter incidental. Yet it is the latter that primarily determines the various kinds of counterpoint used from the Middle Ages to the present day and therefore serves as the means for classification (in terms of evolution). This does not mean that the other aspects—evolution of melodic lines and of rhythmic coordination—are less important, but only that, owing to their more complex character, they take second place in a systematic study.

II. *Theory.* The earliest designations for polyphonic music were *organum and discantus (*c.* 900–1300). The term *punctus contra punctum* was used first in the treatise of Petrus dictus Palma ociosa of 1336 [see *SIM* xv, 508, 513]. About 1350 the term *contrapunctus* appeared in various treatises, some of which describe it as *nota contra notam* [see *CS* iii, 12, 23]. Throughout the 14th century *contrapunctus* meant note-against-note style. Thus, the author of the *Ars contrapunctus secundum Philippum de Vitriaco* (de Vitry lived from *c.* 1290 to 1361) distinguished between *contrapunctus* and *cantus fractibilis,* admitting only in the latter the use of several notes against one [*CS* iii, 23]. Tinctoris in his *Diffinitorium* (*c.* 1475) called both types *contrapunctus,* distinguishing them as *simplex* and *diminutus* [*CS* iv, 180].

Up to 1300, the intervals admitted in theoretical treatises were unison, octave, fifth, and fourth, together with the third as an "imperfect consonance." In three-voice counterpoint (first discussed by Franco) the governing principle was that the *triplum* must be added in consonance with either the tenor or the *duplum,* though not necessarily with both. Thus, vertical combinations such as 1–4–5, 1–4–7, 1–3–4 were permissible and actually occur in musical practice. Johannes de Muris, however, stated that all three parts must be consonant [see *CS* iii, 68]. Four-part counterpoint is discussed in a "Tractatus de musica figurata et de contrapuncto" from the second half of the 15th century and is illustrated by a table showing the admissible combinations [*CS* iv, 447ff]. The earliest document for florid counterpoint is the Vatican treatise from *c.* 1150 [*Ottob. lat. 3025;* in F. Zaminer, *Der Vatikanische Organum Traktat* (1959)], which contains about 350 examples showing how to write a melismatic upper part above the various intervallic progressions (c-d, c-e, etc.) of the tenor. A similar, much later document is Conrad Paumann's "Fundamentum organisandi" (1452). The first theorist to discuss florid counterpoint and give definite rules concerning dissonance treatment, etc., is Tinctoris (*Liber de arte contrapuncti*, 1477; see *ReMR*, pp. 140ff). Johannes Cochlaeus (*Musica,* 1507) and Pietro Aaron (*Libri tres de institutione harmonica,* 1516) state that all the parts are best composed simultaneously, not in *successive counterpoint. Giovanni Lanfranco, in his *Scintille di musica* (1533), distinguishes four *species of counterpoint that are essentially identical with those of J. J. Fux. The equal importance of both the linear and the vertical aspect of counterpoint is emphasized by Vicentino (*L'Antica Musica,* 1555) and even more by Zarlino, whose *Istitutioni harmoniche* (vol. iii, 1558) is the first comprehensive study of counterpoint. Zarlino was also the first to deal systematically with imitation, canon, double counterpoint, and other *obblighi,* a subject presented in a more limited manner by H. Buchner [in his "Fundamentum" of *c.* 1525; repr. in *VMW* v].

In the 17th century traditional counterpoint as taught by Zarlino (today usually referred to as Palestrina counterpoint) was called *contrappunto osservato* and was retained as the basis of instruction. The main objective of theorists such as Diruta, Cerone, Zacconi, Banchieri, Berardi, and numerous others was to present the rules in a simplified form. The final link in this development in Fux's *Gradus ad Parnassum* (1725), a work that contains hardly anything new but has served to perpetuate the tradition of the *stile osservato* to the present day [see Species]. The actual contrapuntal practice of the baroque period differed from the rules, mainly in the much freer treatment of dissonances. As early as

the 1580's Vincenzo Galilei (*c.* 1520–91) wrote two treatises, "Il Primo Libro della prattica del contrapunto intorno all' uso delle consonanze" and "Discorso intorno all' uso delle dissonanze" (not published), in which he admits dissonances on the strong beat, upward resolutions, multiple appoggiaturas, diminished fourths and augmented fifths, seventh chords, and other formations characteristic of the *seconda pratica* or, as it is generally called today, Bach counterpoint. The only other author dealing with this type of counterpoint is Christoph Bernhard (1627–92) in his "Tractatus compositionis augmentatus" and "Ausführlicher Bericht vom Gebrauche der Con- und Dissonantien" (*c.* 1660), which also remained in manuscript.

In the 18th century, what little was written about counterpoint (e.g., J. P. Kirnberger's *Die Kunst des reinen Satzes in der Musik,* 1774–79) shows counterpoint in complete subservience to harmony. J. G. Albrechtsberger, in his *Gründliche Anweisung zur Komposition* (1790, 1818) returned to the species used by J. J. Fux, admitting much more freedom in the treatment of dissonances. In L. Cherubini's *Cours de contrepoint et de fugue* (1835) and H. Bellermann's *Der Kontrapunkt* (1862), the strict counterpoint of the late 16th century was revived.

III. *Practice.* By and large, contrapuntal practice developed along the same lines as theory, though usually preceding it by a considerable number of years. Thus, thirds occur in practical sources as early as *c.* 1150; four-part counterpoint sporadically *c.* 1200 (Perotinus) and *c.* 1330 (*Messe Notre Dame* of Machaut), and continuously from 1400 on (Dufay, Ockeghem); and imitation quite frequently throughout the 15th century. Only V. Galilei's explanation of 17th-century counterpoint seemed to inaugurate a new phase rather than summarize practice. Examples illustrating contrapuntal practice up to 1200 are given under Organum. The subsequent development up to *c.* 1620 is illustrated by the examples on the next page.

The last example illustrates an isolated case of "deliberate revolt" rather than common practice. By and large, 17th-century compositions are based on the principles known as "Bach counterpoint," which differs from "Palestrina counterpoint" mainly in that it is based on "tonal" (instead of "modal") harmonies, admitting six-four chords, seventh chords, and diminished seventh chords. After Bach the emphasis shifted to accompanied melody. However, contrapuntal passages are found in the late works

1. Perotinus (?), organum triplum "Jacet." Three-voice counterpoint admitting "dissonant concordances" such as 1–4–7 on strong beats (see meas. 3).   2. Machaut, "Comment puet." Considerable dissonance between widely spaced 1–5–8 consonances. Separation of the voice ranges.   3. Dunstable, "Sancta Maria." Panconsonant counterpoint with full triads, often in I, IV, V positions.   4. Ockeghem, Missa Mi-Mi. Counterpoint in four parts of similar design and equal importance. Note the "irregular" resolutions (*).   5. Josquin, "Laudate pueri Dominum." Imitative counterpoint in stile osservato, which, however, Josquin does not always "observe."   6. Frescobaldi, Capriccio cromatico con ligature al contrario. All appoggiaturas (ligature) are resolved upward, i.e., contrary (al contrario) to the rules of the stile osservato.

of Haydn and Mozart as well as in Beethoven, Schumann, Mendelssohn, Liszt, Brahms, Franck, and other 19th-century composers. In contrast to the harmonically oriented counterpoint of this period is the dissonant counterpoint of the 20th century, where the linear aspect rules supreme and the vertical is almost meaningless. See also Canon; Discant; Fugue; Invertible counterpoint; Linear counterpoint; Polyphony; Texture.

Lit.: J. J. Fux, *Gradus ad Parnassum* (1725; trans. A. Mann, *Steps to Parnassus,* 1944); R. O. Morris, *Introduction to Counterpoint* (1944); id., *Contrapuntal Technique in the Sixteenth Century,* rev. ed. (1944); K. Jeppesen, *Counterpoint* (1939); A. T. Merritt, *Sixteenth-Century Polyphony* (1939); W. Piston, *Counterpoint* (1947); G. P. Soderlund, *Direct Approach to Counterpoint in 16th-Century Style* (1947); A. I. McHose, *The Contrapuntal Harmonic Technique of the 18th*

Century (1947); E. Krenek, *Modal Counterpoint in the Style of the Sixteenth Century* [1959]; *id.*, *Tonal Counterpoint in the Style of the Eighteenth Century* [1958]; *id.*, *Studies in Counterpoint Based on the Twelve-Tone Technique* [1940]; H. Searle, *Twentieth-Century Counterpoint* (1954); R. H. Robbins, *Beiträge zur Geschichte des Kontrapunkts von Zarlino bis Schütz* (1938); F. Wright, *The Essentials of Strict Counterpoint* (1935); S. I. Taneiev, *Convertible Counterpoint in the Strict Style,* Eng. trans. [1962]; R. Wood, "Modern Counterpoint" (*ML* xiii, 312); C. L. Seeger, "On Dissonant Counterpoint" (*MM* vii, no. 4); K. Jeppesen, in *MQ* xxi.

Countersubject. See under Fugue I (c).

Countertenor. Old name for (male) *alto, derived from *contratenor altus* [see Contratenor].

Country dance. A generic term for English dances of folk origin, of which there are a great variety. They differ in the arrangement of the dancers as well as in the steps and gestures, but all are group dances. The dancers usually stand in two long lines, men and women facing each other, and move forward and back in figures that change with every eight-measure phrase of the music. There is a definite similarity (if not direct connection) between these English dances, which flourished especially throughout the 17th and 18th centuries, and the French *branles of the 16th century. The melodies written for these dances all are simple, gay tunes with a marked rhythm and in symmetrical eight-measure phrases. The authoritative source for the country dances is Playford's *The English Dancing Master* (1651; fac. repr., 1957), which contains more than a hundred charming tunes, each accompanied by directions and figures for the dancers. Enlarged editions of this book continued to appear until 1728. Throughout the 18th century and early 19th century (till 1830) numerous publications of country dances were issued, frequently in booklets small enough to fit in the dancing master's pocket. Recently there has been a considerable revival of country dances, in England as well as in the United States. See *Contredanse;* Dance music III.

Lit.: C. F. Sharp, ‡*The Country Dance Book* (6 parts, 1909–22); *id.*, ‡*Country Dance Tunes* (11 parts, 1909–22); F. Kidson, ed., ‡*Old English Country Dances* (1890).

Coup d'archet [F.]. Bow stroke.

Coup de langue [F.]. Tonguing.

Coupler [G. *Koppel*]. See under Organ IV.

Couplet [F.]. In French poetry, the stanza of a poem (not two rhyming lines, like the English couplet). The corresponding Spanish term, *copla, denotes the various stanzas of the *villancico*, which alternate with the refrain (*estribillo*). In music, the term *couplet* is used mainly for the various sections of the 17th-century rondeau, which are connected by the reiterated refrain [see Rondeau (2); also Rondo]. In 18th and 19th-century light opera (Singspiel, operetta) *couplet* means a strophic song of a witty character. Properly these should be called *couplets* (stanzas), but the singular form was generally adopted in Germany (Johann Strauss), where it was also used, from about 1890 to 1910, for popular refrain songs of a light and humorous character. Today the couplet is found in musical comedy, burlesque, and popular songs.

Courante [F.; It. *corrente, coranto*]. A dance that originated in the 16th century and became, in the mid-17th century, one of the standard movements of the suite. Arbeau, in his *Orchésographie* (1589), describes it as a dance (in duple time!) with jumping movements and a great variety of figures, according to the dancer's ability and fancy. T. Morley, on the other hand, describes it as "travising and running" [*A Plaine and Easie Introduction to Practicall Musicke* (1597), p. 181], in contrast to the leaps of the *volta*. The earliest known musical example, "La corante du roy" in B. Schmid's tablature of 1577 [see W. Merian, *Der Tanz in den deutschen Tabulaturbüchern* (1927), p. 112], does not show any differences from the *saltarello. However, a number of "Corrantos" of the Fitzwilliam Virginal Book vaguely foreshadow the 17th-century courante with their generally lighter texture and short "running" figures. In the 17th century the dance became stylized as two types, the Italian corrente and the French courante [for a similar case, see under Gigue (2)].

(a) The Italian corrente is in quick triple time (3/4, sometimes 3/8), with continuous running figures in a melody-accompaniment texture. It appears to be the direct outgrowth of the late 16th-century type as exemplified in the Fitzwilliam Virginal Book. It also must be considered the earlier of the two types, since it appears already clearly established in Schein's *Banchetto musicale* (1617), Frescobaldi's *Toccate e partite d'intavolatura di cimbalo* (2nd ed., 1615–16), and S. Scheidt's *Tabulatura nova* (1624).

Later examples are in M. Cazzati's *Corrente e Balletti* (1662, '63; the distinction made here between *c. alla francese* and *c. alla italiana* is scarcely borne out by a difference in style), in the *Sonate da camera* by Corelli (op. 2, 4), in the keyboard suites of Zipoli (*Sonate d'Intavolatura per Organo*, 1716), etc.

(b) The French courante is much more refined. It is in moderate 3/2 or 6/4 time, with a frequent shift from one of these meters to the other (i.e., from the accents 1̄ 2 3̄ 4 5̄ 6 to the accents 1̄ 2 3 4̄ 5 6; see Hemiola II). The resulting instability of rhythm is typical of the courante. Equally subtle is its texture, a free contrapuntal fabric in which the melodic interest frequently shifts temporarily from the upper to one of the lower parts. More than any other type of baroque music, the courante gives the impression of "blurred contours" that is a typical romantic feature in music history [see Romanticism]. Quite properly it has been compared to the quickly changing movements of a fish [Écorcheville]. Examples abound in the works of Chambonnières, L. Couperin, Froberger, D'Anglebert, F. Couperin, and others. The two accompanying examples illustrate the corrente [Ex. 1, Frescobaldi] and the courante [Ex. 2, Chambonnières].

The courantes of Bach's suites are usually of the French type. Especially remarkable for its rhythmic ambiguity is the courante of the English Suite no. 2; in others, the change from 3/2 to 6/4 occurs chiefly in the final measure of each section. The Italian type occurs in the French Suites nos. 2, 4, 5, 6 and in the Partitas nos. 1, 3, 5, 6. In the original edition of the Partitas [*Clavier-Übung* i, 1731] the distinction between courantes and correntes is carefully indicated by Bach; unfortunately, later editors, including those of the *BG*, have substituted the name Courante for some or all of the correntes. See Dance music III. See C. Sachs, *World History of the Dance* (1937), pp. 361ff.

Course [F. *chœur;* G. (*Saiten*)*chor;* It. *coro;* Sp. *orden*]. In stringed instruments, chiefly those of the lute type, a group of strings tuned in unison or in the octave and plucked simultaneously in order to obtain increased volume. On the 16th-century lutes double-courses were used for the lower strings, as follows: G–g c–c′ f–f′ a–a d′–d′ g′ (also G–G c–c f–f a–d d′–d′ g′). In order to simplify the terminology, the single string g″ is also called a "course," so that the 16th-century lute would have 11 strings in 6 courses. A bass-course is a string (single or double) that runs alongside the fingerboard without crossing the frets; hence, it is invariable in pitch. See Lute. Unison courses of two or three strings are used for the higher ranges of the piano and harp.

Courtaud, courtall. Same as curtall [see Oboe family III].

Covered fifths, octaves. Same as hidden fifths, octaves. See under Parallel fifths, octaves.

Cow bells [G. *Kuhglocken*]. Instruments similar in shape and sound to the bells worn by cows in the Alps, but without clapper and struck with a drumstick. They were used by R. Strauss in his *Alpensinfonie* (op. 64; 1915) and are also used in dance bands.

1. *Corrente (Frescobaldi).*   2. *Courante (Chambonnières).*

Crab motion, crab canon [G. *Krebsgang, Krebskanon*]. See Retrograde; Canon (1), I.

Cracovienne [F.]. See *Krakowiak.*

Crash cymbal. Two large circular brass plates made slightly convex so that only the edges will touch when they are struck together. See Cymbals.

Creation, The [G. *Die Schöpfung*]. Oratorio by Haydn, composed in 1797. It is based on a poem compiled by Lidley from Milton's *Paradise Lost,* which was suggested to Haydn by the concert-manager Salomon during his second stay in London (1794–95). Upon Haydn's return to Vienna, the text was translated into German by his friend, Baron van Swieten, and this translation (*Die Schöpfung*) became the basis of the oratorio, which was first performed in Vienna in 1798.

Creation Mass. Popular name for Haydn's Mass in B-flat (1801), used because a theme from his oratorio, *The Creation,* appears in the "Qui tollis."

Creatures of Prometheus. See *Geschöpfe des Prometheus.*

Crécelle [F.]. Rattle.

Credo [L.]. The third item of the Ordinary of the Mass. In plainsong, the first phrase, "Credo in unum Deum," is sung by the officiating priest, and the chorus enters at "Patrem omnipotentem." The Credo (*Symbolum apostolicum*) became part of the Mozarabic liturgy as early as 589 (Council of Toledo) and was officially prescribed from the Frankish liturgy in 798. It was the last of five Ordinary chants to be incorporated into the Roman Mass (in 1014 at the insistence of Emperor Henry II). Even today, the Credo melodies are grouped separately from other items [*LU,* pp. 64ff]. The oldest melody [*LU,* p. 64, no. 1], often called the "authentic Credo," is found in MSS of the 11th century, but because of its formal structure it is generally thought to be of earlier origin [see *ApGC,* pp. 412ff].

Early polyphonic settings (14th to 16th centuries) nearly always begin with "Patrem omnipotentem" and are often indexed under "Patrem" in modern editions. In polyphonic Mass compositions of the 17th and 18th centuries the Credo is usually treated in a majestic and forceful style, expressing unshaking belief in the creed of the Church. A contrasting expression, however, is given to the sections "Et incarnatus est" and *"Crucifixus" [see Mass III]. See R. Hannas, "Concerning Deletions in the Polyphonic Mass Credo" (*JAMS* v); M. Huglo, "Origine de la

mélodie du Credo 'authentique' de la Vaticane" (*RG* xxx). See Creed.

Creed. Name for three texts of the Roman and Anglican rites. (1) Nicene Creed (named after the Council of Nicea, A.D. 325), used in the *Credo of the Mass. (2) Apostle's Creed, *Credo in Deum Patrem omnipotentem,* formerly used in the Offices, either monotoned (Anglican Offices) or said "secretly," i.e., silently except for the initial words and the final versicle and response (Anglican monasteries and Roman Catholic churches). (3) Athanasian Creed, *Quicumque vult salvus esse* (Whosoever wants to be saved), used particularly on Trinity Sunday at the Office of Prime (*LU* p. 227). See F. J. Badcock, *The History of Creeds* (1930).

Crembalum [L.]. *Jew's-harp.

Crescendo, decrescendo, abbr. *cresc., decresc.,* or *decr.;* indicated by the signs $<$ and $>$. The usual terms and signs for increasing or decreasing volume. For the latter, the word *diminuendo* (*dim.*) is also used. For their history, see Expression marks.

Crescendo pedal. See under Organ VII.

Crescent. See Turkish crescent.

Cretic meter. In ancient Greek music, name for *quintuple meter.

Criticism. See Music criticism.

Croche [F.]. Eighth note. See under Notes; also Crotchet.

Croiser les mains. See *Croisez.*

Croisez, croisement [F.]. Indication to cross the hands in piano playing.

Croma [It.]. Eighth note. See under Notes.

Cromatico [It.]. Chromatic. See especially under Chromatic (4).

Cromorne. See under Oboe family III. See C. Sachs, in *SIM* xi, 590ff.

Crook or shank. See under Wind instruments IV (b); Horn II; Trumpet II.

Crooning. A style of singing softly and sentimentally, with sliding and moaning effects, that was introduced about 1930 by popular American radio singers (e.g., Bing Crosby, Rudy Vallee).

Cross fingering [F. *doigté fourchu;* G. *Gabelgriff*]. In playing wind instruments with side holes, any fingering in which open holes alternate with closed ones, in contrast to "normal" fingering, in which all open holes are at the lower end of the pipe and all closed ones at the upper end. While the normal fingering produces most of the diatonic tones of the main octave, cross fingering is necessary for the semitones and the tones of the higher octave. On modern instruments (flutes, clarinets, oboes) cross fingering is largely avoided owing to the elaborate system of keys (*Böhm action).

Cross flute [F. *flûte traversière;* G. *Querflöte;* It. *flauto traverso;* Sp. *flauta traversa*]. Older name for the present-day flute, so called because it is held crosswise to the body. See Transverse flute.

Cross relation [F. *fausse relation;* G. *Querstand*]. Cross relation (or false relation) is the appearance in different voices of two tones that, owing to their mutually contradictory character (e.g., major and minor third of the same triad), would normally be placed as a melodic progression in one voice. In other words, cross relation means the use in "diagonal" position of what properly is a "horizontal" element of musical texture [see Texture]. The most important progression of this kind is the chromatic progression, e.g., E^b–E, which is so strikingly "horizontal" that the ear is disturbed if it hears the first tone in one voice and the second in another [Ex. 1]. In classical harmony and counterpoint, such progres-

sions are considered bad (false) and the rule prohibiting them helps prevent the student from making such an error. Nevertheless, in numerous instances the disturbing effect is sufficiently mitigated to make cross relation acceptable, e.g., if it occurs between inner voices [Ex. 2] and,

particularly, if the "false" relation between one voice and another is rectified by a strikingly "good" relation in each of these voices, i.e., if there is enough melodic (contrapuntal) individuality in each voice to distract the listener's attention from the diagonal clash [Ex. 3; Mozart]. Another, considerably weaker type of cross relation is that involving the tritone (e.g., E–B^b); it is usually avoided between two outer voices [Ex. 4].

Although cross relations generally are not used in "classical" harmony and counterpoint, they are frequently found in earlier music. In the 16th century, the normal manner of proceeding from A major to F major was to place the C-sharp and C-natural in different voice-parts [Ex. 5]. The compositions of Byrd, Gibbons, and Frescobaldi contain numerous interesting examples of cross relation [Ex. 6, 7], and also of what might be called, somewhat antithetically, "vertical cross relation," i.e., the simultaneous sounding of two chromatic tones [Ex. 8; other examples under *Musica ficta*]. In modern music, cross relations are, of course, very common, the impression of "falsity" diminishing with the increasing disintegration of the harmonic system of the 19th century.

Cross rhythm. The simultaneous use of conflicting rhythmic patterns, e.g., three notes against four, or of conflicting accents, e.g., 3/4 meter against 4/4 meter. See Polyrhythm.

Crot. See Crwth.

Crotales [F.], **crotalum** [Gr.–L.]. The *crotalum* of Greek and Latin antiquity was a rattle or clapper similar to the castanets, consisting of two wooden or metal shells held in one hand. The French *crotales* usually means a clapper, specifically the castanets. See under Cymbals.

Crotchet. In British terminology, the quarter note. This is the old *semiminima*, which in black notation was written with a flag attached to the stem [see Notation, Ex. 6, no. 15] and therefore occasionally called *crochata* (hooked; see Crook), e.g., by Anon. I [*CS* iii, 337a]. In white notation, however, the hook appeared with the *fusa*, hence the French *croche* for the eighth note.

Crouth, crowd, cruit. See Crwth.

Crucible, The. Opera in four acts by R. Ward (libretto by B. Stambler, after A. Miller's play), produced in New York, 1961. Setting: Salem, Mass., 1692.

Crucifixus. A section of the Credo of the Mass. In Mass compositions it frequently appears as a separate movement of sorrowful expression, as in Bach's B-minor Mass.

Crumhorn. Cromorne. See Oboe family III.

Crwth. A six-stringed bowed stringed instrument probably of ancient Celtic descent. It is conspicuous for its rectangular shape, which is strongly reminiscent of the Greek *kithara. The oldest illustrations (11th century) show the instrument without a fingerboard and played like a harp. It was used with a bow from the 12th or 13th century, and later a fingerboard was added, whereby it became associated with the violin family [see ill. under Lyra; also in *GD*, ii, opp. 542, and v, opp. 514; *GDB*, iv, opp. 90, and viii, opp. 146]. The instrument was still used in Wales in the early years of the 19th century. It is also known by the anglicized name *crowd* and the Irish names *crot* and *cruit*. A medieval Latin name, used in the 11th to the 14th centuries, is *chorus* [see *SaRM*, p. 80]. The medieval form, without fingerboard, is usually called *rotta* or *rotte*. The *chrotta,* mentioned by Venantius Fortunatus (6th century), was probably the same as the rotta [see *MaMI*, p. 134f].

Lit.: N. Bessaraboff, *Ancient European Musical Instruments* (1941), pp. 314ff; H. Panum, *The Stringed Instruments of the Middle Ages,* rev. and ed. J. Pulver [n.d.]; F. W. Galpin, *Old English Instruments of Music,* rev. ed. T. Dart (1965); A. Baines, ed., *Musical Instruments through the Ages* (1961); O. Anderson, *The Bowed-Harp,* ed. K. Schlesinger (1930).

C.s. [It.]. Abbr. for *colla sinistra,* with the left hand.

Csárdás [Hung.]. A Hungarian dance of the early 19th century, first recorded about 1835. Although it was claimed to be of rustic origin, it probably represents a ballroom variant of the old *verbunkos. It is in rapid 2/4 time, considerably faster than the *friss* (fast) sections of the verbunkos. The slow *lassu* sections were not incorporated into the *csárdás.*

C sol fa ut. See under Hexachord III.

Cuando [Sp.]. One of the oldest Latin American dance forms still popular, mainly in Argentina and Chile. Its similarity to the *minuet confirms its European origin.   J.O-S.

Cuba. Little is known about musical activity in Cuba during the 16th century. The earliest known native musician was Miguel Velásquez, who was organist in the Cathedral of Santiago (1544). In 1682 the post of musical director of the Cathedral of Santiago was established and was filled by Domingo de Flores. Not until the second half of the 18th century did Cuba produce a major composer, Esteban Salas (1725–1803), a native of Havana and a prolific composer of church and secular music, influenced partly by the European late baroque and partly by the early classic school. Among his more than ninety liturgical compositions are several Masses, litanies, psalms, and a Stabat Mater. In addition, he wrote almost two hundred *villancicos* with Spanish texts, some of which are called *cantadas* or *pastorelas.*

Salas was succeeded at Santiago by Francisco José Hierrezuelo (1763–1824), who in turn was followed by Juan Paris (1759–1845), a native of Barcelona; a few of his compositions, written in Viennese classic style, have been preserved. Other composers of the period included Antonio Raffelin (1796–1882), who wrote a Mass and three symphonies; Manuel Saumell (1817–70), who wrote numerous *contradanzas* for piano in the Cuban popular vein; Laureano Fuentes (1825–98), composer of sacred music, several *Sinfonias* (overtures), chamber compositions, and an opera, *Seila* (1865); Nicolas Ruiz Espadero (1832–90), a pianist who wrote a considerable number of virtuoso compositions for his instrument; and Gaspar Villate (1851–1912), who wrote several operas (*Angelo,* 1867; *Zilia,* 1881; *Baltazar,* 1885) and an unfinished music drama, *Cristobal Colón.*

The most outstanding musician of the second half of the 19th century was Ignacio Cervantes (1847–1905), who studied first in Havana and then in Paris, where he absorbed all the influences of the Second Empire. Of his compositions, the most important are his twenty-one *Danzas* for piano, written between 1875 and 1895, which represent the first skillful stylization of Cuban folk music.

Nationalism in the 20th century is brilliantly represented by Amadeo Roldán (1900–39) and Alejandro García Caturla (1906–40), who mingled elements of European music with the spirit of Cuban folk music. José Ardévol (b. 1911) became a prominent leader of modern music in Cuba. In addition to producing a vast number of compositions, especially chamber music, Ardévol has been an outstanding teacher and promoter of contemporary music, through both the *Grupo Renovación* and the Havana Chamber

Orchestra, which he established. In 1922 Gonzalo Roig (b. 1890), author of the well-known lyric comedy *Cecilia Valdéz*, founded the Havana Symphony Orchestra, and two years later the Philharmonic Orchestra was established under the direction of Pedro Sanjuán (b. 1886).

Of Ardévol's pupils, the best known are Harold Gramatges (b. 1918), Edgardo Martín (b. 1915), Serafin Pró (b. 1906), Juan Antonio Cámara (b. 1917), Gisela Herñandez (b. 1910), and Argeliers León (b. 1918). Their contemporaries, Enrique Gonzalez Mantici (b. 1912), Natalio Galán (b. 1919), Hilario Gonzãlez Iñiguez (b. 1920), Carlo Borbolla, and Fabio Landa (b. 1924) have also contributed outstanding works. Of this generation, Julián Orbón (b. 1925) and Aurelio de la Vega (b. 1925) are the best known outside Cuba. Orbón has combined the Spanish tradition with contemporary techniques, notably in such works as his *Tres Versiones Sinfónicas* (1953), Concerto Grosso (1955), string quartet (1951), and *Tres Cantigas del Rey* (1960). De la Vega has moved from the neoromanticism of an early trio (1949) to the atonal idiom of his string quartet (1957), symphony in four parts (1960), *Estructuras* (1963), and *Coordinates* (1964), the last-named an electronic piece. Juan Blanco (b. 1920) has produced *musique concrète* and *electronic music, while Leo Brower (b. 1939) has written some skillful serial compositions.

A prominent composer of light music and musical comedies is Cuba's internationally recognized Ernesto Lecuona (1896–1964).

Cuban folk music stems from two main traditions, Spanish and African. The Spanish tradition is strongly reflected in the rural songs generically known as *punto. This type developed from the Spanish *contradanza,* which by the mid-19th century acquired characteristics far different from its original models, leading to the *habanera, *guajira, *guaracha, *tonada, and *bolero. African influences are more evident in urban folk music, which differs from that of Spanish origin mainly in its wide use of syncopation. Such types include the *danzón,* *rumba, *son, *macumba, and *conga. The *tumba was introduced to Cuba from Haiti.

Lit.: A. Carpentier, *La Música en Cuba* (1946); P. Hernandez Balaguer, *Breve Historia de la Música Cubana* (1964); *id., Música en la Catedral de Santiago de Cuba* (1965); Z. Lapique Becali, *Catalogación y Clasificación de la Música Cubana* (1963); A. León, *Música Folklorica Cubana* (1964); A. Carpentier, "Music in Cuba" (*MQ* xxxiii). Also see under Latin America. J.O-S.

Cue. In orchestral parts including a long rest, a short passage taken from another leading instrument and printed in small notes, in order to warn the player of the entry of his part.

Cueca, zamacueca [Sp.]. The most popular Latin American dance in Chile. It is always based on alternations of 3/4 and 6/8 meter in fast tempo, and generally employs eight-syllable quatrains followed by improvised dialogues similar to the *relaciones* in the Argentinian *gato. The first section of the tune is sometimes slow and in the minor mode, followed by another section in rapid tempo in a major mode whose melody always ends in a cadence on the third or fifth degree of the scale. The melody is usually sung in parallel thirds. Hand claps by singers and dancers underline the simple chordal accompaniment of guitars, which uses only tonic and dominant chords. The *cueca* is danced by a couple, with the woman constantly trying to attract her partner's attention and then escaping his pursuit. See P. Garrido, *Biografía de la Cueca* (1943). J.O-S.

Cuivre [F.]. *Instruments de cuivre* or simply *les cuivres* are the brass instruments of the orchestra. *Cuivré* calls for a forced, harsh tone in playing, especially of the horn [see Horn I].

Cumbia. Afro-Panamanian dance form, in duple meter, moderately syncopated and performed either as a purely instrumental piece or as a song accompanied by a *mejoranera. Two varieties are known in Panama: the *cumbia plebeya,* of a rustic and sensual character, and the *cumbia de salón,* performed with steps and figures similar to those used in the polka. J.O-S.

Cunning Vixen, The [Cz. *Lišky Příhody Bystroušky*]. Opera in three acts by L. Janáček (to his own libretto), produced in Brno, 1924. Setting: fairy tale.

Currende [G.]. In the 16th and 17th centuries, name for the choruses of Latin schools (*Gymnasium*) in Germany. Their members were usually boys lacking in funds who, by singing in the streets and for special occasions such as funerals and weddings, helped provide for their support. There has been a revival of this custom in various German towns. See Quempas. See G. Schünemann, *Geschichte der deutschen Schulmusik* (1928); W. Nicolai, in *Bach-Jahrbuch* (1914).

Currentes. Same as *conjunctura* or, at least, the quick diamond-shaped notes of the *conjunctura.*

Cursive and tonic. Terms applied to the termination formulas of Gregorian recitatives (psalm tones, Introit tones, responsorial tones), depending on whether they are invariable or subject to modification (insertion of extra notes for additional syllables of the text). The more ornate terminations (used for the verses of Introits and Responsories) are usually cursive, while the simple ones (for the psalms and canticles) are tonic. The cursive endings consist of five units (single notes or short groups of notes) to which the last five syllables of the text are sung, regardless of their accentual structure, whether ´×× ´ × or ××´ ×× or ´×´ ××, etc. In tonic terminations the accented syllables always fall on the same unit. See *ApGC,* pp. 215 (Fig. 49), 231 (Fig. 55).

Cursus. In classical Latin, a principle of rhythmic structure used in the closing words of a sentence and designed to give prose a certain poetic quality (Cicero, Quintilian). The most important scheme was the *cursus planus,* which consisted of a trochee and a palimbacchius: − ∪ | − − ∪, e.g., *mēmbră fīrmāntŭr.* In accordance with the principles of Latin poetry, this and other combinations (*cursus tardus, cursus velox*) are based on the quantity (measuring) of syllables [see Poetic meter III] and hence are called metrical *cursus.* According to a theory advanced at Solesmes, these were replaced, after 400, by rhythmical *cursus,* which is based on the quality (speech accent) of the syllables. The rhythmical *cursus planus* would be: ´×× ´ ×, e.g., *mémbra firmántur.* Dom Mocquereau tried to show that the rhythmic *cursus* plays an important role in Gregorian chant, i.e., that the accented syllables are sung to a higher pitch (tonic accent). This theory, to which he devoted the major part of vol. iv of the *Paléographie musicale,* cannot be considered valid. Equally untenable is the theory advanced by Dom P. Ferretti (*Il cursus metrico e il ritmo delle melodie gregoriane,* 1913) that the cadential formations of Gregorian chant were influenced by the metrical *cursus.* See H. B. Briggs, in *PMA* xxiv; H. Bewerunge, in *ZIM* xii; *ApGC,* pp. 297ff.

Curtain tune. Same as act tune [see Entr'acte].

Curtal(l). See under Oboe family III.

Custos [L.]. See under Direct.

Cycle. (1) In musical acoustics, designation for a double vibration [see Acoustics I]. (2) Designation for various systems of equal temperament, i.e., systems whose tonal material is obtained by dividing the octave into a number of equal intervals. The simplest is the twelve-tone division, which is the basis of present-day music. Its justification lies in the fact that twelve pure fifths

($\frac{3}{2}$ = 702 cents; see table under Intervals, calculation of) are very close to seven octaves. Its "error" is $12 \times 702 - 7 \times 1200 = 24$ (more nearly 23) cents (Pythagorean *comma). The error is much smaller in the 53-division, called Mercator cycle (after Nicolas Mercator, *c.* 1620–87), which is based on the fact that 53 pure fifths are equal to 31 octaves with an error of only 3.62 cents. This system had been proposed in China as early as 40 B.C., by Jing Farng [see China]. It has the advantage of having practically perfect fifths (701.9 as against 702) and thirds (384.9 as against 386). However, the large number of notes involved renders it useless for practical purposes. Another cycle, named after Christian Huygens (1629–95), has 31 tones to the octaves. It proceeds from the fact that 31 pure thirds are equal to 10 octaves with an error of 34 cents. Its thirds (387 cents) are even more perfect than those of the Mercator cycle but its fifths less so (697 cents). This division was used (approximately) in Vicentino's *arcicembalo. A 19-division was discussed by Zarlino and Salinas and is expressly called for in a "chromatic" chanson by Costeley [see K. J. Levy, in *AnnM* iii, esp. pp. 216ff]. It is the only one that could be put to practical use. See J. M. Barbour, *Tuning and Temperament* (1951), pp. 113ff.

Cyclic, cyclical. (1) Generally, term for any musical form including several movements; thus, the sonata, suite, toccata, cantata, etc., are cyclic forms. (2) Specifically (and preferably), compositions—usually sonatas or symphonies—in which related thematic material is used in all or in some of the movements. One example of cyclic treatment is Schubert's *Fantasie* op. 15 ("Wanderer"). Still more conspicuous is the use of identical material in Berlioz' *Symphonie Fantastique.* Cyclic treatment was used by Bruckner, who in several of his symphonies restates the initial theme of the first movement in the closing climax of the last. It was more clearly established as a principle of composition by César Franck, Vincent d'Indy, Saint-Saëns, Fauré, and Dukas. Statements regarding the presence of cyclical treatment in Beethoven's sonatas, etc., should be accepted cautiously, except, of course, in those obvious cases where a movement shows the insertion (usually in the character of a reminiscence) of a short section from another movement, as, e.g., in the Fifth Symphony, the piano sonata op. 101, and the Ninth Symphony. Cyclic treatment is, however, clearly indicated in many Masses of the 15th and 16th centuries, all of whose movements are based on the same tenor or begin with identical opening measures (*cantus firmus* cycle, motto cycle; see Mass B II c). It is also present in the variation canzona [see Canzona (5), I] and, to some extent, in early baroque compositions (canzonas, sonatas) showing a rounded structure, A B C . . . A [see Sonata B I; *HAM*, nos. 191, 208].

Cylinder. See Valve.

Cymbalon. See Cimbalum.

Cymbals. A percussion instrument (idiophone) consisting of two metal plates struck together. Cymbals in the form of two small saucers attached to handles or held by means of leather straps were used in ancient Egypt, Greece, and Rome (*crotalum*). Similar instruments have been introduced by Debussy (*cymbales antiques*) and Ravel (*crotales*). These are small cymbals of thick metal that can be tuned to a definite pitch. The normal orchestral cymbals are much larger, of thin metal, and of indefinite pitch; see Percussion instruments B, 6. Choke cymbals and sizzle cymbals are varieties used in jazz bands. See H. Hickmann, *Cymbales et crotales dans l'Égypte ancienne* (*Extrait des Annales du Service d'Antiquités de l'Égypte*, vol. xlix, Cairo, 1949).

Cymbalum [L.; pl. *cymbala*]. In the Middle Ages, a small bell. Such bells were made in graded sizes, from four to eight, and hung on a frame to be used as chimes. They were also called *nolae, campanae,* and *tintinnabula.* Various writers give detailed prescriptions for the amount of metal to be used for each bell. See J. Smits van Waesberghe, *Cymbala* (*Bells in the Middle Ages*) (1951).

Cythara. Medieval spelling of *kithara but used as a generic designation for stringed instruments.

Cythringen. See under Guitar family.

Czakan [G. *Stockflöte*]. An early 19th-century contraption made for the enjoyment of music during a walk in the country. It was in the form of a walking stick whose upper part consisted of, or contained, a detachable flute (or recorder?). It was popular in Austria and Hungary from about 1800 to 1850.

Czardas. Erroneous spelling for *csárdás.

Czechoslovakia. The earliest known Czech musical culture dates from the conversion to Christianity in the first half of the 9th century. The missionaries Cyril and Methodius, who arrived there in 863 or 864, established the liturgy of the Eastern Church. From the beginning of the 10th century Gregorian chant spread throughout Bohemia, Moravia, and Slovakia. Important documents of Gregorian chant on Czech soil are the Prague Troper (1235), the Evangeliář (Gospel) of 1293, and the Tobíáš Agenda of Bishop Tobíáš of Bechyně (1294). The oldest surviving Czech religious song is the famous "Hospodine, pomiluj ny" (Lord have mercy on us), written in 1055. It became so popular that it was used at coronations of Czech kings. "Svatý Václave" (St. Wenceslaus) from the 12th century is a secular prayer that was sung at important state functions and before battles, and "Jezu Kriste, ščedrý kněže" (Jesus Christ, noble prince) was later used by Jan Hus. St. Vitus' Cathedral in Prague was the center of musical activity, and in 1259 a cathedral choir of twenty-four priests and twelve choir boys ("bonifantes"—*boni infantes*) was formed.

In the 13th and 14th centuries the minnesingers Heinrich von Meissen (Frauenlob) lived at the Prague court under Wenceslaus II (reigned 1278–1305), and Heinrich von Mügeln (d. *c.* 1371) during the reign of John of Luxemburg (1310–46). During the reign of Charles IV (1346–78), who founded Charles University, there lived three composers of Czech religious and secular songs: the Dominican monk Domaslaus; the Magister Záviš of Zap (*c.* 1350–1411), a few of whose monophonic songs have been preserved; and the Archbishop of Prague, Jan of Jenštejn (1350–1400), whose compositions reveal French influence. Dramatic plays for Christmas and Easter became very popular. In the "Plankty" (Laments of the Virgin Mary) and especially in the satirical Easter play *Mastikář* (The Quack) Czech was preferred to the Latin text. As a result of the Reformation, led by Jan Hus (*c.* 1371–1415), all polyphonic and ornate singing was banned. Religious songs were turned into war songs. The Taborites especially used bold and forceful revolutionary battle songs, the best known of which is "Ktož jsú Boží bojovnici" (Ye Who Are God's Warriors), which still lives in 19th- and 20th-century Czech compositions [e.g., Smetana's *Má Vlast*, Dvořák's "Husitská" overture, etc.]. Most of the Hussite songs are preserved in the *Jistebnice Cantionale* (*c.* 1420). From the Hussite songs there developed, in the second half of the 16th century, the *Rorate* chants [see Rorantists].

The Hussite tradition was continued from the second half of the 15th century by the Bohemian (later Moravian) Brethren. Their spiritual songs were collected in beautifully illustrated books (*cantionales*) containing hymns, canticles, and historical songs. The oldest is the *Mladoboleslav Kancional* (1501), and the most important the *Šamotulský* (1561). The rich musical tradition of the Brethren was ended in their homeland by religious persecution, but it was continued abroad. Jan Amos Komenský (Comenius, 1592–1670) produced the *Amsterdam Cantionale* (printed 1659), which contains 150 psalms and 430 songs. In the early 18th century the Brethren moved to America and other countries.

Vocal polyphony was cultivated especially by the Literary Brethren (*fraternitates literatorum*), who organized choral singing in many Czech towns somewhat in the manner of guilds. The most interesting of their splendidly illuminated song books is the *Hradec Králové* [Königgrätz] *Speciálník* of 1611, which contains 300 compositions, mostly motets and Mass sections. The high point of polyphony came during the Counter-Reformation at the splendid court of Rudolph II (1552–1612), the last Hapsburg emperor to reside in Prague. He employed outstanding composers from England, the Netherlands, Spain, Italy, and Germany, among them Charles Luython, Philipp de Monte, Jacob Regnart, Lambert de Sayve, Jacobus de Kerle, Jakob Hassler, and especially Jacobus Gallus (Jacob Handl, 1550–91). Representatives of the native polyphonic school were Jan Trajan Turnovský, sometimes called the "Bohemian Palestrina," Jiří Rychnovský, and especially Kryštof (Christof) Harant of Polžic (1564–1621), who combined the native style with that of the French, Venetian, and Netherlands schools.

The development of Czech music came to a sudden halt with the defeat of the Protestants in the battle of White Mountain (near Prague) in 1620. In the baroque era it came, belatedly, under the influence of the Italian madrigal and Florentine monody, except in church music. During this time numerous native composers of German parentage left their homeland, among them Christoph Demantius (1567–1643), Andreas Hammerschmidt (1612–75), and the famous violinist Heinrich Ignaz Franz Biber (1644–1704), who together with Pavel Josef Vejvanovský (*c.* 1643–93) was employed by the Archbishop Karl Liechtenstein-Kastelkorn in Kremsier (Moravia). Johann Sigmund Kusser (Cousser, 1660–1727) left his native Bratislava (Pressburg) and later played an important part in the early Hamburg Opera. Composers who remained in their homeland wrote mostly baroque church music. The most important were Adam Michna of Otradovice (*c.* 1600–70), Jan Dismas Zelenka (1679–1745), who studied counterpoint with J. J. Fux in Vienna, the Minorite monk Bohuslav Matěj Černohorský (1684–1742), and František Václav Miča (1694–1744), head of the orchestra of Count Questenberg in Jaroměřice, who wrote cantatas and operas (*L'Origine de Jaromeriz in Moravia*). Černohorský's pupils included Jan (Johann) Zach (1699–1773?) and František Tůma (1704–74), who also studied with Fux. Both wrote, besides Masses and Requiems, a great many secular instrumental works, and they influenced the early style of Mozart. Another important pupil of Černohorský's was the organist Joseph Seeger (1716–82), who in turn counted among his pupils Antonín Koželuch (1738–1814), Václav (Wenzl) Pichl (1741–1804), and Jan Vaňhal (Johann Wanhal, 1739–1813).

The 18th century saw an enormous emigration of Czech musicians, mostly for economic reasons. In Mannheim, Jan Václav Stamic (Johann W. A. Stamitz, 1717–57) developed a new orchestral style together with his countrymen Franz Xaver Richter (1709–89), Jiří Čart (1708–89), Antonín Fils (Filtz, 1730–60), and Karl Stamitz (1745–1801). For religious reasons the entire Benda family (Protestant) went to Berlin. Its most prominent member, Georg (Jiří) Benda (1722–95), originator of the staged *melodrama, settled in Gotha. In Paris lived the piano virtuoso and composer Jan Ladislav Dusík (Johann Dussek, 1760–1812), the horn player Jan Václav Stich (Giovanni Punto, 1746–1803), and Antonín Rejcha (Reicha, 1770–1836), who wrote, among other things, chamber music for wind instruments and many works on music theory, and was the teacher of Berlioz, Gounod, and Franck at the Paris Conservatory. The emigration to Italy was headed by Josef Mysliveček (1737–81), called "Il Boemo," who wrote many operas in Italian style.

The greatest number of Czech musicians in the 18th century moved to Vienna, beginning with František Tůma. Florian Gassmann (1729–74) studied in Italy and wrote operas, both *seria* and *buffa* (*La Contessina*). J. Antonín Štěpán (Joseph Anton Steffan, 1726–97) was court pianist and wrote many piano compositions. Jan Vaňhal (Wanhal, 1739–1813), like most of the Czech composers in Vienna, contributed to the development of the preclassical style. Wagenseil's successor at the Vienna court was the versatile teacher and composer Leopold Koželuch (1752–1818). Many *Singspiele and the romantic opera *Oberon* were written by Pavel Vranický (Paul Wranitzky, 1756–1808), a friend to Haydn, Mozart, and especially Beethoven. František Krommer-Kramář (1759–1831) wrote excellent concertos for violin, oboe, and clarinet, as well as chamber music. The Singspiel composers included Wenzel Müller (1767–1835, *Die Schwestern von Prag*), Ferdinand Kauer (1751–1831, *Das Donauweibchen*), and Vojtěch Jírovec (Adalbert Gyrowetz, 1763–1850), who wrote the opera *Agnes Sorel* for the Congress of Vienna. One of the most talented piano composers and a friend of Beethoven's was Jan Hugo Voříšek (Johann Hugo Woržischek, 1791–1825), who influenced both Schubert's and Smetana's piano music. In Prague František Xaver Dušek (Franz Dussek, 1731–99) wrote piano, chamber, and orchestra music. Jan Václav Tomášek (Tomaschek, 1774–1850), nicknamed the "music Pope" of Prague, was a great teacher and composer of piano and vocal music. Characteristic of the late classical and early romantic tradition was Jakub Jan Ryba (1765–1815), with his great output of secular orchestral and church music. Best known are his pastoral Christmas Masses, using simple folk tunes and Czech texts. František Škroup (1801–62) wrote the first Czech romantic opera, *Dráteník* (The Tinker), and also the Czech national anthem. He was the first Czech opera conductor, succeeding Carl Maria von Weber.

The founder of Czech national music was Bedřich Smetana (1824–84). He created the classical form of Czech serious opera (*The Brandenburgs in Bohemia, Dalibor, Libuše*) and folk opera (the world-famous *Bartered Bride, The Kiss, The Two Widows,* and *The Secret*). He also wrote numerous symphonic poems, and chamber, choral, and piano compositions. Antonín Dvořák (1841–1904) represents the climax of full-blooded Bohemian musicianship. In many of his Slavonic dances, rhapsodies, and scherzo movements he used the *furiant,* and in adagios of chamber music the *dumka, both Slavic dances. While the neoromantic Smetana wrote mostly operas and symphonic poems, Dvořák was more interested in nonprogrammatic music (nine symphonies, twelve string quartets and other chamber works, concertos for piano, violin, and cello). His choral and piano music and also his best opera, *Rusálka,* are mostly nationalist in character. Zdeněk Fibich (1850–1900), a quite sophisticated romanticist influenced by Wagner, reflects little of the nationalist

tradition. He wrote mostly operas (*The Bride of Messina*) and melodramas (the trilogy *Hippodamia*). Leoš Janáček (1854–1928), creator of musical realism, was influenced by Borodin and Mussorgsky. Arranger of many Moravian folksongs, he studied the melodic speech inflections of his people and thus arrived at a new declamatory vocal style. He wrote for every medium but most important are his operas (*Jenufa, Katja Kabanova,* etc.) and his *Glagolitic Mass.* The older Janáček grew, the more modern his music became. The link between the classical and modern Czech generation was Joseph B. Foerster (1859–1951), who wrote psychologic-spiritual operas (*Eva*). Dvořák's foremost pupils were Josef Suk (1874–1935), his son-in-law, who as a member of the famous Bohemian String Quartet wrote much chamber music (*Meditation on the Chorale "St. Wenceslaus"* for string quartet), and a symphonic cantata *Epilogue;* and Vítěslav Novák (1870–1949), who composed a symphonic cantata, *The Storm,* and a piano cycle, *Pan.* They continued the legacy of their teacher but were also influenced by French impressionism and brought a new national expression to neoromanticism. Otakar Ostrčil (1879–1935) was influenced by Gustav Mahler (1860–1911), who, although born in Bohemia, is considered in connection with German music. Vítěslav Novák had many pupils, of whom the most important were Ladislav Vycpálek (b. 1882), Boleslav Vomáčka (b. 1887), Jaroslav Křička (b. 1887), Emil Axman (1887–1949), Jan Kunc (b. 1883), Vilém Petrželka (b. 1889), and Václav Kaprál (1889–1947).

Jaroslav Jeremiáš (1859–1918) and his brother Otakar Jeremiáš (1892–1962) continued the tradition of Smetana, while Jaroslav Kvapil (1892–1958) and Karel B. Jirák (b. 1891; since 1947 in the U.S.) were influenced by Mahler and R. Strauss. A happy amalgamation of national elements and a moderately modern idiom is found in Jaromír Weinberger's (b. 1896) opera *Schwanda, the Bagpiper* (1927), which had international success. Janáček's most talented pupil was Pavel Haas (1899–1944), who died in a concentration camp (opera *The Charlatan,* in avantgarde vein). The champion of atonal and quarter-tone music is Alois Hába (b. 1893; opera *The Mother*); his brother Karel Hába (b. 1898), a viola virtuoso, also writes quarter-tone music. Avant-garde composers include Karel Reiner (b. 1910) and Václav Kašlík (b. 1917). Music for the very advanced modern stage was written by Emil F. Burián (1904–59) and Jaroslav Ježek

(1906–42), who wrote political satire.

Bohuslav Martinů (1890–1959), although he left Prague in 1923 to study with Roussel in Paris and lived many of his last years in the United States, is still considered one of the outstanding Czech composers of the 20th century. He combined a melodic Czech folk idiom with French impressionist tendencies; his earlier works were much influenced by Stravinsky. Of his ten operas, the short *Comedy on a Bridge* is the most performed.

Neoclassicism is represented by Pavel Bořkovec (b. 1894), whose pupils include Jiří Pauer (b. 1919), Viktor Kalabis (b. 1923), and Miloslav Ištván (b. 1928).

Iša Krejčí (b. 1904) has written three excellent symphonies, orchestral variations on the folksong "Good Night," and a successful comic opera, *The Revolt at Ephesus.* Václav Dobiáš (b. 1909) wrote a cantata, *The Czech Polka.* Miloslav Kabeláč (b. 1908), like many of his contemporaries, wrote polemic music against the Nazis, such as the cantata *Do Not Give Way* (1938), and also a passacaglia for large orchestra, *The Mystery of Time* (1957).

The first important Slovak composer was the neoromantic Ján Levoslav Bella (1843–1936). Influenced by Liszt and Wagner, he composed a four-part chorus, "Our Father," for the 1000th anniversary of the arrival of Saints Cyril and Methodius in Slovakia. Contributors to the development of Slovak national music and the preservation of folksong include Mikuláš Moyzes (1872–1944), Viliam Figuš-Bystrý (1875–1937), and Mikuláš Schneider-Trnavský (1881–1958). Outstanding modern Slovak composers are Eugen Suchoň (b. 1908) who wrote an unusual dramatic opera, *Krutňava* (The Whirlpool), Ján Cikker (b. 1911; opera *Juro Janošík*), and Alexander Moyzes (b. 1906).

Lit.: R. Newmarch, *The Music of Czechoslovakia* (1942); V. Štěpánek and B. Karásek, *An Outline of Czech and Slovak Music* (1964); J. Racek, *Česká hudba* (1958; Czech music to c. 1800; résumé in German, pp. 277–93 by P. Eisner, extensive bibl.); Z. Nejedlý, *Dějiny ceské hudby* (Prague, 1903; history of Czech music, no trans.); V. E. Helfert and E. Steinhard, *Geschichte der Musik in der Tschechoslovakischen Republik* (1936; '38, French trans.); R. Batka, *Die Musik in Böhmen* [1906]; *id., Geschichte der Musik in Böhmen* (1906); P. Nettl, *Beiträge zur böhmischen und mährischen Musikgeschichte* (1927); H. Lindlar, ed., "Tschechische Komponisten" (*Musik der Zeit* viii, 1954); ‡*Musica Antiqua Bohemica,* 65 vols. (1937–64); J. Pohanka, ‡*Dějiny České hudby v příkladech* (1958; history of Czech music in examples); R. P. Kafka, "Music in Bohemia" (*ReMR*); Z. Nejedlý, "Magister Záviše and seine Schule" (*SIM* vii); D. Orel, "Stilarten der Mehrstimmigkeit des 15. und 16. Jahrhunderts in Böhmen" (*CP Adler*); *id.,* "Tschechoslowaken" (*AdHM* ii, 1156ff); J. Bužga, "Zur musikalischen Problematik der alttschechischen Kantionalen" (*MF* xii); P. Nettl, "The Czechs in Eighteenth-Century Music" (*ML* xxi, 362ff); *id.,* "Schubert's Czech Predecessors" (*ML* xxii, 61ff); J. Racek and J. Vysloužil, "Problems of Style in 20th-Century Czech Music" (*LBCM*). E.V.

Czimbalom. See Cimbalom.

D

D. See Pitch names; Letter notation; Hexachord. In 16th-century *partbooks D stands for *discantus* (soprano). In harmonic analysis D means dominant.

Da capo [It.], abbr. *D.C.* From the beginning. Indication that the piece is to be repeated from the beginning to the end or to a place marked *fine* (*da capo al fine*). It is most frequently found at the end of the trio to a scherzo (or minuet), indicating that the latter is to be repeated after the trio. *Da capo senza repetizione* means that the repetitions within the scherzo should be omitted, as is usually done even without this indication. *Da capo e poi la coda,* see Coda; see also *Dal segno.*

Da capo aria. See under Aria IV.

Dactyl, dactylic. See under Poetic meter I.

Daily hours. See under Office.

Dal segno [It.], abbr. *D.S.* Indication for repetition, not from the beginning [see *Da capo*] but from another place (frequently near the beginning) marked by the sign §.

Dame blanche, La [F., The White Lady]. Opera in three acts by Boieldieu (libretto by A. E. Scribe, based on Sir Walter Scott's *Guy Mannering* and *The Monastery*), produced in Paris, 1825. Setting: Scotland, 17th century.

Damenization. See under Solmization III.

Damnation de Faust, La [F., The Damnation of Faust]. Dramatic legend in five acts by Berlioz (libretto by the composer and A. Gandonnière, based on G. de Nerval's version of Goethe's *Faust*). Produced (in concert form) in Paris, 1846; stage version (adapted by R. Gunsbourg) in Monte Carlo, 1893. One of the best known numbers is the *Rákóczi March.

Damper [F. *étouffoir;* G. *Dämpfer;* It. *sordino;* Sp. *sordina*]. In pianos and harpsichords, the part of the mechanism that terminates the vibration of the string—hence, the sound—at the moment the key is released. The piano dampers are small pieces of wood, their underside covered with felt, that are placed above the strings. See Piano I; also Mute.

Damper pedal. See under Piano I; also Sordino (2).

Dämpfer [G.]. (1) The *dampers of the piano. (2) The *mutes of the violin. The term *dämpfen* (to damp) is also used for the muting of the horn and other instruments.

Dance music. I. In prehistoric times as well as in many primitive cultures (Africa), dance was primarily ritualistic, often containing erotic symbolism and serving to invoke magic, propitiate gods, induce hypnosis and fear, or heal illness. Dances were performed by the medicine man or a select group of warriors. Frequently women were not allowed to dance but only to beat the drums. On the other hand, almost all primitive or truly old cultures (Spain, Frisian and Scandinavian territories, American Indians, etc.) have in their repertory dances for women only. In more refined cultures dance took on a symbolic significance. The ancient Egyptians and Chinese (*c.* 1000 B.C.) had highly stylized ceremonial dances, with strictly regulated movements. In Greece, dance for the first time developed into an "art," i.e., an expression of beauty for its own sake, although it still retained religious significance. In the last centuries of the pre-Christian era, there appeared in Greece as well as in Rome a large influx of Oriental dances that were strongly erotic and frequently obscene. Dance became the occupation not of priests but of prostitutes. Little is known about dancing in the early Middle Ages. The Church strongly opposed dancing, which it considered heathenish and lascivious. Nevertheless, the very number of edicts against dancing issued by clerical authorities [see, e.g., L. Gougard, "La Danse dans les églises," in *Revue d'histoire ecclésiastique* xv (1914)] is in itself evidence that the continuity of dance among the people as well as the aristocracy was never really disrupted. In the later Middle Ages there is considerable evidence of ritual dancing [see Religious dances], which survives to the present day in Spain [see *Seises*]. In the 14th century, the convulsive dances of the flagellants expressed the fright and despair of a population tortured by plague, fire, wars, and religious scruples.

II. Beginning *c.* 1300, we find a repertory—at first sporadic, later more and more continuous—of dance music. Among the earliest examples are a number of instrumental pieces—some monophonic, some in two parts—of French or English derivation, all of which have the structure of the *estampie* or *ductia* [see *HAM*, nos. 40, 41]. To the same type belong some 14th-century Italian dances (all monophonic) called *istampita* or *saltarello* [see *HAM*, no. 59]. Dance melodies also occur in tenors, called "Chose Tassin" or "Chose Loyset," of late 13th-century motets [Codex Montpellier, nos. 270, 292, 294, 297].

In the 15th century dance as courtly entertainment and also as an art form reached its first great peak. All over Europe the stately *basse danse* (bassadanza) and the more intricate *balli* were taught by choreographers of renown, and the dancing master was as esteemed a member of any princely household as the court musician or chapel singer. More than 200 court dances from the 15th and early 16th centuries with all their choreographic details are preserved in contemporary dance instruction books (Domenico da Piacenza, "Arte del ballo"; Guglielmo Ebreo, "De pratica seu arte tripudii vulgare opusculum"; Antonio Cornazano, "Libro del art del danzare"; the magnificent Burgundian basse danse MS; Michel Toulouze's printed dance book of *c.* 1486; etc.), whereas the music for these dances is much less precisely documented. The dance treatises themselves contain approximately 100 melodies without accompaniment. In actual performance these skeleton melodies served as a *cantus firmus* of improvised additional voices and percussion (known from iconography of the time as well as literary references to dance bands, courtly and municipal accounts, etc.). Some four-part instrumental pieces, such as "Der Ratten Schwantz" (The Rat's Tail), "Der Pawir Schwantz" (pawir = peasant), "Der Phoben Swanz" (The Peacock's Tail, possibly an early reference to the pavane) and "Der schwartze Knab Dantz" (Dance of the Black Fellow = moresca!) from the Glogauer Liederbuch of *c.* 1480 [see Liederbuch], the Lochamer Liederbuch, the Buxheim Organ Book, and others give some idea of the structure of dance compositions in the 15th and early 16th centuries but were not necessarily used for actual dance accompaniment.

The increasingly diverse repertory of dances in the 16th century is reflected in the large variety of dance compositions in the collections of lute, keyboard, and ensemble music of the time. As in the 15th century, the starting point was usually a twin arrangement of a slow-moving main dance followed by a lively jumping dance (Nachtanz, tripla, Proportz, Hupfauf, saltarello). Among such pairs are the Italian bassadanza–saltarello and the Franco-Burgundian basse-danse–pas de breban (*c.* 1400–1550), and the later Italian passamezzo–saltarello (*c.* 1550–1600), as well as suitelike combinations such as basse danse–recoupe–tourdion (Attaingnant), pavana–saltarello–piva (Petrucci), etc. An important source of information about 16th-century dances in France is the *Orchésographie* of Thoinot Arbeau, an anagram of his real name, Jehan Tabourot (1589; new Eng. ed. by C. W. Beaumont, 1925; M. S. Evans, 1948), a church dignitary from Langres, France, who gave detailed and lively descriptions of the dances above as well as many others, particularly the various *branles. A good cross-section of the Italian repertory of the 16th century is given in the dance treatises by Fabritio Caroso (*Il Ballarino,* 1581; *Nobiltà di dame,* 1600) and Cesare Negri (*Nuove Inventioni di Balli,* 1604); the musical accompaniment for each dance or suite of dances is given in lute tablature, with or without the addition of a *superius* in mensural notation.

III. In the last decades of the 16th century the English virginalists (Byrd, Bull, Gibbons) brought the pavane and galliard to a high point of artistic perfection, comparable to that reached in the allemandes and sarabandes in Bach's suites. At the same time appeared new dances that were to play a prominent part in the art music of the 17th century, the (German) *allemande, the (French) *courante, the (Spanish) *saraband, and the (English) *jig or *gigue. About 1650 these dances became the standard movements of the *suite, which until then had employed earlier types, such as the *padovana, gagliarda, intrada, etc. At the same time a host of new dances, considerably more refined, grew up under the favorable auspices of the French court at Versailles, where Louis XIV patronized dance and ballet to an extent unparalleled in history. Most of them were originally peasant dances of the French provinces, e.g., the *bourrée (from Auvergne), the *gavotte (from Dauphiné), the *passepied (from Brittany), the *rigaudon (from Provence), the *loure (from Normandy), and, most important of all, the *minuet (from Poitou). Together with certain dances of foreign origin, such as the *anglaise, *hornpipe, and *polonaise, and the *canarie (from the Canary Islands), they played a prominent part in the ballets and operas of Lully, Purcell, and Rameau, and became, about 1700, the constituents of the optional group of the suite. An important national type of the 17th century is the English *country dance.

IV. The 18th century cultivated particularly the minuet and did not add much to the repertory of dance music until the end of the century. Then Vienna became a new center of dance music, and the first modern types of dance appeared, the vigorous *écossaise (Beethoven) and the soft swaying *Ländler (Schubert), which soon changed into one of the most famous dances of all time, the *waltz. Between 1830 and 1850 a number of dances quickly superseded one another in popularity, e.g., the Polish *mazurka (Chopin), the *quadrille, the Bohemian *polka, and the *galop (Offenbach). All of them were launched in Paris, confirming the fame of this city as a center of entertainment. The rise of nationalism led to the discovery by composers of a wealth of national dances, among which the Spanish dances figure prominently in variety and individuality of character [see Spain III]. In the early part of the 20th century, the Americas made their contribution to dance music with *ragtime, *jazz, and the *conga, *rumba, *tango, *samba, etc. See also Ballet; Suite. Also under Africa, Bali, China, etc.

Lit. A. *Dance:* A. Chujoy, *The Dance Encyclopedia* [1949]; S. Y. Belknap, *Guide to Dance Periodicals* (1950—); C. Sachs, *A World History of the Dance* (1937); E. B. Long and M. McKee, *A Bibliography of Music for the Dance* (1936); P. D. Magriel, *A Bibliography of Dancing* (1936); *id.*, *Chronicles of the American Dance* [1948]; C. W. Beaumont, *A Bibliography of Dancing* (1929); E. Porter, *Music through the Dance* [1937]; P. Hooreman, *Danseurs à travers les temps* [1953]; V. Junk, *Handbuch des Tanzes* (1930).

B. *Dance music:* P. Nettl, *The Dance in Classical Music* [1963]; *id.*, *The Story of Dance Music* [1947]; F. M. Böhme, *Geschichte des Tanzes in Deutschland,* 2 vols. (1886); T. Arbeau, *Orchésographie* (1589; trans. by C. W. Beaumont, 1925; by M. S. Evans, 1948); *LavE,* ii.5, 3082ff; M. Dolmetsch, *Dances of England and France from 1450 to 1600* [1949]; M. Wood, *Some Historical Dances* (1952); J. Dieckmann, *Die in deutscher Lautentabulatur überlieferten Tänze des 16. Jahrhunderts* [1931]; R. Carrieri, *La Danza in Italia* [1946]; I. Brainard, "Die Choreographie der Hoftänze in Burgund, Frankreich und Italien im 15. Jahrhundert" (diss. Göttingen, 1956); L. Moe, "Dance Music in Printed Lute Tablatures from 1507–1611" (diss. Harvard Univ., 1956); D. Heartz, "Sources and Forms of the French Instrumental Dance in the 16th Century" (diss. Harvard Univ., 1957); J. Wolf, "Die Tänze des Mittelalters" (*AMW* i); O. Gombosi, "About Dance and Dance Music in the Late Middle Ages" (*MQ* xxvii); *id.*, "Der Hoftanz" (*AM* vii); J. Pulver, "The Ancient Dance-Forms" (*PMA* xxxix, xl); O. Kinkeldey, "Dance Tunes of the Fifteenth Century," in *Instrumental Music,* ed. D. Hughes (1959); L. Schrade, "Tänze aus einer anonymen italienischen Tabulatur" (*ZMW* x); P. Nettl, "Die Wiener Tanzkomposition in der zweiten Hälfte des siebzehnten Jahrhunderts" (*StM* viii).

C. *Collections of dance music:* P. Aubry, *Estampies et danses royales* (1907); R. Eitner, "Tänze des 15. bis 17. Jahrhunderts" (*MfM* vii, Supp.); W. Merian, *Der Tanz in den deutschen Tabulaturbüchern* (1927); *Editions XI, 8; C. Gervaise, *Danceries* [*Editions XXV, 23]; E. Halbig, *Klaviertänze des 16. Jahrhunderts* (Cotta); *Wiener Tanzmusik* (*c.* 1650–1700; *DTO* 56).

See also under Religious dances; Suite; Ballet; individual dance types.   rev. I.B.

Dance of death. Death as a dancer or as a gruesome fiddler of dance tunes was a favorite subject of 15th- and 16th-century artists (Holbein, Dürer), who took their inspiration from medieval or contemporary dances incorporating dancers disguised as skeletons. Augustus Nörmiger's tablature of 1598 contains a piece entitled "Matasin oder Toden Tantz," whose peculiar syncopated rhythm was meant to express fear and trembling. In the 19th century two composers used the "Dies irae" as the basis of compositions portraying the idea of the dance of death (Liszt: *Totentanz* for piano and orchestra, 1849, rev. 1853–59; Saint-Saëns: *Danse macabre*). For a 14th-century Spanish example, see O. Ursprung, in *ZMW* iv, 141ff.

Danse macabre [F.]. (1) *Dance of death. (2) Symphonic poem by Saint-Saëns, op. 40 (1874), that depicts Death playing the violin and dancing in a graveyard at midnight. The music includes the "Dies irae" from the Requiem Mass.

Dante Symphony. *Program symphony with choral ending by Liszt (1856; full title: *Eine Symphonie zu Dantes Divina commedia*), based on Dante's *Divina commedia.* It is in two movements, entitled "Inferno" (see also under "Dies irae") and "Purgatorio."

Danza tedesca [It.]. The *Ländler* or the early *waltz (*c.* 1800).

Danzón [Sp.]. A Cuban dance of urban origin that belongs to the "danza" group, which probably developed from the *contradanza.* It is in 2/4 meter, with frequent use of the rhythmic pattern ♪♫♫. Its classic form is that of a rondo: A B A C A D A, with an 8-measure refrain (A) and three episodes of 16, 32, and 32 measures respectively. The first episode (B) is called "clarinet trio"; the second (C), originally a "trio de metales" (brass trio), but now played by a violin, is in slower tempo; the third (D) employs brief rhythmic patterns similar to those of the *rumba. Today the *danzón* is performed by an ensemble consisting of a flute, one or two clarinets, piano, violin, double bass, small kettledrums, and güiro [see *Reco-reco*]. The earliest known examples were written in 1789 by a Cuban composer, Miguel Failde.   J.O-S.

Daphnis et Chloé [F.]. Ballet by Ravel (choreography by M. Fokine), produced in Paris, 1912. It is based on the Greek legend. Two suites from the ballet music, arranged by the composer, are frequently played in orchestral concerts.

Daseian notation [G. *Daseia-Notation*]. A notational system of the 9th and 10th centuries in which the tones of the scale are represented by signs derived from the *prosodia daseia*, i.e., the aspirate sign in ancient Greek [Ex. a]. The signs

in Ex. b indicate the tetrachord d–e–f–g, while others (derived largely from these by turning them upside down or reversing from right to left) indicate one lower and two-and-one-half higher tetrachords that repeat the basic tetrachord in exact transpositions of the fifth. There results a curious scale that avoids diminished fifths but, as a consequence, includes augmented octaves: G A B♭ C | d e f g | a b c′ d′ | e′ f′♯ g′ a′ | b′ c″♯. This notation is used in 9th-century treatises ("Musica enchiriadis," "Scholia enchiriadis," "Commemoratio brevis"; see *GS* i, 152ff, 173ff, 213ff; also *CS* ii, 81) for writing down monophonic melodies (psalm tones, etc.) as well as examples of *organum [see *ApNPM*, pp. 204ff].

Lit.: E. J. Grutchfield, "Hucbald: A Millenary Commemoration" (*The Musical Times* lxxi, 507ff, 704ff); P. Spitta, "Die Musica enchiriadis und ihr Zeitalter" (*VWM* v); *WoHN* i, 31ff.

Dastgah. See under Persia II.

Daughter of the Regiment, The. See *Fille du Régiment*.

Davidsbündler Tänze [G., Dances of the David-leaguers]. Robert Schumann's cycle of eighteen *character pieces for piano, op. 6, composed in 1837. The title refers to an imaginary "League of David" frequently mentioned in Schumann's writings on music, to which he entrusted the task of fighting the musical "Philistines" of his day, that is, the mediocre drawing-room music then in vogue. Each piece is signed E. or F., for Eusebius and Florestan, imaginary characters representing respectively the pensive introverted and the impulsive extroverted sides of Schumann's own personality. They also appear in his *Carnaval*, together with a "March of the David-leaguers against the Philistines."

D. C. Abbr. for *da capo.

Deaconing. See Lining.

Dead interval. An interval between the last note of a melodic phrase and the first note of the next,

often involving separation by a rest. The term was introduced in teaching counterpoint in order to justify such intervals as the chromatic semitone or the augmented fifth, which in strict theory are not permitted within the course of a phrase but may well occur between phrases.

Deagan marimbaphone, madimba, etc. Xylophone-like instruments invented by J. C. Deagan (d. 1936); they are used in P. Grainger's suite *In a Nutshell* [see *MaMI*].

Death and the Maiden. See *Tod und das Mädchen*.

Death and Transfiguration. See *Tod und Verklärung*.

Decalogue. The Ten Commandments, particularly when substituted for the Kyrie in the Anglican service. Each commandment is followed by a people's response, which is a troped form of the Kyrie.

Decani and cantoris [L.]. In Anglican church music, two groups of the choir, one by the dean's stall (right side facing the altar), the other close to the cantor (left side). Late 16th-century composers (Tallis, Farrant, Byrd) often employed the groups antiphonally, separately, or jointly to obtain special effects of tone color and sonority, usually without increasing the actual number of parts. See Polychoral style.

Deceptive cadence. See under Cadence I.

Déchant [F.]. *Discant. *Déchant sur le livre,* see *Discantus supra librum. Déchant de viole,* descant viol.

Decibel. See Bel.

Decrescendo, abbr. *decr., decresc.* See *Crescendo.*

Degree. Term used in harmonic analysis; see Scale degrees.

Degrees and diplomas. The degrees most commonly awarded to music students are:

1. *B.A.* (with major in music). The Bachelor of Arts degree is given for completion of a liberal arts course (normally four years) in which music is stressed but in which nonmusical studies predominate. Graduation with honors means that the student has done some special work during his senior year, generally a paper or original composition of some magnitude, and has maintained a high scholastic average.

2. *B.Mus.* The Bachelor of Music degree is given for completion of a course of study (normally four years) in which musical studies

(piano, voice, violin, etc., or composition, theory, opera, music history and literature) predominate and a minimum of nonmusical studies is required.

3. *M.A.* (in music). The Master of Arts degree represents the logical continuation of the B.A. course of study. In some institutions it is limited to such areas as musicology, theory, or composition. Residence requirements vary from one to two years. Most schools require a thesis that calls for some research. In most instances the student must demonstrate reasonable ability in piano playing, sight reading, and similar musical skills.

4. *M.Mus.* In the Master of Music degree as in the B.Mus., the emphasis is less on nonmusical subjects and more on musical ones. This degree is given chiefly by conservatories and schools of music. M.Mus. degrees are given in various fields of concentration—performance, theory, composition, history and literature, aesthetics, conducting, etc. The special requirements vary greatly among the various schools. Most schools require a thesis or its equivalent, such as a long composition, or public concerts in the case of a performing major.

5. *Ph.D.* (in music). In the United States, the Doctor of Philosophy degree is an "academic" degree in the sense that the major field is usually within the areas of theory, musicology, or music education. One to three years of residence are required or customary. The candidate must submit an acceptable dissertation showing distinctly original work. In addition, he normally must pass an oral examination covering all branches and fields of music. Some institutions grant Ph.D. degrees in musical composition, in which case a composition of some scope is substituted for the dissertation.

6. *Mus.D.* The Doctor of Music, originally a purely honorary degree in the United States, is now an earned degree in a small number of institutions. It may be earned in the applied areas, for example, in voice, piano, strings, composition, conducting, and the like. The requirements are generally similar to those for the Ph.D., except that performances may replace the dissertation, or at least a portion of it. The examination procedures are similar to those for the Ph.D.

7. *D.M.A.* The Doctor of Musical Arts degree is similar in requirements and purpose to the earned Mus.D. degree. Although the examination procedures are similar to those for the Ph.D., performances usually satisfy a considerable portion of the dissertation requirement.

8. *Education degrees:* B.Mus.Ed.; B.Pub. School Mus.; M.M.Ed. These degrees are generally given by state universities and schools of music to students preparing to teach in the public schools. The Mus.Ed.D. degree has in many respects become similar to the Ph.D. in music. In some institutions it is identical to the Ph.D. in music education, except that no foreign languages are required; in others it is designed as a preparation for teaching at the college level; in still others, for teaching or supervising music in the public schools.

9. *Diplomas, certificates, etc.:* It is impossible to describe all the various awards of this kind that are made throughout the United States. State teaching certificates are required of public-school music teachers, and requirements vary somewhat from state to state. Music schools in particular give out a variety of diplomas, certificates, and the like. Since each individual school sets the standard, the value of such awards depends directly upon the excellence of the school granting them. In some schools the term "artist's diploma" is used to indicate that it is given for excellence in performance.

10. *Foreign degrees:* (a) *Great Britain.* The British system of degrees is most similar to the American. Mus.B., Mus.M., and Mus.D. degrees are given, the requirements varying somewhat among the various universities. The Mus.B. candidate is expected to have already received the B.A. degree, or to pass preliminary examinations of equivalent difficulty. In this respect the British degrees are different from the American. The Mus.M. is seldom given. All the British degrees in music are concerned primarily with the candidate's possession of a technique of composition, although in a few universities performance or musicological research may be substituted. Several universities give Litt.B., Litt.D., or Ph.D. degrees for work in musical research. A great number and variety of diplomas are granted by various music schools in Great Britain (see P. Scholes, *Oxford Companion* [1955], p. 283f). In general three grades are observed—Associateship, Licentiateship, and Fellowship. The latter, being the highest, is sometimes purely honorary.

(b) *Germany and Austria.* The only degree given is the Dr. Phil. (Ph.D.). Since this is so, the German Ph.D. in many instances represents a lesser achievement than the American Ph.D. Indeed, some of the German dissertations are no longer and contain little more information than an American master's thesis, although others are splendid contributions to musical research and often are full-size books. In addition to writing a dissertation, the candidate must pass various examinations, in music as well as in one or two secondary fields (e.g., philosophy, mathematics, acoustics).

(c) *Other European countries.* The remaining countries of Europe do not lay so much stress on academic degrees. In France the Doctor of Letters (D. ès Lettres) may be awarded for musicological research. Degrees in musicology are given by the universities of Paris and Strasbourg. The Paris Conservatory, however, and similar schools (Brussels, for example) have systems of recognizing achievement by means of first and second prizes, certificates, and diplomas of various sorts.   E.B.H.; add. by W.C.

Dehors, en [F.]. Emphasized.

Delasol(re), de la sol (re). See under Hexachord III.

Démancher [F.]. In string playing, the shifting of the left hand from one position to another.

Demi- [F.]. Half. *Demi-jeu,* see *Pleinjeu; demi-pause, demi-soupir,* see Notes; *demi-ton,* semitone; *demi-voix* or *mezza voce,* see Mezzo.

Demisemiquaver. See under Notes.

Denkmäler der Tonkunst. See Editions XIII, XIV, XV.

Denmark. Very little is known about early Danish music, although the *lur, a beautiful long S-shaped trumpet [see ill. under Brass instruments] of the latter part of the Nordic Bronze Age (c. 1100–600 B.C.), has been discovered more often in Denmark than anywhere else. The Norse sagas mention the harp, and this instrument is depicted in both its triangular and rounded forms—the latter probably an ancestor of the *crwth—on monuments in the Scandinavian lands. A 10th-century Arab traveler described the ritual singing of the heathen inhabitants of Schleswig as "bestial." Toward the end of this century Christianity was established in Denmark and plainsong hymns and sequences were imported or composed, including the Office of St. Canute found in a 13th-century MS, Codex Kiloniensis (*S.H./84/8vo,* Univ. Lib., Kiel). During the 12th and 13th centuries Danish clerics regularly studied in Paris, where they came in contact with the polyphonic music of Notre Dame. At the Danish court during the later Middle Ages (c. 1250–1350) the folksong ballad (*folkevise*) was extensively cultivated and many MS collections of the verses are extant.

The earliest printed ballad-verse was Anders Sørensen Vedel's *It hundrede udvalde danske viser* (1590), but few folk melodies are recorded before 1800, one exception being a fragment of tune and words at the end of a late 13th-century MS, Codex Runicus (*AM./8vo/28,* in the Arnamagnaean Collection, Univ. Lib., Copenhagen). After the Reformation (completed in Denmark by the mid-16th century) a series of printed service books appeared, the tunes being mostly of German Lutheran origin. During the 16th century a number of English and Flemish or Netherlands composers came to Denmark, among them Adrianus Petit Coclico, who served the court from 1556 to 1562, and John Dowland, court lutenist to Christian IV from 1598 to 1606. Among the earliest Danish composers known to us by name are Mogens Pedersøn (*Pratum spirituale,* 1620) and Hans Nielsen (c. 1580–after 1626), who both studied with G. Gabrieli in Venice [see Editions VIII, 35]. During the 17th and 18th centuries music in Denmark seems to have been almost completely dominated by Italian, French, and German musicians; however, one of the greatest of North European musicians, Dietrich Buxtehude (c. 1637–1707), was almost certainly of Danish parentage and spent the first 30 years of his life in Danish territory [also see under Germany].

A new Danish development began when a German composer, J. A. P. Schulz (1747–1800), court musical director at Copenhagen from 1787 to 1795, established opera by writing *Singspiele in Danish (*Høstgildet, Peters Bryllup, Indtoget*). He was followed by three other German-born composers: F. L. A. Kunzen (1761–1817), grand operas *Holger Danske* (1789), *Erik Ejegod* (1798), and several *Singspiele;* C. E. F. Weyse (1774–1842), the great master of Danish romantic song, whose work in this field was continued by Peter A. Heise (1830–79); and Friedrich Kuhlau (1786–1832), the well-known composer of piano sonatinas and flute music, who wrote the Singspiel *Elverhøj* (1828), still popular in Denmark.

Niels W. Gade (1817–90), the first important Danish-born composer of the 19th century (symphonies, overtures, chamber and choral works), is the Danish counterpart of Schumann and perhaps even more of Mendelssohn, whose romantic lyricism he tinged with a distinctive touch of Nordic color. He is as characteristic of Danish refinement and sensitivity as Grieg is of Norwegian vigor and ruggedness. A contemporary of Gade's, less known outside Denmark, was J. P. E. Hartmann (1805–1900), who wrote sonatas, symphonies, and music for several ballets devised by August Bournonville on national romantic subjects; he is not to be confused with his grandfather, J. E. Hartmann, to whom is attributed the Danish national song, "Kong Christian stod ved højen Mast."

The most important among more recent Danish composers is Carl Nielsen (1865–1931), who, mainly through his six symphonies, has attained an international reputation almost comparable to that of his contemporary, Finland's Jean Sibelius. Practically all 20th-century Danish composers show the influence of Nielsen's original treatment of symphonic form, combining it with impressionist or neoclassical tendencies, e.g., Jørgen Bentzon (1897–1951), Knudåge Riisager (b. 1897), and Finn Høffding (b. 1899). Of the next generation, Vagn Holmboe (b. 1909), an outstanding composer of symphonies and chamber music, Jørgen Jersild (b. 1913), a distinguished teacher as well as a composer of fine craftmanship, and Niels Viggo Bentzon (b. 1919), a prolific writer of works for piano, orchestra, and chamber ensembles, all deserve mention. Still younger composers of importance are Bernhard Lewkowitch (b. 1927), best known for his Masses and other choral works, and Per Nørgård (b. 1932), a pupil of Holmboe and Høffding, who has developed an individual style based on free serial and improvisatory procedures.

Lit.: J. Horton, *Scandinavian Music* [1963]; N. M. Jensen, *Den Danske Romance 1800–1850* (1964); J. Balzer, *Bibliografi over Danske Komponister* (1932); A. Hammerich, *Dansk Musikhistorie indtil ca. 1700* (1921); K. Jeppesen, ed. ‡*Dania sonans,* vol. i (1933; works of M. Pedersøn); H. Thuren, "Das dänische Volkslied" (*ZIM* ix); A. Hammerich, "Musical Relations between England and Denmark in the XVII. Century" (*CP 1911*); B. Wallner, "Scandinavian Music after the Second World War," in *LBCM; AdHM* ii, 1106 (bibl., p. 1112); *LavE* i.5, 2594; *MGG,* "Dänemark," bibl.   rev. J.H.

Déploration [F.]. A 15th- and 16th-century name for a composition written on the death of a musician, usually by one of his pupils. See Lament (2).

De profundis [L.]. Psalm 129 (130). See Penitential psalms.

Derb [G.]. Robust, rough.

Des, deses [G.]. D-flat, d-double-flat. See Pitch names.

Descant. Anglicized form of L. *discantus* and a variant of *discant. Throughout the Middle Ages the term was used indiscriminately with other terms, such as *descaunt.* In the 17th century it took on special connotations in instrumental practice. *Descant viol* and *descant recorder* are names for the highest-pitched instruments, a fourth or a fifth above the treble size [see Viol II; Recorder]. *Descant clef* is an older name for the soprano clef [see Clef, *history*]. In certain 17th-century writings descant takes on the special connotation of ornamentation or variation, whenever such devices are employed in the melody. Finally, in modern hymn-singing, an obbligato part that soars above the tune is known as a descant. While formerly such descants were improvised, the modern practice is to supply them in the printed hymnals. The same method is also known by the wholly inappropriate name "fauxbourdon" or "faburden" [see Fauxbourdon (3)].   rev. S.K.

Descort [F.]. See under Lai.

Descriptive music. See Program music; Word painting.

Desolre(ut), de sol re (ut). See under Hexachord III.

Dessus [F.]. Old term corresponding to *treble, while *par-dessus* corresponds to *descant. Thus, *dessus de viole,* treble viol; *par-dessus de viole,* descant viol.

Détaché [F.]. See under Bowing (b).

Detonieren [G.]. To sing off pitch; to waver in pitch.

Deuterus [Gr.]. See under Church modes II.

Deutlich [G.]. Clear, distinct.

Deutsches Requiem, Ein. A work for solo voices, chorus, and orchestra by Johannes Brahms, op. 45, composed 1857–68, after the death of his mother. It consists of seven movements based on German texts freely selected from the Scriptures, instead of the authoritative Latin text of the liturgical Requiem Mass [see Requiem Mass]. Its first complete performance was in 1869 in Leipzig.

Deux Journées, Les [F., The Two Days]. Opera in three acts by Cherubini (libretto by J.-N. Bouilly, produced in Paris, 1800. Setting: Paris and environs, 1617.

Development. A term carrying two meanings in musical structure: (1) The treatment of musical materials to convey a sense of expansion (increased scope of structure) or exploration (significant shifts in harmonic direction); (2) the section in sonata form that is devoted to such treatment, i.e., the development section.

(1) Development procedures are generally distinguished from the exposition or statement of musical materials. The exposition presents musical ideas; development involves working over these ideas in a variety of ways. The material may: (a) be divided into smaller figures (this creates an effect of stretto, or compressed action, often leading to considerable extensions in structure, as in the beginning of the development section of the first movement of Mozart's Symphony no. 41); (b) have its motifs or figures regrouped into new phrases (this presents the original material in a new light, with a different rhetorical effect, as in the first movement of Beethoven's Symphony no. 8); (c) have the contour or character of its motifs altered (this often imparts a different expressive value to the original material, as in the fugato of the development of the first movement of Beethoven's Quartet in F major op. 18, no. 1); (d) be associated with harmonic explorations and digressions (this creates a sense of continuous and even unpredictable movement, and provides a basis for the use of a, b, and c. Such harmonic activity can be found in virtually any development section of a classical or romantic sonata form). These are only a few of the ways development may take place; there are many more.

The function of development in musical structure has changed from period to period. The sharpest distinction between exposition and development of musical material is found in music of the 18th and early 19th centuries. In this period the exposition tends to consist of well-defined and relatively complete statements, in which the component figures and phrases complement each other on various levels, conveying an impression of over-all symmetry. To support this symmetry there is a strong and stable sense of key, secured by a series of cadences, the last of which is often an authentic cadence. Whenever this symmetry is seriously disrupted, particularly on higher levels of structure (phrase and period), development may be said to take place. Development can be used in moving from one important structural area to another, e.g., in the development section proper of sonata form (see below), in the transition from

the first key to the second in sonata form; also, it may be used to expand an area of the structure through harmonic digressions (first or second key areas in sonata form, the coda of any extended movement). In the classical treatment of development, the centrifugal motion with which the process begins is balanced later by an emphatic arrival at a harmonic objective, an opposing centripetal action. This gives rise to periods of considerable length, carrying great musical intensity. Development can be incorporated into any form, such as *introduction* (Mozart, Prague Symphony); *minuet* (Haydn, Symphony no. 102, second reprise); *rondo* (Beethoven, Quartet op. 18, no. 1, finale, second large episode); *variation* (Beethoven, Quartet op. 18, no. 5, third movement, coda); *fantasia* (Mozart, Fantasia in C minor, K. 475, opening section).

In the baroque period melodic material characteristically undergoes intensive manipulation throughout a movement; there is constant play of a small number of motifs, within rather narrow harmonic limits. In the first movement of his Brandenburg Concerto no. 3, Bach carries out a relentless development of the figures presented in the opening tutti.

Development in romantic music is epitomized in the Prelude to Wagner's opera *Tristan und Isolde.* Here, development employs freely constructed sequences on rising dynamic curves, building to peaks of great expressive intensity. In contrast to classical techniques, the counterbalance of a strong drive to a cadence is lacking; instead, there generally is a sudden drop in tension so that a new line of developmental action may begin. Still another treatment of development is found in the variations and transformation of themes, used by Liszt (Sonata in B minor) and Richard Strauss (*Till Eulenspiegel*) in the 19th century and by the tone-row school in the 20th century (Schoenberg, Quartet no. 4 op. 37). Here the theme undergoes drastic transformations of style and function. It may be used as a main theme, auxiliary figure, or chord while retaining something of its original contour or intervallic relationships.

(2) The development section in *sonata form generally consists of a more intensive working over of material than any other part of the form. Within the sonata form as a whole, it serves to carry the action, through expansions and digressions, from one important structural point to another. Basically, the development stands as a link between the confirmation of the second key at the end of the exposition and the return to

the tonic at the recapitulation. The object of the development section, common to all sonata-form movements of the classical era, is to lead back to the home key. The obligation to arrive at the tonic and create a strong sense of expectation for that arrival imposes restraints on harmonic exploration. Following the cadence that ends the exposition, we hear an increased rate of key change; sooner or later the harmony reaches a point of furthest remove from the home key, the apex of the centrifugal motion. It may be a strong cadence upon a distant degree of the scale or it may comprise a phrase or period in a fairly remote key that stabilizes the harmony momentarily. (Often, the point of furthest remove will be a cadence or a section in the mediant or submediant areas if the home key is major, e.g., Mozart, Sonata in D major, K. 576, first movement.) Then the harmonies will shift direction toward the tonic. Two examples are given below. (The point of furthest remove is underlined twice):

Mozart, Sonata in D major, K. 576, first movement:

a   <u>V of B^b</u>   <u>B^b</u>   <u>g</u>   <u>a</u>   <u>V of B</u>   e   A (as V of D)

(rising action)   (falling circle of fifths)

Beethoven, Quartet in C minor op. 18, no. 4, first movement:

<u>g</u>   <u>c</u>   <u>F</u>   <u>f</u>   G (as V of C)

(f–G–c represents a broad authentic cadence to the home key)

The development section generally makes some reference to melodic material from the exposition. The Beethoven movement cited above paraphrases the exposition, working over the principal theme from each key area of the exposition. The Mozart movement is concerned with the motifs from the first and last phrases of the exposition. At times Mozart introduces new material in the development section (Quartet in B^b major, K. 458, first movement) as does Beethoven (first movements of Symphonies no. 3 and 4). In some development sections there is little or no reference to previously heard material (e.g., Mozart, Quartet in E^b, K. 428, first movement).

In the 18th century, development processes were used throughout the various sections of sonata form; the development section itself was not necessarily the most critical part of the form. However, in the later works of Haydn and Mozart and especially in the works of Bee-

thoven, the development section gradually took on greater scope, becoming the crucial area of the structure, where the flight away from the tonic and dominant keys went far afield and assumed a dramatic power that eventually, in the 19th century, colored every aspect of sonata form. Also see Sonata form.   L.G.R.

Devil and Daniel Webster, The. Opera in one act by D. Moore (libretto by S. V. Benét, based on his story), produced in New York, 1939. Setting: New Hampshire, the 1840's.

Devil's Trill Sonata. A violin sonata by Tartini (MS now lost), said to have been inspired by a dream in which the devil appeared to him. The long trill for which it is named occurs in the last movement.

Devisenarie [G.]. See under Motto.

Dezime [G.]. The interval of the tenth.

Diabelli Variations. Beethoven's op. 120 (1823), consisting of a series of 33 variations on a waltz by Diabelli (full title: *33 Veränderungen über einen Walzer von A. Diabelli*). They were written in response to a request, sent by Diabelli (Viennese publisher) to 51 composers, to contribute one variation each to a collective set that was meant to represent a cross-section of the composition in Austria of his day. The entire collection was published under the title *Vaterländischer Künstlerverein* (Society of Artists of the Fatherland) in two volumes, the first of which contained the variations of Beethoven, the second those of the 50 other composers (Schubert, Moscheles, Kalkbrenner, Liszt—who was then eleven years old—and others). For the complete list, see *GD* v, 457; *GDB* viii, 690–91.

Diabolus in musica [L.]. Late medieval nickname for the *tritone, which in musical theory was regarded as the "most dangerous" interval. See Mi-fa.

Diacisma, diaschisma. A microtonic interval in medieval theory, defined as one-half of the *semitonium minus* (*diesis*). See *GS* ii, 313n (Boethius); *CS* iv, 181 (Tinctoris). See Comma, schisma.

Dialogue [F.; G. *Dialog;* It. *dialogo;* Sp. *diálogo*]. A 17th-century vocal composition whose text is in the form of question and answer, or contains such portions. Dialogues are usually written for two singers whose parts alternate. In a way, they represent the vocal counterpart of the *stile concertante* of 17th-century instrumental music. In addition to their frequent use in operas, there are various collections of cantatas written in the style of dialogues, so-called *dialoghi fuor di scena* (dialogues without stage performance), e.g.: O. Vecchi, *Dialoghi* (1608); M. da Gagliano, *Dialogo di ninfa e pastore* (1611; *RiHM* ii.2, 33); G. F. Capello, *Motetti e dialoghi* (1615; *SchGMB*, no. 180); A. Hammerschmidt, *Dialogi oder Gespräche zwischen Gott und einer gläubigen Seelen* (1645; new ed. *DTO* 16; *HAM,* no. 213); J. R. Ahle, *Erster Teil geistlicher Dialogen* (1648; selections in *DdT* 5); Henry Lawes, *Ayres and Dialogues* (1653, '55, '58). The dialogue technique was frequently used in choruses and arias of oratorios, Passions, etc.; see M.-A. Charpentier's short "sacred history," *Dialogue entre Madeleine et Jésus* (*HAM,* no. 226, where it is mistakenly said to be from another work, *Le Reniement de St.-Pierre*). Famous examples are the initial chorus, "Kommt, ihr Töchter," and the alto aria, "Sehet, Jesus hat die Hand" from Bach's St. Matthew Passion, in which the chorus comes in with such questions as "Wen?" "Wie?" "Wohin?" "Wo?"

In French 17th-century organ music the title "Dialogue" is commonly given to pieces employing contrasting registrations in alternation for phrases of eight and four measures (N.-A. Lebègue and others; see, e.g., Editions I, 9, p. 18).

The history of the dialogue in music begins with the so-called dialogue tropes of the 10th and 11th centuries, e.g., the Christmas trope "Hodie cantandus est" and the Easter trope "Quem quaeritis" [see Liturgical drama]. Some of the *caccie* of the 14th century include lively dialogue passages. In the 16th century, dialogue technique was used in the *frottola, lauda* (dialogue *lauda*), chanson (Le Jeune), and quite often in the madrigal (Verdelot, Willaert, Lassus, and others).

Lit.: T. Kroyer, "Dialog und Echo in der alten Chormusik" (*JMP* xvi); I. Spink, "English Seventeenth-Century Dialogues" (*ML* xxxviii); A. Dolmetsch, ‡*Select English Songs and Dialogues of the 16th and 17th Centuries,* 2 vols. (1898, 1912).

Dialogues des Carmélites, Les [F., The Dialogues of the Carmelites]. Opera in three acts by F. Poulenc (libretto by G. Bernanos), produced in Milan, 1957. Setting: France, 1789.

Diapason. (1) In Greek and medieval theory, the interval that includes "all the tones," i.e., the octave [see *Diapente; Diatessaron;* Interval]. Derived meanings, chiefly used in French ter-

minology, are: (2) range of voice; (3) concert pitch (usually *diapason normal;* see Pitch 2) or tuning fork (also *diapason à branches*). (4) The main foundation stop of the organ, also called principal. See Organ IX.

Diapente [Gr.]. Ancient Greek and medieval name for the fifth *Epidiapente,* fifth above; *subdiapente* or *hypodiapente,* fifth below; *canon in epidiapente,* canon at the fifth above.

Diaphonia, diaphony. (1) In Greek theory, dissonance, in contrast to **symphonia,* consonance. This meaning survives in various medieval writings: Isidore of Seville (d. 636; *GS* i, 21); Marchetto da Padua (c. 1320; *GS* iii, 80); Tinctoris (c. 1480; *CS* iv, 182). (2) More commonly, the term is used by theorists of the 9th to 12th centuries to mean two-part polyphony: "Musica enchiriadis" (c. 900; *GS* i, 165); Guido d' Arezzo, "Micrologus" (c. 1030; ch. xviii: "De diaphonia"). The term *discantus* is probably the Latin translation of *diaphonia.* (3) *Diaphonia basilica* is a term used by Johannes de Muris (c. 1320; *GS* iii, 239) for the *organum duplum* in which the tenor consists of long-held notes. The name is derived not from Gr. *basileus,* king (giving rise to the mistranslation "royal counterpoint") but from Gr. *basis,* base, foundation.

Diaschisma. Same as *diacisma.

Diastematic. See under Neumes II.

Diatessaron [Gr.]. Greek and medieval name for the interval of the fourth. *Epidiatessaron,* fourth above; *subdiatessaron, hypodiatessaron,* fourth below. See also *Diapente.*

Diatonic. The natural scale, consisting of five whole tones and two semitones, as it is produced on the white keys of the keyboard. There is, of course, a corresponding scale in each key. Music is called "diatonic" if it is confined to the notes of this scale, to the exclusion of chromatic tones. For instance, in C major, the melodic progression c–d–e and the chord d a c' are diatonic, while c–d♯–e and d a♭ c' are chromatic. "Diatonicism" means music whose tonality is predominantly diatonic, i.e., nonchromatic, such as the works of Haydn and Mozart. For a recent modification of diatonicism, see Pandiatonicism. For the diatonic genus of Greek theory, see Greece II. For diatonic semitone, see Semitone.

Dice music. See Aleatory music.

Dichterliebe [G., Poet's Love]. See under Song cycle.

Dictionaries of music. These are of several types: (1) those that offer merely the pronunciation, translation, and brief definition of foreign musical terms (e.g., T. Baker, *A Dictionary of Musical Terms*); (2) those that cover the entire field of music with emphasis on separate entries and definitions (e.g., H. Riemann, *Musiklexikon*) or on longer articles including all aspects of the topics (e.g., Grove's *Dictionary of Music and Musicians*); (3) those that cover all periods and fields of composition but are restricted to biographies only (e.g., *Baker's Biographical Dictionary of Musicians*), or to topics without biographical entries (e.g., M. Brenet, *Dictionnaire pratique et historique de la musique*); and (4) those that are limited to a particular period (e.g., A. Eaglefield-Hull, *A Dictionary of Modern Music and Musicians*), a particular country (e.g., E. Refardt, *Historisch-biographisches Musikerlexikon der Schweiz*), or a field (e.g., W. W. Cobbett, *Cobbett's Cyclopedic Survey of Chamber Music*).

The following list groups the dictionaries under three headings: I. General dictionaries (including types 1, 2, and 3 above) published after 1870; II. Special dictionaries (including type 4) published after 1870; III. Earlier dictionaries.

I. *General dictionaries after 1870.*

A. United States: J. W. Moore, *A Dictionary of Musical Information* (1876). J. D. Champlin, Jr. and W. F. Apthorp, *Cyclopedia of Music and Musicians*, 3 vols. (1888–90). T. Baker, *A Dictionary of Musical Terms* (1895; 25th ed., 1939). *Id., Baker's Biographical Dictionary of Musicians* (1900; 5th ed., comp. rev. by N. Slonimsky, 1958; suppl. 1965). W. L. Hubbard, *The American History and Encyclopedia of Music,* 12 vols. (1910). W. S. Pratt, *The New Encyclopedia of Music and Musicians* (1924, originally planned as abridgment of Grove; rev. ed., 1929). O. Thompson, *The International Cyclopedia of Music and Musicians* (1939; 7th ed. rev. by N. Slonimsky, 1956). W. Apel, *Harvard Dictionary of Music* (1944; rev. ed. 1969). *Id.* and R. T. Daniel, *The Harvard Brief Dictionary of Music* (1960). M. Cooper, ed., *The Concise Encyclopedia of Music and Musicians* [1958].

B. England: G. Grove, *A Dictionary of Music and Musicians,* 4 vols. (1879–89, Index, 1890; 4th ed., H. C. Colles, 5 vols., 1940; 5th ed., E. Blom, 9 vols., 1954, Suppl. Vol., 1961; American Suppl., ed. W. S. Pratt, published for 2nd and 3rd ed.). P. Scholes, *The Oxford Companion to Music* (1938; 9th rev. ed. 1955). *Id., The Con-*cise *Oxford Dictionary of Music* (1952). E. Blom, *Everyman's Dictionary of Music* (1946; 2d rev. ed. 1954). J. A. Westrup and F. L. Harrison, *The New College Encyclopedia of Music* (1960). W. J. Smith, *A Dictionary of Musical Terms in 4 Languages* (1961).

C. France: R. Vannes, *Essai de terminologie musicale* (1925). M. Brenet, *Dictionnaire pratique et historique* (1926; new ed., 1930). N. Dufourcq, ed., *Larousse de la musique,* 2 vols. (1957). F. Michel, ed., *Encyclopédie de la musique,* 3 vols. (1958–61).

D. Germany: H. Mendel, *Musikalisches Conversations-Lexikon,* 11 vols. (1870–79; vol. 12, suppl., 1883). H. Riemann, *Musik-Lexikon* (1882; 12th ed., W. Gurlitt, 3 vols., 1959). R. Eitner, *Biographisch-bibliographisches Quellen-Lexikon der Musiker und Musikgelehrten bis zur Mitte des neunzehnten Jahrhunderts,* 10 vols. (1900–04; vol. 11, suppl. *Miscellanea musicae bio-bibliographica,* ed. H. Springer and others, 1912–16; reprint with additions, 11 vols. in 6, 1959). H. Abert *et al., Illustriertes Musik-Lexikon* (1927). H. J. Moser, *Musiklexikon* (1935; rev. ed., 2 vols., 1955). F. Blume, ed., *Die Musik in Geschichte und Gegenwart, c.* 12 vols. (1949—).

E. Italy: C. Schmidl, *Dizionario universale dei musicisti* (1890; 2 vols., 1926; suppl. 1938). A. della Corte and G. M. Gatti, *Dizionario di musica* (1925; 5th ed., 1956). C. Sartori, ed., *Dizionario Ricordi della musica e dei musicisti* (1959).

F. Spain: F. Pedrell, *Diccionario técnico de la música* (1894). A. Albert Torrellas and J. Pahissa, *Diccionario de la música ilustrado,* 2 vols. [1927, '29]. A. Albert Torrellas, *Diccionario enciclopédico de la música,* 4 vols. (1947–52). J. Pena and H. Anglés, *Diccionario de la música Labor,* 2 vols. (1954).

G. Other countries (this list gives at least one recent dictionary for each of the following countries).

Belgium: R. Vannes and A. Souris, *Dictionnaire des musiciens (compositeurs)* (Brussels, 1947).

Canada: Sœurs de Sainte-Anne, *Dictionnaire biographique des musiciens Canadiens* (1935).

Czechoslovakia: G. Černušák, *et al., Československý hudební slovník,* 2 vols. (Prague, 1963–65).

Denmark: H. Panum and W. Behrend, *Illustreret Musiklexikon* (1924–26).

Finland: S. Ranta, *Suomen säveltäjiä puolentoista vuosisadan ajalta* (1945).

Latvia: W. Neumann, *Lexikon baltischer Tonkünstler* (Riga, 1909).

Netherlands: L. M. G. Arntzenius, *et al.*, *Encyclopedie van de Muziek*, 2 vols. (1956).

Norway: O. Gurvin and Ø. Anker, *Musikkleksikon* [1948–49].

Poland: J. W. Reiss, *Podręczna encyklopedia Muzyki* (1949–50).

Portugal: E. Vieira, *Diccionario biografico de musicos portuguezes*, 2 vols. (Lisbon, 1900).

Sweden: N. Broman, J. Norrby, *et al.*, ed., *Tonkonsten*, 2 vols. (1955, '57).

Switzerland: E. Refardt, *Historisch-biographisches Musikerlexikon der Schweiz* (Leipzig-Zurich, 1928). W. Schuh, *et al.*, *Schweizer Musiker-Lexikon; Dictionnaire des musiciens suisses* (1964).

U.S.S.R.: S. A. Pavliuchenko, *Kratkiĭ Muzykal 'nyĭ Slovar'* (1950). A. Vodarsky-Shiraeff, *Russian Composers and Musicians, A Biographical Dictionary* (New York, 1940). G. B. Bernandt and A. Dolzhanskii, *Sovietskie kompository; kratkiĭ biograficheskii spravochnik* (Moscow, 1957).

II. *Special dictionaries after 1870.*

A. United States and Great Britain: J. Julian, *A Dictionary of Hymnology* (1892; 2nd rev. ed. with suppl. 1907; reprinted, 2 vols., 1957). J. Towers, *Dictionary-Catalogue of Operas and Operettas* (1910). J. Pulver, *A Dictionary of Old English Music & Musical Instruments* (1923). *Id.*, *A Biographical Dictionary of Old English Music* (1927). W. W. Cobbett, *Cobbett's Cyclopedic Survey of Chamber Music,* 2 vols. (1929–30; 2nd ed., 3 vols., 1963, last vol. ed. by Colin Wilson). N. Slonimsky, "Concise Biographical Dictionary of Twentieth-Century Musicians," in *Music Since 1900* (1937; 3rd ed. 1949). *Who's Who in Music* (annual, 1937–41). C. Reis, *Composers in America* (1938; rev. and enlarged 1947). *Bio-bibliographical Index of Musicians in the United States Since Colonial Times* (District of Columbia Historical Records Survey 1941; 2nd. ed. 1956). D. Ewen, *Living Musicians* (i.e., performers; 1940). *Id.*, *The Book of Modern Composers* (1942; 2nd ed., 1950). *Id.*, *European Composers Today* (1954). G. Saleski, *Famous Musicians of Jewish Origin* (1949). C. Hopkinson, *A Dictionary of Parisian Music Publishers 1700–1950* (1954). D. H. Boalch, *Makers of the Harpsichord and Clavichord 1440–1840* (1956). K. Jalovec, *Italian Violin Makers* (1957). S. Marcuse, *Musical Instruments, A Comprehensive Dictionary* (1964).

B. France: F. Clément and P. A. Larousse, *Dictionnaire lyrique ou histoire des opéras* (1869?;

rev. ed. *Dictionnaire des opéras* [*Dictionnaire lyrique*], A. Pougin, 1905). R. Vannes, *Dictionnaire universel des luthiers* (1932; 2nd rev. ed., 2 vols., 1951, '59). R. Wright, *Dictionnaire des instruments de musique* (1941).

C. Germany: U. Kornmüller, *Lexikon der kirchlichen Tonkunst* (1870; rev. ed. 2 vols., 1891, '95). S. Kümmerle, *Encyklopädie der evangelischen Kirchenmusik*, 4 vols. (1888–95). W. L. von Lütgendorff, *Die Geigen- und Lautenmacher vom Mittelalter bis zur Gegenwart* (1904; 6th ed., 2 vols., 1922). C. Sachs, *Real-Lexikon der Musikinstrumente* (1913, rev. ed. 1964). J. Zuth, *Handbuch der Laute und Gitarre* (1926). A. Weissenbäck, *Sacra Musica: Lexikon der katholischen Kirchenmusik* (1937). S. Longstreet and A. M. Dauer, *Knaurs Jazzlexikon* (1957). F. K. Prieberg, *Lexikon der neuen Musik* (1958).

D. Italy: C. Dassori, *Opere e operisti (dizionario lirico 1541–1902)* (1903). A. de Angelis, *L'Italia musicale d'oggi. Dizionario dei musicisti* (1918; 3rd ed., 1928). U. Manferrari, *Dizionario universale delle opere melodrammatiche*, 3 vols. (1954–55). C. Sartori, *Dizionario degli editori musicali italiani* (1958).

III. *Earlier dictionaries.*

Some music entries are found in such early dictionaries as the 10th-cent. *Kitab al-Aghani al-Kabir,* compiled by al-Ishbahani, Abu al-Faraj, 'Ali bin al Hussein, 897–967 (mod. ed. Nashr al-Hurini, Bulak, 1868), and the *Dictionarius metricus* ascribed to J. de Garlandia (ed. A. Scheler, Leipzig, 1867) from the early 13th century. The earliest music dictionary is an 11th-cent. *Vocabularium musicum* (repr. in J.-A.-L. de La Fage, *Essais de diphtérographie musicale,* 1864, i, 404–8). Much more complete is J. Tinctoris' *Terminorum musicae diffinitorium, c.* 1475 (repr. in *CS* iv, 177ff; German trans. by H. Bellermann in *JMW* i, 55–114; French trans. by A. Machabey, *Lexique de la musique, XVe siècle,* 1951; English trans. by C. Parrish, *Dictionary of Musical Terms,* 1963). This was followed, but only after more than two centuries, by the *Clavis ad thesaurum magnae artis musicae* (Prague, 1701) of the Bohemian organist T. B. Janowka, and by the *Dictionnaire de musique* (Paris, 1703) of Sébastien de Brossard.

France. From Brossard, who was not familiar with Janowka's work, stems the line of French music dictionaries continued most notably by: J. J. Rousseau, *Dictionnaire de musique* (Geneva, 1767; 2 vols., 1825); N. É. Framery and P. L. Ginguené, *Musique*, 2 vols. (Paris, 1791, 1818), contained in the *Encyclopédie méthodique* (vols. 185–186); A. E. Choron and F.-J.-M. Fayolle, *Dictionnaire historique des musiciens,* 2 vols. (Paris, 1810, '11), the first French biographical dictionary of musicians; F.-H.-J. (Castil-Blaze), *Dictionnaire de musique moderne* (Paris, 1821; 2nd ed., 2 vols. 1825; rev., 1 vol., 1828); F.-J. Fétis, *Biographie universelle des musiciens et bibliographie générale de la musique,* 8 vols. (Paris, 1835–44; 2nd ed. rev., 10 vols., 1860–70; 2-vol suppl. by A. Pougin, 1878, '80); and the still useful compilation, L. Escudier, *Dictionnaire de musique d'après les théoriciens, historiens et critiques les plus célèbres,* 2 vols. (Paris, 1844; 5th ed., 1872).

Germany. The German dictionaries begin with M. Praetorius' *Syntagma musicum,* vol. iii (1619; repr. 1916; fac. ed. W. Gurlitt, 1958) and continue with lists appended to a number of treatises, e.g., C. Demantius' *Isagoge artis musicae* (8th ed., 1632; see *MF* x, 48ff), J. A. Herbst's *Musica practica* (1642), etc. The earliest independent dictionary was J. G. Walther's topical and biographical *Musikalisches Lexikon* (Leipzig, 1732; fac. ed. R. Schaal, 1953). This was followed (in addition to biographical and other material found in J. Mattheson's writings, especially his *Grundlage einer Ehren-Pforte,* Hamburg, 1740; new ed. M. Schneider, 1910) chiefly by: E. L. Gerber, *Historisch-biographisches Lexicon der Tonkünstler,* 2 vols. (Leipzig, 1790, '92; rev. ed., 4 vols., Leipzig, 1812–14); H. C. Koch, *Musikalisches Lexicon* (Frankfurt-am-Main, 1802; rev., Heidelberg, 1865); G. Schilling, *Universal-Lexicon der Tonkunst,* 6 vols. (Stuttgart, 1835–38; suppl., 1842).

England. Following an unimportant volume entitled *A Short Explication of Such Foreign Words as Are Made Use of in Musick Books* (London, 1724), England's first significant music lexicon is J. Grassineau, *A Musical Dictionary* (London, 1740; 2nd ed., 1769), an expanded translation of Brossard's *Dictionnaire de musique.* A slightly later topical dictionary is T. Busby, *A Complete Dictionary of Music* (London [1786? 1800?]; 4th ed., 1813), while the first biographical dictionary of musicians is J. S. Sainsbury's *A Dictionary of Musicians,* 2 vols. (London, 1824; 2nd ed., 1827).

Italy. Italy's first dictionary of music was that of P. Gianelli, *Dizionario della musica sacra e profana,* 3 vols. (Venice, 1801; 3rd ed., 7 vols., 1820), superseded by P. Lichtenthal, *Dizionario e bibliografia della musica,* 4 vols. (Milan, 1826).

United States. Although Busby's dictionary (see under England above) had been published in America in 1827, the most important early American dictionary is J. W. Moore, *Complete Encyclopaedia of Music* (Boston [1852]; App., 1875).

Works in other languages are: B. Saldoni, *Diccionario biográfico-bibliográfico de efemérides de músicos de españoles,* 4 vols. (Madrid, 1868–81); J. de Vasconcellos, *Os musicos portuguezes,* 2 vols. (Oporto, 1870); W. Sowinski, *Les Musiciens polonais et slaves, anciens et modernes* (Paris, 1857; in Polish, Paris, 1874); J. Verschuere-Reynvaan, *Muzijkaal kunstwoordenboek* (Amsterdam, 1795, incompl.; Vlissingen, compl., 1805; new ed., Amsterdam, 1847); C. Envallson, *Svenskt musikaliskt lexikon* (Stockholm, 1802).

For completion of the list above, see J. B. Coover, *Music Lexicography* (1958; this is a later edition of *A Bibliography of Music Dictionaries,* 1952); E. Magni-Dufflocq, "Dizionari di musica" (*Bolletino bibliografico musicale* viii), and s.v. "Dictionaries" in *GDB* and "Lexika" in *MGG.*   L.H.; add. by C.G.R.

Dido and Aeneas. Opera in three acts by Purcell (libretto by Nahum Tate, after Virgil's poem), produced about 1689 at Josias Priest's boarding school for girls in Chelsea (London). Setting: Carthage, after the fall of Troy. The moving simplicity of the plot, together with Purcell's expressive music, make *Dido and Aeneas* an important work of early opera, midway between Monteverdi and Gluck. Particularly famous is Dido's "Lament" before her death, a *chaconne based on a chromatic modification of the descending tetrachord.

Didymic comma. See under Comma.

Dièse [F.]. The sharp sign [see Accidentals; Pitch names]. In the 17th century, also used to indicate the major mode, e.g., *mi dièse,* E major.

Dies irae [L.]. A rhymed sequence [see Sequence II, B], probably by Thomas of Celano (d. 1256), which is among the most impressive products of late medieval poetry and music. It is one of the five sequences still surviving in the Roman liturgy, being sung in the Requiem Mass [*LU,* p. 1810]. Its plainsong melody, which is a good example of a mixed mode [see Church modes III], shows the characteristic structure of the sequence, aa bb cc; it is sung three times and is *Amen*). It may have originated as a trope to the responsory *Libera me* (from the Burial Service; *LU,* p. 1767; also *HAM,* no. 14), particularly its second verse: *Dies illa, dies irae, calamitatis et miseriae*.... Not until the mid-16th century did it become an integral part of the Requiem Mass. Brumel's *Missa pro defunctis* includes the earliest (?) polyphonic composition of the "Dies irae," later examples being found in the Requiem Masses of O. Vecchi, G. F. Anerio, and others. More recent composers have usually retained only the text and have written for it free music of a highly dramatic character (Mozart, Cherubini, Verdi). However, the old melody has frequently been incorporated into program compositions having death or damnation as their subject, e.g., Berlioz' *Symphonie fantastique* (last movement: "Dream of a Witches' Sab-

Di - es i - rae, di - es il - la, Sol - vet saec - lum

in fa - vil - la, Tes - te Da - vid cum Si - bil - la.

bath"), Liszt's *Totentanz* and *Dante Symphony, Saint-Saëns' *Danse macabre. See J. Yasser, "Dies Irae, The Famous Medieval Chant" (*Musical Courier,* Oct. 6, 1927).

Diesis [Gr.]. (1) In early Greek theory (Pythagoras), the diatonic semitone of the *Pythagorean scale. This meaning survives in many medieval treatises, in which *diesis* is explained as the *semitonium minus* [see Semitone]. (2) In later Greek theory, the quarter tone of the enharmonic genus. This meaning survives in Martianus Capella (*c.* 400), who says that the *diatessaron* consists of five *hemitonia* or of ten *dieses.* It reappears in the writings of Vicentino (1555), who tried to restore the Greek system. Other writers explain the *diesis* still differently, e.g., as a fifth of a tone (Marchettus; *GS* iii, 73). Tinctoris, in his *Diffinitorium,* lists seven different meanings of *diesis* (*CS* iv, 182). (3) In some 15th-century treatises the term is used for the sharp sign, e.g., by Nicolaus Capuanus (*Compendium musicale,* 1415; see H. Riemann, *Geschichte der Musiktheorie,* 2nd ed. [1920], p. 252; see also *CS* iv, 444). This meaning survives to the present day in Italian and French terminology [see *Dièse*]. (4) In modern writings on acoustics the term is occasionally used to designate certain theoretical intervals, about a quarter tone in size. The difference between four minor thirds (of

just intonation) and the octave is called *great diesis* $((\%)^4:2 = {}^{648}\%_{25} = 63$ cents$)$, while that between the octave and three major thirds is called *minor diesis* or *enharmonic diesis* $(2:(\%)^3 = {}^{128}\%_{125} = 41$ cents$)$; see Enharmonic (2).

Diferencia [Sp.]. A 16th-century name for a variation. The *diferencias* of Luis de Narváez' *Delphín de música* (1538; see *HAM,* no. 122; *ApMZ* ii) are among the earliest preserved examples of variations [see Variations IV (1)]. Cabezón wrote outstanding *diferencias* for keyboard instruments [repr. in Editions XX, 3, 4, 7 and 8]. Examples in *HAM,* nos. 122, 124, 134. See also Glosa.

Difference tone, differential tone. See Combination tone.

Differentiae [L.]. The various endings of a psalm tone. See Euouae.

Diluendo [It.]. Fading away.

Dimeter. See under Poetic meter.

Diminished intervals. See under Interval.

Diminished seventh chord. See Seventh chord.

Diminished triad. See Triad.

Diminuendo [It.], abbr. *dim.* or *dimin.* Same as decrescendo.

Diminution [L. *diminutio*]. (1) Term in counterpoint and in mensural notation; see Augmentation and diminution. (2) The breaking up of the notes of a melody into quick figures, as is frequently done in variations; hence, synonymous with figuration or ornamentation. See Ornamentation I; also Division.

Diphona [Gr.]. See under *Bicinium.*

Diplomas. See Degrees and diplomas 9.

Direct. A mark ($\sim\!\!\!\!\wedge$) that in early manuscripts and publications is given at the end of each staff (or only of the page) to warn the player of the first note of the following staff (or page). The Latin name is *custos.* Its earliest occurrence, in 11th-century MSS of Gregorian chant, is an indication of the transition from chironomic to (approximately) diastematic neumes.

Directaneus. See under Psalmody I.

Dirge. A vocal or instrumental composition designed to be performed at a funeral or at memorial rites. The name is derived from L.

Dirige Domine, an antiphon from the Office for the Dead [see *LU,* p. 1782].

Dirigent, dirigieren [G.]. Conductor, to conduct.

Dis, disis [G.]. D-sharp, d-double-sharp; see Pitch names. In earlier music, *dis* often stands for e-flat, e.g., in Bach's St. Matthew Passion: "Wiederhole den Choral aus dem Dis" (Repeat the chorale in e-flat). As late as 1805, Beethoven's *Eroica* Symphony was described, at the first performance, as being "in Dis."

Discant. (1) A 12th- to 15th-century term for certain types of polyphonic music in which a part was composed against the plainsong, or in some cases perhaps improvised. It may be a translation of Gr. *diaphonia,* which until *c.* 1100 (John Cotton) was synonymous with organum. However, by *c.* 1175, when various sections of organum began to be stylistically differentiated, a 12th-century "Tractatus de Musica" [in J.-A.-L. de La Fage, *Essais de diphthérographie musicale,* 2 vols. (1864), i, 355], strictly distinguished discant from organum, the former designating two-voice polyphony in note-against-note style, the latter a more elaborate setting employing (or at least including) melismas in the upper part (melismatic organum; see Organum III). Perotinus was skilled in the art of discant, being described as "optimus discantor," while Leoninus was called "optimus organista." In the 13th century, Garlandia even distinguished a third style, *copula,* midway between discant and organum (*CS* i, 114, 175). The term "discant" originated as a designation for the upper voice only, the lower part being called "cantus" (*cantus* = voice; *discantus* = second, or counter, voice). However, the term also was used—and commonly is today—for the combination of both parts, and its original connotation has appeared in the terms *descant, descaunt,* *déchant, déschant,* and *discantus.* In the 13th century, discant continued to denote nonmelismatic music (one or only a few notes against each note of the cantus), but with the emphasis on strict measurement in modal rhythm [see Modes, rhythmic]. Thus, Garlandia says (*CS* i, 106), "Discant is the concurrence of various parts according to the principles of modal meter and of the equivalence of note values." It thus denotes the style used in the so-called discant sections of the organa of Notre Dame and in the two types of polyphony that originated from these, the *clausula* and *motet.* Stylistically, the *conductus* also belongs to the cate-

gory of discant. Its opposite is the "organal" sections, in which the upper part moves in long melismas (with less strict adherence, if any, to the rhythmic modes) above a few sustained notes of the tenor. For examples of 12th- and 13th-century discantus, see respectively under Organum (Ex. 4) and Clausula. As appears from these examples, the two parts move mainly in contrary motion. The ideal of contrary motion was mentioned in the 13th-century "Tractatus de Discantu" (in J.-A.-L. de la Fage, *Essais,* i, 358; *CS* i, 311) but became an essential characteristic of discant theory only at the end of the 13th century, when modal rhythm was replaced by mensural rhythm.

The 13th- to 15th-century treatises on discant deal chiefly with the rules of consonance and voice-leading in part music. In the 14th century, discant was equated with the expressions "nota contra notam" or "punctus contra punctum"; hence the abbreviated form "contrapunctus" or "counterpoint." Thus, discant adopted the connotation of counterpoint, and it continued to be used in that sense by both English and Continental writers through the 15th century.

(2) "English discant" is a recently introduced term (by M. Bukofzer) for a 15th-century style of three-part writing characterized by (a) the extensive use of sixth chords, often in succession (parallel), and (b) the lowest part's being a *cantus firmus.* The term is meant to distinguish this style from authentic discant as described in treatises from the 12th century on, which treated of perfect consonances and the principle of contrary motion. It should be noted, however, that none of the 15th-century English treatises on discant contains a clear reference to a distinct "English discant" as defined above, but they adhere closely to the traditional connotation of the term "discant" as counterpoint. Perhaps it would be advisable to replace the term "English discant" with designations such as "sixth-chord style with *cantus firmus* in the lowest part." Bukofzer also used the term "English discant" to distinguish one English practice from Continental *fauxbourdon,* in which the borrowed melody is in the highest part. See Ex. (close of the Te Deum melody; *c.* 1300). However, the insistence on the position of the *cantus firmus*

In te   Do - mi - ne spe - ra - vi

limits the usefulness of the term, since there are numerous compositions (or sections of compositions) in the same musical style that have the *cantus firmus* in the upper part (e.g., an English Sanctus from *c.* 1300; see G. Schmidt, in *AMW* xv, 238), in the middle part, or, often, no *cantus firmus* at all (e.g., the Gloria in *HAM,* no. 57b). The confusion between discant as practiced in England and a technique of parallel sixth chords stems in part from the treatise *c.* 1480 of the Italian (?) Guilelmus Monachus, who described what appears to have been an improvisory technique as a *modus faulxbourdon* practiced in England [*CS* iii, 288]. Also see *Discantus supra librum.*

(3) Name for the uppermost part (soprano, treble) of a polyphonic composition; used frequently today in connection with 14th- and 15th-century compositions in which a *cantus firmus* appears in the upper part (rather than in the tenor), nearly always in an embellished form (paraphrase). This technique was applied to hymns (Codex Apt, late 14th century; Dufay and others, 15th century), Marian antiphons (Dunstable, Dufay; see *HAM,* no. 65), Masses or Mass sections (see Discant Mass), etc. See also *Descant.*

Lit.: *ReMMA,* pp. 398ff; W. G. Waite, *The Rhythm of Twelfth-Century Polyphony* (1954); "Discant or Measured Music," in *OH,* i, ch. vi; S. W. Kenney, *Walter Frye and the "Contenance angloise"* (1964), ch. 5; E. Apfel, *Studien zur Satztechnik der mittelalterlichen englischen Musik,* 2 vols. (1959); M. Bukofzer, *Geschichte des englischen Diskants und des Fauxbourdons* (1936); T. Georgiades, *Englische Diskanttraktate aus der ersten Hälfte des 15. Jahrhunderts* (1937); R. Crocker, "Discant, Counterpoint, and Harmony" (*JAMS* xv); S. B. Meech, "Three Musical Treatises in English from a Fifteenth-century MS" (*Speculum* x); J. Handschin, "Zur Notre Dame-Rhythmik" (*ZMW* vii); id., "Zur Geschichte der Lehre vom Organum" (*ZMW* viii); E. Apfel, "Der klangliche Satz und der freie Diskantsatz im 15. Jahrhundert" (*AMW* xii); E. H. Sanders, in *MD* xix.   rev. s.k.

Discant Mass [G. *Diskantmesse*]. A recent term for Masses or Mass sections of the fourteenth and fifteenth centuries in which the borrowed *cantus firmus* does not appear, as is usual, in the tenor but in the upper part, often in an embellished form. Among the earliest examples is an English Sanctus from *c.* 1300 [reprinted in Schmidt, *AMW* xv, 238]. In a Credo by Zacha-

rias de Teramo of *c.* 1400 [*DTO* 61, p. 16], the melody of Credo I alternates in the two upper parts, with only a few notes added here and there. In Dufay's Missa Sancti Jacobi of *c.* 1428 several sections (end of the Introit, third Kyrie, Communion) have the Gregorian melody in the upper part, slightly embellished. More fully paraphrased plainsongs are used in a number of sections of a Mass by Reginald Liebert [*DTO* 53, p. 1; see the analysis on pp. 95ff]. In Ockeghem's Requiem Mass also the various liturgical melodies (Introit, Kyrie, etc.) appear mostly in the discant. On the whole it seems that discant treatment was employed for individual Mass sections rather than for a complete Mass. The term "discant Mass" is therefore somewhat misleading. Furthermore, the same practice is found in other categories, such as hymns and Marian antiphons.

Assigning certain earlier Mass compositions (Gloria, Credo of the Mass of Tournai; Credo of Machaut's Mass) to this type is based on the (questionable) assumption that their seemingly free upper parts actually are highly elaborate *paraphrases of liturgical melodies [see R. von Ficker, in *StM* vii; J. Handschin, in *ZMW* x and *KJ* xxv]. For a refutation of these assertions, see M. F. Bukofzer, *Studies in Medieval and Renaissance Music* [1950], p. 52.

Discantus. See Discant.

Discantus supra librum [L.; F. *déchant sur le livre*]. Designation for methods of improvising polyphony (or rather, harmony) on the basis of a single notated melody found "in the book," i.e., the book of Gregorian chant. The *organum of the 9th and 10th centuries, proceeding largely in parallel fourths or fifths, may be considered an early type of *discantus supra librum,* since its rules enabled a singer to improvise a second voice (*vox organalis*) to the plainsong melody (*vox principalis*). Usually, the term is applied to more elaborate methods of improvised harmonization of the 14th and 15th centuries. One of these, described (not quite clearly) by Simon Tunstede [*CS* iv, 294a], seems to be a "modernization" of the early organum of the fifth. Four singers perform doubled parallel fifths, while a fifth singer, the "discantor," introduces thirds, sixths (?), and tenths; see Ex. 1, in which the "part from the book" is indicated by black notes, the doubling parts by white notes, and the discantor's part by lozenges.

To the same category of improvised harmonization belongs a method described by an anonymous early 15th-century English writer (Brit. Mus. *Lansdowne 763*) as *faburden. Here also, only one part is notated and two singers improvise melodies resulting in sixth chords with occasional open triads (1–5–8). According to the most recent explanations [by B. Trowell, in *MD* xiii] the method was as follows: one singer sings the melody as written, e.g., d–e–f–g–f–e–d; another singer (treble) duplicates the melody at the upper fourth, g–a–b–c′–b–a–g; a third singer (faburdener) derives from the written melody a modified one by replacing each of its tones, except the first and last, by its upper third, d–g–a–b–a–g–d, but actually singing it a fifth lower, G–c–d–e–d–c–G. The result is sixth-chord harmony with the *cantus firmus* in the middle [see Ex. 2].

Very similar to this is a method described *c.* 1480 by the Italian (?) Guilelmus Monachus as a *modus faulxbourdon* practiced in England [*CS* iii, 288]. Here the derivative melody moves a third *below* the written melody and is transposed by one singer to the upper fifth and by another to the upper octave. The result is sixth-chord harmony with the *cantus firmus* in the lowest part [see Ex. 3]. As can easily be seen, the upper-third modification of the melody can also be used to produce sixth-chord progressions with the *cantus firmus* in the topmost part by singing it at the lower octave and doubling the original melody at the lower fourth. The result is shown in Ex. 4.

Finally, it should be mentioned that Tunstede's method has been interpreted as calling not for 1–5–8–12 but for 1–3–6–10 progressions, therefore as in Ex. 3 with a fourth part added a fifth above the third [Ex. 5, transcribed by W. Apel; see M. F. Bukofzer, *Geschichte des englischen Diskants* (1936), p. 20; B. Trowell, "Faburden and Fauxbourdon" (*MD* xiii)]. See

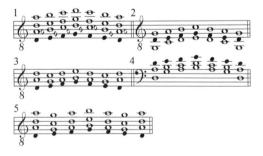

Abbé Jean Prim, "*Chant sur le livre* in French Churches in the 18th Century" (*JAMS* xiv). See also Fauxbourdon; Sixth-chord style.

Discantus visibilis. See under Sight.

Discord. See Concord, discord.

Disinvolto [It.]. Jaunty, unconstrained.

Disjunct. See Conjunct, disjunct.

Diskant [G.]. Soprano; see Discant. *Diskantmesse,* see Discant Mass.

Disposition. The arrangement of stops, manuals, pedals, couplers, etc., of an organ.

Dissonance. See Consonance, dissonance.

Dital harp. See Harp lute.

Dithyramb [Gr. *dithyrambos*]. A song in honor of the Greek god Dionysus. Originally it probably was a strophic song sung by a chorus or by the whole crowd attending the feast of the god. From the 6th to the 4th century B.C. it grew more elaborate, with the inclusion of *aulos accompaniment, soloists, and dancing groups. Thus it became a compound form consisting of various "movements," which has been compared to the cantata. It also adopted a dramatic and emotional character, full of unbridled passion. Toward the end of the 4th century B.C. it degenerated into a kind of theatrical performance in which various characters were frequently portrayed by a single actor.

Modern composers have occasionally used the word as a title for compositions of a free and passionate nature. See *ReMMA*, pp. 12ff; *RiHM* i.1, 129; *AdHM* i, 58; T. Reinach, *La Musique grecque* (1926), p. 149.

Ditonus [L.]. Medieval name for the major third, equal to two whole tones. For ditonic scale, see under Pentatonic scale (b).

Div. Abbr. for *divisi.

Divertimento [It.]. (1) Fugal episode. (2) A term frequently used in the 18th century, especially in Austria, for an instrumental composition written primarily for entertainment and hence in a rather light vein. The title Divertimento (or *Divertissement*) was given to an enormous variety of types. Usually, however, such compositions were written for small ensembles (strings, winds, or mixed groups; three to eight or more players) and consisted of a number (three to ten) of relatively short movements, some of which are modeled after the sonata while others are dances (especially minuets), marches, or variations. Among the composers of divertimenti are I. Holzbauer, Leopold Mozart [see *DTB* 17],

G. C. Wagenseil, J. C. Monn [see *DTO* 39], J. Starzer [see *DTO* 31], K. Ditters von Dittersdorf, Michael Haydn [see *DTO* 29], and, most prominently, F. J. Haydn and W. A. Mozart. In one of his autograph catalogs Haydn used the title Divertimento for 162 compositions, among them his Baryton trios. More than 50 of them are divertimenti as defined here. Mozart wrote 37 compositions called Divertimento. Later examples include Schubert's *Divertissement à l'Hongroise* (op. 54, for piano, 4 hands), A. Roussel's *Divertimenta* (op. 6, for 5 winds and piano), and F. Busoni's *Divertimento* (op. 52, for flute and orchestra). Compositions such as Beethoven's Septet op. 20 and Schubert's Octet op. 166 belong to the same category. Closely related types are the *cassation, *Feldmusik,* and *serenade. See G. Hausswald, "Der Divertimento-Begriff bei Georg Christoph Wagenseil" (*AMW* ix).

Divertissement [F.]. (1) Fugal episode. (2) A musical potpourri, frequently in the form of pieces extracted from an opera. (3) In French baroque opera, the ballets, dances, entr'actes, etc.—in short, all those pieces that served merely to entertain without being essential to the plot. (4) Same as *divertimento.

Divided stop. A device of organ building that makes it possible to use different registrations for the upper and lower halves of the manual. It was frequently found in organs of the 17th century, especially in Spain, where all stops were divided stops. Contemporary terms are half-stop (Purcell or Blow), *registro spezzato* [It.], *registre coupé* or *rompu* [F.; in Brit. Mus. *add. MS 29486*], *medio registro* [Sp.], and *meyo (meio) registo* [Port.]. Spanish organ composers often prescribed this device in their works, making a distinction between *registro alto, de tiple, de dos tiples* (solo part in the upper half) and *registro baxo, vajo, dos vajos* (solo part in the lower half). See Editions XI, 14 (Francisco Peraza, S. Aguilera de Heredia), and XXXII, 6, 12 (F. Correa de Araujo).

Divisi [It.], abbr. *div.* Used in orchestral scores to indicate that an instrumental body, e.g., the first violins, is to be divided into two groups for rendering passages that include full chords, doubling in thirds, etc. See under *A due;* also Gymel (2).

Divisio [L.]. (1) In 13th-century notation *divisio modi* is a small vertical dash of indefinite length that is regularly placed at the end of an *ordo,* i.e., a melodic phrase in modal meter. It is equivalent to a rest. (2) In 14th-century Italian notation, *divisiones* are metrical schemes comparable to our 4/8, 6/8, 9/8, 12/8, etc. meters, so called because they are arrived at by dividing a long note (*brevis*) into smaller values. See *ApNPM*, pp. 370ff.

Division. A 17th- and 18th-century term for *figuration, that is, the breaking up of a melody into quick figures and passages [see also Ornamentation I; Coloratura]. In particular, the term refers to the predominantly English practice of a harpsichordist's playing a ground bass (with its thoroughbass chords) to which a viol or flute player, "having the said Ground before his eyes, as his Theme or Subject, plays such a variety of Descant or Division in Concordance thereto, as his skill and present invention do then suggest unto him" [C. Simpson, *The Division-Violist,* 1659]. Such music, chiefly extemporized, was called "divisions upon a ground." Important English publications besides Simpson's are: John Playford, *The Division Violin* (1684); *The Division Flute* (anon., 1722). See Improvisation III; *Partimento.*

A modern counterpart of the 17th-century method of divisions exists in *boogie-woogie.

Division viol. See under Viol IV, 2.

D la sol (re). See under Hexachord III.

Dixie. A song by Daniel D. Emmett (1815–1904), written in 1859 for his Negro minstrel shows. Ironically, it was adopted by the Confederate troops during the Civil War.

Do, doh. See under Solmization I; Tonic sol-fa.

Doctrine of affections. See Affections, doctrine of.

Doctrine of figures. See Figures, doctrine of.

Documenta polyphoniae liturgicae sanctae ecclesiae Romanae. See Editions XVa.

Dodecachordon. An important theoretical book by H. Glareanus (original name Heinrich Loris, 1488–1563), published in 1547, in which the traditional system of eight *church modes is enlarged to a system of twelve. The book is also remarkable for its highly judicious and comprehensive analysis of the works of Josquin and other masters of the early 16th century. A German translation by P. Bohn appeared in 1888 [Editions XLVII, 16]. See C. A. Miller, "The *Dodecachordon* of Heinrich Glarean" (diss. Univ. of Michigan, 1950); *id.*, in *MD* xv;

A. Schering, "Die Notenbeispiele in Glarean's Dodekachordon" (*SIM* xiii). The name was used by Claude Le Jeune (d. 1606) as a title for a cycle of motets based on the twelve modes of Glareanus [see Editions XXV, 11].

Dodecaphonic. Pertaining to *twelve-tone technique or compositions [see Serial music].

Dodecuple scale. The chromatic scale in its modern interpretation, as used in the twelve-tone technique [see Serial music].

Doigté [F.]. Fingering. *Doigté fourchu,* cross fingering.

Dolce [It.]. Sweetly, softly.

Dolcino, dolcian. See under Oboe family III.

Dolente, doloroso [It.]. Sorrowful.

Domchor [G.]. The choir of a German cathedral (*Dom*), either Protestant or Roman Catholic.

Domestic Symphony. See *Symphonia domestica.*

Dominant. (1) The fifth degree of the major or minor scale, so called on account of its "dominating" position in harmony as well as in melody. Many melodies show the fifth as a tone second in importance only to the first degree, the tonic. However, the fifth degree is even more important in harmony as a bass tone, i.e., the root of the dominant triad (g–b–d′ in C major). In *harmonic analysis, this triad is indicated by the numeral V or the letter D. It is most frequently resolved into the tonic triad (I) [see Cadence I]. Other chords with dominant function are the dominant seventh and the dominant ninth [see Seventh chord; Ninth chord]. Of particular importance in harmonic practice are the so-called "secondary dominants," i.e., the dominants of any degree of the scale other than the tonic. These chords account for the majority of accidentals found in music that is essentially diatonic. The designation for such chords is: V of II (V/II), V of III (V/III), etc. [see Ex.]. The early history of the V–I progression is briefly described under Cadence II. (2) For the dominant of the modes, see Church modes II.

V/III   III   V/II   II   V   I

Dominant seventh chord. See under Seventh chord; Dominant.

Dominica [L.]. Sunday [see under *Feria*].

Dominican Republic. The indigenous music of the island of Hispaniola at the time of the Spanish conquest was described by two 16th-century chroniclers, Father Bartolomé de las Casas and Gonzalo Fernandez de Oviedo, Columbus' official historian. Both wrote about dance-songs called *areitos* as performed by the Tainan Indians of the Antilles. Father Las Casas was the first to celebrate a High Mass with the participation of a chorus in the New World (1510). Cristóbal de Llerena (1540–c. 1600) of Santo Domingo was the first musician trained in European music to be appointed to the Cathedral of La Vega.

By the beginning of the 17th century secular music was represented by the *villancico and such dances as the *zarabanda* and *calenda,* and later the *fandinguete* and *tumba.*

Not until the 19th century did a native school of art music begin to develop. This development began with Juan Bautista Alfonseca (1810–75), a native of Puerto Rico who composed instrumental dances in the popular vein, as well as two Masses. His pupil, José Reyes (1835–1905), also a church and dance music composer, wrote the Dominican national anthem (1883). A contemporary of his, José María Arredondo (1840–1924), composed the music for several *zarzuelas.* The foremost figure in the second half of the 19th century was Pablo Claudio (c. 1855–99), who wrote two music dramas, *América* and *Maria de Cuellar,* as well as a great number of instrumental pieces in native dance forms. Other composers of the period were Arredondo's son, Clodomiro Arredondo Murra (1864–1935), who wrote liturgical music and songs, and José María Rodríguez Arresón (b. 1875), composer of a *Sinfonia quasi una Fantasia,* choral music, and dance music.

The link between late 19th-century romanticism and a nationalist school of composition is represented by four composers who used materials from folk music as a basis for larger forms. They are José de Jesús Ravelo (1876–1952), who composed sacred music such as the oratorios *La Muerte de Cristo* (1939) and *La Resurección de Cristo* (1942), in addition to symphonic compositions and a string quartet; Manuel de Jesús Lovelace (b. 1871), composer of *Escenas Dominicanas* for orchestra; Gabriel del Orbe (b. 1888), composer of art songs and chamber music; and

Augusto Vega (b. 1885), composer of more than three hundred works, including an opera, *Indigena.*

The pioneers of modern music in the Dominican Republic include Esteban Peña Morell (1897–1939), a renowned folk-music collector, composer of a *Sinfonia Bárbara* (1923) and an opera, *Embrujo-Antellano* (1928), and Juan Francisco García (b. 1892), who has consistently employed folk materials in works such as his three symphonies, the overture *Advenimiento, Scherzo Clásico* (1941), several works for band, string quartets, and art songs. By combining several Dominican dance forms he established a new form that he called *sambumbia.* To these two men a younger group of nationalists owe much of their inspiration: Enrique Mejía-Arredondo (1901–51); Luís Emilio Meña (1895–1965), composer of a *Sinfonia Giocosa;* José Dolores Cerón (b. 1897); Rafael Ignacio (b. 1897); Julio Alberto Hernandez (b. 1900); Ramón Diaz (b. 1901); Luís Rivera (b. 1902); and Enrique de Marchena (b. 1908), the best-known Dominican composer abroad, whose works include a Concertino for flute and orchestra, a Concerto for violin and orchestra, and a *Suite Imágenes.*

With the arrival, in 1940, of the Spanish-born composer Enrique Casal Chapí (b. 1909), more progressive paths were opened. Among the most outstanding followers of his ideas are Ninon de Boroüwer (b. 1907), Manuel Simó (b. 1916), and Antonio Morel Guzmán. In addition, there is a large group of composers of dance music, of whom Rafael Petitón Guzmán (b. 1894) is the best known for his *merengues, danzas,* and *criollas,* and Juan Bautista Espínola (1894–1923) for his more than five hundred pieces of popular music.

The folksongs of the Dominican Republic are best represented by the *tonada* and by a number of Spanish-influenced examples such as the *plena* (working song), *criolla* (serenade), *arení* and *trocha* (children's game-songs), *vela* and *calvarios* (religious songs), etc. Most of the folk dances have evolved from African and Spanish prototypes, the most popular being the *merengue,* its derivative the *pambiche,* and the *baile de palos, carabiné, *mangulina, *sarambo,* and *bolero,* the last imported from Cuba.

Lit.: J. M. Coopersmith, *Music and Musicians of the Dominican Republic* (1949); J. F. Garcia, *Panorama de la Música Dominicana* (1947); id., "Formas de la música folklórica dominicana" (*Bol. folk. dom.* i); F. de Nolasco, *La Música en Santo Domingo* (1939); J. M. Coopersmith, "Music and Musicians of the Dom. Rep. A Survey" (*MQ* xxxi, 71, 212). Also see under Latin America.   J.O-S.

Don Carlos. Opera in four acts by Verdi (libretto, in French, by F. J. Méry and C. DuLocle, based on Schiller's drama; It. trans. by A. Ghislanzoni), produced in Paris, 1867, rev. It. version in Milan, 1884, Setting: Spain, mid-16th century.

Domp(e). See Dump.

Domra. A Russian long-necked lute [see Lute II] of the 16th and 17th centuries, the forerunner of the *balalaika. See A. S. Faminzin, *The Domra* (1891; Russian); *LavE* i.5, 2493ff.

Don Giovanni [It., Don Juan]. *Dramma giocoso* in two acts by Mozart (libretto by L. da Ponte), produced in Prague, 1787. Setting: Seville, 17th century. The original title, *Il Dissoluto punito,* is rarely used today.

Don Juan. Symphonic poem by R. Strauss, op. 20 (1881–89), based on a dramatic poem by Lenau.

Donnermaschine [G.]. *Thunder machine.

Don Pasquale. Opera in three acts by Donizetti (libretto by the composer and G. Ruffini), produced in Paris, 1843. Setting: Rome, early 19th century.

Don Quixote. Symphonic poem by R. Strauss, op. 35 (1897), based on the novel by Cervantes and composed in the form of an Introduction, Theme with Variations, and Finale. The variations describe ten adventures of Don Quixote, and the finale depicts his death. In addition to the main "theme of a knightly character," there is a lyrical one portraying Don Quixote in love and a comic one for Sancho Panza.

Don Rodrigo. Opera in three acts by A. Ginastera (libretto by A. Cassona), produced in Buenos Aires, 1964.

Doppel [G.]. Double. *Doppel-Be,* double flat; *Doppelchor,* double chorus; *Doppelfuge,* double fugue; *Doppelgriff,* double stop; *Doppelkreuz,* double sharp; *Doppelpedal,* double pedal; *Doppelschlag,* turn; *Doppeltriller,* double trill; *Doppelzunge,* double-tonguing. In regard to instruments, the term usually denotes *duplex instruments [see *SaRM,* pp. 114–17].

Doppelt so schnell [G.]. Twice as fast.

Doppio [It.]. Double. *Doppio bemolle,* double flat; *doppio diesis,* double sharp; *doppio movimento (tempo),* double speed; *doppio pedale,* double pedal.

Dorian. See under Greece II (c); Church modes I; Modality. The Dorian sixth is the major sixth used in a minor key (e.g., in C minor: c–e♭–f–g–a–g), so called because it appears in the Dorian church mode (d–f–g–a–b–a). See A. J. Hipkins, "Dorian and Phrygian" (*SIM* iv).

Dorian Toccata and Fugue. A Toccata and Fugue in D minor by Bach for organ, written without the customary B-flat in the key signature and therefore having the appearance of a composition in the Dorian mode. Actually, however, the accidentals for D minor are supplied throughout. The use of key signatures with one flat less than is used today (e.g., one flat for G minor, two flats for C minor) was a common practice throughout the 17th century.

Dot [F. *point;* G. *Punkt;* It. *punto;* Sp. *puntillo*]. In present-day musical notation a dot is used: (a) after a note, to indicate augmentation of its value by one-half [see Dotted notes]; (b) above a note, to indicate *staccato or *portato. In Italian and French keyboard sources of the early 16th century, a dot above or below a note indicates chromatic alteration [see *ApNPM* pp. 4, 6]. See also *Punctus.*

Dotted notes. I. *Present usage.* A dot placed after a note adds to it one-half of its value. Thus, a dotted half note equals three quarter notes [Ex. 1a]. Two dots after a note add to it one-half plus one-fourth of its value. Thus, a double-dotted half note equals seven (4 + 2 + 1) eighth notes [Ex. 1b]. In modern practice, dotted notes

1

are used only if their value does not extend over a bar line; otherwise tied notes are used [Ex. 1c]. Brahms revived an older practice when he wrote dotted rhythm as shown in Ex. 1d.

II. *In baroque music.* Prior to 1750, the dot was frequently used in a different manner, which has been the object of much investigation and controversy. The only proper conclusion is that in the baroque period the dot indicated a prolongation of undetermined value depending on various factors, such as the character of the

piece, the rhythm of the other parts, the tempo, the performer's interpretation, etc. Statements to this effect are found in practically all theory books written between *c.* 1680 and 1750. J. J. Quantz, in his *Versuch einer Anweisung die Flöte traversière zu spielen* (1752), seems to have been the first to use the double dot, thus paving the way for a clearer indication of different degrees of prolongation. The following cases of the freely used dot are noteworthy:

(a) If dotted notes are used in conjunction with triplets, the dotted rhythm may be modified (attenuated) into a triplet rhythm [Ex. 2; Bach, Partita no. 1]. According to contemporary writers, however, this modification was not obligatory but was left to the performer's discretion. An interesting illustration is the gavotte from Bach's Partita no. 6 [Ex. 3], where neither

the exact nor the assimilated rhythm can be consistently maintained, since the same dotted figure appears in conjunction with triplet groups as well as with groups of four notes. Consistency in this matter (as in many others) concerned Bach much less than it does the student of today. Dotted notes against or in alternation with triplets are very common in the piano compositions of Schubert, probably with the same meaning as in Bach, since the notation ♩ $_3$ ♪ does not occur in these works (was it ever used by Schubert?). See S. Babitz, in *MQ* xxxviii, 533ff; E. R. Jacobi, in *MF* xiii, 268ff; G. Horn, in *RdM* 1935, pp. 27ff; E. Harich-Schneider, in *MF* xii, 35ff (the first two writers in favor of assimilation, the others against it).

(b) According to French writers of the early 18th century, compositions written in "French style" (i.e., the style of the slow section in Lully's French *overture) call for a more pronounced rhythm than is indicated in writing, so that a dotted note should be performed almost as a double-dotted value, as in Ex. 4. This rendition, if used with taste and moderation, helps bring out the pompous quality of the French overture style and should be applied, though without ostentatious exaggeration, to pieces such as the

prelude to Bach's Partita no. 6 and the Prelude in E-flat minor from his *Well-Tempered Clavier* vol. i, a composition whose true character is far different from the gentle, somewhat boring lyricism with which it is usually interpreted. On the other hand, some modern writers and performers have gone too far in recommending strict double dotted execution for all sorts of pieces that show a remote resemblance to the style of the French overture (e.g., the D-major Fugue of the *Well-Tempered Clavier,* vol. i).

(c) Another free use of the dot, but less likely to lead to confusion, is illustrated in Ex. 5 (used as early as Kotter's tablature, *c.* 1515; see *ApNPM,* p. 30).

(d) About 1700 dotted rhythm was also applied to passages written in equal notes. See *Inégales.*

III. *Inverted dotting.* The rhythm that is the reverse of the ordinary dotted rhythm; in other words, a dotted note that is preceded, not followed, by its complementary short value (e.g., ♪ ♩.). This rhythm is generally known as "Scotch snap," because it is a typical feature of the *strathspey and other Scottish folk tunes. Its use, however, is far more widespread. It is a typical feature of American Negro music and of jazz, and it has been maintained that the syncopated effects of jazz have their origin in the Scotch snap [see under Jig]. On the other hand, inverted dotting is also very common in non-Western music, where the normal dotted rhythm is rather rare. In this connection it is interesting to note that Jacobus of Liège ("Speculum musicae," *c.* 1330), in defending the *ars antiqua* against the refinements of the *ars nova,* maintains that iambic rhythm (♪♩) is preferable to

trochaic rhythm (♩♪) because it is "a rhythm full of strength and harmonizing with nature which is always stronger at the end than at the beginning."

In art music, inverted dotting appears first in French songs of the late 16th century to indicate correct pronunciation [see *ApNPM,* p. 129]. It is extremely common in Italian music of the early 17th century and, in fact, represents one of the most typical embodiments of the exaggerated expressiveness of early baroque music (examples in Caccini, *Nuove Musiche* (1601); toccatas of Trabaci, A. Mayone, Frescobaldi). Italian terms for inverted dotted rhythm are *alla *zoppa* and *stile lombardo* (Lombardic style). Exceptionally clear examples are found in the works of Sammartini and J. C. Bach, who both lived in Milan, the capital of Lombardy. This rhythm also figures prominently in English music of the 17th century (Blow, Purcell), where it is used effectively to bring out the short but accented first syllables that occur in so many English dissyllabics.

Double. (1) The French word *double* is a 17th- and 18th-century term for a simple type of variation, consisting chiefly of the addition of embellishments. It occurs especially in certain dances of the suite (Bach, English Suite no. 1: courante with two *doubles;* English Suite no. 6: sarabande with *double*). See M. Reimann, in *MF* v, vi. (2) The English word "double" indicates either instruments of lower pitch or a combination of two instruments in one. The former meaning, which is derived from the double octave, is exemplified by double bass, double-bass clarinet, double-bass trombone, double bassoon, etc., and the latter by double horn, double trumpet, and double flageolet. See Duplex instruments.

Doublé [F.]. Term used by the French clavecinists for the *turn.

Double appoggiatura. See Appoggiatura, double.

Double aria. See under Aria V.

Double bass [F. *contrebasse;* G. *Kontrabass;* It. *contrabasso;* Sp. *contrabajo*]. Also called *bass viol, contrabass.* The largest member of the *violin family, serving in the orchestra somewhat as a 16-foot organ stop and frequently doubling the cellos in the lower octave. The modern instrument has four strings tuned E_1 A_1 D G, notated an octave higher (E A d g). Some instruments have a fifth string, tuned C_1, and some have a mechanical device controlled by levers that extends the range of the E string down to C_1. The upper limit for orchestral parts is a (notated a'), although virtuosos extend the range of the instrument considerably by the use of harmonics. Famous double-bass players have been D. Dragonetti (1763–1846), G. Bottesini (1821–89), and S. Koussevitzky (1874–1951).

More than any other instrument of the violin family, the double bass has been subjected to modification and experiment in shape, size, number and tuning of the strings, etc. As a matter of fact, the principles of violin-building have never been fully applied to this instrument, which to the present day retains various features of the viol family, e.g., sloping shoulders, flat back, tuning of the strings in fourths rather than fifths, etc. This ancestry is evident also in the names "bass viol" and "double bass," both abbreviated versions of the full name "double-bass viol" [see Viol IV, 1]. In the 19th century, instruments with three strings, tuned A_1 D G or G_1 D A, were in great favor. What these lose in compass they gain in brightness of tone on account of the smaller pressure on the table. Even today there are players (particularly in Europe) who hold the bow in the manner of viol-playing, i.e., with the hand underneath the stick. See M. Grodner, *Comprehensive Catalogue of Literature for the String Bass*, rev. ed. (1964); R. Elgar, *Introduction to the Double Bass* (1960); *id.*, *More about the Double Bass* (1963); E. Halfpenny, "A Note on the Genealogy of the Double Bass" (*GSJ* i).

Double-bass clarinet, trombone. See under Clarinet family II; Trombone I (d).

Double bassoon. See under Oboe family I D.

Double C (D, etc.). See under Pitch names II.

Double cadence [F.]. A compound ornament, frequently introduced at cadences in music of the 17th and 18th centuries and consisting of a *cadence,* or trill, upon each of two successive notes. The interpretation of the *double cadence* was quite flexible, its details being left to the discretion of the performer, but the following sequence of notes, in which the first trill is reduced to a five-note turn, is typical:

Ex. a shows how the *double cadence* is indicated in 17th-century music (Chambonnières, D'An-

glebert, etc.), while Ex. b represents the 18th-century notation (Bach, Handel, F. Couperin, Rameau) of the same ornament. The name *double cadence* (or its abbreviation, *doublé*) was often applied to the turn alone.   P.A.

Double chorus. Use of two choruses in alternation. See Polychoral style.

Double concerto. A concerto for two solo instruments and orchestra, such as Mozart's Concerto for violin and viola, K. 364.

Double corde [F.]. Double stop.

Double counterpoint. See Invertible counterpoint.

Double croche [F.]. Sixteenth note. See under Notes.

Double cursus. Term for the immediate repeat of a melody, used particularly in connection with medieval music, e.g., for the repeated sections of a sequence or the restatement of a tenor melody in clausulae or motets.

Double flat. See under Accidentals.

Double fugue. A fugue with two subjects. The term is applied to two different types. (a) A genuine double fugue consists of three distinct sections, each complete in itself: a fugue on the first subject (I), a fugue on the second subject (II), and a fugue on both subjects in contrapuntal combination (I + II). Probably the earliest examples are among the ricercars of Andrea Gabrieli (e.g., *Il Terzo Libro de ricercari*, 1596, nos. 3, 4, 6). Bach employed this structure in the great harpsichord fugue in A minor, in the fugue of the organ toccata in F major, and in the G-sharp minor fugue of the *Well-Tempered Clavier,* vol. ii. The fugue in C-sharp minor from the *Well-Tempered Clavier,* vol. i, represents a somewhat simplified scheme, including the sections I and I + II. His **Art of Fugue* contains not only double fugues (nos. 9, 10) but also triple fugues of a similar scheme (nos. 8, 11) and an (unfinished) quadruple fugue. (b) Usually, the term is applied to a much simpler type, i.e., a fugue in which the countersubject has an individual character and is consistently used throughout the piece, combined with the main subject; in other words, fugues represented by the last section only of scheme (a). Examples of this type are quite common but usually they treat the secondary theme more freely than is the case in the double fugue proper. For an example see the *Well-Tempered Clavier,* vol. i, no. 14 (F-sharp minor). See Double theme.

Double pedal. In organ playing, the use of both feet simultaneously (rather than, as usual, in alternation) for rendering intervals or two parts. This technique is documented as far back as 1448 [see W. Apel, "Die Tabulatur des Adam Ileborgh" (*ZMW* xvi)]. As early as *c.* 1520 Arnolt Schlick wrote a composition, "Ascendo al patrem," in ten parts, six for the hands and four for the feet, each foot playing thirds [see M. S. Kastner, ed., *Hommage à l'empereur Charles-quint,* 1954]. While this was a singular achievement, the double-pedal technique was generally practiced and fully developed by the North German organ masters of the 17th century (Tunder, Reincken, Lübeck) and by Bach, whose organ chorales on "Aus tiefer Not" and "An Wasserflüssen Babylons" have a complete part for each foot. In modern organ pieces octave-doubling is very common. It is also used by organists to exploit the limited resources of smaller organs.

Double sharp. See under Accidentals.

Double stop. The execution of two or more simultaneous tones (intervals, chords, passages in two or more parts) on the violin and similar instruments. Double-stop technique is already used to a remarkable degree in Ganassi's "ricercares" for viola da gamba (1552; see *HAM,* no. 119) and in the earliest violin sonatas (Biagio Marini [1626]; see *SchGMB,* no. 183). It reaches the peak of artistic perfection in Bach's sonatas for violin solo and the height of brilliant virtuosity in the compositions of Paganini.

Double structure. A term describing compositions, mostly of the 15th century, having a *cantus firmus* in two parts simultaneously. There are two main types of double structure: one formed by two different *cantus firmi,* the other by the same *cantus firmus* in canonic imitation. The first type is practically identical with what is generally called a *quodlibet.* An early example is Dufay's motet "Ecclesiae militantis," in which the beginning of the Antiphon "Ecce nomen Domini" [*LU,* p. 317] is supplemented by the first four notes of the Antiphon "Gabriel angelus" [*LU,* p. 1417]; see Ex. A much more complex double structure is found in an anonymous "Alma Redemptoris Mater," which has the complete Gregorian melody in the discant, while the first section of the tenor includes three statements of the passage "tuum sanctorum

Gabriel

Ecce nomen

genitorem" from the "Alma" and the second section the beginning of "Ave regina" [*DTO* 53, p. 37; see A. Orel, in *StM* vii, 69; J. Handschin, in *MD* v, 102]. A famous example is Josquin's motet "O bone et dulcis," based on a combination of "Pater noster" and "Ave Maria." See also *Quodlibet.* Canonic (or freely imitative) double structure is present in several "L'Homme armé" Masses, e.g., those by Faugues and B. Vacqueras [Editions XXXI, Series I, no. 1; see W. Apel, in *Speculum* xxv]. Josquin's motet "Nimphes, nappés" is based on a canon of the plainsong "Circumdederunt," which recurs in his "Christus mortuus" and "Sic Deus dilexit."

Another example of double structure occurs in what has been termed *Diskant-Tenormesse* [see R. Ficker, in *StM* vii, 22], i.e., a Mass (more accurately, a Mass section) characterized "by the simultaneous use of two *cantus firmi,* one of them ornamented in the upper part, the other usually unchanged in the tenor" [*ibid.,* p. 27]. This type is much more problematic than the others, since its existence rests on the often questionable assumption that a seemingly free upper part actually is a highly elaborate paraphrase of a liturgical melody [see under Discant Mass]. Of the various examples cited by Ficker and others, perhaps the most convincing is the Gloria of an anonymous "O rosa bella" Mass [*DTO* 22, p. 34], which uses both the discant and the tenor of Dunstable's chanson not simultaneously but successively. A similar construction occurs in Dunstable's "Veni sancte spiritus," in which the melody of "Veni creator spiritus" is used alternately in the discant and in the tenor. For another meaning of double structure, see *NOH* iii, 187 (Bukofzer).

Double theme. A fugal theme that continues beyond the entrance of the answer, including also the counterpoint to the answer, which is treated as a second theme. This method is frequently employed in early ricercars, by Andrea

T_1 T_2

T_1

Gabrieli [see Ex.; *Ricercari . . . Libro secondo* (1595), no. 13], Frescobaldi, and others. The fugues described under *double fugue (b) might better be called fugues with a double theme.

Double-tonguing. See Tonguing.

Double touch. A modern principle of organ construction, devised by Hope-Jones, which allows the keys of the organ to be depressed in two successive degrees, so that different registrations become available simultaneously on the same manual, e.g., a small group of accompaniment stops on the first touch, and a solo stop on the second. Its application is confined to theater organs. See also Harmonium II.

Double trill. A simultaneous trill on two different notes, usually a third apart. Its perfect and rapid execution is one of the most difficult technical feats on the piano as well as on the violin. For the latter instrument it appears as early as the middle 17th century [J. Schop; see A. Moser, in *CP Kretzschmar*]. For the piano, the long double trills in Beethoven's Piano Concerto in G major, op. 58, are among the earliest examples.

Doucement [F.]. Gently, smoothly.

Douloureux [F.]. Sorrowful.

Down in the Valley. Folk drama in one act by K. Weill (libretto by A. Sundgaard), produced at Indiana University, 1948. Setting: America, the present.

Doxology. An expression of the glory of God. In the Roman liturgy, the name of two important texts, the Lesser Doxology: "Gloria patri (et filio et spiritui sancto, sicut erat in principio, et nunc et semper et in saeculum saeculorum. Amen)"; and the Greater Doxology: "Gloria in excelsis deo (et in terra pax hominibus bonae voluntatis," etc.). The Greater Doxology is the *Gloria of the Mass. The Lesser Doxology (D) is a part of all the Introits, which follow the scheme A V D A [see Psalmody III]. It also is added as a final verse to all psalms and nearly all canticles, its last six syllables being indicated by their vowels only, thus: *Euouae [see also Psalm tones]. It is also used elsewhere, e.g., in connection with the "Asperges me" [*LU*, p. 11].

In the Anglican rites, doxology usually means the metrical verse "Praise God from whom all blessings flow," which is widely sung to the *Old Hundredth tune. Also, the last verses of many hymns, as well as the addition to the *"Pater noster" beginning with "For thine is the king-

dom," are included in the term. See E. Werner, "The Doxology in Synagogue and Church, A Liturgico-Musical Study" (*Hebrew Union College Annual* xix, 1946, pp. 275ff).

Drag. See under Percussion instruments B, 1.

Dragma [Gr.]. A note form of the late 14th century consisting of a double-stemmed semibreve. It is used, with a variety of meanings, in the theoretical and practical sources of the period. See *ApNPM, passim*.

Dramatic music. Music written for a drama or play (*incidental music), particularly incidental music written by Henry Purcell, in order to distinguish it from his only complete opera, *Dido and Aeneas*. See J. S. Manifold, *The Music in English Drama* [1956]; E. D. Rendall, in *ML* i, 135ff; W. Barclay Squire, in *SIM* v.

Drame lyrique [F.], **dramma lirico** [It.]. Modern terms for opera, not necessarily of a lyrical character. The English term "lyrical drama" is used in the same way.

Dramma per musica [It.]. The earliest name for Italian operas (17th century), particularly serious ones (the later *opera seria*). Bach used the term for secular cantatas in dialogue form that were designed for a modest stage performance (*Der Streit zwischen Phöbus und Pan, Kaffeekantate,* etc.).

Drängend [G.]. Pressing on.

Dreher [G.]. An Austrian dance, similar to the *Ländler.

Drehleier [G.]. *Hurdy-gurdy.

Drehorgel [G.]. Street organ.

Dreigroschenoper, Die [G., The Threepenny Opera]. A play with music by Kurt Weill (libretto by Bertolt Brecht), produced in Berlin, 1928. Setting: London, early 18th century. It is a modern *ballad opera, based on the plot of John Gay's *The Beggar's Opera* (1728), with attractive music in a sophisticated jazz style.

Dreiklang [G.]. *Triad.

Dreitaktig [G.]. In phrases of three measures.

Drone. (1) The low pipes of the *bagpipe. (2) A primitive bagpipe, capable of playing only a few low tones and used to accompany other instruments or voices. (3) In musical composition, long sustained notes, usually in the lowest part (drone bass). See Pedal point; *Bourdon*.

Drum. I. Generic name for instruments consisting of skin stretched over a frame or vessel and struck with the hands or a stick (or sticks). Drums therefore are practically identical with the category "membranophones" [see Instruments II]. In some primitive cultures, however, there are drums that have no membrane, consisting simply of a tree trunk hollowed out through a narrow longitudinal slit (slit-drum; see *SaHMI*, p. 29f). These are classified as "idiophones."

II. The membranophonous drums are among the oldest and most widespread of all instruments. They are found in all cultures, among the most primitive African and South American tribes as well as in China, India, Arabia, etc. A gigantic, man-size bass drum is depicted on a Sumerian vase of the third millennium B.C. [see *SaHMI*, pl. IV]. Egyptian drums from about 1800 B.C. have been preserved, and drums are mentioned in one of the earliest Chinese poems, dating from 1135 B.C. Drums existed and still exist in a large variety of sizes and shapes, in the form of a barrel, a cylinder, an hourglass, a goblet, etc.

From the Orient the drum was introduced to the Western world via Greece, where the use of the "tympanon" was restricted to the orgiastic cult of Dionysus and Cybele, and later to medieval Europe, where the earliest evidence is an English 12th-century miniature showing a juggler disguised as a bear and striking with his hands a barrel drum hung around his neck. A famous Spanish miniature of the 13th century [see *Cantiga*] shows the player of an hourglass drum, which he carries on his shoulder. Such forms were probably imported from the Orient during the Crusades. Of greater importance was the introduction, before 1300, of the Arabian *nagarah* (naqqarah), small kettledrums used in pairs and called *nacaires* in France, *nakers* in England, *naccheroni* in Italy. The cylindrical drum appeared about the same time under the name *tabor* or, later, *tambourin. In the 15th century kettledrums as well as side drums were adopted by armies as an indispensable part of military equipment. They remained restricted to this sphere until the 17th century, when kettledrums were first used in the orchestra. For the modern orchestral drums, see Percussion instruments A, 1; B, 1–4.

Drum-Roll Symphony. Popular name for Haydn's Symphony no. 103 in E-flat (*Salomon Symphonies no. 11), composed in 1795, so called

because of the drum roll in the opening measure of the Introduction.

Drum Stroke Symphony. See Surprise Symphony.

D.S. [It.]. Abbr. for *dal segno.*

Dualism, dualistic theory. A theory according to which the tonalities of major and minor are not in the relationship of "primary" and "secondary" but are phenomena of equal value, one being the inversion of the other. The theory is based on the fact that by reckoning downward the intervals of the major triad, the tones of the minor triad are reached: e.g., c′–e′–g′ becomes, by strict inversion, c′–ab–f. The dualistic principle is foreshadowed in Zarlino's explanation of the major and minor triad [see Arithmetic and harmonic mean]. It was clearly stated by Rameau (1737), Vallotti (1779), and M. Hauptmann (1853). A. von Oettingen (*Harmoniesystem in dualer Entwickelung*, 1866; *Das Duale Harmoniesystem*, 1913) and H. Riemann (*Das Problem des harmonischen Dualismus* [1905] and his other books on harmony) developed this principle to the fullest extent and made it the basis of harmonic analysis. The accompanying example

serves as an illustration. It will be noted that the "minor dominant" corresponds to the "major subdominant," and vice versa. The greatest shortcoming of the theory lies in the fact that in a minor mode the triad is determined not by its lowest but by its highest tone, i.e., the fifth. Hence, the first chord on the lower staff must not be read: f (fundamental)–ab (minor third)–c′ (fifth), but downward: c′ (fundamental)–ab (major third)–f (fifth). This awkward explanation contradicts the most elementary facts of acoustics and musical experience. The theory has not gained much ground except within the school of Riemann.

Lit.: A. von Oettingen, *Das duale Harmoniesystem* (1913); S. Karg-Elert, *Polaristische Klang- und Tonalitätslehre* [1931]; D. Jorgenson, "A

Résumé of Harmonic Dualism" (*ML* xliv); H. Westerby, in *PMA* xxix; O. Ortmann, "The Fallacy of Harmonic Dualism" (*MQ* x); C. Dahlhaus, "War Zarlino Dualist?" (*MF* x).

Ductia. A medieval instrumental form (13th century) that, according to Johannes de Grocheo, is a shorter *stantipes* [see *Estampie*], i.e., with three to four *puncti* [see Punctus (2)] instead of five or more. The term does not occur in musical sources. However, examples of the type exist in the "Dansse Real" of the *Chansonnier du roy* [see P. Aubry, *Estampies et danses royales,* 1907] and in several two-part instrumental pieces from the MS Brit. Mus. *Harleian 978* [see *ApNPM*, p. 239f]. Examples in *HAM*, nos. 40a, 41.

Dudelsack [G.]. *Bagpipe.

Due [It.]. Two. *Due corde,* two strings, indicates in violin music that the same tone should be sounded on two strings, for greater volume; in piano music, see *Una corda.* See also *A due.*

Duenna, The [Rus. *Obruchenie v monastyre,* Betrothal in a Monastery]. Opera in four acts by Prokofiev (libretto by the composer and M. Mendelssohn, based on R. B. Sheridan's play), produced in Leningrad, 1946. Setting: Seville, 18th century.

Duet [F. *duo;* G. *Duett, Duo;* It. *duetto;* Sp. *dúo*]. A composition for two performers of equal importance, with or without accompaniment. The most important types are: (a) the vocal duet, i.e., songs or arias for two voices with accompaniment [G. *Duett*]. These play a prominent part in operas, particularly "love duets" (practically the whole second act of Wagner's *Tristan* is a "love duet"). Nonoperatic duets occur in the songs of Schubert, Schumann, Brahms, and many others. An early type of unaccompanied vocal duet is the *bicinium of the 16th century. A famous operatic duet of early date is the finale of Monteverdi's *L'Incoronazione di Poppea* (1642; see *SchGMB*, no. 178). In the 17th century the chamber duet (chamber cantata for two singers, with accompaniment) was a much cultivated type. Early examples are by Monteverdi, Marco da Gagliano, and Frescobaldi. See K. Jeppesen, *La Flora* (1949), iii, nos. 27ff; L. Landshoff, ‡*Alte Meister des Bel canto*, 2 vols. [n.d.]; E. Schmitz, in *JMP* xxiii; also *RiHM*, ii.2 and ii.3. There are numerous duets by Steffani (some pub. in Chrysander's edition of Handel and in *DTB* 11) and Durante (some pub. by Cherubini). Examples in *HAM*, nos. 209 (Landi),

257 (Campra), 273 (Durante), 287 (Pergolesi). (b) The instrumental duet, for example, for two violins with or without piano accompaniment [G. *Duo*]. Only a few composers (Rode, Spohr, Romberg) have written such pieces, in which the piano part is usually mere chord-filling. Works in which this part has individual significance, as, for example, in the sonatas by Bach, are called *trio sonatas. (c) The piano duet, i.e., music for two pianists (four hands), either on the same or on two instruments [see Piano duet].

Dugazon. See under Soubrette.

Duke Bluebeard's Castle. See *Bluebeard's Castle.*

Dulce melos. See under Echiquier.

Dulcimer [F. *tympanon;* G. *Hackbrett;* It. *salterio tedesco*]. (1) Medieval stringed instrument, a variety of *psaltery and almost identical to it in shape but having a flat soundboard, often triangular, with ten or more parallel strings that are struck by small hammers (the psaltery is plucked). Thus the dulcimer and psaltery are related to each other as are their ultimate descendants, the piano and harpsichord. The dulcimer originated in the Middle East (Assyria, Persia), whence it migrated in three directions: (a) to Spain and western Europe, where it appeared as early as the 12th century, as seen in the reliefs of the cathedral in Santiago de Compostela (1184); (b) to Turkey and thence to Hungary, where it still is used by Gypsies under the name *cimbalom; (c) to China, where it appeared about 1800 and was called yangchyn, i.e., "foreign zither." In the early 18th century Pantaleon Hebenstreit revived the instrument in a greatly enlarged and improved form, the so-called *pantaleon. Also see Instruments IV, A, 1, b. See *MaMI*.

(2) A plucked folk instrument of uncertain ancestry but with features derived from the German Scheitholt and the Swedish *hummel, played in the southern Appalachian Mountains of the U.S. It consists of an elongated oval sound box of wood, about a yard long and nine inches wide, on which is mounted a narrow fretted fingerboard. In a three-string instrument, one string, tuned C, may be the melody string, while the other two strings, tuned G, sound as a drone bass to the melody. The player lays the instrument flat, across his knees or on a table. Traditionally the strings are plucked with a goose quill. The dulcimer, also called "dulcimore," is generally used to accompany singing and only rarely as a solo instrument.

Lit. *For* (2): J. F. Putnam, *The Plucked Dulci-*

mer of the Southern Mountains, rev. ed. (1961); A. W. Jeffreys, Tuning and Playing the Appalachian Dulcimer (1958); C. Seeger, "The Appalachian Dulcimer" (Journal of American Folklore, 1958, p. 50f); H. C. Mercer, "The Zithers of the Pennsylvania Germans" (Papers, Bucks County Historical Society, v, 1926, 483–497).

(2) by E.C.K.

Dulcina. Same as dolcino [see Oboe family III].

Dulcitone. A variety of celesta, with tuning forks instead of steel plates.

Dulzian [G.]. Same as dolcino [see Oboe family III].

Dumbarton Oaks. Concerto for fifteen instruments by Stravinsky (1938), written in the style of a modern concerto grosso. The name refers to the residence of R. W. Bliss near Washington, D.C.

Dumka [Rus.; also dumki, dumky]. (1) A Slavic (especially Ukrainian) folk ballad, poem, or meditation describing heroic deeds. It is generally thoughtful or melancholy in character. (2) A type of vocal music, probably first introduced by K. Kurpiński in "Dumka włościan Jabłonny" (Dumka of the Jabłonna Peasants; text by J. D. Minasowicz), which he published in his Tygodnik Muzyczny (Musical Weekly; 1821). (3) A type of instrumental music involving sudden changes from melancholy to exuberance. Well-known examples are Dvořák's piano trio op. 90 (1891; called Dumky-Trio), his Dumka (Elegy) op. 35 (1876), and his Furiant with Dumka op. 12 (1884).

Dump, domp. A type of English 16th-century music known through 15 examples, all instrumental, for keyboard (3), lute (9), or viol (3). The oldest and most celebrated example is "My Lady Careys Dompe" from c. 1525 [see HAM, no. 103], a series of continuous variations on a tonic-dominant harmony (T T D D). Nearly all the others show a similar structure, with ground patterns such as T T D T, D T D T, T S D T, etc., one of the exceptions being the "Irishe Dumpe" found in the Fitzwilliam Virginal Book [new ed. ii, 236]. There is no recognizable connection between these pieces and the dump mentioned in literary sources, usually as a lamenting song. See J. Ward, in JAMS iv.

Duo [F., G., Sp.]. *Duet.

Duodecuple scale. See Dodecuple scale.

Duodezime [G.]. The interval of the twelfth.

Duo imitation. See Paired imitation.

Duole [G.], **duolet** [F.]. *Duplet.

Dupla [L.]. In early musical treatises, the relation 2 : 1, hence, the octave. For proportio dupla, see Proportions.

Duplet [F. duolet; G. Duole; Sp. dosillo]. A group of two notes to be played in the time of three.

Duplex instruments. Instruments, usually of the brass family, that are a combination of two instruments. The two most important members of the class are: (a) The double euphonium, which has a wide euphonium bell and a narrow Saxtromba bell, either of which may be used by manipulating a controlling valve that directs the windstream through one or the other of the bells; thus two different tone qualities are available on one instrument. (b) The double horn in F and B-flat, which combines two instruments of the same timbre but of different pitch. The change is effected by an additional valve. Numerous other combinations, mostly of an experimental nature and ephemeral importance, are mentioned in SaRM, p. 123f (also pp. 115–17). See also LavE ii.3, 1461f.

Duplex longa. A 13th-century name for the maxima [see Mensural notation I].

Duplum. In the organa and clausulae of the school of Notre Dame [see Ars antiqua], the part above the tenor. In 13th-century motets this part was called motetus because here the duplum was provided with mots [F., words, i.e., text]. Triplum and quadruplum are other parts above the tenor, frequently of the same range as the duplum. See Organum (2).

Dur, moll [G.]. Major and minor. C-dur, C major; A-moll, A minor; Dur- (Moll-) tonart, major (minor) tonality; Dur- (Moll-) akkord, major (minor) chord; Dur- (Moll-) dreiklang, major (minor) triad. Originally, the names Dur and Moll stemmed from two different forms of the letter b, the b durum (so called on account of its angular shape) and the b molle (round shape). Andreas Werckmeister (Die nothwendigsten Anmerckungen und Regeln . . . , 1698) seems to have been the first to use the terms Dur and Moll with their present-day meaning. See C. Dahlhaus, in AMW xii.

Duramente [It.]. Harshly.

Durchbrochene Arbeit [G.]. A technique of writing in which fragments of a melody are given to different instruments in turn [see Ex.; Haydn]. This technique, which is frequently used in symphonies, quartets, etc., appeared first in the

works of the Mannheim school [see *RiHM* ii.3, 147ff]. A medieval version of this technique is the *hocket. See also Antecedent and consequent.

Durchführung [G.]. The term is used with two different, almost opposite meanings according to whether it refers to sonata form or the fugue. In the former case it means development; in the latter, exposition. Thus, sonata form follows the scheme *Themenaufstellung* (exposition), *Durchführung* (development), *Reprise* (recapitulation), while the scheme of the fugue is *Durchführung* (exposition), *Zwischenspiel* (episode), *Durchführung, Zwischenspiel*, etc.

Durchgangsnote [G.]. Passing note.

Durchimitation [G.]. *Through-imitation.

Durchkomponiert [G.]. *Through-composed.

Duret, duretto. A dance mentioned in some English masque texts (e.g., *Masque of Flowers*,

1614) as well as in Michael Praetorius' *Terpsichore* (1612; p. x), where it is described as a courante named after its composer. The two durettos in *Terpsichore* (nos. 37, 103) and the one in Benjamin Cosyn's Virginal Book are the same composition (in different keys). In some 17th-century German sources *Durett* means **durezza*.

Durezza [It.]. In modern music, *con durezza* means to play with an expression of harshness and determination. In the 17th century, *durezza* meant dissonance. Hence, *toccata di durezza e ligature* (Frescobaldi) meant toccata with dissonances and with tied notes, in a sense, a study in appoggiaturas. The earliest examples occur in the works of G. Macque (d. 1614) and his pupil G. Trabaci, both members of the early *Neapolitan school of keyboard music.

Dux, comes [L.]. In imitative compositions (fugue, canon), the statement and answer of the theme, also called antecedent and consequent.

Dynamic marks. The words, abbreviations, and signs that indicate degrees of volume. The most common are: pianissimo (pp); piano (p); mezzopiano (mp); mezzoforte (mf); forte (f); and fortissimo (ff); crescendo (cresc., <) and decrescendo or diminuendo (decr., dim., >); sforzato (sf); forte-piano (fp). See the various entries. For the use of dynamic marks in music prior to 1750, see Expression marks.

E

E. See Letter notation; Pitch names; Hexachord.

Ear training. An important field of elementary instruction designed to teach the student to recognize and write down musical intervals and rhythms. See Solfège.

Ecclesiastical dances. See Religious dances.

Ecclesiastical modes. See Church modes.

Échappée. See under Nonharmonic tones I.

Échappement [F.]. Escapement (of the piano).

Echegiatta [It.]. Baroque term for a composition using *echo effects.

Échelette [F.]. Xylophone.

Échelle [F.]. *Scale.

Echiquier [also *eschiquier, eschequier, eschaquier, escacherium, exaquir*]. An early stringed keyboard instrument mentioned in various literary sources of the 14th and 15th centuries. In a letter written by King John I of Aragon, who tried to obtain such an instrument from Duke Philip the Bold of Burgundy (1387), it is described as an "istrument semblans d'orguens qui sona ab cordes" (similar to the organ but sounding with strings). The same instrument is probably meant by the English *chekker* and German *Schacht-brett* (i.e., *Schaftbrett,* quillboard, not chessboard as has frequently been suggested) which is mentioned in a poem, "Der Minne Regeln," by Eberhard Cersne (1404). Both the etymology of the name and the nature of the instrument are obscure. According to C. Sachs it was an upright harpsichord [see *SaHMI,* p. 336f], while F. W. Galpin identifies it with a 15th-century instrument called *dulce melos,* for which he readopts the theory advanced by Bottée de Toulmon (*Dissertation sur les instruments de musique,* 1840) that it was a clavichord with a hammer action anticipating that of the piano [see *GD,* Suppl. Vol., p. 118; *GDB* ii, 194–95]. In the original description, however, no hammers, only a checking device, are mentioned. See W. H. Grattan Flood, in *ML* vi, 151; G. Le Cerf, in *RdM* 1931, p. 1.

Echo. Echolike effects occur frequently in the polyphonic works of Josquin and his followers, as the result of a special technique called *paired imitation. However, it was not until the end of the 16th century that the echo was exploited as a source of variety and of realistic effects. One of the earliest examples is Marenzio's madrigal "O tu che fra le selve," in which the line "Mi risponde, non son d'amanti esempio" is answered by the echo "Empio" (". . . example," "empty"). Lassus, in his famous "O la, o che bon eccho" (*Libro de villanelle,* 1581; F. X. Haberl and A. Sandberger, ed., ‡*Orlando di Lasso. Säm(m)tliche Werke,* 21 vols. [1894–1926], x, 140ff) exploits the humorous effect of a constantly repeated echo in a most skillful manner. Echolike repetitions of short motifs, often marked *f* and *p,* are among the most typical devices of the organ style of Sweelinck, Tunder, Reinken, Buxtehude, Nivers, Gigault, etc. A number of unpretentious Echoes for organ are found in the *Liber fratrum cruciferorum Leodiensium* of 1617 [*Editions I, 10]. Of particular interest are the echo effects in 17th-century vocal pieces (operatic arias, cantatas) in which the personified Echo answers the laments of the deserted lover, the distressed fugitive, etc. A beautiful example is in Carissimi's oratorio *Jephthe* [see *SchGMB,* no. 198; also *RiHM* ii.2, 35ff]. A charming instrumental echo piece by J. K. F. Fischer is reproduced in *DdT* 10, p. 84.

For an echo effect in Bach, see the last movement (Echo) of his Partita in B minor (*Clavier-Übung,* vol. ii, 1735). Mozart wrote a very ingenious *Notturno en Écho* (1777) in which four groups of players produce a quadruple echo. Numerous 19th-century opera composers used the echo repetition of military signals, hunting calls, etc. (Beethoven, *Fidelio;* Wagner, *Tristan*). See T. Kroyer, "Dialog und Echo in der alten Chormusik" (*JMP* xvi).

Echo attachment. A special valve attached to brass instruments (horns, trumpets, cornets) whereby a bell with a smaller opening is brought into use. The tones thus produced sound as if they were played from a great distance.

Echos [pl. *echoi*]. In ancient Syrian and Byzantine chant, a system of tonal classification that corresponds to the system of modes [see Church modes] of Roman chant. The *echoi* existed in the same number—eight—as the Western church modes and were collectively referred to as *oktoechos* (eight *echoi*). They differed from the modes in that they were not abstract scale formations but melodic formulas that included the characteristic features (tonic, cadential endings, typical progressions) of all the melodies written in one *echos.* Thus they are *melody types.

The earliest mention of the *oktoechos* is found in a Syrian source of about 515 [see Syrian chant], 300 years before the earliest account of the eight church modes, which were probably derived from the Syrian (or Byzantine) *echoi,* possibly by amalgamation with the ancient Greek system of octave species (*tonoi;* see Greece II). Various other Eastern churches, e.g., the *Armenian, *Russian, and Serbian, still use a classification based on *echoi,* i.e., melodic formulas, rather than modes, i.e., scales [see *ReMMA,* p. 101f; *GD,* Suppl. Vol., p. 174f, 181; *GDB,* ii, 863f, 870].

It is believed that some traces of the early *echoi* are preserved in the *enechemata* of 12th- and 13th-century Byzantine MSS, which were sung as an intonation to the chant proper much as a pianist sometimes strikes a few chords in order to "establish the key." Each *enechema* was sung to certain syllables whose meaning is obscure; e.g., the *enechema* of the first plagal mode was d–f–e–d and was sung to the "word" *Aneanes* [see *ReMMA,* p. 87; see also Anenaiki; Noeane; Solmization].

Lit.: E. Werner, "The Oldest Sources of Octave and Octoechos" (*AM* xx); *id.,* "New Studies in the History of the Early Octoechos"

(*CP* 1952); E. Wellesz, "Die Struktur des serbischen Oktoechos" (*ZMW* ii); C. Høeg, "L'Octoechus byzantin" (*CP 1950,* p. 107); P. J. Thibaut, in *RMC* i; O. Strunk, "Intonations and Signatures of the Byzantine Modes" (*MQ* xxxi); *id.*, "The Antiphons of the Oktoechos" (*JAMS* xiii).

Éclatant [F.]. Brilliant, sparkling.

Eclogue. An idyllic poem in which shepherds converse (after the model of Virgil's ten *Bucolic Eclogues*). In the 16th century such poems were frequently written in the form of dramatic plays and performed on the stage, particularly in Spain. These presentations, which probably involved music, are believed to be among the precursors of opera. See A. Salazar, in *PAMS* 1938, pp. 98ff. Modern composers have used the term "eclogue" (eglogue) as a title for compositions of an idyllic, pastoral character.

Eco [It.]. Echo.

École d'Arcueil. A group of 20th-century French musicians (Henri Sauguet, Roger Desormière, Maxime Jacob, Henri Cliquet-Pleyel) named after Arcueil, the home of Erik Satie, whom they considered their leader. The group was founded in 1923 [see N. Slonimsky, *Music Since 1900* (1937), p. 236]. See also *Six, Les.*

Écossaise [F.]. A dance that, despite its name, has nothing in common with genuine Scottish dance music [*reel, *strathspey], but belongs to the category of English *country dances. It appeared about 1780 in England and France and was very popular in the early 19th century. Beethoven as well as Schubert wrote collections of *écossaises,* all in quick 2/4 time. See Dance music IV.

Ecphonetic notation. Term for certain primitive systems of musical notation, consisting only of a limited number of conventional signs designed for the solemn reading of a liturgical text. Originally they were simply signs added to the text in order to clarify its sentence structure, comparable to present-day punctuation marks. Signs also were added to individual syllables or words of importance that were to be emphasized. Later these signs adopted a musical significance. The punctuating signs developed into more or less elaborate musical formulas whose exact nature is now obscure, while the accentuating signs became associated with a raising or lowering of pitch [see Neumes II]. Unlike the neumes of Roman, Byzantine, and Mozarabic chant, the ecphonetic signs do not indicate a continuous

melody of free design, since they occur only sporadically, usually at the beginning and end of a phrase. They probably represent a type of singing similar to Gregorian psalmody.

Ecphonetic signs occur in Syrian, Jewish, Byzantine, Armenian, and Coptic manuscripts from *c.* 600 to 1000 and later. In Jewish chant they developed into fuller musical notation, the *ta'amim,* which is used to the present day [see Jewish music]. Especially important are the Byzantine signs, e.g. / $\sim$ \\ +, whose meaning has been greatly clarified by C. Høeg [see the reproduction in *BeMMR,* p. 32]. See Notation II; Byzantine chant III.

Lit.: J. B. Thibaut, *Monuments de la notation ekphonétique et neumatique de l'église latine* (1912); C. Høeg, *La Notation ekphonétique* (1935); *WoHN* i, 61ff; E. Wellesz, "Die byzantinischen Lektionszeichen" (*ZMW* xi).

Ecuador. The history of European music in Ecuador dates from the establishment in Quito of a Flemish Franciscan order (1535), where Fray Jodoco taught Indians how to play keyboard and various stringed and wind instruments, as well as giving instruction in mensural notation and plainchant. In 1555 the Franciscans founded the Colegio de San Andrés, where the first native musicians were trained. One of them was Diego Lobato (*c.* 1538–*c.* 1610), who became the musical director of the Cathedral of Quito in 1574. His *motetes* and *chanzonetas* are mentioned in some documents of the period but have not yet been found. In 1588 he was succeeded by Gutierre Fernandez Hidalgo (1553–*c.* 1620), who had previously served two years as musical director in Bogotá [see Colombia] and was re-engaged in 1590. After him a long series of organists, choirmasters, and composers occupied this position until 1682, when a distinguished composer, Manuel Blasco, was appointed. Blasco was the foremost figure of music in colonial Ecuador after Fernandez Hidalgo. His works include an *Officium defunctorum* (1681), *Laudate Dominum, a 12* (1683), Magnificat, *Sedet a dextris meis,* and two *villancicos,* preserved in Bogotá. José Ortuño de Larrea (d. 1722), member of a large family of musicians that had had a monopoly of the cathedral posts in Quito during the 17th century, succeeded Blasco in 1696.

During the 18th century Quito was replaced by Guayaquil as the center for church music. The 19th century was musically unproductive, with only a few exceptions, such as Agustin

Baldeón (d. 1847), the first Ecuadorian to write symphonic music. In 1870, a musician of German ancestry, Antonio Neumann (1818–*c.* 1890), wrote the national anthem and became the first director of the Conservatorio Nacional de Música at Quito, founded in the same year.

The first composer to employ native elements in art music was an Italian, Domenico Brescia, who was director of the Conservatory from 1903 to 1911. His works include a successful *Sinfonia Ecuatoriana.* Two of his disciples, Segundo Luis Moreno (b. 1882), who wrote numerous piano compositions, songs, and orchestral works inspired by native idioms, and Luis H. Salgado (b. 1903), composer of the symphonic suite *Atahualpa,* a concerto for viola and orchestra (1955), the operetta *Ensueños de Amor,* and many other works, are the leading figures of contemporary Ecuadorian music. A contemporary of theirs, Pedro Traversari (b. 1874), has written music in the romantic tradition, in some cases using subjects based on native legends, as in his melodramas, *Cumanda, The Prophecy of Huiracocha,* and *Kizkiz.* A representative of the younger generation is Mesías Maiguascha (b. 1938), who studied in Buenos Aires with Ginastera and has written a Suite for string quartet that is largely atonal and shows no use of folk elements.

The traditions of Indian music are well preserved in Ecuador. European influences have brought only slight modifications to the aboriginal scales and rhythms and to the choreography of dances as described by the first Spanish chroniclers. The **cachullapi, danzante,* and *sanjuanito* (or **huaiño*) are highland dances that still preserve many elements of their original Indian models, namely, the use of short motifs in duple meter and the prevalence of the pentatonic scale. In the coastal areas the Hispano-Creole traditions are more often encountered in such forms as the **pasacalle, *pasillo,* and **zamba.* They tend to use 6/8 meter in alternating divisions of two and three pulsations to a measure.

Lit.: R. Stevenson, *Music in Quito: Four Centuries* (1963); S. L. Moreno, "La Música en el Ecuador" (*Orellana* ii). Also see under Latin America.   J.O-S.

Editio Medicea; Ratisbonensis; Vaticana. See under Liturgical books II.

Editions, historical. Under this heading, which corresponds to the German term *Denkmäler,* is a list of important serial publications of early music. Volume titles are in roman, but are in italics for books not containing music. Editorial information is found in brackets. For spellings of titles of works and composers' names, the sources themselves have been followed exactly. B indicates ballet; I, instrumental; K, keyboard; L, lute; M, masque; Op, opera; Or, oratorio; S, song (solo, cantata, duet, etc.); V, vocal.

Also see A. H. Heyer, *Historical Sets, Collected Editions and Monuments of Music: A Guide to their Contents* (1957); L. B. Spiess, *Historical Musicology* (1963), bibl.

I. *Archives des maîtres de l'orgue* [10 vols., ed. A. Guilmant and A. Pirro, 1898–1910, organ compositions].
1. J. Titelouze, Oeuvres complètes d'orgue.
2. A. Raison, Livre d'orgue.
3. F. Roberday, Fugues et caprices; L. Marchand, Pièces choisies pour l'orgue; L.-N. Clérambault, Premier Livre d'orgue; P. Du Mage, Premier Livre d'orgue; L.-C. d'Aquin, Livre de noëls.
4. N. Gigault, Livre de musique pour l'orgue.
5. N. de Grigny, Oeuvres d'orgue; F. Couperin (de Crouilly), Pièces d'orgue; L. Marchand, pièces d'orgue.
6. J. Boyvin, Oeuvres complètes d'orgue.
7. J.-F. Dandrieu, Premier Livre de pièces d'orgue.
8. S. A. Scherer, Oeuvres d'orgue.
9. N.-A. Lebègue, Oeuvres complètes d'orgue.
10. J. Guilain, Pièces d'orgue pour le magnificat.

II. *Archivium musices metropolitanum mediolanense* [11 vols., ed. L. Migliavacca, 1958—; after vol. 5, no numbering system. The remaining volume numbers are taken from the prospectus for this edition].
1/2;3. F. Gaffurio, Messe i, ii, iii, ed. A. Bortone.
4. F. Gaffurio, Magnificat, ed. F. Fano.
5. F. Gaffurio, Mottetti, ed. L. Migliavacca.
6. Anonymous, Messe, ed. F. Fano [in prep.].
7. Anonymous, Magnificat, ed. F. Fano.
8. Anonymous, Mottetti, ed. L. Migliavacca [in prep.].
9. Anonymous, Mottetti, ed. L. Migliavacca.
10. H. Isaac, Messe, ed. F. Fano.
11. G. van Werbeke, Messe e mottetti, ed. G. Tintori.
12. J. Martini, Magnificat e Messe, ed. B. Disertori.
13. L. Compère, Messe, Magnificat e motteti, ed. D. Faggion.

III. *L'Arte musicale in Italia* [7 vols., ed. L. Torchi, 1897–1908; reprinted with corrections, n.d., *c.* 1958].

1. Composizioni sacre e profane a più voci, secoli XIV, XV e XVI [mainly motets, madrigals, frottole, *c.* 1500–90, V].
2. Composizioni sacre e profane a più voci, secolo XVI [mainly motets, madrigals, *c.* 1580–1625, V].
3. Composizioni per organo o cembalo, secoli XVI, XVII e XVIII [K].
4. Composizioni a più voci—secolo XVII [V].
5. Composizioni ad una e più voci—secolo XVII [scenes from S. Landi, *Il Sant' Alessio,* Op; Anon., *Daniele,* Or; solo cantatas and arias, 17th cent.].
6. La Musica scenica—secolo XVII [J. Peri, *Euridice,* Op; C. Monteverdi, *Il Combattimento di Tancredi e Clorinda,* V; *Il Ballo delle ingrate,* V].
7. Musica instrumentale—secolo XVII [I].

IV. Biblioteca de Catalunya: Biblioteca central, *Publicaciones de la sección de música,* Barcelona [19 vols., ed. H. Anglés and others, 1921—. In library catalogs this may be listed under Barcelona, Biblioteca, *Publicaciones,* etc.].

1. Juan Brudieu, Els Madrigals i la Missa de Difunts, ed. F. Pedrell and H. Anglès, [V].
2. Catàleg dels manuscrits musicals de la col·lecció Pedrell.
3;7. J. Pujol, Opera omnia [i, ii; V].
4;8;13;17. J. Cabanilles, Opera omnia [i-iv; K].
5. El Canto mozárabe, ed. C. Rojo and G. Prado.
6. El Còdex musical de Las Huelgas [3 vols., V].
9. A. Soler, Sis Quintets per a instruments d'arc i orgue o clave obligat.
10. La Música a Catalunya fins al segle xiii.
11. J. Hildalgo (text by Calderón), Celos aun del aire matan, ed. J. Subirá [Op].
12. V. Ripollès, El Villancico i la cantata del segle xviii a València [V].
14. D. Terradellas, La Merope, ed. R. Gerhard [Op].
15;18;19. La Música de las cantigas de Santa María del Rey Alfonso el Sabio [ii, transcriptions; iii in 2 vols., commentary; i, facsimile].
16. M. Flecha, Las Ensaladas [V].

V. *Biblioteca di rarità musicali* [9 vols., some lacking title pages, ed. O. Chilesotti, 1884–1915].

1. F. Caroso and C. Negri, Danze del secolo XVI [L].
2. G. Picchi, Balli d'arpicordo [K].
3. G. Stefani, Canzonette del 1600 [*Affetti amorosi,* S].
4. B. Marcello, Arianna [Op].
5. O. Vecchi [Arie, canzonette e balli; arias, canzonettas, and dances, V].
6. G. Frescobaldi [Partite sopra *La Romanesca, La Monicha, Ruggiero e La Follia;* K].
7. J.-B. Besard [Airs de court (Secolo XVI) dal *Thesaurus Harmonicus;* L arr. for S].
8. Musica del passato (da intavolature antiche); 1536–*c.* 1750 [L arr. for K].
9. J.-B. Besard [Madrigali, villanelle, ed arie di danza del cinquecento; L arr. for K].

VI. *Capolavori polifonici del secolo XVI* [6 vols., ed. B. Somma, 1939—; the Italian predecessors of opera].

1. A. Banchieri, Festino nella sera del giovedi grasso avanti cena [V].
2. O. Vecchi, Le Veglie di Siena [V].
3. G. Croce, Triaca musicale, ed. A. Schinelli [V].
4. A. Striggio, Il Cicalamento delle donne al bucato [V].
5. O. Vecchi, L'Amfiparnaso [comedia harmonica, V].
6. A. Banchieri, La Pazzia senile [V].
7. G. Torelli, I Fidi amanti [in prep., Op].
8. O. Vecchi, Convito musicale [in prep., V].

VII. *Chefs-d'oeuvre [classiques] de l'opéra français* [40 vols., unnumbered, of a projected *c.* 60-vol. series, various editors, *c.* 1880; piano reductions of baroque operas].

B. de Beaujoyeux, Le Ballet-comique de la Reine [L. de Beaulieu, J. Salmon, collaborators].

R. Cambert, Les Peines & les plaisirs de l'amour; Pomone.

A. Campra, L'Europe galante; Les Fêstes vénitiennes; Tancrède.

C.-S. Catel, Les Bayadères.

P. Colasse, Les Saisons (with Lully); Thétis et Pélée.

A.-C. Destouches, Issé; Omphale.

A. Grétry, La Caravane du Caire; Céphale & Procris.

M.-R. de Lalande and A.-C. Destouches, Les Éléménts.

J. F. Le Sueur, Ossian ou Les Bardes.

J.-B. Lully, Alceste; Armide; Atys; Bellérophon; Cadmus et Hermione; Isis; Persée; Phaéton; Proserpine; Psyché; Thésée.

F. A. Philidor, Ernelinde.

N. Piccinni, Didon; Roland.

J.-P. Rameau, Castor & Pollux; Dardanus; Les Festes d'Hébé; Hippolyte et Aricie; Les Indes galantes; Platée (ou Junon Jalouse); Zoroastre.

A. Sacchini, Chimène ou Le Cid; Renaud.

A. Salieri, Les Danaïdes; Tarare.

VIII. *Das Chorwerk* [107 vols., 1–106, 108, of 15th- to 18th-century vocal music, ed. F. Blume and, beginning with vol. 53, K. Gudewill, 1929—. Composers are listed alphabetically; collective volumes are placed at the end. Items in brackets are those forthcoming to which a serial number has been assigned].

106. S. Aguilera de Heredia, Drei Magnificat.

56. Anonymous, Missa anonyma II aus dem Codex Breslau Ms. 2016.

31. J. Aulen, Missa.

99. J. L. Bach, Zwei Motetten.

66. A. Beber, Markus-Passion.

16;107. C. Bernhard and J. Theile, Zwei Kurzmessen; C. Bernhard, Eine Kurzmesse und eine Motette [in prep.].

22. G. Binchois, Sechzehn weltliche Lieder.

68. A. Brumel, Missa pro defunctis.

25. A. Caldara, Ein Madrigal und achtzehn Kanons.

82. P. Certon, Zehn Chansons.

72. J. Clemens non Papa, Drei Motetten.

55. L. Compère, Missa alles regrets.

27;36;39. C. Demantius, Passion nach dem Evangelisten Johannes; and J. H. Schein, Der 116. Psalm; Vier deutsche Motetten.

83. A. Divitis, Missa quem dicunt homines.

28. G. Dressler, Fünf Motetten.

19;49. G. Dufay, Zwölf geistliche und weltliche Werke; Sämtliche Hymnen.

97. R. Fayrfax, Missa tecum principium.

9;21. H. Finck, Acht Hymnen; Missa in summis; Zwölf Hymnen.

24;38;53. M. Franck, Fünf Hohelied-Motetten; Musikalische Bergreihen; Drei Quodlibets.

78/79. F. Funcke, Matthäus Passion.

96. A. Gabrieli, Drei Motetten.

10;67. G. Gabrieli, Drei Motetten; Drei Motetten, II.

75. A. Gosswin, Newe teutsche Lieder.

103. C. Goudimel, Vier Festmotetten.

40. A. Grandi, Drei konzertierende Motetten.

87. M. Greiter, Sämtliche weltliche Lieder.

44;85. J. Hähnel (Galliculus) [J. Handl (Gallus)], Ostermesse; Drei Weihnachtsmagnificat.

98. H. Hartmann, Vier deutsche Motetten.

47. B. Harzer (Resinarius), Summa passionis secundum Johannem.

7;81;100. H. Isaac, Missa carminum; Introiten i; Vier Marienmotetten.

73. C. Janequin, Zehn Chansons.

1;3;18;20;23;33;42;57;64. Josquin des Près, Missa pange lingua; Weltliche Lieder; Vier Motetten; Missa da pacem; Drei Evangelien-Motetten; Drei Psalmen; Missa de Beata Virgine; Drei Motetten; Zwei Psalmen.

71. D. Köler, Drei deutsche Psalmen.

50. J. G. Kühnhausen, Passion nach dem Evangelisten Matthäus.

11;91. P. de La Rue, Requiem und eine Motette; Vier Motetten.

13;34;37;41;48. O. di Lasso, Madrigale und chansons; Busstränen des heiligen Petrus i, ii, iii; Prophetiae Sibyllarum.

15. J. Lupi, Zehn weltliche Lieder.

46. J. Martini, Drei geistliche Gesänge.

95. D. Mazzocchi, Sechs Madrigale.

70;76. J. Mouton, Missa alleluya; Fünf Motetten.

110. J. Nucius, Vier Motetten [in prep.].

4. J. Ockeghem, Missa mi-mi.

52. A. Pfleger, Passionsmusik über die sieben Worte Jesu Christi am Kreuz.

93. C. Porta, Missa la sol fa re mi.

51. M. Praetorius and L. de Sayne [Sayve], Teutsche Liedlein.

17. H. Purcell, Fünf geistliche Chöre.

101. A. M. Rener, Missa carminum.

51;86. L. de Sayve and M. Praetorius, Teutsche Liedlein; L. de Sayve, Vier Motetten.

65. A. Scandello, Missa super epitaphium Mauritii.

12;36. J. H. Schein, Sechs deutsche Motetten; C. Demantius, Der 116. Psalm.

26;90. T. Selle, Passion nach dem Evangelisten Johannes; Zwei Kurzmessen.

62. L. Senfl, Zwei Marien-Motetten.

84. J. Sheppard, Sechs Responsorien.

6;74. T. Stoltzer, Der 37. Psalm, Erzürne dich nicht; Ostermesse.

104. G. P. Telemann, Vier Motetten.

16. J. Theile and C. Bernhard, Zwei Kurzmessen.

2. J. Vaet, Sechs Motetten.

108. O. Vecchi, Missa in resurrectione domini.

109. G. de Wert, Vier Madrigale und drei Kanzonetten [in prep.].

59;105. A. Willaert, Drei Motetten; Fünf Madrigale um Adrian Willaert.

77. G. Zarlino, Drei Motetten und ein geistliches Madrigal.

Collective volumes:

5. Italienische Madrigale [A. Willaert, P. Verdelot, J. Arcadelt, C. de Rore].

8. Volkstümliche italienische Lieder [A. Willaert, O. di Lasso, G. da Nola, and others].

14. Sieben chromatische Motetten des Barock [O. di Lasso, H. L. Hassler, J. H. Schein, J. P. Sweelinck, H. Praetorius].

29. Fünfzehn deutsche Lieder [P. Schöffer, printer, 1513].

30. Acht Lied- und Choralmotetten [Josquin des Prés and others].

32. Zwölf Hymnen [A. von Fulda, H. Finck, V. Florigal, B. Hartzer, U. Kungsperger].

35. Neun Madrigale, Nordische Gabrieli-Schüler [J. Grabbe, M. Pedersøn, H. Nielsen].

43. Karnevalslieder der Renaissance [H. Isaac, Michele Pesenti, L. Compère, and others].

45. Deutsche Lieder des 15. Jahrhunderts aus fremden Quellen [Magister Alanus, Egidius de Rhenis, Pyllois, E. Koler].

54. Fünf Vergil-Motetten [Josquin des Prez and others].

58. Sechs italienische Madrigale [J. Arcadelt and others].

60. Spanisches Hymnar um 1500.

61. Zwölf französische Lieder aus Jacques Moderne: *Le Parangon des chansons* (1538) [orig. ed. J. Moderne].

63. Zehn weltliche Lieder aus Georg Forster: *Frische teutsche Liedlein* (Teil III bis V) [orig. ed. G. Forster].

69. Drei Motetten [G. Hemmerley and others].

80. Vier Madrigale von Mantuaner Komponisten [G. de Wert and others].

88. Fünf Madrigale auf Texte von Francesco Petrarca [G. Nasco, S. Rossetti, P. Taglia].

89. Vier Motetten der Bachschule [J. L. Krebs and others].

92. Fünfzehn flämische Lieder der Renaissance [Benedictus Appenzeller, N. Faignient, J. Verdonck, and others].

94. Drei Motetten [J. Richafort and others].

102. Drei Te Deum-Kompositionen des 16. Jahrhunderts [T. Crequillon and others].

IX. *I Classici della musica italiana* [36 vols., ed.-in-chief G. d'Annunzio, (1918–21). The titles do not always correctly indicate the contents].

1. A. Banchieri, Musiche corali, ed. F. Vatielli [V].

2. G. B. Bassani, Canzoni, ed. F. Malipiero [S].

3. L. Boccherini, Sonate, ed. A. Toni [I].

4. G. Caccini, Arie, ed. C. Perinello [S].

5. G. Carissimi, Oratorii, ed. B. Pratella [Or].

6. G. Cavazzoni, Musica sacra, ricercari e canzoni, ed. G. Benvenuti [K].

7. L. Cherubini, Arie [volume contains 4 operatic overtures], ed. A. Toni [arr. for K].

8. M. Clementi, Sonate, ed. G. C. Paribeni [K].

9. A. Corelli, Sonate, ed. A. Toni [I].

10. E. del Cavalieri, La Rappresentazione di anima e di corpo, ed. F. Malipiero [Or].

11. F. Durante, Sonate, toccate e divertimenti, ed. I. Pizzetti [K].

12. G. Frescobaldi, Sonate, ed. A. Casella [K].

13. B. Galuppi, Il Filosofo di campagna, ed. F. Malipiero [Op].

14. C. Gesualdo, Madrigali, ed. I. Pizzetti [V].

15. N. Jommelli, La Passione di Gesù Cristo, ed. F. Malipiero [Or].

16. P. Locatelli and F. Bertoni, Composizioni, ed. A. Toni [I].

17. B. Marcello, Cantate, ed. F. Malipiero.

18. G. Martini, Sonate, ed. A. Lualdi [K].

19. C. Monteverdi, Il Combattimento di Tancredi e Clorinda, ed. A. Toni [V].

20. G. Paisiello, La Pazza per amore, ed. C. Perinello [Op].

21. G. P. de Palestrina, Canzonette e madrigali, ed. C. Perinello [V].

22. P. D. Paradisi, Sonate, ed. G. Benvenuti and D. Cipollini [K].

23. G. B. Pergolesi, Opere, ed. A. Toni [Op, V].

24. J. Peri, L'Euridice, ed. C. Perinello [Op].

25. N. A. Porpora, Sonate, ed. A. Toni [I].

26. M. A. Rossi, Composizioni, ed. A. Toni [K].

27. G. M. Rutini, Sonate, ed. B. Pratella [K].

28. G. B. Sammartini, Sonate notturne, ed. C. Perinello and E. Polo [I].

29. P. G. Sandoni and G. Serini, Sonate, ed. B. Pratella [K].

30. A. Scarlatti, Cantate, ed. A. Toni and G. Marinuzzi.

31. D. Scarlatti, Composizioni, ed. G. Ferranti [K].

32. G. Tartini, Sonate, ed. F. Malipiero [I].

33. F. Turrini, Sonate, ed. C. Pedron [K].

34. F. M. Veracini, Sonate, ed. I. Pizzetti and M. Corti [I].
35. A. Vivaldi, Le Stagioni, ed. A. Toni [I].
36. D. Zipoli, Composizioni, ed. A. Toni [K].

X. *I Classici musicali italiani* [15 vols., ed. G. Benvenuti and others, vols. 1–13, 15, 1941–43; vol. 14, 1956].

1. M. A. Cavazzoni, Ricercari, motetti, canzoni; J. Fogliano, G. Segni, and others (anon.), Ricercari e ricercate, ed. G. Benvenuti [K].
2. B. Marcello, Cantate per contralto e per soprano, ed. G. Benvenuti [S].
3. F. Giardini, Sonate per cembalo con violino o flauto traverso, op. 3, ed. E. Polo [I].
4. L. Boccherini, Sonate per cembalo con violino obbligato, op. 5, ed. E. Polo [K, I].
5. A. Gabrieli, Musiche di chiesa da cinque a sedici voci, ed. G. D'Alessi [V].
6. F. Giardini, Quartetti, Op. 23 n. 3 e 4, ed. A. Poltronieri [I].
7. N. Piccinni, La Buona Figliola, ed. G. Benvenuti [Op].
8. B. Marcello, Gioàz, ed. G. Benvenuti and F. Calusio [Or].
9. C. Monteverdi, L'Orfeo, ed. G. Benvenuti [Op].
10. S. d'India, Madrigali a cinque voci, libro I, ed. F. Mompellio [V].
11. G. Martini, Concerti per cembalo e orchestra, ed. G. Agosti [K, I].
12. G. Grazioli, Dodici Sonate per cembalo, ed. R. Gerlin [K].
13. A. Scarlatti, Primo e secondo libro di toccate, ed. R. Gerlin [K].
14. P. Locatelli, Sei Sonate de camera per violino e basso, dall' Op. 6, ed. G. Benvenuti and E. Polo [I].
15. C. Graziani, Sei Sonate per violoncello e basso continuo, op. 3, ed. G. Benvenuti and G. Crepax [I].

XI. *Corpus of Early Keyboard Music* [19 vols. to date, ed.-in-chief W. Apel, 1963—].

1. Keyboard Music of the Fourteenth and Fifteenth Centuries, ed. W. Apel.
2. M. Facoli, Collected Works, ed. W. Apel.
3. G. Salvatore, Collected Keyboard Works, ed. B. Hudson.
4. H. Praetorius, Organ Magnificats, ed. C. G. Rayner.
5. B. Pasquini, Collected Works for Keyboard, ed. M. B. Haynes [7 vols.].

6. Johannes of Lublin, Tablature of Keyboard Music, ed. J. R. White [6 vols.].
7. B. Storace, Selva di varie compositioni d'intavolatura per cimbalo ed organo, ed. B. Hudson.
8. Keyboard Dances from the Earlier Sixteenth Century, ed. D. Heartz.
9. C. Antegnati, L'Antegnata Intavolatura de ricercari d'organo, 1608, ed. W. Apel.
10. Keyboard Music from Polish Manuscripts [4 vols., N. Hasse, H. Scheidemann, F. Tunder, J. Podbielski, M. Wartecki and others], ed. J. Golos and A. Sutkowski.
11. G. Strozzi, *Caprici da sonare cembali et organi*, ed. B. Hudson.
12. E. Pasquini, Collected Keyboard Works, ed. W. R. Shindle.
13. J. U. Steigleder, Compositions for keyboard, ed. W. Apel and others [in prep.].
14. Spanish organ music after A. Cabezón, ed. W. Apel [in prep.].
15. M. A. Rossi, Works for Keyboard, ed. J. R. White.
16. A. Reinken, Collected keyboard works, ed. W. Apel.
17. Tablature of Celle, *c.* 1600, ed. W. Apel [in prep.].
18. C. Gibbons, Keyboard compositions, ed. C. G. Rayner.
24. Neapolitan keyboard composers: Stella, Lambardo and others, ed. R. Jackson.
27. S. Mareschal, Selected Works, ed. J.-M. Bonhote.
30. Unpublished keyboard works of Frescobaldi, ed. W. R. Shindle, [3 vols.].
32. 17th-century Keyboard Music in the Chigi Manuscripts of the Vatican Library [3 vols.].

XII. *Corpus mensurabilis musicae* [ed.-in-chief A. Carapetyan, 1947—; mostly collected works of 15th- and 16th-cent. composers in process of publication].

1. G. Dufay, Opera omnia, ed. G. de Van and H. Besseler [1–6, supplement to 3. Vol. 2 appeared with several numberings; the final vol. 2 contains 6 Masses].
2. G. de Machaut, Opera [*La Messe de Nostre Dame*], ed. G. de Van.
3. A. Willaert, Opera omnia, ed. H. Zenck and W. Gerstenberg [1–5, 7, 13; *c.* 15 vols. proj.].
4. J. Clemens non Papa, Opera omnia, ed. K. P. B. Kempers [1 in 4 fascicles, 2–15, 5 suppl. bound with 5; *c.* 21 vols. proj.].

5. A. Brumel, Opera omnia, ed. A. Carapetyan [1, 2 fascicles so far; *c.* 8 vols. proj.].
6. N. Gombert, Opera omnia, ed. J. Schmidt-Görg [7; *c.* 12 vols. proj.].
7. J. Barbireau, Opera omnia, ed. B. Meier [2 vols.].
8. The Music of Fourteenth-century Italy, ed. N. Pirrotta [5 vols.].
9. J. Regis, Opera omnia, ed. C. W. H. Lindenburg [2 vols.].
10. F. Gafurius, Collected Musical Works, ed. L. Finscher [2 vols.].
11. Early Fifteenth-century Music, ed. G. Reaney [3 vols.].
12. G. Gabrieli, Opera omnia, ed. D. Arnold [4; *c.* 10 vols. proj.].
13. Missa Tornacensis [Tournai Mass], ed. C. Van den Borren.
14. C. de Rore, Opera omnia, ed. B. Meier [1–3, 7; *c.* 10 vols. proj.].
15. L. Compère, Opera omnia, ed. L. Finscher [4; *c.* 6 vols. proj.].
16. R. Carver, Collected Works, ed. D. Stevens [1; *c.* 5 vols. proj.].
17. R. Fayrfax, Collected Works, ed. E. B. Warren [3 vols.].
18. J. Tinctoris, Opera omnia [Missa 3 vocum], ed. F. Feldmann.
19. W. Frye, Collected Works, ed. S. W. Kenney.
20. P. Attaingnant, Transcriptions of Chansons for Keyboard, ed. A. Seay.
21. The Cypriot-French Repertory of the Manuscript Torino, Biblioteca nazionale, J. II. 9, ed. R. H. Hoppin [4 vols.].
22. A. Agricola, Opera omnia, ed. E. R. Lerner [4; *c.* 5 vols. proj.].
23. J. Ghiselin-Verbonnet, Opera omnia, ed. C. Gottwald [3; *c.* 4 vols. proj.].
24. G. de Wert, Collected Works, ed. C. MacClintock and M. Bernstein [6; *c.* 12 vols. proj.].
25. C. Festa, Opera omnia, ed. A. Main [1; *c.* 10 vols. proj.].
26. N. Vicentino, Opera omnia, ed. H. W. Kaufmann.
27. N. Ludford, Collected Works, ed. J. D. Bergsagel [1; *c.* 3 vols. proj.].
28. P. Verdelot, Opera omnia, ed. A.-M. Bragard [1 vol. so far].
29. Fourteenth-century Mass Music in France, ed. H. Stäblein-Harder. [Companion vol. of critical text, *Musicological Studies and Documents, No. 7* (A. I. M.)].
30. The Works of Jehan de Lescurel, ed. N. Wilkins.
31. J. Arcadelt, Opera omnia, ed. A. Seay [7; *c.* 12 vols. proj.].
32. Music of the Florentine Renaissance, ed. F. D'Accone.
33. J. Hothby, The Musical Works of John Hothby, ed. A. Seay.
34. M. Pipelare, Opera omnia, ed. R. Cross [3 vols.].
35. J. Brassart, Opera omnia, ed. K. E. Mixter [1; *c.* 2 vols. proj.].
36. A 14th-century Repertory from the Codex Reina, ed. N. Wilkins.
37. A 15th-century Repertory from the Codex Reina, ed. N. Wilkins.
38. Canons in the Trent Codices, ed. R. Loyan.
39. The Motets of the Manuscripts Chantilly, musée condé, 564 (*olim* 1047) and Modena, Biblioteca estense, *α.* M. 5, 24 (*olim* lat. 568), ed. U. Günther.
40. The Music of the Pepys MS 1236, ed. S. R. Charles.
41. J. Pullois, Opera omnia, ed. P. Gülke.
42. The Unica in the Chansonnier Cordiforme (Paris, Bibliothèque Nationale, Rothschild 2973), ed. E. Kottick.
44. Adam de la Halle. The Lyric Works of Adam de la Halle: Chansons, Jeuxpartis, Rondeaux, Motets, ed. N. Wilkins.
45. Passereau, Opera omnia, ed. G. Dottin.

XIII. *Denkmäler deutscher Tonkunst* [*DdT;* 65 vols., ed. R. von Liliencron, 1892–1912, H. Kretzschmar to 1924, H. Abert to 1927, A. Schering to 1931; new revised edition, ed. H. J. Moser, 1957–1961. Composers are listed alphabetically; collective volumes are placed at the end].

5. J. R. Ahle, Ausgewählte Gesangswerke, ed. J. Wolf [V].
12/13. H. Albert, Arien [arias], ed. E. Bernoulli [S].
56. J. C. F. Bach, Die Kindheit Jesu; Die Auferweckunk Lazarus, ed. G. Schünemann [Or].
48. J. E. Bach, Passionsoratorium, ed. J. Kromolicki [Or].
42. J. E. Bach, Sammlung auserlesener Fabeln, ed. H. Kretzschmar [S].
64. G. Benda, Der Jahrmarkt, ed. T. W. Werner [Op].
6. C. Bernhard, Solokantaten und Chorwerke mit Instrumentalbegleitung, ed. M. Seiffert [S, V].
45. G. Böhm, Heinrich Elmenhorsts [text]

258

Geistliche Lieder, ed. J. Kromolicki and W. Krabbe [S].

14. D. Buxtehude, Abendmusiken und Kirchenkantaten, ed. M. Seiffert [S + I].

11. D. Buxtehude, Instrumentalwerke, ed. C. Stiehl [I].

43/44. F. Deller, Ausgewählte Ballette Stuttgarter Meister aus der 2. Hälfte des 18. Jahrhunderts, ed. H. Abert [B].

31;41. P. Dulichius, Prima [Secunda] Pars Centuriae octonum et septenum vocum stetini 1607, ed. R. Schwartz [V].

46/47. P. H. Erlebach, Harmonische Freude musikalischer Freunde [parts I and II], ed. O. Kinkeldey [S].

10. J. C. F. Fischer, Orchestermusik des XVII. Jahrhunderts [*Le Journal du printemps*], ed. E. von Werra [I].

45. J. W. Franck, Heinrich Elmenhorsts [text] geistliche Lieder, ed. J. Kromolicki and W. Krabbe [S].

16. M. Franck, Ausgewählte Instrumentalwerke, ed. F. Bölsche [I].

57. J. V. Görner, Sammlung neuer Oden und Lieder, ed. W. Krabbe and J. Kromolicki [S].

15. K. H. Graun, Montezuma, ed. A. Mayer-Reinach [Op].

51/52. C. Graupner, Ausgewählte Kantaten, ed. F. Noack [S].

40. A. Hammerschmidt, Ausgewählte Werke, ed. H. Leichtentritt [V].

20. J. A. Hasse, La Conversione di Sant' Agostino, ed. A. Schering [Or].

2. H. L. Hassler, Cantiones sacrae, ed. H. Gehrmann [V].

7. H. L. Hassler, Messen, ed. J. Auer [V].

24/25. H. L. Hassler, Sacri concentus, ed. J. Auer [V].

16. V. Haussmann, Ausgewählte Instrumentalwerke, ed. F. Bölsche [I].

42. V. Herbing, Musikalischer Versuch, ed. H. Kretzschmar [S].

8/9. I. Holzbauer, Günther von Schwarzburg, ed. H. Kretzschmar [Op].

32/33. N. Jommelli, Fetonte, ed. H. Abert [Op].

37/38. R. Keiser, Der hochmütige, gestürzte und wieder erhabene Croesus; Erlesene Sätze aus L'Inganno fedele, ed. M. Schneider [Op].

58/59. S. Knüpfer, Ausgewählte Kirchenkantaten, ed. A. Schering [S].

19. A. Krieger, Arien, ed. A. Heuss [S].

53/54. J. P. Krieger, 21 Ausgewählte Kirchenkompositionen, ed. M. Seiffert [V].

58/59. J. Kuhnau, Ausgewählte Kirchenkantaten, ed. A. Schering [S].

4. J. Kuhnau, Klavierwerke, ed. K. Päsler [K].

60. A. Lotti, Messen, ed. H. Müller [V].

55. C. Pallavicino, La Gerusalemme liberata, ed. H. Abert [Op].

63. J. C. Pezel, Turmmusiken und Suiten, ed. A. Schering [I].

23. H. Praetorius, Ausgewählte Werke, ed. H. Leichtentritt [V].

18. J. Rosenmüller, Sonate da camera, ed. K. Nef [I].

43/44. J. J. Rudolph, Ausgewählte Ballette Stuttgarter Meister aus der 2. Hälfte des 18. Jahrhunderts, ed. H. Abert [B].

1. S. Scheidt, Tabulatura nova, ed. M. Seiffert [K].

58/59. J. Schelle, Ausgewählte Kirchenkantaten, ed. A. Schering [S].

10. J. A. S[chmierer], Orchestermusik des XVII. Jahrhunderts [*Zodiaci musici*], ed. E. von Werra [I].

39. J. Schobert, Ausgewählte Werke, ed. H. Riemann [I].

17. J. Sebastiani, Passionsmusiken, ed. F. Zelle [V].

35/36. Sperontes [pseud. for J. S. Scholze], Singende Muse an der Pleisse, ed. E. Buhle [S].

65. T. Stoltzer, Sämtliche lateinische Hymnen und Psalmen, ed. H. Albrecht and O. Gombosi [V].

61/62. G. P. Telemann, Tafelmusik [*Musique de table*], ed. M. Seiffert [I].

28. G. P. Telemann, Der Tag des Gerichts [Or], Ino [S], ed. M. Schneider.

57. G. P. Telemann, Vierundzwanzig Oden, ed. W. Krabbe and J. Kromolicki [S].

17. J. Theile, Passionsmusiken, ed. F. Zelle.

3. F. Tunder, Gesangswerke, ed. M. Seiffert [V].

26/27. J. G. Walther, Gesammelte Werke für Orgel, ed. M. Seiffert [K].

6. M. Weckmann, Solokantaten und Chorwerke mit Instrumentalbegleitung, ed. M. Seiffert [S + I].

45. P. L. Wockenfuss, Heinrich Elmenhorsts [text] Geistliche Lieder, ed. J. Kromolicki and W. Krabbe [V].

21/22. F. W. Zachow, Gesammelte Werke, ed. M. Seiffert [V, I, K].

Collective volumes:

29/30. Instrumentalkonzerte deutscher Meister [J. G. Pisendel, J. A. Hasse, C. P. E. Bach,

G. P. Telemann, C. Graupner, G. H. Stölzel, K. F. Hurlebusch], ed. A. Schering [I].

34. Newe deudsche geistliche Gesenge für die gemeinen Schulen [orig. ed. G. Rhau, 1544, numerous composers], ed. J. Wolf [S].

49/50. Thüringische Motetten der ersten Hälfte des 18. Jahrhunderts [Arnoldi, J. M. Bach, P. H. Erlebach, Flender, G. P. Telemann, and others], ed. M. Seiffert [V].

XIV. *Denkmäler der Tonkunst in Bayern* [*DTB;* published as *Denkmäler deutscher Tonkunst,* zweite Folge; 36 vols., ed. A. Sandberger, 1900–1931; new rev. ed., 36 vols., 3 vols. to date, 9, 20 (ed. C. R. Crosby, Jr.), 22 (ed. O. Kaul), 1962—; *neue Folge* (new series in 2 parts: main series and special series of book-size volumes (*Sonderbände*), 1 vol. in each part to date, 1967—. Vol. numbers of new rev. ed. are listed first; old *Jahrgang* and *Band* numbers are in parentheses. Composers are listed alphabetically; collective vols. appear next; *neue Folge* vols. and projections are placed at the end. Cross-references are to vol. numbers.

1;16 (1;9.i). E. F. dall'Abaco, Ausgewählte Werke, ed. A. Sandberger [I].

18 (10.i). G. Aichinger, Ausgewählte Werke [selected works], ed. T. Kroyer [V].

7 (4.ii). C. Erbach, Ausgewählte Werke, ed. F. von Werra [K].

26 (14.ii). C. W. Gluck, Le Nozze d'Ercole e d'Ebe, ed. H. Abert [Op].

19 (10.ii). A. Gumpelzhaimer, Ausgewählte Werke, ed. O. Mayr [V].

8. (5.i). H. L. Hassler, *Bermerkungen zur Biographie Hans Leo Hasslers und seiner Brüder,* by A. Sandberger.

9. (5.ii). H. L. Hassler, Werke Hans Leo Hasslers, Canzonette von 1590 und neue teutsche Gesang von 1596, ed. R. Schwartz [V; 8 and 9 bound together in first edition].

20 (11.i). H. L. Hassler, Werke Hans Leo Hasslers, Madrigale zu 5, 6, 7 und 8 Stimmen von 1596, ed. R. Schwartz [V].

7 (4.ii). H. L. Hassler and J. Hassler, Ausgewählte Werke, ed. E. von Werra [K].

34 (26). J. de Kerle, Ausgewählte Werke, die "Preces speciales etc." für das Konzil von Trient, ed. O. Ursprung [V].

3 (2.ii). J. K. Kerll, Ausgewählte Werke, ed. A. Sandberger [K, V, I].

24;32 (13;21–24). J. E. Kindermann, Ausgewählte Werke, ed. F. Schreiber [V; K, V, I].

30 (18). J. and J. P. Krieger, Gesammelte Werke für Klavier und Orgel, ed. M. Seiffert [K].

17 (9.ii). L. Mozart, Ausgewählte Werke, ed. M. Seiffert [K, I, S, V].

30 (18). F. X. A. Murschhauser, Gesammelte Werke für Klavier und Orgel, ed. M. Seiffert [K].

2;6 (2.i;4.i). J. and W. H. Pachelbel, Klavierwerke; Orgelkompositionen, ed. M. Seiffert [K].

35 (27/28). J. C. Pez, Ausgewählte Werke, ed. B. A. Wallner [I, Op, V].

36 (29/30). A. Raselius, Cantiones sacrae, ed. L. Roselius [V].

33 (25). F. A. Rosetti, Ausgewählte Kammermusikwerke nebst einem Instrumentalkonzert, ed. O. Kaul [I].

22 (12.i). F. A. Rosetti, Ausgewählte Sinfonien, ed. O. Kaul.

5 (3.ii). L. Senfl, Ludwig Senfls Werke [motets and Magnificat], ed. T. Kroyer [V].

12;14 (7.i;8.i). J. Staden, Ausgewählte Werke, ed. E. Schmitz [V; V, S, I].

21 (11.ii). A. Steffani, Ausgewählte Werke, Alarico, ed. H. Riemann [Op].

23 (12.ii). A. Steffani, Ausgewählte Werke, ed. H. Riemann [Op].

11 (6.ii). A. Steffani, Ausgewählte Werke, ed. A. Einstein and A. Sandberger [S, V].

31 (19/20). P. Torri, Ausgewählte Werke, ed. H. Junker [Op].

25;29 (14.i;17). T. Traetta, Ausgewählte Szenen, ed. H. Goldschmidt [Op].

Collective volumes:

4;13;15 (3.i;7.ii;8.ii). Sinfonien der Pfalzbayerischen Schule [J. Stamitz, F. X. Richter, A. Filtz, I. Holzbauer, J. B. Toeschi, C. Cannabich, F. Beck, A. Stamitz, K. Stamitz, E. Eichner], ed. H. Riemann [I].

10 (6.i). Nürnberger Meister der zweiten Hälfte des 17. Jahrhunderts, geistliche Konzerte und Kirchenkantaten [P. Hainlein, H. Schwemmer, G. K. Wecker, J. Pachelbel, J. P. Krieger, J. Krieger], ed. M. Seiffert [V].

27;28 (15;16). Mannheimer Kammermusik des 18. Jahrhunderts [F. X. Richter, I. Holzbauer, J. Toeschi, C. Cannabich, K. Stamitz, A. Stamitz, J. Stamitz, and others], ed. H. Riemann [I].

Neue Folge, main series:

1. E. F. dall'Abaco, Ausgewählte Werke iii, ed. H. Schmid based on the estate of A. Sandberger.

J. de Kerle, Ausgewählte Werke ii, ed.

R. Machold, based on the estate of O. Ursprung [in prep.].

Kompositionen von Angehorigen der Bayerischen Hofkapollo zur Zeit Orlando di Lassos, ed. H. Leuchtmann [in prep.].

Aus dem Repertoire der Nürnberger Aegidien-Kirche um 1600, ed. W. Rubsamen [in prep.].

Philothea seu Anima Deum amans. Comoedia sacra (1643), ed. H. Schmid [in prep.].

F. X. A. Murschhauser, (10) Vesperpsalmen und Magnificat, ed. R. Walter [in prep.].

Aus dem Repertoire des Grafen Rudolf Franz Erwein von Schönborn-Wiesentheid, ed. F. Zobeley [in prep.].

J. V. Rathgeber, Chelys sonora, opus VI, (25) Instrumentalkonzerte (1728) selection, ed. F. Krautwurst [in prep.].

I. de Vento, Ausgewählte Werke, ed. M.-L. Göllner, based on the estate of K. Huber [in prep.].

G. Plàtti, Ausgewählte Werke, ed. F. Zobeley and O. Kaul [in prep.].

Kirchenmusik der Mannheimer Schule i: Die älteren Mannheimer, ed. E. Schmitt [in prep.].

T. Traetta, Ausgewählte Werke iii, ed. S. Kunze [in prep.].

Instrumentalkonzerte um 1800, ed. R. Münster [in prep.].

Neue Folge, Sonderbände:

1. Die flötnerschen Spielkarten und andere Curiosa der Musiküberlieferung des 16. Jahrhundert aus Franken, ed. C. R. Crosby, Jr.

Das Lochamer Liederbuch, ed. C. Petzsch and W. Salmen [in prep.].

Die lateinischen Gesänge und Lieder des Moosburger Graduale der Universitätsbibliothek zu München, ed. B. Stäblein [in prep.].

XV. *Denkmäler der Tonkunst in Österreich* [*DTO;* 115 vols. to date, ed. G. Adler to vol. 83, ed. E. Schenk from vol. 85; new ed. of vols. 1–83, 1959—. Volume (*Band*) numbers are listed first with numbers of annual issues (*Jahrgänge*), usually two per year, in parentheses, composers are listed alphabetically; collective volumes are placed at the end; cross-references are to volume numbers].

33 (16.ii). J. G. Albrechtsberger, Instrumentalwerke, ed. O. Kapp [I].

73 (38.i). B. Amon, Kirchenwerke I, ed. P. C. Huigens [V].

20 (10.i). O. Benevoli, Festmesse und Hymnus, ed. G. Adler [V].

69 (36.i). S. Bernardi, Kirchenwerke, ed. K. A. Rosenthal [V].

11;25 (5.ii;12.ii). H. I. F. Biber, Acht Violinsonaten, ed. G. Adler; Sechzehn Violinsonaten, ed. E. Luntz [I].

92. H. I. F. Biber, Harmonia artificiosa-ariosa, ed. P. Nettl and F. Reidinger [I].

96;97. H. I. F. Biber, Mensa sonora [I], Fidicinium sacro-profanum [I], ed. E. Schenk.

106/107. H. I. F. Biber, Sonatae tam aris quam aulis servientes (1676), ed. E. Schenk [I].

99. A. von Bruck, Sämtliche lateinische Motetten und andere unedierte Werke, ed. O. Wessely [V].

91. A. Caldara, Dafne, ed. C. Schneider and R. John [Op].

75 (39). A. Caldara, Kammermusik für Gesang: Kantaten, Madrigale, Kanons, ed. E. Mandyczewski [S, V].

26 (13.i). A. Caldara, Kirchenwerke, ed. E. Mandyczewski [V].

6;9 (3.ii,4.ii). M. A. Cesti, Il Pomo d'oro, ed. G. Adler [Op].

81 (43.ii). K. D. von Dittersdorf, Drei Sinfonien, eine Serenata, ed. V. Luithlen [I].

46 (23.i). A. Draghi, Kirchenwerke, ed. G. Adler [V].

55 (28.i). J. E. Eberlin, Oratorium, der blutschwitzende Jesus nebst Anhang: Stücke aus anderen Oratorien, ed. R. Haas [Or].

67 (35.i). E. A. Förster, Zwei Quartette, drei Quintette, ed. K. Weigl [I].

8;13;21 (4.i;6.ii;10.ii). J. J. Froberger, Zwölf Toccaten, sechs Fantasien, sechs Canzonen, acht Capriccios, sechs Ricercare für Orgel und Clavier; Suiten für Clavier; Dreizehn Toccaten—zehn Capriccios—sieben [8] Ricercare—zwei Fantasien—zwei Suiten und Suitensätze, ed. G. Adler [K].

47 (23.ii). J. J. Fux, Concentus musico-instrumentalis, ed. H. Rietsch [I].

34/35 (17). J. J. Fux, Costanza e fortezza, ed. E. Wellesz [Op].

19 (9.ii). J. J. Fux, Instrumentalwerke, ed. G. Adler [I].

1 (1.i). J. J. Fux, Messen, ed. J. E. Habert and G. A. Glossner [V].

3 (2.i). J. J. Fux, Motetten, ed. J. E. Habert [V].

85. J. J. Fux, Werke für Tasteninstrumente, ed. E. Schenk [K].

94/95;117. J. Gallus [see J. Handl].

42–44 (21.i). F. L. Gassmann, La Contessina (Die junge Gräfin), ed. R. Haas [Op].

83 (45). F. L. Gassmann, Kirchenwerke, ed. F. Kosch [V].

60 (30.ii). C. W. Gluck, Don Juan, ed. R. Haas [B].

82 (44). C. W. Gluck, L'Innocenza giustificata (Der Triumph der Unschuld), ed. A. Einstein [Op].

44a (21.ii). C. W. Gluck, Orfeo ed Euridice, ed. H. Abert [Op].

16 (8.i). A. Hammerschmidt, Dialogi oder Gespräche einer gläubigen Seele mit Gott, ed. A. W. Schmidt [V].

12;24;30;40;48;51/52 (6.i;12.i;15.i;20.i;24;26). J. Handl [Gallus], Opus musicum, ed. E. Bezecny and J. Mantuani [V].

78 (42.i);94/95;117. J. Handl [Gallus], Sechs Messen; Fünf Messen zu acht und sieben Stimmen; Drei Messen zu sechs Stimmen, ed. P. A. Pisk [V].

29 (14.ii). M. Haydn, Instrumentalwerke I, ed. L. H. Perger [I].

62 (32.i). M. Haydn, Kirchenwerke, ed. A. M. Klafsky [V].

45 (22). M. Haydn, Missa Sti. Francisci, Missa in dominica palmarum, Missa tempore quadragesimae, ed. A. M. Klafsky [V].

10;32 (5.i;16.i). H. Isaac, Choralis Constantinus i, ed. E. Bezecny and W. Rabl; ii, ed. A. von Webern [V].

28;32 (14.i;16.i). H. Isaac, Weltliche Werke, Nachtrag zu Jahrgang XIV, Band 1 [supplement of secular works], ed. J. Wolf [V, I, K].

65 (33.ii). J. Lanner, Ländler und Walzer, ed. A. Orel.

110. T. Massaino, Liber primus cantionum ecclesiasticarum (1592); Drei Instrumentalcanzonen (1608), ed. R. Monterosso [V, I].

57 (29.i). C. Monteverdi, Il Ritorno d'Ulisse in patria, ed. R. Haas [Op].

89. Georg Muffat, "Armonico tributo" 1682, "Exquisitioris harmoniae instrumentalis gravi—jucundae selectus primus" 1701, ed. E. Schenk [I].

23 (11.ii). Georg Muffat, Auserlesene . . . Instrumental musik. 1701; Armonico tributo, ed. E. Luntz [I].

2;4 (1.ii;2.ii). Georg Muffat, Florilegium primum; Florilegium secundum, ed. H. Rietsch [I].

7 (3.iii). Gottlieb Muffat, Componimenti musicali per il cembalo, ed. G. Adler [K].

58 (29.ii). Gottlieb Muffat, Zwölf Toccaten und 72 Versetl [12 toccatas and 72 versets or fugues], ed. G. Adler [K].

71 (37.i). Neidhart von Reuenthal, Lieder von Neidhart [von Reuental], ed. W. Schmieder.

17 (8.ii). J. Pachelbel, 94 [95] Kompositionen Fugen über das Magnificat für Orgel oder Klavier [95 compositions, mostly fugues on the Magnificat], ed. H. Botstiber and M. Seiffert [K].

70 (36.ii). P. Peuerl, Neue Paduanen 1611; Weltspiegel 1613; Ganz neue Paduanen 1625, ed. K. Geiringer [I, V].

70 (36.ii). I. Posch, Musikalische Tafelfreud 1621, ed. K. Geiringer [I, V].

88. G. Reutter d. J., Kirchenwerke [church compositions], ed. P. N. Hofer [V].

66 (34). J. Schenk, Der Dorfbarbier, ed. R. Haas [Op].

105. J. H. Schmelzer, Duodena selectarum sonatarum (1659), Werke handschriftlicher Überlieferung, ed. E. Schenk [I].

111/112. J. H. Schmelzer, Sacro-profanus concentus musicus, Fidium aliorumque instrumentorum (1662), ed. E. Schenk [I].

93. J. H. Schmelzer, "Sonatae unarum fidium" 1664, Violinsonaten handschriftlicher Überlieferung, ed. E. Schenk [I].

5 (3.i). J. Stadlmayr, Hymnen, ed. J. E. Habert [V].

68 (35.ii). J. Strauss d. Ä., Acht Walzer, ed. H. Gál [I].

63 (32.ii). J. Strauss d. J., Drei Walzer, ed. H. Gál [I].

74 (38.ii). Josef Strauss, Drei Walzer, ed. H. Botstiber [I].

115. F. M. Techelmann, Suiten für Tasteninstrumente, ed. H. Knaus [K].

36 (18.i). I. Umlauf, Die Bergknappen, ed. R. Haas [Op].

98; 100; 103/104; 108/109; 113/114; 116. J. Vaet, Sämtliche Werke I, II, III, IV, V, VI, ed. M. Steinhardt [V].

18 (9.i). O. von Wolkenstein, Geistliche und weltliche Lieder, ed. J. Schatz and O. Koller [S].

87. N. Zangius, Geistliche und weltliche Gesänge, ed. H. Sachs and A. Pfalz [S].

Collective volumes:

14/15;22;38;53;61;76 (7;11.i;19.i;27.i;31;40). Sechs [Sieben] Trienter Codices [6 (7) Trent Codices], ed. G. Adler and O. Koller; ed. R. Ficker and A. Orel [53]; ed. R. Ficker [61, 76] [V].

27 (13.ii) Wiener Klavier- und Orgelwerke aus der zweiten Hälfte des 17. Jahrhunderts [A. Poglietti, G. Reutter d. Ä., F. T. Richter, *c.* 1650–1700], ed. H. Botstiber [K].

31;39 (15.ii;19.ii). Wiener Instrumentalmusik vor und um 1750, ed. K. Horwitz and K. Riedel; ed. W. Fischer [I].

37;50 (18.ii;25.ii). Österreichische Lautenmusik im XVI. Jahrhundert . . . zwischen 1650 und 1720, ed. A. Koczirz [L].

41 (20.ii). Gesänge von Frauenlob, Reinmar v. Zweter, und Alexander, ed. H. Rietsch [S].

49. Messen von H. Biber, H. Schmeltzer, J. C. Kerll, ed. G. Adler [V].

54;79 (27.ii;42.ii). Das Wiener Lied von 1778 bis Mozarts Tod; Das Wiener Lied von 1792 bis 1815, ed. M. Ansion and I. Schlaffenberg; ed. H. Maschek and H. Kraus [S].

56 (28.ii). Wiener Tanzmusik in der zweiten Hälfte des siebzehnten Jahrhunderts, ed. P. Nettl [I].

59. Drei Requiem für Soli, Chor, Orchester aus dem 17. Jahrhundert: C. Strauss, F. H. Biber, J. C. Kerll, ed. G. Adler [V].

64 (33.i). Deutsche Komödienarien, 1754–58, ed. R. Haas [S].

72 (37.ii). Das deutsche Gesellschaftslied in Österreich von 1480–1550, ed. L. Nowak and A. Koczirz [S].

77 (41). Italienische Musiker und das Kaiserhaus, ed. A. Einstein [V].

80 (43.i). Salzburger Kirchenkomponisten [K. Biber, M. S. Biechteler, J. E. Eberlin, A. Adlgasser], ed. K. A. Rosenthal and C. Schneider [V].

84. Wiener Lautenmusik im 18. Jahrhundert, ed. K. Schnürl with material from A. Koczirz and J. Klima [L].

86. Tiroler Instrumentalmusik im 18. Jahrhundert, ed. W. Senn [I].

90. Niederländische und italienische Musiker der Grazer Hofkapelle Karls II. 1564—1590, ed. H. Federhofer and R. John [V].

101/102. Geistliche Solomotetten des 18. Jahrhunderts, ed. C. Schoenbaum [V].

XVa. *Documenta polyphoniae liturgicae sanctae ecclesiae Romanae* [13 vols., 1947—; practical edition with modern clefs and signs; proposed, series II, *Proprium missae* and series III, *Divinum officium*].

Series I. A., Ordinarium missae:

1. G. Dufay, Fragmentum missae.

2. L. Power, Missa super "Alma redemptoris mater."

3. G. Dufay, Et in terra "ad modum tube."

4. G. Dufay, Missa de sanctissima trinitate.

5. G. Binchois, Missa de angelis.

6. Standley, Missa ad fugam reservatam.

7. G. Dufay, 2 Kyrie et 1 Gloria in dominicis diebus.

8. J. Dunstable, Gloria e Credo (Jesu Christe Fili Dei vivi).

9. Leonel, Messa super fuit homo missus.

10. G. Dufay, Et in terra de quaremiaux.

11. J. Franchoys?, Gloria e Credo.

Series I. B., Ordinarium missae, 6 voices:

1. P. de La Rue, Missa ave sanctissima.

Series IV, Motecta:

1. Standley?, Quae est ista (Fuga reservata) [I].

XVI. *The English Madrigal School* [36 vols., ed. E. H. Fellowes, 3 editions, 1913–24; new rev. ed., *The English Madrigalists,* 27 vols. to date, ed. T. Dart, *c.* 1958—. Revised edition has slightly different titles].

1. T. Morley, The First Book of Canzonets to Two Voices; Canzonets or Little Short Songs to Three Voices.

2. T. Morley, First Book of Madrigals to Four Voices; Two Canzonets to Four Voices.

3. T. Morley, Canzonets or Little Short Airs to Five and Six Voices; Two Madrigals.

4. T. Morley, First Book of Ballets to Five Voices.

5. O. Gibbons, First Set of Madrigals and Motets of Five Parts.

6. J. Wilbye, First Set of Madrigals to 3. 4. 5. and 6 Voices [includes madrigal pub. 1601 and 2 motets pub. 1614].

7. J. Wilbye, Second Set of Madrigals to 3. 4. 5. and 6 Voices.

8. J. Farmer, First Set of Madrigals to Four Voices [includes a madrigal pub. 1601].

9. T. Weelkes, Madrigals to 3. 4. 5. and 6 Voices.

10. T. Weelkes, Ballets and Madrigals to Five Voices.

11. T. Weelkes, Madrigals of Five Parts.

12. T. Weelkes, Madrigals of Six Parts.

13. T. Weelkes, Airs or Fantastic Spirits to Three Voices [includes a madrigal pub. 1601].

14. W. Byrd, Psalms, Sonnets, and Songs of

Sadness and Piety to Five Parts; Two Madrigals.

15. W. Byrd, Songs of Sundry Natures to 3. 4. 5. and 6. Parts.
16. W. Byrd, Psalms Songs and Sonnets, Some Solemn Others Joyful to 3. 4. 5. and 6. Parts [includes a madrigal from 1590].
17. H. Lichfild, First Set of Madrigals of Five Parts.
18. T. Tomkins, Songs of 3. 4. 5. and 6. Parts [includes a madrigal pub. 1601].
19. J. Ward, Madrigals to 3. 4. 5. and 6. Parts.
20. G. Farnaby, Canzonets to Four Voices.
21. T. Bateson, First Set of Madrigals.
22. T. Bateson, Second Set of Madrigals.
23. J. Bennet, Madrigals to Four Voices [includes madrigal pub. 1601 and 2 songs pub. 1614].
24. G. Kirbye, Madrigals to 4. 5. and 6. Voices [includes a madrigal pub. 1601].
25. F. Pilkington, First Set of Madrigals and Pastorals of 3. 4. and 5. Parts.
26. F. Pilkington, Second Set of Madrigals and Pastorals of 3. 4. 5. and 6. Parts.
27. R. Carlton, Madrigals to Five Voices [includes madrigal pub. 1601].
28. H. Youll, Canzonets to Three Voices.
29. M. East, Madrigals to 3. 4. and 5. Parts.
30. M. East, Madrigals to 3. 4. and 5. Parts [includes a madrigal pub. 1601].
31. M. East, Madrigals Contained in The Third Set of Books [31A in rev. ed.]; Madrigals Contained in The Fourth Set of Books [31B in rev. ed.].
32. T. Morley [publisher], Madrigals, The Triumphs of Oriana to 5. and 6. Voices.
33. R. Alison, An Hour's Recreation in Music.
34. T. Vautor, Songs of Divers Airs and Natures.
35. R. Jones, The First Set of Madrigals of 3. 4. 5. 6. 7. 8. Parts [includes a madrigal pub. 1601; 35A in rev. ed.]; J. Mundy, Madrigals Included by him in his Songs and Psalms Composed into 3. 4. and 5. Parts [includes a madrigal pub. 1601; 35B in rev. ed.].
36. M. Cavendish, Madrigals to 5. Voices [includes a madrigal pub. 1601]; T. Greaves, Madrigals for Five Voices; W. Holborne, Airs to Three Voices.

XVII. *The English School of Lutenist Song Writers* [two series of 16 vols. each, ed. E. H. Fellowes, *c.* 1920–32; *The English Lute-Songs,* rev. ed. of both series—vol. 17 added to series 1, 4 vols. to date; vols. 17 and 18 added to series 2, 3 vols. to date—ed. T. Dart, 1958—. Some of the original collections are subdivided; binding may vary. Punctuation of titles varies].

First series:

1;2. J. Dowland, First Book of Airs. 1597.
3. T. Ford, Airs to the Lute, from Musicke of Sundrie Kindes, 1607.
4;13. T. Campion, Songs from Rosseter's [ed.] Book of Airs. 1601.
5;6. J. Dowland, Second Book of Airs. 1600.
7;15. F. Pilkington, First Book of Songs or Airs. 1605.
8;9. P. Rosseter, Songs from Rosseter's [ed. and composer] Book of Airs, 1601.
10;11. J. Dowland, Third Book of Airs. 1603.
12;14. J. Dowland, A Pilgrimes Solace (Fourth Book of Airs, 1612) [in addition, 3 songs included in R. Dowland's [composer] *A Musicall Banquet, 1610*].
16. T. Morley, First Book of Airs. 1600.
17. J. Coperario, Funeral Teares (1606), Songs of Mourning (1613), The Masque of Squires (1614), ed. T. Dart and G. Hendrie.
18. T. Maynard, *The Twelve Wonders of the World,* 1612 [in prep.].
19. Lutenist songs from manuscript [in prep.].

Second Series:

1. T. Campion, First Book of Airs. Circa 1613.
2. T. Campion, Second Book of Airs. Circa 1613.
3. J. Bartlet, A Booke of Ayres. 1606.
4. R. Jones, First Booke of Songes and Ayres (1600).
5. R. Jones, Second Booke of Ayres (1601).
6. R. Jones, Ultimum Vale, Third Booke of Ayres (1608).
7. M. Cavendish, Songs included in Michael Cavendish's Booke of Ayres and Madrigalles (1598).
8. J. Danyel, Songs for the Lute, Viol and Voice (1606).
9. J. Attey, First Booke of Ayres 1622.
10. T. Campion, Third Booke of Ayres circa 1617.
11. T. Campion, Fourth Booke of Ayres, circa 1617.
12. W. Corkine, First Booke of Ayres 1610.
13. W. Corkine, Second Booke of Ayres 1612.
14. R. Jones, A Musicall Dreame or Fourth Booke of Ayres 1609.
15. R. Jones, The Muses Gardin for Delights or Fifth Booke of Ayres 1610.
16. A. Ferrabosco the younger, Ayres 1609.

17. R. Johnson, Ayres, Songs and Dialogues, ed. Ian Spink.

18. T. Greaves, G. Mason, J. Earsden, Songs (1604) and Ayres (1618), ed. Ian Spink.

XVIII. *Das Erbe deutscher Musik* [Continuation of *DdT*, various editors, 1935—; earlier volumes in the process of being reprinted. Two series: *Reichsdenkmale*, i.e., documents of general importance; *Landschaftsdenkmale*, i.e., documents of chiefly local importance, discontinued 1942].

A. *Reichsdenkmale* has two numbering systems: (1) by the consecutive numbering of the whole *Reichsdenkmale*. This numbering is listed first. (2) By 10 regular and one special series (orchestral music, Orch; motets and Masses, M-M; Middle Ages, MA; opera and song, Op-S; chamber music, Cham; oratorio and cantata, Or-Cant; polyphonic vocal music, Poly V; organ/keyboard/lute, O/K/L; early romantic, E Rom; selections of one composer, Select of; special or miscellaneous series, Sp Ser). The vols. of each series are numbered consecutively, though not always correctly. After volume 23, with the exception of 25, the name *Reichsdenkmale* is abandoned.

1 (Sp Ser 1). Altbachisches Archiv, ester Teil: Motetten und Chorlieder, ed. M. Schneider [V].

2 (Sp Ser 2). Altbachisches Archiv, zweiter Teil: Kantaten, ed. M. Schneider [S].

3 (Cham 1). J. C. Bach, Sechs Quintette/Op. 11, ed. R. Steglich [I].

4 (MA 1). Das Glogauer Liederbuch, ester Teil: deutsche Lieder und Spielstücke, ed. H. Ringmann [V, I].

5 (M-M 1). L. Senfl, Sieben Messen zu vier bis sechs Stimmen, ed. E. Löhrer und O. Ursprung [V].

6 (Op-S 1). G. P. Telemann, Pimpinone oder Die ungleiche Heirat, ed. T. W. Werner [Op].

7 (Solo music 1, also MA 2). Trompeterfanfaren, Sonaten und Feldstücke … des 16./17. Jahrhunderts, ed. G. Schünemann [I].

8 (MA 2, is MA 3). Das Glogauer Liederbuch, zweiter Teil: ausgewählte lateinische Sätze, ed. H. Ringmann and J. Klapper [V].

9. (O/K/L 1). Orgelchoräle um Joh. Seb. Bach [numerous composers], ed. G. Frotscher [K].

10 (Poly V 1). L. Senfl, Deutsche Lieder, erster Teil: Lieder aus handschriftlichen Quellen bis etwa 1533, ed. A. Geering and W. Altwegg [S].

11 (Orch 1). Gruppenkonzerte der Bachzeit [J. F. Fasch, J. D. Heinichen, G. P. Telemann], ed. K. M. Komma [I].

12 (O/K/L 2). Lautenmusik des 17./18. Jahrhunderts [E. Reusner and S. L. Weiss], ed. H. Neemann [L].

13 (M-M 2). L. Senfl, Motetten, erster Teil: Gelegenheitsmotetten und Psalmvertonungen, ed. W. Gerstenberg [V].

14 (Cham 2). Deutsche Bläsermusik vom Barock bis zur Klassik [numerous composers], ed. H. Schultz [I].

15 (Poly V 2). L. Senfl, Deutsche Lieder, zweiter Teil: Lieder aus Hans Otts erstem Liederbuch von 1534, ed. A. Geering and W. Altwegg [S].

16 (Select of 1). C. Othmayr, Ausgewählte Werke, erster Teil: Symbola, ed. H. Albrecht [V].

17 (Cham 3). J. J. Walther, Scherzi da violino solo con il basso continuo, 1676, ed. G. Beckmann [I].

18 (Orch 2). C. P. E. Bach, Vier Orchestersinfonien mit zwölf obligaten Stimmen, ed. R. Steglich [I].

19 (Op-S 2). Ohrenvergnügendes und gemüthergötzendes Tafelconfect [V. Rathgeber, J. C. Seyfert, probable composers; 1733–46], ed. H. J. Moser [V, S].

20 (Poly V 3). G. Forster, orig. ed., Frische teutsche Liedlein (1539–1556), erster Teil: Ein Auszug guter alter und neuer teutscher Liedlein (1539) [numerous composers], ed. K. Gudewill and W. Heiske [S].

21 (M-M 3). G. Rhau, orig. ed., Sacrorum hymnorum liber primus, erster Teil: Proprium de tempore [H. Finck, T. Stoltzer and others], ed. R. Gerber [V].

22 (Select of 2). T. Stoltzer, Ausgewählte Werke, ester Teil, ed. H. Albrecht (V, I).

23 (Select of 3). S. Dietrich, Ausgewählte Werke, erster Teil: Hymnen (1545), erste Abteilung, ed. H. Zenck [V].

24 (Cham 4). I. Holzbauer, Instrumentale Kammermusik [selected chamber music], ed. U. Lehmann [T].

25 (M-M 4). G. Rhau, Sacrorum hymnorum liber primus, zweiter Teil: Proprium et commune sanctorum [H. Finck, T. Stoltzer, B. Hartzer and others], ed. R. Gerber [V].

26 (Select of 4). C. Othmayr, Ausgewählte Werke, zweiter Teil: Cantilenae (1546),

Epitaphium D. Martini Lutheri (1546), Bicinia (1547?), Tricinia (1549), einzelne Werke aus verstreuten Quellen, ed. H. Albrecht [V].

27 (Op-S 3). J. A. Hasse, Arminio [i], ed. R. Gerber [Op].

28 (Op-S 4). J. A. Hasse, Arminio ii, ed. R. Gerber [Op].

29 (Poly V 4). J. Jeep, Studentengärtlein, ed. R. Gerber [V]; J. Steffens, Neue teutsche weltliche Madrigalia und Balletten, ed. G. Fock [V].

30 (Orch 3). J. C. Bach, Fünf Sinfonien, ed. F. Stein [I].

31 (Cham 5). G. J. Werner, Musikalischer Instrumental-Kalender, ed. F. Stein [I].

32;33 (MA 4; MA 5). Der Mensuralkodex des Nikolaus Apel (MS 1494 der Universitätsbibliothek Leipzig) Teil I; Teil II, ed. R. Gerber [V].

34 (MA 6). Der Mensuralkodex des Nikolaus Apel (MS 1494 der Universitätsbibliothek Leipzig) Teil III, ed. R. Gerber and L. Finscher [in prep.].

35 (Or-Cant 1). G. Kirchhoff and J. G. Goldberg, Kirchenkantaten, ed. A. Dürr [S].

36 (O/K/L 3). Die Lüneburger Orgeltabulatur KN 208[1], ed. M. Reimann [K].

37;38;39 (MA 7; MA 8; MA 9). Das Buxheimer Orgelbuch, ed. B. A. Wallner [K].

40 (MA 10). Das Liederbuch des Dr. Hartmann Schedel, ed. H. Besseler [in prep., S].

41 (Orch 4). Klarinetten-Konzerte des 18. Jahrhunderts [J. M. Molter, F. X. Pokorny], ed. H. Becker [I].

42 (M-M 5). A. P. Coclico, Consolationes piae, Musica reservata (Nürnberg 1552), ed. M. Ruhnke [V].

43 (Op-S 5). A. Hammerschmidt, Weltliche Oden oder Liebesgesänge (Freiberg 1642 und 1643, Leipzig 1649), ed. H. J. Moser [S].

44 (Cham 6). J. Schenk, Le Nymphe di Rheno für zwei Solo-Gamben, ed. K. H. Pauls [I].

45;46 (Or-Cant 2; Or-Cant 3). Geistliche Konzerte um 1660–1700 i, ii, Chorkonzerte, ed. H. J. Moser [in prep.].

47 (M-M 6). L. Daser, Motetten, ed. A. Schneiders [V].

48 (Select of 5). C. Geist, Kirchenkonzerte, ed. B. Lundgren [V, S].

49 (Cham 7). A. Hammerschmidt, "Erster Fleiss" Instrumentalwerke zu 5 und 3 Stimmen, ed. H. Mönkemeyer [I].

50 (Or-Cant 4). A. Pfleger, Geistliche Konzerte Nr. 1–11, ed. F. Stein [V].

51 (Orch 5). Flöten-Konzerte der Mannheimer Schule [A. Filtz, F. X. Richter, J. W. A. Stamitz, K. Stamitz, A. Stamitz, K. J. Toeschi], ed. W. Lebermann.

52 (M-M 6?). J. P. Förtsch, Motetten, ed. H. Kümmerling [in prep., V].

53 (Op-S 6). J. A. P. Schulz, Athalia, ed. H. Gottwaldt [in prep., Op].

54;55 (O/K/L 4; O/K/L 5). H. Buchner, Sämtliche Orgelwerke i, ii, ed. J.-H. Schmidt [in prep., K].

56 (Orch 7?). J. C. Bach, Konzertante Sinfonien, ed. E. J. Simon [in prep., I].

57 (Select of 6). H. Finck, Ausgewählte Werke, erster Teil, Messen und Motetten zum Proprium Missae, ed. L. Hoffmann-Erbrecht [V].

58 (E Rom 1). J. F. Reichardt, Goethes Lieder, Oden, Balladen und Romanzen mit Musik, Teil I, 1. und 2. Abteilung, ed. W. Salmen [S].

59 (E Rom 2). J. F. Reichardt, Goethes Lieder, Oden, Balladen und Romanzen mit Musik, Teil II, ed. W. Salmen [in prep., S].

60;61 (Poly V 5; Poly V 6). G. Forster, orig. ed., Frische teutsche Liedlein ii, iii, ed. K. Gudewill and H. Siuts [in prep., S].

64 (Or-Cant 5). A. Pfleger, Geistliche Konzerte Nr. 12–23 aus dem Evangelien-Jahrgang, ed. F. Stein [S].

Sonderreihe, no over-all numbering:

1. C. Demantius, Neue teutsche weltliche Lieder 1595; Convivalium concentuum farrago 1609, ed. K. Stangl [S, V]; reprint of vol. 15 of *Landschaftsdenkmale.*

2. J. Kugelmann, Concentus novi 1540, ed. H. Engel [V].

3. E. Widmann, Ausgewählte Werke, ed. G. Reichert [I, V].

4. J. Schobert, Sechs Sinfonien für Cembalo [Op. 9 and 10], ed. G. Becking [I].

C. H. Abel: Erstlinge musikalischer Blumen, ed. H. Krause-Graumnitz [in prep.].
J. Vierdanck: Geistliche Konzerte und Instrumentalmusik, ed. G. Weiss [in prep.].

B. *Landschaftsdenkmale* [extension of *DTB,* ceased publication in 1942, reprints of these vols. will appear as part of the *Sonderreihe* listed above. The first two vols. listed retain the *DTB* numbering system (*Band,* then *Jahrgang*) and in addition have the new system: regional name followed by vol. no. within the individual regional series. The numbers in brackets are not original and are to assist in cross-reference].

[1] 37 (31–36) Bayern [Bavaria], 1. R. I. Mayr, Ausgewählte Kirchenmusik, ed. K. G. Fellerer [V].

[2] 38 (37/38) Bayern [Bavaria], 2. J. W. Franck, Die drey Töchter Cecrops', ed. G. F. Schmidt [Op].

[3] Kurhessen [Electorate of Hessen], 1. M. Landgraf von Hessen, Ausgewählte Werke, erster Teil: 16 Pavanen, Gagliarden und Intraden; . . . zweiter Teil: Vier Fugen und fünf Madrigale, ed. W. Dane [I, V].

[4] Niedersachsen [Lower Saxony], 1. J. Schultz, Musikalischer Lüstgarte 1622, ed. H. Zenck [V, I].

[5] Niedersachsen [Lower Saxony], 2. A. Crappius, Ausgewählte Werke, ed. T. W. Werner [V].

[6] Mecklenburg und Pommern [Mecklenburg and Pomerania], 1. Hochzeitsarien und Kantaten Stettiner Meister nach 1700, [F. G. Klingenberg, M. Rohde], ed. H. Engel and W. Freytag [S].

[7] Mecklenburg und Pommern [Mecklenburg and Pomerania], 2. D. Friderici, Ausgewählte geistliche Gesänge, ed. E. Schenk and W. Voll [V].

[8] Rhein-Main-Gebiet [Rhine-Main area], 1. J. A. Herbst, Drei mehrchörige Festkonzerte für die freie Reichsstadt Frankfurt a. M., ed. R. Gerber [I].

[9;10] Schleswig-Holstein und Hansestädte [Schleswig-Holstein and Hanseatic cities], 1, 2. N. Bruhns, Gesammelte Werke, erster Teil: Kirchenkantaten Nr. 1–7; . . ., zweiter Teil: Kirchenkantaten Nr. 8–12, Orgelwerke, ed. F. Stein [S, K].

[11] Schleswig-Holstein und Hansestädte [Schleswig-Holstein and Hanseatic cities], 3. J. S. Kusser, Arien, Duette und Chöre aus Erindo oder Die unsträfliche Liebe, ed. H. Osthoff [Op].

[12] Schleswig-Holstein und Hansestädte [Schleswig-Holstein and Hanseatic cities], 4. M. Weckmann, Gesammelte Werke, ed. G. Ilgner [I, K, S].

[13] Mitteldeutschland [Middle Germany], 1. F. W. Rust, Werke für Klavier und Streichinstrumente, ed. R. Czach [K, I].

[14] Ostpreussen und Danzig [East Prussia and Danzig], 1. Preussische Festlieder, Zeit-genössische Kompositionen zu Dichtungen Simon Dachs [composers: J. Stobäus, G. Kolb, H. Albert, J. Weichmann, J. Sebastiani, K. Matthäi, C. Kaldenbach], ed. J. Müller-Blattau [S].

[15] Sudetenland, Böhmen und Mähren [Sudetenland, Bohemia and Moravia], 1. C. Demantius, Neue teutsche weltliche Lieder 1595; Convivalium concentuum farrago 1609, ed. K. Stangl [S, V; has appeared in reprint as Sonderreihe, 1].

[16] Alpen- und Donau—Reichsgaue [Imperial district of Alps and Danube], 1. Wiener Lautenmusik im 18. Jahrhundert [F. Ginter, Graf Logi, J. G. Weichenberger and others], ed. A. Koczirz [L, I, S; pub. 1942, originally intended as vol. 84 of DTO, which has the same title but different music].

XIX. *Florilège du concert vocal de la renaissance* [8 vols., often bound in one, ed. H. Expert, 1928/29].

1. C. Janequin, Chantons, sonnons, trompetes. J'atens le temps. Sy celle-la. Il s'en va tard. Ouvrez-moy l'huis [Chansons].

2. O. de Lassus, O temps divers. Sçais-tu dir' l'Ave. Quand un Cordier. Qui bien se mire. Petite folle. En m'oyant. J'ay de vous voir [Chansons].

3. C. Janequin, Les Cris de Paris (1529) [Chanson].

4. G. Costeley, Arreste un peu, mon coeur. Voicy la saison plaisante. Dessoubz le may, près la fleur esglantine [Chansons].

5. P. Bonnet, Airs et villanelles [S].

6. C. Le Jeune, Las! où vas-tu sans moy. Je pleure, je me deux. Comment pensés-vous que je vive. Nostre vicaire, un jour de feste [Chansons].

7. J. Mauduit, Psaumes mesurés à l'antique de J.-A. de Baïf [S].

8. C. de Sermisy, Peletier, G. de Heurteur, and A. Gardano, Duos [V].

XX. *Hispaniae schola musica sacra* [8 vols., 4–7 may be bound together, ed. F. Pedrell, 1894–98; subtitle to series: Opera varia (saecul. XV, XVI, XVII et XVIII)].

1. Christophorus Morales [Magnificat, motets, Masses, laments].

2. Franciscus Guerrero [compositions, V].

3;4;7;8. Antonius a Cabezón [*Obras de música, 1578*, i–iv, duos, intermezzi, fauxbourdons, tientos or ricercars, variations, etc., K].

5. Joannes Ginesius Pérez [compositions, V].
6. Psalmodia modulata (vulgo fabordones) a diversiis auctoribus, inter quos Fr. Thomas a Sancta María, Franciscus Guerrero, Thome Ludovici a Victoria, Ceballos, aliique incerti aut ignotis [V].

XXI. *Instituta et monumenta* [3 vols., ed. S. Bassi, 1954—; Series I: *Monumenta;* Series II: *Instituta,* projected].

Monumenta:

1. O. dei Petrucci, orig. pub., Le Frottole [books 1–3], ed. G. Cesari, R. Monterosso, and B. Disertori [S].
2. Sacre rappresentazioni nel manoscritto 201 della bibliothèque municipale di Orléans [liturgical dramas, MS 201, "The Fleury Play Book," Orléans], ed. G. Tintori and R. Monterosso.
3. A. Vivaldi, La Fida Ninfa, ed. R. Monterosso [Op].

XXII. *Istituto italiano per la storia della musica* [publications of, 1941—].

I. *Antologie e raccolte:*

1. Giovanni de Antiquis and others, Villanelle alla Napolitana a tre voci di musicisti baresi del secolo XVI, ed. S. A. Luciani [V].

II. *Monumenti:*

1.i; 1.ii; 1.iii–vi. Don C. Gesualdo, Madrigali, ed. F. Vatielli [1.i and 1.ii sometimes bound together, V].
2.i. P. Nenna, Madrigali, ed. E. Dagnino [V].
3.i. G. Carissimi, Historia di Job, Historia di Ezechia, ed. C. dall'Argine, F. Ghisi, R. Lupi [Or].
3.ii. G. Carissimi, Historia di Abraham et Isaac; Vir frugi et pater familias, ed. L. Bianchi [Or].
3.iii. G. Carissimi, Historia di Baltazar, ed. L. Bianchi [Or].
3.iv. G. Carissimi, Iudicium extremum, ed. L. Bianchi [Or].
3.v. G. Carissimi, Historia divitis (Dives malus), ed. L. Bianchi [Or].
3.vi. G. Carissimi, Tolle, Sponsa; Historia dei Pellegrini di Emmaus, ed. L. Bianchi [Or].
3.viii. G. Carissimi, Oratorio della SS.ma Vergine, ed. L. Bianchi [Or].

XXIII. *Istituzioni e monumenti dell'arte musicale italiana* [6 vols., 1931–39; nuova serie, 3 vols., 1956—].

1. A. and G. Gabrieli, Andrea e Giovanni Gabrieli e la musica strumentale in San Marco, tomo I, Musiche strumentali e "per cantar et sonar" sino al 1590, ed. G. Benvenuti [V, I].
2. A. and G. Gabrieli, Andrea e Giovanni Gabrieli e la musica strumentale in San Marco, tomo II, Canzoni e sonate a più strumenti di Giovanni Gabrieli contenute nelle "Sacrae symphoniae" del 1597, ed. G. Benvenuti and G. Cesari [I].
3. Giacomo and Gaudenzio Battistini, Le Cappelle musicali di Novara dal secolo xvi a'primordi dell'ottocento, ed. V. Fedeli [V].
4. V. Galilei, La Camerata Fiorentina, La sua opera d'artista e di teorico come espressione di nuove idealità musicali, ed. F. Fano [V, L].
5. L'Oratorio dei Filippini e la scuola musicale di Napoli, tomo I [G. D. Montella, G. M. Trabaci and C. Gesualdol], ed. G. Pannain [Or, V].
6. M. A. Ingegneri and C. Monteverdi, La Musica in Cremona nella seconda metà del secolo XVI e i primordi dell'arte Monteverdiana, ed. G. Cesari and G. Pannain [V].

New Series:

1. Matteo da Perugia, La Cappella musicale del Duomo di Milano, Le Origini e il primo maestro di cappella: Matteo da Perugia, ed. G. Cesari and F. Fano [V].
2. Giovanni Benedetto Platti e la sonata moderna, ed. F. Torrefranca [K].
3. F. Bossinensis, Le Frottole per canto e liuto intabulate da Franciscus Bossinensis, ed. B. Disertori [S + L].

XXIV. *Lira sacro-hispana* [10 vols., ed. M. H. Eslava, 1869; Spanish sacred music, chiefly motets; detailed list of contents in *GD* ii, 177; *GDB* ii, 970].

Mainly 16th century, 2 vols. [A. de Fevin, C. de Morales, F. Guerrero, T. L. de Victoria and others].
Mainly 17th century, 2 vols. [J. B. Comes, A. Lobo, S. Aquilera de Heredia, G. Salazar and others].
Mainly 18th century, 2 vols. [J. de Bravo, D. Muelas, Padre A. Soler, A. da Ripa and others].
Mainly 19th century, 4 vols. [F. J. García, F. Secanilla, N. Ledesma, M. H. Eslava y Elizondo and others].

XXV. *Les Maîtres musiciens de la renaissance française* [23 vols., ed. H. Expert, 1894–1908; French vocal music of the 16th century. A few separate octavo issues exist; some are contained in the regular series, some present new music].

1. O. de Lassus, Premier Fascicule des mélanges.
2;4;6. C. Goudimel, 1er Fasc. des 150 Psaumes (Éd. de 1580); 2e Fasc. des . . . ; 3e Fasc. des . . . .
3;18;19. G. Costeley, Musique.—Premier fascicule; Musique.—Deuxième fascicule; Musique.—Troisième fascicule.
5. P. Attaingnant [pub.], Trente et une chansons musicales [C. de Sermisy, Consilium, Deslouges, Janequin and others].
7. C. Janequin, Chansons (Attaingnant, 1529?).
8. A. Brumel and P. de La Rue, Liber quindecim missarum, Brumel, Missa "De beata virgine," P. de La Rue, Missa "Ave maria."
9. J. Mouton and A. de Févim [Fevin], Liber quindecim missarum, Io. Mouton, Missa "Alma redemptoris," Févim, Missa "Mente tota."
10. J. Mauduit, Chansonnettes mesurées de Ian-Antoine de Baïf.
11. C. Le Jeune, Dodecacorde (1er fascicule) [12 Psalms].
12;13;14. C. Le Jeune, Le Printemps (1er fascicule); . . . (2e fascicule); . . . (3e fascicule) [i–iii].
15. F. Regnard, Poésies de P. de Ronsard et autres poètes.
16. C. Le Jeune, Mélanges (premier fascicule).
17. F.-E. Du Caurroy, Mélanges (premier fascicule).
20;21;22. C. Le Jeune, Pseaumes en vers mezurez—(1er fascicule); . . . (2e fascicule); . . . 3e fascicule).
23. C. Gervaise, E. Du Tertre and anon., Danceries (1er volume) [I].

Bibliographie thématique [H. Expert, ed.; projected set of 15 vols., only 2 published, 1900].

3. Trente et une chansons musicales (Attaingnant, 1529).
8. Trente et sept chansons musicales (Attaingnant, 1528–30?).

XXVI. *Mestres de l'Escolania de Montserrat* [5 vols., ed Dom D. Pujol, 1930–36; musical works by the monks of the monastery of Montserrat 1500–1800].

Vocal Music:

1. Joan Cererols, I [Vesper Psalms, hymns, canticles, Compline Psalms, anthems].
2. Joan Cererols, II ["Asperges me," antiphon, 4 Masses].
3. Joan Cererols, III [34 villancicos, tonos, romances].

Instrumental Music:

1. Música instrumental [M. López, llenos, versets; N. Casanoves, fugues, sonatas, I, K].
2. Música instrumental [A. della Viola, concerto for bassoon obbligato and orchestra; F. Rodríguez, sonatas, rondo; J. Vinyals, sonatas; I, K].

XXVII. *Monumenta musica neerlandica* [7 vols., Vereniging voor Nederlandse Muziekgeschiedenis, 1959—].

1. P. Hellendaal, Concerti grossi, Opus III, ed. H. B. Buys [I].
2. Klavierboek Anna Maria van Eijl [composers; Steenwick, G. Berff and others], ed. F. Noske [K].
3. Nederlandse klaviermuziek uit de 16e en 17e eeuw, ed. A. Curtis [K].
4. P. Locatelli, Opera quarta, prima parte, sei introduttioni teatrali, ed. A. Koole [I].
5. C. T. Padbrué, Nederlandse madrigalen, ed. F. Noske [V].
6. The Utrecht Prosarium, ed. N. de Goede [S].
7. Het geestelijk lied van Noord-Nederland in de vijftiende eeuw, ed. E. Bruning, M. Veldhuyzen, H. Wagenaar-Nolthenius [V].

XXVIII. *Monumenta musicae belgicae* [ed. J. Watelet, vols. 1–7; ed. R. B. Lenaerts, vols. 8–10, 1938—].

1. J.-B. Loeillet, Werken voor clavecimbel [K].
2. A. van den Kerckhoven, Werken voor orgel [K].
3. J.-H. Fiocco, Werken voor clavecimbel [K].
4. C. Guillet, G. Macque, C. Luython, Werken voor orgel of voor vier speeltuigen [K, I].
5. J. Boutmy, Werken voor klavecimbel [K].
6. D. Raick and C.-J. van Helmont, Werken voor orgel en/of voor clavecimbel [K].
7. G. Havingha, Werken voor clavecimbel [K].
8. P. de La Rue, Drie Missen van Pierre de La Rue, ed. R. B. Lenaerts and J. Robijns [V].
9. Nederlandse Polyfonie uit Spaanse bronnen

[3 Masses by N. Bauldewijn, M. Gascongne, T. Verelst; 1 chanson by Bauldewijn], ed. R. B. Lenaerts [V].

10. E. Adriaenssen, Luitmuziek [Fantasies, Danses, Madrigals from Pratum Musicum (1584), Novum Pratum (1592), Pratum Musicum II (1600)], ed. G. Spiessens [L].

XXIX. *Monumenta musicae byzantinae* [ed. C. Høeg, H. J. W. Tillyard and E. Wellesz, 1935—; liturgical music of the Eastern Orthodox Church].

A. *Principia* [facsimiles]:

1. Sticherarium [Codex Delassinos of Vienna National Library].
2. Hirmologium Athoum [Hirmologium of Mt. Athos].
3. Hirmologium e codice cryptensi, E. γ. II; Hirmologium Cryptense, Codex Cryptensis E. γ. II [Codex Cryptensis of Grottaferrata, 2 vols., one contains the facsimile, 1950; the other the index, ed. L. Tardo, 1951].
4. Contacarium Ashburnhamense [Codex Ashburnham of Laurentian Library, Florence].
5a;5b. Fragmenta Chiliandarica Palaeoslavica, A. Sticherarium; B. Hirmologium [early Slavic fragments from the Chilandri Monastery].
6. Contacarium Palaeoslavicum Mosquense [Early Slavic Contacarium of Moscow], ed. A. Bugge.
7. Specimina Notationum Antiquiorum [selected pages from various 10th-, 11th-, 12th-century MSS], ed. O. Strunk.
8. Hirmologium Sabbaiticum [Codex Saba 83], ed. J. Raasted [in prep.].

B. *Subsidia* [books on subjects related to the facsimiles]:

1.i. H. J. W. Tillyard, *Handbook of the Middle Byzantine Musical Notation.*
1.ii. C. Høeg, *La Notation ekphonétique.*
2 (Am. series 1). E. Wellesz, *Eastern Elements in Western Chant.*
3. R. P. Verdeil, *La Musique byzantine chez les Bulgares et les Russes (du IXᵉ au XIVᵉ siècle).*
4;4 suppl. M. M. Velimirović, *Byzantine Elements in Early Slavic Chant: The Hirmologion* [4 suppl. contains appendices].
5. R. P. B. di Salvo, *Canti ecclesiastici della tradizione italo-albanese, I canti della Sicilia* [in prep.].
6. R. Jakobson, ed., *Studies on the Fragmenta*

Chilian-darica Palaeoslavica. II: Fundamental Problems of Early Slavic Music and Poetry [in prep.].
7. J. Raasted, *Intonation Formulas and Modal Signatures in Byzantine Musical Manuscripts.*
8. C. Thodberg, *Der byzantinische Alleluiarionzyklus.*

C. *Transcripta:*

1. Die Hymnen des Sticherarium für September, ed. E. Wellesz.
2. The Hymns of the Sticherarium for November, ed. H. J. W. Tillyard.
3;5. The Hymns of the Octoechus [i; ii], ed. H. J. W. Tillyard.
4 (Am. series 2). Twenty Canons from the Trinity Hirmologium, ed. H. J. W. Tillyard.
6;8. The Hymns of the Hirmologium [i; iii 2], ed. A. Ayoutanti, M. Stöhr and C. Høeg; ed. A. Ayoutanti, H. J. W. Tillyard.
7. The Hymns of the Pentecostarium, ed. H. J. W. Tillyard.
9. The Akathistos Hymn, ed. E. Wellesz.
10. The Hymns of the Sticherarium for January, ed. H. J. W. Tillyard [in prep.].

D. *Lectionaria* [religious texts containing neumes]:

1. Prophetologium, i–v, ed. C. Høeg and G. Zuntz [vi in prep.].
2. Evangeliarium, ed. E. C. Colwell and S. Lake [in prep.].

XXX. *Monumenta polyphoniae italicae* [3 vols., ed. Pontif. instituto musicae sacrae, 1930—].

1. Missa cantantibus organis, Caecilia, 12 vocibus [various 16th-century composers], ed. R. Casimiri [V].
2. C. Festa, Sacrae cantiones 3, 4, 5, 6 vocibus, ed. E. Dagnino [V].
3. C. Festa, Hymni per totum annum 3, 4, 5, 6 vocibus, ed. G. Haydon [V].

XXXI. *Monumenta polyphoniae liturgicae sanctae ecclesiae Romanae* [ed. L. Feininger, 1947—. Each fascicle has a separate title page. Generally all fascicles of each vol. will be bound together].

Series I: Ordinarium missae [on cover only, not on title page].

1. Missa super L'Homme armé [from fascicle title p., no vol. title p.; Masses on *L'Homme armé*. 10 fascicles: G. Dufay, A. Busnois,

P. Caron, G. Faugues, J. Regis, J. Ockeghem, M. de Orto, Philippe Basiron, J. Tinctoris, Vaqueras].

2. Missa caput, Veterem hominem et Christus surrexit; Missa se la face ay pale, Sine nomine et Pax vobis ego sum; Missa ave regina celorum, La Mort de Saint Gothardo; Missa ecce ancilla domini, Puisque ie vis [eight Masses and two fragments in 4 fascicles, Dufay and anon.].
3.i. Missa prima super L'Homme armé [anon.].
3.ii. Missa secunda super L'Homme armé [anon.].
3.iii. Missa III super L'Homme armé [anon.].
3.iv. Missa IV super L'Homme armé [anon.].
3.v. Missa V super L'Homme armé [anon.].
4.i. G. Faugues, Missa Vinnus vina.

Series II: Proprium missae.

1. Missarum propria XVI [16 Propers of the Mass; anon., 11 are ascribed to G. Dufay].

XXXII. *Monumentos de la música española* [24 vols. to date, ed. H. Anglés and others, 1941—; rev. ed. in progress, vol. 2, 1965].

1;5;10;14-1;14-2. La música en la corte de los reyes católicos, I, Polifonía religiosa; II; III, Polifonia, profana, Cancionero musical de palacio (siglos XV–XVI); IV–1; IV–2, Cancionero musical de Palacio (siglos XV–XVI), vols. I, II, III ed. by H. Anglés, and vols. IV–1, IV–2 ed. by J. R. Figueras [V].
2. L. Venegas de Henestrosa, La música en la corte de Carlos V, con la transcripción del "Libro de cifra nueva para tecla, harpa y vihuela," ed. H. Anglés [K].
3. L. de Narvaez, Los seys libros del Delphin de música de cifra para tañer vihuela, ed. E. Pujol [L].
4. J. Vásquez, "Recopilación de sonetos y villancicos a quatro y a cinco," ed. H. Anglés [V].
6;12. F. Correa de Araujo, Libro de tientos y discursos . . . intitulado Facultad Orgánica [i, ii], ed. S. Kastner [K].
7. A. Mudarra, Tres libros de música en cifras para vihuela, ed. E. Pujol [L].
8;9. Cancionero musical de la Casa de Medinaceli (siglo XVI), I Polifonía profana, ed. M. Querol Gavaldá [V].
11;13;15;17;20;21;24. C. de Morales, Opera omnia, i, Missarum liber primus; ii, Motetes I–XXV; iii, vi, Missarum liber secundus;

iv, XVI Magnificat; v, Motetes XXVI–L; vii, Misas XVII–XXI, ed. H. Anglés [V].
16;19. F. Guerrero, Opera omnia i, ii, Canciones y villanescas espirituales, ed. V. García and M. Querol Gavaldá [incomplete V].
18. Romances y letras a tres vozes (siglo XVII), ed. M. Querol Gavaldá.
22/23. E. de Valderrábano, Libro de música de vihuela, intitulado Silva de Sirenas, ed. E. Pujol [S + L].
25;26. T. Luis de Victoria, Opera omnia, i, Missarum liber primus; ii, Motetes I–XXI, ed. H. Anglés [V].
27/28/29. A. de Cabezón, Obras de música para tecla, arpa y vihuela . . . , i, ii, iii, ed. H. Anglés.

XXXIII. *Monuments de la musique française au temps de la renaissance* [11 vols., ed. H. Expert, 1924–29, vol. 11 in 1958; sacred and secular vocal works. Sometimes bound singly or 1–3, 4–7, 8–10].

1. C. Le Jeune, Octonaires de la vanité et inconstance du monde (I–VIII).
2. P. Certon, Messes à quatre voix: *Sus le pont d'Avignon—Adiuva me—Regnum mundi.*
3. D. Le Blanc [orig. ed.], Airs de plusieurs musiciens réduits à quatre parties.
4;5. A. de Bertrand, Premier Livre des amours de Pierre de Ronsard (I–XIX); . . . (XX–XXXV).
6. A. de Bertrand, Second Livre des amours de Pierre de Ronsard.
7. A. de Bertrand, Troisième Livre de chansons.
8. C. Le Jeune, Octonaires de la vanité et inconstance du monde (IX–XII); Pseaumes des Meslanges de 1612; Dialogue à sept parties (1564) [or *Dix Pseaumes de David*].
9. C. Goudimel, Messes à quatre voix: *Audi filia.—Tant plus ie metz.—De mes ennuys.*
10;11. P. de l'Estocart, Premier (Second) Livre des octonaires de la vanité du monde [i, ii].

XXXIV. *Musica Britannica* [various editors, 1951—; rev. ed., 1958—, only a few vols. have changes, 1, 4, and 9; the remainder are reprints].

1. The Mulliner Book, ed. D. Stevens [K].
2. M. Locke and C. Gibbons, Cupid and Death, ed. E. Dent [M].
3. T. A. Arne, Comus, ed. J. Herbage [M].
4. Mediæval Carols, ed. J. Stevens [V].
5. T. Tomkins, Keyboard Music, ed. S. D. Tuttle [K].

6. J. Dowland, Ayres for Four Voices, transcribed by E. H. Fellowes, ed. T. Dart and N. Fortune [S].
7. J. Blow, Coronation Anthems; Anthems with Strings, ed. A. Lewis and H. W. Shaw [V].
8. J. Dunstable, Complete Works, ed. M. Bukofzer [V].
9. Jacobean Consort Music [J. Ward, O. Gibbons, T. Tomkins, A. Holborne and others], ed. T. Dart and W. Coates [I].
10;11;12. The Eton Choirbook: I;II;III [J. Browne, R. Davy, R. Fayrfax, G. Banester and others], ed. F. L. Harrison [V].
13. W. Boyce, Overtures, ed. G. Finzi [I].
14;19. J. Bull, Keyboard Music I;II, ed. J. Steele, F. Cameron and T. Dart [K].
15. Music of Scotland 1500–1700, ed. K. Elliott and H. M. Shire [V, I].
16. S. Storace, No Song, No Supper, ed. R. Fiske [Op].
17. J. Field, Piano Concertos, ed. F. Merrick [K + I].
18. Music at the Court of Henry VIII, ed. J. Stevens [V, I, S].
20. O. Gibbons, Keyboard Music, ed. G. Hendrie [K].
21. W. Lawes, Select Consort Music, ed. M. Lefkowitz [I].
22. Consort Songs, ed. P. Brett [I, V, S].
23. T. Weelkes, Collected Anthems, ed. D. Brown, W. Collins, P. Le Huray [V].
24. G. and R. Farnaby, Keyboard Music, ed. R. Marlow [K].
25. W. Boyce, Trio-Sonatas [in prep., I].
26. R. Dering, Secular Vocal Music [in prep., V].

XXXV. *Musica divina.* Sive thesaurus concentuum selectissimorum omni cultui divino totius anni . . . [10 vols., ed. C. Proske, J. Schrems and F. X. Haberl, 1853–1878; contains selections of 16th-century sacred vocal music; 8 vols. in 2 *Anni,* 2 extra vols.]

Annus primus; Harmonias iv. vocum continens, ed. C. Proske.

Annus secundus; Harmonias iv vel v etc. voc. continens, ed. F. X. Haberl and J. Schrems.

Selectus novus missarum [new series of Masses]; ed. C. Proske, 1855–1861.

1. Octo missas iv. v. vi et viii vocum continens [in 2 vols.].

2. Octo missas iv. v. vi. et viii vocum continens [in 2 vols.].

XXXVI. *Musica sacra; Sammlung der besten Meisterwerke des [16.,] 17. und [18.] Jahrhunderts,* also has Latin subtitle *Cantiones [XVI,] XVII, [XVIII] saeculorum praestantissimas . . .* [28 vols., ed. F. Commer, *c.* 1839–1887; sacred music, mostly 16th and 17th centuries; rev. ed., 2 vols., ed. H. F. Redlich, vol. 1 has subtitle *Meister des Orgelbarock,* 1931, vol. 2 has subtitle of orig. series, 1932].

Other publications with the same name:

Musica sacra; Sammlung religiöser Gesänge älterer und neuester Zeit [and other subtitles; *c.* 12 vols., ed. H. A. Neithardt and others, *c.* 1851–*c.* 1896, vols. numbered 5–16. Parallel series to the one above, contains church music. Numbered in prospectus (see vol. 2 of series above) as vols. 5–14; intended as a continuation of the first four vols. of series above. The content and numbering of vols. 14–16 vary with different libraries].

Italia sacra musica [3 vols., ed. K. Jeppesen, 1962—; Italian church music from the first half of the 16th century].

Musica sacra, Sammlung berühmter Kirchenmusik [2 vols., ed. A. Dörffel, 1889?].

XXXVII. *Musical Antiquarian Society* [publications of, 19 vols., *c.* 1840–*c.* 1848; vols. are unnumbered. Has been reprinted. The numbering system used here is that found in most other sources].

1. W. Byrd, A Mass for Five Voices, ed. E. F. Rimbault [V].
2. J. Wilbye, The First Set of Madrigals, ed. J. Turle [V].
3. O. Gibbons, Madrigals and Motets, ed. G. Smart [V].
4. H. Purcell, Dido and Aeneas, ed. G. A. Macfarren [Op].
5. T. Morley, The First Set of Ballets, ed. E. F. Rimbault [V].
6. W. Byrd, Book 1, of Cantiones sacrae, for Five Voices, ed. W. Horsley [V].
7. H. Purcell, Bonduca [music for the play, *Bonduca*], ed. E. F. Rimbault [Op].
8. T. Weelkes, The First Set of Madrigals, ed. E. J. Hopkins [V].
9. O. Gibbons, Fantasies in Three Parts, Composed for Viols, ed. E. F. Rimbault [I].

10. H. Purcell, King Arthur, ed. E. Taylor [Op].
11. T. East, orig. pub., The Whole Book of Psalms, ed. E. F. Rimbault [V].
12. J. Dowland, The First Set of Songs, ed. W. Chappell [S].
13. J. Hilton, Ayres or Fa las, ed. J. Warren [S].
14. A Collection of Anthems [M. East, T. Ford, T. Weelkes, T. Bateson], ed. E. F. Rimbault [V, I].
15. J. Bennet, Madrigals for Four Voices, ed. E. J. Hopkins [V].
16. J. Wilbye, The Works of John Wilbye [second set of madrigals and appendix], ed. G. W. Budd [V].
17. T. Bateson, [The First Set of English Madrigales; title page lacking], ed. E. F. Rimbault [V].
18. Parthenia, or the First Musick ever Printed for the Virginals (W. Byrd, J. Bull, O. Gibbons), ed. E. F. Rimbault [K].
19. H. Purcell, Ode, Composed for the Anniversary of St. Cecilia's Day, A.D. 1692, ed. E. F. Rimbault [S].

XXXVIII. *Musikalische Denkmäler* [6 vols., Kommission für Musikwissenschaft, Akademie der Wissenschaften und der Literatur in Mainz, 1955—].

1. Oberitalienische Figuralpassionen des 16. Jahrhunderts [Maistre Jan (Nasco), C. de Rore, Jachet von Mantua, G. M. Asola], ed. A. Schmitz [V].
2. G. Binchois, Die Chansons von Gilles Binchois (1400–1460), ed. W. Rehm [S].
3. 46 Choräle für Orgel von J. P. Sweelinck und seinen deutschen Schülern [J. P. Sweelinck, A. Düben, P. Hasse, J. Praetorius, H. Scheidemann, G. Scheidt and others], ed. G. Gerdes [K].
4. G. Frescobaldi, Arie musicali (Florenz 1630), ed. H. Spohr [S].
5. G. Mainerio, Il Primo Libro de balli (Venedig 1578), ed. M. Schuler [I].
6. Mehrstimmige Lamentationen aus der ersten Hälfte des 16. Jahrhunderts [anon., C. de Sermisy, J. Gardano, T. Crecquillon and others], ed. G. Massenkeil [V].

XXXIX. *Das Musikwerk; eine Beispielsammlung zur Musikgeschichte* [31 vols., some unnumbered, ed. K. G. Fellerer, 1951—; *Anthology of Music*, 1959—, reprint with introductions in English, vols. 1–21 available. Titles are for the German edition. In most cases the number of composers represented in each vol. is too large to list individually].

[1]. 400 Jahre europäischer Klaviermusik, ed. W. Georgii [K].
[2]. Troubadours, Trouvères, Minne- und Meistergesang, ed. F. Gennrich [S].
[3]. Das mehrstimmige Lied des 16. Jahrhunderts in Italien, Frankreich und England, ed. H. Engel [A rev. German version, 1952, includes Spanish composers as well. New edition is given a volume number].
4. Europäischer Volksgesang, Gemeinsame Formen in charakteristischen Abwandlungen, ed. W. Wiora [S].
[5]. Die Oper von den Anfängen bis zum Beginn des 19. Jahrhunderts [G. Caccini, C. W. Gluck, Mozart, L. Spohr and others], ed. A. A. Abert [Op].
[6]. Die musikalische Klassik [G. B. Sammartini, J. J. Quantz, Haydn, Mozart and others], ed. K. Stephenson [K, I, K arr.].
[7]. Die italienische Triosonate [F. Turini, A. Caldara, G. Pugnani and others], ed. E. Schenk [I].
[8]. Das Charakterstück, ed. W. Kahl [K, L, I].
[9]. Die mittelalterliche Mehrstimmigkeit, ed. H. Husmann [V].
[10]. Das deutsche Chorlied vom 16. Jahrhundert bis zur Gegenwart [H. Finck, C. Othmayr, J. S. Bach, F. Schubert, M. Reger and others], ed. H. Osthoff [V].
[11]. Die Variation, ed. K. von Fischer [K, I, L].
[12]. Die Improvisation in Beispielen aus neun Jahrhunderten abendländischer Musik, ed. E. T. Ferand [I, V].
13. Die Musik der Byzantinischen Kirche, ed. E. Wellesz [V].
14/15. Das deutsche Sololied und die Ballade, ed. H. J. Moser [S].
15. Die Solosonate, ed. F. Giegling [K, I].
16. Das ausserdeutsche Sololied 1500–1900, ed. F. Noske [S].
[17]. Die Tokkata, ed. E. Valentin [L, K].
18. Der Gregorianische Choral, ed. F. Tack [S].
19. Die Fuge, Heft I, von den Anfängen bis zu Johann Sebastian Bach, ed. A. Adrio [K].
20. Hebräische Musik, ed. E. Werner [V].
21. Romantik in der Tonkunst, ed. K. Stephenson [K, S].
22. Die Kunst der Niederländer, ed. R. B. Lenaerts [V, K, L, I].
23. Das Concerto Grosso, ed. H. Engel [I].

24. Geschichte der Instrumentation, ed. H. Becker [I].
25. Das Solokonzert, ed. H. Engel [I].
26. Die Suite, ed. H. Beck [I, K].
27. Der Tanz, ed. G. Reichert.
28. Altklassische Polyphonie, ed. K. G. Fellerer [V].
29. Die Sinfonie, ed. L. Hoffmann-Erbrecht [I].
30. Geschichte der Messe, ed. J. Schmidt-Görg [V].
32. Die Kantate, ed. R. Jakoby.

XL. *The Old English Edition* [25 vols., ed. G. E. P. Arkwright, 1889–1902; reprinted 1965, bound together or individually].

1. T. Campion, T. Lupo, and T. Giles, Masque in Honour of the Marriage of Lord Hayes (1607) [M].
2. T. A. Arne, Six Songs [S].
3–5. G. Kirbye, Six Madrigals to Four Voices; Twelve Madrigals to Five Voices; Six Madrigals to Six Voices [V].
6–9. W. Byrd, Songs of Sundry Natures, Nine Songs to Four Voices; ... Twelve Songs to Five Voices; ... Fourteen Songs to Three Voices; ... Ten Songs to Six Voices [S].
10. C. Tye, Mass to Six Voices, "Euge bone" [V].
11–12. A. Ferrabosco (the elder), Nine Madrigals to Five Voices, from Musica transalpina, 1588; Five Madrigals to Six Voices ... [V].
13–15. T. Weelkes, Eight Ballets and Madrigals [V].
16–17. T. Weelkes, Airs or Fantastic Spirits [S].
18–20. F. Pilkington, The First Book of Songs or Airs of Four Parts [S].
21. R. White, G. Kirbye, J. Wilbye and W. Daman, Anthems and Motets [V].
22. J. Milton, Six Anthems [V].
23. J. Blow, Six Songs ... selected from the Amphion Anglicus, 1700 [S].
24. H. Purcell, Six Songs ... selected from the Orpheus Britannicus [S].
25. J. Blow, "Venus and Adonis." A Masque [M].

XLI. *Organum; ausgewählte ältere vokale und instrumentale Meisterwerke* [ed. M. Seiffert, †1948, ed. A. Albrecht, †1961, ed. L. Hoffmann-Erbrecht from 1960; 1924—. In 5 series; usually each vol. is devoted to a single composer, earlier vols. being reprinted].

Reihe [series] 1: Geistliche Gesangsmusik für Solo- oder Chorstimmen mit oder ohne Begleitung; [33 vols., ed. M. Seiffert, vols. 1–24, ed. H. Albrecht from vol. 25; 1924—. M. Weckmann, J. P. Krieger, F. Tunder, D. Buxtehude, G. H. Stölzel, J. C. Frauenholtz, and others; Melodeyen-Gesangbuch of 1604 (vols. 25–27); Niederländische Bildmotetten aus dem 16. Jahrhundert i, ii (vols. 19, 20; motets, pictures, sources given)].

Reihe [series] 2: Weltliche Gesangsmusik für Solo- oder Chorstimmen mit oder ohne Begleitung; [20 vols., ed. M. Seiffert, 1924–39. J. P. Sweelinck, G. F. Handel, H. Schütz, and others].

Reihe [series] 3: Kammermusik; [69 vols., ed. M. Seiffert, vols. 1–34; ed. H. Albrecht from vol. 35—, ed. L. Hoffmann-Erbrecht from 1960; 1924—. A. Corelli, G. P. Telemann, J. P. Krieger, P. H. Erlebach, I. Pleyel, M. Haydn, and others].

Reihe [series] 4: Orgelmusik; [22 vols., ed. M. Seiffert, 1925—. G. Böhm, F. Tunder, N. Bruhns, J. Pachelbel, J. Krieger, and others].

Reihe [series] 5: Klaviermusik; [34 vols., ed. H. Albrecht and L. Hoffmann-Erbrecht, 1950—. M. Clementi, K. P. E. Bach, J. L. Dussek, L. A. Koželuch, E. W. Wolf, J. N. Hummel, D. G. Türk, J. B. Cramer, and others].

XLII. *Paléographie musicale* [19 vols., ed. the Benedictines of *Solesmes, Dom A. Mocquereau to 1930, Dom J. Gajard since 1931; 1889—. Contains facsimiles and studies of plainsong MSS. Subtitle for series: *Les Principaux Manuscrits de chant grégorien, ambrosien, mozarabe, gallican*].

A. *First Series:*

1. Le Codex 339 de la bibliothèque de Saint-Gall (xe siècle), Antiphonale missarum sancti Gregorii.
2;3. Le Répons-Graduel Justus ut palma.
4. Le Codex 121 de la bibliothèque d'Einsiedeln (x^e-xie siècle), Antiphonale missarum sancti Gregorii.
5;6. Antiphonarium Ambrosianum du musée britannique (xiie siècle), Codex additional 34209.
7;8. Antiphonarium tonale missarum, xie siècle, Codex H. 159, de la bibliothèque de l'école de médecine de Montpellier.
9. Antiphonaire monastique, xiie siècle, Codex

601 de la bibliothèque capitulaire de Lucques.

10. Antiphonale missarum Sancti Gregorii, ixᵉ-xᵉ siècle, Codex 239 de la bibliothèque de Laon.

11. Antiphonale missarum Sancti Gregorii, xᵉ siècle, Codex 47 de la bibliothèque de Chartres.

12. Antiphonaire monastique, xiiiᵉ siècle, Codex F. 160 de la bibliothèque de la cathédrale de Worcester.

13. Le Codex 903 de la bibliothèque nationale de Paris (xiᵉ siècle), Graduel de Saint-Yrieix.

14. Le Codex 10673 de la bibliothèque vaticane, fonds Latin (xiᵉ siècle), Graduel Bénéventain.

15. Le Codex VI. 34 de la bibliothèque capitulaire de Bénévent (xiᵉ-xiiᵉ siècle), Graduel de Bénévent avec prosaire et tropaire.

16. Le Manuscrit du Mont-Renaud, xᵉ siècle, Graduel et antiphonaire de Noyon.

17. [No title page, manuscripts of liturgical chant (miscellaneous), Chartres].

B. *Second Series* (Monumentale); vol. 1, 1900, vol. 2, 1924:

1. B. Hartker [scribe], Antiphonale officii monastici écrit par le B. Hartker, no. 390–391, de la bibliothèque de Saint-Gall.

2. Cantatorium, ixᵉ siècle, no. 359 de la bibliothèque de Saint-Gall.

XLIII. *Plainsong and Mediaeval Music Society* [1890—. The publications are not issued as a set and are unnumbered. A selection from the numerous publications has been chosen, mainly the facsimiles and scholarly dissertations, rather than the transcriptions for English school and church use or the explanations for plainsong performance. (For a complete listing through 1959 see Dom A. Hughes, *Septuagesima*, 1959.) The numbering system used is for cross-reference purposes only. The volumes are arranged in the order of publication date].

1. [Muscial Notation of the Middle Ages; no title page, some facsimiles], ed. H. B. Briggs.

2. A Collection of Songs and Madrigals . . . of the Close of the Fifteenth Century [transcriptions of English secular vocal music; no music before 1500, no madrigals].

3. Graduale Sarisburiense [facsimile i, bound with 5], ed. W. H. Frere.

4. Madrigals . . . of the Close of the Fifteenth Century [6 transcriptions of English secular vocal music; no music before 1500, no madrigals].

5. Graduale Sarisburiense [facsimile ii and introduction, bound with 3], ed. W. H. Frere.

6. Bibliotheca musico-liturgica [i, ii; list of musical and Latin-liturgical MSS of the Middle Ages in the British Isles], ed. W. H. Frere.

7. The Sarum Gradual and Gregorian Antiphonale Missarum [reprint of intro. to 3 and 5], ed. W. H. Frere.

8. Early English Harmony from the 10th to the 15th Century [i, facsimiles], ed. H. E. Wooldridge.

9. Antiphonale Sarisburiense [3 vols. of facsimile of Mm.ii.9 and an introductory vol.; introductory vol. reissued in 1927], ed. W. H. Frere.

10. T. Petri, orig. pub., Piae cantiones [collection of chiefly ancient Swedish church and school songs, 1582], ed. G. R. Woodward.

11. Early English Harmony from the 11th to the 15th Century [ii, transcriptions and notes], ed. H. V. Hughes.

12. Pars Antiphonarii [facsimiles of incomplete MS B.iii.II at Durham], ed. W. H. Frere.

13. Mass "O quam suavis" for Five Voices [transcription of Cambridge MS Nn.vi.46], ed. H. B. Collins.

14. Worcester Mediaeval Harmony of the Thirteenth & Fourteenth Centuries [transcriptions of 13th- and 14th-century sources, facsimiles, notes], ed. Dom A. Hughes.

15. The Old Hall Manuscript [i–iii, transcription, a few facsimiles], ed. A. Ramsbotham, H. B. Collins and Dom A. Hughes.

16. Polyphonia sacra [transcriptions of 15th-century vocal music from the Bodleian MS Canonici misc. 213], ed. C. Van den Borren.

17. Anglo-French Sequelae [from the collection of H. M. Bannister], ed. Dom A. Hughes.

18. Early English Organ Music (16th Century), ed. M. Glyn.

19. The Play of Daniel [liturgical drama transcribed], ed. W. L. Smolden.

XLIV. *Portugaliae musica* [10 vols., ed. M. S. Kastner, M. Joaquim and others, 1959—; 16th- to mid-19th century Portuguese masters; may be numbered and/or grouped by series A and B].

1 (A);3 (A). M. R. Coelho, Flores de musica pera o instrumento de tecla & harpa [i, book of tentos or ricercars, appendix contains 3rd

tento of the first tone; ii, compositions on liturgical themes], ed. M. S. Kastner [K].

2 (B). J. de Sousa Carvalho, L'Amore industrioso [overture], ed. F. de Sousa [I, score and parts].

4 (A). E. Lopes Morago, Várias obras de música religiosa "a cappella," ed. M. Joaquim [V].

5 (A);6 (A). M. Cardoso, Liber primus missarum [i; ii], ed. J. A. Alegria [V].

7 (A). J. da Costa de Lisboa, G. dos Reis and others, Tenção [selections from], ed. C. R. Fernandes [K].

8 (B). J. D. Bomtempo, Symphonia No. 1/ Opus 11, ed. F. de Sousa [I; score and parts].

9 (B). M. Portugal, Il Duca di foix [overture], ed. M. de Sampayo Ribeiro [I, score and parts].

10 (A). C. Seixas, 80 Sonatas para instrumentos de tecla, ed. M. S. Kastner [K].

J. Rodrigues Esteves, Stabat mater; Miserere, ed. M. de Sampayo Ribeiro [in prep., V].

V. Lusitano, Obras completas, ed. M. A. Barbosa [in prep.].

XLV. *Publications of Medieval Music Manuscripts* [*Veröffentlichungen mittelalterlicher Musikhandschriften,* 11 vols., 1957—; facsimile reproductions of MSS. This edition may be listed under Institute of Medieval Music in some libraries. Titles given in both German and English on volume].

1. Facsimile Reproduction of the Manuscript Madrid 20486 [intro. by L. Dittmer].

2. Facsimile Reproduction of the Manuscript Wolfenbüttel 1099 (1206) [intro. by L. Dittmer].

3. *A Central Source of Notre-Dame Polyphony* [by L. Dittmer].

4. Paris 13521 & 11411, Facsimile, Introduction, Index and Transcriptions from the Manuscripts Paris. Bibl. nat. nouv. acq. fr. 13521 (La Clayette) and lat. 11411 [by L. Dittmer].

5. Worcester Add. 68, Westminster Abbey 33327, Madrid, Bibl. nac. 192, Facsimile, Introduction, Index and Transcriptions [by L. Dittmer].

6. Oxford, Latin liturgical D 20, London, Add. MS 25031, Chicago, MS 654 App., Facsimile, Introduction, Index and Transcriptions [by L. Dittmer].

7. Opera omnia Faugues, Facsimile of the compositions of Faugues from the Manuscripts . . . [intro. by G. Schuetze, Jr.].

8. Facsimile Reproduction of the Manuscripts Sevilla 5-1-53 & Paris N. A. Fr. 4379 (Pt. 1) [intro. by D. Plamenac].

9. Carmina Burana, Facsimile Reproduction of the Manuscript Clm 4660 and Clm 4660a, ed. B. Bischoff.

10;11. Firenze, Biblioteca mediceo-laurenziana, pluteo 29, I, ed. L. Dittmer.

XLVI. *Publikationen älterer Musik* [ed. T. Kroyer and H. Schultz, 1926–40, reprinted 1967—, vols. 2, 3ii, 4i, 6, 8, 11 available. The first number is *Jahrgang,* the second *Teil.* Volumes containing the same composer's works have consecutive *Band* numbers, found in brackets].

1.i. G. de Machaut, Musikalische Werke, erster Band, Balladen, Rondeaux und Virelais, ed. F. Ludwig [V].

1.ii. J. Ockeghem, Sämtliche Werke, erster Band, Messen I–VIII, ed. D. Plamenac. [*Band* ii of Ockeghem's works was at the printer's in 1930 but was not published until 1947 by American Musicological Society, without the series title, V].

2. L. Milán, Libro de música de vihuela de mano, ed. L. Schrade [L]. Also numbered as vols. 4 and 5 of Sächs. Staatliche Forschungsinstitut für Musikwissenschaft.

3.i. G. de Machaut, *Musikalische Werke, zweiter Band, Einleitung zu I. Balladen, Rondeaux und Virelais II. Motetten III. Messe und Lais* [musical works ii; preface to vols. i, iii, and iv by F. Ludwig]. Also vol. 6 of SSFM, see entry above.

3.ii. *Sixtus Dietrich, Ein Beitrag zur Musik und Musikanschauung im Zeitalter der Reformation* [S. Dietrich, composer, a contribution to the music and the conception of music in the time of the Reformation by H. Zenck]. Also vol. 7 of SSFM, Abhandlungen 1.

4.i;6. L. Marenzio, Sämtliche Werke, erster Band, Madrigale für fünf Stimmen, Buch I–III; . . . zweiter Band, Madrigale für fünf Stimmen, Buch IV–VI, ed. A. Einstein [V].

4.ii. G. de Machaut, Musikalische Werke, dritter Band, Motetten, ed. F. Ludwig. Also vol. 8 of SSFM [V].

5;7. Das Graduale der St. Thomaskirche zu Leipzig (14. Jahrhundert) als Zeuge deutscher Choralüberlieferung, erster Band, von Advent bis Christi Himmelfahrt; . . . zweiter

Band, von Christi Himmelfahrt bis Advent, sanctorale und ordinarium Missae, ed. P. Wagner. Also vols. 9 and 10 of SSFM [V].

8. O. Petrucci [orig. pub.], Frottole, Buch I und IV nach den Erstlings-Drucken von 1504 und 1505 (?), ed. R. Schwartz. Also vol. 11 of SSFM [V].

9. A. Willaert, Sämtliche Werke, erster Band, Motetten zu 4 Stimmen, I. und II. Buch (1539 und 1545), ed. H. Zenck [V].

10. *Das Madrigal als Formideal; Eine stilkundliche Untersuchung mit Belegen aus dem Schaffen des Andrea Gabrieli*. Also 13 of SSFM, Abhandlungen 2.

11. Die drei- und vierstimmigen Notre-Dame-Organa, Kritische Gesamtausgabe (mit Einleitung), ed. H. Husmann. Also vol. 14 of SSFM [V].

[12]. G. de Machaut, Musikalische Werke, vierter Band, Messe und Lais [from Ludwig's MSS, ed. H. Besseler, 1943—destroyed in print. Reprinted 1954 as vol. 4 of the *Opera omnia* with no ref. to the *Publ. ält. Mus.;* vols. 1–3 of the *Opera omnia* also reprinted 1954 with indication that earlier they were part of the *Publ. ält. Mus.*]

XLVII. *Publikationen älterer praktischer und theoretischer Musikwerke* [29 vols. or 33 *Jahrgänge;* ed. R. Eitner, 1873–1905; reprinted, 1965. Numbers in parentheses are *Jahrgang* numbers. Numbers in brackets are *Jahrgang* numbers that do not appear on the volumes themselves but can be inferred from the sequence. May also be listed under Gesellschaft für Musikforschung in some libraries. Vols. may be bound together].

1–3;4 (1–3;4). J. Ott, orig. ed., Ein Hundert fünfzehn weltliche u. einige geistliche Lieder [H. Isaac, L. Senfl, T. Stoltzer, S. Mahu and others]; 4, *Einleitung, Biographieen, Melodieen und Gedichte zu Johann Ott's Liedersammlung von 1544* [preface, biographies, texts and melodies for 1–3], ed. R. Eitner, L. Erk and O. Kade [V].

5 (4.ii). P. A. Schubiger [author], *Musikalische Spicilegien über das liturgische Drama, Orgelbau und Orgelspiel, das ausserliturgische Lied und die Instrumentalmusik des Mittelalters* [about the liturgical drama, organ building, organ playing, the nonliturgical song, the instrumental music of the Middle Ages].

6 (5). Josquin Desprès, Iodocus pratensis

(1440 oder 50 bis 1521). Eine Sammlung ausgewählter Kompositionen [selected compositions, 1 Mass, motets, Psalms and chansons], ed. R. Schlecht and R. Eitner [V].

7 [6]. J. Walther, Wittembergisch geistlich Gesangbuch von 1524, ed. O. Kade [V].

8 (7). Heinrich and Hermann Finck, Eine Sammlung ausgewählter Kompositionen [selected compositions, German sacred and secular part songs, hymns, motets], ed. R. Eitner [V].

9 (8). E. Oeglin [orig. ed.], Liederbuch zu vier Stimmen, Augsburg 1512 [anon. but possibly P. Hofhaimer, H. Isaac, A. Rener and others], ed. R. Eitner and J. J. Maier.

10 (9). G. Caccini, M. da Gagliano, C. Monteverdi, Die Oper von ihren ersten Anfängen bis zur Mitte des 18. Jahrhunderts. Erster Thiel: Einleitung, Caccini's Euridice, Gagliano's Dafne und Monteverde's Orfeo, ed. R. Eitner [Op].

11 [10]. S. Virdung, Musica getutscht und auszgezogen [facsimile], ed. R. Eitner.

12 [11]. P. F. Cavalli, M. A. Cesti, Die Oper von ihren ersten Anfängen bis zur Mitte des 18. Jahrhunderts. Zweiter Theil: Francesco Cavalli's Il Giasone (1649) und Marc' Antonio Cesti's La Dori (1663), ed. R. Eitner [Op].

13 [12]. M. Praetorius, Syntagma. II. Teil, Von den Instrumenten. Wolfenbüttel 1618, ed. R. Eitner.

14 [13]. J. B. Lully, Die Oper von ihren ersten Anfängen bis zur Mitte des 18. Jahrhunderts. Dritter Theil: Jean Baptiste de Lully's Armide, ed. R. Eitner [Op].

14.ii (14). A. Scarlatti, La Rosaura, ed. R. Eitner [Op].

15 (15). H. L. Hassler, Lustgarten. Eine Sammlung deutsche Lieder . . . nebst elf Instrumentalsätzen, ed. F. Zelle [V, I].

16 (16–18). H. Glareanus, Dodecachordon, Basileae MDXLVII, ed. P. Bohn.

17 (19). G. K. Schürmann, Die Oper von ihren ersten Anfängen bis zur Mitte des 18. Jahrhunderts. Vierter Theil: Georg Caspar Schürmann: Ludovicus Pius oder Ludewig der Fromme, ed. H. Sommer [Op].

18 [20–22]. R. Keiser, Die Oper von ihren ersten Anfängen bis zur Mitte des 18. Jahrhunderts. Fünfter Theil: Reinhard Keiser: Der lächerliche Prinz Jodelet, ed. F. Zelle [Op].

19 (23). J. Regnart, L. Lechner, J. Regnart's Deutsche dreistimmige Lieder nach Art der

Neapolitanen nebst L. Lechner's Fünfstimmiger Bearbeitung, ed. R. Eitner [V].

20 (24). M. Agricola [author], Musica instrumentalis deudsch, erste und vierte Ausgabe [facsimile], ed. R. Eitner.

21 [25]. J. Eccard, Neue geistliche und weltliche Lieder . . . Königsberg 1589, ed. R. Eitner [V].

22 (26). J. Burck, Zwanzig deutsche geistliche vierstimmige Lieder, Erfurt 1575. Die Passion nach dem Evangelisten Johannes zu vier Stimmen. Wittenberg 1568 und Die Passion nach dem 22. Psalmen Davids (1574), ed. A. Halm and R. Eitner [V].

23 (27). P. Attaingnant, orig. pub., 60 Chansons [J. Arcadelt, P. Certon, P. Sandrin, C. de Sermisy and others], ed. R. Eitner [S].

24 (28). G. Dressler, XVII Motetten, ed. A. Halm and R. Eitner [V].

25 [29]. H. G. Lange, Eine ausgewählte Sammlung Motetten [24 motets from his *Cantiones sacrae*], ed. R. Starke [V].

26 [30]. O. Vecchi, L'Amfiparnaso, ed. R. Eitner [Op].

27 [31]. J. M. Leclair (the elder), Zwölf Sonaten für Violine und Generalbass nebst einem Trio für Violine, Violoncell und Generalbass. 2. Buch der Sonaten, ed. R. Eitner [I].

28 [32]. M. Zeuner, 82 geistliche Kirchenlieder, ed. R. Eitner [V].

29 (33). G. Forster, orig. ed., Der zweite Teil der kurtzweiligen guten frischen teutschen Liedlein [A. von Bruck, G. Forster, L. Senfl and others], ed. R. Eitner [S].

XLVIII. *Smith College Music Archives* [15 vols., ed. R. L. Finney, 1935—].

1. F. Geminiani, Twelve Sonatas for Violin and Piano, ed. R. L. Finney [I + K].

2. J. J. Fux, Costanza e fortezza, ed. G. P. Smith [Op].

3. L. Boccherini, Concerto for Cello and String Orchestra, ed. M. DeRonde [I].

4. A. Antico, orig. pub., Canzoni sonetti strambotti et frottole, libro tertio, ed. A. Einstein [S].

5. J. Arcadelt, The Chansons of Jacques Arcadelt, ed. E. B. Helm [S].

6. C. de Rore, The Madrigals of Cipriano de Rore for 3 and 4 Voices, ed. G. P. Smith [V].

7. F. Caccini, La Liberazione di Ruggiero dal l'isola d'Alcina, ed. D. Silbert [B].

8. V. Galilei, Contrapunti a due voci 1584, ed. L. Rood [I].

9. G. Tartini, Concerto in A Minor; Concerto in F Major for Solo Violin and String Orchestra, ed. G. Ross [I].

10. J. Haydn, Symphony No. 87 in A Major, ed. A. Einstein [I].

11. A. Steffani, 8 Songs for Solo Voice, One or Two Woodwinds and Continuo, ed. G. P. Smith [S + I].

12. T. A. Vitali, Concerto di sonate, Opus 4 for Violin, Violoncello, and Continuo, ed. D. Silbert, G. P. Smith and L. Rood [I].

13. P. Quagliati, La Sfera armoniosa and Il Carro di fedeltà d'amore, ed. V. D. Gotwals and P. Keppler [Op].

14. G. B. Vitali, Artifici musicali, Opus XIII [canons], ed. L. Rood and G. P. Smith [V, I].

15. J. Brahms, 28 Folk Songs, Canons, and Songs arr. for Womens Voices [Drinker MSS], ed. V. Gotwals and P. Keppler [S].

XLIX. *Société française de musicologie, Publications* [28 vols., 3 series, various editors, 1925—].

Series I, Monuments de la musique ancienne:

1. P. Attaingnant [orig. ed.], Deux Livres d'orgue parus chez Pierre Attaingnant en 1531, ed. Y. Rokseth [K].

2. Beethoven, Oeuvres inédites de Beethoven, ed. G. de Saint-Foix [K, I].

3–4. [Falsely designated 4–5]. Chansons au luth et airs de cour français du xvie siècle, ed. L. de la Laurencie, A. Mairy and G. Thibault [S, L].

5. P. Attaingnant [orig. ed.], Treize motets et un prélude pour orgue parus chez Pierre Attaingnant en 1531, ed. Y. Rokseth [K].

6;7. D. Gaultier, La Rhétorique des dieux et autres pièces de luth, ed. A. Tessier and J. Cordey [L].

8. J.-H. d'Anglebert, Pièces de clavecin, ed. M. Roesgen-Champion [K].

9. J.-J. Cassanea de Mondonville, Pièces de clavecin en sonates, ed. M. Pincherle [K].

10. Le Manuscrit de musique du trésor d'Apt (XIVe–XVe siècle) [Codex Apt, MS of polyphonic music], ed. A. Gastoué [V].

11;12. A. Boieldieu, Sonates pour le pianoforte, ed. G. Favre [K].

13. G. Jullien, Premier Livre d'orgue, ed. N. Dufourcq [K].

14. G.-G. Nivers, Troisième Livre d'orgue, ed. N. Dufourcq [K].

15. G. de Coinci, Les Chansons à la Vierge, ed. J. Chailley [S].
16. Airs de cour pour voix et luth (1603–1643), ed. A. Verchaly [S + L].
17. Anthologie du motet latin polyphonique en France (1609–1661), ed. D. Launay [V].

Series II. Documents et catalogues [1930—]:

1-2. *Inventaire critique du fonds Blancheton de la Bibliothèque du Conservatoire de Musique Paris,* ed. L. de la Laurencie.
3-4. *Mélanges de musicologie,* ed. L. de la Laurencie.
5-6. *Documents inédits relatifs à l'orgue français* i, ii, ed. N. Dufourcq.
7. *Catalogue des livres de musique (manuscrits et imprimés) de la Bibliothèque de l'Arsenal à Paris,* ed. L. de la Laurencie and A. Gastoué.
8. *Bibliographie des poésies de P. de Ronsard mises en musique au xvie siècle,* ed. G. Thibault and L. Perceau.
9. *Bibliographie des éditions d'Adrian Le Roy et Robert Ballard,* ed. F. Lesure and G. Thibault.
10. *La Musique dans les congrès internationaux (1835–1939),* ed. M. Briquet.
11. *Les Facteurs de clavecins parisiens; notices biographiques et documents (1550–1793),* ed. C. Samoyault-Verlet.

Series III, Etudes [1951—]:

1. C. Marot, *Les Chansons de Clément Marot, étude historique et bibliographique,* ed. J. Rollin.

L. *Trésor musical* [Collection authentique de musique sacrée & profane des anciens maîtres belges, 58 vols.; or 29 années (years) each with 2 separate parts titled *Musique religieuse* and *Musique profane,* ed. R.-J. van Maldeghem, 1865–93; contains sacred and secular music mostly of the 16th century; reprinted 1965 in 6 vols. Detailed index in *GD* v, 377ff (not in *GDB*); for corrections see G. Reese, "Maldeghem and his Buried Treasure," *Notes,* Series 2, vi, 75ff].

1. Musique profane [années 1–12].
2. Musique profane [années 13–29].
3. Musique religieuse [années 1–12].
4. Musique religieuse [années 13–29].
5. Musique profane [individual voice parts pub. between 1881–93].

6. Musique religieuse [individual voice parts, pub. between 1882–93].

LI. *Tudor Church Music* [10 vols. and 1 supplementary vol., various editors, 1922–29, 1948; vocal church music of 16th- and 17th-century England. Some vols. have only the series title and the name of composer, no individual title].

1. J. Taverner, Part I [Masses].
2. W. Byrd, English Church Music: Part I.
3. J. Taverner, Part II [motets, Magnificats, Masses, etc.].
4. O. Gibbons [anthems, Psalms, services, etc.].
5. R. White [motets, Magnificats, lamentations, anthems, etc.].
6. T. Tallis [Masses, Magnificats, motets, etc.].
7. W. Byrd, Gradualia, Books I and II [sacred part songs].
8. T. Tomkins, Part I: Services.
9. W. Byrd, Masses, Cantiones [sacred part songs], and Motets.
10. H. Aston, J. Marbeck, O. Parsley [Masses, motets, etc.].

Appendix with Supplementary Notes [by E. H. Fellowes], 1948.

LII. *Ver[e]eniging voor [Noord-] Nederlands[che] Muziekgeschiedenis* [46 vols., 1869–1955; most vols. have both score and parts. The complete works of Sweelinck, ed. M. Seiffert, Obrecht, ed. J. Wolf, and Josquin des Prez, ed. A. Smijers, are also published by this society. This series may also be catalogued under Maatschappij tot bevordering der toonkunst (Society for the Advancement of Music)].

1. J. P. Sweelinck, Regina coeli (1619), ed. H. A. Viotta [V].
2. A. Valerius, Oud-Nederlandsche Liederen uit den "Nederlandtschen Gedenck-clank," ed. A. D. Loman [S].
3. J. P. Sweelinck, Zeven Orgelstukken, ed. R. Eitner [K].
4. Twaalf Geuzeliedjes uit de Geusen Liedenboecxkens van 1588 en later, ed. A. D. Loman [S].
5. C. Schuijt [Schuyt], Drie madrigalen; J. P. Sweelinck, Twee chansons; ed. R. Eitner [V].
6. J. P. Sweelinck, Acht zes-stemmige Psalmen, ed. R. Eitner [V].
7. J. P. Sweelinck, Chanson [S].
8. J. Wanning, Bloemlezing uit de 52 Sententiae, ed. R. Eitner [V].

9. J. Obrecht, Missa fortuna desperata, ed. R. Eitner [V].
10. Oud-Nederlandsche danswijzen, ed. J. C. M. van Riemsdijk [arr. for K].
[11]. C. Huygens, Correspondance et oeuvre musicales de Constantin Huygens [contains preface, correspondence and *Pathodia sacra et profana occupati*], ed. W. J. A. Jonckbloet and J. P. N. Land [S]. No. vol. number and issued as part of a French series, libraries and prospectus list as part of this series.
12. J. P. Sweelinck, Zes vierstemmige Psalmen, ed. R. Eitner [V].
13. J. A. Reinken, Hortus musicus, ed. J. C. M. van Riemsdijk [I].
14. J. A. Reinken, Partite diverse sopra l'aria: Schweiget mir von Weiber nehmen [K].
15. J. P. Sweelinck, Cantio sacra, "Hodie Christus natus est" (vijfstemmig) [V].
16. Vier en twintig Liederen uit de 15de en 16de eeuw, ed. J. C. M. van Diemsdijk [S].
17. J. P. Sweelinck, Psalm 150 (achtstemmig) [V].
18. J. Obrecht, Passio domini nostri Jesu Christi secundum Matthaeum (vierstemmig), ed. D. de Lange [V].
19. A. van Noordt, Tabulatuur-Boeck van Psalmen en Fantasyen, Amsterdam 1659, ed. M. Seiffert [K].
20/23/33/36. Oud-Hollandsche Boerenliedjes en Contradansen, ed. J. Röntgen [I].
21. Marschen in gebruik bij het Nederlandsche Leger gedurende den Spaanschen successie-oorlog 1702–1713, ed. J. W. Enschedé [arr. for K].
22. C. Boscoop, 50 Psalmen Davids met vier partijen, ed. M. Seiffert [V].
24. J. Tollius Zesstemmige Madrigalen, ed. M. Seiffert [V].
25;27. Nederlandsche Dansen der 16de eeuw, ed. J. Röntgen [arr. for K].
26. Een duytsch musyck Boeck naar de uitgave van 1572 in partituur gebracht, ed. F. van Duyse [V].
28. J. Schenck, Scherzi muzicali per la viola da gamba con basso continuo ad libitum, ed. H. Leichtentritt [I].
29. T. Susato, Het ierste musyck boexken, ed. F. van Duyse [V].
30. 25 Driestemmige Oud-Nederlandsche Liederen uit het einde der vijftiende eeuw, ed. J. Wolf [S].
31. P. Locatelli, Twee sonates, ed. J. Röntgen [I].

32. C. F. Hurlebusch, Compositioni musicali per il cembalo, ed. M. Seiffert [K].
34. Orkestcomposities van Nederlandsche Meesters van het begin der 17de eeuw [M. Borchgreving, B. Grep and N. Gistow], ed. H. F. Wirth [I].
35. A. Willaert, Missa super benedicta, ed. A. Auerkamp.
37. Oud-Nederlandsche Klaviermuziek uit het Muziekboek van Anna Maria van Eijl (Anno 1671), ed. J. Röntgen [K].
38. P. de Monte, Missa ad modulum benedicta es sex vocum, ed. A. Smijers [V].
39. *Wat leeren ons de schilderijen en prenten der zestiende eeuw over de instrumentale begeleiding van den zang* [by M. Seiffert].
40. Lente-film composities, Nederlandsche Boerendansen, ed. J. Röntgen [arr. for K].
41. P. Hellendaal, Vier sonates voor violoncel en becijferde bas, ed. J. Röntgen [I].
42. C. Padbrué, J. van den Vondels [poet] Kruisbergh, ed. A. Smijers [V].
43. De muzikale handschriften van Alphons Diepenbrock, ed. E. Reeser.
44. Drie oud-Nederlandse motetten [J. Obrecht, J. des Prez, J. Clemens non Papa], ed. E. Reeser [V].
45. C. Schuyt, Vijfstemmige Madrigalen, ed. A. Smijers [V].
46. Rynoldus Popma van Oevering, VI Suittes voort' Clavier, ed. H. B. Buys [K].

LIII. *Wydawnictwo dawnej muzyki polskiej* [*Publication[s] de musique ancienne polonaise,* ed. A. Chybiński [1928]–1950; *Éditions de l'ancienne musique polonaise,* ed. A. Chybiński 1951, ed. H. Feicht 1953–56, continuation of Publication[s] . . .; Éditions de la musique polonaise ancienne, ed. H. Feicht 1957—, and from 1964 Z. M. Szweykowskiego as well. Rev. ed. of vols. 1–21, ed. H. Feicht c. 1957—, also called Éditions de la musique polonaise ancienne. Polish name does not change. Many vols. have instr. parts].

1. S. S. Szarzyński, Sonata a due violini e basso pro organo [I].
2. M. Mielczewski, Deus in nomine tuo, concerto a 4 [S + I].
3. J. Różycki, Hymni ecclesiastici (quatuor vocibus concinendi) [V].
4. B. Pękiel, "Audite mortales" a 2 canti, 2 alti, tenore, basso . . . [V + I].
5. S. S. Szardyński, Pariendo non gravaris, concerto a 3 [S + I].

6. M. Mielczewski, Canzona a 3, doi violini e fagotto o viola con basso continuo [I].
7. G. G. Gorczycki, Missa paschalis quatuor vocibus cantanda [V].
8. Anonymous, "Duma" na 4 instrumenty [I].
9. W. z Szamotuł, "In te domine speravi" (Psalmus XXX) [V].
10. S. S. Szarzyński, Jesu, spes mea, concerto a 3 [S + I].
11. A. Jarzębski, Tamburetta a tre voci con basso continuo [I].
12. M. Zieleński, "Vox in Rama," Communio [V].
13. P. Damian, Veni consolator, concerto a 2 [S + I].
14. G. G. Gorczycki, "Illuxit sol," motetto de martyribus [V].
15. A. Jarzębski, Nova casa a tre voci con basso continuo [I].
16. J. Różycki, "Magnificemus in cantico," concerto de sanctis à 3 voci: due canti e basso con basso d'organo.
17. B. Pękiel, Missa pulcherrima a canto, alto, tenore e basso [V].
18. J. Podbielski, Praeludium organum vel clavicymbalum [K].
19. B. Pękiel, Dwie koledy łacinskie (2 Latin carols) [in prep.].
20. J. z Lublina, 36 Tańców z tabulatury organowej [K].
21. A. Jarzębski, "Chromatica," concerto a 3 [I].
22. J. Polak [J. Reys], Preludia, fantazje i tańce na lutnię [L].
23. W. Długoraj, Fantazje i wilanele na lutnię [L].
24. D. Cato, Preludia, fantazje, tańce i madrygały na lutnię [L].
25. S. S. Szarzyński, Ave Regina, antyfona [S + I].
26. S. S. Szarzyński, Ad hymnos ad cantus, motetto pleno [V + I].
27. A. Jarzębski, Bentrovata, concerto a 3 [I].
28. W. z Szamotuł, Pieśni na 4-głosowy chór a cappella [V].
29. M. Mielczewski, Canzona a 2, doi violini e basso [I].
30. B. Pękiel, 40 utworów na lutnię [L].
31. M. Zieleński, "Domus mea," communio ad cantum organi per quattuor voces [V].
32. A. Jarzębski, Sentinella, concerto a 3 [I].
33. T. Szadek, Officium "Dies est laetitiae," quatuor vocibus concinendi [V].
34. C. Bazylik, Pieśni na 4-głosowy chór mieszany a cappella [V].
35. M. Leopolita, Missa paschalis na 5-głosowy chór mieszany a cappella [V].
36. M. Zieleński, Exiit sermo inter fratres; Si consurrexistis cum Christo [S].
37. G. G. Gorczycki, Laetatus sum, concerto a 9 [V + I].
38. M. Mielczewski, Veni domine, concerto a 3 [V].
39. A. Jarzębski, Canzoni a quattro voci con basso continuo [I].
40. F. Lilius, Iubilate Deo omnis terra, motetto a 11 [V].
41. M. Zieleński, Iustus ut palma florebit, Offertorium per septem voces et organum [V].
42. M. Mielczewski, Vesperae dominicales na głosy solowe, chór, zespól instrumentalny i b.c. [in prep.].
43. A. Rohaczewski, Canzon a 4 per organo o quattro stromenti [I].
44. J. Różycki, Exsultemus omnes, concerto a 3 [V].
45. M. Zieleński, Communiones per canto solo cum organo [S].
46. A. Rohaczewski, Crucifixus surrexit, motetto a nove voci.
47;48;49. M. Gomółka, Melodie na psałterz polski, psalmi quattuor vocibus concinendi I;.II; III [in prep., V].
50. S. S. Szarzyński, Veni sancte spiritus, concerto a 3 [S + I].
51. A. Jarzębski, Concerti a 2, I, due voci con basso continuo [I].
52. B. Pękiel, 2 Patrem per chorum quattuor vocum [V].
53. M. Zieleński, In monte Oliveti per chorum quinque vocum con organo [V].
54. J. Różycki, Magnificat [V + I].
55. J. Kobierkowicz, Ego mater, canto, alto, tenore, basso, due violini, con basso continuo [V + I].
56. F. Lilius, Tua Jesu dilectio a canto e basso con basso continuo [S].
57. A. Jarzębski, Concerti a 2, II, na 2 instrumenty i b.c. [I].
58. B. Pękiel, Missa paschalis na 4-głosowy chór mieszany a cappella (songs for 4-part choruses) [V].
59. A. Jarzębski, Concerto a 3, tre voci con basso continuo [I].
60. J. Różycki, Confitebor [V + I].
61. M. Mielzewski, Canzoni a 3 [I].
62. B. Pękiel, Missa brevis [V].
63. G. G. Gorczycki, Os iusti meditabitur; Iustus ut palma florebit [V + I].

64. Zebrowski, Magnificat [V].
65. G. G. Gorczycki, Missa a rorate [V].

Education. See Music education.

Eglogue. *Eclogue.

Egmont. Incidental music, op. 84, composed by Beethoven in 1810 for Goethe's play. The overture is often played alone.

Eguale. See Equale.

Egypt. Archaeological findings and pictorial representations (mainly tomb paintings and reliefs) provide a surprisingly complete story of Egyptian music for a period of several thousand years. As early as the 4th millennium B.C. clappers and rattles give evidence of a primitive ritualistic music that served primarily to exorcise evil spirits. During the Old Kingdom (3rd to 10th dynasties; *c.* 2778–*c.* 2160 B.C.) harps with small bow-shaped resonators, long vertical flutes (end-blown, without a fipple), and double clarinets appeared. Tomb reliefs and paintings show groups of players together with singers, dancers, and men making signs with their hands or fingers, to indicate either some melodic motion or rhythm, possibly in connection with a primitive type of polyphony. From the Middle Kingdom (11th to 17th dynasties; *c.* 2160–*c.* 1580 B.C.) evidence of barrel-shaped drums and asymmetrical lyres has been found, the former perhaps imported from sub-Saharan Africa, the latter from Asia. Studies of flutes dating from about 1800 B.C. suggest melodies moving in rather large intervals, e.g., d–f–a–b [see C. Sachs, in *AMW* ii]. Toward the end of this period the long-necked lute appeared. The New Kingdom (18th to 20th dynasties; *c.* 1580–*c.* 1085 B.C.) saw a great flowering of music. The older instruments appeared in new forms, often splendidly decorated. A wall-painting from the tomb of Paser (*c.* 1450) shows an upright harp as tall as a man as well as a *kithara. Among the new instruments are double oboes, trumpets, short lutes, and the *sistrum. Particularly famous are the silver and gold trumpets found in the tomb of Tut-ankh-amen (fl. *c.* 1350 B.C.). Melodies seem to have moved in smaller intervals than before. Evidence of antiphonal and responsorial singing, of men's and women's choruses, of strophic songs and of liturgical music has been found. During the so-called Late Period (21st to 30th dynasties; 1085–332 B.C.) Egypt was dominated by foreign rulers—Libyan, Ethiopian, Assyrian, and Persian. There is relatively little information about the music of this period. Under Persian rule (525 B.C. and later) attempts were made to eliminate foreign influences and restore the old tradition, but they led merely to stagnation. Hieroglyphic inscriptions indicate the names and occupations of numerous musicians, one of the earliest being Chufu'Ankh, a singer, flutist, and director of court music *c.* 2500 B.C.

Following its conquest by Alexander the Great in 332 B.C., Egypt came under Greek domination. To what extent Egyptian music was influenced by Greek music is difficult to estimate. The Greeks, however, adopted a number of Egyptian instruments, notably the sistrum, when they took over the Isis cult. A notable event of the Ptolemaic period was the invention of the *hydraulos, constructed by a Greek engineer working in Alexandria. From 30 B.C. to A.D. 395 Egypt was a Roman colony, and from A.D. 395 to 640 a part of the Byzantine Empire. In the early Christian era, Alexandria was an important center of Christian worship and psalm-singing (Clement of Alexandria, *c.* 150–*c.* 220). Eventually the *Coptic Church was established. From 640 to 1517 Egypt was dominated by the Arabs, and from 1517 to 1873 by the Turks. During this long period Egyptian music was almost completely under Arab influence, but in time it developed certain indigenous traits, e.g., a scale consisting of 24 quarter tones (established about 1860 by M. Meschāqa in Damascus, introduced in Egypt in 1905 by Kamel al-Kholay). In 1871, the opening of Cairo's new Opera House was celebrated with the first performance of Verdi's *Aida.* In the 20th century Egypt's music came under the influence of Western Europe. However, a conservative group continues to cultivate the older Arab styles [see Arab music].

Lit.: A. Hemsi, *La Musique orientale en Égypte* (1930); H. Hickmann, *Musique et vie musicale sous les pharaons* (1955); id., *Musicologie pharaonique* (1956); id., *Ägypten* (*Musikgeschichte in Bildern*, ed. H. Besseler and M. Schneider, ii, 1 [1961]); id., and Charles Grégoire, Duc de Mecklembourg, *Musique égyptienne* (1958); *NOH* i, 255ff; C. Sachs, *The Rise of Music in the Ancient World* [1943], pp. 71ff; *ReMMA*, pp. 6ff (bibl., p. 426); J. Pulver, "The Music of Ancient Egypt" (PMA xlviii); C. Sachs, "Die Tonkunst der alten Aegypter" (*AMW* ii); *id.*, "Die Namen der altägyptischen Musikinstrumente" (*ZMW* i); H. Hickmann, "Abrégé de l'histoire de la musique en Égypte" (*RdM* 1950, p. 8); *id.*, "Une Scène de musique pharaonique" (*RBM* x); *id.*, "Rhythme, mètre et mesure" (*AM* xxxii).

Eighteen-Twelve Overture. A festival overture by Tchaikovsky, op. 49, composed in 1882, in commemoration of the 70th anniversary of Napoleon's retreat from Moscow (1812).

Eight-foot. See under Foot (2).

Eilend, mit Eile [G.]. Hurrying.

Eingestrichen [G.]. One-line (octave, c', d', etc.).

Einklang [G.]. *Unison.

Einleitung [G.]. Introduction.

Einsatz [G.]. (1) Attack. (2) Entrance of an orchestral part.

Einstimmig [G.]. Monophonic.

Eintritt [G.]. Entrance, particularly of a fugal subject [see *Einsatz*].

Eis, eisis [G.]. E-sharp, E-double-sharp; see Pitch names.

Eisteddfod. See under Bards; Pennillion.

Eklogen [G.]. *Eclogue.

Ekphonetic. See Ecphonetic notation.

E la (mi); elami. See under Hexachord III.

El Amor Brujo. See *Amor brujo.*

Élargissent [F.] Broadening in speed.

Electronic instruments. Generic term for musical instruments in which the tone is produced, modified, or amplified by electronic circuits. Electronic instruments are a comparatively recent development. The first such instrument, the Telharmonium of Thaddeus Cahill, was made about 1904, and truly practical types only began to appear in the 1920's.

Electronic instruments may be divided into two groups: those in which the tone is generated by electronic circuits and those in which the tone is generated by such conventional means as strings or reeds and then subjected to modifications in loudness and timbre by electronic circuitry. A third group of instruments comprises those used in *electronic music; since these devices generally are not played by performers but are employed by the composer in the creation of the music itself, they are discussed in that article rather than here. [See also Computer; Synthesizer.]

I. *Instruments using conventional tone generators.* The more familiar electronic instruments are mostly members of the second group. In some types, such as the electronic flute and electronic saxophone, a small microphone is mounted on the instrument. The output of this microphone is conducted by cables to an amplifier that increases its strength (and often modifies its character) and then to a loudspeaker that converts the electrical signal back into sound waves. In such stringed instruments as electric guitars, the vibrations of the strings are converted to electrical signals by either of two types of pickup. In the electromagnetic system, a tiny coil is mounted near the string, but far enough from it to prevent contact as the string vibrates. When the string is plucked, its vibrations generate alternating current in the coil. In the electrostatic system, the coil is replaced by a simple conductor and the string itself is charged. As the string vibrates, variation of the distance between it and the conductor generates alternating current. In both systems, the signal produced by the pickup is amplified and converted into sound waves in the manner described above.

Electronic amplification makes it possible not only to obtain great volume from a small instrument but also to control the characteristics of its tone. Harmonics may be altered in intensity or omitted altogether, thus changing the timbre of the original sound, and the dynamic envelope of the tone may be controlled to vary the apparent manner of generation and decay—e.g., the percussive impact of a finger or a piano hammer on the string may be eliminated so that the tone builds up gradually. By such means, a plucked string may be made to produce sonorities resembling those of a bowed string or even a wind instrument. In addition, the sustaining power of the instrument may be greatly increased.

Because the electromagnetic and electrostatic

pickup systems do not rely on the vibration of a conventional soundboard, electronic instruments can be built that are much smaller and less expensive than such conventional instruments as pianos and double basses. Electronic stringed instruments (violins, violas, cellos, basses) usually consist of skeleton frameworks just sufficient to support the fingerboard, bridge, and strings (and to afford some guidance to the player's hand), with nonmicrophonic (usually electrostatic) pickups attached to the bridge. In one type of electronic piano, struck reeds replace the strings. A chromatic kettledrum invented by B. F. Miessner consists of thirteen short bass viol strings that are stretched over a rectangular frame and tuned in semitones. When the strings are struck with ordinary kettledrum sticks their vibrations, picked up electrostatically and amplified through a suitable loudspeaker, produce sounds closely resembling those of conventional kettledrums.

Electronics makes it possible to obtain from small and inexpensive devices sounds resembling those produced by bells weighing many tons. One form of electronic carillon consists of a set of coiled steel reeds similar to those used in clocks. It is played in the same manner as the piano, and an amplifying system increases the volume to any degree desired. Another form utilizes loosely suspended lengths of piano wire. The latter has proved especially successful in reproducing the nonharmonic partials characteristic of bells.

II. *Instruments using electronic tone generators.* The purely electronic instruments, with only a few exceptions—of which the Hammond organ is the most important—use electronic oscillators (circuits capable of producing an alternating current of a given frequency) as tone generators. The instruments of this type may be divided into two subgroups, those in which there are a number of oscillators, which permit the performance of polyphonic music, and those in which the frequency of a single oscillator is varied to produce different pitches; the instruments of the second subgroup are capable only of performing monophonic music. Most of the instruments of both types have keyboards, and the *Ondes Martenot* (or *Ondes musicales*), a monophonic instrument, has, in addition, a sliding ribbon that permits glissandi and the sounding of intermediate pitches.

The *Hammond organ* generally resembles a spinet in size and shape but has two manuals and a pedal board. It generates electrical oscillations by means of small, motor-driven rotary generators that produce alternating current at frequencies corresponding to those of the tempered scale. The instrument has harmonic controls that provide a very large number of timbres, some of which are preset.

The *novachord,* a single-manual instrument that also resembles the spinet in form, employs a purely electronic tone-generating system. Twelve vacuum-tube oscillators operate at the frequencies of the highest octave of the instrument. There is a separate oscillator for each note of the chromatic scale, and associated with each oscillator are five frequency-dividing circuits, each of which operates at one-half the frequency of the preceding tube. Thus one oscillator and the five dividers associated with it supply the six octaves of one note of the scale. Controls mounted on a panel above the keyboard provide different tone colors and vary the tonal envelope to produce either percussive effects, similar to those of the piano, or sustained tones, similar to those of stringed or wind instruments. The principles of the novachord are employed in a number of different electronic organs.

One of the first electronic instruments to attract public attention was the *Theremin,* invented about 1924 by the Russian scientist whose name it bears. This instrument uses a radio-frequency beat system of tone generation based on the interference between the outputs of two oscillators. One oscillator operates at a fixed frequency and the other at varying frequencies determined by the proximity of the player's hand to a short rod antenna, which is charged with alternating current from the second oscillator. The difference between the frequencies of the two oscillators produces a "beat"—i.e., a third frequency, which is the audio-frequency that operates the loudspeaker. The volume of sound is controlled in a similar manner by the player's other hand. A serious defect of this instrument in its earliest form was its inability to change from one pitch to another without an intervening glissando, but that defect was remedied to some extent in later models by means of an improved volume control. The Ondes Martinot operates on a similar principle, as does the *Trautonium.* Originally, the Trautonium was operated by the hands in the same manner as the Theremin, but later a metal string was placed over a metal rail having marks to indicate where the string should be pressed on the rail for the correct pitches of the tempered scale.

Lit.: A. L. Douglas, *The Electrical Production of Music* [1957]; *id., The Electronic Musical*

Instrument Manual, rev. ed. (1961); K. S. Lewis, *Electronic Musical Instruments* (1948); R. H. Dorf, *Electronic Musical Instruments,* rev. ed. [1959]; *Internationaler Kongress "Musik und Electroakustik,"* Gravesano, Switzerland, 1954 [1955]; N. H. Crowhurst, *Electronic Musical Instrument Handbook* [1962]: R. W. Young, "A Decade of Musical Acoustics (*Proceedings of the 4th International Congress on Acoustics,* 1962, Part II); B. F. Miessner, "The Electronic Piano" (*Proceedings, Music Teachers' National Association,* 1937); *id.,* "Electronic Music and Instruments" (*Proceedings, Institute of Radio Engineers,* 1936); L. Stokowski, "New Vistas in Radio" (*The Atlantic Monthly,* Jan. 1935); J. M. Barbour, "Music and Electricity" (*PAMS,* 1937); V. Ussachevsky, "The Processes of Experimental Music" (*Journal, Acoustical Society of America* vi, 202ff); A. Douglas, "The Electrical Production of Music" (*Journal, Acoustical Society of America* vi, 146ff); H. Bode, "European Electronic Music Instrument Design" (*Journal, Acoustical Society of America* ix, 267ff); F. C. Judd, "Electronic Music: Sound Sources and Treatment" (*Wireless World* lxvii, 483ff).

E.M.R.

Electronic music. Music made by producing, modifying, and recording sound, and reproducing it by electroacoustical means. Electronic music has become very important since World War II, both because of the new techniques it uses [see III below] and because its new resources are linked with new concepts of music and aesthetics.

Electronic music traditionally means music made up of sounds created exclusively by electronic means, as distinct from *musique concrète,* which is made by recording sounds that already exist. However, this distinction is not always clear, because today composers may combine the use of both natural and electronically produced sounds. [See *Musique concrète* for further differences.]

I. *History.* Electronic music in Europe grew out of research by the post-Webern generation in the years 1950–54 and was, at least in the beginning, closely tied to *serial music. Its chief pioneers were the composers K. H. Stockhausen, H. Eimert, G. Ligeti, and G. M. Koenig at the West German Radio studio in Cologne, L. Berio and B. Maderna in the Italian Radio studio at Milan, and H. Pousseur at both centers. The scholars W. Meyer-Eppler, F. Winckel, and A. Lietti contributed greatly, both technically and theoretically, to their research. The *musique*

concrète studio of the French Radio in Paris, although not involved with the concerns of the first electronic composers, nevertheless greatly assisted in the creation of electronic-music studios, not only because it preceded them (1948) but also because it had already examined some important problems relating to the new methods.

In the United States, after independent research that in the early 1950's was called "tape music," involving such pioneers as V. Ussachevsky, L. and B. Baron, J. Cage, and others, several studios were formed, the most important of which was at Columbia University in New York, directed by Ussachevsky and Otto Luening. This studio, which actually included three studios of complementary equipment, was open to all directions of research and composition, including serial music, notably that of M. Babbitt. Among the other important American centers are the studios of the University of Illinois at Urbana, the San Francisco Tape Center, and the studio of Brandeis University. In Europe, important studios are in Munich, Brussels, Warsaw, and elsewhere, and in Japan the electronic-music studio of the NKH in Tokyo is very active.

II. *Principles.* The reasons behind the use of electronic methods of composition are multiple, even divergent, and may be formulated in a new and different way with each work. In the beginning, however, a fundamental idea inspired electronic music, the idea of the unity of musical thought and musical material. It was then—and is now—a matter of the sounds themselves generating the structure of a composition. To go beyond fixed scales (notably the well-tempered scale) and create specific scales for each work, to compose sound spectra, thus giving a necessary structural role to the timbre, to realize with maximum precision the demands of a new musical syntax, especially with regard to the duration of intensities, the differentiation of which goes beyond the capabilities of the performer—these were some of the motives that at first justified recourse to the field of electronic music. This field in turn revealed latent resources that musical theory had to absorb and exploit, which in turn influenced the studios to the point of a radical revision. Today the need for going beyond static principles is making itself felt in most of the studios. It is only when automation is extended to all dimensions of sound and all stages of composition, made possible through the introduction of new electronic devices, that electronic music will reach a complexity comparable to that of nature. Some European and American studios are currently moving in this direction.

III. *Equipment and techniques.* Owing to considerable differences in concepts, equipment, and development among the studios throughout the world, the installations and basic techniques of electronic music can be described only in a very general way. They include, theoretically, three essential steps that correspond to the phases of creation of a composition: (1) generation of material; (2) transformation of material; and (3) recording. All these steps are, of course, simultaneous.

(1) The generation of electronic material (to which nonelectronic material may be added) is of two kinds: synthetic and analytic. The first uses sinus tones furnished by oscillators as wanted. The synthesis of the sinus tones, variable in number, duration, and intensity, allows the creation of more or less complex spectra. Different modifications can intervene at this stage. The second method, which can be combined with the first, calls for "white noise," a statistical mixture of all audible frequencies furnished by a white-noise generator. By means of electroacoustical filters, more or less wide frequency bands can be isolated from this spectrum, even to the selection of a single frequency; this process hence is the inverse of the first.

(2) The transformation of materials is of several kinds: variation of speed of the magnetic tape, simple (causing a variation in frequency of the recorded sound) or of the Springer type (without variation in frequency); filtering the frequency (filtering the octave, the third, the pass-band) and the amplitude; modulations (of frequency, of amplitude, etc.); reverberation (natural echo chambers or electronic ones), etc.

(3) Recording on tape recorders. The base speed of the output of the tapes in electronic studios today is virtually standard, at 15 inches per second. Tape recorders are synchronized at one, two, or four channels of independent amplification.

The techniques now in use tend more and more to bring about simultaneity in these three operations and to substitute automation for manual putting together of their results. One of the first attempts in this direction was made by the studio of Columbia University-Princeton in New York with the *synthesizer,* which uses a rudimentary system of programming on a perforated tape. Recent interest centers on the use of electronic computers for this purpose.

Electronic music poses important problems with respect to the listener. A traditional concert-hall performance appears inadequate to many composers. The new music seems to call for new listening conditions that are more appropriate to its stereophonic dimensions, and even more important, allow freer modes of audience contact in both time and space (permanent diffusion, free entry and exit, free movement of the audience inside the auditorium), conditions that have already been clearly expressed by numerous composers.

Lit.: M. Wilkinson, *An Introduction to Electronic Music* (1960); F. C. Judd, *Electronic Music and Musique concrète* (1961); P. Schaeffer, *Traité des objets musicaux* [1966]; A. P. Basart, *Serial Music, A Classified Bibliography of Writings on Twelve-Tone and Electronic Music* (1961); F. K. Prieberg, *Musica ex Machina* [1960]; *Die Reihe* (German ed., 1955—, English ed., 1958—), *passim; RBM* xiii (*Musique expérimentale;* articles by Boulez, Eimert, Stockhausen, *et al.*); *Revue musicale,* nos. 236 [n.d.] and 244 [n.d.]; *Perspectives of New Music* [1962—], *passim; Incontri musicali* nos. 1–4 (1956–60), *passim;* H. Davies, "A Discography of Electronic Music and Musique Concrète" (*Recorded Sound,* no. 14, April 1964); V. Ussachevsky, "Notes on a Piece for Tape Recorder" (*MQ* xlvi); K. Stockhausen, "Electronic and Instrumental Music" (*Die Reihe* v, English ed. [1961]); J. Xenakis, "Le Corbusier's 'Electronic Poem'—the Philips Pavilion" (*Gravesaner Blätter,* ser. iii, ix, pp. 51ff); M. V. Mathews, J. R. Pierce, and N. Guttman, "Musical Sounds from Digital Computers" (*Gravesaner Blätter,* ser. vi, xxiii/xxiv, pp. 119ff, 129); M. V. Mathews, "The Computer Music Record Supplement" (*Gravesaner Blätter,* ser. vi, xxvi, p. 117, and including a disk recording of musical examples). For additional bibl. see Electronic instruments.   A.B.

Electropneumatic action. In organs, a system of key action, developed in the late 19th century and widely prevalent today, in which the pipe valves in the wind chest are opened by pneumatic motors actuated by electrical impulses from the keys. See Organ II, XI.   C.B.F.

Elegie für Junge Liebende [G., Elegy for Young Lovers]. Opera in three acts by H. W. Henze (libretto by W. H. Auden and C. Kallman), produced (in German) in Schwetzingen, 1961. Setting: Austrian Alps, early 20th century.

Elegy [G. *Elegie*]. A plaintive poem; hence, a musical composition of a mournful character.

Elektra. Opera in one act by R. Strauss (libretto by H. von Hofmannsthal, based on Sophocles' tragedy), produced in Dresden, 1909. Setting: courtyard in royal palace of Mycenae, after Trojan War. Strauss has set this story of hate and murder to most brutal and violent music, a relentless piling up of intense orchestral effects from which there is only occasional relief, as in the scene of recognition between Elektra and Orestes.

Elevation [L. *elevatio;* It. *elevazione*]. (1) The music played during the Elevation of the Host. It consists of either a motet or an organ piece. A "Toccata per l'elevazione" and other similar pieces are in Frescobaldi's *Fiori musicali* (1635). See Offertory. (2) See Appoggiatura, double II.

Eleventh. See under Interval. Eleventh chord, see under Ninth chord.

Elijah. [G. *Elias*]. Oratorio by Mendelssohn to words from the Old Testament, produced in the English version at the Birmingham Festival, 1846, and in the German version at Hamburg, 1847.

Elisir d'amore, L' [It., The Elixir of Love]. Opera in two acts by Donizetti (libretto by F. Romani), produced in Milan, 1832. Setting: Italian village, early 19th century.

Elmuahim, elmuarifa. Terms used by 13th-century theorists [see *CS* i, 339, 341] to denote the *semibrevis,* which has the shape of a rhombus. They come from Arabic *al ma' luma* and *al ma' rufa,* "the known thing," terms meaning "rhombus" that were used in Arabic translations of Euclid. See J. Handschin, in *ZMW* xiv, 321, 322n; J. Chailley, in *CP Apel;* H. G. Farmer, in *Journal of the Royal Asiatic Society* (1925), p. 76.

El Salvador. Art music in El Salvador dates from the mid-19th century. The first composer trained in European music was José Escolástico Andrino, a native of Guatemala who came to El Salvador in 1845 and the next year organized the first symphony orchestra. During the second half of the 19th century a number of Italian-born musicians came to El Salvador, among them Juan Aberle, who wrote the music for the national anthem and in 1883 established a fortnightly music review, *Ilustración Musical Centro-Americana.*

The first native composer of importance was Wenceslao García, who wrote an opera, *Adela.* Many of his contemporaries and immediate successors wrote short instrumental dances, most of them for piano, and popular songs and marches.

The most distinguished Salvadoran composers of the 20th century are Cirìaco Jesús Alas (1866–1952), composer of an *Obertura Patriotica* for band; Domingo Santos (1892–1951), who wrote six Requiem Masses, three piano sonatas, two overtures, and several instrumental marches; María de Baratta (b. 1894), an outstanding scholar of folk music whose numerous compositions of native inspiration include an opera-ballet (*El Fuego Nuevo*), and *Nahualismo* and *Danza Sagrada,* both for orchestra; and Esteban Servellón (b. 1921), who is also the conductor of the El Salvador Symphony Orchestra, established in 1922, and author of a Suite for strings, a symphonic poem, *Falton,* and several compositions for piano. An outstanding representative of the young generation is Gilberto Orellana (b. 1942).

Folk music in El Salvador is very much like that of the rest of Central America. The *danza,* *pasillo,* and *marcha* are the most popular forms. Also see under Latin America.   J.O-S.

Embellishment. (1) Same as ornamentation. (2) Same as auxiliary tone; see Nonharmonic tones I.

Embolada [Port.]. A type of Brazilian folk singing that involves alliteration and onomatopoeias sung very fast and requiring enormous skill in diction. Each syllable of the text is set to one note in patterns of rapid sixteenth notes. Villa-Lobos frequently used the term as a title for instrumental pieces written in a fast toccata-like manner.   J.O-S.

Embouchure [F.]. (1) The proper position of the lips in the playing of wind instruments (also called "lip," "lipping"). It is sometimes misspelled "embrochure." (2) The mouthpiece of a wind instrument, especially of the brass instruments and the flute.

Emiola, emiolia. See Hemiola.

Emmeles [Gr.]. Early medieval term of uncertain or at least variable significance. In the 10th-century *Alia musica* it is explained as a whole tone that may be sung below or above the octave, fifth, or fourth [see *GS* i, 129a]. This would include the use of the *subtonium* and formations such as d–a–b–a (beginning of many antiphons of the first mode). According to Engelbert of Admont, *emmeles* is the difference between two consonances, such as a fifth and a fourth [*GS* ii, 320]. Hugo Riemann's statement that *emmeles* is a term for the fifth and fourth is without foundation [see H. Riemann, *Geschichte der Musiktheorie im IX.-XIX. Jahrhundert,* 2nd ed. (1918), p. 338; English translation by R. H. Haggh (1962), p. 289].

Emperor Concerto. Popular name for Beethoven's Piano Concerto in E-flat, op. 73 (1809), suggested by the grandeur of the work. The first movement opens with an unusual improvisatory introduction played by the pianist and has a written-out *cadenza. Particularly noteworthy is the transitional passage linking the slow and the final movements.

Emperor Quartet [G. *Kaiserquartett*]. Haydn's String Quartet in C, op. 76, no. 3, so called because the slow movement consists of variations on the "Emperor's Hymn," formerly the national anthem of Austria, which was composed by Haydn (as a four-part chorus) in 1797.

Empfindsamer Stil [G.]. The North German style of the second half of the 18th century, represented by W. F. Bach, K. P. E. Bach, Quantz, G. Benda, Reichardt, and others who, in the period *c.* 1750–80, tried to arrive at an expression of "true and natural" feelings, to some extent anticipating 19th-century romanticism. A basic tenet of this school was to replace the baroque idea of maintaining an "affection" throughout a composition (or a sonata movement) by a constant change of affection or expression, together with changes of dynamics, etc. A piece such as K. P. E. Bach's Fantasia [*HAM* ii, no. 296] is especially characteristic of this style. Somewhat simpler manifestations are the *Volkstümliches Lied and *Singspiel. See P. H. Lang, *Music in Western Civilization* [1941], pp. 585ff; W. S. Newman, *The Sonata in the Classic Era* [1963]; *GrHWM.*

Empfindung, mit [G.]. With feeling.

Empressé [F.]. Hurrying.

Ému [F.]. With emotion, with feeling.

Emyolia. See Hemiola.

Enchaînement [F.]. Voice-leading, proper connection of chords and/or parts.

Enchaînez [F.]. Same as *segue.

Enchiriadis, enchiridion [Gr.]. Medieval terms for handbook, manual. Examples are the *"Musica enchiriadis" of the 9th century and "Enchiridion musices" of the 10th century [see Theory II, A, 3, 5]. *Enchiridion* is the title

of several early publications of Protestant chorales, especially the so-called *Erfurt Enchiridion,* published in Erfurt, 1524.

Enclume [F.]. Anvil.

Encore. In a public performance, the repetition of a piece, or an extra piece played in response to applause by the audience. The practice of encores started in the 17th century with the rise of the operatic virtuoso singers. Haydn had turned against this practice by 1799; on the occasion of the first performance of his *Creation* (1798), in a note printed on the program, he begged the audience not to insist upon the repetition of any number. The French and Italian equivalent is *bis.*

En dehors [F.]. See *Dehors.*

Endings. See under *Differentiae.*

Enechema. See under *Echos.*

Enfance du Christ, L' [F., The Childhood of Christ]. Oratorio by Berlioz, op. 25 (1854), for solo voices, chorus, and orchestra.

Enfant et les sortilèges, L' [F., The Child and the Sorceries; sometimes trans. The Bewitched Child]. Opera in one act by Ravel (libretto by Colette), produced in Monte Carlo, 1925. Setting: contemporary French country house.

Enfant prodigue, L' [F., The Prodigal Son]. (1) Cantata (lyric scene) by Debussy (libretto by E. Guinand), composed in 1884 for the Prix de Rome; produced as an opera in London, 1910. (2) Ballet by Prokofiev, produced in Paris, 1929.

Engführung [G.]. Stretto of fugues.

England. I. Although English music history, like that of other nations, reflects the economic, political, religious and social life of the nation, certain tendencies do seem to have been peculiar to England. One constant factor has been the conservatism that preserved old traditions even in periods of experiment. When subjected to powerful foreign influences—e.g., during the formative period of the Elizabethan madrigal or the period of absorption of the Notre Dame repertory—the English conservative tradition was strong enough to transform borrowed styles and genres until they became suitable for genuine native expression.

The high points of English music history have generally coincided with the lifespan of one preeminent composer or school. They are the "Age of Dunstable" (*c.* 1400–60); "Tudor Age" (i.e., that of Tallis, Byrd, and Gibbons, *c.* 1600); "Restoration" or "Purcellian period" (1660–1710); "Handelian Era" (1710–60); the period of T. A. Arne (1710–88) and W. Boyce (1710–79), overlapping Handel's and extending a few decades beyond; and the modern renascence, dominated by Benjamin Britten (b. 1913), although the achievements of both his predecessors and the succeeding generation must not be discounted.

II. Gregorian chant was established in England by Pope Gregory himself, who in 596 sent to Canterbury his own emissary, Augustine of Kent, with 40 monks and priests, to introduce the Roman Catholic rite. Augustine, the first Bishop of Canterbury, re-established Christianity in southern England so successfully that by 664 Kentish Christians were able to defeat their Celtic colleagues at the Synod of Whitby, firmly establishing priority for the Roman Catholic liturgy. In 680 a skilled singer was brought from Rome to Wearmouth and Jarrow, where his teaching ensured authentic Gregorian practices, which were further strengthened by the Council of Clovesho in 747. The *Sarum use, developed at Salisbury Cathedral, established an English variant of Gregorian chant, which in due course was to influence all English and some Continental music. Also, the art of organ building began to develop, especially in Anglo-Saxon areas, reaching an early climax with the construction *c.* 950 of an enormous organ at Winchester [see Organ XII]. Important contemporaneous developments at Winchester include the quasidramatic performance of the Easter *trope, *Quem quaeritis* [cf. *Concordia Regularis* of Bishop Ethelwold], the copying of the Winchester fragments (Oxford Bodleian MS 775) and the first English experiments in polyphony in the form of two-voice organa.

With the Norman conquest (1066) England's musical and religious ties with northern France and the Low Countries became stronger. More and more cloisters and cathedrals in the new Norman style were built. Musical activity manifested itself in the Winchester Troper [see Troper], in the development of early polyphony, and in the "Musica" (*c.* 1100?) of John Cotton (possibly a Belgian). Important English theorists of the time include Johannes de Garlandia (b. *c.* 1195, active in Paris), Anonymous IV [see Anonymous], and Walter Odington (fl. early 14th century; "De speculatione musice"). Two of the most important achievements of this period were

the composition of *"Sumer is icumen in" and the earliest copying of portions of the Notre Dame repertory (from *"Magnus liber organi") in MS Wolfenbüttel 677, which was prepared for the Priory of St. Andrews in Scotland. Like Brit. Mus. MS Harl. 978, this MS includes Notre Dame organa, but it also contains (facs. 11) some two-part tropes, sequences, and Offertories unique to English sources. The "English" or "peripheral" style of these is also reflected in a few motets in the Codex Montpellier that are notable for their use of *voice exchange [see *HAM* i, no. 33a].

III. A recognizably "English" repertory began to take shape in several fragmentary sources, mainly originating at Worcester *c.* 1300. The pieces in these are polyphonic tropes, motets, conductus, and the like, a few borrowed from the Notre Dame repertory but many of English origin. On the whole they are in a simple, conductus-like style that seems very conservative compared to contemporary French compositions. A remarkable trait is the extensive use of voice exchange as a structural device. There also are several passages of "parallel six-three chords," foreshadowing the *fauxbourdon of a later period. Perhaps related to an earlier improvisatory English practice of singing in thirds and sixths mentioned by Giraldus Cambrensis [see Gymel; Sixth-chord style; Discant (2)], this English penchant for imperfect consonances may have been one factor leading to the establishment of the *third as a basic interval of counterpoint. Little music of the late 14th century has survived, but Chaucer and Lydgate refer frequently to a large variety of musical instruments, so very likely instrumental music was developing rapidly.

The early 15th century was a period of flourishing activity. Several MSS, of both native [Old Hall MSS, see Sources, no. 25] and Continental origin [see Sources, nos. 20, 22; also Trent Codices], survive. The two groups of sources represent different composers, different areas, and different musical styles, which gave rise to the assumption that there were two English schools, an insular school of strictly conservative trends (Sturgeon, Typp, *et al.*) and a Continental school of progressive tendencies (J. Dunstable, Lionel Power, J. Bedyngham, J. Benet, *et al.*). However, Bukofzer has shown that such a hypothesis is untenable. [See Editions XXXIV, 8.] Dunstable (*c.* 1370–1453) and Power (d. 1445) were clearly the most important composers. Dunstable's greatness was recognized in his own time, and his invigorating influence on the French music of the 15th century (*Burgundian school) is attested in a poem by Martin Le Franc, "Le Champion des dames" (c. 1441–42), which says that Dufay and Binchois" . . . ont prins de la contenance Angloise et ensuy Dunstable pour quoy merveilleuse plaisance rend leur chant joyeux et notable" (The English guise they wear with grace, they follow Dunstable aright, and thereby have they learned apace to make their music gay and bright; see *ReMR*, pp. 12–13). The most striking traits of this "English guise" are a fully consonant harmonic idiom and a beautiful style of melody based on the degrees of the triad [see Third]. Dunstable's contemporary, Lionel Power (d. 1445), wrote a *Missa Alma redemptoris mater* that is the earliest known example of the *cantus firmus* Mass [see Mass C II b]. After Dunstable, Walter Frye (fl. mid- to late 15th century) carried on the tradition, along with Robert Morton (c. 1440–75), who also was a member of the Burgundian school. Developments in England at this time are reflected in MS Egerton 3307 (c. 1450; also called Windsor MS), which contains, among other items, the two earliest known polyphonic *Passions as well as a number of native English *carols, twenty-two Latin *cantilenas, and a goliardic drinking song set parodistically, in isorhythmic fashion [see *ReMR*, p. 764].

IV. The recently discovered Eton MS [*Editions XXXIV, 10–12], dating from shortly after 1500, contains a large repertory of sacred compositions (Magnificat, "Salve regina," Marian motets) that apparently were used at St. George's Chapel, Windsor [*ReMMA*, p. 410]. Their most unusual feature is their many-voiced polyphony, generally for five or six but occasionally for as many as eight or even eleven parts. The very advanced "choral arranging" foreshadows the *polychoral style of the late 16th century. Of the twenty-five composers represented in the collection, John Browne (b. 1452) stands out as the most important. Others are Walter Lambe (1452–c. 1500), Richard Davy (c. 1467–c. 1516), Robert Wilkinson (Master of the Choristers at Eton, 1500–15), Robert Fayrfax (1464–1521), and William Cornyshe (c. 1468–1523). Fayrfax, Cornyshe, and their royal patron, King Henry VIII (reigned 1509–47), wrote secular part songs to English or French texts that were frequently humorous or even satirical [see *HAM* i, no. 86].

After the Anglican Reformation (1534) there was a gradual change to compositions with English texts as the Sarum use became nation-ally established under the leadership of John Marbeck (c. 1510–c. 1585) and the three "T's" of early Tudor music: John Taverner (c. 1495–1545), Christopher Tye (c. 1500–c.1572), and Thomas Tallis (c. 1505–85) [see Editions LI]. Marbeck is noted chiefly for his *The Booke of Common Praier Noted* (1550), while Tye and Tallis were the most important composers of anthems and services with English texts. These men laid the groundwork for the golden age of Elizabethan music, brilliantly represented in the works of Tallis' pupil, William Byrd (1543–1623), and the English madrigalists [see under Editions XVI]. The 16th century also saw the rise of English keyboard music, the composers of which made original contributions in their patterned variations, suites, and some dances representing the earliest English use of the *ground (in the strikingly advanced "Hornpype" by Hugh Aston, 1480?–1522?, and in "My Lady Carey's Dompe"). There is also a large repertory of liturgical organ music (settings of antiphons, hymns, offertories, psalm verses, etc.; see Felix namque; In nomine) by John Redford (d. 1547), Thomas Preston (c. 1564), William Blitheman (c. 1510–91) and many others [see the Mulliner Book in Editions XXXIV, 1]. In the equally impressive repertory of the English virginalists—William Byrd, John Bull (c. 1562–1628), Giles Farnaby (c. 1560–1640), John Munday (d. 1630), Peter Philips (1561–1628), and Orlando Gibbons (1583–1625)—the emphasis is on secular keyboard music, especially dances and variations. Their pavanes and galliards are among the most beautiful products of the 16th century. English Renaissance music, vocal as well as instrumental, achieved a subtle refinement in the works of Orlando Gibbons and the compositions of lutenist-songwriters like John Dowland (1562–1626) and poet-composer-theorist Thomas Campion (1567–1620) [see Editions XVII]. During this period English chamber music came to equal that of any in Europe. At first English composers and players were famous chiefly for viol consort music, as represented by the fancies of John Coperario (c. 1575–1626), Alfonso Ferrabosco II (c. 1575–1628), Tobias Hume (d. 1645), and Robert Jones II (fl. 1601–7) [see Browning; Fancy; "In nomine"; Consort]. But within a short time the English "broken consort" became equally popular (see Morley's *The First Booke of Consort Lessons,* 1599, and Adson's *Courtly Masquing Ayres,* 1611) as did the wind consort.

V. About 1625, with the death of nearly all

the Elizabethan composers, these promising developments in vocal and keyboard music slackened. Only chamber music continued to flourish, with such composers as John Jenkins (1592–1678), William Lawes (1602–45), Henry Lawes (1596–1662), William Young (d. 1671), and Matthew Locke (c. 1630–77). Roger North, in his interesting account of 17th-century English musical life ("Memoires of Musick," 1728; pub. 1846, ed. by E. F. Rimbault), tells us that Locke's consorts were "the last of the kind that hath been made."

During the early Caroline period Nicholas Laniere (1588–1666), Henry Lawes, and William Lawes experimented with the new Monteverdian recitative style, and might have succeeded in adapting it to the English language had conditions permitted. John Jenkins and William Lawes modernized the style of instrumental "consort" music, as did Thomas Tomkins in his keyboard compositions. John Wilson (1595–1674) and the younger John Hilton (1599–1657), along with some of the above-named composers, also introduced new stylistic developments in English solo and part-song composition, while Charles Coleman, Hilton, the Lawes brothers, and Matthew Locke experimented with new "baroque" styles in church music composition.

With the rebellion and subsequent establishment of the Commonwealth in 1649, many of these developments were cut short. That is not to say that Cromwell suppressed music itself. Indeed, the reforms instituted by his government emphasized and enhanced the development of those kinds of music not proscribed by the Puritans. Vocal and instrumental chamber music prospered, and a new phase of musical activity, the public concert, made its first tentative beginnings. All tended to usher in a broader if more amateurish musical culture, which was to grow apace in the remaining decades of the 17th century.

The Restoration of Charles II and the Stuart monarchy introduced a vogue for new musical styles, forms, and media. During his travels on the Continent (1646–60), Charles had acquired a taste for the music performed at the court of Louis XIV, much of it directed by J.-B. Lully (1632–87). Here vocal and instrumental ensembles achieved standards of performance more splendid than any yet known in Europe. The "Vingt-quatre (24) violons du Roi" and "Mr. Baptist's vein" (as Lully's style of composition was referred to in England) became universally famous by the last quarter of the 17th century.

Charles soon established his own "Royal violins," modeling his court musical establishment after the French court's and even sending Pelham Humfrey (1647–74) and others to study in France and Italy. He placed in charge of his musical forces men like Captain Henry Cooke (c. 1615–72) and Nicholas Staggins (d. 1700), who had studied abroad, and he hired foreign musicians, such as Louis Grabu and G. B. Draghi (fl. 1667–1706), to fill important posts, often to the chagrin of capable British musicians, notably John Banister (1630–79) and Matthew Locke.

In the 1670's a new generation of native English composers—of whom the most important were John Blow (1648/9–1708) and Michael Wise (c. 1648–87)—adapted the Franco-Italian continuo styles and forms, paving the way for Henry Purcell (c. 1659–95), who was to demonstrate mastery not only of the new imported forms and styles (opera, cantata, oratorio, sonata, etc.) but of traditional English genres as well (fancy, anthem, catch, masque). After his highly successfully dramatic 17th-century opera, *Dido and Aeneas,* Purcell experimented with an English hybrid form, the semiopera, a combined opera, stage play, masque, and ballet, e.g., *Dioclesian* (1690), *King Arthur* (1691), *The Fairy Queen* (1692), and *The Indian Queen* (1695). Between 1680 and 1695 he also wrote incidental music, consisting of instrumental pieces, songs, and masques, for some 44 plays. His greatest achievement, however, was his masterful setting of the English language to music—a difficult feat most conspicuously achieved in his songs (e.g., in the posthumous collection *Orpheus britannicus,* 1698–1702). None of Purcell's successors, such as Daniel Purcell (c. 1660–1717), Jeremiah Clarke (c. 1673–1707), John Eccles (c. 1650–1735), or John Weldon (1676–1736), was of sufficient stature to check the decline that followed Purcell's death.

VI. Not until 1710, when G. F. Handel (1685–1759) arrived there, did England possess another outstanding composer. His efforts to establish an Italian operatic tradition failed, although his operas represent some of his most brilliant works. But his oratorios, organ concertos, St. Cecilia odes, and Chandos Anthems breathe the spirit of the English high baroque and at the same time establish Handel as the only composer of the late baroque who can be compared to J. S. Bach.

After Handel's death came a period of less brilliant activity, based on native forms such as the *ballad opera, *glee, and *voluntary. The more important composers of this era include Thomas Arne (1710–78; numerous operas, glees); William Boyce (1710–79; anthems, publication of *Cathedral Music,* 3 vols., 1760–78), Benjamin Cooke (1734–93; odes, glees, catches), and Samuel Webbe (1740–1816; glees, catches). Samuel Wesley (1766–1837), famous for his organ improvisation as well as his efforts on behalf of Bach's music, was a competent composer of anthems and services as well as Masses, motets (he joined the Roman Catholic Church in 1784), and organ music. His son, Samuel Sebastian Wesley (1810–76), who was influenced by Mendelssohn and Schumann, helped raise the low standard of English church music with his excellent anthems and services. Romanticism is more clearly represented by John Field (1782–1837; nocturnes) and William Sterndale Bennett (1816–75; piano and orchestral music). In 1880 English operetta found its outstanding representative in Arthur S. Sullivan (1842–1900).

VII. About the turn of the century began the modern renascence of British music. The development from 1880 to 1966 may be divided into three main periods: that of German influence, that of nationalist and impressionist tendencies, and that comprising the three most recent generations of British composers.

To the first period belong C. H. Parry (1848–1918), C. V. Stanford (1852–1924), and Edward Elgar (1857–1934). Parry and Stanford were influenced by Schumann, Wagner, and Brahms, although individual traits are by no means absent, particularly in some works of Stanford, in which elements of his native Ireland are prominent. Elgar wrote in a rich, emotional style with strong native English associations. Though sometimes tending to be ostentatious, his music ushered in the modern flowering of English music. The second period was that of the "nationalist" composers, such as Frederick Delius (1862–1934), Ralph Vaughan Williams (1872–1958), Arnold Bax (1883–1953), Gustav Holst (1874–1934), the "impressionist" Cyril Scott (b. 1879), and Arthur Bliss (b. 1891), known particularly for his *A Colour Symphony* (1922; rev. 1932). Vaughan Williams took an active part in the revival of English folksong and in the efforts of the Purcell Society to publish the complete works of the *Orpheus britannicus.* From these he adapted archaic idioms for many of his compositions. Bax, part Irish, had a penchant for romantically colored mysticism and wistfulness that earned him the title of "Yeats in

music." Holst's earlier works (*The Planets,* perf. 1918) are notable for their brilliant orchestration, to which the austere linearity of his late compositions offers a striking contrast. Of the composers of the third group, the most outstanding are Alan Bush (b. 1900), Edmund Rubbra (b. 1901), William Walton (b. 1902), Michael Tippett (b. 1905), Alan Rawsthorne (b. 1905), and Benjamin Britten (b. 1913). The last in particular has become internationally known through his operas (*Peter Grimes,* 1945; *The Rape of Lucretia,* 1946; *Billy Budd,* 1951; *The Turn of the Screw,* 1954), written in an easy but technically reliable, eclectic and yet personal style. Equally famous are his choral works (*A Ceremony of Carols,* 1942; *War Requiem,* 1962), and perhaps best known of all his *Young Person's Guide to the Orchestra* (op. 34), variations and fugue on a theme by Purcell. The twelve-tone technique has been used by Elisabeth Lutyens (b. 1906) and Humphrey Searle (b. 1915).

Of the most recent generation of British composers, the most outstanding are Richard Rodney Bennett (b. 1936), Harrison Birtwhistle (b. 1934), Peter Maxwell Davies (b. 1934), Alexander Goehr (b. 1932), Alan Hoddinott (b. 1929), Nicholas Maw (b. 1935), Anthony Milner (b. 1925), Thea Musgrave (b. 1928), and Malcolm Williamson (b. 1931).

Lit. *General:* E. Walker, *A History of Music in England,* rev. ed. by J. Westrup (1952); H. Davey, *History of English Music,* rev. ed. (1921); E. D. Mackerness, *A Social History of English Music* (1964). *For II–IV:* J. Pulver, *A Dictionary of Old English Music and Musical Instruments* (1923); id., *A Biographical Dictionary of Old English Music* (1927); F. L. Harrison, *Music in Medieval Britain* (1958); S. Kenney, *Walter Frye and the "Contenance Angloise"* (1964); W. H. Grattan Flood, *Early Tudor Composers* (1925); F. W. Galpin, *Old English Instruments of Music,* rev. ed. T. Dart (1965); E. Apfel, *Studien zur Satztechnik der mittelalterlichen englischen Musik,* 2 vols. (1959); *ReMMA,* pp. 387ff; *ReMR,* pp. 763ff; *Early English Harmony,* vol. i, facsimiles, by H. E. Wooldridge (1897), vol. ii, transcriptions, by H. V. Hughes (1913); J. Stainer, ed., ‡*Early Bodleian Music,* vols. ii, iii (1901, '13); *Editions XVI, XVII, XXXIV, XXXVII, XL, XLIII, LI; J. Handschin, in *The Musical Times,* 1932, pp. 510–13; 1933, pp. 697–704 (MS Wolfenbüttel 677); K. J. Levy, in *JAMS* iv, 220 (early motets); M. Bukofzer, in *ML* xvii, 225 (first motet); id., in *ML* xix, 119 (first chanson); J. B. Trend, in *ML* ix, 111 (songs); D. Attwater, in *ML* ix, 129 (folksong); A. H. Fox Strangways, in *ML* v, 293 (folksong); F. L. Harrison, in *CP 1952* and *AnnM* i (Eton Choirbook). See also under Carol; "In nomine"; Worcester; "Sumer is icumen in"; Discant. *For V–VII: BuMBE,* pp. 180ff; G. Cecil, *The History of Opera in England* (1930); E. H. Meyer, *English Chamber Music . . . to Purcell* (1946); C. L. Day and E. B. Murrie, *English Song Books 1651–1702: A Bibliography* (1940); J. A. Fuller-Maitland, *English Music in the XIXth Century* (1902); C. Forsyth, *Music and Nationalism: A Study of English Opera* (1911); H. Davey, *English Music, 1604–1904* (1906); F. Kidson and M. Neal, *English Folk Song and Dance* (1915); C. J. Sharp, ed., ‡*English County Folk Songs,* 5 vols. (1908–12; repr. 1 vol., 1961); J. Mark, in *ML* v, 247 (Dryden and opera); H. Reichenbach, in *ML* xix, 268 (tonality of folksong); J. Pulver, in *AM* vi, 169 (Commonwealth); C. L. Cudworth, in *PMA* lxxviii (18th-century symphonists); E. J. Dent, in *PMA* lxxi (Italian opera in London); F. C. Woods, in *PMA* xxii (18th-cent. dances); *id.*, in *PMA* xxiii (18th-cent. songs); A. Porter, in *LBCM,* also *MQ* li (see especially the articles from *The Musical Times* on young British composers mentioned here).   rev. F.B.Z.

English discant. See under Discant.

English flute. An 18th-century name for the end-blown flutes (*recorder or flageolet), as distinct from the side-blown type (transverse flute), which was known as German flute. See Whistle flute.

English horn. See under Oboe family I, B.

English Madrigal School, The. See Editions XVI.

English School of Lutenist Song Writers, The. See Editions XVII.

English Suites. Six suites for the harpsichord by Bach, composed in Köthen (1720?). Each opens with an extended prelude, often in the general style of the first movement of a concerto grosso. The name "English," not used by Bach himself, may stem from the fact that a manuscript in the possession of his son, Johann Christian, contained the inscription "fait pour les Anglais."

English violet. See under Viola d'amore.

Enharmonic. (1) In Greek music, a tonality (scale, tetrachord, genus) that includes quarter tones [see Greece II; see H. Husmann, in *JMP* xliv; C. del Grande, in *RMI* xxxvi].

 (2) In modern theory, tones that are actually

one and the same degree of the chromatic scale but are named and written differently, e.g., g♯ and a♭, c♯ and d♭, etc., according to the key in which they occur. Enharmonic intervals are intervals consisting of the same tones but "spelled" differently, e.g.:

A well-known example of "enharmonic equivalents" is the diminished seventh chord, which can be written in four or more different ways. Enharmonic change is the change of meaning of a tone or a chord (frequently a diminished seventh chord) from sharp to flat, or vice versa, as is frequently the case in modulations, e.g. (one of the earlier instances, from Handel's *Samson*):

his might-y griefs   re-dress

Enharmonic tones are identical in pitch in the modern system of well-tempered tuning, but not in other systems of either theoretical or historical significance (Pythagorean system, *just intonation, mean-tone systems; see Temperament). In just intonation, e.g., c♯ (upper third of a) is $^{25}/_{24}$ while d♭ (lower third of f) is $^{16}/_{15}$; the difference between these tones is the enharmonic **diesis,* $^{128}/_{125} = 41$ cents (very near one-fifth of a whole tone). While pianists have fully adopted the view that enharmonic tones are identical in pitch, violinists and singers frequently insist that they differ and that this difference should be brought out in performance. Thus, in the example (a) below, the d♭ would sound nearly a quarter tone

lower than the preceding c♯. The main objection to this procedure is that it introduces an arbitrary adjustment [see Just intonation] into a performance that in all other respects is based on equal temperament, e.g., in the intonation of the triad. Moreover, in an example like (b), the recommended distinction is obviously impossible since the "changeable" tone is tied over. Finally, it should be noted that the enharmonic change is by no means restricted to chromatic tones such as c♯ and d♭, but that it may occur also on any of the diatonic degrees of the scale. For instance, example (a) in exact transposition a major third upward becomes example (c). However, even the most sensitive violinist would probably not think of playing this passage as it should be played in enharmonically correct intonation, that is, as indicated under (d).

(3) Enharmonic instruments are keyboard instruments that have separate keys and strings (pipes, etc.) for the different enharmonic tones. In this category was Bosanquet's harmonium, specially constructed (c. 1873) to produce 53 microtones to the octave [see R. H. M. Bosanquet, in *PMA* i, 139]. For a 16th-century construction, see Arcicembalo.

Lit.: M. Vogel, *Die Enharmonik der Griechen,* 2 vols. (1963); E. Seidel, *Die Enharmonik in den harmonischen Grossformen Franz Schuberts* (1963); R. P. Winnington-Ingram, in *MF* xviii, 60; W. Dupont, *Geschichte der musikalischen Temperatur* (1935).

Enigmatic canon. See under Canon II. Enigmatic scale, see *Scala enigmatica.*

Enigma Variations. Theme with variations for orchestra by Elgar, op. 36 (1899), so called because each variation depicts one of his friends, who are enigmatically indicated by their initials or by a nickname.

Ensalada [Sp.]. A term known mainly through a publication, *Las Ensaladas de Flecha* (1581), that contains six long four-part vocal compositions by Mateo Flecha (1481–1553), his nephew Mateo Flecha (1530–1604), and others. It has an essentially literary meaning, implying a humorous or satirical mixture of various texts, somewhat in the nature of the textual *quodlibet* [see *Quodlibet* III]. Musically these *ensaladas* are very similar to Janequin's program chansons. There seems to be no basis for the current opinion that the *ensalada* was necessarily a musical *quodlibet.* Flecha's *Ensaladas* (pub. by H. Anglés, 1954) include a "La Guerra" (The Battle), "El Fuego" (The Fire), and "La Bomba" (The Fire Pump). Aguilera de Heredia (b. c. 1560) used the designation for an extended organ composition of a playful character and of varied contents [see Editions XI, 14].

Ensemble [F.]. A group of musicians performing together. One speaks (1) of a "good" or "bad" ensemble with reference to the balance and unification attained in the performance of a string quartet, etc. (2) In opera, ensemble is a piece for more than two singers (duet) or for the soloists together with the chorus. Such pieces usually occur at the end of an act (finale).

(3) In early music (prior to 1600), a distinction between ensemble music (music for more than one performer) and solo music (music for a single performer) is of fundamental importance, since it explains many features of style and clarifies various problems of *performance practice, e.g., the question of improvised coloraturas, which are possible only in solo music, either monophonic (e.g., the solo portions of Gregorian chant) or polyphonic (i.e., keyboard and lute music). Similarly, *Freistimmigkeit is restricted to (polyphonic) solo music, as was free variability of tempo [see Expression]. It may be noted, however, that the "soloist versus ensemble" viewpoint can also be applied to the question of how ensemble music should be performed. In fact, motets or chansons may be reproduced either in "ensemble performance," i.e., with more than one singer to each part, or in "solo performance," i.e., with only one singer to the part. While ensemble performance calls for strict adherence to the music as written, solo performance leaves the singer free to insert improvised coloraturas, particularly in the highest part. There is ample evidence to show that, toward the end of the 16th century, ensemble performance of motets was frequently superseded by solo performance (including improvised coloraturas), a procedure that evidently foreshadows the monodic style of the 17th century.

The distinction between ensemble and solo music is basic in the study of the notation of polyphonic music [see Notation V]. It also may be recommended to supplant the customary but unsatisfactory classification of early polyphonic music as "vocal music" and "instrumental music." This classification has several drawbacks: (a) Prior to 1550 (i.e., prior to the period of strict a cappella music), instrumental participation was frequently called for, or admitted, in the performance of "vocal" music; this admixture is particularly conspicuous in the accompanied songs (*ballades,* etc.) of the 14th century, and in the *frottole* of the early 16th century. (b) Several publications of the 16th century [e.g., A. Willaert, *Fantasie recercari contrapunti a tre voci* (1559)] contain the remark: "da cantare e suonare d'ogni sorte di stromenti," showing that such textless pieces could be sung (in *vocalization) as well as played on any type of melody instrument (viols, recorders, cornettos). Evidently such pieces cannot be classified as either instrumental or vocal music; however, they are definitely "ensemble music." (c) The field of "instrumental music" includes such heterogeneous styles as that of a free-voice keyboard toccata and a lute prelude on the one hand, and, on the other, a ricercar by Willaert or Padovano strictly written in three or four voice-parts. This contrast of style is easily explained if it is recalled that the former types are solo music and the latter ensemble music. It may be noted in passing that ensemble music may well be changed into solo music, a method that was generally known in the 16th century as *intabulation. This practice, however, does not invalidate the basic distinction between genuine ensemble music and genuine solo music, no more than the existence of 19th-century arrangements (e.g., of a Beethoven string quartet) invalidates the distinction between chamber music and piano music.

(4) In a large choral work or piano (violin, cello, etc.) concerto, "solo" refers to the soloist's part as opposed to the part of the chorus and/or orchestra (ensemble).

See *ApNPM*, p. xxif; L. Hibberd, in *MQ* xxxii, no.1.

Enté [F.]. *Motet enté* is a special type of 13th-century motet whose upper part is constructed by inserting a new text (and melody) between portions of a preexisting text (and melody). The "old material" is usually one of the numerous popular refrains taken from the *ballades,* rondeaux, etc., of the trouvères and split into two or more portions between which new words are interpolated. For instance, the refrain "E ai! Ke ferai! Je mur d'amouretes, comant garirai?" of a trouvère *ballade* [see F. Gennrich, *Rondeaux, Virelais und Balladen,* 2 vols. (1921, '27), i, 148f] leads to the following triplum of a motet: "He, ha, que ferais? Belle, je vous ai Tant amée... Et nuit et jour pens et chant: *Je muir d'amouretes!* Se vostre amour n'ai ... ou je languirai, *Et coument en garrai?*" [see Y. Rokseth, *Polyphonies du xiii*ᵉ *siècle,* 4 vols. (1936–39), iii, 52]. For another example ("*Hé amours... avoir merci*") see *AdHM* i, 242. Obviously this method of textual amplification is derived from the identical procedure used in liturgical *tropes. See Refrain III; Farce.

Entführung aus dem Serail, Die [G., The Abduction from the Seraglio]. Opera in three acts by Mozart (libretto by G. Stephanie, based on C. F. Bretzner's play), produced in Vienna, 1782. Setting: Turkey, 16th century. It is Mozart's first real opera in German and also the first German opera of significance. It was written as a wedding gift for Constanze Weber, whom he married a month after its production. See Janizary music.

Entr'acte. A piece (usually instrumental) performed between the acts of a play or opera, e.g., Beethoven's compositions for Goethe's play *Egmont,* or Bizet's entr'actes for his opera *Carmen.* The music of Lully's *comédie-ballets* is mostly in the form of entr'actes (*intermèdes*) for Molière's plays, e.g., *Le Bourgeois Gentilhomme.* Purcell's instrumental entr'actes are known as act tunes or curtain tunes. The term *intermezzo is sometimes used for entr'acte.

Entrada [Sp.], **entrata** [It.]. See Intrada; Entrée.

Entrée. In Lully's operas and similar works, a marchlike piece that was played for the entrance of a dancing group or important personage. The term is also used for nonoperatic compositions of a similar character, e.g., in Bach's Suite in A for violin and harpsichord [see Intrada]. In French ballet of the 17th and 18th centuries, an entrée is a subdivision of an act, roughly corresponding to a "scene" in opera [see Quadrille (2)]. It also is used as equivalent to "act," e.g., in Rameau's *Les Indes galantes;* in these works, each entrée has its own plot, unconnected with that of any other entrée.   D.J.G.

Entremes [Sp.]. The Spanish variety of the operatic *intermezzo.

Entremet [F.]. In the French and Burgundian courts of the 14th and 15th centuries, a short entertainment performed between the courses of a banquet, often including dancing to vocal or instrumental accompaniment.

Entry. The "entrance" of the theme in the different parts of a fugue, at the beginning as well as in the later expositions, particularly if preceded by a rest, as is frequently the case.

Entschieden, entschlossen [G.] Determined, resolute.

Enunciation. A term occasionally used as a synonym for "exposition" in the sonata form.

Envoi, envoy [F.]. In strophic trouvère songs, a

short stanza added at the end as a "send-off." It corresponds to the second half of the full stanzas and is therefore sung to the closing phrases of the full melody [see, e.g., J.-B. Beck, *Le Chansonnier Cangé* (1927), ii, 109]. The Provençal (troubadour) term is *tornada,* while the Italian is *commiato.*

Éoliphone [F.]. *Wind machine (e.g., in Ravel's *Daphnis et Chloé*).

Epechema. Same as *enechema;* see under *Echos.*

Epidiapente, epidiatessaron. See Diapente; Diatessaron.

Epilogue. Synonym for *coda (in sonatas, etc.).

Épinette [F.]. Spinet, harpsichord.

Epiphonus. See under Neumes I (table).

Episema [Gr.]. In some 9th- and 10th-century manuscripts that were written in chironomic neumes, a subsidiary sign in the form of a dash attached to a neume. It occurs most frequently in connection with the *virga* and the *clivis,* as illustrated in Ex. a. It indicates a prolonged note value and therefore is important in the study of Gregorian rhythm [see Gregorian chant VI]. In the modern Solesmes editions it is represented (though not consistently) as shown in Ex. b.

These editions also make extensive use of the "vertical episema" [Ex. c], which is meant to indicate the *ictus. This does not exist in the medieval sources. The term "episema" is also occasionally used for other subsidiary signs of neumatic notation, e.g., those indicating quarter tones [see *WoHN* i, 45].

Episode. A secondary passage or section forming a digression from the main theme. The term is used mainly for a section of a *fugue that does not include a statement of the subject and for the subsidiary sections of the *rondo. Early examples of fugal episodes occur in some ricercars by Girolamo Cavazzoni. Giovanni Gabrieli was the first to employ contrasting material for episodes [see his Ricercar del X. tono, in *RiMB* no. 52 and in *TaAM* ii, 76]. Episodic form is another name for rondo form. However, this term is also used for loosely constructed pieces consisting "only of episodes," like the third movement of Franck's Violin Sonata.

Epistle. A selection, usually from the Epistles of the New Testament (especially those of St. Paul), read or sung between the Collect and Gospel of the Roman Mass (or the Anglican Communion). In the Roman liturgy a special Tone for the Epistle (*tonus epistolae;* see *LU,* pp. 104ff) is used, consisting of a simple recitation with inflections at the ends of sentences.

Epistle sonata. A 17th- and 18th-century instrumental piece designed to be played in church before or after the reading of the *Epistle. Mozart composed several for organ and violin, etc. See R. S. Tangeman, in *MQ* xxxii.

Epithalamium [It. *epitalamio*]. In Greek poetry (Sappho), a poem to be sung by a chorus at weddings; hence music intended for use at weddings. J. J. Kuhnau's program composition "Jacob's Heyrat" (*Biblische Historien,* 1700) contains an *epitalamio.*

Epitritus. Greek for *sesquitertia,* i.e., the ratio $4 : 3$; hence, name for the interval of the fourth [see Acoustics III].

Epogdous, epogdoa [Gr.]. Terms meaning *sesquioctava,* i.e., the ratio $9 : 8$ [see Sesqui-]; hence, name for the Pythagorean whole tone [see Acoustics III].

Equale [*aequale, eguale*]. A composition for *equal voices, i.e., all male or all female, or for equal instruments. In particular, a composition for four trombones, written for solemn occasions. Beethoven composed three such pieces (1812), which, arranged for male chorus, were performed at his funeral.

Equal temperament. See under Temperament III.

Equal voices. Indication for men's voices only or for women's voices only, as opposed to mixed voices. Less frequently, it is used to mean for soprano voices (or others) only. See Equale.

Erbe deutscher Musik, Das. See Editions XVIII.

Ergriffen [G.]. Deeply moved.

Erhöhungszeichen, Erniedrigungszeichen [G.] Sharp, flat.

Erlöschend [G.]. Fading away.

Ermattend [G.]. Tiring, weakening.

Ernani. Opera in four acts by Verdi (libretto by F. M. Piave, after V. Hugo's play), produced in Venice, 1844. Setting: Spain and Aix-la-Chapelle, about 1519.

Ernst, ernsthaft [G.]. Serious.

Eroica. Beethoven's Third Symphony in E-flat major, op. 55, composed in 1803–4. It was written in homage to Napoleon, but Beethoven withdrew the planned dedication when Napoleon took the title of emperor, changing the work's title from "Sinfonia grande: Buonaparte" to "Sinfonia eroica composta per festeggiar il sovvenire d'un gran uomo" (Heroic symphony composed to celebrate the memory of a great man). The programmatic idea suggested by the title and the original dedication is realized only in the most general way, except for the slow movement, marked *Marcia funebre* (funeral march). The last movement is a series of free variations, also including fugal sections, all based on a dancelike theme that Beethoven had used in three earlier compositions: *Contredanses,* no. 7; *Die *Geschöpfe des Prometheus* (a ballet); *Eroica* Variations.

Eroica Variations. Variations for piano by Beethoven, in E-flat major, op. 35 (1802), so called because the theme is the same as the one he employed later in the last movement of the *Eroica Symphony. Another name is *Prometheus Variations,* after the ballet, *Die *Geschöpfe des Prometheus,* in which the theme occurred for the first time.

Eroticon. A love song, or an instrumental piece portraying passionate love.

Ersatzklausel [G.]. Substitute clausula. See Clausula.

Ersterbend [G.]. Fading away.

Erwartung [G., Expectation]. Monodrama in one act by Schoenberg (libretto by M. Pappenheim), completed in 1909 but not produced until 1924, in Prague. Setting: the edge of a forest, timeless. The orchestral accompaniment is in the near *atonal style the composer developed in this period.

Erzähler [G.]. Narrator.

Erzlaute [G.]. Archlute.

Es, eses [G.]. E-flat, e-double-flat; see Pitch names.

Escapement. See under Piano.

Escape note. Same as *échappée* [see Nonharmonic tones I].

Eschequier. See Echiquier.

Esercizio [It.]. Exercise, etude.

Eskimo music. Lit.: H. Thuren and W. Thalbitzer, *The Eskimo Music* (1911; repr. from *Meddelelser øm Gronland* xl, avdeling I); E. Vogeler, *Lieder der Eskimos* (1931); W. Thalbitzer, *Légendes et chants esquimaux du Groenland* (1929); H. H. Roberts and D. Jenness, *Eskimo Songs. Songs of the Copper-Eskimos* (1925); D. Jenness, in *MQ* viii; W. Thalbitzer and H. Thuren, in *ZIM* xii, *BSIM* vii, 36–56; Z. Estreicher, in *Anthropos* xlv (1950), 659; *id.,* in *Bulletin de la Societé neuchâteloise de géographie* liv (1948), 1–54. Also see under American Indian music; Ethnomusicology.

Espinette [F.]. A 16th-century term for a type of harpsichord; see Spinet.

Espressivo [It.]. Expressively; abbreviated *espr.*

Espringale. Medieval name for a jumping dance as distinguished from *carole,* a round dance.

Esquinazo [Sp.]. A Chilean type of serenade, most often sung at Christmas or at special celebrations such as a birthday or saint's day. It sometimes includes a short coda, called *cogollo,* in which words are improvised to dedicate the song to a particular person.   J.O-S.

Estampes [F.]. A set of three piano pieces by Debussy (1903): "Pagodes" (Pagodas); "Soirée dans Grenade" (Evening in Granada); "Jardins sous la pluie" (Gardens in the Rain).

Estampie, estampida, istanpitta, stampita. The most important instrumental form of the 13th and 14th centuries. Similar to the (vocal) sequence [see Sequence II] from which it was evidently derived, it consists of four to seven sections called *puncta,* each of which is repeated: a a, b b, c c, etc. Different endings, called *ouvert* and *clos* [It. *aperto* and *chiuso*], are provided for the first and second statement of each *punctum,* as in the modern *prima* and *seconda volta.* In some cases the same two endings are used for all the *puncta,* so that the following scheme results: a + x, a + y; b + x, b + y; c + x, c + y; etc.

The earliest known example of this form is the troubadour song "Kalenda maya" (The Month of May; see *HAM,* no. 18d; *AdHM* i, 190), whose text supposedly was written by the troubadour Raimbaut de Vaqueiras (fl. 1180–1207) to the melody of an "estampida" played by two "joglar de Fransa" (French jongleurs) on their vielles. All the other existing examples are purely instrumental pieces. Eight monophonic *estampies* are contained in the 13th-century *Chansonnier Roy* [see Sources, no. 12], while the 14th-century MS Brit. Mus. *Add. 29987* contains a number of "istanpittas," some with subtitles such as "Lamento di tristano," "La manfredina," "Salterello," "Isabella," "Tre fontane" [Ex. in *HAM*, nos. 40c, 59; *SchGMB,* no. 28]. These charming pieces are in the character of idealized dances, suggesting that the *estampie* originally was a true dance. The earliest source of keyboard music, the so-called Robertsbridge Fragment of *c.* 1320, contains three extended two-part compositions (one incomplete) in the form of an *estampie* [*HAM,* no. 58]. There also exist two-voice examples of *estampie* (or *ductia*) [*HAM,* no. 41].

Owing to the similarity of name and structure, the *estampie* is usually identified with the *stantipes,* a form described by Johannes de Grocheo (*c.* 1300) as consisting of from five to seven "puncta." This theory, however, has not remained unchallenged (C. Sachs). Grocheo distinguishes the *stantipes* from the **ductia,* characterizing the latter as having four (or fewer) *puncta.* It may be noted, however, that the so-called *estampida* "Kalenda maya" has only three *puncta.* The problem is further complicated by the fact that two 14th-century treatises on poetry describe a "vocal" *estampie* that apparently lacked the *puncta* but possessed a refrain.

Lit.: P. Aubry, ‡*Estampies et danses royales* (1906); C. Sachs, *A World History of the Dance* (1937), pp. 292ff; L. Hibberd, "Estampie and Stantipes" (*Speculum,* 1944); J. Wolf, "Die Tänze des Mittelalters" (*AMW* i); J. Handschin, "Über Estampie und Sequenz" (*ZMW* xii); H. J. Moser, "Stantipes und Ductia" (*ZMW* ii).

Estey organ. See under Harmonium III.

Esthetics. See Aesthetics of music.

Estilo [Sp.]. A typical song of the Argentine pampas consisting of an initial section in slow duple meter (2/4 or 4/4) and a fast section in triple meter (3/4 or 6/8), after which the first section is repeated. Its text is based on a stanza of ten eight-syllable lines and almost always deals with life in the Argentine plains.   J.O-S.

Estinto [It.]. Barely audible.

Estribillo [Sp.]. See under *Villancico*.

Éteint [F.]. Barely audible.

Ethiopian church music. Lit.: J. M. Harden, *The Anaphoras of the Ethiopic Liturgy* (1928); M. Cohen, *Chants éthiopiques* (1931); E. Wellesz, in *Oriens Christianus* (1920); L. Picken, in *AM* xxix, 41; *GD,* Suppl. Vol. p. 179f; *GDB,* ii, 868f; *AdHM* i, 138.

Ethnomusicology. A term coined by J. Kunst to replace "comparative musicology" (G. *vergleichende Musikwissenschaft*) on the ground that the comparative method is employed in every scientific discipline. Ethnomusicology is an approach to the study of *any* music, not only in terms of itself but also in relation to its cultural context. Currently the term has two broad applications: (1) the study of all music outside the European art tradition, including survivals of earlier forms of that tradition in Europe and elsewhere; (2) the study of all varieties of music found in one locale or region, e.g., the "ethnomusicology" of Tokyo or Los Angeles or Santiago would comprise the study in that locality of all types of European art music, the music of ethnic enclaves, folk, popular and commercial music, musical hybrids, etc.; in other words, all music being used by the people of a given area.

In the 18th and 19th centuries an interest in what was then termed "exotic music" led to studies in Chinese music (J. B. du Halde, 1735; J. M. Amiot, 1779) and Arab music (Andres, 1787; R. G. Kiesewetter, 1842). As early as 1768, the *Dictionnaire de musique* of Jean-Jacques Rousseau contained examples of Chinese, Canadian Indian, Swiss, and Persian music. It was not until the end of the 19th century, however, that a few writers began to realize that the musical cultures of the non-Western world merited the same serious scholarship that was being focused on the European art tradition (e.g., C. R. Day, *The Music and Musical Instruments of Southern India and The Deccan,* 1891, with an Introduction by A. J. Hipkins; F. T. Piggott, *The Music and Musical Instruments of Japan,* 1893; F. Bose in *AMW* xxiii, 239ff).

About the same time, two developments provided essential tools for the ethnomusicologist: the Ellis cent system and the phonograph. In 1884–85 the British mathematician and philologist, Alexander John Ellis, aided by A. J. Hipkins, demonstrated that there are a great variety of tuning systems and scales built on different principles from those known in western Europe. He showed that these are accepted by accustomed ears as normal and logical. His method in these studies was based on the arbitrary division of the tempered octave into 1,200 parts or "cents" [see Cents]. The first phonographic field recordings were made in America by J. W. Fewkes in 1890 and transcribed by B. I. Gilman in 1891 ["Zuni Melodies," in *Journal of American Archaeology and Ethnology* i, 68]. In 1900 C. Stumpf and O. Abraham made the first German recordings of this kind when a court orchestra from Thailand and musicians from South Africa visited Berlin. Today innumerable collections have been amassed by universities, state-supported institutions, and centers for research all over the world, with the tape recorder having largely replaced the phonograph.

In Germany the term *vergleichende Musikwissenschaft* became associated with the systematic studies inspired by Stumpf and Abraham and subsequently led by E. M. von Hornbostel. The interest of German scholars was concentrated on acoustics, psychology, and physiology in an effort to understand principles of tuning systems, scales, and organology, leading to a number of speculative theories founded on the *Kulturkreislehre*. In the United States studies in comparative musicology, pioneered by Fewkes and Gilman and carried on by Frances Densmore and others, showed the influence of anthropological interest in the American Indian. The methods developed under Hornbostel's brilliant leadership were introduced in the United States in 1928 by one of his pupils, G. Herzog ("The Yuman Musical Style," *Journal of American Folklore* xli, 183–231). Both German and American scholars emphasized cross-cultural comparisons.

An early concern with comparative method, before the subjects under comparison could be understood, led to some imaginative theories but provided very little accurate information. Nonmusical standards relating to economic status, technology, and relative social isolation were responsible for the general use of such terms as "primitive music" and "exotic music." It was not until 1928 that M. E. Metfessel documented the need for a device that could register musical sounds objectively, independent of the aural prejudice of the transcriber, showing subtleties of pitch, duration, attack, release, and other details of performance style that resist transcription in Western music notation (*Phonophotography in Folk Music*, 1928). Various approaches to this problem have been undertaken in Japan, Norway, Israel, and the United States.

In 1941 C. Seeger wrote that actual performance of music of another culture must carry far more weight than mere listening to it ["Music and Culture," MTNA, *Proceedings*, 35th series, pp. 112–22], an observation made a few years earlier by P. R. Kirby [Preface, *The Musical Instruments of the Native Races of South Africa*, 1934; repr. Johannesburg, 1953]. Foreshadowed by Seeger and Kirby, a new kind of program that has had a profound effect on training and research elsewhere in the United States and abroad was begun in 1954 at the University of California, Los Angeles. The program includes training in basic musicianship of non-Western musical cultures in order to provide a firm foundation in the performance skills of specific African, Oriental, and other types of music. Also, as Manfred Bukofzer indicated in 1956 ["Observations on the Study of Non-Western Music," *Les Colloques de Wégimont*, Brussels, Elsevier, 1956, p. 35] and as practical studies in performance have borne out, the research methods of Western historical musicology are inadequate for non-Western studies. As a result, new field and laboratory methods are rapidly being developed. The basic elements of music—rhythm, melody, harmony, tone color—have developed differently and with varying degrees of emphasis in different cultures. In the Middle East, Africa, South and Southeast Asia, and the Far East, rhythm and melody are expressed in subtle, rich, and complex forms. Among the gong-chime cultures of Southeast Asia orchestras composed of bronze instruments have developed a rich harmonic texture founded on the principle of orchestration known as stratification. In Western music, the primary emphasis on harmonic development represents an entirely different utilization of the basic elements of music. A comparison of the rhythm and melody of India with those elements in European art music (or American jazz, for that matter) serving as models is no more enlightening than a comparison of Tamil with Latin and Greek.

Recent studies not only document Ellis' assertion regarding the "musical scale" but also indicate that the musical practices, cultural contexts, and value systems of cultures throughout the world are highly individual, varying often in principle and always in detail from region to region and locale to locale (e.g., see under Bali, Java, Thailand, Vietnam, etc.). A vast number of musical cultures of the non-Western world are yet to be studied systematically and the music of the European art tradition re-examined in the light of newly emerging concepts before comparative methods can "give musicology a truly world-wide perspective."

Lit.: For bibl. through 1958, see J. Kunst, *Ethnomusicology,* 3rd ed. (1959) and Suppl. (1960). Also see E. M. Hornbostel, *Opera Omnia,* ed. K. Wachsmann (in preparation, 1966); C. Sachs, *The Wellsprings of Music,* ed. J. Kunst (1962); A. P. Merriam, *The Anthropology of Music* (1964); B. Nettl, *Theory and Method in Ethnomusicology* [1964]; id., *Reference Materials in Ethnomusicology* [1961]; G. Herzog, *Research in Primitive and Folk Music in the United States, a Survey* (1936); C. Seeger, "Systematic Musicology: Viewpoints, Orientations and Methods" (*Journal of the American Musicological Society* iv, 240–48); id., "Semantic, Logical and Political Considerations Bearing Upon Research in Ethnomusicology" (*Ethnomusicology* v, 77–80); id., "Music as a Tradition of Communication Discipline and Play" (*Ethnomusicology* vi, 156–63); M. Hood, "Music, the Unknown," in *Musicology* (1963).   M.H.

Ethos [Gr.]. In ancient Greek music, the "ethical" character of the various scales. The (Greek) Dorian (similar to our Phrygian) was considered manly and strong, representing the ancient tradition; the Phrygian, ecstatic and passionate; the Lydian, feminine and lascivious; the Mixolydian, sad and mournful. Similar characterizations, doubtless influenced by the Greek ideas, are found in medieval and later discussions of the church modes. See Key characteristics.

Lit.: *ReMMA,* pp. 44ff; L. Harap, in *MQ* xxiv; E. M. von Hornbostel, in *CP Wolf;* C. Sachs, *The Rise of Music in the Ancient World* [1943].

Et in terra pax. See under Gloria.

Étouffé [F.]. Damped, muted (kettledrums, violins). *Étouffoir,* piano damper.

Etude. A piece designed to aid the student of an instrument in developing his mechanical and technical ability. An etude is usually devoted entirely to one of the special problems of instrumental technique, such as scales, arpeggios, octaves, double stops, trills, etc. Whereas etudes are written in the form of a complete piece, finger exercises are short formulas that have to be repeated many times, either on the same pitch or moving through the degrees of the scale. Many modern teachers prefer finger exercises because they are more efficient than etudes.

Finger exercises were already known in the early 16th century. The tablature of Oswald Holtzach (1515, Univ. Bibl. Basel) contains sequential passages in sixteenth notes, entitled: "Lauffwerck, mit beiden Händen zu bruchen"

("running passages, to be used with both hands"). A similar piece is contained in Leonard Kleber's tablature (*c.* 1520, St. Bibl. Berlin). Toward the end of the 17th century the Italian toccata became a sort of etude, owing to the extended use of stereotyped passages and the deterioration of the musical quality (A. Scarlatti, B. Pasquini). A publication by F. Durante (1684–1755), *6 Sonate per cembalo divisi in studii e divertimenti,* contains six "sonatas," each consisting of a "studio" and "divertimento," the former being somewhat serious and difficult to play, the latter in the lighter vein of the "gallant style" [see Editions IX, 11]. The originator of the modern etude is Muzio Clementi (1752–1832), whose *Préludes et Exercices* (1790) and *Gradus ad Parnassum* (1817–26) mark the beginning of the enormous literature of the 19th-century etude. Outstanding collections of etudes for the piano were written by Cramer, Czerny, Moscheles, and Bertini, and for the violin by Kreutzer, Rode, Paganini, d'Alard, and Bériot. Chopin, in his 27 Etudes (op. 10, op. 25, and three single pieces), created the concert etude, which is designed not only for study but also for public performance and which combines technical difficulty with high artistic quality. His example was followed by F. Liszt (*Études d'exécution transcendante,* and others), Scriabin (op. 8, op. 42, op. 65), and Debussy (twelve *Études,* dedicated to the memory of Chopin, 1915). See E. Gork, "Die Entwicklung der Klavieretüde von Mozart bis Liszt" (diss. Vienna, 1930).

Études d'exécution transcendante [F., Transcendental Etudes]. Twelve concert etudes by Liszt, published 1852. The title refers to their great technical difficulty.

Études symphoniques [F., Symphonic Etudes]. A set of twelve piano pieces by Schumann, op. 13 (1834), in the form of a theme (by Fricken) with variations and a concluding finale. The term "symphonic" probably refers to the highly virtuoso treatment of the piano, occasionally with distinctly "orchestral" effects. The variation technique is extremely advanced for the time [see under Variations IV (3)], and some of the pieces have, at best, a very tenuous connection with the theme. This probably is the reason why Schumann discarded the original title, *Études en forme de variations.*

Eugen Onegin [Rus. *Yevgeny Onyegin*]. Opera in three acts by Tchaikovsky (libretto by K. S. Shilovsky and the composer, after a poem by

Pushkin), produced in Moscow, 1879. Setting: Russia, about 1820.

Eunuch flute. See Mirliton.

Euouae. In the liturgical books of the Roman rites, the usual abbreviation for "seculorum. Amen" (consisting of the vowels of these two words), the closing words of the "Gloria Patri" [see Doxology]. It is given at the end of introits and antiphons in order to indicate the proper ending (*differentia*), which leads back to the final repetition of the introit or antiphon. For more details, see Psalm tones. The spelling *Evovae*, frequently found in older books, has been confused by some writers (among them F. X. Haberl, in *Cäcilien-Kalender*, 1885, p. 32b) with the ancient Greek word *Evoe*, an interpretation that aroused surprise and indignation over the use in the Roman service of a bacchanalian exclamation of joy.

Euphonium. See under Brass instruments III (d).

Euridice, L'. Title of the two earliest extant operas, one by Peri (1600), the other by Caccini (1602), both produced at Florence and based on the same libretto (by O. Rinuccini), which relates the story of Orpheus and Eurydice. Setting: ancient Greece. The music consists almost entirely of recitative, which, although not free from monotony, is remarkable for its austere expressiveness, particularly in Peri's opera.

Evangeliary [L. *evangeliarium*]. See under Liturgical books I (9).

Evangelist. In a Passion, the narrator who recites the text of the Gospel.

Evangelium [G.]. Gospel.

Evensong. The sung form of the Evening Prayer of the Anglican Church, corresponding to the Roman Catholic Vespers. See Anglican church music.

Evirato [It.]. Same as *castrato*.

Evovae. See Euouae.

Exaquir. See Echiquier.

Exchange of voice-parts. See Voice exchange.

Exequiae [L.]. Exequies, i.e., music for funeral rites.

Exotic music. Archaic term for non-Western music. See Ethnomusicology.

Exposition. In the *sonata* form, the first section, containing the statement of the themes [G. *Themenaufstellung*]. In a fugue, the first as well as subsequent sections containing the imitative presentation of the theme [G. *Durchführung*]; see *Fugue I (d), (f).

Expression [F.; G. *Ausdruck;* It. *espressione;* Sp. *expresión*].

I. *In composition.* Musical expression may be described as the quality that accounts for the peculiar emotional effect of music—much more than the other arts—on human beings. In fact, expression is usually regarded as a basic and universal attribute of music. However, while most music known and heard today is expressive, there are numerous compositions—generally from earlier periods—that are more notable for their formal organization, intricate design, fascinating figurations, playful elements [G. *Spielmusik*], and similar features resulting from a detached, objective, impersonal, and even intellectual approach to composition. To regard an organum by Perotinus, a conductus of the 13th century, a motet by Machaut, an echo-fantasia by Sweelinck, or even Stravinsky's octet for wind instruments as expressive would simply render the term meaningless. On the other hand, some early music is more or less expressive, e.g.; Gregorian chant, a *ballade* by Machaut, a motet by Josquin, a madrigal or an opera by Monteverdi, a lament by Froberger, a cantata by Buxtehude or Bach. Baroque vocal music is often highly expressive, while baroque instrumental music tends to appeal to present-day listeners because of its detached, nonexpressive character.

An important step toward expressiveness in instrumental music was taken by the members of the *Mannheim school (c. 1750). It was in their symphonies that devices of dynamic expression such as sudden *ff* and *pp* and long crescendos and decrescendos were first exploited. While in these works the details of expression are not always justified by the music itself, often appearing as a somewhat extraneous addition, a complete amalgamation of "expression" and "composition" is achieved in the works of Haydn, Mozart, Beethoven, and Schubert. Here expression is in complete agreement with the musical substance, which has become expressive in itself. In the romantic movement, the possibilities of expression were exploited to the fullest. An immense array of shades of subtlety appeared, and composers invested vast ingenuity in the invention of new nuances as well as words or signs to indicate them. Although this tendency has greatly enriched the musical palette, it has not always enhanced artistic quality. The anti-romantic movement of the 20th century brought a marked reversal of attitude. Erik Satie was probably the first to write intentionally unexpressive (dry) music, and to ridicule the romantic tendencies with ironic expression marks, such as: "corpulentus," "caeremoniosus," "devenez pâle," etc. Composers such as Poulenc, Stravinsky, and Hindemith also frequently wrote in an intentionally unexpressive style, using expression signs very sparingly and sometimes indicating their intentions through remarks such as "sans expression," "Mit wenig Ausdruck." Recent composers, especially Boulez and Carter, have provided their scores with an incredible number of novel signs to indicate minute details of performance.

II. *In performance.* Usually expression refers less to composition than to performance, as appears from statements such as "Expression [is] the creative element in musical performance [*GDB, s.v.* "Expression"] or "Ausdruck nennt man die feinere Nüancierung im Vortrage musikalischer Kunstwerke" [*Riemanns Musiklexikon, s.v.* "Ausdruck"]. It is the performer who must transform the composer's work from the printed page into vital communication. This process involves details of tempo, rhythm, dynamics, phrasing, accentuation, touch, and bowing as well as subjective interpretation. The ideal performer is one who succeeds in bestowing on the composition a personal and original expression within the stylistic frame of the work and in full compliance with the intentions indicated by the composer. Unfortunately, the second part of this postulate is not always realized, and it is the arbitrariness of so many virtuosos that has been partly responsible for the excess of expression marks found in the works of composers who thus hoped to forestall distortion and misinterpretation. Yet complete control over the performer is not only impossible but undesirable. The only remedy is to improve the education of performers in matters of musical style and taste. The most common fault is the application of a romantic, i.e., a highly expressive, treatment to nonromantic music, such as the works of Bach, Haydn, Mozart, and Beethoven. The deplorable result is an exaggeration of all nuances: the use of prestissimo instead of allegro, of larghissimo instead of adagio, of *fff* and *ppp* instead of *f* and *p*, of frequent crescendos

and decrescendos instead of an even level of sonority, of numerous rubatos, ritardandos, and accelerandos instead of strictly kept tempo, etc. Even more disastrous is the application of such methods to works of the Middle Ages or the Renaissance, works that demand clarity above all. See also Expression marks.

Lit.: E. Sorantin, *The Problem of Musical Expression* (1932); C. C. Pratt, *The Meaning of Music* (1931); T. Dart, *The Interpretation of Music* [1954]; R. Donington, *The Interpretation of Early Music* [1963]; G. Haydon, "On the Problem of Expression in Baroque Music" (*JAMS* iii).

Expressionism. Term taken over from the visual arts and used, more or less metaphorically, for music written in a deeply subjective and introspective style. The composition of such music is roughly coeval and linked in inspiration with the German school of expressionist painters (Nolde, Kirchner, Ernst, Kokoschka, *et al.*), who worked in Munich, Berlin, Vienna, and other important German and Austrian centers from about 1905 to about 1930. These painters sought to go beyond the purely visual appearance and to depict the artist's subjective interpretation of reality, using distortion, exaggeration, symbolism, etc. This approach is opposed to that of the *impressionist painters, who sought to depict the moving appearance of things in given settings of light and color as seen through a highly sensitive but objective eye, with total disregard for the psychological or emotional aspects of the subject.

Musical expressionism in the early 20th century is the result of a gradual development rather than an abrupt reaction (against impressionism). Its roots lie in romanticism, which continued to dominate the creative arts in Germany. Indeed, the "expressionist" music produced in Germany in the 1910's and 1920's may be considered the last desperate cry of romanticism in its decline.

The composers most often identified as "expressionists" are Schoenberg (who was also a talented painter) and Berg, to some extent Webern, and, in some of their works, Krenek, Hindemith, and others. Schoenberg's *Verklärte Nacht, Pierrot Lunaire,* and *Erwartung,* along with Berg's operas *Wozzeck* and *Lulu,* are the masterpieces of expressionist music. [Also see Atonality.] Whether musical expressionism ends where neoclassicism begins is open to question. Its actual end seems rather to coincide with the beginnings of Nazism in Germany and Austria.

The Nazi condemnation of so-called *entartete Kunst* (perverted art) was directed against those works of painting and music that are most representative of expressionism.

Lit.: L. Rognoni, *La Scuola musicale di Vienna* [1966]; L. Cammarota, *L'Espressionismo e Schönberg* [1965]; A. Schering, *Die expressionistische Bewegung der Musik,* in *Einführung in die Kunst der Gegenwart* (1922); T. W. Adorno, *Philosophie der neuen Musik* (1949); A. Berg, *Écrits,* ed. H. Pousseur [1957].   A.B.

Expression marks. Signs or words (sometimes abbreviated) used to indicate details of performance. The most basic types are *tempo marks and *dynamic marks. In addition there are signs for *legato and *staccato, for various kinds of *bowing, for *articulation and *phrasing, for the use of the piano *pedals, etc., and finally, numerous terms such as "passionato," "dolce," and "con brio" that are intended to describe the general character or mood of a composition, section, or passage.

No expression marks of any kind from before 1500 have been found. The earliest dynamic indication is a *tocca pian piano* (play very softly) in "Non ti spiaqua l'ascoltar" of the so-called Capirola lute book of *c.* 1517 (ed. by O. Gombosi, p. 85). Tempo indications first appear in the vihuela book *El Maestro* (1535) by Luis Milán, who prescribes for certain passages of his fantasias "apriessa" (quick), and for others "a espacio" (slow). It is significant that the earliest expression marks are found in music for a single player. About the end of the 16th century, the novel style of contrasting sonorities [see Concertato; Echo] led to the use of the terms *forte* and *piano.* The earliest compositions with these indications are G. Gabrieli's *Sonata pian e forte,* 1597 [see *SchGMB,* no. 148; *HAM,* no. 173], the upper part of a Kyrie published in the same year [see *ReMR,* p. 498], Adriano Banchieri's madrigal comedy *La Pazzia senile,* 1598 [*Editions VI, no. 6] and some pieces in his *L'Organo suonarino* (1605–22). A little later the abbreviating letters must have come into use, since Domenico Mazzocchi, in the preface to his *Madrigali* (1638), says that the letters F. P. E. t.—for Forte, Piano, Echo, trill—are commonly known.

The monodic style of the early 17th century made musicians aware of the importance of subtly shaded expression. Caccini, in the preface of *Le Nuove musiche* (1601), illustrated the new style of singing through examples bearing remarks such as "Esclamazione spiritosa," "senza misura quasi favellando," etc. Banchieri used a variety of tempo indications, such as presto, più presto, prestissimo, in addition to allegro and adagio [see *ApMfZ* i, 27ff]. At the same time, Frescobaldi gave detailed information regarding free tempo in the preface of his *Toccate e partite d'intavolatura di cembalo* [1615–16; see C. Sartori, *Bibliografia della musica strumentale italiana* (1952), pp. 206f, 218f]. In the second half of the 17th century such terms as grave, largo, vivace, and others were not uncommon. About 1720 François Couperin described the character of his harpsichord pieces with such subtly shaded expression marks as "gravement sans lenteur" or "gracieusement et légèrement."

Prior to the middle of the 18th century crescendo and decrescendo were used chiefly for the vocal performance of single sustained tones [see *Messa di voce*]. Mazzocchi seems to have been the first to indicate these effects with signs, a *V* for a crescendo (called by him *messa di voce*), and a *C* for a crescendo followed by a diminuendo (the *messa di voce* proper; see Harding, p. 91). The modern signs for crescendo and diminuendo appeared much later, the earliest known instance being in Geminiani's *Prime Sonate* of 1739. Crescendos and diminuendos extending over lengthy musical phrases were also known throughout the 17th century but were always indicated with prescriptions such as "forte, piano, pianissimo" (Mazzocchi), or "Lowd, Soft, Softer" (M. Locke), or "lowder by degrees" (M. Locke, Curtain Tune in *The Tempest,* 1675). The members of the Mannheim school were the first to use all dynamic effects in the modern way, for the purpose of orchestral coloring and climatic or anticlimatic effects.

Expression marks in Bach are in effect limited to a handful of pieces in which degrees of sonority are indicated by *f, p,* and *pp.* In view of the excessive number of expression marks found in modern editions of Bach, it should be noted that the entire manuscript of *The Well-Tempered Clavier* contains nothing but the notes and signs of ornamentation, except for some *f* and *p* (usually disregarded in modern editions) in the G♯-minor prelude of Part II.

Lit.: R. E. M. Harding, *Origins of Musical Time and Expression* (1938); D. Boyden, "Dynamics in Seventeenth- and Eighteenth-Century Music" (*CP Davison*); G. Langley, in *PMA* xxxviii; A. Heuss, "Die Dynamik der Mannheimer Schule" (*ZMW* ii); M. Brenet, "Sur l'Origine du 'crescendo'" (*BSIM,* 1910).

Expressive organ [F. *orgue expressif*]. See under Harmonium II.

Exsultet. See under *Praeconium paschale.*

Extemporization. See Improvisation.

Extravaganza. Term sometimes used for a musical caricature [see Satire]. Gilbert and Sullivan used it as a subtitle for *Trial by Jury.*

Exultet. See under *Praeconium paschale.*

Eye music [G. *Augenmusik*]. Certain 15th- and 16th-century compositions in which the affective meaning of the music is made visible to the eye by the use of special methods of notation. By far the most common device is the use of blackened notes for texts expressing grief or lament as well as for individual words such as "night," "dark," "shade," etc. An early instance is found in Ockeghem's *Missa Mi-Mi,* where black notation

is used at the end of the Credo for the word "mortuorum" (also, however, for the continuation: "et vitam venturi saeculi. Amen," which has the opposite connotation). A more striking example is Josquin's *lament on the death of Ockeghem, *Nymphes des bois,* written entirely in black notes. Numerous examples occur in the madrigals of the second half of the 16th century, especially those of Luca Marenzio. Since the notational significance of blackened notes is a change from duple to triple rhythm [coloration; see Mensural notation V], the "dark" passages appear in modern transcription as triplet formations.

The term "eye music" is also applied to examples of *word painting, particularly those that employ ascending or descending motion, thus giving to the reader or performer a visual impression of the meaning of words such as "heaven" or "dying." See A. Einstein, *The Italian Madrigal* (1949), i, 234ff; *id.,* in *ZIM* xiv.

F

F. (1) See Pitch names; Letter notation; Hexachord. (2) Abbr. for forte; ff (fff), abbr. for fortissimo. (3) F clef, see Clef. F-hole, see Sound hole.

Fa. See Pitch names; Solmization; Hexachord. *Fa fictum* means, in systems of hexachord and mutation, the *fa* (fourth degree) of the *hexachordum molle* (beginning with f), i.e., b-flat; or, the same degree of the transposed hexachord starting on b-flat, i.e., e-flat'. Both tones belong to *musica ficta.

Faberdon. German 16th-century corruption of F. *fauxbourdon.* The term had no real significance but acquired a legendary connotation concerning Pythagoras, who is said to have "invented" music by listening to the sounds of smith's hammers of various sizes (L. *faber,* smith, and G. *Don* [*Ton*], sound; see Pythagorean hammers). The humanist Latinization *fabrisonus* also was used (e.g., in H. Buchner's "Fundamentum" of *c.* 1520–30).

Fabordón. Spanish 16th-century corruption of

F. *fauxbourdon,* used to denote four-part harmonization of the psalm tones [see *Falsobordone*]. See also Glosa.

Faburden. (1) A term used in an English MS of the early 15th century (Brit. Mus. *Lansdowne 763*) to describe a method of improvised sixth-chord harmonization; see *Discantus supra librum.* It involves the use of a derivative melody that is generally a third above but occasionally in unison with the *cantus firmus.* (2) In English organ music of the early 16th century (John Redford, *et al.*), a "verse on the faburden" is a polyphonic setting not of the original plainsong but of a derivative melody that is generally a sixth or occasionally an octave below the plainsong [see Redford's *O Lux, on the fabourden* in C. Pfatteicher's *John Redford* (1934), music section, p. 50; see Ex. a, original melody;

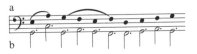

b, faburden melody. This faburden is the same as that described by the 15th-century anonymous writer who uses it transposed to the lower fifth, whereas in the example here it is transposed to the lower octave]. In other organ pieces by Redford the derivative melody is used untransposed, and in still others he uses a derivative melody forming lower thirds and occasional unisons with the *cantus firmus*. This modification is the same as in the *modus faulxbourdon* described by Guilielmus Monachus in his "De preceptis artis" of *c.* 1485 (*CS*, iii, 288); see *Discantus supra librum*. For the relationship between faburden and fauxbourdon, see Fauxbourdon. See H. Miller, in *MQ* xxvi. (3) See *Falsobordone*.

Fackeltanz [G.]. A traditional dance of Prussian court ceremonies of the 19th century, consisting of a slow torchlight procession [G. *Fackel,* torch]. Spontini, Flotow, and Meyerbeer have written music for such occasions.

Fado, fadinho [Port.]. The popular music par excellence of the cities of Portugal, frequently heard in cafés and on the streets. It consists of song and dance accompanied by the guitar. It originated in Lisbon, in time spreading to other cities, with noticeable differences in style and spirit. See G. Chase, *The Music of Spain* (1941), p. 241; R. Gallop, in *MQ* xix, xx, and in *ML* xiv, 222ff, 343ff.

Fa fictum. See under Fa.

Fagott [G.], **fagotto** [It.]. Bassoon. *Fagottino* [It.] is the tenor oboe (tenoroon), *fagottone* [It.] the contrabassoon. *Fagottgeige* [G.] is a large 18th-century viol whose strings were overspun with silk and therefore produced a buzzing sound reminiscent of the Fagott. *Fagottzug* [G.] is a stop mechanism of old pianos (*c.* 1800) that produced a buzzing effect by means of a paper strip rubbing against the strings.

Fair of Sorochinsk, The [Rus. *Sorochinskaya Yarmarka*]. Unfinished opera in three acts by Mussorgsky (to his own libretto, based on a short story by Gogol). Revised and completed by several composers, it is occasionally performed in a version by Nicolas Tcherepnin (1923). Produced (in concert form) in St. Petersburg, 1911. Setting: the Ukraine, mid-19th century.

Fakes, musical. See Spurious compositions.

Fa-la, fa-la-la. A special type of 16th-century song in which the syllables "fa la la" or similar ones are used as a refrain, e.g.: "Now is the month of Maying, When merry lads are playing, Fa la la la . . . , fa la la la . . ." (T. Morley). An early example, with the refrain "tan tan tan tarira," occurs in Baldassare Donato's *Il Primo Libro di canzon villanesche alla napolitana* (1550?); numerous others are found in the works of G. Gastoldi, Lasso, Orazio Vecchi, and others. Through Gastoldi's *Balletti . . . per cantare sonare & ballare* (1591) the fa-la's became known in England (Morley, Weelkes, Hilton) and in Germany (H. L. Hassler, E. Widman, J. Staden, D. Friderici). Ex. in *HAM*, nos. 158, 159.

Falsa [Sp., Port.]. Dissonance. In 17th-century organ music, *obra* (or *tiento*) *de falsas* is a composition making deliberate use of dissonances, as in the Italian *durezze e ligature*. A large number of *falsas* were written by Aguilera de Heredia, Correa de Arauxo (*Libro de tientes,* 1626), Bruna, Joséph Jiménez, Cabanilles, and others. See Editions XI, 14; H. Anglés, in *CP Wagner*.

Falsa musica. See *Musica ficta*.

False. *False cadence,* same as deceptive cadence. *False fifth* (*triad*), old term for the diminished fifth (triad). *False modulation,* see Modulation. *False relation,* see Cross relation.

Falsetto. [It.]. An artificial method of singing used by male singers, particularly tenors, to reach notes above their ordinary range. Actually falsetto is an action: the deliberate limitation of the tone-making apparatus. Since such tones are rather weak compared to the normal tones of a voice, falsetto is usually considered to be of inferior quality. In early music, however, falsetto singing was highly esteemed and was much used for the higher parts of polyphonic Masses and motets when boy singers were not available. In England, particularly, falsetto singing was widely practiced [see Alto]. In fact, a well-trained falsetto voice, though lacking the powerful volume and dramatic expressiveness of a tenor, has its own charm. It stands in the same relationship to the normal tenor voice as the recorder to the flute, the viol to the violin. See C. Anthon, in *Etude* lxiii, 615; R. S. Tatnell, *The Consort,* no. 22, 1965.

Falsobordone [It., from F. *fauxbourdon*]. A 16th-century term for simple four-part harmonizations of psalm tones or other liturgical recitatives (Magnificat, Lamentations, etc.). This style was cultivated particularly in Spain, where it was called *fabordón*. A. de Cabezón (1510–66) wrote *fabordones* for organ, and F. Guerrero (1528–99) for chorus [see Editions XX, 2, 3]. These are settings of psalm or Magnificat verses that were used alternately with verses in plainsong [see Magnificat]. For an Italian example (from Cesare de Zaccaria, *Intonationes cum Psalmodiis*, 1594) see *ReMR*, p. 492. Heinrich Schütz, in the preface to his *Historie von der ... Auferstehung* (1623), speaks of the instrumental accompaniment to the Evangelist's recitations as *falsobordone*. The use of *falsobordone* compositions (particularly in Palestrina's *Lamentations) in alternation with Gregorian chant was authorized for special occasions by Pius X in his *Motu proprio* (1903).

For a plausible explanation of the transition from 15th-century fauxbourdon to 16th-century *falsobordone*, see E. Trumble, in *JAMS* viii, 71.

Falstaff. Opera in three acts by Verdi (libretto by A. Boito, based on Shakespeare's *Henry IV* and *The Merry Wives of Windsor*), produced at Milan, 1893. Setting: Windsor, early 15th century. Together with *Otello* (1887), this opera represents the climax of Verdi's work. Influenced by Wagner's music drama, Verdi largely abandoned here the "number style" of his earlier works [see Number opera] and adopted something like Wagner's unending recitative. However, he remained completely untouched by the harmonic innovations of Wagner, whose chromatic harmonies (*Tristan und Isolde*, 1865) are conspicuously absent in *Falstaff*.

Familiar style [It. *stile familiare*]. A term used for vocal music in which the voices (usually four) move uniformly in regard to note values as well as to syllables of the text, as in a church hymn. From the point of view of musical texture, familiar style is equivalent to note-against-note style (and other designations, e.g., homorhythmic), the only difference being that the latter term is not restricted to vocal music and hence carries no implication of textual treatment.

The term *stile familiare* probably originated in the 16th century. G. Baini, in his *Memorie . . . di Palestrina* (1828; ii, 415), speaks of "lo stile semplice di nota e sillaba, che fu denominato *familiare*" and mentions Josquin's Mass *D'ung aultre amer* as the first model. Actually there are much earlier manifestations of the same principle of composition; see Homorhythmic.

Fanciulla del West, La [It., The Girl of the Golden West]. Opera in three acts by Puccini (libretto by G. Civinini and C. Zangarini, based on a play by D. Belasco), produced in New York, 1910. Setting: California during the Gold Rush (1849–50).

Fancy (fantasy). A 16th- and 17th-century term for certain lute, keyboard, and instrumental ensemble music of English origin. The fancy stems from the Italian fantasia [see Fantasia (5)]. Until the middle of the 17th century the contrapuntal style of the Italian fantasia was rather strictly adopted by the English musicians, but by about 1680 the influence of the new Italian melodic style (Carissimi) was strongly felt. The earliest type of fancy is described by Morley [*A Plaine and Easy Introduction . . .* (1597), p. 181; ed. R. A. Harman (1952), p. 296]: "The most principal and chiefest kind of music which is made without a ditty is the Fancy, that is when a musician taketh a point at his pleasure and wresteth and turneth it as he list . . ."

In general, fancies are fairly long compositions in which several themes (Morley's "point") are treated in imitation. Thus, they consist of several thematic sections, which, however, usually overlap, as in a ricercar. For an example of this type, by Byrd, see Editions XVI, 16, p. 71. Another composition by Byrd (*ibid.*, p. 166) shows more varied treatment, e.g., sections in triple meter. In the early 17th century the sections are often clearly separated, contrasting in character, and based on more specifically instrumental themes or motifs. Several examples by A. Ferrabosco, William Lawes, and J. Jenkins are reproduced in E. H. Meyer's *English Chamber Music* (1946; Appendix). Toward the middle of the 17th century the fancy acquired suitelike features by the inclusion of dance movements modeled after the pavane, galliard, allemande, sarabande, etc. This type is represented by the fancies of M. Locke and Purcell.

The most important composers of fancies were William Byrd (1543–1623), Thomas Morley (1557–1602), John Coperario (*c.* 1575–1626), Alfonso Ferrabosco (*c.* 1575–1628), Richard Deering (*c.* 1580–1629/30), Orlando Gibbons (1583–1625), Thomas Lupo (d. before 1628), Thomas Tomkins (1572–1656), William Lawes (1602–45), John Jenkins (1592–1678), and Henry Purcell (*c.* 1659–95). Their works constitute a treasure of early chamber music, which Roger North, in his *Musicall Gramarian* (*c.* 1728), aptly characterized: "If ye musick was not so Ayery, it was sound and good." Also see Fantasia.

Lit.: E. H. Meyer, *Die mehrstimmige Spiel-musik des 17. Jahrhunderts in nord- und mittel-europa* (1934); *id.*, *English Chamber Music* (1946); C. Arnold and M. Johnson, "The English Fantasy Suite" (*PMA* lxxxii); E. H. Walker, "An Oxford Book of Fancies" (*MA* iii); R. Erlebach, in *PMA* lix (W. Lawes); C. W. Hughes, in *MQ* xxvii (R. Deering); H. J. Sleeper, in *BAMS* iv (Jenkins); D. Stevens, in *ML* xxxiii (Purcell); *Editions XXXIV 9, 21; Purcell, ‡*Fantazias and Other Instrumental Music* (*The Works of Henry Purcell* xxxi); E. Fellowes, ‡*Nine Fantasias . . . by Orlando Gibbons* [1924]; H. J. Sleeper, ‡*John Jenkins, Fancies and Ayres* (1950); P. Warlock and A. Mangeot, ‡*Six String Quartets by Mat-thew Locke* [1932]; *id.*, ‡*Purcell: Three, Four and Five Part Fantasias for Strings* (1927); E. H. Meyer, ‡*Englische Fantasien* (1934); A. Man-geot, ‡*Three Fancies for String Quartet* [1936].

Fandango. A Spanish dance in moderate to quick triple time with rhythms such as Ex. 1, danced by a couple to the accompaniment of guitar and castanets, in alternation with sung couplets. The fandango appeared in Spain in

the early 18th century. A popular melody [Ex. 2] was used by Gluck in his ballet *Don Juan* (1761), as well as by Mozart in *Le Nozze di Figaro* (1786; finale of Act III, section in 3/4 time). More re-cently, Rimsky-Korsakov (*Capriccio espagnol*, 1887) and E. Granados (*Goyescas*, no. 3, 1912) have written fandangos. Local varieties of the dance are the *Malagueña* (from Malaga), the *Granadina* (from Granada), the *Murciana* (from Murcia), the *Rondeña* (from Ronda), etc.

Fanfare. (1) French term for a brass band, either military or civilian. (2) A short tune for trumpets, used as a signal for ceremonial, military, or hunting purposes. Since they are intended for natural instruments, they include the tones of the triad only. The various nations possess a large repertory of such melodies.

Fanfare-like motifs have been frequently used in art music. As early as the 14th century they occur in a *caccia* by Ghirardello (Gherardellus)

to the words "sounded his horn" [see Ex. a; see *HAM*, no. 52] and in a virelai "Or sus vous dor-mez trop" (Awake, you sleep too long; Ex. b).

suo cor-no so - na-va

A famous example is Dufay's *Et in terra* "ad modum tubae," a long canon accompanied throughout by fanfare motifs played by two trombones in alternation [Ex. c]. Later instances are found in Josquin's *Vive le roy* [*SchGMB*, no. 62a], in Janequin's program chanson "La Guerre" (*c.* 1528) and in other *battaglie*, in the introductory "toccata" of Monteverdi's *Orfeo* (1607), and in Bach's *Capriccio sopra la lon-tananza del suo fratello dilettissimo*. Various operatic composers have made highly effective use of the fanfare, e.g., Beethoven in *Fidelio* (Act II, arrival of the governor), Wagner in the horn-call scene of *Tristan* (introduction to the first scene of Act II).

Lit.: H. de la Porte, *Les Fanfares des équipages français*, rev. ed. (1930); K. Taut, *Die Anfänge der Jagdmusik* (1926); G. Schünemann, ed., ‡*Trompeterfanfaren, Sonaten und Feldstücke* (1936; see Editions XVIII A 7); *id.*, in *ZMW* xvii.

Fantasia [It.; F. *fantaisie;* G. *Fantasie, Phantasie*]. Generally speaking, a composition in which the "free flight of fancy" prevails over contemporary conventions of form, style, etc. Naturally, the term covers a great variety of types, which may be tentatively classified as five groups.

(1) Pieces of a markedly improvisory char-acter; written records, as it were, of the impro-visation technique of the various masters. Examples are Bach's Chromatic Fantasia and his lesser-known Fantasia in A minor for harpsi-chord (*BG* xxxvi, 81–87; ed. Peters, iv, 22–29), Mozart's Fantasia in D minor for piano, and Beethoven's Fantasia op. 77. The numerous *Fantasien* by K. P. E. Bach also belong to this category [see *HAM*, no. 296].

(2) *Character pieces of the romantic era. Here, "fantasia" is one of the various titles used to indicate a dreamlike mood or some other fanciful whim. Examples are Brahms' *Fantasien* op. 116.

(3) Sonatas in freer form, or of a special character; e.g., Beethoven's op. 27, nos. 1, 2, both entitled "Sonata quasi una fantasia" and deviating in various respects from the conventional sonata form and style; Schubert's *Wanderer Fantasie* op. 15, in which a song of his ("Der Wanderer") is used as the main subject for all the movements [see Cyclic]; Schumann's *Fantasie* op. 17, which is a romantic hybrid of sonata form.

(4) Operatic potpourris of a free and somewhat improvisory treatment, as if written in remembrance of a performance; e.g., Liszt's *Réminiscences de "Don Juan"* (1841).

(5) In the 16th and 17th centuries, a term for instrumental music that was sometimes used interchangeably with ricercar, *tiento,* and even *praeambulum.* Fantasias were written for the lute, for keyboard instruments, and for instrumental ensembles. There is a large repertory of lute and vihuela fantasias in the music of Marco d'Aquila (1536; *SchGMB,* no. 94), Luis Milán (1535; *HAM,* no. 121), Francesco da Milano (1547; *SchGMB,* no. 115), Miguel de Fuenllana (1554), and others.

The great majority of 16th-century fantasias are for lute, vihuela, guitar, and other stringed instruments, but the keyboard fantasia has a considerably longer development. The term "fantasia" first appears *c.* 1520 in the tablatures of Hans Kotter and Leonhard Kleber. Kotter's *Fantasia* [see W. Merian, *Der Tanz in den deutschen Tabulaturbüchern* (1927), p. 58] is a prelude and fugue. Kleber's two fantasias employ various motifs in free imitation, sequential treatment, paired imitation, etc. One of them ("Fantasy in Fa," *Orgeltabulaturbuch,* fol. 56a, 1524) opens with a homophonic introduction and closes with an extended running passage over an F-pedal. Andrea Gabrieli's *Fantasia allegra* [*Editions III, 3] shows a free mixture of imitation and figuration. A larger repertory of keyboard fantasias is preserved in English sources from *c.* 1600, especially in the Fitzwilliam Virginal Book, which contains fantasias by Byrd (4), Bull (2), Farnaby (10), Munday (2), Philipps (2), and others. Some of these are intabulated madrigals or chansons [Fuller Maitland-Squire ed., ii, 333, 340]. The majority are sectional compositions, beginning with a section in contrapuntal style and continuing with passagework, figurations, short imitations, dance movements, etc. In the 17th century the keyboard fantasia was cultivated mainly by Sweelinck, Frescobaldi, and Froberger. Each of these masters developed his own type, which differs considerably from the others. The meaning of the term instrumental (more properly, *ensemble) fantasia, in publications such as *Fantasie et recerchari a tre voci* (1549) and *Fantasie recercari contrapunti a tre voci* (1551), is not fixed, and the titles in these books (containing mostly compositions by Tiburtino and Willaert) seem to be used interchangeably. *Fantaisies* by Claude Le Jeune and F. E. du Caurroy (*c.* 1610; ed. H. Expert [1910?]) and by Charles Guillet (1610; see Editions XXVIII, 4) are strictly imitative. In the 17th century the ensemble fantasia was cultivated mainly in England; see Fancy.

Lit.: O. Deffner, *Über die Entwicklung der Fantasie für Tasten-Instrumente (bis J. P. Sweelinck)* (1927); E. H. Meyer, *Die mehrstimmige Spielmusik des 17. Jahrhunderts in Nord- und Mitteleuropa* (1934); H. Colin Slim, "The Keyboard Ricercar and Fantasia in Italy, *c.* 1500–1550" (diss. Harvard Univ., 1960); M. Reimann, "Zur Deutung des Begriffs Fantasia" (*AMW* x): P. Hamburger, "Die Fantasien in Emanuel Adriansens Pratum musicum (1600)" (*ZMW* xii). See also under Fancy.

Fantasiestück [G.]. See under Fantasia (2).

Fantastic Symphony. See *Symphonie fantastique.*

Fantasy. (1) See Fantasia; Fancy. (2) The development section (fantasy section) in *sonata form.

Farandole. A Provençal dance performed by men and women who, holding hands, form a long chain and follow the leader through a great variety of figures to music played on the *pipe and tabor. The dance seems to be of very ancient origin (symbolic celebration of Theseus' escape from the labyrinth?) and is still danced today. Similar dances are the *branle and *cotillon. The music of the farandole is usually in moderate 6/8 meter. The dance has been introduced into opera by Bizet (*L'Arlésienne*) and Gounod (*Mireille*). See G. Beaucaire, in *RMC* v.

Farbenklavier [G.]. *Color organ.

Farce [It. *farsa*]. (1) Originally, an interpolation, as in a *trope. (2) In plays and operas, chiefly of the 18th century, farcing means the introduction of alien elements, usually of a humorous, comical, or even lascivious nature [see Intermezzo]. This meaning persists in present-day usage, in which farce is a light comedy, sometimes vulgar, frequently a travesty of a serious model. About 1800, Italian comic operas in one act were called *farsa,* e.g., Rossini's *La Cambiale di matrimonio* (1810).

Farewell Sonata. See *Adieux, Les.*

Farewell Symphony. See *Abschieds-Symphonie.*

Fasola. A system of *solmization, much used in England and in America during the 17th and 18th centuries, in which only four of the six Guidonian syllables are used, the syllables *fa sol la* being applied to c–d–e as well as to the identical progression f–g–a, and the *mi* being used for the seventh degree, b. Before 1800 the fasola method was used in certain American tune books, the letters F, S, L, F, S, L, M being placed on a staff (e.g., in John Tuft's *An Introduction to the Singing of Psalm-Tunes,* 1721). In 1802 William Little (*The Easy Instructor*) introduced four different shapes of note for each of the syllables, a method known as buckwheat, four-shape, shape-note, or character notation [see Ex.], which proved very successful in the rural districts of the South.

fa   sol   la   fa   sol   la   mi   fa

Lit.: I. Lowens, *Music and Musicians in Early America* (1964), pp. 58–88; D. Horn, "Shape Note Hymnals and the Art Music of Early America" (master's thesis, Rochester Univ., 1942); G. P. Jackson, "Buckwheat Notes" (*MQ* xix); C. Seeger, "Contrapuntal Style in the Three-voice Shape-note Hymns" (*MQ* xxvi); K. P. Fuller, in *Etude* lvii, 501.

Fastoso [It.]. Pompous.

Fausse relation [F.]. False relation [see Cross relation].

Faust. Opera in five acts by Gounod (libretto by J. Barbier and M. Carré, based on Goethe's tragedy), produced in Paris, 1859. Revised version with accompanied recitatives and ballet produced in Paris, 1869. Setting: Germany, 16th century.

Fauxbourdon [F.]. (1) Historically and properly, fauxbourdon is a 15th-century French technique of composition in which a plainsong melody transposed to the upper octave is notated together with a contrapuntal part moving along at the lower sixth or occasionally at the octave, while a middle part is extemporized by a singer doubling the melody at the lower fourth through-

out [see Ex., from Dufay's "Juvenis qui puellam"; see *WoGM* ii, 57ff, and iii, 87]. According to recent studies (Besseler), fauxbourdon was invented by Dufay about 1428, its first use being in the Communion of his *Missa Sancti Jacobi.*

Cantus. Faulxbourdon.   Contratenor

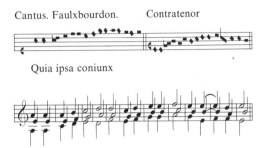

Quia ipsa coniunx

Here as well as in other compositions by Dufay, notably a number of hymns [see Editions VIII, 49], the fauxbourdon technique is used throughout either the entire composition or a self-contained section, resulting inevitably in a certain monotony. Quite properly, Dufay and Binchois [see J. Marix, *Les Musiciens de la cour de Bourgogne* (1937), pp. 131ff] used it mainly for what might be called *Gebrauchsmusik* associated with the lay devotional movement (hymns, psalms, Magnificats).

The term "fauxbourdon" has recently been explained as referring to the middle part added a fourth below the *superius* (Besseler; see under *Bourdon*), an explanation hardly more satisfactory than the older one, according to which it referred to the lowest part, this being regarded as a "false bass" because it was a secondary contrapuntal part and not the *cantus firmus.* Since about 1950 fauxbourdon has become the subject of studies and controversies, claims and counterclaims (mainly concerning its relationship to the English *faburden), to an extent hardly commensurate with its relatively minor importance. Of real importance was the incorporation of the sixth chord into the musical vocabulary [see Sixth chord], not the invention of one or another artificial method producing nothing but parallel sixth chords. Also see related articles: Discant; *Discantus supra librum; Faberdon; Fabordón;* Faburden; *Falsobordone.*

(2) In modern usage, a general designation for harmonic progressions based on parallel sixth chords, such as occur not only in old music but in the works of Bach, Beethoven, and others. In scholarly writings the designation *sixth-chord style (or six-three writing) is preferable.

(3) In present-day English usage, "a means of giving interest to hymn-singing by supplying the choir sopranos with a freely written part, which often soars above the hymn-tune as sung by the congregation" [see P. A. Scholes, *The Oxford Companion to Music* (1955), p. 342]. This would seem to be one of the various newer meanings of the term resulting from a misunderstanding of its proper connotation. A more appropriate name for this method of singing is *descant.

Lit.: M. Bukofzer, *Geschichte des englischen Diskants und des Fauxbourdons* (1936); T. Georgiades, *Englische Diskanttraktate aus der ersten Hälfte des 15. Jahrhunderts* (1937); E. Trumble, *Fauxbourdon* [1959]; H. Besseler, *Bourdon und Fauxbourdon* (1950); *id.*, in *AM* xx, *MF* i, *AM* xxvi; R. von Ficker, in *AM* xxiii, *AM* xxv; M. F. Bukofzer, in *MQ* xxxviii; S. Clercx, in *RdM* 1957, p. 151; S. W. Kenney, in *MQ* xlv; B. Trowell, in *MD* xiii; F. L. Harrison, in *MD* xvi; E. Trumble, in *RBM* xiv. The etymology of fauxbourdon and faburden is discussed by H. M. Flasdieck in *AM* xxv and *Anglia* lxxiv, 188; G. Kirchner, in *AM* xxvi; N. L. Wallin, in *CP 1953*.

Favola d'Orfeo, La. [It., The Fable of Orpheus]. Opera in a prologue and four acts by Monteverdi (libretto by A. Striggio), produced in Mantua, 1607. Setting: ancient Greece. Combining the archaic style of the earliest operas [see *Nuove musiche*] with great expressiveness and dramatic impact, *Orfeo* is a landmark in the history of opera [see also under Orchestra]. It has been revived with considerable success.

Feeders. In organ building, small bellows employed to supply the large bellows with wind. See Organ I.

Fe fa ut, Fefaut. See under Hexachord III.

Feierlich [G.]. Solemn.

Feldmusik [G.]. A 17th- and 18th-century designation for brass music for open-air performance; such pieces were also called *Feldstücke, Feldsonaten, Feldpartiten,* etc. Originally these were fanfares in four-part harmony played by the *Feldtrompeter,* i.e., the military trumpeters as distinguished from the *Kammertrompeter,* who were members of the orchestra [see *SaHMI,* p. 328]. See Lit. under Fanfare. J. P. Krieger wrote a *Lustige Feld-Musik* (1704) and Haydn a number of *Feldpartiten.*

Felix namque. Title of numerous English organ compositions, mostly from the 16th century, so called because they are polyphonic elaborations of the Offertory "Felix namque es," for certain feasts of the Virgin Mary [*LU*, p. 1271; a more accurate source is the Sarum Gradual]. Some settings omit the intonation "Felix" and begin with "namque" a–g–c′–d′–e′–d′–c′–e′–d′–c′. The "Felix namque" enjoyed great popularity in England, second only to the *"In nomine." The earliest known setting is in a recently discovered fragment from *c.* 1400 [see T. Dart, in *ML* xxxv, 201]. A setting from the early 16th century (Brit. Mus., *Roy. App. 56*) is interesting because it is in *quintuple meter. Others are by Redford, Preston, Blitheman, Shelby, Tallis, and T. Tomkins [see C. F. Pfatteicher, *John Redford* (1934); *Editions XXXIV, 1; Fitzwilliam Virginal Book, see Virginal music (b)].

Fellowships. See Scholarships, fellowships, and prizes.

Feminine cadence. See Masculine, feminine cadence.

Feria, ferial. Any weekday in the calendar of the Roman Catholic Church on which no feast occurs. This meaning is the reverse of the original meaning of L. *feria,* i.e., festival day. The reversal came about by extending the use of the word from Sunday to the other days, Sunday being named *feria prima,* Monday *feria secunda,* Tuesday *tertia,* etc. Later, Sunday was called *Dominica,* whereas for Saturday the Hebrew name *Sabbato* was kept. It should be noted that the adjective "ferial" (days, rites) is used in a meaning closer to the original, i.e., including Sunday, provided no special feast occurs. The opposite is festal (days, rites), which refers to feasts on weekdays or Sundays.

Fermata [It.]. In Italian, pedal point. In American and German usage, *fermata* means pause [It. *corona*].

Ferne, wie aus der [G.]. As if from a distance.

Fernwerk [G.]. Echo organ.

Fes [G.]. F-flat. See under Pitch names.

Festal. See under *Feria.*

Feste Romane [It.]. See under Symphonic poem IV.

Festivals. The earliest instances of musical festivals are the French *puys, which originated with the troubadours of the 13th century and continued until the 16th century. The *Sängerkriege* of the German minnesingers, of which Wagner gives a lively picture in his *Tannhäuser* *und der Sängerkrieg auf der Wartburg,* were an imitation of the *puys.* Of similar age are the Eisteddfod of the Welsh bards.

I. *England.* A new development started in England in the 17th century with the *Festival of the Sons of the Clergy,* which was founded in 1655 and still continues, in the form of a musical service on grand lines. There followed, in 1724, the *Three Choirs Festival,* which combines the choral forces of Gloucester, Worcester, and Hereford and lasts several days. Others are the *Birmingham Festival* (1768–1912), *Norwich Festival* (1770—since 1824 triennially), and *Leeds Festival* (1858, since 1874 triennially), all of which are held for the benefit of local charitable institutions. The *Handel Festivals* in the Crystal Palace began in 1857 but ended in 1936, when the Palace was damaged by fire. Also notable is the *Glyndebourne Opera Festival,* Sussex, founded in 1934 by A. and J. Christie.

II. *United States.* The earliest American festivals on record are those of the Handel and Haydn Society of Boston (triennial; 1857–83) and at Worcester (1858). In 1869 P. S. Gilmore organized his huge festival *Peace Jubilee,* as a celebration of the conclusion of the Civil War, employing an orchestra of 1,000 and a chorus of 10,000. In his *World's Peace Jubilee* of 1872 he doubled these forces and added electrically fired cannons, chimes, and powerful organs. The *Worcester Festivals* became an established annual institution in 1869, and Cincinnati followed with its biennial *Cincinnati Music Festival,* commonly called May Festivals, in 1873 (founded by T. Thomas). The *Ann Arbor May Festivals* of the University of Michigan were founded in 1893. At Bethany College in Lindsborg, Kansas, annual performances of *The Messiah* were begun in 1882 and have developed into a festival week. The *Bethlehem Bach Choir* of Bethlehem, Pa. was founded in 1898 and has given numerous festivals, each including a performance of Bach's B-minor Mass. At Northwestern University festivals were established in 1909 as the *Evanston North Shore Festival* and, after a lapse in 1932, were revived in 1937. In the same year (1909) began the *Spring Festivals of Cornell University,* now held at irregular intervals. Outstanding among subsequent developments are: *Berkshire Festival of Chamber Music* at Pittsfield, Mass. (established 1918 by Elizabeth Sprague Coolidge, transferred to the Library of Congress after 1924 and also known as *Coolidge Chamber Music Festival,* which featured numerous first performances of chamber works); *Westchester County Music Festival* (1925, now at White Plains, N.Y.); *Eastman School Festival of American Music* at Rochester, N.Y. (1930, founded by Howard Hanson); *Westminster Festival* at Princeton, N.J. (1936; programs of American music); *Berkshire Symphonic Festival* at Lenox, Mass. (founded by Henry K. Hadley at Stockbridge in 1934, since 1936 in connection with the Boston Symphony Orchestra; since 1940 held at Tanglewood); and *Marlboro Music Festival* at Marlboro, Vt. (founded by A. Busch and R. Serkin in 1951; offers instruction and concerts).

For detailed information on these and other festivals, see Pierre Key's *Music Year Book* and the *Calendar of Music Activities in the United States of America* published by the President's Music Committee of the People-to-People Program.

III. *Other countries.* Outside the United States and England, music festivals are found mainly in Germany and Austria. Among these the *Niederrheinische Musikfeste* (founded 1817; held alternately in Cologne, Düsseldorf, and Aachen) are most like the American or English choral festivals. More important from the artistic point of view were the *Tonkünstlerfeste* of the *Allgemeiner deutscher Musikverein,* founded by F. Liszt in 1861 and held annually in different cities, the last (1932) in Zurich. Celebrations of great German composers are frequently held in their native cities, e.g., the *Beethovenfeste* in Bonn, the *Bachfeste* in Eisenach, the *Mozartfeste* in Salzburg, Austria. Most famous among these are the **Bayreuther Festspiele,* devoted to Wagner's operas. The *Kammermusikfeste* at Donaueschingen, founded in 1921, have been very important in the development of modern music [see *Gebrauchsmusik*]. Similar in purpose are the festivals of the *International Society for Contemporary Music,* held since 1923 in various places all over the world (complete programs are given in Slonimsky's *Music since 1900*). More recent festivals that have attracted much attention are the *Maggio musicale Fiorentino* of Florence (since 1933) and the *Internationale Musikfestwoche* in Lucerne (since 1938).

Lit.: D. Stoll, *Music Festivals of Europe* (1938); G. Gavazzeni, *Le Feste musicali* (1944); J. Feschotte, *Les Hauts Lieux de la musique* (1949); W. A. Fischer, *Music Festivals in USA* (1933); F. Ghisi, *Feste musicali Medicee* (1939); H. M. Schletterer, in *MfM* xxii, 181–96 (16th century).

Festoso [It.]. Festive.

Festschrift [G.]. General designation for publications (not necessarily German) usually presented as a tribute to outstanding scholars on the occasion of their 60th, 70th, etc. birthday. They contain contributions from colleagues, pupils, scholars in the same (or an allied) field, etc. Many musicologists, and occasionally composers and conductors, have been honored in this way. The *Festschriften* referred to in this dictionary are listed in the Abbreviations under Collective Publications. Others have been published (under various titles) for: J. Écorcheville (1916), C. Engel (1943), W. Fischer (1956), M. Friedländer, (1922), J. Handschin (1962), K. Jeppesen (1962), Z. Kodály (1953, 1957), I. Krohn (1927), R. Lach (1954), R. Münnich (1947, 1957), E. Newman (1955), F. Pedrell (1911), P. Raabe (1942), A. Schoenberg (1924, 1934), A. Schweitzer (1946), J. Smend (1927), and F. Weingartner (1933). See W. Gerboth, "Index of Festschriften and Some Similar Publications" (*CP Reese*).

Festspiel [G.]. See under Festivals III; also *Bühne*.

Ff. Abbr. for fortissimo.

F fa ut. See under Hexachord III.

F-hole. See Sound hole.

Fiato [It.]. Breath. *Stromenti da fiato,* wind instruments.

Fiddle. Colloquial for the violin and stringed instruments resembling it, particularly the folk varieties used to accompany dancing. Also, the primitive ancestors of the violin, as found in many Oriental cultures. See Violin II.

Fidelio [G.]. Opera in two acts by Beethoven (libretto by J. Sonnleithner and G. F. Treitschke after Bouilly), first produced in Vienna in 1805 as *Fidelio oder die eheliche Liebe* in three acts, rev. 1806 as *Lenore* in two acts, final rev. 1814. Setting: a state prison in Spain, 18th century. For the various overtures, see Lenore Overtures. See also under Melodrama.

Fidicen [L. *fides,* string]. Humanist (16th-century) name for a string player.

Fiedel [G.]. (1) Colloquial for violin and the like. (2) Generic term for medieval violins (*vielle, fidula*) and modern imitations thereof.

Fiero [It.]. High-spirited, bold.

Fife. A small flute with six to eight finger holes and usually no key, used chiefly in military bands. It has been replaced in the drum corps by the piccolo. For ill. see under Flute.

Fifre [F.]. Fife.

Fifteenth. In organs, name for foundation stops sounding two octaves (fifteen notes) above normal. Hence, 2-foot stops.

Fifth. See under Intervals. Also Blown fifth; Consonance; Circle of fifths; Parallel fifths; Organum (2) I; Triad. Concerning the relative importance of the fifth and the fourth, see under Fourth.

Figaro, The Marriage of. See *Nozze di Figaro, Le.*

Figlia del Regimento, La. See *Fille du Régiment, La.*

Figura [L.]. (1) In medieval theory, generic name for the notational signs. Franco (*CS* i, 119) distinguishes the *figurae simplices,* i.e., the single notes (*longa, brevis, semibrevis*), from the *figurae compositae,* i.e., the ligatures. *Figura obliqua* means the oblique form of *ligatures. (2) See Figures, doctrine of.

Figural, figurate, figured [G. *figuriert*]. The terms are rather indiscriminately used with two different though related meanings. (1) As a translation of L. *musica figurata,* a 15th- and 16th-century term for any polyphonic music as opposed to *musica plana,* plainsong. In particular, the term figural music or style [G. *Figuralmusik, figurierter Stil*] denotes the highly florid polyphonic style of the early Flemish composers, such as Ockeghem and Obrecht, as distinguished from the less complex style of Josquin and his successors [see *Musica reservata*]. (2) Applied to 17th- and 18th-century music, the terms mean the use of stereotyped figures or motifs, particularly in variations or in the accompanying parts of organ chorales [see Figuration; Figured chorale]. The ambiguous and inconsistent use of these terms is to be deplored, particularly since "figured" has still another meaning in the term *figured bass. Tentatively the following distinctions are recommended: Figurate = florid [see Webster]; figural = using musical figures; figured = provided with numerals. Hence: figurate melody; figural variation or chorale; figured bass. See the subsequent articles.

Figuralpassion [G.]. Same as motet Passion; see Passion music B.

Figuration. The use of stereotyped figures, particularly in variations on a theme. See Figural (2); Variations III [Ex. var. 1].

Figure. See under Motif.

Figured bass. A bass part provided with figures (numerals) to indicate harmonies [see Thorough-bass].

Figured chorale [G. *Figurierter Choral*]. A species of *organ chorale (chorale prelude) in which a certain figure (i.e., a short and characteristic group of notes) is used consistently, in one or several of the contrapuntal parts, against the plain notes of the chorale, which usually is in the soprano. Most of the chorales in Bach's *Orgel-büchlein* belong to this category, e.g., "Alle Menschen müssen sterben," "Der Tag, der ist so freudenreich," and "Jesu, meine Freude." "Ich ruf' zu dir" is an especially good example. A more appropriate term would be "figural chorale" [see Figural].

Figured melody. Ornamented or florid melody. A more appropriate term would be "figurate melody" [see Figural].

Figures, doctrine of [G. *Figurenlehre*]. A 17th- and 18th-century theory of musical composition based on the idea that music is an art analogous to rhetoric, i.e., the art of speech and literature. This idea is carried out mainly through an elaborate system of *figurae* (established in rhetoric by Aristotle and Quintilian), i.e., standard devices that differ from ordinary speech and are introduced to render oratory more expressive and impressive. Examples are *anaphora* (repeating the same word at the beginning of successive sentences), *aposiopesis* (sudden stopping, silence), *pathopoeia* (expression of hate, wrath, pity), *hypallage* (mixture of two constructions), *hypotyposis* (use of illustrative examples), *noëma* (reference to something generally known), etc. Among the numerous writers who applied these "figures" to music were Joachim Burmeister (1599, 1606), Johannes Nucius (1613), Joachim Thuringus (1625), Christoph Bernhard (*c.* 1660), Johann Gottfried Walther (1708, 1732), and Johann Mattheson (1739). While some of the rhetorical figures could be adopted with the same or a very similar significance (e.g., *aposiopesis, pathopoeia,* the latter in the general meaning of expression of passions, hence also chromaticism), others could be applied to music only with a more or less different meaning. Thus, *hypallage* was used as a term for imitation by inversion (mixture of theme and inverted theme), *noëma* as a designation for chordal style, and *hypotosis* as a generic term for word painting. Others were interpreted

differently by various writers. Thus, *anaphora* is explained by Burmeister as a sort of fugal imitation, by Thuringus as a repeat of the bass (*basso ostinato?*), and by Nucius and others as repeat in general, while Mattheson comes closest to its proper meaning by saying that it means the use of the same formula (e.g., g–a–b–c') at the beginning of several successive melodic phrases [see Lit., Lenneberg, p. 203]. In addition to terms borrowed from rhetoric, the above-mentioned writers also introduced into "musical rhetoric" numerous *figurae* of purely musical significance, such as *anabasis* (ascent), *catabasis* (descent), *circulatio* (turning motion, f–g–a–g), *saltus* (jump), *diminutio, fuga, syncopatio,* etc. Together with the others they formed a veritable "vocabulary of musical speech."

Another aspect of musical rhetoric is represented by the *loci topici*. In rhetoric these are conventional topics (arguments) used by the orator or writer to argue his case and prove his point. Examples are the *locus notationis* (argument derived from the name, e.g., "Music"), *locus oppositorum* (contrasting "Music" and "Science"), *locus exemplorum* (argument by means of examples), etc. In music these became devices to stimulate and facilitate invention. Mattheson, who treats this matter at length, interprets the *locus notationis* to include devices suggested by musical "notation" (use of different time values, inversion, fugal answer, etc.), the *locus oppositorum* as the category of contrast (change of meter and tempo, use of high and low notes), and the *locus exemplorum* as imitation of other composers.

Lit.: H. H. Unger, *Die Beziehungen zwischen Musik und Rhetorik im 16.–18. Jahrhundert* (1941); H. Brandes, *Studien zur musikalische Figurenlehre im 16. Jahrhundert* (1935); J. M. Müller-Blattau, *Die Kompositionslehre Schützens in der Fassung seines Schülers Christoph Bernhard* (1926); A. Schering, "Die Lehre von den musikalischen Figuren" (*KJ* xxi [1908]); H. Lenneberg, in *Journal of Music Theory* ii, 47ff, 193ff (trans. Mattheson); A. Schmitz, in *AMW* ix (Walther); F. Feldmann, in *AMW* xv (Thuringus, Nucius); H. H. Eggebrecht, in *AMW* xvi; C. O. Dreger, in *BJ* 1934 (Bach); K. Ziebler, in *ZMW* xv; A. Schmitz, in *CP 1950a* (Bach).

Filar il tuono [It.], **filer le son** [F.]. An 18th-century term, properly a synonym of *messa di voce*. Modern writers and singers, however, frequently interpret it as calling for sustained notes without the crescendo and decrescendo implied by *messa di voce.*

Fille du Régiment, La [F., The Daughter of the Regiment; It. *La Figlia del Regimento*]. Opera in two acts by Donizetti (libretto by J. F. A. Bayard and J. H. Vernoy de Saint-Georges), produced in Paris, 1840. Setting: Bologna, early 19th century. It is Donizetti's first opera in French, and one of his most popular.

Film music. In the early days of silent films, music, played by a pianist, was considered mainly a means to drown out the noise of the projector. A pianist would play well-known melodies or improvise. Often he was assisted by a percussion man who would produce tonal effects appropriate to the action: gunfire, birdsong, railway, airplane, thunderstorm, etc. By about 1920 orchestras appeared in theaters in larger cities, and various film companies began to provide them with music suitable for the action on the screen. A great many short descriptive pieces were written under titles such as "Help, Help," "The Slimy Viper," "Love's Response," or "Broken Vows." A. Schoenberg contributed to this repertory his *Begleitmusik zu einer Lichtspielszene,* op. 34 (1930), consisting of "Drohende Gefahr," "Angst," and "Katastrophe." From about 1925 on it became customary to have music composed expressly for individual films. The earliest example on record is the music M.-F. Gaillard wrote for *El Dorado* in 1921. At this time some important composers of reputation became interested in writing music for the movies, e.g., Satie (*Entr'acte,* 1924) and R. Strauss (*Rosenkavalier,* film version, 1925). Honegger wrote film music in 1922 that later became his orchestral work, *Pacific 231.* The 1920's were the era of the great movie orchestras, often led by well-known conductors. Nevertheless, the majority of theaters did not have orchestras capable of performing such ambitious scores. The decisive change came with the introduction, about 1929, of the soundtrack. Originally the music was recorded simultaneously with the picture, but this method proved unsatisfactory. The common practice now is to make a separate soundtrack that is then played back on the camera film.

The composer's approach to the peculiar demands and problems of the medium varies greatly. In the great majority of so-called commercial American films, the music is late romantic in style (Rachmaninoff, Strauss, Delius) and frankly descriptive in purpose, regarding physical situations (forest, mountains, desert, sunset)

as well as psychological ones (love, distress, fright). Often extensive use is made of leitmotivs. The music is continuous (or nearly so), accompanying the picture from the beginning to the end and thus automatically relegating itself to a background role.

In contrast to such routine works there are numerous film scores of intrinsic musical interest or value, written by well-known composers. Many of these, it should be noted, were not written for the entertainment industry (feature films), but belong to the nonfiction field (documentaries, here abbreviated as "Doc"), an area that tends to be less circumscribed in its tastes and range of styles. Among the notable scores are: A. Copland, *The City* (1939; Doc), *Our Town* (1940), *The Heiress* (1949); V. Thomson, *The River* (1938; Doc), *Louisiana Story* (1948; Doc); W. Walton, *Spitfire* (1942; Doc), *Henry V* (1944), *Hamlet* (1948); S. Prokofiev, *Lieutenant Kijé* (1934), *Alexander Nevsky* (1938), *Ivan the Terrible* (1945); R. Vaughan Williams, *Coastal Command* (1942; Doc), *Scott of the Antarctic* (1948; incorporated in his *Sinfonia Antarctica*), *Vision of William Blake* (1958; Doc); H. Villa Lobos, *Green Mansions* (1959); L. Bernstein, *On the Waterfront* (1954); G. Auric, *À Nous la liberté* (1931), *Le Sang d'un Poète* (1931), *Moulin Rouge* (1953), *Les Mystères de Picasso* (1957; Doc); A. Honegger, *L'Idée* (1934; Doc), *Pygmalion* (1938); D. Milhaud, *L'Hippocampe* (1934; Doc), *Dreams That Money Can Buy* (1948; with Hindemith, Cage, Varèse, P. Bowles, L. Applebaum); G. Kubik, *Memphis Belle* (1944; Doc), *Gerald McBoing Boing* (1950; cartoon); R. Vlad, *Leonardo da Vinci* (1952), *Romeo and Juliet* (1954); and J. Cage, *Works of Calder* (1950; Doc). Although it is no longer fashionable to use existing musical works as background for films, a striking impression was achieved in Jean Cocteau's *Les Enfants terribles,* with the music of Vivaldi.

In the 1960's film music entered a new stage. Financially, the cinema felt increasingly the competition of television, and the majority of serious composers, ranging in age from Stravinsky to Boulez, tended to complement their composing activities by conducting rather than by writing film music. Recent film scores tend to use more and more such devices as **musique concrète,* *electronic music, etc., and the widespread use of the magnetic tape may in time mean the death of the large studio orchestra, conducted by a studio musical director, performing scores for a conventional symphony orchestra.

Lit.: L. L. Sabaneev, *Music for the Film* (1935);

K. London, *Film Music* (1936); H. Eisler, *Composing for the Film* (1947); J. Huntley, *British Film Music* [1947]; L. Levy, *Music for the Movies* (1948); J. Huntley and R. Manvell, *The Technique of Film Music* [1957]; G. Hacquard, *La Musique et le cinéma* (1959); Z. Lissa, *Aesthetik der Film Musik* (1965); F. W. Sternfeld, "Music and the Cinema," in *Twentieth Century Music,* ed. R. H. Myers [1960], pp. 95–111; Z. Lissa, "Formprobleme der Film Musik" (*CP Fellerer*); F. W. Sternfeld, in *MQ* xxxvii, 161 (Copland); *id.,* in *MQ* xxxiii, 517; C. Austin, in *ML* v, 177; E. Irving, in *ML* xxiv, 223. Additional literature in *GDB* and *MGG.*   F.W.S.

Final, finalis. See under Church modes I.

Finale [It.]. (1) The last movement of a sonata or any of the related forms, i.e., symphony, quartet, etc. In the classical sonata it is usually a fast movement in either rondo or sonata form; occasionally it is written as a theme with variations (Beethoven, piano sonata op. 111; Brahms, clarinet quintet op. 115). While Haydn and Mozart planned their finales as a "happy ending," Beethoven frequently gave his a character of final triumph and apotheosis. In this respect, Bruckner followed and even surpassed him. (2) The last piece of an operatic act. Operatic finales are usually longer and more elaborate than the other pieces (arias), since a good deal of the dramatic action is likely to take place at the end of an act. They frequently include various sections of contrasting character [e.g., the finales in Mozart's *Figaro*]. Alessandro Scarlatti is considered the originator of the dramatic finale. Niccolò Piccinni (1728–1800) introduced the sectional construction, including change of tempo, key, etc.

Lit.: M. Fuchs, "Die Entwicklung des Finales in der opera buffa vor Mozart" (diss. Vienna, 1932); A. O. Lorenz, "Das Finale in Mozart's Meisteropern" (*DM* xix.9); E. J. Dent, "Ensembles and Finales in 18th-Century Italian Opera" (*SIM* xi, xii).

Fin' al segno [It.]. "As far as the sign," indicating repetition from the beginning to the sign §.

Fine [It.]. End, close.

Fingerboard. In stringed instruments, a long strip of hardwood (ebony) fixed to the neck, over which the strings are stretched. The fingerboards of older instruments, such as the lute, guitar, viola da gamba, lyra, etc., were provided with frets, as are the present-day guitar and ukulele.

Finger exercise. See under Etude.

Fingerfertigkeit [G.]. Agility of the fingers, virtuosity.

Fingering [F. *doigté;* G. *Fingersatz, Applicatur* (obs.); It. *diteggiatura, tocco;* Sp. *digitación*]. The methodical use of the fingers in playing instruments. More than any other instrument, the piano has what might be called a "natural system of fingering," owing to the natural conformity between the arrangement of the fingers and the keys. There are three chief types of fingering: (1) normal fingering. This applies to passages involving no more than five keys, e.g.,

$$\text{c e g d f e c}$$
$$\text{1 3 5 2 4 3 1}$$

(2) contracted or expanded fingering, e.g.,

$$\text{g' g a b c' a f g c}$$
$$\text{5 1 3 4 5 4 2 3 1}$$

This fingering usually leads to a "shift of position," that is, the thumb does not return to its original key. It is very common in extended passages of "zigzag" design (bent figures) that have no more than five tones in either direction (e.g., in Chopin's etude op. 10, no. 1); (3) passing fingering, i.e., the thumb passes under a finger (second, third, fourth) or one of these fingers passes over the thumb. This fingering must be used whenever there are more than five tones in the same direction, as in scales.

The modern principles of fingering are relatively new, their definite establishment by M. Clementi (1752–1832) being practically simultaneous with the replacement of the harpsichord and clavichord by the piano. The earlier fingering is distinguished from the modern method chiefly by the very sparing use of the thumb and fifth finger in scale passages. Throughout the 16th and 17th centuries, scales were played with a fingering such as:

$$\text{c d e f g a b a g f e d c}$$
$$\text{2 3 2 3 2 3 4 3 2 3 2 3 2}$$

[see Ex.; also A. Guilmant, "La Musique d'orgue," in *LavE* ii.2, 1149ff, and Weitzmann-Seifert, *Geschichte der Klaviermusik* (1899), pp. 11, 13, 70, 82, 84, 160, etc.]. This method of passing one finger over the other, which from the modern point of view appears extremely clumsy, was entirely appropriate on the old instruments, whose keys had a smaller "fall" than those of the piano and required a much lighter touch. Particularly on the clavichord, passages sound

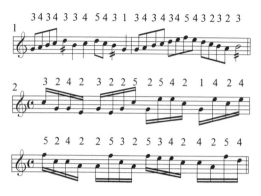

more even if played without the thumb. The normal position of the hand was with the middle fingers lying almost flat on the keys and with the thumb hanging down in front of the keyboard. However, as early as 1565 Thomás de Sancta María, in his *Libro Lamàdo Arte de tañer fanta-sia,* indicates the fingering 4 3 2 1 4 3 2 1 4 for the descending scale [see O. Kinkeldey, *Orgel und Klavier in der Musik des 16. Jahrhunderts* (1910), p. 36]. The modern fingering for the descending scale (5 4 3 2 1 3 2 1) occurs in the keyboard works of A. Scarlatti with each finger represented by a special symbol, *, /, etc. [see the modern edition by Shedlock]. J. S. Bach was one of the first to make systematic use of the thumb and to develop more modern methods of fingering [see his *Klavierbüchlein für Friedemann Bach,* new ed. H. Keller (1927), pp. 15, 23]. He played with curved fingers and brought the thumb to the surface of the keyboard. An interesting document is Johann Kirnberger's *Klavierübungen mit der Bachischen Applikatur* (1762–63). Another step toward modern fingering was taken by Bach's son K. P. E. Bach [see his *Versuch über die wahre Art das Klavier zu spielen* vol. i, 1753]. The next in line was Clementi.

Until recently, English musicians used an older method of numbering the fingers, known as English fingering, x 1 2 3 4, i.e., with an "x" for the thumb and with 1 for the index finger (as in violin playing). This has now been almost completely abandoned for the "German fingering" 1 2 3 4 5. Oddly enough, the "English system" was widely used in Germany as well as in other countries during the 18th century, while the first record of "German fingering" is in English virginal books (*c.* 1600). Purcell used English fingering but in reverse order for the left hand, i.e., with the x for the fifth finger. For the system of fingering for stringed instruments,

see Positions. See H. Gleason, "Organ Instruction before Bach" (*BAMS* iv).

Finland. Finland possesses a large wealth of folksongs, ancient and modern. The earliest type, called *joiku,* is a kind of improvised lament. Next follow the *runot* (sing. *runo;* sung to traditional legendary verses), which are melodic and rhythmically vigorous, often employing a 5/4 meter. Between 1835 and 1849 Elias Lönnrot worked these narrative folksongs into a full-length epic, *Kalevala,* which has been used by numerous Finnish composers as a basis for songs or symphonic poems (Sibelius). There is also a considerable body of folksong originating in the Swedish-speaking districts of Finland and closely related in verse and melodic forms to the folksong of the Scandinavian peninsula. The traditional Finnish folk instrument is the kantele, a *psaltery shaped like a bird's wing, originally with 5 but today with 20 to 30 strings.

Medieval liturgical MSS in the Helsinki University Library testify to the spread of Gregorian chant in the diocese of Åbo (Turku) during the period 1100–1500. Some of the religious songs of the Swedish *Piae cantiones* of 1582 [*Editions XLIII, 10] may be of native Finnish origin. The earliest Finnish composer of general renown was B. H. Crusell (1775–1838), who was a virtuoso on the clarinet and wrote concertos for it. A continuous development started about 1850 with the activity of German musicians, e.g., Fredrik Pacius (1809–91; born in Hamburg; professor of music at Helsingfors University from 1834; composer of the opera *Kung Karls jakt,* 1852, and of the Finnish national anthem "Maame") and Richard Faltin (1835–1918; professor at Helsingfors Conservatory, 1871–96; compiler of a collection of Finnish folksongs). A native-born composer was Martin Wagelius (1846–1906), who in 1882 became director of the new Helsingfors Conservatory (now Sibelius Academy) and who wrote a number of theoretical books (in Swedish). Robert Kajanus (1856–1933) used Finnish coloring in his symphonic poems *Aino* and *Kullervo,* but it was Jean Sibelius (1865–1957) who established the national Finnish style and gave Finnish music international importance. His symphonic poems (*Finlandia,* 1899; *Pohjola's Daughter,* 1906; *Tapiola,* 1926, etc.; see Symphonic poem IV), seven symphonies, and violin concerto have become part of the standard repertory, particularly in America and England. Contemporaries of Sibelius include Ilmari Krohn (1867–

1960; opera, oratorios, Passion; also author of
textbooks and editor of hymns and folksongs),
Oskar Merikanto (1868–1924; opera, part songs,
organ music), and Armas Järnefelt (1869–1958;
symphonic poems *Korsholma, Luvattu maa,* and
the popular orchestral *Praeludium* and *Berceuse*).
There followed Erkki Melartin (1875–1937;
opera *Aino;* symphonies, symphonic poems,
chamber music, etc.); Selim Palmgren (1878–
1951; opera *Daniel Hjort;* five piano concertos
including "The River" and "Metamorphoses";
numerous lyrical piano pieces); Leevi Madetoja
(1887–1947; symphonies, numerous symphonic
poems; operas *Pohjalaisia* and *Juha*); Armas
Launis (b. 1884; operas, orchestral and piano
music; also scholar and writer; see Lit.); and
Toivo Kuula (1883–1918; orchestral works,
chamber music). Representatives of a later generation, influenced by the trends of 20th-century
music, are Yryö Kilpinen (1892–1959; songs),
Aarre Merikanto (1893–1958; much symphonic
and chamber music), and Väinö Raitio (1891–
1945; ten symphonic poems, five operas, some
chamber music). Prominent Finnish composers
born in the 20th century include Uuno Klami
(1900–61; symphonies, concertos, and various
orchestral works); Sulho Ranta (1901–60);
Tauno Pylkkänen (b. 1918); Ahti Sonninen
(b. 1914); Lauri Saikkola (b. 1906); Erik Berg-
man (b. 1911); Einar Englund (b. 1916); Eino-
juhani Rautavaara (b. 1928); and Joonas Kok-
konen (b. 1920).

Lit.: A. Launis, *Über Art, Entstehung und
Verbreitung der estnisch-finnischen Runenmelo-
dien* (1913); I. Krohn, *Über die Art . . . Geistliche
Volksmelodien in Finnland* (1899); *AdHM* ii,
1122ff; *LavE* i.5, 2586f; V. Helasvuo, *Sibelius and
The Music of Finland* (1952); J. Horton, *Scandi-
navian Music* (1963); K. Flodin, "Die Erweckung
. . . in der Finnischen Musik" (*DM* 1903/04);
F. Bose, "Typen der Volksmusik in Karelien"
(*AMF* iii); O. Andersson, "The Introduction
of Orchestral Music into Finland" (*CP 1911*);
H. Pudor, in *SIM* ii; B. Wallner, "Scandinavian
Music after the Second World War," in *LBCM,*
also *MQ* li.   rev. J.H.

Finlandia. See under Symphonic poem IV.

Fioritura [It.]. Embellishment, either written out
or improvised. See Ornamentation.

Fipple flute. *Whistle flute.

Firebird, The. See *Oiseau de feu, L'.*

First-movement form. Same as *sonata form.

The term is unfortunate, since the same form
frequently also occurs in the slow and in the final
movement of a sonata.

Fis, fisis [G.]. F-sharp, f-double-sharp. See Pitch
names.

Fistelstimme [G.]. Falsetto.

Fistula [L.]. Medieval name for flute and, particularly, organ pipe (*fistula organica*). Several
treatises (Notker Labeo, *GS* i, 101f; "Alia
musica," *GS* i, 147f; Odo, *GS* i, 303; Bernelinus,
GS i, 329f; Aribo, *GS* ii, 222ff; Eberhard von
Freising, *GS* ii, 279ff) give detailed instructions
for making organ pipes. Of particular interest
is the point that originally they all had the same
diameter ("eiusdem amplitudinis omnes esse
debent"; Notker) and hence a variable scaling
[see Organ XII]. *Fistula panis, f. anglia, f. germanica* are humanist names for panpipe, English flute (recorder), German flute (transverse
flute) respectively.

Fitzwilliam Virginal Book. See under Virginal
music.

Five, The. Designation for a group of five Russian composers who, about 1875, united their
efforts in order to create a truly national school
of Russian music. The original name, coined in
a newspaper article in 1867, was *Moguchaya
Kuchka* (The Mighty Handful). They were
César A. Cui (1835–1918), Alexander P. Borodin
1833–87), Mily A. Balakirev (1837–1910), Modest P. Mussorgsky (1839–81), and Nicolay A.
Rimsky-Korsakov (1844–1908). See Russia II.
See M. O. Zetlin, *The Five* (1959).

Five-three chord. The common triad, so called
because in figured bass it is indicated by the
figures $^5_3$ (third and fifth) above the root.

Fixed-do(h). See under Movable do(h).

Flagellant songs. See *Geisslerlieder.*

Flageolet. See under Whistle flute. For ill. see
under Flute. Flageolet tones, see *Flageolett-töne.*

Flageolett-töne. German term for the *harmonics of stringed instruments. The English
term "flageolet tones" is rarely used.

Flam. See under Percussion instruments B, 1
(side drum).

Flamenco. A south Spanish (Andalusian) type
of song, midway between folk and art music,
performed by specially trained singers to the

accompaniment of a guitar. Characteristic traits are an E-minor tonality vacillating between f and f-sharp and g and g-sharp (sometimes including the g♯–f–e progression of *Gypsy music), narrow range, absence of strict meter, expressive ornamentation, repetition of short phrases,

A - ha - y, tri - hin tri - hi - hi - hi - - y, a - y - hy

melancholy mood, etc. The songs often begin with the plaintive exclamation "Ay."

The *cante flamenco* is believed to have developed from an early 19th-century *cante hondo* (*jondo,* deep song), a highly emotional and tragic song cultivated among prisoners (*carcelera*), which in turn may have had an Oriental (Arab? Hindu? Jewish?) background. Late in the 19th century the *cante hondo* was adopted, under the name *cante flamenco,* by the Gypsies, who made it even more expressive and florid. See D. E. Pohren, *The Art of Flamenco* [1962]; D. Duff, in *MM* xvii, 214; M. de Falla, in *LRM* xi; M. G. Matos, in *AnM* v.

Flat [F. *bémol;* G. *Be;* It. *bemolle;* Sp. *bemol*]. The sign ♭, which indicates the lowering of the pitch of a note by a half-step. See Accidentals; Pitch names. The term is also used to indicate incorrect intonation on the underside.

Flatté, flattement [F.]. In French 17th-century viol music, an *agrément* equivalent to the *pincé* of the clavecinistes [see Mordent]. After the middle of the 18th century the term is occasionally applied to the *Schleifer* [see Appoggiatura, double II], probably due to a mistaken translation.

Flatterzunge [G.]. Flutter-tonguing. See Tonguing.

Flautando, flautato. See Bowing (l).

Flautino [It.]. A small flute, either the flageolet or the descant flute.

Flauto [It.]. Flute. *Flauto a becco, flauto diritto, flauto dolce,* *recorder; flauto d'amore,* see Flute II (b); *flautone,* alto flute or bass flute; *flauto piccolo,* piccolo (flute). Until the middle of the 18th century, e.g., in Bach, *flauto* always meant

the recorder, the flute being called *flauto traverso* [see Flute III]. In the same period, *flauto piccolo* meant not the transverse piccolo but a small recorder.

Flaviol. A small, one-handed Spanish flute, used for dance music. See Pipe (2).

Fledermaus, Die [G., The Bat]. Operetta in three acts by Johann Strauss, Jr. (libretto by C. Haffner and R. Genée, derived from a French farce, *Le Reveillon,* by H. Meilhac and L. Halévy after R. Benedix's *Das Gefängnis*), produced in Vienna, 1874. Setting: Bad Ischl, Austria, 1874.

Flemish school. I. The leading school of the Renaissance period, active *c.* 1450–1600, after the *Burgundian school. It includes a long succession of outstanding composers—many of them the undisputed leaders of their day—who came from the southern Netherlands, approximately present-day Belgium (Antwerp, Bruges—the Flemish north; Liège, Mons—the Walloon south) and the adjoining region of northern France. It is often called the Second and Third Netherlands school [see Netherlands schools]; in English-speaking countries the designation "Flemish" is usually connected with the history of painting, referring to the northern part of Belgium. A further semantic problem is raised by the fact that in present-day Belgium, the Dutch and French languages are spoken, the former by people known as Flemings (Flemish) and the latter by Walloons (Walloon; see R. B. Lenaerts, in *Editions XXXIX, 22). Some writers feel that it is misleading to apply the term "Flemish" to Renaissance music, in which composers from Flanders, southern Belgium, and northern France all played a role. Nevertheless, it is preferable to Franco-Flemish or Franco-Netherlandish [see *ReMR,* p. 9]. Although its members came from the same area, the Flemish school, as it will be called in this dictionary, is not a national one in the proper sense of the word—as, e.g., the French or the Italian *ars nova*—but an international movement of extraordinary dimensions. This characteristic is due to the fact that the composers in question seldom stayed in their homeland but emigrated to other countries, where they held high positions in church choirs and in the chapels of princes. In the 15th century they were the leaders of the musical development in France. In the first half of the 16th century their influence stimulated the rise of national talent in France, Germany, Austria, Italy, England, Spain, Poland, and Hungary.

The second half of the 16th century saw both rivalry and cooperation between the Flemish teachers and their "foreign" pupils.

II. The earliest known composer of Netherlands extraction is Johannes Ciconia (born in Liège; c. 1335–1411), who was active not only in his native city but also in Padua, thus foreshadowing the typical wanderlust of his 16th-century compatriots. Other early Flemish composers were Johannes de Limburgia, Reginald Liebert (?), Arnold and Hugo de Lantins (Lantin, province of Liège), and Hayne van Gizeghem. However, the Flemish school (as understood here) begins with the great master Johannes Ockeghem (born in Hainaut; c. 1430–95), who created a musical style entirely different from that of his predecessors (Dufay, Burgundian school). His approach to problems of polyphonic texture, form, and expression was so novel that scholars have tried to trace its "origin" but without success. Very possibly, it was truly original.

Following is a list of the most important Flemish composers, arranged according to generations; some "Franco-Flemish" composers (marked Fr.) are included.

1425: Johannes Ockeghem (1430–95); Antoine Busnois (Fr.; d. 1492); Jacques Barbireau (c. 1408–91); Philippe Basiron (?).

1450: Jacob Obrecht (a Netherlander, b. Berg-op-Zoom; 1452–1505); Gaspar van Weerbecke (c. 1445–after 1514); Heinrich Isaac (c. 1450–1517); Josquin des Prez (c. 1450–1521); Pierre de la Rue (Fr.; d. 1518); Loyset Compère (Fr.; c. 1455–1518).

1475: Jean Mouton (c. 1470–1522); Antoine de Fevin (Fr.; 1474–1512); Adrian Willaert (c. 1490–1562); Nicolas Gombert (c. 1490–1556); Jean Richafort (c. 1480–1548).

1500: Jachet Berchem (?–?); Jachet of Mantua (Fr.; c. 1495–1559); Jacques Buus (d. 1565); Jacob Arcadelt (c. 1505–c. 1560); Jacobus Clemens (Clemens non Papa; c. 1510–c. 1556); Philippe Verdelot (d. c. 1550).

1525: Cipriano de Rore (1516–65); Philippe de Monte (1521–1603); Jacobus de Kerle (1531/32–91); Orlando di Lasso (1532–94); Giaches de Wert (1535–96).

1550: Jacob Regnart (c. 1540–99); Charles Luython (c. 1556–1620); Giovanni (Jean de) Macque (c. 1550–1614).

The great contribution of the Flemish masters was the establishment of a new polyphonic style characterized by (ideally) the equality of all the parts and, beginning with Josquin, the consistent use of imitation as the chief means to achieve this

equality. This tendency appears even in those compositions in which a *cantus firmus* stands apart from and in balance to the contrapuntal web of the other voices (tenor Masses and motets of the 15th century). Masses and motets are the backbone of the vast repertory of Flemish composers; to these were gradually added the various "national" types of secular music, the (French) *chanson, the (Italian) *madrigal, the (German) *lied, and finally the many popular forms of *villanella, *canzonet, *balletto, etc., that indicate approaching decadence.

III. Following is a brief account of the development within this general framework. The main difference between the Burgundian school (Dufay) and the first Flemish masters (Ockeghem, Obrecht) is the change from three-part writing to four-part writing; from a relatively high and narrow range to a considerably lower and fuller range (first appearance of the bass); from a medieval timbre (*sound ideal) of contrasting sounds to a full vocal sonority, probably *a cappella;* from clear phrases and cadences to an "unending melody"; from an early manifestation of the major mode to the somber colors of modal harmonies; from a (decorated) chordal style, frequently of the melody-accompaniment type, to a truly polyphonic style with highly embroidered lines in all the parts; from aristocratic subtlety and refinement to pious devotion and mystic expression.

Although Ockeghem and Obrecht are usually named in one breath, the difference between their styles is considerable. Of the two, Ockeghem is by far more purely Flemish and presents a much stronger contrast to Dufay than Obrecht, who frequently introduced chordal passages, full cadences, and sectional treatment. In fact, these two attitudes can be traced throughout the entire development of Flemish music: the former (strictly polyphonic, continuous, noncadential, uniform sonority) being represented by Ockeghem, Isaac, La Rue, Gombert, de Monte; the latter (partly chordal, sectional, cadential, using contrasting sonorities) by Obrecht, Josquin, Willaert, and G. Gabrieli [for the use of chordal style in Flemish music, see Familiar style]. Although the Flemish composers occasionally used proportional complications and canonic riddles [see Proportions; Canon III] in their Masses, it is misleading to emphasize this feature as the principal distinguishing characteristic. Almost to the present day, books have been published in which Ockeghem is represented only by a 36-voice canon (probably not his) or his *Missa cuiusvis toni* [see Catholicon], and Josquin by his early canonic *Missa L'Homme armé*. Actually, English composers of the mid-15th century far surpassed their colleagues from the Low Countries in devising canonic enigmas, and the notational complications in the works of Ockeghem, Isaac, and Josquin are only a modest remainder of those encountered in French music of the late 14th century. See also Imitation; Mass; Motet; *Musica reservata*.

Lit.: A. W. Ambros, *Geschichte der Musik*, vols. ii, iii (1864, '68); A. Pirro, *Histoire de la musique de la fin du XIVe siècle à la fin XVIe* (1940); H. Wolff, *Die Musik der alten Niederländer* (1956); C. van den Borren, *Études sur le quinzième siècle musical* (1941); A. Smijers, ed., ‡*Van Ockeghem tot Sweelinck*, 7 vols. (1949–56); *Editions XXXIX, 22; P. Lang, "The So-called Netherlands Schools" (*MQ* xxv); H. Besseler, "Von Dufay bis Josquin" (*ZMW* xi); J. Wolf, "Der niederländische Einfluss in der mehrstimmigen Musik bis zum Jahre 1480" (*TV* vi, vii); G. d'Alessi, "Maestri e cantori fiamminghi nella Capella . . . di Treviso (1411–1561)" (*TV* xv); H. Anglés, "Els Cantors i organistes Franco-Flamencs i Alemanys a Catalunya" (*CP Scheurleer*); A. Hammerich, "Niederländische Musiker in Dänemark im 16.–17. Jahrhundert" (*CP Scheurleer*).

Flex, flexa. (1) See under Psalm tones. (2) Same as *clivis* (also *punctus flexus*); see Neumes I, table.

Flick-kanzone [G.]. *Quilt canzona.

Flicorno [It.]. An Italian variety of Flügelhorn.

Fliegende Holländer, Der [G., The Flying Dutchman]. Opera in three acts by Richard Wagner (to his own libretto after Heine's *Memoiren des Herrn von Schnabelewopski*), produced at Dresden, 1843. Setting: medieval, legendary time. One of Wagner's earliest works, it is allied, through its supernatural subject, with the romantic opera of Weber (*Der *Freischütz*) and Marschner. The music shows similar antecedents, both in the broad melodic style and in the rich and colorful orchestral accompaniment. Wagnerian features such as the use of *leitmotivs, continuous melody, and symphonic treatment of the orchestra are not yet evident.

Fliessend, fliessender [G.]. Flowing, more flowing.

Florid. Ornamented, embroidered, decorated, figurated, etc., chiefly with reference to contrapuntal music in which the lines move largely in relatively quick notes from one beat to the next.

Thus, the works of the early Flemish masters (Ockeghem, Obrecht, Isaac) are said to be in florid style [see *HAM*, no. 73b; *SchGMB*, nos. 52, 55]. Florid counterpoint specifically means the use of ornamented lines in teaching counterpoint.

Florilège du concert vocal de la renaissance. See Editions XIX.

Flos [L.]. A 13th-century term for embellishments, somewhat like the trill, mordent, or vibrato. Jerome of Moravia (*CS* i, 91) likens the *flos harmonicus* to the rippled surface of water moved by a gentle wind.

Flöte [G.]. Flute.

Flötenuhr [G.]. See under Mechanical instruments III.

Flott [G.]. Briskly, without hesitation.

Flourish. (1) A trumpet call or fanfare. (2) A somewhat showy decorative passage, often one added by the performer.

Flue pipes (stops, work). See under Organ VIII, IX.

Flügel [G.]. The grand piano.

Flügelhorn. See under Brass instruments III (b).

Flüssig [G.]. Flowing.

Flute. For the general characteristics of the flutes, see under Wind instruments. I. *Present forms.* (a) Flute [F. *flûte;* G. *Flöte;* It. *flauto;* Sp. *flauta*]. The modern flute is a cylindrical tube closed at the upper end. At this end is a side hole (embouchure) across which the player blows, thus making the column of air inside the tube vibrate. The lowest octave of the fundamental scale is overblown by increased wind pressure, thus providing the second octave. The remainder of its three-octave range is produced by further overblowing and by *cross fingering. The modern flute was largely developed by T. Böhm [see Böhm system], who devised the instrument described above. It is generally made of silver, though older instruments were of wood, and gold is occasionally used. The timbre varies considerably at different levels, the lowest tones being thick and breathy, the higher ones becoming brighter and more penetrating. The flute is extremely agile. Trills are possible on nearly every note, and rapid reiterations of a pitch are easily executed by means of *tonguing. Its range is shown in Ex. 1, although some instruments

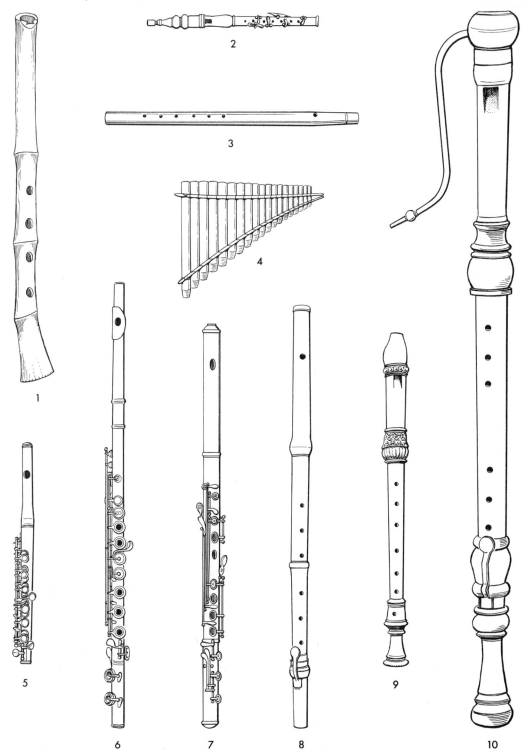

Flutes: *1. Shakuhachi.* *2. Keyed flageolet.* *3. Fife.* *4. Panpipes.* *5. Piccolo.* *6. Metal flute.*
7. Wooden flute. *8. Flute (18th century).* *9. Alto recorder.* *10. Bass recorder.*

seem to have had the low B♭, and the high C♯ and D are occasionally written. (b) Piccolo [F. *petite flûte;* G. *kleine Flöte, Pickelflöte;* It. *flauto piccolo, ottavino;* Sp. *flautín*]. A small flute, pitched an octave above the flute. Its written range is shown in Ex. 2, sounding an octave higher. It is one of the brightest, most penetrating instruments of the orchestra, and its upper register must be used with care. (c) Alto flute [F. *flûte alto;* G. *Altflöte;* It. *flautone;* Sp. *flauta bajo*], sometimes called bass flute. An instrument built in G, i.e., a perfect fourth lower than the normal flute, with a range from g to c'''. It is notated as a transposing instrument, a fourth above its actual sound (c' to f'''). (d) Bass flute, sometimes called contrabass flute. An instrument built an octave below the regular flute. Another kind of flute is the *Albisiphone* (invented by A. Albisi, 1911). This instrument is held vertically, the extension being shortened by means of a double U-tube between the embouchure and the tuning slide. The mouth part is bent horizontally to form the top of a T. The fingering is that of the regular Böhm system. The compass is from B to f''♯. See also Giorgi flute.

II. *Obsolete forms.* (a) *Terzflöte* [G.; Third flute]. So called from being built in E♭, a minor third higher than the standard instrument. (b) Flûte d'amour [G. *Liebesflöte;* It. *flauto d'amore;* Sp. *flauta de amor*]. A flute built a third lower than the regular flute. The alto flute [see I (c)] is sometimes called by this name.

III. *History.* Flutes are among the most ancient and widespread of all instruments. They existed in Sumeria, Egypt, and Palestine, as well as in Mexico and South America, where they were frequently made from clay. In Europe, the first evidence of the transverse flute is a miniature in the *Hortus Deliciarum,* an encyclopedia from the end of the 12th century, where it is called *swegel* [see Schwegel]. Throughout the Middle Ages, Renaissance, and early baroque period, the transverse flute was mainly a military instrument (fife) associated particularly with Germany, so it was generally known as the German flute. For artistic purposes, the end-blown flute, or *recorder, was preferred. About 1650 the instrument, which formerly had a cylindrical bore, was provided with a conical bore, a change that made for a much smoother

tone. Before 1750 the *flûte traversière* became, for the first time, an important solo instrument, as shown by the appearance of Quantz's epochal treatise, *Versuch einer Anweisung die Flöte traversiere zu spielen* (1752). It may be noted that in Bach and Handel the plain name *flauto* still invariably meant the recorder, the transverse flute being called *flauto traverso* or *traverso.* Lully was probably the first composer to use the flute in the orchestra, but not until the time of Haydn did the flute become a permanent member. Beginning *c.* 1800, attempts were made to improve the instrument, chiefly to compensate for the position of the side holes, which were cut to conform to the reach of the fingers rather than the laws of acoustics. The final step in this development was the system of Böhm, who also changed the bore back to its earlier cylindrical shape. This change made the pitch more accurate but detracted from the "sweet sound" of the conical flute. See also Fife; Whistle flute (flageolet); Panpipes; Japan VI (*shakuhachi*).

Outstanding compositions for the flute include J. S. Bach's unaccompanied Sonata in A and 6 sonatas for flute and accompaniment; K. P. E. Bach, numerous sonatas; Handel, sonatas; Mozart, concerto (K. 285c); Schubert, Introduction and Variations on "Ihr Blümlein alle," op. 160; Debussy, *Syrinx* (1912); Prokofiev, Sonata in D, op. 94; Hindemith, sonata (1936) and *Acht Stücke* (1927) for flute solo; Honegger, *Danse de la chèvre* (1932); and Varèse, *Density 21.5.*

Lit.: T. Boehm, *The Flute and Flute-Playing,* rev. ed. [1964]; C. Welch, *History of the Boehm Flute,* rev. ed. (1896); D. C. Miller, *Catalogue of Books . . . Relating to the Flute* (1935); H.-P. Schmitz, *Querflöte . . . in Deutschland während des Barockzeitalters,* rev. ed. [1958]; L. Gilliam and W. Lichtenwanger, *The Dayton C. Miller Flute Collection: A Checklist of the Instruments* (1961); J. J. Quantz, *Versuch einer Anweisung die Flöte traversière zu spielen* (1752), fac. of 1789 ed. (1953), Eng. trans. [1966]; A. Veenstra, "The Classification of the Flute" (*GSJ* xvii).

Flûte [F.]. Flute. *Flûte traversière, allemande,* transverse flute, i.e., flute. *Flûte à bec, flûte douce,* *recorder. *Flûte d'amour,* see Flute II (b).

Flutter-tonguing. See Tonguing.

Flying Dutchman, The. See *Fliegende Holländer, Der.*

Folia, follia, folies d'Espagne. (1) A dance, probably of Portuguese origin, mentioned in

Portuguese documents of the late 15th century. In all probability it was a "fool's dance" similar to the *moresca. No music from this early period survives. (2) A harmonic pattern related to the *passamezzo antico and the *romanesca, used by a great many composers in the 17th and 18th centuries, and by a few in the 19th and 20th centuries, as the skeletal structure for continuous variations. As is true of the *bergamasca and the *romanesca, one discant melody became attached to the skeletal bass in the 17th century and is found in many of the compositions written on the pattern.

Folia variations were written by Farinelli [see Playford's *The Division Violin*, 1685], D'Anglebert (for harpsichord, 1689; see *TaAM* vii, 122), A. Scarlatti (for harpsichord; see *TaAM* ix, 112), M. Marais (for viola da gamba; *Pièces de viole*, 1681), J. P. Förtsch (in the opera *Die grossmächtige Thalestris*, 1690), Corelli (for violin, op. 5, no. 12, 1700), Keiser (overture to *Der lächerliche Prinz Jodelet*, 1726), J. S. Bach (*Bauernkantate*, 1742), K. P. E. Bach (for piano, 1778; see K. von Fischer, in *RBM* vi, 206f), Grétry (in the opera *L'Amant Jaloux*, 1778), Cherubini (overture to *L'Hôtellerie portugaise*, 1798), Liszt (*Rapsodie espagnole*, 1863), Carl Nielsen (opera *Maskarade*, 1906), and Rachmaninoff (*Variations on a Theme by Corelli*, op. 42, 1932).

As with all the Renaissance harmonic patterns (*passamezzo antico* and *moderno*, *romanesca*, *bergamasca*, etc.), the isometric form developed over a long period. Adumbrated forms of the *folia* appear in late 15th- and early 16th-century MSS in Spain and Italy (e.g., "Cancionero musical de Palacio," in Editions XXXII, 10, p. 171; "Adorámoste, Señor Dios," by F. de la Torre; and "Dindiri din," Montecassino MS 871 in *RBM* ii, 14). In the 16th century, many variants developed. The most popular was the one known as "La Cara Cosa" or "La Gamba" in Italy (e.g., D. Bianchini, *Intabolatura de lauto*, 1546, no. 4), "Mes Pas semez" in France (e.g., arr. for voice and guitar by A. Le Roy, *Second Livre de guiterre*, 1555, f. 8), "Blame not my lute" in England

(a song by Wyatt, in Washington, D.C., Folger Shakespeare Library MS 448.16, f. 4), and simply "Pavana" in Spain (e.g., E. Enriquez de Valderrábano, *Libro de música, Silva de Sirenas*, 1547, ff. 94^v and 95^v; D. Pisador, *Libro de música de vihuela*, 1552, f. 4; and L. Venegas de Henestrosa's *Libro de cifra nueva*, 1557; ed. H. Anglés, 1944, p. 191, in musical examples). D. Ortiz, in his *Tratado de glosas* (1553), used "La Cara Cosa" as the basis of two "recercada" (ed. M. Schneider, 1913, pp. 117, 130).

Lit.: O. Gombosi, in *AM* viii; *id.*, in *MGG* iv, 479–84; J. Ward, in *CP 1952*, 415–22; J. Subirá, *Historia de la música española e hispanoamericana* [1953].   L.H.M.

Folk music, folksong. I. The musical repertory and tradition of communities (particularly rural), as opposed to art music, which is the work of musically trained composers. It generally develops anonymously, usually among the uneducated classes, and originally was (and may still be) transmitted aurally, thereby becoming subject to modification. Folk music exists in practically every part of the world and constitutes a vast body whose study often requires special methods [see Ethnomusicology]. By far the greatest part of this repertory involves singing and thus is known as folksong. The present article is confined to a consideration of the tradition of folksong in Western culture.

Western folksong developed together with artless poems dealing with various aspects of daily life: work songs, love songs, cradle songs, drinking songs, patriotic songs, dancing songs, mourning songs, narrative and epic songs, etc. Folksongs of different nations have certain characteristic features that, although difficult to describe, are clearly felt to represent the general national traits of the people. The examples here, showing an Anglo-American (1), Italian (2), German (3), Russian (4), and Hungarian (5) folksong, demonstrate this point. On the other hand, numerous examples of melodies found among widely separated nations show a striking similarity of melodic or rhythmic design. Certain Hungarian folksongs, for example, have been found to be almost identical to melodies sung in Anatolia, Scotch folk tunes have been said to be similar in some respects to those of Arabia, and Russian Gypsy songs are surprisingly like Brazilian melodies. While in many cases such similarity may be coincidental, it may point to a common origin of such melodies, which are thought to date from before the time when the peoples involved migrated to different places. In this way (applicable in the case of Hungary and Anatolia, but certainly not in the case of Scotland and Arabia or Russia and Brazil), it has been possible to establish the age of certain folksongs. This point is particularly important in view of the fact that nowhere have guesswork and even pure fancy been given such free rein as in some studies of folk music, where melodies that show unmistakable traces of 17th-

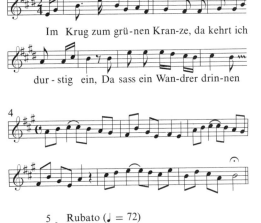

Im Krug zum grü-nen Kran-ze, da kehrt ich

dur - stig ein, Da sass ein Wan-drer drin-nen

T'aie fat - ta la gon - nel - laAn - to-ni - a

a. Te l'a - ie fat - ta col - la cre - den - za

1. A version of the "Cherry Tree Carol." 2. Example of Italian folksong.

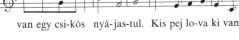

5. Rubato (♩ = 72)

Ti-szán in-nen, Du-nán. túl, túl a Ti-szán

van egy csi-kós nyá-jas-tul. Kis pej lo-va ki van

köt-ve szür-kö-tél-lel, pok-róc nél-kül, gaz-dás-tul.

3. German folksong. 4. "The Bridegroom's Plea," a Russian wedding song, a variant of which was used by Stravinsky in L'Oiseau de feu. 5. "Tiszán innen Dunán túl" (Hungarian).

or 18th-century origin are ascribed to pre-Christian times. Actually, most of the folk melodies of the Western nations are of relatively recent origin. For instance, practically all the folksongs in current use in Germany date from about 1800. Those of Italy are still more recent, while the English ones frequently show traits of a somewhat earlier origin (16th, 17th centuries).

II. The great majority of Western folksongs as they exist today belong to what might be termed "civilized" folksong, i.e., folksongs that show the influence of art music. This becomes clear by comparing any of them to a truly "aboriginal" folksong, such as those found in primitive cul-

tures and occasionally in remote regions, such as parts of the Balkan peninsula, Finland, Scotland, etc. Strict meter and measure, clear and regular phrases, well-defined tonality (sometimes with traces of modality), definite form, triadic intervals, etc., are features that have their origin in the rationalized vocabulary of art music and that have, in the course of one or two centuries, reached the lower classes in a characteristic process of seepage [G. *abgesunkenes Kulturgut*]. (An interesting example illustrating the "city influence" on Spanish folksong is given by H. Anglés in *AMF* iii, 350.) The recognition of this influence as "from above to below" is, of course, in diametrical opposition to the still largely current opinion that folksong is the "foundation" of all music, an opinion reflected in many books on music history that begin with an introductory chapter on folksong. Such a procedure would have some justification if examples of really primitive folk music were discussed instead of folksongs that clearly date from the 17th and 18th centuries.

The process of seepage has had much more effect on the texts than on the melodies of folksongs. Numerous texts of folksongs have been shown to be merely modified or distorted versions of art poems. Similar examples are rare, however, where the melodies are concerned. Here the influence "from above" is of a more general nature, establishing the general framework of style and design only, but admitting original creativity within this frame.

Regarding the question of authorship, modern scholars take a much more sober view than earlier writers who surrounded the folksong with an aura of "divine origin," mystic "self-conception," or "collective creation." Each folksong is, of course, the product of an individual, and the "collective" point of view is justifiable only in so far as the "original" song has, in the course of decades, centuries, or millennia, been modified by others.

III. Perhaps the earliest true folksongs traceable in written form are Icelandic songs and the Polish war song *Bogurodzica,* which are preserved in 13th-century MSS [see Iceland; Poland I]. While the melodies in 15th-century monophonic sources (Lochamer Liederbuch, MS of Bayeux) are too elaborate to be considered folksongs, a number of true folk (or, at least, popular) melodies are probably preserved in the tenors (occasionally upper parts) of polyphonic compositions, e.g., "La Belle se siet" (Dufay), *L'Homme armé," "T'saat een meskin" (Obrecht; *HAM,* no. 78), "T'Andernaken" (Obrecht), "Es leit ein Schloss in Österreich" (Glogauer Liederbuch; see Editions XVIII, 4, p. 16) and "Ich stund an einem Morgen" (H. Finck). Other interesting sources of 15th- and 16th-century folksongs are the *quodlibets* and *Souterliedekens.* Some early (14th-century?) Spanish melodies are recorded in Salinas' *De musica libri septem* (1577), among them "Calvi vi calvi calvi arabi" (Arabic "Qalbi bi qalbi, qalbi arabi," "Heart, oh my heart, 'tis the heart of an Arab"; see *ReMMA,* p. 375). One of the most beautiful German folksongs of the present day, "Innsbruck ich muss dich lassen," is a composition by Heinrich Isaac (*c.* 1450–1517). Particularly interesting is a Hungarian melody preserved in Tinodi's *Cronica* of 1554 because it is the earliest folksong showing unmis-

takable "national" traits [see *LavE* i.5, 2615f]. A number of charming English folk tunes ("Goe from my window," "John come kisse me now") are preserved in the Fitzwilliam Virginal Book (*c.* 1600), where they are used as themes for variations. Most of the English folk melodies date from the 16th century, while those of Germany originated mostly around and after 1800. Many of the most popular "folksongs" are of traceable authorship, e.g., the "Lorelei" (German; text by Heine, music by F. Silcher, 1789–1860), "Dixie" (Daniel D. Emmett, 1859), or "Estrellita" (Mexico; Manuel Ponce, 1913). For the folksongs of the United States, a clear line of distinction must be drawn between the melodies of the American Indians and the folksongs of the white settlers and Negroes. For the former, see American Indian music; for the latter, Shanty; Negro music.

Lit. (selection of books and collections of a general nature): W. Danckert, *Das europäische Volkslied* (1939); W. Wiora, *Das echte Volkslied* (1950); *LavE* ii.5, 2866–3014 (bibl.); B. Nettl, *Theory and Method in Ethnomusicology* [1964]; id., *An Introduction to Folk Music in the United States* (1960); F. J. Gillis, "An Annotated Bibliography of Theses and Dissertations in Ethnomusicology and Folk Music" (*Ethnomusicology* vi, 3); K. P. Wachsmann, *International Catalogue of Published Records of Folk Music* (International Folk Music Council, 1960); H. Mersmann, "Grundlagen einer musikalischen Volksliedforschung" (*AMW* iv, v).

Bibliographical studies for Anglo-American: D. K. Wilgus, *Anglo-American Folksong Scholarship since 1898* (1959); C. Haywood, *A Bibliography of North American Folklore and Folksong,* rev. ed., 2 vols. (1961); G. M. Laws, *Native American Balladry,* rev. ed. (1964); R. M. Lawless, *Folksingers and Folksongs in America,* rev. ed. [1965]; A. Lomax and S. R. Crowell, *American Folk Song and Folklore, A Regional Bibliography* (1942); M. E. Henry, *A Bibliography for the Study of American Folk Songs* (1937).

Collections of folksongs: (a) *International:* F. H. Botsford, *Folk Songs of Many Peoples,* 3 vols. (1921); M. Karpeles, *Folk Songs of Europe* [1956]; W. Wiora, *Europäische Volksmusik* [1957]; H. Möller, *Das Lied der Völker,* 3 vols. [n.d.; 1930?]. (b) *National:* B. H. Bronson, *The Traditional Tunes of the Child Ballads,* 2 vols. to date (1959—); H. H. Flanders, *Ancient Ballads Traditionally Sung in New England,* 4 vols. to date [1960—]; C. J. Sharp, *English County Folk Songs,* rev. ed. [1961]; Ilmari Krohn, *Suomen kansan sävelmiä* (Finnish), 4 vols. (1893–1912); "List of Authoritative French Folk Music, Records" (*Ethnomusicology,* vi, 1); C. M. Barbeau, *Jongleur Songs of Old Quebec* [1962]; J. Canteloube, *Anthologie des Chants populaires français,* 4 vols. [n.d.; 1951?]; J. Tiersot, *Sixty Folksongs of France* [1915]; *Volkslieder aus Deutschen Landschaften,* ed. by Institut für Volkskunstforschung beim Zentralhaus für Volkskunst, 6 vols. [n.d.; 1957?]; L. Erk, *Deutscher Liederhort,* rev. F. Böhme, 3 vols. (1893–94); *id., Deutscher Liederschatz* (German), 3 vols. (1859–72); B. Bartók and Z. Kodály, *Corpus Musical Popularis Hungaricae* (1951—); W. A. Fisher, *Sixty Irish Songs* [1915]; D. de Lange, *et al., Nederlandsch Volksliederenboek* (1896); O. Gurvin, *Norsk Folkemusikk,* 4 vols. (1958—); E. Grieg, *Norges Melodier* (Norway); O. M. Sandvik, *Norske Religiøse Folketoner,* 2 vols. (1960—); F. V. Sokolov, *Gusli Zvonchatyie* (Moscow, 1959); E. Lineff, *Folk Songs of the Ukraine* [1958]; N. A. Rimsky-Korsakov, *100 Chants populaires russes* [1877–?]; A. Moffat, *The Minstrelsy of the Scottish Highlands* (1907); *id., The Minstrelsy of England* (1901); K. Schindler, *Folk Music and Poetry of Spain and Portugal* (1941); G. Hägg, *Songs of Sweden* [1937]. For more bibl. on American folksong see under Ballad; Negro music; American Indian music. For English folksong, see D. Attwater, in *ML* ix, 129; A. H. Fox Strangways, in *ML* v, 293.

Follia. See *Folia.*

Fonds d'orgue [F.]. Foundation stops of the organ.

Fontane di Roma. See under Symphonic poem IV.

Foot. (1) In versification, see Poetic meter.

(2) In organ building, terms such as eight-foot (written 8-ft. or 8′), four-foot (4′), sixteen-foot (16′), thirty-two-foot (32′), etc., are used to differentiate stops that sound at the pitch indicated by the corresponding key from others sounding higher or lower octaves or even other intervals. If, e.g., the key c′ is touched, an 8′-stop sounds c′, while a 4′-stop sounds c″ and a 16′-stop sounds c. The terminology is derived from the fact that, in a normally pitched flue stop, such as 8′-principal, the length of the pipe sounding c measures about 8 feet (the other pipes of the same stop being, of course, correspondingly shorter), whereas, in a stop of the 4′-class, the pipe sounded by the same key is only half as long, etc. [see Organ V]. In mutation stops, i.e., stops designed to reinforce the harmonics of the unison stops [see Organ VI, IX(e)], still other foot-measurements occur. For instance $2\frac{2}{3}'$ is a pipe of one-third ($2\frac{2}{3} = \frac{8}{3}$) the length of the normal pipes; it therefore produces the third partial, i.e., the twelfth (g″ for the key c′); $5\frac{1}{3}'$ ($= \frac{16}{3}$) sounds the lower octave of this, g′, and $1\frac{1}{3}'$ ($= \frac{4}{3}$) the higher one, g‴. Similarly, $1\frac{3}{5}'$ ($= \frac{8}{5}$) gives the fifth partial, i.e., the third two octaves above the fundamental, e‴, while multiples of this fraction, such as $3\frac{1}{5}'$ ($= \frac{16}{5}$) and $6\frac{2}{5}'$ ($= \frac{32}{5}$) give lower thirds, e″, e′, and $\frac{4}{5}'$, $\frac{2}{5}'$ still higher ones, e⁗, e′′′′′. The seventh partial appears in stops such as $1\frac{1}{7}'$ ($= \frac{8}{7}$), etc. This terminology has been borrowed for similar distinctions in other fields, e.g., for the designation of octaves (8-ft. octave, 4-ft. octave) or of instruments, e.g., 4-ft. instrument for the piccolo flute, etc.

Forefall. See Backfall, forefall.

Forgeries. See Spurious compositions.

Forlana, furlana. A dance from northern Italy (*Friuli*). In dance collections of the 16th century (Phalèse, *Chorearum molliorum Collectanea,* 1583) it is similar to the *passamezzo* (in duple meter), whereas in the baroque period it is a gay dance in triple meter (6/4, 6/8) with dotted rhythms and characteristic repeats of motifs. It became associated with festive activities in Venice, e.g., in the ballets of Campra (*L'Europe galante,* 1697; *Le Carnaval de Venise,* 1699; *Les Festes Vénitiennes,* 1710). Bach's orchestral Suite in C major includes a *forlane.* In 1914 attempts were made (ostensibly under the auspices of the Pope) to revive the *forlana* in place of the "offensive" tango, although the *forlana* was far from "innocent." See J. Écorcheville, in *BSIM* x; P. Nettl, in *RM* xiv, 191–95.

Form. A term that has different meanings depending on whether it refers to "form *in* music" or "form(s) *of* music." The former has a very general and loose meaning, simply expressing the basic fact that music, like all art, is not a chaotic conglomeration of sounds but consists of elements arranged in orderly fashion according to numerous obvious principles as well as a still greater number of subtle and hidden relationships. In this sense, form is so essential to music that it is difficult to imagine how it could be avoided. Even the simplest melody shows relationships of pitch (intervals), time values (rhythm), grouping (phrases), etc., in other words, has "form." "Forms *of* music," however, refers to the existence of certain schemes that govern the over-all structure of a composition and were traditionally used in various periods of music history, e.g., the fugue or the sonata.

As might be expected, the ambiguity of the term "form" has led to numerous misunderstandings and futile argument. Much of this could be avoided if, in speaking of a specific composition, a clear distinction were made between the "form *in* this composition" and the "form *of* this composition." The question of "form vs. content" is a good example. Consider, e.g., a typical statement such as: "In the last analysis form and content cannot be wholly independent of each other." This is entirely correct if form here means "form *in* a composition." In fact, in this case one might say "the form *in* a composition is entirely dependent on its content." If, however, form here meant "form *of* a composition," the almost exact opposite would be correct, i.e., "the form *of* a composition (if it has a 'form') is essentially independent of its content." If we conceive of sound as a somewhat amorphous substance comparable to the flesh and cells of a body, then form might be said to be the support that holds and shapes this substance. This support is of two kinds, one forming a highly complicated inner structure comparable to the bones and muscles (form *in* a composition), the other determining its outer contour, somewhat like the skin (form *of* a composition).

"Form *in* music" includes practically all the theoretical and compositional principles of music, i.e., tones, intervals, scales, tonality, consonance and dissonance, meter, rhythm, phrase, theme, motif, repetition, variation, modification, transposition, modulation, sequence, inversion, and all the higher devices of counterpoint. There are separate entries for most of these categories. For "forms *of* music," see Forms, musical. See K. Westphal, *Der Begriff der musikalischen Form* (1935). Also see bibl. under Forms, musical.

Formant. See under Tone color.

Formes fixes [F.]. Collective designation for the three chief forms of late medieval French poetry and music: *ballade*, *virelai*, and *rondeau*. Their main period was the 14th century, under the poet-composer Guillaume de Machaut (c. 1300–77) and his literary successors, Eustache Deschamps, Charles d'Orléans, Alain Chartier, and Christine de Pizan (d. 1430). After 1450 they gradually declined in importance, being replaced by freer and more varied forms [see Chanson]. All three forms have a *refrain, which, however, has an entirely different function in the rondeau (inner refrain) from that in the two other forms (final refrain). The presence of a refrain as well as etymological considerations (*ballare,* to dance; *virer,* to turn around; *rond,* round) suggest that originally they may have been dancing songs. F. Gennrich has tried to establish a morphological genealogy, rondeau → virelai → ballade [see, e.g., *ReMMA,* pp. 221ff], a construction that involves a good deal of arbitrary manipulation. See F. Gennrich, *Rondeaux, Virelais und Balladen,* 3 vols. (1921–63); *id.*, *Grundriss einer Formenlehre des mittelalterlichen Liedes* (1932); G. Reaney, in *MD* vi; W. Apel, in *JAMS* vii; R. H. Perrin, in *JAMS* viii, 77.

Forms, musical. The general principles and schemes that govern the over-all structure of a composition [see under Form]. In other words, a musical form is the structural outline—comparable to an architect's ground plan—in the composer's mind when he sets out to write, say, a fugue or a sonata. In almost every period of Western music (much less so in Oriental music) certain formal schemes have become traditionally established and have been used by the composers as molds, setting the general frame for their creative imagination. The most important —at least, the most clearly defined—forms may be classified as follows:

I. Single forms
- A. Repeat forms
  - (1) a a' a" . . .   *Variation form.
  - (2) ‖: a :‖: b :‖   *Binary form.
  - (3) ‖: a :‖: b a :‖   Rounded binary form.
  - (4) ‖: a :‖ b a   *Sonata form.
  - (5) a b a   Ternary form.
  - (6) a b a c a   Five-part form (also called *rondo form)
  - (7) a b a c a b a   *Rondo form (rondo-sonata form)
  - (8) a b a c a d . . . a   Rondeau [see Rondeau (2)]
  - (9) Medieval forms: see *Ballade;* Rondeau (1); Virelai (*Ballata*)

For the forms (2) to (5) see Binary and ternary form; also *Bar* form. The forms (3) to (7) have a structure similar to an arch ("arch form" or "bow form"; G. *Bogenform*), while (1) and the *sequence resemble the structure of a chain ("chain form"; G. *Kettenform, Reihenform*). Forms such as (8) combine both structures.

B. Continuation forms
   (1) *Cantus firmus* forms: *organum; 13th-century *motet; chorale compositions
   (2) Imitative forms: 16th-century *motet; *ricercar; *fugue

II. Compound forms (consisting of various "movements")
   A. Instrumental: *sonata; *concerto; *suite; *toccata
   B. Vocal: *cantata; *Mass; *Passion; *oratorio; *opera

Naturally this list is not complete nor without some unavoidable defects, and it should be regarded only as a general outline of the subject. There are a large number of "hybrids" that do not fit into the classification or that represent borderline cases. For instance, the fugue, which is classified above as a continuation form, might also be considered a kind of repetition form, owing to the characteristic alternation of expositions and episodes. In other cases—in fact, in most of them—historical development must be taken into account. For instance, the toccata, which in Bach's time was a compound form consisting usually of five distinct movements, began, about 1550, as a single continuation form (A. Gabrieli), and gradually acquired sectional character (Merulo, *c.* 1600), which finally led to the breaking up into movements.

The interpretation above of "forms of music" as a composer's ground plan does not claim to be a generally accepted definition. In fact, it would be impossible to find a definition likely to meet with the universal approval of musicians and scholars. Many writers use the term in a wider sense, including in it what might more properly be termed "stylistic types," e.g., the chaconne and the passacaglia (which are stylistic types of variation form), or the allemande, courante, etc. (which are stylistic types of binary form). Others prefer to use it in a narrower sense, restricting its application to the schemes based on the principle of repetition [see I, A, in the classification above]. Such restricted usage has a certain advantage. No doubt the repetition forms are not only more clearly defined than the continuation forms but also conform more fully to the general notion of form as a "pre-existing mold." For the continuation types, the name "procedure" has been suggested and indeed might be appropriate. Thus, in the case of a fugue, one would speak of "fugal procedure" rather than "fugal form."

Although with the fugue one might argue whether it is a form or a procedure (or both combined), the appropriateness of the latter term is more clearly indicated in many types of vocal music, namely those in which the text provides the sole "ground plan" of the composer, as in the recitative, the through-composed song, in Wagner's "unending melody," etc. A similar situation exists with regard to the "compound vocal forms" [II, B, above] and the symphonic poem, in which the composer "proceeds" on the basis of the programmatic idea.

There is a widespread tendency among modern composers and writers to deny, or at least minimize, the importance of musical forms, the view being that each composition creates not only its own inner form (form *within* the composition; see under Form) but also its outer structure (form *of* the composition). As far as the repertory of classical music and the greater portion of early music are concerned, such a statement is obviously wrong. It finds justification mainly in the numerous examples of 19th- and 20th-century program music, and in the attempts of recent composers to modify, particularly in their symphonies, the traditional scheme of the sonata. Nonetheless, even such compositions as the symphonies of Sibelius and Shostakovitch or the piano sonatas of Hindemith clearly show that the composers, in writing them, were thinking in terms of the traditional principles of sonata writing.

Lit.: L. Stein, *Structure and Style* [1962]; id., ‡*Anthology of Musical Forms* (1962); E. C. Bairstow, *The Evolution of Musical Form* (1943); H. Leichtentritt, *Musical Form* (1951); S. Macpherson, *Form in Music* (1908); M. H. Glyn, *Analysis of the Evolution of Musical Form* (1909); R. Stöhr, *et al.*, *Formenlehre der Musik* (1933); R. von Lobel, *Die Formenwelt der klassischen Instrumentalmusik* (1935); W. H. Hadow, "Form and Formalism in Music" (*PMA* xxiv); E. J. Dent, "Binary and Ternary Forms" (*ML* xvii, 309); A. Lourié, "The Crisis in Form" (*MM* viii, no. 4); R. Ficker, "Formprobleme der mittelalterlichen Musik" (*ZMW* vii); "Form in Baroque Music" (*BuMBE*, pp. 351ff); M. Bauer, "Formprobleme des späten Beethoven" (*ZMW* ix); H. Mersmann, "Zur Geschichte des Formbegriffs" (*JMP* xxxvii). See also under Sonata; Fugue.

Forte [It.], abbr. *f*, loud; *fortissimo*, abbr. *ff* (*fff*), very loud; *più forte*, louder; *forte-piano*, abbr. *fp*, loud followed by soft; *mezzoforte*, abbr. *mf*, medium loud. For the history, see Expression marks.

Fortepiano [It.]. (1) See under *Forte*. (2) Older name for piano.

Fortspinnung [G.]. In melodic construction, the process of continuation, development, or working out of material, as opposed to repetition in a symmetrical arrangement. Modern writers on melodic analysis (W. Fischer) frequently distinguish between *Fortspinnungstypus* and *Liedtypus*, terms that might be translated "continuation type" and "repetition type." A melody of the latter type is symmetrical in design and structure, whereas one of the former proceeds differently, often from longer phrases to shorter ones. These types are illustrated by the two themes given here [Ex. a, last movement of

Mozart's Symphony in G minor; Ex. b, scherzo of Beethoven's Fifth], which are usually cited as an example of "identical material" (even of plagiarism) but are more noteworthy as an example of "contrasting treatment of the same material," the former in repetition, the latter in continuation. Other terms for the same two types are "static" and "dynamic" melody (E. Kurth). See W. Fischer, in *StM* iii.

Forty-eight, The. Popular name for the 48 preludes and fugues of Bach's *Well-Tempered Clavier* i and ii (24 in each).

Forza del Destino, La [It., The Force of Destiny]. Opera in four acts by Verdi (libretto by F. M. Piave), produced in St. Petersburg, 1862. Setting: Spain and Italy, 18th century.

Forzando, forzato [It.]. Forcing, forced, accented.

Foundation stops. Designation for the unison- and octave-sounding (8′, 16′, 4′, 2′) ranks of the organ, especially those of the diapason chorus. See Organ VI.

Fountains of Rome [It. *Fontane di Roma*]. See under Symphonic poem IV.

Fourniture [F.]. Mixture stop of the organ.

Four Saints in Three Acts. Opera in four acts by Virgil Thomson (libretto by Gertrude Stein), produced in Hartford, Conn., 1934. Setting: Spain, 16th century. There being more than a dozen saints and four acts, the title is a bit of whimsy. The text is in stream-of-consciousness style, the juxtaposition of interesting word sounds being a primary objective. The music, which includes a number of ballets, is in a clear, crisp rhythmic style somewhat reminiscent of jazz, with simple harmonies and a great deal of monotone recitation of the text.

Four-shape note. See Fasola.

Fourth. The interval of the fourth was of basic importance in Greek music [see Tetrachord] and in early medieval polyphony, which was essentially an *organum of the fourth, not of the fifth. As late as *c.* 1030, Guido of Arezzo ruled out the fifth (together with the semitone) from what he called *nostra mollis diaphonia,* "our sweet diaphony." In the 12th century, however, the fifth began to take priority over the fourth, and in the late 15th century Tinctoris said that "the fourth was considered by the ancients the foremost of all consonances, but actually, taken by itself, it is not a consonance but an intolerable dissonance, which can be used only with the third or the fifth" [*CS* iv, 85]. In the 15th century there existed a harmonic style in which the fourth was completely avoided [see *ReMR*, p. 103f]. The fourth has once more acquired basic importance in modern harmony [see Fourth chord].

Fourth chord. Any of various chords consisting of superimposed fourths, e.g., c–f–b♭, c–f♯–b–e′, or of fourths in dissonant combinations with other intervals. These chords play an important role in the harmonic idiom of modern composers (Scriabin, Casella, Hindemith, Bartók), replacing the traditional harmonies resulting from the superimposition of thirds (triad, seventh chord, ninth chord). Scriabin was the first to make deliberate use of fourth chords. Several of his compositions are based on a single fourth-chord combination, e.g., the so-called *mystic chord, c–f♯–b♭–e′–a′–d″. See Quartal harmony; Harmony II (9). See O. Beer, in *DM* xxii.2.

Fox trot. An American ballroom dance dating from about 1915 that became the basis for most subsequent dance steps in duple time with the exception of such importations as the rumba, tango, etc. Varieties are the *Charleston, black bottom, and *shimmy.

Fp. Short for forte-piano [see under *Forte*].

Française. See *Contredanse*.

France. The history of French music includes three periods of particular importance: an early one (1150–1450), during which France was the undisputed leader in musical development; another of about 100 years, during the baroque era (Chambonnières, Lully, Couperin, Rameau); and a third one, that of modern French music, beginning with Berlioz.

I. During the 5th, 6th, and 7th centuries there existed in France a special branch of Christian worship, the Gallican rite, which had special music known as *Gallican chant. After the establishment of the Roman rite (by Pepin, 714–68) the Cathedral of Metz became the leading French center of Gregorian chant, known particularly for its neumatic manuscripts written in a special type of neume, the Messine neumes [see Neumes II]. Possibly, what is known today as Gregorian chant developed in the Franco-German empire of Pepin, Charlemagne (742–814), and his successors [see Gregorian chant VII]. In the 9th and 10th centuries the Monastery of St. Martial in Limoges played a leading part in the early development of the *trope and the *sequence, a development that reached its culmination in Adam de St. Victor (d. 1192). Also preserved from the 9th century are a number of songs in Latin, which, of course, can be claimed with equal right as "French" or "German" (e.g., the "Planctus Karoli"; see *GD* v, 1; *AdHM* i, 160). The oldest song in the Provençal language is a "Hora vos dic vera raizun" of the 10th century [see P. Aubry, *Les Plus Anciens Monuments de la musique française* (1905), pl. I]. Of later date is the *Sponsus* play with a mixed Latin and Provençal text, and the northern French Daniel play (from Beauvais).

II. The great period of medieval French music began about 1100, developing along two parallel lines of equal importance: monophonic secular music, represented by the *troubadours and *trouvères, and polyphonic music, represented by the anonymous composers of the schools of Chartres (*c.* 1100) and *St. Martial (*c.* 1150), by the school of *Notre Dame with Leoninus and Perotinus (before and after 1200), by the composers of the *ars antiqua of the 13th century, and by the *ars nova of the 14th century

(Philippe de Vitry, 1291–1361; Guillaume de Machaut, *c.* 1300–77). After a transitional period (late 14th century: Solage, Selesses, Cordier, *et al.;* early 15th: Carmen, Césaris, Tapissier, *et al.*) came the final culmination of medieval music in the work of the *Burgundian school, with Dufay (*c.* 1400–74) and Binchois (*c.* 1400–60). In the second half of the 15th century, French composers such as Busnois (d. 1492), Barbireau, Regis, Caron, and Faugues came under the influence of the *Flemish school. A happy fusion of Flemish and French elements characterizes the music of the great Renaissance composer, Josquin des Prez (*c.* 1450–1521), and his contemporaries, Pierre de La Rue (d. 1518), Compère (d. 1518), and Brumel (fl. 1483–1520).

The so-called Parisian *chanson—as opposed to the Netherlands type of the late 15th century—originated with a group of composers active in and around the French capital during the first half of the 16th century. Chief among these were Claude de Sermisy (*c.* 1490–1562) and Clément Janequin (*c.* 1485–*c.* 1560). If the witty, often frivolous chanson of this school established France's leadership in the field of amorous and worldly music, it also marked the end of her artistic eminence. An interesting although short-lived product of the academic movement in France was the *musique mesurée* of Claude Le Jeune (1528–1600), Jacques Mauduit (1557–1627), and others, written for the *vers mesurés of Antoine Baïf and his associates of the *Académie de Musique et de Poésie*. A large repertory of 16th-century French lute music (mostly dances and arrangements of chansons) exists in the lute books of Attaingnant (1530), Morlaye (*c.* 1550), Adrian Le Roy (*c.* 1550), and others [see Lute music], and a few remnants of 16th-century French organ music have been preserved in the organ books published by Attaingnant about 1530.

III. In the 17th century, French music was entirely under the patronage of the royal court (Louis XIII, reigned 1610–43; Louis XIV, reigned 1643–1715), whose pomp and splendor were enhanced by the ballet (Cambefort, 1605–61; Lully, 1632–87; Campra, 1660–1744) and opera (Cambert, *c.* 1628–77; Lully; Campra; Rameau, 1683–1764; see Opera IV). Here originated the *minuet, *gavotte, *bourrée, and numerous other dances that later became part of the suite. Of great artistic significance is the French lute music of the 17th century, represented chiefly by Denis Gaultier (*c.* 1600–72), and the harpsichord music that leads from the reserved dignity of Chambonnières (*c.* 1602–72) and Louis Couperin (*c.* 1626–61) over the baroque peak of D'Anglebert (*c.* 1628–91) to the rococo worldliness of François Couperin (1668–1733), coming to its close in the masterpieces of Rameau (1683–1764), with their remarkable traits of ingenious characterization and dramatic surprise. French organ music of the baroque started with J. Titelouze (1563–1633), an important composer with traditional leanings; continued with N. Gigault (*c.* 1625–1707), G.-G. Nivers (1632–1714), N.-A. Lebègue (1631–1702), A. Raison (*c.* 1645–1714), J. Boyvin (*c.* 1653–1706), and others whose work is more notable for ventures in registration than for artistic achievement; and culminated with Nicolas de Grigny (1672–1703). Music for viols was cultivated by Marais (1656–1728) and for violin by Leclair (1697–1764). Less known but important contributions were made in the fields of the motet (Charpentier, Lully, and others; see Motet C) and cantata (Campra and others; see Cantata II). French song literature of this period includes the *air de cour, *brunette,* and other types; see Chanson.

The invasion of the Italian *opera buffa* (1752; *War of the Buffoons) marked the end of the French baroque opera and the beginning of the less significant *opéra comique.* For a hundred years, from 1750 to 1850, the history of French music was practically restricted to efforts to build up a new "grand opera," efforts in which the German Gluck (1714–87), the Italians Cherubini (1760–1842) and Rossini (1792–1868), and the German Meyerbeer (1791–1864) participated along with French composers such as Grétry (1741–1813), Méhul (1763–1817), Boieldieu (1775–1834), Auber (1782–1871), and Halévy (1799–1862).

IV. Much more important than these operas is the symphonic work of Hector Berlioz (1803–69), heir to the tradition of Beethoven and perhaps the greatest figure in 19th-century French music. With all their "flaws," his compositions show an originality, passion, and vigor rarely encountered in French music. César Franck (1822–90) amalgamated the classical forms of the symphony, quartet, variations, etc., with a romantic vocabulary of harmonies and elements derived from a thorough study of counterpoint. Charles Gounod (1818–93) and Georges Bizet (1838–75) are known mainly for their operas, *Faust* (1859) and *Carmen* (1873–4). Camille Saint-Saëns' (1835–1921) numerous works, in a late classical style, are distinguished by technical mastery but are somewhat lacking in inspiration. *Danse macabre* (1874), *Le Carnaval des animaux* (1886), and the Third Symphony (with organ, 1886) are his best-known compositions. Academic and dogmatic leanings are present in the work of Vincent d'Indy (1851–1931), who, with others, in 1896 founded the *Schola cantorum,* devoted to the tradition of Franck and the study of Gregorian chant and 16th-century counterpoint.

A tendency toward greater subjectivism, more lyrical expressiveness, a richer orchestral palette, and a typically French exquisiteness of taste appear in the works of Gabriel Fauré (1845–1924), creator of the modern French song (*mélodie),* and of Henri Duparc (1848–1933), Ernest Chausson (1855–99), and Paul Dukas (1865–1935). Unfortunately, each of them produced only a few works of importance. To the foregoing may be added Florent Schmitt (1870–1958), who, more than any other French composer, was influenced by the emotional exuberance of German romanticism. Modern French music found its most characteristic expression in *impressionism, which was foreshadowed by Édouard Lalo (1823–92) and Emmanuel Chabrier (1841–94) and brought to full flowering in certain works of Claude Debussy (1862–1918) and Maurice Ravel (1875–1937). Debussy may be considered among the founders of modern music in the same sense as Stravinsky and Schoenberg. He emancipated harmony and created a new kind of sound based on the sonorities themselves.

The revolutionary tendencies of the postwar period brought a strong reaction against the refinements of the impressionist style, a reaction that found its clearest formulation in the words of Cocteau: "After the music with the silk brush, the music with the ax." In this movement Erik Satie (1866–1925) was the spiritual leader of the group known as Les Six [see *Six*], which included the most prominent contemporary French composers, notably Darius Milhaud (b. 1892), Arthur Honegger (1892–1955), Francis Poulenc (1899–1963), and Georges Auric (b. 1899). A separate place must be reserved for Albert Roussel (1869–1937) who, though influenced successively by D'Indy, Debussy, and Stravinsky, developed a highly personal style, basically contrapuntal but greatly varying from one composition to the next.

Highly diversified trends appear in the works of the composers born after 1900. André Jolivet (b. 1905) writes in a sort of neoprimitive style;

Olivier Messiaen (b. 1908) tends toward a religious mysticism influenced by Scriabin, Oriental music (Hindu rhythms), bird song, and serial techniques, which he was the first to apply to all elements of music (duration, intensity, etc.). René Leibowitz (b. 1913) writes twelve-tone music; the music of Jean Françaix (b. 1912) is precise, clever, and frankly amusing. In 1936 Jolivet, Messiaen, Yves Baudrier (b. 1906), and Daniel Lesur (b. 1908) formed a group known as "La Jeune France." Today's avant-garde is represented by Pierre Boulez (b. 1925) who, influenced by Webern, has introduced twelve-tone techniques in France. *Musique concrète* and electronic music are represented by Pierre Schaeffer, Jean Barraqué (b. 1928) and others.

Lit.: P. Lasserre, *L'Esprit de la musique française* (1917; trans. 1921); M. Hargrave, *The Earlier French Musicians, 1632–1834* (1917); A. Hervey, *French Music in the XIXth Century* (1903); A. W. Locke, *Music and the Romantic Movement in France* (1920); E. B. Hill, *Modern French Music* (1924); G. Jean-Aubry, *French Music of Today* (1919); M. Cooper, *French Music from the Death of Berlioz to the Death of Fauré* (1951); P. Barbier and F. Vernillat, ‡*Histoire de France par les chansons,* 7 vols. (1956—); H. Grace, *French Organ Music, Past and Present* (1919); N. Dufourcq, *La Musique française* (1949); *id., La Musique d'orgue française de Jehan Titelouze à Jehan Alaine* (1941); A. Coeuroy, *La Musique française moderne* (1922); C. Rostand, *La Musique française contemporaine* (1952); A. Cortot, *La Musique française de piano,* 3 vols. (1930–32); L. de La Laurencie, *L'École française de violon,* 3 vols. (1922–24); *LavE* i.3, 1176ff (to 1814), ii.1, 56ff (modern); P. Daval, *La Musique en France au XVIIIe siècle* (1961); A. Goléa, "French Music since 1945," in *LBCM.* For the earlier periods, see under *Ars antiqua, Ars nova,* Chanson, etc. Also see Editions XXV, XXXIII, XLIX.

Franco-Flemish school. See Flemish school.

Fraudulent compositions. See Spurious compositions.

Frauenchor [G.]. Women's chorus.

Frauenliebe und Leben [G., Woman's Love and Life]. A cycle of eight songs by Schumann, op. 42 (1840), based on a group of poems by Adalbert von Chamisso (published under the same title). It was composed shortly after Schumann married Clara Wieck.

Frau ohne Schatten, Die [G., The Woman without a Shadow]. Opera in three acts by R. Strauss (libretto by H. von Hofmannsthal), produced in Vienna, 1919. Setting: fairy tale.

Fredon [F.]. A rather indefinite term applied by 17th-century French musicians to a trill or a short *roulade.* In the 18th century it was generally used in a derogatory sense for excessive ornamentation.

Freemason music. The Freemason movement began with the foundation of the Grand Lodge of London in 1717. From England it spread to France, Germany, America, and many other countries. Among the Freemasons have been numerous composers, e.g., Boyce, Arne, Wesley, Haydn, Mozart, Löwe, Spohr, Cherubini, Liszt, Irving Berlin. Music played an important role in the Masonic meetings, which often included performances by outstanding artists. Essential to the Masonic rites is the singing of songs, many of which were published in collections such as *Recueil de chansons des Franc-Maçons* (1750), *La Lire maçonne* (1763), *A Selection of Masonic Songs* (by Smollet Holden; 1796), and *The Masonick Minstrel* (Dedham, U.S.A., 1816). Most of the songs are popular tunes, dance tunes, or operatic melodies provided with a suitable text and thoroughbass accompaniment. The most important composer of Masonic music was Mozart, whose works include at least four written specifically for the Freemasons of Vienna: *Gesellenreise* (1785; K. 468); *Die Maurerfreude* (1785; K. 471); *Maurerische Trauermusik* (1785; K. 477); and *Freimaurerkantate* (1791; K. 623). His *Die Zauberflöte* contains numerous elements borrowed from Masonic rites: the Egyptian background, the priests, the ordeal by fire and water, the evil Queen of the Night, the serpent, etc.

Lit.: P. Nettl, *Mozart and Masonry* (1957); *id., Mozart und die königliche Kunst* (1932); *id.,* in *MQ* xvi; O. E. Deutsch, *Mozart und die Wiener Logen* (1932); M. Friedländer, *Das deutsche Lied im 18. Jahrhundert* (1902).

Frei [G.]. Free, with freedom.

Freischütz, Der [G., The Freeshooter]. Opera in three acts by Weber (libretto by F. Kind), produced at Berlin, 1821. Setting: Bohemia, after the Seven Years' War. *Der Freischütz* marks both the beginning and the peak of German romantic opera. Folklore, nature, and superstition are the subjects given a musical setting that is admirable for the charm of its folklike melodies and dance tunes as well as touches of dramatic tension and excitement. Particularly remarkable is the bold use of wind instruments: the horns that capture the atmosphere of the "German forest"; the trombones that accompany the hermit; the clarinet that characterizes Agathe; and the low register of the flute, which portrays Samiel. See also under Melodrama.

Freistimmigkeit [G.]. Modern German term, sometimes translated as "free voice-leading," for a pseudocontrapuntal style in which there is no strict adherence to a given number of parts, i.e., voices are free to enter or drop out, and chordal elements also occur. The natural idiom for such a style lies in music for keyboard instruments or for the lute. Indeed, *Freistimmigkeit* is a characteristic of solo music as opposed to ensemble music [see Ensemble (3)]. The earliest keyboard pieces (Robertsbridge Fragment, *c.* 1320; *Fundamentum organisandi,* 1452) are in two parts but occasionally include single chords or short passages in three parts. More typically *freistimmig* are the organ compositions in the collections of Attaingnant (*c.* 1530; *Editions XLIX, 1) and in the publications of Marco Antonio (da Bologna) Cavazzoni (1524; *Editions X, 1) and of Girolamo Cavazzoni (1542; *Editions IX, 6). *Freistimmigkeit* is highly characteristic of the keyboard style of Frescobaldi [see Ex.] and Froberger. Unfortunately, modern editors have shown a tendency to "correct" this flexible idiom by the insertion of rests, use of double-stemmed notes, and similar devices. As late as about 1700, fugues and ricercars were written without strict adherence to a given number of parts [see, e.g.,

Krieger, in *HAM,* no. 249a]. Naturally, the contrapuntal writing in 19th-century compositions, such as Beethoven's sonatas, is always more or less *freistimmig.* Lute music is almost of necessity *freistimmig.* See also Texture.

French chanson. See under Chanson (2).

French harp. Older name for the mouth organ.

French horn. The horn, as opposed to the English horn, which is a member of the *oboe family. See Horn.

French overture. See under Overture I; Suite V.

French sixth. See Sixth chord.

French Suites. Six suites for harpsichord by Bach, composed about 1720 (in Köthen). The name "French" (not by Bach) has little significance, since French elements are present here to the same extent as in all the suites of Bach and his German predecessors (Pachelbel, Froberger). See under Suite.

Frequency. See under Acoustics I.

Fret [F. *touche;* G. *Bund,* pl. *Bünde;* It. *tasto;* Sp. *traste*]. A thin strip of material placed across the fingerboard of certain instruments (lute, guitar, viols, balalaika, banjo, and various Indian and Arab instruments) that marks the position for stopping the strings. Formerly frets were made from pieces of catgut that were tied tightly around the neck. In more modern instruments they are narrow strips of wood or metal fixed on the fingerboard. On European instruments the frets are always arranged so as to give a succession of semitones [see Tablature III].

Frettoloso [It.]. Hurried.

Fricassée [F.] French name for *quodlibet. Examples including many textual and musical quotations are found in various 16th-century collections of chansons. A *Fricassée* by Henri Fresneau (in J. Moderne, *Le Parangon des chansons,* iii, 1538) contains almost one hundred quotations. See J. Jacquot, ed., ‡*Musique et poésie au XVIe siècle* (1954), pp. 174, 179.

Friss, friszka. See *Csárdás; Verbunkos.*

Frog. A slightly raised ridge fastened to the upper end of the neck of stringed instruments (violin, etc.). It serves to raise the strings over the fingerboard. The British term for frog is *nut.* Also see Bow.

Fröhlich [G.]. Joyful.

From My Life. Smetana's name for each of his two string quartets, in E minor (1876) and in D minor (1882), both of them autobiographical. Today the name is used particularly for the E-minor quartet, which describes the happy experiences of his youthful life but contains in the finale a long-drawn high note that he heard for many years before he became deaf.

From the New World. See New World Symphony.

Frottola [It.]. (1) Generic name for various types of Italian secular song of the late 15th and early 16th centuries. The most important source consists of the eleven books of *frottole* published by Petrucci (1504–14; book X is lost). The *frottole* are often in a simple, essentially chordal style in three or four parts, with the upper part standing out as a melody. Since only the upper part has a text, they were probably performed as accompanied songs, the lower parts being played on instruments (viols, lute, harpsichord, etc.). However, purely vocal performance cannot be ruled out, particularly for the numerous examples written in a strictly homorhythmic style. The *frottola* developed under the aegis of the courts of northern Italy, particularly at Mantua, where the two most outstanding composers of *frottole,* Marco Cara (d. after 1525) and Bartolomeo Tromboncino (d. after 1535), worked under the patronage of Isabella d'Este. The prevailingly chordal style and the simple harmonic idiom (V–I, IV–I) of the *frottole* probably account for the appearance of similar traits in the works of contemporary Flemish composers (Obrecht, Isaac, Josquin). The late *frottole* are of interest as forerunners of the *madrigal.

(2) Specifically, *frottola* is one of the various poetic-musical types represented in Petrucci's collections, also known as *barzelletta.* Others are the *capitolo, *villota, canzona* [see Canzona (4)], *oda,* and *strambotto.* The *frottola* is a late offspring of the 14th-century *ballata.* Similar to this form (and even more so to the Spanish *villancico* of *c.* 1500), it frequently consists of an initial four-line stanza and several six-line (occasionally eight-line) stanzas between which the first half of the initial stanza is repeated as a refrain. The most common musical form is the following (each letter represents two lines of the poem; refrain in capital letters):

Ab   aab   A—   aab   A—...

The music as printed consists of two sections, one for the first stanza (A b), the other for its first half as used as a refrain (A—). A— is essentially the same as A but includes a codalike extension. Frequently the second half of A (music for the second single line) is similar or identical to the first half of b (music for the third single line; see the examples in *HAM*, no. 95). Although the scheme described above is the one most frequently encountered, there are many other but related formal patterns.

Lit.: A. Einstein, *The Italian Madrigal* i (1949), pp. 35ff; W. H. Rubsamen, *Literary Sources of Secular Music in Italy* (1943); *ReMR,* pp. 156ff; B. Disertori, *La Frottola nella storia della musica* (1954); *id., Le Frottole per canto e linto intabulate da Franciscus Bossinensis* [1964]; F. Torrefranca, *Il Segreto del quattrocento* (1939); *Editions XXI, 1 (Petrucci I–III); *Editions XLVI, 8 (Petrucci I, IV); *Editions XLVIII, 4 (Antico); E. B. Helm, in *MQ* xxvii; E. T. Ferand, in *MQ* xxvii; A. Einstein, in *MQ* xxxvii; R. Schwartz, in *VMW* ii, *JMP* xxxi, *CP Kroyer;* A. Einstein, in *ZMW* x; E. T. Ferand, in *AM* x; K. Jeppesen, in *AM* xi and *PAMS* 1939; H. Rosenberg, in *AM* xviii, xix; H. Engel, in *CP 1952;* A. Pirro, in *RdM* 1922, p. 3; R. Gandolfi, in *RMI* xviii; F. Vatielli, in *RMI* xxviii; G. Cesari, in *RMI* xix; B. Disertori, in *RMI* li.

Fuga [L.; It.]. (1) Italian for fugue. In earlier practice, also for fugal theme, e.g., *[Ricercar del] Primo tono con tre fughe* (Trabaci, *Ricercate,* 1603). (2) The original meaning of *fuga* [L.] is not fugue but what today is called canon. In this sense the term occurs in the "Speculum musicae" of *c.* 1330 (*in conductis, motettis, fugis, cantilenis, rondellis;* see *CS* ii, 395a), in the *Fugae* of Oswald von Wolkenstein, in Buchner's "Fundamentum" of *c.* 1525 (*cantus fugat in alto et tenore*), in Glareanus' *Dodecachordon* (1547; p. 445; *iiii vocum fuga ex unica;* see *ApNPM,* p. 180f), in Antonio de Cabezón (*Editions XX, 7, p. 20), in Vincenzo Galilei [*Editions XXIII, 4, p. 12), etc. About 1600 the word *fuga* took on its present meaning as a generic term for pieces in the fugal style, either *canzonas* [see B. Schmid, *Tabulaturbuch* (1607): "Fugen oder wie es die Italiäner nennen, Canzoni alla Francese"], extended *ricercars* [S. Scheidt, *Tabulatura nova* (1624); see *DdT* i, 99], or any of the precursors of the fugue proper.

Fugato. A passage in fugal style that is part of a primarily nonfugal composition. Such passages frequently occur in the development sections of symphonies, sonatas, and quartets.

Fuge tune, fuging tune. A form of hymn or psalm tune developed in New England during the late 18th and early 19th centuries. It commonly begins with a homophonic section, usually cadencing in the tonic and followed by a phrase in which the voices enter in succession (the order varies), which is in turn followed by a concluding homophonic phrase. Two misconceptions are that it represents a crude attempt to write a real fugue, and that it is a native American form originating with Billings. It is, in fact, based on an English form common in the 17th and early 18th centuries, of which Tye's "Laudate nomen Domini" is perhaps the best-known example. English fuging tunes are found as early as 1592 (in T. East's *The Whole Booke of Psalmes*), and 17th-century Scottish psalters contained similar pieces called "reports" (from F. *rapporter,* to carry back). The American fuging tunes thus are a last manifestation of an old form, and are generally somewhat freer in style. Aside from this, the only significant difference is that the English examples "fuged" on the last line, and the American ones on the next-to-last line. Fuging tunes were written for and extensively used in the singing schools organized toward the end of the 18th century in an attempt to improve the bad state of singing in the non-liturgical churches, the writers almost always being singing masters. Among the most gifted of these were William Billings (1746–1800), Daniel Read (1757–1836), Jeremiah Ingalls (1764–1828), Timothy Swan (1758–1842), and Andrew Law (1749–1821).

Lit.: W. Billings, *The Continental Harmony* (1794; fac. ed. 1961); F. J. Metcalf, *American Writers and Compilers of Sacred Music* [1925]; I. Lowens, in *JAMS* vi; *id.,* in *Notes* ix, 233–48; *id.,* in *The Hymn,* April 1952; E. H. Pierce, in *MQ* xvi; A. P. Britton, in *JAMS* iii, 286; C. E. Lindstrom, in *MQ* xxv. See also United States I; Hymn, English; Tune book.   B.J.O.

Fughetta [It.]. A short fugue.

Fugue [F. *fugue;* G. *Fuge;* It., Sp. *fuga*]. The latest and most mature form of imitative counterpoint, developed during the 17th century and brought to perfection by J. S. Bach.

I. *Structure.* The main characteristics of a fugue are: (a) It is always written in contrapuntal style, i.e., with a texture consisting of a number of individual voices, usually three or four. (b) It is based on a short melody, called *subject* or *theme,* which is stated at the beginning of the fugue by one voice alone, being taken up ("imitated") by the other voices in close succession and reappearing throughout the entire piece in all the voices at different places according to principles explained below. (c) In each voice the space between one statement of the subject and the next is filled in by a freely invented counterpoint, which, however, is usually unified by the use of recurrent motifs. These motifs are derived either from the subject itself, or, more usually, from its continuation, which forms the counterpoint to the first imitation (second statement) of the subject, near the beginning of

the fugue. Frequently, but not always, this continuation takes a rather definite form, almost equal to the subject in individuality and importance. In such cases it is called *countersubject* and reappears throughout the fugue in a manner similar to the main subject, though less rigidly. (d) A section in which the theme appears at least once in each voice is called *exposition.* The exposition may include one more statement than the number of parts, e.g., four in a three-voice fugue, the subject being stated again by the voice in which it first appeared. However, this does not usually happen in the first exposition, which in other respects as well is the most rigid in structure. Sometimes the term exposition is restricted to the first exposition, without any special name being applied to later sections of similar construction. The accompanying example (J. K. F. Fischer, *Ariadne Musica, c.* 1700) illustrates the

beginning of a fugue. (e) A section of the fugue that does not include a statement of the subject is called an *episode.* The episodes are based chiefly on short motifs derived from the subject or its continuation (countersubject). They frequently use sequential treatment [see Sequence I]. (f) The over-all structure of a fugue is an alternation of expositions and episodes. The episodes, although still in strict counterpoint, are somewhat freer and "lighter in weight." A fugue may have three, four, or more expositions, separated from one another by episodes. The middle expositions usually involve modulations into other keys, such as the relative minor, dominant, or subdominant, with return to the main key in the last exposition. (g) While in the first exposition the statements of the subject follow in rather close succession, in the later expositions they usually are more widely spaced, separated by what might be called secondary episodes. For instance, the first fugue from the second book of Bach's *Well-Tempered Clavier* has two secondary episodes within its second exposition (see the accompanying diagram, which shows the basic structure of the fugue). The three subjects of the initial expo-

	Exposition 1	Episode 1	Exposition 2			Episode 2	Exposition 3	Coda
soprano	S₂ —		S —	Episode	Episode	S —	S —	
alto	S₁ —			S —		S —	
bass		S₁ —		S —			S —	
meas. no.	1 5 9	13	25 29 39 43	47 51	55	68 72 76	80 83

sition are designated S₁ and S₂ in order to indicate that they appear in two keys, tonic (S₁) and dominant (S₂). Because of this tonal relationship they are referred to as "subject and answer," or "antecedent and consequent," or "*dux* (leader) and *comes* (follower)." Usually the answer is not an exact transposition but involves the modification of certain steps, e.g., the replacement of a fifth (c–g) by a fourth (g–c', instead of g–d') [see Tonal and real]. The fugue usually closes with a *coda, which often has a pedal point.

It must be noted that the scheme above represents a "student's fugue" rather than a "composer's fugue," such as those by Bach, few of which fit the theoretical description in every detail. Interestingly enough, Bach treated the fugue much more freely than Mozart, Haydn, and Beethoven treated the sonata. The question may well be raised whether there really is such a thing as the "fugue form" and whether it would not be more proper to speak of "fugal procedure" rather than "fugal form" [see Forms, musical]. At any rate, the statement of numerous authors that "a fugue is a three-part form" is rather misleading.

While the explanations above describe the basic principles of the fugue, fugal style includes many special devices of lesser or greater complexity, which contribute interest, variety, and intensity. Most of these are found under separate entries [see Augmentation and diminution; Inversion (2); Stretto; Double fugue; see also *Art of Fugue*].

II. *History.* The principle of imitative counterpoint, which is the basis of the fugue, can be traced back as far as *c.* 1200 [see Imitation]. However, it was not until the late 15th century that composers became fully aware of the importance of imitation as a structural element of polyphonic music (Obrecht, Isaac, Josquin). The style and form of Josquin's and Gombert's motet, characterized by many relatively short "expositions" (points), each based on a different subject and following one another in a dovetailing fashion, were imitated in the organ *ricercar (Cavazzoni, *c.* 1540). However, the ricercar had modifications that foreshadow future tendencies, e.g., reduction of the number of points (i.e.,

themes) and expansion of each point into a well-defined section including a greater number (up to 15 or more) of statements of the subject. Besides these "polythematic" ricercars, which are quite long, there also are shorter "monothematic" ricercars (e.g., by A. Gabrieli; see W. Apel, in *MD* iii). Another important forerunner of the fugue is the organ *canzona, which is similar in form to the polythematic ricercar but livelier and freer. The ricercar style persists in slow fugues, such as nos. 4 and 22 of the *Well-Tempered Clavier* i, and the canzona type in the more flexible and individual subjects of the faster fugues [see Soggetto].

The details of the development leading from the ricercar and canzona of about 1600 to the fugue of Bach have never been thoroughly investigated and clearly outlined. The problem is difficult indeed, owing to the enormous wealth of material and the variety of trends and schools. Restricting ourselves to the keyboard fugue (i.e., omitting the fugal compositions in instrumental and vocal music), it can be said that this development took place chiefly in Germany ("fugues" by Frescobaldi, which have been frequently reprinted in modern collections, e.g., L. Oesterle, ed., ‡*Early Keyboard Music* i, p. 59, are definitely spurious) and that slowly and gradually the typical features of the Bach fugue appeared, such as adherence to a given number of parts, relative shortness, restriction to one theme, consistent alternation of expositions and episodes, modulatory principles, I–V–I–V entries in the first exposition [see the Ex. by Fischer above, which has I–V–V–I entries], etc. This process is illustrated by the following examples, contained in A. Ritter, *Zur Geschichte des Orgelspiels,* vol. ii (1884): Simon Loher, *c.* 1550–1611 (p. 106); Wolfgang Carl Briegel, 1626–1710 (p. 206); Georg Caspar Wecker, 1632–95 (p. 120); Johann Christoph Bach, 1643–1703 (p. 172). See also *HAM,* nos. 195b (Scheidemann), 215 (Tunder), 234 (Buxtehude), 237 (J. C. Bach), 247 (J. K. F. Fischer), 249b (Krieger), 251 (Pachelbel). The fugues in Johann Krieger's *Anmuthige Clavier-Übung* (1699; new ed. in *DTB* 18) contain practically all the elements of fugal style used by Bach.

The excellence of Bach's fugues compared

to those of his predecessors lies in various factors: greater contrapuntal skill, clarification of the formal structure, more advanced methods of harmonic treatment, etc. While all these traits represent progress by degrees, one trait puts Bach's fugues into a class of their own, namely, the incomparable artistic quality of the themes [see Melody III]. The great master of the fugue after Bach was Beethoven, who in various movements of his latest piano sonatas (op. 106, 110), quartets, and other works showed that the potentialities of the form had by no means been exhausted by the baroque masters. Composers after Beethoven seldom used the fugue as a serious art form. Recently, however, the *neoclassical tendencies of the 20th century have stimulated a new creative interest in this form (Hindemith and others).

Lit. *A. Instructive:* A. Mann, *The Study of Fugue* (1958); C. H. Kitson, *The Elements of Fugal Construction* (1929); J. Knorr, *Lehrbuch der Fugenkomposition* (1911); A. Gédalge, *Treatise on Fugue,* trans. A. Levin (1964); W. Apel, *Die Fuge* (1932); S. Levarie, "Fugue and Form" (*BAMS* vii).

B. Historical: *Editions XXXIX, 19; J. Müller-Blattau, *Geschichte der Fuge,* rev. ed. (1963); W. Wesely, "Die Entwicklung der Fuge bis Bach" (diss. Prague, 1928); K. Trapp, *Die Fuge in der Romantik von Schubert bis Reger* (1958); W. L. Graves, *Twentieth Century Fugue; a Handbook* (1962); U. Unger, *Die Klavierfuge im zwanzigsten Jahrhundert* (1956); O. Roy, ‡*Die Fuge* (1963); E. P. Schwartz, "Die Entstehung und Entwicklung der Themenbeantwortung in der Fuge vor J. S. Bach" (diss. Vienna, 1932); J. S. Shedlock, "The Evolution of the Fugue" (*PMA* xxiv); F. Deutsch, "Die Fugenarbeit in den Werken Beethovens" (*StM* xiv); M. Zulauf, "Zur Frage der Quintbeantwortung bei J. S. Bach" (*ZMW* vi); A. Ghislanzoni, "La Genesi storica della fuga" (*RMI* xlviii).

Fugue tune, fuguing tune. See Fuge tune.

Füllstimme [G.]. A mere "filling" part, without independent importance.

Functional harmony [G. *Funktionslehre*]. A relatively new system of harmonic analysis, developed chiefly by H. Riemann, that attempts both to simplify traditional methods and to give clearer insight into the essentials of harmonic progressions. It is based on the idea that in a given key there are only three "functionally" different chords, namely, tonic (I), dominant (V), and subdominant (IV). All other chordal com-

binations, even the most complex and chromatic, are variants of one of these three chords, i.e., they have a tonic-function, dominant-function, or subdominant-function. The chief substitute for each of the three principal triads is its relative minor; thus VI stands for I; III for V; II for IV. However, the "upper relative" may also serve as a substitute: III for I; VII for V; VI for IV. The resulting ambiguity in meaning of, e.g., III (which may appear in tonic-function or in dominant-function) is an essential feature of the system in which a chord is determined not as an isolated phenomenon by its degree (as in the current system of harmonic analysis) but by its function within a series of progressions. The subdominant in particular has many substitutes; among these is the *Neapolitan sixth, which in functional harmony is simply a (doubly altered) S, while in the orthodox system it is the first inversion of the lowered supertonic. Another example of functional interpretation is the six-four chord of the first degree (I_4^6), which functionally is nearly always a plain dominant (V) involving a double appoggiatura.

Riemann's system has hardly gained a foothold outside Germany. Although one might argue about the advisability of its full acceptance, it certainly deserves more recognition as a corrective of the traditional system with its somewhat dogmatic method of labeling, which is not always conducive to an understanding of harmony. The accompanying example (Schumann) illustrates the traditional and "functional" methods.

$B^\flat{:}V$ V^2 $\natural\,IV$ $\natural\,/I$ $\sharp\,/I$
$G^\flat{:}V^7$ $V^2\,I^6\,D^\flat{:}\,V^6\,E^\flat{:}V^6\,F{:}V^6$ I

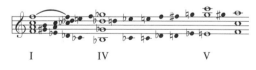

I   IV   V

Lit.: H. Riemann, *Vereinfachte Harmonielehre* (1893); E. Kirsch, *Wesen und Aufbau der Lehre von den harmonischen Funktionen* (1928); H. Distler, *Funktionelle Harmonielehre* (1941); H. Moser, in *ZMW* i.

Fundamental, fundamental tone. The lowest tone, i.e., the bass note of a chord. Also, the first harmonic.

Fundamental bass [F. *basse fondamentale*]. In J. P. Rameau's theory, *basse fondamentale* is a fictitious bass line that consists of the roots of the chords occurring in a succession of harmonies. Only if a chord is in root position does the *basse fondamentale* coincide with the real bass. Rameau used the *basse fondamentale* in order to demonstrate his then novel theory of inverted chords.

Fundament-instrument [G.]. In the *thorough-bass period, all instruments used for playing the bass part, either the written part only (violone, viola da gamba, cello, bassoon, etc.), or with accompanying chords (organ, harpsichord, chitarrone, theorbo, etc.).

Fundamentum. Title used by 15th- and 16th-century German composers for collections of pieces designed to teach composition of keyboard music. They consist of theoretical *cantus firmi* (*ascensus* and *descensus,* i.e., ascending and descending scale formations) to which figurate counterpoint is added. For early examples, dating from *c.* 1440–50, see Editions XI, 1, pp. 13, 24, 25. The most famous example (for organ) is Conrad Paumann's "Fundamentum organisandi" of 1452 [fac. ed., together with the Lochamer *Liederbuch, by K. Ameln, 1925; transcr. in *JMW* ii and in Editions XI, 1, p. 32]. The *Buxheim Organ Book contains four or five greatly enlarged collections, including pieces in three-voice counterpoint. Hans Buchner's (1483–1538) "Fundamentum" of *c.* 1520–30 gives instruction in three- and four-voice counterpoint as well as in imitation [see C. Päsler, in *VMW* v]. In the organ tablature of Johannes de Lublin (*c.* 1540) the same techniques are illustrated by almost 800 examples.

Funktionslehre [G.]. See Functional harmony.

Fuoco, con [It.]. With fire.

Furiant. A rapid and fiery Bohemian dance, in 3/4 time, with frequently shifting accents. It has been used repeatedly by Dvořák [op. 12, *Dumka and Furiant;* op. 42, *Two Furiants;* also in his chamber music] and by Smetana [*The Bartered Bride; Czech Dances*]. An early description of a "Furie" is found in Türk's *Klavierschule* (1789; p. 400).

Furlana. See *Forlana.*

Furniture stop. Same as mixture stop.

Fusa [L.; G. *Fusela, Fusel*]. See under Mensural notation I.

Futurism. The term *futurismo* was introduced by the Italian writer Marinetti in 1909 to describe extreme radicalism in literature and in all the arts. His ideas were applied to music at least theoretically by Francesco Pratella, in his *Musica futurista* (1912), which contains the following characteristic sentences: "To present the musical soul of the masses, of the great factories, of the railways, of the transatlantic liners, of the battleships, of the automobiles and airplanes. To add to the great central themes of the musical poem the domain of the machine and the victorious kingdom of Electricity" [see the full text in N. Slonimsky, *Music Since 1900,* rev. ed. (1949), pp. 642ff]. Pratella also gives a detailed description of a composition for an "orchestra" consisting of machine guns, sirens, steam-whistles, etc. His music, however, is not more than a mild Debussyism, mingled with Puccinian idioms. Another champion of futurism was the painter Luigi Russolo, who actually is the author of the description quoted above. See W. Austin, "The Idea of Evolution in the Music of the 20th Century" (*MQ* xxxix, esp. 30ff).

Fz. [It.]. Abbr. for *forzando, forzato,* same as *sforzando* (*sf, sfz*).

G

G. See Pitch names; Letter notation; Hexachord. For G clef, see Clef.

Gabelgriff [G.]. *Cross fingering.

Gagaku [Jap.]. The orchestral music of the Japanese court, founded in the 8th century and preserved to the present day with little change. It also includes vocal pieces, e.g., *saibara* and *rōei* [see Japan III]. The term *gagaku* is also used for a type of orchestral music of continental Asia, particularly China and Korea, which is the predecessor of the Japanese *gagaku.*

The frequent visits of foreign musicians to Japan, particularly Koreans and Chinese, during the 5th to 8th centuries culminated in 701 in the establishment of *Gagaku-ryō,* the Imperial Music Bureau. During the 8th century, repertories of different origins were blended and modified into a Japanese style, resulting in *gagaku* as it is known today. It reached its height in the Heian Period (894–1192). After the 12th century the tradition was barely continued by the musicians at the Imperial Court and at a few shrines and temples but was revived after World War II.

Gagaku performed alone is called *kangen;* when it accompanies a dance it is called *bugaku.* Both types are further divided into left music and right music (or dance). The left music is of Chinese or Indian origin or reflects their influence, while the style of right music is like that of Korea and other northern countries. The left and the right use different sets of instruments. An orchestra of the left music consists of *ryūteki* (or *wōteki,* a 7-holed flute), *hichiriki* [see Oboe family III], and *shō* (a mouth organ); *biwa* (a lute derived from the *pyiba) and the *gakusō* (of the *koto* family); and *taiko* (a big drum), *shōko* (a metal drum), and *kakko* (a horizontal drum with two side surfaces). The right music substitutes *komabue* (a 6-holed flute) for *ryūteki,* and *sanno-tsuzumi* for *kakko,* and omits the *shō,* which provides a "harmonic" background for the left music. [See Ex.] [For the scale system in *gagaku,* see Japan IX.]

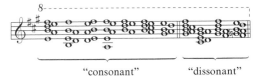

"consonant"   "dissonant"

Except in some free-rhythm passages (introduction or postlude), percussion instruments indicate strong (S) and weak (w) beats throughout the piece. The chief patterns are S w w w, S w w w w w w w, S w S w, S w S w w w, and S w S w w. Two winds, *ryūteki* (or *komabue*) and *hichiriki,* play melodic parts and often create a *heterophonic effect. Sometimes, in the right music, the two may play entirely different melodies. The strings have a percussive function rather than a melodic one.

The most frequently found form for a *bugaku* is in three sections: *jo* (a slow introduction), *ha* (moderate tempo), and *kyū* (a fast ending). This form is also found in various types of Japanese music in later periods. See Japan.

Lit.: R. A. Garfias, *Gagaku* (1959); ‡*Score of Gagaku,* transcr. by S. Shiba, 2 vols. (1955, '56); E. Harich-Schneider, in *MQ* xxxix, 49–74; S. Kishibe and L. Traynor, in *Tōyō Ongaku Kenkyū* (Tokyo) ix, 26–53.   M.K.

Gagliard, gaillarde. See Galliard.

Gaïta. See Bagpipe.

Gaitilla. A Spanish 17th-century organ stop with a nasal sound, in imitation of the gaïta. Also (rarely), a composition whose solo part was played on this stop.

Galanterien [G.]. An 18th-century name for short entertaining pieces in homophonic (nonfugal) style, including airs, variations, dances. The term is used particularly for the more recent dances in the optional group of the suite, such as the bourrée, passepied, gavotte, etc., which are composed in a lighter style than the traditional allemande, courante, saraband, and gigue. Note the title of the first part of Bach's *Clavier-Übung:* ". . . Sarabanden, Giguen, Menuetten und anderen Galanterien." See Gallant style.

Lit.: W. Dahms, "The 'Gallant' Style of Music" (*MQ* xi, 356); P. Gradenwitz, "Mid-Eighteenth-Century Transformations of Style" (*ML* xviii, 265); E. Bücken, "Der galante Stil" (*ZMW* vi, 418); see also under Rococo.

Galerón [Sp.]. A ballad form in octosyllabic quatrains popular in the Colombian plains. Its melody has a limited range, and its rhythm follows the text in a recitative-like manner. At the end of each stanza, refrains in slightly quicker tempo and contrasting with the predominantly narrative character of the stanzas are interpolated.   J.O-S.

Gallant style [F. *style galant;* G. *galanter Stil*]. In the 18th century, the light, elegant style of the rococo, as opposed to the serious, elaborate style of the baroque. The appearance of this style accompanied the shift from church to salon as the cultural center, from fugal treatment (polyphonic) to accompanied melody (homophonic), from church music to secular music. This change is already evident in the harpsichord compositions of J. K. F. Fischer, F. Couperin, Telemann, and G. T. Muffat, as well as in the optional dances (minuets, bourrées, gavottes, etc.; see

Galanterien) of Bach's suites [also the (spurious?) dances—minuets, marches, polonaises—in the *Notenbüchlein der Anna Magdalena Bach*]. The gallant style is clearly present in the violin concertos and sonatas of Tartini [see *HAM*, no. 275] and in Pergolesi's *La *Serva padrona* (1733). The adoption of the new style led, about 1750, to a deterioration in musical quality, notably in some works of Italian composers such as Rutini, Paganelli, and Pescetti, and in England. In the second half of the 18th century, Bach's sons Wilhelm Friedemann and Karl Philipp Emanuel endowed the gallant style with a new expressiveness [see *Empfindsamer Stil*], so that the word "gallant" was no longer applicable. The same was true of Mozart's works, which are directly derived from the gallant style of the Italians (including Johann Christian Bach). See Rococo; Haffner collection.

Lit.: W. Dahms, "The 'Gallant' Style of Music" (*MQ* xi); P. Gradenwitz, "Mid-Eighteenth-Century Transformations of Style" (*ML* xviii); E. Bücken, "Der galante Stil" (*ZMW* vi). See also under Rococo.

Gallarda [Sp.]. A 17th-century Spanish type of continuous variations based on a theme of 8, 10, or more measures in 4/4 time. There are five examples in the works of Cabanilles (ed. H. Anglés, ii, 62ff). The *gallarda* also was a dance. Its movements are described in a late 17th-century *Libro de danzar* [see *AnM* v, 193].

Galliard [F. *gaillarde;* It. *gagliarda;* Sp. *gallarda*]. A gay, rollicking 16th-century dance of Italian origin. The music is characterized by a predominantly compound duple (6/8) meter interspersed with hemiola (3/4) measures. The dance step of the galliard is similar to that of the 16th-century *saltarello*. Both use variations of the same basic five steps (*cinquepace* or *cinq pas*). The only difference is in the execution. The galliard is danced more vigorously, and the leap on the fifth beat of the measure is higher for the galliard than for the *saltarello*. The music for both dances is indistinguishable in style. Either dance is frequently coupled to a *pavane* or a *passamezzo*. Early examples are preserved in Attaingnant's *Six Gaillardes et six pavanes* [1529]; his *Quatorze Gaillardes, neuf pavannes* [1531]; in J. Abondante's *Intabolatura sopra el lauto* (1546); and in A. Rotta's *Intabolatura de lauto* (1546).   L.H.M.

Gallican chant. The French branch or "dialect" of plainsong of the medieval Western Church

[see Chant]. It was in use in France until the introduction of the Roman chant and rite under Pepin [see France I]. Its liturgical structure has much in common with *Mozarabic and *Ambrosian chant. The chants of the Mass consisted of the following items (Gregorian equivalents in parentheses): *Praelegendum* (Introit); *Aius* (*Trishagion,* Gloria); *Kyrie; Benedictus* (canticle of Zachary); *Responsorium* (Gradual); *Preces; Laudes* (Alleluia); *Sonus* (Offertory); *Confractio* [see Confractorium] and *Trecanum* (Communion). Unfortunately, only a few melodies survive in manuscripts of the 11th century. Certain portions of the Gallican chant were incorporated into the Roman liturgy, e.g., the *Improperia* and the hymns "Crux fidelis" and "Pange lingua ...certamnis" (*LU*, p. 742).

Lit.: A. Gastoué, *Histoire du chant liturgique à Paris* (1904); *id., Le Chant gallican* (1939; also pub. in *RCG* xli–xliii; H. Anglés, in *NOH* ii, 75ff. For additional bibl. see *ReMMA*, p. 436.

Galop. A quick round dance of the mid-19th century (*c.* 1825–75) with rhythms such as those

$$| \frac{2}{4} \, \flat \, | \, \sqrt{}\hspace{-1.2em}\int\!\!\int . \; \flat \, | \, \sqrt{}\hspace{-1.2em}\int\!\!\int .$$

shown in the illustration. It was executed with many changes of steps and hopping movements. Offenbach parodied it in his *Orphée aux Enfers* (1858). Liszt wrote a *Grand Galop Chromatique* (1838) and a *Galop de Bal* (*c.* 1840). See Dance music IV.

Galoubet. See under Pipe (1).

Gamba, gambe [G.]. Abbr. for *viola da gamba.

Gambang (saron). An Indonesian idiophone, consisting of a number of wood, bamboo, or metal bars resting on a large trough resonator. See J. Kunst, *Music in Java*, rev. ed., 2 vols. (1949). Also see under Java. For ill. see under Percussion.

Gambenwerk [G.]. An 18th-century name for bowed keyboard instruments. Same as *Geigenwerk*. See Sostenente piano.

Gamelan. Generic term for an Indonesian orchestra. See under Bali; Java.

Game of Cards, The. See *Jeu de cartes, Le.*

Gamma [Gr.]. In medieval theory, the lowest tone of the scale, G of the modern scale. In Guidonian terminology it was called *gamma-ut* [see Hexachord III]. Later, the term was meta-phorically used for "all the tones from gamma," i.e., the entire scale. This meaning persists in the Italian *gamma* and the French *gamme* for scale, as well as in the English *gamut* for scale or range.

Gamme [F.]. *Scale. See under Gamma. *Gamme des physiciens* (i.e., of the physicists), the "natural" scale derived from just intonation.

Gamut. See under Gamma.

Ganze Note, ganze Pause [G.]. Whole note, whole-note rest. See Notes.

Ganzton [G.]. Whole tone. *Ganztonleiter,* whole-tone scale.

Ganzschluss [G.]. Full cadence.

Gapped scale. A scale that is derived from a more complete system of tones by omitting some of them. Thus, the pentatonic scale is a gapped scale of the diatonic system, and this in turn can be considered a gapped scale of the chro-matic system. Another selection of notes from the chromatic system results in the chromatic scale of ancient Greek theory. Most of the scales of Oriental music are gapped scales, since the tones used in actual music are only a small selec-tion from a more complete system that is de-signed only for theoretical demonstration (e.g., the 22 *sruti* and the 7-tone scales, *sa-grama* and *ma-grama,* of *India).

Garbato, con garbo [It.]. Graceful, elegant.

Gaspard de la nuit [F.]. A set of three piano pieces by Ravel (1908) inspired by the collected poems of Bertrand, which were published under the same title (literally, Caspar of the Night, a nickname for Satan): (1) *Ondine,* a water nymph; (2) *Le Gibet* (gallows); (3) *Scarbo* (clown of the Punch and Judy show).

Gassenhauer [G.]. In present German usage, a vulgar street song. In publications of the 16th century, e.g., in Egenolff's *Gassenhawerlin* and *Reutterliedlin* (1535; fac. ed. by H. J. Moser, 1927), it simply means popular song, without any implication of vulgarity. In fact, these collections include some of the most beautiful songs of Isaac, Hofhaimer, and Senfl.

Gathering note. In hymn singing, a note sounded by the organist as a signal to the congregation, to give them the correct pitch of the hymn.

Gato [Sp.]. One of the most important rural dances of Argentina, generally danced in circular

movements by two couples, who emphasize its lively rhythms by finger-snapping, shoe-tapping, and the so-called *escobilleo* (i.e., swinging each foot in turn, back and forth). The music, which is sung to the accompaniment of the guitar, follows rhythmic patterns alternating between 6/8 and 3/4 meter. J.O-S.

Gaukler [G.]. See Minstrel.

Gavotte. A French dance of the 17th century whose name is said to be derived from "Gavots," the inhabitants of the Pays de Gap in Dauphiné. The dance is in moderate 4/4 time, with an up-beat of two quarter notes, and with the phrases usually ending and beginning in the middle of a measure. Earlier examples, however, are frequently notated without upbeat [see Ex.,

D'Anglebert, *Pièces de clavecin,* 1689]. The dance is mentioned in Arbeau's *Orchésographie* (1589) as a *recueil de branles.* Several examples (for lute) are contained in the *Trésor d'Orphée* (1600) by Antoine Francisque, but apparently the dance did not come into vogue until the middle of the 17th century, when Lully introduced it into his ballets and operas. From here it found its way into the *ordres* of D'Anglebert and F. Couperin and the German suites of Pachelbel and J. K. F. Fischer. Bach often used it as one of the optional dances in his instrumental and keyboard suites. See Dance music III.

Gebrauchsmusik [G.]. A term originated in the 1920's (by Hindemith?) meaning "music for use," i.e., music intended for practical use by amateurs, in the home or at informal gatherings, as opposed to music written "for its own sake" (*l'art pour l'art*) and intended chiefly for concert performance by professionals. Characteristic traits of *Gebrauchsmusik* are: forms of moderate length; simplicity and clarity of style; small ensembles; avoidance of technical difficulties; parts of equal interest and so designed that they can be played on whatever instruments are available; soberness and moderation of expression; emphasis on "good workmanship." The rise of *Gebrauchsmusik* is typical of the neoclassical reaction against the exaggerated individualism and *fin de siècle* refinement of late romanticism and impressionism. The movement, which was begun by Hindemith and others in the festivals of Donaueschingen [see Festivals III], was supported by the socialist elements in post-war Germany and by the revival of interest in early music, particularly Bach's. In fact, Bach's cantatas were frequently cited as the earliest examples of *Gebrauchsmusik* in the sense of "music written for immediate consumption or on commission" (Bach had to write a cantata for every Sunday). While 19th-century composers would have regarded such a demand as interfering with the artist's free creative inspiration, musicians such as Hindemith and Krenek adopted the less aloof attitude that was natural to the masters of earlier periods. Hindemith's introductory notes to his *Plöner Musiktag* (1932) and to *Wir bauen eine Stadt* (1931) contain many pertinent remarks on *Gebrauchsmusik*. See J. Willett, *The Theatre of Bertolt Brecht* [1959]; *DM* xxi.6 and xxiv.3; H. Closson, "The Case against Gebrauchsmusik" (*MM* vii).

Gebrochener Akkord [G.]. Broken chord.

Gebunden [G.]. Legato.

Gebundener Stil [G.]. The strict contrapuntal style of the 17th and early 18th centuries (fugues), as opposed to *freier Stil* (free style), i.e., either accompanied melody or *Freistimmigkeit*.

Gedackt [Old G.], **gedeckt** [G.]. Stopped. The former term is used for an organ register consisting of stopped pipes, the latter for the modern "stopped" instruments, such as the clarinet. See Stop; Wind instruments III.

Gedämpft [G.]. Muted, muffled.

Gedehnt [G.]. Stretched out, slow.

Gefährte [G.] The answer of a fugal subject.

Gefühlvoll [G.]. With feeling.

Gegenbewegung [G.]. Contrary motion (between two voices); sometimes used as synonym of inversion (of a subject).

Gegenfuge [G.]. Counterfugue.

Gegensatz [G.]. Contrast. In older writings, a countersubject or second theme.

Gegenthema [G.]. Countersubject (of a fugue) or second theme (of a sonata movement).

Gehalten [G.]. Held out, sustained.

Gehend [G.]. Moving, andante.

Gehender Bass [G.]. Running bass.

Geige [G.]. Violin; see under Gigue (1). *Geigenwerk,* see under Sostenente pianoforte.

Geisslerlieder [G.]. German 14th-century songs that were sung during the penitential processions of the flagellants, particularly in the year of the Black Death, 1349. Melodically and structurally they anticipate to some degree the Lutheran chorale. See P. Runge, *Die Lieder und Melodien der Geissler des Jahres 1349* (1900); *ReMMA*, p. 239.

Geisstriller [G.]. *Goat's trill.

Geistlich [G.]. Sacred, religious, spiritual. *Geistliche Konzerte* (Schütz) are pieces (vocal and instrumental) for church use; see Concerto III.

Gekkin. A Japanese guitar; see under Guitar family.

Gekoppelt [G.]. Coupled.

Geläufigkeit [G.]. Technical fluency.

Gelassen [G.]. Quiet, calm.

Gemächlich [G.]. Comfortable, leisurely.

Gemässigt [G.]. Moderate.

Gemeindelied [G.]. Congregational hymn, chorale.

Gemell. Same as *gymel.

Gemendo [It.]. Lamenting.

Gemessen [G.]. Restrained.

Gemischte Stimmen [G.]. Mixed voices.

Gendèr. A Javanese metallophone, consisting of thin bronze slabs over resonating bamboo tubes [see Java; Bali].

Genera. Plural of L. *genus.* See Greece II.

Generalbass [G.]. Thoroughbass.

Generalpause [G.], abbr. *G.P.* In orchestral works, a rest for the entire orchestra, coming unexpectedly after a climactic passage. This effect was one of the startling innovations of the *Mannheim school.

Generalprobe [G.]. Dress rehearsal of orchestra concerts, usually open to the public.

Genus [L.; pl. *genera*]. See under Greece II.

German flute. An 18th-century name for the transverse (cross) flute, as distinguished from the English flute, i.e., the recorder.

German Requiem, A. See *Deutsches Requiem, Ein.*

German sixth. See Sixth chord.

Germany. The development of music in Germany, compared to France, England, and Italy, began quite late. In the field of polyphonic music in particular, it was not until the middle of the 15th century—that is, when the great period of medieval French music was coming to a close—that Germany came to the fore. From then on, however, German music progressed in a continuous line that, even aside from its many outstanding summits, maintained an exceptionally high level to the present day, thus making Germany the leading nation in the more recent era of music history.

I. *Prehistory and Middle Ages.* The *lurer, beautiful long trumpets of the Nordic Bronze Age [see Denmark], are evidence of a high standard of bronze founding rather than of "prehistoric German music," as has occasionally been claimed. Late Roman and early medieval writers often commented unfavorably on the musical ability of the ancient Germans, particularly about their singing. In the 9th century the monastery of St. Gall (founded by Irish monks) became one of the most important centers of cultivation of Gregorian chant, particularly remarkable for its contribution to the development of the *sequence (Notker Balbulus, c. 840–912; Tuotilo, d. 915; Wipo of Burgundy, c. 1000–50) and musical theory (Notker Labeo, d. 1022; Hermannus Contractus, 1013–54). The oldest surviving song in the German language is the 9th-century *Petruslied,* "Unsar trohtin" [see Müller-Blattau, in *ZMW* xvii, 129ff; O. Ursprung, in *MF* v]. In the 12th century the Provençal troubadour movement spread to Germany, leading to a first flowering of German secular song among the *minnesingers, among whom Neithart von Reuenthal (c. 1180–c. 1240) was outstanding from the musical point of view. Toward the end of the 15th cent. their tradition was continued by the * Meistersinger, with Hans Sachs (1494–1576) as the main representative.

Meanwhile, polyphonic music had made a late and slow start in the primitive pieces (written in the style of 11th-century organum) of the 14th-century Codex Engelberg 314 [see F. Ludwig, in *KJ* xxi, 48–61, and in *AMW* v, 305ff], and in the slightly less archaic pieces of the Münch of Salzburg (fl. *c.* 1375) and Oswald von Wolkenstein (1377–1445; see *BeMMR,* p. 180; *SchGMB,* no. 46; complete works in *DTO* 18). Three MSS of *c.* 1460–70, the Lochamer, Münchner (Schedel'sche), and Glogauer *Liederbuch, preserve, besides Flemish, French, and Italian compositions, a number of German compositions, polyphonic *Lieder,* attractive ensemble dances, *quodlibets, etc. Closely related to the Lochamer MS is the *"Fundamentum organisandi" (1452) of Conrad Paumann (1410–73), an important source of German organ music, preceded by the tablature of Adam Ileborgh (1448; see W. Apel, in *ZMW* xvi) and followed by the *"Buxheim Organ Book" of *c.* 1470.

II. *Renaissance.* The late 15th century saw the rise of the first important school of German polyphonic music, represented by Adam von Fulda (c. 1445–1505; see W. Niemann, in *KJ* 1902), Heinrich Finck (1445–1527; see Editions VIII, 9, 21, 32), and Alexander Agricola (c. 1446–1506). The Flemish master Heinrich Isaac (c. 1450–1517) played a leading role in this development, particularly in the field of the German part song ("Innsbruck ich muss dich lassen"), to which Paul Hofhaimer (1459–1537), court organist to Maximilian I, Thomas Stoltzer (c. 1480–1526), and Ludwig Senfl (c. 1490–1543), a Swiss, also contributed many examples of great beauty [see H. J. Moser, *Paulus Hofhaimer* (1929); *DTO* 72; *DdT* 34]. Senfl's *quodlibets are an interesting source for the study of early German folksong. Of particular importance is the German organ music of the early 16th century, represented by the great master Arnolt Schlick (c. 1460–after 1517), Hofhaimer, H. Buchner (1483–1538), and others [see Organ music I]. Schlick's *Tabulaturen etlicher Lobgesang und Lidlein* [1512] also contain some compositions for the lute (the earliest lute songs). Among the numerous other German lutenists, Hans Judenkünig and Hans Newsidler deserve special mention [see Lute music]. About the middle of the 16th century the autochthonous development of German music was interrupted somewhat by the great influx of Flemish composers who held key positions in all the musical centers (De Monte in Prague; Le Maistre and Scandellus in Dresden; Lasso in Munich), until their German pupils, such as Jacobus Gallus

(Handl, 1550–91), Leonhard Lechner (c. 1550–1606), and Hans Leo Hassler (1564–1612), were ready to take up the tradition. Gallus and Hassler, together with Hieronymus Praetorius (1560–1629) and Michael Praetorius (1571–1621), also cultivated the Venetian polychoral style. Toward the end of the century a number of musicians known as *colorists were active in the field of keyboard music.

III. *Baroque.* The 17th century found German composers active in practically every field of vocal and instrumental music and soon leading in church music (particularly cantatas, Passions) and organ compositions. Here the Lutheran chorale provided a basis of tradition as well as progress, which largely accounts for the spiritual integrity and, as a result, the high artistic quality of German baroque music. An idea of the scope of German baroque music can be gained by glancing through the list of German *Denkmäler* [see Editions XIII, XIV, XV]. The most outstanding figures were (arranged in groups of contemporaries):

Schütz, Schein, Scheidt (b. c. 1585, 100 years before Bach)
Tunder, Froberger, Rosenmüller (b. c. 1615)
Buxtehude, Georg Muffat, Biber (b. c. 1640)
Johann P. Krieger, Fischer, Pachelbel (b. c. 1650)
Böhm, Bruhns, Kuhnau (b. c. 1660)
Telemann, Walther, Handel, J. S. Bach (b. c. 1685).

The beginning of the 17th century saw interesting developments in the instrumental dance and *suite, represented by Johann Hermann Schein (1586–1630), Valentin Haussmann, Isaac Posch, and Paul Peuerl. Simultaneously Heinrich Schütz (1585–1672) brought vocal church music (*Passion, *oratorio) to an artistic height comparable to Bach's, while Hieronymus Praetorius (1560–1629), Michael Praetorius (1571–1621), and Samuel Scheidt (1587–1654) laid the foundation for the development of German organ music [see Organ music II A; Organ chorale; etc.]. The next generation saw the rise of harpsichord music under Johann Jacob Froberger (1616–67; see Suite III), and about 1650 the church cantata emerged as an exclusively German product [see Cantata III]. Lute music reached an artistic climax in the works of Esajas Reusner (1636–79) and Sylvius Weiss (1686–1750), while violin music was cultivated by Johann Schop (c. 1590–1667), Nicolaus Adam Strungk (1640–1700), and Heinrich Biber (1644–1704), masters whose virtuosity paved the way

for Bach's pieces for solo violin. In orchestral music Johann Rosenmüller (c. 1620–84) stands out as an early master, while later composers such as Georg Muffat (1653–1704) and Philipp Erlebach (1657–1714) incorporated elements of the Italian and French orchestral styles. The German baroque lied found an outstanding master in Adam Krieger (1634–66; see Lied III), and only in opera did German musicians fail to compete successfully with other countries. In all these fields except the last two, the development reached a climax with J. S. Bach (1685–1750).

IV. *Rococo.* Contemporaries of Bach, such as Georg Philipp Telemann (1681–1767), Johann Valentin Rathgeber (1682–1750), and Gottlieb Muffat (1690–1770), were quick to embrace the novel style of the *rococo, and "progressive" writers such as Johann Mattheson (1681–1764) helped overthrow the last vestiges of a tradition that they considered oldfashioned and useless. After a comparatively short period of low ebb, German music took a new start in two directions: one toward a novel type of expressiveness, the *Empfindsamer Stil; the other toward the exploitation of modern orchestral resources and the formal development of the classical sonata, symphony, and string quartet. In the former field Bach's sons Wilhelm Friedemann Bach (1710–84) and Karl Philipp Emanuel Bach (1714–88) are outstanding; in the latter were the numerous musicians of the *Mannheim school. Concomitant with this development is the rise of the *Singspiel, and of the *volkstümliches Lied [see also Berlin school].

V. *Classicism, romanticism, and modernism.* The man who molded the formal and stylistic elements of the late rococo into a new art, thus laying the foundation for *classicism, was Franz Joseph Haydn (1732–1809). From 1770 on, his symphonies and string quartets, as well as those of Mozart (1756–91), show more and more the full mastery and maturity that led to the designation "classical." No less immortal are Haydn's oratorios and Mozart's operas. Beethoven (1770–1827) brought this development to its acme and, in his latest works, prepared for *romanticism, side by side with Franz Schubert (1797–1828), the great master of the lied. The romantic spirit is more patent still in the operas and piano works of Carl Maria von Weber (1786–1826) and was wholeheartedly embraced by Robert Schumann (1810–56), who more than any other composer represents romanticism with all its novel wonders as well as its inherent flaws.

The history of German music from 1830 to

1930 follows in the form of a chronological list of the important compositions produced in each decade:

1830–40: The romantic decade *par excellence,* including practically all the important works of Schumann and Mendelssohn.

1840–50: Schumann's last works (Piano Concerto), and Wagner's (1813–83) first operas: *Der fliegende Holländer, Tannhäuser, Lohengrin.*

1850–60: Wagner's *Rheingold, Walküre, Tristan.* Liszt (1811–86) establishes the *symphonic poem (*Faust* and *Dante* symphonies, *Mazeppa, Hunnenschlacht*) and writes his *Études d'exécution transcendante* and most of the Hungarian Rhapsodies. Brahms (1833–97) produces his piano sonatas (op. 1, 2, 5) and D-minor Concerto, op. 15.

1860–70: Wagner and Brahms still dominate the scene, the former with *Siegfried* and *Meistersinger,* the latter with op. 18–50, including the Handel Variations, the Magelone Songs, and the *Deutsches Requiem.*

1870–80: Wagner's *Götterdämmerung,* the last music drama of the *Ring des Nibelungen.* Brahms writes his first two symphonies and chamber music (up to op. 86). Bruckner (1824–96) appears with his symphonies nos. 2–6.

1880–90: Wagner produces his final music drama, *Parsifal;* Bruckner and Brahms produce their symphonies nos. 7–9 and 3–4 respectively. Brahms writes his last chamber works and the Piano Concerto in B-flat. Richard Strauss (1864–1949) brings new life to the symphonic poem with *Don Juan* and *Tod und Verklärung.* Hugo Wolf (1860–1903) writes most of his songs.

1890–1900: The last works of Brahms (op. 114–121). High point of Strauss' symphonic poems: *Till Eulenspiegel, Zarathustra, Don Quixote.* Gustav Mahler's (1860–1911) symphonies nos. 2–4.

1900–10: The romantic movement comes to a close with Mahler's symphonies nos. 5–10 and *Das Lied von der Erde,* Strauss' operas *Salome* and *Elektra,* and the chamber music of Max Reger (1873–1916). Arnold Schoenberg (1874–1951), after his impressionist *Pelleas und Melisande,* writes the atonal *Drei Klavierstücke* (1909), the first examples of a radical break with the past.

1910–20: Vestiges of the romantic tradition in Strauss' *Rosenkavalier* and *Alpensinfonie,* in Pfitzner's opera *Palestrina,* and in Schreker's

1878–1934) operas *Der ferne Klang* and *Der Schatzgräber.* Schoenberg's *Pierrot Lunaire* and the completely atonal *Sechs kleine Klavierstücke.* Ferruccio Busoni (1866–1924) writes the first *neoclassic pieces (sonatinas and *Fantasia contrappuntistica*).

1920–30: The heterogeneous post-war decade with its experiments in twelve-tone technique, jazz idioms, primitive rhythms, neoclassic forms, etc., brings to the fore a group of composers striving toward new means of expression, notably Alban Berg (1885–1935) with his two *expressionist operas *Wozzeck* (1914–25) and *Lulu* (1928–34); A. von Webern (1883–1945) with his *serial techniques; Paul Hindemith (1895–1963) with neoclassical sonatas, string quartets, and the song cycle *Das Marienleben* (1924); Ernst Krenek (b. 1900) with highly dissonant piano and chamber music, as well as the jazz opera *Jonny spielt auf* (1925–26); and Kurt Weill (1900–50) with his highly successful *Dreigroschenoper* (1928).

Side by side with these composers were others, most of them under the influence of the "back-to-Bach" idea: Heinrich Kaminsky (1886–1946) with "neo-Gothic" compositions filled with expression of religious ecstasy and mysticism; J. Nepomuk David (b. 1895), who reverted to the Flemish polyphony in works such as *Ricercare in C minor* (1927), *Fantasia super L'Homme armé* (1929), organ chorales, toccatas, etc.; and Hugo Herrmann (b. 1896), who used a linear style approaching atonality.

This development was suddenly interrupted by Hitler's coming to power in 1933. Schoenberg, Krenek, Hindemith, and Weill fled to the United States, and for the next twelve years musical activity and production in Germany were determined by a totalitarian regime hostile to all progress in the arts. Among the composers who pursued their work secretly was Anton von Webern (1883–1945), who developed Schoenberg's twelve-tone technique into a highly sensitive idiom of fragmentary sounds [see Serial music] that foreshadows the techniques of *musique concrète* and *electronic music. After World War II there emerged a new generation of great vitality and wide scope of activity. The neoclassical group comprises Ernst Pepping (b. 1901), Wilhelm Maler (b. 1902), Kurt Thomas (b. 1904), and also Wolfgang Fortner (b. 1907), whose more recent compositions show influence of serial techniques. Werner Egk (b. 1901) and Gottfried von Einem (b. 1918) have been successful in the field of opera, the former with *Zaubergeige* (1935, *Peer Gynt* (1938) and *Circe* (1948), the latter with *Dantons Tod* (1947). Boris Blacher (b. 1903) has written music strongly influenced by novel dance rhythms (variable meters). Carl Orff (b. 1895) has written the highly successful *Carmina burana* (1936), a scenic oratorio presenting pseudomedieval melodies in a clever, attractive garb. Giselher Klebe (b. 1925) is a leading twelve-tone composer, and Hans Werner Henze (b. 1926) has produced notable works for the stage (*König Hirsch,* 1956; *Undine,* 1959). Karl Heinz Stockhausen (b. 1928) is a pioneer of electronic music.

Lit.: H. J. Moser, *Geschichte der deutschen Musik,* 3 vols. (1920–24); *id., Die Musik der deutschen Stämme* (1957); H. von der Pfordten, *Deutsche Musik* (1920); A. Schering, *Deutsche Musikgeschichte im Umriss* (1917); R. Malsch, *Geschichte der deutschen Musik* (1926); H. Mersmann, *Eine deutsche Musikgeschichte* [1934]; J. Müller-Blattau, *Das deutsche Volkslied* [1932]; L. Schiedermaier, *Die deutsche Oper* (1930); *AdHM* ii, 1002–38 ("Die Moderne"; bibl.); W.-E. von Lewinski, "The Variety of Trends in Modern Music," in *LBCM,* also *MQ* li.

Ges, geses [G.]. See under Pitch names.

Gesamtausgabe [G.]. Complete edition. Most of the German *Gesamtausgaben* have been published by Breitkopf and Härtel, Leipzig.

Gesang [G.]. Song.

Gesangbuch [G.]. Hymn book, either of the Roman Catholic or of the Protestant Church. For the earliest publication of Protestant hymn books, see Chorale.

Gesangvoll [G.]. Songlike, cantabile.

Geschöpfe des Prometheus, Die [G., The Creatures of Prometheus]. Ballet by Beethoven (choreography by S. Vigano), produced in Vienna, 1801. It is remembered chiefly for its overture and for a theme in the finale that Beethoven used in three other compositions [see under *Eroica*].

Geschwind [G.]. Quick, nimble.

Gesellschaftslied [G.]. Musicologic term for a song that belongs to the middle classes, as opposed to *Hoflied* (court song) or *Volkslied* (folksong). The term is used particularly for the German 16th-century polyphonic songs of Hofhaimer, Senfl, and others, but it may also be used for the Italian madrigal, French chanson, etc.

Ge sol re ut, gesolreut. See under Hexachord III.

Gesteigert [G.]. Increased.

Gestopft [G.]. The stopped notes of the horn. See Horn I.

Geteilt [G.]. Divided. See Divisi.

Getragen [G.]. Sustained, slow.

Gewandhaus [G.]. See under Orchestras III.

Ghimel. See Gymel.

Ghironda [It.]. *Hurdy-gurdy.

Gianni Schicchi. See under *Trittico.*

Gigelira [It.]. *Xylophone.

Gigue. (1) Medieval name for stringed instruments, perhaps specifically the rebab [see Rabab], whose pear-shaped form is similar to a *gigot* [F., leg of lamb]. In the late 13th century a French poem mentions the "gigueours de l'Allemaigne," i.e., the gigue players of Germany [see *GéHM,* p. 400]. Probably the German *Geige* [Old G. *gîge*], violin, is derived from the French *gigue.*

(2) In the suites of 1650–1750 the gigue [It. *giga*] is one of the four constituent dance movements, usually the final one [see Suite; Dance music III]. The gigue evolved from the 16th-century Irish or English *jig, which on the Continent developed differently in France and in Italy. The French type (Gaultier, Chambonnières) is characterized by compound duple time (6/8, 6/4), dotted rhythm, wide intervals (sixths, sevenths, octaves), and fugal writing, usually with the inverted subject [see Inversion (2)] used for the second section. [See Ex., from Bach, French suite, no. 4.] The less common Italian type, the *giga,* is much quicker (presto gigue) and nonfugal, with running passages over a harmonic basis [for a similar case, see Courante]. This type occurs in the works of G. B. Vitali [*Balletti, corrente, gighe, allemande, e sarabande* 1668–71], Corelli, and Zipoli [see Editions

IX, 36]. It survives in the 6/8–presto pieces of the 18th century [see a gigue by K. H. Graun, 1701–59, in W. Niemann, ‡*Alte Meister des Klaviers*], which in turn are the model of such movements as the presto finale of Beethoven's Piano Sonata op. 2, no. 1.

The gigues in the suites of Froberger, Handel, and Bach are usually of the French type. However, a number of gigues by Froberger are in 4/4 meter, and some of Bach's suites (e.g., in the Partita no. 1 and English Suite no. 2) are modeled on the Italian type.

Lit.: W. Danckert, *Geschichte der Gigue* (1924); F. Pulver, in *PMA* xl.

Gimel. See Gymel.

Gioconda, La. Opera in four acts by A. Ponchielli (libretto by A. Boito, based on V. Hugo's play), produced in Milan, 1876. Setting: Venice, 17th century.

Giocoso [It.]. Jocose, humorous.

Gioioso [It.]. Joyous, cheerful.

Giorgi flute. A flute invented by Giorgi (1888) that has finger holes for each chromatic tone, thus making cross fingering unnecessary. It was blown at the end rather than across the bore. See *SaRM*, p. 158; H. Standish, in *PMA* xxiv.

Gipsy music. See Gypsy music.

Giraffe piano [G. *Giraffenklavier*]. An early 19th-century variety of piano, somewhat like the grand piano but with the wing-shaped part of the case put upright, thus vaguely resembling the neck of a giraffe.

Girl of the Golden West. See *Fanciulla del West, La.*

Giro [It.]. *Turn.

Gis, gisis [G.]. G-sharp, g-double-sharp. See Pitch names.

Giselle. Ballet by Adolphe Adam (choreography by Jean Corali, based on a story by H. Heine), first produced in Paris, 1841.

Gitana, alla [It.]. In the *Gypsy style.

Gittern. See under Guitar family.

Giulio Cesare in Egitto [It., Julius Caesar in Egypt]. Opera in three acts by G. F. Handel (libretto by N. Haym), produced in London, 1724. Setting: Egypt, 48 B.C.

Giustiniana. See under Villanella.

Giusto [It.]. Just, right. *Tempo giusto,* fitting tempo or strict tempo.

Glass harmonica [G. *Glasharmonika*]. An instrument that Benjamin Franklin invented in 1763 and called "armonica." It consists of a series of glass basins of graded sizes fixed on a horizontal spindle, which is made to revolve by a treadle operated by the player's foot. The spindle is fitted into a trough filled with water so that the glasses are kept wet. [For ill. see under Percussion.] The sound is produced by delicate rubbing of the fingers against the glasses [ill. in *SaRM*, p. 159]. The instrument was extraordinarily popular, particularly in Germany and Austria where, together with the *Aeolian harp, *nail violin, and other "ethereal" instruments, it became a characteristic vehicle of *Empfindsamkeit.* Among various compositions for the glass harmonica, Mozart's Adagio in C major (K. 356) and Adagio and Rondo (K. 617) for harmonica, flute, oboe, viola, and cello, both composed in 1791, are the most interesting [see comp. ed., x]. They seem to require an instrument equipped with a keyboard mechanism such as that constructed in 1784. Beethoven used the glass harmonica in a melodrama, *Leonora Prohaska,* composed in 1814 [suppl. vol. of B. and H. ed.]. Other composers who wrote for the instrument were J. G. Naumann, Padre Martini, Hasse, Galuppi, and Jommelli. About 1830 the instrument fell into oblivion but was reintroduced by R. Strauss in his opera *Die Frau ohne Schatten* (1917).

The use of glass as a sound-producing material is quite old. Musical glasses were known in Persia in the 14th century. About 1743 Richard Pockrich (Puckeridge), an Irishman, constructed an "angelick organ" consisting of a number of drinking glasses that were tuned by being filled with varying amounts of water. There is a report from 1760 saying that "Pockrich played Handel's Water Music on the glasses." In 1746 Gluck played in London on "twenty-six glasses filled with spring water." In 1761 in London Benjamin Franklin attended a recital on musical glasses, and subsequently he invented the glass harmonica.

A newer glass instrument is the glass harp [G. *Glasharfe*] constructed by B. Hoffmann in 1929. Similar to the musical glasses of England, it consists of 46 individually tuned glasses fixed on a resonant table.

Lit.: H. W. Geissler, *Die Glasharmonika* (1953); C. F. Pohl, *Cursory Notices on the Origin and History of the Glass Harmonica* (1862); A. H.

King, "The Musical Glasses and Glass Harmonica" (*PMA* lxxii, 97); B. Hoffmann, "Glasharmonika und Glasharfe" (*Schweizerische Musikzeitung,* 1951).

Glee. An 18th-century genre of English choral music, unaccompanied, in three or more parts, for solo men's voices (including a male alto), comparatively brief, sectionally constructed, and homophonic (chordal) rather than polyphonic. The glee was one of two wholly English 18th-century forms (the other being the *ballad opera). In the latter part of the century societies including both amateur and professional members devoted themselves to composing and performing glees. Among these were the Noblemen's and Gentlemen's Catch Club, the Anacreontic Society, the Glee Club, and the Concentores Sodales. During the first half of the 19th century glee singing was much in vogue, but in time its best qualities merged with the part song while the glee's artistic virtues were reduced to a shadow by Victorian composers of the shorter choral forms. Among the most celebrated glee writers were Benjamin Cooke (1734–93); Samuel Webbe (1740–1816), perhaps the most typical glee composer, who wrote more than three hundred glees and whose "Glorious Apollo" invariably opened the programs of the glee clubs; Stephen Paxton (1735–87); and John Callcott (1766–1821). Representative glees are in Novello's *Standard Glee Book, A Collection of the most favorite Glees* [n.d.]

The term "glee" is derived from the Anglo-Saxon *gliw* or *gléo* (entertainment, fun), especially as connected with minstrelsy—playing, singing, dancing, and perhaps even acrobatic feats. Until fairly recent times it was in this spirit that American college glee clubs, with rare exceptions, interpreted the term. About 1918, after a few years in which programs were made up of a mixture of popular, college, and classical music, the Harvard Glee Club began to devote itself to classical music exclusively, at the same time severing its connection with the Instrumental Clubs made up of banjos and mandolins. This step initiated a wave of interest in the singing of serious music by college choral organizations and also had a marked effect on the quality of music sung by secondary-school glee clubs. See also Catch.

Lit.: W. A. Barrett, *English Glees and Part-songs* (1886); D. Baptie, *Sketches of the English Glee Composers* (1896); J. Spencer-Curwen, "Regarding English Glees" (*ZIM* vi); J. M. Knapp,

"Samuel Webbe and the Glee" (*ML* xxxiii, 346); B. F. Wright, "The Glee" (*The Monthly Musical Record* lxxxix, 226).   A.T.D.

Gleemen. See under Minstrels.

Gleichmässig [G.]. Even.

Gli Scherzi. See *Scherzi, Gli.*

Glissando [It.]. The execution of rapid scales by a sliding movement. In piano playing, the nail of the thumb or of the third finger is drawn rapidly over the white keys. The same technique can also be used on the black keys. A much more difficult feat is the glissando in parallel thirds, sixths, or octaves, which is performed by a sliding movement of the hand with two fingers held rigid. Surprisingly enough, Mozart already used a glissando in parallel sixths in the cadenza of his piano variations "Lison dormait." It should be noted, however, that the glissando was much easier to perform on the old keyboard instruments with their light action. This fact also explains the octave glissandi in the last movement of Beethoven's Waldstein Sonata, which are almost impossible to perform on modern instruments. The first example of glissando is in a publication by Moyreau, *Pièces de clavecin . . . Œuvre Ier* [n.d.]. Glissando is much used in the playing of the harp. On the violin the glissando is a difficult virtuoso effect produced by a rapid succession of minute distinct movements of the hand. This effect should not be confused with the *portamento, which is easily produced by a continuous movement of the hand.

Glocke [G.]. Bell.

Glockenspiel. The modern celesta [see Percussion instruments A, 4]. The portable glockenspiel of military bands consists of steel bars fixed on a frame in the shape of the ancient Greek lyre; hence the name "bell lyre" [G. *Lyra*]. In German the word *Glockenspiel* [lit. bell-play] is also used for a set of bells, i.e., a *carillon. In the late 18th century some glockenspiels were played from a keyboard, similar to the modern celesta. This is probably the instrument called for in Mozart's *Die Zauberflöte* by the name *strumento d'acciaio* (steel instrument).

Glogauer Liederbuch. See under Liederbuch.

Gloria (in excelsis). The second item of the Ordinary of the Mass, also known as Greater *Doxology. See Mass A. C III. In plainsong the first phrase, "Gloria in excelsis Deo," is sung by the officiating priest, and the chorus enters at

"Et in terra pax." Early (15th-century) polyphonic settings of the Gloria therefore begin
with the latter phrase and are usually indexed
under *Et in terra* in modern editions. See
D. Bosse, *Untersuchung einstimmiger mittelalterlichen Melodien zum "Gloria in excelsis deo"*
(1954); *ApGC,* pp. 409ff.

Gloria patri. See Doxology.

Glosa [Sp.]. A 16th-century name used for
diminutions [see Ornamentation I]. Diego Ortiz'
Trattado de Glosas sobre clausulas (1553; repr. by
M. Schneider, 1913, '36) contains many instructive examples of methods of ornamenting a
cadential formula (clausula). Cabezón (*Obras de
música,* 1578) uses the term for simple figurative
variations of harmonized psalm tones (*fabordon
y glosas;* see *ApMZ* ii, 18), while more elaborate
variations are called **diferencias.*

Glückliche Hand, Die [G., The Lucky Hand].
Monodrama in one act by Schoenberg (to his
own libretto), published in 1913, first performed
in Vienna, 1924. Only one character sings (baritone), supported by a chorus of six men and
women whose heads appear through holes in a
backdrop and who comment on the action in
*Sprechstimme.

G.O. In French organ music, abbr. for *grand
orgue.*

Goat's trill [F. *chèvrotement;* G. *Bockstriller,
Geisstriller;* It. *trillo caprino;* Sp. *trino de cabra*].
Generally, a poorly performed trill, reminiscent
of a goat's bleating. J. F. Agricola, in his *Anleitung zur Singkunst,* 1757 (trans. of Tosi's *Opinioni
de' cantori,* 1723), says a trill is called a *Bockstriller* if its two tones are less than a semitone
apart or if they are sung with unequal speed or
force. L. Mozart, in his *Versuch einer gründlichen
Violinschule* (1756, p. 221), warns against performing the trill too fast, lest it become "unver-
ständlich, meckerend [bleating] oder ein soge-
nannter Geisstriller." Later (Spohr, *Violinschule,*
1832) the *Bockstriller* was described as a trill at
the unison, i.e., a **tremolo.*

Goldberg Variations. A series of 30 variations by
J. S. Bach, commissioned by the Russian Count
Kayserling and named after Bach's pupil,
Johann Gottlieb Goldberg (*c.* 1727–56), who was
in the count's service as a harpsichordist. Bach
published them in the fourth part of the
*Clavier-Übung (1742). The work, which is
among the greatest of its kind, is written according to a special plan: two variations in free style

(frequently of a highly virtuoso character) are
always followed by a canonic variation (nos. 3, 6,
9, etc.). The latter are unsurpassed masterpieces
of canon technique, being canons at different
intervals within the same harmonic frame. The
final variation is a **quodlibet.*

Golden Cockerel, The [Rus. *Zolotoy Pyetushok*].
Opera-ballet in three acts by Rimsky-Korsakov
(libretto by V. I. Byelsky, based on a fairy tale
by Pushkin), produced in Moscow, 1909, one
year after the composer's death. A well-known
selection is the "Hymn to the Sun."

Golden sequence. Popular name for the **sequence *Veni Sancte Spiritus.*

Goliard songs. Latin poems of the 10th to 13th
centuries written by goliards, wandering students or young ecclesiastics who played an
important part in the cultural life of that period.
The most famous collection is the *Carmina
Burana* (named after the monastery of Benedict-
beuren in southwest Germany, where the manuscript was preserved). Some of these poems are
provided with staffless neumes that cannot be
deciphered. However, *c.* 40 melodies can be
read with the help of other sources (e.g., the
St. Martial MSS). The oldest known melody is
that for the 10th-century poem "O admirabile
Veneris ydolum" [*BeMMR,* p. 72]. See *ReMMA,*
p. 200; H. Spanke, in *ZMW* xiii; W. Lipphardt,
in *AMW* xii; *id.,* in *CP Besseler;* A. Machabey,
in *Cahiers de civilisation médiévale, Université de
Poitiers,* vii, 257.

Gondola song [G. *Gondellied;* It. *gondoliera*]. See
Barcarole.

Gong. See under Percussion instruments B, 7.
See also under China; Java.

Gopak, hopak. A lively dance of Byelorussia
(Little Russia), in duple time. A well-known
example is in Mussorgsky's unfinished opera
The Fair at Sorochinsk.

Gorgia [It.]. Generic term for the art of improvised ornamentation, particularly as practiced
c. 1600 in the performance of madrigals, motets,
etc. (L. Zacconi, *Prattica di musica,* 1592; see
F. Chrysander, in *VMW* vii, ix, x). Detailed
explanations of the *gorgia* practice with its
various types of ornamentation (*passaggi, ac-
centi, esclamatione, trillo, groppo*) are given by
Caccini in the preface to his *Nuove Musiche* of
1601 [see *SSR,* pp. 377ff]. *Gorgheggio* is a modern term for very rapid vocal passages.

Gospel [L. *Evangelium*]. In the Roman Catholic rites, a passage from one of the four Gospels, chanted at Mass in monotone with inflections (*Tonus Evangelii;* see *LU*, p. 106). Gospel canticles are the three major *canticles. For Gospel hymn, see Hymn, English. Texts from the Gospels have often been set to music, in motets (Gospel motet, *Evangelienmotette*), Passions, oratorios, and cantatas. See H. J. Moser, *Die mehrstimmige Vertonung des Evangeliums* [1931].

Gothic music. A term used by various modern writers to denote music contemporary with or culturally related to the Gothic era in architecture, sculpture, and painting. It is usually understood to embrace the period from 1150 (Perotinus) to 1450 (Dufay), that is, before the beginning of the Renaissance [see History of music]. The term also has a geographical connotation, referring to north European cultures (northern France, England, the Netherlands, Germany) rather than those of the south. In fact, the music of the Italian *ars nova* is perhaps too "earthy" and "lively" (too "proto-Renaissance") to be termed Gothic.

Metaphorically, the word Gothic is also applied to later works showing traits suggestive of Gothic spirituality and otherworldliness, for instance, the "transcendental" organ toccatas of Buxtehude or Bach. Modern works showing similar traits have been called neo-Gothic (Hindemith, Kaminsky).

Götterdämmerung. See *Ring des Nibelungen.*

Goyescas. Two sets of piano pieces by Enrique Granados (1911), inspired by etchings of Francisco Goya (1746–1828). Granados also wrote an opera *Goyescas* (1916) that includes material from the piano pieces.

G.P. In German orchestral scores, abbr. for *Generalpause*. In French organ music, abbr. for *grand positif,* i.e., great and choir organ coupled.

G.R. In French organ music, abbr. for *grand récitatif,* i.e., great and swell organ coupled.

Grace. Term used by early English musicians for any musical ornament, whether written out in notes, indicated by sign, or improvised by the performer. In lute and viol playing a distinction was made between smooth graces, produced by siiding the finger along the fingerboard (appoggiaturas, slides, and *Nachschläge*), and shaked graces, for which the finger is shaken, producing several repercussions of the same tone (trills, relishes, and beats). Another distinction is that between open graces, which involve a whole fret (semitone), and closed graces, which involve a smaller interval (vibrato). P.A.

Grace note. A note printed in small type to indicate that its time value is not counted in the rhythm of the bar and must be subtracted from that of an adjacent note. Large groups of grace notes sometimes represent an exception to this rule in that together they fill up the time value of a single note that has been omitted from the score (as in the so-called "cadenzas" by Chopin and other romantic composers), in which case the rhythm of the grace notes is flexible and not subject to a strict beat. Most grace notes are used to represent *graces, or musical ornaments. P.A.

Gradatamente [It.]. Gradually.

Gradevole [It.]. Pleasant, pleasing.

Gradual [L. *graduale*]. (1) The second item of the Proper of the *Mass. The Graduals are responsorial chants, consisting of respond and verse [for the full form, see Psalmody II]. They have highly florid melodies, usually including long melismas in the respond as well as in the verse. They are almost entirely limited to the four authentic modes, except for a group of closely related melodies, usually designated as "gradual-type Justus ut palma" and assigned to mode 2 [see *ApGC*, pp. 344ff]. The name "gradual" is thought to be derived from L. *gradus,* step, the explanation being that the chant was a *responsorium graduale,* i.e., a responsory sung from the steps of the altar. However, early treatises have the form *gradale,* which could mean "graded," "distinguished" (the *Alia musica* of c. 900 also has the term *antiphona gradalis* for the Introit; see *ApGC*, p. 24). (2) The *liturgical book containing the musical items of the Mass, as distinguished from the *antiphonal. Originally such a book was called *antiphonale missarum,* and *graduale* may have had the meaning of *cantatorium,* i.e., a book containing only the responsorial (solo) items of the Mass, i.e., Graduals, Alleluias, and Tracts. The six earliest graduals (8th–9th centuries), which contain only the texts of the Mass chants (without neumatic notation), have been published by Dom R. J. Hesbert under the title *Antiphonale missarum sextuplex* (1935).

Gradus ad Parnassum [L.]. Title of two publications designed to lead to the highest perfection in their fields: a treatise on counterpoint by J. J. Fux (1725) and a collection of piano etudes by M. Clementi (1817).

Grail. English name for *Gradual, used in the Anglican Church.

Gramophone [G. *Grammophon*]. See under Phonograph and recorded music.

Gran cassa, gran tamburo [It.]. Bass drum.

Grand [F.]. *Grand jeu, grand orgue,* full organ; *grand opéra,* an opera (always serious) with fully composed text, as distinct from *opéra comique.*

Grandezza, con [It.]. With grandeur, grandiose.

Grandsire. See under Change ringing.

Grave [It.]. Grave, solemn.

Gravicembalo [It.]. Italian 17th-century name for the harpsichord, possibly for a large variety used especially for orchestral accompaniment. The name may be a corruption of clavicembalo, or it may refer to the presence of a "grave" 16-foot stop.

Great antiphons. Same as *O antiphons.

Greater perfect system. See under Greece II.

Great Fugue. See *Grosse Fuge.*

Greece. Of ancient Greek music, only some twenty written pieces survive, mostly fragmentary and widely scattered in date. An incomplete treatise by Aristoxenus (*c.* 320 B.C.) contains a valuable analysis of some basic principles of music as he knew it. Other theoretical treatises are preserved, but while they use certain terms and schematic figures derived from musical practice, their actual subject is the science of "harmonics," a mathematical discipline concerned with acoustical phenomena as such and studied independently of the art of music [see H. I. Marrou, *History of Education in Antiquity*]. Their relevance to music history is therefore limited and indirect. On the other hand, there is considerable direct source material from the composers themselves, for in archaic and classical Greece the poet was his own composer, and the term *mousikē (musica)* comprised both the music and the verse. Lyric and choric poetry shows the rhythmic patterns of the music, which followed the verse exactly. The poet-composers sometimes describe musical performances, occasionally their own style or orchestration. In particular, the comedies of Aristophanes are full of musical criticism and parody, which the words can often convey even though his music is lost. Plato's writings contain penetrating observations about contemporary musical change.

Greek vase-painters contribute many scenes of music in social life—school lessons, solos, concerts, dances, wine and song parties. The vases yield especially important evidence about Greek instruments, of which very few specimens have been discovered, none of them intact.

I. *History.* Four stages can be roughly distinguished. (a) The archaic music, as first seen in Homer (8th century B.C.), was already a sophisticated art, although primitive or rustic forms also existed. Some Oriental influence may be surmised but cannot be assessed; in general, Greek music was unlike Eastern: it was not bound by liturgical formulas; new works were composed for every public performance; composers were highly competitive and individual in style. In Homer's world every class practiced music, on almost every social occasion. Epics of war and adventure were intoned by professional bards and by high personages, to their own accompaniment on the lyre (phorminx; the *kithara was a later and larger type). Homer also knew wedding hymns, maiden songs, dirges of keening women, shanties for harvest or vintage, pipings of shepherds on the *syrinx (panpipes), dances of boys and girls accompanied by lyre or *aulos, or simply by their own hand-claps or castanets. The lyric forms continued, with songs of love and hate, drink and politics. In the 7th century B.C. Sparta was the great center, drawing musicians from elsewhere—the semilegendary Terpander of Lesbos (*c.* 675 B.C.), Alcman, and Tyrtaeus, the composer of marching-songs. Then the primacy passed to Sappho and Alcaeus of Lesbos (b. *c.* 620 B.C.). Religious festivals often included musical competitions for larger works, e.g., the Pythian *nomos,* a genre celebrating Apollo the dragon-slayer, or the dithyramb, a choral song with aulos accompaniment, dedicated to the god Dionysus.

(b) The classical music proper was perfected in the 5th century B.C. by Pindar in variously orchestrated odes (among other lyric forms) and by the new Athenian dramatists, both tragic and comic, using a chorus of amateur citizens supported by an aulos. At Athens the vast production of new music was balanced by private repetition of the old, learned by ear at school and sung at home to one's own lyre or at wine-parties with a hired aulos-girl. Aristophanes' audience could recognize his quotations and parodies of music, ancient or modern; its best memorial is his *Frogs* (405 B.C.), staging a competition in Hades between the early classical composer Aeschylus and the modernist Euripides. Different poetic forms were served by different musical idioms and tunings (*harmoniae*), called by ethnic names (Dorian, Phrygian, Ionian, Lydian, etc.), but by the end of the century only the Dorian and Phrygian are attested in serious music. In the Dorian, a clear-cut precision of tuning was associated with music of a sober and disciplined character (*ethos*); the Phrygian manner, assimilated to the unstable intonation of the aulos, was especially used for the emotional and ecstatic dithyramb.

(c) Later in the 5th century B.C. a musical revolution started from a school of dithyrambists and culminated, after the fall of Athens (404 B.C.), in Philoxenus and Timotheus of Milet (447–357 B.C.), who rejected all tradition and broke the old associations of poetic and musical forms. Instrumental improvisations, with sound-effects imitating nature, overshadowed the vocal part that had dominated Greek music; modulation, coloratura, and wobbly tuning so undermined the old tonality that by 320 B.C., according to Aristoxenus, few musicians knew or understood the classics. Instead, the talented and deliberately popular works of Philoxenus and Timotheus were repeated for two centuries, never rivaled by later composers. Music, though widely enjoyed, lost its cultural prestige and its place in higher education (above children's schooling); it was left to professional virtuosos of high technical skill—judging from their enormous fees—but low intellectual standards. Two surviving Delphic Hymns, of the later 2nd century B.C., seem to be samples of the music of this epoch in decline.

(d) Music continued not as a creative art but as an adjunct to rites, ceremonies, theatrical shows, or banquets. Only Mesomedes of Crete, at Hadrian's court, had any pretensions as a composer; generally, musicians ranked as craftsmen, well paid and encouraged by public prize competitions but socially despised. Extant fragments tell little of this later Greco-Roman music. The hypothesis that it passed into the medieval traditions of Europe or Byzantium is now discarded.

II. *Elements of music.* The fundamental tetrachord was bounded by the "fixed notes" of the perfect fourth; between them, two "movable

notes" were placed in three *genera*, roughly as in the example above. Thus, the highest of the three intervals of the tetrachord was widened from a whole tone, a–g [Ex. c, diatonic], into an interval of three semitones, a–f♯ [Ex. b, chromatic], or four semitones, a–f [Ex. a, enharmonic]. The remaining interval (f♯–e, or f–e) was halved, a procedure that, in the latter case, produced two quarter tones.

In all three the notes were called, in descending order, *Mese(a), Lichanos, Parhypate, Hypate.* Above was placed another tetrachord either "disjunct" (*e′* to *b*, leaving the whole tone *a* to *b* between tetrachords; notes named in descending order *Nete, Paranete, Trite, Paramese*) or "conjunct" (*d′* to *a*; notes in descending order named *Nete, Paranete, Trite*—without *Paramese*). All the "fixed notes" had functional priority; there was no paramount "tonic."

A two-octave "Greater Perfect System" was formed, as in the illustration below, of two pairs of conjunct tetrachords with a disjunctive tone between and an added bottom tone (*Proslambanomenos*).

Nete hyperbolaeon	a′ ⎞	I. Tetr.
Paranete hyperbolaeon	g′ ⎟	hyperbolaeon
Trite hyperbolaeon	f′ ⎟	
Nete diezeugmenon	e′ ⎠	
Paranete diezeugmenon	d ⎞	II. Tetr.
Trite diezeugmenon	c ⎟	diezeugmenon
Paramese	b ⎠	
Mese	a ⎞	III. Tetr.
Lichanos meson	g ⎟	meson
Parhypate meson	f ⎠	
Hypate meson	e ⎞	
Lichanos hypaton	d ⎟	IV. Tetr.
Parhypate hypaton	c ⎟	hypaton
Hypate hypaton	B ⎠	
Proslambanomenos	A	

Judging from the names of the tetrachords, III was the nucleus of the system; the name of II ("disjunct") refers to the fact that its lowest tone lies above the highest of the other. The name "hypaton" (highest) for IV is probably explained by the fact that the kithara players tilted their instrument so that the strings lowest in pitch were in the highest position (an analogous phenomenon exists in the 16th-century Italian lute tablatures; see under Tablature III). The names for the single tones also show that the whole system developed from the playing of the kithara: *nete* (*chorde*) means lowest strings (actually the highest in pitch); *paranete,* next to the lowest; *trite,* the third, etc.

Modulation was typified by a "Lesser Perfect System" of three conjunct tetrachords, but these were abstract theoretical constructions. The tetrachord added conjunctly above is called *synomenon,* "hooked," and provides the tones (a), b♭, c′ and d′. In the tetrachord of practical music the enharmonic *genus* (often called the "*harmonia*") was for Aristoxenus the tuning of the best classical music and may represent the old Dorian. Its essential feature was not the pair of microtones but the progression from *Mese* to a *Lichanos* tuned a whole ditone below it. In the 4th century *Lichanos* was tuned higher, within the chromatic *genus.* The Delphic Hymns are in one of these two *genera;* later extant pieces are diatonic. The old variety of modal idioms (*harmoniae*) disappears in the 4th century.

Modulation within a fixed vocal register, a fashion of 4th-century music, became a preoccupation for harmonic theorists. They calculated it by transposing their standard scale to other degrees of its own tonal sequence. A sample is given here, using the diatonic *genus* favored by theorists.

I (Dorian)   a′ g′ f′ | e′ d′ c′ b♭ a g f e | d c B A
                          T T S T T T S

II (Phrygian) a′ g′ f♯′ | e′ d′ c♯′ b a g f♯ e | d c B A
                            T S T T T S T

Within the octave e′–e, between the bars—symbolizing the melody in its fixed vocal register—scale I presents the sequence of tones (T) and semitones (S): T T S T T T S. The same sequence, at f♯′–f♯, is the core of the identical but transposed scale II. The transposition automatically places a different sequence, T S T T T S T, in the central register; and similar transposed scales at each diatonic degree will produce the seven segments, or "species," of the octave. These octave species and their corresponding double-octave scales (*tonoi*) were named:

a′–a: Hypodorian (Hyperphrygian, Aeolian, Locrian)
g′–g: Hypophrygian (Hyperlydian, Ionian, Iastian)
f′–f: Hypolydian
e′–e: Dorian
d′–d: Phrygian
c′–c: Lydian
b–B: Mixolydian (Hyperdorian)

They can be indicated in modern notation by the addition of various key signatures to the scale on e:

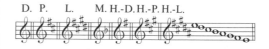

D. P. L.   M. H.-D. H.-P. H.-L.

Some theorists inferred that the species were the obsolete *harmoniae;* they were interpreted as musical "modes" by medieval scholars, and some still hold this opinion. It should have been refuted by correct understanding of Ptolemy. The scale of melodic function (*dynamis*) is always the Dorian. The other species are merely artificial redistributions of the Dorian octave T T S T T T S; e.g., in scale II the top tone is transferred to the bottom of the central register, and functional *Mese* is transposed from *a* to *b,* without modal change. The species serve to define the relative position (*thesis*) of the *tonoi* in the mathematical system, which is abstract and pitchless.

Some scholars, while admitting that Ptolemy's *tonos* system is pitchless, believe that other sets of *tonoi,* placed on each semitone, represented real pitch-keys. But Ptolemy, arguing that the extra *tonoi* are a logical error, presupposed that they, too, were abstract theoretical figures. Two of the old *harmoniae* were associated with relatively high or low voices (of either sex), but for the hypothesis that an absolute pitch-standard was recognized the evidence is inadequate.

In Greek music the voice was paramount, except in the revolutionary phase, and only the vocal part was transmitted to memory. Instrumental accompaniments were sometimes heterophonic improvisations, but harmony and counterpoint were unknown, though choirs occasionally doubled at the octave. Instrumental solos were rare, and the role of instruments in the development of the music should not be exaggerated.

III. *Notation and documents.* On the two notations (called by late writers "vocal" and "instrumental," but not consistently so used), see *WoHN* i, and C. Sachs in *ZMW* vi, vii. Sachs' hypothesis that they were tablatures for the kithara, pentatonically tuned, has been criticized by R. P. Winnington-Ingram in *The Classical Quarterly,* new series vi (1956), and rests on the unwarranted assumption that written music was used by performers. Some inferior theorists employed notation, but musical compositions were seldom written down; transmission was oral and precarious. Of the few written pieces extant, one of the two earliest (*c.* 250 B.C.) contains words from Euripides, but the music may be a later setting. The two hymns to Apollo from Delphi (one dated to 127 B.C.) are long fragments of prize compositions, academic in manner. The undated Seikilos Song is rhythmically alien to any known Greek music. Two hymns to the Muse, and the hymns to Nemesis and the Sun (ascribed to Mesomedes) may be ancient, but a Byzantine origin is possible.

See also Aulos; *Chroai; Chronos;* Dithyramb; Enharmonic; Ethos; Hydraulos; Hyporchema; Kithara; Lyra; Magadis; Pyknon; Pythagorean scale.

IV. *Modern.* Nothing is known of Greek music between *c.* 200 and 1800 of the Christian era, when Greece was dominated successively by Rome, Byzantium, and, from 1456 to 1830, by the Turks. Of interest is the fact that *c.* 1000 many elements of Greek theory were incorporated into Arab music. On the other hand, Greek folksong seems to have been greatly influenced by the music of the Near East.

The development of modern Greek music began about 1850 under the influence of Italian opera. The first composer of modern Greece was Nikolaos Mantzaros (1795–1872), who is now chiefly remembered for his setting of the Greek national anthem. He was followed by Spyridon Xyndas (1812–96) and others. Particularly successful was Spyros Samaras (1861–1917), a pupil of Delibes, with the opera *Flora Mirabilis* (1886). A national movement started with the songs of George Lambelet (1875–1945) and found more definite expression in the works of Manolis Kalomiris (1883–1962), whose opera *Protomastoras* (1916) has been compared to Glinka's *A Life for the Czar.* The national element is also prominent in the works of Mario Varvoglis (b. 1885) and some of the younger composers, e.g., M. Theodorakis (b. 1925) and Manos Hadjidakis (b. 1925), who cultivate a sort of neofolk music. Neoclassical influences characterize the works of Petro Petridis (b. 1892) and Georges Poniridis (b. 1892). Of the composers born after 1900, Nikos Skalkottas (1904–49) is by far the most important. A pupil of P. Jarnach and A. Schoenberg, he introduced serial music into Greece, an idiom that has also been adopted in varying degrees by Yiannis Papaioannou (b. 1910), Yorgos Sisilianos (b. 1922), Yannis

Xenakis (b. 1922; see his *Musique Formelles; Nouveaux Principes Formels de Composition Musicale* [1963]; also articles in *RM* no. 257 [1963]); Arghyris Kounadis (b. 1924), and Janis Christou (b. 1926; see J. G. Papaioannou, in *Greek Heritage* i, no. 2, 52–54 [1964]).

For Greek church music, see Byzantine chant.

Lit. *For I–III:* T. Reinach, *La Musique grecque* (1926); J. F. Mountford, in Powell and Barber, *New Chapters in Greek Literature II* (1929; transcriptions of most of the fragments); I. Düring, *Ptolemaios und Porphyrios über die Musik* (1934; G. trans. and notes); R. P. Winnington-Ingram, *Mode in Ancient Greek Music* (1936); E. A. Lippman, *Musical Thought in Ancient Greece* (1964); O. Gombosi, *Tonarten und Stimmungen der antiken Musik* (1939); C. Sachs, *The Rise of Music in the Ancient World East and West* (1943); I. Henderson, in *NOH* i, 336ff; J. Chailley, "Le Mythe des modes grecs" (*AM* xxviii); J. M. Barbour, "The Principles of Greek Notation" (*JAMS* xiii, 1ff). Additional bibl. in *ReMMA*, 427ff, and *NOH* i, 495ff.

For IV: P. L. Dacios, *Concise History of Music from Ancient Times to Our Days* (1934); S. Michaēlidēs, *Hē Neoellēnikē mousikē* (1952; in Greek); S. G. Motsenigos, *Neoellēnikē Mousikē* (1958; in Greek); T. N. Synadinos, *History of Neo-Hellenic Music* (1919; in Greek; covers 1824–1919); N. Slonimsky, "New Music in Greece," in *LBCM*; R. L. Finney, "Music in Greece" (*Perspectives of New Music* [1965], 169–70); I. Xenakis, in *RM* no. 253–4, 1963.

Folk music: S. Michaēlidēs, *The Neohellenic Folk-Music* (1948); S. Baud-Bovy, *La Chanson populaire grecque du Dodécanèse* (1936); *id., ‡Chansons du Dodécanèse,* 2 vols. (1935, '38); *id., Chansons populaires grecques du Dodécanèse* [1946]; P. E. Formozis [Phormozes], *Contribution a l'étude de la chanson et de la musique populaire grecque* (1938); G. Lambelet, *La Musique populaire grecque* (1934); D. Petropulos, *La Comparaison dans la chanson populaire grecque* (1954); P. Tzermias, *Die volkstümliche Musik Griechenlands* (1962).   I–III by I.H.

Greghesca [It., pl. *Greghesche*]. See under Villanella.

Gregorian chant. The liturgical chant of the Roman Catholic Church. It is named after Pope Gregory I (reigned 590–604), who was believed to have developed it. Between 750 and 850 the chant probably reached its final form as preserved in MSS of the 10th and subsequent centuries. The term "Gregorian chant" has the disadvantage of excluding, strictly speaking, the early development leading up to the Gregorian period, as well as the additions and changes introduced afterward. Moreover, Gregory's alleged role in the formation of the chant is now generally considered more or less legendary [see VII]. Another common name is plainsong [L. *cantus planus*]; this, however, originally had a different meaning [see *Cantus planus*] and is now frequently used in a wider and more technical sense [see Plainsong]. A more appropriate name is "Roman chant," because it indicates the chant's age-long connection with the Church of Rome, as distinct from other bodies of Western chant in Milan (*Ambrosian), Spain (*Mozarabic or Visigothic), and ancient Gaul (*Gallican). Recent investigations, however, have led to the theory that the Roman chant received its final form in France during the 8th and 9th centuries (hence the designation "Franco-Roman chant") and that from the historical point of view the name "Roman" would be more correctly applied to yet another repertory, now usually called *Old Roman chant. Therefore the term Gregorian chant ought to be retained.

Whereas some former musicians disdained Gregorian chant, particularly because it lacked harmony, it is now more and more fully recognized as an unsurpassed treasure of purely melodic music. Its freely flowing rhythm, far from being chaotic, shows subtleties of structure and organization that are superior to the hackneyed rhythmic devices of some harmonized music, with its meter, measures, beats, regular phrases, etc. The current repertory of Gregorian chant consists of nearly 3,000 melodies, all monophonic, rhythmically free, and sung partly both chorally (by the *schola, i.e., choir) and solo (by the *cantor). The following will be considered below in this order: I. Liturgical categories; II. Text; III. Style; IV. Forms; V. Tonality; VI. Rhythmic interpretation; VII. Historical development.

I. *Liturgical categories*. The calendar of the Roman Church includes a large number of holy days. These fall into three categories: (a) feasts of the Lord (Proper of the Time, *Proprium de tempore*, also *Temporale*), i.e., all Sundays and the special occasions commemorating Jesus' life, such as the Nativity, Easter, Ascension; (b) feasts of individual Saints (Proper of the Saints, *Proprium Sanctorum*), e.g., of the Virgin Mary, St. Andrew, St. Peter, St. Paul; (c) feasts of special groups of Saints (Common of Saints, *Commune Sanctorum*), such

as Apostles, Martyrs, Confessors, etc. Categories (b) and (c) form the *Sanctorale*. The services on a given day consist of the *Office and the *Mass. The chants for the former are found in the *antiphonal, those for the latter in the *gradual [see also Liturgical books]. Both are conveniently combined (with many omissions and additions) in the *Liber usualis* [*LU*]. Within the entire repertory a division is made between *Ordinary and *Proper chants. The main sections of *LU* are: Ordinary chants of the Mass (pp. 11–111; this includes what is commonly called the Mass Ordinary: Kyrie, Gloria, Sanctus, Credo, Agnus Dei); Ordinary chants of the Office (pp. 112–316; this includes mostly the Office Psalms); Proper of the Time (pp. 317–1110); Common of Saints (pp. 1111–1272); and Proper of the Saints (pp. 1303–1762). The three last-named sections include the Proper chants for the respective categories of feasts [see under Proper].

II. *Text*. By far the greater part of the chants are based on prose texts, and of these the great majority are taken from the Book of *Psalms. Entire Psalms sung to a *psalm tone form a regular part of the Office; single Psalm verses are used in the "verses" ($\mathbb{V}$.) of the Introits, Graduals, Alleluias, and Tracts, as well as in the opening antiphons and responds of these chants and in the Communions and Offertories [see Psalmody]. Nonpsalmodic scriptural texts occur in the *canticles and in the *responsories of Matins; many of the latter take their texts from the historical books of the Old Testament, such as Genesis, Kings, etc. In the liturgical books, *Ps.* (in the Introits) always denotes a verse from the Psalms, while $\mathbb{V}$. indicates a verse either from the Psalms or from other scriptural texts. The outstanding nonscriptural prose texts are those of the Ordinary of the Mass. The chants based on poetic texts (medieval) are the *hymns and the *sequences. A semipoetic text occurs in the four Antiphons B.M.V., particularly in the "Ave regina." An invaluable help for the study of the Gregorian texts is C. Marbach, *Carmina Scripturarum* (1907), which gives many of the sources for the scriptural texts of the Gregorian chant.

III. *Style*. Three melodic styles of the prose chants are usually distinguished by modern writers: (a) syllabic style; (b) neumatic or group style; and (c) melismatic style. (a) Chants in *syllabic style* [Ex. a] have one note to each syllable of the text; occasionally a group of two or three notes will be sung to one syllable. To this type belong the various recitation tones of the Office (psalm tones, lesson tones) and of the

Mass, as well as numerous antiphons of the Office, the hymns, and the various melodies for the Credo. The recitation tones are inflected *monotones, whereas the other chants have fully developed melodies. (b) In the chants in *group style* [Ex. b] there is more frequent use of groups of two to four or more notes to one syllable. The most important chants of this kind are the Introits and the Communions; also the melodies for the Sanctus and Agnus Dei, the Marian antiphons, etc. (c) The chants in *melismatic style* [Ex. b] include one or more melismas, groups of ten to twenty or more notes sung on

1

a

Cre-do in u-num De-um, Pa-trem om-ni-po-ten-tem

b

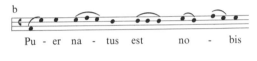

Pu - er na - tus est   no - bis

c

Al - le - lu - ia

one syllable. Here we find most of the Kyries, Graduals, Alleluias, Offertories, Tracts, and responsories.

The rather strict adherence to a given style in any of the liturgical categories is one of the most remarkable traits of Gregorian chant. According to a carefully laid out plan, each type of chant receives the treatment that conforms to its liturgical position and significance. Even the same text is set to music in totally different styles according to whether it is used as an antiphon, a Gradual, or for some other purpose. A famous example is the psalm verse *Justus ut palma,* for which more than 20 different melodies exist, ranging from the simplest to the most ornate.

IV. *Forms.* Structurally, the chants can be roughly divided into three categories: (a) *Through-composed chants.* In this category are the Glorias, Sanctus, and Credos of the Ordinary of the Mass, as well as the Offertories and Communions of the Proper of the Mass [for the last two, see Psalmody II, III]. Naturally, to classify these chants as through-composed does not preclude the occasional repetition of motifs or longer phrases (see, e.g., the passages "Benedici-

mus te," "Adoramus te," "Glorificamus te" in the *Gloria X* [*LU* p. 43f]; such reiterations are a peculiarity of the individual chants, not of the category to which they belong). (b) *Strophic chants.* To this class belong mainly the hymns, and also the Psalms, every verse of which is sung, with minor modifications, to the same melody. (c) *Repetitive forms.* Simple repetitive structures are used for the *Kyries, *Agnus Dei, and *sequences. All these are chants of the late Middle Ages (11th to 13th centuries). More interesting and more typical of Gregorian art are the various repeat forms found in the Introits, Alleluias, Graduals, and responsories, and formerly also in Offertories and Communions. All these are reductions of the rondolike structure of early psalmody, responsorial or antiphonal. They are discussed separately under Psalmody. Particularly intricate repeat structures are found in the *Tracts.

V. *Tonality.* The tonal basis of Gregorian chant is the system of the eight *church modes. In the modern liturgical books, the mode of each chant is indicated at the beginning, e.g., *Grad. 7* (Gradual in mode 7; similarly in the index). The most frequently used modes are 1 and 8, the least used 5 and 6. Among the most notable aspects of Gregorian tonality is the fact that the Tracts are limited to modes 2 and 8, and the Graduals to the four authentic modes except for a special group in mode 2, usually referred to as the "Gradual-type Justus ut palma." Although the great majority of Gregorian melodies conform to the general requirements of their respective modes, some do deviate from the normal scheme. Deviations are: (a) The use of the b-flat. This is often introduced in order to avoid the tritone (f–g–a–b) or the major sixth (d–a–b–a). It should be noted, however, that numerous flats given in the modern editions are not authentic. This remark applies particularly to the formula d–a–b–a, which occurs at the beginning of many chants of mode 1. The chants of modes 3 and 4 often include cadential formations with the general outline f–b–e, which, it will be noted, results in a tritone whether or not the b is flatted. (b) Transposed chants. A number of chants close on one of the *affinales (a, b, c'), instead of on one of the four finals (d, e, f, g). Most of these were transposed, not to bring them into a more convenient range but because they included chromatic pitches (e-flat or f-sharp) that could only be represented in this way within the plainsong system. For instance, d–e–f–e♭–f could only be represented in a transposition to the upper fifth as a–b–c'–b♭–a, and e–f–g–f♯–e only in transposition to the upper fourth as a–b♭–c'–b–a, because b and b-flat was the only "chromatic pair" available in the medieval scale. (c) Excessive range. This category includes chants whose range exceeds the authentic as well as the plagal ambitus. An example is the Gradual "Timete Dominum" [*LU*, p. 1726], which closes on d and extends from A to c'. Later theorists (e.g., Marchetto da Padua, in his *Lucidarium* of *c.* 1318; see Strunk, in *La Rassegna Musicale* xx [1950], 314) accounted for this phenomenon by introducing various kinds of "mixed modes" combining the range of the authentic (d–d') with that of the plagal (A–a). The best way of dealing with this problem is to renounce the distinction between authentic and plagal and classify the chant only according to its final, as *protus, deuterus, tritus,* or *tetrardus* [see Maneria]. This is also advisable in the case of chants with a limited range, e.g., the Communions "Amen dico" [*LU*, p. 1206] and "Dominus Jesus" [*LU*, p. 679]. Although both have the range c–a, the former is assigned to mode 1 and the latter to mode 2. It must be noted, however, that in the case of antiphons a decision has to be made, because the mode of the antiphon determines the psalm tone to be used for the subsequent Psalm. (Originally this was true of the Communions as well.)

An interesting phenomenon in a number of chants is a certain tonal instability. This occurs particularly in the chants of the *deuterus,* which often begin and continue with phrases suggestive of various other tonal realms, until they finally and quite unexpectedly close on e. Recently much attention has been given to the "pentatonic background" of the Gregorian melodies. Although the sweeping contention that all these melodies are essentially "pentatonic melodies with ornamental *pien tones*" [see the reference in *ReMMA,* p. 160] is without foundation, the fact remains that a considerable number of chants are clearly pentatonic [see Ex. 2, from the Communion "In splendoribus"; *LU,* p. 395]. Such examples deserve mention

because they may indicate an earlier stage in the evolution of the complete modes.

VI. *Rhythmic interpretation.* This remains the most disputed area of Gregorian chant. It arises from the fact that the notation of the chants contains no clear indication of temporal values [see Neumes; also Monophonic notation] and that, by the 13th century, the oral tradition of the rhythmic performance had been lost. Unsuccessful attempts at reconstruction were made in the 19th century when in reprints of the "Editio Medicea" [see Liturgical books II] the neumatic signs of plainsong were wrongly interpreted as mensural notes and ligatures (*longa, brevis, semibrevis,* etc.; see Notation; also Square notation). The result is illustrated in Ex. 3. Still more distorted is the interpretation of H. Riemann,

Ky-ri - e

who applied his principle of *Vierhebigkeit* to Gregorian melodies [see *RiHM* i.2, 39]. Today, scholars agree that Gregorian rhythm belongs to the category termed "multimetric" [see Rhythm II (b)], in particular to the *chronos protos* variety. There are, however, two sharply divided schools of thought, one of which maintains that in Gregorian rhythm there exists practically only one time value, say, the eighth note, while the other admits the existence of two time values, the eighth note and its double (quarter note), and possibly also its triple (dotted quarter note).

To the former school belong the *accentualists* (Dom Pothier), who consider the textual accent and, in melismas, the first note of a neume the organizing factors within the succession of uniform time values. Their interpretation is called "free oratoric rhythm." In opposition to Pothier, Dom Mocquereau developed what has become known as the *Solesmes system or "free musical rhythm." He completely discards the text and the neumatic notation as a basis of interpretation, and also opposes the idea of accent. Instead, he regards the melody as a motion consisting of *élan* and *repos* (rise and fall), dividing it into an irregular succession of groups of two and three notes [see Ictus]. Occasionally, a slight lengthening of certain notes (*nuance*) is indicated by a horizontal stroke (horizontal *episema*). Doubled values, indicated by a dot (*punctum-mora*) occur, with rare exceptions, only at the end of a phrase.

In splen-do-ri-bus sanc-to - rum, ex u - te - ro

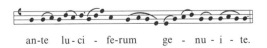

an-te lu - ci - fe-rum   ge - nu - i - te.

Among the adherents of the second school (generally called *mensuralists*), the admission of two time values naturally leads to considerable disagreement as to which notes of the chants are long and which short. Here the various scholars (A. Dechevrens, P. Wagner, J. Jeannin, E. Jammers, W. Lipphardt, J. W. A. Vollaerts) differ mainly concerning the correct interpretation and relative importance of early theorists as well as of certain special signs found in the early neumatic manuscripts, such as the *episema,* the *Romanus letters, the *virga* and *punctum* [see Neumes], etc. Ex. 4 illustrates some of the various methods of interpretation (a. Solesmes; b. Wagner; c. Jeannin). See also *ReMMA*, p. 148.

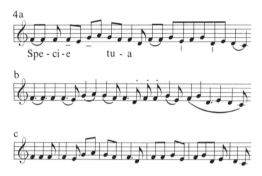

4a

Spe - ci - e   tu - a

b

c

The mensuralists "have an impressive amount of historical evidence on their side" [*ReMMA*, p. 146], while the Solesmes interpretation seems to derive its main justification from results in actual performance and recordings that, so far at least, have not been challenged by similar attempts on the part of the mensuralists. Regarding the historical accuracy of the Solesmes interpretation, it has been said that it probably stands in the same relation to its medieval counterpart as a Romanesque church of 1880 to its 11th-century model [*BeMMR*, p. 15]. A recent study by J. W. A. Vollaerts [see Lit.] has been widely recognized as an important step in the right direction.

VII. *History.* There has been extensive controversy regarding the origin of Gregorian chant. Formerly opinion was divided among those who traced it to Greek roots and those who pointed to the tradition of the Jewish synagogue. Today the latter view prevails, and the theory of Greek origin has been almost completely discarded. The very fact that practically all the early texts of the Roman Church are taken from the Psalms points to a strong Jewish influence; also, the Office Hours of the Church are modeled after the prayer hours of the Jewish synagogue. This point of view gained considerable support in the investigations of A. Idelsohn [see *ZMW* iv, 515], who showed that melodies still sung today by Jewish peoples living in isolated places (South Arabia, Iran) are strikingly similar to lection tones of the Roman Church.

Early development of Gregorian chant took place in the East, particularly in Jerusalem and Antioch (Syria). A report from *c.* 385, known as the "Peregrinatio ad loca sancta" (pilgrimage to the holy place), contains detailed information about the liturgy at Jerusalem and also about the singing of hymns and Psalms. With Pope Damasus I (reigned A.D. 366–84) the center of development shifted to Rome. He was the first of a line of Popes who are reported to have instituted a *cantus annalis,* a cycle of chants for the liturgical year. The list also includes Gregory I (reigned 590–604), who certainly played an outstanding role in the organization of the Roman chant. However, the idea that the melodies as preserved in MSS of the 10th and 11th centuries are "Gregorian" in the proper sense of the word is generally considered untenable today. According to recent research (H. Hucke, W. Apel), what is known now as Gregorian chant received its final form under the Frankish rulers Pepin the Short (714–68) and Charlemagne (742?–814), mainly at Metz. In Rome there developed a different repertory, the so-called *Old Roman chant. From the 14th through 19th centuries the history of plainsong is one of increasing deterioration, first in rhythmic interpretation, later also in the melodies themselves [*Editio Medicea, Ratisbonensis;* see under Liturgical books; see also *Machicotage; Plain-chant musical*]. Simultaneously, the monophonic chants were increasingly replaced by polyphonic settings, first by the 13th-century organa, clausulae, and motets (compositions for portions of the Proper of the Mass), later by compositions for the Ordinary of the Mass (14th and subsequent centuries), for the hymns (15th century, Dunstable, Dufay, and successors), and for the psalm tones (16th century; see *Falsobordone;* Verset). The return to the medieval tradition of unaccompanied chant is largely the work of the monks of *Solesmes.

See also (substantial articles are italicized): Alleluia; Antiphon; Benedicamus Domino; Benediction; Benedictus qui venit; Canticle; Cantus planus; Cecilian movement; Chant; *Church modes;* Communion; Cursus; Dies irae; Doxology; Euouae; Gradual; Hymn; Ictus;

Improperia; Incipit; Introit; Jubilus; Lamentations; Litany; *Liturgical books;* Machicotage; Magníficat; *Mass;* Miserere; Missa; Motu proprio; Neuma; *Neumes;* Offertory; *Office;* Ordinary and Proper; Plain-chant musical; Proper; Psalm; *Psalmody; Psalm tones;* Requiem Mass; Responsory; Salve Regina; Sarum use; Sequence II; Solesmes; Te Deum; Tenebrae; Tract; Tris(h)agion; Trope.

Lit. *Practical:* Dom Dominicus Johner, *A New School of Gregorian Chant,* trans. H. S. Butterfield, rev. ed. (1925); A. Robertson, *The Interpretation of Plainchant* (1937); J. Schrembs, *The Gregorian Chant Manual* (1935); G. Suñol, *Text Book of Gregorian Chant* (1930).

Historical: ApGC; D. J. Keller, *Fundamentals of Gregorian Chant* (1959); P. Wagner, *Einführung in die gregorianischen Melodien,* 3 vols. (1895–21; vol. i appeared in English as *Introduction to the Gregorian Melodies, Part I* [1901]); *id.,* in *AdHM* i, 75ff; Dom A. Mocquereau, *Le Nombre musical grégorien ou Rhythmique grégorienne,* 2 vols. (1908, '27); J. W. A. Vollaerts, *Rhythmic Proportions in Early Medieval Ecclesiastical Chant* (1958); J. Rayburn, *Gregorian Chant: A History of the Controversy Concerning Its Rhythm* (1964); G. Murray, *Gregorian Chant According to the Manuscripts* (1963); Dom J. Gajard, *Notions sur la rythmique grégorienne* [n.d.]; Dom J. Jeannin, *Études sur le rhythme grégorien* (1926); E. Jammers, *Der gregorianische Rhythmus* (1937); W. Apel, "The Central Problem of Gregorian Chant" (*JAMS* ix); G. Stevens, in *MQ* xxx; C. H. Phillips, "The Aesthetics of Plainsong" (*ML* xv, no. 2); E. Wellesz, "Some Exotic Elements of Plainsong" (*ML* iv, no. 3); H. Hucke, "Die Einführung des Gregorianischen Gesangs im Frankenreich" (*Römische Quartalschrift für Christliche Altertumskunde* xlix, 172ff); P. Wagner, "Zur Rhythmik der Neumen" (*JMP* xvii); L. Bonvin, "The 'Measure' in Gregorian Music" (*MQ* xv); J. Jeannin, "Il mensuralismo Gregoriano" (*RMI* xxviii, xxix, xxx). See also Editions XLII; Neumes. Fuller bibl. in *ReMMA,* pp. 437ff.

Groppo [It.]. See *Gruppetto.*

Gross, grosse [G.]. Large, great. *Grosse Flöte,* the ordinary flute. *Grosses Orchester,* full orchestra. *Grosse Trommel,* bass drum. *Grosse Sext (Terz),* major sixth (third); *Grosse Quinte (Quarte),* perfect fifth (fourth). *Grosse Oktave,* great octave.

Grosse caisse [F.]. Bass drum.

Grosse Fuge [G., Great Fugue]. Beethoven's long and complex fugue for string quartet, op. 133. It was composed in 1825 as the last movement of his String Quartet op. 130 but later was published as a separate composition. It is remarkable for the boldness of its theme and for the treatment, which is "tantôt libre, tantôt recherchée" (partly free, partly studied).

Ground, ground bass. A short melodic phrase (normally four to eight measures) that is repeated over and over again as a bass line, with varying music for the upper parts. The resulting composition is also called a "ground." The contrast between the fixed scheme of the bass and the free display of imagination in the upper part or parts lends particular charm to this form. However, the bass melody is not always entirely "fixed," but may occur with modifications or in another key. The ground bass or *basso ostinato* [It.] may vary from such simple formations as the descending tetrachord: a–g–f–e (one note to

the measure; see Ex. under Chaconne) to full-length melodies, as in the accompanying example (Purcell). The ground is a characteristic form of baroque music and was cultivated especially in England, frequently with improvisation of the upper parts [see Division]. The name was first (?) used in keyboard composition by William Byrd. For earlier manifestations of the same principle, see Ostinato.

The ground belongs to the general category of continuous variations [see Variations I]. In particular, all the passacaglias (as defined under Chaconne and passacaglia) can be considered grounds, even if their ostinato motif is occasionally transferred to an upper voice-part, as in Bach's passacaglia. For a somewhat different type of reiterated bass, see Strophic bass.

Lit.: L. Nowak, *Grundzüge einer Geschichte des Basso ostinato* (1932); L. Propper, "Der Basso ostinato" (diss. Berlin, 1926); R. Litterscheid, Zur Geschichte des basso ostinato" (diss. Marburg, 1928); L. Walter, "Die konstructive und thematische Ostinatotechnik des 17. und 18. Jahrhunderts" (diss. Würzburg, 1939); H. Riemann, "Basso ostinato und basso *quasi* ostinato" (*CP Liliencron*); *id.*, in *SIM* xiii; H. Shaw, "Blow's Use of the Ground Bass" (*MQ* xxiv); O. Gombosi, "Italia: Patria del basso ostinato" (*LRM* vii); W. Greenhouse Allt, "The Treatment of Ground" (*PMA* lxxii, 73); H. M. Miller, "Henry Purcell and the Ground Bass" (*ML* xxix, 340).

Grund- [G.]. *Grundlage,* root position. *Grundstimmen,* the 8-foot registers of the organ. *Grundton,* root of a chord. *Grundtonart,* main key.

Gruppetto, gruppo, groppo [It.]. Italian 16th-century names for an ornament like a *trill. See Ornamentation I.

G.S., GS. Abbr. for Gerbert's *Scriptores.* See under *Scriptores.*

G sol re ut (G solreut). See under Hexachord III.

Gsp. Abbr. for glockenspiel.

Guajira [Sp.]. Term derived from *guajiro* ("hillbilly"), name given to people of the interior of Cuba, which more properly applies to a rural style of song of prevailingly Spanish influence than to a definite type of folk expression. Many devices of Latin American music are characteristic of the *guajira* style, among them the alternate use of 3/4 and 6/8 meter, use of the guitar or *tiple* (high-pitched guitar without the lower strings) to accompany the solo voice, harmonies centering around the dominant seventh chord, etc. The *punto* is one of the most typical present-day forms of *guajira.*   J.O-S.

Guaracha [Sp.]. Cuban folksong originating from a sequence of quatrains sung alternately by a chorus and a solo voice. Improvisation and topical allusions were included in the solo sections. This older form of *guaracha* developed into the present-day two-section form, consisting of an introduction followed by a faster section. Symmetrical rhythms as well as syncopation are employed within either 3/4 and 6/8 or 2/4 meter. The most characteristic feature is the use of mischievous, equivocal texts.   J.O-S.

Guaranía [Sp.]. Paraguayan ballad in slow waltz tempo and usually in a minor mode, created by José Asuncion Flores in the late 1920's [see Paraguay] in an attempt to promote a new popular song form of native character. This form soon became popular and is now regarded as part of the country's folk music.   J.O-S.

Guárdame las vacas [Sp.]. Title of 16th-century Spanish variations (L. de Narváez, 1538; A. Mudarra, 1546; Enriquez de Valderrabano, 1547; A. de Cabezón) on a theme that is identical to the *romanesca.* The title (Let us watch over the cows) suggests that it was a popular Spanish song. In the *Libro de tientos . . . Facultad Organica* of F. Correa de Araujo (1626; new ed. by S. Kastner, ii, 213) it is designated as *seculorum del primero tono,* obviously because the melodic outline a–g–f–e–d is also the termination formula of the first psalm tone.

Guasa [Sp.]. Satirical Venezuelan folksong based on many different poetical structures. Musically, almost every *guasa* is binary in form, in 6/8 meter, and based on the following rhythmic pattern:

J.O-S.

Guatemala. In 1554 the Spanish-born composer Hernando Franco (1532–85) arrived in Guatemala and remained there until 1573, when he moved to Mexico City [see Mexico]. From 1534, when the Guatemala Cathedral was provided with an organist and precentor, European music had played an important role in the conversion of Guatemalans. Despite the scarcity of information about colonial Guatemala's musical life, there is evidence enough to show that Guatemala was not far behind Mexico and Peru in 16th- and 17th-century music. Nine 16th- and early 17th-century codices containing works by outstanding Spanish and Flemish composers of the Renaissance have been assembled in Huehuetenango, near Guatemala City. Two of them, compiled before 1600, contain *coplas* and *villancicos* in Spanish, signed by Tomas Pascual and Francisco de Leon.

One of the most important composers of a later period was Vicente Sáenz (1756–1841), who wrote *Villancicos de Pascua* that were very popular in his day. His son, Benedicto Sáenz (d. 1831), was at one time the organist of the Cathedral of Guatemala City, and his son, also named Benedicto Sáenz, had several compositions published in France. José Escolástico Andrino, a noted violinist from Guatemala, lived in El Salvador from 1845 on. Of his compositions, two symphonies, three Masses, and an opera (*La Mora Generosa*) are preserved.

Luis Felipe Arias (1870–1908), who received his musical training in Europe, wrote short piano pieces and songs inspired by Guatemalan folk idioms. His immediate follower, Jesús Castillo

(1877–1946), a noted scholar of Indian music, wrote two operas based on folk idioms, *Quiché Vinak* (1924) and *Nicté,* as well as a ballet (*Guatema*), an *Obertura Indígena* and *Obertura Tecum,* and a collection of piano pieces published in France under the title *Popol Buj.* His half-brother, Ricardo Castillo (b. 1894), studied in France, where he lived for ten years. He has written incidental music for various native plays, two ballets, a *Sinfonietta,* several orchestral works, and piano compositions. Of the same generation are José Castañeda (b. 1898), an experimenter in modern trends of composition, conductor, and theoretician; Franz Ippisch (b. 1883), an Austrian-born composer; José Molina Pinillo (b. 1889), who studied in Mexico and Berlin; and Raúl Paniagua (b. 1898), composer of a well-known orchestral composition, *La Leyenda Maya.*

In the succeeding generation the most important figures are Miguel Sandovál (1903–53), a pianist and composer, mainly of film music; Salvador Ley (b. 1907), a noted pianist, director of the Conservatorio Nacional de Música in Guatemala (1934–54), and composer of a number of orchestral, piano, and chamber works; and Enrique Solares (b. 1910), a pianist, diplomat, and composer who writes in the neoclassical vein.

Best known among the youngest generation of composers are Manuel Herrarte (b. 1924); Joaquin Orellana (b. 1935), who has written chamber music, incidental pieces for orchestra and choral compositions; and Jorge Sarmientos, who is also a conductor.

Jesús Castillo, in his valuable study *La Música Maya-Quiché* (1941), classifies native Guatemalan melodies as following six clearly differentiated scales, some of which, he claims, are imitations of the song of a Guatemalan bird, the *cenzontle.* The only native dance that is largely free of European influences is the **Son Chapin,* also known as *Son Guatemalteco.*

Lit.: V. M. Diaz, *Las Bellas Artes en Guatemala, La Música* (1934); J. Sáenz Poggio, *Historia de la música guatemalteca desde la monarquía española, hasta fines de año de 1877* (1878; 1947 reprint in *Anales de la sociedad de geografia e historia de Guatemala* xxii, nos. 1–2); S. Ley, *Cultural Aspects of Musical Life in Guatemala* (1952); J. Castillo, *La Música Maya-Quiché* (1941); R. Stevenson, *European Music in 16th-Century Guatemala* (1964). Also see under Latin America.   J.O-S.

Guerre des bouffons [F.], **guerra dei buffoni** [It.]. See War of the Buffoons. The preferred French designation is *querelle* (quarrel) *des bouffons.*

Guida [It.]. (1) Subject (*dux*) of a fugue. (2) A **direct. (3) An abbreviated orchestral score [see *Conducteur*].

Guidon [F.]. A **direct.

Guidonian hand. A sketch of the human hand with the notes from G to e″ in various parts of the skeleton, intended as an aid for memorizing the scale and its solmization syllables. It acquired an almost supernatural significance as the symbol of the complete mastery of the medieval system of **hexachord and mutation— indeed, of the entire system of church modes. Thus, for instance, chromaticism was strongly objected to as late as the 16th century because it was not contained "in the hand" (*non est in manu*). In the accompanying sketch the tones are indicated by the modern pitch names instead of the composite solmization names (Gamma ut, A re, B mi, etc.; see Hexachord II) that are used in the early treatises.

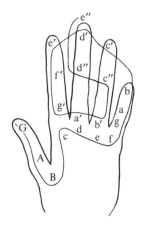

The Guidonian hand is not present in the works of Guido d'Arezzo (*c.* 990–1050), nor is the complete system of **solmization. It is found for the first time in treatises of the late 13th century (Engelbert, Elias Salomon, Hieronymus de Moravia; see *GS* ii, 292, iii, 22; *CS* i, 21). Until the end of the 15th century it was called *manus musicalis.* The name *manus Guidonis* appears in the *Musica practica* of B. Ramos de Pareja (1482; ed. by J. Wolf, p. 13).

Guillaume Tell [F., William Tell]. Opera in four acts by Rossini, produced in Paris, 1829. Setting: Switzerland, early 14th century. The overture was a popular orchestral concert selection until made banal by association with various radio programs and motion pictures.

Guimbarde [F.]. *Jew's-harp.

Guïro. See under Percussion instruments B, 8.

Guitar. [F. *guitare;* G. *Gitarre;* It. *chitarra;* Sp. *guitarra*]. A plucked stringed instrument, similar to the lute but with a flat back and built-up, inward-curved ribs, somewhat like the violin. [For ill. see Guitar family.] The modern guitar has metal frets and six strings tuned E A d g b e'. The music is notated one octave higher than it sounds. Today the guitar is chiefly a popular instrument used to provide a simple chordal accompaniment to a dance or a song, especially folksong, the chords being indicated in a manner similar to the principles that are followed in 16th-century lute tablatures. Most of the great guitar virtuosos have been Spanish: Dionisio Aguado (1784–1849), who established the principles of modern guitar playing in a method written in 1825 and still used today; Fernando Sor (1778–1839), who aroused the admiration of Méhul, Cherubini, and Fétis, and who wrote numerous brilliant compositions for the guitar; Francisco Tárrega (1852–1909), the greatest of all guitar players, who initiated the present-day revival of the instrument; and the noted Andrés Segovia (b. 1893), who has made the instrument known all over the world and who has contributed much to a revival of old (16th-century) guitar (vihuela) music. Modern composers for the guitar include Manuel de Falla, Joaquín Turina, Rodolfo Halffter, Albert Roussel, Alexander Tansman, and others. Percy Grainger has used it in several compositions [see C. Forsyth, *Orchestration,* rev. ed. (1936), p. 480].

In 16th-century Spain at least three types of guitar were in use: (1) the six-course *vihuela, an instrument equal in artistic importance to the contemporaneous lute and for which seven books of tablature were published, one each by L. Milán, L. de Narvaez, A. Mudarra, E. Enriquez, de Valderrábano, D. Pisador, M. de Fuenllana, and E. Daza, containing a great many fantasias, variations (*diferencias*), duets, songs (*villancicos, romances*), a few dances, and many intabulations; (2) the four-course *guitarra,* a popular instrument for which Mudarra and Fuenllana composed a few pieces; and (3) the five-course *guitarra española,* whose vogue at the end of the century and throughout the 17th century was in part responsible for the eclipse of the lute and whose music usually consisted of chordal accompaniment only. G. Montesardo, in his *Nuova Inventione d'Intavolatura per sonare li Balletti sopra la Chitarra Spagnuola* (1606), invented a new notation (stenographic indication of the chords), which was broadened by other guitarists, such as Pietro Milioni (1627), Caliginoso (1626), and Lucas Ruiz de Ribayaz (1677; see *WoHN* ii, 174, 175, 201).

In the 17th century, when lute music reached the height of artistic perfection under Denis Gaultier, Esaias Reusner, Robert de Visée, and others, the guitar rose to prominence as an instrument much easier to play and, consequently, of greater popular appeal. In the late 17th century the instrument came into vogue in French court circles, and fashionable painters like Watteau depicted it in the hands of beautiful ladies and clowns. Boccherini used the guitar in some of his chamber music, as did other composers of the 18th century. Schubert's so-called Guitar Quartet, however, is only an adaptation of a trio for flute, violin, and guitar by a Bohemian, W. Matiegka, published in 1807. See also Guitar family; Electronic instruments I.

Lit.: A. P. Sharpe, *The Story of the Spanish Guitar,* rev. ed. (1959); J. de Azpiazu, *La Guitarra y los Guitarristas* (1961); D. Prat, *Diccionario . . . de guitarristas* (1934); B. Terzi, *Dizionario dei chitarristi e liutai Italiani* (1937); J. Zuth, *Handbuch der Laute und Gitarre* (1926); *LavE* ii.3, 1997–2035; *WoHN* ii, 157–218, A. Koczirz, "Die Fantasien des Melchior de Barberis" (*ZMW* iv); *id.,* "Die Gitarrenkompositionen in Miguel de Fuenllana's *Orphénica lyra* (1554)" (*AMW* iv); F. Lesure, "La Guitare en France au XVIe siècle" (*MD* iv); T. Usher, "The Spanish Guitar in the Nineteenth and Twentieth Centuries" (*GSJ* ix); D. Heartz, "Parisian Music Publishing . . . Four Recently Discovered Guitar Books" (*MQ* xlvi); E. Schmitz, "Guitarrentabulaturen" (*MfM* xxxv); O. Chilesotti, "La Chitarra francese" (*RMI* xiv); M. R. Brondi, "Il Liuto e la chitarra" (*RMI* xxxii, xxxiii).

Guitar family. This category is here understood to include instruments that have the general characteristics of the lute family but have the flat body of the guitar. Like the lute, the guitar is of Oriental origin. It appears in various shapes in the famous miniatures of the 13th-century

Guitars: 1. Yuehchyn. 2. Bandurria. 3. Banjo. 4. Ukulele. 5. Balalaika. 6. Chitarra battente.
7. Cittern. 8. Guitar.

Cantigas MS of the Escorial. Several such instruments existed in the 16th and 17th centuries under different names. The most important of these was the *cittern* (also *cithren, cister, cistre, cither, cithara, cetera, cistola, citole*), which had an oval belly and back, similar to that of the lute, and wire strings. The *Cythringen* (*Cithrinchen*) on which the miller Veit Bach, J. S. Bach's great-great-grandfather, is reported to have entertained himself while grinding flour, was a smaller instrument of this type. In the 18th century the cittern was much used in England under the name *English guitar*. See T. Dart, "The Cittern

and Its English Music" (*GSJ* i). A direct derivative of the cittern is the *bandurria* and its larger variety, the *bandolon* [see *MaMI*]. The name of these instruments (probably also that of the modern *banjo) comes from the 16th-century *bandora* (sometimes called *pandora*). The *gittern*, which had gut strings, is another early member of the guitar family, but the name *quinterne* (probably from *guitterne*) was applied to other instruments as well. A Portuguese guitar, much used in the Azores, is the *machete*, which is the ancestor of the modern *ukulele*. The *chitarra battente* is an Italian form of guitar. Of the various guitar instruments of Russia only the *bala-laika* survives today. A circular guitar with a short neck is used in China under the name *yuehchyn* and in Japan under the name *gekkin* [see *MaMI*]. The Japanese *shamisen* (*samisen*) is sometimes considered a guitar, but is more closely related to the lute [see Lute, Japan VI]. See also *Vihuela*.

Gurre-Lieder [G.]. A song cycle ("Great Cantata") by Schoenberg to poems (originally in Danish) by J. P. Jacobsen, for 5 solo voices, 3 four-part male choruses, 1 eight-part mixed chorus, narrator, and large orchestra, begun 1901–02 but not finished until 1911. The musical style represents the climax of late romanticism.

Gusle. A primitive one-stringed instrument, played with a primitive bow. It is used almost exclusively to accompany and support the chanting of the epic poems of the southern Slavs (Serbs, Montenegrins, Macedonians, and, less frequently, Bulgarians). Pear-shaped, it is covered with skin and has a long neck ending with a decorative carving, usually in the shape of an animal's head. The single string usually is made of twisted horsehair, which also is used for the bow. [For ill. see Violin.] A two-stringed variant is known in Bosnia. In Macedonia it may have three strings and resembles the Bulgarian *gadulka* as well as the Byzantine *lyra*, a variant of which is still in use in southern Dalmatia, where it is known as *lijerica.* The gusle player is called *guslar* and is regarded as the carrier of traditional epic poems. The Russian *gusli* is a zitherlike instrument [see Psaltery] quite unrelated to the Balkan gusle. See W. Wünsch, *Die Geigentechnik der südslawischen Guslaren* (1934); *id.,* in *MGG* v.   M.V.

Gusto, con [It.]. With style, with zest.

Gymel, gimel, gemell. (1) A late medieval term for two-part polyphony based on thirds, sixths, and tenths. The term is derived from the *Latin gemellus,* meaning twin. Guilelmus Monachus described it (*c.* 1480) as a style used in England

and employing upper as well as lower thirds ("habet consonantias tertias tam altas quam bassas . . ."; see *CS* iii, 289a). This would require a crossing of parts, e.g., e–d–c–d–e as counterpoint to c–d–e–f–g. A number of English compositions from *c.* 1300 are in this style, e.g., *Jesu Cristes milde moder* (*ReMMA,* p. 389), *Edi beo* (*NOH* ii, 342), and *Foweles in the frith* (*NOH* ii, 343; here the two voices are an octave apart, so that the upper and lower third become tenths and sixths). The term is also used for two-part polyphony in parallel thirds. A famous example of this style is the 13th-century hymn "Nobilis humilis" written in praise of St. Magnus, the patron saint of the Orkneys (*HAM,* no. 25c). It should be noted, however, that parallel thirds were used in France as early as *c.* 1150 [see Third]. Perhaps the "crossing" gymel may more properly be considered to be of English origin than the "parallel" variety. See M. Bukofzer, "The Gymel, the Earliest Form of English Polyphony" (*ML* xvi, 77); *ReMMA,* p. 388. (2) In English musical sources of the 15th century, "gymel" means *divisi,* i.e., to indicate that a part is temporarily divided into two.

Gypsy music. Whether the Gypsies ever possessed a musical tradition of their own is a matter of doubt. What is generally called Gypsy music actually is Hungarian music of fairly recent origin, composed by Hungarians of the upper middle class but performed by Gypsies (according to Bartók). The so-called Gypsy scale, c–d–e♭–f♯–g–a♭–b–c′ [see Scale I], with two augmented seconds, is probably of Indian origin and was introduced by the Gypsies into eastern Europe, particularly into Hungary, where it became a pseudonationalist feature [see Hungary]. It also is common in modern Turkish and Jewish music as well as in Greek church music. The Gypsies have also played a role in the cultural and musical life of Spain [see *Flamenco*]. See *LavE* i.5, 2646ff; B. Bartók, "Gypsy Music or Hungarian Music?" (*MQ* xxxiii); W. Starkie, "The Gipsy in Andalusian Folk-Lore and Folk-music" (*PMA* lxii).

H

H. See Pitch names; Letter notation. Abbr. for horn (in orchestral scores). *H dur* (*moll*), German for B major (minor).

Habanera [Sp.]. A Cuban dance of Spanish origin that is rarely performed today despite its considerable historic importance. It is the ancestor of many new dance forms, e.g., the Argentine *tango. At the time of the Spanish-American War, the *habanera* was the most popular dance of the New World. Examples were sung in music halls throughout Europe, often modified according to the traditional styles of each country. At the time Bizet wrote his famous *habanera* (*Carmen*, 1875) the form was already well known outside Cuba. Many other European composers were inspired by its rhythm, among them Debussy, Albéniz, Auber, Chabrier, De Falla, and Ravel. Always in 2/4 meter in moderate tempo, the habanera uses a variety of rhythmic patterns, the two most common being

J.O-S.

Hackbrett [G.]. See Dulcimer.

Haffner collection. An important collection of early piano (harpsichord) sonatas, published by Johann Ulrich Haffner from 1755 to 1766. The complete collection consists of three publications entitled *Oeuvres mêlées, Raccolta musicale,* and *Collection récréative.* It contains 114 sonatas by K. P. E. Bach, Bertoni, Galuppi, Marpurg, L. Mozart, Paganelli, Rutini, Scheibe, Schobert, Wagenseil, and others. Eighteen sonatas from the *Raccolta musicale* have been republished by G. Benvenuti under the title *Cembalisti Italiani del Settecento* (G. Ricordi). See Sonata B III (a) and (b).

Haffner Serenade. Mozart's Serenade in D [K. 250], composed in 1776 for a wedding in the family of Sigmund Haffner, burgomaster of Salzburg. His Haffner Symphony in D [K. 385] was composed in 1782 for another festive occasion.

Haiti. Music during the early Spanish colonization of what is now the Republic of Haiti developed along the same lines as in the rest of the island of Hispaniola [see Dominican Republic]. Not until the end of the 17th century, when the French colonized the western third of the island, did an independent development begin.

Art music in Haiti dates from the beginning of the 20th century. Most Haitian composers have written works using some native elements but lacking the forceful expression of their original models. Occide Jeanty (1860–1936) is the earliest Haitian-born composer. He studied in Paris and in 1886 returned to Haiti as musical director of the Republic. Ludovic Lamothe (b. 1882) devoted himself to the study of folk music and then became a noted pianist and composer, especially of songs and short piano compositions. Justin Elie (1883–1931) also studied in Paris, and from 1922 until his death he lived in New York. He wrote a well-known *Aboriginal Suite* for orchestra and numerous compositions for piano, violin, and voice.

The traditional music of Haiti is largely a mixture of African, French, and Spanish elements, since the original Indian population disappeared under Spanish rule and none of its influences remains clearly traceable. Most Haitian songs and dances are dominated by the religious and social framework of the *vodoum* or *voodoo and are characterized by freedom of measure and rhythm. This is true of the *baboule, bamboche, bumba, salongo, monsondi,* and many other types mentioned by Courlander [see Lit.].

Lit.: L. Bowman, *The Voice of Haiti* (1938); H. Courlander, *Haiti Singing* (1939). Also see under Latin America. J.O-S.

Hakenneumen [G.]. Hook neumes; see Neumes II.

Halb, halbe [G.]. Half. *Halbe Note* (*Pause*), half note (-rest). *Halbinstrument,* half-tube instrument. *Halbschluss,* half-cadence. *Halbsopran,* mezzosoprano. *Halbton,* semitone.

Half. Half-close, imperfect cadence. Half-fall, see Appoggiatura. Half-shift, the first shift on the violin. Half-step, semitone. Half-stop, see Divided stop. Half-tube instruments, see Wind instruments II.

Hallelujah. A Biblical word, expressing joyful praise of God. For its use in Gregorian chant, see Alleluia. The original spelling is retained in Ambrosian chant. In choral compositions of the

17th and 18th centuries the word "Hallelujah" frequently serves as the text for an extensive final movement in fugal style. Famous examples are the Hallelujah choruses in Bach's cantata *Christ lag in Todesbanden* and in Handel's *Messiah* (close of Part II). See E. Gerson-Kiwi, "Halleluia and Jubilus in Hebrew-Oriental Chant" (*CP Besseler*).

Halling. A fast, lively Norwegian folk dance in 2/4 or 4/4 meter. It is a strenuous solo dance for men in which one person in the middle of the room holds a man's hat on a long pole. Several men in turn try to kick the hat off the pole. Grieg has used the dance in several of his *Lyric Pieces*. See T. Knudsen and A. Sommerfelt, ed., *Norsk riksmålsordbok* i (1937).

Hammerklavier [G.]. Early 19th-century name for the piano. Beethoven used it for his sonatas op. 101 and 106 (the latter is widely known as the Hammerklavier Sonata), probably for no other reason than to avoid the Italian word *pianoforte*.

Hammers, Pythagorean. See Pythagorean hammers.

Hammond organ. See under Electronic instruments II.

Handel Variations. Twenty variations (and a fugue) for piano by Brahms, op. 24 (1861), based on a theme by Handel (the "Air" from his harpsichord suite in B-flat). The fugue is based on a theme freely derived from the initial notes of the tune.

Hand horn. See under Horn II.

Hand organ. Term for two mechanical instruments similar in construction but different in purpose: the English barrel organ, formerly used in small churches, and the street organ of the Italian organ grinders.

Handstück [G.]. Late 18th-century name for an instructive piano piece.

Handtrommel [G.]. Tambourine.

Hänsel und Gretel. Opera in three acts by Humperdinck, produced in Weimar, 1893. The libretto, written by his sister, Adelheid Wette, is based on one of Grimm's *Fairy Tales*. Setting: the Harz Mountains, Germany. Although lacking in originality, the music provides a suitable background for the plot with its folklike simplicity and warmth of feeling.

Hardingfele, Hardanger fiddle. A Norwegian folk instrument shaped somewhat like the violin but slightly smaller and with a flatter bridge. [For ill. see under Violin.] It has four gut strings above four or five metal sympathetic strings in various tunings, such as a–d'–a'–e'' or a–e'–a'–c''♯ for the former, b–d'–e'–f'♯–a' or c'♯–d'–e'–f'♯–a' for the latter. The music is highly ornamented and generally is in two voice-parts in addition to the drone effect produced by the sympathetic strings. Dissonances of the second, augmented fourth, seventh, and ninth are common. The instrument probably was modeled after the ancient Norwegian *gigja* and *fidla* as well as the viola d'amore (probably brought from the British Isles). It is used to accompany folk dances such as the *halling, ganger,* and *springar*. See O. Gurvin, ed., ‡*Norsk folkemusikk*, 4 vols. (1958–63).

Harfe [G.]. Harp.

Harmonia. A Greek word, whose original meaning is "a fitting together," often implying the combination and unification of diverse elements (Plato). The Greeks used it for music in general, for scale formations (*harmoniae;* see Greece II), and for a well-ordered melody, but also in the sense of "harmony of the world" or "harmony of body and soul." In medieval treatises on music the term usually means "beautiful music" in a general sense, without specific reference to chords or simultaneous sounds. The definition given in the *Musica enchiriadis* ("Harmonia est diversarum vocum apta coadunatio"; *GS* i, 159a) is not found in the discussion of organum and therefore probably refers to monophonic music. It is quoted in Marchettus' *Lucidarium* (*GS* iii, 81a), which is devoted exclusively to plainsong. Walter Odington distinguished between an *armonica simplex* (plainsong), and an *armonica multiplex* (diaphony; *CS* i, 212b). The meaning harmonia = harmony appears clearly in Gafurius' *Practica Musice* (1496), where *harmonia* is said to consist of a high, a low, and a middle sound (*conficitur ex acuto gravi et medio*).

Harmoniae. See under Greece II.

Harmonic. See under Acoustics IV; Harmonics.

Harmonica. (1) The *glass harmonica. (2) The mouth harmonica or mouth organ [F. *harmonica à bouche;* G. *Mundharmonika;* It. *armonica a bocca;* Sp. *armónica*]. A popular instrument that consists of a small, flat metal box with slitlike openings on one of its long sides. Each slit leads to a pair of reeds of the same pitch inside the box, one of which works by means of pressure and the other by means of suction. The player places the instrument against his lips and, moving it back and forth according to the notes desired, blows into or inhales against the slits. For ill. see under Wind instruments. Many harmonica bands have been formed in the United States and elsewhere, and some players have achieved a remarkable degree of virtuosity. One modern form of the instrument was invented by F. Buschmann in 1821 [see *SaHMI*, p. 406]. Sir Charles Wheatstone is also mentioned as the inventor (his was called Aeolina, 1829; see *GDB* v, 919). (3) In French and German the name is also used for a variety of instruments of the xylophone type, i.e., consisting of tuned strips of wood (*harmonica de bois, Holzharmonika*), steel (*harmonica à lames d'acier, Stahlharmonika,* i.e., **glockenspiel*), stone (*harmonica à lames de pierre,* e.g., the Chinese *bianchinq*), etc. The *Ziehharmonika* [G.] is the accordion.

Harmonic analysis. I. *General.* Harmonic analysis is the study of the individual chords or harmonies in a piece of music, together with their use in succession to form larger units of phrases, periods, sections, or whole compositions. It is applicable to all Western music that has a harmonic aspect. Although such study is necessary to understand music of other periods, it is particularly applicable to the tonal music of the 18th and 19th centuries; in this area it still forms the initial basis of training for the young musician.

II. *Triads.* The basis of tonal harmony is the triad. Each of the seven degrees of the major and minor scale can serve as the **root* of a **triad*. The triads on the "tonal" degrees of the scale, I, IV and V, are the most important for establishing the tonality of a piece, and occur more frequently than those on the "modal" degrees, II, III, and VI. The triad on VII tends to be used least of all. The four kinds of triad (major, minor, diminished, augmented) possible in the major and minor mode are illustrated in Ex. 1.

Besides the practice of exchange of chords from one mode to the other, which in itself makes the two modes practically identical, certain other changes have come into use that further color, and therefore confuse, the two modes; in the late 19th century practically any note of any chord could be sharped or flatted,

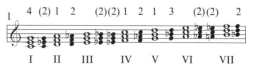

Chords written in white notes are used in the major key; those in black notes are used in the minor key, with the following exceptions: those marked 1 are common to both modes; those marked 2 are often borrowed from the minor mode to be used in the major; that marked 3 is used only under certain circumstances even in the minor; that marked 4 is sometimes used as a final chord in pieces in the minor, in which case the chord is said to have a Picardy third; and those marked (2), which can be borrowed from the minor for use in the major, were mostly so used in the 19th century.

and if this were done judiciously the feeling of a central tonality could still be preserved, although it might not be possible to determine whether the resulting tonality was major or minor.

III. *Seventh and ninth chords.* Besides the triads illustrated above, music of the 18th and 19th centuries makes much use of seventh chords. These chords are triads with still another diatonic third superposed. Ninth chords, used more commonly in the 19th century than previously, are seventh chords with yet another diatonic third superposed. Seventh chords and ninth chords are designated by adding the Arabic figure 7 or 9 to the Roman numeral indicating the root, thus: I^7, I^9. The symbol I^9_7 means a tonic ninth chord with the seventh degree flatted. [See Ex. 2.] For more details see Seventh chord; Ninth chord.

IV. *Root position and inversion.* When any chord built of superposed thirds stands in its original position it is said to be in root position, since the note on which the structure is built, the **root*, lies in the bass or lowest part. Thus a chord built on C, whether it be a triad, a seventh, a ninth chord, or even greater, is in root position so long as C remains in the bass, no matter how the notes above are arranged or how many notes there are in the chord. All the chords in Ex. 1 and Ex. 2 are in root position.

If the third of the chord, E in the examples above, lies in the bass, the chord is said to be in first inversion; if the fifth, G in the examples above, is in the bass, the chord is in second inversion; and if the seventh is in the bass, it is in third inversion. In harmonic analysis the Arabic figures indicate the characteristic intervals between the lowest note (bass note, not the root) and those above it. Thus, the designation for the first inversion, known as sixth chord, is I^6 (properly I_3^6) and for the second inversion, known as six-four chord, I_4^6; similar symbols are used for the inversion of the seventh chord [Ex. 3]. See Inversion; Sixth chord; Six-four chord; Seventh chord.

V. *Altered chords.* These are chords in which one or more notes are chromatically altered by accidentals foreign to the key. (The sharping of a note often serves to give that note a tendency to rise; the flatting of a note tends to make it descend.) The mutual borrowing of chords between the major and minor modes cannot rightly be said to involve alteration (see Ex. 1); nor does the formation of *secondary dominants constitute alteration, but rather momentary borrowing.

The most common altered chords with their usual resolutions are illustrated in Ex. 4. They are: (a) the Neapolitan sixth, built on II; (b) the augmented sixths, built on II and IV; (c) altered II and VI. For purposes of illustration each is reckoned in the key of C.

VI. *Modulation.* Modulation, one of the most valuable devices in tonal music, is accomplished by means of pivot chords. The C-major triad, for instance, is not only I in the key of C major, but also IV in G, V in F, III in A minor, VI in

E minor, the Neapolitan II in B, and VII in D minor. Treated as a secondary dominant, its functions are wider yet, since it can be considered V of III in D minor, V of III in D-flat, V of V in B-flat, and so on. The diminished seventh and the augmented sixth chords are also valuable as pivots since enharmonically each can be found in a variety of keys. These pivot chords serve as connections or hinges between different keys, and it is by means of them that modulation is effected. See Modulation.

VII. *Nonharmonic tones.* These are tones dissonant to the harmonies with which or after which they are sounded; they usually serve the purpose of providing smoothness of melodic flow and embellishment as well as color. They are of two main types, accented and unaccented. The unaccented nonharmonic tones include (1) passing tones, (2) auxiliary tones, (3) anticipations, (4) échappées, and (5) cambiatas, while the accented ones are (6) appoggiaturas and (7) suspensions, although the last has no rhythmic accent on the note itself at the moment it causes dissonance. All the nonharmonic tones may be found either ascending or descending, and in any voice part. See Nonharmonic tones.

VIII. *Harmonic rhythm.* Harmonic rhythm is the rate of speed with which harmonies change in the course of a phrase or series of phrases. In some phrases the harmonies change more quickly than in others, and certain parts of single phrases likewise have faster-moving harmonies than other parts. The tendency in single phrases is to have faster harmonic change in the latter part than in the first, but this depends on the structure of the piece as a whole and the effect the composer wishes to convey. See Harmonic rhythm.

See also Harmony; Functional harmony; Texture; Dualism.

Lit. (attempt at a selection from hundreds of texts): W. Piston, *Harmony,* rev. ed. [1962]; *id., Principles of Harmonic Analysis* (1933); P. Hindemith, *A Concentrated Course in Traditional Harmony* [1943]; R. Sessions, *Harmonic Practice* [1951]; A. Schoenberg, *Structural Functions of Harmony* [1954]; H. A. Murphy and E. J. Stringham, *Creative Harmony* (1951); W. J. Mitchell, *Elementary Harmony,* rev. ed. (1948); A. Forte, *Tonal Harmony in Concept and Practice* [1962]; H. Tischler, *Practical Harmony* (1964); S. Levarie, *Fundamentals of Harmony,* rev. ed. [1962]; N. Rimsky-Korsakov, *Practical Manual of Harmony* (1930); H. A. Miller, *New Harmonic Devices* [1930]; R. Lenormand, *A Study of*

Modern Harmony (1915); A. F. Barnes, *Practice in Modern Harmony* [1937]; C. Koechlin, *Traité de la harmonie,* 3 vols. [1928–30]. For historical studies, see under Harmony.   A.T.M.

Harmonic inversion. See under Inversion (1).

Harmonic mean. See Arithmetic and harmonic mean.

Harmonic minor (scale). See Major, minor.

Harmonice musices odhecaton. See Odhecaton.

Harmonic rhythm. The rhythmic pattern provided by the changes in harmony. The pattern of the harmonic rhythm of a given piece of music, found by noting the root changes as they occur, reveals important and distinctive features of style and texture. For example, there may be no change of harmony over several measures of music, as in the opening of Beethoven's Ninth Symphony. A contrast to this is a rapid succession of root changes, a different chord appearing with each note of the melody, as in Ex. 1 (Chopin, Mazurka op. 59, no. 2). Between these extremes all variations can be found. In general, contrapuntal music uses fewer chord changes than do other types.

The pattern of harmonic changes is made up of strong and weak rhythmic quantities. Certain root progressions, such as II to V, are regarded as strong progressions, that is, having the rhythmic effect of weak to strong. Others, like III to V, are weak progressions, with strong to weak, or even static rhythm [Ex. 2]. Usually, however, a pattern contains several root progressions, so that evaluating their comparative rhythmic values involves consideration of other factors. The most important influence on the rhythmic

stress is the element of time. Long time values are generally accepted as being heavy, or strong, in comparison with shorter values [Ex. 3]. A dissonant chord with its resolution may constitute either a weak or a strong progression [Ex. 4]. Dynamic indications usually underline the natural rhythm of the music but are sometimes used by composers in a contrary sense, to give an accent where one would not normally occur.

The strong beats of the harmonic rhythm are commonly in agreement with the first beats of the measures, thus coinciding with what one feels to be the pulse of the music, although this is by no means always the case. The pattern of harmonic changes may be quite independent of the meter and of the various melodic rhythms for which it forms the background. Ex. 5 (Beethoven, Sonata op. 31, no.3) serves as an illustration. In this example it should be noted that the harmonic rhythm, while it is the product of the combination of the melodic lines, is unlike any one of the melodic rhythm patterns and does not agree with the regularity of the meter.

The resource of harmonic rhythm has been largely abandoned by some 20th-century composers who have been inclined toward purely contrapuntal music. This accounts for a certain static quality in some modern music. Increased

melodic and contrapuntal rhythmic complexity and the use of irregular and changing meters are in some instances a compensation for the loss in rhythmic interest and vitality due to the absence of harmonic rhythm. See Harmonic analysis VIII.   W.P.

Harmonics. The term is used with two different though related meanings: (a) a general acoustical phenomenon [see Acoustics IV]; (b) its application to stringed instruments.

The harmonics of the violin (and other stringed instruments), sometimes called flageolet tones [G. *Flageolett-Töne;* F. *sons harmoniques*], are high tones of a flutelike timbre that are produced by lightly touching the string at one of its nodes (exact fractional points) instead of pressing it down as in ordinary stopping. Touching a string lightly at its half-way point will produce a harmonic an octave higher than the open string. Ex. 1 shows the vibration of (a) an open string, (b) a stopped string, and (c) a lightly

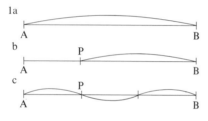

touched string. If the open string sounds g, stopping at P, in our example at one-third of the entire length, produces the fifth d' (vibrating length ⅔), while light touch will produce the harmonic d" (vibrating length ⅓). The formula for the determination of the harmonics is $\frac{1}{h} = 1 - \frac{1}{t}$, h and t being the relative frequencies of the harmonic and the normal tone produced at the same point. For instance, in determining the harmonic obtained by lightly touching the c of the g-string, t is ⅘ (relative frequency of the fourth; see Intervals, calculation of); therefore, $\frac{1}{h} = 1 - \frac{3}{4} = \frac{1}{4}$, and $h = 4$, i.e., the frequency of the second octave; hence, the harmonic is g". In Ex. 2 the lozenges indicate, as customary, the point of touch, and the black notes the pitch of the resulting harmonic. The practical results do not always agree with the theory. For example, if the g-string is touched at e, the harmonic b' is less likely to be heard than its first overtone, b".

Stopping and light touch can be used simultaneously. The tones thus obtained are called "artificial harmonics," the others "natural harmonics." In compositions for violin (or cello), the latter are indicated by a small circle placed over the desired tone, while for the artificial harmonics the method shown in Ex. 3 is used, where the position of the fingers as well as the resultant tones are indicated.

The introduction of harmonics has been variously ascribed to Domenico Ferrari (1722–80), a pupil of Tartini, and to Jean de Mondonville (1711–72). The latter seems to have made the first practical application of harmonics in his six sonatas, *Les Sons harmoniques,* op. 4 [*c.* 1735]. See also Chyn; Tromba marina; Harp I. See W. Kirkendale, "Segreto comunicato da Paganini" (*JAMS* xviii).

Harmonic (minor) scale. See under Major, minor; Scale I.

Harmonic series. The series of the acoustical harmonics [see Acoustics IV].

Harmonie [F., G.]. Harmony. In French usage the term also means the wind section of the orchestra, or a special wind band. *Cor d'harmonie,* French horn.

Harmonie der Welt [G., Harmony of the World]. (1) A symphony by Hindemith, composed in 1951. As in the case of **Mathis der Maler,* the three movements were derived from the composer's opera of the same title before the opera was finished and performed. The titles of the movements are "Musica Instrumentalis," "Musica Humana," and "Musica Mundana." (2) Opera in five acts by Hindemith (to his own libretto), produced in Munich, 1957. Setting: Central Europe, between 1608 and 1630.

Harmonika [G.]. Either the *Mundharmonika,* mouth harmonica [see Harmonica (2)], or the *Ziehharmonika,* i.e., *accordion. B. Franklin's harmonica is called *Glasharmonika.* See also Harmonica (3).

Harmonious Blacksmith. Air with variations from Handel's Harpsichord Suite No. 5, in E

(1720). There is no plausible explanation for the name, which is spurious.

Harmonium. I. A keyboard instrument that sounds by means of thin metal tongues being set in vibration by a steady current of air, which is provided by a pair of pedal-operated bellows. The metal tongues act as free reeds [see Reed]. The harmonium was long considered a popular substitute for the organ, which it resembles in some features, e.g., the wind supply, keyboard, *ad libitum* sustained tones, and stops that provide a variety of timbre. Properly used, however, the modern harmonium is an instrument in its own right. It can produce "expressive" gradations of sound by means of the expression stop, which puts the pressure in the bellows under direct control of the player's feet. This device, though unsuitable for the works of Bach, lends itself well to rendering many organ compositions of the 19th century (Mendelssohn, Schumann, Liszt, Reger) as well as pieces written especially for the harmonium (Karg-Elert, Dvořák, Reger, César Franck).

II. The harmonium was developed in the 19th century from Grenié's *orgue expressif* (1810) and a number of more or less experimental instruments (Organo-violine, *c.* 1814; Aeoline, *c.* 1818; Physharmonica, 1818; Aeolodicon, *c.* 1820; Aérophone, *c.* 1829; Séraphine, 1834; Mélophone, 1837; and many others) to the first real harmonium (A. Debain, 1840), which combined numerous useful devices found separately in the earlier instruments. Important improvements made afterward are: the *percussion* (small hammers like those of the piano, acting upon the tongues and causing a quicker and more precise "start" of the sound); the *prolongement,* by which single tones can be automatically prolonged (pedal points); the *melody attachment,* which puts the highest notes in relief over the others; the *pedal substitute,* by which the lowest note of a chord can be made to stand out; the *double touch* (1855), which permits a certain gradation of sound by a slighter or greater depression of the key; and the *expression* (invented by Mustel, 1854), by which the volume of sound is controlled directly by the player's feet—a delicate device that calls for considerable skill to operate. The *Mustel organ* is very popular in France and England.

III. An important variety of harmonium is the *American organ,* in which the wind is not forced out through the reeds by compression but is drawn in by evacuation of the air in the bellows. The reeds of this instrument are smaller and more curved than those of the harmonium. All these devices produce a softer, more organ like tone that lacks, however, the expressive quality of the harmonium. Modern instruments have an electric wind supply, leaving the feet of the player free to operate a pedal-keyboard like that of the organ. The principle of the American organ was invented about 1835 by a workman in the harmonium factory of J. Alexandre, Paris, who subsequently emigrated to America. Here his ideas were put into practical form by Estey of Brattleboro, Vt. (*Estey organ,* 1856), and by Mason and Hamlin of Boston (1861). For a 16th-century type of harmonium, see Regal.

Lit.: A. Mustel, *L'Orgue expressif ou l'harmonium,* 2 vols. (1903); *LavE* ii.2, 1375ff; L. Hartmann, *Das Harmonium* (1913; bibl.).

Harmony. The chordal (or vertical) structure of a musical composition, in contrast to counterpoint, i.e., the melodic (or horizontal) structure [see Texture]. The principles of harmony predominant in the 18th and 19th centuries are explained under Harmonic analysis. In this article the subject is treated historically.

I. Harmony came to be appreciated considerably later than counterpoint. Although even in the early days of counterpoint (9th–12th centuries; see Organum) it was apparent that certain intervals sounded better simultaneously than others and although the ensuing progress of counterpoint necessarily entailed an increased consideration of harmony, it was not until the mid-16th century that musicians began to think of harmonies as a primary building material of music. In fact, it was not until the early 18th century that Rameau (1722), Fux (1725), and others formally recognized them as structural and compositional elements. This late recognition is all the more striking in view of the extensive use of simple chordal progressions in various periods of early music history [see Familiar style] and, particularly, in view of the 17th-century practice of *thoroughbass, which is essentially harmonic in nature. Actually, the recognition of the harmonies as building elements depended on another concept that did not evolve until after 1650, namely, *tonality, which superseded polyphonic modality and made possible an over-all conception of a piece of music from the harmonic point of view. Only when tonality was firmly established could the relative importance of chords built on the different degrees of the scale be determined in relation to a key center or tonic; only when this was accomplished could a logical departure from this tonic into other keys and return from those keys to it—modulation—be achieved.

When chords came to be conceived as entities it became possible to enlarge the small chords, such as the triad with its inversions, to bigger ones with three or more thirds (seventh chords; ninth chords). For the sake of color, moreover, it was possible to raise or lower the various notes of these chords without allowing them to lose their identity and their relationship with the central tonic. From the beginning of the 18th century on, the beauty of melodic lines depended largely on the effective arrangement of the harmonies underlying them.

But the very concept of tonality contained the seeds of its own weakening. In time, with the increasing boldness of composers in modulating to ever more distant keys and in coloring, or altering, the notes of their chords more and more, the strength of the single tonal center became diluted. In addition, the 19th-century composers tended increasingly to fuse the major and minor modes, using chords typical of one mode in the other (Schubert), and to avoid strong tonal cadences and to substitute for them all kinds of deceptive cadences that in turn veiled contours of phrases (Liszt and Wagner), giving their music a far less definite feeling of tonality than the compositions of the 18th century possessed. Another practice undermining the strength of classical tonality was the use by certain late 19th-century nationalist composers of a preponderance of modal degrees of the scale in the harmonization of the folk or folklike melodies in their compositions (Dvořák, Mussorgsky). This, with its logical complement of writing consecutively a number of chords on adjacent scale degrees (*parallel chords; Debussy), led harmony back in many respects to the paths it had followed in the period of modality. Some 20th-century composers have abandoned tonality altogether and once again depended on the conjunction of melodic lines to form their harmonies (*atonality; Schoenberg), while others retain only the triad as the basic chord with which phrases must begin and end, and allow varying combinations of notes to form the harmonies in the course of the phrases, so long as they are arranged logically in regard to increasing and decreasing dissonance as the phrase proceeds, an arrangement called "harmonic fluctuation" (Hindemith).

II. Regarding the triad as the most important

chord, harmonic music may be divided into three main periods: a central period in which the third (triad) is sovereign (period of tertian harmony, c. 1450–1900); an earlier period in which the potentialities of the triad have not yet been exploited (period of pre-tertian harmony, c. 900–1450); and a period in which, after the exhaustion of the triad, new combinations were sought after (period of post-tertian harmony, c. 1900—).

A. *Pre-tertian harmony* (900–1450).

(1) 900–1050: Parallel fourths or fifths; also unisons, seconds, and thirds at the beginning and end of phrases. See Organum, Ex. 1, 2.

(2) 1050–1200: Unisons, octaves, fifths, and fourths as chief consonances of two-part writing in contrary and in parallel motion, interspersed with seconds, thirds, and sevenths, hardly ever with sixths. See Organum, Ex. 3, 4.

(3) 1200–1300: Open triads (1–5–8), including those with a diminished fifth, as the main consonances in three-part writing; full triads (1–3–5) in weak positions, and occasionally also "dissonant concordances" such as 4–5 or 1–4–7 [see Counterpoint II]; harsh dissonances (consecutive seconds, etc.) freely admitted as passing notes. Ex. 1 (motet, c. 1250).

(4) 1300–1450: Open triads continue as the main harmony; full triads more frequent, also at the beginning and end of (inner) phrases; first appearance of the sixth chord, as single harmony (De Vitry, Machaut), successively in cadential motion (Landini), or as the prevailing harmony (in England, also Dufay, Binchois; see Sixthchord style). Frequent use of the *Lydian

cadence with a leading tone before the fifth and the octave. Dissonances between consonant "pillars" occur often in Machaut and even more in the works of late 14th-century French composers. See also Landini cadence; Ex. 2 (Machaut, "Plourez dames"); Ex. 3 (Landini, "El mio dolce sospir").

B. *Tertian harmony* (1450–1900).

(5) 1450–1600: Full triads and first inversions in four or more parts; dissonances used sparingly in an essentially panconsonant idiom; the roots of the triads moving preferably in modal sequence (I–II, I–III, I–VI) except at cadential points, where IV–I and V–I are commonly used. Ex. 4 (Ockeghem, the "Christe" of *Missa L'Homme armé*); Ex. 5 (Palestrina, "Adjuro vos").

(6) 1600–1750: Triads and seventh chords with all their inversions, in four parts or in free chordal style; increasing predominance of the first, fifth, and fourth degrees as the central chords (tonic, dominant, subdominant), leading to the establishment of the major and minor tonality in all the keys (*The Well-Tempered Clavier*, 1722) and to modest modulations; appearance of altered chords such as the diminished seventh and Neapolitan sixth; occasionally extensive use of chromatic progressions;

enharmonic change. Ex. 6 (M. Weckmann, Symphonia from the "Motetto concertato 'Weine nicht' "); Ex. 7 (J. S. Bach, Organ Fantasy and Fugue in G minor.)

(7) 1750–1825: Reduction of the harmonic vocabulary of the late baroque to its bare "essentials," the tonic, dominant, and subdominant, which are used functionally as the carriers of extended melodies and as the vehicle of development (*Mannheim school; Viennese classics). Distant modulations, with or without pivot chords. Ex. 8 (Schubert, Piano Sonata no. 13 in C minor).

(8) 1825–1900: The period of romantic harmony; fullest exploitation of the triadic system to its farthest limits; extensive use of chromatic alterations, of unprepared and—toward the end of the century—unresolved appoggiatura chords; free modulation into distant keys [see under I]. Gradual disintegration of tonality. Ex. 9 (Chopin, Nocturne no. 17); Ex. 10 (Wagner, *Tristan*).

C. *Post-tertian harmony.*

(9) 1900—: Deliberate violation of the harmonic system by the use of *parallel chords (Debussy), *fourth chords (Scriabin), etc., leading to the complete abandonment of harmonic

restrictions, i.e., *atonality (Schoenberg; *c.* 1910) and to a period of unlimited experimentation that produced frequently novel practices, frequently of a contrapuntal kind, such as *bitonality, *serial techniques, and *pandiatonicism. The recent development known as *musique concrète* indicates a trend toward methods of composition in which harmony no longer enters into consideration.

III. The theoretical treatment of harmony began with Zarlino's *Le Istitutioni harmoniche* of 1558. Zarlino was the first to analyze music on the basis of full chords ("corpo pieno di consonanze e di harmonie") instead of consonant intervals, which led him to recognize the basic importance of the major and minor triad [see Arithmetic and harmonic mean]. Rameau's main contribution was the recognition of sixth chords and six-four chords as *inversions of the triad, together with the seventh chord and its inversions. Gottfried Weber, in his *Versuch einer geordneten Theorie der Tonsetzkunst* (3 vols., 1817–21), seems to have been the first to use the present-day system of designating chords by Roman numerals, with traditional figured-bass symbols to indicate inversions.

Lit.: R. F. Goldman, *Harmony in Western Music* [1965]; C. Macpherson, *A Short History of Harmony* (1917); H. Schenker, *Harmony*, ed. O. Jonas [1954]; M. Shirlaw, *The Theory of Harmony . . . from Rameau to the Present Day* [n.d.]; L. Ratner, *Harmony: Structure and Style* [1962]; E. A. Lippman, "Hellenic Conceptions of Harmony" (*JAMS* xvi); A. Hughes, "The Origins of Harmony, with Special Reference to an Old St. Andrews Ms." (*MQ* xxiv); G. Reany, "14th-Century Harmony and the Ballades, Rondeaux and Virelais of Guillaume de Machaut" (*MD* vii); B. Meier, "Die Harmonik im cantus firmushaltigen Satz des 15. Jahrhunderts" (*AMW* ix); H. Leichtentritt, "Harmonic Daring in the 16th Century" (*MM* v, no. 1); *id.*, "Handel's Harmonic Art" (*MQ* xxi); A. Liess, "L'Harmonie dans les oeuvres de Claude Debussy" (*RM* 1931, no. 111); G. Knosp, "Essai d'harmonie exotique" (*RMI* xxxviii, xxxix). See also under Harmonic analysis; Romanticism; Twentieth-century music.

Harmony of the spheres [G. *Sphärenharmonie*]. The Pythagorean concept of the cosmos as consisting of separate spheres, one each for the planets, moon, and sun, which move around the earth at different velocities, producing different sounds. Later the seven spheres (Moon, Mercury, Venus, Sun, Mars, Jupiter, Saturn) were thought to produce the seven notes of the scale (Cicero and others). This concept persisted through the Middle Ages under the name *musica mundana* (music of the world): "The music of the world is that produced by the concordance of sounds caused by the motion of the heavenly bodies" (Boethius). A different interpretation of cosmic harmony was given by Johannes Kepler (1571–1630), who found that the aphelions and perihelions of the six planets (moving around the sun in elliptical orbits) are in the same ratios as the basic musical intervals: $\frac{4}{5}$ (major third) for Saturn; $\frac{5}{6}$ (minor third) for Jupiter; $\frac{2}{3}$ (fifth) for Mars; $\frac{15}{16}$ (half-tone) for the earth; $\frac{24}{25}$ (*diesis*) for Venus; $\frac{5}{12}$ (octave plus minor third) for Mercury. See A. Moberg, in *Svensk Tidskrift for Musikforskning,* 1937; M. Schneider, in *AM* xxxii.

Harold en Italie [F., Harold in Italy]. A program symphony by Berlioz, op. 16, written in 1834 at the request of Paganini, who wanted a work that would feature an exceptional viola he had just acquired. The symphony, which has a prominent viola part, is in four movements, after portions from Byron's *Childe Harold:* (1) Harold aux Montagnes (Harold in the Mountains); (2) Marche de Pélerins (Pilgrims' March and Prayer); (3) Sérénade (Serenade of an Abruzzi Mountaineer to his Sweetheart); (4) Orgie de Brigands (Orgy of the Brigands).

Harp [F. *harpe;* G. *Harfe;* It., Sp. *arpa*]. Generic name for chordophones in which the plane of the strings is perpendicular to the soundboard (not parallel as in, e.g., the zither and piano); see Instruments IV, D. It is nearly always plucked.

1. *The double action harp.* The double action (or double pedal) harp used in modern orchestras was introduced about 1810 by Sébastien Érard. It has a large triangular frame that consists of an upright pillar, a hollow tapered back (with the soundboard), and a curved neck. The strings are attached to the neck and extend down to the soundboard. It has a range of six octaves and a fifth, with seven strings to the octave, tuned normally in the key of C^b major, i.e., from C_1^b to g''''^b. At the foot of the instrument are seven pedals, one controlling all the C-strings, one all the D-strings, etc. Each pedal can be depressed to two notches—"double action"—and each time the corresponding strings are shortened to sound one semitone higher than normally. Thus, the C-pedal in high position gives the tone C^b, in the first notch the tone C, and in

the second notch the tone C♯. With all the pedals in the first notch the tuning of the instrument is C major; with all in the second, C♯ major. Operation of single pedals makes all the major and minor keys available as well as altered chords so long as they do not involve "cross-relations," i.e., the simultaneous use of C♮ and C♯, or E♭ and E♮. Special effects can be obtained by enharmonic substitutions. For instance, the tuning c d♯ e♭ f♯ g♭ a b♯ c makes it possible to produce the diminished seventh chord c–e♭–f♯–a in a rapid glissando over all the strings. Of special charm are the harmonics of the harp, which are produced by resting part of the hand on the middle of the string while plucking with the thumb. The resulting tone is, of course, the higher octave of the normal tone, but with a different, mysterious timbre. Still another timbre can be obtained by plucking the strings close to the soundboard.

II. *The chromatic harp.* This harp was introduced in 1897 by the Parisian firm of Pleyel. It abandons the pedal mechanism entirely, substituting a string for each semitone of the octave. Despite certain advantages (there is no restriction with regard to the simultaneous use of natural and chromatic degrees, so that anything playable on the piano is playable on the chromatic harp) it has not been generally accepted and has only a small repertory of music.

III. *History.* Harps are among the oldest instruments. In *Mesopotamia they are documented as far back as *c.* 3000 B.C., and a great variety of forms existed there as well as in *Egypt. In spite of many Biblical references to King David's "playing the harp," it is not certain whether the Hebrews had a harp. King David's instrument, the *kinnor,* was not a harp but a lyre, similar perhaps to the Greek kithara [see *SaHMI,* p. 106f]. In Greece there were various types of harp, such as the *pektis* and the *magadis.*

In Europe, harps made their first appearance in Ireland, which still uses the Irish harp (*clarsech*) as its heraldic symbol. Whether the instruments represented on Irish stone crosses of the 9th and 10th centuries were harps or lyres is still a matter of controversy among scholars [see *SaHMI,* p. 262; N. Bessaraboff, *Ancient European Musical Instruments* (1941), p. 215; also p. 418, 460n, 461n. On the other hand, the ancient English *rotta* probably was a harp. In Wales harps (*telyn*) were known before A.D. 1000. In the 12th century the harp spread to the Continent, where it was held in high esteem by the troubadours, trouvères, and minnesingers. In

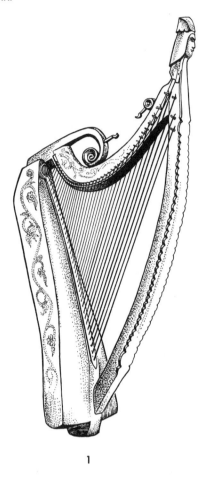

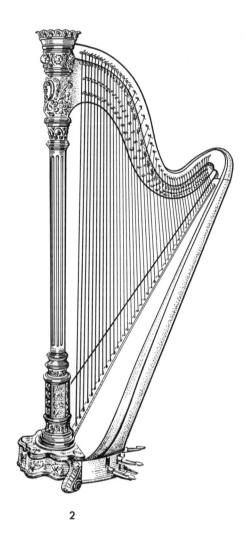

1

2

1. Irish harp. 2. Harp.

the 16th and 17th centuries harp playing was cultivated particularly in Spain and Italy. Harps of the late 17th century had hooklike gadgets in the neck whereby the pitch of the strings could be raised a semitone. In 1720 C. Hochbrucker introduced five pedals to operate the hooks, each pedal altering the tuning of a string and its octaves.

IV. *Repertory.* The earliest extant sources for harp music are the *Libro de cifra nueva* published by Venegas des Henestrosa (1557) and Antonio de Cabezón's *Obras de música* (1578). Both bear the remark "para tecla, harpa, y vihuela," indicating that the compositions (**tientos*, liturgical pieces, variations) could be played on keyboard instruments, harps, or lutes. Compositions written expressly for the harp are found among the keyboard works of the Neapolitan composers Trabaci and Mayone [see Neapolitan school II]. Mayone's *Secondo libro di diversi capricci* of 1609 contains a "Ricercar sopra il Canto Fermo di Costantio Festa, et per sonar all'Arpa" [see Spagna]; Trabaci's *Il Secondo Libro de Ricercate* of 1615 a "Toccata . . . per l'Arpa" and "Ancidetemi pur, Per l'Arpa." All these pieces show a high degree of virtuosity; probably they were written for Giovanni Leonardo dell'Arpa, who belonged to the group of musicians around Gesualdo. A much later and artistically rather inferior repertory of solo pieces for the harp begins with the compositions of J. B. Krumpholz (1745–90) and M.-M. de Marin (1769–1861). Harp virtuosos of the early 19th century, such as Martin-Pierre Dalvimare (1772–1839), Robert-Nicolas Bochsa (1789–1856), and Elias Parish-Alvars (1808–49), obligingly tendered to the demands of the harp-playing ladies in the salons of Paris and London. It was not until the end of the 19th century that music of artistic merit was written for the harp, mainly by French composers such as Saint-Saëns (*Fantaisie* for violin and harp), Debussy (Sonata for flute, viola, and harp), Ravel (*Introduction et Allegro* for harp, string quartet, flute, clarinet), Roussel (Serenade for flute, violin, viola, cello, and harp), Florent Schmitt (*Andante et Scherzo* for harp and string quartet), and Ingelbrecht (Sonatina for flute and harp; Quintet for strings and harp). Other chamber works calling for the harp are by D. G. Mason (3 pieces for flute, harp, string quartet), Bax (Sonata for viola and harp), and Carlos Salzedo.

The harp was occasionally used in Italian opera of the early 17th century (Monteverdi, *Orfeo,* 1607; see Orchestration II, Orchestra II),

and then almost disappeared from the orchestra. Occasionally it was employed for the rendition of thoroughbass. Handel and Gluck used it a few times, the former in *Esther* (1720), the latter in *Orfeo* (1762). Mozart wrote a Concerto for flute and harp (K. 299) and Beethoven used the harp in *Prometheus.* Berlioz, Liszt, Wagner, and most later composers included the harp in their orchestral scores, and composers such as Debussy and Ravel used it prominently as a vehicle of impressionist coloring, often writing parts for two harps.

Lit.: M. L. Tournier, *The Harp* [1959]; R. Rensch, *The Harp* [1950]; C. Salzedo, *Modern Study of the Harp* (1921); A. N. Schirinzi, *L'Arpa* [1961]; H. J. Zingel, *Harfe und Harfenspiel vom Beginn des 16. bis ins zweite Drittel des 18. Jahrhunderts* (1932); *LavE* ii.3, 1892–1971; A. Kastner, "The Harp as a Solo Instrument and in the Orchestra" (*PMA* xxxv); *id.,* "The Use of the Modern Harp" (*ZIM* xiii); F. W. Galpin, "The Sumerian Harp of Ur, *c.* 3500 B.C." (*ML* x, 108ff); *id.,* "The Origin of the Clarsech or Irish Harp" (*CP 1911,* p. 317); M. S. Kastner, in *CP Jeppesen* (17th-cent. Spain); H. Hickmann, "Das Harfenspiel im alten Ägypten" (*MF* v); *id.,* in *CP 1952,* pp. 233ff; H. Panum, "Harfe und Lyra im alten Nordeuropa" (*SIM* vii); H. J. Zingel, in *MF* ii, *AM* vii, *AMF* ii, *ZMW* xvii; J. Rimmer, in *PMA* xc (baroque), *GSJ* xvii (Irish), *GSJ* xviii (triple harp).   I-II by W.D.D.

Harpa [It.]. *Harp.

Harp lute. (1) An early 19th-century instrument combining features of the guitar (rather than the lute) and harp. It looks like a guitar that, instead of the neck, has a harplike structure attached to the top of the body, thus providing space for a greater number of strings. Similar constructions were the *Dital harp* and *Harp-lute guitar.* See ill. in *GD* ii, opp. 70, 542; *GDB* viii, opp. 146, iv, opp. 90. (2) Name for a small harp built by Pleyel in the early 20th century and used by De Falla in his *El Retablo de Maese Pedro.*

Harp Quartet. Popular name for Beethoven's Quartet in E-flat op. 74, so called on account of some pizzicato arpeggios in the first movement.

Harpsichord [F. *clavecin;* G. *Cembalo (Clavicimbel, Kielflügel);* It. *clavicembalo;* Sp. *clávicémbalo*]. I. A stringed keyboard instrument in use from the 16th through 18th centuries and similar in shape to the modern grand piano, the strings being roughly parallel to the long side of the case. Each string was plucked by a plectrum of crow quill mounted in the pivoted tongue of a fork-shaped jack, which stood on the rear end of the key lever. Depressing the key raised the jack until the horizontally projecting plectrum plucked the string. Upon release of the key, the jack fell back until the underside of the plectrum touched the string, causing the tongue to rotate on its pivot. As the jack continued to fall the plectrum was tilted upward and back until its point passed below the string. A string of boar's bristle mounted at the rear of the jack then returned the tongue to its original position so that the jack was again ready to pluck. A damper made of woven woolen cloth was inserted into a slot sawed in one tine of the forked jack, its bottom edge just above the level of the plectrum. When the key was at rest the damper touched the string, but the slightest depression of the key raised the damper, leaving the string free to vibrate. Thus the string of the harpsichord, like the pipe of an organ, could continue sounding only so long as the player held a key down.

Each rank of jacks was carried in a pair of mortised battens mounted vertically over one another. The lower batten (lower guide) was fixed, but the upper batten (slide or register) was movable, usually by means of hand stops. Thus each rank of jacks could be moved slightly toward or away from its choir of strings, engaging or disengaging the plectra. In this way "stops" or ranks of jacks could be silenced or added to the ensemble.

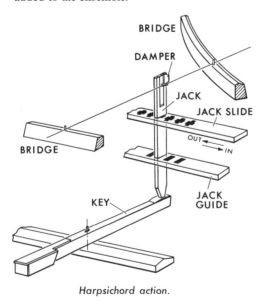

Harpsichord action.

The typical 18th-century harpsichord had three choirs of strings, two of which were tuned to 8' pitch and one an octave higher at 4' pitch [see Foot]. (Very rarely a fourth choir at 16' pitch might be added.) Such a harpsichord would ordinarily have three ranks of jacks, one for each choir. Frequently there were two keyboards, the upper of which might have only one 8' stop. The lower manual usually sounded the other 8' stop and the 4' stop. The upper manual normally could be coupled to the lower, making all three stops available from the lower keyboard.

The choirs of strings were used singly or in various combinations to provide variations in loudness and timbre, much as the stops of the organ are employed. The more nasal sound of a string plucked near one end is noticeable in the upper manual (front) 8' stop of the typical harpsichord as compared to the darker, more center-plucked sound of the lower manual 8'. Sometimes a special rank of jacks was provided to pluck the upper manual choir of 8' strings at its extreme end to produce an even more nasal timbre (lute stop). Buff leather pads were used to partially damp one choir of strings, giving a harplike effect (buff stop).

Many modern harpsichords do not resemble their antique prototypes in the most essential details. Especially during the first years of the 20th-century revival of the harpsichord, there was a tendency to employ concepts of design and aesthetic more germane to the piano or organ than to the harpsichord. The ability of the harpsichord to vary its timbre has been exploited more than in earlier centuries, and for many years nearly all harpsichords seen in concert halls had several pedals provided to change the stops. Recently, however, several players of the first rank have returned to hand stops. The 16' stop for a time was almost universally fitted to concert instruments despite the fact that in early times it was found only in Germany during the 18th century, and even there only rarely. Most of these modern instruments were constructed far more heavily than the early instruments, with longer treble strings and shorter bass strings, often overspun in the manner of the bass strings of the piano. Plectra were of leather instead of the quill almost invariably found in early times. All of these changes tended to produce a more sustained but weaker tone of less harmonic complexity than that typical of antique instruments.

Since about 1950 many makers in several countries have returned to the early principles, and harpsichords are now being made that not only closely resemble those for which the keyboard music of the Renaissance and baroque was composed, but which to their enthusiasts seem to have solved many of the performance problems that seemed insurmountable to harpsichordists of the first half of the century. At present the field is still being contested by the proponents of the modern and antique styles of instrument.

Throughout the baroque period the harpsichord was the chief instrument for the realization of *thoroughbass accompaniment, always in chamber music and occasionally (in place of the organ) in church music. Its ability to blend with other instruments while providing a slight impulse at the moment of ictus makes it unsurpassed for this purpose. Although the harpsichord cannot produce a gradation of sound by lighter or stronger touch, this limitation is not felt in the context of baroque style. For contrapuntal music it is definitely superior to the piano, since the middle and lower parts of a composition stand out with amazing clarity.

II. *History.* The earliest records of what may have been a harpsichord-like instrument date from the 14th century, when sources in England, France, Spain, and Burgundy mention an *echiquier that was described in 1387 as "an instrument like an organ which sounds by means of strings." A drawing of the harpsichord in plan view and several suggested mechanisms for jacks with a discussion of their operation is contained in the mid-15th-century manuscript of Henri Arnaut de Zwolle, a member of the retinue of the Duke of Burgundy. Other early representations are French, German, and English in origin [see *SaHMI,* pp. 334–43, for a discussion of the early history of the harpsichord]. One of the earliest of all detailed treatments of the harpsichord is preserved in S. Virdung's *Musica getutscht* of 1511. Virdung provides extremely crude illustrations of what he calls a virginal, clavicimbalum, and claviciterium. The distinction between the first two is not clear since both appear to have been small rectangular instruments. The claviciterium was a small upright harpsichord looking very much like the small portative organs of the period.

Although nearly all of the early written descriptions of the harpsichord were made north of the Alps, the oldest extant instruments are Italian. Boalch has provided the names of several 15th-century Italian makers who were active as early as 1419, but the oldest harpsichord to have survived was made in Rome in 1521. Italian harpsichords from this date until late in the 18th century generally resembled this instrument very closely. Their construction was very light, of unfinished cypress ornamented by elegant moldings. The elongated and deeply incurved harpsichords were enclosed in outer boxes ornamented according to the prevailing fashion. Usually there were two 8' stops and a single manual of four octaves, range C–c''', with a *short octave in the bass. The lack of development of the Italian type of harpsichord can perhaps be explained by the Italian emphasis on its role as a continuo instrument in the baroque. The transparent but rhythmically emphatic tone of the Italian instrument could hardly be improved upon for that purpose.

The demands of the solo keyboard literature developing north of the Alps produced a much more elaborate instrument. The earliest extant northern instruments were made in Antwerp toward the end of the 16th century, especially by the Ruckers family. Much heavier in construction than the Italian instruments, with painted exteriors and interiors covered with block-printed paper, this Flemish type influenced all subsequent schools of harpsichord-making north of the Alps. At first single manual instruments C–c''' (short octave) with two stops, $1 \times 8'$, $1 \times 4'$, the Flemish harpsichords later are found with $2 \times 8'$ and occasionally $2 \times 8'$, $1 \times 4'$. About the middle of the 17th century a second manual was first fitted for expressive purposes (originally it was used merely as a transposing device), probably developed by French makers. Flemish harpsichords were imitated and rebuilt throughout the 18th century in Germany, England, and especially France. During the 18th century each of these countries developed a characteristic national style that nevertheless owed a great deal to the Antwerp makers of the previous centuries.

Between 1500 and 1800 there were a variety of shapes and constructions under names that cannot always be identified with a given type. There were instruments in the shape of a long wing called harpsichord, clavicembalo, clavecin, Flügel, virginal, épinette; a rectangular box— virginal, Instrument, spinetta; an upright wing —clavicytherium; and a short wing extending diagonally—spinet, épinette à l'Italienne [ill. in *GD* i, opp. 664; ii, opp. 546; v, opp. 552; *GBD* iv, opp. 96, 102]. See Arcicembalo; Arpicordo; Clavicytherium; Spinet; Virginal; also under Pedal piano.

In the late 18th century the harpsichord was gradually displaced by the piano. It is interesting to note that the original editions of almost all the Beethoven sonatas up to op. 27 bear the inscription: "Pour le Clavecin ou Pianoforte." This does not mean that such essentially pianistic works were composed for the harpsichord, but it does show that harpsichords were still widely in use about 1800 and that the publishers (who in all probability were chiefly responsible for such inscriptions) were anxious to accommodate the players and owners of the old instrument as well as those of the newer one.

Lit.: F. Hubbard, *Three Centuries of Harpsichord Making* (1965); R. Russell, *The Harpsichord and Clavichord* (1959); D. A. Boalch, *Makers of the Harpsichord and Clavichord, 1440 to 1840* (1956); E. Harich-Schneider, *The Harpsichord: An Introduction to Technique, Style and the Historical Sources* [1954]; H. Neupert, *Harpsichord Manual* (1960). See also under Keyboard Instruments.   F.H.

Harpsichord music. Throughout the 16th and 17th centuries it is difficult to draw clear lines of demarcation among compositions for the organ, harpsichord, and clavichord. See the explanations under Keyboard music.

I. *Renaissance* (to 1600). Practically all keyboard music written prior to 1500 is organ music. Clearly secular compositions, such as the numerous intabulations of Italian, French, or German songs in the Codex Faenza and the Buxheim Organ Book, could *a priori* be claimed for the harpsichord, but it is more than doubtful whether this instrument was generally known in Italy about 1400 (Codex Faenza) or in Germany about 1470 (Buxheim Organ Book). In the 16th century we find a large repertory of keyboard dances, and these may well be considered the beginning of the literature for the stringed instruments, primarily the harpsichord. The earliest examples are in the MS book of Hans Kotter (*c.* 1515), in P. Attaingnant's *Quatorze Gaillards* (1529), and in an English MS of *c.* 1525 [see Dump; Hornpipe]. Some of them also show traces of an idiomatic harpsichord style, such as quick tone repetition and "percussive" chords [see Ex., from Hans Weck's *Spanyöler Tancz; HAM,* no. 102]. Similar elements occur in the dances found in the *Intabolatura nova di varie sorte di balli* of 1551 and in the late 16th-century books of the German *colorists. Dances and variations figure prominently in the repertory of the English virginalists, who were the first to develop an idiomatic harpsichord style based on

quick "pianistic" figurations (broken-chord passages, parallel thirds, quick scales, etc.). See also *Basse danse; Passamezzo;* Pavane; Variations IV (1).

II. *Baroque* (1600–1750). As in the preceding period, the harpsichord literature consists mainly of dances, now arranged in suites, and of variations. Gradually certain types of organ music, such as the toccata and the fugal forms (ricercar, canzona, capriccio, fugue), took on stylistic features that made them suitable for stringed keyboard instruments as well. In Italy we find, about 1600, a school of composers working in Naples [see Neapolitan school II] who were the first to prefer the harpsichord to the organ. A. Valente published, in 1576, an *Intavolatura de cimbalo,* and G. M. Trabaci said, in his publication of 1615, that "the harpsichord is the sovereign of all the instruments in the world, and upon it all music can be played easily" [see W. Apel, in *MQ* xxiv, 425]. These Neapolitan masters represent the transition to Frescobaldi (1583–1643), whose numerous partitas (variations) could well be claimed for the harpsichord although, like Sweelinck's variations, they also belong to the literature for the organ. Frescobaldi abandoned the strictly contrapuntal texture of the earlier period for a freer and more idiomatic keyboard style in which the voices are allowed to come and go freely [see *Freistimmigkeit*]. His pupil Froberger (1616–67) went even further in this direction, being influenced by the free style of French lute music (Denis Gaultier). Johann Caspar Kerll (1627–93), Alessandro Poglietti (d. 1683), and Johann Kuhnau (1660–1722) contributed some amusing program pieces, the last-named particularly known for his *Musikalische Vorstellung einiger Biblischen Historien* (1700) and his attempts to transfer the trio sonata to the harpsichord (*Clavier-Übung* ii, 1692). A large repertory of preludes, fugues, suites, toccatas, etc., was created by numerous 17th-century German composers mentioned under Organ music II. Bach's compositions for the harpsichord include such immortal works as the Inventions, *Well-Tempered Clavier,* English and French Suites, Partitas, Chromatic Fantasy and Fugue, Italian Concerto, French Overture, and Goldberg Variations.

An important school of harpsichord composers (clavecinists) existed in France, from Chambonnières (c. 1602–72) to Rameau (1683–1764) [see France III]. François Couperin (1668–1733) created the *character piece, a genre that Rameau endowed with traits of ingenious characterization. In England Henry Purcell (c. 1659–95) and Handel (1685–1759) made important contributions, mainly to the suite. In Italy the toccata took on features of a somewhat superficial virtuosity with Bernardo Pasquini (1637–1710) and Alessandro Scarlatti (1660–1725), while Domenico Zipoli (1688–1726) pursued a more serious line in his toccatas, fugues, and suites. The greatest Italian keyboard composer of this period was Domenico Scarlatti (1685–1757), who wrote more than 400 pieces, called sonatas, in which he exhibited a highly remarkable display of ingenuity, introducing such special devices as the crossing of the hands and extended rapid scales. His style was imitated by the Spanish padre Antonio Soler (1729–83). A contemporary of Scarlatti's, Francesco Durante (1684–1755), represents the transition to the rococo style of the 18th century.

III. *Rococo* (1730–80). While Bach was writing his masterpieces, the apex of a glorious tradition, other composers eagerly adopted the facile methods of the *gallant style and produced quantities of mediocre works that even today fill volumes euphemistically entitled "The Early Masters of the Piano." Italian composers such as Durante, Porpora, Antonio Rossi (frequently confused with Frescobaldi's pupil Michelangelo Rossi), Paradisi, Galuppi, Grazioli, Sacchini, and Rutini wrote numerous harpsichord sonatas that, however slight in quality, are historically important as the precursors of the classical sonata [see Sonata B, III; also Haffner collection]. Padre Martini's (1706–84) sonatas are of a more serious nature but tend to be academic.

The end of the harpsichord literature can be seen in the works of Bach's sons. Karl Philipp Emanuel published in 1742 and 1744 two collections entitled *Sei Sonate per Cembalo* (the Prussian and Württemberg Sonatas), but his later keyboard compositions are for the clavichord (*Sechs Sonaten für Clavier,* 1760) and his latest for the piano (*Clavier-Sonaten . . . fürs Fortepiano,* 1780, '81). Wilhelm Friedemann also published *Sei Sonate per il Cembalo* in 1745, while his *12 Polonaises* (1765?) are written in a highly expressive style that calls for the clavichord or piano. Johann Christian Bach's compositions nearly always are marked "pour le clavecin ou le piano forte" (sonatas, 1770; concertos, 1777), as is an early publication of Haydn's Variations in F minor (1799), obviously as a publisher's advertisement. None of Mozart's compositions was written for the harpsichord. Not until the 20th century did composers again write for the harpsichord, mostly concertos with a small orchestra. The first work of this kind was by De Falla (1923), followed by others by Poulenc, Martinu, Orff, and Hugo Hermann.

Lit.: M. Kenyon, *Harpsichord Music* (1949); W. Landowska, *Music of the Past,* trans. W. A. Bradley (1924); E. Harich-Schneider, *Die Kunst des Cembalo-Spiels* [1939]; A. Pirro, *Les Clavecinistes* [1925]; O. Kinkeldey, *Orgel und Klavier in der Musik des 16. Jahrhunderts* (1910); R. Kirkpatrick, *Domenico Scarlatti* (1953); E. Bodky, *The Interpretation of Bach's Keyboard Works* (1960); W. Apel, *Geschichte der Orgel- und Klaviermusik bis 1700* (1967); W. Merian, ‡*Der Tanz in den deutschen Tabulaturbüchern* (1927); W. Apel, ‡*Musik aus früher Zeit für Klavier,* 2 vols. [1934]; R. Buchmayer, ‡*Aus Richard Buchmayers historischen Klavierkonzerten,* 5 vols. [1927]; J. Epstein, ‡*Alte Meisterstücke für Klavier,* 4 vols. [n.d.]; L. Oesterle, ‡*Early Keyboard Music,* 2 vols. [1904]; W. Apel, "Early Spanish Music for Lute and Keyboard Instruments" (*MQ* xx), id., "Early German Keyboard Music" (*MQ* xxiii); id., "Neapolitan Links between Cabezón and Frescobaldi" (*MQ* xxiv); C. van den Borren, "La Musique de clavier au XVIIe siècle" (*RM* 1921, no. 6); J. S. Shedlock, "The Harpsichord Music of Alessandro Scarlatti" (*SIM* vi); G. Abraham, "Handel's Clavier Music" (*ML* xvi, 278ff); F. Müller, "Vom Cembalo in Joh. Seb. Bachs Kirchenmusik" (*AM* x); M. Steinberg, "Some Observations on the Harpsichord in Twentieth Century Music" (*Perspectives of New Music* i). See also Keyboard music; Piano music.

Harp-way tuning. See under Viol IV, 3 (lyra viol).

Hasosra. A Biblical trumpet. See Jewish music I; Brass instruments V (a).

Hastig [G.]. With haste, hurrying.

Haupt- [G.]. Chief, principal. *Hauptstimme,* principal part (usually soprano); *Haupttonart,* principal key, i.e., the original key returned to after a modulation; *Hauptwerk,* great organ;

Hauptsatz, first theme (or section) in the sonata form [see under *Satz*].

Hausmusik [G.]. Music for home use, as opposed to music for public performance. See *Gebrauchsmusik.*

Haut, haute [F.]. High. *Haute-contre,* high tenor, male *alto, usually replaced by a female contralto. *Haut-dessus,* high treble, soprano.

Hautbois, hautboy [F.]. *Oboe.

Haydn Quartets. Familiar name of six string quartets by Mozart (K. 387, 421, 428, 458, 464, 465), composed 1782–85 and all dedicated to Haydn. They are listed as nos. 14 to 19 in the complete series of Mozart's string quartets.

Haye, hay, heye. A dance figure or dance of the late 16th century. Arbeau, in his *Orchésographie* (1589), speaks of the "passage de la haye" in the dances of the *bouffons* (*matasins*). It was well known in England during the Elizabethan period. In the 17th century it was identified with the *canarie (John Playford's *Musick's Handmaid* of 1678 includes an air entitled "The Canaries or the Hay"). The name may be derived from F. *haie,* hedge, because the dancers are aligned in two hedgelike rows, probably in imitation of a battle.

Hb. Abbr. for F. *hautbois* (oboe).

Headvoice. Higher register of a voice; cf. *chest voice. See Register (2).

Hebrew music. See Jewish music.

Hebriden, Die, or **Fingals Höhle** [G., The Hebrides, or Fingal's Cave]. Concert overture by Mendelssohn (B minor, op. 26, 1830). The composition was inspired by a visit to the famous cave in Scotland during his first tour through the British Isles.

Hebung [G.]. See under Arsis and thesis.

Heckel-clarina, Heckelphonklarinette [sometimes misspelled *heckel-clarind*]. See Clarinet family II.

Heckelphone. See under Oboe family II, E.

Heftig [G.]. Violent.

Heirmos. See Hirmos.

Heiter [G.]. Cheerful.

Heldenleben, Ein [G., A Hero's Life]. Symphonic poem by R. Strauss, op. 40, completed 1898. The work describes the composer's own strug-

gles to achieve recognition, depicting the jibes of the critics (by a dissonant "adversaries' section" and a noisy "battle scene") and the unceasing devotion of his wife (by an extended violin cadenza).

Heldentenor [G.]. A tenor voice of great brilliancy and volume, well suited for operatic parts of the "hero," e.g., Siegfried.

Helicon. See under Brass instruments III (e).

Hemidemisemiquaver. See under Notes.

Hemiola, hemiolia [Gr.]. In early theory the term had two meanings, both implying the ratio 3 : 2. (1) If applied to pitches, *hemiola* meant the fifth, since the lengths of two strings sounding this interval are in the ratio 3 : 2 [see Acoustics III]. (2) In treatises on mensural notation (15th, 16th centuries) the term is applied to time values that are in the relationship 3 : 2, particularly to the use of blackened notes in *tempus perfectum* [see Mensural notation V], or, in modern terms, of three half notes instead of two dotted half notes: ${}^6_4\text{♩.♩.}|\text{♩♩♩}|$ or ${}^3_4\text{♩.♩.}|\text{♩.♩♩♩}|$. This change from 6/4 to 3/2 or vice versa is found very frequently in the works of Dunstable, Dufay, and other 15th-century composers, as well as in music of the baroque period [see H. H. Wintersgill, "Handel's Two-length Bar," in *ML* xvii, no. 1]. It is a typical trait of the *courante. In the 19th century it was rediscovered by Schumann (*Spanische Liebes-Lieder,* op. 138, no. 6) and used frequently by Brahms [see Ex., from Symphony no. 2]. See

Polo. See M. B. Collins, "The Performance of Sesquialtera and Hemiolia in the 16th Century" (*JAMS* xvii); K. P. Bernet-Kempers, "Hemiolenrhythmik bei Mozart" (*CP Osthoff*).

Hemitonium [Gr.-L.]. Semitone.

Heptachord. A term occasionally used to distinguish the concept of the modern octave, which consists of seven different tones, from the earlier *hexachord, which includes only six. Ramos de Pareja (*Musica practica,* 1482) used *heptachordum* to mean the interval of the seventh [see ed. by J. Wolf, p. 49].

Hermannus letters. A system of letters used by Hermannus Contractus (d. 1054) in order to clarify the intervals in nondiastematic MSS (*e = equalis,* i.e., unison, *s* = semitone, *t* = tone, etc.). See A. Mocquereau, in *CP Riemann.*

Hermeneutics. The term, which properly means interpretation of the Scriptures, was introduced into musical aesthetics by H. Kretzschmar (*c.* 1900) for his method of "interpreting" musical motifs as the expression of human emotions, etc. This method, which was also adopted by R. Lach and A. Schering, is similar in principle to the *Affektenlehre* of the 18th century but places more emphasis on scientific method and systematic investigation based on the study of intervals, motion, rhythm, rests, etc. See Aesthetics of music III (a). See H. Kretzschmar, in *JMP* ix, xii; A. Schering, in *Bericht: Kongress für Aesthetik und allgemeine Kunstwissenschaft* (1914); *id.,* in *KJ* xxi; *id.,* in *Zeitschrift für Ästhetik und allgemeine Kunstwissenschaft* ix (1914); R. Lach, in *CP Kretzschmar.*

Hero's Life, A. See *Heldenleben, Ein.*

Hervorgehoben [G.]. Emphasized.

Hesitation waltz. See Boston.

Heterophony. A term used by Plato (*Laws* vii, 812 D) and adopted by modern musicologists (first by C. Stumpf) to describe an improvisational type of polyphony, namely, the simultaneous use of slightly or elaborately modified versions of the same melody by two (or more) performers, e.g., a singer and an instrumentalist adding a few extra tones or ornaments to the singer's melody. In addition to other polyphonic forms, heterophonic treatment plays an important role in many genres of primitive, folk, and non-Western art music (Chinese, Japanese, Javanese, etc.). Javanese and Balinese orchestral (gamelan) music in particular is largely based on a complex and highly sophisticated form of this technique. See Java III and the illustration, p. 438f. See also *HAM,* nos. 2 (Japan) and 3 (Siam).

Adopting the term as a convenient designation for a rather well-defined type of non-harmonic polyphony in which the intent is mono-melodic and horizontal is not tantamount to answering the question of what Plato meant in the passage indicated above. The basic meaning of Plato's text is that "the heterophony and diversity of the lyre, with the tune of the chords being different from the poet's melody, the use of tightness and looseness [small and wide inter-

vals?], of speed and slowness, of height and depth [pitches?]—all these in 'symphony' or 'antiphony' [agreement or contrast?]—, also the diversity of rhythm in the sounds of the lyre: are not suitable for the education of young people." From this description it is clear that ancient Greek heterophony involved a difference between the melody of the lyre and that of the singer. Whether the subsequent references to different intervals, speeds, pitches, and rhythms are details of heterophony or elements of "Greek polyphony" is not clear.

Lit.: H. Görgemanns and A. J. Neubecker, in *AMW* xxiii; C. Sachs, *The Rise of Music* [1943], pp. 256ff; *id., The Wellsprings of Music* (1962), pp. 185ff; J. Handschin, *Musikgeschichte,* p. 61; P. Barry, in *MQ* v; G. Adler, in *JMP* xv; A. Dechevrens, "Étude sur le système musical chinois" (*SIM* ii).

Heure espagnole, L' [F., The Spanish Hour]. Opera in one act by Ravel (libretto by Franc-Nohain, based on his own comedy), produced in Paris, 1911. Setting: Toledo, Spain, 18th century. The music is in a delicate impressionist style.

Hexachord. I. In medieval theory, a group of six tones following each other in the intervallic sequence of *t t s t t,* (*t = tonus,* whole tone; *s = semitonus,* half tone), e.g., c d e f g a. In the diatonic (C major) scale there are two—and only two—hexachords, one beginning with c, the other with g. If, however, the b-flat is added, there is a third hexachord, starting on f. The hexachord on c was called *hexachordum naturale;* that on g *hexachordum durum,* because it included the *b durum,* i.e., b natural [see Letter notation]; that on f *hexachordum molle,* because it included the *b molle,* i.e., b-flat. Since medieval theory did not consider tones of higher or lower octaves "identical," there were seven hexachords in the scale from G to e":

molle:

G A B c d e f g a♮ c' d' e' f' g' a♮ c" d" e"
$b\flat$ ... b ... $b'\flat$ ... b'

durum:
naturale:

In medieval theory the compass of tones was obtained not by joined octaves but by overlapping hexachords. This method, although generally considered inferior to the modern practice, is actually superior in that it produces the scale without at the same time establishing a preference regarding tonality. Indeed, in the modern system the initial tone c automatically becomes a tonal center (in other words, our diatonic scale is necessarily a "C-major scale"), whereas in the system of the hexachord such a fixation is avoided.

II. As an aid for memorizing, Guido d'Arezzo (c. 990–1050) designated the six tones of the hexachord by the vocables [L. *voces, voces musicales*] ut, re, mi, fa, sol, la. These are the initial syllables of the first six lines of a hymn to St. John [see *LU*, p. 1504], whose melody (probably invented by Guido himself) has the peculiarity of beginning one tone higher in each successive line:

c d f de d *Ut* queant la- xis	d d cde e *Re*-sonare fibris
efg e d c d *Mi*- ra ges:orum	f gagfd d *Fa*-muli tu-orum
gag e f g d *Sol*- ve polluti	a gafga a *La*-bi-i re-a tum, gf d c e d Sancte Johannes.

(That with relaxed voices thy servants may be able to sing the wonders of thy deeds, remove the sin from their polluted lips, O holy John.) These syllables were used as a "movable solmization," being applied to each of the seven hexachords. Thus, the tone d was *sol* (fifth) in the hexachord on G, and *re* (second) in that on c.

III. To indicate the various "functions" of a given tone, compound names were devised so as to include the tone's pitch letter as well as all its syllables, e.g., D sol re (Desolre), thus indicating that the tone d may appear either as a *sol* or a *re*. Following is a chart of the complete nomenclature (D. = *durum;* N. = *naturale;* M. = *molle*):

e''				la	E la (Ela)
d''				sol	D la sol (Delasol)
c''				fa	C sol fa (Cesolfa)
b'				mi	B mi (Bemi)
bb'			fa		B fa (Befa)
a'			la	mi	re A la mi re (Alamire)
g'			sol	re	ut G sol re ut (Gesolreut)
f'			fa	ut	D. F fa ut (Fefaut)
e'		la	mi		M. E la mi (Elami)
d'	la	sol	re		D la sol re (Delasolre)
c'	sol	fa	ut		C sol fa ut (Cesolfaut)
b	mi				N. B mi (Bemi)
bb		fa			B fa (Befa)
a		la	mi	re	A la mi re (Alamire)
g		sol	re	ut	G sol re ut (Gesolreut)
f		fa	ut	D.	F fa ut (Fefaut)
e	la	mi		M.	E la mi (Elami)
d	sol	re			D sol re (Desolre)
c	fa	ut			C fa ut (Cefaut)
B	mi	N.			B mi (Bemi)
A	re				A re (Are)
G	ut D.				G ut (Gamma ut)

To a certain extent the compound names served to differentiate octaves, e.g., C fa ut (c), C sol fa ut (c'), and C sol fa (c'').

IV. In order to accommodate melodic progressions exceeding the compass of one hexachord, two (or more) hexachords were inter-

locked by a process of transition, called *mutation*. For example, in order to interpret the melody c e d g a b a, the tone g was considered a pivot tone, being *sol* in the lower hexachord c–a and *ut* in the higher hexachord g–e'. Hence, the solmization of this melody would be: *ut mi re sol* (= *ut*) *re mi re*. If, however, the melody were c e d g a b♭ a, the mutation would have to be made into the hexachord f–d': *ut mi re sol* (= *re*) *mi fa mi.* According to Engelbert (c. 1250–1331) the mutation was made preferably on e, a, e' or a' (*GS* ii, 324), while Johannes de Garlandia and Marchetto da Padua said that it could be made "in any tone having two or three *voces*" (*CS* i, 160; *GS* iii, 90). The accompanying figure shows a mutation passage from an instructive two-part composition found in the Codex Huelgas of c. 1300 (ed. Anglés, iii, 405).

molle   naturale

ut mi   re fa mi sol   fa la   sol ut   fa fa

V. The hexachord system superseded the Greek (and early medieval) system of the *tetrachord, in which a group of four tones served as the generating segment for the construction of the entire scale. The development of the hexachord system began with Guido (c. 990–1050), who in his "Epistola ad Michaelem Monachum: de ignoto cantu" introduced the syllables *ut, re, mi*, etc.) for the tones c to a (*GS* ii, 45). He also called attention to the identity of intervallic construction between G–e and c–a but did not apply the syllables to the former (*GS* ii, 47a). Nor did he mention the segment f–d' (*hexachordum molle*), probably because of the "irregular" nature (*minus regulare*) of the b-flat. No details concerning the post-Guidonian development seem to be known. The system appeared in its full form (three hexachords, compound pitch names, mutation, *Guidonian hand, etc.) about 1300 in the writings of Hieronymus de Moravia (*CS* i, 21ff, 83ff). The term "hexachord" seems to be of a rather late date (16th century?). Tinctoris does not include it in his *Diffinitorium.* Medieval writers used designations such as *sex voces* (Tunstede, d. 1369; see *CS* iv, 220).

VI. The six tones of the hexachord have repeatedly been used as a *cantus firmus* or thematic subject for compositions, both vocal and instrumental. There are hexachord Masses

(*Missa Ut re mi fa sol la*) by A. Brumel (?), Morales, and Palestrina, the last-named being particularly noteworthy for an ingenious presentation of the basic material. Byrd, Bull, Sweelinck, and Frescobaldi used it as a subject for organ fantasias. Bull's composition (Fitzwilliam Virginal Book, i, 183ff) is especially interesting on account of its modulatory scheme, the hexachord (ascending and descending) being successively used in the keys of G, A, B, D♭, E♭, F and A♭, B♭, C, D, E, F♯ [see Arcicembalo]. See also Solmization; Mi-fa; *Soggetto cavato; voces musicales* under Vox.

Lit.: H. Riemann, *Geschichte der Musiktheorie,* rev. ed. [1920]; *id., History of Music Theory,* trans. R. H. Haggh (1962); *RiHM* 1.2, 173ff.

Hexameter. See under Poetic meter II.

Hey. See Haye.

Hichiriki. A Japanese oboe. See *Gagaku;* Oboe family III.

Hidden fifths, octaves. See under Parallel fifths, octaves.

High fidelity, abbr. *hi-fi.* The term refers to a standard of excellence in the reproduction of sound on discs, tape, and film. Recording companies and manufacturers of recording equipment have made great progress in this respect since 1945. See under Phonograph and recorded music.

Hilfslinie [G.]. Ledger line.

Hinaufstrich [G.]. See Bowing (a).

Hindu music. See India.

Hinsterbend [G.]. Fading away.

Hintersatz [G.]. Old term for organ mixture stop, so called because of the arrangement of the pipes one behind (*hinter*) the other.

Hirmos (Heirmos). In early *Byzantine music (9th–12th centuries), a melody composed for the first stanza of a hymn and repeated with subsequent stanzas, in a strophic song. Naturally, the procedure was more flexible than with a modern strophic chant, admitting adjustments to the varying number of syllables in the different stanzas, like the method used with the psalm tones. Most of the *hirmoi* (which were collected in books called *hirmologion*) were composed in the 7th and 8th centuries, and were later used for other hymns modeled on the earlier music.

Lit.: H. Gaïsser, *Les "Heirmoi" de Pâques dans l'Office grec* (1905; also in *RMC* ii); A. Gastoué, *Les Origines du chant romain* (1907), pp. 60ff. See also general bibl. under Byzantine chant.

Hirtenflöte [G.]. Shepherd's flute. *Hirtenlied,* shepherd's song.

His [G.]. See under Pitch names.

Hispaniae schola musica sacra. See Editions XX.

Histoire du soldat, L' [F., The Soldier's Tale]. A play with music and dance by Stravinsky (libretto by C. F. Ramuz), produced in Lausanne, 1918. Setting: fairy tale. It is somewhat like a *ballet d'action,* combining ballet performance with a story told in dialogue by the characters and a narrator. The music, in acrid dissonances and pungent rhythms, consists of a number of *character pieces such as Marche, Tango, Valse, Ragtime, and Choral, composed for a chamber orchestra of six instruments and percussion.

History of music. This article is devoted to a survey of epochs, schools, and musical forms, with cross-references to relevant articles elsewhere in this dictionary.

Nothing certain is known about the music of earliest man, but there is no reason to doubt that some kind of music was practiced even by Stone Age peoples. Some ancient peoples, especially those of *Egypt, *China, and *Mesopotamia, have a musical tradition that can be traced back about three thousand years before the birth of Jesus. No music from these remote times has been preserved, but numerous archaeological findings and pictorial representations of instruments from different periods give evidence of musical activity and development long before the beginning of Western music. Somewhat later, other civilizations, e.g., those of *Japan and *India, developed.

Western music, on the other hand, began at a much later time, and, aside from scattered archaeological data [see, e.g., Lur], its history is recorded essentially in musical documents supplemented by theoretical writings. Moreover, it is a history that can be continuously traced from *c.* A.D. 800 to the present.

I. *The main periods.* Three times during its development, at intervals of 300 years, the evolution of Western music produced changes so strikingly novel that contemporary writers used the term "new" to describe them: the *ars nova* of 1300, the *nuove musiche* of 1600, and the *new music of 1900. To these "landmarks of innovation" we might add the year 1000, which marks one of the most important inventions in music, the musical *staff (Guido and his predecessors). Other landmarks of equal importance occur almost exactly at the midpoint of each of the 300-year periods. The year 1750 marked the death of J. S. Bach. About 1450 came the rise of the *Flemish school, marking the end of medieval music and the beginning of the Renaissance; and about 1150 arose the first important school of polyphonic music, the school of St. Martial. Finally, the middle of the 9th century can be regarded as the "beginning of polyphony," judging from the earliest preserved records. The 150-year periods so derived can be conveniently described by terms long used in the visual arts:

but remarkable changes of style. About 1150 the school of *St. Martial stands out as an important landmark in this evolution, being followed, about 1175, by the even more important school of *Notre Dame, which, with its two masters, Leoninus and Perotinus, is usually considered the beginning of the *ars antiqua (13th century). Secondary forms developed by this school were the nonliturgical *conductus and the *clausulae—fragments, as it were, of organa that acquired particular importance as the starting point of the *motet, the most characteristic form of the ars antiqua proper (Franco of Cologne, Petrus de Cruce). The early Gothic period also saw the rise of secular music under the Provençal *troubadours (c. 1100–1300), who were followed, half a century later, by the northern French *trouvères (c. 1150–1300) and the

850: Beginning of polyphony	Early *Middle Ages
1000: Invention of the staff	Romanesque ⎫ Later
1150: School of St. Martial	Early *Gothic ⎬ Middle
1300: *Ars nova	Late Gothic ⎭ Ages
1450: Rise of *Flemish school	*Renaissance
1600: *Nuove musiche	*Baroque
1750: Death of Bach	*Rococo, *classicism, *romanticism
1900: *New music	*Twentieth-century music

It goes without saying that in reality these periods are not as neatly marked off as the table above suggests. However, it does serve as a useful outline.

II. *To 1300.* For want of information, the history of pre-Christian music in Europe is practically limited to that of Greek music [see also under Rome]. The early Christian era saw the rise of Christian chant (plainsong), which appears to be rooted chiefly in the tradition of the *Jewish synagogue. The most important branch of Christian chant [see Chant], that of the Roman Catholic Church, probably developed into its final form relatively late, approximately between 750 and 850 [see Gregorian chant]. Parallel developments led to the formation of *Old Roman, *Ambrosian, *Gallican, *Mozarabic, and *Byzantine chant. About 850 (Romanesque period) began a period of amplification of the traditional repertory, leading to the *tropes, *sequences, and finally *liturgical drama. More important than this "horizontal" broadening is the simultaneous rise of polyphonic music, which, in its early period, might be described as "vertical" broadening of the chant, i.e., as polyphonic settings of plainsong *cantus firmi. In the ensuing three centuries these settings, known as organa, underwent slow

German *minnesingers (c. 1150–1350). The latter tradition continued to live in the *Meistersinger (c. 1400–1600), the last representatives of monophonic music, aside from folksong, which, of course, was not restricted to any single period. Monophonic music also had a relatively short period of flowering, chiefly during the 13th century, in Spain (*cantigas) and in Italy (*laude).

III. *1300–1450.* With the advent of the late Gothic period or, in musical terms, of the *ars nova, the emphasis in music underwent a striking change from the sacred to the secular, a change that engendered the appearance of an entirely new repertory, the polyphonic *ballades, *rondeaux, and *virelais in France (Machaut), and the *madrigals, *caccie, and *ballate in Italy (Jacopo da Bologna, Francesco Landini). The motet continued to be cultivated in France, growing in dimensions and acquiring peculiar structural features [see Isorhythmic]. Toward the end of the 14th century the development led to a highly mannered style of great rhythmic complexity and intricate dissonance treatment (Matheo da Perugia, Solage, and others). Gothic music was brought to a glorious climax by England's Dunstable, whose great genius left scant traces in his own country [see England III] but became all the more important as the inspiring force of the renovation of French music, culminating in the *Burgundian school of Dufay and Binchois.

IV. *1450–1600.* The middle of the 15th century (*Renaissance) saw a renewed emphasis on sacred music under the first masters of the *Flemish school (or schools), Ockeghem and Obrecht. Although their Masses and motets, particularly those of the former, are far removed from what the term "Renaissance" suggests, Renaissance-like features—the "sun of Italy," as it were—appeared in the secular compositions of Obrecht and still more so in those of his great successor, Josquin. In the early 16th century as in the early 14th century, numerous secular forms arose: the Italian *frottola, the German polyphonic *lied, the Spanish *villancico, the Italian *madrigal. The tradition of sacred music, however, continued in the numerous Masses and motets, reaching a peak under Palestrina, Lasso, Byrd, and Victoria. The beginning of the Renaissance also marks the starting point of a continuous development of *instrumental music, for *ensemble as well as for the organ and, somewhat later, the lute [see Prelude; Intabulation; Ricercar; Canzona (5); Fantasia; Toccata; Variations; Dance music; the last-mentioned with interesting forerunners in the 13th and 14th centuries (*estampie)]. The Renaissance came to an impressive close with the pompous splendor of the Venetian *polychoral style of G. Gabrieli [see Venetian school].

V. *1600–1750.* In spite of attempts by various scholars to show that "nothing new happened" about 1600 (baroque), this year remains one of the most important landmarks in music history [see *Nuove musiche;* Baroque music], witnessing the rise of the *recitative, the *monodic style, and the *thoroughbass, together with such novel forms as the *opera, *oratorio, *cantata, and *basso ostinato* forms (*chaconne and passacaglia), and leading quickly to a development of instrumental music equal in importance to that of contemporary vocal music. The fact that most of these styles and forms can be traced back to earlier roots again warns us that not all of the lines demarcating periods are hard and fast. Witness the continued influence of the Venetian as well as the *Roman schools of the 16th century, or the fact that the two chief forms of baroque instrumental music, the *suite and *sonata, both are rooted in 16th-century developments [see Canzona (5)], while the contrast style of the *concerto is more exclusively a feature of the baroque. In a way, the baroque period is the most "international" period in music history, with Italy, Germany, and France competing on almost equal terms and England not far behind. No other period can boast of such a variety of forms, so many great composers, or a summit such as that represented by Bach.

VI. *1750–1900.* Although the changes following Bach's death (1750) are well known, there actually is more (at least, just as much) "transition" here than elsewhere, namely in the *rococo movement that began in France (Couperin) about 1700 and continued, under the name *gallant style, chiefly in Italy and Germany. In the latter country it took on, in the hands of W. F. and K. P. E. Bach, a greater expressiveness [see *Empfindsamer Stil;* also Berlin school] that heralds the achievements of the classical and even the romantic period. At the same time the members of the *Mannheim school (and other composers also) laid the foundations for the formal development of the *sonata, the dominant form of the 19th century, with its orchestral and chamber varieties, the *symphony and *quartet. Vienna became the musical center of the world under the masters Haydn, Mozart, Beethoven, and Schubert [see Classicism]. The last-named, the great master of the *lied, also represents the transition to the *romanticism of the 19th century. The early romanticists (Schumann, Mendelssohn, Chopin) cultivated particularly the *character piece for piano, in which they achieved better results than in the large forms of the classical period. The symphonic tradition was revived, however (c. 1870–90), in the symphonies of Bruckner, Brahms, Tchaikovsky, and C. Franck, coming to a close with those of Mahler (c. 1890–1910). About 1850 the *symphonic poem developed as a novel type of symphonic music, and the opera took a new direction under Wagner. Against the dominant position of German music there arose, about 1860, the national schools [see Nationalism] of the "peripheral" nations (Bohemia, Norway, Russia, Spain, England), and, about 1900, the *impressionism that brought France back into the spotlight.

VII. *After 1900.* Impressionism was the first manifestation of a quickly growing reaction against romanticism and the musical tradition of the 19th century in general. The ensuing revolutionary tendencies, summed up under the term *twentieth-century music, embrace a variety of attempts, experiments, and tendencies for which there is no parallel in the entire history of music.

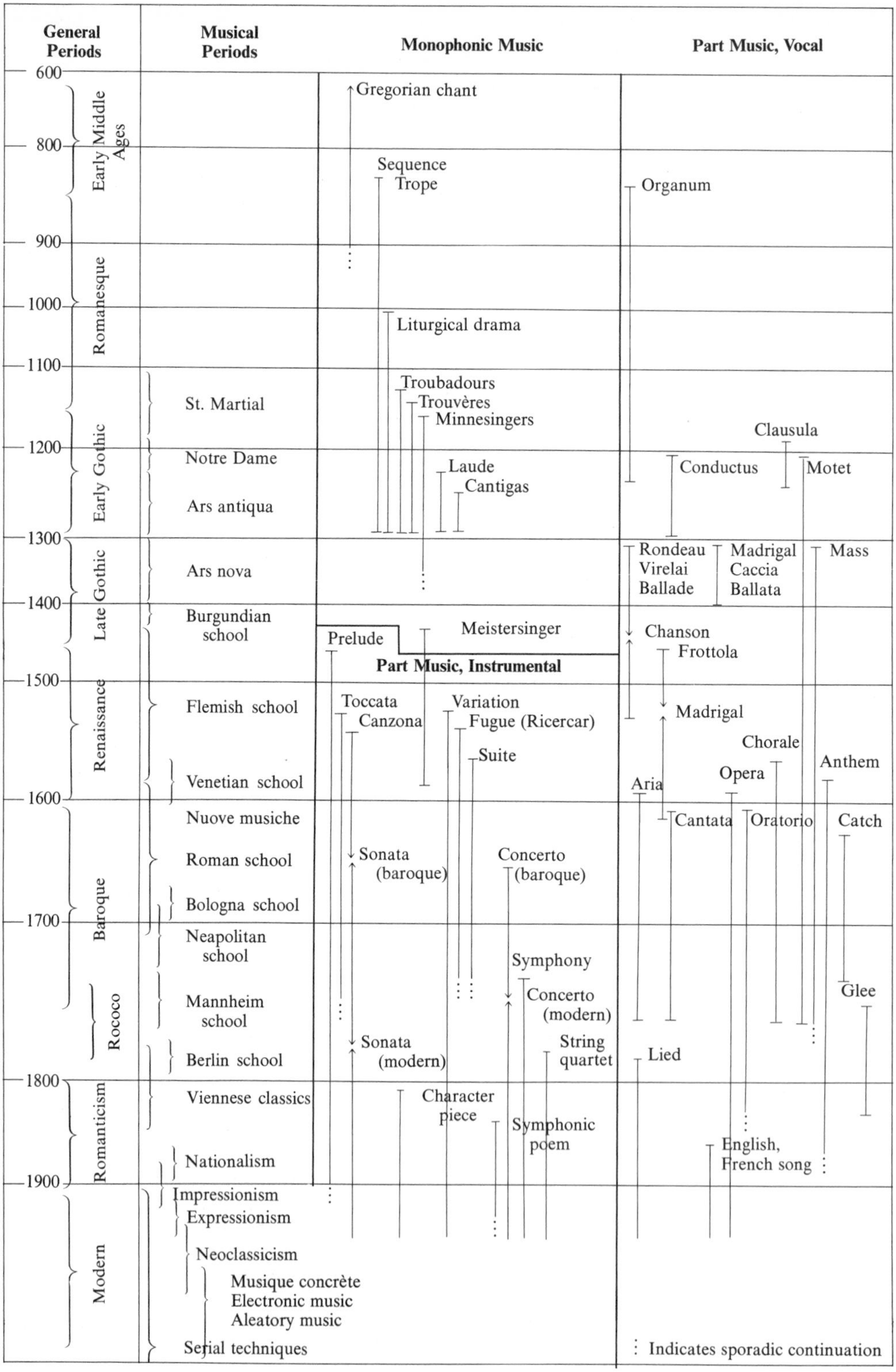

General Periods	Musical Periods	Monophonic Music	Part Music, Vocal

Timeline years (left axis): 600, 800, 900, 1000, 1100, 1200, 1300, 1400, 1500, 1600, 1700, 1800, 1900

General Periods:
Early Middle Ages
Romanesque
Early Gothic
Late Gothic
Renaissance
Baroque
Rococo
Romanticism
Modern

Musical Periods:
St. Martial
Notre Dame
Ars antiqua
Ars nova
Burgundian school
Flemish school
Venetian school
Nuove musiche
Roman school
Bologna school
Neapolitan school
Mannheim school
Berlin school
Viennese classics
Nationalism
Impressionism
Expressionism
Neoclassicism
Musique concrète
Electronic music
Aleatory music
Serial techniques

Monophonic Music:
Gregorian chant
Sequence
Trope
Liturgical drama
Troubadours
Trouvères
Minnesingers
Laude
Cantigas
Meistersinger

Part Music, Instrumental:
Prelude
Toccata
Canzona
Variation
Fugue (Ricercar)
Suite
Sonata (baroque)
Concerto (baroque)
Symphony
Concerto (modern)
Sonata (modern)
String quartet
Character piece
Symphonic poem

Part Music, Vocal:
Organum
Clausula
Conductus
Motet
Rondeau
Virelai
Ballade
Madrigal
Caccia
Ballata
Mass
Chanson
Frottola
Madrigal
Chorale
Aria
Opera
Anthem
Cantata
Oratorio
Catch
Glee
Lied
English, French song

⋮ Indicates sporadic continuation

Among the most clearly established trends are *serial music and *neoclassicism. Even today the outlook still changes every five or ten years, the most important recent innovations being *musique concrète and *electronic music.

The preceding table illustrates the development of the most important forms of music (straight lines indicate their main period, dotted lines a more sporadic continuation).

Lit.: Oxford History of Music, 2nd ed., 7 vols. (1929–38; for the medieval period, vols. i and ii of first ed., 1901, are preferable); NOH; GrHWM; A. Robertson and D. Stevens, ed.; The Pelican History of Music, 2 vols. (1960, '63); W. Wiora, The Four Ages of Music, trans. H. Norton [1965]; C. Sachs, Our Musical Heritage (1948); H. Prunières, A New History of Music (1943); P. Lang, Music in Western Civilization (1941); D. N. Ferguson, A Short History of Music (1947); id., A History of Musical Thought, rev. ed. (1948); A. Einstein, A Short History of Music, rev. ed. (1947); K. Nef, An Outline of the History of Music (1935); H. M. Miller, History of Music (College Outline Series), rev. ed. (1960). Other languages: A. W. Ambros, Geschichte der Musik, rev. ed., 4 vols. (1887–1911); BüHM; AdHM; RiHM; J. Handschin, Musikgeschichte im Überblick, rev. ed. (1964); A. Schering, Tabellen zur Musikgeschichte, 5th ed. (1962); LavE; J. Combarieu, Histoire de la musique, 5 vols. (1948–60; vols. 4 and 5 by R. Dumesnil); N. Dufourcq, La Musique des origines à nos jours (1946); A. della Corte and G. Pannain, Storia della musica, 3 vols. (1942).

Collections of Examples: HAM; C. Parrish and J. F. Ohl, Masterpieces of Music before 1750 (1951); E. Creuzburg, Geschichte der Musik in Beispielen (1953); SchGMB; EiBM; K. G. Fellerer, ed.-in-chief, Beiträge zur rheinischen Musikgeschichte, 60 vols. [1952–65]; RiMB. For collections of pictorial representations see under Iconography; of recordings, under Phonograph.

Articles: G. Malipiero, "The History of Music and the Music of History" (MQ ix); A. Mendel, "Spengler's Quarrel with the Methods of Music History" (MQ xx); A. Lorenz, "Periodizität in der Musikgeschichte" (DM xxi.9); A. Schering, "Historische und nationale Klangstile" (JMP, 1927); H. Osthoff, "Die Anfänge der Musikgeschichtsschreibung in Deutschland" (AM v, no. 3); C. van den Borren, "Une Conception nouvelle de l'histoire de la musique" (RM 1928, no. 11).

Hoboe. Old spelling for oboe.

Hoch Kammerton [G.]. See under Pitch.

Hocket [L. hoketus, oketus, ochetus; F. hocquet, hoquet; It. ochetto]. In medieval polyphony (13th and 14th centuries), a peculiar device consisting of the rapid alternation of two (rarely three) voices with single notes or short groups of notes, one part having a rest while the other sounds. See the accompanying examples: (1) motet In Bethlehem, c. 1280; (2) French *chace, c. 1320. Numerous motets of the period (Petrus de Cruce, De Vitry, Machaut) include passages in hocket style [see HAM, nos. 32e, 35]. Theorists of the 13th century mention hoketus not only as a technique to be used within a composition but also as an independent musical form. They probably mean pieces in which hocket technique is used consistently between the two upper parts. Six compositions of this type are in the Codex Bamberg [see P. Aubry, Cent motets, nos. 102, 103, 104, 106, 107, 108] and one among the works of Machaut (Hoquetus David, so called because the tenor employs the melisma DAVID from the Alleluia Nativitas (today Alleluia Solemnitas, LU, p. 1676a). All these are "motets" for instrumental performance, probably on wind instruments, which are more appropriate for playing single notes or short fragments than strings. Such hockets are the earliest type of *instrumental music known to us.

Some of the 17th-century *catches show a fragmentary alternation of voices similar to the

hocket technique. See M. Schneider, in *ZMW* xi; H. Husmann, in *AMW* xi, 296.

Hoflied [G.]. See under *Gesellschaftslied.*

Hoftanz [G.]. A 16th-century German dance, possibly a German variety of the French *basse danse*. About 50 examples are found in lute and keyboard tablatures of the 16th century, the earliest in the lute books of Judenkünig of 1515 and 1523 [*DTO* 37]. A "Hoftanz mit durchstraichen" (strumming all the strings of the lute, resulting in full chords) by Hans Newsidler is reproduced in *HAM,* no. 105a. Like other dances of the 16th century [see Spagna; *Passamezzo*], the majority of *Hoftänze* are based on traditional melodies ("Der schwarze Knab," "Bentzenauer"]. See O. Gombosi, in *AM* vii; D. Heartz, "Hoftanz and Basse dance" (*JAMS* xix).

Ho-hoane. Corruption of Irish "ochone," i.e., *lament. The Fitzwilliam Virginal Book contains a piece labeled "The Irish Hohoane" [ed. Barclay-Squire, i, 87].

Hold. Same as *pause.

Holz- [G.]. Wood. *Holzblasinstrumente,* woodwinds. *Holzblaser,* player of woodwinds. *Holzharmonika, Holzstabspiel,* xylophone. *Holzschlegel,* wooden drumstick. *Holztrompete,* see Clarinet family II; also *SaRM,* p. 181.

Homme armé, L'. See *L'Homme armé.*

Homo-, iso-. Prefixes that both mean "same" or "equal to." In musical terminology, particularly concerning rhythm, they are useful in distinguishing two different kinds of "identity" or "similarity," one vertical and the other horizontal. Thus, *homorhythmic means the simultaneous use of the same rhythm in different parts of a contrapuntal texture, while *isorhythmic means the successive use of the same rhythm in one part. A similar distinction can be made between homoperiodic and isoperiodic. Homoperiodicity is found in many clausulae and 13th-century motets [see, e.g., Aubry, *Cent motets,* no. 60] and isoperiodicity in those of the 14th century. See Poly-, multi-.

Homophony. Music in which one voice leads melodically, being supported by an accompaniment in chordal or a slightly more elaborate style. Practically all music of the 19th century is homophonic. Homophony is the opposite of polyphony, music in which all parts contribute more or less equally to the musical fabric.

However, the term is also applied to a kind of polyphonic (or part) music in which all the voices move in the same rhythm, thus producing a succession of intervals (in two-part writing) or chords (in three- or four-part writing). Hence, homophonic is synonymous with "strict chordal style" or familiar style. A more suitable term for this style is *homorhythmic.

In French usage *homophonie* means (1) monophonic music; (2) enharmonic equivalence.

Homorhythmic. Designation for a type of polyphonic (or part) music in which all the voices move in the same rhythm, thus producing a succession of intervals (in two-part writing) or of chords (in three- or four-part writing; see under Homo-, iso-). The best-known examples are the four-part harmonizations of hymn or chorale melodies. Such music is commonly described as being in *chordal style, *familiar style, *homophonic, *isometric, note-against-note, or even harmonic. Since, however, homorhythmic texture has been used since the beginning of polyphony, terms implying the presence of chords or harmony are misleading.

The early organum, from its beginnings about 850 to *c.* 1100, is strictly homorhythmic. So are most of the conductus of the 13th century, written in two to four parts; hence the term "conductus style" as yet another synonym for homorhythmic, used preferably with reference to 13th- and 14th-century music. In the 15th-century *fauxbourdon and the 16th-century *falsobordone, homorhythmic writing takes on the function of harmonization. In the Masses and motets of Obrecht, Josquin, and later 16th-century composers the prevailing polyphonic (more properly, *polyrhythmic) texture is often balanced by sections in homorhythmic style. This style was also used for the more popular types of 16th-century music, such as the *frottola, musique mesurée,* villanella, etc. After 1600 it persisted chiefly in harmonized hymns and chorales. As a rule, homorhythmic treatment goes hand in hand with a strictly syllabic setting of the text.

Lit.: H. Bush, "The Emergence of the Chordal Concept" (diss. Cornell Univ., 1939); K. Jeppesen, "Das isometrische Moment in der Vokalpolyphonic" (*CP Wagner*); U. Teuber, "Bemerkungen zur Homophonie im 16. Jh." (*CP 1952*).

Honduras. Despite various efforts made at different times, musical life in Honduras has remained relatively undeveloped. Since the establishment of the first military band in 1876, musical activity has been confined to a fairly small number of native conductors and composers. These include Ignacio Villanueva Galeano (b. 1885), composer of several military marches, Camilo Rivera (b. 1878), Ramón Ruiz (b. 1894), and Francisco R. Diaz Zelaya (b. 1898), as well as Manuel de Adalid y Gamero (b. 1872), the most prominent member of the group, composer of numerous orchestral, chamber, and solo instrumental works. Younger Honduran composers are Roberto Dominguez, Modesto Martinez, and Rafael Coello Ramos.

In the mid-1930's Leonidas Rodriguez founded an academy of music in Tegucigalpa, and in 1951 the *Escuela Nacional de Música* was established by government decree.

Leading in ethnomusicologic research has been Rafael Manzanares, director of the *Officina del Folklore Nacional.* According to him, folk music in Honduras reflects three main traditions: the indigenous, especially in the northwest areas of the country; the Creole or mestizo in the urban centers; and the Afro-Honduran. Typical of the indigenous tradition is music played on the native instrument known as *zambumbia* or *caramba. La correa* is a popular dance of Spanish origin, and the *iancunú* or *baile de máscaros* reflects African influences.

Lit.: R. Manzanares, *Songs of Honduras* (1960); M. de Adalid y Gamero, "La Música en Honduras" (*Revista del archivo y biblioteca nacionales* xvii). Also see under Latin America.

J.O-S.

Hook neumes. See under Neumes II.

Hopak. See Gopak.

Hopper. See under Piano I.

Hoquet, hoquetus. See Hocket.

Horizontal. See under Texture.

Horn [F. *cor;* G. *Horn;* It. *corno;* Sp. *trompa*]. I. The modern orchestral instrument, called French horn (in order to distinguish it from the English horn, a member of the *oboe family), is a *brass instrument with a funnel-shaped mouthpiece and a narrow conical bore wound into a spiral and ending in a large flaring bell. It has three valves (usually rotary, though in England piston valves are used) and is therefore also called valve horn [F. *cor-à-pistons, cor chromatique;* G. *Ventilhorn;* It. *corno ventile, corno a macchina;* Sp. *trompa de pistón*] to distinguish it from the early valveless instruments [see II]. See ill. under Brass instruments.

For the basic principles of tone production on the horn, see Wind instruments.

Normally the horn is pitched in F, and the series of its natural tones is F_1 F c f a c' f' g' a', etc. Owing to the narrow bore, however, the lowest tone of this series (pedal tone) is practically unobtainable, so that the series starts with F. By operating the valves a complete chromatic scale from B_1 to f ", etc., becomes available (the highest tones, however, being of little use). The horn is notated as a transposing instrument, written a fifth higher than it sounds. For the lowest notes the bass clef is used, usually (in older scores always) with the notes written a fourth lower—instead of a fifth higher—than their actual sound [see Ex.]. In older scores key signatures are avoided for the horn parts, the chromatic alterations being given with each single note; but today horn parts are commonly written with a key signature, which, owing to the transposed notation, has one flat less or one sharp more than that of nontransposing instruments, e.g., the violins (E-flat for a composition in A-flat, etc.).

The horn has the reputation of being the most difficult of all the orchestral instruments. Horn playing requires several special methods of tone production. The most important of these is stopping [F. *bouché;* G. *gestopft;* It. *chiuso;* Sp. *tapada*], achieved by inserting the hand into the bell. Formerly, on the natural (valveless) horn the missing tones of the natural series were produced by inserting the hand flat into the bell and closing it ¼, ½, or ¾. This gave a continuous scale mostly of diatonic tones, which, however, was not very satisfactory since the stopping changed the timbre. Nowadays stopping is used only to obtain a special effect. Blocking the bell with the hand and sharply increasing the wind pressure cause the tone to rise approximately a semitone. Stopped tones are indicated thus: +. To a limited extent (mainly in the lower two octaves) stopping can also be used to lower the pitch by as much as a semitone. The different methods of stopping depend largely on the individual player.

The mute [F. *sourdine;* G. *Dämpfer;* It., Sp. *sordina*] is a pear-shaped piece of metal, wood, or cardboard that is inserted into the bell in order to obtain yet another timbre (muted horns). Modern mutes are nontransposing, while the older ones, smaller and shaped slightly differently, raised the pitch. Muting may also be done with the player's hand.

"Brassy" tones [F. *cuivré;* G. *schmetternd*] are obtained by increased wind pressure and can be produced either open, stopped, or muted.

Horns are also built and occasionally demanded in other sizes, e.g., E, E^b, D, low C, low B^b, and also in high B^b, an octave above the largest size. More recently a "double horn" has come into use, a combination of the horns in F and B^b alto [see Duplex instruments].

The solo and chamber music literature for the horn includes: Haydn, two concertos for one horn (maybe a third); Mozart, four concertos, and a quintet for horn, violin, two violas, and cello; Beethoven, Sonata for piano and French horn, op. 17, Sextet for two horns and strings, op. 81b; Schumann, Adagio und Allegro for horn and piano, op. 70, *Concertstück* for four horns and orchestra, op. 86; Brahms, Horn Trio, op. 40; R. Strauss, Concerto for horn, op. 11; Hindemith, Sonata (1939) and Concerto (1949); Britten, Serenade for tenor, horn, and strings.

II. *History.* The discussion here deals only with the modern horn's most immediate predecessors, the other members of the horn family being treated under Brass instruments. The earliest type was the hunting horn, a plain pipe that was coiled in a circle large enough to permit carrying over the shoulder. It had a shallow mouthpiece like that of a trumpet and therefore a loud and brilliant tone. Toward the end of the 17th century the instrument, having undergone various changes (smaller size, wider bell, etc.), began to be used in the orchestra. It was similar in most respects to the modern horn, except that it had no valves or crooks [see below], so that only the tones of a single harmonic series could be obtained. The details of the development leading from the hunting horn to the natural horn [F. *cor. d'harmonie;* G. *Naturhorn, Waldhorn;* It. *corno naturale*] are difficult to trace. Throughout the first half of the 18th century the orchestral horns had a trumpetlike sound and were frequently criticized as coarse and vulgar. Not until 1750 did the instrument take on proportions that gave it its typical "mellow" timbre.

About 1760 the Bohemian Kölbel constructed an instrument called *Amorschall,* a horn with a modified bell and with lateral holes covered by keys, the first instance of a keyed brass instrument. Also *c.* 1760 the horn player Hampel of Dresden found that the natural tones of the horn could be lowered a semitone or whole tone by placing the open hand with closed fingers into the bell. This technique made it possible for the first time to produce "artificial" horn tones, thus bridging to some extent the gaps between the natural tones. The natural horns thus played were called *hand horn* [It. *corno a mano*].

In the 18th century horns were provided with *crooks, additional lengths of tubing whereby the instrument's pitch could be changed. Thus, a horn in F could be made into a horn in E or E^b, etc. At first the crooks were inserted immediately under the mouthpiece. This method, however, made the instrument inconveniently long, especially for hand-stopping. The above-mentioned Hampel is credited with the invention of curved sliding crooks, called "inventions," and hence the name *Inventionshorn* for instruments using them. The use of crooks together with stopped notes made the horn an almost completely chromatic instrument. However, the stopped notes differed in timbre from the natural notes and changing crooks was a time-consuming process. The invention, *c.* 1815, of *valves by F. Blühmel (or H. Stölzel?) did away with these inconveniences and revolutionized horn playing. The first part for the valve horn is in Halévy's *La Juive* (1835). The hand horn, however, continued to be used along with the modern type, owing to its more brilliant tone. See ill. under Brass instruments.

Lit.: R. Morley-Pegge, *The French Horn* [1960]; R. Gregory, *The Horn* [1961]; K. Taut, *Beiträge zur Geschichte der Jagdmusik* (1927); F. Piersig, *Die Einführung des Hornes in die Kunstmusik . . . bis zum Tode Joh. Seb. Bachs* (1927); H. Fitzpatrick, "Some Historical Notes on the Horn in Germany and Austria" (*GSJ* xvi); *id.,* "An Eighteenth-Century School of Horn-Makers in Bohemia" (*GSJ* xvii).

Horn fifths [G. *Hornquinten*]. See under Parallel fifths.

Hornpipe. (1) An obsolete wind instrument, probably identical with the pibgorn [see Clarinet family IV; Reed II]. (2) A dance popular in England from the 16th through 19th centuries [see Dance music III], which, at least in its later development, was performed as a solo dance by sailors, with folded arms and many characteristic steps and gestures. The earliest preserved hornpipe ("hornepype") is a composition by

Hugh Aston, dating from *c.* 1525 [repr. in J. Stafford Smith, *Musica Antiqua* (1812), in J. Wolf, *Sing- und Spielmusik,* rev. ed. (1931), and (slightly abridged) in *ApMZ* ii]. It is one of the most remarkable early keyboard compositions, noteworthy for its sheer flow of melodic inspiration above an extremely simple harmonic scheme, i.e., alternation of tonic and dominant [see Ostinato]. The numerous hornpipes of the 17th and 18th centuries are usually in moderate 3/2 time, later in 4/4 time, with a characteristic "Scotch snap" rhythm [see Ex.]. Examples are found in the theatrical works of Purcell, Handel's Concerto Grosso no. 7, Gottlieb Muffat's *Componimenti Musicali* (1739), *A Col-*

lection of Original Lancashire Hornpipes (1705), and the various books of *country dances.

Hornquinten, Hornsatz [G.]. Horn fifths.

Horn Trio. A celebrated trio by Brahms, op. 40 (1865), for horn, violin, and piano.

Hornwerk. In Austria in the Gothic period and Renaissance, a set of organ pipes set on their own chest in a tower. The pipes, which all sounded together continuously so long as the mechanically operated bellows supplied wind, announced the hours of the day, the beginning of Mass and Vespers, etc. Later the Hornwerk was connected to a pinned barrel whereby tunes were inserted. The only intact surviving example is the *Stierorgel* (bull organ) at Hohe Feste, Salzburg, built in 1502. Others (only partly preserved) are at Rein (near Graz) and Heiligenkreuz (near Vienna). See R. Quoika, *Altösterreichische Hornwerke* [1959].

Hosanna, Osanna. A Hebrew word expressing triumph and glorification. In the phrase "Hosanna in excelsis" it occurs in the Sanctus of the Ordinary of the Mass [see Mass C, III]. In polyphonic Masses the phrase is always treated as a brilliant coda.

Hptw. [G.]. Abbr. for *Hauptwerk* (in organ music).

Hr. Abbr. for Horn.

Huaiño [Sp.]. Lively dance of Bolivia, Ecuador, and Peru. Also written *wainyio* and *guaiño,* it is usually in 2/4 meter and moderate tempo and

consists of two four-measure phrases that are constantly repeated. Originally, at the time of the Spanish conquest, the name *huaiño* was used by the Quechuan Indians for funeral dances.

J.O-S.

Huapango [Sp.]. Generic name for tunes played and danced at the *Bailes de Huapango,* a kind of popular festivity common mainly along the shores of the Gulf of Mexico. Fast and complicated steps danced to intricate cross-rhythms are characteristic of these dances, as well as the juxtaposition of 2/4, 3/4, and 6/8 meter. It is performed by instrumental ensembles that range from duos of harp and guitar to a full *mariachi band.

J.O-S.

Huehuetl [Sp.]. Generic name for a series of ancient Mexican upright drums made from hollowed logs. A jaguar skin that can be tightened or loosened to raise or lower the pitch covers the single drumhead. The player uses his fingers rather than mallets. Also see *MaMI.*

J.O-S.

Hufnagelschrift [G.]. See *Nagelschrift.*

Huguenots, Les [F., The Huguenots]. Opera in five acts by Meyerbeer (libretto by E. Scribe), produced in Paris, 1836. Setting: Paris and Touraine, 1572.

Humanism, humanist music. Music of the 16th century that was influenced by humanism in literature, especially the revival of interest in the Greek and Roman classics. Its clearest musical expressions are in the composition of Horatian *odes, in *vers mesuré,* in the revival of Greek theory, and in the resulting experiments with chromaticism and *enharmonic tones. The term is also used more broadly to describe the entire school of early 16th-century composers (chiefly German and French) who had close contact with the leading humanist writers and thinkers (Erasmus, Ulrich von Hutten, Johann Reuchlin, Ronsard, Baïf) and who adopted the humanist emphasis on refinement, balance, and restraint (Hofhaimer, Senfl, Janequin, Claudin). A popular practice of this period was the use of scholarly names, such as *prooemium* [L.] or *anabole* [Gr.] for prelude [see W. Merian, *Der Tanz in den deutschen Tabulaturbüchern* (1927), pp. 60, 62, 63]. See Renaissance.

Lit.: D. P. Walker, *Der musikalische Humanismus* (1949; also in *MR* ii, iii); H. J. Moser, *Geschichte der deutschen Musik,* rev. ed. (1930), i, 379; *LavE* i.3, 1298.

Hummel [G.]. (1) A Swedish zither with frets, widely used during the 18th century. See S. Walin, *Die schwedische Hummel* (1952). (2) In German, older designation for the drone of bagpipes and perhaps also for a primitive bagpipe itself.

Humoreske [G.], **humoresque** [F.]. A 19th-century name for instrumental compositions of a humorous, fanciful, or simply good-humored nature. R. Schumann (op. 20) used it for a long composition in which the expression frequently changes from one extreme to another.

Hungarian Dances [G. Ungarische Tänze]. A collection of twenty-one dances by Brahms, for piano, four hands, published in four volumes (1852–69). Some of them employ genuine Hungarian melodies, while others are freely invented in the Hungarian Gypsy style.

Hungarian Rhapsodies. See *Rhapsodies hongroises.*

Hungary. I. The oldest stratum of Hungarian music is represented by folk music discovered after 1905 by Bartók and Kodály, which, according to recent findings, extends eastward to the Cheremis tribe around the Volga, to the Bashkirs, and to the Mongols as far as the Yellow Sea. This music is pentatonic, with characteristic rhythms and melodies. Gregorian chant was introduced during the Middle Ages. The earliest recorded sources (Codex Hahót, Codex Albensis, Codex Pray), dating from the 11th century, show by their notation that they are related to the Frankish, North Italian, and St. Gall repertories. Soon afterward Hungarianized "popular" versions of Gregorian melodies with Hungarian texts appeared. During the late Middle Ages (*c.* 1200–1480) the courtly and popular music of the minstrels flourished. Literary sources indicate that this tradition was closely connected with specific instruments— the *kobuz* (a short lute), viol, horn, bagpipe. Toward the end of the Middle Ages, e.g., at the court of Matthias Corvinus (1443?–90), this indigenous tradition gave way to more international influences, in part mingled with the practices of wandering players.

The 16th century brought the flowering of epic song, developed by traveling singers, among them some schoolmasters trained in the humanist tradition. Their long historical or Biblical epics were usually sung with some instrumental accompaniment. The most important of them is Sebastian Tinódi (1505?–56), whose *Cronica* of

1554 includes rhymed verses as well as some melodies. Particularly remarkable is the song commemorating the siege of Eger (1389) because of its unmistakable "national" traits [see *LavE* 1.5, 2615]. At the same time there developed, under the influence of the Reformation, an indigenous repertory of religious choral music. Beginning in 1607, the melodies of the French Huguenot Psalter were underlaid with Hungarian texts and partly displaced the earlier Hungarian hymns.

Traces of instrumental dance music are found in German and Italian collections of keyboard or lute music, which contain pieces such as "Ungaresca," "Ungarischer Tanz," "Ballo ongaro," etc. The most important representative of Hungarian lute music is Bálint (Valentin) Bakfark (1507–76), who worked mostly at the French and Polish courts and won international recognition. Between 1552 and 1565 he published four books of lute music, containing ricercars, fantasias, and intabulations of motets and chansons [see Editions XV, 37].

An interesting repertory of 17th-century harpsichord music is preserved in four manuscripts (Codex Kájoni, Codex Vietórisz, Sopron MS by J. J. Stark, Löese MS), which contain arrangements of songs, dances, suites, etc., originally scored for instrumental ensembles. In Transylvania the Franciscan monk János Kájoni (1629/30–87) collected Hungarian, Rumanian, and Gypsy dances, together with Italian monodic pieces, German choral compositions, and French suites. In 1711 Prince Pál (Paul) Esterházy (1635–1713) had published, under the title *Harmonia Caelestis,* a collection of 55 sacred compositions ("Concertos") for voices and instruments. Traces of the 17th-century repertory also are present in popular melodies known as *kuruc* songs, which appeared about 1800, at the time of the anti-Hapsburg uprisings, and represent an effort to restore the old national tradition.

II. In the middle of the 18th century student choirs were established, especially encouraged by Professor Georg Maróthi of Debreczin, who published (1743) Goudimel's Psalter with Hungarian texts by Albert Szenczi Molnér. This tradition of religious choral polyphony was carried over to secular songs, and between 1780 and 1820 the repertory of numerous provincial schools was included in several "Melodaria" (MS Liederbücher). In these the influence of rococo dance forms played an important role. The 18th century also saw the development of a new Hungarian folksong, which links the old Oriental tradition with new forms, melodies, and tonalities. Simultaneously there appeared a new style of dance music, the so-called *verbunkos* [from G. *Werbung,* draft], which were used to recruit soldiers. This dance type became so popular that in 19th-century western Europe it was regarded as *the* national music of Hungary, and the type was imitated by Haydn, Mozart, Schubert, Weber, and Brahms. The *verbunkos* and its offspring, the *csárdás,* are the most important achievements of Hungarian romanticism, an inspiration for all 19th-century Hungarian composers.

In opera, cultivated since the beginning of the 19th century, Franz (Ferenc) Erkel (1810–93) became the leading composer. His nationalist operas (*Hunyadi László,* 1844; *Bánk Bán,* 1861; *Brankovics György,* 1874; etc.) represent the new romantic style, as do the Hungarian Rhapsodies of Franz Liszt (1811–86) and the symphonic works of Mihály Mosonyi (1814–70). Liszt's importance, however, transcends nationalist romanticism. His innovations in style, form [see Symphonic poem], and harmony mark a new direction for the entire development of late romantic music, as well as the beginnings of 20th-century Hungarian music.

III. About 1900, some of the late romantic composers such as Jenö Hubay (1858–1937), Ernst von Dohnányi (1877–1960) and Leo Weiner (1885–1960) attempted to combine the native tradition with contemporary European trends. These efforts produced wholly new results after 1905, in the works of Béla Bartók (1881–1945) and Zoltán Kodály (1882–1967). Setting themselves apart from the romantic conventions and striving for international contacts, they created a new Hungarian idiom based on the old folk material they had discovered. Bartók's research extended far beyond the borders of Hungary, into the folk music of Rumania, Slovakia, the Ukraine, Bulgaria, Turkey, etc. He is generally regarded as one of the outstanding composers of the 20th century. Kodály achieved a fusion of Hungarian folk tradition and European art music. Among the followers of Bartók and Kodály are László Lajtha (1891–1963) and numerous younger composers who, like them, strive for a synthesis of the Hungarian tradition with the most recent trends (Ferenc Szabó, Endre Szervánszky, Pál Kadosa, Pál Járdányi, György Ranki, Ferenc Farkas, Emil Petrovics, György Kurtág, András Mihály, Rezsö Sugár, and others).

Lit.: B. Szabolcsi, *A Concise History of Hungarian Music* [1964]; B. Bartók, *Hungarian Folk Music* (1931); Z. Kodály, *Folk Music of Hungary* [1960]; E. Haraszti, *La Musique hongroise* (1933); J. Vigué and J. Gergely, *La Musique hongroise* (1959); B. Rajeczky, ed., ‡*Melodiarium hungaricae medii aevi, i: Hymnen und Sequenzen* (1956); B. Bartók, "Hungarian Peasant Music" (*MQ* xix); O. Gombosi, "Music in Hungary" (*ReMR,* pp. 714ff.); id., "Vita musicale alla corte di re Mattia" (*Corvina* xvii [1929], 110ff.); id., "Die ältesten Denkmäler der mehrstimmigen Vokalmusik aus Ungarn" (*Ungarische Jahrbücher* xi, 84ff); B. Szabolsci, "Ungarische Chorpartituren des 18. Jahrhunderts" (*ZMW* xi); id., "Die ungarischen Spielleute den Mittelalters" (*CP Abert*); Z. Falvy, "Spielleute im mittelalterlichen Ungarn" (*Studia musicologica* i, 29–64); D. Bartha, in *AMF* ii; E. Haraszti, in *RdM* 1929, 159ff, *RdM* 1930, 176ff; B. Szabolcsi, "Probleme der alten ungarischen Musikgeschichte" (*ZMW* vii, viii); I. Fábián, "Modern Hungarian Music" in *LBCM,* also in *MQ* li.

B.S. trans. W.A.

Hunnenschlacht, Die [G., The Battle (Slaughter) of the Huns]. Symphonic poem by Liszt (1857), inspired by a painting by Kaulbach.

Hunting horn. See under Horn II.

Hunt music [G. *Jagdmusik*]. See K. Taut, "Beiträge zur Geschichte der Jagdmusik" (diss. Leipzig, 1927). See Fanfare.

Hunt Quartet. (1) Popular name for Mozart's String Quartet in B-flat, K. 458 (no. 3 of the *Haydn Quartets), also called *La Chasse,* with reference to the hunting-horn motif in the opening theme. (2) Popular name for Haydn's String Quartet in B-flat, generally considered his first quartet, first published in 1762.

Hunt Symphony. Haydn's Symphony in D major, no. 73 (1781), also called *La Chasse,* with reference to the last movement, which was originally composed to depict a hunting scene in his opera *La Fedeltà premiata* (1780).

Hupfauf [G.]. See under *Nachtanz*.

Hurdy-gurdy [F. *vielle (à roue);* G. *Drehleier;* It. *ghironda;* Sp. *zanfoña*]. A medieval stringed instrument, shaped somewhat like a lute or viol, whose strings are put in vibration not by a bow but by a rotating rosined wheel operated by a handle at the lower end of the body. The instrument usually had two to four unfingered bass-strings that were allowed to sound continuously, producing a drone harmony (c–g–c'), and two melody strings (tuned in unison) running over the fingerboard, which were stopped by tangents connected with a keyboard. The instrument was very popular from the 10th to 14th centuries; later it was disdained as a street musician's instrument. Praetorius, in *Syntagma Musicum* (1615), expressly declines to speak of the "Bauern- und umlaufenden Weiber-Leyer" (the lyre of peasants and itinerant wenches). However, in the 17th century it, together with the musette, became fashionable in French society [see Musette]. Haydn wrote five concertos and seven *notturnos for two hurdy-gurdies. He called the instrument *lyra* or *lira organizzata,* a name that has been erroneously interpreted as lira da braccio. Some 18th-century specimens of hurdy-gurdy have a small number of organ pipes attached in the body, and it is probably to these that the term "organizzata" refers. The name "lyra" as well as the use of a crank has also led to confusion with the street-organ [G. *Leier-kasten]*. Schubert's well-known song "Der Leiermann" portrays the player of a hurdy-gurdy, not a street-organ. See ill. under Violin.

The hurdy-gurdy is described in a 10th-century treatise entitled *Quomodo organistrum construatur* (*GS* i, 303, where it is attributed to Oddo of Cluny). Pictures from the 12th and 13th centuries show a much larger instrument (held and played by two men) than the later type. The original name *organistrum* was replaced about 1300 by the names *armonia* and *symphonia,* the latter of which was corrupted into *chifonie, cinfonia, zanfonja, zampugna, *sambuca,* etc. In the 15th century the instrument was given the name *vielle,* after the old *vielle (a fiddle) had become obsolete. See *SaHMI,* pp. 271f; E. de Bricqueville, in *BSIM* 1909, p. 735.

Hurtig [G.]. Quick, nimble.

Hydraulos [F. *orgue hydraulique;* G. *Wasseror-gel*]. The organ of ancient Greece, invented by Ktesibios of Alexandria (*c.* 300–250 B.C.). It differed from the pneumatic organ mainly in the wind supply, which was provided by water instead of bellows. The water did not, as older writers fancifully said, run through the pipes, but was enclosed in a separate container and served to conduct hydraulic pressure provided by hand pumps. The instrument was very accurately described by Hero of Alexander (*c.* 120 B.C.) and Vitruvius Pollio (*c.* 14 B.C.). A clay model found in the ruins of Carthage and

portions of an actual instrument discovered in 1931 at Aquincum, near Budapest, have shown additional details of its construction. The hydraulos was not, as is frequently stated, a "loud and noisy" instrument. Cicero, who describes its use at banquets, calls its sound a sensation "as delectable to the ears as is the most delicious fish to the palate" (*Tusculan Disputations,* iii, 43). It was originally and predominantly for home use but later was also used to accompany gladiator contests in Rome. The most remarkable feature of the hydraulos was its playing mechanism, which consisted of small hinged keys that could easily be depressed with one finger and that automatically returned to their normal position

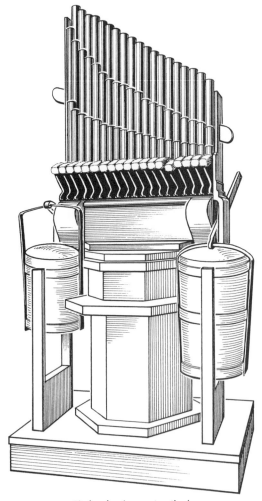

Hydraulos (reconstruction)

by means of springs. It was not until the 10th century that this keyboard mechanism was rediscovered and used in organs. See Organ XII; Magrepha.

Lit.: H. Degering, *Die Orgel . . . bis zur Karolingerzeit* (1905); E. Buhle, *Die Blasinstrumente in den Miniaturen des frühen Mittelalters* (1903); H. G. Farmer, *The Organ of the Ancients from Eastern Sources* (1931); *SaHMI*, p. 143; W. Apel, "Early History of the Organ" (*Speculum* xxiii); C. Maclean, in *SIM* vi; J. W. Warman, in *PMA* xxx; L. Nagy, *Az Aquincumi orgona* (1934; in Hungarian, summ. in German); W. W. Hyde, in *Transactions and Proceedings of the American Philological Association* lxix (1938); K. Schlesinger, in *SIM* ii; T. Schneider, in *MF* vii; P. Tannery and C. de Vaux, in *Revue des études grecques* xxi.

Hymn. A song of praise or adoration of God (originally, in honor of Apollo; two hymns to Apollo of *c.* 150 B.C. are among the most complete remnants of Greek music; see *HAM*, no. 7a, b). In the early Christian era, the term "hymn" was applied to all songs in praise of the Lord; later it was restricted to newly written poems, as distinguished from the scriptural Psalms and canticles [see Gregorian chant II].

I. *Hymns of the Eastern churches.* Antioch (Syria) and Constantinople (Byzantine Empire) were the earliest centers of hymn writing (hymnody). The movement apparently started among the Gnostics, a sect that flourished in the 2nd century. Bardesanes (154–*c.* 222) and his son (or disciple?) Harmonius wrote a complete Gnostic Psalter, a collection of poetic paraphrases of the Psalms. Its great popular success (cf. the *Psalters of the 16th century) led to imitations among the Christians. Saint Ephraem (d. 378?) of Syria is usually considered the father of Christian hymnody. The Eastern churches (Syrian, Byzantine, Armenian) gave hymns a much more prominent part in the service than they ever attained in the Western church [see Byzantine chant; Armenia; Syrian chant]. The earliest preserved hymn melody is the *Oxyrhynchos Hymn of *c.* A.D. 300. See H. J. W. Tillyard, *Byzantine Music and Hymnography* (1923); Editions XXIX.

II. *Latin hymns.* St. Hilary, Bishop of Poitiers (d. *c.* 367), is credited with having written the first Latin hymns, in imitation of the Syrian and Greek hymns of the early Eastern churches. Their style (three survive) is rather involved and obscure. It was left to St. Ambrose (*c.* 340–397) to introduce a type of hymn that, because of its clarity and regularity, became immensely popular and gained a firm foothold in the Milanese as well as the Roman rites [see Ambrosian hymns]. Among his successors were Aurelius Prudentius (348–after 405), Caelius Sedulius (mid-5th century), Venantius Fortunatus (530–609), Paulus Diaconus (d. 799), Theodulphus (d. 821), Hrabanus (Rhabanus) Maurus (d. 856), and many poets of succeeding centuries. The 55 volumes of the *Analecta hymnica* (ed. by G. M. Dreves and C. Blume) contain a very large though not complete collection of medieval hymn texts; a useful index for quick reference is U. Chevalier's *Repertorium hymnologicum.* Of the innumerable hymns written between A.D. 400 and 1400 (if not later), about 120 are still in use.

The earliest sources of hymn melodies (hymnaries) date from the 11th or 12th century. To assume (as is frequently done) that any of these melodies dates from the time of St. Ambrose is entirely gratuitous. Equally unwarranted are reconstructions purporting to show the "original" form of such melodies, i.e., strictly syllabic and in triple meter. The great majority of the preserved melodies employ groups of two to four notes that fall just as frequently on the strong as on the weak syllable. Obviously they do not admit a strictly metrical rendering [see P. Wagner, *Einführung in die Gregorianischen Melodien,* iii, 462, and *ApGC*, p. 428f].

III. *Polyphonic hymns.* From before 1400 there exist only a few scattered examples of polyphonic hymns, among them the famous 13th-century Hymn to St. Magnus, written in parallel thirds (*HAM*, no. 25c). The earliest source containing a number of polyphonic hymns is the Codex Apt [see Sources, no. 19]. They are in a simple homorhythmic style, usually with the plainsong melody in the highest part. Dunstable wrote one hymn ("Ave maris stella"), Dufay a cycle of 21 hymns in a similar though slightly more ornate style [ed. by R. Gerber, *Das Chorwerk,* no. 49]. In the 15th-century MSS most of the hymn settings follow the alternation principle whereby the odd-numbered strophes are sung to the chant melody and a single polyphonic setting is provided for the even-numbered stanzas. The cycle of hymns in the Codex Capella Sixtina 15 (*c.* 1500), however, provides a new polyphonic setting based on the same *cantus firmus* for each of the alternate strophes, thus setting a pattern that was to become more or less standard for a long series of hymn collections by individual composers through the next two centuries. The four complete sets of Vespers hymns by Carpentras, C. Festa, A. Willaert, and F. B. Corteccia, written before the middle of the 16th century, were followed by similar cycles by such composers as J. de Kerle, D. Ortiz, G. M. Asola, T. M. de Victoria, G. P. Palestrina, C. Porta, and O. Lassus—to mention only a few. Organ hymns were written by H. Buchner, G. Cavazzoni (1543), T. Tallis, A. de Cabezón, J. Titelouze, and others; see Organ chorale I.

IV. *German hymns.* Long before any other nation, the Germans began to sing hymns in their native language. As early as *c.* 1300 some Latin sequences had German versions, e.g., "Christ ist erstanden" (after Wipo's Easter sequence, *Victimae paschali laudes*) or "Komm, heiliger Geist" (Whitsun sequence, *Veni sancte spiritus*). The Münch (Monk) of Salzburg (fl. *c.* 1400) and Heinrich Laufenberg (*c.* 1390–1460) translated a large number of hymns into German. Along with these original compositions of great beauty were written, e.g., the Crusader's song "In Gottes Namen fahren wir" and cradle-songs for the Nativity, remarkable for their C-major melodies and lulling rhythm in triple meter ("Joseph, lieber Joseph mein" and "In dulci jubilo"). A Marian hymn, "Maria zart," has survived in a Mass by Obrecht and in two settings by Arnolt Schlick, one for organ [*HAM*, no. 101] and the other for lute. These are only a few examples from a large repertory that became the point of departure for the ensuing development of the German Protestant hymn [see Chorale].

V. *English hymns.* See next entry.

Lit.: *For I:* See under Byzantine chant, etc. *For II:* G. M. Dreves and C. Blume, *Analecta hymnica,* 55 vols. (1886–1922); U. Chevalier, *Repertorium hymnologicum,* 6 vols. (1892–1921); ‡*Monumenta monodica medii aevi* (vol. i, *Hymnen*), ed. B. Stäblein (1956); A. S. Walpole, *Early Latin Hymns* (1922); M. Britt, *The Hymns of the Breviary and Missal* (1922, '24); G. M. Dreves, *Ein Jahrtausend lateinischer Hymnendichtung,* 2 vols. (1909); C.-A. Moberg, *Die liturgischen Hymnen in Schweden* (1947); *ApGC,* pp. 421ff. *For III:* R. Gerber, "Römische Hymnenzyklen des späten 15. Jahrhunderts" (*AMW* xii); *id.,* "Spanische Hymnensätze um 1500" (*AMW* x); *id.,* "Die Hymnen des Apelschen Kodex" (*CP Schering*); *id.,* in *MGG* vi, 1018–30; G. Haydon, in *Enciclopedia della musica,* ii, 467–9; *Editions VIII,* 9 (Finck), 32 (Adam von Fulda, *et al.*), 49 (Dufay); *Editions XVIII,* 32–34 (Codex Apel).

For IV: W. Bäumker, *Das katholische deutsche Kirchenlied in seinen Singweisen,* 4 vols. (1883–1911); M. C. Pfleger, "Untersuchungen am deutschen geistlichen Lied des 13. bis 16. Jahrhunderts" (diss. Berlin, 1937); M. John Bosco Connor, *Gregorian Chant and Medieval Hymn Tunes in the Works of J. S. Bach* (1957).

Hymn, English. I. From evidence in literary works, it appears that sacred ballads and carols were sung outside the church in the late 15th and 16th centuries. Some of the ballads circulated in broadsides; the *Song made by F.B.P.,* "Jerusalem my happy home," dates from 1571. By 1540 echoes of Continental hymn singing had reached the British Isles. Sometime in the 1540's John Wedderburn, a Scottish priest, published *Gude and Godlie Ballates,* which contained a translation of Luther's hymn, "Vom Himmel hoch." About 1543, Miles Coverdale's *Goostly Psalmes and Spirituall Songes* was published, containing words and music of 40 hymns, many of them English translations from the German, including the tunes used in Germany, as, e.g., "Ein' feste Burg." The collection was proscribed and burned in 1546.

Music editions of the Sternhold and Hopkins metrical psalms date from 1560, although an English collection was published four years earlier in Geneva. All of these collections, apart from containing the 150 psalms set in meter, also had a few hymns or metrical prayers appended.

The English Psalters suffered musically by comparison with the French or Genevan Psalter and the German *chorale melodies because of the limited number of regular meters to which the texts were set. This continued well into the 18th century, even after the New Version of the metrical psalms by Tate and Brady had appeared (1696). Another inhibiting factor was the illiteracy of most congregations; this required each hymn to be *lined-out; a precentor, clerk, or deacon, as he was variously called, sang one line of the hymn at a time and then waited while the congregation sang it after him before singing the second line, etc. The result was that by 1725 many congregations knew fewer than ten tunes and sang most of the hymns to those tunes.

After the Psalters published by John Day (1522–84), significant collections with new tunes were published by Thomas East (1591, '92), Thomas Ravenscroft (1621), and John Playford (1671, '77). The new style of hymn texts by Isaac Watts (1674–1748) and Charles Wesley (1707–

1788) inspired many newer tunes with more rhythmic freedom and wider use of intervals than in the older psalm tunes. Because of their association with singing at Wesleyan services, they have been referred to as "Methodist tunes."

Significant English *tune books of the 18th century were *Lyra Davidica* (1708); John Arnold's *The Compleat Psalmodist* (1741); John Wesley's *A Collection of Tunes ... sung at the Foundery* (1742); *Psalms, Hymns and Anthems of the Foundling Hospital* (1774); and Martin Madan's *A Collection of Psalm and Hymn Tunes* (1769). There was some provision for three or four parts in these books, but basically they were intended for unison singing by the congregation. It should be noted that from the earliest printing until the mid-19th century, tune books contained either no text at all or merely the first stanza; singers had to use a separate hymnal for the words.

Composers such as J. B. Dykes in the mid-19th century wrote tunes with four-part harmony that were miniature part songs. These, introduced in successive editions of *Hymns Ancient and Modern* (1861–1950), completely changed the character of hymn singing. Other significant musical editions of the period were Arthur Sullivan's *Church Hymns with Tunes* (1874) and Joseph Barnby's *The Hymnary* (1872). Important collections of the 20th century are *The English Hymnal* (1906) and *Songs of Praise* (1925), both of which have come out in recent editions.

II. In America, apart from a few tunes bound in the back of successive editions of *The Bay Psalm Book,* the first tune book to be published was James Lyon's *Urania* (1761), followed shortly by Francis Hopkinson's *A Collection of Psalm Tunes* (1763) and Josiah Flagg's *A Collection of the best Psalm Tunes ... to which are added some Hymns and Anthems; the greater part of them never before printed in America* (1764; on plates engraved by Paul Revere). By 1800, more than 130 such collections had been published along the Atlantic coast. In the 19th century, collections such as Lowell Mason's *Carmina Sacra* went through thirteen editions between 1841 and 1860, selling more than 500,000 copies. During the same years, Joseph Funk, a Mennonite, brought out about twenty editions of his *Genuine Church Music* (later called *Harmonia Sacra*) in the Shenandoah Valley of Virginia.

Today, each major denomination has its own hymnal, sharing nearly half its hymns and tunes

with other denominations and adapting the remainder to its own traditions. Musically, the Episcopal *Hymnal 1940* perhaps has the broadest interest; its 600 tunes include plainsong melodies, German chorale melodies, tunes from the Genevan Psalter and the early English Psalters, part-song tunes of the Victorian era, folksongs (apart from the Christmas carols), broad modern unison melodies, and 44 newly composed tunes.

One phenomenon connected with American congregational song of the latter part of the 19th century was the gospel song. Many of its texts were closely connected with the doctrine of salvation by grace, and their content sometimes seems to be an irritatingly priggish assumption of Christian superiority. Both as literature and as music they plumbed the depths of commonness, but nevertheless their influence extended beyond the confines of the revival meeting into the regular services of the church. The tunes were pallid imitations of popular songs, always using a refrain that in practice was frequently sung several times between stanzas.

Lit.: W. Douglas, *Church Music in History and Practice,* rev. ed. by L. Ellinwood (1962); J. T. Lightwood, *Hymn-Tunes and Their Story* [1906]; *id., The Music of the English Methodist Hymn Book* (1935); F. J. Metcalf, *American Psalmody* (1917); *id., American Writers and Compilers of Sacred Music* [1925]; M. Frost, *English and Scottish Psalm & Hymn Tunes c. 1543–1677* (1953); *id., Historical Companion to Hymns Ancient & Modern,* rev. ed. [1962]; A. P. Britton, *Bibl. of Early Religious American Music* (microfilm, 1949); M. Patrick, *Four Centuries of Scottish Psalmody* (1949); R. G. McCutchan, *Hymn Tune Names* (1957); G. Dearmer, "The Fall and Rise of the Hymn Tune" (*ML* vi, 35); *The Hymnal 1940 Companion,* 3rd ed. (1955); and handbooks to other contemporary hymnals.

A.T.D; rev. L.E.

Hypate [Gr.]. See under Greece II.

Hyper-, hypo- [Gr.]. Prefixes denoting higher and lower pitches respectively. *Hyper- (hypo-) diatessaron* is the upper (lower) fourth; *hyper-(hypo-) diapente,* the higher (lower) fifth. In Greek theory, terms such as Hyperdorian and Hypodorian signify modes (more properly, octave species) that start a fifth above and below the initial tone of the original octave, e.g., Dorian on e, Hyperdorian on b, Hypodorian on A [see Greece II]. In the medieval system of church modes the prefix *hypo-* denotes modes whose range (*ambitus*) is a fourth below that of the corresponding primary (authentic) mode [see Church modes I].

Hyporchema [Gr.]. An ancient Greek dancing song from Crete.

I

I. This letter was introduced by Kirnberger to denote the natural seventh, i.e., the seventh harmonic, such as that produced on the natural horn. Its pitch (7/4 = 969 cents) is noticeably lower than that of the well-tempered seventh (1000 cents) and that of the seventh in *just intonation (996 cents).

Iamb, iambic. See under Poetic meter; also Modes, rhythmic.

Iastian. See under Greece II.

Iberia [L.]. Twelve piano pieces, in four sets of three each, by Albéniz, published 1906–08. Each is based on a Spanish theme or locale. For Debussy's *Ibéria,* see under *Images.*

Iceland. The Icelanders possess a remarkable tradition of folk music that probably antedates all the other European folk traditions [see Folk music III]. A comparison of medieval manuscripts (Arnamagnæan collection, University Library of Copenhagen; see *WoHN* i, 119) with recent collections shows that types of folk music have not changed much during the last 600 years. A characteristic feature of the *rímur* (dancing songs, ballads) is frequent change of meter accompanied by a change of tune (*Kvædalög*). Particularly interesting is the *tvisöngur* (twin song), i.e., two-part singing in parallel fifths, which is evidently a remnant of the parallel organum of the 9th century and was still practiced until comparatively recent times [see *ReMMA,* p. 270f]. Modern composers include Jon Leifs (b. 1899), who incorporates both *rímur* and *tvisöngur* in his work, and Páll Isólfsson (b. 1893), an organist-composer whose work reflects the Lutheran background of Icelandic music.

Lit.: B. Thorsteinsson, *Islenzk Thjódlög* (1906–09); J. Leifs, *Isländische Volkslied* (1929); S. Sveinbjörnsson, *Icelandic Folksongs,* rev. ed.

(1949); A. Hammerich, in *SIM* i; E. M. von Hornbostel, "Phonographierte isländische Zwiegesänge" (*Deutsche Islandforschung,* 1930); J. Leifs, in *ZMW* xi and *DM* xvi.1.

Iconography of music. The representation of musical instruments, musicians, and the like in painting, sculpture, mosaics, coins, and other media is a very important repository, particularly for music of ancient times, for which it is practically the only source of information. Knowledge of Babylonian, Assyrian, and Egyptian music is based almost entirely on iconographic material. Medieval representations such as the illuminations for the *cantiga MS of the 13th century are the main source of information about the early development of European instruments. Even where other information is available, pictorial representations often provide additional evidence, showing, e.g., how the organ was played in the 15th century or how the violin and bow were held in the 18th century. In a broader sense, iconography includes also the portraits of composers, conductors, and performers, reproductions of concert halls, operatic stagings, music titles, etc.

The most important collections of pictorial material are: G. Kinsky, *A History of Music in Pictures* (1930); M. Pincherle, *An Illustrated History of Music* [1959]; A. Buchner, *Musical Instruments through the Ages* [1956?]; A. G. Hess, *Italian Renaissance Paintings with Musical Subjects* (1955); H. Besseler and M. Schneider, ed., *Musikgeschichte in Bildern* (1961—); M. Sauerlandt, *Die Musik in fünf Jahrhunderten der europäischer Malerei* [1922]; C. Moreck, *Die Musik in der Malerei* (1924); G. Kanth, *Bilder-Atlas zur Musikgeschichte von Bach bis Strauss* [1912]; G. F. Schorer, *Bildnis der Musik* (1955); K. Andorfer and R. Epstein, *Musica in nummis* (1907; on coins); E. Buhle, *Die musi-*

kalischen Instrumente in den Miniaturen des frühen Mittelalters (1903); L. Parigi, *La Musica nelle Gallerie di Milano* (1935); id., *I disegni musicali del gabinetto degli "Uffizi" . . . a Firenze* (1951); H. Lavoix *fils*, *La Musique dans l'ymagerie du moyen âge* (1875); P. Collaer and A. Vander Linden, *Atlas historique de la musique* [1960]; E. Valdruche, *Iconographie des titres de musique au xviiie et xixe siècle* (1912); D. F. Scheurleer, *Iconographie des instruments de musique* (1914); E. Reuter, *Les Représentations de la musique dans la sculpture romane en France* (1938); V. Denis, *De muziekinstrumenten in de Nederlanden en in Italië naar hun afbeelding in de 15e-eeuwsche kunst* (1944); P. Lang and O. Bettmann, *A Pictorial History of Music* [1960]; Ris-Paquot, *La Céramique musicale et instrumentale* (1889); W. von Zur Westen, *Musiktitel aus vier Jahrhunderten* (1921); A. H. King, "English Pictorial Music Title-Pages: 1820–1885" (*The Library* [1950]).

Lit.: F. Auerbach, *Tonkunst und bildende Kunst* (1924); E. Hohne, *Music in Art* (1965); H. Leichtentritt, in *CP 1906;* id., in *SIM* vii (14th–17th cent.); M. Seiffert, in *AMW* i (16th cent.); H. Besseler, in *AMW* xvi (16th cent.); C. Sachs, in *AMW* i; E. Winternitz, in *CP 1961;* P. Egan, in *JAMS* xiv (Ital. Renais.).

Ictus. In prosody, a stress or accent. The term was introduced in music by the monks of *Solesmes as an integral part of their rhythmic interpretation and performance of Gregorian chant [see Gregorian chant VI]. The ictus serves primarily to mark off those groups of two and three notes that form the basis of their rendition of the chant. The ictus has nothing to do with the speech accent (tonic accent); it often falls on the weak syllable [see Ex.]. The monks of Solesmes make it a point that, in actual performance, the

Ky - ri - e   e - - le - i - son

ictus should not be rendered as an increase in intensity ("ictus nullam cum intensitate connectionem habet"), nor by sustaining the tone (in the Solesmes rhythm all notes have the same duration unless dotted or marked with horizontal episema). Thus, its actual meaning remains rather obscure. Probably the perception of alternating high and low points (aided by chironomic representations and analogies such as the

waves of the sea) helped the singer produce the effect. See the authoritative explanation in *LU*, pp. xxviff. Also all the Solesmes books [Dom Mocquereau, *Le Nombre musical grégorien,* etc.; particularly, Dom Gajard, *Notions sur le rhythme grégorien* (1935)].

Idée fixe. Berlioz' name for the principal subject of his *Symphonie fantastique.* It occurs in all the movements [see Cyclic], representing the artist at various stages of his life. It is considered an important forerunner of Wagner's *leitmotiv.

Idiomatic style. A style appropriate for the instrument for which particular music is written. To write idiomatically is a matter of prime concern for modern composers, particularly in orchestral scoring, since the quality of the score is judged largely by the degree to which the various parts exploit the technical and sonorous resources of the instruments without exceeding them. In early music, however, including that of Bach, the question of "idiomatic style" is often controversial, since examples abound in which the style does not conform to the technical properties of the instrument or voice. For example, a piece such as the E-major Fugue from *The Well-Tempered Clavier,* vol. ii, is neither in harpsichord style nor in clavichord style, but in organ style or even instrumental ensemble style (string quartet). Examples like this show that idiomatic writing cannot always be considered a valid criterion for evaluating a composition or composer.

Idiomelon [Gr.]. In Byzantine chant, a hymn (*kontakion, kanon, sticheron,* etc.) having its own melody, as opposed to *prosomoion,* a hymn text sung to a borrowed melody [see *Contrafactum*]. A select group of *idiomela* whose melodies were used for *prosomoia* are known as *automela* (sing. *automelon*).

Idiophone. See under Instruments I.

Idomeneo. Opera in three acts by Mozart (libretto by G. B. Varesco), produced in Munich, 1781. Setting: Crete in legendary times.

Images [F.]. Title used by Debussy for two cycles of compositions. (1) Six piano pieces in two sets of three each: I (1905), *Reflets dans l'eau, Hommage à Rameau,* and *Mouvement;* II (1907), *Cloches à travers les feuilles, Et la Lune descend sur le temple qui fut, Poissons d'or.* (2) Three symphonic poems (*Images pour orchestre,* 1906–11): *Rondes de printemps, Ibéria, Gigues.* The second, *Ibéria,* consists of three movements:

Par les rues et par les chemins, Les Parfums de la nuit, and *Le Matin d'un jour de fête.*

Imbroglio [It.]. An operatic scene in which the idea of utter confusion is artfully carried out by giving the singers and players parts that, although properly coordinated harmonically, are deliberately incongruous and contrasting in rhythm and meter. The three orchestras in the ballroom scene of Mozart's *Don Giovanni* [end of Act I] and the street scene of Wagner's *Die Meistersinger* [end of Act II] are famous examples.

Imitation. The restatement in close succession of a melody (theme, motif) in different parts of a contrapuntal texture. This device is most consistently employed in the *canon, in which a whole voice-part is imitated in another (canonic imitation). Imitation of themes (subjects) is an essential feature of the *fugue (fugal imitation) as well as the 16th-century motet and the various prefugal forms, the *ricercar, *canzona, *fantasia, and *capriccio. While in a fugue the imitation is normally restricted to one theme, the earlier forms usually have a number of themes.

Imitation is predicated on the presence of two (or more) equivalent voice-parts, and it is interesting to note that its history begins with the earliest type of composition meeting this requirement, the *organa tripla* and *quadrupla* of the school of Notre Dame, c. 1200 [Ex. 1]. Imitation, sometimes quite extensive, occurs also in a few three-voice motets of the 13th century, always in connection with an identical text (i.e., an identical phrase occurring within the essentially different texts of the two upper parts; see Y. Rokseth, *Polyphonies du XIIIe siècle,* nos. 104, 105, 325). A thorough study of the numerous conductus is likely to yield many additional examples of imitation in their **caudae.* In the 14th century, imitation found its first systematic realization in the Italian *caccia and French **chace,* which are extended two- and three-part canons. Of greater importance to the development of imitation (which is essentially the development of fugal, not canonic imitation) are imitative passages found in a number of Italian madrigals and *ballate* of the 14th century, particularly in the works of Lorenzo Masini and Paolo Tenorista. In some of the motets by Jean Ciconia (*c.* 1335–1411) imitation takes on a structural significance. In the 15th century Hugo de Lantins made frequent use of imitation, much more so than his contemporary, Dufay, or than Ocke-

ghem, who has quite wrongly been called the "father of imitation." The works of Obrecht, Isaac, and Josquin show more and more deliberate use of imitation, which *c.* 1500 became an essential element of musical style. The development reached its climax with Nicolas Gombert (*c.* 1490–1556), who established the *through-imitative style commonly associated with the 16th-century motet. Throughout the 16th century and the baroque period imitation remained a basic element of contrapuntal writing (*imitative counterpoint). The various learned devices of imitation—augmentation, diminution, inversion, double counterpoint, combination of two and three themes—were developed in the *ricercar, particularly by Andrea Gabrieli. Prior to 1700, fugal imitation at the interval of a fourth (lower fifth) was much more common than that of a fifth. Bach was one of the first to establish imitation at the interval of a fifth as a characteristic feature of fugal writing [cf. Ex. 2 and 3].

In the rococo period (*c.* 1725–75) came a sharp reaction against the fugal style of the baroque era [see Gallant style]. However, free use of imitation made a comeback in Haydn's and Mozart's later symphonies and quartets, and has

1. Organum triplum, Descendit, c. 1200. 2. Josquin, Cueurs desolez, c. 1500.

3. Bach, Well-Tempered Clavier, vol. ii, 1744.

since remained an important technique of composition, particularly in the development section of symphonies, quartets, sonatas, etc.

Lit.: G. Adler, "Die Wiederholung und Nachahmung in der Mehrstimmigkeit" (*VMW* ii); M. Schneider, "Zur Satztechnik der Notre-Dame Schule" (*ZMW* xiv); W. Apel, "Imitation in the Thirteenth and Fourteenth Centuries" *CP Davison*); C. van den Borren, "Quelques Reflexions à propos du style imitatif syntaxique" (*RBM* i); J. Kerman, "Byrd, Tallis, and the Art of Imitation" (*CP Reese*). See also literature under Fugue; Canon.

Imitative counterpoint. Contrapuntal music based on *imitation, i.e., the use of the same thematic material in all the parts. There are three chief types: *canon (imitation of an entire voice-part); *fugue (imitation throughout the piece of an initial subject); and *motet (imitation of several subjects, each one being used for one point of imitation; see Through-imitation). The preludes in Bach's *Well-Tempered Clavier* offer many interesting examples of "free imitative counterpoint" (e.g., vol. ii, no. 19).

Imperfect. See Perfect, imperfect.

Impressionism. An artistic movement of the late 19th and early 20th centuries, represented in music chiefly by Debussy (1862–1918). The term

is borrowed from painting, indicating the close relationship of contemporary trends in the various arts. The paintings of the French impressionists (Monet, Manet, Renoir) and the refined poetry of Verlaine, Baudelaire, and Mallarmé suggested to Debussy a new type of music, eminently French in character: a music that hints rather than states; in which successions of colors take the place of dynamic development, and "atmospheric" sensations supersede heroic pathos; a music that is vague and intangible as the changing light of day. The implementation of these ideas led to the partial abandonment of such "German" achievements as sonata, symphony, thematic material, and development technique, and led to the introduction of various novel devices that represent the antithesis of the principal features of classical and romantic harmony. Prominent in the impressionist vocabulary are unresolved dissonances, mostly triads with added seconds, fourths, sixths, sevenths; the use of chords, consonant as well as dissonant, in parallel motion (*parallel or gliding chords); the *whole-tone scale in melodic as well as chordal combinations; frequent use of the tritone; modality, particularly avoidance of the leading tone; avoidance of "direction" in the melodic contour (preference of vague "zigzag" design); and irregular and fragmentary construction of phrases.

Foreshadowed in the works of Edouard Lalo and Emmanuel Chabrier [see France IV], impressionism found its first full realization in Debussy's *Prélude à l'après-midi d'un faune* (1892–94) and still more so in his ensuing works, such as the three *Nocturnes* for orchestra (1893–99), the orchestral suite *La Mer* (1903–05), the opera *Pelléas et Mélisande* (1902), or the collections for piano *Images* (1905, '07) and *Préludes* (1910–13). After Debussy, Ravel became the main exponent of impressionism, although his classical inclinations, general feeling for form, dancelike rhythms and elegance are traits hardly compatible with impressionism in the purest sense. In fact, except for its founder, impressionism has not found any full-fledged representative, but it has left its imprint upon the works of many composers, e.g., the Frenchmen Dukas, Roussel, De Séverac; the Englishmen Delius, Bax, Cyril Scott; the Germans Gräner, Schreker, Niemann; the Americans Loeffler, Carpenter, Griffes; the Spaniard De Falla; the Italian Respighi; and the Czech Novak.

After a relatively short time impressionism began to lose much of its original fascination. Its overrefinement and fin-de-siècle character were not conducive to active development. In his latest works (*Études, En blanc et noir,* 3 Sonatas), written 1915–17, Debussy himself—who, incidentally, objected to being called an impressionist—developed a more impersonal style indicative of neoclassical trends. His friend Erik Satie did much to discredit the rich impressionist palette with his whimsical and barren sketches, which seem like a cynical caricature of impressionist technique (e.g., his *Embryons desséchés*). It was the French writer Cocteau who pronounced the death sentence on impressionism: "After the music with the silk brush, the music with the axe." Ironically, Debussy's work today appears to some not as he intended—the negation of romanticism—but as part of it, indeed its acme and conclusion. On the other hand, some impressionist devices have been adopted, with characteristic modifications, in *twentieth-century music, particularly the parallel chords, modified from a coloristic into a rhythmic effect [see Parallel chords].

Lit.: E. B. Hill, *Modern French Music* (1924); R. Lyr, *Les Musiciens impressionistes* (1938); H. G. Schulz, "Zur Phänomenologie des musikalischen Impressionismus" (diss. Würzburg, 1938); H. F. Kölsch, *Der Impressionismus bei Debussy* (1937); O. Wartisch, *Studien zur Harmonik des musikalischen Impressionismus* (1930); E. Evans, "French Music of Today" (*PMA* xxxvi); P. Landormy, "Le Déclin de l'impressionnisme" (*RM* ii); W. Danckert, "Liszt als Vorläufer des musikalischen Impressionismus" (*DM* xxi.5); A. Capri, "Le Origini dell' impressionismo musicale" (*LRM* xi).

Impromptu [F.]. Fanciful name for 19th-century *character pieces of the romantic period. The best-known examples are Schubert's Impromptus op. 90 and op. 142 (probably their title is not Schubert's but that of his publisher, Haslinger) and Chopin's Impromptus op. 29, 36, 51, 66. The title does not refer to elements of improvisation in these pieces (they all are in straightforward style and form) but is meant to describe their somewhat casual origin in the composer's mind. Several years before Schubert wrote his Impromptus a collection of *Impromptus* (1820) by H. Wozzischeck was published.

Improperia [L.]. In the Roman Catholic liturgy, chants for Good Friday Mass. They consist of three passages from the Prophets ("Popule meus quid feci tibi"; "Quia eduxi te per desertum"; "Quid ultra debui facere tibi"), each of which is

followed by the *Trisagion and a number of other short texts, sung in alternation with "Popule meus" [see *LU*, pp. 737ff]. A vestige of the long suppressed *Gallican rites, the *improperia* were adopted in Roman liturgy *c.* 1200. Palestrina set them in *falsobordone* style for double chorus. His settings, whose artistic quality has been much overrated, have been regularly performed since 1560 in the Sistine Chapel on Good Friday. Victoria, Anerio, and Ingegneri composed the text in the same style as Palestrina.

Improvisation, extemporization. I. The art of performing music spontaneously, without the aid of manuscript, sketches, or memory. Also, in a more restricted sense, the art of introducing improvised details into written compositions. The former is a phenomenon so evanescent that it defies documentation and detailed description. This is true, at least, of the great days of improvisation, when masters such as Bach, Handel, Mozart, and Beethoven were as famous for their improvising as for their written compositions. Today, the tape recorder could readily make a permanent record of such performances. However, the great art of improvisation has been lost, since it is no longer practiced by composers and survives chiefly among organ virtuosos.

II. Early musicians famous for their improvisation were Francesco Landini and Paulus Hofhaimer. In the 16th century the ability to improvise in fugal style was a common requirement for an appointment as organist [see Fantasia (5)]. Important information about this practice is given in the *Arte de tañer fantasia* of the Spanish theorist Tomás de Santa María [see O. Kinkeldey, *Orgel und Klavier* (1910)]. In the 17th century the organ improvisations of Sweelinck, Frescobaldi, and Buxtehude attracted people from far-distant places. Bach is known to have improvised a prelude and a fugue, an organ trio (i.e., a piece in three obbligato parts), a chorale prelude, and a final fugue, all on a single hymn tune. In 1747, on visiting Frederick the Great in Potsdam, he extemporized a fugue on the "royal theme" that he subsequently worked out in his *Musikalisches Opfer*. John Hawkins is one of several writers who have vividly described the effect of Handel's extemporization. Mozart frequently extemporized fugues or variations on a given theme. There are a number of enthusiastic accounts of Beethoven's fascinating improvisation [see *Thayer's Life of Beethoven* ed. E. Forbes (1964), i, 367f]. In the romantic period, Moscheles, Liszt, Franck, and Bruckner were famous for their improvisations, which frequently were included in their concert programs.

III. The introduction of improvised details in a written composition is a more tangible phenomenon. It probably played an important role in the emergence of the more ornate (melismatic) types of Gregorian chant [see Ornamentation I]. It is more clearly discernible in the 14th- and 15th-century practice of improvised harmonization [see *Discantus supra librum*]. Tinctoris, in his *Liber de arte contrapuncti* (1477), distinguished between improvisation (*supra librum cantare*) and composition (*res facta*). In the 16th century *contrapunctus* often meant improvised counterpoint (also called *sortisatio*) in contrast to written out counterpoint, which was called *compositio*. In the second half of the 16th century interest turned from contrapuntal (vertical) to melodic (horizontal) improvisation, i.e., the improvised rendition of ornaments and coloraturas (*diminution; *glosa), which played an important part in musical instruction and practice [see Diego Ortiz, *Trattado de glosas* (1553); Agostino Agazzari, *Del sonare sopra il basso* (1607); see Ornamentation II; also under Ensemble (3)]. "Melodic" improvisation continued particularly in the English *divisions of the 17th century, while a new, very important practice arose in the "harmonic" improvisation of the *thoroughbass [see also *Partimento*]. In the 18th century the improvised coloraturas of vocal virtuosos led to the *cadenzas of the classical concerto. An interesting revival of improvisation is the jam session of contemporary *jazz. See also Pennillion.

Lit.: T. C. Whitmer, *The Art of Improvisation* [1922]; A. M. Richardson, *Extempore Playing* (1922); J. Tobin, *How to Improvise Piano Accompaniments* [1956]; G. P. Wollner, *Improvisation in Music* [1963]; M. Dupré, *Traité d'improvisation à l'orgue* (1925); A. Rowley, *Extemporisation: A Treatise for Organists* [1955]; G. F. Wehle, *Die Kunst der Improvisation,* 3 vols. (1925–32); E. Ferand, *Die Improvisation in der Musik* [1938; historical]; *id.,* *Editions XXXIX, 12; P. Rosenfeld, "A Plea for Improvisation" (*MM* xix, no. 1); E. Haraszti, "La Technique des improvisateurs ... au Quattrocento" (*RBM* ix, 12); I. Horsley, "Improvised Embellishment in the Performance of Renaissance Polyphonic Music" (*JAMS* iv); E. T. Ferand, "Improvisation in Music History and Education" (*PAMS* 1940, p. 115); *id.,* "Improvised Vocal Counterpoint in the Late Renaissance and Early Ba-

roque" (*AnnM* iv); *id.,* "Embellished 'Parody Cantatas' in the Early 18th Century" (*MQ* xliv). See also under *Sortisatio,* Ornamentation.

Im Takt. See *Takt.*

Incalzando [It.]. Pressing, hurrying.

In campo aperto [L.]. See under Neumes II.

Incantation. A spell that is sung in a magic ritual. In opera, a scene in which spirits are conjured. Famous examples are the song of Medea in Cavalli's *Il Giasone* of 1649 [see *SchGMB,* no. 201] and a scene in Massenet's *Roy de Lahore* of 1877.

Incatenura [It.]. Italian term for *quodlibet.*

Incidental music. Music to be used in connection with a play. It may consist of occasional songs, marches, dances, and background music for monologues and dialogues, as well as instrumental music before and after each act. The Greek theater and the *liturgical dramas of the Middle Ages made ample use of incidental music [for the latter, see E. Coussemaker, *Drames liturgiques du moyen âge* (1860)]. Shakespeare frequently prescribed incidental music, e.g., at the beginning of *Twelfth Night.* Nearly all of Purcell's dramatic music is incidental music for plays. Later examples are Beethoven's music to Goethe's *Egmont* and to Kotzebue's *Die Ruinen von Athen,* Mendelssohn's music to *A Midsummer Night's Dream,* Bizet's music to Daudet's *L'Arlésienne* (1872), and Grieg's music to Ibsen's *Peer Gynt* (1875).

Lit.: N. O'Neill, "Music to Stage Plays" (*Musical Times,* 1914); *LavE* ii.5, 3373; A. Aber, *Die Musik im Schauspiel* (1926); J. Manifold, "Theatre Music in the Sixteenth and Seventeenth Centuries" (*ML* xxix, 366); A. Salazar, "Music in the Primitive Spanish Theatre before Lope de Vega" (*PAMS* 1938, p. 94). See also Dramatic music.

Incipit [L.]. (1) In Gregorian chant, the first words of a liturgical text (also called "intonation") sung by the cantor before the chorus enters at the place indicated by an asterisk; e.g., "Ad te levavi *animam meam" [*GR,* p. 1]. (2) In psalm tones, etc., same as *initium (inceptio).* (3) In the *cantus firmus* motets of the 13th and 14th centuries, a word or two given at the beginning of the tenor and serving as a reference to the chant from which the tenor is taken, e.g., *Manere,* referring to the melisma on the word "manere," which occurs in the Gradual "Exiit sermo" (inter fratres . . . moritur. ℣. Sed: sic eum volo *manere* . . .) [*GR*, p. 39]; see Motet I. Long lists of incipits are found in P. Aubry and A. Gastoué, *Recherches sur les "Tenors" latins* (1907); P. Aubry, *Recherches sur les "Tenors" français* (1907); Y. Rokseth, *Polyphonies du XIIIe siècle* (1936–39), iv, 152; F. Ludwig, ed., *Guillaume de Machaut, Musikalische Werke,* ii, 58ff (*Editions XLVI 3.i; see also Editions XLVI 1.i, 4.ii, 12); A. Rosenthal, in *AnnM* i, 129f, supp. by M. Bukofzer in *AnnM* iv, 255–58.

Incoronazione di Poppea, L' [It., The Coronation of Poppea]. Opera in three acts by Monteverdi (libretto by G. F. Busenello), produced in Venice, 1642. Setting: Rome during Nero's reign, A.D. 62. It is Monteverdi's last opera, and the first to deal with a historical (rather than Biblical or mythological) subject.

India. The music of India can be divided into four periods: the Vedic period, beginning in the 2nd (or even 4th) millennium B.C.; the classical period, beginning with the 2nd century A.D., a time of the evolution of elaborate theoretical systems and the creation of the *rāga* concept; the medieval period, beginning with the Islamic invasions in the 11th and 12th centuries, the time of division between northern and southern music; and the modern period, beginning with the 18th century, when the northern and southern systems were crystallized.

I. *Vedic chant.* The Vedic sacrificial ceremonies are remarkable for their strict and correctly performed textual and musical formulas. Any mistake in the enunciation and intonation of the sacred formulas was believed to upset the balance of the universe. Of the four Vedas only three are chanted; the Yajur Veda was recited on one note only. The Rigvedic hymns were chanted according to the textual accents, on a middle note (*udātta*), a low note (*anudātta*), and a high note (*svarita*), usually at the distance of a whole tone. The Sāmaveda, chanted comparatively rarely and only at large offerings and sacrifices, shows a wider range of notes, in some schools extending to one octave. The scales of Sāmavedic chant were considered in descending order. The Sāmavedic text, derived mainly from the Rigveda, was embellished with additional syllables and extended vowels and required comparatively florid melodies. Sāmavedic chants were and still are performed by three Brahmins.

Research in Vedic chant has been greatly hampered by Brahmin secrecy, as well as by the complex traditions, different schools and inter-pretations, and present "anti-Brahmin" trend among the people, offering little hope that this great art will be preserved.

II. *The classical system.* The oldest source of Indian music theory is the *Bharatanātyaśāstra* (ch. xxviii-xxxiii), a work probably written *c.* 200 B.C. (though some authorities say A.D. 200 and others even A.D. 500). The chapters on music state that there are seven degrees in the scale, named *SA, RI, GA, MA, PA, DHA, NI* (abbr. of *Ṣaḍja, Ṛṣabha, Gāndhāra, Madhyama, Pañcama, Dhaivata, Niṣāda*). The distances between these degrees are measured by means of twenty-two *śrutis* (Sanskr. *śru,* to hear), theoretically slightly unequal but for all practical purposes equal microtonal intervals, each roughly equal to a quarter tone. There are two basic scales (*grāmas*): the *SA-grāma,* defined in its rising form by a sequence of 4 3 2 4 4 4 3 2 *śrutis,* and the *MA-grāma,* by 4 3 4 2 4 3 2 *śrutis* (if the latter scale begins with *MA*). If the *MA-grāma* is transposed to *SA* (by maintaining the original scale degrees), the two *grāmas* differ in their third scale degrees: the *SA-grāma* shows a minor third and the *MA-grāma* a major third. Later authors (Nārada, Śārṅgadeva) mention a third basic scale, the *GA-grāma,* with the *srutis* 4 3 3 3 4 3 2, which was never used "on earth."

Numerous Sanskrit accounts are vague in describing scales, failing to state whether the *śrutis* are placed below or above the seven notes. Generally it is assumed (or known, e.g., Śārṅgadeva) that there are four *śrutis* below *SA,* three *śrutis* below *RI,* and so on. This method is contradicted in later centuries when *SA* is represented by the first rather than the fourth *śruti,* a procedure that alters the form of the scale. There are seven *murchanās* (scales) from the *SA-grāma* and another seven from the *MA-grāma.* The first notes of each *murchanā* group are listed in a descending order, e.g., the first three *murchanās* derived from the *SA-grāma* are: *Uttaramandrā* beginning with *SA, Rajanī* beginning with *NI, Uttarāyatā* beginning with *DHA,* etc. This practice seems to be the only link with the much older Sāmavedic scale types. Of the fourteen *murchanās,* seven are called *jātis.* They are distinguished from the *murchanās* by having "strong" and "weak" notes, referring to initial, central, and final notes. The use of these notes and several other features shows that *jātis* are indeed the forerunners of the *rāgas.*

The word *rāga* appears for the first time as a musical term in the *Bṛhaddeśi,* a Sanskrit work by Mataṅga (*c.* A.D. 5th century). Mataṅga groups his *gītis* (melodies) into several types, among which the *rāga-gītis* are listed together with subordinate forms (*bhāsā-gītis*). Mataṅga is fully aware of the distinct moods (*rasas*) created by the performance of his *rāga-gītis*. He discusses their functions and use in Sanskrit drama, stating that certain *gītis* have to be used at the beginning, others in the middle and for the climax, and still others during the intermissions.

Another author, Nārada (7th century), groups the *rāgas* into male and subordinate female types (*rāginīs*) and assigns fixed performance times to them.

III. *The medieval period. A. North.* With the Mohammedan invasions there began a new phase of Indian music, characterized by further elaboration of the *rāgas*, the fusion of Mohammedan and Hindu elements in the music of the North, and, particularly, a division between northern and southern musical styles. Among the important musician-theorists of the North was Locanakavi or Lochana-Kavi (*Rāga-Tarangini*, 12th century), who wrote of 12 *melas* (a southern term referring to basic scales and *rāgas*) and 77 *janya* (subordinate) *rāgas*. One of the most famous musicians and theorists was Śārṅgadeva (a northerner), author of the oft-quoted *Saṅgīta-Ratnākara* (13th century). He is vague in describing scales, and later authors who quoted him contributed much to the confusion in theory. Śārṅgadeva links some of the *rāgas* of which he lists five groups, with gods and patron saints, and seasons. Pārśvadeva (*Saṅgīta-Samayasāra*, c. 13th–14th centuries), groups the *rāgas* into head- and "imitation" (*āṅga*) types. In another list he classifies the *rāgas* musically as seven-, six-, and five-tone types. Amir Khosru (1254–1325), a Mohammedan poet, was one of the important experimenters who fused *Persian *maqamat* and Hindu *rāgas* [see Persia]. Khosru Indianized Persian melodies and supposedly is the creator of several famous Indian *rāgas*, such as *Yaman-kalyan*, *Kafi*, *Sazgiri*, *Bahar*, etc. Puṇḍarika Viṭṭhala (17th century) wrote three books, in which he groups the *rāgas* into male (*purusa*), female (*bhāryā*) and offspring (*putra*) types. He calls the head scales *thāta-melas* (*thāta* being a northern and *mela* a southern term). Another Nārada (16th century) groups the *rāgas* into *janakas* (parent) and *janyas* (derivative). Both terms are southern. He also offers brief pictorial descriptions of the *rāgas*. Dāmodara Miśra (17th century) groups his *rāgas* into head and subordinate forms and states their perform-

ance times in detail (morning, afternoon, etc.). Somanātha (17th century) determines the *srutis* by referring to divisions of strings of the *vina*. His *rāgas* are grouped into *melas* and *janyas*.

B. South. Up to the time of Śārṅgadeva there were few differences between the systems of the north and south. Numerous Sanskrit works appear to deal with both styles, and opinion about which they refer to is divided. The term "Carnatic music," meaning the music of the south, appears for the first time in the *Mānosallāsa*, a dictionary of the 12th century. Rāmāmatya (16th century) groups the *rāgas* into *melas* and *janyas*. His basic scale, the ancient *Mukhari*, corresponding to the modern *Kanakangi*, is C D^b E^{bb} F G A^b B^{bb} c. These notes are the *shuddha svaras*, the "naturals" of the southern system, and all other scales are derived from them. Rāmāmatya indicates performance times of his *rāgas*. Govinda Dīkṣit (17th century) and especially Venkatamakhin (17th century) laid the foundation of the modern system of the south.

IV. *Modern period. A. North.* In the north, Muhammed Rezza Khan of Patna (*Naqmat-e-Asaphi*, 1813) declared the grouping of *rāgas* into male and female types utterly absurd and presented for the first time a new classification based on the tonal material of the various scales. He adopted as the basic scale (*shuddha* scale) that of *rāga Bilaval* (approximately C D E F G A B c) and thus paved the way for the eminent Pandit V. N. Bhatkhande, author of several works, most notably the *Hindusthani Sangit Paddhati* (1934–41). Bhatkhande grouped all northern *rāgas*, entirely on a musical basis, under the headings of ten fundamental scales (*thātas*) and created the modern system of North Indian music.

B. South. In the south another Govinda, author of the *Samgraha-Cūda-Mani* (late 18th century) elaborated the Carnatic system of 72 *melas* and numerous subordinate *janyas*. Two systems evolved: the so-called *Kanakambari-Phenadyuti* and the *Kanakangi-Ratnangi*. The latter became the modern system of the south. The 72 *melas* are grouped into twelve *chakras* ("wheels"), each containing six *melas*. The scales of the *melas* are arranged in an orderly manner whereby the same or similar sequences of notes appear and show rotating modifications. The names of the *melas* are related to their numbers (1–72) by their first two consonants. These consonants are numbered according to their appearance in the Sanskrit (and related) alphabet and its four letter groups. For example, in the *mela* name *Kiravani* the letters K and R are the first two consonants; K is the first letter of the *ka* group, R the second letter of the *ya* group. The resulting numbers are 1 and 2. If reversed to 2 1 the correct number of *mela Kiravani* in the system of the 72 *melas* is obtained. This rule of deriving the *mela* number from the two consonant numbers of the alphabet (in reverse order) applies to the majority of the 72 *mela* names. There are, however, a few exceptions.

V. *Rāga and performance practice.* Bharata established ten characteristics of the *jātis:* initial note; central note; final note; secondary final note; height and depth (ambitus); "muchness" and "fewness" of notes (five, six, or seven); six-tone form; and five-tone form (the seven-tone form is not specifically mentioned). Today North Indian music recognizes only the *vādi* and *samvādi,* the central and secondary central notes and, occasionally, a *vishrantisthan* that has a function similar to the *vādi.* The scales may consist of five, six, or seven tones. The tone material of the majority of *rāgas* can be demonstrated by scales. Some *rāgas,* however, have *vakra* (zigzag) features in their scales.

Each *rāga* must be accompanied by a drone that consists of the constant sounding of the basic note of the scale (*SA*) together with its fifth (*PA*). If the scale of the *rāga* does not contain a fifth, the fourth (*MA*) is used. If the scale possesses neither fourth nor fifth, the major seventh (*NI*) is employed. If, e.g., the basic note is C, the following drone types, usually performed on a *tambura, are possible:

PA SA   MA SA   NI SA

Each *rāga* has its own, fixed, unalterable tone material, which must be used throughout its performance. Modulations are strictly forbidden. In contrast to a plain scale, a *rāga* has "strong" and "weak" notes, which together with special intonations, typical phrases, etc., form the physiognomy of the *rāga.* After the basic note (*SA*), the *vādi* (the "speaker"), or *aṁsa,* is the predominant note. Most melodies and phrases end either with *SA* or the *vādi,* or, at times, with the secondary central note, the *samvādi,* generally a fourth or fifth distant from the *vādi.* The importance of these "strong" notes is further shown by the fact that they have to

coincide with a similarly "strong" beat (*sam*) on the drums.

Below are the formulas of two different *rāgas* that use the anhemitonic pentatonic tone material c' d' e' g' a' c''. The use of half, quarter, eighth, etc., notes in the examples indicates not rhythmic values but the relative melodic importance of the notes in the design of the *rāga:*

Rāga Bhupali

vādi

Rāga Deshkar

vādi
vishrantistan

There is little doubt that the constant use of certain notes in one *rāga* creates a certain mood or atmosphere (*rasa*). The step from the recognition of a specific mood to the deification and personification of a *rāga* is small, and so it is no wonder that numerous *rāgas* are represented pictorially (*rāga-māla*). In the 16th century a considerable iconography of *rāga-mālas* evolved. Further, *rāgas* were believed to possess magic powers, such as creating rain (*Mallar rāgas*), fire (*Dipak*), healing of diseases and melting stones (*Kedar*), etc.

The compositions are not rigidly fixed. The performer is aware of all essential features of the *rāga* he is presenting and will improvise within the often very tightly knit framework of the given rules: scale, strong and weak notes, characteristic phrases, special intonations, plus the careful observation of rhythm and formal structure. Today melodies can be found in notated form, but they usually constitute only the skeleton for an elaborate performance that generally varies from one occasion to the next.

Southern *rāgas* have the same or similar features as the *rāgas* of the North. Musicians of the South prefer the term *aṁsa,* which does not necessarily represent one but may represent several notes.

VI. *Tāla (rhythm).* The term *mārga tāla,* derived from Sanskrit prose, refers to the free recitation of the Vedic texts, while *desī tāla* refers to secular music. Northern as well as Carnatic music inclines toward the additive formation of *tālas* in which a fixed group of bars (*āvarta*) is repeated over and over. For instance, *Dhamār-tāla* consists of the repetition of the following four bars, which constitute an *āvarta:*

This *āvarta,* containing four *vibhāgas* (bars) of five, two, three, and four metrical units respectively, occurs throughout the performance. The first beat (*sam*) is notated with an X, the sixth beat (the first of the second bar) with 2, the eighth (the first of the third bar) with 0 (the *khālī,* the "open" beat), and the eleventh beat (the first of the fourth bar) with 3. Particularly *sam* and *khālī* require special drumbeats and thus provide the soloist with acoustical signposts through his often complex performance. Some of the most commonly used northern *tālas* are:

Chautāl	|1 2 |3 4 |5 6 |7 8 |9 10 |11 12 | |X |0 |2 |0 |3 |4 |
Dādra	|1 2 3 |4 5 6| |X |0 |
Dhamār	(see above)
Ektāl	the same number of beats as *Chautāl* but with different types of drumbeat
Rūpak	|1 2 3 |4 5 |6 7| |X |2 |3 |
Tintāl (Tritāl)	|1 2 3 4 |5 6 7 8 |9 10 11 12 |13 14 15 16| |X |2 |0 |3 |

The southern *tālas* are similar to those of the north but are organized into groups. Southern musicians speak of seven basic *tālas,* each of which can be performed in five forms (*jātis*). The following table shows the seven basic *tālas* in two *jātis: Trisra* (based on three rhythmic units) and *Chatusra* (based on four). The other three *jātis* (*Khanda, Misra, Sankirna*) have the same basic organization but are based on, respectively, five, seven, and nine rhythmic units.

Basic tālas:	Jātis Trisra	Chatusra
Eka	3	4
Rūpaka	2 + 3	2 + 4
Jhampa	3 + 1 + 2	4 + 1 + 2
Tripuṭa	3 + 2 + 2	4 + 2 + 2
Mātya	3 + 2 + 3	4 + 2 + 4
Dhruva	3 + 2 + 3 + 3	4 + 2 + 4 + 4
Āṭa	3 + 3 + 2 + 2	4 + 4 + 2 + 2

Another frequently used *tāla* is *Ādi-tāla* (4 + 2 + 2), which is simply *Tripuṭa tāla* in its *chatusra jāti* form.

VII. *Musical forms. A. North.* The ancient Hindu form, not influenced by Mohammedan types, is the *Dhrūpad.* The name is derived from *dhruva,* "firm," and *pāda,* "quarter-verse," the latter referring to a recurring verse somewhat similar to the Western rondo. *Dhrūpad* performances today are extremely rare and it is said that a singer must have the strength of five buffalos in order to accomplish this musical *tour de force.* A *dhrūpad* performance is free from all ornaments and is believed to show the *rāga* in its purest form. It may last for several hours. *Dhrūpads* are always sung in a slow and dignified tempo and only a few *tālas* can be employed: *Chautāl, Dhamār, Surphakta* (2 + 2 + 2 + 2 + 2), and *Tevra* (3 + 2 + 3). The drum used in *dhrūpad* performances is the ancient *mridanga.* The structure of the *dhrūpad* is: (a) *Ālāp,* a rhythmically free prelude in which the singer presents the essential features of the *rāga.* This is performed to the drone of the tambura but without drumming; (b) *Asthayi* (*Sthāyī*), the first part of the song, usually emphasizes the notes of the lower tetrachord. It is accompanied by the drummer (and, of course, by the tambura); (c) *Antara,* the second part of the song, emphasizes the notes of the upper tetrachord; (d) *Sanchāri,* the third part, deals with the notes of the entire range; (e) *Ābhog,* the fourth part, is usually a return to the *Asthayi;* occasionally it introduces a new, fast melody. The recurring melody (of the *Asthayi*) appears not only in the *Abhog* but is interpolated between the other parts of the song. Occasionally the end of the *dhrūpad* appears in the form of a fast "stretto" that may be subdivided into several, rhythmically differing sections (*Āḍ, Chaugan, Kuar*).

The *Khyāl,* created by both Hindu and Mohammedan musicians, is the comparatively modern and very frequently used form of northern art music. The name is derived from *khyāl karo,* "Do imagine!" or "Fancy this!" which musicians would say to each other when performing something newly created. The *khyāl* consists of: (a) *Ālāp;* (b) *Asthayi;* (c) *Antara* plus a repetition of a part (usually the first line) of the *Asthayi;* (d) *Ālāp* proper, an elaborate *ālāp* performed with the drummer; (e) repetition of *Asthayi* and *Antara;* (f) *Bol-tāns,* fast passages, fiorituras, and variations, sung to textual syllables (the term is derived from *bolna,* "to speak"); (g) repetition of the *Asthayi* and *Antara;*

(h) *Tāns* proper, *tāns* without text, sung on "ah" or "na"—this is the virtuoso part of the song; (i) conclusion, either a repetition of the *Asthayi* or a new, fast melody.

Other northern forms are *Thumri*, a Hindu love song; *Ghazal*, a Mohammedan love song with Urdu or Persian text; *Sargam*, a song that uses the tone syllables *SA, RI, GA*, etc., as text; *Tarana*, a song that uses drum words as text; *Tappa*, a Mohammedan love song, usually with Hindi text. All these and numerous other forms follow the *Asthayi-Antara* sequence but avoid the complicated *tāns*.

B. *South*. The musical forms of the south are similar to those of the north. The *Kīrtana* consists of four parts: *Pallavi, Anupallavi, Charana*, and a return to the *Pallavi*. The four parts have the same significances as the four parts of the *dhrūpad* and the basic sections of the *khyāl*. The *kīrtanas*, however, are more flexible than the *khyāls;* textually and musically they are simple and can be sung by persons who do not have a thorough musical education. The *Krti*, however, having more or less the structure of the *kīrtana*, shows elegant virtuoso features and can be performed only by trained singers. In addition, Carnatic music uses a large number of smaller forms such as the *Namavali, Mangalam, Nirupanam*, etc.

VIII. *Instruments*. The ancient vīṇa, a stick zither, often fretted, has two resonance gourds in the north and usually one in the south, although there are several exceptions. There are various forms of the vīṇa with different names. The instrument has four strings strung across the frets and generally three open bourdon strings. The tuning is in fourths and/or fifths. The sitar (setar) is a long-necked lute with movable frets. Sitars have three to seven strings. Below the strings are a dozen (or thirteen) thin, sympathetic wire strings. The tuning is similar to that of the vīṇa. The sarod, either plucked or bowed, has a pear-shaped body and one resonance gourd below the peg-box. It has six gut strings and about twelve thin sympathetic wire strings below the main strings. The tambura (tanbura, tanpura) is a long-necked lute with four wire strings. The instrument is not fretted and is used only for producing the drone sounds in *dhrūpad* and *khyāl* performances. The sarangi, a popular fiddle with three thick gut strings, has numerous sympathetic wire strings below the main strings. The instrument is played with a short bow. The dilruba (and esraj) is a fretted long-necked fiddle with three or four main strings and numerous sympathetic wire strings strung below the main strings.

India possesses a large number of flutes, mostly made of bamboo with a varying number of holes. A popular double reed instrument is the shannai (sānāyī). A horn (conical bore) in the shape of the letter S appears often in folk music.

The mridanga, the ancient barrel drum of India, has two heads and is used in *dhrūpad* performances in the north and is still favored in certain districts of the south. Extremely popular are the tablas, a pair of small kettledrums (actually one is a kettle, the other a barrel), both with single heads. The tablas are used in art and popular music, and occasionally also in folk music. In addition, numerous other drums (khol, dholaka, etc.) are used, chiefly in folk music.

India possesses a large number of bells, cymbals, gongs, clappers, rattles, etc., in a great variety of shapes and sizes. Of interest is the jaltarang, a set of china cups filled with water and tuned to the scale of the *rāga* to be performed. The cups are beaten with small sticks.

Lit. *Works in Sanskrit:* Bharata, *Nātyaśāstra* (Benares, 1926; Kashi Sanskrit Series, no. 60); V. N. Bhatkhande, *Hindusthani Sangit Paddhati*, 6 vols. (Bombay, 1939–40); Damodara, *Saṅgīta-Darpaṇa* (Paris, 1930); Mataṅga, *Bṛhaddeśi* (Trivandrum, 1928; Trivandrum Sanskrit Series, no. 94); Śārṅgadeva, *Saṅgīta-Ratnākara* (Madras, 1943); Venkaṭamakhin, *Caturdaṇḍi-Prakāśika* [Madras, 1934].

Others: Swāmī Prajñānānanda, *Historical Development of Indian Music* (1960); *id., A Historical Study of Indian Music* (1965); B. A. Pingle, *History of Indian Music*, rev. ed. (Calcutta, 1962; 1st ed., 1894); H. A. Popley, *The Music of India* (1921, '50); C. Sachs, *The Rise of Music in the Ancient World* (1943), pp. 157ff; P. Sambamoorthy, *South Indian Music*, 5 vols. (Madras, 1951–54); O. Gosvami, *The Story of Indian Music* (Bombay, 1957); A. Bake, in *MGG* vi, cols. 1150–85; *id.*, in *GDB* iv, 456–60; J.-M. van der Hoogt, *The Vedic Chant* (1929); A. Daniélou, *Northern Indian Music*, 2 vols. (1949, '54); *id., Introduction to the Study of Musical Scales* (1943); A. H. Fox-Strangways, *The Music of Hindostan* (1914); E. Felber, *Die indische Musik der vedischen und der klassischen Zeit* (1912); W. Kaufmann, *The Musical Notations of the Orient* (1967); *id.*, "The Classification of Indian Ragas" (*Asia and the Humanities*, Indiana Univ., 1959); *id.*, in *CP Apel* (notation of Vedic chant); *id.*, "Folk-songs of the Gond and Baiga" (*MQ* xxvii, 280–88); *id.*, "The Forms of the *Dhrūpad* and *Khyal* in Indian Art Music" (*The Canadian Music Journal* iii, 25–35); *id.*, "The Songs of the Hill Maria, Jhoria Muria and Bastar Muria Gond Tribes" (*Ethnomusicology* iv, 115–28); *id.*, "The Musical Instruments of the Hill Maria, Jhoria, and Bastar Muria Gond Tribes" (*Ethnomusicology* v, 1–9); *id.*, "Rasa, Rāga-mālā and Performance Times in North Indian Rāgas" (*Ethnomusicology* ix, 272–91); H. S. Powers, "Mode and Raga" (*MQ* xliv).   w.k.

Indian music. See American Indian music; India.

Indirectum [L.; properly, *in directum*]. See under Psalmody I.

Indo-China. See Vietnam; under Thailand (Cambodia). Also see G. Knosp, "Notes sur la musique Indo-Chinoise" (*RMI* xvi, 821, and xvii, 415); *id.*, "Histoire de la musique dans l'Indo-Chine" (*LavE* i.5); M. Humbert-Sauvageot, "La Musique à travers la vie laotienne" (*Zeitschrift für vergleichende Musikwissenschaft* ii, 14ff).

Indonesia. See Java; Bali.

Inégales [F.; abbr. for *notes inégales*]. The practice of performing certain evenly written notes "unequally," with alternation of longer and shorter values. This manner crystallized in France during Lully's age into a distinct convention that, elaborately codified, lasted with little apparent change to the eve of the French Revolution (1789). The earliest mention of this practice is in Loys Bourgeois' *Le droict chemin de Musique* (1550), which was followed by a few scattered references in other Latin countries (Tomás de Santa Maria, Pedro or Pietro Cerone, Frescobaldi). After 1615 foreign sources grew silent, while in 17th-century France the sources lagged behind the practice. Though clearly documented as part of the Lully style by its German chronicler, Georg Muffat (*Florilegium Primum, Secundum*, 1695, '98; particularly the latter), references in Lully's lifetime are sporadic and not too specific. The first detailed account is presented by E. Loulié in his *Eléments ou principes de musique* (1696). After Loulié the sources rapidly multiply, and during the 18th century at least 40 French writers recorded the convention with remarkable unanimity.

Inequality was definitely long-short only and applied generally speaking to the fastest prevailing notes: in duple meter to the fourfold subdivision of the metrical unit such as ♪ in 4/4,

♪ in 2/4; in triple meters to twofold subdivisions: ♪ in 3/4, ♪ in 3/8; to shorter notes, if they occurred, but never to longer ones. It applied to melodies that moved by and large in stepwise progression; it was limited to French music written in the French style, hence excluding works patterned after foreign models such as Italianate sonatas or concertos. The composer could cancel inequality by such words as *détaché* or *marqué*, or by dots or dashes above the notes. The degree of unevenness was left up to the performer, varying from a slight lilt (*louré*) to a more pronounced inequality (*pointé* or *piqué*) that could approach, but only rarely reached, the full meaning of a dot.

A dotted note in a setting of inégales. The dot here takes the place of the long note of a long-short pair. This practice is probably the source of the mistaken theory of a "French style" of overdotting.

The only known non-French reference in the 18th century is a passage in Quantz' treatise of 1752, where this advocate of a "mixed style" endorses the *inégales* convention. The passage has become the mainstay of a widely accepted theory that the *inégales* were a universal "baroque practice" that applied to German masters, including Bach, as well as to the French. Based on a misinterpretation, this mistaken theory was compounded by the frequent confusion of the *inégales* with other types of unevenness of genuinely international currency, such as agogic accents, the accentual pattern of the so-called "good" and "bad" notes, and the occasional assimilation of duple to triple meter:

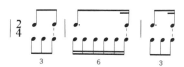

which was a makeshift for the not yet common notation of $\sharp^3\flat$ with no implication of rhythmic freedom.

Lit.: C. Jacobs, *La Interpretación de la música española* (1959), pp. 43ff; E. Borrel, *L'Interprétation de la Musique française* (1934), pp. 150ff; *id.*, in *RdM* 1931, pp. 278ff; R. Donington, *The Interpretation of Early Music* (1963), pp. 386ff; F. Neumann, in *JAMS* xviii; S. Babitz, in *MQ* xxxviii; N. Powell, "Rhythmic Freedom in the Performance of French Music from 1650 to 1735" (diss. Stanford Univ., 1958); G. Scheck, in *DM* xxxi.8; E. Schenk, in *DM* xxxi.11.   F.N.

Inflection, inflexion. See under Monotone.

Inganno [It.]. Deceptive cadence. In earlier practice the term was used for a "deceptive" modification of a fugal subject, e.g., by Trabaci, who in his ricercars of 1615 often marked certain fugal entries as "inganno della fuga."

Ingressa. The *Introitus* in *Ambrosian chant.

Initium [L.]. The two or three opening notes of a *psalm tone.

Innig [G.]. Heartfelt, tender.

Inno [It.]. Hymn.

In nomine [L.]. Title of a large number of English instrumental pieces (for viols, lute, or keyboard) based on a *cantus firmus:* d f d d d c f g f g a .... This *cantus firmus* has nothing to do with the Introit "In nomine Jesu" (*LU,* p. 446) but is quite similar to the melody of the Vespers antiphon of Trinity Sunday "Gloria tibi Trinitas" (*LU,* p. 914). The seemingly wrong designation

Glo - ri - a ti - bi Tri - ni - tas ae - qua - lis

is explained by the fact that the species originated with and developed from the "In nomine" section ("Benedictus qui venit in nomine Domini"; from the Sanctus) of Taverner's *Missa Gloria tibi Trinitas* [see Editions LI, i, 126]. This section (like many others in this Mass) employs the melody of "Gloria tibi Trinitas" as a *cantus firmus,* while the upper parts are sung to the words "In nomine Domini." The Mulliner Book of *c.* 1560 contains a keyboard transcription of this section, which is quite properly called "In nomine" [*Editions XXXIV, i, no. 35]. Later composers wrote different settings of the anti-

phon melody, emulating Taverner's example even to the extent of retaining, through respect or perhaps ignorance, a title that was correct only for the prototype. Some earlier "In nomine" compositions are correctly designated "Gloria tibi Trinitas" (e.g., John Bull, The Fitzwilliam Virginal Book i, 160). An "In nomine" by Allwood (Mulliner Book, no. 23) is not based on the antiphon melody.

The "In nomine" was the most favored type of *cantus firmus* composition in England after *c.* 1550, replacing the *"Felix namque," which was cultivated mainly before that date. The Mulliner Book contains, in addition to Taverner's piece, seven settings for organ, among them six by Blitheman, all entitled "Gloria tibi Trinitas." Even more "In nomine" compositions were written for viols [ex., by Tomkins, in *HAM,* no. 176]. Purcell's two "In nomine" compositions represent a late attempt at revival of the form. For an interesting description by Roger North (1728), see P. A. Scholes, *The Oxford Companion to Music* (1955), p. 516f.

Lit.: G. Reese, "The Origin of the English *In Nomine*" (*JAMS* ii); R. Donington and T. Dart, "The Origin of the In Nomine" (*ML* xxx, 101); D. Stevens, "Les Sources de l' 'In Nomine'" (*La Musique instrumentale de la Renaissance,* 1955); E. H. Meyer, *Die mehrstimmige Spielmusik des 17. Jahrhunderts* (1934), pp. 133ff; *id.,* "The 'In Nomine'" (*ML* xvii, 25).

In seculum. One of the most popular tenors of 13th-century clausulae and motets, taken from the Easter Gradual "Haec dies" [see *LU,* p. 778] and beginning: c c B c d e c B c c B [see *HAM,* nos. 30d, 32d, 30e]. This *cantus firmus* is particularly interesting because it also occurs in a number of "instrumental motets" in the Bamberg Codex [see P. Aubry, *Cent Motets du XIIIe siècle* (1908), ii. nos. 104–8]. One of them, reproduced in *SchGMB,* no. 20, bears the inscription "In seculum viellatoris," possibly with reference to a well-known *vielle player who composed it [see *ReMMA,* p. 325]. See H. Gleason, in *BAMS* vi.

Instituta et monumenta. See Editions XXI.

Instrument [G.]. Aside from its general meaning [see Instruments], the term was used in Germany during the 17th and 18th centuries as a specific designation for a keyboard instrument, usually (always?) the clavichord. The title of B. Schultheiss' *Clavier-Lust* (1679) contains a reference to "Instrument, Spinet, oder Clavicymbel," in which "Instrument" obviously stands in opposition to spinet and clavicymbel (both harpsichords). In the preface to his *Musicalisches Blumen-Büschlein* (1698), Johann Caspar Fischer says that the pieces are "stillere Music, . . . allein auf das Clavicordium, oder Instrument eingerichte" (more quiet music proper only for the clavichord or Instrument), a remark in which "Instrument" is clearly a synonym for "Clavicordium." In the early 19th century the name was often used for the piano.

Instrumental music. Music performed on instruments, as opposed to music performed by voices (*vocal or *choral music). Since in mixed participation the voices are usually treated as the more important body, compositions for voices and instruments (cantatas, operas, etc.) are usually classified as vocal music. There are two main types of instrumental music: ensemble (chamber and orchestral music) and solo (piano, organ, lute, etc.). Often the term "instrumental music" is used for the former only. Below is a brief summary of the development of instrumental music (both ensemble and soloist), divided into three periods in which instrumental music was (A) of lesser, (B) of equal, (C) of greater importance than vocal music.

A. *Period of lesser importance (1250–1600).* 13th century: French *estampies;* instrumental motets *"In seculum"; *hockets. 14th century: Italian *estampies;* arrangements [see Intabulation]; liturgical organ pieces [see Organ music I]. 15th century: German instrumental pieces and dances [Glogauer *Liederbuch]; *preludes; liturgical organ music; *intabulations for keyboard [Ileborgh, Paumann, *Buxheim Organ Book]; *carmina* and other instrumental pieces by Isaac [*DTO* 28]. 16th century: numerous dances for keyboard [see Dance music III], lute [see Lute music], and ensemble; *ricercar; *fantasia; *canzona; *toccata; *variations; a large repertory of liturgical organ music including organ Masses, organ hymns, verses for the Psalms and the *Magnificat, etc.

B. *Period of equal importance (1600–1750).* Chamber music: instrumental *canzona; *fancy; *sonata da camera; sonata da chiesa; *trio sonata; *ground. Orchestral music: operatic *overture and *sinfonia; orchestral *suite; *concerto grosso. Keyboard music: *suite, *toccata; *fugue; *chaconne and passacaglia; *variations; *organ chorale.

C. *Period of greater importance (1750—).* Chamber music: *string quartet and other types

of modern chamber music; violin sonata. Orchestral music: *cassation; *divertimento; *symphony; *concerto; *symphonic poem. Piano music: *sonata; *variations; *character pieces.

Lit. *For A:* H. M. Brown, *Instrumental Music Printed before 1600: A Bibliography* (1965); L. Schrade, *Die handschriftliche Ueberlieferung der ältesten Instrumentalmusik* (1931); J. Wolf, "Die Tänze des Mittelalters" (*AMW* i); W. J. von Wasielewski, *Geschichte der Instrumentalmusik in XVI. Jahrhundert* (1878); J. Jacquot, ed., *La Musique instrumentale de la Renaissance* (1955). *For B:* C. Sartori, *Bibliografia della musica strumentale italiana stampata in Italia fino al 1700* (1952); L. Torchi, *La Musica istrumentale in Italia nei secoli XVI, XVII e XVIII* (*RMI,* 1897–1901; pub. separately in 1901); K. Nef, *Zur Geschichte der deutschen Instrumentalmusik . . . des 17. Jahrhunderts* (1902); E. H. Meyer, *Die mehrstimmige Spielmusik des 17. Jahrhunderts* (1934). *For C:* W. Altmann, *Orchester-Literatur-Katalog; Verzeichnis von seit 1850 erschienenen Orchester-Werken,* 2 vols. (1924, '36). See the literature under the various forms; also under Organ music; Piano music; Violin music; Lute music; Dance music.

Instrumentation. The art of using instruments in a composition. Instrumentation is essentially the same as orchestration, since it is particularly in writing for the orchestra that the composer must select and combine various instruments. See Orchestra; Orchestration.

Instruments. Generic name for all mechanisms producing musical sounds and hence for all musical media with the exception of the human voice.

Classification. Studies of musical instruments used to be restricted to those of European art music, but the scope of investigation was widened considerably in the 1920's by the inclusion of non-Western (Oriental, African, etc.) instruments, which far outnumber the others. The Western instruments were (and usually still are) grouped in three categories: *stringed instruments, wind instruments,* and *percussion instruments.* The members of the first group are called *chordophones* [Gr. *chordos,* string; *phonos,* sound]; the second, *aerophones* [Gr. *aeros,* air, wind]; the third, which are extremely numerous in non-Western music, are divided into two classes, *idiophones* [Gr. *idios,* self], instruments that consist simply of elastic material (metal, wood) capable of producing sound, and *membrano-*

phones [L. *membranum,* skin], instruments in which a stretched skin is the sound-producing agent. To these four classes a fifth has recently been added, the *electrophones,* in which the acoustical vibrations are produced by electric contrivances. Each of these categories is further subdivided. The following survey is based on the classification established by C. Sachs and E. M. von Hornbostel [see *SaHMI,* pp. 455ff].

I. *Idiophones.*

A. Struck: triangle; gong; *bell; *chimes; *glockenspiel; *cymbals; *xylophone; celesta; *castanets [see Percussion instruments]. Also numerous non-Western instruments, e.g., the Javanese *gambang (xylophone) and the Chinese chinq (stone chimes).

B. Shaken: *rattle; *sistrum; crescent.

C. Plucked: *Jew's-harp; also the music box.

D. Rubbed: *glass harmonica; *nail violin.

II. *Membranophones.* Chiefly *drums. Classifications can be made according to shape (tubular drums, kettledrums, frame drums) or material (wood, metal, coconut, gourd, etc.), fastening of the skin, etc. The *mirliton is a membranophone that is not a drum.

III. *Aerophones.*

A. Free aerophones. Instruments that act on the principle of the free (more properly, idiophonous) *reed: *harmonium; *accordion; *regal; *sheng; the reed section of the organ [see Organ X].

B. *Wind instruments. Instruments in which the sound-generating medium is an enclosed column of air. According to the device that sets the air into vibration, the following classes are distinguished:

1. Trumpets and horns. The device is the compressed lips of the player: lip-vibrated aerophones, commonly called *brass instruments.

2. Flutes. The device is the sharp edge of a mouth-hole.

   a. Vertical flutes. The mouth-hole is formed by the upper aperture of the pipe. Found occasionally in Egypt and Arabia; *panpipes.

   b. Transverse flute. The mouth-hole is cut in the side of the pipe. Flute proper; see Flute.

   c. Whistle flutes. The player blows from the upper end through a flue against the sharp edge cut in the side; *recorder; flageolet; the flue section of the organ [see Organ IX].

3. Reed pipes. The device is a (heterophonous) reed.

   a. A single reed: clarinets. See Clarinet family.

   b. A double reed: oboes. See Oboe family.

IV. *Chordophones.*

A. Zithers. The strings are stretched between the two ends of a flat body, such as a board or a stick.

1. Board zithers. The body has the shape of a flat board.

   a. Psalteries. The strings are plucked: *psaltery; *zither; kantele; *kanum. Keyboard psalteries: *harpsichord; *virginal; *spinet.

   b. Dulcimers. The strings are struck with a hammer: *dulcimer; *cimbalom; *pantaleon. Keyboard dulcimer: *piano.

   c. The strings are touched by tangents: *clavichord.

2. Stick zithers. The body has the shape of a stick: several non-Western instruments, notably the Hindu *vīna.

3. Long zithers. The body has the shape of a long board with a slightly curved surface (originally made from the longitudinal segment of a bamboo pipe): the Chinese *chyn (Japanese koto).

B. Lutes. Instruments having a body with a neck. The following families can be roughly distinguished:

1. Plucked: *lute family (round back); *guitar family (flat back).

2. Bowed: fiddles; *violin family; *viols; *vielle; *hurdy-gurdy; *tromba marina.

C. Lyres. Instruments having a yoke, i.e., two projecting arms connected at their upper end by a crossbar: *kithara, *lyra, *crwth, kinnor.

D. Harps. Instruments in which the plane of the strings is perpendicular rather than parallel to the soundboard. See Harp.

V. *Electrophones.* See Electronic instruments.

Another classification of instruments, considerably wider in scope and taking into account various other aspects (e.g., the relationship between instrument and player) is given in H. H. Dräger, *Prinzip einer Systematik der Musikinstrumente* (1948).

History. Restricting ourselves to Western culture, the most important pre-Christian instruments were the various instruments of the Bible [see Jewish music], the *kithara, *lyra, *hydraulos, and *aulos of the Greeks, and the *tuba (salpinx) and *lituus in Rome (used chiefly for military purposes). The fact that, in the late Roman Empire, instruments were mainly in the hands of the *mimus* (actors), *joculares* (jongleurs), dancers, and other entertainers provoked a general prejudice against the actual use of instruments in the medieval Christian Church, although they are frequently mentioned in the writings of the church fathers as religious symbols. Nonetheless, there existed—outside the Church—a variety of instruments, as shown in numerous pictorial representations ranging from the 6th to the 13th centuries. Of these, the organ is the most important as well as the best documented. Particularly informative are the famous miniatures of the 13th-century Spanish Codex of *cantigas* (numerous reproductions in *GD*). The medieval instruments included plucked instruments such as the *harp, *lyra, *psaltery, *lute, and chrotta [see Crwth]; bowed instruments such as the rebec, rubeba [see Rabab], *hurdy-gurdy, and *tromba marina; various wind instruments (trumpets, horns, flutes, shawms, bagpipes); the *portative (organ) and the *echiquier (clavichord or harpsichord); bells and bell chimes, drums (nacaire), and castanets. Most of these instruments came from the Orient, probably through the Arabs via Spain. Except for the organ and vielle, they were used chiefly for the improvised (or, at least, unrecorded) accompaniment of singers and dancers.

During the 15th and 16th centuries most of the types above continued to be used, developing into more elegant forms. For the 15th century, our knowledge is in the main restricted to what has been recorded in paintings and drawings, particularly in numerous representations of "celestial harmony" showing beautifully shaped and decorated instruments in the hands of angels (Van Eyck, Memling; see, e.g., *SaHMI*, p. 304). In the 16th century there developed an independent repertory of music for the organ, harpsichord, and lute [see Instrumental music]. Many other instruments, however, were built and used, as shown in the writings of Sebastian Virdung (*Musica getutscht,* i.e., "Music Germanicized," 1511); Martin Agricola (*Musica instrumentalis deudsch,* 1528); and Michael Praetorius (*Syntagma musicum,* vol. ii, 1618). These books, together with evidence such as, e.g., surviving lists of instrument collections, show

that the 16th century placed a marked emphasis on wind instruments. The collection of 381 instruments left by King Henry VIII of England comprised 272 wind instruments (cross flutes, recorders, shawms, cromornes, horns, cornets, organs, bagpipes) and 109 stringed instruments (virginals, lutes, viols, guitars, clavichords). An important feature of this period was the building of instruments in families; in fact, the playing of music in homogeneous groups, e.g., on four recorders, four viols, four trombones, replaced to a large extent the mixed ensembles of the 15th century, which had preferred the simultaneous sound of contrasting timbres [see Sound ideal].

The 17th century (baroque) brought a marked trend toward the stringed instruments: the soft viol, the delicate lute, the "singing" violin. The lute, especially, existed in a great variety of sizes and types, such as the chitarrone, theorbo, cittern, mandola, etc. [see Lute; Guitar family]. Special types of viol were the *viola d'amore, baryton, and *viola pomposa. Among the wind instruments of the baroque, the recorder and oboe were prominent, with the trumpet and horn coming into use after 1700. For the ensuing history and current classification of the modern orchestral instruments, see Orchestra and Orchestration.

Lit.: C. Sachs, *The History of Musical Instruments* (1940); *id., Handbuch der Musikinstrumentenkunde,* rev. ed. (1930); *id., Real-Lexikon der Musikinstrumente,* rev. ed. (1964); F. W. Galpin, *A Textbook of European Musical Instruments* (1937); *MaMI,* passim; R. Donington, *The Instruments of Music,* rev. ed. [1951]; N. Bessaraboff, *Ancient European Musical Instruments* (1941); H. W. Schwartz, *The Story of Musical Instruments* (1938); F. Bonanni, *The Showcase of Musical Instruments* (1964; 152 illustrations from a 1723 print); K. Schlesinger, *A Bibliography of Musical Instruments and Archaeology* (1912); M. Mersenne, *Harmonie universelle: The Books on Instruments,* trans. R. E. Chapman (1957); K. Geiringer, *Musical Instruments, Their History* [1943]; A. Baines, *European and American Musical Instruments* [1966]; *id., Musical Instruments through the Ages* [1961]; D. Darlow, *Musical Instruments* [1962]; A. Buchner, *Musical Instruments through the Ages* [1956?]; F. Harrison and J. Rimmer, *European Musical Instruments* (1964); F. W. Galpin, *Old English Instruments of Music,* rev. ed., [1965]; A. Schaeffner, *Origine des instruments de musique* (1936); W. Heinitz, *Instrumen-*

tenkunde (*BüHM* 1929); H. H. Dräger, *Prinzip einer Systematik der Musikinstrumente* (1948); E. Buhle, *Die musikalischen Instrumente in den Miniaturen des frühen Mittelalters: I. Die Blasinstrumente* (1903); K. Reinhard, "Beiträge zu einer neuen Systematik der Musikinstrumente" (*MF* xiii); E. A. Bowles, "Haut and Bas" (*MD* viii). For specific literature, see the various instruments; also bibl. in *SaHMI* and in Bessaraboff.

Inszenierung [G.]. Staging [F. *mis en scène*] of an opera or play.

Intabulation [G. *Intabulierung;* It. *intavolatura*]. Designation for a keyboard or lute *arrangement of vocal music from the 14th to the 16th centuries. The term, derived from L. *tabula* (table), refers to the change from the original notation in single parts (*mensural notation) to the scorelike (tabular, vertical) notation used for the *tablatures of the solo instruments, the organ and lute. The intabulation of a motet or chanson by Josquin is the 16th-century counterpart of the piano arrangement of a modern symphony or quartet. The chief difference between the early and modern procedures is the

Original version

Intabulation

greater freedom of the former. Not only were original parts omitted or differently distributed wherever their range was inconvenient for the reach of the hand, but the texture was enriched by the addition of coloraturas, passing notes, etc. [see Ex.].

The documented history of intabulation begins with the earliest extant source of keyboard music, the so-called Robertsbridge Fragment of *c.* 1320, which includes three intabulations of contemporary motets, two of them preserved in the *Roman de Fauvel.* The next source, the Codex Faenza (*c.* 1400), consists largely of arrangements of 14th-century *ballades,* madrigals, etc., by Machaut, Landini, and others, while the *Buxheim Organ Book of *c.* 1460 contains nearly 200 arrangements of French chansons (by Dunstable, Dufay, Binchois) and German lieder. All these pieces show the characteristic trait of the intabulation, the liberal addition of ornamental figurations. In the 16th century intabulations of motets, Mass compositions, chansons, and madrigals appeared in ever-increasing quantity in the numerous publications of keyboard and lute music. The artistic importance of this sometimes overwhelmingly large repertory is very slight. It is interesting, however, from the sociologic viewpoint, since it indicates an ever-growing desire on the part of music lovers to have favorite pieces of their time available for domestic use. In the late 16th and early 17th centuries some composers of intabulations replaced the routine ornaments of the earlier specimens with freely invented and often very ingenious figurations. One of the earliest examples of this type is Hernando de Cabezón's "Suzanne un jour," which he included in his edition of the works of his father (*Obras de música,* 1578; *Editions XX). Equally interesting are intabulations by Peter Phillips (in the Fitzwilliam Virginal Book), Coelho (*Flores de música,* 1620) and Frescobaldi (Arcadelt's "Ancidetemi pur," in *Toccate* ii, 1627). These are among the latest that were written.

Musicologists have drawn on the intabulations chiefly for the study of *musica ficta* [E. Frerichs, in *ZMW* vii; W. Apel, *Accidentien und Tonalität in den Musikdenkmälern des 15. und 16. Jahrhunderts* (1936)], and ornamentation [A. Schering, *Studien zur Musikgeschichte der Frührenaissance* (1914); O. Kinkeldey, *Orgel und Klavier in . . . 16. Jahrhunderts* (1910)]. See Arrangement. Examples in *HAM,* nos. 145, 160; *SchGMB,* nos. 35/36 and 62b/63a. For additional examples (original plus intabulation), see

WoGM iii, 191 (Robertsbridge Fragment; D. Plamenac, in *JAMS* iv, 190 (Codex Faenza); A. Schering, *Studien zur Musikgeschichte der Frührenaissance* [1914; Buxheim Organ Book]; Y. Rokseth, *Treize Motets . . . parus chez Pierre Attaingnant* (1930; motets and Mass compositions by Obrecht, Compère, Févin, *et al.;* also *Editions XLIX, 5); O. Kinkeldey, *Orgel und Klavier* (1910), pp. 245 (ensemble ricercar by Buus), 260, 264 (French chansons).

Intavolatura [It.]. See Intabulation. In titles of Italian publications of keyboard music (16th–17th centuries) the designation "Toccate (Canzone, Capricci, etc.) d'intavolatura" indicates that the music is notated on two staves (piano score), as distinguished from "di partitura" (or "spartiti"), i.e., with a separate staff for each part, as in the open score.

Integer valor [L.]. In mensural notation of the 15th and 16th centuries, the normal value of a note (*brevis, semibrevis*), as distinguished from the reduced or enlarged values caused by the proportions. See Proportions.

Interchange of voices. See Voice exchange.

Interference. See under Acoustics VI.

Interlude. Any kind of inserted music [see Entr'acte; Intermezzo]. Specifically, name for short organ pieces played between the various verses of a hymn or a psalm. These were usually improvised and hence are rarely found in printed books except in those of the early 19th century, when the art of improvisation had begun to decline. One of the few early books containing interludes is Daniel Purcell's *The Psalms Set Full for the Organ or Harpsichord . . . as also with their Interludes of Great Variety* (pub. 1718; see Nagel, in *MfM* xxx, 47). The low standard of the later interludes is illustrated by an example from Gresham, *Psalmody Improved* (c. 1780), which is reproduced in P. A. Scholes, *The Oxford Companion to Music* (1955), pl. 86 (opp. p. 503). In the German Protestant service short interlude-like passages were inserted between the various lines of the chorale rather than after a complete stanza. Certain organ chorales by Bach illustrate this procedure, e.g., his *In dulci jubilo* (*BG* xl, 74).

Intermedium [L.], **intermède** [F.], **intermedio** [It., Sp.]. See Intermezzo (1).

Intermezzo. (1) A light theatrical entertainment introduced between the acts of a serious play or opera (interpolations consisting only of instrumental music are more properly termed *entr'actes). Twice in music history intermezzi have led to new forms: the 16th-century *intermedi* of stage plays are among the forerunners of the opera [see Opera II], and the 18th-century intermezzi of operas were the predecessors of the *opera buffa* [see Comic opera II B]. A similar process took place in the 13th century when certain *tropes (in a sense, intermezzi of Gregorian chant) developed into the medieval *liturgical drama.

As early as the last quarter of the 15th century, musical interludes were used with presentations of plays based on ancient Greek and Latin themes. In 1471 an *Orfeo* was performed at Mantua with music consisting of a *canzone*, choruses of dryads and bacchantes, and a prayer of Orfeo's [see *ReMR*, p. 173]. In 1502, at the wedding of Lucrezia Borgia and Alfonso d'Este, Plautus' *Asinaria* was presented with *intermedi* by Tromboncini and others. At the marriage of Cosimo de' Medici and Eleonora of Toledo in 1539, a play by Antonio Landi, *Il Commodo,* was performed, with *intermedi* for which Corteccia composed the music, which has been preserved [see F. Ghisi, *Feste musicali*]. In 1565, Corteccia and Striggio provided music for *intermedi* representing the story of Cupid and Psyche, which were played between the acts of a comedy, *La Cofanaria*. The music is lost, but an account that survives includes a detailed description of the instruments employed [see Orchestra II]. A particularly sumptuous entertainment took place at Florence in 1589, at the wedding of Ferdinand de' Medici and Christine of Lorraine. On this occasion *intermedi* composed by Cavalieri, Malvezzi, Marenzio, and Caccini were performed with a comedy, *La Pellegrina*. The pieces—a *Sinfonia* by Marenzio, madrigals, solo songs, and ballets, with considerable instrumental accompaniment—had no connection with the main play nor among themselves, but represented individual scenes such as "The Harmony of Spheres," "The Strife between the Pierides and the Muses," and "The Combat between Apollo and the Dragon" [see A. Della Corte and G. Pannain, *Storia della musica* i, 339ff]. Similar presentations also took place in France, culminating in the *Balet comique de la royne* of 1581 [see Ballet I].

In the latter part of the 17th century most of the Italian operas performed at Paris were furnished with *intermèdes* (ballets and vocal music) by French composers, especially Lully [see H. Prunières, *L'Opéra italien en France avant Lulli* (1913)]. In Italy itself the intermezzi developed along a particularly important line that can be traced back to 1623, when an opera, *L'Amorosa innocenza,* was performed in Bologna with intermezzi that, although inserted between different acts, formed a little continuous opera of their own called *Coronazione di Apollo.* This was the beginning of a practice of "interwoven twin operas" that continued throughout the 17th century, uniting a serious plot and a lighter one into a unique kind of entertainment. In the Neapolitan opera of the early 18th century the comic intermezzi so appealed to the public that they became a dangerous rival of the main operas, with their somewhat stereotyped plots. The final stage of this development is represented by Pergolesi's *La Serva padrona,* which, originally performed as an intermezzo to the composer's serious opera *Il Prigionero superbo* (1733), was so successful that it continued to exist independently as an *opera buffa* [see Comic opera II, B]. See also Masque.

(2) One of the numerous titles of 19th-century *character pieces, suggestive of the somewhat casual origin of a piece, as if it were composed between works of greater importance (Schumann, Brahms).

Lit. for (1): D. P. Walker, ed., *Les Fêtes du mariage de Ferdinand de Médicis et de Christine de Lorraine, Florence 1589,* 2 vols. (1963—); *id., Musique des Intermèdes de "La Pellegrina"* (1963); L. Schrade, *La Représentation d'Edipo tiranno au teatro olimpico (Vicence 1585)* (1960); A. Della Corte and G. Pannain, *Storia della musica* (1944), i, 332ff; O. Kinkeldey, *Orgel und Klavier in der Musik des 16. Jahrhunderts* (1910), pp. 163ff; F. Ghisi, *Feste musicali della Firenze*

O. Sonneck, in *MA* iii (*Cofanaria*); H. Engel, "Nochmals die Intermedien von Florenz 1589" (*CP Schneider*); W. F. Weichlein, in *JAMS* xi, 85. For the intermezzi of the 17th and 18th centuries, see Comic opera.

International Musical Society. For this organization, Internationale Musikgesellschaft, and others, see under Societies III.

Interpretation. The personal and creative element in the performance of music, which, as in drama, depends on a middleman between the composer and the audience (except in *electronic music). The player or conductor, while studying a composition, absorbs it and, consciously or unconsciously, models it according to his own general ideas and taste [see also Expression]. A personal interpretation is the performer's great privilege, granted him by the composer. A really fine performer is always aware of the responsibility toward the work that this privilege imposes.

In early music, interpretation is primarily a matter of study of standards and styles entirely different from those of the current repertory. Even Bach presents many problems of interpretation that are not in the main questions of personal taste but of historical fact. See Performance practice. See G. Brelet, *L'Interprétation créatrice,* 2 vols. (1951).

Interrupted cadence. See under Cadence I.

Interval. The distance in pitch between two tones. The name of each interval indicates the number of tones of the diatonic scale it includes. Following are these names in English, German, French, Italian, Spanish, and Latin (medieval):

	c–c	c–d	c–e	c–f	c–g	c–a	c–b	c–c′
E.	unison (prime)	second	third	fourth	fifth	sixth	seventh	octave
G.	Prime	Sekunde	Terz	Quarte	Quinte	Sexte	Septime	Oktave
F.	unisson	seconde	tierce	quarte	quinte	sixte	septième	octave
It.	prima	seconda	terza	quarta	quinta	sesta	settima	ottava
Sp.	unísono	segunda	tercera	cuarta	quinta	sexta	séptima	octava
L.	unisonus	tonus	ditonus	diatessaron	diapente	tonus cum diapente	ditonus cum diapente	diapason

medicea (1480–1589) (1939); R. G. Kiesewetter, *Schicksale und Beschaffenheit des weltlichen Gesanges* (1841), pp. 65ff (examples from the *intermedi* of 1539 and 1589); articles by L. Schrade, D. P. Walker, and F. Ghisi in *Les Fêtes de la Renaissance,* J. Jacquot, ed., i (1956);

The intervals larger than an octave are called *compound intervals.* The first four of these also have special names: c–d′, ninth or compound second [F. *neuvième;* G. *None;* It. *nona;* Sp. *novena*]; c–e′, tenth or compound third [F. *dixième;* G. *Dezime;* It. *decima;* Sp. *décima*];

c–f′, eleventh or compound fourth [F. *onzième;* G. *Undezime;* It. *undicesima;* Sp. *undécima*]; c–g′, twelfth or compound fifth [F. *douzième;* G. *Duodezime;* It. *duodecima;* Sp. *duodécima*]. The same intervals occur between any two notes, e.g., f–a is a third, g–d′ is a fifth, b–c′ is a second. Intervals leading down from a note are described as "lower"; e.g., the lower fifth of c is F, etc. See also Complement; Inversion (1).

Although, e.g., a third always includes three tones, there are various kinds of third, according to whether the tones are whole tones or semitones, i.e., according to the number of chromatic steps contained in the interval. The following table shows the classification and terminology (the numbers in parentheses indicate the number of semitones in each interval):

	Diminished	Minor	Major	Augmented
Second	c♯–d♭ (0)	c–d♭ (1)	c–d (2)	c–d♯ (3)
Third	c♯–e♭ (2)	c–e♭ (3)	c–e (4)	c–e♯ (5)
Sixth	c♯–a♭ (7)	c–a♭ (8)	c–a (9)	c–a♯ (10)
Seventh	c♯–b♭ (9)	c–b♭ (10)	c–b (11)	c–b♯ (12)

		Perfect	
Fourth	c♯–f (4)	c–f (5)	c–f♯ (6)
Fifth	c♯–g (6)	c–g (7)	c–g♯ (8)
Octave	c♯–c′(11)	c–c′ (12)	c–c♯′ (13)

Intervals, calculation of. The following explanation presupposes some knowledge of algebra, including powers, roots, and (optionally) logarithms.

I. The pitch of a tone is determined by its frequency, i.e., the number of vibrations per second produced by the tone [see Acoustics I]. The interval between two tones is determined by the quotient or ratio (not the difference; see under IV) of the two frequencies. For instance, the interval between the tones 500 and 800 is $800:500 = 1.6$; that between the tones 512 and 1024 is $1024:512 = 2$ (the octave); the interval between 512 and 728 is the same as that between 384 and 546, i.e., 1.42. In the calculations of intervals the actual pitches are, of course, immaterial. An arbitrary tone, usually c, is chosen as the point of departure and is designated by the frequency 1.

II. Practically all calculations of intervals are based on three elementary intervals, the octave (O), the fifth (F), and the major third (T). Experiments already begun by Pythagoras (6th century B.C.) produced the following laws: (1) If the frequency of a tone is n, those of the octave, fifth, and (major) third are $2n$, $\frac{3}{2}n$, and $\frac{5}{4}n$ respectively. In terms of intervals (initial tone = 1) this means that the octave (O) is 2, the fifth (F) $\frac{3}{2}$, the third (T) $\frac{5}{4}$ i.e., $O = 2$; $F = \frac{3}{2}$; $T = \frac{5}{4}$. (2) Intervals are added by multiplying their respective fractions. Thus, the interval of the twelfth (upper fifth) is $F + O = \frac{3}{2} \times 2 = 3$; that of the major seventh is $F + T = \frac{3}{2} \times \frac{5}{4} = \frac{15}{8}$; that of the third octave is $O + O + O = 2 \times 2 \times 2 = 8$; etc. (3) An interval is subtracted by multiplying with its inverted fractions: $-O = \frac{1}{2}$; $-F = \frac{2}{3}$; $-T = \frac{4}{5}$. Thus, the fourth is $O - F = 2 \times \frac{2}{3} = \frac{4}{3}$; the minor third is $F - T = \frac{3}{2} \times \frac{4}{5} = \frac{6}{5}$; the major sixth is $2 \times \frac{5}{6} = \frac{5}{3}$ (octave minus minor third); etc.

III. The calculation of intervals, particularly of the more complicated ones, can be considerably simplified by disregarding the octave, i.e., the factor 2. In doing so, the fifth becomes 3 (actually the twelfth), the third becomes 5 (actually the second higher third): $F = 3$; $T = 5$. Naturally, when using these figures the results are not correct in terms of their octave position; however, they can easily be corrected by multiplying them by such a power of 2 (2, 4, 8, ½, ¼, ⅛) as will cause the product to lie between 1 and 2. Examples: (1) Calculation of the major seventh, i.e., fifth plus third: $F + T = 5 \times 3 = 15$; multiplied by ⅛, hence $\frac{15}{8}$. (2) Calculation of the fourth, i.e., lower fifth: $-F = \frac{1}{3}$; to be multiplied by 4, hence $\frac{4}{3}$. (3) Find the syntonic comma, i.e., the difference between the tone e of the *Pythagorean system (fourth consecutive fifth) and the natural third: $4F - T = 3^4:5 = \frac{81}{5}$, to be multiplied by $\frac{1}{16}$, hence $\frac{81}{80}$. This method is especially convenient for the reverse calculations, i.e., determining the interval if the ratio is given. Examples: (4) Which interval is represented by $\frac{9}{8}$? Disregarding all powers of two $(8 = 2 \times 2 \times 2)$ we find that the interval is 3×3, i.e., $F + F = 2F$, hence the second consecutive fifth, d. (The fact that the original figure lies between 1 and 2 is enough to show that this is the d within the normal octave, hence, the second.) (5) Determine the interval $^{25}\!/_{18}$. Solution: $\dfrac{5 \times 5}{3 \times 3 \times 2} = 2T - 2F$, hence two consecutive thirds minus two consecutive fifths, that is, f-sharp. (6) Determine the interval $^{45}\!/_{32}$. Solution (the denominator contains only powers of 2, $2^5 = 32$): $3 \times 3 \times 5 = 2F + T$, that is, f-sharp. Naturally, this f-sharp is not exactly the same as the one before; the difference between them is again the syntonic comma, as can easily be found by dividing the two figures (a quicker method is to subtract the two "symbols": $(2F + T) - (2T - 2F) = 2F + T - 2T + 2F = 4F - T$, a quantity that always indicates the syntonic comma).

IV. *Logarithmic intervals.* Several drawbacks of the method above are avoided if logarithms are used. According to the fundamental equation of logarithms, $\log a \times b = \log a + \log b$, the logarithm of a product is equal to the sum of the logarithms of the factors (e.g., $\log 15 = \log 3 + \log 5$). If, therefore, two intervals i_1 and i_2 are represented, not by their frequency ratios f_1 and f_2 but by the logarithms of these figures, $\log f_1$ and $\log f_2$, the compound interval $i_1 + i_2$ is represented, not as before by $f_1 \times f_2$ but by $\log (f_1 \times f_2) = \log f_1 + \log f_2$. It follows that, if logarithmic intervals are used, "addition" or "subtraction" of intervals is done by actually adding and subtracting figures instead of multiplying or dividing them. The chief advantage of logarithmic frequencies is that equal musical intervals are represented by equal distances on a geometric scale. For instance, in the usual logarithmic scale of *cents, the various octaves are indicated by the equidistant figures 0, 1200, 2400, 3600 [Ex. b], while in ordinary frequencies they are indicated by the figures 1, 2, 4, 8, etc. [Ex. a]:

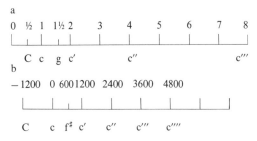

a

| 0 | ½ | 1 | 1½ | 2 | | 3 | | 4 | | 5 | | 6 | | 7 | | 8 |

C c g c' c'' c'''

b

-1200 0 600 1200 2400 3600 4800

C c f♯ c' c'' c''' c''''

Note that in the ordinary measurement the fifth g (1½, 3, 6) lies exactly in the middle of the octave, although this place should actually be occupied by the well-tempered f-sharp, as it is in the logarithmic scale.

V. Logarithmic frequencies are particularly important—in fact, indispensable—in all calculations concerning tempered intervals or microtonic intervals (non-Western scales). The well-tempered scale consists of twelve equal intervals (semitones) within one octave. If the interval of the semitone were i, the successive tones of the chromatic scale would have the frequencies: 1 (c), i (c♯), i^2 (d), i^3 (d♯), etc., until i^{12} (c'). Since, on the other hand, the octave has the frequency 2, we have the equation $i^{12} = 2$; hence $i = \sqrt[12]{2} = 1.05946$. The successive powers of this figure give the relative frequencies of the successive tones of the well-tempered scale (e.g., d would be $1.05946 \times 1.05946 = 1.12246$, etc.). In using logarithms, the intervals of the well-tempered scale are found much more easily as the multiples of $\log i = 0.0251$: $c = 0$; c♯ $= 0.0251$; $d = 0.0502$; d♯ $= 0.0753$; ... $c' = 12 \times 0.0251 = 0.3010$ ($= \log 2$). The only flaw in this scale is that the important interval of the octave is represented by the rather cumbersome figure 0.3010. This defect, however, can easily be corrected by multiplying the scale by a convenient factor. Various such "enlarged logarithmic scales" are in use; the most widely adopted one is that suggested by Ellis, in which the enlarging factor is $\dfrac{1200}{\log 2}$, so that the octave becomes exactly 1200. The unit of this measurement is called *cent;* each chromatic semitone equals 100 cents [see Cents]. The formula for the conversion of interval ratios (i) into cents (c) is: $c = \dfrac{1200}{\log 2} \times \log i = 3986 \times \log i$. For nearly all purposes the factor 3986 can be replaced by 4000. Thus, the calculation of the fifth is as follows: $F = 4000 \times \log \frac{3}{2} = 0.1761 \times 4000 = 704.4 \approx 704$ cents. If very accurate results are desired, the following correction should be made: Subtract from the result 0, 1, 2, 3, or 4, according to whether the interval lies next to c, e^{b}, f♯, a, or c'. Therefore, the accurate figure for F is 702 cents. A similar calculation for T is $T = \log \frac{5}{4} \times 4000 = 0.0969 \times 4000 = 387$ cents, corrected to 386. With these figures for F and T, all the other intervals of *just intonation and of the *Pythagorean system can easily be calculated. For instance, the major seventh $T + F$ is $702 + 386 = 1088$. This result shows that the major seventh of just intonation is 12 cents lower that that of equal temperament, 1100.

VI. The accompanying table gives the most important intervals in relative frequencies and in cents. The letters P, E, and J indicate the tones

	P	E	J
Semitone	$256/243 = 90$	$i = 100$	$16/15 = 112$ (C–D♭); $135/128 = 92$ (C–C♯)
Whole tone	$9/8 = 204$	$i^2 = 200$	$9/8 = 204$ (C–D); $10/9 = 182$ (D–E)
Minor third	$32/27 = 294$	$i^3 = 300$	$6/5 = 316$
Major third	$81/64 = 408$	$i^4 = 400$	$5/4 = 386$
Fourth	$4/3 = 498$	$i^5 = 500$	$4/3 = 498$
Aug. fourth	$729/512 = 612$	$i^6 = 600$	$45/32 = 590$
Dim. fifth	$1024/729 = 588$	$i^6 = 600$	$64/45 = 610$
Fifth	$3/2 = 702$	$i^7 = 700$	$3/2 = 702$
Minor sixth	$128/81 = 792$	$i^8 = 800$	$8/5 = 814$
Major sixth	$27/16 = 906$	$i^9 = 900$	$5/3 = 884$
Minor seventh	$16/9 = 996$	$i^{10} = 1000$	$16/9 = 996$ (D–C); $9/5 = 1018$ (E–D)
Major seventh	$243/128 = 1110$	$i^{11} = 1100$	$15/8 = 1088$ (C–B); $256/135 = 1108$ (C–C♭)
Octave	$2 = 1200$	$i^{12} = 1200$	$2 = 1200$

of the systems of Pythagoras (factors 3 and 2), equal temperament (powers of i), and just intonation (factors 3, 5, and 2). For a graphic table, see Temperament III.

It must be understood that the systems P and J actually consist of an infinite number of tones within one octave (P one-dimensional, J two-dimensional); only the simplest of these are given in the table.

Unfortunately, the measurement based on cents is not the only one in use; various others are employed, all of them logarithmic but differing in the enlarging factor and, therefore, in the number of units contained in the octave. Some of these other systems are:

Savart (301 to the octave) $= 1000 \times \log i \approx$ ¼ cent (1 savart = approximately 4 cents).

Millioctave (1000 to the octave) $= \dfrac{1000}{\log 2} \times$ $\log i = \tfrac{5}{6}$ cent (1 millioctave = $\tfrac{6}{5}$ cents).

Centitone (600 to the octave) $= \dfrac{600}{\log 2} \times$ $\log i = \tfrac{1}{2}$ cent (1 centitone = 2 cents).

For example, the well-tempered fifth is 700 cents = 175.6 savarts = 583.3 millioctaves = 350 centitones.

See Pythagorean scale; Just intonation; Microtone; Temperament; Comma; Cents.

Lit.: R. W. Young, *A Table Relating Frequency to Cents* (1939); H. Husmann, *Fünf- und siebenstellige Centstafeln zur Berechnung musikalischer Intervalle* (1951); A. Daniélou, *Tableau comparatif des intervalles musicaux* (*Publications de L'Institut français d'Indologie* viii [1958]).

Intolleranza 1960. Opera-oratorio by L. Nono (libretto by the composer after A. M. Ripellino), produced in Venice, 1961. Setting: the present.

Intonation. (1) In ensemble performance, intonation means singing or playing in tune. Correct intonation in violin (and all string) playing results from a combination of exact listening, technical facility, and a good instrument. The violinist generally uses the well-tempered scale when accompanied by the piano but has greater freedom to modify leading tones, raise thirds, etc., with a string group. See C. Heman, *Intonation auf Streichinstrumenten* (1964); K. G. Mostrass, *Die Intonation auf der Violine* (1961). (2) In Gregorian chant, the opening notes of a *psalm tone or other recitation tones. (3) See Just intonation.

Intonatione. A 16th-century Italian name for a prelude, designed chiefly for liturgical use. The best-known examples are those in *Intonationi d'organo di Andrea Gabrieli, et di Gio. suo nepote* of 1593. This publication contains eight *intonationi* by A. Gabrieli, one for each of the eight church modes (*del primo, secondo, . . . tono*), and eleven by G. Gabrieli, one for each of Glareanus' enlarged system of twelve modes, except for modes 3 and 4, which are represented by a single *Intonatio del terzo et quarto tono* (the actual number of pieces is twenty-two, since each is also given in transposition to the fourth or fifth). B. Schmid's *Tabulatur Buch* of 1607 ascribes eight *intonationi* to G. Gabrieli and the group of twenty-two to A. Gabrieli. The term was occasionally used by later composers, e.g., F. X. Murschhauser and S. A. Scherer.

Intrada, entrada [It.]. A 16th- and 17th-century name for an opening piece of a festive or marchlike character, written in full homophonic style. A number of intradas for five to six instruments (the earliest in existence?) are in a publication of 1597 by Alessandro Orologio. Intradas in duple or triple meter figure prominently among the dance types of the German orchestral suites of the early 17th century, in which they usually (but not always) appear at the beginning [see the suites of M. Franck and V. Haussmann, in *DdT* 16; J. H. Schein, *Banchetto musicale* (1617), new ed. by A. Prüfer, vol. i; *SchGMB,* nos. 153, 154, 157; *RiHM* ii.2, 173]. Mozart (*Bastien und Bastienne*) and Beethoven (*Wellingtons Sieg*) used the name for short overtures. See M. Reimann, in *MF* x.

Introduction. A slow section frequently found at the beginning of symphonies, quartets, sonatas, etc. An unusually long and elaborate introduction is that of Beethoven's Seventh Symphony.

Introit [L. *introitus*]. (1) The initial chant of the (Proper of the) *Mass. It is an antiphonal chant [see under Antiphon (3)] and is usually in a moderately ornate style. For the form of the Introit, see Psalmody III. The Introit was introduced by Pope Celestine I (reigned 422–32) as a chant accompanying the entrance of the priest to the altar [cf. the Ambrosian analogue *ingressa*] and consisted originally of an entire psalm sung antiphonally. The text, particularly its first section (antiphon), frequently refers to the occasion, e.g., the Christmas Introit "Puer natus est nobis" [see *GR,* p. 33]. Several Sundays are named for the initial word of their Introit, e.g., Laetare Sunday (fourth Sunday in Lent) from the text: "Laetare Jerusalem" [*GR,* p. 138]; see also Requiem Mass. (2) In isorhythmic motets of the 14th and 15th centuries, an *introitus* is an introductory section that stands outside the isorhythmic structure. Usually the tenor is silent during this section. Two motets by P. de Vitry, "In arboris" and "Virtutibus laudabilis" (ed. L. Schrade, in *Polyphonic Music of the Fourteenth Century* [1956], i), five by G. de Machaut (ed. F. Ludwig, *Editions XLVI,* 4.ii, nos. 9, 19, 21, 22, 23), seven by G. Dufay (ed. G. de Van, nos. 1, 3, 4, 5, 7, 12, 13), and many others (J. Ciconia, N. Grenon, J. Dunstable) begin with an *introitus.* Sometimes it is composed as a canon (e.g., Dufay, nos. 4, 7, 13). Occasionally the *introitus* has no text, becoming an instrumental introduction (Dufay, no. 3).

Invention. A rarely used term but familiar to every musician through Bach's collection (1723) of 15 keyboard pieces in two parts, called "Inventiones," and 15 pieces in three parts, called "Sinfoniae." (In the *Klavierbüchlein für Wilhelm Friedemann Bach* they are called "Praeambulum" and "Fantasia" respectively.) The usual

names, "two-part invention" and "three-part invention," are not authentic but seem justifiable on account of the similarity of style in both groups. Bach's reason for choosing these terms is entirely obscure. The word "sinfonia" was widely used in his day, but for an entirely different type of music [see Sinfonia]. The designation "invention" was used by G.-B. Vitali for pieces involving special tricks ("inventioni curiose," 1689; see Editions III, 7) and by F. A. Bonporti as a synonym for suites (partitas) in a work (op. 10) published under different titles at various times (1712, '25). Four of Bonporti's "inventions" have been reprinted as works of Bach in *BG* [vol. xlv, pp. 172–89; see W. Wolffheim, in *BJ,* 1911; C. Bouvet, in *RdM* 1918]. No less obscure than the origin of the name is the development leading to the type represented by Bach's inventions and sinfonias, which might best be described as "studies in double or triple counterpoint." Possibly an investigation of the numerous 17th-century Italian publications of two-part "ricercares" [see Ricercar II (d); *inventio* = translation of ricercar?] would throw light on whether or not Bach "invented the inventions." It may be noted that the invention style is very common in the preludes of Bach's *Well-Tempered Clavier* (e.g., vol. i, nos. 3, 9, 11, 13, 15, 18, 19, 20), and is used also in the preludes of the first three partitas [see Suite I].

Inventions-horn. See under Horn II.

Inversion. Substitution of higher for lower tones and vice versa. There are two main types of inversion, harmonic inversion and melodic inversion. In harmonic inversion, the lower note (of an interval) or the root (of a chord) is in an upper part instead of in the bass. In melodic inversion, the successive intervals of the melody are inverted.

(1) *Harmonic inversion.* An interval is inverted by transferring its lower note into the higher octave, or its higher note into the lower octave, e.g., the inversion of d–a is a–d' or A–d. By inversion, a fifth changes into a fourth, a third into a sixth, etc. (the sum of the numbers indicated in the names of the two intervals is always nine, e.g., $5 + 4 = 9$; $3 + 6 = 9$). Both intervals together form an octave [see Complement]. Major intervals become minor, augmented intervals become diminished, while a perfect interval produces another perfect interval. See the table shown on p. 419, in which inverted intervals can easily be found by looking for two figures whose sum is twelve, the number of semitones in the

octave, e.g., major third and minor sixth $(4 + 8 = 12)$ or augmented second and diminished seventh $(3 + 9 = 12)$ [Ex. la]. A chord (triad, etc.) is inverted by applying the principle just explained to the lowest tone, e.g., changing g–b–d′ into b–d′–g′. For more details, see Harmonic analysis IV.

a. Inverted intervals. b. Inverted chords. c. Inverted counterpoint.

In counterpoint, the principle of harmonic inversion leads to an exchange of higher and lower parts by means of octave transposition. For more details see Invertible counterpoint. The term "inverted pedal (point)" means a sustained note (pedal) in a higher part rather than in the bass [see Pedal point].

(2) *Melodic inversion.* A melody (subject) is inverted by changing each ascending interval into the corresponding descending interval, and vice versa. By this process, an ascending fifth c–g changes into a descending fifth c–F, the ascending progression c–d′–e′ into the descending progressions c–b–a. The result is a mirrorlike exchange of upward and downward movements [Ex. 2, from Bach's *Well-Tempered Clavier*, vol. i; in the illustration here the second line of music has been transposed a fourth higher than the original (from meas. 20ff) for purposes of comparison]. Inversion is said to be strict (or real) if the original and inverted intervals agree

2

exactly with regard to semitonal distance. Thus the strict inversion of c–d′–e′ is c–b♭–a♭. However, since this procedure destroys the tonality, it is practically never used except in the twelve-tone system, in which tonality has no place [see

Serial music]. Normally, inversion is "tonal," i.e., it utilizes the degrees of the scale of the key. Thus c–d′–e′ would become c–b–a, preserving the tonality. Inversion plays an important part in fugues [see Counterfugue], in *gigues, and in the development sections of sonatas and symphonies [Ex. 3, Bruckner, Symphony no. 7].

3

Melodic inversion appears in the works of Ciconia [see under Isomelic] and in the tenors of 15th-century Masses and motets, where it is indicated by canons such as "Subverte lineam" (Dunstable; see *ApNPM*, p. 187), "Per antifrasim canta" (Obrecht, *Missa L'Homme armé*), or "Qui se exaltat humiliabitur, et qui se humiliat exaltabitur" (Obrecht, *Missa Graecorum*). As a device of fugal composition, it was first exploited by Andrea Gabrieli [see W. Apel, in *MD*, iii].

Inverted canon. Canon either by (melodic) inversion or by retrograde motion; see Canon I (d), (e).

Inverted fugue. *Counterfugue.

Inverted mordent [G. *Schneller*]. An 18th-century ornament involving alternation of the written note with the note immediately above it, to be performed as a short, rapid trill beginning on the beat. The inverted mordent was not one of the French *agréments,* having been introduced after 1750 by K. P. E. Bach, who always indicated it by two small grace notes [Ex. a]. Later composers often designated the inverted mordent with a short wavy line [Ex. b], which originally indicated a somewhat different ornament called *Pralltriller.* This is a rapid trill of four notes, beginning with the upper auxiliary, as was customary with trills in that period. This trill was used only on the lower note of a descending second and tied to the preceding note, sometimes giving the erroneous impression that the *Pralltriller* begins with the main note. The *Schneller,* on the other hand, can occur only on a detached note, that is, the upper note of a descending second, so that the position of the sign (b) usually indicates whether a *Schneller* [Ex. c] or a *Pralltriller* [Ex. d] is meant.

After 1800 the *Pralltriller* dropped out of use so that the sign (b) always indicates the *Schneller*. Simultaneously, however, the name *Schneller* dropped out of use and the ornament illustrated under (c) became known as *Pralltriller,* the current German term for the inverted mordent.

2

double counterpoint, if to three (four) parts, triple (quadruple) counterpoint [Ex. 2; Beethoven, op. 10, no. 3].

Occasionally double counterpoint is treated in a more elaborate manner, involving transposition at intervals other than the octave. For instance, in double counterpoint at the fifth (tenth, twelfth) one part is transposed to the

The former restriction regarding its position on the first note of a descending second has, of course, been long abandoned, and the inverted mordent is frequently found in connection with skips to which it adds crispness and a determined attack [last movement of Beethoven's "Hammerklavier" Sonata op. 106]. About 1830 (Hummel, Moscheles) the inverted mordent began to be performed before the main note, and today this is generally considered the proper manner of execution. As late as in Chopin, however, examples abound in which the old method appears to be preferable, owing to its greater expressiveness [Ex. e, Valse in A-flat]. For some questionable cases, see P. Aldrich, in *MQ* xlix.   P.A.

Invertible counterpoint. A passage in contrapuntal texture so designed that, by means of transposition (usually of an octave) the lower part may become the higher part, or the higher the lower [Ex. 1]. This is an application of the principle of harmonic inversion [see Inversion (1)]. If applied to two parts, the method is called

upper fifth (tenth, twelfth) while the other remains at the same pitch or is merely transposed an octave. Several examples of this technique occur in S. Scheidt's *Tabulatura nova* of 1624 [Ex. 3, "Bicinium duplici contrapuncto"; see *DdT* 1, 130]. Particularly remarkable is its application in J. S. Bach's *Einige kanonische Veränderungen über . . .* "*Vom Himmel hoch, da komm ich her*" [Ex. 4; here transposed up one octave for clarification]. Other examples are found in the canons of Bach's *Art of Fugue*. This technique is in general somewhat less "labored" than it is frequently thought to be. A comparison of the various intervals (unison, second, third, etc.) with their equivalents in, e.g., double counterpoint at the fifth (fifth, sixth, seventh, etc.) readily reveals which intervals will make good consonances in the original as well as in the inverted position. Extensive studies of these and other, more complicated devices (usually combinations of the double counterpoint with canonic treatment) are found in most books on counterpoint. See S. I. Taneiev, *Convertible Counterpoint in the Strict Style* [1962].

1

Exceptionally early examples of double counterpoint occur in the *caudae* of some 13th-century conductus. They are all the more remarkable because they involve transposition at the fourth and fifth [see Y. Rokseth, "Le Contrepoint double vers 1248," in *CP Laurencie*]. In the 16th century double counterpoint became established as a standard technique of contrapuntal stye. It is treated by Vicentino (1555), and with special attention by Zarlino in his *Le istitutioni harmoniche,* vol. iii (1558).

The term "invertible counterpoint" is occasionally used to mean melodic inversion [see Inversion (2)]. This usage is unfortunate, particularly because melodic inversion, although frequently found in contrapuntal writing, does not in any way involve counterpoint but applies essentially to a single melody. See Mirror composition. For the exchange of parts without transposition, see Voice exchange. Also see Y. Rokseth, "Le Contrepoint double vers 1248" (*Editions XLIX, ser. ii, 3–4).

Invitation to the Dance. See *Aufforderung zum Tanz.*

Invitatory [L. *invitatorium*]. In the Roman Catholic rites, the opening chant of Matins [see Office], consisting of Psalm 94 (*psalmus invitatorius*) "Venite, exsultemus Domino" (Psalm 95 of the King James Version: "O come let us sing unto the Lord"), sung with varying antiphons (invitatory antiphons). The invitatory is one of the few remaining examples of the original structure of antiphonal psalmody [see Psalmody III], the antiphon being sung not only at its beginning and end but also between each pair of verses. The psalm is sung to a number of tones considerably more elaborate than the ordinary psalm tones [see *Liber responsorialis*, pp. 6ff; for more details, see *ApGC*, pp. 241ff], and the antiphons are equally elaborate. Being a chant of Matins, the *invitatorium* is given in the *Liber usualis* only for Christmas, Whitsuntide, Corpus Christi, and the Office for the Dead [*LU*, pp. 368, 863, 918, 1779]. It is more fully represented in the *Liber responsorialis.*

In the Anglican rites the "Venite" with proper antiphons forms a part of every Morning Prayer, being sung either in plainsong or in Anglican chant [see Service]. The antiphon is sung only at the beginning and end. The Lutheran and Methodist churches also include the "Venite" set to Anglican chant in their morning services, the former with antiphons and the latter without.

Ionian. See under Church modes; Greece II.

Iphigénie. Two operas by Gluck, *Iphigénie en Aulide* (F. *Iphigenia in Aulis;* libretto by F. L. G. Lebland du Roullet, based on Racine's tragedy), produced in Paris, 1774, and *Iphigénie en Tauride* (F. *Iphigenia in Tauris;* libretto by N. F. Guillard), produced in Paris, 1779. Both are based on dramas by Euripides. Setting: ancient Greece.

Ireland. Historically, Ireland's most important musical achievements were in folksong and early medieval music. In the early Middle Ages, Irish monks were among the first to foster Gregorian chant, both at home and abroad. For example, in 614 St. Gall, an Irish hermit, built a cell near the site of the town in Switzerland named after him (Sankt-Gallen). After his death in 640, a monastic community developed there, and in the year 719 the Abbot Othmar founded a Benedictine cloister at St. Gall. By the mid-8th century this foundation had become a regular establishment and a leading center for plainsong.

In the 9th century, Joannes Scotus (called Erigena; *c.* 815–*c.* 877) wrote his "De Divisione Naturae," which contains interesting remarks about music [see J. Handschin, in *ZMW* ix]. The oldest representations of Irish instruments (lyres? harps?; see Harp III) are reliefs on stone crosses of the 8th and 9th centuries, whose presence perhaps explains why the harp became Ireland's national instrument and heraldic symbol. In the 12th century Giraldus Cambrensis frequently referred to the achievements of Irish instrumentalists and their influence on Scottish and Welsh music [see *ReMMA*, p. 392]. Various claims for the precedence and eminence of early Irish music, advanced by G. Flood and others, have not been substantiated. Apart from J. de Garlandia, Dowland, and Purcell, all three alleged by Flood to be of Irish descent, prominent composers from Ireland include Thomas Roseingrave (1690–1766), John Field (1782–1837), Michael W. Balfe (1808–70, composer of the opera *The Bohemian Girl*), William V. Wallace (1812–65), Charles V. Stanford (1852–1924), Hamilton Harty (1879–1914), and Arnold E. T. Bax (1883–1953; of Irish descent, born in England). Also see England.

Lit. A. G. Fleischmann, *Music in Ireland* (1952); W. H. Grattan Flood, *A History of Irish Music* (1905; not wholly trustworthy); R. Honebry, *A Handbook of Irish Music* (1928); C. M. Fox, *Annals of the Irish Harpers* (1911); H. Hughes, ‡*Irish Country Songs; id., ‡Historical Songs and Ballads of Ireland;* A. W. Patterson, "The Folk-Music of Ireland" (*MQ* vi); W. L.

Lawrence, "Early Irish Ballad Opera and Comic Opera" (*MQ* viii); J. Travis, "Irish National Music" (*MQ* xxiv); F. St. John Lacy, in *PMA* xvi; A. W. Patterson, in *PMA* xxiii; J. S. Bumpus, "Irish Church Composers" (*PMA* xxvi); W. H. Grattan Flood, "Irish Musical Bibliography" (*SIM* xiii; also *CP 1911,* p. 359).

rev. F.B.Z.

Irish harp. See under Harp.

Isomelic. Term for a device found in isorhythmic motets of the time of Ciconia to Dufay (*c.* 1400–50), i.e., the use of the same or similar melodic material in the upper parts at corresponding places (measures) of their isorhythmic structure. A clear distinction must be made according to whether the "corresponding places" occur from *talea* to *talea* (of the same *color*) or from *color* to *color.* The former type seems to be the older, since it is used in several motets by Ciconia. Because corresponding measures of different *taleae* usually have different pitches in the tenor, isomelic recurrence normally involves transposition or some other modification (e.g., inversion). Ex. 1 shows two isomelic passages from Ciconia's panisorhythmic motet, "Ut per te omnes" [see Van den Borren, *Polyphonia sacra,*

p. 180]. Similar examples occur in some motets by Dunstable (e.g., "Veni sancte spiritus," meas. 22–24 = 67–69) and Dufay (e.g., "Fulgens iubar," motetus meas. 4–10 = 52–58, 97–98 = 113–114; in *Opera Omnia,* I², 52). The other type of isomelic correspondence, relating to the *colores* of a motet, means that hand in hand with the restatement of the tenor melody (*cantus firmus*) the upper parts also make use of the same melodic material. This recurrence is usually on a broader scale than the *talea* recurrence but also much less exact, involving considerable variation [see Ex. 2, from Dufay's "Fulgens iubar"; for another example, from "Nuper rosarum flores," see *ReMR,* p. 80]. It is usually in this sense that the term isomelic is employed by musicologists. Less commendable is the use of the term isomelic for certain Masses

that employ the same *cantus firmus* in their various movements but in rhythmic variants [see E. Reeser, "Een 'isomelische mis' uit den tijd van Dufay" (*TV* xvi, 151); see, e.g., the *Missa O rosa bella* in *DTO* 22, p. 28]. In this meaning, the term is practically synonymous with cyclic [Mass cycle; see Mass C II] and, moreover, fails to indicate, as it should, different rhythm rather than unchanged melody. See *BeMMR,* p. 206; *ReMR,* pp. 80, 92; W. Stephan, *Die burgundisch-niederländische Motette zur Zeit Ockeghems* (1937), p. 12; M. F. Bukofzer, *Studies in Medieval and Renaissance Music* [1950], pp. 65ff; S. E. Brown, "New Evidence of Isomelic Design in Dufay's Isorhythmic Motets" (*JAMS* x).

Isometric. Term used for polyphonic compositions in which all the voice-parts move simultaneously in the same rhythmic values, thus forming a succession of chords. See *Homo-, iso-, where it is advocated that a better name for this style would be "homometric" or, preferably, *homorhythmic. The term "isometric" might then be used to describe horizontal identity of meter, i.e., continued presence of the same meter, as opposed to *polymetric, i.e., varying meter. See K. Jeppesen, "Das isometrische Moment in der Vokalpolyphonie" (*CP Wagner*); K. P. Bernet Kempers, "Isometrische Begriffe und die Musik des 19. Jahrhunderts" (*CP Blume*).

Isoperiodic. See under Isorhythmic.

Isorhythmic. A term introduced by F. Ludwig [*SIM* iv, 16–69] to denote a structural principle frequently used in 14th-century motets, particularly in the tenors. Its main feature is the use of a reiterated scheme of time values for the presentation of a liturgical *cantus firmus.* The tenor of

G. de Machaut's motet "Hé Mors—Fine Amour—Quare non sum mortuus" [see *Guillaume de Machaut, Musikalische Werke,* ed. F. Ludwig, iii, 9] serves as an example [Ex. 1].

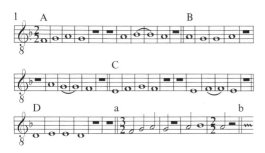

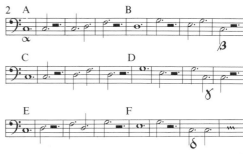

The repeated scheme of time values used in sections A, B, C, and (half of it) D is called *talea* in 14th-century treatises. Beginning with (a), the entire liturgical melody, the so-called *color,* is repeated in halved values (diminution), a procedure normally employed in isorhythmic motets. Two typical schemes of 14th-century tenor structure are: [c/3t] × 2 (2:1) and [c/2t] × 3 (3:2:1). In the first, the *color* (c) is divided into three *taleae* (t), this being restated in halved values. Similarly, in the second formula there are three statements of the *color* in progressive diminutions, each divided into two *taleae.*

The isorhythmic principle, although usually thought of as a characteristic feature of the *ars nova,* is the logical development of the modal rhythm of the 13th century. Modal patterns such as:

[see *SchGMB,* no. 12] differ from the 14th-century *taleae* only in length. Particularly interesting are examples in which the number of notes in *color* and *talea* (i.e., in the melodic and in the rhythmic pattern) are not in proportion, thus leading to the repetition of the melody in different rhythmic patterns. The tenor of an Alleluia which was written about 1200 serves as an illustration [Ex. 2]. Since here the *color* (α, β, γ, etc.) includes nine notes and the *talea* (A, B, C, etc.) five, the *color* would have to be repeated five times until both schemes would come to a simultaneous close. Actually, the piece stops after the fourth *color,* leaving the last *talea* incomplete. Such configurations, involving overlapping of *taleae* and *colores* ([2c/3t],

[3c/5t], etc.), also are found in some 14th-century motets.

In the 14th century the isorhythmic principle was not only the chief method for the rhythmic organization of the tenors but was also applied—more freely—to the upper parts [for an example by P. de Vitry, see *ReMMA,* p. 338]. In most of Machaut's motets the upper parts have identical rests at corresponding places of the *talea,* so that the periods within one *talea* are of the same length as those within the others (isoperiodicity). Moreover, they usually are partly isorhythmic, i.e., a passage of three or four measures recurs isorhythmically in some or all of the subsequent *taleae.* The culmination of this development is the panisorhythmic motet, in which every voice-part is strictly isorhythmic. (It may be noted that often the term "isorhythmic" is employed in the specific meaning more clearly indicated by "panisorhythmic".) A panisorhythmic motet may be said to consist of a number of "melody-variations" of a fixed rhythmic theme. This type, represented in Machaut by only two motets, is the one normally used by the latest composers of isorhythmic motets, Ciconia, Dunstable, and Dufay. In the late 14th century isorhythm was occasionally applied to the two sections of the rondeau [see W. Apel, *French Secular Music of the Late 14th Century,* p. 7a]. In some motets of about 1400 the upper parts only are isorhythmic, the tenor being free [see C. van den Borren, *Polyphonia sacra,* no. 25]. After 1450 the isorhythmic principle survived in various attenuated modifications [see R. Dammann, "Spätformen der isorhythmischen Motette im 16. Jahrhundert" (*AMW* x)]. See Isomelic.

Isosyllabic. Term for a principle of versification based solely on the number of syllables, without regard for either quantity or quality [see Poetic meter]. It was discovered by F. J. Mone (*Lateinische Hymnen des Mittelalters* ii, 1854) and independently by Cardinal J. B. Pitra (*Hymno-*

graphie de l'Église grecque, 1867) in connection with the Byzantine *kontakia* and *kanons,* which until then had been regarded as prose. This principle was already used in ancient Syrian poetry (St. Ephraem, St. Romanus) and may even be of pre-Christian origin. St. Romanus' "Hymn on the Nativity", for example, has the structure 7 8 7 8/8 5 8 5 8 5/7 [see E. Wellesz, *A History of Byzantine Music and Hymnography,* rev. ed. (1961), p. 188].

Israel in Egypt. Oratorio by Handel (to a scriptural text), composed in 1738.

Istampita, istanpitta. See *Estampie.*

Istar Variations. Seven orchestral variations by V. d'Indy, op. 42 (1896), which are a unique example of "variation in the reverse," starting with the most complex variation and ending with the theme in octaves. This process of "disrobing" is implied in the title, Istar being the Babylonian goddess of passion.

Istesso tempo [It.]. Indication that, even though the meter changes, the duration of the beat remains unaltered. For example, it means $\downarrow = \downarrow.$ if there is a change from 2/4 to 6/8; $\downarrow = \downarrow$ if the time changes from 2/4 to 3/4. The situation is different, of course, if the tempo is so fast that the half note becomes the beat. In this case, a change from 2/4 to 3/4 would have to be interpreted $\downarrow = \downarrow.$; in any case, exact indications of equivalent note values are a much more definite indication than the somewhat vague term *istesso tempo.*

Istituto italiano per la storia della musica. See Editions XXII.

Istituzioni e monumenti dell' arte musicale italiana. See Editions XXIII.

Italiana in Algeri, L' [It., The Italian Woman in Algiers]. Opera in two acts by Rossini (libretto by A. Anelli), produced in Venice, 1813.

Italian Concerto. A composition for harpsichord by Bach, so called because it is in the form and style of the instrumental concertos of the early 18th-century Italian school (Vivaldi); see Concerto III (b).

Italian overture. See under Overture I.

Italian sixth. See Sixth chord.

Italian Symphony. Mendelssohn's Symphony no. 4 in A major, op. 90 (1831–33), begun in Italy and containing allusions to Italian folk music,

particularly in the last movement, entitled "Saltarello."

Italy. I. Among the leading musical nations, Italy has the distinction of having the longest recorded music history and, after France, the most influential position. Perhaps its most important contribution is the development of Christian chant, which took place in Rome (*cantus romanus,* Roman chant) and is usually referred to as *Gregorian chant in recognition of the role Pope Gregory I (reigned 590–604) played in its evolution. While the final development of this chant probably took place outside Italy, there has recently come to light another chant repertory known as *Old Roman chant, which undoubtedly developed in Italy and was used in Rome. Even 200 years before Gregory, St. Ambrose (333–97) had established a rite that today is used only in Milan (*Ambrosian chant, Milanese chant), though his hymns [see Ambrosian hymns] were incorporated into the Roman repertory. The contributions of Italy to the development of the *sequences and *tropes seem to have been restricted to their latest period, the 13th century, when Thomas of Celano wrote the "Dies irae," Thomas Aquinas the "Lauda Sion," and Jacopone the "Stabat mater" [see Sequence II D]. Guido d'Arezzo (*c.* 990–1050) not only made (or established) the epochal invention of the *staff but also discussed, in his "Micrologus," the primitive polyphony of his day [see Organum I]. Nonetheless, until the end of the 13th century the development of polyphonic music remained in the hands of France [see France II], and Italy's contribution to the music of the *ars antiqua* was restricted to monophonic religious songs, the *laude.* The 14th century saw the first flowering of Italian polyphony in the *caccie and *madrigals of Giovanni da Cascia (or de Florentia) and Jacopo da Bologna (fl. *c.* 1350), culminating in the work of the blind Francesco Landini (1325–97), whose *ballate* represent an amalgamation of French polyphony with Italian melody [see Ars nova III]. Other composers of Landini's time are Laurentius de Florentia and Paolo tenorista, whose works are noteworthy for the frequent use of *imitation. The development of Italian music about and after 1400 is not wholly clear. Composers such as Matheus de Perusio, Antonellus and Filipoctus de Caserta, Bartolomeo de Bononia, and Nicolaus Zacharias wrote mainly secular pieces of French derivation (*ballades, virelais, rondeaux,* frequently with French texts) in a highly complex and even mannered style.

The central figure of this period was Johannes Ciconia (*c.* 1340–1411), a Walloon who worked in Padua. He wrote sacred music (motets, Mass items) in a dignified and "festive" style, similar to that of Dunstable, as did his younger contemporary, Antonius Romanus [see *SchGMB,* nos. 29, 30; for additional examples, see *WoGM* ii, iii, nos. 30ff]. Important theorists were Marchettus de Padua ("Pomerium," *c.* 1325), Theodoricus de Campo (*c.* 1350), and Prosdocimus de Beldemandis (*c.* 1400).

II. *Renaissance.* During the 15th century Italian musical development declined, at least so far as we know. Only recently have some traces of musical activity come to light. Of particular interest is the discovery of a number of choirbooks from Modena containing simple homorhythmic settings of psalms and hymns for two alternating choruses, the earliest known examples of this kind [see Bukofzer, *Studies in Medieval and Renaissance Music,* pp. 181ff]. Northern composers such as Dufay, Obrecht, Isaac, and Josquin traveled to the south, and features of harmony and balance found in their works have frequently, though with doubtful authenticity, been ascribed to "sunny Italy." While art music declined, popular music seems to have flourished [see *Villota*], and it is this field that, toward the end of the 15th century, gave Italian music new life, in the *frottola* (Marco Cara, Tromboncino) and the *canti carnascialeschi.* Once more, Flemish masters took the lead in raising these unpretentious songs to the high standard of the *madrigal, but after 1550 we find Italian composers such as Costanzo Festa, Andrea Gabrieli, Luca Marenzio, and Gesualdo in successful competition with the *oltramontani.* Rome became the center of sacred music (*motet, *Mass) through Palestrina (*c.* 1525–94) and his numerous successors [see Roman school], while in Venice Giovanni Gabrieli (*c.* 1555–1612), uniting large choral and instrumental sonorities, attained unparalleled pomp and splendor [see Venetian school]. Hardly less important were the contributions of 16th-century Italian organ composers (Cavazzoni, Andrea Gabrieli, Claudio Merulo), who created the *ricercar, *canzona, and *toccata.

III. *Baroque.* From about 1600, during the early baroque era, we meet with terms such as *Camerata, *nuove musiche, *monody, *thoroughbass (*basso continuo*), *opera, *oratorio, *cantata—all exclusively Italian—and names such as Caccini, Peri, E. del Cavalieri and, above all, Monteverdi, whose *I & II Prattica* of the

8 Books of Madrigals epitomizes the evolution from Renaissance polyphony to *stile recitativo e rappresentativo.* To the numerous masters of vocal forms (Caccini, Peri, Banchieri, Monteverdi, Carissimi, Cavalli, Grandi, Cesti, Legrenzi, Stradella, G. B. Bassani, A. Scarlatti, Caldara, B. Marcello, Leo, Pergolesi, Piccinni, Sacchini) must be added composers of instrumental music (*sonata, *concerto, *concerto grosso, *sinfonia: L. Viadana, M. A. Rossi, B. Marini, Legrenzi, Torelli, G. B. Vitali, Vivaldi, Corelli, Bonporti, Durante, Veracini, Geminiani, Porpora; see Bologna school) and keyboard music (Trabaci, A. Mayone [see Neapolitan school], Frescobaldi, M. A. Rossi, B. Pasquini, Zipoli, D. Scarlatti). About 1750, when Italian vocal music declined into empty virtuosity, composers such as Sammartini, Locatelli, and Piatti worked to develop a new style in instrumental music, simultaneously with the *Mannheim school of Germany. The leadership, however, soon fell to Germany, and Italian music remained in the hands of academics such as Padre Martini (who taught the young Mozart) or cheap entertainers such as Paradisi, Rutini, and Paganelli [see Rococo; Gallant style]. Muzio Clementi (1752–1832), one of the founders of modern piano technique (*Gradus ad Parnassum*) lived and worked abroad. A survey of Italian baroque music would be incomplete without mentioning such outstanding achievements in musical reproduction as *bel canto [see also *Castrato*] and the building of violins [see Violin].

IV. *Opera, 1760–present.* About 1760 the leadership in instrumental music passed from Italy to Germany and for about 100 years Italian composers devoted themselves almost exclusively to opera (Jommelli, Galuppi, Cimarosa, Paisiello). Instead of building up a national opera, however, most of them were attracted by the operatic centers outside Italy, especially Paris. It was in Paris that Niccolò Piccinni (1728–1800) became a dangerous rival of Gluck and that Antonio Sacchini (1730–86) competed with Piccinni. Antonio Salieri, the teacher of Beethoven and Schubert, worked in Vienna and Paris, and Maria Luigi Cherubini (1760–1842) became the central figure in French music during the Napoleonic era, while Gasparo Spontini (1774–1851) played a similar role at the court of Berlin. Gioacchino Rossini (1792–1868) was the first to write another great Italian opera, his *Il Barbiere di Siviglia* (1816). His *Guillaume Tell* (1829), written for Paris, marks the beginning of the *grand opéra,* which was continued by Gaetano Donizetti (1797–1848) and Vincenzo Bellini (1801–35), and can be considered the first to show signs of *romanticism.

In marked contrast to the above-mentioned stands Giuseppe Verdi (1813–1901), who devoted his long life to the establishment of a national opera. From his early *Nabucodonosor* (1842) to the mature masterpieces (*Rigoletto, Il Trovatore, La Traviata*) and his late *Otello* (1887) and *Falstaff* (1893), his style shows a steady progress to great artistic heights, a progress all the more remarkable in that he managed to escape the all-pervading influence of Wagner. He was followed by three composers who each wrote only one successful opera: Arrigo Boito (1842–1918; *Mefistofele*, 1868), Pietro Mascagni (1863–1945; *Cavalleria rusticana*, 1890), and Ruggiero Leoncavallo (1858–1919; *Pagliacci*, 1892), the last two being known as the founders of *verismo*. Italian opera took on a more lyrical and slightly sentimental tinge with Giacomo Puccini's (1858–1924) world successes, *La Bohème* (1896) and *Madama Butterfly* (1904). Among more recent operatic composers, Italo Montemezzi (1875–1952; *L'Amore dei tre re*, 1913) and Ildebrando Pizzetti (b. 1880; *Debora e Jaele*, 1922) are outstanding.

V. *20th century*. Not until the late 19th century was activity in instrumental music renewed in Italy. Giovanni Sgambati (1841–1914) wrote symphonies and chamber music in the style of Brahms, as did Giuseppe Martucci (1856–1909). Neither they, however, nor their successors, such as Enrico Bossi (1861–1925) or Leone Sinigaglia (1868–1944), succeeded in breaking the all-powerful position of opera, and not until 1910 did tendencies toward a more universal and cosmopolitan attitude emerge. This reorientation of Italian music was first promoted by F. Busoni (1866–1924) and then continued by O. Respighi (1879–1936), I. Pizzetti (b. 1880), G. F. Malipiero (b. 1882), A. Casella (1883–1947), and G. F. Ghedini (b. 1892). The first two cultivated an eclectic, neoromantic style, variously influenced by Rimsky-Korsakov, R. Strauss, and Ravel, while the last three often drew inspiration from the works of early Italian masters (chiefly Monteverdi, Scarlatti, Frescobaldi). The main representatives of the next generation are Luigi Dallapiccola (b. 1904), who introduced the twelve-tone technique into Italy and, like Busoni, was oriented toward the German tradition, and Goffredo Petrassi (b. 1904), who was strongly influenced by Stravinsky in his early works and combines neoclassical with baroque

influences. Both helped give Italian music an important place on the European scene, preparing the way for further developments, which, through the works of Bruno Maderna (b. 1920), Luigi Nono (b. 1924), Luciano Berio (b. 1925), F. Donatoni (b. 1927), and others suggests that Italian instrumental music has definitely regained a prominent place in contemporary music.

Lit.: S. Chiereghin, *Storia della musica italiana* (1937); *LavE* i.2, 611–910; *Editions III, V, VI, IX, X, XXI, XXII, XXIII, XXX. For Middle Ages and Renaissance: ReMMA*, pp. 360ff (bibl., 458ff; records, 476f); *ReMR;* K. von Fischer, *Studien zur italienischen Musik des Trecento und frühen quattro cento* (1956); id., in *MQ* xlvii; K. Jeppesen, *Italia sacra musica* (1962); C. Gallico, *Un Canzoniere musicale italiano del cinquecento* (1961); W. Korte, *Studie zur Geschichte der Musik in Italien im 1. Viertel des 15. Jahrhunderts* (1933); F. Torrefranca, *Il Segreto del quattrocento* (1939); E. Dent, *Music of the Renaissance in Italy* (1933); N. de Robeck, *Music of the Italian Renaissance* (1928); E. R. Lerner, "The Polyphonic Magnificat in 15th-century Italy (*MQ* l); see also under *Laude, Frottola,* Madrigal. *For 1600–1800:* C. Sartori, *Bibliografia della musica strumentale italiana stampata in Italia fino al 1700* (1952); L. Torchi, *La Musica instrumentale in Italia nei secoli XVI, XVII e XVIII* (1901; also in *RMI*, iv–viii); F. Florimo, *La Scuola musicale di Napoli e i suoi Conservatori*, 4 vols. (1880–81); F. Torrefranca, *Le Origini italiane del Romanticismo musicale* (1930); see also under *Nuove musiche*, Oratorio, Cantata, Opera, etc. *For 1800–present:* LavE ii.1, 146ff; *AdHM* ii, 1087ff; D. de Paoli, *La Crisi musicale italiana 1900–1930* (1939); F. D'Amico, *I Casi della musica* [1962]; M. Mila, *Cronache musicale, 1955–1959* (1959); M. Bortolotto, "The New Music in Italy" (*LBCM*); J. C. G. Waterhouse, "The Italian Avant-Garde and National Tradition" (*Tempo*, no. 68, 14); M. Laghezza Ricagni, *Studi sul canto lirico monostrofico popolare italiano* (1963); E. Desderi, "Le Tendenze attuali della musica" (*RMI* xxxv–xxxviii).

Ite missa est. The concluding salutation of the *Mass: "Ite, missa est, Deo gratias" (Go, [the congregation] is dismissed; thanks to the Lord). It is from this salutation that the word "Mass" [L. *missa*] is probably derived. In Masses lacking the Gloria it is replaced by the *"Benedicamus Domino." See W. Fischer, "Die Herkunft des 'Ite, Missa est' V. toni" (*CP Orel*).

J

Jácara [Sp., Port.]. A popular ballad or dance tune. Originally (17th century) *jácara* (or *xácara*) was a picaresque comic interlude inserted into stage plays and describing the antics of some objectionable person. In time it developed into the *tonadilla. The term also has been used for a dance, for the popular songs of coachmen and cart drivers, etc. A *jácara* for three sopranos and chorus is published in F. Pedrell's *Cancionero musical popular español,* 4 vols. (1918–22), iv, no. 101. There are some *jácaras* for keyboard, written as a continuous variation of a short ostinato theme, similar to the chaconne; see H. Anglés, ed., *Johannis Cabanilles opera omnia,* 3 vols. (1927–36), ii, 146; M. S. Kastner, ed., *Silva ibérica* [n. d.], nos. 8, 9 (anonymous, Bertolomieu de Olagué). For a description of the dance, see *AnM* v, 194.

Jack. See under *Harpsichord I.*

Jagd- [G.]. Hunt. *Jagdhorn,* hunting horn; *Jagdmusik,* hunting music. Also see under *Hunt music.*

Jahreszeiten, Die. See *Seasons, The.*

Jale. See under Solmization III.

Jaleo [Sp.]. An Andalusian solo dance in moderate 3/8 time, accompanied by rhythmic handclapping of the spectators.

Jam. Jazz musicians' term for improvisation, used until *c.* 1945. At a jam session, a group of musicians choose a familiar tune and improvise, both together and as soloists. Jamming is thus distinguished from the "hot chorus" or "takeoff," in which an improvised solo is played against a written or memorized accompaniment performed by the whole group.

Janizary music [G. *Janitscharenmusik*]. Music of the Janizary, the military bodyguard of the Turkish sovereigns (*c.* 1400–1826), or pieces written in imitation thereof. The characteristic instruments of the Janizary were big drums, cymbals, triangles, and the *Turkish crescent. About 1800, this type of music was extremely popular in Europe [see Military music]. Haydn imitated it in his "Military" Symphony (no. 100); Mozart in his *Entführung aus dem Serail* and the Rondo "alla Turca" of his Piano Sonata in A (K. 331); Beethoven in *Die Ruinen von Athen* (also his Variations op. 76) and, most effectively, in the finale of his Ninth Symphony (tenor solo: "Froh wie Deine Sonnen fliegen"). The harpsichords and pianos of the late 18th century were frequently provided with a *Janitscharenzug* (Janizary stop), which produced a rattling noise. See N. Bessaraboff, *Ancient European Musical Instruments* (1941), pp. 20ff; P. Panoff, "Das musikalische Erbe der Janitscharen" (*Atlantis* x); W. Lichtenwanger, "The Military Music of the Ottoman Turks" (*BAMS,* nos. 1–13, pp. 55ff).

Janko keyboard. See under Keyboard III. See R. Hansmann, in *ZIM* v.

Japan. There are two distinct traditions in Japanese music, folk music and art music. The latter can further be divided according to the historic periods [see I–VII below].

I. *Before A.D. 612.* Concerning Japanese music prior to the introduction of Continental Asian culture, early historic documents, both Japanese and Chinese, as well as archaeological findings confirm the use of the five-stringed *wagon* (of the *koto family), the *yamato-bue* (a flute), drums, etc. Music was frequently associated with dances or with ceremony; one type of music, for example, performed at a Shinto ritual, is known by the generic term *kagura,* but surviving examples of *kagura* are of later date.

II. *612 to the end of Nara period (794).* Although the earliest known record of the introduction of Continental Asian music dates from A.D. 453, when eighty musicians were sent to Japan by the ruler of Silla (a small Korean kingdom), it was only after a Korean scholar, Mimashi, imported the *gigaku* (Chinese dance and music) in 612 that the Japanese really began to learn the foreign music. During the succeeding years, music from Korea, India (via the Chinese), etc., was frequently introduced to Japan, and this active exchange finally culminated in the establishment in 701 of *Gagaku-ryō,* or the Imperial Music Bureau, which at its inception included 250 Japanese musicians and dancers, 72 Chinese, 72 Koreans, and a few others. A collection of instruments, used at the celebration for the completion of the Great Buddha of Tōdaiji Temple (752), is still preserved in the Imperial Treasury of Shōsōin in Nara.

III. *Heian period (794–1192).* The repertories of these court musicians of different origin were soon modified into a Japanese-style instrumental ensemble, with or without dances, known as *gagaku,* which flourished during the Heian period and still exists today in only slightly changed form. Among vocal types belonging to gagaku, there were *saibara* (art song based on popular song) and *rōei* (singing of a Chinese-style poem). Besides *gagaku,* there were also *gigaku* and *sangaku* (the latter an acrobatic entertainment). Also imported from China during this period were theories of music, which included the invention of a twelve-tone system by a Pythagorean-like method. Toward the end of the Heian period, the recitation of Buddhist *sutras* (scriptural narratives), imported earlier from China, became popular, establishing a vocal style called *shōmyō.* Two Buddhist sects, Shingon and Tendai, became famous for this genre.

IV. *Kamakura period (1192–1333).* The *shōmyō* continued its popularity during the Kamakura period, thanks to two important masters, Kanchō (936–98) of the Shingon sect and Ryōnin (1073–1132) of the Tendai sect. Buddhist priests also performed the *ennen* (primarily dances), while secular music included the *dengaku* (evolved from a ceremony in the rice fields) and *sarugaku* (derived from the *sangaku*). However, the most characteristic product of this period was *heikyoku,* sung by a blind storyteller with a *biwa* (a four-stringed lute derived from the Chinese *pyiba,* or *p'i-p'a*), played with a large plectrum. In a *heikyoku* piece, the oldest example of narrative (*katarimono*) style [see VI below], the instrument is not used to accompany the voice but to insert instrumental interludes between the vocal parts.

V. *Muromachi and Azuchi-Momoyama periods (1333–1600).* The major entertainment of this period is the *noh* drama, derived from *sarugaku.* *Kyōgen,* a comic play either inserted between the acts of a *noh* or performed independently, often included popular tunes of the time. A treatise by Zeami (*Kadensho,* 1402) represents a significant essay on aesthetics. During the late 15th and 16th centuries, beggar priests, who played a short, vertical bamboo flute called *hitoyogiri* (the later *shakuhachi*), frequently performed in the streets.

VI. *Edo period (1600–1868).* The *zokusō,* *shakuhachi,* and *shamisen* (samisen) were the three representative instruments of this period. The *zokusō* (or simply *koto*) is a rectangular instrument made of paulownia wood with thirteen silk strings set on movable bridges and

played with ivory picks. It became popular after Yatsuhashi-Kengyō (1614–85) composed the earliest *kumiuta,* a vocal piece composed of several short poetic texts. The instrument can be tuned in various ways [see Ex. 1], *hira-jōshi* [1a], *kumoi-jōshi* [1b], and *kokin-jōshi* [1c] being the

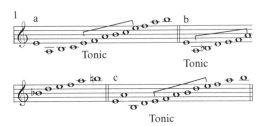

most common tunings. *Sōkyoku,* or music for *zokusō,* may be either purely instrumental or, far more often, have a vocal part. In the latter category, the most important is *jiuta,* and the most important music form *tegotomono,* both derived from early *shamisen* music. *Tegotomono* normally consists of three parts: *maeuta,* or fore-song (S); *tegoto,* an instrumental interlude (I); and *atouta,* an after-song (S); sometimes this form is extended to S I S I S, or even to S I S I S I S. The purely instrumental *sōkoyu* is represented by *danmono* (free-style variations, e.g., the famous six-part "Rokudan"). Later, the tradition of the instrument was carried on by two major schools: the Ikuta school of Kyoto, founded by Ikuta-Kengyō c. 1700, and the Yamada school of Edo (i.e. Tokyo), founded by Yamada-Kengyō c. 1800.

The *shakuhachi* is a vertical bamboo flute with five finger holes, four in front and one in back. [For ill. see under Flute.] It was played solo by *komusō* (mendicant Buddhist priests), and its tradition was carried on by the Kinko school, founded by Kurosawa Kinko (1710–71).

The *shamisen* (*samisen* or *sangen*) is a long-necked three-stringed instrument with a square wooden sound box, covered on the top and bottom with catskin. It is played with a large ivory plectrum. The three principal tunings are 1–4–8, 1–5–8 and 1–4–7 (minor). The *shamisen* normally accompanies a vocal part, either solo or in ensemble. There are numerous schools of *shamisen* music, which differ both in the nature of the text and music they play and in the size and shape of the instruments they use; a major distinction is between narrative (*katarimono*) and lyric (*utaimono*) types. The former is represented by a style called *jōruri,* which includes *gidayū,* founded by Takemoto Gidayū (1651–1714) and used in a puppet play called *bunraku;* the other principal existing *jōruri* are *kiyomoto, shinnai,* and *tokiwazu,* played for the *kabuki* theater. Early examples of the lyric type include *kumiuta* and *jiuta* (just like *sōkyoku* above), while *nagauta* became indispensable to the *kabuki* dance, often with *hayashi* ensemble (a flute and drums).

Sankyoku, an ensemble for *koto, shamisen,* and *kokyū* (a rarely played, bowed stringed instrument) that became popular during the 19th century, represents a rare instance of Japanese instrumental ensemble; sometimes *kokyū* was replaced by *shakuhachi.* The *tegotomono* form, as used in *sōkyoku* or in *shamisen* pieces, is also popular among the *sankyoku* repertory.

VII. *Modern.* The drastic reforms of Emperor Meiji (reigned 1868–1912) included the adoption of European music in the Japanese educational system, with the result that European music soon became a part of Japanese life. The first among modern composers is Kōsaku Yamada (1886–1966), who produced symphonic works, operas, songs, etc. The generation between world wars includes Kiyoshi Nobutoki (b. 1887), Syūkichi Mitsukuri (b. 1895), Akira Ifukube (b. 1914), and Yorinori Matsudaira (b. 1907). Michio Miyagi (1894–1957) is known for his adaptation of European styles in his compositions for *zokusō.* The post-war generation is represented by Ikuma Dan (b. 1924), Yasushi Akutagawa (b. 1925), Toshirō Mayuzumi (b. 1929), Kan Ishii (b. 1921), Makoto Moroi (b. 1930), Hikaru Hayashi (b. 1931), and Akira Miyoshi (b. 1933).

VIII. *Folk music.* Japanese folksongs are normally associated with work (e.g., rice planting, fishing), dance, ceremony, feasts, etc. They were sung with or without the accompaniment of hand-clapping or instruments (flute, *shamisen,* *shakuhachi,* drums, etc.). The form used is frequently strophic. The instrumental pieces are usually for dances or for local ceremonies; the instruments often include the *fue* (a flute), *taiko* (a drum), *dōbyōshi* (small cymbal), *bin-zasara* (bamboo clappers), *suri-zasara* (bamboo scraper), *suzu* (bell), etc. The Ainus in Hokkaidō and the Okinawans in the Ryūkyū Islands have their own folk tradition, some of which is related to Japanese music.

IX. *Scales.* A twelve-tone system introduced from China has been known since the Heian period. In actual performance, the scales mostly consist of five or seven notes; the more impor-

tant are the *ryō-sen* and *ritsu-sen* system, used in *gagaku,* and the *yō-sen* and *in-sen* system, found in the music of the Edo period. The former consists of two scales, each with five basic notes and two auxiliary notes [Ex. 2, a and b]. The latter includes two pentatonic scales, *yō* and *in,* of which the second makes a characteristic use of semitones [Ex. 2, c and d].

2

a *Ryō* scale

Kyū Shō Kaku Hen - chi chi U Hen - kyū (Kyū)

b *Ritsu* scale

Kyū Shō Ei - shō Kaku Chi U Ei - u (Kyū)

c *Yō* scale

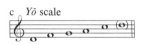

d *In* scale

X. Examples. It is impossible to summarize the styles of Japanese music in a few words, but the examples chosen below may give the readers some idea of some of the more representative styles. Ex. 3 is a *gagaku* passage (*Sekai Ongaku Zenshū,* xviii, 10), illustrating the heterophonic treatment of the principal melody by two wind instruments, the "harmony" by *shō,* the accelerating beats of *kakko,* and typical patterns of the string accompaniment. Ex. 4, a recitative in *noh* (*ibid.,* xxv, 3), has a melody confined to few notes, is rhythmically rather free, and has a few ornaments; also characteristic is the sparse use of drums. Ex. 5, from the *sōkyoku,* "Rokudan" (*ibid.,* xxv, 199), has a typical melodic line with big skips and intervals of a fourth and a second. Ex. 6 shows a typical treatment of voice and shamisen, in which the melodic lines, basically heterophonic, are rhythmically shifted by a half beat to one another, creating occasional intervals of seconds, thirds, fourths, etc. Ex. 7, taken from a folksong of a northern district, illustrates an elaborate melodic line on an *in* scale, with a declamatory quality and with many ornaments.

Lit.: H. Tanabe, *Japanese Music,* rev. ed.

JAPAN

(1959); *LavE* i.1, 242; W. P. Malm, *Japanese Music and Musical Instruments* [1959]; *id.*, *Nagauta; the Heart of Kabuki Music* [1963]; F. T. Piggott, *The Music and Musical Instruments of Japan,* rev. ed. (1909); K. Sunaga, *Japanese Music* [1936]; C. Leroux, *La Musique classique japonaise* (1910); S. Kishibe, *The Traditional Music of Japan* (1966); Tsunezō Yoshida, ed., ‡*Tendai Shōmyō Taisei,* 2 vols. (1935, '55); Kashkō Machida, *et al.,* ed., ‡*Nihon Min'yō Taikan* (*Anthology of Japanese Folksongs;* 5 vols. to date, Tokyo, 1953–66); Chūichirō Takeda, ed., ‡*Tōhoku Min'yō Shū* (*Anthology of Folksongs in Tōhoku;* 6 vols. 1956–63); ‡*Sekai Ongaku Zenshū* (*Collection of the World's Music;* 1930—), ed. by H. Tanabe, *et al.,* vols. 17, 18, 22, 25, 27, 34, 43, 48; D. Arima, *Japanische Musikgeschichte auf Grund der Quellenkunde* (*c.* 1960); E. Cunningham, in *MQ* xxxiv; E. Harich-Schneider, in *MQ* xxxix; *id.,* "Rōei; the Medieval Court Songs of Japan" (*Monumenta Nipponica* xiii–xv); J. F. Embree, "Japanese Peasant Songs," (*Memoirs, American Folklore Society* xxxviii [1943]); O. Abraham and E. M. von Hornbostel, in *SIM* iv; E. Kikkawa, in *SIM* xiv–xv; F. Y. Nomura, in *AM* xxxv, 47–53; F. T. Piggott, in *PMA* xviii, 103–20; K. Takano, in *LRM* xii, 107–24, 165–71. Also see under *Gagaku; Koto; Noh.*

For Okinawan music, see Kikuko Kanai, ‡*Ryūkyū no min'yō* [1954]; J. LaRue, "The Okinawan Classical Songs: An Analytical and Comparative Study" (diss. Harvard Univ., 1952); *id.,* in *JAMS* iv, 27ff.

For further bibl. see *Notes* vii, 266ff; *K.B.S. Bibliography of Standard Reference Books for Japanese Studies with Descriptive Notes,* vii (B), "Theatre. Dance and Music" (Tokyo, 1960).

M.K.

Jarabe [Sp.]. Traditional Mexican dance, binary in form and moderate in tempo, derived from the Spanish *zapateado* and musically similar to the *mazurka.* Within its basic 3/4 meter the *jarabe* shifts occasionally to 6/8 meter. As in the Chilean *cueca,* the dancing is based on the idea of a man pursuing a girl who gracefully eludes him.

J.O-S.

Jarana [Sp.]. A hybrid dance type from the state of Yucatan, involving Mexican and West Indian rhythms. Examples using 3/4 or 6/8 meter have been traced, as well as others using both alternately. The *jarana* requires very agile movements. The dancers scrape the floor with their shoes, continuing the rhythm during the sudden stops in the music. Improvised short poems,

recited either in Spanish or in the Mayan language, are often inserted.

J.O-S.

Java. I. *History.* Of all the highly diversified societies that inhabit more than 3,000 islands in the Republic of Indonesia, the peoples of Java and *Bali have attained the richest cultural development. For more than 2,000 years, compatible influences from the mainland of Southeast Asia, China, India, and the Middle East have affected religion, social institutions, government, literature, language, architecture, and other modes of cultural expression. These were rapidly assimilated and became distinctly Indonesian in character. The mainstream of musical evolution, on the other hand, appears to be an autochthonous development that responded to and became integrated with the development of other cultural institutions. The relatively incompatible pressures of various Western countries during the past three centuries have had little or no effect on the principal musical traditions of Java and Bali. Although on both of these islands there persists a great variety of musical genres, it is the music of numerous types of gamelan orchestra that remains the overwhelmingly dominant tradition. The singular importance of music in relationship to religion, functions of state, literature, and various forms of puppetry and dance drama has been fostered by the royal courts and emulated by cities, towns, and even the remotest villages since at least the 8th century and has continued to the present day—notwithstanding the fact that in Java the adoption of a mystical form of Islam has been nearly universal since the 16th century.

The most ancient form of gamelan, known as *gamelan Munggang,* has only three tones, and extant ensembles more than 1,000 years old are still in use on special state occasions. It appears likely that from an original three-tone gamelan of this type there were two lines of development, one that led to the five-tone sléndro system, established by the 8th century or earlier, and another that became successively a four-tone system, a six-tone system, and finally, by the 16th century or earlier, the seven-tone pélog system. Archaic ensembles representing all these stages of development still survive and are in use [see Lit., M. Hood, "The Effects of Medieval Technology"]. In the course of the past four or five centuries three distinct musical traditions and types of ensemble have been developed from this common origin: one by the Javanese in Central and East Java, one by the Sundanese in West Java, and one by the Balinese in Bali [see Bali].

II. *Tuning systems and mode.* The Javanese recognize eighteen species or basic types of tuning, nine in sléndro and nine in pélog. Beyond this general classification of tuning system and species, no two gamelan have precisely the same intervallic structure. It appears that the individuality of each gamelan tuning derives in part from the practice of stretching or compressing octaves throughout the six-octave compass of the orchestra, so that a unique "tuning pattern" is responsible for the particular character of each ensemble [see Lit., M. Hood, "Sléndro and Pélog Redefined"]. Both sléndro and pélog are composed of nonequidistant intervals, those of the former ranging from slightly less than 200 cents to slightly less than 300 cents, those of the latter ranging from less than 100 cents to more than 300 cents [see Cents]. The tuning pattern of a gamelan produces a different intervallic structure for each octave. The examples given below represent the intervallic structure of octaves iii, iv, v, and vi taken from the sléndro and pélog halves of the *gamelan Kjai Mendung* ("Venerable Dark Cloud"). The five pitches of sléndro are numbered according to the Javanese cipher notation, 1, 2, 3, 5, 6 and those of pélog 1, 2, 3, 4, 5, 6, 7. The size of the intervals between pitches is given in cents.

Sléndro

Octave	1	2	3	5	6	1
vi		246	241	219	254	246
v		245	237	234	245	267
iv		218	255	248	233	259
iii		220	280	236	242	248

Pélog

Octave	1	2	3	4	5	6	7	1
vi		131	163	252	126	131	173	—
v		140	143	275	127	116	204	222
iv		125	141	297	113	124	165	255
iii		120	144	297	117	126	155	246

There are three modes or *paṭet* in sléndro (*paṭet nem, paṭet sanga, paṭet manjura*) and four modes in pélog (*paṭet lima, paṭet nem, paṭet barang,* [*pélog*] *paṭet manjura*). Each mode is governed by a hierarchy of five pitches; melodic movement is guided by a primary and a secondary interval of the sléndro or pélog fifth, and melodic resolution is achieved through the use of typical cadential formulas outlining the primary interval of the fifth. The modes are also associated with certain times of the day or night and specific time periods in the presentation of puppet plays and dance dramas based on the

literature of the Mahabharata, Ramayana, Pandji cycle, and historical subjects. The pélog system has more flexibility than the sléndro system because each five-tone mode, representing a particular selection from the available seven pitches, may employ either of the two omitted tones as *sorogan* or exchange tones to effect modulation to auxiliary scales lying a pélog fifth higher or lower than the principal scale [see Lit., M. Hood, *The Nuclear Theme as a Determinant*]. In both tuning systems "vocal tones" are added to the basic supply of pitches by a bowed lute, flute, and voices; in Central Java five additional vocal tones are recognized in sléndro and two vocal tones in pélog. Occasionally, these "vocal" parts in sléndro may borrow a pitch from pélog, or vice versa. In West Java the Sundanese have carried the development of vocal tones to a more complex and formal system of submodes known as *surupan* [see Lit., J. Kunst, *Music in Java*].

III. *Orchestras and musical practice.* The generic term *gamelan* includes a great variety of ensembles in Java, differing in size, function, and musical style. A gamelan is a particular set of instruments that is valued with increasing age as its individual characteristic beauty of sound develops, i.e., as the crystalline structure of the bronze instruments stabilizes through being played. Frequently a gamelan has its own proper name. During the past few decades in West Java the Sundanese have begun to favor smaller ensembles. The largest gamelan are found among the royal courts and princely residences of Central and East Java. A complete gamelan, *sapangkon,* is a double set of instruments, one tuned to sléndro, the other to pélog, and may consist of as many as seventy-five to eighty instruments. There are two styles of playing: (1) the soft style, a subtle, mystical, and seemingly timeless flow of sound, associated with singing and the *alus* or refined style of dance (or puppet) characterization; (2) the strong style, a virile and powerfully resonant battery of sound associated with the *gagah* or strong, "heroic" dance characterization. [See Lit., M. Hood, "The Enduring Tradition"]. The players are seated cross-legged on mats with the sléndro instruments in front of them and the corresponding pélog instruments arranged on one side or the other. A principle of orchestration that may be termed "polyphonic stratification" supports the group improvisation of about thirty instrumentalists, a male chorus of approximately fifteen, and three female soloists in realizing a complex musical fabric of as many as twenty-five distinct strata of sound. Each orchestral composition or *gending* consists of a fixed and unique melody that serves as the foundation for all strata of improvisation. This melody is more than a *cantus firmus* in the Western sense; it *is* the *gending* itself and bears an individual name, e.g., "Udan Mas" ("Golden Rain"), "Pangkur," etc. The melody may be in long regular note values, or it may consist of relatively short note values with frequent rhythmic irregularities. *Gending* are known in a great variety of traditional musical forms determined by the particular periodicity of various members of the gong family and basic drumming patterns [see J. Kunst, *Music in Java*]. Principal instruments of this family are the large hanging gongs, *gong ageng;* the *kenong,* a number of large bronze inverted kettles suspended on crossed cords; the *kempul,* a series of smaller hanging gongs; the *keṭuk,* a small inverted kettle; and a pair of small kettles known in sléndro as *engkok* and *kemong* and in pélog as *kempyang.* The drums come in four sizes: the large *kenḍang gending,* the small *ketipung,* the *batangan* or *tjiblon*—the dance drum, and, finally, a very large double-ended barrel-shaped drum known as the *beḍug.* The fixed melody of the piece is carried by a family of instruments found in three sizes, each consisting of six or seven bronze slabs over a trough-resonator: the *saron demung,* the *saron barung,* the *saron panerus* or *peking.* Simultaneous variations of the fixed melody are executed by a family of instruments occurring in three sizes known as the *bonang,* each consisting of a double row of kettles suspended on crossed cords: the *bonang panembung,* the *bonang barung,* the *bonang panerus.* These instruments, together with the *gendèr panembung,* described below, form the strong-playing ensemble. In soft playing, highly complex simultaneous variations are added: by a family of gendèr, found in three sizes and consisting of thin bronze slabs suspended over bamboo or metal resonators, the single-octave *gendèr panembung* or *slenṭem,* the multioctave *gendèr barung* and *gendèr panerus;* by the *gambang,* a xylophone; by the *tjelempung,* a thirteen-double-course zither plucked with the thumbnails; by the *suling,* an end-blown flute; and by the *rebab,* a two-stringed, bowed lute played by the leader of the gamelan. In strong playing he delegates his responsibility to the drummer.

Several forms of basic notation have developed during the past two centuries, usually providing only the colotomic structure (played by the gong family), the basic drumming patterns, indications of tempo and tempo change, the fixed melody, and sometimes additional indications as a guide to register for the bonang family. Collections of such notation are maintained at the principal courts as a means of preserving individual pieces that might otherwise fade from the musician's memory. In recent times a cipher notation has been used for instruction in three different conservatories of gamelan study in an attempt to replace the traditional method of instruction by imitation and rote learning. Neither students nor professional gamelan players, however, perform from written music but entirely from memory and improvisation. The accompanying transcription by Hardja Susilo is a fragment of the gending in *ladrang* form called "Sriredjeki" as played in pélog paṭet nem.

Lit.: J. Kunst, *Music in Java,* 2 vols., rev. ed. (1949); *id., Hindoe-Javaansche muziekinstrumenten, speciaal die van Oost Java* (*Studien over Javaansche en andere Indonesische muziek,* Deel II, 1927); *id., De Waardeering van exotische Muziek in den Loop der Eeuwen* (1942); Mangkunagara VII of Surakarta, KGPAA, *On the Wajang Kulit* (*Purwa*) *and Its Symbolic and Mystical Elements* (1957); D. A. Lentz, *The Gamelan Music of Java and Bali* [1965]; E. Jacobson and J. H. van Hasselt, *De Gong-fabricatie te Semarang* (1907); Ki Hadjar Déwantara, *Leidraad behoorende bij den Cursus over de Javaansche Muziek* (1930); J. R. Brandon, *Theatre in Southeast Asia* (1967); M. Hood, *The Nuclear Theme as a Determinant of Paṭet in Javanese Music* (1954); *id.,* "Changing Patterns in the Arts of Java" (*Bulletin of the Institute of Traditional Cultures,* 1959); *id.,* "The Challenge of 'Bi-Musicality'" (*Ethnomusicology* iv); *id.,* "The Reliability of Oral Tradition" (*JAMS* xii); *id.,* "The Enduring Tradition: Music and Theatre in Java and Bali" (R. T. McVey, ed., *Indonesia* [Southeast Asia Studies no. 12], 1963); *id.,* "The Effects of Medieval Technology on Musical Style in the Orient" (*Essays on Music and History in Africa and Asia,* Royal Anthropological Institute, London, 1966); *id.,* "Sléndro and Pélog Redefined" (*Selected Reports,* Institute of Ethnomusicology. University of California at Los Angeles, 1966); J. Kunst, "Waar komt de Gong vandaan?" (*Cultureel Indië* iv); *id.,* and R. Toemenggoeng Wiranatakoesoema, "Een en ander over Soendaneesche Muziek" (*Djawa* i); J. Kunst and C. J. A. Kunst-van Wely, "Over Toonschalen en Instrumenten van West Java"

S R I R E D J E K I

Kendangan Ladrang Kendang 2, Pélog Patet Nem; transcribed by Hardja Susilo.

In this fragment the fixed melody is being played by Saron I–II, Demung I–II. Saron III–IV are playing one style of imbal; other styles include the alternation of the tone of the fixed melody with either upper or lower neighbor tones. Western pitches indicated are only an approximation of the pélog tones.

(*Djawa* iii); J. S. Brandts Buys, in *Djawa* i, ii, iv, xx; A. Brandts Buys-van Zijp, in *Djawa* viii, xiv, xv, xvi.　　　　　　　　　　　　　　M.H.

Jazz. A kind of indigenous American music of the 20th century, originally identified with social dancing, featuring rhythmic patterns peculiar to the "jazz beat." The origin of the word "jazz," which first appeared in print in 1917, is obscure. [See, e.g., R. Blesh, *Shining Trumpets* (rev. ed. 1958), p. 328; M. Stearns, *The Story of Jazz* (1956; corr. pr. 1962), p. 154.]

I. Jazz grew out of several kinds of earlier American music: minstrel-show music, early brass bands, early string bands (fiddle, guitar, banjo or mandolin, double bass or "lard stand"), *ragtime (*c.* 1890–*c.* 1915), and *blues (*c.* 1910—). In the 1910's and 1920's jazz was loosely connected with the popular songs of Tin Pan Alley. However, jazz titles indicate closer ties with ragtime and minstrel music.

Jazz music is closely allied with ragtime (the names are sometimes used interchangeably) and blues. Although ragtime was easily notated, early jazz was rarely written, the instrumental parts being composed spontaneously by performers who often could not read notes. Ragtime was an outgrowth of the minstrel-show bands and music for dancing at "pleasure houses" (bordellos). The ragtime pianist was in great demand around the turn of the century. For many years he performed in the music departments of the larger ten-cent stores. Important figures who appeared in various sections of the country were Buddy Bolden (*c.* 1878–1931) and his band in New Orleans, pianists Louis Chauvin and Tom Turpin in St. Louis, and Scott Joplin (1868–1917) in Sedalia, Missouri. Joplin organized the Queen City Negro Band in Sedalia in 1896. From this band he took six instruments (clarinet, E-flat tuba, cornet, baritone, drums, and piano) to form a hot dance band.

Publication of ragtime piano music began about 1900. Sedalia especially encouraged ragtime players and their publications, and Joplin, before he moved to New York, had published there his most famous composition, "Maple Leaf Rag," in 1899. The first rag, "Harlem Rag," by Tom Turpin, may have been published in 1895. H. A. French, of Nashville, Tennessee, published several ragtime pieces, among them Thomas Broady's "Mandy's Broadway Stroll" (1898), "A Tennessee Jubilee" (1899), and "Whitling Remus" (1900). Throughout the period Zes Confrey published ragtime instruction books as well as "Kitten on the Keys" (1921).

The distinguishing characteristic of ragtime is its persistent syncopation, as opposed to the incidental syncopation found in classical music. In the piano versions ragtime figures are usually played by the right hand accompanied by a harmonic figure in duple meter in the left. For two decades ragtime was the principal music of Broadway musicals and vaudeville. Joplin, who was the most prominent pioneer composer of the period, wrote two operas using the ragtime idiom, *A Guest of Honor* (1903) and *Treemonisha* (1907); neither of them enjoyed much popularity. [See also Ragtime.]

The unwritten folk *blues, a precursor and a rich ingredient of jazz, emerged in the 20th century, although many have placed the origin earlier. W. C. Handy, an unusually sensitive band man who traveled widely, first heard the blues in the early 1900's [see Niles, *Blues*, p. 20]. Gertrude "Ma" Rainey, Bessie Smith, and Ethel Waters were also associated with the early blues. The first published blues were Jelly Roll Morton's "Jelly Roll Blues" (1905; © 1915), Handy's "Memphis Blues" (1912), and "St. Louis Blues" (1919; first pub. 1913 as "Jogo Blues").

Unlike ragtime, which had a standard form of 8, 16, or 32 measures, the folk blues had a 12-measure mold divided into three 4-measure phrases. The first phrase was usually a melody over a tonic chord. The second, using the same text, was accompanied by a subdominant chord cadencing on the tonic, while the third was accompanied by the dominant chord closing on the tonic. In the rural South, where blues originated, the principal accompaniment is the guitar. The text often does not last the full 4-measure phrase, but the dance-rhythm must be continued by the guitar on each beat. Filling in a measure following an incomplete text is an important function of the accompaniment. These "fill-ins" (similar to "episodes" in fugal music) were called "riffs" and were an essential part of the music.

The derivation of jazz from blues is obvious, but in jazz the band replaces the single instrument accompanying the singer, and each instrument improvises free rhythms and idiomatic counterpoint at each performance. A striking example of a piano, cornet, and trombone accompaniment is heard in the Bessie Smith recording of "Standin' in the Rain Blues" (14338–D Columbia). Subsequent verses have variants—not repetitions—of the accompaniment. The true blues singer likewise sings a variant for each new verse. Blues, usually sung in slow tempo, are in 4/4 meter although the accompaniment often plays in 12/8. The rhythm of the words avoids a straight marchlike meter and replaces it with the "jazz beat," where the emphasis is shifted from the strong beat and frequently falls on fragments of the beat. It is characterized by anticipations of the beat and of the afterbeat. This style, which makes accurate notation difficult, depends on the experience, tradition, and sensitivity of the performer. The authentic melodic style of the blues singer involves the use of "blue notes" (the flatted third and seventh in the major keys), slurs, and portamentos. The instrumental accompanists also added sevenths to the chords and enriched the harmony considerably. When the ragtime bands began to use the style they had learned from playing blues, jazz was born. [See also Blues.]

II. Just when jazz emerged as an identifiable entity has not been determined. Marshall Stearns suggests 1900, while earlier historians placed the point of origin in New Orleans, stressing the importance of Joe "King" Oliver (1885–1938) and Ferdinand "Jelly Roll" Morton (1885–1941) and their bands, as well as local pleasure houses such as Storyville, which provided employment for jazz musicians. The success of the Original Dixieland Jazz Band (1912—) and the fame of such jazz musicians as Sidney Bechet, Edward Ory, Robert ("Baby") Dodds, Bunk Johnson, Alphonse Picou and, especially, Louis Armstrong, strengthened this claim. Later studies, however, have shown that the development taking place in New Orleans occurred simultaneously elsewhere, in Kansas City, Chicago, Memphis, and New York City.

One reliable chronicler of the growth of dance-band music and of the music heard in the early 1900's was W. C. Handy. Another report on early jazz comes from Robert Goffin, who describes the impact of Louis Mitchell's loud Southern Symphony Quintet on New York in 1912 and on Europe in 1914 [see Lit.]. Dance music in Baltimore is described by Leonard Feather, who quotes Eubie Blake, composer and ragtime player of an earlier era. In New York about 1912, Will Marion Cook and James Reese Europe at the Clef Club were playing exciting music.

In the early stages, jazz was highly improvisory, depending for its appeal more on the skill, intuition, and experience of the individual performers than on the written note. Most of the early jazz performers were not formally trained but were apprenticed musicians who relied on the traditional idioms of the style or created new ones.

III. After World War I, the growing popularity of recorded jazz music, the development of commercial radio, and the enthusiasm of the American people for public dancing ushered in the "Jazz Age" of the 1920's. Jazz now became big business. Important hotels replaced salon orchestras with jazz bands. Conservatory-trained musicians, who were already skilled in instrumental techniques, invaded the field. Their jazz was learned from jazz-band recordings, performances, and rehearsals. Jam sessions, occasions when jazz musicians gathered informally to play for themselves and to experiment [R. Blesh, *Shining Trumpets,* p. 237], were eagerly sought out.

In 1918, when Joe "King" Oliver began his reign in Chicago, his famous Creole Jazz Band consisted of a cornet, trombone, drums, clarinet, bass, and piano. Other jazz bands used the same instruments, sometimes adding a banjo. Gradually the band began to expand; a tuba was added, a second cornet, then a tenor saxophone. Later a first and second alto saxophone became essential for the "big" jazz band [L. Feather, *The Book of Jazz,* p. 94]. In the 1930's the addition of another cornet (or trumpet) and trombone resulted in the "five brass" idea. A fourth saxophone, the replacement of the banjo by the guitar, and the replacement of the tuba by the string bass gave the big band its characteristic sound.

In the earliest forms of jazz the leader "stomped off" the tempo (gave it by tapping his foot), and the ensemble played a refrain maintaining some faithfulness to the melody. Then each soloist was given a refrain for his individual expression. The background for these solos was generally provided by the piano player, sometimes a spur-of-the-moment idea of an idle side man. The "solo" continued as long as the leader wished to let the people dance. In conclusion came the "out" chorus, in which the entire band played ecstatic excursions of music within the harmonic framework of the composition.

Whereas the jazz band had presented a musical product that was more or less spontaneous and therefore quite flexible, the big dance band presented a contrived, rigid composition. A solo passage was presented within a written framework that was the same at every playing, thus diminishing spontaneity of expression. The era of the "arranger" and "arrangement" had been launched, and the real jazz band was temporarily relegated to the background.

An example of improvisation, transcribed by John W. Work from "Royal Garden Blues" by Clarence Williams. 1. Original version. 2. Improvisation.

Perhaps the greatest musician during the transition from the jazz band to the big band was Fletcher Henderson (1898–1952). He gave impetus to the contrived music but at the same time played individual, exciting, organized jazz. His arrangement and recording of "Sugar Foot Stomp" (including the then sensational new trumpeter, Louis Armstrong) became, with a few changes, a hit for Benny Goodman some fifteen years later. Paul Whiteman (1890–1967) "king of jazz," who assembled a large orchestra of expert performers and supplied them with attractive arrangements of jazz pieces, called his music "symphonic jazz." Until then, jazz had been music to which people danced. Whiteman taught his audiences to listen to it. Whether he applied jazz rhythms to classical melodies (Rimsky-Korsakov's "Song of India") or to Tin Pan Alley tunes, he emphasized the idea that jazz was not a kind of music but a way of performing it. The culminating event in Whiteman's career was a concert at Aeolian Hall in 1924, which attracted a highly intellectual audience. The highlight of the concert was the now famous *Rhapsody in Blue* by George Gershwin.

Concurrent with the big-band style, the Chicago style (small groups of four to seven men) was continued by Eddie Condon, Bud Freeman, and Dave Tough. Among this group was Louis Armstrong, a trumpet virtuoso and scat singer from New Orleans. Largely under his influence there arose (*c.* 1925) the style known as "hot" jazz. Bix Beiderbecke, among others, was strongly influenced by him. Armstrong's vibrato and short expressive phrases were imitated on the clarinet, saxophone, trombone, and piano. The harmonies remained simpler than the big-band chords, rhythms were more pronounced, easily singable melodies were abandoned, and, above all, advance preparation and arrangements were taboo.

In the late 1920's and early 1930's the Duke Ellington band created a new style of jazz music, neither true jazz nor totally contrived. It was a band of individualists, ingeniously welded together, who created the well-known Ellington sound. Ellington's greatest talent was his ability to blend different instruments into a beautiful or unusual sound. A great stylist, he was probably the first leader to have special rehearsals for his rhythm section. As a result, his music was eminently danceable, unlike the music of some later bands.

In the big band the arranger was the most important individual at the leader's command. For the sparkling spontaneity and unlimited individual expression found in early jazz, the arranger substituted a technical brilliance and fine concerted playing that were unheard of before. True jazz was now in the background and a new dance music, "swing," had come to the fore. The great names in swing were Benny Goodman, Artie Shaw, the Dorsey Bands, Harry James, and others. In the midst of this big-band era Benny Goodman introduced a swing combo: Teddy Wilson, piano; Gene Krupa, drums; Lionel Hampton, Vibraharp; and Benny Goodman, clarinet. Dancers welcomed swing with a frenzy. In 1938 at the Randall's Island concert in New York, called "A Carnival of Swing," a crowd estimated at more than 20,000 listened for five and a half hours with unrestrained glee.

In the 1920's and 1930's jazz assumed the function of entertainment as well as furnishing dance music. Many instrumentalists provided antics to entertain listeners, while others performed skits (e.g., Fred Waring's Pennsylvanians). Vocalists who sang in a style called "crooning," such as Bing Crosby, Rudy Vallee, and Frank Sinatra, began their singing careers with these jazz bands. At the same time, many band leaders contributed significantly to jazz music: Louis Armstrong, Count Basie, Bix Beiderbecke, Cab Calloway, Bob Crosby, Jimmy Dorsey, Tommy Dorsey, Duke Ellington, Benny Goodman, Lionel Hampton, Fletcher Henderson, Woody Herman, Earl "Father" Hines, Gene Krupa, Guy Lombardo, Vincent Lopez, Glenn Miller, Red Nichols, Ben Pollack, William McKinney, Don Redman, Thomas "Fats" Waller, Fred Waring, Chick Webb, and Paul Whiteman.

While some people regard only the music of Joe "King" Oliver's band and the Original Dixieland Band as pure jazz, others call all music performed by a jazz band "jazz": accompaniments to popular songs, boogie woogie, rock and roll, rhythm and blues, Afro-Cuban music, and bop as well as "progressive jazz." Both these interpretations represent extreme points of view.

IV. As the bands grew smaller and their personnel and locale changed, changes in jazz music were inevitable. In 1938 there was a revival of New Orleans (Dixieland) jazz (Mezz Mezzrow, Bunk Johnson). However, in the 1940's four great jazz musicians appeared on the scene and brought still another revolution. They were Charlie "Bird" Parker, tenor saxophonist; Dizzy Gillespie, trumpeter; Miles Davis, trumpeter; and Art Tatum, pianist. The loudness of the old jazz band was reduced, small combos began to displace the big bands, new rhythms replaced the four- or eight-beat pattern, and melodies became more florid and complex. Dissonant, strange harmonies bewildered audiences, who were more listening- than dance-oriented. This was the era of *bop [M. Stearns, *The Story of Jazz*, p. 227; also see Historical Masterpieces, album of three records of Charlie Parker's bop, issued by the Charles Parker Corporation].

Bop developed into "progressive jazz," whose principal exponents are Thelonious Monk, Stan Kenton, Dave Brubeck, Jerry Mulligan, John Lewis, and Gil Evans. The performance demands of "progressive jazz" and its harmonic and contrapuntal concepts are so severe that they have made membership in any of the progressive groups, such as the Modern Jazz Quartet, very exclusive. The success of the Modern Jazz Quartet and of Thelonious Monk indicate that the big band is unwieldy and therefore incapable of the subtleties required for "progressive jazz." Progressive jazz men have turned completely away from dancing, which to their music is nearly impossible.

A blending of the new music with classical forms is found in the music of the John Lewis Piano Combo. Instead of the older minstrel-music titles and the "stomps," their titles seem to be derived from European impressionism, e.g., "Harlequin," "The Bad and the Beautiful," "Warmeland," "Pierrot," and "Colombine." Some composers have combined jazz with the European art music tradition. In this area only George Gershwin has produced a number of successful serious compositions. A new movement called "third stream," led by Gunther Schuller in the 1960's, combines "progressive jazz" with the classical tradition. John Coltrane (b. 1926, tenor saxophonist) is the leader of the newest movement in jazz.

Jazz has also occasionally been used in Protestant churches. On Dec. 27, 1965, Duke Ellington and his jazz band played at the Fifth Avenue Presbyterian Church, New York City. Others have followed his example. On April 24, 1966, the Emmanuel Church of Boston offered a Service in Jazz based on the themes from the ancient Apostolic Tradition of Hippolytus (A.D. 217). A jazz suite on texts of the English Mass has been composed by Lalo Schifrin, while Vince Guaraldi has set the Eucharist for organ, choir, and his own jazz trio.

Various composers have incorporated jazz forms or styles into their works, through either direct imitation or subtle allusions. A few such works are: 1908, Claude Debussy, "Golliwog's Cake Walk" (From *Children's Corner*); 1918, Igor Stravinsky, *Ragtime* for eleven instruments; 1922, Paul Hindemith, *1922 Suite für Klavier* (movements "Shimmy" and "Ragtime"); 1923, Milhaud's *La Création du Monde* (blues intonations); 1925–26, E. Krenek's opera, *Jonny spielt auf* ("Shimmy," "Blues," "Spiritual"); 1928, Kurt Weill, *Die Dreigroschenoper;* 1935, G. Gershwin, *Porgy and Bess;* 1954, R. Liebermann, *Concerto for Jazz Band and Symphony Orchestra*.

Lit.: See references in text. S. G. Charters, *Jazz: New Orleans 1885–1963: An Index to Negro Musicians of New Orleans,* rev. ed. (1963); L. Feather, *The Book of Jazz: A Guide to the Entire Field,* rev. ed. (1965); id., *The Encyclopedia of Jazz,* rev. ed. (1960); R. Gold, *A Jazz Lexicon* (1964); J. Goldberg, *Jazz Masters of the Fifties* (1965); W. C. Handy, *Father of the Blues: An Autobiography,* ed. A. Bontemps (1941); B. McRae, *The Jazz Cataclysm* (1967); J. F. Mehegan, *Jazz Improvisation,* 4 vols. (1959, '62, '64, '65); A. P. Merriam and R. J. Benford, *A Bibliography of Jazz* (1954); L. Ostransky, *The Anatomy of Jazz* (1960); R. G. Reisner, *The Literature of Jazz: A Selective Bibliography,* rev. ed. (1959); W. Sargeant, *Jazz: A History* (1964); G. Schuller, *Early Jazz: Its Roots and Musical Development* (1968); R. de Toledano, *Frontiers of Jazz,* 2d ed. (1962); B. Ulanov, *A History of Jazz in America* (1952); D. Heckman, "What Next for Jazz" (*Downbeat,* 10th Year Book, 1965).　　　　　　　　J.W.W.

Jeanne d'Arc au Bûcher [F., Joan of Arc at the Stake]. Dramatic oratorio by A. Honegger with a prelude and ten scenes (libretto by P. Claudel), produced in Basel, 1938. Setting: Rouen, 15th century.

Jena Symphony. A symphony discovered at Jena, Germany, in 1909. Once acclaimed as an early work of Beethoven, it was not generally accepted as such. H. C. Robbins Landon (in *MR* xviii, pp. 109ff) has fairly convincingly established that it was composed by Friederich Witt (1770–1837).

Jeng (also spelled cheng, tseng). (1) A Chinese stringed instrument similar to the *chyn but without frets. See W. D. Sheepers, in *Folklorist* vi, 396. (2) A shallow, basin-shaped Chinese gong corresponding to the Korean *ching.
　　　　　　　　　　　　　　　　　　　　　R.C.P.

Jenufa [Cz.; orig. title *Jerí Pastorkyna,* Her Foster-daughter]. Opera in three acts by L. Janáček (libretto by the composer after G. Preissová), produced in Brno, 1904. Setting: village in Moravia.

Jephtha. (1) Handel's last oratorio (English text by Thomas Morell), produced in London, 1752. (2) Oratorio by Carissimi (Latin text from the Scriptures), composed about 1650.

Jeté [F.]. See under Bowing (e).

Jeu [F.]. In organ music, stop; *jeu de fonds,* foundation stop; *jeu de mutation,* mutation stop; *jeu à bouche,* flue stop; *jeu d'anche,* reed stop. *Jeu de timbres,* *glockenspiel. *Jeu-parti,* see Tenso.

Jeu de cartes, Le [F., The Card Game]. Ballet "in Three Deals" by Stravinsky, produced in New York, 1937. The dancers represent the chief cards in a poker game that proceeds through three deals, each successively more complex.

Jeune France, La. A group of French composers, formed in 1936, consisting of Yves Baudrier (b. 1906), André Jolivet (b. 1905), Daniel Lesur (b. 1908), and Oliver Messiaen (b. 1908). They were united in their common objective of "sincerity, generosity, and artistic good faith."

Jewish music. I. *The original tradition.* The frequent references in the Bible to musical instruments have been reconstructed by modern scholars (Idelsohn) into a lively, interesting picture. The music of the Temple (the center of the Jewish religion in Jerusalem, comparable to St. Peter's in Rome) was in the hands of professional musicians, the Levites. Instruments such as the hasosra (chatzotzra, a silver trumpet, used in numbers up to 120 in Solomon's time), *magrepha (organ), tzilzal (cymbals), and others apparently served chiefly for signaling, i.e., to announce the entrance of the priests, give the sign for the congregation to prostrate themselves, etc. Many instruments mentioned in the Scriptures have an Egyptian ancestry, e.g., the nevel (nebel, probably a large harp, played with the fingers), the kinnor (a lyre, played with a plectrum, similar to the Greek kithara; see Harp III), the halil (probably a double-oboe and, like the Greek aulos, used for highly exciting and virtuoso-like music; it had to be banned from ritual use), etc. The only instrument to survive up to the present is the *shofar, a ram's horn that also was (and still is) used as a signaling instrument [see ill. under Brass instruments; see also the detailed study of the Biblical instruments in *SaHMI*, pp. 106–27].

The instrumental music of the Temple fell into oblivion after its destruction in A.D. 70. However, the chanting of the Bible (believed to have been established in the 5th century B.C.) has survived in the various synagogues to the present day, representing the oldest extant type of Jewish music [see under II below]. Particular interest attaches to the singing of the psalms, which is expressly indicated in inscriptions such as "To the chief Musician on Neginoth" [for a correct interpretation of these inscriptions, see Psalm]. The singing was entrusted to professional musicians. A number of psalms, however, show that the congregation occasionally participated in their performance by responding "Hallelujah" or "Amen" after each verse. Some early sources also refer to choral singing in two answering groups, i.e., *antiphonal singing.

Although no manuscripts of early Jewish music exist, the state of music in the late pre-Christian era has been clarified considerably by Idelsohn, who examined the musical tradition of Jewish tribes in Yemen, Babylonia, Persia, Syria, etc. A startling similarity was found among the chants sung by these tribes, who, living in strict isolation, had no contact with one another after leaving Palestine. Therefore these melodies probably antedate the destruction of the Temple and have been preserved for 2,000 years with only slight alterations. They thus are thought to approximate very closely the Jewish chant of the pre-Christian era. No less interesting is the close resemblance between some of these melodies and certain melodies of Gregorian chant. For instance, a chant used by the Jews of Yemen for the recitation of the Pentateuch (as well as of certain psalms) shows a striking similarity to the Gregorian psalm tones [Ex. 1].

1

II. *The main types of Jewish chant.* The oldest type of Jewish ritual music is the chant used for reading the prose books of the Bible, such as the Pentateuch, Prophets, Ruth, etc. This chant, usually called "cantillation," consists of a succession of stereotyped melodic formulas, each of which is represented by a sign written above or below the scriptural text. These signs, called *ta'amim* (accents), no doubt developed from an earlier system of accents designed to assist the reader in the proper emphasis and rendition of the important words of the text [see Ecphonetic notation]. The oldest extant sources for the *ta'amim* date from the 9th century (for 11th- and 12th-century MSS, see A. Gastoué, in *TG* xxii). For almost 1,000 years the meaning of these signs was handed down orally by the Jewish singers and, therefore, was exposed to considerable variation in different periods and localities. Fortunately their late medieval status was recorded by Johannes Reuchlin (*De accentibus et orthographia linguae hebraicae* [1518]) and S. Münster (*Institutiones grammaticae in Hebraeam linguam* [1524]). Ex. 2 shows one of these

2

signs, the *t'lishá* (*talsá*) *gadolá* ("major drawing out") in four variants: (a) as recorded by Münster; (b) as sung today in northern Europe; (c) from Morocco; (d) from Egypt and Syria.

Even within a single rite, e.g., that of the North European (Ashkenasic) Jews, a given sign indicates different melodic formulas depending on which book of the Bible is chanted. Each book has its own mode, usually based on a tetrachordal scale (e.g., d–g, g–c'), so that the rendition of the *ta'amim* varies in pitch and other details from one book to another. Ex. 3 shows

3

the same text sung (a) in the ordinary Penta-teuchal mode, (b) in the penitential Pentateuchal mode, and (c) in the Prophetal mode. Long tables of the *ta'amim* are given in *The Jewish Encyclopedia* under "Cantillation" and in Idel-sohn's *Jewish Music,* p. 44; see also F. L. Cohen, in *PMA* xix; S. Rosowsky, in *PMA* lx. Ex. in *HAM,* no. 6.

Second oldest after the cantillation of the Bible is that of the prayers, which is not based on a set of stereotyped melodic formulas indicated by signs but belongs to the general category of *melody types. For each service there are cer-tain traditional themes or motifs, but the actual singing is a free vocal fantasia, frequently of a highly virtuoso character, which retains only the barest outline of the prayer motif (mainly in the closing formula). These more or less freely created melodies are known as *hazzanut,* a word derived from *chazzan,* the name for the profes-sional cantor to whom the singing of the prayers is entrusted. From the Middle Ages through the end of the 19th century the *chazzanim* were the main carriers of Jewish ritual music. They were chosen mainly for their beautiful voices and their ability to improvise on the prayer motifs. Until the middle of the 19th century, even the most famous among them had no formal education in music and were unable to read notes.

Finally, there are a number of melodically fixed chants. These represent the most recent development of ritual music, starting after the 9th century. Most of the melodies show evidence of contact with various kinds of non-Jewish music, e.g., the famous Kol Nidre, partly bor-rowed from Gregorian chant; the beginning of Maoz Zur, taken from the Protestant chorale "Nun freut Euch Ihr frommen Christen"; and one of the melodies for Adonai Melek, borrowed from Verdi's *La Traviata.*

III. *Semireligious music and folksong.* To the former category belong the *zmiroth,* the chants used at home for singing grace at meals or, e.g., for reciting the Haggadah, the account of the Hebrews' captivity in and deliverance from Egypt. An important repertory of semireligious songs are the Hasidic melodies, created by the Hasidim, a pietist sect that originated in the early 18th century in Poland and Russia. Music played an important part in their creed as a means of ecstatic communication with God.

The Jews of eastern Europe possess a large repertory of domestic songs, including love songs, work songs, lullabies, wedding tunes, dance melodies, etc. Some 3,000 such songs have been gathered under the auspices of the Petrograd Jewish Folk-Song Society, founded by pupils of Rimsky-Korsakov's. Outstanding among the collectors of Jewish folksong was A. Z. Idelsohn, whose *Hebräisch-orientalischer Melodienschatz* (10 vols., 1914ff) includes the results of his studies in Morocco, Yemen, Persia, Palestine, Poland, etc.

IV. *The European development.* Shortly after 1500, Jews for the first time participated in mu-sical life outside the ghetto. Abramo dall'Arpa Ebreo was a famous singer at the court of Man-tua from 1542 to 1566. Allegro Porto published his *Nuove musiche* in 1619 and two collections of madrigals, one (without title page) probably in 1622, the other in 1625. The most important of these Jewish composers was Salomone Rossi (*c.* 1587–1630), who was one of the pioneers of violin music [see Sonata B, I; *Romanesca; Rug-giero*] and the first to compose polyphonic music for the Jewish service, in his *Hashirim Asher Li'Shlomo* (The Songs of Solomon; 1622). Need-less to say, these compositions, written for chorus and soloists, completely break away from the Jewish tradition.

About 1700 some of the wealthier German synagogues employed instrumental music for the Friday-evening service and installed organs, and choirs were fairly generally employed. Since there was no traditional music for such per-formances, the contemporary repertory of non-Jewish music was used, including secular and even operatic elements, dance tunes, and rococo arias. Ahron Beer (1738–1821), one of the first *chazzans* to possess some musical knowledge, made an extensive collection of compositions for the service and of traditional Jewish songs, including two versions of the Kol Nidre, marked 1720 and 1783. A different line was followed by Israel Jacobson (1768–1828), who was an ex-ponent of the Reform movement and who, in the first Reform temple (Seesen, Westphalia, 1810), not only used organ and bells but also German chorales provided with Hebrew texts [see Idelsohn, p. 237]. The consequent reaction against this Christianization of the Jewish serv-ice led to the moderate reform of Salomon Sulzer (1804–90), who declared that the "restora-tion should remain on historical grounds" and that "the old tunes should be improved, selected and adjusted to the rules of art" (*Denkschrift,* 1876). Although Sulzer succeeded in bestowing on the musical service a fundamental dignity and appropriateness, his compositions and ver-sions of songs tend to represent current Euro-pean idioms rather than Jewish tradition. The same was true of Louis Lewandowski (1821–

1904), whose thorough training in musical theory, harmony, etc., enabled him to write choruses in Mendelssohn's oratorio style. His complete service, *Kol Rinnah* (1871), with its facile and pleasing tunes, has been widely adopted. In America, synagogue music started by imitating the current European models (Alois Kaiser of Baltimore; Max Spicker and William Sparger of New York; Edward Starck of San Francisco). Recently, however, there has been a remarkable movement toward independent development, represented by a number of choral compositions of a distinctly Hebraic character, mostly for the Sabbath service. Among the contributors have been Ernest Bloch, Frederick Jacobi, Lazare Saminsky, and Isadore Freed.

Throughout the 19th and 20th centuries, Jews played an active part in the development of European music, as composers (Giacomo Meyerbeer, 1791–1864; Jacques Halévy, 1799–1862; Felix Mendelssohn, 1809–47; Jacques Offenbach, 1819–80; Karl Goldmark, 1830–1915; Gustav Mahler, 1860–1911; Arnold Schoenberg, 1874–1951; Ernest Bloch, 1880–1959; Darius Milhaud, b. 1892; George Gershwin, 1898–1937; Aaron Copland, b. 1900; and many others), and even more prominently as performers and conductors (Joachim, Kreisler, Heifetz, Menuhin, Godowsky, Schnabel, Serkin, Myra Hess, Damrosch, Bruno Walter, Klemperer, to name only the most outstanding).

Since about 1915 there has been a movement to create a "Jewish national music," comparable to the national music of other countries. The leader of this movement was Ernest Bloch who, in his symphony *Israel* (1912–16), *Schelomo* (1915–16), *Sacred Service* (1930–33), and other works, used distinctly Hebraic idioms. The establishment, after World War II, of the national state of Israel has given further impetus to this trend. In 1936 Bronislaw Huberman founded the Palestine Orchestra, which gave its first performance under Toscanini. A considerable number of operas have been performed in Hebrew. Musical education has reached high standards under the guidance of L. Kestenberg. Composers working in Israel include Paul Ben-Haim (b. 1897), Joseph Tal (b. 1910), Ödön Partos (b. 1907), Herbert Brün (b. 1918), and others.

Lit.: A. Z. Idelsohn, *Jewish Music in Its Historical Development* [1929]; id., ‡*Hebräisch-orientalischer Melodienschatz*, 10 vols. (1914ff); S. B. Finesinger, *Musical Instruments in the Old Testament* (1926); L. Saminsky, *Music of the Ghetto and the Bible* (1934); E. Werner, *The Sacred Bridge* (1959); M. Wohlberg, *The Music of the Synagogue* (1963); P. Gradenwitz, *The Music of Israel* [1949]; M. T. Cohen, *The Jews in Music* [1939]; A. Holde, *Jews in Music* [1959]; Richard Wagner, *Judaism in Music* (1850 and 1869; trans. 1910); A. Sendrey, *Bibliography of Jewish Music* (1951); J. Yasser, *Bibliography of Books and Articles on Jewish Music* (1955); S. Rosowsky, *The Cantillation of the Bible* (1957); C. Sachs, *The Rise of Music in the Ancient World* (1943), pp. 79–95; *NOH* i, 283–335; *LavE* i.1, 67–76; ii.4, 2287–2314; C. Vinaver, ‡*Anthology of Jewish Music* [1955]; A. Ringer, "Musical Composition in Modern Israel" (*LBCM*, also in *MQ* li); E. Werner, *Mendelssohn* (1963); id., "The Oldest Sources of Synagogal Chant" (*Proc. of the American Academy for Jewish Research* xvi, 225); B. J. Cohon, "The Structure of the Synagogue Prayer-Chant" (*JAMS* iii); E. Gerson-Kiwi, "Musicology in Israel" (*AM* xxx; bibl.); O. Kinkeldey, "A Jewish Musician of the 15th Century" (*Studies in Jewish Bibliography and Related Subjects,* A. S. Freidus memorial volume, 1929; also pub. separately); L. Sabaneev, "The Jewish National School in Music" (*MQ* xv); A. Z. Idelsohn, "Parallelen zwischen gregorianischen und hebräisch-orientalischen Gesangsweisen" (*ZMW* iv); id., "Parallels between the Old-French and the Jewish Song" (*AM* v, vi); id., "Deutsche Elemente im alten Synagogengesang Deutschlands" (*ZMW* xv); id., in *ZMW* viii; H. Loewenstein, in *ZMW* xii. Extensive bibl. in *Notes* v, 354–62.

Jew's-harp or trump [F. *guimbarde;* G. *Maultrommel*]. A primitive instrument consisting of an elastic strip of metal, one end of which is attached to a small horseshoe-shaped frame of metal or wood. The frame is held between the teeth (the name Jew's-harp may be a corruption of jaw's-harp), and the elastic strip is plucked with the fingers, causing it to vibrate in the player's mouth. Although the instrument as such produces only one sound, different harmonics can be obtained by changing the position of lips, cheeks, and tongue. The instrument is very ancient and widespread. It is mentioned and depicted in a Chinese book of the 12th century, and specimens have been found in Japan, Borneo, Siberia, North Germany (14th century), Norway, etc. In the early 19th century it was temporarily revived by virtuosos who used larger instruments with several vibrating reeds. [For ill. see under Percussion instruments.] See *MaMI; SaHMI*, bibl., p. 471; M. Heymann, "La Guimbarde" (*RM* 1923, no. 6).

Jig. (1) An English popular dance of the 16th century, which is especially important as the forerunner of the *gigue. Names such as "Kemp's Jig" and "Slaggin's Jig" refer to famous comedians of the English stage. The "Nobody's Jigg" that appears in various sources is the jig of the comedian R. Reynolds, who played "Nobody" in the popular comedy *Somebody and Nobody.* The English comedians who, in the early 17th century, invaded the Netherlands, Scandinavia, and Germany, introduced the jig there. According to a recent theory, jigs were also introduced in America, where they were imitated by Negroes and gradually transformed into the grotesque dances of the minstrel shows; in this respect, note the jazzlike rhythm [see Dotted notes III] in the Ex. ["Mr. Slaggin's Jigg," from *The Dancing Master* (1686); see W. Danckert, *Geschichte der Gigue* (1924), p. 17].

(2) A type of English stage entertainment (also spelled "jigg"), a kind of low comedy nearly always dealing with indecent subjects, that was popular in England from the late 16th to the early 18th centuries. A forerunner of the *ballad opera, it consisted of verses sung to well-known tunes, interspersed with lively dances. The Elizabethan comedian Nicholas Tarleton played an important role in the early development of this entertainment. His pupils (William Kemp, Robert Reynolds, Thomas Sackville) popularized it not only in England but also on the Continent (Holland, Germany). See C. R. Baskerville, *The Elizabethan Jig* (1929); P. E. Mueller, "The Influence and Activities of English Musicians on the Continent" (diss. Indiana Univ., 1954).

Jingling John(ny). See Turkish crescent.

Jodel. See Yodel.

Jongleur. See Minstrel; Troubadour; also reference under *Estampie.*

Jonny spielt auf. Opera in two parts by E. Krenek (to his own libretto), produced in Leipzig, 1927. Setting: the present.

Joropo [Sp.]. The most typical of all Venezuelan folk dance-songs. It is always performed by a couple using steps and figures quite similar to those employed in the Colombian *pasillo and *bambuco. The *joropo,* in fast 3/4 meter, employs

short melodic phrases in rhythmic patterns such as:

The accompaniment supports the melody with strongly accentuated quarter notes, resulting in a rhythmic conflict. As a rule the texts consist of quatrains in eight-syllable lines.   J.O-S.

Jota [Sp.]. A dance of Aragon (northeast Spain) in rapid triple time, performed by one or more couples and accompanied by castanets. One of the most popular melodies has been used by Liszt in his *Rhapsodie espagnole* no. 16 (*Folies d'Espagne et jota aragonese*) and by Glinka in his orchestral overture *Jota aragonesa.* Other examples occur in De Falla's *El Sombrero de tres picos* and in compositions by Saint-Saëns, Albéniz, *et al.* Statements regarding the medieval or Arab origin of the *jota* [see J. Ribera y Tarragó, *La Música de la jota aragonesa,* 1928] are entirely unfounded. See G. B. Brown, in *BAMS* ii; M. Arnaudas Larrodé, *La Jota aragonese* (1933); A. de Larrea, in *AnM* ii; Ex. in *LavE* i.4, 2373ff.

Jubilus. In the Gregorian Alleluias, the melisma sung to the final vowel of the first word "Alleluia," which invariably stands at the beginning of this chant. The melisma of the jubilus often recurs at the end of the verse. It often shows repeat forms such as a a b, a a b b c, etc. After the verse, the word Alleluia with its jubilus is repeated. See *ApGC,* p. 386. Also see Alleluia.

Judas Maccabaeus. Oratorio by Handel (libretto by T. Morell), produced in London, 1747.

Jupiter Symphony. Nickname of Mozart's last symphony, in C major, no. 41 (K. 551), composed in 1788. The name appears to refer to the "majestic" opening of the first movement.

Justiniana. Same as *giustiniana;* see under Villanella.

Just intonation [G. *Reine* or *natürliche Stimmung*]. A system of intonation and tuning in which all the intervals are derived from the natural (pure) fifth and the natural (pure) third [see Acoustics III]. Therefore, all the intervals of just intonation are contained in the formula $m \times F + n \times T$ (F = fifth, T = third). The formula for the relative frequencies is therefore $(\frac{3}{2})^m \times (\frac{5}{4})^n$. They are easy to calculate if [as explained under Intervals, calculation of III] the octaves, i.e., all the factors 2, are disregarded at first, so that the formula for the relative frequencies becomes $3^m \times 5^n$, in which m and n designate the number of fifths and thirds contained in the interval in question. There result the following values for the C-major scale:

$$
\begin{array}{llll}
c & d(= 2F) & e(= T) & f(= -F) & g(= F) \\
1 & 9 & 5 & \frac{1}{3} & 3 \\
a = (T - F) & b(= T + F) \\
\frac{5}{3} & 15
\end{array}
$$

Reduced into the normal octave, they become:

	c	d	e	f	g	a	b	c′
c = 1:	1	⁹⁄₈	⁵⁄₄	⁴⁄₃	³⁄₂	⁵⁄₃	¹⁵⁄₈	2
c = 24:	24	27	30	32	36	40	45	48
Intervals:		⁹⁄₈	¹⁰⁄₉	¹⁶⁄₁₅	⁹⁄₈	¹⁰⁄₉	⁹⁄₈	¹⁶⁄₁₅

Owing to the presence of two constituents (F and T) the complete system of just intonation forms a two-dimensional infinite set of tones [G. *Tongewebe;* see C. Eitz, *Das mathematisch-reine Tonsystem,* 1891]. A selection of these tones is given under Intervals, calculation of, VI.

Just intonation has the advantage of giving the three fundamental triads, c–e–g, f–a–c′, and g–b–d′, as "natural triads" (characterized by the ratio 4:5:6; e.g., 24:30:36 = 4:5:6), which are more "euphonious" than those in *Pythagorean or well-tempered tuning [see Temperament III]. However, its disadvantages are much more numerous and, in fact, so serious as to make it practically useless. The chief ones are: (a) The tones of the C-major scale include one "dissonant" fifth, namely d–a, which is ⁴⁰⁄₂₇ (⁸⁰⁄₅₄) instead of ³⁄₂ (⁸¹⁄₅₄). (b) The C-major scale has two different whole tones, ⁹⁄₈ (major tone) and ¹⁰⁄₉ (minor tone); their difference is the syntonic *comma ⁸¹⁄₈₀. (c) Modulation is impossible; the first three tones of the G-major scale, g–a–b, already have different intervals from those of the C-major scale, c–d–e. Hence, two different tones a would be necessary, one for the sixth of c, the other for the second of g. The difficulties would rapidly increase with the introduction of chromatic tones. (d) In chordal music, just

intonation produces pure triads and has, therefore, been considered ideal for *a cappella* music in the style of Palestrina, etc. However, the principle of pure triads can be maintained only at the expense of a constant lowering in pitch. For instance, if the succession of chords indicated in our example were sung in pure triads, the notes indicated in black would have the following frequencies: $c' = 1$; $a' = \frac{5}{3}$; $d'' = \frac{5}{3} \times \frac{4}{3} = \frac{20}{9}$; $g' = \frac{20}{9} \times \frac{2}{3} = \frac{40}{27}$; $c' = \frac{40}{27} \times \frac{2}{3} = \frac{80}{81}$, i.e., the syntonic comma (⁸¹⁄₈₀) lower than the initial c. Since harmonies including the supertonic (this chord is responsible for the lowering of pitch) are particularly common in the Palestrina style, just intonation proves unsatisfactory for exactly the type of music for which it has frequently been recommended. Thus, just intonation is primarily of theoretical importance. Its practical application is probably limited to violin music, for which it was recommended as early as the 18th century by P. Prelleur (*The Modern Musick-Master,* 1731), Geminiani, Tosi, and Tartini. It may be noted, however, that the tendency of modern violinists to play sharps higher than their equivalent flats (e.g., C-sharp and D-flat) cannot be justified by invoking the authority of just intonation, as is usually done. In just intonation the sharps are actually lower than the flats [see the table under Intervals, calculation of, first line under J].

Lit.: A. D. Fokker, *Just Intonation* (1949); J. M. Barbour, *Tuning and Temperament* (1951); *id.* and F. A. Kuttner, *The Theory and Practice of Just Intonation* (record and booklet, 1958); *id.,* "Just Intonation Confuted" (*ML* xix, 48); *id.,* in *BAMS* ii; L. S. Lloyd, "Just Temperament" (*ML* xx, 365ff); D. D. Boyden, "Prelleur, Geminiani, and Just Intonation" (*JAMS* iv). See also under Acoustics; Intervals, calculation of; Temperament.

K

K., K.V. Abbr. for *Köchel-Verzeichnis,* i.e., the chronological list of all the works of Mozart made by L. von Köchel (publ. 1862, rev. by Einstein, 1937, '47; by Giegling, Weinmann, and Sievers, 1964). Mozart's compositions are usually referred to by the numbers of this list, e.g.,

K. 357 or K.V. 357. See A. Hyatt King, "Das neue Köchel-Verzeichnis" (*MF* xviii).

Kadenz [G.]. (1) *Cadence; (2) *cadenza.

Kaffeekantate [G.]. See Coffee Cantata.

Kaiserquartett [G.]. See Emperor Quartet.

Kalevala. The Finnish national epic [see Finland], dating from the 13th and 14th centuries. Several symphonic poems by Sibelius (and other Finnish composers) are based on legends from this epic, e.g., *Lemminkäinen's Homecoming, *Pohjola's Daughter, *Swan of Tuonela, *Tapiola.

Kamānja, kemânğe. See Arab music. For ill. see under Violin.

Kammer- [G.]. Chamber. *Kammerton,* chamber pitch [see Pitch (2)]; *Kammermusik,* chamber music; *Kammerkantate,* chamber cantata; etc.

Kanon. (1) German for *canon. (2) A type of medieval Byzantine poetry [see Byzantine chant II]. (3) In ancient Greek music, name for the *monochord [see Canon (2); Kanun].

Kantate [G.]. *Cantata.

Kantele. See under Finland. For ill. see under Zither.

Kantional [G.]. See Cantionale.

Kantorei [G.]. In the 15th and 16th centuries, a group of professional singers employed by a church or at a prince's court; later also groups of amateurs who provided music for their communities.

Kanun (*qānūn*). Arab name for a psaltery shaped like a trapezoid and mounted with numerous strings (as many as 64 in the 14th century). [For ill. see under Zither.] The name, derived from the Greek *kanón* [monochord; see Canon (2)], occurs as early as the 10th century in a story of the *Arabian Nights.* Later (11th century?) the instrument was imported into Europe. See Psaltery.

Kanzone [G.]. (1) *Canzona. (2) *Canzo.

Kapelle [G.]. *Chapel, usually with the connotation of "private or small orchestra," e.g., *Hofkapelle* (court orchestra), *Militärkapelle* (military band). *Kapellmeister,* originally an honorable title (Bach served as *Kapellmeister* to Prince Ernst of Cöthen from 1717 to 1723), is now an old-fashioned provincialism for *Dirigent* (conductor). *Kapellmeistermusik* is a pejorative designation for compositions of formally correct design but lacking in imagination and originality—as the pieces of the *Kapellmeister* often were.

Kapodaster [G.]. *Capotasto.

Karelia. Orchestral overture (op. 10) and Suite (op. 11) by Sibelius, composed in 1893. Karelia is the southern province of Finland, where the composer lived at the time.

Káta Kabanová. Opera in three acts by L. Janáček (libretto by V. Červinka, after a story by A. N. Ostrovsky), produced in Brno, 1921. Setting: Kalinow, a small town on the Volga, about 1860.

Katerina Ismailova. See *Lady Macbeth of Mtsensk.*

Katzenmusik [G.]. *Charivari.

Kazoo. See Mirliton.

Kehraus [G.]. The last dance at a ball.

Kemânğe. *Kamānja.

Kent bugle, Kent horn. Key bugle; see under Brass instruments V (c).

Kerabe [G.]. Old term for *Kehraus,* used to denote a 16th-century *Nachtanz.

Kesselpauke, Kesseltrommel [G.]. Kettledrum.

Kettenform [G.]. See under Forms (after I, A).

Kettledrum. See under Percussion instruments A, I; also Drum II.

Key. (1) On keyboard instruments, the visible parts of the action [F. *touche;* G. *Taste;* It. *tasto;* Sp. *tecla*], which are depressed by the player's fingers [see Keyboard]. In woodwinds the term applies to comparable devices, i.e., the levers covering the side holes [F. *clef;* G. *Klappe;* It. *chiave;* Sp. *llave*].

(2) By specialization, the term came to mean the "main" key of a composition, i.e., the main note or "tonal center" to which all its notes are related and finally, by extension, the meaning of the entire tonal material itself in relation to its center. Thus, "key" is practically synonymous with *tonality. There is, however, a distinct difference between key and scale, since numerous notes extraneous to the scale can be used in the key, e.g., as chromatic variants or in connection with modulations.

Corresponding to the 12 tones of the chromatic scale, there are 12 keys, one on C, one on C-sharp, etc. (this number is increased to 14 or 15 by the notational distinction between *enharmonic keys, such as C-sharp and D-flat, or G-sharp and A-flat). With any given key there is a choice of *modality, i.e., of certain alterations of the tones that form the scale. Thus, in C there is the choice between major (mode): c d e f g a b c'; minor (mode): c d e^b f g a(^{b}) b c';

Lydian mode: c d e f♯ g a b c'; and others derived from the *church modes. Of these, only the first two are usually considered and are actually (though not quite logically) distinguished as different keys, thus leading to a total number of 24 keys, one major and one minor on each tone of the chromatic scale. See Key signature; Key relationship. See W. W. Roberts, "Key Quality" (*ML* xi, 58).

Keyboard. I. The whole set of keys in pianos, organs, harpsichords, etc. (*keyboard instruments). The modern piano keyboard usually includes 88 keys for seven full octaves, from C_1 to c''''', and a quarter octave added at the lower end of the compass. (The organ has 61; the harpsichord varies.) In each octave there are seven white and five black keys, arranged as illustrated in Ex. 1. This arrangement is the natural result of the fact that the fundamental

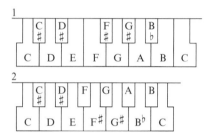

scale of Western music consists of seven tones, which are given to the white keys. Except for the steps e–f and b–c' the intervals between these tones are whole tones, each of which admits the introduction of a semitone in between, represented by a black key. Although the introduction of equal temperament, which permits unlimited transposition, seriously weakened the dominating position of the white keys, the old "C-major keyboard" has proved fully capable of adapting itself to the new system and has to the present day successfully withstood all attempts at reform, e.g., the adoption of the truly "chromatic keyboard" [Ex. 2], in which all scales beginning on a white key would have the same arrangement and consequently the same fingering (as would all those beginning on a black key).

II. *History.* The earliest keyed instrument was the organ. According to Galpin's reconstruction of the Greek *hydraulos, this instrument had 19 keys about 8 inches long and 2 inches wide. Organs of the 9th and 10th centuries had a number (8 to 10) of large keys called *linguae* (tongues), which were pulled out and pushed in.

Reports that keys of organs were so large and heavy that they were played with the fist seem of rather dubious authenticity. About 1200, the keyboard covered nearly three octaves (from G to e''; see Hexachord). From then on, its compass as well as the number of chromatic keys steadily increased. The early 14th-century organ pieces from the Robertsbridge Codex (Brit. Mus. *Add. 28550*) make use of all the chromatic tones in at least one octave. A normal device of all the old keyboards was the *short octave. The 16th-century experiments with enharmonic music (Vicentino) led to the construction of keyboards with separate keys for C♯ and D♭, etc. [see Arcicembalo]. In the 17th century, keyboards had an average compass of four octaves, with all the chromatic notes except for the lowest range. Bach's harpsichord had more than five octaves. Broadwood, in 1794, made the first piano keyboard with six octaves, from C_1 to c''''; this was the compass of the Broadwood instrument used by Beethoven from 1817 on.

III. *Modern reforms.* Since about 1875 various unsuccessful attempts have been made to improve the keyboard. The *Janko keyboard* (patented 1882) had six rows of short keys arranged somewhat like a typewriter keyboard. Each row included the keys for a whole-tone scale, that beginning with C in rows 1, 3, 5, and that beginning with C♯ in rows 2, 4, 6. Thus, each octave had 36 keys, three for each tone of the chromatic scale. In spite of certain advantages and its initial success (Liszt and Rubinstein recommended it), the Janko keyboard failed to supersede the traditional one. Later modifications and simplifications (*Adam keyboard, Durand keyboard, Clavier Hans*) met with the same fate. *Mangeot's keyboard,* called "piano à doubles claviers renversés" (1878), had two keyboards, the lower of which, intended for the right hand, had the usual arrangement, while the higher, for the left hand, had the reverse arrangement, i.e., with the keys for high notes on the left side. The advantage claimed for this innovation was identical fingering of, e.g., the ascending scale, for both hands. In the *Clutsam keyboard* (1907) the keys were arranged in a slightly curved instead of a straight line, taking into account the fact that the player's arms move in arcs. This arrangement has been widely adopted for organ pedals. Moor's *Duplex Coupler Grand Piano* imitates the two manuals of the harpsichord. The upper of the two keyboards, otherwise normal, gives the tones of the higher octave and can be coupled with the lower. This keyboard greatly facilitates the execution of the usual virtuoso effects and permits the execution of many others not possible on the usual keyboard. Its failure to win acceptance might be ascribed to decreasing interest in purely virtuoso playing. If invented 50 years earlier it would probably have been a great success. Another use of two keyboards is made in the *quarter-tone keyboards* (Haba, 1923; Stoehr, 1924), in which the upper keyboard is a quarter tone higher than the lower. At present, it would seem that attempts to enlarge the traditional keyboard are less likely to succeed than those leading in the opposite direction, i.e., eliminating the highest and lowest tones, which, being seldom used in music played at home, unnecessarily increase the size and price of the instrument.

Keyboard instruments. Instruments having a keyboard, i.e., the piano, organ, harpsichord, and clavichord. The term is used particularly for instruments used before *c.* 1750, when there was often no clear distinction among works written for the three last-named instruments [see Keyboard music]. The piano, harpsichord, and clavichord have an important technical feature in common, i.e., the use of strings, and therefore they are often grouped together in studies dealing with their history and their music.

Lit.: A. J. Hipkins, *A Description and History of the Pianoforte and of the Older Keyboard Stringed Instruments* (1896); P. James, *Early Keyboard Instruments from Their Beginnings to the Year 1820* (1930); F. J. Hirt, *Meisterwerke des Klavierbaus: Geschichte der Saitenklaviere von 1440 bis 1800* (1955); J. Wörsching, *Die historischen Saitenklaviere und der moderne Klavichord- und Cembalobau* (1946); H. Brunner, *Das Klavierklangideal Mozarts und die Klaviere seiner Zeit* (1933); P. James, "Early Keyboard Instruments" (*PMA* lvii); V. G. Woodhouse, "Old Keyed Instruments and Their Music" (*ML* i, 45ff); C. Krebs, "Die besaiteten Klavierinstrumente bis zum Anfang des 17. Jahrhunderts" (*VMW* viii). See also under Instruments; Clavichord; Harpsichord; Organ; Piano.

Keyboard music. Music for *keyboard instruments, particularly prior to 1750, when there was often no clear distinction among works for the organ, harpsichord, or clavichord. The 16th-century (and modern) Spanish term is *tecla* [see A. de Cabezón's *Obras de música para tecla arpa y vihuela* (1578; Musical works for keyboard, harp, and vihuela)]. Italians occasionally used the term *istrumenti perfetti* or *istrumenti da tasti*. The lack of distinction among keyboard instruments is most clearly indicated in titles such as "du jeu orgues, espinettes, manicordions" (P. Attaingnant, ed., (*Quatorze gaillardes*, 1531), or ". . . per ogni sorte di stromenti da tasti" (A. Gabrieli, 1595), ". . . auff Orgeln und Instrumenten zugebrauchen" (B. Schmid, 1607), or "di cimbalo et organo" (Frescobaldi, *Il primo libro d'intavolatura*, 1628), Storace (*Selva di varie compositioni d'intavolatura per cimbalo ed organo*, 1664), G. Strozzi, *Capricci da sonare cembali et organi*, 1687). Modern demarcations are usually based on the various types of music. Liturgical compositions, such as Masses, hymns, and versets for psalms or the Magnificat, are obviously organ music, while dances clearly belong to the domain of the harpsichord or clavichord. Variations on secular tunes are primarily harpsichord music, although they may also have been played (and often sound best) on the organ (e.g., Sweelinck's variations on "Mein junges Leben hat ein End"). Occasionally, considerations of style are helpful or decisive, e.g., in some ricercars that employ the theme in quadruple augmentation, involving long notes that can be sustained only on the organ (A. Gabrieli). Canzonas are usually designated "Canzona d'organo" and must be considered primarily organ music, despite their "secular" background and character.

Such problems are not confined to the keyboard music of the 16th and 17th centuries. Indeed, they exist in connection with the keyboard music of Bach. To the present day it is not known whether his *Well-Tempered Clavier* was written for harpsichord, clavichord, or both instruments, or even some pieces for the one instrument and some for the other. See E. Bodky, *Der Vortrag alter Klaviermusik* [1932]; *id.*, in *DM* xxiv, no. 2; L. A. Coon, in *PAMS* 1936; N. Wilkinson, in *ML* iv, 162ff; R. Buchmayr, in *BJ* 1908; various authors in *BJ* 1910.

Lit.: W. Apel, *Masters of the Keyboard* (1947); G. S. Bedbrook, *Keyboard Music from the Middle Ages to the Beginnings of the Baroque* (1949); J. Gillespie, *Five Centuries of Keyboard Music* (1965); M. Seiffert, *Geschichte der Klaviermusik* (1899); W. Apel, *Geschichte der Orgel- und Klaviermusik bis 1700* (1967); F. W. Riedel, *Quellenkundliche Beiträge zur Geschichte der Musik für Tasteninstrumente in der zweiten Hälfte des 17. Jahrhunderts* (1960).

Key bugle. See under Brass instruments V (c).

Key characteristics. A branch of musical aesthetics concerned with what might be called the "psychological properties" of a given key (usually, a given scale). In ancient Greek music each *harmonia* had a specific ethical connotation [see *Ethos*]. Guido was probably familiar with this doctrine when he said, "The diversity of the tropes [i.e., church modes] corresponds to the diversity of feelings so much that one man may delight in the broken jumps (*fractis saltibus*) of mode 2, another prefer the voluptuousness of mode 5, another approve of the suavity of mode 8" (*Micrologus;* ed. Smits van Waesberghe, p. 159). Johannes Cotto (*Afflighemensis*) also assigns specific characterizations to each mode, some of which are obscure (*De Musica,* cap. 16; ed. Smits. van Waesberghe, pp. 109ff). How different his concept is from the present-day correlation of major = joyful, minor = sad, is seen in his designation of mode 4 as *adulatorius* (flattering), mode 6 as *lacrimosus* (tearful). Almost 400 years later, Ramos de Pareia correlated the four *maneriae* to four kinds of temperament and their "colors" (*Musica practica;* ed. J. Wolf, p. 56):

protus:	*phlegmaticus; color cristalinus* (crystal)
deuterus:	*colericus; color igneus* (fire)
tritus:	*sangunineus; color sanguineus* (blood)
tetrardus:	*melancholicus; color luteus* (yellow, orange-red)

In addition, he ascribed to each mode characteristics similar to Cotto's. In the 16th century these concepts underwent significant changes, as appears from a comparison of Ramos with Diruta (*Il Transilvano,* pt. II, book 4), who probably copied Zacconi. Particularly interesting are the Phrygian and Hypophrygian modes:

	Ramos	Diruta
mode 3:	*severus, incitatus*	*commovere al pianto*
mode 4:	*blandus, adulatorius*	*lamentavole, mesta*

For Ramos mode 3 is exciting, mode 4 bland and ingratiating; for Diruta, both are plaintive and sad.

Today, one point on which there is general agreement is the difference in feeling between major and minor. It is interesting, however, that Mattheson did not accept what in his day had already become a trivial convention. In *Das Neu-Eröffnete Orchestre* (1713) he rejects the view that minor is sad and major gay, or that flat keys are "soft" and sharp keys "hard." Among his interesting characterizations the following are particularly noteworthy: "E major expresses a desperate and deadly sadness"; "B

major (*H dur*) . . . seems to have a disgusting, harsh and unpleasant, also somewhat desperate quality."

In the 19th century the "feeling" of the keys was usually expressed by correlation with colors; see Color and music. Cf. also the *rāgas* of *Indian music and, at the other end of the scale, the preface to Hindemith's *Marienleben.*

Lit.: J. Handschin, *Der Toncharakter* [1948]; H. Stephani, *Der Charakter der Tonarten* (1923); P. Mies, *Der Charakter der Tonarten* (1948); E. M. von Hornbostel, "Tonart und Ethos" (*CP Wolf*); R. Wustmann, "Tonartensymbolik zu Bachs Zeit" (*BJ* 1911); A. Montani, "Psicologia dei moderni modi musicali" (*RMI* xliv); F. Monfort, Jr.; "L'Éthos des tonalités" (*CP Borren*).

Keynote. Same as *tonic.

Key relationship. The degree of relationship between two keys. All keys are related, but in different degrees. The order of relationship generally follows that of the tones in the series from consonant to dissonant: fifth (dominant), fourth (subdominant), third (mediant), etc. The most important such relationships are as follows: (a) *parallel keys*—major and minor key with the same tonic (C major and C minor); (b) *relative keys*—major and minor key with the same signature (C major and A minor; C minor and E-flat major); (c) *related keys*—keys whose signature differs by not more than one sharp or flat from that of the main key (in C major: A minor, G major, E minor, F major, D minor; in A minor: C major, E minor, G major, D minor, F major). See W. H. Frere, "Key-relationship in Early Medieval Music" (*PMA* xxxvii; also in *CP 1911,* p. 114).

Key signature. The sharps or flats appearing at the beginning of each staff to indicate the *key of a composition. A given signature indicates one of two keys, a major key or its relative minor key; these are shown in the accompanying illus-

tration by a white and a black note respectively. Normally there are 12 key signatures, corresponding to the 12 chromatic tones of the octave.

There may, however, be 13, 14, or even 15 if a notational distinction is made between *enharmonic keys, e.g., C-sharp and D-flat. See also Circle of fifths.

In early music the use of key signatures is very limited. Until the late 15th century the only signature occurring frequently is one flat, and this is used mostly in the lower voices only [see Partial signature]. In the 16th century the increased use of transposed modes produced signatures (usually partial) with two flats. Not until the middle of the 17th century were sharps generally adopted as signatures. Actually, the scope of keys in use was somewhat wider than the variety of signatures, since the keys were usually written with fewer signs in the signature than they are today, and with more accidentals during the course of the composition. Thus, the minor keys with flats (D minor, G minor, C minor) were usually notated with one flat less than in modern practice, the flat for the sixth being omitted. One of the numerous examples of this practice is an organ toccata and fugue by Bach, actually in D minor throughout but written without a B-flat in the signature and therefore (quite wrongly) nicknamed "Dorian Toccata." Likewise, the major keys (G major, D major, A major) are sometimes notated without a sharp for the leading tone in the signature. A well-known example is Handel's Harpsichord Suite in E (containing the so-called "Harmonious Blacksmith"), which in the original has only three sharps.

Key trumpet. See under Trumpet II.

Khovanshchina. Opera in five acts by M. Mussorgsky (to his own libretto), produced in St. Petersburg, 1886. Setting: Moscow and environs, 1682–89.

Kielflügel [G.]. Old name for harpsichord.

Kin. Japanese name for a smaller *koto. K'in is used in German for the Chinese *chyn (ch'in).

Kinderscenen [G., Scenes from Childhood]. A composition by Schumann, op. 15 (1838), consisting of 13 short and simple *character pieces for piano. The familiar "Träumerei" (Dreams) is no. 7 in the group.

Kindertotenlieder [G., Children's Death Songs]. A cycle of five songs with orchestra or piano by Mahler (poems by Rückert), composed 1901–04. The poems are an elegy on the death of Rückert's child. The songs are masterpieces of melodic invention and artistic simplicity. The orchestra is

treated throughout as a large chamber ensemble rather than as a mass of sound.

King David. See *Roi David, Le.*

Kinnor. See under Harp III; Jewish music I.

Kirchen- [G.]. Church. *Kirchenjahr,* church year; *Kirchenkantate,* church cantata; *Kirchenmusik,* church music; *Kirchenschluss,* plagal cadence; *Kirchensonate,* church sonata (*sonata da chiesa*); *Kirchenton,* church mode; *Kirchenlied,* church song, either a Protestant *chorale or a Roman Catholic hymn written in German (in contradistinction to the older Latin hymn; see Hymn IV).

Kit [F. *pochette;* G. *Taschengeige;* It. *sordino*]. A tiny fiddle to be carried in the pocket, used by the dancing masters of the 17th and 18th centuries. There were two different types, one a diminutive violin, the other a descendant of the medieval *rebec. See ill. under Violin.

Kithara. The foremost instrument of ancient Greece, consisting of a square wooden soundbox and two curved arms connected by a crossbar. A number of strings, varying from five (8th century B.C.) to seven (7th century B.C.) and finally eleven or more (5th century B.C.), were stretched between the soundbox and the crossbar. They were plucked with a plectrum. The tuning of the traditional type with six strings was anhemitonic: e g a b d' e'. The tuning of the outer strings could be changed to f and f' [see Greece II]; the additional strings of the later periods seem to have been mainly octave-duplications of the original ones. The additional tones required for the various tetrachords—diatonic as well as chromatic and enharmonic—were obtained by pressing a piece of hardwood shaped like a finger against a string at a place near its lower end, thereby increasing its tension. Thus, the pitch of a string could be raised a quarter tone, a semitone, or a whole tone [see O. Gombosi, in *CP 1939*]. It was this practice that led to the curious system of Greek instrumental notation, as has been convincingly shown by C. Sachs [see *Musik des Altertums* (1924); also *AdHM* i, 45].

Instruments closely resembling the kithara existed in Mesopotamia and about 1500 B.C. in Egypt. In Greece the kithara became the symbol of Apollo, in whose hands it represented the Greek ideal of *kalokagathia* (harmonious moderation), as contrasted with the "emotional" *aulos, associated with Dionysus. See ill. under Lyra.

Kl. [G.]. In orchestral scores, abbr. for Klarinette.

Klagend [G.]. Lamenting.

Klang [G.]. Sound, sonority. *Klangboden,* sounding board; *Klangfarbe,* tone color, timbre; *Klangfolge,* chord progression; *Klanggeschlecht,* mode (major or minor); *Klangideal,* see Sound ideal.

Klangfarbenmelodie [G.]. A term suggested by Schoenberg in his *Harmonielehre* (1911, p. 470f) in a discussion of the possibility of composing "melodically" with varying tone colors, on a single pitch level as well as with varying pitch, duration, and intensity. The term attempts to establish timbre as a structural element comparable in importance to pitch, duration, etc. If Schoenberg did not apply this theory to one sustained note, nevertheless his concern with timbre as a structural element became evident in the *Five Orchestral Pieces* op. 16 (1909, rev. 1949), especially the third of these. The concept of melodic writing with successive points of tone color was explored almost obsessively by Schoenberg's pupil Anton Webern, beginning with his first chamber and orchestral works. A striking example of Webern's concept of *Klangfarbenmelodie* is found in the first of his *Five Pieces for Orchestra* op. 10 (1913). Webern also

applied this pointillistic procedure, characteristic of his mature style, to a remarkable orchestral transcription of the six-voice ricercar from Bach's *Musikalisches Opfer.* The technique has been much exploited by his followers in *serial composition and by *electronic composers. For interesting examples of *Klangfarbenmelodie* applied to a single pitch, see Alban Berg's Theme and Variations, Act III, *Wozzeck* (op. 7), and Elliott Carter's *Eight Etudes and a Fantasy for Woodwind Quintet* (1950).   J.R.W.

Klappe [G.]. Key of wind instruments. *Klappenhorn, -trompete,* key bugle, key trumpet.

Klar [G.]. Clear, distinct.

Klarinette [G.]. *Clarinet.

Klausel [G.]. (1) Cadence, particularly those in 16th-century polyphonic music. (2) *Clausula (2).

Klaviatur [G.]. Keyboard.

Klavier [G.]. Piano. *Klavierauszug,* piano arrangement; *Klavierstück,* piano piece; *Klavierspiel,* piano playing. In historical studies *Klavier* is the generic designation for stringed keyboard instruments, as distinct from the organ. Sometimes the term means manual (*Orgel mit 2, 3, Klavieren*). Prior to the introduction of the piano, i.e., until about 1775, *Klavier* (then usually spelled *Clavier*) meant the harpsichord and/or clavichord. Hence, titles such as *Clavier-Übung* or *Wohltemperiertes Clavier* do not reveal which instrument was intended. To K. P. E. Bach and his contemporaries *Clavier* usually meant the clavichord. See also Clavier.

Kleine Nachtmusik, Eine [G., A Little Night Music, or Serenade]. A celebrated composition for string orchestra by Mozart (K. 525), composed in 1787. It is in four movements, similar to those of a symphony.

Kleine Oktave [G.]. The "small octave," from c to b. See Pitch names.

Kl. Fl. [G.]. Abbr. for *kleine Flöte,* piccolo.

Kl. Tr. [G.]. Abbr. for *kleine Trommel,* side drum. See Percussion inst. B, I.

Kluge, Die [G., The Clever Girl]. Opera in one act by C. Orff (to his own libretto, after a Grimm fairy tale), produced in Frankfurt, 1943. Setting: fairy tale.

Knaben Wunderhorn, Des [G., The Youth's Magic Horn]. A group of songs by Mahler, based on texts of German folksongs collected and published under the title *Des Knaben Wunderhorn* by Achim von Arnim and Clemens Brentano (*c.* 1820). The group includes nine songs with piano, ten songs with orchestra, and three songs as parts of symphonies. One of them, "Urlicht," was incorporated into the *Resurrection Symphony.

Knarre [G.]. *Rattle.

Kniegeige [G.]. Viola da gamba.

Knyaz Igor. See *Prince Igor.*

Koboz. Old Hungarian name (mentioned first in 1326) for the short-necked lute.

Köchel-Verzeichnis. See under K.

Koleda, kolenda. A Bohemian, Rumanian, or Polish song for Christmas and other feasts, comparable to the English *carol. The earliest examples (without music) date from the 12th century. Large collections of the 16th, 17th, and 18th centuries indicate the great popularity of the custom of singing *koledy*. See J. Kuckertz, *Gestaltvariation in den von Bartók gesammelten rumänischen Colinden,* 2 vols. (1963).

Kollektivzug [G.]. Composition stop or combination stop of the organ. See Organ IV.

Kolorieren [G.]. To introduce coloraturas, i.e., ornaments into a composition, as was done in the *intabulations of the 16th century. For *Koloristen,* see Colorists.

Komplementärfigur [G.]. An important device of early keyboard music, consisting of a figure that alternates among the various voice-parts. The technique was used by Cabezón [see Ex.,

"Obras diferencias de Vacas," from *Obras de música,* 1578], Sweelinck, and particularly by Sweelinck's German pupils (Scheidt, Scheidemann, etc.). See *Spielfigur.*

Kondakarion. In Russian church music, manuscripts of the 12th and 13th centuries containing collections of short hymns of praise (*kondak,* from *kontakion?*). They contain melodies written in an early type of notation, the so-called *kondakarny* notation, which has not yet been deciphered. See Russia I. See also *ReMMA,* p. 96; *WoHN* i, 90.

König Hirsch, Der [G., The Stag King]. Opera in three acts by H. W. Henze (libretto by H. von Cramer, after C. Gozzi), produced in Berlin, 1956. Setting: in the South, any time.

Königskinder, Die [G., The King's Children]. Opera in three acts by E. Humperdinck (libretto by E. Rosmer), produced in New York, 1910. Setting: Germany, Middle Ages.

Kontakion. See under Byzantine chant II.

Kontra- [G.] *Kontrabass,* double bass; *-factur, *contrafactum; -fagott,* contrabassoon; *-bassklarinette,* double-bass clarinet; *-oktave,* contra octave [see Pitch names]; *-punkt,* counterpoint; *-subjekt,* countersubject.

Kontretanz [G.]. *Contredanse.

Konzert [G.]. Concert or concerto. *Konzertmeister,* concertmaster.

Konzertstück [G.]. See under Concertino (2).

Kopfstimme [G.]. Head voice.

Koppel [G.]. Coupler.

Korea. I. *History.* Probably the earliest historical reference to Korean music is found in the *Annals of the Three Kingdoms,* a Chinese history of the 3rd century: "The Mahan [a Korean tribe] always end the planting in the 5th month by acknowledging the spirits. They gather together, sing, dance, carouse not stopping for day or night . . . ." The music for these festivities undoubtedly had North Asian roots and is ancestor to present-day Korean folk music. In early times (to the end of Silla) a steady stream of musical instruments and music came in from China, and the dichotomy between *tarngak* (*tangak*)—music from Tarng (T'ang) China—and *hyangak*—Korean music—was established at this time. That the flow of ideas was not entirely one-sided is shown by the presence of a Korean orchestra at the Tarng court. Korean music in turn exerted a direct influence on *Japanese music, presumably still seen in the present-day *komagaku.* The large number of *tsyr* (*ch'ü*) melodies of Sonq (Sung) times mentioned in the *Koryo-sa* (history of the Koryo dynasty) suggest their popularity during this period, when they apparently superseded the earlier Tarng music. Of these melodies, *Bohoja* (*Po-hŭcha*) and *Nakyangch'un* (*Nak-yan-chun*) are still performed by the orchestra of the National Traditional Music Institute. Some of the *hyangak* melodies mentioned in the *Koryo-sa* have been preserved in the later Yi dynasty notation, and others were reworked and given new titles, particularly at the beginning of the Yi dynasty.

With the resurgence of Confucianism during the later Tarng and Sonq periods, interest was revived in Confucian music, which appeared in Korea during the reign of Yejong (12th century). Musical contact between China and Korea was reduced to a minimum from the time of the Yuan dynasty (considered a barbarian dynasty by the Koreans as well as the Chinese), although a noteworthy exception was the introduction of the *yanggum* or *yang-kŭm* (dulcimer) to Korea during the coeval Ching (China) and Yi (Korea) periods. At this time Korean court music became decidedly nationalist. Under Sejong, the most enlightened of the Yi monarchs, imperial shrine music commemorating the founding of the dynasty was newly created, as was music for the court epic *Yong-bi-o-ch'on ga,* the first literary work to employ the Korean alphabet. In general the dichotomy between *tarngak* and *hyangak* broke down, and the repertory became largely Koreanized. This process was abetted by the introduction of aristocratic music into the court in the latter half of the dynasty. During this period Pak Yon helped restore Confucian music to something of its original purity (an example of musical humanism antedating the Florentine Camerata by more than a century) and Song Hyon published the musical treatise *Akhak kwebom* (*Ak-hak-koe-pum*). Equally important were the developments in music not sponsored by the court, particularly vocal music associated with the major literary forms and, in the 19th century, the solo instrumental repertory known as *sanjo,* but documentation for these categories is sparse.

II. *Kinds of music.* The main kinds of traditional music that have survived are:

I. Court music. A. Ritual music: 1. Confucian music; 2. Imperial shrine music. B. Banquet music: 1. *Tarngak;* 2. *Hyangak.* C. Military music.

II. Non-court music. A. Instrumental music: 1. Aristocratic chamber music; 2. Virtuoso solo music with drum accompaniment; 3. Agricultural music; 4. Shamanist music. B. Vocal music: 1. *Kagok;* 2. *Kasa;* 3. *Sijo;* 4. *P'ansori;* 5. *Japka;* 6. *Sonsori;* 7. Folksong; 8. Buddhist chant.

In Confucian music two orchestras are used, and the instruments and style are unique to the category. Two orchestras also are used in the imperial shrine music. The ritual associated with this music is divided into the following sections: ushering in of the spirit; offering of tribute; offering of food; offering of the first cup of wine; the second cup; the third cup; withdrawal of tribute; ushering out of the spirit. The majority of pieces of the court repertory belong to the category of banquet music. Mention should be made of *Sujech'on,* probably the most highly regarded piece in the repertory, and *Yomillak* (*Yu-min-ak*), the instrumental version of the previously mentioned court epic. *Sijo,* the most important Korean poetic form (all Korean poetic forms, it should be noted, are associated with music), is a three-line verse with a secondary pause within each line. In a musical performance the singer is accompanied by a *janggo,* and the three lines have the following metrical subdivision: 5 8 8 5 8, 5 8 8 5 8, 5 8 5 8. *Sijo*

texts also are employed in *kagok,* where they are divided into five sections with an instrumental interlude and postlude. (The secondary pause in the first *sijo* line marks the division between the first and second *kagok* lines, and the secondary pause in the third line marks the division between the fourth and fifth lines.) *Sijo* are sung mainly by amateurs, whereas *kagok,* with richer scales and instrumental accompaniment, are sung only by professional musicians. *P'ansori* is sung drama; originally all the parts were sung by a single performer accompanied only by a *puk,* a barrel-shaped drum. The vocal techniques and pyrotechnics employed are astonishing, ranging from patter and various types of onomatopoeia to something that is a good approximation of white noise. All these techniques serve for dramatic expression, and the over-all effect of a *p'ansori* such as *Sim Ch'ong ga* is of surpassing tragic grandeur.

III. *Notation.* The twelve-tone Chinese character notation known as the *yulja* (*yul-cha-po*) notation is the most widely used. The following are the Korean readings of the characters with Western equivalents arbitrarily chosen to indicate the relative values: *hwang* (F), *tae* (F♯), *t'ae* (G), *hyop* or *hyŭp* (A♭), *ko* (A), *jung* or *chung* (B♭), *yu* (B), *yim* or *im* (C), *yi* (C♯), *nam* (D), *mu* (E♭), *ung* (E). The *kong-ch'ak* (*kong-chuk-po*) notation, which is in part an absolute pitch and in part a scale-degree notation without cognizance of octave equivalence, and the simple five-tone notation, which is a kind of number notation, are both found in the historical notation books. Mnemonic notations for the various instruments, a tablature notation for the *komungo* (*komunko*), and a kind of neumatic notation for *kagok* also exist. Rhythm is indicated by columns of squares, with each square representing a beat and each column a measure. Subdivisions of the measure are indicated by heavy lines, and subdivisions of the beat are indicated by appropriate placement of the characters within the squares.

IV. *Theory.* The majority of pieces in the court repertory employ a five-tone scale, *jung, yim, nam, hwang, t'ae* (B♭, c, d, f, g), which can be generated only by a fourth (or fifth) and takes the following form in terms of fourths: *jung, hwang, yim, t'ae, nam.* This is also a rough indication of the pitch hierarchy, although some writers consider *hwang* the most important note. The scale yields the following intervals: 4 perfect fourths, 3 major seconds, 2 minor thirds, and 1 major third. This also represents a fair approximation of the frequency with which the intervals occur, at least for some of the pieces. The Korean fourth tends to be flat, and there is perhaps some indication of a gravitation toward equidistance. In addition to the above, the following transpositions occur: *mu, jung, hwang, yim, t'ae; hwang, yim, t'ae, nam, ko; hyop, mu, jung, hwang, yim.* The *yanggum* [see under V below], which contains eight pitches disregarding octaves, seems to set the limit for the number of transpositions, at least in the *hyangak* category. In earlier periods, six-tone and seven-tone scales were widely used. The *Akhak-kwebom* describes a system of sixty seven-tone modes. Pieces employing seven-tone melodies are also notated in the same work. At present a seven-tone scale is employed in the Confucian music. With the virtual obliteration of the *tarngak* portion of the repertory, however, the seven-tone scale has otherwise fallen almost into complete disuse. The situation of the *hyangak* modes is complicated and seems to vary according to period. In general, four modes are recognized, and they apparently hold a relationship with the transpositions mentioned above. Fortunately the *Yang gum shin bo* (*Yang-kŭm- shin-po*), a *komungo* tablature of 1610, contains the piece *Jung-dae-yop* (*Chung-tae-yŭp*) in the four modes, throwing light at least on the modal practice of its period. Ex. 1 gives the first two lines of each modal version in He-gu Yi's (Hie-ku Lee) transcription. Ex. 2 indicates the structure of the modes as derived by Yi (Lee) from a comparison of the four versions.

The ornamentation of Korean music is very rich, including a characteristic slow vibrato as well as many kinds of figuration. The rate of dynamic change also tends to be very high. Korean music, both court and non-court, is notable for its large, compound, symmetrical metric structures. The vast majority of pieces in

1
a P'yongjo

b P'yongjo-kyemyonjo

c Ujo-kyemyonjo

d Ujo

2
a P'yongjo   b Ujo

yim nam hwang t'ae ko yim hwang t'ae jung yim

c P'yongjo-kyemyonjo

nam hwang   yim   mu   hwang t'ae jung yim

d Ujo-kyemyonjo

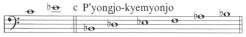

hwang hyop jung   yim mu hwang

the historical notations have the metrical structure 3 + 2 + 3 [see Ex. 1]. This was apparently associated with extremely slow tempos. The present court repertory, however, displays considerably more metrical variety. Non-court music is remarkable for the large number of compound triple meters. (Triple meter is apparently quite rare in both China and Japan.) Ex. 3 gives some of these meters with their names, transcribed by Sa-hoon Chang.

3 Jinyang jo (upper notes indicate bamboo strokes,

lower notes bare hand on the janggo)

Jungmori   Jungjung mori
b   c

Jajin mori   Hui mori
d   e

Kut kori   Ot jung mori
f   g

V. *Instruments.* Two classification systems have been employed for instruments. One is according to the material of manufacture, as in China, and the other according to function in the repertory (*a-ak* [*ah-ak*] or ritual music, *tarngak,* and *hyangak*). The main instruments in use today are the *kayagum* (*kaya-kǔm*), a plucked zither with 12 strings related to the Japanese **koto* and Chinese **cheng; komungo,* a fretted 6-stringed zither played with a stick plectrum; *a-jaeng,* a bowed 7-stringed zither, the bow consisting of a bare stick that is resined; *haegum* (*hae-kǔm*), a two-stringed fiddle with horsehair bow; *yanggum* (*yang-kǔm*), a zither with 14 quadruple strings, played with only one hammer; *piri,* a double reed with 8 finger holes, which comes in several different types; *t'aep'-yong-so,* a conical double reed with brass funnel; *taegum,* a horizontal flute with one of the holes covered with a membrane, producing a buzz when actuated (this flute comes in three sizes); *tanso,* a vertical notched flute; *janggo* (*chang-ko*), an hourglass-shaped drum, one head of which is played with a bamboo stick and the other with the bare hand; *p'yon-kyong,* a set of tuned stones; *p'yon-jong,* a set of tuned bronze bells; and *pak,* clappers in the shape of a fan.

Lit.: He-gu Yi (Hie-ku Lee), *Studies in Korean Music* (*Hanguk Ǔmak Yǒngu*) (1957); id., *Yang gum shin bo* (1959; fac. ed. of the 1610 *komungo* tablature); Sa-hoon Chang, *Kukak Kaeyo* (1961; Eng. trans., mimeographed ed., *A Glossary of Korean Music*); id., *Kukak-kye ui Jo-sul mit Nonmun* (1963; extensive bibl. of writings since World War II; Kyǒng-nin Sǒng, *Hanguk Akbo Haeje* (1965; inventory of all extant historical notation books). D.S.

Kornett [G.]. See under Cornet.

Kortholt [Low G.]. According to Praetorius (*Syntagma musicum* ii, 1619), a short double-reed instrument with a reed cap. Later the term seems to have been applied to double-reed instruments that, like the bassoon, have a tube doubled back on itself, thus being shortened. For this instrument the English name is *curtal* [see Oboe family III].

Koto [Jap.]. A Japanese stringed instrument, usually classified as a zither. It has a rectangular wooden body and 7 to 13 silk strings. It is placed horizontally on the floor and is plucked with the fingers, sometimes assisted by artificial nails. [See ill. under Zither.] Sometimes the name *koto* is specifically used for the *zokusō,* an instrument popular during the Edo period (see Japan VI). There are two types of *koto: sō* (or Chinese **jeng*), with movable bridges; and *kin* (or Chinese **chyn*) without such bridges and usually with seven strings. The representative types of *sō* are the *gakusō,* used in **gagaku;* the *tsukushi-goto,* which was popular in the late 16th century in the Kyūshū district; and the *zokusō.* All of these have 13 strings, while the *wagon,* an ancient Japanese instrument, today has six strings. The modern addition to the *sō* family is the *shinsō,* or new *sō;* which has 17 strings. See S. Isawa, ed., ‡*Collection of Koto Music* (Tokyo, 1888). M.K.

Kräftig [G.]. Strong, vigorous.

Krakowiak [F. *Cracovienne*]. A Polish dance named after the city of Cracow (Krakow). The music is in 2/4 time and employs simple syncopated patterns. The *krakowiak* was danced by large groups, with shouting, improvised singing, and striking of the heels together. It was in vogue in the early part of the 19th century and became known all over the world through the stage performances of Fanny Elssler. Chopin wrote a "Krakowiak" for piano and orchestra (op. 14).

Krebskanon [G.]. Crab canon; *krebsgängig,* in retrograde motion.

Kreisleriana. Schumann's cycle of eight piano pieces (op. 16, 1838), which are in strongly contrasting moods [see under Character piece]. The title refers to the whimsical and fantastic figure of the "Kapellmeister Kreisler," invented by the German novelist E. T. A. Hoffmann.

Kreutzer Sonata. Popular name for Beethoven's Violin Sonata op. 47 (1803), dedicated to the French composer and violin virtuoso Rodolphe Kreutzer (1766–1831) but originally composed for the English violinist George Bridgetower (c. 1780–1860), whom Beethoven accompanied at the first performance in 1803. The first movement is notable for its forceful expression of intense emotion. In Tolstoy's story "The Kreutzer Sonata," the composition symbolizes the destruction of morals caused by violently emotional music.

Kreuz [G.]. Sharp.

Kreuzflöte [G.]. **Transverse flute.

Kriuki, krjuki. See under Russia I; Znamenny chant.

Krummhorn [G.]. Cromorne; see under Oboe family III. Also, an organ stop; see Organ XI.

Kuhreigen [G.]. **Ranz des vaches.*

Kujawiak. A Polish dance from the province of Kujawy. It is a rapid variety of the **mazurka.* Chopin's mazurkas op. 33, no. 3, and op. 41, no. 2, are *kujawiaks.*

Kunst der Fuge, Die. See *Art of Fugue, The.*

Kunstlied [G.]. Term used in American (rather than German) literature for art song, especially those of German composers such as Schubert, Schumann, and Brahms, in contrast to German folksongs. It is also applied to 16th-century polyphonic songs with a German text (Hofhaimer, Senfl).

Kurz [G.]. Short. *Kurz Oktave,* *short octave. *Kurzer Vorschlag,* short appoggiatura.

K.V. See K.

Kyrial [L. *kyriale*]. See under Liturgical books I (6).

Kyrie [Gr.]. The first item of the Ordinary of the *Mass. Its full text is: *Kyrie eleison; Christe eleison; Kyrie eleison* (Lord, have mercy, etc.). Each of these three invocations is sung three times, usually with the melodies repeated according to the scheme: aaa bbb ccc′ (c′ indicates an extension or variant of c), or aaa bbb

aaa′. Other schemes are aba cdc efe and aaa aaa aaa′, the former probably of a later date, the latter an earlier type represented in the present-day collection only by the Kyrie of the Mass for the Dead [*LU,* p. 1807]. Originally (4th century) the Kyrie was employed in connection with litanies, a usage that survives in the archaic Mass of Holy Saturday [*LU,* p. 756] and in the procession of Rogation Days [*LU,* p. 835]. Not until about 800 is it described as consisting of "three times three" acclamations. In the 10th and 11th centuries the Kyries were frequently troped (farced Kyrie) by the interspersion of attributes, e.g., Kyrie *lux et origo* eleison [see Trope (3)]. Although these tropes have disappeared, the Kyries are still named after them, e.g., *Kyrie lux et origo* (Mass I, *LU,* p. 16). See *ApGC,* p. 405; M. Melnicki, *Das einstimmige Kyrie des lateinischen Mittelalters* (1954).

The Church of England adopted the Kyrie in the response "Lord, have mercy upon us, and incline our hearts to keep this Law" after the recitation of the Ten Commandments.

Kyrieleis [G.]. See *Leise.*

L

L. Abbr. for left or [G.] *links;* L. H., left hand, [G.] *linke Hand.*

La. See under Solmization; Pitch names; Hexachord II.

Labial pipes [G. *Labialpfeifen*]. Same as flue stops. See Organ VIII, IX.

Lacrimoso [It.]. Mournful.

Lady Macbeth of Mtsensk [Rus. *Lady Macbeth Mtsenskago Uyezda*]. Opera in four acts by Shostakovitch (libretto by A. Preis and the composer, based on a novel by N. S. Lyeskov), produced in Moscow, 1934. Setting: a village in Russia, 1840. The opera became notorious because of some unpleasant scenes that represent the *verismo technique at its most degenerate. Although these scenes were omitted from later performances, the opera was officially condemned by the Soviet government in 1936 as "bourgeois and formalistic." It was revised after the official decree was rescinded (1958) and was produced under the title *Katerina Ismailova* (1962).

Lage [G.]. Position with reference to (1) violin playing (*erste, zweite,* . . . *Lage,* i.e., first, second, . . . position); (2) chords (*enge* or *weite Lage,* i.e., close or open position); (3) ranges of voices and instruments (*hohe* or *tiefe Lage,* i.e., high or low range).

Lagnoso [It.]. Lamenting.

Lai, lay [G. *Leich;* not to be confused with *leis(e)* or *laisse*]. A form of medieval French poetry and music developed mainly in northern France during the 13th century by the trouvères. The lai was also cultivated in southern France, but only two or three troubadour (Provençal) lais are preserved with music. The development ended with Machaut, who wrote 18 lais. The texts of the lais are poems (usually addressed to the Virgin or to a lady) consisting of 60, 100, or more lines of 4 to 8 syllables each, divided into irregular stanzas of 6 to 16 or more lines. Each stanza is based on one or two rhyme-syllables, and there is a great variety in the schemes of meter and rhyme to be found in the various stanzas, e.g., a^4 a^4 b^7 a^4 a^4 b^7 a^4 a^4 b^7 b^7 b^7 b^7 b^7 b^7 b^7 (the letters indicate lines with the same rhyme; the figures give the number of syllables in the line).

The musical structure of the lai is essentially that of the sequence [see Sequence II], from which it evidently stems, but it has certain traits of elaboration or modification. Instead of the double versicles of the sequence, there are triple versicles and quadruple versicles (a melody repeated three or four times), as well as single versicles involving no repetition. Following is the scheme of one of the shortest lais, Guillaume le Vinier's "Espris d'ire et d'amour" [A. Jeanroy, *Lais et descorts français du XIIIe siècle* (1901), p. 87; cf. *HAM,* no. 19i]:

		II	III	
A	B	C	D	E
a a	b_1 b_2 b_1 b_2	c c	d d d	e_1 e_2 e_1 e_2

	V	
F	G H	I
f f	g h h h	i

(a, b, etc., are the versicle melodies; A, B, etc., the musical sections; I, II, etc., the poetic stanzas, according to Jeanroy; b_1, b_2, different endings for the same melody.) Another name for the lai is *descort* ("disorder"), a term thought to refer to its highly variable structure in contrast to the *formes fixes,* such as the *ballade,* rondeau, etc.; or to a discord between the lover and his lady; or to some other irregularity [see *ReMMA,* p. 225]. In Machaut's lais the musical scheme is somewhat less irregular because all the versicles are either double or quadruple. Of particular interest are his "Lay de la fonteinne," in which all the even-numbered sections are three-part *chaces,* and the "Lay de confort," which is composed entirely in three-part polyphony, every section being a *chace.*

The German counterpart of the lai is the 14th-century *Leich.* Here the double-versicle structure of the sequence is, as a rule, rigidly observed. For example, Heinrich Frauenlob's "Unser Frauen Leich" [see Runge, p. 1] consists of 44 stanzas (*Lieder*) sung to 22 melodies (*Töne*).

Lit.: A. Jeanroy, L. Brandin, and P. Aubry, ed., ‡*Lais et descorts français du XIIIe siècle* (1901); F. Ludwig, ed., ‡*Guillaume de Machaut, Musikalische Werke* iv (ed. H. Besseler, 1954); L. Schrade, ed., ‡*Polyphonic Music of the Fourteenth Century,* vol. ii (Machaut); P. Runge, ed., ‡*Die Sangesweisen der Colmarer Handschrift* (1896; *Leich*); G. Holz, F. Saran, and E. Bernoulli, ed., ‡*Die Jenaer Liederhandschrift,* 2 vols., (1901; *Leich*); *DTO* 41 (Frauenlob, *et al.*);

F. Wolf, *Über die Lais, Sequenzen und Leiche* (1841); G. Hase, *Der Minneleich Meister Alexanders* (1921); F. Gennrich, "Das Formproblem des Minnesangs" (*Deutsche Vierteljahrsschrift für Literaturwissenschaft und Geistesgeschichte* ix [1931]); *id.,* in *Studi medievali,* new series xv (1942; Provençal lais); J. Handschin, in *ZMW* xii, xiii; H. Spanke, in *ZMW* xiv; G. Reaney, in *ML* xxxix (origins of lai); *id.,* in *PMA* lxxxii (Machaut); J. Maillard, in *MD* xvii (Ernoul). See also general bibl. under Trouvère; Minnesinger.

Laisse. See under *Chanson de geste.*

Lakmé. Opera in three acts by Delibes (libretto by E. Gondinet and P. Gille), produced in Paris, 1883. Setting: India, 19th century.

Lament. (1) In Scottish and Irish music, a piece for bagpipes or a song used at clan funerals or other mournful occasions. Each clan has its traditional tune, which is often performed with a number of more or less irregular variations. See also Ho-hoane.

(2) General designation for compositions commemorating the death of a famous person. The earliest examples are a "Planctus Karoli" lamenting the death of Charlemagne (814) and another *planctus* for his son Hugo (844), both preserved with melodies in an early neumatic script that has not been deciphered. A late 12th-century troubadour *planc* (*planh*) by Gaucelm Faudit deplores the death of Richard the Lion-Hearted (1199). From the 14th to 17th centuries laments, called *déplorations, tombeaux, plaintes,* or *apothéoses,* were often written for great composers by their pupils. The oldest known example is a *ballade,* "Armes, amours," written by Deschamps and composed by F. Andrieu on the death of Machaut in 1377 [see F. Ludwig's edition of Machaut, i, 49ff]. From the 15th or 16th century comes a lament by Ockeghem for Binchois ("Mort tu as navré"; see J. Marix, *Les Musiciens de la cour de Bourgogne* [1937], pp. 83ff), by Josquin for Ockeghem ("Nymphes des bois," with the Introit "Requiem aeternam" as a *cantus firmus,* the entire composition being written in black notes; see Eye music), by Gombert for Josquin ("Musae Jovis"), and others [see *ReMR,* index, s.v. Lament]. A great number of laments, often very moving expressions of grief, exist in the French literature of the 17th century, e.g., *tombeaux* by Denis Gaultier for the Seigneur de Lenclos, by Raquette for Gaultier, and by L. Couperin and D'Anglebert for their teacher Chambonnières. F. Couperin

wrote two *apothéoses* in the form of sonatas, one for Lully and one for Corelli. Froberger's *lamentation* for Ferdinand IV [see *DTO* 13, p. 32], *tombeau* for Monsieur Blancheroche [*DTO* 21, p. 14], and *lamentation* for Ferdinand III [*DTO* 21, p. 116] should be added to a repertory in which the romanticism of the 17th century is most beautifully expressed. Many of these compositions are written in the form and style of a *pavane. Comparable pieces are Blow's setting of Dryden's ode on the death of Purcell, "Mark how the Lark and Linnet sing," Purcell's elegy for Locke, "What hope for us Remains now he is gone," and similar works of late 17th-century England. A well-known modern example is Ravel's *Le Tombeau de Couperin*. See M. Brenet, in *RMC* iii.

Lamentations. Music set to the Lamentations of Jeremiah. In the Roman Catholic service the Lamentations are sung, in place of the three lessons, during the first Nocturn of Matins on Thursday, Friday, and Saturday of Holy Week (*Tenebrae), in a simple recitation tone [*LU*, pp. 631, 692, 754]. A characteristic feature of the text, taken over from the Bible, is the enumeration of the verses by Hebrew letters: "ALEPH. Quo modo sedit . . . BETH. Plorans ploravit," etc.

From the late 15th through the 17th centuries the famous text was often composed polyphonically, usually in a simple homorhythmic style, except for the Hebrew letters, which often received a more elaborate treatment. Probably the earliest extant example is a four-part composition of a portion of the text, "Patres nostri peccaverunt" (Lesson III from Holy Saturday; see *LU*, p. 759) by the Spaniard (Italian?) Johannes Cornago (fl. *c.* 1450–70; see *ReMR*, p. 576). In 1506 Petrucci published two volumes, *Lamentationum Jeremiae prophetae liber primus; . . . liber secundus,* that include settings by Johannes Tinctoris, de Orto, Tromboncino, and others. In 1532 a setting by Carpentras (pseud. of Elzéar Genet, *c.* 1475–1548) was published that was used until 1587 by the Papal Chapel in place of the ancient plainsong. In 1557, LeRoy and Ballard published a collection of settings (*Piissimae ac sacratissimae lamentationes Jeremiae Prophetae*) that, in addition to Carpentras' composition, included others by Pierre de La Rue, Févin, Arcadelt, Festa, and Claude Le Jeune. In 1588, Palestrina published his *Lamentationum Hieremiae Prophetae, liber primus* [comp. ed., vol. xxv], which supplanted Carpentras' composition in the service of the

Papal Chapel [for more details, see *GD* iii, 80; *GDB* v, 34f.]. Other settings are by Stephan Mahu, Gaspar van Werbecke [*SchGMB*, no. 58], Cristobal Morales (1564), Tallis, Byrd, Händl [*DTO* 30], Giovanni Maria Nanini, and Gregorio Allegri. In 1640, Allegri's composition was added to the setting of Palestrina, which did not include the complete text. The Sistine Choir still uses the settings of these two composers. For Palestrina's complete and original composition, see R. Casimiri, *Il "Codice 59" dell'Archivio musicale lateranense* (1919). In the 17th century the text was composed in a highly expressive aria style, e.g., by J. Rosenmüller [see *HAM*, no. 218] and F. Couperin. A recent setting is Stravinsky's *Threni* (1958).

Lit.: G. Massenkeil, *Mehrstimmige Lamentationen aus der ersten Hälfte des 16. Jahrhunderts* [1965]; A. E. Schröder, "Les Origines des lamentations" (*CP 1952*); G. Watkins, "Three Books of Polyphonic Lamentations of Jeremiah" (diss. Univ. of Rochester, 1953); R. P. Rojo, "The Gregorian Antiphonary of Silos and the Spanish Melody of the Lamentations" (*Speculum* v); G. Massenkeil, "Eine spanische Choralmelodie in mehrstimmigen Lamentationskompositionen des 16. Jahrhunderts" (*AMW* xix/xx); *id.,* in *AMW* xvii.

Lamento. Music of an elegiac, mournful character. For unknown reasons a dance of the 14th century bears the title *Lamento di Tristano* [*SchGMB,* no. 28]. In 17th-century opera the *lamento* is a scene expressing utter despair, usually placed shortly before the unexpected "turn to the happy end." This type was inaugurated by Monteverdi's famous "Lamento d'Arianna" of 1608 [*SchGMB,* no. 177]. See A. Westrup, in *MR* i. See also Lament.

Lancio, con [It.]. With vigor.

Landini cadence. A cadence, named after Francesco Landini (1325–97), in which the sixth

degree (a, "Landini sixth") is inserted between the leading tone (b) and the octave (c'). Frequently the altered fourth (f♯) appears in the middle part, as a leading tone to the dominant (g) [see Ex. a], a formation that properly belongs to the Lydian mode [Ex. b]. The use of this cadence is much wider than is suggested by the name. It occurs in the works of Machaut (*c.* 1300–77; see, e.g., *SchGMB,* no. 26, "loyaument"), was used frequently by Landini, and is a characteristic feature of the music of the *Burgundian school, usually in the ornamented form shown in Ex. c. There are cases, however, in which the "flatted" formula [Ex. d] would seem to be required [see *ApNPM,* p. 106]. The 7–6–8 progression, which is the characteristic trait of the Landini cadence, was used sporadically throughout the 16th century, e.g., by Josquin (*Missa de Beata Virgine,* close of Kyrie I), Schlick (*Salve regina*), Palestrina (only in the middle parts; see K. Jeppesen, *The Style of Palestrina and the Dissonance,* rev. ed., [1946], p. 194), and Victoria [see *HAM,* no. 149]. It was still employed in the recitative of the early 17th century, e.g., in Monteverdi's *Orfeo,* where the words "De la bell'Euri-dice" (in "In questo lieto e fortunato giorno") are sung to f♯ . . . f♯ e–g g. See Cadence II.

Ländler. An Austrian dance much like a slow waltz. It was very popular in the early 19th century, before the *waltz came into vogue. Mozart (K. 606), Beethoven (11 *Mödlinger Tänze,* 1819), and Schubert (op. 171) wrote collections of *Ländler.* See Dance music IV.

Langaus [G.]. An Austrian dance of the late 18th century, danced in such a wild manner that it was prohibited by the police. The music was similar to that of the waltz or *Ländler.* See P. Nettl, *The Story of Dance Music* [1947], p. 242; E. Schenk, in *Studia musicologica* iii, 301ff.

Langsam [G.]. Slow.

Laos. See under Thailand.

Larga [L.]. In mensural notation, rare name for the *maxima* (Verulus de Anagnia; see *CS* iii, 135f).

Largamente [It.]. Broadly.

Largando. Same as *allargando.

Larghetto [It.]. The diminutive of *largo, therefore somewhat faster than this tempo. Also, title for pieces in such a tempo.

Largo [It.]. (1) Very slow in tempo, usually combined with great expressiveness. See Tempo marks. (2) Popular name for a famous composition by Handel, originally the aria "Ombra mai fù" ("Shade never was") from his opera *Serse* (*Xerxes*) but usually played in an arrangement for organ or other instruments. The title is taken from the original tempo indication for the piece.

Lark Quartet. Popular name for Haydn's String Quartet in D major (op. 64, no. 5), so called because of the high passage of the first violin "soaring like a lark" at the opening of the first movement.

Lassu. See under *Verbunkos; Csárdás.*

Latin America. See individual entries Argentina, Bolivia, Brazil, etc.

Lit.: G. Chase, *A Guide to the Music of Latin America,* rev. ed. (1962); L. Saminsky, *Living Music of the Americas* [1949]; N. Slonimsky, *Music of Latin America* [1945]; R. V. García, L. C. Croatto, and A. A. Martin, *Historia de la Música Latino-americana* (1938); G. Duran, *Recordings of Latin American Songs and Dances,* rev. ed. (1950); J. Orrego-Salas, *The Young Generation of Latin American Composers* (1963).

Laube Sonata. See Moonlight Sonata.

Lauda [It., pl. *laude;* the less correct forms *laude* (sing.), *laudi* (pl.), are also used]. Hymns of praise and devotion in the Italian language, which from the 13th century to the middle of the 19th century played an important part in the religious life of the Italian people. Their origin and early development were closely connected with St. Francis of Assisi (*c.* 1182–1226) as well as with the many penitential fraternities (flagellants; see *Geisslerlieder*) of the 13th and 14th centuries. Later, numerous congregations, called *Companie de Laudesi* (or *Laudisti*), were founded to foster devotional singing among the Italian people. The musical and dramatic presentations held in their meeting halls led, in the 16th century, to the development of the *oratorio. Till the mid-19th century the *laudesi* continued to be centers of religious life.

The *laude* of the 13th century are monophonic songs that to some extent show the influence of French troubadour music. Their textual structure is that of a refrain poem, consisting of several (two to ten or more) stanzas (S) of four or six lines each, alternating with a refrain (*ritornello, R) of usually two lines: R S R S . . . S R. Music is provided for the refrain and the stanza, the latter usually including the former or a part of it, in a great variety of schemes, e.g., A B a b a b, A B c d a b, A B c d e b, A B c c d b, A B c c a b (capital letters indicate the refrain). The last scheme, which may also be represented as A b b a (or, with repetition of the refrain, A b b a A) is that of the French *virelai (or the Italian *ballata*). This form, however, plays a much less prominent part in the *laude* than some scholars have maintained. Only about a dozen *laude* are in the form of the virelai, and most of these show considerable modifications in the repeated phrases, which are not found in the virelai proper [see "Sancto Lorenzo" in *HAM*, no. 21c]. One of the few examples of strict virelai form is given in *HAM*, no. 21b. The usual transcription in 4/4 meter [Liuzzi; *BeMMR*, p. 153f] is, to say the least, hypothetical [see Y. Rokseth, in *Romania* (Paris) lxv, 383; see also under *Vierhebigkeit*]. The original MSS give no indications for rhythm [see Monophonic notation].

The *lauda* poetry flourished in the 15th century, but only few remnants of the music— some monophonic, some in two parts—have survived. A new period of *lauda* composition began with Petrucci's two books of *Laude* (1507, '08), containing *laude* by some of the *frottola* composers (Tromboncino, Marco Cara, Fogliano) as well as by an otherwise unknown composer, Dammonis. These are all polyphonic, in three or four parts, and in a simple chordal style borrowed from the *frottola* [ex. in *HAM*, no. 94]. In the second half of the 16th century Fra Serafino Razzi inaugurated a vast literature of *laude* in the popular styles of the *villanella* and *canzonetta* [ex. by G. Animuccia in *SchGMB*, no. 120]. Frequently, folksongs and dance melodies were used with the religious texts. The numerous publications of the 17th century are important sources of early Italian folksong [see under *Ruggiero*].

Lit.: F. Liuzzi, ‡*La Lauda e i primordi della melodia italiana*, 2 vols. (1935); G. Cattin, *Contributi alla storia della lauda spirituale* (1958); K. Jeppesen, *Die mehrstimmige italienische Laude um 1500* (1935); id., "Die neuentdeckten Bücher der Lauden des ... Petrucci" (*ZMW* xii); id., "Ein venezianisches Laudenmanuskript" (*CP Kroyer*); D. Alaleona, "Le Laudi ... nei secoli XVI e XVII" (*RMI* xvi; E. J. Dent, "The Laudi Spirituali" (*PMA* xliii); L. Cervelli, "Le Laudi spirituali di Gio. Animuccia" (*LRM* xx); J. Handschin, in *AM* x (review of Liuzzi's publication); F. Ghisi, in *CP Jeppesen* (14th and early 15th cent.); H. Anglés, in *CP Apel*.

Laudes [L.]. (1) Latin for *Lauds. (2) Name for Gloria tropes. (3) In the *Gallican and *Mozarabic rites, the counterpart of the Roman Catholic Alleluia. (4) *Laudes regiae* (Praises of the king) is a medieval chant celebrating Jesus as the ruler of the world. It begins with the acclamation *Christus vincit, Christus regnat, Christus imperat.* See E. H. Kantorowicz and M. F. Bukofzer, *Laudes regiae* (1946).

Laudon Symphony. Haydn's Symphony no. 69 in C (*c.* 1778), composed in honor of the Austrian field marshal Baron von Laudon (1717–90).

Lauds. The second of the canonical hours. See under Office.

Lauf [G.; pl. *Läufe*]. A rapid passage, particularly in scales. For *Laufwerk*, see under Mechanical instruments III.

Launeddas. A Sardinian triple clarinet thought to be of Oriental (Phoenician?) origin [see Clarinet family IV]. It consists of three pipes made of cane and provided with single reeds. The two outer pipes are melody pipes with five or six holes, while the center pipe is an unchangeable bourdon. The music played on the launeddas, therefore, is in two parts over a sustained pedal. See G. Fara, in *RMI* xx, xxi, xxv. For the peculiar technique of blowing, see *SaHMI*, p. 91; also Oboe family III.

Laute [G.]. Lute. *Lautentabulatur,* lute tablature. *Lautenclavicymbel,* see Lute harpsichord.

Lavolta. See under Volta (1).

Lay. See Lai.

Leader. (1) Conductor (in America) or concertmaster (in England). (2) See Fugue I (g).

Leading motive, motif. See Leitmotiv.

Leading tone, note [F. *note sensible;* G. *Leitton;* It. *sensibile;* Sp. *sensible*]. The seventh degree of the scale, a semitone below the tonic, so called because of its strong tendency to "lead up" (resolve upward) to the tonic. This progression (b–c′) is the characteristic step of the regular cadence in major as well as minor [see Ex. a] and therefore is extremely common in music of the 17th to 19th centuries.

The consistent and compulsory use of the leading tone is one of the chief features of modern major and minor, as opposed to the modes, most of which (Dorian, Phrygian, Mixolydian, Aeolian) have a whole tone (*subtonium*) below the tonic, not a semitone (*subsemitonium*) [see Ex. b]. The leading tone is practically nonexistent in Gregorian chant. Although in modal music the *subsemitonium*, i.e., the leading tone, could be introduced by sharping the *subtonium,* this did not result in a complete suppression of the diatonic seventh [see *Musica ficta*]. Thus, earlier music usually wavers between the natural and sharped varieties, as illustrated in Ex. c. In the 14th and early 15th centuries the sharped degrees were used more than during the ensuing period of Flemish music (1450–1600; see Landini cadence). See M. L. Mackey, "The Evolution of the Leading Tone in Western European Music to *circa* 1600 A.D." (diss. Catholic Univ. of America, 1962); L. H. Skrbensky. "Leitton und Alteration in der abendländischen Musik" (diss. Prague, 1928).

League of Composers. See under Societies I, 4.

Lebendig, lebhaft [G.]. Lively.

Lectio [L.]. See Lesson (1).

Lectionary [L. *lectionarium*] See under Liturgical books I (9).

Ledger lines. Short lines drawn through the stem of notes that are too high or too low to be represented on the staff. In early music they are usually avoided by introducing lower or higher clefs. The earliest source in which they are extensively used is M. A. Cavazzoni's organ book *Ricercari, motetti, canzoni* of 1523 [see *ApNPM,* pp. 3ff].

Leere Saite [G.]. Open string.

Legato [It.]. To be played without any perceptible interruption between the notes [Ex. a], as opposed to *leggiero* or nonlegato [Ex. b], *portato* [Ex. c], and *staccato* [Ex. d]. *Legatissimo,* indi-

cated by the word and not with notational symbols, is either a more forceful indication of legato, or a sort of super-legato in which the preceding note is held for a short moment together with the following one (Ex. e). The first line in the illustration shows the notes as written; the second line shows the approximate effect.

In the musical practice of earlier centuries, legato playing was not always the normal manner of performance, as it is today. For organ and violin music of the 17th and 18th centuries slightly detached playing is more suitable than a full legato.

Legende, légende [G., F.]. Romantic name for compositions based on, or suggestive of, a devotional or legendary narrative.

Leger lines. See Ledger lines.

Leggèro, leggiero [It.]. Light, nimble.

Legno [It.]. Wood. *Col legno* means, in violin playing, tapping the strings with the stick of the bow instead of bowing them. *Stromenti di legno,* woodwind instruments.

Lehrstück [G.]. Name for a type of German musical play of the 1920's designed to be educational for a working-class audience, particularly within the youth movement of that period. Typical examples are Hindemith's *Wir bauen eine Stadt* (We Build a Town) and Kurt Weill's *Der Jasager* (The Yes-Sayer).

Leich [G.]. See under Lai.

Leidenschaftlich [G.]. Passionate.

Leier [G.]. Usually, the *lyre. In earlier usage, the *hurdy-gurdy (*Drehleier, Radleier, Bettlerleier*). Schubert's song, "Der Leiermann," portrays a player of the hurdy-gurdy (not of the street organ, called *Leierkasten*).

Leierkasten [G.]. Street organ.

Leise [G.]. (1) Soft. (2) Medieval congregational hymns in the German language, so called because of their refrain, kyrie *eleis*(on), which was abbreviated to *kirleis* or *leis.* The oldest specimen, *Unsar trohtin,* dates from the 9th century. Several Protestant chorales belong to this category, e.g., *Nun bitten wir den heiligen Geist,* and *Christ ist erstanden* [see *AdHM,* p. 448]. There is frequent confusion of the terms *Leise* and *Leich* [see *GD* i, 636; *GDB* ii, 270]. See O. Ursprung, in *MF* v.

Leiter [G.]. (1) Scale (*Tonleiter*); *leitereigen,* proper to the scale, diatonic. (2) Leader of an orchestra.

Leitmotiv, leitmotif [G.]. A term coined by R. Wagner's friend H. von Wolzogen ["Die Motive in Wagner's *Götterdämmerung*" (*Musikalisches Wochenblatt* ix, 1878)] to denote the fundamental method of composition in Wagner's later operas, that is, the representation of

characters, typical situations, and recurrent ideas by musical motifs. (Wagner himself had used the term *Grundthema,* basic theme.) In *Der Ring des Nibelungen,* for instance, there are motifs characterizing the Ring (Ex. 1), the Contract (Ex. 2), Valhalla (Ex. 3), the Sword (Ex. 4), etc. These leitmotivs are not rigidly fixed melodies but are used very flexibly with modifications in rhythm, intervals, etc., according to the requirement of the particular situation [see Transformation of themes]. It should be noted that the extensive "Tables of Leitmotivs" usually found in popular editions of Wagner's operas are not by him, nor are any of the names they bear.

Although Wagner was the first to make consistent use of the leitmotiv, his method is adumbrated in various earlier compositions. In Grétry's *Richard Coeur-de-Lion* (1784) the theme "Une fièvre brûlante" [see *AdHM,* p. 747; Beethoven wrote variations on it] appears nine times. In Méhul's *Ariodant* (1799) a characteristic theme called *cri de fureur* is used repeatedly to express the vengeance of the deceived lover [see *AdHM,* p. 748]. A well-known example outside opera is the **idée fixe* of Berlioz' *Symphonie fantastique.* There is also recurrent use of thematic material in Karl Loewe's *Balladen.* Many of the post-Wagnerian operatic composers (R. Strauss, Debussy, Pfitzner, D'Indy) adopted Wagner's procedure, which also had an influence on symphonic music, particularly the symphonic poem.

Lit.: R. Donington, *Wagner's Ring and Its Symbols* [1963]; D. Cooke, *The Language of Music* (1959); L. Windsperger, *Das Buch der Motive und Themen . . . Richard Wagner's,* 2 vols. [19—]; K. Wörner, "Beiträge zur Geschichte des Leitmotivs in der Oper" (diss. Berlin, 1931); *id.,* in *ZMW* xiv; M. Lamm, "Beiträge zur Entwicklung des musikalischen Motivs in den Tondramen Richard Wagners" (diss. Vienna, 1932); L. Sabaneev, "Remarks on the Leit-motif" (*ML* xiii, 200); G. E. H. Abraham, "The Leitmotif since Wagner" (*ML* vi, 175); E. Haraszti, "Le Problème du Leit-Motiv" (*RM* iv).

Leitton [G.]. Leading tone.

Lemminkäinen's Homecoming. Symphonic poem by Jean Sibelius, op. 22, no. 4 (1893–95, describing (after a story from the *Kalevala) the hero's journey home from Pohjola [see *Pohjola's Daughter*].

Leningrad Symphony. A title sometimes used for Shostakovitch's Symphony no. 7, op. 60, composed in 1941, when Leningrad was besieged by the Germans.

Lento [It.]. Slow. See under Tempo marks.

Leonore Overtures. The overtures Beethoven wrote for his opera *Fidelio,* prior to the final overture, known as Fidelio Overture (or, incorrectly, as Leonore Overture no. 4). Leonore nos. 1 and 2 were written in 1805, no. 3 in 1806. The name refers to the original title of the opera, *Leonore.* The *Fidelio* overture was written in 1814. See H. Braunstein, *Beethoven's Leonore-Ouvertüren* (1927).

Les Adieux, l'absence, et le retour [F.]. See *Adieux, Les.*

Lesson [L. *lectio*]. (1) In the Roman Catholic rites, a reading from the Scriptures and other sources, e.g., the writings of the church fathers. Matins includes nine lessons, three for each Nocturn. Mass includes two, one before the Gradual, the other after the Alleluia. The former is usually taken from the Epistles (*Lectio Epistolae . . .*) and so is called Epistle; the latter nearly always comes from the Gospels (*Sequentia sancti Evangelii . . . ; sequentia* here means "continuation"), and so is called Gospel. (2) A 17th- and 18th-century name for a type of English instrumental piece, particularly for harpsichord or organ. The term does not imply any special form or style, nor necessarily a pedagogical purpose; in fact, it seems to have been just as general as the modern term "piece." In the 17th century the term was frequently used for a suite (Suite of Lessons), e.g., in Matthew Locke's *Melothesia . . . A Choice Collection of Lessons for the Harpsichord and the Organ* (1673). In the 18th century some organ verses as well as sonata-like compositions were called "lessons."

Letter notation. The use of letters for the indication of tones is restricted today to theoretical and instructive purposes; see Pitch names. In earlier periods they were also used for writing down music, e.g., in ancient Greece [see Notation II], in Arab and Persian music of the 13th century [see *NOH* i, 453], and in the German organ tablature [see Tablature I]. Letters are also used in the French lute tablature, but here they indicate finger positions, not pitches [see Tablature IV].

In the Middle Ages there were several systems of letter notation based on the Roman alphabet. Several of these are shown here:

1.		A	B	C	E	H	I	M	O		X	Y	CC	DD	FF	KK	LL
2.		A	B	C	D	E	F	G	H		I	K	L	M	N	O	P
3.				A	B	C	D	E	F		G	H	I	K	L	M	N	O	P
4.	E	F	G	A	B	C	D	E	F		G	A	B	C	D	E	F

																			a	b	c
5.	Γ	A	B	C	D	E	F	G	a	b	♮	c	d	e	f	g	a	b	c
Modern	G	A	B	c	d	e	f	g	a	b♭	b	c'	d'	e'	f'	g'	a'	b'	c''

System (1) is found in the "De institutione musica" of Boethius (*c.* 480–524) and may therefore be called *Boethian notation* (the missing letters, D, F, G, etc., are used for the additional tones of the chromatic and enharmonic genera of ancient Greek music). Systems (2) and (3) employ the letters from A to P for two octaves, the former from A to a', the latter from c to c''. The A-to-P series also occurs in Boethius but without reference to definite pitches [see *ReMMA,* p. 135n]. Hence the name "Boethian notation" is hardly justifiable for system (2), for which it is often used. In system (4) only the letters from A to G are used, without distinguishing higher or lower octaves. In both (3) and (4) the letter A stands for the present-day c. This method seems to have been employed chiefly in connection with certain instruments, such as the monochord, organ, or sets of bells (*nolae, tintinnabulae*). System (5), often called *Guidonian letters,* was used more than 100 years before Guido in a treatise by Odo of Clugny and therefore should be termed *Oddonic letters.* It includes two shapes of the letter b, one for b natural, the other for b-flat [see Accidentals II]. This system was universally adopted and, with certain modifications, persists to the present day. Of the others, system (2) is of particular interest because it was employed in various MSS of Gregorian chant to clarify the pitches of the neumatic signs, e.g., in the "bilingual" Codex Montpellier *H. 159* [see Editions XLII A, 7 and 8; also *WoHN* i, opp. p. 44], as well as for writing down a famous two-part composition of the 11th cen-

tury, *Ut tuo propitiatus* [see *ApNPM,* p. 207f]. For source references for the various systems described above, see *ApNPM,* p. 21, and A. Auda, *Les Gammes musicales* [1947], p. 310. For other systems see Romanus letters; Hermannus letters.

Lit.: J. Smits van Waesberghe, *Muziekgeschiedenis der Middeleeuwen* (1939–42), vol. ii.

Leuto [It.]. Old spelling for *lauto,* lute.

Levalto. See under Volta (1).

Levare, levate [It.]. To take off (organ stops, mutes). *Si levano i sordini,* take off the mutes.

Levatio [L.], **elevazione, levazione** [It.]. *Elevation.

L.H. Abbr. for left hand.

L'Homme armé [F.]. A 15th-century melody that became famous because of its frequent use as a tenor of polyphonic Masses [see Mass C, IIb, IIe]. The tune, with its recently discovered text [see D. Plamenac, in *Annales de la Fédération archéologique et historique de Belgique* (Bruges, 1925), p. 229f], is here reproduced. Pietro Aron (*Il Toscanello,* 1523) ascribed the tune to Busnois,

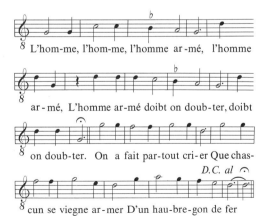

8 L'hom-me, l'hom-me, l'homme ar -mé, l'homme

8 ar - mé, L'homme ar-mé doibt on doub-ter, doibt

8 on doub-ter. On a fait par-tout cri-er Que chas-

D.C. al ⌒

8 cun se viegne ar-mer D'un hau-bre-gon de fer

(d. c. 1490), but it is used in a chanson that very likely was written c. 1430–40 [see M. Bukofzer in *MQ* xxviii, 19]. There are more than thirty Masses based on this melody (*Missa L'Homme armé*). Among their composers are Dufay [see *HAM,* no. 66], Busnois, Caron, Ockeghem [*HAM*, no. 73], Obrecht, Tinctoris, Josquin [*HAM*, no. 89], Brumel, de La Rue [*HAM*, no. 92], Pipelare, Senfl, de Orto, Morales, Palestrina, and, in the 17th century, Carissimi [see O. Gombosi, *Jacob Obrecht,* p. 47]. In 1930, J. N. David composed a *Fantasia super L'Homme armé.* Ten 15th-century Masses are published in *Editions XXXI. See M. Brenet, in *MfM* xxx; O. Gombosi and D. Plamenac, in *ZMW* x, xi, xii; O. Strunk, in *BAMS* ii; W. Apel, "Imitation Canons on L'Homme armé" (*Speculum* xxv).

Liber usualis [L.]. See under Liturgical books I, 5.

Libraries. Most of the great music libraries are located in western Europe, with a growing concentration in the United States and few collections of real importance elsewhere. In recent years, the books and manuscripts dating back through the centuries have been supplemented by valuable new resources such as photostats, microfilms, and phonograph and tape recordings. The International Association of Music Libraries (AIBM) is currently updating R. Eitner's *Quellen-Lexikon* [see under Bibliography] as an *International Inventory of Musical Sources* [see *RISM*]. The Music Library Association, founded in 1931, is of particular importance in North America, with its quarterly *Notes* (1934—). Important and useful listings are: S. De Ricci, ed., *Census of Medieval and Renaissance Manuscripts in the United States and Canada,* 3 vols. (1935–40; suppl. 1962); M. B. Stillwell, *Incunabula and Americana, 1450–1800* (1931); *id., Incunabula in American Libraries* (1940); O. E. Albrecht, *A Census of Autograph Music Manuscripts of European Composers in American Libraries* (1953). Extensive lists of music libraries and their catalogues have been made by A. Ott in *MGG* ix, 1034ff, by C. Cudworth in *GDB* v, 160ff, and by V. Duckles in *Music Reference and Research Materials,* 2nd ed. (1967). See also the lists of contributing libraries in the volumes of the *International Inventory* (mentioned above). There follows a list of the most important libraries and collections with significant musical holdings of special interest. They are arranged in alphabetical order of countries within each continent (North America,

Central and South America, Europe, Asia,) and by cities within each country.

NORTH AMERICA.
CANADA. See M. Duchow, "Canadian Music Libraries: Some Observations" (*Notes* xviii).

Montreal: McGill University, Conservatory, music representative of 19th-cent. life in Montreal.

Ottawa: National Library.

UNITED STATES.

Ann Arbor, Mich.: University of Michigan, Stellfeld collection [see L. E. Cuyler, G. A. Sutherland, and H. T. David, "The University of Michigan's Purchase of the Stellfeld Music Library" (*Notes* xii)]. Early American music.

Berea, Ohio: Baldwin-Wallace College, Riemenschneider Memorial Bach Library [S. Kenney, *Catalog* (1960)].

Berkeley, Calif.: University of California Music Library, primary sources in early opera scores and librettos (Cortot opera collection), early Italian instrumental music [V. Duckles and M. Elmer, *Thematic Catalog of a Manuscript Collection of Eighteenth-Century Italian Instrumental Music* (1963)]; reference collections of Alfred Einstein and Manfred Bukofzer; MSS of Ernest Bloch [*Autograph Manuscripts of Ernest Bloch at the University of California* (n.d.)].

Bethlehem, Pa.: Archives of the Moravian Church [A. G. Rau and H. T. David, *A Catalogue of Music by American Moravians, 1724–1842* (1938)].

Bloomington, Ind.: Indiana University School of Music, photostats of keyboard sources.

Boston, Mass.: Public Library, Allen A. Brown Reference Collection [*Catalogue,* 3 vols. and suppl. (1910–16)].

Cambridge, Mass.: Harvard University, Isham Memorial Library, microfilms and photostats of MSS and prints of music from the 12th to 18th centuries; originally concerned with early keyboard music, but enlarged to include all kinds of monophonic and polyphonic vocal and instrumental, sacred and secular (early sample listing by W. Apel in *MD* i); Eda Kuhn Loeb Music Library, a strong reference collection of books, scores, recordings. The Houghton Library of rare books at Harvard University contains many music rarities.

Charlottesville, Va.: University of Virginia, Alderman Library, MacKay Smith Collection, strong in 18th-cent. chamber music, trio sonatas.

Chicago, Ill.: Newberry Library, hymnology,

theory, important rarities [*Handbook of the Newberry Library* (1933)].

Cincinnati, Ohio: Hebrew Union College, Jewish music.

Los Angeles, Calif.: University of California at Los Angeles, W. A. Clark Memorial Library, ballad opera, 17th–18th-cent. English music; University Music Library, 17th–18th-cent. librettos, ethnomusicology, American sheet music from 1800.

New Haven, Conn.: Yale University Library, American songbooks, folksongs, carols; Yale Music School Library, Lowell Mason collection, with hundreds of keyboard manuscripts from the library of J. C. Rinck.

New York, N.Y.: Music Division of the Research Library of the Performing Arts (at Lincoln Center), a very comprehensive collection, including early printed music, Americana, and musical portraits [*Catalogue of Jos. W. Drexel's Musical Library* (1869); *Dictionary Catalog of the Music Collection,* 33 vols. (1964), suppl. i (1966); [C. S. Smith], *Early Psalmody in America,* series 1–3 (1938–39); O. Kinkeldey, in *The Library Journal* xl]. Bartók Archives [V. Bator, *The Béla Bartók Archives, History and Catalogue* (1963)]. Columbia University, Music Department, Béla Bartók deposit of southeast European folk music. The Heineman Foundation music collection [E. Waters, in *Notes* vii].

Northampton, Mass.: Smith College, Philip Hale and Alfred Einstein collections (includes Einstein's MS scores of 16th- and 17th-cent. partbooks).

Philadelphia, Pa.: Curtis Institute, Burrell Wagner collection (Ileborgh keyboard tablature); Free Library, Edwin A. Fleisher music collection [*A Descriptive Catalogue,* rev. ed. (1965—)]. Library Company [E. Wolf, *American Song Sheets, Slip Ballads and Poetical Broadsides, 1850–1870* (1963)].

Pittsburgh, Pa.: Carnegie Library; University of Pittsburgh Library; St. Vincent's College [T. Finney, *A Union Catalogue of Music and Books on Music Printed before 1801 in Pittsburgh Libraries,* rev. ed. (1963), suppl. (1964)].

Rochester, N.Y.: Eastman School of Music, Sibley Library, chamber music, French and Russian music, folksong, literature on the violin, rich in primary source materials.

St. Louis, Mo.: St. Louis University, Pope Pius XII Memorial Library [E. C. Krohn, "Music in the Vatican Film Library at Saint Louis University" (*Notes* xiv)].

Salem, Mass.: Essex Institute, Americana [H. E. Johnson, in *Notes* v].

San Francisco, Calif.: San Francisco State College, Frank V. De Bellis collection of Italian music, MSS, early printed music, theoretical works by Italian musicians.

San Marino, Calif.: Huntington Library and Art Gallery, incunabula, early English printed music, Americana [E. N. Backus, *Catalogue of Music in the Huntington Library Printed before 1801* (1949)].

Stanford, Calif.: Stanford University, Memorial Library of Music [N. van Patten, *A Memorial Library of Music* (1950)]. Stanford University Archive of Recorded Sound.

Washington, D.C.: Library of Congress, Music Division (est. 1897), the most notable music collection in the United States. A copyright deposit, it possesses many important manuscripts, old prints, opera scores and librettos, musical Americana, autographs of contemporary composers, as well as many sound recordings of American folk and primitive music. [Special catalogues: *Dramatic Music . . . Full Scores* (1908); *Orchestral Music . . . Scores* (1912); *Catalogue of Early Books on Music (before 1800)* (1913), suppl. (1944); *Catalogue of Opera Librettos Printed before 1800,* 2 vols. (1914)]. Notable acquisitions are cited in the *Report of the Librarian of Congress* (1903—), and in occasional special articles in the Library's *Quarterly Journal of Current Acquisitions* (1943—). The Library issues a series of monumental bibliographical tools in its *A Catalog of Books Represented by Library of Congress Printed Cards,* 167 vols., its *The National Union Catalog,* which maintains a separate cumulative listing of *Music and Phonorecords* (1953—), and its *Catalog of Copyright Entries, Part 3: Musical Compositions* (1906—), in which both published and unpublished music submitted for copyright registration is listed. [F. R. Goff, "Early Music Books in the Rare Books Division of the Library of Congress" (*Notes* vi); George Herzog, *Research in Primitive and Folk Music in the United States* (1936); *Check List of Recorded Songs in the English Language . . . to July 1940,* 3 vols. (1942)]. The Folger Shakespeare Library, Elizabethan printed music, MSS of operas and music related to Shakespeare and his time. Pan-American Union, music of North and South America, particularly folk music.

Watertown, Mass.: Perkins School for the Blind, information on blind musicians of the past, music in Braille circulated nationally.

Worcester, Mass.: American Antiquarian Society, Americana, especially hymn books.

CENTRAL AND SOUTH AMERICA. Cathedral and monastery archives in Mexico, at Mexico City, Morelia, and Puebla, and at Lima, Peru; 16th–18th-cent. church music [E. T. Stanford and L. B. Spiess, *Some Preliminary Information Concerning Mexican Musical Archives* (1966)]. The resources of these archives have been described in part by Robert Stevenson in *Music in Mexico* [1952] and *id., The Music of Peru* [1960].

Rio de Janeiro, Brazil: Biblioteca Nacional [F. C. Lange, in *Revista de estudios musicales* i; C. S. Smith, "Music Publications in Brazil" (*Notes* iv)].

Santiago, Cuba: Cathedral archives [P. Hernández Balaguer, *Catálogo de Música de los Archivos de la Catedral de Santiago de Cuba y del Museo Bacardí* (1961)].

EUROPE.
AUSTRIA

Admont: Stiftsbibliothek, MS missals [J. Köck, *Handschriftliche Missalien in Steiermark* (1916)].

Göttweig: Benedictine Abbey, 16th-cent. Meistersinger MSS, 18th-cent. MSS, Merulo keyboard music, portions of the library of Aloys Fuchs [P. L. Koller, "Inventar der Göttweiger Kantorei 1612" (*Das Waldviertel,* 1955)].

Graz: University Library [A. Kern, *Die Handschriften der Universitätsbibliothek Graz* (1939–40, 1956)].

Klosterneuburg: Stiftsbibliothek, 12th–16th-cent. MSS, 16th-cent. printed music [H. Pfeiffer and B. Černík, *Catalogus codicum manu scriptorum,* 2 vols. (1922–31)].

Kremsmünster: Benedictine Abbey, liturgical music, 16th-cent. MSS and printed music, tablatures [R. Flotzinger, *Die Lautentabulaturen des Stiftes Kremsmünster* (1965); other sources cited in A. Kellner, *Musikgeschichte des Stiftes Kremsmünster* (1956)].

Melk: Benedictine Monastery Library, 13th–14th-cent. liturgical MSS, 16th-cent. Mass MSS, J. Haydn collection [*Catalogus codicum manu scriptorum,* i (1889)].

St. Paul (Lavant Valley): Benedictine Monastery Library, troubadour MSS, early treatises [H. Federhofer, in *KJ* xxxv].

Salzburg: Cathedral Chapter, MSS of 16th-cent. vocal polyphony; Mozart Museum and Mozarteum, Mozart MSS [*Katalog des Mozart-Museums,* 4th ed. (1906)]; Abbey of St. Peter, compositions by M. Haydn; Museum Carolino-Augusteum [J. Gassner, *Die Musikaliensammlung im Salzburger Museum Carolino Augusteum* (1962)], Mozart MSS, Benevoli's 53-voice Mass.

Tulln: Church of St. Stephan [K. Schnürl, *Das alte Musikarchiv der Pfarrkirche St. Stephan in Tulln* (1964)].

Vienna: National Library [L. Nowak, "Die Musiksammlungen der Oesterreichischen National-Bibliothek" (*Musikerziehung* vi); *id.,* "Die Musikhandschriften" (*Die Oesterreichische Nationalbibliothek. Festschrift* (1948)]. Important holdings such as the Fugger music collection [R. Schaal, "Die Musikbibliothek von Raimund Fugger d. J." (*AM* xxix], the d'Este music collection [R. Haas, *Die Estensischen Musikalien: thematisches Verzeichnis* (1927)], the Palatine Library [J. Mantuani, *Tabulae codicum manuscriptorum . . . in Bibliotheca Palatina Vindobonensi asservatorum* (1864–99), especially vols. ix and x]; an archive established by Heinrich Schenker and Anthony van Hoboken containing photofacsimiles of the works of the major Viennese composers. Gesellschaft der Musikfreunde, MSS, letters, portraits, etc., of Viennese masters [K. Geiringer, history of the collection, in *Anbruch: Monatsschrift für moderne Musik* xix; E. Mandyczewski, in *Zusatz-Band zur Geschichte der K.K. Gesellschaft der Musikfreunde in Wien* (1912), surveys the contents of the library, museum, and archive]. Schottenkloster, early liturgical MSS, 16th-cent. MSS and printings [A. Hübl, *Catalogus codicum manuscriptorum qui in bibliotheca Monasterii B.M.V. ad Scotos Vindobonae servantur* (1899); *id., Die Inkunabeln der Bibliothek des Stiftes Schotten in Wien* (1904)]. University Library, 16th–17th-cent. lute music and theoretical works. City Library, Schubert MSS and 19th-cent. dance music. Minoritenkonvent, MSS and printed 17th-cent. organ and vocal music [F. W. Riedel, *Das Musikarchiv im Minoritenkonvent zu Wien* (1963), in *Catalogus musicus* i]. St. Peter's Church [C. Rouland, *Katalog des Musik-Archives der St. Peterskirche in Wien* (1908)].

BELGIUM. For general information, see J.-G. Prod'homme, "Les Institutions musicales (Bibliothèques et Archives) en Belgique et en Hollande" (*SIM* xv); C. van den Borren, "Inventaire des manuscrits de musique polyphonique qui se trouvent en Belgique" (*AM* v–vi); S. Clercx, in *Alumni* (Brussels) xvi.

Brussels: Royal Library, collections of C. J. E. van Hulthem [C. A. Voisin, *Bibliotheca Hulthemiana*, 6 vols. (1836–37)] and F. J. Fétis [*Catalogue de la Bibliothèque de F. J. Fétis* (1877)], MSS from monastery libraries and the Dukes of Burgundy [J. van den Gheyn, *Catalogue des manuscrits*, 12 vols. (1901–36); B. Huys, *Catalogue des imprimés musicaux des XVe, XVIe et XVIIe siècles* (1965)]. Conservatoire Royal de Musique, MSS, 16th-cent. opera librettos, K. P. E. Bach collection [A. Wotquenne, *Catalogue de la bibliothèque*, 4 vols. and suppl., incompl., (1898–1912)]; Holtenfeltz collection [C. van den Borren, "Les Fonds de musique ancienne de la Collégiale SS. Michel et Gudule à Bruxelles" (*Annuaire du Conservatoire*, 1930)].

Liège: Conservatoire Royal de Musique, Grétry collection, 17th–18th-cent. local composers, Fonds Terry [E. Monseur, *Catalogue*, 4 vols. in one (n.d.)].

Oudenarde: St. Walpurgakerk, 18th-cent. church music [*Liste générale de la musique appartenant à l'église parochiale de St. Walpurga à Audenarde* (n.d.)].

CZECHOSLOVAKIA. For general information, see D. Plamenac, "Music Libraries in Eastern Europe" (*Notes* xix). The University Library at Brün (Brno) publishes an accessions list for the principal music libraries of Czechoslovakia [*Přírůstky hudebnin v československých knihovnách* (1956—)]. M. J. Terrayová has compiled thematic catalogues of MSS in two Czech music archives, the Pfarrkirche of Púchov and the archive of the Prílesky-Ostrolúcky family [*Hudobnovedné Stúdie* iv, 1960].

Prague: University Library, MSS and printings of 11th–17th-cent. treatises, Bohemian songs, and 14th–16th-cent. Easter Mysteries, lute books, Kubelik violin collection, Lobkowitz Archive [P. Nettl, "Musicalia der fürstlich Lobkowitzschen Bibliothek in Raudnitz" (Verein für Geschichte der Deutschen in Bóhmen, *Mitteilungen des Vereines* . . . lviii)]; National Museum, music library of Emilián Troldy [*Hudební sbírka Emiliána Troldy*, catalogue by A. Buchner (1954)]; Conservatory of Music [R. Procházka, *Aus fünf Jahrhunderten: Musikschätze des Prager Konservatoriums* (1911)]; Municipal Library, Smetana Music Library, 78,000 printings of music, mostly Slavic; Cathedral Chapter Library [A. Podlaha, *Catalogus collectionis operum artis musicae* (1926)].

DENMARK.

Aarhus: Statsbibliothek, copyright deposit library [*Fagkataloger 3: Musikalier,* rev. ed. (1951–57); 4: *Musik,* rev. ed. (1946—)].

Copenhagen: Royal Library, organ tablature, rare Antwerp and Copenhagen printings [E. Jørgensen, *Catalogus codicum latinorum medii ævi Bibliothecæ Regiæ Hafniensis,* 2 parts (1923, '26)]; University Library [A. Krarup, *Katalog over Universitetsbibliotekets Haandskrifter,* 2 vols. (1929–35)]; Museum of Music History, collection of historical musical instruments [A. Hammerich, *Das Musikhistorische Museum . . . beschreibender Katalog* (1911)]; Kommunebibliotekerne (Public Library) [*Katalog over musik og musiklitteratur,* 5 vols. (1954–56)].

ENGLAND. See GREAT BRITAIN.

FINLAND.

Helsinki: University Library, collection of fragmentary MSS from medieval liturgical books [T. E. Haapanen, *Verzeichnis der mittelalterlichen Handschriftenfragmente in der Universitätsbibliothek zu Helsingfors,* I. Missalia (1922), II. Gradualia, Lectionaria Missae (1925), III. Breviaria (1932)].

FRANCE. For general bibl. see: *Catalogue général des manuscrits des bibliothèques publiques de France,* I. *Paris* (various dates); II. *Départements* (old series, 1849–85; new series, 1886—); N. Bridgman, "Musique profane italienne des 16e et 17e siècles dans les bibliothèques françaises" (*Fontes artis musicae* [1955], 40ff); P. Chaillon, "Les fonds musicaux de quelques bibliothèques de province" (*Fontes artis musicae* [1955], 151ff); E. H. Fellowes, "The Philidor Manuscripts: Paris, Versailles, Tenbury" (*ML* xii); F. Lesure, "Richesses musicologiques des bibliothèques provinciales de France" (*RdM* [1950], 109–18).

Aix-en-Provence: Bibliothèque Mejanes, troubadour MS and lute songs [*Catalogue général des manuscrits . . . (Départements)* xvi and suppl. in xl, xlv, xlix].

Amiens: Bibliothèque Communale. 17th-cent. treatises and psalters, 18th-cent. operas and songs [for MSS, *Catalogue général des manuscrits . . . (Départments)* xix and suppl. in xl].

Cambrai: Bibliothèque Municipale, Burgundian and Flemish church music and part songs [A. J. Le Glay, *Catalogue . . . des manuscrits de la Bibliothèque de Cambrai* (1831); E. de Coussemaker, *Notice sur les collections musicales de la*

Bibliothèque de Cambrai et des autres villes du Département du Nord (1843)].

Chantilly: Musée Condé, 16th-cent. collections, partly from Cigogne.

Colmar: Consistoire Protestant, 16th-cent. psalters in all languages.

Lille: Bibliothèque Municipale, 17th–19th-cent. opera scores, MSS (severe losses from fire in 1916) [*Catalogue des ouvrages sur la musique et des compositions musicales de la Bibliothèque de Lille* (1879)].

Marseilles: Bibliothèque de la Ville, 12th-cent. liturgical MSS [*Catalogue général des manuscrits . . . (Départements)* xv and suppl. xlii]; Sainte-Madeleine, 12th-cent. liturgical MSS.

Montpellier: Bibliothèque de la Faculté de Médecine, 9th-cent. antiphonary, 13th-cent. motets, 14th-cent. chansons [*Catalogue général des manuscrits . . . (Dèpartements)* i (old series, 1849) and suppl. xlii (new series)].

Orléans: Bibliothèque de la Ville, 12th-cent. mystery plays, 16th-cent. sacred and secular music [*Catalogue général des manuscrits . . . (Départements)* xii and suppl. xlii].

Paris: For general information, see E. Leroy, *Guide pratique des Bibliothèques de Paris* (1937). Bibliothèque Nationale, extremely rich for all periods from the earliest, including 9th-cent. MSS with notation, troubadour songs, French and Italian 14th-cent. music, 15th–16th-cent. *chansonniers;* copyright deposit [J. Écorcheville, *Catalogue du fonds de musique ancienne de la Bibliothèque Nationale,* 8 vols. (1910–14); P. Lauer, *Catalogue général des manuscrits latins,* 4 vols., (1939–58)]; Bibliothèque du Conservatoire, in the *Réserve,* has 10,000 unique, valuable printed music and MSS, autographs, scores and rarities, Philidor MSS of early French instrumental music [J. B. Weckerlin, *Bibliothèque du Conservatoire national . . . catalogue bibliographique . . . de la Réserve* (1885)]; Fonds Blancheton, instrumental music pre-1750 [L. de la Laurencie, *Inventaire critique du Fonds Blancheton,* 2 vols. (1930–31)]; Bibliothèque de l'Opéra, MSS of operas, librettos, history of the lyric theater [T. de Lajarte, *Catalogue historique, chronologique, anecdotique,* 2 vols. (1878)]; Bibliothèque de l'Arsenal, MSS, 13th-cent. *chansonnier* [*Catalogue général des manuscrits . . . (Paris)* i–ix; suppl. in *Catalogue général des manuscrits . . . (Départements)* xliii, xlv; L. de Laurencie and A. Gastoué, *Catalogue des livres de musique de la Bibliothèque de l'Arsenal* (1936)]; Bibliothèque Ste. Geneviève [C. Kohler, *Catalogue des manuscrits,* 3 vols. (1893–98)]; Institut

de Musicologie, medieval music, folklore, Aubry and Guilmant collections; Société des Concerts, library and archives of the 18th-cent. *concert spirituel;* Private collection of Geneviève Thibault, 16th-cent. printed music, French and Italian, MSS of 17th-cent. Italian cantatas; Private collection of André Meyer [F. Lesure, *Collection musicale André Meyer* (1961)].

Strasbourg: Bibliothèque de l'Institut de Musicologie, University Faculty of Letters, autographs, O. Jahn and G. Jacobsthal collections [F. Ludwig, *Die älteren Musikwerke der . . . Bibliothek des "Akademischen Gesang-vereins" Strassburg* (1913)].

Tours: Bibliothèque de la Ville, 9th–10th-cent. MSS with neumes, 12th-cent. mystery plays, J. de Muris MS, 15th–18th-cent. liturgies, 17th-cent. motets, organ music (800 of 2,000 MSS remained after 1940 fire) [A. J. Dorange, *Catalogue descriptif . . . des manuscrits de la Bibliothèque de Tours* (1875); *Catalogue général des manuscrits . . . (Départements)* xxxvii; H. Quittard, "Un musicien oublié du XVIIe siècle français: G. Bouzignac" (*SIM* vi)].

Valenciennes: Bibliothèque Municipale, 9th-cent. treatises [*Catalogue général des manuscrits . . . (Départements)* xxv; E. de Coussemaker, *Notices sur les collections musicales de la Bibliothèque de Cambrai et des autres villes du Département du Nord* (1843)].

Versailles: Bibliothèque Municipale, 17th–18th-cent. MSS, 16th–19th-cent. prints [*Catalogue général des manuscrits . . . (Départements)* ix and suppl. xliii; *Manuscrits musicaux de la Bibliothèque de Versailles* (1884); A. Tessier, "Un Catalogue de la Bibliothèque de la Musique du Roi" (*RdM* [1931], 106–17, 172–89)].

GERMANY. General information in the *Deutscher Gesamtkatalog* (1935—); *Deutsche Musikbibliographie,* monthly with annual cumulations, *Jahresverzeichnis der deutschen Musikalien und Musikschriften* (complete except vol. xciii, 1944). W. Kahl and W. Martin Luther, *Repertorium der Musikwissenschaft* (1953), a union catalogue of musicological literature in German libraries. For wartime losses see Georg Leyh, *Die deutschen wissenschaftlichen Bibliotheken nach dem Krieg* (1947).

Augsburg: Staats- und Stadtbibliothek, MSS and printed music from monasteries and the library of Raimund Fugger [R. Schaal, "Die Musikbibliothek von Raimund Fugger d. J." (*AM* xxix); H. M. Schletterer, in suppl. to *MfM* x, xi; *id.,* "Aktenmaterial aus dem städtischen

Archiv zu Augsburg" (*MfM* xxv, xxx)]; Bibliothek des bischöflichen Ordinariats [B. Kraft, *Die Handschriften der Bischöfl. Ordinariatsbibliothek* (1934)].

Bamberg: Staatliche Bibliothek, liturgical MSS with neumes; 13th-cent. motet MS [F. Leitschuh and H. Fischer, *Katalog der Handschriften der Königlichen Bibliothek zu Bamberg*, 3 vols. (1887–1912)].

Bayreuth: Haus Wahnfried, Wagner archives.

Berlin: Deutsche (formerly Preussische) Staatsbibliothek (this library, now in the East sector of Berlin, has not regained all of its great prewar music collection; many of its holdings are in Marburg and Tübingen [R. S. Hill, "The Former Prussian State Library," (*Notes* iii); M. Cremer, in *Zweiter Weltkongress der Musikbibliotheken, 1950* (1951); for prewar holdings [W. Altmann, in *ZMW* ii-ix; J. Wolf, "Neuerwerbungen der Musikabteilung der Staatsbibliothek Berlin 1928–1931," (*AM* iii); *id., Zur Geschichte der Musikabteilung der Staatsbibliothek* (1929); K.-H. Köhler, "Die Musikabteilung," *Deutsche Staatsbibliothek, 1661–1961*, 2 vols. (1961)]; The Amalienbibliothek, a collection formed in the late 18th century by a sister of Frederick the Great, is contained, in part, in the Deutsche Staatsbibliothek [E. R. Blechschmidt, *Die Amalien-Bibliothek, Musikbibliothek der Prinzessin Anna Amalia von Preussen* (1965)]; Hochschule für Musik, in West sector, MSS of *c.* 1500, Spitta library, rare 17th–18th-cent. prints; Akademie für deutsche Kirchen- und Schulmusik, school-music collection now in Hochschule für Musik Library, sacred music now in East Berlin. Destroyed or heavily damaged during World War II; Bibliothek zum Grauen Kloster, Königliche Hausbibliothek, Joachimsthalisches Gymnasium.

Bonn: Library of the Musicological Institute [W. Virneisel, *Ch.B. Klein und seine Sammlungen musikalischer Handschriften* (1924)]; University Library [T. Clasen, "Die musikalischen Autographen der Universitäts-Bibliothek Bonn" (*CP Schmidt-Görg*)]; Beethoven House and Archive [J. Schmidt-Görg, *Katalog der Handschriften des Beethoven-Hauses und Beethoven-Archivs Bonn* (1935)].

Breslau: See Wroclaw, Poland.

Cologne: Cathedral Chapter Library [G. Göller, *Die Leiblsche Sammlung, Katalog der Musikalien der Kölner Domcapelle* (1964)]; Universitäts- und Stadtbibliothek, unique Lassus works, 16th-cent. tablatures and printed music [W. Kahl, *Katalog der in der Universitäts- und Stadtbibliothek Köln vorhandenen Musikdrucke* (1958); *id., Die alten Musikalien der Kölner Universitäts- und Stadtbibliothek* (1953), repr. from *Jahrbuch des Kölnischen Geschichtsverein*].

Darmstadt: Hofbibliothek, MSS and printed music, 15th–18th-cent. [F. W. E. Roth, in *MfM* xx]; Internationales Musikinstitut (Kranichsteiner Musikinstitut), a library of contemporary music [E. Thomas, *Katalog* (1966)].

Donaueschingen: Library of Prince Fürstenberg, 2,200 musical MSS [C. A. Barack. *Die Handschriften der Fürstlich-Fürstenbergischen Hofbibliothek zu Donaueschingen* (1865)].

Dresden: Sächsische Landesbibliothek, 7,555 musical MSS remain from the war [R. Eitner and O. Kade, *Katalog* (suppl. to *MfM* xxi, xxii); L. Schmidt and A. Reichert, *Katalog der Handschriften der Königl. öffentlichen Bibliothek* iv (1923)].

Eisenach: Richard Wagner library, Wagner literature and documents [N. Oesterlein, *Katalog einer Richard Wagner-Bibliothek*, 4 vols. (1882–95)].

Erlangen: University Library, valuable MSS and printed material [*Katalog der Handschriften der Universitätsbibliothek Erlangen*, rev. ed. (1928—); F. Krautwurst, *Die Heilbronner Chorbücher der Universitätsbibliothek Erlangen* (1956)].

Frankfurt: Stadt- und Universitätsbibliothek, which houses surviving local libraries [C. Süss, *Kirchliche Musikhandschriften des XVII. und XVIII. Jahrhunderts* (1926); *Jahrbuch der Musikwelt* (1949–50)].

Freiberg: See O. Kade, *Die älteren Musikalien der Stadt Freiberg in Sachsen* (suppl. to *MfM* xx).

Göttingen: University Library, rare 15th–16th-cent. works, 1,000 17th-cent. song books [A. Quantz, *Die Musikwerke der Kgl. Universitäts-Bibliothek in Göttingen* (suppl. to *MfM* xv)].

Halle: Händel-Haus, scores, documents and iconography related to Handel and his contemporaries [*Katalog zu den Sammlungen des Händel-Hauses in Halle*, 3 vols. (1961–64)]; University, Musicological Seminar library, Robert Franz collection [*MfM* xxvi, 42]; Waisenhausbibliothek, 17th–18th-cent. hymnals, music and theory; Kirchenmusikalische Bibliothek, 7,000 vols. on church music [*Werkverzeichnis 1925, 1930, 1936; Jahrbuch der Musikwelt* (1949–50)].

Hamburg: Staats- und Universitätsbibliothek (heavy war damage), 16th-cent. theoretical works, English music; Völkerkunde-Museum, exotic and primitive music and instruments;

Landeskirchliche Musikbücherei; Hamburger Musikbücherei, theater music [A. Eckhoff, *Oper, Operette, Singspiel: ein Katalog* (1965)].

Jena: University Library, 14th–16th-cent. songs, liturgical MSS [K. E. Roediger, *Die geistlichen Musikhandschriften der Universitäts-Bibliothek Jena,* 2 vols. (1935)].

Kassel: Landesbibliothek, 16th–17th-cent. MSS and printed books [C. Israël, *Uebersichtlicher Katalog der Musikalien der ständischen Landesbibliothek zu Cassel* (1881)]. Deutsches Musikgeschichtliches Archiv, central collection of early musical scores and books in microfilm [H. Heckmann, *Katalog der Filmsammlung,* 7 vols. (1955–65)].

Kiel: Schleswig-Holsteinische Landesbibliothek, University Library, and Musicological Seminar Library [all three libraries catalogued in K. Hortschansky, *Katalog der Kieler Musiksammlungen* (1963)].

Königsberg: Staats- und Universitätsbibliothek, Bibliotheca Gottholdiana, 55,000 vols. MSS and printed music, 16th–19th cent. [J. Müller, *Die musikalischen Schätze . . . zu Königsberg in Pr. aus dem Nachlasse F. A. Gotthold's* (1870)].

Leipzig: Musikbibliothek Peters, MSS and rare prints, 15th–18th cent. [R. Schwartz, in *JMP* xxvi; E. Schmitz, in *JMP* xlvi–xlvii]; Town Library, Bach, Wagner, Breitkopf und Härtel collections; University Library, librettos, theoretical works; St. Thomas Church Archives, MSS.

Lübeck: Bibliothek der Hansestadt, *c.* 13,000 vols., including Buxtehude, Tunder, Frederick the Great [C. Stiehl, *Katalog der Musiksammlung auf der Stadtbibliothek zu Lübeck* (1893); *id.,* "Die Stadtbibliothek in Lübeck" (*MfM* xvi); W. Stahl, *Musik Bücher der Lübecker Stadtbibliothek* (1927); *id., Die Musik-abteilung der Lübecker Stadtbibliothek in ihren älteren Beständen* (1931); *Jahrbuch der Musikwelt* (1949–50)]; Marienkirche collection [C. Stiehl, "Musiksammlung der St. Marienkirche," in *Einladung zu den . . . Prüfungen und Redeübungen der Schüler des Katharineums zu Lübeck* (1893)].

Lüneburg: Town Library, 16th–19th-cent. MSS and printed material, 17th-cent. North German organ tablatures, motets, and theatrical works [F. Welter, *Katalog der Musikalien der Ratsbücherei Lüneburg* (1950)].

Mainz: Town Library, 15th–16th-cent. partbooks; 16th–18th-cent. theoretical works [F. W. E. Roth, in *MfM* xxi].

Marburg: Westdeutsche Bibliothek, 170,000 vols. from the former Prussian State Library music collection [see Berlin, Deutsche Staatsbibliothek].

Munich: Bayerische Staatsbibliothek, 15th–17th-cent. MSS and printed works, first editions from the classical and romantic periods [J. J. Maier, *Die musikalischen Handschriften der K. Hof- und Staatsbibliothek in Muenchen* (1879)]; Städtische Musikbibliothek, folksong collection, Bavarian music MSS; Frauenkirche, 16th–19th-cent. prints and MS choirbooks [J. Jenne, *Die Chorbibliothek der Münchener Frauenkirche* (1950), typescript; K. G. Fellerer, in *CP Wagner*]; Bayerisches Hauptstaatsarchiv, documents on music history; Staatstheater, early 19th-cent. theater music, librettos, etc. [R. Schaal, "Die vor 1801 gedruckten Libretti des Theatermuseums München" (*MF* x–xiv)].

Münster: Bischöfl. Dios. Archiv, Santini collection [F. Santini, *Catalogo della musica esistente presso Fortunato Santini in Roma* (1820); J. Killing, *Kirchenmusikalische Schätze der Bibliothek des Abbate Fortunato Santini,* (1910); K. G. Fellerer, *Die musikalischen Schätze der Santinischen Sammlung: Führer durch die Ausstellung der Universitäts-Bibliothek* (1929); *id.,* "Verzeichnis der kirchenmusikalischen Werke der Santinischen Sammlung" (*KJ* xxvi–xxxiii)].

Regensburg (Ratisbon): Staatliche Bibliothek, old MSS and printed works [C. T. Gmeiner, *Kurze Beschreibung der Handschriften in der Stadtbibliothek* (1780?)]; Proske Music Library, 13th–18th-cent. MSS [K. Weinmann, "Die Proskesche Musikbibliothek in Regensburg" (*KJ* xxiv)]; Court Library of Prince Thurn und Taxis, MSS of late 18th-cent. court music [S. Färber, *Verzeichnis der vollständigen Opern, Melodramen und Ballette, wie auch der Operntextbücher der fürstlich Thurn und Taxisschen Hofbibliothek* (1936)]; Institut für Musikforschung, choral and folk music [F. Hoerburger, *Katalog der europäischen Volksmusik im Schallarchiv* (1952)].

Stuttgart: Württembergische Landesbibliothek, 2,500 MSS and 7,500 printed volumes [C. Gottwald, *Die Handschriften der Württembergischen Landesbibliothek Stuttgart* (1964); A. Halm, catalog of 16th–17th-cent. MSS, in suppl. to *MfM* xxxiv–xxxv; H. Marquardt, *Die Stuttgarter Chorbücher* (1936)].

Tübingen: University Library, autographs and several old printings of theory formerly in the Prussian State Library [see under Berlin, Deutsche Staatsbibliothek].

Wolfenbüttel: Herzog-August-Bibliothek, two 13th-cent. MSS of organa [O. von Heinemann, *Die Handschriften der Herzoglichen Bibliothek zu Wolfenbüttel,* 4 vols. (1884–1913); E. Vogel, *Die Handschriften nebst den älteren Druckwerken der Musikabtheilung* (1890)].

Zwickau: Robert Schumann Museum; Ratsschulbibliothek [R. Vollhardt, *Bibliographie der Musik-werke in der Ratsschulbibliothek zu Zwickau* (suppl. to *MfM* xxv–xxviii)].

GREAT BRITAIN. General: W. H. Frere, *Bibliotheca Musico-Liturgica, a Descriptive Hand List of the Musical and Latin-liturgical MSS of the Middle Ages Preserved in the Libraries of Great Britain and Ireland,* 2 vols. (1901–32); E. B. Schnapper, *The British Union-Catalogue of Early Music Printed before the year 1801,* 2 vols. (1957).

Cambridge: For general information, see J. Vlasto, in *MR* xii; V. Duckles, "Some Observations of Music Libraries at Cambridge" (*Notes* ix). University Library, MSS dating from the 11th cent., English lute tablatures, F. T. Arnold collection of works on thoroughbass practice, early printings [*Catalog of the Manuscripts preserved in the Library of the University of Cambridge,* 6 vols. (1856–67)]; Clare College, Cecil Sharp folksong collection, 18th-cent. English organ music; Corpus Christi College [M. R. James, *A Descriptive Catalogue of the Manuscripts,* 2 vols. (1909–12)]; Christ's College [*M. R.* James, *A Descriptive Catalogue of the Western Manuscripts* (1905)]; Jesus College [M. R. James, *A Descriptive Catalogue of the Manuscripts in the Library of Jesus College* (1895)]; Magdalene College, psalters, 16th-cent. vocal MSS, the library of Samuel Pepys [*Bibliotheca Pepysiana,* 4 vols. (1914–40)]; Pembroke College [M. R. James, *A Descriptive Catalogue of the Manuscripts* (1905)]; Pendlebury Library, University Faculty of Music; Peterhouse College, 16th–17th-cent. sacred vocal MSS, 17th-cent. MS organ music [A. Hughes, *Catalogue of the Musical Manuscripts at Peterhouse* (1953)]; Trinity College [M. R. James, *The Western Manuscripts in the Library of Trinity College,* 4 vols. (1900–04)]; the Union Society, Erskine Allan collection; Fitzwilliam Museum, MSS of 17th–18th-cent. harpsichord music, French operas and motets, Italian cantatas, Handel collection [J. A. Fuller-Maitland and A. H. Mann, *Catalogue of the Music in the Fitzwilliam Museum* (1893); M. R. James, *A Descriptive Catalogue of the Manuscripts* (1895)].

Dundee: Free Library, Wighton collection of works relating to Scottish music.

Edinburgh: University Library, old Scottish music, Gaelic song records [C. R. Borland, *A Descriptive Catalogue of the Western Mediæval Manuscripts* (1916)]; Reid Music Library of the University Music Faculty, Tovey, Niecks, and Weiss collections [H. Gál, *Catalogue of Manuscripts, Printed Music and Books on Music up to 1850 in the . . . (Reid Library)* (1941)]; National Library of Scotland, MSS of bagpipe and country dance music, Glen collection [*Catalogue of Manuscripts Acquired since 1925* (1938—)].

Glasgow: University Library, Euing collection of old music [*Catalogue of the Musical Library of the Late Wm. Euing, Esq.* (1878)]; Farmer collections of Scottish music and Oriental music, from 9th century on, and Stillie, Zavertal, and Drysdale collections.

London: British Museum, numerous collections, MSS and printed music [A. Hughes-Hughes, *A Catalogue of Manuscript Music in the British Museum,* 3 vols. (1906–09), repr. (1964–65); [*List*] now *Catalogue of Additions to the Manuscripts in the British Museum,* for years 1836–1920 (1843–1933); W. Barclay Squire, *Catalogue of Printed Music Published between 1487 and 1800 now in the British Museum,* 2 vols. and 2 suppl. (1912—); K. Meyer and P. Hirsch, *Katalog der Musikbibliothek Paul Hirsch,* 4 vols. (1928–47); *Accessions, Part 53: Music in the Hirsch Library* (1951); *Accessions, 3rd series— Part 291B: Books in the Hirsch Library with supplementary List of Music* (1959)]; Royal Music Library, now part of the permanent collection of the British Museum [W. Barclay Squire and H. Andrews, *Catalogue of the King's Music Library,* 3 vols. (1927–29)]; Royal College of Music [W. Barclay Squire, *Catalogue of Printed Music in the Library of the Royal College of Music* (1909); *id., Catalogue of the Manuscripts in the Library* (1931), typescript catalogue of more than 4,000 MSS; W. H. Husk, *Catalogue of the Library of the Sacred Harmonic Society* (1872), now incorporated into the Royal College collection]; Royal Academy of Music, autograph MSS, glees, rare 18th-cent. instrumental music [*A Catalogue of the Angelina Goetz Library* (1904); F. Corder, *A History of the Royal Academy of Music* (1922)]; Trinity College of Music, Fletcher collection of old instruments; Westminster Abbey, 17th–18th-cent. English and Italian MSS [W. Barclay Squire, *Musik-katalog der Bibliothek der Westminster-Abtei in London* (suppl. to *MfM* xxxv)]; Lambeth Palace, sacred music [M. R. James and C. Jenkins, *A Descriptive Catalogue of the Manuscripts in the Library of Lambeth Palace* (1930–32)]; Guildhall Library, Gresham Music Library [*A Catalogue of the Printed Books and Manuscripts deposited in Guildhall Library* (1965)].

Manchester: Henry Watson Music Library, 18th-cent. MSS and printed music, Newman Flower Handel collection.

Oxford: Bodleian Library, MSS dating from the 10th cent., including the Burgundian school [Dom Anselm Hughes, *Medieval Polyphony in the Bodleian Library* (1951); W. Frere, *Bibliotheca Musico-Liturgica* i (1901); N. G. Wilson and D. I. Stefanović, *Manuscripts of Byzantine Chant in Oxford* (1963)]; 16th–18th-cent. MSS [F. Madan, *A Summary Catalogue of Western Manuscripts in the Bodleian Library,* 7 vols. (1895–1953)], and rare printed works, especially English; Faculty of Music, Terry Bach collection, Heron-Allen violin collection, and portrait collections; Christ Church College, old English MSS [G. E. P. Arkwright, *Catalogue of Music in the Library of Christ Church, Oxford,* 2 vols. (1915–23); A. Hiff, *Catalogue of printed music published prior to 1801 now in the Library of Christ Church, Oxford* (1919)]; Oriel College, 17th–18th-cent. printed music.

Tenbury: St. Michael's College, Gore Ouseley collection of rare treatises and old English MSS, Toulouse-Philidor collection of 17th–19th-cent. French operatic works and motets [E. H. Fellowes, *The Catalogue of Manuscripts . . . of St. Michael's College, Tenbury* (1934); E. H. Fellowes, in *ML* xii].

GREECE.

Athens: The Gennadion, Byzantine MSS, Greek church and folk music.

Mount Athos: Monasteries, important Byzantine musical MSS.

Patmos: St. John's Monastery, Byzantine MSS.

HUNGARY.

Budapest: National Széchénhi Library, Esterházy Archive of Haydn scores and documents, autograph letters of Haydn, Liszt, and Hungarian musicians [D. Bartha and L. Somfai, "Catalogue raisonné der Esterházy-Opernsammlung" (*Haydn als Opernkapellmeister,* 1960)]; J. Vécsey, *Haydns Werke in der Musiksammlung der Nationalbibliothek Széchényi in Budapest* (1959); O. Gombosi, "Die Musikalien der Pfarrkirche zu St. Aegidi in Bártfa" (*CP Wolf*)]; Hungarian Academy of Sciences, Bartók-Kodály collections of Hungarian folk music.

IRELAND.

Dublin: National Library, Irish and Scottish books of songs and country dances, early ballad operas and songsheets (mostly 18th-cent.); Irish Academy of Music, Antient Concerts Society library; St. Patrick's Cathedral, Archbishop Marsh's Library, MSS and printed music, 16th–17th cent., lute pieces and instrumental fantasies [N. J. D. White and J. R. Scott, *Catalogue of the Manuscripts remaining in Marsh's Library* (1913); N. J. D. White, *An Account of Archbishop Marsh's Library, Dublin . . . with a Note on Autographs by Newport B. White* (1926)]; Trinity College, Ebenezer Prout Library; copyright deposit [T. K. Abbott, *Catalogue of the Manuscripts in the Library* (1900)].

ITALY. For contents of important musical collections, see the Bulletins (*Bollettino* or *Pubblicazioni*) of the *Associazione dei Musicologi Italiani* (1909–41?). For MSS, see A. Sorbelli and others, *Inventari dei manoscritti delle biblioteche d'Italia* (1890—), partial index in lxvi, and G. Gabrieli, *Notizie statistiche, storiche, bibliografiche delle collezioni di manoscritti oggi conservati nelle biblioteche italiane* (1936).

Bologna: Civico Museo Bibliografico Musicale (G. B. Martini Music Library), one of the most important music libraries, especially for Italian publications [G. Gaspari and U. Sesini, *Catalogo della Biblioteca del Liceo Musicale di Bologna,* 5 vols. (1890–1943) repr., 4 vols. (1961); F. Vatielli, *La Biblioteca del Liceo Musicale di Bologna* (1916)]; Biblioteca Universitaria, 11th- and 15th-cent. MSS [F. X. Haberl, "Wilhelm du Fay" (*VMW* i, 475ff); A. Sorbelli and others, *Inventari dei manoscritti delle biblioteche d'Italia* xix; F. Liuzzi, "I codici musicali conservati nella Biblioteca Universitaria di Bologna" (*La Rinascita Musicale* i [1909]); L. Frati, in *RMI* xxiii]; San Petronio, church archives, 16th-cent. vocal polyphony, 17th–18th-cent. music for strings and solo instruments [A. Bonora and E. Giani, *Catalogo delle opere musicali . . . città di Bologna,* in *Pubblicazioni dell'Associazione dei musicologi italiani,* series ii (1914–39); L. Frati, *I Corali della Basilica di S. Petronio in Bologna* (1896); J. Berger, in *MQ* xxxvii; K. Jeppesen, in *AM* xiii, 30]; Archinginnasio [A. Sorbelli and others, *Inventari dei manoscritti delle biblioteche d'Italia* xxx, liii].

Florence: Biblioteca Nazionale Centrale,

Magliabechiana and Palatina collections, 12th–15th-cent. theoretical works, 13th-cent. *laude*, 15th–18th-cent. sacred and secular works [A. Sorbelli and others, *Inventari dei manoscritti delle biblioteche d'Italia* vii–xiii; B. Becherini, *Catalogo dei manoscritti musicali della Biblioteca Nazionale di Firenze* (1959)]; Biblioteca Mediceo-Laurenziana, liturgical MSS, Squarcialupi Codex, Magnus Liber Organi, 10th–15th-cent. Ashburnham MSS [C. Paoli, *I codici Ashburnhamiani della R. Biblioteca Mediceo-Laurenziana* i (1887–89)]; Bibliotheca Riccardiana *Catalogus codicum manuscriptorum qui in Bibliotheca Riccardiana Florentiniae adservantur* (1756); R. Morpurgo, *I Manoscritti della R. Biblioteca Riccardiana* i (1893–1900)]; Conservatorio Luigi Cherubini, 15th–17th-cent. MSS, rare theoretical and practical works, musical instruments [R. Gandolfi, C. Cordara and A. Bonaventura, *Catalogo delle opere musicali . . . città di Firenze*, in *Pubblicazioni dell'Associazione dei musicologi italiani*, series iv (1929); B. Becherini, "I manoscritti e le stampe rare della Biblioteca del Conservatorio 'L. Cherubini' di Firenze" (*La Bibliofilia* lxvi); A. Damerini, *Il R. Conservatorio di Musica "Luigi Cherubini" di Firenze* (1941)]; Biblioteca Marucelliana, early 16th-cent. printings [E. Vogel, *Bibliothek der gedruckten Weltliche Vokalmusik Italiens* ii (1892), rev. ed. (1962)].

Lucca: Biblioteca Bovernativa, 11th–15th-cent. MSS, 15th–18-cent. printings; Biblioteca del Seminario, 16th–19th-cent. MSS and printed music [E. Maggini, *Catalogo delle musiche stampate e manoscritte del fondo antico* (1965); A. Bonaccorsi, "Catalogo con notizie biografiche delle musiche . . . nelle biblioteche di Lucca" (*Collectanea Historiae Musicae* ii)].

Milan: [For general information, see *Le biblioteche milanesi* (1914); W. Rubsamen, "Music Research in Italian Libraries . . . Second Installment" (*Notes* vi)]. Biblioteca Ambrosiana, 10th–13th-cent. liturgical MSS, 16th–17th-cent. sacred printings, autographs [*Catalogo delle opere musicali . . . città di Milan*, in *Pubblicazioni dell'Associazione dei musicologi italiani*, series iii (1910–11)]; Conservatorio "G. Verdi," 16th-cent. printed sacred vocal music, autographs; copyright deposit [E. de' Guarinoni, *Indice generale dell'Archivio Musicale Noseda . . . alla Biblioteca del R. Conservatorio di Musica di Milano* (1897)]; Cathedral Archive, 15th–18th-cent. MSS [C. Sartori, *La Cappella musicale del duomo di Milano. Catalogo delle musiche dell'archivio* (1957)]; La Scala, theatrical museum, auto-

graphs and pictures [S. Vittadini, *Catalogo del Museo teatrale alla Scala* (1940–58)].

Modena: Biblioteca Estense, 15th–18th-cent. MSS and prints [P. Lodi, *Catalogo delle opere musicali . . . città di Modena*, in *Bollettino dell'Associazione dei musicologi italiani*, series viii (n.d.); V. Finzi, "Bibliografia delle stampe musicali della R. Biblioteca Estense" (*Rivista delle biblioteche* iii–v); E. J. Luin, in *La Bibliofilia* xxxviii].

Monte Cassino: Monastery Library, liturgical MSS and treatises, Neapolitan operas [E. Dagnino, "L'Archivo musicale di Montecassino" (*Casinensia* i [1929]); P. Ferretti, "I manoscritti musicali gregoriani dell' archivio di Montecassino" (*Casinensia* i, 1929)].

Naples: Biblioteca Nazionale, 12th–13th-cent. liturgical MSS, 13th–15th-cent. Byzantine MSS, 16th–17th-cent. printings [A. Mondolfi, "Il fondo musicale cinquecentesco della Biblioteca nazionale di Napoli" (*Collectanea Historiae Musicae* ii)]; Regio conservatorio di musica (Conservatorio di San Pietro a Maiella), 16th–18th-cent. printings, 18th–19th-cent. Neapolitan operatic MSS [*Il Museo storico musicale di "S. Pietro a Majella"* (1930)]; Oratorio dei Filippini, 16th–17th-cent. church music [G. Gasperini and F. Gallo, *Catalogo generale . . . città di Napoli*, in *Pubblicazioni dell'Associazione dei musicologi italiani*, series x (1918–34); E. Mandarini, *I codici manoscritti della Biblioteca Oratoriana di Napoli* (1897)].

Padua: Biblioteca Nazionale, 16th–17th-cent. printings; Biblioteca Capitolare [A. Garbelotto, "Codici musicali della biblioteca capitolare di Padova" (*RMI* liii–liv)]; University Library, 14th-cent. French and Italian songs, MS organ tablatures [W. Rubsamen, "Music Research in Italian Libraries . . . Second [Third] Installment," (*Notes* vi, viii)]; Cathedral of San Antonio, Tartini printings and autographs [G. Tebaldini, *L'Archivio musicale della Cappella Antoniana* (1895); L. M. Minciotti, *Catalogo dei codici manoscritti* (1842)].

Parma: Conservatorio "Arrigo Boito," 16th–17th-cent. partbooks, MSS and early theory [R. Allorto, "Biblioteche musicali in Italia: La Biblioteca del Conservatorio di Parma e un fondo di edizioni dei sec. XVI e XVII non compiese nel catalogo a stampa" (*Fontes Artis Musicae*, 1955); M. Medici, "Osservazione sulla Biblioteca Musicale di Parma" (*Aurea Parma*, May–August 1964)].

Rome: Vatican Library, 10th–15th-cent. treatises, MSS, Barberini and Chigi collections, archives of San Pietro, Sistine Chapel [J. M. Llorens, *Capellae Sixtinae Codices musicis notis instructi sivi manu scripti sive praelo excussi* (1960); supersedes an earlier catalogue by F. X. Haberl (1885–88)]; Julian Chapel [see St. Louis University for microfilms and card catalogue of Vatican collection; H. Stevenson, *Bibliotheca Apostolica Vaticana . . . Inventario dei libri stampati Palatino-Vaticani,* 2 vols. (1886–91); G. B. de Rossi, *La biblioteca della Sede Apostolica ed i cataloghi dei suoi manoscritti* (1884)]; Archives of St. John Lateran, Santa Maria Maggiore, and Santa Maria sopra Minerva; Biblioteca Corsiniana, Accademia Nazionale dei Lincei [V. Raeli, in *RMI* xxv–xxvii]; Biblioteca Casanatense, Baini collection, 11th–14th-cent. liturgies, 16th–17th-cent. printings; Accademia nazionale di S. Cecilia and Biblioteca del Conservatorio, copyright deposit, also rich in printed music and librettos [*Catalogo delle opere musicali . . . città di Roma,* in *Pubblicazioni dell'Associazione dei musicologi italiani,* series v (1912–13), theoretical works only; *Elenco delle opere musicali* (1896); *Catalogo delle opere di musica . . . della Congregazione ed Accademia di Santa Cecilia di Roma* (1846)]; Biblioteca Nazionale Centrale, 15th–17th-cent. liturgical music, 16th–19th-cent. MSS; Rolandi collection of librettos and vocal scores [U. Rolandi, *Il libretto per musica* (1951)]; Basilica Liberiana [V. Raeli, in *Musica d'oggi* (old series) ii]. The German Historical Institute in Rome maintains a well-stocked music reference collection.

Trent: Seven 15th-cent. codices [*DTO* 14/15, 22, 38, 53, 61, 76].

Turin: Biblioteca Nazionale, madrigal prints, 17th-cent. ballets, Foà and Giordano collections, 17th-cent. German organ tablature [*Esposizione nazionale di Torino M. DCCC. XCVIII: Manoscritti e libri a stampa musicati esposti dalla Biblioteca Nazionale di Torino* (1898); O. Mischiati, "L'Intavolatura d'organo tedesca della Biblioteca Nazionale di Torino. Catalogo ragionato" (*L'Organo* iv); A. Gentili, "La raccolta di antiche musiche Renzo Giordano alla Biblioteca Nazionale di Torino" (*Accademie e biblioteche d'Italia* ix); id., "La raccolta Mauro Foà nella biblioteca nazionale di Torino" (*RMI* xxxiv)]; Accademia Filarmonica [A. della Corte, *Catalogo dell'archivio di musica* (1926)]; Cathedral, MS and printed 16th–18th-cent. sacred vocal music.

Venice: Biblioteca Marciana, MSS, madrigal partbooks, early Venetian operas, Canal and Contarini collections [*Catalogo delle opere mu-*

sicali . . . città di Venezia, in *Pubblicazioni dell'Associazione dei musicologi italiani,* series vi (1915–41); T. Wiel, *I codici musicali Contariniani del secolo XVII nella R. Biblioteca di San Marco* (1888); *Biblioteca musicale del Prof. P. Canal in Crespano Veneto* (1885)]; Biblioteca del Palazzo Giustinian Lolin [S. Cisilino, *Stampe e manoscritti preziosi e rari della Biblioteca del Palazzo Giustinian Lolin a San Vidal* (1966)]; Conservatorio Benedetto Marcello, later Venetian MSS of vocal and instrumental pieces; Biblioteca Querini-Stampaglia, late 17th-cent. vocal MSS [*Catalogo delle opere musicali . . . città di Venezia,* in *Pubblicazioni dell'Associazione dei musicologi italiani,* series vi (1913)].

Important music MSS are also at Aosta, Castell'Arquato, Faenza, Ivrea, and Monza.

NETHERLANDS.

Amsterdam: Library of the Dutch Musicological Society housed in the Public Library [*Catalogus van de bibliotheek der Vereeniging voor Nederlandsche Muziekgeschiedenis* (1919)].

The Hague: Scheurleer collection [*Muziekhistorisch Museum van Dr. D. F. Scheurleer, Catalogus,* 3 vols. (1923–25)].

Leyden: University Library, 10th–15th-cent. MSS, Souterliedekens [P. C. Molhuysen, *et al., Codices manuscripti,* 7 vols. (1910—)]; Town Archives, five 16th-cent. choirbooks from St. Pieterskerk; Bibliotheca Thysiana, lute music.

Utrecht: University Library, 12th–15th-cent. liturgical MSS [P. A. Tiele, *Catalogus codicum manu scriptorum Bibliothecae Universitatis Rheno-Trajectinae,* 2 vols. (1887–1909)].

POLAND. For general information, see D. Plamenac, in *Notes* xix.

Krakow: See A. Chybinski, "Die Musikbestände der Krakauer Bibliotheken von 1500–1650" (*SIM* xiii). University Library, 16th-cent. organ tablature, autographs [J. Reiss, *Ksiażki o muzyce,* illustrated catalogue of 15th–16th-cent. music, 3 fasc. (1924–38)].

Warsaw: Biblioteka Narodowa, microfilm archive of the music holdings of numerous Polish libraries [*Katalog mikrofilmów muzycznich* (1956—)].

Wroclaw (formerly Breslau): University Library, 16th–17th-cent. printings, collections from former Town Library and Brieg Gymnasium [E. Bohn, *Bibliographie der Musik-Druckwerke bis 1700* (1883); id., *Die musikalischen Handschriften des XVI. und XVII. Jahrhunderts in der Stadtbibliothek zu Breslau* (1890); E. Kirsch, *Die Bibliothek des Musikalischen In-*

stituts bei der Universität Breslau (1922)]. The Musicological Institute has the collections of the Domstift and St. Elizabeth-Kirche.

PORTUGAL.

Coimbra: University Library [S. Kastner, *Inventário dos inéditos e empressos musicais* (1937); M. de Sampayo Ribeiro, *Os manuscritos musicais* (1941)].

Lisbon: Biblioteca da Ajuda, 17th–18th-cent. Portuguese and Italian operas [M. A. Machado Santos, *Catálogo de música manuscrita,* 6 vols., 1958–63; *Inventário dos códices alcobacenses,* 5 vols. (1930–32)]; Cathedral archives, Portuguese church music; Biblioteca Nacional, MSS of Portuguese composers; Library of João IV, King of Portugal, valuable collection destroyed in the earthquake of 1775 [P. Craesbeck, *Primeira parte do index da livaria de musica... 1649,* fac. ed. (1874)].

Oporto: Public Library [*Catalogo da Bibliotheca publica municipal do Porto,* 10 parts (1879–96)].

RUMANIA. Brasov: Honterus Gymnasium, MSS, keyboard tablature [E. H. Müller, *Die Musiksammlung der Bibliothek zu Kronstadt* (1930)].

RUSSIA. See Union of Soviet Socialist Republics.

SPAIN. Barcelona: Biblioteca Musical (Central) de la Diputació, MSS and printings of the 16th cent., Spanish vocal music, keyboard MSS [F. Pedrell, *Catàlech de la Biblioteca Musical,* 2 vols. (1908–09)]; Pedrell collection [H. Anglés, *Catàleg dels Manuscrits Musicals de la Collecció Pedrell* (1920)]; Orféo Catalá, 15th-cent. MSS; University Library, 16th-cent. keyboard and theoretical printings.

El Escorial: Monastery Library, 12th–16th-cent. vocal, instrumental, and theoretical MSS and printings [G. Antolín, *Catálogo de los Códices latinos,* 5 vols. (1910–23)]; Monastery Chapel, MS choirbooks, 17th–18th-cent. vocal and organ music [P. Aubry, "Iter Hispanicum" (*SIM* viii, 517ff)].

Madrid: Biblioteca Nacional, 9th–18th-cent. vocal, instrumental, and operatic MSS, 16th–18th-cent. printings, especially for vihuela and guitar [H. Anglés and J. Subirá, *Catálogo Musical de la Biblioteca Nacional de Madrid,* 3 vols. (1946–51)]; Alba Collection, largely destroyed [J. Subirá, *La Música en la casa de Alba* (1927)]; Biblioteca Medinaceli, MS Spanish madrigals [J. B. Trend, "Catalogue of the music

in the Biblioteca Medinaceli, Madrid" (*Revue Hispanique* lxxi)]; Palacio Nacional, music archive [J. G. Marcellan, *Catálogo del Archivo de Música de la Real Capilla de Palacio* (n.d.)]; Biblioteca Musical circulante, 18th-cent. *tonadillas,* incidental music, church music [*Catálogo de la Biblioteca Musical* (1946)].

Montserrat: Monastery, 12th-cent. liturgical MSS, 16th–19th-cent. Spanish music [*Música sacra española* [1941–47], *passim;* catalogue in preparation].

Seville: Cathedral, Biblioteca del Coro, 16th-cent. MSS and printings; Biblioteca Columbina, 15th–16th-cent. song MSS and printings [H. Anglés, "La Musica conservada en la Biblioteca Colombina y en la Catedral de Sevilla" (*AnM* ii)].

Toledo: Cathedral, Mozarabic and polyphonic MSS [F. Rubio Piqueras, *Códices polifónicos Toledanos* (1925)]; Biblioteca Capitolar [R. Lenaerts, "Les manuscrits polyphoniques de la Bibliothèque Capitulaire de Tolède" (*CP 1952*)].

Valencia: Cathedral [E. Olmos y Canalda, *Catálogo descriptivo de los códices* (1927, '28); *id., Códices de la Catedral de Valencia* (1943)]; Colegio del Patriarca or Colegio de Corpus Christi, MS Partbooks, sacred prints [V. Ripollés, catalogue in *Boletín de la Sociedad Castellonense de Cultura,* mainly in vii].

Valladolid: Cathedral Library, MSS and early printed books [H. Anglés, "El Archivo Musical de la Catedral de Valladolid" (*AnM* iii)].

SWEDEN. See Å. Davidsson, *Catalogue... des imprimés de musique... conservés dans les bibliothèques suédoises* (1952); *id., Catalogue critique et descriptif des ouvrages théoriques sur la musique... conservés dans les bibliothèques suédoises* (1953).

Stockholm: Kungliga Musikaliska Akedemien, 18th-cent. MSS and printings, guitar music [C. F. Hennerberg, "Kungl. Musikaliska Akademiens Bibliotek" (*Nordisk Tidskrift för Bok- och Biblioteksväsen* xiv)]; Musikhistoriska Museet [*Instrumentsamling* (1902); *Musikhistoriska Museet, dess upkomst, utveckling och systemål* (1910)].

Upsala: University Library, 16th–17th-cent. printings of sacred and secular music, 17th–18th-cent. MSS [R. Mitjana and Å. Davidsson, *Catalogue... des imprimés de musique... de l'Université royale d'Upsala,* 3 vols. (1911–51); C. Stiehl, in *MfM* xxi; R. Mitjana y Gordón, in *La Bibliofilia,* 1909–10]; Gimo Collection, 18th-cent. Italian instrumental music [Å. Davidsson, *Catalogue of the Gimo Collection of Italian* manuscript music in the University Library of Uppsala (1963)].

SWITZERLAND. Basel: University Library, 13th–15th-cent. liturgical MSS, medieval treatises, keyboard tablatures, 18th-cent. symphonies and chamber music [J. Richter, *Katalog der Musik-Sammlung auf der Universitäts-Bibliothek in Basel* (suppl. to *MfM* xxiii–xxiv); E. Refardt, *Katalog der Musikabteilung . . . und der in ihr enthaltenen Schweizerischen Musikbibliothek. I. Musikalische Kompositionen* (1925); id., *Thematischer Katalog der Instrumentalmusik des 18. Jahrhunderts in den Handschriften der Universitätsbibliothek Basel* (1957)].

Bern: Schweizerische Landesbibliothek, 19th-cent. music by Swiss composers [K. Joss, *Katalog der Schweizerischen Landesbibliothek, Musik* (1927)].

Einsiedeln: Monastery Library, 10th–15th-cent. treatises, J. C. Bach collection [G. Meier, *Catalogus codicum manu scriptorum* (1899)].

Lucerne: Theater- und Musik-Liebhabergesellschaft, Haydn collection [W. Jerger, *Die Haydndrucke aus dem Archiv der Theater- und Musik-Liebhabergesellschaft zu Luzern* (1959)].

St. Gall: Monastery Library, 9th–18th-cent. liturgical MSS and treatises [G. Scherrer, *Verzeichniss der Handschriften* (1875); id., *Verzeichniss der Incunabeln* (1880)]; Town Library, lute books.

Zurich: Zentralbibliothek, 10th–15th-cent. liturgical MSS, Swiss autographs, 16th-cent. organ music and treatises [W. Nagel, in *MfM* xxii, 67ff, 94ff; id., in *MfM* xxiii, 71ff; T. Odinga, in *MfM* xxii, 213f; C. Mohlberg, *Katalog der Handschriften der Zentralbibliothek Zürich: Mittelalterliche Handschriften* (1931)]; Bibliothek der Allgemeinen Musikgesellschaft Zürich, 17th–18th-cent. German and Italian printings, autographs [G. Walter, *Katalog der gedruckten und handschriftlichen Musikalien des 17. bis 19. Jahrhunderts im Besitze der Allgemeinen Musikgesellschaft Zürich* (1960)].

UNION OF SOVIET SOCIALIST REPUBLICS. See M. Elmer, in *Notes* xviii.

Leningrad: Saltykow-Shedrin Library, formerly the Royal Public Library, Russian vocal music, opera scores, composers' legacies; Central Music Library, Russian MSS, theater music. See I. V. Golubovskiĭ, "Biblioteki i muzei" (*Muzykal'nyĭ Leningrad,* 1958) for a general description of the musical contents of 14 Leningrad libraries and 12 museums.

Moscow: Synod School Library, 15th–19th-cent. MSS of Russian church music in various notations, Razumovskii and Odoevskii collections [I. M. Kudryavtzev, *Sobraniya D. V. Razumovskovo* (catalogue, 1960)].

ASIA.

INDIA. Calcutta: Santi Niketan Library, Indian classical music, some very old, both sacred and secular.

JAPAN. Tokyo: Nanki Music Library, 4,500 vols., including 454 from the W. H. Cummings collection [*Catalog of the Nanki Music Library,* 2 vols., rev. ed. (1920); *Catalogue of the W. H. Cummings' collection in the Nanki Music Library* (1925)].

TURKEY. Istanbul: List of Istanbul library collections, 36 vols. (1882–93); history-geography MSS (1943—); Divan MSS (1947—).

Lit.: E. T. Bryant, *Music Librarianship: A Practical Guide* [1959]; V. Duckles, ed., *Music Libraries and Librarianship* (*Library Trends* viii, no. 4, April 1960); G. Kinsky, "Musikbibliotheken: ein Überblick über die wichtigsten öffentlichen und privaten Musiksammlungen" (*Philobiblon* [Vienna] vi); L. R. McColvin and H. Reeves, *Music Libraries,* rev. ed. by J. Dove, 2 vols. [1965]; A. Ott, "Die Musikbibliotheken" (in F. Milkau's *Handbuch der Bibliothekswissenschaft* ii, rev. ed., 1959; E. Vogel, "Musikbibliotheken nach ihrem wesentlichsten Bestande aufgeführt" (*JMP* i).   rev. V.H.D.

Libretto [It.]. The text of an opera, oratorio, etc. Famous writers of librettos (librettists) include Ottavio Rinuccini (1562–1621; for Peri, Caccini, Monteverdi); Philippe Quinault (1635–88; for Lully); Pietro Metastasio (1698–1782; for A. Scarlatti, Hasse, Handel, Mozart); Ranieri di Calzabigi (1714–95; for Gluck); Lorenzo da Ponte (1749–1838; for Mozart's *Le Nozze di Figaro, Così fan tutte,* and *Don Giovanni*); Eugène Scribe (1791–1861; for Auber, Meyerbeer, Halévy, Boieldieu); Arrigo Boito (1842–1918; for Verdi's *Otello* and *Falstaff*); Hugo von Hofmannsthal (1874–1929; for R. Strauss); W. S. Gilbert (1836–1911; for A. Sullivan). Richard Wagner began a new practice by writing his own texts and by insisting upon a degree of unification between text and music theretofore unknown. His example was followed by Cornelius, Pfitzner, Schreker, Menotti, and others.

Large collections of librettos of early operas (17th and 18th centuries) are at the Library of Congress (Collection A. Schatz) and in the libraries of Berlin, Vienna, Brussels, Paris, Bologna, Munich, Venice, etc.

Lit.: O. G. T. Sonneck, *Catalogue of Opera Librettos Printed before* 1800, 2 vols. (1914); E. Istel, *The Art of Writing Opera-librettos* [1922]; E. de Bricqueville, *Le Livret d'opéra français de Lully à Gluck* (1887); M. Ehrenhaus, *Die Operndichtung der deutschen Romantik* (1918); A. Wotquenne, *Libretti d'opéras et d'oratorios italiens du XVIIe siècle (Catalogue de la Bibliothèque du Conservatoire ... de Bruxelles,* Annexe I, 1901); I. Pizzetti, *Musica e dramma* (1945); U. Rolandi, *Il Libretto per musica attraverso i tempi* (1951); A. della Corte, *Il Libretto e il melodramma* (1951); F. Vatielli, "Operistilibrettisti dei secoli XVII e XVIII" (*RMI* xliii); H. Prunières, "I Libretti dell' opera veneziana nel secolo XVII" (*LRM* iii); T. M. Baroni, in *RMI* xii (Metastasio); M. Callegori, in *RMI* xxvi, xxviii (Metastasio).

Libre Vermell. See Llibre Vermell.

Licenza, con alcuna [It.]. Indication for some license in performance, or in composition, e.g., *canone con alcuna licenza.* In the 17th and 18th centuries *licenza* meant a passage or cadenza inserted by the performer; also, an operatic prologue designed as a dedication to a noble patron [see Prologue], such dedication being considered a "liberty" taken by the composer.

Liceo [It.]. Name of various Italian conservatories, e.g., Liceo Padre Martini (Bologna, also known simply as Liceo Musicale, famous for its library; see under Libraries), Liceo Rossini (Pesaro), Liceo B. Marcello (Venice), Liceo Verdi (Turin), etc.

Lichanos [Gr.]. See under Greece II.

Liebesgeige; -oboe [G.]. Viola d'amore; oboe d'amore.

Liebeslieder [G., Love Songs]. Two groups of eighteen (op. 52, 1869) and fifteen (*Neue Liebeslieder,* op. 65, 1875) short pieces by Brahms. Each is in the character of a waltz, for vocal quartet and piano duet in a chamber-music relationship. The texts are taken from Daumer's *Polydora,* except for the last song in op. 65, which is by Goethe.

Lied [G.; Pl. *Lieder*]. A song in the German vernacular. The history of the lied can be divided into the following periods: I. Minnesingers and Meistersinger (*c.* 1250–1550); II. Polyphonic lied (15th–16th century); III. Accompanied lied

("Generalbass-lied") of the baroque (1600–1750); IV. "Volkstümliches lied" (1775–1825); V. The "German lied" of the 19th century.

I. See Minnesinger; Meistersinger.

II. The 15th-century composers Oswald von Wolkenstein (1377–1445) and the Münch von Salzburg (fl. *c.* 1400) were the first to write polyphonic songs, rather primitive imitations of 14th-century French models or still earlier styles [see O. Ursprung, in *AMW* iv, v; *DTO* 18]. Important collections of 15th-century folksongs, some monophonic, some in polyphonic setting, are the Glogauer, Münchner, and Lochamer Liederbücher [see Liederbuch]. The polyphonic songs of Adam von Fulda (*c.* 1445–1505) and Heinrich Finck (1445–1527) show remarkable progress in style (true polyphonic treatment, imitation), thus leading to the masterly compositions of Heinrich Isaac (*c.* 1450–1517; see *DTO* 28; *HAM,* no. 87), Paul Hofhaimer (1459–1537; see H. J. Moser, *Paul Hofhaimer,* 1929; *HAM,* no. 93), Stoltzer (*c.* 1475–1526; see *DdT* 65; *HAM,* no. 108), and Ludwig Senfl (*c.* 1490–1543; see *DdT,* no. 34; *Editions XVIII A, 10; HAM,* no. 110). Isaac's "Innsbruck ich muss dich lassen" is one of the oldest and most beautiful German folksongs. Important sources of real German folksong are Senfl's **quodlibets,* in which many popular songs of his day are cited. Important collections of polyphonic songs are G. Forster's five books *Ein Ausszug guter alter und newer teutscher Liedlein* (Nuremberg, 1539–56; the second book, *Frische teutsche Liedlein,* repub. by Eitner; *Editions XLVII, 29), and J. Ott's *115 guter newer Liedlein* (1544, repub. by Eitner; *Editions XLVII, 1–4). In the second half of the 16th century Orlando di Lasso composed numerous German texts with consummate imagination and dexterity [see *Newe Teütsche Liedlein mit fünff Stimmen,* 3 vols., 1567, '72, '76; *Newe Teutsche Lieder ... mit vier Stimmen,* 1583, etc.; see compl. ed., vols. xviii, xx]. In the works of the foreigners, Mattheus Le Maistre (*c.* 1505–77), Antonio Scandello (1517–80), and Jacob Regnart (*c.* 1540–99), the lighter vein of the Italian *canzonette* and the *Bauernharmonie* (peasant harmony) of the **villanella* superseded the polyphonic style of the earlier period [see Editions XLVII, 19; *SchGMB,* no. 139]. The two great masters from the end of the 16th century, Leonhard Lechner (*c.* 1550–1606; *Neue Teutsche Lieder,* 1582, new ed. by E. F. Schmid, 1926) and Hans Leo Hassler (1564–1612; *Canzonette a quatro voci,* 1590, and *Neue teutsche Gesäng,* 1596, new ed. in *DTB* 9; *Lustgarten,* 1601, new ed., see Editions XLVII, 15) combine refinement of technique with depth of feeling and expression. The development of the polyphonic lied came to an end with Johann Hermann Schein (1586–1630; *Venus Kräntzlein,* 1609; *Musica boscareccia,* 1621, '26, '28; see comp. ed. by A. Prüfer, vols. i, ii; also *SchGMB,* nos. 187, 188).

III. The accompanied solo lied of the baroque period ("Generalbass-lied," song with thorough-bass accompaniment) first appeared in J. Nauwach's (*c.* 1595–*c.* 1630) *Erster Theil teütscher Villanellen mit 1, 2 und 3 Stimmen* (1627), J. Staden's (1581–1634) *Hertzentrosts-Musica* (1630) and *Geistlicher Music-Klang* (1633), and T. Selle's (1599–1663) *Deliciarum Juvenilium decas Harmonica-bivocalis* (1634) and *Monophonetica* (1636) [see H. J. Moser, ed., ‡*Alte Meister des deutschen Liedes,* 1931]. With H. Albert's (1604–51) *Arien* (1638–50; *DdT* 12, 13; see also *HAM,* no. 205; *SchGMB,* no. 193) and A. Hammerschmidt's *Weltliche Oden* (1642–49; see Moser, *Alte Meister; SchGMB,* no. 194) it freed itself from the Italian model and became a truly German type, combining popular simplicity with artistic taste. This development reached its high point in the inspired songs of A. Krieger (1634–66; see *DdT* 19; H. Osthoff, *Adam Krieger,* 1929; *HAM,* no. 228; *SchGMB,* no. 209), who used the instrumental ritornello to be played at the end of each stanza. This "ritornello-lied" was also cultivated by J. E. Kindermann (1616–55; see *DTB* 21–24), J. Theile (1646–1724; see *SchGMB,* no. 210), and P. H. Erlebach (1657–1714; see *DdT* 46/47). Toward the end of the century the religious song found a master in J. W. Franck (1641–*c.* 1710; *Geistliche Lieder,* 1681–1700; new ed. *DdT* 45). The arias of Bach and Handel deserve only passing mention here since they do not properly belong to the category of lied. In fact, during the first half of the 18th century the lied practically ceased to exist, giving way to the elaborate treatment of the aria. On the other hand, a great number of lieder were written, under the name "aria," in the operas of J. S. Cousser [*SchGMB,* no. 250], R. Keiser [*SchGMB,* nos. 268, 269], Telemann, etc. Sperontes' *Singende Muse an der Pleisse* (1736–45; *DdT* 35/36; see *SchGMB,* no. 289) gives a good cross-section of the period of deterioration and disintegration of the *Generalbass-lied.* See also *DdT* 57 for songs (*Oden*) by Telemann and Görner.

IV. Matters took a new turn after 1750 when J. A. Hiller (1728–1804), the founder of the *Singspiel, replaced the worn-out pathos of the late baroque with an affected naïveté in songs that were often addressed to children [*Lieder für Kinder* (1769); *Fünfzig geistliche Lieder für Kinder* (1774); *Sammlung der Lieder aus dem Kinderfreunde* (1782); see Moser, *Alte Meister*]. J. A. P. Schulz (1747–1800) found a more genuine expression of folklike simplicity (*Lieder im Volkston;* see Volkstümliches lied), while other members of the second *Berlin school, such as J. F. Reichardt (1752–1814) and K. F. Zelter (1758–1832), introduced a new lyricism, particularly in their settings of Goethe's poems. In the songs of Haydn, Mozart ("Das Veilchen"), and the early Beethoven, this movement came to its artistic climax and end. See *DTO* 54 and 79 for a survey of the Viennese lied from 1778 to 1815.

V. The greatest period of the German lied began with Schubert (1797–1828), who, after a few preliminary songs in traditional style, opened a new era with his "Gretchen am Spinnrade" (Oct. 19, 1814, "the birthday of the German lied"), a miracle of musical art as well as of psychological intuition, being the work of a seventeen-year-old. There soon followed a flood of immortal masterworks, including the "Erlkönig" (1815), "Wanderer's Nachtlied" (1815), "Der Tod und das Mädchen" (1817), and "Der Wanderer" (1819), then the song cycles *Die Schöne Müllerin* (1823) and *Winterreise* (1827), and finally the collection *Schwanengesang* (1828). Measured by the artistic perfection of these songs, even the most beautiful lieder of Schumann and Brahms seem somewhat slight in imagination, and only Hugo Wolf's compositions stand the proof of comparison. For a complete outline of the development of the romantic lied, one must also add Mendelssohn, Liszt, Wagner, R. Franz (1815–92), P. Cornelius (1824–74), Mahler (1860–1911), R. Strauss (1864–1949), H. Pfitzner (1869–1949), and M. Reger (1873–1916).

The revolutionary tendencies of the 20th century found their first clear expression in Schoenberg's 15 Poems for high voice from *Das Buch der Längenden Gärten* by Stefan George (op. 15, 1908 and later) which, in addition to their novel harmonic style, show a new type of vocal (or, rather, unvocal) line, a speechlike declamation in which the rise and fall of the speaking voice is reflected. Anton von Webern, Josef Hauer, and Ernst Krenek have written songs in a similar vein, sometimes using serial techniques. In contrast to these is Hindemith's *Marienleben* (op. 27, 1924), which is inspired by the structural concept and polyphonic style of Bach. Traditional and progressive elements are combined in the songs of Hermann Reutter, Ernst Pepping, and Wolfgang Fortner.

Lit.: O. Bie, *Das deutsche Lied* (1926); E. Bücken, *Das deutsche Lied* (1939); H. J. Moser, *Das deutsche Lied seit Mozart*, 2 vols. (1937); H. Bischoff, *Das deutsche Lied* [n.d.]; M. Friedländer, *Das deutsche Lied im 18. Jahrhundert*, 2 vols. in 3 (1902); H. Kretzschmar, *Geschichte des neuen deutschen Liedes i: Von Albert bis Zelter* (1911); W. K. von Jolizza, *Das Lied... bis zum Ende des 18. Jahrhunderts* (1910); W. Vetter, *Das frühdeutsche Lied*, 2 vols. (1928); H. H. Rosenwald, "Geschichte des deutschen Liedes zwischen Schubert und Schumann" (diss. Heidelberg, 1930); H. J. Moser, ed., ‡*Alte Meister des deutschen Liedes*, rev. ed. (1931); *id.*, ‡*Corydon*, 2 vols. (1933); M. Breslauer, *Das deutsche Lied . . . bis zum 18ten Jahrhundert* (1908; bibl.); A. Prüfer, *Johann Hermann Schein und das weltliche deutsche Lied* (1908); R. Velten, *Das ältere deutsche Gesellschaftslied unter dem Einfluss der italienischen Musik* (1914); R. Eitner, *Das deutsche Lied des 15. und 16. Jahrhunderts*, 2 vols. (1876, '80); also in *MfM* viii–xv); H. Osthoff, *Die Niederländer und das deutsche Lied, 1400–1640* (1938); H. Rosenberg, *Untersuchungen über die deutsche Liedweise im 15. Jahrhundert* (1931); O. A. Baumann, *Das deutsche Lied und seine Bearbeitungen in den frühen Orgeltabulaturen* (1934).

Periodicals. For 15th cent.: O. Ursprung, in *AMW* iv, v, vi (bibl.); H. Riemann, in *SIM* vii; W. Krabbe, in *AMW* iv; J. Müller-Blattau, in *ZMW* xvii, *AMF* iii; J. Wolf, in *CP Liliencron;* R. Molitor, in *SIM* xii. *16th cent.:* F. Spitta, in *CP Riemann;* A. Becker, in *ZMW* i; E. Radecke, in *VMW* vii (lute music); H. J. Moser, in *JMP* xxxv. *17th cent.:* F. Noack, in *ZMW* 1; P. Epstein, in *ZMW* x; W. Vetter, in *ZMW* x. *18th cent.:* M. Seiffert, in *CP Liliencron;* B. Seyfert, in *VMW* x; H. J. Moser, in *JMP* xxxix; G. Frotscher, in *ZMW* vi. *19th cent.:* E. Hughes, in *MQ* iii (Liszt); R. Gerber, in *JMP* xxxix (Brahms). *20th cent.:* H. Nathan, in *MM* xiv, no. 3. See also under Minnesinger; Meistersinger.

Liederbuch [G.]. A term commonly applied to 15th- and 16th-century collections of German songs, mainly: (a) Lochamer Liederbuch, *c.* 1450 [fac. ed. by K. Ameln, 1925; description with transcriptions in *JMW* ii (1867); improved transcription by K. Escher and W. Lott (1926); see W. Salmen, *Das Lochamer Liederbuch* (1951);

O. Ursprung, in *AMW* iv, v, vi; H. Rosenberg, in *ZMW* xiv; J. Müller-Blattau in *AMF* iii; see also *Fundamentum*]. (b) Glogauer (formerly Berliner) Liederbuch, *c.* 1480 [new ed., see Editions XVIII A, 4 and 8; also in *MfM* vi, no. 5 and viii, Beilage]. (c) Münchener (also Walther's or Schedel's Liederbuch), 1461–67 [*MfM* xii–xv, Beilage; H. Rosenberg, ed., ‡*Das Schedelsche Liederbuch* (1933)].

The Lochamer Liederbuch is the most important source of early German folksong (some monophonic, some in three-voice composition). The Glogauer Liederbuch contains, in addition to vocal pieces, interesting instrumental dances [see Dance music II] and canons. For bibl. see under Lied (15th century); also *BeMMR*, p. 229.

In the 16th century a number of extensive collections of German songs in four (occasionally five) parts were published by: Arnt von Aich, *LXXV hubscher Lieder, c.* 1510 [see H. J. Moser and E. Bernoulli, *Das Liederbuch des Arnt von Aich*, 1930]; Erhart Öglin, 1512, without title [*Editions XLVII, 9]; Peter Schöffer, 1513, without title [fac. ed. 1909; *Editions VIII, 29]; *id.* and M. Apiarius, *Fünff und sechzig teütscher Lieder*, 1536; Johann Ott, *121 neue Lieder*, 1534 [see H. J. Moser, in *AM* vii]; *id.*, *115 guter neuwer Liedlein*, 1544 [*Editions XLVII, nos. 1–4]; Christian Egenolff, *Gassenhawerlin* and *Reutterliedlin*, 1535 [see *Gassenhauer*]; Wolfgang Schmelzl, *Guter, seltzamer und künstreicher teutscher Gesang*, 1544 [see *Quodlibet*]; Georg Forster, *Ein Ausszug guter . . . Liedlein*, 1539–56 [*Editions XVIII A, 20]; *id.*, *Der ander Theil kurtzweiliger . . . Liedlein*, 1540 [*Editions XLVI, 29]; *id.*, *Der dritte Teyl schöner . . . Liedlein*, 1549; *id.*, *Der vierdt Theyl schöner . . . Liedlein*, 1556; *id.*, *Der fünffte Theil schöner . . . Liedlein*, 1556. They contain compositions by Isaac, Senfl, Bruck, Hellinck, Paminger, Stoltzer, Lemlin, Othmayr, and others, as well as numerous anonymous settings.

Liedercyclus, Liederkreis [G.]. *Song cycle.

Lieder eines fahrenden Gesellen [G., Songs of a Wayfarer]. Four songs for contralto and orchestra by Mahler (1883), set to his own poems. They were inspired by his youthful love affair with Johanna Richter.

Lieder ohne Worte [G., Songs without Words]. Forty-eight piano pieces by Mendelssohn, published in eight groups of six each (op. 19b, 30, 38, 53, 62, 67, 85, 102; 1830–45) and written in the form and style of a song, i.e., with a singable melody and a simple, uniform accompaniment. The songlike character is also evident in the absence of contrasting middle sections such as are usually found in the *character pieces of the 19th century. The individual titles given in modern editions ("Spring Song," "Hunting Song," "Spinning Song") are not authentic, except for the three called *Venezianisches Gondellied,* nos. 6, 12, and 29, the *Duetto,* no. 18, and the *Volkslied,* no. 23.

Liedertafel [G.]. A men's singing society, founded by Zelter in 1809, whose members first sat around a table [G. *Tafel*] for refreshments. Various similar societies sprang up during the 19th century.

Liedform [G.]. *Song form.

Liedmotette [G.]. Song motet; see Motet B I.

Lied von der Erde, Das [G., The Song of the Earth]. A symphonic song cycle by Mahler (who called it a symphony), for mezzo-soprano, tenor, and orchestra, set to German translations (by Hans Bethge) of old Chinese poems: 1. *Das Trinklied vom Jammer der Erde* (The Drinking Song of Earth's Woe); 2. *Der Einsame im Herbst* (The Lonely One in Autumn); 3. *Von der Jugend* (Of Youth); 4. *Von der Schönheit* (Of Beauty); 5. *Der Trunkene im Frühling* (The Toper in Spring); 6. *Der Abschied* (The Farewell). The work, Mahler's last, was completed in 1908 and first performed in Munich in 1911, after his death.

Lieto [It.]. Gay, joyful.

Lievo [It.]. Light, easy.

Life for the Czar, A [Rus. *Zhizn za Tsarya*]. Opera in five acts by Glinka (libretto by G. F. Rozen), produced in St. Petersburg, 1836. Setting: Russia, 1612–13. An alternate title in current use in Russia is *Ivan Susanin.* The opera is a landmark in music history because it was the first popular opera in the Russian language, inaugurating a nationalist movement that has continued ever since.

Ligatura [It.]. (1) *Ligature. (2) In the 17th century, a tied note; see under Durezza.

Ligatures. I. Notational signs of the 13th to 16th centuries that combine two or more notes in a single symbol. They developed in the late 12th century as square-shaped modifications of the neumes [see Ex.; see also Notation]. From these they inherited certain graphic peculiarities that

can only be understood if viewed as the result of this evolution, e.g., the initial stroke of the "descending" forms (1 and 3), which is lacking in the "ascending" forms (2 and 4). Although in plainsong and related bodies of monophonic music these signs are but graphic modifications of the neumes [see Monophonic notation], they adopted definite rhythmic meanings in polyphonic music. The first step in this direction was in the modal notation of the school of Notre Dame, in the early 13th century. Here, ligatures are the ordinary notational signs for all the parts, single notes being used only for special reasons (long notes of the tenor). Their rhythmic values depend entirely on their grouping, according to the different rhythmic *modes [see Square notation]. The rise of the *motet (c. 1225) greatly diminished the use of ligatures in the upper parts because they had a full text, whose syllables were sung, as a rule, to single notes. The final step in the development of the ligatures came c. 1250 with Franco of Cologne, who succeeded in assigning an unambiguous metrical significance (independent of the modes) to each of the various shapes. His rules remained unaltered throughout the ensuing period of mensural notation. The discussion below refers mainly to the period of white mensural notation (after 1450).

II. Ligatures are classified according to the number of notes they contain: *ligatura binaria* (two), *ternaria* (three), *quaternaria* (four), etc. In each of these categories there are various types distinguished by the terms *proprietas* and *perfectio.* The former term refers to the modifications concerning the initial notes, the latter to those of the final note. The various types of *ligatura binaria* are illustrated in the accompanying table in which *c.c.* means *cum* (with) *proprietate et cum perfectione; s.c., sine* (without) *proprietate et cum perfectione,* etc., while *c.o.p.* designates a special type, known as *cum opposita proprietate* (B = *brevis;* L = *longa;* S = *semibrevis*):

	Desc.	Asc.	Value	
c.c.			B	L
s.c.			L	L
c.s.			B	B
s.s.			L	B
c.o.p.			S	S

These principles cover also the various types of *ternaria* and *quaternaria,* since the middle notes occurring in these ligatures are (normally) always B.

As a further illustration, an example of ligatures together with a rendition in single notes is given. It should be noted that oblique writing has no rhythmical significance unless it occurs

at the end of a ligature, and that even here it affects only the last of the two notes comprised in its graph.

Lit.: *ApNPM,* pp. 87ff, 231ff, 312ff; L. Dittmer, in *MD* ix (Codex Montpellier); O. Ursprung, in *AM* xi; H. Rietsch, in *ZMW* viii. See also under Mensural notation.

Lilliburlero. A 17th-century political tune whose melody appeared first under the name "Quickstep" in *The Second Book of The Pleasant Musical Companion* (1686). This melody [see *GD* iii, 198; *GDB* v, 237] was, the following year, used with a political text, satirically directed against the Papists and the Irish Roman Catholics, which began as follows:

Ho, broder Teague, dost hear de decree,
Lilliburlero, bullen a la.

The melody has been used for various other texts of the same type. It also appears under the name "A New Irish Tune" in *Musick's Hand-Maid...for the Virginals, Harpsichord, and Spinet* (1689), with H. Purcell given as the composer, of either the tune or the keyboard version. Purcell also used it as a ground in his play, *The Gordian Knot Unty'd* (1691).

Limma [Gr.]. See under Pythagorean scale.

Limoges, school of. Same as school of *St. Martial.

Linear counterpoint. A term introduced by E. Kurth (*Grundlagen des linearen Kontrapunkts,* 1917) in order to emphasize the "linear" or horizontal aspects of counterpoint, as opposed to the harmonic (or vertical) point of view that prevailed at the time the book was published. Today the "linear" character of counterpoint is generally recognized. The term is also used as a designation for what Germans call *rücksichtsloser* (reckless) *Kontrapunkt,* i.e., the modern type of counterpoint that takes little account of harmonic combination and euphony (Hindemith, Stravinsky).

Lining (out). In American and English psalm and hymn singing, the practice of having each line read by the minister or some other person before it is sung by the congregation. This custom, which sprang from people's insufficient familiarity with the texts, died out by about the middle of the 19th century, largely because of the introduction of singing schools and instruments. In England it was known as "deaconing." See Psalter.

Linke Hand [G.]. Left hand.

Linz Symphony. Mozart's Symphony in C, no. 36 (K. 425), composed at Linz, Austria, and first performed there by the private orchestra of Count Thun.

Lip. See Embouchure.

Lippenpfeife [G.]. Labial pipe.

Liquescent neumes. See under Neumes. See H. Freistedt, *Die liqueszierenden Noten des Gregorianischen Chorals* (1929); J. Pothier, in *RCG* ix; L. David, in *RCG* xxxiv; *Paléographie musicale* (Solesmes, 1889—) ii, 37ff; *ApGC,* p. 104.

Lira. A 15th- and 16th-century type of violin having a wide neck with front pegs, drone strings, and a slightly pear-shaped body. The *lira da braccio* was held in the arm, the larger *lira da gamba* (*lirone*) between the knees. See ill. under Violin; also see Violin II. See A. Hajdecki, *Die italienische Lira da braccio* (1892). For Haydn's *lira organizzata,* see Hurdy-gurdy.

Lira sacro-hispana. See Editions XXIV.

Liscio [It.]. Smooth, even.

L'istesso tempo [It.]. Same tempo.

Litany. In the Roman Catholic Church, solemn supplications addressed to God, the Virgin, or the Saints. They open with the *Kyrie eleison, continue with numerous exclamations such as "Mater Christi, ora pro nobis," sung responsively to a short inflected monotone, and close with the *Agnus Dei. The most important litanies are those of Rogation Days [*LU,* p. 835], and the Litany of Loreto (*Litaniae Laurentanae*), named after Loreto, Italy, where it is supposed to have originated in the 13th century; *LU,* p. 1857). The latter is especially popular, being frequently used at processions, the presentation of the sacrament at Benediction, and many popular services where it is sung by the whole congregation (particularly in Italy). It has been frequently composed in a simple chordal style (*falsobordone*), e.g., by Festa, by Palestrina [comp. ed. by Haber (1886), vol. xxvi, and Bianchi (1955), vol. xx], by Lasso, and others. See A. Machabey, "Le Origini asiatiche della Litania cristiana occidentale" (*LRM* xxi, 279); K. A. Rosenthal, "Mozart's Sacramental Litanies and their Forerunners" (*MQ* xxvii).

The Anglican litany has the same basic structure as the Roman Catholic litanies. It consists of petitions interspersed with responses such as "Spare us, good Lord," "Good Lord, deliver us," etc.

Liturgical books. I. The most important books of the Roman Catholic rites are the following: (1) The *missale* (missal) contains all the texts for the Mass, the prayers, lessons, and the texts of the Mass chants. (2) The *breviarium* (breviary) is the corresponding collection of all the texts for the Office. (3) The *graduale* (*gradual) contains the Mass chants, with their music. (4) The *antiphonale* or *antiphonarium* (*antiphonal, antiphonary, or antiphoner) contains the Office chants (except Matins), with their music. (5) The *Liber usualis* is a modern combination of the four books just mentioned, with some additions and many omissions. It includes the spoken texts as well as the musical items for both the Mass and the Office, arranged in their proper order, giving a clear picture of the entire service from day to day. It also includes the service of Matins (for a few of the highest feasts), which is omitted in the *antiphonale* because it is held today only in monastic churches. On the other hand, a number of services that are very important, particularly from the historical point of view, are omitted from the *Liber usualis,* mainly the weekdays of Lent, and the Wednesdays and Fridays of the four Ember weeks. (6) The *kyriale* (kyrial) contains only the chants of the Ordinary of the Mass (beginning with the Kyrie). (7) The *vesperale* (vesperal) contains the service of Vespers and usually that of Compline as well. (8) The *processionale* (processional) is a collection of the chants (mostly responsories and antiphons) sung during processions (within the church) before Mass. Such processions are customary mainly in monastic churches, particularly in France. (9) The *sacramentarium* (sacramentary), a very early type (6th to 8th century), contains only the texts spoken by the priest or the officiating bishop, mainly the prayers and the variable Prefaces for the *Canon of the Mass. In this period the readings from the Scriptures and Gospels were also in separate books, the *lectionarium* (lectionary) and the *evangelarium* (evangeliary or evangelistary). (10) The *tonarium* or *tonale* (*tonary) is a medieval book in which the chants are arranged according to the eight church modes. (11) The *cantatorium* (cantatory), a 9th- to 10th-century prototype of the gradual, contains only the solo chants of the Mass, i.e., Graduals, Alleluias, and Tracts. (12) The *troparium* (*troper) is a medieval book containing *tropes. (13) The *pontificale* (pontifical), contains the services used in functions where a bishop or prelate officiates, e.g., consecration of a church, ordination of priests, etc. (14) The *Liber responsorialis,* a modern compilation, contains mostly *responsories.

Antiphonale originally was the name for a gradual as well as for an antiphonary [see Antiphonal]. The earliest graduals and antiphonals (8th to 10th centuries) contain only the texts of the chants. The six existing graduals of this type are collated in Dom R. J. Hesbert's *Antiphonale missarum sextuplex* (1935).

II. Toward the end of the 16th century various books were published in which the traditional melodies were "reformed," mainly in the direction of simplification and, especially, elimination of the melismas on unaccented syllables. To this category belong a *Graduale* published by Liechtenstein and a *Graduale abbreviatum* published by Giunta (both Venice, 1580), as well as J. Guidetti's *Directorium chori* (Rome, 1582). Even more drastic changes were incorporated in the *Graduale de tempore et de sanctis . . . cum cantu Pauli V. Pont. Max. jussu reformato,* prepared by Anerio and Suriano, published by Raimondi (2 vols., Rome, 1614) and generally known as the "Editio Medicea" (because the press was owned by the Medici family). Throughout the 17th, 18th, and 19th centuries the publications of Liechtenstein and Giunta as well as those by Plantin (Antwerp) and Nivers (Paris) were generally used. The Editio Medicea was unfortunately revived in the so-called Ratisbon edition ("Editio Ratisbonensis"), a series published under the title "Medicea" by Pustet

(Regensburg, 1871). Meanwhile, studies of medieval manuscripts led to attempts to restore the authentic versions of Gregorian chant, the first tangible result being P. Lambillotte's *Antiphonaire de Saint Grégoire* (Brussels, 1851) and *Antiphonarium Romanum* (Paris, 1854). There followed Dom Pothier's *Liber gradualis a Gregorio Magno olim ordinatus* (Tournai, 1883) and *Liber gradualis juxta antiquorum codicum fidem restitutus* (Solesmes, 1895), and finally, under Dom Mocquereau's leadership, the Vatican edition ("Editio Vaticana"). Two of its four volumes are the *Graduale sacrosanctae Romanae ecclesiae* (Rome, Vatican Press, 1907) and the *Antiphonale sacrosanctae Romanae ecclesiae* (*ibid.*, 1912), usually known as *Graduale Romanum* and *Antiphonale Romanum*. Both books also appeared in versions known as the Solesmes editions (pub. by Desclée, Tournai), in which the chants are provided with the rhythmic signs of Solesmes, particularly the vertical stroke (*"episema"*) indicating the *ictus*. The *Liber usualis* also belongs to this group of publications. See Gregorian chant VII; Solesmes; *Motu proprio.*

III. Liturgical books in the Anglican communion are divided into official and semiofficial. Owing to the autonomy of the various national churches, the few official books are binding only for the particular church by which they are issued. The official music books issued by the Protestant Episcopal Church in the U.S.A. include *The Hymnal 1940, The Choral Service, The American Psalter,* and *The Plainsong Psalter.* Among the semiofficial volumes are the American *St. Dunstan Kyrial,* the *Monastic Diurnal Noted* and other editions of C. W. Douglas, the *English Gradual,* and other publications from St. Mary's Convent in England.

Other Protestant churches combine their suggested order of worship with their hymnals. In most cases, this is a further simplification of the Anglican Morning Prayer and Communion Service. See the *Service Book and Hymnal of the Lutheran Church in America* (1958), *The Methodist Hymnal* (1939), *The Pilgrim Hymnal* (1958), etc.   III by V.P.D.

Liturgical dances. See Religious dances; Dance music I.

Liturgical drama. Medieval plays (chiefly 12th- and 13th-century) representing Biblical stories (in Latin) with action and, occasionally, monophonic music. Since they never actually were part of the official liturgy, they might better be called "religious" drama.

Liturgical drama developed during the 10th and 11th centuries from *tropes to the Introits for Christmas and Easter, which were written in the form of a *dialogue (so-called dialogue tropes), i.e., question-and-answer form. One of the earliest examples is the trope "Hodie cantandus est" (possibly by Tuotilo, d. *c.* 915) to the Christmas Introit "Puer natus est" [Schubiger, p. 39; abridged in *SchGMB,* no. 3]. A more fully developed type—in fact, a real play—is the 10th-century trope "Quem queritis" to the Introit "Resurrexi" for Easter Sunday [*SchGMB,* no. 8]. For an account of its performance at Winchester in the middle of the 10th century, see *ReMMA,* p. 194. Later plays, mostly of French origin, deal with the story of Daniel, the massacre of the innocents (containing the "lament" of Rachel), the wise and foolish virgins (the 12th-century play, *Sponsus*), etc. Favorite subjects for other plays were the miracles of various saints, particularly St. Nicholas (the so-called miracle plays).

From the 14th to 16th centuries, liturgical drama developed into the mysteries or mystery plays [corruption of L. *ministerium,* service], coming under secular sponsorship and using the vernacular. These were dramatic representations based on Biblical subjects such as the life of Jesus, the Acts of the Apostles, the Creation, etc., elaborately staged and in some instances continuing over a period of 20 days or longer. They used music only incidentally, for processions, fanfares, and dances, occasionally including plainsong, popular songs, etc. In Italy they were known as *sacre rappresentazioni,* in Spain and Portugal as *autos.* It is chiefly from these plays that European drama developed. See also Opera II.

Lit.: N. Greenberg, ed., ‡*The Play of Daniel* (1959); W. L. Smoldon, ed., ‡*Herod; A Medieval Nativity Play* [1960]; E. Coussemaker, ed., ‡*Drames liturgiques du moyen âge* (1860; fac. ed. Broude Bros., 1964); H. Villetard, ed., ‡*Office de Pierre de Corbeil* (1907); A. Schubiger, in *Editions XLVII, 5 (4.ii); id., Die Sängerschule St. Gallens* (1858); K. Young, *The Drama of the Medieval Church,* 2 vols. [1962]; R. B. Donovan, *The Liturgical Drama in Medieval Spain* (1958); O. E. Albrecht, *Four Latin Plays of St. Nicholas* (1935); W. Lipphardt, *Die Weisen der Lateinischen Osterspiele des 12. und 13. Jahrhunderts* [1948]; E. A. Schuler, *Die Musik der Osterfeiern, Osterspiele und Passionen des Mittelalters* (1951);

L. P. Thomas, *Le Sponsus* (1951); A. della Corte, *Storia della Musica* i (1944), 77ff; *NOH* ii, 175ff; *GéHM*, pp. 232ff; G. Tintori and R. Monterosso, ed., *Sacre rappresentazioni nel manoscritto 201 della Bibliothèque municipale di Orléans* (Cremona, 1958); J. Handschin, "Das Weihnachts-Mysterium von Rouen" (*AM* vii); O. Ursprung, "Das Sponsus-Spiel" (*AMF* iii); J. B. Trend, "The Mystery of Elche" (*ML* i, 145ff); F. Pedrell, "La Festa d'Elche" (*SIM* ii); J. Smits van Waesberghe, "A Dutch Easter Play" (*MD* vii); W. Lipphardt, "Das Herodesspiel von Le Mans" (*CP Waesberghe*); F. Liuzzi, "L'Espressione musicale nel dramma liturgico" (*Studi medievali*, new series ii [1929], 74–109); W. L. Smoldon, "The Music of the Medieval Church Drama" (*MQ* xlviii); *id.*, "The Easter Sepulchre Music-Drama" *ML* (xxvii); E. Bowles, "The Role of Musical Instruments in Medieval Sacred Drama" (*MQ* xlv).

Liturgy. The officially authorized service of the Christian churches, particularly of the Roman Catholic Church, as distinguished from extra-liturgical services, such as the *Benediction. See Gregorian chant; Mass; Office; Liturgical books; also Liturgical drama.

Lituus. (1) A Roman trumpet, possibly of Etruscan origin; see Brass instruments V (a). (2) A 17th-century Latin name for the cornett or cromorne [see Oboe family III]. The two *litui* in Bach's Cantata no. 118 are obviously tenor trumpets in B-flat [see *SaRM*, p. 244]. See C. Sachs, "Die Litui in Bachs Motette 'O Jesu Christ'" (*BJ* 1921).

Liuto [It.]. *Lute.

Livret [F.]. *Libretto.

Lizenza [It.]. "License," freedom.

Llibre Vermell [Cat.]. A late 14th-century Spanish MS from the monastery of Montserrat, containing, in addition to literary texts, a few pages with ten compositions. Among the latter are three entitled *caça*, which are three-part canons similar in structure to the French *chace of the early 14th century. Also of interest is a reference to *religious dancing. In the 19th century the book was bound in red velvet, hence the name [Sp. *vermell*, vermilion]. See H. Anglés, in *AnM* x; O. Ursprung, in *ZMW* iv; *ReMMA*, p. 373f.

Lo [It.]. Abbr. for *loco* [It., place], used to indicate return to the normal octave after *all' ottava* or similar designations.

Lochamer Liederbuch. See under Liederbuch.

Locrian, lokrian. See under Church modes II; Greece II.

Lohengrin. Opera in three acts by Richard Wagner (to his own libretto, based on W. von Eschenbach and medieval legends), produced in Weimar, 1850. Setting: Antwerp, early 10th century. *Lohengrin* marks the transition from Wagner's early operas (*Rienzi, Der Fliegende Holländer, Tannhäuser*) to the late masterpieces (*Ring, Tristan, Meistersinger, Parsifal*). In it Wagner for the first time made consistent use of his "continuous melody" as opposed to the "number" style [see Number opera] that still occurs in *Tannhäuser*. There is also a modest use of *leitmotivs to characterize the most important personages and emotions.

Lombardic style [It. *stile lombardo*]. (1) Unexplained name for inverted dotting; see Dotted notes III. (2) "Howling of the Lombards" is a term derived from the statement made in 1274 by Elias Salomonis that "the singing of the Lombards is like the howling of wolves" [*GS* iii, 60]. It is usually described as being "parallel organum of the second," on the basis of explanations and musical examples given by Gafurius in his *Practica musice* of 1496 (with reference to "Ambrosiani nostri," i.e., singers of the Ambrosian chant of Milan). Actually what is involved is the use of organum of the fourth ("Musica enchiriadis") but beginning and ending with a second rather than with a unison. Anon. IV says that the Lombards sometimes put the last note in unison with the tenor but not always [*CS* i, 358]. The example "Rex coeli" under Organum would illustrate the "Lombardic organum" if the lower part began on b-flat instead of c. See J. Handschin, in *AM* xv, 2; E. Ferand, in *MQ* xxv; H. Riemann, *Geschichte der Musiktheorie*, rev. ed. (1918), p. 348 (Eng. trans., *History of Music Theory*, by R. Haggh [1962], p. 296f); B. Stäblein, in *A Ettore Desderi* (1963).

London Symphonies. (1) Haydn's last twelve symphonies, nos. 93–104, written in 1791–95 for the Salomon Concerts in London [see Concert I], also known as the Salomon Symphonies. Particularly the last of these, no. 104 in D, is known as "The London Symphony." (2) *A London Symphony* is a composition by Ralph Vaughan Williams, composed in 1913. Although written largely in the form of a classical symphony, it incorporates programmatic elements (Westminster chimes, London street cries).

Longa, long. See under Mensural notation I.

Long playing. See under Phonograph and recorded music.

Loop. See under Acoustics V.

Louise. Opera in four acts by Charpentier (to his own libretto), produced in Paris, 1900. Setting: Paris, c. 1900. The opera is closely related to the *verismo movement, particularly to Puccini's *La Bohème*.

Lourd [F.]. Heavy.

Loure [F.]. (1) A 16th- and 17th-century name for bagpipe [see *SaRM*, p. 245]. (2) A 17th-century dance (originally accompanied by the instrument loure?) in moderate 6/4 time and with dotted rhythms leaning heavily on the strong beats [see Dance music III]. Early examples are in Lully's opera *Alceste* of 1677; the *loure* in Bach's French Suite no. 5 is by far the most beautiful example of this dance type.

Louré [F.]. See under Bowing (f).

Love for Three Oranges, The [Rus. *Lyubov k trem Apelsinam*]. Farcical opera in four acts by Prokofiev (to his own libretto, based on a tale by C. Gozzi), produced (in French) in Chicago, 1921. Setting: fairy tale. Numerous set pieces, particularly the March and the Scherzo, have become standard concert works.

Lovesong Waltzes. See *Liebeslieder*.

Low Mass. In the Roman Catholic rites, the Masses of ordinary weekdays, celebrated without singing, as opposed to the High Mass of Sundays [see Mass].

Lucernarium. The first item of Vespers in *Ambrosian chant. The text nearly always includes a reference to "light" [L. *lucerna,* lamp]. *Lucernarium* is an old term for the evening service, held when the lamps were lighted.

Lucia di Lammermoor. Opera in three acts by Donizetti (libretto by Cammarano, after Sir Walter Scott), produced in Naples, 1835. Setting: Scotland, end of 17th century.

Ludus Tonalis [L., Tonal Play]. A work for piano by Hindemith, composed in 1942 and designed as a 20th-century *Well-Tempered Clavier*. It consists of twelve fugues linked by eleven interludes and preceded by a prelude that serves, in retrograde inversion, as a postlude. The fugues are arranged according to Hindemith's principle of decreasing tonal relationship to the tonic of C: C, G, F, A, E, etc., the interludes leading from one tonality to the next. The fugues explore the various contrapuntal devices (accompanied canon, double and triple fugue, crab motion, inversion, etc.) in a modern idiom. The work is one of the most characteristic products of *neoclassicism.

Luftpause [G.]. Breathing rest.

Lulu. Unfinished opera in three acts by Alban Berg (to his own libretto, based on two plays by F. Wedekind), produced in Zurich, 1937. Setting: Germany, early 20th century. The music is in twelve-tone technique based on a single tone row throughout [see Serial music]. Through various devices, Berg succeeds in introducing simple folk melodies as well as involved Wagnerian lines, creating a work of infinite variety and great dramatic sensitivity.

Lundu [Port.]. Rural Brazilian folk dance, originally sung during harvest celebrations. At present this form has become a kind of serenade, also known as *aribú,* that still preserves its basic African characteristics.   J.O-S.

Lur [Dan.; pl. *lurer*]. A prehistoric Nordic trumpet of bronze, preserved (especially in Denmark) in about 50 examples dating from the 12th to 6th centuries B.C. They are in the shape of a long twisted S, ending in a flat ornamental disk, and are usually found in pairs turned in opposite directions, resembling a pair of mammoth tusks. Archaeological evidence suggests that they were used not for military purposes or signaling but in connection with a religious cult. These instruments, being almost the sole evidence of Nordic musical activity of the pre-Christian era, have been the subject of much speculation and exaggerated claims (e.g., "three-voiced harmony, 3,000 years ago" in K. Grunsky, *Der Kampf um deutsche Musik,* 1933), which are generally considered untenable today. The tone of the lur is variously described as "rough and blatant" [*GD* iii, 251; *GDB* v, 43] and (rather euphemistically) as "sanft posaunenartig" [H. J. Moser, *Geschichte der Deutschen Musik* (1930), i, 32]. See ill. under Brass instruments.

Lit.: H. C. Broholm, W. P. Larsen, and G. Skjerne, *The Lures of the Bronze Age* (1949); A. Oldeberg, in *Acta Archaeologica* xviii (1947); H. C. Broholm, *Bronzelurerne i National Museet* (1958; Eng. summ. pp. 113–23); A. Hammerich, in *VMW* x; H. Schmidt, in *Prähistorische Zeitschrift* vii (1915).

Lusingando [It.]. Caressing.

Lustig [G.]. Merry, cheerful.

Lustigen Weiber von Windsor, Die [G., The Merry Wives of Windsor]. Opera in three acts by Otto Nicolai (libretto by S. H. Mosenthal, after Shakespeare's play), produced in Berlin, 1849. Setting: Windsor, 15th century.

Lustige Witwe, Die [G., The Merry Widow]. Operetta in three acts by F. Lehár (libretto by V. Léon and L. Stein), produced in Vienna, 1905. Setting: Paris, early 20th century.

Lute [F. *luth;* G. *Laute;* It. *lauto, liuto, leuto;* Sp. *laúd;* L. *testudo* or *chelys,* i.e., "turtle," a humanist misnomer referring to the tortoise shell of the ancient Greek *lyra].

I. *General.* A plucked stringed instrument with a round body in the shape of a halved pear, a flat neck with 7 or more frets, and a separate pegbox set perpendicular to the neck. The instruments of the 16th century had 11 strings in 6 *courses, tuned (in theory) G–c–f–a–d'–g' or A–d–g–b–e'–a', with the two lowest courses doubled, sometimes in the higher octave, and the three following courses doubled in the unison. (In practice the 16th-century lute was tuned to a convenient pitch, depending on the music to be played.) In the 17th century an increasing number of bass-courses (up to six) were added, running alongside the fingerboard and therefore being unalterable in pitch. They were normally tuned F E D C, etc. About 1640 another system of tuning, introduced by the great lutenist and lute-composer Denis Gaultier (*c.* 1600–72), was generally adopted, A–d–f–a'–d'–f'; called *nouveau ton,* it persisted as long as the lute was used (end of the 18th century).

II. *History.* The history of the lute is unusually long and interesting. There are two main types of early lute, the long lute, with a neck much longer than the body, and the short lute, with a neck slightly shorter than the body. The former is by far the older instrument. It appears on Mesopotamian figurines dating from about 2000 B.C. From Babylon it spread to Egypt (*c.* 1500 B.C.) and Greece, where it was called *pandoura.* This lute had a small body covered with parchment through which the long handle penetrated [see *SaHMI,* p. 102]. The later development of the long lute took place in Persia, where it was called *setār* ("two-strings"), *cartār* ("four-strings"), or *panctār* ("five-strings"), according to the number of strings,

and in Arabia, where it was named **tanbur.* A European offshoot of the Arabian long lute was the *colascione* of the 16th and 17th centuries [see *WoHN* ii, 125], and the Russian **domra (dombra).* The Japanese *shamisen (samisen)* has a nearly square body with rounded corners. It is covered with skin, has a long neck, and three silk strings tuned in fourths or fifths [see Japan VI].

The short lute appears first on Persian clay figures from about 800 B.C. and on Indian reliefs from the first centuries A.D. About the latter time we find it in China, under the name **pyiba* [Jap. *biwa*]. In these early instruments the neck is formed by the tapering body, a shape still present in the Arabic short lute of medieval times, called *'ud* (or *al 'ud,* Sp. *laúd,* hence lute). The transformation into the European lute, an instrument with a distinct neck and a central sound hole (the *'ud* had two crescent-shaped sound holes, like the early viols) probably took place in Spain, not very long before the 15th century. From Spain, the instrument spread to other European countries.

III. *Other types.* Numerous varieties of lute were used during the 16th and 17th centuries. The *mandola* or *mandore* had a long pegbox slightly curved and with a head-scroll reminiscent of the violin's [see *SaHMI,* p. 245; *GD* iii, 252; *GDB* v, 433ff]. A diminutive form of this instrument is the **mandolin.* The *angelica* was a 17th-century variety with 17 different strings for the tones of the diatonic scale, so that stopping was largely avoided. During the 17th century the increasing demand for bass instruments led to the construction of archlutes [G. *Erzlaute;* It. *arciliuto;* Sp. *archilaúd*], i.e., double-neck lutes with a second pegbox that carried the bass-courses. There was a "short" archlute, the *theorbo,* and a "long" archlute, the *chitarrone.* For a third type, the *liuto tiorbato,* see *SaHMI,* p. 372.

All the instruments above have the round back characteristic of the lute. The instruments with a flat back are treated under Guitar family. Only one of them, the Spanish **vihuela,* should be mentioned here because its musical repertory is closely allied to that of the lute [see Lute music; Lute tablature]. The **bandora and the smaller **orpharion have a peculiar scalloped shape, usually forming three lobes (somewhat like an oak leaf).

The term "lute" is also used as a generic name for a large class of stringed instruments. See Instruments IV, B.

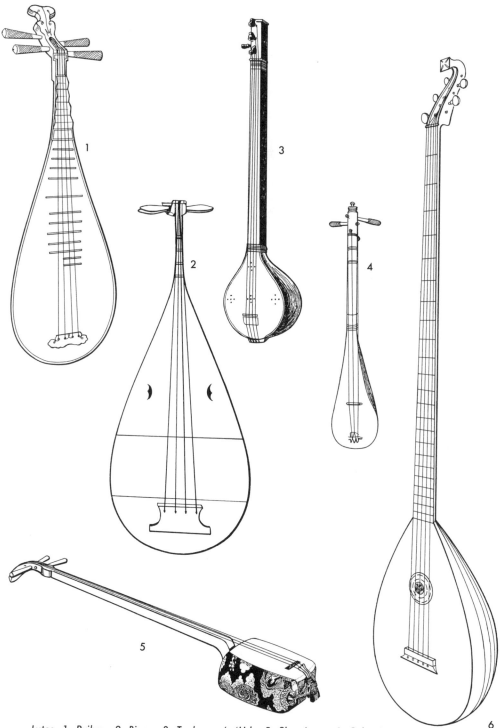

Lutes: 1. Pyiba. 2. Biwa. 3. Tanbur. 4. 'Ud. 5. Shamisen. 6. Colascione.

Lutes: 7. Mandola, 8. Mandolin. 9. Lute. 10. Orpharion. 11. Bandora (pandora). 12. Theorbo. 13. Chitarrone.

Lit.: J. Zuth, *Handbuch der Laute und Gitarre* (1926); N. Bessaraboff, *Ancient European Musical Instruments* (1941), pp. 220ff; J. Jacquot, ed., *Le Luth et Sa Musique* (1958); H. Sommer, *Die Laute in ihrer musikgeschichtlichen, Kultur- und Kunsthistorischen Bedeutung* (1920); H. Farmer, *An Old Moorish Lute Tutor* (1933); W. Stauder, in *CP Osthoff;* K. Geiringer, "Vorgeschichte und Geschichte der europäischen Laute" (*ZMW* x); M. Brenet, "Notes sur l'histoire du luth en France" (*RMI* v, vi); F. Behn, "Die Laute im Altertum und frühen Mittelalter" (*ZMW* i); M. Brondi, "Il Liuto e la chitarra" (*RMI* xxxii, xxxiii); G. Kinsky, "Alessandro Piccinini und sein Arciliuto" (*AM* x).

Lute harpsichord [G. *Lautenclavicymbel*]. A harpsichord with gut strings instead of the usual metal strings. The tone was very much like that produced by the gut strings of the lute (the reference to "checking by a damper of cloth—*GD* iii, 115; *GDB* v, 439—is evidently a confusion with the lute-stop of the ordinary harpsichord). Such harpsichords are mentioned as early as 1511 (Virdung). For the description of an instrument of 1718, see *SaRM*, p. 239f. In 1740 Bach had such an instrument made for his own use, which, according to Adlung (*Musica mechanica organoedi* ii, 139) produced a sound like a theorbo or, if damped by the lute-stop, like a lute. See O. Fleischer, in *ZIM* i.

Lute music. Lute music, as preserved in the numerous lute books (*lute tablatures) of the 16th and 17th centuries, forms an important repertory of early instrumental music, second only to that of the organ and harpsichord. Particularly during the 16th century, the lute was the chief instrument used at home, much as the piano is today.

The surviving literature for the lute extends from 1507 to about 1770. It begins with four books, *Intabulatura de lauto,* published by Petrucci 1507–08 (I and II by Spinaccino, III lost, IV by Joan Ambrosio Dalza), containing intabulations of vocal music, dances, and free compositions called *ricercar and *tastar de corde* (touching of the strings). A recently discovered MS of a slightly later date (*c.* 1517), by Vincenzo Capirola, contains the earliest instances of signs of ornamentation and dynamic indications [see Expression marks]. Beginning in the 1530's there followed a vast number of printed books and manuscripts of Italian, French, German, Spanish, and English origin [see the long lists in *WoHN* ii, 47, 66, 95, and H. M. Brown, *Instrumental Music Printed before 1600* (1965)]. The sources of the 16th century contain dances (*bassadanza,* *pavane, *calata, *piva, *galliard, *passamezzo, *saltarello, etc.), *ricercars and *fantasias (contrapuntal and otherwise), *variations (many in the Spanish guitar books), and free *preludes (called "ricercars" in the earliest Italian books), in addition to a large number of *intabulations of vocal music (motets, chansons, etc.). The most outstanding composers are the *Italians* Alberto da Ripa (Albert de Rippe), Marco d'Aquila, Francesco da Milano, Antonio Rotta, Pietro Paolo Borrono, Giacomo Gorzanis, Vincenzo Galilei, Fabritio Caroso, and Giovanni Antonio Terzi; the *French* Attaingnant (publisher), Adrian le Roy, and Guillaume Morlaye, to whom the *Hungarian* Valentin Bacfarc (pseud. Greff) may be added; the *Germans* Arnolt Schlick, Hans Judenkünig, Hans Gerle, Hans Newsidler, Wolff Heckel, Melchior Newsidler, Matthaeus Waisselius, and Sixtus Kargel; the *English* John Johnson, Anthony Holborne, Francis Cutting, John Dowland, Daniel Bachelor, and Robert Johnson. One might also include the great *Spanish* composers (who, however, wrote specifically for the *vihuela) Luis Milan, Luis de Narváez, Enriquez de Valderrabano, Diego Pisador, and Miguel de Fuellana.

In the 17th century, lute music persisted chiefly in France and in Germany, while Italy and Spain turned to the more popular guitar. The repertory consisted chiefly of preludes and stylized dances (allemandes, courantes, sarabandes, etc.). Whereas in the books of the early 17th century these dances are compiled separately [see Jean-Baptiste Besard, *Thesaurus harmonicus,* 1603, which is divided into ten "books," one each for preludes, allemandes, courantes, etc.], later they were arranged according to keys in groups that resemble the *suite [e.g., Denis Gaultier's *La Rhétorique des dieux,* *c.* 1655; new ed. by A. Tessier]. After 1650 the center of artistic activity shifted to Germany. The suites by Esajas Reusner (1636–79) and the sonatas of Silvius Leopold Weiss (1686–1750)— the latter astonishingly like Bach in style— represent the culmination of the entire literature. J. S. Bach wrote a number of pieces for the lute (ed. by Bruger).

Lit. A. *Collections of music;* D. Heartz, ‡*Preludes, Chansons and Dances for Lute, published by Pierre Attaingnant* (1964); H. D. Bruger, ‡*Alte Lautenkunst aus drei Jahrhunderten* [1923];

id., ‡*Johann Sebastian Bachs Kompositionen für die Laute* (1921); P. Jansen *et al.,* ed. ‡*Oeuvres de Adrian Le Roy,* 3 vols. (1960–62); A. Souris, *et al.,* ed. ‡*Oeuvres de Robert Ballard,* 2 vols. (1963, '64); *id.,* ‡*Oeuvres de Dufaut* (1965); O. Gombosi, ed., ‡*Compositione di meser Vincenzo Capirola, Lute-book (circa 1517)* (1955); H. Quittard, ‡*Le Trésor d'Orphée . . . par Antoine Francisque,* 1600 (1906); G. Gullino, ‡*Gio. Battista della Gostena, Intavolatura di liuto,* 1599 (1949); *id.,* ‡*Joan Maria da Crema, Intavolatura di liuto,* 1596 (1955); *id.,* ‡*Simone Molinaro Genovese, Intavolatura di liuto,* 1599 (1940); *id.,* ‡*Gio. Maria Radino, Intavolatura di balli personar di liuto,* 1592 (1949); D. Lumsden, ‡*An Anthology of English Lute Music (16th century)* (1954); D. Stephens, ‡*The Wickhambrook Lute Manuscript* (1963); *Editions XV, 37, 50 (Austrian lute music); XVII (English lute songs); XVIII A, 12 (Reusner, Weiss); XLIX, Ser. I, 3–4, 6, and 7 (French); V, 1, 7, 8, 9 (Italian, French); LIII, 23 (Długoraj), 24 (Cato).

B. *Bibliography:* O. Körte, *Laute und Lautenmusik bis zur Mitte des 16. Jahrhunderts* (1901); J. Jacquot, ed., *Le Luth et sa musique* (1958; essays); J. Zuth, *Handbuch der Laute und Gitarre* (1926); J. Dieckmann, *Die in deutscher Lautentabulatur überlieferten Tänze des 16. Jahrhunderts* (1931); P. Warlock, *The Lute Music of J. Dowland* (1928); O. Lefkoff, *Five Sixteenth Century Venetian Lute Books* (1960); L. H. Moe, "Dance Music in Printed Italian Lute Tablatures from 1507 to 1611" (diss. Harvard Univ., 1956); D. Lumsden, "The Sources of English Lute Music (1540–1620)" (diss. Cambridge Univ., 1955); W. Boetticher, "Studien zur solistischen Lautenpraxis des 16. und 17. Jahrhunderts" (diss. Berlin, 1943); J. Dodge, in *SIM* ix (ornamentation); O. Chilesotti, in *RMI* xxi (Gorzanis); C. Lozzi, in *RMI* ix (V. Galilei); W. Apel, in *MQ* xx (Spanish); H. M. Fitzgibbon, in *ML* xi, 71 (Ballet, Dallis); R. Newton, in *PMA* lxv (English); A. Koczirz, in *SIM* vi (Judenkünig); O. Gombosi, in *Musicologia hungarica* ii, 1935 (Bacfarc); L. de la Laurencie, in *RM* 1924, pp. 33ff (Jacques Gaultier); *id.,* in *RM* 1923, pp. 224ff (Basset); *id.,* in *RdM* 1926 (Bocquet, Francisque, Besard); J. Lindgren, in *MfM* xxiii (Mouton); D. F. Scheurleer, in *TV* v (Vallet); E. Radecke, in *VMW* vii (German lied); Quittard, in *SIM* viii (*Hortus musarum*); W. Tappert, in *MfM* xviii (Gerle); *id.,* in *MfM* xxxii (Reusner); A. Verchaly, in *RdM* 1947 (Bataille); C. Sartori, in *MQ* xxxiv (Bossinensis); H. Halbig, in *CP Kroyer* (Gorzanis); E. Haraszti, in *RdM* 1929, p. 159 (Bacfarc); O. Chilesotti, in *SIM* iv (Francesco da Milano); H.-J. Schulze, in *MF* xix; H. Neemann, in *ZMW* x (Weiss); *id.,* in *BJ* 1931 (Bach); T. Dart, in *GSJ* xi (Burwell Instruction Book); D. Gill, in *GSJ* xii (Elizabethan 7-course lute); D. Lumsden, in *GSJ* vi (sources of English lute music); L. Picken, in *GSJ* viii (short lute's origin); *The Lute Society Journal, passim.*

Lute tablature. (1) The notational systems used for writing down lute music during the 16th, 17th, and 18th centuries; see Tablature III, IV, V. (2) The manuscripts and books in which this notation is employed; hence, practically all the lute books of the same period [see Lute music].

Lutherie [F.]. The art of making lutes or stringed instruments in general. *Luthier,* the maker of such instruments, today of violins, etc.

Luttuoso [It.]. Mournful.

Lydian. (1) See under Greece II. (2) The fifth *church mode, represented by the segment f–f' of the diatonic scale, with f as the tonic. From the modern point of view it is a major mode (F major) with the augmented fourth (B natural, Lydian fourth, i.e., tritone) instead of the perfect fourth (B-flat). Owing to the presence of the tritone f–b in prominent position, examples of pure Lydian are rare in Gregorian chant. The Antiphon "Domine tu mihi" [*LU*, p. 673]

is one of them [Ex. 1]. Usually, Lydian occurs in Gregorian chant as a "mixed" tonality, using the B natural (preferably for descending motion) as well as the B-flat (for ascending motion). It should be noted, however, that the modern editions of the chant have many flats not found in the original MSS [see *ApGC*, pp. 153ff]. A similar situation exists in polyphonic music from *c.* 1200 to 1500. Ex. 2 shows a purely Lydian passage from a 13th-century motet [see *SchGMB*, no. 19], while Ex. 3 [*c.* 1470; Buxheim Organ Book] illustrates the more frequent occurrence of a tonality of mixed F-major and Lydian idioms, melodic as well as harmonic. This mixed tonality, which is very characteristic of polyphonic music prior to 1500, should not be destroyed by editorial accidentals [see *Musica ficta* (Ex. 8); Partial signature]. An especially important Lydian formula is the Lydian cadence, characterized by the presence of two leading tones, one before the octave, the other before the fifth [see Cadence, Ex. 16–18]. This was used very frequently in 14th-century music (Machaut), usually in transposition on c, g, or d. Similar formulas were used sporadically throughout the 15th and 16th centuries. Probably the latest example is found at the end of F. Tunder's chorale variations on "Jesus Christus unser Heiland" (*c.* 1660), where the piled-up leading tones produce a truly dramatic final intensification [see K. Straube, *Choralvorspiele alter Meister* (1907), p. 135]. Beethoven revived the Lydian mode in the "Dankgesang" (slow movement) of his String Quartet op. 132. As a characteristic of Slavic folksong it appeared in Chopin's mazurkas [see Modality].

Lyra. (1) An ancient Greek stringed instrument, similar to the *kithara but of simpler construction, smaller, and with the soundbox usually made of tortoise shell [see ill.]. It was played with a plectrum. Instruments of the same design

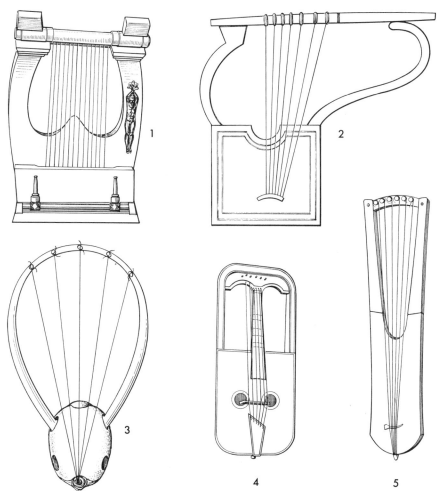

Lyres: 1. Kithara (Greek). 2. Kithara (Egypt, Mesopotamia). 3. Lyra. 4. Crwth. 5. Rotta.

appear on Egyptian wall paintings from *c.* 1500 B.C. See H. Hickmann, *Musicologie pharaonique* (1956), pp. 158ff. In the Middle Ages the name "lyre" was adopted for several instruments only remotely like the Greek lyra, namely: (2) A medieval fiddle similar to the rebec (hence the name *lira for a 16th-century violin; see Violin II). (3) The *hurdy-gurdy, particularly in the names *lyra rustica* (peasant's lyra) and *lyra mendicorum* (beggar's lyra). (4) In modern German usage, the military *glockenspiel, on account of the shape of its frame, which is similar to the Greek lyra. The "Lyra" called for in several compositions by Haydn is not the *lira da braccio* but the *hurdy-gurdy. See also Lyre; Kithara; Crwth; *Rotta.* See H. Panum, "Harfe und Lyra im alten Nordeuropa" (*SIM* vii).

Lyra piano [G. *Lyraflügel*]. An early 19th-century variety of upright piano, with a case shaped like a Greek lyre.

Lyra viol. See under Viol IV, 3. For ill. see under Violin.

Lyra way. See under Viol IV, 3 (lyra viol).

Lyre. As a specific instrument, see Lyra. As a generic term for a class of instruments, see Instruments IV, C, and illustration, p. 495.

Lyric Suite. Suite in six movements for string quartet by Alban Berg (1926). Although all of the movements are in a dissonant and *expressionist idiom, only the first and last adhere throughout to the twelve-tone technique [see Serial music]. A subtle unity is achieved by introducing the main theme of each movement in the preceding movement.

M. In organ music, manual or manualiter. See also Metronome.

Maatschappij. See under Societies II, 6.

Macbeth. (1) Opera in three acts and a prologue by E. Bloch (libretto by E. Fleg, after Shakespeare's play), produced in Paris, 1910. Setting: Scotland, 11th century. (2) Opera in four acts by Verdi (libretto by F. M. Piave, after Shakespeare's play), produced in Florence, 1847; rev. version (in French) in Paris, 1865. Setting: Scotland, 11th century.

Machete. See under Guitar family; Ukulele.

Machicotage [F.]. A French practice of ornamenting plainsong by inserting improvised grace notes or coloraturas between the authentic notes of Gregorian chant. The practice of *machicotage* is documented as far back as 1391 [see F. Godefroy, *Dictionnaire de l'ancienne langue française* (1961)] and continued throughout the 18th and early 19th centuries. Usually *machicotage* was used with the solo songs while the chants of the *schola* (choir) remained unadorned. The adoption of the Solesmes versions ended this practice.

Macumba. Secret religious ceremony accompanied by songs and dances, performed by Brazilian Negroes. It combines Christian symbols with others originating in Africa and passed on by Amazon Indian tribes. The music in these ceremonies is valued for its magical powers rather than its intrinsic beauty. The term *macumba* is employed mainly in the State of Guanabara. In other states these ceremonies are known as *candomblé* (Baia), *babacué* (Pará), *tambo* (Maranhao), and also *catimbó* or *pagelança.*   J.O-S.

Madama Butterfly. Opera in three acts by Puccini (libretto by G. Giacosa and L. Illica, based on a story by John L. Long and D. Belasco's dramatization), produced in Milan, 1904. Setting: near Nagasaki, Japan, about 1900.

Madrasha. See under Syrian chant.

Madrigal. Name for two different types of Italian vocal music, one of the 14th century, the other of the 16th century (to which the term more often refers). A number of etymologies of the name have been given: *mandrialis,* from *mandra,* flock (pastoral song); *materialis,* from *materia,* secular (as opposed to *spiritualis*); *matricalis,* from *mater,* mother (interpreted as "in the mother tongue," "motherly, affectionate," or "belonging to the Mother Church," hence, "of liturgical origin"); cf. *ReMMA,* p. 362; J. Wolf, in *SIM* iii and *PMA* lviii; N. Pirrotta, in *RMI* xlviii, xlix, and *MD* ix; J. Handschin,

Musikgeschichte, p. 207; W. T. Marrocco, in *Speculum* xxvi.

I. *The 14th-century madrigal.* As a poetic form the madrigal consists of two or, more rarely, three strophes of three lines each, which are followed by a final strophe of two lines, called *ritornello. In each strophe, two lines rhyme with one another. The lines are usually in iambic pentameter with 7 or 11 syllables. Below is the beginning of an 8-line (3 + 3 + 2) madrigal by Petrarch as well as its complete rhyme scheme [see *HAM,* no. 49]:

> Non ál so amánte piú Diána piáque
> Quandó per tál ventúra túta núda
> La vídi in méço déle gélid' áque

I	II
... piaque	... cruda
... nuda	... vello
... aque	... chiuda

Ritornello
... cello
... gello

The subject of the madrigal is often amatory and pastoral, as in the example above: "Nor did Diana ever please her lover / So much as when through good fortune he saw her naked / In the midst of the cool waters," etc. Often the poems present fantastic images of animals or birds (white lamb, leopard, lizard, snake, falcon, white peacock) symbolic of men or women in pursuit of love.

Music for these texts was composed usually in two, sometimes in three voice-parts, in a form that closely follows that of the poetry, the same music (a) being provided for the strophes and different music (b) for the ritornello, so that the two-stanza (8-line) madrigal has the form a a b, and the three-stanza (11-line) madrigal the form a a a b (for an example of the latter, see *HAM,* no. 50, where the same music is used for the first and second lines of the ritornello, resulting in the form a a a b b). The normal form, a a b, is similar to but probably not derived from that of the French *ballade [see also *Bar* form]. Madrigals were composed chiefly by the members of the early Italian school, e.g., Jacopo da Bologna and Giovanni da Cascia, whereas in the second half of the 14th century the madrigal was largely abandoned in favor of the *ballata. Landini, for instance, wrote only 12 madrigals and 140 *ballate.*

The style of the *trecento* madrigal is best described as an ornamented *conductus style, contrasting sharply with the genuinely polyrhythmic style of contemporary French music (Machaut). Its impressively designed ornamenting lines foreshadow the Italian coloraturas of the 17th century. Nonetheless, A. Schering's interpretation of the madrigal as "koloriertes Orgelmadrigal" (*SIM* xiii) is historically untenable, regarding both the implied method of "added coloraturas" and the organ as the proper medium. It is interesting to note that Landini, in his nine two-voice madrigals, adheres rather strictly to the type just described but uses a freer treatment in his three-voice examples. These are all through-composed and show French influence in their polyrhythmic texture as well as, in one instance (the wonderful "Musica son"), simultaneous use of three different texts after the fashion of the motet, the three stanzas of the poem being sung at the same time. Examples in: *WoGM* ii, iii, nos. 38–44, 47, 49, 50, 54, 55; L. Ellinwood, ‡*The Works of Francesco Landini* (1939), nos. 1–12; *HAM,* nos. 49, 50, 54; *SchGMB,* no. 22; *ReMMA,* p. 363; *AdHM* i, p. 287; *BeMMR,* p. 156. The "Madrigale" in J. Wolf, ‡*Sing- und Spielmusik aus älterer Zeit* (1931), no. 6, is a *ballata.*

II. *The 16th-century Italian madrigal.* As a literary type, the madrigal of the 16th century is a free imitation, without any strict form, of the 14th-century madrigal, which Italian humanists (Cardinal Bembo and his followers) used as a point of departure in their endeavors to develop a more refined poetry than that of the previous period (*frottola, *strambotto). Although these attempts were not very successful from the literary standpoint, the movement was a great stimulus to musical activity. The musicians of the early 16th century, at first Netherlands composers working in Italy (Verdelot, Willaert, Arcadelt), cooperated with the poets in order to achieve a new style of artistic refinement and expression. Naturally, they did not take their cue from 14th-century music, which was entirely forgotten. In fact, it was only the literary bond that justified the use of the old name for the new compositions. As a musical composition the madrigal of the 16th century is an outgrowth of the *frottola,* more specifically, the canzona [see Canzona (4)]. Indeed, the style of the earliest madrigals, published in *Madrigali de diversi Musici* of 1530 (including pieces by Verdelot, Carlo, C. and S. Festa, *et al.*), differs little from that of the late *frottole* (1531; cf. *SchGMB,* nos. 72 and 98).

The development of the madrigal in Italy is usually divided into three phases. (a) *The early madrigal:* Philippe Verdelot (d. *c.* 1550), Costanzo Festa (*c.* 1490–1545; the first Italian composer of madrigals), Jacob Arcadelt (*c.* 1505–*c.* 1560). The style is, in spite of considerable imitation, prevailingly homophonic; the writing is in three or four parts; the expression is quiet and restrained. (b) *The classic madrigal:* Adrian Willaert (properly intermediate between a and b), Cipriano de Rore, Andrea Gabrieli, Orlando di Lasso, Philippe de Monte, Palestrina (publications 1550–80). Here the writing is in four to six (usually five) parts and the style is more genuinely polyphonic and imitative, approaching that of the contemporary motet, the expression being more intense and closely allied to the text in meaning as well as pronunciation. A collateral type of this period is the *madrigale spirituale,* intended for devotional use (e.g., by Palestrina; compl. ed., vol. xxix). (c) *The late madrigal:* Luca Marenzio, Carlo Gesualdo, Claudio Monteverdi (publications 1580–1620). Here, the development leads to a highly elaborate type of music, even exaggerated and mannered, manifesting all the experimental tendencies of the *fin de siècle*—chromaticism, word-painting, coloristic effects, declamatory monody, virtuosity of the vocal soloist, dramatic effects. Particularly important is the fact that, at this late date, the madrigal was flexible enough to drop its traditional polyphonic texture and adapt itself to the new monodic style. The transition is particularly apparent in the madrigals of Monteverdi, whose books i, ii, iii, and iv (1587, '90, '92, 1603) are purely polyphonic and *a cappella,* whereas in the following books (v, 1605; vi, 1614) the style becomes increasingly soloistic and the accompaniment often requires *basso continuo;* book vii, called *Concerto* (1619), is entirely in *stile rappresentativo* with *basso continuo.* Caccini's *Nuove musiche* of 1602 contains "madrigals" for solo voice that are through-composed, in contrast to his strophic "arias" [see Aria II].

III. *The English madrigal.* Outside Italy, the madrigal was cultivated chiefly in England. A few isolated pieces such as Richard Edwards' "In Going to My Naked Bed" (composed not later than 1564) make it probable that the influence of the Italian madrigal was felt in England shortly after 1550. William Byrd (1543–1623) seems to have been the first English composer to grasp fully the importance of the madrigal [see Editions XVI, 14, 15]. He, together with Thomas Morley (1557–1602), represents the earlier period of the English madrigal, whose style corresponds to a certain extent to that of the second

Italian school. Nevertheless, the English madrigal soon acquired native characteristics resulting from the peculiarities of the English language, the frequent use of false relations and other harmonic acerbities, and a propensity for an unmistakably English touch of merriment or melancholy. The *Musica Transalpina* (a collection of Italian madrigals provided with English text, published by N. Yonge in 1588, a few months after the appearance of Byrd's first book) gave the movement new impetus and a different direction. The younger Englishmen, notably Thomas Weelkes and John Wilbye, leaned further toward Italy and exploited the innovations of Marenzio and Gesualdo, though somewhat more conservatively. The English madrigals appeared under a variety of names, such as Song, Sonet, Canzonet, and Ayre. See Editions XVI.

IV. *Other countries.* In Germany, the influence of the madrigal appears to some extent in the works of Le Maistre, Scandello, Regnart, and Lasso [see Lied II], all foreigners, a fact that may account for the failure of the madrigal to attain the artistic significance it achieved in Italy or England. Hans Leo Hassler [*DTB* 20] is the outstanding German madrigalist, although many of his madrigals have Italian texts. Spanish madrigals were published by Pedro Vila (1561), Juan Brudieu (1585), and Pedro Rimonte (Ruimonte; 1614) [see *LavE* i.4, 2015ff].

Lit. *For I:* W. T. Marrocco, ‡*The Music of Jacopo da Bologna* (1954); N. Pirrotta, ‡*The Music of Fourteenth-century Italy* (1954; see Editions XII, 8); J. R. White, ‡"Music of the Early Italian Ars Nova" (diss. Indiana Univ., 1952); K. von Fischer, *Studien zur italienischen Musik des Trecento* (1956); A. von Königslöw, *Die italienischen Madrigalisten des Trecento* (1940); N. Pirrotta, in *CP Besseler; id.,* in *RMI* xlviii, xlix; L. Biadene, in *ML* xxix; E. Li Gotti, in *Poesia* iii/iv; *id.,* in *Atti della Reale Accademia . . . di Palermo* iv/4, 2; J. Wolf, in *SIM* iii, *PMA* lviii, *JMP* xlv; A. Schering, in *SIM* xiii; W. T. Marrocco, in *Speculum* xxvi. See also under *Ars nova.*

For II: A. Einstein, *The Italian Madrigal,* 3 vols. (1949); E. Magni Duffloq, *Il Madrigale* (1931); G. Cesari, *Die Entstehung des Madrigals im 16. Jahrh.* (1908); T. Kroyer, *Die Anfänge der Chromatik im italienischen Madrigal des XVI. Jahrhunderts* (1902); E. Kiwi, *Studien zur Geschichte des italienischen Liedmadrigals* (1937); H. Schultz, *Das Madrigal als Formideal* (1939); J. Haar, ed., *Chanson & Madrigal, 1480–1530* (1964), esp. ‡appendix; E. B. Helm, "The Beginnings of the Italian Madrigal and the Works of Arcadelt" (diss. Harvard, 1939); H. F. Redlich, *Das Problem des Stilwandels in Monteverdis Madrigalwerk* (1931); W. Klefisch, *Arcadelt als Madrigalist* (1938); F. Keiner, *Die Madrigale Gesualdos von Venosa* (1914); L. Benson, ‡*Albums of Madrigals,* 12 vols. (Edition Laudy; for contents see *ReMR,* p. 904); W. Weismann and G. E. Watkins, ed., ‡*Gesualdo di Venosa, Sämtliche Werke* (1957—); C. McClintock, ‡"The Five-Part Madrigals of Giaches de Wert" (diss. Indiana Univ., 1955); *Editions III, 1, 4 (various composers); IX, 14 (Gesualdo); X, 10 (D'India); XXII, section II, l. i–vi (Gesualdo); XXII, section II, 2.i (Nenna); XLVI, 4.i (Marenzio); XLVIII, 6 (De Rore); R. T. Watanabe, "Five Italian Madrigal Books of the Late 16th Century" (diss. Univ. of Rochester, 1951); E. Helm, "Heralds of the Italian Madrigal (*MQ* xxvii); G. Cesari, "Le Origini del madrigale cinquecentesco" (*RMI* xix); C. van den Borren, "Le Madrigalisme avant le madrigal" (*CP Adler*); H. Engel, "Contributo alla storia del madrigale" (*LRM* iv); H. Redlich, "The Italian Madrigal: A Bibliographical Contribution" (*ML* xxxii); A. Einstein, "Das Madrigal zum Doppelgebrauch" (*AM* vi); *id.,* "Augenmusik im Madrigal" (*ZIM* xiv); *id.,* "Narrative Rhythm in the Madrigal" (*MQ* xxix); E. Dent, "The Musical Form of the Madrigal" (*ML* xi); H. Engel, in *ZMW* xvii (Marenzio); J. Razek, in *RM* xiii (Luzzaschi); O. Kinkeldey, in *SIM* ix (Luzzaschi); P. Wagner, in *VMW* viii (Palestrina); A. Einstein, in *SIM* viii (Verdelot); L. Torri, in *RMI* iii (Ruffo); H. Leichtentritt, in *SIM* xi (Monteverdi); A. Heuss, in *CP Liliencron* (Monteverdi); G. Pannain, in *LRM* v (Monteverdi); E. Schmitz, in *SIM* xi (continuo-madrigal). For original publications see E. Vogel, *Bibliothek der gedruckten weltlichen Vocalmusik Italiens* (1962).

For III: J. Kerman, *The Elizabethan Madrigal* (1962); E. H. Fellowes, *The English Madrigal Composers,* rev. ed. (1948); *id., The English Madrigal* (1925); H. Heurich, *John Wilbye in seinen Madrigalen* (1931); G. Bontoux, *La Chanson en Angleterre au temps d'Élisabeth* (1936); A. Obertello, *Madrigali italiani in Inghilterra* (1949); R. B. Childs, "The Setting of Poetry in the English Madrigal" (diss. Stanford, 1959); *Editions XVI; *Editions XL, 3–5 (Kirby), 11–12 (Ferrabosco), 13–15 (Weelkes); C. van den Borren, "The Aesthetic Value of the English Madrigal" (*PMA* lii); E. Helm, "Italian Traits in the English Madrigal" (*MR* vii); J. Kerman, "Elizabethan Anthologies of Italian Madrigals" (*JAMS* iv); A.

Einstein, in *ML* xxv (*Musica Transalpina*); E. Dent, in *CP Wolf* (Byrd); D. Arnold, in *ML* xxxv; J. Kerman, in *MQ* xxxviii.

For IV: C. van den Borren, in *RM* 1925 (Brudieu); J. B. Trend, in *PMA* lii, *CP 1930, CP Adler;* R. Schwartz, in *VMW* ix.

Madrigal comedy. Modern designation for a late 16th-century type in which an entire play [It. *commedia*] was set to music in the form of madrigals and other kinds of contemporary polyphonic vocal music. Among the first and most famous examples is *L'Amfiparnaso* by Orazio Vecchi (performed in Modena, 1594; printed 1597). It has been suggested that the inner contradiction between the ensemble character of the music, which is in five parts throughout, without instrumental accompaniment, and the soloistic demands of a theatrical performance was resolved by a strange compromise: when the plot called for single characters, the singers of the other parts were made to sing behind a curtain. This surmise, however, is unlikely, not only for practical considerations but because Vecchi states expressly in the Preface that this spectacle (*spettacolo*) appeals to the imagination (*mente*) through the ear (*orecchie*), not the eye (*occhi*). *L'Amfiparnaso,* therefore, is not, as has been alleged, a pre-operatic type, but an idealized presentation of a loosely knit dramatic plot, somewhat comparable to the presentation of an oratorio. The plot is more clearly outlined here than in other, similar works by Vecchi—the *Selva di varia ricreatione* (1590), *Convito musicale* (1597), and *Le Veglie di Siena* (1604)—each of which, however, includes a number of dramatic "scenes." *L'Amfiparnaso* is a mixture of comic and sentimental portions. Alessandro Striggio's *Il Cicalamento delle donne al bucato* (The Babbling of the Women on Washday, 1567) may be considered a predecessor of the former, and Simone Balsamino's *Novellette* (after Tasso's *Aminta,* printed 1594) of the latter. Other models exist in the *greghesche* of Andrea Gabrieli and other Venetian composers. Imitators of Vecchi included, among others, Adriano Banchieri [ex. in *HAM,* no. 186].

Lit.: E. J. Dent, in *SIM* xii; A. Heuss, in *SIM* iv, 175, 404. Republications of *L'Amfiparnaso* and other madrigal comedies in *Editions III, 4, and XLVII, 26; also by Perinello (fac. and transcr., 1938). A.E.

Madrigalism. A term commonly used for word-painting and related devices, such as are found particularly in the madrigals of Luca Marenzio.

Maestoso [It.]. Majestic.

Maestro. Honorary title for distinguished teachers, composers, and conductors.

Magadis. An ancient Greek harp, which seems to have had ten pairs of strings, each pair consisting of the fundamental and its octave. The term "magadizing" is sometimes used to describe singing in octaves, which is considered by some writers the "beginning of polyphony."

Magelone Romances. See *Romanzen aus L. Tieck's Magelone.*

Maggiolata [It.]. Popular song for the month of May. For 16th-century examples composed in the style of the *villanella, see A. Bonaventura, in *RMI* xxiv; F. Ghisi, *Musique et poésie au XVIe siècle* (1954), s.v. "Maggiolata."

Maggiore [It.]. Major key.

Magic Flute, The. See *Zauberflöte, Die.*

Magnificat. The *canticle of the Virgin, text ("Magnificat anima mea Dominum," My soul doth magnify the Lord) from Luke 1:46–55. It consists of twelve verses, including the *Doxology at the end. In the Roman Catholic rites it is sung at the Office of Vespers by alternating choruses to one of eight *toni*, recitation chants similar to the psalm tones [see *LU,* pp. 207ff], in connection with an antiphon (Magnificat antiphon) that is usually somewhat more elaborate in style than the psalm antiphons. See O antiphons.

From the 15th through the 18th centuries the Magnificat was frequently set, for voices or for organ. Aside from an English 14th-century setting, the earliest composers of the Magnificat were Dunstable, Dufay, and Binchois. Each of them composed the entire text, including the Doxology at the end, using one or the other of the Magnificat tones. Thus, Dunstable wrote a *Magnificat secundi toni* (*Editions XXXIV, 8, p. 95); Binchois, Magnificats in tones 1, 2, 3, 4 [see J. Marix, *Les Musiciens de la cour de Bourgogne,* p. 131ff; no. 2 also in *SchGMB,* no. 43]; Dufay, in tones 1, 3, 5, 6, 8 [two in *DTO* 14/15, 169ff]. After 1450 it became customary to compose only the even-numbered verses, the others being sung in plainsong. This practice of alternating occurs in Obrecht (comp. ed. by J. Wolf) and in the numerous Magnificats preserved in the Eton MS from about 1500, and was generally adopted by 16th-century composers such as Senfl, Lasso, Palestrina, J. de Kerle, Le Maistre,

Mahu, and Morales, who often wrote complete sets of Magnificat verses, usually six for each of the eight tones. Later composers of the Magnificat are Schütz, S. Bernardi (*DTO* 69), R. Ahle (*DdT* 5), and J. S. Bach, who composed it as a cantata.

The alternating method of composition, applied to the eight tones, was also used by organ composers. Such Magnificat *versets for the organ occur in Attaingnant's *Magnificat sur les huit tons* (1531; *Editions XLIX, 1); G. Cavazzoni's *Intavolatura* (1543); A. de Cabezón's *Obras de música* (1578); J. Titelouze's organ works (*Editions I, 1); J. E. Kindermann's *Harmonia organica* (1645; *DTB* 32); and J. K. Kerll's *Modulatio organica* (1686). J. Pachelbel's 95 Magnificat fugues (*DTO* 17) are essentially free compositions (not based on the plainsong *toni*), which seem to have served primarily as intonations (preludes), not as versets proper.

The Magnificat in English translation ("My soul doth magnify the Lord") was taken over into the Anglican *Service, where it forms a part of the Evening Prayer. The Magnificat, set to the melody of the *tonus peregrinus* [see Psalm tones], was used for organ chorales by Scheidt, Pachelbel, J. S. Bach, and others.

Lit.: C.-H. Illing, *Zur Technik der Magnificat-Komposition des 16. Jahrhunderts* (1936); J. Meinholz, "Untersuchungen zur Magnificat-Komposition des 15. Jahrhunderts" (diss. Cologne, 1956); J. Schmidt-Görg, in *Gesammelte Aufsätze zur Kulturgeschichte Spaniens* v (1935; Gombert); T. W. Werner, in *AMW* ii (Adam Rener); H. Osthoff, in *AMW* xvi (Josquin); E. R. Lerner, in *MQ* l (15th-cent. Italy); G. Reese, in *JAMS* xiii.

Magnum opus musicum. Title of a publication containing 516 compositions (motets) of O. di Lasso (1532–94), published in 1604 in six volumes by his sons.

Magnus liber organi [L.]. According to Anon. IV (*CS* i, 342), title of the collection of two-voice organa for the entire ecclesiastical year written *c.* 1175 by Leoninus, with additions and modifications by his successor Perotinus (*c.* 1200; see *Ars antiqua*). The full title was "Magnus liber organi de gradali et antiphonario pro servitio divino multiplicando." The complete collection includes 59 pieces for the Mass ("de gradali") and 34 pieces for the Office ("de antiphonario"), all composed "to enrich the divine service." Three 13th-century MSS from Florence and Wolfenbüttel contain the "Magnus liber organi" in a more or less complete form, together with numerous other pieces (three- and four-voice organa, clausulae, conductus, motets). A list based on the collection in the Florentine Codex (Florence, Bibl. Laur. *plut. 29.i* [*F*]) is given in F. Ludwig, *Repertorium organorum . . . et motetorum*, rev. ed. (1964), pp. 65–75, where the letters O and M refer to the pieces for the Office and the Mass respectively [see *ApNPM*, pp. 201, 230n]. The Leoninus collection is transcribed in W. G. Waite, *The Rhythm of Twelfth-Century Polyphony* (1954). See *Ars antiqua;* Mass B; Organum IV; Square notation; Sources, no. 3. Also see W. G. Waite, in *JAMS* xiv; H. Husman, in *JAMS* xvi; id., in *MQ* xlix.

Magrepha. An organ of the ancient Hebrews, used in the last period of the Third Temple as a signaling instrument. See J. Yasser, in *JAMS* xiii.

Magyar music. The indigenous folk music of *Hungary.

Maid as Mistress, The. See *Serva Padrona, La*.

Main [F.]. Hand. *Main droite (gauche)*, right (left) hand. *À deux (trois, quatre) mains,* for two (three, four) hands.

Maîtres musiciens de la renaissance française, Les. See Editions XXV.

Maîtrise [F.]. The choir school and choir of a French church. These institutions, which date from the 15th century if not earlier, were under the direction of a "maître de chapelle" and provided board as well as education, both general and musical. In organization and purpose they resembled the *conservatorii* of Italy. During the French Revolution (1791) they were suppressed and replaced by the *conservatoires*. Today the name means simply "church choir."

Majeur [F.]. Major.

Major, minor [F. *majeur, mineur;* G. *Dur, Moll;* It. *maggiore, minore;* Sp. *mayor, menor*]. Terms used (1) to distinguish intervals, e.g., major second (c–d), and minor second (c–d♭) [see Interval]; (2) for two types of scale, triad, or key, which are distinguished mainly by their third, this being a major third (c–e) in the major scale (triad, key) and a minor third (c–e♭) in the minor scale (triad, key). The major scale is the same ascending and descending [Ex. 1]. The descending minor scale, however, has a flatted seventh (b♭) and sixth (a♭) in addition to the flatted third of the ascending scale [Ex. 2]. The justification for this is that, without the flatted seventh and

sixth, the descending minor scale would sound like a major scale until its sixth tone was reached. Since the minor scale just described rests on melodic considerations (upward and downward movement), it is called "melodic minor scale." There is another minor scale that, ascending as well as descending, combines the flatted sixth with the unaltered seventh [Ex. 3]. This scale is called the "harmonic minor scale" because it is built from the tones contained in the three main harmonies of the minor key [Ex. 5].

A key is called "major" or "minor" according to whether it is based on the major or minor scale. In the major key, the three main triads, tonic (T), dominant (D), and subdominant (S; see Scale degrees), are all major triads [Ex. 4]. In a minor key, T and S are minor, D is major [Ex. 5]. See also Mode.

The definite establishment of major and minor as the tonal basis of music took place during the 17th century [see Harmony II, B (6)]. Prior to this, music was based on the church modes, all of which differ from major or minor in some of their degrees. Glareanus' enlarged system of twelve modes (*Dodecachordon*, 1547) is usually considered the first theoretical system including both major and minor, the former in his Ionian (diatonic scale on c), the latter in his Aeolian (diatonic scale on a). Actually, the latter differs from minor mainly in that it does not have the leading tone (g♯). Zarlino seems to have been the first to recognize that there are only two modes, one with the major third, the other with the minor third (*L'Istitutioni harmoniche*, 1558; see R. W. Wienpahl, in *JAMS* xii, 30). In musical practice the situation was quite different. Particularly in monophonic music it is not difficult to find 12th- and 13th-century examples of major melodies, by the troubadours, trouvères, or minnesingers, either on c (*HAM*, nos. 19b, d, 20a), on f with b-flat (*HAM*, no. 19e), or on g (*HAM*, no. 17b). Their number is greatly increased if, as in many modern editions, editorial accidentals are added, resulting in leading tones such as f♯ to g. A Dorian melody can easily be changed into D minor by the addition of sharps (for c) and flats (for b). Whether or not such changes are admissible is another question. The same statement applies, *a fortiori,* to polyphonic music, in which another problem arises, i.e., whether or not "modal harmonies" (extensive use of the II, III, VI degrees) are compatible with major or minor. Examples in point are the two-part *ductiae* reproduced in *HAM,* no. 41, or the famous *"Sumer is icumen in."* A definite trend toward a major-type of melody and harmony is noticeable in the works of Dunstable and Dufay (*HAM,* nos. 62, 65). It may be noted, however, that often a composition beginning in C major will close in a different tonality, e.g., D minor (*HAM,* no. 62). In the 16th century, particularly during the second half, most compositions were written in an idiom that, aside from the occasional use of modal progressions, is very close to either major or minor. See also Tonality.

Lit.: A. Machabey, *Genèse de la tonalité musicale classique des origines aux xvᵉ siècle* (1955); P. Beyer, *Studien zur Vorgeschichte des Dur-Moll* (1958); C. Sachs, "The Road to Major" (*MQ* xxix); A. H. Fox Strangways, "The Minor Chord" (*ML* iv, 26); Dom J. Jeannin, "Etude sur le mineur et le majeur" (*RMI* xxii); H. J. Moser, "Die Entstehung des Durgedankens, ein kulturgeschichtliches Problem" (*SIM* xv).

Malaguena [Sp.]. According to available information, term for three different types of southern Spanish folk music, all localized in the provinces of Malaga and Murcia: (1) Usually a local variety of the *fandango. (2) A type of highly emotional song, in free style and rhythm [see *LavE,* 1.4, 2390]. (3) An older type of dance music, based on the ostinato-like repetition of the harmonies VIII–VII–VI–V (in minor), played in parallel triads and with an improvised melody on top; thus, a passacaglia on the descending tetrachord, like those written frequently during the 17th century [see Chaconne and passacaglia, Ex. 2].

Malincònico [It.]. Melancholy.

Mamelles de Tirésias, Les [F., The Bosom of Tirésias]. Musical farce in two acts and a prologue by F. Poulenc (libretto by G. Apollinaire, after his play), produced in Paris, 1947.

Ma Mère l'oye [F., *Mother Goose (Suite)*]. Suite by M. Ravel based on fairy tales by C. Perrault (1678–1703). Originally written (1908) for piano

duet, it was scored for orchestra by Ravel and produced as a children's ballet in 1915.

Man. Abbr. for *manual.

Manche [F.]. Neck of the violin, etc.

Mandola, mandora. See under Lute III.

Mandolin. The most recent instrument of the lute family and the only one in general use today, chiefly in southern Italy. The Neapolitan mandolin has four double courses (eight steel strings) tuned g d a e. It is played with a plectrum of tortoise shell or another flexible material. The tones are rendered as a sustained tremolo, which is produced by a quick vibrating movement of the plectrum. See ill. under Lute. The mandolin has been used occasionally in art music, e.g., in Handel's oratorio *Alexander Balus* (1748), Grétry's *L'Amant jaloux* (1778), G. Paisiello's *Il Barbiere di Siviglia* (1782), Mozart's *Don Giovanni* (1787), Verdi's *Otello* (1887), Mahler's Symphony no. 7 (1908), and four pieces by Beethoven for mandolin and piano (two in suppl. vol. of B.-H. ed.; see also *BSIM* viii, no. 12, p. 24). More recent works using the mandolin include Schoenberg's *Serenade* op. 24, Webern's *5 Stücke für Orchester* op. 10, and Stravinsky's *Agon.*

Lit.: P. J. Bone, *The Guitar and Mandolin: Biographies of Celebrated Players and Composers* (1954); K. Wölki, *Die Geschichte der Mandoline* (1940); K. Boss, *Die Mandolinenmusik vor und nach dem (Welt-) Kriege im In- und Auslande* (1924); J. Zuth, "Die Mandolinhandschriften in der Bibliothek der Gesellschaft der Musikfreunde in Wien" (*ZMW* xiv); G. de Saint-Foix, "Un Fonds inconnu de compositions pour mandoline" (*RdM* 1933, p. 129).

Maneria [L.]. A term used by some 12th-century writers on plainsong (Guido of Cherlieu; see *CS* ii, 157a) to denote the *church modes in their authentic as well as plagal variety. Thus there are four *maneriae: protus, deuterus, tritus,* and *tetrardus.* The term is very useful in connection with melodies that, because of their limited or excessive ambitus, cannot be classified as either authentic or plagal. See *ReMMA,* p. 153; *ApGC,* p. 135.

Maneries [L.]. A 13th-century term for *modus,* i.e., rhythmic *mode, mentioned by Garlandia (*CS* i, 175), Pseudo-Aristotle (*CS* i, 279), and Anon. IV (*CS* i, 327).

Manfredina. See Monferrina.

Mangulina [Sp.]. A traditional dance that was popular in the Dominican Republic *c.* 1855. It is said to have evolved from the Spanish *zortziko,* which was in 5/4 and 5/8 meter. Nevertheless, most of the examples preserved and occasionally still performed today show a closer connection with either the Spanish *seguidilla* or the *muiñeira.* Many composers, among them Esteban Peña Morell (1897–1939) and Juan Francisco García (b. 1892), have employed the *mangulina* in art music.   J.O-S.

Manica [It.]. Shift of position in violin playing.

Manico [It.]. Fingerboard of the violin, etc.

Manicordion, manichord. A 16th-century name for *clavichord.

Maniera [It.]. A 16th-century term used by numerous theorists to denote the aesthetic basis of contemporary musical composition. See L. Schrade, in *ZMW* xvi.

Manieren [G.]. An 18th-century name for ornaments of restricted melodic range, approximately equivalent to *agrément.*

Männergesangverein [G.]. Male choral society in Germany, similar to the American *Apollo Club and the French *Orphéon.

Mannheim school. An important group of German composers of the mid-18th century, centered at Mannheim and associated with the orchestra of Karl Theodor (1724–99), Elector of Pfalzbayern (Palatinate), hence also known as *Pfalzbayrische Schule.* Johann Stamitz (1717–57), who joined the orchestra in 1745 and soon became its conductor, inaugurated an entirely novel style of orchestral music and performance, thereby laying the foundation for the symphonic style of the Viennese classical school during the same period when the tradition of baroque music culminated in the late works of Bach and Handel. Conspicuous features of the new style were: melodic prominence of the violins in an essentially homophonic, noncontrapuntal texture; abandonment of imitation and fugal style; presto character of the quick movements; use of dynamic devices such as extended crescendos and unexpected fortes and fortissimos; complete rests (*Generalpausen*); a novel type of subject and figure that quickly rise over a wide range, usually in broken chords, the so-called *Raketen* [G., rockets, Roman candles]; orchestral effects such as the tremolo and broken chords in quick notes; replacement of thoroughbass accompani-

ment by written out orchestral parts. Johann Stamitz' activity was continued by Ignaz Holzbauer (1711–83; came to Mannheim in 1753), Franz Xaver Richter (1709–89; came to Mannheim in 1747), and a younger generation including Anton Filtz (1730–60), Franz Beck (1723–1809), Christian Cannabich (1731–98), and Johann Stamitz' sons Karl Stamitz (1745–1801) and Anton Stamitz (1754–1809).

The importance of the Mannheim composers lies in their historical position as forerunners of the classical period rather than in the intrinsic value of their works. The symphonies of Johann Stamitz, typical products of a single-minded innovator, are artistically even less satisfactory than those of the later Mannheimers, who turned from Stamitz' fragmentary and incoherent mosaic style (somewhat like that of Domenico Scarlatti) to a more continuous and melodic manner, which, however, is not free from the sentimentalities of the gallant style and which, needless to say, is inferior to that of their noted contemporaries, Haydn and Mozart. Mozart's father referred to the extravagant novelties of this school as the "vermanirierte Mannheimer goût" (the mannered Mannheim taste).

The importance of the Mannheim school as the founders of the modern symphony and chamber music was strongly emphasized by their discoverer, H. Riemann. More recently his claims to precedence and superiority have been challenged by other historians who have pointed to similar tendencies in Vienna (Georg Monn, 1717–50; Georg Wagenseil, 1715–77; see G. Adler in preface to *DTO* 31), Italy [see F. Torrefranca, *Le Origini italiane del romanticismo musicale,* 1930], and Bohemia [see V. Helfert, in *AMW* vii]. No doubt the novel ideas of style and form were "in the air" about 1740, and a great many musicians, among whom G. B. Sammartini (1701–75) deserves particular mention, worked in the same direction, laying the foundation for Haydn, Mozart, and Beethoven. Perhaps some of the contradictory claims can be settled if a clearer distinction is made between the various features of the classical sonata or symphony. The early Viennese composers were definitely much more advanced than the Mannheimers in the establishment of the formal principles of the sonata. On the other hand, the importance and true meaning of the new principles of symphonic style [see the description above] were more clearly understood in Mannheim than elsewhere, probably owing to the favorable conditions there. See also Sonata III; Sonata form; Symphony II.

Lit.: R. Fuhrmann, *Mannheimer Klavier-Kammermusik*, 2 vols. (1963); F. Waldkirch, "Die konzertanten Sinfonien der Mannheimer im 18. Jahrhundert" (diss. Heidelberg, 1931); R. Münster, "Die Sinfonien Toeschis. Ein Beitrag zur Geschichte der Mannheimer Sinfonie" (diss. Munich, 1956); H. Boese, "Die Klarinette als Soloinstrument in der Musik der Mannheimer Schule" (diss. Berlin, 1940); G. Schmidt, "Peter Ritter. Ein Beitrag zur Mannheimer Musikgeschichte" (diss. Munich, 1925); P. H. Lang, *Music in Western Civilization* (1941), pp. 608ff; *RiHM* ii.3, 119ff; P. Gradenwitz, "The Symphonies of Johann Stamitz" (*MR* i); *id.*, "Mid-Eighteenth-century Transformations of Style" (*ML* xviii, 265); J. P. Larsen, "Zur Bedeutung der 'Mannheim Schule'" (*CP Fellerer*); W. Fischer, "Zur Entwicklungsgeschichte des Wiener klassischen Stils" (*StM* iii); A. Heuss, "Über die Dynamik der Mannheimer Schule" (*CP Riemann*); *id.*, in *ZMW* ii; *id.*, "Zum Thema: 'Mannheimer Vorhalt'" (*ZIM* ix); R. Sondheimer, "Die Sinfonien Franz Becks" (*ZMW* iv); L. Kamienski, "Mannheim und Italien" (*SIM* x). Re-editions in *DTB* 4, 13, 15, 27, 28; *DdT* 39; *DTO* 31, 39 [see Editions XIV, XV].

Manon. Opera in five acts by Massenet (libretto by H. Meilhac and P. Gille, based on Prévost's novel, *Histoire de Manon Lescaut*), produced in Paris, 1884. Setting: France, early 18th century.

Manon Lescaut. Opera in four acts by Puccini (libretto in Italian by M. Praga, P. Oliva, and L. Illica, based on Prévost's novel), produced in Turin, 1893. Setting: France and Louisiana, early 18th century. (Also, an opera by Auber.)

Manual. On the organ, any of the keyboards provided for the hands, as opposed to the pedal [see Organ III]. The two keyboards of the harpsichord are also distinguished as first and second manual. *Manualiter* means playing with the hands only.

Manualkoppel [G.]. Manual coupler; see Organ IV.

Manubrio [It.]. The knobs and handles of the organ stops.

Manus musicalis [L.]. *Guidonian hand.

Maqam [Arab.; pl. *maqamat*]. See under Arab music; Melody type.

Maraca. A gourd or calabash shell shaker filled with dry seeds, typical of the Caribbean countries but known throughout Latin America under different names, such as *alfandoque, carángano, guazá* (Colombia); *asson, tcha-tcha* (Haiti); *bapó, caracaxá* (Brazil); *chinchin* (Guatemala); *dadoo* (Venezuela); *huada* or *wada* (Chile); *Maruga* (Cuba); *nasisi* (Panama); *sonajas* (Mexico). It is often used in pairs.   J.O-S.

Marcando, marcato [It.]. Marked, stressed.

Marcellus Mass. A famous Mass by Palestrina, named after Pope Marcellus II (*Missa Papae Marcelli*) and long thought to have played a decisive role at the *Council of Trent. The work is exceptional among Palestrina's Masses because it is almost completely in homorhythmic (note-against-note) style, resulting in a clearly audible declamation of the text. According to recent research (Jeppesen, in *AM* xvi–xvii, 38) it was composed 1562–63, long after the death of Marcellus, who ruled for only three weeks in 1555. During his short pontificate Marcellus instructed the singers of the papal choir to sing so that the words could be clearly understood, and this probably explains the name of the Mass. See K. Jeppesen, in *CP Adler* and *AM* xvi–xvii.

March. Music originally designed to promote orderly marching of a large group, especially of soldiers. Marches are generally in simple, strongly marked rhythm and regular phrases. The standard form, derived from the minuet-with-trio, is that of a march repeated after one or several trios of a more melodious character: M T M, or M T M T M. Military marches can be divided into four categories: (1) funeral march; (2) slow march—75 steps per minute, 2 steps per bar; (3) quick march—108 to 128 beats per minute; (4) double-quick march—140 to 160 beats per minute. In the United States the standard military march is the quick march, the finest examples having been written by John Philip Sousa, known as "the March King."

The earliest traces of the march as an art form are the numerous *battaglias of the 16th century. William Byrd wrote a "Battell" (in *My Ladye Nevells Booke;* see Virginal music) consisting of "The March of Horsmen," "The March of Footemen," etc., as well as "The Earle of Oxfords Marche" (in The Fitzwilliam Virginal Book, no. cclix). Many examples of march music, usually dignified and ceremonial rather than military in character, are found in the operas of Lully, Handel, etc. (Handel's *Scipione* contains a march that is to the present day the parade march of the British Grenadier Guards.) There are three charming little marches—probably not by Bach—in the *Klavierbüchlein für Anna Magdalena Bach* of 1725. Similar pieces occur in the suites of J. P. Krieger, J. K. F. Fischer, etc. Mozart used two different types of march music in *Figaro* ("Non più andrai") and *The Magic Flute* (March of the Priests). The movement "Lebhaft. Marschmässig" in Beethoven's Sonata op. 101 is a superb example of stylization. Schubert's *Marches militaires* deserve mention for their admirable variety and ingenuity. The processional march of Wagner's *Die Meistersinger* is a distinguished example of the numerous marches in 19th-century opera. A special type is the funeral march (*marcia funebre*), of which well-known examples occur in Beethoven's *Eroica* and Wagner's *Götterdämmerung*. Among modern composers of marches are Barber (*Commando March*), Shostakovitch ("Festive Overture" op. 96), Prokofiev, Hindemith, Vaughan Williams, and Stravinsky. Also see Band; Military music.

Lit.: J. A. Kappey, *Military Music* (1894); R. F. Goldman, *The Wind Band* (1961); id., *The Concert Band* (1946); id., *The Band's Music* (1938); H. G. Farmer, *The Rise & Development of Military Music* [1912]; G. Kandler, *Deutsche Armeemärsche* (1962); W. C. White, *A History of Military Music in America* (1945); K. Strom, "Beiträge zur Entwicklungsgeschichte des Marsches" (diss. Munich, 1926).

Marcha [Sp.]. In Spain, term used essentially for music designed to accompany marching groups [see March], but in Latin America, name for various kinds of folk dance, in fast or slow tempo and in major or minor mode or following Indian scale patterns. In Brazil the *marcha* is essentially a carnival dance whose steady rhythms are occasionally broken by Afro-Brazilian syncopation. In Haiti the *marche* [F.] is an urban dance considerably more ardent and intense than examples from other places. In Central America the *marcha* is halfway between a military march and a street dance.   J.O-S.

Marche [F.]. *March. Also see under *Marcha*. *Marche harmonique*, F. for *sequence I.

Marcia [It.]. *March. *Marcia funebre*, funeral march. *Alla marcia*, in the manner of a march.

Mariachi [Sp.]. Mexican ensemble of folk musicians, composed of two violins, *jarana* (guitar), *arpón* (harp), and *guitarrón* (large guitar). The number of players is variable, ranging from groups of four players to the size of a regular band. The word *mariachi* or *mariache* is also used for a single folksinger.   J.O-S.

Marian antiphon. Name used for the antiphons B.M.V.; see Antiphon (2).

Marimba. An African and Central and South American *xylophone, consisting of a number of wooden plates of different size and thickness. Underneath the plates are resonators made of gourds. The instrument has been modernized (first by Sebastián Hurtado of Guatemala c. 1895) and is now made with bars of hardwood of uniform thickness and with tuned tubular metal resonators, encompassing up to six or seven octaves. Of warm and mellow tone, it is played with rubber- or felt-headed mallets, often by two to five players. Marimba concertos have been written by Creston (1940) and Milhaud (1949). For ill. see under Percussion instruments.

The marimba is especially popular in Central America and is considered the national instrument of Guatemala, where marimbas of all sizes are made, ranging from those played by a single player to models so large as to need seven players. Sounds produced by the Dominican marimba are low enough to be employed as the bass in the *merengue and other dances.

Lit.: V. Chenoweth, *The Marimbas of Guatemala* (1964); D. Vela, *La Marimba: estudio sobre el instrumento nacional* (1962); S. F. Nadel, *Marimba-Musik* (1931); S. N. Coleman, *The Marimba Book* (1930).   add. by J.O-S.

Marimbaphone. Several varieties of marimba, designed and made by J. C. Deagan of Chicago between 1915 and 1920. Percy Grainger prescribed them in his suite *In a Nutshell* (1916).

Marinera [Sp.]. Dance form that is an offspring of the Chilean *cueca, which was very popular in Peru before the War of the Pacific between the two countries (1879–84). At that time it was known in Peru as *chilena*. The name *marinera* was adopted about 1880 in homage to the marines who fought in the war. On the northern coast of Peru the dance is known as *tondero*.
                                               J.O-S.

Marine trumpet. See Tromba marina.

Marizápalos [Sp.]. According to J. Pena and H. Anglés (*Diccionario de la música labor*, 1954), a popular song (17th-century?) of Spain. Three MSS of c. 1700 (Municipal Lib. of Oporto, Portugal, no. 1577, Loc. B, 5; Martín y Coll, Bibl.

nat., Madrid, *M-1358*, ff. 74ᵛ–75ᵛ, and *M-1359*, pp. 584–87) contain three *marizápalos* for keyboard, all of which have a bass similar to that of the *folia.

Markiert [G.]. Marked, stressed.

Markig [G.]. Vigorous.

Marqué [F.]. Marked, stressed.

Marriage of Figaro, The. See *Nozze di Figaro, Le.*

Marsch [G.]. *March.

Marseillaise, La. See under National anthems.

Martelé [F.]. A special method of violin bowing; see Bowing (c). *Martellando, martellato* [It.] means either the *martelé* of the violin or a somewhat similar technique of piano playing in which the hands act like hammers, usually in rapidly alternating octaves.

Martellement [F.]. In the 17th century, a *mordent performed on stringed instruments. In the 18th century, a mordent or a short trill preceded by a long appoggiatura.

Martha. Opera in four acts by F. von Flotow (libretto by F. W. Riese), produced in Vienna, 1847. Setting: Richmond, England, about 1710.

Martyrion. See under Byzantine chant III.

Mascherata. See under Villanella.

Masculine, feminine cadence. A cadence or ending is called "masculine" if the final chord of a phrase or section occurs on the strong beat [Ex. 1] and "feminine" if it is postponed to fall on a weak beat [Ex. 2, 3]. The masculine ending

must be considered the normal one, while the feminine is preferred in more romantic styles. Feminine endings appeared for the first time about 1600, becoming one of the various novel features of the baroque era. One of the earliest examples is a "Sarabrand" by Gibbons [see Ex. 2 above; see M. H. Glyn, *Orlando Gibbons 1583–1625, Complete Keyboard Works*, vol. ii]. It may well be this novel feature to which Shakespeare alludes in his famous line: "That strain again, it had a dying fall." Feminine endings are common

in Froberger and are a typical feature of the *polonaise. Beethoven showed a marked preference for feminine endings in his late works.

Masked Ball, A. See *Ballo in maschera, Un.*

Masque, mask. A stage production of the 16th and 17th centuries, designed for the entertainment of the nobility and combining poetry, vocal and instrumental music, dancing, acting, etc., lavishly applied to the presentation of mythological and allegorical subjects. The masque originated in Italy and France, where members of the court played an active part in their preparation as well as performance. B. de Beaujoyeulx's famous *Balet comique de la Royne* [see Ballet I], performed in the Louvre in 1581, was one of the first plays with a unified plot that continued through all scenes.

The masque was introduced into England during the 16th century and remained in great favor during the 17th century. The best-known writer of masques was Ben Jonson, who from 1605 to 1631 provided them for the court. A specialty of his plays was the "antimasque," i.e., intermediate scenes of a grotesque character (similar to the operatic *intermezzo). The earliest known composers of music for masques are Thomas Campion (1567–1620), Alfonso Ferrabosco II (1575–1628), Robert Johnson (*c.* 1583–*c.* 1633), and John Coperario (*c.* 1570–1627). Whereas the music for these masques consists of *ayres and *balletti,* later composers, such as Nicholas Laniere (1588–1666), Henry Lawes (1596–1662), and William Lawes (1602–1645), introduced the *stile recitativo.* Henry Lawes wrote the music to Milton's masque *Comus,* produced in 1634 [repub. by the Mermaid Society, 1904; ex. in *HAM,* 204]. After the civil war (*c.* 1660) opera gradually superseded the masques, which deteriorated into mere fancy-dress balls. A late revival was *Freya's Gift,* text by J. Oxenford, music by G. A. Macfarren, which was produced at the wedding of Edward VII (1863). See Opera VI.

Lit.: R. E. Moore, *Henry Purcell & The Restoration Theatre* (1961); H. A. Evans, *English Masques* (1897); E. Welsford, *The Court Masque* (1927); F. S. Boas, *Songs and Lyrics from the English Masques and Light Operas* (1949); W. W. Greg, *A List of Masques* (1902); P. Reyher, *Les Masques anglais, 1512–1640* (1909); R. Brotanek, *Die englischen Maskenspiele* (1902); *Editions XXXIV, 3 (Masque of Comus); *Editions XL, 1 (Masque . . . of Lord Hayes); A. Sabol, ‡*Songs and Dances for the Stuart Masque* (1959); D.

Heartz, "A Spanish 'Masque of Cupid'" (*MQ* xlix); J. P. Cutts, "Jacobean Masque and Stage Music" (*ML* xxxv); J. Mark, "The Jonsonian Masque" (*ML* iii, 358); W. J. Lawrence, "Notes on a Collection of Masque Music" (*ML* iii, 49); O. Gombosi, in *JAMS* i; A. H. D. Prendergast, in *PMA* xxiii; *ReMR*, pp. 881ff; *BuMBE*, pp. 181ff.

Mass [F. *messe;* G. *Messe;* It. *messa;* L. *missa;* Sp. *misa*]. The most solemn service of the Roman Catholic Church, representing the commemoration and mystical repetition of the Last Supper. The name is derived from the words "Ite, missa est (congregatio)"—literally, "Depart, the congregation is dismissed"—sung at the end of the service [see, e.g., *LU*, p. 19]. The discussion following refers to the full form known as High Mass [see Missa solemnis], as opposed to the *Low Mass. Liturgically, the Mass falls into two parts, the Mass of the Catechumens and the Mass of the Faithful; the former ends with the Gospel, while the latter goes from the Offertory to the end. (The Credo, a later addition, belongs to neither.)

A. *The Mass in Gregorian chant.* The Mass consists of a number of items whose texts vary from day to day (Proper of the Mass, *proprium missae*) and others having the same text in every Mass (Ordinary of the Mass, *ordinarium missae*). Another classification can be made according to whether an item is (a) recited to a *monotone or spoken, or (b) sung to a distinct melody. The former category is entrusted to the celebrant priest and his assistants, the latter to the choir (*schola*). The following table shows the normal structure of the Mass, with the items classified under four categories: Ia, Proper sung; Ib, Ordinary sung; IIa, Proper recited (or spoken); IIb, Ordinary spoken.

	Sung		Recited or Spoken	
Ia Proper	Ib Ordinary	IIa Proper	IIb Ordinary
1. Introit			
	2. Kyrie		
	3. Gloria		
		4. Collect	
		5. Epistle	
6. Gradual			
7. Alleluia or Tract			
		8. Gospel	
	9. Credo		
10. Offertory			
		11. Secret	
		12. Preface	
	13. Sanctus		
			14. Canon
	15. Agnus Dei		
16. Communion			
		17. Post-Communion	
	18. Ite missa est or Benedicamus Domino		

For the texts of items Ib and IIb (and other texts not included below), see the *Ordo Missae,* given in *LU,* pp. 1–7. The variable texts (*Collect, *Epistle, etc.) are given with the different Masses, e.g., *LU,* pp. 317ff, while the recitation tones of items 4, 5, 8, and 12 are found in *LU,* pp. 98–111. The items Ia with their melodies are given with the different Masses, e.g., *LU,* pp. 317ff, while those for Ib are found in *LU,* pp. 11–97.

The items of classes Ia and Ib are those of most interest from the musical point of view, and it is to these exclusively that the subsequent discussion refers. What is usually known to music students as "Mass" are the items of the rubric Ib, the (sung) Ordinary of the Mass. The reason for this narrow and actually misleading view is the fact that these alone (with the exception of the "Ite missa est") were composed polyphonically after 1300 [see under B]. From the standpoint of Gregorian chant, the Proper of the Mass (Ia) is much more important and musically interesting. These chants and their texts are much older than those of the Ordinary. Also, many of them are derived from the psalms [see Psalmody]. Thus, the Introit originally was a *psalmus ad introitum,* the Communion a *psalmus ad communionem,* etc. About A.D. 500, the Mass consisted only of the chants of the Proper, alternating with lections from the Epistles, etc. Gradually, the chants of the Ordinary were introduced, probably in the following chronological order: Sanctus, Kyrie, Gloria, Agnus Dei, Credo. A number of Masses have a musical structure differing from the normal one [see *ApGC,* pp. 28ff].

For each item of the Ordinary there exist numerous melodies (e.g., about 300 for the Agnus Dei), the earliest of which date from the 11th century. From this large repertory a small number has been selected for present-day use and organized into eighteen cycles, each of which is assigned to a specific category of feasts and is named after the *trope formerly associated with its Kyrie. Thus, the *Liber usualis* has a "Mass I: In Paschal Time (Lux et origo)," "Mass II: For Solemn Feasts. 1. (Kyrie fons bonitatis)," etc. [see *LU,* pp. 16ff]. The Credos, being late additions, are listed separately [*LU,* pp. 64ff]. The earliest of these cycles, Mass IV (*Cunctipotens Genitor Deus*), dates from the end of the 13th century, others are from the 14th and 15th centuries, and still others were put together at *Solesmes in the 19th century [see *ApGC,* p. 419f].

B. *The polyphonic Mass Proper.* In early polyphonic music, prior to *c.* 1250, the chants of the Mass Proper were composed much more frequently than those of the Ordinary. The MS Reg. 586 of the Vatican Library (originally from Fleury or Tours) contains three Graduals ("Viderunt omnes," "Omnes de Saba." "Gloriosus deus") composed in a style very close to that described in Guido's "Micrologus" of *c.* 1030. The Winchester Troper of *c.* 1050 includes, among its 150 organa, 3 Introits, 53 Alleluias, 19 Tracts, and 7 sequences, in a notation that unfortunately cannot be accurately read. An 11th-century Alleluia from Chartres is reproduced in *HAM,* no. 26c. The "de gradali" section of the *"Magnus liber organi" contains 59 Mass Propers, all Graduals or Alleluias. (For details regarding the composition, see Organum, particularly the scheme for "Viderunt.") Under Perotinus (*c.* 1160–1225), the repertory of compositions for the Proper was considerably enlarged by the numerous *clausulae, many of which were transformed into *motets. Thus, all the clausulae and motets with the tenor *"In seculum" form a part of the Easter Gradual "Haec dies." About 1250, the composition of the Proper practically died out, but it reappeared in the 15th century. The *Trent Codices contain more than 250 settings of the Mass Proper, among them a number of complete cycles consisting of Introit, Gradual, Alleluia, Offertory, and Communion [see Editions XXXI, ser. ii, 1, where several of these cycles are ascribed to Dufay]. See also Plenary Mass. The most famous collection of Mass Propers, all arranged in liturgical cycles, is Isaac's *Choralis Constantinus.* Numerous other settings from about the same period are preserved in two MSS of the University Library of Jena (nos. 30, 35) and in an anonymous publication of 1528, *Contrapunctus seu figurata musica super plano cantu missarum solennium totius anni.* The last publication in this field is William Byrd's *Gradualia* of 1605–07, which includes thirteen almost complete settings of the Mass Proper. In organ music, the Introit and Offertory were composed most frequently, the latter especially in England during the 16th century. See Felix namque.

C. *The polyphonic Mass Ordinary.* I. To 1400. Settings of the Mass Ordinary, mostly Kyries and Glorias, appeared about the same time as the earliest compositions of the Proper but much less frequently. Among the organa of the Winchester Troper are twelve Kyries and eight Glorias, most of them troped. The 11th-century treatise "Ad organum faciendum" contains a Kyrie trope in the style of free organum, i.e., in contrary motion [*HAM,* no. 26]. Two-voice settings of Sanctus and Agnus tropes, probably of English origin, are in fasc. 11 of the Wolfenbüttel Codex W_l [see *HAM,* no. 37]. Two-part compositions of troped and plain Kyries as well as a three-voiced "Et in terra" are in the Codex Huelgas of *c.* 1275 [see H. Anglés, *El Codex Musical de las Huelgas,* 3 vols. (1931)]. The first example of a complete Mass (Ordinary) is the *Messe de Tournai* of *c.* 1300, which, however, is probably a compilation of individual compositions written at different periods [new ed. in E. Coussemaker, *Messe du XIIIe siècle* (1861), and in *Editions XII,* 13; also in L. Schrade, *Polyphonic Music of the Fourteenth Century,* i (1956), which in addition contains two recently discovered cycles known as the Mass of Toulouse and the Mass of Barcelona]. Machaut's Mass (now available in editions by Ludwig-Besseler, De Van, Schrade, Chailley, and Hübsch) was formerly believed to have been composed for the coronation of Charles V in 1364 but is probably one of the earlier works of Machaut, judging from its *ars antiqua* style and some striking similarities to the Mass of Tournai. A considerable number of individual items (Kyries, Glorias, etc.) are preserved in various 14th-century MSS [Codex Ivrea, Apt, Torino, etc.). In England, the practice of writing single Mass movements (sometimes paired, e.g., Gloria and Credo) prevailed throughout the 15th century (Dunstable; numerous composers of the Old Hall MS).

II. 1400–1600. This was the main period of Mass composition, during which the term "Mass" assumed its present-day meaning, i.e., a polyphonic setting of the entire Mass Ordinary. Nearly always the composition was in the form of a "cycle," the various movements being held together by a liturgical association or, more commonly, by some musical device. The earliest indisputable example of a Mass cycle in the proper sense of the word is Lionel Power's *Missa super Alma redemptoris mater,* probably composed shortly after 1400. Dufay (*c.* 1400–74) and Palestrina (*c.* 1525–94) are the first and the last in a long succession of composers who wrote mainly Masses. The following main types of Mass composition can be distinguished:

a. Plainsong Mass [L. *missa choralis*]. This represents the most obvious and natural procedure, i.e., the polyphonic setting of a Gregorian Mass Ordinary, such as the Mass I or the Mass IV [see under A above], with each movement drawing its musical material from the corresponding item of the plainsong Mass. Such a Mass is cyclical from the liturgical point of view, since it fully corresponds to one of the plainsong cycles, each of which is assigned to a specific liturgical situation (Paschal Time, Solemn Feasts, Sundays throughout the Year, etc.). This genre is found throughout the period, but to a far lesser extent than might be expected. Examples are Isaac's *Missa Solemne, Missa Pascale,* etc. [see L. Cuyler, ed., ‡*Five Polyphonic Masses by Heinrich Isaac* (1956)], Josquin's and Morales' *Missa de Beata Virgine,* Palestrina's *Missa pro defunctis* [see Requiem Mass], as well as all the *organ Masses of the 16th century (Girolamo Cavazzoni, Merulo).

b. *Cantus firmus* Mass. This is a Mass in which all the movements are based on one and the same melody, usually in the tenor [see Tenor Mass]. (The terms "plainsong Mass" and "*cantus firmus* Mass" are far from being correct designations; the "plainsong" of the former is a *cantus firmus,* and the "*cantus firmus*" of the latter is frequently taken from plainsong.) This cyclical type is perhaps the most common of all. According to the source of the *cantus firmus,* three species can be distinguished: Masses based on (a) a liturgical, (b) a secular, and (c) an invented *cantus firmus.* Among the liturgical *cantus firmi* the antiphons B.M.V. [see Antiphon (2)] and hymns are most often used. Examples are Lionel Power's *Missa super Alma redemptoris mater,* Dufay's *Missa Ave regina* and *Missa Ecce ancilla Domini,* Ockeghem's *Missa Ecce ancilla Domini,* Josquin's *Missa Pange lingua,* and Palestrina's *Missa Panem nostrum.* This type, although found throughout the period, is more characteristic of the 16th century than the 15th, when secular *cantus firmi* were preferred. Particularly popular were French chansons, above all the famous *L'Homme armé. Other examples are Dufay's *Missa Se la face ay pale,* Ockeghem's *Missa De plus en plus* and Obrecht's *Missa Fortuna desperata.* In England the tune *"Western Wynde" was popular [Shepherd, Taverner, Tye). Isaac's *Missa carminum* is an example of the *quodlibet* Mass, in which several secular melodies are combined. About 1500 "invented" *cantus firmi* were occasionally used, either a *soggetto cavato,* e.g., Josquin's *Missa Hercules Dux Ferrariae,* or the *hexachord, e.g., Palestrina's *Missa Ut re mi fa sol la* (*Missa super voces musicales*).

c. The motto cycle (motto Mass). In this type unification is achieved by—and normally restricted to—the use of an identical motif at the

beginning of each movement. This device occurs in a number of Gloria-Credo pairs from the early 15th century [see Bukofzer, *Studies in Medieval and Renaissance Music* (1950), pp. 219ff] and, applied to a full cycle, in a Mass by Arnold de Lantins [see C. van den Borren, *Polyphonia sacra* (1932), nos. 1–5]. It was also used in conjunction with the *cantus firmus* method, e.g., in Dufay's *Missa Caput.*

d. Parody Mass. See separate entry.

e. The freely invented Mass. For freely invented Masses, which constitute a relatively small group, general designations such as *Missa quarti toni* (Vittoria), *Missa cuiusvis toni* (Ockeghem), *Missa sine nomine* (Obrecht), and *Missa brevis* (Palestrina) were used. It must be noted, however, that the complete originality of any Mass written during the period is open to question, and that a *cantus firmus* is often used where none is indicated in the title. This is especially true for Masses composed after the *Council of Trent, which forbade the use of secular *cantus firmi.* For instance, Palestrina's *Missa quarta* (1582) is based on *L'Homme armé.*

Naturally, within each of these categories the treatment varies considerably according to the period of composition. The earliest type (though by no means restricted to the early period) uses the *cantus firmus,* without alterations, in long notes (*cantus planus*) in the tenor. Later the *cantus firmus* is shared among the other voices but omitted in certain sections, e.g., in the "Christe eleison" and Credo. Another modification is the use of a melodically and rhythmically altered *cantus firmus,* a sort of free variation on the borrowed melody, which was used not only as a tenor but also as a soprano melody [see Discant Mass]. By the end of the 15th century the techniques of variation upon a borrowed tune were extremely highly developed; the *cantus firmus* sometimes was completely absorbed throughout the polyphonic texture, so that a derivative Mass is indistinguishable in style from a freely composed one. A noteworthy example is Josquin's *Missa Pange lingua* [see Paraphrase (3)].

III. 1600–present. After 1600 Mass composition lost its former importance. In Italy [see Roman school] the *a cappella* tradition of Palestrina (*stile antico*) was continued by composers such as Steffano Bernardi (*c.* 1576-1636; see *DTO* 69), Antonio Draghi (1635-1700; see *DTO* 46), and Antonio Lotti (*c.* 1667-1740; see *DdT* 60), while others enlarged the vocal resources to huge choirs of 32 and 48 voice-parts

(Orazio Benevoli, 1605–72; see *DTO* 20). In Germany the development followed more progressive trends with the inclusion of the orchestra and of the 17th-century styles of the concerto, aria, etc. (*stile moderno*). The Masses of Biber, Schmeltzer, and Kerll [see *DTO* 46] are landmarks on the road leading to Bach's B-minor Mass (1733–38). Concomitant with the tendency to a greater variety of styles was the division of the Mass into a greater number of movements, particularly within the Gloria and the Credo. Following is the structure of Bach's Mass:

Kyrie
  Kyrie eleison (Lord, have mercy)
  Christe eleison (Christ, have mercy)
  Kyrie eleison (Lord, have mercy)
Gloria
  Gloria in excelsis Deo (Glory to God in the highest)
  Laudamus te (We praise you)
  Gratias agimus tibi (We give you thanks)
  Domine Deus (Lord God)
  Qui tollis peccata mundi (Who take away the sins of the world)
  Qui sedes ad dexteram patris (Who sit at the right hand of the Father)
  Quoniam tu solus sanctus (For you alone are holy)
  Cum Sancto Spiritu (With the Holy Spirit)
Credo
  Credo in unum Deum (I believe in one God)
  Patrem omnipotentem (Father almighty)
  Et in unum Dominum (And in one Lord)
  Et incarnatus est (And he became flesh)
  Crucifixus (Crucified)
  Et resurrexit (And rose again)
  Et in Spiritum Sanctum (And [I believe] in the Holy Spirit)
  Confiteor unum baptisma [I confess one baptism)
Sanctus
  Sanctus (Holy)
  Hosanna in excelsis (Hosanna in the highest)
  Benedictus qui venit (Blessed is he who comes)
Agnus
  Agnus Dei (Lamb of God)
  Dona nobis pacem (Grant us peace)

The Masses by Francesco Durante (1684–1755), Johann Adolf Hasse (1699–1783), Haydn (1732–1809), and Mozart (1756–91) show the trend toward secularization of the music for the Mass, and not until Beethoven's *Missa solemnis*

(op. 123, 1819–23) was a work created that stands the test of comparison with Bach's Mass. Beethoven treats the text in a more continuous manner than Bach but uses, in the Credo, a separate movement for "Et homo" (after "Et incarnatus") and "Et vitam" (after "Confiteor"), this being treated as an extended closing fugue.

Cherubini (1760–1842) wrote several Masses between 1809 (Mass in F for three voices and orchestra) and 1825 (Coronation Mass) that deserve more attention than is given them, as do the six Masses of Schubert. Mass composition was continued by Weber (2), Liszt (5, including the *Graner Mass,* 1855), Franck (2), and Gounod (9), culminating in the Masses of Bruckner, particularly his F-minor Mass (1866), one of the truly great Mass compositions after Bach and Beethoven. In the 20th century, Masses have been written by Villa-Lobos (Mass of St. Sebastian, 1937), Poulenc (1937), and Stravinsky (1948).

D. The musical items of the Anglican Mass (also called Communion) include all the parts of the Ordinary, often with the *Decalogue as an alternative for the Kyrie. Although the Offertory texts are the only ones of the Proper that are given in the Prayer Books, the places for all the Propers have been retained, and they are widely sung. The Lutheran services retain all of the Ordinary and part of the Proper. The Methodist Communion Service provides for the Kyrie, Sanctus, Agnus Dei, and Gloria. Settings of the Mass in English range from the monophonic versions of John Merbecke's *The Booke of Common Praier noted* (1550) to contemporary compositions, e.g., by Vaughan Williams. See Service.

Lit. *Liturgical:* J. A. Jungmann, *The Mass of the Roman Rite,* 2 vols. (1952); A. Fortesne, *The Mass: A Study of the Roman Liturgy* (1950); A. Cabrol, *The Mass, Its Doctrine and History* (1931); P. Parsch, *The Liturgy of the Mass* (1936); G. Dix, *The Shape of the Liturgy* [1960]. *For A:* P. Wagner, *Introduction to the Gregorian Melodies* (1907); *id., Gregorianische Formenlehre* (1921); *ApGC,* pp. 25ff and *passim;* P. Wagner, *Geschichte der Messe* (1913; also polyphonic to 1600); A. Piovesan, *La Messa nella musica dalle origini al nostro tempo* (1949); R. Hoppin, "Reflections on the Origin of the Cyclic Mass (*CP Borren,* 1964); K. von Fischer, "Neue Quellen zum einstimmigen Ordinariumszyklus" (*CP Borren,* 1964). *For B:* G. Eisenring, *Zur Geschichte des mehrstimmigen Proprium Missae bis um 1560* (1913); W. Lipphardt, *Die Geschichte des mehrstimmigen Proprium Missae* (1950). *For C I:* H. Stäblein-Harder, ‡*Fourteenth-Century Mass Music in France* (1962); B. J. Layton, "Italian Music for the Ordinary of the Mass" (diss. Harvard Univ., 1960); F. Ludwig, "Die mehrstimmige Messe des 14. Jahrhunderts" *AMW* vii, 417–35); H. Harder, "Die Messe von Toulouse" (*MD* vii, 105–28); J. Chailley, "La Messe de Besançon" (*AnnM* ii, 93–103); L. Schrade, "The Mass of Toulouse" (*RBM* viii, 84–96); *id.,* in *JAMS* viii, 66–69. *For C II;* R. von Ficker, "Die frühen Messenkompositionen der Trienter Codices" (*StM* xi, 3–58); *id.,* "Die Kolorierungstechnik der Trienter Messen" (*StM* vii, 5–47); H. B. Collins, in *ML* v, 322–24 (Taverner); F. X. Haberl, in *MfM* iii, 81–89 (Willaert); J. Schmidt, in *ZMW* ix, 129–58 (Clemens non Papa); C. Hamm, "The Reson Mass" (*JAMS* xviii, 5–21); P. Gossett, "Techniques of Unification in Early Cyclic Masses and Mass Pairs" (*JAMS* xix); A. Smijers, "De Missa Carminum van Jacob Hobrecht" (*TV* xvii, 192–94); W. Widmann, in *KJ* xxviii (Palestrina); see also under Parody Mass; Organ Mass. *For C III:* H. A. Sander, *Italienische Messkompositionen des 17. Jahrhunderts* (1934); G. Adler, "Zur Geschichte der Wiener Messkompositionen" (*StM* iv, 5–45). *For C IV:* A. Schnerich, *Messe und Requiem seit Haydn und Mozart* (1909); B. A. Wallner, in *ZMW* viii (Weber).

Mass of the Presanctified. The Mass for Good Friday, so called because the elements (bread and wine) are consecrated the day before. The only musical items for this Mass are two Tracts, the **Improperia,* and the hymn "Crux fidelis" [see *LU,* p. 742].

Mastersingers. See Meistersinger.

Mastersingers of Nuremberg, The. See *Meistersinger von Nürnberg, Die.*

Matasin, matassin, mattachin. A 16th-century dance performed by costumed dancers, representing men in armor or other costume [see *Bouffons;* Dance of death; *Moresca*]. An example called "Mattasin oder Toden Tantz" is in Nörmiger's tablature of 1598 [see W. Merian, *Der Tanz in den deutschen Tabulaturbüchern* (1927), p. 256]. A similar melody, called "Matachina," is found in a French gittern tablature of 1570 [see W. Tappert, *Sang und Klang aus alter Zeit* (1906), p. 39]. The name "matachin" survives in the American Southwest and Mexico as a designation for ritual folk dances of various

kinds (for rain, crops, etc.). See J. D. Robb, in *Western Folklore* xx.

Mathis der Maler [G., Mathias the Painter]. Opera in seven tableaux by Hindemith (to his own libretto), finished in 1934 and produced in Zurich, 1938. Setting: in and near Mainz, Germany, *c.* 1525. The story deals with the life of the German painter, Mathias Grünewald (*c.* 1480–1528), who supported the peasant revolution in the early days of the Protestant Reformation. Three extracts (the overture, the scene at the painter's deathbed, and a crowd scene from the second act) were combined into a three-movement symphony for which Hindemith provided descriptive titles referring to the panels in Grünewald's famous Isenheim Altar in Colmar, Alsace.

Matin, Le: [F., The Morning]. Nickname of Haydn's Symphony no. 6 in D, which, together with *Le Midi* (Noontime), no. 7 in C, and *Le Soir* (The Evening), no. 8 in G, forms a well-known group of Haydn's earliest symphonies, all having been composed about 1761.

Matins. The first of the canonical hours. See Office. In the Anglican Church, Morning Prayer.

Matrimonio Segreto, Il [It., The Secret Marriage]. Opera in two acts by D. Cimarosa (libretto by G. Bertati, after the play *The Clandestine Marriage* by G. Colman and D. Garrick), produced in Vienna, 1792. Setting: Italy, 18th century.

Maultrommel [G.]. *Jew's-harp.

Maundy music. Generally, the Antiphons sung during the ceremony of the Washing of the Feet on Maundy Thursday of Holy Week. The name is a corruption of L. *mandatum,* which in turn refers to the first Antiphon of the ceremony, "Mandatum novum do vobis" [*LU,* p. 671].

Má Vlast [Cz., My Fatherland]. Cycle of six symphonic poems by Smetana, composed 1874–79, based on various subjects pertaining to his country: 1. *Vyšehrad* (the old citadel of Prague); 2. *Vltava* (the river Moldau); 3. *Šárka* (an Amazon of Czech legend); 4. *Z českých luhův a hájuv* (From Bohemia's Meadows and Forests); 5. *Tábor* (an ancient city); 6. *Blaník* (a mountain near Prague where, according to legend, the old heroes slumber, ready to rise again).

Mavra. Opera in one act by Stravinsky (libretto by B. Kochno, based on Pushkin's story "The Little House of Kolomna"), produced in Paris,

1922. Setting: living room in a Russian village long ago. The music is in a *pandiatonic style with many accompanying figures reminiscent of early *opera buffa*. It consists of solo and ensemble numbers without recitative.

Maxima. See under Mensural notation I.

Maxixe [Port.] Old Brazilian urban dance, in moderate duple meter, danced by couples. It is derived from the *lundú*, but today it shows both Negro and Latin American influences, among them that of the Argentine *tango.   J.O-S.

Mazeppa. Symphonic poem by Liszt, composed 1851, based on a poem by Victor Hugo describing the insurrection (1708) and death of the Ukrainian Cossack chief, Mazeppa. The music incorporates elements from Liszt's *Mazeppa Etude* for piano, one of the *Études d'exécution transcendante* (1851).

Mazurka. A family of Polish folk dances. The mazurka is in triple meter and is performed at several speeds from moderately slow to quite rapid. One type is the *kujawiak* (not to be confused with *krakowiak*), so named because it originated in the province of Kujawy. Another is the *obertas*. Characteristic of these dances is the heavy accenting of normally weak beats [see Ex. 1].

1

Mazurkas are generally danced by couples in multiples of four (i.e., eight, twelve, or sixteen couples), with few basic steps and positions but a multitude of variations. A good deal of both musical and choreographic improvisation is traditionally applied. The mazurka spread throughout Europe in the 18th and 19th centuries, first as a dance and later as a source for art music. For the latter, Chopin's piano mazurkas dominate the literature. These pieces are highly stylized, sometimes submerging the folk-dance character; they range from slow, contemplative works (op. 17, no. 4, and op. 68, no. 4) to *kujawiaks* and even *obertas* (op. 56, no. 2), exhibiting modal characteristics and sometimes displaying very advanced chromatic techniques. Many of Chopin's most puzzling expressive pianistic devices appear in the mazurkas.

Outstanding uses of the mazurka by non-Polish composers are in Glinka's *A Life for the Tsar* and Mussorgsky's *Boris Godunov*, where the dance is used to portray what the Russian composers saw as the brilliant decadence of 17th-century Polish court life (during this period Poland was a European power while Muscovy was struggling for stability). In these pieces the composers explored extremes of chromatic expression that even exceed some of Chopin's most daring examples [Ex. 2, from *Boris*, Act III, Scene 2, marked "alla Polacca"].

etc.

Lit.: J. Miketta, *Mazurki Chopina* (1949); *MGG* viii, col. 1856–60; F. Starczewski, "Die polnischen Tänze" (*SIM* ii); T. Norlind, "Zur Geschichte der polnischen Tänze" (*SIM* xii).
                                                                    J.S.

M.d. Abbr. for *main droite* [F.] or *mano destra* [It.], i.e., right hand.

Meane, mene. In 15th- to 17th-century English music, a middle part of a polyphonic composition. See, e.g., the following passage from a 15th-century MS [see G. Schad, *Musik und Musikausdrücke in der mittelenglischen Literatur* (1911), p. 13]: "Primus pastor: 'Let me syng the tenory.' Secundus pastor: 'And I the tryble so hye.' Tertius pastor: 'Then the meyne fallys to me.'" Several organ compositions of the pre-virginalist period show inscriptions such as "Salvator withe a meane." Sometimes such a middle part is written in black notes, in contrast to white notes in the other parts [see *ApNPM*, pp. 10ff]. John Redford (d. 1547) wrote a long poem on the *mene* [in C. Pfatteicher, *John Redford* (1934), p. 64], which unfortunately does little to clarify the term. In most cases the part referred to as *meane* is shared by the right and left hands.

The earliest use of the term is in connection with the 15th-century practice of *sight. It was also applied to instruments (viols) playing the middle part as well as to the two middle strings (small meane, great meane) of the viol.

Mean-tone system. See under Temperament II.

Measure [F. *mesure;* G. *Takt;* It. *misura;* Sp. *compás*]. A group of beats (units of musical time), the first of which normally bears an accent. Such groups, in numbers of two, three, four, or, occasionally, five or more, recur consistently throughout a composition and are marked off from one another by *bar lines. The basic scheme of note values within a measure is called *meter or time (duple, triple, 6/8 meter, etc.). Occasional deviations from the regularity of accent, e.g., *syncopation, emphasize rather than destroy the general scheme of measure and meter.

The concept of measure is based on the principle of regular accent, which is of primary importance in almost all music generally known today. However, music has by no means always embodied this principle. Disregarding dance music, which for obvious reasons is nearly always "measure-music," the history of European music may be divided into four periods alternating between "measure-free music" and "measure-music": (a) 500–1200; no measure (plainsong, *organum purum*); (b) 1200–1450; measure based on the rhythmic *modes, the mensurations, or, in Italy, the *divisiones;* (c) 1450–1600; prevalence of measure-free (Flemish) polyphony; (d) 1600–1920; measure based on the regular (four-measure) melodic phrases that often reflect the influence of dance music. With respect to period (c), the reader must be warned not to confuse "measure-music" (as defined above) with "measured music" in the sense of *mensural music. Mensural music, which prevailed throughout the period in question, embodies the principle of regular groups of beats (*tempus perfectum, imperfectum,* etc.) but frequently lacks the most important characteristic of "measure-music," i.e., the normal accent on the first beat of such a group. See also Bar line; Rhythm II (a).

Mechanical composition. Composing by means of some mechanical device. Athanasius Kircher (1602–80) invented an *arca musarithmica,* a box with slides that was supposed to compose music by means of mathematical combinations. In the second half of the 18th century mechanical composition was a sort of parlor game, in which a polonaise, minuet, or waltz was "composed" from a number of written out measures that were selected by the throwing of dice [see Aleatory music]. Strange as the method might appear, it produced perfectly acceptable results, neither better nor worse than hundreds of traditionally composed minuets of that period. D. N. Winkel (1780–1826), the inventor of the *metronome, built a *componium,* an enormous machine (now in the Brussels Conservatory) that automatically produces variations based on changes in weather and temperature. These innocent jests of the past represent interesting forerunners of the present-day *computer.

Mechanical instruments. I. Appliances designed to produce musical performance mechanically, i.e., without an actual performer. Prior to the end of the 19th century such apparatus was always based on a barrel-and-pin mechanism. The hand, or a mechanical clockwork, turned a cylinder bearing pins acting against levers or similar gadgets, which in turn operated the hammers of a keyboard instrument, the clappers of a set of bells, the mouthpieces of organ pipes, etc. As early as the 14th century, carillons were operated by such a mechanism. In the 16th century the same principle was applied to harpsichords and organs. In the collection of instruments left by Henry VIII at his death in 1547 was a "virginal that goethe with a whele without playing uppon." An instrument sent by Queen Elizabeth to the Sultan of Turkey in 1593 included an organ, a carillon, "trumpeters," "singing byrds," etc., and went into action automatically every six hours. About the same time Hans Leo Hassler took an active interest in the fabrication and sale of musical clockworks. Athanasius Kircher, in his *Musurgia universalis,* vol. ii (1650), pp. 312ff, described various elaborate musical mechanisms, e.g., a *Cylindrum phonotacticum* that could play *Toccatas sive Ricercatas* by Kerll and others. Of particular interest is a mechanical spinet, which is preserved with six pieces from the early 18th century, probably the earliest extant examples of "phonograph" music [see P. Nettl, in *ZMW* ii, 523]. Mozart wrote several compositions for the mechanical organ, an Adagio in F minor and an Allegro in F major (K. 594), a Fantasia in F minor (K. 608), and an Andante in F major (K. 616).

II. The only instrument of the barrel-and-pin type that attained considerable practical importance was the English barrel organ. This was a small organ connected with an arrangement of interchangeable barrels, each containing a number of the most popular psalm and hymn tunes. These automatons enjoyed great popularity in rural English churches during the 18th and 19th centuries. William Mason, in his *Essays, Historical and Critical, on English Church Music* (1795), said he preferred "the mechanical assistance of a Cylindrical or Barrel Organ to the fingers of the best parochial organists," a statement that probably reflects more the skill of the parochial organists than the qualities of the barrel organ. See also Serinette; *Orgue* (*Orgue de barbarie*).

III. Toward the end of the 18th century various small instruments called *Flötenuhr* (fluteclock) were made by P. Niemecz, librarian to Prince Esterhazy. They combined an ordinary clock with a set of small pipes and bellows operated by a clockwork. For these instruments (also called *Laufwerk*) Haydn wrote a number of charming pieces [see E. F. Schmid, ‡*Werke für Laufwerk* (1931), and in *ZMW* xiv].

Passing reference may be made to the wellknown "music boxes" [F. *boîte à musique, tabatière de musique;* G. *Spieldose*], whose high, thin tones have frequently been imitated in piano pieces, e.g., by A. Liadov, T. Leschetizky, and, with irony, by Stravinsky in *Petrouchka* (Valse). A truly remarkable specimen was a "musical bustle" that was presented to Queen Victoria in 1887; it was "so designed as to provide a performance of the National Anthem (God Save the Queen) whenever the wearer sat down."

In the early 19th century a number of instruments were built for the mechanical reproduction of entire orchestras, e.g., J. N. Maelzel's Panharmonicon (1804), for which Beethoven originally wrote the "Sieges-Symphonie" of his *Wellingtons Sieg (1813), the Appollonicon built by Flight and Robson (1817), the Orchestrion of Friedrich Theodor Kaufmann (1851), and numerous others, whose descendants are still found in taverns throughout Europe, playing the same role as the American "jukebox."

IV. An important advance over the barreland-pin mechanism was the perforated paperroll of the late 19th century. A roll of cardboard is pierced with small openings corresponding in position and length to the pitch and duration of the tones of the composition to be reproduced. This passes over a cylinder furnished with numerous small apertures (similar to those of the mouth harmonica), which are connected by pipes to the action of a piano. As often as an opening in the cardboard passes over the cylin-der, a stream of air is pushed (or drawn) through the corresponding pipe, setting the hammer in motion. This principle has been applied with a considerable degree of accomplishment in instruments such as the player piano, the Welte-Mignon, the Pianola, the Phonola, etc. The player-rolls are usually reproductions of performances by famous virtuosos. In most of the instruments the rendition can be modified according to the taste of the player, who can regulate to a certain degree the speed and dynamics. Needless to say, the possibility of beating the speed record of world-famous pianists has added considerably to the commercial value of these instruments. Some modern composers (Hindemith, Toch) have written original compositions for such mechanical pianos, availing themselves of the possibility of producing sound effects not obtainable by a live pianist, e.g., chords consisting of thirty and more notes, or the simultaneous use of the lowest, middle, and highest registers.

The *phonograph and radio have largely eclipsed such attempts at reproduction.

Lit.: R. Mosoriak, *The Curious History of Music Boxes* (1943); John E. T. Clark, *Musical Boxes,* rev. ed. (1961); A. Buchner, *Mechanical Musical Instruments* [1959]; A. Chapuis, *Histoire de la boîte à musique et de la musique mécanique* (1955); A. Protz, *Mechanische Musikinstrumente* (1941); O. E. Deutsch, in *ML* xxix, p. 140; E. Simon, *Mechanische Musikinstrumente früherer Zeiten und ihre Musik* (1960); H. Leichtentritt, in *MQ* xx, p. 15; *LavE* ii.3, 2117; G. C. A. Jonson, in *PMA* xlii, p. 15.

Mechanik [G.]. The action of a piano, etc.

Medesimo tempo [It.]. The same tempo.

Media caña [Sp.]. An urban dance of Argentina that played an important role prior to 1900. Most of the traditional examples preserved consist of five parts and show melodic and rhythmic elements characteristic of other Argentine folk dances, such as the **pericón, zamacueca,* and **gato.*   J.O-S.

Medial cadence. See under Cadence I.

Mediant. See under Scale degrees.

Mediation [L. *mediatio*]. See under Psalm tones.

Medicean edition [L. *Editio Medicea*]. See under Liturgical books II.

Medicinale. See under Psaltery.

Medieval music. See Middle Ages.

Medio registro [Sp.]. *Divided stop.

Medium. *Cantus per medium* is, in 16th-century theory, singing in "halved" values, i.e., in *proportio dupla* [see Proportions] or, in modern parlance, *alla breve.*

Medium, The. Opera in two acts by Gian Carlo Menotti (to his own libretto), produced in 1946 at Columbia University. Setting: outside a large city, the present. The music is accompanied recitative with occasional expressive arias.

Medley. Same as *potpourri. The term was already used by the virginalists.

Meerestille und glückliche Fahrt [G., Calm Sea and Prosperous Voyage]. Orchestral overture by Mendelssohn (op. 27, 1828), based on two short poems by Goethe. The same poems were set by Beethoven as a cantata for chorus and orchestra (op. 112, 1815).

Mehr- [G.]. More, several. *Mehrchörig,* polychoral; *Mehrsätzig,* in several movements; *Mehrstimmig,* in more than one part, i.e., polyphonic; *Mehrstimmigkeit,* polyphony.

Meistersinger [G., mastersinger]. I. A literary and musical movement of the 15th and 16th centuries that was cultivated by the guilds of German craftsmen and represents the middle-class continuation of the aristocratic *minnesingers of the 12th to 14th centuries. The desire of the Meistersinger to emphasize such a lineage led to a store of naïve legends concerning their origin. For example, A. Puschmann, in his *Gründlicher Bericht des deutschen Meistergesanges und der Tabulatur* (1571; new ed. by R. Jonas, 1888), relates that the *Meistergesang* was founded, on the initiative of the Emperor Otto I, at Paris in A.D. 962 by twelve "first masters," among whom were Walther von der Vogelweide and Heinrich Frauenlob—men who actually lived *c.* 1200 and *c.* 1300 respectively. The statement that Heinrich Frauenlob was the first Meistersinger is still frequently found in modern writings, although the accuracy of this tradition was already questioned by the German professor J. C. Wagenseil, in his *De . . . civitate Noribergensi commentatio* (1697), the source for Wagner's *Meistersinger libretto. Actually, it is not until the early 15th century that names such as Muskatblüt, Harder, and Der Zwinger suggest greater participation by commoners. Even Michel Behaim (1416–74), who might be more

properly regarded as the first Meistersinger, falls outside the category proper, since he led a traveling life—like the bards—whereas the Meistersinger were resident members of reputable city guilds, united in local schools. Among the actual Meistersinger were Conrad Nachtigall, Hans Sachs (1494–1576), Georg Hager (1552–1634), Hans Folz (all in Nuremberg), Sebastian Wilde (in Augsburg), and Adam Puschmann (1532–1600, in Breslau). In the 16th century the movement spread over most of Germany, but it declined rapidly during the 17th century. Certain schools existed throughout the 18th century; that of Ulm was dissolved in 1839.

II. Characteristic of the *Meistergesang* were the rigid and pedantic rules that regulated the procedure of their weekly meetings (on Sunday, after church), the establishment of competitions and prizes, the promotion of members into various classes (*Schüler, Schulfreund, Singer, Dichter, Meister,* i.e., pupil, friend, singer, poet, master), etc. The rules were set down in the so-called *Tabulatur* (tablature). The title *Dichter* was given for the invention of a new poem (called *Lied, Gesang*), the title *Meister* for a new melody (called *Ton, Weise*). Most of the numerous poems were sung to standard melodies whose names referred to their composers (e.g., "Brant-weise; Der Wilde Ton") or to other more or less obscure characteristics (e.g., "Rosenton," "Grasmückenweise"—warbler-melody), while names such as "Schwartz-Dintenweis" (black ink melody) and "Kurtze-Affenweis" (short monkey melody) show that the Meistersinger did not wholly lack humor. The whole setup has been vividly (and accurately) described by Wagner in his *Die Meistersinger von Nürnberg* (particularly Act I, David and Kothner).

III. The musical repertory of the Meistersinger, as it is preserved, consists of a large number of melodies, written in *monophonic notation in a more or less free rhythm. Practically all of them are in *Bar form, the traditional form of the minnesingers. Among the songs of Hans Sachs are several attractive melodies [see *HAM*, no. 24; *EiBM*, no. 9; *BeMMR*, p. 271; *SchGMB*, no. 78]. On the whole, however, the Meistersinger melodies are clumsy and barren, often crowded with meaningless coloraturas [G. *Blumen*].

The Meistersinger probably derived elements of their ritual not only from the minnesingers but also from the procedure of medieval doctoral examinations, from pious fraternities similar to the Italian *laudesi* [see *Lauda;* note the prevailingly Biblical repertory of the Meistersinger], and possibly from the French *puys.

Lit.: C. Mey, *Der Meistergesang in Geschichte und Kunst,* rev. ed. (1901); W. Nagel, *Studien zur Geschichte der Meistersänger* (1909); B. Nagel, *Der deutsche Meistergesang* (1952); C. H. Bell, *Georg Hager: A Meistersinger of Nürnberg,* 3 vols. (1947); R. W. Linker, *Music of the Minnesinger and Early Meistersinger; A Bibliography* [1962]; A. Taylor and F. H. Ellis, *A Bibliography of Meistergesang* (Indiana Univ. Studies, no. 113, 1936); *ReMR,* pp. 652ff; H. J. Moser, *Geschichte der deutschen Musik,* rev. ed. (1930), i, 303–18; P. Runge, ‡*Die Colmarer Liederhandschrift* (1896); G. Münzer, ‡*Das Singebuch des Adolf Puschman* (1907); R. Staiger, *Benedikt von Watt* (1914); H. Thompson, *Wagner and Wagenseil* (1927); G. Münzer, "Hans Sachs als Musiker" (*DM* v.19); P. Runge, *et al.,* "Über die Notation des Meistergesangs" (*CP 1906,* p. 17; *CP 1909,* p. 84); *MGG* viii, s.v. "Meistergesang."

Meistersinger von Nürnberg, Die [G., The Mastersingers of Nuremberg]. Opera in three acts by Richard Wagner (to his own libretto, based on Goethe, E. T. A. Hoffmann, and others), produced in Munich, 1868. Setting: Nuremberg, 16th century. The plot, based on careful studies of original sources, presents a true and lively picture of the life and customs in the mastersinger guilds of the 16th century [see Meistersinger]. *Die Meistersinger* represents an artistic peak in Wagner's work. In its balance of means, its "C-major atmosphere," and its variety of scenes and expressions, the opera offers a striking contrast to the earlier *Tristan* (1865), with its exuberant chromaticism and passionate expression of tragic love-madness. The overture, frequently performed in concerts, is one of the great examples of 19th-century instrumental music. See Opera X. See H. Thompson, *Wagner & Wagenseil* (1927).

Mejorana [Sp.]. Song of Spanish origin that was brought to Panama during the 18th century. It may be vocal, in which case it is sung exclusively by men and never danced, or instrumental and danced. Its melodies are mainly descending and proceed by disjunct intervals, using leaps of major sixths, sevenths, and ninths, and frequently also augmented fourths. Characteristic of its harmonic structure is the use of I–IV–V chords, I and IV in inverted position and V in root position. The *mejorana* is in 6/8 meter with a free alternation of duple and triple divisions in a moderate tempo. The vocal *mejorana,* also

called *socavón,* begins with an improvised vocalization, sung partly in falsetto, which is repeated after each stanza of the poem.   J.O-S.

Mejoranera [Sp.]. Panamanian five-stringed guitar that is used to accompany the folksongs and dances of this country and is also a leading instrument in a popular band, along with a *rabel* (three-stringed violin), *tambora* (large drum), *pujador* (medium-sized drum), *repicador* (small drum), *guáracha* (gourd shaker), and *almirez* (brass mortar).   J.O-S.

Melisma. (1) An expressive vocal passage sung to one syllable, as opposed to the virtuoso-like and frequently stereotyped *coloratura. The term is used particularly with reference to Gregorian chant but may also be applied to expressive or characteristic passages in other vocal styles. The distinction between melismatic style and syllabic style is of fundamental importance in Gregorian chant [see Gregorian chant III] as well as in 13th-century polyphonic music [see *ApNPM,* pp. 212ff]. (2) The term has occasionally been used (F. Ludwig) for the more common term *clausula because the clausulae are polyphonic elaborations of plainsong melismas (vocalizing passages in the Graduals and Alleluias).

Mellophone. A brass instrument, similar to an althorn but in circular form, pitched in E^b and F. It was used in marching bands in place of the French horn, which it resembles. See *MaMI.*

Mélodie [F.]. Solo song with accompaniment, corresponding to the German lied. See Song III. See F. Noske, *La Mélodie française de Berlioz à Duparc* (1954).

Melodrama. A stage presentation intermediate between play and opera, consisting of spoken text and background music. If only one or two actors are involved, the terms "monodrama" or "duodrama" may be used. Melodramatic presentation seems to have played an important role in Greek drama. It became very popular in the second half of the 18th century. The earliest known examples are melodramatic scenes in a Latin school play, *Sigismundus,* by J. E. Eberlin (1753; see *DTO* 55). The first full melodrama was J.-J. Rousseau's *Pygmalion* (1762), followed by Georg Benda's *Ariadne auf Naxos* (1775; new ed. by A. Einstein, 1920; see *AdHM* ii, 752) and *Medea* (1778). In all these works, spoken text and music do not sound simultaneously but alternate, the music sometimes being used as a background for pantomime gestures. Benda's plays made quite a sensation and caused Mozart to use two long melodramatic monologues in his *Zaïde* (1780). Well-known examples of melodramatic style are the gravedigging scene in Beethoven's *Fidelio* and the incantation scene in Weber's *Der Freischütz*. In Spain, Tomás de Iriarte (1750–91) wrote a melodrama, *Guzmán el Bueno* (1790). In the early 19th century ballads often were recited to a piano accompaniment. An interesting example, by Beethoven's pupil F. Ries, is reproduced in *TaAM* xiv. Here the music no longer consists of fragments that alternate with words but becomes a continuous background for the delivery of the text, as it is in Schubert's "Abschied von der Erde," Schumann's "Schön Hedwig," and Liszt's "Der traurige Mönch." Modern examples of melodrama include R. Strauss' *Enoch Arden* (1898), Schoenberg's *Erwartung* (1909), and Stravinsky's *Perséphone* (1934), as well as sections of A. Bliss' *Morning Heroes,* D. Milhaud's *Christophe Colomb,* and the part of Joan in A. Honneger's *Jeanne d'Arc au bûcher.* What might be called a semimelodramatic style was introduced by Schoenberg in his *Pierrot Lunaire* (1912), in which he replaced plain speech by a half-musical speech known as *Sprechstimme.*

Lit.: J. F. Mason, *The Melodrama in France* (1912); P. H. Lang, *Music in Western Civilization* (1941), p. 583f; J. van der Veen, *Le Mélodrame musical de Rousseau au Romantisme* (1955); E. Istel, *Die Entstehung des deutschen Melodramas* (1906); *id.,* in *DM* v.9–12; E. C. van Bellen, *Les Origines du mélodrame* (1927); R. Augsten, *Les Premiers Mélodrames français, comparés aux modèles allemands* (1912); M. Steinitzer, *Zur Entwicklungsgeschichte des Melodrams und Mimodrams* (1918); H. Martens, ‡*Das Melodrama* (1932).

Melodramma [It.]. A 17th-century term for opera (not *melodrama).

Melody. I. In the broadest sense, a succession of musical tones, as opposed to *harmony, i.e., musical tones sounded simultaneously. Melody and harmony represent the horizontal and vertical elements of musical *texture. By its very nature melody cannot be separated from rhythm. Each musical sound has two fundamental qualities, pitch and duration, and both of these enter into the successions of pitch-plus-duration values known as melodies. To consider melody and rhythm separate or even mutually exclusive phenomena—as is often done—is mis-

leading. If a distinction between the pitch quality ("high–low") and the time quality ("long–short") is needed, the proper terms are *motion and rhythm. Melody may thus be said to consist of motion plus rhythm, and every melody can be separated into a motion skeleton and a rhythm skeleton, as the accompanying example illustrates.

In musical composition, melody may occur either without any additional element of texture (*monophonic music), or in combination with one or more other melodies (*polyphonic music), or supported by harmonies (*homophonic music). These three categories roughly describe the entire development of music: the first embraces the period from its beginnings through the first millennium of the Christian era (Greek music, Gregorian chant; up to the present in primitive and non-Western music and in folksong); the second, from 1000 to about 1750 (Middle Ages, Renaissance, baroque; see History of music); the third, from 1750 to the present day. In the last period, particularly during the 19th century, there has been an increasing tendency to make melody subservient to harmony, or at least to consider it the mere result of harmonic progressions. The current description of melody as the "surface of harmony" clearly illustrates this point of view. Writers have gone so far as to maintain that a melody that cannot be interpreted harmonically is incomprehensible. It should suffice to point to the great treasure of purely melodic music in Gregorian chant in order to refute so utterly false a conception.

II. Although the present interest in polyphonic music has resulted in a revision of the worst misconceptions, the real importance of melody is still far from being fully and generally recognized. Among the various components of musical composition, such as melody, harmony, rhythm, and orchestration, melody is, from the historical as well as from the creative point of view, by far the most important. The 19th-century development of music, with its growing emphasis on the exploitation of novel harmonies, orchestral colors, and rhythm as an independent element, temporarily obscured the fact that melody is the only element in common to music of all times and all peoples, and that, moreover, it is the cornerstone and touchstone of artistic quality. Harmony, orchestration, and rhythm are subject to certain rational premises, and many composers of mediocre artistic rank have exploited them with great skill. Only true artists, however, possess the imagination and creativity that produce a great melody. It is significant as well as deplorable that since 1900 hundreds of books on harmony and on orchestration have been written, and that courses on these subjects have formed an indispensable part of the curriculum of all educational institutions, while the study of melody has been almost completely neglected.

III. It is encouraging, however, to see that in the past decades several writers have turned their attention to the study of melody, not as mere ornamentation of a harmonic structure but as an element in its own right. General characterizations such as "tuneful," "simple," "touching," "expressive," "dramatic," etc., are not entirely without significance but are too vague to provide a basis for thorough study. A more promising approach—indeed the one most likely to prove successful—is that derived from the fact that a melody consists of successive notes of varying pitch. This leads to a consideration of a melody as a "geometrical" design including upward and downward steps and, still more important, as a "physical" phenomenon reminiscent of a moving body subject to forces that regulate its motion. A very important concept of such a theory is that of "musical gravity," a term implying that the "natural" movement of a musical line is downward [see the scales of *Greek music], while an ascending motion always has the connotation of tension and energy. Of course, practically all melodies combine ascending and descending

movements, but the greater emphasis on or prevalence of one or the other is a point of prime importance, as may readily be seen from a comparison of melodies by Bach and Beethoven with those of Mendelssohn, for example. The preceding illustration [Ex. a, Bach; b, Mendelssohn] shows two graphs of opposite musical gravity, melodies that differ markedly in their physical as well as artistic "weight."

IV. Another consideration of basic importance is that of the steps in which a melody moves, i.e., narrow (conjunct) or wide (disjunct). This distinction is of prime interest in the study of primitive and non-Western music. For instance, Japanese music is prevailingly conjunct —hence, emotional, expressive—while ancient Chinese music is disjunct—hence, static, reserved [cf. also the two scales, *sléndro* and *pélog,* of *Javanese music]. In European folksong it has frequently been noted that the French and Italians prefer narrow steps and ranges, while the northern peoples (English, German, etc.) prefer wider ones.

In art music this dichotomy becomes one between scalar and chordal progressions, i.e., progressions through the tones of the scale or of a chord (triad, seventh chord). Influenced by the current preoccupation with harmony, writers usually consider the latter the more important and often regard scalar progressions as mere passing-notes between main notes forming a chordal progression. In order to refute this point of view, it suffices to point to the theme of Beethoven's first Piano Sonata [Ex. 3a], which, with the "ornamental" notes suppressed [Ex. 3b], loses its character entirely, while it is not fundamentally affected by a substitution of scalar instead of chordal motion for the initial notes [Ex.

3c]. In fact, scalar motion is not only much older and more common than chordal motion but also more important from the musical and artistic point of view. Only the scale possesses that character of "logical continuation," of "variety and unity," that is the lifeblood of melody. In fact, in a progression such as c′–b–a–g–a–b–c′ each tone has a significance and function, leading from one level to another, while a similar chordal progression, such as c'–g–e–c–e–g–c', is, in spite of its greater range, a mere reiteration of one element. Many melodies of the great composers begin with a chordal motion and continue with scalar motion, thus showing a progression from a "static" beginning to a "dynamic" continuation [see Ex. 4–6, by Mozart (Piano Sonata, K. 284b, also K. 309), Beethoven (*Eroica*), and Bruckner (Symphony no. 7)].

Lit.: A. C. Edwards, *The Art of Melody* (1956); J. Smits van Waesberghe, *A Textbook of Melody* (1955); R. Faith, *Creative Musicianship; the Tonal Materials and Rhythmic Structure of Melody* (1941); F. M. Ralston, *Melodic Design* (1930); B. Szabolcsi, *A History of Melody* (1965); W. Woehl, *Melodielehre* (1923); W. Danckert, *Personale Typen des Melodiestils* (1931); id., *Ursymbole melodischer Gestaltung* (1932); E. Hoffmann, *Das Wesen der Melodie* (1925); H. Zingerle, *Zur Entwicklung der Melodik von Bach bis Mozart* (1937); T. Dunhill, "The Evolution of Melody" (*PMA* xxxiv); F. Kidson, "The Vitality of Melody" (*PMA* xxxiv); A. Lourié, "An Inquiry into Melody" (*MM* vii); A. H. Fox Strangways, "Tune" (*ML* iii, 90); H. J. Watt, "Melody" (*ML* v, 272); O. Bie, "Melody" (*MQ* ii, 402).

Melody chorale. A type of *organ chorale in which the chorale tune is placed in the top part, as a clearly audible melody accompanied by contrapuntal parts of individual design. An exceptionally early and also exceptionally beautiful example is Arnolt Schlick's *Maria zart* (in *Tabulaturen etlicher Lobgesang,* 1512; new ed., G. Harms [1957], p. 32). Almost all the chorales of J. S. Bach's *Orgelbüchlein* are melody chorales.

Melody type. A term used in modern writings on non-Western and early European music for a practice of fundamental importance in the more primitive stages of music, i.e., a repertory of traditional melodies, melodic formulas, stereotyped figures, tonal progressions, ornamentations, rhythmic patterns, etc., that serve as a model for the creation of new melodies. Evidently such a procedure is in complete contrast to the modern ideal of "free invention" and "originality." An imaginary school of musicians writing deliberately in "Beethoven-style" would be approximately analogous to what still is the normal procedure among Arab and Indian musicians—a procedure that largely accounts for the absence of the evolutionary element in Oriental music. To the category of melody types belong the ancient Greek *nomos,* the *echos* of Byzantine and Armenian church music, the Syrian *risqolo,* the Javanese *patet,* the Hindu *rāga,* the Arabian *maqam* and, in Europe, the Russian *popievki* and the *Weisen* or *Töne* of the Meistersinger [see the entries Greece, etc.].

Scholars formerly considered the *rāgas, maqamat, echoi,* etc., the "modes" of Hindu, Arab, Byzantine, etc., music. Actually, they represent an earlier stage of development in which the "model" prescribes not only a scale with a given ambitus and center tone—as does a mode—but also typical motifs and tone progressions. [For an example, see under India V; a Syrian example is given in *GD, Sup. Vol.,* p. 175; *GDB* ii, 864.] The medieval system of eight church modes probably developed through a process of rationalization from an earlier system of melody types, possibly from the Byzantine *echos.

Mélophone. A free-reed instrument shaped like a guitar or hurdy-gurdy, about 32 inches long, with a broad neck and bellows housed in the body. The player activates the bellows by pushing and pulling a metal handle with the right hand, while his left hand depresses the desired keys, placed on the neck in seven rows of twelve keys each. The instrument was invented in the 1830's in Paris. See ill. under Wind instruments.

Melopiano. See under Sostenente piano.

Membranophone. See under Instruments.

Memby. Generic name for a set of native wind instruments (pipes, vertical flutes) of the Guarani Indians, which are still widely used in Paraguay and in the Brazilian states of Mato Grosso and Paraná. The instruments belonging to a set are tuned so as to produce perfect fifths or octaves when played together.   J.O-S.

Mendelssohn Scholarship. See under Scholarships II.

Mene. See Meane; also Sight.

Ménestrandise [F.]. Early term for a guild of professional musicians [*ménestrel*, i.e., minstrel]. François Couperin pictured a procession of minstrels, jongleurs, beggars, and acrobats with their bears and monkeys in a piece called "Les Fastes de la grande et ancienne Mxnxstrxndxsx" [see his *Pièces de clavecin*, ed. J. Brahms and F. Chrysander, ii, 208].

Meno [It.]. Less. *Meno mosso*, less quickly.

Mensur [G.]. (1) Meter, mensuration. (2) In organ building, same as scale, *scaling.

Mensural music (also **mensurable, mensurate**). Translation of L. *musica mensurata* (*cantus mensurabilis*), which in early theory (13th–16th centuries) is used in contrast to *musica plana*, i.e., plainsong. It means polyphonic music in which every note has a strictly determined value, as distinct from Gregorian chant with its free rhythm. See Mensural notation; also under Measure.

Mensural notation. The system of musical notation that was established *c.* 1250 by Franco of Cologne and remained in use until 1600. Actually, this period embraces a variety of systems differing from each other in many particulars [see under Notation]. The following discussion concerns the final stage of the development (*c.* 1450–1600), called *white mensural notation*, with reference to the white shapes of the larger note values used instead of the earlier black shapes.

I. *Notational signs.* These fall into two classes; single notes and ligatures. The single notes are

maxima (Mx), *longa* (L), *brevis* (B), *semibrevis* (S), *minima* (M), *semiminima* (Sm), *fusa* (F), and *semifusa* (Sf). The accompanying table shows the single notes and corresponding rests, together with the modern forms derived from them.

For the transcription into modern notation it is advisable not to use the exact equivalents (S = whole note, etc.), but smaller values that

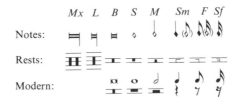

conform more closely to the actual temporal duration of the old signs. In the subsequent description a reduction 1:4 is used so that the S is rendered as a quarter note. For the ligatures, see the separate article.

II. *Mensuration.* Mensuration is the general term for the temporal relationships between the note values, comparable to the different meters of the modern system. Special terms are: *modus (relationship between L and B), tempus (B and S), and prolatio (S and M). While in modern notation a note (unless dotted) is invariably equal to two notes of the next smaller value, in mensural notation the chief notes, namely L, B, and S, may equal either two or three. This dichotomy is indicated by the terms *imperfect* and *perfect*. Omitting the *modus,* which is usually imperfect, there result four combinations of *tempus* and *prolatio* (e.g., *tempus perfectum cum prolatione imperfecta*), which constitute the four main mensurations of mensural notations and are indicated by special signs. They are the exact equivalent of four basic meters of modern notation, as shown below:

Tempus	Prolatio	Sign.	Value of		Example
			B	S	
I. Imperfect	Imperfect	C	◉ = ◊ ◊	◊ = ♩ ♩	C ◉ = ◊ ♩ ♩ = 2/4 ♩ | ♩ ♫ |
II. Perfect	Imperfect	O	◉ = ◊ ◊ ◊	◊ = ♩ ♩	O ◉ = ◊ ♩ ♩ ♩ = 3/4 ♩. | ♩ ♫♩ |
III. Imperfect	Perfect	C·	◉ = ◊ ◊	◊ = ♩ ♩ ♩	C· ◉ = ◊ ♩ ♩ ♩ = 6/8 ♩. | ♩. ♫♩ |
IV. Perfect	Perfect	⊙	◉ = ◊ ◊ ◊	◊ = ♩ ♩ ♩	⊙ ◉ = ◊ ♩ ♩ ♩ ♩ = 9/8 ♩.♩.| ♩. ♫♩♩. |

The subsequent explanations refer chiefly to mensuration II. As a matter of fact, in I the metrical relationships between the various notes are the same as in modern notation; this mensuration, therefore, presents no problems, aside from the use of ligatures and coloration [see V below]. The principles for mensuration III can easily be derived from those for II by replacing each note by the next smaller note, e.g., the B by the S, the *tempus* by the *prolatio,* etc. Mensuration IV practically never occurs in the sources of white notation and is rare even in the 14th century.

III. *Imperfection and alteration.* The normal values of the B and S, i.e., three and one S respectively, are frequently modified according to principles known as imperfection and alteration. By imperfection the B is reduced from three S to two S, and by alteration the value of the S is doubled. The following rules cover the most common cases: If a B is followed by one or by more than three S, it is imperfected. If a B is followed by two S, the second of these S is altered [Ex. 1]. The last of these examples shows that a B may also be imperfected by a preceding S, a

process called *imperfectio a parte ante,* in contrast to the more common *imperfectio a parte post.* Rests cannot be imperfected or altered but may cause imperfection or alteration of a note [Ex. 2].

IV. *Punctus divisionis, punctus additionis.* In order to indicate deviating groupings and also in cases of ambiguity, a dot called *punctus divisionis* is used. This is equivalent to the modern bar line in 3/4 meter, as it always marks off groups of three S (perfection). Other terms, such as *punctus perfectionis, imperfectionis,* or *alterationis,* are both superfluous and confusing. The dot is also used, however, with an entirely different meaning, i.e., as a *punctus additionis,* which is identical to the dot of modern notation. In the accompanying example the first and fifth

dots are *puncti divisionis,* while the others are *puncti additionis.*

V. *Coloration.* Coloration is the use of black notes (B, S, M) instead of the normal white forms (originally, red ink was used for this purpose):

The general principle of coloration is that three black notes are equal to two white notes. The result is different according to whether the black notes replace two imperfect or two perfect notes. In the former case [Ex. a, b] triplets result, while in the latter case [c, d] the effect is a change of rhythm similar to that encountered frequently in the courantes of the 17th century [see *Hemiola*]:

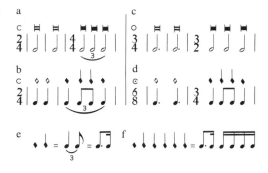

A special case of coloration is the so-called *minor color,* that is, the combination S-M in black notes. Originally, this indicated triplet rhythm, as above under (b). Owing to the shortness of the notes, however, its meaning changed into a dotted rhythm, as illustrated under (e). It is frequently followed by a series of *Sm,* as under (f). In a combination like this it should be observed that, notwithstanding their identity in shape as well as rhythmic value, the first of the stemmed notes is a black M while the others are "white" (i.e., normal) *Sm.*

The following example illustrates the principles explained above. It also includes passages in *proportion. For further details of mensural notation the reader is referred to specialized books on the subject. See also Notation; Score II.

Lit.: *ApNPM,* pp. 85–195; J. Wolf, *Handbuch*

Discantus

Tenor

Transcription

der Notationskunde i (1913), pp. 381–465; H. Bellermann, *Die Mensuralnoten...des XV. und XVI. Jahrhunderts* (1858; rev. ed. 1963, ed. H. Husmann); E. Praetorius, *Die Mensuraltheorie des Franchinus Gafurius* (1905); H. Birtner, "Die Probleme der spätmittelalterlichen Mensuralnotation" (*ZMW* xi); A. M. Michalitschke, "Zur Frage der longa in der Mensuraltheorie des 13. Jahrhunderts" (*ZMW* viii); id., in *ZMW* xii.

Mensuration. See Mensural notation II.

Mensuration canon. See under Canon II.

Mensurstrich [G.]. See under Bar line.

Mente, alla [It.]. Improvised.

Menuet [F.], **Menuett** [G.]. See Minuet.

Mer, La [F., The Sea]. Three symphonic poems by Debussy, composed 1903–05: 1. *De L'Aube à midi sur la mer* (From Dawn to Noon on the Sea); 2. *Jeux de vagues* (Play of the Waves); 3. *Dialogue du vent et de la mer* (Dialogue of the Wind and the Sea). The work represents the culmination of *impressionist pictorialism and

technique, with its tendency toward constant change of melodic material and orchestral color, a technique eminently suited to the rendition of a "musical seascape."

Mère l'oye, Ma. See *Ma Mère l'oye.*

Merengue [Sp.]. One of the most popular dances of Santo Domingo in moderate duple time and with the basic rhythmic pattern:

It consists of two sections of sixteen measures each, the second in the key of the dominant or of the relative minor of the first.

The *merengue* can be traced back to Spanish traditions imported during the Conquest. In the 19th century it took on features of the waltz, the mazurka, and the contredanse, often modified by Negro influence. Because of its sensual character, the upper classes of Santo Domingo were reluctant to adopt it.   J.O-S.

Merry Wives of Windsor, The. See *Lustigen Weiber von Windsor, Die.*

Mescolanza [It.]. *Medley.

Mese. See under Greece II.

Mesopotamia (Babylonia, Sumeria, Assyria). Knowledge of the musical culture of the ancient inhabitants of Mesopotamia is restricted chiefly to information about their musical instruments from pictorial, architectural illustrations and religious texts. The chief instruments of the Sumerian period (*c.* 3000–2000 B.C.) were the harp, usually without forepillar, and the lyre. Both existed in a great variety of shapes and sizes. The music was strictly liturgical. During the Babylonian rule (2000–1000 B.C.) the use of lutes, flutes, oboes, and drums seems to point to greater refinement. During the Assyrian rule (1000–605 B.C.) music and musical instruments were brought in by foreign musicians. C. Sachs' attempt [*AMW* vii] to interpret certain signs on a Babylonian clay tablet dating from about 800 B.C. as harp notation, and his consequent reconstruction of a Babylonian hymn, were withdrawn by him in an article [*MQ* xxvii; also *CP 1939*] in which he also refutes another interpretation given by F. W. Galpin.

Lit.: F. W. Galpin, *The Music of the Sumerians...Babylonians and Assyrians,* rev. ed. (1955); C. Sachs, *The Rise of Music in the Ancient World* [1943]; *ReMMA*, pp. 4ff (bibl. p. 426);

W. Stauder, *Die Harfen und Leiern Vorderasiens in babylonischer und assyrischer Zeit* (1961); H. Hartmann, *Die Musik der Sumerischen Kultur* (1960); M. Duchesne-Guillemin, "Découverte d'une Gamme Babylonienne" (*RdM* 1963, pp. 3–17); bibl. in *Notes* v, 179ff.

Mesotonic. Same as mean-tone (system); see under Temperament II.

Messa di voce [It.]. A special vocal technique of 18th-century *bel canto*, consisting of a gradual crescendo and decrescendo over a sustained tone; see Expression. Modern singers use it extensively for training but sparingly in performance. The term should not be confused with *mezza voce*. See also *Filar il tuono*.

Messanza [It.]. See under *Quodlibet* III.

Messe [F., G.]. Mass. *Messe des morts* [F.], Requiem *Mass.

Messel. Corruption of *mathal,* a term used in Arab theory to indicate fractions of the type $\dfrac{n+1}{n}$, e.g., *mathal wa thuluth* = ⁴⁄₃, *mathal wa subu* = ⁸⁄₇, etc. [see R. d'Erlanger, *La Musique arabe* ii, 264]. It corresponds exactly to the Latin term *sesqui-*. All intervals represented by such fractions were considered consonant by the Arabs. The messel has nothing to do with an early recognition of the third or the sixth as consonances, as was formerly believed (R. G. Kiesewetter, *Die Musik der Araber* [1842] and many others after him). The third (⁵⁄₄) is simply one in the long series of consonant *mathal* intervals, while the sixth (⁵⁄₃) does not occur in this series and hence was not a consonance.

Messiah. Oratorio in three parts by Handel (libretto by C. Jennens, based on various books of the Bible), produced in Dublin, 1742, later revised, and published in 1767. It is Handel's most popular work. Particularly famous are the "Pastoral Symphony" and the alto aria, "He shall feed His flock" from the first part, and the "Hallelujah Chorus" from the end of the second part.

Messine neumes. The neumatic script of Metz. See Neumes II (table, col. I).

Mèsto [It.]. Sad, mournful.

Mestres de l'Escolania de Montserrat. See Editions XXVI.

Mesure [F.]. Measure or meter.

Metamorphosis. See Transformation of themes.

Meter. The pattern of fixed temporal units, called *beats*, by which the timespan of a piece of music or a section thereof is measured [see Rhythm II (a)]. Neither meter nor rhythm is exactly equivalent to patterns of note values [see Rhythm I]. Meter is indicated by *time signatures. For instance, 3/4 meter (or 3/4 time) means that the basic values are quarter notes and that every third quarter note receives an accent.

Such metric groupings are indicated by *bar lines that mark off measures. According to whether there are two, three, or four units to the measure, one speaks of duple (2/2, 2/4, 2/8), triple (3/2, 3/4, 3/8), and quadruple (4/2, 4/4, 4/8) meter, 4/4 also being called "common" meter. All these are simple meters. For 4/4 and 2/2 the signs C and ₵ are used [see *Alla breve*]. Compound meters are simple meters multiplied by three: compound duple (6/2, 6/4, 6/8), compound triple (9/4, 9/8), and compound quadruple (12/4, 12/8, 12/16). *Quintuple meter (5/4) is either 2/4 + 3/4 or 3/4 + 2/4, depending on where the secondary accent lies. An example of septuple meter, written 3/4 + 4/4, occurs in Brahms' *Variations* op. 21, no. 2. For the history of meter, see Rhythm III. See also Poetic meter; Time signatures. For bibl. see under Rhythm.   rev. G.C.

Metrical psalms. See under Psalter.

Metronome. An apparatus that sounds regular beats at adjustable speed and is used to indicate the exact tempo of a composition. The instrument in general use today was invented *c.* 1812 by Dietrich Nikolaus Winkel of Amsterdam but is named after Johannes N. Maelzel, who usurped and exploited Winkel's invention. The Maelzel Metronome (M.M. or M.) is based on the principle of a double pendulum, i.e., an oscillating rod with a weight at each end, the one at the upper end being movable along a scale. By adjusting this weight away from or toward the axis, the oscillations can be made slower or faster respectively. An indication such as M.M. 80 means that the pendulum makes 80 oscillations per minute. In a piece marked M.M. ♩ = 80, the duration of the half note will be $\dfrac{60}{80} = \dfrac{3}{4}$ second.

Metronomic indications can be used to estimate the approximate duration of a piece. The formula is $\dfrac{n \times t}{M}$, where M is the metronome figure, t the number of measures of the piece, and n the number of notes—those to which the metronome figure refers—in a measure. For instance, a piece of 160 measures in 3/4 time with the metronome mark M.M. $\bullet = 90$ will last $\frac{3 \times 160}{90} = 5\frac{1}{3}$ minutes, or 5 minutes and 20 seconds.

The first composer to use the metronome was Beethoven. In 1817 he published metronomic indications for all the movements of his (then) eight symphonies (*Allgemeine Musikalische Zeitung,* no. 51). Unfortunately, the tempi indicated in his "Hammerklavier" Sonata and Ninth Symphony are almost impossibly fast, as are those indicated in the works of Schumann. See Tempo.

After more than a hundred years, during which it kept the pyramid shape fashionable in Napoleonic days, the Maelzel metronome gradually began to be replaced by devices resembling a watch, often built with an electric motor.

Lit.: R. E. M. Harding, *Origins of Musical Time and Expression* (1938); R. Kirkpatrick, "Eighteenth-century Metronomic Indications" (*PAMS* 1938); E. Borrel, "Les Indications métronomiques . . . du xviiie siècle" (*RdM* 1928); D. Kämper, "Zur Frage der Metronombezeichnungen Robert Schumanns" (*AMW* xxi); R. Kolisch, "Tempo and Character in Beethoven's Music" (*MQ* xxix, nos. 2 and 3); J. T. Hanson, "A New Metronome" (*PMA* xx).

Mette [G.]. *Matins.

Mettez [F.]. Draw (an organ stop).

Metzer Neumen [G.]. Messine neumes; see Neumes I.

Mexico. Mexico's history of music can be divided into three main periods: the pre-Columbian, which dates from the rise of the Maya culture *c.* 200 A.D. to the end of the Aztec Empire, marked by Cuauhtemoc's defeat by Cortes (1521); the colonial, from 1521 until the declaration of independence from Spain in 1810; and independence, from 1810 to the present.

Information about pre-Hispanic music comes from the writings of early Spanish chroniclers, as well as from systematic study of native instruments known to have been used before Cortes' arrival and from melodies collected today among Indian groups supposedly not influenced by the European tradition. Such sources have led to the following conclusions: pre-Hispanic music was always linked to ritual and ceremonial occasions; it was monophonic and prevailingly pentatonic; instrumental performance was always combined with singing; certain instruments, e.g., the *huehuetl, *teponaztli, and *tlapitzalli* (a four-hole flute), were considered divine or endowed with supernatural powers and were worshiped as idols; music was a means of communal rather than individual expression. To date no indication of musical notation has been found.

With the arrival of the Spaniards, music in Mexico underwent a profound change. From the very beginning of the Spanish conquest, music was used to help convert the people to Christianity, and European musical methods were introduced along with education in other arts. In 1523 the first school for teaching European music to the Indians was established by a Franciscan missionary, Pedro de Gante (1480–1572). The students were trained in the construction and playing of instruments and were taught the elements of plainchant.

Secular forms of music were developed at the same time by a number of instrumentalists who had accompanied Cortes' first expedition to Mexico. Chronicles mention a guitar player, Juan Ortiz, who shortly after 1521 taught Indians to play the guitar and perform European dances.

A printing press established in Mexico in 1539 issued an *Ordinarium* in 1556, the first book with music printed in the New World. Between 1560 and 1589 eleven more liturgical books, containing portions of the Mass, antiphons, hymns, psalms, and Passion music, were printed in Mexico. This relatively large production indicates the existence of a considerable number of Indian choirs. Besides plainchant, polyphonic psalms, motets, and *villancicos* were performed as far back as 1538. Choirbooks preserved in the cathedrals of Mexico City and Puebla, containing works by the Spanish composers Cristóbal de Morales (*c.* 1500–53) and Francisco Guerrero (1527–99) that were brought to Mexico in manuscript copies before 1550, further indicate that part singing was widely practiced during this period. In 1539 Juan Xuárez, who had come to Mexico in 1530, was appointed the first choir director of the Cathedral of Mexico City.

The repertory of polyphony preserved in the codices of Mexican archives includes works by several noted composers, ranging from the mid-16th century to the early 18th century. Juan de Lienas (16th cent.) is represented in the archives of the Mexico City and Puebla cathedrals and the Convento del Carmen by three Masses (one a Requiem), a Magnificat, sevaral motets, and sets of Lamentations; Hernando Franco (1532–85), by seven Magnificats, two Salve reginas, psalms, hymns, and responsories [see Guatemala]; Fructos del Castillo by one motet; Pedro Bermudez (fl. 1605) by four Salvereginas and one psalm; Bernardo de Peralta (fl. 1640) by a Magnificat; Francisco Lopez y Capilla (fl. 1645) by three Masses, two Magnificats, twelve motets, and a set of Lamentations; Juan de Padilla (fl. 1650) by five Masses, five Magnificats, a Passion according to St. Matthew, motets, and *villancicos;* Antonio de Salazar (fl. 1690), choirmaster at the Cathedral of Mexico from 1685 to 1715, by seven hymns, two psalms, and a number of *villancicos;* and Manuel Zumaya (fl. 1720), composer of the first opera produced in the New World, *La Parténope* (1711), and a musical drama *El Rodrigo* (1708), by three Magnificats, two Misereres, two sets of Lamentations, and several *villancicos.*

Other colonial composers were Miguel Matéo Dallo y Lana (fl. late 17th cent.), musical director in Puebla, known for his part setting of *Sor Juana Ines de la Cruz' Villancicos,* printed in Mexico in 1690; José de Torres (fl. 1703), whose *Missarum Liber* was printed in Madrid in 1703; José María Aldana (d. 1810), composer of *villancicos,* a Mass in D, and instrumental music influenced by late 18th-century Italian examples; and Antonio Juanas (d. 1817).

In the 19th century, music in Mexico was strongly influenced by Italian opera. The predominant types were short theatrical farces and comedies and instrumental pieces based on dances. The former is represented by the *zarzuela,* the latter by the *minuet, contradanza* (*contredanse*), and *jarabe.* During the first half of the century a group of composers, inspired by the spirit of national independence and romanticism, were active. Members of this group were José Mariano Elízaga (1786–1842), author of two books on theory, *Elementos de la Música* (1822) and *Tratado de la Armonía y Melodía* (1835), and composer of two Masses, a Miserere, Lamentations, Responses, and a *Valse y variaciones* for piano; Joaquín Beristaín (1817–39), precocious composer of a *Sinfonia* and an orchestral fantasy, *La Primavera;* Luis Baca (1826–55), the first opera composer after independence; Cenobio Paniagua (1821–82), composer of the operas *Catalina di Guisa* (1845) and *Pietro d'Abano* (1863), the oratorios *Siete Palabras* (1869) and *Tobias* (1870), and several Masses; Melesio

Morales (1838–1908), who wrote the operas *Ildegonga* (1869), *Cleopatra* (1891), and *Anita* (1867), and a large number of piano pieces; Aniceto Ortega (1823–75), a gifted amateur composer of piano music and a short opera, *Guatimozin* (1871); and Tomás León (1826–93), a noted piano virtuoso, teacher, and composer.

During the long period when Porfirio Diaz was in power (1872–1911), Mexican composers continued to produce operas in the Italian style and at the same time cultivated virtuoso pieces, mainly for piano, strongly influenced by European romanticism. Among them were Julio Ituarte (1845–1905), a noted virtuoso and composer of several Fantasias for piano; Ernesto Elorduy (1853–1912), cultivator of the stylized type of Mexican *danza* for solo piano; Felipe Villanueva (1862–93), known for his opera, *Keofar* (1893); Gustavo E. Campa (1863–1934), who followed the French tradition in his piano compositions and his opera, *Le Roi Poète* (1901); and Ricardo Castro (1864–1907), successful pianist and composer of orchestral works, two operas, *Atzimba* (1901) and *La Legende de Rudel* (1906), and numerous compositions for piano.

At the time of the revolt against Porfirio Diaz (1910), two important figures emerged in Mexico's musical life, both pioneers of 20th-century music. One was Julián Carrillo (1875–1965), a noted composer and theorist who devised a microtone system called *Sonido trece,* according to which he wrote a number of chamber and orchestral works, using third, quarter, eighth, and sixteenth tones. In addition, he wrote numerous works in the vein of the coeval German school. His contemporary, Manuel M. Ponce (1882–1948), wrote a large number of compositions in which he gradually proceeded from the French impressionist style to a type of nationalism combined with 20th-century neoclassical elements. In addition to a very popular song, "Estrellita," he wrote more than a hundred songs and as many piano pieces, compositions for solo guitar, several concertos for solo instrument and orchestra, a number of orchestral compositions, and an opera, *El Patio Florido* (1913).

The contemporary Mexican school is headed by two composers of international renown, Silvestre Revueltas (1899–1940), who developed a highly original and unaffected style deeply rooted in Mexican folk music, and Carlos Chávez (b. 1899), who has combined a brilliant career as composer with that of conductor, lecturer, and leader of Mexico's musical life since the late 1920's.

Other important Mexican composers born before 1900 are Juan B. Fuentes (1869–1955), composer of a *Sinfonia Mexicana,* songs, and piano music; Rafael Tello (b. 1872), composer of several operas (*Juno, Nicolas Bravo, Due Amore, El Oidor*) and a *Sonata Trágica* for violin and orchestra; Candelario Huízar (b. 1888), a nationalist who exploited Indian materials in his music, which includes four symphonies, a string quartet, and several tone poems; José Rolón (1883–1945), a disciple of Nadia Boulanger, who wrote orchestral works in the French manner; Estanisalo Mejia (b. 1882), another nationalist; and José F. Vasquez (b. 1895), composer of five operas, ballets, and numerous instrumental works.

Contemporary Mexican music is further represented by a group of composers whose influence began to be felt in the early 1930's. One of them is Miguel Bernal Jimenez (1910–56), composer of church music, an opera, *Tata Vasco* (1941), and orchestral compositions. Another is Spanish-born Rodolfo Halffter (b. 1900), who came to Mexico in 1939 and played an important role as a promoter of contemporary music. He has written a number of orchestral works, chamber and choral music, and solo instrumental compositions in a neoclassical manner. Other notable members of this group are Salvador de Elias (b. 1902), composer of several orchestral works; Luis Sandi (b. 1905), whose works include an opera, *Carlota;* and Vicente T. Mendoza (1894–1964). In addition, there is the well-known *Grupo de los Cuatro* (Group of the Four), all pupils of Chavez who banded together to promote Mexican music: Salvador Contreras (b. 1912), Daniel Ayala (b. 1908), Pablo Moncayo (1912–58), and Blas Galindo (b. 1910), the most important of them all. In his early works, Galindo was strongly attached to nationalist principles; later he gradually turned to more international trends and became considerably freer in his use of harmonies.

Already beginning to win recognition are such members of the younger generation as Mario Kuri-Aldana (b. 1931), Manuel Enriquez (b. 1926), Leonardo Velasquez (b. 1936), Eduardo Mata (b. 1942), and Joaquin Gutierrez Heras (b. 1927).

Many Mexican composers of popular music are extensively recognized abroad. Of these, the best known is Agustín Lara (b. 1900).

Most of the folk dances and songs of contemporary Mexico are of Spanish derivation. The *huapango, *jarabe, *jarana,* and *zandunga*

exemplify the development of original Spanish dance patterns into strongly individual Mexican forms. The same is true of the *corrido,* which is a remarkable native development of the Spanish *romance.* Also characteristically Mexican is the *mariachi,* the typical band that serves to entertain people in cafés and at village and country dances and celebrations.

Lit.: R. M. Stevenson, *Music in Mexico* (1952); O. Mayer-Serra, *The Present State of Music in Mexico* (1946); *id., Panorama de la música mexicana* (1941); G. Saldivar, *Historia de la música en México;* J. Pope, *Documentos relacionados con la historia de la música en México* (1951); V. T. Mendoza, *El Romance español y el corrido mexicano* (1939); J. Bal y Gay, *Tesoro de la Música Polifónica en México* (1952); S. Barwick, *The Franco Codex of the Cathedral of Mexico* (1965); *id.,* "Puebla's Requiem Choirbook" (*CP Davison*); B. Galindo, "Compositores de mi generación" (*Nuestra musica* iii, no. 10, 1948); L. M. Spell, "La Música en la Catedral de México" (*Rev. estud. mus.* ii, no. 4, 1950); L. Sandi, "Cincuenta años de música en México" (*Nuestra musica* vi, no. 23, 1951). Also see under Latin America.   J.O-S.

Meyo (meio) registo [Port.]. See Divided stop.

Mezzo, mezza [It.]. Half. *Mezzo forte* (abbr. *mf*), half loud, moderately forte. *Mezza voce,* with "half voice," i.e., with restrained volume of tone [see, however, *Messa di voce*]. *Mezzo legato,* half legato. *Mezzo-soprano,* see Voices, range of.

Mf. [It.]. Abbr. for *mezzo forte,* half loud.

M.g. [F.]. Abbr. for *main gauche,* left hand.

Mi. See Solmization; Pitch names; Hexachord. As the third degree of the hexachord, *mi* in the Guidonian system takes on the meaning of the leading tone (e, b; see Mi-fa).

Micanon. See under Psaltery.

Mi contra fa. See Mi-fa.

Micrologus. A treatise by Guido d'Arezzo (c. 990–1050) of c. 1030 [*GS* ii, 2ff; new ed. by J. Smits van Waesberghe, 1955; G. trans. M. Hermesdorff, 1876]. It contains a famous description of the principles of melodic motion (*motus;* ch. xvi) and a curious method of inventing melodies on the basis of the text (ch. xvii; see under *Soggetto cavato*). It also is an important source for the development of organum [see Organum I]. It may be noted that Guido's most famous contributions to musical progress, the *hexachord and the *staff, are not in the "Micrologus" but in his "Epistola de ignoto cantu," written in the form of a letter to the monk Michael [*GS* ii, 43–50; *SSR*, pp. 121ff]. The term "Micrologus" was also used by A. Ornithoparchus in his *Musice active micrologus* (1517).

Microtone. An interval smaller than a semitone. Long a structural feature of Asian music, the use of microtones in Western music, although far from new, has been—aside from traditional, empirical performance practice involving microtonal adjustment of intervals for expressive purposes—far less extensive. The enharmonic system of Greek music, which gained temporary importance in the period of Euripides (*c.* 480–06 B.C.), included *quarter tones [see Greece II]. Martianus Capella (fl. 4th to 5th cent.?), in his *De nuptiis Mercurii et Philologiae* or *Satyricon* (Book ix, "De musica"), mentions third tones (*tristemoria*) and quarter tones (*tetrastemoria*) [see ed. F. Eyssenhardt (1866), p. 349; similarly Regino of Prüm, in *GS* i, 232, no. 4]. Several of the "ornamental" neumes of Gregorian chant probably involved quarter tones [see Neumes I]. There is incontestable evidence of the practical use of quarter tones in the 11th-century Gradual of Montpellier [see *WoHN* i, 44f; *ApGC*, p. 122f, pl. vi]. In the 16th century, the enharmonic system of the Greeks was revived by N. Vicentino [see Arcicembalo]. At the end of the 17th century, Christiaan Huygens proposed a division of the octave into thirty-one equal parts, permitting transpositions of the diatonic scales in just intonation.

The adoption of the equal-tempered twelve-note scale for keyboard instruments rendered such efforts as Huygens' supererogatory, and it was not until music began approaching a state of chromatic saturation that composers once again considered the introduction of microtones into the resources of Western music [see Serial music].

In 1895, the Mexican Julián Carrillo wrote a string quartet using quarter tones [see *Sonido trece*]. Between 1903 and 1914 Charles Ives wrote a Quarter-tone Chorale for Strings. In 1907, Busoni was considering the use of third tones (*Entwurf einer neuen Ästhetik der Tonkunst* [1906?]). Ives used quarter tones in at least two other works, Quarter-tone Pieces for Two Pianos and his Fourth Symphony. Similar experiments were made in the first half of the 20th century by Hans Barth (Concerto for quarter-tone piano and strings, 1930), I. Vyshnegradsky (*Dithy-

ramb, 1926; Prelude and Fugue, 1929), and Alois Hába, whose extensive list of compositions includes works using both quarter tones and sixth tones. Both Carrillo and Harry Partch have written a considerable number of pieces using even smaller intervals, Partch dividing the octave into forty-three unequal steps, Carrillo, into ninety-six equal ones. Several Dutch composers (H. Badings, H. Kox, P. Schat, *et al.*), holding, like Partch, that further subdivision of the equal-tempered twelve-note scale merely compounds the harmonic errors inherent in it, have written pieces using the 31-note scale advanced by Huygens and, in this century, by Adriaan Fokker. Recently, many younger composers, stimulated at least in part by *electronic music, have been using microtones to a considerable extent.

Notation of microtones, even in the case of the fairly commonly used quarter tones, has not been standardized. Perhaps the best known system is that established by Hába. His system for quarter tones is found in his String Quartet op. 12, no. 2 [Ex. 1]; for sixth tones, it is found in his String Quartet op. 87, no. 11 [Ex. 2]; another fairly common system for quarter tones is used by Krzystof Penderecki in *Anaklasis*

(1959/60). One typical objection to these systems is that the symbols for the quarter and sixth tones are too easily misread for the conventional sharps and flats. Also, that used by Hába makes it impossible to use both sixth and quarter tones in the same composition, while that used by Krzystof Penderecki makes no provision for sixth tones at all. One system that attempts to overcome these drawbacks prefixes the ordinary accidentals with $\sqrt{}$ and $\rceil$ for quarter tones and $\sqrt{}$ and $\lceil$ for sixth tones (Ezra Sims, *Octet for Strings*, 1964; see Ex. 3). There is also the special system devised by Carrillo for his pieces using sixteenth tones, in which numerical fractions replace conventional staff notation ("Preludio a Cristobal Colón," in *New Music* xvii, no. 3, 1944).

A few instruments for performance of microtonal music have been built. A quarter-tone piano was patented first in 1892 (G. A. Behrens-Senegalden). In 1924, Förster of Löbau/Georgswalde built a piano with two manuals, the second a quarter tone higher than the first; later, Hans Barth, in the United States, built a similar instrument [see N. Slonimsky, *Music since 1900*, rev. ed. (1949), p. 337]. In the Teyler Museum, Haarlem, there is an organ designed for performance of 31-note music [see R. Orton, "The 31-note Organ," *The Musical Times* cvii, 1966]. Both Carrillo and Partch have built special instruments for the performance of their music.

Lit.: A. Hába, *Von der Psychologie der musikalischen Gestaltung . . . eines neuen Musikstils* [1925]; *id., Neue Harmonielehre* (1927); S. Waller, *Die Grundtheorie des Vierteltonsystems*, rev. ed. [1936]; J. Carrillo, *Sistema General de Escritura Musical* (1957); C. Ives, *Essays before a Sonata and Other Writings* [1962]; J. Yasser, *A Theory of Evolving Tonality* (1932); H. Partch, *Genesis of a Music* (1949); I. Vyshnegradsky, in *RM* 1937, no. 171; A. Wellek, in *MQ* xii; H. Carpenter, in *AM* xxxii (16th cent.); A. Holde, in *MQ* xxiv; L. Sabaneev, in *The Musical Times* lxx, 501; H. Kaufmann, in *JMT* v, 32; W. Berard, in *JMT* v, 95; C. Schmidt and D. Kraehenbuehl, in *JMT* vi, 32.   E.S.

Middle Ages, music of the. The music of the period preceding the Renaissance, roughly from 500 to 1450. In view of the length of this period it is helpful to divide it into shorter periods comparable to those of other times, such as the Renaissance and the baroque. See History of music and the separate entries Gregorian chant; *Ars antiqua; Ars nova;* Burgundian school. Also the initial portions of France; Italy; England; etc.

Lit: *ReMMA, passim;* M. F. Bukofzer, *Studies in Medieval and Renaissance Music*

(1950); A. Seay, *Music in the Medieval World* [1965]; H. Gleason, ‡*Examples of Music before 1400* (1942); *BeMMR, passim;* J. Chailley, *Histoire musicale du moyen âge* (1950); *GéHM;* T. Gérold, *La Musique au moyen âge* (1932); J. Smits van Waesberghe, *Muziekgeschiedenis der Middeleeuwen,* 2 vols. (1939–42; theory); G. S. Bedbrook, "The Nature of Medieval Music" (*ML* xxvi, 78–88).

Middle C. The C near the middle of the keyboard, i.e., c′ [see Pitch names]. It is represented on the first ledger line below the violin staff, or on the first ledger line above the bass staff.

Midi, Le [F.]. See under *Matin, Le.*

Midsummer Night's Dream, A. (1) Incidental music by Mendelssohn to Shakespeare's play, first performed in 1843. The overture is the most popular excerpt and is perhaps his most inspired composition, fascinating for its elfin lightness and orchestral colors. (2) Opera in three acts by B. Britten (libretto by the composer and P. Pears, after Shakespeare's play), produced in Aldeburgh, England, 1960. Setting: a wood near Athens and Theseus' palace in Athens, legendary times.

Mi-fa. In the medieval theory of *hexachords, a general expression for cautioning the singer against special or dangerous intervallic progressions. From the following table, showing the mi's and fa's of the three hexachords, it appears that the combination mi-fa designates a semitone if the two syllables are taken from the same hexachord, and a tritone if from successive hexachords (see the diagonal lines):

	Mi	Fa
Hexachordum durum (on G):	B	c
Hexachordum naturale (on C):	e	f
Hexachordum molle (on F):	a	b♭

It is particularly to the *tritone, the *diabolus in musica,* that the warning *mi contra fa* (*mi contra fa, diabolus in musica*) refers.

Mignon. Opera in three acts by A. Thomas (libretto by J. Barbier and M. Carré, based on Goethe's *Wilhelm Meisters Lehrjahre*), produced in Paris, 1866. Setting: Germany and Italy, 18th century.

Migrant cantus firmus. See *Cantus firmus.*

Migrant melisma. A term (introduced by P. Wagner, G. *Wandermelismen*) for phrases in Gregorian chant that recur in a number of melodies of the same type (e.g., the tracts of mode 8), migrating, as it were, from one chant to another. Such phrases are not melismas in the proper sense of the word, but carry a text that, of course, varies from one chant to another. If, however, the variable text is disregarded, a melisma results. See under Cento.

Milanese chant. See Ambrosian chant.

Military music (bands). Music for military purposes (signaling, marching into battle, etc.) was employed by the Jews (hasosra), Romans (*tuba, cornu, *lituus), and other ancient peoples. In the Middle Ages (11th century and later) the Herhorn, Stierhorn, and *oliphant were used to warn of the enemy's arrival. Instrumental groups including trumpets, pipes, drums, and cymbals were used by the Saracens in their battles with the Crusaders, who soon adopted this practice. In Scotland the *pibroch (a kind of bagpipe music) was used to rouse the soldiers' spirit. With the rise of organized armies during the 15th and 16th centuries, certain standard practices developed, e.g., the use of trumpets and kettledrums for the cavalry, and of fifes and drums for the infantry. The military trumpeters were organized in guilds [G. *Feldtrompeter*] and were endowed with many privileges. The kettledrummers used extravagant and affected gestures, such as survive to the present day in the movements of drum majors and majorettes [see *SaHMI*, p. 330]. The music of these groups was limited to a repertory of signals, each for a special purpose [see Fanfare].

Toward the end of the 17th century, melody instruments were introduced, leading to the establishment of military bands and a broader repertory, including marches and similar pieces. The bands of Louis XIV (1638–1715), organized by Lully, consisted of oboes, bassoons, and drums, while those of Frederick II (1712–86) included oboes, clarinets, horns, and bassoons. About 1800, the vogue of Turkish music [see Janizary music] led to the adoption of other percussion instruments, such as cymbals, triangles, the military glockenspiel, and the crescent. Infantry regiments under Napoleon had bands consisting of one piccolo, one high clarinet and sixteen ordinary clarinets, four bassoons, two serpents, two trumpets, one bass trumpet, four horns, three trombones, two side drums, one bass drum, one triangle, two pairs of cymbals, and two crescents. A landmark in the development of military music was a performance given in honor of the Russian Emperor by W. F. Wie-

precht, the organizer of Prussian military music, in Berlin on May 12, 1838, where he conducted the united bands of sixteen infantry and sixteen cavalry regiments, totaling 1,000 wind instruments and 200 drummers. About 1850, Adolphe Sax reorganized the French military bands by introducing his novel valve brass instruments.

The history of military bands in America parallels the European development. The first use of instruments in battle came after the capture of Fort Ticonderoga in 1775, when a fife and drum are reported to have been played. Routine "calls" or "beats" were played by drum alone. Massachusetts regiments were among the first to employ bands in 1792, but it was not until 1812 that the regular army increased its allotment to two musicians for each regiment or company, and not until 1847 was the size of the standard band increased to sixteen men. Outstanding figures in this development were Patrick Sarsfield Gilmore (1829–92) and John Philip Sousa (1854–1932), both bandmasters skilled as promoters as well as musicians. Gilmore took his 22nd Regiment Brass Band on a world tour, and Sousa, after resigning as head of the Marine Band, followed suit with his own group. With little exception the bands of Sousa and Gilmore, as well as the military bands of today, were fairly similar to those developed immediately after the French Revolution. Today's larger groups, connected with or representing specific branches of the armed services, are highly polished ensembles, able to perform deftly the most difficult contemporary wind literature. Indeed, in England, the term "military band" has become synonymous with the "concert" or "symphonic" band of the United States, since only the larger branches of the service can support an adequate instrumentation. Among the outstanding military bands today are those of the Scots Guard Royal Artillery, United States Marines, Army, Navy, and Air Force, as well as the Garde Républicaine band of France.

Lit.: H. G. Farmer, *Military Music* [1950]; id., *History of the Royal Artillery Band 1762–1953* (1954); P. L. Binns, *A Hundred Years of Military Music* (1959); R. F. Goldman, *The Concert Band* (1946); id., *The Wind Band* (1961); W. C. White, *A History of Military Music in America* [1944]; J. A. Kappey, *Military Music. A History of Wind-Instrumental Bands* [19—?]; H. E. Adkins, *Treatise on the Military Band,* rev. ed. (1958); V. F. Safranek, *Complete . . . Manual for Field Trumpets and Drums* (1942); R. B. Reynolds, *Drill and Evolutions of the Band* (1943); M. Brenet, *La Musique militaire* (1917); L. Degele, *Die Militärmusik* (1937); G. Parés, *Traité d'instrumentation . . . des musiques militaires,* 2 vols. (1898); P. Panoff, *Militärmusik in Geschichte und Gegenwart* (1938); G. Dyson, "The Composer and the Military Band" (*ML* ii, 58–66); M. Brenet, "French Military Music in the Reign of Louis XIV" (*MQ* iii, 340–57). See also Brass band.   rev. J.W.

Military Polonaise. Familiar name for Chopin's most popular polonaise, op. 40, no. 1, in A major (pub. 1840).

Military Symphony. Popular name for Haydn's Symphony in G, no. 100 (no. 8 of the *Salomon Symphonies), composed 1794. The second movement, Allegretto, employs triangles, cymbals, and bass drum in imitation of Turkish music [see Janizary music], and also contains a trumpet fanfare.

Milonga [Sp.]. A very popular dance in the suburbs of Buenos Aires during the last decades of the 19th century. Together with the *tango Andaluz* and the **habanera,* it is one of the most important sources of the Argentine *tango, which by 1900 had completely absorbed the *milonga.*   J.O-S.

Mimodrame [F.]. Older name for *pantomime.

Mineur [F.]. Minor.

Miniature score. An open score of orchestral or chamber music, inexpensive and pocket-size, designed chiefly for the student or for the amateur who wants to read the music while listening to a performance. This important and successful publishing enterprise was started by A. Payne in Leipzig and was taken over in 1892 by E. Eulenburg of Leipzig, who developed it greatly. Later publications were issued that include a large number of scores in one volume, e.g., all the symphonies of Beethoven. These are the size of ordinary music but contain on each page four pages of miniature score. See R. Upton, *Index of Miniature Scores* (1956).

Minim [L. *minima*]. (1) British name for the half note. (2) See Mensural notation I.

Minnesinger [G. *Minnesänger*]. German poet-musicians of noble birth who flourished from the 12th to 14th centuries. Inspired by the French *troubadours (not the *trouvères), the minnesingers became the leading—in fact, practically the sole—representatives of German music during the Middle Ages. The start of the move-ment is usually traced to the marriage of Frederick Barbarossa to Beatrix of Burgundy in 1156. The close relationship of the minnesingers to the troubadours is demonstrated by, among others, a Provençal *vers* of the troubadour Guyot de Provins that also exists with a German text by Friedrich von Husen, who flourished in the 12th century [see *BeMMR,* pp. 106, 108]. Following is a tentatively chronological list of the most important minnesingers whose melodies are preserved (1, 2, etc. = number of melodies; *J = Jenaer Handschrift; C = Colmarer Handschrift, Cgm 4997,* in Munich):

Before 1200: Spervogel (3; *J, C*).

Early 13th century: Walther von der Vogelweide, d. 1230 (3 "Töne" with new texts in A. Puschman's "Das Singebuch," in Breslau, *Bohn no. 356;* 3 in *C*); Neidhardt von Reuenthal, *c.* 1180–1240 (55 in *DTO* 71); Brüder Wirner (6; *J*); Meister Alexander (5; *J*).

Mid-13th century: Tannhäuser (3; *C, J*); Konrad von Würzburg (7; *C, J*); Rumsland or Rumelant (10; *J, C*); Der Meissner or Mysnere (17; *J, C*).

Late 13th century: Heinrich von Meissen, called Frauenlob, d. 1318 (28; *C, J*); Wizlav von Rügen, d. 1325 (13; *J*); Hermann der Damen (6; *J*).

14th century: Heinrich von Müglin (4; *C*); Hermann Münch von Salzburg, *c.* 1350–1410 (10; *C*); Hugo von Montfort, 1357–1423. The Münch von Salzburg also wrote the earliest extant German polyphonic pieces, which, like those of Oswald von Wolkenstein (1377–1445), are not part of the minnesinger repertory.

In spite of the French influence, the music of the minnesingers differs considerably from that of the troubadours and trouvères. The texts are narrative rather than amorous or idyllic (Neidhardt von Reuenthal being a notable exception) and usually devotional, many of them being songs in praise of the Virgin. The melodies are more markedly modal (church modes) than the French ones, and many of them make extensive use of the interval of a third [for an example, see under Third]. Textual considerations as well as a certain "massiveness" of the musical line forbid the application of *modal interpretation (3/4 meter) that is generally accepted for the trouvère songs. Finally, the French refrain forms, the *virelai and the *rondeau, are absent in the German repertory, which uses only two forms, the **Bar* form, derived from the French **ballade,* and the *Leich,* derived from the French *lai.

Owing to the large number of surviving songs and the individual charm of his melodies, Neidhardt von Reuenthal stands out as the central figure of minnesinger music, though from the literary point of view he represents a decline from refined courtly lyricism (Walther von der Vogelweide) to a realistic and occasionally slightly vulgar naturalism. Ex. in *HAM*, no. 20.

Lit.: H. Kuhn and G. Reichert, ed., *Minnesang des 13. Jahrhunderts* (1953); K. K. Müller, *Die Jenaer Liederhandschrift* (fac. reprod. 1893); R. W. Linker, *Music of the Minnesinger and Early Meistersinger; A Bibliography* [1962]; F. Saran, G. Holz, and E. Bernoulli, ‡*Die Jenaer Liederhandschrift*, 2 vols. (1901); H. Rietsch, ‡*Gesänge von Frauenlob, Reinmar von Zweter und Alexander* (*DTO* 41); W. Schmieder, ‡*Neidhart, Lieder* (*DTO* 71); P. Runge, ‡*Die Sangesweisen der Colmarer Handschrift und die Liederhandschrift Donaueschingen* (1896); *id., Die Lieder des Hugo von Montfort* (1906); H. Rietsch and F. A. Mayer, *Die Mondsee-Wiener Liederhandschrift* (*Acta Germanica* iii, iv, 1894–96); F. Eberth, *Die Minne- und Meistergesangweisen der Kolmarer Liederhandschrift* [1935]; B. Kippenberg, *Der Rhythmus im Minnesang* (1962); F. Gennrich, *Das Formproblem des Minnegesangs* (1931); H. J. Moser, in *ZMW* vii and *CP 1924;* E. Jammers, in *ZMW* vii; O. Ursprung, in *AMW* v; R. Molitor, "Die Lieder des Münsterer Fragments" (*SIM* xii); C. Weinmann and P. Runge, "Der Minnesang und sein Vortrag" (*MfM* xxxv, 51, 83).

Minor. See Major, minor.

Minstrel. Originally and properly, the professional musician (instrumentalist) of the Middle Ages, especially one employed in a feudal household. Today the term is used generically for the entire field of popular musical entertainment, from the mimes of antiquity to the show business of the present day.

The earliest musical entertainers in Western Europe were the mimes (*mimus*), the actors of the Greek and Roman theater. After the fall of Rome, during the barbarian invasions, the mimes, who in Roman law were already considered outcasts (*infami*), devoted themselves to various activities—frequently of a dubious nature—that included the playing of instruments. The efforts of church and state authorities to suppress them are documented in numerous edicts. Nevertheless, the mimes or, as they were later called, *joculatores* [from L. *jocus,* jest; F. *jongleur;* E. juggler; G. *Gaukler*], survived and

gradually became more secure and respectable—at least those who were willing to abandon their dissolute life. It is reasonable to assume that they were the bearers of a tradition of folk music that occasionally crept into art music. In the 11th and 12th centuries the *jongleurs* were employed by the troubadours and trouvères [see Troubadour]. In the 14th century the name *jongleur* was replaced by *ménestrier,* probably in order to distinguish a class of higher social standing and professional repute. They became organized in guilds known as **ménestrandise,* similar to those of the medieval craftsmen.

In England, a class of acrobat-musicians was known as "gleemen," and in Germany as *Gaukler.* A vivid description of their activities is given in a German report of the 12th century, according to which they were expected "to play the drum, the cymbals, and the hurdy-gurdy; to throw small apples and to catch knives; to perform card-tricks and to jump through four hoops; to play the citole and mandora, the manichord, the guitar, and many other instruments." In the early 14th century the term "minstrel" appeared. Guilds and fraternities were gradually formed, whose history can be traced at least to the beginning of the 17th century [see Wait]. The German counterpart of these guild-musicians were the *Stadtpfeifer.* For the minstrel show, see Negro music I.

To include the **bards in the same category as minstrels is somewhat misleading since they always held a high social position in their countries, notably in Wales and Ireland.

Lit.: E. Duncan, *The Story of Minstrelsy,* rev. ed. (1950); J. J. Jusserand, *English Wayfaring Life in the Middle Ages* (1888 and later); E. Faral, *Les Jongleurs en France au moyen âge* (1910); W. Grossmann, "Frühmittelenglische Zeugnisse über Minstrels" (diss. Berlin, 1906); P. Aubry, in *RMC* iv; *id.,* in *TG* vi; J. Sittard, in *VMW* i; W. Salmen, in *CP Anglés* ii; *ReMMA*, p. 241.

Minuet [F. *menuet;* G. *Menuett;* It. *minuetto;* Sp. *minué, minuete*]. A French country dance that was introduced at the court of Louis XIV about 1650. The King himself is said to have danced "the first" minuet, composed by Lully in 1653. The minuet, with its choreographic floor-pattern in the shape of a Z or S, was soon adopted as the official court dance of the régime of the Sun King, and it quickly spread throughout Europe, completely superseding the older types (courantes, pavanes) and establishing a new period of dance and dance music. The fact that a number of early minuets (e.g., those contained in the Collection *Philidor) include phrases of three measures suggests that the minuet may have been derived from the *branle à mener, or *amener [ex. in HAM, no. 229]. Lully introduced the minuet into his ballets and operas, and G. Muffat, J. Pachelbel, and J. K. F. Fischer used it in their suites (c. 1700). Many of these minuets already show the *alternativement* arrangement of two minuets, M_1–M_2–M_1, which is the origin of the minuet and trio movement of the sonata [see Trio].

The minuet was the only one of the baroque numerous dance types that did not become obsolete after the decline of the suite (c. 1750). The statement that Haydn was the first to introduce the minuet into the symphony is far from correct. The operatic sinfonias of Alessandro Scarlatti (1660–1725) and others usually close with a minuet, as do many of the independent symphonies and sonatas of the pre-Haydn period. The minuet with trio as the next to last movement is found in practically all the symphonies of the *Mannheim school [see Sonata B III (a)].

The minuet is in 3/4 meter and, originally, in moderate tempo. The accompanying example (Lully's minuet "Dans nos bois," as given in D'Anglebert's *Pièces de clavecin* [*Editions

XLIX, I, 8, p. 29]) shows the graceful dignity of the early minuet, which survives in the famous minuet in Mozart's *Don Giovanni*. In the symphonies of Haydn and Mozart, however, the minuet became faster and more humorous or whimsical in character, gradually leading into the *scherzo. See also Dance music III and, for the internal structure of the minuet, Binary and ternary form II. See E. Blom, in *ML* xxii, 162–80.

Minuta [It.]. See under Ornamentation III.

Minute Waltz. Popular name for Chopin's Waltz in D-flat, op. 64, no. 1, derived from the fact that it lasts approximately one minute when played at an excessively rapid tempo.

Miracle play. See under Liturgical drama.

Mirliton [F.]. An instrument consisting of a pipe closed at one end by a membrane. By directing the natural voice against the membrane, the tone is altered, the timbre becoming quite nasal. In the 17th century the instrument was known as *flûte-eunuque* (eunuch flute) and was admired by men of such high standing as Mersenne for its "new charm." Today it is a musical toy, shaped approximately like a cigar and commonly known as "kazoo." See Instruments II.

Miroirs [F., Mirrors]. A group of five piano pieces by Ravel, composed 1905: 1. *Noctuelles* (Moths); 2. *Oiseaux tristes* (Mournful Birds); 3. *Une Barque sur l'océan* (A Boat on the Ocean); 4. *Alborada del gracioso* (Morning Music of a Minstrel-Clown); 5. *La Vallée des cloches* (The Valley of the Bells).

Mirror composition. The principle of mirror reflection can be applied to a composition in two ways: (a) with the mirror placed at the end, producing its retrograde form; (b) with the mirror placed underneath, resulting in its inverted form. Usually but not always the term refers to (b). Thus a mirror composition is one that, if changed according to the principle of melodic inversion [see Inversion (2)] leads to an acceptable result. A mirror canon (mirror fugue) is a canon (fugue) so constructed. Among the few mirror compositions found in actual music is a setting of the chorale "Mit Fried und Freud ich fahr dahin," which Buxtehude included in his *Fried- und freudenreiche Hinfarth*, written in 1674 for the burial of his father [see Ex.]. Much better known are the two mirror fugues in Bach's *Art of Fugue* (*BG*, vol. xxv, pt. i, Contrapunctus

12 [also *BG,* vol. xlvii, no. 18] in four parts; Contrapunctus 13 [no. 16] in three parts, also a Fugue on p. 85 [Contrapunctus 17, p. 93] with the addition of a "non-mirrored" voice). It should be noted that the term "mirror canon" is often used for what is more properly called "canon by inversion" [see Canon I (d)]. Occasionally it is used to mean retrograde canon [see Canon I (e)].

Misattributed compositions. See Spurious compositions.

Miserere [L.]. Psalm 50 [51]: "Miserere mei, Deus, secundum magnam misericordiam tuam" (Have mercy upon me, O God, according to thy loving kindness). In the Roman Catholic rites it is sung as the first psalm of Lauds on Maundy Thursday, Good Friday, and Holy Saturday [see Tenebrae]; also at Lauds of the Office for the Dead and during the Burial Service. It is one of the *penitential psalms and has been composed as such, but also independently, owing to the impressiveness of the text. The earliest example is a setting by Costanzo Festa (1517) for two choruses, one in four parts, the other in five, in familiar style (*falsobordone*). Various other compositions in the same style, usually retaining the "traditional" number of nine parts, were written, among them the celebrated composition by Gregorio Allegri (*c.* 1582–1652) that remained in use at the Papal Chapel until 1870, alongside Palestrina's *Improperiae and *Lamentations for the same service. A host of legends—including that of the young Mozart copying it from memory, against the express law of the Church —have arisen, all intended to elevate this work to the realm of divine inspiration and beauty. Actually it is a rather undistinguished composition in a plain *falsobordone* style whose monotony is somewhat relieved by "abbellimenti" (probably 18th-century additions) at the end of each verse. The mediocrity of Allegri's Miserere does not, of course, prevent it from being very effective when performed with the solemnity of the pontifical rites. A much more beautiful and imaginative composition of the text is the Miserere by Josquin, published in 1519.

Missa [L.]. *Mass. *Missa solemnis* (solemn Mass, High Mass) is the Mass in its full form, with all the items (except for lections, etc.) sung, while in the *Missa lecta* (read Mass, Low Mass) there is no music, except perhaps hymn singing. *Missa cantata* (sung Mass) is, from the musical point of view, identical with the High Mass but is celebrated in a less elaborate manner. From the

above it appears that the title *Missa Solemnis* chosen by Beethoven for his Mass (op. 123) carries no connotation that would not also apply to a Mass by Palestrina or Bach. *Missa pro defunctis,* Mass for the Dead, Requiem Mass. *Missa Papae Marcelli,* see Marcellus Mass. *Missa L'Homme armé,* see *L'Homme armé.*

Missal [L. *missale*]. See under Liturgical books I (1).

Mistaken authorship. See Spurious compositions.

Mistic(h)anza [It.]. *Quodlibet.

Misura [It.]. Measure, beat. *Alla misura,* in strict time; *senza misura,* without strict time.

Mit Andacht. See *Andächtig.*

Mit Ausdruck. See *Ausdrucksvoll.*

Mit Eile. See *Eilend.*

Mit Empfindung. See *Empfindung.*

Mit Wärme. See *Wärme.*

Mixed cadence. See under Cadence I.

Mixed mode. See under Church modes III.

Mixed voices. A combination of men's and women's voices [see Equal voices].

Mixolydian. (1) See under Greece II. (2) The seventh *church mode (*septimus tonus; tetrartus*), represented by the segment g–g′ of the diatonic scale, with g as the tonic. From the modern point of view it is a major mode with a minor seventh (f instead of f♯). See also Modality.

Mixture stop. See under Organ VI, IX (f).

M.M. See under Metronome.

Modal. Pertaining to a mode, either a church mode (e.g., in modal harmony, *modality) or the rhythmic modes of the 13th century (modal notation, modal interpretation, modal rhythm).

Modality. The use of harmonic and melodic formations based on the *church modes, as opposed to those based on the major and minor modes (*tonality). In particular, the term refers to the use of modal idioms in the prevailingly tonal music of the 19th and 20th centuries. This phenomenon may be traced to three different sources: (a) the desire to imitate the tonal language of 16th-century sacred music; (b) the influence of Slavic or other folksong having modal features; (c) a reaction against the system of classical harmony. Examples of (a) are Beetho-ven's "Dankgesang an die Gottheit in der lydischen Tonart" (String Quartet in A minor op. 132, 1825)—probably the earliest example of 19th-century modality—and the composi-tions of Vaughan Williams; examples of (b) occur in Chopin's mazurkas and in numer-ous compositions by Mussorgsky, Tchaikovsky, and other *nationalist composers; the last-mentioned tendency is conspicuous in the works of Debussy [see Impressionism] and 20th-cen-tury neoclassical composers. The accompanying examples illustrate the use of modality. Ex. 1 (Chopin, Mazurka no. 15) is Lydian (B natural instead of B-flat); Ex. 2 (Franck, Symphony) is

because it is based on the system of rhythmic *modes. The parts are written in *ligatures, whose value depends on the mode used. Thus, a single three-note ligature (*ligatura ternaria*) may have the value *L-B-L* in mode 1, *B-L-B* in mode 2, *L-L-L* in mode 5 (*L = longa*, *B = brevis*, corresponding to the quarter note and eighth

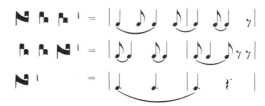

note in modern transcriptions). See Ex. This ambiguity was eliminated in the Franconian notation (*c.* 1260). See Notation III, Ex. 2; also Square notation.

Modal rhythm. A rhythm based on the rhythmic *modes. See also Rhythm III (b).

Modal theory. A theory according to which compositions (mostly of the 13th century) should be interpreted in modal rhythm, although the original notation gives no evidence of such rhythm. This theory has been applied to (a) the *conductus and (b) the melodies of the trouba-dours, trouvères, and minnesingers, nearly all of which are notated in uniform note values [Ex. a] but are thought to have been performed with a regular alternation of long and short values [Ex. b].

The modal theory was proposed simultane-ously (*c.* 1907) by P. Aubry, F. Ludwig, and J. B. Beck (concerning the question of priority, see J. Chailley, in *AMW* x, 213ff). In its original form it called for the strict application of one of the rhythmic modes (in practice only modes 1, 2, and 3), the proper mode to be selected on the basis of the metrical structure of the text (num-ber of syllables, distribution of accents). This, however, is a rather nebulous criterion, since in numerous cases a single melody has been inter-preted differently by different scholars [see, e.g.,

transposed Dorian (major sixth D-sharp instead of minor sixth D); Ex. 3 (Brahms, Symphony no. 4) combines Phrygian (minor second F instead of F-sharp) with Mixolydian (minor seventh D, instead of the leading tone D-sharp); Ex. 4 (Sibelius, Symphony no. 2) is Aeolian (minor sixth and seventh, F and G instead of F-sharp and G-sharp). See J. Vincent, *The Diatonic Modes in Modern Music* (1951); J. d'Almendra, *Les Modes grégoriens dans l'œuvre de Claude Debussy* [1950].

Modal notation. A notational system used mainly in the organa and clausulae of the school of *Notre Dame (*c.* 1175–1250), so called

HAM, no. 18c, showing three versions of Guiraut de Bornelh's *Reis glorios,* to which at least two others could be added]. Originally an ardent champion of modal theory, F. Gennrich has since advocated a freer application of modal rhythm, aiming at an even closer agreement between the musical rhythm and details or variants of the accentual structure of the text. This often involves highly personal judgment as to which word or syllable is strongly accented, particularly since French is not an "accentuating" language like English or German. See Monophonic notation; Poetic meter IV.

Lit.: P. Aubry, *La Rythmique musicale des troubadours et des trouvères* (1907); J. B. Beck, *Die Melodien der Troubadours* (1908); A. Machabey, *Notations musicales non modales* (1959); F. Gennrich, ‡*Troubadours Trouvères Minne- und Meistergesang* (in *Das Musikwerk,* ed. K. G. Fellerer [1951]); F. Ludwig, "Zur 'modalen Interpretation' von Melodien des 12. und 13. Jahrhunderts" (*ZIM* xi); *ReMMA,* pp. 206ff; *ApNPM,* pp. 258ff (conductus); F. Gennrich, in *MF* i, *MF* vii, *CP Anglés* i; H. Husmann, in *AMW* ix, *AMW* xi, *MF* v. See also the summaries by J. Smits van Waesberghe in *KJ* xlvii, 20, and xlviii, 15.

Mode. A term used for two entirely different concepts, both rooted in medieval music, namely (1) one of scale formation, and (2) one of rhythm.

(1) Mode, in the widest sense of the word, denotes the selection of tones, arranged in a scale, that form the basic tonal substance of a composition. In any given key (i.e., for any given center tone or tonic, e.g., E) a large number of modes are possible, some of which are indicated in the accompanying illustration: 1 is the "Dorian mode" (transposed from D to E); 2 is the "Phrygian mode" (untransposed); 3 is the "major mode" (usually called major key); 4 is the "minor mode" (usually called minor key); 5 is a "pentatonic mode"; 6 is the "whole-tone mode." See Scale III. In a narrower sense, the term "mode" refers only to those scales that go back to the medieval *church modes (modes 1

and 2 of the example). It is with reference to these that the terms "modal" and "modality" are commonly used. For the use of the term "mode" with reference to Oriental (Indian, Arab, etc.) music, see Melody type.

(2) See Modes, rhythmic; also *Modus.*

Moderato [It.]. In moderate speed, i.e., between andante and allegro.

Modern music. A term used so loosely that it is virtually meaningless. The dates of the period so described vary with each writer. Some people might agree that modern music started about 1890, when composers such as Elgar, R. Strauss, and Sibelius (all born *c.* 1860) produced their first significant works. Others would restrict it to the music of contemporary (living) composers. See Impressionism; Twentieth-century music; Neoclassicism; Atonality; Expressionism; Serial music; Electronic music; etc. See A. Cohn, *Twentieth-Century Music in Western Europe* [1965]; *LBCM, passim;* J. Machlis, *Introduction to Contemporary Music* (1961); N. Slonimsky, *Music since 1900* (1937); G. Perle, *Serial Composition and Atonality* (1962); W. Austin, *Music in the 20th Century* [1966]; A. Salazar, *Music in Our Time* (1946).

Modes, rhythmic. A 13th-century system of rhythm, characterized by the consistent repetition of certain simple rhythmic patterns in ternary meter. Usually six modes are distinguished, as shown below. The Greek names (added in parentheses) were not used until relatively late (W. Odington, *c.* 1290; see Theory II, 12) and do not imply that the modes are derived from the feet of ancient Greek poetry [see Poetic meter].

In musical compositions, the patterns were reiterated a number of times, depending on the

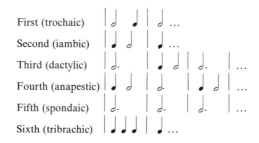

length of the phrase or, in medieval terminology, on the *ordo.* The *ordo* indicated the number of times a pattern was repeated without interruption, e.g.:

First mode,
third ordo

Third mode,
second ordo

The modes are the rhythmic basis of the organa, clausulae, and motets of the 13th century, which are therefore said to be written in *modal notation [see also Square notation]. Usually the first, second, and sixth modes occur in the upper parts (sometimes also the third), and the third and fifth in the lower (the fourth mode was rarely used). In practice, certain modifications of the normal patterns were admitted, such as occasional omission of a weak beat (*extensio modi*) or breaking up of one note into two or three (*fractio modi*). See also under Perfect, imperfect.

Lit.: *ApNPM*, pp. 220ff; A. Michalitschke, *Die Theorie des Modus* (1923); H. Sowa, in *ZMW* xv; H. Husmann, in *AMW* xi; F. Chailley, in *CP Anglés* i; E. H. Sanders, in *JAMS* xvii, 261ff.

Modinha [Port.]. Urban song of European traditions, chiefly Italian opera, that was developed mainly during the 19th century in Brazilian salons. Its music, lyrical and very sentimental, is usually set for a solo voice accompanied by a chamber group and reflects the influences of both Portuguese folksongs and *bel canto*. Since the peak of its development was reached under the Brazilian Empire, it is also known as *modinha imperial*.

J.O-S.

Modulamen, modulatio, modulus. Humanist (16th-cent.) misnomers for motet.

Modulation. Change of key within a composition. Such changes are among the most common devices of harmonic variety and are found in practically every work of some length. For an effective modulation, the initial as well as the new key should be established by a cadence.

I. *Theory.* A modulation is effected by means of a "pivot chord," i.e., a chord that is common to both the initial and the new key. For instance, in Ex. 1, the third chord is the pivot chord, being I in the old key (C) and IV in the new key (G); hence it is designated $\frac{C:I}{G:IV}$. In Ex. 2, the same chord adopts the function of VII in D (properly, D minor), while in Ex. 3, V of C is reinterpreted as III of E (properly, E minor).

Usually three types of modulation are distinguished: diatonic, chromatic, and enharmonic. A diatonic modulation is one made through a chord that is diatonic in both keys. Ex. 1–3 be-

C: I   V⁶   I
G: IV   V⁴₃   I

C:I   V⁶   I
D:VII   V⁶   I

C:I   V⁶
E:III⁶ V   I

C:I   ♭II⁶
A♭: IV⁶ V⁶₅   I

C:I   V⁹♭
A:V⁹♭   I

C:I   IV   V   I
D:III   IV⁄   C:II   II⁶   I⁶₄   V   I

C:I   IV   V   I
D: III   IV⁄   B♭:III II⁶   I⁶₄   V   I

long to this category. A chromatic modulation is one made through a chord that is chromatically altered in one or both keys, a very common example being the modulation through the Neapolitan sixth [Ex. 4]. The field of chromatic modulation is very large, and its exploitation has been one of the main achievements of 19th-century harmony. Enharmonic modulation is one that involves the enharmonic change of one or several notes. This is frequently achieved through the diminished seventh chord [Ex. 5].

If the new key is touched upon only momentarily, leading quickly into a third key, the modulation is said to be "false" or "passing." The former term is used if the third key is the initial key [Ex. 6], the latter if it is still another key [Ex. 7]. The latter occurs mainly in sequential progressions (sequential modulation). Naturally, the interpretation of a modulation as "real," "false," or "passing" depends largely on the impression of permanence (to the second key) and therefore is frequently a subjective judgment.

536

Aside from the above-described "pivot modulations," change of key is often effected simply by juxtaposing the old and new keys, a very effective device that some writers claim is not really "modulation." Ex. 8, by Schubert, under Harmony, illustrates this method, which usually involves a shift of a whole tone or semitone. Even in these cases, however, the harmonic relationships can be analyzed on the basis of pivot chords. See Harmonic analysis VI.

II. *History.* Obrecht (*c.* 1450–1505) and Josquin (*c.* 1450–1521) seem to have been the first composers to make deliberate use of modulation, always in short passages involving five or six passing modulations to the lower fifth, e.g.: D–G–C–F–B♭–E♭–D. Similar passages occur sporadically throughout the 16th century. An interesting early experiment in chromatic (and, in a sense, enharmonic) modulation is Willaert's duo "Quidnam ebrietas" [see J. S. Levitan, in *TV* xv; E. E. Lowinsky, in *TV* xviii]. Naturally, the chromatic madrigals of the late 16th century (Marenzio, Gesualdo, Monteverdi) abound in chromatic modulations of various types. A particularly interesting landmark in the history of modulation is John Bull's organ fantasia *Ut, re, mi, fa, sol, la* [see Hexachord VI], not only because of its unusual modulatory scheme—always a whole tone upward—but also because the modulations serve to establish a succession of different keys, which later was to become their main function. This seems to have taken place chiefly with the establishment of fixed repeat forms, the binary form of the dance movements of the suite and the ternary form of the *da capo* aria [see Aria IV]. With Bach, a modulatory scheme became an essential trait of the fugue. In the late 18th century, the *sonata form was treated (and explained by theorists) primarily as a harmonic-modulating form, involving certain standard changes of key [see Lit., Ratner]. In this period the term "to modulate" [G. *modulieren*] often meant "exploiting a key" rather than "change of key."

Lit.: A. Foote, *Modulation and Related Harmonic Questions* (1919); C. Zöller, *The Art of Modulation* (1930); M. Reger, *On the Theory of Modulation* [trans.; n.d.]; H. O. Rogers, "The Development of a Concept of Modulation in Theory from the 16th to the Early 18th Century" (diss. Indiana Univ., 1955); F. Turrell, "Modulation: An Outline of Its Prehistory from Aristoxenus to Henry Glarean" (diss. Univ. of Southern California, 1956); L. Ratner, "Harmonic Aspects of Classic Form" (*JAMS* ii);

H. Ausubel, "Aspects of Modulation Practice in the Period between 1890 and 1910" (*MR* xvi, 218ff). See also under Harmony.

Modulator. See Tonic sol-fa.

Modus [L.]. (1) *Church mode; see also Tonus (2). *Mode, rhythmic. (3) In *mensural notation, *modus major* (*modus maximarum*) denotes the relationship between the *maxima* and the *longa,* and *modus minor* (*modus longarum*), or simply *modus,* that between the *longa* and the *brevis.* In English books, Morley's translations "greater mood" and "lesser mood" are frequently used in this sense. Both *modi* could be either perfect or imperfect [see Mensural notation II; also Perfect, imperfect]. The *modus longarum* often occurs in the tenors of 14th- and 15th-century motets and Masses, while the *modus maximarum* is much rarer [see *ApNPM,* p. 124]. The *modus longarum* developed from the six rhythmic modes of the 13th century [*ibid.,* pp. 242ff].

Modus lascivus [L.]. Medieval name for the tonality of C major, which was avoided in plainsong but was frequently used in secular music.

Moldau, The. English title of the second (*Vltava*) of Smetana's symphonic poem cycle *Má Vlast.*

Moll [G.]. Minor key; *G moll,* G minor. See *Dur.*

Molto [It.]. Very. *Molto allegro* (*adagio*), very quick (slow).

Moments musicals [F., Musical Moments, correctly *Moments musicaux*]. Title of Schubert's six piano pieces, op. 94 (1828?). See under Character piece.

Monacordo [It.]. A 16th-century name for the *clavichord.

Mondscheinsonate [G.]. *Moonlight Sonata.

Monferrina. A country dance from Piedmont (north Italy) in 6/8 time, which became fashionable in England *c.* 1800, where it usually was called *monfrina, monfreda,* or *manfredina.* Examples are found in Wheatstone's *Country Dances for 1810* and similar collections.

Monochord. A device consisting of a single string stretched over a long wooden resonator to which a movable bridge is attached so that the vibrating length of the string can be varied. The monochord was widely used in antiquity (under the name *kanon) and in the Middle Ages for the investigation and demonstration of the laws of musical acoustics, a purpose for which it is still used today [see Acoustics II]. Detailed descriptions are given by Odo of Clugny [*GS* i, 252], Hieronymus de Moravia [*CS* i, 74], and others. In the later Middle Ages the number of strings was increased to two or three, so that intervals and chords could be made audible. Such monochords, sometimes called "polychords," were the ancestors of the *clavichord, which as late as the 16th century was called *monacordo* in Italy. In the 17th and 18th centuries the monochord was widely used by organ tuners.

Lit.: S. Wantzloeben, *Das Monochord als Instrument und System* (1911); W. Nef, "The Polychord" (*GSJ* iv, 20ff); *GéHM,* p. 407; J. Chailley, "La Monocorde et la théorie musicale" (*CP Waesberghe*).

Monocordo. In violin playing, the performance of a piece or passage on a single string. This effect was used first by Paganini in his Sonata "Napoleon" for the G string.

Monodrama. See under Melodrama.

Monody. A term occasionally used as a synonym of *monophonic music or for accompanied solo song in general, but more properly denoting a particular type of accompanied solo song that developed about 1600 in reaction to the polyphonic style of the 16th century and that is characterized by recitativo-like design of the voice-part and thoroughbass accompaniment.

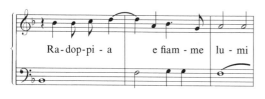

Ra - dop-pi - a   e fiam - me   lu - mi

al me-mo-ra-bil   gior-no Fe - bo ch'il car-ro

d'or ri-vol   —   — gi in-tor - no

The illustration shows one of the earliest examples of true monody, from Caccini's *Le Nuove musiche* (1601; for others, see *HAM,* nos. 182–85; *SchGMB,* nos. 169, 171–73, 176, etc.; see also *Nuove musiche;* Aria III; Cantata; Recitative).

Forerunners of the monodic style are the numerous 16th-century songs with lute or vihuela accompaniment (Schlick, *Tabulaturen etlicher lobgesang und lidlein,* 1512; Milán, *El Maestro,* 1535; Enriquez de Valderrabano, *Libro de música de vihuela,* 1547) and polyphonic madrigals arranged for a solo singer with an accompanist for the lower parts (e.g., Luzzascho Luzzaschi; see *SchGMB,* no. 166). Bottrigari, in his *Desiderio* (1594; new ed. by K. Meyer, 1924), wrote about a widespread practice of solo song in the *laude,* the *intermedii* [see Intermezzo (1)], and in folk singing.

Lit.: P. Aldrich, *Rhythm in Seventeenth-Century Italian Monody* [1966]; N. Fortune, "Italian Secular Song from 1600 to 1635. The Origins and Development of Accompanied Monody" (diss. Cambridge Univ., 1953); *id.,* "Italian Secular Monody from 1600 to 1635" (*MQ* xxxix); A. Schering, "Zur Geschichte des begleiteten Sologesangs im 16. Jahrhundert" (*ZIM* xiii); E. Schmitz, "Zur Frühgeschichte der ... Monodie" (*JMP* xviii); P. Nettl, "Über ein handschriftliches Sammelwerk von Gesängen italienischer Frühmonodie" (*ZMW* ii); C. Mac-Clintock, "The Monodies of Francisco Rasi" (*JAMS* xiv); A. Einstein, "Firenze, prima della monodia" (*LRM* vii); L. Torchi, "Canzoni ... ad una voce nel secolo XVII" (*RMI* i).

Monophonic notation. The notation of early monophonic music, e.g., Chinese, Indian, Greek, Byzantine, Gregorian, sequences, troubadours, trouvères, minnesingers, Meistersinger, etc. Since this repertory has widely differing origins, monophonic notation is simply a generic term for a number of entirely different systems of notation, each of which requires individual study. In Oriental as well as in ancient Greek music the pitches are indicated by symbols derived from the literary script (syllables, letters), while the neumatic notation of Christian and ancient Jewish chant employs special signs of purely musical significance [see Ecphonetic notation; Byzantine chant III; Neumes]. After A.D. 1000 the neumes of Gregorian chant became "heighted" and were written on a staff, a development that led to a permanent solution for notating pitch. The 12th-century neumatic script of France, characterized by the use of square-shaped characters [see Square notation], was adopted for the notation of polyphonic music [see Notation III] as well as for writing down the monophonic repertory of secular songs. The melodies of the troubadours and trouvères and the Italian *laude* and Spanish *cantigas* all are written in this notation, essentially that employed in modern editions of Gregorian chant. Some of the earliest (12th-century) sources of troubadour and trouvère song, especially the Chansonnier de Saint-Germain des Près, employ the somewhat different symbols of Messine script, which was adopted in Germany (minnesingers, Meistersinger).

The main deficiency of these notational systems is their failure to indicate note values. This gives rise to the question of rhythm, not only in Gregorian chant [see Gregorian chant VI] but also for the repertory of secular song, in which, however, it is distinctly different because of the presence of poetic texts. The use of nonmensural symbols for writing down presumably measured melodies has led to various theories, most of them based on a consideration of the poetic meter of the text. While Riemann advocated the principle of *Vierhebigkeit* and duple meter, P. Aubry and others proposed an interpretation in triple meter based on the rhythmic modes of the 13th century [see Modal theory; also Poetic meter IV]. The validity of the modal theory has been challenged by A. Machabey and especially by H. Anglés, who maintains that the Spanish *cantigas,* the Italian *laude,* and some troubadour and trouvère MSS are written in a mensural notation that is partly modal, partly nonmodal (binary meter). This important discovery may well lead to new results in the field of secular song.

Lit.: *WoHN* i, 146–71; 172–97; *RiHM* i.2, 245ff, 260ff; J. B. Beck, *Die Melodien der Troubadours* (1908; see *WoHN* i, 200n); *id., Le Chansonnier Cangé* (1927); P. Aubry, *Trouvères and Troubadours* (1914); A. Machabey, *Notations musicales non modales* (1957); H. Riemann, in *JMP* xii; J. Handschin, in *AM* x and *Medium Aevum* iv (1935); H. J. Moser, in *ZMW* vii, 367ff; E. Jammers, in *ZMW* vii, 265ff; H. Anglés, in *CP 1949,* pp. 45ff, and *CP 1958,* pp. 56ff. See also under Modal theory.

Monophony, monophonic. Music consisting of a single melodic line without additional parts or accompaniment, as opposed to *polyphony, *homophony, etc. [see Texture]. Monophonic music is the purest realization of the melodic element [see Melody]. It is the oldest type of music, being the only kind employed in ancient Greece, in the various branches of early church music (Gregorian chant, Byzantine chant), the music of the troubadours, trouvères, minnesingers, and Meistersinger, the Spanish *cantigas* and Italian *laude* of the 13th century, and universally in non-Western and primitive music as well as in European folk music. Also see remark under Monody.

Monothematic, polythematic. Terms describing compositions based on one theme (e.g., a fugue) or several themes (e.g., a sonata or a movement in sonata form). They are applied particularly to the imitative forms of the 16th and 17th centuries, such as the fantasia, ricercar, etc. It was formerly maintained that the fantasia was monothematic and the ricercar polythematic [see M. Seiffert, *Geschichte der Klaviermusik* (1899), p. 33f]. Actually, both forms may have one or several themes.

Monotone. The recitation of a liturgical text on an unchanged pitch, as in psalms, prayers, lessons (reading from the Scriptures), etc. Usually, monotonic declamation is modified by inflections, i.e., a few ascending or descending tones at the beginning, middle, or end of the phrase of the text. See Psalm tones. The term "inflected monotone" has also been used for rather elaborate chants that have been interpreted as highly ornamented variants of a recitation.

Montirande. A 16th- and 17th-century variety of the *branle, mentioned by Arbeau (*Orchésographie,* 1589) as "branle de monstierandel," and by Mersenne (*Harmonie universelle,* 1636) as "branle de montirandé." A manuscript in Uppsala contains a number of Montirandes for instrumental ensemble, in 4/4 meter and with dotted rhythms. See J. J. S. Mráček, "Seventeenth-Century Instrumental Dances in Uppsala, Univ. Libr. I Mhs 409" (diss. Indiana Univ., 1965).

Montonero [Sp.]. Counterpart of the French minuet that developed in the La Plata River region during the first half of the 19th century. It is also known as *minué montonero* or *el Nacional* (the national). While retaining the a b a structure of the European model, the *montonero* became a characteristic New World dance through the inclusion of numerous folk devices, e.g., the use of shoe-tapping and of many Latin American figures, as well as melodic ornamentation common to folksongs of this area. Examples based on popular melodies and on national anthems have been preserved. A well-known one from 1837 is the *Minué Republicano,* based on Antonio Sáenz's Uruguayan national anthem.

J.O-S.

Montpellier, Codex. Name of two important early manuscripts, both in the library of the *Faculté de médecine* of the University of Montpellier in southern France: (1) *Cod. H 159,* an 11th-century MS of Gregorian chant, unique for its arrangement of the chants according to modes (*Tonale missarum*) and for its double ("bilingual") notation in nondiastematic neumes and *letter notation [*Editions XLII A, 7 and 8]; (2) *H 196,* the most important source of 13th-century motets; see Sources, no. 4.

Monumenta, Monumenti, Monuments. See Editions XXVII to XXXIII.

Mood. See *Modus* (3).

Moonlight Sonata [G. *Mondscheinsonate*]. Popular name for Beethoven's *Sonata quasi una fantasia* op. 27, no. 2. The name probably comes from a review written by Heinrich Rellstab (1799–1860), in which the first movement was likened to a boat floating by moonlight on Lake Lucerne. Another name is *Laube Sonata* [G. *Laube,* "bower"], referring probably to a fancied place of composition. The latter name is not known at all in Germany. See under Mute.

Morceau [F.]. Piece, composition.

Mordent [G.; F. *mordant* (Old F. *pincé, pincement*); It. *mordente;* Sp. *mordiente*]. A musical ornament consisting of the alternation of the written note with the note immediately below it. It is indicated by one of the signs given in Ex. 1 (the third sign is used only in music for bowed

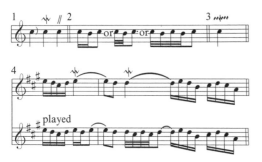

instruments). In performance the mordent always occupies part of the value of the written note and should not be introduced before it. The alternations of the written note and the auxiliary may be either single or double [Ex. 2]; there is a special sign for the latter [Ex. 3], but it is not often used and the choice between these executions is generally left to the performer, who bases his decision chiefly on the duration of the written note. If two mordents occur in close succession, contemporary authorities recommend that one should be made single and the other double, as in Ex. 4 (Bach).

In the works of J. S. Bach the mordent often is fully written out [Ex. 5, Adagio of the C-major organ toccata]. All of Bach's mordents, except for those in pieces with a particularly vigorous rhythm, should be performed comparatively slowly, as in Ex. 6 [a. Italian Concerto; b. *Well-Tempered Clavier* ii, no. 1]. When a mordent and an appoggiatura occur on the same note, the mordent must be delayed until the appoggiatura has been held for its normal duration, as in Bach's chorale prelude, "Wenn wir in höchsten Nöten sein" [Ex. 7]. After 1750 all mordents were performed more rapidly than in Bach's time. The ornament apparently was absorbed by the ordinary notation before the classical period, for it is not found in the works of Mozart and Beethoven.

The mordent occurs in the German organ tablatures of the 15th and 16th centuries, where it is indicated by the signs illustrated (a. Bux-heim Organ Book, *c.* 1470; b. Kotter, Buchner, *c.* 1520). It was executed somewhat differently, however, since the main note was held and only the lower auxiliary was quickly repeated [see

WoHN ii, 24; *ApNPM*, p. 24]. According to Ammerbach (*Orgel oder Instrument Tabulatur-buch,* 1583), the mordent was performed with the lower or upper neighboring note depending on whether it occurred in ascending or descending motion [see *WoHN* ii, 29]:

Also see Inverted mordent. See the general books on ornamentation.   P.A.

Morendo [It.]. Fading away.

Moresca, morisca. A. pantomimic dance of the 15th and 16th centuries, which was executed in Moorish costume and other grotesque disguises, the dancers having their faces blackened and small bells attached to their legs. Arbeau, in his *Orchésographie* (1589), reports that he saw the *moresca* danced in his youthful days (*c.* 1530) by "un garçonnet machuré et noircy, des grelot-tières aux jambes." The *moresca* was easily the most popular dance for the ballets and mum-meries of the Renaissance. There were two types, a solo dance and a dance of two groups that represented a sword fight between Chris-tians and Moslems. The latter was known also as *danse des *bouffons* [see also *Matasin*]. Dances of this kind are still known today in Spain, Cor-sica, and Guatemala. In England they survived under the name "Morris dance," partly in a con-tinuous tradition, partly as the result of a con-scious revival *c.* 1900. The Morris dance was performed chiefly as part of the May games. It included, in addition to six male dancers in two groups, certain solo characters, such as the "Mayde Maryan," represented by a boy dis-guised as a girl, or by a dancer with a hobby-horse. For the vocal *moresca* (Lasso), see under Villanella. See C. Sachs, *World History of the Dance* (1937); O. Gombosi, in *PAMS* 1940, p. 91; P. Nettl, in *AMW* xiv.

Morris dance. See under *Moresca.*

Moses und Aron. Opera in three acts by Schoen-berg (to his own libretto), produced in Ham-burg, 1954, concert performance; Zurich, 1957, stage performance. Setting: Mt. Sinai, Biblical times.

Mòsso [It.]. Moved, agitated.

Motectum. A 16th-century latinized term for motet.

Motellus [L.]. A 13th- and 14th-century term for motet.

Motet. The most important form of early poly-phonic music, particularly during the Middle Ages and Renaissance. Since it underwent numerous changes during the more than five centuries of its existence (*c.* 1220–1750), it is im-possible to formulate a general definition that covers all the phases of its development. As a rule, a motet is an unaccompanied choral com-position based on a Latin sacred text and de-signed to be performed in the Roman Catholic service, chiefly at Vespers. There are, however, side developments into the secular field (13th-century French motet; 15th-century ceremonial motet), as well as motets for soloists (13th-cen-tury motet; also in the late 17th century) or with orchestral accompaniment and to texts in the vernacular (17th century, Germany and France; the English motets of this period are called *anthems). The history of the motet may be divided into three periods: A. medieval motet (*c.* 1220–1450); B. Flemish motet (1450–1600), named for its inaugurators, although it became international property after 1550; C. baroque motet (1600–1750).

A. *The medieval motet.* I. The medieval motet originated in the early 13th century, possibly as early as 1200, through the addition of a full text to the upper part (*duplum*) of the *clausulae of the Perotinus period, a development strikingly similar to the one that, in the 9th century, led from the vocalized melismas of the Alleluias to the full-text sequences. Owing to the addition of "mots," the *duplum* with text was called *motetus,* a name that was adopted for the entire composi-tion. The tenor of a motet (like that of a clausula) is practically always a melismatic (vocalized) passage taken from a Gregorian chant (usually a Gradual, Alleluia, or responsory) and identi-fied by the word or syllable (*incipit,* usually capitalized in modern writings) with which it occurs in the original plainsong. The only change is in rhythm, from the free rhythm of plainsong to a strict modal pattern [see Modes, rhythmic]. The accompanying example shows the motet "O Maria—Nostrum" [see *ApNPM,* p. 285, for a facsimile of the original notation] and the Easter Alleluia [see *LU,* p. 779] from which the tenor NOSTRUM is taken. It is im-

Al-le-lu - ia. ℣. Pas-cha NO - STRUM

O Ma - ri - a de-cus an - ge - lo - rum,

NOSTRUM

ma - ter re - gis re - gi - na coe - lo - rum

portant to realize that originally a motet was not an independent composition but, like the clausulae, a polyphonic interpolation (polyphonic *trope) of the chant to which it is allied by its tenor. The following scheme—a modification of that given under Clausula—shows two motets in their proper liturgical position (ordinary print indicates plainsong; capital letters the motet tenors; italics the added text of the upper part):

O Maria . . .

Alleluia, alleluia. ℣. Pascha NOSTRUM

Radix venie . . .

immo-LATUS   est Christus.

II. There are a few specimens of a 12th-century type of motet, the *organal motet,* so called because it is based on a complete Gregorian melody so that, except for the text of its upper part, it is an organum rather than a clausula. Examples are "*Stirps Jesse*—Benedicamus Domino" and "*Amborum sacrum spiramen*—Benedicamus Domino," the latter remarkable for its text, a medley of Latin and French [see J. Handschin, "Über den Ursprung der Motette," in *CP 1924*]. To this type belongs a version of Perotinus' *organum quadruplum,* "Viderunt omnes," in which the *duplum* is provided with a full text, "Vide prophecie" [see *AdHM* i, 229].

The first step in the development of the 13th-century motet probably was to supply clausulae

with a text that represents a paraphrase of the tenor incipit, e.g., *Domino fidelium omnium* for the tenor DOMINO [see *HAM,* no. 28f]. Frequently, however, not only unrelated Latin texts but also French secular texts were employed. An important step was the addition of a third voice-part (*triplum*), in either Latin or French (a Latin *triplum* was used only in connection with a Latin *motetus*). There also exist a few motets in four parts. A special type is the *conductus motet* in three (occasionally four) parts, in which the upper parts have an identical text and identical rhythm, as in a conductus. Motets with two (three) different texts are called double (triple) motets. The Latin double motet may be regarded as the classical type of 13th-century motet. While most of the earlier motets are based on clausulae, those of a later date (after 1250?) consist of freely invented parts added to the tenor.

The use of a French text in connection with a liturgical tenor is a startling incongruity, since these texts usually deal with amorous and occasionally even lascivious subjects. Needless to say, such motets were never sung in church but served as an entertainment at social gatherings. The Latin motet, on the other hand, far from being incongruous, is a perfect expression of the universalism of Thomas Aquinas and other medieval philosophers. At any rate, the mixture of sacred and secular, the merging of the Gregorian tradition with the trouvère movement, the frequent exchanges and substitutions, both musical and textual, are what make the development of the motet so fascinating. Examples illustrating the extraordinarily manifold relationships within the repertory of the 13th-century motet are found in *AdHM* i, 237, 240 (F. Ludwig), and *HAM,* no. 28h, 28i. A limited number of motets are musical *quodlibets* including combinations of different pre-existent melodies [see Refrain III; *Enté*].

III. The rhythmic structure of the motet is based on the rhythmic *modes, the upper parts frequently employing a quicker pattern (first, second, sixth mode) than the tenor (third, fifth mode), as illustrated (schematically) in our example. In the early motets (before 1250?) sub-

divisions of the breve (represented by a quarter note in the example) into two or three notes (eighth notes, eighth-note triplets) occur only as ornamenting groups sung to one syllable. Franco of Cologne recognized these shorter notes as a new value, the semibreve, thereby introducing a new type, the Franconian motet, in which each semibreve could be sung to a separate syllable, resulting in a more lively declamation [see *HAM*, no. 28i, 2; also no. 33b]. This tendency was carried to an extreme in the Petronian motet of the late 13th century (named after Petrus de Cruce), in which the breve is subdivided into four to seven notes, sung syllabically in a rapid *parlando* style [see *HAM*, nos. 34, 35].

IV. In the 14th century the motet lost its dominant position [see *Ars nova*] but grew in length, elaboration, and rhythmic variety. A feature of special interest is the introduction of the *isorhythmic principle. Practically all the motets of Machaut (*c.* 1300–77) are isorhythmic [ex. in *HAM*, no. 44], and a number of them apply this principle not only to the tenor but also, with a certain amount of freedom, to the upper parts [*see ReMMA*, p. 354]. The final stage of the development is represented by the strictly panisorhythmic motet (in which *all* parts are strictly isorhythmic), used a few times by Machaut but predominantly by his successors until *c.* 1430 (Dunstable, Dufay). There are a considerable number of early 14th-century English motets, many of which combine a conservative 13th-century style with an extended use of *voice exchange [ex. in *HAM*, no. 57a; see Worcester, school of].

Beginning in the 15th century, novel methods of composition were used for motets. The two characteristics of the medieval motet, polytextuality and a *cantus firmus* tenor, were abandoned in favor of free composition with the same text in all the parts. The earliest examples of this type are by J. Ciconia (*c.* 1335–1411), e.g., his "O felix templum," composed *c.* 1406. In the works of Dunstable and Dufay, free motets appear side by side with the last representatives of the isorhythmic type. They are usually in three voice-parts and in *cantilena style, with only the upper part (sometimes the two upper parts) carrying the text. In this period it is very difficult to draw a line between motets on the one hand and polyphonic settings of hymns or Marian antiphons on the other. For instance, an "Ave Regina caelorum" may in one edition be included among the motets [e.g., Bukofzer's edition of Dunstable, in *Editions XXXIV, 8]

but not in another [e.g., De Van and Besseler edition of Dufay].

B. *The Flemish motet.* I. The return to sacred music that characterizes the *Flemish school brought the motet back to prominence as a musical form second in importance only to the Mass. The motet now became a choral setting of a Latin religious text, in four to six or more voice-parts. Its texture became much more unified, all the parts being vocal and having approximately the same degree of rhythmic animation. In not a few motets, however, one part (usually the tenor) is made to stand out from the others by having a *cantus firmus* in slower motion, sometimes in long-held values, e.g., one note to the measure [see *Cantus planus* style]. Such *cantus firmus* motets, as they might be called, often have a different text for the main voice, a striking revival of the polytextuality of the 13th-century motet. Examples are Obrecht's "Laudemus nunc Dominum" (with "Non est hic alius"), Josquin's *Stabat Mater* (with "Comme femme"), and Cristóbal de Morales' "Emendemus in melius" (with "Memento homo"; see *HAM*, no. 128). Others are based on a short motif that is repeated in the manner of an *ostinato. Beginning with Ockeghem, motets are usually divided into two or three sections (*Prima, Secunda, Tertia pars*). In contrast to these fairly long compositions is a type often referred to as "song motet" [G. *Liedmotette*], which was particularly cultivated in the late 15th century and which was shorter and simpler in style [see *ReMR*, p. 94]. For an attempt to distinguish between different types of motet on the basis of their liturgical derivation (sequence, antiphon, responsory), see O. Strunk, in *CP 1939.*

II. The stylistic development of the Flemish motet is of great importance, because from *c.* 1450 to 1550 the motet provided the most fertile soil for all developments and innovations in style. The most interesting aspect is the ever-increasing use of imitation, a process that culminated in the *through-imitative style (also called "pervading imitation"). This style has been so much identified with the motet that it is often referred to as "motet style." Actually, its application was more limited than is usually thought. The motets of the 15th century (Ockeghem, Obrecht) make only sporadic use of imitation. Josquin often introduced full points of imitation [see Point (3)] but in alternation with sections in homophonic (*homorhythmic) style, in free counterpoint, and in *paired imitation. It was Nicolas Gombert (*c.* 1490–1556) who introduced fully imitative treatment in the motet [see *HAM,* no. 114]. In the second half of the 16th century motets were often composed in eight or more voice-parts, particularly in connection with *polychoral treatment. This style led to a new type of motet, the "Venetian motet," so called to distinguish it from the "Netherlands motet."

III. About 1550 the motet spread throughout Europe, and the Flemish masters (Josquin, Gombert, de Monte, Lasso) found disciples of equal rank in Italy (A. Gabrieli, Palestrina, G. Gabrieli), Spain (Morales, Victoria), England (Tallis, Byrd), Germany (Senfl, Handl, Hassler), and France (Goudimel). In England the adoption, *c.* 1560, of texts in the vernacular led to a special type of motet, the *anthem.

Important collections of 16th-century motets are: *Motetti A B C* (printed by O. Petrucci, 1502, '03, '04); *Motetti de la corona,* 4 books (Petrucci, 1514–19); *Motetti del frutto,* 4 collections (A. Gardano, 1538, '39, '49); *Motetti del fiore,* 4 books (J. Moderne, 1532–39); *Novum et insigne opus musicum,* 2 vols. (H. Formschneider, 1537, '38); *Thesaurus musicus,* 5 vols. (J. Montanus and U. Neuber, 1564); *Novus Thesaurus musicus,* 5 vols. (ed. P. Joanelli, 1568); *Promptuarium musicum,* 4 vols. (ed. A. Schade, C. Vincent, 1611–17); *Florilegium selectissimarum cantionum* (ed. E. Bodenschatz, 1603; repub. as *Florilegium Portense,* 1618).

C. *The baroque motet.* After 1600 the style of the motet changed considerably. The pure *a cappella* style was abandoned, and solo voices as well as instrumental accompaniment were used. This does not mean that the 16th-century style was completely forsaken. Both the "stile antico" of Palestrina and the Venetian style with its massive sound were continuously cultivated in the motets of the baroque, sometimes in almost unchanged manner, as, e.g., in numerous motets written by members of the *Roman school (cf. the motets by J. J. Fux, *c.* 1700, in *DTO* 3). Usually, however, the old methods were modified according to the stylistic devices of the 17th century, such as instrumental participation, solo voices, aria style, *basso continuo,* recitativo, etc.

The earliest examples of the new practice are in Viadana's *Concerti ecclesiastici* (1602, '07, '09), containing motets for one, two, three, and four voices with organ accompaniment. While organ accompaniment is already prescribed in the *Concerti di Andrea et di Gio. Gabrieli* (1587) and

the *Concerti ecclesiastici* of A. Banchieri (1595), Viadana's innovation is the use of solo voices instead of chorus, a novelty that is particularly conspicuous in the pieces for one or two voices [see *SchGMB,* no. 168; *HAM,* no. 185]. The solo motet for two or three singers with organ accompaniment prevailed in Italy throughout the baroque era, side by side with the choral style of the Roman or Venetian tradition; not a few motets of this period made use of both styles, such as soloistic treatment in the first part and choral treatment in the second (e.g., G. Carissimi). Antonio Caldara (1670–1736) seems to have been one of the first in Italy to use instruments in addition to the organ [*DTO* 26]. There is a large repertory of 18th-century motets (A. Scarlatti, F. Durante, D. Terradellas, N. Jommelli) about which very little is known. Some of them are written in a highly virtuoso, quasioperatic style [see *HAM,* nos, 298, 299].

More interesting is the development in Germany, whose beginning and end are marked by two composers of the highest rank, Schütz (1585–1672) and J. S. Bach (1685–1750). Schütz' *Symphoniae sacrae* (1629, '47, '50) are a treasure of masterpieces written in a great variety of styles, incorporating instrumental participation, solo voices, expressive coloraturas, characteristic motifs in rapid notes, echolike alternation of two singers or instruments, realistic effects, trumpet calls, etc. Most of these pieces, particularly those from the later collections, are written to German texts, as are the majority of motets written by Schütz' successors. It goes without saying that this practice makes it even more difficult, if not impossible, to draw a line between the German motet and other types of church music, such as the cantata, spiritual song, *geistliche Konzert,* etc. As a rule, the use of the chorus marks the German form, since in Germany (unlike Italy) the motet remained choral and frequently *a cappella.* Continuing with Hammerschmidt, Johann Christoph Bach, Johann Michael Bach, Buxtehude, Pachelbel, and others, the German motet reached its peak in the six motets by J. S. Bach, four of which are written for double chorus of eight voices, while one ("Jesu meine Freude") is for five voices and one ("Lobet den Herrn") for four voices with continuo.

An important but little-known development took place in France, beginning with Charpentier (1634–1704) and continuing with Lully (1632–87), Michel-Richard de Lalande (1657–1726), Campra (1660–1744; see *HAM,* no. 257),

F. Couperin (1668–1733; *HAM,* no. 266), and Rameau (1683–1764). Some of these motets are for one voice and continuo, and others (*grand motet*) for soloists, chorus, orchestra, and organ.

For the development in England, see Anthem.

After J. S. Bach the motet declined. Motets were written by Hasse, Graun, K. P. E. Bach, Mozart ("Ave verum"), Mendelssohn, Schumann, and, particularly, Brahms (op. 29, 74, 110). A somewhat more continuous development took place in France, with Gounod, Saint-Saëns, Théodore Dubois, Franck, Charles Bordes, D'Indy, and other members of the *Schola cantorum.* Twentieth-century composers of motets include Vaughan Williams, H. Distler, Pepping, and Krenek.

Lit. *General:* H. Leichtentritt, *Geschichte der Motette* (1908). *For A. 13th century:* F. Ludwig, *Repertorium . . . motetorum vetustissimi stili* (1910); F. Gennrich, *Bibliographie der ältesten französischen und lateinischen Motetten* (1957); *id., Aus der Frühzeit der Motette,* 2 vols. (1963); F. Matthiassen, *The Style of the Early Motet* (1966); W. Meyer, *Der Ursprung des Motetts* (1898); *NOH* ii, pp. 353ff; G. Kuhlmann, *Die zweistimmigen französischen Motetten des Kodex Montpellier,* 2 vols. (1938); P. Aubry, ‡*Cent motets du xiiie siècle,* 3 vols. (1908; Codex Bamberg); Y. Rokseth, ‡*Polyphonies du xiiie siècle,* 4 vols. (1935–39; Codex Montpellier); A. Auda, *Les "Motets Wallons" du manuscrit de Turin: Vari 42,* 2 vols. [1953]; F. Ludwig, "Die Quellen der Motetten ältesten Stils" (*AMW* v); *id.,* "Über die Entstehung . . . der lateinischen und französischen Motette" (*SIM* vii); J. Handschin, "Über den Ursprung der Motette" (*CP 1924*); H. Besseler, "Die Motette von Franko von Köln bis Philipp von Vitry" (*AMW* viii); H. Husmann, "Die Motetten der Madrider Handschrift" (*AMF* ii) H. Tischler, "English Traits in the Early 13th-Century Motet" (*MQ* xxx); M. Bukofzer, "The First Motet with English Words" (*ML* xvii, 225)—*14th and 15th centuries:* S. E. Brown, "The Motets of Ciconia, Dunstable, and Dufay" (diss. Indiana Univ., 1962); L. Schrade, ‡*Polyphonic Music of the 14th Century,* 4 vols. (1956–58), i (*Roman de Fauvel;* De Vitry), ii, iii (Machaut); F. Ludwig, ‡*Guillaume de Machaut, Musikalische Werke,* vol. iii (1929); M. J. Johnson, ‡ "The Motets of the Codex Ivrea," 2 vols. (diss. Indiana Univ., 1955); R. H. Hoppin, ‡*The Cypriot-French Repertory of the Manuscript Torino . . . J.II.9,* 4 vols. (1960–63; *Editions XII, 21); A. Hughes, ‡*Worcester Mediaeval Harmony* (1928); L. A. Dittmer, ‡*The Worcester Fragments*

(1957); C. van den Borren, ‡*Polyphonia sacra* (1932; MS Oxford, *Can. 213*); Compl. works of Dunstable (*Editions XXXIV, 8), Dufay (*Editions XII, 1); A. Ramsbotham, ‡*The Old Hall Manuscript,* 3 vols. (1933–38); ‡*The Eton Choirbook* [see Editions XXXIV, 10–12]; *DTO* 76 (motets from the Trent Codices); J. Chailley, "Motets inédits du XIVe siècle" (*RdM* 1950, p. 27); G. Zwick, "Deux Motets inédits de Philippe de Vitry et de Guillaume de Machaut" (*RdM* 1948, p. 28); M. Bukofzer, "John Dunstable and the Music of His Time" (*PMA* lxv); U. Günther, "The 14th-Century Motet" (*MD* xii).

For B: Compl. works of Obrecht (ed. J. Wolf), Regis (ed. C. Lindenburg), Josquin (ed. A. Smijers), etc.; *Treize livres de motets parus chez Pierre Attaingnant en 1534 et 1535,* 13 vols. (1934–*c.* 1963; i–vii ed. A. Smijers, viii–xiii ed. A. T. Merritt); W. Stephan, *Die Burgundisch-niederländische Motette zur Zeit Ockeghems* (1937); J. M. Shine, "The Motets of Jean Mouton" (diss. New York Univ., 1953); H. Eppstein, *Nicolas Gombert als Motettenkomponist* (1935); K. P. Bernet Kempers, *Jacobus Clemens non Papa und seine Motetten* (1928); M. Steinhardt, *Jacobus Vaet and his Motets* (1951); L. Dikenmann-Balmer, *Orlando di Lassos Motetten* (1938); A. Orel, "Einige Grundformen der Motettenkomposition im XV. Jahrhundert" (*SIM* vii); O. Strunk, "Some Motet-Types of the 16th Century" (*CP 1939*).

For C: J. E. Richards, "The Grand Motet of the Late Baroque in France" (diss. Univ. of Southern California, 1950).

Motet-chanson. A term for certain 15th-century French chansons employing a Latin text in the tenor, resembling in this respect the French-Latin motet of the 13th and 14th centuries.

Motet style. See under Motet B, II.

Motetus [L.]. (1) Latin for motet. (2) In the medieval motet, the voice above the tenor; see Motet A, I; *Duplum.*

Mother Goose Suite. *See Ma Mère l'oye.*

Motif, motive [F. *motif;* G. *Motiv;* It., Sp. *motivo*]. A short figure of characteristic design that recurs throughout a composition or a section as a unifying element. A motif is distinguished from a theme or subject by being much shorter and generally fragmentary. In fact, motifs are often derived from themes, the latter being broken up into shorter elements. As few as two notes may constitute a motif, if they are sufficiently characteristic melodically and/or rhythmically, e.g., the descending fourth at the beginning of Beethoven's Piano Sonata in A major op. 2, no. 2. More than anyone, Beethoven used a highly developed motif technique, which gives his works a unique quality of logical coherence. His most eminent successor in this respect was Brahms. The technique of motifs is particularly important in sonatas and symphonies, whose development sections often are largely based on motifs derived from the various themes of the exposition. The accompanying example shows the various motifs derived from the main theme of

Beethoven's Pastoral Symphony. An exceptionally early use of motifs as an integrating device is found in the works of Machaut (*c.* 1300–77); see G. Perle, "Integrative Devices in the Music of Machaut" [*MQ* xxxiv]. See also Leitmotiv; Motto.

Motion. The pattern of changing pitch levels (high-low) in the melody, as distinguished from rhythm, which is the pattern of different durations (long-short). Any melody can be separated into a motion-pattern and into a rhythm-pattern, as shown under Melody. Motion may be ascending or descending, in the narrow steps of the scale (conjunct) or in the wider steps of a chord (disjunct). The study of these features is of prime importance in melodic analysis. See Melody I, IV.

The term "motion" is also used to describe the relative changes of pitch in two or more simultaneous voice-parts. Two such parts are said to be in "parallel" motion if they remain in the distance of the same interval [Ex. a]; in "similar" motion if they move in the same direction but change their distance [b]; in "contrary" motion

if they move in opposite directions [c]; in "oblique" motion if one part remains stationary on the same pitch [d].

Motion picture music. See Film music.

Mòto [It.]. Motion. *Andante con moto,* somewhat faster than *andante.*

Motto [It.]. In music, the term is used in connection with (a) 15th- and 16th-century Masses using an identical opening motif ("motto," also called "head-motif") for each of the movements (see Mass C II c); (b) 17th- and 18th-century arias that begin with a preliminary statement of the initial motif of the melody and continue with the full melody. Usually, the initial motif ("motto") appears twice, first sung and then echoed by the instruments. Such a composition is called a *motto aria* [G. *Devisenarie*]. The motto aria occurs sporadically in the cantatas of Luigi Rossi (1597–1653) and became established *c.* 1660 in the cantatas and operas of the Venetian composers Cesti (1623–69) and Legrenzi (1626–90). Many of Bach's arias begin with a motto. See Aria IV. The accompanying example is taken from Cesti's opera *L'Argia* [see

SchGMB, no. 203]. For additional examples, see *HAM,* nos. 244 (Steffani), 258 (A. Scarlatti).

Motu proprio [L.]. Generally, a papal decree concerning the administration of the Church. Particularly, a decree issued by Pope Pius X in 1903 that contained new regulations for the music in the Roman Catholic service. The most important points were: (a) abolition of the theatrical and worldly style of church music that had spread during the 19th century, particularly in the Latin countries; (b) return to Palestrina's music as the model for polyphonic church music; (c) restoration of Gregorian chant according to the principles of the monks of *Solesmes; abolition of the "Editio Medicea" and introduction of the "Editio Vaticana" [see Liturgical books II]; (d) suppression of instrumental music except for special occasions and reduction of organ playing to a modest role; (e) the admission of modern vocal compositions provided their character was in agreement with the spirit of the service and the liturgical functions. For the complete text (English) see N. Slonimsky, *Music Since 1900* (1937), pp. 523ff.

Motus [L.]. See under "Micrologus."

Mount of Olives, The. See *Christus am Ölberge.*

Mouth organ. See Harmonica (2).

Mouthpiece [F. *embouchure;* G. *Mundstück;* It. *bocchino, bochetta;* Sp. *boquilla*]. The part of a wind instrument that is inserted into the player's mouth or applied to his lips. In a way, the mouth-piece is the most characteristic part of an instrument, since it indicates to which family an instrument belongs. Four main types can be distinguished:

(a) Cupped mouthpiece, used for the *brass instruments. This is an enlargement of the bore to which the player's lips are applied to form a kind of double reed. Cupped mouthpieces exist in a great variety of shapes, varying from the true "cup" of the trumpet to the "funnel" of the horn. See ill. in *SaHMI,* p. 418.

(b) Single-reed mouthpiece, used for the *clarinets. This mouthpiece [F. *bec,* G. *Schnabel*] consists of a beak-shaped chamber with an opening on the underside to which a single reed is fixed.

(c) Double-reed mouthpiece, used for the *oboes (usually not considered a "mouthpiece" but included here for the sake of completeness and comparison). It consists of two reeds that form a narrow ( )-shaped slit at the top. Older oboes had much larger reeds (approaching the size of bassoon reeds) than the modern instrument. In certain 16th-century types, e.g., the cromornes, the reed was covered with a wooden cap that acted as a windchest (similar to the reed pipes of the organ; see Reed).

(d) Fipple mouthpiece, used for *recorders. It consists of a beak-shaped chamber that is stopped by a plug, leaving only a narrow flue to conduct air toward the sharp edge of a side hole. The principle is the same as in the flue pipes of the organ.

Mouvement [F.]. (1) Movement. (2) Tempo.

Movable Do(h). Generally, any system of *solmization so designed that the syllables can be used in transposition for any key, as distinguished from Fixed Do(h), in which the syllables correspond to invariable pitches of notes. See also Tonic sol-fa.

Movement [F. *mouvement;* G. *Satz;* It. *movimento;* Sp. *movimiento*]. The various complete and comparatively independent divisions of the *sonata, *symphony, etc. One speaks of a "first" or "second" movement, or a "fast" or "slow" movement. The *suite also consists of various movements, each in the character of a dance. See Cyclic (1).

Movie music. See Film music.

Mozarabic chant. The chant of the medieval Christian Church of Spain [see Chant]. The name refers to the Mozarabs, the Christians living in Spain (particularly in Aragon, Castile, and León) while it was under Mohammedan rule. Another name for it is *Visigothic chant,* referring to the Visigoths, who conquered Spain in the 5th century. St. Leander (d. 599), St. Isidore (*c.* 570–636), and St. Ildefonsus (d. 667) played an important role in the development of the chant, which remained in use, untouched by the Gregorian reforms, until about the 11th century. The Mozarabic liturgy has many details in common with the *Gallican, e.g., the name *praelegendum* for the Introit, and *laudes* for the Alleluia. The music of the Mozarabic rites has been preserved in a number of MSS dating from the 9th to 11th centuries, the most important of which is the celebrated antiphonal (for both Mass and Office) of the Cathedral of León, recently published in a facsimile edition. Unfortunately all these sources are written in a very unusual neumatic notation that has not yet been deciphered. They do, however, reveal a prolixity of style similar to that found in Ambrosian chant. Particularly interesting are the extremely long Alleluia melismas, which often show a clearly discernible repeat structure (aa bb cc . . . ; see fac. ed., f. 187), similar to that of the Gregorian Alleluia melismas (and sequences). Only about twenty chants survive in a legible script, among them a very archaic recitation for the "Pater noster" and a number of *preces.

Lit.: ‡*Antifonario visigótico mozárabe de la Catedral de León* (fac. ed. 1953; ed. of text, 1959); P. Wagner, *Der mozarabische Kirchengesang* (1928); C. Rojo and G. Prado, *El Canto mozárabe* (1929); A. Gastoué, *Cours . . . de chant grégorien* (1917; ex. on pp. 71, 79); C. W. Brockett, "Antiphons, Responsories and Other Chants of the Mozarabic Rite" (diss. Columbia Univ., 1965); *ReMMA,* pp. 110ff (bibl. p. 436); *NOH* ii, 81ff; P. Aubry, in *SIM* ix, 157ff; M. Sablayrolles, in *SIM* xiii; R. P. German Prado, in *Speculum* iii; J. M. Roqueta, in *AnM* v; L. Brou, in *AnM* v, vi, x; *id.,* in *CP 1950,* p. 183; E. Werner, in *CP Anglés* ii.

Mozarteum. An institute at Salzburg, Austria, headquarters of the *Mozart-Gemeinde,* devoted to the memory of Mozart and study of his works.

Mp. [It.]. Abbr. for *mezzo piano.*

M.s. [It.]. Abbr. for *mano sinistra,* left hand.

Muance [F.]. Same as mutation. See Hexachord IV.

Mudanza [Sp.]. See under *Mutazione; Villancico.*

Muineira, muñeira [Sp.]. A dance of the province of Galicia (northwest Spain), in quick 6/8 meter and evenly flowing motion. See *LavE* i.4, 2368.

Mulliner Book. An important source of English organ music of the Tudor period. The MS (Brit. Mus. *add. Ms. 30513*) was compiled *c.* 1550–70 and is named after Thomas Mulliner, who owned it and made additions to the original collection. It contains 120 compositions for organ or harpsichord and 11 pieces for the cittern and gittern, written in lute tablature. Among the composers represented are Redford, Tallis, Blitheman, Shepherd, and Allwood. New ed. by D. Stevens, *The Mulliner Book* (1962; *Editions XXXIV, i) and *Commentary* (1952).

Multimetric. A metric scheme wherein the meter changes frequently, e.g., two measures of 3/4 followed by one measure of 2/4 followed by three measures of 3/8. It is common in the works of Stravinsky, Hindemith, Bartók, and other 20th-century composers. See Poly-, multi-.

Mundharmonika [G.]. Mouth organ. See Harmonica (2).

Muñeira. See *Muiñeira.*

Munter [G.]. Merry, cheerful.

Murciana [Sp.]. A local variety of *fandango named for Murcia, a town in southern Spain.

Murky. An 18th-century name of unknown origin, given to pieces with a bass accompaniment in broken octaves [murky bass; see *SchGMB,* p. 289 (2), from Sperontes (J. H. Scholze), *Die singende Muse an der Pleisse* (1736)]. This unimaginative accompaniment was widely used in the second half of the 18th century (*rococo). An early instance of broken octaves is found in F. Couperin's "La Triomphante" (*Pièces de Clavecin,* ordre X), where it serves a pictorial purpose. It may be compared with the highly dramatic "murky" in the first movement of Beethoven's *Pathétique* Sonata. See C. R. Halski, "Murky: A Polish Musical Freak" (*ML* xxxix, 35ff).

Musette. (1) The French *bagpipe of the 17th and 18th centuries. It had two chanters and a number of drones and arm-operated bellows. The instrument became fashionable, along with the vielle [see Hurdy-gurdy], in French society when, under Louis XIV (1643–1715) and Louis XV (1715–74), the court circles indulged in a sophisticated craze for "Arcadia," dressing up as shepherds and peasants. The instruments of this period were splendidly decorated, the bags being covered with elaborate needlework and the pipes made of ivory and inlaid with precious stones. A selection of pieces for musette and vielles is in H. Expert, *Amusements des musiciens français du XVIIIe siècle* (Sènart, Paris), which includes compositions by Jacques Aubert (1689–1753), Charles Bâton (d. 1758), and Nicolas Chédeville. See also *GDB,* s.v. "Anet"; "Boismortier." (2) Dancelike pieces of a pastoral character with a long-held drone, such as could easily be played on the instrument described above. Well-known examples are found in Bach's English Suites nos. 3 and 6, where they are marked "gavotte." An amusing piece in the same style occurs in Mozart's *Bastien et Bastienne,* where it announces the arrival of the Sorcerer. (3) French name for the flageolet, an instrument similar to the recorder [see Whistle flute].

Lit.: E. Thoinan, *Les Hotteterre et les Chédeville* (1894); De Bricqueville, *Les Musettes* (1894).

Music. The term is derived from Gr. μοῦσα, muse, and more specifically from μουσικὴ τέχνη, the art (technique) of the Muses. Originally this term included all the cultural endeavors represented by the nine Muses but later it became associated with Polyhymnia, the Muse of "many songs." Some medieval writers believed the word to be derived from the Egyptian word *moys* (water), construing from this a connection with Moses (whose name indeed may be derived from *moys*). Besides Moses, Jubal and Pythagoras were considered the "inventors" of music. Of basic importance throughout the Middle Ages was Boethius' concept of music as an all-embracing "harmony of the world," divided into *musica mundana* (harmony of the universe), *musica humana* (harmony of the human soul and body), and *musica instrumentalis* (music as actual sound; see Aesthetics of music II). Boethius' contemporary Cassiodorus (*c.* 485–*c.* 580) took a more down-to-earth view, adopting Plato's distinction between *scientia harmonica* (high and low sounds), *metrica* (different meters), and *rhythmica* (relation to text?). Even closer to musical practice is the classification of

St. Isidore of Seville (*c.* 570–636), with his *musica harmonica* (vocal), *organica* (*ex flatu,* i.e., organ, flutes, trumpets, etc.) and *rhythmica* (*ex pulsis digitorum,* i.e., drums, kithara, etc.). In the 14th century, Theodoricus de Campo divided music into *mundana, humana, vocalis* (animal voices) and *artificialis,* subdividing the latter as follows:

	artificialis			
armonica (vocal)		*instrumentalis*		
prosaica metrica rhythmica		*cordae*	*ventus*	*pulsus*
		strings	wind	percussion

As early as 300 B.C., Aristoxenos had divided music into theoretical and practical music. It was not until about 1500 that this classification, still valid, was reintroduced.

Musica [L.]. Music. The term was used in early writings in the following ways: *Musica divina* or *sacra,* church music; *musica vulgaris,* secular music; *musica mensuralis,* *mensural (measured, i.e., polyphonic) music; *musica plana,* *plain song; *musica figurata,* *figural music; *musica ficta or *falsa,* music involving chromatic tones. See also the classifications under Music.

Musica Britannica. See Editions XXXIV.

Musica divina. See Editions XXXV.

Musica enchiriadis. An important treatise of *c.* 900, formerly attributed to the monk Hucbald (*c.* 840–930), more recently to Hoger of Werden (d. 905), Otger of St. Pons (d. 940), Otgerus of St. Amand, and others [repr. in *GS* i, 152–73]. A companion treatise, written in the form of a dialogue, is the "Scholia enchiriadis" [repr. in *GS* i, 173–212]. They are the earliest treatises dealing with polyphony (called *symphonia*) and containing examples of parallel *organum as well as organum at the fourth with oblique motion. They also provide important information on various aspects of Gregorian chant and include the earliest readable melodies (alleluias, hymns), written in *daseian notation. See Theory II.
   Lit.: H. Müller, *Hucbalds echte und unechte Schriften über Musik* (1884); P. Spitta, in *VMW* v; G. trans. by Schlecht, in *MfM* vi, vii, viii; A. H. Fox-Strangways, in *ML* xiii, 183; H. Sowa, in *ZMW* xvii; *SSR,* pp. 126ff; *ReMMA, passim;* W. Apel, in *RBM* x; L. Spiess, in *JAMS* xii.

Musica ficta, musica falsa [L.]. I. In the music of the 10th to 16th centuries, the theory of the chro-

matic or, more properly, nondiatonic tones, i.e., tones other than those in the diatonic scale. At an early time the B-flat was admitted in practice (Gregorian chant) as well as in theory (Odo of Clugny; see under Letter notation) and was, therefore, frequently regarded as not part of *musica ficta.* The introduction of the nondiatonic tones resulted from melodic modifications or from transpositions of the church modes. For instance, a C-sharp may occur either as an artificial leading tone in (untransposed) Dorian, or as the normal third of Mixolydian, transposed a second above. The distinction between these two provinces is useful, although it was not made in medieval terminology as has been maintained by R. von Ficker, according to whom the former type was called *musica falsa* and the latter *musica ficta* [see his "Beiträge zur Chromatik des 14. bis 16. Jahrhunderts," in *StM* ii]. *Musica falsa* is simply the older term (13th century), which was supplanted by the other in the 14th century, probably because its implication of falseness became objectionable.
   II. The earliest reference to nondiatonic tones is found in the "Scholia enchiriadis" of *c.* 900 [see Musica enchiriadis], where formations such as c–d–e^b–f–g and c–d–e–f$\sharp$–g (also downward) are described under the name *absonia* [L., lit. "off-sound"; see *GS* i, 176f; *WoHN* i, 33]. A slightly later treatise by Odo of Clugny (d. 942) contains a table showing transpositions of the fundamental gamut G–e″, with b-flat and b natural, up a whole tone, a fourth, and a fifth [see *GS* i, 274]. This involves the degrees c$\sharp$, f$\sharp$, and e^b, which, however, Odo always represents by the letter *m* (*mysticum*?), thus emphasizing their speculative character. There is ample evidence that at least the f$\sharp$ and e^b were also used in Gregorian chant [see *ApGC,* pp. 160ff]. Nothing definite is known about the development of the altered tones during the next two centuries, when the name *musica falsa* apparently was introduced. As early as 1250 Pseudo-Aristotle (Magister Lambert) turned against this name, declaring that "falsa musica non est inutilis, immo necessaria"—not useless but even necessary [*CS* i, 258]. Walter Odington (*c.* 1300) already knew the e^b and b^b, as well as c$\sharp$ and f$\sharp$. For more details concerning the treatises on

musica falsa, see *WoGM* i, 109ff. In the 13th century the writers on *musica falsa* discuss the chromatic tones primarily with reference to the single line, emphasizing chiefly the *subsemitonium* (leading tone) and the avoidance of the *tritone in progressions such as: g–f(♯)–g, c–e–f(♯)–g, f–a–b(♭)–a, etc. In the 14th century Johannes de Muris (*c.* 1325) approached the problem from the point of view of simultaneous voice-leading, forbidding the tritone as a

chordal formation [see Tritone] and postulating that the third or sixth before a fifth or octave should be major if the upper voice ascends and minor if it descends [see Ex.; *WoGM* i, 116f].

III. In modern musicological writings, *musica ficta* denotes not so much the theory of early chromaticism but the problems arising from the fact that chromatic alterations rarely are indicated in musical sources prior to 1600. Considering the fact that Odington already discussed most of the chromatic tones, it is disconcerting indeed to find throughout the 15th and 16th centuries many long compositions completely lacking any indication of accidentals. Beginning with H. Riemann, musicologists have shown a strong inclination to emend the original texts by adding accidentals, which, in reliable scholarly editions, are placed above the notes in order to distinguish them from those given in the original sources. Although generally speaking the necessity for such emendations cannot be denied, matters were carried much too far in many editions published between 1900 and 1930. An extreme position was taken by Riemann, who maintained that, except in the rare case of the Phrygian mode, all compositions of the 15th and 16th centuries were either major or minor [see his "Verloren gegangene Selbstverständlichkeiten in der Musik des 15.–16. Jahrhunderts" (1907), in *Musikalisches Magazin* xvii] and accordingly presented Baude Cordier's "Belle bonne" of *c.* 1400 as a composition in D major [see *RiHM* i.2, 354ff, and *HAM*, no. 48b]. Some other editors, although they have not gone to such extremes, have shown a tendency, often clearly formulated in the prefaces of their publications, to translate by means of numerous editorial accidentals the tonal language of the Middle Ages and the Renaissance into that of major and minor. Since about 1940, however, musicolo-

gists have approached the problem from a more critical and, no doubt, historically more accurate point of view by "diminishing the number of suggested accidentals" [see *NOH* ii, 373] or "adding only those which seem to be indispensable" [W. Rehm, *Die Chansons von Gilles Binchois* (1957), p. 14*: "Akzidentien wurden nur hinzugefügt, wo es unbedingt erforderlich schien"].

IV. With a problem of such subtlety and flexibility, it is obviously futile to strive for an answer that would apply equally to Gregorian chant, to music of the *ars antiqua,* and to compositions of the 16th century. Concerning Gregorian chant, it may be noted that the formula d–a–b–a frequently found at the beginning of Introits and antiphons and usually presented as d–a–b♭–a [e.g., *LU*, p. 353] is now recognized as being a purely diatonic progression [see *ApGC*, p. 153] and that, on the whole, the earliest MSS suggest a much more restricted use of the b♭ than the later ones. In the 12th and 13th centuries the tonal resources of polyphonic music are so limited, the harmonies so clearly modal, that very seldom are accidentals needed in addition to those indicated in the original sources [see Partial signature]. Thus, nearly all the sharps and many of the flats suggested in Aubry's edition of the Codex Bamberg (*Cents Motets du xiiie siècle,* 3 vols., 1908) would probably be considered unnecessary by present-day scholars [cf., e.g., motet no. 57 with the version in A. Auda, *Les "Motets Wallons"* (1953), no. 27]. From the 14th century on the situation becomes much more complex, as appears from a comparison of different editions (all recent). For example, the figure a b–a–g–f e, which recurs frequently in the Gloria of Machaut's Mass, appears consistently with a b♭ in the edition of L. Schrade and without it in that of Ludwig and Besseler. The closing passage of the *caccia* "Or qua, compagni" has editorial b-flats and f-sharps in the edition of Marrocco (*Fourteenth-Century Italian Cacce,* 1942), none of which is considered necessary by H. Husmann (*Die mittelalterliche Mehrstimmigkeit, c.* 1955). For further illustration, seven passages of this kind are shown here. (This

1. *Landini, Somma felicità (J. Wolf, Der Squarcialupi-Codex, 1955; without accidentals in L. Ellinwood, The Works of F. Landini, 1939).* 2. *Same.* 3. *Landini, Dappo ch'a te (same).* 4. *Dunstable, Quam pulcra es (Besseler, Capella i, 1959; without accidentals in Bukofzer, *Editions XXXIV, 8).* 5. *Same (Bukofzer; without accidentals in Besseler).* 6. *Ockeghem, Missa Mi-Mi, Sanctus (Plamenac, Johannes Ockeghem, 1947, ii; without accidentals in *Editions VIII, 4, ed. by Besseler).* 7. *Barbireau, Osculetur me (B. Meier, Jacobi Barbireau: Opera omnia, 1957, ii; without accidentals in A. Smijers, Van Ockeghem tot Sweelinck, 1952, ii).*

writer in every case favors the version without the editorial accidentals.) Valuable relevant material is found in the German organ tablatures of the 16th century (Schlick, Kotter, etc.), because they employ a notation that, unlike mensural notation, provides for a largely unequivocal indication of altered tones. Following are some excerpts from these sources showing unusual but entirely legitimate formations. See also Cross relation; Leading tone; Lydian.

Lit.: G. Jacobsthal, *Die chromatische Alteration im liturgischen Gesang der abendländischen Kirche* (1897); *ApGC*, pp. 153ff; W. Apel, *Accidentien und Tonalität in den Musikdenkmälern des 15. und 16. Jahrhunderts* (1937); E. Lowinsky, *Secret Chromatic Art in the Netherlands Motets* (1946); *ApNPM*, pp. 104ff, 120; articles by Schwartz, Kroyer, Wolf, and Bernoulli in *CP 1909*, pp. 109ff; L. Hibberd, "Musica ficta and Instrumental Music" (*MQ* xxviii); C. W. Fox, "Accidentals in Vihuela Tablatures" (*BAMS* iv); E. Lowinsky, in *MQ* xxix; E. St. Willfort, in *ZIM* x; W. Apel, in *BAMS* ii; A. Einstein, in *SIM* viii (Merulo); E. Frerichs, in *ZMW* vii, 99ff (organ tablatures); A. Cauchie, in *CP Kroyer* (French vocal music).

Musical Antiquarian Society. See Editions XXXVII.

Musical bow. A primitive instrument found in widely distant places, including New Mexico, Patagonia, Central and South Africa, etc. Like a hunter's bow, from which it probably was derived, it consists of a flexible stick whose two ends are connected by a string. In order to intensify the sound, a gourd is often attached or the string is held in the mouth. The string is plucked with the hand or struck or scraped with a stick. The musical bow is one of the few chordophones found in primitive cultures. See H. Balfour, *The Natural History of the Musical Bow* (1899).

Musical glasses. See Glass harmonica.

Musical Joke, A. See *Musikalischer Spass, Ein.*

Musical Offering. See *Musikalisches Opfer, Das.*

Music and mathematics. The German philosopher and mathematician Leibnitz described music as an "unconscious exercise in arithmetic" [see Aesthetics of music II]. The relevance of this statement is evident in the fact that all the elements of music are defined numerically: material $= 7$ or 12 tones; measure $= 3$ or 4 beats; staff $= 5$ lines; standard pitch $= 440$ vibrations; fifth $= \frac{2}{3}$, third $= \frac{4}{5}$, whole tone $= \frac{8}{9}$, $\sqrt[12]{2}$, $1,000$ cents; loudness $= 50$ decibels; etc. No less close are the relationships of music to geometry, as appears from the "up and down" character of the scale, or the "horizontal and vertical" aspect of musical *texture. In the Middle Ages, music was quite properly grouped with arithmetic, geometry, and astronomy in the *quadrivium*. Methods of higher mathematics enter into the calculation of *intervals, which require the use of logarithms, and in problems of *temperament, which require the solution (by means of continued fractions) of the equation $2^x \times 3^y \times 5^z = 1$. Still another aspect of this relationship is *number symbolism. Recently, mathematical methods have been applied to musical analysis (works of Bach, Josquin) and to composition [see Aleatory music]. See also Computer; Number symbolism.

Lit.: E. Bindel, *Die Zahlengrundlagen der Musik im Wandel der Zeiten,* 2 vols. (1950, '51); A. D. Fokker, *Les Mathématiques et la musique* (offprint, The Hague, 1947); G. Warrack, "Music and Mathematics" (*ML* xxvi, 21ff); J. M. Barbour, "Music and Ternary Continued Fractions" (*American Mathematics Monthly* lv [1948]); E. Werner, "The Mathematical Foundation of Philippe de Vitri's *Ars Nova*" (*JAMS* ix); E. Souriau, "Le Problème de la notation mathématique de la musique" (*CP Masson*); W. Blankenburg, "Der Harmonie-Begriff in der lutherisch-barocken Musikanschauung" (*AMW* xvl).

Music and medicine. See Music therapy.

Music and painting. See Iconography of music. See C. Moreck [pseud. K. Haemmerling], *Die Musik in der Malerei* [1924].

Music and poetry. See Poetic meter; Text and music.

Music and society. See Sociology of music.

Music appreciation. A type of musical training designed to develop the ability to listen intelligently to music. This type of musical education is very common in the United States and Britain but practically unknown in Germany and France. Courses in music appreciation have been criticized as superficial, but like all academic courses they can be well or poorly devised. The amateur listener has often demonstrated an analytic and critical faculty quite the equal of that of many professional performers. The art of listening with "activity of thought," which is the aim of appreciation courses, can be as demanding and as satisfying as performing. Training in appreciation should begin in elementary school and can continue through a lifetime.

Lit. (chronological): R. D. Welch, *The Appreciation of Music* (1927); D. S. Moore, *Listening to Music,* rev. ed. (1937); E. Toch, *The Shaping Forces of Music* [1948]; K. Liepmann, *The Language of Music* (1953); H. Tischler, *The Perceptive Music Listener* (1955); D. Boyden, *An Introduction to Music* (1956); A. Copland, *What to Listen for in Music,* rev. ed. (1957); L. G. Ratner, *Music: The Listener's Art* (1957); E. J. Stringham, *Listening to Music Creatively,* rev. ed. [1959]; M. Bernstein, *An Introduction to Music,* rev. ed. [1961]; W. S. Newman, *Understanding Music,* rev. ed. [1961]; D. F. Tovey, *Essays in Musical Analysis,* 6 vols. (1935–37); A. H. Fox-Strangways, in *ML* viii, 395.   G.W.W.

Musica reservata or **riservata** [L.]. A term first used by Adrian Coclico in his *Compendium musices* (1552) to describe the music of Josquin and his followers as opposed to that of the preceding period (Ockeghem, Obrecht, Isaac). In the same year Coclico also published a collection of motets under the title *Musica reservata.* The literal meaning of the term has been much disputed. The word *reservata* has been explained as referring to the greater "reserve" (restraint) of the newer style in the use of figurations and ornamental design; or as pointing to some "reserved" secrets of musical technique (improvisation, expression of the text by musical motifs, chromaticism not indicated by accidentals); or as indicating the "reserved" (exclusive) character of music written for audiences of high cultural standing. In later writings the term *musica reservata* occurs as a designation for expressive interpretation of the text (S. Quickelberg, *c.* 1560, with reference to Lassus), for a continuous flow of the melodic line (anon. treatise of Besançon, 1571), etc. [see *ReMR*, pp. 513ff]. Thus no single definite meaning can be assigned to it.

Lit.: M. van Crevel, *Adrianus Petit Coclico* (1940); A. Sandberger, *Beiträge zur Geschichte der bayrischen Hofkapelle unter Orlando di Lasso,* i (1894); T. Kroyer, in *Festschrift für Heinrich Wölfflin* (1935); K. Huber, *Ivo de Vento* (1918); *ReMR,* pp. 511ff; H. Leichtentritt, in *BAMS* vi; E. Lowinsky, in *BAMS* vii; C. Palisca, in *JAMS* vii, 168; *id.,* in *AM* xxxi; F. Federhofer, in *AM* xxiv; B. Meier, in *MF* viii and *AM* xxx; W. B. Clarck, in *RBM* xi; R. Hannas, in *RBM* xii, 107f; R. B. Lenaerts, in *CP Borren* (1964).

Musica sacra. See Editions XXXVI.

Music box. See under Mechanical instruments III.

Music criticism. I. Music criticism today is the reviewing of public performances in a newspaper or periodical. Before describing this important activity, however, we should briefly consider the less conspicuous but no less important criticism of musical compositions found in a number of books. Long before the era of newspapers, Glareanus in his *Dodecachordon* (1547) offered profound critical analyses, still worth reading, of the works of Josquin, Isaac, and other masters. About two centuries later there was a more aggressive type of criticism in Mattheson's *Critica musica* (1722/3, '25), Scheibe's *Der critische Musicus* (1737–40), and Marpurg's *Der critische Musicus an der Spree* (1749–50). Burney wrote an "Essay on Musical Criticism" (prefixed to Book III of his *A General History of Music* [1789]). Johann Adam Hiller founded one of the earliest music *periodicals, the *Wöchentliche Nachrichten und Anmerkungen, die Musik betreffend* (1766–70), in which he wrote for the general public rather than for the learned professionals. F. M. Grimm, a German who lived in Paris, edited (together with Diderot and others) the *Correspondance littéraire* (1753–90), which contains some interesting material about the much discussed question of Italian versus French opera [see War of the Buffoons]. At the beginning of the 19th century came the reviews of E. T. A. Hoffmann (1776–1822), written for the *Allgemeine musikalische Zeitung* (Leipzig, 1809–19), which include admirable analyses of Beethoven's C-minor Symphony, Coriolanus Overture, Trios op. 70, and *Egmont* [see comp.

ed. of Hoffmann, by W. Harich (1921), vol. xii]. An important landmark in the development of music criticism are the reviews of Robert Schumann (in *Neue Leipziger Zeitschrift für Musik*) who, in addition to his creative abilities, had the faculty of understanding and appreciating other artists. In fact, he had uncanny foresight, as is shown by his numerous reviews, favorable or adverse, of an op. 1 or op. 2, including those of Chopin, Berlioz, and Brahms. Other great composers who were also active as critics—although not with so much success as Schumann—were Weber, Berlioz, Liszt, Wagner, Hugo Wolf, and Debussy. Among more modern writers of critical studies D. F. Tovey of England and A. Halm of Germany deserve special mention.

II. Music journalism, i.e., the activity of the professional music critic, represents a quite different phase of music criticism. Whereas books and music journals are addressed mainly to professionals, serious students, or the musical amateur, the newspaper critic speaks to the general public. Until the French Revolution music had developed under the auspices of the church or aristocracy. In the 19th century, however, the middle class became the prime supporter and patron of musical performance, which created a new demand to see public concerts critically discussed in the daily papers. Thus a new profession came into being. Eduard Hanslick, who wrote from 1864 for the *Neue Freie Presse* (Vienna), may justly be called the father of music journalism, if only for the reason that, in his one-sided feelings against Wagner and for Brahms, he introduced into music criticism elements of personal prejudice, which, unfortunately, were imitated by numerous later critics. Hanslick's successor as critic for the *Neue Freie Presse* in 1902 was Julius Korngold, who, until the rise of Hitler, exercised great power.

In the early 20th century Berlin became a world center of music and also of music criticism. The leading Berlin critics were the Wagnerian Wilhelm Tappert, one of the first musicologist-critics; Leopold Schmidt of the *Berliner Tageblatt* and his successor, Alfred Einstein; Adolph Weissmann, a champion of modern music; and Herman Springer of the *Deutsche Tageszeitung.* Authoritative voices in the influential *Frankfurter Zeitung* were those of Karl Holl and Paul Bekker; the latter was later active in New York, until his death in 1937.

Music in London before the turn of the century was subjected to the brilliant invective and enthusiasm of George Bernard Shaw, whose lively style in *The Star* (1888–89) under the pen name "Corno di Bassetto" and in *The World* (1890–94) still makes delightful reading. The activity of Ernest Newman for more than fifty years, principally in the London *Sunday Times* from 1920, and that of Neville Cardus in *The Manchester Guardian* from 1917, represent a consistently high level of views of the English musical scene.

III. American music criticism began with J. S. Dwight, editor of *Dwight's Journal of Music* (1852–81), and William Henry Fry, a musician-writer for the New York *Tribune* who was among the first to express enthusiasm for American composers. About 1900 a galaxy of writers was active in the Eastern cities, with points of view ranging from sober conservatism to intense subjectivity. Among this generation James Huneker (New York *Sun, World*), H. E. Krehbiel (40 years with the *Tribune*), W. J. Henderson (35 years with the *Sun*), Lawrence Gilman, Philip Hale, H. T. Parker, and Richard Aldrich lent great esteem to the profession. The next generation presented a great diversity of views on modern music, musical institutions, and the repertory suitable for American tastes. The important positions in New York were held by Olin Downes (the New York *Times* until his death in 1955, Virgil Thomson (*Herald Tribune,* resigned 1954), Samuel Chotzinoff (New York *World* and *Post*), Leonard Liebling, Oscar Thompson, and Paul Rosenfeld. In addition, music criticism in other cities grew more important, with Alfred Frankenstein (San Francisco), Cecil Smith (Chicago), and John Rosenfield (Dallas) winning positions of authority.

IV. Dr. Burney in his "Essay on Musical Criticism" [see under I] pleaded for "a liberal, enlarged and candid mind," a qualification still called for, though many famous critics have been interesting particularly because of their biases. Criticism is an echo of musical life. Perhaps the critic's main duty is to become involved in the strongest artistic currents, of both composition and performance, and develop a keen sense of public taste. He may interpret either to the other while giving information, opinion, analysis, disagreeing with all, or simply recording events. As Virgil Thomson said, "Nobody has to be right."

Music criticism today is practiced with varying degrees of competence by composers, musicologists, performers, newspapermen, and musical amateurs. The role of critic is as diverse as the backgrounds these men bring to the profession, and no single kind of preparation can

be said to be the best. Efforts to reform this unsystematic profession have been made by various writers. M. D. Calvocoressi described a general method that might separate the three main considerations of a critic's activity: (1) "predispositions"; (2) "direct data"; (3) "indirect data." The critic's predispositions are formed by his personality, temperament, education, experience—the individual taste without which a critic is valueless. Direct information comes from the composition and its performance, with clear distinctions required between these. "Indirect data" include the accessory facts that may illuminate the occasion: the relation of the composer and his work to other composers and other music, the performance to other performances and to tradition, the occasion itself to the social environment of music, past and present. Calvocoressi suggests that the critic's main responsibility is to avoid the undue prevalence of "predisposition" over "data."

Journalistic criticism as it is practiced everywhere falls too often into routine—obligatory notices of debuts, endless repetition of judgments on the standard pieces, descriptive panegyrics of famous personalities. Critics with a sense of the newsworthy might remove some of the faults of the profession by ignoring these formulas in favor of observations worth saying freshly. Such a step would correct the imbalance between the critics' too great authority in a few large musical centers and too little authority in smaller communities where musical taste is still at a formative stage.

For a list of living critics, see Pierre Key's *Music Year Book.*

Lit.: M. D. Calvocoressi, *The Principles and Methods of Musical Criticism*, rev. ed. (1931); N. Cardus, ed., *Samuel Langford Musical Criticisms* (1929); P. Rosenfeld, *Discoveries of a Music Critic* [1936]; O. Thompson, *Practical Musical Criticism* [1934]; R. F. French, ed., *Music and Criticism: A Symposium* (1948); I. Kolodin, *The Critical Composer* (1940); V. Thomson, *The Art of Judging Music* (1948); M. Graf, *Composer and Critic* [1946]; N. Demuth, *An Anthology of Musical Criticism* (1947); N. Slonimsky, *Lexicon of Musical Invective* (1953); A. Machabey, *Traité de la critique musicale* (1947); F. Stege, *Bilder aus der deutschen Musikkritik* [1936]; P. Mies, *Vom Sinn und Praxis der musikalischen Kritik* (1949); H. Andres, "Beiträge zur Geschichte der Musikkritik" (diss. Heidelberg, 1938); Y. Bannard, "Composer-Critics" (*ML* v, 264); W. Wright Roberts, "Berlioz the Critic" (*ML* vii, 62, 133);

J. D. Rorke, "The Personal Note in Musical Criticism" (*MQ* xiii); P. C. Buck, in *PMA* xxxii; A. H. Fox-Strangways, in *PMA* lxv; M. D. Calvocoressi, in *MQ* ix; A. Schering, "Aus der Geschichte der musikalischen Kritik in Deutschland" (*JMP* xxxv); F. Stege, "Die deutsche Musikkritik des 18. Jahrhunderts" (*ZMW* x); A. Damerini, "Gli albori della critica musicale italiana" (*LRM* vi); G. del Valle de Paz, "I primordi della critica musicale in Francia" (*RMI* xxxviii).   H.L.; rev. J.R.W.

Music drama. Designation for Wagnerian type of opera. See Opera X.

Music education in the United States. This article is concerned principally with formal music education in elementary and secondary schools and in institutions of higher learning. Education provided in the home, through group activities in the community, or by private teachers is not included.

I. *History.* Music first became part of the school curriculum in 1838, when Lowell Mason was engaged to teach singing in the Boston schools. During the next two decades other cities followed this example, but progress was slow. Early music education used the methods of the privately operated singing schools, which flourished in many parts of the United States from the early 18th century into the 19th. Although choral singing in colleges had been carried on from the mid-18th century and the first college instrumental society was founded in 1808, music in higher educational institutions during this period continued on an extracurricular basis. The establishment of a professorship in sacred music at Oberlin (1835) was an isolated case.

After the Civil War music education increased concurrently with the acceleration of American musical activity. Between 1865 and 1868 six major conservatories were established (Boston, Cincinnati, New England, Oberlin, Peabody, Chicago Musical College). In 1870 music became a recognized course of study in college (at Harvard); professorships and college departments of music began to multiply. Pioneering efforts in training public-school music teachers at Potsdam, New York (1884) were slowly duplicated by other teachers' colleges and normal schools. The development of private music teaching as a profession is reflected in the founding of the Music Teachers' National Association in 1876. Emphasis in schools in the last quarter of the 19th century was heavily on sightreading

and the development of teaching methods. The growth of music in schools led, of necessity, to an increasing use of general classroom teachers to teach music.

From the last decade of the 19th century the child-study movement and an increased understanding of psychology began to affect educational procedures. This "new education" led to a shift from artificial sightreading exercises to the "song approach." The *Modern Music Series* (1898) reflects this change in emphasis. To meet the growing need for teachers, normal schools and (from 1903) colleges assumed more responsibility for pedagogic training in music and also began to offer summer music courses. In 1900 the first school music magazines appeared, and the professional organization for school music teachers, the Music Supervisors' (now Educators') National Conference, was founded in 1907.

High-school music, aside from isolated extracurricular performance activities, has been largely a 20th-century development. The first comprehensive high-school music course (1906, in Chelsea, Mass.) included credit for both school activities and private study. About this time the music-appreciation movement was gaining support, partly influenced by the development of the phonograph. The second and third decades of the 20th century witnessed notable expansion of high-school music education, particularly in instrumental music. Class instruction, first for the violin, soon was used for all band and orchestral instruments and piano. Bands multiplied after World War I as men trained in service bands entered the teaching profession. Many school administrators were won over to supporting instrumental music by the performance of the first National High School Orchestra (1926). In the 1920's and 1930's the contest-festival movement helped establish performance standards for choirs, bands, orchestras, small ensembles, and soloists.

During the 20th century college music departments and professional schools continued to grow in size and number. Several nationally known conservatories are products of this century, including Eastman (1919), Juilliard (1919), and Curtis (1924), and there was a definite trend toward the affiliation of conservatories with universities. [See Conservatory.] Notable among modern developments are: broadening of the college music curriculum; emphasis on degrees in music [see Degrees and diplomas]; growth of graduate music study; development of courses for the general college student; the opera-work-shop movement; growth of musicology; acceptance of performance study for credit; emphasis on teacher training; and growing size and competence of performing organizations. The National Association of Schools of Music (1924) continues as a standardizing influence in higher education.

Among educators who had considerable influence on music education, Hollis Dann (New York University) influenced a generation of choral teachers, Peter Dykema (Wisconsin and Columbia) and Karl Gehrkens (Oberlin) contributed to music pedagogy, and James Mursell (Columbia) applied psychological insights to the development of a philosophy of music education. In the postwar years, coincident with a growing awareness of music-education methods in other countries, educators have been influenced by C. Orff and E. Jaques-Dalcroze in rhythmic and creative activities, Kodály in the use of folk material, and Suzuki in the teaching of violin to very young children. Growing concern that music instruction has become too professionalized has resulted in a strengthening of courses in music for the non-performing student as a part of general education.

II. *Public and private schools.* Since the responsibility for education in the United States is, by constitutional provision, entrusted to the states, and economic, social, and geographical conditions vary throughout the country, there is considerable diversity among music programs in both public and private schools.

Although singing still occupies a key role throughout elementary school, rhythmic activities involving bodily movement, listening, the writing of simple songs, and the use of simple instruments like *recorders and *zithers have been introduced. From kindergarten through third grade, emphasis tends to be on awakening the child's awareness of and sensitivity to music through rhythmic responses and group singing. At higher levels (grades 4 to 6), activities become more specialized, with the gradual introduction of reading music, part singing, and class instruction in instruments. It is common to have, in addition to one or more choruses, an orchestra or a band.

Because of differences among music educators as to ways of dealing with adolescents, the junior high school does not always effectively facilitate the transition from elementary to secondary school. In the seventh grade music is customarily a required subject, but from the eighth grade into high school the subject becomes optional.

Thus music must compete with "academic" subjects for a place in the curriculum. Recent emphasis on science and technology has been a matter of serious concern to teachers in all areas of the arts.

In the junior and senior high schools, emphasis shifts toward performance. It is common—although by no means universal—practice to hold rehearsals of a chorus, orchestra, or band during school hours. Some of the high-school ensembles attain near-professional standards. Junior groups are available for less experienced musicians, and small vocal and instrumental ensembles provide a variety of experience.

The emphasis on group performance, however, is not exclusive. Courses in "general music," particularly in junior high, stress the historical, theoretical, and cultural aspects of music and provide opportunity for some performance. In this area more attention is given to non-Western music, jazz, and folksong. A high-school program might also include courses in "music appreciation," history of music, harmony, and even orchestration. An encouraging aspect of music education is the use of "live" performances, not only for the benefit of music students but for the whole school. Generous grants, notably from the Ford Foundation, have made it possible for young composers to work among and write for school musicians. Commissions to composers from school and college ensembles, professional organizations, and individuals are increasingly being awarded. Partly as a result of these developments, interest in contemporary music and its performance by educational groups has grown substantially. Finally the socializing influence of music is strengthened through festivals, select performing organizations such as "all-state" ensembles, and a nation-wide network of summer camps devoted to music and the fine arts.

III. *Higher education.* Most advanced music instruction in the United States is now provided by colleges and universities. This system is in contrast to European practice, in which the theoretical and scholarly aspects of the subject are taught at universities while performance and pedagogy are the concern of conservatories [see Degrees and diplomas]. Broadly speaking, advanced instruction in music may be divided into two categories: (1) music for general (liberal arts) education and (2) professional training. In the liberal arts, the emphasis is on presenting music for cultural enrichment as well as on the scholarly or theoretical point of view. Professional training includes performance (instruments, voice, church music, opera, conducting, etc.), theory and composition, history, and allied fields such as therapy and ballet, major attention being directed toward both the preparation of elementary and secondary teachers and performance [see Profession of music I].

An important contribution to the cultural life of the nation is being made through college and university sponsorship of resident string quartets and other chamber groups and the creation of positions for composers- and artists-in-residence. Choirs, orchestras, bands, and glee clubs in institutions of higher learning draw members from the entire student body, the faculty, and the community, thus performing a unifying function. The quality of performance is often high, even when few music majors participate. College music groups not only contribute to cultural life, but also to church services, athletic events, and ceremonial occasions.

IV. *Adult education.* Social changes in American life, especially increasing leisure, favor the growth of adult education and encourage the recreational uses of music. Extension courses in music appreciation and other aspects of music, sponsored by colleges, boards of education, and community organizations, are popular; group lessons in piano, recorder, and other instruments are frequently available. Adults take part widely in nonprofessional community orchestras, concert bands, choral societies, operettas, and small vocal and instrumental ensembles. Public libraries provide record-listening facilities and lend records in the same way as books.

V. *Conclusion.* The rapid growth of music education in the United States is a development without parallel. There has been both enthusiastic praise and searching criticism of the movement. One devastating charge leveled is that much of the music performed is of mediocre quality or worse; another is that the repertory for both performance and listening is limited historically and stylistically. There is severe criticism of the percentage of time spent in purely entertainment functions, of the apparently passive, perhaps eager, acquiescence of teachers in utilitarian music-making under the aegis of education. Critics complain that too much stress in teacher training is placed on developing pedagogical skills and not enough on producing teachers who are musically and academically literate. The product of school and college music courses has been examined by some and found wanting in "musicianship."

Music education is charged on the one hand with neglecting the scholarly and theoretical aspects of music, and on the other with producing graduates whose performing skills do not meet professional standards. The flourishing music industry has received some of the blame for education's shortcomings, although there is considerable evidence of the service rendered by publishers and manufacturers of instruments and equipment. Unfavorable comparisons have been made between the number of students receiving music instruction and the small number of adult performing groups. Some feel that the influence of music should be extended to more students rather than concentrating on ensembles in which relatively few are involved. Music education is seen to be suffering from the lack of a logical and continuous plan.

Some of the most searching criticism has come from music educators themselves. This is an encouraging sign, for it indicates an awareness within the profession of the need for continuous re-examination of means and objectives.

Also see Conservatory; Degrees and diplomas; Scholarships.

Lit.: J. Barzun, *Music in American Life* (1958); E. B. Birge, *History of Public School Music in the United States* (1937): P. W. Dykema and H. M. Cundiff, *School Music Handbook* (1955); W. Earhart, *The Meaning and Teaching of Music* (1935); V. Jones, *Music Education in the College* (1949); K. D. Ernst and C. L. Gary, ed., *Music in General Education* [1965]; C. Leonhard and R. W. House, *Foundations and Principles of Music Education* (1959); W. S. Larson, *Bibliography of Research Studies in Music Education* (1949), suppl. in *J. of Research in Mus. Ed.* (1957); H. N. Morgan, ed., *Music in American Education* (1955); J. L. Mursell, *Education for Musical Growth* (1948); *id.* (with M. Glenn), *The Psychology of School Music Teaching* (1931); National Society for the Study of Education, *Basic Concepts in Music Education* (1958); C. V. Palisca, ed., *Music in Our Schools* [1964]; L. B. Pitts, *The Music Curriculum in a Changing World* (1944); UNESCO, *Music in Education* (1955). Additional bibl. in P. W. Dykema and K. W. Gehrkens, *The Teaching and Administration of High School Music* (1941); "Music Education Materials," in *J. of Research in Mus. Ed.* vii, 1 (1959).

Official publications: MENC *Yearbooks* (1907–40); MTNA *Volumes of Proceedings* (1906–50); *American Music Teacher; Music Educators' Journal.*   R.A.R.

Music history. See History of music.

Musicology. A term adopted from French (*musicologie*) to denote the scholarly study of music. It is the equivalent of the German term *Musikwissenschaft* (science of music), which was introduced by F. Chrysander in the preface to his *Jahrbücher für musikalische Wissenschaft* (1863) to emphasize the idea that musical studies, particularly historical ones, should be raised to the same standards of seriousness and accuracy that had long been adopted for the natural sciences as well as the humanities. Guido Adler, in the first volume of the *Vierteljahrsschrift für Musikwissenschaft* (1885), wrote an article, "Umfang, Methode und Ziel der Musikwissenschaft" (Scope, Method and Aim of the Science of Music), which included a comprehensive table of the entire province of music study. The table included paleography (musical notation), historical art forms, history of composition and of instruments, harmony, rhythm, melody, theory, aesthetics, and teaching, as well as a final category, *Musikologie* (research). Similar programs have been outlined by other writers, e.g., Waldo S. Pratt in "On Behalf of Musicology" (*MQ* i). The modern interpretation of musicology is illustrated by the following quotations: "Musicology must include every conceivable discussion of musical topics" [Pratt, *ibid.,* p. 3]; "the whole body of systematized knowledge about music, which results from the application of a scientific method of investigation or research, or of philosophical speculation and rational systematization to the facts, the processes and the development of musical art, and to the relation of man in general (or even animals) to that art" [O. Kinkeldey, "Musicology," in O. Thompson, *The International Cyclopedia of Music and Musicians,* 1952]; "Musicology unites in its domain all the sciences which deal with the production, appearance and application of the physical phenomenon called sound" [H. Lang; see L. Harap, "On the Nature of Musicology," in *MQ* xxiii].

This wide domain is usually subdivided into three main fields: historical, comparative, and systematic musicology. The first deals with history of music. The second comprises what is now generally known as *ethnomusicology, the study of folk music and non-Western music. The third field includes a variety of more or less independent studies: accoustics, physiology, psychology, aesthetics, sociology, pedagogy, and theory (melody, rhythm, harmony, counterpoint, etc.).

G. Haydon, in his *Introduction to Musicology,* includes comparative musicology among the various subdivisions of systematic musicology.

Briefly, musicology is generally thought to include everything that is not clearly in the domain of "practical" or "applied" music, i.e., composition and performance. Perhaps the most debatable aspect of such a broad concept is the inclusion of musical theory, which means that such elementary disciplines as music notation, sightreading, harmony, and counterpoint are considered part of musicology. The resulting dilemma is illustrated by the fact that in Haydon's above-mentioned book harmony and counterpoint are treated in a chapter somewhat speciously termed "The Theory of Music Theory," as well as under "Musical Pedagogy."

A very important area of musicology is Adler's last-named field, *Musikologie* [*VMW* i, 17], which plays a vital role in all of the musical disciplines and may well be considered the ingredient that turns "musical study" into "musicology." If "musicology" is interpreted as research, then it means work—in any of the areas mentioned—that involves the discovery of unknown or the clarification of obscure matters, an activity comparable to research in the natural sciences. The musicologist, then, is the pioneer of music study. If the result of this research is valid and important, it will, sooner or later, become general usage, i.e., it will pass from the field of musicology to the domain of the theorist, the essayist, the biographer, the performer, and perhaps even the composer. An example illustrating this process is the case of Bach. About 1850, his work was largely forgotten, most of his compositions preserved only in scattered manuscripts. The men who undertook to "discover Bach" (among them K. F. F. Chrysander) were musicologists in the true sense of the word. The result of their research was the complete edition of the Bach-Gesellschaft. A student who now examines, e.g., a partita by Bach, is no more a musicologist than is the performer who plays it or the composer who derives new inspiration from it. This does not mean that musicological study of Bach was finished after the publication of the *BG.* There were—and still are—many aspects of his works that remain to be investigated, examples in point being F. Spitta's studies of their historical background, or E. Kurth's work on Bach's counterpoint, or C. S. Terry's thorough investigation of the details of his life, or the new edition [1954—] based on new research.

Musicology in the sense of historical research was a product of the 18th century. The first attempt in this direction was the *Historische Beschreibung der edlen Sing- und Klingkunst* (1690) of W. K. Printz, written in the form of an anecdotal chronicle. In 1715 Jacques Bonnet published *Histoire de la musique, et de ses effets, depuis son origine jusqu' à présent* (based on the research of his uncle, Abbé Pierre Bourdelot), which deals with the history of the dance and dance music. Padre G. Martini's *Storia della musica* (3 vols., 1757–81) deals only with the music of antiquity, which is treated on the basis of original research and with critical evaluation. M. Gerbert, in his *De cantu et musica sacra* (2 vols., 1774), deals in a similar manner with the history of church music. Deservedly famous are C. Burney's *A General History of Music* (4 vols., 1776–89) and J. Hawkins's *A General History of the Science and Practice of Music* (5 vols., 1776). The latter in particular is remarkable for its historical orientation and scientific approach. Equally universal in scope are J. B. de Laborde's *Essai sur la musique* (4 vols., 1780) and J. N. Forkel's *Allgemeine Geschichte der Musik* (2 vols., 1788, 1801), which, however, carries the development only to about 1500.

All these works suffered from an insufficient knowledge of primary source material, particularly in music from Gregorian chant to Palestrina, which was *terra incognita* mainly because of its unfamiliar notation. The interest in medieval culture that played such an important role in the romantic movement (J. L. Tieck, A. W. von Schlegel) spurred music historians on to specialized studies. The pioneer in this field was R. G. Kiesewetter, who wrote on Guido d'Arezzo, Arab music, and the music of the early Netherlands masters (*Die Verdienste der Niederländer um die Tonkunst,* 1829). A. Bottée de Toulmont published in 1836 a study of the *Chanson en France au moyen-âge* (troubadours, trouvères), and Kiesewetter, in his *Schicksale und Beschaffenheit des weltlichen Gesanges vom frühen Mittelalter bis zu . . . den Anfängen der Oper* (1841), traced the development of secular music from the 12th to 17th centuries, illustrating it with examples of 13th-century motets and compositions by Landini, Machaut, Dufay, Binchois, Busnois, Regis, Marco Cara (*frottola*), and others. On the basis of such investigations and extensive studies of his own, Kiesewetter's nephew, A. W. Ambros, wrote his *Geschichte der Musik* (5 vols., 1862–78; to Frescobaldi), the first music history that comes up to present-day

standards and in some respects is still unsurpassed. The pathfinding work of German scholars such as H. Riemann, H. Kretzschmar, P. Wagner, F. Ludwig, and J. Wolf and the subsequent spread of musicological research to numerous other countries requires no further description.

Lit.: G. Haydon, *Introduction to Musicology* (1941); L. B. Spiess, *Historical Musicology* (1963); F. L. Harrison, *et al., Musicology* (1963); M. F. Bukofzer, *The Place of Musicology in American Institutions of Higher Learning* (1957); A. Mendel, *et al., Some Aspects of Musicology* (1957); H. Riemann, *Grundriss der Musikwissenschaft* (1908); L. Schiedermair, *Einführung in das Studium der Musikgeschichte* (1947); K. G. Fellerer, *Einführung in die Musikwissenschaft* (1953); H. Husmann, *Einführung in die Musikwissenschaft* (1958); J. Chailley, *et al., Précis de musicologie* (1958); A. Machabey, *La Musicologie* (1962); H. Hewitt, *Doctoral Dissertations in Musicology*, rev. ed. (1961); W. S. Pratt, "On Behalf of Musicology" (*MQ* i); P. H. Lang, "Musicology for Music" (*MM* xix, 92–95); R. Sessions, "Musicology and the Composer" (*BAMS* v); L. Hibberd, "Musicology Reconsidered" (*AM* xxxi); C. Seeger, "Systematic Musicology" (*JAMS* iv); W. Wiora, in *MF* i; A. Wellek, in *MF* i; A. Machabey, in *RdM* 1931, pp. 89–98, 161–72.

Music therapy. Music and medicine have been associated since the beginning of recorded history. One of the earliest Egyptian documents on music is, in effect, a prescription for music therapy. The healing powers of music were recognized by the Chinese, Hindus, ancient Greeks, and Arabs, as well as in primitive cultures. Numerous references to these powers are found in both musical and medical writings of the 16th and 17th centuries [see Tarantella]. In 1807 P. Lichtenthal published a famous book, *Der musikalische Artz* (The Musical Physician), which four years later was translated into Italian. Since that time there has been increasing scientific research on the psychophysiological effects of music. Interest in clinical music therapy developed particularly in military hospitals during World Wars I and II. The National Association for Music Therapy, established in 1950, has set up programs for the advancement of research, distribution of helpful information, establishment of training standards for therapists, etc. Several colleges and universities in the United States now offer four-year courses with an additional six months of clinical training leading to a baccalaureate degree in music therapy.

Music is widely used in the treatment of mental illnesses and, to a lesser extent, certain physical ailments, such as cerebral palsy, tuberculosis, infantile paralysis, etc. Such therapy, extensively used for children, is a valuable means for working with patients toward specific therapeutic or rehabilitation goals.

A related aspect of music therapy is the consideration of occupational diseases of musicians, e.g., throat and lung ailments of singers and wind instrumentalists, or skin, muscle, and joint diseases of string players and keyboard performers.

Lit.: *National Association for Music Therapy, Book of Proceedings* (1951–59); D. M. Schullian and M. Schoen, ed., *Music and Medicine* (1948); E. Podolsky, *et al., Music Therapy* (1954); D. Soibelman, *Therapeutic and Industrial Uses of Music* (1948; bibl.); W. Van de Wall, *Music in Hospitals* (1946); S. H. Licht, *Music in Medicine* (1946); A. Pontvik, *Heilen durch Musik* (1955); D. Kerner, *Krankheiten grosser Meister* (1963); A. Machabey, *La Musique et la médecine* (1952); K. Singer, *Diseases of the Musical Profession* (1932); J. Flesch, *Berufs-krankheiten des Musikers* (1925); D. K. Antrim, in *MQ* xxx; E. Werner, in *CP Sachs* (Greece).   A.W.

Musikalische Denkmäler. See Editions XXXVIII.

Musikalischer Spass, Ein [G. A Musical Joke]. A sextet (*divertimento) by Mozart, K. 522 (1787), for strings and two horns, in which he pokes fun at the incompetent provincial musicians of his day by using all sorts of faulty devices, such as dissonances, parallel fifths, etc.

Musikalisches Opfer, Das. [G., The Musical Offering]. One of J. S. Bach's latest works, composed and published in 1747 and dedicated to Frederick the Great of Prussia. It contains a number of highly academic contrapuntal pieces, all based on a theme of the King's invention upon which Bach had extemporized during his visit to Potsdam in 1747. The dedication copy bears the inscription "Regis Iussu Cantio Et Reliqua Canonica Arte Resoluta" (Upon the King's Demand, the Theme and Additions Resolved in Canonic Style), which forms the acrostic RICERCAR, emphasizing the learned character of the work. In fact, together with the **Art of Fugue, Das Musikalisches Opfer* represents the summary and consummation of three centuries of contrapuntal art. The work consists of thirteen compositions: no. 1, *Ricercar a 3;* nos. 2–7, six *Canons;* no. 8, *Fuga canonica:* no. 9, *Ricercar a 6;* no. 10, *Canon a 2 quaerendo invenietis;* no. 11, *Canon a 4;* no. 12, *Trio:* no. 13, *Canone perpetuo.* Five of the canons (nos. 3, 8, 10, 11, 13) involve canonic treatment of the *Thema regium* (royal theme), while the other five (nos. 2, 4, 5, 6, 7) employ the theme as a *cantus firmus* against which two contrapuntal parts form a canon [see Canon II]. The two types might be distinguished as "canon *of* the theme" and "canon *on* the theme."

Das Musikalisches Opfer was composed and printed in four sections (I. nos. 1–2; II. nos. 3–8; III. nos. 9–11; IV. nos. 12–13). Sections I and II seem to constitute the original "Offering," to which the other pieces were added later the same year. Evidently the collection originated without any preconceived plan. Nonetheless, a considerable number of editions have been published in which the pieces are rearranged according to some "higher plan" that is supposed to underlie the work, as has been done with *The Art of Fugue.* In fact, aside from the *BG* edition (vol. 31.2), no edition agrees entirely with the original in this respect.

Lit.: P. Spitta, *Bach,* Eng. trans., iii, 191–97, 233, 292ff; A. Orel, in *DM* xxx, 2 and 3; H. David, in *MQ* xxiii; W. Pfannkuch, in *MF* vii (survey of all the editions).

Musikwerk, Das. See Editions XXXIX.

Musikwissenschaft [G.]. See under Musicology.

Musique concrète [F., concrete music]. A musical development introduced *c.* 1948 by Pierre Schaeffer in Paris, which derived from experiments with recorded sounds and broadcasting in the Studio d'Essai of the French radio. Its basic idea is to replace the traditional material of music (instrumental or vocal sounds) with recorded sounds obtained from many different sources, such as noises, voice, percussion, and others. As a rule this material is subjected to various modifications: a recorded sound may be played backwards, have its attack or resonance cut off, be reverberated in echo chambers, be varied in pitch by changing the speed of the record or playback, be modulated in various ways, etc. The montage of the resulting sounds on a final single or multi-track tape has been compared to the collages of certain 20th-century painters. It eliminates the performer, and hence also the *raison d'être* of a score.

It was Schaeffer who named this development

musique concrète, i.e., music made directly on tape with real sounds, as opposed to *musique abstraite,* where the sounds (of instruments) are notes (pitch abstractions) composed into an abstract system of signs (score). Also, according to Schaeffer, *musique concrète* deals with acoustically evident, directly perceptible phenomena. In *electronic music, on the other hand, the sounds are the result of purely theoretical combinations of sound-parameters (frequency, amplitude, duration), elements that, according to Schaeffer, could by no means alone be responsible for the effect of the whole. Schaeffer's method of investigation, classification, and eventually association of sounds (which is not and does not pretend to be a method of *composition),* called *solfège concret,* is based on description and comparison, in plain language, of the sounds (*objets sonores*) as perceived. This method discards the scientific approach (in terms of physical acoustics) as inadequate; it may be considered one of the first—although still primitive—attempts to arrive at a contemporary "phenomenology of sound" (not to be confused with a phenomenology of music). It is the principle of *solfège concret* that best defines both the theoretical basis of *musique concrète* and how it differs from other contemporary trends in music.

Lit.: F. C. Judd, *Electronic Music and Musique concrète* (1961); A. Moles, *Les Musiques expérimentales* [1960]; P. Schaeffer, *A la Recherche d'une musique concrète* [1952]; id., *Traité des objets musicaux* [1966]; *Incontri musicali* nos. 1–4 (1956–60), *passim;* P. Schaeffer, "Musique concrète et connaissance de l'objet musical" (*RBM* xiii); G.-W. Baruch, "Was ist Musique concrète?" (*Melos,* 1953).   A.B.

Musique mesurée [F.]. See *Vers mesuré.*

Mustel organ. See under Harmonium.

Muta [It.]. Indication for a change of tuning in the orchestral parts for kettledrums and, in earlier scores, a change of crooks for horns and natural trumpets. For instance, "muta in G/d" means that the two kettledrums should be tuned in G and in d.

Mutanza [It.]. Rare 16th-century term for variation.

Mutation. (1) The change from soprano or alto to tenor or bass that takes place in a boy's voice during adolescence, usually between the ages of 14 and 16. (2) The term is occasionally used for the shift in violin playing. (3) See under Hexachord IV.

Mutation stops. See under Organ VI. Also Foot (2).

Mutazione [It.]. A 15th-century term for the *piedi* of the *ballata* or the *barzelletta.* The corresponding Spanish term is *mudanza* [see *Villancico*].

Mute [F. *sourdine;* G. *Dämpfer;* It. *sordino;* Sp. *sordina*]. A device for softening or muffling the tone of a musical instrument. In violins, etc., the mute is a clamp with three (occasionally two or five) prongs that is placed on the bridge and makes the tone veiled and somewhat nasal. It is usually called for by the phrase *con sordini.* It has been frequently used to convey a mysterious or uneasy atmosphere, one of the earliest examples being in Act II, Scenes iii and iv of J.-B. Lully's *Armide* (1686), marked "sourdines." Beethoven used muted violins in the prison scene of *Fidelio,* and Berlioz for the "Ballet des Sylphes" of his *La Damnation de Faust,* to mention only a few of the earlier instances. Muted cellos and double basses are used very effectively at the beginning of Stravinsky's *L'Oiseau de feu.* Brass instruments are muted by inserting a pear-shaped piece of wood or metal into the bell. The French horn, however, is usually muted by inserting the player's hand. Kettledrums were formerly muted by placing a cloth over the parchment; today sponge-headed drumsticks are generally used instead. In pianos, the sound is muted by the left pedal (soft pedal), which causes the whole keyboard with the hammers to shift a little to the right [G. *Verschiebung,* shift], so that the hammers strike only one string instead of two or three (hence the Italian term *una corda,* one string); see Piano I. In upright pianos a similar effect is achieved by reducing the ambit of the hammer.

The term "mute" is often identified or confused with *damper. Properly, a damper is a device that deadens a sound. The difference between mute and damper is particularly clear on the piano, where the left pedal is a mute whereas the right pedal releases the dampers from the string, allowing the string to keep on sounding. The same ambiguity exists with the Italian word *sordino,* which is applied to the muting of violins as well as to the dampers of the piano, while muting the piano is called *una corda.* The confusion has been compounded by editors (German and English) who, reading the indication *senza sordini* in the first movement of Beethoven's Moonlight Sonata, considered it an error and changed it to *con sordini* or *una corda.*

Actually, Beethoven's *sordini* are the dampers of the piano, and his indication *senza sordini* means "without dampers," i.e., "with the right-hand pedal." See *Una corda*.

M.v. [It.]. Abbr. for *mezza voce;* see under *Mezzo*.

My Country (Fatherland). See *Má Vlast*.

Mystery play. See under Liturgical drama.

Mystic chord. A chord invented by A. N. Scriabin, consisting of a series of five fourths: c–f♯–b♭–e′–a′–d″. It forms the harmonic basis of his *Prometheus* (1910), op. 60, and the Seventh Piano Sonata, op. 64. In other compositions Scriabin used similar chord formations, e.g., c–f♯–b–e′ (op. 57, no. 1), and A–d♯–g–c′♯–(f′)–b′–e″ (Eighth Piano Sonata, op. 66). See A. Eaglefield-Hull, in *PMA* xliii. See Fourth chord.

N

Nabla, nablum, nablium. A stringed instrument mentioned by Greek writers, probably the nebel (nevel) of the ancient Hebrews [see Jewish music I].

Nabucco or **Nabucodonosor** [It., Nebuchadnezzar]. Opera in four acts by Verdi (libretto by T. Solera), produced in Milan, 1842. Setting: Jerusalem and Babylon, 568 B.C.

Nacaire. See under Drum II.

Nacchera [It.]. (1) Kettledrum. See Drum II. (2) In present-day usage, *nacchere* (pl. form) means castanets.

Nachahmung [G.]. Imitation.

Nachdrücklich [G.]. Emphatic, expressive.

Nachlassend [G.]. Relaxing, slackening.

Nachschlag [G.]. (1) In modern German terminology, the two terminating notes that are usually played at the end of a trill [see Trill IV].
(2) In 17th- and 18th-century music, an ornament consisting of one or several short notes attached to the preceding main note. The ornamenting notes constitute a melodic movement away from the preceding note and are to be performed as a part of it, i.e., *before* the next main note. Thus the Nachschlag is the exact opposite of the *appoggiatura, which is a melodic movement toward, and a part of, the following note. The accompanying illustration shows the simplest method of notating the Nachschlag, together with the correct rendition.

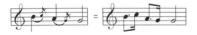

In French music of the 17th and 18th centuries the most common form of Nachschlag is the *agrément* variously called *accent, aspiration,* or *plainte,* which consists of raising the pitch a half-tone or whole tone at the end of a sustained note. The *accent* was indicated by several different signs: an inverted V, a short vertical stroke, or a tiny grace note. All these signs are invariably suppressed in modern editions. Ex. 1, from Rameau's opera *Hyppolyte et Aricie,* shows the notation (on upper line) and the approximate effect of the *accent* (on lower line); its 17th-century English equivalent is called the *springer.* It was used chiefly in music for the lute or viol, and was performed by lightly touching the string at a higher fret (without plucking it again) at the end of a sustained note. The sign for the springer is an ascending oblique stroke placed slightly to the right of the written note (or letter, in the case of tablatures), as in Ex. 2.
The Nachschläge described above were rarely used in Germany, but a similar ornament was used in German music of the baroque period. It always appears between a series of descending thirds and is indicated by a curved hook extending to the right of the main note, as in the accompanying example by J. S. Bach [Ex. 3]. Although this ornament had no sign in French music of the period, its use was taken for granted by French musicians, and it should be inserted, in performance, in all passages where thirds descend in notes of equal value. This practice was known as *couler les tierces.*
A special type of Nachschlag is one that anticipates the following note, i.e., the "anticipation" of modern composition [see Nonharmonic tones]. The descending anticipation was

a very common ornament in the 17th century, known in France as a *cheute* and in England as a *cadent*. Its sign is the same in both countries—a descending oblique line to the right of the written note [Ex. 4] (with proper execution below). In the 18th century the most common use of this type of Nachschlag was as an anticipation of the final note of a phrase [Ex. 5]. The Nachschlag in this position is usually written as an ordinary note or else left to the discretion of the performer. Particularly common was the Nachschlag as the closing note (or notes) of a trill. In modern German usage the term Nachschlag usually refers to this practice [see (1)].

Romantic composers returned to some extent to the earlier custom of writing Nachschläge as grace notes. Since they generally did not bother to slur the grace note to the preceding note, there is some danger of confusing it with an appoggiatura, unless the composer is careful (as Schumann always was) to place the Nachschlag before the bar line [Ex. 6, "Warum"]. There is no strict rule that will eliminate this confusion entirely, but it may at least be assumed that whenever the grace note is identical with the following note (as in Ex. 7, from Chopin's Nocturne op. 32, no. 2) the ornament is a Nachschlag.

P.A.

Nachspiel [G.]. Postlude.

Nachtanz [G.]. After-dance. In the instrumental music of the 16th century, a quick dance in triple meter that immediately followed a slower dance

in duple meter [see Dance music II]. Combinations occurring very often were *basse danse— tourdion* (1530), *pavane—galliard* (c. 1520–1600), and *passamezzo—saltarello* (c. 1550–1620). Other names for such dances were *Sprungk* (jump, jumping dance), *Hupfauf* (hopping up), and *Kerabe* (*Kehrab, Kehraus,* lit. sweep off, sweep out, i.e., closing dance). Frequently the *Nachtanz* is a rhythmic variation of the main dance, employing the same melody but in triple meter. In such instances it was often called **Proportz* or *tripla* with reference to the *proportio tripla* [see Proportions] involved in this modification. Some of the 14th-century *istanpitte* [see *Estampie*] have a *Nachtanz* called **rotta*. Ex. in *HAM*, nos. 83b; 102b; 105a and b; 137, no. 2; 154a; 179.

Nachtmusik [G.]. *Serenade.

Nachtstück [G.]. *Nocturne. The pieces by Schumann and Hindemith (*1922 Suite für Klavier*) bearing this title are much more suggestive of night visions and dreams than Chopin's nocturnes are.

Nagarah. See under Drum II.

Nagelgeige [G.]. *Nail violin.

Nagelschrift, Hufnagelschrift [G.]. A German variety of neumes used during the 14th and 15th centuries, so named because the characters resemble the type of nail used with horseshoes [G. *Nagel,* nail; *Huf,* hoof]. Another name is Gothic neumes. See Neumes II (table, col. V).

Nail violin, nail harmonica. An instrument consisting of a flat, round wooden soundboard with a set of nails or U-shaped iron pins of various lengths driven around the rim. The nails are made to vibrate with a violin bow. The nail violin (invented by J. Wilde, *c.* 1740) belongs to the same period of *Empfindsamkeit* (late 18th and early 19th cent.) that produced the *Aeolian harp and the *glass harmonica as a result of its general penchant for ethereal, supernatural sound. Ill. in *SaHMI,* p. 403, and *AdHM* i, 632. [See ill. under Percussion instruments.] F. W. Rust wrote a quartet for nail violin, two violins, and cello [see Editions XVIII B 13].

Naked fifth. Same as *open fifth.

Nakers, nakeres. See under Drum II.

Napoletana. See under Villanella.

Naquaires. Same as nacaires [see Drum II].

Narrator [It. *testo*]. In oratorios, Passions, cantatas, and occasionally operas, a character who tells the basic story, usually in recitative. In Passions, he is called *Evangelista* or *Chronista*. A famous early example of a stage presentation employing a narrator is Monteverdi's *Combattimento di Tancredi e Clorinda* (1624); a modern one is Stravinsky's *L'Histoire du Soldat* (1918).

National anthems. The songs adopted by various nations to be played on official occasions and to represent them in international gatherings. Those written up to 1830 are given below in chronological order (if both author of the text and composer are known, the former is indicated first, the latter second). *Netherlands:* "Wilhelmus von Nassouwe" (Philip van Marnix, *c.* 1570; music in A. Valerius, *Gedenck-Clanck,* 1626). *England:* "God Save the King" (appeared in its present-day form in *Thesaurus musicus,* London, 1744); its melody is used in the American song "My Country 'Tis of Thee," as well as in the German prewar anthem "Heil dir im Siegerkranz," in the Swiss anthem "Rufst Du, mein Vaterland," and in those of Sweden and Liechtenstein. *Denmark:* "Kong Kristian" (J. Ewald; D. L. Rogart, 1779). *France:* "Allons, enfants de la patrie," known as "La Marseillaise" (text and music by Rouget de Lisle, 1792). *Poland:* "Jeszcze Polska nie zgineta" (J. Wybinski; K. Oginski, *c.* 1795). *Austria:* "Gott erhalte unsern Kaiser" to 1919 (L. L. Haschka; J. Haydn, 1797); Haydn's famous melody was used in Germany with the text "Deutschland, Deutschland über alles," by H. A. Hoffmann von Fallersleben, 1841. *Venezuela:* "Gloria al bravo pueblo" (V. Salias; J. Landaeta, *c.* 1810). *Argentina:* "Oid, mortales" (V. López y Planes; J. Blas Parera, 1813). *United States of America:* "The Star-Spangled Banner" (Francis Scott Key, 1814; tune by England's John Stafford Smith, composed originally for "To Anacreon in Heaven"). *Peru:* "Somos libres, seámos-lo siempre" (J. de la Torre Ugarte; J. Bernardo Alzedo, 1821). *Chile:* "Dulce patria, recibe los votos" (B. de Vera y Pintado, rev. 1847 by E. Lillo; Ramón Carnicer, 1828). *Greece:* "Se gnorizo apo ten kopsi" from 1864 (D. Solomós; N. Mantzaros, 1828). *Belgium:* "Après des siècles d'esclavage," known as "La Brabançonne" (L. A. H. Dechet, pseud. Jenneval; F. van Campenhout, 1830).

The political changes following World Wars I and II have led to a number of new anthems, particularly in the following countries: *Soviet Union:* "Gimn Sovetskogo Susa" (Hymn of the Soviet Union; S. Mikhalkov and E. L. Registan; A. V. Alexandrov, 1943). *West Germany:* "Einigkeit und Recht und Freiheit" (2nd stanza of "Deutschland, Deutschland über alles"; see above, under Austria). *East Germany:* "Auferstanden aus Ruinen" (J. R. Becher; H. Eisler, 1949). *Austria: Land der Berge, Land am Strome* (P. Preradovič; sung to the last part of Mozart's *Kleine Freimaurer-Kantate,* K. 623). *Italy:* "Fratelli d'Italia" (G. Mameli; M. Novaro, 1847).

Lit.: M. Shaw and H. Coleman, *National Anthems of the World* [1960]; P. Nettl, *National Anthems* (1952); S. A. Rousseau, *Les Chants nationaux de tous les pays* (1930); E. Bohn, *Die Nationalhymnen der europäischen Völker* (1908); E. Murillo, ed., ‡*National Anthems of the Countries of North, Central and South America* (1935); D. R. Wakeling and G. de Fraine, "National Anthems" (*MR* iii; complete list); H. Abert, "Eine Nationalhymnen-Sammlung" (*ZIM* ii).

Nationalism. In music, a movement beginning in the second half of the 19th century that is characterized by a strong emphasis on national elements and resources of music. It is based on the idea that the composer should make his work an expression of national and ethnic traits, chiefly by drawing on the folk melodies and dance rhythms of his country and by choosing scenes from his country's history or life as subjects for operas and symphonic poems. Nationalism, therefore, represents a contradiction of what was previously considered one of the chief prerogatives of music, i.e., its universal or international character, which meant that the works of the great masters appealed equally to any audience.

To defend their cause, champions of the nationalist movement hold that music always has been and always will be national. They point out that the music of Bach, Beethoven, Schumann, and Wagner is thoroughly German, that of Scarlatti, Rossini, and Verdi is unmistakably Italian, and that of Byrd or Sullivan is unequivocally English. No doubt there is some truth in such statements. Although it is difficult—maybe impossible—to point out in detail what is German, Italian, or French in musical style and expression, one could perhaps indicate some general characteristics, such as "idealistic" for German music, "corporeal" for Italian, or "spirited" for French. However, such generalizations have nothing to do with nationalism as defined here. Nationalism is essentially a matter of intention. No composer can help inheriting, together with his language, certain national ideas, views, and feelings. The difference between the "international" and "national" composer of, e.g., Italian ancestry, is the difference between someone who cannot help speaking Italian and someone who wants to speak Italian. It is the latter who belongs to the nationalist movement in music.

The nationalist movement began as a reaction against the supremacy of German music. It was started by talented musicians who found themselves forced to compete with men like Beethoven, Wagner, and Brahms, and who, in their national treasure of melodies, dances, etc., found a potentially strong weapon. For this reason the nationalist movement is practically nonexistent in Germany, nor has there been much of one in France. Debussy entered the arena with purely musical weapons, which, though very "French," were in no way nationally inspired. The absence of a strong nationalist movement in Italy has been ascribed to the fact that Italy has no folksong tradition. A more likely reason is that Italy, like Germany and France, had an old musical tradition to draw upon and did not need to resort to the somewhat extraneous resources of the nationalist movement.

Nationalism was principally embraced by the "peripheral" European nations, for which it proved, in most cases, the first opportunity to advance to the center of the musical scene. It found its first full realization in Glinka's opera *A Life for the Czar* (1836). About 1860 the movement gained fresh impulse in Bohemia, Norway, and Russia, with Smetana's *The Bartered Bride* (1866), Grieg's first book of *Lyric Pieces* (op. 12; e.g., "Folk Song," "Norwegian Melody"), and Borodin's *Prince Igor* (1869–87). In Russia, the group known as The *Five formed a strong bulwark of nationalism against the internationally inclined Tchaikovsky and Rubinstein. Mussorgsky's *Boris Godunov* (1872) in particular is a landmark in the nationalist movement. In Bohemia, Smetana's work was carried on to some extent by Dvořák (1841–1904) and more wholeheartedly by Janáček (opera *Her Foster-Daughter*, 1894–1903). Toward the end of the 19th century the movement spread to Spain, where it found ample nourishment in the immense wealth of Spanish dance rhythms and melodies. Albéniz (1860–1909), Granados (1867–1916), and De Falla (1876–1946) are the outstanding representatives. In Finland, Sibelius (1865–1957)

first was an ardent supporter of nationalism but later turned to "absolute" music, which, nonetheless, remained largely Finnish in character. In England the national movement was championed by Elgar (1857–1934) and Vaughan Williams (1872–1958), in Hungary by Bartók (1881–1945) and Kodály (1882–1967), and in Rumania by Georges Enesco (1881–1955). Outstanding nationalist composers of Latin America are Brazil's Heitor Villa-Lobos (1887–1959) and Mexico's Carlos Chávez (b. 1899).

In the United States the nationalist movement started with H. F. Gilbert (1868–1928), whose compositions have a racy flavor derived largely from Negro music (*Negro Rhapsody,* 1913). Frederick Converse (1871–1940) drew inspiration from the American landscape (*California; American Sketches*). Among later composers Roy Harris (b. 1898) and Gershwin (1898–1937) are prominent champions of nationalism.

By about 1930 the nationalist movement had lost its impact nearly everywhere in the world. The pendulum swung back to supranational idioms, so much so that nationalism was called "the last illusion of people without talent" (A. Lourié, in *MQ* xxvii, 241). During its century of life, however, it produced a number of works of undisputed artistic value.

Lit.: C. Forsyth, *Music and Nationalism* (1911); R. Vaughan Williams, *National Music and Other Essays* [1963]; *GrHWM,* pp. 583–97, 612–25; D. Hussey, "Nationalism and Opera" (*ML* vii, 3); G. Seaman, "The National Element in Early Russian Opera, 1779–1800" (*ML* xlii, 252ff); F. Toye, "A Case for Musical Nationalism" (*MQ* iv).

Natural. (1) A note that is neither sharp nor flat, e.g., G natural as opposed to G-sharp or G-flat. (2). The sign ♮, which indicates the natural note in cases where the note would otherwise be altered, according either to the signature or to a previous accidental. See Accidentals.

Natural horn, trumpet. A horn or trumpet consisting only of a pipe without side holes operated by keys or additional tubing operated by valves. Such instruments can produce only the natural tones, aside from certain artificial chromatic alterations produced by stopping (stopped notes). They were used until the end of the 18th century, when the first keyed instruments were invented (key trumpets, key bugle). See Horn II; Trumpet II; Fanfare.

Natural tones. See under Wind instruments II.

Naturhorn, Naturtrompete [G.]. *Natural horn, natural trumpet.

Neannoe. See Noeane.

Neapolitan school. I. "Neapolitan" is a term somewhat loosely applied to a school of composition in the 18th century that is thought to have originated in Naples and cultivated particularly in that city or by composers who studied there. It included a great many composers of greater or lesser importance, e.g., F. Provenzale (1627–1704), A. Scarlatti (1660–1725), N. Porpora (1686–1768), L. Vinci (1690–1730), F. Feo (1691–1761), L. Leo (1694–1744), N. Logroscino (1698–1765), G. B. Pergolesi (1710–36), G. Latilla (1711–91), D. Pérez (1711–78), D. Terradellas (1713–51), N. Jommelli (1714–74), P. Anfossi (1727–97), T. Traetta (1727–79), P. Guglielmi (1728–1804), N. Piccinni (1728–1800), A. Sacchini (1730–86), G. Tritto (1733–1824), G. Paisiello (1740–1816), and D. Cimarosa (1749–1801). A. Scarlatti's German pupil J. A. Hasse (1699–1783) also belongs to this group.

Most of these composers were known chiefly for their operas, and because many of them were born in or near Naples and received their musical education in one of the famous *conservatorii* of that city, the general type of opera they represent has frequently been called "Neapolitan." The composers mentioned, however, were active in many different parts of Europe: Rome (Scarlatti, Anfossi, Piccinni), Lisbon (Pérez), Paris (Piccinni, Sacchini), St. Petersburg (Paisiello), Stuttgart (Jommelli), Vienna, Milan, etc., and there is not sufficient evidence to show that the Italian *opera seria* of the 18th century was peculiar to Naples. It was rather a general type, cultivated all over Italy and extending to other countries, and it underwent gradual changes in style, especially after 1760. Under the poet-dramatists Metastasio and Hasse, its leading representatives toward the middle of the century, the type of plot, number of characters, and musical characteristics were rather rigidly set. In form, it consisted of a series of recitatives alternating with arias (mostly *da capo*), with occasional duets but seldom any larger ensembles. Aria types (*cantabile, mezzo carattere, bravura,* etc.) and the order of their succession were governed by conventional rules. In the latter part of the century the earlier rigidity of form and style was gradually relaxed, especially in the works of Jommelli and Traetta composed for non-Italian audiences, while the influence of the French *tragédie lyrique* became evident in the greater use of choruses and ballets. The 18th-century *opera seria* was the chief medium through which virtuoso singing underwent an unparalleled development, particularly by the famous *castrati* of the period. Comic opera (intermezzo, *opera buffa*) also flourished at Naples from the early 18th century and spread to other centers. See Opera VIII; Comic opera II B; Aria IV; Overture.

II. About 1600 there existed in Naples a school of keyboard composers who represent an important transitional link from the keyboard style of the 16th century (A. Gabrieli, Cabezón) to that of the early baroque (Frescobaldi). To this group belonged A. Valente (publications of 1576, '80), R. Rodio (*c.* 1530–1610), G. Macque (*c.* 1550–1614), S. Stella, F. Lambardi (1587–1642), G. M. Trabaci (*c.* 1580–1647), and A. Mayone (d. 1627). Macque was a Belgian who, after stays in Vienna and Rome, came in 1586 to Naples, where he entered the service of Fabrizio Gesualdo, the father of Carlo Gesualdo. Both Trabaci and Mayone were his pupils, as was Luigi Rossi. The works of Macque and his successors are most remarkable for novel and experimental traits typical of early baroque style and expression.

Lit. *For I:* G. Tintori, *L'Opera napoletana* (1958); A. della Corte, *L'Opera comica italiana nel '700,* 2 vols. (1923); G. Pannain, *Le Origini della scuola musicale napoletana* [1914]; F. Florimo, *La Scuola musicale di Napoli,* 4 vols., rev. ed. (1880–82); M. Scherillo, *L'Opera buffa napoletana durante il settecento; storia letteraria* [1917]; D. J. Grout, *A Short History of Opera,* 2 vols., rev. ed. (1965), ch. xiv and bibl.; E. Downes, "The Operas of Johann Christian Bach" (diss. Harvard Univ., 1958); *id.* and H. Hucke, in *CP 1961;* G. Pannain, in *RMI* xxxv–xxxix; S. di Giacomo, in *RMI* xxii, xxiii; E. Dent, in *ML* xxv (nomenclature).

For II: *Editions XXVIII, 4; I. Fuser, ed. ‡*Antonio Valente, 43 Versi spirituali* (1958); Rocco Rodio, *Cinque Ricercate,* ed. M. S. Kastner (1958); J. Burns, "Neapolitan Keyboard Music from Valente to Frescobaldi" (diss. Harvard Univ., 1953); W. Apel, in *MQ* xxiv (Mayone, Trabaci); J. Burns, in *JAMS* xii (Valente).

I by D.J.G.

Neapolitan sixth. The *sixth chord of the lowered supertonic, f–a♭–d′♭ in C. It is often used in cadential formations of the type IV–V–I, replacing IV [see Functional harmony]. Although frequently found in the works of the *Neapolitan school, the Neapolitan sixth was an established idiom throughout the second half of the 17th century (Carissimi, Corelli). Ex. 1 shows an example from Carissimi's duet "Il mio core," and Ex. 2 one from the "Frost Scene" in Purcell's *King Arthur* (1691). See Harmonic analysis V.

Nebel, neble. See Nabla.

Neben- [G.]. Auxiliary, secondary. *Nebenthema, Nebensatz,* second theme (of a sonata). *Nebendreiklang,* any triad other than I, IV, and V. *Nebennote,* a note other than those conditioned by the harmony, i.e., auxiliary notes, passing notes, appoggiaturas, etc. *Nebentonart,* a key other than the main key of a composition, e.g., the dominant and subdominant, the relative keys, etc. *Nebenstimme,* subordinate or accompanying part.

Neck. The projecting portion of a violin, lute, guitar, etc., by which the instrument is held.

Negro music. I. The term "Negro music" is generally applied to music composed by Negroes, either folk music or pieces by individual composers. It is not to be confused with the Negro-dialect songs that have been composed largely by white men: the "plantation songs" of Stephen Foster, the "coon songs" of the late 19th century, and the commercialized imitations of *blues. However, so many Negro composers work in the commercial "jazz" and "swing" industry that it is often impossible to distinguish between genuine Negro music and its imitation by white men.

References to Negro music date back to the 18th century. The opera, *The Disappointment* [pub. libretto 1767), contains the earliest Negro dialect song. Thomas Jefferson wrote of the

musical talents of the Negro in his *Notes on Virginia* (1784); Aird's *Selection of Scotch, Irish, and Foreign Airs* (Glasgow, 1782) contained a "Negro Jig"; J. Carr of Baltimore published in 1801 a "Negro Song," composed or arranged by Benjamin Carr, an English musician who moved to America in 1793; and Gottlieb Graupner became one of the forerunners of the minstrel show by singing in costume "A Gay Negro Boy" between the acts of a play in Boston in 1799. Thus, white men's descriptions and imitations of Negro singing came into vogue long before Negro music was collected and preserved. The minstrel shows received their impetus directly from the Negro, however. According to tradition, which is partially confirmed by known fact, this type of entertainment was popularized by Thomas Rice, who dressed in clothes borrowed from a Negro and imitated the Negro's manner of singing a song called "Jim Crow." This occurred about 1830, and from that time on the movement spread and dozens of minstrel troupes came into prominence. Most of the songs written for the minstrels were composed by white composers, among them Stephen Foster, and for decades these Negro-dialect songs constituted the chief source of information that many Americans, particularly Northerners, possessed regarding the musical talents of the Negro.

It was not until after the Civil War that native Negro singing and songs became known to the country at large, mainly through a traveling group of Negro singers from Fisk University led by George L. White. As other Negro institutes were founded, notably Hampton and Tuskegee, their student singing groups toured the country and acquainted the nation, particularly the North, with the Negro's own songs. In their programs, the emphasis was principally on the so-called "spirituals," or religious songs, of the Negro.

II. The origin of the Negro's melodies is a controversial subject, particularly as to whether any appreciable number of them have an African background. Comparison is made between the music of African peoples and that of the American Negro. The pentatonic scale is common to both, and each has a decided tendency toward syncopation. Also, the Negro has a love for complex and involved rhythmic combinations, which some students claim derives from an African background. Other authorities, notably George Pullen Jackson in his *White Spirituals in the Southern Uplands* (1933), claim a white origin for many of the Negro songs and point to many convincing examples [see Jig]. It is true, also, that white evangelists and "revivalists" traveled among the southern Negroes and sang to them many of the gospel songs from their own hymn-books. The most tenable theory, perhaps, is that the Negroes brought with them from Africa their own musical traditions and that association with white men and exposure to their customs and music tempered and molded the African idioms into something that represented a combination of the two.

III. The emphasis on Negro religious songs delayed for many years recognition and general knowledge of the secular songs, which cover a wide range, both in type and in mood. These have been collected and distributed only since about 1930, as interest in folklore and balladry became something of a science among American scholars. There are work songs—for cotton-picking, corn-shucking, stevedoring; railroad songs of the section gang; steamboat songs; and prison songs of the chain gang and the rock pile. The Negro's love of balladry is responsible for many songs of the narrative type—"Frankie and Johnnie," Negro versions of "Casey Jones," the story of "John Henry," and many other legends. In addition there are bad men's songs, unprint-able "devil's" songs, and numerous tunes for Negro dances. Of particular importance is the *blues, a type of sorrow-song that has become extremely popular and became one of the main ingredients of jazz.

The 20th century has brought striking innova-tions in Negro folk singing, notably the religious dance, the rhythmic gospel song, and the choral organizations in the folk church. These innova-tions stem largely from the introduction of in-strumental accompaniment into the church service. The accompaniment, provided princi-pally by piano (and tambourine in the Holiness Church service), is not the conventional four-voice hymn accompaniment but highly rhythmic and prominent. Pieces featuring these innova-tions are known as "gospels." An important fea-ture of their appeal is the improvisory style of the singers, who rely little on the printed page. Pioneers in gospel song—the new spiritual—include Thomas A. Dorsey and Roberta Martin of Chicago, and Lucy Campbell of Memphis.

The effect of Negro folk music on the art music of America, as well as the work of serious Negro composers, is discussed under United States II, IV. See also Jazz.

Lit.: H. Courlander, *Negro Folk Music, U.S.A.*

(1963); Z. W. George, *A Guide to Negro Music* (1953); G. P. Jackson, *White and Negro Spirituals* (1944); LeRoi Jones, *Blues People: Negro Music in White America* (1963); H. E. Krehbiel, *Afro-American Folksongs* (1913; repr. 1967); J. B. T. Marsh, *The Story of the Jubilee Singers* (1880); H. W. Odum and G. B. Johnson, *The Negro and His Songs* (1925; repr. 1964); G. D. Pike, *The Jubilee Singers* (1873); R. A. Waterman, in S. Tax, ed., *Acculturation in the Americas* (1952); N. I. White, *American Negro Folk-songs* (1928; repr. 1965); W. F. Allen et al., eds., ‡*Slave Songs of the United States* (1867; rev. ed. 1965); N. G. J. Ballanta, ed., ‡*Saint Helena Island Spirituals* (1925); H. A. Chambers, ed., ‡*The Treasury of Negro Spirituals* (1963); J. H. Cox, ed., ‡*Folk-songs of the South* (1925); G. P. Jackson, ed., ‡*Down-East Spirituals* (1943); R. E. Kennedy, ed., ‡*Mellows, a Chronicle of Unknown Singers* (1925); A. Lomax, ed., ‡*The Folk Songs of North America* (1960); D. Scarborough, ed., ‡*On the Trail of Negro Folk-songs* (1925; repr. 1963); J. W. Work, ed., ‡*American Negro Songs* (1940); D. J. Epstein, in *Notes* xx; D. L. Thieme, in *African Music* ii.   J.T.H.; add. by J.W.W.

Neighbor tone. Same as auxiliary tone; see Non-harmonic tones I.

Nelson Mass. Mass by Haydn in D minor, writ-ten in 1798 while Lord Nelson was engaged in the Battle of the Nile, an event that intrigued Haydn immensely. The Mass is sometimes called "The Imperial."

Neoclassicism. A movement of 20th-century music that is characterized by the inclusion into contemporary style of features derived from the music of the 17th and 18th centuries. It repre-sents the expression of a general reaction against the unrestrained emotionalism of late romanti-cism. Particularly distinct is the influence of Bach, which makes itself felt in the emphasis on contrapuntal texture; in the revival of early forms such as the suite (not the ballet-suite of the late 19th century), toccata, passacaglia, ricercar, concerto grosso, and ground; in the reduction of orchestral resources and colors; in the abandoning of program music; and in a gen-eral tendency toward an objective and detached style. The music of Scarlatti, Pergolesi, Monte-verdi, F. Couperin, and Lully has also left im-prints on contemporary works, particularly by

French and Italian composers who supplemented the "back to Bach" movement with the motto "clarté latine."

Considered a typically neoclassical work is Prokofiev's Classical Symphony (1918), a clever parody of Mozart's style. However, neoclassicism as a general movement did not start until the early 1920's, when Igor Stravinsky startled the musical world with his *Pulcinella,* his opera *Mavra,* and other works written in what was then interpreted as an "18th-century manner" but that proved to be the beginning of a new style in contemporary music. The same idiom prevails in his Sonata (1924), Piano Concerto (1924), Serenade (1925) for piano, his opera-oratorio *Oedipus Rex* (1927), and the ballet *Apollon Musagète* (1928). Although the term neoclassicism seems to have been adopted by musicologists to refer to a stylistic category, most of the composers to whom it could be applied totally refuse to accept it, notably Stravinsky.

Still closer in spirit to Bach than Stravinsky is Paul Hindemith, who, from *c.* 1925 on (Three Concertos, op. 36; Piano Studies, op. 37), has systematically developed a new contrapuntal style, deliberately impersonal and sometimes mechanical, that may well be described as a 20th-century version of Bach. Certain features point to a still more distinct relationship, namely, the dissonant linearity of 14th-century composers such as Machaut [see under *Ars nova* II]. Hindemith is only one of a number of composers who, *c.* 1925, arrived at neoclassicism as their "third period," after earlier periods of first impressionism and then a rather anarchic mixture of primitivism and jazz. In this group are A. Casella, G. F. Malipiero, W. Piston, W. Fortner, and others.

The neoclassical movement has led to the revival of numerous forms and idioms that developed from the 16th to 18th centuries, e.g., the madrigal, ricercar, concerto grosso, number opera, passacaglia, ostinato, counterpoint, polyrhythmic and polymetric devices, etc.

Lit.: K. R. W. Heyman, *The Relation of Ultramodern to Archaic Music* (1921); L. Rognoni, *La Scuola musicale di Vienna* [1966], pp. 135–210; I. Stravinsky, *Chronicle of my Life* (1936); id., *Poétique musicale* [1945]; A. Lourie, " 'Neogothic' and 'Neoclassic' " (*MN* v); A. G. Browne, "Paul Hindemith and the Neo-classic Music" (*ML* xiii, 42).

Neomodal. Pertaining to the use of modal idioms in present-day music. See Modality.

Netherlands. The music history of the Netherlands cannot be described without taking into account the political changes that took place in northwest Europe during the last five centuries. This area was successively a part of France, Burgundy, The Holy Roman Empire, and Spain, until it became an independent state in 1581 (William of Orange), which, from 1815 to 1830, also included present-day Belgium. Such 19th-century historiographers as Kiesewetter, Fétis, Ambros, and Van der Straeten included Belgium in their studies of Netherlands music and even extended their scope to some bordering provinces of northern France (Cambrai), which in the 15th and 16th centuries were politically or culturally related to the Netherlands. Modern scholars distinguish between the northern (now Protestant) and the southern (Roman Catholic) parts of the Low Countries, the former being considered Netherlands or Dutch countries, the latter Belgium or, in earlier times, Flemish countries. Through this distinction, the early history of Netherlands music loses much of the glory with which it has been surrounded by the above-mentioned writers [see Netherlands schools].

The so-called Gruythuyser MS (ed. K. H. Heeroma and C. W. H. Lindenburg, 1966) from the second half of the 14th century contains 147 monophonic songs in the Dutch language [see J. Wolf, in *CP 1924*], while the contemporary MS Prague *XI E 9* includes polyphonic compositions with Dutch titles, such as "Vaer rouwe in dander huys," "Het dunct mi wesen verre," etc. [see F. Kammerer, *Die Musikstücke des Prager Kodex XI E 9* (1931)]. In both sources French influence is apparent. In the 15th century, Jacob Obrecht (1452–1505), the only real Dutchman among the "Netherlands composers" (he was born at Bergen op Zoom in Brabant), wrote not only Masses, motets, and French chansons, but also a number of Dutch songs [see A. Smijers, *Van Ockeghem tot Sweelinck,* vol. iii]. A collection of three-part compositions with full texts, dating from about 1500, has been published by J. Wolf in *Editions LII, 30. An important source of Dutch-Flemish music of the 16th century are the seven *Musyckboexkens* (music booklets) published by Tielman Susato of Antwerp (1551–57). Books 1–2 contain "amoreuse liedekens" (amorous chansons), Book 3 is a collection of dances, and Books 4–7 contain religious songs, the *Souterliedekens* (Psalter songs).

The next important Dutch composer after

Obrecht is Jan Pieterszoon Sweelinck (1562–1621). His main vocal work, the four- to eight-part polyphonic setting of the complete Psalter, appeared in four books, three of them during his lifetime (Amsterdam, 1604–21). Among his instrumental works, nearly all for keyboard instruments, the *Fantasia Chromatica,* with its use of a chromatic style, is a striking exception to Sweelinck's more usual diatonic style. He became famous throughout Europe for his organ playing at the Oude Kerk in Amsterdam, and his pupils included nearly all the leading German organists and organ composers of the early baroque (S. Scheidt, H. Scheidemann, M. Schildt, P. Siefert, J. Praetorius), a fact that won him the name "Der deutsche Organisten-macher" (the maker of German organists). A successor of Sweelinck was A. van Noordt, who published a *Tabulatuur-Boeck van Psalmen en Fantasyen* (1659) containing six keyboard fantasias that represent a significant step in the development from earlier imitative forms to the fugue. Noordt's book is reissued in *Editions LII, 19, which also includes other examples of the development of Netherlands music during the 17th and 18th centuries.

Little can be said about the development of indigenous Netherlands music during the 17th and 18th centuries, when it was influenced first by Italian and later by French music of the time. During the 19th century the influence of German composers such as Mendelssohn and Schumann became prominent, appearing in the works of Johannes Verhulst (1816–91), Richard Hol (1825–1904), and others. Toward the end of the century a period of new creative musical activity was initiated by Alfons Diepenbrock (1862–1921), the most important Dutch composer. A self-taught musician, Diepenbrock was first attracted to both the chromatic harmonics of Wagner and the polymelodic, vocal style of Palestrina, which he combined most successfully in one of his main works, the Te Deum for 4 solo voices, double chorus, and orchestra (1897–1908). In later years he came to admire Debussy, as is seen in his numerous songs, written mostly to French texts, and his stage music for *Marsyas* (a Dutch comedy by Balthasar Verhagen; 1910) and Sophocles' *Electra* (1920). In striking contrast to the subjective mysticism of his music is that of his contemporary Johan Wagenaar (1862–1941), who was rooted in the German tradition of Liszt and R. Strauss.

The later Dutch composers were more inclined toward internationalism of German or,

more frequently, French derivation. Representatives of the latter group include Hendrik Andriessen (b. 1892) and Alexander Voormolen (b. 1895). More advanced, although unmistakably French-oriented, is the work of Daniel Ruyneman (1886–1963) and Willem Pijper (1894–1947), the latter the most original Dutch composer since Diepenbrock. Pijper created a musical language based on the use of polytonality, polymetric and polyrhythmic figures, and the "germ cell," which is often no more than a chord or a single motif, from which is developed organically not only all the motivic and thematic material of a composition but even its form and the duration of its movements. Thus Pijper's music exhibits a highly intellectual structure yet, at the same time, concentrated expressiveness, as in his Piano Sonatinas nos. 2 and 3 (1925) and the Third Symphony (1926). The teacher of most of the leading present-day Dutch composers, he has had a profound influence on Dutch music. Among his pupils are Guillaume Landré (b. 1905), known for his orchestral works and chamber music; Kees van Baaren (b. 1906), who adopted the twelve-tone technique of Schoenberg and the Viennese school in such works as *Variazioni per Orchestra* (1959); Henk Badings (b. 1907), the most prolific contemporary Dutch composer, who clings more to the German tradition of Reger and Hindemith; Rudolf Escher (b. 1912); and Hans Henkemans (b. 1913). The most recent generation is represented by Ton de Leeuw (b. 1926), a pupil of Messiaen, who in his opera *The Dream* (1964) shows a great attachment to Asian idioms, and Peter Schat (b. 1935), disciple of Boulez and Cage, whose most advanced project, *Labyrinth* (1966), is an important attempt at creating a new kind of musical theater.

Lit.: C. van den Borren, *Geschiedenis van de muziek in de .Nederlanden,* 2 vols. (1948–51); H. C. Wolff, *Die Musik der alten Niederländer* (1956); F. van Duyse, *Het oude nederlandsche lied,* 3 vols. (1903–08); J. D. C. van Dokkum, *Honderd jaar muziekleven in Nederland* (1929); E. Reeser, *Een Eeuw Nederlandse Muziek* (1950); S. Dresden, *Het muziekleven in Nederland sinds 1880* (1932); H. Badings, *De hedendaagse Nederlandse muziek* [Amsterdam, n.d.]; C. Backers, *Nederlandse componisten van 1400 tot op onze tijd* (1941); E. Reeser, ed., *Music in Holland* [Amsterdam, n.d.]; J. Wouters, "Dutch Music in the 20th century" (*LBCM*); *Sonorum speculum* (ed. by Donemus Foundation, 1959—).

rev. E.R.

Netherlands schools. A designation introduced by R. G. Kiesewetter, in his *Die Verdienste der Niederländer um die Tonkunst* (1826), for the long series of 15th- and 16th-century musicians of the Low Countries. He distinguished a first, second, and third Netherlands school, which were headed respectively by Dufay (*c.* 1400–74), Ockeghem (1430–95) and Obrecht (1452–1510), and Josquin (*c.* 1450–1521). Today, these terms have been largely discarded, chiefly because only one of the so-called "Netherlands" masters, Obrecht, came from the Netherlands proper, all the others coming from either the southern Lowlands (Belgium), northern France (Cambrai), or Burgundy (Dijon). A more appropriate name for the first Netherlands school is *Burgundian school, while the musicians from Ockeghem to Lasso can be grouped best in various generations of the *Flemish school. See H. C. Wolff, *Die Musik der alten Niederländer* (1956); P. H. Lang, in *MQ* xxv, 48.

Neue Musik [G.]. German term for *twentieth-century music. Also see under New music.

Neue Sachlichkeit [G.]. A term coined in the 1920's for antiromantic tendencies toward an objective [G. *sachlich*] and even nonexpressive type of music.

Neuma. (1) See under Neumes. (2) Medieval term for extended melismatic passages of plainsong, sung to one syllable or simply a vowel [see Vocalization]. In the early Middle Ages, when the Christian service had the character of boundless exultation rather than restrained devotion, the *neuma* had a symbolic significance as expressing a mystic feeling that could not be put into words. In Gregorian chant the term applies mainly to long melismas representing a later insertion, i.e., a nontextual *trope. They occur especially in responsories, the most famous example being the *neuma triplex* of "Descendit de caelis" [see *ApGC*, p. 343]. (3) In the later Middle Ages the name *neuma* was given to instructive melodies devised to show the special characteristics of each mode [see *Noeane*]. Through misuse, however, these melodies were introduced into the Office and sung before or after the antiphons (in Paris as late as 1873). They also served, under the name *Neuma*, as tenors for 13th-century motets [see P. Aubry and A. Gastoué, *Recherches sur les "Tenors" latins* (1907), p. 13].

Neumatic style. See under Gregorian chant III.

Neumes. The notational signs of the Middle Ages (8th–14th centuries), which were used for writing down plainsong. The term means chiefly the signs used for the music of the Roman Catholic Church (Gregorian chant) but is also used for other systems of a similar character, such as the *Byzantine, Mozarabic, or Armenian neumes. This article describes only the first type.

I. Neumatic notation consists of a large number of signs for single tones as well as for groups of two, three, or more tones. The accompanying table shows the most important neumes as they occur in the MSS of St. Gall (9th–10th centuries), together with the modern forms used in present-day liturgical books (Solesmes edition, Vatican edition) and a rendition in ordinary notation.

The neumes may be divided into two main groups, the "basic" neumes (A) and the "special" neumes (B). The former indicate melodic motion only, while the latter also indicate special manners of performance. Category A.1 of the table includes the so-called "simple" neumes, i.e., those having up to three notes. For these, individual names are used, while the neumes with more than three notes (A.2, "compound" neumes) have compound names. The signs under B.1 are the "liquescent" neumes (*semivocales*). They always occur on a diphthong (*au, eu*) or where there are two consonants in succession, such as *ng* (*angelus*), *lm, rn*, etc. According to one theory, they are thought to have called for a particularly smooth transition by means of an interpolated *e*, as, for instance, *in(e)fer(e)ni* instead

in - fer - ni　cir - cum

of *inferni*. The *epiphonus* is the liquescent variety of the *podatus,* the *cephalicus* that of the *clivis,* the *ancus* that of the *climacus.* See the accompanying example, from the Introit "Circumdederunt." The signs under B.2 belong to the class of "ornamenting" neumes. Each of them involved a special manner of performance, whose exact nature is not always clear. The *strophicus* (*apostropha*) occurs usually as a group of two or three signs (*bistropha, tristropha*) of identical pitch and indicates a quick reiteration (repercussion), i.e., a true vocal *tremolo [see *ApGC,* p. 107f]. In present-day practice it is usually rendered as a sustained note of double or triple duration. The original significance of the *oriscus, quilisma, salicus,* and *pressus* is very

A. 1. Punctum				
Virga				
Podatus or Pes				
Clivis or Flexa				
Scandicus				
Climacus				
Torculus				
Porrectus				
2. Scandicus flexus				
Porrectus flexus				
Torculus resupinus				
Pes sub-punctis				
B. 1. Epiphonus				
Cephalicus				
Ancus				
2. Strophicus				
Oriscus				
Quilisma				
Salicus				
Pressus				

obscure, and the explanations in *LU,* pp. xxivff, have little historical validity [see *ApGC,* pp. 110ff]. Another specialized neume frequently found in the earliest MSS of St. Gall is the *trigon,* consisting of three dots forming a triangle. It probably indicated staccato performance of *torculus* formations involving a semitone at the beginning, such as e–f–d or b–c′–a. Possibly, the initial interval was a quarter tone, since later MSS usually represent the *trigon* as a repercussive formation, f–f–d or c′–c′–a. Early writers cite quite a number of other "ornamenting" neumes under names such as *notae vinnulae* ("charming" notes) or *tremulae,* which, we are told, the Franks were unable to sing [see C. Vivell, "Les 'Sons Répercutés' dans le chant Grégorien," in *TG* xviii; also see Vox (1)].

II. There are various theories about the origin of the neumes. The one most generally accepted considers the neumes an outgrowth of accents in the Greek language, signs that indicated not so much accentuation in the modern sense but an inflection of the voice, the *acutus* (a), a raising, and the *gravis* (b), a lowering of the pitch. The former became the *virga* (which, as a rule, is used for a higher note), and the latter the

punctum (which usually indicates a lower tone). Combinations of these accents (c, d, e) led to neumes of two or more notes, the *podatus, clivis, porrectus,* etc. Therefore, all these neumes (group A of the complete table) are called "accent neumes" [G. *Akzentneumen*]. Most of the neumes shown in group B belong to the category called "hook neumes" [G. *Hakenneumen*] because they are drawn with a rounded hook that may have come from the Greek aspirate sign: ʼ.

In the earliest sources (9th–10th centuries) the neumes are written so as to give only the general outline of the melodic motion and not the actual intervals. Thus, the *podatus* may mean an ascending second, third, fifth, etc. Evidently these signs served only as a mnemonic aid for the singer, who knew the melodies by heart, or for the choir leader, who may have interpreted them to his choir by appropriate movements of the hand. These neumes are called *chironomic, staffless, oratorical, or *in campo aperto* ("in the open," i.e., without clear orientation). About A.D. 1000 we find the earliest traces of a more careful arrangement of the neumatic signs so as to give some tentative indication of pitch. Particularly the 11th-century MSS of Italy, written in the so-called Longobardian or Beneventan character, are remarkable for their early use of "heighted" (intervallic, diastematic) neumes, i.e., neumes that are written on a staff, either imagined or actually indicated by one, two, or finally four lines. Slightly later than the Beneventan neumes are the Aquitanian neumes, whose shapes approximated, and finally led to,

the square-shaped characters of the 13th century. These were quickly adopted everywhere except in Germany, where a peculiar variety, the Gothic neumes, remained in use as late as the 16th century. The square-shaped neumes are still used today in the liturgical books of the Roman Catholic Church. The accompanying illustration shows the eight "simple" neumes in five different styles: I. Messine neumes (Monastery of Metz, 9th–10th cent.; G. *Metzer Neumen*); II. Beneventan neumes (Monastery of Benevent in southern Italy, 11th–12th cent.); III. Aquitanian neumes (southern France, 12th–13th cent.); IV. Square neumes from Salisbury, England (Sarum use; 13th cent.); V. Gothic neumes, also called *Nagelschrift* (German MSS, 14th–15th cent.). These may be compared with the St. Gall neumes shown above.

The chironomic neumes as such cannot be deciphered [for a futile attempt, see O. Fleischer, *Die germanischen Neumen* (1923)]; they can only be compared with those of the later sources, which have preserved the old melodies in a clearer system of notation, with the neumes written on an imaginary or real staff of one to four lines. For material showing the development of the neumes see Editions XLII, A, 2 and 3.

III. The question of the rhythmic meaning of neumatic notation is infinitely more difficult than that of pitch. It has been the subject of painstaking research and of sharp controversies that still continue. See Gregorian chant VI.

The neumatic signs in their final shape (square shapes of the 13th century) were also adopted for the notation of two other bodies of early music, secular monophonic melodies (troubadours, trouvères) and polyphonic music (organa, clausulae of the school of Notre Dame). In both cases they present problems of rhythmic interpretation that are entirely different from those of the neumes in Gregorian chant. See Monophonic notation and Square notation; also Notation.

Lit.: G. Suñol, *Introduction à la paléographie musicale grégorienne* (1935); P. Wagner, *Einführung in die gregorianischen Melodien* ii: *Neumenkunde* (1905; rev. ed., 1912); H. M. Bannister, *Monumenti Vaticani* (1913; extensive tables of neumes); E. Jammers, *Tafeln zur Neumenschrift* (1965); *Editions XLII, A 2 and 3 (*Justus ut palma* from more than 200 MSS); M. Huglo, "Les Noms des neumes et leur origine" (*Études grégoriennes* i); J. Handschin, "Eine alte Neumenschrift" (*AM* xxii); see also under Gregorian chant and in *ReMMA*, pp. 440–42; also s.v. "Notation" A. II. and B. I., in *MGG* ix.

Neutöner [G.]. A derogatory term applied, *c.* 1890, to Wagner, Richard Strauss, and other "radicals" of the time.

Nevel. See Nabla.

New music. A term adapted from G. *neue Musik* as a designation for various novel and radical trends in 20th-century music, such as *atonality, *serial techniques, etc. The term, which was introduced *c.* 1925, is interesting historically, since similar names were used for similar reasons both 300 and 600 years ago, i.e., the *nuove musiche* of 1600 and the *ars nova* of 1300 [see also History of music].

New World Symphony. Dvořák's Ninth Symphony (usually called no. 5) in E minor, op. 95 (1893). It was written while Dvořák resided in the United States and incorporates themes modeled after the songs of American Negroes and Indians. Some of this material, however, sounds more Bohemian (Czech) than American.

New Zealand. See under Australia.

Nibelungenring. See *Ring des Nibelungen, Der.*

Nicaragua. Information about native songs and dances in Nicaragua at the time of the Spanish conquest is found in the writings of Columbus' historiographer, Gonzalo Fernandez Oviedo. He described dance festivals involving large numbers of Indians. One of them would act as a leader and answer in antiphonal manner to the singing of the group, supported by the beats of native drums and calabash shakers. These and other native instruments are still in use. The amalgam of Indian rituals and Roman Catholic rites is shown in such examples as the festival plays known as *Güegüence,* which date from colonial times and in which Spanish and Nahuatl dialects are mixed.

Many of the Creole forms of songs and dances that are at present popular in Nicaragua are basically the same as those found in the rest of Central America.

Art music in Nicaragua developed relatively late. Data on some composers born during the last decades of the 19th century has been recently made available. Alejandro Vega Matus (1875–1935) and José de la Cruz Mena (1874–1907), a composer of sacred music, belong to this group. The foremost figure in Nicaraguan music is Luis A. Delgadillo (1887–1964), a prolific composer of more than four hundred works who served as director of the Escuela Nacional de Música, founded in 1950, and conductor of the symphony orchestra of Managua. His works all are in the romantic tradition, and most of them are inspired by native music. Other contemporary composers from Nicaragua are Manuel Ibarra, J. Francisco Rosales, Antonio Zapata, Arturo Picado, Carlos Ramirez Velasquez, and Justo Santos.

Lit.: G. Vega Miranda, "De la Música nicaragüense" (*Elite* vii, 75); L. A. Delgadillo, "La Música indígena y colonial en Nicaragua" (*Rev. estud. mus.* i, 3). Also see under Latin America.

J.O-S.

Nightingale, The [Rus. *Salavei*]. Opera in three acts by Stravinsky (libretto by the composer and S. Mitusov after H. C. Andersen's fairy tale), produced in Paris (in French, as *Le Rossignol*), 1914. Setting: fairy tale (China).

Night on the Bald Mountain. Symphonic poem in variation form by Mussorgsky, inspired by the witches' Sabbath in Gogol's story, "St. John's Eve." Composed in 1867, it was repeatedly revised and eventually incorporated into his un-

finished opera, *Fair at Sorochinsk.* Today it is performed in an orchestral arrangement by Rimsky-Korsakov.

Nights in the Gardens of Spain. See *Noches en los jardines de España.*

Ninth chord. A chord that consists of the third, fifth, seventh, and ninth above the root. It usually occurs as the dominant of the key (dominant ninth chord), e.g., in C major: g–b–d'–f'–a'. Frequently the root (g) is omitted, in which case the chord can also be interpreted as the seventh chord of the seventh degree (b). The principle of superimposed thirds that leads from the triad to the seventh chord and to the ninth chord can be carried on still further, resulting in the eleventh chord (g–b–d'–f'–a'–c'') and thirteenth chord (g–b–d'–f'–a'–c''–e''). This building-up principle is used to produce a very impressive climax in the first movement of Bruckner's Symphony no. 7 [see Ex.]. Usually, the chords mentioned

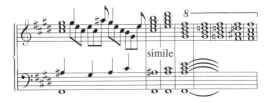

occur in a reduced form and in exchanged position of the higher notes. In such cases they can usually be interpreted as appoggiaturas of simpler chords, e.g., g–f'–b'–e'' as an appoggiatura of g–f'–b'–d''.

Ninth Symphony. Although many composers (e.g., Bruckner, Dvořák, Haydn, Mozart, Mahler) have written nine or more symphonies, the most celebrated ninth is Beethoven's last symphony, also known as the *Choral Symphony.

Nobilissima Visione. Ballet by Hindemith (composed 1938), based on the life of St. Francis of Assisi. Some of the numbers were arranged into an orchestral suite for concert performance.

Noces, Les [F., The Wedding]. Ballet by Stravinsky (choreography by B. Nizhinska), produced in Paris, 1923. It is scored for chorus, soloists, four pianos, and seventeen percussion instruments (including four tympani) and consists of four scenes.

Noches en los jardines de España [Sp., *Nights in the Gardens of Spain*]. Suite for piano and orchestra by Manuel de Falla, finished in 1915. The three movements are (translated titles): (1) In the Generalife; (2) Distant Dance; (3) In the Gardens of the Sierra de Cordoba.

Nocturn [L. *horae nocturnae*]. One of the three parts into which the Office of Matins is divided. See Office.

Nocturne. A romantic *character piece for piano, written in a somewhat melancholy or languid style, with an expressive melody over a broken-chord accompaniment. The first nocturnes were written by the Irishman John Field (1782–1837), from whom F. Chopin adopted the idea and the name. See *Notturno; Nachtstück.*

Nocturnes. Three symphonic poems by Debussy, composed 1893–99: 1. *Nuages* (Clouds); 2. *Fêtes* (Festivals); 3. *Sirènes* (Sirens), with women's voices.

Node. In a vibrating string, the points of rest or of minimum amplitude. Such points occur not only at the two fixed ends of a string, e.g., bridge and fingerboard of a violin, but also at regular points in between, owing to the fact that the string vibrates not only as a whole but also in segments—½, ⅓, ¼, ⅕, etc.—of its length. Harmonics on a violin are produced by touching the string at one of these points. Similarly, in a vibrating air column (pipe), nodes are the points of highest density, where the air particles do not move. The intermediate points of maximum amplitude (string) or movement (pipe) are called loops or antinodes. See Acoustics V.

No drama. See *Noh.*

Noeane, noeagis, etc. Word formations of unknown meaning that appear in various treatises of the 9th and 10th centuries in connection with short melodies called *neuma* and are designed to give the characteristics of the various modes. The "Commemoratio brevis" of *c.* 900 gives a set of eight such neumata, e.g., for the first tone [see *GS* i, 214]:

a   g   f e   g   f e   d c   fga gagf eaf efe d
No- a- no- e- a-   ne

The syllables *no-e-a-no-e-a-ne* were commonly used for modes 1 and 3, *no-e-a-ne* for 5 and 7, and *no-e-a-(g)is* for all the plagal modes. They are mentioned *c.* 850 by Aurelianus Reomenois ("Musica disciplina"; see *GS* i, 41f), who tried to learn their meaning from a Greek and was told that they were merely expressions of joy. They are related to the Byzantine *enechemata* [see

Echos]. See also *Anenaiki;* Solmization. See *ReMMA,* p. 173; *RiHM* i.2, 57; H. Riemann, in *ZIM* xiv; E. Werner, in *MQ* xxviii, L. Kunz, in *KJ* xxx.

Noel [F.]. A popular Christmas song, particularly of French origin [see Carol]. In 1553 Nicolas Denisot published two books called *Cantiques et Noëls,* the second of which includes thirteen melodies. Another important early publication is F. Colletet, *Noëls nouveaux et cantiques spirituels* (1660). Eustache de Caurroy's *Meslanges* (1610) contains polyphonic settings of noels. From the 17th to 19th centuries innumerable noels were published (frequently as sheet music), in which a semireligious text was set to secular melodies, dancing songs, drinking songs, *vaudevilles,* etc. In the 17th century the name was applied to organ pieces designed to be played during the Christmas service. Most of these are simple variations on popular Christmas melodies. Collections of noels were published by Nicolas-Antoine Le Bègue [see *HAM,* no. 231], Nicolas Gigault, Jean F. Dandrieu, Louis-Claude Daquin, A. P. F. Boely, Claude Balbastre, and others.

The earliest known use of the word *noël* [from L. *natalis,* birthday] in musical compositions is in a Christmas motet, "Nova vobis gaudia," by Grenon (*c.* 1420), which includes four (isorhythmic) refrains sung to the word "noël" [see J. Marix, *Les Musiciens de la cour de Bourgogne* (1938), p. 233]. To the same class belong a motet by Busnois sung entirely to this word and Mouton's motet "Noe, noe psallite noe." A number of the 15th-century English carols begin with the word "Nowell" [see Editions XXXIV, 4].

Lit.: F. Hellouin, *Le Noël musical français* (1906); H. Bachelin, *Les Noëls français* (1927); J. R. H. de Smits, *Les Noëls et la tradition populaire* (1932); H. Poulaille, *La Grande et Belle Bible des noëls anciens* [1948].

Noh [Jap.]. A genre of Japanese theater performed by a group of soloists, a chorus, and three or four instrumentalists. It was founded by Kan'ami Kiyotsugu (1333–84?), an author and actor of *sarugaku* [see Japan IV], and his son Zeami Motokiyo (1363–1443?) under the patronage of the shogun Ashikaga Yoshimitsu. A *noh* play is normally in one or two acts and is classified according to subject as god play, battle play, woman's play, secular play, or demon's play. Usually a *kyōgen,* a comic intermezzo, is performed between acts and/or between two *noh* plays. The entire text of *noh* is either sung or recited while that of *kyōgen* is spoken. A passage from a *noh* that is performed as a vocal piece without costume or instrumental accompaniment is called *utai* or *yōkyoku.*

Noh is performed by *shite,* the leading character, who usually wears a mask, and by *waki,* the principal supporting character, who does not. Other minor roles are called *tsure* and *wakizure;* sometimes there is a *kokata,* a role assigned to a young boy. The chorus, consisting of about eight persons, explains the plot or comments on the *shite's* psychological situation. The soloists may recite or sing, while the chorus always sings; the manner of singing is much influenced by *shōmyō* [see Japan III, IV].

The instrumental ensemble in *noh* consists of a bamboo flute (*noh-kan* or *fue*), two drums shaped like an hourglass (the larger, *ōtsuzumi,* rests on the player's left knee, while the smaller, *kotsuzumi,* is held on the right shoulder; both are played with the right hand), and a barrel-shaped drum (*taiko*), played with two wooden sticks. An instrumental passage often occurs at the entrance of the *shite,* at the climactic dances, or at the end of the play, joining in with the vocal parts. Such an instrumental piece, when played independently, is called *hayashi.* In addition to playing the instruments, the drummers often utter vocal exclamations, such as "Yah," "Hah," etc., which in fact are a part of the music.

The scale system used in singing a *noh* centers around three important notes, *jō* (high), *chū* (middle), and *ge* (low), with several less important notes around them. The intervals between these three important notes depend on the manner of singing. In *yowagin* (the "soft" style) each note is a perfect fourth apart, while in *tsuyogin* (the "strong" style) *jō* and *chū* fall on the same note and *ge* is a minor third below.

The descendants of Zeami took the family name Kanze, which also became the name of the school. In addition, there originally were three other schools: Komparu, Hōshō, and Kongō. Later, in the early 17th century, a fifth school, Kita, was founded by Kita Shichidayū. See T. Minagawa, in *JAMS* x, 181–200.   M.K.

Noire [F.]. See under Notes.

Nola [L.]. See under Cymbalum.

Nomos [Gr.]. In early Greek culture, particularly in the Homeric epoch, the traditional melodies used by the singer (*aoidos*) for the recitation of the epics, to the accompaniment of the phorminx. See Greece I; Melody type.

None. (1) German term for the interval of the ninth; *Nonenakkord,* ninth chord. (2) The sixth of the canonical hours. See Office.

Nonet [G. *Nonett;* It. *nonetto;* Sp. *noneto*]. Chamber music for nine instruments, e.g., string quartet and five winds. Nonets have been written by Spohr (op. 31), Rheinberger (op. 139), Stanford (op. 95, for strings and winds), Ravel (*Trois Poèmes de Stéphane Mallarmé,* for voice and nine instruments), Webern (*Concerto* op. 24), and others.

Nonharmonic tones. In *harmonic analysis, generic term for tones that are foreign to the harmony of the moment and occur as melodic "ornamentations" in one of the parts. There are two main categories:

I. Rhythmically weak notes occurring between two "harmonic" notes (i.e., notes that are part of the harmony). There are five such types, four of which are found between harmonic notes of different pitch [in Ex. 1–4, at the interval of a second], and one between harmonic notes of the same pitch [Ex. 5]. These are called: (1) *passing tone;* (2) *anticipation;* (3) *échappée;* (4) *cambiata;* (5) *auxiliary tone* (upper or lower auxiliary; also called embellishment, neighbor tone, returning note, alternating note).

The first four of these may, of course, occur between two harmonic notes forming any ascending or descending interval. The difference between *échappée* and *cambiata* is that in the

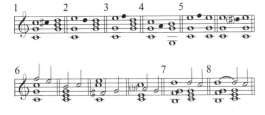

former the motion to the ornamenting tone is contrary to the motion between the harmonic tones, while in the latter these two motions are similar [see Motion]. Thus, with an ascending progression of harmony notes, e.g., e–g, the nonharmonic note d would be an *échappée* (e–d–g), the nonharmonic note A a *cambiata* (e–a–g).

II. Rhythmically strong notes occurring in place of harmonic notes. These are called *appoggiatura* [from It. *appoggiare*, to lean; also neighbor-tone]. An appoggiatura is the tone a second above or below the harmonic tone, played on the beat and resolved to the harmonic tone. The plain triad offers many possibilities for appoggiatura formations [Ex. 6] that are important as sources for dissonant chordal combinations. If the "wrong" note appears in the preceding chord, one speaks of a *prepared appoggiatura* [Ex. 7]; otherwise the appoggiatura is *unprepared*. The former type is the more orthodox, because the previous appearance of the "wrong" note somewhat weakens its dissonant character. This character is still more weakened—in fact, almost eliminated—if the preparing tone is tied to the appoggiatura. This formation is called *suspension* (sometimes retardation; Ex. 8). If two or more appoggiaturas occur simultaneously, one speaks of an appoggiatura chord [Ex. 9, Tchaikovsky, Symphony no. 4, last movt.]. A characteristic idiom of modern music is the extended use of "unresolved appoggiaturas" [Ex. 10, Debussy, *Pelléas et Mélisande,* end of Act I].

III. The classification and terminology above (based on W. Piston's *Harmony,* 1941) differs in various particulars from that used by other authors. This is especially true with respect to the term "appoggiatura," which is frequently restricted to those cases in which the "wrong" note is approached by leap [Ex. 11], the cases of stepwise approach being called *accented passing tone* [Ex. 12]. The advantage of this terminology appears to lie chiefly in its application to historical studies, since accented passing tones occur in practically all periods of music history while the "free" appoggiatura was not much used before *c.* 1750 (it is a characteristic feature of the *Empfindsamer Stil* of K. P. E. Bach; see *SchGMB,* p. 458). Other terms frequently used are *free passing tone* for a passing tone approached by leap [Ex. 13] and *changing notes* for the upper and lower auxiliary in succession [Ex. 14]. See E. Walker, "The Appoggiatura" (*ML* v, 121). See also Cambiata.

Nonnengeige [G.]. Name for *tromba marina.

Non nobis Domine. A celebrated canon that is usually, but without demonstrable evidence, attributed to William Byrd. It is frequently sung as a grace at English banquets. It is remarkable for the great number of solutions it admits, solutions that differ according to the number of parts and to the intervals and distance of the imitating voices. See the article in *GDB*.

Norddeutsche Schule. See Berlin school.

Norma. Opera in four acts by Bellini (libretto by F. Romani), produced in Milan, 1831. Setting: Gaul during the Roman occupation, *c.* 50 B.C.

Norway. Some 12th-century chants in honor of St. Olaf (*c.* 995–1030), patron saint of Norway, are probably the oldest music composed in that country. Giraldus Cambrensis (*c.* 1147–1223), in his well-known description of early part-singing [see *ReMMA,* p. 387], says that this practice may have originated among the Danes and Norwegians. From the Orkney Islands, a Norwegian possession from the 9th century, comes a two-part hymn, "Nobilis, humilis," in praise of their patron saint, St. Magnus (d. 1115), which may well be an example of early Norwegian polyphony. At the time of the Reformation (1537 in Norway), much of the earlier music was forbidden and, as a result, was lost. The songbooks of the Lutheran Church represent a new beginning. Among them were H. Thomissøn's *Salmebog* (1569), T. Kingo's *Graduale* (1699), and later Pontopiddan's *Salmebog* (1742). The first composers of note were Johan Daniel Berlin (1714–87), town musician of Trondheim, and, especially, his son, Johan Henrich Berlin (1741–1807), who composed cantatas, symphonies, concertos, and string quartets in the style of the time. The rise of national art music went hand in hand with political independence, which began in 1814 with the separation from Denmark. Waldemar Thrane's Singspiel *Fjeldeventyret* (1825; first perf. 1850) may be said to mark the beginning of indigenous Norwegian music. Halfdan Kjerulf (1815–68) wrote songs and piano pieces in the style of Mendelssohn and Schumann, though not without a certain Norwegian lyricism. Martin Andreas Udbye (1820–89) composed string quartets and operas. Under the influence of Rikard Nordraak (1842–66), who composed the present Norwegian national anthem, Edvard Hagerup Grieg (1843–1907) created a national style that won universal recognition and fame. Grieg often used melodic and rhythmic patterns derived from folksongs and from the *hardingfele music. Johan Svendsen (1840–1911) and Christian Sinding (1856–1941), contemporaries of Grieg, were exponents of international romanticism rather than national Norwegian music, although traits of the latter are by no means absent. Both cultivated larger symphonic forms as well as the more intimate ones, including songs, piano works, piano-violin pieces, and string quartets. Post-romantic tendencies of German derivation are evident in the works of Hjalmar Borgström (1864–1925), Johan Halvorsen (1864–1935), and Halfdan Cleve (1879–1952). French impressionist influences appeared after 1920 in the works of Alf Hurum (b. 1882), Arvid Kleven (1899–1929), and Pauline Hall (b. 1890). Harald Saeverud (b. 1897), Klaus Egge (b. 1906), and Eivind Groven (b. 1901) combine folk rhythms and melodies with free tonal concepts derived from the melodies themselves. Both Fartein Valen (1887–1952) and Klaus Egge (after World War II) composed in a linear style with free use of serial techniques. Younger composers, among them F. O. Arnestad (b. 1917) and others, followed similar paths, with G, Sønstevold (b. 1912) and K. Wiggen (b. 1927) experimenting with electronic music. Arne Nordheim (b. 1931), Finn Mortensen (b. 1922), and Egil Hovland (b. 1924) employed serial or nonserial techniques emphasizing vertical and coloristic means of expression.

Lit.: K. Lange and A. Østvedt, *Norwegian Music; a Brief Survey* (1958); J. Horton, *Scandinavian Music: A Short History* [1963]; O. M. Sandvik and G. Schjelderup, *Norges musikhistorie,* 2 vols. (1921); O. M. Sandvik, *Norsk Folkemusikk* (1921); G. Reiss, *Det norske rigsarkivs middelalderlige musikhaandskrifter* (1908); A. Hernes, *Impuls og tradisjon i norsk musikk 1500–1800* (1952); G. Abraham, ed., *Grieg: A Symposium* (1948); D. Schjelderup-Ebbe, *A Study of Grieg's Harmony* (1953); O. Gurvin and Ø. Anker, *Musikkleksikon,* rev. ed. (1959); *Festskrift til O. M. Sandvik* (1945); O. Gurvin, ed. ‡*Norsk folkemusikk,* 4 vols. (1958–63); B. Wallner, "Scandinavian Music after the Second World War" (*LBCM;* also *MQ* li); O. Gurvin, in *MGG* ix, cols. 1577–87; F. Mjöen, in *AdHM* ii, 1113–18; O. Andersson, ed., *Musikk og Musikkinstrumenter* (*Nordisk Kultur* xxv). H.-J.H.

Nota cambiata. See Cambiata.

Notation. The method or methods used for writing down music.

I. A fully developed system of notation must be designed so as to indicate the two main properties of a musical sound: its pitch and its duration. The most satisfactory of the numerous symbols that have been devised for this purpose is the note, a pointlike sign that indicates pitch by its position on a *staff provided with a *clef, and duration by a variety of shapes, such as hollow or black heads with or without stems, flags, etc. [see Notes]. Additional symbols of modern notation are *accidentals, *key signature, *time signature, *dynamic marks, *tempo marks, *expression marks, the *tie, the *slur, etc. The modern system of notation dates from the early 17th century. Previously, systems of notation had been used that differ more or less radically from the present one regarding either the indication of rhythm (as in mensural notation) or that of pitch (as in the tablatures). Below is a brief survey of the evolution of notation (in Europe).

II. Greek music was notated by means of letters. Two systems were in use: an older one (used chiefly for instrumental music and evidently devised for the kithara), which included certain ancient symbols (Phoenician letters?) and used these symbols in different positions, upright, reversed, etc. [see under Pyknon]; and a more recent one (used chiefly for vocal music), which employed the Ionic alphabet together with a few additional signs [see *ReMMA* pp. 26, 27; C. Sachs, in *ZMW* vi, vii]. This method left no immediate traces in the musical notation of the Christian era [for a 9th-century revival, see Daseian notation]. The ensuing development and, for that matter, our modern system of notation are rooted not in the notational signs of Greek music but in the much vaguer symbols of Greek and Oriental (Jewish) speech recitation, the grammatical accents [see Accent (3)] of the 2nd century B.C., and similar signs known generically as ecphonetic notation. These developed (c. 800?) into a more elaborate system of stenographic symbols vaguely indicating the outlines of the melodic movement, the *neumes. Far from being "primitive" (as they are frequently described), the neumes are a very sensitive and supple means of recording the innumerable finesses of ancient singing, involving special techniques that today survive only in Oriental music. On the other hand, owing to their failure to clearly indicate pitch as well as rhythm, they are not a fully developed notation but only a mnemonic aid for the oral transmission of the chant. As early as the 9th century various methods were designed to remedy the indefiniteness of the neumes, chiefly by the addition of letters [see Letter notation; Romanus letters]. More important were the modifications that took place during the 11th century, leading from the vague chironomic symbols to shapes that corresponded more accurately to the rise and fall of the melody, the diastematic neumes. This evolution was stabilized by the adoption of staff lines, first one, then two, and finally four. About 1200, the neumes acquired the square shapes that are still used in the liturgical books of the Roman Catholic Church. See Neumes.

III. The square shapes [see Ex. 1] were soon adopted for the notation of monophonic secular melodies [see Monophonic notation] as well as for polyphonic music, where they are known as

1

*ligatures. The introduction of the square shapes was accompanied, shortly before 1200, by the establishment of definite rhythmic values on the basis of the rhythmic *modes. The resulting system is known as *square or *modal notation [Ex. 2]. There followed, during the 13th and 14th

the motet [Ex. 3]; about 1250, the introduction of a smaller note value, called *semibrevis,* two or three of which could be used in place of a *brevis;* about 1260, the unequivocal rhythmic interpretation of the ligatures, independent of the modes (Franco of Cologne; usually considered the beginning of *mensural notation); about 1280, the introduction of more than three semibreves (up to seven) in place of a *brevis* (Petrus de Cruce). Shortly after 1300, the restriction to modal rhythm, i.e., to ternary meter, that prevailed throughout the 13th century [see *Ars antiqua*] was abandoned, and the basic principles of rhythm and notation were radically revised by Philippe de Vitry. The new system, expounded in his treatise "Ars nova" (*c.* 1320), recognized duple and triple rhythm as equally important and applied this dichotomy to all the note values in the different mensurations: *modus* (*longa-brevis*), *tempus* (*brevis-semibrevis*), and *prolatio*

Motet "Ave beatissima," Montpellier, Fac. de Méd. H. 196.

(*semibrevis-minima*). The notational principles of this period remained virtually unchanged until the end of the 16th century, the only modification being the change, *c.* 1450, from black notes (black mensural notation) to white notes (white mensural notation). The explanations of the latter system, found under Mensural notation, therefore cover also the principles (though not the details) of black mensural notation.

2

Organum triplum "Descendit," Wolfenbüttel 1206 (olim Helmstedt 1099).

centuries, an extremely rapid development, involving frequent changes and innovations: the introduction of two different note values, called *longa* and *brevis* (*c.* 1225), which became necessary for the notation of the texted parts of

579

Simultaneously with Vitry's system, however, there developed a different system in Italy (Italian notation) that retained to a greater extent the principles of the late 13th century (particularly the Petronian groups of semibreves, i.e., those of Petrus de Cruce). After 1350 this system incorporated features of the contemporary and more progressive French system, thus leading to a system (Mixed notation) that was used by Francesco Landini and other composers of the second half of the 14th century [Ex. 4].

F. Landini, Nessun ponga sperança, Florence, Bibl. Laur. Pal. 87, Squarcialupi Codex.

coloration ligatures

Pierre de la Rue, Missa L'Homme armé, "Patrem" (Misse Petri de la Rue, Petrucci, 1503).

Toward the end of this century, notation became so complicated that the pieces of this period now represent the most interesting problems in the study of notation (mannered notation).

IV. In the first half of the 15th century (Dufay) these complications were largely abandoned. There resulted what might be called the "classical" system of mensural notation (c. 1450–1600), characterized by the use of white instead of black notes (white mensural notation; Ex. 5). Its principles are the same as those of the French notation of the Machaut period, except for the addition of the *proportions as a notational device and the occasional use of riddle canons [see Canon III]. This is the notation used by the Flemish masters Ockeghem, Obrecht, and their numerous successors. In the latter part of the 16th century triple mensuration (*tempus perfectum, prolatio perfecta*) as well as the ligatures were largely discarded, together with other special methods of mensural notation (proportions). Thus, the system of notation became virtually that of the present day, particularly after the general acceptance of *bar lines and score arrangement [see Score; Partbooks]. Throughout the 17th century, however, remnants of the older system lingered on, particularly the use of blackened notes (coloration) and proportional signs [see Time signatures]. Of these the *alla breve sign is the only one that has survived. The accompanying example illustrates the development of the main notational signs in six periods.

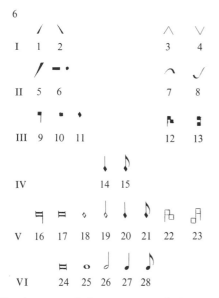

I. Greek accents: *1. Accentus acutus; 2. Acc. gravis; 3. Acc. circumflexis; 4. Hypothetical.* II. Neumes: *5. Virga; 6. Punctum; 7. Podatus; 8. Clivis.* III. Black mensural notation (1250): *9. Longa; 10. Brevis; 11. Semibrevis; 12. Descending ligature; 13. Ascending ligature.* IV. Additional signs of the 14th century: *14. Minima; 15. Semiminima.* V. White mensural notation (1450): *16. =9; 17. =10; 18. =11; 19. =14; 20. =15; 21. Fusa; 22. =12; 23. =13.* VI. Modern notation (after 1600): *24. Breve or double-whole note; 25. Whole note; 26. Half note; 27. Quarter note; 28. Eighth note.*

V. Side by side with the system of mensural notation there existed, particularly in the period 1450–1600, special notational methods known as *tablatures. These were used for writing down keyboard and lute music (generally solo music, while mensural notation was used for ensemble music; see Ensemble). Some of these systems use the ordinary mensural notes, differing from mensural notation only in that the parts are written in score, as in the modern piano score or the modern partitura. These may be designated as keyboard scores or keyboard partituras, as opposed to the tablatures proper, which use letters, figures, or other symbols instead of notes.

Surveys of modern attempts at reform are given in *WoHN* ii, 335ff, and A. Eaglefield-Hull, *A Dictionary of Modern Music* (1924). Entirely novel methods of notation have been devised for *electronic music and *musique concrète.

VI. In the Far East various notational systems were developed, especially in China, Korea, Japan, and India. All these employ pitch symbols derived from literary script, some of them with additional symbols for duration and for special effects (e.g., loud, soft, different manners of plucking stringed instruments or beating drums, etc.). The Tibetan notation of Buddhist chant employs oddly curved symbols that are vaguely reminiscent of the neumatic symbols of Western chant.

See also: Accidentals; Braille music notation; Chevé system; *Chiavette;* Clef; Daseian notation; Ecphonetic notation; Letter notation; Ligatures; Mensural notation; Microtone; Monophonic notation; *Musica ficta; Nagelschrift;* Neumes; Notes; Partbooks; Partial signature; *Plica;* Proportions; *Punctus;* Romanus letters; Score; Square notation; Staff; Staffless notation; Tablature; Tie; Time signatures; Tonic sol-fa.

Lit.: *ApNPM;* C. Parrish, *The Notation of Medieval Music* (1957); *WoHN; WoGM;* J. Wolf, *Musikalische Schrifttafeln* (facsimiles; 1927); *id., Die Tonschriften* (1924); H. Bellermann, *Die Mensuralnoten und Taktzeichen des XV. und XVI. Jahrhunderts* (1858); H. Riemann, *Studien zur Geschichte der Notenschrift* (1878); F. Gennrich, *Abriss der frankonischen Mensuralnotation,* rev. ed. (1956; facsimiles); *id., Abriss der Mensuralnotation des XIV. und ... XV. Jahrhunderts* (1948; facsimiles); E. Thomas, ed., *Notation neuer Musik* (Darmstädter Beiträge zur Neuen Musik, ix); A. Machabey, *La Notation musicale* (1952); A. Tirabassi, *Grammaire de la notation proportionelle* (1930); G. Vecchi, *Átlante paleografico musicale* (facsimiles; 1951).

Modern notation: H. E. Laing and A. W. Brown, *The Standard System of Musical Notation* (1928); J. Chailley, *Les Notations musicales nouvelles* (1950). See also under Mensural notation; Tablature; Square notation; Monophonic notation.

Note-against-note style. See Homorhythmic.

Note nere [It.]. See under Chromatic (4).

Notes. The signs with which music is written on a staff. In British usage the term also means the sound indicated by a note, as well as the key of the piano on which the sound is produced [see under Tone (2)].

The illustration shows the note values with their American names. British, French, German, Italian, and Spanish terms are given below. The

o	[▬]	whole note
𝅗𝅥	[▬]	half note
♩	[𝄽]	quarter note
♪	[𝄾]	eighth note
♬	[𝄿]	sixteenth note
♬	[𝅀]	thirty-second note
♬	[𝅁]	sixty-fourth note

Whole note: Brit. semibreve; F. ronde; G. Ganze (Note); It. semibreve; Sp. redonda. Half note: Brit. minim; F. blanche; G. Halbe (Note); It. bianca; Sp. blanca. Quarter note: Brit. crotchet; F. noire [soupir]; G. Viertel; It. nera; Sp. negra. Eighth note: Brit. quaver; F. croche; G. Achtel; It. croma; Sp. corchea. Sixteenth note: Brit. semiquaver; F. double-croche; G. Sechzehntel; It. semicroma; Sp. semicorchea. Thirty-second note: Brit. demisemiquaver; F. triple-croche; G. Zweiunddreissigstel; It. biscroma; Sp. fusa. Sixty-fourth note: Brit. hemidemisemiquaver; F. quadruple-croche; G. Vierundsechzigstel; It. semibiscroma; Sp. semifusa.

German names for the rests are: ganze (halbe, viertel, etc.) Pause; Italian: pausa di semibreve (bianca, etc.); French: pause, demi-pause, soupir, demi-soupir, quart de soupir, huitième de soupir, seizième de soupir; Spanish: silencio de redonda (blanca, negra, corchea, semicorchea, fusa, semifusa).

Note sensible [F.]. *Leading tone.

Notes inégales [F.]. See *Inégales.*

Nothus [L.]. A term used by Regino of Prüm (d. 915) for certain antiphons (*antiphonae nothae*) of irregular tonal behavior, "beginning in one mode, belonging to another in the middle, and finishing in a third" [GS i, 231]. The examples he cites belong to a type [Gevaert's *thème 29,* in *La Mélopée antique dans le chant de l'église latine* (1895), p. 322] that is represented by more than eighty antiphons. See *Parapter.*

Notre Dame, school of. Designation for a school of French polyphonic music of *c.* 1200, whose leading composers—the only ones known by

name—were Leoninus (second half of the 12th cent.) and Perotinus (*c.* 1160–1220). The name is based on the surmise (a very likely one) that both masters were connected with the famous cathedral of Paris, whose cornerstone was laid in 1163. The repertory of the school of Notre Dame, preserved mainly in the MSS *F, W₁* and *W₂* [see Sources, no. 3], consists of a collection of two-part organa known as the *"Magnus liber organi," additional organa in two, three, and four parts, and numerous *clausulae, *conductus, and early *motets. See *Ars antiqua.*

Lit.: See under *Ars antiqua;* Conductus; Organum. See also J. Handschin, "Zur Geschichte von Notre Dame" (*AM* iv); *id.,* "Was brachte die Notre Dame-Schule Neues?" (*ZMW* vi); *id.,* "Zur Notre Dame-Rhythmik" (*ZMW* vii).

Notturno [It.]. (1) *Nocturne. (2) An 18th-century name for compositions similar to the *serenade, designed to be played as an evening entertainment. Notable examples are Haydn's *Notturni* of 1790, for 2 *lire organizzate* (*hurdy-gurdies), 2 clarinets, 2 horns, 2 violas, and bass; six of them have three movements, one four, and one two. Mozart wrote a *Notturno* for strings and 2 horns (K. 269a).

Nourri, bien [F.]. With a rich sound.

Novachord. See under Electronic instruments II.

Nowell. *Noel.

Nozze di Figaro, Le [It., The Marriage of Figaro]. Opera in four acts by Mozart (libretto by L. da Ponte, after Beaumarchais' play *La Folle Journée ou Le Mariage de Figaro,* sequel to his *Le Barbier de Seville,* the source of Rossini's *Barbiere di Siviglia*), produced in Vienna, 1786. Setting: castle near Seville, 18th century. *Figaro* and *Don Giovanni* generally are considered Mozart's finest operas.

Nuances [F.]. Subtle modifications of intensity, tempo, touch, phrasing, etc. The term is also used as a translation of the Greek *chroai,* and for other microtonic intervals.

Number opera [G. *Nummernoper*]. An opera written in single "numbers," i.e., separate pieces such as arias, duets, ensembles, and ballets, interspersed with recitative or spoken dialogue. This type of opera prevailed until the early 19th century. It was vehemently opposed by Wagner, who supplanted it with continuous music that follows the action without interruption. His procedure has been adopted by practically all subsequent operatic composers. It must be noted, however, that replacement of the "number style" with continuous writing began as early as the operas of Jommelli, Traetta, Gluck, and particularly Mozart, whose late operas (*Le Nozze di Figaro, Don Giovanni*) contain several long sections in which various numbers are linked together by transitional passages to make a complete, well-rounded musical whole. This tendency is still more pronounced in the operas of Beethoven, Weber, and Meyerbeer, while French and Italian composers such as Auber, Rossini, Bellini, and Donizetti generally adhered to the number opera. Some composers of the 20th century have deliberately revived the form of the number opera, examples being Hindemith's *Cardillac* (1926; rev. 1952), and Stravinsky's *The Rake's Progress* (1951). See Opera VIII, XI.

Number symbolism. Secret numerical relationships supposed to exist in the works of great masters, especially Bach. Attempts to find such relationships are based on one or another system of assigning numbers, e.g., A = 1, B = 2, etc. According to this system the letters BACH total 14, while J. S. BACH totals 41; in his last work, the organ chorale *Vor deinen Thron,* the first line of the melody has 14 notes, the entire melody 41. See M. Jansen, "Bachs Zahlensymbolik" (*BJ* 1937).

Nunc dimittis. See under Canticle.

Nuove musiche [It.]. (1) Title of a publication of 1601 by Giulio Caccini (*c.* 1546–1618), containing arias and madrigals in the then new style of monodic recitative with thoroughbass accompaniment. For the difference between aria and madrigal in this work, see Aria II.

(2) Today, the term is used for music of the whole period around 1600, which is one of the most important landmarks in music history since it marks the origin of the opera, oratorio, cantata, and the baroque period in general [see History of music]. The leading idea of the new movement was to abolish the Flemish tradition of the 16th century, with its emphasis on counterpoint and artful elaboration. Particularly objectionable was the obscuring of the text that resulted from polyphonic treatment and from the motet style, with its characteristic points of imitation. The reaction against this style led, in the course of a few decades, to a complete reversal of the relationship between music and

text, as was clearly expressed by Monteverdi (*Scherzi musicali,* 1607): "L'orazione sia padrona dell' armonia e non serva" (The text should be the master, not the servant, of the music). As a result, the polyphonic *a cappella* style was replaced by accompanied solo song (*aria, *monody, *recitative).

These tendencies found strong theoretical support in classical studies of Greek theory, which, about 1580, were pursued by Vincenzo Galilei (1520–91) and others known as the *Camerata. Although they could not decipher the remnants of Greek music then available and so relied on ancient writings, these men formed a picture of the role that music had played in the ancient Greek drama, and made the perfect union of words and music (in Greek music always a monophonic rendition of the text) their own goal. Although accompanied solo songs in rather plain homophonic style had been written in Spain as early as 1530 (vihuela songs by Milán, E. de Valderrábano), it was not until the last years of the century that the open break with the tradition occurred, in the earliest operas of Peri and Caccini [see Opera III], which were based exclusively on the principle of monody. Caccini in his *Nuove musiche* applied the new style to short lyrics, giving it a subtler, more expressive design. Cavalieri, another pioneer of the new style, used it in his *La *Rappresentazione di anima e di corpo* of 1600 [see Oratorio II], a work that, owing to its inclusion of choral passages [see *SchGMB,* no. 169], is less radical but actually more progressive than those of Peri and Caccini. In fact, the limitations of the *stile rappresentativo* soon became patent. Music could not, for any length of time, be completely subjugated to the role of a mere servant, and musicians began to resume some of the trends that had too abruptly been halted. As early as 1607 Monteverdi's *Orfeo* showed that mixture of old and new ideas upon which the imposing structure of the baroque was to be built. See R. Paoli, "Difesa del primo melodramma" (*LRM* 1950, xx, 93); M. Mila, in *LRM* 1933, vi, 219 (Peri); M. Feller, in *CP* 1958 (Caccini); C. Palisca, in *MQ* xlvi (Galilei). (See also under Baroque music; Camerata.

Nut. See under Frog.

Nutcracker Suite. Orchestral suite in six movements by Tchaikovsky, op. 71a (1891), arranged from his ballet *The Nutcracker* [F. *Cassenoisette*], based on E. T. A. Hoffmann's fairy tale, *The Nutcracker and the Mouse King.*

O

O. This or similar signs (circle; zero) are used as follows: (1) In music for violins, etc., to indicate the open string. (2) In English *fingering for keyboard, as a sign for the thumb. (3) In thorough-bass parts, as a sign for *tasto solo;* see Thoroughbass 6. (4) In *mensural notation, as a sign for *tempus perfectum* (circle). (5) In medieval tonaries, as a sign for the seventh church mode, e.g. in the Codex Hartker.

O antiphons. Antiphons used for the Magnificat during the week preceding the Nativity, so called because they all begin with the exclamation "O": *O sapientia, O Adonai, O Radix Jesse,* etc. [see *LU*, pp. 340ff]. Also known as Great Antiphons, they all are sung to a standard melody of the second mode. The late 14th-century Codex Torino Bibl. Naz. *J II 9* [see Sources, no. 18] contains polyphonic settings of these chants. See A. Cabaniss, "A Note on the Date of the Great Advent Antiphons" (*Speculum* xxii).

Obbligato [It.]. Obligatory, usually with reference to an instrument (*violino obbligato*) or part that must not be omitted; the opposite is *ad libitum.* Unfortunately, through misunderstanding or carelessness, the term has come to mean a mere accompanying part that may be omitted if necessary. As a result, one must decide in each individual case whether obbligato means "obbligato" or "ad libitum"; usually it means the former in early music and the latter in more recent pieces. For *accompanimento obbligato,* see under Accompaniment.

Obbligo, obligo [It.]. In 17th- and 18th-century counterpoint, *con obbligo* means a manner of writing that involves certain "obligations," such as canon, double counterpoint, inversion, etc. Early examples are Frescobaldi's "Capriccio di obligo di cantare la quinta parte" (calling for the addition of a short melody at suitable places) and his "Recercar ottavo, obligo di non uscir mai di grado" (obligation to avoid conjunct motion), both in *Il primo libro di capricci* (1626).

Oberdominante [G.]. Dominant, as opposed to *Unterdominante,* subdominant.

Oberstimme [G.]. Upper part.

Obertas [Pol.]. A Polish round dance in quick triple meter and performed very vigorously, like a wild waltz. Examples are in Wieniawski's *Mazurka Charactéristique* no. 1 (for violin) and in the first act of Boito's *Mefistofele.* Chopin's Mazurka op. 56, no. 2 is in the character of an *obertas.* A modern example is in A. Tansman's *Quatre Danses Polonaises* [1932] for orchestra. Another name, more commonly used today, is *oberek.*

Obertaste [G.]. See *Taste.*

Oberton, Obertöne [G.]. Upper harmonic(s).

Oberwerk [G.]. Swell organ.

Obligat [G.]. *Obbligato.

Oblique motion. See Motion.

Oboe family. A large group of *wind instruments having a double reed [see Reed; Mouthpiece], in contrast to the *clarinet family, comprising the wind instruments with a single reed. Strictly speaking, the oboe, English horn, bassoon, etc., constitute families of their own, since each of these instruments existed in various sizes [see N. Bessaraboff, *Ancient European Musical Instruments* (1941), p. 111]. In the present article these distinctions will be disregarded. The instruments of the present-day orchestra are discussed below under I, and those that are rarely used or obsolete under II, while a historical survey is given under III. All these instruments (with the exception of some old types) have a conical bore, in contrast to the cylindrical bore of the clarinets.

I. *Present-day forms.* A. Oboe [F. *hautbois*]. The oboe consists of a conical pipe made of wood (usually in three sections: top joint, lower joint, and bell) with a double reed fixed to the upper end. The scale produced when the six finger holes are opened in succession is D (as is that of the flute); nevertheless, the oboe is not treated as a transposing instrument and hence is considered to be in the key of C. Owing to its conical bore, the oboe overblows at the octave, as do all the other members of the family. For the difference in timbre between the oboe and the clarinet, see Clarinet family I.

The oboe seems to have originated in the mid-17th century. Cambert's *Pomone* (1671) has a part for "Hautbois." The repertory for oboe includes concertos by Handel and K. P. E. Bach, Schumann's *Drei Romanzen* op. 94, Piston's *Suite* (1934), Hindemith's Sonata (1939), and

Nielsen's *Fantasiestücke* op. 2. For bibl. see end of section III.

B. The English horn [F. *cor anglais;* G. *englisches Horn;* It. *corno inglese;* Sp. *corno inglés*]. An alto oboe, pitched a fifth below the oboe. To facilitate the handling of this rather long instrument, the double reed may be carried on a small metal tube attached to the upper end and bent back toward the player's mouth. Its bell is pear-shaped, with a rather small opening [see II, A], which accounts for its soft, somewhat melancholy timbre. It is treated as a transposing instrument, the parts sounding a fifth lower than written. Early instruments of this size were curved like an animal's horn, a fact that explains half of its name; it is not known why it is called "English" [see II, B]. In the early part of the 19th century, the English horn is thought to have gradually replaced the older *oboe da caccia.* Early uses of the English horn are in Jommelli's *Ezio* (1741), J. A. Hasse's *Il Trionfo di Clelia* (1762), and Haydn's Symphony no. 22. By about 1830 the instrument was generally accepted into the orchestra; Rossini used it in *Guillaume Tell* (1829) and Meyerbeer in *Robert le diable* (1831).

C. Bassoon [F. *basson;* G. *Fagott;* It. *fagotto;* Sp. *fagote*]. The bass of the oboe family. Owing to the great length of the tube, it is bent back on itself, first descending and then ascending. The instrument consists of five sections: the *crook*

Normal ranges: a. Oboe.   b. English horn.   c. Bassoon.   d. Contrabassoon.

(bocal), a narrow, curved metal tube to which the reed is attached; the *wing* or *tenor joint,* which forms the descending section of the pipe; the *butt* or *double joint,* the bottom section, in the shape of a U; the *bass* or *long joint,* which forms the ascending pipe; and the *bell.* The instrument is remarkably even in tone color, although the lowest fifth of its range tends to be rather thick and reedy and the highest fifth is somewhat "pinched" and terse. It has a wide dynamic range, and all kinds of legato and staccato figures can easily be performed on it. It blends well with the French horns, with which it is often used, but is equally valuable as a solo instrument or as a bass to the woodwind section. The bassoon is specified in several compositions by Schütz (e.g.,

Symphoniae sacrae, 1629). In 1645, A. Bertali published nine "Sonatas" for bassoon solo (*Compositioni musicali fatte per sonare col fagotto solo*). Vivaldi wrote a great many concertos for bassoon alone or with other solo instruments. Bassoon concertos were written by Mozart (K. 191) and Weber (op. 75), and a sonata by Hindemith (1938). See L. G. Langwill, *The Bassoon and Contrabassoon* [1965]; W. Heckel, *Der Fagott,* rev. ed. (1931); W. Spencer, *The Art of Bassoon Playing* (1958); E. Halfpenny, "The Evolution of the Bassoon in England, 1750–1800" (*GSJ* x).

D. Contrabassoon or double bassoon [F. *contrebasson;* G. *Kontrafagott;* It. *contrafagotto;* Sp. *contrafagot*]. This instrument is pitched an octave below the bassoon. Its modern form, which was developed by Heckel (*c.* 1880), has a tube more than sixteen feet long that is doubled on itself four times. The bell points down instead of up, as in the bassoon. It is notated an octave above the actual sound (in Wagner's *Parsifal* it is written at its true pitch). Both the lowest and highest tones of its range are rather unsatisfactory and therefore are less frequently used. An older form of double bassoon was used by Handel in the *Coronation Anthem* (1727) and in *L'Allegro* (1740). Haydn scored for it in *The Creation,* and Beethoven used it in his Fifth and Ninth Symphonies. In 1739 a giant instrument, three times the size of the normal one, was built [see E. Halfpenny, in *ML* xxxiv, 41ff]. See L. G. Langwill, "The Double-Bassoon" (*PMA* lxix, 1ff).

II. *Rare and obsolete forms.* The oboes of the 18th and early 19th centuries were much more strident and piercing in sound than the modern instruments, a statement even more true of still earlier instruments [see under Aulos].

A. Oboe d'amore. A mezzo-soprano instrument pitched a minor third below the ordinary oboe and having the characteristic pear-shaped bell [G. *Liebesfuss*] of today's English horn. The name probably refers to its sound, which was "sweeter" than that of the other oboes of the day. It was invented *c.* 1720, one of its earliest uses being in Bach's cantata no. 37, "Wer da glaubet" (*c.* 1727). A reconstructed form is called for in R. Strauss's *Sinfonia Domestica* to characterize the "dreaming child."

B. Oboe da caccia. Probably an alto oboe in F, with an expanding bell or, more frequently, a pear-shaped bell that rendered the sound less strident. The instrument was built in the shape of a curved hunting horn and may have been the

OBOE FAMILY

1. Double bassoon or contrabassoon. 2. Bassoon. 3. English horn. 4. Oboe. 5. Heckelphone.
6. Sarrusophone.

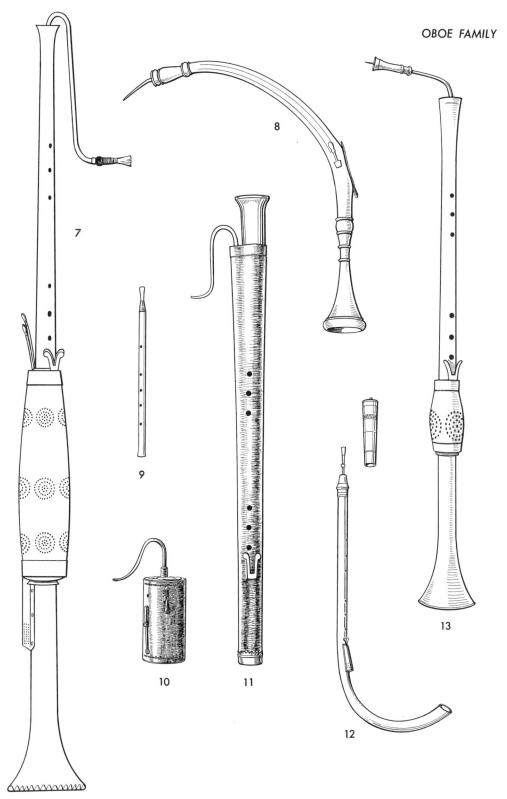

7. Shawm (bass). 8. Oboe da caccia. 9. Aulos. 10. Racket. 11. Curtal, double. 12. Crumhorn (tenor). 13. Shawm (tenor).

model for the old, curved form of the English horn.

C. Tenoroon. A small bassoon pitched a fifth above the ordinary bassoon. Invented and used in the first half of the 19th century, it is now obsolete.

D. Quartfagott, Quintfagott. According to M. Praetorius (*De Organographia*, 1619), instruments pitched respectively a fourth and a fifth below the ordinary bassoon. In the 18th and 19th centuries the names were used for small bassoons pitched a fourth or a fifth above the ordinary bassoon, like the tenoroon [see above].

E. Heckelphone. A baritone oboe invented by Heckel in 1904 and pitched an octave below the oboe. Built in a straight shape with a bulb-shaped bell, it has a bore much wider than the oboe's. In spite of its full, rich sound it has been little used (R. Strauss, *Salome;* Delius).

F. Sarrusophone. A whole family of double-reed brass instruments, invented by the French bandmaster Sarrus (patented 1856) and made in eight sizes, from sopranino to subcontrabass. The only sarrusophone used in the orchestra is a contrabass size in C that has the same compass as the contrabassoon and has been preferred by numerous French composers to the contra-bassoon. The smaller sizes are obsolete, but the larger ones continue to be used in some wind and rhythm bands, especially in Italy.

III. *History.* Double-reed instruments are very ancient and widespread, much more so than single-reed instruments (clarinets). They usually occur in pairs (double oboe), the longer pipe probably being used to provide a drone or, perhaps, some tones missing in the shorter one. Sumerian double oboes are documented as far back as 2800 B.C., and similar instruments common in Egypt, Israel (*halil;* see Jewish music I), Greece (*aulos), and Rome (*tibia*). They are found in practically all the countries of Asia, where they are usually provided with a metal disk against which the player's lips are stretched (he takes the reed entirely into his mouth—not, as in European practice, between his lips). Because Egyptian oboe players blow continuously, they must breathe exclusively through the nose [see *Launeddas*]. The indigenous oboe of China (*kuan*) and Japan (*hichiriki*) is cylindrical. A conical type is an importation from India, where oboe music "is in great demand at weddings, ceremonials, processions and festivals. Expert performers are paid fabulous sums" [see *SaHMI,* p. 230].

The early European ancestor of the oboe is the *shawm,* which was used until the 17th century. In France it was called *bombarde, chalemie;* in Germany, *Pommern (Bomhart, Pumhart),* except for the highest member of the group, which was known as *Schalmei;* in Italy, *piffaro;* in Spain, *chirimia.* The earliest reference to such an instrument is in French literary sources of the 13th century. Probably introduced from the Near East in the 12th century, it consisted of a single piece of wood curving in a bell. By the 16th century shawms existed in all sizes, ranging from sopranino (Praetorius' *Klein-Schalmey*) to double bass (*Gross-Bass-Pommer*), the name "shawm" being reserved for the soprano instrument while the lower-pitched instruments were called *bombard.* The bombards (all straight tubes) were soon abandoned in favor of shortened shapes called *curtals* [F. *courtaut;* G. **Kortholt,* "short wood," referring to the instrument's shortened form, i.e., with folded tube]. These instruments [F. *basson, fagot;* G. *Dulzian, Fagott;* It. *fagotto;* Sp. *bajón*] were forerunners of the modern bassoon but were made from a single block of wood with two parallel bores, one descending and one ascending.

Numerous other types of double-reed instrument are described by Praetorius under names such as *Sordune, Schryari,* and *Bassanelli.* The *Sordune* [F. *sourdines*] had a channel running down and up two or three times within the same piece of wood, ending in a lateral hole [see *SaHMI,* p. 317f]. More important are the *crumhorns* [F. *cromorne, tournebout;* G. *Krummhorn;* It. *storto;* Sp. *orlo*], which are depicted in paintings of the 15th and 16th centuries as held by angels. Their tube was nearly cylindrical, curved upward like a J, and a pierced cap (wind cap) covered the reed so that the player could not touch it [see ill. in *SaHMI,* p. 320]. The cap served as a wind chamber, so that the reed was set in vibration much as in the reed pipes of the organ. Thus the sound was as unchangeable as that of an organ pipe, i.e., overblowing was impossible. The instrument was used until about the mid-17th century. One of the strangest instruments is the *racket* [G. *Rackett, Rankett*], a short, thick cylinder of solid wood pierced lengthwise by ten cylindrical channels connected so as to form a continuous tube. Praetorius described four sizes of racket. Toward the end of the 17th century a new version was devised with a conical tube and bore and a bassoon-like bell. It came to be known as racket bassoon or sausage bassoon [G. *Wurstfagott*]. See H. Seidl, "Das Rackett" (diss. Leipzig, 1959).

Lit. (for Oboe): P. Bate, *The Oboe* [1956]; R. Sprenkle and D. Ledet, *The Art of Oboe Playing* [1961]; E. Halfpenny, "The English 2- and 3-keyed Hautboy" (*GSJ* ii); *id.*, "The 'Tenner Hoboy'" (*GSJ* v); *id.*, "The French Hautboy: A Technical Survey" (*GSJ* vi and viii); J. Marx, "The Tone of the Baroque Oboe" (*GSJ* iv). I by W.D.D.

Obra [Sp.]. General designation for work, as in the *Obras de música* (1578) by Antonio de Cabezón. Specifically, a **tiento*, e.g., *Obra de 8° tono* (Jiménez).

Ocarina. A popular instrument in the shape of an egg, a bird, or a sweet potato (the last name commonly used in the U.S.), with a mouth-hole and a number of finger holes. It is classified as a globular flute, a type with an interesting ancestry in China and Africa [see *SaHMI*, p. 166f].

Occursus [L.]. In the 9th- and 10th-century organum of the fourth, the unison-confluence of the two parts employed at the beginning and end of phrases (converging organum; see Organum I). The term is used (for the first time?) in Guido's "Micrologus," ch. xviii: "De Diaphonia."

Octave. (1) The eighth tone of the diatonic scale [see Interval]. Acoustically, the tone with twice the frequency of the home tone (ratio 1:2; e.g., $a' = 440$; $a'' = 880$). The octave is the most perfect consonance, so perfect that it gives the impression of duplicating the original tone, a phenomenon for which no convincing explanation has ever been found. Its singularity becomes apparent if the acoustical frequencies are compared with the series of color frequencies (spectrum), which does not show any such duplication [see Color and music]. The fundamental importance of the octave appears also from the fact that it is the only interval common to practically all the scales ever evolved, regardless of the number or pitch of the intermediate steps. For the designation of the various octaves, see Pitch names.

(2) In ecclesiastical terminology, the eighth day or the entire week after a feast.

Octave species [G. *Oktavgattungen*]. See under Greece II.

Octavier [F.]. See under Wind instruments III.

Octet. Chamber music for eight instruments, either all strings (Mendelssohn, Gade, Enesco), all winds (Beethoven, op. 103; Stravinsky), or mixed (Schubert, Spohr).

Octobasse. See under Violin family (j).

Octoechos. See *Echos*.

Oda [It.]. A 14th- and 15th-century type of Italian poetry consisting of a number of four-line stanzas with the rhyme scheme *a a a b* (repeated) or *a b b c c d d e e f f g* . . . . Petrucci's collections of **frottole* include several *ode*, composed as strophic songs. See A. Einstein, *The Italian Madrigal*, 3 vols. (1949), i, 91f; E. B. Helm, in *MQ* xxvii, 308.

Oddonic letters. See Letter notation.

Ode. (1) In poetry (ancient Greek and Latin as well as modern), a poem in free meter and verse structure, frequently addressed to a deity. Odes are usually composed in a free form similar to that of the cantata, including several movements or sections for chorus, soloist, and orchestra. Dryden's "Ode on St. Cecilia's Day" (set by Handel) and Schiller's "Ode to Joy" (set by Beethoven, Ninth Symphony) are well-known examples.

In the 16th century the Horatian odes were frequently set to music in strict chordal style and in a rhythm dictated by the poetic meter, e.g.:

Mǣē - cē - nās ǎ - tǎ - vīs ē - dī - tě rē - gǐ - būs

This practice was inaugurated by Konrad Celtis, professor of poetry at the University of Ingolstadt (1492–97). Among the earliest publications of such odes are: Petronius Tritonius, *Melopoiae sive harmoniae tetracenticae super xxii genera carminum heroicorum* (1507); Paulus Hofhaimer, *Harmoniae poeticae* (1539), Ludwig Senfl, *Varia carminum genera* (1534), and Claude Goudimel, *Q. Horatii Flacci poetae lyrici odae . . . ad rhythmos musicos redactae* (1555). Examples for the lute occur in Judenkünig's *Ain schone kunstliche Underweisung* of 1523 [see *DTO* 56; *ApMZ* i]. In France this poetic modification of musical rhythm [see Rhythm II (b)] led to the **vers mesuré*. See Humanism.

(2) In Byzantine chant, *ode* is one of the nine sections of the *kanon*, each written in imitation of a scriptural canticle. See Byzantine chant II.

Lit.: R. von Liliencron, in *VMW* iii; P. Masson, in *RMC* vi; H. J. Moser, *Paul Hofhaimer* (1929), Appendix, pp. 112ff; *id.*, *Geschichte der deutschen Musik* i (1920), 406ff.

Ode to Napoleon Buonaparte. Composition by A. Schoenberg, op. 41b (1942), based on Byron's poem, scored for string orchestra, piano, and a reciting voice. The text is a bitter comment on the downfall of dictators. The work is organized as an opera without action, with an overture, arias, and recitatives, and, for its significance at the time of composition, a quotation of the opening "Victory" theme from Beethoven's Fifth Symphony.

Odhecaton. Title (complete form: *Harmonice musices Odhecaton A*) of a printed collection of "100 songs" (actually only 96) published by Petrucci in 1501. The book is the earliest printed publication of polyphonic music [see Printing of music] and of great importance as a collection of secular polyphonic music of the period c. 1470–1500. Similar collections, *Canti B* and *Canti C*, appeared in 1502 and 1504. The composers represented include Hayne van Ghizeghem [see Burgundian school], Ockeghem (1430–95), Obrecht (1452–1505), Isaac (c. 1450–1517), Alexander Agricola (c. 1446–1506), Josquin (c. 1450–1521), and many others. The fact that only nine pieces have a text does not necessarily prove that the contents of these books was exclusively instrumental music; indeed, a considerable number of the compositions are preserved in other sources (manuscripts) with a text, at least in the discant. On the other hand the omission of the texts, although perhaps conditioned by practical considerations (typographic problems), illustrates the latitude of 16th-century musical practice, which readily admitted instrumental performance of vocal pieces. It is, of course, impossible to assume that all the readers of these books were familiar with the texts of more than 300 compositions.

Lit.: ‡*Harmonice musices Odhecaton* (fac. ed. pub. by *Bollettino bibliografico musicale*, 1932); H. Hewitt, ed., ‡*Harmonice musices Odhecaton A* (1942); C. L. W. Boer, *Chansonvormen op het Einde van de XVde Eeuw* (1938); G. Reese, in *MQ* xx; M. Cauchie, "L'Odhecaton, recueil de musique instrumentale" (*RdM* 1925, p. 148); J. Marix, in *RdM* 1935, p. 236; B. Disertori, in *RMI* li.

Odoistic notation. Same as Oddonic notation; see Letter notation.

Oedipus Rex [L., King Oedipus]. Opera-oratorio in two acts by Stravinsky (libretto in Latin by J. Cocteau and J. Daniélou, based on Sophocles' tragedy), produced in Paris, 1927. Setting: ancient Thebes. The extensive use of the chorus for commentary, the use of a narrator, the reduction of the action to entrances and exists, and the minimal scenery all are reminiscent of ancient Greek tragedy and prevent the work from being called an opera in the usual sense. The underlying principles are similar to those of Cavalieri's *La *Rappresentazione di anima e di corpo* (1600).

Oeuvre [F.]. *Opus.

Offertory [L. *offertorium*]. In the Roman Catholic liturgy, the fourth item of the Proper of the Mass, accompanying the placing on the altar of the elements (bread and wine). Originally it was a psalm with antiphon (*antiphona ad offerendum*); today only the antiphon remains. However, the verses (published in C. Ott, *Offertoriale sive versus offertoriorum*, 1935) are of great stylistic interest [see *ApGC*, pp. 363ff; also R. Steiner, in *JAMS* xix]. Unlike the other antiphonal chants of the Mass (Introit, Communion), the Offertory acquired a highly developed melismatic style, thus becoming a responsorial chant.

Polyphonic settings of Offertories, based on the plainsong melodies, are found sporadically in 15th-century sources (Trent Codices). In England, the Offertory *"Felix namque" for Lady-Masses was set for organ as early as c. 1400 and frequently during the 16th century. Toward the end of the 16th century, Lassus (in *Sacrae cantiones*, 1582, '85) and Palestrina (In *Offertoria per totum annum*, 1593) published complete cycles of Offertories written as free motets, without use of the plainsong melodies. In the 17th century, the ceremony of offering became the most suitable occasion for organ playing. Frescobaldi wrote several pieces "per l'Elevazione" [see Elevation], and numerous *Offertoires* for organ with or without other instruments were composed by Lebègue, Grigny, F. Couperin, and others.

Office, Divine [L. *officium*]. In the Roman Catholic liturgy, the service of the canonical or daily hours (as distinct from that of the Mass), including *psalms, *canticles, *antiphons, *responsories, *hymns, *versicles, lessons (lections, readings), and prayers. The Offices are celebrated eight times a day: (1) *Matins* [L. *matutinum*], held during the night, usually between midnight and dawn; (2) *Lauds* [*laudes*], immediately following Matins, originally at sunrise; (3) *Prime* [*ad primam*], c. 6 a.m.; (4) *Terce* [*ad tertiam*], c. 9 a.m.; (5) *Sext* [*ad sextam*], c. noon; (6) *None* [*ad nonam*], c. 3 p.m.; (7) *Vespers* [*vesperae*], sunset; (8) *Compline* [*completorium*], immediately after Vespers or before retiring. The Mass follows Terce except on ordinary weekdays, when it follows Sext, or on fast days, when it follows None.

From the musical point of view the most important Offices are Matins, Vespers, Lauds, and Compline. The service of Matins consists of the *invitatory and three divisions called *nocturns,* each of which includes three psalms with antiphons and three lessons, each followed by a responsory. The last responsory is usually replaced by the *Te Deum. Matins is now held regularly only in monastic churches and is therefore not included in the *Antiphonale Romanum* [see Liturgical books II]. The *Liber usualis* includes Matins of Nativity [*LU,* pp. 368ff], Maundy Thursday [pp. 626ff], Good Friday [pp. 688ff], Holy Saturday [pp. 752ff], Pentecost [pp. 863ff], Corpus Christi [pp. 917ff], and the Office of the Dead [pp. 1779ff].

Vespers includes five psalms, each with an antiphon, a hymn, and the *Magnificat. It is the only Office for which music other than Gregorian chant is admitted. Beginning in the 16th century the evening psalms were frequently treated in four-voice harmony (so-called *fauxbourdon), and the Magnificat in particular has been given very elaborate settings by numerous great composers. Motets also find their place chiefly at Vespers. Mozart wrote two Vespers (K. 321 and 339) for voices, orchestra, and organ, each comprising five psalms and the Magnificat.

Lauds has the same structure as Vespers, but with the Canticle of Zachary ("Benedictus Dominus Deus Israel") instead of the Magnificat (Canticle of the Virgin), and with the fourth psalm replaced by one of the lesser *canticles, two of them being assigned to each day of the week—one for normal use, the other during Lent. The *Liber Usualis* includes the general order of Lauds of feasts (*LU,* pp. 221–23), as well as the special Lauds for the feasts named under Matins. The full service of Lauds is given in the *Antiphonale Romanum.*

Compline includes three psalms enframed by a single antiphon, a hymn, the Canticle of Simeon ("Nunc dimittis"), and the four Marian antiphons [see Antiphon (2)], one for each season of the year. The other hours—Prime to None—each include a hymn and three psalms enframed by a single antiphon.

The service for the hours on an ordinary Sunday is given in *LU,* pp. 224ff (without Matins and Lauds). See also *ApGC,* pp. 19ff; P. Batiffol, *Histoire du Bréviaire Romain* (1911); J. Pascher,

Das Stundengebet der röm. Kirche (1954); J. A. Jungmann, *Der Gottesdienst der Kirche* (1955), pp. 167–98; *id., Brevierstudien* (1958).

O I OU E A E. In the Anglican liturgical books, the usual abbreviation for "world without end, Amen" (i.e., the vowels from this phrase analogous to the Roman *E u o u a e).

Oiseau de feu, L' [F., The Firebird]. Ballet by Stravinsky, produced by the Ballets Russes (Diaghilev and Fokine) in Paris in 1910. The story, taken from Russian legend, concerns Prince Ivan who captures the fabulous Firebird. *L'Oiseau de feu* is an outstanding product of Stravinsky's early period, when the composer was following the nationalist tradition of his teacher, Rimsky-Korsakov. Three versions of a suite taken from the ballet have been made by the composer, the last (1945) identical with the first (1911), but for a smaller orchestra.

Oketus. See Hocket.

Oktave [G.]. Octave. Applied to instruments, it means sizes an octave above the normal size (e.g., *Oktavflöte,* piccolo flute), or below it (e.g., *Oktavfagott,* contrabassoon). *Oktavgattung,* Octave species.

Oktavieren [G.]. See under Wind instruments III.

Oktoechos. See *Echos.*

Old English Edition, The. See Editions XL.

Old Hall MS. See Sources, no. 25.

Old Hundredth. An old hymn tune that was used in Béza's *Genevan Psalter* (1554) for the 134th Psalm, in Knox's *Anglo-Genevan Psalter* (1556) for the 3rd Psalm, and in Sternhold and Hopkins' *Psalter* (1562) for the 100th Psalm (hence the name). See W. H. Havergal, *A History of the Old Hundredth Psalm Tune* (1854); *GDB* vi, 184f.

Old Maid and the Thief, The. Opera in one act by Menotti (to his own libretto), produced by N.B.C. radio in New York, 1939, stage premiere, Philadelphia, 1941. Setting: a small American town in the present.

Old Roman chant. A repertory of chant discovered *c.* 1890 and preserved in five MSS (the earliest dated 1071), all of which were written in Rome. Liturgically, it is very similar to Gregorian chant in both the structure of Mass and Office and the texts prescribed for the various services. However, the melodies are essentially different, although occasionally their outlines agree with those of the corresponding Gregorian melodies. Dom Mocquereau, who was the first to call attention to this special group of manuscripts (*Editions XLII, A, 2, pp. 4ff), considered the melodies variants from a decadent epoch. Dom Andoyer, on the contrary, maintained that they were older than the Gregorian melodies and designated them "pre-Gregorian," whereas B. Stäblein considered them "Gregorian," assigning the so-called Gregorian repertory to the second half of the 7th century. According to the most recent theory, the two repertories represent different locales rather than different periods, the Old Roman being connected with Rome and the Gregorian with the Frankish kingdom and empire of Pepin and Charlemagne. See *ApGC*, pp. 77ff, 484ff.

Olé. See under Polo.

Oliphant. A medieval instrument for signaling, made from an elephant's tusk, often beautifully carved.

Ombra scene [It.]. In early operas, designation for a scene that takes place in Hades or in which ghosts are conjured up. Every opera dealing with the subject of *Orpheus has an *ombra* scene.

Ondeggiando, ondulé [It., F.]. In violin playing, an undulating movement of the bow [see Bowing (n)]. It is used for arpeggio-like figures but also on one note in order to produce a slight fluctuation of intensity. In earlier music (c. 1650–1750; Purcell, Stamitz) the latter effect, which is actually a *tremolo, was rather common, being indicated by a wavy line [see ill. accompanying Ornamentation].

Ondes Martenot [F.]. See Electronic instruments II.

One-step. American dance of the period c. 1910–20, in quick duple meter, similar to the *fox trot. It was superseded, c. 1920, by the slower two-step (slow-fox).

Ongarese, all' [It.]. In Hungarian style.

Onion flute. Same as eunuch flute. See Mirliton.

Onzième [F.]. The interval of the eleventh.

Op. Abbr. for *opus.

Open fifth, open triad. A fifth or triad without the third, e.g., c–g–c'.

Open graces. See under Grace.

Open harmony. See under Spacing.

Open notes. (1) On wind instruments, same as natural notes. (2) On stringed instruments, the tones produced on the *open strings.

Open pipe. See under Wind instruments III.

Open strings. The unstopped strings of violins, lutes, etc. Their use is sometimes prescribed by the sign O.

Opera [It.; F. *opéra;* G. *Oper;* Sp. *ópera*]. "A drama in which music is the essential factor comprising songs with orchestral accompaniment (as *recitative, aria, chorus*) and orchestral preludes and interludes" (*Webster's Third New International Dictionary*).

I. *General.* Opera is the most important of the forms that combine music and theatrical representation. It is highly complex, involving many different arts—music (both instrumental and vocal), drama, poetry, acting, dance, stage design, costuming, etc.—and this fact accounts in part both for its widespread appeal and for the equally widespread objection that it is artistically impure. The classic statement of this critical attitude is Saint Evremond's definition of opera as "a bizarre affair made up of poetry and music, in which the poet and the musician, each equally obstructed by the other, give themselves no end of trouble to produce a wretched result" [*Oeuvres* (1740 ed. of Des Maizeau) iii, 248]. Because opera is, of all musical or dramatic forms, the most difficult and expensive to produce, it has been associated with the upper social strata, thus making it a "status symbol" for the public as well as an object of particular attraction for many ambitious composers and singers. Most operas have been composed by specialists in the form, the composers who have distinguished themselves equally in opera and other branches of music being exceedingly few—Monteverdi, Handel, Mozart, R. Strauss, Berlioz, Prokofiev, Britten, and Stravinsky being outstanding in this respect. On the other hand, composers such as Bach, Schubert, Schumann, Mendelssohn, Brahms, and Bruckner either did not attempt opera at all or did so without conspicuous success, while the achievements of Beethoven and Debussy are limited to one work each, albeit a masterpiece in both cases.

Like all art forms, opera is founded on certain conventions, the most important of which is that the characters express their thoughts and feelings in song rather than speech. Since it usually takes longer to develop ideas in music than in words, either or both of the following devices are often used: (1) a noticeable stretching out and consequent slow pace of the action (as in Wagner's music dramas); (2) alternating periods of action and repose, the action being carried on in *recitative (with a minimum of music) and being periodically interrupted by musical "numbers" (arias, ensembles, ballets, etc.; see Number opera), all of which are, from the dramatic standpoint, likely to be merely episodic or at best unnecessarily long elaborations of certain moments of the action. Such a slow tempo of the action or such frequent interruptions, which would be regarded as serious defects in a spoken play, are hardly avoidable in opera. From these basic necessities arise many of the features of opera that persons unaccustomed to the form may find difficult to accept, such as frequent text repetitions, prolonged emotional scenes, dying speeches, and so on. While it is true that many operas are cheaply sentimental, silly, or melodramatic, the same charge may be made against many plays. These faults are not inherent in the form, though the skillful use of music may cause the ordinary listener to forgive their presence in opera more readily than in a play.

II. *Prehistory.* Although the first work now known as an opera dates from 1597, the combining of music and drama is undoubtedly of very early origin. Ancient Greek drama incorporated the choral songs and dances of the earlier *dithyrambs, in a tradition that may go back to the still older rites of the Bacchic cults. The tragedies of Aeschylus, Sophocles, and Euripides all give a large place to the chorus, and it is known from theoretical treatises (e.g., Aristotle's *Poetics*) that music was an essential element of the form, though unfortunately only a single mutilated specimen of Greek dramatic music has survived (fragment of a chorus from Euripides' *Orestes*).

In the Middle Ages the Church fostered dramatic music in the *liturgical dramas (11th–13th centuries) and mystery plays (14th–16th centuries). While medieval religious drama had no direct historical connection with the earliest operas, its tradition may still be traced in some of the operas on religious subjects at Rome and in Germany during the 17th century.

The immediate predecessors of opera are various types of secular dramatic entertainment with music that appeared during the 16th century. These are of two basic categories: (1) works in which music was an adjunct to scenery and dancing, the definitive form in this

class being the *ballet, brought from Italy to France, where it later exercised a determining influence on the French opera [see below]; (2) works in which music served as a diversion from spoken drama, the musical portions usually appearing as *intermezzi between the acts of a play. However, the creation of opera itself had to await the discovery of a kind of drama that would lend itself to the continuous use of music and of a kind of music that would be suitable for dramatic expression. The necessary poetic form was found in the pastorale, which toward the end of the 16th century displaced practically all earlier dramatic types in Italy and culminated in T. Tasso's *Aminta* (1573) and B. Guarini's *Il Pastor fido* (1581–90). The earliest opera-poems are pastorales modeled on these two works [see also Eclogue]. A musical style suitable for opera was developed by the Florentine *Camerata [see also *Nuove musiche* (2); Monody]. The *madrigal comedies of O. Vecchi, which are frequently mentioned as preoperatic types, have only a subsidiary place in the history of the opera.

The history of opera may be divided into five periods:

1590–1680. Development of dramatic style in music and of appropriate dramatic and musical forms [sections III–VII below].

1680–1760. Utilization of established style and forms in serious operas of a standard type; rise of comic opera as an independent genre [VII–VIII].

1760–1850. Introduction of new subject matter and loosening of traditional forms in the interest of a more direct connection between dramatic content and musical expression [IX]; rise of national types of opera.

1850–1920. Rejection of set forms and formal divisions in favor of continuous music, with recurrence of characteristic motifs; the music drama [X].

1920—. Reaction against romantic subject matter and musical amorphousness of the music drama; fusion of opera with oratorio and other dramatic forms; revival of the 18th-century "number" opera in 20th-century musical idioms [XI].

III. *Early Italian opera.* The earliest operas, all performed at Florence, were: *Dafne,* poem by Rinuccini, music by J. Peri (1597; music lost); *Euridice,* poem by Rinuccini, music by G. Caccini (perf. 1602; in *Editions XLVII, 10); *Euridice,* poem by Rinuccini, music by Peri and

Caccini (1600; in *Editions III, 6, and IX, 24). The music of the Florentine operas consists mostly of recitative over a thoroughbass whose somewhat colorless harmonies were realized by a small instrumental ensemble. Conforming to the ideal of imitation of Greek drama, the vocal line aims at close adherence to the natural rhythm and accent of the spoken word; therefore, although flawless in declamation and occasionally expressive in detail, it is lacking in any distinct melodic character or any clear principle of musical organization. Exceptions to this style occur in the occasional metrical songs and choruses, usually with dancing, which are placed at the end of the principal scenes. However, the almost total exclusion of counterpoint and the neglect of instrumental music led, as soon as the novelty of the new *stile recitativo* had worn off, to an unbearable monotony of effect. It was Monteverdi who introduced into opera the full resources of the art of music. His *La Favola d'Orfeo* (Mantua, 1607; poem by Alessandro Striggio) is on the same subject and in the same general style as the earlier Florentine *Euridice* operas, but it shows notable advances in both dramatic characterization and musical form. Monteverdi's harmony is incomparably richer and more varied than that of Peri or Caccini. The recitative is more expressive and is frequently organized by means of repetitions, sequential passages, etc., into distinct musical patterns. The remarkable aria "Possente spirto" in Act III consists of six strophes of elaborately ornamented vocal solo, each with a different orchestral accompaniment. The large orchestra is another feature of this work, as well as the number of instrumental pieces (26 in all), including the introductory "toccata" (the earliest operatic *overture) and the frequent ritornellos, which, by their recurrence, give musical unity to long sections of the opera.

In the third decade of the 17th century the center of operatic interest shifted to Rome (S. Landi, D. Mazzocchi, M. A. Rossi, L. Vittori, L. Rossi). Mazzocchi's *La Catena d'Adone* (1626) and Landi's *Il Sant' Alessio* (1632; *Editions III, 5) show the gradual differentiation between recitative and aria styles, with the use of tuneful melodies in the latter, as well as continued progress toward formal clarity. In Landi's work the "canzona" type of overture appears, while the "sinfonia" before the second act is an early example of the three-movement arrangement (fast–slow–fast) of the later Italian overture. The Roman operas are distinguished by

extensive use of vocal ensembles. This school was also the first to produce *comic operas.

IV. *Later 17th-century Italian opera.* An important historical event was the opening at Venice in 1637 of the first public opera house (Teatro San Cassiano). The transformation of opera from a courtly entertainment for invited guests to a public spectacle for a general audience had important consequences for both music and libretto. The earliest composers at Venice were Monteverdi with *Il Ritorno d'Ulisse in Patria,* 1641 (*DTO* 57), and *L'Incoronazione di Poppea,* 1642; and P. F. Cavalli with *Giasone,* 1649 (*Editions XLVII, 12), and *Xerse,* 1654. The recitatives in Monteverdi's *Incoronazione* are the apotheosis of the Florentine monodic style. Combined with more regular aria forms, they make for one of the most beautiful operatic scores of the entire 17th century. The works of Cavalli and M. A. Cesti show the influence of public taste on operatic form in their greater size, more lavish staging [see especially Burnacini's stage designs for *Il Pomo d'oro* in *DTO* 6 and 9], greater number of characters, plot complications, and use of burlesque comic episodes. Musical effects become less subtle than in earlier works. The virtuoso soloist begins to be featured. Recitative and aria become completely distinct and the latter crystallizes into standard forms (strophic, ostinato-bass, *da capo*). There are many arias in light, popular, melodic style, as well as more serious types. The use of an orchestral introduction to the aria, repeated at the close ("ritornello" principle), as well as short orchestral interludes between the sections, becomes established. There are important orchestral overtures and sinfonias, but vocal ensembles (except duets) are much less prominent than in operas from the first half of the century.

The course of Italian opera in the later 17th century is difficult to follow because few scores are available in modern editions. Venice remained the principal but by no means the only center of production, the leading composers there being Antonio Sartorio (*L'Adelaide,* 1672) and Giovanni Legrenzi (*Totila,* 1677). Other notable figures in Italy were M. A. Cesti, active in various cities, who produced *La Dori* at Florence in 1661 (*Editions XLVII, 12) and *Il Pomo d'oro* (*DTO* 6 and 9) at Vienna in 1661, A. Stradella (*La Forza dell'Amor paterno,* 1678), and F. Provenzale, one of the first composers of opera at Naples. Among Italians resident at South German centers were C. Pallavicino (*La Gerusalemme liberata,* 1687; see *DdT* 55) and especially Agostino Steffani (*Alarico il Baltha,* 1687; *Henrico Leone,* 1689; see *DTB* 21, 23), whose works achieved a perfect reconciliation of the monodic and contrapuntal principles and laid the foundation for the operatic style of Handel.

By the end of the 17th century Italian opera was firmly established in its native land as a leading musical institution. Moreover, the forms of music and drama that had developed by then remained basic to the further evolution of Italian opera over the next two centuries and had a far-reaching influence on opera in other countries as well.

V. *French opera, 1670–1750.* French national opera was founded by Robert Cambert (*Pomone,* 1671) and Jean-Baptiste Lully (*Cadmus et Hermione,* 1673; *Atys,* 1676; *Amadis,* 1684; *Armide,* 1686). Although there had been performances of Italian opera in Paris between 1645 and 1662 (notably Luigi Rossi's *L'Orfeo* in 1647; first perf.), the French were slow to adopt the form, partly because in their own classical tragedy (Corneille, Racine) and in the *ballet they had already perfected two types of stage production with which they were satisfied and which they did not believe could be successfully merged. It is a tribute to Lully's skill that he was able to take certain features of each of these established forms, along with some elements of the pastorale, and combine them in a form of opera he called *tragédie lyrique.* Compared to contemporary Italian works, the French opera was distinguished by (1) the relatively greater importance of the drama; (2) the exceptionally large place given to ballets, choruses, and spectacular scenes in general; (3) the greater use of instrumental music; (4) the use of short and simple songs, mostly of a dancelike character (*airs) rather than elaborate arias; (5) a special type of *recitative; and (6) a special type of *overture known as "French overture." This type of opera remained essentially unchanged in the hands of Lully's successors, including Rameau (*Hippolyte et Aricie,* 1733; *Castor et Pollux,* 1737), whose operas represent the high point of this form in France before Gluck. [For reprints of French operas, see Editions VII.]

VI. *English opera.* As French opera grew out of the ballet, so English opera developed from the *masque, though not without difficulty owing to the prejudice against stage entertainments during the Commonwealth (1649–60). John Blow's *Venus and Adonis* (*c.* 1684?), although entitled "a masque," is the first genuine opera to be produced in England in this period. The only great figure of English opera is Henry Purcell, whose *Dido and Aeneas* (*c.* 1689) is a masterpiece in miniature. Though not free from French influence (form of overture, care for clear text declamation, certain rhythmic mannerisms, prominence of dancing, instrumental pieces, and choruses), it nevertheless combines these features with highly original and characteristically English melodies, rhythms, and harmonies, together with a degree of tragic expressiveness (Dido's lament, "When I am laid in earth") that has hardly been surpassed in opera. The same qualities may be found in much of Purcell's other theater music, which is in the form of incidental music to plays (*Dioclesian,* 1690; *King Arthur,* 1691). With Purcell's early death, the writing of serious operas by English composers of the first rank practically ceased until the 20th century.

VII. *German opera.* With the exception of Heinrich Schütz's *Dafne* (1627 at Torgau; music lost), the early history of opera in Germany is predominantly the history of Italian composers at German courts: Pallavicini at Dresden, A. Draghi at Vienna, A. Steffani at Munich and Hanover, and a host of others. Their influence was such that for the next hundred years even native German masters were content to write in the Italian style and to Italian texts (J. J. Fux, J. A. Hasse, Gluck, Mozart). The only important native German school was at Hamburg, where the titles of the first Singspiele (e.g., J. Theile's *Der erschaffene, gefallene und aufgerichtete Mensch* 1678) show the connection with the tradition of "school dramas" (plays with music, usually about Biblical subjects, intended for the edification and instruction of pupils in schools. An earlier example is S. T. Staden's "spiritual pastorale" *Seelewig,* Nuremberg, 1644; see *MfM* xiii; SchGMB, no. 195). German operas on secular subjects, both serious and comic, soon made their appearance. The chief composer of the Hamburg school was Reinhard Keiser, of whose reputed 120 operas only 18 have been preserved (*Croesus,* 1711, rev. 1730, in *DdT* 37/38; *Octavia,* 1705, in vol. vi of sup. to Händelgesellschaft ed. of Handel's works; *Der laecherliche Printz Jodelet,* 1726, in *Editions XLVII, 18). Keiser not only was the best composer of early German opera but had a direct influence on Handel, whose first four operatic works were produced at Hamburg (1705–06). Keiser's operatic style is essentially like that of Steffani, its outstanding features being the skill of his orchestral writing and the variety of instrumental combinations he employed for accompanying solo arias. After Keiser, German opera degenerated and by the middle of the 18th century had entirely disappeared.

VIII. *Italian 18th-century opera.* The prevailing type of 18th-century Italian *opera seria* was cultivated in all countries (except France) by native and Italian composers alike. Because many of its early composers worked chiefly at Naples, this type of opera has sometimes been called "Neapolitan" [see Neapolitan school], although in fact Naples was but one center among many. Much of the usual criticism of *opera seria* rises from not understanding the principles of the form or from concentrating on its abuses while ignoring its virtues. *Opera seria* was based on a rationalist ideal of drama, realized through the reforms of A. Zeno and his more famous successor, P. Metastasio, who purged the chaotic 17th-century opera libretto of irrelevant elements (e.g., comic and fantastic episodes) and created a unified, close-knit three-act dramatic structure, with characters and subjects drawn principally from ancient history or legend (seldom from mythology). Formally, each scene consists of two distinct parts, the first comprising the action and the second devoted to the expression of the reflections, feelings, or resolves of the principal character, which are a consequence of the action just preceding. Thus the libretto presents a constant alternation of active and reflective portions, the former being interpreted musically as recitative (mostly *recitativo secco*) and the latter as aria. Choruses are practically nonexistent. As for the orchestra, its function, except for the overture [see Overture I] and an occasional march or other incidental piece, is decidedly subordinate, though in the hands of an able composer the ritornellos and accompaniments to the arias may be of considerable interest and importance. But the center of attention and the basic structural unit of these operas was the aria, of which there were many different types (*aria cantabile, aria parlante, aria di bravura,* etc.), practically all of them in the *da capo* form. There were fairly rigid conventions as to the number and order of the different types of aria and their distribution among the members of the cast, and the popularity of Metastasio (his 27 librettos were set to music more than 1,000 times in the 18th century) is in large part attributable to his ability to meet the peculiar requirements of the form without undue sacrifice of dramatic force

and continuity. Corollary to the concept of the aria as the essential structural unit were two phenomena characteristic of 18th-century opera: (1) the high development of vocal technique [see *Bel canto*], particularly by the **castrati;* (2) the prevalent custom of borrowing arias from one opera for use in another, whether or not by the same composer (**pasticcio*). Since there were no printed scores and no copyright restrictions, an opera was seldom performed the same way in any two places or at any two times, and the changes were sometimes so extensive that it is no longer possible to reconstruct the original version.

Alessandro Scarlatti, who has sometimes been called the founder of the 18th-century *opera seria,* is probably better regarded as a composer in the late baroque tradition. The lighter, more vivacious, more purely melodic preclassical style characteristic of the *opera seria* began to predominate from about 1720, the principal early composers being N. A. Porpora, L. Vinci, L. Leo, and J. A. Hasse. Unquestionably the greatest composer of Italian opera in this period was G. F. Handel, who from 1711 to 1740 produced at London some works that have never been surpassed in nobility of style or profundity of dramatic insight (*Giulio Cesare in Egitto,* 1724; *Tamerlano,* 1724; *Rodelinda,* 1725). Later composers of *opera seria* include G. Latilla, N. Piccinni, G. Sarti, A. Sacchini, A. Salieri, Gluck (early works), J. C. Bach, and Mozart (*Idomeneo,* 1781). Growing objections to the rigidity of the form and the abuses resulting from the overbearing vanity of singers [see B. Marcello's satire *Il Teatro alla moda,* 1720] led to efforts at reform, in which N. Jommelli (*Fetonte,* 1768; in *DdT* 32/33) and T. Traetta (in *DTB* 25, 29) were prominent. Credit for the final reform of Italian 18th-century opera is generally given to Gluck, in spite of the fact that of his "reform" operas only two (*Orfeo ed Euridice,* 1762; *Alceste,* 1767, pub. 1769) were composed originally to Italian librettos, and these were later revised and adapted to French texts at Paris. His other late operas (*Iphigénie en Aulide,* 1774; *Armide,* 1777; *Iphigénie en Tauride,* 1779) on French poems were designed for and performed at Paris, and moreover they embodied many of the features that had been characteristic of French opera from the time of Rameau and Lully: comparative subordination of music to drama, avoidance of mere vocal display, flexibility of musical forms, closer approximation of style between recitative and aria, and general simplicity both of subject and treatment. (These are the points stressed in the famous dedicatory preface to *Alceste*.) To these features may be added another detail common to Rameau and Gluck but not common in Italian operas before the late 18th century: the use of large choral and ballet scenes connected with the action. In short, the direct reform of Gluck lay in his injection of renewed dramatic vigor into French opera, though indirectly his success at Paris and the subsequent steadily growing influence of the French capital in operatic affairs made later Italian composers more ready to adopt practices calculated to win Parisian approval, thus leading to a closer *rapprochement* of the two national styles. Other influences working toward a reform of *opera seria* in the late 18th century were the cult of naturalness set forth in the writings of Rousseau and the increasing importance of popular comic operas, which by the end of the century had in all countries attained artistic equality with serious opera. See Comic opera: Number opera.

IX. *From Mozart to Wagner.* The climax of later 18th-century Italian opera is reached in the works of Mozart (*Le Nozze di Figaro*, 1786; *Don Giovanni*, 1787; *Così fan tutte*, 1790), and it is significant that his three Italian masterpieces were of the comic or semicomic variety (his *opera seria*, *La Clemenza di Tito*, 1791, is of less importance). Mozart's operas are outstanding in sharpness and subtlety of characterization, integration of vocal and instrumental factors, and the adaptation of the classical symphonic style in their ensemble finales. His *Die Entführung aus dem Serail* (1782) is one of the finest examples of the *Singspiel, and *Die Zauberflöte* (1791) is an important forerunner of 19th-century German romantic opera.

The influence of Gluck was evident in a school of large-scale "heroic" opera centering at Paris, represented by such works as A. Sacchini's *Dardanus* (1784) and *Oedipe à Colone* (1786), A. Salieri's *Les Danaïdes* (1784), Cherubini's *Médée* (1797), G. Spontini's *La Vestale* (1807), and E.-N. Méhul's *Joseph* (1807). The continuation of this school was the 19th-century "grand opera," of which the most famous examples are G. Rossini's *Guillaume Tell* (1829), J. Halévy's *La Juive* (1835), G. Meyerbeer's *Les Huguenots* (1836) and *Le Prophète* (1849), R. Wagner's *Rienzi* (1842), and H. Berlioz' *Les Troyens à Carthage* (2nd pt. 1863; whole work, 1890). In contrast to this style was opera with more realistic, often melodramatic subjects, a charac-

teristic form being the "rescue opera" (Cherubini's *Les Deux Journées*, 1800; Beethoven's *Fidelio*, 1805, '06, '14). The works mentioned so far constitute what may be called the international opera of the early 19th century. Less pretentious at first in scope and subject matter but of greater eventual importance historically were the various national schools.

In Italy the leading composers were Rossini (best known for his comic opera *Almaviva*, better known as *Il Barbiere di Siviglia*, 1816), Bellini (*Norma*, 1831), Donizetti (*Lucrezia Borgia*, 1833; *Lucia di Lammermoor*, 1835), and Verdi (*Rigoletto*, 1851; *Il Trovatore*, *La Traviata*, 1853; *La Forza del Destino*, 1862; *Aida*, 1871; *Otello*, 1887; *Falstaff*, 1893). The crowning point of typical Italian opera, characterized by melodramatic plots, popular-type melodies, and concentration on "effective" vocal numbers [see Number opera], is reached in Verdi's works of the 1850's. *Aida*, a work in the "grand opera" tradition, shows unmistakable signs of the changes in style that were fully realized in *Otello* and *Falstaff*: better libretto, continuity of presentation, a more flexible rhythm, more varied harmony, and closer approach to equality between vocal and instrumental elements— though still retaining the classical Italian qualities of clarity, dramatic simplicity, and profound comprehension of the expressive possibilities of the solo voice.

In France, besides "grand opera" the early 19th century was taken up with the *opéra comique*, a form and style inherited from the preceding period that gradually developed into the lyric opera of Gounod (*Faust*, 1859) and A. Thomas (*Mignon*, 1866), both showing Italian influence. Later 19th-century French opera is represented by Bizet (*Carmen*, 1875), Delibes (*Lakmé*, 1883), Chabrier (*Gwendoline*, 1886, obviously indebted to Wagner's *Tristan und Isolde*, 1865), Massenet (*Manon*, 1884), D'Indy (*Fervaal*, 1897), and other composers (see below).

In Russia a national school of opera was definitively launched with the performance of Glinka's *A Life for the Czar* in 1836. Its chief representative was Mussorgsky, who in *Boris Godunov* (1874) created a work that combined nationalist subject matter and musical material with originality and great dramatic power. Other composers of Russian opera who should be mentioned are Borodin (*Prince Igor*, 1890) and Rimsky-Korsakov (*The Snow Maiden*, 1882; *Sadko*, 1898). Tchaikovsky's works in operatic form (*Yevgeny Onyegin,* or *Eugen Onegin,* 1879; *The Queen of Spades,* 1890) are in the romantic style but are not nationalist.

The background of romantic opera in Germany is found in the *Singspiel of the late 18th and early 19th centuries. An important early composer is L. Spohr (*Faust,* 1816; *Jessonda,* 1823), Weber's *Der Freischütz* (1821) and *Euryanthe* (1823) established the fundamental characteristics of the school: (1) romantic treatment of subjects derived from national legend and folklore; (2) a deep feeling for nature and the use of natural phenomena as an essential element in the drama; (3) the acceptance of supernatural agencies as a means of dramatic development; and (4) nationalism. Musically, *Der Freischütz* marks an important stage in the discovery of romantic expressive effects (introduction to the Overture, the Wolf's Glen scene), as well as in the use of folksong-like melodies side by side with more conventional operatic arias. The operas of Marschner (*Der Vampyr,* 1828; *Hans Heiling,* 1833) continue the general type established by Weber, and the latter's influence is strongly evident in Wagner's *Der fliegende Holländer* (1843) and even *Lohengrin* (1850).

X. *The music drama.* Wagner's next two operas after *Der fliegende Holländer* are steps in the evolution toward the music drama. *Tannhäuser* (1845) still retains the old-fashioned division into "numbers" and has some unessential display scenes, but in *Lohengrin* (composed 1846–48) these irrelevancies are dismissed. Music and drama are more closely unified, greater continuity is achieved, and the symbolic meaning of the drama is made clearly evident. The vocal line begins to be emancipated from the older periodic rhythm, approaching the free melodic style of the late works. Wagner employed the early years of his exile (1849–64) in completing the libretto and part of the music of *Der Ring des Nibelungen* and in writing various essays, of which the most important is *Oper und Drama* (1851). In this work he developed the theoretical basis for the music drama, whose practical application appears in the four dramas of the *Ring* (first complete perf. at Bayreuth, 1876), *Tristan und Isolde* (composed 1857–59, perf. 1865), *Die Meistersinger von Nürnberg* (comp. 1862–67, perf. 1868), and *Parsifal* (comp. 1877–82; perf. 1882).

These works all are based on a concept of the music drama as a universal art form (*Gesamtkunstwerk*) in which all the constituent arts are transfigured, sacrificing their individual identity

and some of their special characteristics for the larger possibilities of development opened up by the new association. The myth is held to be the ideal subject, not merely because it is entertaining but also because it is significant; its meaning is expressed in poetry (speech), but it is inevitably impelled to song, since only music is capable of conveying the intensity of feeling to which the ideas of the poem give rise. This song is flexible (nonperiodic rhythm) and free (no formal divisions into recitative, aria, etc.); it implies a polyphonic substructure that is realized by the orchestra and that embodies the "inner action" of the drama (i.e., the feelings) as the words embody its "outer action" (i.e., the precise ideas with which the feelings are associated). The orchestral music is continuous throughout an act, the technical concomitant of this being the avoidance of double bars and perfect cadences and the continual shifting of the tonal center; it is unified by the use of *leitmotivs, short musical themes, each connected with a particular person, thing, or idea (or all three, as in the case of Siegfried's horn call), and recurring, varying, or developing musically in accord with the recurrence, variation, or development of the corresponding object in the drama. Wagner's music is the incarnation of the full, rich sound ideal of the late romantic period, deriving a peculiar intensity of expression from skillful orchestration, freedom and variety of the harmonic progressions, and effective use of suspensions and appoggiaturas. The continuing popularity of his works is undoubtedly due more to their musical qualities and their sheer dramatic effectiveness than to any general acceptance of the theory of the *Gesamtkunstwerk,* with its manifold implications.

XI. *The 20th century.* Wagner's musical style and his ideal of continuous melody influenced the composers of opera in the late 19th and early 20th centuries, particularly Richard Strauss (*Salome,* 1905; *Der Rosenkavalier,* 1911). At the same time, the music drama provoked a reaction in favor of so-called "realism" in subject matter and compression and simplicity of musical treatment. This reaction took such forms as the "realism" of the French Bizet (*Carmen,* 1875), the *verismo of the Italians Mascagni, Leoncavallo, and Puccini (*La Bohème,* 1896; *Tosca,* 1900), and the "naturalism" of the French Bruneau (*Messidor,* 1897) and Charpentier (*Louise,* 1900). Another reaction to 19th-century styles was impressionism. Debussy's *Pelléas et Mélisande* (1902) is a unique application of the *impressionist technique to opera and comes closer than any other modern work to realizing the Florentine ideal of music as an almost imperceptible support and setting for the poetry. Dukas' *Ariane et Barbe-Bleue* (1907) and Bartók's *Duke Bluebeard's Castle* (comp. 1911, perf. 1918), both based on a Maeterlinck drama, were strongly influenced by Debussy. Maurice Ravel's *L'Heure espagnole* (1911) and Fauré's *Pénélope* (1913) are lesser-known operas in the French impressionist style. In Italian opera immediately before World War I, both French and German influences began to replace the *verismo* style (I. Montemezzi, *L'Amore dei tre re,* 1913).

In the period following World War I, the established opera houses still leaned heavily on the standard repertory from Mozart to Puccini. Despite such experiments as Alban Berg's atonal *Wozzeck* (1925) and Schoenberg's uncompleted masterpiece *Moses und Aron* (acts I and II completed 1932, radio perf. 1954), many composers retained traditional subjects, forms, and musical styles (R. Strauss, *Die Frau ohne Schatten,* 1919). Among the most significant operas of the 1920's are Janáček's *Káta Kabanová* (1921) and *The Cunning Vixen* (1924), and Prokofiev's *The Love for Three Oranges* (1921). Jazz influenced Krenek's *Jonny spielt auf* (1927). The only serial opera that has found public acceptance is Berg's *Lulu* (1937). Schoenberg's *Moses und Aron* (less successful because of enormous staging difficulties) exemplifies an important tendency in this period to combine the characteristics of opera and oratorio in works of serious ethical purpose with huge musical and stage resources. Other examples of this tendency are Arthur Honegger's *Jeanne d'Arc au bûcher* (1938), Paul Hindemith's *Mathis der Maler* (1938), and Darius Milhaud's *Christophe Colomb* (1930). Other operas of the 1930's are Virgil Thomson's *Four Saints in Three Acts* (1934), an opera in a simple musical style set to a text by Gertrude Stein, and Shostakovitch's *Lady Macbeth of Mtsensk* (1934).

Since World War II there have been a large number of new, successful operas. Numerous works in traditional styles achieved some public success: G. C. Menotti's *The Medium* (1946), *The Consul* (1950), *Amahl and the Night Visitors* (1951) and *Le dernier Sauvage* (1963); S. Barber's *Vanessa* (1958); W. Walton's *Troilus and Cressida* (1954); and A. Copland's *The Tender Land* (1954). In a somewhat more venturesome vein were Britten's *Peter Grimes* (1945), *The Turn of*

the Screw (1954), *A Midsummer Night's Dream* (1960), and *Curlew River* (1964). Operas on a very large scale are Prokofiev's *War and Peace* (1955), Hindemith's *Die Harmonie der Welt* (1957), Milhaud's *David* (1954), and Ginastera's *Don Rodrigo* (1964). Interesting formal experiments, on a more modest scale and with elements adapted from folklore, are the early musico-dramatic works of Carl Orff, including *Die Kluge* (1943). His *Antigonae* (1949) and *Oedipus der Tyrann* (1959) combine stylized speech and chant with melismatic phrases against a percussive orchestral background. Along with the tendency toward the fusion of opera and oratorio came an opposite trend toward opera as straightforward dramatic entertainment, serious or comic, in a neoclassical revival of the 18th-century principle of the *number opera; the outstanding example is Stravinsky's *The Rake's Progress* (1951). Another important work of this type is Poulenc's *Les Dialogues des Carmélites* (1957). Serial techniques were used by Luigi Nono for *Intoleranza 1960* (1961).

In the United States *The Ballad of Baby Doe* (1956) by Douglas Moore and *Susannah* (1955) by Carlisle Floyd are examples of folk operas that have been fairly successful. Other American operas are *Montezuma* (first perf. in Berlin, 1964) by Roger Sessions, *The Crucible* (1961) by Robert Ward, *The Mother of Us All* (1947) by Virgil Thomson, and *The Wings of the Dove* (1961) by Douglas Moore. A hopeful sign for the future of opera in the United States is the growing number of new works produced under the patronage of civic and community groups, colleges, and music schools.

See also Comic opera; Operetta; Ballad opera; Ballet in opera; Singspiel; Libretto; *Opera seria; Verismo;* Number opera; Aria IV, V; Madrigal comedy; Masque; Liturgical drama; Recitative; *Bel canto; Pasticcio; Leitmotiv.*

Lit. (selected). A. *Lexicons:* J. Towers, *Dictionary—Catalogue of Operas and Operettas* [1910]; H. Riemann, *Opern-Handbuch* (1887); F. Clément, *Dictionnaire des opéras (Dictionnaire lyrique),* rev. A. Pougin [1905]; C. Dassori, *Opere e operisti* (1903); Library of Congress, *Catalogue of Opera Librettos Printed Before 1800,* 2 vols. (1914); W. Altmann, *Katalog der seit 1861 . . . theatralischen Musik.* 5 vols. (1935–39); A. Loewenberg, *Annals of Opera, 1597–1940,* rev. ed. 2 vols., [1955]; U. Manferrari, *Dizionario universale delle opere melodrammatiche,* 3 vols.

(1954–55); H. Rosenthal and J. Warrack, *Concise Oxford Dictionary of Opera* (1964).

B. *Plots of operas:* G. Kobbé, *Kobbé's Complete Opera Book*, ed. The Earl of Harewood, rev. ed. [1954]; H. E. Krehbiel, *A Book of Operas* (1919); O. Downes, *The Home Book of the Opera* (1937); E. Newman, *Seventeen Famous Operas* (1955); *id., Great Operas, the Definitive Treatment of Their History, Stories, and Music* (1958).

C. *General history:* E. Dent, *Opera,* rev. ed. [1951]; D. J. Grout, *A Short History of Opera,* rev. ed. 2 vols., (1965); H. Kretzschmar, *Geschichte der Oper* (1919; most useful for pre-1800); O. Bie, *Die Oper* (1923); H. Graf, *The Opera and Its Future in America* [1941].

D. *Special history:* A. Solerti, *Gli Albori del melodramma,* 3 vols. [1904–05]; H. Goldschmidt, *Studien zur Geschichte der italienischen Oper im 17. Jahrhundert,* 2 vols. (1901, '04); R. Rolland, *Les Origines du théâtre lyrique moderne: Histoire de l'opéra en Europe avant Lully et Scarlatti,* rev. ed. (1931); S. T. Worsthorne, *Venetian Opera in the Seventeenth Century* (1954); H. C. Wolff, *Die venezianische Oper in der zweiten Hälfte des 17. Jahrhunderts* (1937); H. Prunières, *L'Opéra italien en France avant Lulli* (1913); *id., Cavalli et l'opéra vénitien au XVIIe siècle* [1931]; E. Wellesz, *Essays on Opera* [n.d.; 1950?]; A. A. Abert, *Claudio Monteverdi und das musikalische Drama* (1954); H. C. Wolff, *Die Barockoper in Hamburg, 1678–1738,* 2 vols. (1957); P. M. Masson *L'Opéra de Rameau* (1930); E. Dent, *Alessandro Scarlatti,* rev. ed. [1960]; *id., Foundations of English Opera* (1928); *id., Mozart's Operas,* rev. ed. (1947); A. Einstein, *Mozart, His Character, His Work* (1945); H. Schletterer, *Das deutsche Singspiel* [1863?]; H. Leichtentritt, *Reinhard Keiser in seinen Opern* (1901); G. F. Schmidt, *Die frühdeutsche Oper und die musikdramatische Kunst Georg Caspar Schürmann's,* 2 vols. (1933, '34); H. Abert, *Niccolo Jommelli als Opernkomponist* (1908); F. Florimo, *La Scuola musicale di Napoli,* 4 vols. (1880–82); A. B. Marx, *Gluck und die Oper,* 2 vols. (1863); E. Newman, *Gluck and the Opera* (1895); M. Cooper, *Gluck* (1935); L. Schiedermair, *Die deutsche Oper,* rev. ed. [1940]; W. L. Crosten, *French Grand Opera: An Art and A Business* (1948); H. Weinstock, *Donizetti and the World of Opera in Italy, Paris and Vienna in the First Half of the Nineteenth Century* [1963]; F. Toye, *Giuseppe Verdi* [1931]; F. Walker, *The Man Verdi* (1962); E. Newman, *The Wagner Operas* (1949); A. Lorenz, *Das Geheimnis der Form bei Richard Wagner,* 4 vols. [1924–33];

R. Wagner, *Wagner on Music and Drama: A Compendium of Richard Wagner's Prose Works,* ed. A. Goldman and E. Sprinchorn (1964); R. Newmarch, *The Russian Opera* [n.d.; 1914?]; M. Cooper, *French Music: From the Death of Berlioz to the Death of Fauré* (1951).

E. *Periodicals* (grouped according to the divisions of the article). *II* (*Prehistory*): A. Solerti, in *RMI* x; W. Smoldon, in *MQ* xlviii; R. Weaver, in *MQ* xlvii; E. Bowles, in *MQ* xlv; C. Palisca, in *MQ* xl. *III* (*early Italian opera*): O. G. Sonneck, in *SIM* xv (*Dafne*); L. Torchi, in *RMI* i, ii (instrumental accompaniment); S. Reiner, in *MR* xxii (*Chi soffre speri*). *IV* (*later 17th-cent. Italian opera*): A. Sandberger, in *JMP* xxxi, xxxii (Venetian opera); H. Kretzschmar, in *VMW* viii (Venetian opera, Cavalli, Cesti); *id.,* in *JMP* xiv, xvii, xviii (Venetian opera); A. Solerti, in *RMI* ix (1571–1605 in Venice); H. Hess, in *Publikationen der internationalen Musikgesellschaft,* Beihefte (1906), ii.3 (Stradella); N. Pirrotta, in *MQ* xli (*commedia dell'arte,* opera); H. Goldschmidt, in *SIM* vii (F. Provenzale); E. Wellesz, in *StM* vi (operas, oratorios, in Vienna 1660–1708); M. Neuhaus, in *StM* i (A. Draghi). *V.* (*French opera*): D. J. Grout, in *ML* xxii (forerunners of Lully); *RM, Numéro spécial* (January 1925; Lully); H. Prunières, in *SIM* xii (French overture). *VI* (*English opera*): J. Mark, in *ML* v (Dryden); O. Gombosi, in *JAMS* i (masques); W. Barclay Squire, in *SIM* v (Purcell); A. Nicoll, in *Anglia. Zeitschrift für englische Philologie* xlvi (1922; Italian opera in England, first five years); I. Lowens, in *MQ* xlv (London opera, 1728); R. Babcock, in *ML* xxiv, and also O. E. Deutsch letter, in *ML* xxv, 126 (Coleman's "Register of Operas"). *VII* (*German opera*): L. Schiedermair, in *JMP* xvii (early German opera); G. F. Schmidt, in *ZMW* v, vi (1627–1750); A. Sandberger, in *AMW* i (Nuremberg, *c.* 1650–*c.* 1700); P. A. Merbach, in *AMW* vi (Hamburg, 1718–50); W. Kleefeld, in *SIM* i (Hamburg, 1678–1738). *VIII* (*Opera seria*): E. J. Dent, in *ML* xxv (nomenclature); W. Vetter, in *AMW* vi and *ZMW* vii (Gluck); K. Wörner, in *ZMW* xiii (Gluck); H. Welti, in *VMW* vii (Gluck); W. Vetter, in *ZMW* xiv (Vienna, 1750); M. Callegari, in *RMI* xxvi, xxvii (Metastasio); R. Giazotto, in *RMI* xlviii–li (Zeno and Metastasio); N. Burt, in *MQ* xli (Arcadian opera, Zeno and Metastasio); W. Vetter, in *Deutsches Jahrbuch der Musikwissenschaft für 1959* iv (1960; Metastasio); O. Sonneck, in *SIM* xii (*pasticcio*); F. Walker, in *MQ* xxxviii (*pasticcio*); E. Dent, in *SIM* viii (L. Leo), *MA* iv (L. Vinci);

H. Abert, in *ZMW* i (J. C. Bach); E. Kurth, in *StM* i (Gluck). *IX* (*Mozart to Wagner*): H. Kretzschmar, in *JMP* xii (Mozart); H. Strobel, in *ZMW* vi (Méhul); H. Leichtentritt, in *MQ* xiv (Schubert); W. Altmann, in *SIM* iv (Spontini); G. Schünemann, in *ZMW* v (Mendelssohn); S. Goddard, in *ML* x (*Boris Godunov*); H. Engel, in *Mozart—Jahrbuch 1954* (Mozart); B. Szabolcsi, in *Studia musicologica* i (1961; Mozart); F. Walker, in *ML* xxxiii-xxxiv (Mercadante, Verdi); G. Roncaglia, in *RMI* xlvii (Verdi). *X* (*music drama*), *XI* (*20th century*): Since it is impossible to make a short representative selection of periodical articles for these divisions, the reader is referred to D. J. Grout, *A Short History of Opera,* 2 vols., rev. ed. (1965), pp. 686ff, and footnotes to ch. 23, 26, 27.   D.J.G.

Opéra bouffe [F.]. See Comic opera.

Opera buffa [It.]. See Comic opera.

Opéra comique [F.]. See Comic opera.

Opera houses. The first public opera house was the Teatro San Cassiano in Venice, opened in 1637; previously, opera performances had been given in private homes and for invited guests only. There followed the establishment of opera houses in London (1656), Paris (1669), Rome (1671), and Hamburg (1678). After 1700, opera houses became common in all the musical centers of Europe. The most important opera houses of today are listed below.

I. United States. New York: *Metropolitan Opera* (*Lincoln Center*). Chicago: *Civic Opera House* (*Lyric Opera*). San Francisco: *War Memorial Opera House* (*San Francisco Opera*).

II. South America. Buenos Aires: *Teatro Colón.* Rio de Janeiro: *Teatro Municipal.*

III. Austria. Vienna: *Staatsoper; Volksoper.*

IV. England. London: *Royal Opera House* (*Covent Garden*).

V. Germany. Berlin: *Deutsche Staatsoper* (E. Berlin); *Städtische Oper* (W. Berlin). Dresden: *Staatstheater.* Hamburg: *Staatsoper.* Munich: *Prinzregententheater; Bayerische Staatsoper.* Bayreuth: *Bühnenfestspielhaus* (Wagner operas). There are about 30 more opera houses in smaller German cities; see *Opera Annual,* ed. H. Rosenthal [1960].

VI. France. Paris: *Théâtre national de l'Opéra; Théâtre national de l'Opéra-Comique.*

VII. Italy. Rome: *Teatro dell'Opera;* Milan: *Teatro alla Scala.* Venice: *Teatro la Fenice.* Turin: *Teatro nuovo.* Naples: *Teatro San Carlo.*

For more detailed information see Pierre Key's *Music Year Book* (1927–28). See also S. Hughes, *Great Opera Houses* [1956]; E. Krause, *Die grossen Opernbühnen Europas* (1966).

Opera seria, semiseria [It.]. *Opera seria* refers to 18th-century Italian operas based on a "serious" plot and divided into three acts, as opposed to the *opera buffa,* the comic opera consisting of two acts. Mozart's *Idomeneo* is an example of *opera seria. Opera semiseria* is a serious opera including comic elements, e.g., Mozart's *Le Nozze di Figaro.* Also see Opera VIII.

Operetta. In the 18th century, a short opera; in the 19th and 20th centuries, a theatrical piece of light and sentimental character in simple and popular style, containing spoken dialogue, music, dancing, etc. The modern operetta originated in Vienna with Franz von Suppé (1819–95; *c.* 30 operettas from 1860 to his death) and in Paris with Jacques Offenbach (1819–80; *c.* 90 operettas from 1855 to his death). The latter's *Orphée aux enfers* (1858), and *La Belle Hélène* (1864) are famous for their satirical treatment of Greek mythology. Johann Strauss the Younger (1825–99) raised the Viennese operetta to international fame with about 16 operettas written between 1871 and 1897, among which *Die Fledermaus* (1874) has remained in the repertory to the present day. The Viennese tradition was continued by Franz Lehár (1870–1948) with *Die lustige Witwe* (1905). In England Sir Arthur Sullivan wrote operettas (mostly to librettos by W. S. Gilbert) that represent the first high point in English dramatic music since Purcell.

In the United States operettas were written mainly by Victor Herbert (1859–1924), composer of *Mlle. Modiste* (1905), *Naughty Marietta* (1910), and many other operettas, and by H. L. Reginald de Koven (1859–1920), remembered chiefly for his *Robin Hood* (1890). Other works that might be mentioned are *The Doctor of Alcantara* (pub. libretto 1862) by J. Eichberg, *The Firefly* (1912) by Rudolf Friml, *The Student Prince* (1924) by Sigmund Romberg, and G. W. Chadwick's *Tabasco* (1894). During the late 1920's the sentimental operetta began to change (e.g., Jerome Kern's *Showboat,* 1927) into what is now called a "musical comedy," "musical play," or simply "musical." Political and social satire appeared in *Of Thee I Sing* by George Gershwin (1931; first musical to win a Pulitzer Prize), K. Weill's *Die Dreigroschenoper* (text by B. Brecht, 1928; as *The Threepenny Opera,* 1933), and Richard Rodgers'

Pal Joey (text by L. Hart, 1940). Although Irving Berlin's musicals continued the more traditional vein (*Annie Get Your Gun,* 1946), a more unified format developed in the 1940's, exemplified by Richard Rodgers' *Oklahoma!* (1943; Pulitzer Prize 1944) and *South Pacific* (1949), and Cole Porter's *Kiss Me Kate* (1948). Leonard Bernstein's *Candide* (1956) is noteworthy for its musical content, and his *West Side Story* (1957) for the emphasis on choreography, while *My Fair Lady* (1956) by Frederick Loewe (lyrics by Alan Jay Lerner) will probably remain a model of the genre, Also se Comic opera.

Lit.: M. S. Mackinlay, *Origin & Development of Light Opera* [1927]; F. A. Beach, *Preparation and Presentation of the Operetta* [1930; for public schools]; K. R. Umfleet, *School Operettas and Their Production* [1929]; O. Keller, *Die Operette in ihrer geschichtlichen Entwicklung* (1926); G. Hughes, *Composers of Operetta* (1962); S. Green, *The World of Musical Comedy* [1960]; F. Hadamowsky and H. Otte, *Die Wiener Operette* [1947].

Ophicleide. See under Brass instruments V (c).

Opus [L.; F. *oeuvre*]. Term, abbr. op., used to indicate the chronological position of a composition within a composer's entire output (e.g., op. 1, op. 2). Opus numbers are not always reliable because they are usually applied in the order of publication rather than composition. Perhaps the first composer to use opus numbers was Adriano Banchieri (1567–1634), whose *L'Organo suonarino* of 1605 was designated op. 13. Another early composer using opus numbers was Biagio Marini (*Affetti musicali,* op. 1, 1617). Bach never numbered his compositions, and with both Haydn and Mozart the opus numbers are applied so inconsistently and haphazardly (frequently by the publisher rather than the composer) that they are practically useless. Beethoven was the first to use opus numbers with some consistency, at least for his more important works.

Oratio [L.]. The prayer of the Roman Catholic Mass, also called *Collect.

Oratoric(al) neumes. Same as staffless neumes; see Neumes II.

Oratoric rhythm. Term used for Dom Pothier's rhythmic interpretation of Gregorian chant, according to which the accentual structure of the Latin text is a basic factor in the rendition of the melodies. Another name for this type of interpretation is "accentualist" [see Gregorian chant VI].

Oratorio. I. *Definition.* A composition with a long libretto of religious or contemplative character that is performed in a concert hall or church without scenery, costumes, or action, by solo voices, chorus, and orchestra. This definition applies to most but not all oratorios. For example, the earliest oratorios were usually performed with scenery and costumes, the chief distinguishing characteristic from opera being a more contemplative, less dramatic libretto. Other features distinguishing the oratorio from opera are greater emphasis on the chorus, absence of quick dialogue (question and answer in rapid succession), and, frequently, use of a narrator [It. *testo*] who introduces the characters and connects their parts. Compositions of a similar nature but based on a scriptural or liturgical text (Mass, Requiem, Passion) are usually not considered oratorios. There are, however, Passion oratorios, in which the story of the Passion is freely told. The oratorio is distinguished from the sacred cantata (Bach) by greater length and a more narrative libretto.

II. *History to 1650.* Forerunners of the oratorio include such early types of dramatic music as the *liturgical dramas of the later Middle Ages and the mystery plays of the 14th and 15th centuries. More properly, the history of the oratorio begins in the mid-16th century when Filippo Neri inaugurated, in Rome, a special order called *oratoriani* and established a building called *oratorio* in which regular services of a popular character were held. These included reading from the Scriptures, a sermon, and the singing of *laude. A special type of *laude* were the "dialogue-*laude,*" religious poems in the form of a dialogue between God and the Soul, Heaven and Hell, etc. Being written in three or four parts, they were performed by different groups of singers who may have dressed up as the characters they represented. It is from these presentations (called *rappresentazione, storia, esempio, misterio*) that the oratorio proper developed, supported, no doubt, by the popularizing tendencies of the Counter-Reformation. Palestrina as well as other famous 16th-century composers is supposed to have written music for such occasions, but nothing has been preserved prior to Emilio del Cavalieri's (*c.* 1550–1602) **Rappresentazione di anima e di corpo* (1600; *Editions IX, 10; also *SchGMB,* 169, 170; *HAM,* no. 183), a work that in terms of both date and style is close to the earliest operas (Peri, Caccini). In fact, some modern writers (Alaleone, see Lit.) have denied it a place in the history of the oratorio and, mainly on account of its elaborate stage production (including the simultaneous [*sic*] representation of Heaven, Earth, and Hell, splendid costumes and ballets; see *GD* iii, 70; *GDB* vi, 247ff), have called it a "spiritual opera," a later example of which is S. Landi's *Il Sant' Alessio* (1632). At any rate, this work appears to have been an isolated attempt that failed to establish a tradition. More successful was the *Teatro Armonico Spirituale* (1619) of Giovanni Francesco Anerio (*c.* 1567–1630), in which a refined madrigal style is used for the choral portions, alternating with monody for the solo parts, which included a narrator. Another important work, greatly celebrated in its day, was Domenico Mazzocchi's (1592–1665) *Querimonia di S. Maria Maddalena* (*c.* 1640?). It is an example of the *oratorio volgare*, i.e., written in the vernacular.

III. *1650–1800.* About the middle of the 17th century the oratorio entered a new phase with G. Carissimi (1605–74), who in such works as *Jephtha, Judicium Salomonis, Jonas,* and *Extremum Judicium* [*Editions IX, 5] created the first oratorios fully deserving of the name [ex. in *HAM,* no. 207]. Most of his oratorios have a Latin text (*oratorio latino*) and were directed at a more educated audience. Carissimi's successors included A. Draghi (1635–1700; *c.* 40 oratorios); A. Stradella (1642–82), with his oratorios *S. Giovanni Battista* and *Susanna* [see *SchGMB,* no. 230]; and A. Scarlatti (1660–1725), who wrote a large number of oratorios (eighteen are preserved with the music) that approximate rather closely the style of his operas but are, on the whole, much less successful. The oratorios of A. Lotti (*c.* 1667–1740) and A. Caldara (1670–1736), both representatives of the Roman-Venetian tradition, are more reserved in style, combining dignity with slightly sentimental pathos, while L. Leo (1694–1744), J. A. Hasse (1699–1783; *La Conversione di Sant Agostino, DdT* 20; *HAM,* no. 281), and N. Jommelli (1714–74; *La Passione;* see Editions IX, 15) continued the Neapolitan emphasis on virtuosity and vocal display, thus removing the oratorio even further from its ideal.

The first German oratorio composer was Heinrich Schütz, with his *Historia der Auferstehung* (1623) and his Christmas Oratorio (*Historia von der . . . Geburt Christi,* 1664), a work of no less artistic significance than Bach's Christ-

mas Oratorio written a century later. Oratorios by Selle (1642), Theile (1672), and Sebastiani (1672) belong to the special category of the Passion [see Passion music], and later composers such as Weckmann, Buxtehude, and Rosenmüller preferred the smaller form of the cantata. J. S. Bach was the first to resume the tradition of Schütz in his great Christmas Oratorio (1733–34) and in the less important Easter Oratorio (1736?). There followed J. E. Eberlin with *Der blutschwitzende Jesus* (*DTO* 55), G. P. Telemann (1681–1767) with his highly dramatic *Der Tag des Gerichts* of 1761 (*DdT* 28; *HAM,* no. 272), and Johann Christoph Friedrich Bach (1732–95) with *Die Kindheit Jesu* and *Die Auferweckung des Lazarus* (*DdT* 56). This development came to a fitting close with the truly remarkable oratorios of K. P. E. Bach (*Die Israeliten in der Wüste,* 1775; *Die Auferstehung und Himmelfahrt Jesu,* 1787), which, in their mixtures of styles, reflect the influence of his father but also foreshadow Haydn [see the study by W. H. Hadow, in *OH* v].

The English oratorio is represented by Handel who, after a few early works (*La Resurrezione,* 1708), turned mainly to oratorio writing after becoming dissatisfied with opera, and whose *Israel in Egypt* (1737), *Messiah* (1742), *Judas Maccabeus* (1746), and *Jephtha* (1751) are lasting monuments to his greatness. In contrast to Bach's devotional attitude, Handel approached the oratorio more subjectively, using it to express his own dynamic personality and incorporating the elements of his dramatic opera style. It is interesting that his oratorios were intended to be performed during Lent, when theatrical performances were forbidden by law. The practice of composing Lenten oratorios was continued by J. C. Smith (1712–95), J. Stanley (1713–86), and others. T. Arne (1710–78), in his *Abel* (1744) and *Judith* (1764), succeeded in not succumbing totally to Handelian influence, but after Arne's death the English oratorio entered "on a century of artistic darkness, over which brooded from first to last the elephantine shadow of Handel, to which was added in the final thirty years the almost equally universal though less ostentatiously ponderous shadow of Mendelssohn. The composers of these tons of oratorios were 'all honourable men': . . . but . . . their music is nothing worse than intolerably dull" (*GD* iii, 721f, *GDB* vi, 260f).

An important though little-known development took place in France with Carissimi's pupil M.-A. Charpentier (1634–1704) whose works, so-called *histoires sacrées* (*Judicium Salomonis,*

Filius prodigus, Le Reniement de St. Pierre, etc.), all with Latin texts, combine masterly technique with depth of feeling and dramatic expression [see *HAM,* no. 226]. Unfortunately he had no successors in his country.

IV. *1800–Present.* Haydn (1732–1809), after his *Il Ritorno di Tobia* (1775; said to be "the finest example of 18th-century Italian oratorio that exists" [*GD* iii, 718; *GDB* vi, 257]) and his highly expressive *Seven Last Words on the Cross (1797), wrote two works that inaugurated a new era in oratorio writing, *Die Schöpfung (The Creation,* 1797) and *Die Jahreszeiten (The Seasons,* 1801). The latter, though justly called an oratorio, is more secular than religious. Compared to these works, which stand at the summit of a long life of creative activity, Beethoven's early *Christus am Ölberge* (op. 85, comp. 1800, pub. 1811) is insignificant. In the first half of the 19th century Germany underwent a period of oratorio worship similar to that of England, and the works of L. Spohr (1784–1859; *Das jüngste Gericht*), F. Schneider (1786–1853), and Karl Loewe (1796–1869; *Hiob,* 1848) enjoyed a popularity that is hardly justified by their artistic merits but continued until Mendelssohn (1809–47) appeared with his *St. Paul* (1836) and *Elijah* (1846). These two oratorios, with their romantically colored Bach-Handel style, have retained a lasting place of honor, particularly in England. Schumann wrote two secular oratorios, *Das Paradies und die Peri* (1843) and *Der Rose Pilgerfahrt* (1851).

In the second half of the 19th century quite a number of composers produced oratorios (Wagner, *Das Liebesmahl der Apostel,* 1844; Liszt, *Die Legende von der heiligen Elisabeth,* 1862, and *Christus,* 1866; Dvořák, *St. Ludmila,* 1886; Berlioz, *L'Enfance du Christ,* 1854; Franck, *Les Béatitudes,* 1879, *Rebecca,* 1881, etc.; D'Indy, *La Légende de Saint-Christophe,* properly a stage work), but on the whole with conspicuous lack of success. The only great contribution of this period was Brahms' *Ein Deutsches Requiem* (op. 45, 1857–68), a work that, although not an oratorio in the strict sense of the word (it is based on scriptural passages rather than a free text), cannot be omitted in a description of this form. England saw, after more than a century of mediocrity, a notable revival in oratorios such as H. Parry's *Judith* (1888), *Job* (1892), and *King Saul* (1894); Elgar's *The Dream of Gerontius* (1900), *The Apostles* (1903), and *The Kingdom* (1906); W. Davies' *Everyman* (1904); and W. Walton's *Belshazzar's Feast* (1931)—nearly all compositions written for and performed at one of the British Festivals. Of American oratorios, H. Parker's *The Legend of St. Christopher* and *Hora novissima* as well as Paine's *St. Peter* must be mentioned.

In the 20th century, A. Honegger opened new possibilities for the oratorio in his *Le Roi David* (1923) by abandoning the emotionalism of the romantic oratorio and incorporating archaic idioms that give the work an impressive touch of "biblical greatness." Other composers have cultivated the secular oratorio, e.g., Stravinsky in *Oedipus Rex* (1927, with stage action), Hindemith in *Das Unaufhörliche* (1931), and Hermann Reutter in *Der grosse Kalender* (1933). Recent examples of the religious oratorio are Malipiero's *La Passione* (1935), Driessler's *Dein Reich komme* (1948/9; first perf. 1950), Dallapiccola's *Job* (1950), Stravinsky's *Threni* (1958), and Orff's *Comœdia de Christi resurrectione* (1956).

Lit.: A. Schering, *Geschichte des Oratoriums* (1911); K. H. Bitter, *Beiträge zur Geschichte des Oratoriums* (1872); G. Pasquetti, *L'Oratorio musicale in Italia* (1906); *LavE* i.3, 1546ff (French oratorio); D. Alaleona, *Storia dell'oratorio musicale in Italia* (1945); G. Pannain, *L'oratorio dei Filippini* (1934); E. Vogl, "Die Oratorientechnik Carissimis" (diss. Prague, 1928); H. W. Hitchcock, "The Latin Oratorios of Marc-Antoine Charpentier" (diss. Univ. of Michigan, 1954); A. Schering, in *JMP* 1903, *SIM* viii; K. Meyer, "Das Offizium und seine Beziehung zum Oratorium" (*AMW* iii); E. J. Dent, "La Rappresentazione di Anima e di Corpo" (*CP 1939*); M. Brenet, "Les Oratoires de Carissimi" (*RMI* iv); H. Vogel, "Das Oratorium in Wien, 1725–40" (*StM* xiv).

Orchésographie. Title of T. Arbeau's important treatise (1589) on the dance. See under Dance music II.

Orchestra. I. *General.* In its common meaning, a large ensemble of instruments, as distinct from small ensembles (one player to the part) used for chamber music or from ensembles consisting of special instruments, called *band. The modern symphony orchestra consists of about 100 instruments divided into four main sections: strings, woodwinds, brass, and percussion:

Strings: violin I (18); violin II (16); viola (12); cello (10); double bass (8); harp (2). *Woodwinds:* flute (3); piccolo (1); oboe (3); English horn (1); clarinet (3); bass clarinet (1); bassoon (3); double bassoon (1). *Brass:* horn (6); trumpet (4); trombone (4); tuba (1). *Percussion:* kettledrums (4);

glockenspiel, tenor drum, bass drum, chimes, xylophones, celesta, cymbals, etc., according to requirements. To these may be added organ, piano, saxophones, mandolins, and other special instruments.

The orchestra just described is that generally called for in compositions of the late 19th century (Wagner, Brahms, Bruckner, Tchaikovsky, R. Strauss). In the early decades of the 20th century composers often wrote for considerably larger groups. For instance, Mahler in his Eighth Symphony ("Symphony of a Thousand," 1910) calls for the following: 2 piccolos, 4 flutes, 4 oboes, English horn, 2 E-flat clarinets, 3 B-flat clarinets, bass clarinet, 4 bassoons, contrabassoon; 8 horns, 4 trumpets, 4 trombones, tuba; timpani, bass drum, 3 pairs of cymbals, tam-tam, triangle, chimes, glockenspiel, celesta; piano, harmonium, organ, 2 harps, mandolin; 4 trumpets and 3 trombones as a supplementary fanfare group; first violins, second violins, violas, cellos, double basses; first and second soprano, first and second alto, tenor, baritone, and bass soloists, two mixed choruses, and boys' choir. The musical revolution that got underway after World War I naturally brought with it fundamental changes in orchestral technique and resources. The giant orchestra of the Mahler period was replaced by small groups, frequently approaching the size of a chamber orchestra but in highly individual combinations that differ greatly from one work to another. The change may be illustrated by comparing two works of Stravinsky's: the one, his *Le Sacre du printemps* (1911–13), utilizes an instrumental group even larger than the list above (though without vocalists), while his *Histoire du soldat* (1918) is scored for violin, double bass, clarinet, bassoon, cornet, trombone, and 8 percussion instruments handled by one player.

II. *History.* The music of the Middle Ages and early Renaissance that can be identified as "instrumental" [see Instrumental music; Instruments, *History*] was chamber rather than orchestral music. Larger ensembles did exist, but they were used mainly for ceremonial and festive occasions, such as welcoming royalty, weddings, and banquets. During the 16th century orchestral groups of fairly large sizes were used in the *intermezzi. The presentation, in 1565, of a comedy, *La Cofanaria,* with music by Corteccia and Striggio, involved, among others, 4 harpsichords, 4 viols, 2 trombones, 2 tenor recorders (*tenori di flauti*), 2 *cornetts (*cornetti*), 4 flutes (*traverse*), 2 lutes, 1 bass viol (*sotto basso*

di viola), 5 *storte,* and also *dozaina, lirone,* and *tamburi* [see Sonneck, in *MA* iii; A. della Corte, *Storia della musica,* i, 271ff]. During the latter part of the 16th century many-voiced motets were occasionally performed by orchestral groups of considerable size. Thus, Massimo Troiano (*Dialoghi,* 1569) reports that Striggio's motet "Ecce beatam lucem," written in forty parts for four choirs, was performed at a marriage ceremony of the Bavarian court by 8 *tromboni,* 8 *viole da arco,* 8 *flauti grossi,* 1 *instrumento da penna* (harpsichord), and 1 *liuto grosso* (large lute). Giovanni Gabrieli's *Sacrae symphoniae* of 1597 are the first compositions to indicate a specific instrument for each part, namely, *cornetti,* trombones, and violins [see Editions XXIII, 2, nos. 6, 11, 12, 16]. One of these compositions, the famous *Sonata pian' e forte,* employs two instrumental groups, one consisting of *cornetto* and 3 trombones, the other of violin and 3 trombones. The apotheosis of the Renaissance orchestra is represented by the instrumentation for Monteverdi's *Orfeo* of 1607. It consisted of: 2 harpsichords (*gravicembani*), 2 double-bass viols (*contrabassi de viola*), 10 viols (*viole da brazzo*), 1 harp (*arpa doppia*), 2 violins (*violini piccoli alla francese*), 2 bass lutes (*chitaroni*), 2 organs with wooden pipes (*organi di legno*), 3 bass viols (*bassi da gamba*), 4 trombones, 1 *regal, 2 cornetts, 1 small recorder (*flauto alla vigesima seconda*), 1 high trumpet (*clarino*), and 3 "soft" trumpets (*trombe sordine*), the trumpets having the usual (though unspecified) kettledrum support, at least in the overture. Praetorius carefully designated kettledrums in his *Polyhymnia caduceatrix* (1619).

In the 17th century, instrumental groups were usually small and variable. Music of the *basso continuo* type was performed by violins (for the upper parts) and a group of foundation instruments, such as harpsichord (or organ), bass viol, harp, lute, and theorbo, for the continuo [see the Sinfonia of Landi's *Il Sant' Alessio, c.* 1632; repr. in *HAM,* no. 208]. Contrapuntal music, such as instrumental canzonas, was played by what instruments were available. Occasionally, instruments are specified, as, e.g., in Legrenzi's "sonata" *La Buscha* (1655), scored for two *cornetti, fagotto,* 2 *violini,* and *viola da brazzo* [see *HAM,* no. 220]. The most famous orchestra of the 17th century was that established by Lully under the name "Les vingt-quatre violons du Roi," which, as the name implies, consisted mainly of strings. About 1700, this included a well-defined group of wind instruments, flutes, oboes, and horns, in addition to the violins, which by this time had replaced the earlier viols.

In the 18th century, trumpets and kettledrums were occasionally required. Bach's cantata, "Preise, Jerusalem, den Herrn" (1723), composed for the election of the city council of Leipzig (*Ratswahlkantate*), utilizes the following: 4 voice-parts, 4 trumpets, 2 timpani, 2 flutes, 3 oboes, 2 *oboi da caccia*, first and second violins, violas, and continuo, the last to be played by cellos and an organ. Under Johann Stamitz (1717–57), the main representative of the Mannheim school, the orchestra became more standardized: string section and doubled wind instruments, flutes, oboes, horns, and bassoons [see *HAM,* no. 294]. By the end of the 18th century this was amplified into the standard orchestra of the Viennese classics, consisting of 2 flutes, 2 oboes, 2 clarinets, 2 bassoons, 2 horns, 2 trumpets, 2 timpani, and the string group (first and second violins, violas, cellos, and double basses). In the 19th century, Weber, Berlioz, Meyerbeer, and Wagner contributed most to the development of orchestral resources. Berlioz in his *Grand Traité d'instrumentation et d'orchestration* (1843) discusses, in addition to the above-mentioned instruments, the harp, guitar, mandolin, piano, English horn, contrabassoon, bass clarinet, piccolo, organ, various sizes of trombone, bass tuba, glockenspiel, bass drum, tamtam, cymbals, side drum, triangle, castanets, saxophones, saxhorns, and various instruments that have dropped out of use. He describes the make-up of what he considers an ideal concert orchestra, containing 121 players, and, for giant festivals, a 465-member orchestra. Wagner designed and introduced the tubas (actually horns) named after him, which were later employed by Bruckner and R. Strauss. Shortly before 1900 the xylophone (Saint-Saëns' *Danse macabre*) and celesta (Tchaikovsky's *Nutcracker*) were added to the percussion section and soon were accorded full symphony status, along with other instruments, by Mahler. See Orchestration.

Lit.: P. Bekker, *The Story of the Orchestra* (1936); A. Elson, *Orchestral Instruments and Their Use* (1923); Johnstone and Stringham, *Instruments of the Modern Symphony Orchestra* (1928); F. Howes, *Full Orchestra*, rev. ed. (1947); G. F. Malipiero, *The Orchestra*, trans. G. Blom [1921]; R. Nettel, *The Orchestra in England*, rev. ed. [1956]; A. Carse, *The Orchestra in the 18th Century* (1940); *id., The Orchestra from Beethoven to Berlioz* (1949); J. Eppelsheim, *Das Orchester in den Werken Jean-Baptiste Lullys*

(1961); W. Kleefeld, "Die Orchester der Hamburger Oper, 1678–1738" (*SIM* i); H. Goldschmidt, "Das Orchester der italienischen Oper im 17. Jahrhundert" (*SIM* ii); K. Nef, "Zur Instrumentation im 17. Jahrhundert" (*JMP* xxxv); J. Lawrence, "The English Theatre Orchestra" (*MQ* iii); A. Carse, "17th Century Orchestral Instruments" (*ML* i, 334); R. Haas, "Zur Frage der Orchesterbesetzung in der zweiten Hälfte des 18. Jahrhunderts" (*CP 1909*, p. 159); A. Carse, "Brass Instruments in the Orchestra, Historical Sketch" (*ML* iii); G. F. Malipiero, in *RMI* xxiii, xxiv.

Orchestras. Following is a selected list of important orchestras (with date of establishment).

I. *United States:* Baltimore Symphony O. (1916); Boston Symphony O. (1881); Chicago Symphony O. (1891); Cincinnati Symphony O. (1895); Cleveland O. (1918); Detroit Symphony O. (1914); Indianapolis Symphony O. (1930); Los Angeles Philharmonic O. (1919); Minneapolis Symphony O. (1903); New York, Philharmonic Symphony O. (1842); Philadelphia O. (1900); Pittsburgh Symphony O. (1926); Rochester Philharmonic O. (1922); St. Louis Symphony O. (1907); San Francisco Symphony O. (1911); Washington, National Symphony O. (1931).

II. *Latin America:* Bogotá (Colombia), Orquesta Sinfónica de Colombia (1936); Buenos Aires (Argentina), Orquesta del Teatro Colón (1908); Caracas (Venezuela), Orquesta Sinfónica Venezuela (1935); Guatemala, Orquesta Sinfónica Nacional (1944); Havana (Cuba), Orquesta Filarmónica (1924); Lima (Peru), Orquesta Sinfónica Nacional (1938); Mexico, Orquesta Sinfónica Nacional (1928); Montevideo (Uruguay), Orquesta Sinfónica del Servicio Oficial de Dufusión Radio Electrica, abbr. Ossodre (1931); Rio de Janeiro (Brazil), Orquesta Sinfónica Municipal, Orquesta Sinfónica Brasileira (1940); Santiago (Chile), Orquesta Sinfónica de Chile (1922).

III *Europe:* Amsterdam, Concertgebouw Orchestra (1883); Berlin, Philharmonisches Orchester (1882); Brussels, Orchestre National Belge (1895); Geneva, Orchestre de la Suisse Romande (1918); Leipzig, Gewandhaus Konzerte (1781); London, London Philharmonic Orchestra (1932), London Symphony Orchestra (1904); Munich, Bayrisches Staatsorchester (1911), Konzertverein or Philharmoniker; Paris, Concerts du Conservatoire (1792), Concerts Colonne (1873), Concerts Pasdeloup (1920);

Rome, Concerti del Augusteo (1908); Vienna, Wiener Philharmonische Konzerte (1842).

IV. In the 1930's radio broadcasting orchestras were founded all over the world, not only in the great centers of music but also in numerous other places (Australia, Canada, New Zealand, etc.). The most outstanding were those of the National Broadcasting Company (NBC) and the British Broadcasting Company (BBC).

Lit.: M. Grant and H. S. Hettinger, *American Symphony Orchestras* (1940); J. H. Mueller, *The American Symphony Orchestra* (1951); *Pierre Key's Music Year Book* (1927–28); A. Eaglefield-Hull, *A Dictionary of Modern Music* (1924), s.v. "Orchestras"; A. Einstein, *Das Neue Musiklexikon* (1926), *s.v.* "Orchester"; R. Nettel, *The Orchestra in England,* rev. ed. [1956]; E. Chateau, *Histoire . . . des orchestres symphoniques aux États-Unis* (1933).

Orchestration. The art of employing, in an instrumental composition, the various instruments in accordance with (a) their individual properties and (b) the composer's concept of the sonorous effect of his work. It involves a detailed knowledge of the playing mechanism of each instrument, its range, tone quality, loudness, limitations, etc.

I. *Standard practice.* In traditional music, the *strings* are the backbone of the orchestra and, in general, are given the most important melodic parts of the score. Highly expressive, adaptable, and not too "individual," they are used throughout the composition with only short interruptions. Next in importance as melody instruments are *woodwinds,* each of which has a very characteristic timbre. The woodwinds are generally used sparingly as color effects imposed on the basic drawing of the violins. In the *brass* group, the horns (French horn) are rather similar in character and use to the woodwinds. Particularly in early symphonies (Haydn, Mozart) they are usually combined with the oboes. The trumpets and trombones, the "heavy artillery" of the orchestra, serve chiefly as a reinforcement for the climaxes of massed sound. They are also valuable for soft effects and as solo instruments, the trombones to express solemn grandeur, the trumpets for brilliant passages of a military or other character. The *percussion* group contributes rhythmic life and also special effects (triangle, cymbals, celesta).

II. *To 1700.* Until the end of the 16th century instrumental music was hardly ever written for or performed by specific instruments. Among

the rare exceptions are Dufay's "Gloria ad modum tubae," a vocal canon accompanied by two *tubae* (trumpets) sounding a fanfare ostinato, and A. Busnois' motet "Anthoni usque limina," which calls for the sounding of a bell (*campana*) in every second measure. G. Gabrieli was the first to prescribe specific instruments in his *Sacrae symphoniae* of 1597 [see Orchestra II], but little distinction is made between the capabilities of the various instruments. Monteverdi was perhaps the first to realize what color effects could be obtained by the judicious employment of one instrument or another. On the title page of his *Orfeo* (1607) the large orchestra employed for the first performance is indicated [see Orchestra II]. Although, in conformity with the then novel practice of *thoroughbass, the score consists largely of the vocal parts and the bass part, the accompanying written directions giving an idea of the desired orchestral effects. For instance, in Act III Caronte (Charon) is always accompanied by the regal and Orfeo by the *organo di legno* [see *HAM,* no. 187]. Also noteworthy is the use of the violin pizzicato and measured tremolo in Monteverdi's *Combattimento di Tancredi e Clorinda* [see *HAM,* no. 189].

The 17th-century emphasis on bowed instruments and the prevailing practice of thoroughbass scoring (melody and bass only) were not conducive to progress in the use of orchestral resources. The main place for a variety of instruments was the continuo part, which, in addition to harpsichord and double bass, could be performed by harps, lutes, theorbos, and other "foundation" instruments. This, however, was largely an early baroque practice that disappeared after 1650.

III. *18th century.* By the time of Bach (1685–1750), instruments and techniques of instrumental performance had been improved and various effective combinations worked out. Bach's basic method of orchestration consisted of an impartial distribution of interchangeable parts among string and wind instruments; each of the four fundamental parts—as opposed to the three or five of the 17th century—is independent, melodic, essential, and conceived in general rather than individual instrumental terms. Thus a part, whether for voice, flute, oboe, violins, or even brass, can scarcely be identified save by range. Wholesale duplication of the fundamental parts is common. In arias, where smaller groups of instruments are used, these, as well as special effects such as pizzicato and *con sordino,* are carried through the entire number, the contrast being from number to number rather than within a piece.

Handel, who had a keener sense of orchestral effect, treated his instrumental forces in a more broadly contrasting style than Bach yet without departing from "contrapuntal orchestration." His occasional use of the small recorder, contrabassoon, trombone, and harp in operas and cantatas is exceptional for the period, while his purely instrumental compositions are often for groups much more conventional than those of Bach. That the makeup of the orchestra was not yet standardized is obvious from an examination of Bach's *Brandenburg Concertos and four Orchestral Suites.

Although the orchestra as such remained largely unchanged throughout the 18th century, important progress was made in its treatment. Perhaps the first composer to give each instrument a distinct part of its own was J.-P. Rameau (1683–1764). He introduced interesting and unexpected passages on the flutes, oboes, and bassoons, opening the path to the coloristic treatment of the modern orchestra, and he, along with Arne, J. C. Bach, and Gluck, helped the clarinets achieve permanent status. Johann Stamitz (1717–57), leader of the Mannheim orchestra [see Mannheim school], developed the dramatic resources of the orchestra, chiefly the string section, by the use of dynamic variations such as sudden ff and pp, sustained crescendos, etc. The four symphonies written by K. P. E. Bach *c.* 1776 may be said to represent the final phase of orchestration prior to the masterworks of Haydn and Mozart. They are scored for two flutes, two oboes, one or two bassoons, two horns, and the usual group of strings. The interchangeable instrumental part of the past gives way to a part characteristic for the instrument for which it is written, though features of the older style remain in the frequent unison of the first and second violins and the near identity of viola, cello, and bass parts, including the harpsichord.

IV. *From Haydn to the present.* During the time of Haydn and Mozart the stringed instruments became entrenched as the foundation of the orchestra, and their numbers grew larger in proportion to the number of performers in the entire group. Each wind instrument was regarded as fully capable of assuming the main melodic line if the occasion demanded, as well as aiding in supplying the harmonic background, since the keyboard instrument was no longer used for that purpose. Ordinarily, instruments were no longer omitted from entire movements of a work, except in the trio of the minuet, and the orchestral color changed on a moment-to-moment basis, emphasizing the changes of subjects and the alternation of motifs. Beethoven, in his middle and late symphonies, occasionally augmented the orchestra with a piccolo, contrabassoon, third and fourth horn, and trombones; the last three symphonies also require the timpani to be tuned to notes other than tonic and dominant, and the Ninth has one section that uses triangle, cymbals, and bass drum.

The 19th century benefited enormously from improvements in instrument-making, most notably the key mechanisms for woodwinds and the valve systems for horns and trumpets. It also owed much to Berlioz regarding the use of instruments for their particular tone quality, and his ambitious and imaginative compositions greatly influenced such later composers as Liszt, Wagner, and R. Strauss. Berlioz seems to have risen suddenly as an innovator during the 1830's, but if one considers earlier composers, largely of the French school, it is evident that his work is partly founded on the coloristic efforts of Gluck, Cherubini, Méhul, Spontini, Boieldieu, and Weber.

In the second half of the 19th century there developed certain standard practices well known through the works of Wagner, Brahms, Tchaikovsky, Dvořák, and others [see I above]. A notable exception was Bruckner, who employed methods that have been somewhat contemptuously termed "organ orchestration" but that are well suited to the style of his symphonies. The complex scoring of R. Strauss outdid that of all previous composers in technical difficulty. Mahler, too, demanded a virtuoso orchestra and wrote with consummate skill for both small and mammoth forces. In strong contrast, Debussy introduced new methods of utter refinement and a highly developed coloristic technique for which the characteristic name "orchestral palette" has been widely adopted [see Impressionism].

The musical revolution of the 20th century has naturally brought with it many changes in orchestration techniques. One reaction against the 19th-century principles of orchestration was the shift from the huge forces of Strauss and Mahler to smaller groups (chamber orchestra), a change observable in the successive works of Stravinsky and Schoenberg. The breakdown of the standard orchestra was also spurred by the search for new timbres and combinations. One method was "perverted orchestration," e.g., giving the melody to the brass and using the strings for percussive effects; often used by Stravinsky, it has been widely employed for many purposes, including parody. Other approaches included the eliciting of new sounds from standard instruments, especially percussion and harp (Carlos Salzedo); the scoring largely or exclusively for percussion (Stravinsky's *Les Noces;* Varèse's *Hyperprism* and *Ionisation*); the adoption of Latin American or other exotic instruments (such as the Hungarian cimbalom, used not only by Bartók and Kodály but also in Stravinsky's *Renard* and *Ragtime*); the employment of unusual sound-effect instruments (big iron chains in Schoenberg's *Gurrelieder;* sirens, roulette wheel, typewriter, rattle, pistol shots, water splashes, etc. in Satie's *Parade*); and the use of newly invented instruments (Vibraphone in Berg's *Lulu,* the Ondes Martenot in many French works). Anton Webern introduced a new technique known as *Klangfarbenmelodie,* which became the point of departure for the avant-garde orchestration employed in *musique concrète* and *electronic music,* an "orchestration without orchestra."

Lit.: C. Forsyth, *Orchestration* (1935); S. Lockwood, *Elementary Orchestration* [1926]; D. J. Rauscher, *Orchestration* [1963]; N. Rimsky-Korsakov, *Principles of Orchestration* (1922); J. Wagner, *Orchestration* (1959); H. Berlioz, *Treatise on Instrumentation,* rev. and enlarged by R. Strauss (Eng. trans., 1948); A. Carse, *The History of Orchestration* (1925); L. A. Coerne, *The Evolution of Modern Orchestration* (1908); C. S. Terry, *Bach's Orchestra* (1932); G. Read, *Thesaurus of Orchestral Devices* (1953); C. Koechlin, *Traité d'orchestration,* 5 vols. (1955); K. Kennan, *The Technique of Orchestration* (1952); id., *Orchestration Workbook* (1952); W. Piston, *Orchestration* (1958). See also Editions XXXIX, 24.   w.d.d.; rev. w.a. and c.t.

Orchestrion. See under Mechanical instruments III.

Ordinary and **Proper** [L. *ordinarium, proprium*]. In the Roman Catholic rites, the Ordinary is the portion of the service that remains the same no matter what day it is performed, while the Proper includes all the variable texts and chants. The distinction is particularly important with the Mass [see Mass A]. Other services, however, also contain invariable and variable portions, e.g.,

the *Magnificat* is a part of the Ordinary of Vespers.

Ordo [L., pl. *ordines*]. See under Modes, rhythmic.

Ordo Romanus [L.]. Designation for early liturgical books (7th–9th centuries) containing descriptions of the liturgy as celebrated by the Pope. Their contents include important information concerning the early form of Mass chants, e.g., the Introit with numerous verses [see *ApGC,* pp. 52f, 190]. They are edited in M. Andrieu, *Les Ordines romani du haut moyen âge,* 3 vols. (1931–35).

Ordre [F.]. In F. Couperin's *Pièces de Clavecin* (1713–30), name for his suitelike collections of pieces in the same key. An *ordre* usually begins with a few pieces in the style of an allemande, courante, and sarabande, but also includes a great many other pieces with fanciful or descriptive titles. See Suite III.

Orfeo. See *Favola d'Orfeo, La* (Monteverdi); *Orphée aux Enfers;* Orpheus and Eurydice.

Orfeo ed Euridice. Opera in three acts by Gluck (libretto by R. di Calzabigi), produced in Vienna, 1762 (produced in Paris, as *Orphée,* 1774, with French text). Setting: Greece, legendary times. The story is essentially the same as that of Monteverdi's La *Favola d'Orfeo,* the main difference being that the tragic and heroic close of Monteverdi's work is replaced by a happy ending (Amor, the god of Love, appears and restores Euridice to life). *Orfeo* is the first of Gluck's reform operas.

Organ [F. *orgue;* G. *Orgel;* It. *organo;* L. *organum;* Sp. *órgano*]. I. *General description.* The organ is a keyboard instrument, operated by the player's hands and feet, that consists of a series of pipes standing on a wind chest. The wind chest is fitted with valves connected to the keys, either by a direct mechanical linkage or by electrical and/or pneumatic intermediaries. Means also are provided for delivering a constant supply of air under pressure to the chest. Traditionally the wind was supplied by *feeders or bellows; since about 1915 the source of supply has been an electric rotary blower, in which case the bellows serve merely as a reservoir whose top is weighted or sprung to ensure a steady pressure. The simplest organ consists of one set of pipes, each pipe corresponding to one key of the keyboard. However, to make available a variety of tone colors for the performer, organs usually have several sets (*ranks) of pipes, known as *stops or *registers, which can be brought into play or retired—i.e., "stopped"—at will.

II. *Mechanism.* In all organs, ancient or modern, the sounding of a desired pipe is effected by a combination of two mechanisms that operate crosswise in the manner of Cartesian coordinates. One of these, the "abscissa" (*x*), is actuated by depressing a key, while the other, the "ordinate" (*y*), is actuated by drawing a stop. In geometry an ordered pair of numbers (*x, y*) is required to determine a point; in organ playing a key must be depressed and a stop be drawn if a particular pipe is to speak. The means for effecting these two types of control vary. Prior to the mid-19th century the mechanism was a mechanical linkage, a system of levers known as *tracker action. Thereafter pneumatic and/or electric mechanisms became increasingly common until the second quarter of the 20th century, when tracker key action began to reappear.

(a) Tracker organ. In a hypothetical miniature organ with three ranks and seven keys, there will be 21 pipes and 21 holes arranged in three lines of 7 each in the upper board (table) of the wind chest. For each rank there is a thin strip (slider) of wood or plastic bored with seven holes and arranged so as to slide freely beneath a stationary toe board, also bored with seven holes, over each of which stands a pipe. Drawing a knob (stop, drawstop) adjacent to the keyboard aligns the holes of table, slider, and toe board, thereby setting one rank of pipes in readiness to sound. To each key is linked a hinged valve (pallet) that, when opened by the player's depressing the key, allows air to pass from the constant wind supply into a narrow rectangular note channel (key chamber) running crosswise beneath the three sliders. In order to obtain a desired tone, say, that of the pipe C of the rank Principal, the player draws the knob labeled "principal," thereby placing that register in readiness, and presses the key C, which pulls on the trace rod (tracker) connecting the key with the C pallet, causing the pallet to move down on its hinge. Air then passes into the C note channel and upward through the C hole in table, slider, and toe board into the C pipe of the principal, which sounds.

(b) Electropneumatic organ. In the electropneumatic organ each pipe has its own individual valve, which is mounted on a leather pneumatic (pouch) that is inflated when the valve is in off (closed) position and the pipe is not sounding. When the pouch is deflated, the valve opens and the pipe above speaks. In this type of action the depression of a key closes an electric circuit that activates a magnet. The minute armature of the magnet acts as a pneumatic valve, which, unless intercepted by the stop action, exhausts all the pouches controlled by the key. In like manner, the drawing of a stop exhausts a channel that allows the key action to take effect. Thus, as with the slider chest, it is only when the key and stop mechanisms intersect at right angles that a pipe speaks. There are many variants of electric action, some of which are illustrated in Audsley, *The Art of Organ Building* [see Lit.]. In the case of key action, the tracker mechanism has certain advantages [see section XI below].

III. *Keyboards and divisions.* An organ meeting the minimum requirement for a proper rendition of the literature will have two keyboards (*manuals), each controlling a separate division of five or six stops, and a keyboard for the feet (pedal) commanding two to five stops. Organs having four manuals and pedal with fifty to one hundred stops are common, however, and even five to seven manuals have been employed. The divisions, or "organs," connected with the various keyboards are called *pedal organ, great organ, swell organ, choir organ, positive organ, solo organ,* and *echo organ.* (Foreign names such as *Hauptwerk, Rückpositiv* [G.] and *récit* [F.] are occasionally used.) Their allotment to the different manuals varies a great deal (except, of course, for the pedal organ), and so does the selection of pipes connected with each of them.

IV. *Couplers, etc.* Practically every organ possesses devices that make the various divisions available on keyboards other than their own. These are the so-called couplers. For instance, coupler swell-to-great makes the swell organ available on the manual for the great organ, so that stops from both can be sounded simultaneously. Similarly, any manual can be coupled to the pedal. Suboctave couplers and superoctave couplers connect one manual with the lower or higher octave of another manual or of itself. [See also Divided stop.]

Changes in *registration are sometimes desired at moments when the player's hands are too occupied on the keyboard to manipulate a number of stops. To facilitate such changes, special controls are provided in the form of thumb buttons or toe studs. Each of these so-called pistons controls an *ad libitum* selection of stops, which the player can arrange in advance and then can instantly bring into play by a single touch on the piston.

V. *Compass.* The normal compass of the modern organ manual is sixty-one notes or five complete octaves extending from C to c''''. That of the pedal keyboard is thirty-two notes or two and one-half octaves extending from C to g'. The compass has not always been so large. Bach's organs usually had one octave less on the manuals (C to c''') and five keys less on the pedal (C to d'); on the other hand, the English organ of Purcell and Handel, lacking pedals entirely, had a deeper manual compass (G_1 to f'''). The actual pitch range of the organ is much greater than the compass of its keyboards, owing to the fact that there are, in addition to the pipe ranks of normal (unison) pitch (comparable to that of the piano), others whose pitch is one or two octaves lower or higher. The normal pitch is called unison and is indicated by the symbol 8' [read eight-foot; see Foot (2)], the suboctave pitch is 16', and there are three superoctave pitches, designated 4', 2', and 1'. On the pedal the normal pitch, being an octave below that of the manual, is known as 16' pitch, its suboctave being 32'. The frequency of 32' C is approximately 16 vibrations per second while that of the top C of a manual 2' stop is more than 8,000. Thus the real compass of the instrument extends over nine complete octaves.

VI. *Mutation and mixture stops.* In addition to the various octave pitches, called *foundation stops,* there are the so-called *mutation stops,* whose pitch corresponds to one of the harmonics of the unison pitch. For instance, a mutation stop 2⅔' is tuned to the third harmonic (twelfth) and hence will sound g' if the key of c is depressed [see explanation under Foot (2)]. Such stops are not to be played alone (which would result in transposition) or with a unison stop of about the same loudness (which would result in parallel fifths), but together with a unison stop of considerably greater force, in which case the mutation stop ceases to be heard individually and merely serves as an artificial harmonic, thus modifying the timbre of the unison stop. Finally there are *mixture stops* (also called *compound stops*), i.e., stops that combine a selection of unison and mutation ranks. These serve the same purpose as the mutation stops just described and must also be drawn together with a sufficiently strong unison stop. Mutation and mixture stops, if properly used, are among the organist's most valuable resources for obtaining a variety of tone color and clear articulation.

VII. *The organ case; expression.* By the 15th century it was customary to place the wind chests, pipes, and mechanism of the organ in a large wooden cabinet, known as the organ case, closed on all sides but the front. The keyboards and stop controls were centered in front at floor level, while the show pipes (open diapason, principal, prestant, montre) stood in the opening above the keyboards and together with decorative carvings formed a perforated screen through which the sound from pipes inside the cabinet could pass. An important (and original) purpose of the organ case was to protect the delicate pipes and mechanism, but the case was also of musical value in (1) blending the sound, (2) imparting its own cavity-resonances to it, and (3) projecting sound toward the listener. In old organs, both case and wind chest acted as blending agencies, each making use of the tendency of two organ pipes, especially those speaking in unison or octaves, to "draw" or "pull," i.e., to synchronize pitch, in so far as they are able to "hear" each other, either through their common note channel [see II] or via the concentrated sound field inside the case. Cavity-resonances in the case were responsible for an attractive burgeoning of the sound in tenor or bass octaves even from pipes of slender scale, an effect similar to the baritone bloom in antique harpsichords although derived differently, i.e., by air resonance rather than timbre resonance. For sound projection the close-fitting cabinet acted as a band-shell, giving the organ good attack even in highly reverberant buildings. In the 17th century, when organs grew to the point of having several divisions, each division was likely to be given its own tone cabinet in the over-all complex of the organ case, and at least one division, the *Rückpositiv* or chair organ, was nearly always separately situated at the gallery railing below the main body of the instrument and behind the player. In performing on such an organ, to change from one manual to another is to move the source of sound from one cabinet to another, producing a stereophonic effect that, when heightened by differences in registration and cabinet resonance, is eminently in keeping with the terraced dynamics of the baroque style. The principle according to which an organ is thus visibly divided into cabinets, each relating to a keyboard, is known as the *Werk* principle, a system of organization that became unfashionable during the 18th century but that has been revived in the 20th. A tone cabinet that survived the abandonment of the *Werk* principle is the expression chamber or swell box, in effect a cabinet whose opening is covered by a set of Venetian shutters that can be opened or closed in varying degrees by a foot pedal. Though artificial, this is for the organ the only possible means for varying dynamics, other than the stepwise addition or subtraction of stops.

VIII. *Organ pipes in general.* There are two distinct classes of organ pipe: flue and reed. The flue pipe closely resembles the ordinary tin whistle [see Whistle flute], in which a vibrating air sheet sets up vibrations in the column of air surrounded by the pipe. The complete flue pipe is made up of the following parts: the "body," the cylindrical portion that encloses the column of air; the "foot," usually a tapered cone connecting the body to the wind supply from the chest; and the "mouth," a rectangular opening cut from the body at the point where the foot joins it. At the mouth, the cylindrical body and the conical foot are flattened, and the straight edge thus formed at the top of the mouth is called the "upper lip." Similarly, the so-called "lower lip" is the straight, flattened portion of the foot just below the mouth. The "languid" is a flat piece of metal forming an internal partition between foot and body; along its front edge it is beveled and arranged so as to form, with the lower lip, a narrow slit known as the "flue," through which the wind sheet issues. When a pipe is sounding, the wind sheet, as it rises from flue toward upper lip, flexes in and out of the mouth in a complex way, exciting the resonant air column within the body of the pipe. Flue pipes are extremely sensitive to their geometry at the mouth, so that shaping and adjusting the languid and lips, known as "voicing," requires considerable skill. Of particular interest in voicing is the so-called "nicking," a row of serrations or nicks cut into the edges of the languid and lower lip where they form the flue. An unvoiced metal organ pipe whose flue is not closed up to a hair's breadth produces, when first winded, a strong transient, onomatopoeically known as the "chiff," followed by a coarse and unstable note displaying many nonharmonic overtones. Other conditions being favorable, a small number of shallow nicks will purify and steady the note without dispelling the chiff. Deepening the nicks and increasing their number eventually eliminates the chiff entirely, at the same time tending to make the steady note dull and lifeless. Although the chiff was anathema to 19th-century musicians, used in moderation it was not unfavorably regarded in earlier times and is perhaps better thought of today than ever before, owing to current interest in the horizontal aspect of

music, i.e., the clarification of contrapuntal line, to which the chiff undoubtedly contributes. In tracker organs the chiff can be controlled to a limited extent by the player according to the speed with which he depresses the key.

Flue pipes are tuned by lengthening or shortening the pipe. This is accomplished at the top of the pipe by a sliding sleeve (tuning slide), or by rolling down a strip of metal from the top, or by "coning" the top of the pipe in or out so as to make the top opening smaller or larger.

The type of reed pipe used almost exclusively in the organ is known as the *beating reed* and must not be confused with the free reed employed in the harmonium or reed organ [see Reed II]. The beating reed consists of a vibrating brass tongue, slightly curved, which rolls down over a long opening in the side of a brass tube, or "shallot." The lower end of the shallot is closed so that when the tongue rolls down flat against the carefully flattened surface surrounding the opening no air can pass into the shallot. The upper end of the shallot is connected to the lower end of a resonator or horn, usually conical or cylindrical, whose upper end is open to the air. Shallot and tongue are held firmly together in a heavy block of metal or wood; the resonator is inserted into the top of the block, while the block in turn is inserted into a socket that conveys the wind up from the wind chest. When wind is admitted to the socket it surrounds tongue and shallot, causing the tongue to commence vibrating, which, by alternately opening and closing, sends pulses of air via the shallot into the resonator, thereby exciting the air column enclosed within the resonator and causing a note to issue from its open end. The tone of a reed pipe is extremely sensitive to the shape of its shallot and shallot opening, and especially to the thickness and curvature of the tongue, whose proper adjustment is perhaps the most refined skill in organ building. Tuning and loudness are regulated jointly at two points, first by lengthening or shortening the resonator at its upper end, and second, by a tuning wire in the block that controls the free vibrating length of the tongue.

IX. *Flue pipes.* There are two fundamental kinds of flue pipe: the "principals" and the "flutes." The basic difference between them is the way they are voiced, i.e., adjusted at the mouth, and one speaks of a pipe as being voiced to operate in "principal mode" or in "flute mode." In principal mode the wind sheet vibrates in such a way as to develop in about equal strength the first and second harmonics, while in flute mode only the first harmonic (fundamental) is emphasized. For a particular pipe to operate in principal mode, either the mouth height (cut-up) must be relatively low or the volume of air passing through the pipe must be large. The same pipe may be voiced in flute mode by reducing the flow of air, or by increasing the cut-up, or both. Principal mode also requires a higher setting of the languid than does flute mode.

(a) Diapason or principal tone. The bodies or resonators of organ flue pipes are made in a large variety of shapes, but the most common is that of the so-called diapason or principal, a cylindrical tube of moderate scale [see Scaling], open at the top. The concerted sound of these pipes is characteristic of the organ alone, and it is the diapason chorus that accounts largely for the sonority known as "full organ." Diapasons may occur at all possible pitches. In an organ of moderate size they are likely to be found at 8', 4', 2⅔' and 2' pitches on the manuals, at 16', 8', 5⅓' and 4' on the pedals, and in practically all mixtures [see IX (f) below]. Usually only the 16' and 8' members of the chorus are labeled diapason, those of higher pitch simply being labeled according to their position in the diatonic scale relative to unison, e.g., octave 4', twelfth 2⅔', fifteenth 2'.

Diapason pipes operate in principal mode. The tone of a single rank is apt to be somewhat assertive and moderately full, with a moderate harmonic development. A considerable variety of diapason tone exists: the violin diapason is of smaller scale and tends toward the string side, while the montre of an 18th-century French organ is quite full and fluty in character.

(b) Flute tone. The most common variety of organ flute is the stopped flute [G. *gedackt,* F. *bourdon*], whose large-scale cylindrical bodies are made of wood or metal with a stopper or plug in the upper end. The stopper has two effects: (1) it acoustically doubles the length of the body so that the note spoken is an octave lower than it would be with the end open; (2) it attenuates the even-numbered harmonics (second, fourth, sixth, etc.). The latter effect, in conjunction with the natural emphasis on first harmonic given by flute-mode operation, causes the stopped flute to produce mainly fundamental (first harmonic) with but a trace of "quint" (third harmonic). An emphasis on fundamental is the hallmark of organ flutes; with their marked quickness of speech, flutes are ideal for rapid passages, particularly when com-

bined with mutations [see (e) below] or a quiet mixture [see (f)].

The *chimney flute* has a small-diameter open tube extending upward from its stopper, while *koppel* and *spindle flute* substitute a form of open-topped, cone-shaped extension for the stopper. All three have greater harmonic development than the stopped flute, owing partly to the encouragement of even-numbered harmonics by the small opening at the top. Stopped and half-stopped flutes occur frequently at 8' and 4' pitches on the manuals and at 16', 8', and 4' on the pedal.

Large-scale open flutes having no stopper, such as the *nighthorn* and *block flute,* are often used at 4' and 2' pitches and as mutations [see (e)]. These do not have the "quinty" sound of the stopped flutes but have greater carrying power and stability in the treble. The harmonic flute, a large-scale open flute of double length with an octave hole drilled at the midpoint of the body, represents an effort to imitate the orchestral traverse flute. It occurs occasionally at 8' though more usually at 4' pitch.

(c) String tone. String-toned stops such as the *cello, viola, salicional,* and *gamba* have a high harmonic development, causing the tone to be thin and cutting. String tone is actually an extreme form of principal tone; it is produced by using pipe scales that are narrower than normal principal scale and voicing techniques that emphasize the intrinsically bright character of principal mode. Because of their narrow scale, strings articulate with difficulty. They are therefore unsuitable for rapid passages and indeed were never fully developed as organ stops until the 19th century, when sonority replaced agility as the most important feature of a musical instrument. String stops produce a distinctive sonority, particularly when they occur in pairs that are intentionally tuned one sharp to the other so as to produce a slow undulation. Such a pair may be labeled *voix céleste* or *unda maris.*

(d) Hybrids. *Spitzflute* and *gemshorn* ranks commonly have pipe bodies in the form of an inverted cone. This construction brings into prominence the second harmonic, and, according to scale, amount of taper, and the mode of vibration used at the mouth, the tone lies either between principal and flute or between string and flute. Because of its hybrid nature, this class of tone often appears on a small organ or small division where a single stop must do the work of both a flute and a principal. Mutation stops of

2⅔′, 1⅗′, and 1⅓′ pitches are successfully constructed as hybrids.

(e) Mutations. The mutation stop is characteristic of the organ, its chief use being with a unison or octave rank or a combination of such stops to alter the tonal character by artificially bringing into prominence a particular overtone. Mutation ranks greatly increase the tonal variety of the instrument, since each new way of combining them with unisons and octaves produces a strikingly different result. They thus are useful for producing solo combinations and for giving an individual character to each voice line in contrapuntal music of several keyboards, e.g., trios for two manuals and pedal. When the mutation stops called *nazard* 2⅔′ and *tierce* 1⅗′ are combined with three flutes of 8′, 4′, and 2′ pitches respectively, the effect toward the treble is reminiscent of a trumpet and is known as the *cornet*. Traditionally the cornet is a solo voice for use either by itself or with a trumpet stop, in which case it serves to strengthen the treble register of the latter.

(f) Mixture stops. Mixtures, or compound stops, usually comprise from two to seven principal pipes per note of the keyboard arranged to speak certain harmonics of the note. There are a great many varieties of mixture, but normally the ranks employed speak only octaves and fifths (quints). A typical mixture for a great division might be laid out as follows:

	row I	row II	row III	row IV
C to B :	1⅓′	1′	⅔′	½′
c to b :	2′	1⅓′	1′	⅔′
c′ to b′ :	2⅔′	2′	1⅓′	1′
c″ to b″ :	4′	2⅔′	2′	1⅓′
c‴ to c⁗:	8′	4′	2⅔′	2′

Here the pitch of each rank is as usual indicated by the length of the C pipe [see Foot]. (In the case of those ranks that do not extend down to C, e.g., the 2′ rank, the pipe length given is the one the C pipe would have if the rank were carried all the way down.) Breaks occur here between each B and C, where the highest-pitched rank is discontinued and a new low-pitched rank is introduced. A practical reason for the breaks is the impossibility in the treble of even hearing high-pitched ranks such as the ⅔′ and ½′; a musical reason is that high-pitched pipes used in the bass give attack and definition to slow-speaking diapason basses, while multitudinous pipes of comparable length lend mass to the treble. Each division of a well-appointed organ of moderate size will have a diapason chorus capped by one or more mixtures. Mixtures composed of octaves and quints may bear names such as *mixture, plein jeu, fourniture, Scharf,* and *cymbal.* Mixtures containing also third-sounding ranks (*tièrces*) may appear under labels such as *sesquialtera, tertian,* and *terzcimbel.* All sorts of scaling may occur, from very wide to very narrow.

X. *Reed pipes.* There are three kinds of reed pipe: *chorus reeds; semichorus reeds;* and *solo* or *orchestral reeds.* Chorus reeds belong chiefly to the trumpet family and appear in the modern organ on both manual and pedal divisions at subunison, unison, and octave pitches. *Posaunes, trombones, trumpets, cornopeans,* and *clarions* are in this category. Although their names suggest orchestral tones, they differ in quality considerably from their orchestral prototypes. They are purely organ voices and are used to add power and vigor to the ensemble. They may also be employed for solo work. The trumpet family have conical resonators of full length, i.e., 8′ C has a resonator of approximately 8′ length.

Semichorus reeds come to us largely from the baroque period and are not imitative, although their names may suggest an orchestral background. The *cromorne, schalmei,* and *rankett* are typical examples. The term "semichorus" is used because they may function as chorus reeds, solo stops, or merely timbre creators in combination with other voices. The resonators of this class of reed are often cylindrical and short. They may be half-, quarter-, or even an eighth-length.

The solo or orchestral reeds are imitative of various orchestral instruments, such as the *bassoon, English horn, clarinet,* and orchestral *oboe.* They are used largely as solo stops.

XI. *Tonal structure of the organ.* The organ is unique among instruments in that the choice of voices (i.e., stops) that go into its makeup is arbitrary. The list of the stops in an organ, called the "specification," varies greatly from one organ to another, especially if organs of different periods are taken into consideration. In earlier times, an organ was designed for performing a limited repertory consisting mainly of music of its period. The wide range of the modern repertory, however, has required great emphasis on designing organs on which the music of all periods can be played. This is by no means an easy task when one considers the long lifespan of the instrument. A conscientiously eclectic sample specification might be:

GREAT	POSITIVE
Quintaten 16′ (wood)	Gedackt 8′
Principal 8′	Dulciana 8′
Spitzflöte 8′	Principal 4′
Octave 4′	Koppelflöte 4′
Rohrflöte 4′	Nazard 2⅔′
Quint 2⅔′	Octave 2′
Super octave 2′	Tierce 1⅗′
Nachthorn 2′	Larigot 1⅓′
Mixture IV–V ranks	Super octave 1′
Scharf III–IV ranks	Scharf IV ranks
Cornet II–V ranks	Cymbel III ranks
Double trumpet 16′	Dulcian 16′
Trumpet 8′	Krummhorn 8′
Clarion 4′	

SWELL (enclosed)	PEDAL
Geigen principal 8′	Principal 16′
Viole-de-gambe 8′	Bourdon 16′
Viole céleste 8′	Octave 8′
Chimney flute 8′	Spillflöte 8′
Principal 4′	Quint 5⅓′
Lieblich flute 4′	Choralbass 4′
Fifteenth 2′	Nachthorn 4′
Sesquialtera II ranks	Blockflöte 2′
Plein jeu IV–VI ranks	Mixture IV ranks
Contre hautbois 16′	Bassoon 32′
Trompette 8′	Posaune 16′
Vox humana 8′	Trompette 8′
Clairon 4′	Schalmei 4′
Tremulant	

Although this specification might be acceptable to many organists and organ builders, opinion is presently divided over the basic principles of organ construction. Two widely differing principles are in use today, the so-called tracker principle and the electropneumatic principle. The names derive from the kind of key action used, but the differences go beyond any question of key action.

In its purest form, the modern tracker organ embodies the following characteristics: (1) only mechanical connections between keys and valves [see II (a)] and therefore, (2) proximity of key desk and wind chests; (3) a functional and often decorative wooden organ case—essentially a large piece of furniture—standing freely within the auditorium [see VII]; (4) slider wind chests throughout; (5) low wind pressures; (6) use of the *Werk* principle [see VII]. The modern tracker organ thus retains a geometry and a tonal ideal already firmly established in the 17th century, though employing modern materials for the effective operation of its mechanism and often

drawing on registers and sonorities from later periods, e.g., the voix célestes. By contrast, the modern electropneumatic organ, while adopting many sonorities and registers from the 17th century, employs a less predictable geometry. It is usually characterized by: (1) electrical connections between keys and pipe valves, and therefore, (2) free choice of placement for the key desk with respect to the wind chests; (3) free arrangements of the pipes on the wind chests; (4) wind chests having a separate valve for each pipe [see II (b)]; (5) freedom to use both low and high wind pressures; (6) emphasis on the decorative possibilities presented by freely exposed masses of pipes, with minimal adherence to the *Werk* principle, and often with part of the organ recessed in chambers.

A well-built tracker action affords the player a sense of immediacy (through "feedback") that is totally unattainable with electropneumatic action. Taken all together, the unifying effect of a slider chest, a shallow focusing tone cabinet, pipework voiced with a modicum of chiff, and an uncoupled tracker action produces a precision of attack and release akin to that of the harpsichord and piano and invaluable in the performance of contrapuntal music. By contrast, electropneumatic action, while lacking the preciseness that makes for a good keyboard instrument, provides the best means for controlling a very large organ, when attention necessarily focuses on variety and expansiveness of sonority rather than on subtle keyboard articulation. It also provides a means of adapting the pipe organ to the impractical physical arrangements often presented to the organ builder by church and auditorium architects.

XII. *History.* Legend traces the organ back to the "Syrinx" (panpipes) and similar primitive wind instruments consisting of a group of pipes or reeds of varying pitches (rather than a single pipe bored with finger holes). If we regard the organ as a wind instrument that, besides having multiple pipes of fixed pitches, is mechanically supplied with air under pressure and played from a keyboard, then it dates from *c.* 250 B.C., when the Greek engineer Ktesibios of Alexandria is supposed to have invented the *hydraulos (as recorded in Hero's *Pneumatika, c.* 120 B.C.). The hydraulos had a set of fixed-pitch pipes, a crude keyboard of limited compass, and a mechanical wind supply regulated by water pressure. While Hero's account is the first recorded instance of a "modern" organ, the hydraulos doubtless had even more primitive antecedents. The hydraulos was used at least until the end of the 5th century.

Its uses were entirely secular, and it was popular at festivals and in outdoor arenas, suggesting that it made a loud sound.

The pneumatic (as opposed to hydraulically regulated) organ made its first recorded appearance *c.* A.D. 120, when an organ supplied with wind by means of a simple bellows is mentioned in a passage from J. Pollux's *Onomastikon.* Another early reference to this type of organ is found in an epigram of the Roman Emperor Julian the Apostate (A.D. 331–63). Elaborate Byzantine organs with gilded and silvered pipes are described in reports from A.D. 867 to 946. Such instruments were sometimes made as royal gifts. In 757 the Byzantine Emperor Constantine Copronymus is said to have presented one to the Frankish King Pepin, and in 812 Charlemagne received a similar instrument.

In England the organ was known as early as the 7th century, as appears from the writings of Bishop Aldhelm (*c.* 640–709), who repeatedly praised it for its "mighty voice." A large organ is recorded by the monk Wolstan as having been erected at Winchester Cathedral under the Bishop Elphege (d. 951). It supposedly had 400 pipes and 26 bellows, was played by two organists on two keyboards of 20 keys each, and had an exceedingly powerful sound. During the early Middle Ages virtually all English and Continental organs were built by ecclesiastics.

The hydraulos and all recorded early pneumatic organs up to as late as 1100 had a very crude key mechanism consisting of slides that were simply pulled out or pushed in to open the pipes. In a more advanced model, such slides were connected to large hinged "keys," which were either pushed down like the keys of a carillon or, as Michael Praetorius suggests in his *Syntagma musicum,* vol. ii (1619) struck with the fists. This type of action employed a return spring that facilitated playing.

Prior to the 15th century there was no means of controlling individual ranks of pipes, so that the color or intensity of the sound produced could not be varied. The very earliest organs (i.e., the hydraulos and the most primitive pneumatic organs) had only one set of pipes and, if one is to believe contemporary descriptions, there was no notion of scaling the pipes [see Scaling] such as developed later. According to these early accounts, all pipes of the set were about the same diameter, varying only in length with their pitch. Such a practice would make the longer pipes tend toward a stringlike sound while the treble pipes gave flutelike sounds. The tonal conse-

quences of this were not too serious, since until the 14th century the compass of organs was never more than three octaves, and often less. Eventually builders began to vary the scaling (diameter) of the pipes along with the pitch length to produce a more even timbre throughout the compass. Also, as larger organs were adopted for church use, the number of ranks of pipes began to increase. As a result, the medieval organ developed as a large mixture [F. *grand jeu;* G. *Werck, Hintersatz;* Neth. *Blokwerk*]. To the pipes of the fundamental (8′) pitch were added others of higher unison pitches (4′, 2′, 1′) as well as those sounding the fifth (2⅔′, 1⅓′), which reinforced and brightened the total harmonic structure.

Increasing the number of ranks necessitated the invention of a more efficient playing action than the old slide system. The modern barred wind chest [see Tracker action] had its inception in the 14th century, and from that time on the key control was achieved by opening a spring-loaded valve (pallet) that admitted wind from a common supply into a note-channel communicating with all the pipes for any given note. By the 14th century, the keyboard had become smaller, ranging up to three octaves in compass and having semitones, particularly in the middle range. The earliest preserved examples of *organ music (in the Robertsbridge Codex in 1325) require a complete chromatic middle octave.

The next step in the organ's development was the provision of means to vary the loudness and timbre of the sound produced. Organs having more than one keyboard had already appeared; that built in 1361 in Halberstadt, Germany, had three manuals and a primitive pedal, twenty bellows worked by ten men, and pipes as long as 31′ (approx. C_2). As far as can be determined, however, each division of this and similar organs was but a mixture, and those variations of color that were possible were due purely to differences in the strength and timbre of the separate divisions.

During the 14th century, along with the development of large but still cumbersome church organs, there appeared a parallel development of a smaller, more refined, and more tractable instrument called a *positive.* This instrument was a self-contained organ small enough to be moved like a piece of furniture. It had one keyboard, no pedals, and no exceptionally large or loud pipes, since it was often used in small rooms or for accompaniment purposes. Smaller than the great church organs, it had a narrower and more manageable keyboard, which was understandably favored by performers. Positives began to be placed in the chancel area of churches to assist the singing of plainsong by the clergy. Soon afterward some organists began to place a positive organ close to the keyboard of the great organ (by now generally located in the rear or side gallery of the church), making it possible to play both loudly and softly. From this it was but a short step to connect a small (positive) organ to the great organ so that both might be played from adjacent keyboards. The positive division so created came to be located on the gallery rail, immediately behind the organist's back (hence the German name, *Rückpositiv*), the keyboards of both organs being located in the front of the main organ.

The use of separate *stops, whereby the player could select different ranks of pipes to play while others remained mute, seems to have begun in Italy during the first half of the 15th century. The oldest surviving organ with stops, built in 1470, is in the Church of St. Petronio in Bologna. As this development gradually spread across the Continent, an intermediate type of instrument appeared in Germany, having a great organ consisting of an undivided mixture and a smaller positive organ with stops. Gradually, individual stops began to be added to, or detached from, the main mixture of the great organ, leaving in the end individual stops of different timbres and pitches and one or more stops controlling grouped smaller pipes of higher unison and harmonic pitches. This last vestige of the *Blokwerk* survives in the harmonic-corroborating mixture stops of present-day organs in a much refined and improved form. Examples of these intermediate *Blokwerk*-and-positive organs, dating from the 16th century, are in the Abbey Church of Klosterneuburg (near Vienna) and in St. Nicolai, Utrecht (organ moved to the Koorkerk of Middelburg, Holland, in 1885). A. Schlick, in his *Spiegel der Orgelmacher und Organisten* (1511), describes in detail a church organ of the 15th century that has individual and contrasting registers separately controllable, including diapasons (*Prinzipale*) from 8' to 2' pitch, mixtures of differing compositions (*Zimbel, Rauschpfeife*), various flute colors, *Gemshörner,* and reed stops (*Trompeten*). Reed stops seem to have appeared scarcely a century before this time. Mechanically, the organ of Schlick's era had almost reached its final form. It had a regulated wind supply and a fairly sophisticated tracker action. It had barred chests and stop controls that put

stops on and off, either by the now common means of sliders or else by the ventil method [G. *Springlade*].

While the Gothic church organ and the positive organ are the true ancestors of the modern organ, two other instruments developed during the 14th century also deserve mention. These were the *portative organ,* or organetto, and the *regal.* Both were quite small, the former having a set of ordinary pipes of high pitch and a short-compass keyboard, the latter producing sound by means of beating or free reeds. The regal was actually the ancestor of the modern reed organ or *harmonium. Both the portative and the regal could be carried by means of a strap around the neck, so that the player could work the bellows with his left hand and play on the keyboard with his right.

Beginning in the 16th century, national schools of organ building began to develop, and these took distinct form during the 17th and early 18th centuries, that remarkable golden age of the organ, and continued a separate evolution until well into the 19th century.

A. The German and Netherlands school of organ building was the first to develop a large organ having more than one manual keyboard, a versatile pedal keyboard, and an advanced and quite varied collection of stops of different pitches and colors, including many varieties of flute and reed stops and complex mixture stops. By Praetorius' time a well-developed polyphonic instrument, controlled by an easily manipulated action and keyboards close in size to modern ones, was ready for the genius of Pachelbel, Buxtehude, and J. S. Bach. This was the much lauded baroque organ of Germany and the Netherlands, many outstanding examples of which have been preserved. Of a number of highly gifted builders who worked in this period, the North German Arp Schnitger stands out. During the late 17th and early 18th centuries, the equally brilliant Gottfried Silbermann flourished in South Germany. After the death of J. S. Bach (1750), both organ composition and organ building began a slow decline in Germany and an even slower one in the more conservative Netherlands. During the 19th century German organ builders swept headlong into decadence, seeking novelties for their own sake and cultivating a generally gross tonal quality along with an emphasis on orchestrally imitative stops.

B. By 1600 the French school had developed a versatile and unique type of organ that lasted in remarkably unaltered form until the late 18th century. Like the German organ, it had a well-developed great organ and a colorful positive organ, but additional manual divisions were likely to be very limited or specialized and short in compass. While French organs probably possessed pedal divisions as early as German organs did, they never became as complete or independent. France's high point came early in the 18th century, which produced two illustrious builders, François Henri Clicquot and Andreas Silbermann (the brother of Gottfried). It was for the rich, silvery instruments of this period with their splendid reed stops and colorful mutations that F. Couperin, P. Du Mage (*c.* 1676–1751), J. F. Dandrieu, and N. de Grigny (1672–1703) wrote their unique organ Masses and Noëls. During the 19th century a new romantic school of builders sprang up almost full-blown in a few scant decades, led by the gifted Aristide Cavaillé-Coll. The French romantic organ, while largely indebted to the orchestral concept of organ tone, was also outstanding in its own right, and it had a profound influence on the organ of the 20th century.

C. Partly because of the ravages of the Commonwealth period, there remain no complete English organs of the 16th or early 17th centuries. The English organ received its first great impetus from Bernard Smith and Renatus Harris, who did the bulk of their important work *c.* 1680–1710 and influenced even foreign-born builders such as C. Shrider and J. Snetzler, as well as all English work up to the early 19th century. Tonally, the 18th-century English organ bore many similarities to the French organ of the same period, especially with regard to the chorus work and the use of the tierce mutation, but it tended to be lighter and gentler. The characteristic that differentiated it most from Continental organs was its lack of a pedal. This was partially compensated for by a keyboard compass that extended down to (10⅔') G_1 and sometimes F_1 below the normal low 8' C of Continental (and modern) manual divisions. The English 18th-century style continued well into the 19th century. Early in the 18th century a primitive swellbox was introduced, and early in the 19th equally primitive pedal boards. Like the French, the English moved somewhat abruptly into the romantic era, beginning with the work of William Hill (d. 1871) in the 1830's and culminating in the great mid- and late 19th-century cathedral and concert-hall organs of the first Henry Willis, whose style still influences English organ building.

D. The Italian organ took shape early in the 16th century and remained little changed for the next three centuries. While they were among the first organs to have stops, Italian instruments of the 16th through mid-19th centuries seldom had more than one keyboard. Some had pedal boards, but often these were simply permanently coupled to the manual, having no independent pipes of their own. Although they had no mixture stops, they possessed a great variety of separately drawing mutations, commonly including the 22nd and sometimes extending even to the 36th. These mutations, especially the higher-pitched ones, broke back when the pipes became too small. They thus functioned in the chorus as the ranks of a mixture and were largely unsuited for solo use. Flute stops also appeared at several pitches, but reeds were almost non-existent. A distinctive stop found in many early Italian organs was the *voce umana* (*fiffaro*), consisting of two ranks of mild principal pipes (tuned one sharper than the other, thus producing an undulating sound similar to that of modern celeste stops). The tone of Italian organs tended to be warm but not particularly loud, despite the complex chorus of mutations. The leading Italian builders were mostly members of the Antegnati family, which flourished in Brescia in the 16th and 17th centuries.

E. The Spanish and Portuguese school had a development similar to the Italian and, like it, halted fairly early, in this case in the early 17th century. Spanish organs tended to be somewhat larger and louder than Italian ones. While they, too, had only crude coupled pedals, after the 16th century they often had two and occasionally three manuals, whose stops were commonly divided at c'. What distinguished Iberian organs from all others, however, was their rich and brilliant reed stops, which in most organs of any size were mounted horizontally from the front (*en chamade*) of the case. The first non-Iberian organ builder to see the possibilities in horizontal reeds was France's Cavaillé-Coll. From France their use spread to other countries, and today such reeds can be found all over America and Europe.

F. The earliest organs in America were either imported from Spain or built by imported organ builders in the 16th and 17th centuries for the cathedrals and monasteries of Mexico and Central and South America. There are records of organs being used in Quebec churches as early at the 1660's, at least one of which was sent from Paris. In the early 18th century the German colonists in Pennsylvania and the surrounding areas began to import small chamber organs and positives from their homeland, and shortly thereafter organs of English make began to appear in New England, New York, and Virginia. By the mid-18th century two indigenous schools of organ building had begun to develop, in eastern Pennsylvania and around Boston. The dominant figure of this period was David Tannenberg (1728–1804) of Lititz, Pennsylvania, who built a number of excellent organs, including at least one with three manuals. After his death the Pennsylvania school rapidly waned, to be superseded by the fast-growing New York and Boston schools. During the first half of the 19th century Henry Erben (1800–84) and George Jardine (1801–c. 1883) were the undisputed leaders of the former, while William M. Goodrich (1777–1833), Thomas Appleton (1785–1872), and the Hook brothers (Elias, 1805–81; and George G., 1807–80) distinguished themselves in the latter. Whereas the Pennsylvania school had built a distinctly German organ in the South German tradition, the Boston school was thoroughly English in its orientation, as was the New York school. Indeed, the Boston group continued to build in almost pure 18th-century English style until the mid-1850's, when the new romantic movement finally began to be felt. By the 1870's and 1880's the revolution in concept and assimilation of European ideas was fully accomplished. Leaders in this new movement were Hilborne Roosevelt (1849–86) in New York, George Hutchings (1835–1913) in Boston, and the Casavant brothers in Montreal. The advent of electropneumatic action at the turn of the century gave free rein to innovators such as John T. Austin, Ernest M. Skinner, and the Englishman Robert Hope-Jones. The last-named was the inventor of the unit organ and the father of the "theatre organ," a totally orchestrally oriented instrument developed for the performance of popular music and the accompaniment of silent movies. Although Albert Schweitzer issued a plea for an "organ reform" as early as the first decade of the 20th century [see Organ reform], it was not heeded in America for at least twenty years. Then came pioneers such as W. Lynnwood Farnam, who commanded world-wide attention by playing the complete works of Bach in recital during the 1920's, and the organ builders G. Donald Harrison (1889–1956) and Walter Holtkamp, who began to explore the way back to traditional organ tone in the 1930's. From the efforts of such individuals and their many successors the organ in the next three decades regained much of its former stature as a unique instrument with its own literature, both in America and abroad.

Lit. *For I–XI:* F. Bedos de Celles, *L'Art du Facteur d'Orgues,* 4 vols. (1766; repr. 1934, '63); G. A. Audsley, *The Art of Organ-Building* (1905; repr. 1965); *id., Organ Stops and Their Artistic Registration* (1921); J. G. Töpfer, *Lehrbuch der Orgelbaukunst,* (1855; repr. 1955, vol. i); P.-G. Anderson, *Orgelbogen* (1955); J. Adlung, *Musica Mechanica Organoedi* (1768); M. Praetorius, *Syntagma Musicum,* part ii (1618; Eng. trans. 1949); C. Antegnati, *L'Arte Organica* (1608; repr. 1938); H. Norman and H. J. Norman, *The Organ Today* (1966); J. I. Wedgwood, *A Comprehensive Dictionary of Organ Stops,* rev. ed. (1907); N. A. Bonavia-Hunt, *The Organ Reed* (1951); J. Blanton, *The Organ in Church Design* (1956); *id., The Revival of the Organ Case* (1966); W. & T. Lewis, *Modern Organ Building* (1939); G. Frotscher, *Deutsche Orgeldispositionen aus 5 Jahrhunderten* (1939); J. B. Jamison, *Organ Design and Appraisal* (1959); H. Klotz, *Über die Orgelkunst des Gotik* (1934); J. Broadhouse, *The Organ Viewed from Within* [1914]; H. Smith, *Modern Organ Tuning* [1902]; J. Matthews, *The Restoration of Organs* (1920).

For XII: W. L. Sumner, *The Organ,* rev. ed. (1962); P. Williams, *The European Organ, 1450–1850* (1966); C. F. A. Williams, *The Story of the Organ* (1903); E. J. Hopkins and E. F. Rimbault, *The Organ: Its History and Construction* (1855; 3rd ed., 1877); C. Clutton and G. Dixon, *The Organ: Its Tonal Structure and Registration* (1950); C. Clutton and A. Niland, *The British Organ* (1963); J. Fesperman, *The Organ as Musical Medium* (1962); A. Schweitzer, *Deutsche und Französische Orgelbaukunst und Orgelkunst* (1927); A. Bouman, *Orgels in Nederland,* rev. ed. (1956); A. G. Hill, *The Organ-Cases and Organs of the Middle Ages and Renaissance,* 2 vols. (1883, '91); M. A. Vente, *Die Brabanter Orgel* (1958); A. Werckmeister, *Erweiterte und verbesserte Orgelprobe* (1698; fac. repr. 1927); A. Schlick, *Spiegel der Orgelmacher und Organisten* (1511; repr. 1951); H. G. Farmer, *The Organ of the Ancients* (1931); R. Quoika, *Das Positiv in Geschichte und Gegenwart* (1957); W. Supper, *Kleines Orgelbrevier für Architekten* (1959); F. Munger, *Schweitzer Orgeln von der Gotik bis zur Gegenwart* (1961); N. Dufourcq, *Documents inédits relatifs a l'orgue français,* 2 vols. (1934, '35); G. Moortgat, *Oude Orgels in Vlaanderen,* 2 vols. (1964, '65); W. Haacke,

Orgeln in Aller Welt (1965); A. Cellier and H. Bachelin, *L'Orgue* (1933); J. L. C. Huré, *L'Esthétique de l'orgue* (1923). See also Organ music; Organ playing.

I–XI by C.B.F., E.W.F., and J.F.; XII by B.J.O.

Organ chorale. A polyphonic composition for organ based on a *chorale melody (excluding simple harmonizations such as those suitable for accompanying congregational singing). Although the term is commonly used only for the polyphonic settings of German Protestant chorales, the earlier organ settings of hymns of the Roman Catholic Church must also be considered.

I. *Roman Catholic hymn settings.* Beginning in the early 15th century (Codex Faenza), various items of the service that until then had been performed in the traditional plainsong were replaced by organ compositions. Among them were items of the Mass Ordinary [see Organ Mass], the Magnificat, antiphons, and some items of the Mass Proper, notably Introits and Offertories. The hymns also were subject to this process, which, although it hastened the decline of Gregorian chant, became the chief impetus for the development of organ music. The earliest extant organ hymns are found in Paumann's "Fundamentum organisandi" (1452) and in the Buxheim Organ Book (*c.* 1460–70). These sources include several settings of two German hymns, "Benedicite Allmächtiger Gott" and "Christ ist erstanden," as well as compositions of Latin hymns such as "Veni creator spiritus," "O gloriosa Domina," "Dies est leticie," etc. The original melodies usually appear in the lowest part (tenor), frequently ornamented or paraphrased. Arnolt Schlick's *Tabulaturen etlicher Lobgesangk* (1512) contains a setting of the German hymn "Maria zart" in which, for the first time, the melody is made to stand out clearly in the soprano [see *HAM,* no. 101]. It is a remarkably early example of the so-called melody chorale, one of the standard types of the 17th-century Protestant organ chorale or organ prelude. Leonhard Kleber's tablature of *c.* 1517 includes a "Maria zart" by Buchner (designated *Fuga optima*) that may be regarded as an early example of the chorale motet, since every phrase of the melody is treated in imitation. Hans Buchner's "Fundamentum" (*c.* 1525) contains settings of "Veni creator spiritus" and others, treated in *cantus planus style or in imitation. An anonymous "In dulci jubilo" from Sicher's tablature [repr. in H. Moser, *Frühmeister der*

deutschen Orgelkunst (1930), p. 7] is interesting in that its canonic treatment is remarkably similar to that in J. S. Bach's setting of the same hymn.

The hymns of A. de Cabezón (1510–66) are noteworthy for their strict adherence to the liturgical melodies ("Ave maris stella," "Pange lingua," etc.), which are usually presented in strict *cantus planus* style, without figuration or *Vorimitation*. Five of his settings are chorale motets [*Editions XX, 3, pp. 50ff]. Cavazzoni's *Intavolatura* (1542) contains twelve hymns, most of which are also in *cantus planus* style but in faster values (semibreves, instead of Cabezón's breves) and always with *Vorimitation* [see *SchGMB,* no. 103]. His "Pange lingua" is a particularly impressive chorale motet. John Redford (*c.* 1485–1545; see *HAM,* no. 120) often replaces the original plainsong with a derivative melody resulting from the use of faburden technique [see Faburden (2)] or elaborate paraphrasing. The Mulliner Book of *c.* 1560 [*Editions XXXIV, 1] contains organ hymns by Allwood, John Blitheman, and Thomas Tallis. Blitheman's "Eterne rerum conditor" is an early example of chorale variation, as is John Bull's "Telluris ingens conditor" [*Editions XXXIV 14, p. 134]. The main development of the Roman Catholic organ hymn ended with the *Hymnes de l'Église* (1623) of Jean Titelouze, which contains twelve hymns, each treated as a series of three or four variations called "versets" and obviously meant to be played in alternation with verses (i.e., hymn stanzas) sung in plainsong. Some of the variations are in *cantus planus* style, some in motet style, and still others in the form of a canon above the *cantus firmus*.

II. *The Protestant organ chorale.* In the German Protestant Church the organ chorale assumed a role quite different from that in the Roman Catholic service. In the latter, it served as a substitute for plainsong, from which it inherited its liturgical function. In the Protestant Church, the singing of the chorale became the privilege of the congregation, and it was the organist's duty not only to accompany the singing but also to play the chorale beforehand on the organ as an introduction (hence the German organ chorale is often called *chorale prelude). This novel function stimulated the development of new techniques of composition. Former devices such as elaborate paraphrasing or faburden technique, as well as the tendency to place the melody in the tenor as a *cantus planus* having structural rather than melodic significance, were largely discarded. The Lutheran chorales, differing from the Gregorian chants mainly in that they consisted of several clearly marked phrases, were made to stand out in the soprano (melody chorale), sometimes provided with figurative or (later) expressive ornamentation (ornamented chorale), and even in chorale motets were treated so as to be readily recognizable to the congregation.

The outset of this development is marked by a collection of *c.* 20 compositions in E. Nicolaus Ammerbach's *Orgel oder Instrument Tabulatur* (1571, '83) and 77 compositions in the "Tabulaturbuch auff dem Instrumente" (1598) by Augustus Nörmiger. All these settings have a texture similar to that of the final chorales in J. S. Bach's cantatas, i.e., essentially homophonic but interspersed with polyphonic elements. Considerably longer and more elaborate settings, approaching the chorale motet and even the *chorale fantasia, are found in the Tablature of Celle (1601). Entirely different are the organ chorales of the Dutch composer J. P. Sweelinck, who cultivated exclusively the chorale variation, a type rarely used before. Sweelinck's contemporary, Michael Praetorius, composed (in addition to six Latin hymns) three Lutheran chorales —"Ein feste Burg," "Christ unser Herr," "Wir glauben all"—as magnificent chorale motets of huge dimensions and complexity. Sweelinck's immediate German successor was Samuel Scheidt, who adopted his master's preference for the chorale variation. Exceptional is his fantasia (actually a chorale motet) "Ich ruf zu Dir," one of the outstanding works of the entire literature, which anticipates in form, style, and expression such works as Bach's *chorale motet "Jesus Christus unser Heiland" (*BG* xxv). The historical development between Scheidt and Bach followed two lines, a North German and a Middle German (for the composers, see Organ music II A; the South German organ composers, being Roman Catholic, naturally made no contribution to the repertory). In North Germany there was a distinct preference for extended treatment and for the free, rhapsodic type known as chorale fantasia, while the organ chorales of the Middle German masters are shorter and simpler, chiefly *chorale fugues, melody chorales, or chorale variations (partitas).

Bach utilized all the forms of the past and, needless to say, attained in them new heights of expression and artistic perfection. The following types can be clearly distinguished: (a) *cantus firmus* (more properly, *cantus planus*) *chorale—*

the chorale melody in long notes usually in the bass (*BG* iii, 224; *BG* iii, 234; *NBA* iv/2, 3); (b) *chorale motet—*each line of the chorale is treated in imitation, resulting in a succession of "fugues" (*BG* xxv or *NBA* iv/2, 87; *NBA* iv/2, 212); (c) *chorale fugue—*the first line or the initial phrase of the chorale is treated as a fugue (*BG* iii, 205; *BG* iii, 239; *NBA* iv/3, 65); (d) *melody chorale—*the chorale appears as a continuous melody in the soprano, accompanied by contrapuntal parts that usually proceed in definite figures (most of the chorales from the *Orgelbüchlein;* see Figured chorale); (e) *ornamented chorale—*the chorale is used in the soprano with elaborate and expressive ornamentation (*NBA* iv/2, 55; *Orgelbüchlein* in *BG* xxv², 57); (f) *chorale canon* (*Orgelbüchlein* in *BG* xxv², 45; *BG* xxv², 12); (g) *chorale fantasia—*free, North German treatment (*NBA* iv/3, 16; *NBA* iv/3, 24); (h) *chorale variations* (*partitas*)—a number of variations (corresponding to the number of stanzas of the text) on the chorale melody (*NBA* iv/2, 38). Naturally, these methods of treatment frequently overlap, e.g., the chorale prelude "Num komm der Heiden Heiland" (*NBA* iv/2, 55) and many others combine the principle of imitation, as in the motet, with the ornamented treatment for the final statement of the "subject."

Among later contributions to the repertory, the chorale preludes of Brahms (op. 122) and H. Kaminsky merit special mention.

Lit.: G. Kittler, *Geschichte des protestantischen Orgelchorals* (1931); F. Dietrich, *Geschichte des deutschen Orgelchorals im 17. Jahrhundert* (1932); Stainton de B. Taylor, *The Chorale Preludes of J. S. Bach* (1942); W. Apel, "Die Celler Orgeltabulatur von 1601" (*MF* xix); W. Breig, in *AMW* xvii (Sweelinck); W. H. Frere, "Bach's *Vorspiele* of 1739" (*ML* i, 218); C. Macpherson, "Choral-Preludes" (*PMA* xxxix); E. Fisher-Krückeberg, "Johann Crügers Choralbearbeitungen" (*ZMW* xiv). Also see under Organ music.

Organetto [It.]. A 14th-century name for portative organ; see Organ XII.

Organ hymn. See Organ chorale I.

Organicen, organoedus. Humanist names for organ player, organist.

Organista [L.]. Organ player, organist. However, the term "optimus organista," conferred on Leoninus (*c.* 1200; see *Ars antiqua*) by the late 13th-century Anon. IV of *CS* i characterizes this master as a "great composer of organa" [see Organum (2)], not as a "very able organist."

Organistrum [L.]. Medieval name for *hurdy-gurdy.

Organ Mass [G. *Orgelmesse*]. Polyphonic composition of the Mass, nearly always the Ordinary, for organ. The Codex Faenza of *c.* 1400 contains a single Kyrie as well as two Kyrie-Gloria sets, all based on the corresponding items of the Gregorian Mass IV [see Mass A] and composed according to a structural principle encountered in nearly all organ Masses, i.e., alternation of organ music and plainsong [see Alternation]. The pieces are in two parts, the *cantus firmus* appearing in long notes [see *Cantus planus* style] in the tenor against an upper part in lively motion. Similar settings of the Gloria, Credo, and Kyrie are preserved in German sources from *c.* 1430–50 [see Editions XI, 1]. The Buxheim Organ Book (*c.* 1460–70) contains a number of items composed in a more advanced style, among them a Kyrie in four-part chordal style. In the 16th century we find complete organ Masses including all five items (sometimes without the Credo), each composed according to the alternation principle, in Germany (Buchner, "Fundamentum," *c.* 1525), France (Attaingnant, *Tabulature pour le jeu d'orgues*, 1531), England (Philipp ap Rhys, in Brit. Mus. *Add. 29996, c.* 1540) and Italy (Giaches Buus, in a manuscript from Castell'Arquato, *c.* 1540). G. Cavazzoni's *Intabolatura d'organo* (1543?) contains three such Masses, one for feasts of the Lord (*Missa Dominicalis*), one for feasts of Saints (*Missa Apostolorum;* see *HAM,* no. 117), and one for feasts of the Virgin (*Missa de Beata Virgine*). The same three Masses were composed by Merulo (*Messe d'intavolatura,* 1568). All organ Masses belong to the type known as plainsong Mass [see Mass C II a]. The Mass Proper is represented by a number of Introits (Buxheim Organ Book, H. Buchner), Offertories (Redford and other English composers; see Felix namque), and a singular composition by Preston, consisting of the Introit, Gradual, Alleluia, and sequence for Easter Sunday.

In the 17th century the organ Mass was cultivated mainly in Italy and France. Frescobaldi, in his *Fiori musicali* of 1635, provided music for the same three Masses as Cavazzoni and Merulo. However, only the Kyrie is fully represented by a number of plainsong settings, to which are added a number of free organ pieces to be played at the beginning of the Mass (*Toccata avanti la Messa*), after the reading of the Epistle (*Canzona dopo l'Epistola*), after the Credo

(*Ricercare dopo il Credo*), during the Elevation of the Host (*Toccata cromatica per l'elevazione*), and after the Communion (*Canzona post il Communio*). French organ Masses by Nivers (1667), Gigault (1685), Lebègue (1687), F. Couperin (1690), N. de Grigny (1699), and Corrette (1703) are structurally similar to those of the 16th century, consisting of the required number of pieces for the Kyrie, Gloria, Sanctus, and Agnus, usually with the addition of an *Offertoire*. The pieces for the Kyrie are often based on the Kyrie IV [see *LU*, p. 25], while the others are freely composed. Bach wrote what has been called a "German organ Mass" in his *Clavier-Übung*, pt. iii.

According to A. Schering (*Die Niederländische Orgelmesse,* 1912), numerous Masses of the Flemish masters that are commonly regarded as vocal compositions were actually intended to be organ music. That this theory is untenable is evident in Schering's renditions for organ [see his *Alte Meister aus der Frühzeit des Orgelspiels* (1913); also *SchGMB*, no. 57]; their highly complex texture is totally contrary to the organ style of the 15th century (Paumann, Buxheim Organ Book).

Lit.: A. C. Howell, ‡*Five French Baroque Organ Masses* (1961); D. Plamenac, in *CP 1952* (Codex Faenza); L. Schrade, in *AMF* i and *MQ* xxviii (15th-cent. Masses); C. Paesler, in *VMW* v (Buchner); D. Stevens, in *MD* vi (Philipp ap Rhys), *ML* xxxix, 29 (Preston); K. Jeppesen, in *AMW* xii (Castell'Arquato); A. Schering, "Zur alternatim Orgelmesse" (*ZMW* xvii); A. Tessier, "Les Messes d'orgue de Couperin" (*RM* 1924, no. 1).

Organ music. I. *Middle Ages and Renaissance.* Prior to 1300, the organ was played by alternately pushing in and pulling out handles with both hands [see Organ XII]. As a result, organ music could be no more than a monophonic succession of fairly sustained notes. There is evidence, however, of two organists' playing simultaneously and thus performing two-part *organum. Organs were probably also used to assist singers in performing the long-held notes in the tenors of the organa of Leoninus and Perotinus (*c.* 1200), and possibly also for the rendition of the tenors of 13th-century motets. The earliest preserved examples of organ music (*c.* 1325) are *intabulations of motets and *estampies in the MS Brit. Mus. *Add. 28550,* the so-called Robertsbridge Codex [see Editions XI, 1]. They are usually assumed to be of English origin, although certain features, particularly the notation, would seem to point to Italy or perhaps France. A newly discovered source of great interest is the Codex Faenza (c. 1400), which contains some pieces for the *organ Mass and a large number of intabulations, mostly of secular music (Machaut, Landini, Jacopo da Bologna, et al; see D. Plamenac, in *JAMS* iv). Organ music of the 15th century is preserved only in various German tablatures [*Editions XI, 1], among which the Ileborgh tablature of 1448 [see W. Apel, in *ZMW* xvi] is remarkable for its free *preludes, Paumann's "Fundamentum organisandi" of 1452 for its elaborations of German songs and instructive pieces [see Counterpoint II], and the *Buxheim Organ Book of c. 1460–70 for its preludes, Mass compositions, and arrangements or transcriptions of German songs and French chansons. Toward the end of the 15th century Paulus Hofhaimer was famous for his organ playing and improvisation, but only two or three of his organ pieces have survived, along with compositions of his pupils Kotter, Sicher, Buchner, and Kleber [see Lit., Moser, *Frühmeister*]. German organ music reached its first peak in the great master Arnolt Schlick, whose *Tabulaturen etlicher Lobgesangk* (1512; new ed. by G. Harms, 1957) contains a "Salve Regina," "Maria zart," and other liturgical compositions. A recently discovered MS contains, among others, a composition in ten voice-parts, four of them to be played on the pedal [see M.S. Kastner, *Arnolt Schlick, Hommage à l'Empereur Charles-Quint* (1954)]. The German tradition of this period is continued in some extensive tablatures of Polish origin, written c. 1550 [see Poland].

In the 16th century other important developments took place in Italy, Spain, England, and France. The *Recerchari motetti canzoni* of 1523 by M. A. Cavazzoni (Marcoantonio da Bologna) contains the earliest extant organ ricercars [see Ricercar II (b)]. The compositions of his son, Girolamo Cavazzoni—organ Masses, hymns, Magnificats, imitative ricercars, as well as the earliest organ canzonas [see Canzona I]—represent the artistic culmination of Italian 16th-century organ music. M. A. Cavazzoni's works are republished in K. Jeppesen, *Die italienische Orgelmusik am Anfang des Cinquecento* and in *Editions X, no. 1; those of Girolamo Cavazzoni in *Editions III, 3 and complete in IX, 6. Andrea Gabrieli (c. 1520–86) made important contributions to the development of the ricercar [see Ricercar I (b)] and wrote the first *toccatas,

a form whose artistic possibilities were more fully realized by C. Merulo (1533–1604). The earliest extant source of Spanish organ music, a *Libro de cifra nueva* published by Venegas de Henestrosa in 1557 [*Editions XXXII, 2], contains mostly *tientos, some of them by the great master A. de Cabezón (1510–66). Other organ works by Cabezón—hymns, versets for the Psalms and the Magnificat, variations, and instructive pieces of rare excellence—are contained in the posthumous *Obras de música* of 1578 [*Editions XX, 3, 4, 7, 8].

In England there flourished before 1550 a remarkable school of organ composers represented chiefly by J. Redford (c. 1485-1547; see C. Pfatteicher, *John Redford* [1934]), whose numerous liturgical pieces (organ hymns) include some outstanding pieces in motet style. The Mulliner Book of c. 1560 [*Editions XXXIV, 1] contains liturgical organ compositions by Allwood, Blitheman (c. 1510–91), and Tallis (c. 1505–85) [see "Felix namque"; "In nomine"]. Finally, two French publications of 1531 (Attaingnant; see Editions XLIX, Sec. I, 5) give evidence of an early activity whose succession is unfortunately lost for nearly 100 years, the next oldest source of French organ music preserved being the organ books by Titelouze (1563–1633) issued in 1623 and 1626 [*Editions I, 1].

II. *Baroque.* While Titelouze's organ hymns represent the late Renaissance, the works of his contemporary, Jan Pieterszoon Sweelinck (1562–1621), inaugurated the organ music of the baroque, establishing a new style characterized mainly by extensive use of lively figurations and precise motifs in ever-varying contours and rhythms. Sweelinck wrote long monothematic fantasias [see Fantasia (5)], some of which exploit the *echo effect of the organ, and also chorale variations based on German Protestant hymn tunes [see Organ chorale II].

A. *Germany.* Of Sweelinck's numerous pupils, Samuel Scheidt (1587–1654) is the most outstanding (*Tabulatura nova*, 1624; new ed. *DdT* 1). His organ compositions—chorale variations of Latin and German hymns, Magnificats, and fugal compositions (*Fuga, Fantasia*)---are somewhat less imaginative than those of his teacher but mark the beginning of a new development of German organ music that was to continue until the death of Bach. This development may be divided into three branches: North German, Middle German, and South German. In the first are H. Praetorius (1560-1629), M. Praetorius (1571–1621), M. Schildt (1592/3–1667), H. Scheidemann (*c.* 1596–1663), D. Strungk (1601–94), F. Tunder (1614–67), M. Weckmann (1619–74), J. A. Reinken (1623–1722), J. N. Hanff (1630–1711); D. Buxtehude (*c.* 1637–1707), V. Lübeck (1654–1740), G. Böhm (1661–1733), and N. Bruhns (1665–97)—composers who developed especially the large forms of organ music (toccata, chorale fantasia, prelude, and fugue) and evolved a free, highly imaginative style that has been termed *Gothic. The Middle German composers, in Thuringia and North Bavaria, worked with more modest and intimate means and contributed chiefly to the development of the chorale fugue and melody chorale. This line fittingly begins with Bach's great-uncle Heinrich Bach (1615–92), his uncles Johann Christoph (1645–93) and Johann Michael (1648–94; organ chorales in Ritter), and continues with J. Krieger (1651–1735; *DTB* 30), J. Pachelbel (1653–1706; *DTB* 6), J. Kuhnau (1660–1722), J. H. Buttstett (1666–1727), and J. G. Walther (1684–1748; *DdT* 26/27).

An early South German school of organ music is represented by H. L. Hassler (1564–1612; *DTB* 7), C. Erbach (1573–1635; *DTB* 7), J. U. Steigleder (1593–1635; interesting variations on the *Vater unser;* ricercars, ed. by Emsheimer, 1928), W. Ebner (1612–65), and J. E. Kindermann (1616–55; *DTB* 32). Italian contrapuntal style and Italian forms such as the ricercar and canzona are important in their works. A new development began with J. J. Froberger (1616–67), who, as a pupil of Frescobaldi and a friend of French lutenists and clavecinists (Gaultier, Chambonnières), brought to German organ music many new ideas derived from Frescobaldi's novel forms (toccata, variation canzona, *capriccio) and free, idiomatic keyboard style [see *Freistimmigkeit*], while French influence is seen chiefly in his harpsichord music (suite). The repertory of the later South German composers, such as J. K. Kerll (1627–93; *DTB* 3), Georg Muffat (1653–1704), G. von Reutter (1656–1738), F. X. Murschhauser (1663–1738; *DTB* 30), J. K. F. Fischer (*c.* 1665–1746; new ed. by E. von Werra, 1901), and Gottlieb Muffat (1690–1770; *DTO* 58), also has an "Italian division" of ricercars, canzonas, toccatas, and versets, and a "French division" of harpsichord music.

B. *Italy.* The Italian organ music of the baroque began with the *Neapolitans G. M. Trabaci (*c.* 1580–1647) and A. Mayone (d. 1627), who are important links between Cabezón and Frescobaldi [see Neapolitan school II]. Fresco-

baldi (1583–1643), a unique combination of intellectual scholar and highly imaginative artist, is one of the greatest and most fascinating composers of organ music. A predecessor of Frescobaldi's was E. Pasquini (d. *c.* 1620), and an immediate successor was M. A. Rossi (publication of 1657). Later Italian organ composers are G. Salvatore (early 17th cent.–*c.* 1688; *Editions XI, 3), B. Storace (publication of 1664; *Editions XI, 7), and D. Zipoli (1688–1726; *Editions IX, 36).

C. *France.* French organ music of the 17th century is represented by H. Dumont (1610–84), G. Nivers (1632–1714), N. Gigault (*c.* 1625–1707), N.-A. Lebègue (1631–1702), A. Raison (d. 1719); Jacques Boyvin (*c.* 1653–1706), F. Couperin (1668–1733), N. de Grigny (1672–1702), L. Marchand (1669–1732), J.-F. Dandrieu (1628–1738), and L.-C. Daquin (1694–1772). Most of their compositions are liturgical pieces in a style that became increasingly secular and "operatic" during the course of the period. They are noteworthy for their emphasis on registration, which is usually carefully indicated [*Editions I].

D. *England.* None of the Continental forms of organ music was cultivated in England during the 17th century. Instead, composers such as C. Gibbons (1615–76), M. Locke (*c.* 1630–77), J. Blow (1648/9–1708), H. Purcell (*c.* 1658–95), J. Clarke (*c.* 1673–1707), and W. Croft (1678–1727) wrote verses and *voluntaries in a variety of styles and forms. Quite frequently these took the form of "fugue and postlude," or sometimes that of two fugues followed by a postlude. The fugues are written in a rather perfunctory manner, rapid figurations and homophonic measures appearing side by side with imitative passages. Handel's contribution to the organ repertory consists of his famous twenty concertos for organ and orchestra.

E. *Spain and Portugal.* The Iberian Peninsula produced a huge repertory of organ music whose importance has only begun to be recognized. The Spaniards Sebastian A. de Heredia (*c.* 1565–after 1620) and F. Correa de Araujo (*c.* 1576–after 1633; *Libro de tientos,* 1626, new ed. by M. S. Kastner, 1948) wrote mostly *tientos, the former in a transitional style, the latter in a colorful baroque style in which the imitative element is almost suppressed by a luxuriant growth of ever-changing and often highly erratic figurations. The Portuguese M. R. Coelho (b. 1583) published *Flores de música* (1620; new ed. by M. S. Kastner, 2 vols. [1959, '61]) containing *tientos* similar to those of Correa de Araujo as well as organ hymns, versets for the psalms and the Magnificat [see *HAM,* no. 200], and Kyries. Organ compositions by Pablo Bruna and others, probably born *c.* 1600–20, are preserved in MSS in El Escorial and Barcelona [see W. Apel, in *AnM* xvii]. The great master of the second half of the 17th century was J. B. J. Cabanilles (1644–1712), whose pupil, José Elias (1675–1749), said: "Ante ruet mundus quam surget Cabanilles secundus" (The world will go to ruins before another Cabanilles will arise). His hundreds of organ compositions (about one-half published in H. Anglés, *Joannis Cabanilles Opera omnia,* i–iv) display a fascinating command of a great variety of forms and stylistic devices. Many hundreds of additional organ pieces in Portuguese and Spanish MSS (Bibl. municipal of Oporto, *Libro de cyfra, Livro de obras de orgao;* Madrid, Bibl. nac., 5 vols. compiled by A. Martíny Coll, 1706–09) have only begun to be investigated [see K. Speer, "A Portuguese Manuscript of Keyboard Music," diss. Indiana Univ., 1956; B. Hudson, "A Portuguese Source of Seventeenth-Century Iberian Organ Music," diss. Indiana Univ., 1961].

F. *Bach.* In organ music more than any other field, Bach represents the consummate peak of baroque music and, for that matter, of the entire literature. Here as elsewhere, his achievement was principally artistic perfection rather than innovation. Building on the forms and methods of his predecessors, he conferred on the chorale prelude an incomparable expressiveness and on the toccata and fugue a unique architectural structure, while his organ sonatas represent the apotheosis of three-voice counterpoint.

III. *1750 to present.* After Bach, organ music suffered a decline from which it did not recover until *c.* 1840. The low ebb of organ music *c.* 1800 is beyond description (for examples, see an article by H. Müller, in *KJ* 1901). Mendelssohn was one of the first to compose organ music of artistic significance. However, his six Sonatas (1844–45), although incorporating elements of Bach's style (fugues, chorales), clearly show the detrimental influence of romanticism on organ composition. Liszt's organ works opened a new period of organ composition, owing to their exploitation of the orchestral and coloristic resources of the instrument. This path was pursued further by France's A. Guilmant (1837–1911), C. M. Widor (1844–1937), and L. Vierne (1870–1937), outstanding organ virtuosos who wrote veritable symphonies for the organ.

Franck's organ pieces, particularly his *Trois Chorales* of 1890, are in a similar style, modified by the spiritual influence of Bach. Much closer to Bach in style and spirit are Brahms' *Chorale Preludes* (*Elf Choralvorspiele* op. 122, 1896). With Reger (1873–1916) romantic organ music came to an imposing close. Huge forms are filled with an exuberance of ideas and a profusion of technical display but bound by great contrapuntal skill in the tradition of Bach. The neoclassical tendencies of the 1920's brought a more sincere revival of the polyphonic tradition of the baroque. H. Kaminski's (1886–1946) compositions are pervaded by a Gothic mysticism, while Kurt Thomas (b. 1904) and Hindemith (three organ sonatas, 1937, '40) represent the tendencies toward objectivism and linear design. In France, a similar trend led to the mysticism and sonorous visions of C. Tournemire, O. Messiaen, and J. Alain. To these should be added the Belgian organ composer Flor Peeters.

Lit.: A. C. D. de Brisay, *The Organ and Its Music* (1935); W. Apel, *Geschichte der Orgel-und Klaviermusik bis 1700* (1967); G. Frotscher, *Geschichte des Orgelspiels und der Orgelkomposition,* 2 vols. (1935, '36); *LavE* ii.2, 1181–1374; A. Ritter, *Zur Geschichte des Orgelspiels* (1884); O. Kinkeldey, *Orgel und Klavier in der Musik des 16. Jahrhunderts* (1910); N. Dufourcq, *La Musique d'orgue française de Jehan Titelouze à Jehan Alain* (1941); M. Fischer, *Die organistische Improvisation im 17. Jahrhundert* (1929); H. Kelletat, *Zur Geschichte der deutschen Orgelmusik in der Frühklassik* (1933); B. Weigl, *Handbuch der Orgelliteratur* (1931); [G. A. C. de Graaf], *Literature on the Organ* [1957]; J. Wolf, "Zur Geschichte der Orgelmusik im vierzehnten Jahrhundert" (*KJ* 1899, p. 14); W. Apel, "Du Nouveau sur la musique française pour orgue au XVIe siècle" (*RM* 1937, no. 172); J. E. West, "Old English Organ Music" (*PMA* xxxvii); F. Raugel, "The Ancient French Organ School" (*MQ* xi); K. G. Fellerer, "Zur italienischen Orgelmusik des 17./18. Jahrhunderts" (*JMP* xlv); O. Mansfield, "Mozart's Organ Sonatas" (*MQ* viii); H. Grace, "Modern French Organ Music" (*PMA* xliv); N. Dufourcq, "Panorame de la musique d'orgue française au XXe siècle" (*RM* 1938, nos. 184–86; 1939, no. 189).

Collections of old organ music: *Editions XI, 1 (14th–15th cent.); J. Klein, *The First Four Centuries of Music for the Organ,* 2 vols. [1948]; H. J. Moser, *Frühmeister der deutschen Orgelkunst* (1930); K. Straube, *Alte Meister* [n.d.]; *id., Alte Meister des Orgelspiels,* 2 vols. [1929, '53]; *id.,*

Choralvorspiele alter Meister [1907; repub. 1951]; *Editions XLI, ser. 4; E. Kaller, *et al.*, *Liber organi*, 10 vols. [1931–58]; G. Gerdes, *46 Choräle für Orgel* [1957]; *Editions XVIII, 9; H. J. Moser, *Choralbearbeitungen und freie Orgelstücke der deutschen Sweelinck-Schule*, 2 vols. (1954, '55); E. Kraus, *Cantantibus organis*, 12 vols. [1959–64]; *Editions III, 3 (Italy); *Editions I, 1–10 (France); F. Raugel, *Les Maîtres français de l'orgue*, 2 vols. [1951]; J. E. West, *Old English Organ Music*, 3 vols. (1906); D. Stevens, *Altenglische Orgelmusik* (1953); F. Pedrell, *Antologia de organistas clásicos españoles;* L. Villalba Muñoz, *Antología de organistas clásicos españoles* (1914). See also Organ chorale; Organ Mass.

Organ playing. For a short historical account, see Organ XII.

Lit. (selected; see also under Organ): H. Gleason, *Method of Organ Playing*, rev. ed. (1962); S. Irwin, *Dictionary of Pipe Organ Stops* [1962]; E. H. Geer, *Organ Registration in Theory and Practice* [1957]; C. N. Boyd, *Organ Registration and Accompaniment*, 2 vols. (1932); N. A. B. Hunt, *Modern Organ Stops* (1923); C. Dickinson, *The Technique and Art of Organ Playing* (1922); H. F. Ellingford, *The Art of Transcribing for the Organ* (1922); H. Grace, *The Complete Organist* (1920); G. B. Nevin, *A Primer of Organ Registration* (1920); E. Bruggaier, *Studien zur Geschichte des Orgelpedalspiels* (1959); T. Schneider, *Die Namen der Orgelregister* (1958); H. Gleason, "Organ Instruction before Bach" (*BAMS* iv); P. Hardouin, "Essai d'une sémantique des jeux de l'orgue" (*AM* xxxiv).

Organ point. See Pedal point.

Organ reform [G. *Orgelbewegung*]. A movement to reform methods of organ building, begun *c.* 1900 by Albert Schweitzer and others. Its aim is to reestablish in modern practice many of the techniques of 17th- and 18th-century organ building that are considered essential in an organ for the proper interpretation of polyphonic music, particularly that of Bach and his predecessors. Another aim is to foster new growth in organ composition. See Organ XI, XII.   C.B.F.

Organ stops. See under Organ VIII–XI. For bibl., see under Organ; Organ playing.

Organ tablature. (1) The various notational systems that were used to write down early organ music (prior to 1600). They are usually distinguished as Italian, German, Spanish, etc., organ tablature. However, in Italy as well as in France and England, organ music was notated in virtually the same way as it is today, except for minor details, such as variations in the number of staff lines. Only in Germany and in Spain was organ music (more generally, keyboard music) written in systems that could truly be called "tablature." See Tablature. (2) The manuscripts and printed books of early organ music. As under (1), the name should be restricted to German and Spanish sources. Long lists of organ tablatures (French, Italian, English, German, and Spanish) are given in *WoHN* ii, 32ff, 270ff, 278.

Organum. (1) Latin for organ. In early writings (church fathers, lives of Saints) the term "organum" has as great a variety of meanings as the English word "organ" (part of the body, medium, etc.). Failure to recognize this fact has led to unwarranted conclusions concerning the use of the organ in the 6th to 8th centuries. St. Augustine (A.D. 354–430) says in two different passages that "organum is the name for all musical instruments," adding in one, "not only for that which is big and is inflated by bellows," and in the other, "although it has become customary to use it properly for those which are inflated by bellows" [see W. Apel, in *Speculum* xxiii, 201].

(2) Name for the earliest types of polyphonic music, from the 9th century ("Musica enchiriadis") to *c.* 1200 (Leoninus, Perotinus). The question of a connection between *organum* = polyphony and *organum* = organ is usually answered in the negative. The fact that until 1100 (if not later) the "push-and-pull" mechanism of organs permitted playing only one line [see Organ XII] seems to rule out this possibility. There is, however, literary and pictorial evidence that organs were occasionally played by two organists in a sort of "four-hand" performance, resulting in the simultaneous sounding of two melodies—i.e., a primitive type of polyphony.

In the broadest sense, organum is a composition consisting of a liturgical (plainsong) tenor to which one or more contrapuntal parts (*duplum, triplum, quadruplum*) are added. In earlier organum (prior to 1150) there was, judging from the relatively few preserved examples, no restriction as to the type of plainsong chosen as the basis for organum; syllabic hymns and sequences seem to have been preferred. In this period, therefore, organum means a general technique of composition. In the school of Notre Dame, organum treatment became restricted to a few types of plainsong, mainly Graduals, Alleluias, and responsories, resulting in a much narrower meaning for the term [see V]. The following phases of the development can be distinguished:

I. *Parallel organum* (c. 900–1050). To the main part, called *vox principalis,* is added a *vox organalis* at the lower fifth or fourth, note against note. Either or both parts can be duplicated at the octave, so that the sound d–a is amplified to A–d–a, d–a–d', D–d–a, d–a–a', d–a–d'–a', etc. (composite organum). In the organum at the fourth the parallelism of the parts is usually observed only in the middle of the phrase, while at the beginning and end the parts move in oblique motion, starting and ending in unison [*occursus; see Tritone]. This type, the converging organum at the fourth [Ex. 2], probably is much more representative of the earliest polyphony than the organum at the fifth [Ex. 1], which may have been primarily a theoretical speculation. Of the various sources—*"Musica (and Scholia) enchiriadis," treatises of Cologne, Paris, Bamberg, Guido's "Micrologus" of c. 1040—the first-mentioned is the only one that discusses organum at the fifth. For "organum at the second," see under Lombardic style; for "organum at the third," see Gymel.

II. *Free and contrary organum* (c. 1050–1150). In the second half of the 11th century, contrary motion began to be used side by side with parallel motion (in fourths, fifths, occasionally even thirds) and oblique motion. This type may be called "free organum." In addition to theoretical sources (*Ad organum faciendum,* in Milan [Ex. 3]; short treatise of Montpellier) there are long compositions written in this style, especially the famous "Ut tuo propitiatus" [*HAM,* no. 26b] and five Alleluias in Chartres *MS 109* [*HAM,* no. 26c]. The numerous organa in the 11th-century Winchester Troper are written in neumes that make exact reading impossible. The often repeated statement that this source shows clear evidence of contrary motion is very questionable. John Cotton, in his "Musica" of c. 1100, emphasizes the importance of contrary motion, saying that "whenever the original melody rises, the organal part should descend, and vice versa" [Ex. 4]. This method, which may be termed "contrary organum," became the foundation of the subsequent development of polyphony. As a concomitant, the fourth tends to disappear, or at least be replaced by the fifth as the main consonance after the unison and the octave. The two parts frequently cross.

III. *Melismatic organum* (mid-12th century). This type is characterized by the use of groups of notes in the added part against a single note of the original part, the length of such a group varying from a few notes to long melismas. As a result, the original becomes a succession of "held" tones and came to be called *tenor. The new style continued to be called "organum," the older note-against-note style now being termed *discant. The melismatic treatment, of course, greatly lengthens the composition [cf. *HAM,* nos. 28a and b; also nos. 26a and 27b]. Examples of pure melismatic organum occur particularly in the Codex Calixtinus from *Compostela [Ex. 5]. The organa of *St. Martial often have sections in organal style side by side with others in discant style [see *HAM,* no. 27a].

IV. *Measured organum* (before and after 1200). In the organa of the school of Notre Dame, the alternation of organal and discant sections became a standard practice and was usually applied so that the syllabic or neumatic sections of the plainsong were composed in a profuse style (up to 40 or more notes against one) and its melismatic sections in a concise style (one to three notes against one). Of the greatest importance was the introduction of measured rhythm,

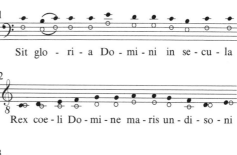

1. **Parallel organum at the fifth ("Musica enchiriadis").** 2. **Converging organum at the fourth** (ibid.). 3. **Free organum (Milanese treatise).** 4. **Contrary organum (Cotton).**

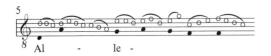

Al - le -

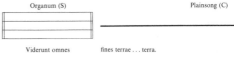

Organum (S)   Plainsong (C)

Viderunt omnes   fines terrae . . . terra.

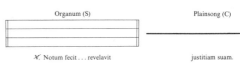

Organum (S)   Plainsong (C)

℣. Notum fecit . . . revelavit   justitiam suam.

Hec

5. Melismatic organum (Compostela). **6.** Measured organum (Notre Dame; two rhythmic versions, see HAM, no. 29, and Waite, The Rhythm of Twelfth-Century Polyphony, p. 120).

according to the rhythmic *modes. In the earliest Notre Dame organa, all in two parts and presumably composed by Leoninus [see "Magnus liber organi"], modal rhythm is clearly present in the discant sections, though less clearly in the others [Ex. 6; see *HAM*, nos. 28c, 29]. This type of organum is referred to by theorists as *organum duplum, organum purum,* or *organum per se.* Modal rhythm became fully established in the works of Perotinus, who wrote numerous organa in three parts (*organum triplum;* see *HAM,* no. 31) as well as two gigantic *organa quadrupla,* which represent the acme of organum as well as the end of the development.

V. In the school of Notre Dame (partly already in the earlier schools), polyphonic treatment and, therefore, the term "organum" was restricted to certain types of plainsong, mainly Graduals, Alleluias, responsories, and the *"Benedicamus Domino." Note that only the soloist sections of such a chant were used as a basis for polyphonic composition. For example, in a Gradual only the *Incipit* of the respond and the entire verse, except for its conclusion, were composed polyphonically, the remaining portions being supplied by the choir in plainsong [for the structure of the Graduals, see Psalmody II]. This practice strongly suggests that the organum (i.e., polyphonic) sections were performed by a small number of soloists, not a full chorus. The scheme below illustrates the performance of Perotinus' Christmas gradual "Viderunt" in the Cathedral of Notre Dame, *c.* 1200 (S = soloists, C = choir).

Lit.: *OH* i, *passim; ReMMA, passim,* bibl. 451–56; W. Krüger, *Die authentische Klangform des primitiven Organum* (1958); A. Geering, *Die Organa und mehrstimmigen Conductus* [1952]; F. Ludwig, *Repertorium organorum recentioris et motetorum vetustissimi stili* (1910); L. B. Spiess, "Polyphony in Theory and Practice from the Ninth to the Close of the Thirteenth Century" (diss. Harvard Univ., 1942; rev. 1948); W. G. Waite, ‡*The Rhythm of Twelfth-Century Polyphony* (1954; *organa dupla*); T. Göllner, *Formen früher Mehrstimmigkeit in deutschen Handschriften des späten Mittelalters* (1961); H. Husmann, ‡*Die drei- und vierstimmigen Notre-Dame-Organa* (1940); *id., Die dreistimmigen Organa der Notre Dame-Schule* (1935); Helmut Schmidt, ‡*Drei Benedicamus Domino-Organa* (1933); F. Spreitzer, "Studien zum Formaufbau der dreistimmigen Organumkompositionen" (diss. Freiburg, 1951); W. Waite, "Discantus, Copula, Organum" (*JAMS* v); J. Handschin, "Zur Geschichte der Lehre vom Organum" (*ZMW* viii); *id.,* "L'Organum à l'église" (*RCG* xl, xli); P. Wagner, "Über die Anfänge des mehrstimmigen Gesangs" (*ZMW* ix); W. Apel, "The Earliest Polyphonic Composition" (*RBM* x); *id.,* "Bemerkungen zu den Organa von St. Martial" (*CP Anglés* i); J. Handschin, "Der Organum-Traktat von Montpellier" (*CP Adler*); *id.,* "Zur Geschichte der Lehre vom Organum" (*ZMW* viii); R. Ficker, "Der Organumtraktat der Vatikanischen Bibliothek" (*KJ* 1932). See also under Notre Dame, school of; St. Martial, school of; Musica enchiriadis; "Magnus liber organi."

Organ vers. See Verset.

Orgel [G.]. Organ. *Orgelmesse,* *organ Mass. Orgelpunkt,* pedal point. *Orgelwalze,* barrel organ [see Mechanical instruments II].

Orgelbüchlein [G.]. Original title of a manuscript by J. S. Bach that contains forty-five organ chorales but was intended to include many more, since numerous pages are empty except for the name of the chorale. All the compositions are short settings, mostly of the melody-chorale type. The collection was probably made toward the end of Bach's stay in Weimar (1708–17). According to the title inscription, it was designed "to instruct a beginning organist how to set a chorale in diverse manners and also how to acquaint himself with the pedal, this being treated fully *obligato*."

Orgue [F.]. Organ. *Orgue de Barbarie,* the barrel organ of the Italian organ grinder, consisting of one or two rows of small organ pipes in a small portable case, operated by turning a handle. *Barbarie* is a corruption of the name of an 18th-century instrument-maker, Giovanni Barberi of Modena. See A. Schaeffner, "L'Orgue de Barbari de Rameau" (*CP Masson*). *Orgue expressif,* *harmonium. *Orgue positif,* positive organ [see Organ XII].

Oriental music. Generic term for the music of the Near and Far East: Arabia, China, India, etc. [see under individual countries; also Ethnomusicology]. Oriental music represents a cultural development comparable to that of Western music, the basic difference being that in the former the emphasis has been on melody and rhythm and in the latter on counterpoint and harmony. "Polyphonic" traits are not uncommon in the music of the East but are limited to rhythmic accompaniment, drones, and *heterophonic elements.

Oriental music has influenced Western music chiefly through two channels: (1) the Jews and the early Christian Church; and (2) the Arabs in Spain. The former influence persists in Gregorian chant, and the latter in many musical instruments and certain elements of theory and acoustics [see Arab music].

Lit.: C. Sachs, *The Rise of Music* [1943]; Hirosi Endo, *Bibliography of Oriental and Primitive Music* (1929); R. Lachmann, *Musik des Orients* (1929); *id.,* in *BüHM* xii; R. Lach, "Die Musik der Natur- und orientalischen Kulturvölker" (*AdHM*); separate articles in *LavE, NOH* i. See also under Ethnomusicology and specific countries.

Ornamentation. Musical ornamentation originated as a spontaneous act by the interpreter who, in performing a written or traditional melody, enlivened, expanded, or varied it through his technique of improvisation. The more or less stereotyped melodic figures that, in

the course of this process, have been substituted for or added to the original notes of the melody are known as ornaments. Throughout the history of music there have been three kinds of ornamentation: I. that left entirely to the improvisation of the performers; II. that in which definite ornaments are indicated by some sort of written sign; III. that in which the ornaments are written out in notes.

I. *Improvised ornamentation.* There is evidence that the early singers of Gregorian chant indulged in extemporaneous ornamentation of the traditional melodies, and that some of the variations created in this manner were eventually incorporated in the MSS. Tunstede (*c.* 1370) describes a type of improvised harmonization [see *Discantus supra librum*] that also calls for the introduction of improvised figurations [see *CS* iv, p. 294]. In the 16th century improvised ornamentation, known as *diminutio,* had its center at the papal chapel in Rome, where the singers ornamented and completely transformed works by Willaert, Lassus, Palestrina, *et al.* All the voices of a polyphonic composition were susceptible to ornamentation. Hermann Finck, in his *Practica Musica* (1556), states that "the character of the coloratura depends upon the skill and the individuality of the executant. My own view is that all voices must be ornamented, but not simultaneously, so that each voice will be brought out in turn." Zacconi (*Prattica di musica,* 1592) writes that the art of diminution, also known as *gorgia,* "charms the listener, especially when in four-, five-, or six-part pieces two voices stand out and sing solos together. It is a delight when one part of the piece is sung with improvised diminutions and the rest played upon instruments." There are a number of manuals for teaching the art of improvised diminution. The two earliest are Sylvestro Ganassi's *Opera intitulata Fontegara* (1535) and Diego Ortiz's *Tratado de glosas* (1553). Ex. 1 shows diminutions by G. dalla Casa (*Il vero modo di diminuir,* 1584) to Palestrina's madrigal "Vestiva i colli." Diminutions (known in Spain as *glosas,* in England as *divisions) were also used in purely instrumental performance. The fame of Merulo, the two Gabrielis, and Cabézon rested largely on the free and vivid improvisation with which they inspired seemingly dry pieces.

In many of the 16th-century treatises specific name are used for certain small melodic formulas that consist of either the repetition of a single note or the rapid alternation of two (or three) adjacent notes. To the former type belongs the

Handel's *Messiah* [Ex. 3] and a flute sonata by Quantz [Ex. 4] illustrate typical 18th-century practice.

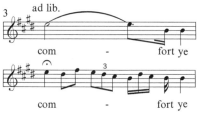

Italian *trillo* (an accelerated *tremolo); to the latter (*trills), the *tremolo, groppo,* and *ribattuta,* as well as the Spanish *redoble* and *quiebro* and the English *relish [see Ex. 2]. Caccini, Cavalieri, and

other 17th-century Italian musicians urged using these small ornaments, which they call *effetti,* as a special means of expression. It was in France, however, and under the name *agréments* that these ornaments finally became stereotyped and were systematized to the extent that it was possible to indicate them by signs or abbreviations and to establish definite rules for introducing them extemporaneously.

Improvised ornamentation and divisions continued to play a large part in musical performance throughout the 17th and 18th centuries. During this period singers probably never executed a solo part as it was written. Corelli [see *HAM,* no. 252], Handel, Tartini, and their contemporaries made their written parts of sonatas for strings mere sketches of what the player should do. The accompanying fragments from

Beginning with Gluck, composers gradually suppressed most improvised ornamentation. One important relic of the earlier practice, which persists even in the operas of Mozart and Gluck, is the appoggiatura in recitative. From the time of Alessandro Scarlatti it was customary for composers to write the appoggiatura that appears at the end of almost every phrase of recitative as a harmony note, in order to make the underlying harmony clear to the accompanist [see Ex. 5, where the upper system shows the customary notation and the lower the correct performance; Ex. 6 shows a standard cadence (a) as written and (b) as performed].

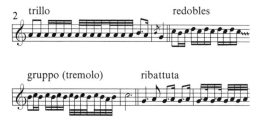

II. *Ornamentation as indicated by signs.* Some musical ornaments are so subtle and flexible in rhythm and pitch that they defy expression in ordinary musical notation and can only be represented by signs. The MSS of Gregorian chant contain special signs (sometimes appearing as modifications of the neumes) that probably indicate special effects such as tremolos, stressed notes, vibratos, portamentos, and smothered notes (liquescent neumes; see Neumes I). The only frequently recurring sign for an ornament in the music of the later Middle Ages is the *plica, which was derived from the liquescent neumes.

During the 16th century the indication of ornaments by signs was restricted almost entirely to keyboard music. The Germans used special signs for the *mordent, and in the English virginal books there is a profusion of single and double oblique strokes through the stem of the note, denoting ornaments whose exact nature has not been established. The Italian *groppo* and *tremolo* are sometimes indicated by *g* and *t* in the keyboard pieces of Valente [see *ApNPM,* fac. no. 16, p. 51], Mayone, Trabaci, Strozzi, B. Pasquini, and others. The Spaniard Correa de Araujo used the letter *R* for *redobles.*

By far the most important of all signs for ornaments are those of the French *agréments,* which were systematized during the 17th century and remained in continuous use by all European musicians until the beginning of the romantic period. It should be noted that they were used to the same extent in French harpsichord and organ music, a clear refutation of the common notion that their main purpose was to prolong the sound of the harpsichord. The correct interpretation of these signs constitutes a considerable problem in performing the music of this period, owing to the fact that the nomenclature and signs used for the individual *agréments* lacked uniformity and consistency. Identical ornaments were often called by different names and represented by different signs, while the same name and sign were sometimes given to different *agréments.* The *agréments,* in general, may be divided into the following categories: (1) appoggiatura (also double appoggiatura); (2) trill; (3) turn; (4) mordent; (5) Nachschlag; (6) arpeggio; (7) vibrato. [See the separate entries for each.] The first three types were regarded as essential *agréments,* in that their use was obligatory in certain positions of the musical phrase whether their signs appeared in the score or not. The others were left to the discretion of the performer. It is significant that the only signs to be found in the works of

Mozart and Beethoven are the tiny note representing the appoggiatura, the ~ for the turn, and the *tr* or *t* with a wavy line (*t̃*), indicating the trill. The other *agréments* had by then been absorbed by the ordinary notation. Rossini was probably the first composer who—much to the indignation of Stendhal—deliberately abandoned the signs for *agréments,* writing out what he considered necessary in notes (in his opera *Elisabetta,* 1815).

For a detailed study of the baroque ornaments, the tables of signs given with a number of publications are indispensable [e.g., D'Anglebert, in *TaAM* vii, 111; F. Couperin, in *TaAM* x, 78f; Kuhnau, in *TaAM* x, 2f; Georg Muffat, in *DTO* 4, p. 52; Gottlieb Muffat, in *DTO* 7, p. 89]. Very helpful also are the realizations in the modern edition of Loeillet [*Editions XXVIII, 1; the trill is often wrongly indicated to begin with the main note], Fiocco [*Editions XXVIII, 3], and in an article by A. Dolmetsch (theme of Bach's Goldberg Variations, "Un Cas d'ornamentation chez Bach," *BSIM* viii, 24–30). The accompanying table shows (without claim to completeness) a variety of signs used for the different types of ornamentation. A long list of signs is given in *GDB* vi, 441ff.

III. *Written out ornamentation.* The embellishment of a simple melody became, at an early date, one of the regular procedures of composition. Frequently, melismatic chants of the Gregorian repertory have been interpreted as ornamented versions of simpler skeleton melodies, e.g., of monotones [see *GDB* vii, 130]. Definite evidence of ornamentation technique has been found in the music, monophonic or polyphonic,

I. Dashes.

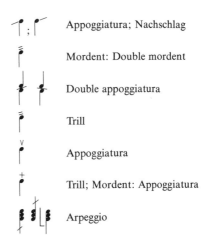

Appoggiatura; Nachschlag

Mordent: Double mordent

Double appoggiatura

Trill

Appoggiatura

Trill; Mordent: Appoggiatura

Arpeggio

II. Zigzag Lines.

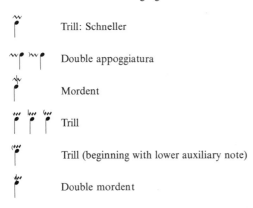

Trill: Schneller	
Double appoggiatura	
Mordent	
Trill	
Trill (beginning with lower auxiliary note)	
Double mordent	

III. Curved Lines.

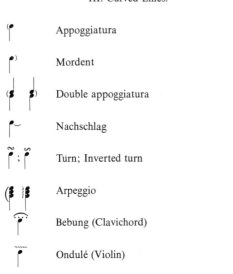

Appoggiatura	
Mordent	
Double appoggiatura	
Nachschlag	
Turn; Inverted turn	
Arpeggio	
Bebung (Clavichord)	
Ondulé (Violin)	

IV. Letters.

t   Trill; Schneller

tr t....   Trill

of the 12th to 14th centuries [see Lit., Hand-schin]. The upper voice of 15th-century *discant compositions (hymns, Mass sections, etc., by Dunstable, Dufay, *et al.*) is usually an orna-mented version of a Gregorian chorale. The accompanying example (Gloria by Dunstable; see Editions XXXIV, 8, pp. 16ff) illustrates the free and highly imaginative treatment that was customary at that time [see also Dufay, in *HAM,*

bo - nae vo - lun - ta - tis

no. 65]. Numerous other examples exist in the *melody chorales of the baroque period, particu-larly in those of Buxtehude [see *HAM,* no. 190b] and Bach (e.g., "Wenn wir in höchsten Nöten sein").

The transcription of vocal works for instru-mental performance on the keyboard, lute, or instrumental ensembles is another area where written out ornamentation played an important role, especially during the 16th and 17th cen-turies [see Intabulation]. Furthermore, many 16th-century pieces for keyboard or lute (whether transcription or independent compo-sition) contain *groppi, tremoli, minute, *tirades,* etc.—ornaments that were customarily impro-vised by singers and by players of melodic in-struments but that, in the case of keyboard and lute music, were written out in groups of rapid notes, as in the accompanying example from Sweelinck's *Fantasia chromatica.* Some of these

minuta   tirata   groppo

formulas gradually became more and more stereotyped until finally they were incorporated in the system of *agréments* and indicated by signs or left to the improvisation of the performer.

Between 1650 and 1750 the practice of writing ornaments in notes was frowned on as detrimen-tal to the visual clarity of the melodic line. J. S. Bach, for instance, was severely criticized by at least one contemporary musician on the ground that "he writes down in actual notes the orna-ments and embellishments that performers are accustomed to supply instinctively, a habit which not only sacrifices the harmonic beauty of his music but also makes the melody totally in-distinct" (J. A. Scheibe, in *Der Critische Musicus,* May 14, 1737). The example here given (from W. Landowska, *Music of the Past* [1924], pp. 131ff) shows how a passage from the Andante of the Italian Concerto would appear had it been written in the more conventional notation of Bach's time [(a) *Doppelschlag* (turn); (b) *Schleifer*

(double appoggiatura); (c) mordent; (d) *passaggio;* (e) *tirade*]. It must be noted, however, that Bach did not invariably adhere to this unorthodox practice; his keyboard suites, for instance, are provided with numerous traditional signs for *agréments.*

Since the late 18th century the pendulum has swung in the other direction, and composers have endeavored to indicate their intentions as precisely as possible, using a minimum of signs and expressing all complex ornaments in such a way that there can be no doubt as to what notes are to be performed, even though, in certain cases, the rhythm of those notes be free, as in the so-called "cadenzas" written in tiny grace notes by Chopin and other romantic composers.

Lit.: E. Dannreuther, *Musical Ornamentation,* 2 vols. (1893); A. Dolmetsch, *The Interpretation of the Music of the 17th and 18th Centuries,* 2 vols. (1915); E. Fowles, *Studies in Musical Graces* (1907); R. Donington, *The Interpretation of Early Music* [1963]; P. Aldrich, *Musical Ornamentation in the 17th/18th Centuries* (1951); id., "The Principal Agréments of the 17th and 18th Centuries" (diss. Harvard Univ., 1942); M. Kuhn, *Die Verzierung in der Gesangskunst des 16.–17. Jahrhunderts* (1902); H. Goldschmidt, *Die Lehre von der vokalen Ornamentik* (1907); W. Georgii, *Die Verzierungen in der Musik* (1957); H.-P. Schmitz, *Die Kunst der Verzierung im 18. Jahrhundert* (1955); K. P. E. Bach, *Essay on . . . Playing Keyboard Instruments,* trans. W. Mitchell [1949]; P. Brunold, *Traité des signes et agréments employés par les clavecinistes français des 17. and 18. siècles* (1935); J. Arger, *Les Agréments et le rythme dans la musique vocale française du 18e siècle* [n.d., 1917?]; P. Aldrich, *Ornamentation in J. S. Bach's Organ Works* (1950); E. Bodky, *The Interpretation of Bach's Keyboard Works* (1960); W. Emery, *Bach's Ornaments* (1953); F. Couperin, *L'Art de toucher le clavecin* (1760); H. Ehrlich, *Die Ornamentik in Beethoven's Klaviersonaten* (1896); J. P. Dunn, *Ornamentation in the Works of Frederick Chopin* (1921); C. G. Hamilton, *Ornaments in Classical and Modern Music* [1929]; A. Dechevrens, in *SIM* xiv (Gregorian chant); J. Handschin, in *ZMW* x (Middle Ages); R. von Ficker, in *StM* vii (Trent Codices); J. Dodge, in *SIM* ix (lute tablatures); I. Horsley, in *JAMS* iv (improvised, 16th cent.); G. Thibault and others, in *CP 1961;* A. Moser, in *ZMW* i (Corelli); H. Prunières, in *RM* 1932 (baroque, vocal); P. Aldrich, in *MQ* xxxv, *MQ* xlix, *The Inchoirer,* Sept. 1939–Feb. 1940 (Bach); S. Salter, in *MQ* vi (Bach); E. Lockspeiser, in *ML* xvi, 312 (Bach, French); T. Dart, in *GSJ* xiv (Jacobean lute and viol); V. Duckles, in *AnnM* v (English 16th–17th cent.); A. Schering, in *SIM* vii (18th cent.); H. Lungershausen, in *ZMW* xvi (18th cent.); M. Seiffert, in *SIM* viii (*Messiah*); F. Salzer, in *ZMW* xii (K. P. E. Bach); H. Mersmann, in *AMW* ii (preclassical. P.A.

Orpharion. An instrument of the lute family that was in use *c.* 1600. It was shaped like the *bandora but smaller in size, and had six or more double courses tuned F–G–c–f–a–d'–g'. William Barley's *A new Booke of Tabliture* (1596) contains pieces for this instrument. [For ill. see under Lute.] See W. W. Newcomb, *Lute Music of Shakespeare's Time* (1966); D. Gill, in *GSJ* xii.

Orphée aux Enfers [F., Orpheus in the Underworld]. Operetta in two acts by Offenbach (libretto by H. Crémieux and L. Halévy), produced in Paris, 1858. Setting: Greece, legendary times. It is an amusing burlesque of the famous Greek legend [see under Orpheus and Eurydice].

Orphéon. Name used by French male choral societies, similar to the American *Apollo Clubs and German *Männergesangvereine. The members are chiefly farmers, workers, and middle-class people. The movement started *c.* 1835 and spread rapidly. By 1910 there were about 1,200 *Orphéons* in France. A system of public competitions called *Concours Orphéoniques* was inaugurated by Bocquillon-Wilhelm in 1842. Gounod conducted the Orphéon of Paris from 1852 to 1860.

Orpheoreon. Same as *orpharion.

Orpheus and Eurydice. The touching fable of the "inventor of music" recovering his beloved Eurydice from Hades and losing her again in the moment of their reunion has been used as an operatic libretto more frequently than any other subject. Among the numerous operas based on this story, Monteverdi's *La *Favola d'Orfeo*

(1607), Gluck's *Orfeo ed Euridice* (1762), and Offenbach's parody *Orphée aux Enfers* (1858) are immortal. A more recent version is E. Krenek's *Orpheus und Eurydike* (1926). It is interesting to note the difference between the tragic close of Monteverdi's opera and the happy ending of Gluck's. In the former, Orpheus loses Eurydice but, as a reward for his great love, is transferred to the stars by Apollo; in the latter, Amor appears and restores Eurydice to life.

Orpheus in the Underworld. See *Orphée aux Enfers.*

Orphica. A variety of piano, invented by K. L. Röllig of Vienna, 1795.

Osanna. See Hosanna.

Ossia [It.]. Indication for an alternate version, usually one that is easier to execute.

Ostinato. A clearly defined phrase that is repeated persistently, usually in immediate succession, throughout a composition or a section. The ostinato differs from other devices of repetition, such as *imitation and *sequence [see Repetition (2)], in that it is reiterated in the same voice and usually at the same pitch. It is this feature of "persistent" repeat that accounts for the name [It., obstinate].

The earliest examples of ostinato occur in compositions of the 13th century, e.g., in the motet "En mon chant—Omnes" (MS Munich, gallo-rom., *42; c.* 1230), whose *duplum* consists of nine repetitions of a two-measure phrase [Ex. 1]. Several other examples occur among the motets of the Codex Montpellier [see Y. Rokseth, *Polyphonies du XIIIe siècle*, iv, 202], among them one ("Amor potest conqueri") with the short ostinato figure shown in Ex. 2. In another, a street cry, "Frese nouvele, muere france" (Fresh strawberries, wild blackberries) is repeated four times [see *HAM*, no. 33b]. A well-known English example is the *pes* of *"Sumer is icumen in." In the 14th and early 15th centuries the ostinato seems to have been little used, a notable exception being Dufay's *Gloria ad modum tubae*, in which two trumpets constantly alternate with a fanfare motif [Ex. 3]. Ostinato reappeared after 1450 in a large number of motets (*ostinato motets*) in which the tenor consists of short restated phrases. The impression of ostinato, however, is weakened by the use of fairly long rests between the statements and by the fact that these often involve transposition. In Busnois' motet "In hydraulis" the entire tenor consists of the motif

d–c–d [Ex .4], starting on d, a, d', a, g, a, the whole sung (or played) four times. In Josquin's motet "Salve Regina" the beginning of the plainsong (a–g–a–d) is sung alternately on g' and on d'. Stepwise transposition of a motif occurs in Compère's "Royne du ciel" [*HAM*, no. 79], in which the bass sings the beginning of the Marian antiphon "Regina coeli" successively on c, d, e, and f. The same method is used more extensively in Josquin's "Miserere," in which a psalm-tone motif, e–e–e–e–e–f–e, recurs eight times on

successively lower degrees from e' to e and then upward through the same steps. A famous ostinato motet by Morales is his "Emendemus in melius" [*HAM*, no. 128].

A different manifestation of the ostinato technique is the so-called *discanto ostinato,* i.e., an upper part consisting of (or including) numerous restatements of a motif, at irregular intervals and in free modifications. Examples occur in the works of Isaac [see *RiHM* ii.1, p. 166] and particularly in English compositions, such as Taverner's Mass *The Western Wynde* [see *HAM*, no. 112] and several organ pieces by Redford [see C. Pfatteicher, *John Redford*, p. 40; *HAM*, no. 120b]. Frescobaldi employed this technique with great virtuosity in his *Capriccio sopro il Cucho* and *Capriccio sopra La Sol Fa Re Mi* [*Primo libro de Capricci,* 1624; see Ex. 5].

In the 16th century the ostinato technique received a fresh impulse from dance music, possibly from Oriental dances, in which it is still prominent today. The Oriental element is particularly conspicuous in a Fantasia for two vihuelas by E. Enriquez de Valderrabano in which the second vihuela plays a one-measure ostinato throughout the entire composition [Ex. 6; see W. Apel, in *MQ* xx, 300]. Two English dances from *c.* 1525, "My Lady Careys Dompe" [*HAM,* no. 103] and a "Hornepype" by Hugh Aston, are based on a tonic-dominant ostinato and are the earliest examples of the *basso ostinato* or *ground. A 19th-century example of a tonic-dominant ostinato is Chopin's Berceuse. See also Chaconne and passacaglia; Aria III.

The ostinato has been revived in music of the 20th century. Composers such as Hindemith and Bartók have been attracted by its polyphonic and rhythmic possibilities as well as its antiromantic precision and straightforwardness [Ex. 7, Hindemith, *Konzert* op. 38, 4th movt.]. For bibl. see under Ground.

Otello [It., *Othello*]. Opera in four acts by Verdi (libretto by A. Boito after Shakespeare), produced in Milan, 1887. Setting: Cyprus, late 15th century. *Otello,* together with **Falstaff* (1893), represents the climax of Verdi's achievement. In these operas Verdi abandoned the aria style of his earlier operas (*Aida, etc.*) and adopted something like Wagner's principle of continuous composition without, however, sacrificing the peculiarities of his personal style.

Ôtez, ôter [F.]. Take off (a stop or the violin mutes).

Ottava [It.]. Octave, abbr. *8va* (*8*). *All'ottava, ottava alta, ottava sopra,* or simply *8va* written above the notes indicates playing one octave higher than written; *ottava bassa, ottava sotto,* or *8va* written below the notes (usually in the bass part) calls for the lower octave. *Coll'ottava* means doubling in the higher (or lower) octave.

Ottava rima. See under *Strambotto.*

Ottavino [It.]. The piccolo flute.

Ottoni, stromenti d'ottone [It.]. *Brass instruments.

Ours, L' [F., The Bear]. Popular name for Haydn's Symphony no. 82, in C (1786), the first of the Paris Symphonies. The name is suggested by the opening theme of the last movement, a "growling" theme in the bass.

Ouvert and clos [F.]. In the **ballades,* *estampies,* and *virelais* of the 14th century, *ouvert* and *clos* [L. *apertum, clausum;* It. *aperto, chiuso*] indicate different endings for repeated sections, corresponding to the modern *prima volta, seconda volta.*

Ouverture [F.]. *Overture.

Overblowing. See under Wind instruments II, III.

Overtones. See under Acoustics IV. Overtones play an important role in music theory, where they have been used to explain the phenomenon of *consonance, and also as a means for deriving the entire tonal material (scale) from a single sound [e.g., Hindemith, *The Craft of Musical Composition,* 2 vols. (1941, '45)]. See G. Albersheim, "Overtones and Music Theory" (*BAMS* 1948, p. 69).

Overture. An instrumental composition intended as an introduction to an opera, oratorio, or similar work. I. *The operatic overture.* The earliest operas, which usually began with a *prologue, had no overture, or at most a flourish of instruments such as the "Toccata" of Monteverdi's *Orfeo* (1607). Among the first more elaborate overtures are the three *Sinfonie that precede the three acts of S. Landi's *Il Sant' Alessio* [*Editions III, 5; the second in *HAM,* no. 208], each in the form of a canzona with several short sections. The "canzona" overture [see Canzona (5) II] was a favorite type in the Venetian opera, where it is usually in the form of an introductory slow movement in duple rhythm followed by a fast movement in triple rhythm (Cavalli, *Giasone,* 1649). Other overtures, hardly different in form, are called "Sonata" (e.g., Cesti, *Il pomo d'oro,* 1667). The Venetian type of overture was the model for Lully's famous French overture (earliest example in his ballet *Alcidiane,* 1658), which became the first standard type of overture. It consists of a slow introduction in pompous style with dotted rhythm, followed by an allegro in imitative style on a short, canzona-like subject, though the imitative treatment is not strictly maintained [see *HAM,* no. 224]. Sometimes the second movement of the French overture ends with a broad adagio passage, which has led to the erroneous idea that this is a three-movement form; this view is not in accordance with the actual examples, in which the closing section (if present at all) is an "allargando" coda to the allegro rather than a separate movement. There are, however, later examples of the French overture in which the closing passage is extended into a "third movement," e.g., that which opens Bach's so-called French Overture (really a French overture followed by a suite; see Suite V). Handel's overture to *Rinaldo* (1711; see SchGMB, no. 278) illustrates other methods of amplification, merging with the *sonata da chiesa.*

In the late 17th century Alessandro Scarlatti introduced another type of overture, the Italian overture (earliest example in *Dal male i bene,* overture, *c.* 1696), consisting of three sections, allegro, adagio, and allegro, an early adumbration of the three movements of the sonata. These sections are in simple homophonic style except the first, which introduces some imitative treatment for the entrances of the voices. The usual name for this type is "sinfonia" [see Sinfonia; ex. in *HAM,* no. 259]. During the first half of the 18th century the French and the Italian types existed side by side. Cases of Italian operas and oratorios with a French overture—which surpassed the other in artistic quality—are not rare (e.g., Handel). The French overture disappeared *c.* 1750 as a result of the rapidly growing importance of the symphony and sonata as standard forms.

An important feature of the ensuing development was the emphasis on a closer connection of the overture with the opera itself, mainly by incorporation into the overture of material from the opera. This procedure was used in Cesti's *Il Pomo d'oro* and Rameau's *Castor et Pollux* (1735) but did not become accepted practice until after 1750. Still more important is the idea of using the overture to prepare for the mood of the first scene of the play. Perhaps the first example is the overture to Gluck's *Iphigénie en Tauride* (1778), in which the overture announces the approaching thunderstorm of the opening scene. Famous examples of using the overture to set the emotional background for the plot are those to Haydn's *Creation,* Mozart's *Don Giovanni* and *Zauberflöte,* Beethoven's *Leonore* Overtures (not the final *Fidelio* overture), Weber's *Freischütz,* and practically all the overtures by Wagner and his successors. Wagner abandoned the sonata-like structure of the overture in favor of a free *Vorspiel* directly leading into the first scene. His precedent has been followed by most modern composers of opera. In strong contrast to this romantic type is the overture to the 19th century *grand opéra* of French derivation (Rossini, Boieldieu, Auber,

Meyerbeer), which usually is a potpourri of the most prominent melodies of the opera.

II. *The French overture as a suite.* See Suite V.

III. *The concert-overture.* This 19th-century type is an independent orchestral composition written along the same lines as the operatic overture, either as a single movement in sonata form or as a free *Vorspiel.* Well-known examples are Mendelssohn's *Die *Hebriden,* Berlioz' *Le Carnaval romain,* and Brahms' *Akademische Festouvertüre.* In this category may also be included the overtures written as an introduction to spoken plays and frequently performed as concert pieces, such as Beethoven's overture to Goethe's *Egmont* and Mendelssohn's overture to *A Midsummer Night's Dream.*

Lit.: H. Botstiber, *Geschichte der Ouverture* (1913); H. S. Livingston, "The Italian Overture from A. Scarlatti to Mozart" (diss. Univ. of North Carolina, 1952); A. Heuss, "Die Venetianischen Opernsinfonien" (*SIM* iv); H. Prunières, "Notes sur l'origine de l'ouverture française" (*SIM* xii).

Oxford Symphony. Haydn's Symphony no. 92, in G, composed in 1788. It was performed at Oxford in 1791, when Haydn was there to receive an honorary degree from the university.

Oxyrhynchos Hymn. The earliest Christian hymn (*c.* A.D. 300) for which the music is preserved. It takes its name from Oxyrhynchos, in Egypt, where the papyrus on which it is written was found. The text is in Greek, and the melody is written in Greek vocal notation [see Notation II]. The melody (most recent transcription in E. Wellesz, *A History of Byzantine Music and Hymnography,* p. 126) is essentially Greek in style (descending fifths and sixths) except for the closing "Amen, amen," which shows the smooth melodic motion of a "Gregorian" cadence. Facsimile and six transcriptions in *MGG* iv, 1052. See A. S. Hunt, *The Oxyrhynchos Papyri* (1928); T. Reinach, *La Musique grecque* (1926); H. Abert, in *ZMW* iv; O. Ursprung, in *BüHM* ix, 12.

P

P. Abbr. for piano; for pedal (in organ and piano music); or for [F.] *positif,* i.e., choir organ.

Pacato [It.]. Calm.

Pacific 231. Symphonic poem ("Mouvement symphonique") by Honegger (1923), named for an American type of locomotive and suggesting its motion from start to full speed to stop.

Padiglione [It.]. The bell of a wind instrument. *Padiglione cinese,* Chinese crescent.

Padovana, padoana. A 16th-century title that is difficult to define owing to its diverse applications. Etymologically, it means a dance from Padua. In practice it had two meanings: (1) In the first half of the 16th century it was used as a generic term for dances of the **pavane-*passamezzo* species. The nine dances labeled *pavana* in Dalza's *Intabulatura de lauto* (Petrucci, iv, 1508) are described as *padoane diversi* on the title page of the collection, as are the *passamezzi* in Da Crema's *Intabolatura de lauto* (1546). Dances of the same type in Capirola's lute book (*c.* 1517; see Gombosi ed., 1955) and, anachronistically, in J. C. Barbetta's *Intavolatura de liuto* (1585) and J. Abondante's *Il Quinto Libro de tabolatura da liuto* (1587) are labeled *padoana.* (2) Toward the middle and in the second half of the 16th century, the term *padovana* or *padoana* was usually applied to a quick dance in quadruple compound meter (12/8) resembling a **piva.* Such dances appear in lute tablatures by D. Bianchini (1546), Antonio Rotta (1546), Gorzanis (1561, '63, '64, '6?), Barbetta (1585), Abondante (1587), Radino (1592), and Terzi (1599).

For the most part the inconsistent use of the term in Italian collections is duplicated in German ones, but in Spanish and French sources, with few exceptions, the word *pavana* (pavane, or *pavenne*) is employed as a generic term for dances of both the pavane-*passamezzo* and padoana-*piva* types. In German sources of the 17th century, the title reverts to its earlier 16th-century meaning, and introductory dances of the pavane-*passamezzo* species in suites of Isaac, Posch, Peurl, Schein, and Scheidt are labeled *paduana.*

For detailed description and bibl. see L. H. Moe, in *MGG* x, 566–68.   L.H.M.

Paean. Originally a name for Apollo, the term came to mean a song in praise of this god, or a song of praise in general.

Paganini Etudes. Six concert etudes for piano by Liszt, based on Paganini's *Capricci* for violin (except no. 3, which is taken from Paganini's *La Campanella*). Schumann also wrote twelve etudes on themes from Paganini's *Capricci.*

Paganini Variations. Variations (in two sets) for piano by Brahms, op. 35 (1866), on a theme by Paganini, the same that Liszt had used in no. 6 of his **Paganini Etudes.* Brahms' variations combine the utmost technical difficulty with an emotional detachment that is very unusual in the piano literature of the period.

Pagliacci, I [It., The Players]. Opera in two acts and prologue by Leoncavallo (to his own libretto), produced in Milan, 1892. Setting: Montalto Calabria, Aug. 15, 1865. Together with Mascagni's **Cavalleria rusticana, Pagliacci* is the outstanding example of the **verismo* movement. Particularly famous is the prologue in which Tonio explains the idea of the plot—an intentional revival of the **prologue of 17th-century opera.

Paired imitation [G. *paarige Imitation*]. A special type of imitative treatment, in which the four statements of the theme are arranged so that 1 and 2 appear in close succession, while 3 and 4 enter later in the same combination (except for octave transposition). It is very characteristic of Josquin's style [see Ex. 1, from the motet "Memor esto," meas. 203]. Sometimes the

second pair is made to vary from the first through use of double counterpoint at the octave, fifth, or fourth. The term "paired imitation" is also used for another device, equally common in the works of Josquin, in which each pair consists of two different melodies [Ex. 2, from "Ave Maria," meas. 19]. This device might perhaps be distinguished from true paired imitation by calling it "duo imitation." Both methods are occasionally found in earlier compositions, e.g., by Busnois.

Paléographie musicale. See Editions XLII.

Palestrina. Opera in three acts by H. Pfitzner (to his own libretto), produced in Munich, 1917. Setting: Rome and Trent, 1563.

Palestrina style. A polyphonic *a cappella* style based on the principles of counterpoint, imitation, melodic movement, and consonance and dissonance as used in the music of Palestrina. As early as the 17th century this style, known by such names as *stile antico* or *stile osservato,* had become "classical" in the *Roman school. It was revived by Baini (1775–1844) in the early 19th century, and later by the *Cecilian movement. Pope Pius X, through his *motu proprio,* gave it new status in church composition. Today the Palestrina style is an important aspect of the study of counterpoint [see K. Jeppesen, *Counterpoint* (1939); A. T. Merritt, *Sixteenth-Century Polyphony* (1940)].
    Lit.: K. Jeppesen, *The Style of Palestrina and the Dissonance* (1927); O. Ursprung, *Restauration und Palestrina-renaissance in der katholischen Kirchenmusik der letzten zwei Jahrhunderte* (1924); K. G. Fellerer, *Der Palestrinastil und seine Bedeutung in der vokalen Kirchenmusik des achtzehnten Jahrhunderts* [1929].

Pallet. See under Organ II.

Panama. Panama's folk music combines the Spanish tradition of the coast, the indigenous inland forms, the African elements brought by Negro slaves, and the internationalism of Panama City. The pentatonic structure of pre-Columbian music survives in the rituals of the Tule Indians, who still use rudimentary flutes and drums similar to those described by early Spanish chroniclers. The Spanish traditions in Panama were untouched by the influences of Italian opera and 19th-century salon dance music, which so strongly affected most Latin American folk music. Native forms such as the *mejorana* or *socavón* and the *punto* remained unchanged, and the *tamborito* and *cumbia* retain their African character to the present day.

Art music developed relatively late in Panama, although information concerning the musical history of Panama City Cathedral is available from the time of Juan de Araujo (1646–1714), who served as music director until 1670 (when he was appointed to the Lima Cathedral; see Peru).

A group of composers born during the last decades of the 19th century produced the first art music composed by native Panamanians. Most of them were amateurs who wrote popular songs and dances, short instrumental pieces in the national vein, and band music. Among them was Jorge Santos (1870–1941), who composed the national anthem. The most outstanding member of this group is Alfredo Saint-Malo (b. 1898), a noted violinist educated in Paris, who at one time was director of the *Conservatorio Nacional* of Panama. Ricardo Fábrega (b. 1905) has won recognition for songs and dances composed in the native manner. The first professionally trained musician of stature was Herbert de Castro (b. 1906), who wrote a number of works in prevailingly impressionist style and became a strong promoter of contemporary music in Panama.

Panama's most distinguished contemporary composer is Roque Cordero (b. 1917), whose works have projected a genuine Panamanian idiom into international music. In addition to writing three symphonies, a Concerto for violin and orchestra, *Capricho Interiorano,* and several solo and chamber works, he has been active as an educator (head of the *Instituto Nacional de Música*) and conductor (of the *Orquesta Sinfónica de Panamá*). Other contemporary Panamanian composers are Gonzalo Brenes, a noted ethnomusicologist whose compositions include a ballet, *Mariana del Monte;* José Luis Cajar, composer of a *Preludio* for orchestra and a Quintet for winds; and Marina Saiz Salazar (b. 1930), composer of a Sonata for piano and *Sejatpar* for orchestra.
    Lit.: N. Garay, *Tradiciones y Cantares de Panamá* (1930); G. Chase, *Composed by Cordero* (1958); N. Slonimsky, "Music, Where the Amer-

icas Meet" (*Christian Science Monitor,* June 8, 1940); R. Cordero, "Actualidad musical en Panamá" (*Buenos Aires Musical* xii, no. 197, Oct. 1957). Also see under Latin America.   J.O-S.

Panconsonant. A term introduced by M. Bukofzer for a style inaugurated *c.* 1420 by Dunstable, in which triads are predominant and dissonances are ornamental (*cambiata* or *échappée;* see Nonharmonic tones I) rather than structural [see under *Ars nova* II]. See M. Bukofzer, in *MGG,* s.v. "Dunstable."

Pandean pipes. See Panpipes.

Pandiatonicism. A term introduced by N. Slonimsky to describe an important technique in 20th-century music, i.e., the use of the diatonic scale instead of the chromatic scale as a tonal basis without conventional harmonic limitations. The accompanying example (Stravinsky, Piano Concerto) illustrates this style, in which the absence of functional harmony usually results in a certain tonal staticity, offset by a greater interest

in counterpoint, rhythm, and chord spacing. Historically, however, pandiatonicism represents a reaction against both the "panchromaticism" of atonality and the "harmonic chromaticism" of the late 19th century. In fact, a page from, e.g., Stravinsky's Serenade (1925) or Poulenc's Suite (1920) with their C-major appearance offers a striking contrast to the piling up of sharps and flats in a page from Ravel or Schoenberg.

Pandiatonic style is clearly present in many of Satie's whimsical pieces, written *c.* 1910 (e.g., *Embryons desséchés*), Debussy's "Doctor Gradus ad Parnassum" (in *Children's Corner* [*Coin des enfants*], 1910), and portions of Stravinsky's *Petrushka* (1911). It became more fully established about 1925 as a concomitant of the *neoclassical movement. See N. Slonimsky, *Music Since 1900,* rev. ed. (1949), p. xxiv.

Pandora. See Bandora.

Pandoura, pandura. A long-necked lute of ancient Greece and Rome [see Lute II].

Pandura. See Bandurria.

Panduri, pandur. A small, bottle-shaped fiddle used in the Caucasus.

Panharmonicon. See under Mechanical instruments III.

Pan-isorhythmic. A term introduced by W. Apel for 14th- and early 15th-century motets in which isorhythmic technique is applied to all the voice-parts, not only to the tenor. See Isorhythmic. See W. Apel, "Remarks about the Isorhythmic Motet" (*Les Colloques de Wégimont* ii [1955]).

Panpipes, pandean pipes. A primitive wind instrument consisting of a number of tuned pipes (vertical flutes; see Instruments III) of different size, which are bound or glued together, usually in the form of a raft. The pipes, usually stopped at one end, are blown across the top, as in the mouth organ. [See ill. under Flute.] The panpipes are among the oldest instruments. They were used in ancient Greece, where they were called *syrinx,* attributed to the god Pan, and played by shepherds, as well as in China, Rumania, and South America. The Peruvian panpipes are called *antara* and those of Ecuador (made of 33 pipes of cane) *rondador.*

The Chinese panpipes, called *pai-hsiao,* consist of sixteen (formerly twelve) pipes arranged in two whole-tone scales [see Ex.]. It is a ritualistic and symbolic instrument, its shape representing the outspread wings of the mystic bird phoenix, and the arrangement of its pipes in two

groups standing for the male and female elements (the tones of the left half are the *yang lü,* i.e., masculine tones; those of the right half, the *yin lü,* i.e., feminine tones). See China II. See A. H. Fox-Strangways, in *ML* x; J. Tregenna, *The Pipes of Pan* (1926); *SaHMI;* E. M. von Hornbostel, in *Festschrift für P. W. Schmidt* (1928).

Pantaleon. An enlarged *dulcimer invented *c.* 1697 by Pantaleon Hebenstreit, who also was a virtuoso on this instrument. It reportedly had 186 strings and was played by means of two small hammers. The last virtuoso on the instrument was one Georg Nölli (Noel), who gave performances in England (1767) on an instrument with 276 strings. Toward the end of the 18th century the name was used for a piano with down-striking action.

Pantomime. A silent dramatic performance in which the action is revealed by facial expression, movements, and gestures, with musical accompaniment. The pantomime is distinguished from *ballet in that it emphasizes dramatic movements rather than dancing; however, the *ballet d'action* is very close to pantomime. Pantomime played an important part in ancient Greece. Toward the end of the pre-Christian era pantomime developed into a virtuoso show, in which a single actor performed entire plays, representing different personages by using masks. Throughout the 18th century, pantomime was extremely popular, with the stock characters Harlequin, Pantaloon, Clown, the Old Man and his Pretty Daughter taken from the Italian *commedia dell'arte*. For these popular entertainments, music was occasionally written by composers of some renown, such as the two Arnes, Dibdib, *et al.* A revival of greater musical significance was inaugurated by André Wormser's *L'Enfant prodigue* (1890). Later examples are R. Strauss' *Josephslegende* (1914) and *Schlagobers* (1924), as well as Stravinsky's *L'Histoire du soldat* (1917) and Bartók's *Der wunderbare Mandarin* (1926). See R. J. Broadbent, *A History of Pantomime* (1901); A. E. Wilson, *The Story of Pantomime,* 2 vols. (1949).

Pantonality, pantonal. The inclusion of all tones on an equal basis. The terms are sometimes used instead of *atonality and atonal.

Papadike. See under Byzantine chant III.

Papillons [F., Butterflies]. Fanciful title used by Schumann for a set of twelve short piano pieces (op. 2, 1829–31), "butterflies of different colors," as it were. The final piece suggests the end of a ball early in the morning, with the clock striking six. See also under Character piece.

Paraguay. The earliest musical accomplishments in Paraguay are associated with the first Jesuit missions in northern Paraná. Soon after the founding of La Asunción (1537), chronicles mention two Spaniards, Juan Gabriel Lezcano and Rodrigo Melgarejo, who taught the Guaraní Indians to perform plainchant and instrumental music. In 1609 the Jesuit mission of San Ignacio Guazú was established, and by 1620 it included a school of music organized by Father Pedro Comental (1595–*c.* 1670), a Neapolitan mathematician and musician. His work was carried on by a Frenchman, Father Luis Berger (1588–1639), an accomplished violinist who settled in Paraguay in 1616 and later moved to Buenos Aires [see Argentina]. Little is known about musical life during the remainder of the colonial period.

After independence from Spain (1811), Paraguay underwent a long period of dictatorship and isolation, which is reflected in the country's musical development. European salon music acquired new characteristics in Paraguay, quite different from those in the rest of 19-century Latin America. The waltz, polka (polka Paraguaya), and galop developed rhythmic and metrical variations peculiar to Paraguay, and the extensive use of the Guaraní language was reflected in certain characteristic features in folksongs of Spanish origin, as in the Paraguayan *canción* known also as *purajhei*. This tradition was later revived by José Asuncion Flores (b. 1904) in a type of ballad song called *guarania*, which many of his followers have also cultivated.

The first important native Paraguayan composer was Agustín Pio Barrios (1885–1944), who wrote mainly for the guitar. Other prominent composers of the 20th century are Fernando Centurion de Zayas (b. 1886), also a conductor and educator; Remberto Gimenez (b. 1899), composer of a *Rapsodia Paraguaya* and of the official version of the national anthem; and Juan Carlos Moreno (b. 1912), who has written piano, chamber, and orchestral works, some based on elements drawn from Paraguayan native music.

Primitive instruments of the Guaraní Indians are still used in Paraguay. Most of them belong to the *memby* family, a group of wind instruments. A trumpet called *inubia* and several kinds of drum, such as the *trocano, matapú,* and *curugú,* are also used, in addition to the *mbaracá* [see Maraca] and *congoerá*.

Lit.: J. M. Boettner, *Música y músicos del Paraguay* (1957?); J. C. Moreno Gonzales, "Los Guaraníes y la música" (*Boletín latino-americano de música* iv, 1938). Also see under Latin America.   J.O-S.

Parallel chords. The successive sounding of a fixed chordal combination, consonant or dissonant, through various degrees of the scale. In classical harmony this device is admissible only for the sixth chord and diminished seventh chord, being strictly prohibited for triads, seventh chords, etc., on account of the parallel fifths that would result. In deliberate violation of these principles, French composers, particularly Debussy, introduced parallelism for triads and seventh chords as well as for any dissonant combination involving seconds, fourths, etc. [Ex. 1, *Danse sacrée*, 1904; Ex. 2, *Et la lune descend*, 1907]. This technique, one of the most character-

istic features of *impressionist music, is in opposition to traditional harmony not only because it violates the rule of parallel fifths and introduces unresolved dissonances but, chiefly, because it rejects the fundamental concept of traditional harmony, i.e., the functional character of the chords. Instead, it establishes the chord as a mere sensuous and sonorous factor. Later composers, such as Stravinsky, Bartók, and Casella, have exploited the percussive quality of parallel chords by using them in rapid succession and in pronounced rhythm [Ex. 3, *Petrushka*].

Although Debussy is rightfully credited with establishing parallelism as a technique, occa-

sional examples are found in other 19th-century works (by Rossini, Mussorgsky, Lalo, Délibes; see *LavE* ii.1, 72ff, 632ff). Parallel fourth chords are found in Satie's *Le Fils des étoiles* of 1891 [Ex. 4], and "percussive" parallelism prevails in the introduction to Act II of Puccini's *La Bohème*, 1896 [Ex. 5]. In the 16th century, parallel 1-5-8 chords were quite common in keyboard dances [see Editions XI, 8], and parallel triads were used parodistically in the *villanella. A "serious" example of remarkable boldness occurs in Monteverdi [see H. Leichtentritt, in *MM* v, 16]. In compositions of the period c. 1400 there are instances of parallel triads without parallel motion [Ex. 6, schematic; see W. Apel, *French Secular Music of the Late Fourteenth Century*, p. 13a].

Parallel (consecutive) fifths, octaves. The duplication of the melodic progression of a part (e.g., c-d) by another part at the distance of a fifth (g-a) or octave (c′-d′). Such voice-leading [see Ex. 1, 2] is considered faulty and is strictly prohibited in classical counterpoint. Its avoidance is

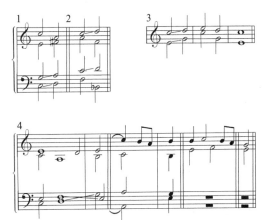

a basic feature of the contrapuntal style from the 15th through 19th centuries.

A fifth (or octave) that is reached not in parallel but in similar motion is referred to as a "hidden (covered) fifth" (or octave). This kind of voice-leading is usually admissible, except for certain extreme cases, e.g., when large intervals are involved in both voices, e.g., $\frac{g-c'}{B-f}$. Particularly common (and entirely legitimate) is the progression illustrated in Ex. 3. This is called "horn fifths" because it is characteristic of the writing for natural horns.

Parallel fifths and octaves are basic in the early *organum (10th century) and occur frequently in compositions of the subsequent centuries, e.g., 13th-century motets. The younger Johannes de Garlandia, in his "Optima introductio in contrapunctum" (*c.* 1300; *CS* iii, 12) was the first to state that "two perfect consonances of the same type should never follow one after the other." Nevertheless, consecutive fifths and octaves are still common in the works of Machaut. From the 15th century on the rule was generally observed, although not always as strictly as later theorists demanded. Ex. 4 shows three cases of unorthodox treatment in Josquin's "Tu pauperum refugium" [*HAM,* no. 90]. Even Bach and Mozart occasionally admitted parallel fifths and octaves. Theorists and writers of the 18th and 19th centuries treated this rule as a "strict law" on the basis of which they not only discovered many "stylistic faults" in Bach but also condemned as crude such early musical styles as the parallel organum of the 9th century or the motets of the 13th century, sometimes even going so far as to object to the mixture stops of the organ [see Organ VI]. Today this narrow view has been largely abandoned.

Lit.: F. T. Arnold, "J. S. Bach and Consecutives in Accompaniment" (*ML* xiv, 318); F. E. Gladstone, in *PMA* viii; M. G. Sewall, "Hucbald, Schoenberg and Others on Parallel Octaves and Fifths" (*MQ* xii); M. Shirlaw, "Aesthetics and Consecutive Fifths" (*MR* x, 89ff).

Parallel key. See Key relationship.

Parallel motion. See Motion.

Parallel seconds. See under Lombardic style.

Parallel thirds. See under Gymel.

Paralleltonart [G.]. Relative (not parallel) key.

Paramese, paranete. See under Greece II.

Parameter. A mathematical term denoting special variables, e.g., the variable amplitude in a group of sine curves [see Acoustics VI and accompanying Ex.]. The term has been introduced into contemporary music (*serial music, *electronic music) to indicate variabilities of pitch, rhythm, volume, timbre, etc.

Paraphonia. In late Greek and early medieval theory, term used for the intervals of the fifth and fourth, as opposed to *symphonia (unison) and *antiphonia* (octave). The fact that *paraphonistae* are mentioned in writings of the 1st and 7th centuries (Longinus; *Ordo Romanus I*) has been interpreted as evidence of parallel organum long before the "Musica enchiriadis." See P. Wagner, in *RdM,* 1928, pp. 15ff; 1929, p. 4; A. Gastoué, in *RdM,* 1928, pp. 61ff; C.-A. Moberg, in *ZMW* xii, 220; *ReMMA,* p. 252.

Paraphrase. A free rendition or elaboration. In music the term may mean: (1) A textual paraphrase, i.e., a free rewriting of a text; e.g., a psalm paraphrase is a new wording of a psalm, usually in poetic language (metrical psalm; see Psalter). See under *Contrafactum.* (2) A reworking and free arrangement of well-known melodies, such as Liszt's concert paraphrases of Wagnerian operas.

(3) In early music (14th–16th centuries), a free elaboration of a plainsong melody, comparable to the ornamentation of chorale melodies found in many organ chorales by Buxtehude and Bach. Unlike ornamentation, which is easily recognized as such because it involves smaller note values, paraphrase is a more subtle transformation in which original and additional notes blend into a new melody of homogeneous design. The accompanying Ex. shows a passage from a Gloria (based on the Gregorian Gloria IX) by Dunstable, who was one of the first composers to make extensive use of this technique, which is the opposite of *cantus planus style. The same technique is employed in Dufay's *Alma redemptoris mater* [*HAM,* no. 65], as well as in 15th- and 16th-century organ music (Buxheim Organ Book, John Redford). The term "paraphrase Mass" has been applied to 15th-century Masses

Tu so - lus Al - tis - si - mus

(usually single Mass items) having a paraphrased plainsong in one voice-part, as well as to 16th-century Masses in which a paraphrased plainsong (usually a hymn melody) or portions thereof are used in all the voices, producing points of imitation. Probably the earliest example is Josquin's *Missa Pange lingua.* In later compositions of this type (Palestrina) the paraphrase sometimes involves simplification rather than amplification of the plainsong.

In true paraphrase the original notes (often marked *x* in modern editions) appear in a normal distribution, approximately one to each measure.

Attempts to interpret upper parts of certain Masses as paraphrases involving highly irregular distribution of the plainsong melody—e.g., three or more notes in one measure and the next note perhaps ten measures later—are not authentic [see Discant Mass]. See J. Handschin, "Die melodische Paraphrase im Mittelalter" (*ZMW* x); R. Ficker, "Die frühen Messenkompositionen der Trienter Codices" (*StM* xi); R. L. Marshall, "The Paraphrase Technique of Palestrina" (*JAMS* xvi); *ReMR, passim.*

Parapter. Term used in a few medieval treatises for tonally irregular antiphons and, possibly, for four irregular modes to be added to the eight normal church modes. Hucbald, in his *De harmonica institutione* ("De modis"; *GS* i, 148), enumerates four *parapteres,* two of which can be identified with two well-known groups of irregular antiphons: the *parapter tertius* with what Regino calls *antiphonae nothae* [see Nothus; Gevaert's *thème 29,* in *La Melopée antique,* 1895], the *parapter quartus* with the *tonus-peregrinus* antiphons (*thème 28;* see *ApGC,* p. 399f). See A. Auda, *Les Gammes musicales* [1947], pp. 153ff [his reconstruction of the modes, p. 158, is not convincing]; P. Wagner, in *CP Adler.*

Pardessus de viole. See Dessus.

Parhypate. See under Greece II.

Paris Symphonies. Six symphonies by Haydn, nos. 82–87, composed 1785–86 for the *Concerts de la Loge Olympique* in Paris. Three of them have individual names: *L'Ours* (no. 82), *La Poule* (no. 83), and *La Reine* (no. 85).

Paris Symphony. Mozart's Symphony in D (K. 297), written in 1778 during his stay in Paris and performed there at the *Concerts spirituels.*

Parlando, parlante [It.]. In singing, an indication that the voice must approximate speech; in a sense, "spoken music," as distinguished from the "musical speech" of the *recitative. Parlando occurs particularly in rapid tempo when the syllables of the text change with every note; see Patter song. In instrumental music, parlando (*parlante*) calls for an expressive declamation, suggestive of speech or song. See Beethoven's *Bagatellen* op. 33, no. 6: "Con una certa espressione parlante."

Parlato [It.]. Same as *parlando, but also used to distinguish the spoken sections in comic opera (ballad opera, Singspiel) from those that are sung.

Parody. (1) In present-day usage, a satirical imitation, such as may be created in music either by replacing the original text with a comic one or by changing the composition itself in a comic manner [see Satire]. (2) In early practice, replacement of the text, with or (more often) without the implication of caricature. This procedure, although often referred to as parody (e.g., parodies of Lully's operas), is more properly termed *contrafactum* to distinguish it from the "musical" parody described below.

(3) Before 1600 and occasionally in the 17th century, parody means a serious reworking of a composition, involving additions to or essential modifications of the original. The most important use of this technique was in the Mass [see Parody Mass]. However, it was also used in other fields, especially in transferring vocal compositions to lute or keyboard instruments, a process that often involved more than mere *intabulation. One method was to borrow themes from a vocal composition and treat them in a new, usually more expanded manner. An example in point is G. Cavazzoni's keyboard canzona "Falte d'argens," a parody of Josquin's chanson "Faulte d'argent" [see *HAM,* nos. 91, 118]. The same method is used in A. de Cabezón's "Tiento sobre Cum sancto spiritu" (*Editions XX, 7) a composition based on themes from the "Cum sancto spiritu" section (end of the Gloria) of Josquin's *Missa de Beata virgine.* A different method of parody is exemplified by a "Glosa sobre el 'Cum sancto spiritu'" by the Spanish vihuela composer Mudarra (*Editions XXXII, 7, p. 59), in which the same composition by Josquin is divided into three sections marked "Josquin," each of which is preceded by a freely invented section marked "Glosa."

Lit. *For (2):* See under Contrafactum. *For (3):* W. Steinecke, *Die Parodie in der Musik* (1934); M. Steinhardt, *Jacobus Vaet and His Motets* (1951), pp. 54–59; L. Lockwood, in *CP Reese* (16th cent.); J. Ward, in *JAMS* v and *CP Sachs* (16th-cent. instrumental music); F. Reimann, in *MF* viii (North German tablatures). See also under Paraphrase; Parody Mass; Satire; Villanella.

Parody Mass [L. *missa parodia*]. Term for an important practice in 15th- and 16th-century Mass composition, i.e., incorporating into the Mass material derived from various voice-parts or from entire sections of a polyphonic composition (motet, chanson, madrigal). This extensive borrowing distinguishes the parody Mass from the *cantus firmus* Mass, which employs only one voice-part (tenor or *superius*) of its model [see Mass C II b]. Whereas in the *cantus firmus* Masses there is a fairly uniform practice of employing the borrowed melody as the tenor of each Mass item, in the parody Masses a large variety of methods is used, in regard to both the amount and the treatment of the borrowed material.

The earliest incontrovertible examples of parody Mass are by two late 14th-century Italian composers, Bartolomeo da Bologna and Antonio Zacara of Teramo. The former reworked his *ballata*, "Vince con lena" [Stainer, *Dufay and His Contemporaries,* p. 60] into a Gloria [Van den Borren, *Polyphonia sacra,* pp. 37ff; see especially the "Gratias agimus"]; Zacara wrote an "Et in terra *Rosetta,*" "Et in terra *Fior gentil,*" and "Patrem *Deus deorum,*" in which he incorporated his *ballate* "Rosetta" and "Fior gentil" with the Gloria, and "Deus deorum" with the Credo [see F. Ghisi and N. Pirrotta, in *CP 1950,* pp. 308ff, 315ff]. In the 15th century the parody technique was applied to entire Masses. Among the earliest instances are Faugue's (Ockeghem's?) *Missa Le Serviteur,* which draws on all the parts of Dufay's chanson of the same name [see the table in *ReMR,* p. 113], and Ockeghem's similarly constructed *Missa Fors seulement* [*ReMR,* p. 127]. Several Masses by Obrecht are essentially *cantus firmus* Masses, being based on the tenor of a chanson, but incorporate additional material from the chanson, sometimes entire segments, into the sections during which the tenor pauses (*Missa Fortuna desperata, Si dedero, Rose playsant,* etc.).

The 16th-century parody Mass incorporates not fragments taken from individual parts but entire polyphonic segments of the model, in this period usually a motet. A sort of minimum procedure was to use three segments, from the beginning, the middle (often beginning of Part II), and the close of the motet, and employ these in the same position in each Mass movement, with the middle segment serving for the beginning of subsections (Kyrie II, Qui tollis, Et in spiritum, Osanna, Agnus II). These segments are connected by newly composed material, in a manner very similar to that used in the *tropes of the 10th and 11th centuries. Most of the Masses of Gombert and Clemens non Papa belong to this type. Later composers went even further, breaking up the entire motet into segments and incorporating them, usually in the same order, into the Mass movements. About three-fourths of the Masses of Palestrina and Lassus are parody Masses. Examples are in *HAM,* no. 146b (de Monte), and *ReMR,* pp. 478 (Palestrina) and 607 (Victoria).

Lit.: F. Ghisi and N. Pirrotta, in *CP 1950* (14th cent.); L. Schrade, in *AM* xxvii (14th cent.); W. H. Rubsamen, in *BAMS* iv (16th cent.); R. B. Lenaerts, in *MQ* xxxvi (16th cent.); J. Schmidt-Görg, in *KJ* xxv (16th cent.); P. Pisk, in *StM* v (Gallus); J. Klassen, in *KJ* xxxvii–xxxix (Palestrina); H.-C. Wolff, in *CP Anglés* ii (16th cent.).

Parsifal. Opera in three acts by Richard Wagner (to his own libretto), produced at Bayreuth, 1882, for the dedication of the *Festspielhaus* [see *Bühne*] and performed there almost exclusively for thirty years. Setting: in and near Montsalvat, Spanish Pyrenees, Middle Ages. The first performance elsewhere was at Munich in 1884 (private). Stage productions produced in violation of the Bayreuth privilege were first held in New York, 1903, and at Amsterdam, 1905. *Parsifal,* Wagner's last work, is written according to the principles of the music drama [see Opera X].

Part. (1) In orchestral or chamber music, the music for a particular instrument, such as violin, flute, piano, etc. (2) In contrapuntal music, the single melodic line of the contrapuntal web (fugue in three, four parts). The modern names for such parts, also called voices, are soprano, alto, tenor, and bass. Early designations are: *vox principalis, vox organalis* (9th–11th cent.); *cantus, discantus* or *cantus, organum* (12th cent.); *tenor, duplum (motetus), triplum, quadruplum* (13th cent.); *discantus, tenor, contratenor* (1300–1450); *superius, altus, tenor, bassus,* additional parts being called *quinta vox, sexta vox, vagans* (1450–1600). See also Treble; Meane. (3) A section of a composition, as in three-part song form.

Partbooks [G. *Stimmbücher*]. The manuscript or printed books of the 15th and 16th centuries, each containing the music for an individual voice of a polyphonic composition [see under Score II]. The earliest source of this kind is the Glogauer Liederbuch of *c.* 1480, written in three partbooks. The usual number of partbooks is four: *Cantus (Discantus, Superius); Altus; Tenor; Bassus (Basis),* abbr. *C (D, S); A; T; B.* Books for additional parts were marked either *Cantus I, Cantus II,* or *Quinta Vox* (V), *Sexta Vox* (VI), etc.

Publication in partbooks clearly indicates that the music thus written or published is *ensemble music, either vocal, or instrumental, or mixed.

Parte [It.]. (1) Voice-part [see Colla]. (2) 17th-century term for variation [see *Partita;* Parthie].

Parthenia. A printed collection of *virginal music, published *c.* 1611 (1613, 1646, and many later editions). According to the title, it was "the first musicke that euer was printed for the Virginalls." It contains twenty-one compositions "by three famous Masters William Byrd, Dr. John Bull and Orlando Gibbons." New editions were published by Rimbault (1847), Farrenc (*Trésor des pianistes,* 1863), M. Glynn (1927), and K. Stone [1951]. A facsimile edition by O. E. Deutsch appeared in 1943. A companion work is the *Parthenia inviolata,* which contains anonymous pieces ("dances and tunes") for virginal and bass viol (only preserved copy in the New York Public Library).

Parthie, Partia, Partie [G.]. 17th- and 18th-century names for suite; see Partita (2). The French word *partie* means voice-part (*fugue à 3 parties*) or section, movement (*sonate en 4 parties*).

Partial. See under Acoustics IV.

Partial signature. The use of a signature, practically always b-flat, in some but not all the voices of a polyphonic composition (also called conflicting signature). Prior to 1500 such signatures are extremely common—indeed, much more so than "full" signatures. As a rule, the highest part carries no signature, the b-flat being indicated only with the lower parts. Typical combinations are: ♮, ♭, for two-voice pieces (13th cent.); ♮, ♮, ♭, or ♮, ♭, ♭, for three-voice pieces (13th, 14th cent.); ♮, ♮, ♭, ♭, for four-voice pieces (15th cent.). This method of notation does not, as some writers assume, represent an oversight or a meaningless tradition. It has been explained as the adequate expression of a sort of contrapuntal bitonality (Apel, Johnson) or bimodality (Hoppin) and, in contrast to these views, as the practical reflection of the various cadential formations of the period (Lowinsky). See W. Apel, in *AM* x, xi; *id.,* in *ApNPM,* pp. 102ff, 140; E. Lowinsky, in *MQ* xxxi, *JAMS* vii; R. H. Hoppin, in *JAMS* vi, ix; M. Johnson, in *Hamline Studies in Musicology* ii (1947; Landini).

Partie [G., F.]. See under Parthie.

Partimen [Prov.]. See *Tenso.*

Partimento [It.]. A 17th- and 18th-century practice of improvising melodies and complete pieces above a written bass; thus, a broadening of the practice of thoroughbass in which the bass as well as the melody is given. The English *divisions upon a ground belong to the field of *partimento* playing, which was extensively cultivated in the later baroque period as a means of musical instruction. Gaetano Greco (b. 1680), Francesco Durante (1684–1755), and Giacomo Tritto (1733–1824) wrote *partimenti.* See K. G. Fellerer, *Der Partimento-Spieler* (1940); *id.,* "Gebundene Improvisation" (*DM* xxxi.6).

Partita [It.]. (1) The original and proper meaning of the term, as applied to music, is variation. A MS from 1584, containing lute compositions by Vincenzo Galilei, includes a *Romanesca con cento parti,* each *parte* being a variation. In A. Mayone's *Primo libro di diversi capricci* (1603), Trabaci's *Ricercate, canzone . . . partite diverse* (1603), Frescobaldi's *Toccate e partite d'intavolatura* (1615), the autographs of Pasquini, and elsewhere, *partita* always means a variation, the entire composition being correctly called *partite* (plural). In Germany, the term occurs in connection with Froberger's variations "Auff die Mayerin," as well as chorale variations by Georg Böhm ("Freu dich sehr o meine Seele") and Bach ("O Gott, du frommer Gott" and two others). The modern practice of using the singular form *partita* for the entire composition (e.g., "Partita über die Arie"; see J. Wolgast, *Georg Böhm, Sämtliche Werke* [1952], i, 69), is wrong, both grammatically and historically. See F. Torrefranca, in *CP 1953.* (2) To the present-day reader, a *partita* is a suite, a meaning based on the six Partitas in Bach's *Clavier-Übung* i (1731). Possibly this term is derived from the French word *partie,* since in the 1690's suites were occasionally termed *Parthien* (Froberger, 1693; Kuhnau, 1693; Krieger, 1697). Bach's three suites for violin solo are termed *Partia* (not Partita) in the autograph. (3) Occasionally, the term *partite* means "pieces," e.g., in the posthumous publication *Diverse . . . Partite di toccate, ricercate, capricci e fantasie . . . di Froberger* (1693).

Partition [F.], **Partitur** [G.], **partitura** [It.]. *Score. See also under Intavolatura.

Part song. A choral composition in homophonic style, i.e., with the top part the sole carrier of the melody. The term is commonly understood as an antonym of the madrigal, with its emphasis on polyphonic texture, and therefore applies chiefly to choral works of the 19th century, such as were written by Schumann, Mendelssohn, Parry,

Stanford, Elgar, and many others. See also Glee. Sometimes the term is used quite differently, i.e., for the truly polyphonic songs of the pre-madrigal period. Thus, Isaac's "Innsbruck ich muss dich lassen" is designated as a "German part song." See A. Vogel, "The English Part-Song around 1500" (*BAMS* 1940).

Parture [F.]. See under *Tenso.*

Pasacalle [Sp.]. A Bolivian serenade of gay character, in 2/4 meter, usually performed in the streets by couples who dance either holding hands or separately.   J.O-S.

Paseos [Sp.]. A term used by Cabanilles (1644-1712) for compositions very much like a chaconne. Ex. in *HAM*, no. 239.

Pasillo [Sp.]. Originally, a Colombian ballroom dance similar to the waltz, but today a dance performed mainly in rural areas. Like the waltz it is in moderate 3/4 meter, but it often employs a characteristic rhythmic pattern with a dotted quarter note on the first beat and a strong accent on the third.   J.O-S.

Paso doble [Sp.]. A kind of one-step (though the name means "double-step") in 6/8 meter that became popular about 1926.

Paspy. Another name for *passepied.*

Passacaglia [It.], **passacaille** [F.]. See Chaconne and passacaglia.

Passage. A term loosely used for a short section of a composition much as in literature (a passage from the Bible). More specifically, passages or passage work refers to sections that contain a brilliant display of virtuosity rather than important musical ideas. Thus, one speaks of "scale passages," "arpeggio passages."

Passaggio [It.]. (1) Transition, modulation. (2) Passage work. (3) In the 16th-century art of diminution [see Ornamentation], a generic term for improvised ornaments, usually other than plain scale passages or trill-like figurations.

Passamezzo, pass'e mezzo. An Italian dance of the 16th and early 17th centuries similar to a *pavane; indeed, the musical style of the common pavane cannot be distinguished from a *passamezzo*. The dance steps must also have been similar. Arbeau (*Orchésographie,* 1589, f. 33) describes the *passamezzo* as a "pavana played less heavily to a lighter beat," and M. F. Caroso's choreographies for the two dances have the same stylistic characteristics (*Il Ballarino,*

1581, and *Nobiltà di Dame,* 1600). Furthermore, Gervaise (*Sixième livre de danseries,* 1555) uses the term *pavanne-passemaize.* In all probability the *passamezzo* was a type of pavane. Like the pavane, it was usually coupled to a *saltarello,* a galliard, or a *padovana.* Dances coupled together were composed on the same melodic and/or harmonic patterns.

The earliest extant example appears in H. Newsidler's *Ein newgeordent künstlich Lautenbuch* (1536) listed as "Welscher tantz Wascha mesa" (Italian dance *Wascha mesa*). The curious *Wascha mesa* is explained in a later collection by Newsidler [*Ein newes Lautenbüchlein,* 1540), in which it is supplanted by the title "Passa mesa: Ein Welscher tantz." The title is not found in Italian books until 1546 (lute tablatures by G. Abondante, D. Bianchini, da Crema, and A. Rotta), but it must have existed earlier, since Newsidler cited it as an Italian dance. It did not occur in Spain but is found in England by the middle of the century (London, Brit. Mus. MS *Roy. App. 74,* f.38). It also appears in the Flemish collections of Phalèse as early as 1546 and in France in the Gervaise collection printed by Attaingnant in 1555.

A large proportion of *passamezzi,* a few pavanes, and at least one-fifth of all 16th-century dances (including *saltarelli,* galliards, *padovane,* etc.) are composed on two harmonic patterns known as the *passamezzo antico* [Ex. 1] and the *passamezzo moderno (commune, novo;*

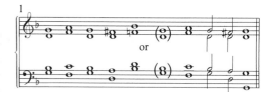

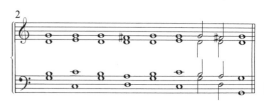

Ex. 2). No particular discant melody was associated with the two harmonic patterns. See O. Gombosi, "Italia: Patria del basso ostinato" (*LRM* vii); id., "Stephen Foster and 'Gregory Walker'" (*MQ* xxx; showing the survival of the *passamezzo* patterns in 19th- and 20th-century

popular music); I. Horsley, "The 16th-Century Variation" (*JAMS* xii); G. Reichert, "Der Passamezzo" (*CP* 1950a); J. Ward, in *MGG* x, 877–80.
L.H.M.

Passecaille [F.]. Passacaglia.

Passepied [F.]. A gay, spirited dance in rather quick 3/8 or 6/8 meter that was very popular at the French court under Louis XIV and Louis XV [see Dance music III]. It is said to have come from Brittany. Examples occur in the French

operas (e.g., Campra, *L'Europe galante,* 1697; see Ex.) and in the suites of German composers (J. K. F. Fischer; J. S. Bach, English Suite no. 5).

Passing tone [F. *note de passage;* G. *Durchgangsnote;* It. *nota di passaggio;* Sp. *nota de paso*]. See under Nonharmonic tones I.

Passion music. A musical setting of the text of the Passion (*Passio Domini nostri Jesu Christi*) according to one of the four Evangelists. In the Roman Catholic rites, the Passion according to St. Matthew is read during Mass on Palm Sunday, that according to St. Mark on the following Tuesday, that of St. Luke on Wednesday, and that of St. John on Good Friday.

Musical settings of the Passion, ranging from the 10th to 18th centuries, naturally show a great variety of styles. A considerable number of terms have been suggested for the purpose of classification—dramatic, oratoric, choral, motet-like, figural, scenic, through-composed, responsorial, etc.—some of which are used with entirely different meanings by different writers. The most useful and least ambiguous of these are discussed below.

A. *The plainsong Passion.* In the Middle Ages the Passions were sung in a manner designed to bring out the contrast between the participants of the story: Jesus, the Jews (*turba Judaeorum*), and the narrator (*Evangelista, Chronista*). This was done by using a recitation at three different pitch levels and speeds: low and solemn for the words of Jesus (recitation on f, with inflections down to c), medium and in normal speed for those of the Evangelist (on c′, down to f), high and with pronounced agitation for the Jews (on f′, down to c′). The earliest MSS (9th, 10th cent.) distinguish only between the words of Jesus and other text by marking the former *t* (*tarde,*

slowly), the latter *c* (*celeriter,* quick). Later the letter *s* (*sursum,* high) was added to characterize the Jews. Eventually, the letter *t* was interpreted as the sign of the Cross, †, and the two others adopted different meanings, C for *Chronista* and S for *Synagoga.* The music is found in the *Cantorinus Vaticanus* and also in the *Officium et Missa ultimi tridui* (for Good Friday).

B. *The polyphonic Passion.* The earliest polyphonic settings known today are found in an English MS from *c.* 1450 [see G. S. McPeek, ed. ‡*The British Museum Manuscript Egerton 3307* (1963)]. Here only the *turba* sections (also the words of individuals, such as John, Peter, Pilate) are polyphonically composed, those of Christ and the Evangelist being sung in plainsong. Because of the dramatic effect of the contrast of plainsong with polyphony, this type of Passion is called "dramatic Passion" (also "scenic," "responsorial"). Other examples are the Passions in MS Modena, Bibl. Est. *lat. 454/5* (*c.* 1480) and those by Davy (*c.* 1490), Sermisy (1534), Lassus (1575 and later), Guerrero (1585), Asola, Victoria, and Byrd (1607). The polyphonic portions are usually simple settings (often in *falsobordone* style) of the plainsong melody (in the tenor). In some Italian Passions of the 16th century, the words of Jesus are also composed, plainsong being used only for the Evangelist [see K. von Fischer, in *AMW* xi, 203]. In Germany, the Reformation led to the adoption of the vernacular and, occasionally, to modifications of the traditional plainsong, e.g., the use of an elaborate melisma for Jesus' cry: "Eli, eli, lama asabthani." The earliest Passion of this type, by Johann Walther (St. Matthew, 1550) was very popular and was still performed in 1806 at Nuremberg. Among many other composers who used the same method are A. Scandello (*c.* 1550), Jacob Mailand (St. John, 1568; St. Matthew, 1570), Thomas Mencken (1610), Matthias Vulpius (1612), Christian Schultze-Delitzsch (1653), and Christian Flor (1667).

Side by side with this tradition was another, musically more elaborate treatment, i.e., the composition of the entire text of the Passion in motet style (motet Passion; also through-composed Passion). The earliest known example is one by Longaval (*c.* 1510; formerly attributed to Obrecht), whose text is derived from all four Gospels. Others are by Galliculus (1538), Cypriano de Rore (1557), Joachim a Burgk (1568; *Editions XLVII, 22), Jacobus Gallus (1587), and Leonard Lechner (1594). As a rule, the liturgical plainsong is preserved as a *cantus* *firmus* in these polyphonic settings, at least in the earlier works, while later composers adhered less strictly to this principle and occasionally abandoned it altogether.

C. *The baroque Passion.* The 17th century saw the application to the Passion of all the dramatic innovations of the baroque era, such as *stile recitativo,* the aria, the orchestra, etc., together with a freer treatment of the authentic text, which was either paraphrased or broadened by free poetic interpolations, thus approaching the oratorio (oratoric Passion). An early work indicative of these new tendencies is the Passion according to St. John by Thomas Selle (1643; *Editions VIII, 26). Interesting features are the *recitativo* passages, the introduction of "intermedii," i.e., choral settings of interpolated texts (psalms and Protestant chorales), and the use of different instrumentation for the Evangelist and for Christ. The great figure in this period is Heinrich Schütz (1585–1672). Late in life (*c.* 1665–72) he wrote three Passions (Matthew, Luke, and John; a fourth, according to Mark, is spurious) in a remarkably austere and even archaic style. Technically they belong to the "dramatic" type of the 16th century, since they employ *a cappella* polyphony for the *turbae* and unaccompanied recitation for the rest of the text. However, Schütz replaced the traditional plainsong by a "neo-Gregorian" recitative of his own invention [see *SchGMB,* no. 192]. Other Passions of this period are interesting chiefly for their progressive tendencies, such as the use of the orchestra and the introducton of chorales and arias (C. Flor, 1667; J. Sebastiani, 1672; J. Theile, 1673; see *DdT* 17).

D. *The Passion oratorio.* After 1700 the authentic text of the Bible was abandoned in favor of rhymed paraphrases in the sentimental and allegorical style of the day. Particularly popular were C. F. Hunold-Menante's *Der blutige und sterbende Jesus* (composed by Keiser, 1704) and Brockes' *Der für die Sünden der Welt gemarterte und sterbende Jesus.* The latter was set to music by many composers, among them Keiser, Telemann, Handel, and Mattheson. Hand in hand with this textual deterioration went a decline in musical taste, leading to a style that approximates opera more closely than oratorio.

Against this background, Bach's St. John Passion (1723) and, particularly, his St. Matthew Passion (1729) represent a return to proper and dignified Passion style that is no less remarkable than their artistic superiority. Both Passions use the Biblical text as a basic narrative, set in recitative or (for the *turbae*) in short choruses. Poetic texts (by Brockes for the St. John Passion, by Picander for the St. Matthew Passion) are used for the arias and large choruses. The form may be described as a succession of cantatas, each closing with a chorale. According to the earliest catalog of Bach's works (1754), he wrote five Passions. However, aside from the two mentioned above, only portions of the St. Mark Passion remain in the *Trauer-Ode* of 1727. A St. Luke Passion, published in *BG* xlv, is spurious.

The ensuing history of the Passion includes such works as Telemann's *St. John Passion* (1741); Passion oratorios by Caldara (1730), Jommelli (1742), and Paisiello (1784), all based on a text by Metastasio (*La Passione di Jesù Cristo*); Johann Ernst Bach's (1722–77) *Passionsoratorium* [*DdT* 48]; two Passions by K. P. E. Bach (1787, '88); and oratorios dealing with the Passion story, such as K. H. Graun's *Der Tod Jesu* (1755), Haydn's *Die sieben Worte am Kreuz* (1785), Beethoven's *Christus am Ölberge* (1803), and Spohr's *Des Heilands letzte Stunden* (1835). Compositions of the *Stabat Mater and the *Seven (Last) Words also are in this category.

The 20th-century Bach revival brought about a remarkable rekindling of the true Passion spirit in works such as the *Markus-Passion* of Kurth Thomas and the *Choralpassion* of Hugo Distler.

Lit.: O. Kade, *Die ältere Passionskomposition bis zum Jahre 1631* (1893); H. J. Moser, *Die mehrstimmige Vertonung des Evangeliums,* 2 vols. (1931, '34); F. Spitta, *Die Passionen von Heinrich Schütz* (1886); P. Spitta, *Die Passionen nach den vier Evangelisten von Heinrich Schütz* (1893); A. Schmitz, ed., ‡*Oberitalienische Figuralpassionen des 16. Jahrhunderts* [1955]; W. Braun, *Die mitteldeutsche Choralpassion im achtzehnten Jahrhundert* [1960]; Y. Rokseth, "La Liturgie de la Passion vers la fin du Xe siècle" (*RdM* 1949, p. 1); A. Smijers, "De Mattheus-Passie van Jacob Obrecht" (*TV* xiv); W. Lott, "Zur Geschichte der Passionskomposition von 1650–1800" (*AMW* iii, vii); P. Epstein, "Zur Geschichte der deutschen Choralpassion" (*JMP* 1929); *id.,* in *BJ* 1930; K. Nef, "Schweizerische Passionsmusiken" (*Schweizer Jahrbuch für Musikwissenschaft* v); H. J. Moser, "Aus der Frühzeit der deutschen Generalbasspassion" (*JMP* xxvii); H. M. Adams, "Passion Music before 1724" (*ML* vii, 258ff); C. S. Terry, "The Spurious Bach Lucaspassion" (*ML* xiv, 207ff); R. Haas, "Zu Walthers

Choralpassion nach Matthäus" (*AMW* iv); K. Nef, "Die Passionsoratorien Jean-François Lesueurs" (*CP Laurencie*); *id.*, "Beiträge zur Geschichte der Passion in Italien" (*ZMW* xvii); H. H. Eggebrecht, "Die Matthäus-Passion von Melchior Vulpius" (*MF* iii); K. von Fischer, "Zur Geschichte der Passionskomposition des 16. Jahrhunderts in Italien" (*AMW* xi); A. Schmitz, "Italienische Quellen zur Figuralpassion des 16. Jahrhunderts" (*CP Schneider*); G. Schmidt, "Grundsätzliche Bemerkungen zur Geschichte der Passionhistorie" (*AMW* xvii).

Passy-measure. Old term for *passamezzo.

Pasticcio [It.]. (1) A musical work consisting of contributions by two or more composers. The earliest known example is an ornamented intabulation of Ferabosco's madrigal "Io mi son giovinetta," written by Scipione Stella, G. D. Montella, and Ascanio Mayone (in Mayone, *Secondo libro di diversi capricci*, 1609; new ed. by M. S. Kastner, in *Orgue et Liturgie*, nos. 63 [1964], 65 [1965]). Later examples are the opera *Muzio Scevola* (1721), to which Amadei (sometimes called Pippo), G. B. Bononcini, and Handel contributed one act each; the oratorio *Die Schuldigkeit des ersten Gebotes*, written by Mozart, Adlgasser, and Michael Haydn; Diabelli's *Vaterländischer Künstlerverein* (1823–24), containing, in addition to Beethoven's Diabelli Variations, variations by fifty other composers [see *GD* v, 456; *GDB* viii, 690ff]; the *Hexameron* (1837), a similar collection of variations by Liszt, Thalberg, Pixis, Herz, Czerny, and Chopin; a violin sonata for J. Joachim for which Schumann, Brahms, and Dietrich each wrote a movement; and, for a modern example, *L'Éventail de Jeanne*, a ballet written by ten French composers (1927). See M. Reimann, "Pasticcios und Parodien in norddeutschen Klaviertabulaturen" (*MF* viii).

(2) An operatic medley of the 18th century whose music was selected by the arranger or producer from the works of famous composers in order to entertain the audience with an uninterrupted succession of their favorite songs, a procedure that became immensely popular. See also Opera VIII. See O. G. Sonneck, *Miscellaneous Studies in the History of Music* (1921), pp. 111–79; *id.*, in *SIM* xii.

Pastorale. (1) An instrumental or vocal piece written in imitation of the music of shepherds, their shawms and pipes. With reference to the Biblical shepherds who attended the birth of Jesus, the pastorale took on the character of idyllic Christmas music. Typical features are 6/8 or 12/8 meter in moderate time, suggestive of a lullaby; a tender, flowing melody; and long-held drones. The pastorale (as well as the almost identical *siciliana) originated in Italy, where the rural shepherds (*pifferari;* see *Piffero*) had an old tradition of coming to town on Christmas morning and playing on their shawms. Among the many beautiful examples of this type of composition (one of the earliest being by Frescobaldi) are Bach's Pastorale for organ, the Sinfonia that opens the second part of his Christmas Oratorio, the Sinfonia pastorale in Handel's *Messiah*, and the last movement of Beethoven's *Pastoral Symphony.

(2) In the 16th century, a dramatic performance with an idyllic plot. These were among the most important forerunners of *opera. In the 17th century this genre was cultivated particularly in France. Several of the early French operas, e.g., Cambert's *Les Peines et les plaisirs de l'amour* (1672) and Lully's *Les Festes de l'Amour et de Bacchus* (1672), bear the title Pastorale. See L. de la Laurencie, "Les Pastorales ... avant Lully" (*CP 1911,* p. 139).

Pastoral Symphony. Beethoven's Symphony no. 6, in F major, op. 68, published in 1809 under the title "Sinfonie Pastorale, No. 6." The five movements portray, according to Beethoven's inscriptions (in translation): (1) Awakening of Cheerful Feelings on Arrival in the Country; (2) Scene by the Brook; (3) Merrymaking of the Country Folk; (4) Storm; (5) Song of the Shepherds, Joy and Gratitude after the Storm. Beethoven expressly distinguished this work from the more obvious type of program music of his day (battle pieces, etc.) with the remark: "Mehr Ausdruck der Empfindung als Mahlerey" (Expression of feeling rather than painting).

Pastoris. See *Reisado.*

Pastourelle [F.], **pastorela** [Prov.]. A chanson of the troubadours and trouvères whose subject is a rural love scene, frequently including licentious allusions. The term is of purely literary significance.

Pater noster [L.]. Our Father (The Lord's Prayer). A prayer of the Roman Catholic (also, perhaps originally, the *Mozarabic and Gallican) rites, said near the end of the Canon of the Mass. Polyphonic settings, drawing on the plainsong melody (in *Missale Romanum,* 1920, p. 346), include Josquin's motet "O bone et dulcis Domine Jesu" with the tenor "Pater noster" (and the bass "Ave Maria"), and Palestrina's *Missa Pater noster.*

Paṭet. See under Melody type; Java.

Patètico [It.]. With great emotion.

Pathétique. (1) Popular name for Beethoven's Piano sonata op. 13 (1799). Tchaikovsky chose the name *Symphonie Pathétique* for his last symphony, no. 6, op. 74 (1893). (2) [F.]. With great emotion.

Pathetisch [G.]. With great emotion.

Patter song. "A kind of song, the humour of which consists in getting the greatest number of words uttered in the shortest possible time" (*GDB*). This rapid *parlando style has often been used for comical effects in operas (Mozart's *Don Giovanni,* "Catalogue Aria"; Rossini's *Barbiere di Siviglia,* Act I, sc. ii, "Largo al factotum") and plays an important part in the comic operas of Gilbert and Sullivan.

Pauke [G.]. Kettledrum [see Percussion instruments A, 1].

Pause [F. *point d'orgue;* G. *Fermate;* It. *fermata;* Sp. *calderón*]. The sign ⌒, also known as "hold" or *fermata,* indicating that the note (or rest) over which it appears is to be prolonged. As a rule, a duration approximately (but not exactly) twice the normal value will prove appropriate. Note that the foreign terms *pause* [F.], *Pause* [G.], and *pausa* [It.] always mean a rest.

The pause is by far the oldest of all the "tempo marks" of present-day musical notation. As early as the 14th century it was used not only for the final note but also for short passages of block harmony designed to underline the significance of especially important portions of the text. Among the earliest examples (late 14th century) are Cuvelier's *ballade* "Se Galaas" [*WoGM* ii, 115] and Franciscus' "De Narcissus" [W. Apel, *French Secular Music of the Late Fourteenth Century,* p. 90]. The passage "ex Maria virgine" in the Credo of Machaut's Mass, often reproduced in modern editions as *fermata* chords, is actually written in *maximae.* In the early 15th century, *fermata*-marked harmonies occur frequently in the works of Dufay, e.g., in his motet "Supremum est mortalibus" (celebrating the peace between Pope Eugene IV and King Sigismund, 1433), to the words: "Eugenius et rex Sigismundus." For an example by Arnold de Lantins, see *ReMR,* p. 40.

Pavane, pavenne [F.; It., Sp. *pavana;* anglicized *pavan, paven, pavin*]. A 16th-century court dance of Italian provenance. The word is derived from Pava, a dialect form of Padua; music and literature as well as dances from Pava or in the Paduan style were described as *alla pavana.* The earliest extant examples of pavane are found in Dalza's *Intabulatura de lauto* (Petrucci, iv, 1508). The dance became popular early in the century and quickly spread throughout Europe. Other early examples are found in Germany in Judenkünig's *Ain schone kunstliche Underweisung* (1523), in France in Attaingnant's *Dixhuit basses dances* (1529), and in Spain in Milán's *El Maestro* (1535). The dance remained in vogue for most of the century, although its popularity abated somewhat in the last quarter of the period. However, it was restored and revitalized in idealized musical form and attained its highest point of artistic perfection under the aegis of the English virginalists Byrd, Bull, Gibbons, Tomkins, Morley, Farnaby, Philips, Dowland, and others. Under the title *paduana* it flourished briefly in Germany in the early 17th century, where it was used as the introductory movement of the German suite. More recent examples, actually recreations of the earlier idealized dance form, have been written by Saint-Saëns ("Pavane," in *Étienne Marcel*), Ravel ("Pavane de la belle," in *Ma Mère l'oye* and "Pavane pour une infante défunte"), and Vaughan Williams ("Pavane," in *Job*).

The pavane is a slow, processional type of dance, for the most part employing a continuous repetition of basic step patterns: two single and one double step forward followed by two single and one double backward. There are few extant choreographic sources. F. Caroso describes a sophisticated *pavana* with more intricate steps in his *Il Ballarino* (1581). Usually the pavane is followed by one of the faster dances, the *saltarello, *galliard, *padovana,* or *piva.* Most dances of the genre are in a simple quadruple meter (4/4 or 4/2). Musically they resemble the *passamezzo;* indeed, it is often difficult to distinguish the music of a *passamezzo* from that of a pavane.

A few pavanes are in a simple triple meter (3/4 or 3/2), but this form of the dance is rare [see Milán's *El Maestro,* f.Gv^v; Abondante's *Intabolatura sopra el lauto* (1546), no. 26; Mudarra's *Tres libros de música,* 1546, bk. 1, f.19^v; Attaingnant's *Six gaillardes et six pavanes* (1529), no. 2].

For a detailed description and bibl. see L. H. Moe in *MGG* x, 974–77.   L.H.M.

Pavillon [F.]. The bell of wind instruments. *Pavillon chinois,* the crescent.

Pavin. A 16th-century English name for pavane.

Peal. See under Change ringing.

Peasant Cantata. See *Bauernkantate.*

Pêcheurs de Perles, Les [F., The Pearl Fishers]. Opera in three acts by Bizet (libretto by E. Cor-' mon and M. Carré), produced in Paris, 1863. Setting: Ceylon, in the past.

Pedal. (1) In musical instruments, an action that is operated by the feet. See Organ III, XI, XII; Piano; Harpsichord; Harp. (2) Short for *pedal point.

Pedal clarinet. Older name for the double-bass clarinet.

Pedalflügel [G.]. See Pedal piano.

Pedal harp. The modern chromatic harp.

Pedal harpsichord. A harpsichord that is equipped with a pedal board, similar to that of the organ, so that the bass can be played with the feet. Several 16th- and 17th-century Italian harpsichords are extant that once had pedal boards pulling down the keys of the manual by means of cords. The pedal boards ranged from eight to fifteen notes all based on C (short octave).

Many traces of French pedal-board harpsichords of the 17th and 18th centuries exist. For example, Jean Denis owned one in 1686, as did Jean LeBègue in 1684. The organist Nicolas Gigault in 1701 possessed an instrument described as "Un clavecin à double claviers a l'unison . . . un clavecin de pedalles a l'octave le tout au ton de chambre" (A harpsichord with two keyboards at the unison [eight-foot pitch] . . . a pedal harpsichord at four-foot pitch, both at chamber pitch). [See F. Hubbard, *Three Centuries of Harpsichord Making* (1965), p. 111.] The harpsichord was probably three-choired, $2 \times 8'$, $1 \times 4'$. The pedal harpsichord may have had only a single 4' choir. It will be noted that it is no longer a question of a pedal board operating through pull-downs, but of a separate instrument lying on the floor under the harpsichord. Toward the end of the 18th century French makers began to place pedal boards operating a piano action under their harpsichords.

Both the pull-down and separate-instrument

types of pedal harpsichord are discussed by J. Adlung, who preferred the latter and admitted the former only for the sake of economy (*Anleitung zu der musikalischen Gelahrtheit* [1758], p. 556; *id., Musica mechanica organœdi* [1768] ii, 158–61). See J. S. Halle, *Werkstäte der heutigen Künste* (1764), iii, 363.

No genuine pedal harpsichords or harpsichords with pull-down pedal boards have survived, although many extant instruments from several countries show traces of once having been attached to pull-down pedal boards. Analogous systems were also in use to apply the pedal board to the clavichord. See Pedal piano.
                F.H.

Pedalier [F.]. (1) The pedal board of the organ, or a similar apparatus attached to a piano. (2) See Pedal piano.

Pedalklavier [G.]. *Pedal piano.

Pedalkoppel [G.]. The pedal coupler of the organ; see Organ IV.

Pedalpauke [G.]. Kettledrums tuned by pedals. See Percussion instruments A, 1.

Pedal piano [G. *Pedalflügel, Pedalklavier;* F. *piano à pedalier*]. A piano equipped with a pedal board, similar to that of the organ, so that the bass can be played with the feet. The *Pedalflügel,* which had but fleeting success, is known chiefly through the series of "Studien" and "Skizzen" that Schumann wrote for it (op. 56, 58). There also are compositions for this instrument by Alkan and Gounod [see *GD* iv, 95; *GDB* vi, 609]. See J. Handschin, "Das Pedalklavier" (*ZMW* xvii). See Pedal harpsichord.

Pedal point [F. *point d'orgue;* G. *Orgelpunkt;* It. *pedale;* Sp. *bajo de órgano*]. A long-held note, normally in the bass, sounding with changing harmonies in the other parts. Sometimes the word "pedal" alone is used. The pedal point represents one of the most natural sources of dissonance, inasmuch as the held note blends easily with every chordal combination (e.g., low C with a D-flat or a B-flat triad; see Ex.). According to

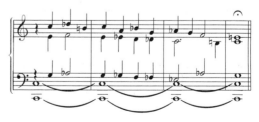

the scale degree of the held note, a distinction is made among tonic pedal, dominant pedal, and subdominant pedal (long note on the tonic, dominant, or subdominant of the key). The terms "inverted pedal" and "internal pedal" denote pedal points that appear not in the bass but in the soprano or middle part.

The pedal point (also called *bourdon or *drone) is one of the earliest devices of polyphony—perhaps the earliest—as may be concluded from its extensive use in non-Western music. In Western music it first appears in the organa of the 12th and 13th centuries (schools of St. Martial and Notre Dame), in which the notes of the original plainsong are frequently extended as long-held tones, one each serving as a basis for an entire section. A monumental example of a 13th-century pedal point is the beginning of Perotinus' *organum quadruplum* "Viderunt omnes" [see *AdHM* i, 229], which has been called the "F-major toccata of the 13th century" (with reference to Bach's composition of this name). The term *punctus organicus* (organ point, G. *Orgelpunkt*) probably refers to these organa rather than to the organ. As an organ device, the pedal point appears first in certain compositions by Frescobaldi, e.g., his *Capriccio Pastorale*. Its importance in the organ works of Buxtehude, Bach, etc., is well known. Among later composers, Tchaikovsky showed a particular predilection for pedal points.

Pedal tone. See under Wind instruments II; Horn I.

Peer Gynt Suite. Two orchestral suites by Grieg, op. 46 and 55, arranged from his incidental music to Ibsen's play *Peer Gynt*.

Peine entendu, à [F.]. Barely audible.

Peking opera. See under China I.

Pelléas et Mélisande. Opera in five acts by Claude Debussy (to his own libretto, after Maeterlinck's play of the same name), produced in 1902. Setting: a mythical kingdom, Allemonde, in the Middle Ages. The story is told in a succession of scenes filled with mystic and symbolic meanings, scenes that are not meant to form a continuous plot and that have about the same relation to the closely knit action of Wagnerian opera as Debussy's aphoristic *impressionism does to the sweep and pathos of Wagner's musical style. As the only significant opera that impressionism has produced, *Pelléas et Mélisande* stands in a class by itself. In reaction

against Wagnerian opera, Debussy's score deliberately avoids emotional stress, providing only a "tonal envelope" of pale colors and incorporeal transparency. Also see under Recitative.

Pélog. See under Java.

Penitential psalms. Psalms 6, 31[32], 37[38], 50[51], 101[102], 129[130], and 142[143]. For the system of numbering, see Psalm. In music history the penitential psalms are famous particularly through Orlando di Lasso's composition of the whole series of texts (*Psalmi Davidis poenitentiales*, 1560). The same project was carried out by L. Lechner (1587) and others. Later composers have been particularly attracted by the dramatic greatness of Psalm 129[130], "De profundis," and Psalm 50[51], *"Miserere."

Pennillion [sing. *pennill*]. An ancient form of Welsh musical performance executed by a harper and a singer (*bards), the former playing a well-known harp air and the latter extemporizing words and a somewhat different melody to suit the harper's tune and harmonies. The harper can change his tune as often as he wishes; the singer, after a measure or two, is expected to join with proper words and music, in accordance with the dictates of tradition. The pennillion are probably the last relics of those legendary contests in which the heroes fought against one another not only with weapons but with their wits, solving puzzles and competing with musical instruments. See W. S. Gwynn Williams, ‡*Penillion in English* (1925); E. Jones, ‡*Musical and Poetical Relicks of the Welsh Bards* (1794), pp. 60–74.

Pentachord. A five-tone segment of the scale, e.g., from c to g. It is intermediate between the Greek *tetrachord and the Guidonian *hexachord, not only technically but perhaps also historically, since the *pentachordum* forms the basis of theoretical demonstrations in the "Musica enchiriadis" of c. 900 [see *GS* i, 175ff].

Pentatonic scale. A scale that has five tones to the octave. Among the numerous scales of this kind the following are of special importance: (a) The *tonal* [G. *anhemitonisch*] *pentatonic scale*, i.e., a five-tone scale that has no semitones. Properly speaking, there is only one such scale (aside from transpositions): c d . f g a . c'. However, by using different tones as a tonic, five different "modes" can be derived from it, e.g., c d . f g a . c' d', or *f* g a . c' d' . *f*', etc. On the piano, such scales can easily be reproduced by playing the black keys only. The tonal pentatonic scale, usually in its "first mode" (on c), occurs in the music of nearly all ancient cultures —China, Polynesia, Africa—as well as that of the American Indians, Celts, and Scots. The ancient Chinese construed it as a succession of ascending fifths and descending fourths: f–c'–g–d'–a [see China II B]. A considerable number of Gregorian melodies are purely pentatonic, and others may have originally been so. (b) The *semitonal* [G. *hemitonisch*] *pentatonic scale* results from omitting the second and the sixth or the second and the fifth degrees of the diatonic scale: c . e f g . b c', or: c . e f . a b c'. Since these scales include two major thirds (*ditonus*) they are also called "ditonic." The second form is of special interest since this is the scale that, in descending motion, prevailed in ancient Greece: e' . c' b a . f e. Semitonal pentatonic scales frequently occur in modern *Japanese music. (c) A pentatonic scale with equidistant steps is the *Javanese *sléndro*. This has been used, under the name "pentaphonic" scale, by Alaleona [see A. Eaglefield Hull, in *Monthly Musical Record,* Sept. 1922, p. 212]. See J. Yasser, *A Theory of Evolving Tonality* (1932); B. Szabolcsi, in *AM* xv; W. Wiora, "Älter als die Pentatonik" (*CP Bartók*).

Percussion instruments. Generic name for instruments that are sounded by shaking or striking one object with another. In the general classification of instruments they are divided into two categories, *membranophones* and *idiophones* [see Instruments I, II]. Membranophones are by far the oldest of all instruments and exist in enormous variety all over the world [see Drum II]. The following discussion deals with the percussion instruments of the orchestra. They can be divided into two groups, those that produce a sound of definite pitch and those that do not.

A. *Of definite pitch.* 1. *Kettledrum* [G. *Pauke;* F. *timbale;* It. *timpano;* Sp. *timbal*]. The kettledrum is the most important percussion instrument. It consists of a basin-shaped shell of copper or brass over which is stretched a head of calfskin whose tension can be adjusted by screws fixed to the shell, thereby changing the pitch. The instrument is played with two sticks with a wooden handle and a head, usually of hard felt covered with a layer of soft felt, although for special effects different materials may be used. Traditionally kettledrums were used in pairs, one small and one large, which were tuned to the tonic and dominant of the key of the composition. A third drum was added in the early 19th century. Today a number of sizes of kettledrum

are used, four being most common: 30" (D–A), 28" (F–c), 25" (B♭–f), and 23" (d–a). Each instrument can exceed its basic range of a fifth by several half-tones at either end. The kettledrums may be muffled or muted [see Mute]. Various methods of tuning the drums mechanically by a controlling pedal (pedal drums or pedal timpani; G. *Pedalpauke*) or other device have been invented. Such instruments, which allow the pitch to be changed quickly, are required in, e.g., *Salome* by R. Strauss or Bartók's *Music for Strings, Percussion and Celesta,* where glissandos are performed by the kettledrums.

The introduction of the kettledrum into the orchestra took place in the 17th century. The opening toccata of Monteverdi's *Orfeo* (1607) has what was surely a kettledrum part. M. Praetorius authorized them in certain numbers of his *Polyhymnia Caduceatrix & Panegyrica* (1619), and O. Benevoli's Mass for 53 voices (*Saltzburger Festmesse,* 1628) seems to be the first instance of a clearly labeled written out part. Bach often used kettledrums in his cantatas to express joy or triumph.

Lit.: H. W. Taylor, *The Art and Science of the Timpani* (1964); P. R. Kirby, "Kettledrums: An Historical Survey" (*ML* ix, 34); P. A. Browne, "The Orchestral Treatment of the Timpani" (*ML* iv, 334); C. Titcomb, "The Kettledrums in Western Europe" (diss. Harvard Univ., 1952); *id.,* in *GSJ* ix, 56ff.

2. *Glockenspiel* [E.; G.; F. *carillon;* It. *campanette;* Sp. *campanólogo*]. An instrument composed of a series of tuned steel bars of varying length, with or without resonators, arranged in two rows, roughly like a piano keyboard, and struck with two, three, or four small-headed mallets made of rubber, glass, brass, etc. It is generally made in a chromatic range of 2½ octaves, written as in Ex. 1 but sounding two octaves higher. Its most notable characteristic is its

1. Glockenspiel.   2. Xylophone (not largest size).
3. Celesta.

bright, penetrating tone color. Wagner used the glockenspiel in the "Dance of the Apprentices" in *Die Meistersinger,* and Tchaikovsky in the "Chinese Dance" of his *Nutcracker Suite* (1892).

3. *Xylophone.* An instrument resembling the

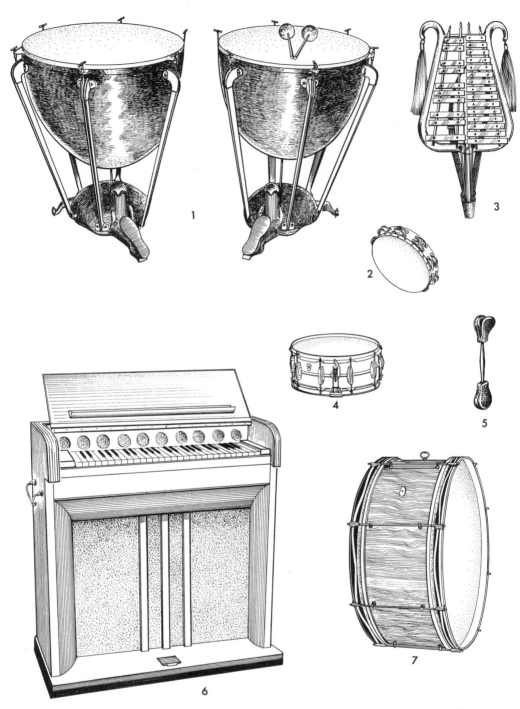

Percussion instruments (orchestra and band):   1. Timpani (pedal).   2. Tambourine.   3. Glockenspiel.
4. Snare drum.   5. Castanets.   6. Celesta.   7. Bass drum.

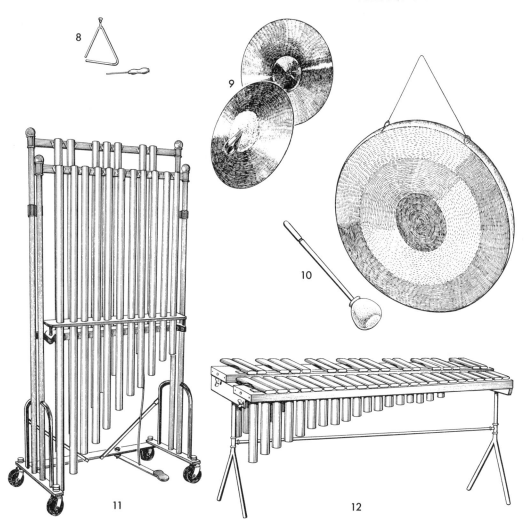

Percussion instruments (orchestra and band): 8. *Triangle.* 9. *Cymbals.* 10. *Gong.* 11. *Chimes.* 12. *Xylophone.*

glockenspiel in basic construction, except that its bars are wooden. The largest size has a range of 3½ octaves, written as in Ex. 2 but sounding one octave higher. In tone quality it is dry and "wooden," without lasting resonance. See also Xylophone.

4. *Celesta.* An instrument invented in 1886 that looks like a small upright piano. It may be considered a "keyboard-glockenspiel," since the tone is produced by the striking of steel bars with hammers connected to a keyboard by a simplified piano action. Music for the celesta is notated

on two staves, like piano music, with a written range as in Ex. 3, sounding an octave higher. It is most suitable for light and graceful effects. The instrument was introduced by Tchaikovsky for the "Dance of the Fairy Dragee" of his *Nutcracker Suite* (1892). A more recent variety is the *dulcitone.*

5. *Chimes or tubular bells* [F. *cloches tubulaires;* G. *Röhrenglocken;* It. *campana tubolare*]. A set of metal tubes, vertically suspended in a frame, tuned chromatically from c′ to f″, and struck with one or two wooden mallets. They are

655

employed in the orchestra to produce the effect of church bells, e.g., in the finale of Tchaikovsky's "1812" Overture, in Mahler's Symphony no. 2, in Sibelius' Symphony no. 4 (fourth movement), and in many operas.

6. Other percussion instruments of definite pitch are the *anvil, *marimba, *tubaphone, and *vibraharp.

B. *Of indefinite pitch.* 1. *Snare drum* or *side drum* [F. *caisse claire, tambour militaire, petit tambour;* G. *kleine Trommel;* It. *tamburo militare, cassa;* Sp. *tambor, caja*]. A small cylindrical drum with two heads stretched over a shell of metal. The upper head, which is struck with two drumsticks, is called the "batter head"; the lower, across which are stretched the taut snares (a group of gut or silk strings, in appearance not unlike violin strings, bound with wire), is called the "snare head." The brilliant tone quality of the side drum results largely from the vibrations of the snarehead against the snares. The instrument may be muffled by placing a cloth on the batter head (*coperto*). By loosening the snares a dull sound is obtained. In addition to the roll, which produces a tremolo, there are two other strokes commonly used on the side drum: the flam, consisting of two notes [Ex. 4], and the drag, a series of strokes fused into a sort of in-

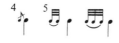

4. Flam. 5. Drag (ruff).

stantaneous roll, preceding an accented note [Ex. 5].

2. *Tenor drum* [F. *caisse roulante;* G. *Rührtrommel;* It. *cassa rullante;* Sp. *redoblante*]. A drum with a wooden shell that is deeper (in relation to its diameter) and larger than the side drum. It has no snares.

3. *Bass drum* [F. *grosse caisse:* G. *grosse Trommel;* It. *gran cassa* or *cassa grande;* Sp. *bombo*]. A large, two-headed cylindrical drum that varies considerably in size, in both width and diameter. It is played with a single large, padded stick. The sound produced is low and heavy. A roll can be performed by two timpani sticks or by a two-headed *tampon. The bass drum was used by Mozart in his *Die Entführung aus dem Serail* and by Beethoven in the finale of his Ninth Symphony.

4. *Tambourine* [F. *tambour de Basque;* G. *Schellentrommel, Tamburin;* It. *tamburino, tam-*

buro basso; Sp. *panderete*]. A small, shallow, single-headed drum into whose wooden shell loosely hanging "jingles" (circular metal disks) are inserted, usually in pairs. The instrument is played: (a) by striking the head with knuckles, closed fist, back of hand, or player's knee, which gives detached sounds and simple rhythmical figures; (b) by grasping the shell firmly and shaking it, which gives a "roll" of the jingles; (c) by rubbing the thumb along the edge of the head, which gives a tremolo of the jingles; and (d) with the instrument flat, head up, on the player's lap, playing near the rim with fingers or drumsticks.

5. *Triangle* [F; G. *Triangel;* It. *triangolo;* Sp. *triángulo*]. A small cylindrical bar of steel bent in the shape of an equilateral triangle, open at one end, struck with a short metal rod. Early uses include that in Gluck's *Iphigénie en Tauride* (1779) and in Mozart's *Die Entführung aus dem Serail* (1782) in order to obtain an exotic "Turkish" atmosphere [see Janizary music]. Beethoven used it in the finale of his Ninth Symphony for the "Turkish" variation of the theme, and Haydn in his "Military" Symphony no. 100. For a prominent solo part, see the Piano Concerto in E-flat by Liszt.

6. *Cymbals* [F. *cymbales;* G. *Becken;* It. *piatti, cinelli;* Sp. *platillos*]. Large circular brass plates of various sizes, made slightly convex so that only the edges touch when they are struck together. In the center of each cymbal is a deep saucerlike depression with a hole through which a strap is attached, enabling the player to hold it. They are played: (a) by clashing them together with a brushing movement—the ordinary way of playing single notes; (b) by clashing the two cymbals against each other in quick repetition by means of a rotating motion, called "two-plate roll"; (c) by striking a single cymbal (suspended on a stand) with a hard snare-drum stick or a soft timpani stick; (d) by suspending one cymbal and performing a roll on it with two hard snare-drum sticks or two soft timpani sticks; (e) by fastening one cymbal to the top of the bass drum and clashing the other against it, while the player uses his other hand to play the bass drum. See also Cymbals.

7. *Tamtam* or *gong.* A broad circular disk of metal, slightly convex, with the rim turned down, giving it the appearance of a shallow plate with low vertical sides. It is hung vertically, and struck in the center with a soft-headed beater.

8. Other percussion instruments of indefinite

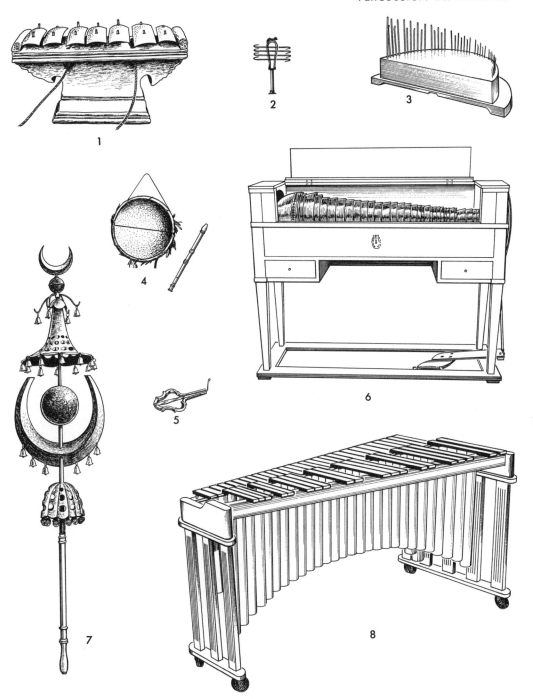

Other percussion instruments: 1. Gangsa gambang (saron). 2. Sistrum. 3. Nail violin. 4. Pipe and tabor. 5. Jew's-harp (shown three times actual size in relation to others). 6. Glass harmonica. 7. Turkish crescent. 8. Marimba.

pitch, more rarely used in orchestral scores, are the *castanets, *rattle, wood block, *Chinese temple block, and *thunder machine. Modern composers have devised many unusual percussive and noise-producing effects. Non-Western instruments, such as the Latin American *maracas, *claves, and guïro (a notched gourd scraped with a stick), have been used by Prokofiev (*Alexander Nevsky*) and Stravinsky (*Le Sacre du printemps*). An interesting instance of a purely percussive score is Edgar Varèse's *Ionisation* (1931).

For nonorchestral percussion instruments, see Gambang; Glass harmonica; Jew's-harp; Marimba; Nail violin; Pipe (1); Sistrum; Turkish crescent.

Lit.: C. Bavin, *The Percussion Band from A to Z*, rev. ed. (1953); J. Blades, *Orchestral Percussion Technique* (1961); E. B. Gangware, "The History and Use of Percussion Instruments in Orchestration" (diss. Northwestern Univ., 1962).

W.D.D.

Perfect, imperfect. See Cadence; Interval; Mensural notation II. The *modus perfectus* and *imperfectus* of mensural notation are entirely different from the *modus perfectus* and *imperfectus* of the 13th-century theory of rhythmic *modes. In the former the terms indicate the ternary or binary value of the *longa* ($L = 3 B$ or $= 2 B$); in the latter they refer to the final note in the pattern of a mode, this final note being present in the *modus perfectus* and absent (replaced by a rest) in the *modus imperfectus*. The *modi imperfecti*, although discussed at length by theorists (Anon. IV; see *ReMMA*, p. 280), have no practical significance [see *ApNPM*, pp. 223, 445].

Performance practice [G. *Aufführungspraxis*]. The study of how early music, from the Middle Ages to Bach, was performed and the many problems connected with attempts to restore its original sound in modern performance. The problems of performance practice vary, of course, according to the period in question. In medieval music the foremost question is that of vocal versus instrumental performance, since long passages and even entire voice-parts of apparently vocal compositions are found without a text, e.g., the tenors of 13th-century organa and motets or the "melismatic" *caudae* of many conductus from the same period. The existence of numerous instruments is well documented by literary sources and particularly by pictorial evidence [see under *Cantiga*], but the musical

sources contain no reference to them. A plausible explanation would be that the compositions are essentially vocal in all their parts and sections, but that occasionally instruments were used in addition to (rather than as a substitute for) voices [see Vocalization]. The secular compositions of the 14th century (French *ballades,* Italian madrigals) often include what in the original appear to be extended vocalizations [see, e.g., *HAM*, nos. 50, 51]. To interpret these as "instrumental preludes, interludes, postludes" can be done only by rearranging the syllables of the text and by artificially interrupting the musical lines. Compositions of the early 15th century, however, frequently include textless passages separated by rests, and these in all probability are intended to be played on instruments, most likely by the singer himself [see, e.g., Dunstable's "O rosa bella" and Dufay's "Mon chier ami"; *HAM*, nos. 61, 67].

Another difficulty results from the fact that the instruments of these periods, such as the psaltery, rotta, vielle, and rebec of the 14th century, or the viol, cornett, and theorbo of the 15th and 16th centuries, all are obsolete. It is only through patient experiments with modern reproductions of these instruments that one may hope to gain a clearer idea of the intended sound of old music. Generally speaking, the lack of clear and unequivocal indications of instruments, accidentals, etc., is not mere negligence by the composer or carelessness by the scribe but an adequate expression—in fact, the necessary concomitant—of the intrinsically antirational viewpoint of the Middle Ages and Renaissance. The idea of writing music for a specific instrument was just as foreign to the 15th-century musician as the idea of using one "correct" spelling for a word was foreign to a writer of this period. For both the only concern was the substance, which remained the same regardless of how it was realized.

In the 16th and 17th centuries the problems of performance practice are relatively simpler. Among them are the correct execution of *thoroughbass, the performance of *ornaments, either improvised or abbreviated, the size of the orchestra, and the specifications of tempo and dynamics. Most of these questions have been quite satisfactorily clarified by musicologists. A work such as Bach's St. Matthew Passion should be performed by about twenty players (flutes, oboes, strings, organ, harpsichord) and a similar number of singers; it should be played at moderate speeds, ranging from allegro to adagio, and with a clear distinction of forte and piano, rather than fortissimo and pianissimo with continual crescendos and decrescendos. Although historically oriented performance groups such as *collegia musica* have generally adopted the principles of performance practice, conductors of standard orchestras are still reluctant to do so. In the period after Bach the problems of performance practice largely disappear, owing to the more specific directions of composers for clearly indicating their intentions. See also Ensemble (3).

Lit.: T. Dart, *The Interpretation of Music* (1954); F. Dorian, *The History of Music in Performance* (1942); R. Donington, *The Interpretation of Early Music* (1963; bibl.); F. Rothschild, *Musical Performance in the Times of Mozart and Beethoven* [1961]; A. Dolmetsch, *The Interpretation of the Music of the XVII and XVIII Centuries Revealed in Contemporary Evidence,* rev. ed. (1946); R. Haas, *Aufführungspraxis der Musik* (in *BüHM*); A. Schering, *Aufführungspraxis alter Musik* (1931); C. Döbereiner, *Zur Renaissance alter Musik* (1950); H. P. Schmitz, *Prinzipien der Aufführungspraxis alter Musik* [1950]; B. Aulich, *Alte Musik, recht verstanden* (1957); G. Frotscher, *Aufführungspraxis alter Musik* [1963]; W. Kolneder, *Aufführungspraxis bei Vivaldi* [1955]; E. Borrel, *L'Interprétation de la musique française (de Lully à la Révolution)* (1934); R. Albrecht, "Die Aufführungspraxis der italienischen Musik des 14. Jahrhunderts" (diss. Berlin, 1925); H. Leichtentritt, in *CP 1909*, p. 147 (17th cent.); G. Reaney, in *RBM* x (Machaut); *id.,* in *CP Reese* (medieval); A. Pirro, in *CP 1930*, p. 55 (*c.* 1400); W. Krüger, in *MF* ix, x, xi (13th cent.); H. Mersmann, in *AMW* ii (preclassical chamber music); P. Aldrich, in *CP Davison* (baroque); D. D. Boyden, *ibid.* (dynamics); D. J. Grout, *ibid.* (historical authenticity).

Périchole, La. Satirical comedy in two acts by J. Offenbach (libretto by H. Meilhac and L. Halévy), produced in Paris, 1868.

Pericón [Sp.]. Traditional Argentine dance, very popular in the days of the War of Independence. It consists of fourteen eight-measure sections, each alternating between the tonic and dominant chords within a steady 3/8 meter. Each section employs a different rhythmic pattern, and in some sections the mode changes from major to minor. The *pericón* is danced by a group of couples facing one another.   J.O-S.

Period. In traditional music, a division of time, i.e., a group of measures comprising a natural division of the melody; usually regarded as comprising two or more contrasting or complementary phrases and ending with a cadence. Some more recent composers, especially of the *serial school, extend the concept of period to all elements of traditional music. Thus, sound, as opposed to noise, is actually made up of *periodic vibration*; triads represent the most periodic vibrations of chords; harmony is as periodical as melody, e.g., I–V–I. Similarly, rhythm on various levels—beats, measures, phrases—can be considered periodic, and so can form, notably A B A form, *rondo form, *sonata form, etc. The very tonal system itself can be regarded in this way, octaves being the periodic organization of the pitch-space.   H.P.

Periodicals, music. I. *Historical survey.* Among the earliest music periodicals (leaving out of account periodical publications of music, etc.) are Mizler's *Neu eröffnete Musikalische Bibliothek* (1735–54), Scheibe's *Der Critische Musicus* (1737–40), *Journal de musique française et italienne* (1764–68), and J. A. Hiller's *Wöchentliche Nachrichten* (1766–70). The most important periodicals thereafter are: *Allgemeine musikalische Zeitung* (Leipzig, Breitkopf und Härtel, 1798–1848, 1863–82); Fétis' *La Revue musicale* (1827–80; merged with *Gazette musicale de Paris* and became the *Revue et Gazette musicale de Paris*); *Le Ménestrel* (Paris, 1833–1940); *Neue Zeitschrift für Musik* (founded by Robert Schumann, 1834; now issued as *Zeitschrift für Musik;* see under IV); *Signale für die musikalische Welt* (Leipzig, 1843–1941); *The Musical Times* (London, 1844—); *Dwight's Journal of Music* (Boston, 1852–81); *Le Guide musicale* (Brussels, 1855–1914, Paris, 1917–18); *The Musical Standard* (London, 1862–1933); *Music* (Chicago, 1891–1902).

There follows a selected list of periodicals still issued (or issued until World War II), classified according to countries, with a special group (VIII) reserved for musicologic publications. Also see the periodicals in the list of abbreviations for this dictionary.

II. *United States. Musical Courier* (Philadelphia, New York, 1880—). *The Etude* (Philadelphia, 1883–1957). *The Musician* (Philadelphia, 1896–1917; New York, 1918—). *Musical America* (New York, 1898—). *Music Educators' Journal* (Madison, Wis., 1914–34; Chicago, 1934—). *The Musical Quarterly* (New York,

1915—; see also VIII). *Modern Music* (New York, 1924—). *American Music Lover* (New York, 1935—). *Perspectives of New Music* (New York, 1962—).

III. *England.* The *Monthly Musical Record* (London, 1871—). *Musical Opinion* (London, 1877—). *The Strad* (London, 1890—). *R. C. M. Magazine* (London, 1904—). *The Chesterian* (London, 1915—). *Music and Letters* (London, 1920—; see also VIII). *The Gramophone* (London, 1923—). *Music Review* (Cambridge, 1940; see also VIII).

IV. *Austria, Germany, Switzerland. Allgemeine [deutsche] Musikzeitung* (Berlin, 1874–1943). *Die Musik* (Berlin, 1901–15; Stuttgart, 1922–43). *[Musikblätter des] Anbruch* (Vienna, 1919–37). *Melos* (Mainz, 1920–34, 1934–36, 1946—). *Schweizerische Musikzeitung* (Zurich, 1861—). *Österreichische Musikzeitschrift* (Vienna, 1946—). *Dissonances* (Geneva, 1923—). *Die Reihe* (Ger. ed., Vienna, 1955—, Eng. ed., Bryn Mawr, Penn., 1958—).

V. *Belgium, France. Le Ménestrel* (Paris, 1833–1940). *La Revue musicale* (Paris, 1920–40, 1946–49; 1952—; see also VIII). *La Revue musicale belge* (Brussels, 1925—). *Contrepoints* (Paris, 1946—). *La Revue internationale de musique* (Brussels, 1938–40, 1950—). *Polyphonie* (Brussels, 1947–1956).

VI. *Italy. Rivista musicale italiana* (Turin, 1894–1932, 1936–44, 1947—; see also VIII). *La Rassegna musicale* (Turin, 1928–43, 1947). *Musica d'oggi* (Milan, 1919—). *Bollettino bibliografico musicale* (Milan, 1926–33). *Musica e dischi* (Milan, 1945—). *L'Approdo musicale* (Turin, 1958—).

VII. *Other countries.* A. Europe. *Ritmo: Revista musical ilustrada* (Madrid, 1942—). *Música: Revista mensual ilustrada* (Madrid, 1944—). *De Muziek* (Amsterdam, 1926–33). *Muziekwereld* (Amsterdam, 1936—). *Mens[ch] en melodie* (Utrecht, 1946—). *Tijdschift voor muziekwetenschap* (formerly *T. der Vereeniging voor Nederlandsche muziekgeschedenis;* Amsterdam, 1882–1946; 1948—). *Norsk musikkgransknig* (Oslo, 1937—). *Dansk Musiktidsskrift* (Copenhagen, 1925—). *Svensk Tidskrift för Musikforskning* (Stockholm, 1919—). *Sovetskaia muzyka* (Moscow, 1933–41, 1946—). *Musike kinesis* (Athens, 1949—). *Muzika* (Sofia, 1948—). *Muzsika* (Budapest, 1958—).

B. Latin America. *Correio musical brasileiro* (São Paulo, 1921—). *Revista brasileira de música* (Rio de Janeiro, 1934—). *Revista musical chilena* (Santiago, 1945). *Brasil musical* (1944–49). *Nues-tra Música* (Mexico, 1946–52). *Arte musical* (Buenos Aires, 1946—). *Boletín del Conservatorio nacional de música* (Lima, 1943—). *Boletín interamericano de música* (Washington, D.C., Pan-American Union, 1957—).

C. Asia. *Toyō Ongaku Kenkyū* (Tokyo, 1937–46, 1951—). *Musica hebraica* (Jerusalem, 1938–?).

VIII. *Musicologic periodicals.* See abbreviations for this dictionary. Also, *Fontes Artis Musicae* (Kassel, 1954—): *The Journal of Musicology* (Greenfield, Ohio, 1939—); *Note d'archivo per la storia musicale* (Rome, 1924–43). See also *GDB,* "Periodicals."

Lit.: A. *General:* H. Koch, "Die deutschen musikalischen Fachzeitschriften des 18. Jahrhunderts" (diss. Halle, 1923); W. Freystätter, *Die musikalischen Zeitschriften* (1884); E. Rohlfs, *Die deutschsprachigen Musikperiodica, 1945–1957* (1961); E. van der Straeten, *Nos Périodiques musicaux* (1893); A. Riedel, *Répertoire des périodiques musicaux* (1954); O. Sonneck, "Die musikalischen Zeitschriften-Literatur" (*ZIM* i); E. O'Meara, "Music in the 17th and 18th Century Periodicals" (*Notes* iv); L. Fairley, "A Check-List of Recent Latin American Music Periodicals" (*Notes* ii, 120–23); J. T. Windle, "Report on the Project for Indexing Music Periodicals" (*Notes* ix); H. E. Johnson, "Early New England Periodicals devoted to Music" (*MQ* xxvi).

B. *Indexes to periodical literature:* E. C. Krohn, *The History of Music: An Index to . . . a Selected Group of Publications* (1952); D. H. Daugherty, *A Bibliography of Periodical Literature in Musicology* (1940—); K. Taut, *Bibliographie des Musikschrifttums* (1937–61); J. B. Coover, "A Bibliography of East European Music Periodicals" (*Fontes Artis Musicae* iii–vii, ix).

Perpetuum mobile [L.]. A term used by Paganini (*Moto perpetuo,* op. 11), Weber (last movement of Piano Sonata op. 24), and others to denote pieces that proceed from beginning to end in the same rapid motion, e.g., sixteenth notes in presto. Pieces of this type, although not labeled as such, occur also in Chopin's Études.

Persia I. *History.* Of major importance in the history of Persian music is the long political and cultural contact between Persia and ancient Greece, which lasted from the 5th century B.C. well into the 3rd century of the Christian era. The Persian expeditions into Greece were followed by Alexander the Great's decisive conquest of the Achaemenid Empire in 330 B.C., a century of Greek rule in Persia, and four centuries of continued Hellenic influence. During this time, it is not unlikely that a significant musical interchange occurred. To the present day, Persian art music, composed by *melody types, is still monophonic and organized in tetrachords. Further, Persian music theory (like *Arab) is Greek in origin. The treatises of the medieval Islamic theorists were modeled after those of Euclid, Aristoxenus, Ptolemy, and others, which were translated into Arabic at Baghdad during the 9th century [see Arab music].

The earliest descriptions of Persian music appear in writings of Greek historians, Herodotus and Xenophon among them. For the Sassanid period (A.D. 226–642) there are sources giving the names of musicians and their compositions, while players of instruments are included in the numerous bas-reliefs and engraved metal plates that survive from this artistic time. With the Arab conquest of Persia in the 7th century, there was such a blending of Persian and Arab music, instruments, and terminology that the question of which music most influenced the other is still debated. Many scientific treatises on music appeared as part of the extensive philosophical writings produced at Baghdad, an intellectual capital of the early medieval world. Of the great music theorists, two were Persian: Ibn Sina (Avicenna, 980–1037), and Safi al-Din (d. 1294). Side by side with great activity in theory, however, was the Islamic disapproval of music in practice that tended to discourage progress in both Persian and Arab music for at least a millennium.

During the Mongol and Timurid periods (1221–1501) the Persians discarded many aspects of Arab culture, and the musical treatises of Shirazi (d. 1310) and Ghaibi (d. 1435) were written in the Persian language. Although the next dynasty, the Safavid (1501–1736), brought forth a rebirth of Persian culture, the renewed religious fervor occasioned by adoption of the Shia sect of Islam as the state religion again discouraged the practice of music. This antimusical atmosphere lasted until about 1900, when public concerts gradually became sanctioned and musicians were no longer considered socially inferior. Today Persian music has entered a new period of development. Stimulated by the introduction of Western music and by extensive patronage of music by the state, considerable attention is now given to the collection and preservation of native Persian music.

II. *Melody types and rhythm.* Contemporary Persian art music is organized into seven *dastgah,* melody types similar to the Arabic *maqamat* and Indian *rāgas.* Although their names are mentioned by theorists as early as the 9th century, the exact configuration of the scales of these melody types is not known until the 13th-century writings of Safi al-Din. In the next seven centuries, variation in the names and structures occurred, and, even today, under the influence of Western music, they are not completely stable. The version of the scales of the *dastgah* given by most contemporary theorists is represented below, transposed to start on the note C. The sign P (*koron*) designates a flat of approximately one-quarter tone (the *sori,* $\sharp$, designates a half-sharp).

Shour and Nava	C	DP	E^b	F	G	A^b	B^b	C
Homayoun	C	DP	E	F	G	A^b	B^b	C
Segah	C	D	EP	F	G	AP	B^b	C
Chahargah	C	DP	E	F	G	AP	B	C
Mahour and Rast								
Panjgah	C	D	E	F	G	A	B	C

Related to the Shour are four auxiliary *dastgah* (*avaz* or *naghmeh*)—Abu Ata, Dashti, Afshari, and Bayote Tork—and related to Homayoun is the auxiliary *dastgah* of Esfahan, making a total of twelve melody types.

Each *dastgah* and *naghmeh* possesses twenty to fifty short melodies or melodic formulas (*gousheh*) that the composer-performer uses as the basis for improvisation. For a performance, the singer or instrumentalist selects a number of *goushehs* within a single *dastgah,* treating them with considerable freedom. The entire collection of melodies in all seven *dastgah* and five *naghmeh,* now numbering about 500, is called the *radif.* Handed down orally for many centuries, it has been transcribed during the past fifty years by several masters and published in Western notation [see Ex., a *gousheh* from the *dastgah* of Shour].

Rhythm in Persian music, unlike Arab and Indian music, is no longer systematized into the

rhythmic modes (*iqa'at*) described by medieval Persian theorists. Most traditional art music is, in fact, unmeasured and performed in a free rubato manner. The strongest rhythmic factor in music of the *radif* comes from poetry. Like the music of ancient Greece, Persian music is closely allied with poetry. Generally one couplet of classical verse is set to a single *gousheh,* with long melismatic sections and instrumental rhapsodizing between the various *gousheh.* Thus the meter of the poetry imparts a kind of recurrent rhythmic structure to the otherwise unmeasured composition.

III. *Instruments and forms.* Although Western instruments are widely used in Persia, some native instruments are favored for performances of traditional music. The most popular plucked stringed instruments are the *setar,* a long-necked three-stringed lute with pear-shaped wooden body, and its larger counterpart, the *tar,* which has a double belly, covered with a sheepskin membrane. The Persian dulcimer, the *santour* (Arab. *santir*), is also prominent. These three native instruments are comparable to the lute ('ud) and psaltery (kanun), the native instruments most often played today in Arab countries but used only rarely in Iran. The Persian *nay* (flute) and *kamanche* (a spike fiddle held on the player's knee), still used in the provinces, have been replaced by their Western counterparts in the cities. The Persian drum is the *tombak,* held on the player's knee and struck with the palms and fingers of both hands.

Classical Persian music is solo or chamber music, usually performed by a soloist or a small ensemble consisting of singer, instrumentalist, and drummer. In the latter, the texture is *heterophonic, the instrumentalist and drummer following the lead of the singer. Semiclassical music, of more recent origin, is composed and notated. Played by chamber orchestras of mixed native and Western instruments, these vocal and instrumental pieces (*pish-daramad, tasnif,* and *reng*) often have conservative Western harmony and counterpoint.

Lit. (the first four books are in Persian, with useful musical examples): Ruhollah Khaleqi, *Nazari be Musiqui* (1938), vol. ii; *id., Sargozasht-e Musiqui-ye Iran* (1954), vol. i; Ali Naqi Vaziri, *Musiqui-ye Nazari* (1934); *id.,* ‡*Dastur-e Tar* (1913); Mehdi Barkechli and Moussa Ma'aroufi, ‡*La Musique traditionelle de l'Iran* (1963); Khatchi Khatchi, *Der Dastgāh* (1962); R. d'Erlanger, *La Musique arabe* (1930–39), vols. i–iv; H. Farmer, "An Outline History of Music and

Musical Theory," in *A Survey of Persian Art,* A. U. Pope, ed. (1939), iii, pp. 2783–2894; E. Gerson-Kiwi, *The Persian Doctrine of Dastga-Composition* (1963); E. Zonis, in *MQ* li, 636–48; *id.,* in *Ethnomusicology* viii, 303ff; C. Huart, "Musique Persane," in *LavE* 1.5, 3065ff; M. Barkechli, "La Musique iranienne," in *L'Encyclopédie de la Pléiade* (1960); *Folkways* (record) 8831 and 8832 (A Study Recording of the Twelve Dastgah).   E.Z.

Peru. Long before the Spanish conquest (1526), Peru had a highly developed civilization, the vast Inca empire, which ruled most of northwest South America. Evidence of a fairly sophisticated musical culture is found in the oral tradition of the Incas' descendants and in the numerous panpipes, flutes, bells, shell and tubular trumpets, and drums preserved to the present day. The earliest Peruvian composer of distinction was Gutierre Fernández Hidalgo (*c.* 1553–1618), who wrote Masses, Magnificats, hymns, music for the offices of Holy Week, and motets. He was active not only in Peru, but also in Colombia, Ecuador, and Bolivia. The outstanding masters in Lima during the early 17th century were Estacio de la Serna and Miguel de Bobadilla. Juan de Araujo (*c.* 1646–1714) was a composer of liturgical part songs and *villancicos, and Tomás de Torrejón y Velasco (1644–1728) is most famous for his opera, *La Púrpura de la rosa,* with a libretto by Calderón de la Barca, produced at the Viceroy's palace in Lima in 1701. José de Orejón y Aparicio (d. 1765), the first native Peruvian appointed to the Cathedral of Lima (1742), composed several hymns, psalms, and Masses. Roque Ceruti (d. 1760) was an Italian-born musician who came to Peru as conductor of the Viceroy's private orchestra and also was the palace composer.

José Bernardo Alzedo (1798–1878) is the best-known composer from the early period of independence, primarily because he wrote the Peruvian national anthem (1821). By the end of the 19th century a group of composers in the romantic tradition became the first to support musical nationalism. Among them were Claudio Rebagliati (1843–1909), an Italian who settled in Lima, José María Valle-Riestra (1859–1925), composer of the opera *Ollanta* (1901), and Luis Duncker Lavalle (1874–1922).

Several composers from succeeding generations shared this nationalist tradition but combined it with the aesthetics of early 20th-century music. Prominent among them are Daniel

Alomias Robles (1871–1942), Luis Pacheco de Céspedes (b. 1893), Teodoro Valcárcel (1902–42), Roberto Carpio Valdes (b. 1900), Andrés Sás (b. 1900; also a well-known musicologist), Pablo Chávez Aguilar (b. 1899), Carlos Sánchez Malaga (b. 1904), and Raoul de Verneuil (b. 1899). German-born Rodolfo Holzman (Rudolph Holzmann), opened the doors to more progressive styles of composition. Many of Holzman's disciples became part of a group of internationally recognized avant-garde composers. Important among them are Enrique Pinilla (b. 1927), Enrique Iturriaga (b. 1918), Celso Garrido-Lecca (b. 1926), Francisco Pulgar Vidal (b. 1929), Olga Pozzi Escot (b. 1931), Edgar Valcárcel (b. 1932), and José Malsio.

Peruvian folk music from the highlands represents to a large extent a direct survival of pre-Columbian traditions. Primarily pentatonic, its melodies have a descending character and are usually in duple meter. The *cachua is a typical form from this region. Songs and dances from the lower coastal regions, such as the *marinera, tonero, *cumbia, socavón [see Mejorana], and similar Creole songs are derived from Spanish models that were transformed by African influences. In many ways this music is similar to Chilean, Argentinian, Bolivian, and Ecuadorian folksongs.

Lit.: R. Stevenson, The Music of Peru [1960]; C. Raygada, Guia Musical del Peru (1957); R. and M. d'Harcourt, La Música de los Incas, rev. ed. (1957); R. Klatovsky, "Music in the Realm of the Incas" (Musical Times lxxv, 696ff); C. Vega, "Tonleitern mit Halbtönen in der Musik der alten Peruaner" (AM ix); A. Sas, "Ensayo sobre la música Inca" (Boletín latino-americano de música i); C. Raygada, "Panorama musical del Perú" (ibid. ii); C. Sánchez Malaga, "La Música en el Peru" (Nuestra Música ii, 72–77 [1947]). Also see under Latin America.   J.O-S.

Pes [L.]. (1) Same as podatus; see Neumes I, table. (2) Name for the tenor in English 13th- and 14th-century MSS, particularly also for the two lower parts of *"Sumer is icumen in."

Pesca [It.]. See under Caccia.

Peter and the Wolf. An orchestral fairy tale for children by Prokofiev (op. 67, completed in 1936), for a small orchestra and narrator. The narrator tells the story of a boy's capturing a large and ferocious wolf with the aid of friendly animals. Each character (cat, duck, Peter, etc.) is associated with a specific instrument and melodic phrase, making the work an excellent introduction to the orchestra for young children.

Peter Grimes. Opera in three acts by Britten (libretto by M. Slater, based on G. Crabbe's poem, The Borough), produced in London, 1945. Setting: the Borough, a fishing village on the east coast of England, about 1830.

Petrushka. Ballet by Stravinsky (choreography by M. Fokine), produced in Paris, 1911, by Diaghilev's Russian Ballet. The work, often heard in the form of an orchestral suite at concerts, is one of the landmarks of 20th-century music. Among the many notable features are the percussive parallel chords in the opening scene, the clever caricature of a sentimental valse, and the bold use of bitonality, particularly in the "Petrushka chord" [see under Bitonality].

Peu, un [F.]. A little, somewhat.

Pezzo [It.]. Piece, composition.

Pf. In orchestral scores, etc., abbr. for pianoforte (piano). As a dynamic sign, abbr. for "piano followed by forte."

Pfeife [G.]. Fife; organ pipe.

Pfundnoten [G.]. The long notes [G. Pfund, pound—each, as it were, weighing a pound] that occur in the cantus firmi of innumerable polyphonic compositions, from the 13th-century organa to Bach's cantus firmus chorales. See Cantus planus style.

Phagotus. A curious instrument invented in the early 16th century by Afranio Albonese. It is worth mentioning only because it has erroneously been considered the predecessor of the *fagott, i.e., bassoon. Actually it was a fanciful and impractical version of bagpipe. See L. F. Valdrighi, Il Phagotus di Afranio (Musurgiana, ser. 1, no. 5, 1881); GD iv, opp. 132; F. W. Galpin, in PMA lxvii, 57–72.

Phantasie [G.]. See Fantasia. Phantasiestücke, Phantasiebilder, etc., are romantic titles for imaginative, fanciful pieces with a slight programmatic connotation. See Character piece. Phantasieren means "to improvise."

Phantasy. Title of English chamber works that were written for the Cobbett Competitions, established in 1906. According to the rules of the competition, they had to be in one movement. More than forty such compositions were written between 1905 and 1930. R. Vaughan Williams, W. H. Hurlstone, Frank Bridge, John Ireland,

and Thomas Dunhill were among the contributors. See C. Maclean, in *ZIM* xii.

Philidor, Collection. A large MS collection of 17th-century music (chiefly French), compiled by André Philidor (Danican; *c.* 1647–1730). The collection contains many dance tunes and airs, all the ballets and operas of Lully and a few other composers, as well as all the sacred music in use at the French court chapel. A large part of the collection is now at St. Michael's College in Tenbury, England, and another in the library of the Paris Conservatory. See J. W. Wasielewski, in *VMW* i, 531–45; E. H. Fellowes, in *ML* xii, 116–29; A. Tessier, in *RM* xii [1931], 295–302.

Philippines. For about nine-tenths of the Philippine population, a musical tradition nurtured by three centuries (1565–1898) of cultural contact with Spain is exemplified in songs and dances (*kundiman, balitao, pandango, cariñosa, tinikling,* etc.) with a melody in major and minor, duple and triple meters, and a harmonic accompaniment played by guitar, piano, or an ensemble of steel strings (*rondalla*). Together with brass bands playing marches, overtures, and selections from Italian opera, this type of music constitutes an

cal," "popular," or "jazz."

Generally unknown to the larger audience is a rich variety of aboriginal Malayan music still performed in remote areas that had little or no contact with Western ways. Principally in three regions—northern Luzon; Mindoro; and Palawan, Mindanao, and Sulu—the music is similar to that heard in the islands of Indonesia and the hills of southeast Asia. This whole complex comprises one cultural unit. In the northern Philippines, music is used for festivities such as a peace pact, a head-hunting celebration, or a prestige ceremony, and in the south for a wedding, a thanksgiving for a bountiful harvest, or an Islamic ritual.

Among the mountain people of northern Luzon, gong music that accompanies dancing by couples and groups plays an important role in celebrations. Flat gongs without a boss (*gangsa*), not found elsewhere in the islands, are played in various instrumental combinations (6 gongs; 2 gongs and 1 cylindrical drum; 2 gongs, 2 conical drums, and a pair of iron bars). They are beaten with padded sticks. Among the Kalinga six performers tapping and sliding their palms on six gongs of diminishing size produce a music that might be notated as follows:

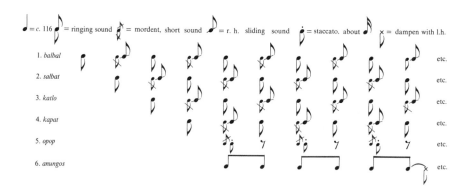

important part of the repertory used for celebrations, school programs and, especially, fiestas in honor of a patron saint. Toward the end of the 19th century, in Manila particularly, there were Spanish *zarzuelas,* visiting Italian opera companies, and performances by local and foreign artists attended by a well-informed public. Later, with the introduction of modern schools and symphony orchestras, composition and performance included more complex European forms. Today, music in various segments of Philippine society simply means Western music—"classi-

Other musical instruments in this region are the bamboo tube, xylophone blades, tube zither, buzzer, quill-shaped tube, panpipes, flutes (nose, lip-valley, whistle), brass and bamboo Jew's-harp, row of sticks, and musical bow (among the Negrito). A syllabic style of singing with reiterations on pivotal tones is used for song debates, work songs, medicine-man songs, songs for peace pacts, epics, etc., sung either by a leader and chorus or a soloist, in ritual as well as recreational surroundings.

Music in Mindoro shows some Western influences—harmonic patterns played on a miniature guitar, and diatonic melodies performed on a small violin and a transverse flute.

In the southern Philippines, except for leader-chorus singing in Palawan, musical forms are generally similar to one another. Most valued is a large suspended gong with a wide rim (*agung*), played together with various instruments, such as one or more of the following: another *agung*, cylindrical drum, gongs suspended in a frame, gongs in a row, bamboo zither, two-stringed lute, and other types of gong. The music for the *kulintang* ensemble with five instruments may be written as follows:

of the Magindanao in the Philippines" (diss. Univ. of California, Los Angeles, 1963); *id.*, "Chants from Sagada Mountain Province, Philippines" (*Ethnomusicology* ii, 2; ii, 3); L. Reid, "Dancing and Music (in Guinaang, Mountain Province)" (*Philippine Sociological Review* ix, 55–82); M. Schneider, "Música Filipina" (*AnM* vi); W. R. Pfeiffer, "A Musical Analysis of Some Ritual Songs of the Manobo of North Central Cotabato" (master's thesis, Univ. of Hawaii, 1965); R. D. Trimillos, "Some Social and Musical Aspects of the Music of the Taosug in Sulu, Philippines" (master's thesis, Univ. of Hawaii, 1965); *Bayanihan Philippine Dance Company*,

Generally, the *kulintang* is tuned to a "flexible" pentatonic scale (two small gaps, one big gap, and one small gap of varying dimensions). Other musical instruments of the area are various flutes (ring, lip-valley, beak-type), bamboo horn, reed pipe, shell trumpet, bamboo zither, spike fiddle, violin, small gongs with shallow boss, percussion beams, log drum, Jew's-harp, slit drum, bamboo scraper, stamping tube, and xylophone. Syllabic recitations on key tones of a scale are frequently employed in songs—legends, epics, lullabies, courting or wedding songs, etc.—or in prayers to drive bad spirits from a sick person's body. Among peoples influenced by Islamic culture, melismatic songs are found in Islamic rituals—Friday-noon service, Maolud, Ramadan—or in long narratives (*sindil, baat*) sung by special singers. Solo songs are the norm, but some singers are accompanied by the bamboo zither, the lute, and, especially, the xylophone and violin among the Taosug of Sulu.

Lit.: F. R. Aquino, *Philippine Folk Dances*, 2 vols. (1950, '53); P. Magdamo, ed., ‡*Philippine Folk Songs: Songs of the Visayas*, 6 vols. (1957–58); F. Santiago and E. Reysio-Cruz, ed., ‡*Filipino Folk Songs* (1950); J. Maceda, "The Music

Record MF 322 (Monitor Records, New York, 1959); J. Maceda, *The Music of the Magindanao*, 2 records, FE 4536 (Folkways Records, New York, 1962); *id.* and H. Conklin, *Hanunoo Music*, Record 4466 (Folkways Records, New York, 1955).   J.M.

Phoebus and Pan. See *Streit zwischen Phöbus und Pan.*

Phonograph and recorded music. The origin of the phonograph traces back to Thomas A. Edison, who in 1877 produced a record made of tin foil on which his own voice could be heard reciting "Mary had a little lamb." This record was a cylinder, as were the all commercial records made by Edison for many years. The invention of practicable disc records (introduced commercially *c.* 1896) and the beginnings of mass production and marketing of recordings owed much to Emil Berliner, who held the patents on which the Improved Gramophone was based. This machine did not become practicable until the invention of a suitable motor by E. R. Johnson, a Camden, New Jersey mechanic whose factory supplied motors and later entire machines for the enterprise. The marketing was done by F. Seaman (under contract to Berliner). Eventually internal dissension and lawsuits from competitors broke up this alliance, and Johnson, who developed a new and much better method of making discs, set up his own company, Victor, in cooperation with Berliner.

The types of phonograph and record remained generally the same until 1925, when the Ortho-phonic Victrola and electric recording were introduced. These instruments, featuring more sonorous sound chambers than those of the earlier machines, were able to bring more music from the records than had been heard before, and the new method of recording, utilizing the microphone that had come into being with radio, marked a tremendous advance in the range and faithfulness of reproduction. The next few years saw the development of the electric phonograph, in which the sound is reproduced entirely by electricity. The next major innovation, compara-ble in importance to the replacement of the old cylinder by discs, was changing the speed of the turntable from 78 revolutions per minute (RPM) to 33⅓ or 45 RPM. The slower speed combined with more grooves on the surface of the disc made possible a period of about twenty to thirty minutes of uninterrupted performance as com-pared to a previous maximum of about five minutes. This advantage of the long-playing (LP, originally a Columbia trademark) record, in addition to greater convenience of storage and transportation, made the older 78 RPM discs obsolete. Fortunately, many of the older discs have been transferred onto LP discs.

Of great importance to the recording industry was the development of magnetic-tape record-ing, introduced commercially in the 1940's. Recording companies were quick to seize on the many advantages of this medium: longer unin-terrupted playing time; freedom from many kinds of distortion inherent in disc recording; potentially lower noise levels; and, especially, the possibility of editing and splicing short sections of tape, an impossibility in disc recording. Mis-takes and extraneous noises could be easily eliminated by making a composite recording from portions of several separate recordings (or "takes"). The great majority of commercial recordings of music are made in this fashion, producing a musical result technically more per-fect but frequently less spontaneous than a "live" musical performance. Owing to its technical superiority, virtually all sound recordings are now made on tape and then transferred to the desired medium (disc, tape, or film). Because high-quality tape recorders can be made quite compact and portable, this recording method has become an indispensable research tool for *ethnomusicology.

Except for a few experiments, all discs issued up to 1958 were monaural (or monophonic), i.e., they employed only one sound channel. But human hearing is binaural, the separation of the two ears enabling the listener to perceive the direction of sound. Although stereophonic re-cording is easily accomplished on a single mag-netic tape (by placing two or more channels side by side), it is much more difficult to achieve on discs. Experimental techniques had been devel-oped as early as c. 1935, but it was only in 1958 that the technical problems of combining two sound channels in a single record groove were finally overcome and stereophonic ("stereo") discs were commercially introduced.

The repertory for the phonograph has under-gone considerable change since the early days. Edison's original intention was to produce liter-ally a talking machine, and the musical possi-bilities of the new instrument were not at first apparent. The earliest repertory of the commer-cial phonograph, therefore, consisted mostly of vaudeville sketches and monologues. These were gradually supplemented with band records and sentimental songs, for it was possible to repro-duce wind instruments with reasonable clarity, and the singing voice emerged recognizably from the wax. Celebrated singers soon began to record their voices, and by the 1890's this prac-tice was quite fashionable. Recordings made from the first Paris performance of *Parsifal* (1882) are believed to be the oldest preserved. About 1900 the record companies in Europe be-gan to see the commercial possibilities of the idea, and a new period in phonograph history began. The first American celebrity recordings were announced in 1903 by the Columbia Com-pany, the list including discs by Marcella Sem-brich, Edouard de Reszke, Ernestine Schumann-Heink, Giuseppe Campanari, Antonio Scotti, Charles Gilibert, and Suzanna Adams. Victor was not slow to follow, building up an impressive "Red Seal" catalog to which most of the feted vocalists and instrumentalists of the day con-tributed. The singers recorded mostly operatic arias, occasionally branching out into the song repertory, and the violinists, cellists, and pianists gave their versions of the lighter classics. At first all accompaniments were played on the piano, but about 1905 many of the singers were busy remaking their selections with orchestra. Owing to the limitations of reproduction at that time, all kinds of alteration were made in the orchestrations of arias and the instruments were necessarily few in number, but the voices as recorded were unmistakably those of their famous prototypes. Today, collecting early celebrity recordings is a major hobby, and several societies have been formed for the purpose of re-recording or re-pressing old masters on a subscription basis.

In 1913 the Gramophone Company in Europe completed the last of a series of orchestral recordings, securing the services of Arthur Nikisch, who conducted the Berlin Philharmonic Orchestra in Beethoven's Fifth Symphony, and the London Symphony Orchestra in a series of standard works. In the same year the Columbia Company in the United States engaged Felix Weingartner and enlarged its staff orchestra for several recordings under his direction. The first of these were cut versions of the "Liebestod" from *Tristan* and the conductor's arrangement of Weber's "Aufforderung zum Tanz." Several years later (1917) Columbia engaged the Chicago Symphony, conducted by Frederick Stock, the Cincinnati Orchestra under Kunwald, and the New York Philharmonic under Stransky. Victor followed a year later with a series of recordings of Karl Muck and the Boston Symphony, and shortly thereafter Leopold Stokowski began his long series with the Philadelphia Orchestra. The year 1919 saw the first serious attempts at recording chamber music in this country when the Flonzaley Quartet made for Victor a series of abbreviated movements from their repertory.

The issuing of complete symphonies and other larger works received its greatest impetus in Europe. As early as 1907 and 1908 Victor was issuing complete performances of operas (including *Pagliacci* made under the direction of the composer) recorded by the La Scala company in Milan, but it was not until the establishment of electrical recording that the American catalog began to fill up with records made for the sake of the music rather than the artist. After a period of decline, attributed to the competition of radio, records began to enjoy a new popularity comparable to that of the great days of celebrity discs. In the first decade of electric recording the usual repertory of standard works, both instrumental and vocal, had been pretty well covered, and the enterprise of some of the companies, particularly in Europe, made it possible for the phonograph owner to come to know a great deal of music he might never otherwise have had a chance to hear. This fact has certainly been in no

small measure responsible for the general rebirth of interest in the music of the 16th and 17th centuries. Societies were formed for the recording of music whose appeal was expected to be limited, but many of the sets so issued proved sufficiently popular to be subsequently released in the regular commercial catalogues. The music of men like Delius, Hugo Wolf, Sibelius, Kilpinen, and Purcell was issued in such sets, as well as the sonatas of Beethoven, various works of Bach, and several operas of Mozart. A further development has been the issue of records of chamber music with one of the instrumental parts missing, and of accompaniments to songs, for the benefit of amateurs who lack the necessary partners for musical performance.

The amazing growth of interest in records is seen in the amount of literature published on the subject. *The Gramophone* in England and *The American Music Lover* (now *The American Record Guide*) in the United States are magazines devoted entirely to recorded music, and various dealers publish critical bulletins. Many general magazines and newspapers have instituted record-review columns, and in 1936 The Gramophone Shop in New York published an *Encyclopedia of Recorded Music* (new editions of which appeared in 1942 and 1948). Most modern books on music include lists of records, and several critical surveys of recorded music have been brought out.

Another important development has been the introduction of record collections in libraries throughout the world. A project of the Carnegie Corporation has been the assembling of "music sets" for colleges and schools, and the free distribution of these records, books, and scores to selected institutions. Steps are being taken to establish record archives in various libraries, not only to provide the public with a place to listen to music but to preserve many of the important discs no longer on the market. The voices of such singers as E. Caruso, E. Eames, Lilli Lehmann, Victor Maurel, Adelina Patti, Melba, Tamagno, De Lucia, Tetrazzini, and Fremstad, and the playing of Paderewski, Kreisler, Ysaÿe, Pachmann, and many others will thus be preserved for posterity.

The output of recorded music includes, needless to say, the entire standard concert repertory and many compositions that are seldom heard in the concert hall. Particularly worth mentioning is the attention that has been given to the music of Bach and the masters of still earlier periods. Most of the latter have been recorded in sets covering the entire history of music or special phases thereof. The most important of these are: *L'Anthologie Sonore* (Parlophone-Odeon; ed. C. Sachs); *The Columbia History of Music by Ear and Eye* (Columbia 78; ed. P. Scholes); *The History of Music in Sound* (RCA Victor); *Masterpieces of Music before 1750* (Haydn Society); *A Treasury of Early Music* (Haydn Society); *2000 Years of Music*, ed. C. Sachs (orig. Decca 78, then LP, then Folkways LP); *Anthologie de la Musique d'Orgue* (Ducretet-Thomson); *Archiv* series (Deutsche Grammophon Gesellschaft). For recordings of medieval music, see the Record List in *ReMMA,* pp. 465ff, and J. Coover and R. Colvig, *Medieval and Renaissance Music on Longplaying Records* (1964).

Lit.: F. F. Clough and G. J. Cuming, *The World's Encyclopaedia of Recorded Music* [1952], supp. [1951, '53, '57]; D. Hall, *Records* (1950); *The Gramophone Shop Encyclopedia of Recorded Music* (1936, '42, '48, with supplements); I. Kolodin, *The New Guide to Recorded Music* (1950); B. Lebow, *American Record Index* (1950); M. Smith, *Selective Record Guide* (1950); H. C. Schonberg, *The Guide to Long-Playing Records: Chamber and Solo Instrument Music* (1955); E. Greenfield, I. March, and D. Stevens, ed., *The Stereo Record Guide*, 2 vols. (1960, '61); O. Read and W. L. Welch, *From Tin Foil to Stereo; Evolution of the Phonograph* [1959]; P. Gammond, *Music on Record: A Critical Guide,* 2 vols. [1962]; R. Bauer, *The New Catalogue of Historical Records,* 1898–1908/09 [1947]; K. Myers, *Record Ratings* (1956—); *Schwann Long Playing Record Catalogue* (monthly).—Periodicals: *The American Record Guide; The New Records; High Fidelity; Recorded Sound; The Gramophone.*   P.L.M.

Phonola. See under Mechanical instruments IV.

Phorminx [Gr.]. Homeric name for the *kithara, or *lyra.

Phrase. A division of the musical line, somewhat comparable to a clause or a sentence in prose. Other terms used for such divisions are period, half-phrase, double phrase, etc. There is no consistency in applying these terms nor can there be, in view of the infinite variety of situations and conditions found in music. Only with melodies of a very simple type, especially those of some dances, can the terms be used with some consistency, e.g., half-phrase for a unit of two measures, phrase for one of four, double phrase or period for one of eight, double period for one of sixteen. Music of the era from *c.* 1600 to 1900 often

shows a "regular" phrase structure in units of four measures; see *Vierhebigkeit.*

Phrasing and articulation. Terms used to describe clear and meaningful rendition of music (chiefly of melodies), comparable to an intelligent reading of poetry. The main (though not the only) means of achieving this goal is the separation of the continuous melodic line into smaller units varying in length from a group of measures to single notes. Properly speaking, phrasing refers to the separation of a melody into its constituent *phrases, whereas articulation refers to the subdivision of a phrase into smaller units. Often, however, it is difficult to distinguish between the two, partly owing to the vagueness of the term "phrase." Moreover, in practice the term "phrasing" is often applied to what is properly termed "articulation."

The earliest use of phrasing marks (other than written out rests) occurs in Cavalieri's *La Rappresentazione di anima e di corpo* (1600), where the sign ⅌ is placed above the final note of a phrase [Ex. 1; see *SchGMB,* p. 183]. F. Couperin, in Books 3 and 4 of his *Pièces de clavecin* (1722, '30), used a comma in order to indicate what, in the foreword to these publications, he called "la terminaison des Chants ou de nos Phrases harmoniques." In some cases, the comma serves as a sign of articulation rather than phrasing [Ex. 2; cf. ed. by J. Brahms and K. F. Chrysander, iii, 280]. None of the later composers (Mozart, Beethoven) paid special attention to

Nel In-fer-no vi stan-no Le spe-lun-chee le grot-te

phrasing, apparently taking it for granted that the performer would know how to divide melodies into phrases. On the other hand, signs of articulation, such as the various signs for *legato and *staccato, are not uncommon in compositions from *c.* 1620 to 1750 and occur with increasing attention to detail in the works of the classical, and later, romantic composers. An early example is a passage from Carlo Farina's *Capriccio stravagante* (1627) for violin, noteworthy for its capricious alternation of downbeat and upbeat slurs [Ex. 3; see Keller, p. 45]. J. S. Bach's indications are open to a variety of interpretations. Indeed, his melodies are so complex in structure and so rich in relationships on numerous levels that any indication of phrasing is bound to be one-sided and misleading.

One of the earliest theorists to write about phrasing was Mattheson, who in his *Kern melodischer Wissenschaft* (1737) described it as "the most remarkable and least noticed aspect" of musical language [G. *Klangrede*]. J. A. P. Schulz was perhaps the first to observe (in Sulzer's *Allgemeine Theorie der schönen Künste,* 2 vols., 1771, '74) that phrases often extend over the bar line. In the late 19th century H. Riemann published a number of books dealing in minute detail with all aspects of phrasing and articulation. In his edition of Beethoven's *Sonaten für Klavier* (3 vols., 1885) phrasing and articulation are practically the only stylistic elements considered, and his numerous *Phrasierungsausgaben* of compositions by Bach and other masters [see his *Altmeister des Klavierspiels,* 2 vols. (1890?), nos. 96, 97] are provided with such a large number and variety of marks as to make them practically useless (in fact, almost illegible). Riemann's ideas were applied, with more moderation, by numerous editors to works ranging from the 16th century [see *TaAM* i, ii, etc.] to Mozart and Beethoven. Special attention was paid to one particular "law" of phrasing, i.e., Riemann's thesis that every musical phrase begins with an upbeat [G. *Auftakt*]. Undoubtedly this is a principle of considerable importance, but it has been carried *ad absurdum,* often in clear violation of the composer's intentions. Good phrasing and articulation involve the separation of larger and smaller units, but also such other factors as proper accentuation, variety of attack, and subtle crescendos and decrescendos, all of which contribute to the meaningful shaping of a melody. See also Bowing; Expression; Expression marks; Piano playing; Style.

Lit.: H. Keller, *Phrasing and Articulation* (1965); A. H. Fox-Strangways, in *ML* ix, 1ff; F. Rosenthal, in *ZMW* viii, 262ff; K. Speer, in *The Diapason,* Oct. and Nov. 1959 (organ music); *id.,* in *BJ* 1954 (Bach's organ works).

Phrygian. (1) In ancient Greek theory, the octave species d'–d [see Greece II]. (2) In the system of

*church modes, the segment e–e' of the diatonic scale, with e as the tonic (*finalis*). From the modern point of view, it appears as a variety of minor (E minor), the characteristic distinguishing feature being the minor second: e f g a, instead of e f♯ g a. In compositions in the Phrygian mode,

this characteristic step appears most conspicuously in the cadences (Phrygian cadence; see Ex.). To the harmonically minded, such formulas seem to be not so much a full close in E (VII–I) as a half-cadence in A (IV–V). In this sense the Phrygian cadence is frequently found in the sonatas of Corelli, Handel, and others as a transition from one movement to the next. For an example of Phrygian in modern music, see Modality.

In Gregorian chant, the Phrygian mode (modes 3 and 4; *deuterus*) is represented by a large number of chants, many of which, however, show a tendency toward tonal instability, the E-tonality not being established until the end [see *ApGC,* p. 142]. Also noteworthy is the frequent occurrence of a b-flat, particularly in cadences with the general outline f–b♭–e [e.g., the Communion *Qui meditabitur, LU,* p. 529]. In polyphonic music, the Phrygian mode was "discovered" by Ockeghem in his *Missa Mi-mi* and frequently used by Josquin as a vehicle for somber expression, e.g., in his motet, "Tu pauperum refugium" [*HAM,* no. 90]. See also *HAM,* nos. 93 (Hofhaimer), 111 ("Aus tiefer Not").

Physharmonica. See under Harmonium II.

Piacere, a [It.]. See *A piacere.*

Piacevole [It.]. Pleasing, agreeable.

Pianamente [It.]. Smoothly, softly.

Pianino [G.]. Upright piano

Piano, abbr. *p* [It.]. Soft; pianissimo (abbr. *pp*), very soft. See Dynamic marks.

Piano, pianoforte. A stringed instrument whose strings are struck by hammers activated by keys, and which, since the end of the 18th century, has been the principal domestic keyboard instrument in Europe and America. It was originally called *pianoforte* [It. soft-loud; also *forte-piano*] because, in contrast to the earlier harpsichord, the loudness of its sound could be varied by the

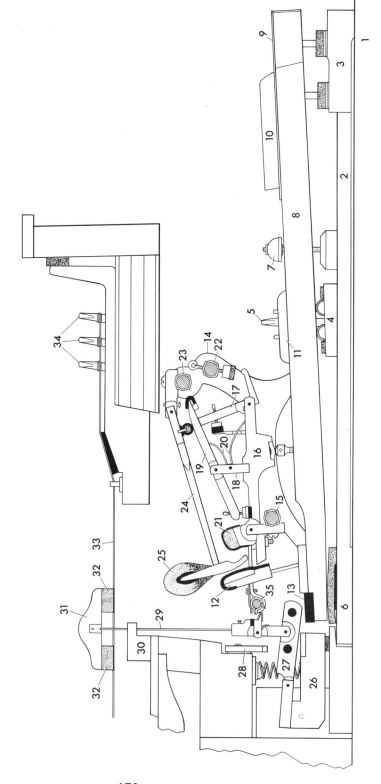

Cross section of grand piano action: 1. Keybed. 2. Keyframe. 3. Front rail. 4. Balance rail. 5. Balance rail stud. 6. Back rail. 7. Key stop rail. 8. White key. 9. Key covering. 10. Black key. 11. Key button. 12. Backcheck. 13. Underlever key cushion. 14. Action hanger. 15. Support rail. 16. Support. 17. Fly. 18. Support top flange. 19. Balancer. 20. Repetition spring. 21. Hammer rest. 22. Regulating rail. 23. Hammer rail. 24. Hammershank. 25. Hammer. 26. Underlever frame. 27. Underlever. 28. Damper stop rail. 29. Damper wire. 30. Damper guide rail. 31. Damper head. 32. Damper felts. 33. String. 34. Tuning pin. 35. Sostenuto rod. Courtesy of Steinway & Sons touch of the fingers. Today the abbreviated name "piano" is more commonly used.

I. *General.* The piano is, with the single exception of the organ, the most complex of all conventional instruments. It has a greater range than any other instrument—usually more than seven octaves, from A_2 to c'''''—and a dynamic range that, again, is exceeded only by the organ's. The complexity of the piano arises from the fact that the soft felt hammer cannot merely be lifted toward the string like the tangent of the *clavichord or carried past the string like the plucking mechanism of the *harpsichord. Instead, the hammer must be thrown up and must immediately rebound from the string so that it will not damp out the vibrations it initiates. Since the hammer must be thrown instead of being lifted, it must move faster than the key that activates it, requiring a lever system (called an *action*) between it and the key. If the action is to give the performer good dynamic control, the distance over which the hammer is thrown after the motion of the key is arrested must be kept small. On the other hand, the hammer must fall far enough away from the string after striking it so that there will be no possibility of its bouncing back up and accidentally restriking the string. This requirement is met by the provision of a device that catches the hammer as it falls (a *backcheck*) and, more important, by an *escapement,* by means of which the lever that lifts the hammer is moved aside just before the hammer's impact on the string. The hammer then falls back farther than it was thrown upward, even while the key is still held down. An action meeting all of these requirements still does not permit rapid repetition of a note, especially when playing softly. This need was met only by the still more complicated *repetition action* or *double escapement,* developed in 1821 by Sébastien Érard (1752–1831). In this action, the hammer falls to an intermediate position and can be thrown upward again before the key returns all the way to its original resting position.

In addition to activating the hammers, the keys of a piano must also control felt-covered dampers, lifting them as a note is struck and allowing them to fall back to silence the strings when the keys are released. Generally, three strings per note are provided in the treble, two in the tenor, and one in the bass. The aggregate tension imposed by these strings, which approaches eighteen tons, is borne by a massive cast-iron frame.

The modern piano is equipped with two or (especially in America) three pedals, the damper or "loud" pedal at the right, the *una corde* or "soft" pedal at the left, and (if present) the sostenuto pedal in the center. On being depressed, the damper pedal raises all the dampers, allowing all the strings to vibrate regardless of what keys are being depressed; this produces a characteristic coloring of the tone and permits legato performance of notes that do not lie beneath the hand. The *una corda* pedal shifts the entire keyboard and action to the right so that each hammer strikes only two of its three unison strings in the treble and only one of its two strings in the tenor. In addition to a reduction in volume, this pedal also produces a characteristic tone color. The sostenuto pedal operates to sustain only those tones whose dampers are already raised by the action of the keys. Thus, it permits the sustaining of single notes (e.g., a pedal point in the bass) while both hands are occupied elsewhere, and also provides the means of producing various coloristic effects.

II. *History.* Although interest in providing the harpsichord with some sort of hammer mechanism seems to have been fairly widespread in the first years of the 18th century—perhaps owing to the phenomenal success of Pantaleon Hebenstreit (1669–1750) and his large dulcimer, the *pantaleon—the piano was created essentially single-handed by Bartolommeo Cristofori (1655–1730) of Florence, shortly before 1709. Cristofori's *gravicembalo col piano e forte* was conceived, as its name implies, as a new variety of harpsichord, whose hammer action could provide gradations of loudness instead of the ordinary harpsichord's "terrace dynamics." The perfection of Cristofori's piano action of 1720, which included both an escapement and hammer check, was such that it was not significantly improved upon for nearly a century, and no instruments even comparable in quality, except for direct copies like those by Gottfried Silbermann (1683–1753), were made until the 1770's. Cristofori's invention was not much appreciated in his homeland, but the description of it published by Scipione Maffei (1711) and printed in German translation in Mattheson's *Critica musica* (1725) appears to have inspired a number of Germans besides Silbermann to experiment with hammer mechanisms. The point of departure for most of the German builders seems to have been the clavichord rather than the harpsichord, and the German piano of the 18th century is, in both conception and tone quality, far more like a loud clavichord than a dynamically flexible harpsichord. Most of the mid-18th-century German pianos were in fact built in the "square" form of the clavichord (in contrast to Cristofori's and Silbermann's, which were wing-shaped "grands"). The German builders employed a very simple action, radically different from Cristofori's, whose appears to have dropped from sight only to be essentially reinvented in England in the last quarter of the 18th century. In the typical German action, the hammer is pivoted in a fork at the back of the key rather than hinged from a rail fixed above the keys as in Cristofori's design. Most of the early German actions lacked an escapement, which was first incorporated by Johann Andreas Stein (1728–92) c. 1770. This so-called Viennese action yielded a touch that was lighter and shallower than that of Cristofori's instrument and greatly facilitated performance of the sparkling passagework characteristic of piano music before Beethoven's time.

The English piano appears to have descended from Cristofori's in a highly indirect fashion, the first pianos in England having been built by a German expatriate, Johann Zumpe, c. 1765. Zumpe's square pianos employed an escapementless action that was like Cristofori's only in having the hammers hinged from an overhead rail; this action was provided with an escapement, probably c. 1772 by Americus Backers, John Broadwood, and Robert Stodart, and later was to be the point of departure for Érard. Thus, the English action is the ancestor of that found in all modern pianos. It required a touch heavier than that of the delicate Viennese action, but it proved capable of giving greater volume and a wider dynamic range to the performer.

The history of the piano after the perfection of the double-escapement action is largely concerned with the development of metal bracing that could withstand the ever-increasing tension imposed by the thicker strings required for increased loudness and brilliance. The greatest single advance was the invention in 1825 of the one-piece cast-iron frame by Alpheus Babcock, who also was the first to conceive of *cross-stringing,* an arrangement in which the strings of treble and middle registers fan out over most of the soundboard while the bass strings cross over them, forming a separate fan at a higher level. These two features were given what is essentially their present form in the grand piano exhibited in 1855 by Steinway and Sons of New York.

III. *Modern types.* Of the horizontal piano

designs, the clavichord-shaped "square" and the wing-shaped "grand," only the latter has continued to be built in the 20th century. Modern grand pianos range in size from the 9-foot "concert grand" down to 5-foot, 2-inch "baby grands." (These sizes are the normal extremes; there are instruments as long as 11 feet and shorter than 5 feet.) Pianos with their strings arranged in a vertical plane have been built since the middle of the 18th century. The earliest examples appear to have been either "pyramid" pianos, in which the strings were housed in a case that formed a tall isosceles triangle above the keyboard, or "giraffe" pianos, which were essentially grand pianos set on end. The 19th century saw the introduction of "cabinet" pianos with tall rectangular cases, as well as the diagonally strung "cottage" piano of Robert Wornum (1811), which is the true ancestor of the modern upright. Large upright pianos more than 4 feet high have been largely superseded by lower instruments: the "studio upright" (about 46 inches high), the "console" (about 40 inches high), and the "spinet" (about 36 inches high). The spinet frequently differs from the others in having a special action that operates from below the keys. See also Keyboard; Pedal piano; Sostenente piano; Electronic instruments.

Lit.: R. E. M. Harding, *The Pianoforte* (1933; bibl.); E. A. Wier, *The Piano* (1940); L. Nalder, *The Modern Piano* (1927); P. James, *Early Keyboard Instruments . . . to the Year 1820* (1930); D. Spillane, *History of the American Pianoforte* (1890); A. Loesser, *Men, Women and Pianos* (1955); F. J. Hirt, *Meisterwerke des Klavierbaus* (1955); S. Hansing, *Das Pianoforte in seinen akustischen Anlagen* (1950); H. Brunner, *Das Klavierklangideal Mozarts und die Klaviere seiner Zeit* (1933); "Experimental Pianofortes" (*PMA* lvii); *id.,* in *CP 1930;* S. M. Cleeve, "The Future of the Piano" (*Musical Times* lxxxvii, 201, July 1946); C. Parrish, "Criticisms of the Piano When It Was New" (*MQ* xxx). See also under Keyboard instruments.   E.M.R.

Piano arrangement. See Arrangement.

Piano concerto. See Concerto II, III (c).

Piano duet. A composition for two pianists playing on either one or two instruments. Such compositions are also called "for four hands" [F. *à quatre mains;* G. *vierhändig;* It. *a quattro mani;* Sp. *a cuatro manos*].

(a) *Duets for one instrument* (organ, harpsichord, piano). As early as the 8th century some organ music was performed by two organists, each playing one melody (with the hands alternating in pulling out and pushing in slides), both together performing organum [see Organum (2)]. From *c.* 1600 there is a "three-hand" organ composition, *Ut re my fa sol la,* by William Byrd, bearing the remark: "The playnesong Breifes To Be played by a second person" [see S. Tuttle, *William Byrd, 45 Pieces for Keyboard Instruments,* pp. 86ff], as well as two four-hand compositions, an *In nomine* by Nicholas Carleton [see H. Miller, in *MQ* xxix] and a Fancy by Thomas Tomkins [*Two Elizabethan Keyboard Duets,* ed. F. Dawes (1949)]. A continuous tradition, however, did not begin until the late 18th century. A famous picture of 1762 shows the young Mozart and his sister playing together. Among the earliest extant compositions are six sonatas by Johann Christian Bach (1735–82), Mozart's four-hand Sonata in D (K. 381; 1772), Burney's *Four Sonatas or Duets for two Performers on One Piano Forte or Harpsichord* (1777), Haydn's *Il Maestro e lo scolare* (1778), and seven compositions (six sonatas, K. 19d, K. 381, K. 358, K. 497, K. 521, K. 357; one set of variations, K. 501) by Mozart, composed between 1765 and 1787. Besides Mozart, the only great composer who was seriously interested in four-hand music was Schubert. Brahms wrote a set of variations on a theme by Schumann (op. 23); Max Reger *12 Walzer-Capricen* (op. 9), *Sechs Burlesken* (op. 58), *Sechs Stücke* (op. 94), and others; and Hindemith a *Sonate* (1938).

(b) *Duets for two instruments.* The *Libro de cifra nueva* by Venegas de Henestrosa (1557) contains a chanson, "Belle sans paire," by Crecquillon, arranged "a doce para dos instrumentos," i.e., in twelve voice-parts for two harpsichords or organs [*Editions XXXII, 2, p. 158]. An English example from the late 16th century is "For two Virginals" by Giles Farnaby [see Fitzwilliam Virginal Book, i, 202]. Bernardo Pasquini (1637–1710) wrote 14 three-movement sonatas for two harpsichords, each consisting of two figured basses only. In France, *pièces à deux clavecins* were written by F. Couperin ("Allemande à deux Clavecins," several other pieces; see new ed. by Brahms-Chrysander, 4 vols., ii, 160; iii, 250, 262, 264, 284) and by Gaspard Le Roux (*Pièces de clavessin,* 1705). A sonata for two harpsichords reproduced in the complete works of Bach (*BG,* vol. 43.i, p. 47), but actually composed by his son W. F. Bach, has received little attention. The present-day repertory begins with Mozart, whose Sonata in D (K. 448; 1781) is one of the

most famous pieces for two pianos. Other notable compositions are his Fugue in C minor (K. 426; 1783), two Sonatas by Clementi (op. 12, 46), Schumann's Andante and Variations in B$^\flat$ major (op. 46), a Rondo by Chopin in C major (op. 73), Variations by Sinding, several compositions by Busoni, Debussy's *En Blanc et noir* (1915), and, among later contributions, a Sonata by Hindemith (1942) and a Concerto and Sonata by Stravinsky (1935, 1944). More numerous are arrangements for two pianos, among which those made by the composers themselves are particularly worth mentioning (Brahms, F-minor Quintet and Variations on a Theme by Haydn; Busoni, *Fantasia contrappuntistica,* originally written for piano solo).

Lit.: A. Rowley, *Four Hands—One Piano* (1940); H. Moldenhauer, *Duo-pianism* [1950]; K. Ganzer and L. Kusche, *Vierhändig* (1937, '55); W. Georgii, *Klaviermusik,* rev. ed. [1950], pp. 531–610; W. Altmann, *Verzeichnis von Werken für Klavier vier- und sechshändig sowie für zwei und mehr Klaviere* (1943); A. M. Henderson, in *PMA* lii; F. Niecks, in *ZIM* v; H. Miller, in *MQ* xxix.

Pianola. See under Mechanical instruments IV.

Piano music. The literature proper for the piano starts with the sonatas that Clementi, Haydn, and Mozart wrote from *c.* 1775 on, and includes among its contributors practically all the composers of the 19th and 20th centuries. Nobody would think of excluding from this repertory the works of J. S. Bach, although they were written for the harpsichord and clavichord. The sonatas of Domenico Scarlatti have likewise joined the piano repertory. There are, moreover, numerous earlier keyboard composers—Byrd, Sweelinck, Frescobaldi, D'Anglebert, and others—whose works could well be performed on the piano, provided they were played with a proper regard for style [see W. Apel, *Masters of the Keyboard,* p. 5].

I. *The beginnings.* The earliest known pieces for the piano (though written in true harpsichord style) are by Lodovico Giustini, who in 1732 published sonatas for the "cembal di piano e forte detto volgarmente di martelletti" ("... commonly called the one with hammers"; see R. Harding, in *ML* xiii; new ed. by R. Harding, 1933). These, however, remained as isolated as Cristofori's instrument [see Piano II], and it was not until about forty years later that the piano began its triumphal career. One of its first champions was J. F. Edelmann (1749–94) in Paris. Clementi's first sonatas of 1773 are perhaps the earliest pieces to make use of the distinctive powers of the instrument. Of K. P. E. Bach's six publications "für Kenner und Liebhaber," the first (1779) is called "Sechs Clavier-Sonaten," probably indicating free use of any of the three keyboard instruments, while the others (1780–87) expressly call "fürs Forte piano." On the other hand, the original editions of almost all the Beethoven sonatas up to op. 27 (including the "Moonlight" Sonata) bear the inscription "Pour le clavecin ou pianoforte," an inscription for which the publishers probably were responsible [see Harpsichord II].

II. *Classicism (1780–1830)*. This is the greatest and best-known period of piano music, and too extensive to describe in detail. One might point out a few of the most obvious advances in exploiting the resources of the instrument, such as the amazing degree of virtuosity attained in Beethoven's Waldstein Sonata, Appassionata, and piano concertos, the transcendental technique of his latest sonatas (op. 106ff), and the "orchestral coloring" that appears in Schubert's great but somewhat neglected sonatas. Beethoven's Bagatelles mark the beginning of an important type of 19th-century piano music, the *character piece.

III. *Romanticism (1830–1910)*. This period, too, is too rich and familiar to describe in detail. The piano pieces by Schumann, Chopin, Liszt, and Brahms form the standard repertory, and indeed overshadow many other compositions that would be equally or more worthy of attention (particularly Schubert). Mendelssohn, formerly the most favored composer, has fallen into a not entirely deserved eclipse from which he seems to be re-emerging. Weber's sonatas also could be put to use as a relief from the monotony of many recital programs.

About 1870 the national composers began to make their novel contribution to the piano repertory, with Edvard Grieg as the pioneer. Relatively easy to play and yet highly effective, his pieces, as well as those of Dvořák, Smetana, MacDowell, Albéniz, Granados, and De Falla, are greatly favored by players and listeners. The contrary can be said of Max Reger and Ferruccio Busoni. Grandiose compositions such as the former's *Variations and Fugue on a Theme by Bach* or the latter's *Fantasia Contrappuntistica*, though extremely interesting, make technical and intellectual demands on the performer that are out of proportion to their general appeal.

Alexander Scriabin's Etudes and Sonatas are largely in the same category. Debussy, on the other hand, developed a very attractive piano style and succeeded in exploiting entirely novel resources of the instrument [see Impressionism]. His coloristic technique left its imprint on the works of Ravel as well as numerous other composers of the 20th century.

IV. *The 20th century*. At the outset of this period stand Arnold Schoenberg's *Drei Klavierstücke* op. 11 (1909), whose *atonality shocked the musical world of the time, as did his *Sechs kleine Klavierstücke* op. 19 (1911). The piano literature of the ensuing three decades reflects, of course, the general trends that characterize this extremely tumultuous and varied period. A central position is held by Béla Bartók, who as early as 1908 (*14 Bagatellen* op. 6) exploited the "percussive" effects of the piano (see also his *Allegro barbaro* of 1911), and whose *Mikrokosmos* (6 vols., 1926–37), consisting of 153 short pieces, is a veritable manual of 20th-century pianism in all its aspects. Other outstanding contributions include Hindemith's *Reihe kleiner Stücke* op. 37 (1927), three Sonatas (1936), and *Ludus tonalis* (1943), and Stravinsky's Sonata (1924) and *Serenade en la* (1925). The avant-garde tendencies of serial and electronic music are reflected in the extremely complicated piano scores of O. Messiaen, P. Boulez, and K. Stockhausen (1950 and later).

Lit. *General:* H. Westerby, *The History of Pianoforte Music* (1924); C. G. Hamilton, *Piano Music, Its Composers and Characteristics* (1925); W. Apel, *Masters of the Keyboard* (1947); J. Friskin and I. Freundlich, *Music for the Piano ... 1580 to 1952* [1954]; A. Ruthardt, *Wegweiser durch die Klavier-Literatur* (1925); K. Dale, *Nineteenth-Century Piano Music* (1954); W. Georgii, *Klaviermusik,* rev. ed., 2 vols. (1950); G. Schünemann, *Geschichte der Klaviermusik,* rev. ed. (1953); A. Prosniz, *Handbuch der Klavier-Literatur,* 2 vols. (1907, '08); A. Cortot, *La Musique française de piano,* 3 vols. (1944).

For I: C. F. H. Parent, *Répertoire encyclopédique du pianiste,* 2 vols. (1900, '07); F. Torrefranca, *Le Origini italiane del romanticismo musicale* (1930); C. Parrish, "The Early Piano" (diss. Harvard Univ., 1939); R. Harding, "The Earliest Pianoforte Music" (*ML* xiii, 195); G. de Saint-Foix, "Les Premiers Pianistes parisiens" (*RM* 1922, no. 10; 1923, no. 6; 1924, no. 8; 1925, nos. 8, 10). *For II:* H. Abert, "Joseph Haydns Klavierwerke" (*ZMW* ii); *id.,* "Joseph Haydns Klaviersonaten" (*ZMW* iii); John F. Porte,

"Mozart's Pianoforte Works" (*ML* vii, 374). *For III:* K. Westphal, "Der romantische Klavierstil" (*DM* xxii, no. 2). *For IV:* R. Teichmüller and K. Herrmann, *Internationale moderne Klaviermusik* (1927); W. Apel, "Neue Klaviermusik" (*DM* xxiv, nos. 3, 7); E. J. Dent, "The Pianoforte and Its Influence on Modern Music" (*MQ* ii). See also under Harpsichord music; Keyboard music; Organ music; Sonata; Concerto; Character piece.

Piano playing. Although there is some disagreement among artists and teachers as to how the piano should be played, many basic, universally accepted rules for pianism have been determined. It is surprising, therefore, that many piano teachers (and, as a result, many pianists) are ignorant of some of these basic principles, particularly those that have been developed and accepted in the last hundred years.

I. *The playing apparatus.* The pianist uses a flexible system of levers (fingers, hand, forearm, upper arm, torso) connected by four joints (knuckles, wrist, elbow, shoulder). Sound is produced by moving: (a) the fingers from the knuckles; (b) the hand from the wrist; (c) the forearm from the elbow; (d) the upper arm from the shoulder. The first of these, the *finger action,* is by far the most important and is the basis of piano technique. The second, *wrist action,* is useful for playing passages in light, quick staccato, e.g., rapid octaves. The elbow is important mainly because it permits a rocking action of the forearm necessary for tremolos and Alberti bass figures. In the older school a straight downward movement of the forearm, called "elbow staccato," was taught, but this is of little value since it causes the fingers to make a circular motion. Such waste is avoided by using *arm action,* in which the whole arm moves from the shoulder, enabling the hand to rise vertically above the keys and then drop from a greater or lesser distance. This technique is important for the execution of powerful fortissimo chords. While the other actions (finger, wrist, and elbow) require muscular activity, arm action is executed by relaxing the muscles and using the weight of the arm.

II. *Basic piano technique.* In addition to the four actions described above, there is a fifth method of producing sound, which might be called "minimized arm action": the finger is placed on the key, and the arm is slightly raised and then relaxed as in the visible arm action. This method produces a "singing" tone and

allows for minute control of dynamic nuances not otherwise obtained. This action is by no means restricted to producing single tones, but can be used for rapid passages if it is combined with "minimized finger action" (the fingers constantly touching the keys) and with a transfer of the arm's weight from one finger to the next. This "close technique" (which is much easier to learn than to describe) is the basic technique of truly accomplished piano playing. Only through this technique do melodies sound like a "living organism" rather than the dead sum of so many single notes, which is the inevitable result of pure finger action. If it is combined with a rotating movement of the hand, rapid figures (e.g., quick turns), difficult and unsatisfactory when played by the fingers alone, become easy. In fact, all the other movements of levers and joints find their proper place naturally and easily within the basic frame of this technique. Thus the stiffness so often found in older methods of playing is eliminated at the outset.

Although the systematic teaching of the close-finger and arm-weight techniques is relatively new, there is no doubt that the great pianists of earlier periods used them. Particularly informative in this respect is Forkel's description of Bach's playing (*Ueber Johann Sebastian Bachs Leben, Kunst und Kunstwerke,* 1802; new ed. 1925, pp. 28ff): "According to Bach's manner ... the five fingers are curved so that ... each of them is placed immediately above its respective key. This position requires that the finger should not *fall down* on the key nor (as is frequently done) be *thrown,* but merely should be *carried* through the movement with a certain feeling of security and mastery."

The discovery of arm-weight playing and its revolutionary possibilities led some pedagogues to an extreme reaction against the pure finger method of the older school. Such a radical point of view, however, is unwise. Finger development is the most important factor in piano playing, and thus the finger exercises of the old school still have a legitimate place in modern piano instruction, their main function being to develop strong, independent fingers that can support the arm's weight and direct it to the individual key. There are, however, cases in which more active finger participation (i.e., lifting them higher) is desirable in order to bring out, e.g., the crispness and brilliancy required by Mozart or the dry and percussive sound called for in the music of Bartók, Hindemith, Stravinsky, and others. The trill is perhaps the only figure that calls for pure finger action. Its brilliant execution is therefore one of the most difficult feats of piano playing.

III. *The wrist.* The proper use of the wrist in piano playing is often neglected. The smooth combination of a supple, flexible wrist with pre-hensile fingers is indispensable. One of the most useful functions of the wrist is in shaping a musical phrase. The general principle is to begin a phrase with the wrist at keyboard level, gradually lift the wrist as the phrase develops, and drop it again as the phrase comes to an end. With a tapering phrase, however, the wrist should be lifted toward the end. Sideways motions of the wrist are also important. They are used mainly for widely spaced broken-chord figures, e.g., in Chopin's A-flat Etude. The principle is to move the wrist (almost ahead of the fingers) in such a way that each finger, if called into action, forms the straight prolongation of the arm. In playing chords the wrist acts as a shock absorber. For percussive and harsh effects, a stiff wrist may be used, but as a rule the wrist should be flexible and elastic to make the sound full and sonorous. In octave-playing the wrist may be used in one of two ways: light, quick octaves require an up-and-down movement of a flexible wrist (particularly for octave repetitions on the same keys), while octave passages in forte or fortissimo call for arm action combined with a fixed wrist.

IV. *Sense of touch.* Many difficulties in elementary piano instruction result from the teacher's failure to develop the pupil's sense of touch on the keys. Beginners, trying to find a note, may fall into the habit of shifting their eyes constantly up and down between music page and keyboard. The hesitations that mar the playing of otherwise promising students are often caused by this habit. While trying to avoid such hesitations, students may develop the even more detrimental habit of haphazardly playing from memory. The only remedy is to show the pupil how to find the intervals (third, fifth, octave, etc.) through his sense of touch, i.e., without looking at the keys. Wide jumps (which for this reason should be avoided in the first two or three years of piano playing) are an exception to the rule. How much a well-developed sense of touch facilitates sight-reading is obvious [see Sight-reading III].

V. *Touch and tone quality.* The word "touch" is widely used in piano teaching to denote (somewhat vaguely) the method of producing different tone qualities, ranging from soft and lyrical to harsh and percussive. The theory of touch assumes that the piano permits not only dynamic gradations of sound (*pp, p, mf,* etc.), but at a given

intensity, additional variations of timbre so that *mf* may be, e.g., "lyrical," "decisive," or "percussive." Whether this is possible or not is a hotly contested issue. One group holds that the percussive noise accompanying the attack of a tone determines its quality (timbre) and proposes that, by varying the speed and force of finger action, different timbres can be produced in each dynamic register. The other group holds that no such variation is possible with a single sound ("a piano key struck by Paderewski and the same key struck by an umbrella sound absolutely the same"), and that the varieties of timbre noticeable in the playing of accomplished pianists result from the relationship of varying intensities produced either simultaneously (as in chords) or successively (as in melodies). In any case, the perception of tone quality, even if not scientifically measurable, is an important illusion.

VI. *Mental approach.* Certain mental processes are as important as the purely technical methods: "Brains as well as hands play the piano" [see T. Fielden, in *PMA* lix]. Particularly important is a "look-ahead" attitude, a mental anticipation of the actual playing by the fingers. A well-developed sense of touch is the first step in this direction. Difficult passages are mastered by "positioning" the hand, i.e., analyzing the changing hand positions needed for a passage, and using preparatory hand movements that lead to the new position while the fingers are still occupied in the old one. Another application of the same principle is the so-called "long hand," or "pre"-formation of wide skips often encountered in left-hand accompaniments.

VII. *History.* Information about 16th-century keyboard technique (clavichord, organ) is contained in Tomás de Santa María's *Llibro llamado arte de tañer Fantasia* (1565; see O. Kinkeldey, *Orgel und Klavier in der Musik des 16. Jahrhunderts,* 1910) and in Girolamo Diruta's *Il Transilvano* (1593, 1609). Extremely difficult passages occur in the works of the *virginal composers, particularly those of John Bull (rapid scales in parallel thirds for the left hand, repeated notes, etc.). J. S. Bach contributed to the development of a modern fingering system [see Fingering], whereas his contemporary, Domenico Scarlatti (1685–1757), explored the virtuoso resources of the harpsichord to the fullest (crossing hands, wide skips, extensive arpeggios).

The "old school" of piano playing (emphasizing finger technique) is represented by M. Clementi (1752–1832), J. N. Hummel (1778–1837), and C. Czerny (1791–1857). Beethoven, Chopin,

Liszt, and Anton Rubinstein were probably in full command of the advanced methods of modern pianism, but Ludwig Deppe (1828–90) was the first to point out the importance of armweight [see Amy Fay, *Music-Study in Germany, c.* 1880]. T. Leschetizky (1830–1915) established systematic training in the new playing style. R. Breithaupt (1873–1945) introduced the principles of relaxation, *Rollung* (rolling and rotating hand movements), positioning, and coordination of finger and arm, but had a tendency to underestimate the importance of finger training. The same applied to the relaxation school of T. Matthay (1858–1945) who, with his emphasis on freedom and suppleness, to some extent discredited a good cause. See Fingering.

Lit.: G. Gát, *The Technique of Piano Playing* [1958]; W. S. Newman, *The Pianist's Problems* (1950); M. Brée, *The Groundwork of the Leschetitzky Method,* rev. ed. (1905); R. M. Breithaupt, *Natural Pianotechnic* (1909; original G. ed. 1905); T. A. Matthay, *The Act of Touch in All Its Diversity* (1903); *id., The Visible and Invisible in Pianoforte Technique* (1932); O. R. Ortmann, *The Physiological Mechanics of Piano Technique* (1929); M. Levinskaya, *The Levinskaya System of Pianoforte Technique and Tone-colour* (1930); Arnold Schultz, *The Riddle of the Pianist's Finger* (1936); Y. Bowen, *Pedalling the Modern Pianoforte* (1936); J. Dichler, *Der Weg zum künstlerischen Klavierspiel* [1948]; C. A. Martienssen, *Die individuelle Klaviertechnik* (1930); W. Bardas, *Zur Psychologie der Klaviertechnik* (1927); F. A. Steinhausen, *Ueber die physiologischen Fehler und die Umgestaltung der Klaviertechnik* (1905); H. Klose, *Die Deppesche Lehre des Klavierspiels* (1886); T. Fielden, "The History of the Evolution of Pianoforte Technique" (*PMA* lix).

Piano quartet. See under Quartet.

Piano-violin. See Sostenente piano.

Piatti [It.]. Cymbals.

Pibgorn, pibcorn. See under Clarinet family IV; Reed II. See H. L. Balfour, in *Journal of the Anthropological Institute* xx, 142ff.

Pibroch. A type of Scottish bagpipe music consisting of highly ornamented variations on a theme called *urlar.* They were formerly written in a curious notation called *canntaireachd,* in which syllables such as *em, en, dari, dili,* etc. stand for tones or stereotyped motifs. See J. P. Grant, in *ML* vi, 54–63; A. Mackay, *A Collection of Ancient Piobaireachd,* rev. ed. (1839; repr. 1899).

Picardy third [F. *tierce de Picardie*]. The major third as used for the final chord of a composition in a minor key. This practice originated *c.* 1500 when, for the first time, the third was admitted in the final chord of a piece. An early example is in Tromboncino's *frottola* "Non val aqua" of *c.* 1500 [see *HAM,* no. 95]. The extent to which it was used prior to 1550 is difficult to assess, this being largely a problem of **musica ficta.* In the second half of the 16th century the practice became fairly common. In A. Willaert's *Musica nova* of 1559 the final chord always includes the major third, in plagal as well as in authentic cadences. The Picardy third continued to be used until the end of the baroque period (*c.* 1750). No plausible explanation has been found for the name "tierce de Picardie," first used in J.-J. Rousseau's *Dictionnaire de musique* (1767).

Piccolo [It.]. Abbr. for piccolo flute; see Flute I (b).

Pickelflöte [G.]. Older name for piccolo flute. The modern German name is *kleine Flöte.*

Pictures at an Exhibition. Collection of descriptive piano pieces by M. P. Mussorgsky, composed in 1874. Each piece illustrates a picture by the Russian painter Victor A. Hartmann (d. 1873) shown at a memorial exhibition of his paintings in 1874. The highly "picturesque" pieces are preceded and connected by a recurring "promenade" theme suggesting the walk from one picture to the next. The work is usually heard in an orchestral version by Ravel.

Piedi [It.]. See under *Ballata.*

Pien. In *Chinese music *pien* (pronounced *biann*) denotes the two tones that are a semitone below the fifth degree and the octave note respectively on a diatonic scale. Thus they are f♯ and b on a scale from c to c′. The term is often used by modern writers with reference to other kinds of music [see Gregorian chant V] in which certain degrees of the scale are considered less important than others and therefore are treated as mere ornamental or passing tones.   R.C.P.

Pièno [It.]. Full; *organo pieno,* full organ; *a voce piena,* with full voice.

Pierrot lunaire [F., Pierrot in the Moonlight]. Cycle of twenty-one short pieces for a "singing narrator" (*Sprechstimme) and chamber orchestra (flute, violin, clarinet, cello, piano, etc.) by

A. Schoenberg, op. 21 (1912), based on poems by A. Giraud in a German translation by O. E. Hartleben. The poems, highly decadent and macabre (one of them describes Pierrot contentedly smoking tobacco out of a human skull), are composed in a novel melodramatic style, accompanied at times by the full group of instruments and sometimes by only one or two.

Piffero [It.]. Old term for various popular wind instruments, such as the shawm, fife, and bagpipe, all of which were used by shepherds. Hence, the name *pifferari* for the peasants who, in the 18th century, went to Rome every Christmas morning to play there in imitation of the Biblical shepherds. Berlioz still heard them. For *pifferari*, see Pastorale.

Pincé [F.]. (1) See under Mordent. (2) Term for plucked instruments (lute, harp, etc.) and for pizzicato.

Pini di Roma [It., Pines of Rome]. Symphonic poem by Respighi (1924), depicting four musical "landscapes" near Rome (the Villa Borghese, a catacomb, the Janiculum [a hill named after the god Janus], and the Appian Way). In the third section a recording of the song of an actual nightingale is introduced.

Piobaireachd [Gael.]. *Pibroch.

P'ip'a. See Pyiba.

Pipe. (1) A small instrument of the recorder type that was held and played with the left hand only, while the right hand played the tabor, a small drum. [For ill. see under Percussion instruments.] The playing of the pipe and tabor [Prov. *galoubet* and *tambourin*; Sp. *flaviol* and *tamboril;* Cat. *fluviol* and *tambori*] was popular as early as the 13th century, as is shown by the famous miniatures of the Cantigas MSS of the Escorial [ill. in *GDB* iii, opp. p. 176; iv, opp. p. 500]. It was the usual accompaniment to the *farandole* and the English morris dance, and is still used for the Spanish *sardana*. See D. Fryklund, *Le Galoubet provençal* (1939). (2) Generic name for various groups of instruments: all the *wind instruments; the woodwinds; the flutes; the pipes of the organ; primitive instruments in the shape of a simple tube.

Pique Dame [F.]. See *Queen of Spades, The.*

Piston. Piston valve [see Valve].

Pitch. (1) [F. *hauteur;* G. *Tonhöhe;* It. *intonazione;* Sp. *entonación*]. The location of a musical sound in the tonal scale, proceeding from low to high. The exact determination of pitch is by frequency (number of vibrations per second) of the sound; see Acoustics I. Pitch as a physiological sensation also depends to a small degree on other factors (e.g., intensity), which are, however, negligible from the musical point of view; see Stevens and Davis, *Hearing* (1938).

(2) [F. *diapason;* G. *Kammerton, Stimmung;* It. *diapason;* Sp. *diapasón*]. The absolute pitch of one specific note, standardized for the purpose of obtaining identical pitches on all instruments. The present-day standard of pitch is a′ = 440 (double) vibrations (cycles) per second. This standard was universally adopted in 1939 by an international conference held in London under the auspices of the International Standards Association. It replaced the old standard of 435 that had been fixed by the Paris Academy in 1859 (*diapason normal*) and confirmed, under the term "international pitch," at a conference held in Vienna in 1885.

Before these agreements there was a confusing variety of pitches. Bach frequently had to transpose his orchestral and choral parts owing to different tuning of organs in various churches, or had to score woodwind parts in C, for example, while the parts for organ, voices, and strings were scored in A (a different scoring for voices and strings was unnecessary since these could easily be adapted to the pitch of the organ). These discrepancies resulted from the use throughout the baroque period of different pitch levels for different ensembles: *Kammerton* (chamber pitch) for domestic instrumental music; *Chorton* (choir pitch, organ pitch) for church organs and, consequently, for sacred choral music; *Cornett-ton* for the brass instruments used by town musicians. The confusion in this matter has been compounded by numerous modern writers concerned more with terminology than with historical fact [see, e.g., the contradictory statements in H. Riemann, *Musiklexikon,* 11th ed., 1929, pp. 316 and 856]. By far the clearest account, though not trustworthy in every detail, is found in N. Bessaraboff, *Ancient European Musical Instruments* (1941), pp. 357–59, 377–78, and 442. Following his suggestion, the different pitches are represented below by pitch names (disregarding microtonic deviations), the standard pitch of the present day (a′ = 440) being represented by the key of C. The standard pitches used during the baroque period were as follows:

	Praetorius (*De Organographia,* 1619)	Common designation after Praetorius
B♭	*Tertia minore*	*Tief Kammerton*
B	*Chorton*	*Hoch Kammerton*
C♯	*Kammerton*	*Chorton*
D	*Cornett-ton*	*Cornett-ton*

The names in the right column are used below.

The *hoch Kammerton* must be regarded as the standard instrumental pitch from *c.* 1700 to *c.* 1820. Thus, Bach's instrumental compositions (as well as the symphonies of Haydn, Mozart, and Beethoven) sounded a semitone lower than they do when performed today [see Absolute pitch]. On the other hand, his organ works and cantatas (which involved organ participation) sounded a semitone or even a whole tone higher than today. Following is a list of some characteristic data covering the period from *c.* 1700 to 1850:

	Pitch	Date	Source
B♭	396	1716	Strasbourg, Silbermann organ
B	422	1751	Handel's tuning fork
	422	1780	Mozart's tuning fork
	427	1811	Paris, *Grand opéra*
C	440	1834	Scheibler (Stuttgart pitch)
	446	1856	Paris, *Grand opéra*

Long lists given by A. J. Ellis and N. Bessaraboff also include pitches from earlier centuries but their accuracy is highly questionable. For instance, Ellis' calculations of the "low" and "high" organ pitch in Arnolt Schlick's *Spiegel der Orgelmacher* (1511) have been rejected by Kendall, and Kendall's calculations by Mendel. Lit.: A. J. Ellis, *The History of Musical Pitch* 1880); N. Bessaraboff [see above]; W. L. Sumner, "A History of Musical Pitch" (*Hinrichsen's Musical Year Book* vii [1952], 233ff); R. Kendall, "Notes on Arnold Schlick" (*AM* xi); R. Mendel, "Pitch in the 16th and Early 17th Centuries" (four parts in *MQ* xxxiv); *id.*, "On the Pitches in Use in Bach's Time" (two parts in *MQ* xli, 332ff, 466ff).

Pitch aggregate. A collection or cluster of pitches (usually, but not necessarily, simultaneous). See under Aleatory music.

Pitch names. I. The accompanying table gives the English, German, French, Italian, and Spanish names for the tones of an octave.

English:	C	D	E	F	G	A	B
German:	C	D	E	F	G	A	H
French:	ut	ré	mi	fa	sol	la	si
Italian:	do	re	mi	fa	sol	la	si
Spanish:	do	re	mi	fa	sol	la	si

English:	C-sharp	C-flat
German:	cis	ces
French:	ut dièse	ut bémol
Italïan:	do diesis	do bemolle
Spanish:	do sostenido	do bemol

English:	C-double-sharp	C-double-flat
German:	cisis	ceses
French:	ut double-dièse	ut double-bémol
Italian:	do doppio diesis	do doppio bemolle
Spanish:	do doble sostenido	do doble bemol

Note that in German a sharp is denoted by the suffix *-is* and a flat by the suffix *-es,* a double-sharp by *-isis* and a double-flat by *-eses.* Irregular formations are: *B,* B-flat, instead of *Hes; Es,* E-flat, instead of *Ees; As,* A-flat, instead of *Aes.* Note particularly that the English B is in German *H* (pronounced *hah*), and that the English B-flat is in German *B.*

II. Unfortunately there is no uniform practice for indicating different octaves. The accompanying table shows the system employed in this dictionary and widely used elsewhere (1), together with two others, (2) and (3). The chief source of confusion is that some writers designate middle c (the C in the middle of the keyboard) by c′ and

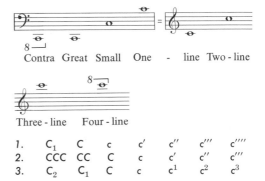

1.	C₁	C	c	c′	c″	c‴	c⁗
2.	CCC	CC	C	c	c′	c″	c‴
3.	C₂	C₁	C	c	c¹	c²	c³

others by c. Method (3) is perhaps the simplest and most logical; however, it has not been widely accepted. See R. W. Young, in *Journal of Musicology* i, no. 2, pp. 5–8.

For other systems of pitch designation, see Solmization; Letter notation.

Pitch pipe. (A device used since the 18th (17th?) century to set the pitch for a choir or to tune stringed instruments. In its early form it was a wooden pipe with a movable stopper that made it possible to raise or lower the sound according to graduated marks. Present-day pitch pipes, used mostly by amateurs, are in the form of a disk containing a free reed whose length can be regulated, or consist of a number of pipes giving the pitches of, e.g., the strings of a guitar. The most accurate device, used for professional tuning, is the tuning fork.

Più [It.]. More; *più allegro,* more quickly; *piuttosto allegro,* rather quick.

Più tosto. See *Tosto.*

Piva. (1) An Italian term for bagpipe. (2) The fastest measure (*misura*) or step unit of the *bassa dansa* (*basse danse*). It consisted of a series of rapid steps (*passetti presti*) embellished by leaps and turns. In one of the dances, Domenico da Piacenza suggested that three measures of the *piva* be danced in a herringbone or zigzag pattern. (3) One of the fastest dances of the early 16th century. Seven examples of music survive in Dalza's *Intabulatura de lauto* (Petrucci, iv, 1508), where they appear as the third dance of a suite including a *pavane, a *saltarello,* and a *piva.* All are in compound quadruple meter (12/8). The last dances of the other two suites in the collection are of the same genre as the *piva* but are called *spingardo.* One isolated *piva* in the *Intabolatura di lauto* of M. Barberüs (ix, 1549) is in the 6/8 meter of a *saltarello* or galliard.

For a detailed description and bibl., see L. H. Moe in *MGG* x, 1313–15.   L.H.M.

Pivot chord. See under Modulation.

Pizzicato [It.; abbr. *pizz.*]. For violins (violas, etc.), indication that the string is to be plucked with the finger, as it regularly is in guitars, harps, etc. The earliest known use of pizzicato occurs in Monteverdi's *Combattimento di Tancredi e Clorinda* (1624), where it is indicated by the remark: "Qui si lascia l'arco e si strappano le corde con duoi ditti" (Here the bow is laid aside and the strings are plucked with two fingers; see *HAM,* no. 189). Other early instances of the technique occur in Reinhard Keiser's *Adonis* (1697) and Handel's operas *Agrippina* (1709) and *Il Pastor fido* (1712), Paganini introduced the virtuoso technique of plucking the strings with the left hand in alternation or simultaneously with bowed tones.

Placido [It.]. Calm, tranquil.

Plagal cadence [G. *Plagalschluss*]. The cadence with the subdominant preceding the tonic: IV–I. This cadence, also known as the Amen cadence because it was traditionally used for the "Amen" at the end of hymns, was prominent in early music (15th, 16th centuries). It became obsolete or archaic during the 18th and 19th centuries and again became important in 20th-century music, particularly in the works of Hindemith. This revival is concomitant with the modern aversion to the leading tone, which is the characteristic note of the authentic cadence. See Cadence.

Plagalis, plagius [L.]. A plagal mode; e.g., *primus plagius,* first plagal mode. See Church modes.

Plainchant. Another name for; see plainsong, Gregorian chant.

Plain-chant musical [F.]. A 17th-century French type of plainsong, characterized by the use of more "expressive" melodic progressions than in Gregorian chant, of accidentals (leading tone), and of strictly measured note values (half and quarter notes) in the free arrangement of "multimetric rhythm" [see Rhythm II (b)]. The rhythmic principles in *plain-chant musical* are obviously derived from the *vers mesuré* of the 16th century. *Plain-chant musical* originated *c.* 1620 and spread all over France in the 17th and 18th centuries but is now extinct. Henri Dumont (*Cinq Messes en plein-chant,* 1701), F. Bourgoing, Chastelain, and G. Nivers wrote many melodies

Kyrie

(all monophonic) in this style [see Ex.: beginning of a "Messe royale" by Dumont, which was included as "Missa regia" in the *Liber gradualis* of 1895, ed. Dom Pothier]. See A. Gastoué, in *TG* ix, 81–92; *id., Cours . . . de chant grégorien* (1917), pp. 84ff; H. Quittard, *Un Musicien en France . . . Henry du Mont* (1906), pp. 175ff.

Plainsong. Term derived from *cantus planus,* a 13th-century name for *Gregorian chant. It is used synonymously with the latter, but also is employed as a generic term for the ancient style of monophonic and rhythmically free melody that is common to various Western liturgies (Gregorian, *Ambrosian, *Gallican, *Mozarabic chant) as well as of those of the East (Byzantine, Syrian, Armenian chant). It may also be used for similar kinds of non-Christian liturgical music (Jewish, Hindu) in order to indicate that this music is neither harmonic nor strictly measured.

Plainsong and Mediaeval Music Society. See Editions XLIII.

Plainsong Mass. In the proper sense of the word, a monophonic Gregorian Mass, either the Proper, the Ordinary, or both combined. Usually, however, the term is used for a special type of polyphonic Mass composition in which each movement is based on a corresponding item of a Gregorian Mass Ordinary; see Mass C II a. Occasionally it is used for a *cantus firmus* Mass [see Mass C II b] based on any plainsong melody, e.g., *Alma redemptoris mater.*

Plainsong notation. The notation of Gregorian chant; see Neumes. The term has also been used for the notation of medieval secular monophony [G. *Choralnotation*]; see Monophonic notation.

Plainte [F.]. (1) See Lament (2). (2) A baroque ornament, either a *portamento (in 17th-century viol music) or a *Nachschlag.

Plaisanterie [F.]. Name for a playful movement in the suites of the 18th century; also, a collection of pieces in the light style of *rococo.

Planc, planh [Prov.], **planctus** [L.]. See Lament (2).

Planets, The. Programmatic suite for orchestra, organ, and women's chorus by G. Holst (1914–16), describing in successive movements the astrological nature of seven planets.

Plantation songs. See under Negro music.

Plaqué [F.]. Indication for notes of a chord to be played simultaneously, as opposed to *arpeggio.

Plate numbers. A device used by publishers to keep track of the engraved metal plates from which music was printed. The plate numbers appear as small figures, usually at the bottom of pages. Some publishers, e.g., Pleyel, also used letters to identify their plates. Plate numbers often enable musicologists to date a composition fairly precisely when no other chronological evidence is available.

Lit.: O. E. Deutsch, *Music Publishers' Numbers* (1946; G. ed. 1961); O. W. Neighbour and A. Tyson, *English Music Publishers' Plate Numbers in the First Half of the Nineteenth Century* (1965); A. Zakin, "Pleyel's Plate Numbers" (New York Public Library, 1966); R. S. Hill, "The Plate Numbers of C. F. Peters' Predecessors" (*PAMS* 1938); K. Meyer and I. M. Christensen, "Artaria Plate Numbers" (*Notes,* no. 15); W. B. Squire, "Publishers' Numbers" (*SIM* xv).   J.LaR.

Platerspiel [G.]. Old term for bladder pipe; see Bagpipe.

Player piano. See under Mechanical instruments IV. Also see S. Grew, *The Art of the Player-Piano* (1922).

Plectrum. A small piece of horn, tortoise shell, wood, ivory, metal, etc., used to pluck certain stringed instruments, such as the Greek lyre and the modern mandolin and zither. The quills of the harpsichord are a mechanized form of plectrum.

Plein-jeu [F.]. Full organ. Also, name for pieces written for the full organ. *Demi-jeu,* half organ, i.e., softer registration.

Plena [Sp.]. In Santo Domingo, name used for certain work songs consisting of short lines (sometimes an entire quatrain) sung by a leader and answered by a chorus in meaningless syllables called *chuins.* In Puerto Rico the *plena* shows strong Negro influence, as it does in Santo Domingo, but has developed into a narrative folk ballad about a real event. After each stanza, sung by a soloist, the chorus answers with the same refrain. The music of the Puerto Rican *plena* is in 2/4 meter and usually employs the following rhythmic pattern:

J.O-S.

Plenary Mass [G. *Plenarmesse*]. A polyphonic Mass composition that includes both the Ordinary and the Proper. All *Requiem Masses belong to this type, which otherwise is very rare. Examples are Dufay's *Missa Sancti Jacobi* and the Mass (for Marian feasts) by Reginald Liebert [*DTO* 53], both from the early 15th century.

Plica [L.]. A notational sign of the 13th century calling for an ornamental tone to be inserted following the note to which it is connected. The sign for the *plica* is an upward or downward dash that is attached to single notes (*longa, brevis*) as well as to the final note of a ligature (*ligatura plicata*). The direction of the dash indicates whether the grace note is higher or lower than the main note (usually a second or, more rarely, a third, depending on the position of the next note). The accompanying example shows three *plicae longae*

	Poetic	Musical
Iamb	⌣ – ⌣ –	
Trochee	– ⌣ – ⌣	
Dactyl	– ⌣⌣ – ⌣⌣	
Anapest	⌣⌣ – ⌣⌣ –	
Spondee	– – – –	
Tribrach	⌣⌣⌣ ⌣⌣⌣	

The sign ⌣ indicates a short syllable, the sign — a long one. Each of the examples here includes two feet.

[1, 2, 4], characterized by a longer dash on the right side, two *plicae breves* [3, 7] with a longer dash on the left side or two dashes of about equal length, and two *ligaturae plicatae* [5, 6]. See *ApNPM, passim.*

The *plica* developed from the liquescent *neumes of Gregorian chant. According to 13th-century theorists (Pseudo-Aristoteles; see *GS* i, 173ff) it was sung in a special manner, probably a tremolo [see Tremolo III]. The theory advanced by H. Riemann (*Mus. Wochenblatt,* 1897, p. 17), and adopted by P. Runge (*Die Sanges-weisen der Colmarer Handschrift,* 1896), that the *plica* played a prominent part in the music of the minnesingers is erroneous. The German scribes of the 14th and 15th centuries used notational characters shaped like the *plica* notes of 13th-century music but without their meaning. See H. Anglés, in *CP Fellerer.*

Plut. [L.]. Abbr. for *pluteus,* shelf (of a library).

Pneuma. See *Neuma* (2).

Pneumatic action. See under Organ II.

Pochette [F.]. *Kit.

Poco, un poco [It.]. Little; a little, somewhat. Derivative forms are *pochetto, pochettino, pochissimo.*

Podatus. See under Neumes I.

Poetic meter. I. Poetic meter, with its regular patterns of accented (strong) and unaccented (weak) syllables or, in ancient Greek terminology, of *thesis* and *arsis, is very similar to musical meter with its various schemes of accented and unaccented notes. The terminology of ancient Greek poetry therefore is frequently used for corresponding schemes of musical rhythm. The chief patterns (called "feet") of the Greek system are:

This terminology is used particularly for the 13th-century system of rhythmic modes, in which, however, nearly all the musical schemes differ in some detail from those indicated above [see Modes, rhythmic].

II. According to the number of feet contained in a line of verse, one distinguishes between *dimeter* (two feet), *trimeter* (three), *tetrameter* (four), *pentameter* (five), and *hexameter* (six). For instance, dactylic hexameter (Homer) consists of six dactyls, the last of which usually lacks one *arsis* (*katalectic*): – ⌣ ⌣ – ⌣ ⌣ – ⌣ ⌣ – ⌣ ⌣ – ⌣ ⌣ – ⌣. In classical verse, in the case of an iambic or trochaic foot, however, the numbering proceeds in pairs of feet (*dipody,* i.e., two feet). Thus, a line including four iambs, ⌣ – ⌣ – ⌣ – ⌣ –, is called iambic dimeter (not tetrameter). In hymnody certain standard meters have special names, e.g., *common meter,* indicated thus: 8 6 8 6 (the figures give the numbers of syllables in each line). Here each line may be considered an iambic dimeter, the lines "8" complete, the lines "6" katalectic, with one *arsis* and *thesis* missing at the end.

III. In applying metrical schemes to words (versification), there are two principles that determine on which syllables the *thesis* falls and on which the *arsis,* one ancient and one modern. In ancient poetry the division of lines into feet was quantitative, based on the principle of short and long syllables [G. *Silbenmessung*], whereas in modern poetry the division is accentual, based on the principle of weak and strong syllables [G. *Silbenwägung*]. The former method is indicated by the signs ⌣ –, the latter by × ′.

In modern poetry the *thesis* and *arsis* syllables are essentially the same as they are in prose; in other words, poetic accentuation follows the natural accent of the words, e.g. (for the sake of clarity, secondary accents are omitted here):

´ × × ´ × ´ × ´ × ´ ×
Meantime we shall express our darker purpose

[See *Cursus.*] In Greek and Latin poetry, however, *thesis* and *arsis* were not determined by accent, as the following example shows:

× ´ × ´ × × ´ × × ´ × ×
Prose accent: Maecenas atavis edite regibus

Poetic meter: _ _ _ ◡◡ _| _ ◡◡ _ ◡ ◡

(For the rules governing ancient poetry, see any Greek or Latin grammar.) The early Christian hymns, e.g., those of St. Ambrose, are essentially quantitative, although not always strictly so. Often they are written so that the accents are both quantitative and accentual. The rhymed sequences of the 12th and 13th centuries (Adam de St. Victor; *Stabat mater*) are purely accentual.

IV. The musical sources of the 13th and later centuries often show a disregard for the natural accent. Thus, the iambic verse, "O nátió nefándi génerís," whose poetic structure would suggest the first mode, is cited in the "Discantus positio vulgaris" of *c.* 1225 as an example of the third

´ × × ´ × × ´
mode. hence a dactylic verse: "O nati-o nefan-di

× × ´
gene-ris" [see *CS* i, 96–97]; similarly, Franco of Cologne quotes the verse "Eximie pater et regie," changing the accentuation from × ´ × × ´ × × ´ × × to ´ × × ´ × × ´ × × ´

There are similar ambiguities in the poems of the troubadours and trouvères, owing to the peculiar indifference to accentuation of medieval (and, to some extent, modern) French, in contrast to English or German. Practically all poems in decasyllabic (ten-syllable) lines can be read either as iambic pentameter or as dactylic tetrameter, e.g.:

(a)   × ´ × ´ × ´ ×   ´   × ´
     Quar eusse je cent mile mars d'argent

(b)   ´ × × ´ × × ´ ×   × ´

While (a) is no doubt the correct literary accentuation, the notation of the melody as found in the "Chansonnier Cangé" clearly shows the pattern of the third mode, as under (b) [see J.-B. Beck, *Die Melodien der Troubadours* (1908), pp. 132, 138]. Since the majority of troubadour and trouvère melodies are notated without indication of note values, this ambiguity often presents great difficulties in determining the "cor-

rect" rhythm [see Monophonic notation]. An example in point is the *Reis glorios* of Guiraut de Bornelh (d. *c.* 1250), which has been interpreted both in the first and in the third mode [see *HAM,* no. 18c, versions 1 and 3]. See also Modal theory.

Lit.: C. F. Abdy Williams, "The Aristoxenian Theory of the Rhythmical Foot" (*MA* ii); I. Krohn, "Der metrische Taktfuss in der modernen Musik" (*AMW* iv); F. Rosenthal, "Probleme der musikalischen Metrik" (*ZMW* viii).

Pohjola's Daughter. Symphonic poem by J. Sibelius, op. 49 (1906), based on a story from the *Kalevala.

Poi [It.]. Then, afterward. *Poi la coda,* "then the coda," usually given at the end of the trio to indicate that the resumption of the scherzo is to be followed by the coda: S–T–S–C.

Point. (1) The upper end of the violin bow. (2) Point of perfection, of division, etc. [see *Punctus*]. (3) In the motets of the 16th century, *point of imitation* means a section of the polyphonic texture in which a single subject, connected with a small division of the text, is treated in imitation. These points are the structural parts of the motet, which consists of a succession of them. They are usually marked off diagonally rather than vertically, so that the conclusion of one point overlaps the beginning of the next. Ex. in *HAM,* no. 114; *SchGMB,* no. 107.

Point d'orgue [F.]. (1) The *pause and its sign. (2) *Pedal point. (3) A *cadenza in a concerto, so called because its beginning is customarily indicated by a pause sign placed above the preceding chord of the composition proper.

Pointing. See under Anglican chant.

Polacca [It.]. Generic name for Polish dances, usually the polonaise. However, the "Polacca" in Bach's Brandenburg Concerto no. 1 shows hardly any affinity to the polonaise. See Polonaise.

Poland. I. *To 1600.* Aside from liturgical books, the earliest example of Polish music is the famous war song, "Bogurodzica" (Mother of God), dating from the 13th century [see *MGG* x, 1388]. The earliest known Polish composer is Mikolaj z Radomia (Nicolas of Radom; early 15th cent.), who wrote a Magnificat, three Glorias, and three Credos, all in three-part writing [see F. Ludwig, in *AMW* vii, 430]. A continuous development in Polish music began in the 16th century with Sebastian of Felsztyn (b. *c.* 1480), who wrote motets, hymns, and a Mass, all in Flemish style, and published several theoretical books between 1519 and 1543. He was followed by Waclaw Szamotulczyk (psalms), Martinus Leopolita (Martin Lwowczyk; 1540–89), Thomas Szadek, and Mikolaj Gomolka (*c.* 1535–1609), all brought up in the tradition of the Flemish school or, later, of Palestrina. In 1543, King Sigismund I founded the *Rorantists chapel. Three organ tablatures (Tablature of Johannes of Lublin, 1537–48; Tablature of Cracow, 1548; Tablature of Warsaw [Krasinski Libr.], also called T. of Martin Leopolita, *c.* 1580) contain *c.* 400 keyboard compositions, liturgical organ music, intabulations of vocal music, preludes, dances, etc. Toward the end of the 16th century Polish dances appeared at the Saxon court, as is shown by a number of pieces ("Polnischer Tantz") contained in the tablature of Nörmiger of 1599 [see Colorists]. Their music, however, does not show any specific national traits.

II. *1600–1900.* Under King Sigismund III (1587–1632), Venetian polychoral music was cultivated at the Warsaw court and at numerous private chapels of the nobility. About 1625, opera was established at the court, under the direction of Marco Scacchi (1602–*c.* 1685) of Rome. Noteworthy composers of vocal and instrumental music were M. Zieleński, A. Jarzębski, M. Mielczewski, B. Pękiel, J. Rózycki, S. Szarzyński, and G. G. Gorczycki (*c.* 1664–1734). About 1700, many Christmas songs were written [see Koleda].

During the first half of the 18th century, when Poland was ruled by the Kings of Saxony (Augustus II, Augustus III), musical activity declined considerably. The Polish opera came to new life under Mathias Kamienski (1734–1821), who between 1780 and 1800 composed numerous operas in the style of the *Singspiel. Josef Kozlowski (1757–1821) is interesting mainly as a composer of numerous *polonaises, as is his pupil, Prince Michael Oginski (1765–1833). Joseph Elsner, known mainly for being Chopin's teacher, wrote numerous operas of which only the titles have been preserved, as well as symphonies, chamber music, songs, and a famous Passion oratorio. He also founded the first conservatory at Warsaw (1820), where Chopin studied. Even more important was Karol Kurpinski (1785–1857), a composer of operas, conductor, and teacher. The foremost instrumental composer of the "classical" period of Polish

music was Ignacy Feliks Dobrzyński (1807–67; two symphonies, chamber music).

Frédéric Chopin (1810–49), whose father was French and mother Polish, was the first to make Polish music famous throughout the world. Along with Schumann and Mendelssohn he founded romanticism, to which he imparted a distinct national tinge, particularly in his polonaises and *mazurkas. Stanislaw Moniuszko (1819–72) wrote numerous songs, many of which became a part of the national treasure of Poland. His opera *Halka* (1848; expanded 1858) is the first Polish national opera. Five of his fifteen operas belong to the permanent repertory of Polish opera houses. His most important successor was Wladyslaw Zelenski (1837–1921), who composed operas of some merit but deserves mention mainly for his chamber music in a moderately romantic style, influenced by Schumann and Mendelssohn. Henryk Wieniawski (1835–80) became world-famous as a violin virtuoso and composed two well-known violin concertos as well as other pieces for his instrument. Ignacy Jan Paderewski (1860–1941) occupied a similar place in piano music, to say nothing of his outstanding position in Polish political life.

III. *1900—.* The next generation is represented mainly by Karol Szymanowski (1882–1937), an outstanding modern composer. Successively influenced by R. Strauss, Scriabin, and, after World War I, Debussy, he arrived, *c.* 1920, at a mature style of his own, a mixture of romantic and impressionist elements but at the same time consciously Polish, and in his latest works, tending towards atonality and constructivism. Among his most important works are a Stabat mater, the ballet *Harnasie* (1926), a Symphonie Concertante for piano and orchestra, and his Second Violin Concerto (1933). Ludomir Rózycki (1883–1953) was celebrated as both teacher and composer. Other important modern composers are Karol Rathaus (1895–1954) and Aleksander Tansman (b. 1897), who both emigrated to the U.S. in the 1940's, Stanislaw Wiechowicz (1893–1963) and Tadeusz Szeligowski (b. 1896), who became interested in neoclassicism, as did Jerzy Fitelberg (1903–51), Roman Palester (b. 1907), and Michal Spisak (b. 1914). Witold Lutoslawski (b. 1913) is a popular present-day composer of Poland. Since 1955 a number of composers have taken advantage of more open contact with the West. Lutoslawski, T. Baird, K. Serocki, and others have incorporated the new influences into their styles. The avant-garde, represented by W. Szalonek (b. 1927), W. Kilar (b. 1932), H. Górecki (b. 1933), and K. Penderecki (b. 1933), have been strongly influenced by Western developments yet continue to show imagination and individuality in their compositions.

Lit.: E. Rayson, *Polish Music and Chopin Its Laureate* (1916); Z. Lissa, *Music in Poland, 1945–55* (1955); *LavE* i.5, 2568–85; A. Wieniawski, *La Musique polonaise* (1937); H. Opienski, *La Musique polonaise* (1918, '29); M. Glinskiego, *Muzyka polska* (1927); Z. Jachimecki, *Historja muzyki polskiej* (1920); id., "Polish Music" (*MQ* vi). For I: ReMR, pp. 741–57; J. M. Chomiński and Z. Lissa, ‡*Music of the Polish Renaissance* (1955); *Editions LIII; *Editions XI, 6; A. Chybiński, "Über die polnische mehrstimmige Musik des 16. Jahrhunderts" (*CP Riemann*); id., "Polnische Musik ... des 16. Jahrhunderts in ihren Beziehungen zu Deutschland" (*SIM* xiii); id., "Die Musikbestände der Krakauer Bibliotheken von 1500–1650" (*SIM* xiii); id., ‡*36 Tänze aus der Orgeltabulatur des Johannes de Lublin* (1950); Z. Jachimecki, "Eine polnische Orgeltabulatur aus dem Jahre 1548" (*ZMW* ii); J. W. Reiss, "N. Gomołka und seine Psalmen-Melodien" (*ZIM* xiii); F. Starczewski, in *SIM* ii (dances); T. Norlind, in *SIM* xii (dances); J. R. White, in *MD* xvii (Lublin tablature). For II: H. Opienski, in *CP 1911*, pp. 146–49, and in *RdM* 1929, pp. 92–8 (opera); id., in *RdM* 1934, pp. 193–96 (symphony). For III: Z. Jachimecki, in *AdHM* ii, 1144–51; M. Glinski, "La Jeune Musique polonaise" (*RM* 1931, no. 117); S. Jarociński, "Polish Music after World War II" (*LBCM,* also *MQ* li).

rev. J.S.

Polka. A Bohemian dance in quick duple meter with characteristic rhythms. It originated *c.* 1830 in Bohemia and soon spread to the European salons, causing a veritable "polkamania" that lasted until the end of the century. The polka was introduced into art music by Smetana (*The Bartered Bride; From My Life; Bohemian Dances*), Dvořák, and others. See Dance music IV..

The polka Paraguaya is an offshoot of the European polka in which the accompaniment has triplet rhythm against the binary meter used in the melody. A common pattern is the following:

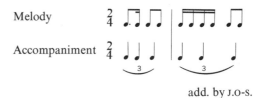

add. by J.O-S.

Polo. An Andalusian (south Spanish) dance in moderate 3/8 meter with frequent syncopations of the *hemiola* type [see Ex.] and rapid coloraturas sung to words such as "Ay," "Olé," etc. The dance movements show Oriental influence, being movements of the body rather than of the feet. Two famous polos were written by Manuel Garcia (1775–1832), "Yo soy el contrabandista"

and "Cuerpo bueno" [see *LavE* i.4, 2293ff], the latter of which was used by Bizet in the prelude to Act IV of *Carmen.* A modern example is found in De Falla's *Seven Spanish Popular Songs,* no. 7.

Polonaise [F.]. A Polish national dance of a stately and festive character. The music (a) is always in moderate triple meter, (b) consists of (usually) phrases without upbeat and with feminine ending, and (c) often includes measures containing a short repeated rhythmic motif. About 1800 it acquired its classic form, which, in addition to the features named above, is characterized by the specific rhythmic pattern shown in Ex. 1.

An example of this type is Beethoven's Polonaise op. 89, shown in Ex. 2.

The origin and early history of the polonaise are obscure. It seems to have originated in connection with court ceremonies and processions. Beginning in the late 16th century, dances entitled "Polnischer Tanz," "Chorea polonica," "Polacca," etc., appear in various sources, e.g., a manuscript by Löffelholtz (1585; see W. Merian, *Der Tanz in den deutschen Tabulaturbüchern* [1927], p. 187), the "Tabulaturbuch" by Nörmiger (1598; see *ibid.*, pp. 241ff), Besard's *Thesaurus harmonicus* (1603), Biagio Marini's *Sonate, symphonie, canzoni* (1629; see *BuMBE*, p. 44), etc. None of these, however, bears any resemblance to the polonaise. The earliest known examples with the above-mentioned

traits (a), (b), and (c) are polonaises written by J. S. Bach (French Suite no. 6, see Ex. 3; Orchestral Suite no. 2). A large number of vocal polonaises are found in Sperontes' *Singende Muse an der Pleisse* [DdT 35/36]. J. G. Goldberg (for whom Bach wrote the *Goldberg Variations) composed 24 polonaises in a routine rococo style, while W. F. Bach wrote 12 polonaises in a highly idealized style with great artistic imagination.

The classic polonaise, characterized by the rhythmic pattern in Ex. 1, emerged *c.* 1800 in Poland in the works of J. Kozlowski (1757–1831) and Prince M. Oginski (1765–1833). Well-known 19th-century examples are by Beethoven [Ex. 2], Schubert (*Polonaises* for four hands, op. 61, 75), Weber (op. 21, 72), Liszt (*Deux Polonaises*, 1851), Mussorgsky (in *Boris Godunov*), Tchaikovsky (in *Eugene Onegin*), and above all, Chopin, who made the polonaise the symbol of Polish heroism and chivalry.

In the 17th and 18th centuries, under such titles as *polonez, polonesse, *polska, *polacca, taniec polski, galanterie polone*, etc., there appeared throughout Europe a variety of pieces in numerous media, which occasionally but not necessarily bear some resemblance to the classic polonaise.

The polonaise also plays an important role in Polish folk music. The earliest known examples

are in a MS collection by Joseph Sychra from 1772, considerably later than those found in art music.

Lit.: H. Dorabialska, *Polonez przed Chopinem* (The Polonaise before Chopin; 1938); A. Lindgren, in *CP 1901;* F. Starczewski, in *SIM* ii; T. Norlind, in *SIM* xii; Z. Steszewska, in *Muzyka* v, no. 2; J. W. Reiss, in *Poradnik Muzyka* 1950, no. 12, 1951, nos. 1, 2. See also under Mazurka.

Polska. A Swedish dance, probably of Polish origin, similar to the mazurka rather than the polonaise. Ex. in *GD* iv, 219, *GDB* vi, 848, and W. Niemann, in *SIM* v, 99. See E. Ala-Könni, *Die Polska-Tänze in Finnland* (1956).

Poly-, multi-. Prefixes meaning "many" or "diverse." Applied to music, they are often used indiscriminately but could be employed to differentiate two kinds of "diversity," vertical and horizontal. Thus, "polyrhythmic" or "polymetric" would mean the simultaneous use of different rhythms or meters, and "multirhythmic" or "multimetric" their successive occurrence. Similarly for polytonal and multitonal. See Homo-, iso-; also Multimetric, Polymetric.

Polychoral style. Term used for compositions in which the ensemble (chorus with or without the orchestra) is divided into several (usually two or

three) distinct groups performing singly (in alternation) as well as jointly. Italian terms are *coro battente* and *coro spezzato* (broken choir), the latter of which also implies separate placement of the groups. The earliest known examples of this technique are in the works of Ruffino Bartolucci, who was musical director at the Cathedral of Padua from 1510 to 1520. Willaert used it in his *salmi spezzati* (broken psalms) found in publications of 1550 and 1557. The common notion that G. Zarlino in his *Istituzioni armoniche* (1558) credited Willaert with the invention of the *coro spezzato* is not correct. Zarlino merely says that Willaert formulated some rules for composing pieces employing *coro spezzato*. The polychoral style was also cultivated by Andrea Gabrieli (*c.* 1520–86), who wrote a *Deus misereatur nostri* for three four-part choruses, and was fully exploited by G. Gabrieli (*c.* 1557–1612; see Ex.). It is a characteristic feature of the *Venetian school. Its development was furthered by the alternate playing on the two organs of St. Mark's at Venice, which were installed in the two apses of the cathedral. Accordingly, different choruses were placed with the organs and elsewhere in the building. The polychoral style persisted throughout the baroque period, particularly in Rome (Orazio Benevoli; see Roman school) and Germany (Händl, Hassler, Schütz), the latest examples being found in Bach (first movement of the St. Matthew Passion).

The term "polychoral" is also used, less appropriately, for compositions performed by two groups that merely alternate, without joining forces. The earliest record of this method is an Italian MS from the second half of the 15th century (Modena, Bibl. Est. *lat. 454/455*). Such pieces should be called "antiphonal" rather than "polychoral." Nor is "polychoral" a wholly accurate term for the *decani* and *cantoris* choirs of the Anglican rites. These sing alternately as well as together, but in the latter case merely duplicate their parts, so that the result is an increase of volume rather than voice-parts.

Lit.: L. Reitter, *Doppelchortechnik bei Heinrich Schütz* (1937); A. E. Ray, "The Double-Choir Music of Juan de Padilla" (diss. Univ. of Southern California, 1953); E. Hertzmann, in *ZMW* xii; H. Zenck, in *CP 1949* and *MF ii* (Willaert); G. d'Alessi, in *JAMS* v (Bartolucci); W. Boetticher, in *AMW* xii (Lasso); M. Bukofzer, in *Studies in Medieval and Renaissance Music* (1950), pp. 181–84 (cod. Modena); D. Launay, in *RdM* 1957, p. 173 (France, 17th cent.); D. Arnold, in *ML* xl, 4, and *MF* xii (A. Gabrieli).

Polychord. See under Monochord.

Polychronion. See under Acclamation.

Polymetric. Term used for modern editions of 16th-century vocal music in which the bar lines are placed at irregular intervals according to the requirements of the musical and textual phrases, resulting in a succession of different meters. This practice might better be called "multimetric," while "polymetric" would be reserved for the simultaneous use of different meters, e.g., 2/4 against 3/4 or 6/8 [see under Polyrhythm]. See Poly-, multi-.

Polyphony [F. *polyphonie;* G. *Mehrstimmigkeit;* It. *polifonia;* Sp. *polifonía*]. Music that combines several simultaneous voice-parts of individual design, in contrast to *monophonic music, which consists of a single melody, or *homophonic music, which combines several voice-parts of similar, rhythmically identical design [see also Heterophony]. The prefix "poly-" [from Gr. *polys,* many] should not be taken literally, since as few as two parts can make perfect polyphony —better, indeed, than six or eight. Polyphony is largely synonymous with counterpoint, except for a difference of emphasis [see Counterpoint].

There are numerous theories regarding the "origin of polyphony," but none is more than hypothetical. Some scholars regard the earliest extant examples of polyphony (*c.* 900) not as a beginning but as a "first culmination" of a development whose origin, they believe, lies in Oriental and primitive music [see *ReMMA,* pp. 249ff].

Lit.: M. Schneider, *Geschichte der Mehrstimmigkeit,* i, ii (1934–35); L. B. Spiess, "Polyphony in Theory and Practice from the Ninth Century to the Close of the Thirteenth Century" (diss. Harvard Univ., 1942; rev. 1947); P. Wagner, "Über die Anfänge des mehrstimmigen Gesanges" (*ZMW* ix); E. Steinhard, "Zur Frühgeschichte der Mehrstimmigkeit" (*AMW* iii); F. Ludwig, "Die mehrstimmige Musik des 14. Jahrhunderts" (*SIM* iv); *id.,* "Studien über die Geschichte der mehrstimmigen Musik im Mittelalter" (*SIM* v); M. Schneider, "Kaukasische Parallelen zur mittelalterlichen Mehrstimmigkeit" (*AM* xii); P. Collaer, "Polyphonies de tradition populaire en Europe méditerranéenne" (*AM* xxxii); for additional bibl. see *ReMMA,* p. 451f.

Polyrhythm. The simultaneous use of strikingly contrasted rhythms in different parts of the musical fabric. In a sense, all truly contrapuntal or polyphonic music is polyrhythmic, since rhythmic variety in simultaneous parts more than anything else gives the voice-parts the individuality that is essential to polyphonic style [see Texture].

Generally, however, the term is restricted to cases in which rhythmic variety is introduced as a special effect that is often called "cross rhythm." Two types can be distinguished: contrasting rhythms within the same scheme of accents (meter) [Ex. 1, a and b]; contrasting rhythms involving a conflict of meter or accents [Ex. 1, c and d]. The latter is sometimes termed "poly-

metric." Polyrhythmic designs play a prominent role in music of about 1400 and in 20th-century music. A passage from Baude Cordier's "Amans ames secretement" of *c.* 1400 [Ex. 2; *ApNPM,* p. 175] and one from Hindemith's *Klaviermusik,* op. 37 [Ex. 3] serve as illustrations. The bass part of the latter actually is in 3/8 meter but is written in 4/8 for the sake of easier reading.

Polytextuality. The simultaneous use of different texts in various parts of a composition. Polytextuality is a characteristic trait of the early motets, from *c.* 1225 to 1400 [see Motet A, I and II]. It is implicitly present in the *cantus firmus* Masses of the 15th century, particularly those based on a liturgical *cantus firmus.* Thus, in Regis' *Missa Ecce ancilla Domini* and in Obrecht's *Missa Sub tuum praesidium* the text and melody of the respective antiphons are retained. In addition, there are other *cantus firmus* texts and melodies used as well as the Mass Ordinary text; they may occur together, in sequence, or in alternation [see *ReMR,* p. 195]. In the *Missa L'Homme armé* by Regis the *cantus firmus* carries the text "Dum sacrum mysterium." However, in Morales' Mass on the Spanish song *Tristezas me matan,* the original Spanish text is retained. Both Josquin and Morales wrote a number of "bilingual" motets; see Motet B I. See also Motet-chanson; *Quodlibet* III.

Polythematic. See Monothematic, polythematic.

Polytonality. See Bitonality, polytonality.

Pommer, Pomhart [G.]. Corruptions of *bombarde [see Oboe family III].

Pomp and Circumstance. Five concert marches for orchestra by Elgar, op. 39 (nos. 1 to 4 composed 1901–07, no. 5 in 1930). The title is taken from Shakespeare's *Othello,* Act III: "Pride, pomp and circumstance of glorious war."

Ponticello [It.]. The bridge of stringed instruments. *Sul ponticello,* see Bowing (k).

Pontifical [L. *pontificale*]. See under Liturgical books I (13).

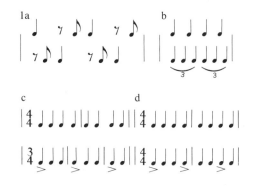

Porgy and Bess. Opera in three acts by George Gershwin (libretto by D. B. Heyward, adapted from D. B. and D. Heyward's play, *Porgy,* with lyrics by Ira Gershwin), produced in New York, 1935. Setting: Charleston, S.C., in the recent past. The music features the styles of blues, jazz, and Negro spirituals.

Porrectus. See under Neumes I.

Port. Old Scottish term for an instrumental piece, usually for the harp. See *GD* iv, 232; *GDB* vi, 882.

Portamento [It.]. (1) A special manner of singing in which the voice glides gradually from one tone to the next through all the intermediate pitches. A similar effect, frequently but erroneously called *glissando, can be obtained on the violin and trombone. In vocal compositions the portamento is indicated by a slur connecting two notes of different pitch when the notes have different syllables; otherwise the slur means repetition of the same vowel. If the effect of portamento is desired on the interval with one vowel, the word "portamento" is printed. See Portato. (2) The term is also used for anticipation or appoggiatura.

Portative organ. A small portable organ of the late Middle Ages (12th–15th cent.). It was held with the left arm and resting on the left knee, in such a way that the keyboard was nearly at a right angle to the upper body. Thus it could be played only with the right hand (the small bellows were operated by the left hand) and therefore was a pure melody instrument, like the recorder or panpipes. An Italian 14th-century name is *organetto.* The blind master Francesco Landini was celebrated for his playing of the organetto. The famous illumination from the Squarcialupi Codex [see, e.g., *BeMMR,* opp. p. 168] shows him with this instrument. Giovanni da Prato, in his *Paradiso degli Alberti* (*c.* 1389), gives a vivid description of Landini's playing, saying it was "so beautiful that even the birds listened to it." Paintings of the 14th and 15th centuries frequently show the organetto in the hands of angels [see *SaHMI,* pl. XVI, opp. p. 272, and pl. XVIII, opp. p. 304]. See H. Hickmann, *Das Portativ* (1936); H. Wolff, in *ZMW* xv; L. Parigi, in *LRM* 1949, p. 40.

Portato [It.]. A manner of performance halfway between legato and staccato [see Legato]. The use of the term *portamento for this is misleading and should be avoided.

Port de voix [F.]. (1) In modern French, same as *portamento. (2) One of the most important French *agréments* of the 17th and 18th centuries. Essentially it is an upward-resolved suspension or appoggiatura, generally expressed by sign or a particular notation [see Appoggiatura (2)]. Usually, however, both appoggiatura and resolution are repeated, so that the ornament consists of four notes, the last three forming a *pincé* (*mordent). In keyboard music this fuller execution is usually indicated by combining the sign for *port de voix* with that for the *pincé* [see Ex., J.-H.

1. Port de voix. 2. Port de voix pincé.

d'Anglebert, *Pieces de clavecin* (1689)]. In music for the voice and all other instruments the *pincé* was taken for granted. P.A.

Portée [F.]. Staff.

Porter (portez) la voix. See *Port de voix* (1).

Portugaliae musica. See Editions XLIV.

Portugal. I. *To 1700.* In the 13th century Kings Alfonso III (reigned 1248–79) and Diniz (Denis; reigned 1279–1325) attracted Provençal troubadours to their courts. Very likely they aroused interest and following among native musicians, one of whom, Martim Codax (late 13th cent.), is known through seven songs that were discovered in 1914 in the binding of a 14th-century MS of Cicero's *De officiis* [see *ML* v, 29f; I. Pope, in *Speculum* ix]. John I (reigned 1385–1433) was a munificent and lavish ruler who kept a large orchestra at his court for festivities and ceremonial occasions. A collection of anonymous three-part songs from *c.* 1500 is preserved in the Cancioneiro of Elvas [see Cancionero (2)]. In the 16th century Portuguese musicians such as Damião de Goes (1501–74; well known as a historian, diplomat, and traveler), Cosme Delgado (*c.* 1530–96), and Manuel Mendes (*c.* 1550–1605) came under the influence of Flemish polyphony, but very little of their work has been preserved (a motet, "Ne laetaris," by Goes in Glareanus' *Dodecachordon*).

About 1600 a splendid school of Portuguese polyphonic music emerged, known as the school of Évora. To this belong Duarte Lobo (*c.* 1565–1646), Manuel Cardoso (1571–1650), Felipe de Magalhães (d. 1648), João Lourenço Rebello

(1609–61), and Diogo Dias Melgaz (1638–1700). To these must be added King John IV (1604–56), who studied music under Rebello, composed many works for church use (of which two motets are preserved), wrote a book and pamphlet in defense of Palestrina, and founded the world-famous library whose destruction in the Lisbon earthquake of 1755 meant the loss of innumerable priceless musical works. A contemporary of Lobo's was Manuel Rodrigues Coelho (b. 1583), who in 1620 published an important collection of organ music (*Flores de música;* *Editions XLIV, 1 and 3), containing *tentos* (ricercars) and liturgical compositions [see *HAM,* no. 200]. Recently, several extensive MS collections of Portuguese organ music from the end of the 17th century have come to light, among them a *Libro de cyfra* and a *Livro de obras de orgão* of 1695 (both in the Bibl. Mun. of Porto). They contain *tentos, jogos de versos, entradas, batalhas,* and other pieces [see Lit., B. Hudson, K. Speer].

II. *1700–present.* Under King John V (1706–50) Portuguese music came under the influence of Italian musicians. Domenico Scarlatti stayed at the Portuguese court from 1721 to 1729, and his influence is seen in the works of Carlos de Seixas (1704–42), who wrote numerous "toccatas" and "sonatas," some of which are interesting forerunners of sonata form [see S. Kastner, *Cravistas Portuguezes*]. Even more penetrating was the Italian influence on opera, which came entirely under the domination of Neapolitan composers. Among the first Portuguese composers of operas was Francisco Antonio de Almeida (d. *c.* 1755). He was followed by João de Sousa Carvalho (1709–98), whose pupil, Marcos Portugal (1762–1830), became the greatest Portuguese opera composer. João Domingos Bomtempo (1775–1842) was Portugal's first composer of symphonies, writing orchestral works in the style of Haydn and Mozart. Unfortunately he had no followers of note.

In the 20th century, José Vianna de Motta (Mota; 1868–1948) was a champion of nationalism (*Portuguese Scenes; The Lusiades* for chorus and orchestra). Freitas Branco (1890–1955) combined impressionist idioms with national elements. Ruy Coelho (b. 1892) has written many operas, ballets, and symphonic and chamber works in the national tradition. Frederico de Freitas (b. 1902) composed orchestral and instrumental pieces in the impressionist vein. Other important modern composers include Oscar da Silva (b. 1870), Cláudio Carneyro (b. 1895), Croner de Vasconcelos, Armando Fernandes,

Fernando Lopes Graça (b. 1906), Joly Braga Santos, and Ivo Cruz (b. 1901). Among modernists interested in serial or electronic music are Filipe Pires, Jorge Peixinho, and Alvaro Cassuto.

Lit.: G. Chase, *The Music of Spain,* rev. ed. (1959), ch. xviii; *LavE* i.4, 2401ff; J. de Vasconcellos, *Os músicos portuguezes* (1870); J. de Freitas Branco, *História de música portuguesa* (1959); A. Soubis, *La Musique au Portugal* (1890); S. Corbin, *Essai sur la musique religieuse Portugaise . . . (1100–1385)* (1952); S. Kastner, *Contribucion al estudio de la música española y portuguesa* (1941); *id., Carlos de Seixas* [1947]; A. Pinto, *Música moderna portuguesa* (1930); M. de Sampayo Ribeiro, *A Música em Portugal nos séculos xvii e xix* (1938); J. E. dos Santos, ‡*A Polifonia clássica portuguesa* (1938); M. Joaquim, ed., *Composições polifón de Duarte Lôbo,* vol. i (1945); B. Hudson, "A Portuguese Source of Seventeenth-Century Iberian Music" (diss. Indiana Univ., 1961); K. Speer, "A Portuguese Manuscript of Keyboard Music from the Late Seventeenth Century" (diss., Indiana Univ., 1956); S. Kastner, ‡*Cravistas Portuguezes;* A. T. Luper, "Portuguese Polyphony in the Sixteenth and Early Seventeenth Centuries" (*JAMS* iii); F. D. Perkins, "Music in Portugal Today" (*LBCM,* also *MQ* li); *Editions XLIV. For Portuguese folk music, see under *Fado.*

Portuguese hymn. The hymn "Adeste fideles" (O come, all ye faithful), so called because it was frequently used, *c.* 1800, in the Portuguese chapel at London.

Pos. Abbr. for *position, or [F.] *positif, or [G.] *Posaune.*

Posaune [G.]. Trombone.

Positif [F.]. *Choir organ.

Position. (1) With reference to chords (close, open position), see Spacing. (2) On the violin, etc., positions are the places on the fingerboard to which the left hand shifts in order to obtain higher or lower tones. Thus, on the G-string the first position covers the fifth from g to d', g being the open string and the four successive notes, a, b, c', d', being stopped by the four fingers. The second position starts with the first finger on b and ends with the fifth finger on e', third position starts on c', etc. Moving from one position into another is known as a "shift." Both terms apply also to the trombone with reference to the position of the slide. The home position is called the first, and each successive position lowers the pitch a semitone.

Positive organ [F. *orgue positif;* G. *Positiv*]. A medium-sized medieval organ, which was not built into the walls of the church but was a self-contained instrument that could be moved by two or four men. It had one manual, no pedal, and only flue pipes, often in two rows (4' and 2'). A famous illustration is found on Van Eyck's Altar of Ghent. There also was a very small positive that was set on a table. It was as "portable" as the *portative, but differed from it in that it was played with both hands, the bellows being worked by an assistant. It was exclusively a domestic instrument.

Later the name was used for a special section of the church organ in which there were flue stops (principal, etc.) suitable for the accompaniment of the choir; hence, synonymous with *choir organ, *Positif* [F.], *Rückpositif* [G.]. See Organ III, VII, XII. See H. Bornefeld, *Das Positiv* (1947); E. Bonitz, *Das Positiv und die Zukunft* (1951); R. Quoicka, *Das Positiv in Geschichte und Gegenwart* (1957); F. W. Galpin, in *MA* iv.

Post Epistolam [L.]. Alternative name for the Hallelujah of the Ambrosian Mass; see Ambrosian chant.

Post Evangelium [L.]. An item of the Ambrosian Mass; see Ambrosian chant.

Postlude. An organ piece played at the conclusion of the service, during the exit of the congregation. It is usually improvised. The term is also used for a *coda.

Potpourri [F.]. A medley of popular tunes, operatic airs, patriotic songs, etc., which are played in succession, connected by a few measures of introduction or modulation. The name (literally "rotten pot," i.e., a dish made of many ingredients) was used as early as C. Ballard's collection of *brunettes* (*Brunetes ou petits airs tendres,* 3 vols., 1703–11). J. B. Cramer was the first to use it for the 19th-century drawing-room piece.

Poule, La [F., The Hen]. Popular name for Haydn's Symphony no. 83, in G minor (1785), no. 2 of the *Paris Symphonies. The name seems to refer to the second theme of the first movement, which vaguely suggests a hen cackling.

Poussé, poussez [F.]. Up-bow; see Bowing (a).

Pp. Abbr. for pianissimo. Sometimes ppp and pppp are used to indicate still greater degrees of softness.

P. R. In French organ music, abbr. for *Positif-Récit,* i.e., choir organ and swell organ coupled.

Praeambulum [L.]. A 15th- and 16th-century name for *prelude.

Praeconium paschale [L.]. Name for the *Exsultet jam Angelica turba* [see *Psalmus idioticus*], which is sung on Holy Saturday during the Blessing of the Paschal Candle (Easter Vigil). The text is given in *LU,* p. 776M; a melody (obviously of a relatively late date) is in the *Officium et Missa ultimi tridui* (1947), p. 227. For older melodies, see P. Wagner, *Einführung in die gregorianischen Melodien,* vol. iii (1921), pp. 229ff. See *Psalmus idioticus.*

Praefatio [L.]. See Preface.

Praelegenda [L.]. Name for the Introit in *Gallican and *Mozarabic chant.

Praeludium [L.]. See Prelude.

Prague Symphony. Mozart's Symphony in D (K. 504), composed in 1786 in Vienna and first performed (1787) in Prague, where it was enthusiastically received. It has no minuet.

Pralltriller [G.]. See under Inverted mordent.

Préambule [F.], **preambulum** [L.]. Same as *prelude.

Precentor. (1) The director of music in a cathedral or monastic church. (2) Deacon, elder, or "chorister" in the Puritan churches of New England in the 17th and 18th centuries who "lined out" the psalm and hymn tunes. See Lining.

Preces [L.]. In the rites of the Latin and Anglican churches, name for supplications in the form of versicles and responses. They play an important role in the *Gallican and *Mozarabic rites, where they were sung during the Mass on certain penitential days. Several Mozarabic *preces* are reproduced, with the designation "ex Liturgia Gothica," in the publication *Variae Preces* (rev. ed., 1939, pp. 112, 114, 135, 264; in this title the word "Preces" has no specific significance). Many Gallican *preces* (*Variae Preces,* p. 266) are preserved, and these make up the largest remnant of Gallican chant. Both the Mozarabic and the Gallican *preces* usually have a refrain form, R V_1 R V_2 R V_3.... In the Roman Catholic rite the *preces* play a much lesser role, being confined to the Office of Prime on ordinary Sundays [*LU,* p. 231]. However, the *litanies belong to the same type of chant. In the Anglican Prayer Books, *preces* means the portion of Morning and Evening Prayer that begins with the versicle "O Lord, open Thou our lips." There are polyphonic settings of the Preces by Tallis, Morley, and others, that by Tallis being the one most widely used [see *The Hymnal 1940*, p. 699]. See Suffrages. See W. Meyer, "Die Preces der mozarabischen Liturgie" (*Abhandlungen der Königlichen Gesellschaft der Wissenschaften zu Göttingen*, Philologisch-historische Klasse. Neue Folge, vol. xv, no. 3, 1914); R. P. G. Prado, "Mozarabic Melodics" (*Speculum* iii).

Precipitando [It.]. Rushing, impetuous.

Preface [L. *praefatio*]. In the Roman Catholic Mass, a solemn declaration of praise beginning (after short versicles and replies) with the words "Vere dignum et justum est." It is, together with the immediately following Sanctus, an introduction to the Canon of the Mass, hence the name [see Mass A, table, nos. 12–14]. In addition to the Common preface [*LU*, p. 3f] there are a number of Proper prefaces for special feasts, all beginning with the same words [*LU*, pp. 8ff]. The "Tones for the Prefaces" given in *LU*, p. 109f are used for the initial versicles and replies. An example of a recitation tone for the preface itself is found in *Officium hebdomadae sanctae et octavae paschae* (1962), pp. 456, 458.

Prelude [L. *praeludium;* F. *prélude;* G. *Präludium, Vorspiel;* It., Sp. *preludio*]. A piece of music designed to be played as an introduction, e.g., to a liturgical ceremony or, more usually, to another composition, such as a fugue or suite. This connotation, which prevails throughout the entire early history of the prelude [see below], was lost in the 19th century, when Chopin, Scriabin, and Debussy used the word as one of numerous noncommittal titles for piano pieces [see Character piece]. How completely the term lost its proper meaning is evident in the fact that even the most pedantic listeners do not seem to have objected to twenty-four preludes being played in succession. With few exceptions the prelude has always been restricted to instrumental solo music, that is, to keyboard instruments and the lute [see Ensemble (3)].

The history of the prelude is of particular interest since it represents *the* earliest type of idiomatic keyboard music as opposed to types based on or modeled after vocal music (liturgical organ music, intabulations, ricercars, and canzonas). Its history can be divided into three periods. In the first period (c. 1450–1650) the prelude is a single composition that may be used for any suitable purpose, sacred or secular; in the second period (c. 1650–1750) the prelude becomes the "first movement" of a special composition to which it is inseparably connected; in the third period (19th century) it becomes an independent piece to which no function or other composition is attached.

I. The preludes of the 15th and early 16th centuries are mostly short pieces (ten to twenty measures long) remarkable for their free keyboard style, made up of passages and chords, in marked contrast to the strict contrapuntal style of contemporary vocal music. This repertory includes about fifty pieces (*praeambula*) in the Ileborgh tablature (1448); in C. Paumann's *"Fundamentum organisandi"* (1452); in the *Buxheim Organ Book* (c. 1460–70); in H. Kotter's tablature (c. 1520); and in L. Kleber's tablature (c. 1520; ex. in *HAM*, no. 84; *MQ* xxiii, 213; *ApMZ* i). Similar although frequently longer are the lute preludes in the tablatures of F. Spinaccino and J. A. Dalza (*Intabulatura de lauto* i, ii, iv, 1507–08; pub. by Petrucci), Judenkünig (1523), Hans Newsidler (1536), H. Gerle (1552), and others. The preludes of the Petrucci publications are called *recercari* [see Ricercar II (a)] or *tastar de corde* [Ex. in *HAM*, no. 99; *SchGMB*, nos. 63b, 93; *ApMZ* i, 20]. Toward the end of the century John Bull wrote a number of preludes [see *HAM*, no. 178] that are noteworthy for their virtuoso character and to which the simultaneous lute pieces by J. B. Besard (*Thesaurus harmonicus*, 1603; see *ApMZ* ii, 24) offer a striking contrast of style and expression. See also *Intonatione*.

II. About 1650 composers began to combine the prelude with a special composition. The prelude as an introduction to suites or a suite-like series of pieces was used by Louis Couperin, who created a unique type of prelude, completely free in rhythm and, therefore, notated without the conventional note values [see rev. ed. by P. Brunold and T. Dart [1959]; also *TaAM* viii, 40, where the "Transcription" on p. 43 completely obscures the basic character of the composition; for a similar prelude by D'Anglebert, see *HAM*, no. 232]. Particularly remarkable are the preludes to the lute suites of E. Reusner (1636–79; ex. in *HAM*, no. 233, and *RiMB;* see also H. Riemann, in *SIM* vi). Handel preferred a prelude in a free, improvisory style for his suites, whereas Bach's introductory pieces to suites and partitas are full-sized *concerto grosso* movements, overtures, toccatas, or sinfonias. The combination of the prelude with a fugue that became classic with Bach can be traced to organ preludes of the early 17th century, which, after a section in free style, continue and close with a short fugal section. A piece such as the "Praeludium" of Heinrich Scheidemann (*c.* 1596–1663) in *Editions XLI (*Vierte Reihe,* i, p. 16) or the "Praeludium" by F. Tunder (1614–67) in *HAM,* no. 215, may be considered the beginning of this interesting development, which, half a century later, led to the monumental "Praeludium cum Fuga" of Buxtehude [Ex. in *HAM,* no. 234] and finally to those of Bach. For a closely related form of keyboard music, see Toccata. For the chorale prelude, see Organ chorale II.

III. The 19th-century prelude is represented by the preludes of Chopin and his numerous imitators, chiefly Scriabin (90 preludes), Debussy (24 in two books), and Rachmaninoff (op. 23). These are essentially pianistic character pieces. Except for those of Debussy, they are usually based on a short figure or motif that is exploited by means of harmonic modulations. See L. Hibberd, "The Early Keyboard Prelude" (diss. Harvard Univ., 1941); W. Apel, "Der Anfang des Präludiums in Deutschland und Polen" (*The Book of the First International Musicological Congress . . . of Frederick Chopin,* ed. Z. Lissa [Warsaw, 1963], p. 495).

Prélude à l'après-midi d'un faune. See *Après-midi d'un faune, L'.*

Préludes, Les. Symphonic poem by Liszt (first perf. 1854), based on a poem of the same title by Lamartine.

Preparation. A harmonic device whereby the impact of a dissonant note in a chord is softened by first sounding it as a consonant note in the preceding chord. In the strict counterpoint of the Palestrina style dissonant notes always are prepared, while in Bach's this principle is largely discarded. See Nonharmonic tones, particularly appoggiatura.

Prepared piano. A piano whose sound is artificially altered by various devices, e.g., metal clips or metal bolts attached to the strings; strips of paper, rubber, felt, etc., inserted across the strings; altered tuning of the unison strings, etc. The prepared piano was introduced by John Cage (b. 1912).

Presa [It.]. In canons, a sign, usually like an S, to indicate the place where the imitating voice or voices enter.

Pressante [It.]; **pressez** [F.]. Urgent, hurrying.

Pressus. An ornamenting neume; see Neumes I (table).

Presto [It.]. Very fast, faster than allegro. *Prestissimo* denotes the greatest possible speed. See Tempo marks.

Priamel [G.]. A 16th-century misspelling of *Praeambel,* i.e., prelude. The explanation in Brenet's *Dictionnaire de musique* is erroneous.

Prick song. A 16th- and 17th-century English term for a written or printed composition, distinguishing it from the oral tradition of plainsong, folksong, popular dance music, etc., as well as from improvised music.

Prim [G.]. *Prime (1).

Prima donna [It.]. Originally, the singer of the principal female role of an opera, as distinguished from the *primo uomo,* the leading male singer, and the *seconda donna,* the second female singer. These parts were basic in the plot construction of 18th-century operas, as can be seen, e.g., in Mozart's *Don Giovanni* and *Figaro.* In the 19th century the term came to mean a conceited, jealous, capricious operatic star, a meaning also extended to her male counterpart, both in performing and conducting. See H. S. Edwards, *The Prima Donna,* 2 vols. (1888); K. Homolka, *Die grossen Primadonnen* (1960).

Prima (seconda) prattica [It.]. Early 17th-century terms used (first by Monteverdi?) to distinguish the polyphonic style of the 16th century from the monodic style of the 17th. Synonyms are *stile antico* and *stile moderno.*

Prima vista [It.]. Playing without previous study. See Sight-reading.

Prima volta, seconda volta [It.]. The different endings for the first and second performances of a repeated section. In scores, abbreviations such as ⌐1. and ⌐2. are used. The practice of using different endings occurs occasionally in Gregorian chant, e.g., in the Offertory "Eripe me . . . Domine," which in its full form with two verses [see C. Ott, *Offertoriale,* no. 30] can be diagramed as $O-e_1 \ V_1 \ O-e_1 \ V_2 \ O-e_2$ (O = Offertory; V = verse; e = ending), with e_1 closing on the "dominant" b and e_2 on the tonic e. It appears fully established in the *ballades* and virelais of Machaut; see *Ouvert* and *clos.*

Prime (1) The interval "zero," i.e., unison. (2) The third of the canonical hours. See Office.

Primgeiger [G.]. First violinist, also concert-master.

Primitive music. See Ethnomusicology.

Prince Igor [Rus. *Knyaz Igor*]. Opera in four acts by Borodin (to his own libretto), composed between 1871 and 1887, the year of his death, completed by Rimsky-Korsakov and Glazunov, produced in St. Petersburg, 1890. Setting: semilegendary Russia, 1185. Best known are the Polovtsian Dances, which are often heard in concerts, and the selections adapted for the Broadway musical *Kismet*.

Principal. In German organs, the "open diapason," in 8', 16', 32', and 4' [see Foot]. In American and British organs, a 4'-open diapason only, or an 8'-open diapason on the pedal.

Printing of music. The printing of music began soon after the invention of movable letter type (Gutenberg's Bible, *c.* 1455). A *Psalterium*, printed in 1457 by Gutenberg's associates, Johann Fust and Peter Schöffer, has printed staves on which the notes were written by hand. The earliest method used for the complete reproduction of music was *double printing*, in which the staff lines and notes were printed in two different processes, usually the former in red and the latter in black. Various printers of the 15th century used this method for liturgical books (missals), e.g., Ulrich Han (Rome, 1476), Jörg Reyser (Würzburg, 1481), Octavianus Scotto (Venice, 1482), J. Sensenschmidt (1485), and Erhard Ratdolt (1487). In the early 16th century it was perfected by O. dei Petrucci (first printed book, the *Odhecaton*, 1501), the only music printer who can be compared to Gutenberg. Equally skilled was Peter Schöffer, who printed the beautiful publication of Arnolt Schlick's *Tabulaturen* (1512). Most printers, however, found double printing too difficult and replaced it with two other methods, which, with many variations and improvements, have persisted side by side until the present day: (a) *block* or *sheet printing*, and (b) *type printing*.

(a) In *block printing*, the block for the entire page of music is prepared as a whole. While woodcuts, such as those used in N. Burtius' *Musices opusculum* (1487; printed by De Rugeriis in Bologna), yielded extremely clumsy results [ill. in *GD* iv, 254; *GDB* vi, 929], hand-engraved metal plates proved very satisfactory, as is shown by the beautiful publications of the Roman printers Simone Verovio (*Diletto spirituale*, 1586; C. Merulo's *Toccate*, 1597, 1604), and

Nicola Borbone (Frescobaldi's *Toccate*, 1637), by the *Parthenia*, etc. Not infrequently the composers themselves engraved their music, as, for instance, Johann Ulrich Steigleder (*Ricercar Tabulatura*, 1624) and probably also Bach (*Clavier-Übung* iii). Throughout the 17th and 18th centuries engraving was the most common method of printing. American publishers imported engraved plates from England (as early as 1690), Paul Revere being the first American to engrave music (*c.* 1760). An important advance was made in the early 18th century by John Walsh who *c.* 1710 (1730?) mechanized the process of engraving with the use of punches, long tools having a note or other character at one end, which were struck with a hammer. A combination of punching and hand-engraving (e.g., for long lines) is still used today. About 1800, Senefelder's lithographic process (writing on a smooth stone with a greasy ink) was used for music publications; C. M. von Weber helped perfect this method and in 1800 lithographed his op. 2 himself. Later the stone was replaced with a copper plate covered with beeswax on which the musical signs were scratched. When the plate was etched with acid, the signs appeared as grooves in the copper plate. In the modern *offset process* (also called *photolithography*) the characters are first hand-engraved (with the aid of punches) on a lead plate from which a clear proof on paper is drawn. Eight or sixteen such proofs are pasted on a large sheet and a negative photograph is made. The negative is reproduced photographically on a sensitive zinc plate (covered with a photographic emulsion), which, after treatment with acid, shows the signs engraved.

(b) In *type printing*, movable type, comparable in size to letter type, is put together in order to prepare the block for the printing. In the 16th century such type consisted of a note combined with a small section of the staff, as illustrated.

Although this method proved successful for printing *partbooks (vocal music), in which each staff carried only one melodic line, it was very tedious and costly for keyboard music, which frequently included chords. Examples of keyboard music printed in this manner are Attaingnant's books of 1529. Type printing was largely abandoned after 1600 but was reintroduced, greatly improved, by J. G. I. Breitkopf (1755), who used tiny pieces of type, one each for note-heads, stems, flags, etc., that were put together in a complicated mosaic. This troublesome method is used today chiefly for short musical examples inserted in printed books and for plainsong.

Lit.: W. Gamble, *Music Engraving and Printing* (1923); A. H. Littleton, *A Catalogue . . . Illustrating the History of Music Printing* (1911); H. M. Brown, *Instrumental Music Printed before 1600* (1965); G. Marco, *The Earliest Music Printers of Continental Europe* [1962]; K. Meyer-Baer, *Liturgical Music Incunabula* (1962); A. H. King, *Four Hundred Years of Music Printing* (1964); D. B. Updike, *Printing Types, Their History, Form, and Use*, rev. ed. (1962); R. Steele, *The Earliest English Music Printing* (1903); K. Meyer, "The Printing of Music, 1473–1934" (*The Dolphin*, 1935); O. Kinkeldey, *Music and Music Printing in Incunabula* (1932; repr. from *Papers of the Bibliographical Society of America* xxvi); M. Foss, in *ML* iv, 340; L. M. Spell, "The First Music Books Printed in America" (*MQ* xv); K. Meyer, "The Liturgical Music Incunabula in the British Museum" (*The Library* xx [1939], 272–94); W. H. Cummings, in *PMA* xi; A. Thurlings, in *VMW* viii; H. Springer, in *CP 1906*, p. 37; M. Donà, *La Stampa musicale a Milano fino all'anno 1700* (1961); *WoHN* ii, 475ff.

Prix de Rome. See under Scholarships II.

Prizes. See Scholarships.

Processional [L. *processionale*]. See under Liturgical books I (8).

Prodaná Nevěsta. See *Bartered Bride, The.*

Prodigal Son, The. See *Enfant prodigue, L'.*

Profession of music. I. *Teaching.* The largest number of opportunities for a musical career are in teaching, which also is the surest and steadiest method of earning an income.

a. Public schools. Teaching in public elementary and high schools usually requires a teaching certificate based on completion of a degree program in an accredited institution. Often the teacher is asked to give instruction in one or more subjects besides music.

b. Private schools, elementary and secondary. The requirements for teachers in private schools vary greatly. Most private schools require a B.A. and often an M.A. degree. In some instances a single teacher is employed for all classroom teaching—theory, history, solfège, appreciation, etc. He may also be required to teach an instru-

ment or voice, direct a chorus or band, etc., or to teach another subject in addition to music.

c. Colleges and universities. The B.A. degree is prerequisite (or B.S., or B.Mus.). The M.A. is more and more widely required, while the Ph.D. is indispensable for obtaining positions in top-ranking colleges and universities. A balance of musical knowledge (theory and history) with performing ability is ideal, the one or the other being stressed according to the teacher's special abilities. A knowledge of the other arts is receiving wider recognition as an important part of the understanding of music.

d. Music schools. Here the emphasis is more specifically on performance. Although the better music schools include on their staffs teachers of theory and history, they also have a place for the virtuoso, whose interest is primarily in performance and in training performers.

e. The private music teacher. Except for a few "stars" who have become famous as performers, the private teacher's career tends to be uncertain. Moreover, anyone who wishes to do so may take on pupils, with the result that many incompetent persons set themselves up as teachers. More security results from cooperation with high schools and colleges, which may refer students to private teachers for instruction. Private teaching often is done on a part-time basis, e.g., by church organists, orchestra players, and occasionally by school music teachers. In addition, recognized concert artists frequently accept a few gifted pupils.

II. *Performing.* Performing as a soloist on the concert or operatic stage is the most "glamorous" profession, but the number of such opportunities is limited compared to the quantity and quality of talented performers available. Frequently performance is combined with teaching. Conducting is an even more limited field. There may be a good future for local concert artists—performers who appear principally in a given region, where they also participate, as teachers or otherwise, in the musical life of the community.

Symphony orchestras (and a few opera and ballet companies) provide employment for good instrumental players, and the growth in recent years of good orchestras in smaller cities has created new opportunities. Musical shows and operettas offer employment to orchestral players but seldom on a permanent basis. Many musicians find semipermanent work in small groups, playing popular and dance music.

Churches employ a large number of musicians and singers, usually for quite a small fee. Many churches, however, pay their organist and choir-master enough to enable him (usually with the help of private lessons) to support himself.

III. Various other activities are open to professional musicians. Some of them, such as composition, offer little in material returns. Others, such as writing and arranging for motion pictures, radio, or television, recording for the phonograph, acting as commentator for radio programs, or making arrangements for popular bands or folk singers generally pay handsomely but employ a relatively small number of persons. Newspaper criticism pays very little, with a few important exceptions. Opportunities for music librarians have increased during the past few years and may become even broader in the future.

Lit.: W. R. Anderson, *Music As A Career* (1939); E. B. Helm, *Music (Vocational Monographs, no. 6, 1940)*; W. Martin, *The Conditions of Life and Work of Musicians,* 2 vols. (1924); K. Singer, *Diseases of the Music Profession* (1937); H. Taubman, *Music as a Profession* (1939); H. Johnson, *Your Career in Music* (1945). E.B.H.

Program chanson. See under Chanson (2); Program music III.

Program music. I. *General.* Music inspired by a program, i.e., a nonmusical idea, which is usually indicated in the title and sometimes described in explanatory remarks or a preface. Thus, program music is the opposite of *absolute music. Although examples of program music are found in nearly all periods from at least the 14th century, it was not until the 19th century that it became a serious rival of absolute music, to the point of ousting the latter—at least temporarily—from its dominating position. About 1900, many persons, particularly writers on music, believed that in order to be understandable music must "express something" or "tell a story." In pursuit of this idea, Bach's Forty-eight Preludes and Fugues were given descriptive titles (Queen Carmen Sylva of Rumania), and some writers maintained that the word *giocoso* at the head of a sonata movement indicated a particular mood of the composer and hence a program (F. Niecks). Today such views are a thing of the past, and it is generally agreed that music is an art in its own right, that it must work with its own tools, and that too great a reliance on outside program will weaken rather than enhance a composition's artistic merit [see Aesthetics of music III]. In fact, one cannot help feeling that a good deal of the

interest of composers in program music is owing to a lack of purely musical imagination, a lack for which they try to compensate with an interesting program. In the last analysis, there are two types of program music: music that is good regardless of the program, and music that is mediocre or poor although it is a skillful rendition of the program. Although the former category includes such outstanding compositions as Beethoven's *Pastoral Symphony and Berlioz' *Symphonie fantastique,* as well as such remarkable works as R. Strauss' *Till Eulenspiegel* and Debussy's *Prélude à l'après-midi d'un faune,* the great majority of program compositions tend to fall into the second category.

Programmatic ideas are frequently found in the works of 17th- and 18th-century composers. F. Couperin with his numerous program pieces [see below] and Bach with his word painting in arias and choral preludes have frequently been cited to support the cause of 19th-century program music. The old masters, however, did not identify themselves with the programmatic thought but used it only as a point of departure, from which they derived not much more than the

So schnell _____ ein

rau _____ schend Was - ser schiesst

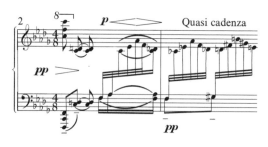

general design of the initial theme. A comparison of Bach's aria "So schnell ein rauschend Wasser schiesst," from the cantata *Ach wie flüchtig* [Ex. 1], with Debussy's *Reflets dans l'eau* [Ex. 2], both "interpreting" water, clearly illustrates this difference. Moreover, early program pieces in which the programmatic idea is pursued as thoroughly as in modern examples are usually mediocre from the musical point of view. This is particularly true of the program chansons of Janequin and the battle pieces [see *Battaglia*] of Byrd, Kerll, and others, among which Beethoven's *Wellingtons Sieg* is no exception.

II. *Methods.* In the history of program music, a general trend from the pictorial (objective) to the psychological (subjective) approach can be observed. Prior to 1600, composers limited themselves to imitating natural sounds (birds, battlecries, thunder, trumpet fanfares, etc.), bodily movements (flight, running, hobbling, throwing, falling, stopping), and words closely associated with movement (e.g., heaven = high; death = fall; see Word painting). Beginning in the 17th century, basic emotions or feelings were "translated" into music through associated movements or sounds. Thus, anguish is portrayed by a trembling or staggering motion, confidence by secure and wide steps, joy by a melody reminiscent of laughter, sorrow by descending steps in chromatic succession [see Chromaticism], etc. These examples illustrate the two basic methods of program music, imitation of sounds and imitation of movements, each used either directly or indirectly by way of association. These devices remained the chief vehicles of 19th-century program music, although they came to be used with much greater subtlety and refinement. In addition, the modern orchestral palette offered greater possibilities for convincing portrayal and faithful imitation. While Beethoven's Pastoral Symphony introduces the musical cries of the nightingale, cuckoo, and quail, Wagner very skillfully imitated the toad and serpent (in *Das Rheingold*), and R. Strauss a flock of sheep (*Don Quixote*). The climax of this trend (and, in a sense, the *reductio ad absurdum* of program music) is found in Respighi's *The Pines of Rome,* where the problem of imitating the nightingale is solved by simply using a recording of an actual nightingale's song.

III. *History.* Several of the Italian *caccie* of the late 14th century show an attempt to imitate in music the vivid scenes described in their texts, e.g., street cries, sounds of horns, the general commotion of a hunting scene, a fishing trip, a fire. From the same period dates a "bird motet" by Jean Vaillant, which recurs, with a German text ("Der May"), among the compositions of Oswald von Wolkenstein [Ex. 3; see *HAM,* no. 60]. More deliberate in approach but much less imaginative are the program chansons by Jane-

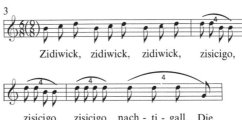

Zidiwick, zidiwick, zidiwick, zisicigo,

zisicigo, zisicigo, nach - ti - gall, Die

quin (*c.* 1528)—"Le Chant des Oyseaux," "La Chasse," "L'Alouette," "La Guerre"—the last of which, suggested by the famous battle of Marignano (1515), was followed by a host of imitations [*Editions XXV, 7; *HAM,* no. 107]. H. Newsidler's "Der Judentanz" (1544; *ApMZ* i, no. 10) is an amusing example of caricature [see Satire in music], and Byrd's *The Bells* is remarkable for its artistic ingenuity, far superior to the naïve attempts of John Munday to imitate "Lightning," "Thunder," and "Faire Wether" [see *Fitzwilliam Virginal Book* i, 274 and 23]. Passing over the numerous instances of programmatic portrayal in operas, oratorios, etc., some outstanding examples of instrumental program music of the baroque period are Froberger's beautiful *Lamento sopra la dolorosa perdita della Real Maestà di Ferdinando IV* [see *HAM,* no. 216; see also Lament]; Poglietti's satirical *Aria allemagna con alcuni variazioni* [*DTO* 27; also *TaAM* viii], J. Kuhnau's *Biblische Historien* (depicting the fight between David and Goliath, the marriage of Jacob, etc.; see *DdT* 4; *HAM,* no. 262); the numerous descriptive pieces by F. Couperin (*Pièces de clavecin,* 1713–30; see *HAM,* no. 265), including an interesting anticipation of Schumann's *Carnaval* [see *Ménestrandise*]; Rameau's "La Poule" and "Les Cyclopes" (*Pièces de clavecin,* 1706) or "Ramage des oiseaux" [*HAM,* no. 27]; and Bach's "Capriccio sopra la lontananza del suo fratello dilettissimo" (Capriccio on the departure of his beloved brother; *c.* 1704), a successful imitation of Kuhnau's program pieces. Perhaps the most startling example of baroque program music is a "Tableau de l'opération de la taille" for viol and harpsichord by Marais (1717), describing the painful details of a surgical operation [reproduced in *LavE* ii.3, p. 1776]. Between 1750 and 1800 mediocre musicians served an easily satisfied audience with battle pieces of very low quality [see *Battaglia*].

Beethoven's *Pastoral Symphony of 1807–08 marks the beginning of 19th-century program music. His remark, "Expression of feelings rather than painting," also applies to Schumann's approach (*Kinderscenen,* etc.), except for pieces such as *Carnaval,* with its realistic references to the scenes of a masked ball. There followed Berlioz, with his autobiographical *Symphonie fantastique* (1830–31), and Liszt, who in his numerous symphonic poems created the type of program music that was to become dominant in the ensuing decades of the 19th century [see Symphonic poem]. The 20th-century development brought a sharp reaction against program music as a goal in itself, employing musical portrayal chiefly for the purpose of caricature and jest [see Satire].

Lit.: F. Niecks, *Programme Music in the Last Four Centuries* [1906]; W. Klatte, *Zur Geschichte der Programmusik* [n.d.]; O. Klauwell, *Geschichte der Programmusik* (1910); N.-E. Ringbom, *Über die Deutbarkeit der Tonkunst* [1955]; A. Wellek, "Doppelempfinden und Programmusik" (diss. Vienna, 1928); W. P. James, "Music Pure and Applied" (*ML* ii, 373); H. Antcliffe, in *PMA* xxxvii; M. D. Calvocoressi, "Esquisse d'une esthétique de la musique à programme" (*SIM* ix); M. Brenet, "Essai sur les origines de la musique descriptive" (*RMI* xiv, xv); K. Schubert, ‡*Die Programm-Musik* [1933].

Program symphony. A composition written in the general form of a symphony (in several movements) and based on a programmatic idea [see Program music]. Examples are Beethoven's *Pastoral Symphony, Berlioz' *Symphonie fantastique,* Liszt's *Faust Symphony,* and R. Strauss' *Alpensinfonie.* Each movement of these symphonies has its own title, indicating one aspect of the general program. See Symphonic poem I.

Prolation [L. *prolatio*]. See Mensural notation II. In the early 14th century the term meant either all the mensurations (*modus, tempus,* and *prolatio*) or the four combinations of *tempus* and *prolatio* (Vitry's "quatre prolacions"). The latter meaning exists in Ockeghem's *Missa prolationum,* so called because each of the four voices sings in a different mensuration (in modern terms, 2/4, 3/4, 6/8, 9/8).

Prologue. In early operas and ballets, an introductory scene in which one or several narrators, representing deities, virtues, etc., give a brief summary of the opera or of its symbolic meaning. The prologue sometimes developed into a small play with an entirely independent action, designed to serve as a dedication to or eulogy of the royal or noble patron. An example is the pro-

logue of Lully's *Phaëton* (1683), which consists of an overture plus twelve different pieces. The simple narrative prologue of the earliest operas (Caccini's and Peri's *Euridice,* 1600; Monteverdi's *Orfeo,* 1607) was successfully revived by Leoncavallo in *I Pagliacci* (1892). See H. Leichtentritt, in *PAMS* 1936.

Prolongement [F.]. The sostenuto pedal of the piano.

Prometheus. (1) Ballet by Beethoven; see *Geschöpfe des Prometheus.* (2) A symphonic poem by Scriabin, *Prometheus, Poem of Fire* (op. 60, 1910), for large orchestra, piano, organ, choruses, and *color organ. The first (and only?) performance with color organ took place in New York in 1915. The music is based on the so-called mystic (Promethean) chord [see under Fourth chord].

Pronunciation. See A. J. Ellis, *Pronunciation for Singers* (1877; E., F., G., It.); C. J. Brennan, *Words in Singing* [1905]; E. Wilcke, *German Diction in Singing* [1930]; M. Marshall, *The Singer's Manual of English Diction* (1953).

Prooemium [L.]. Humanist (16th-century) name for prelude.

Proper [L. *proprium*]. In the Roman Catholic liturgy, a term used in two ways: (1) In the classification of feasts, the Proper of Saints (*Proprium Sanctorum*) includes the feasts in honor of a specific Saint (St. Andrew, St. Lawrence), while the Common of Saints (*Commune Sanctorum*) includes those in honor of lesser Saints grouped in categories such as Martyrs, Doctors, Virgins, etc. The feasts of the Lord are set apart as Proper of the Time (*Proprium de Tempore*), "time" meaning the time or life of the Lord. (2) In the classification of chants for any of the above-mentioned feasts, some are classed as Proper and others as Ordinary; see Ordinary and Proper. The section in *LU,* pp. 317–1110, contains mostly the proper chants for the Proper of the Time.

Prophecies. Lessons from the Book of Prophets in the Old Testament. In the Roman Catholic rites they are read (or chanted; see the Tone for the Prophecy, *LU,* p. 102f) chiefly on the four Ember Days and on Monday, Tuesday, and Wednesday of Holy Week, as a part of the Mass. The longest readings are the nine (formerly twelve) Prophecies of Holy Saturday [*LU,* pp. 754ff], some of which, however, are from other books of the Scriptures. In Anglican churches, these are sung on Saturday evening.

Proportional notation. Same as *mensural notation. The term refers to the use of note values in the proportion of 2 to 1 (imperfect) or 3 to 1 (perfect).

Proportions. (1) In *mensural notation, the diminution or (more rarely) augmentation of the normal note values in arithmetic ratios. For example, the sign ¾ indicates that, in the subsequent passage, each note is reduced to three-fourths of its normal value (the so-called *integer valor*), in other words, four notes of this passage are equal in duration to three notes of the preceding passage [Ex. 1].

The most important proportions are *proportio dupla, tripla,* and *sesquialtera,* which call respectively for a diminution of the note values in the ratios of 1:2, 1:3, and 2:3. The first is usually indicated by a vertical dash drawn through the sign of mensuration, ₵, φ, [Ex. 2a], and the others by figures [Ex. 3a; 4a]. In the accompanying illustrations, Ex. 2 shows *proportio dupla* (2 *S prop.* = 1 *S int. val.*); Ex. 3, *proportio tripla* (3 *S prop.* = 1 *S int. val.*); Ex. 4, *proportio sesquialtera* (3 *S prop.* = 2 *S int. val.*). In Ex. 2 under the sign ₵ the beat (*tactus,* rendered as a quarter

note) is represented by the *brevis,* while under the normal signs of mensuration, ₵, φ, it falls on the *semibrevis.* Therefore the latter were called *alla semibreve* and the former *alla breve,* a name that persists as the only vestige of the proportional system. The reduction indicated by *sesquialtera* could also be produced by *coloration. Regarding *proportio tripla,* see Proportz. See also Time signatures.

The system of proportions, although relatively simple in principle, presents certain difficulties for which the reader is referred to special studies on mensural notation (*WoHN; ApNPM*). Occasionally composers went quite far in devising proportional tricks, combined with canonic riddles. Nonetheless, these cases are on the whole not numerous or typical enough to justify any sweeping statements regarding the speculative and "purely intellectual" character of early Flemish music. The normal use of proportions was, through training and experience, just as familiar to the choir singer of the 15th century as operatic roles are to the modern singer. In their more complex applications they offered a combination of intellectual and artistic enjoyment for which there is no analogy today.

(2) In early treatises on musical acoustics the proportions indicate the relationships of vibrating strings and hence denote intervals. For example, *dupla* 2:1 is the octave, *tripla* 3:1 the twelfth (compound fifth), *sesquialtera* 3:2 the fifth, *sesquitertia* 4:3 the fourth. See Acoustics III.

Proportz, Proportio [G.]. In the German dance literature of the 16th century, a *Nachtanz* in quick triple time that follows a main dance in slower duple time. Both dances have the same melody in different meters. This is actually implied in the name, which indicates the application of a *proportion to the original melody. Nominally this proportion was *proportio tripla* (another name for such a *Nachtanz* was *Tripla*); actually, however, it was *proportio sesquialtera.* Therefore, three notes of the *Proportz* equal in duration two notes of the main dance. The accompanying example (Ammerbach, *Herzog Moritz-Tanz*) shows the exact rhythmic relation-

ship between the two [see W. Merian, *Der Tanz in den deutschen Tabulaturbüchern* (1927), p. 77]. See H. Riemann, "Tänze des 16. Jahrhunderts à double emploi" (*DM* vi.3).

Proposta [It.]. The subject (*dux*) of a fugue, as opposed to *risposta,* the answer (*comes*).

Proprietas. See under Ligatures II.

Proprium missae [L.]. The Proper of the Mass. See Mass A, B.

Prosa [L.], **prose** [F.]. Medieval name, retained to the present day in France, for the *sequence. Originally it seems to have been used specifically for the sequence texts, as opposed to their music; hence the designations *sequentia cum prosa* or *prosa ad sequentium,* found in some early French MSS. The *prosae* were not in any measured poetic meter, so that the term, given its older meaning ("elevated diction"), is quite logical. *Prosarium* [F. *prosaire*] is a medieval book containing sequences. See *Prosula.* See H. Husmann, "Sequenz und Prosa" (*AnnM* ii, 61–91).

Proslambanomenos [Gr.]. The lowest tone, A (not G), of the Greek scale, so called because it was added below the lowest tetrachord, e–d–c–B. See Greece.

Prosomoion. See *Idiomelon.*

Prosula [L.]. Medieval term for certain kinds of textual trope, i.e., for textual insertions adapted to the melismas of the original chant, resulting in a syllabic setting. In MSS of the 11th century they are indicated by *Prosl.* or *Psl.* They are found mostly in Alleluias and Offertories. The oldest example is a 9th-century "Psalle modulamina" underlaid to the verse of the Alleluia "Christus resurgens." An Alleluia-*prosula* (or Alleluia-trope) differs from the sequence (*prosa*) in that the former is an Alleluia with an amplified text (the original words of the verse are skillfully worked into the fuller text), while the sequence is an addition to the Alleluia that often shows no musical relationship to the mother chant. See Trope. See *ApGC*, p. 433; J. Smits von Waesberghe, in *CP 1958,* p. 251.

Protestant church music (German). Martin Luther (1483–1546), who founded the German Protestant Church, retained many elements of the Roman Catholic liturgy, particularly the Mass Ordinary (also the Gradual and Communion), but replaced the Latin texts with German translations. To these he added the sermon and his great contribution to the development of music, the *Kirchenlied,* known as the German Protestant *chorale. Important developments of the 17th century are the *organ chorale and church cantata [see Cantata III]. L. Senfl (*c.* 1490–1543), H. Schütz (1585–1672), and J. S. Bach (1685–1750) are probably the greatest of the many great masters who contributed to the development of Protestant Church music. See

Church music III (also for bibl.); Psalter; Anglican chant; Anglican church music.

Protus [Gr.]. See under Church modes I.

Prussian Quartets. (1) A set of three string quartets by Mozart, in D, B-flat, and F (K. 575, 589, 590), composed 1789–90 and dedicated to Friedrich Wilhelm II, King of Prussia, who in 1789 had invited him to Berlin. The cello parts are unusually elaborate, obviously intended to please the King, who played this instrument. (2) The name is also used for Haydn's string quartets op. 50, nos. 1–6, for which the title page of the Artaria first edition (1787) bears a dedication to Friedrich Wilhelm II.

Ps. Abbr. for *Psalm. In German scores, abbr. for *Posaune,* i.e., trombone.

Psallenda. An item of the Vesper service of *Ambrosian chant, somewhat comparable to the Magnificat antiphons of the Roman rites.

Psalm [F. *psaume;* G. *Psalm;* It., Sp. *salmo*]. The Book of Psalms has been, no doubt, the single most important source of text in music history. In their original form the psalms were not pure poetry but songs, perhaps with instrumental accompaniment. However, the inscriptions of many psalms do not, as was formerly assumed, refer to instruments but to standard melodies to be used for a given psalm. For instance, the inscription translated in the King James Version as "To the chief musician upon Gittith (Shoshannim, etc.)" [see Ps. 8, 45] actually means: "To be sung to the main melody 'Wine-press' ('Lilies,' etc.)," terms that indicate *melody types similar to the Arab *maqamat* [see *SaHMI,* pp. 124ff].

The Book of Psalms contains 150 poems. The numbering system in the Latin version of the Bible, used in the Roman Catholic services, differs slightly from that of the English version. The English nos. 9 and 10 correspond to no. 9 of the Vulgate (Latin version) and the English no. 147 corresponds to nos. 146 and 147 of the Vulgate. Therefore, for all the psalms between nos. 10 and 147 the English number is one digit higher than the Vulgate's. References in this dictionary are to the Latin number, with the English number (if needed) added in parentheses (or brackets), e.g., Psalm 49 (50).

In the original Hebrew, the psalms are poems based mostly on the principle of accentuation. Each psalm consists of a number of verses (marked ℣ in the liturgical books of the Roman Catholic Church), each of which consists of two (sometimes three) parts that correspond to each other, often expressing the same thought or contrasting thoughts. They were sung to music somewhat similar to that of the Gregorian psalm tones, which are obviously derived from ancient Hebrew models such as exist to the present day among Jewish communities in the Near East [see Jewish music I].

The psalms were used as texts for the music of many Christian Churches, except for the Lutheran, whose music is based on *chorale texts. For the psalm music of the Roman Catholic Church, see Psalmody; Psalm tones; for that of the Anglican, see Anglican chant; for that of the Reformed Churches, see Psalter; for the polyphonic composition of psalm texts, see Psalm composition. See also Penitential psalms.

Psalm composition. The psalms have often been used as texts for polyphonic compositions. Aside from early polyphonic settings of Graduals and Alleluias (Winchester Troper, school of Notre Dame), whose texts are nearly always taken from psalms, this activity began in the 15th century. The earliest example is Binchois' fauxbourdon-like setting of the entire Psalm 113 (114), "In exitu Israel" [see J. Marix, *Les Musiciens de la cour de Bourgogne,* p. 196]. Simple homophonic settings of the psalms were widely used throughout the period from *c.* 1450 to 1600. Examples are the three-part settings for alternating choruses in MS Modena, Bibl. Est. *lat 454–455* (*c.* 1450–1500); the numerous four-part settings in *falsobordone* style in MS Jena, Univ. Bibl. *34* (*c.* 1500–20); Willaert's *polychoral *Salmi spezzati* (1550); and the Spanish *fabordones* for voices (Guerrero, Victoria, and others; see Editions XX, 6) or for organ (A. de Cabezón; see *ibid.,* 3, pp. 32ff).

Of greater musical interest are the 16th-century settings of psalm texts in motet style (psalm motets). Probably the first and, at the same time, the greatest master in this field was Josquin, who used psalm texts for more than thirty of his motets ("De profundis," "Dominus regnavit," "Domine, ne in furore"; see Editions VIII, 33). Among the later contributions, Lasso's *Psalmi Davidis poenitentiales* of 1560 [see Penitential psalms] are noteworthy. In the field of organ music, Cabezón was the first to write a complete set of psalm *versets, four versets for each psalm tone [see Alternation]. Most of the *anthems use psalm texts in English translation.

In the 17th and 18th centuries paraphrased psalm texts were used, e.g., in Schütz's *Psalmen Davids* (1619) and Benedetto Marcello's *Estro *poetico-armonico* (8 vols., 1724–26). Often single psalm verses were composed. Examples are Viadana's *Exaudi me* (Ps. 69:16) and F. Couperin's *Qui dat nivem* (Ps. 145:16); see *HAM,* nos. 185, 266. In Germany, cantatas were occasionally based on psalm texts, e.g., by Andreas Hammerschmidt, Tunder, and Buxtehude. Bach used psalms for his motets "Lobet den Herrn, alle Heiden" (Ps. 116 [117] and "Singet dem Herrn" (Ps. 148 [149] and 149 [150]), as well as for his early cantata, "Der Herr denket an uns" (Ps. 114 [115]: 12–15). In some of his later cantatas he based the initial chorus on a psalm verse, e.g., "Du Hirte Israel, höre" (Ps. 79 [80]: 1) and "Herr, gehe nicht ins Gericht" (Ps. 142 [143]: 2).

Among 19th-century psalm compositions, those by Schubert (Ps. 23, op. 132), Mendelssohn (cantatas and motets), Brahms (op. 29, no. 2), Liszt (Ps. 13, for tenor solo, chorus, and orchestra), and Bruckner (Ps. 150) are outstanding. Important 20th-century compositions are Reger's *Der 100. Psalm* (1908), Kodály's *Psalmus Hungaricus* (1923), Honegger's *Le Roi David* (1921), Stravinsky's *Symphonie des Psaumes* (1930), Milhaud's various works based on psalm texts, and Britten's *Psalm 150.* See also Penitential psalms; Miserere; Psalter; Bay Psalm Book.

Lit.: M. Cauchie, "Les Psaumes de Janequin" (*CP Laurencie*); B. Widmann, "Die Kompositionen der Psalmen von Statius Olthof" (*VMW* v).

Psalmellus. In *Ambrosian chant, name for the Gradual.

Psalmody, Gregorian. The psalms are by far the most important texts used in Gregorian chant [see Gregorian chant II]. In the early days of Christian worship the service consisted only of psalm singing, and in spite of the many fundamental changes that took place in ensuing centuries the psalms retained their dominant position in the Roman liturgy. This development, which may have taken place between the years 400 and 800, led to a variety of forms and types for the different items of the chant, each item receiving the structure proper to it from the standpoint of the liturgy. All these forms stem from three original types: direct psalmody, responsorial psalmody, and antiphonal psalmody. The last two terms originally meant two different methods of performance, alternation between soloist and chorus (responsorial) and alternation between two half-choruses (antiphonal). However, this distinction is no longer valid [see Responsorial singing] and the terms have only historical and stylistic significance, the responsorial types being the more elaborate of the two.

I. *Direct psalmody* means singing a psalm (or a number of verses thereof) without any textual addition or modification. This method survives in two types, one for the Mass and the other for the Office for the Dead. The former is the *Tract. The latter is known as *psalmus directaneus* (*in directum, indirectum*) and means singing a psalm to a psalm tone but without antiphon [see under III below]. For this method, which is rarely used, special psalm tones called *tonus in directum* are provided.

II. *Responsorial psalmody* was directly taken over from the Jewish service. Originally, the entire psalm was sung by a soloist (*cantor*), with the chorus (congregation; eventually the church choir, or *schola*) responding after each verse with a short affirmative phrase such as Amen, Alleluia, etc. (A direct model for this exists in Ps. 135 [136], in which each verse ends with the sentence: "For his mercy endureth forever.") The resulting form may be indicated as follows:

$$(\underset{\cdots}{R}) \; \underset{\cdots}{V} \; \underline{R} \; \underset{\cdots}{V} \; \underline{R} \; \underset{\cdots}{V} \; \text{etc.} \; \underline{R}$$

(R is the recurrent *respond, V stands for the verses of the Psalm; straight underlining indicates choral performance; dotted lines mean solo performance; the length of the underlines, i.e., long or short, and the number of dots, i.e., one to four, indicate the relative length of the section.) Although originally the singing of the cantor consisted of a simple recitation in the style of an inflected monotone, similar to that of the psalm tones, there developed, probably in the 4th to 6th centuries, more elaborate methods of singing that finally led to a highly melismatic style of singing psalm verses. A similar development took place with the responds, which, originally sung by the congregation, eventually passed over to the trained chorus (*schola*) and grew considerably longer, both in text and music. Naturally the increase in length of the single sections, verses as well as respond, necessitated a drastic reduction in the number of sections (a similar development is that leading from the *canzona to the *sonata). Instead of singing an entire psalm, single verses were selected, varying in number from four to one. The respond was also cut, so that it was not repeated in full after each verse but in a reduced form, its initial half (or third) being omitted.

It is in these more or less radically reduced forms that responsorial psalmody entered the Gregorian repertory. In only a few special chants does the original scheme survive to some extent. An unusually full example is the responsory "Aspiciens a longe" for Matins on the First Sunday in Advent [see *Processionale monasticum*, p. 18]. Its scheme is:

$$\underset{\cdots}{R} \; \underset{\cdots}{V_1} \; \underline{R}' \; \underset{\cdots}{V_2} \; \underline{R}'' \; \underset{\cdots}{V_3} \; \underline{R}''' \; \underline{D} \; \underline{R}$$

R is the respond: *Aspiciens a longe, ecce video Dei potentiam venientem, et nebulam totam terram tegentem.* **Ite obviam ei, et dicite:* †*Nuntia nobis si tu es ipse* ‡*qui regnaturus es in populo Israel.* In the repetitions of the respond, this is successively shortened from the beginning, as indicated by the signs *, †, ‡ (R': *Ite*, etc.; R'': *Nuntia*, etc.; R''': *qui regnaturus*, etc.). The letter D stands for the Lesser *Doxology, the first part of which, *Gloria patri et filio et spiritui sancto*, is frequently added in the forms of responsorial (and antiphonal) psalmody as a final "verse." A chant of almost equally complete structure is the responsory "Libera me," sung at the Burial Service [*LU*, p. 1767; *HAM*, no. 14]. Yet another responsory showing the rondo structure of the early responsorial psalmody is the "Subvenite" of the Burial Service [*LU*, p. 1765].

Aside from such isolated examples, the surviving categories of responsorial chant are still shorter. The most important of these types are the *responsory, the short responsory (*responsorium breve*), the *Gradual, and the *Alleluia. The following table shows the usual form of these chants:

(1) Responsory: $\underline{R} \; \underset{\cdots}{V} \; R'$ or $\underline{R} \; \underset{\cdots}{V} \; R' \; \underline{R}$ or $\underline{R} \; \underset{\cdots}{V} \; R' \; D \; \underline{R}$

(2) Short responsory: $\underline{R} \; \underline{R} \; \underset{\cdots}{V} \; R' \; D \; \underline{R}$

(3) Alleluia: $R' \; \underline{R} \; \underset{\cdots}{V} \; \underline{R}$

(4) Gradual: $\underline{R} \; \underset{\cdots}{V}$ or $\underline{R} \; \underset{\cdots}{V} \; \underline{R}$

The signs · – and · · · – indicate respectively soloist beginning (*incipit of a choral section) and choral conclusion of a solo section. Examples for (1) are found in *LU*, pp. 725ff, 721ff, 375. The short responsory has a fairly long (somewhat variable) scheme, but short and simple melodies in each section. The accompanying example of a short responsory [*LU*, p. 229] will also help clarify the structure of the other, more melismatic chants. In the Alleluias the response consists of the word "Alleluia" only. This is sung first by the soloist (R'), after which the chorus repeats it and continues with the *jubilus on (*allelui*)a—(R). With the Graduals the repetition

1. R. Chri-ste Fi-li De-i vi-vi * Mi-se-re - re no-bis
2. R. Chri-ste Fi-li De-i vi-vi Mi-se-re - re no-bis
4. Mi-se-re - re no-bis
6. R. Chri-ste Fi-li De-i vi-vi Mi-se-re - re no-bis

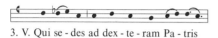

3. V. Qui se - des ad dex - te - ram Pa - tris

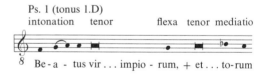

5. D. Glo-ri-a Pa-tri, et Fi-li-o, et Spi-ri-tu-i Sanc-to.

of the respond is optional [see *LU*, p. 320f].

III. *Antiphonal psalmody* originally consisted of the psalms sung by two alternating half-choruses. This method was introduced into the Western Church by St. Ambrose (A.D. 1333–97) in imitation of Syrian models. The exact procedure in the early antiphonal psalmody is not known; there may have been alternating performance for the two halves of each single verse, or (more likely) for each pair of verses [see Antiphon, *History*].

The antiphonal method of psalm singing was at an early time enriched by the addition of a short sentence sung by the whole chorus (perhaps originally the congregation) after every two verses, which was called antiphon (A). There resulted a rondo-like scheme: A V$_1$ V$_2$ A V$_3$ V$_4$ A etc. A, similar in structure to that of early responsorial psalmody. As in the latter, the full scheme survives only in special chants, such as the *invitatory at the beginning of Matins, in which Ps. 94, "Venite exultemus Domino" (Ps. 95, O come, let us sing unto the Lord) is sung according to the following scheme [see *LU*, p. 368; also pp. 765, 863, 918, 1779]: A̲ A̲ V̲$_1$ V̲$_2$ A V̲$_3$ V̲$_4$ A̲' V̲$_5$ V̲$_6$ V̲$_7$ A V̲$_8$ V̲$_9$ A̲' V̲$_{10}$ V̲$_{11}$ A̲ D A̲'A̲. (A is the antiphon *Christus natus est nobis, Venite adoremus;* A' stands for the second half alone; the verses of the Latin text [here, the Itala Bible] do not always agree with the divisions of the English version). A similarly extended structure (A V$_1$ A V$_2$ A V$_3$ A D$_1$ A D$_2$ A) occurs in the antiphon *Lumen ad revelationem gentium,* sung in alternation with the verses of the canticle *Nunc dimittis* during the distribution of the candles on the feast of Purification [*LU*, p. 1357].

Aside from such special chants, there are four standard types of chant that are considered derivatives of antiphonal psalmody, the Office psalms and the *Introit, *Offertory, and *Communion of the Mass. The Office psalms are complete psalms sung to a psalm tone (the same for each verse) and introduced and closed by a short antiphon: A V$_1$ V$_2$ etc. V$_n$ A [see Psalm tones]. The form of the Introit is A̲ V̲ D̲ A̲ (D is the Lesser Doxology; see above). In the Offertory and Communion the verse has been entirely lost, so that only the antiphon remains. In the *Ordo Romanus primus* from *c.* 775 both Introit and Communion are described as consisting of several verses sung in alternation with the antiphon, the doxology appearing in the middle rather than at the end. The Offertories had one, two, or three verses as late as the 11th or 12th century [see C. Ott, *Offertoriale sive versus offertoriorum*]. See *ApGC*, pp. 179ff; H. Avenary, "Formal Structure of Psalms and Canticles in Early Jewish and Christian Chant" (*MD* vii).

Psalm tones. In Gregorian chant, the recitation melodies used for singing (complete) psalms during the Office [see Psalmody III]. There are eight such tones, one for each church mode, and all in the character of an inflected *monotone. The main note of the recitation, called *tenor (repercussio, tuba,* reciting note), is always the fifth degree of the mode [see Church modes II]. In

Ps. 1 (tonus 1.D)

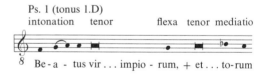

Be - a - tus vir ... impio - rum, + et ... to-rum

non ste - tit et ... - lenti - ae non se - dit,

accordance with the binary structure of the psalm verses, the psalm tone falls into halves, the first half consisting of intonation, tenor, and mediation, and the second of tenor and termination. If the first half is too long to be sung in one breath, there is another slight inflection at the breathing point, the *flex.* The accompanying example (verse 1 of Ps.1: *Beatus vir, qui non abiit in consilio impiorum,* †*et in via peccatorum non stetit,* *et in cathedra pestilentiae non sedit;* see *LU*, p. 923) shows all these details.

Each psalm is sung with an enframing *antiphon that occurs in full at the end and is reduced to its first word or two (incipit only) at the beginning, except on greater feasts ("Doubles"), when the whole antiphon is sung before as well as after. The antiphon determines not only the psalm tone, which must be in the same mode as the antiphon, but also its termination, for which a number of different formulas called *differentiae* (differences) are provided. The one to be chosen is designed so as to lead back smoothly to the initial note of the antiphon, as sung after the last verse of the psalm. It is indicated, e.g., as follows: Ant. 8.c (mode 8 with the ending on c). Since the *Gloria patri . . . seculorum amen* [see Doxology] invariably serves as a last verse of the psalm, the liturgical books give the *differentia* with the syllables *E u o u a e* (= *seculorum Amen*). The antiphon *Beatus populus* with some verses of Psalm 143 serves as an example (note that the intonation is sung only with the first psalm verse). See also *HAM,* no. 11.

Ant. 8c

Be - a - tus po - pu - lus.

Ps. 143   diff. c

1. De - us canticum . . .psal - lam ti - bi.
2.   Qui das . . . e - ri - pe me.
10.   Gloria . . . tu - i Sanc-to.
11.   Sicut . . . lo - rum. A - men.

Ant.

Be-a-tus po-pu-lus cu-jus Do-mi-nus De-us e-jus.

An exceptional psalm tone is the *tonus peregrinus,* which has different tenors for its first and second halves. It is used for the psalm *In exitu Israel* [*LU,* p. 160]. See H. Gaïsser, in *TG* vii, p. 129. For *tonus directaneus* see Psalmody I.

Psalmus idioticus [L.]. A literary production of the 3rd and 4th centuries consisting of texts written in imitation of the psalms. Among the few surviving examples are the Gloria of the Mass, the Te Deum, and the "Exsultet" [see *Praeconium paschale*].

Psalter. Name for the Book of Psalms translated into the vernacular (English, French, Dutch Psalter), frequently in rhymed versions (metrical

Psalter) and provided with music for congregational singing [for a Psalter of the 3rd century, see Hymn I]. Collections of prose psalms set to *Anglican chant are also known as psalters.

For all branches of the Christian faith as well as for Judaism, the Book of Psalms has been a perennial resource. It was natural, therefore, that the Reformed Churches should, with one exception (the German), turn to it for texts. The earliest and most influential of the psalters was the French or Genevan Psalter, begun in Strasbourg in 1539 and completed, with metrical versions by Marot and Bèze and music by Bourgeois, in Geneva in 1562. Bourgeois adapted existing melodies, some of them from secular sources, and composed others to fit the various meters. In conformity with the Protestant trend toward musical simplification, the settings are almost uniformly one note to a syllable. Calvin opposed the setting of psalter melodies in parts, but it was inevitable, of course, that they should be so treated. Among the composers who contributed part settings of the French Psalter were Bourgeois (1547, 1560), Goudimel (1564, 1565), Claude Le Jeune (1564; also settings in *vers mesuré,* 1606), Mauduit, and the Dutchman Sweelinck (1604–21). Ex. in *HAM,* nos. 126, 132.

The Dutch Psalter is represented by the *Souterliedekens collections of 1540 (S. Cock) and 1556–57 (Susato). In 1566 the French Psalter was adopted in the Netherlands, replacing the Dutch versions.

During the persecutions under Queen Mary, about the middle of the 16th century, many English Protestants fled to Geneva, where they came under the influence of the French Psalter. As a result, the so-called Anglo-Genevan Psalter was published with the help of both Englishmen and Scots. The French style is strongly represented in this work, and even after the refugees returned to Britain the Scottish Psalter of 1564 perpetuated the French influence, whereas the English Psalter pursued a quite different course with regard to both verse and music. Among the better-known English Psalters are the "Old Version" of Sternhold and Hopkins, completed and published by Day in 1562; Ravenscroft (1621); Playford (1671; another in 1673); and the "New Version" of Tate and Brady (1696). The English type of psalm tune consists of a number of shorter notes between two longer ones. Such a fixed pattern tends, after many repetitions, to be monotonous, and it compares most unfavorably with the free-flowing and infinitely varied melodies of the French prototype.

Another group of refugees came under the influence of the French form, this time in Amsterdam, where Henry Ainsworth in 1612 brought out a Psalter for the benefit of the English "Separatists" called The Ainsworth Psalter. Thence it traveled to America with the Pilgrims in 1620. Its hold on its devotees must have been remarkable, for though the highly influential *Bay Psalm Book appeared in 1640, Ainsworth's Psalter was not entirely displaced for many years thereafter.

In the early 18th century in both England and America, the grace or ornament became popular in psalm singing. Clerical protests against this practice are similar to other attempts in music history to preserve a medium that was becoming outmoded. The music of the Psalter was, if praiseworthy for its dignity, very monotonous. Aside from the fact that the pace was probably painfully slow, the custom of *"lining out" disrupted the sense of the text and destroyed musical continuity. In the 18th century the *hymn began to make its way among English-speaking Protestant congregations. Its eventual adoption with a corresponding neglect of psalm singing was neither completely profitable nor wholly to be deplored. However, Scottish devotion to the Psalter remained so strong that not until 1861 did the Established Church of Scotland authorize the singing of hymns.

Lit.: A. C. Welch, *The Psalter in Life, Worship and History* (1926); E. B. Cross, *Modern Worship and the Psalter* (1932); C. C. Keet, *A Liturgical Study of the Psalter* [1928]; F. J. Metcalf, *American Psalmody* (1917); W. S. Pratt, *The Music of the French Psalter of 1562* (1939); C. Schneider, *La Musique originelle des psaumes huguenots* (1934); H. Expert, *Le Psautier huguenot du XVIe siècle* (1902); P. Pidoux, *Le Psautier huguenot du XVIe siècle,* 2 vols. (1962); M. Frost, *English and Scottish Psalm and Hymn Tunes, c. 1543–1677* (1953); M. Patrick, *Four Centuries of Scottish Psalmody* (1949); N. Livingston, *The Scottish Metrical Psalter of 1635* (1864); C. S. Smith, ‡*The Ainsworth Psalter* (1938); J. Warrington, *Short Titles of Books Relating to or Illustrating the History and Practice of Psalmody in the United States, 1620–1820* (1898); S. J. Lenselink, *De nederlandse psalmberijmingen* (1959); G. R. Woodward, "The Genevan Psalter of 1562" (*PMA* xliv); W. Truron, "The Rhythm of Metrical Psalm-Tunes" (*ML* ix, 29); W. S. Pratt, "The Importance of the Early French Psalter" (*MQ* xxi); L. Ellinwood, "Tallis' Tunes and Tudor Psalmody" (*MD* ii).

A.T.D.

Psaltery. A class of ancient and medieval instruments (also called *zithers) consisting of a flat soundboard over which a number of strings are stretched. They are plucked with the fingers or a plectrum. This manner of playing distinguishes the psaltery from the *dulcimer, which is struck with hammers. In the general classification of instruments, the term is used for a group that includes, among others, the harpsichord, a keyed psaltery [see Instruments IV, A, 1, a].

The name *psalterion* is encountered in Greek literature, probably meaning a harp [see *SaHMI*, p. 136, also p. 115f]. In a letter attributed to St. Jerome (*c.* 330–420) a *psalterium decacordum* (ten-stringed psaltery) depicted in the shape of a rectangle is interpreted symbolically, the strings representing the Ten Commandments and the sides of the frame the four Gospels. From the 14th to 16th centuries psalteries of various shapes were used. One of the most common was shaped like a symmetrical trapezoid, sometimes with the slanting sides curved inward. Such instruments were called *caño* or *canon,* after their Arab model, the *kanun.* Another type, shaped like half of a trapezoid, was called *medio canon* or *micanon* (sometimes corrupted into *medicinale*). This shape, which persisted in the winged form of the harpsichord and piano, slightly resembled a pig's head and so was called *istromento di porco* by M. Praetorius (*Organographia,* 1619). Among the more recent types of psaltery are the Austrian *zither and Finnish kantele. See also Bell harp. See ill. under Zither.

Psychology of music. The study of the relationship of music to the human mind. From very early times people have been aware of such a relationship and have described in more or less definite terms how the human mind is affected by music [see Affections]. Specifically the term applies to a relatively new field involving the use of scientific methods of investigation. The first impulse for such studies came from Helmholtz' *On the Sensation of Tones* (*Die Lehre von den Tonempfindungen,* 1863), primarily a physiological study. Carl Stumpf (1848–1936) was the first to apply the scientific method (experiments, tests, statistics) to musical-psychological phenomena—particularly to the problem of consonance and dissonance—in his *Tonpsychologie* (2 vols., 1883, '90) and other publications. Another important step was taken by Ernst Kurth who, in his *Musikpsychologie* [1931], proceeded from the "psychology of tone" to a more penetrating "psychology of music" based not only on the perceptive but also on the interpretative faculties of the human mind (*Gestaltlehre,* psychological dynamics, tension, anticipation, etc.). Stumpf's experimental approach to the problem was continued and enlarged by G. Révész, C. E. Seashore, A. Wellek, and many others.

Among the main fields of research today are: sound perception, especially the problem presented by the phenomenon of the *octave; consonance and dissonance (Stumpf's theory of *Tonverschmelzung;* see Consonance, dissonance I d); *absolute pitch; *key characteristics; tone and color synesthesia [see Color and music]; musical talent and aptitude [see Tests and measurements in music]; special aptitudes of the child prodigy, the blind, the deaf; heredity and musical talent; *music therapy; reading of music; and sexual and psychoanalytical aspects of music.

Lit.: G. Révész, *Introduction to the Psychology of Music* [1953]; M. Schoen, *The Psychology of Music* [1940]; *id., The Understanding of Music* [1945]; R. P. Farnsworth, *The Social Psychology of Music* [1958]; C. E. Seashore, *Psychology of Music* (1938); R. W. Lundin, *An Objective Psychology of Music* [1953]; J. L. Mursell, *The Psychology of Music* [1937]; H.-P. Reinecke, *Experimentelle Beiträge zur Psychologie des musikalischen Hörens* (1964); A. Wellek, *Musikpsychologie und Musikästhetik* (1963); J. Handschin, *Der Toncharakter* [1948]; A. Wellek, "Der gegenwärtige Stand der Musikpsychologie" (*CP 1961*); C. Stumpf, "Musikpsychologie in England" (*VMW* i, 266, 299). Additional bibl. in books above; also in D. H. Daugherty, *A Bibliography of Periodical Literature in Musicology* (1940), pp. 108ff.

Publicaciones, Publications, etc. See Editions XLV–XLVII.

Public school music. See Music education in the United States II. See also article in O. Thompson, *The International Cyclopedia of Music and Musicians* (1939), bibl. pp. 2270ff.

Publishing, music. Music publishing began with Octavianus Scotus of Venice, who in 1481 printed the first *Missale Romanum* with music, and Ottaviano dei Petrucci of Venice, who in 1498 obtained from the Seignory a twenty years' monopoly on the printing of music (other than plainsong). Petrucci's first publication was the famous *Odhecaton of 1501, which was followed by a score of important books of Masses, motets,

and *frottole.* Thirty years later, Pierre Attaingnant founded a publishing house at Paris, which from 1528 to 1550 issued books of lute music, organ music, motets, Masses, and thirty-five books of chansons. In the latter part of the 16th century, as a result of generally improving economic conditions and the increase in music production and consumption, quite a number of music publishers were at work: The Gardano firm in Venice (1538–1685); Verovio in Rome (1586–1608; the first publisher of engraved music; see Printing of music); Jacques Moderne at Lyons (1532–67); Christophe Plantin at Antwerp (1578–1639); Nicolas du Chemin at Paris (1549–76); Pierre Phalèse at Louvain, later Antwerp (1545–1674); Tielman Susato at Antwerp (1543–60 and later); and the firm of Ballard and Le Roy at Paris, which, founded in 1551, continued to exist until *c.* 1814, using its first type for more than 200 years. In England Tallis and Byrd were granted a monopoly on music printing in 1575, which in 1598 was transferred to Morley. The publishing, however, was done by Thomas and Michael East, who issued practically all the books of English madrigals from 1587 till 1638. There followed Playford, from 1648 to 1700, and in the 18th century, the house of Walsh (*c.* 1695–1766), the first music publisher to use "high-pressure" methods, including a good deal of pirating [see Lit., Pincherle]. At the same time the house of Roger flourished in Amsterdam and that of Haffner in Nuremberg [see Haffner collection]. About 1750 the world-famous house of Breitkopf (later Breitkopf & Härtel) published its first music books, using a new typographic method that revolutionized the printing of music [see Printing of music (b)]. In 1773 the house of Schott (Mainz) was founded, which together with Artaria (1778, Vienna) published many of Beethoven's works. There followed Simrock of Berlin (1790), Peters of Leipzig (1814), Bote and Bock of Berlin (1838), and Steingräber of Leipzig (1878). Modern music publishing in England started with Novello (1811) and continued with Augener (1853), Chester (1860), and numerous others.

Music publishing in the United States began in the last two decades of the 18th century. Publishing houses known to have existed before 1790 include John Aitken (1785), Thomas Dobson (1785), and Alexander Reinagle (1787), in Philadelphia; and Thomas Dobson (1787) and George Gilfert (1787) in New York. In the following decade about twenty more names were added to the list, e.g., Joseph Carr (1794) in Baltimore, and

G. Graupner (1800) in Boston. [See H. Dichter and E. Shapiro, *Early American Sheet Music* (1941), pp. 165ff.] The first publishing house of importance was Ditson in Boston (1835). There followed Schirmer (Beer & Schirmer, 1861; Schirmer, 1866), and Carl Fischer (1872) of New York, Theodore Presser (1884) of Philadelphia, and many others.

Lit.: G. Dunn, *Methods of Music Publishing* (1931); F. Kidson, *British Music Publishers* [1900]; W. A. Fisher, *150 Years of Music Publishing in the United States* (1934); C. Humphries and W. C. Smith, *Music Publishing in the British Isles . . . to the Middle of the Nineteenth Century* [1954]; C. Hopkinson, *A Dictionary of Parisian Music Publishers, 1700–1950* (1954); A. Weinmann, *Wiener Musikverleger . . . von Mozarts Zeit bis gegen 1860* (1956); C. Sartori, *Dizionario degli editori musicali italiani* (1958); O. E. Deutsch, *Music Publishers' Numbers . . . 1710–1900* (1946); W. C. Smith, *A Bibliography of the Musical Works Published by John Walsh During the Years 1695–1720* (1948); F. Lesure and G. Thibault, *Bibliographie des éditions d'Adrian Le Roy et Robert Ballard, 1551–1598* (1955); C. Sartori, *Bibliografia delle opere musicali stampate da Ottavian Petrucci* (1948); J. A. Stellfeld, *Bibliographie des éditions musicales plantiniennes* [1949]; M. Donà, *La Stampa musicale a milano fino all'anno 1700* (1961); C. Hopkinson, *Notes on Russian Music Publishers* (1959); F. Lesure and G. Thibault, "Bibliographie des éditions musicales publiées par Nicolas du Chemin, 1549–1576" (*AnnM* i); R. Eitner, "Buch- und Musikalien-Händler, Buch- und Musikaliendrucker" (*MfM*, 1904, suppl.); F. Kidson, "John Playford" (*MQ* iv); *id.*, "Handel's Publisher, John Walsh" (*MQ* vi); M. Brenet, "La Librairie musicale en France de 1653 à 1790" (*SIM* viii); G. Cucuel, ". . . La Librairie musicale au XVIIIe siècle" (*SIM* xiii); M. Pincherle, "De la Piraterie . . . aux environs de 1700" (*RdM* 1933, p. 136). See also Bibliography of music; Printing of music; Plate numbers.

Puerto Rico. Material concerning Puerto Rico's four and one-half centuries of music history (since its discovery in 1493) deals mainly with folk music. Early 16th-century chroniclers report performances of a dance called *el Puertorrico* in Peru, Chile, and other South American Spanish colonies. This was most likely the forerunner of the **seis,* a dance familiar to the islanders during the 16th, 17th, and 18th centuries. Further evolution of this form resulted in the *contradanza* [see

Contredanse], which has inspired many composers from the 19th century to the present. Among the earliest of them were Aurelio Dueño (d. 1870) and Carlos Segnet (*c.* 1837–87). By the end of the 19th century this dance showed the additional influences of both Italian opera and French romanticism, and, in the hands of such composers as Manuel Gregorio Tavárez (1843–83), it became a stylized form used by such composers as Julian Andino (1845–1926), Casimiro Duchesne (1852–1906), and Federico Ramos (1857–1927).

The most famous 19th-century Puerto Rican composer is Juan Morel Campos (1857–96), whose creative output went far beyond the *contradanza,* including music for the church, theater, and instrumental ensembles. He also helped train a large number of composers who reflected his influence in their cultivation of the *danza puertorriqueña;* the most prominent of these were Juan Peña Reyes (1898–1948), Juan Rios Ovalle (*c.* 1863–1928), and Juan F. Acosta (b. 1893). Their contemporaries and successors, Braulio Dueño Colón (1854–1934), Jesús Figueroa (b. 1878), José E. Pedreira (1904–59), Narciso Figueroa (b. 1906), and José J. Quintón (1881–1925), also produced major forms, especially chamber music and solo instrumental music.

Puerto Rico's 20th-century music still reflects the influences of the traditional dance forms, even in abstract works by such composers as Amaury Veray (b. 1922), Russian-born Jack Delano (b. 1914), and Luis Antonio Ramírez (b. 1923). The best-known Puerto Rican contemporary composer is Hector Campos-Parsi (b. 1922), who studied in both the United States and France and whose works have won international recognition.

In addition to the traditional **seis* and *contradanza,* the **plena* and *sonduro* are exclusively Puerto Rican folk forms whose popularity equals that of the **guaracha,* **bolero,* **son,* and **punto,* all forms of Cuban origin that were adopted in Puerto Rico as a result of the continual contact between the two islands.

Puerto Rico also has an outstanding composer of popular songs, Rafael Hernández, who became well known in New York shortly after World War I.

Lit.: M. Deliz, *Renadio del cantar folklórico de Puerto Rico* (1952). Also see under Latin America.   J.O-S.

Pui. See *Puy.*

Pulcinella. Ballet by Stravinsky, produced in Paris, 1920. The music is a modern setting of numerous passages from anonymous works formerly thought to be by the 18th-century composer Pergolesi. Many of the melodies are intact, while the accompaniment is cleverly altered into a sophisticated 20th-century idiom that is often *pandiatonic. See Neoclassicism.

Pumhart [G.]. Old term for bombarde; see Oboe family III.

Punctum. (1) See under Neumes I. (2) Same as *punctus.*

Punctus [L.]. (1) In *mensural notation, a sign like the dot of modern notation and having the same meaning, but also having a function somewhat like that of the modern bar line. In its first meaning it is called *punctus additionis* or *augmentationis* and is used for binary (imperfect) notes to which it adds one-half of their value. In the latter meaning it is called *punctus divisionis* and is used only in triple meter (*tempus perfectum, prolatio perfecta*) in order to mark off groups of perfections (i.e., of three semibreves, or three minims) for the sake of clarity. In the accompanying example, the second, third, and fifth dots are *puncti additionis* while the others are *puncti divisionis.*

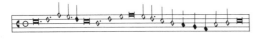

The system of *puncti* has been unnecessarily complicated by early theorists who deal in detail with a number of other *puncti,* such as *punctus perfectionis, imperfectionis, alterationis, syncopationis,* etc. Unfortunately these unnecessary complications have been perpetuated by modern writers. Especially misleading is the "simplified" explanation [see S. T. Warner, in *PMA* xlv] that distinguishes only between the *punctus divisionis* and *punctus perfectionis,* since a further distinction must be made between the *punctus perfectionis* in perfect mensuration and the *punctus "perfectionis"*—properly, *additionis*—in imperfect mensuration. For a fuller explanation, see *ApNPM, passim.*

(2) In the *estampies* of the 13th and 14th centuries the various sections, each of which is repeated, are called *punctus (primus punctus, secundus punctus,* etc.).

Punta, punto [It.]. Point. *A punta d'arco,* with the point of the bow (of the violin); *punto d'organo,* the pause and its sign.

Punto [Sp.]. Gay rural Cuban folksong of Spanish origin, usually sung to the accompaniment of the *bandurria* and *claves.* It is generally in 3/4 meter unexpectedly alternating with 6/8, and rarely in 2/4 meter with occasional shifts to 3/4 and 6/8. It has a short melody that is repeated for each line of a quatrain, alternating with short instrumental interludes. The music is always in the major mode, with seventh chords predominating over the tonic. Freedom of expression and use of descending vocal portamentos are characteristic of the form.   J.O-S.

Purajhei. Paraguayan folksong that musically reflects strong European 19th-century influences but is sung to Guaraní texts, whose euphonic character gives the songs a highly individual, flowing sweetness.   J.O-S.

Purfling. The inlaid border of violins, etc., consisting of three small slips of wood, the middle one black, the other two white. Besides its ornamental value, it helps prevent chipping of the edges.

Puritani di Scozia, I [It., The Puritans of Scotland]. Opera in three acts by Bellini (libretto by C. Pepoli, based on a play by F. Ancelot and X. B. Saintine), produced in Paris, 1835. Setting: near Plymouth, during the English Civil War.

Puritans and music. See under United States. Also see P. Scholes, *The Puritans and Their Music in England and New England* (1934); W. S. Pratt, *The Music of the Pilgrims* (1901).

Puy, pui. Name for medieval French societies that sponsored literary and musical festivals, held regularly with competitions and prizes. They are documented as far back as the 11th century (earliest troubadours) and existed as late as the 16th century. The most famous was the *Puy d'Èvreux,* held annually on St. Cecilia's Day from 1570 till 1614 (founded by Guillaume Costeley and others). Among its laureates (*roy du puy*) were Orlando di Lasso, Titelouze, and Du Caurroy. The *puys* of the troubadours served as a model for similar competitions of the German minnesingers, such as the "Sängerkrieg auf der Wartburg," which Wagner used as the basis for *Tannhäuser.* See also Meistersinger III; Tenso.

Puzzle canon. Riddle canon [see Canon II].

Pyiba, pyipar (*p'i-pa, p'i-p'a*). A Chinese pear-shaped short lute with a rather flat body and four strings [see ill. under Lute], usually tuned A–d–e–a. On the traditional model the frets, when pressed over the A-string will produce the notes B–c–c♯–d–e–f–f♯–g–a–b–c$^{+'}$–d'–e'–f♯'–g$^{+'}$–a'. The pyiba player uses a variety of finger techniques. Some distinctive features of pyiba music are the sustained rolls on one or more strings, the long portamento, the gradual crescendo and decrescendo, and numerous kinds of percussive effect. The repertory ranges from pieces expressing deep pathos to comical parodies.

The name pyiba was used in the 3rd century for a hand-plucked stringed instrument with a long neck and round body. In the 6th century a short lute with a crooked neck, played with a large plectrum, was introduced into China from the Middle East. This instrument survives in its original form in the present-day *biwa* of Japan, where 8th-century specimens can still be seen. In China, it went through modifications in shape and arrangement of the frets. It is now played mainly with the fingers instead of a plectrum. The pyiba figured prominently in Tarng (T'ang) dynasty (618–906) orchestras. It was also used to accompany songs and dances and as a solo instrument. Numerous romantic anecdotes and poems have been written about it. Unlike the *chyn, which traditionally belongs to the scholars and philosophers, the pyiba has always been associated with popular entertainment. Today, the pyiba is played as a solo instrument, in instrumental ensembles, and as accompaniment to singing in certain theatrical performances. Although it has popular appeal, its demanding technique keeps it from being readily accessible to dilettantes and amateurs.

Since the 1920's there have been serious efforts to revise interest in the pyiba. A notable exponent was Liou Tianhwa (1895–1932), a virtuoso pyiba player and composer of a few widely known pieces for it. Other outstanding contemporary players today are Lii Tyngsong, Tsaur Anher, Suen Peirjang, Leu Jennyuan (Lui Tsun-yuen), and Leu Peiryuan. One result of the revival has been a change in the positions of some of the frets; on the newer models they have been rearranged to produce a complete chromatic scale.

As far as is known, there are about ten pyiba music collections in existence. Most of these have been published, the earliest in 1819. Besides descriptive pieces, they also include lengthy works in the form of a medley or variations on a theme or on a group of thematic materials. The traditional notation for the pyiba consists of pitch symbols and abbreviated Chinese characters indicating the finger techniques. In all these collections, beats indicating larger units of time are given. At the beginning of the 20th century, a manuscript with twenty-five pyiba compositions dating from sometime before the mid-10th century was discovered in the Duenhwang caves of northwest China. The notation is a tablature indicating strings and frets closely related to the notation still used for the biwa and the mouth organ (shō) in gagaku today.

Lit.: Hayashi Kenzō, "Study on Explication of Ancient Musical Score of P'i-p'a" (*Bulletin*, Nara Gakugei University, v, no. 1, Dec. 1955, based on Jap. article in *Gekkan Gakufu* [1938], pp. 23–58); S. Kishibe, "Origin of the P'i-pa" (*Transactions of the Asiatic Society of Japan* xv [1940], pp. 259–304); L. Picken, "Origin of the Short Lute" (*GSJ* viii, 32ff); *SaHMI*, pp. 189ff.   R.C.P.

Pyknon [Gr.]. In the ancient Greek scale [see Greece II], the lower segment of the enharmonic and chromatic tetrachords, containing the two microtones or semitones. In either case, this segment was smaller than the interval above it. Its three notes were sometimes described (in descending order) as *oxypyknon, mesopyknon,* and *barypyknon*. The theory of Sachs, connecting these notes with a fixed pentatonic tuning of the lyre and with the structure of Greek notation, is dubious [see Greece IV], though it is generally possible that these and other notes were rendered on the lyre by stopping strings.   I.H.

Pythagorean hammers. Pythagoras is said to have discovered the basic laws of music by listening to the sound of four smith's hammers, which produced agreeable consonances. They turned out to weigh 12, 9, 8, and 6 pounds respectively. From these figures he derived the octave ($12:6 = 2:1$), fifth ($12:8 = 9:6 = 3:2$), fourth ($12:9 = 4:3$) and whole tone ($9:8$). See, e.g., Guido's "Micrologus," ch. xx (ed. Smits van Waesberghe, p. 228).

Pythagorean scale. A scale, said to have been invented by Pythagoras (*c.* 550 B.C.), that derives all the tones from the interval of the pure fifth, ⅔ [see Acoustics III]. The tones of the diatonic scale are obtained as a series of five successive upper fifths and one lower fifth:

F	c	g	d'	a'	e''	b''
$\frac{2}{3}$	1	$\frac{3}{2}$	$\left(\frac{3}{2}\right)^2$	$\left(\frac{3}{2}\right)^3$	$\left(\frac{3}{2}\right)^4$	$\left(\frac{3}{2}\right)^5$

By reducing these tones to a single octave (c–b), the following scale results:

	c	d	e	f	g	a	b	c'
Frequency:	1	$\frac{9}{8}$	$\frac{81}{64}$	$\frac{4}{3}$	$\frac{3}{2}$	$\frac{27}{16}$	$\frac{243}{128}$	2

Intervals: $\frac{9}{8}$ $\frac{9}{8}$ $\frac{256}{243}$ $\frac{9}{8}$ $\frac{9}{8}$ $\frac{9}{8}$ $\frac{256}{243}$

[For the calculation of the frequencies and intervals, see Intervals, calculation of, I–III; see also the tables under Intervals and under Temperament.] The Pythagorean whole tone is slightly larger than that of the well-tempered scale (204 cents instead of 200), while the semitone is considerably smaller (90 instead of 100). Likewise, the Pythagorean third is 8 cents higher than the well-tempered third, which in turn is higher than the "pure" third (408, 400, and 386 cents).

The Pythagorean semitone was called *limma* (left over) or *diesis* (difference) because it was obtained by subtracting two whole tones from the fourth. Like all tones of the Pythagorean system, it can be represented by powers of 3 and 2:

diesis

$$\frac{2^2}{3} : \left(\frac{3^2}{2^3}\right)^2 = \frac{2^2}{3} \times \frac{2^6}{3^4} = \frac{2^8}{3^5} = \frac{256}{243} = 90 \text{ cents}$$

The difference between the whole tone and the semitone was called *apotome* (cut off). Its value is:

apotome

$$\frac{3^2}{2^3} : \frac{2^8}{3^5} = \frac{3^2}{2^3} \times \frac{3^5}{2^8} = \frac{3^7}{2^{11}} = \frac{2187}{2048} = 114 \text{ cents}$$

In the Greek scale it appears as the interval between b-flat and b natural. It is slightly larger than the *diesis*. In medieval theory these two semitones were distinguished as *semitonium majus* (*apotome*) and *semitonium minus* (*diesis*). Their difference—or that between the whole tone and two *dieses*—is the Pythagorean comma:

comma

$$\frac{3^7}{2^{11}} : \frac{2^8}{3^5} = \frac{3^7}{2^{11}} \times \frac{3^5}{2^8} = \frac{3^{12}}{2^{19}} = \frac{531441}{524288}$$
$$= 23 \text{ cents}$$

The accompanying diagram illustrates the processes just described.

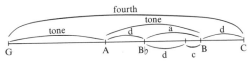

a = *apotome.* c = *comma.* d = *diesis* (*limma*).

The succession of Pythagorean fifths can be continued beyond the tone b, leading to chromatic tones f♯, c♯, etc., and finally to b♯♯, which is slightly higher than c, the interval between the two pitches again being the Pythagorean comma of $\frac{3^{12}}{2^{19}}$ (the ratio of 12 fifths to 7 octaves). See under Circle of fifths. The Pythagorean system was also known in China [see China II], possibly earlier than in Greece [see F. Kuttner, in *CP 1958*, p. 174]. See E. Krenek, "Proportionen und pythagoräische Hämmer" (*Musica* xiv, 708ff).

Q

Qānūn. See Kanūn.

Q.-L. Customary abbr. for R. Eitner's *Quellen-Lexikon* [see under *RISM*].

Quadran pavan. English name (late 16th cent.) for the *passamezzo moderno,* used by Bull, Morley, and other Elizabethans, probably so called because it was in the major mode using B natural (B *quadratum*) whereas the *passamezzo antico* was in the minor and used B-flat. See O. Gombosi, in *MQ* xxx, 145.

Quadratnotation [G.]. *Square notation.

Quadreble. See under Sight.

Quadrille [F.]. (1) A French dance of the early 19th century performed by two or four couples moving in a square. It consisted of five figures (*Le Pantalon, L'Été, La Poule, La Trénise* and *La Pastourelle, Finale*), the music for which, alternating between 6/8 and 2/4 meter, was chosen from popular tunes, operatic airs, and even sacred music. The dance was very popular during the Napoleonic era and remained fashionable until it was replaced by the *polka. (2) In 17th- and 18th-century French ballet (Campra, Lully), *quadrille* is the name of the group of dancers (4, 6, 8, or 12) who performed the figures of an *entrée. See Dance music IV.

Quadrivium. In the medieval system of education, the four "mathematical arts"—arithmetic, geometry, music, and astronomy—as opposed to the *trivium* of "rhetorical arts"—grammar, logic, and rhetoric. In this scheme music was not considered an art in the modern sense but a science allied with mathematics and physics (acoustics).

Quadruple counterpoint. See Invertible counterpoint.

Quadruple-croche [F.]. See under Notes.

Quadruple fugue. A fugue with four different subjects, such as the last (unfinished) piece of Bach's *Art of Fugue. See Double fugue.

Quadruple meter, time. See Meter.

Quadruplet. A group of four notes, to be played in the time of three.

Quadruplum. See Duplum.

Quality. (1) Tone quality; see Tone color. (2) As opposed to quantity, see Poetic meter III.

Quantity. See under Poetic meter III.

Quarrel of the Buffoons. See War of the Buffoons.

Quart, Quarte [G.]. The interval of the fourth. As a prefix in the names of instruments, it indicates that the instrument is a fourth higher (*Quartflöte, Quartgeige*) or a fourth lower (*Quartfagott;* see Oboe family II, D) than the normal instrument.

Quartal harmony. Term for a harmonic system based on the *fourth, as distinguished from the common system of *tertian harmony, based on the third. Quartal harmonies have been recommended for replacing tertian harmonies in harmonizations of Gregorian chant [see J. Yasser,

Mediaeval Quartal Harmony (1938); also in *MQ* xxiii, xxiv]. See Accompaniment V.

Quarter note. See under Notes.

Quarter tone. An interval equal to one-half semitone, there being twenty-four quarter tones to the octave. See Microtone. Quarter tones have been frequently used since World War II by serial composers such as Boulez, Stockhausen, and others. Boulez has demonstrated how a serial principle of organization, which can be generalized to any number of elements (i.e., not necessarily restricted to the twelve chromatic semitones), can accommodate quarter tones. See P. Boulez, *Penser la musique aujourd'hui* [1964]; *id.,* "Eventuellement . . ." (*RM* 1952, no. 212). Also see under Microtone.   E.S.

Quartet [F. *quatuor;* G. *Quartett;* It. *quartetto;* Sp. *cuarteto*]. A composition for four instruments or voices. Also, the four performers organized to play or sing such compositions. By far the most important combination is the *string quartet. A number of piano quartets (for piano, violin, viola, and cello) have been written: 2 by Mozart, 4 by Beethoven, 3 by Mendelssohn, 2 by Schumann, 3 by Brahms, 2 by Dvořák, 2 by Fauré, 1 by Chausson, 1 by Copland, etc. See J. Saam, *Zur Geschichte des Klavierquartetts* (1933); W. Altmann, *Handbuch für Klavierquartettspieler* (1937).

The "vocal quartet," i.e., a polyphonic composition for four voices, was established *c.* 1450 by the early Flemish composers, although there are isolated earlier examples, such as Perotinus' *organa quadrupla* [see Organum; *Ars antiqua*] and Machaut's Mass. Much of the music of the 16th century (motets, Masses, madrigals, chansons, etc.) is written in four parts, although there was a tendency toward increasing the number of parts to five, six, and more. In the 17th century four-part writing was limited chiefly to the English *glee and the German *chorale. In the 19th century the *a cappella* quartet was extensively cultivated by glee clubs, *Liedertafel*, etc. Four-part writing has traditionally served as the basis for studies in harmony and counterpoint.

Quartfagott, Quartflöte, Quartgeige [G.]. See under Quart; also Violin family (a).

Quartole [G.], **quartolet** [F.]. *Quadruplet.

Quartsextakkord [G.]. The second inversion of the triad (six-four chord).

Quatreble. See under Sight.

Quattro [It.]. Four. *Quattro mani,* four hands; *quattro voci,* four voices.

Quatuor [F.]. *Quartet.

Quaver. See under Notes.

Queen, The. See *Reine, La.*

Queen of Spades, The [Rus. *Pikovaya Dama*]. Opera in three acts by P. Tchaikovsky (libretto by M. Tchaikovsky, rev. by the composer, based on a story by Pushkin), produced in St. Petersburg, 1890. Setting: St. Petersburg, end of the 18th century.

Quempas. Abbr. for L. *Quem pastores laudavere* (He, whom the shepherds praised), a Christmas song that was popular in Germany in the 16th century. The term was used as a generic designation for Christmas songs, particularly in the term *Quempas Singen,* i.e., the singing of carols by students in Latin schools, an activity in which Luther participated. The alms earned by singing from house to house were often a welcome addition to a student's meager income [see *Currende*]. *Quempasheft* was the collection of carols that every student copied for himself.

Quer- [G.]. Cross, transverse. *Querflöte* (transverse) flute; *Querpfeife,* fife; *Querstand,* false relation.

Querelle des bouffons [F.]. See War of the Buffoons.

Queue [F.]. The stem of a note. *Piano à queue,* grand piano.

Quick-step. In military parlance, a *march in quick steps (*c.* 108 per minute). Also, music for such a march.

Quiebro. See under Ornamentation I.

Quilisma [L.]. The most important of the early "ornamental" neumes; see Neumes I (table). See C. Vivell, in *Gregorianische Rundschau* iv, v (several installments); *ApGC,* pp. 113ff.

Quilt canzona. English equivalent of G. *Flickkanzone* (patch canzona), a term introduced by H. Riemann for a type of canzona consisting of rapidly changing, extremely short sections in contrasting styles. An example of this relatively rare type is a canzona by J. H. Schein [see comp. ed. by Prüfer, i, 41]. For another example, by G. B. Grillo (1608), see *RiHM* ii.2, 127.

Quindezime [G.]. The interval of the fifteenth, i.e., the double octave.

Quinta falsa [L.]. False (i.e., diminished) fifth.

Quinta vox [L.]. See under Part (2); Partbooks.

Quinte [F.]. (1) Interval of the fifth. (2) Obsolete French name for viola (*quinte de viole*).

Quinte, Quint [G.]. Fifth. *Quintenparallelen,* parallel fifths. *Quintenzirkel,* *circle of fifths.

Quintern [G.]. A 16th- and 17th-century name for the guitar or similar instruments. See K. Geiringer, in *AMW* vi.

Quintet [F. *quintette,* formerly *quintuor;* G. *Quintett;* It. *quintetto;* Sp. *quinteto*]. Chamber music for five players. The string quintet is usually for two violins, two violas, and cello (the repertory includes 12 by Boccherini, 6 by Mozart, 3 by Beethoven, 2 by Mendelssohn, 2 by Brahms, 1 by Bruckner, 1 by Vaughan Williams, etc.). The less usual combination of two violins, viola, and two cellos prevailed in Boccherini (113) but survived only in Schubert's famous Quintet in C, op. 163. A piano (clarinet, etc.) quintet is a composition for piano (clarinet, etc.) and string quartet. The literature of piano quintets includes Schubert's op. 114 (Trout Quintet, for piano, violin, viola, cello, double bass), Schumann's op. 44, Brahms' op. 34, and compositions by Dvořák, Franck, Reger, Pfitzner, Fauré, Elgar, Hindemith, Bloch (in quarter tones), Shostakovitch, *et al.* See W. Altmann, *Handbuch für Klavierquintettspieler* (1936).

Vocal quintets are usually for two sopranos, alto, tenor, and bass. There is a large literature of vocal music in five parts in the madrigals, *balletti,* etc., of the late 16th century (Lasso, Lechner, English madrigalists).

Quintfagott [G.]. See under Oboe family II, C.

Quintierend [G.]. See under Wind instruments III.

Quintole [G.], **quintolet** [F.]. Quintuplet.

Quinton [F.]. According to some authorities (Sachs, Bessaraboff), a violin with five (instead of four) strings tuned g d' a' d" g"; according to others, a French 17th-century viol (*pardessus de viole*) with five (instead of six) strings tuned g c' e' a' d".

Quintoyer [F.]. See under Wind instruments III.

Quintsaite [G.]. E-string of the violin.

Quintsextakkord [G.]. Six-five chord; see under Seventh chord.

Quintuor [F.]. Old name for quintet.

Quintuple meter. The measure of five beats. Quintuple meter can usually be considered a compound of 2/4 and 3/4, or, less frequently, of 3/4 and 2/4. Examples are found in Chopin's Sonata op. 4, Tchaikovsky's Symphony no. 6 [Ex. 1], Wagner's *Tristan,* Act III, Scene 2 [Ex. 2], and K. Loewe's ballad "Prinz Eugen." Quintuple meter is used very frequently in 20th-century music, e.g., in Rachmaninoff's *The Isle of the Dead* (1909).

Quintuple meter was known in ancient Greek music as Cretic meter [see the "First Delphic Hymn," *HAM,* no. 7a]. In Western polyphony it appeared in the late 14th century, resulting from the juxtaposition of a perfect and an imperfect value (black and white *semibrevis;* see the anonymous *Fortune* discussed in *ApNPM,* p. 400f). In the Sanctus of Isaac's *Missa paschalis* the same rhythm is expressed by half-blackened breves, each equal to a black plus a white *semibrevis* [see *WoHN* i, 420]. Sequential passages based on five-beat patterns are not uncommon in the works of Obrecht and Isaac. In all these instances quintuple meter is used in one part only and therefore is likely to be obscured by the regular pulse of the other parts. One of the earliest compositions written entirely in quintuple time (5 = 4 + 1) is a *"Felix namque" in the English MS Brit. Mus. *Roy. App. 56* (c. 1530). Other examples are found in Spanish music, e.g., in several pieces in the *Cancionero de Palacio* of *c.* 1500 (*Editions XXXII, 5; see nos. 59, 102, 151, probably not correctly transcribed by Anglés), in the *tientos* of Correa de Araujo, 1626 (*Editions XXXII, 12, p. 31), and in the *zortziko.*

Quintuplet. A group of five notes played in the duration of (normally) four.

Quire. Obsolete spelling for choir.

Qui tollis [L.]. Section of the *Agnus Dei of the Mass [see under Mass]. Medieval settings of the Agnus Dei frequently begin with these words, the initial words being sung in plainsong.

Quodlibet [L.]. A humorous type of music in which well-known melodies or texts are combined in an advisedly incongruous manner. The following types can be distinguished:

I. *The polyphonic quodlibet.* In this type, by far the most interesting one, different melodies or snatches of melodies are used simultaneously in different voice-parts of a polyphonic composition. This method appears in some 13th-century motets, in which refrains of trouvère songs occur in the upper voice against the liturgical melody (borrowed from Gregorian chant) in the tenor [see Refrain III; also Motet II]. A particularly interesting example is no. 178 of the Codex Montpellier. In the 15th and 16th centuries numerous *quodlibets* were written in which different folk tunes are combined contrapuntally, the only license being that the time values may be lengthened or shortened according to the requirements of consonance. One of the earliest examples, in the Glogauer Liederbuch of *c.* 1480 [see Liederbuch], contrasts the then famous "O rosa bella" melody with snatches of German folksongs [see *HAM,* nos. 80, 82]. A composition by Tinctoris (*Proportionale musices; CS* iv, 173) combines fragments of "O rosa bella," "L'Homme armé," "Robinet tu m'as la mort donné," and other material. Several *quodlibets* are found in the Chansonnier of Seville [see D. Plamenac, in *MQ* xxxvii, xxxviii]. An outstanding composer of *quodlibets* was Ludwig Senfl [see *SchGMB,* no. 85], and comprehensive collections were published by Wolfgang Schmelzl (*Guter, seltzamer und künstreicher teutscher Gesang,* 1544) and Melchior Franck (*Musicalischer Grillenvertreiber,* 1622). These pieces proved extremely valuable sources of 16th-century German folksong [see Lied II]. The best-known example of this type is the final variation of Bach's *Goldberg Variations, in which two popular melodies of his day, "Ich bin so lang nicht bei dir g'west" (Long have I been away from thee) and "Kraut und Rüben" (Cabbage and turnips) are artfully combined within the harmonic frame of the theme [see Ex.].

(a) Ich bin so lang nicht bei dir g'west

(b) Kraut und   Rü - ben

ha-ben mich ver-trie - ben

Of a more serious nature are *quodlibets* combining different liturgical melodies. Several examples are found in the *Mensuralkodex des Nikolaus Apel* [*Editions XVIII A, 32], e.g., one combining the hymn "Exsultet caelum" with the antiphon "Vos eritis" (no. 12). Particularly famous is a motet by Gombert, which combines the "Salve Regina," "Ave Regina," "Alma redemptoris mater," and four other chants [see *ReMR*, p. 345]. Its title, "Diversi diversa orant," reveals the prayerlike significance of the liturgical *quodlibet*. To the same category belongs a composition by Kindermann, based on three Protestant chorales [see *DTB* 32, p. 13].

II. *The successive quodlibet.* A simpler type of *quodlibet* is that in which various melodies are quoted in succession, as in a potpourri. This technique is used in several of the above-mentioned *quodlibets*, e.g., in the upper part of the motet from the Codex Montpellier and in the lower parts of the "O rosa bella" *quodlibet* from the Glogauer Liederbuch. Several compositions in the collections of Schmelzl and Franck also are of this type.

III. *The textual quodlibet.* The term *quodlibet* is also used for pieces that contain a mixture of borrowed texts without involving borrowed musical material. As in the musical *quodlibet*, the texts may occur simultaneously or successively. The polytextual motet of the 13th century is frequently cited as an example of textual *quodlibet*, but it should be observed that in all such motets (except in a special type, the refrain motet) the texts of the upper parts are not borrowed but freely invented, while the tenor has no full text but only an *incipit. Clearer examples of the textual *quodlibet* are certain 15th-century

Masses mentioned in the entry Polytextuality and the motets by Josquin and Morales quoted under Motet B 1 (e.g., Josquin's *Stabat mater* with "Comme femme"). The text of a number of 18th-century pieces consists of a nonsensical succession of jocose and deliberately incongruous sentences. To this type belongs a *quodlibet* believed to be an early work of J. S. Bach's [pub. by M. Schneider, in *Veröffentlichungen der Neuen Bachgesellschaft*, xxxii.2]. It consists of a large number of short texts (the "seafaring allusions" mentioned by C. S. Terry in an article in *ML* xiv have a clearly obscene meaning) set to music evidently without using pre-existing melodies. Possibly this piece, rather than the truly polyphonic *quodlibet* from the Goldberg Variations, illustrates the "improvised *quodlibet* singing" that, according to K. P. E. Bach, was traditional in his family for many generations. Numerous examples of the same type are found in Valentin Rathgeber's *Tafelconfekt* of 1733 (*Editions XVIII, A, 19). See also Moser, Lit.

Other terms for *quodlibet* are *cento or *centone*, *fricassée* [F.], and *incatenatura* [It.]. The Italian terms *misticanza* and *messanza*, as well as the Spanish *ensalada*, seem to mean "potpourri" rather than *quodlibet*. See also Pasticcio. For *quodlibet* Mass, see Mass C, II, b.

Lit.: K. Jeppesen, in *CP 1939* (Venetian *centone*); D. Plamenac, in *CP Sachs* (Seville Chansonnier, *quodlibet*); R. Becherini, in *Collectanea historiae musicae* i (*incatenatura*); E. Bienenfeld in *SIM* vi (Schmeltzl Liederbuch); K. Gudewill, in *CP 1961* (origin); R. Eitner, in *MfM* viii, ix, Beilage (Germany, 15th–16th cent.); H. J. Moser, ‡*Corydon*, 2 vols. (1933).

R

R. In early orchestral music, *ripieno;* in French organ music, *récit;* in Gregorian chant (℟), *responsory.

Rabab. Arabic name for various bowed string instruments found in Islamic countries. They occur in various shapes, e.g., elongated boat, halved pear, trapezoid, rectangle, etc., and usually have three strings. With the spread of Islam the rabab was carried both eastward, to Malaya and Indonesia (early 15th century), where it is called *rebab,* and westward, via Spain into Europe (8th or 9th cent.), where it was known as *rabec, rabeca, rebec, rebelle, ribibe, ribible* (Chaucer), *rubeba, rubèbe* (Machaut), *rybybe*, etc. Jerome of Moravia, in his "Tractatus de musica" (*c.* 1280), describes the rubeba as having two strings tuned a fifth apart and played with a bow [*CS* i, 152]. The most common European form was in the shape of an elongated pear and its most common name was *rebec*. In France it was used as late as the 18th century by street fiddlers, who were forbidden to use the violin. A genuine specimen, dating from the 15th century, is preserved in Bologna [see B. Disertori, in *RMI* xlii]. See ill. under Violin.

Rabel. See *Mejoranera.*

Racket. See under Oboe family III.

Raddolcendo [It.]. Becoming softer.

Raddoppiare [It.]. To double, usually at the lower octave.

Radel [G.]. A 14th-century name for a canon or *round. See *ReMMA,* p. 377; also *Rota (2).

Radical bass. Same as *fundamental bass.

Radio and television broadcasting. Although radio broadcasting as a regular public service in the United States was inaugurated in November, 1920, it was not until large networks were established (National Broadcasting Company [NBC], 1926; Columbia Broadcasting System [CBS], 1927; and others) that broadcasts of serious music became available to a wide audience. Some years earlier, Walter Damrosch had made his first broadcast (a lecture-recital on Beethoven, Oct. 29, 1923), which led to a decade-long nationally broadcast "Music Appreciation Hour."

(1) *"Live" performances.* Many serious music broadcasts are performances that are only incidentally relayed to radio listeners or television viewers. The two annual series that have endured the longest and secured the most loyal group of listeners are the Sunday afternoon subscription concerts of the New York Philharmonic Society (heard since 1930) and the Saturday matinee performances of the Metropolitan Opera Association of New York (since 1931). Intermission time at the Philharmonic concerts is used for talks about the music being presented. Originally the orchestra's official annotator, Lawrence Gilman, was in charge. In the mid-1930's talks of a lighter nature were given by Deems Taylor. In recent seasons these intervals have been used for taped musical productions usually not directly connected with the concert.

The Opera series has offered a fairly conservative repertory (*c.* 80 operas, mostly in their original languages) in thirty seasons. Beginning in the 1950's, television has been increasingly turning to the concert hall. Leonard Bernstein and the New York Philharmonic have televised Young People's concerts, and the Boston Symphony is seen eight times a year, with each concert repeated at least once.

(2) *Performances for broadcasts.* Since the early 1930's all the networks have made significant contributions in music performances designed especially for radio listeners. NBC arranged 110 programs of "Music of the Americas"; the Mutual network presented long sequences devoted to Bach cantatas, Mozart concertos and operas, and American stage works; and for several years CBS presented Sunday morning organ recitals by E. Power Biggs playing in Harvard University's Busch-Reisinger Museum. In 1938 NBC assembled an excellent orchestra especially for radio concerts, conducted by Arturo Toscanini. After Toscanini's retirement in 1954, the orchestra continued to exist for several seasons as the Symphony of the Air but was eventually disbanded. Sporadically, leading composers have received commissions for works written especially for broadcasting. CBS was active in commissioning such men as R. Harris, A. Copland, W. Piston, L. Gruenberg, and R. Thompson. Gian-Carlo Menotti's *The Old Maid and the Thief,* the first opera commissioned for broadcasting (NBC, 1939), has also proved one of the most durable works in this medium. After a hiatus during World War II the practice of awarding special commissions was revived. For example, conductor-composer Daniel Pinkham received a foundation grant to compose four choral works for first performance on the WGBH educational network founded by WGBH in Boston, and younger composers, such as Rorem, Kay, Flanagan, and Wuorinen, have received similar commissions.

Numerous television stations have offered segments and sequences from the standard operatic repertory. In addition, NBC formed an opera company (founded by Samuel Chotzinoff) to create productions especially for the new medium. The company offered three or four television performances a year and for two seasons tried national tours of live performances. Here, too, Menotti scored a success with an opera created specifically for the medium, *Amahl and the Night Visitors* (NBC, 1951), which has replaced *Hänsel und Gretel* as the Christmas favorite of opera groups, both amateur and professional, all over America.

(3) *Recorded music.* Broadcasting recorded music not only has gained widespread public acceptance but has had enormous influence on listening habits and tastes. Station WQXR in New York pioneered in this development, devoting more than 80 per cent of its broadcasting time to recordings of serious music, and for several years even having its own resident string quartet. Many educational stations, founded and supported by colleges and universities, have followed this pattern. An important development for the broadcasting of recorded music was the invention of FM (frequency modulation) radio, which had a vastly superior sound, free from static and with a much wider frequency response, i.e., the listener could hear both higher and lower pitches, making the broadcasts sound much more like the original source. Unfortunately, many FM radio stations, opened before and during World War II, failed owing to lack of funds. In 1949 Columbia Records released its first "Long Playing" records, which contained nearly ten times the amount of music and had much greater fidelity of sound than the older, faster-rotating records. This development led to a widespread demand for high-quality home playbacks and simultaneously a renewed interest in FM radio. [See phonograph and recorded music.] The availability of a wide repertory of serious music through FM radio and records has altered listening habits and added to the public's musical sophistication. Listeners no longer ask for Gershwin's *Rhapsody in Blue* or Grofé's *Grand Canyon Suite,* favorites of the 1930's and 1940's. Instead, requests may range from Obrecht to Dittersdorf to Messiaen. Since many radio stations devote themselves exclusively to broadcasting recorded music, live performances arranged for radio are rare. There are, of course, exceptions. WNYC in New York has an annual American music festival between Lincoln's and Washington's birthdays, which still offers first performances. WGBH in Boston has also been active in presenting studio performances, in both radio and television. [See (2).]

(4) Educational broadcasts *about* serious music have been important since the early days. During the 1930's and 1940's CBS presented series such as "Exploring Music," "Essays in Music," and "The Story of Song." G. Wallace Woodworth of Harvard University has conducted radio "listener-rehearsals" preparing

audiences in the Boston area for the broadcasts by the Boston Symphony Orchestra, as well as teaching a television course for college credit called "Two Centuries of Symphony."

R.A.; rev. W.H.C.

Radleyer [G.]. *Hurdy-gurdy.

Raffrenando [It.]. Slowing down.

Rāga. See under India; Melody type.

Ragtime. A style of American popular music that reached its peak *c.* 1910–15. Its harmony is conventional, based largely on the tonic, dominant, and subdominant triads of the major mode, with a regular phraseology. However, ragtime was created (often by improvisation) and performed primarily by pianists (who rejected, as in later jazz, subtler pedal effects in favor of a percussive tone), with or without a group of additional instruments. Hence its

Examples from a set of ragtime pieces published c. 1898–1901.

melody became more instrumental in style (most of the rags had no text). Ragtime was made popular by the pianist Ben Harvey, who published his *Ragtime Instructor* in 1897. Also see Jazz.

Raindrop Prelude. Popular name for Chopin's Prelude in D-flat op. 28, no. 15, so called because the continuously repeated note A^b ($G\sharp$ in the middle section) suggests the dripping of rain.

Rake's Progress, The. Opera in three acts by Stravinsky (libretto by W. H. Auden and C. Kallman, inspired by the set of prints by Hogarth), produced in Venice, 1951. Setting:

England, 18th century. The libretto, generally admired for its excellence, combines elements of *Don Giovanni* and *Faust.* The work is a modern revitalization of late 18th- and early 19th-century opera (Mozart to Bellini), with recitative and other similarities to scores of that period.

Rákóczi March. A Hungarian national air, composed by Janos Bihari in 1809, in homage to Prince Ferencz Rákóczi (1676–1735), who led the Hungarians in a revolt against Austria. The melody was used by Berlioz in his *La Damnation de Faust* and *Marche hongroise,* as well as by Liszt in his *Rhapsodie hongroise,* no. 15.

Ralentir [F.]. To slow down.

Rallentando, abbr. *rall.* Same as **ritardando.*

Range. See Voices, range of.

Rank. In organs, a complete set of pipes of the same type, controlled by one *stop knob or tablet. A mixture stop, however, has several ranks, according to the number of pipes combined in the production of a single tone. See Organ II; Register.

Rankett. See under Oboe family III.

Rant. Name for a 17th-century dance found, e.g., in the fantasies (suites) of John Jenkins and in Matthew Locke's *Melothesia* (1673). Judging from the music, the term may well be an abbreviation of *corranto,* i.e., **courante.*

Ranz des vaches [F.; G. *Kuhreigen, Kuhreihen*]. A type of Swiss mountain melody sung or played on the *alphorn by herdsmen to summon their cows. About fifty such melodies are traditionally used in various districts of the Alps. They all show the irregularity of rhythm and melodic design that is the hallmark of ancient folk music. Indeed, one of them, beginning with the words "Lobe, Lobe," occurs as early as 1545, in Rhaw's *Bicinia.* A *Kuhreigen* of 1710 (in T. Zwinger, *Fasciculus dissertationum medicarum*) is reproduced in the B. & H. edition of Franz Liszt, *Pianofortewerke* iv, p. iv. It shows the augmented fourth, another characteristic trait of these melodies.

The *ranz des vaches* has been repeatedly used in operas about Swiss subjects, e.g., in the overtures of Grétry's and Rossini's *Guillaume Tell,* and in W. Kienzl's *Der Kuhreigen.* See A. H. King, in *MQ* xxxi; A. Glück, in *VMW* viii.

Rape of Lucretia, The. Opera in two acts by Britten (libretto by R. Duncan after A. Obey's

play), produced in Glyndebourne, 1946. Setting: Rome, 510 B.C. The work is organized in the manner of a Greek tragedy, with two characters representing the male and female choruses, who comment on the action from the viewpoint of each sex. The score is of chamber-music dimensions, calling for only seventeen instruments.

Rappresentativo. See under *Stile rappresentativo.*

Rappresentazione di anima e di corpo, La [It., The Representation of Soul and Body]. Stage work by Emilio del Cavalieri, produced in Rome, 1600. It is usually regarded as the first *oratorio. The music consists almost exclusively of recitative and short choruses.

Rapsodie Espagnole [F., Spanish Rhapsody]. Descriptive suite for orchestra by Ravel, composed in 1907. Its four movements are: (1) Prélude à la nuit; (2) Malagueña; (3) Habanera; (4) Feria. The third movement is an orchestral version of an unpublished "Habanera" for two pianos, written in 1895.

Rasch [G.]. Quick.

Rasgado, rasgueado [Sp.]. In guitar playing, strumming the strings with a finger to produce an arpeggio.

Ratisbon Edition. See under Liturgical books II.

Ratsche [G.]. Cog *rattle.

Rätselkanon [G.]. Riddle canon. See Canon III.

Ratswahlkantate [G.]. A cantata (no. 71) by J. S. Bach, "Gott ist mein König," written in 1708 for the election of the town council of Mühlhausen (Thuringia), where he was organist (1707–08).

Rattenando, rattenuto [It.]. Holding back.

Rattle. An instrument of the percussion family, similar to the toy of that name, consisting of a wooden cogwheel that revolves against a flexible strip of wood or metal. It is used in R. Strauss' *Till Eulenspiegel.* In the classification of instruments, "rattle" is a generic term for shaken idiophones [see Instruments I, B]. These are among the oldest and most widely distributed instruments. An example is the Latin American *maraca, consisting of a gourd filled with pebbles or dry seeds and shaken by means of a wooden handle.

Rauscher [G.]. An 18th-century term for the French *batterie* [see Batterie (3)] or for a quick figure involving repeated notes.

Ravvivando [It.]. Quickening.

Razor Quartet. Popular name for Haydn's String Quartet, no. 61 (op. 55, no. 2), in F minor, composed in 1788. Haydn jokingly gave it to his publisher, Bland, in exchange for a new razor.

Razumovsky Quartets. See Russian Quartets.

Re. See under Solmization.

Reading Rota. Another name for *"Sumer is icumen in," a *rota that may have been composed by a monk from Reading.

Real answer, real fugue. See under Tonal and real.

Rebab. See Rabab.

Rebee. See Rabab. For ill. see under violin.

Rebube [F.]. Obsolete name for *Jew's-harp.

Recapitulation. See under Sonata form.

Recercada, recercar. Same as *ricercar.

Récit [F.]. A 17th-century term, derived from *récitative, for a vocal solo piece, usually in aria style; e.g., *récit de basse,* bass aria. In organs, the term is used similarly, i.e., for a solo organ stop and for the entire solo organ (*clavier de récit*); also as a title for an organ piece with a distinct melodic part (as opposed to earlier, contrapuntal organ music). An inscription such as *Récit de tierce en taille* means solo passage (*récit*) in a middle part (*taille*) for the left hand, played on the organ stop tierce.

Recital. A public performance by one or two players (as opposed to concert, used for a group of three or more). The term was first used for performances by F. Liszt in London in 1840.

Recitative [F. *récitative;* G. *Rezitativ;* It., Sp. *recitativo*]. I. A vocal style designed to imitate and emphasize the natural inflections of speech. It is usually employed with more or less narrative prose texts, particularly in operas, where it serves to carry the action from one aria (ensemble, chorus) to another. In the recitative, the purely musical principles of vocal melody, phrase, and rhythm are largely disregarded, being replaced by speechlike reiteration of the same note, slight inflections, irregular rhythms, purely syllabic treatment of the text, etc. Despite the intrinsic limitation of recitative style, a large variety of types have developed, which are briefly discussed below.

II. The recitative plays a very important role in Gregorian chant, where it is employed for the speechlike singing of psalms [see Psalm tones], prayers, readings from the Prophets, Epistles, Gospels, etc. There is no doubt that this method is of Jewish origin [see Jewish music I]. About 1600 a new type of recitative appeared in secular music, not through the influence of the Gregorian recitative but as a result of attempts to revive the chorus of ancient Greek drama. [See *Nuove musiche;* Monody; Opera III.] The earliest operas (Peri's, Caccini's *Euridice,* 1600) were written throughout in a carefully and impressively designed declamatory style, which is quite different from the later *parlando. The accompanying example from Caccini's *Euridice* (1600) is typical of this early Florentine recitative [Ex. 1]. During the 17th century this *recitativo arioso* [see Arioso] developed in a number of directions:

(a) Taking on more distinct phrasing, melodic character, and definite form, it grew into the aria; there are examples in Monteverdi and the Roman and Venetian composers, though not yet fully set apart from the recitative portions (e.g., P. Cavalli's *Il Giasone,* 1649).

Nin-fa, deh sii con - ten-ta ri-dir per-chè t'af-

fan-ni, che ta-ciu-to mar-tir trop-po tor-men - ti.

(b) With the development of the aria as a distinct type, the recitative gradually became faster and less melodic. Examples of this style are already present in M. A. Cesti (*Il Pomo d'oro,* 1667) and C. Pallavicino (*La Gerusalemme liberata,* 1687). It was not until the 18th century, however, that this parlando style was generally introduced into opera. It was known as *recitativo secco* [It. *secco,* dry—with reference to its lack of expressiveness]. This type remained in use throughout Italian 18th-century *opera seria* and in the operas of Mozart and Rossini [see Ex. 2, from Mozart's *Don Giovanni*].

(c) Whereas both the early Florentine and the *recitativo secco* were sung to thoroughbass accompaniment only, a fuller accompaniment (including strings) was introduced for recitatives of special importance. Monteverdi was one of

G: A-mi-co, che ti par?

L: Mi par ch'ab-bia-te un'

Va là, che se'il gran gon-zo

a-ni-ma di bron-zo.

language, on a principle similar to the 16th-century *vers mesuré* [see also Rhythm II (b)].

En-fin il est en ma puis-san-ce, ce fa-tal en-ne-

mi, ce sup - per - be vain - queur.

the first to use this device in the closing measures of his famous "Possenti spirto" (in *Orfeo*, 1607), and Schütz used it similarly for the part of the Evangelist in his *Historia der Auferstehung Jesu Christi* (1623). The use of ensemble accompaniment naturally led to a more strictly measured recitative, dramatic rather than declamatory, the *recitativo accompagnato* or *stromentato*. It assumed considerable importance in 18th-century opera, where it was usually reserved for the climactic scenes of the drama and served to introduce the most brilliant arias of the work. Bach, in his St. Matthew Passion, used it consistently for the part of Christ and for the recitatives preceding an aria [Ex. 3].

(d) A special type of recitative, involving frequent changes of meter (4/4, 3/4, 2/4), developed in France under Lully [Ex. 4] and spread, with necessary adaptation to the language, to England (Purcell). This recitative represented an attempt to set down in exact note values the rhythm, accents, and inflections of the French

(e) Finally, Schütz in his latest works, the Passions, developed a highly impressive "archaic" type of recitative, entirely unaccompanied, a baroque revival of the Gregorian *psalm tones [see *SchGMB*, no. 192].

The most outspoken adversary of Italian opera and its stereotyped parlando recitative, Richard Wagner, revived the truly musical recitative: his "unending melody" is actually a highly dramatic and expressive recitative. An interesting contrast to the emotionalism of Wagner's recitative is the subdued recitative of Debussy's *Pelléas et Mélisande*.

The free character of the recitative has repeatedly been imitated in instrumental music. Examples occur in J. Kuhnau's *Musicalische Vorstellung einiger biblischer Historien* (1698), Bach's *Chromatic Fantasy and Fugue*, Beethoven's Piano Sonata op. 31, no. 2 (first movement, recapitulation) and op. 110 (slow movement), Schumann's *Kinderscenen* ("The Poet Speaks"), etc.

Lit.: F. H. Neumann, *Die Ästhetik des Rezitativs* (1962); C. Spitz, "Die Entwicklung des 'Stile Recitativo'" (*AMW* iii); S. Wilson, "The Recitatives of the St. Matthew Passion" (*ML* xvi); E. Borrel, "L'Interprétation de l'ancien recitatif français" (*RdM* 1931, p. 13); E. O. Downes, "*Secco* Recitative in Early Classical Opera Seria (1720–80)" (*JAMS* xiv); J. A. Westrup, "The Cadence in Baroque Recitative (*CP Jeppesen*). D.J.G. and W.A.

Reciting note. See under Psalm tones.

Recorded music. See Phonograph and recorded music.

Recorder [F. *flûte à bec;* G. *Blockflöte;* It. *flauto diritto;* Sp. *flauta de pico*]. The most important type of whistle (or fipple) flute, i.e., end-blown, with a "whistle" mouthpiece [see Whistle flute]. Its tone quality is highly individual, soft and slightly reedy, in part produced by a wide, tapering conical bore. The recorder attained virtually its final form in the late Middle Ages; by the 16th century it formed a complete family of instruments from treble to bass that played an important part in the music of the late Renaissance. By the early 18th century only three or four sizes of recorder remained in use. Parts for recorder were marked "flauto" by J. S. Bach and most of his contemporaries, the cross flute (the modern instrument) being called "German flute," "flûte traversière," or "flauto traverso." Bach and Handel occasionally made use of a "flauto piccolo" or "flautino," a small recorder usually an octave higher in pitch than the flauto. After 1750 the recorder gradually passed out of use.

In the early 20th century a revival took place, begun by Arnold Dolmetsch in England and followed after 1918 by German manufacturers using mass-production methods, and finally, on a much smaller scale, by makers in the United States. Modern instruments are generally made in four sizes, named by German and British makers as follows:

German	British	Range
Soprano	Descant	c″–d‴′
Alto	Treble	f′–g‴
Tenor	Tenor	c′–d‴
Bass	Bass	f–g″

Two systems of boring finger holes are used in modern instruments; one used by certain German makers, with a lowered fifth hole, usually called "German" fingering, has not gained wide acceptance, and the 18th-century system, called "English" or "baroque" fingering, is now most used. For the alto (treble), widely popular as a chamber-music instrument in the 18th century, there is an important literature written expressly for it by composers of nearly every nationality; much of this music has been reprinted. See ill. under Flute.

Lit.: A. Rowland-Jones, *Recorder Technique* [1963]; H. Alker, *Blockflöten-bibliographie* (1960); L. H. von Winterfeld and H. Kunz, *Handbuch der Blockflöten-Literatur* (1959); H. Peter, *The Recorder,* Eng. trans. [1958]; *id.,* ed., *Sylvestro Ganassi . . . Schule des Kunstvollen Flötenspiels . . . Venedig 1535* (1956); E. Hunt, *The Recorder and Its Music* (1962); A. G. Hess, ‡*800 Years of Music for Recorders* [1945]; F. J. Giesbert, *Schule für die Altblockflöte in f* [1937]; R. Cotte, *Méthode complète de flûte à bec* (1958); Jacques Hotteterre, *Principes de la flûte . . . à bec*

(1707; fac. ed. 1958); H. M. Fitzgibbon, "Of Flutes and Soft Recorders" (*MQ* xx); C. F. Dolmetsch, in *ML* xxii, 67; A. Carse, "Fingering the Recorder" (*MR* i); C. Welch, "Literature Relating to the Recorder" (*PMA* xxiv); E. Halfpenny, in *GSJ* ix.   J.F.O.

Reco-reco. Brazilian native scraper, made of a notched gourd, or of a bamboo cane with carved transverse notches, or of a cylindrical metal tube with a piece of corrugated tin fixed to it. The instrument is scraped with a small wooden or metal stick. It is also known by the names *reque-reque* and *caracaxá.* A similar type of scraper called *güiro* is used in the Antilles.   J.O-S.

Recoupe [F.]. See under *Basse danse.*

Recte et retro [It.]. See under Retrograde.

Recueilli [F.]. Meditative, contemplative.

Redobles [Sp.]. See under Ornamentation I.

Redowa, rejdowak. A Bohemian dance in moderately quick triple meter, similar to the mazurka. It became popular *c.* 1850.

Réduction [F.]. Arrangement. *Réduction pour le piano,* arrangement for piano.

Reed [F. *anche;* G. *Zunge, Blatt, Rohrblatt;* It. *ancia;* Sp. *lengüeta*]. I. A thin, elongated piece of cane, metal, or other material that is fixed at one end and is free to vibrate at the other end. The reed is the sound-producing agent in various musical instruments, chiefly the woodwinds, bagpipes, harmonium, accordion, harmonica, and the reed stops of the organ. The best cane reeds are made from *Arundo donax,* a species of tall grass that is grown in southern France (Fréjus region).

There are two principal types of reed, *idiophonic* and *heterophonic* [G. *harte* and *weiche Zungen*]. Idiophonic [Gr., own sound] reeds are made of a hard, heavy material, usually metal, and can produce a sound of one pitch only, this being determined by their length and thickness (similar to, e.g., a tuning fork). Such reeds are used in the *harmonium, *accordion, *harmonica, Chinese *sheng, *regal, and in organ reed stops. In the last they are combined with a pipe that serves to reinforce the sound [see Organ VIII]. Heterophonic [Gr., other sound] reeds are made of a flexible, light material, usually cane, and can produce a wide range of pitches but only if they are attached to a pipe whose length determines the pitches. In instruments such as the oboe or clarinet, the sounding length of the pipe can be varied by covering different holes, so that a whole scale can be obtained from the reed.

II. There are two main kinds of heterophonic reed, *single reeds* (clarinet, saxophone) and *double reeds* (oboe, bassoon). With the former only one reed vibrates against a slot of the pipe; with the latter two reeds, separated by a slight opening, vibrate against each other. In a sense the lips of the trumpet or horn player form a pair of heterophonic double reeds.

Another distinction is that between *free* and *beating reeds.* In the former type, used in the harmonium, the reeds move in and out of a slot just wide enough to let the reed pass "freely"; in the latter type, used chiefly in the organ, the opening of the slot is somewhat smaller than the reed so that the reed "beats" against the frame [see Organ VIII]. The reed of the clarinet also is a beating reed.

A special type of reed is the *covered reed,* a reed (single or double) enclosed in a cap perforated by a hole into which the player blows, thus controlling the reed indirectly. This device, which precludes expressive and dynamic nuances, was used in various early instruments, e.g., in the cromornes, while in the *pibgorn the reed is enclosed in a funnel-shaped mouthpiece that is pressed tightly around the lips.

Reed pipes, stops. See under Organ VIII, X.

Reel. A dance performed by two or more couples facing one another and performing figures of eight. It is common in northern Europe and North America, the American variety being known as "Virginia reel." The music consists of four or eight measures in moderately quick duple meter, which are repeated over and over again. See under Strathspey.

Réexposition [F.]. Recapitulation.

Reformation Symphony. Mendelssohn's Symphony no. 5, op. 107, in D minor, composed in 1830 for the tercentennial of the Augsburg Conference, where Luther openly declared the establishment of the German Reformed (i.e., Protestant) Church.

Refrain. I. In poetry, one or two identical lines recurring at the end of each stanza of a strophic poem. It is equivalent to the musical term "burden." In a musical composition, each repetition of the refrain is, of course, set to the same melody, so that the term refers to both textual and musical repetition. The refrain is often called "chorus," since it is often sung by the full chorus while the stanzas (verses) are solo.

II. In the antiphonal and responsorial singing of the early Christian Church, an exclamation such as Amen, Alleluia, or a short phrase was repeated by the congregation or choir after each psalm verse or pair of verses [see Psalmody II, III]. The refrain poem, cultivated in the 12th and 13th centuries by the *trouvères, was the basis for various refrain forms. The simplest of them was the *ballade,* usually a poem with three stanzas of eight lines each (the last two lines constituting the refrain), the musical scheme for a stanza being a a b C. (Refrain texts are usually printed in italics. In the schemes shown here, one letter, large or small, denotes the same music; capital letters indicate the same text as well as music, therefore a refrain; small letters indicate different texts.) Another 13th-century refrain form is the *virelai, with the stanza structure A b b a A, in which the closing refrain serves also as the initial refrain for the next stanza. The medieval rondeau, unlike the other forms, normally has only one stanza—A B a A a b A B [see Rondeau (1)]—in which the textual and musical repetition takes place. In the Italian 14th-century *ballata the refrain is called *ripresa, and in the Spanish *villancico it is *estribillo.

III. The refrain texts, particularly for the rondeaux, were often lines taken from earlier poems that, owing to their popularity, were so well known as to be part of a courtly education. Thus, the term "refrain" may mean a line of text taken from some other literary work. In the first half of the 13th century there was a large stock of well-known refrains, usually of amorous character, such as "C'est la fin koi que nus die, j'amerais," or "En ma dame ai mis mon cuer, et ma pensée" [see *HAM,* nos. 19f and 28i; also nos. 19d and 32d], which were freely borrowed for new songs as well as for the upper parts of French motets. Three examples of their use are: (a) The *chanson avec des refrains,* a strophic song, concluded each stanza with a different refrain, i.e., one of the stock refrains [ex. in *AdHM* i, 195 f]. (b) The *refrain motet* included refrain quotations in the text of the upper parts, usually at the end. This was a common practice in French motets from *c.* 1250. (c) The *motet enté* began with the first half of a refrain, which was followed by new material and concluded with the second half of the refrain [see Enté]. There are even a few motet texts (and one conductus text) that consist entirely of refrains [ex. in *AdHM* i, 240, E], in the manner of a *cento. While philologists have fully investigated textual borrowing in motets, the extent of musical borrowing has not yet been completely studied. In some instances, a refrain was incorporated into a motet along with a tenor melody borrowed from plainsong (a *quodlibet* technique). The reverse—borrowing from a motet (first phrase of the *duplum*) to create a refrain—was also common. Borrowing refrains continued until the late 15th century [see M. F. Bukofzer, in *MQ* xxviii, 33]. A complete list of 13th-century refrains is given in F. Gennrich, *Bibliographisches Verzeichnis der französischen Refrains des 12. und 13. Jahrhunderts* (1964).

Alternation between variable and repeated portions of a composition reappears in the 17th-century instrumental *ritornello* as well as in the rondeaux of the French clavecinists [see Rondeau (2); Rondo].

Lit.: F. Gennrich, *Musikwissenschaft und Romanische Philologie* (1918).

Regal. A small portable organ, probably invented *c.* 1450 and much used during the 16th and 17th centuries, which had reed pipes only [see Reed]. The reproduction in *GDB* vi, 288 shows how it was built. The origin of the name is uncertain [see the conjectures in *GDB; SaHMI,* p. 308; *SaRM,* p. 318]. By the 16th century, the reed pipes of the regal had been incorporated into the organ, which until then had had only flue pipes, and the term "regal" came to mean the ranks of reed pipes, which were given such names as *Geigenregal, Trichterregal,* etc. Monteverdi prescribed the regal in his *Orfeo* (1607) to accompany the song of Charon. A particularly

small type of regal was the *bible regal,* so called because it could be folded together like a book. See *SaHMI,* p. 309.

Regina caeli laetare [L.]. One of the four antiphons B.V.M. See Antiphon (2).

Regisseur [F.,G.]. The artistic or stage director of an opera. The G. *Regie* corresponds generally to "production"; the *Regiebuch* contains the operatic text with indications for the stage setting.

Register. (1) In organs, the full set of pipes controlled by one stop; hence, practically identical with organ *stop. A register may include one or (in mixture stops, etc.) several *ranks. (2) In the human voice, the different portions of the range, which are distinguished, according to their place of production and sound quality, as "head register," "chest register," etc. There is considerable disagreement among singers and voice teachers regarding vocal registers. Some say the voice has two registers, high and low; many claim three registers, high (head), middle (throat), and low (chest); others subdivide still further. Formerly the registers played a prominent part in teaching and writing about singing, but today the whole idea is generally considered of little importance.

Registration [G. *Registrierung*]. The art of using and combining organ registers. While modern organ composers frequently indicate the registration of their compositions (at least in a

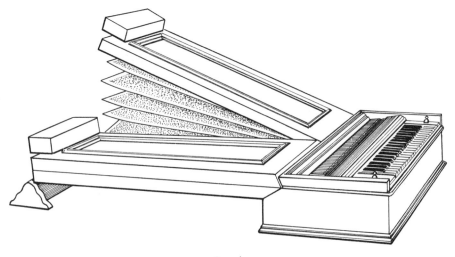

Regal.

general way), such indications are rare in early organ music. Before 1700 French organ composers were practically alone in prescribing specific registrations, employing titles such as "Récit de cromorne en taille" (Cromorne as solo stop for the tenor part). Authentic details regarding Bach's registration are available in a few pieces, notably the chorale preludes "Ein' feste Burg" (Peters ed. vi, no. 22: *Rückpositiv* and *Oberwerk*), "Christ lag in Todesbanden (Peters vi, no. 15: *piano* and *forte*), and the "Dorian" Toccata (Peters iii: *Oberwerk* and *Positiv*). See E. H. Geer, *Organ Registration in Theory and Practice* (1957). See also under Organ; Organ playing.

Regola dell' ottava [It.]. In the thoroughbass practice of the 17th and 18th centuries, a scheme

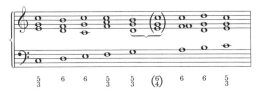

$$\begin{array}{cccccccccc} \frac{5}{3} & 6 & 6 & \frac{5}{3} & \frac{5}{3} & (\frac{6}{4}) & 6 & 6 & \frac{5}{3} \end{array}$$

whereby each tone of the octave is provided with a suitable chord, as in the accompanying example. Such schemes were helpful for the realization of simple basses that had no figures indicating more elaborate chords. See E. Borrel, in *TG* xxi, 175ff; A. Tirabassi, in *CP 1924* and *CP Borren.*

Rehab. See Rabab.

Reigen [G.]. Round dance.

Reimofficium [G.]. Rhymed versions of the liturgical texts for the Offices of Saints. They were very popular from the 11th through 16th centuries, until they were abolished by the Council of Trent (1545–63). See *AdHM* i, 89; P. Wagner, *Einführung in die Gregorianischen Melodien* i, 300ff; K. Meyer, in *AMW* iii.

Reimsequenz [G.]. The rhymed sequence of the 12th century. See Sequence II B.

Reine, La [F., The Queen]. Nickname for Haydn's Symphony no. 85, in B flat (no. 4 of the *Paris Symphonies), composed *c.* 1786. The name refers to Queen Marie Antoinette, who is said to have been particularly fond of this work.

Reine Stimmung [G.]. *Just intonation.

Reisado [Port.]. A native Brazilian play commemorating the journey of the Magi to Bethlehem, similar in many ways to the *Pastoris,* which depict the shepherds' adoration of the infant Jesus. Music and dance were an important part of these plays. A dance known as *Bumba meu Boi* (My Good Ox), which was added to the *reisado* as a kind of epilogue, is still performed in certain rural areas of Brazil.   J.O-S.

Réjouissance [F.]. In 18th-century music (Bach, Orchestral Suite no. 4), name for a light, playful piece, generally in quick triple meter.

Related key, relative keys. See Key relationship.

Relative pitch. (1) The pitch of a tone (e.g., E) in relation to a standard tone or given key (e.g., C). It may be expressed as an interval (major third), or by means of solmization syllables (mi), or by relative frequencies (⅝). (2) The ability to recognize and indicate relative pitch, e.g., to recognize the tone E as the major third above C, or to sing this tone if the major third above C is demanded. This faculty is a fundamental requirement for a musician, much more important than *absolute pitch.

Religious dances. Dignified ceremonial dances, performed by clergy in connection with some part of the service, were not uncommon in France and Spain from the 12th to 14th centuries. An early 14th-century MS from Sens contains a responsory for the feast of St. Stephen with the inscription: "ad processionem in navi ecclesie Senonum precentor debet ballare" (to [during?] the procession through the nave of the church of Sens the precentor should dance), as well as a responsory for the feast of St. Columba with a similar inscription [see Lit., Chailley]. The Spanish *"Llibre Vermell" contains a two-part composition, "Stella splendens" [see *AnM* x, 72f], in a simple style and in the form aa' bb aa', with the remark: "Sequitur alia cantilena . . . ad trepudium rotundum" (Here follows another song . . . for a sacred round dance). It also says that the pilgrims should avoid "cantilenas vanas atque tripudia inhonesta" [see Anglés, p. 54]. Religious dancing has survived to the present day in the Cathedral of Seville; see *Seises.*

Lit.: E. L. Backman, *Religious Dances in the Christian Church* (1952); R. Foatelli, *Les Danses religieuses dans le christianisme* (1939); L. Gougaud, "La Danse dans les églises" (*Revue d'Histoire ecclésiastique* xv [1914]); H. Spanke, "Tanzmusik in der Kirche des Mittelalters" (*Neuphilologische Mitteilungen* xxxi [1930]); Y. Rokseth,

"Danses cléricales du XIIIe siècle" (*Publications de la Faculté des Lettres de l'Université de Strasbourg,* fasc. 106 [1945]); H. Anglés, "El Llibre vermell . . . y la danza sacra" (*AnM* x); J. Chailley, "Un Document nouveau sur la danse ecclésiastique" (*AM* xxi); J. Amades, "Danses rituals d'iniciació" (*CP Anglés* i).

Relish. An ornament used in performing early English music for lute, viol, and keyboard. The term "single relish" was used for any ornament formed by the alternation of two adjacent notes. The "double relish," a complex ornament similar to the French *double cadence,* consists

essentially of a trill upon each of two successive notes [see Ex.].   P.A.

Remettez [F.]. In organ music, indication to take off a stop.

Renaissance, music of the. The music of the period *c.* 1430–1650, preceded by the Middle Ages and followed by the baroque. There is little disagreement about when it ended, since 1600 is one of the clearest landmarks in music history [see History of music; Baroque music]. However, there is much less unanimity about its beginning, which has been placed as early as 1300 (H. Riemann, H. Besseler) and as late as 1520 (C. van den Borren). Today most musicologists agree that 1430 marks the approximate beginning of Renaissance music, making it nearly coeval with the Renaissance in the visual arts (*c.* 1400: Ghiberti's bronze doors of the Baptistry of Florence). Thus Dunstable (*c.* 1385–1453), Dufay (*c.* 1400–74), and Binchois (*c.* 1400–67) would be the first representatives of Renaissance music. However, the traits usually regarded as characteristic of the Renaissance as a broad cultural movement (rebirth of classical art and learning, independence of thought, humanist tendencies, etc.) were not present in music, at least not in the initial stage. Moreover, whereas the Renaissance in literature and the visual arts was originally (and for a long time) exclusively Italian, Renaissance music originated and developed exclusively in northern France and Belgium. Music flourished in Italy in the 14th century but declined during the era of Fra Angelico (1387–1455), Donatello (1386–1466), Brunelleschi (1379–1446), and their successors.

Renaissance music, therefore, represents a movement that initially had no connection with the Renaissance in general. Like the term *baroque, the term Renaissance serves mainly to place an important and well-defined period of music history within the over-all cultural development. That a new musical development did begin in the second quarter of the 15th century is certainly true. Tinctoris, writing *c.* 1476, speaks of an *ars nova* that began forty years ago, adding that music written before that time was not worth hearing.

By and large, Renaissance music shows the general traits of "classicism" in contrast to the "romantic" tendencies of the 14th and 17th centuries [see Classicism]. Clarity, balance, euphony, and expressiveness within well-regulated limits are among its characteristic features, especially in its later development. Its most outstanding technical achievements are the development of a *panconsonant style; a gradual tendency toward functional harmony with prepared cadences; four-part polyphony with equal participation of all the voice-parts; imitation; and, in the 16th century, methodical treatment of dissonances, close consideration of the text, etc. See Burgundian school; Flemish school; Humanism; *Musica reservata.*

Lit.: *ReMR, passim;* L. Schrade, in *CP 1952;* H. C. Wolff, in *CP 1952;* R. E. Wolf, in *RBM* ix; H. Besseler, in *AMW* xxiii.

Renforcer [F.]. To reinforce, to increase in loudness.

Renversement [F.]. Inversion (of intervals, chords, subjects).

Repeat. The signs ‖: at the beginning and :‖ at the end of a section, which call for repetition of this section. If the latter sign alone appears, the repetition is to start from the beginning of the composition (e.g., the exposition of sonata form).

Repercussio, repercusa [L.]. Names for the reciting note (tenor) of *psalm tones. Neumes such as *bistropha, tristropha* [see Neumes I] are called repercussive neumes because they involve repeat of the same tone.

Répertoire International des sources musicales. See *RISM.*

Repetenda [L.]. In Gregorian chant, *repetenda* or *versus ad repetendum* designates psalm verses that were added *ad libitum* to a chant when the occasion required. They were used at least from the 8th through the 11th centuries, particularly for Introits and Communions, since the opening and closing ceremonial of the Mass took a varying amount of time. Thus, the Introit of Easter Sunday appears in the early sources as follows: Ant. *Resurrexi;* Psalm. *Domine probasti;* Ad repet. *Tu cognovisti.* The term is also used for the refrain in hymns, such as the *Gloria laus* of Palm Sunday.

Repetitio [L.]. Besides meaning "repetition," the term is sometimes used for a concluding section, e.g., the *Abgesang* of a *Bar* form [see *HAM*, no. 81a]. See under Ritornello (1).

Repetition. (1) A special device of the piano action that permits the quick repetition of a tone (invented by S. Érard). See Piano I.

(2) In musical composition, repetition is one of the most important principles of structure. Its importance becomes clear when one considers that repetition of a musical idea or a motif includes such devices as sequential treatment, imitation, ostinato, variation, and repeat of entire sections. The last is the basis of nearly all musical forms (A B A; A A B A; A B A C A D A; etc.; see Forms, musical). In a broader sense, repetition also includes such basic concerns as the equal length and comparable rhythm of phrases (four measures); in fact, the very presence of uniform meter throughout a piece constitutes an element of repetition.

In contrapuntal music four principal devices of repetition are used: repetition in the same part at the same pitch (*ostinato); repetition in the same part at a different pitch (*sequence); repetition in a different part at the same pitch (*Stimmtausch); repetition in a different part at a different pitch (*imitation).

Lit.: C. A. Harris, "The Element of Repetition in Nature and the Arts" (*MQ* xvii); R. Lach, "Das Konstructionsprinzip der Wiederholung" (*Sitzungsberichte der Akademie der Wissenschaften in Wien,* vol. cci [1925]).

Répétition [F.], **ripetizione** [It.]. Rehearsal. *Répétition générale* [F.], dress rehearsal.

Repicador. See under *Mejoranera.*

Replica [It.]. Repeat. *Senza replica* indicates omission of the repeats, as, e.g., of the sections of the minuet or scherzo after the trio.

Répons [F.]. *Responsory.

Réponse [F.]. Fugal answer.

Reports. A 17th-century English term for *points of imitation or some other kind of contrapuntal treatment. Playford's *Introduction to the Skill of Music* (12th ed., 1694) mentions "imitation or reports," and the Scottish Psalter of 1635 contains tunes treated in the style of an anthem and inscribed "Psalmes in Reports."

Reprise [E., F., G.]. (1) Repetition. The term is used particularly in connection with *sonata form, but unfortunately with two different meanings. Originally, it referred to the repetition of the exposition before the development, usually indicated by the *repeat sign. This meaning is intended in K. P. E. Bach's *Sechs Sonaten für Clavier mit veränderten Reprisen* (1760), in which the repetition of the exposition is written out in a varied form. Today, however, the term usually means the recapitulation, i.e., the repetition of the exposition after the development section [see under *Durchführung*]. (2) In 17th-century French music, the second section of pieces in binary form is called *reprise,* e.g., in practically all the dances in the suites of Chambonnières and D'Anglebert. See under Ritornello (1).

Reprisenbar [G.]. See under *Bar* form II.

Reproaches. See *Improperia.*

Requiem Mass. A musical setting of the Mass for the Dead (*Missa pro defunctis*), so called because it begins with the Introit "Requiem aeternam dona eis Domine" (Give them eternal rest, O Lord). The liturgical structure of this Mass is essentially like that of any other *Mass, except that the joyful portions of the Ordinary (Gloria and Credo) are omitted and the Alleluia is replaced by a Tract, after which the sequence "Dies irae" (by Thomas of Celano, 13th cent.) is added. For the plainsong music of this Mass, see *LU*, pp. 1807ff.

The polyphonic composition of the Mass for the Dead differs from the normal Mass chiefly in that it includes not only the items of the Ordinary (Kyrie, Sanctus, Agnus Dei), but also, and in fact more prominently, those of the Proper (Introit, Gradual, etc.). Thus it is of the type known as *plenary Mass. It should be noted that rarely (if ever) were all the items of the Gregorian Mass included in the polyphonic composition. The selection varied greatly, although in the 16th century there were certain standard practices in Italy, Spain, and the Netherlands.

Since a Requiem by Dufay (mentioned in his will) has been lost, the earliest extant example is one by Ockeghem. It consists only of Introit,

Kyrie, Gradual (the old "Si ambulem" instead of the later "Requiem aeternam"), Tract ("Sicut cervus" instead of "Absolve Domine"), and Offertory. A large number of 16th-century settings exist, among them those by La Rue [*Editions VIII, 11], J. Prioris (pub. by Attaingnant, 1532), A. de Fevin, Morales [*Editions XX, 1], Guerrero (*Liber primus missarum,* 1566), Palestrina (*Missarum liber primus,* 1554), Lasso (1589), and finally, Victoria's great *Officium defunctorum,* written in 1603 for the death of the Spanish Empress María. In all these works the "Dies irae" is not composed but sung in plainsong, as are the opening intonations of the various portions, while the composed sections use the liturgical melodies more or less freely as a *cantus firmus.* The 17th-century composers were particularly attracted by the dramatic words of the "Dies irae." The 17th-century Requiems of C. Straus (*c.* 1575–1631), H. I. F. von Biber (1644–1704), and J. K. Kerll (1627–93), reproduced in *DTO* 59, all use tremolo effects for the words "Quantus tremor." Among the 18th-century settings for chorus and orchestra, Jommelli's and, above all, Mozart's Requiem are outstanding. Among 19th-century composers of the Requiem are Cherubini, Berlioz, Dvořák, Bruckner, Verdi, Saint-Saëns, and Fauré. Brahms' *Ein deutsches Requiem* (op. 45, 1868) is an impressive work based on German texts freely chosen from the Scriptures. Important 20th-century examples are M. Duruflé's Requiem, op. 9 (1947) and B. Britten's *War Requiem,* op. 66 (1961). See C. W. Fox, "The Polyphonic Requiem before about 1615" (*BAMS* vii); R. J. Snow, in *JAMS* xi.

Rescue opera. See under Opera IX.

Reservata. See *Musica reservata.*

Res facta [L.]. A term used by modern musicologists for a type of composition (usually 15th-century) that is fully written out in all parts, as distinguished from improvised counterpoint, such as *discantus supra librum.* The term was introduced by J. Tinctoris, but his explanations (*Liber de arte contrapuncti, CS* iv, 85; *Diffinitorium, CS* iv, 187) are somewhat contradictory and do not agree with the interpretation above. Perhaps the term should be abandoned altogether. See E. T. Ferand, in *JAMS* x.

Resolution. In harmonic analysis, the succession of a dissonant note, e.g., an appoggiatura, by the corresponding consonant note [Ex. 1]; or of a dissonant chord, e.g., a seventh chord, by a con-

sonant chord. If the seventh chord is followed by the tonic, the resolution is regular [Ex. 2]; otherwise it is irregular [Ex. 3]. Ex. 4 illustrates the

resolution into another dissonance, a very common and important means of obtaining "harmonic flow."

Resonance. The transmission of vibrations from a vibrating body to another body. This phenomenon takes place only when the two bodies are capable of vibrating at the same frequency (or a harmonic thereof). If, e.g., two tuning forks of the same frequency (i.e., same pitch) are placed close together and one of them is struck with a hammer, the other will immediately vibrate and emit the same sound. In the case of vibrating strings, the possibilities for resonance are considerably wider, owing to the presence of harmonics. On the piano, e.g., the string C sets up resonant vibrations in the strings c, g, c', e', etc., as seen in an experiment described under Acoustics IV). The resonance of the piano strings causes the change in timbre that occurs when, by means of the damper pedal, the dampers are lifted from the strings. Another name for this effect is sympathetic vibration. See also Sympathetic string.

Important to musical instruments are the "general resonators," bodies that react with sounds of any frequency or pitch. To this type belong the soundboard of the piano and the belly and back of the violin, which co-vibrate and reinforce any sound produced on the strings. Resonance is one of the factors in the study of *architectural acoustics [see this entry and also Acoustics for bibl.]. See A. Seiffert, in *ZMW* xi.

Resonanzsaiten [G.]. *Sympathetic strings.

Resonator. Any acoustical implement, usually in the shape of a hollow vessel, that serves to reinforce sounds by resonance. Resonators in the form of a glass globe with a small opening were used by H. Helmholtz to prove the existence of harmonics. Others, shaped like hollow cylinders, are used with the Javanese xylophones and *marimba. Using the term as a synonym for globular flute results from (or leads to) confusion with Helmholtz' scientific devices.

Respond. A term meaning *responsory, *response, or, preferably, the main section of a responsorial chant (corresponding to the antiphon section of antiphonal chants) as opposed to the verse. Thus, a responsory or a Gradual consists of respond and verse. See Psalmody II.

Response. (1) In Anglican churches, the choral or congregational reply to the versicles (in the *preces and *suffrages), the petitions (in the *litany), and the Commandments of the *Decalogue. The term "Festal Responses" usually refers to the five-part harmonizations in Tallis' *Preces* and *Responses,* with the plainsong melody in the tenor. See Versicle. (2) In the Reformed churches, a short piece such as "Hear our prayer, O Lord" or a manifold Amen, sung by the choir, usually after a pastoral prayer. These are more in the nature of independent compositions, since the tradition in Reformed churches does not include singing of the minister's portions.   V.P.D.

Responsorial singing. In Gregorian chant, the performance of a chant by one or more soloists (*cantor, cantores*) in alternation with the choir (*schola*), as opposed to performance by two alternating half-choruses, known as *antiphonal singing. Originally each method was restricted to particular portions of the liturgy, the responsorial to the elaborate chants (responsories, Graduals, Alleluias, Offertories) and the antiphonal to the simpler ones (psalms, Introits, Communions); see Psalmody II, III. Today all these chants are sung responsorially, antiphonal performance being used only for certain nonpsalmodic chants, e.g., the Kyrie, Gloria, or the bilingual Sanctus on Good Friday [*LU,* p. 737]. For the book called *Liber responsorialis,* see Liturgical books I, 14. See C. Gindele, "Doppelchor und Psalmvortrag im Frühmittelalter" (*MF* vi); *ApGC,* pp. 196ff.

Responsory [L. *responsorium*]. In the Roman Catholic rites, a type of chant sung principally at Matins as a musical postlude to a lesson. Since Matins includes nine lessons (three for each Nocturn), it has nine responsories, the last of which is usually replaced on Sundays and feast days by the *Te Deum. More than a thousand responsories are found in 12th- and 13th-century MSS. A few of these, from the Matins of Nativity, Maundy Thursday, Good Friday, Holy Saturday, Pentecost, Corpus Christi, and the Office of the Dead, are included in the *Liber usualis.* Many more are found in the *Liber res-*

ponsorialis (1895), which, in accordance with monastic usage, has twelve responsories for each Matins. Responsories are also sung during Processions, e.g., that of Palm Sunday, and the *Processionale monasticum* (1893) contains processional responsories for all the major feasts. All these responsories are long, elaborate chants, consisting of respond, one or more verses, and the doxology. They are known as great responsories (*responsoria prolixa*), in distinction to the much simpler short responsories (*responsoria brevia*), which are sung after the short lesson (the so-called chapter) of the daytime hours [see, e.g., *LU,* p. 229]. These are indexed in the *Antiphonale Romanum,* but not in the *Liber usualis.* The formal structure of both types is outlined under Psalmody II. For *responsorium graduale,* see Gradual.

In the 16th century the great responsories were frequently composed as motets (responsory motets), with the respond in the *prima pars* and the verse and repeated portion (second half) of the respond in the *secunda pars.* Such motets usually are in the form ab cb (a = first, b = second half of the respond, c = verse). Tallis' setting of "Audivi vocem" (*Processionale monasticum,* p. 236) is based on the very old principle—consistently employed in the organa of Notre Dame [see Organum V]—of composing the solo sections only, the choral sections being added in plainsong [see *HAM,* no. 127].

Ressortir [F.]. To emphasize.

Rest [F. *pause, silence;* G. *Pause;* It. *pausa;* Sp. *silencio*]. See under Notes.

Restatement. Same as recapitulation in *sonata form.

Resultant bass. Name for organ pipes in which the acoustical phenomenon of resultant (differential) tones is used to produce the lowest registers; also called acoustic bass. See Combination tone.

Resultant tones. Same as *combination tones.

Resurrection Symphony. Mahler's Symphony no. 2, in C minor, completed in 1894. The fourth movement is a setting for alto solo and orchestra of "Urlicht" (Primordial Light, a song from *Des Knaben Wunderhorn*); the fifth and last movement is a setting of Klopstock's poem "Auferstehung" (Resurrection), for soprano solo, chorus, and orchestra.

Retardation. An uncommon term for suspension, particularly a suspension resolving upward.

Retirada [It.]. In Italian ballets and suites of the 17th century, a closing movement, as opposed to the *intrada*. Biagio Marini wrote suites consisting of *Entrata–Ballo–Gagliarda–Corrente–Retirada* [see P. Nettl, in *ZMW* ix, 538].

Retroensa [Prov.]. *Rotrouenge.*

Retrograde. A melody read backward, i.e., beginning with the last note and ending with the first. Synonymous terms are crab motion, *cancrizans* [L.], *Krebsgang* [G.], *al rovescio,* and *recte et retro* [It.]. See Ex. 1.

Although this procedure (unlike *inversion) completely obscures the original melody for the listener, it has not infrequently been used as a structural device. The earliest example is a 13th-century clausula, "Nusmido," in which the tenor has the liturgical melody "Dominus" in retrograde motion [see F. Ludwig, *Repertorium* (1910), i, 80]. Retrograde motion is one of the most common procedures of the 14th- and 15th-century riddle canons. It is indicated by inscriptions such as as: "Ma fin est mon commencement" (Machaut), "Ubi α ibi ω" (with reference to the first and last letters of the Greek alphabet), "Cancriza" (walk like a crab), "Canit more Hebraeorum" (sing as the Hebrews read, i.e., from right to left), "Vade retro Satanas" (Retreat, Satan), or a word spelled backward, e.g., "Ronet." In the 18th century Haydn used crab motion as a humorous trick in a "Menuet al Roverso," third movement, Symphony no. 47 (also in his A-major Violin Sonata, no. 4, and the

A-major Piano Sonata, B. & H. edition, no. 26). The minuet consists of a ten-measure phrase, ending on the dominant, which is played in retrograde to form the second half of the minuet (dominant to tonic). The trio is constructed in the same manner (two twelve-measure sections). The whole two-phrase minuet is then repeated in retrograde ("al rovescio"), which, however, sounds exactly the same as the original minuet. [See *GDB* vii, 267; also see *Rovescio*.] For a retrograde minuet by K. P. E. Bach, see *Nagel's Musik-Archiv* No. 65, no. 6a. Beethoven used

crab motion in the final fugue of the Hammerklavier Sonata, op. 106.

Retrograde inversion is the combination of retrograde motion and inversion [see Ex. 2]. The Postlude in Hindemith's *Ludus tonalis* is the retrograde inversion of its Prelude. Retrograde motion and inversion are of basic importance in *serial music. For retrograde canons, i.e., the simultaneous use of a melody and its retrograde form (*recte et retro*), see Canon I.

Revolutionary Etude. Nickname for Chopin's Etude in C minor, op. 10, no. 12, written in 1831 after he heard that Warsaw had been captured by the Russians.

Rf., rfz. [It.]. Abbr. for *rinforzando.

Rhapsodie aus Goethe's 'Harzreise im Winter' [G., Alto Rhapsody]. Composition by Brahms, op. 53 (1869), for contralto, men's chorus, and orchestra, based on a fragment from Goethe's *Harzreise im Winter* (Winter Journey through the Hartz Mountains).

Rhapsodies hongroises [F., Hungarian Rhapsodies]. A group of about twenty piano compositions by Liszt, in the character of free fantasies based on Hungarian themes. Most of them open with a slow introduction and continue with a fast, dancelike movement in imitation of the Hungarian *csárdás.

Rhapsody. Originally, a section of a Greek epic (e.g., the *Iliad*) or a free medley of such sections sung in succession. Musicians have used the term with different meanings, chiefly for free fantasies of an epic, heroic, or national character (F. Liszt, *Rhapsodies hongroises;* J. J. Raff; É. Lalo; A. Dvořák; B. Bartók). In Brahms' *Rhapsodien* for piano (op. 79 and op. 119, no. 4) the name seems to refer to their *ballade*-like character, whereas in his *Rhapsodie* in C, op. 53, for contralto, male chorus, and orchestra, the title may refer to the fact that it is written to a section of Goethe's *Harzreise im Winter*. The free, "rhapsodic" element appears to be emphasized in Gershwin's *Rhapsody in Blue*. See V. Jankelevitch, *La Rhapsodie* [1955].

Rheingold, Das. See *Ring des Nibelungen, Der.*

Rhenish Symphony. Schumann's Symphony no. 3, in E-flat, op. 97, composed in 1850 after a trip along the Rhine. The fourth movement was inspired by a ceremony in Cologne Cathedral.

Rhetoric. See Figures, doctrine of.

Rhumba. *Rumba.

Rhyme, musical. A term used for a composition consisting of sections having an identical ending: a+e b+e. Early examples occur in Gregorian chant, notably in some hymns (e.g., "Te lucis"; *LU,* pp. 367, 540) in the *Alleluias, and in the Offertories with verses [see *ApGC,* p. 373; see also *ReMMA,* p. 107f, for an example from Ambrosian chant]. Musical rhyme is an essential feature of the *estampies* and is frequently present in the *ballades* of Machaut and his successors [see *HAM,* nos. 45, 47].

Rhythm. I. *General.* In its primary sense, the whole feeling of movement in music, with a strong implication of both regularity and differentiation. Thus, breathing (inhalation vs. exhalation), pulse (systole vs. diastole), and tides (ebb vs. flow) all are examples of rhythm.

Rhythm and *motion may be analytically distinguished, the former meaning movement in time and the latter movement in space (pitch). A melody can be separated into a rhythm skeleton and a motion skeleton, but each qualifies the other. In Ex. 1, a particular pattern of note values is given five different rhythmic meanings through five different relationships to meter.

On the other hand, the two melodic fragments in E-flat major [see Ex. 2] have the same rhythm in the sense of relative note values and accent, but in the more general sense of the feeling of movement they are by no means alike. In Ex. 2a the

rhythm is qualified by the relative finality of leading-tone-to-tonic; in Ex. 2b the rhythm implies further movement (flow) toward the note G. Nevertheless, "foot rhythms" such as ♩|♩, short–long, with the long note accented, and related phenomena (e.g., dotted rhythm, modal rhythm) constitute perhaps the only particular cases for which the general term "rhythm" will be acceptable to most—perhaps all—musicians.

II. *Classification.* There are two main categories of rhythm, isometric and multimetric.

(a) In *isometric rhythm, every time value is a multiple (or fraction) of a beat, and the measures are equal and are normally accented on the first beat. In modern notation, the measures are marked off from one another by bar lines. See Ex. 1a–d. This is, aside from exceptions mentioned below, *the* rhythm of traditional Western music.

In isometric music, phrasing usually becomes a metric as well as a formal phenomenon. Especially in dance music and in music based on dance rhythms, there is a strong tendency to group the measures in two's and powers of two (2, 4, 8, etc.). Regularity of phrasing produces a meter on a higher level, so that isometric groups of measures become units of time, and the space of time measured by these units may in turn become a unit in a yet larger group, and so on.

(b) In multimetric rhythm [see Poly-, multi-], every time value is a multiple (or fraction) of a beat, but there is no regularly recurrent accent, owing to free alternation of different measures [see Ex.1e]. This type is much more important in music history than is generally recognized. Gregorian chant, in its Solesmes rendition as well as the "mensuralist" interpretation [see Gregorian chant VI], belongs to this category (the common idea that Gregorian rhythm is "free" is actually misleading; a certain freedom of performance, involving ritardandos and accelerandos, may be applied to any type of rhythm and meter). The same is true of modern Russian and *Syrian chant, as well as the humanist *ode and *vers mesuré* of the 16th century, the *plain-chant musical,* and the French *recitative of the 17th century. Multimeter became prominent in the works of modern composers such as Stravinsky, Bartók, and Hindemith, in which it frequently is notated as *syncopation, i.e., a temporary displacement of regular meter and accent.

The measurement of time is not always by means of a rhythm rationalized in terms of beats and multiples and fractions thereof. So-called "free" rhythm is like multimetric rhythm without a fixed unit of time: measure is by groups of notes, but the relative lengths of the notes themselves are not measured. Such free rhythm appears in various Oriental (Indian, etc.) songs and some ancient European folk music, e.g., Hungarian. Obviously, such rhythm cannot be expressed in Western musical notation, which is essentially based on the idea of a common unit of time. For an interesting attempt to escape the rhythmic fetters of Western notation, see under Prelude II (L. Couperin). Free rhythm is also present whenever a striking deviation from strict rhythm is demanded, e.g., by rallentando, accelerando, rubato.

III. *History.* (a) Prehistory. Practically all the extant examples of Greek music are isometric. Some of them employ irregular meters, such as 5/8 and 8/8 + 7/8 [see *HAM,* no. 7]. The early Christian hymns, especially those of St. Ambrose, are usually thought to have been sung in ternary meter (long plus short), but the evidence for this theory is somewhat doubtful [see Ambrosian chant]. The same applies to numerous hymns of later centuries, all of which are written in strictly measured verses, e.g., "O sálutáris hóstiá," but are sung to melodies that often have several notes per syllable and therefore are not easily adaptable to rendition in strict meter [see Ex. 3]. Similar problems arise in connection with

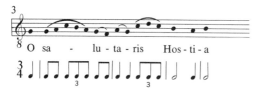

the rhymed sequences of Adam de St. Victor (d. 1177 or 1192) and the repertory of the troubadours, trouvères, minnesingers, etc. See Monophonic notation; Modal theory.

(b) Modal rhythm. Not until shortly before 1200 did isometric rhythm become definitely established through the modal rhythm [see Modes, rhythmic] of the organa, clausulae, etc., of the school of Notre Dame. Credit for this important innovation must be ascribed to Leoninus. While his organa (*dupla*) seem to represent an intermediate type, including sections in

modal rhythm along with others in the free rhythm of the earlier period (*St. Martial), his successor, Perotinus, established the exclusive use of modal (hence metric) rhythm [see Organum (2), IV; also *Ars antiqua* II]. The system of six rhythmic modes and their associated *ordines,* which developed shortly after 1200, is the first attempt at a methodical treatment of rhythm and meter. It prevailed for the rest of the century, later being broadened by the introduction of smaller values (two to seven semibreves) in the place of one breve (the quarter note of 3/4 meter).

(c) Rhythm in the polyphonic era, 1300–1600. About 1250 the first attempts to introduce duple meter were made. A remark in a contemporary treatise (Pseudo-Aristotle; see *CS* i, 271) refers not only to this daring innovation but to the strength of contemporary opposition: ". . . If somebody were to ask whether a song can be formed by imperfect [i.e., duple] *longae* [half notes] exclusively just as it can be formed by perfect *longae* [triple or dotted half notes], the approved answer is no; since nobody can sing a succession of pure imperfect *longae.*" In order to understand this position, it must be remembered that, to the 13th-century musician, triple meter was "perfect" because it had a "beginning," "middle," and "end"; duple meter, on the other hand, had a "beginning" and "middle" but no "end" and was therefore "imperfect." Musicians, however, did not bow to such scholastic reasoning, and shortly after 1300 duple and triple meter were recognized as equal in all degrees, from the *maxima* to the *semiminima* or, as one might say today, from the whole note to the quarter note, so that all meters, 2/4, 3/4, 6/8, 9/8, became available. This system, which is the basis of *mensural notation, was established by Philippe de Vitry (*c.* 1320). Hand in hand with this freedom of meter went a rapid advance in the use of rhythmic subtleties and finesses, such as dotted rhythm, triplets, *hemiola formations, *syncopation, and *polyrhythms [see under *Poly-, multi-]. Toward the end of the 14th century polyphonic music achieved a complexity of rhythm and meter that has never again been paralleled in all history [see Polyrhythm, Ex. 1]. These complexities largely disappeared in the Burgundian school (Dufay) and the subsequent Flemish schools (Ockeghem, Obrecht, Josquin). While composers of the 15th century preferred ternary meter, those of the 16th adopted binary meter as their standard meter and, within this framework, developed the technique of contrapuntal rhythms that is the very essence of true counterpoint [see Texture]. However, irregular groupings and phrases are common, particularly in the works of the early Flemish masters (Ockeghem, Obrecht), so that the underlying meter is often obscured. In modern transcription this results in syncopation, but actually the formations are multimetric [see Ex., from the Kyrie of Ockeghem's *Missa Mi-mi*].

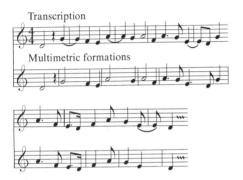

Transcription

Multimetric formations

(d) Classical rhythm. With the abandoning of polyphonic music and the introduction of accompanied melody (1600; see Baroque music), isometric rhythm superseded the multimetric. This change, which had extensive antecedents in the dance music and the more popular vocal music of the late Renaissance, had two results: (1) the effect of the measure-to-measure rhythm became much simpler, because of the strong accents in regular recurrence that pervade and regulate the entire fabric; and (2) the regularly recurring pattern was used over greater spans of time than before, which in turn (with the important help of tonality) led to the emergence of the large piece. This classical rhythm, which is most simply and clearly realized in the dance, became the matrix for rhythmic development in all music from *c.* 1600 to 1900. About 1700 there arose, particularly with Antonio Vivaldi (d. 1741), a precise and energetic rhythm in quick notes that is well known from many fugal themes of Handel and, especially, from Bach's Brandenburg Concertos. After 1750, metric developments are relatively uninteresting until Beethoven, who in his late piano sonatas employed complete syncopation as a means of escaping from the "tyranny of the bar line" [see Syncopation]. His example was followed by Schumann and Brahms, who, familiar with the music of earlier periods, often used *hemiola formations.

(e) The 20th century. The 20th century has seen a tremendous rise of interest in rhythmic

and metric variety. Multimetric music has been regenerated. Slavic dances with their lively rhythms, jazz with its complicated syncopations, the modern machine with its relentless motorism, neoclassicism with its return to polyphonic styles, and the general tendency to explore to the limit whatever was neglected in the 19th century —all these contribute to giving variety of rhythm and meter a place in contemporary music such as it had not had for many centuries [see Serial music IV]. For more details see Jazz; Syncopation; Polyrhythm.

Finally, those readers whose concept of rhythm is primarily derived from the temporal phenomena of measure-music [see Measure] are referred to the entry Meter.

Related articles: Agogic; Beat; Measure; Meter; Modes; Poetic meter; Polyrhythm; Proportions; Rubato; Syncopation; Tactus; Tempo; Tempus; Time signatures.

Lit.: C. Sachs, *Rhythm and Tempo* (1953); G. W. Cooper and L. B. Meyer, *The Rhythmic Structure of Music* [1960]; M. H. Glyn, *The Rhythmic Conception of Music* (1907); E. Jaques-Dalcroze, *Rhythm, Music and Education* (1921); M. Lussy, *A Short Treatise on Musical Rhythm* (1909); C. F. A. Williams, *The Rhythm of Modern Music* (1909); H. Cowell, *New Musical Resources* (1930); W. G. Waite, *The Rhythm of Twelfth-Century Polyphony* (1954); P. Aldrich, *Rhythm in Seventeenth-Century Italian Monody* [1966]; F. Rothschild, *The Lost Tradition in Music,* vol. i [1953; Bach]; H. Riemann, *System der musikalischen Rhythmik und Metrik* (1903); G. Becking, *Der musikalische Rhythmus als Erkenntnisquelle* (1928); R. Dumesnil, *Le Rythme musical,* rev. ed. [1949]; G. L. Howle, "The Musical Measure...from 1650 to 1800" (diss. Stanford Univ., 1960); K. M. Wilson, in *ML* viii; M. Lussy, in *VMW* i; L. Schrade, in *RM1* lvi; H. Cowell, in *MM* v, no. 4.   rev. G.C.

Rhythmic modes. See Modes, rhythmic.

Ribattuta [It.]. See under Ornamentation I.

Ribeba [It.]. *Jew's-harp.

Ribibe, ribible. See Rabab.

Ribs. The sides of instruments of the violin family, connecting the back and the table.

Ricercar(e), ricercata, recercada [It.]. Terms that, during the 16th and 17th centuries, were used for various types of instrumental music that differ considerably in style and purpose. By far the most important of these is the imitative ricercar [see I]. The other connotations, however, should not be overlooked in order to understand fully the general meaning of this term, for which the word "study" is a reasonably good equivalent. Such a "study" may be contrapuntal [I] or technical or instructive [II]. It should be noted that 16th-century prints and MSS often present the term ricercar interchangeably with fantasia, tiento, and preamble.

I. *The imitative (contrapuntal) ricercar.* This is, to a certain extent, the instrumental counterpart of the (vocal) motet. Its chief characteristic is the imitative treatment of one or more themes, the themes sometimes being slow and lacking rhythmic as well as melodic individuality (e.g., theme of the E-major fugue from Bach's *Well-Tempered Clavier,* vol. ii). Such pieces were written for instrumental (occasionally even vocal) ensembles and for the organ. The former were published in partbooks, the latter in scores, either on two staves (*intavolatura*) or (in the 16th and 17th centuries) occasionally on four staves (*partitura*). There is, however, evidence that the ensemble ricercar was occasionally also played on keyboard instruments in the Veggio MS at Castell' Arquato [see H. C. Slim, in *JAMS* xv], and in the arrangements from the *Musica nova* of 1540 (new ed. H. C. Slim [1964], nos. XI–XIII). These arrangements appear as keyboard compositions (*tientos*) in the *Libro de cifra nueva* of 1557 [*Editions XXXII, 2].

(a) The ensemblè ricercar. Instrumental pieces in the style of the motet were written by Isaac (*c.* 1450–1517) and Hofhaimer (1459–1537). Some of Isaac's "Instrumentalsätze" [e.g. *DTO* 28, nos. 42, 51] and Hofhaimer's "Carmen in re" ("in sol"; see H. J. Moser, *Paul Hofhaimer* [1929], nos. 22–23) might well be considered the point of departure for the ricercar. The earliest ensemble pieces called "ricercar" are found in the *Musica nova* of 1540 (Willaert, Julio da Modena) and in publications by Jacques Buus (1547, '49), Giuliano Tiburtino (1549; also eight by Willaert), Willaert (1551, '59), and Annibale Padovano (1556). Stylistically, these are very similar to motets, being written in a vocal ambitus and in a continuous texture with numerous overlapping points of imitation, frequent crossing of voice-parts, without ornamentation and passagework, etc. The close relation to vocal practice is indicated by titles such as "per cantar et sonar" (*Musica nova*), "da cantare et sonare" (Buus, 1547), or "da cantare a quattro voci" (Merulo, 1607), inscriptions indicating that these ricercars could be sung (in *vocalization)

as well as played on viols, recorders, cornetts, etc. Moreover, singers frequently utilized ricercars by adding solmization syllables (Tiburtino, 1549; Fuenllana, *Orphenica lyra,* 1554; P. Vinci, *Motetti e ricercari,* 1591). The ensemble ricercar was cultivated until about 1620, the latest (?) publication being by Antonio Cifra (1619). Others are by Palestrina (?; see Lit., Ritter), Merulo (1574, 1607), Malvezzi (1577), and Stivori (1589, '99).

(b) The organ ricercar. The history of the imitative ricercar for keyboard begins with the four ricercars in Girolamo Cavazzoni's *Intavolatura cioè recercari canzoni himni magnificati* of 1542/43 [see *HAM,* no. 116]. They show many of those peculiarities of style and structure that make the organ ricercar a type in its own right, not a mere "textless motet," as is largely the case with the ensemble ricercar. The most important trait is the employment of a relatively small number of themes, each of them extensively treated in a lengthy section that comes to a full stop. Other traits, not found in the ensemble ricercar, are free-voice writing, cadential coloraturas, and passages in toccata style. Andrea Gabrieli wrote a number of ricercars (pub. posthumously, 1595, '96), in which the tendency towards elaborate treatment of a small number of themes becomes even more apparent. Five of these ricercars are monothematic; others are based on two or three themes. In addition, Gabrieli made extensive use of special contrapuntal devices such as augmentation, diminution, inversion, double counterpoint, and combination of different themes, thus bestowing on the ricercar the character of learnedness that was later to be associated with it. In Italy the organ ricercar was also cultivated by Merulo (1567), Mayone (1603, '09), Antegnati (1608; *Editions XI, 9), Trabaci (1603, '15), Frescobaldi (1615; also some in the *Fiori musicali,* 1635), Salvatore (1641), Storace (1664), Battiferri (1669), Fontana (1677), and Pasquini (*Editions XI, 5). German (chiefly South German) composers of ricercars were H. L. Hassler (*c.* 25 ricercars; some in *DTB* 7), Erbach (*c.* 35 ricercars; some in *DTB* 7), Steigleder (1624), Froberger (*DTO* 8), Krieger [see *HAM,* no. 249a], Poglietti, and Pachelbel (*DTB* 6). Bach ended the development with his famous ricercar (acrostic: *Regis Iussu Cantio Et Reliqua Arte Canonica Resoluta* —Upon the King's Demand, the Theme and Additions Resolved in Canonic Style) from *Das *Musikalisches Opfer,* 1747.

II. *The nonimitative ricercar.* Numerous 16th- and 17th-century compositions bearing the name ricercar are quite different in style and form from the type described above. In a way, they may be characterized as "studies" in technique and instruction rather than counterpoint.

(a) For the lute. The earliest pieces called "ricercar" are the lute ricercars in Petrucci's *Intabulatura de lauto* i, ii, iv (1507/8; iii is lost). Unrelated to the motet, they are short pieces in free lute style, consisting chiefly of sequential passages and chords, much like a prelude. Counterpoint is reduced to a bare minimum, and imitation is usually absent [see *HAM*, no. 99; *SchGMB*, no. 63b]. However, not all these pieces are preludes (as suggested by various writers), because several pieces by Dalza in Petrucci's Book iv consist of a "tastar de corde" (touching of the strings), a "ricercar dietro" (ricercar thereafter), and a "Recercar detto coda." Here the *tastar* evidently takes the place of the prelude proper; in fact, the ricercar is, by comparison, somewhat more "constructed" and may have served to exploit the technical resources of the lute [see *HAM*, no. 99]. Certainly an early function of the ricercar was an associative one: those by Bossinensis (Petrucci, bks. i and ii, 1509, '11) are designated by a system of letters to be played with his arrangements of *frottole* for solo voice and lute. In the later literature for the lute (Francesco da Milano, 1536, '46, '47, etc; Simon Gintzler, 1547 [see *DTO*, 37]; Valentin Bacfarc, 1552; Vincenzo Galilei [for original lute pieces from *Fronimo*, 1584, see Editions XXIII, 4]), the ricercar more and more approaches the style of the imitative ricercar, apparently owing to the greater skill of the lutenists, who by then regarded the polyphonic style as idiomatic for their instrument. The practice of incorporating preexistent polyphonic music in ricercars resulted in the parody ricercar [see J. Ward, in *CP Sachs*, pp. 208–28].

(b) For the organ. The earliest organ pieces called ricercar are found in Marco Antonio Cavazzoni's *Recerchari, motetti, canzoni* (1523). Like the lute pieces, they have no connection with the motet. They are long compositions showing a mixture of chordal elements, passagework, and sporadic imitation of short motifs. In spite of their length they apparently served somewhat as a prelude, each of the two ricercars being followed by a piece in the same key, a *Salve virgo* and an *O stella maris*—evidently the "motets" of the title. Four ricercars by Giacomo Fogliano (*Editions X, 1) and those by Claudio Veggio [see Lit., article by Slim] show increased use of imitation and represent the transition to

the imitative ricercar of Girolamo Cavazzoni.

(c) For viols, etc. Theorists such as Silvestro Ganassi (*Regola Rubertina*, 1542/3; ed. by M. Schneider, 1924) and Diego Ortiz (*Tratado de glosas*, 1553; rev. ed. by M. Schneider, 1936) use the term "ricercar" for instructive pieces designed to demonstrate the skillful playing of the viola da gamba. Ganassi's pieces are interesting for their extensive use of double stops [see *HAM*, no. 119], while those by Ortiz illustrate the art of variation and ornamentation. Clearly in the same category are 17th-century ricercars for cello solo (without accompaniment) by Giovanni Battista degl'Antonii (op. 5, 1690) and Domenico Gabrielli (1689; see *SchGMB*, no. 228).

(d) For voice. A pedagogic purpose is clearly indicated in an extensive repertory of 16th- and 17th-century "ricercari a due voci" (F. Guami, 1588; G. Metallo, 1603 and later editions; C. Gentile, 1642; C. Piochi, 1671), i.e., two-voice untexted compositions designed primarily for singers, since in several of the publications above they are referred to as vocal exercises, to be performed, of course, in *vocalization. Orlando di Lasso's "Cantiones sine textu" [see comp. ed. i, 8ff] belong to the same category. As late as 1774, G. Martini in his *Esemplare ossia saggio* (p. 295) speaks of "the masters who compose ricercars and solfeggios." These pieces are particularly interesting as potential predecessors of Bach's two-part inventions.

The neoclassical movement of the 20th century has led to a revival of the ricercar, e.g., in B. Martinu's *Tre Ricercari*, in A. Casella's *Due Ricercari sul nome di Bach*, and in Stravinsky's *Cantata*.

Lit.: W. J. V. Wasielewski, *Geschichte der Instrumentalmusik im XVI. Jahrhundert* (1878), suppl. (nos. 12–15 for lute; 17–18 for ensemble; 20, 21, 24 for organ); O. Kinkeldey, ‡*Orgel und Klavier in der Musik des 16. Jahrhunderts* (1910); R. M. Murphy, "Fantaisie et recercare dans les premières tablatures de luth du XVIe siècle," in *Le Luth et sa musique*, ed. J. Jacquot (1958); R. S. Douglass, "The Keyboard Ricercare in the Baroque Era" (diss. North Texas State Univ., 1963); H. C. Slim, "The Keyboard Ricercar and Fantasia in Italy *c.* 1500–1550," 2 vols. (diss. Harvard Univ., 1960); W. Apel, "The Early Development of the Organ Ricercar" (*MD* iii); G. Sutherland, "The Ricercari of Jacques Buus" (*MQ* xxxi); H. H. Eggebrecht, "Terminus 'Ricercar'" (*AMW* ix); A. G. Ritter, "Die 'Ricercari sopra li Toni' von G. P. Palestrina (?)" (*MfM* vi); H. Opienski, "Quelques Considerations sur l'origine des ricercari pour luth" (*CP Lauren-cie*); A. Einstein, "Vincenzo Galilei e il duetto didattico" (*LRM* xi); H. C. Slim, "Keyboard Music at Castell' Arquato by an Early Madrigalist" (*JAMS* xv); J. Ward, "Parody Technique in 16th-century Instrumental Music" (*CP Sachs*).   rev. H.C.S.

Ricochet [F.]. See under Bowing (e).

Riddle canon. See under Canon (1), III.

Ridotto [It.]. Reduced, i.e., arranged (for piano, etc.).

Riduzione [It.]. Arrangement.

Rienzi. Opera in five acts by Wagner (full title, *Cola Rienzi, der Letzte der Tribunen;* libretto by the composer, based on Bulwer-Lytton's novel), produced in Dresden, 1842. Setting: Rome, about 1350. An early work, it reflects the styles of Italian and French opera.

Rigaudon, rigadoon. A Provençal dance of the 17th century [see Dance music III] used in the operatic ballets of Lully, Campra, and Rameau, and also introduced in the optional group of the suite (Pachelbel, Bach). Among the earliest extant examples is a Rigadoon by Purcell (*c.* 1659–

95; see Ex.). The *rigaudon* also occurs in the suites of modern composers (Grieg, *From Holberg's Time;* Ravel, *Le Tombeau de Couperin*). See V. Alford, in *MQ* xxx, no. 3.

Rigo [It.]. Staff.

Rigoletto. Opera in three acts by Verdi (libretto by F. M. Piave, after Victor Hugo's drama *Le Roi s'amuse*), produced in Venice, 1851. Setting: Mantua and environs, 16th century. Its gruesome plot places *Rigoletto* in the category of the "horror opera," which had a great vogue around 1850. However, the action is full of moments of genuine dramatic tension, and the music elevates the opera far beyond the level of, e.g., Meyerbeer's *Robert-le-Diable.* Together with *Il Trovatore* (1853) and *La Traviata* (1853), *Rigoletto* represents the high point of Italian opera with melodramatic plots, popular melodies, and emphasis on "effective" vocal numbers.

Rilasciando [It.]. Slowing down.

Rinforzando, abbr. *rf, rfz, rinf.* [It.]. A sudden accent on a single note or chord, practically synonymous with **sforzando.* In early orchestral music (J. W. A. Stamitz) the term is used for a short but strong crescendo.

Ring des Nibelungen, Der [G., The Ring of the Nibelung]. Tetralogy by Richard Wagner, consisting of four operas: *Das Rheingold* (The Rhine Gold, 1853–54; designated by Wagner as *Vorspiel,* i.e., prologue); *Die Walküre* (The Valkyrie, 1854–56); *Siegfried* (1856–71); and *Götterdämmerung* (The Twlight of the Gods, 1873–74). The libretto is by Wagner, based on legends from the Scandinavian Edda and the Nibelungenlied. The first performance of the entire *Ring* took place in Bayreuth, 1876, for the dedication of the Bayreuth Festspielhaus. Setting: Germanic mythology.

In order to forge together his large, complicated plot, Wagner here more than in any of his other operas relies on **leitmotivs* as a means of unification. Not only has each of the characters his own specific motif, but basic ideas, such as "the curse," "the ring," and "the sword," are also represented in this way. Moreover, in contrast to such earlier operas as *Tannhäuser* and *Lohengrin,* Wagner here completely discards the last remnants of the aria or lied as an ingredient of operatic structure, replacing it with an "unending melody" that, intentionally avoiding definite cadences and sectional construction, continues almost from the beginning to the end of each act in an uninterrupted flow [see Opera X; Recitative; Leitmotiv].

Ripieno [It.]. In the 17th- and 18th-century orchestral music, particularly in the **concerto grosso,* the "reinforcing section" of the orchestra, comparable to the "rear section" of the violins, etc., in the modern orchestra. Therefore, *ripieni* indicates the full orchestra (*tutti, concerto grosso*) as distinguished from the soloists (*concertino*). However, *senza ripieni* (without *ripieni*) does not mean "orchestra silent" but calls for the leading orchestra players only, i.e., a smaller ensemble used for the accompaniment of the soloists (*concertino*). A *ripienista* is an orchestral player.

Riposato [It.]. With a feeling of repose.

Riprendere [It.]. To take up (the original tempo).

Ripresa [It.]. (1) Repeat or repetition (also of a performance, opera, etc.). (2) Recapitulation (in sonata form). (3) In the 14th-century **ballata* (and its descendant, the *frottola), the refrain. (4) In 16th- and 17th-century music, a varied repeat of a dance [see T. Norlind, in SIM vii, 172], or a closing section of a dance or a tune [see HAM, no. 154, Ammerbach; no. 192, Frescobaldi]; see under Ritornello (1).

Riservata [It.]. Variant spelling of reservata. See Musica reservata.

RISM. Abbr. for Répertoire International des sources musicales, an exhaustive inventory of musical sources intended to replace R. Eitner's Biographisch-Bibliographisches Quellen-lexikon (1900–04). The project was initiated in 1952 by F. Blume (chairman) and other musicologists. It consists (or will consist) of two main sections: A. an alphabetical catalog of authors (composers, writers, theorists, etc.); B. a number of catalogs arranged chronologically or systematically, each dealing with a specific subject, e.g., "Printed Collections of the 16th–17th Centuries," "Manuscripts of Tropes and Sequences," etc. The following volumes (all for section B) have appeared: F. Lesure, Recueils imprimés, XVIe–XVIIe siècles: I. Liste chronologique [1960]; id., Recueils imprimés, XVIIIe siècle [1964]; J. S. van Waesberghe, P. Fischer, and C. Maas, The Theory of Music from the Carolingian Era up to 1400, vol. i. [1961]; H. Husmann, Tropen- und Sequenzenhandschriften [1964]; G. Reaney, Manuscripts of Polyphonic Music, 11th–Early 14th Century [1966]. See F. Blume, in JAMS xvii, 415ff.

Rispetto [It.]. A form of early Italian poetry, usually in eight lines with the rhyme scheme a b a b c c d d. Several 14th-century madrigals have texts in rispetto form [see W. T. Marrocco, The Music of Jacopo da Bologna (1954), p. 16].

Risposta [It.]. Fugal answer.

Risqolo. See under Syrian chant; Melody type.

Ritardando, abbr. rit., ritard. [It.]. Gradually slackening in speed, also indicated by rallentando. Ritenuto properly calls for immediate reduction of speed.

Ritenuto [It.]. See under Ritardando.

Rite of Spring, The. See Sacre du printemps, Le.

Ritmo [It.]. *Rhythm. For Beethoven's indication "ritmo di tre [quattro] battute," see Battuta.

Ritornello [It.]. (1) In the 14th-century *caccia and *madrigal, the couplet at the end of the

poem, which usually expresses the "thought" derived from the preceding "description." In musical composition, it is treated as a separate section, usually involving a change of meter. The ritornello is not a refrain. The name ("little return") may indicate that the ritornello restates the content of the main stanza in modified form. Cf. the terms *repetitio, *reprise, and ripresa [see Ripresa (3) and (4)], all of which mean "conclusion."

(2) In 17th-century Italian operas and cantatas, the term has essentially the same meaning but is applied to short instrumental conclusions added to an aria or a song [see HAM, no. 183, Cavalieri; no. 209, Landi; no. 221, Cesti]. Sometimes the ritornello also occurs at the beginning of the song, an example being the famous ritornello for Orfeo's song "Vi ricorda," in Monteverdi's Orfeo (1607) [for another example, by Stradella, see HAM, no. 241]. Aside from the *sinfonias, which serve a different purpose, the ritornelli are the only instrumental pieces in early operas. The ritornello instrumental refrain is a standard feature of German 17th-century strophic songs (arias). See the arias of Johann Erasmus Kindermann in DTB 32 and Adam Krieger in DdT 19.

(3) See Ritornello form. See also Ritournelle.

Ritornello form. A term often used for the typical form of the first and frequently also the last movement of the baroque concerto, particularly the *concerto grosso. Such movements consist of an alternation of tutti and solo sections, the tutti sections being based on identical material while the solo sections vary. The tutti sections therefore form the ritornello.

Ritournelle [F.]. A 17th-century dance in quick triple time, by far the most common dance type in the ballets of Lully. Like the *ritornello, it serves as the conclusion of a song.

Riverso, rivolto [It.]. Terms that mean *inversion (of intervals, chords, or parts) but also are used to denote *retrograde motion. See Rovescio.

Rococo. In painting, architecture, and other visual and decorative arts, designation for an 18th-century style in which light, ornate decoration (especially in the form of scrolls, shells, etc.), and emphasis on frivolous elegance and luxury replace the massive structures of the baroque. Its counterpart in 18th-century music is the so-called *gallant style, which, with its emphasis on pleasantness and prettiness, is in marked contrast to the impressive grandeur of the *baroque style. The main flowering of rococo was from 1725 to 1775. However, the movement began considerably earlier in France, where François Couperin (1668–1733) represents the musical counterpart of the first major rococo painter, Watteau (1684–1721). From France it spread to Germany (Telemann, 1681–1767; Mattheson, 1681–1764) and Italy (D. Scarlatti, 1685–1757). The wholehearted adoption of the rococo style led to a deterioration of artistic standards under musicians such as Balbastre, Daquin, C. Nichelmann, G. B. I. Grazioli, Sacchini, and many others who fill volumes euphemistically called "The Old Masters of the Pianoforte." Although as early as 1740 Johann W. A. Stamitz, founder of the *Mannheim school, established a novel style of a more vigorous nature, rococo elements are still present in the works of K. P. E. Bach, Haydn, and Mozart. See Gallant style; *Empfindsamer Stil.* See P. H. Lang, *Music in Western Civilization* (1941), pp. 530ff; *GrHWM,* pp. 416–26.

Rogue's March. A tune of English origin that was used when a soldier was expelled from the army. See *GD* iv, 416, and iii, 316; *GDB* vii, 207.

Rohrblatt [G.]. The *reed of the clarinet, oboe, etc., instruments called *Rohrblattinstrumente.*

Rohrstimmen, Rohrwerk [G.]. The reeds of the organ.

Roi David, Le [F., King David]. Opera (Dramatic psalm) in two parts by Honegger (libretto by R. Morax), produced in Mézières, Switzerland, 1921, and produced as an oratorio in New York, 1925. In the latter form, the orchestra is considerably enlarged, and a narrator relates the dramatic events between musical selections. Comprising 27 pieces, it describes the life of David from his youth as a shepherd boy until his death.

Rolle [G.]. An 18th-century term (used by D. G. Türk) for the *turn.

Rollschweller [G.]. The crescendo pedal of the organ.

Roman Carnival, The. See *Carnaval romain, Le.*

Romance [F., Sp.], **Romanze** [G.], **romanza** [It.]. (1) The Spanish *romances* are long poems in four-line stanzas dealing primarily with historical or legendary subjects. Their origin can be traced back to the 14th century. The *Cancionero musical de palacio* [*Editions XXXII, 5] contains polyphonic settings of several *romances,* e.g.,

"En memoria d'Alixandre" (Anchieta) and "Pésame de vos, el Conde" (J. del Encina). Settings to lute (vihuela) accompaniment are found in the lute (vihuela) books of Narvaez [*Editions XXXII, 3; e.g., "Paseábase el rey moro"], Luis Milán [*Editions XLVI, 2; e.g., "Durandarte"], and Mudarra [*Editions XXXII, 7; e.g., "Triste estaua el rey David"]. A large number of 17th- and 18th-century *romances* are preserved in various Cancioneros and other sources [*Editions XXXII, 18]. Among the numerous composers of *romances* were M. Romero, G. Diáz, J. Pujol, and the brothers Francisco and José Ruiz Samaniego. To the present day, the *romance* is extensively cultivated in Spanish folk music.

(2) The French *romance* is a short strophic song of lyrical character, usually dealing with love but also with historical events. An early publication is the *Recueil des romances historiques, tendres et burlesques* by M. Delusse (1767). Well-known composers of *romances* were H. Duparc, G. Fauré (instrumental), and others.

(3) The German *Romanze* is primarily an instrumental composition of a lyrical character (Haydn's symphony, *La Reine;* Mozart, Piano Concerto in D minor, K. 466; Beethoven, *Romance,* op. 40, 50; Schumann, *Albumblätter,* no. 11). In Schumann's *Drei Romanzen* op. 28, only the second is in an idyllic style, the other two being highly dramatic. Vocal *Romanzen* occur mostly in operas, a famous example being Pedrillo's "Romanza" in Mozart's *Die Entführung aus dem Serail.*

Roman chant [L. *cantus Romanus, cantilena Romana*]. The liturgical chant of the Roman Catholic Church, i.e., *Gregorian chant. Although this chant developed in Rome, it probably received its final form—the only one known today—in the Frankish empire during the 8th and 9th centuries. More properly "Roman" is a different repertory known as *Old Roman chant.

Roman de Fauvel. See Sources, no. 8.

Romanesca. A harmonic bass, widely used for the composition of *arie per cantar* and dance

variations from the middle of the 16th through the early 17th centuries [see Ex. 1]. Its provenance is uncertain; extant sources indicate that musicians in both Italy and Spain played a significant role in its early history. Because, in *arie per cantar,* singers improvised discant tunes to the bass pattern, many different discant melodies are found in extant versions of the *romanesca.*

The isometric pattern cited above developed over a long period. Many late 15th- and early 16th-century sources in both Italy and Spain include adumbrated examples that are more complicated rhythmically than the isometric pattern. Indeed, numerous variants existed side by side with the isometric pattern, under such titles as *Favorita, El poverin, La desperata, La comadrina, L'Herba fresca* [see Ex. 2], *La pigna, La meza notte, La canella, Todeschin,* etc. [see Ex. 2, *L'Herba fresca* bass].

Among the earliest examples of pieces written on the isometric bass pattern are a "Gaillarde" in Attaingnant's *Dixhuit basses dances* (1529; f.24), a set of variations on "O guárdame las vacas" in Narvaez's *Los Seys Libros del Delphin* (1538; vi, f.82ᵛ), "Ein gutter venetianer Tantz" in H. Newsidler's lute tablature (1540; f.E4), and a "Pass'e mezo alla villana" in Rotta's lute tablature (1546; no. 20). The earliest extant appearances of the title *Romanesca* with the bass pattern are in Mudarra's *Tres libros de música* (1546; ff.17, 24, "Romanesca o guardáme las vacas") and in Phalèse's *Carminum quae chely vel testudine* (1546; f.164, "Romanescha"). Settings also appear in 16th-century collections by Valderrábano (1547; see *HAM,* no. 124), F. Bianchini (1546), Pisador (1552), Ortiz (1553), Balletti (1554), Becchi (1568), Le Roy (1568), Phalèse (1568, '74), Valente (1576), Cabezón (1578), Caroso (1583), and many others.

In the 17th century, keyboard variations were written by Trabaci (1603), Mayone (1609), and Frescobaldi [see *HAM,* no. 192]; strophic bass arias [see Aria III] by Caccini (*Le Nuove Musiche;* see *BüHM, Barock,* p. 45), Monteverdi (*Madrigali,* bk. vii), Landi (*RiHM,* ii.2, 91f), and Kaspar Kittel (*ibid.,* p. 353); and violin variations by Marini (*HAM,* no. 199) and Salomone Rossi (*RiHM,* ii.2, 88f). The pattern was also used for countless compositions in collections for the guitar. See O. Gombosi, in *LRM* vii, 14–25; J. Ward, in *MGG* xi, 778–79.   L.H.M.

Romanian letters. See Romanus letters.

Roman school. A term used with reference to the *a cappella* church music established in Rome by Palestrina (*c.* 1525–94; see Palestrina style) and continued, with incorporation of the polychoral elements of the *Venetian style, by a long line of strongly conservative musicians, mostly in Rome, among them G. M. Nanino (*c.* 1545–1607), F. Suriano (1549–after 1621), R. Giovannelli (1560–1625), F. Anerio (*c.* 1560–1614), G. Allegri (*c.* 1582–1652), D. Mazzocchi (1592–1665), V. Massocchi (1597–1646), F. Foggia (*c.* 1604–88), O. Benevoli (1605–72), E. Bernabei (*c.* 1620–87), T. Bai (*c.* 1660–1714), G. Pitoni (1657–1743), and Caldara (1670–1736). In general, these musicians rejected the current styles and forms of baroque music (aria, recitative, oratorio, cantata, opera, sonata, toccata, etc.) and devoted themselves to the composition of strictly liturgical music (Masses, motets, Requiems, psalms, etc.). Based on the principles of vocal style of the Palestrina period, their technique tended toward scholarly treatment (canonic contrivances) as well as pompous display; thus Masses for 16, 24, and more voice-parts are no rarity in what has aptly been called the "colossal baroque," and some composers used up to eight choruses, which were placed throughout St. Peter's [see the 54-voice Mass by Benevoli in *DTO* 20]. For the later development of this style, which continued throughout the 18th century, see K. G. Fellerer, *Der Palestrinastil . . . des achtzehnten Jahrhunderts* [1929]; also O. Ursprung, in *ZMW* vii. See *A cappella;* Palestrina style.

Romanticism [F. *romantisme;* G. *Romantik;* It., Sp. *romanticismo*]. An important movement of the 19th century, continuing until *c.* 1910. Foreshadowed in the late works—particularly the piano sonatas—of Beethoven (1770–1827), it found its first champions in Weber (1786–1826) and Schubert (1797–1828) and its fullest realization in the works of six composers, all born within a single decade: Berlioz (1803–69), Mendelssohn (1809–47), Schumann (1810–56), Chopin (1810–49), Liszt (1811–86), and Wagner (1813–83). Berlioz, Mendelssohn, Schumann, and Chopin worked principally from 1820 to 1850, a period often designated as early romanticism. Liszt and Wagner, who lived much longer, produced their most important works after 1850, as did Franck (1822–90), Bruckner (1824–96), Smetana (1824–84), Brahms (1833–97), Mussorgsky (1839–81), Tchaikovsky (1840–93), Dvořák (1841–1904), and Grieg (1843–1907).

They represent the middle period of romanticism, from about 1850 to 1890. The last phase of the movement, known as late (or neo-) romanticism, from *c.* 1890 to 1910, is represented by a large number of composers born between 1850 and 1880, among them Elgar (1857–1934), Puccini (1858–1924), Mahler (1860–1911), R. Strauss (1864–1949), Sibelius (1865–1957), and Reger (1873–1916). Other late romantic composers, like Grieg, Dvořák, and Albéniz, are identified especially with *nationalism in music.

The romantic movement in the arts began in literature during the second half of the 18th century. Jean-Jacques Rousseau (1712–78) and others, reacting against the intellectual, formalistic classical tradition, demanded a return to simplicity and naturalism, with a greater emphasis on man's instincts and feelings than on his intellect. In music, romanticism was characterized by emphasis on subjective, emotional qualities and greater freedom of form. These traits need not imply that nonromantic music lacks emotional appeal. Nor does it mean that the romanticists were not form-conscious; if anything, they were more so, sometimes to the point of becoming formalistic (Chopin's later mazurkas, Schumann's Symphony in D minor, Liszt's Sonata in B minor). The greatest works of the romantic era, like those of all periods, are those that derive substance and balance from traditional principles of form and structure. Shortly after 1900 there began a reaction against romanticism that gained such impetus that antiromanticism became the most tangible element of the early modern era. Whereas Debussy's *impressionism, directed largely against German romantic music (especially Wagner), did not introduce any radical innovations, other *twentieth-century music was a violent negation of romanticism in all its aspects, technical as well as philosophic.

In spite of its limitations, romanticism has supplied a large portion of the repertory of modern pianists and conductors. In the province of musical forms, romanticism's three outstanding contributions are the *character piece for piano, the art song for voice and piano, and the *symphonic poem for orchestra. Romantic composers have contributed much to the development of harmony and of orchestral colors. Finally, they have done much to break down some of the artificial barriers between the arts. For example, their combined use of literature and music is seen in such terms as "symphonic poem" or "tone poem," in the choice of literary subjects

for program pieces (*Mazeppa, Till Eulenspiegel*), and, most clearly, in Wagner's concept of the opera as a *Gesamtkunstwerk*. An important romantic device in such music is the *leitmotiv.

Certain earlier periods of music history bear general resemblance to 19th-century romanticism and therefore might be termed "romantic," in contrast to others that might be considered "classical" periods [see under Classicism for a discussion of this idea].

Lit.: A. Einstein, *Music in the Romantic Era* (1947); D. G. Mason, *The Romantic Composers* (1930); W. H. Hadow, *Studies in Modern Music*, 2 vols., rev. ed. (1921); *GrHWM*, pp. 492–609; P. H. Lang, *Music in Western Civilization* (1941), pp. 734ff; E. Istel, *Die Blütezeit der musikalischen Romantik in Deutschland* (1909); R. Dumesnil, *Musiciens romantiques* (1928); C. Laforêt, *La Vie musicale au temps romantique* (1929); E. Kurth, *Romantische Harmonik und ihre Krise in Wagners "Tristan"*, rev. ed. (1923); K. Roeseling, *Beitrage zur Untersuchung der Grundhaltung romantischer Melodik* [n.d., *c.* 1928]; H. Eckardt, *Die Musikanschauung der französischen Romantik* (1935); G. Knepler, *Musikgeschichte des 19. Jahrhunderts,* 2 vols. (1961); W. Mellers, *Romanticism and the 20th Century (from 1800),* (1957); G. Abraham, *A Hundred Years of Music,* rev. ed. [1964]; K. Dale, *Nineteenth-century Piano Music* (1954); *OH* vi; *BüHM* v; E. J. Dent, "The Romantic Spirit in Music" (*PMA* lix); A. Schering, "Kritik des romantischen Musikbegriffs" (*JMP* xliv, 9); A. Farinelli, "Il Romanticismo e la musica" (*RMI* xxxiii, 161); H. Költzsch, in *ML* xx, 130 (Schubert); E. Lockspeiser, in *ML* xv, 26 (Berlioz); V. Basch, in *RM* 1924, vi, no. 2 (Schumann); R. Gorer, in *ML* xvii, 13 (Weber); P. Lang, in *MQ* xxii, 314 (Liszt).   rev. ED.

Romantic Symphony. (1) Popular name for Bruckner's Symphony no. 4, in E-flat major, composed in 1874 (rev. 1878, 1880). (2) Name for Hanson's Symphony no. 2, composed 1928–30.

Romanus letters, Romanian letters [G. *Romanus-Buchstaben*]. A system of letters said to have been invented by a legendary 8th-century papal singer named Romanus. The system is explained by Notker (Balbulus; *GS* i, 95) and others, and is used in various neumatic MSS from St. Gall, Metz, and Chartres. The letters were to be used with the neumes in order to clarify details of pitch, rhythm, or performance not indicated by the neumes themselves. Of the numerous letters mentioned by Notker, only a few attained practical significance, chiefly those concerning temporal values: *c* (*celeriter*, quick), *t* (*tenere*, slow), and *m* (*mediocriter*). They play a central part in present-day discussions of Gregorian rhythm [see Gregorian chant VI]. See *WoHN* i, 140; *ReMMA,* pp. 140ff; *ApGC,* p. 117; L. Kunz, "Die Romanusbuchstaben c und t" (*KJ* xxxiv).

Romanze, [G.]. See under *Romance*.

Romanzen aus L. Tieck's Magelone [G., Magelone Romances]. A cycle of fifteen songs by Brahms, op. 33 (1861–68), set to poems by L. Tieck.

Rome. For a full account of what little is known about the music of the ancient Romans, see *ReMMA,* pp. 51ff, and *GéHM,* pp. 114ff. See also Hydraulos; Lituus (1); Tuba (1); Buccina. See *NOH* i, 404; H. Antcliffe, in *ML* xxx, 337; P. R. Coleman-Norton, in *JAMS* i (Cicero); G. Wille, in *AMW* xi, 71.

Romeo and Juliet. Among the many compositions based on Shakespeare's play are: (1) Dramatic symphony by Berlioz, op. 17 (1839), for solo voices, chorus, and orchestra; (2) opera by Gounod (1867); (3) symphonic poem (Fantasy Overture) by Tchaikovsky (1869); (4) ballet by Prokofiev, op. 64 (1935).

Rondador. See under Panpipes.

Ronde [F.]. See under Notes. Also, a round dance.

Rondeau. (1) An important form of medieval French poetry and music. In its simplest, 13th-century form, it consists of eight short lines with a rather artificial repeat structure, line 1 being identical with lines 4 and 7, and line 2 with line 8. Lines 1 and 2 therefore form a refrain that recurs in part in the middle and complete at the end. Music is composed for the refrain only (line 1 = a, line 2 = b) and is repeated according to the scheme A B a A a b A B (capital letters indicate the refrain). In the 14th and 15th centuries the refrain (and correspondingly the entire poem) was expanded from two lines to three (2 plus 1, *rondeau tercet*), four (2 plus 2, *quatrain*), or five (3 plus 2, *cinquain*), but the musical structure remained the same. The accompanying example shows a 13th-century rondeau in the usual modern arrangement. The rondeau is one of the three *formes fixes*.

A considerable number of 13th-century rondeaux, all monophonic, exist. However, they are not found in the chansonniers of the trou-

vères, their texts occurring in purely literary sources such as the "Roman de la Rose" of *c.* 1200 or in large collections of poems such as Bibl. nat. *f. fr. 12786.* In a number of cases the music can be reconstructed because the refrains are preserved elsewhere with music, e.g., in 13th-century refrain motets. For example, the text of the accompanying example is in the above-

1.4.7. En ma dame ai mis mon coeur
3. N'en par - ti - roi a nul fuer
5. Si m'ont sor - pris si vair oeil

2.8. Et mon pen - ser.
6. Ri - ant et clair

mentioned MS, and its refrain with music at the end of the motet "Trop souvent–Brunete–In seculum" [*HAM,* no. 32d]. Polyphonic settings, usually for voice and two instrumental parts, were composed by Adam de la Hale (*c.* 1240–87), Machaut (*c.* 1300–77) and his successors, and in the 15th century by Dufay, Binchois, Hayne van Ghizeghem, Busnois, Ockeghem, and many others. Of the *formes fixes,* the rondeau was the only one widely used after 1400. It figures prominently in the *Odhecaton* and its companion books, *Canti B* and *Canti C.* Examples in *HAM,* nos. 19d, 19e, 36b, 48, 68, 69, 71, 72, 79. For the origin of the rondeau, see *Rondellus* (2).

The literary form of the rondeau survives in modern poetry as the *triolet.*

Lit.: F. Gennrich, *Rondeaux, Virelais und Balladen,* 2 vols. (1921, '27); P. Aubry; "Refrains et rondeaux du XIIIe siècle" (*CP Riemann*); W. Apel, "Rondeaux, Virelais, and Ballades" (*JAMS* vii); G. Reaney, "The Poetic Form of Machaut's Musical Works" (*MD* xiii).

(2) An instrumental form of the 17th century, consisting of a reiterated *refrain and different "couplets": A B A C A D . . . A. Whether this form is an outgrowth of the medieval rondeau is, to say the least, doubtful; no connection between the two is known. The rondeau is the form used most by the French clavecinists (Chambonnières, L. Couperin, D'Anglebert, F. Couperin, Rameau), as well as in contemporary orchestral and operatic music (Lully). The refrain as well as each couplet is a well-marked strain of 8 or 16 measures. Each couplet

usually emphasizes a different key, e.g., the first, tonic; the second, dominant; the third, relative minor; etc. [ex. in *HAM,* no. 277]. In the late 18th century, the 17th-century rondeau developed into the *rondo form of the sonata.

Rondellus [L.]. (1) Medieval name (used by W. Odington, *c.* 1300) for a triple or duple *voice exchange. (2) Modern (or medieval?) name for a type of Latin song that is structurally similar to the medieval rondeau [see Rondeau (1)]. Such songs, which date from the 12th century, are interesting as the forerunners of the French rondeau. They are found occasionally in the MSS of St. Martial, but the most important source is a collection of 60 *rondelli* in the last fascicle of the Notre Dame MS Florence, Bibl. Laur., *plut. 29.i* (*F*) [see "Magnus liber organi"; Sources, no. 3]. They are written in various repeat forms, the most common being that of the French rondeau without the initial refrain: a A a b A B. Actually, this is a simple binary form: ‖: a :‖: a b :‖ . For an example, see *HAM,* no. 17b. See H. Spanke, "Das lateinische Rondeau" (*Zeitschrift für französische Sprache und Litteratur* liii, 27); P. Aubry, "Iter hispanicum" (*SIM* ix, 41); *id.,* in *CP Riemann.*

Rondeña. See Fandango.

Rondo, rondo form, rondo-sonata form. A form frequently used in classical sonatas, symphonies, and concertos for the final movement. It was developed from the *rondeau of the French clavecinists by reducing the number of "couplets" to three, by using the same material for the first and third couplets, and by elaborating the middle couplet in the style of a development section, so that the following scheme results: R A R B R A' R. In this form the rondeau is similar to sonata form, inasmuch as A and A' correspond to the exposition and recapitulation, and B to the development. The recurrent section is usually called "rondo," and the intermediate sections "episode" or "diversion." The rondo form has often been used for the last movements of sonatas and concertos as a joyful or playful conclusion. Numerous examples are found in the final movements of Beethoven's earlier piano sonatas (op. 2, no. 3; op. 13; etc.) and in practically all the concertos of the Viennese classics. Earlier, less developed examples occur in the sonatas of Johann Christian Bach (e.g., no. 6 of the new ed. by L. Landshoff), the independent rondos of K. P. E. Bach (e.g., *Clavier-Sonaten nebst einigen Rondos fürs Pianoforte,* 1780), and

the early works of Haydn (e.g., Sonata no. 24, op. 17, no. 3). See Sonata B III (b).

The term "rondo form" is also used, particularly by English writers, for two alternation schemes shorter than the true rondo, the ternary form A B A and the five-part form A B A B A (or A B A C A). These are called respectively "first" and "second" rondo form, in distinction to the "third" rondo form discussed above. This terminology is objectionable from the historical standpoint, since only the "third" rondo form developed from the rondeau. The "first" rondo form is the ternary form [see Binary and ternary form], while the "second" rondo form represents an expanded ternary form. See Forms, musical.

Lit.: F. Piersig, ‡*Das Rondo* [n.d.]; W. Chrzanowski, "Das instrumentale Rondo und die Rondo-formen des 18 Jahrhunderts" (diss. Leipzig, 1911); C. F. Abdy Williams, in *PMA* xvii; S. Clercx, in *RDM* 1935, p. 148 (K. P. E. Bach).

Room acoustics. See Architectural acoustics.

Root. The generating note of a triad or any of its inversions and modifications (seventh chord). For example, in the following chords the root is always C:

A triad, seventh chord, etc. is said to be in root position if the root is the lowest note; otherwise, it is in *inversion. See Harmonic analysis IV.

Rorantists. A chapel choir (of nine singers and a cleric, *Collegium Rorantistarum*) founded in 1543 at Cracow by King Sigismund I of Poland (1467–1548) for the cultivation of *a cappella* music. Its name was derived from the Czech *Rorate* chants, a repertory of 16th-century songs for Advent that are named for the Introit for Advent, *Rorate coeli.* The Rorantist chapel existed until the 18th century.

Rosalia. A pejorative term for a schematic, unimaginative sequential treatment, such as was frequently used by second-rate composers of the period 1750–1850. It applies in particular to sequences that, owing to the exact repetition of the intervals, involve modulation of the key to the higher second, e.g., G–C–A–D–B–E, etc. The

inferiority of such passages lies in their facile symmetry of melody, harmony, and phrasing. The name comes from an Italian popular song, "Rosalia, mia cara," in which this device occurs. The German equivalent is *Schusterfleck* (cobbler's patch).

Rosamunde. Incidental music by Schubert for a play by Helmina von Chézy, produced in Vienna, 1823. It contains, in addition to some choral numbers, an overture (originally written for a melodrama, *Die Zauberharfe*), three entr'actes, and two ballets that are often played in concert form.

Rose. Ornamental decoration in the circular sound hole of instruments such as lutes, guitars, and early harpsichords, often serving as the maker's trademark. See Sound hole.

Rosenkavalier, Der [G., The Knight of the Rose]. Opera in three acts by R. Strauss (libretto by H. von Hofmannsthal), produced in Dresden, 1911. Setting: Vienna, mid-18th century. The music is well known through numerous orchestral excerpts, particularly the waltzes.

Rosin, resin. A preparation made from gum of turpentine that is applied to the hair of the violin bow in order to give it the necessary grip on the strings.

Rota [L.]. (1) Medieval name for a round, particularly *"Sumer is icumen in," probably with reference to the "turnover" of the melody in the different parts [see also Round]. See F. L. Harrison, in *PMA* lxxxvi; J. Handschin, in *MD* iii, 82ff. (2) See Rotta (1).

Rote. See Rotta (1).

Rotrouenge, rotruenge. A form of French 13th-century poetry that has been the subject of various philologic as well as musicologic studies. Seven poems, consisting of three to seven stanzas, can be definitely identified as *rotrouenges* on the basis of textual references such as "Ma rotruenge finira . . . ." Only one of them, "Chanter m'estuet" (Raynaud, no. 636), is preserved with music; it has the structure a a a B c, B being an internal refrain, "Oiés pour quoi." From this evidence it has been hypothesized (by Gennrich)

that the musical form of the *rotrouenge* was characterized by repetition of the same melody for all the lines of the stanza except the last two or the last one, e.g.: a a a a B [see *AdHM*, p. 195]. However, this assumption is unwarranted. A musical form "rotrouenge" does not exist. See F. Gennrich, *Die altfranzösische Rotrouenge* (1925); *id.*, in *Deutsche Vierteljahrsschrift für Literaturgeschichte* ix, 306; W. Apel, in *JAMS* vii, 129f; R. H. Perrin, in *JAMS* viii, 77.

Rotta, rotte, rota. (1) A medieval instrument mentioned in numerous literary sources (8th to 14th cent.). Most likely it was a psaltery. Possibly the name is a variant of cruit. For ill. see under Lyra. See H. Steger, *Die Rotte* (1961); *MaMI*, p. 133f; *SaHMI*, p. 262 (where it is said to be a harp). (2) In 14th-century Italian dances, the *rotta* is an after-dance that is a rhythmic variant of the main dance [see *HAM*, no. 59a; *SchGMB*, no. 28]. Mario Fabrizio Caroso's *La Nobiltà di dame* (1581, 1605) contains a *rotta* for lute (Balletto–Gagliarda–La Rotta–Canario; see *Editions V, 1, p. 35) in triple meter, similar to the *padovana*. Here the name may refer to Antonio Rotta, whose publication of 1546 contains the earliest *padovanae*.

Rotulus [L.]. Name for medieval MSS in the form of a long sheet of parchment that was rolled from top to bottom (like the Jewish Torah, which is rolled from left to right). Two or three *rotuli* with music exist, containing mostly early 14th-century motets (Brussels, Bibl. Royale, *19606;* Paris, Bibl. nat., *Coll. de Pic. 67*). An illustration found in one of the Machaut MSS shows a group of singers reading from a *rotulus* [see *ReMMA*, opp. p. 364]. See R. Hoppin, in *RBM* ix, 131 (MS Brussels).

Roulade [F.]. A vocal melisma or a highly ornamented melody. In German, the term has a pejorative implication, being used for meaningless coloraturas in operatic arias. Originally, *roulade* meant an ornament consisting of rapid passing notes inserted between two principal melodic notes.

Round. Common name for a circle canon, i.e., a canon in which each singer returns from the conclusion of the melody to its beginning, repeating it *ad libitum*. The scheme of a three-voice round is:

I	a	b	c ‖	a	b	c	‖
II		a	b ‖	c	a	b	‖
III			a ‖	b	c	a	‖

The melody of a round always consists of sections of equal length that are designed to make good harmony with each other. Accompanying is an example (by M. Praetorius, 1571–1621) together with the resulting harmony. The earliest and most famous round is *"Sumer is icumen in," which, however, is not designed to

Vi-va vi-va la   Mu-si-ca

be repeated *ad libitum.* Rounds were very popular in England, particularly the variety known as catch. For bibl. see under Catch.

Rounded chanson. Same as G. *Rundkanzone.* See *Bar* form II.

Roundelay. A 14th-century anglicization of the French term *rondelet,* i.e., *rondeau (1).

Round O. A 17th-century anglicization of rondeau (rondo), used by Matthew Locke (*Melothesia,* 1673), G. B. Draghi (*Six Select Suites of Lessons, c.* 1700), and others.

Rovescio [It.]. Retrograde motion or inversion. For example, "Menuet(to) al rovescio" in Haydn's Sonata no. 4 for piano and violin (identical to his Symphony no. 47, 3rd movt. ["al roverso"], and also Piano Sonata no. 26, B. & H. edition) is to be played backward, in retrograde motion [see Retrograde], whereas that in Mozart's Serenade K. 388 uses imitation in the inversion.

Row. Same as tone row. See Serial music.

Roxelane, La. Popular name for Haydn's Symphony no. 63, in C, composed in 1777. The second movement is a set of variations on the French tune "La Roxelane."

Royal counterpoint. See under *Diaphonia.*

Rubab. See Rabab.

Rubato [It.]. (1) An elastic, flexible tempo involving slight accelerandos and ritardandos that alternate according to the requirements of musical expression. There has been a great deal of discussion about tempo rubato, and some

writers maintain that it is the most difficult of musical terms to define. Actually, these difficulties disappear if a clear distinction is made between two types of rubato, one that affects the melody only and another that affects the whole musical texture.

The first type has become well known through its use in jazz. However, it also was used during the second half of the 18th century. Tosi (1723), Quantz (1752), K. P. E. Bach (1753), Leopold Mozart (1756), and D. G. Türk (1789) maintain that rubato applies only to the melody and should not affect the accompaniment. Chopin is reported to have taught this type of rubato, which may extend over several measures, after which the melodic and harmonic accents should again coincide.

The second type of rubato, which affects the whole musical fabric, would need no further explanation were it not for the fact that several writers, having studied the above-mentioned books, have applied the "give-and-take" principle of the 18th- (and 20th-) century type to the "full" rubato of Liszt or Chopin. They maintain that here, too, the accelerandos and ritardandos must complement one another, so that, after six or seven measures in free tempo, the player arrives at exactly the same moment in time that he would have reached had he played in rigid tempo. This interpretation has led to heated controversy.

The preface to Frescobaldi's *Fiori musicali* (1630) contains interesting remarks about the rubato performance of his toccatas [see *TaAM* iv, p. x].

(2) About 1800 the term "rubato" was used to indicate modifications of dynamics rather than tempo, e.g., accents on normally weak beats, such as the second and fourth in a 4/4 measure (Türk, 1789; H. C. Koch, 1808; see Lit., Bruck). It is possible that Chopin meant this manner of performance when he prescribed "rubato" in his compositions, since he used the term almost exclusively in mazurkas or melodies in mazurka style (e.g., F-minor Concerto, last movement). The strict rhythm of the mazurka would seem to exclude modifications of tempo yet readily admits unexpected accents on the second or third beat.

Lit.: Henry T. Finck, *Musical Progress* [1923], ch. vi; John B. McEwen, *Tempo Rubato; or, Time-variation in Musical Performance* (1928); J. A. Johnstone, *Rubato* [1925]; B. Bruck, *Wandlungen des Begriffes Tempo rubato* [n.d., *c.* 1928]; L. Kamienski, "Zum Tempo rubato" (*AMW* i).

Rubeba, rubible. See Rabab.

Rückpositif [G.]. A division of an organ separated from the main portion of the instrument and usually located on the gallery railing at the organist's back. It was almost always played from the lowest keyboard of the main console, although in some organs of the 16th century it had its own keyboard, requiring the organist to turn completely around in order to play it. Other names for it are *positiv* [F.], *Rugwerk* [Neth.], and *chaire* or *chair* [Eng.]. It was very common in German, Dutch, French, and English organs up to the early 19th century, and is now being revived in England and America. Also see *Positif;* Organ II, VII, XII.   B.J.O.

Rücksichtslos [G.]. Inconsiderate. *Rücksichtsloser Kontrapunkt,* the modern "reckless" counterpoint, without regard for harmonic considerations.

Rueda. A Spanish (Castilian) round dance in fast quintuple time. See *Zortziko.* See H. Collet, "La Musique espagnole moderne" (*BSIM* iv).

Rugby. "Symphonic movement" by Honegger (1928), suggested by the English sport.

Ruggiero. A harmonic bass of Italian provenance, popular from the mid-16th through the early 17th centuries [see Ex.]. A. Einstein has suggested that the title comes from the first word of a verse from L. Ariosto's *Orlando furioso:* "Ruggier, qual sempre fui, tal' esser voglio" [see *SIM* xiii; the word *Fedele* is sometimes substituted for *Ruggiero* and the piece labeled *Aria sopra Fedele*]. The practice of chanting epic poetry to a skeletal bass is an old one; examples of its most developed form are found in Italian collections under the title "Aria per cantar ottave." A singer usually improvised a discant tune to the harmonic pattern represented by the bass, a fact that accounts for the many different discant melodies found in extant versions.

Many settings of the *ruggiero* have survived. An early example is the final *recercada* for viola' da gamba and harpsichord in D. Ortiz's *Tratado de glosas* of 1553 (ed. M. Schneider, p. 134).

Others include keyboard variations by the Neapolitan composers G. Macque (*c.* 1580; *Editions XXVIII, 4), G. M. Trabaci (1603), Ascanio Mayone (1603), Frescobaldi ("Capriccio sopra l'aria di ruggiero," 1624; "Capriccio . . . Fra Jacopino" and "Partite 12," 1637; ed. Pidoux, ii, 48; iii, 86; iii, 60), lute settings by V. Galilei, English collections from *c.* 1600 [see *ReMR,* p. 848, 130n], a violin sonata by Salomone Rossi (1613; see *RiHM,* ii.2, 94), a two-voice aria by Antonio Cifra (*Scherzi,* 1613), a "Canzon Ruggiero" by Tarquinio Merula (1637; see H. Riemann, *Old Chamber Music* iii), and a virtuoso solo aria by Kaspar Kittel (*RiHM,* ii.2, 349). Other musical formulas for singing verses of the *Orlando,* some of them titled Ruggiero, are found in 16th-century sources, but the pattern shown above was the most popular. See J. Ward, in *MGG* xi, 1086–88, for a more detailed description and bibl.; A. Einstein, in *RMI* xli; D. Plamenac, in *PAMS* 1941, 150ff.   L.H.M.

Rührtrommel [G.]. Tenor drum; see Percussion instruments B, 2.

Ruinen von Athen, Die [G., The Ruins of Athens]. Incidental music by Beethoven, op. 113, for a play by Kotzebue, produced in Budapest, 1812. It contains, among other movements, an overture and a Turkish march (the latter adapted from a Theme with Variations for piano, op. 76, composed 1809).

Rule of the octave. See *Regola dell'ottava.*

Rumania. Rumania has a large repertory of folksong that is remarkably free from the influence of art music. Typical traits are the use of portamenti, rubatos, Scotch snaps, recitations, long melismas, standard ornaments, descending fourths, mixtures of pentatonic elements and various modes (Dorian, Phrygian, etc.), and combinations of major and minor. Johann Anton Sulzer included some Rumanian folksongs and dances in his *Geschichte des transalpinischen Dakiens* (1781; L. *Dacia,* Rumania), but the true nature and wide range of Rumanian folk music were revealed in the 20th century through the research of G. Weigand (*Dialekte der Bukowina und Bessarabiens,* 1904), Pompiliu Parvescu (*Hora din Cartal,* 1908), Béla Bartók (*Chansons populaires du département de Bihor,* 1913), and Constantin Brailoiu (1893–1958). Two important types are the *doina,* or shepherd songs, which are free ornamented songs, and the *kolinde,* or Christmas songs, which are in strict meter and rhythm [see *Koleda*]. Dance music is mostly instrumental (fiddle, bagpipe, shepherd flute) and shows the influence of neighboring peoples, especially the Yugoslavs.

The development of art music in Rumania is relatively recent. Although some Western influence was noticeable in the second half of the 18th century, it was not until the end of Turkish rule (1822) that German and Italian music became influential. In 1838 Prince Alexander Ghika, governor of Wallachia, dismissed his Turkish band and brought a Viennese musician, L. A. Wiest (1819–89), to Bucharest. Edward Wachiman (1836–1909), trained in Paris, organized the first regular series of symphony concerts in Bucharest. Queen Elizabeth of Rumania (1843–1916), who used the pseudonym Carmen Sylva, greatly encouraged Rumanian art and letters and became widely known for her poetic descriptions of Bach's *Well-Tempered Clavier*. Representatives of modern Rumanian music are Georges Enesco (1881–1955), internationally known violinist, composer, and conductor, and Dinu Lipatti (1917–50), pianist and composer. The compositions of Alfred Alessandrescu (b. 1893) show the influence of Debussy and Dukas, while Michal Andrico (b. 1894) cultivated a nationalist style based on Rumanian folk music. The Rumanian composers Stan Golestan (1872–1956) and Marcel Mihalovici (b. 1898), like Enesco, worked largely in Paris.

Lit.: *LavE* i.5, 2656ff; *AdHM* ii, 1182ff; B. Bartók, *Melodien der rumänischen Colinde* (*Weihnachtslieder*) (1935); L. Cassini, *Music in Rumania* [1954]; N. Slonimsky, "Modern Composition in Rumania" (*LBCM;* also *MQ* li); B. Bartók, "Volkmusik der Rumänen von Maramures" (*Sammelbände für vergleichende Musikwissenschaft* iv); id., "Der Musikdialekt der Rumänen von Hunyad" (*ZMW* ii); E. Riegler, "Das rumänische Volkslied und die Instrumentalmusik der Bauern" (*CP 1927*). See also *CP Bartók*, 17ff [note summary].

Rumba [Sp.]. Urban Afro-Cuban dance that is always performed by instrumental ensembles and a singer using meaningless phrases and syllables. It consists either of a single theme, usually eight measures long, that is constantly repeated, or of two shorter themes, the second a variation of the first. Its tempo is fast, and it is danced by separate partners, with only slight movements of the feet but marked movements of the hips and shoulders. After 1930 rumba

rhythms were incorporated into jazz. A typical rhythmic rumba pattern is:

J.O-S.

Rundkanzone [G.]. See under *Bar* form II.

Russia. I. Prior to *c.* 1700 musical activity in Russia was, aside from folk music, restricted mainly to the church. The liturgy in Slavonic, a practice begun by the southern Slavs, was borrowed from the Byzantine liturgy of the late 9th or early 10th century and continued to be influenced by Greek sources until the Mongol invasion of Russia (13th century). The Byzantine hymn texts, as well as their melodies, modal system, and notation, were taken over almost literally. Three of the four principal collections of early Byzantine chant—the Sticherarion [see *Sticheron*], Hirmologion [see *Hirmos*] and Asmatikon—have Slavic counterparts with 11th- or 12th-century notation (only the Slavic counterpart for the Greek Psaltikon is still unknown). The earliest Slavic syllabic chants, known as *Znamenny chant and notated in neumatic symbols called *kriuki* (hooks), are derived from the Sticherarion and Hirmologion [see M. Velimirović, *Editions XXIX, B, 4]. The earliest Slavic melismatic chants (11th–13th centuries), preserved in the *Kondakarion and notated in the elaborate symbols of "kondakarion notation," are derived from the Byzantine Asmatikon and related sources [see K. Levy in *MQ* xlvii, 554–58, and *JAMS* xvi, 127–75]. The melismatic chants fell out of use in the 13th century, while the simpler Znamenny chant, gradually moving away from Byzantine models, continued. In the 16th century the notation was improved by I. Shaidurov, who added letters in red ink ("cinnabar letters") that fixed the intervallic meaning of the *kriuki,* a development comparable to that from staffless to intervallic neumes of Gregorian chant [see Neumes II]. However, by the 16th century Znamenny chant deteriorated through the interpolation of coloraturas by various rival singers [see Anenaiki]. In 1668 A. Mesenetz reformed the chant by codifying it and adopting a five-line staff with distinctive notes ("Kiev signs"; see *WoHN* i, 120f). About the same time, polyphonic singing was officially adopted by the Russian church (for early Russian polyphony, known as *strochny* chant, see V. Beliaev, in *CP Bartók,* pp. 307ff).

All these reforms were rejected, however, by the *raskolniki* (Old Believers), who still use the old chant and *kriuki* notation. Most Russian chant is based on a system of eight *echoi* [see Echos], each of which has stock melodic figures (*popievki*) that are used only for chants written in that particular *echos* [see Melody type].

Peter the Great helped introduce Western opera. Under Catherine II (reigned 1762–96) music in St. Petersburg was dominated by Italian composers, such as F. Manfredini, B. Galuppi, T. Traetta, and G. Paisiello, who controlled the Imperial Opera from 1776 to 1784. The earliest Russian composers, such as Maximus Beresovsky (1745–77), Dimitri Bortniansky (1751–1825), and E. I. Fomin (1761–1800), studied with Italians and wrote operas in the Italian style, while Alexey Titov (1769–1827) imitated Mozart. His son, Nikolay Titov (1800–75), and Alexander Varlamov (1801–48) wrote many very popular songs, e.g., Varlamov's "The Red Sarafan." Alexey Verstovsky (1799–1862) was a forerunner of the first great Russian composer, Glinka.

II. The spirit of Russian folk music dominated the evolution of both vocal and instrumental art music. The earliest collection of folksongs was published by V. Trutovsky (4 vols., 1776–95), and soon after, I. Pratch, a Czech residing in Russia, published a collection of songs (2 vols., 1790, 1806). The first composer to use the unusual melodic and rhythmic inflections of Russian folksong was Mikhail Glinka (1804–57), popularly known as "the father of Russian music." He wrote the first national opera, *A Life for the Czar* (1836), also called *Ivan Sussanin,* the name of its patriot hero. In his second opera, *Russlan and Ludmilla* (1842), Glinka introduced Oriental elements and other colorful devices. Glinka's tradition of Russian nationalism was continued by Alexander Dargomyzhsky (1813–69), whose operas *Rusalka* (1856) and *The Stone Guest* (first perf. 1872) contain early examples of realism in recitative. Alexander Serov (1820–71), on the other hand, represented Western trends. His Biblical opera *Judith* (1863) is in German oratorio style, although his later operas, *Rogneda* (1865) and *Evil Power* (1871), are nationalist. Anton Rubinstein (1829–94), known primarily as a virtuoso pianist, also composed operas, among them *Demon* (1875), which is still popular in Russia. The first great Russian symphonist was Peter Tchaikovsky (1840–93), of whose six symphonies the last (*Pathétique,* 1893) is the most profound and best known. Also part of the standard repertory are his symphonic fantasies *Romeo and Juliet* (final version, 1880) and *Francesca da Rimini* (1876); his Piano Concerto no. 1 (1875); his Violin Concerto (1879); and his ballets *Swan Lake* (1877) and *The Nutcracker* (1892). His two operas, *Eugen Onegin* (1879) and *The Queen of Spades* (1890), are favorites in Russia but are not often performed abroad. Tchaikovsky's tradition was continued by the piano virtuoso Sergey Rachmaninoff (1873–1943), whose Piano Concerto no. 2 is widely performed. Minor followers of Tchaikovsky's include Anton Arensky (1861–1906) and Vassili Kalinnikov (1866–1901).

The melancholy tone of Tchaikovsky's music, reflected in his wide use of minor keys, found a sharp contrast in the vigorous national style of the so-called *Five: Alexander Borodin (1833–87), César Cui (1835–1918), Mily Balakirev (1837–1910), Modest Mussorgsky (1839–81), and Nicolay Rimsky-Korsakov (1844–1908). Mussorgsky's opera *Boris Godunov* (1874) influenced not only Russian composition but music everywhere, while his unfinished opera *Marriage* (written 1868, 1st stage perf. 1909) anticipates the modern comic opera. Balakirev is noted for his skillful use of Oriental melodic materials, especially in his symphonic poem *Tamara* and the brilliant piano fantasia *Islamey.* Borodin composed two symphonies and the historical opera *Prince Igor* (posthumously perf. 1890). Rimsky-Korsakov, the most prolific of the Five, wrote nine operas, of which *The Snow Maiden* (1882), *Sadko* (1898), and *The Tale of Czar Saltan* (1900) are the most frequently performed in Russia. His last three operas, *Kashchey the Immortal* (1902), *The Invisible City of Kitezh* (1907), and *The Golden Cockerel* (1909), represent a transition from traditional to modern Russian music, while his symphonic poem *Scheherazade* (comp. 1888) is an outstanding example of coloristic use of the orchestra. César Cui, of French ancestry, was a romantic composer whose association with the Russian national school was a historical accident. Other important composers in the Russian national tradition were Alexander Glazunov (1865–1936; eight symphonies, concertos, chamber music, ballets) and Anatol Liadov (1855–1914), whose symphonic fairy tales are miniature masterpieces. Mikhail Ippolitov-Ivanov (1859–1935), Alexander Gretchaninov (1864–1956), Sergey Vasilenko (1872–1956), Nicolas Tcherepnin (1873–1945), and Reinhold Glière (1875–

1956) also composed in the Russian national style.

The early modern school is represented by Alexander Scriabin (1872–1915) and Nicolai Medtner (1880–1951). Scriabin, a mystic, is an isolated phenomenon in Russian music. His symphonic style stems from Wagner and Liszt, while his sonatas, preludes, and piano etudes owe their inspiration to Chopin. However, his harmonic idiom is far more advanced than his models, and his melodic writing approaches atonality. His symphonic poem *Prometheus* (1910) is built on a six-note *mystic chord.

Igor Stravinsky (b. 1882) lived in Paris from 1910 and in the United States from 1939. One of the great figures in 20th-century music, he had more influence on European and American composers than on his compatriots. In Paris he was associated with the ballet impresario Sergei Diaghilev, for whom he wrote his greatest scores, *L'Oiseau de feu* (1911) and *Le Sacre du printemps* (1913). The former work shows the influence of Rimsky-Korsakov, but *Le Sacre du printemps* breaks with all tradition, although it retains elements of Russian folk melos (it is subtitled *Tableaux de la Russie païenne*). Stravinsky returned to Russian subjects in several later works, but in the 1920's he abandoned his national style in favor of neoclassicism, and in the 1950's he adopted serial techniques.

Sergey Prokofiev (1891–1953) lived in Paris and America from 1918 to 1932 and then returned to Russia. His early works are aggressively modernistic, full of vitality, wit, and irony. A brilliant pianist, he initiated a new percussive genre of piano composition. His works include piano concertos, sonatas, and suites; the operas *Love for Three Oranges* (1921) and *War and Peace* (concert perf., 1944); the ballets *Romeo and Juliet* (1938) and *Cinderella* (1945); the cantata *Alexander Nevsky* (1939); seven symphonies, of which the first, named *Classical Symphony* (1918), is the most famous; *Lieutenant Kijé*, and numerous other instrumental compositions. His symphonic fairy tale, *Peter and the Wolf* (1936), is a perennial favorite.

Prokofiev's contemporaries included Nicolai Miaskovsky (1881–1950), who wrote twenty-seven symphonies in a neoromantic style; Mikhail Gnessin (1883–1957), who used Jewish subjects; and the brothers Alekandr A. Krein (1883–1951) and Grigory A. Krein (1880–1955), who also contributed compositions inspired by Jewish music.

Among composers of the Soviet generation, the most renowned is Dmitri Shostakovitch (b. 1906). His first symphony, written while a student at the Leningrad Conservatory, established him as a highly gifted composer and became his most frequently performed composition. His Symphony no. 7, written during the siege of Leningrad (1941), was acclaimed as a great patriotic work. In addition to thirteen symphonies, Shostakovitch has written ten string quartets, two piano concertos, a violin concerto, and many piano compositions. His operas *The Nose* (1930) and *Lady Macbeth of Mtsensk* (1934), criticized by Soviets for their use of dissonance, have rarely been performed.

Other significant Soviet composers are Aram Khatchaturian (b. 1903; ballet *Gayane,* with the famous *Saber Dance,* piano concerto, violin concerto); Dmitri Kabalevsky (b. 1904; operas, instrumental concertos, piano music); Ivan Dzerzhinsky (b. 1909; known mostly for his operas); Tikhon Khrennikov (b. 1913; operas, instrumental music); Vissarion Shebalin (1902–63; five symphonies, nine string quartets, etc.); and Georgy Sviridov (b. 1915; oratorios and other choral works).

Soviet philosophy dictates that art must serve society, but the attempts of the Russian Association of Proletarian Musicians to govern composers failed, and the government disbanded it in 1932. The slogan "Socialist Realism," launched in the 1930's, promulgated a national style in an accessible idiom. In a famous assault on Shostakovitch, a *Pravda* editorial of 1936 denounced modernism in Soviet music and condemned the vaguely defined formalism of Western music. A 1949 decree of the Central Committee of the Communist Party of the U.S.S.R. renewed this attack, specifically accusing Prokofiev and Shostakovitch. The decree was rescinded in 1958 but at the same time reasserted "Socialist Realism" as the governing principle of Soviet music.

With the relaxation of stylistic strictures in the 1960's, a group of young Soviet composers began to write music using serial techniques, and some even applied *aleatory methods of the Western avant-garde. Among these composers was Andrey Volkonsky (b. 1933), born in Geneva and living in Russia since 1950. His unrestrained modernism was sharply criticized, but his music was admitted for performance in 1965. Other members of the Soviet avant-garde are Edison Denisov (b. 1929), Sergey Slonimsky (b. 1932), Leonid Grabovsky (b. 1935), and Valentin Silvestrov (b. 1937).

Lit.: R. Leonard, *A History of Russian Music* (1957); B. V. Asafiev, *Russian Music from the Beginning of the 19th Century* (1953); G. Abraham, *Studies in Russian Music* (1936); *id., On Russian Music* (1939); M. D. Calvocoressi and G. Abraham, *Masters of Russian Music* (1936); M. Montagu-Nathan, *A History of Russian Music* (1914); *id., Contemporary Russian Composers* (1917); R. Newmarch, *The Russian Opera* (1914); L. Sabaneyev, *Modern Russian Composers* (1927); *LavE* i.5, 2485ff, ii.1, 159ff (modern), ii.4, 2355ff (church music), ii.5, 2945ff (folk music); P. Souvtchinsky, *et al., Musique russe* (1953); R. Hofmann, *Un Siècle d'opéra russe* (1946); R.-A. Mooser, *Annales de la musique et des musiciens en Russie au XVIIIe siècle*, 3 vols. (1948–51); *id., Opéras . . . joués en Russie durant le XVIIIe siècle* (1945); K. Laux, *Die Musik in Russland und in der Sowjetunion* (1958); R. Trautmann, *Altrussische Helden- und Spielmannslieder* (1948); S. Ginzburg, ‡*Istoriya Russkoy Muzyki v notnykh obraztsakh* (Russian music in examples; 1940); M. Balakirev, ed., ‡*Sbornik' Russkikh' Narodnykh' Piesen'* (Russian folksongs; 1891); E. Lineva, ‡*Velikorusskie Pesni* (Russian folksongs; 1904, '09); Akademiya Nauk, Institut istorii iskusst, *Istoriya russkoĭ sovetskoĭ muzyki*, 2 vols. (history of Soviet Russian music; 1956, '59); G. Bernandt and A. Dolzhansky, *Sovietskiye Compository* (Soviet composers; 1957); G. Bernandt, *Slovar Oper* (dictionary of operas; 1962); L. Danilevitch, *Kniga o sovetskoĭ muzyke* (book on Soviet music; 1962); J. Handschin, "Le Chant ecclésiastique russe" (*AM* xxiv); G. Abraham, "The Elements of Russian Music" (*ML* ix, 51–58); *id.,* "The Foundation-Stone of Russian Music" (*ML* xviii, 50–62); R. Newmarch, "The Development of National Opera in Russia" (*PMA* xxviii–xxxi); G. Seaman, "Russian Folksong in the Eighteenth Century" (*ML* xl, 253ff); N. Findeisen, "The Earliest Russian Operas" (*MQ* xix); *id.,* in *SIM* ii; E. Oliphant, "A Survey of Russian Song" (*MQ* xii); A. Lourié, "The Russian School" (*MQ* xviii); L. Sabaneyev, "Music and Musicians in the U.S.S.R." (*ML* xv); W. J. Birbeck, "Some Notes upon Russian Ecclesiastical Music" (*PMA* xvii); V. Belaiev, "The Folk-Music of Georgia" (*MQ* xix); P. Panoff, "Die Volksmusik der Grossrussen" (*DM* xxi, no. 5); B. Schwarz, "Soviet Music Since the Second World War" (*LBCM;* also *MQ* li). For detailed bibl. see G. Orlov, *Muzykal'naia Literatura* (1935). I rev. K.L.; II by N.S.

Russian bassoon. A 19th-century upright serpent, now obsolete. It was made of wood in three or four detachable sections, ending in a brass bell. It also had six finger holes and three or four keys. See Brass instruments V (b).

Russian horn. A Russian hunting horn, straight or slightly bent, used from *c.* 1750 to *c.* 1826 in bands of 30 to 60, each horn playing a single note only, i.e., without making use of the overblown tones. The first of these bands, which have been compared to a live organ, was established by a Czech horn player, J. A. Maresch, in 1751, and attained a high degree of perfection, as appears from the rather complicated pieces it played. Two examples are reproduced in *LavE* i.5, 2499. See J. C. Hinrichs, *Entstehung, Fortgang und jetzige Beschaffenheit der russichen Jagdmusik* (Petersburg, 1796).

Russian Quartets. Beethoven's string quartets, op. 59, nos. 1–3, composed in 1805–1806, also known as "Razumovsky Quartets" because they were commissioned by the Russian Count Razumovsky. In nos. 1 and 2 Beethoven used a "Thème Russe" that he took from a collection of 150 songs published by Iwan Pratsch in 1790. The name is also used for Haydn's quartets nos. 37–42, op. 33, which follow the *Sonnenquartette,* nos. 31–36. See *Scherzi, Gli.*

Russlan and Ludmilla [Rus. *Ruslan i Lyudmila*]. Opera in five acts by Glinka (libretto by V. F. Shirkov and V. A. Bakhturin, based on a poem by Pushkin), produced in St. Petersburg, 1842. Setting: Russia, legendary times.

Rute [G.]. A kind of birch brush called for by R. Strauss and others to obtain a special effect on the bass drum.

Rybebe. See Rabab.

S

S. (1) Abbr. for **segno, *sinistra, subito.* (2) In liturgical books, abbr. for **schola,* i.e., choir. (3) In H. Riemann's system of harmonic analysis [see Functional harmony], abbr. for subdominant. (4) In 16th-century **partbooks, abbr. for *superius,* i.e., soprano. (5) Abbr. for W. Schmieder's catalog of Bach's works; see *BWV.*

Saccadé [F.]. Abrupt, jerky.

Sackbut, sagbut, saqueboute, sacabuche. Names for the medieval trombone. See Trombone II.

Sackgeige [G.]. **Kit.

Sackpfeife [G.]. Bagpipe.

Sacramentary [L. *sacramentarium*]. See under Liturgical books I, 9.

Sacre du printemps, Le [F. The Rite of Spring]. Ballet by Stravinsky (choreography by Nijinsky), produced in Paris, 1913. It represents an ancient pagan rite. The two parts (I. *L' Adoration de la terre;* II. *Le Sacrifice*), now often performed as a concert piece, are divided into several scenes. The work is one of the major landmarks in 20th-century music, establishing Stravinsky's revolutionary dynamism. Its harsh sounds and wild rhythms, willingly accepted and admired today, caused a riot of indignation at the first performance.

Saeta [Sp.]. An Andalusian folksong sung during Lent or the Feast of the Nativity to accompany street processions and other outdoor devotional or penitential activities. *Saetas* vary greatly in form and style, ranging from simple syllabic melodies to highly ornamented ones. See A. de Larrea, in *AnM* iv; A. Salazar, in *Nuestra música* vi, 29ff (Mexico); ex. in F. Pedrell, ‡*Cancionero musical popular español,* 4 vols. (1918–22), i, 119ff; also M. Schneider, in *AnM* i, 80ff.

Sagbut. **Sackbut. See Trombone II.

Sainete [Sp.]. A Spanish type of comic opera of the late 18th century, portraying scenes from everyday life and often approaching low comedy. Among the composers of *sainetes* were Antonio Soler (1729–83) and Blas Laserna (1751–1816).

St. Anne's Fugue. Popular name for Bach's great organ fugue in E-flat, from the **Clavier-Übung*

iii (1739), so called because its theme is similar to the beginning of an English hymn tune called "St. Anne" (usually sung to the verses beginning "O God, our help in ages past"). Bach, of course, did not know the hymn, nor Sperindio Bertoldo's Ricercar on the sixth tone (1591), which employs Bach's theme (in C).

St. John Passion. See under Passion music.

St. Martial, school of. An important school of the 10th to 12th centuries located at the Abbey of St. Martial in Limoges (also known as the school of Limoges). Aside from composing many **sequences and *tropes (chiefly 10th and 11th centuries), it is important mainly for its contribution to the development of **organum, in which the polyphonic school of St. Martial (c. 1100–50) immediately preceded **Notre Dame. Ex. in *HAM,* no. 27a.

Lit.: J. Chailley, *L'École musicale de Saint Martial de Limoges* [1960]; J. Handschin, in *ZMW* vi; R. L. Crocker, in *JAMS* xi (proses); P. Hooreman, "Saint-Martial de Limoges au temps de l'abbé Odolric" (*RBM* iii); L. Treitler, in *JAMS* xvii (polyphony); J. M. Marshall, in *JAMS* xv (hidden polyphony); G. Schmidt, in *MF* xv (structural problems); W. Apel, "From St. Martial to Notre Dame" (*JAMS* ii); id., in *CP Anglés* (organa); H. Spanke, in *Zeitschrift für französische Sprache und Literatur* liv, lvi; id., in *Butlletí de la Biblioteca de Catalunya* viii, 280ff (London MS); H. Anglés, *ibid.,* pp. 301ff (London MS); id., in *CP Besseler* (polyphony); B. Stäblein, in *CP Blume* (modal rhythm); J. Handschin, in *CP 1924* (motets).

St. Matthew Passion. Bach's last and greatest Passion, based on the Gospel according to St. Matthew, with free poetic insertions by Picander, first performed at St. Thomas' Church, Leipzig, on Good Friday, 1729. The first performance after Bach's death, produced in Berlin by Mendelssohn in 1829, was the decisive step toward the "rediscovery" of Bach. See Passion music.

St. Paul. Oratorio by Mendelssohn, op. 36, produced in Düsseldorf, 1836.

Saite [G.]. String. *Saitenchor,* **course of strings. *Saiteninstrument,* stringed instrument.

Salicus. See under Neumes I.

Salmo [It.]. Psalm, psalm composition.

Salome. Opera in one act by R. Strauss (libretto by H. Lachmann, translated from Oscar Wilde's play), produced in Dresden, 1905. Setting: Terrace of Herod's palace, Galilee, about A.D. 30. Except for the passages associated with Jochanaan (John the Baptist), the music is some of the most intensely emotional ever written.

Salomon Symphonies. Haydn's last twelve symphonies, nos. 93 to 104, written 1791–95 in London for the concerts managed by Johann Peter Salomon. They are also known as *London Symphonies, although the name London Symphony specifically applies to no. 104 (also sometimes called the Salomon Symphony). Others in this group are the *Surprise (no. 94), *Military (no. 100), *Clock (no. 101), and *Drum-Roll (no. 103). It should be noted that the numbering of the complete series of Haydn's symphonies is not in agreement with the numbering within this group; nos. 94 and 104 of the complete series are nos. 3 and 7 (rather than 2 and 12) of the Salomon Symphonies.

Salón México, El. Descriptive piece for orchestra by Copland, composed 1933–36, inspired by the composer's visit to Mexico in 1932. It uses several popular Mexican melodies such as might be heard in a dance hall (*El Salón México*).

Salpinx. See under Brass instruments V (a).

Saltarello. A gay, sprightly dance of Italian provenance.

(1) *14th century*. The music of four saltarelli without choreographies is preserved in Brit. Mus. MS *Add. 29987*. In varying meters (6/8, 3/4, 6/8, 4/4), all are monophonic pieces cast in the four-repeated-phrase form of the *estampie.

(2) *15th century* [F. *pas de breban* (Brabant); Sp. *alta danza*]. One of the faster measures (*misura*) or step units of the *bassa dansa* (*basse danse*). The term was sometimes applied to the *quadernaria,* another step unit of the *basse danse* family that, because of its popularity in Germany, was known to the Italians as the *saltarello tedesco.*

(3) *16th century* [F. *sauterelle, tordion, tourdion;* G. *Hupfauf,* *Proportz, Sprung,* *Nachtanz*]. The music of the *saltarello* is indistinguishable from that of the *galliard. The difference between the two is in the style of dancing as suggested by the respective titles: *saltarello,* a small leap; galliard, vigorous. The galliard is simply a more vigorous version of the *saltarello.* A galliard or a *saltarello*

is usually coupled either to a *pavane or a *passamezzo,* and the coupled dances all are composed on the same musical material (harmonic patterns, melodies, etc.).

The *saltarello* continued in vogue until late in the 19th century. Indeed, its basic steps are still used in present-day folk dances. However, by the 17th century any function it had as an elegant court dance waned in favor of a dance of the common people. As a folk dance, its movements were executed more rapidly and with greater violence. The *saltarelli* in the last movement of Mendelssohn's Italian Symphony are stylized apotheoses of the dance, but they do suggest its hopping and jumping movement. For detailed descriptions and bibl. see L. H. Moe in *MGG* xi, 1315–18.   L.H.M.

Saltato, saltando [It.]. Same as *sautillé* [see Bowing (d)].

Saltbox. A popular noise-producing instrument in the form of a box with a revolving mechanism. It was used by clowns in 18th-century England.

Salterio [It., Sp.]. *Psaltery, *dulcimer.

Salve Regina [L.]. One of the four antiphons B.V.M. [see Antiphon (2)], probably written and composed by Hermannus Contractus (1013–54). The chant, actually a hymn with a free poetic text sung to a first-mode melody of great beauty [*LU,* p. 276], soon became famous, particularly among the religious societies of the 14th to 16th centuries whose main object was the worship of the Virgin (Salve Societies). Polyphonic compositions of the text, with or without use of the plainsong melody, are fairly numerous (e.g., Dunstable, see Editions XXXIV, 8, p. 152; Ockeghem, see *BeMMR,* p. 238; Obrecht; Josquin). Of particular interest are the compositions for organ (Buxheim Organ Book, Hofhaimer, Kotter, Schlick; see H. J. Moser, *Frühmeister des deutschen Orgelkunst,* 1930), which usually include only the odd-numbered verses (*Salve Regina; Ad te clamamus; Eia ergo; O clemens; O dulcis*), the others (*Vita dulcedo; Ad te suspiramus; Et Jesum; O pia*) being sung *alternatim* in plainsong. Later settings for organ are by John Bull [*Editions XXXIV, 14], Pieter Cornet [*Editions I, 10], and numerous 17th-century Spanish composers, e.g., Aguileria de Heredia, Jimenez, and Bruna. See *HAM,* nos. 100, 139.

Lit.: J. Maier, *Studien zur Geschichte der Marienantiphon Salve Regina* (1939); K. Dèzes, in *ZMW* x; P. Runge, in *CP Liliencron;* A. Orel, in *StM* vii, 48–101.

Samba [Port.]. A Brazilian style of folk dance characterized by the use of syncopated rhythmic patterns within a 2/4 meter. Two types of samba are performed today, a rural type, which is more violent and somewhat faster, similar to the *batuque,* and an urban variety, derived from the *maxixe,* which is more moderate in tempo and less strongly syncopated. In Rio de Janeiro the samba is the most characteristic carnival music, and at these festivities it is generally performed in groups forming a circle. Otherwise, it is danced by couples.   J.O-S.

Sambuca [Gr. *sambykē*]. A name used for a variety of old instruments, among them a harp or psaltery of ancient Rome, a medieval chordophone commonly known as the *crwth, and also a woodwind made from the elder tree [L. *sambucus*]. In the Middle Ages the *hurdy-gurdy was sometimes called *sambuca rotata.* In the early 17th century, Fabio Colonna, also known as Linceo (*c.* 1567–1650), invented an enharmonic harpsichord called *sambuca lincea.* It had 17 notes to the octave and a total of 50 strings (hence its other name, *pentecontachordon*). Colonna described it in his *La Sambuca lincea* (Naples, 1618).

Samisen. Same as shamisen. See Japan; Lute.

Sampogna. Same as *zampogna.

Samson et Dalila [F., Samson and Delilah]. Opera in three acts by Saint-Saëns (libretto by F. Lemaire, based on the Bible), produced in Weimar, 1877. Setting: Gaza, Palestine, 1150 B.C.

Sanctorale [L.]. In the Roman rite, generic name for the feasts of Saints, as opposed to the *Temporale, the feasts of the Lord. It is subdivided into the *Proprium sanctorum* and *Commune sanctorum;* see Gregorian chant I.

Sanctus. [L.]. The fourth item of the Ordinary of the *Mass. The text consists of three sections, *Sanctus . . . , Pleni sunt caeli . . . ,* and *Benedictus qui venit . . . .* Polyphonic compositions usually fall into three corresponding sections, or at least two, Sanctus and Benedictus. In later Mass compositions (17th, 18th centuries) the Benedictus is usually written in a lyrical style. See P. J. Thannabaur, *Das einstimmige Sanctus* (1962), which includes Sanctus melodies.

Sanft [G.]. Soft, gentle.

Sanglot. [F.]. An 18th-century name for an appoggiatura or passing tone sung to plaintive words such as "Oh" or "Hélas."

Sangsaite. [G.]. See Cantino.

Saqueboute [F.]. *Sackbut. See Trombone II.

Saraband [F. *sarabande;* Sp. *zarabanda*]. A 17th- and 18th-century dance [see Dance music III] in slow triple meter and dignified style, usually without upbeat, frequently with an accent or prolonged tone on the second beat and with feminine endings of the phrases.

The saraband probably came from Mexico (not Persia, as was formerly believed) and appeared in Spain in the early 16th century. Originally it was probably a wild and even lascivious love dance, for it is described and severely attacked as such by various writers, among them Cervantes. Particularly characteristic is the following passage from a *Tratado contra los juegos públicos* (Treatise against public amusements) of Juan de Mariana (1536–1624): "A dance and song, so lascivious in its words, so ugly in its movements, that it is enough to inflame even very honest people." The dance was officially suppressed in Spain (*c.* 1590) by Philip II but continued to exist under the name *zarabanda* throughout the 17th and 18th centuries as a quick dance with a characteristic alternation of 3/4 and 3/8 meter. [See *LavE* i.4, 2098, 2247.] As late as 1676, Thomas Mace, in his *Musick's Monument,* wrote "Serabands, are of the shortest triple-time; but are more toyish and light, than corantes; and commonly of Two Strains."

About 1600 the saraband appeared in France and England. An early example is a "Sarabrand" by Orlando Gibbons that, being faster and gayer than the classical type, may represent the transition from the original dance to its later dignified

form (similar examples appear in Michael Praetorius, *C. Terpsichore,* 1612). Examples of the slower type occur in Chambonnières (Bauyn MS, *c.* 1650). At the same time (Froberger) it became a standard dance of the *suite. The accompanying example (from Handel's Suite no. 7) illustrates the normal type of saraband, whereas the saraband from Bach's Partita no. 6 shows it in its final stage of artistic idealization. See R. Stevenson, "The First Dated Mention of the Sarabande" (*JAMS* v); D. Devoto, "La folle Sarabande" (*RdM* 1960, p. 3; 1961, p. 145).

Sarambo [Sp.]. A traditional dance form, very popular in the Dominican Republic, that evolved from the Andalusian *zapateado* and is also known as *zapateo*. It is essentially a fast 6/8 tap dance in which solo and group dancing alternate. Three instruments are always used, the *acordeon, güiro* [see *Reco-reco*], and **tambora* (played without sticks). In the group episodes, called *callao* (lit., silent), the melodic instruments cease playing and only percussion continues. Rhythmically the *sarambo* is built on a one-measure pattern with strong accents on the weak beats.   J.O-S.

Sārangī. See under Violin II.

Sardana. The national dance of Catalonia, usually in quick 6/8 meter and danced in a circle to the accompaniment of the *pipe and tabor. See *LavE* i.4, 2379.

Saron. See *Gambang.* For ill. see under Percussion instruments.

Sarrusophone. See under Oboe family II, F.

Sarum use. (1) The ritual used in the Cathedral of Salisbury, England, which differed in certain details from the Roman liturgy. It prevailed during the later Middle Ages throughout much of England, until it was abolished by decree in 1547. Two plainsong MSS dating from the 13th century have been published in facsimile by W. H. Frere under the titles *Graduale Sarisburiense* (1894) and *Antiphonale Sarisburiense* (1901–25). See his *The Sarum Gradual* and the *Gregorian Antiphonale Missarum* (1895).

French composers of the 15th century repeatedly based their compositions on the Sarum use rather than the Gregorian version of chants. Examples are the three *Caput* Masses, and some motets by Binchois and Josquin [see *ReMR,* pp. 68, 90, 114, 255].

(2) When compared to the older Gregorian form, the final form of the Sarum melodies (*c.* 1500) included many new or rewritten compositions showing economy of range, balance of cadence, a more advanced sense of musical form, and some transposition for effect or contrast. Much of the Gradual remained closer to the Gregorian form of the melodies than the Antiphonal did. Alleluia verses and hymns varied the most, with new melodies being written continuously until the suppression of the English monasteries. The hymns varied in transmission as do folksongs. The modern revival of plainsong in Anglican churches has used the Sarum more than the Gregorian form of the melodies. See F. L. Harrison, "Music for the Sarum Rite" (*AnnM* vi).   (2) by L.E.

Sassofone [It.]. Saxophone.

Satire. Satire, irony, and caricature are by no means foreign to music. Although 19th-century philosophers and aestheticians "proved" that such distortions have no place in musical expression, the 20th century brought forth abundant evidence to the contrary. In fact no account of the revolutionary movement of the early 20th century would be complete without pointing to the important role that satire, irony, and caricature played in the effort to overthrow the tradition of the 19th century. French composers in particular used ridicule as a weapon, notably Erik Satie in numerous pieces bearing such satirical titles as "Embryons desséchés." The new harmonic style with its unlimited exploitation of discord naturally offered unprecedented opportunities for caricaturing effects. Examples are Debussy's "Golliwogg's Cakewalk" (from *Children's Corner*), with its allusion to the Tristan theme; Stravinsky's *Petrouchka,* with the caricaturing *Valse;* A. Casella's *Pupazzetti;* E. Goossens' *Kaleidoscope;* and Shostakovitch's *Polka* (from *The Golden Age*), which satirizes the Geneva disarmament conference.

Satire is usually effected by deliberate violation of the rules or by stylistic distortion. Such an effect is probably intended in Lorenzo Masini's madrigal "Dolgomi a voi" of *c.* 1350, in which he uses a strikingly dissonant and awkward style (involving parallel fifths) as the text complains about "qui che guastan tutte nostre note" (those who make a mess of all our notes). A rondeau by Solage, "Fumeux fume" (written *c.* 1380), exceptional for its low range and tonal vagaries, appears to ridicule the *fumeurs,* a group of late 14th-century Bohemians in Paris [see W. Apel, *French Secular Music of the Late 14th*

Century, no. 40; also Commentary]. An especially effective example of musical caricature is Hans Newsidler's "Der Judentanz" of 1544 [see *HAM,* no. 105b]. In the late 16th century parallel fifths were deliberately used in the *villanella in order to enhance the textual parody. Aside from innumerable examples in opera, in which the satire usually lies mainly in the text and action, other examples of essentially musical satire are Mozart's charming *Ein musikalischer Spass* (1787; K. 522), with its good-natured mockery of provincial music; the Beckmesser Scene of Wagner's *Meistersinger,* which is an acid satire on the untalented musician; and Berlioz' *Symphonie fantastique,* in which the distorted presentation of the *Dies irae portrays hellish despair and fiendish laughter. One of the first modern composers to write satirical music for its own sake was Enrico Bossi (*Pezzi satirici*).

Lit.: H. F. Gilbert, "Humor in Music" (*MQ* xii); R. D. Chennevière, "Erik Satie and the Music of Irony" (*MQ* v); A. Einstein, "Die Parodie in der Villanella" (*ZMW* ii); Z. Lissa, "Die Kategorie des Komischen in der Musik" (*CP 1958*).

Satz [G.]. (1) Movement (of a sonata, symphony, etc.); e.g., *erster Satz,* first movement. However, *Hauptsatz,* and *Seitensatz* (*Nebensatz*) denote the first and second theme within a movement. (2) Style, manner of writing; e.g., *strenger* (*freier*) *Satz,* strict (free) style.

Saul. Oratorio by Handel, produced in London, 1739.

Sausage bassoon [G. *Wurstfagott*]. See under Oboe family III (end).

Sauterelle [F.]. See *Saltarello* (3).

Sautillé [F.]. See under Bowing (d).

Savart. Unit of a system of logarithmic pitch determination introduced by Félix Savart (1791–1841) of France. It is based on the fact that the logarithm of 2 (ratio of frequencies of two tones an octave apart) is 0.30103, so that the logarithmic intervals of all tones lie between 0 and 0.30103. For convenience all figures are multiplied by 1,000, so that the octave measures 301 savarts. The system is very useful, particularly since for all practical purposes the figure 301 can be replaced by 300, so that each semitone equals 25 savarts. It was later supplanted by A. J. Ellis' system of *cents, in which all the figures are approximately four times as large

(1 savart = 3.99 cents). See Intervals, calculation of, VI.

Saxhorn. See under Brass instruments III (f).

Saxophone [G. *Saxophon;* It. *sassofone;* Sp. *saxófono*]. A family of hybrid instruments invented by Adolphe Sax of Brussels *c.* 1840 (patented 1846). They are played with a single beating reed, as are the clarinets, but are conical in bore, as are the oboes. Their key arrangement also resembles that of the oboes, but their mouthpiece is like that of the clarinets. The body of the instrument is of metal, as in the brass instruments. [For ill. see under Clarinet family.] The saxophones are especially valuable in bands, in which they blend well with either the woodwinds or the brasses. The complete family numbers eight instruments, alternately in E-flat and B-flat, as follows: (1) sopranino in E-flat; (2) soprano in B-flat; (3) alto in E-flat; (4) tenor in B-flat; (5) baritone in E-flat; (6) bass in B-flat; (7) contrabass in E-flat; (8) subcontrabass in B-flat. All are treated as transposing instruments, written in the treble clef and with the written chromatic compass shown [see Ex.]. The sopranino sounds a minor third higher than written, the soprano a major second lower than

written, etc. Nos. 3 to 5 are the most popular of the group.

The sound of the saxophone is extremely variable. Its timbre being intermediate between those of wood and brass, it passes from the softness of the flute over the broad, mellow tone of the cello to the metallic strength of the cornet. These properties, together with its great flexibility, have given it a prominent place in jazz bands. The principal member of the family is the alto saxophone (also made in F), which has been employed for solos by many French composers, first by J. G. Kastner in *Le dernier Roi de Juda* (1844) and subsequently by Delibes, Thomas, Saint-Saëns, Bizet, and D'Indy. Richard Strauss introduced a quartet of saxophones in his *Sinfonia Domestica,* and Hindemith used the saxophone in his opera *Cardillac.* Compositions for saxophone include Debussy's *Rapsodie pour Saxophone et piano* (1903–05), Ibert's *Concertino da camera* for saxophone and orchestra (1935), Milhaud's *Scaramouche* for saxophone and piano (1942), and Villa-Lobos' *Fantasia* for saxophone and orchestra (1948). See J. Kool, *Das Saxophon* [1931].   W.D.D.

Sax(o)tromba. A group of valved brass instruments devised by Adolphe Sax (patented 1845) with a bore intermediate between that of the trombone and saxhorn. They are seldom used today.

Saxtuba. A circular valved brass instrument invented by Adolphe Sax (1852).

Saynète [F.]. *Sainete.

Scala [It.]. *Scale.

Scala, La. See under Opera houses VII.

Scala enigmatica. An arbitrary scale, c–d♭–e–f♯–g♯–a♯–b–c′, used by Verdi in his "Ave Maria" (1898).

Scale [F. *gamme;* G. *Skala, Tonleiter;* It. *scala;* Sp. *escala, gama*]. I. The tonal material of music arranged in an order of rising pitches. Since the tonal material varies greatly in different periods as well as different countries (e.g., China) there are a large number of scales. The basic scale of European music is the *diatonic scale.* It consists of five whole tones (t) and two semitones (s) in the following arrangement: t t s t t t s (e.g., c, d, e, f, g, a, b, c′). This scale is usually referred to as a *major scale* (properly C-major scale; see III) as distinguished from the *minor scale,* in which the arrangement of intervals is t s t t t t s (e.g., c d e♭ f g a b c′). For more details, see Major, minor. Both major and minor scales may be transposed, starting on any one of the twelve notes in an octave, e.g., d e f♯ g a b c′♯ d′, or d e f g a b c′♯ d′. Thus there are twelve major scales and twelve minor scales, one in each *key. All the tones found in any of the scales above can be combined in one scale, the *chromatic scale,* which consists of twelve semitones. This all-inclusive scale, also known as the *dodecuple scale, is the tonal foundation of modern music, the other scales now being considered selections thereof [see Gapped scale]. Naturally, numerous other selections are possible and occasionally have been employed, particularly the *whole-tone scale,* the so-called *gypsy scale,* and the *pentatonic scale.* The accompanying table shows how they are set up.

Chromatic	c	c♯	d	d♯	e	f	f♯	g	g♯	a	a♯ b c′
Major	c		d		e	f		g		a	b c′
Minor, melodic											
ascending	c		d e♭		f			g		a	b c′
descending	c		d e♭		f			g a♭			b♭ c′
Minor, harmonic	c		d e♭		f			g a♭			b c′
Whole tone	c		d				f♯	g♯		a♯	c′
Gypsy	c		d e♭				f♯ g a♭				b c′
Pentatonic	c		d			f		g		a	c′

In the 20th century attempts have been made to broaden the tonal material of music by the introduction of *quarter tones, resulting in a quarter-tone scale of twenty-four tones to the octave [see also Microtone].

II. All the scales described above can be derived from the diatonic scale, which was already used by the ancient Greeks. Upon closer examination, however, it appears that this scale underwent minute changes owing to the different systems of intonation (tuning) used in the various periods from about 500 B.C. to A.D. 1750. Thus, the Greek diatonic scale was based on the *Pythagorean system, while in the Middle Ages certain intervals of *just intonation crept in (particularly, the *third), a fact that in turn necessitated the adoption of various systems of *temperament. The last of these was that of equal temperament, established in the time of Bach. (For tables showing the differences among these scales, see Temperament; also Intervals, calculation of.) Still greater deviations are found in the numerous non-Western scales, such as the *sléndro* and *pélog* of *Java, the *SA-grāma* of *India, etc.

III. Still another consideration in the concept of "scale" is the center tone (tonic, home tone), whereby the various tones of the scale are not considered equally important but are related and subordinated to one of them. Thus, the diatonic scale is usually interpreted as a "C-major scale," because C is its initial tone (for an ingenious method of constructing the diatonic scale without preference given to one tone, see Hexachord). Actually, any of the tones of the diatonic scale (as well as of other scales) can be designated as the center tone, as in the medieval *church modes. For the sake of clarity, the term "scale" should be avoided for these centralized scales, which are better termed modes. Thus, the C-major scale would be called the "C-mode of the major (or diatonic) scale," the Lydian scale the "F-mode of the major scale," etc. Each mode of any scale may also begin on various pitch levels. This leads to what is generally called transposed scales but might better be termed keys. Thus, the F-sharp minor scale would be the "F-sharp key of the C-mode of the minor scale." The same terminology can be applied to other scales, e.g., "D-mode of the pentatonic scale," etc.

The medieval modes (as well as the Greek "scales") included yet another element of limitation, i.e., *ambitus. Thus, the medieval Hypolydian might be considered the c-c′ segment of the F-mode of the diatonic scale.

Lit.: A. Daniélou, *Introduction to the Study of Musical Scales* [1943]; A. Auda, *Les Gammes musicales* [1947]; H. Pfrogner, *Die Zwölfordnung der Töne* [1953]; A. H. Fox Strangways, in *ML* vii; L. S. Lloyd, in *MQ* xxviii; *id.*, in *ML* xxvii; V. de Rubertis, in *RMI* xxix and xxx.

Scale degrees. Special names and signs used in *harmonic analysis to denote the various tones of the scale when they occur as the roots of triads, seventh chords, etc. These names are: tonic (I), supertonic (II), mediant (III), subdominant (IV), dominant (V), submediant or superdominant (VI), and subtonic or leading tone (VII). The most important are the *tonic, *dominant, and *subdominant.

Scaling, scale [G. *Mensur*]. The proportion of diameter to length in an *organ pipe or, more generally, in a rank of pipes. In the modern German system of scaling, all pipe diameters are compared to a single standard scale known as *Normalmensur,* in which the diameters for the c pipes are: C (8-foot c) = 6⅛ in., c = 3⅜ in., c′ = 2⅛ in., c″ = 1¼ in., c‴ = ¾ in., c⁗ = 1/16 in. In practice the foregoing represents a usable scale for a diapason (or principal) 8-foot. Wider scaling (i.e., pipe diameters larger than *Normalmensur*) tends to produce flute tone (characterized by few audible harmonics), while narrower scaling tends to produce string tone (more audible harmonics). Reed pipes are scaled by a different method. Also see Organ VIII.

Scampata [It.]. Same as *charivari.

Scandicus. See under Neumes I (table).

Scandinavia. See Denmark; Finland; Iceland; Norway; Sweden. See J. Horton, Scandinavian Music [1963]; B. Wallner, "Scandinavian Music after the Second World War" (*LBCM;* also *MQ* li).

Scat singing. In jazz, the interpolation of nonsense syllables and other peculiar vocal effects, introduced in the 1920's by Cab Calloway

(b. 1907) and Louis Armstrong (b. 1900). See Jazz III.

Scenario. A skeleton libretto of a play or an opera that indicates the characters, number, and general nature of the scenes. The German term *Scenarium,* however, means a full libretto with detailed directions for the scenery.

Schachtbrett [G.]. Old term for *echiquier.

Schalkhaft [G.]. Roguish.

Schall [G.]. Sound, chiefly acoustical. *Schallbecken,* cymbals. *Schalloch,* sound hole. *Schallplatte,* record. *Schallwellen,* acoustical waves.

Schalmei [G.]. See under Oboe family III.

Scheherazade. Symphonic suite by Rimsky-Korsakov, op. 35 (1888), based on some tales from the *Arabian Nights* and named for the woman who tells the stories. In 1910 it was presented in Paris as a ballet by the Russian Ballet under Fokine. See also *Shéhérazade* (Ravel).

Schellen [G.]. Tambourine. *Schellenbaum,* *Turkish crescent. *Schellentrommel,* tambourine.

Schenker system. A system of musical analysis and interpretation developed by Heinrich Schenker (1868–1935). It represents an attempt to reveal the organic structure of music by showing that every composition is the elaboration of some simple tone structure that guarantees its continuity and coherence.

Schenker's point of departure is "nature," i.e., the overtone series through the fifth partial, from which man derives not only the major triad but all intervals, scales, and basic structures of music. The overtones (1, 2, 3, 5; i.e., unison, octave, fifth, major third) constitute the *Klang* (sound, sonority) or natural triad, which may appear in its vertical or horizontal position. The horizontal projection of the *Klang* determines the melody as well as the bass. In the latter it appears as *Grundbrechung* or *Bassbrechung* (broken ground), mainly as a succession of I and V; in the former as *Urlinie* (primordial, fundamental line), in which the basic tones, I, III, V, are filled in with others. *Urlinie* and *Grundbrechung* together constitute the *Ursatz* (fundamental setting), which is the basic structure, the "background" of the composition.

Schenker's approach to musical analysis is a process of stepwise reduction, leading from the actual composition (foreground) over an intermediate stage (middle ground) to the *Ursatz* (background). The middle ground is a simplified version of the foreground, including the essential elements or the raw materials of the composition. In Ex. 1, the theme from the last movement

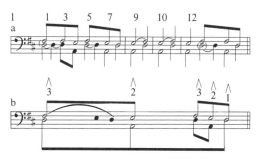

of Beethoven's Ninth Symphony, the melody itself is the foreground. Ex. 1a shows the middle ground, which represents the first phase of the reduction of the actual music to its basic structure (the Arabic numerals refer to the measures of the original melody). The reduction leads from this stage to the background shown in Ex. 1b; this is the *Ursatz*. Important elements of this (and every) structural pattern are the "motions" (*Züge*) of the upper part or parts (here a "motion of a third [*Terz-Zug*]; the numerals 3̂, 2̂, 1̂, signify scale degrees) and the "breaking up" of an otherwise continuous tonic by a 1̂–5̂–1̂ movement of the bass (*Bassbrechung*).

The purpose of this kind of analysis is not to show that all compositions can be reduced to a few types of "fundamental structure," but to demonstrate how a few basic patterns unfold into the infinite variety, the broad and rich life of the actual compositions. Accordingly, its main interest is not in the background itself but in *how* background and foreground are connected, i.e., the middle ground. For instance, an analysis of the second song from Schumann's "Dichterliebe" leads to the same *Ursatz* as Beethoven's melody. The difference lies in the middle ground, which appears more complex here—so complex, indeed, that two successive reductions become necessary, resulting in two levels of middle ground. It is in the middle ground that genius is distinguished from lesser talent. Only a great master can produce such interesting middle-ground pictures as that in Ex. 2 (Bach, 12 Little Preludes, no. 3). Schenker applied his analysis mostly to compositions of the period from Bach through Brahms (excluding Wagner). His pupils have shown that his principles can also be applied to medieval and 20th-century music.

Lit.: F. Salzer, *Structural Hearing* (1952); *id.*, *Sinn und Wesen der abendländischen Mehrstimmigkeit* (1935); A. T. Katz, *Challenge to Musical Tradition* (1945); H. Schenker, *Das Meisterwerk in der Musik,* 3 vols. (1925–30); *id.*, *Der freie Satz*, rev. ed., 2 vols., in *Neue musikalische Theorien und Phantasien*, iii (1956); *id.*, ‡*Fünf Urlinie-Tafeln* (1932); O. Jonas, *Das Wesen des musikalischen Kunstwerks* (1934); A. T. Katz, in *MQ* xxi; R. Sessions, in *MM* xii, 170; M. Mann, in *MR* x; W. Riezler, in *DM* xxii, no. 7; A. Forte, in *Journal of Music Theory* iii.
                                                                                              v.z.

Scherzando [It.], **Scherzhaft** [G.]. Playful.

Scherzi, Gli. Popular name for Haydn's six string quartets, op. 33, so called because the minuets bear the inscription "Scherzo" or "Scherzando" and accordingly are faster than the usual minuets of the period [see under Scherzo]. They are also known as the Russian Quartets (because they were dedicated to the Grand Duke Pavel Petrowitsch, who visited Vienna in 1781) and as Maiden Quartets [G. *Jungfern-Quartette*] because the title page of the 1782 edition shows a female figure [G. *Jungfer*].

Scherzo [It.]. (1) A movement, usually the third, of sonatas, symphonies, and quartets (rarely concertos), which was introduced by Beethoven to replace the *minuet. Like it, the scherzo is followed by a *trio after which the scherzo is repeated. Occasionally (e.g., Beethoven, Symphony no. 7) the scheme of alternation is extended to S T S T S. The distinguishing features of the scherzo are rapid tempo in 3/4 meter, vigorous rhythm, a certain abruptness of thought involving elements of surprise and whim, and a kind of bustling humor that ranges from the playful to the sinister (e.g., Beethoven's Symphony no. 5). The demarcation between minuet and scherzo is by no means always clear. Some late minuets of Haydn's approximate the scherzo, as do minuets by Beethoven, e.g., in his first piano sonata; on the other hand, Haydn used the term "scherzo" in some of his earlier works (*Gli *Scherzi*) for pieces scarcely different from his minuets. The great masters of the scherzo were Beethoven, Schubert, and Bruckner. Nationalist composers have frequently used it as a vehicle for the introduction of national dances, with the result that many composers have produced a moderately good scherzo in an otherwise mediocre symphony. For the internal structure of the scherzo, see Binary and ternary form II.

(2) Chopin and Brahms (op. 4) employed the term "scherzo" for independent pieces in which highly dramatic, somewhat gloomy sections (scherzo) alternate with more lyrical ones (trio).

(3) In the baroque period "scherzo" was used for vocal pieces in a lighter vein (C. Monteverdi, *Scherzi musicali*, 1607; A. Cifra, *Scherzi sacri*, 1616; B. Marini, *Scherzi e canzonette a una, e due voci*, 1622), as well as for instrumental pieces of a somewhat fanciful character similar to the *capriccio. (A. Troilo, *Sinfonie, scherzi*, 1608; Jean [Johann] Schenk, *Scherzi musicali*, *c.* 1700, for viola da gamba and bass [*Editions LII, 28]; J. S. Bach, in Partita no. 3). See G. Becking, *Studien zu Beethovens Personalstil: Das Scherzothema* (1921).

Schicksalslied [G., Song of Destiny]. Setting by Brahms for chorus and orchestra, op. 54 (1871), of a poem from Hölderlin's *Hyperion*.

Schiettamente [It.]. Openly, simply.

Schillinger system. A system of composition introduced by J. Schillinger (1895–1943) and published posthumously (*The Schillinger System of Musical Composition*, 2 vols., 1946). It amounts to an exhaustive presentation of all possible tonal and rhythmic combinations, conceived in arithmetic terms and described in confusing, pseudomathematical language. It has become a manual for trade musicians who have found in it novel combinations, mostly rhythmic.

Schisma. See Comma, schisma.

Schlag [G.]. Beat. *Schlaginstrumente, Schlagzeug*, percussion instruments.

Schlagzither [G.]. The modern plucked *zither (not the dulcimer), as opposed to earlier bowed zithers (*Streichzither*).

Schlegel [G.]. Drumstick.

Schleifer [G.]. See under Appoggiatura, double II.

Schleppend [G.]. Dragging, heavy.

Schlummerlied [G.]. Slumber song.

Schluss [G.]. Conclusion, cadence. *Schluss-satz*, final movement.

Schlüssel [G.]. Clef.

Schnabel [G.]. The mouthpiece of the clarinet and recorder; see Mouthpiece (b), (d).

Schnabelflöte [G.]. Old name for *recorder.

Schnadahupfl [G.]. A Bavarian-Austrian folksong, frequently with improvised humorous texts between an iterated refrain. See K. Rotter, *Der Schnadahupfl-Rhythmus* (1912).

Schnarre [G.]. Rattle. *Schnarrtrommel*, snare drum. *Schnarrwerk*, old term for reed section of the organ.

Schnell [G.]. Fast.

Schneller [G.]. See Inverted mordent.

Schola (cantorum) [L.]. Originally, the papal choir and singing school, possibly organized (or reorganized) by St. Gregory (590–605) but first mentioned in 780 by Paul Diacre (Paulus Diaconus). It became the central body for the propagation of Roman chant, as the singers were sent to other churches and monasteries [see Sistine choir]. In the papal bull *Motu proprio* (1903) of Pius X, new impetus was given to the establishment of *scholae cantorum* in even the smallest churches. The name has also been adopted by certain institutions outside the Church, of which that founded in Paris in 1894 by Vincent d'Indy, Bordes, and Guilmant is the most important. Originally planned as an institution for church music, it developed *c.* 1900 into a general music school with an intensive training program based on Gregorian chant and counterpoint. The name *schola* has come to imply the conservative and academic trends in French music, represented by César Franck and his spiritual successors.

Scholarships, fellowships, and prizes. I. *United States*. Scholarships and fellowships are awards of money granted by institutions or corporations to applicants of unusual ability for further study, research, or composition. A fellowship usually has higher monetary value and represents a greater honor than a scholarship. In awarding scholarships, the applicant's financial need is generally taken into consideration, whereas it usually has no bearing on fellowships.

Scholarships and fellowships fall roughly into two classes: those maintained by funds from a specific bequest (usually bearing the donor's name) and those supplied from a general fund and administered according to prevailing policy or circumstances. The former sometimes contain definite stipulations as to the applicant's qualifications and the use to which the scholarship or fellowship is to be put.

1. Scholarships and student aid. These terms are often used synonymously to designate grants of money for study in the institution granting the awards. A common way of administering such funds is through "tuition scholarships," which take the form of a remission of part or all of the tuition. Unfortunately such a practice has led to abuse in some instances; the granting of tuition scholarships has been only a means of reducing prices to compete with other schools. The fairest method of awarding scholarships is by competition, and this method is used, especially in musical performance, by some of the larger schools.

2. Fellowships. These are granted principally by universities or corporations. Generally they bear a name, have a fixed value, and specify in what field the holder shall work. Most fellowships carry a large enough stipend to enable the holder to live modestly. They are awarded for advanced work in various fields of music— musicology, composition, performance, education, etc. Resident fellowships are given for work in a specific institution, traveling fellowships for work abroad. Most fellowships are granted primarily to enable an advanced student to continue his education.

Full information on scholarships, fellowships, and other grants-in-aid can be secured by writing to the Music Scholarship Chairman of the various colleges and conservatories. Information on fellowships for music study abroad can be secured by writing to the Institute of International Education, New York City. Information on special scholarships not identified with particular institutions is carried regularly in such magazines as *The Music Journal,* the *American Musician, Etude,* and others. The Guggenheim Foundation grants fellowships in composition or in musical research, usually to persons who have passed the student age and have proved their ability. The Fulbright scholarships are given for work outside the United States. There are two categories, one for students to do research, the other for professors to give lectures. The American Academy in Rome offers several fellowships in music, usually granted to young composers of special promise. They require that the candidate reside at the Academy in Rome.

II. *Other countries.* 1. Prix de Rome. Awarded annually (since 1803) by the Académie des Beaux-Arts of Paris after difficult competitive examination, including the composition of a cantata or one-act opera. The first prize consists of a four-year stay in the Villa Medici in Rome; the second is a gold medal. Winners of the "Grand Prix de Rome" have included Halévy (1819), Berlioz (1830), Bizet (1857), Debussy (1884), G. Charpentier (1887), and Florent Schmitt (1900). Ravel was among those who failed to win it. Belgium also has a Prix de Rome, awarded biennially.

2. The most important English prize is the *Mendelssohn Scholarship,* founded in 1847 and awarded annually for composition. It is a cash award. Except for A. S. Sullivan (1856–60) and Eugène d'Albert (1881–82), no outstanding composer appears on the list of the holders [see *GD;* also Sup. Vol.; *GDB*].

3. For the German prizes s.v. "Preise" in Moser's *Musiklexikon.*   E.B.H.

Scholia enchiriadis. See Musica enchiriadis; Theory II, 3.

Schöne Müllerin, Die [G., The Fair Maid of the Mill]. Cycle of twenty songs by Schubert, op. 25, composed in 1823 to poems by Wilhelm Müller.

Schools of music. See Music education in the United States.

Schöpfung, Die [G.]. German title of Haydn's oratorio *The *Creation.*

Schöpfungsmesse [G.]. Haydn's Mass in B-flat (1801), so called on account of the similarity of a theme in the "Qui tollis" with one in his oratorio, *The Creation* [G. *Die Schöpfung*].

Schottische [G.]. A mid-19th-century round dance similar to a slow polka, not to be confused with the much faster *écossaise.* It was also known in England as the "German polka."

Schrammelquartet [G.]. A type of instrumental ensemble, inaugurated in 1877 by the Viennese violinist Johann Schrammel, which became very popular in Vienna and elsewhere for the performance of light music (waltzes, etc.). The original quartet consisted of two violins, clarinet, and guitar; the clarinet was later replaced by the accordion. A Schrammel orchestra is an enlarged ensemble of a similar type.

Schrittmässig [G.]. Measured.

Schübler Chorales. Collection of six chorale preludes by Bach, published about 1747 by Schübler. Four of them are based on arias from cantatas arranged for the organ.

Schuhplattler [G.]. A Bavarian dance in which the dancers slap their knees and soles with their hands. The music is that of the *Ländler* or similar dances.

Schusterfleck [G.]. See under Rosalia.

Schwanda the Bagpiper [Cz. *Švanda Dudák*]. Folk opera in two acts by Jaromir Weinberger (libretto by M. Karesch), produced in Prague, 1927. Setting: fairy tale. The opera, although translated into more than ten languages, is little known in America except for two excerpts, the Polka and the Fugue, which are frequently played in orchestral concerts.

Schwanendreher, Der. Concerto by Hindemith for viola and small orchestra (the only strings used are cellos and basses), composed 1935. The music is a skillful elaboration of four old German songs, in three movements: I. A setting of "Zwischen Berg und tiefem Tal" (*c.* 1500); II. an introduction on "Nun laube, Lindlein, laube" (16th cent.) and a fugato on "Der Gutzgauch auf dem Zaune sass" (by Lemlin, *c.* 1520); III. a set of variations on "Seid Ihr nicht der Schwanendreher?" The name, literally "swan turner," may refer to an organ grinder who had a swan turning on the top of his instrument.

Schwanengesang [G., Swan song]. Schubert's last songs (composed 1828), to seven poems by Rellstab, six by Heine, and one by Seidl, published posthumously by T. Haslinger (Vienna), who chose the title. They are often performed as a song cycle, although they do not properly belong to that category.

Schwärmer [G.]. See under Tremolo I.

Schwebelpfeif [G.]. See under Schwegel.

Schwebungen [G.]. *Beats.

Schwegel, Schwegelpfeife [G.]. Obsolete name for a flute, either transverse or vertical [see also Flute III]. In Poglietti's *Aria allemagna con alcune variazoni* (*c.* 1680; see *TaAM* viii) it appears as *Schwebelpfeif,* meaning a variation in which the quick and high passages of the fife are imitated.

Schweller [G.]. *Swell.

Schwellkasten. Swell box. *Schwellwerk,* swell organ.

Schwingung [G.]. Vibration.

Schwungvoll [G.]. Animated, spirited.

Scialumo [It.]. See Chalumeau (2).

Sciolto [It.]. Easy, unconstrained.

Scordatura [It.]. Abnormal tuning of a stringed instrument in order to obtain unusual chords, facilitate difficult passages, or change the tone color. Scordatura was frequently used in the lute music of the 16th and 17th centuries, the most common procedure being to lower the lowest string from A to G [G. *Laute im Abzug;* It. *bordone descordato;* see *WoHN* ii, 63]. The *Intabulatura de lauto, libro quarto* by J. A. Dalza (Petrucci, 1508) includes two "Pavana alla ferrarese in scordatura," the first in G–c–g–b–e'–a', the second in G–d–g–b–e'–a' (normal tuning: A–d–g–b–e'–a'). A very unusual scordatura, A–e–e–b–e'–g♯', is used for the "Judentantz" in Hans Newsidler's *Ein new künstlich Lautten Buch* (1544; *HAM,* no. 105b; see also *ApNPM,* p. 78). In the early part of the 17th century there virtually was no "normal" tuning for the lute, consequently making it difficult to consider any tuning of this period a scordatura. Often, the particular tuning to be used with a given piece, called *accord [It. *accordatura*], was indicated at the beginning.

Scordatura was also much used in the violin music of the 17th century, particularly by Heinrich von Biber [see *DTO* 11 and 25; the transcriptions are not always correct (see Lit., Schneider)]. His violin sonata, "Surrexit Christus hodie" [*HAM,* no. 238], requires the tuning g–g'–d'–d" (instead of g–d'–a'–e'), whereas a♭–e♭'–g'–d" is required for "Christi Gebet" (*SchGMB,* no. 238). The accompanying example

(beginning of Bach's Suite no. 5 for cello solo) illustrates the notation. The "accord" at the beginning shows that the A-string is to be lowered one tone. The notes indicate not the actual sound but the position of the fingers in the usual manner, and the natural in the signature directs the player always to play g–a–b♭ on the highest string, which actually sounds f–g–a♭. In later music for strings (from Mozart on) the most common instance of scordatura is tuning the lowest string a semitone or whole tone lower in order to increase the range, or a tone higher in order to increase the brilliance of the sound. In Bartók's *Contrasts,* last movement, the violin has sections tuned g♯–d′–a′–e♭″, so that the two tritones can be played on open strings.

Lit.: T. Russel, in *MQ* xxiv; A. Moser, in *AMW* i; M. Schneider, in *ZIM* viii; G. Adler, in *ZIM* ix; E. Lesser, in *AM* iv, nos. 3 and 4; G. Reader, *Thesaurus of Orchestral Devices* [1953], pp. 573ff.

Score [F. *partition;* G. *Partitur;* It., Sp. *partitura*]. I. A notation showing all the parts of an ensemble (orchestra or chamber music) arranged one underneath the other on different staves (full score, orchestral score). A vocal score is the score of a choral work (opera, oratorio) that shows the vocal parts on separate staves but the instrumental parts in a piano reduction. A piano score is the reduction of an orchestral score to a version for piano, on two staves.

Since about the mid-19th century it has been the practice to lay out an orchestral score in the following order, starting at the top of the page: woodwind, brass, percussion, strings. If a harp is used, it is placed immediately above the strings, but should voices and organ also be included, they are written between the harp and strings. In general, the instruments of each group are arranged in order of descending pitch. Following is the arrangement in Brahms' Symphony no. 2:

2 flutes 2 oboes 2 clarinets in A 2 bassoons	Woodwinds
2 horns in D 2 horns in E 2 trumpets in D 3 trombones and bass tuba	Brass
Kettledrums in D and A}	Percussion
Violin I Violin II Viola Cello Double bass	Strings

II. Before *c.* 1225, score arrangement was used exclusively for writing down polyphonic music. All the organa, conductus, and clausulae, i.e., the entire repertory of the schools of St. Martial and Notre Dame, were notated in this fashion. With the development of the motet (*c.* 1225) this arrangement was discarded for part arrangement, in which the parts are notated separately on one or, usually, two facing pages of the book [see *ApNPM,* p. 283]. This method saved space, since there was a great difference in length between the texted upper parts of the

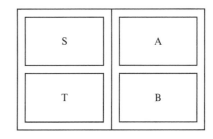

motet and the textless tenor with its few and long notes written in ligatures. The accompanying drawing shows an arrangement of music in four parts as used in the *choirbooks of the 15th and 16th centuries. The choirbook arrangement persisted until the mid-16th century but was gradually superseded by arrangement in *partbooks [G. *Stimmbücher*], i.e., separate books for soprano, alto, etc. The earliest MS partbooks date from *c.* 1480 (Glogauer *Liederbuch). This method was particularly advantageous for printing and, in fact, was almost exclusively employed in the printed books of 16th-century ensemble music, both vocal and instrumental. Solo music (organ, lute), on the other hand, was always written or printed in a scorelike arrangement [see *ApNPM,* p. xx].

Because the large repertory of 13th- to 16th-century vocal music—motets, Masses, secular songs—has survived only in the form of individual parts, one might wonder how musicians could compose such strictly polyphonic and highly complex works (often involving riddle canons and intricate notational devices) without making a score. Obviously they must have used some makeshift scoring, probably writing out sections on a wax tablet, slate, or some other material. Even when parchment or paper was used, the scoring was considered only a sketch without permanent value and therefore was destroyed. The earliest surviving scores date from *c.* 1560.

About 1600 the development of orchestral

music and the acceptance of the thoroughbass led to the general adoption of the score with bar lines (earliest example in Cipriano de Rore's *Madrigali,* 1577). Indeed, one of the largest scores ever written is that of a 54-voice Mass by Benevoli, composed in 1628 for the opening of the new cathedral at Salzburg [*DTO* 20; see Roman school]. Partbook scoring still survives, e.g., in the four volumes containing the parts of Beethoven's string quartets. See R. Schwartz, "Zur Partitur im 16. Jahrhundert" (*AMW* ii); E. Lowinsky, in *JAMS* i, xiii (early scores; cf. *ibid.* ii, 130ff; S. Clercx, in *CP Masson* i.

Score reading. The ability to grasp from a chamber, vocal, or orchestral score the essential features of melodic and harmonic structure and, sometimes, to reproduce these on the piano. This is fairly easy in the case of, e.g., a string quartet of the classical period, where it will often suffice to read the melody part (usually Violin I) and the bass, and to supplement these with the traditional harmonies. Reading a 20th-century string quartet, however, requires much more skill and versatility. Reading an orchestral score becomes even more difficult owing to the use of the old alto and tenor clefs and the transposed notation for numerous wind instruments [see Transposing instruments]. Although precise score reading can be mastered only after long study, the amateur who merely wishes to "follow" a performance with a score can content himself with acquiring facility in glancing quickly over the page and picking out the momentarily leading melody from its general melodic contour and rhythm. See H. Gal, *Directions for Score-Reading* (1924); M. Bernstein, *Score Reading* (1932); H. Creuzburg, *Partiturspiel,* 4 vols. (1956–60).

Scorrendo, scorrevole [It.]. Flowing, gliding.

Scotch snap. See under Dotted notes III.

Scotch (Scottish) Symphony. Mendelssohn's Symphony no. 3, in A minor, op. 56, inspired by a visit to Scotland in 1829. It was begun in Italy in 1830 and finished in Berlin in 1842.

Scotland. The earliest information about music in Scotland is supplied by Giraldus Cambrensis, who in his *Topographia Hibernica* (*c.* 1190) says that "in the opinion of many, Scotland has not only equalled Ireland, her teacher in music, but has . . . surpassed her." The MS Wolfenbüttel 677 (*c.* 1250), the earliest source for the repertory of the school of *Notre Dame [see also "Magnus liber organi"], originally belonged to the mon-

astery of St. Andrews and may have been written for that monastery, since it includes a responsory for its patron saint (f. 18v: "Vir perfecte . . . nos Andrea fac consortes. . . ."). Not until the 16th century are sources of Scottish music encountered, among them a MS known as the "Scone Antiphoner," presently in the Advocates' Library of the National Library of Scotland (Edinburgh), and a MS set of four partbooks known as the St. Andrews Psalter (or Wood's partbooks), now scattered in Edinburgh, Dublin, and London. The former contains Masses, motets, and Magnificats, several of these by Robert Carver, Canon of Carver (1487–after 1546); the latter, dated 1566, contains psalm tunes, Latin motets, and canticles, by Robert Johnson (*c.* 1583–1633), David Peebles (d. 1579), and others. Other composers of this period were Patrick Douglas, of whom a few motets remain in a MS at Christ Church, Oxford, and John Fetny (*c.* 1480–1550). A considerable number of songs, many of them with lute or harpsichord accompaniment, as well as instrumental pieces, mostly pavanes and galliards, survive in various sources [see Editions XXXIV, 15].

The accession of James VI of Scotland to the English throne (James I, 1603) seems to have brought a considerable decline of musical activity in Scotland. Among the few publications of the 17th century are Edward Millar's Psalter of 1635 (Edinburgh) and J. Forbes' *Songs and Fancies 3–5 v. Apt for Voices and Viols* (Aberdeen, 1662, '66, '82). During the 18th century, English ballad operas were introduced in Scotland. An important event was the foundation of the Edinburgh Musical Society, which, from 1725 on, gave regular concerts. Few Scottish composers became famous until the end of the 19th century, when A. C. MacKenzie (1847–1935), J. B. McEwen (1868–1948), and William Wallace (1860–1940) participated in the current revival of music in Britain. Important Scottish composers who, unlike these three, actually worked in Scotland, include David Stephen (1869–1946), Ian Whyte (b. 1901), Cedric Thorpe Davie (b. 1913), and Erik Chisholm (1904–65), settled in South Africa. See Strathspey; Lament (1); Pibroch.

Lit.: H. G. Farmer, *A History of Music in Scotland* (1947); M. Patrick, *Four Centuries of Scottish Psalmody* (1949); D. Baptie, *Musical Scotland: Dictionary of Scottish Musicians from about 1400* (1894); J. Love, *Scottish Church Music* (1891); J. Glen, *Early Scottish Melodies*

(1900); F. Harrison, *Music in Medieval Britain* [1958]; H. G. Farmer, *Music in Mediaeval Scotland* (1930; also in *PMA* 56); *Editions XXXIV, 15; N. Diem, "Beiträge zur Geschichte der schottischen Musik im XVII. Jahrhundert" (diss. Leipzig, 1919); A. Carmichael, *Carmina gadelica,* 5 vols. (1900–54); [H. G. Farmer], "Some Early Scottish Composers" (*MA* ii); J. Beveridge, "Two Scottish 13th-century Songs" (*ML* xx, 352ff); G. Abraham, "Burns and the Scottish Folksong" (*ML* iv, 71ff).

Scriptores [L.]. Abbr. for two important publications of medieval treatises on music: (a) *Scriptores ecclesiastici de musica sacra potissimum,* 3 vols., ed. M. Gerbert (1784; fac. ed. 1931); and (b) *Scriptorum de musica medii aevi nova series,* 4 vols., ed. E. Coussemaker (1864–76; fac. ed. 1963). The collections are usually designated *Gerbert Scriptores* (*GS, G.S.,* or *G.Scr.*) and *Coussemaker Scriptores* (*CS, C.S.,* or *C.Scr.*). Both are indispensable sources for medieval musicological research. The *Gerbert Scriptores* contain chiefly the earliest treatises (9th–11th cent.) and the *Coussemaker Scriptores* those of the 13th and 14th centuries [for partial contents, see Theory]. The contents are given in full in *GD* and *GDB,* together with those of *Musici scriptores graeci,* ed. K. von Jan (1895; sup. vol. 1899), a collection of writings on Greek music.

Scrittura [It.]. Commission to write an opera for the next season, usually granted by an opera company.

Scucito [It.]. Unconnected, *non legato.*

Seashore tests. See under Tests and measurements in music.

Seasons, The. (1) Oratorio by Haydn, composed 1798–1801, with a German libretto (original title: *Die Jahreszeiten*) by G. van Swieten, based on an English poem by J. Thomson. Its four parts portray spring, summer, fall, and winter. (2) Collective title (original, "Le quattro Stagioni") of the first four concertos of Antonio Vivaldi's *Il Cimento dell' Armonia e dell' Inventione,* op. 8, for violin, strings, and continuo. Each concerto is based on a descriptive sonnet.

Sea Symphony. Vaughan Williams' Symphony no. 1 (1910), for solo voices, chorus, and orchestra, based on texts from Walt Whitman's *Leaves of Grass.*

Sea trumpet. Erroneous translation of *tromba marina.*

Sebell. Rare spelling for *cibell.

Secco recitative. See under Recitative.

Sechzehntel [G.]. See under Notes.

Second [F. *seconde;* G. *Sekunde*]. See under Interval.

Seconda prattica [It.]. Term used *c.* 1600 for the then novel style of monody (recitative, aria, opera; see *Nuove musiche*), as opposed to the *prima prattica,* the polyphonic style of the 16th century. Monteverdi, in the preface to Book V of his Madrigals (1605), said that he adopted "seconda pratica, overo perfetione della moderna musica." See also *SSR,* pp. 405ff.

Secondary dominants. See under Dominant (1).

Seconda volta [It.]. See under *Prima volta.*

Seconde rhétorique [F.]. In the 14th and 15th centuries, designation for poetry, as opposed to *première rhétorique,* i.e., prose. All the texts of Machaut's *ballades,* for example, fall under *seconde rhétorique.* See M. Bukofzer, in *MQ* xxviii, p. 33f.

Seelenamt [G.]. *Requiem Mass.

Seelenvoll [G.]. Soulful.

Segno [It.]. A sign in the form of :S: used to indicate the beginning or end of a section to be repeated. In the former case, the indication *dal segno, dal S.,* or *D.S.* appears at the end of the section; in the latter case, *al segno* (to the sign), *sin' al segno* (until the sign), or *fin' al segno* (end at the sign) is stated. See also under *Da capo.*

Segreto di Susanna, Il [It., The Secret of Suzanne]. Opera in one act by E. Wolf-Ferrari (libretto by E. Golisciani), produced (in German) in Munich, 1909. Setting: Piedmont, *c.* 1910.

Segue [It.]. Instruction to the performer to play the following movement without break (*segue l'aria segue la coda*). It may also mean to continue in the same manner, e.g., with a certain pattern of broken chords that is written out in full only at the beginning [see Ex. i under Abbreviations].

Seguidilla. A dance of southern Spain (Madrid, Murcia, Seville, etc.), with a text based on four-line poems (usually 7.5.7.5), whose lines are freely repeated or broken up in actual performance, as well as interspersed with passages played on the guitar. The music is in moderately fast triple meter. In Act I of Bizet's *Carmen* there is a *seguidilla,* which, however, is not typical.

Seikilos Song. One of the few remnants of ancient Greek music, a short song from the 2nd or 1st century B.C. that begins with the words "Hoson zes" (While you live). It is engraved on a tombstone (discovered in 1883), as an epitaph by Seikilos for his wife. Because of the similarity of its melody (perhaps also its first word) to the Gregorian antiphon "Hosanna David" [*LU,* p. 578], it has been cited as evidence that Gregorian chant is derived from ancient Greek music. However, this theory has been almost completely discredited today [see Gregorian chant VII]. The Seikilos Song is shown in *SchGMB,* no. 1; *HAM,* no. 7c; and, together with "Hosanna David," *ReMMA,* p. 115.

Seis [Sp.]. Traditional dance-song of Spanish origin, popular in the Dominican Republic. It uses 6/8 and 3/4 meter alternately, in animated tempo. The text consists of ten-line stanzas [Sp. *décimas*] in eight-syllable verse. It is always sung by a solo singer, either man or woman, to the accompaniment of guitars, but is danced by groups of couples. Yodeling and the use of meaningless syllables is quite common, and the *Phrygian cadence is often used.   J.O-S.

Seises [Sp.]. A group of six (or more) choir boys who perform dances with singing and clapping of castanets before the high altar of the Cathedral of Seville (formerly also in other churches of Spain) on great festival days. The *seises* were established in the 15th century. Victoria, Guerrero, Morales, and others have written music for them, but the music now used is more recent and mediocre in quality. See J. Moraleda y Esteban, *Los Seises de la catedral de Toledo* (1911); J. B. Trend, in *ML* ii, 10; R. H. Stein, "Die Kirchentänze in Sevilla" (*DM* xv, no. 1).

Seiten- [G.]. Side. *Seitenbewegung,* oblique motion. *Seitenthema, Seitensatz,* the second theme of a movement in sonata form, or of other forms.

Sekunde [G.]. Second. *Sekundakkord* [see under Seventh chord].

Semi- [L.]. Half. *Semibiscroma, semibreve* (*semibrevis*), *semicroma, semifusa, semiminima, semiquaver,* see Notes; also Mensural notation. *Semichorus,* half-chorus. *Semidiapente,* diminished fifth. *Semiditonus,* the minor third. *Semiditas,* in mensural notation (*proportions), same as *proportio dupla.*

Semiramide. (1) *Semiramide riconosciuta,* opera in three acts by Gluck (libretto by Metastasio), produced in Vienna, 1748. (2) Opera in two acts by Rossini (libretto by G. Rossi, based on Voltaire), produced in Venice, 1823. Setting (for both): Babylon, legendary times.

Semiseria [It.]. An 18th-century term for an *opera seria* that contained a number of comic scenes.

Semitone. One-half of a whole tone, the smallest interval in traditional Western music. (Smaller intervals are called *microtones.) The octave consists of twelve semitones and the diatonic scale includes two semitones (between e and f, and b and c'). The exact measurement of a semitone varies slightly according to the system of tuning. In equal temperament [see Temperament] each semitone equals exactly 100 *cents, whereas in other systems there are semitones of different sizes. For instance, in the *Pythagorean system the "diatonic" semitone (e–f, b–c'; Gr. *diesis* or *limma,* medieval *semitonus minor*) is equivalent to 90 cents, and the "chromatic" semitone (b^b–b; Gr. *apotome,* medieval *semitonus maior*) to 114 cents. In *just intonation these values are almost reversed, e–f being 112 cents and b^b–b 92 cents.

Semplice [It.]. Simple, unaffected.

Sempre [It.]. Always; e.g., *sempre legato,* always legato.

Senario [It.]. Zarlino's designation for the first six numbers and the ratios between them, 1:2:3:4:5:6. From these he derives all the consonances: octave (2:1), fifth (3:2), fourth (4:3), major third (5:4), minor third (6:5), and major sixth (5:3). See R. W. Wienpahl, "Zarlino, the Senario, and Tonality" (*JAMS* xii).

Senhal [Prov.]. In Provençal poetry, a wordplay whereby a name, usually that of a woman, is concealed in the text. This device was also used in the Italian madrigals of the 14th century, e.g., Landini's *Non a Nnarcisso* (*Anna*).

Senkung [G.]. See under Arsis and thesis.

Sennet (also written *Sennate, Synnet, Cynet,* etc.). In the stage directions of Elizabethan plays, a term meaning that music is to be played. The indication "Trumpets sound a florish, and then a sennate" (Thomas Dekker, *Satiromastix*) calls for a flourish (fanfare) followed by a somewhat longer piece played on brass instruments.

The term is probably derived from sonata [see Sonata B, I]. For a similar term, see Tucket.

Sensible [F.]. The leading tone.

Sentito [It.]. Expressive.

Senza [It.]. Without. *Senza tempo, senza misura,* without strict measure. For *senza sordini,* see Mute.

Sepolcro [It.]. See Sepulchrum play.

Septet. Chamber music for seven players, usually strings and wind mixed. Besides Beethoven's well-known Septet op. 20, there are others by Spohr, Hummel, Saint-Saëns, and Ravel.

Septième [F.], **Septime** [G.]. The interval of the seventh. See Interval.

Septimenakkord [G.]. *Seventh chord.

Septuor [F.]. *Septet.

Septuplet [G. *Septole*]. A group of seven notes played in the time of four or six. Examples occur under proportional designations such as *dupla sesquitercia* (7/3), *tripla hemiolia* (7/2), or *proportio septupla* (7/1), the first two in the late 14th-century Codex Torino, Bibl. Naz. *J. II. 9* [see *WoHN* i, 373ff] and the last in Correa de Araujo's *Libro de Tientos* of 1626 [*Editions XXXII, no. 6, ii, 149].

Sepulchrum play. A medieval play portraying the burial of Jesus. See Liturgical drama. It was revived in the 17th-century *sepolcro,* a special oratorio performed, particularly in Vienna, during Holy Week before a representation of the Holy Sepulchre in the church. See A. Schering. *Geschichte des Oratoriums,* pp. 131ff.

Sequela. Term sometimes used for the preexisting melodies of sequences [see Sequence II C], the term "sequence" being reserved for the combination of these melodies with the text. See Dom A. Hughes, ed., *Anglo-French Sequelae* (1934).

Sequence [G. *Sequenz*]. I. In composition, the repetition in a single part of a short musical phrase at another pitch, usually at the second above or below, more rarely at the third [see Repetition]. A sequence is called *melodic* (or *monophonic*) when the repetition occurs in the melody only (as in monophonic music or when the lower parts are not involved in the procedure); it is called *harmonic* (or *polyphonic*) if similar repetitions occur in all the parts. If the repetitions are made without accidentals (change

of key) the sequence is *tonal* or *diatonic* [Ex. 1a]. This procedure necessarily implies that some of the intervals become larger or smaller by a semitone (minor instead of major third, diminished instead of pure fifth, etc.). If, on the other hand, the intervals of the model are preserved exactly, the sequence is *real* [Ex. 1b; see Tonal and real]. In practice most sequences are of a mixed type called *modulatory* or *chromatic* [Ex. 1c].

In spite of its stereotyped construction, the sequence is highly important as an element of logical continuation. This is particularly true of the tonal sequence (in its exact or slightly modified form), which combines unity of key with variety of intervallic repetition. From the point of view of harmonic analysis, the sequence is interesting because it often produces chordal combinations otherwise not admitted in strict style (diminished fifths, secondary seventh chords, etc.).

Short sequential passages occasionally are found in Gregorian chant, e.g., in a standard cadence of the responsories of mode 8 [Ex. 2a; see "Verbum caro," *LU*, p. 390f], which, like all sequential formations of plainsong, is slightly irregular (note the grouping of the neumes). Very rigid polyphonic sequences are a characteristic trait of the 12th-century organa of St. Martial and of Santiago de Compostela. Usually one part is the inversion of the other [Ex. 2b, from the St. Martial organum *Omnis curet;* cf. a similar passage in *HAM*, no. 27a]. The long coloraturas frequently found in 14th-century madrigals or *caccie* often include sequential passages [see, e.g., *ReMMA*, p. 365]. Imitative sequences appear in the works of Paolo Tenorista [Ex. 2c, from *Tra verdi frondi*] and Johannes Ciconia. In the 15th century, Obrecht

stands out for his masterly handling of the sequence in a large variety of ways. Ex. 2d shows an instance occurring in the Gloria of his *Missa Je ne demande*. The harmonic sequence became an important means of formal development and continuation in many compositions of the 17th to 19th centuries, frequently used in the episodes of the fugue and the development section of the sonata. In the late 18th century mediocre composers made abundant use of an inferior type of sequence known as *rosalia.

II. *Gregorian chant.* A. Origin. The origin of the sequence has been the subject of much study and dispute. [For its relationship to the trope, see under Trope (3).] There is good reason to assume that the sequences originally were long melismas (*melodiae longissimae*) sung without text after the word Alleluia, and that the term *prosa ad sequentia* refers to these purely musical additions. Later these melismas were underlaid with a text, which was called *prosa;* hence the designation *sequentia cum prosa,* i.e., melody with text. An idea of how the sequence originated can be inferred from the report (often misrepresented or, without justification, considered untrustworthy) of Notker (Balbulus), a German monk of St. Gall (*c.* 840–912), who

said that as a young man he had to sing *longissimae melodiae,* which he found difficult to remember. A monk from the monastery of Jumièges (near Rouen) came to St. Gall with a book in which some verses were adapted to the sequences. However, Notker did not find these satisfactory and began to write some of his own. Finally, his teacher, Iso, advised him that it would be best to have only one tone to each syllable of the text. From this it appears that: (1) the sequences were originally without text; (2) the addition of a text (*prosa*) was practiced in northern France *c.* 900; (3) Notker perfected the French method by providing a syllable for each tone of the melisma, so that the *sequentia cum prosa* acquired the fully syllabic style it long retained.

The remainder of this discussion deals separately with the textual and musical aspects of the sequence (hereafter the term will mean sequence *with* text), although in the actual development they are closely interlocked.

B. Text. The sequence texts are long poems in a free style, usually in the form a, bb, cc, dd, ... jj, k; that is, they begin and end with a single line (a, k) between which are a number (four to ten or more) of double-line stanzas. The two lines of each stanza are identical in the number and accentuation of syllables, but usually there is a marked variation from one stanza to the next. For instance, Notker's sequence "Psallat ecclesia" has the following syllabic scheme: 28; 14, 14; 20, 20 [21]; 8, 8; 19, 19; 13, 13; 9, 9; 17 [see *ApGC*, p. 445]. The irregular length of the stanzas and the absence of strict poetic meter suggest Byzantine origin. In fact, a few of the Byzantine *kontakia,* particularly the famous *Akathistos hymn, contain stanzas with similar verse structures. However, the sequence as a species is not derived from the *kontakion,* which has an entirely different form [see Byzantine chant II]. The French sequences, for which the name *prosa was customary, also include a sort of rhyme. In most of them, each line ends on *a* (or *at, am,* etc.), in assonance with the final vowel of "Alleluia." They also often begin with the word "Alleluia," which is rarely true of the German sequences.

C. Music. The music is parallel to the textual structure, there being a single line at the beginning and the end, and repeated lines for each of the double stanzas: a bb cc dd ... jj k. This form is particularly evident in several MSS containing the melodies without text [see *Sequela*]. In these, the first and last section are marked x ($= semel$, once), and the others are marked d ($= duplex$, double). The sequences (and sequelae) often have strange names, such as "Puella turbata" (Disturbed girl), "Cignea" (Swanlike), or "Cithara." In some cases the title refers to the parent Alleluia [see II A above], e.g., "Laetatus sum" (Alleluia Laetatus sum, for the second Sunday of Advent) or "Adorabo" (Alleluia Adorabo, for the dedication of a church). However, the relationship between the sequence melody and the Alleluia melody is by no means wholly clear. In most cases the sequence begins with the phrase for the word "Alleluia" but thereafter it continues freely, without using the melody of the Jubilus and the verse [ex. in *HAM*, no. 16a]. Reconstructions designed to show that the entire sequence is borrowed from the Alleluia are of doubtful validity [see, e.g., *BeMMR*, pp. 84ff].

An interesting trait of many sequences is the use of different ranges and tonal realms in the various sections. Another novelty is the extensive, and often exclusive, use of a rising cadence (f–g) instead of the falling cadence (a–g) that prevails in Gregorian chant.

D. *Later development.* The development of the sequence is usually divided into three phases. The early sequence, described above, was followed about a hundred years later by the "intermediate" sequence. It is characterized by more regular versification, the lines becoming more nearly equal in length, often showing strictly poetic meter (iambic, dactylic) and occasionally employing actual rhyme. The most famous example of this type is the Easter sequence "Victimae paschali laudes," by Wipo of Burgundy (*c.* 1000–50; see *HAM*, no. 16b; *LU*, p. 665f). The third, final stage is the rhymed sequence [G. *Reimsequenz;* F. *proses*], represented mainly by the numerous sequences of Adam de St. Victor (d. 1177 or 1192). Textually, his sequences are indistinguishable from strictly versified hymns of ten, twelve, or more stanzas, and only the musical treatment makes them sequences. Whereas in a hymn all the stanzas are sung to the same melody, Adam gave the first half of each stanza a new melody, the second half being sung to the same melody [see *HAM*, no. 16c]. His sequences thus are in the double-versicle form aa bb cc . . . jj, without single lines at the beginning and end. Although Adam's Latin is admirably elegant, his music is inferior to that of the older sequences. His procedure led to an enormous output of rhymed sequences, which in ensuing centuries threatened to over-

shadow the traditional Gregorian repertory. A drastic step was taken at the *Council of Trent (1545–63), which abolished all but four of these sequences: Wipo of Burgundy's Easter sequence "Victimae paschali laudes" (the only remnant of the older type); the sequence for Whitsunday, "Veni sancte spiritus" (Golden Sequence, attributed to Innocent III, late 12th cent.); Thomas Aquinas' sequence for Corpus Christi, "Lauda Sion" (*c.* 1261); and Thomas of Celano's sequence for the *Requiem Mass, "Dies irae" (*c.* 1200). In 1727 a fifth sequence was adopted for liturgical use, Jacopone da Todi's celebrated *"Stabat Mater." The Christmas sequence "Laetabundus" [see *ZMW* xi, 274ff] is still used in the service of the Dominican monks. Derivatives of the sequence are the *estampie* and the *lai.

E. *Sequence composition.* Sequences appear to have played a considerable role in the earliest days of polyphony. The longest example of organum in the "Musica enchiriadis" of *c.* 900, "Rex coeli Domine" [*HAM*, no. 25b, 2], is a fragment of a sequence [see J. Handschin, in *ZMW* xiii, pp. 113ff], and what may be called the earliest polyphonic composition is based on the sequence "Benedicta sit [see W. Apel, in *RBM* x, p. 134; melody in A. Hughes, *Anglo-French Sequelae*, p. 28]. The 11th-century Winchester Troper contains several two-voice sequences. In subsequent centuries the sequence was used less frequently until Dufay, who composed "Victimae paschali," "Laetabundus," and "Veni Sancte Spiritus" in alternatim form [see under Alternation], one of the double stanzas being in plainsong. From the same period come two settings of "Veni Sancte Spiritus" by Dunstable. A considerable number of sequences are included in the Mass Propers of Isaac's *Choralis Constantinus*. While most of these are in alternatim form, Josquin and other 16th-century composers employed the entire text as the basis for motets [see *HAM*, no. 113, for Willaert's *Victimae*, Pars I; see also *HAM*, no. 299, for a setting of a portion by Jommelli].

Lit. For I: All books on *Harmony; H. A. Mishkin, "The Function of the Episodic Sequence in Baroque Instrumental Music" (diss. Harvard Univ., 1938); M. G. Dann, "Elgar's Use of the Sequence" (*ML*, xix, 255ff); M. van Crevel, "Verwante Sequensmodulaties bij Obrecht, Josquin en Coclico" (*TV* xvi. 107ff).

For II: ApGC, 442ff; G. M. Dreves, ed., *Analecta Hymnita Medii Aevi*, 55 vols. (1886–

1922), vii, l, liii, liv (collection of texts); F. Wolf, *Über die Lais, Sequenzen, und Leiche* (1841); A. Schubiger, ‡*Die Sängerschule St. Gallens* (1858); Dom A. Hughes, ed., *Anglo-French Sequelae* (1934); E. Misset and P. Aubry, ‡*Les Proses d'Adam de Saint-Victor* (1900); C. A. Moberg, ‡*Über die schwedischen Sequenzen* (1927); G. Zwick, ‡*Les Proses en usage à l'église de Saint-Nicolas à Fribourg* (1950); K. Blume, "Vom Alleluja zur Sequenz" (*KJ* xxiv); A. Gastoué, "Sur les Origines de la forme 'sequentia'" (*CP 1906*); H. Spanke, "Aus der Vorgeschichte . . . der Sequenz" (*Zeitschrift für deutsches Altertum und deutsche Literatur* lxxi); *id.*, "Die Kompositionskunst der Sequenzen Adams von St. Victor" (*Studi Medievali*, Nuova Serie, xiv); G. Reichert, "Strukturprobleme der älteren Sequenze" (*Deutsche Vierteljahrsschrift für Literaturwissenschaft* xxiii); E. Jammers, "Rhythmische und tonale Studien zur älteren Sequenz" (*AM* xxiii); H. Husmann, "Sequenz und Prosa" (*AnnM* ii); *id.*, "Die St. Galler Sequenztradition bei Notker und Ekkehard" (*AM* xxvi); *id.*, "Alleluia, Vers und Sequenz" (*AnnM* iv); *id.*, "Notre-Dame und Saint-Victor" (*AM* xxxvi); B. Stäblein, "Zur Frühgeschichte der Sequenz" (*AMW* xviii); L. E. Cuyler, in *JAMS* iii (Isaac).

Sequentia [L.]. Term for sequence, properly one without text; see Sequence II A. For another meaning, see Lesson (1).

Séraphine. See under Harmonium II.

Serenade. Evening music, vocal or instrumental. The former (song of a lover beneath his lady's window) is common in opera (Mozart, Don Giovanni's aria "Deh, vieni alla finestra") and in the song repertory. The opposite is **aubade,* i.e., morning music.

More important is the instrumental serenade, which, losing its "utilitarian" function, developed *c.* 1770 into a purely musical type similar to the *cassation, *divertimento, and *notturno. As a form, the serenade is characterized by a mixture of elements taken from the suite, particularly marches and minuets, and from the sonata. The style likewise is about midway between that of the suite and the symphony. Serenades usually are written for a small ensemble consisting of a limited number of strings and a few wind instruments, as would be suitable for an open-air performance. The most famous examples are Mozart's *"Haffner" Serenade (K. 250) and *Eine kleine Nachtmusik* (K. 525). Others are

by Haydn, Beethoven (op. 8, 25; also op. 41, 42, which are arrangements of the earlier ones), Brahms (op. 16), Dvořák (op. 22, 44), and Elgar (op. 20).

Serenata [It.]. (1) *Serenade. (2) Name for 18th-century short operatic works written to celebrate the birthdays of royal persons (particularly at the Viennese court) and performed (in the evening?) in a reception room with costumes and modest scenery. They might best be described as dramatic cantatas. Well-known examples are Handel's *Acis and Galatea* (1720) and his earlier *Aci, Galatea e Polifemo* (Naples, 1708). A *serenata* by Stradella is reprinted in the Handel Edition, sup. vol. iii.

Serial music. General term describing 20th-century compositions in which the traditional rules and conventions governing all aspects of music—tonality, melody, harmony, rhythm, etc.—are discarded, to be replaced by various new rules and principles. The most general such principle, which radically distinguishes serial music from traditional tonality, is the distribution of structural importance over many (possibly all) elements of musical development, and, as a result, the multiplication of structural characters through their reciprocal "relativization" (and, at the same time, limitation and illumination). The first important attempt to effect such a distribution is represented by generalized asymmetry and nonperiodicity [see section IV].

I. *Origins.* About 1910, numerous composers were experimenting with many different innovations, which nonetheless had one feature in common: they all questioned certain fundamental aspects of the musical language of the West. The works of Arnold Schoenberg in particular attacked the very heart of this language, the tonal structure of harmony. His conclusions have their immediate origin in: (1) the steady increase, in postromantic music, of dissonances, ever less justifiable in the traditional framework, and the more and more frequent use of several successive dissonances chromatically related to one another; (2) a revival of contrapuntal writing, in which the thematic figures, constantly undergoing variation, produce and control the totality of sonorous textures, including elements that had previously been considered only secondary. From these trends sprung new hypotheses that were in flagrant contradiction to the conventions of cadence. In those of his works that are called *atonal (from op. 10 to op. 22), Schoenberg explicitly suspends the traditional harmonic functions. Not content with simply failing to take them into account, he systematically strives to avoid them. This led him to a style based on the most strained dissonances (for his time) and on a generalized chromaticism, which involves the elimination of consonant chords, octaves, and all figures that have a potential for tonal polarization. In his most radical works, such as the op. 16 orchestral pieces and the monodrama *Erwartung,* he succeeds to a large extent in eliminating prolonged rhythmic periodicities, structures with a constant polyphonic density, and motifs with a strong coefficient of repetition—all these being phenomena that confirm tonal organization. One of the most important theoretical concepts Schoenberg formulated at this time was that of generalized nonrepetition. At its extreme, his style produces "sound events," i.e., materials that (for their time) are as discontinuous, as nonformalized, as "concrete" as possible.

II. *Schoenberg's twelve-tone system.* Schoenberg, however, was seeking an organizing principle that could put order into the "chaos" he believed he had created. The result was the *dodecaphonic* or *twelve-tone* system, whose roots lie in his atonal works but which he applied in practice only after a silence of almost ten years (c. 1913–23).

The twelve-tone system consists of using a series of intervals (or tone row; G. *Reihe, Grundgestalt*) involving in turn all twelve tones of the chromatic scale in any order chosen by the composer. No tone may be repeated until the other eleven have appeared. The order of the series remains unchanged throughout the composition except for the following permissible modifications: (1) the octave position of any tone of the series can be changed; (2) in addition to its original form (S) the series is available also in inverted form (S^i), in retrograde form (S^r), and in retrograde inversion (S^{ri}); (3) all four forms of the series can be used in transposition to any step of the chromatic scale, thus making available 48 (12 × 4) modifications. The total development of a composition thus is based on the variations (in rhythm, octave, etc.) of one of these figures, which assumes the role of a "supertheme." The beginning of the Trio from Schoenberg's Suite op. 25 [Ex. a] shows the series of this piece, together with its three basic modifications. The composition begins with four full statements of the series, the third

and fourth in transposition. The continuation is based on three four-tone sections of the series, marked 1, 2, 3. In the series shown here, section 3 is identical (aside from transposition) to its retrograde inversion, 3^{ri}. In the *Klavierstück* op. 33a [Ex. b] measure 1 presents the entire series in three chords of four tones each, and measure 2 uses the same treatment for the retrograde inversion of the series, transposed a semitone down. In the next three measures the *ri*-form of the series appears in the right hand, again divided into three sections, each of which is simultaneously stated by the left hand in its normal form.

The twelve-tone technique was adopted by Alban Berg, who used it intermittently, frequently combining it with methods that are

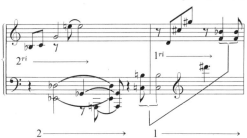

Schoenberg's language has its roots in the music of the 18th and 19th centuries, to which other aspects of his work—e.g., rhythm, phrasing, rhetoric—are more closely related. However, through the very dissonance in his harmony, enhanced by the seemingly contradictory presence of more consonant formations, Schoenberg's music expresses a state of distortion and disintegration that is a remarkable (and typically *expressionist) testimonial to an era of violent crisis.

Other composers who have used the twelve-tone technique are E. Krenek, L. Dallapiccola, W. Fortner, M. Babbitt, and N. Skalkottas.

III. *Webern and serial music.* Well before he adopted the twelve-tone technique, Anton Webern, who with Berg was Schoenberg's principal disciple, carried his master's conclusion even further. Having developed as far as possible the principle of generalized asymmetry, Webern soon defined in his works the principles and requisites for a new harmony, based on the equal harmonic value of all the notes, and, to accomplish this, the pre-eminence of a new kind of chromaticism. Unlike Schoenberg, Webern neither denied nor ignored the polarizing power of the intervals. Instead, he used it in a new, diverging way, giving each sound a maximum presence, specific and irreducible. The nature of the intervals (abundance of major sevenths, etc.) and their arrangement in different octaves thus fulfill a "spreading" function, for it is with these that Webern organizes all other aspects of musical articulation: (a) the variable density and interrupted structure of polyphony; (b) the importance of oblique relations (e.g., interlocking structures); (c) numerous dynamic steps, emphasized by the use of intermittent instrumentation; and (d) rhythmic irregularity, applied to both small and large temporal units, the former emphasized in his earlier works (especially op. 7 to op. 13) and the latter in his later ones.

founded in tonality. In his Violin Concerto (1935) the series is constructed so as to include major and minor triads [Ex. c]. The "vertical" aspect (chord structure) may be just as directly inferred from a series as the "horizontal" aspect (linear structure), but the coordination of these two dimensions poses both theoretical and practical problems.

The twelve-tone method reveals two apparently antithetical tendencies. On the one hand, perpetual utilization of the chromatic total (all twelve tones) manifests the rupture of tonal coherence. In the foreground are those intervals or groups of intervals that are least compatible with tonality. Further, nonrepetition is applied in a very basic way: a note cannot be heard again until the eleven others have appeared (even if only theoretically). On the other hand, the processes used to organize and control the resulting asymmetry, i.e., the variation techniques, necessarily stem from tonal music. Moreover, there is indeed repetition, since the variations are always based on the same source; thus identity takes pre-eminence over difference.

Having carried the search for an absolute asymmetry as far as possible, Webern found symmetry and asymmetry to be not opposites but complementary (a fact classicism recognized when it subordinated one to another, e.g., dissonance to consonance). With this background, Webern turned to twelve-tone serial music. With Schoenberg, the series retains the appearance of a theme, at first always strongly realized and with all else necessarily subordinate to it. With Webern, the series, still the basis for all elements of the composition, is not actual (i.e., not explicit) and so is truly general and generative. No *Ur* or *Grundform,* no version any more "original" than another, no structure is regarded as *the* model series. It is not reducible to a given sequence of twelve notes. Rather, it represents the idea of multiple possible sequences, or better, multiple fields of distribution, at once successive and simultaneous. See Ex. d, showing different forms (in the orthodox sense: retrograde, inversion, transposition) from the series of Webern's Concerto op. 24.

5 (retrograde of 4): b   a   d   c
                      ←   ←   ←   ←

6 (retrograde of 3): c   d   a   b
                      ←   ←   ←   ←

7 (retrograde of 2): d   c   b   a
                      ↑   ↑   ↑   ↑

8 (retrograde of 1): d   c   b   a
                      ←   ←   ←   ←

1. "Original" series (hypothetically) contains four similar groups of three notes: (a) original; (b) retrograde inversion; (c) retrograde; (d) inversion. 2. Retrograde inversion of (1), but also retrograde motion of each group of three notes. 3. Retrograde of (1) transposed a tritone, and also the groups exchanged two by two. 4. Same as (2) but transposed a tritone; also, halves of row exchanged two by two. 5. Retrograde of (4); also inversion of (1); combines operations (2) and (3), i.e., retaining the retrograde of the groups of three notes (2) and the exchange of the groups two by two (3). 6. Retrograde of (3); also transposition at the tritone of (1); combines operations (2) and (4), i.e., retrograde of notes, exchange of halves. 7. Retrograde of (2); the other inversion of (1) a tritone from (5); combines operations (3) and (4), i.e., exchange of groups and of halves. 8. Retrograde of (1); combines operations (2), (3), and (4).

IV. *Post-Webern serial music.* In 1945, a wartime accident put an end to Webern's quest, which he had pursued in almost total isolation. At the same time, young musicians from various countries began to discover, thanks to the postwar resumption of communication, the importance and originality of Webern's contribution. Affected by the atmosphere of the war years, they were still oriented toward relentless criticism of the traditional idioms. Pierre Boulez (b. 1925) was the first composer to take a bold initiative, combining the rhythmic innovations of his master. Olivier Messiaen, with the fruit of the Viennese examples. At a very early stage he took as his principal model the serial techniques of Webern—only to tear them to pieces. Boulez' aesthetic (shared by others of his generation, such as Stockhausen, Berio, and Pousseur, in their own interpretations) is an aesthetic of unpredictability, of irreversible movement, of the pre-eminence of discontinuity, or, musically, of *generalized nonperiodicity* [see Period]. It is as a true generator of asymmetry that the series will function. The stress will be on perpetual variation, whose control, theoretically, is rendered possible by the presence of the row. Applying this to all aspects (pitch, rhythm, dynamics, timbre, etc.) and levels of musical discourse (up to the over-all form), composers will at first attempt to create music in which asymmetry is as general as possible.

Boulez has described the first attempts at generalizing the series, a sort of "zero degree" of musical articulation. The principle of perpetual renewal is at first applied note by note, engendering a music in which each note is distinguished from its neighbors in numerous respects, the lowest notes continually followed by the highest, the shortest by the longest, etc. As all the extremes are rapidly exhausted, the next transformation can only be produced within a more limited field, and so it becomes less and less striking, less and less novel. At the lowest level, the potential for variation is almost entirely exhausted. As it diminishes (e.g., simply in the course of a work's growing longer), there results the danger of monotony and of a static quality. This represents the exact opposite of the sought-after asymmetry and perpetual renewal and is all the more flagrant in that the serial permutations, which are difficult to identify owing to their intricacy, become definable only in terms of chance and probability.

Serial composers aware of these results strive to overcome such problems. Boulez' first book of *Structures* for two pianos (1951–52) already offers the first example of what will later be called a "technique of groups," which consists of treating serially not just isolated notes but entire sections of sonorous material—an entire group of sounds, more or less compact, being opposed to another by this or that *total* character. This naturally presupposes that all the elements making up a group have a particular character in common and present anew a certain degree of relative similarity, recognizability, and symmetry, over and over again.

Thus the present-day—and, no doubt, future—serial composer is concerned with the progressive development of a new synthesis of elements traditionally considered antithetical, a tendency shown in a series of remarkable landmarks, e.g., Boulez' *Le Marteau sans Maître* (1955) and *Pli selon Pli* (1960); Stockhausen's *Zeitmasse* (1956), *Gruppen* (1958), and *Kontakte* (1960); Berio's *Allelujah* I and II (1956; 1956–8) and *Tempi concertati* (1959). This new stage in the history of serial music will manifest itself in the increasing overthrow of taboos (e.g., prohibition of octaves) that serial composers originally felt obliged to establish. All kinds of material—both traditional and wholly new—will come to be used integrally. A number of branches, momentarily diverging, in which musicians of many nationalities are collaborating, have come to enrich the common current. Among them are K. Stockhausen (Germany), H. Pousseur (Belgium), M. Kagel (Argentina), L. Berio, B. Maderna, and L. Nono (Italy), and recently also Stravinsky.

Certain of the serial composers have taken part in investigating highly unusual areas (which the early serialists had initiated), notably that of noise (the accumulation of dissonances), and that of chance, in which some young Americans grouped around John Cage have been working. Noise, which lends itself to extreme differentiation, rich in innumerable "colors," had already been used in instrumental music (e.g., the orchestral masses of Stravinsky's *Le *Sacre du printemps,* the giant percussions of Varèse, the chromatic frictions of Webern's op. 9, no. 5). But it is electronic music, governed by serial methods (although **musique concrete* has undeniably pointed out to it certain paths) that will have the task of fully utilizing noise. [See Aleatory music; Electronic music.] These important lines of research directly affect the techniques of interpretation, conferring on the performer a share of creative responsibility ("open" or "mobile"

forms), a trend whose first signs are implied in Webern's serial treatment.

Research in these fields presumes a solid theoretical background, and serial composers have often relied on modern information and communications theories [see Computer], acoustics and structural linguistics, probability and games theory, the psychology of form, etc. It would seem that a vast system is now beginning to emerge, able to assimilate all the earlier systems that have contributed to its development (including, e.g., the tonal system). If this is true, the theoretical basis for a new and truly collective language will have been found.

Lit.: A. Schoenberg, *Style and Idea* (1950); R. Leibowitz, *Schoenberg and His School,* trans. D. Newlin (1949); R. R. Reti, *Tonality, Atonality, Pantonality* [1958]; E. Krenek, *Music Here and Now* (1939); id., *Studies in Counterpoint Based on the Twelve-Tone Technique* (1940); L. Spinner, *A Short Introduction to the Technique of Twelve-Tone Composition* [1960]; J. Rufer, *Composition with Twelve Notes* [1954]; G. Perle, *Serial Composition and Atonality* (1962); A. Basart, *Serial Music: A Classified Bibliography* (1961); P. Boulez, *Relevés d'apprenti* (1965); id., *Penser la musique aujourd'hui* [1964]; T. W. Adorno, *Philosophie der neuen Musik,* rev. ed. [1958]; K. Stockhausen, *Texte,* 2 vols. [1963, '64]; W. Zillig, *Variationen über neue Musik* [1959]; H. Eimert, *Lehrbuch der Zwölftontechnik* (1952); id., *Grundlagen der musikalischen Reihentechnik* [1964]; H. Pfrogner, *Die Zwölfordnung der Töne* (1953); L. Rognoni, *La Scuola musicale di Vienna* [1966]; W. Kolneder, *Anton Webern. Einführung in Werk und Stil* [1961]; R. Vlad, *Storia della dodecafonia* [1958]; L. Cammarota, *L'Espressionismo e Schönberg* [1965]; R. Leibowitz, *Introduction à la musique de douze sons* [1949]; A. Webern, "Schönbergs Musik," in *Arnold Schönberg* (1912); *Die Reihe* (German ed., 1955—, Eng. ed., 1958—), *passim; Perspectives of New Music* [1962—], *passim; Incontri musicali,* nos. 1–4 (1956–60), *passim;* R. S. Hill, "Schoenberg's Tone-Rows" (*MQ* xxii, 14ff); E. Krenek, "New Developments of the Twelve-Tone Technique" (*MR* iv); G. Perle, "Evolution of the Tone-Row" (*MR* ii); id., "Schönberg's Late Style" (*MR* xiii); id., "The Harmonic Problem in Twelve-tone Music" (*MR* xv); H. Nathan, "The Twelve-Tone Compositions of Luigi Dallapiccola" (*MQ* xliv); R. Erickson, "Krenek's Later Music (1930–1947)" (*MR* ix); W. Wirtz, "The Problem of Notation in the Twelve-Tone Technique" (*MR* vii); M. Babbitt, "Some

Aspects of Twelve-Tone Composition" (*The Score and I.M.A. Magazine,* June, 1955); Z. Lissa, "Geschichtliche Vorform der Zwölftontechnik" (*AM* vii); W. Reich, "Zur Geschichte der Zwölftonmusik" (*CP Orel*).   H.P.

Serinette [F.]. A miniature barrel organ formerly used to teach canaries (*serin*) to sing, through frequent repetition of a tune.

Serpent. See under Cornett; also Brass instruments V (b).

Serse. See *Xerxes.*

Serva padrona, La [It., The Maid as Mistress]. Opera in two acts by Pergolesi (libretto by G. A. Federico), produced in Naples, 1733, as an *intermezzo between the three acts of his serious opera, *Il Prigionier superbo* (The Haughty Prisoner). Setting: Naples, 1733. A delightful miniature employing only three characters, *La Serva padrona* is an important landmark not only in the field of opera [see Comic opera; War of the Buffoons] but in the general development of musical style, anticipating some practices of the later 18th century.

Service. The group of musical settings of the *canticles and other items (Kyrie, Creed, etc.) from the Book of Common Prayer of the Church of England. A morning service consists of "Venite exultemus," *"Te Deum," and "Benedictus," or the alternatives "Benedictus es" [see under "Benedictus Dominus Deus Israel"], "Benedicite," and "Jubilate." The evening service includes the "Magnificat" and "Nunc dimittis," or the alternatives "Cantate Domino" and "Deus misereatur." The Communion service begins with the *Decalogue (or Responses after the Commandments) and/or the *Kyrie, and continues with settings of the Creed, Sanctus, *Benedictus qui venit, *Agnus Dei, and *Gloria in excelsis. Each canticle is traditionally referred to by the original Latin incipit, although all are sung in English. A complete service includes most of the items listed above, usually composed in the same key and therefore commonly referred to by simply the name of the composer and the key, e.g., Ouseley in B minor. In the 20th century, particularly in the United States, many of the canticles have been composed singly rather than as complete or partial services. The terms "short service" and "great service," used chiefly in the 16th and early 17th centuries, refer to the shorter, syllabic style of the former and the richer, contrapuntal style of the latter, with its repetition of textual phrases.

The history of the service proper begins with Christopher Tye (*c.* 1500–*c.* 1572) and Thomas Tallis (*c.* 1505–85). Tye's *Evening Service* and Tallis' *Short Service* are both in the simple homophonic style recommended by Archbishop Cranmer. William Byrd (1543–1623) used the older, polyphonic style in his *Great Service;* in his *Second Short Service with Verses to the Organs* he introduced "verse" or solo passages with organ accompaniment to contrast with the "full" choral passages. Other composers of services before the Commonwealth government were Thomas Morley (1557–1602), Thomas Tomkins (1572–1656), Thomas Weelkes (*c.* 1575–1623), and Orlando Gibbons (1583–1625). It should be noted that the Communion service quickly lost the importance that its model, the *Mass, has always maintained in the Roman Catholic Church, and that interest concentrated on the morning and evening services until the late 19th century.

During the Commonwealth (1642–60) under Oliver Cromwell, the cathedrals were closed, choirs disbanded, organs mutilated, and music books destroyed. During the Restoration, services by men such as William Child (1606–97), Benjamin Rodgers (1614–98), Jeremiah Clarke (*c.* 1673–1707), and John Blow (1648/9–1708) remained conservative. Those by Henry Purcell (*c.* 1659–95) are more progressive but are inferior to his anthems. His *Te Deum* and *Jubilate in D,* for St. Cecilia's Day, 1694, like those of Handel, were written for special festive occasions rather than for the daily services. Such 18th-century composers as William Croft (1678–1727), Maurice Greene (1695–1775), William Boyce (1710–79), John Travers (*c.* 1703–58), Jonathan Battishill (1738–1801), Thomas Attwood (1765–1838), and John Clarke (1770–1836) continued to write better *anthems than services.

Victorian composers, partly influenced by the Oxford movement, which restored the use of the Communion service in parish churches, gave new life to the form by writing independent organ parts. "Venite exultemus" was no longer set for choir but was sung to Anglican chant. Samuel Sebastian Wesley (1810–76), T. A. Walmisley (1814–56), F. A. G. Ouseley (1825–89), and George M. Garrett (1834–97) led the way. The otherwise inferior work of John Stainer (1840–1901) is distinguished by its aptness for the acoustics of St. Paul's Cathedral, London, where he served from 1872 to 1888. Charles Villiers Stanford (1852–1924) made by far the most important contributions of this time. His services, symphonic in conception, are very effectively laid out for choir and organ.

Significant composers of service music in the 20th century include Charles Wood (1866–1926), Edward Bairstow (1874–1946), Harold Darke (b. 1888), Basil Harwood (1859–1949), Henry Walford Davies (1869–1941), John Ireland (1879–1962), Herbert Howells (b. 1892), and Ralph Vaughan Williams (1872–1958), as well as the Canadian, Healey Willan (b. 1880), followed by Edmund Rubbra (b. 1901), Michael Tippett (b. 1905), and Benjamin Britten (b. 1913). Britten's Te Deum in C is built in a most striking manner, using only the C-major triad until it reaches a climax at the words "Holy, Holy, Holy."

Lit.: Dom A. Hughes, "Sixteenth Century Service Music" (*ML* v, 145ff); W. G. Whittaker, "Byrd's Great Service" (*MQ* xxvii, 474ff). See also under Anglican church music; Anthem.

L.E.

Sesqui- [L.]. Prefix used to denote fractions whose numerator is larger by one than the denominator, e.g., *sesquialtera*: 3/2 (one plus one half); *sesquitertia*: 4/3; *sesquiquarta*: 5/4; *sesquioctava*: 9/8; etc. In early music theory these terms were used for either ratios of vibrations (i.e., intervals) or ratios of time values (i.e., *proportions*). For instance, in discussions of the intervals, sesquialtera means the fifth [see Acoustics III], whereas in treatises dealing with proportions it means temporal values corresponding to modern triplet notes (three triplet notes equal two normal notes). The former meaning occurs also in the organ stop "sesquialtera," originally a mixture stop combining the octave with the fifth but usually also including other harmonics, such as the third in various octaves. Another term for sesquialtera is *hemiola.

Sestetto [It.]. *Sextet.

Setzart [G.]. Style of composition.

Seven (Last) Words, The. The seven last words of Christ (compiled from the four Gospels) have occasionally been used as a text for *Passion music, e.g., by Heinrich Schütz (*Die Sieben Worte, c.* 1645), Haydn (1785), and Gounod (*Les Sept Paroles du Christ sur la Croix,* 1855). Haydn's composition, commissioned by the Bishop of Cadiz, is not a choral setting of the text but a series of seven instrumental "sonatas," each to be played after the recitation of one of the "words." It appeared in three versions: first

for orchestra (op. 47), then for string quartet (op. 48, nos. 51–57), and finally for piano (op. 49). See A. Sandberger, in *JMP* x, 45ff. There also is a choral version in the form of a cantata, possibly by Haydn's brother Michael.

Seventh. See under Interval.

Seventh chord. A chord consisting of the third, fifth, and seventh above the fundamental. In a given key there are seven such chords, one on each degree of the scale, e.g., in C major: c–e–g–b (I⁷), d–f–a–c′ (II⁷), e–g–b–d′ (III⁷), etc. By far the most important of these is that on the fifth degree, the so-called dominant seventh: g–b–d′–f′ (V⁷). Each seventh chord is capable of three inversions, according to whether its lowest tone is the third, fifth, or seventh. Shown here are the dominant seventh chord and its three inversions, together with the designations in *harmonic analysis and corresponding German terms.

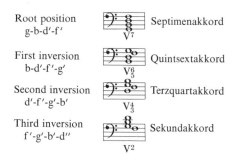

Root position g-b-d′-f′	Septimenakkord V⁷
First inversion b-d′-f′-g′	Quintsextakkord V⁶₅
Second inversion d′-f′-g′-b′	Terzquartakkord V⁴₃
Third inversion f′-g′-b′-d″	Sekundakkord V²

Note that the dominant seventh chord is enharmonically identical with the so-called "German" augmented sixth chord [see Sixth chord], e.g.: g–b–d′–f′ = g–b–d′–e♯′. The natural resolution of the former chord is into the triad on C, and that of the latter into the triad on F-sharp.

While each of the seven "diatonic" seventh chords contains major as well as minor thirds (in various arrangements), there also is an important seventh chord consisting of minor thirds only, the *diminished seventh chord.* It usually appears on the seventh degree of the scale, e.g., b–d′–f′–a♭′ in C (major or minor). The normal resolution of this chord is into the tonic triad (c′–e′–g′). On account of its dominant character, it is frequently called a dominant ninth chord (g–b–d′–f′–a♭′) with the root (g) omitted. Owing to its equidistant construction, any of its tones can be considered the home tone, so that a single chord may serve as a dominant to four different keys. In each case the chord must, of course, be written differently, as shown in Ex. 1. Still other resolutions result from the fact that the chord can also be interpreted as the seventh chord of the raised supertonic, as in Ex. 2. Owing

to its protean nature the diminished seventh chord is frequently used for quick modulation into far-distant keys, e.g., from G into C-sharp [Ex. 3]. See Harmonic analysis III; Ninth chord.

Sext. (1) The fifth canonical hour; see Office. (2) German term (also *Sexte*) for the interval of the *sixth. *Sextakkord,* see under Triad.

Sextet [F. *sextette, sextuor;* G. *Sextett;* It. *sestetto;* Sp. *sexteto*]. Chamber music for six performers, in various combinations, e.g., two violins, two violas, and two cellos (Brahms, op. 18, op. 36; Dvořák, op. 48), string quartet and two horns (Beethoven, op. 81b), two clarinets, two horns, two bassoons (Beethoven, op. 71), etc. A vocal sextet is a composition for six singers with or without instrumental accompaniment.

Sextolet [F.; G. *Sextole;* It. *sestina;* Sp. *seisillo*]. A group of six notes played in the time of four ordinary notes. There should be a clear indica-

tion in writing as to whether the six notes are meant to form three groups of two each, or two groups of three each.

Sfoggiando [It.]. Ostentatiously.

Sforzando, sforzato, abbr. *sf, sfz* [It.]. Forcing, i.e., with a sudden strong accent on a single note or chord. *Sfp, sforzando* followed immediately by *piano.*

Shake. Older name for the trill. For closed and open shake, see under Grace. A shaked beat is a repeated lower appoggiatura; a shaked cadent is a repeated *Nachschlag.*   P.A.

Shakers, music of the. See E. D. Andrews, *The Gift to Be Simple* [1962].

Shakuhachi [Jap.]. See under Japan; for ill. see under Flute.

Shamisen [Jap.]. See under Japan; Lute.

Shank. See under Wind instruments IV (b).

Shanty, chanty, chantey. Names for work songs of English and American sailors, sung while pulling ropes or performing other work requiring concerted effort. Well-known shanties are "The Wide Missouri," "The Banks of Sacramento," and "The Rio Grande."

Lit.: F. Rickaby, *Ballads and Songs of the Shanty-Boy* (1926); J. C. Colcord, *Songs of American Sailormen* (1938); R. R. Terry, *The Shanty Book,* 2 vols. (1921, '26); W. M. Doerflinger, ed., ‡*Shantymen and Shantyboys* (1951); F. P. Harlow, *Chanteying Aboard American Ships* (1962); S. Hugill, *Shanties from the Seven Seas* (1961); R. R. Terry, in *ML* i, 35ff, 256ff; *id.,* in *PMA* xli; H. Whates, in *ML* xviii, no. 3.

Shape-note. See Fasola.

Sharp [F. *dièse;* G. *Kreuz;* It. *diesis;* Sp. *sostenido*]. A musical note or tone one-half step higher than the tone named, indicated by the sign ♯. For its origin and use in early music, see Accidentals II. In the notation of the 16th to 18th centuries the sharp frequently occurs in a diagonal position [see Accidentals II]. The term "sharp" also was used to mean the "sharped," i.e., the major third of a key. For instance, Burney used the term "key E-sharp" in the meaning of "key E major," and Beethoven inscribed his Leonore Overture no. 1, op. 138 (in C major) "Ouverture in C♯." Foreign terms for C-sharp, etc., are given under Pitch names.

Shawm [F. *chalemie;* G. *Schalmei;* It. *piffaro*]. See under Oboe family III.

Shéhérazade. Song cycle by Ravel (to poems by T. Klingsor, inspired by the *Arabian Nights*), composed in 1903 and containing three songs: "Asie," "La Flûte enchantée," and "L'Indifférente." See also *Scheherazade* (Rimsky-Korsakov).

Sheng. A Chinese mouth organ that consists of a bowl-shaped wind chest (originally a gourd or calabash, today made of wood) into which a number of bamboo pipes (12–17) are inserted, arranged in the form of a circle. The pipes are fitted with free reeds made of metal, set in motion by inhalation or, less often, exhalation through a mouthpiece fitted to the wind chest. Not all of the pipes speak, i.e., have reeds; typically, 13 of a set of 17 speak. Each pipe has a small hole, just above the edge of the wind chest, that the player must cover for the pipe to sound. The player holds the instrument cupped in both hands, enabling him to cover several holes at the same time. The music, consisting of chords, usually moves in parallel fifths or triads. [Ex. in R. Lachmann, *Musik des Orients* (1929), p. 108.] The sheng is thought to be the oldest free-reed instrument. See ill. under Wind instruments.

Shift. Movement in violin playing; see Position (2).

Shimmy. A type of dance music popular in America after World War I. It was like a fast fox trot, danced with shaking movements of the shoulders or entire body. Hindemith was one of several German composers who used the dance in art music, in his *Suite 1922,* op. 26, for piano.

Shivaree. U.S. corruption of *charivari.

Sho. Japanese name for *sheng. See E. Harich-Schneider, in *MQ* xxxix.

Shofar. An ancient Jewish instrument made from a ram's horn and used to the present day in Jewish rites for the celebration of the New Year. It has no separate mouthpiece and produces only two crude and awe-inspiring sounds, roughly corresponding to the second and third harmonic. See H. Avenary, "Magic . . . of the Old-Hebrew Sound-Instruments" (*Collectanea Historiae Musicae* ii [1956], 21ff.

Short octave. A special arrangement of the keys in the lowest octave of early organs, harpsichords, etc. The fact that the lowest chromatic tones (C♯, D♯, F♯, G♯) were almost never needed in keyboard music prior to *c.* 1700 naturally led to the omission of the corresponding pipes or strings, a procedure that was particularly desirable in view of the great cost of the large organ pipes. On the keyboard, instead of omitting the four corresponding black keys, the keys for the remaining eight tones were arranged in a "shortened" octave that extended only to the key normally occupied by E. The keys for the tones F, G, A, B♭, and B were usually left in their normal position, and the three remaining keys (normally E, F♯, G♯) were allotted to the tones C, D, and E in arrangements such as

	(a)				(b)			
Black	C	D	B♭		D	E	B♭	
White	E	F	G	A	B	C	F	G A B

An additional advantage of this arrangement was that it enabled playing certain widely spaced chords, e.g., E–B–e–g♯, with the left hand alone [see Fitzwilliam Virginal Book, i, xviif and 287]. As a matter of fact, in arrangement (b) this chord is produced by the keys G♯ B e g♯, which are within easy reach. The often discussed tenth E–g at the end of J. S. Bach's Toccata in E minor for harpsichord does not support Spitta's and Schweitzer's contention that this toccata is an organ piece (the theory being that the low E calls for the organ pedal), since it can easily be played with the left hand on the short octave (b). Similar widely spaced chords occur in the works of Froberger and other early keyboard composers. A later (19th-century) arrangement on pianos was the *broken octave.* Here the lowest octave was complete with twelve keys, except that C♯ was replaced by the more useful note A₁ from below. See also Pedal piano. See *GD* v, 92ff (spinet); *GDB* vi, 296 (organ); G. Kinsky, in *ZMW* ii.

Short service. See under Service.

Si. See under Pitch names; Solmization.

Siam. See Thailand.

Siciliana, siciliano. A 17th- and 18th-century dance of Sicilian origin, in very moderate 6/8 or 12/8 meter, usually with a flowing broken-chord accompaniment and a soft, lyrical melody with dotted rhythms—very similar if not identical to the *pastorale. A characteristic trait is the Neapolitan sixth (flattened supertonic) at cadences. The *siciliana* occurs as a slow movement in early sonatas (Corelli, Bach, Padre Martini) as well as in vocal music (operas, cantatas) whenever gentle pastoral scenes are to be represented musically.

Side drum. Same as snare drum; see Percussion instruments B, 1.

Siegfried. See *Ring des Nibelungen, Der.* *Siegfried Idyll* is the scene (Act II) frequently played in symphonic concerts.

Siegfried Idyll. A composition for small orchestra by Wagner, composed in 1870 and first performed in his home at Triebschen (hence also called *Triebschen Idyll*) on the birthday of his wife, Cosima. The title refers to their son, Siegfried, then just over one year old. It is based on themes from Wagner's opera *Siegfried* but also includes the cradle song "Schlaf, Kindchen, schlaf" (Sleep, baby, sleep).

Sight. In English 15th-century treatises, a term indicating the ranges and permissible intervals of the voice-parts added above a plainsong, primarily in connection with improvised counterpoint. There are "three degrees of discant: meane, treble, quatreble," beginning respectively a fifth, eighth, and twelfth above the tenor. The meane comprises the consonant intervals (third, fourth, fifth, sixth, octave) between 3 and 8, the treble those between 5 and 13, and the quatreble those between 8 and 15. A secondary meaning of the term involves transposition. Some writers give examples in which the added voice (meane) is written a fifth lower than it

should sound [see Ex.; tenor in black notes]. This method may have been used for instruction and also because the sights, particularly the higher ones (treble, quatreble), could be conveniently written on the same staff as the tenor. Alternate names are *discantus visibilis, fictus visus,* and *perfectio ocularis.* See M. F. Bukofzer, *Geschichte des englischen Diskants* (1936), pp. 22ff and *passim;* S. W. Kenney, in *MQ* xlv, 36ff.

Sight-reading, -singing [F. *à livre ouvert;* G. *vom-Blatt-Spiel;* It. *prima vista*]. I. The ability to read and perform music at first sight, i.e., without preparatory study of the piece. This type of playing makes entirely different demands on the performer from those of ordinary finished playing. In fact, from the technical as well as the psychological point of view, it is its very opposite, so that accomplished pianists and virtuosos are frequently very poor at sight-reading. Unfortunately, this may be true not only of concert pianists, who can, perhaps, afford to neglect sight-reading, but also of numerous students and amateurs, who would benefit greatly from facile sight-reading. This is no doubt a serious fault of their present musical education; indeed, many music teachers do not realize the importance of sight-reading.

The problems of sight-reading differ somewhat in various areas of musical activity. Sight-singing, for example, involves elements of association, habit, memory, theoretical understanding, and imagery, which must be learned over a period of time. In recent years this basic study has been emphasized in a number of music schools where it is taught under the name *solfège. An important means of obtaining facility

in sight-singing is ensemble participation. There has been a considerable movement to facilitate sight-singing by the use of *solmization systems in place of ordinary musical notation. Methods such as the English *Tonic sol-fa avoid many of the complications inherent in traditional musical notation (clefs, signatures, accidentals, etc.), but they restrict the student to a limited field of music, whereas familiarity with ordinary notation opens to the student the entire field of music, choral as well as instrumental and orchestral.

II. The situation of the violinist is similar to the singer's since his music is likewise largely restricted to melodic progression in one line. As in singing, the facility of grasping immediately the significance of intervals and of rhythmic figures is prerequisite for playing at sight. As in singing, ensemble performance is very important.

III. The pianist's sight-reading problems are considerably greater, owing to the greater complexity of piano music. The greatest enemy of sight-playing is playing from memory, which, although today considered indispensable for any "finished performance"—with dubious justification, incidentally—causes the player to rely on memory and on looking at his fingers. In sight-reading, however, the player is expected to rely not on his memory but on his faculty of rapid perception; moreover, his eyes must be fixed not on his hands but on the music. Proficiency of sight-reading therefore depends on a student's ability to guide his fingers by the sense of touch. Simple exercises, such as playing an octave, a fifth, a triad, or a seventh chord without looking at the keys will gradually give the feeling of tactile security that is both the basis of sight-playing on the piano and an important factor in piano playing in general [see Piano playing IV].

Still greater are the intellectual demands of playing chamber or orchestral music from a score. See Score reading.

Lit.: R. W. Ottman, *Music for Sight-Singing* (1956); A. I. McHose and R. N. Tibbs, *Sight-Singing Manual,* rev. ed. (1947); S. Berkowitz, G. Fontrier, and L. Kraft, *A New Approach to Sight Singing* [1960]; A. Fish and N. Lloyd, *Fundamentals of Sight Singing and Ear Training* (1964); W. G. McNaught, "The Psychology of Sight-Singing" (*PMA* xxvi); H. Lowery, "Recent Researches in Score-reading" (*Hinrichsen's Year Book,* 1947–48); M. Vidor, "Musical Notation in the Light of Psychology" (*MR* i, no. 3); F. Clark, L. Goss, and D. Kraehenbuehl,

"Reference Book for Piano Teachers," pp. 80–86 (The New School for Music Study, 1963).

rev. K.N.

Signal. See Fanfare; Military music.

Signature. Signs placed at the beginning of a composition, indicating the key [see Key signature] or meter [see Time signatures].

Signet. *Sennet.

Silence [F.]. Rest.

Sillet [F.]. Nut (of the violin).

Similar motion. See Motion.

Simile, simili [It.]. Indication to continue "in the same way," e.g., with the same kind of bowing, or with the same type of broken-chord figure, etc.

Simon Boccanegra. Opera in three acts and a prologue by Verdi (libretto by F. M. Piave, rev. by A. Boito, based on a play by A. Gutiérrez), produced in Venice, 1857; rev. version in Milan, 1881. Setting: Genoa and environs, mid-14th century.

Sin al fine (segno) [It.]. Until the end (sign). See *Segno.*

Sincopa [It.]. *Syncopation.

Sincopas. See *Cinque-pace.*

Sinfonia. (1) [It.]. Symphony. (2) A name chosen by Bach for his three-part *inventions.

(3) In the baroque period (1600–1750), name for orchestral pieces of Italian origin, designed to serve as an introduction to: (a) an opera or operatic scene (Monteverdi, *Orfeo,* 1607, and *L'Incoronazione di Poppea,* 1642; S. Landi, *Il Sant' Alessio,* 1634 [see *HAM,* no. 208; *RiHM* ii.2, 255, 263]; M. A. Rossi, *Erminia sul Giordano,* 1633); (b) an orchestral suite (S. Rossi, *Sinfonie e gagliarde,* 1607, '08; J. J. Löwe von Eisenach, *Synfonien, Gagliarden, Arien,* 1658; J. Rosenmüller, *Sonate da camera cioè Sinfonie Alemande, Correnti,* 1670; J. J. Fux, *Concentus* [see *DTO* 47]); or (c) a cantata (e.g., two cantatas by Provenzale [see *RiHM* ii.2, 385f]; Bach, *Christ lag in Todesbanden*). Bach also wrote a sinfonia for harpsichord, in his Partita no. 2.

No fixed form or style attaches to these pieces. In this period, "sinfonia" is simply one of various names used for an introductory instrumental piece [see Overture], others being sonata, toccata, etc. On the other hand, independent canzonas and sonatas were also designated "sinfonia." Possibly the term had the connota-tion of orchestral performance, not necessarily implied by the others. Not until *c.* 1690 did the operatic sinfonia become standardized (by A. Scarlatti; for later ex., see *HAM,* no. 259, *La Griselda,* 1721) into what is usually called "Italian overture" [see Overture], one of the ancestors of the modern symphony. Examples of 17th-century sinfonias are in *SchGMB,* nos. 151, 191, 211, 220, 223, 224, 229. The last of these shows the merging of the sinfonia with the trio sonata. For an unusually early example of "symphonia" (15th cent.), strikingly similar in style and form to the Toccata in Monteverdi's *Orfeo,* see *RiHM* ii.1, 42 and 207ff.

Sinfonia concertante [It.]. Term used by Mozart and others for a symphony with one or more solo instruments.

Sinfonie pastorale. See Pastoral Symphony.

Sinfonietta [It.]. A small symphony, usually also for a smaller orchestra.

Sinfonische Dichtung [G.]. *Symphonic poem.

Singakademie [G.] A society for concert-giving founded at Berlin in 1791 by C. F. C. Fasch. Today it is mainly known through its concert hall.

Singing. I. Singing is no doubt the most widespread kind of music-making, being the only one (besides whistling) that does not depend on an instrument. The human vocal apparatus can be used in very different ways, depending in part on anatomic differences among various peoples (European, Asian, African) and, even more important, on differences in training and taste. Even in Western music history the "timbre" of the voice has not remained the same. There is reason to believe that the singers of ancient Gregorian chant preferred a somewhat nasal timbre (still frequently heard in churches). The strikingly high range of much 14th- and 15th-century music is accounted for by the extensive use of *falsetto. The celebrated *castrati* of the 17th and 18th centuries probably possessed a vocal timbre that few today would consider ideal. About 1800 the purity and brilliance of *bel canto* were abandoned in favor of the expressive, dramatic voice generally favored today. However, the deliberately unexpressive *Sprechstimme* and the special manners of singing used in modern jazz once more demonstrate the variability of vocal timbre.

II. An infinitely greater variety exists in details of style and performance. Particularly noteworthy is the ample use made, from pre-Christian times through the 17th century and later, of *vocalization. The singing of Gregorian chant involved numerous ornaments, such as *vibrato, *tremolo, and *portamento, some of which were indicated by special neumatic signs [see Neumes]. In the 13th century, Magister Lambert (probably the same as Pseudo-Aristotle) tells us that the *plica, a derivative of "liquescent" neumes, is to be performed "by the partial closing of the epiglottis combined with a subtle repercussion of the throat" [CS i, 273a]. Similarly, some writers hold that the Jewish word "alleluia" originated as a phonetic formation derived from trilling the tongue against the roof of the mouth (1–1–1), a vocal technique still widely used in Asia. Among the most striking features of early vocal music, Gregorian as well as polyphonic, is the seeming indifference to correct underlaying of the text, frequently leading to wrong accentuation. In many cases, however, this procedure was not the result of indifference but of principles contrary to those of modern singing but nonetheless aesthetically valid [see Text and music].

III. Vocal ranges also have varied greatly. Although there presumably always have been voices of high, medium, or low range, in early music they were not exploited to nearly the extent they are today. The average range (ambitus) of Gregorian chant is from c to e′, i.e., the range of the tenor voice. Nearly all 13th-century polyphonic music is within this range in all parts (usually three), while in many compositions of the 14th century (Machaut, Landini) the vocal part goes up to c″ and in the early 15th century (Dufay) to f″, calling for the use of falsetto, even though the actual pitches were about a third below the written ones, because of the lower standard of pitch then in use. A noteworthy contrast to the generally high pitch employed in this period is provided by a few exceptionally low-pitched compositions, e.g., Solage's "Fumeux fume," with an over-all range from E to d, and Binchois' "Beata nobis," with an over-all range from G to f. About 1450, with the rise of the *Flemish school, an important change took place, the texture of polyphonic music being separated into four distinct ranges, corresponding to bass, tenor, contralto, and mezzo-soprano. Since practically all music surviving from this period is sacred, it was performed by men exclusively, perhaps occasionally with boys singing the highest part. Even in the secular repertory of the Middle Ages and

Renaissance there is nothing to indicate performance by women, aside from rare pieces like the liturgical drama of the Resurrection (c. 1100), which includes a dialogue between the Angel and the women watching Christ's tomb [see SchGMB, no. 8]. The rise of opera in the 17th century brought about a decisive change, the various roles now being given to voices of appropriate range. The leading hero (primo uomo) was a castrato, the leading heroine (prima donna) a high soprano, the secondo uomo a bass, and the seconda donna a contralto—a scheme that, of course, was sometimes modified [see Prima donna].

IV. In the 19th century began the "scientific" study of the vocal apparatus and of singing. Manuel Garcia (1805–1906) laid the foundation for this study in his Mémoire sur la voix humaine, which he presented to the French Academy of Sciences in 1840 and which was followed in 1847 by his Traité complet de l'art du chant. Among his pupils were Jenny Lind, Mathilde Marchesi de Castrone, Julius Stockhausen, and others, who in turn taught later generations of celebrated singers. Garcia's scientific studies were continued by Lilli Lehmann and Mathilde Marchesi. In the last analysis, however, such studies have benefited the physiologist more than the singer. Most singing teachers prefer to depend on practical experience and personal influence.

For more details about the technical aspects of voice production, see Voice. Related articles: Voices, range of; Register (2); Bel canto; Castrato; Falsetto; Vocalization; Solfège; Song; Tremolo; Vibrato; Text and music; Vocal music; Word painting.

Lit. A. Historical: H. Pleasants, The Great Singers (1966); D. Stevens, A History of Song [1960]; P. A. Duey, Bel Canto in Its Golden Age (1951); C. L. Reid, Bel Canto; Principles and Practices (1950); W. J. Henderson, Early History of Singing (1921); id., The Art of Singing (1938); Gabriele Fantoni, Storia universale del canto (1873); H. Biehle, Die Stimmkunst, i (1931); T. Gérold, L'Art du chant en France au XVIIe siècle (1921); E. R. M. Hoegg, Die Gesangskunst der Faustina Hasse (1931); B. Ulrich, "Über die Grundsätze der Stimmbildung 1474–1640" (diss. Berlin, 1910); P. Marquardt, "Der Gesang und seine Erscheinungsformen im Mittelalter" (diss. Berlin, 1936); H. Biehle, "Die aesthetischen Grundlagen der französischen Gesangskunst im 17 und 18 Jahrhundert" (ZMW xii); F. Chrysander, "Lodovico Zacconi als Lehrer des Kunstgesanges" (*VMW* vii); H. J. Moser, "Aus der Geschichte der deutschen Gesangskunst" (*CP 1939*); N. Fortune, "Italian 17th-Century Singing" (*ML* xxxv, 206ff).

B. *Practical:* W. Vennard, *Singing, The Mechanism and the Technique* (1964); A. Rose, *The Singer and the Voice* [1962]; V. A. Fields, *Training the Singing Voice* (1947); V. A. Christy, *Foundations in Singing* (1965); Lotte Lehmann, *More Than Singing* [1945]; S. Kagen, *On Studying Singing* [1950]; D. Dossert, *Sound Sense for Singers* [1932]; W. S. Drew, *Voice Training* (1924); P. M. Marafiotti, *Caruso's Method of Voice Production* (1922); W. Shakespeare, *The Art of Singing* [1910]; D. C. Taylor, *The Psychology of Singing* (1908); B. Coffin, *Singer's Repertoire,* rev. ed. (1960).

C. *Scientific:* R. Luchsinger and G. Arnold, *Voice, Speech, Language* (1965); V. E. Negus, *The Mechanism of the Larynx* (1928); R. Curry, *The Mechanism of the Human Voice* (1940); J. Tarneaud, *Traité pratique de phonologie et de phoniatrie* (1961).

Singing saw. An ordinary handsaw, held between the knees and set in vibration by either a violin bow or drumsticks. Its special effect is a gradual modification of pitch (similar to the *portamento of the violin) obtained by bending the free end of the blade with the left hand. The instrument has been used in jazz and other popular music.

Singing school. See under United States.

Singspiel [G.]. About 1700, the German equivalent for *dramma per musica* (drama with music), i.e., opera, applied alike to serious and comic operas (e.g., Keiser's *Croesus,* 1710). Later (c. 1750) the term was restricted to comic operas with spoken dialogue, written on the models of the English *ballad opera or the French *opéra comique.* Charles Coffey's ballad operas, *The Devil to Pay* (1728) and *The Merry Cobbler* (1735), were translated by C. F. Weisse (*Der Teufel ist los* and *Der lustige Schuster*) and then set to new music by J. C. Standfuss (c. 1750). J. A. Hiller (1728–1804) wrote operas to the same two librettos and many others (*Lisuart und Dariolette,* 1766; *Die Jagd,* 1770), representing the high point of the Leipzig Singspiel. From Leipzig the movement spread elsewhere, chiefly to Berlin and Vienna. Most of the members of the *Berlin school wrote Singspiele, notably Georg Benda (*Der Jahrmarkt,* 1775; see *DdT* 64). In Vienna, where as early as 1751 the young

Haydn wrote *Der krumme Teufel* (lost; see *DTO* 64), the Singspiel reached its artistic peak in Mozart's *Die Entführung aus dem Serail* (1782). Other important examples are Ignaz Umlauf's *Die Bergknappen* (1778; *DTO* 36), Dittersdorf's *Doktor und Apotheker* (1786), Johann Schenk's *Der Dorfbarbier* (1796; *DTO* 66), and Schubert's *Die Zwillingsbrüder* (1819). As a distinctive national type of popular opera, the Singspiel played somewhat the same social role in Germany as the *opéra comique* in France and the ballad opera in England. Also, the romantic character of many of the librettos, especially in North Germany, made the Singspiel one of the principal ancestors of German romantic opera.

Operatic works with spoken dialogue were written as early as the 17th century, e.g., S. T. Staden's *Seelewig* (1644; see *MfM* xiii, nos. 4, 5, 6) and J. W. Franck's *Die drey Töchter Cecrops* (1679; see *AMF* iv). Also see Opera VII; Comic opera II E.

Lit.: H. M. Schletterer, *Das deutsche Singspiel* [1863?]; H. Graf, *Das Repertoire der öffentlichen Opern- und Singspielbühnen in Berlin seit dem Jahre 1771* (1934); G. Calmus, *Die ersten deutschen Singspiele von Standfuss und Hiller* (1908); O. Beer, *Mozart und das Wiener Singspiel* (1932); R. Krott, *Die Singspiele Schuberts* (1921); R. Eitner, in *MfM* xiii (*Seelewig*); G. Schmidt, in *AMF* iv (*Cecrops*); W. Stauder, in *AMF* i (J. André); P. Nettl, in *ZMW* vi (*Singballett*); V. Helfert, in *ZMW* v (Viennese Singspiel); F. Brückner, in *SIM* v (Benda).   D.J.G.

Sinistra [It.]. Left (hand).

Sink-a-pace, sinqua-pace. *Cinque-pace.*

Sirvente(s) [Prov.]. A type of troubadour poetry dealing not with love but with political events, questions of morals, etc. According to the *Doctrina de compondre dictatz,* they borrowed their verse structure and melody from some chanson. The only example preserved with music is Peire Cardenal's "Un Sirventes novel."

Sistine choir (chapel). The present name of the papal choir of thirty-two singers who provide the music for services in which the Pope officiates in person. It developed from the ancient *schola cantorum* and received its present name from the *Cappella Sixtina,* the chapel built by Pope Sixtus IV in 1471–84. Since 1480 another choir has existed, the *Cappella Giulia* (richly endowed by Pope Julian II), which performs at St. Peter's and has often been mistakenly called Sistine choir. Both bodies have been greatly admired for the excellence of their vocal technique, involving long crescendos and decrescendos and numerous refinements. However, their performances of Palestrina, etc., are historically incorrect, laden with romantic sentimentality and much inferior to those of other bodies, such as the *Schola Cantorum* of Paris.

Lit.: F. X. Haberl, *Die römische "Schola Cantorum"* (1887; also in *VMW* iii); R. R. Terry, in *MA* iii; E. Celani, in *RMI* xiv; K. Weinmann, in *AMW* ii; R. Casimiri, "I Diarii Sistini" (*Note d'Archivio* i, iii, iv, ix–xvii).

Sistre. Same as cistre. See under Guitar family.

Sistrum. An ancient Egyptian rattle used in the worship of Isis. It consisted of a handle and a horseshoe-shaped metal frame with loose crossbars that rattled when the instrument was shaken. Often, the rattling noise was augmented by loose metal disks strung along the cross-bars. Similar instruments, in the shape of a U, were used in Sumeria, perhaps as early as the third millennium B.C. [For ill. see under Percussion instruments.]

Sitar. See under India VIII.

Sitole. Same as cistre, etc. See under Guitar family.

Six, Les [F.]. A name applied in 1920 to a group of six French composers—Louis Durey, Arthur Honegger, Darius Milhaud, Germaine Tailleferre, Georges Auric, and Francis Poulenc—who c. 1916 formed a loose association based on their acceptance of the aesthetic ideals of Erik Satie. Although their individual styles differed considerably, they all opposed the vagueness of impressionism and endorsed the simplicity, clarity, and other characteristics of the then dawning *neoclassic movement. They found an eloquent advocate in Jean Cocteau. An earlier group, called *Les Nouveaux Jeunes,* included A. Roland-Manuel but not Durey and Milhaud [see N. Slonimsky, *Music Since 1900,* rev. ed. (1949), pp. 181, 201]. A later group of a similar kind was the *École d'Arcueil. See S. M. Trickey, "Les Six" (diss. North Texas State College, 1955); E. Vuillermoz, in *MM* i; R. Manuel, in *MM* ii; V. Rašín, "'Les Six' and Jean Cocteau" (*ML* xxxviii, 164ff); also D. Milhaud, *Notes Without Music,* ed. R. H. Myers, trans. D. Evans (1953).

Six-four chord. The second inversion of the triad, e.g., g–c'–e', indicated I$^6_4$, II$^6_4$, etc., in modern harmonic analysis, and $^6_4$ in figured-bass parts. It normally occurs in strong position followed by

I   I^6 IV   I$^6_4$ IV^6 IV   I$^6_4$ V   I

the dominant (V), as shown in measure 4 of the accompanying example, but may also occur in weak position, as in measure 2. One of the first composers to make deliberate use of the six-four chord was Willaert. See G. Haydon, *The Evolution of the Six-Four Chord* (1933); L. Matossi, in *DM* x, 356ff.

Sixteen-foot. See Foot (2).

Sixth [F. *sixième;* G. *Sexte;* It. *sesta;* Sp. *sexta*]. See Interval. In early music the sixth was regarded as the least perfect consonance, and often even as a dissonance. Thus, Anon. IV (*c.* 1280) speaks of "that vile and loathsome discord which is the sixth" [*CS* i, 359a].

Sixth chord. The first inversion of the triad, e.g., e–g–c', indicated I^6, II^6, etc., and in modern harmonic analysis, 6 or $^6_3$ in figured-bass parts. In four-part harmony, doubling of the fundamental is generally avoided (e–c'–g'–c'', not e–e'–g'–c'') because the e can only be resolved upward to the f, so that, with doubled e, parallel octaves (e–f, e'–f') would result. The sixth chord is used on every degree of the scale and often occurs in parallel progressions [see Sixth-chord style]. An especially interesting chord is the *Neapolitan sixth, f–a^b–d$^{b'}$ in C major, which is usually described as the first inversion of the triad on the lowered supertonic, d^b–f–a^b [see, however, Functional harmony]. Among the numerous chromatic variations on the chord of the sixth, those containing an augmented sixth, e.g., a^b–f$\sharp'$, deserve special mention. There are four common ones: the augmented sixth, the augmented six-five-three, the augmented six-four-three, and the doubly augmented six-four-three. The first three are sometimes called

IV IV^{6+} V   IV^7 IV$^{6+}_3$ V   II^7 II$^{6+}_{4+}$ V

II^7 II$^{6+}_{4++}$ I$^6_4$

(rather pointlessly) "Italian," "German," and "French" sixth respectively. Their derivations and common resolutions are shown in the example (+ and + + indicate augmented and doubly augmented intervals). See P. Miller, "The Augmented Sixth Chord" (*Journal of Musicology* i). See also Added sixth.

Sixth-chord style. Designation for passages formed of consecutive sixth chords. Such passages are often called "fauxbourdon," but this term should be restricted to one particular manifestation of sixth-chord style, described under *fauxbourdon. Rapid sixth-chord progressions occur in the works of Bach [see Ex. 1, from the cantata *Ach wie flüchtig*], Mozart, Beethoven (Piano Sonata op. 2, no. 3, last movement), Brahms, and others. However, sixth-chord style plays a much more important role in the music

of the late Middle Ages (c. 1300–1450). It probably originated in England. In fact, the earliest instances are found in English MSS of c. 1300, when French music was still based on perfect consonances and the principle of contrary motion. For examples, see *ReMMA*, p. 399; *HAM*, no. 57b; see also Discant. Short progressions in sixth chords are quite common in the works of Landini, especially in cadences [see *HAM*, no. 53]. The sixth-chord style reached its culmination in the compositions of Dunstable, Dufay, and Binchois, which often included long passages and even entire sections in sixth chords [Ex. 2]. An extreme case is Binchois' *In exitu Israel* [J. Marix, *Les Musiciens de la cour de Bourgogne* (1937), pp. 196ff], which, from beginning to end, is written in sixth chords. In this period there also developed two special methods of singing in $\frac{6}{3}$ harmonies, both involving some sort of improvisation, namely, Dufay's *fauxbourdon and what Guilelmus Monachus called *Anglorum modus faulxbourdon* [see *Discantus supra librum*]. In the former, the lowest and

highest parts are notated and the middle part "improvised," whereas in the latter only the lowest part is notated.

Sixth tone. An interval equal to one-third semitone, there being thirty-six sixth tones to the octave. See Microtone.

Skala [G.]. *Scale.

Skolie [G.]. Name used by Schubert and others for a drinking song.

Slancio, con [It.]. With dash.

Slargando [It.]. Slowing down.

Slavic music. See Bulgaria, Czechoslovakia, Poland, Russia, Yugoslavia, etc.

Sleeping Beauty, The. Ballet by Tchaikovsky (choreography by M. Petipa), produced in St. Petersburg (now Leningrad), 1890. It is based on the familiar fairy tale.

Sléndro. See under Java.

Slentando [It.]. Slackening, slowing down.

Slide. (1) In violin playing, a slight *portamento used to pass quickly from one note to another, usually at the distance of a third or a fourth. It produces a matchless legato as well as a special effect of expressiveness. Paganini introduced a virtuoso type of slide by executing chromatic passages, singly or in thirds, entirely with the same finger. (2) The movable portion of the *trombone. See also Wind instruments IV (a); Slide trumpet. (3) An ornament consisting of two or more notes approaching the main note by conjunct motion; see Appoggiatura, double II.

Slider. See under Organ II.

Slide trumpet. See under Trumpet II.

Slur. (1) A curved line placed above or below a group of notes to indicate that they are to be played legato, e.g., with one stroke of the violin bow, or with one breath in singing. If the notes to be found under the slur have staccato dots, the meaning of the combined signs is *portato. A slur connecting two notes of equal pitch is properly called *tie or bind. (2) An ornament resembling the French *tierce coulée* [see Appoggiatura, double II].

Sly Vixen, The. See *Cunning Vixen, The.*

Sminuendo [It.]. Same as diminuendo.

Smith College Music Archives. See Editions XLVIII.

Smorzando [It.]. Fading away.

Snare drum. See under Percussion instruments B, 1.

Snèllo [It.]. Nimble, agile.

Soave [It.]. Gentle, sweet.

Sociéte française de musicologie, Publications. See Editions XLIX.

Societies, musical. I. *United States.* Some of the more important musical organizations of national scope are the following:

1. A.G.O. (American Guild of Organists). A national association of church organists, founded in 1896, having as its purposes: (1) improvement of music in churches; (2) maintenance of high standards among organists; and (3) exchange of views and information among members through periodic meetings. The *American Guild of Organists Quarterly* has been published since 1956, and its monthly journal, *The Diapason,* since 1909.

2. A.M.S. (American Musicological Society). An organization, founded in 1934, for "the advancement of research in the various fields of music as a branch of learning" (from its constitution). The society is divided into regional chapters that hold regular meetings where papers of musicologic interest are read. A national convention is traditionally held each year, formerly in connection with the M.T.N.A. convention [see 6] and now with the C.M.S. [see 9]. Two yearly publications, *Papers of the A.M.S.* (*PAMS*) and *Bulletin of the A.M.S.* (*BAMS*), issued from 1936, were superseded by the *Journal of the American Musicological Society* (*JAMS,* 1948—).

3. I.S.C.M. (International Society for Contemporary Music). The society was begun in Europe in 1922; the United States section was founded in 1923. Its purpose is to discover and encourage talent in composition and to provide opportunities for performance of contemporary works. To this end, it holds annual Festivals of Contemporary Music, where works selected by an international jury are performed. See below, under III.

4. League of Composers. An organization, founded in 1923, for promoting modern music through the performance and commissioning of new works, and through its official organ, *Modern Music.* The League was for a number of years primarily a New York organization, but sub-

sequently chapters were founded in various sections of the country.

5. M.E.N.C. (Music Educators National Conference). This organization began in 1907 as the Music Supervisors National Conference. The present name was adopted in 1936. Its purpose is to foster cooperation among public-school teachers, especially supervisors, with a view to raising standards of music in the schools and securing a better place for music in the curriculum of the schools.

6. M.T.N.A. (Music Teachers' National Association). An organization, founded in 1876, interested primarily in the practical problems of musical education. The chief activity of the M.T.N.A. is its annual convention, where papers are read and discussions carried on by educators from all sections of the country and all branches of music education. *Papers and Proceedings of the M.T.N.A.,* published annually from 1906 to 1950, contains reprints of the papers read at the conventions.

7. N.A.S.M. (National Association of Schools of Music). An organization of professional music schools whose aim is to unify curriculum, maintain standards, and serve as an accrediting organization for music schools. Annual meetings are held in conjunction with the M.T.N.A. [see 6]. Much of the credit for the N.A.S.M.'s development belongs to Howard Hanson.

8. Society for Ethnomusicology. Formally founded in 1956, this society publishes the journal *Ethnomusicology.*

9. C.M.S. (College Music Society). Formed in 1958, this society publishes *College Music Symposium,* which first appeared in 1961.

II. *Europe.* 1. Allgemeiner Deutscher Musikverein. Founded in 1861 by Franz Liszt and Karl Franz Brendel, for the purpose of: (1) furthering in a progressive sense the musical life of Germany; (2) looking after the interests of professional musicians and composers; (3) supporting needy composers and their families. The society has given more than sixty festivals (*Tonkünstlerfeste*) in various cities of Germany.

2. Bach-Gesellschaft. A German society founded in 1850 (centenary of Bach's death) with the object of publishing a complete critical edition of Bach's works. This edition, which includes forty-six volumes, is referred to by the abbreviation *BG.* The society was dissolved in 1900 after the last volume had been issued. Simultaneously, a "Neue Bach-Gesellschaft" was founded to carry on the work of completing the original edition by publishing revisions and

practical scores. Since 1904 this society has issued an annual *Bach-Jahrbuch* (*BJ*) containing articles on Bach and related subjects.

3. British Music Society. Founded in 1918 by Dr. A. Eaglefield-Hull, reorganized in 1921. Its object was furthering of the interests of musicians throughout Great Britain. It was disbanded in 1933 but a few local branches survive, notably the Contemporary Music Centre, which acts as the British section of the International Society for Contemporary Music [see III, 3].

4. Gesellschaft der Musikfreunde. The oldest and most important musical society of Austria (Vienna), founded in 1812, largely through the efforts of J. F. Sonnleithner. It has been active in various directions: (a) conservatory, founded 1817, first director Antonio Salieri; (b) *Singverein,* an amateur choral society of outstanding rank, founded 1858; (c) *Gesellschaftsorchester* (today *Orchester Verein*), an orchestral society, first amateur, later professional, founded in 1859; (d) music library, founded 1819 [see Libraries, Austria, Vienna]; (e) museum, containing autographs, letters, pictures, musical instruments (Haydn's piano), and musical curios (Beethoven's ear trumpets).

5. Incorporated Society of Musicians. An English society founded in 1882 by James Dawber and Henry Hiles for furthering the following aims: (1) uniting the musical profession in a representative society; (2) providing opportunities for discussion; (3) improving musical education; (4) organizing musicians; and (5) obtaining legal recognition for qualified teachers of music.

6. Maatschappij tot Bevordering der Toonkunst. The largest musical society in Holland, founded in 1829 and located in Amsterdam. It is active mainly in choral singing. The society has also been active in editing old music [see Editions LII].

7. Société des Concerts du Conservatoire. Founded by F.-A. Habeneck in Paris, probably c. 1828, for the purpose of giving concerts [see Concert II]. It has continued to the present day, giving concerts with conservative programs.

8. Société Nationale de Musique. Founded in Paris, 1871, by Romain Busine and C. Saint-Saëns, for the purpose of performing works by living French composers.

III. *International.* 1. Internationale Gesellschaft für Musikwissenschaft (International Musicological Society; Société Internationale de Musicologie). A society founded in 1927 to further musicologic activities, in place of the former

Internationale Musikgesellschaft [see III, 2]. The headquarters are at Basel. Congresses are arranged every few years [see *CP 1930,* etc., in Abbreviations listed at the front of this book] and a periodical, *Acta Musicologica* (*AM*), has been published since 1928.

2. Internationale Musikgesellschaft (International Musical Society). A society founded in 1899 by O. Fleischer, whose aim was a federation of musicians and musical connoisseurs of all countries and which has been instrumental mainly in furthering musicological research. It issued: *Zeitschrift der Internationalen Musikgesellschaft* (*ZIM*), a monthly periodical; *Sammelbände der Internationalen Musikgesellschaft* (*SIM*), a quarterly, for longer articles; and books under the collective title *Publikationen der Internationalen Musikgesellschaft.* Congresses were held in 1904 (Leipzig), 1906 (Basel), 1909 (Vienna), 1911 (London), and 1914 (Paris), and reports were published under titles such as *Kongress der Internationalen Musikgesellschaft* [see *CP 1904,* etc., in Abbreviations listed at front of this book]. The society was disbanded in September, 1914.

3. International Society for Contemporary Music, founded at Salzburg in 1922, with headquarters in London since 1923. Its object is furthering contemporary music. See under Festivals III. National societies were formed in various countries; see above, I, 3, and II, 3.

See also Academy; Apollo Club; *Männergesangverein; *Orphéon; Singakademie.* For more complete and detailed information about the American societies, see Pierre Key's *International Music Year Book,* rev. ed. (1928); regarding the others, see A. Einstein, *Das neue Musiklexikon* (1926), s.v. "Vereine," and H. Riemann, *Musiklexikon* (11th ed., 1929), pp. 1920ff. E.B.H.

Sociology of music. A discipline concerned with the relationship between music and society. The systematic aspect of this relationship, which is implied by the term "sociology," is as yet undeveloped with respect to both general principles and the analysis of contemporary problems. Thus the field consists essentially of the social history of music, which presumably is viewed in the light of sociologic concepts and larger trends. Studies of Oriental and primitive music are considered in the province of *ethnomusicology, even when their interest is sociological.

A social point of view is particularly valuable in the case of music because of its intimate and highly ramified connections with society. Perhaps more than any other art, music is able to unite and sway masses of people, especially if they are active participants rather than listeners. An operatic production today can hardly be financed without public support. Audiences vary in social composition, size, and diversity, extending from private gatherings of connoisseurs to the huge groups of people that can be reached by electronic media. Style is surprisingly responsive to audience, and extends correspondingly from subtleties of chromaticism, polyphony, and dynamics to monophonic and homophonic textures *al fresco*. Even in the case of modern technologic means of dissemination like television, each style of music has its own audience; the idea of mass culture is largely an illusion. Musical types and forms also are greatly influenced by social forces, generated by and flourishing in response to particular social conditions and functional demands.

Characteristic sociologic subjects of investigation include the social and economic position of the musician, the dissemination of music (including the role of technology), musical organizations and institutions, public musical life, taste and criticism, the social determination of style, the music of specifically social purpose and of lower social strata (types often neglected by a stylistic orientation), the musical interaction of the various strata of society, and particular genres of music (ballet, opera, church music, choral music, convivial music, military music) that are shaped considerably by social forces. The influence of music upon society is as much a part of the field as is the influence of society upon music.

In ancient *Greece, as in all ancient civilizations, the educative and social influence of music was thought to be immense; only in the totalitarian governments of the 20th century did music again become a political instrument of comparable power. The pedagogic ceremonial, military, and religious functions of specific genres were explicitly defined: the communal choral dance, the military music of Sparta, the dithyramb, the *skolion*. Roman music was even more clearly bound to various social contexts: amphitheater games, the pantomime, the theater, the dinner party, military life, funerals.

The styles and forms of *Gregorian chant were molded by their subservience to religious function. Tonal and musical attractiveness were restricted and regarded with suspicion. The chant was an important factor, however, in creating a community of spiritual devotion, even

when it was largely performed by professional singers. Its unifying power was particularly evident in cloister life; and it served as the focal point of the curriculum and of educational ideals in both monastic and cathedral schools. Except during the political ascendancy of the Church, when secular elements were admitted to liturgical music, the official attitude towards instruments and popular melody was one of hostility. The free employment of secular features was characteristic of the Renaissance and still more so of the *baroque [see History of music V]. In Lutheranism this stylistic tolerance was a persistent trait; the communal force of congregational song was strengthened by a folklike quality, and a complex art of *chorale variation was developed for the organ and enlisted in the same cause of enhancing devotion [see Chorale].

The 13th-century *motet, on the other hand, reflects the sophistication of a society of clerics. The *polyphonic music of the *trecento* belongs to a thoroughly secular courtly society, while the lower classes, like the old aristocracy, undoubtedly expressed their musical predilections in *monody. Courtly love is also the basic motivation for the refined art of Machaut, with its retrospective tendencies. In the *Renaissance, although the composer remains a performer, his work gradually takes on the value of personal distinctiveness, and the musical composition correspondingly becomes a *res facta* destined for preservation and looked to for its special aesthetic properties and workmanship. In spite of more popular predecessors and parodies, the *madrigal, like the Flemish *chanson, was music for a closed group of discriminating performers. The Parisian chanson, by contrast, was cast in a more popular mold, and took full advantage of the wide dissemination afforded by music *printing.

The rise of Italian *opera was the most striking social manifestation of baroque music. It combined with foreign forms such as the *ballet de cour* and slowly became diversified in accordance with the variety of social settings in which it found its place. Outside France, the audience changed from a purely aristocratic to a stratified one through the addition of the commercial and lower classes, especially in Venice and Hamburg; yet in the 18th century, as part of a generalized critical reaction, national operatic types arose in specific response to the demands of a wider and less cultivated public. Alongside Italian opera in Germany, the international influence of aristocratic art can also be seen in the imitation of the dance *suites of Lully, which, by way of contrast, are made up to a considerable extent of the courtly stylization of French provincial dances. [Also see Dance music.]

In the 18th century, the major social development apart from *comic opera was the formation of a public musical life, manifested most clearly in concert societies and *music criticism. These activities expanded during the 19th century and were joined by other phases of musical life appealing to still larger masses of people, such as the institution of choral societies, the composition of a large quantity of four-hand *piano music for convivial purposes, and the even more widespread publication of superficial salon music for piano, including facile etudes and variations and arrangements of operatic airs. The diversification of musical life during the 20th century is still more remarkable. Concerts increasingly became presentations of an established repertory attended by a very diverse audience rather than contemporary production involving a conversant and interested group, although a number of special kinds of concert appeared around mid-century, each with its specific audience. At the same time, there was a marked increase in the number of functional and social types of music, which now included commercial music, *jazz, *folk music, and many other varieties.

During the latter part of the 19th century, performers gradually became members of trade unions, the modern descendants of guilds (*Meistersinger), and secured the benefits of steadier employment and adequate income. Composers had ceased to find regular positions in the service of church or nobility during the earlier 19th century; their defined place in society had given way to freedom as well as specialization, and even to the isolation and prophetic mission described in German romantic literature. Rather belatedly, however, it was only in the 20th century that the value of originality was finally recognized in terms of legal protection against plagiarism, as well as by royalties on the sale and performance of music [see Copyright]. It would seem, nevertheless, that the communal constituents of a personal style will always remain considerable; they not only are conspicuous in older music, but can also be discerned without much difficulty in the 19th and 20th centuries.

The modern availability and ubiquity of music of all kinds has undoubtedly had important effects on the role of amateur performance, on the nature of the listening experience, on musicianship, and even on musical scholarship. Technology would seem to have impersonalized and generalized musical response, placing more emphasis on mass reactions.

Lit.: W. Mellers, *Music and Society* (1950); E. Siegmeister, *Music and Society* (1938); M. Weber, *The Rational and Social Foundations of Music* (1958); A. Hauser, *The Social History of Art*, 2 vols. (1951), trans. S. Godman (4 vols, repr. 1958); A. Loesser, *Men, Women, and Pianos: A Social History* (1954); E. D. Mackerness, *A Social History of English Music* [1964]; J. H. Mueller, *The American Symphony Orchestra* (1951); A. R. Oliver, *The Encyclopedists as Critics of Music* (1947); T. W. Adorno, *Einleitung in die Musiksoziologie* [1962]; H. Engel, *Musik und Gesellschaft* [1960]; F. Buchholz, *Von Bindung und Freiheit der Musik und des Musikers in der Gemeinde* (1955); E. H. Meyer, *Musik im Zeitgeschehen* (1952); E. Preussner, *Die bürgerliche Musikkultur*, rev. ed. [1950]; A. Silbermann, *Wovon lebt die Musik?* [1957]; W. Wiora, *Komponist und Mitwelt* (1964); M. Belvianes, *Sociologie de la musique* (1951); E. Eggli, *Probleme der musikalischen Wertästhetik im 19. Jahrhundert* (1965); E. Rebling, *Die soziologischen Grundlagen der Stilwandlung der Musik in Deutschland um die Mitte des 18. Jahrhunderts* [1935]; C. Lalo, *L'Art et la vie sociale* (1921); F. Lesure, ed., *Musik und Gesellschaft im Bild* (1966); A. Loft, *Musicians' Guild and Union: A Consideration of the Evolution of Protective Organization among Musicians* (1950); *BuMBE*, ch. 12; E. Newman, *The Life of Richard Wagner* i, ch. 8 [1933]; R. Michels, "Die Soziologie des Nationalliedes," in *Der Patriotismus* (1929); E. Lowinsky, in *Journal of the History of Ideas* xv (Renaissance); H. Besseler, in *AMW* xvi (16th cent.); H. Engel, in *Der Musik-Almanach* (1949); id., in *ZMW* xvii; id., in *CP 1962*; id., in *Von Deutscher Tonkunst: zu Peter Raabes 70. Geburtstag* [1942]; id., in *CP 1950a* (Bach); J. Kindermann, in *MF* xix; T. Kneif, in *AM* xxxviii; H. Mersmann, in *AMW* x; H. Reinold, in *MF* viii; W. Serauky in *ZMW* xvi. Additional bibl. in *MGG*, s.v. "Soziologie der Musik."   E.A.L.

Soggetto [It.]. Subject or theme [Ex. 1]. In 18th-century theory the term is used in a more special sense, for a fugal theme of a traditional character, similar to the subjects of the 16th-century *ricercar. It is thus distinguished from the *andamento* [Ex. 2], a longer theme, usually falling

into two phrases, and from the *attacco,* a short motif such as used in motets or in the episodic sections of fugues. The subjects of the fugues in C-sharp minor and G major from *The Well-Tempered Clavier,* vol. i, illustrate the difference between a *soggetto* and *andamento.* See Tonal and real.

Soggetto cavato [It., carved subject]. In 16th-century theory (G. Zarlino, *Le Istitutioni har-moniche,* 1558), a musical subject derived by "carving out" vowels [*cavato delli vocali*] from a sentence and transforming them into a melody by means of the solmization syllables of the Guidonian hexachord. An example is Josquin's Mass, He*rcu*les *D*ux *F*er*ra*rie (dedicated to Hercules, Duke of Ferrara), whose main subject is *e u e u e a i e;* or, in corresponding solmization syllables, *re ut re ut re fa mi re;* or, in modern notes, d c d c d f e d. Another example is the motto "Vive le roi" (*V = u,* i.e., *ut*), whose musical realization (*ut mi ut re re sol mi,* i.e., c e c d d g e) is the tenor of an instrumental piece that Josquin wrote for a festive occasion, possibly for the accession of Louis XII to the throne of France (1498; see *SchGMB,* no. 62a). Two Masses by C. de Rore are based on longer "Hercules" mottoes [see *ReMR,* p. 375]. See A. Thürlings, in *CP 1906.*

An early realization of the same principle is implied in a method recommended by Guido d'Arezzo in his "Micrologus," ch. xvii, entitled "Quod ad cantum redigitur omne quod dicitur" (How anything spoken can be turned into music). Without having recourse to his own solmization syllables, he assigns the vowels *a e i o u* to five successive notes of the scale, e.g., c d e f g, so that the text "Sancte Johannes meritorum tuorum" receives, through the syllables *a e o a e e i o u u o u,* the melody c d f c d d e f g g f g. The method is refined by the optional assignment of some of the five vowels to a neighboring pentachord.

Sogitha. See under Syrian chant.

Soir, Le. See under *Matin, Le.*

Sol. See under Pitch names; Solmization.

Soldier's Tale, The. See *Histoire du soldat, L'.*

Soleá. An Andalusian folksong, with stanzas of three eight-syllable lines, the first and third in rhyme. It is plaintive in character and is basically a form of *cante jondo* [see Flamenco]. For an example, see *LavE* i.4, 2394.

Solemn Mass. See *Missa.*

Solesmes. The Benedictine monks of Solesmes (a village near Le Mans, France) have become famous through their work of restoring Gregorian chant. They have produced an edition of a reasonably correct text of Gregorian chant at the high point of its development (9th, 10th cent.), an edition that was officially adopted in 1904 under the name "Editio Vaticana" to replace the corrupt versions of the "Editio Medicea" (17th cent.) and the similar "Ratisbon edition" of the late 19th century [see Liturgical books II]. Another important achievement was their attempt to solve the problem of the chant's rhythm. The Solesmes interpretation of Gregorian rhythm has won wide acclaim, as well as official Church recognition. However, it has also met with serious criticism from various musicologists [see Gregorian chant VI]. The leading personalities of Solesmes were Dom Guéranger (1805-75), Dom Pothier (1835-1923), and Dom Mocquereau (1849-1930). The last-named inaugurated the publication of early neumatic MSS, called *Paléographie musicale* [see Editions XLII], and was also the chief champion of the Solesmes theory of Gregorian rhythm (*Le Nombre musical grégorien ou rhythmique grégorienne,* 1908). The present leader is Dom Joseph Gajard (b. 1885). A periodical, *Revue grégorienne,* is published bimonthly; also, since 1954, *Etudes grégoriennes* at irregular intervals. See N. Rousseau, *L'École grégorienne de Solesmes: 1833-1910* (1910); J. Gajard, *The Solesmes Method* [1960].

Sol-fa. See Tonic sol-fa.

Solfège [F.], **solfeggio** [It.]. (1) Vocal exercises sung to a vowel (*a, o, u*) or to the syllables of *solmization (*ut* [*do*], *re, mi,* etc.), which are used instead of a text. The latter method, which was the earlier, combines the purpose of acquiring vocal technique with one of elementary instruction [see (2)] since the student is supposed to recognize the notes and intervals, a requirement of basic importance for *sight-reading. Vocal exercises sung to a vowel are properly called *vocalises* [F.], *vocalizzi* [It.], but the name *solfeggio* also has come into common use for this procedure, which includes highly difficult virtuoso exercises and frequently involves passages too rapid to be "*sol-fa*-ed."

Vocal exercises without text from the 17th century survive in great number under the name "ricercari" [see Ricercar II (d)]. In 1786 a book called *Solfèges d'Italie* was published in Paris. It contained exercises by Scarlatti, J. A. Hasse, L. Leo, Porpora, Carfaro, and others, to be treated as either *solfeggi* or *vocalizzi*. A famous collection is the *Solfèges du Conservatoire,* which contains contributions by Cherubini and other professors of the Paris Conservatory. An outstanding collection of recent date is the *Répertoire moderne de vocalises-études,* which includes contributions by Fauré, D'Indy, Ravel, and others. Perhaps the most widely used collection is A. Danhauser, L. Lemoine, and A. Lavignac, *Solfège des Solfèges,* 3 vols. [1910–51].

(2) The term also has come to mean instruction in the rudiments of music, i.e., the study of intervals, rhythm, clefs, signatures, etc., usually employing solmization and having as its goal the ability to translate symbols (notation) into an aural image immediately and accurately. Extensive courses in solfège, sometimes covering four years of study, were first introduced in France and Belgium and have been adopted recently by some American institutions. See R. Longy-Miquelle, *Principles of Musical Theory* (1925); P. Hindemith, *Elementary Training for Musicians* (1946); A. Fisk and N. Lloyd, *Fundamentals of Sight Singing and Ear Training* (1964); A. Danhauser, *Théorie de la musique* (1872 and many later editions); H. Villa-Lobos, *Solfejos* (1940); W. Earhart, *Music to the Listening Ear* (1932); O. Ortmann, *Problems in the Elements of Ear-Dictation* (1934); G. A. Wedge, *Advanced Ear-Training and Sight-Singing* (1922).

Solfegietto [It.]. Title used by some composers in the meaning of "little study." The best known example, by K. P. E. Bach, is a work in C minor originally entitled "Solfeggio" (in *Musikalisches Vielerley* [1770], p. 19).

Solmization. I. General term for systems of designating the degrees of the scale by syllables instead of letters. The syllables mostly used today are: *do* (or *doh*), *re, mi, fa, sol, la, si* (*ti*). There are two current methods of applying these syllables to the scale degrees, known as "fixed do" and "movable do." In the former, the syllables are applied to "fixed" notes, i.e., those of the C major scale (*do* = C; *re* = D; etc.). In the latter, they are applicable to any major scale, so that *do, re, mi,* etc., denote tonic, supertonic, mediant, etc. (e.g., in D major: D, E, F♯, etc.). The former system is essentially identical with the current system of tone letters, since there is an exact and unchangeable correspondence between the letters (C, D, E . . .) and the syllables (*do, re, mi* . . .). The syllables have certain advantages, however, chiefly in that they lend themselves better to singing [see Solfège] and that they have more "individuality." They are used mainly in France and Italy. The movable syllables can be used to great advantage in elementary studies, such as scales, clefs, intervals, simple modulations, etc. A modern system of "movable do" is the *tonic sol-fa, which is widely used in England. See Sight-reading.

II. The use of syllables for designating tones is very old. The Chinese had such a system, and tone syllables are still used in Indian music. The ancient Greeks employed the syllables *tah, tā, toh, teh* (τα, τη, τω, τε) for the tones of the descending tetrachord (e.g., a, g, f, e). It is probably from similar syllables (να, νη, νω, νε) that the Byzantine *enechemata* [see Echos] and the *noeane* of Western medieval theory were derived. The modern system of solmization originated with Guido d'Arezzo (*c.* 990–1050), who introduced the syllables *ut re mi fa sol la* as names for the tones c to a. Later they were also used for the two other hexachords [see Hexachord]. The name "solmization" [L. *solmisatio*] is derived from the combination *sol-mi,* which, however, denotes not g–e but g–a, the syllable *mi* being understood as belonging to the hexachord on f. Thus, it denotes not only the Guidonian syllables as such, but the principle of mutation (change from one hexachord into another). The Guidonian syllables were also used as the basis of a "fixed do" terminology, i.e., in the compound terms *C-fa-ut, D-sol-re,* etc. [see Hexachord III].

III. The medieval system remained unaltered until the end of the 16th century, when increasingly wider use of chromatic tones and transposed keys rendered it less and less suitable. About 1600, French musicians began to use the Guidonian syllables in a fixed position, *ut* for C, etc. In order to complete the octave, the syllable *si* (probably derived from the last words *S-ancte I-oannes* of Guido's hymn) was introduced, and *c.* 1650 the rather unsingable syllable *ut* was replaced by *do* [Otto Gibelius, *Seminarium modulatoriae vocalis* (1645)]. Simultaneously, various attempts were made to introduce new systems designed for the heptachord, e.g., the "voces belgicae" of Hubert Waelrant (*c.* 1517–95): *bo ce di ga lo ma ni* (known as "Bocedization"), or Daniel Hitzler's (1575–1635) "Bebization" *la be ce de me fe ge,* or Karl Heinrich Graun's (1704–59) "Damenization" *da me ni po tu la be*—all fleeting attempts occasionally classified as "Bobizations." In the United States a simplified system of solmization known as *fasola was widely used during the 18th century. More recently, attempts at reform have been made in England and Germany, with the idea of making the solmization syllables more useful in elementary instruction and sight-singing [see Tonic sol-fa; Tonika]. Karl A. Eitz (1848–1924) invented a *Tonwort* system for Bosanquet's 53-tone scale, which was simplified in the *Jale* system of R. Münnich [see his *Jale* (1930)].

Lit.: G. Lange, "Zur Geschichte der Solmisation" (*SIM* i); F. Ring, "Zur altgriechischen Solmisationslehre" (*AMF* iii); C. E. Ruelle, "La Solmisation chez les anciens Grecs" (*SIM* ix); H. Müller, "Solmisations-siben in der Medicäischen Choralausgabe" (*AMW* i); C.-A. Moberg, "Die Musik in Guido von Arezzos Solmisationshymne" (*AMW* xvi); *RiHM* i.2, 167ff.

Solo. (1) A piece executed by one performer, either alone (piano solo; violin solo; e.g., Bach's Sonatas for violin solo), or with accompaniment by piano, organ, orchestra, etc. (2) In orchestral scores, a passage intended to stand out. (3) In concertos, designation for the soloist, in distinction from the orchestra (tutti). (4) In the early concerto (Bach, Handel), the orchestral part for passages to be played *senza ripieni* [see *Ripieno*]. See also Ensemble (3).

Solo organ. See under Organ III.

Solo pitch. A pitch slightly higher than normal; it is used occasionally to obtain a more brilliant tone.

Sombrero de tres picos, El [Sp., The Three-Cornered Hat]. Comedy-ballet by De Falla, produced in London, 1919, based on a novel by Alarcón. The music, largely from Andalusian sources, has a strong Spanish flavor, and some of the dances (particularly the Miller's Dance) have become popular concert pieces.

Son (1) [F.]. Sound. *Son bouché,* stopped note (of a horn; see Horn I); *son ouvert,* open (natural) note of a wind instrument.

(2) [Sp.]. A folk dance that originated in Cuba's Oriente Province and reflects strong Afro-Cuban traditions. Its tempo is moderate and its form consists of an exposition, usually sung by a solo voice, followed by two statements of a contrasting melody based on motifs sung by the chorus. The most common accompanying rhythmic patterns used are:

A sort of hybrid form known as *bolero-son,* combining elements of both dances [see Bolero], has recently been developed.   (2) by J.O-S.

Sonata. A. *General.* The sonata is a composition for piano (piano sonata), or for violin, cello, flute, etc., usually with piano accompaniment (violin sonata, cello sonata, etc.), which consists of three or four separate sections called movements. Almost all features of the sonata are also found in other types of instrumental music, i.e., the symphony, chamber music (quartet, trio, quintet, etc.), and, with some modifications, the concerto. The main difference lies in the performing bodies: the symphony is a "sonata" for orchestra, the quartet a "sonata" for four strings, the concerto a "sonata" for a soloist with orchestra, etc. The sonata principle has dominated instrumental music since the late 18th century, including the great majority of works in the present-day concert repertory, from Haydn and Mozart to Brahms, Bruckner, and many 20th-century composers.

The normal scheme for the movements of a sonata (symphony, etc.) is Allegro–Adagio–Scherzo (or Minuet)–Allegro. A slow introduction sometimes precedes the opening Allegro. While Allegro (Allegro molto, Presto) and Adagio (Largo, Lento) merely mean "quick" and "slow," the Scherzo or Minuet has a dance-like character. This movement is sometimes missing, particularly in Mozart's sonatas as well as in most concertos. Notable exceptions to the normal scheme are Beethoven's *Moonlight Sonata* op. 27, no. 2 (designated by Beethoven as *Sonata quasi una fantasia*), consisting of Adagio, Allegretto (a scherzo movement), and Presto; his op. 111, consisting of Maestoso (an introduction), Allegro, and Arietta (an Adagio in variation form); and Liszt's Sonata in B minor, in which the several sections of a single movement function as contrasting sections.

Both the sonata as a whole and its individual

movements are subject to certain principles of formal structure, which are adhered to with varying strictness by different composers. The first movement (Allegro) is almost always in the so-called *sonata form; the second (Adagio) is often in sonata form or ternary form but may be in *binary or variation form; the third movement is normally in ternary form, Minuet (*Scherzo)–Trio–Minuet (Scherzo); the last movement (Allegro, Presto) is in sonata form or *rondo form (occasionally in variation form). See Forms, musical.

B. *History.* I. Until 1650. The history of the sonata as a form is not identical with the history of the name "sonata." Originally, the term simply meant "sound-piece" and was used for various types of instrumental music. In literary sources, variants of the term *sonnade* occur at least as early as the 12th century [see Lit., Newman, *Sonata in the Baroque Era*]. Luis Milán, in his vihuela book *El Maestro* (1535), mentions "villancicos y sonadas," the latter being dances (pavanes) or fantasias. G. Gorzanis used the title "sonata" for a *passamezzo* and *padovana* for lute (*Intabolatura di liuto . . . libro primo,* 1561). Giovanni Gabrieli's well-known *Sonata pian'e forte* [*HAM,* no. 173] and *Sonata octavi toni* (1597; *Editions XXIII, 2) are likewise compositions that have a solely nominal connection with the sonata in its present-day meaning. The former, scored for violin, cornett, and 6 trombones, may be related to the "sonatas" of the military trumpeters, the German *Turmsonaten or the English *sennets. A. Banchieri's *L'Organo suonarino* (1605) contains eight pieces called "Sonata," mostly short imitative pieces in two parts, whereas the fourteen "Sonate di cimbalo" in Gianpietro Del Buono's *Canoni oblighi et sonate* (1641) are different elaborations of the same *cantus firmus* (*Ave maris stella*). As late as 1702, Bernardo Pasquini used the title "Sonate per Gravicembalo" for an autograph containing ricercars, suites, toccatas, etc., but not a single sonata.

The most fundamental aspect of the present-day sonata—i.e., the contrast provided by its different movements—can be traced to instrumental compositions of the late 16th century that fall into a number of short sections in contrasting styles. Among the earliest examples are a "Ricercare del 12° tono" for four instruments by Andrea Gabrieli (*c.* 1520–86; see *HAM,* no. 136); a "Canzon Primi toni" for eight instruments by Giovanni Gabrieli [see Editions XXIII, 2]; and organ canzonas by Vincenzo

Pellegrini (in *Canzoni de intavolatura d'organo,* 1599). During the first half of the 17th century a large number of compositions for instrumental ensemble called "canzone da sonar" or, occasionally, "sonate" (e.g., S. Rossi, *Il quarto libro de varie sonate,* 1622), were published. These pieces fall into five or more short sections in contrasting styles, frequently alternating fairly long sections in imitative style with shorter ones in homophonic texture and slower tempo. For more details, see Canzona (5).

Beginning about 1635, the sections tended to decrease in number and increase in length, thus acquiring the character of "movements." An early example is Tarquinio Merula's canzona "La Gallina" (1637), which has three distinct movements, the first and last based on the same theme [see H. Riemann, *Old Chamber Music,* vol. iii]. Other composers who contributed to this development were Salomone Rossi, B. Marini, G. B. Fontana, M. Neri, and G. B. Buonamente, all of whom published before 1655 [ex. in *RiMB,* nos. 98, 99; J. W. Wasielewski, *Instrumentalsätze;* *Editions III, 7].

II. 1650–1750. After 1650 a fairly standard structure developed, mainly in Venice under Legrenzi (1626–90). It consisted of an initial Allegro movement in fugal style, a homophonic second movement in dancelike triple meter, and a final movement similar to the first and often based on identical or related material. Often this three-part scheme was enlarged to four or five movements by the addition of short "Adagios" before and/or after the middle movement. The four-movement scheme is seen in Legrenzi's "La Torriana" (1655; see *RiMB,* no. 102), and the five-movement form in his "La Buscha" (1677; see *HAM,* no. 220). The "symmetrical" structure Allegro–Adagio–Dance–Adagio–Allegro was used also by G. B. Vitali (*c.* 1644–92; see his sonata of 1667 in H. Riemann, *Old Chamber Music,* iv, 146). Arcangelo Corelli (1653–1713) used, in his *Sonate a trè,* op. 1, op. 3 (1681, '89), a new four-movement plan, Adagio (or Grave)–Allegro–Adagio–Allegro, which was generally adopted as the standard form of the *sonata da chiesa* [see under *Sonata da camera*]. In op. 5 (1700) Corelli returned to the earlier six-movement form, retaining an Adagio at the beginning. Numerous pieces of the *sonata da chiesa* structure (i.e., with a scheme of four movements, slow–fast–slow–fast) were written by non-Italian composers, such as Bach, Handel, Jean Marie Leclair (1697–1764; see Editions XLVII, 27), while the Italians of this period frequently preferred longer or shorter schemes. Thus, Veracini's (1690–c. 1750) violin sonatas have five to eight movements [see Editions IX, 34]; Tartini's (1692–1770) usually have three: slow–fast–very fast [see Editions IX, 32]; and Locatelli's (1695–1764) almost always have three: Andante–Allegro–Minuet (or Aria con variazioni).

According to medium of performance, the baroque sonata may be divided into four categories: those written in one part, in two parts (*a due*), in three parts (*a tre*), and in four or more parts. The most famous examples in one part are Bach's unaccompanied sonatas for violin or for cello [for earlier compositions of this type, see Violin music; Cello]. The "sonatas a due" usually call for three performers, one for the melody (most commonly violin) and two for the realization of the thoroughbass. This type (often called "violin sonata" or even "solo violin sonata") was cultivated as early as 1617 by Marini (*Affetti musicali*) in a strikingly virtuoso style, employing trills, rapid runs, double-stops, etc. [see *SchGMB*, nos. 182, 183]. The virtuoso element is even more prominent in the sonatas of J. H. Schmelzer (*c.* 1623–80) and H. I. F. von Biber (1644–1704; see *SchGMB*, no. 238). The "sonata a tre" or trio sonata, the most important type of all, was performed by one, two, or four players, practically never by three [see Trio sonata], while the "sonata a quatro" and "a cinque" probably were for small orchestral ensembles [see Sinfonia (3)]. The earliest known keyboard compositions written in distinct movements are three *Canzone francese* by Giovanni Salvatore published in 1641 [see Editions XI, 3]. A publication by Gregorio Strozzi of 1687 [*Editions XI, 11] contains three pieces called "Sonata" in three or four movements, the first of which bears the remark, "detta da altri impropriamente Canzona francese" (improperly called by others canzona francese). Five years later, Johann Kuhnau (1660–1722) published, with his *Neüer Clavier-Übung*, pt. ii [1692], a "Sonata aus dem B" that earned him the somewhat undeserved title of "inventor of the piano sonata." Seven other sonatas followed in his *Frische Clavier Früchte* (1696). Bernardo Pasquini (1637–1710) used the term "sonata" as a generic designation for a variety of keyboard compositions [see above], but also for twelve "sonatas" in three or four movements written in the form of two thoroughbass parts to be performed on two harpsichords.

III. 1750–90. The emergence of the "Viennese classical sonata" of Haydn, Mozart, and Beethoven marks one of the most striking developments in music history. The change from the baroque sonata to the classical sonata is not simply a change from a four-movement scheme, Adagio–Allegro–Adagio–Allegro, to a three-movement scheme, Allegro–Adagio–Allegro, or another four-movement scheme, Allegro–Adagio–Scherzo–Allegro. Fundamental changes of style and structure within the movements are involved as well. Further, the repertory now divided into the solo sonata (piano, violin, flute, etc., sonata), chamber sonata (quartet, quintet), and orchestral sonata (symphony), each of which follows a separate line of development. The following discussion deals mainly with the first category from three aspects: (a) over-all form; (b) single-movement form; (c) style. [For the others, see String quartet; Symphony.]

(a) Over-all form. The three-movement plan Allegro–Adagio–Allegro was standardized in the Italian overture of Alessandro Scarlatti [see Overture I]. Bach employed this form in all but the first of his *Brandenburg Concertos, in the "Italian Concerto," and in the six organ sonatas, which are among the first sonatas written in this form. The Italian composers of harpsichord sonatas (G. B. Sammartini, 1701–75; B. Galuppi, 1706–85; P. D. Paradies, 1707–92; G. M. Rutini, 1723–97; see Editions IX, 22, 27, 28) wrote some sonatas in two movements, e.g., Allegro–Andante, or vice versa (Paradies) or Allegro–Minuet (Sammartini). Domenico Scarlatti wrote more than 550 one-movement sonatas, which, in his first publication, *Essercizi per Gravicembalo* (1738), were called "essercizio." Some, if not all, of these pieces were intended to be combined in two- or three-movement sonatas. G. Platti's sonatas (pub. between 1742 and *c.* 1746) are mostly in four movements but frequently include dances, e.g., Larghetto–Allegro–Siciliana–Presto, or Adagio–Allegretto–Grave–Minuet. In the *Haffner collections (1755–66) the sonatas have various plans: Andantino–Allegro–Presto; Larghetto–Allegro–Minuetto; Allegro–Minuetto, etc. The "classical" scheme Allegro–Adagio–Allegro was used consistently in the piano sonatas of K. P. E. Bach (Prussian Sonatas, 1742; Württemberg Sonatas, 1744), Haydn (except some of the earliest), and Mozart. The four-movement scheme Allegro–Adagio–Minuet–Allegro was already used by Johann W. A. Stamitz (1717–57) of the *Mannheim school. Although Haydn and Mozart generally adopted it for their string quartets and symphonies, Beethoven was the first to use it in his sonatas, replacing the Minuet with a Scherzo.

(b) Single-movement form. In the mid-18th-century rococo sonata (Sammartini, G. M. Rutini) practically all the movements are in binary form, A B, with both sections repeated. For the relationship of this form to the first-movement sonata form, see Sonata form II. Forms other than binary were very rare. The Haffner collections contain one example of ternary form for a slow movement (Aria from Sonata 8 by Paradies) and one example of *rondo form (Sonata 16 by G. B. Serini). The slow movements in the sonatas of K. P. E. Bach are usually in free form. Haydn seems to have been the first to make extensive use of the rondo form for the final movement.

(c) Style. The change from the contrapuntal baroque style to a homophonic texture already appears in the final movements of Corelli's sonatas. Vivaldi's style is highly rhythmic, and Tartini's is brilliant, while the rococo composers used a somewhat facile melodic style [see Gallant style], derived from opera. The change to more dramatic expression is usually credited to the Mannheim school and their Viennese contemporaries (Wagenseil), although Italian composers (particularly Sammartini) worked in the same direction. K. P. E. Bach wrote in a highly expressive style [see *Empfindsamer Stil*] that considerably influenced the young Haydn, while the Italianate style of Johann Christian Bach became a model for Mozart. Muzio Clementi's sonatas anticipate the virtuosity and dramatic elements of the Beethoven sonatas.

IV. 1790—. This period, the greatest in the development of the sonata, opens with Beethoven's sonatas for piano, violin, and cello. In his last piano sonatas (op. 81, 90, 101, 106, 109, 110, 111) he expanded the traditional form in various ways and often replaced the intensely dramatic style of his earlier works with a transcendent lyricism. In op. 106, 110, and the cello sonata op. 102, no. 2, the last movement is a fugue. Franz Schubert's piano sonatas, in a lyric, often songlike style, have only recently won the recognition due them. Schumann's sonatas, while not as tightly constructed as those of other composers, show skillful use of counterpoint and rhythm. Chopin's two sonatas in B-flat minor and in B minor, together with Liszt's B-minor Sonata, are outstanding examples of the romantic sonata. Brahms' three piano sonatas (op. 1, 2, 5) and violin sonatas (op. 78, 100, 108) are among the few important works in this genre written in the second half of the 19th century. The early 20th-century composers sometimes

avoided the sonata because it was so representative of 19th-century tradition. Some composers, such as Busoni and Ravel, turned to the *sonatina as a less pretentious type. The emergence of *neoclassicism (*c.* 1920) led to a revival of the sonata, with Stravinsky, Bartók, and Hindemith the most outstanding contributors. Other 20th-century composers of sonatas are C. Ives, Milhaud, Prokofiev, and E. Carter.

Lit. *General:* W. H. Hadow, *Sonata Form* [18??]; J. S. Shedlock, *The Pianoforte Sonata* (1895); O. Klauwell, *Geschichte der Sonate* [1899?]; B. Selva, *La Sonate . . .* (1913); J. P. Larsen, in *CP Blume;* P. T. Barford, in *MR* xiii, 255ff.

For I and II: W. S. Newman, *The Sonata in the Baroque* [1959]; J. W. von Wasielewski, *Die Violine im XVII. Jahrhundert und die Anfänge der Instrumentalcomposition* (1874); id., ‡*Instrumentalsätze vom Ende des XVI. bis Ende des XVII. Jahrhunderts* [n.d., 1920?]; A. Schlossberg, *Die Italienische Sonata . . . im 17. Jahrhundert* (1932); E. H. Meyer, *Die mehrstimmige Spielmusik des 17. Jahrhunderts* (1934); G. Beckmann, *Das Violinspiel in Deutschland vor 1700* (1918); E. C. Crocker, "An Introductory Study of the Italian Canzona . . . and Its Influence upon the Baroque Sonata" (diss. Radcliffe, 1943); A. Schering, "Zur Geschichte der Solo Sonate" (*CP Riemann*); W. S. Newman, "A Checklist of the Earliest Keyboard 'Sonatas' (1641–1738)" (*Notes* xi); S. Clercx, "Johann Kuhnau et la sonate" (*RM* 1934, no. 147, 88–110). *For III:* W. S. Newman, *The Sonata in the Classic Era* [1963]; D. Stone, "The Italian Sonata for Harpsichord and Pianoforte . . . (1730–1790)," 3 vols. (diss. Harvard Univ., 1952); M. Lange, *Beiträge zur Entstehung der südwestdeutschen Klaviersonate im 18. Jahrhundert* (1930); F. Torrefranca, *Le Origini italiane del romanticismo musicale* (1930); B. Studeny, *Beiträge zur Geschichte der Violinsonate im 18. Jahrhundert* (1911); A. Stauch, *Muzio Clementi's Klavier-Sonaten* [1930]; E. Stilz, *Die Berliner Klaviersonate zur Zeit Friedrichs des Grossen* (1930); E. Reeser, *De Klaviersonate met vioolbegeleiding . . . ten tijde van Mozart* (1939); V. Helfert, "Zur Entwickelungsgeschichte der Sonatenform" (*AMW* vii); F. Tutenberg, "Die Durchführungsfrage in der vorneuklassischen Sinfonie" (*ZMW* ix); R. Kamien, "Style Change in the Mid-18th-Century Keyboard Sonata" (*JAMS* xix).

For IV: P. Egert, *Die Klaviersonate im Zeitalter der Romantik* i: *Die Klaviersonate der Frühromantiker* (1934); *Editions XXIII, new series, 2;

O. Schulte-Bunert, *Die deutsche Klaviersonate des zwanzigsten Jahrhunderts* (1963); F. Salzer, "Die Sonatenform bei Schubert" (*StM* xv); V. Urbantschitsch, "Die Entwicklung der Sonatenform bei Brahms" (*StM* xiv).

Sonata da camera, sonata da chiesa [It.]. Baroque terms meaning chamber or court sonata and church sonata respectively. Originally, these terms indicated place of performance, not a specific type or form. They first appear in Tarquinio Merula's *Canzoni, overo sonate concertate per chiesa, e camera,* op. 12 (1637), which contains canzonas and dancelike pieces (*Ballo, Chiacona, Ruggiero*). The former are probably *da chiesa* and the latter *da camera*. Later publications entitled *da chiesa e da camera* are: M. Uccellini, *Sonate correnti Et Arie,* Book 4 (1645; sonatas, *corrente,* arias); G. A. Pandolfi Mealli, *Sonate* (1660; sonatas); M. Cazzati, *Varii e diversi capricci* (1669; capriccios, dances). Between 1670 and 1690 the two terms gradually became associated with larger forms rather than with single pieces. Arcangelo Corelli standardized the *sonata da chiesa* as a piece consisting of four movements, slow–fast–slow–fast (op. 1, op. 3), and the *sonata da camera* as a suite consisting of an introduction and three or four dances, e.g., Allemande, Sarabande, Gigue (op. 2, op. 4). It may be noted that the designation *Sonate da chiesa* appears only in some reprints of his op. 1 (1683, '95). The original editions of both op. 1 (1681) and op. 3 (1689) are entitled *Sonate a trè.* Also noteworthy is the fact that Veracini's *Sonate da camera,* op. 3 (1696) actually contain "church sonatas," e.g., Grave–Vivace–Largo–Vivace.

Sonata form. A term that designates not the over-all form of the sonata [see Sonata A] but a form frequently used for single movements of sonatas (symphonies; quartets; overtures, e.g., Mozart, *Don Giovanni, Zauberflöte;* etc.). Since it is the form most used for first movements of sonatas, it is also known as *first-movement form* or *sonata-allegro form.* These terms, too, are misleading, since the form is often used for the slow or the final movements of sonatas. The form has been used continuously since the time of Haydn and Mozart, although since 1900 it has been so freely treated that sometimes it is scarcely recognizable.

I. A movement written in sonata form consists of three sections—exposition, development, and recapitulation (also called statement, fantasia section, and restatement), the last usually followed by a coda. In the exposition the com-

poser introduces the musical ideas, consisting of a number of themes; in the development section he "develops" this material [see Development]; and in the recapitulation he repeats the exposition with certain modifications. In practically all early sonatas the exposition is repeated, indicated by a repeat sign. The structure, therefore, of sonata form can be indicated by the scheme A A B A. There is no doubt that composers wanted the exposition to be repeated since they frequently wrote two different endings (*prima* and *seconda volta*) for this purpose. This repetition is also aesthetically important, since it helps the listener remember the themes on which the whole movement is based. Beethoven occasionally omitted the repeat (e.g., in the *Appassionata,* 1st movt.) and about 1870 it was generally discarded, mainly on account of the larger dimensions of each section (in the music of Bruckner, Franck, Mahler, *et al.*).

The exposition contains a first and second theme connected by a bridge (modulating) passage. Other melodies in the exposition are considered continuations of the two main themes. Usually there is a difference between the first and second themes, the former being, e.g., dramatic, the latter lyrical. The second theme is in a different key from the first, normally the key of the dominant if the tonic is major, or the relative key if the tonic is minor. After the second theme there is often a more or less distinct "closing theme." In later sonatas or symphonies (Brahms and Bruckner, in particular) this theme becomes as important as the two main themes. Some movements contain many themes (Beethoven's Symphony no. 3, first movt.) while others often concentrate on one main theme (Haydn's later works; e.g., Symphony no. 104, first movt.; F-major Quartet op. 77, no. 2, finale). Occasionally the most vivid contrasts are found within a single theme (Mozart's Jupiter Symphony, K. 551, first movt.). Thematic material was built in a number of ways: as a tune (Mozart, B^b-major Quartet, K. 458, first movt., opening theme); as a group of motifs (Haydn, D-major Quartet op. 76, no. 5, finale); as patterned figuration (Beethoven, *Appassionata,* finale).

The development is the central section of the movement, in position as well as emotional impact. In style and treatment it differs radically from the exposition. Many devices and procedures are used to produce the special character of "development," "dynamic tension," "increased temperature," "fighting forces," etc., one or both of the themes from the exposition being used as the point of departure [see Development]. Two important techniques are melodic fragmentation and rapid harmonic modulation. Other devices are imitation of melodic motifs (fugal style), contrapuntal combination of different motifs, use of themes or motifs in *inversion or *diminution. There are, of course, no set rules for this procedure. In the development section more than anywhere else, the composer is free to use his ingenuity and imagination. Occasionally new themes and material are used in the development (Mozart, B♭-major Quartet, K. 458, first movt.; Beethoven, Piano Sonata op. 2, no. 1, last movt.; Symphonies nos. 3 and 4, first movts.), but this is an exceptional procedure.

The recapitulation normally contains all the material of the exposition, though usually with certain modifications in the bridge passages. One modification is obligatory, namely, that the second theme appear in the tonic (not, as before, in the dominant). Thus the whole movement closes in the tonic. In some symphonies (Sibelius) the recapitulation is shortened, e.g., to a restatement of the first theme only.

The coda, usually a closing statement of moderate length, sometimes assumes considerable proportions and even becomes another development section (e.g., in Beethoven's *Eroica,* first movt.).

The fully developed sonata form may be diagrammed thus:

‖:Exp.   :‖Dev. Recap.   Coda
  I II (III)   I II (III)
  T D   T T

[For a clear example, see Beethoven's C-minor Quartet op. 18, no. 4, first movt.]

Each phase of action tends to be longer than the preceding one. Many sonata forms have a rather brief first key area, establishing the home key. The remainder of the exposition requires more time, both for the second key to overcome the impression of the tonic and for confirming the second key. Similarly, the development must erase the effect of the second key, reach the tonic, and establish it.

Naturally, the standard sonata form described above is sometimes modified. Some modifications and variants are: (1) substitution of an episode for the development (Mozart, Overture to *Die Entführung aus dem Serail;* Beethoven, F-minor Sonata op. 2, no. 1, finale); (2) delay in the establishment of an important key (Beethoven, F-major Quartet op. 59, no. 1, first movt., first key established at measure 43; F-major

Quartet op. 18, no. 1, first movt., second key delayed; Schubert, Symphony no. 7, finale, recapitulation begins in E♭ instead of C); (3) reversal of the order of events, i.e., return to opening theme before the development (Brahms, Symphonies nos. 1 and 3, finales); (4) combination of single-movement sonata form with elements of multimovement layout (Liszt, B-minor Sonata; Beethoven, *Grosse Fuge*).

II. *Early development.* Unlike the baroque sonata (*sonata da chiesa*), the rococo sonata (mostly for harpsichord) begins with an allegro movement. With few exceptions, these movements are in "rounded binary form," ‖: A :‖: BA :‖, which by 1720 was well established in suite movements [see Binary and ternary form]. Alternations between tutti and solo, forte and piano, vigorous and lyric passages (common features of baroque and rococo styles) were the origin of thematic contrast in the sonata form. The first-movement allegros in binary form were often in styles derived from the baroque concerto (Vivaldi), the *opera buffa* (Pergolesi), the so-called Neapolitan opera, the French overture, and many other forms. In time allegros became longer and more complex in thematic (or motivic) substance. Principles of tonal structure that stemmed from the binary dance movements were still essential characteristics of sonata form as late as 1800. Various writers of the 1780's and 1790's (G. J. Vogler, J. G. Portmann, H. C. Koch, A. F. C. Kollmann; see Lit., Ratner) describe sonata form in terms of harmony— *section I* (later the exposition): (1) tonic key with transition to dominant; (2) dominant key (or relative major key) with close on dominant (or relative major); *section II* (later the development and recapitulation): (3) harmonic digressions leading back to first key; (4) restatement of 1 and 2 (or only 2) in tonic key. Note that in this definition the writers are not actually describing the fully developed sonata form of their own time. The use of themes and a thematic development, so important in the fully developed sonata form, is not mentioned and, in fact, is of relatively little significance in preclassical examples. Many early pieces begin with a more or less well-defined theme but continue with motivic rather than thematic material. The harmonic digressions in subsection (3) are usually sequential restatements of a phrase. Often section II begins with the initial theme (in a different key), in which case this material may be omitted from subsection (4). Some binary movements treat the second half of the form as a mirror image of the first:

	Section I	Section II
Key	I V	V I
Thematic material	A B	B A

B in Section II generally incorporates some development procedures (J. C. Bach, E-major Sonata). The practice of starting section II with a full statement of the initial theme was still used by K. P. E. Bach and in Haydn's earlier works. The repeat of both sections, instead of just the first, is indicated in many works by Haydn, Mozart (regularly in his string quartets), and even in Beethoven's Piano Sonata in F-sharp (op. 78). Although some early 18th-century movements fully restate two themes in the tonic (F. B. Conti, *Overture to Pallade Trionfante,* 1722; Bach, *Well-Tempered Clavier* ii, Prelude in D major), the complete recapitulation did not become standard until after 1750. (Note, e.g., the change in Mozart's symphonies.)

Thus, the emergence of sonata form was a gradual development, not the achievement of any single "inventor," as has been proposed by H. Riemann (J. W. A. Stamitz); G. Adler (G. M. Monn); V. Helffert (Czech composers); F. Torrefranca (G. Platti). Stamitz, for instance, instead of developing motifs, uses a mosaic-like alternation of recurring fragments similar to the structure of Domenico Scarlatti's sonatas. A symphony of 1740 by the Viennese composer G. M. Monn [*DTO* 31, p. 37] uses, in a rudimentary manner, the basic sonata form—exposition, development, and recapitulation, as well as two distinct themes in the exposition. A better example is the first movement of a Trio attributed (wrongly) to Pergolesi (1710–36), reprinted in H. Riemann's *Collegium musicum,* no. 30.

It is interesting to note that the basic structure of sonata form occurs, on a much smaller scale, in the scherzos and minuets of sonatas, as well as in many folksongs [see Binary and ternary form II].

Possibly the first theorist to use the term "sonata form" in musical analysis was A. B. Marx in his *Die Lehre von der musikalischen Komposition* (1837–47). Marx and his contemporaries (Riemann, Jadassohn, Prout, Lobe, *et al.*) established the present concept of sonata form as a characteristic order and treatment of themes.

III. *Later development.* The best-known classical examples of sonata form are found in the works of Haydn and Mozart. Beethoven, Schubert, and Brahms expanded the form. The works of Beethoven's middle period (particu-

larly Symphony no. 3, first movt.) have lengthy expositions and recapitulations as well as a wide harmonic range. For example, in Symphony no. 3, Beethoven arrives at E minor, the furthest removed point, and introduces a new theme to emphasize this harmonic region. As a result of this digression, the development section is twice as long as the exposition or recapitulation. The recapitulation alone was no longer sufficient to establish the home key. Therefore the lengthy coda has a section in the home key that counterbalances the E-minor episode in the development.

The 19th-century sonata generally has fewer movements, often very long (Schubert, Bruckner, Mahler). Here sonata form reflects the influence of romanticism. The two key areas for the exposition are more colorful (the use of third-related key shifts: Beethoven, *Waldstein* sonata, first movt.; Brahms, Symphony no. 3, first movt.; Schubert, C-major Quintet, first movt.). Thematic groups and principal themes are more sharply delineated (Tchaikovsky, Symphony no. 6, first movt.). Separation of the exposition into contrasting sections is especially noticeable in movements that have three distinct themes, each in a different key (Beethoven, Sonata *Appassionata,* first movt., F minor, A♭, A♭ minor; Schubert, C-major Quintet, first movt., C, E♭, G; Brahms, Symphony no. 3, first movt., F, A, A minor).

In the 19th century, development techniques were more freely used than in the classical period. Material might be developed following its initial presentation in the exposition, and the development section itself is usually much more complex than those of Haydn and Mozart (e.g., Beethoven's *Eroica*). However, the influence of the 18th-century sonata form is evident, e.g., in Mendelssohn's Symphony no. 3, 2nd movt., and Smetana's Overture to *The Bartered Bride.* The rise to the dominant is unbroken, with only limited melodic contrast.

In the 20th century various aspects of sonata form have been adapted to new techniques of composition. Schoenberg, in his Quartet no. 4, 1st movt., builds two large thematic groups, clearly contrasted in style, using the twelve-tone series. Bartók, in his *Music for String Instruments, Percussion, and Celesta,* 2nd movt., organizes the sonata form around the tonal center C, with G as a contrasting key area. Other 20th-century composers who have used sonata form include Stravinsky, Copland, Richard Strauss, Piston, Sessions, Hindemith, and Bloch.

Lit.: D. Tovey, *Essays in Musical Analysis* (1935–43); *id., Musical Articles from the Encyclopaedia Britannica* (1944); W. S. Newman, *The Sonata in the Classic Era* (1963; extensive bibl.); R. von Tobel, *Die Formenwelt der klassischen Instrumentalmusik* (1935); F. Tutenberg, *Die Sinfonik Johann Christian Bachs* (1928); W. S. Newman, "The Recognition of Sonata Form by Theorists of the Eighteenth and Nineteenth Centuries" (*PAMS* 1941, pp. 21–9); L. Ratner, "Harmonic Aspects of Classic Form" (*JAMS* ii); *id.,* "Eighteenth-Century Theories of Musical Period Structure" (*MQ* xlii); J. P. Larsen, "Sonatenform-Probleme" (*CP Blume*); W. Fischer, "Zur Entwicklungsgeschichte des Wiener klassischen Stils" (*StM* iii [1915]). See also under Sonata, Lit. for III.

Sonatina. A diminutive sonata, with fewer and shorter movements than the normal type and also usually simpler, designed for instruction (Clementi, Kuhlau). However, such composers as Busoni, Ravel, Bartók, Chávez, and Milhaud have written sonatinas of considerable technical difficulty and artistic merit. Although usually associated with the piano, sonatinas are also written for other instruments, both solo and in combinations. See under Sonata B IV.

Son Chapín. The most popular dance of Guatemala. Also known as *son guatemalteco,* it is in binary form and is basically in 3/4 meter with occasional interpolations of 6/8. Derived from European ballroom dances brought to the New World during the 19th century, it differs radically from the Cuban *son,* whose syncopated patterns, reflecting Negro influences, are nonexistent in the Guatemalan model.   J.O-S.

Song. A song is a short composition for solo voice, usually but not necessarily accompanied, and written in a fairly simple style. Based on a poetic text, it is designed so as to enhance rather than overshadow the text.

The song is the oldest musical form and is found in all periods and places. The rest of this article is concerned with the Western secular art song, excluding *folksong, the songs of Africa, China, etc., as well as religious and liturgical songs (chants, chorales, hymns, etc).

I. *To 1600.* Among the few remnants of Greek vocal music is a charming lyrical song, the *Seikilos Song. A few examples of medieval Latin lyrical songs have been preserved, notably the 10th-century lovesong "O admirabile Veneris idolum" [see *BeMMR*, p. 72], whose melody is interesting on account of its clear G-major tonality. The "Planctus Karoli," a lament for the death of Charlemagne (814), is written in neumes that cannot be deciphered [see fac. and attempt at transcription in *GD* v, 1f]. The most notable body of Latin songs is the 12th- and early 13th-century *Carmina burana* [see Goliard songs]. About 1100 a great flowering of song started with the French *troubadours and *trouvères, and continued with the German *minnesingers and *Meistersinger. The devotional songs of Italy and Spain, known as *laude* and *cantigas,* may also be mentioned. All the songs previously mentioned are unaccompanied, but songs with instrumental accompaniment figure prominently in the music of 14th-century France and Italy [see *Ars nova; Ballata;* Madrigal I; Rondeau; Virelai]. This development reached a climax in the numerous chansons of the *Burgundian masters Dufay and Binchois (both born *c.* 1400). In the second half of the 15th century the song with instrumental accompaniment was gradually replaced by the *part song, for three or four voices. Notable composers were Ockeghem, Obrecht (some with Dutch texts), Isaac (French, Italian, German texts), and Josquin. In the 16th century innumerable French chansons were written by Sermisy, Janequin [see Program chanson], Certon, Crécquillon, and a long line of other composers, closing with Orlando di Lasso. The German part song was culvitated by Hofhaimer, Finck, Senfl, and others. The Spanish *villancicos* and Italian *frottole* of the early 16th century may well be regarded as songs, but the madrigals are too elaborate to be so considered. An interesting repertory is made up of the lute songs by Arnolt Schlick (*Tabulaturen etlicher Lobgesang,* 1512) and vihuela songs by Luis Milán (*El Maestro,* 1535), Enriques de Valderrabano (*Silva de Sirenas,* 1547; *Éditions XXXII, 22/23), and other Spaniards [see *Villancico*]. A large number of beautiful lute songs (*ayres) were written in England *c.* 1600 by John Dowland, Thomas Morley, and many others [see Editions XVII]. At the same time the *air de cour* was developed in France, to be supplanted, during the 17th and 18th centuries, by the more popular types known as *vaudevilles, *pastourelles, *bergerettes, and *brunettes.*

II. *Baroque.* The rise of *monody, *c.* 1600, brought with it fresh impetus for song composition, with its declamatory style and its reduction of the accompaniment to bare essentials. In Italy, where this movement originated, monody produced no lasting tradition of songwriting because the chief focus was on opera, which required a more elaborate type of vocal music, the *aria. In Germany, however, the new trends brought about an early flowering that led almost without interruption to the songs of Schubert, Schumann, and Brahms [see Lied].

III. *Modern song.* Long after the German lied had reached its peak (Schubert), interest in song composition was renewed elsewhere, particularly in France, where composers of rank, inspired by the poetry of Verlaine and Baudelaire, inaugurated a typically French tradition of song (*mélodie*). Among the earliest and most impressive examples are the sixteen songs by Duparc (1848–1933), composed 1868–77. About the same time Fauré (1845–1924) began to write songs, mostly in cycles [see Song cycle] such as *La Bonne Chanson* (1892–93), *La Chanson d'Eve* (1907), *Le Jardin clos* (1915–18), and *L'Horizon chimérique* (1921). In the meantime Debussy (1862–1918) had composed his sensational *Chansons de Bilitis* (1897), which decisively turned away from German models toward a typically French (impressionist) style. The songs of Ravel and Albert Roussel follow the same general trend. Later 20th-century French vocal writing shifted from impressionism toward neoclassicism or toward a sophisticated type of pseudo-popular chanson. However, the *mélodies* of Poulenc indicate a return to the expressive and meaningful treatment of Debussy and Fauré.

The Russians, beginning with Glinka, evolved a highly effective type of romance, usually in symmetrical (ternary) song form. The songs of Tchaikovsky, Rachmaninoff, Gretchaninov, and Glière are mostly lyrical and somewhat sentimental, with texts taken from mediocre contemporary poets. Mussorgsky created a vigorous and unacademic type of song, often employing an expressive and realistic recitative, a style that influenced not only Russian but also French and Spanish songwriters. Rimsky-Korsakov, Balakirev, and Borodin wrote numerous songs in a strongly nationalist idiom, with emphasis on elaborate accompaniment. The Soviet school largely followed the Mussorgsky-Borodin tradition, but Tchaikovsky's influence is also apparent.

The Italian song literature of the 19th century consists of a large number of popular and sentimental songs, for the most part of low quality. The preoccupation with opera apparently proved fatal for the song until about 1910. While the songs of Ottorino Respighi are written in the sensuous style of late romanticism, there

followed a trend toward simplification and even archaism, based on the study of Italian song types of the 16th century (Casella, Malipiero, Petrassi).

In England, too, scarcely any songs of importance were written during the 19th century. Among modern English composers who have been active in this genre are Vaughan Williams, Holst, Bax, Goossens, John Ireland, Philip Heseltine (known as Peter Warlock), Benjamin Britten, and Roger Quilter.

In the United States, Stephen Foster was the creator of a national type of song, and many of his songs have become folksongs. In the development of art song Henry F. Gilbert and Horatio W. Parker were pioneers. The romantic song is represented by MacDowell, Hadley, Carpenter, Cadman, and others; the impressionist by Loeffler and Griffes; the modern song has found an impressive representative in Charles E. Ives.

Lit.: D. W. Stevens, *A History of Song* (1960); J. H. Hall, *The Art Song* (1953); H. T. Finck, *Songs and Song Writers* (1900); J. J. Geller, *Famous Songs and Their Stories* (1931); G. Kobbé, *Famous American Songs* (1906); W. T. Upton, *Art-Song in America* (1930); P. L. Miller, *The Ring of Words* (1963); H. C. Colles, *Voice and Verse* (1928); H. P. Greene, "Stanford's Songs" (*ML* ii, 96ff); *id.*, "The Future of the English Song" (*ML* i, 19ff, 123ff); M. Cooper, "Liszt as a Song Writer" (*ML* xix, 171ff); E. Walker, "The Songs of Schumann and Brahms" (*ML* iii, 9ff); H. Bedford, "Unaccompanied Song" (*ML* iii, 262ff); E. H. C. Oliphant, "A Survey of Russian Song" (*MQ* xii). See also Ayre; Ballad; Folk music; Lied; Shanty; Text and music.

Song cycle [G. *Liederkreis*]. A group of related songs designed to form a musical entity. Examples include Beethoven's *An die ferne Geliebte,* op. 98 (composed 1816 to words by A. Jeitteles); Schubert's *Die schöne Müllerin* (1823; words by W. Müller) and *Winterreise* (1827; also by Müller); Schumann's *Frauenliebe und -leben* (1840; poems by Chamisso) and *Dichterliebe* (1840; poems by Heine); Brahms' *Magelone* (1861–68; poems by Tieck); Fauré's *La Bonne Chanson* (1892–93; poems by Verlaine); Debussy's *Chansons de Bilitis* (1897; poems by Pierre Louÿs). Among the numerous song cycles of the 20th century, Hindemith's *Das Marienleben* (1922–23, rev. 1948; poems by Rilke) is outstanding.

The idea of the song cycle is present in 16th-century cycles of madrigals and canzonas, such as G. de Wert's settings of twelve stanzas from Tasso's *Gerusalemme liberata* (1581) or C. de Rore's set of madrigals based on Petrarch's *Vergine bella* and *A la dolc'ombra*. There are several English song cycles from the 17th and 18th centuries. See D. L. Earl, "The Solo Song Cycle in Germany, 1800–1850" (diss. Indiana Univ., 1952); J. Mark, "The Song Cycle in England" (*Musical Times* lxvi, 325ff).

Song form [G. *Liedform*]. The simple ternary form A B A, a form that actually is much more common in instrumental (particularly piano) music than songs. The term was used first (by B. Marx; *GD* iii, 195; *GDB* vii, 962) to designate the M T M form of the minuet with trio, a species for which the term "ternary form" is preferable in view of the wide discrepancy in style between these dancelike pieces and a song. The term "song form" sometimes is also used for *binary form, a distinction being made between ternary song form and binary song form; in this usage the word "song" might just as well be omitted.

Song-motet. See under Motet B I.

Song of Destiny. See *Schicksalslied*.

Song of the Earth. See *Lied von der Erde, Das*.

Songs of a Wayfarer. See *Lieder eines fahrenden Gesellen*.

Songs without Words. See *Lieder ohne Worte*.

Sonido trece [Sp.]. Name given by the Mexican composer and theorist Julián Carrillo (1875–1965) to his method of using microtone intervals. In most of the compositions he wrote after 1922, Carmillo employs ⅓, ¼, ⅛, or ¹⁄₁₆ of whole tones. Special pianos and a harp tuned to these intervals were manufactured by him and used to play his works.   J.O-S.

Sonnambula, La [It., The Sleepwalker]. Opera in two acts by Bellini (libretto by F. Romani), produced in Milan, 1831. Setting: a Swiss village, early 19th century.

Sonnenquartette. See Sun Quartets.

Sonneries [F.]. Signals given by trumpets or by church bells.

Sonus. In the *Gallican and *Mozarabic Mass, an item corresponding to the Roman Offertory.

Sopra [It.]. Above. *Come sopra*, as above. *M.d.* (or *M.s.*) *sopra*, right (or left) hand above the other (in piano playing). See *Sotto*.

Soprano. The highest female voice; see Voices, range of. Soprano soloists are classified as dramatic, lyric, or coloratura. Voices of similar range are the unchanged boy's voice ("boy soprano") and the "male soprano," i.e., either a *falsetto or, formerly, a *castrato. The term is also used for certain instruments to denote the highest member of a family, e.g., soprano recorder.

Soprano clef. See under Clef.

Sorcerer's Apprentice, The. See *Apprenti sorcier, L'*.

Sordino [It.]. (1) See Mute. (2) Old name for the *kit or *clavichord.

Sordune. See under Oboe family III.

Sorochinskaya Yarmarka, Sorotchintsy Fair. See *Fair of Sorochinsk*.

Sortisatio [L.]. A 16th-century term for improvised counterpoint, as opposed to *compositio*, written out counterpoint. The earliest known mention occurs in the "Opus aureum" (1501) by Nicolaus Wollick, who says that *sortisare* is "cantum diversis melodiis improvise ordinare." Similar definitions are given by A. Ornithoparchus ("Musice active micrologus," 1517) and H. Faber ("Compendiolum musicae," 1548), while in later writings (e.g., J. Thuringus, *Opusculum bipartium*, 1625) the term has the connotation of popular music (*Bergreyen, *villanella). Two examples given by Faber are in note-against-note style with occasional progressions in unison and in parallel fifths. See A. Hammerich, in *SIM* i, 352; W. Gurlitt, in *TV* xvi, 194ff; E. T. Ferand, in *CP 1949*, pp. 103ff, and *MQ* xxxvii.

Sospirando [It.]. Sighing, plaintive.

Sostenente (sostinente) piano. Generic name for a keyboard instrument that produces a sustained sound like that of the violin or organ. A great many such instruments, all more or less ephemeral, have been invented. There are four principal means of obtaining such an effect: (1) by currents of air directed against the strings; (2) by repeating hammers; (3) by a bowing mechanism; (4) by means of electricity. The first method was used in Jean Schnell's *Anémocorde* [see under Aeolian harp]. The second, in

796

which rapidly striking hammers produce a tremolo, was invented by Hawkins in 1800, improved in the *Melopiano* of *c.* 1873 (Caldara and Brossi), and patented in a new form by E. Moor in 1931 and by Cloetens in 1932. The third is realized in a large number of instruments generically called *piano-violin* [G. *Bogenklavier, Streichklavier, Geigenwerk*], all descendants of the *hurdy-gurdy. Usually, the "bow" consists of one or more wheels bearing rosined strings and set in rotation by a pedal mechanism, while the strings are pressed against the wheel by a key mechanism. The first successful instrument of this type was Hans Heyden's *Geigenwerk* (*c.* 1575; described in Praetorius' *De Organographia* [1619; vol. ii, *Syntagma musicum*] and its supplement, *Teatrum Instrumentorum* [1620]). Later constructions frequently used complete violins, violas, etc., which were placed inside a big circular bow and pressed against it, in different positions, by a mechanism connected with the keyboard. In 1817 H. R. Mott of England patented a "Sostinente Piano Forte" in which rollers acting on silk threads transmitted vibrations to the strings. For the fourth category, see Electronic instruments. See G. Kinsky, "Hans Haiden" (*ZMW* vi); also *SaRM; MaMI*.

Sostenuto, sostenendo [It.]. Sustaining the tone to or beyond nominal value, i.e., slackening the tempo. *Andante sostenuto* calls for a slow andante.

Sostenuto pedal. See under Piano I.

Sotto [It.]. Under. *Sotto voce* (under the voice) means performance, vocal or instrumental, "in an undertone," i.e., with subdued sound. *M.d.* (*M.s.*) *sotto* means right (left) hand underneath the other (in piano playing); see *Sopra*.

Soubrette [F.]. A light operatic soprano, often playing a somewhat comical role, e.g., Zerlina in Mozart's *Don Giovanni*. The corresponding French term is *dugazon*, after a famous singer, Louise Dugazon (1755–1821), who excelled in such roles.

Soundboard [F. *table d'harmonie;* G. *Resonanzboden;* It. *piano armonico, tavola armonica;* Sp. *caja armónica*]. In pianos, the wooden surface over which the strings are stretched, which serves as a resonator (also called *belly). Most defects in sound, which often develop in pianos after a number of years, are due to cracking or bending of the soundboard.

Sound hole [F. *ouïe;* G. *Schalloch;* It. *occhi;* Sp. *abertura acústica*]. An opening of various shapes cut in the table of violins and other stringed instruments. Such an opening permits freer movement of the central part of the table, thus helping it reinforce the tones produced by the strings. F. Savart's (1791–1841) experiments showed that in violins, violas, etc., the traditional F-shape of the holes (F-holes) is superior to any other shape. In earlier stringed instruments (viols) the holes were in the shape of a sickle or half-moon (C-holes), whereas the apertures of lutes and guitars are in the shape of a circle in the center of the table [see Rose]. In the latter, the shape and position of the holes result in prolongation of the sound, whereas the F-holes of the violins have the opposite effect.

Sound ideal. [G. *Klangideal*] A term used by musicologists for the characteristic "sonorities" of various periods of music, particularly the earlier ones. For instance, the sound ideal of the *Burgundian school (early 15th cent.) is a light, multicolored combination of vocal sound with many instrumental timbres of a somewhat nasal character, extremely rich in overtones and rather harsh and piercing. See *Spaltklang*. This sonority is in striking contrast to that of the early *Flemish school (late 15th cent.), which is darker in color, lower in range, relatively uniform in timbre, and preferably vocal. See A. Schering, in *JMP* xxxiv; G. Pietzsch, in *AM* iv, nos. 2 and 3; K. G. Fellerer, in *JMP* xliv; H. Brunner, *Das Klavierklangideal Mozarts* (1933).

Sound post [F. *âme;* G. *Seele, Stimmstock;* It. *anima;* Sp. *alma*]. In violins, etc., a small pillar of pine set between the table and back. It serves both to counter the heavy pressure of the bridge on the table (its original purpose) and, chiefly, to convey the vibrations of the table to the back of the instrument and to bring the various vibrating sections into conformity with each other. The correct position of the sound post is slightly behind the right foot of the bridge. Attempts to change the material or shape of the sound post have proved unsuccessful. See W. Huggins, *On the Function of the Sound-post* (1883).

Soupir [F.]. See under Notes.

Soupirant [F.]. Sighing, plaintive.

Sources, musical (pre-1450). There are four categories: Gregorian chant; secular monophony; organ music; polyphonic music. For the first category, see Editions XLII. For the second, see under Chansonnier; Minnesinger; *Lauda; Cantiga.* For the third, see under Organ music I. The most important sources of polyphonic music prior to 1450 are listed below.

Before 1100. *"Musica enchiriadis" and other treatises dealing with *organum [see also Theory, nos. 3 to 7]. Winchester Troper [see Troper].

12th century. 1. *MSS* of *St. Martial, *c.* 1150: Paris, Bibl. Nat. *lat. 1139, 3719, 3549;* London, Brit. Mus. *Add. 36881.* Contents: 2-voice organa. See H. Spanke and H. Anglés, *Die Londoner St. Martial-Conductushandschrift* (1935); H. Spanke, in *Zeitschrift für französische Sprache und Literatur* liv, 282ff, 385ff; J. M. Marshall, "The Repertory of the St. Martial Manuscript" (diss. Yale Univ., 1961).

2. Codex Calixtinus, also called Liber Sancti Jacobi, Compostela, Spain. Contents: 2-voice organa (also conductus) of the school of *Compostela. New ed., 2 vols., by W. M. Whitehill and G. Prado (1944); the music section in P. Wagner, *Die Gesänge der Jakobusliturgie zu Santiago de Compostela aus dem sogennanten Codex Calixtinus* (1931); W. Krüger, in *MF* xvii (also *MF* xix, 180).

13th century. 3. Various MSS containing the repertory of the school of *Notre Dame: organa, clausulae, conductus, motets, *"Magnus liber organi." The four most important are (1) Wolfenbüttel *677* (formerly Helmstedt *628*) W$_1$; fac. ed. in J. H. Baxter, *An Old St. Andrews Music Book* (1931); the organa in W. Waite, *The Rhythm of Twelfth-Century Polyphony* (1954). (2) Florence, Bibl. Laur. *plut. 29.1* (*F*). (3) Wolfenbüttel *1206* (formerly Helmstedt *1099*) W$_2$; fac. ed. by L. Dittmer [1960]; also see E. Thurston, "The *Conductus* Compositions in Manuscript Wolfenbüttel 1206," 2 vols. (diss. New York Univ., 1954); J. Knapp, "The *Conductus* of the Notre Dame School," 4 vols. (diss. Yale Univ., 1961). (4) Madrid, Bibl. Nac. *20486* (formerly *Hh 167; Ma*); fac. ed. by L. Dittmer [1957]. For other sources, see F. Ludwig, *Repertorium organorum,* rev. ed. (1964).

4. Codex *Montpellier, Montpellier, Faculté de médecine *H 196* (*Mo*). Contents: motets. New ed. in Y. Rokseth, *Polyphonies du XIIIe siècle,* 4 vols. (1935–39; facsimiles, transcriptions, commentary).

5. Codex Bamberg, Bamberg, Staatsbibl. *Ed. IV.6* (*Ba*). Contents: motets, **In seculum* compositions. New ed. in P. Aubry, *Cent motets du XIIIe siècle,* 3 vols. (1908; facsimiles, transcriptions, commentary).

6. Codex Huelgas or Burgos, Monastery of Las Huelgas near Burgos (*Hu*). Contents: motets and monophonic hymns. New ed. in H. Anglés, *El Còdex musical de Las Huelgas,* 3 vols. (1931; facsimiles, transcriptions, commentary).

7. Torino, Bibl. Reale *man. var. N. 42* (*c.* 1300). Contents: motets. New ed. in A. Auda, *Les "Motets Wallons" du manuscrit de Turin: vari 42,* 2 vols. [1953].

Note: The motet repertory in nos. 3–7 (and some pieces in no. 8, below) may be found in F. Gennrich, *Bibliographie der ältesten französischen und lateinischen Motetten* (1957), and the conductus repertory of the Notre Dame MSS is indexed in E. Gröninger, *Repertoire-Untersuchungen zum mehrstimmigen Notre Dame-Conductus* (1939).

14th century. 8. Roman de Fauvel, Paris, Bibl. Nat. *fr. 146* (*c.* 1315). Contents: motets and monophonic songs inserted in a continuous narrative. Fac. ed. in P. Aubry, *Le Roman de Fauvel* (1907); transcriptions in L. Schrade, *Polyphonic Music of the 14th Century,* vol. i [1956]. See G. A. Harrison, "The Monophonic Music in the Roman de Fauvel" (diss. Stanford Univ., 1963).

9. Codex Ivrea (Italy), Library of the Chapter. Contents: motets and *chaces. See M. J. Johnson, "The Motets of the Codex Ivrea," 2 vols. (diss. Indiana Univ., 1955; commentary and transcriptions).

10. Machaut MSS of the Bibl. Nat., Paris. Contents: complete works of G. de Machaut (*c.* 1300–77). New ed. in F. Ludwig, *G. de Machaut, musikalische Werke,* 4 vols. (1926–29; vol. iv ed. by H. Besseler [1954]); also in L. Schrade, *Polyphonic Music of the 14th Century,* vols. ii, iii [1956]. Also see R. Hoppin, in *Notes* xv and in *MD* xii, xiv.

11. Florence, Bibl. Naz. *Panciatichi 26.* Contents: madrigals, *caccie, ballate,* by early Italian composers. See *WoGM* i, 244 (for correction of the various lists of contents given in *WoGM,* see F. Ludwig, in *SIM* iv).

Note: Collation of nos. 11–15 in K. von Fischer, *Studien zur italienischen Musik des Trecento und frühen Quattrocento* (1956). For complete Italian 14th-century corpus, see Editions XII, 8.

12. London, Brit. Mus. *Add. 29987.* Contents: Italian compositions of the 14th century; also instrumental **estampies. See *WoGM* i, 268.

13. Codex Squarcialupi, Florence, Bibl. Laur. *Pal. 87.* Contents: works of Francesco Landini and numerous other 14th-century Italian com-

posers (madrigals, *ballate, caccie*). See *WoGM* i, 228; new ed. in J. Wolf, *Der Squarcialupi-Codex* (1955).

14. Paris, Bibl. Nat. *ital. 568.* Contents: Italian compositions of the 14th century. See *WoGM* i, 250; G. Reany, in *MD* xiv.

15. Codex Reina, Paris, Bibl. Nat. *fonds fr. nouv. acq. 6771.* Contents: Italian 14th-century pieces; French 14th-century pieces; compositions of the period of Dufay. See *WoGM* i, 260; K. von Fischer, in *MD* xi, xvii; N. Williams, in *MD* xvii.

16. Modena, Bibl. Estense *L. 568.* Contents: French and Italian compositions of the late 14th century. See *WoGM* i, 335.

17. Chantilly, Musée Condé *1047.* Contents: French compositions of the late 14th century. See *WoGM* i, 328; G. Reany, in *MD* viii.

18. Torino, Bibl. Naz. *J II 9.* Contents: Mass items, motets, French secular compositions, all unique and anonymous. See H. Besseler, in *AMW* vii, 210; R. Hoppin, in *MD* xi. New ed. in *Editions XII, 21.

19. Codex Apt, Apt (France), Library of the Chapter, *c.* 1400. Contents: chiefly Mass items. See H. Besseler, in *AMW* vii, 201. New ed. in *Editions XLIX, Ser. I, 10. See the review by G. de Van, in *AM* xii, 64; also A. Elling, "Die Messen, Hymnen und Motetten der Handschrift von Apt" (diss. Göttingen, 1924).

15th century. 20. Bologna, Lic. Mus. *Q 15* (formerly *37;BL*). Contents: compositions by Ciconia, Dunstable, Dufay, J. de Limburgia, *et al.* See G. de Van, in *MD* ii, 231ff.

21. Modena, Bibl. Estense *lat. 471 (ModB).* Contents: similar to no. 20. See H. Besseler, in *AMW* vii, 236.

22. Bologna, Bibl. Univ. *2216 (BU).* Contents: similar to no. 20. See H. Besseler, in *MD* vi.

23. Codex Aosta, Aosta (Italy), Seminary Library (*Ao*). Contents: similar to no. 20. See G. de Van, in *MD* ii, 5ff.

24. Canonici MS, Oxford, Bodl. Libr. *MS. Can. misc. 213* (*c.* 1450). Contents: Mass items, motets, chansons. New ed. of secular pieces in J. Stainer, *Dufay and His Contemporaries* (1898), and in *Editions XII, 11; of sacred pieces, in C. van den Borren, *Polyphonia sacra* (1932). See S. W. Spurbeck, "A Study of the Canonici Manuscript" (diss. Univ. of Rochester, 1943); G. Reany, in *MD* ix; E. Dannemann, *Die Spätgothische Musiktradition* (1936).

25. Old Hall MS, Catholic College of St. Edmunds, Old Hall, England (*c.* 1425). Contents: Mass compositions, motets, hymns. New ed.

by A. Ramsbotham and H. B. Collins, 3 vols. (1935–38). See M. Bukofzer, in *MQ* xxxiv, xxxv; *id., Studies in Medieval and Renaissance Music* [1950].

26. Trent Codices. See separate entry.

27. Cancionero musical, Madrid, Bibl. del Palacio, *MS 2, 1–5* (*c.* 1500). Contents: 463 Spanish accompanied songs, mostly *villancicos.* New ed. in *Editions XXXII, 5, 10.

See also Chansonnier; Liederbuch. For more complete lists see *ApNPM,* pp. 201ff (12th–14th cent.); *WoHN* i, 351ff and 444ff (14th–16th cent.); *AMW* vii, 245 (14th–15th cent.).

Sourd [F.]. Muffled, muted.

Sourdine [F.]. (1) *Mute (*sordine*). (2) An obsolete wind instrument [It. *sordone*] of the late Renaissance, similar to an early form of bassoon, with a soft, muffled sound; see Oboe family III.

Sousaphone. See under Brass instruments III (e).

Souterliedekens [Dutch]. A 16th-century Netherlands collection of 159 monophonic psalm tunes, published in 1540 (by Symon Cock at Antwerp) and reprinted in more than thirty editions. The publication is the earliest complete translation (rhymed) of the psalms into the vernacular [see Psalter]. The melodies are not newly composed but were taken from popular or folk melodies of the period, mostly Dutch, and the editor has indicated with each melody the beginning of the original secular text, thus preserving numerous early folk melodies. There also is a MS collection from 1537. Tielman Susato of Amsterdam published, in his *Musyck Boexken,* iv–vii (1556–57), 62 three-voice settings of the same melodies by Clemens non Papa [ex. in *ReMR,* p. 358]. Clemens' pupil, Gerardus Mes, composed them in four parts (1561).

Lit.: E. Mincoff-Marriage, ed., ‡*Souterliedekens . . . van 1540* (1922); D. F. Scheurleer, ‡*Die Souterliedekens* (1898); H. F. Commer, ed., ‡*Collectio operum musicorum Batavorum,* 12 vols., xi (*c.* 1850; Clemens non Papa; F. van Duyse, ‡*Oude nederlandsche liederen: melodieen uit de Souterliedekens* (1889); H. A. Bruinsma, "The Souterliedekens and Its Relation to Psalmody in the Netherlands" (diss. Univ. of Michigan, 1949); K. P. Bernet Kempers, "Die 'Souterliedekens' des Jacobus Clemens non Papa" (*TV* xii, xiii, xv); E. Mincoff-Marriage, "Unveröffentlichtes aus der Weimarer Liederhandschrift v. J. 1537" (*Tijdschrift voor nederlandsche taal- en letterkunde* xxxviii, new ser. xxx); W. Wiora,

"Die Melodien der 'Souterliedekens' und ihre deutschen Parallelen" (*CP 1952*).

South America. See under Latin America and individual countries.

South American Indian music. See under American Indian music.

Soviet Union. See Russia.

Sp. [G.]. Abbr. for *Spitze* (point), indicating, in violin music, the point of the bow, and in organ music, the toe of the foot.

Spacing. Arrangement of the notes of a chord according to the demands of the single voices. When the three upper voices are as close together as possible, the spacing is described as "close position" or "close harmony" [Ex. 1, 2]; sometimes the term is reserved for positions not ex-

ceeding a twelfth [Ex. 3, 4]. The other arrangements, common in vocal music, are called open position or open harmony [Ex. 5, 6].

Spagna [It.]. A famous *basse danse* melody, entitled "Il Re di Spagna" (The King of Spain), preserved as a monophonic melody in the *basse danse* MSS of the 15th century and used very frequently as the basis of polyphonic compositions. According to a recent study (O. Gombosi) there are nearly 250 settings for instruments, keyboard, or lute, under such names as "Basa Castiglya," "La Spagna," "Spanyol" [*HAM*, no. 102], etc. After 1550 C. Festa transformed the tune into a *cantus firmus* for contrapuntal exercises [see Lit., Gombosi]. H. Isaac composed a *Missa La Spagna* (Petrucci, 1506). The melody is also used in the "Alta" by F. de la Torre [*HAM*, no. 102a]. See O. Gombosi, ed., ‡*Compositione di Meser Vincenzo Capirola: Lute-Book* (1955), pp. xxxvi–lxiii; O. Kinkeldey, "Dance Tunes of the Fifteenth Century," in *Instrumental Music*, ed. D. C. Hughes (1959); M. F. Bukofzer, *Studies in Medieval and Renaissance Music* [1950], pp. 190ff; W. Apel, in *MD* i.

Spain. From earliest times to the present, Spanish music has mingled popular and artistic elements. The establishment of several separate cultural centers within Spain led to a regionalism

that, over a period of time, combined with many outside influences to create a unique musical heritage.

I. *Before 1500.* The Christianization of Spain, which took place during the 4th century, led to the introduction of so-called Visigothic chant, the Spanish counterpart of Gregorian (Roman) chant, which persisted until it was superseded by Gregorian chant in the latter part of the 11th century. Because it remained in use during the Arab domination (711–1085) it is usually known as *Mozarabic chant [see also Chant]. Before the Arab conquest, Seville, Toledo, and Saragossa were centers of musical culture, particularly under the bishops St. Leander (d. 599) and St. Isidore (c. 560–636). The latter's writings contain valuable information concerning contemporary performance of church music [see *ReMMA*, p. 110]. There also are a number of secular songs, unfortunately notated in neumes that cannot be deciphered, although the melodic outline of one nonliturgical Latin song, the "Song of the Sibyl," is known [see *ReMMA*, p. 199]. Probably the earliest known version appears in a Spanish MS of the mid-10th century. The earliest decipherable examples of Iberian secular monody in the vernacular are Galician songs, *Siete canciones de amor,* attributed to the early 13th-century troubadour or *jongleur* Martim Codex. One of the most disputed features of early Spanish music is the *Arab element, which according to some scholars (Farmer, Ribera) exercised a basic influence not only on Spanish music but on all European music. However, such sweeping claims can scarcely be supported. A very important source of more than four hundred monodic devotional songs is the collection known as *Cantigas de Santa María,* written for (and partly by) Alfonso X (the Wise), King of Castile and León (1252–84). The MSS of the *cantigas* contain rich illuminations showing musicians in Arab dress playing on instruments of Arab origin [see *Cantiga*].

In the 12th century the monastery of Santiago de Compostela in the Pyrenees was a leading center of polyphonic music, side by side with the school of St. Martial. The remarkable Codex Calixtinus of Santiago (c. 1140) shows strong evidence of French origin and contains what is apparently the oldest three-part composition known [see Compostela; Sources no. 2; *ReMMa*, p. 267f; *AdHM*, p. 181f; *ApNPM*, pp. 212ff]. One of the sources of the Notre Dame repertory, the MS Madrid (or Toledo Codex), Bibl. Nac. *20486* [see Sources, no. 3], was probably written in Spain. The influence of French polyphonic music is also apparent in the Codex musical de las Huelgas (or Codex Burgos; see Sources, no. 6), which contains original Spanish pieces, monophonic as well as polyphonic. Johannes Roderici (Rodriguez) is repeatedly mentioned as a composer or editor in this MS, which, though inscribed during the early part of the 14th century, also contains 13th-century works. Evidence of musical activity in 14th-century Catalonia includes a list of some six hundred musicians who served at the court of Catalonia-Aragon at the time and a 14th-century MS at Montserrat, the *Llibre Vermell (Red Book), containing dances, "pilgrim songs" (folk tunes with sacred texts), and other short polyphonic and monodic pieces. John I of Aragon (1350–96) not only composed music himself but also sought the best European musicians, musical instruments, and books for his court.

Probably the earliest Spanish composer whose compositions survive is Johannes Cornago (fl. 1455–after 1466), known for his *Missa signor de la mapa mundi* and about a dozen shorter pieces. Juan de Anchieta (1462–1523) and Francisco de Peñalosa (c. 1470–1535) wrote Masses, motets, hymns, and secular songs. A vast repertory of Spanish songs, mostly in three parts, is preserved in a number of late 15th- and early 16th-century *cancioneros, of which the *Cancionero musical de Palacio* [see Sources, no. 27], containing 463 compositions (mostly *villancicos), is the most important. The composers represented in this collection include Cornago, Anchieta, Peñalosa, Francisco de la Torre, Juan Urreda (Johannes Wreede, a Fleming), and Juan del Encina (1468–1529; also famous as a poet and writer). An important theorist of the same period was B. Ramos de Pareja (c. 1440–after 1491).

II. *1500–1800.* The 16th century was the golden age of Spanish music. In sacred vocal polyphony, organ music, and vihuela music Spain produced masters of the first rank. Outstanding in the first field were Cristóbal de Morales (c. 1500–53), his pupil Francisco Guerrero (1527–99), and the "Spanish Palestrina," Tomás Luis de Victoria (c. 1549–1611). Each wrote about twenty Masses in addition to Magnificats, hymns, and motets. Guerrero composed more than one hundred motets, Morales about ninety, and Victoria forty-six. Guerrero also wrote more than a dozen secular songs and some sixty popular religious polyphonic pieces with vernacular lyrics. Besides these three major composers,

more than forty composers were active in local centers throughout Spain under Philip II, producing an extremely rich repertory.

The *Libro de Cifra Nueva para tecla, harpa, y vihuela* (1557), compiled by Venegas de Henestrosa, is particularly noteworthy as an anthology of mid-16th-century Spanish and Italian instrumental music. Among the organists represented in this collection are Francisco Perez Palero, Pedro Vila, Pedro de Soto, and the great master Antonio de Cabezón. The main source for Cabezón's organ music (hymns, Magnificats, *tientos, *fabordones, *diferencias) is the *Obras de música* of 1578 [*Editions XX, 3, 4, 7, 8], published posthumously by his son, Hernando.

In 16th-century Spain the vihuela de mano, a six-course guitar tuned like the lute, was widely used, but no Spanish music calling specifically for lute has been preserved. Outstanding vihuela composers include Luis Milán, Luis de Narváez, Enriquez de Valderrábano, Miguel de Fuenllana, Diego Pisador, and Esteban Daza, who published tablature books between 1536 and 1576 [see Vihuela]. In addition, a number of musicians were known chiefly as theorists: Juan Bermudo (*Declaración de instrumentos musicales,* 1555), Tomás de Santa María [see O. Kinkeldey, *Orgel und Klavier* (1910)], Diego Ortiz (*Tratado de glosas,* 1553, new ed. by M. Schneider [1913]), and Francisco de Salinas (*De música libri septem,* 1577, fac. ed. by Kastner [1958]). See also Madrigal IV; *Ensalada.*

During the 17th century Spanish church composers continued the polyphonic tradition, largely in the conservative *stile antico* that persisted well into the 18th century. Representative composers include Juan Pujol (c. 1573–1626; some sacred works ed. by H. Anglés [1926–32]), Juan Comes (1568–1643), Mateo Romero (d. 1647), and Carlos Patiño (d. 1683). The school of Montserrat is known largely through the publication of the works (Masses, motets, *villancicos) of Joan Cererols [in D. Pujol, *Mestres de l'Escolania de Montserrat,* 3 vols. of vocal music (1931–32)]. The *Cancionero de Sablonara* (78 songs) is a 17th-century collection of *villancicos,* chiefly by Romero and Jean de Castro (c.1540–c. 1610). Numerous 17th-century Spanish composers wrote for the theater [see Lit., Cotarelo]. Organ music of this time is represented by S. Aguilera de Heredia (c. 1565–after 1620), Correa de Araujo (c. 1576–after 1663), José Jiménez (17th cent.), Pablo Bruna (17th cent.), Juan Cabanilles (1644–1712), and his pupil José Elías (c. 1680–c. 1749), of whom more than three hundred compositions are preserved in Spanish libraries [see Organ music E].

The middle of the 17th century saw the rise of the *zarzuela, a unique type of opera. After 1750 it was replaced by more popular types of lyric theater, the *tonadilla and *sainete. During the 18th century Italian influence became more and more prominent, owing much to the unlimited power given the Italian castrato Farinelli, favorite of King Philip V. Operas by Neapolitan composers were performed at the royal theater, and, at the same time, two Spanish musicians became famous abroad as composers of Italian opera—Domingo Terradellas (Italianized name Domenico Terradeglias, 1713–51), who went to Naples as a boy, and V. Martín y Soler (1754–1806; frequently confused with Antonio Soler), who from 1780 on lived in Florence, Vienna, and St. Petersburg. The latter is remembered mainly for his opera *Una Cosa rara* (1786), from which Mozart quoted in the final scene of *Don Giovanni*, a remarkable circumstance in view of the fact that Soler's opera had for a time completely eclipsed Mozart's *Figaro*.

Naples-born Domenico Scarlatti, who lived in Madrid under royal patronage from 1729 until his death (1757), was the chief harpsichord composer in Spain at this time. His style was adopted by his pupil, Padre Antonio Soler (1729–83), who wrote many kinds of music, carrying on the tradition of Cabanilles and Elías in his organ works. Other notable composers of this period include Mateo Albéniz (d. 1831), Manuel Blasco Nebra (1750–84; see *HAM*, no. 308), and Mateo Ferrer (1788–1864). Chamber works were written by such men as Tomás de Iriarte (1750–91), Manuel Canales, José Herrando (pupil of Corelli), and Luis Misón (d. 1766), who also wrote *tonadillas.

III. *1800—*. Ramón Carnicer (1789–1855), Baltasar Saldoni (1807–89), and Miguel Hilarión Eslava y Elizondo (1807–78) were active during the first half of the 19th century. However, Bellini, Donizetti, and Rossini reigned supreme on the operatic stage, until the popular *zarzuela*, in the form of short comic operas with spoken dialogue, was revived by Basilio Basili (1803–95) and F. A. Barbieri (1823–94). Felipe Pedrell (1841–1922), Tomás Bretón y Hernández (1850–1923), and Ruperto Chapí y Lorente (1851–1909) gradually worked toward a more artistic and nationalist Spanish opera.

The founders of modern Spanish music were Pedrell and Isaac Albéniz (1860–1909). Albéniz is famous mainly for his *Iberia* (1906–09), a collection of twelve piano pieces using Spanish dance rhythms with great imagination and a virtuoso piano technique. Enrique Granados (1867–1916) wrote the piano suite *Goyescas* (after scenes from Goya, 1911–14), which was expanded into an opera and first produced at the New York Metropolitan Opera in 1916. Although lacking the exuberant spirit of Albéniz' music, Granados' more introspective works are typically Spanish in their graceful elegance. Manuel de Falla (1876–1946) is probably the most representative Spanish composer since Spain's golden age. Such works as his *Noches en los Jardines de España* and the ballet *El Sombrero de tres picos* (1919) are both impressionist and nationalist. His *El Retablo de Maese Pedro* (1923) and harpsichord concerto in particular greatly influenced younger Spanish composers. Less important is the mannered descriptive music of Joaquín Turina (1882–1949). The impressionist Federico Mompou (b. 1893) is known for his short poetic piano pieces. Composers who are little known outside Spain include José María Usandizaga (1887–1915), Jesús Guridi (b. 1886), and Conrado del Campo y Zabaleta (1879–1953). Ernesto Halffter (b. 1905), a pupil of De Falla, has used folk elements in his music, although neoclassical tendencies are apparent in his Sinfonietta (1923–27). His brother Rodolfo (b. 1900, later moved to Mexico) has a more cerebral approach; with fine craftsmanship he treats popular and traditional material in a highly original manner. Later he turned to serial techniques. Joaquín Rodrigo (b. 1902), highly prolific, has shown a many-sided nationalism, drawing sparingly on folk elements but endeavoring to embrace the whole tradition of Hispanic music. The Catalonian composer Jaime Pahissa (b. 1880, later moved to Buenos Aires) developed a personal system of composition, based exclusively on unisons and multiple octaves that produce a polyphonic effect through contrary motion (*Suite intertonal,* 1926). Oscar Esplá (b. 1886) is distinguished as a theorist as well as a composer. Julian Bautista (b. 1901, moved to Buenos Aires) has composed modern pieces outside the national tradition, whereas Carlos Surinach (b. 1915) combines a nationalist approach with more progressive technique.

Present-day Spanish composers tend to avoid explicit nationalism in order to achieve the "universalization" of Spanish music. Folk elements have been strongly rejected by the leading group of young musicians, who have embraced serial techniques. Among the most important of them are Cristóbal Halffter (b. 1930; nephew of Ernesto and Rodolfo), Luis de Pablo (b. 1930), Ramón Barce, Manuel Carra, Gerardo Gombau, and Enrique Franco.

More than any other country, Spain possesses a wealth of national dances that have inspired many composers. See *Alalá; Alborada; Aurresku;* Bolero; *Canto de órgano;* Fandango; Flamenco; *Folia* (2); *Guajira; Habanera; Jaleo; Jota; Muineira; Murciana;* Pavane; Polo; *Rueda; Saeta;* Saraband; *Sardana; Seguidilla; Seises; Soleá; Zortziko.* Also *Auto; Sainete; Tonadilla; Zarzuela;* Madrigal IV.

Lit. *General:* G. Chase, *The Music of Spain,* rev. ed. [1959; bibl.]; W. Starkie, *Spain,* 2 vols. [1958]; J. Subirá, *Historia de la música española e hispanoamericana* [1953]; A. Araiz, *Historia de la música religiosa en España* [1942]; A. Soubies, *Histoire de la musique: Espagne,* 3 vols. (1899–1900); *LavE* i.4, pp. 1913–2400; J. B. Trend, *The Music of Spanish History to 1600* (1926); E. M. Barreda, *Música española de los siglos XIII al XVIII* (1942); J. Subirá and A.-E. Cherbuliez, *Musikgeschichte von Spanien, Portugal, Lateinamerika* [1957]; P.-M. Masson, in *RdM* 1936, 113–23.

For I: *Editions IV, 10; H. Anglés, in *CP 1927* (polyphony before 1400); P. Aubry, "Iter hispanicum" (*SIM* viii, ix); I. Pope, in *Speculum* ix (13th-cent. songs); O. Ursprung, in *ZMW* iv (14th-cent. songs); H. Anglés, in *CP Kroyer* (15th-cent. songs); R. Gerber, in *AMW* x hymns, *c.* 1500); R. Stevenson, *Spanish Music in the Age of Columbus* (1960); G. Chase, in *ML* xx, 420 (Encina). See also under Mozarabic chant; *Cantiga; Villancico.*

For II: R. Stevenson, *Spanish Cathedral Music in the Golden Age* (1961); H. Collet, *Le Mysticisme musical espagnol au XVIe siècle* (1913); J. Lopez Calo, *La Música en la Catedral de Granada en el siglo XVI,* 2 vols. (1963); *Editions IV, XX, XXIV, XXVI, XXXII; S. Rubio, ed., ‡Antología polifónica sacra,* 2 vols. (1954, '56); O. Tiby, in *MD* ii (S. Raval); O. Ursprung, in *BUM* v (J. Brudieu); W. Apel, in *MQ* xx (lute and keyboard music). See also under Organ music; *Tonadilla; Zarzuela.*

For III: C. Van Vechten, *The Music of Spain* (1920); F. Sopeña, *Historia de la música española contemporánea* (1958); E. Cotarelo y Mori, *Orígenes y establecimiento de la ópera... hasta 1800* (1917); *id., Historia de la Zarzuela* (1934); H. Collet, *L'Essor de la musique espagnole au XXe siècle* (1929); G. Chase, in *ML* xx (Barbieri);

A. Custer, in *LBCM* (also *MQ* li).

Folk music: K. Schindler, ‡*Folk Music and Poetry of Spain and Portugal* (1941); F. Pedrell, ‡*Cancionero musical popular español,* 4 vols. [*c.* 1918–22; new ed., 2 vols., n.d.]; E. Martínez Torner, *Cancionero musical* (1920); C. Rice, *Dancing in Spain* (1931); H. Anglés, "Das spanische Volkslied" (*AMF* iii); J. B. Trend, "Salinas: A Sixteenth-Century Collector of Folk Songs" (*ML* viii, 13ff); F. Pedrell, "Folk-lore musical castillan du XVIe siècle" (*SIM* i); P. Aubry, "Folk-lore musical d'Espagne" (*SIM* ix).   rev. S.B.

Spaltklang [G.]. Name for a sonority resulting from simultaneous use of contrasting timbres. The term is used with reference to 14th- and 15th-century music (Machaut, Dufay), whose polyphonic character is emphasized by the simultaneous sound of, e.g., voice, shawm, and trombone. The Gothic organ also was based on the *sound ideal of *Spaltklang.*

Spanisches Liederbuch [G., Spanish Song Book]. A collection of forty-four songs by Hugo Wolf, composed 1889–90, to German translations, by E. Geibel and Paul Heyse, of Spanish poetry of the 16th and 17th centuries. See F. Walker, in *ML* xxv, 194.

Spanish Rhapsody. See *Rapsodie Espagnole.*

Spanish Song Book. See *Spanisches Liederbuch.*

Sparte [G.]; **sparta, spartita** [It.]. Partition score. *Spartieren* [G.] means to write a full *score or put into score. The term is used specifically with reference to early vocal music (prior to 1600), which was originally written in single parts. Therefore, it is synonymous with transcribing early music, a process requiring knowledge of *mensural notation.

Spatium [L.]. The space between two lines of a staff.

Speaker key. In wind instruments, a key that facilitates the production of tones by overblowing. It opens a small hole that causes the air column to vibrate in one-half or one-third of its entire length. The oboe usually has two such keys, used to overblow different portions of the scale at the octave, while the clarinet has only one, producing the twelfth.

Speaking stop. In organs, any stop that produces sounds, as distinct from others that merely operate couplers, etc.

Species. A method of teaching counterpoint known mainly through J. J. Fux's *Gradus ad Parnassum* (1725). Fux distinguished five species, i.e., different ways of adding contrapuntal voice-parts above and below a given *cantus firmus* (*c.f.*); (1) note against note; (2) two notes against each note of the *c.f.;* (3) four notes against each note of the *c.f.;* (4) notes in syncopated position; and (5) florid counterpoint, consisting of a combination of the other species and progressions in eighth notes. [See Ex.] This method of teaching can be traced back as far as 1533 (G. M. Lanfranco, *Scintille de musica;* see Counterpoint

II). Fux's five species are found in L. Zacconi's *Prattica di musica* ii (1619), together with other "species," such as *contrappunto fugato, ostinato, doppio.* See K. Jeppesen, *Counterpoint* (1930; Eng. trans. 1939).

Speech song. See *Sprechstimme.*

Sperdendosi [It.]. Fading away.

Spezzato [It.]. Split, broken. *Coro spezzato,* divided chorus [see Polychoral style]; *registro spezzato,* divided register [see Divided stop]. M. Pesenti, in his *Il Secondo Libro delle correnti alla francese ... con alcune correnti spezzate a tre* (1630) uses the indication "spezzata" for a style probably similar to the French **style brisé.*

Spianato [It.]. Smooth, even.

Spiccato [It.]. See Bowing (d).

Spiegelfuge [G.]. Same as mirror fugue [see Mirror composition].

Spieldose [G.]. Music box.

Spielfigur [G.]. A term used particularly in connection with the keyboard music of composers such as Bull, Sweelinck, and Scheidemann, who often employed short, lively, playful motifs, such as shown in the accompanying example (Sweelinck, Toccata). Frequently these

figures alternate among the various voice-parts, in which case they are called **Komplementärfiguren.*

Spieloper [G.]. Name for the German 19th-century *comic opera (Lortzing, Marschner).

Spinet [F. *épinett;* G. *Spinett;* It. *spinetta;* Sp. *espineta*]. (1) A type of small harpsichord. Originally the Italian and French terms referred to any jack-action keyboard instrument [see Harpsichord], but later they were limited to any small, single-choired jack-action instrument in which the strings ran more or less transversely. The German term was used mainly to refer to the oblong instruments with transverse strings that in England were called virginals. In Dutch it was used to distinguish virginals with the keyboard displaced toward the left from those in which it was displaced toward the right (*muselar*). During the 18th century the term was applied in England to small instruments having a single transverse choir of strings and a short bent side to the right. In modern English, the spinet is distinguished from the oblong virginals. Generally speaking, any single-choired harpsichord-like instrument that is neither oblong nor of the characteristic harpsichord wing-shape may properly be called a spinet. Acoustically it differs from the virginal, in which both ends of the vibrating section of the strings are supported by bridges mounted on the soundboard, in that one end of each string of the spinet is supported by a bridge glued to the solid wrestplank. In this it resembles the harpsichord. The resulting tone is less hollow than that of the virginal.

(2) A piano with strings perpendicular to the keyboard (as in an upright piano) but with an indirect action. See Piano III.   (1) by F.H.

Spingardo. A dance of the early 16th century, known only from two examples in J. A. Dalza's *Intabolatura de lauto* (Petrucci, 1508), where it occurs in two suites, *passamezzo–saltarello–spingardo*, instead of the normal suite, *passamezzo–saltarello–piva*. It would appear to be just another name for the **piva*.

Spiritoso [It.]. Spirited.

Spirituals. See Negro music I. See G. P. Jackson, "Pennsylvania Dutch Spirituals" (*MQ* xxxviii, 80ff).

Sponsus play. See under Liturgical drama.

Sprechstimme, Sprechgesang [G.]. A type of voice production halfway between song and speech. It consists of recitation on higher or lower pitches, which, however, are merely hinted at in a subdued manner. *Sprechstimme* is usually notated on a staff by means of crosslike symbols instead of notes. Both the method and notation of *Sprechstimme* [lit., speech song] were introduced by Humperdinck in his melodrama *Königskinder* (1897). Schoenberg used it in *Pierrot Lunaire* (1912) and *Die Glückliche Hand* (1913), and Alban Berg in *Wozzeck* and *Lulu*. See R. Stephan, "Zur jüngsten Geschichte des Melodrams" (*AMW* xvii); H. Keller, in *Tempo*, no. 75 [1965/66], pp. 12–17.

Sprezzatura. Term used by G. Caccini (*Le Nuove musiche*, 1601) for a "nonchalant" type of singing, very likely a rubato. See *RiHM* ii.2, 526; *BuMBE*, pp. 28, 371f; F. Torrefranca, in *CP 1952*, p. 412.

Springbogen [G.]. *Sautillé, saltando;* see Bowing (d).

Springer. An *agrément* used in 17th-century English lute and viol music and belonging to the category of **Nachschlag*.

Sprung(k) [G.]. A 16th-century designation for a **Nachtanz* (after-dance).

Spurious compositions. Their number being legion, the reader is referred to C. L. Cudworth, "Ye Olde Spuriosity Shoppe" (*Notes* xii, 25ff, 533ff), as well as the following literature. Considerable emphasis is placed on Haydn and Mozart simply because so much research has been done concerning these two composers.

Lit.: H. C. Robbins Landon, *The Symphonies of Joseph Haydn* [1955]; *id., Supplement to "The Symphonies of Joseph Haydn"* [1961]; *id.,* "Two Orchestral Works Wrongly Attributed to Mozart" (*MR* xvii); *id.,* "The *Jena* Symphony" (*MR* xviii); *id.,* "Doubtful and Spurious Quartets and Quintets Attributed to Haydn" (*MR* xviii); A. Main, "Maximilian's Second-Hand Funeral Motet" (*MQ* xlviii); J. La Rue, "Major and Minor Mysteries of Identification in the 18th-Century Symphony" (*JAMS* xiii); *id.,* "A New Figure in the Haydn Masquerade" (*ML* xl); C. Cudworth and F. B. Zimmerman, "The Trumpet Voluntary" (*ML* xli); D. E. Deutsch, "Unfortunately Not By Me" (*MR* xix; trans. M. J. E. Brown); H. T. David, "A Lesser Secret of J. S. Bach Uncovered" (*JAMS* xiv); W. Kirkendale, "More Slow Introductions by Mozart to Fugues of J. S. Bach?" (*JAMS* xvii); J. Reid, "The 'Gastein' Symphony Reconsidered" (*ML* xl); A. M. Owen, "The Authorship of Bach's Cantata No. 15" (*ML* xli); F. Hudson and A. Dürr, "An Investigation into the Authenticity of Bach's 'Kleine Magnificat'" (*ML* xxxvi); J. M. Barbour, "Pokorny Vindicated" (*MQ* xlix); A. Tyson, "Haydn and Two Stolen Trios" (*MR* xxii); H. C. Robbins Landon, "Problems of Authenticity in Eighteenth-Century Music," in *Instrumental Music*, ed. D. G. Hughes (1959).

Squarcialupi, Codex. See Sources, no. 13.

Square neumes [G. *Quadratneumen*]. A neumatic script of the 12th century, characterized by the use of small squares (rather than dots, dashes, etc.) to indicate pitches. It developed in northern France and was later universally adopted for the notation of Gregorian chant [see Neumes II] as well as secular monophony (trouvères, *laude*), except in Germany, where **Nagelschrift* remained in use up to 1500. See also Square notation.

Square notation [G. *Quadratnotation*]. Term introduced by F. Ludwig (*Repertorium organorum* [1910], i, pt. l) to designate the notation of the school of **Notre Dame* (*c.* 1175–1250), which was the first to use square shapes for the notes and ligatures (derived from the **square neumes*), instead of the less definitely drawn, neumelike symbols of earlier periods (school of **St. Martial*). The chief sources of square notation are the MSS containing the "Magnus liber organi" [see Sources, no. 3].

Some writers prefer the term *modal notation. However, this term implies that the notational signs are to be interpreted in modal meter, i.e., in the scheme of the rhythmic *modes, an implication that is not wholly valid. The pieces written in square notation belong to several categories, of which only one—the repertory of *organa, tripla, quadrupla,* and clausulae—deserves the name "modal." With others, such as the earlier *organa dupla* (Leoninus), conductus, and monophonic songs, modal interpretation is at least doubtful. For an example of square (or modal) notation, see Notation, Ex. 2. See *ApNPM,* pp. 215–81; *WoHN* i, 198–250.

St. See under Saint.

Stabat Mater [L.] A 13th-century sequence (*Stabat mater dolorosa*), probably written by the Franciscan Jacopone da Todi (*c.* 1228–1306). It was officially added to the Roman Catholic liturgy in 1727 and is still sung today at the Feast of the Seven Dolors (Sept. 15; for the text and liturgical melody, see *LU,* p. 1634^v). The poem has been set by Josquin, Palestrina, Lasso, Steffani, d'Astorga (ed. by R. Franz), A. Scarlatti, D. Scarlatti, Caldara, Pergolesi, Haydn, Rossini, Schubert, Verdi, Dvorák, Dohnányi, Stanford, Szymanowski, Poulenc, Thomson, Persichetti, and others.

Lit.: K. H. Bitter, *Studie zum Stabat Mater* (1883); *ApGC,* pp. 31, 424, 464; E. Schmitz, *Das Madonnen-Ideal in der Tonkunst* [1918]; C. B. Edgar, in *SIM* ii; P. Mies, in *KJ* 1932; W. Baeumker, in *KJ* 1883, p. 59.

Stabreim [G.]. *Alliteration.

Staccato. A manner of performance indicated by a dot or the sign ▼ placed over the note, calling for a reduction of its written duration with a rest substituted for half or more of its value. Thus, a quarter note will be reduced to perhaps a sixteenth note, followed by three sixteenth rests. In piano and violin playing as well as in singing, there are various types of staccato, produced by different touch, bowing, attack, etc. [see Bowing (g)]. Earlier composers, such as K. P. E. Bach, Haydn, and Beethoven, normally indicated staccato with the wedge [see Schencker's ed. of Beethoven's piano sonatas], reserving the dot for a less rigid staccato (portato), preferably in slow movements. In *Die Bedeutung der Zeichen Keil, Strich und Punkt bei Mozart* (ed. H. Albrecht, 1957), five scholars (H. Keller, H. Unverricht, O. Jonas, A. Kreutz, E. Zimmermann) investigate the significance of

the wedge, vertical stroke, and dot in Mozart's autographs and first editions, with more or less differing results. See also P. Mies, in *MF* xi. Today the dot is used as the normal sign, and the dash for a more pronounced staccato. See A. Pochon, *Le Rôle du point en musique* (1947).

Staff, stave [F. *portée;* G. *Liniensystem, System;* It. *rigo;* Sp. *pentagrama, pauta*]. A series of horizontal lines, today always five in number, on and between which musical notes are written, thereby indicating (in connection with a *clef) their pitch. The positions of the notes on the staff give a satisfactory image of the pitches, although they fail to indicate the difference between whole tones and semitones, as well as the modifications of pitch produced by accidentals (e.g., C-double-sharp is actually higher in pitch but lower on the staff than D-flat).

The first use of horizontal lines for the representation of pitches appears in *"Musica enchiriadis" (*c.* 900). However, only the spaces between the lines are used, with the syllables of the text written in at their proper place [see *ApNPM,* fac. 42a, 42b]. The invention of the staff proper is ascribed to Guido d'Arezzo (*c.* 990–1050), who in *Regulae de ignoto cantu* [*GS* ii, 34ff] recommends the use of three or four lines, denoting f a c' or d f a c' (the use of one or two lines, red for f and yellow for c', occurred in slightly earlier MSS). The four-line staff has been preserved to the present day for the notation of Gregorian chant. For notating polyphonic music the five-line staff was used as early as the 13th century [see *ApNPM,* fac. 46]. For compositions in simple note-against-note style (*conductus) the different staves were frequently written so close together that they give the impression of a single staff of ten or more lines [see *ApNPM,* fac. 47]; however, the fact that on such a staff the same clef letter (c') is used simultaneously in different positions clearly shows that this is a juxtaposition of several staves rather than a single staff. Six-line staves were occasionally used in the 14th century (e.g., in the Italian Codex Rossi, *c.* 1340), in early 15th-century contratenors of wide range (Dufay, Binchois; see H. Besseler, *Bourdon und Fauxbourdon* [1950], pp. 45ff), and in numerous 16th-century scores of keyboard music [see *ApNPM,* fac. 1, 3, 4, 5].

Lute music and Spanish keyboard music of the 16th century are written on a series of lines that look exactly like the staff but have an entirely different meaning. In the former they represent the strings of the lute and in the latter the voice-parts of a composition. See Tablature II and III. For modern reforms of the staff, see *WoHN* ii, 347ff.

Staffless neumes. See under Neumes II.

Staffless notation. General term for methods of notation in which the tones are indicated by letters or similar symbols rather than by notes on a staff. An old method of this type is the German organ and lute tablature [see Tablature I and V]; a newer one is the *tonic sol-fa.

Stahlspiel [G.]. The military *glockenspiel [see Lyra (4)].

Stampita, stantipes. See *Estampie.*

Ständchen [G.]. *Serenade.

Star-Spangled Banner, The. The national anthem of the United States, officially adopted in a bill passed on March 3, 1931. The words were written by Francis Scott Key (1779–1843) in September, 1814, while he watched the British bombardment of Fort McHenry, near Baltimore. It is sung to a tune by John Stafford Smith (*c.* 1750–1836), an Englishman who originally composed the music for a poem beginning "To Anacreon in Heaven." It is not known whether Key had this tune in mind when he wrote the poem, or whether text and music were united later (possibly by Joseph Hopper Nicholson). See O. G. T. Sonneck, *The Star Spangled Banner* (1914); J. Muller, *The Star Spangled Banner* (1935).

Steel band. A type of instrumental ensemble that has developed since *c.* 1910 in the Caribbean. The instruments are old oil drums whose heads are embossed and indented in such a manner that each head will produce several different notes, depending on where it is struck. It is used extensively in *calypso and *merengue music.

Steg [G.]. Bridge of the violin, etc. See Bowing (k).

Stegreif [G.]. Improvisation, or performance without preparation. *Stegreifkomödien,* farcical plays with improvised dialogue, were extremely popular in Vienna toward the end of the 18th century. See *DTO* 64.

Stendendo [It.]. Slowing down.

Steppes of Central Asia, In the [Rus. *V Srednei Azii*]. Symphonic poem by Borodin, composed

in 1880. Its Russian title means simply *In Central Asia.*

Steso [It.]. Slow.

Sticheron. In Byzantine church music [see Byzantine chant] of the 8th century and later, poetic intercalations between the verses (*stichos*) of a psalm; in other words, psalm tropes. A collection of such hymns was called *sticherarion.*

Stil [G.], **stile** [It.], **stilus** [L.]. See Style.

Stile concertante. See under Concerto III.

Stile concertato. See *Concertato.*

Stile concitato. See under Style.

Stile familiare. See Familiar style.

Stile rappresentativo [It.]. Passages of melody in vocal or instrumental music characterized by freedom of rhythm, irregularity of phrasing, frequent pauses, and other traits of *recitative [see also Arioso].   D.J.G.

Stimm- [G.]. Voice. *Stimmbänder,* vocal cords; *Stimmbildung,* voice training; *Stimmbruch,* mutation; *Stimmbücher,* partbooks; *Stimmgabel,* tuning fork; *Stimmhorn,* a tool in the shape of a hollow cone used in tuning organ pipes; *Stimmführung,* *voice-leading; *Stimmbrücke,* *tuning wire; *Stimmkreuzung,* crossing of parts; *Stimmpfeife,* *pitch pipe; *Stimmritze,* glottis; *Stimmstock,* sound post; *Stimmtausch,* *voice exchange; *Stimmumfang,* range; *Stimmwechsel,* mutation (of the voice); *Stimmzug,* slide (of trombones).

Stimme [G.]. (1) Voice. (2) Voice-part.

Stimmen [G.]. (1) Plural of *Stimme. (2) To tune.

Stimmung [G.]. (1) Mood; thus, *Stimmungsbild,* title for pieces meant to express some definite mood. (2) Tuning, intonation, e.g., *reine Stimmung,* just intonation.

Sting. See under Vibrato (1).

Stinguendo [It.]. Fading away.

Stiracchiando, stirato [It.]. Drawing out, slowing down.

Stockflöte [G.]. See Czakan.

Stockhorn. *Pibgorn.

Stollen [G.]. See under *Bar* form. Sometimes used as a term for exposition, which, in *sonata form, corresponds to the *Stollen* of the medieval *Bar.*

Stop. (1) In the organ, the mechanical device by which the player can draw on or shut off the various registers. Depending on the style of organ console, this device may be in the form of either a stop knob (draw bar) or stop tab; also, the stop action may be mechanical (using draw knobs or levers) or electric (using tabs or knobs). See Organ II, III. The term is also used for the rank (ranks) of pipes controlled by the mechanism mentioned above. (2) In the harpsichord, stops are chromatic sets of strings that correspond to the keys of the keyboard. Stops have various tone colors and pitch levels. See Harpsichord. (3) A special device frequently used in 17th-century organs and harpsichords was the short stop (half-stop), with which the pipes or strings that it governs do not extend through the total compass of the keyboard. See Divided stop.

Lit.: W. L. Sumner, *The Organ*, rev. ed. (1958); S. Irwin, *Dictionary of Pipe Organ Stops* (1962); R. Russell, *The Harpsichord and Clavichord* (1959), pp. 14ff.

Stopped notes. See under Horn I.

Stopped pipe. Any pipe closed at one end. For stopped flute, see Organ IX; also Wind instruments III.

Stopping. (1) In stringed instruments (violins, lutes), placing the fingertips of the left hand so that they shorten the vibrating length of the string. See Double stop. (2) On the natural horn, see Horn.

Storm and Stress. See *Sturm und Drang*.

Storta [It.]. A 16th-century term [lit., twisted] for the cromorne or a very similar instrument. It is mentioned in the descriptions of instruments used for several 16th-century intermezzi.

Strad. Abbr. for Stradivarius violin; see Violin I.

Straff [G.]. Rigid, firm.

Straight organ. An organ having a separate and distinct row of pipes for every stop control at the keydesk. A straight organ has more pipes than a *unit organ with the same number of stop controls. See Organ II (b).   C.B.F.

Strambotto. A form of 15th-century Italian poetry, consisting of eight-line stanzas in iambic pentameter with the rhyme scheme ab ab ab ab, or, more frequently, ab ab ab cc (the latter is known as *ottava rima;* see, e.g., Byron's *Don Juan*). In Petrucci's *Frottole* (1504–14) *strambotti* are composed in strophic form, the music

of the first two lines being repeated four times [ex. in *RiHM* ii.1, 356]. Later examples are through-composed, in the manner of the madrigal. For bibl. see under *Frottola*.

Strascicando, strascinando [It.]. Dragging.

Strathspey. A slow Scottish dance in 4/4 meter, with many dotted notes, frequently in the inverted arrangement of the Scotch snap. The name, derived from the strath (valley) of the Spey, was originally synonymous with *reel; later, "reel" was used for somewhat faster dances in more smoothly flowing rhythm, lacking dotted notes. Important early collections of strathspeys (reels) are: A. Cummings, *A Collection of Strathspeys or Old-Highland Reels* (Strathspey, 1780); Niel Gow, *Collection [A Second . . . Sixth] of Strathspey Reels* (Dunkeld, 1784–1822). Niel Gow (1727–1807) was the most famous performer of strathspeys and reels.

Stravaganza [It.]. General term for a piece in free style or involving some sort of fanciful treatment. As early as the end of the 16th century the name was used by G. Macque (*c.* 1550–1614) for compositions employing "extravagant" harmonies, modulations, dissonances, etc. See his *Consonanze stravaganti* in *HAM,* no. 174 [see also Editions XXVIII, 4, pp. 60, 69].

Straw fiddle. See under Xylophone.

Straziante [It.]. Anguished.

Street cries. As early as the late 13th century, street cries were incorporated into compositions, e.g., in the motet "On parole–A Paris–Frèse nouvele," which describes the gay life of Paris and appropriately employs in the tenor a vendor's cry: "Frèse nouvele! Muere france!" (Fresh strawberries! Wild blackberries!), repeating it four times as an ostinato [*HAM,* no. 33b]. Later, English composers were attracted by the street cries of London. About 1600, Weelkes, Gibbons, and Deering each wrote a composition in which the text (and probably also the music) consists exclusively of the cries of itinerant vendors, as, "New oysters, new walfleet oysters, New mussels . . . , New cockles . . . , Hott mutton pyes . . . ," etc. In Ravenscroft's *Pammelia* (1609) and *Melismata* (1611) a number of street cries are cleverly arranged as rounds. Handel used contemporary street cries in one of the movements of his opera *Xerxes* (1738). Numerous street cries are preserved in 18th-century prints or engravings, representing all sorts of vendors [see P. A.

Scholes, *The Oxford Companion to Music* (1955), facing p. 992].

Street organ, hand organ. A *mechanical instrument based on the barrel-and-pin principle in which the pins operate reed pipes similar to those of the organ. A crank turns the barrel and also operates a bellows, which furnishes air to make the reeds vibrate. The instrument, which is associated with the Italian street musician and his monkey, is popularly but erroneously called *hurdy-gurdy.

Streich- [G.]. Bow. *Streichinstrumente,* bowed instruments. *Streichquartett (-quintett),* string quartet (quintet). *Streichklavier,* piano-violin [see Sostenente piano].

Streit zwischen Phöbus und Pan, Der [G., The Struggle between Phoebus and Pan]. Secular cantata by J. S. Bach (1732), text by Picander, based on Ovid's account of the musical contest between Phoebus Apollo and Pan. The work is probably a satire directed against Bach's critic, Scheibe (represented by the character Midas).

Strepitoso [It.]. Noisy, boisterous.

Stretta [It.]. Same as *stretto (2).

Stretto [It.]. (1) In a fugue, the imitation of the subject in close succession, with the answer entering before the subject is completed [G. *Engführung*]. The resulting dovetailing of the subject and its imitation produces an increased intensity that is particularly suitable for the close of the fugue [see Ex., from the Fugue in D

major, *Well-Tempered Clavier* ii]. Stretto, although used as early as 1400 [see, e.g., Dunstable's *O rosa bella; HAM,* no. 61, meas. 7–9], was used as a special device of theme presentation in the 16th-century ricercar by Girolamo Cavazzoni and, particularly, Andrea Gabrieli and the later ricercar composers. (2) In nonfugal compositions, stretto (stretta) is a concluding section in faster tempo, as, e.g., at the end of the last movement of Beethoven's Fifth Symphony.

Strich [G.]. Bow stroke.

Stringed instruments. Instruments in which the sound-producing agent is a stretched string. The scientific name for this category is chordophone [see under Instruments IV]. The most important members of this large group are the *violin (and its family), *harpsichord, *harp, and *piano. In each of these instruments the sound is produced by different means, i.e., bowing, plucking, and striking with a hammer. Ordinarily, the name "stringed instruments" ("strings") is reserved for members of the violin family. See H. Panum, *The Stringed Instruments of the Middle Ages* (1941); A. J. Rühlmann, *Geschichte der Bogeninstrumente* (1882); W. Bachmann, *Die Anfänge des Streichinstrumentenspiels* (1966).

String quartet [F. *quatuor à cordes;* G. *Streichquartett;* It. *quartetto di corde;* Sp. *cuarteto de cuerdas*]. Chamber music for four strings, practically always first and second violin, viola, and cello. The string quartet is the main type of *chamber music and is frequently considered, by serious musicians as well as amateurs, the ideal type because it "always says what is necessary, and never too much." For its form, see under Sonata.

I. *The present repertory.* The present-day repertory of string quartets begins with the later quartets of Haydn, written between 1770 and 1790, and those written by Mozart in the same decades. In these works Haydn and Mozart established the string quartet not only as a definite ensemble but as the stylistic realization of the ideal of "four-fold companionship" that has remained—despite stylistic changes and some "side-stepping" in the late 19th century—the basic principle of quartet composition. Beethoven's earlier works (op. 18, nos. 1–6, 1801; op. 59, Russian Quartets, 1808) are what might be termed "Haydn quartets in Beethoven's language," but his late quartets (op. 127, op. 130–33, op. 135) transform a distinguished entertainment into music of far greater complexity and profundity. Beethoven's successor was Franz Schubert, whose late quartets (A minor, D minor) were seldom performed until relatively recently. While the quartets of the period immediately following (Cherubini, Schumann, Mendelssohn) are of secondary importance, a new peak was reached in the quartets of Brahms (op. 51, op. 67), which used the traditional form to express restrained romanticism. The romantic string quartet came to its conclusion with the works of Dvořák (eight quartets, 1874–95), Franck (D minor, 1889), D'Indy (op. 35, 1891; op. 45, 1898; op. 96, 1930), and Max Reger (op. 54, op. 74, op. 109, op. 121).

French impressionism, with its emphasis on coloristic effects, and the turbulent decades of the early 20th century were not particularly favorable to the cultivation of so traditional a form as the quartet. Nonetheless, the quartets of this period are interesting documents, showing attempts to utilize the medium of strings as a vehicle for impressionist methods (Debussy, Ravel); atonality (Schoenberg, Berg, Webern); twelve-tone technique (Schoenberg, op. 30); motoric and percussive rhythms (Bartók, nos. 3 and 4); neoclassic idiom (Stravinsky, Sessions, Piston); quarter-tone technique (Bartók, no. 6, 3rd movt., Burletta section); etc.

II. *History.* The string quartet is a relatively recent type. To trace it to the 16th or early 17th century is a misguided effort. In the first place, the four-voice chamber music of this period (*ricercars and similar pieces by Isaac, Hofhaimer, Senfl, Willaert, and A. Padovano; instrumental *canzonas by Maschera and many others) is entirely different from the modern quartet in form and style. Moreover, it has no historical connection with the latter since the medium of four stringed instruments was largely abandoned in the baroque period except in England, where the *fancy was cultivated until *c.* 1680. A composition by Gregorio Allegri (*c.* 1582–1652), which has been called "the first work for four stringed instruments," owes this distinction merely to the fact that Athanasius Kircher, in his *Musurgia* of 1650, reproduced it with the designation "duoi violini, alto, e basso di viola" [see J. W. von Wasielewski, *Die Violine im 17. Jahrhundert, Instrumentalsätze,* Suppl., p. 26]. During the first half of the 17th century numerous four-voice instrumental pieces were written in Italy and Germany; these, however, seem to have been intended for small string orchestras rather than a quartet [see Sonata B II, close]. About 1675 the four-part ensemble was largely abandoned, and the *trio sonata became the chief type of chamber music during the later baroque period.

Certain sonatas by Alessandro Scarlatti (1659–1725) bear the (authentic?) remark *per due violini, violetta, e violon-cello,* the earliest extant indication, after Kircher's, of the modern string quartet. Its actual history, however, does not begin much before 1750. The question of precedence is very difficult to settle since various claimants lived at the same time (Tartini, 1692–1770; Sammartini, 1701–75; F. X. Richter, 1709–89; see *DTB* 27), while others (Starzer; see *DTO* 31; Pugnani; Boccherini; M. Canales; Karl Stamitz; Anton Stamitz; Gyrowetz) belong to the generation of Haydn (b. 1732). In general, the earliest string quartets (including those of the young Haydn) are orchestral rather than chamber music, since they were performed by several players to the part. Their form is frequently that of the *divertimento. Haydn wrote 83 quartets, Boccherini 102, and Gyrowetz 60.

Lit.: W. Altmann, *Handbuch für Streichquartettspieler,* 4 vols. (1928–31); M. D. Herter Norton, *String Quartet Playing* (1925); E. Heimeran and B. Aulich, *The Well-Tempered String Quartet* (1938); J. de Marliave, *Études Musicales* (1917), pp. 215ff; J. Kramarz, *Das Streichquartett* (1961); A. E. Hull, "The Earliest Known String-Quartet" (*MQ* xv); E. J. Dent, "The Earliest String Quartets" (*Monthly Musical Record* xxxiii [1903], 202–04); G. Roncaglia, in *LRM* vi, vii (Cambini); M. Pincherle, "On the Origins of the String Quartet" (*MQ* xv); M. Scott, "Haydn's '83'" (*ML* xi, 207ff); E. Goossens, "The String Quartet since Brahms" (*ML* iii, 335ff); G. Roncaglia, in *LRM* ii and vi. See also Chamber music.

String quintet. Chamber music for five strings. See Quintet.

Strings. Colloquial abbr. for the stringed instruments of the orchestra (string section) or the string quartet, quintet, etc.

String trio. Chamber music for three strings. See Trio (3).

Strisciando [It.]. The correct Italian term for what is usually called *glissando.

Stroboconn. Trade name for an electronic-stroboscopic frequency meter used to measure acoustical frequencies. It can measure frequencies over the entire range of the piano keyboard (27.5 to 4,066 cycles per second), a range that can be extended to 50,000 cycles per second with the use of external frequency dividers. In musical-acoustical research, the Stroboconn is used for defining pitches, intervals, scales, etc., especially of ancient and non-Western music, as well as tunings, temperaments, and instrumental and vocal intonations. It is also useful in studies of the physiology and psychology of hearing, in tuning keyboard and other instruments, and in measuring the frequencies of harmonics, acoustical transients, and vibrato phenomena. The instrument's main advantage is its high precision, being accurate within 1 cent (i.e., .05 per cent). The Stroboconn does not, however, record (write or print out) its results, as some other, far less precise meters do.

Patented in 1942, the Stroboconn became generally available in the late 1940's and is now produced in several models for industrial or musical applications. Measurements are read in *cents as deviations from equal-temperament intonations [see Temperament]; the readings can then be converted from cents into cycles per second by using tables such as found in R. W. Young, *A Table Relating Frequency to Cents* (1939). See also F. A. Kuttner, in *MF* vi, 235ff.   F.A.K.

Strohfiedel [G.]. Straw fiddle [see Xylophone].

Stroh violin (cello). Instrument invented by Charles Stroh in 1901 for the purpose of recording, in which the usual body is replaced by an aluminum plate connected to an amplifying horn.

Stromento [It.]. Instrument. *Stromentato,* instrumented, accompanied by instruments; see Recitative. *Stromenti a corde,* stringed instruments; *s. d'arco,* bowed instruments; *s. di legno,* woodwind instruments; *s. d'ottone* or *di metallo,* brass instruments; *s. a percossa,* percussion instruments; *s. a fiato, s. di vento,* wind instruments; *s. da tasto,* keyboard instruments.

Strophenbass [G.]. See Strophic bass.

Strophenlied [G.]. Strophic song.

Strophic. Designation for a song in which all stanzas of the text are sung to the same music, in contrast to a song with new music for each stanza [*through-composed]. Generally the former method is preferred for simple lyrical texts and the latter for highly dramatic texts or more refined lyrics involving subtle shades of mood and expression.

Strophic bass. Designation for a technique, often found in early 17th-century monody, of using the same bass line for all the stanzas of a song, with varying melodies in the upper part. The strophic bass is distinguished from the *ground (basso ostinato) by its greater length and its definite ending. Thus, *basso ostinato* and strophic bass are examples of continuous and sectional variation respectively [see Variations]. Among the earliest examples is the Prologue of Monteverdi's *Orfeo* (1609), whose five stanzas are sung to varied recitatives over the same bass.

Peri's *Varie musiche* (1610) contains three monodies (nos. 13–15) on the same bass, each consisting of recitative, aria, and ritornello. From *c.* 1620 to 1630, most cantatas are strophic-bass arias, e.g., those in Alessandro Grandi's *Cantade et Arie a voce sola* (1620). Grandi repeats the bass exactly [ex. in *RiHM* ii.2, 39f], whereas in the earlier examples it usually undergoes slight modifications. Frescobaldi's *Primo libro d'Arie musicali* of 1630 [new ed. by H. Spohr (1960), in *Musikalische Denkmäler* iv] contains several strophic-bass arias, e.g., "Dunque dovrò," entitled *Aria di romanesca* because its bass is derived from the *romanesca. Kaspar Kittel's *Arien und Kantaten* of 1638 contain twelve strophic-bass arias, among them one on the *ruggiero bass [see *RiHM* ii.2, 349ff]. See Cantata I; Aria III.

Strophic song. See under Through-composed.

Strophicus. See under Neumes I (table).

Strumento d'acciaio. Same as *instrumento d'acciaio.* See under Glockenspiel.

Stück [G.]. Piece, composition.

Stufe [G.]. Degree (of the scale).

Stundenofficium [G.]. Hours of the *Office.

Sturm und Drang [G.]. A movement in German literature [lit., storm and stress], *c.* 1770–85, represented by Reinhold Lenz (1751–92), F. M. Klinger (1752–1831), and others, and named after Klinger's play, *Sturm und Drang* (1776). It embodied the vehement attack of the younger generation on social and artistic conventions. In music, the term has been used with reference to the "forced" expressiveness that appears as early as 1753 in K. P. E. Bach's *Versuch über die wahre Art, das Clavier zu spielen.* Johann Gottfried Müthel (1718–88) and Johann Gottfried Eckard (1735–1809) represent the same tendencies. See H. H. Eggebrecht, in *Deutsche Vierteljahresschrift für Literaturwissenschaft und Geistesgeschichte* xxix (1955), pp. 323ff; L. Hoffmann-Erbrecht, in *MF* x.

Stürze [G.]. Bell of the horn. *Stürze hoch,* the bell turned upward.

Stutzflügel [G.]. Baby grand piano.

Style [F. *style;* G. *Stil;* It. *stile;* Sp. *estilo*]. In the arts, mode of expression or of performance. In a musical composition, "style" refers to the methods of treating all the elements—*form, *melody, *rhythm, etc. In practice, the term may be applied to single works (e.g., the style of *Tristan* compared to that of *Die Meistersinger*); to composers (the style of Wagner compared to that of Beethoven); to types of composition (operatic style, symphonic style, motet style, church style); to media (instrumental style, vocal style, keyboard style); to methods of composition (contrapuntal style, homophonic style, monodic style); to nations (French style, German style); to periods (baroque style, romantic style); etc. Also, such terms are sometimes used in combination, e.g., "Beethoven's symphonic style," "German romantic style," "instrumental style of the baroque," etc. The founder of modern *style analysis is Guido Adler (1855–1941).

The study of musical style was introduced by Italian writers of the early 17th century, who invented a remarkable vocabulary for the various "languages" of the music of their time. The strict contrapuntal style of Palestrina, which predominated throughout the 17th century in Rome [see Roman school], was called *stile antico* (*obbligato, grave, osservato, romano*). The monodic style of the early 17th century [see *Nuove musiche*], in which the recitative served as the vehicle of expressive declamation, received designations such as *stile nuovo, moderno, espressivo, recitativo, rappresentativo* [see *Stile rappresentativo*]. Latin equivalents used by Christoph Bernhard (1627–92) are *stilus gravis* (or *antiquus*) and *stilus luxurians* (or *modernus*). *Stile concertante* is the style of concerto-like treatment, i.e., of rivaling instruments [see Concerto III], while *stile concitato* is the style of dramatic expression and excitement (Monteverdi, *Il Combattimento di Tancredi e Clorinda,* 1624; see W. Kreidler, *H. Schütz und der Stile concitato von Claudio Monteverdi* [1934]).

Lit.: G. Adler, *Der Stil in der Musik* (1911); *id., Prinzipien und Arten des musikalischen Stils,* rev. ed. (1929); E. Katz, *Die musikalischen Stilbegriffe des 17. Jahrhunderts* (1926); C. H. H. Parry, *Style in Musical Art* (1911); R. Crocker, *A History of Musical Style* [1966]; E. Closson, "Du Style" (*AM* iii, no. 3); K. Meyer, "Zum Stilproblem in der Musik" (*ZMW* v); A. Schering, "Historische und nationale Klangstile" (*JMP* xxxiv); L. Hibberd, "A Note on Musical Styles" (*MR* xix); H. Mersmann, "Zur Stilgeschichte der Musik" (*JMP* xxix); H. L. Clarke, "Toward a Musical Periodization of Music" (*JAMS* ix); E. A. Lippman, "Stil" (*MGG* xii). Also see under Style analysis.

Style analysis. The identification of characteristic features in the music of composers and schools by comprehensive analysis of harmony, rhythm, melody, and sound (all acoustical elements, such as timbre and texture), as well as form. Within these categories, style analysis considers all ramifications appropriate to the music examined, applying analytical procedures in all dimensions, from small details to comparisons of whole movements and cycles, and distinguishing significant from coincidental phenomena by systematic and consistent frames of reference. This approach, which deals concretely with the musical notes themselves, complements aesthetic and historical considerations of style.

Lit.: G. W. Cooper and L. B. Meyer, *The Rhythmic Structure of Music* (1960); G. S. Dickinson, *A Handbook of Music* (1965); J. LaRue, *Guidelines for Style Analysis* (in prep.); W. Fischer, "Zur Entwicklungsgeschichte des Wiener klassischen Stils" (*StM* iii); G. Adler, "Style Criticism" (*MQ* xx); F. Blume, "Fortspinnung und Entwicklung" (*JMP* xxxvi); H. Rosenberg, "On the Analysis of Style" (*AM* ix); R. H. Rowen, "Some 18th-Century Classifications of Musical Style" (*MQ* xxxiii); H. Truscott, "Style in Music" (*MR* xix); J. LaRue, "On Style Analysis" (*JMT* vi, no. 1). J.LaR.

Style brisé [F.]. Term for the characteristic style of 17th-century French lute music (especially that of Denis Gaultier, *c.* 1600–72), in which melody and bass notes are sounded not simultaneously but one after the other, as e.g., f'–a–g–e' d'–f–e–c' [see *BuMBE,* p. 165f]. This style greatly influenced the harpsichord music of the French clavecinists and Froberger. Similar to the *style brisé* are certain formations in "contrapuntal" compositions written for a melody instrument, especially in Bach's compositions for unaccompanied violin and cello. See *Spezzato*.

Style galant [F.]. *Gallant style.

Subdiapente; subdiatessaron. See *Diapente; Diatessaron*.

Subdominant. The fourth degree of the scale (f in C major or C minor), so called because this tone is a fifth below the tonic, just as the dominant is a fifth above it [see Scale degrees]. In harmonic analysis the triad of the subdominant is indicated IV or S. It occurs chiefly in the combination IV–V–I, i.e., as the antepenultimate chord in cadences. In early music it frequently occurs as the penultimate chord IV–I, a combination known as plagal cadence. More than any other triad, the subdominant is capable of modifications that, in the current system of *harmonic analysis, are regarded and labeled as different chords with different roots [see Ex.],

$$\text{IV} \quad \text{IV}^b \quad \text{II}^6_5 \quad \text{II}^6_5 \quad \text{II}^{6b}_5 \quad \text{V}^6_5\!\!\big/\text{V} \quad \text{V}^6_5\!\!\big/^b\!\!\text{V} \quad \text{V}^9_9\!\!\big/\text{V} \quad \text{V} \quad \text{I}$$

although from a functional point of view they are essentially identical [see Functional harmony].

Subfinalis [L.]. See under Church modes I.

Subject [F. *sujet, thème;* G. *Thema;* It. *tema, soggetto;* Sp. *tema*]. A melody that, by virtue of its characteristic design, prominent position, or special treatment, becomes a basic factor in the structure of the composition. The subject (or, if there is more than one, the main subject) is always stated at the outset of the composition. In *sonata form there normally are two subjects or, in longer examples, two groups of subjects. A fugue usually has only one subject, except in special types such as the double or triple fugue.

 In the course of music history the subject has become increasingly important, particularly as a unifying element. In early music (prior to 1500) there is no subject unless the borrowed *cantus firmi,* which form the basis of numerous compositions (Masses, motets), are regarded as such. During the second half of the 15th century (Ockeghem, Isaac) characteristic figures (motifs) were gradually adopted as material for short passages, in imitation, sequential treatment, or occasionally as *ostinatos. The use of identical or similar motifs for the beginning of all the movements of a Mass also indicates a tendency toward unification [see Mass C, II]. The fully developed imitative style of the Josquin period use numerous subjects in succession, one for each *point of imitation. The ricercars of this period usually reduce the number of such subjects and make more extensive use of each. In fact, they can already be considered "fugues in several sections," each fugue being based on one theme. An important step was taken in the variation canzonas of Frescobaldi, which use rhythmic modifications of a single subject for the different sections of the piece [see Canzona (5) I]. The fugues of the 17th century usually

employ themes lacking individuality or deficient in details of design. Bach's main contribution to the development of the fugue was the creation of themes of the highest artistic quality. The accompanying example shows two somewhat similar themes [Ex. a, Buxtehude, "Praeludium und Fuga" in F-sharp minor for organ; Ex. b, *Well-Tempered Clavier* ii, Fugue in A minor]

that illustrate this point. The sonata required a different type of subject, but the details of the development from the "continuous melody" of the *sonata da chiesa* (Bach, Handel) to the individualized subjects of the late works of Haydn and Mozart (*c.* 1780) and the highly dramatic themes of Beethoven are too complex for a brief summary. Suffice it to mention D. Scarlatti, Pergolesi, J. W. A. Stamitz, and Johann Christian Bach as some of the numerous composers who contributed to this development.

Subito [It.]. Suddenly.

Subjugalis [L.]. Early designation for a plagal mode.

Submediant. See under Scale degrees.

Subsemitonium. See *Subtonium.*

Subsidiary subject. A subject of lesser importance, particularly one of those subjects that, in the fully developed examples of sonata form, follow after the "first subject" or the "second subject," thus forming the "first group" or the "second group."

Subtonic. See under Scale degrees.

Subtonium [L.]. The tone added below the normal range of a church mode (*subtonium modi*), hence, c in mode 1, G in mode 2, etc. [see Church modes I]. It is especially important in the authentic modes, in which it represents the tone below the final (*subfinalis*) and therefore is often used in cadences. Later *subtonium* came to mean the tone below the final in both the authentic and the plagal modes. In the 16th century, the term meant "whole tone below the final," as opposed to *subsemitonium,* half-tone below the final. All modes except the Lydian and Ionian have the *subtonium.* The replacement of the *subtonium* by the *subsemitonium* in any of the other modes (e.g., the use of f♯ in Mixolydian) was considered *musica ficta.

Succentor [L.]. In 16th- and 17th-century German church music, the leader of Chorus II in antiphonal singing, deputy to the *precentor.

Successive counterpoint. The writing of contrapuntal music in separate lines rather than in a simultaneous process of composition. From the beginning of polyphony through at least the end of the 13th century, music was always composed successively. For instance, in a 13th-century motet the process would start with the selection of a chant melody, which would be organized rhythmically by consistent application of some rhythmic pattern [see Modes, rhythmic]. This would be used as the tenor, to which was added the *duplum* (*motetus*) and, often by another composer, the *triplum.* The isorhythmic motets of the 14th century were written in the same manner, as were the *cantus firmus* Masses of the 15th century. In secular compositions of the 14th century, such as the *ballades* of Machaut, the process probably started with the *superius,* to which was added first the tenor and then the contratenor. Possibly *superius* and tenor were written more or less simultaneously, but the *contra* is always clearly recognizable as a later addition. In not a few cases the same composition survives with two different contratenors. In the 15th century successive counterpoint was gradually abandoned. Pietro Aaron, in his "De institutione harmonica" of 1516, after describing the successive mode of composition, *secundum veterum morem* (he gives the order *cantus,* tenor, bass, alto), says that modern composers conceive the four parts together, and that in this way the composition becomes more harmonious. See E. Lowinsky, in *PAMS* 1941, pp. 67f.

Suffrages. In the rites of the Anglican Communion, suffrage means an "intercessory prayer or petition" (Webster). There seems to be no clear distinction among the Western liturgies between the terms *preces* and suffrages. For example, *preces* as found in the Latin offices are called suffrages in the *Anglican Diurnal Noted* and the *American Lutheran Service* books. In the Anglican Prayer Books the versicles and responses following the Creed in Morning and Evening Prayer are called the suffrages. A number of musical settings exist, among them two by Tallis. See *The Choral Service* (1929); *The Hymnal of the Protestant Episcopal Church in the United States* (1940), nos. 601, 602.   V.P.D.

Suite. An important instrumental form of baroque music, consisting of a number of movements, each in the character of a dance and all in the same key.

I. *Bach's suite.* The standard scheme of the suite used by Bach is A–C–S–O–G, with A standing for *allemande, C for *courante, S for *saraband, G for *gigue, and O for what is called optional dance or optional group, i.e., one or several dances of various types, chiefly the *minuet, *bourrée, *gavotte, *passepied, *polonaise, *anglaise, *loure, and *air. For the harpsichord, Bach wrote, besides some single suites, six "English Suites," six "French Suites," and six "Partitas." The terms "English" and "French" are both unauthentic and irrelevant; for the term "Partitas," see *Partita.* The English Suites and Partitas are preceded by an introductory piece (prelude), which, in the English Suites is (except for the first) similar to a *concerto grosso* movement. Those of the first three partitas are modeled after the *Inventions, that of the fourth is a French overture [see Overture I], and the last two borrow their style from the *toccata. The dance movements are invariably in binary form, either symmetrical (i.e., with both sections of about the same length) or asymmetrical, i.e., with the second section expanded in a manner foreshadowing sonata form [see Binary and ternary form; Sonata form]. Stylistically the dances of the optional group form a contrast to the others, being simpler in style and more clearly suggestive of dance types. The reason for this important difference is that the allemande, courante, saraband, and gigue are much older types, which originated in the 16th century and, by the time they were adopted into the suite (c. 1650), had lost their dance connotation and become idealized types, rhythmically weakened but elaborate in texture and style. The optional dances, on the other hand, originated in the French ballets of the late 17th century (Lully) and retained the character of actual dance music.

II. *The modern suite.* The suite became practically extinct after 1750, leaving only traces in the *divertimento and *cassation as well as in the minuet of the classical *sonata (symphony). Franz Lachner (1803–90) tried to revive the form with his eight orchestral suites, written in a learned contrapuntal style. More important was the establishment of a modern suite in which the traditional dances were replaced by a free succession of movements of different character, frequently by national dances or ballet dances. This type of orchestral music gained favor in the 1880's and 1890's. Particularly common are orchestral suites arranged from operas and ballets, e.g., Bizet's *L'Arlésienne* no. 1 (from the play with incidental music, 1872), Grieg's *Peer Gynt Suite* (from the incidental music to Ibsen's play, 1876), Tchaikovsky's *Suite from The Nutcracker* (from the ballet, 1892), Stravinsky's *Suite from Petrushka* (from the ballet, 1911). The neoclassical movement of the 20th century led to a deliberate revival of the abstract (non-operatic) suite, and Bach's example occasionally served as a pretext for introducing jazz dances into art music (Hindemith, *Suite 1922;* E. Krenek, E. Schulhoff, Conrad Beck).

III. *The suite before Bach.* The development culminating in Bach's suites represents an interesting example of international cooperation. Italy contributed the early development (16th century), England the gigue, Spain the saraband, France the great wealth of 17th-century dance types, and Germany the allemande as well as concept of the suite as a unified and definite musical form.

The origin of the suite is usually sought in the combinations of two dances, one in duple time, the other in triple time, that occur throughout the 16th century, e.g., pavane–galliard or *passamezzo–saltarello* [see Nachtanz]. Even more important than these pairings are the combinations, not uncommon in 16th-century lute books, of three or more dances played in succession. Examples are the combination *pavana–saltarello–piva* (or *spingardo*) in J. A. Dalza's lute book (1508), *basse danse–recoupe–tordion* in the lute books of P. Attaingnant (1529), *passamezzo–gagliarda–padovana* in that of Antonio Rotta (1546), or *passamezzo–padovana–saltarello–ripresa* in that of M. Waisselius (1573). After 1600 this course was further pursued by such German composers as P. Peuerl, I. Posch (both in *DTO* 70), S. Scheidt (1587–1654), and J. H. Schein (1586–1630), each of whom established his own standard form, e.g., *Paduana–Intrada–Dantz–Gagliard* (Peuerl, 1611; see *EiBM,* no. 26), or *Pavana–Galliarde–Courante–Allemanda–Tripla* (Schein, *Banchetto musicale,* 1617; see *HAM,* no. 197). While the idea of the suite as a unified musical form is clearly present in these compositions, it is lacking in the works of French composers such as Jean-Baptiste Besard (b. 1567), Chambonnières (*c.* 1602–72), Louis Couperin (*c.* 1626–61) and D'Anglebert (*c.* 1628–91), who merely arranged the dances either according to types (Besard, *Thesaurus harmonicus,* 1603; one "Livre" of allemandes, another

of courantes, etc.) or, later, according to keys, but in such large numbers as to exclude the idea of a definite form. For example, a "suite" by Chambonnières in the Bauyn-MSS (*c.* 1760) includes five allemandes, eleven courantes, four sarabands, two gigues, five courantes, one chaconne—all in C major. This loose aggregation still exists in the harpsichord works of François Couperin (pub. 1713–30) who, perhaps deliberately, avoids the name "suite" used as early as 1687 by Lebègue in his *Pièces de Clavecin,* ii) and instead uses the term "Ordre," which might well be also applied in the case of the earlier French composers. The important contribution of the French clavecinists was to transform the allemande, courante, gigue, and saraband from their 16th-century plainness to baroque refinement (the *courante is particularly interesting in this respect), and to enlarge the repertory by those numerous dances that were adopted, *c.* 1700, into the optional group of the suite.

The creation of the classical suite is the work of J. J. Froberger (1616–67) who, born in Stuttgart, educated partly in Rome, and spending the last part of his life in France, was eminently suited for the task of imbuing the German "Renaissance" suite of Peuerl and Schein with the stylistic achievements of the French baroque. About 1650, the prevailing type of suite had only three movements: A–C–S. Many suites of Froberger have this scheme, as do all those by Kindermann (*c.* 1645; see *DTB* 32) and nearly all the instrumental suites of the Kassel MS (ed. by J. Écorcheville, *Vingt Suites d'Orchestre,* 1906). The gigue was introduced somewhat later as an "optional" dance, either before or after the courante, with the saraband retaining its position as the concluding movement: A–C–G–S or A–G–C–S. In Froberger's autograph MSS his four-movement suites invariably close with the saraband, as do, e.g., J. Rosenmüller's *Sonate da camera* of 1670 [*DdT* 18] and some of the suites in M. Locke's *Melothesia* (1673). Not until after Froberger's death were the positions of the saraband and gigue exchanged, as appears from the earliest printed edition of his suites (published posthumously in 1693), which bears the remark, "mis en meilleur ordre" (put in better order). Other examples of the A–C–S–G arrangement are in the suites of Georg Böhm (1661–1733).

The development of the suite was completed by the addition of the prelude and optional dances (minuet, gavotte, bourrée, etc.). Elaborate preludes precede some of the lute suites of E. Reusner (*Delicie testudinis,* 1667; *Neue Lautenfrüchte,* 1676). Some of the suites in Locke's *Melothesia* include a prelude at the beginning and/or an optional dance at the end, e.g., P–A–C–S–Rant or A–C–S–Hornepipe. All the harpsichord suites by Purcell begin with a prelude but lack a gigue. Most of them are in the form P–A–C–S, but occasionally the saraband is replaced by a minuet. Some of Johann Krieger's suites (*Sechs musikalische Partien,* 1697; *DTB* 30; see *Partita*) also employ the optional dance as a closing movement (A–C–S–G–O) while suites ascribed to Pachelbel have it in the middle (A–C–O–S–G). Suites by G. B. Draghi (*Select Suites of Lessons,* 1700) are in the form P–A–C–S–O–G, with the optional dance (or dances) as the penultimate movement, an arrangement that is standard in the suites of Bach.

IV. *The sonata da camera.* Side by side with this central development were others of a somewhat freer character, chiefly in chamber and orchestral music. In Italy the suite was cultivated mainly as a form of chamber music. G. B. Buonamente's *Il quinto libro de varie Sonate, Sinfonie, Gagliarde, Corrente* (1629) contains two suites, *Sinfonia–Gagliarda–La sua Corrente,* and in his *Settimo libro* (1637) this structure is enlarged by the addition of a *Brando* after the *Sinfonia* [see P. Nettl, in *ZMW* ix, 528ff]. Possibly the *Sinfonia* is not an abstract movement like the prelude but an idealized pavane. The usual designation for the Italian instrumental suite of the 17th century is **sonata da camera.* Originally, this term meant any kind of dance music, mostly single dances, but later it was applied to suitelike formations such as *Ballo–Corrente* (M. Cazzati, *Trattenimenti,* 1660), *Balletto–Corrente–Gigha–Sarabanda* (Bassani, 1677, '79, '80; in the last two publications the order is . . . *Sarabanda–Gigha,* corresponding to the simultaneous change from A–C–G–S to A–C–S–G in Germany), or *Balletto–Giga–Minuet–Borea* (G. B. Vitali, 1685). In most of these suites, *balletto* is probably just another name for the allemande [see *Balletto* (2)]. A. Corelli's *Sonate da camera,* op. 2 (1685) and op. 4 (1694), contain twelve suites each, mostly in four movements, such as *Preludio–Allemanda–Corrente* (or *Sarabanda*)–*Giga* (or *Gavotta*). G. Torelli's *Concerto da camera* (1686) contains twelve suites, each in three movements, e.g., *Alemanda–Corrente–Sarabanda; Balletto–Gigha–Sarabanda;* etc. Antonio Veracini's *Sonate da*

camera, op. 1 (1692) show a tendency toward amalgamation with the *sonata da chiesa* through the inclusion of free movements, e.g., *Fantasia–Allegro–Allemanda–Pastorale–Giga.* Thus in Italy the suite appears not to have been standardized, as it was in Germany.

V. *The French overture.* Still another type of suite, designed for orchestral performance, originated (presumably) in a practice similar to that exemplified in, e.g., Tchaikovsky's *Suite from the Nutcracker,* i.e., the performance of Lully's operas or stage ballets "in abstracto," as a succession of their most successful dance numbers preceded by the operatic overture (ballet suite). This idea was taken over by numerous German composers, who wrote orchestral suites consisting of a French overture [see Overture I] followed by a series of "modern" dances, such as rigaudon, marche, chaconne, bourrée, traquenard, and others. Such suites, briefly called "Ouverture," were written by Johann J. S. Kusser (*Composition . . . suivant la méthode française,* 1682), Georg Muffat (*Florilegium,* 1695/98; *DTO* 2, 4), J. K. F. Fischer (*Le Journal du Printems,* 1695; *DdT* 10), J. A. Schmierer (*Zodiacus Musicus,* 1698; *ibid.*), J. J. Fux (*Concentus musico-instrumentalis,* 1701; *DTO* 47), G. P. Telemann (*Musique de table,* 1733); *DdT* 61/62), and J. S. Bach (4 Orchestral Suites). Bach also transferred this type to the keyboard in his *Französische Ouvertüre* (contained in the **Clavier-Ubung* ii, 1734), as Georg Böhm had done earlier [see his *Sämtliche Werke* i (1927), no. 2]. In its use of "modern" dances this suite comes much closer to the 19th-century type than the idealized "classical" suite.

Lit.: K. Nef, *Geschichte der Sinfonie und der Suite* (1921); F. Blume, *Studien zur Vorgeschichte der Orchestersuite im 15. und 16. Jahrhundert* (1925); E. Epstein, *Der französische Einfluss auf die deutsche Klaviersuite im 17. Jahrhundert* (1940); M. Reimann, *Untersuchungen zur Formgeschichte der französischen Klavier-Suite* (1940); G. Oberst, *Die englischen Orchester Suiten um 1600* (1929); *AdHM* i, 563ff; E. Noack, "Ein Beitrag zur Geschichte der älteren deutschen Suite" (*AMW* ii); T. Norlind, "Zur Geschichte der Suite" (*SIM* vii); G. Adler, in *RMI* iii (Muffat); B. Wójciówna, in *ZMW* v (Fischer).

Suite Bergamasque. Piano composition by Debussy, consisting of Prélude, Menuet, **Clair de lune,* and Passepied. Its title is probably derived from a line in Verlaine's poem *Clair de lune,* ". . . masques et bergamasques."

Sul [It.]. On, at. *Sul* G, on the G-string of the violin. *Sul ponticello,* bowing near the bridge; *sul tasto, sulla tastiera,* bowing near the finger-board. See Bowing (k), (l).

Sumeria. See under Mesopotamia.

Sumer is icumen in. A famous composition of the 13th century, preserved in MS Brit. Mus. *Harleian 978* (fac. repr. in *GD* v, frontispiece; *GDB* vii, frontispiece; *OH* i, 326f, 333ff; and elsewhere), written in the form of a four-voice canon supported by a two-voice **rondellus* (called *pes* in the original). The melody of the canon comprises twenty-four measures and is imitated (at the unison) after two measures. The melody of the *pes* consists of two two-measure phrases sung in voice exchange. In the scheme below, each figure or letter stands for two measures (in 6/8 meter):

```
1 2 3 4 5 .... 12  ⌉
  1 2 3 4 .... 11  │ 12                canon
    1 2 3 .... 10  │ 11 12
      1 2 .... 9   │ 10 11 12⌋

a b a b a .... a   ⌉ b  a  b⌉  rondellus
b a b a b .... b   ⌋ a  b  a⌋
```

Some writers (Wooldridge, in *OH* i, 327f; Apel, in *HAM,* no. 42; Bukofzer, see Lit.) assume that the performance stopped before the vertical line (where all the imitating parts arrive at the word "Cucu"), while others (Schering, in *SchGMB,* no. 17) would let it continue until each part has sung the complete melody. This composition, called **rota* in the original, is the oldest surviving canon and an exceptionally early example of many-voiced texture and full sonority. Its artistic significance, however, has often been overrated. A statement such as that quoted in *GD* v, 191 ("Artistically we may say that nothing written for two hundred years after-wards can touch it") cannot be taken seriously.

"Sumer is icumen in" has been assumed to have been written about *c.* 1225–60 at Reading Abbey (hence the name "Reading rota"). How-ever, in 1944 M. F. Bukofzer maintained that it could not have been written before 1280, that it probably was composed as late as 1310, and that it is in duple meter (4/4) rather than triple (6/8). His findings have not been generally accepted. A sacred text (beginning "Perspice Christicola") probably was added to make the work suitable for performance.

Brahms imitated the construction of "Sumer is icumen in" in his canon op. 113, no. 13.

Lit.: *OH* i, 326ff; M. F. Bukofzer, *Sumer is icumen in: A Revision* (1944); J. Hurry, *Sumer is icumen in,* rev. ed. (1914); B. Schofield, in *MR* ix; N. Pirrotta, in *MD* ii; J. Handschin, in *MD* iii.

Summation(al) tone. See Combination tone.

Sumponyah. A name found in the Book of Daniel (ch. 3:5, 7, 10, 15) in the description of pagan worship under Nebuchadnezzar that has been translated variously as sackbut and trigon. It probably is the Greek word *symphonia,* pos-sibly a designation for bagpipe [see Symphonia (2)], or merely used as an adjective (*sumponyah psantrin* = symphonious psaltery).

Sun Quartets [G. *Sonnenquartette*]. Popular name for Haydn's six string quartets op. 20, nos. 1–6, composed in 1772. An early edition had an engraving of the rising sun as part of its frontispiece.

Suor Angelica. See under *Trittico.*

Superdominant. See under Scale degrees.

Superius. See under Partbooks.

Supertonic. See under Scale degrees.

Supplying. See under Verset.

Surprise Symphony. Haydn's Symphony no. 94, in G major (no. 2 of the **Salomon Symphonies*), composed in 1791, so called because of a loud chord in the middle of the quiet first theme of the second movement (Haydn said it would make the ladies jump).

Susannah. Opera in two acts by C. Floyd, pro-duced at Florida State University, 1955. Setting: Tennessee mountain valley.

Suspension. (1) See under Nonharmonic tones II. (2) An 18th-century *agrément* in which the writ-ten note is slightly delayed by a short rest:

$$\widehat{\vphantom{P}}\!\!P \;=\; \gamma\, \widehat{\vphantom{P}}\!\!P$$

Suspirium [L.]. Old name for the rest having the value of a *minima.* See Mensural notation I.

Sussurando [It.]. Whispering.

Sustaining pedal. The sostenuto pedal (middle pedal) of the **piano.* The term is sometimes used for the damper pedal (right pedal).

Svelto [It.]. Quick, nimble.

Svolgimento [It.]. Development.

Sw. Abbr. for *swell organ* [see under Swell].

Swan Lake, The. Ballet by Tchaikovsky (choreography by M. Petipa and L. Ivanov), composed in 1876. It tells the story of Prince Siegfried's fight against the Evil Power in his attempt to woo the Swan Queen, Odette. The ballet is one of the first to utilize the *leitmotiv technique, with a specific melody representing the Queen.

Swan of Tuonela. Symphonic poem by Sibelius, op. 22 (1893), based on a legend from the *Kalevala. Tuonela, the Finnish Hades, is surrounded by a river of black water on which a swan swims majestically and sings. In the music, sustained strings represent the dark waters and the gliding movements of the swan, while a solo English horn presents the swan's song.

Swan Song. See *Schwanengesang*.

Sweden. The tradition of Gregorian chant led, in the 13th century, to a national production of sequences and hymns [see Lit., Moberg]. Aside from this, very little is known about music in Sweden before 1600. The Reformation led to Olaus Petri's adaptation of Latin and German hymnody for Swedish use, but the Royal Chapel was maintained under Gustavus Vasa and his successors, Eric XIV (himself a composer of polyphonic settings) and John III. In the 14th century rhymed Offices for St. Birgitta were written by Archbishop Birger Gregersson (d. 1383) and Bishop Nils Hermansson (d. 1391), with music adapted from well-known melodies. In 1582, Theodoricus Petri published in Greifswald (Pomerania, then part of Sweden) *Piae cantiones* [*Editions XLIII, 10], a collection of religious songs written in one to four parts, which, according to the introduction, were much used in the schools of Sweden and Finland. Some of them probably date as far back as the 13th century, while others are similar to Lutheran hymns. In the reigns of Gustavus Adolphus (1611–32) and his daughter Christina (1632–54) music was liberally encouraged at the court of Stockholm. During this period and until well into the 18th century, several members of the Düben family were active in Stockholm. Andreas Düben (*c.* 1590–1662) is known only for one composition (*Pugna triumphalis*) in Venetian polychoral style, composed for the burial of Gustavus Adolphus (1634), and a *Miserere,* composed for the burial of Karl X (1660). His son, Gustaf (1624–90), compiled a famous MS collection of music, including works by Buxtehude, now in the library of Uppsala.

Gustaf's son, Gustaf Düben (the younger), succeeded his father as a court conductor.

During the 18th century there was considerable musical activity at the University of Uppsala. Prominent figures were Olof Rudbeck (1630–1702), who held office as rector, and Harald Vallerius, professor of mathematics and *director musices.* An important composer was Johan Helmich Roman (1694–1758), who studied in London under Ariosti and Pepusch, and possibly also under Handel. He became director of court music in 1729 and wrote a considerable number of instrumental and vocal pieces in the style of Handel. Court opera houses were built during the 18th century (the one at Drottningholm is still in use), and under Gustaf III (1772–92) the growth of opera was much encouraged. The German Johann Gottlieb Naumann (1741–1801) wrote two successful operas, *Amphion* (1778) and *Gustaf Wasa* (1786), both produced in Stockholm. Other Germans who played a role in Swedish music were G. J. Vogler (Abbé Vogler, 1749–1814; opera *Gustaf Adolph och Ebba Brahe,* 1788) and his pupil J. Martin Kraus (1756–92; symphonies, operas). Particularly successful was the French-Swiss Jean-Baptiste-Edouard du Puy (*c.* 1770–1822) with his opera *Ungdom og Galskab* (1806), which was in the repertory of the Copenhagen and Stockholm operas throughout the 19th century. A unique personality in 18th-century Swedish society was C. M. Bellman (1740–95), who enjoyed the patronage of Gustavus III and frequented the taverns of Stockholm, where he sang his matchless lyrics to tunes he adapted or composed; collections of these songs were published under the titles *Fredmans epistlar* (1790) and *Fredmans Sånger* (1791).

Franz Berwald (1796–1868) deserves mention as a composer of symphonies, string quartets, and other chamber music. Ivar Hallström (1826–1901) gained a reputation as a composer of operas, some of which use clearly national idioms, earning him the title of "the Swedish Glinka." August Söderman (1832–76) encouraged the nationalist movement in his opera *Ett bondbröllop* (A Country Wedding). This movement was widely supported by the public and by music societies but never found a champion comparable in stature to Norway's Grieg. Andreas Hallén (1846–1925) wrote operas (*Harald Viking,* 1881) and symphonic poems in the styles of Wagner and Liszt, whereas Emil Sjögren (1853–1918) wrote songs and piano pieces in a late romantic style. W. Stenhammar

(1871–1927) wrote some distinguished string quartets and piano concertos, and H. Alfven (1872–1960) wrote symphonies and symphonic poems with strong nationalist-romantic coloring.

Late romantic and partly impressionist tendencies characterize the works of Adolf Wiklund (1879–1950), Edvin Kallstenius (b. 1881), Natanaël Berg (1879–1957), Ture Rangström (1884–1947), and Kurt Atterberg (b. 1887). The leaders of mid-20th-century Swedish music are Hilding Rosenberg (b. 1892), Gösta Nyström (b. 1890), Moses Pergament (b. 1893), Lars-Erik Larsson (b. 1908), Dag Wiren (b. 1905), Karl-Birger Blomdahl (b. 1916), Sven-Erik Bäck (b. 1919), Ingvar Lidholm (b. 1921), Bengt Hambraeus (b. 1928), and Bo Nilsson (b. 1937).

Lit.: Å. Davidsson, *Bibliografi över Svensk Musiklitteratur 1800–1945* (1948); *LavE* i.5, 2587ff; *AdHM* ii, 1118ff (modern); B. Alander, *Swedish Music* (1956); J. Horton, *Scandinavian Music* (1963); C. A. Moberg, *Über die schwedischen Sequenzen*, 2 vols. (1927); *id.*, *Die liturgischen Hymnen in Schweden*, i (1947); S. A. F. Walin, *Beiträge zur Geschichte der schwedischen Sinfonie* (1941); K. Valentin, *Studien über die schwedischen Volksmelodien* (1885); A. Soubies, "La Musique scandinave avant le xixe siècle" (*RMI* viii); C. A. Moberg, "Der gregorianische Gesang in Schweden" (*KJ* 1932); *id.*, "Essais d'opéras en Suède sous Charles XII" (*CP Laurencie*); T. Norlind, "Die Musikgeschichte Schwedens in den Jahren 1630–1730" (*SIM* i); *id.*, in *SIM* ii and *CP Wolf;* B. Wallner, "Scandinavian Music after the Second World War" (*LBCM;* also *MQ* li). rev. J.H.

Swell. In organs, mechanism for obtaining a gradation of sound, crescendo and diminuendo. It consists of a large room (swell box) built around one or more divisions of the pipes and provided with shutters similar to Venetian blinds, whence comes the name Venetian swell [G. *Jalousieschweller*]. The chief enclosed division is called *swell organ,* a name that also applies to the manual from which it is played. The swell box is opened and closed by a swell pedal, operated by the feet. The first practical swell mechanism, invented in 1769 by Shudi, was used in harpsichords before it was adopted for the organ.

Swing. See under Jazz III.

Switzerland. In the early Middle Ages the monastery of St. Gall was one of the chief centers of Gregorian chant. According to legend,

formal musical activity dates from *c.* 790, when Romanus, an emissary of Pope Hadrian I, fell ill at the monastery of St. Gall and, in gratitude for his recovery, taught the monks Gregorian chant. The MSS of the monastery, written in the so-called St. Gall neumes [see Neumes I], are among the most valuable sources of Gregorian chant [see Editions XLII A 1, B 1, 2]. In the 9th and 10th centuries St. Gall became prominent in the writing of *sequences (Notker, Tuotilo), and Hermannus Contractus (1013–54) and Berno "Augiensis" (d. 1048), both monks of the Abbey of Reichenau, wrote important treatises [*GS* ii].

From the 11th century on, the monasteries of Einsiedeln, Rheinau, and St. Gall produced many liturgical plays, and by the 13th century the Passion and Easter plays were often given in the vernacular. By 1289 music was formally taught in convents, monasteries, and divinity schools, and in the 15th century daily music lessons were an accepted part of the public school curriculum. Organ building and organ playing soon flourished in Switzerland, which in the early 16th century had an important group of organ composers, Hans Kotter in Bern, Fridolin Sicher in St. Gall, and Hans Buchner in Basel [see Organ music I]. Outstanding were Henricus Glareanus (Heinrich Loris, 1488–1563), author of the *Dodecachordon* (1547), and Ludwig Senfl (1490–1543), born in Zurich. Benedictus Appenzeller [see W. Barclay Squire, in *SIM* xiii], Sixtus Dietrich (*c.* 1492–1548), and Gregor Meyer (frequently mentioned and quoted in the *Dodecachordon*) were followers of Josquin, while Johannes Wannenmacher (d. 1551) is noted particularly for his *Biciniasive duo germanica ad aequales* (1553). The 17th century produced Johann Melchior Gletle (1626–84), a prolific composer of Masses, psalms, motets, and also some pieces for *tromba marina. Heinrich Weissenberg (fl. 1700), commonly known as Henricus Albicastro, wrote trio sonatas and concertos.

Strongly influenced by the educational philosophy of Heinrich Pestalozzi (1746–1827) and Jean-Jacques Rousseau (1712–78), Johann Georg Nägeli (1773–1836) gave new impetus to choral singing, which in turn inspired many outstanding compositions for male chorus, notably by Karl Attenhofer (1837–1914) and Friedrich Hegar (1841–1927). The end of the 19th century saw the development of a new music-education movement founded by Émile Jaques-Dalcroze (1865–1950). In 1892 he introduced a solfège-rhythmic method at the Conservatory of Geneva that is still used throughout the world.

Most representative of the older generation of Swiss composers is the lieder composer Othmar Schoeck (1886–1957), who achieved a perfect union of music and poetry. Ernest Bloch (1880–1959), for many years active in the United States, was a champion of Jewish liturgical music. Frank Martin (b. 1890) was originally influenced by Ravel, later (c. 1930) by Schoenberg. His most important works are *Le Vin herbé* (1938–41), *In Terra Pax* (1944), and *Golgotha* (1945–48).

In the forefront of Swiss music stands Arthur Honegger (1892–1955). Although born in France (of Swiss parents), where he lived most of his life, he also studied and worked in Switzerland. His best-known compositions are *Le Roi David* (1921), *Pacific 231* (1923), *Jeanne d'Arc au Bûcher* (1935), his five symphonies (1930–50), and *Monopartita* (1951). [Also see under France IV; *Six, Les.*]

Wladimir Vogel (b. 1896), of German-Russian parentage but Swiss by choice, is the best-known Swiss serial composer. Albert Moeschinger (b. 1897) began as a champion of late romanticism but soon developed an independent style in such works as his violin concerto op. 40, *Fantasie 1944* for strings, op. 64, and Symphony no. 3, op. 76. Willy Burkhard (1900–55) wrote more than ninety works, of which probably the best known are the oratorio *Das Gesicht Jesajahs* (The Vision of Isaiah; 1935) and the opera *Die schwarze Spinne* (The Black Spider), based on a story by Jeremias Gotthelf. The compositions of Conrad Beck (b. 1901), who studied in Paris, cover a wide field, including chamber and other instrumental music as well as choral works. Rolf Liebermann (b. 1910), a pupil of Wladimir Vogel's, developed a very personal kind of twelve-tone technique. His best-known works include a cantata for baritone, *Une des Fins du monde* (1945), and two operas, *Leonora 40/45* and *Penelope*. Among the younger generation of Swiss composers are Jacques Wildberger (b. 1922) and Rudolf Kelterborn (b. 1931).

Lit.: G. Becker, *La Musique en Suisse depuis les temps les plus reculés jusqu'à la fin du dix-huitième siècle*, rev. ed. (1923); E. Refardt, *Musik in der Schweiz* (1952); id., *Historisch-biographisches Musikerlexikon der Schweiz* (1928): A.-E. Cherbuliez, *Die Schweiz in der deutschen Musikgeschichte* [1932]; A. Geering, "Die Vokalmusik in der Schweiz zur Zeit der Reformation" (*SJ* vi, 1933); id., "Vom speziellen Beitrag der Schweiz zur allgemeinen Musikforschung" (*MF* iii, 97ff); K. Nef, ‡*Musikalische Werke schweizerischer Komponisten des XVI., XVII. & XVIII. Jahrhunderts,* 3 vols. [1927–34]; *LavE* i.5, 2665–75; *AdHM* ii, 1038ff, 1077ff; R.-A. Mooser, *Panorama de la musique contemporaine, 1947–1953* [1953]; H. Ehinger, ed.-in-chief, *Der schweizerische Tonkünstlerverein im zweiter Vierteljahrhundert seines Bestehens* [1950]; F. Labhardt, *Das Sequentiar, Cod. 546 der Stiftsbibliothek von St. Gallen und seine Quellen,* 2 vols. [1959, '63]; W. Reich, "On Swiss Musical Composition of the Present" (*LBCM,* also *MQ* li); P. Budry, *La Suisse qui chante* [1932]. rev. A.G.

Syllabic style. See under Gregorian chant III.

Symbolum. Name for the Credo in Ambrosian chant. *Symbolum Apostolicum* is the Apostles' Creed [see Creed (2)].

Sympathetic string. A string that is not played on but serves to reinforce the sound of the bowed or plucked strings by vibrating along with them [see Resonance]. Numerous instruments have such strings, e.g., the *viola d'amore, *viola bastarda, *baryton, *hardingfele, and *tromba marina. They sometimes are added to the highest register of pianos, where they are called *aliquot strings. See T. L. Southgate, in *PMA* xlii.

Symphonia [Gr.]. (1) Ancient Greek term for unison, as distinguished from *antiphonia,* the octave [see Antiphon] and *paraphonia,* the fifth. (2) In the Middle Ages (possibly also in late Greek writings), *symphonia* means consonance as opposed to *diaphonia,* dissonance (Cassiodorus; *GS* i, 16b). Later the term was applied to various instruments such as the drum (Isidore of Seville, d. 636), *hurdy-gurdy, also called *cinfonie* (J. de Muris, c. 1290–c. 1351), bagpipe (hence the modern name *zampogna?), and a type of clavichord (16th cent.). (3) Beginning in the 17th century the name was used for various types of orchestral music that eventually led to the modern symphony. To avoid confusion, they are discussed under Sinfonia.

Symphonia domestica. A programmatic symphony [see Program symphony; Program music] by R. Strauss, op. 53, completed in 1903 and first heard in New York the following year. It is in one continuous movement divided into three sections.

Symphonic band, concert band. A term used in American secondary schools and colleges to distinguish the strictly musical functions of the typical school wind band from bands playing at pep rallies, half-time shows, athletic events, and so on. Such a distinction was prompted by the growing repertory of serious wind literature since the 1920's. The symphonic band consists of woodwind, brass, and percussion instruments. A typical example might be: 2 piccolos, 6 flutes, 2 E^b clarinets, 4 oboes, 1 English horn, 24 B^b clarinets, 2 alto clarinets, 2 bass clarinets, 4 bassoons, 2 alto saxophones, 1 tenor saxophone, 1 baritone saxophone, 6 cornets, 4 trumpets, 8 horns, 2 baritone horns, 4 trombones, 5 tubas, and 6 percussion. In addition, cellos and contrabasses are sometimes used.

The origin of the symphonic band is inseparable from that of the *military band. The town band of the 16th and 17th centuries had disappeared by the early 18th century, probably because no standard intonation or timbre had been developed by the instrument makers. About 1763 the instrumentation of the Prussian regimental bands was stabilized by Frederick the Great as 2 oboes, 2 clarinets, 2 horns, and 2 bassoons, and literature by Haydn, Mozart, K. P. E. Bach, and Beethoven exists for this "standard" band of the late 18 century. The reorganization of the French bands by Sax in 1854 and the German bands by Wieprecht in 1845 led to great versatility, owing not only to the adoption of valved brass instruments but also to variation in instrumentation. By the latter half of the 19th century, however, serious band literature was virtually nonexistent. Bands played marches, popular arias, and transcriptions. Notable exceptions are the *Grande Symphonie Funèbre et Triomphale* (1840) by Berlioz, *Trauermarsch zur Beisetzung C. M. von Webers* (1844) and *Huldigungsmarsch* (1864) by Wagner, and a *Military Overture*, op, 24 (1824) by Mendelssohn.

In the United States the symphonic band performed the same type of music as its European counterpart. The first mixed wind band of concert-giving stature was the Marine Band, founded in 1792. Notable civilian bands were the Allentown Band from Allentown, Pennsylvania, founded in 1828, Gilmore's Grand Boston Band, founded in 1859, and Sousa's famous band, founded in 1892. Gilmore, famous as an organizer of huge musical festivals, is regarded as the father of the symphonic band in America. His work with the 22nd Regiment Band of New York was known throughout Europe.

The recent revival of the symphonic band owes much to the compositions of Gustav Holst and Ralph Vaughan Williams. Holst's *First Suite for Band in E^b* (1909), *Second Suite in F* (c. 1911), and *Hammersmith: Prelude and Scherzo* (1930), and Vaughan Williams' *English Folk Song Suite* (1924) and *Toccata Marziale* (1924) furthered the concept of a repertory specifically for band. Other composers of specifically band music include P. Hindemith, S. Prokofiev, E. Krenek, I. Stravinsky, D. Milhaud, and A. Schoenberg. Other 20th-century American composers who have written for band are S. Barber, M. Gould, N. Lockwood, and V. Persichetti.

Lit.: R. F. Goldman, *The Concert Band* (1946); *id., The Wind Band* (1961); K. Berger, *The Band in the United States* (1961); *id.*, ed., *Band Encyclopedia* (1960).   J.W.

Symphonic Etudes. See *Études symphoniques*.

Symphonic poem. I. A type of 19th- and 20th-century orchestral music based on an extra-musical idea, either poetic or realistic. The symphonic poem, also called tone poem, belongs to the general category of *program music, representing its most recent and most sophisticated embodiment. Usually the term is reserved for compositions in one movement, in distinction to the *program symphony. The German equivalent, *Symphonische Dichtung*, was first used in 1854, in connection with a performance of Liszt's *Tasso* in Weimar.

II. The symphonic poem proper was inaugurated by Liszt in his one-movement compositions *Ce qu'on entend sur la montagne* (1848, after a poem of Victor Hugo), *Tasso (1849, after Byron), *Les Préludes* (1848, after Lamartine's *Méditations poétiques*), *Mazeppa (1851, after Hugo), *Die Ideale* (1857, after Schiller), *Hunnenschlacht (after a painting by Kaulbach, showing the slaughter of the Huns), *Hamlet* (1857), etc. Usually these compositions follow, somewhat freely, the form of the first movement of a symphony [see Sonata form]. A composition such as Beethoven's *Coriolan Overture* (1807) may be regarded as a predecessor of the symphonic poem. Liszt's innovation was eagerly seized upon by a large number of composers to whom literary, pictorial, and other ideas presented new sources of inspiration. Particularly favored were works descriptive of national life and scenery, for the symphonic poem came into being about the same time as musical *nationalism. The first contributions in this province were Smetana's six symphonic poems *Mà Vlast* (My Fatherland), composed 1874–79 (earlier symphonic poems of his were *Richard III*, 1858; *Wallenstein's Camp*, 1858; and *Hakon Jarl*, 1861). He had a host of successors, and there is scarcely a country that has not been described in music. Compositions such as Borodin's *In the *Steppes of Central Asia* (1880), Saint-Saën's *Africa* (1891), Sibelius' *Finlandia* (1899), Vaughan Williams' *A *London Symphony* (1914), Respighi's *Fontane di Roma* (1917), F. Grofé's *Grand Canyon Suite* (1931), and E. Bloch's *America* (1928) illustrate the scope of the "musical atlas," which, however, includes few pictures of Germany and France, where nationalism never became a great force.

The poetic model of Liszt was followed by, among others, Tchaikovsky, with *Romeo and Juliet* (1869), *Francesca da Rimini* (1876), and *Hamlet* (1888); Saint-Saëns with *Omphale's Spinning Wheel* (1871) and *Phaeton* (1873); Franck with *Les Éolides* (1876), *Le *Chasseur maudit* (1882), *Les Djinns* (1885), and *Psyché* (1886, with chorus).

III. A new period of the symphonic poem began in 1895 when Richard Strauss, after some earlier works of less importance (*Aus Italien*, 1887; *Don Juan*, 1889; *Macbeth*, 1890), produced his outstanding *Tod und Verklärung* (Death and Transfiguration). His realistic approach and extremely bold, skillful handling of the orchestra made this work famous, although it first aroused violent criticism from professional writers and a large section of the public. In 1895 he wrote *Till Eulenspiegel* and there followed *Also sprach Zarathustra* (Thus Spake Zarathustra, after Nietzsche, 1896); *Don Quixote* (1897), a series of free variations that include such realistic effects as the bleating of sheep; wind machine to represent an imaginary flight through the air; and *Ein *Heldenleben* (A Hero's Life, first perf. 1899), a musical autobiography. His *Sinfonia Domestica* (1903) describes, with realistic rather than musical success, a day in the composer's family life, and his *Alpensinfonie* (1915) is a detailed description of a day of climbing the Alps.

IV. Shortly before 1900 two important symphonic poems were written in France, Debussy's impressionist *Prélude à l'*Après-midi d'un faune* (1894) and Paul Dukas' realistic *L'*Apprenti sorcier* (1897). Sibelius wrote a number of tone poems, mostly based on the Kalevala, the Finnish national epic: *En Saga* (1892), *Kullervo* (1892), *The *Swan of Tuonela* (1893), *Lemmin-*

käinen and the Maidens of Saari (1895), *Lemminkäinen in Tuonela* (1895). *Lemminkäinen's Homecoming* (1895), *Pohjola's Daughter* (1906), *Nightride and Sunrise* (1909), *The Bard* (1913), *Luonnotar* (1913), *The Oceanides* (1914), *Tapiola* (1926). The 20th-century repertory includes Debussy's *La *Mer* (1903–05); Stravinsky's *Feu d'artifice* (1908); C. Loeffler's *A Pagan Poem* (c. 1908), based on an Eclogue by Virgil; Elgar's *Falstaff* (1913), perhaps the most detailed musical description of a literary subject; Respighi's Roman trilogy *Fontane di Roma* (The Fountains of Rome, 1917), *Pini di Roma* (The Pines of Rome, 1924), and *Feste Romane* (Roman Festivals, 1929); and G. Gershwin's *An American in Paris* (1928). A. Honegger's *Pacific 231* (1923) and *Rugby* (1928), realistic glorifications of the modern age, represent, both in subject and in their percussive and motoric idiom, an attempt to bring new life to the symphonic poem, which, sensuous and overrefined, had outlived its time. On the whole, this attempt did not prove successful. The neoclassical tendencies of the present day with their emphasis on purely musical forms and styles appear to have brought the symphonic poem to the end of its development. See J. Chantavoine, *Le Poème Symphonique* (1950); R. Mendl, "The Art of the Symphonic Poem" (*MQ* xviii).

Symphonic Variations. See *Variations symphoniques.*

Symphonie fantastique. Symphony by Hector Berlioz (1803–69), composed in 1831, which holds a prominent place in the symphonic literature of the 19th century owing to its outstanding artistic qualities as well as its historic importance in the field of program music [see also Symphonic poem] and in the development of the *leitmotiv. The five sections of the symphony (subtitled *Episode de la vie d'un artiste*) are united by the use of a recurring theme, called *idée fixe.* In the fifth section the *"Dies irae" melody appears in caricature.

Symphonie pathétique. See under Pathétique.

Symphony. In the broadest sense, a symphony is a sonata for orchestra. Its "modern" history may be said to begin with the first symphony of Haydn (1759), though similar works with the same title had become increasingly numerous during the period of coexistence of baroque and classical (c. 1725–1760), and symphonies are still being written today. Since the symphony represents a microcosm of the history and development of musical style since 1760, and since the immense variety of works called "symphony" would lead one into nearly every aspect of musical history and aesthetics, this article is limited to a summary of the literature and a sketch of the main stylistic changes. [Also see such related articles as Sonata; Sonata form; Rondo; Minuet; Scherzo; Orchestra; Nationalism; Program music; Program symphony; etc.]

I. *Origins.* The symphony emerged from the style changes and cross-currents characterizing the waning *baroque and the advancing *classical. Its counterpart in chamber music and solo keyboard music is the *sonata. The sources of the new form are the *concerto grosso* and *trio sonata, as well as the Italian operatic *overture or prelude, sometimes called *Sinfonia avanti l'opera,* which, *c.* 1700, had become standardized in three sections—fast, slow, fast. The baroque concerto contributed to the style of the symphonic slow movement and two-four finale, and the trio sonata is a direct forerunner of the symphony for strings in three parts. The operatic overture, more lyrical and less contrapuntal in texture, more closely approximates the later classical style, although Churgin [see Lit.] points out that Sammartini's early symphonies (1734–40) are much more contrapuntal than the typical operatic overture of that time. The overture melodies are in a conventional singing style; the symphonies are more "thematic." The overtures show very little *sonata-form construction; the symphonies, especially those of Sammartini, contain real sonata-form movements.

During the 1740's a "symphonic style" became more clearly defined, and the four-movement design began to rival the three-movement sequence. The period of experimentation ended largely in the 1750's. The most important composers, many of whom lived about the same time as Haydn and Mozart, were: G. B. Sammartini (1700/1–75), whose first symphony (1734) antedates Haydn's no. 1 by twenty-five years; J. Stamitz (1717–57) and I. Holzbauer (1711–83), of the *Mannheim school; J. C. Bach (1735–82); K. P. E. Bach (1714–88); and the Viennese composers G. M. Monn (1717–50), Wagenseil (1715–77), and Dittersdorf (1739–99). It is the Mannheim orchestra that is largely responsible both for standardizing the makeup of the orchestra and popularizing it. Appropriately, the first movement of Haydn's First Symphony opens with a striking "Mannheim crescendo."

II. *Classicism.* Haydn and Mozart were contemporaries, though Haydn (1732–1809) was born earlier and died later than Mozart (1756–91). Haydn wrote 104 symphonies (1759–95), Mozart 41 (1764–88). The early symphonies of both men, in many respects preclassical, rival each other in variety and originality. In their later works, the results of long experimentation, the symphonic form is definitively established.

The classical symphony normally consists of four movements: an opening allegro, sometimes with a slow introduction; a lyrical slow movement; a minuet and trio, sometimes omitted; and a brisk and virtuoso finale. The instrumentation was built up gradually from a basic choir of two oboes, two bassoons, and strings, through the addition of (1) two horns, (2) two trumpets and drums, and (3) one or two flutes, and finally, (4) two clarinets. The horns served equally as members of the woodwind choir and the brass choir. The trumpets and drums were invariably associated, never one without the other. The double basses duplicated the cello part an octave lower. The orchestra for opera and church music of this period is often more irregular and varied, notably by the inclusion of trombones.

The grand plan of the first movement and sometimes the finale is *sonata form. The slow movement took a variety of lyrical forms, though its key scheme is often that of sonata form; the third movement is a strict *minuet and trio; and the finale might follow the principles—at least the key scheme—of sonata form, or might be more closely related to the *rondo, or, often, represented some mixture of these two.

Other basic practices of the art of composition were perfected by Haydn and Mozart: the presentation of distinct opening ideas and closing material, the manipulation or development of motifs, and the standardization of techniques for transitions, harmonic motion, modulation, and orchestration. Above all, each movement of the symphony, slow as well as fast, was dynamic, "a succession of impulses that converge toward a definite point of repose" (Stravinsky).

Beethoven, whose first symphony (1800) was written roughly a decade after the last symphonies of Haydn and Mozart, stands at the end of the classical period and the beginning of romanticism. Beethoven expanded almost every aspect of symphonic composition. In form, he lengthened the coda, *development, and introductions; he replaced the minuet with the scherzo; and he made far more use than Haydn or Mozart of the variations and the fugue. His manipulations and developments of musical material are more dramatic, as are the points of articulation between themes. His melodic material, his rhythmic drive and cross-accents, and his dynamics all represent innovations. In harmonic and contrapuntal style the advances over his predecessors are fewer. In orchestration, however, the addition in the later symphonies of piccolo, double bassoon, three trombones, triangle, bass drum and cymbals, and finally, soloists and chorus, paved the way for the great orchestral advances of the 19th century.

III. *Romanticism.* There are two mainstreams in the 19th-century symphony—the German, particularly Viennese, and the more revolutionary romanticism of Berlioz and his followers. Aside from minor figures like M. Clementi, L. Cherubini, C. M. von Weber, and L. Spohr (9 sym.), the German tradition was carried on by F. Schubert (8 sym., 1813–28), F. Mendelssohn (4 sym., 1824–41, plus a symphonic cantata, *Lobgesang,* 1840), and R. Schumann (4 sym., 1841–51). Each in large measure adhered to the form and the traditions. Mendelssohn had by far the greatest gift for classical construction, dynamic propulsive movement, and the manipulation of ideas. Schubert had a similar feeling for rhythmic steadiness and perpetual motion at all speeds, fast and slow, whereas Schumann reveled in *tempo rubato.* Each in his own way manifested the first full flower of German romanticism.

Berlioz considered himself the natural successor of Beethoven in freeing the symphony from its classical straitjacket. The *Symphonie fantastique,* op. 14 (1830), has five movements with titles like those in Beethoven's *Pastoral Symphony; *Harold en Italie,* op. 16 (1834), with viola solo, is based on literary scenes and the evocation of nature; *Romeo and Juliet,* op. 17 (1839), called *Symphonie dramatique,* makes use of solos and chorus, as in Beethoven's Ninth; and the *Symphonie funèbre et triomphale,* op. 15 (1840), is obviously concerned with those great confrontations of opposites that have always been a favorite of the romanticists. The legacy of Berlioz, which affected all composers of the 19th century with only a few notable exceptions (e.g., Brahms), consisted of: the musical delineation of romantic moods, and the relaxing of symphonic form to allow for such expression; a much expanded orchestra, not only through the use of new instruments (cornets, bells, antique cymbals, harps, etc.) but even more through the use of effects requiring a large number of players (e.g., four bassoons, cellos "at least fourteen," etc.). Berlioz opened the full

range of orchestral sound to later composers, and he brought to the symphony the whole technical apparatus of romanticism: rubato; frequent tempo changes; the *idée fixe;* chromatic melody and harmony; the transformation of theme; and the cyclic idea, leading directly to a one-movement form, the *symphonic poem.

It is only a step from Berlioz to Liszt's *Eine Symphonie zu Dante's Divina commedia* (1855) and his *Eine *Faust-Symphonie* (1854–57; dedicated to Berlioz), a symphony of three movements with titles (Faust, Gretchen, Mephistopheles), each a character sketch, actually a series of three symphonic poems linked by the transformation of themes. It is another small step to Liszt's symphonic poems and the large repertory of these works, truly poems and truly symphonic, in the latter 19th century.

After the *Faust-Symphonie* (1857) there is a curious fifteen-year hiatus. Minor composers such as Anton Rubinstein (6 sym.) and J. J. Raff (11 sym.) were popular in their day but have been dropped from the modern repertory. However, a promising series of first symphonies began to appear in the late 1860's: N. Rimsky-Korsakov and Dvořák in 1865, Bruckner in 1866, Borodin and Tchaikovsky in 1867, and finally Brahms' Symphony no. 1 in 1876.

With four symphonies (1876–85) Brahms marks a return to the classical ideals of craftsmanship in structure and in the manipulation of musical ideas, and a basic interest in music alone rather than extramusical programs, character sketches, and literary allusions. Although strictly in the Beethoven-Viennese tradition, Brahms has a romantic warmth of melody and harmony and rhythmic specialties all his own. His melody and harmony and rhythm, i.e., the stuff of his music, are romantic; he is classic in his concern for grand plans (even baroque in the Passacaglia of the Fourth Symphony), and in the presentation and working out of his material.

Anton Dvořák (9 sym., 1865–93), was deeply devoted, personally and in musical style, to Brahms and the Viennese tradition. Yet the national music of Bohemia flowed through his veins and he was one of the first of the musical *nationalists [also see Czechoslovakia]. Dvořák's use of folksong and folk dance, the pentatonic scale, and a peasant-like naïveté were combined with a superb mastery of the orchestra in the Schubert-Brahms tradition and virtuosity in creating effects—grandiose, sentimental, or bizarre—in the Berlioz tradition.

Tchaikovsky's six symphonies (1867–93), showing his mastery of solid structure, brilliant orchestration, and melancholy romanticism, make him the pre-eminent Russian symphonic composer of the century. Four streams of 19th-century art meet in him: the Beethoven tradition of clear and powerful form; the Berlioz love of the ultradramatic; a unique gift for orchestration, at once transparent and supremely brilliant; and a strain of Russian nationalism. The primarily nationalist Russian composers of symphonies were Borodin (3 sym., last incomp.), Rimsky-Korsakov (3), Balakirev (2), and Glazunov (8).

Three Americans, George Chadwick (3 sym.), John Knowles Paine (2 sym.), and Horatio Parker (1 sym.), exemplify the late 19th-century school in the United States, dominated largely by the German romanticists.

Anton Bruckner (10 sym., no. 9 incomp., 1866–96) and Gustav Mahler (10 sym., no. 10 incomp., 1884–1910) represent the twilight of German romanticism in radically different ways. Both followed the cult of the gigantic, and the works of both are pervaded with alternate simplicity and nostalgia on the one hand, and the grandiose or majestic on the other. Bruckner was strongly influenced by Wagner and, more remotely, by Schubert and Beethoven. His huge symphonies combine deep religious feeling and heartfelt pathos, yet they are static rather than dynamic. Though the skeleton of classic structure is often apparent, Bruckner's chief concerns were expression and delineation. A busy conductor all his life, Mahler barely found time to compose his nine gigantic symphonies. He commanded an endless variety of orchestral effects, and the instrumental parts are peppered with minute directions describing exactly how every note should be played. The frequently thin and linear texture foreshadows the neoclassicists' return to polyphonic style, but the "messages" of each symphony are spiritual, highly subjective experiences.

A nationalist but highly individual in his symphonies was Sibelius (7 sym., 1899–1925). Though related to Tchaikovsky in his first two symphonies, he struck out on his own with no. 3 (1907), and there followed five works, which (though currently neglected) are among the highest achievements in the literature. Sibelius clearly knew all about classical form, the apparatus of romantic expression, and the craft of orchestration, but his techniques remain intensely personal.

From the 1870's to the mid-1930's, there was hardly a composer who did not write at least one symphony. Notable exceptions are Wagner (if one disregards his youthful symphony of 1832), Debussy, Ravel, and the serial composers. Some of the symphonies written between 1870 and 1930 remain staples of the repertory; others have vanished, either because the composer's nonsymphonic works have assumed larger importance or because his star has, perhaps temporarily, set.

IV. *20th century.* For the sake of convenience, the composers of the modern era are grouped here by nationality.

France. French composers after Berlioz neglected the symphony. There are two examples by Bizet (1855, at the age of 17; 1860–68), one each by E. Chausson (*c.* 1890), P. Dukas (1896), and the Belgian-Parisian César Franck (1888), and three by V. d'Indy. Saint-Saëns wrote three symphonies, all with classical clarity and French elegance, the third (1886), a tour de force with organ and piano for four hands as well as orchestra. In the 1920's the genre was revived by A. Honegger, D. Milhaud, and A. Roussel. Of Roussel's symphonies, the first (1906) is a late romantic work akin to D'Indy's, whereas his last three symphonies are thoroughly postwar 20th-century works. Milhaud wrote five brief symphonies for very small chamber orchestra (1917–22), and then, after a long interval, twelve symphonies for large orchestra (1940–62). Honegger (5 sym., 1931–51) is possibly the most gifted, but the works of all three are substantial examples of the universal 20th-century style—dissonance, classical craftsmanship, counterpoint, driving rhythm, and striking orchestral sonorities, as well as the French national specialties of clarity, simplicity, directness, and lack of pretense. Of younger French composers, there are two symphonies of H. Dutilleux and one by O. Messiaen in ten movements.

Germany. Richard Strauss wrote two youthful symphonies (1881, '84), antedating his rapid succession of superb symphonic poems of the 1890's. His remaining symphonies, *Sinfonia domestica* (1902–03) and the *Alpensinfonie* (1915), are *program symphonies. Schoenberg's chamber symphony for fifteen instruments (op. 9, 1906), with a version for large orchestra in 1935, Webern's symphony of 1928 for chamber orchestra, and Schoenberg's second chamber symphony (op. 38, 1939) constitute the complete contribution of the founders of serial music to the symphonic form. Paul Hindemith has made notable contributions to the *neoclassical symphony. Besides two sinfoniettas (1924, '50), he wrote the symphony *Mathis der Maler* (1934), Symphony in E-flat (1940), *Symphonic Metamorphosis* of themes by Carl Maria von Weber (1943), *Symphonia serena* (1946), Symphony in B-flat for Band (1951), and Symphony "Die Harmonie der Welt" (1951).

Russia. Tchaikovsky and the nationalist composers were followed by V. S. Kalinnikov, A. S. Taneyev, S. I. Taneyev, A. N. Scriabin (3), S. Rachmaninoff (3), A. K. Glazunov (8), N. Y. Miaskovsky (27)—whose works are rarely heard today. However, after World War I Prokofiev, Shostakovitch, and Stravinsky produced first-class additions to the symphonic repertory of the 20th century. Prokofiev's Classical Symphony (op. 25, 1916–17) is one of the first landmarks of neoclassicism. Neoclassic in that it is "the organization of original material within a framework of the past," it is also anticlassical in many of its melodic ideas, harmonies, tonalities, dynamics, and rhythms. Prokofiev's later symphonies (1928–52) are touched with Soviet philosophy and "meaning" as well as by his highly individual style. Shostakovitch's 13 symphonies (1925–62) are marked from the start by the three most significant characteristics of Soviet music: simplicity, the rejection of any complexities and sophistication that could not be understood by the common people; emotionalism, conveyed in the most powerful and direct communication; and ardor, the belief that "there can be no music without idealogy." The Shostakovitch style is lyric above all, strongly and simply rhythmic, simple in texture, and conventional in harmony and tonality with an overlay of pepper and spice. It is not traditionally Russian in its use of folksong and folk dance, but more international, with strong Germanic traits especially in the scherzos. The orchestration is masterly.

Stravinsky's Symphony no. 1 (1905–07) is not followed by another (except by the Symphonies for Wind Instruments, 1920, in which the title assumes the Renaissance and baroque meaning of sinfonia, a soundpiece for instruments) until the cantata-like Symphony of Psalms (1930) and his great Symphony in C (1940) and Symphony in Three Movements (1945). The last two works as well as the Symphony of Psalms comprise a virtual compendium of Stravinsky's abstract and classical style and rank among the masterpieces of the century.

England. The English symphony is represented by E. Elgar (2 large-scale symphonies, 1908, 1910), C. V. Stanford (7), Ralph Vaughan Williams (9; 1910–57), and Arnold Bax (7; 1922–39), along with scattered works by G. Holst, W. Walton, L. Berkeley, M. Tippett, and B. Britten. Of these, Vaughan Williams' works are outstanding. They include a choral-orchestral Sea Symphony (words by Walt Whitman), a Pastoral Symphony, the London Symphony, a highly dissonant Symphony in F minor, and then, ten years later (1945), five more symphonies full of originality, variety, a native idiom nurtured in folksong and dance, and a deep spiritual kinship with the great music of Tudor England.

Others. An individualist like Sibelius but far more simple and naïve was the Danish composer Carl Nielsen (6 sym., 1894–1925); in the mid-20th century his works began to enjoy an increasing vogue. Other European composers worthy of note are the Italian G. F. Malipiero (9 sym., 1934–51), the Dutch Willem Pijper (3 sym., 1917–26), the Czech B. Martinu (6 sym., 1942–55), and the Polish Karol Szymanowski (3 sym., 1907–16). Neither Kodály nor Bartók wrote symphonies, though Bartók's concertos, especially the Concerto for Orchestra, are thoroughly symphonic.

United States. Charles Ives (4 sym., 1898–1916, with fragments of an uncompleted "Universe Symphony") is unique here as he is in every other area of composition. His Fourth Symphony finally reached public performance nearly half a century after its composition, in April, 1965. Other outstanding composers are Walter Piston (8 sym., 1938–65), Aaron Copland (3 sym., also *A Dance Symphony,* 1925–46), Roy Harris (10 sym., 1934–65), and William Schuman (8 sym., 1936–62). Somewhat less prominent in symphony composition are E. B. Hill, Randall Thompson, Howard Hanson, Roger Sessions, Peter Mennin, David Diamond, Paul Creston, Samuel Barber, Irving Fine, and Easley Blackwood. All the cross-currents of 20th-century style are present in the rich and varied production of these composers—from jazz to canon, fugue, and passacaglia; from a romantic urgency to communicate mood, thought, and idea to a single-minded interest in craftsmanship and development of musical ideas for their own sake. Two qualities would appear to be universal: a wealth of dissonance, and an endless quest for new orchestral sonorities.

Younger American composers are represented by Elliott Carter with a single symphony (1942) and Gunther Schuller with a symphony for brass and percussion (1950) and his Symphony no. 1 (1965). The youngest generation, devoted to post-Webern *serial techniques and *electronic music, prefer chamber music and small forms. Indeed, there are predictions that the new music of the second half of the 20th century has no place for the grand design of the symphony, nor even for the orchestra as a medium for composition. Whatever the future, the symphony has proved durable from 1750 to 1950 and the 20th-century contributions of Sibelius, Vaughan Williams, Hindemith, Honegger, Copland, Piston, and Stravinsky would seem to equal those of any other half-century in its history.

Lit.: R. Sondheimer, *Die Theorie der Sinfonie* (1925); A. Carse, *18th Century Symphonies* [1951]; K. Nef, *Geschichte der Sinfonie und Suite* (1921); ‡*DTB* 4, 13, 15; B. Brook, *La Symphonie française dans la seconde moitié du XVIIIᵉ siècle*, 3 vols. (1962); H. C. R. Landon, *The Symphonies of Joseph Haydn* [1955]; id., *Supplement to The Symphonies of Joseph Haydn* [1961]; P. Bekker, *Die Sinfonie von Beethoven bis Mahler* [1918]; R. Kloiber, *Handbuch der klassischen und romantischen Symphonie* (1964); D. Tovey, *Essays in Musical Analysis*, i, ii (1935); B. Churgin, "The Symphonies of G. B. Sammartini," 2 vols. (diss. Harvard Univ., 1963); G. Wolf and J. LaRue, "A Bibliographical Index to Robert Sondheimer's *Die Theorie der Sinfonie*" (*AM* xxxvii); R. Sondheimer, "Die formale Entwicklung der vorklassischen Sinfonie" (*AMW* iv, 85–99; 123–39); id., "Die Sinfonien Franz Becks" (*ZMW* iv); id., in *RMI* xxvii (Boccherini); P. Gradenwitz, in *MR* i (Stamitz); J. Tiersot, "La Symphonie en France" (*ZIM* iii); L. de la Laurencie and G. de Saint-Foix, "Contribution à l'histoire de la symphonie française vers 1750" (*L'année musicale*, 1911); F. Torrefranca, "Le Origini della sinfonia" (*RMI* xx, xxi, xxii).

G.W.W.

Symphony of Psalms. A work for chorus and orchestra (without violins or violas) by Stravinsky, completed in 1930. Its three movements are based on psalms (in Latin): I. Psalm 38, v. 13–14, treated in an archaic chordal style; II. Psalm 39, v. 12–13, a double fugue with one subject for the orchestra, the other for the chorus; III. Psalm 150, in a free, sectionalized form.

Syncopation. Syncopation is, generally speaking, any deliberate disturbance of the normal pulse of meter, accent, and rhythm. The principal system of rhythm in Western music is based on the grouping of equal beats into two's and

three's with a regularly recurrent accent on the first beat of each group [see Rhythm II (a)]. Any deviation from this scheme is perceived as a disturbance or contradiction between the underlying (normal) pulse and the actual (abnormal) rhythm.

Ex. 1 shows the three most common methods of shifting the accent to the normally weak beats of the measure, by: (a) holding on over the strong beat; (b) having rests on the strong beats;

(c) placing a stress on the weak beat. The examples in Ex. 2 show the practical application of these methods [a. Beethoven, Piano Sonata op. 28, no. 1; b. Beethoven, Piano Sonata, op. 57, "Appassionata"; c. Beethoven, String Quartet, op. 18, no. 4].

Normally, syncopation is only "partial," i.e., it occurs in one part only (either the melody or the bass), while other parts maintain and emphasize the normal pulse of the meter. In his late works Beethoven, however, becomes the first to use "complete syncopation," i.e., the displacement

of accents in the entire texture [Ex. 3, Piano Sonata, op. 101]. This procedure creates a complete imbalance in the listener's feeling of rhythmic security, an effect that occurs in romantic music (Schumann) in the sense of blurring, and in modern music (jazz) in the sense of a shock. Still another type of syncopation, resulting not from a displaced accent in unchanged meter but from a sudden change of the meter itself, is common in the works of modern composers, notably Stravinsky [Ex. 4, *L'Histoire du soldat*].

Syncopation first was used in the French *ars nova* (Machaut) and reached its all-time peak of complication in the music of the late 14th century (Cunelier, Grimace, B. Cordier, Solage, *et al.*). In 14th-century theory, syncopation was not explained as it is today (such an explanation would have been impossible since dynamic accent or strong beat are concepts foreign to early theorists), but as a separation of a normal

group of notes by the insertion of larger values, e.g., as in Ex. 5a. Instead of rendering this rhythm by tied notes in unchanged meter [Ex. 5b], a rendition similar to the methods employed by contemporary composers [Ex. 4] is preferable in order to convey the true meaning of early syncopation, as in Ex. 5c. For the original notation of 14th-century syncopation, see *ApNPM*, pp. 395ff.

Synemmenon [Gr.]. In ancient Greek theory, name for an additional tetrachord, whereby the b-flat was introduced into the scale [see Greece II]. In medieval theory, the term was used for the b-flat, and later (13th cent.) also as a general indication of chromatic alteration, e.g., *deuterus synemmenon,* or e-flat [*MS Mensura Monochordi Boetii de Musica; CS* i, 345].

Synthesizer. An electronic instrument (tool) of great versatility and complexity that translates the composer's desires into actual sound. The RCA electronic music synthesizer consists of thousands of individual electronic circuits that generate simple wave forms and then modify them (by changing frequency, intensity, duration, etc.) and combine them to synthesize more complex wave forms characteristic of musical sounds (the Hammond organ also synthesizes its tones but with considerably less flexibility). The numerous functions of the RCA synthesizer are controlled by a punched paper tape. The output of the instrument is preserved on a phonograph record or on magnetic tape. A completed composition usually consists of several such synthesizer outputs mixed together. See also Computer. Additional bibl. under Electronic instruments.

Syrian chant. Syria, being one of the first countries converted to Christianity, has a long history of church music. The entire early development of Christian hymnody took place in Syria, beginning with the Gnostic Psalter (hymnlike versions of the psalms, embodying the Gnostic doctrine) of Bardesanes (d. 223) and his son, Harmonios (fl. 3rd cent.), and continuing with the hymns, still used today, of St. Ephraim (306–73), which mark the beginning of Orthodox hymnody. Antiphonal psalmody also was developed in the heretical Church of Syria, whence the monks Flavianus and Diodorus imported it into the Orthodox Church of Antiochia (*c.* 350). Both hymns and antiphonal psalmody were brought from Syria to Milan by St. Ambrose (*c.* 333–97). Important successors of Ephraim were Narses of Edessa (fl. end of 5th cent.), Jacob of Serugh (451–521), and Simeon of Gesir, the Potter (after 500). The two chief types of ancient Syrian poetry are the *madrasha* (ode), consisting of a number of stanzas for a soloist with a refrain for chorus, and the *sogitha* (hymn), which was performed antiphonally by two choruses, with soloist leaders.

Since no early MSS of Syrian chant have been preserved, the present practice of Syrian chant is the only material available for study. Modern Syrian chant is based on multimetric rhythm [see Rhythm II (b)], as appears from the accompanying example. It is a good deal more rhythmic and syllabic than Gregorian chant. To what degree modern Syrian chant is representative of

the early chant is a matter of conjecture. Contentions to the effect that Syrian chant shows Hellenic influence [see *BeMMR*, p. 48] seem rather farfetched. Such rational features as are evident in Syrian chant may well be the result of 18th- and 19th-century Occidental influence [see *ReMMA*, p. 70]. A characteristic trait of Syrian church music is the use of standard melodies for a number of different poems of a similar verse pattern. Such standard melodies (which allow for a certain amount of rhythmic modification) are known as *risqolo* (for similar methods used in other musical traditions, see Melody type). In a Syrian MS of *c.* 515, the "Plerophoriai," we find the earliest mention of the *oktoechos* [see *Echos*].

Lit.: *NOH* ii, 7ff; *ReMMA*, pp. 67ff, 432; J. Jeannin, *Mélodies liturgiques syriennes et chaldéennes*, 2 vols. (1926, '28); L. Bonvin, "On Syrian Liturgical Chant" (*MQ* iv); H. Husmann, "The Practice of Organum . . . of the Syrian Churches" (*CP Reese*); A. Z. Idelsohn, "Der Kirchengesang der Jakobiten" (*AMW* iv); J. Jeannin and J. Puyade, "L'Octoëchos syrien" (*Oriens Christianus*, New Series iii, 82ff, 277ff); S. Jargy, "La Musique liturgique syrienne" (*CP 1950*). Bibl. in *Notes* vi, 133ff.

Syrinx. Greek name for *panpipes (perhaps also for a single flute).

System. The collection of staves, two or more, as used for musical notation.

T

T. Abbr. for tonic, *tutti*, toe (in pedal parts of organ pieces), trill (in 17th-century music, usually a mordent only). In 16th-century *part-books, abbr. for tenor.

Ta'amim. Notation symbols in Jewish chant. See Jewish music II; Ecphonetic notation.

Tabarro, Il. See under *Trittico*.

Tabatière de musique [F.]. See under Mechanical instruments III.

Tablature [G. *Tabulatur;* It. *intavolatura;* Sp. *tablatura*]. (1) The set of rules that regulated the musical activities of the *Meistersinger.

(2) General name for the various early (15th–17th cent.) systems of notation (for keyboard instruments, lute, guitar, viol, flute, etc.), in which the tones are indicated by letters, figures, or other symbols instead of notes on a staff (as in the contemporary *mensural notation for vocal music). The most important are the keyboard (organ) tablatures and lute tablatures. There are two types of keyboard tablature, the German and the Spanish, and three types of lute tablature, the Italian (also used in Spain, for the vihuela), the French (used everywhere after 1600), and the German. What are sometimes called French, Italian, and English organ tabla-

tures (e.g., in *WoHN* ii) are written entirely in notes on two staves in practically the same manner as the modern piano score. Although they were called *intavolatura* in the 16th century, they are not tablatures in the present-day meaning of the term.

I. *German keyboard tablatures.* Ex. 1 (Buxheim Organ Book, *c.* 1460–70) and Ex. 2 (B. Schmid, *Tabulatur Buch,* 1607), illustrate the "old" and "new" German keyboard tablature. The former, which employs notes for the upper part and letters for the lower parts, was used prior to 1550; the latter, written in letters exclusively, was used after 1550 (as late as 1720 Bach reverted to this system in his *Orgelbüchlein* when there was not enough space on a page to complete the piece in ordinary staff notation; see *ApNPM*,

1a

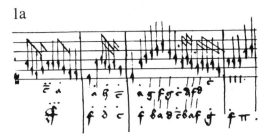

fac. 13). The letters a, b, c, etc., mean the same as they do today; however, in German terminology b means B-flat, B natural being indicated by the letter h [see the entry B (1)]. Chromatic

2 a

alterations are indicated by adding a loop or hook to the letter. This was the stenographic sign for the Latin syllable *is* (e.g., *arbor-is*) so that *c* with a loop means *cis,* German for C-sharp. The tones of the higher octave (usually from c′ to b′; in some sources from a to g′) are marked with a dash above the letter: c (one-line c). Rhythmic values are indicated by the signs

c

illustrated [Ex. 2c], standing for (left to right) a *semibrevis, minima, semiminima,* and *fusa.*

II. *Spanish keyboard tablature.* Here a number of lines (three, four, five) represent the different voice-parts of a composition [Ex. 3, Cabezón, *Obras de música,* 1578]. The figures 1 to 7 stand

for the notes of the diatonic scale beginning with f (1 = f; 2 = g; 3 = a; 4 = b or b♭, according to whether the sign ♮ or B is given at the beginning of the piece; 5 = c′; etc.). Higher and lower octaves are marked by special signs, e.g., a tick on the 3 = A [see the third symbol on the bottom line of Ex. 3a]; the plain figure 3 = a; a dot beside it = a′; a prime beside it, a″. A comma (,) indicates tying of the preceding note; a diagonal slash (/) indicates a rest.

III. *Italian (Spanish) lute tablatures.* All lute tablatures are based on the idea, revived in certain modern instruments (ukulele, zither, guitar), of directing the player's fingers to the position necessary for the desired tone or chord. Thus they avoid the entire matter of "solfège" (pitch, interval, scale, key, accidentals, etc.). They are a "finger notation" [G. *Griffschrift*], as distinguished from the usual "pitch notation" [G. *Tonschrift*]. In the Italian system, a form of which was also used for the *vihuela, six horizontal lines represent the six courses of the lute, tuned (in theory) G–c–f–a–d′–g′, in reverse order, so that the highest line represents course G (only in Milán's *El Maestro* of 1535 is the highest line used for the highest course; see also under IV). On each line, figures from 0 to 9 indicate the fret on which the player is supposed to put his finger, with 0 signifying the open string, 1 the first fret, etc. Since these frets proceed in semitones, the figures 1, 2, 3, etc., represent tones that are one, two, three, etc., semitones higher than the open string; thus, 3 on the second line from the top indicates c (second open string) plus 3 semitones, i.e., d♯ or e♭. The rhythmic values are indicated above the staff by the accompanying signs [Ex. 3c], the first of which represents the *semibrevis* (usually transcribed as a half note). Despite the contrapuntal character of 16th- and

c

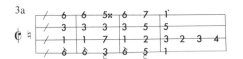

17th-century lute music, no distinction is made between the different temporal values of simultaneous sounds, e.g., between an eighth note in the upper part against a simultaneous half note in a lower part. The rhythmic signs merely give the shortest of all the simultaneous notes, e.g., the eighth note; further, in most later tablatures a rhythmic sign is to be repeated until replaced by another note value [Ex. 4a, Fuenllana, *Libro de Música . . . Orphenica Lyra,* 1554]. The two transcriptions [Ex. 4b, 4c] illustrate the "exact"

4a

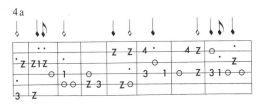

rendition together with the contrapuntal interpretation usually preferred in modern editions [see *ApNPM,* pp. 59ff].

IV. *French lute tablature.* This system differs from the Italian only in details. The staff has only five lines, which represent the five highest courses in their natural order (as in Milán), while the lowest course is represented underneath on short ledger lines. Instead of figures, letters (*a, b, c,* etc.) are used, with *a* standing for the open course [Ex. 5a, G. Bataille, *Third Book of Airs,* 1611]. After 1600 this system of notation underwent various modifications that, *c.* 1650, led to a new system based on Denis Gaultier's novel method of tuning (*nouveau ton*),

5a

A–d–f–a–d′–f′. Here, the Italian staff of six lines is used for the six courses that cross the frets, while the signs

$$\text{a,} \quad \bar{\text{a}}, \quad \bar{\bar{\text{a}}}, \quad \bar{\bar{\bar{\text{a}}}}, \quad 4$$

written underneath the staff indicate the bass courses, tuned (normally) G, F, E, D, C, which are unalterable in pitch.

V. *German lute tablature.* This system is much more awkward than the others, mainly because it was originally designed (15th cent.) for a lute with only five courses and was broadened later (16th cent.) by the inclusion of signs for the sixth (lowest) course. The table here shows the most common system of designation: figures 1–5 for the open courses (read from bottom to top); the letters of the alphabet (completed by two special signs designated here * and **) for the frets 1–5; the same letters with dashes for the higher frets. The table shows that, e.g., the sign h denotes the

Courses		Frets							
		0	1	2	3	4	5	6	7
	g′	5	e	k	p	v	**	$\bar{e}$	$\bar{k}$
	d′	4	d	i	o	t	*	$\bar{d}$	$\bar{i}$
	a	3	c	h	n	s	z	$\bar{c}$	$\bar{h}$
	f	2	b	g	m	r	y	$\bar{b}$	$\bar{g}$
	c	1	a	f	l	q	x	$\bar{a}$	$\bar{f}$
	G	$\bar{1}$	$\bar{2}$	$\bar{3}$	$\bar{4}$	$\bar{5}$	$\bar{6}$	$\bar{7}$	$\bar{8}$

tone b (two semitones above a), and the sign x the tone f (five semitones above c). See Ex. 6, H. Gerle, *Ein neues . . . Lautenbuch,* 1552.

6

VI. *Modern tablatures.* Tablature notation is used today for several popular instruments that are much easier to play when the notation directs the player's fingers to the desired place. The notation of the modern guitar resembles the 16th-century lute tablatures, and a similar method is used for the four-stringed ukulele.

Lit.: *ApNPM*, pp. 21–81; *WoHN* ii, 1–247; *GD, GDB, s.v.* "Tablature."

Tabor, taborel, tabour, tabourin, tabret. See Tambourin; also Pipe (1). For ill. see under Percussion instruments.

Tabulatur [G.]. See Tablature.

Tace [It.]**, tacet** [L.]. Be (is) silent. Term used in orchestral scores for parts not needed for a movement or a long section.

Tact [G.]. See *Takt.*

Tactus [L.]. The 15th- and 16th-century term for beat, both with its temporal meaning and as in "conductor's beat." However, the tactus is a relatively fixed duration of time, about M.M. 60–70 (one second), whereas the modern beat may take on any value within broad limits, according to the tempo and character of the composition. This means that throughout the 16th century there was a uniform "normal" tempo from which only slight deviations were possible. Since the tactus was normally represented by the *semibrevis* (S), the proper tempo of the motets of Obrecht, Josquin, and Palestrina can be expressed by the metronomic mark: S = M.M. 60–70. For a discussion of complications caused by the use of the *alla breve* sign ₵ instead of the *alla semibreve* sign C, see *ApNPM,* pp. 188–95. See also Tempo marks.

From the 13th to the late 15th centuries there were similar units of time, called **tempus* (e.g., Franco of Cologne), which were of considerably shorter duration and which changed somewhat during the course of this period. There also was a successive shift in the note values used to represent the "normal" beat, from the *longa* (c. 1200, school of Notre Dame) to the *brevis* (13th cent.), the *semibrevis* (14th–16th cent.), the *minima* (c. 1550), and finally the *semiminima,* i.e., the modern quarter note (during the 17th century). For a tentative table of the changes in tempo prior to 1400, see *ApNPM,* p. 343.

Lit.: A. Auda, *Théorie et pratique du tactus* (1964); E. Praetorius, *Die Mensuraltheorie des Franchinus Gafurius* (1905), pp. 68ff, in *Publikationen der Internationalen Musikgesellschaft,* supp., series ii, vol. ii; A. Chybiński, *Beiträge zur Geschichte des Taktschlagens* (1908); G. Schünemann, *Geschichte des Dirigierens* (1913),

ch. iii; A. Auda, "Le 'Tactus' dans la Messe 'L'Homme armé' de Palestrina" (*AM* xiv); C. Dahlhaus, "Zur Theorie des Tactus im 16. Jahrhundert" (*AMW* xvii).

Tafelmusik [G.]. Table music, i.e., music to be performed at a banquet, e.g., Telemann's *Musique de table* (*DdT* 61/62) and J. A Reutter's *Servizio di tavola* (*DTO* 31).

Tagelied [G.]. See under *Alba.*

Tagliato [It.]. Obsolete term for the **alla breve* sign.

Taille [F.]. Old name for a middle voice, particularly the tenor. See *Récit.* The term was also used for instruments performing such a part, e.g., *taille de basson,* tenor oboe; *taille de violon* or simply *taille,* viola. The indication *taille* in some of Bach's cantatas appears always to call for the tenor oboe (oboe da caccia, English horn).

Takt [G.]. (1) Beat (*schwerer, leichter Takt,* i.e., strong, weak beat). (2) Measure (*nach 10 Takten,* after 10 measures). (3) Meter, time (3/4 *Takt,* 3/4 meter). *Im Takt,* in strict tempo and meter; *Taktart,* meter; *taktmässig,* in strict meter; *Taktmesser,* metronome; *Taktstock,* baton; *Taktstrich,* bar line; *Taktvorzeichnung,* time signature; *Taktwechsel,* change of meter; *Taktzeichen,* time signature; *taktieren,* to indicate the beat.

Talea. See under Isorhythmic.

Tales of Hoffmann, The. See *Contes d'Hoffmann, Les.*

Talon [F.]. The nut of the violin bow [see Bow].

Tambora [Sp.]. Two-headed drum constructed from the hollowed trunk of the *lana* tree. It is considered the national instrument of the Dominican Republic. A male goatskin is used for the top head and a female one for the bottom. These are mounted on three hoops and held in place by additional sets of hoops tied to the body with a cord. The drum is played with the palm and fingers of the left hand and with a *palito* (small stick) held in the right hand.   J.O-S.

Tamborito [Sp.]. A Panamanian dance of African origin, in which a solo singer (always a woman, called *cantaora alante*) alternates with a chorus singing an unchanging refrain. The melody is mainly syllabic, usually in the major, in the Phrygian or Hypodorian modes, and proceeding by disjunct thirds and fourths. It is always in duple meter and involves a fair amount of syncopation. The *tamborito* is usually sung and danced to the accompaniment of percussion and handclapping. Toward the end of the piece, the drums often shift from 2/4 to 6/8 meter, gradually increasing the tempo. *Tamboritos* danced in street parades are known as *tunas*.   J.O-S.

Tambour [F.]. Drum; also, drummer. *Tambour militaire*, snare drum; *tambour de Basque*, tambourine (the modern percussion instrument).

Tambourin [F.]. (1) A small (occasionally tiny) two-headed medieval drum, cylindrical in shape, with both heads covered with skin. It is mentioned as early as *c.* 1080 in the *Roman de Roland* as a *tabor*, which is of Arab origin. It was played together with the *galoubet*, a small flute (pipe and tabor; Sp. *flaviol* and *tamboril*; see Pipe (1). D.-F.-E. Auber used the tambourin in his opera, *Le Philtre* (1831). However, in modern scores the term usually means *tambourine. (2) An old Provençal dance, originally accompanied by pipe and tambourin (or tambour de Basque, i.e., tambourine), in lively 2/4 meter. Rameau's operas contain many tambourins, in which the drum is represented by a monotonous bass accompaniment. A famous example, found among his harpsichord pieces, is from his opera *Les Fêtes d'Hébé* (1739).

Tambourine. See under Percussion instruments B, 4. In early music, the term usually means *tambourin.

Tambur. A long-necked, round-bodied lute of Afghanistan, also called *rabab. Also see Tanbur.

Tambura (also *tanbura, tanpura*). Long-necked, unfretted, round-bodied drone lute of India. It has four metal strings that are plucked with one finger. See India VIII.

Tamburin [G.], **tamburino** [It.]. Usually, the modern tambourine; rarely, the obsolete *tambourin.

Tamburo [It.]. Drum, kettledrum; *t. grande, grosso*, old name for bass drum; *t. rullante*, tenor drum; *t. militaire*, snare drum.

Taming of the Shrew, The. Opera in three acts by V. Giannini (libretto by the composer and D. Fee, based on Shakespeare's play), produced in Cincinnati, 1953. Setting: Padua, 16th century.

Tampon [F.]. Two-headed drumstick used to produce a roll on the bass drum. It is held in the middle and moved by shaking the wrist.

Tamtam. Same as gong [see Percussion instruments B,7]. Not to be confused with *tom-tom.

Tanbur. A long-necked lute with a pear-shaped body that is found throughout the Balkans and Near East. It has a variable number of metal strings. See Lute II.

Tanbura. See Tambura.

Tañer [Sp.]. See under *Tastar*.

Tangent [G. *Tangente*]. See under Clavichord.

Tango [Sp.]. An urban modern dance of Argentina, performed by couples, which had adopted its characteristic features by the first decade of the 20th century in Buenos Aires. Before then it was a hybrid form, combining elements of the Andalusian tango, *habanera, and *milonga. It consists of two sections of equal length (14–20 measures), with the second generally in the dominant or relative minor of the original key. It is based on syncopated patterns within a 2/4 meter. Its texts usually deal with urban topics, often melodramatic or pathetic.   J.O-S.

Tannhäuser, or *Der Sängerkrieg auf Wartburg* [G., The Singers' Contest at Wartburg]. Opera in three acts by Wagner (to his own libretto, after a medieval legend), produced in Dresden, 1845. Setting: Venusberg and in and around Wartburg, near Eisenach, early 13th century. The formal structure is essentially that of the traditional *number opera, with distinct arias, numerous choruses, and even a ballet (first scene), although the actual numbering of the different items is abandoned. The harmonic style also is fairly traditional. It is by reason of its expressive and emotional qualities that *Tannhäuser* opens a new period in the history of opera.

Tanpura. See Tambura.

Tanz [G.]. Dance.

Tape recording. See under Phonograph and recorded music.

Tapiola. Symphonic poem by Sibelius, op. 112 (1926). The name is based on Tapio, the forest god of Finnish legend (*Kalevala).

Tarantella. A Neapolitan dance in rapid 6/8 meter, probably named for Taranto in southern Italy, or, according to popular legend, for the tarantula spider whose poisonous bite the dance was believed to cure. In the mid-19th century it was frequently composed (Chopin, Liszt, S. Heller, Auber, Weber, Thalberg) in the style of a brilliant *perpetuum mobile.* See M. Schneider, "La Danza de espadas y la tarantela" (*AnM* ii).

Tardo, tardamente [It.]. Slow, slowly. *Tardando,* slowing.

Tarogato. Hungarian instrument of ancient origin, originally a wooden *cornett having only natural tones. It was used for sounding military signals such as occur in the well-known Rákóczy march. Later, the name was used for a wooden shawm (oboe mouthpiece) with five or more holes. The modern tarogato, built by W. J. Schunda, is a wooden saxophone, i.e., with a clarinet mouthpiece. It has a somewhat darker timbre than the normal saxophone. See ill. accompanying Clarinet family.

Tartini's tone. Same as differential tone [see Combination tone].

Tartold. A strange instrument mentioned in the inventory of the ducal collection at Schloss Ambras in the Austrian Tyrol (1596): "Tartold wie Drackhen [dragons] geformirt" [see J. Schlosser, *Die Sammlung alter Musikinstrumente* (1920), p. 85, Tafel XL]. Five instruments have been preserved (now in Vienna, Kunsthistorisches Museum, nos. 219–23). They are rackets with metal bodies of dragon shape and painted red, green, and gold. Probably they were used in masquerades.

Tasche [It.]. Popular name for festivals celebrated at Lucca for several centuries until *c.* 1800. Boccherini was among those who wrote music for them. See A. Bonaventura, in *RMI* xxxvi (Boccherini); U. Rolandi, in *Bollettino bibliografico musicale* vii.

Taschengeige [G.]. *Kit.

Tasso. Symphonic poem by Liszt, based on a poem by Byron, composed 1849–51 and first performed as an overture to Goethe's drama, *Torquato Tasso.*

Tastar [It.]. Italian 16th-century term for a lute piece in the style of a free prelude (*tastar de corde,* "touching of the strings"). Ex. in *HAM,* no. 99a, and in *ApMZ* i, 20. The Spanish equivalent was *tañer* (Milán). See Ricercar II (a).

Taste [G.]. Key (of piano, organ, etc.). *Untertaste,* white key; *Obertaste,* black key.

Tastiera [It.]. Keyboard. For the *tastiera per luce* (*clavier à lumières*) in Scriabin's *Prometheus,* see Color organ.

Tasto [It.]. (1) The key of a keyboard. For *tasto solo* (*t.s.*), see Thoroughbass I, 6. (2) Fingerboard of the violin, etc. For *sul tasto,* see Bowing (l).

Tattoo [F. *rappel;* G. *Zapfenstreich;* It. *ritirata;* Sp. *retreta*]. The military signals sounded on bugles and drums for recalling soldiers to their quarters at night.

Tecla [Sp.]. A 16th- and 17th-century term for key and keyboard. *Música para tecla* (e.g., Cabezón's *Obras de música,* 1578) is music for keyboard instruments.

Tedesca [It.]. In the 17th century, name for the *allemande. About 1800, name for the *Ländler* and similar dances in rather quick triple meter (e.g., Beethoven, op. 79, op. 130).

Te Deum. A celebrated song of praise and rejoicing, "Te Deum laudamus" (We praise Thee, O God), also known as the hymn of thanksgiving. It was formerly attributed to St. Ambrose (hence the designation Ambrosian hymn). It may have been written by Nicetus (or Nicetius; d. 568), bishop of Remesiana (now Nish in Yugoslavia), but certain lines are taken from the *De mortalitate* of St. Cyprian (A.D. 272). It is one of the few remaining examples of the *psalmus idioticus.* In the Roman Catholic liturgy it usually replaces the last responsory of Matins on feast days and Sundays [see *LU,* pp. 876, 939] and also may be sung as a hymn of thanksgiving on various occasions. Its present-day form is the result of various changes and intercalations, rarely encountered in the tradition of Gregorian chant [see P. Wagner, *Einführung in die Gregorianischen Melodien* (1911–21; repr. 1962), iii, 224ff]. It is sung to a highly archaic psalmodic melody [*LU,* p. 1832], employing formulas almost the same as some in Yemenite cantillations of the Torah.

The Te Deum has often been composed. One of its verses, "Tu patris sempiternus es filius," is used in the *"Musica enchiriadis" (*c.* 900) as an instructive example of organum of the fifth. The closing verse, "In te Domine speravi," was set in English discant *c.* 1300 [see Discant (2)]. Binchois composed the entire melody in a simple fauxbourdon style. There are 16th-century contrapuntal settings, all based on the Gregorian melody, by Hugh Aston [*Editions LI, 10; also a *Missa Te Deum*], Festa, Palestrina, Anerio, Kerle, and Vaet, and settings for organ in Attaingnant's *Magnificat sur les huit tons avec Te Deum laudamus* (1530) and in the *"Mulliner Book" (W. Blitheman). Since 1549 it has been

one of the canticles of Morning Prayer in *Anglican church music. In the 17th century and later
the Te Deum became a hymn of thanksgiving for
special occasions (e.g., a great victory) and was
composed in a festive and grandiose style,
frequently for double chorus with orchestra
(Purcell, 1694; Handel, for the Peace of Utrecht,
1713, and the victory at Dettingen, 1743; K. H.
Graun, 1757, battle of Prague; Berlioz, for the
Paris Exhibition of 1855; Bruckner, 1884;
Dvořák, 1896; Verdi, 1898; Sullivan, for Queen
Victoria's Diamond Jubilee, 1897).

The German translation (by Luther) is "Herr
Gott, dich loben wir." Under this title J. S. Bach
wrote a long organ piece (hardly to be classified
as a "chorale prelude") in which he shows great
ingenuity in providing different polyphonic settings for the frequently repeated phrases of the
(somewhat simplified) plainsong melody. Settings of the 20th century include those of Britten
(1945), Kodály (1936), Pepping (1956), and
Vaughan Williams (1937). See E. Kähler, *Studien
zum Te Deum* (1958).

Telephone, The. Opera in one act by Menotti, a
companion piece to his *Medium,* produced in
New York, 1947. Setting: Lucy's apartment, the
present.

Telharmonium. See under Electronic instruments.

Telyn. Welsh harp. See Harp III.

Tema [It., Sp.]. *Theme, subject.

Temperament [G. *Temperatur*]. I. *General.* A
system of tuning in which the intervals deviate
from the "pure" (i.e., acoustically correct)
intervals of the *Pythagorean system and *just
intonation. The deviations are necessary because
these two systems, although perfect within a
small range of tones (mainly those of the
C-major scale), become increasingly inadequate
with the successive introduction of the chromatic
tones. For instance, the acoustically perfect fifth
[see Acoustics III] might well be used to obtain
a succession of five or six fifths, c, g, d, a, e, b.
However, if tones such as f♯, c♯, g♯, d♯ are added
in the same manner, the resulting tones cannot
be satisfactorily used for melodies such as
d e f♯ g, or d♯ f g g♯ (meaning e♭ f g a♭). Moreover, the twelfth tone of the succession of fifths,
b♯, is noticeably higher than the tone c it would
represent in our system of notation [see Circle
of fifths]. Thus, it is necessary to devise methods
that, instead of being perfect in the simple keys

and intolerably wrong in the others, spread the
inevitable inaccuracy over all the tones and keys.
The most consistent realization of this principle
is the equal temperament [see III] universally
used today. Prior to its general acceptance,
various other systems of tempered intervals,
generally referred to as "unequal temperament,"
were in use, among which the mean-tone system
was the only one to attain practical significance.

II. *The mean-tone system.* This system, which
was in use c. 1500 (A. Schlick, *Spiegel der . . .
Organisten,* 1511; fully explained in P. Aaron's
Thoscanello de la Musica, 1523) is based on a
fifth that is one-fourth of the syntonic *comma
(c. 22 cents) smaller than the perfect fifth (697,
instead of 702 cents), the result being that four
such fifths in succession (c–g–d'–a'–e'') lead to a
major third (e''). In the simple keys with one
or two sharps or flats, the mean-tone scale is
very satisfactory both melodically and harmonically. In fact, owing to the presence of a perfect
third and an almost perfect fifth, the triads sound
much purer than in equal temperament. However, the continuation of the series of mean-tone
fifths leads to a very noticeable discrepancy
between sharp and flat tones, indeed a difference
of almost a quarter tone (42 cents) between any
two enharmonic tones (e.g., G♯ = 772, A♭ =
814); this difference is known as the "wolf."
Having to choose between these two tones (the
corresponding choice between C♯ and D♭, or
between D♯ and E♭, being relatively easier, i.e.,
in favor of C♯ and of E♭), Schlick interestingly
enough preferred the A♭, in order to obtain
the "süss und fremd lautende Konkordanz"
(sweet and strange-sounding consonance) of the
triad on A-flat, which actually occurs in his "Da
Pacem" [new ed. by G. Harms (1957), p. 37; all
the pieces here are transposed down a fourth].
Since this tone could not be used to represent
G♯, Schlick recommends avoiding the G♯ or
concealing it with a quick ornament [see
G. Frotscher, *Geschichte des Orgelspiels* i, 93f].
A better expedient is the use of divided keys,
which, as a matter of fact, were not infrequently
used in organs of the 16th century. However,
even this improvement did not meet the needs
of the more fully developed harmonies, modulations, and keys used during the 17th century. The
increased use of keys with three to six sharps
and flats necessarily led to the system of equal
temperament.

III. *Equal temperament.* The principle of equal
temperament is to divide the octave into twelve
equal semitones. Since the frequency ratio of the

octave is 2, the frequency ratio s of this semitone is given by the equation: $s^{12} = 2$; $s = \sqrt[12]{2} = 1.05946$. The successive powers of this figure give the frequency ratios for the tones of the chromatic scale, e.g., $c = 1$; $c\sharp = 1.05946$; $d = 1.05946^2 = 1.12246$; $d\sharp = e^b = 1.05946^3 = 1.18921$; etc. Usually a logarithmic measurement is used in which the whole octave equals 1,200 cents and each semitone 100 cents [see Intervals, calculation of, IV, V].

In equal temperament no interval other than the octave is acoustically correct or pure. The deviation of the fifth (2 cents) is too small to be perceived. With the thirds, the difference is considerably greater, the well-tempered third (400 cents) being 14 cents (one-eighth semitone) larger than the pure third (386 cents). However, the modern ear has become completely accustomed to this "error," and the advantages of the system far outweigh its flaws. The following table shows the actual frequency ratios of the Pythagorean system (P), of just intonation (J), and of the tempered tones (E):

	c″	d″	e″	f″	g″	a″	b″	c‴
P.	520	585	658	693	780	877	987	1040
J.	520	585	650	693	780	867	975	1040
E.	520	584	655	694	779	874	982	1040

The accompanying illustration shows the difference between E and J in cents.

major and minor keys, *The Well-Tempered Clavier* (1722, '44), or its less complete predecessor, J. K. F. Fischer's *Ariadne musica* (1715), referred to equal temperament or merely a close approximation is not entirely clear. At any rate, the system was not universally adopted in Germany until *c.* 1800, and in France and England until *c.* 1850. Other systems of temperament, such as that of the mathematician Leonardt Euler (1707–83) and of J. P. Kirnberger (1721–83), never attained practical significance. See also Cycle.

Lit.: J. M. Barbour, *Tuning and Temperament* (1951); *id.,* "Equal Temperament: Its History from Ramis (1482) to Rameau (1737)" (diss. Cornell Univ., 1932); W. Dupont, *Geschichte der musikalischen Temperatur* (1935); P. Garnault, *Le Tempérament, son histoire et influence sur la musique du xviiie siècle* (1929); J. M. Barbour, "Bach and *The Art of Temperament*" (*MQ* xxxiii); *id.,* "Irregular Systems of Temperament" (*JAMS* i, no. 3); H. J. Watt, in *ML* iv, 246ff; L. S. Lloyd, in *ML* xix, 443ff, xx, 365ff, xxi, 347ff; *id.,* in *MR* v, no. 4 (mean-tone tuning); J. Handschin, in *Schweizer Jahrbuch für Musikwissenschaft* ii; K. Hasse, in *ZMW* xiii.

Temperatur [G.] *Temperament. Gleichschwebende, ungleichschwebende T.,* equal, unequal temperament.

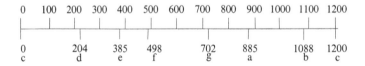

Equal temperament is usually said to have been invented by Andreas Werckmeister *c.* 1700. However, the history of equal temperament can be traced back at least to 1518, when H. Grammateus recommended dividing the octave into ten equal semitones and two of somewhat smaller size. V. Galilei, in his *Dialogo* (1581), proposed using a semitone of the frequency $^{18}\!/_{17}$ (99.3 cents), a close approximation of the well-tempered semitone. The principle of equal temperament was clearly expounded by the Chinese Prince Tsai-yu in 1596 and by Mersenne in 1635. Contrary to common belief, Werckmeister never stated equal temperament correctly. The introduction of equal temperament into musical practice was very slow. Whether Bach's famous collection of pieces in all the

Tempo. The speed of a composition or a section thereof, ranging from very slow to very fast, as indicated by tempo marks such as largo, adagio, andante, moderato, allegro, presto, prestissimo. More accurate are *metronome indications, such as ♩ = M.M. 100, i.e., the quarter note lasts $\frac{1}{100}$ of a minute. The practical limits for the duration of the beat are M.M. 50 and M.M. 120. M.M. 60–80 represents a "normal" tempo that agrees with various natural paces, e.g., moderate walking or the human pulse. The question of the "right" tempo for a piece is a favorite one among musicians, listeners, and critics. Discrepancies in tempo among performances of a particular work are often explained as being conditioned by external factors, e.g., the size and reverberations of the concert hall, the sonority of the instruments, or the size of the orchestra. Such explanations, however, account for only minute modifications and not the startling differences often found among performances. These are purely a matter of interpretation, and the differences encountered in the interpretation of tempo are no greater than those in style, phrasing, and orchestral treatment. Generally, it can be said that, where the classical repertory is concerned (Mozart, Beethoven, and especially Bach), modern conductors and performers play the fast movements too fast and the slow ones too slowly. See also Tempo marks. For tempo in early music, see Tactus.

Lit.: C. Sachs, *Rhythm and Tempo* (1953); S. A. Aronowsky, *Performing Times of Orchestral Works* (1959); R. Donnington, *Tempo and Rhythm in Bach's Organ Music* [1960]; C. Jacobs, ‡*Tempo Notation in Renaissance Spain* [1964]; E. Barthe, *Takt und Tempo* (1960); I. Herrmann-Bengen, *Tempobezeichnungen . . . im 17. und 18. Jahrhundert* (1959); S. Gullo, *Das Tempo . . . des XIII. und XIV. Jahrhunderts* (1964); E. O. Turner, "Tempo Variation" (*ML* xix, 308ff); H. Gál, "The Right Tempo" (*Monthly Musical Record* lxix, 174ff); R. Kolisch, "Tempo and Character in Beethoven's Music" (*MQ* xxix). See also under Metronome.

Tempo giusto. See *Giusto*.

Tempo marks. To indicate the tempo of a piece, a number of Italian terms are used, the most important of which are given here, in order of slowest to quickest: *largo* (broad), *lento* (slow), *adagio* (slow; lit., at ease), *andante* (walking), *moderato* (moderate), *allegretto, allegro* (fast; lit., cheerful), *presto* (very fast), *prestissimo* (as fast as possible). In addition to these are terms calling for gradual change of speed, mainly *ritardando* (slackening) and *accelerando* (quickening); *rubato* indicates a deliberate unsteadiness of tempo.

With the use of tempo marks, the duration of any given note value becomes variable within large limits. In actual practice, the range of variation is much larger even than one might assume, owing to the practice of writing quick pieces in the larger values (whole to eighth notes) and slow pieces in the smaller ones (quarter to sixty-fourth notes). The first two examples [Ex. 1, Mozart, Piano Concerto, A major, K. 488, last movt.; Ex. 2, Beethoven, Piano Sonata op. 10, no. 3, slow movt.] show that the duration of the half note may vary from less than half a second to four seconds. The difference between "ex-

1. Allegro assai

2. Largo e mesto

3. ♩ = 70   4. ♩ = 70

tremely quick" and "extremely slow" is clear if the two examples are written according to the "natural" principle of using small values for quick notes and large values for long notes [Ex. 3, 4]. If this principle were accepted, tempo marks would become practically obsolete.

Prior to 1600, tempo marks were practically unknown, since the pace of a composition was expressed in the notation itself, the note values then used having absolute durations that were variable only within small limits [see Tactus]. An isolated early example of tempo indication is in the vihuela book *El Maestro* (1935) of Luis Milán [*Editions XLVI, 2], who points out that certain sections of his fantasias must be played *apriessa* (quick) and others *espacio* (slow). One of the first composers to use modern tempo marks was Adriano Banchieri (1568–1634), who in his *Organo suonarino* (1611, '22) prescribes *adagio, allegro, veloce, presto, più presto,* and *prestissimo* [see *ApMZ* i, 27ff]. In the 17th and 18th centuries *presto* did not have the present-day meaning of "extremely fast" but only meant "fast." Thus, players of Bach's E-minor Prelude from *The Well-Tempered Clavier* i commit a grave error if they try to play its final section in a speed comparable to that of a *presto* etude by Chopin. It was not until the time of Mozart that *presto* had its present-day meaning.

Temporale. In the Roman Catholic rite, generic designation for the feasts of the Lord, as opposed to the Sanctorale, the feasts of Saints. They are also called *de tempore,* i.e., feasts referring to the "time" (life) of the Lord. See Gregorian chant I.

Temps [F.]. Beat; *temps fort (faible),* strong (weak) beat. *Temps premier,* see under *Chronos.*

Tempus [L.]. In 13th-century theory, the unit of musical time, comparable to the *tactus* of the 16th century. Franco of Cologne describes it as "minimum in plenitudine vocis," i.e., the smallest time in which a "full sound" can be conveniently produced (*c.* M.M. 80). In the 13th century this duration was represented by the *brevis,* whereas with the beginning of the *ars nova* the *semibrevis* was used instead. However, the term *tempus* continued to indicate the mensuration of the *brevis,* whether it was equal to three or to two semibreves (*tempus perfectum, imperfectum*). See Mensural notation II. See S. Gullo, *Das Tempo in der Musik des XIII. und XIV. Jahrhunderts* [1964].

Ten. Abbr. for *tenuto.*

Tender Land, The. Folk drama in three acts by A. Copland (libretto by H. Everett), produced in New York, 1954. Setting: Midwestern farm, early 1930's.

Tenebrae [L.]. In the Roman Catholic liturgy, the service of Matins and Lauds on Thursday, Friday, and Saturday of Holy Week. It is so called [lit., darkness] because of the gradual extinguishing of the candles, one after each psalm of Matins and Lauds on Thursday [*LU,* pp. 626ff]. At the first nocturn of Matins the *Lamentations of Jeremiah are sung; at the beginning of Lauds, the *Miserere (Ps. 50).

Teneramento [It.]. Tenderly, gently.

Tenor. (1) In early polyphony (*c.* 1200 to 1500 and later), the part that carries the *cantus firmus* and therefore is the basis for the addition of other parts [see Successive counterpoint]. In the earliest stages of polyphony this part was called *vox principalis* (*"Musica enchiriadis," c.* 900) or *cantus* (11th cent.; see Part [2]). It came to be called "tenor" (from L. *tenere,* to hold) in connection with the development of melismatic organum, in which the notes of the *cantus* were drawn out and sustained. In the motets of the 13th and 14th centuries the tenor usually carries only a single syllable or word, such as NOSTRUM, IN SECULUM, GO, because its melody is taken from a melisma (not a fully texted section) of a chant [see Clausula; Motet A I].

(2) With the development of four-part writing (*c.* 1450), "tenor" came to mean second-lowest part, since the *bassus* (originally *contratenor bassus*) was added below it.

(3) The highest natural voice of men, of approximately the same range as the contrapuntal tenor requires [see Voices, range of].

(4) An instrument of about the same range as the vocal tenor, as tenor trombone, tenor horn, tenor saxhorn, tenor violin, etc.

(5) In plainsong psalmody, the "held" (i.e., repeated) recitation tone; see Psalm tones.

Tenorgeige [G.]. Tenor violin [see under Violin family (f)].

Tenor horn. Same as tenor tuba; see Tuba.

Tenorhorn [G.]. Baritone; see Brass instruments III (c).

Tenor Mass. A polyphonic Mass based on a *cantus firmus* that is used as a tenor. Most *cantus firmus* Masses of the 15th and 16th centuries are of this type [see Mass C II b]. See also Discant Mass.

Tenoroon. See under Oboe family II, C.

Tenorschlüssel [G.]. Tenor clef. See Clef.

Tenor violin. See under Violin family (f).

Tenso. A form of troubadour and trouvère poetry, in the nature of a dialogue or debate (real or feigned) about politics or other controversial subjects. A similar form was the *jeu-parti* (*parture;* Prov. *partimen*), an actual dialogue, usually about love [see *ReMMA,* p. 213f]. They played an important part in the competitions of the troubadours (*puys*) and the *minnesingers (Sängerkriege).

Tenth. See under Interval.

Tento [Port.]. *Tiento.*

Tenuto [It.]. Held, sustained; usually equivalent to legato.

Teponaztli. A pre-Columbian wooden drum in the shape of a barrel, enclosed at both ends and with an H-shaped slit on top that creates two tongues facing each other. When the player strikes the drum, using a pair of rubber-tipped mallets, the tongues vibrate and the body acts as a resonator, while a rectangular opening cut on the bottom serves to increase the volume. The inside is cut away in layers so as to produce different pitches. In Central America, three- and four-key *teponaztlis* have been found.   J.O-S.

Terce. The fourth of the canonical hours. See Office.

Teretism. See under Anenaiki.

Ternary form. See Binary and ternary form.

Ter Sanctus [L.]. Term used with reference to the "Sanctus, sanctus, sanctus" (Holy, holy, holy) of the *Trisagion, of the Sanctus of the Mass, or of the *Te Deum.

Tertian harmony. A harmonic system based on the third, i.e., the triad; hence, the common Western system of harmony as opposed to, e.g., *quartal harmony. See also under Third.

Terz [G.]. Third. *Terzdezime,* a thirteenth, i.e., upper sixth. *Terzquartakkord,* see under Seventh chord. *Terzverwandtschaft,* the relationship between keys a third apart, e.g., C and E, or C and E♭. *Terzflöte (Terzfagott),* a flute (oboe) in E.

Terzett [G.], **terzetto** [It.]. A vocal composition for three voices. An instrumental piece in three parts is called *trio.

Terzina [It.]. Triplet.

Terzo suono [It.]. Tartini's name for the *combination tones discovered by him.

Tessitura [It.]. The general "lie" of a vocal part, whether high or low in its average pitch. It differs from range in that it does not take into account a few isolated notes of extraordinarily high or low pitch.

Testo [It.]. *Narrator (in oratorios, Passions, etc.).

Tests and measurements in music. Psychological tests in all fields had their inception at the time of World War I. The history of the development of tests of musical capacities and abilities has paralleled that of psychological tests. Tests in music have been devised to measure efficiency of teaching, general musical knowledge and achievement, musical taste or preference, and innate musical capacity. They may be divided into two groups: (a) tests and measurements of musical capacities; (b) tests and measurements of musical abilities. The former are independent of training, whereas the latter depend on capacity and training. (*Capacity* means undeveloped, innate, native talent, receptive powers, i.e., potentiality for development; *ability* denotes acquisition of knowledge, skills, and techniques, i.e., development of a capacity.)

(a) *Tests and measurements of musical capacities.* Research in music tests began with experiments by C. E. Seashore in the Psychological Laboratory at the University of Iowa at the beginning of the 20th century. In 1919 the original phonograph recordings known as the Seashore Measures of Musical Talent were released for use. This set of six records purports to measure innate sense for the following musical factors: pitch, intensity, time, consonance, tonal memory, and rhythm. The 1939 revision consists of two series. Series A is suggested for group surveys to discover talent. Series B constitutes an individual measurement where greater reliability is desired and is suggested as a basic entrance requirement for admission to music schools, assignment to musical instruments, and diagnosis of special problems. Both revised series measure the same factors: pitch, loudness, time, timbre, rhythm, and tonal memory. The 1956 revision retains Series A but discontinues the more difficult Series B of the 1939 revision.

The Kwalwasser-Dykema Music Test, developed by J. Kwalwasser and P. W. Dykema, has been available since 1930. It consists of phonograph records measuring the following abilities and capacities: tonal memory, quality discrimination, intensity discrimination, feeling for tonal movement, time discrimination, rhythm discrimination, pitch discrimination, melodic tastes, and rhythm imagery. The Kwalwasser Music Talent Test of 1953 presents three tones that are repeated with changes in pitch, time, loudness, or rhythm. The subject must determine which variable has been changed. There are two forms: Form A has forty items; Form B, the more difficult test, has fifty items.

The Wing Standardized Tests of Musical Intelligence (1939–60), which became available in 1948 on ten records, included chord analysis, pitch change, memory, rhythmic accent, harmony, and intensity phrasing. Piano music was used in an attempt to place each of these tests in an integral musical setting. The 1957–58 revision was in the form of two types of tape recording, standard and long-playing. German and French editions, as well as an edition for the blind, have been made available.

All the capacity tests are measures of auditory perception and may be given in groups or individually for the purpose of individual diagnosis and prognosis. They can be given to persons musically trained or untrained, to adults and to children as young as nine years or in the fifth grade. Early research substantiated by later investigations proved that records of musical capacities do not vary with age, training, and general intelligence. A high Intelligence Quotient is no assurance of keen pitch discrimination or superior talent in any other musical factor. Training is effective in developing the power to use a fixed capacity. Variation with age may be attributed to an increase in maturity, and may therefore mean that there is no improvement in the physiologic limit of pitch discrimination itself.

As would be expected, ratings determined by capacity measures have been high for successful musicians or students who have made satisfactory or outstanding progress in music. This and other reasons have been considered evidence of the validity of the measures of musical capacity and justify their use in vocational and avocational guidance in music. The reliability and validity of all psychological measures depend on the training and experience of the examiner. It is generally agreed that no one should assume responsibility for the administration, interpretation, and application of tests and results without knowledge of the nature of the psychology of music, principles of testing, and principles of musical interpretation and guidance.

(b) *Tests and measurements of musical abilities.* Tests in this group may be classified as (1) those measuring appreciation and information, and (2) those measuring performance. Tests of appreciation and information based on knowledge acquired in elementary school, high school, and college measure general information, recognition, and comprehension of music from notation, musical symbols, terms, musical instruments, composers, artists, and melodies. These are largely written tests in the form of completion, multiple choice, true and false, or answer to a direct question. Tests measuring performance include tests of sight-singing ability, melodic and rhythmic dictation (writing in musical notation what one has heard played), and the analysis of musical performances directly or from phonograph recordings by means of later developments in phonophotography (see Lit., *The Vibrato,* Seashore, ed.). Many college music departments have devised placement tests in music that are given to applicants in order to estimate the extent and quality of their previous musical training. These tests often combine tests of appreciation and information and tests of performance.

Lit.: C. E. Seashore, *The Psychology of Musical Talent* [1919]; *id., Psychology of Music* (1938); *id.,* ed., *The Vibrato* [1932]; H. M. Stanton, *Measurement of Musical Talent* (1935); J. L. Mursell, *The Psychology of Music* [1937]; C. W. Flemming and M. Flagg, *A Descriptive Bibliography of Prognostic and Achievement Tests in Music* (1936); S. K. Gernet, *Musical Discrimination at Various Age and Grade Levels* (1939); V. R. Ross, *Relationships between Intelligence, Scholastic Achievement, and Musical Talent* [1937]; W. E. Whybrew, *Measurement and Evaluation in Music* (1962); E. Franklin, *Tonality As A Basis for the Study of Musical Talent* (1956); H. Lowery, in

PMA lxvii; C. E. Seashore, in *MQ* i; J. C. Moos, "The Yardstick Applied to Musical Talent" (*MQ* xvi). For miscellaneous discussions, see *Mental Measurements Yearbooks* (1938—), which form a comprehensive bibliography of tests for use in education, psychology, and industry.   D.D.

Testudo [L., tortoise]. (1) The ancient Greek *lyra, which was frequently made of tortoise shell. (2) A 16th-century humanist name for the lute (e.g., L. Fuhrmann, *Testudo Gallo-Germanica,* 1615).

Tetrachord. In ancient Greek music, succession of four descending pitches, at the intervals of a whole tone, whole tone, semitone (*t–t–s*), e.g., e′–d′–c′–b, or a–g–f–e. By joining several tetrachords the entire diatonic scale from e′ down to B was obtained [see Greece]. In Greek theory, a tetrachord always has the structure above; groups of four tones with a semitone at another place (e.g., d′–c′–b–a, c′–b–a–g, etc., which some writers call Phrygian, Lydian, etc., tetrachord) did not exist in the Greek system. There were, however, chromatic modifications of the tetrachord, the chromatic tetrachord e′–c′♯–c′–b and the enharmonic tetrachord e′–c′–x–b (*x* designating the quarter tone between c′ and b).

The tetrachord was adopted by medieval theorists, although in a modified form, always ascending and sometimes with a different intervallic structure. According to the *"Musica enchiriadis," the scale consists of four tetrachords of the type *t–s–t,* beginning respectively on G, d, a, e′ and designated *tetrachordum gravium, finalium, superiorum, excellentium* [*GS* i, 153f]. J. Tinctoris distinguishes seven tetrachords of the type *t–t–s,* each forming the first four notes of a hexachord, hence beginning on G, c, f (with b-flat), g, c′, f′, g′ [*CS* iv, 220f].

Tetrardus [Gr.]. See under Church modes I.

Tetrastemorium. Term used by Regino of Prüm (d. 915) in his "Epistola de Harmonica Institutione" for *quarter tone [see *GS* i, 232b]. The term is a corruption of *tetarton morion* [Gr., the fourth part]. He also used *tristemorium* [Gr. *triton morion,* the third part] for $\frac{1}{3}$ of a tone.

Text and music. In vocal music, particularly songs, the text is one of the prime considerations of the modern composer. Correct accentuation, clarity of pronunciation, emphasis of important words, etc., are basic requirements of good vocal style and indispensable to the main object of conveying musically the general character of the text as well as subtle nuances. Any song, from

Schubert's to those of the present day, will show the composer's concern about text. In fact, from 1880 on, one finds a tendency to emphasize text at the expense of melody, the latter frequently being reduced to a mere "recitation" (Hugo Wolf, Debussy, Schoenberg). Modern composers have been very discriminating in their selection of poetic texts, choosing only those of outstanding literary value. Such 19th-century poets as Goethe, Heine, Mörike, Baudelaire, and Mallarmé gave great impetus to the composition of songs. On the other hand, this has not always been the case; indeed, Bach wrote some of his greatest arias to inferior texts.

The principles of textual treatment developed gradually in the 16th century. Earlier composers seem to have been less interested in these matters, which they often considered irrelevant. Two examples are an *Ave regina* by Dufay, in which the following accentuation occurs: *ra-díx, ăn-gé-lŏ-rúm, ré-gĭ-ná;* and a motet from the Roman de Fauvel (*c.* 1300), in which an almost deliberately absurd declamation is used with Ovidian hexameter: *In nova fert animus* [see *ApNPM*, pp. 117ff, 336]. It was not until the *musica reservata* of the 16th century that the attitude toward textual accent changed. Of Josquin, it has been said that "Latin accents are not infrequently mishandled even in his latest works, although, inconsistently, at other times great care seems to be exercised in this matter" [*ReMR*, p. 245]. Naturally, the use of texts in the vernacular emphasized the need for more care in textual treatment. This is especially true of the Italian madrigal, which, almost from its inception, is characterized by precise and beautiful declamation of the text in all the voice-parts. Equal care was exercised by the English composers. Byrd's anthems contain many examples of a most careful interpretation of the text, J. Wilbye's "rhythmic rendition of the prosody is invariably just as regards accent and quantity" [*ReMR*, p. 829], and the declamation in Purcell's dramatic works is generally admired as a model. German composers were slower to adopt the new point of view. A striking example of misdeclamation—not lacking, however, a certain forcefulness of expression—occurs at the end of Schütz's Christmas Oratorio (1664), where the accentuation *mít Schăl-lé* is consistently used instead of the correct *mĭt Schăllĕ* [cf. also *spá-de* side by side with *spá-dĕ* in Monteverdi's *Il Combattimento; HAM,* no. 189]. This cannot be considered wholly negligence or error, but a de-

liberate attempt to avoid the weakness of feminine endings. The same was true of Bach, e.g., in the tenor aria, "Geduld, Geduld" of the St. Matthew Passion, where the accentuation *răchén* is used instead of *răchén.* In other cases in Bach's music, however, such lapses result from his preoccupation with purely musical (melodic) considerations, e.g., in his cantata no. 105 (*BWV*), *Hérr géhĕ nĭcht íns Gĕrícht,* instead of *Hérr, gĕhĕ nĭcht ĭns Gĕrícht.*

Carelessness in text underlaying is very common in early sources, particularly those of the 14th and 15th centuries. A striking exception, however, is presented by the Italian MSS of the 14th century, in the works of Giovanni da Cascia, Jacopo da Bologna, Francesco Landini, and others. Possibly the difference between these and contemporary French sources is the result of negligence on the part of the copyists rather than the composers. In the earliest printed collection of vocal music, the *Odhecaton* (1501), only the incipits of the texts are given, obviously because of the typographical difficulties involved in presenting music together with words. The Parisian publisher Attaingnant was probably the first printer to place the words carefully under their corresponding notes. For the numerous problems concerning the text (more properly, the absence or scarcity of text) in 15th-century Masses, the reader is referred to special studies. The modern editorial practice of repeating words for passages lacking a text in the original (e.g., "Kyrie eleison" ten times, instead of once or, perhaps, thrice) is of very doubtful authenticity. Long *vocalizations (on the syllable *e* of Kyrie) are much more plausible from the musical as well as the liturgical point of view. See also Word painting.

Lit.: A. T. Davison, *Words and Music* (1954); R. Hinton Thomas, *Poetry and Song in the German Baroque* (1963); N. Frye, ed., *Sound and Poetry* (1957); J. Müller-Blattau, *Das Verhältnis von Wort und Ton in der Geschichte der Musik* (1952); J. Jacquot, ed., *Musique et Poésie au XVIe siècle* (1954); L. Gamberini, *La Parola e la musica nell'antichità* (1962); H. E. Wooldridge, "The Treatment of Words in Polyphonic Music" (*MA* i); H. Monro, "Words to Music" (*ML* i); G. Adler, "Über Textlegung in den 'Trienter Codices'" (*CP Riemann*); K. Jeppesen, "Die Textlegung in der Chansonmusik des späteren 15. Jahrhunderts" (*CP 1927*); E. Wellesz, "Words and Music in Byzantine Liturgy" (*MQ* xxxiii). For extensive bibl., see *BeMMR*, p. 319.

Texture. Much like woven fabric, music consists of horizontal ("woof") and vertical ("warp") elements. The former are the successive sounds forming melodies, the latter the simultaneous sounds forming harmonies [see also Counterpoint I]. It is these elements that make up the texture. The texture stands out particularly clearly in part music, i.e., music written in a given number of parts. Each part represents a horizontal line of individual design, connected with the other lines by the (vertical) relationship of consonance or harmony. Such music is said to have a *contrapuntal* or *polyphonic* texture. In accompanied melody, on the other hand, the texture is primarily vertical, based on a succession of chords that are horizontally connected by a top melody. This texture is called *chordal* or *homophonic*. Ex. 1a and 1b illustrate the two kinds of treatment of a single melody.

Between the two extremes of strictly polyphonic and strictly homophonic music lie a large variety of intermediate textures. Ex. 2 [Beethoven, Piano Sonata op. 106] illustrates a mixture

ven, Piano Sonata op. 106] illustrates a mixture of horizontal and vertical elements that is particularly common in 19th-century piano music (Beethoven, Brahms). As early as the 16th century the strictly contrapuntal texture of the polyphonic era was often modified into a pseudo-contrapuntal texture described as *freistimmig*. Distinctive of contrapuntal music is the rhyth-

mic relationship between the parts. There are two types of polyphonic texture, one in which the four parts move in identical rhythm (as in a church hymn), and another in which they are rhythmically wholly independent (as is frequently the case in Palestrina or Bach). Only the latter texture, known as *polyrhythmic, is truly contrapuntal. The former, called *homorhythmic, borders on chordal texture, and indeed is often called *strict chordal style* (as opposed to *free chordal style,* where the number of notes in a chord is not fixed and there is usually no horizontal movement except in the top melody.

One may also distinguish between *light* and *heavy* texture. Light texture results from the use of few instruments, or instruments of light color (e.g., flute), or both. G. Gabrieli's *polychoral compositions and Sibelius' symphonies exemplify heavy texture; Dufay's chansons and Stravinsky's *L'Histoire du soldat* are light. Many 20th-century composers prefer light texture (e.g., Stravinsky, Hindemith). See G. Dyson, "The Texture of Modern Music" (*ML* iv, 107ff, 203ff, 293ff).

Thailand. During the past six hundred years, Thai music has absorbed instruments and musical ideas from neighboring cultures into its indigenous musical culture. The strongest influences came from China, where the Thai resided before migrating in the 13th century into present-day Thailand, and from the Khmer at Angkor in Cambodia, through whom also came indirect influences from India and Indonesia. Because of the rich interchange among Laos, Cambodia, and Thailand, the traditional music and instruments of these countries are essentially similar today.

Three main ensembles are used in Thai traditional music: (1) the *pi phat,* consisting of xylophones, metallophones, sets of gong-kettles, hand cymbals, gong, drum, and the *pi,* a double-reed wind instrument; (2) the *khruang sai,* composed of various stringed instruments, rhythmic percussion, and a bamboo flute; (3) the *mahori,* consisting of melodic and rhythmic percussion, stringed instruments, and the flute.

In the Thai musical system, the octave is divided into seven relatively equidistant intervals. The instrumental music consists of a main melody combined simultaneously with variations of itself, a practice that may be termed "polyphonic stratification," each layer usually being performed by only one instrument and having characteristics idiomatic to that instrument. Music in a definite tempo is always in duple meter, emphasized by accented and unaccented beats played by the small hand cymbals in patterns indicating the form of the piece. Melodies are created mainly out of a repertory of standard melodic species and cadential formulas. The rhythmic emphasis falls on beats two and four of the groups, shorter or longer, of four beats. The pitches falling on the fourth beat of each period (usually two or four measures) form a pattern that indicates the mood or mode of a piece.

Of the seven available pitches, five are used at any one time to form the principal scale; music in "Thai" style is therefore basically pentatonic. In another style, called *mon* (pronounced mawn), the other two pitches are used more freely as passing tones. Melodies, basically conjunct, are in one of two styles: motivic, the older style, in which the rhythms are simple and in which standard patterns are employed, and lyric, the more modern style, in which the melody is spun out in a variety of rhythms. The melodic line may shift from one pitch level to another, usually to a level a fifth above or below the preceding one.

Thai music does not employ many forms. The majority of pieces are through-composed, with elementary use of repetition and sequential treatment. A type of variation form was developed during the late 19th and early 20th centuries: a previously existing piece is enlarged to twice its original length and contracted to one-half its original length according to specific principles. The extended version may be played alone, or the extended, middle (original), and short versions may be played in that order as a three-part suite, with or without alternating vocal sections.

Vocal music uses a voice quality rich in partials with much ornamentation. Although vocal sections are used between the main divisions of the variation form described above, vocal techniques are most broadly represented in theater music, where speech, semichants, chants, simple and elaborate songs—solos, as well as leader and chorus styles—are used. Solo music for stringed and wind instruments is also characterized by much ornamentation, similar to that for the voice, often making use of pitches not in the fixed tuning system.

Within relatively limited means, Thai traditional music exhibits great variety. However, because of the restrictions imposed by the principles of the music and the discontinuance in 1932 of the royal households under whose aegis it evolved, this music has probably reached its apogee of development, beyond which it cannot go without a broadening of its strict organizational principles and the stimulation of new musical ideas. Nevertheless, although it has reached an impasse and may soon become a museum piece, Thai traditional music (together with that of Laos and Cambodia) stands as one of the high musical cultures of Asia.

There is much folk music in Southeast Asia that has not yet been fully studied. Characteristic types include ensembles of gongs and long drums used in processions, serenades, and love songs accompanied by stringed or wind instruments, and unaccompanied, extemporaneous rhymed verses, usually humorous and often bawdy, generally created by members of two opposing groups in friendly competition. Although there has been little if any influence from Western music in Thai traditional music, contemporary popular Thai music does show such influence, the melodies, generally pentatonic, being harmonized principally by primary triads.

Lit.: (Phra) Chen Duriyanga, *Thai Music* (Thailand Culture Series, no. 8, 4th ed. [1955]); D. Yupho, *Thai Musical Instruments* [1960]; A. Daniélou, *La Musique du Cambodge et du Laos* (1957); D. Morton, "The Traditional Instrumental Music of Thailand" (diss. U.C.L.A., 1964); K. Pringsheim, "Music of Thailand" (*Contemporary Japan* xiii, 745–67).   D.M.

Theater music. See Incidental music.

Theme [F. *thème;* G. *Thema;* It., Sp. *tema*]. A musical idea that is the point of departure for a composition, especially a sonata (symphony, string quartet, etc.), fugue, or set of variations. In sonatas and fugues it is also called *subject. An important field of musical scholarship is the *thematic catalog,* which shows the themes (beginnings) of the works of a given composer, e.g., those of Bach (by W. Schmieder), Mozart (Köchel-Einstein), or Beethoven (M. G. Nottebohm; replaced by Kinsky-Halm). Attempts have been made to create a general catalog of musical themes, in which the themes of all compositions (or a large segment) would be listed according to some "alphabetical" system so that they could be looked up and identified.

Lit.: R. Reti, *The Thematic Process in Music* (1951); *A Check List of Thematic Catalogues* (1954); H. Barlow and S. Morgenstern, *A Dictionary of Musical Themes* (1948); *id., A Diction-

ary of Vocal Themes (1950); W. Altmann, "Über thematische Kataloge" (*CP 1927*); O. Koller, in *SIM* iv; I. Krohn, *ibid.;* N. Bridgman, in *MD* iv; W. Heinitz, in *AMW* iii.

Themenaufstellung [G.]. Exposition.

Theorbo. See under Lute III. See H. Quittard, "La Théorbe comme instrument d'accompagnement" (*BSIM* i, 221ff, 362ff).

Theory, musical. I. *General.* The theory of music as taught today includes elementary studies classified as fundamentals, music writing, *solfège, and advanced studies in harmony [see Harmonic analysis], as well as *counterpoint, *form, and *orchestration. In this curriculum at least one important study is missing, that of *melody. Other aspects of musical theory, closely bound up with melody, are *rhythm and *phrasing. More scientific in approach are the studies of *acoustics, *intervals (calculation of), *scales, etc., while the philosophical and speculative aspects are in the province of musical *aesthetics. See also Musicology.

II. *History.* The rest of this article is devoted to a survey of fourteen centuries of Western musical theory (*c.* 500–1900) through a list of representative treatises. Many of these are briefly described (with bibl.) in G. Reese, *Fourscore Classics of Music Literature* (1957). *SSR* (1950) contains translated excerpts; see also *RISM* B III.

A. *500–1200.*

1. Boethius (*c.* 480–524). *De institutione arithmetica libri duo; De institutione musica libri quinque* (ed. G. Friedlein, 1867; *SSR,* pp. 79ff). Transmits Greek theory; considered authoritative source through the Middle Ages.

2. Aurelianus Reomensis (mid-9th cent.). *Musica disciplina* (*GS* i, 27ff). Early writing concerning the organization and character of the church modes.

3. *"Musica enchiriadis," with commentary, "Scholia enchiriadis," *c.* 900, formerly ascribed to Hucbald (*GS* i, 152ff, 173ff; G. trans. by R. Schlecht, in *MfM* vi, vii, viii; *SSR,* pp. 126ff; L. B. Spiess, in *JAMS* xii). Earliest detailed account of *organum and *Daseian notation.

4. Regino of Prüm (d. 915). *Epistola de harmonica institutione* (*GS* i, 230ff); *Tonarius* (*CS* ii, 1ff). Discusses music as one of the seven liberal arts.

5. Odo de Clugny (d. 942). *Dialogus de musica* or *Enchiridion musices* (*GS* i, 252ff; G. trans. by P. Bohn, in *MfM,* xii; *SSR,* pp. 103ff); *Into-*

narium (*CS* ii, 117). Presents a *letter notation beginning with great G (Γ) and extending upward to a' (*aa*).

6. Guido d'Arezzo (*c.* 990–1050). *Micrologus de disciplina artis musicae* (*GS* ii, 2ff; new ed. by J. Smits van Waesberghe, 1955; G. trans. by M. Hermesdorff, 1876); *Item aliae Regulae de ignoto cantu: Prologus in antiphonario* (*GS* ii, 34ff; *SSR,* pp. 117ff); *Epistola de ignoto cantu* (*GS* ii, 43ff; *SSR,* pp. 121ff). Essential text; establishes the hexachordal system of *solmization using the six syllables *ut, re, mi, fa, sol, la;* introduces a staff similar to the modern staff.

7. Anonymous [J.-A.-L. de la Fage], *Tractatus de musica, c.* 1150 (J.-A.-L. de la Fage, *Essais de diphthérographie musicale,* 2 vols. [1864], i, 335ff). Describes six species of *discant.

B. *1200–1400.*

8. *Discantus positio vulgaris, c.* 1225 (*CS* i, 94ff; F. trans. in part in E. Coussemaker, *Histoire de l'harmonie au moyen âge* [1852], pp. 247ff; E. trans. J. Knapp in *JMT* vi [1962]). Description and commentary of the various species of discant in use at Notre Dame in the early 13th century; particularly emphasizes the motet. One of earliest treatises to discuss modal rhythm as a factor in polyphonic compositions.

9. Johannes de Garlandia (*c.* 1195–*c.* 1272). *De musica mensurabili positio* (*CS* i, 97ff; another version, Vatican Codex, in *CS* i, 175ff). Describes six rhythmic modes; codifies and discusses in detail concordance and discordance.

10. Franco of Cologne. *Ars cantus mensurabilis, c.* 1260 (*CS* i, 117ff; *GS* iii, 1ff; *SSR,* pp. 139ff). Improvement and standardization of system for mensural notation. Remained authoritative text for nearly a century.

11. Anonymous IV. *De mensuris et discantu, c.* 1275 (*CS* i, 327ff; new ed. with E. trans. by L. Dittmer, 1959). Deals with premensural notation; describes the literature and mentions composers of the *Notre Dame school of 1180–1240.

12. Walter Odington. *De speculatione musicae, c.* 1300 (*CS* i, 182ff; new ed. and commentary by F. Hammond, diss. Yale Univ., 1965). Comprehensive coverage of 13th-century compositional practice in England.

13. Jacques de Liège. *Speculum musicae, c.* 1330 (Books vi, vii in *CS* ii, 193ff; comp. ed. by R. Bragard, *Corpus scriptorum de musica* 3, 1955—; *SSR,* pp. 180ff). Plea for a return to the security of "Franconian" principles.

14. Philippe de Vitry (1291–1361). *Ars nova, c.* 1325 (*CS* iii, 13ff; new ed. by Reaney, Gilles,

and Maillard, in *MD* x, xi, xii, xiv [1956–60] includes F. trans.; G. trans. by P. Bohn, in *MfM* xxii; E. trans. by L. Plantinga, in *JMT* v). *Ars perfecta in musica, c.* 1350 (*CS* iii, 28ff). Speaks for the inclusion of duple mensuration and presents symbols for indicating *Modus, Tempus, Prolatio.*

15. Marchetto da Padua. *Lucidarium in arte musicae planae, c.* 1318 (*GS* iii, 64ff); *Pomerium in arte musicae mensuratae, c.* 1319 (*GS* iii, 121ff; G. Vecchi, *Corpus scriptorum de musica* 6 [1961]; *SSR,* pp. 160ff). An account of contemporary practices in Italy. Earliest text accepting duple mensuration.

C. *1400–1600.*

16. Prosdocimus de Beldemandis (*c.* 1380). *Tractatus practice de musica mensurabili,* 1408 (*CS* iii, 200ff); *Tractatus de contrapuncto,* 1412 (*CS* iii, 193ff; G. trans. by R. Schlecht, in *MfM* ix); *Tractatus practice de musica mensurabili ad modum Italicorum,* 1412 (*CS* iii, 228ff; new ed. in C. Sartori, *La Notazione italiana del trecento* [1938]). Summarizes practices in Italian notation and prescribes use of chromatics that produce a complete chromatic scale.

17. Johannes Tinctoris (1436–1511). *Terminorum musicae diffinitorium, c.* 1475, printed *c.* 1494 (*CS* iv, 177ff; new ed. with F. trans. by A. Machabey, 1951; G. trans. by H. Bellermann, in *JMW* i; E. trans. by C. Parrish, 1963); *Proportionale musices, c.* 1474 (*CS* iv, 153ff; *SSR,* pp. 193ff; E. trans. by A. Seay, in *JMT* i [1957]); *Liber de arte contrapuncti,* 1477 (*CS* iv, 76ff; *SSR,* pp. 197ff; E. trans. by A. Seay, in *Musicological Studies and Documents* 5 [1961]); *De inventione et usu musicae, c.* 1485 (new ed. K. Weinmann, *Johannes Tinctoris und sein unbekannter Traktat,* 1917). Eight other treatises (all in *CS* iv) are described in *ReMR,* p. 140. The twelve treatises present a sequential exposition of musical knowledge of the time.

18. Bartoloméo Ramos de Pareja (*c.* 1440– after 1491). *Musica practica,* 1482 (ed. J. Wolf, 1901; *SSR,* pp. 200ff). Presents a simpler method of dividing a string than that transmitted by Boethius. Uses the just major third. This intonation was discouraged by Gafurius, championed by Foglianus.

19. Guilielmus Monachus. *De preceptis artis musicae, c.* 1485 (*CS* iii, 273ff; new ed. by A. Seay, in *Corpus scriptorum de musica* 11 [1965]). Discusses fauxbourdon and gymel.

20. Franchinus Gafurius (1451–1522). *Practica musicae,* 1496; *Theorica musicae,* 1492 (fac. ed., G. Cesari, 1934; see also P. Hirsch, in *CP*

Wolf; MGG iv, cols. 1237–43). Unlike his predecessors, Gafurius did not depend on Boethius but read Latin translations of Quintilian, Ptolemy, and other Greek writers.

21. Pietro Aaron (1480–1545). *Libri tres de institutione harmonica,* 1516; *Thoscanello de la musica,* 1523; *Trattato della natura et cognitione di tutti gli tuoni di canto figurato,* 1525 (*SSR,* pp. 205ff); *Lucidario in musica,* 1545. Reports the abandonment of the successive manner of composing parts.

22. Lodovicos Fogliani (d. 1538). *Musica theorica,* 1529 (partly in Riemann, *History of Music Theory,* ch. xii). Describes syntonic diatonic tuning requiring just major third made up of a major and a minor whole tone.

23. Giovanni Maria Lanfranco (d. 1545). *Scintille di musica,* 1533 (trans. and comm. by B. Lee, diss. Cornell Univ., 1961). An excellent example of the Renaissance primer on music.

24. Henricus Glareanus (Heinrich Loris; 1488–1563). *Isagoge in musicen,* 1516 (E. trans. by F. Turrell, in *JMT* iii [1959]); **Dodecachordon,* 1547 (G. trans. by P. Bohn, in **Editions* XLVII, 16; *SSR,* pp. 219ff; E. trans. by C. Miller, in *Musicological Studies and Documents* 6, 2 vols. [1965]). In *Dodecachordon* the number of modal scales is increased to twelve.

25. Nicola Vicentino (1511–72). *L'Antica musica ridotta alla moderna prattica,* 1555 (fac. repr. ed. E. Lowinsky, 1959); *Descrizione dell'arciorgano,* 1561 (E. trans. by H. Kaufmann, in *JMT* v [1961]). Describes a tuning system and gives specifications for building an instrument with 36 pitches (in practice only 34 keys) within each octave, providing intervals of ancient Greek diatonic, chromatic, and enharmonic genera in addition to just and mean-tone scale requirements.

26. Gioseffo Zarlino (1517–90). *Le istitutioni harmoniche,* 1558 (fac. repr. by Broude, 1965; *SSR,* pp. 228ff; G. Marco, diss. Univ. of Chicago, 1956; *ReMR,* p. 377). Notes natural opposition of major and minor triads; renumbers Glareanus' twelve modes, placing Ionian first.

27. Francisco de Salinas (1513–90). *De musica libri septem,* 1577 (fac. repr. M. Kastner, 1958). A comprehensive statement of contemporary knowledge of music, supporting the work of Zarlino and Glareanus.

28. Vincenzo Galilei (*c.* 1520–91). *Dialogo della musica antica e della moderna,* 1581 (*SSR,* pp. 302ff). Musical mentor of Florentine "Camerati."

29. Giovanni M. Artusi (*c.* 1540–1613). *L'Arte*

del contraponto, 1586–89. Clear statement of fundamental rules of counterpoint as taught in late 16th century.

30. Ludovico Zacconi (1555–1627). *Prattica di musica,* 2 vols., 1592, 1622. Extensive description of instruments of his time and directions for executing ornaments.

31. Ercole Bottrigari (1531–1612). *Il desiderio, overo de' concerti di varii strumenti musicali,* 1594 (fac. ed. K. Meyer, 1924; E. trans. by C. MacClintock, in *Musicological Studies and Documents* 9 [1962]). Discusses combinations of instruments.

32. Thomas Morley (1557–1602). *A Plaine and Easie Introduction to Practicall Musicke,* 1597 (mod. ed. R. A. Harman, 1952; *SSR,* pp. 274ff). An excellent book describing forms and compositional techniques.

33. Girolamo Diruta (b. 1550). *Il Transilvano,* 2 vols., 1593, 1609 (part in G. trans. by C. Krebs, in *VMW* viii). Significant for consideration of aesthetic as well as technical aspects of performance; includes many musical examples.

D. *1600–1800.*

34. Michael Praetorius (1571–1621). *Syntagma musicum,* 3 vols., 1615, '18, '19 (vol. ii, *Organographia,* repr. in *Editions XLVII, 13; fac. ed. W. Gurlitt, 1929; repr. 1958–59; E. trans. of pts. 1, 2 of vol. ii by H. Blumenfeld, 1949; vol. iii, new ed. E. Bernoulli, 1916; E. trans. of vol. iii by H. Lampl, diss., Univ. of Southern California, 1957). Encyclopedic effort. Vol. iii describes secular composition.

35. Camillo Angleria (*c.* 1580–*c.* 1630). *La regola del contraponto e della compositione,* 1622. The subtitle states "in which is treated briefly everything about consonance and dissonance with examples in 2, 3, and 4 parts." Uses the eight church modes.

36. Charles Butler (d. *c.* 1647). *The Principles of Musick,* 1636 (*Short Title Catalogue*). Though based on Morley's work, an interesting attempt to codify the author's later observations concerning the practice of composition and the development of the concept of harmony.

37. Marin Mersenne (1588–1648). *Harmonie universelle,* 1636 (fac. ed. F. Lesure, 1963; E. trans. "The Books on Instruments," R. Chapman, 1957). Extensive coverage of experiments on physical properties of sound. Full description of contemporary instruments.

38. Adriano Banchieri (1568–1634). *L'Organo suonarino,* 1605. Several editions; 2nd ed. includes detailed discussion of figured bass and performance practice.

39. Antoine Parran (1587–1650). *Traité de la musique théorique et pratique,* 1639. Excellent text on 17th-century techniques of composition employing the twelve modes of Glareanus as renumbered by Zarlino.

40. Christoph Bernhard (1627–92). *Von der Singe-Kunst oder Manier; Tractatus compositionis augmentatis* (both MSS, *c.* 1657; in J. Müller-Blattau, *Die Kompositionslehre Heinrich Schutzens,* 1926). Describes motifs and compositional procedures in accordance with the doctrine of affections.

41. Christopher Simpson (*c.* 1610–69). *The principles of Practical Musick* [*Delivered in a Compendious, Easie, and New Method*], 1665. Under the title *A Compendium of Practical Musick in Five Parts,* this book (1st ed., 1667) was reprinted in at least nine editions. The five parts are: 1. The rudiments of song. 2. The principles of composition. 3. The use of discords. 4. The form of figurate descant. 5. The contrivance of canon.

42. Giovanni Maria Bononcini (1642–78). *Musico prattico,* 1673. Deals with counterpoint, consonance, dissonance, the twelve tones, composition in two, three, and four parts.

43. Lorenzo Penna (1613–93). *Li primi albori musicali per li principianti della musica figurata,* 1st ed. 1656, 2nd ed. corrected and enlarged by author, 1679 (actually issued 1694). Includes three books: 1. The principles of singing. 2. The rules of counterpoint. 3. Fundamentals of playing from a figured bass.

44. John Playford (1623–86). *A Breefe introduction to the skill of musick for song & violl.,* 1654. Nineteen numbered and six unnumbered editions of this popular work appeared between 1654 and 1730.

45. Jean Rousseau (late 17th cent.). *Méthode claire, certaine et facile pour apprendre à chanter la musique,* 1678. In this little book on the art of singing the seventh syllable *si* appears as a normal part of the solmization system.

46. Angelo Berardi (*c.* 1653–*c.* 1700). *Il perchè musicale,* 1693. Detailed and clear rules "in which reason dissolves difficulty, examples demonstrate how to avoid errors and to weave with artifice the components of music."

47. Andreas Werckmeister (1645–1706). *Harmonologia musica,* 1702. This short book deals with composition and describes techniques of improvisation.

48. Zaccaria Tevo (1651–between 1709–12). *Il musico testore,* 1706. The work is divided into four parts, of which the last two deal extensively

with the materials and procedures of composition. The last part includes examples of composition for voices and instruments, double counterpoint, fugue.

49. Alexandre Frère. *Transpositions de musique,* 1706. An attempt to provide proper signatures for all keys and particularly a single basis for minor scale signatures.

50. Alexander Malcolm (b. 1687). *A Treatise of Musick, Speculative, Practical, and Historical,* 1721. Concerned mainly with elementary matters but notable for including the first "correct" table of key signatures, essential to the full development of the major-minor key system.

51. Jean-Philippe Rameau (1683–1764). *Traité de l'harmonie reduite à ses principes naturels,* 1722 (*SSR,* pp. 564ff; fac. Broude Bros., 1965). A text of prime importance to the history of music theory. Rameau's concept of *centre harmonique* firmly establishes the major-minor system. *Nouveau système de musique theorique,* 1726; *Génération harmonique ou Traité de musique theorique et pratique,* 1737; *Démonstration du principe de l'harmonie,* 1750; and *Nouvelles réflexions sur sa demonstration du principe de l'harmonie,* 1752 (all available in fac.) with numerous letters and articles. These consistently expound a belief in the *corps sonore* as the source, musical practice as the means, and psychological response as the arbiter.

52. Johann Joseph Fux (1660–1741). **Gradus ad Parnassum,* 1725 (E. trans. A. Mann, *Steps to Parnassus,* 1943). An 18th-century codification of contrapuntal practice, still used as a manual for the development of compositional skills.

53. Johann Mattheson (1681–1764). *Grosse General-Bass-Schule,* 1731; *Kleine General-Bass-Schule,* 1735; *Der vollkommene Capellmeister,* 1739 (fac. M. Reimann, 1954; partly trans. by H. Lenneberg, in *JMT* ii, 1 and 2; B. C. Cannon, *Johann Mattheson,* 1947). A well-organized presentation of essential theoretical knowledge and, in the last book, a complete presentation of the doctrine of *affections.

54. Giuseppe Tartini (1692–1770). *Trattato di musica secondo la vera scienza dell'armonia,* 1754 (A. Planchart, in *JMT* iv, 32). Uses phenomena of "third sound" (difference tone) to explain harmonic relation.

55. Georg Joseph Vogler (Abbé; 1749–1814). *Tonwissenschaft und Tonsetzkunst,* 1776. Systematic but complicated derivation of harmonies from the first 32 partials. He is better known for producing low-pitched organ tones by combining two higher-pitched pipes.

E. *1800–1900.* Of the numerous texts that appeared during the 18th century after Rameau's basic work, most were of a decidedly practical nature. Similarly, after 1800 only a few are concerned with purely theoretical problems. Among these are:

56. Gottfried Weber (1779–1839). *Versuch einer geordneten Theorie der Tonsetzkunst,* 1817–21. Practical and nonacoustical approach. Remembered for advancing the use of Roman numerals for chord identification within key structures; also contributed evaluation of harmonic constructs on artistic grounds.

57. Anton Reicha (1770–1836). *Cours de Composition Musicale,* 1818. A friend of Beethoven's and a composer of some repute. His pupils included Berlioz, Gounod, and Franck.

58. François-Joseph Fétis (1784–1871). *Traité complet de la théorie et de la pratique de l'harmonie,* 1844. Rejects mathematical and acoustical bases of harmony. The first to employ the term tonality (*tonalité*) to explain, in almost identical terms, the *centre harmonique* described by Rameau in 1722.

59. Moritz Hauptmann (1792–1868). *Die Natur der Harmonik und der Metrik zur Theorie der Musik,* 1853. Based on the philosophical method of Hegel. Though severely criticized, warrants consideration.

60. Abramo Basevi (1818–85). *Introduzione ad un nuovo Sistema d'Armonia,* 1862. Directs attention to sensation and perception. The work is mentioned by Helmholtz in *On the Sensations of Tone.*

61. Hermann (Ludwig Ferdinand) von Helmholtz (1821–94). *Die Lehre von den Tonempfindungen als physiologische Grundlage für die Theorie der Musik,* 1863 (E. trans. *On the Sensations of Tone,* A. J. Ellis, 1885; repr. 1954). Major contribution to knowledge of musical materials on physical and physiologic grounds.

62. Hugo Riemann (1849–1919). Though most important as the author of *Geschichte der Musiktheorie im IX.–XIX. Jahrhundert,* 1898 (E. trans. of books I and II [2nd ed.] by R. Haggh, 1962), Riemann wrote several additional texts on music theory, including *Musikalische Logik,* 1873; *Musikalische Syntaxis,* 1877; *Die Natur der Harmonik,* 1882; and *Vereinfachte Harmonielehre,* 1893 (E. trans. by Bewerunge, 1896). For systematic presentation of fundamental knowledge, Riemann's work is outstanding although colored by 19th-century positivism.

Among modern contributions to musical theory, the writings of Heinrich Schenker

(1868–1935; see Schenker system), Charles Koechlin (1867–1950), and Paul Hindemith (1895–1963) are noteworthy. Intentional expansion of existing tonal systems are the basis of the writings of Alois Hába (b. 1893; *Neue Harmonielehre des diatonischen, chromatischen . . . Tonsystems,* 1927); Joseph Yasser (b. 1893; *A Theory of Evolving Tonality,* 1932); and Olivier Messiaen (b. 1908; *Technique de mon langage musical,* 1944; E. trans. J. Satterfield, 1956). For serial techniques, the work of J. Rufer (b. 1893; *Die Komposition mit zwölf Tönen,* 1952; E. trans. H. Searle, 1954) is basic.

Lit.: H. Riemann, *Geschichte der Musiktheorie im IX.–XIX. Jahrhundert* (1898; 2nd ed. 1921; Eng. trans. bks. I and II, R. Haggh, 1962); G. Pietzsch, *Die Klassifikation der Musik von Boetius bis Ugolino von Orvieto* (1929); A. Hughes, in *OH* 1929, Introductory Volume; *AdHM* ii, 1232ff (bibl.); *LavE* i.1, 566ff; *ReMMA,* pp. 17ff (Greek), 125ff (medieval); *ReMR,* pp. 178ff, 185f, 586f; *ApNPM,* pp. 201ff; J. Smits van Waesberghe, ed., *The Theory of Music from the Carolingian Era up to 1400,* i [1961]; A. Davidsson, *Bibliographie der musiktheoretischen Drucke des 16. Jahrhunderts* (1962); E. Coussemaker, *L'Art harmonique aux XIIᵉ et XIIIᵉ siècles* (1865; repr. 1964); M. Shirlaw, *The Theory of Harmony* [1917; repr. B. Coar, 1955]; J. B. Coover, "Music Theory in Translation: A Bibliography" (*JMT* iii, 70); A. Basart, *Serial Music; A Classified Bibliography of Writings on Twelve-Tone and Electronic Music* (1961); H. Boatwright, *Introduction to the Theory of Music* [1956]; G. Reaney, "The Question of Authorship in the Medieval Treatises on Music" (*MD* xviii), J. Wolf, "Early English Musical Theorists" (*MQ* xxv); *id.,* "Die Musiktheorie des Mittelalters" (*AM* iii, 63f; bibl.); U. Kornmüller, "Die alten Musiktheoretiker" (*KJ* 1891, 1899, 1903); D. von Bartha, "Studien zum musikalischen Schrifttum des 15. Jahrhunderts" (*AMF* i); A. Mann, *The Study of Fugue* (1958; paperback ed. 1966); *Deutsches Musikgeschichtliches Archiv Kassel. Katalog der Filmsammlung* I–VI (sect. ii), 1955–1963; K. Eschman, *Changing Forms in Modern Music* [1945].   N.P.

Theremin. See under Electronic instruments.

Theresienmesse [G., Theresa's Mass]. Popular name (unexplained) for Haydn's Mass in B-flat, composed in 1799.

Thesis. See Arsis and thesis.

Third [F. *tierce;* G. *Terz;* It. *terza;* Sp. *tercera*]. The third degree of a scale, and the interval thus formed with the first degree [see Interval]. The third is the most characteristic interval of the Western harmonic system, which, indeed, might be called the system of triadic (or *tertian) harmony (*c.* 1400–1900), as distinguished from an earlier period (*c.* 900–1400) when the third was not fully admitted, and from a later one (*c.* 1900—) in which it has lost its former important position [see Harmony II].

Guido d'Arezzo in his "Micrologus" (ch. xviii) admits both the major and the minor third as *concordiae* of the *diaphonia* (organum), and both intervals occur in his instructive examples. They also occur sporadically in the early 12th-century organa of Fleury and Chartres, occasionally even in groups of three parallel thirds. In the five organa from Chartres *130* [see Bannister, in *RG* i, 29ff] the third actually is the most common of all intervals (66 thirds, 63 unisons, 46 fourths, etc.). The St. Martial organum *Senescente mundano filio* (*c.* 1150) contains an entire section in parallel thirds [see Ex.; see W. Apel, in *CP Anglés* i, 66; also Handschin, in *CP Adler,* p. 57. Whereas these findings invalidate the customary

Di - gna   di - gnis   pa - rat   o - spi - ci - a

view that the third is "of English origin," there is evidence of an English (or Scandinavian) predilection for thirds, beginning with the well-known hymn for St. Magnus, "Nobilis, humilis" (*HAM,* no. 25c), which may date from the 12th century. In French treatises of the 13th century the third is regarded as an imperfect consonance, but Anon. IV says that "in the part of England called *Westcuntre* they are considered as excellent consonances" (*optime concordiante;* see *CS* i, 358b). This statement is supported by a number of English compositions written in *gymel and in *sixth-chord style. An interesting early example of a tertian and, at the same time, pentatonic melody is Neidhardt von Reuenthal's "Der May," written *c.* 1225 [see Ex., from *HAM,* no. 20c]. Melodies outlining a major triad play an important role in the works of Dunstable [see *HAM,* no. 62; *SchGMB,* nos. 34, 35]. Prior to 1500, the third was not admitted in the final chord [see Picardy third].

In the Pythagorean system the major third is obtained as the fourth consecutive fifth (c–g–d'–a'–e''), with the frequency ⁸¹⁄₆₄, and the minor

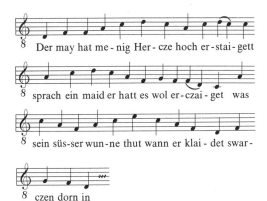

Der may hat me - nig Her - cze hoch er - stai - gett

sprach ein maid er hatt es wol er - czai - get was

sein süs-ser wun-ne thut wann er klai - det swar-

czen dorn in

third as the third consecutive fourth (c–f–b^b'–e^b") with the frequency $^{32}\!/_{27}$. The consonant (pure) third of *just intonation, ⁵⁄₄, was already known to Aristoxenos (b. *c.* 354 B.C.) but does not appear in medieval theory until *c.* 1300, in W. Odington's "De speculatione musicae." The difference (in cents) between the thirds of the various systems is shown in the following table:

	Minor third	Major third
Pythagorean	294	408
Just intonation	315	386
Mean-tone system	315	386
Equal temperament	300	400

The difference between the tempered and pure major third can easily be demonstrated on the organ by playing on one manual the tone e″ with a normal 8′ register, and on the second manual the tone c with a mutation stop (1⅗′) which produces the fifth harmonic e″ in just intonation.

Thirteenth, chord of the. See under Ninth chord.

Thirty-second note. See under Notes.

Thirty-two foot stop. See under Foot (2).

Thoroughbass, figured bass [F. *basse chiffrée, continue, figurée;* G. *Generalbass, bezifferter Bass;* It. *basso continuo;* Sp. *bajo cifrado*]. Note: "thorough" (old spelling for "through") means the same as *continuo,* i.e., continuing throughout the piece.

I. A method of indicating an accompanying part by the bass notes only, together with figures designating the chief intervals and chords to be played above the bass notes. This stenographic system was universally used in the baroque period (1600–1750). The chief principles of the fully developed system (*c.* 1700) are:

1. A figure given with a bass note calls for the corresponding interval above this note in the key indicated by the signature. For instance, in A^b major, a 6 written under (or above) g indicates E^b, and the figures ⁶₅ indicate D^b and E^b.

2. The intervals of the third, fifth, and octave often are not indicated by figures (3, 5, 8), it being understood that these were to be added where suitable.

3. Chromatic alterations are indicated by a sharp or flat placed in front of (occasionally behind) the figure. A sharp or flat without a figure calls respectively for the major or minor third. The natural sign is used in a similar way. Sharping is frequently indicated by a diagonal stroke through the figure or by an apostrophe.

4. A horizontal dash following a figure or a vertical group of figures indicates that the notes of the right hand are to be held, even if the bass proceeds to other tones.

5. A small diagonal dash indicates repetition of the same figures above a changed bass note, i.e., sequential transposition of the chord.

6. The figure *0* indicates *tasto solo,* i.e., no accompaniment other than the bass note.

7. Frequently, two or more successive figures do not indicate chords proper but only voice-leading, appoggiaturas, or passing tones, e.g., 4 3, or 9 8, or 5 4 3.

The accompanying examples illustrate these principles.

II. The principles above constitute only the rudiments of a very difficult art. A good thoroughbass accompaniment is considerably more than a mere translation of figures into musical notes. At the proper places, the musical material used in the solo parts (voice, violin) should be incorporated into the accompaniment, in free imitation, or in doubling thirds, or in contrapuntal contrast. How far this should be carried is a difficult and controversial question. Obviously, different situations are presented by different compositions and in different periods. Between the years 1600 and 1750, the style of improvised accompaniment changed from simple homophony to real counterpoint. Thus an elaborately contrapuntal realization for, e.g., arias of the mid-17th century is clearly inappropriate.

Bach himself left two records of his own thoroughbass improvisation, one in the second aria of the solo cantata *Amore traditore* and another in the second movement of his sonata in B minor for flute and harpsichord. Although both parts are designated *Cembalo obbligato*, their style differs markedly from that of other written out parts and so probably indicates his style of thoroughbass improvisation [see M. Schneider, in *JMP* xxi/xxii]. Another informative example of written out thoroughbass accompaniment is in a sonata by Handel for viola da gamba and harpsichord [Händelgesellschaft ed., xlviii, 112–17].

In addition to the accompanying harpsichordist, the realization of a thoroughbass part calls for a cello or viola da gamba that reinforces the bass line. It would be entirely in keeping with baroque *performance practice for the players of such instruments to simplify the written part somewhat whenever it includes rapid figures, intelligently underlining the contours instead of disturbing the equilibrium with a forced display of virtuosity.

III. The thoroughbass practice of the baroque grew out of the improvisation techniques of the 16th century. About 1600, motets were occasionally accompanied on the organ by a *bassus pro organo*, a separate bass part from which the organist played the harmonies. The earliest known instance of this method is in a forty-part motet of 1587, "Ecce beatam lucem," by A. Striggio [see M. Schneider, p. 67]. A similar bass part, printed for Giovanni Croce's *Motetti* of 1594, has ♯ and ♭ above the notes in order to indicate major or minor triads (thirds). The earliest examples of a *basso continuo* with figures

are Cavalieri's *Rappresentazione* and (less completely) Peri's and Caccini's operas *Euridice,* all from 1600. Here as well as in numerous later works, different figures are used for the different octaves, e.g., 10 for the tenth (upper third), 15 for the double octave [see, e.g., *WoHN* ii, 315]. Among the numerous 17th- and 18th-century writers on *basso continuo* are A. Agazzari, *Del sonare sopra'l basso,* 1607 (fac. ed. by Bollettino Bibliografico Musicale, 1933); M. Praetorius, in *Syntagma musicum* iii, 1619 (ch. vi: *De basso generali seu continuo*); M. Locke, *Melothesia, or Certain General Rules for playing upon a Continued-bass,* 1673; M. de Saint-Lambert, *Nouveau Traité de l'accompagnement* (1707); J. D. Heinichen, *Der General-Bass in der Composition,* 1728; J. Mattheson, *Grosse General-Bass-Schule,* 1731; G. P. Telemann, *Singe-, Spiel-, und Generalbass Übungen* 1733/4 (new ed. by M. Seiffert, 1914); K. P. E. Bach, *Versuch über die wahre Art das Clavier zu spielen,* 1753 (trans. W. J. Mitchell, 1949); D. G. Türk, *Kurze Anweisung zum Generalbassspielen,* 1791. See also *Partimento.*

Lit.: F. T. Arnold, *The Art of Accompaniment from a Thorough-bass* (1931); H. Keller, *Thoroughbass Method* [1965]; F. Oberdörffer, *Der Generalbass in der Instrumentalmusik des ausgehenden 18. Jahrhunderts* (1939); G. Kirchner, *Der Generalbass bei Heinrich Schütz* (1960); E. Ulrich, *Studien zur deutschen Generalbass-Praxis ... des 18. Jahrhunderts* (1932); M. Schneider, *Die Anfänge des Basso continuo und seiner Bezifferung* (1918); G. J. Buelow, in *AM* xxxv; L. Landshoff, in *CP Sandberger; RiHM* ii.2, 72ff; E. Stilz, in *ZMW* xiii; L. Torchi, in *RMI* i, ii; A. Toni, in *RMI* xxvi; H. H. Eggebrecht, "Arten des Generalbasses" (*AMW* xiv); *WoHN* ii, 314ff.

Three-Cornered Hat, The. See *Sombrero de tres picos, El.*

Threepenny Opera. See *Dreigroschenoper, Die.* Also see under Ballad opera.

Through-composed. This term, which is widely accepted as a translation of G. *durchkomponiert,* is applied to songs in which new music is provided for each stanza. Its opposite is "strophic song," a song in which every stanza is sung to the same melody. The latter method is frequently used for simple lyrics, while the former is preferred for dramatic or narrative texts in which the situation changes with every stanza, e.g., Schubert's "Der Erlkönig." Schubert and Karl Loewe [see *Ballade* (G.)] were among the first to employ the through-composed style. Since then it has been almost universally adopted for lyrical songs.

The term also applies, in a more general sense, to the use of new music where musical repeat would be possible or normal. Thus, in most church hymns the individual stanza is through-composed, but some use repeat forms such as a a b c. From the over-all view, of course, they are strophic since the music is repeated in each stanza. Similarly, in troubadour and trouvère songs, the individual stanza may be through-composed or have initial repeat [see Canzo].

Through-imitation [F. *imitation syntaxique;* G. *Durchimititation*]. The procedure of basing a composition entirely on the principle of imitation. In this sense, Bach's fugues are through-imitative. However, the term is chiefly applied to the fully imitative polyphony of the 16th-century motet [see Motet B II], in distinction to earlier compositions based on a *cantus firmus* or employing imitation only sporadically. Although some pieces by A. Busnois, L. Compère, and Josquin come fairly close to being through-imitative, it was Gombert (*c.* 1490–1556) who established through-imitation (or, as it is also called, "pervading imitation") as the standard method of motet composition. See C. van den Borren, "Quelques Réflexions à propos du style imitatif syntaxique" (*RBM* i).

Thunder machine [G. *Donnermaschine*]. A device introduced by R. Strauss in his *Alpensinfonie,* op. 64 (1915), to imitate thunder. It consists of a big rotating drum with hard balls inside that strike against the drumhead.

Thus Spake Zarathustra. See *Also Sprach Zarathustra.*

Tibet. Since World War II, a considerable amount of research has been done on Tibetan music. The liturgical chant traditionally practiced in the numerous monasteries (especially in the capital, Lhasa) is a kind of recitative of a very low bass range (E to G) in an unstressed rhythm of equal pulses, accompanied by metallophones, drums, and an even lower drone held by long trumpets, often extending like telescopes to a length of twelve or more feet. There are also religious performances with dancing by large groups of masked performers, often lasting several days and making use of large orchestras similar to those of ancient China. Secular music is cultivated by touring troupes performing

plays with music, somewhat similar to Chinese opera. There is a large repertory of folk dances, folksongs, work songs, etc. A detailed description of Tibetan music is found in *GDB* viii, 456ff. Tibetan musical notation consists of elaborate scrolls of a highly ornamental design; ex. in L. A. Waddell, *The Buddhism of Tibet,* rev. ed. (1934). See also *LavE* i.5, 3084ff (examples doubtful); *NOH* i, 137ff; T. H. Somervell, in C. G. Bruce, *The Assault on Mount Everest 1922* (1923), ch. xiv; T. H. Somervell, in *Musical Times* lxiv, 107f; W. Graf, in *Studia musicologica* (Budapest) iii, 133ff.

Tibia [L.]. Name for the Greek *aulos; see Oboe family III. *Tibicen* [L.], flute player.

Tie, bind. A curved line, identical in appearance to the *slur, that connects two successive notes of the same pitch and has the function of uniting them into a single sound equal to their combined durations. The tie is used (1) to connect two notes separated by a bar line; (2) to produce values that cannot be indicated by a single note, e.g., the value of seven eighth notes:

$$\text{♩ ♩.} \quad (7 = 4 + 3).$$

The tie, together with the bar line, is the most conspicuous achievement of modern notation over the earlier system of *mensural notation, where it does not exist (the earliest known instance occurs in a keyboard score of 1523, *Recerchari motetti, canzoni* of Marco Antonio Cavazzoni [da Bologna]; see *ApNPM,* p. 5). Owing to the nonexistence of the tie in mensural notation, a note equaling five units was never used in duple meter (*tempus imperfectum*) in any vocal composition prior to *c.* 1600; only in triple meter (*tempus perfectum*) could such a value be obtained, by subtracting one from six (imperfection).

Occasionally a tie calls not for a complete suppression but for a subtle repetition of the second note; see under Tremolo I.

Tiento [Sp.], **tento** [Port.]. A 16th- and 17th-century form that is the Iberian counterpart of the Italian ricercar (not, as has been stated, of the toccata). Like the ricercar, it originated in vihuela (lute) music (Milán, *Libro de música . . . El Maestro,* 1535–36) as a free "study" [see Ricercar II] in idiomatic style for the instrument and was later used for organ music (L. Venegas de Henestrosa, A. Cabezón; see Editions XXXII, 2, and XX, 3, 4, 7, 8), where it became a study in imitative counterpoint. However, the erudite formal treatment often found in the ricercar is rarely present in the *tientos,* which also are usually much shorter than the contemporary ricercars. *Tientos* continued to be composed throughout the 17th century, mainly by Manuel R. Coelho (*Flores de música,* 1620), F. Correa de Araujo (*Libro de tientos,* 1626; *Editions XXXII, 6), and Juan Cabanilles (1644–1712; *Opera omnia,* ed. by Anglés). Most of these are long compositions in which imitation appears only at the beginning, the thematic material serving only as the springboard for a wealth of playful motifs, lively figurations, and picturesque ideas.

Tierce [F.]. (1) Third. *Tierce de Picardie,* see Picardy third. (2) An organ stop of the mutation type that sounds a note two octaves and a major third above the key played. See Organ. (3) *Tierce coulé.* See Appoggiatura, double II.

Till Eulenspiegels lustige Streiche [G., Till Eulenspiegel's Merry Pranks]. Symphonic poem by R. Strauss, op. 28 (1895), based on the 16th-century German folk tale of Till Eulenspiegel. The music develops, in a free rondo form, around two themes, one representing Till as a popular hero, the other as a vagabond and prankster. There are no specific programmatic connotations except at the end, where the sentencing and hanging of Till are clearly suggested.

Timbale [F.], **timpano** or **timballo** [It.]. Kettledrum [see Percussion instruments A, 1].

Timbre [F.]. (1) Medieval name for *tambourin. (2) Same as *tone color. (3) A standard melody, especially for popular tunes underlaid with new texts (*opéra comique,* vaudeville). See also the "Catalogue des timbres" in E. Misset and P. Aubry, *Les Proses d'Adam de Saint-Victor,* pp. 119ff.

Timbrel. Old name for *tambourine.

Time. Term used loosely to indicate *meter, tempo, or the duration of a given note.

Time signatures. The time (meter) is indicated at the beginning of a piece by two numbers, one above the other; the lower indicates the chosen unit of measurement (half note, quarter note, etc.), while the upper indicates the number of such units comprised in a measure. See Meter.

Early time signatures and their proportional modifications are explained under Mensural notation II and Proportions. Two of them survive, the sign C for 4/4, and the sign ¢ for 2/2

(*alla breve). In the sources of the 17th century more complicated signs such as C_3, C_2^3 are still common, often puzzling the modern reader to whom a combination of C (4/4) and 3/2, 6/4, 8/9 [sic] seems contradictory and senseless. Such signs actually combine two meanings, the older proportional meaning with the more recent metrical one. Thus, the sign C_4^6 [see Froberger, Suite no. 5, in *DTO* 13] means that (a) each measure contains six quarter notes, and (b) these six notes are equal in duration to the four notes of the preceding section. These signs have a strictly metronomic significance (relative to the normal tempo of the piece), a fact usually overlooked by modern readers. Particularly noteworthy is the signature C_3 (3, $\frac{3}{1}$), which is very frequently used for sections containing three whole notes to the measure [see Froberger, Suites nos. 1–5, *DTO* 13]. Although this may suggest a very slow tempo, the correct speed for such pieces is moderately quick, since these three whole notes will have to be played in the time normally consumed by one whole note:

If, however, the composition is notated in *alla breve* (as is usual in 16th-century vocal music; Palestrina), then the relationship is not 3:1 but 3:2 [see *ApNPM,* pp. 193ff].

Time signatures such as 8/9 or 8/12, found, e.g., in Frescobaldi [see *HAM,* no. 193] do not mean "eight ninth or twelfth notes," but serve—in accordance with 15th-century theory—to cancel previous proportional indications, 9/8 or 12/8. See explanation in *HAM* ii, 281.

About 1700 the symbol Φ was used to indicate measures of double length, i.e., 8/4 instead of 4/4 (e.g., Bach, Partita no. 6, Gigue), a method of designation that was still used by Schubert (¢ ¢; = 4/2) in his Impromptu op. 90, no. 3.

Timing [F. *minutage*]. The duration of a performance, a matter of importance in planning programs, particularly for radio and television. See S. Aronowsky, *Performing Times of Orchestral Works* (1959); W. Reddick, *The Standard Musical Repertoire, with Accurate Timings* (1947); T. C. York, *How Long does It Play?* (1929).

Timpan. (1) A medieval stringed instrument (psaltery? bowed harp?). (2) Kettledrum [see Timpani].

Timpani [It.]. Kettledrums. *Timpani coperti, t. sordi,* muffled kettledrums. For ill. see under Percussion instruments.

Tin Pan Alley. Slang term for anything connected with popular song publishing in the United States. The term originated in the early 1900's, when the popular music trade was concentrated on West 28th Street, New York City; it is now largely outmoded. See I. Goldberg, *Tin Pan Alley* (1930); A. Shaw, "The Vocabulary of Tin-Pan Alley Explained" (*Notes,* 2nd series, vii).

Tintinnabulum [L.]. Medieval term for bell.

Tiorba [It., Sp.]. Theorbo. See Lute III.

Tiple [Sp.]. Soprano, upper voice. Also, a small guitar. The meaning of titles such as "Tiple a tre" (A. Falconieri, *c.* 1620; see L. Torchi, *L'Arte Musicale in Italia* vii, 128, 143, 151) is not clear.

Tipping. See Tonguing.

Tirade [F.], **tirata** [It.]. Baroque ornament consisting of a scale passage of more than three notes that serves as a transition between two principal melody notes. It was written out or

indicated by the sign illustrated in Ex. 1 but often was improvised to fill in large intervals. *Tirades* are typical of the French overture style [see Ex. 2, from Bach's Goldberg Variations]. A late example appears in the fourth measure of Beethoven's Piano Concerto no. 4 in G major, op. 58.   P.A.

Tirana. A type of Andalusian dance-song. Blas Laserna (1751–1816; see *Tonadilla*) wrote a "Tirana del Tripidi" that was famous throughout 19th-century Europe.

Tirare [It.]. To draw. *Tira tutti* [draw all], full organ. *Tirarsi* [to be drawn], sliding mechanism of the *trombone. *Tirando,* slowing of tempo.

Tirasse [F.]. Originally, the pedals of a small organ that had no separate pipes but were mechanically connected (coupled) to the manual keys. Hence, a pedal coupler of the organ, e.g., *Tirasse du Positif* (*Tir. P.*), coupler "choir to pedal."

Tirer, tirez, tiré [F.]. Indication for downstroke of the bow [see Bowing], the drawing of organ stops, or slowing of tempo.

Toada. See *Tonada.*

Toccata. (1) A keyboard (organ, harpsichord) composition in free, idiomatic keyboard style, employing full chords and running passages, with or without the inclusion of sections in imitative style (fugues). The earliest toccatas, by A. Gabrieli [*Editions III, 3], consist of full chords and interlacing scale passages only. To consider them merely virtuoso pieces (as many writers have) is scarcely appropriate, since the passages are decidedly expressive, particularly if played in the free tempo typical of the toccata [see reference to Frescobaldi under Rubato (1)]. With Claudio Merulo (1533–1604) the toccata became organized into alternating toccata (free, idiomatic keyboard style) and fugal sections, usually arranged T F T F T. Frescobaldi's (1583–1643) toccatas are written in a series of short sections, exhibiting a variety of moods in rapid succession. A special type (already written by his predecessors, Trabaci and Ascanio Mayone; see W. Apel, in *MQ* xx) is the short liturgical toccata (e.g., "Toccata avanti l'elevazione," to be played before the Elevation of the Host; see Offertory), which is a short prelude in dignified style. With Bernardo Pasquini (1637–1710) and Alessandro Scarlatti (1660–1725) the Italian toccata became the arena for empty keyboard virtuosity and soon declined into a *perpetuum mobile type very similar to the etudes of the early 19th century (Clementi).

The development of the toccata in Germany was twofold. The South German composers (Froberger, Kerll, Muffat) followed the Italian model (Frescobaldi), enriching its stylistic resources and enlivening its contents. More important is the North German development, which led to an entirely novel, rhapsodic toccata that has sometimes been termed *Gothic. The new style appeared first in the toccatas of Matthias Weckmann (1619–74) and was developed with great artistry by Dietrich Buxtehude (*c.* 1637–1707), Nicolaus Bruhns (1665–97), and J. S. Bach (1685–1750). Most of these toccatas, particularly those of Bach, retain Merulo's five-section scheme alternating between free and contrapuntal style. Bach's great organ toccata in F major, however, combines the large dimensions of the North German type with the rhythmic precision of the late Italian toccata (Pasquini). The toccata style is also frequently used for preludes of fugues, e.g., Bach's organ fugue in A minor.

Both the North German and Italian toccatas survive in a few isolated romantic and modern works. Schumann, Debussy (in *Pour le Piano,* 1901), Honegger, Prokofiev, and Casella have written toccatas of the *perpetuum mobile* type, whereas the free, rhapsodic style appears in the toccatas of Busoni (1921) and Petyrek (1934).

(2) About 1600, the name toccata was also used for a festive brass fanfare, e.g., in the introduction of Monteverdi's *Orfeo* (1607). The reason for using the name for pieces so different from the keyboard toccata is not clear. Possibly the latter connotation is bound up with the use of kettledrums for the bass part of such pieces [see Toccatina; Toccato; *Touche* (4); Tucket; *Tusch*].

Lit.: E. Valentin, *Die Entwicklung der Tokkata im 17. und 18. Jahrhundert* (1930); L. Schrade, "Ein Beitrag zur Geschichte der Tokkata" (*ZMW* viii); O. Gombosi, "Zur Vorgeschichte der Tokkate" (*AM* vi, no. 2); S. Clercx, "La Toccata, Principe du style symphonique" (*La Musique instrumentale de la Renaissance,* ed. J. Jacquot [1955]); L. Torchi, ‡*L'Arte musicale in Italia* iii; F. Boghen, ‡*Antichi Maestri Italiani: Toccate* [1918]; E. Valentin, ‡*Die Tokkata* (1958).

Toccatina. A short toccata, serving as a prelude to a suite. Examples by J. K. F. Fischer and Murschhauser show a style closer to that of the orchestral toccata [see Toccata (2)] than the free style of the keyboard toccata [Toccata (1)].

Toccato. In 17th-century music for trumpets, the bass part of a trumpet piece, so called probably because it was originally played on, or together with, kettledrums. See bibl. under Clarino (2). See also Toccata (2).

Tod und das Mädchen, Der [G., Death and the Maiden]. Schubert's String Quartet no. 14 in D minor (1826), whose second movement consists of variations on his song of the same name (1817).

Tod und Verklärung [G., Death and Transfiguration]. The second of R. Strauss' six famous symphonic poems, completed in 1889. The music, in four sections, depicts the fevered fantasies of a patient at the crisis of a fatal illness.

Tokkate [G.]. Toccata.

Tombeau [F.]. See Lament (2).

Tom-tom. Set of high-pitched drums used in dance bands. The drums, which can be tuned to

a definite pitch, may be double-headed or single-headed, and represent an imitation of African drums.

Ton [F.]. (1) Pitch; *donner le ton,* to give the pitch. (2) *Pitch pipe. (3) Key or mode; *ton d'ut,* key of C; *ton majeur,* major key; *ton d'église,* church mode. (4) Whole tone, as distinct from *demiton,* semitone. (5) Crook; *ton du cor, ton de rechange,* crook of the horn.

Ton [G.]. *Tone, chiefly in the meanings (1) and (3).

Tonabstand [G.]. *Interval.

Tonada [Sp.]., **toada** [Port]. Almost any folksong of prevailingly lyrical character, set to four-, five- or ten-line stanzas, or to quatrains with refrain. Whenever the setting is for a text in the last of these forms, contrasting tempos between a slow refrain and a lively quatrain are employed, usually a slow 3/4 meter and a fast 6/8 meter.

J.O-S.

Tonadilla [Sp.]. A short, Spanish, popular comic opera, with one to four characters, consisting of solo song and, occasionally, choruses. Its origins were short scenic interludes performed between the acts of a play or serious opera, but (like the Italian *opera buffa*) it later became an independent piece. It flourished from about the middle of the 18th to the early 19th centuries. One of the first *tonadillas* is a comic musical dialogue between a woman innkeeper and an itinerant Bohemian, written in 1757 by Luis Misón (d. 1766). Besides Misón, the chief composers of *tonadillas* are Pablo Esteve (b. *c.* 1730) and Blas Laserna (1751–1816). The *tonadilla* superseded the older *zarzuela, which was an elaborately staged serious opera, usually based on mythological subjects.

Lit.: *LavE* i.4, 2227–57; J. Subirá, *La Tonadilla escénica* (1933); F. Pedrell, *Teatro lírico español anterior al siglo XIX,* 5 vols. (1897–98); M. N. Hamilton, *Music in Eighteenth Century Spain* (1937); J. Subirá, in *CP Laurencie.*   D.J.G.

Tonal and real. In a fugue, an answer is "real" if it is an exact (diatonic) transposition of the subject and "tonal" if certain steps are modified. Such modifications frequently take place if the subject contains the interval of the fifth (d–a), this being answered not by the transposed fifth (a–e′) but by the fourth (a–d′), as illustrated in the accompanying example from Bach's *The Art of Fugue.* The purpose of this procedure is to avoid sudden oscillations between the keys of

the tonic and dominant. In fact, with the theme in question the "real answer" a-e'-c' . . . would result in a somewhat irritating clash between the low d in the subject and the high e in the answer. It is difficult to formulate rules as to when tonal and real answer is properly used. In general, the fugal themes called *soggetto lend themselves more readily to tonal treatment, whereas the newer types of subject called *andamento are frequently too "individual" and well defined to admit any modification. In early music, before c. 1550, most fugal answers are real, if only because they are usually at the unison or the fourth. Also, the themes rarely include the fifth. An early instance of a tonal answer, by A. Gabrieli, appears in the instance given under Double theme.

The tonal-real dichotomy has also been applied to entire fugues, a fugue being called tonal if the answer is tonal and real if it is real. This distinction, however, implies that in a fugue one or the other type of answer is strictly maintained. Whereas there are numerous examples of tonal fugues, there are scarcely any of real ones.

The terms "tonal" and "real" are also used in connection with imitation at intervals other than the fifth, particularly with the imitation at the higher or lower second that occurs in sequential passages [see Sequence I]. This is called real if the intervals are imitated exactly, thus involving modulation, and tonal if it stays within the key.

Tonale [L.]. See Tonary.

Tonalität [G.]. *Tonality in the sense of "loyalty to a key," but admitting modulations into another key that are not necessarily included in the German term Tonart. Thus, the beginning of Beethoven's Waldstein Sonata, op. 53, shows the Tonarten of C, G, B-flat, F, and C in quick succession but has only one Tonalität, C major.

Tonality. Loyalty to a tonic, in the broadest sense of the word. One of the most striking phenomena of music is the fact that, throughout its evolution—in non-Western cultures, in Gregorian chant, and in harmonized music—practically every single piece gives preference to one tone (the tonic), making this the tonal center to which all other tones are related. [Also see Key (2); Atonality.]

Although nearly all music in this sense of the word is tonal, the means of achieving tonality have greatly varied throughout history. Whereas in Gregorian chant and other monophonic music the relationships are purely melodic, a much more complex situation is encountered in harmonized music. About 1700 came general acceptance of a system of tonal functions based on the establishment of three main chords—the tonic, the dominant, and the subdominant triads—as the carriers of harmonic as well as melodic movements. Broadened by the ample use of chromatic alterations and modulation into other keys, this system prevailed throughout the 18th and 19th centuries. For subsequent developments, see Atonality.

In current usage the terms "tonality" and "modality" are mutually exclusive, the former referring to music written in a "key" (major or minor mode) and the latter to pieces written in, or showing the influence of, the church modes [see Modality]. This usage is obviously not compatible with the broad definition of tonality above, which includes all tonal relationships, whether "tonal" or "modal." If the explanation of mode as the constituent scale is accepted [see Mode (1)], then tonality exists in different "modal" varieties, based, e.g., on the church modes, the major and minor modes, the pentatonic mode, the whole-tone mode, the diatonic mode [see Pandiatonicism] or, as in some modern music, the chromatic mode. Tonality also exists in the quarter-tone mode (e.g., in the Greek enharmonic genus), although modern *quarter-tone music tends to be atonal.

Other uses of the term "tonality," e.g., in the sense of "tonal system" (almost synonymous with what has been termed modality above), or in the sense of major-and-minor tonality (as opposed to modality in the accepted meaning of the term), also have become firmly entrenched in current usage.

Lit.: J. Yasser, *A Theory of Evolving Tonality* (1932); E. E. Lowinsky, *Tonality and Atonality in Sixteenth-Century Music* (1961); A. Machabey, *Genèse de la tonalité musicale classique* (1955); J. Chailley, *Traité historique d'analyse musicale* (1951); F. Neumann, *Tonalität und Atonalität* (1955); D. F. Tovey, "Tonality" (*ML* ix, 341ff); J. Yasser, "The Future of Tonality" (*MM* viii); H. Reichenbach, "The Tonality of English and Gaelic Folksong" (*ML* xix, 268ff); W. H. Frere, "Key-relationship in Early Mediaeval Music" (*SIM* xiii; also in *CP 1911*, p. 114); L. Hibberd, "'Tonality' and Related Problems in Terminology" (*MR* xxii); M. Touzé, "La Tonalité chromatique" (*RM* 1922, no. 9). W. Margraff, "Tonalität in Machaut und Dufay" (*AMW* xxiii). Also see under Atonality.

Tonart [G.]. Key.

Tonary [L. *tonarium, tonarius, tonale*]. A medieval book similar to a "thematic catalog" [see Theme] in which the chants are listed (with their beginnings) according to mode, and often with subdivisions within each mode. Tonaries contain the chants that are (or were) connected with a psalm verse sung to one of the various recitation tones organized into a system of eight tones [see Tone (3)], e.g., antiphons, responsories, Introits, Communions. The purpose of the tonaries was to show the mode of a chant, a matter of great practical importance, since the selection of the proper tone (e.g., first psalm tone, third Introit tone) depended on the mode of the antiphon, Introit, etc. The subdivisions fulfilled the even more urgent need for determining the correct termination of the tone. The most important tonaries are those by Regino of Prüm (*c.* 900), Odo de Clugny (10th century), and one ascribed to Guido d'Arezzo (11th century), all published in *CS* ii, 1ff, 78ff, 117ff. Theoretical writings of a similar nature are the *Tonarius Bernonis* (*GS* ii, 79ff) and the *Commemoratio brevis de tonis et psalmis modulandis* (*GS* i, 213ff).

Different from these is the so-called Mass Tonary (*tonale missarum*) of Montpellier [*Editions XLII A, 7 and 8], which contains all the chants of the Mass, fully written out (with an additional *letter notation) and arranged according to their modes. See F. X. Mathias, *Die Tonarien* (1903); W. Lipphardt, *Der Karolingische Tonar von Metz* (1965); M. Runge, in *MfM* xxxv.

Tonbuchstaben [G.]. Tone letters [see Letter notation].

Tondichtung [G.]. Tone poem; also, any composition of a poetic character. See Symphonic poem.

Tone [F. *ton;* G. *Ton;* It., Sp. *tono*]. (1) A sound of definite pitch and duration, as distinct from noise and from less definite phenomena, such as the violin *portamento. (2) The interval of a major second, i.e., a whole tone, as distinct from a semitone (minor second). This is the usual British meaning of the term, the word "note" being used for (1).
(3) In Gregorian chant, tone [L. *tonus*] is the generic name for all recitation formulas, such

as lesson tones, prayer tones, gospel tones, psalm tones, canticle tones, Introit tones, responsorial tones, etc. All these consist essentially of a recitation on one pitch (reciting tone, reciting note, repercussion, tenor, tuba), which probably explains the name *tonus*. The Introit tones are used for the verses of the Introits, the responsorial tones for those of the great responsories. Both are organized as a system of eight tones, one for each mode, as are the *psalm tones and the canticle (or *Magnificat) tones.

Tone cluster. A strongly dissonant group of tones lying close together and produced, usually on the piano, by depressing a segment of the keyboard with the fist, forearm, or a board of specified length. The term was invented by Henry Cowell, who, along with Charles Ives ("Concord" Sonata), used the device extensively. See H. Cowell, *New Musical Resources* (1930), pp. 117ff.

Tone color [F. *timbre* (also in Eng. usage); G. *Klangfarbe*]. The quality ("color") of a tone as produced on a specific instrument, as distinct from the different quality of the same tone if played on some other instrument. As shown by H. Helmholtz and others, tone color is determined by the harmonics, or, more precisely, the greater or lesser prominence of one or another harmonic. Thus, the c of the cello and the c of the horn have the same harmonics (c', g', c'', e'', g'', ...), but their intensities differ widely.

The sound of a tuning fork and of the stopped diapason of the organ have practically no harmonics; the "pure sound" of the flute results from its lack of nearly all the harmonics except the first (octave); the rich and mellow timbre of the clarinet result from the lack of even-numbered harmonics (c', c'') and the prominence of the odd-numbered harmonics (g', e'' ...). The pungent, nasal sound of the oboe is caused by the presence of practically all the harmonics, which also appear, in different degrees, in the tones of the violin.

The classical theory of tone color, as outlined above, has been modified to some extent by the recent theory of the *formant.* According to the former, the characteristic constituents of, e.g., a tone on a violin, are in a fixed relation to the fundamental tone and, therefore, are shifted up or down if the fundamental changes. For example, if for the violin tone g the characteristic partials are g'' and b'', the violin tone d' would have the (much higher) characteristic partials d''' and f'''. According to more recent investigations, however, the characteristic partials of a violin tone lie within an absolutely fixed range of rather narrow limits, regardless of the pitch of the fundamental. This characteristic "absolute range of partials" is called the formant. In most violins the formant lies between 3,000 and 6,000 cycles per second. The formant theory also plays an important part in explaining the different "timbre" of the vowels in singing. For each vowel, the human voice represents a different "instrument" with the formant in a different region. See the modern books under Acoustics; *SaHMI*, p. 354; W. T. Bartholomew, "Voice Research at Peabody Conservatory" (*BAMS* vi).

Tone poem. *Symphonic poem.

Tone row [G. *Tonreihe*]. See under Serial music.

Tonfarbe [G.]. *Tone color.

Tongeschlecht [G.]. Distinction of a chord or key, whether major or minor.

Tonguing. In playing wind instruments, the use of the tongue for greater articulation. It consists of momentary interruption of the windstream by an action of the tongue as if pronouncing the letter *t* or *k*. Three types of tonguing are distinguished: single tonguing (*t–t* . . .), double tonguing (*t–k t–k* . . .), and triple tonguing (*t–k t–k t–t–k* . . .). The first is employed in slower passages, the last two in rapid passages in groups of two or three notes. Single tonguing is used for practically all the wind instruments; double and triple tonguing is used chiefly for brass instruments (trumpet, horn, etc.) as well as the flute. A special type of tonguing called *Flatterzunge* (fluttertonguing) was introduced by R. Strauss. It calls for a rolling movement of the tongue, as if pronouncing *d–r–r–r*.

Tonhöhe [G.]. *Pitch.

Tonic. The first and main note of a key, hence, the keynote. See Scale degrees; Tonality.

Tonic accent. An accent caused by a higher pitch, rather than a stress or a larger note value, e.g.,

Domine, not *Dómine* or *Do—mine.*

The last two kinds of accent are called *dynamic* and *agogic* respectively. The term "tonic accent" is also applied to a melody to indicate that a strong syllable of the text receives a note of higher pitch than the surrounding weak syllables. The tonic accent plays an important role in

the discussion of Gregorian chant [see *ApGC*, pp. 289ff].

Tonic sol-fa. An English method of solmization designed primarily to facilitate sight singing. It was developed from earlier methods (Lancashire system) by Sarah A. Glover and perfected *c.* 1840 by John Curwen (1816–80). It is widely used for teaching in England, and has also become known in some other countries, e.g., in Germany (as *Tonika-do*).

Tonic sol-fa is a system of "movable do," i.e., the tone syllables *do, re, mi, fa, sol, la, ti* are used with reference to the key of a piece or any section thereof where there is a change of key. The syllables, or rather, their initial consonants, d r m f s l t, are also used for notation in a manner reminiscent of the German keyboard tablatures of the 16th century. Octave repetitions are indicated for the higher octave thus: $\overline{d} \overline{r} \overline{m}$ or d' r' m'; for the lower octave thus: $\underline{d} \underline{r} \underline{m}$ or d, r, m,. For the minor scale the third degree becomes *do*, owing to the changed intervals of this scale: l t d r m f s l. Actually this succession represents the Aeolian scale (white keys from A, or any transposition). In order to arrive at the minor scale, the sixth and seventh degrees must be sharped. Sharped tones are usually indicated by changing the vowel to e (*de, re, fe, se, le*), flatted tones by changing it to a (*ra, ma, la, ta*). [For exceptions, see *GDB* viii, 504ff.] For the sixth degree of the ascending melodic minor scale a separate syllable *ba* is introduced, since the use of *fe* would suggest a half-step to the next note, whereas actually a whole-step follows (to *se*). Therefore the melodic minor scale is designated (up and down): l t d r m ba se l; l s f m r d t l. The tones and their relation to each other are shown in a chart called *Modulator*.

If the piece modulates into another key, the new key is indicated (in various ways), and the tone syllables are now reckoned in the new key. For the indication of meter and rhythm, additional signs (horizontal strokes, single dots, colons, commas, etc.) are used.

Lit.: J. Curwen, *The New Standard Course of Lessons and Exercises in the Tonica Sol-fa Method* (3rd ed., 1872); W. R. Phillips, *A Dictionary of the Tonic Sol-fa System* (1909); W. G. Whittaker, in *ML* v, 313, and vi, 46, 161; *id.*, in *MQ* viii; J. Taylor, J. C. Ward, in *PMA* xxiii; C. A. Harris, in *MQ* iv; J. A. Fuller-Maitland, in *MQ* vii.

Tonika [G.]. Tonic. *Tonika-do,* German modification of *tonic sol-fa.

Tonkunst [G.]. Music. *Tonkünstler,* composer.

Tonleiter [G.]. *Scale.

Tonmalerei [G.]. *Word painting or descriptive music.

Tono [It.]. Tone; whole tone; key; mode. *Primo* (*secondo,* etc.) *tono,* first (second, etc.) church mode.

Tono llanero [Sp.]. Folksong of the Venezuelan plains that shows many early Spanish influences intact without any trace of the Negro influences that dominate the coastal region of the country. The music, for voices without instrumental accompaniment, uses inverted chords and plagal cadences, as well as long melodic phrases and melismatic sections.   J.O-S.

Tonos, pl. **tonoi** [Gr.]. See under Greece II.

Tonsatz [G.]. Composition. *Tonsetzer,* composer.

Tonschrift [G.]. Notation.

Tonysystem [G.]. System of tones, i.e., *tonality, used mainly in combinations such as *Europäisches Tonsystem, javanisches Tonsystem, Pythagoräisches Tonsystem.* See E. M. von Hornbostel, "Musikalische Tonsysteme" (in H. Geiger, *Handbuch der Physik,* vol. viii [1927]).

Tonus [L.]. (1) Whole tone. (2) Generic name for the plainsong recitation formulas, such as *tonus lectionum, toni psalmorum, tonus peregrinus, toni v. Gloria Patri ad introitum,* etc. [see Tone (3)].
   (3) Church mode, e.g., *primus tonus, tonus authenticus, tonus plagalis.* Medieval writers used three designations for the church modes: *tonus, tropus,* and *modus.* The earliest writers, Flaccus Alcuinus (*c.* 753–804) and Aurelianus Reomensis (whose text incorporated all of Alcuin's) used the term *tonus.* The latter used the term in a general sense, i.e., "tone" = discrete musical pitch, as well as specifically, i.e., whole tone, and further, to mean church mode and recitation formula. In the last sense it has as a synonym *tenor,* owing to the long-standing use of both terms by Latin grammarians to refer to syllabic accent (stress or musical). Consequently, both *tonus* and *tenor* may also mean the reciting tone of a psalm formula. While both these terms (with their translations into modern languages) survive into the Renaissance and later, *tropus* in this meaning passes out of use in the later Middle Ages.
   Tonus in directum (*indirectum*), see Psalmody I; *tonus mixtus, commixtus, perfectus, imper-*

fectus, see Church modes III; *tonus peregrinus,* see Psalm tones. See K. Speer, in *CP Apel;* O. Gombosi, "Studien zur Tonartenlehre" (*AM* x, xi, xii).   rev. L.G.

Tonverschmelzung [G.]. See under Consonance, dissonance I (d).

Tonwort [G.]. A method of solmization invented in 1892 by K. A. Eitz, designed for a 53-note scale with particular reference to chromatic progressions and enharmonic changes. See M. Koch, *Einführung in das Tonwort* (1925).

Torbellino [Sp.]. Traditional Colombian dance in 3/4 meter with heavy accents on the strong beats and usually with elaborate fast accompaniments to vocal melodies sung in parallel thirds. Long pauses are often made on the upbeat and are used by the instrumentalists for certain tonal elaborations.   J.O-S.

Torculus. See under Neumes I (table).

Tordion. See under *Basse danse.*

Tornada. See under Envoi.

Tosca. Opera in three acts by Puccini (libretto by G. Giacosa and L. Illica, based on V. Sardou's drama of the same title), produced in Rome, 1900. Setting: Rome, June 1800.

Tosto [It.]. Quickly, at once. *Più tosto* means either "more quickly" or the same as *piuttòsto,* "rather."

Tost Quartets. Twelve quartets by Haydn, written 1789–90 and dedicated to Johann Tost, Viennese merchant and violinist. They comprise op. 54, nos. 1–3; op. 55, nos. 1–3; op. 64, nos. 1–6.

Touch [G. *Anschlag*]. See under Piano playing (particularly IV and V).

Touche [F]. (1) Key of the piano. (2) Fingerboard of the violin [see Bowing (1)]. (3) A 16th-century term for fret (of a lute, guitar). (4) A 17th-century term (also used in English sources) for the "orchestral" toccata [see Toccata (2)].

Tour de gosier [F.]. A vocal ornament of the 17th and 18th centuries, consisting of a turn composed of five notes. The term is also applied to the closing notes of the trill.   P.A.

Tourdion [F.]. Tordion. See under *Basse danse.*

Tourte bow. A violin bow made by F. Tourte (1747–1835), famous bowmaker. See Bow.

Toye. Title for a short light composition for virginal.

Toy Symphony. A playful composition often ascribed to Haydn and scored, aside from the first and second violins and double bass, for toy instruments such as cuckoo, quail, nightingale, trumpet, drum, rattle, and triangle. It is now thought to be the work of Mozart's father, Leopold (1719–87), or of Michael Haydn. See K. Geiringer, *Haydn,* rev. ed. (1963), p. 316.

Tpt. Abbr. for trumpet.

Tr. Abbr. for trill, treble, transpose.

Tracker action. In organs, the purely mechanical system of key action used in most organs constructed before 1900. It derives its name from the tracker, a wooden trace rod connecting the key to the pipe valve in the windchest. See Organ II, XI.   C.B.F.

Tract [L. *tractus*]. In Gregorian chant, an item of the Proper of the *Mass, used instead of the Alleluia for various feasts during Lent, for Ember days, and for the Requiem Mass. It consists of two to fourteen psalm verses, without the addition of an antiphon or response, and thus is one of the few remaining examples of direct psalmody [see Psalmody I]. All the Tracts are in either the second or eighth mode, a restriction not elsewhere encountered in Gregorian chant. Also, the Tracts are sung to a limited number of standard melodies (actually, standard phrases), which are used, with minor modifications, for a large number of texts. The principle is illustrated in the two subsequent schemes, (1) for the Tract "Attende caelum," (2) for "Sicut cervus" (I, II, etc., indicate the different verses; a, b, etc., various musical phrases):

	I	II	III	IV	V
(1)	a b c	d e c	e c	d e c	d f
(2)	a e c	d e c g	d e c f		

This method, called centonization [see Cento], is reminiscent of the use of *melody types in many kinds of non-Western music and probably reflects a very early stage in the development of the chant. In the recent edition of the *Liber usualis* some tracts (e.g., "Attende caelum," "Sicut cervus," and "Cantemus Domino" [*LU,* pp. 776U; 776BB; 776R]) are named canticles, and others (e.g., those of Good Friday) responsories. See H. Riemann, in *SIM* ix; *ApGC,* pp. 312ff.

Tragic Symphony. Subtitle provided by Schubert for his Symphony no. 4, in C minor, composed in 1816. The work is clearly more somber than his first three symphonies.

Tragische Ouvertüre [G., *Tragic Overture*]. Orchestral composition by Brahms, op. 81, composed in 1880 as a companion piece to the *Akademische Festouvertüre.*

Trait [F.]. *Tract.

Trakt [G.]. *Tract.

Traktur [G.]. *Tracker action.

Transcendental Etudes. See *Études d'exécution transcendante.*

Transcription. See Arrangement.

Transfigured Night. See *Verklärte Nacht.*

Transformation of themes. The modification of a musical subject with a view to "changing its personality." This is a 19th-century device that differs markedly from earlier, more "technical" methods of modification, as, e.g., the augmentation and diminution of a fugal subject, or the ornamentation of a theme. A characteristic example is the various appearances of the *idée fixe* in Berlioz' *Symphonie fantastique.* Liszt exploited

the principles of "transformation des thèmes" in his symphonic poems, and Wagner applied it to the *leitmotiv of his operas [see Ex. 1a, 1b, both from *Götterdämmerung*]. In Sibelius' symphonies the metamorphosis is more abstract, as shown in Ex. 2a, b, c (Symphony no. 5, first movt.).

Transient modulation. Same as passing *modulation.

Transition. (1) Same as passing *modulation. (2) A lasting change of key effected abruptly rather than through regular modulation. (3) A passage (bridge) that leads from one main section to another, e.g., from the first to the second theme of a movement.

Transitorium. An item of the Ambrosian Mass [see Ambrosian chant], corresponding to the Roman Communion.

Transmutatio [L.]. In the 13th-century theory of rhythmic modes, *transmutatio modi* means the transfer of a given composition (clausula, motet, hocket, conductus) from one mode to another, most frequently from mode 1 to mode 2 or vice versa. This practice is mentioned by Anonymous IV [*CS* i, 350] and other late 13th-century theorists. See *AdHM* i, 237; M. F. Bukofzer, in *AnnM* i, 90.

Transposing instruments. Instruments for which the music is written in a key or octave other than that of their actual sound. This method is widely used for wind instruments, such as the clarinet in B♭, whose natural tones are the harmonics of B♭. Since for the player of this instrument B♭ is the simplest key, it has become customary to present this key to him in the simplest notation, i.e., C major. The transposition to be made from the written part to the actual sound is indicated by the interval from C to the pitch note of the instrument, e.g., to B♭ in the case of the B♭ clarinet, A in that of the A clarinet [see Ex., Bruckner, Symphony no. 7]. With certain instruments the transposition includes a change to the lower octave, e.g., for the horn in E♭.

Clarinet in A: 1. As written. 2. As it sounds.

The use of transposing instruments or, more accurately, transposing notation, dates from the time when only natural tones were available (18th cent.). With the introduction of valves and keys the difference in facility for playing various keys was greatly diminished and eventually almost eliminated. As a result, today transposed notation might in a sense be considered obsolete. However, in cases where the *tone color of a particularly pitched instrument is desired (e.g., the same pitch on a B♭ trumpet is "richer" than on a D trumpet) transposed notation is much more convenient for the player although, of course, it presents an obstacle to the conductor, who may have to read as many as six or seven different types of transposed notation in a single orchestral score.

Nearly all the wind instruments not pitched in C are transposing instruments, except for the trombones, which, although pitched to E♭, B♭, etc., are written as they sound. The term is also used for instruments such as the piccolo flute, which is, quite sensibly, notated an octave lower than it sounds, to avoid ledger lines. Here, the use of a special clef such as $\phi \atop 8$ would exclude the instrument from the category of transposing instruments. A number of 20th-century composers (Prokofiev, Schoenberg, Berg, Webern, *et al.*) have published nontransposed scores. Berg has even notated piccolo, contrabassoon, and double bass parts in their actual octaves. Many recent compositions are published in concert-pitch scores.

Transposition. I. *General.* Rewriting or *ex tempore* performance of a composition in another key, e.g., E-flat instead of the original D, etc. This practice is particularly common with songs in order to accommodate different voice ranges. A skilled accompanist can extemporize transposition. The easiest transposition is that of a semitone, e.g., from F to F-sharp, or from E to E-flat, since here most of the written notes remain unaltered and only a different signature has to be imagined. Transposition of a third or fourth calls for a thorough knowledge of harmonies, intervals, etc., and becomes increasingly difficult with music involving many modulations, chromatic alterations, etc.

II. *History.* Transposition is a basic part of ancient Greek theory [see Greece]. The Gregorian repertory contains a number of transposed chants, which close on one of the *affinales,* a, b, and c′. These were originally a fifth or a fourth lower and were transposed because they involved the semitonal cluster, f–f♯–g♯ or e♭–e–f (not, of course, in immediate succession), which could be notated only as b♭–b–c′, a fourth or a fifth higher [see *ApGC,* pp. 157ff]. The author of "Musica enchiriadis" repeatedly emphasizes the possibility of "diatonic" transposition at the distance of a whole tone or semitone [*GS* i, 156, 165]. This method is used in Josquin's *Missa L'Homme armé super voces musicales,* in which the "L'Homme armé" melody appears in six diatonic transpositions. In the 16th century, organists were expected to be proficient in transposing compositions. Detailed instruction for transposition is given in J. Bermudo's *Declaración de instrumentos musicales* (1555); O. Kinkeldey, *Orgel und Klavier* (1910), p. 17 and *passim;* G. Diruta's *Il Transilvano,* part ii (1609); and elsewhere. Giovanni Paolo Cima, in his *Partito de ricercari e canzoni alla Francese* (1606), gives instructions and examples for transposition through all the degrees of the chromatic scale. See A. Mendel, "Devices for Transposition in the Organ before 1600" (*AM* xxi).

Transverse flute [F. *flute traversière;* G. *Querflöte;* It. *flauto traverso;* Sp. *flauta traversa*]. The modern flute, as opposed to the recorder. See Flute.

Traps. (1) In dance or theater orchestras, devices used for special effects (e.g., whistles, whip crack, ratchet, cowbell, etc.), usually notated for the percussion section, although many of the devices are not, strictly speaking, percussion instruments. (2) In jazz, term for both the devices in (1) and the complete "set of drums," which then includes such devices along with actual percussion instruments.

Traquenard. A dance found in German orchestral suites [see Suite V] of the late 17th century, e.g., by Georg Muffat [see *DTO* 4, p. 188], J. K. F. Fischer [see *DdT* 10, p. 54], P. H. Erlebach, J. P. Krieger, and others. In French *traquenard* means a horse's ambling gait, and the dotted rhythm of the music, usually in *alla breve,* evidently imitates this movement. See P. Nettl, in *StM* viii, 93f.

Trascinando [It.]. Dragging, slowing.

Trattenuto [It.]. Delayed, slowed down.

Trauermusik [G.]. Funeral music. *Trauermarsch,* funeral march.

Trauer-Ode [G., Funeral Ode.]. Choral work by Bach, written in 1727 on the death of the Electress Christiane of Saxony. It is based on an ode by Gottsched and is in the form of a cantata.

Trauer-Symphonie [G., Mourning Symphony]. Popular name (because of its somber character)

for Haydn's Symphony no. 44 (*c.* 1771), in E minor.

Träumerisch [G.]. Dreamy.

Trautonium. See under Electronic instruments.

Traverso [It.], **traversière** [F.], **Traversflöte** [G.]. See under Flute III.

Traviata, La [It., The Erring One]. Opera in three acts by Verdi (libretto by F. M. Piave after Dumas' *La Dame aux camélias*), produced in Venice, 1853. Setting: Paris and environs, about 1850. *Traviata* is one of the earliest instances of the use of a contemporary plot in opera, a practice that became established, *c.* 1890, by the *verismo movement. Musically it follows the tradition of the *grand opéra,* a mixture of lyrical and pathetic elements, with popular melodies and concentration on effective vocal numbers. *Rigoletto and *Trovatore belong to the same category.

Traynour. According to the 14th-century theorist Philippus de Caserta, the use of conflicting rhythmic groupings in different voice-parts, e.g., nine or three notes against two, four notes against three, etc. [see *CS* iii, 123]. This was a common practice toward the end of the 14th century. See *ReMR,* p. 31f; W. Apel, *French Secular Music of the Late Fourteenth Century* (1950), p. 8.

Tre [It.]. Three. *A tre voci,* in three parts. *Tre corde,* see *Una corda.*

Treble. The highest part of a choral composition, hence synonym of soprano. However, treble clef is not the same as soprano clef [see Clef]. For treble viol, recorder, see under Descant. For the early (15th cent.) meaning of the term, see under Sight.

Trecanum. An item of the *Gallican Mass, corresponding to the Roman Communion.

Tredezime [G.]. The interval of the thirteenth, i.e., the compound *sixth.

Treibend [G.]. Hurrying.

Tremblement. The most important of the French *agréments* of the 17th and 18th centuries, more commonly known as *trill.   P.A.

Tremolo [It.]. I. In stringed instruments, the quick reiteration of the same tone, produced by a rapid up-and-down movement of the bow, indicated as in Ex. a. The string tremolo is an important orchestral effect, widely used for dramatic passages or for the purpose of orchestral coloring. It appeared in some of the earliest compositions for the violin (B. Marini, *Affetti musicali*, 1617; see *RiHM* ii.2, 101). Monteverdi, in his *Combattimento di Tancredi e Clorinda* (1624; *HAM,* no. 189), used it to express excitement and danger, for which it has since been used innumerable times, e.g., in Bach's St. Matthew Passion ("Und siehe da, der Vorhang im Tempel zerriss in zwei Stück"), in the oracle scene of Gluck's *Alceste,* etc. The term is also used for rapid alternation between two notes of a chord, usually a third apart, as in Ex. b, this being called a "fingered tremolo." Some 18th-century names for the string tremolo are *bombo* [It.] and *Schwärmer* [G.].

In violin music of the 18th century (J. W. A. Stamitz, Gluck, Haydn) a special tremolo, known as "undulating tremolo" [It. *ondeggiando;* F. *ondulé*], is much used. It produces a series of moderately fast pulses, usually four to a note. It was indicated by a wavy line extending over repeated eighth or quarter notes [see table under Ornamentation], a sign that is sometimes misinterpreted as indicating a vibrato. Beethoven used the undulating tremolo several times, e.g., in the theme of his Great Fugue, op. 133, where it is indicated by placing a tie over two successive notes of the same pitch [see Ex. c].

II. In keyboard instruments the tremolo is of much less importance. In organ music a tremolo effect is produced by the *tremulant stop, which changes the steady wind pressure into a pulsating one. In piano music the genuine tremolo is a device used mainly in highly virtuoso compositions, such as Liszt's *La Campanella,* where it also occurs in the form of quickly repeated octaves. In piano arrangements of orchestral compositions the tremolo of the strings is imitated by the rapid alternation of a note and its octave, sometimes also of its third and fifth. A famous passage in the third movement of Beethoven's Piano Sonata op. 110, which is usually referred to as an example of *Bebung, actually is an imitation of the undulating string tremolo,

indicated in the same manner as in the example from the Great Fugue [see Ex. d].

III. In singing, "tremolo" commonly means the excessive vibrato that leads to deviation of pitch. It usually results from lack of breath control and faulty control of singing muscles (in jaw, base of tongue). The true vocal tremolo, i.e., the quick reiteration of the same pitch, is an effect that is practically never used today. In early music, however, it was one of the most important ornaments. The *bistropha* and *tristropha* of Gregorian chant, which often occur in groups of five, six, or more notes of the same pitch [see, e.g., the Offertory "Anima nostra"; *LU,* p. 430], were originally performed as a rapid tremolo; indeed, Aurelianus Reomensis says that the *tristropha* is sung "as a rapid beat, like a vibrating hand" [*GS* i, 57]. Other 13th-century terms, such as *repercussio gutturis* and *reverberatio* [see *CS* i, 91], seem to indicate a vocal tremolo [also see *Plica*]. In the early 17th century the vocal tremolo was widely used; called *trillo,* it was usually written out in quick notes [see Ex. e, from Benedetto Ferrari's *Musiche varie a voce sola,* books i–iii (1633–41); see also *GD* v, 20 (Caccini); *GD* iv, 234, *GDB* vi, 885 (Walter Porter); *RiHM* ii.2, 28, 297 (Caccini, C. Saracini)]. During this period, the term *tremolo* meant a trill; see Ornamentation I.

In the 18th century the vocal tremolo fell into disuse and was henceforth known by such derogatory names as *chevrotement* [F.] and *Bockstriller* [G.], which liken it to the bleating of a goat.

Tremulant. An organ stop producing alternating increases and decreases of wind pressure, thus causing a rapid fluctuation of pitch, an expressive effect similar to the violinist's vibrato. Although considerably abused during the period of the theater and orchestral organ, to the point where it became anathema to purists, it existed in French and German organs of the baroque period and, when properly regulated and judiciously used, it has a legitimate musical function in the literature of the baroque, romantic, and contemporary periods.   rev. B.J.O.

Trenchmore. An English country dance of the 16th and 17th centuries, in lively triple meter with dotted rhythms. An amusing description from 1689, showing that its only rival in popularity at the court of King Charles was the cushion dance, is quoted in *GD* (and *GDB*).

Trent, Council of. See Council of Trent.

Trent Codices [G. *Trienter Codices*]. Seven MS volumes of 15th-century polyphonic music, the first six of which were discovered by F. X. Haberl in the library of the Cathedral of Trent (in northern Italy, also famous for the *Council of Trent) and described in his *Bausteine für Musikgeschichte: I. Wilhelm du Fay* (1885). In 1891 they were purchased by the Austrian government but became Italian state property through the Treaty of St. Germain of 1918 and are now back in Trent (Castel del Buonconsiglio). The first six volumes (Cod. 87–92) contain 1,585 compositions, mostly from the mid-15th century; a seventh volume, discovered later, contains mostly duplicates. The major part of the collection was copied by Johannes Wiser for Bishop Johannes Hinderbach. This collection, by far the most extensive source of 15th-century music, contains compositions by about 75 French, English, Italian, and German composers, e.g., Dunstable, Lionel Power, Reginald Liebert, J. Ciconia, J. Brassart, Dufay, Binchois, Ockeghem, Busnois, and Isaac. A large selection has been published in six volumes of *DTO* [*Editions XV]: nos. 14/15 and 22 (all the French, Italian, and German secular songs); 38 (five complete Masses); 53 (Mass of Reginald Liebert, motets, antiphons, hymns); 61 (Masses and Mass sections by various composers); 76 (sacred and secular motets by Dunstable, Dufay, Brassart, De Vitry, and others).

Lit.: G. Adler, "Über Textlegung in den 'Trienter Codices'" (*CP Riemann*); R. von Ficker, "Die Kolorierungstechnik der Trienter Messen" (*StM* vii); A. Orel, "Einige Grundformen der Motettkomposition im XV. Jahrhundert" (*StM* vii); R. Wolkan, "Die Heimat der Trienter Musikhandschriften" (*StM* viii).

Trepak. A Cossack dance in quick duple time.

Trésor musical. See Editions L.

Trezza. A dance in some German suites of the 17th century, e.g., the ballets of J. H. Schmelzer [see *DTO* 56, p. 9]. It is similar to the *courante or *galliard.

Triad [G. *Dreiklang*]. A chord of three notes consisting of a root and the third and fifth above it. There are four kinds of triad: major (major plus minor third); minor (minor plus major third); diminished (minor plus minor third); and augmented (major plus major third). The first two are consonant and the last two dissonant chords. Each triad (e.g., c–e–g) has two inver-

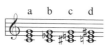

Triads: a. major. b. minor. c. diminished. d. augmented.

sions, the *sixth chord (e–g–c') and the *six-four chord (g–c'–e').

The triad is the basis of the harmonic practice of the 17th to 19th centuries. See Harmony II; Harmonic analysis II. In the earliest three-part writing (13th-century organa, motets, conductus) the harmonic structure consists mainly of pure consonances, 1–5–5, 1–1–5, 1–5–8; full triads occur only sporadically. Thus, the *organum triplum* "Hec dies" (Perotinus?; see *HAM*, no. 31) contains, among *c.* two hundred chords, eleven triads. However, the Englishman Walter Odington was the only theorist writing about 13th-century practices to recognize the triad, both major and minor, as a consonant chord [*CS* i, 202b]. English compositions from *c.* 1300 use considerably more triads [see, e.g., "Alleluia psallat"; *HAM*, no. 57]. One of them, a four-voice "Pro beati Pauli," closes with 1–3–5–1, and *"Sumer is icumen in" has a 1–3–5–8 in nearly every measure. French compositions of the 14th century also used more triads, but rarely at the end of phrases and almost never at the end of a composition. As late as 1500 the inclusion of the third in the final chord was unusual [see Picardy third]. A remarkable exception is the *Missa Virgo Parens Christo* by Jacques Barbireau (*c.* 1408–91), in which every movement closes with a full triad [*Editions XII, 7].

Trial of Lucullus, The. One-act opera by R. Sessions (libretto by B. Brecht), produced in Berkeley, California, 1947.

Triangle. See under Percussion instruments B, 5.

Tricesimoprimal temperament. Division of the octave into thirty-one equal steps, advocated in the 17th century by Christiaan Huygens and revived, mainly by Dutch composers and theorists, in the 20th. See Microtone.   E.S.

Tricinium [L.]. A 16th-century name for a vocal composition in three parts. There is a large repertory of such works in publications such as G. Rhaw, *Tricinia . . . Latina, Germanica, Brabantica, et Gallica* (1542); J. Montanus and U. Neuber, *Selectissimorum triciniorum discantus* (1560); Sethus Calvisius, *Tricinium* (1603; see *SchGMB*, no. 160); Melchior Franck, *Tricinia* *nova* (1611); Michael Praetorius, *Musae Sionae* (9 vols., 1605–10; vol. ix); and elsewhere. Praetorius' three-voice elaborations of chorale melodies in particular are true gems.

Trienter Codices [G.]. *Trent Codices.

Trigon. See under Neumes I.

Trihori(s). See Triori.

Trill [E., formerly *shake;* F. *cadence, tremblement;* G. *Triller;* It. *trillo;* Sp. *trino*]. A musical ornament consisting of the rapid alternation of a given note with the diatonic second above it.

I. The trill originated in the 16th century as an ornamental resolution of a suspension dissonance at a cadence. Ex. 1 shows various forms of the 16th-century trill: 1a and 1b represent the typical vocal cadence found in the works of Palestrina, Lassus, etc. The other variants occur

frequently in instrumental transcriptions of vocal works and in independent keyboard compositions. It is probable, however, that even in vocal performances the singers of this period customarily embellished the simple written cadence in this more elaborate manner.

The cadence formulas given above have the following characteristics in common: (1) the trill begins on the penultimate strong beat of the phrase, with a dissonant note (suspension or appoggiatura); (2) it consists chiefly of the alternation of that dissonant note with its resolution; (3) the dissonant note receives the accent throughout, since it coincides with the accented subdivisions of the beat; (4) the note below the resolution may be introduced, near either the beginning or the end of the trill.

These characteristics became the basis of the most important *agrément* of the 17th century, the French *cadence* or *tremblement,* which was adopted in Germany as the *Triller,* in England as the *shake,* and in Italy as the *trillo* [for the early meaning of this term, see Tremolo III]. As the French name implies, the ornament was at first (early 17th cent.) invariably associated with

cadences. Later it was freely introduced at other positions in the musical phrase, but until the end of the 18th century it retained its primary function as the ornamental resolution of a dissonance.

II. In music of the 17th and 18th centuries the trill, instead of being written out in notes or left to the improvisation of the performer (as had hitherto been the case), was often indicated in the score by one of the following signs:

$$tr \quad t \quad \text{ᴛᴡ} \quad \text{ᴍᴡ} \quad \text{ᴡ} \quad +$$

These signs are exactly synonymous; the use of one instead of another has no meaning in the performance of the ornament and reveals nothing but the composer's personal preference. Since the sign is always placed over the harmony note, the accent must always fall on the upper auxiliary, which, as the dissonance, requires the greater emphasis. Apart from this factor, which is constant throughout the period, the execution of the trill was varied considerably in individual cases by adding prefixes or terminations and by varying the number and rhythm of the notes comprising the ornament. In the time of Bach and Handel, three ways of ending the trill were almost equally popular [Ex. 2]. The use of a simple sign (t, tr) for the trill left the performer free to choose interpretation a, b, or c. If the composer desired a particular execution as at 2b or 2c, he used one of the notations shown here:

The number and rhythmic distribution of the notes comprising the trill were generally left entirely to the performer's discretion. Ex. 3

shows several realizations of a cadence formula that is particularly common in the works of J. S. Bach and his contemporaries. All these interpretations are equally correct according to the traditions of Bach's time; the choice among them should depend on the tempo and character of the passage in which the trill occurs. Obviously a greater number of notes should be used for a trill on a long note than for one on a short note. Interpretations in Ex. 3e and 3f are therefore more appropriate for a rapid tempo, and Ex. 3b, 3c, and 3d for a slow tempo. Also, the most expressive interpretations are those giving the most weight to the initial dissonance, as in Ex. 3d and 3e. Sometimes the composer expressly indicates dwelling on the introductory note of the trill, known in French as *tremblement appuyé* and in German as *vorbereiteter Triller,* by (1) inserting the sign for an appoggiatura, (2) prefixing a vertical stroke to the sign for the trill, or (3) writing the introductory appoggiatura as an ordinary note. The excerpts in Ex. 4 show J. S. Bach's use of all three procedures.

In the music of this period, trills on very short notes are best rendered as four notes of equal value, or, if the tempo is too rapid to permit this, the trill should rather be abbreviated to two notes, i.e., a single appoggiatura, with which it is, in a sense, synonymous. In no case must the

trill be reduced to a triplet beginning with the main note, for the accent would then fall on the wrong note. [See under Turn.]

III. The beginning of a trill is often varied by the addition of a prefix, which may be indicated by one or more small notes or by a modification of the ordinary sign for the trill. The number of small notes used in the notation of the prefix

does not affect the interpretation. A hook extending down from the beginning of the trill sign indicates a prefix starting below the main note; a hook extending up represents an introductory turn beginning with the upper auxiliary [Ex. 5]. The prefix from below is especially

common; indeed, throughout the 18th century, it was customary to start a long trill with such a prefix, even when not indicated, whenever the main note was approached conjunctly from below, as in the illustrated passage from Beethoven's Piano Sonata op. 10, no. 3 [Ex. 6].

IV. The modern trill, which begins with the main note, was first introduced early in the 19th century by the Viennese pianists J. N. Hummel, Czerny, and Moscheles. It is usually played with a two-note termination [G. *Nachschlag*]. This

trill no longer fulfills the appoggiatura function with which the ornament had been associated for nearly two centuries; it is a virtuoso effect and serves merely to accentuate the main note or add brilliance or color to the performance, as shown in Ex. 7 [a. Chopin, *Bolero;* b. Liszt, *Hungarian Rhapsody* no. 14].

The "main note" trill did not entirely supplant the traditional form, which often appears in the works of Chopin, Schumann, and Liszt. It is customary, however, in the romantic and modern periods, for the composer to indicate the first note of the trill by means of a small grace note. In the absence of such an indication the trill should begin on the main note.

The "main note" trill also occurs in early Italian music, usually as an ornamenting prolongation of a single pitch, as in Ex. 8 (Mayone, 1603). In a MS from about 1620 it occurs repeat-

8

edly in its 19th-century form, leading to the upper second and therefore including an uneven number of notes [Ex. 8b, c].   P.A.; add. by W.A.

Triller [G.]. *Trill. Trillerkette,* chain or series of trills.

Trillo [It.]. *Trill. In the 17th century, the true vocal tremolo [see Tremolo III].

Trinklied [G.]. Drinking song.

Trio [It.]. (1) Originally, a contrapuntal composition in three parts. This meaning applies to Bach's six sonatas for the organ [see Trio sonata] as well as the three-voice pieces in Hindemith's *Reihe kleiner Stücke,* op. 37.

(2) In the scherzo or minuet movement of the *sonata, the middle section played between the scherzo (minuet) and its repetition [see Scherzo]. For its use in the march, see March. The term "trio" comes from the 17th-century custom of writing minuets and other dances in three parts, frequently for two oboes and bassoon (Lully), a treatment that was used particularly for the second of two dances played alternately, resulting in the arrangement *Menuet, Menuet en trio, Menuet.* A good example is Bach's Brandenburg Concerto no. 1, in which the minuet is fully orchestrated whereas the trio is written for two oboes and bassoon. The accompanying example, from Bach's French Suite no. 6, shows the use of the same type of trio for harpsichord. As late as Haydn, Mozart, and Beethoven (e.g., Symphony no. 7), the trio

usually retained the lighter texture and woodwind character of Lully's trio. Schubert and others used the term for the middle section of compositions in ternary form. See E. Blom, in *ML* xxii, 162ff.

(3) Chamber music for three players. The most important type is the piano trio, for piano, violin, and cello. In most of Haydn's 31 trios the violin and cello are chiefly reinforcements for the piano part. Mozart's 7 piano trios (K. 254, K. 496, K. 498, K. 502, K. 542, K. 548, K. 564) show greater individuality of the parts, paving the way for such great works as Beethoven's op. 70 and op. 97, and Schubert's op. 99 and op. 100. The standard trio repertory also includes those of Schumann (3), Mendelssohn (2), Brahms (3), Dvořák (3), Franck (4), Fauré (1), Ravel (1), and others. The string trio, usually for violin, viola, and cello, has attracted far fewer composers. After Haydn's 20 trios (for two violins and cello) came a divertimento by Mozart (K. 563), Beethoven's op. 3, 9, 87, and a few later compositions. See W. Altmann, *Handbuch für Klaviertriospieler; Wegweiser durch die Trios für Klavier, Violine und Violoncell* (1934).

Triole [G.], **triolet** [F.]. *Triplet.

Trionfo di Afrodite [It., Triumph of Aphrodite]. *Concerto scenico* by C. Orff (to his own Latin and Greek libretto, after Catullus, Sappho, and Euripides), produced in Milan, 1953. Setting: timeless.

Trionfo di Dori, Il. See under *Triumphes of Oriana.*

Triori (also *trihory, trihoris,* etc.). A 16th-century Breton dance, described by Arbeau in his *Orchésographie* (1589) as a kind of branle in duple meter.

Trio sonata. The most important type of baroque chamber music, written in three parts, two upper parts of similar range and design and a supporting figured-bass part. The trio sonata is usually performed on four instruments, two violins (or, in the earlier period, viols, cornetti) for the two upper parts, a cello (viola da gamba, violone) for the bass part, and a harpsichord (organ, theorbo) for the bass part together with the realization of the thoroughbass accompaniment. Other instrumentation was occasionally employed, e.g., in Biagio Marini's Sonatas for violin and organ, op. 8 (1626), in which the organ has two written parts; in Bach's six organ trios, written for organ alone in three parts without thoroughbass figures; and in G. B. Bononcini's op. 4 (1686), for which there are five partbooks, first and second violin, cello, theorbo, and organ. Throughout the 17th century there were trio sonatas written in four voices, the cello part becoming somewhat different from the bass part for the harpsichord [see Tommaso A. Vitali, *Sonate a tre*, 1693]. There even were orchestral trio sonatas, sometimes entitled Sinfonia. In all these cases, however, the writing is essentially in three parts, and it is this texture that is indicated in the customary designation *a tre*.

Early three-voice compositions, mostly in the form and style of the instrumental *canzona, were written by Salomone Rossi (*Il Terzo Libro de varie sonate*, 1623), G. B. Buonamente (Books 4, 5, 7 of *Sonate*, 1626–37), Tarquinio Merula, Marini, and others [see Editions III, 7]. Toward the end of the 17th century two types of trio sonata developed, the *sonata da chiesa* (church sonata) and the *sonata da camera* (chamber sonata). The trio style became popular particularly in France, where it was known as *sonate en trio*. The form persisted into the classical period, the last examples being by Gluck (1746), the *Mannheim school, and Haydn [*Six Sonates à deux violins & basse*, op. 8, *c.* 1766]. Thereafter it changed into the classical trio for three instruments, with a fully written out part for piano [see Trio (3)].

The literature of the trio sonata includes most of the illustrious names of the late baroque, among them Corelli (48, op. 1–4), Purcell (12), Buxtehude, Handel (28, 6 of which are for two oboes and bass), F. Couperin (14), and Vivaldi (12). Bach wrote only a few trio sonatas of the standard type (i.e., for two melody instruments and thoroughbass accompaniment), one in the *Musikalisches Opfer* and several others. His sonatas for two violins and harpsichord as well as his organ sonatas represent the trio sonata with three obbligato parts, i.e., without thoroughbass accompaniment. However, the fact that the opening measures of the third movement of one (*BWV* 1036) have thoroughbass figures suggests (along with some other considerations) that a second, "accompanying" harpsichord was used to play the main notes of the bass part and improvise the chordal accompaniment. See H. Hoffmann, *Die Norddeutsche Triosonate* (1929). See also under Sonata.

Tripla. (1) Term in mensural notation, i.e., *proportio tripla;* see Proportions. (2) Same as *Proportz.* (3) Plural of *triplum* [see *Duplum*].

Triple concerto. A concerto for three solo instruments, such as Bach's two concertos for three harpsichords, and Beethoven's concerto for violin, cello, and piano, op. 56.

Triple counterpoint. See Invertible counterpoint.

Triple-croche [F.]. See under Notes.

Triple fugue. See under Double fugue.

Triplet [F. *triolet;* G. *Triole;* It. *terzina;* Sp. *tresillo*] A group of three notes to be performed in place of two of the same kind, indicated by a 3 and, usually, a slur:

$$\flat\flat = \overset{3}{\flat\flat\flat}$$

For the indication of triplet rhythm by dotted notes, see Dotted notes II (a).

Triple time. Triple meter [see Meter].

Triplum. See under *Duplum.*

Tris(h)agion [Gr.]. The Sanctus in its original, Greek version, which in turn is derived from the Jewish *kadusha,* the threefold "Kadosh" (Holy) from the Book of Isaiah 6:3. As early as *c.* A.D. 90, Pope Clement I mentioned in a letter "Hagios, Hagios, Hagios." About 500 it passed from the Greek to the Mozarabic and Gallican rites, where it was known as *Aius.* In the Roman rite it is used during the Adoration of the Cross on Good Friday, as a part of the *Improperia* [*LU*, p. 737]. It consists of three acclamations in Greek (*Agios o Theos,* etc.), each of which is answered antiphonally and to the same melody in the Latin translation (*Sanctus Deus,* etc.).

Tristan und Isolde. Opera in three acts by Richard Wagner (to his own libretto, based on G. von Strassburg), produced in Munich, 1865. Setting: aboard a ship, Cornwall, Brittany, in legendary times. *Tristan* is without doubt the fullest incarnation of romantic love ever presented in opera. Practically the whole second and third acts are an "unending love duet," in which every feeling and sensation, ranging from the tenderest to the most passionate, is portrayed. Owing to the relative simplicity of the plot, the *leitmotiv plays a secondary role in this opera (as compared with the *Ring), and the most conspicuous features of the music are the "unending melody" and a harmonic vocabulary full of daring chromatic progressions and bold appoggiaturas. In fact, so conspicuous are these traits that "Tristan melody" and "Tristan harmony" have become common terms.

Triste [Sp.]. Melancholy love song of Peruvian origin adopted in northern Argentina by the second half of the 19th century. The melody is predominantly pentatonic, although occasionally it follows patterns based on the European seven-note scale. The texts frequently combine Indian and Spanish words.   J.O-S.

Tristropha. See under Neumes I.

Trite [Gr.]. See under Greece II.

Tritone. The interval of the augmented fourth (c–f♯) or diminished fifth (c–g♭), so called because it spans three whole tones. It has always been considered a "dangerous" interval, to be avoided or treated with great caution [see *Diabolus in musica*]. As a melodic progression it was rarely used before 1900, except in combinations such as c–f♯–g, where f♯ is the leading tone before g. In modern music, however, it is a legitimate interval, e.g., in the *whole-tone scale or in various experimental devices based on the fact that the tritone is exactly one-half of the octave.

Tritonic progressions such as f–a–b–a are not uncommon in Gregorian chant, but most of them were later eliminated by the use of a B♭. Of particular interest is a standard cadential formula of the Graduals of mode 3, having the outline f–b–e and therefore involving a tritone whether sung with or without B♭ [see, e.g., "Eripe me," *LU*, p. 570f]. The formula f′–d′–b occurs in practically every Gradual of mode 2 [e.g., *Haec dies, LU*, p. 778f, on "e–a"]. Probably the first writer to forbid the melodic tritone was Guido d'Arezzo, who said that the *b rotundum* (B-flat) was added to the scale because the F has no *concordiam* with its fourth, being at the distance of a *tritonium* (*Micrologus*, ch. viii; in *GS* ii, 8). Later the tritone was subsumed under the rule *Mi contra fa, diabolus in musica* [see Mi-fa].

The vertical tritone plays an important role in the early organum of the fourth ("Musica enchiriadis," c. 900), where its *inconsonantia* led to the replacement of strictly parallel motion

[Ex. b] by oblique motion [Ex. a]. However, the sources of 13th- and 14th-century polyphonic music contain numerous instances like that in Ex. c. Ramos de Pareja said that using the tritone is not a "deadly sin" (*peccatum mortale*) but a necessity (*Musica practica*, 1482; ed. J. Wolf,

p. 50f). In classical harmony the tritone is allowed only in combination with other intervals, mainly in the seventh chord (c–e–g–b♭) and its inversions, the second of which is sometimes called tritone because it usually contains the interval in a particularly conspicuous position (e–b♭–c′–g′).

Trittico [It., Triptych]. A cycle of three independent one-act operas by Puccini, first produced together in New York, 1918: *Suor Angelica* (Sister Angelica; libretto by G. Forzano; setting, a convent near Siena, 17th century); *Gianni Schicchi* (libretto by G. Forzano, based on Dante; setting, bedroom of a house in Florence, 1299); *Il Tabarro* (The Cloak; libretto by G. Adami, after D. Gold's play *La Houppelande;* setting, a barge on the Seine, 19th century).

Tritus [L.]. See under Church modes I.

Triumphes of Oriana, The. A collection of English madrigals, published by Morley in imitation of an Italian collection of madrigals, *Il Trionfo di Dori* (1592), and dedicated to Queen Elizabeth. The book was scheduled to appear in 1601 but was not published until 1603, after the Queen's death. It contains twenty-nine madrigals in five or six parts, by Morley, Weelkes, Ellis Gibbons, and others, all of which close with the refrain "Long live fair Oriana" (in imitation of the refrain "Viva la bella Dori" in the *Trionfo*), except for the last three, which have the refrain "In Heaven lives Oriana." List of contents in *GD* v, 385; *GDB* viii, 550; repr. in *Editions XVI, 32.

Trochee, trochaic. See under Poetic meter I; Modes, rhythmic.

Trojans, The. See *Troyens, Les.*

Tromba [It.]. Trumpet, bugle. *T. a macchina* (*ventile*), valve trumpet. *T. bassa*, bass trumpet. *T. da tirarsi, t. spezzata* slide trumpet [see Trumpet II].

Tromba marina [It.]. A late medieval bowed instrument, still in use in the 18th century, that consisted of a tapering three-sided body, 5 to 6 feet long, over which a single string was stretched. The string was not stopped, as in violin playing, but lightly touched with one finger to produce harmonic notes, the bow playing above the "stopping" point (between it and the nut). Inside the long soundbox were a large number (up to twenty or more) of sympathetic strings that were tuned in unison with the playing string [see ill. accompanying Violin]. The most peculiar feature was the bridge, in the shape of a wide inverted U whose left foot, shorter than the right, was free to vibrate against the soundboard, resulting in a drumming noise (hence G. *Trumscheit,* drum log). While its trumpetlike sound probably accounts for the *tromba* part of the name, no explanation for *marina* has been found. The fantastic identification of *marina* with "marine" may have led to the name "sea-trumpet." The instrument was frequently used by nuns and hence another German name, *Nonnengeige* (nun's fiddle). The tenor marked "Trompette" in Pierre Fontaine's chanson "J'ayme bien celui" (*c.* 1400) was probably written for the tromba marina. [See P. Aubry, in *SIM* viii, 525f.] Antonio Vivaldi (*c.* 1669–1741) wrote solo parts for two tromba marinas in one of his concertos [see A. Schering, *Geschichte des Instrumentalkonzerts* (1905), p. 62], and the Swiss Johann M. Gletle (1626–84) wrote duets for the instrument (new ed. in A. Stern and W. Schuh, *Schweizer Sing- und Spielmusik* vi). A *Mémoire sur la trompette marine* by J. B. Prin of 1742 is reprinted in *BSIM* iv.2, 1176ff. For a detailed description of the instrument, see N. Bessaraboff, *Ancient European Musical Instruments* (1941), 317ff; also *SaHMI* 290ff [pl. XVIII, opp. p. 304]; *GD,* s.v. "Tromba marina"; *GDB,* s.v. "Trumpet marine."

Lit.: F. W. Galpin, "Monsieur Prin and his Trumpet Marine" (*ML* xiv, 18ff); *LavE* ii.3, 1757ff (bibl.); P. Garnault, *La Trompette marine* (1926).

Trombetta [It.]. Old name, used by Dante, for a small trumpet.

Trombone [G. *Posaune;* Sp. *trombón*]. I. The modern orchestral trombone is a brass instrument with a cylindrical bore except for the lower third of its length, which gradually expands into the bell, and a cup-shaped mouthpiece. It consists of two separate pieces, one made up of the mouthpiece, cylindrical bore, and bell, held together by a crossbar, and the other of a U-shaped middle piece that, by means of another crossbar, can be moved toward and away from the player and therefore is called slide. [See ill. under Brass instruments.] The slide takes the place of the valves used with other brass instruments and, like them, fills in the gaps of the natural tones [see Wind instruments IV (a)]. There are seven recognized positions (six plus the original one) of the slide, each a semitone lower, changing the natural tuning of the trombone successively from, e.g., B-flat to A, A-flat, etc. The range for each position is about two octaves (B_1^b–B^b–b^b for the normal position), but the lowest note of this series, called pedal tone, is difficult to produce in the three lowest positions. Since the movement from position to position requires a certain amount of time, a true legato cannot be executed on the trombone. On the other hand, a *glissando (properly termed *portamento) can. This effect has been used by some composers for comic purposes.

The trombone may be regarded as the bass of the trumpet although its tone is more dignified and solemn and less brilliant. This difference in tone color is due mainly to the trombone's larger mouthpiece. Trombones have been made in many sizes, ranging from soprano to contrabass, and in many keys. The four types used in the modern orchestra are:

(a) Tenor trombone. It is pitched in B-flat and has a complete chromatic compass as shown in Ex. a, in addition to which four pedal tones,

shown in Ex. b, are available. It is notated at its sounding pitch (not transposing as, e.g., the horn).

(b) Bass trombone. It is pitched in F, although instruments pitched in G or E-flat may be used in England. Its compass is a fourth below that of the tenor trombone. Owing to the great length of the pipe the slides are difficult to handle, and today the instrument is generally replaced by the tenor-bass trombone.

(c) Tenor-bass trombone. It has the size (and pitch) of the tenor trombone but the bore of the bass trombone, which facilitates playing pedal tones and makes the sound similar to the bass trombone's. It has a single valve that lowers the pitch a fourth (B^b to F), i.e., to that of the bass trombone. The tenor-bass trombone has virtually supplanted the bass trombone in the modern orchestra.

(d) Contrabass trombone. It is pitched an octave below the tenor trombone (British instruments are sometimes pitched in C). The difficulty caused by the great length of its pipe was overcome in 1816 (by Gottfried Weber) with the invention of the "double slide," the pipe being bent into four parallel tubes. Wagner used it in his *Ring des Nibelungen* and other composers have followed his example (e.g., D'Indy in *Jour d'été à la montagne*). It is, however, very tiring to play, owing to the great strain on the player's lungs and lips.

Occasionally valve trombones have been made (used by D'Indy in *Le Chant de la cloche*). Their tone, however, is less noble than that of the slide trombone.

II. *History*. The trombone was the first of the modern orchestral instruments to appear in its present shape. It developed in the 15th century from a large trumpet (hence the name *trombone*, i.e., large *tromba*) through the addition of a slide, and the earliest representations, in paintings of the late 15th century, show all the essentials of the present instrument. The German name *Posaune* points to another line of descent, the large and straight *buisine*, a name that in turn goes back to L. **buccina* [see E. A. Bowles, *AMW* xviii, 63ff]. The medieval name for the trombone was *sackbut* (derived from the old Spanish *sacabuche*, "draw tube," or from old French *sacqueboute*, "pull-push"). Throughout the 16th century trombones were commonly used in the ceremonial bands of princes and large cities as well as in churches. Their sliding mechanism made them suitable for performing art music at a time when horns and trumpets were still limited to the performance of military signals. Owing to the narrower bell of the old trombones, their sound was relatively soft and therefore combined well with voices and other instruments. They were, no doubt, often used for the performance of sustained tenors in the isorhythmic motets of the 14th and 15th centuries. Several compositions of the early 15th century have lower parts marked *trompetta* or *tuba* [see H. Besseler, "Die Entstehung der Posaune," in *AM* xxii]. G. Gabrieli's *Sacrae symphoniae* of 1597 are scored for cornetti, trombones, bassoons, and strings [see Orchestra II]. Michael Praetorius, in his *Theatrum instrumentorum* (1620), *Syntagma musicum,* ii, part 6, included illustrations of alto, tenor, and bass

trombones, called *Alt Posaun, Rechte gemeine* (right common) *Posaun,* and *Quart-Posaun* respectively. Bach and Handel used the instrument occasionally, but mostly in unison with voices for the sake of greater sonority. Gluck was perhaps the first to make effective use of the trombone for accompanying chords, e.g., in the aria "Divinité du Styx" from *Alceste,* and Mozart gave the trombones a prominent place in his *Zauberflöte* and *Don Giovanni.* Beethoven introduced the trombones into symphonic music in the final movement of his Fifth Symphony, but it was not until after 1850, with Berlioz and Wagner, that the trombone became firmly established as a member of the orchestra. In the 20th century the trombone has been used as a solo instrument with orchestra and in chamber music combinations by A. Hovhaness, H. Cowell, Stravinsky, Poulenc, and Hindemith.

Lit.: W. Worthmüller, *Die Instrumente der Nürnberger Trompeten- und Posaunenmacher* (*Mitteilungen des Vereins für Geschichte der Stadt Nürnberg,* 1955); id., *Die Nürnberger Trompeten- und Posaunenmacher des 17. und 18. Jhs.* (*Mitteilungen des Vereins für Geschichte der Stadt Nürnberg,* 1954); H. Besseler, "Die Entstehung der Posaune" (*AM* xxii); C. Sachs, "Chromatic Trumpets in the Renaissance" (*MQ* xxxvi); F. W. Galpin, "The Sackbut, Its Evolution and History" (*PMA* xxxiii); F. Jahn, "Die Nürnberger Trompeten- und Posaunenmacher im 16. Jahrhundert" (*AMW* vii).

Trommel [G.]. Drum [see Percussion instruments B, 1–3]. *Trommelschlegel,* drumstick.

Trommelbass [G.]. Pejorative name for stereotyped bass figures, such as the piano tremolo in octaves.

Trompete [G.], **trompette** [F.]. Trumpet. *Trompette à coulisse,* slide trumpet.

Trompetengeige [G.]. **Tromba marina.*

Troparia. See under Byzantine chant II.

Troparium [L.]. See Troper.

Trope [L. *tropus*]. (1) In certain medieval treatises, designation for church mode: see Tonus (3), Tropus. (2) Term used by J. M. Hauer (b. 1883) in a kind of twelve-tone system devised by him. In his *Zwölftontechnik* (1926), which differs from that of Schoenberg [see Serial music] and has not been generally accepted, Hauer divides each series of twelve notes into two hexachords and groups all the series having the same notes in each of the hexachords into a class called *trope.* Thus, one such trope (no. 44) contains all series beginning with the tones c d e f♯ g♯ a♯ (in any order) and closing with c♯ d♯ f g a b (in any order). There are 44 tropes, and each represents, in a sense, a key with two fundamental chords, the change from one trope to another then being comparable to modulation.

(3) A category of plainchant that flourished from the 10th through the 12th centuries, comprising musical and textual additions to the established repertory of Mass (both Proper and Ordinary) and Office chants. The classic definition is that of Léon Gautier, "l'interpolation d'un texte liturgique" [*Les Tropes,* 1886]. The methods of interpolation are now often designated [e.g., in *ApGC*] as: (a) the addition of a new text to a melisma of a traditional "Gregorian" chant; (b) the composition of a new melody and text, which is then sung together with a traditional chant in various ways, before and/or after it, or by alternation of the phrases of the trope with those of the original chant, or, in the case of a short text like the "Benedicamus Domino," embedding the few original words or their synonyms in an elaborate new melody and text; (c) an independently composed melody without text added to an item of the standard repertory. However, such a precise classification falsely implies a far greater knowledge of the quite large and still not thoroughly studied repertory of medieval tropes, not to speak of their prehistory, than we actually possess. It is particularly difficult to apply it to the highly original (in melody and text) and numerous group of Ordinary tropes (especially, but not only, the Kyrie), which first appeared in musical notation in late 10th- or early 11th-century chant books. Before this there may have been a primitive unadorned melody to which the trope was added, but this assumption cannot be proved. The question arises whether the *entire* text and melody may not have been first composed in the elaborate, troped form. It should be observed that, although the unadorned Ordinary texts are very old and were surely used liturgically before Carolingian times, by either the *schola* or the congregation, the music of the simple Ordinary chants also may be considered an accretion to the traditional sung liturgy; such untroped Ordinary chants appear no earlier than the tropes, and in the same collections.

The practice of appending or interpolating long untexted melismas to pre-existing liturgical chant is thought by some scholars (e.g., B. Stäb-

lein, J. Handschin) to date from long before the 9th century. In any event, Amalar of Metz (*c.* 775–*c.* 850) provides, in various works between A.D. 823 and 844, the first substantial evidence for what appear to be tropes of the Alleluia (i.e., sequences, probably without text), Kyrie ("Kyrie eleison Domine pater miserere"), and responsory (a *neuma triplex,* i.e., a thrice-repeated melisma, is mentioned as having been transferred from its original use with the responsory "In medio ecclesiae" to the responsory "Descendit de caelis"). The first composers of tropes known by name are two monks of St. Gall, Notker (Balbulus; *c.* 840–912) and Tuotilo (d. 915). The former is associated with the *sequence, which, although it is a trope in a broad sense, has been studied separately, perhaps because it rapidly became an independent component of the Mass. The best known of Tuotilo's works is the trope "Hodie cantandus" [*SchGMB,* no. 3] to the Introit for the third Mass of Christmas; it has often been cited as a forerunner of the *liturgical drama. It is clear that Notker was no innovator, but rather a refiner of a technique transmitted to St. Gall from northern France about the middle of the 9th century. This may also be true of Tuotilo's work. Some 19th-century scholars overemphasized the originality of St. Gall; shortly after 1900 the situation was reversed [cf. particularly the introductory essay by C. Blume and H. Bannister to *Analecta hymnica* liii] and since then France, with special but not exclusive emphasis on St. Martial de Limoges, has been considered the cradle of the sequence, and possibly also the trope. The existence of very early (10th-century) *tropers from Aquitaine is a significant point of evidence; however, there is a group of important early tropers from St. Gall as well. The later history of the trope parallels that of the sequence, particularly in the increased degree of poetic and tonal regularity. All the tropes were abolished by the *Council of Trent. Their traces survive, however, in the present-day names of many Kyries [see Kyrie] and the corresponding Mass Ordinaries, e.g., *Missa Cunctipotens genitor* for Mass IV [see Mass A]. It should be observed that, in the Middle Ages, an Ordinary chant in its troped form was often proper to a particular feast or local saint.

(4) In musicological research, the term "troping" is also used in connection with the polyphonic elaborations of liturgical chants. For instance, the early motet may be considered a "polyphonic trope" (or "vertical trope"), since

here a new text, elaborating upon the idea of the original chant in the tenor, is used for the upper parts. Finally, the process of troping can also be observed in trouvère music, in which new texts were interpolated between the two halves of a refrain, a procedure that is believed to have been the origin of the *rondeau (Gennrich) and that is clearly evident in the *motets entés* [see Enté]. See *Prosula*.   (1) and (3) rev. L.G.

Lit.: *ApGC*, pp. 429ff; J. Chailley, *L'École musicale de Saint Martial de Limoges* [1960]; J. Handschin, in *NOH* ii (1954), pp. 128–74; *id.*, in *ZMW* x; R. Weakland, in *MQ* xliv (beginnings); H.-J. Holman, in *JAMS* xvi (responsory tropes); P. Evans, in *JAMS* xiv (origin); B. Stäblein, in *CP 1961* (text underlay); *id.*, in *AM* xxxv ("classical" tropes). See the summaries (Waesberghe) in *KJ* 1962, p. 68, *KJ* 1963, p. 17, *KJ* 1964, p. 131. Also see Troper.
(1) and (3) rev. L.G.

Troper [L. *troparium*]. A liturgical book containing tropes. The oldest extant tropers are those from St. Martial (10th, 11th centuries). An 11th-century English MS known as the Winchester Troper (Cambridge, Corpus Christi College, MS *473*) is of particular importance because it contains, in a separate section entitled *Melliflua organorum modulamina*, organa for more than 150 chants, making it by far the most extensive source of early organum. Unfortunately, it is written in nondiastematic neumes that cannot be deciphered with total certainty. See W. H. Frere, ed., *The Winchester Troper* (1894); H. Husmann, *Tropen- und Sequenzenhandschriften* (*RISM*, ser. B, i [1954]); J. Handschin, "The Two Winchester Tropers" (*Journal of Theological Studies* xxxvii); A. Machabey, "Remarques sur le Winchester Troper" (*CP Besseler*); G. Weiss, "Zum Problem der Gruppierung südfranzösischer Tropare" (*AMW* xxi).

Troppo [It.]. Too (much). *Allegro non troppo*, not too fast.

Tropus. In medieval treatises, designation for mode or scale. See *Tonus*.

Troubadour. Name for any of a large number of 12th- and 13th-century poet-musicians of southern France (Provence), who were the first in Western history to establish a tradition of songs in the vernacular. Their Provençal name was *trobador*, possibly derived from *tropator*, i.e., writer of tropes. The movement was begun by Guilhem IX, seventh Count of Poitiers

(fl. 1087–1127), and included members of the French nobility as well as commoners, all devoted to poetry and music in the service of chivalrous love. In the mid-12th century it spread to northern France (*trouvères) and Germany (*minnesingers). Scholars do not agree about the origins of this movement. Arab-Spanish models as well as Carolingian love lyrics and liturgical hymns in honor of the Virgin Mary all have been cited as sources. Very likely each contributed certain elements. Another question is to what extent the noblemen were assisted by jongleurs. Probably the practice varied in different cases. Among the troubadours whose melodies survive are Guilhem IX, Marcabru, a commoner (d. *c.* 1150), Bernart de Ventadorn (*c.* 1127–95), Peire Vidal, a commoner (d. 1215), Rambault de Vaqueiras (d. 1207), Folquet de Marseille (*c.* 1155–1231), Raimon de Miraval (d. *c.* 1220), Aimeric de Peguillan (1205–75), and Guiraut Riquier (d. 1294), the "last of the troubadours."

About three hundred troubadour poems (*c.* thirty with devotional texts) are preserved with melodies. The main sources are listed under Chansonnier. The texts of most of the songs are love lyrics. Special types are the *alba, pastorela* [see Pastourelle], *planc* [see Lament (2)], *partimen* [see *Tenso*], and *sirventes. Practically all of them are strophic poems, normally with five or six stanzas and a concluding half-stanza (*tornada;* see Envoi). Most often the stanza is throughcomposed, but the form with initial repeat, a a b, also occurs [see *Canzo*]. Of *c.* 270 lyrical songs, about 90 are in a a b form, but it is significant that nearly one-half of the latter are found among the works of the "last" troubadour, Riquier, who probably was influenced by trouvère music, in which the repeat form far outweighs the other. Two Provençal *lais also survive. The melodies of the troubadours (and of the trouvères) all are monophonic and were never accompanied in the modern sense of the word. Instrumental participation in the performance, suggested by some pictures showing a singer holding a fiddle or being assisted by an instrumentalist, was restricted to a strict or slightly varied unison duplication of the melody [see Heterophony] or, perhaps, to some short extemporization in the way of a prelude, interlude, or postlude. For the notation and rhythmic interpretation of the troubadour songs, see under Trouvère. Ex. in *HAM*, no. 18.

Lit.: J.-B. Beck, *Die Melodien der Troubadours and Trouvères* (1908); *id.*, *La Musique des trouba-*

dours [1910]; H. G. Farmer, *Historical Facts for the Arabian Musical Influence* (1930); R. Briffault, *Les Troubadours et le sentiment romanesque* (1945); F. Gennrich, ‡*Der musikalische Nachlass der Troubadours,* 3 vols. (1958–65; comp. ed. of all the melodies); U. Sesini, *Le Melodie trobadoriche . . . della Biblioteca Ambrosiana* (1942); C. Appel, *Die Singweisen Bernart de Ventadorn* (1934); A. Jeanroy, *Le Jeu de Sainte Agnès* (1931); B. Stäblein, "Zur Stilistik der Troubadour-Melodien" (*AM* xxxviii); R. H. Perrin, "Some Notes on Troubadour Melodic Types" (*JAMS* ix); B. Smythe, "Troubadour Songs" (*ML* ii, 263); A. Restori, "Per la Storia musicale dei Trovatori provenzali" (*RMI* ii, iii); P. Aubry, in *TG* x (Marcabru); H. Anglés, in *Estudis Universitaris Catalans* xi (Riquier); *id.,* in *AnM* xiv.

Literary studies: A. Pillet, *Bibliographie der Troubadours* [1933]; H. J. Chaytor, *The Troubadours* (1912); R. Croft-Cooke, *Troubadour* (1930); A. Jeanroy, *Bibliographie sommaire des chansonniers provençaux* (1916). See also Trouvère.

Trout Quintet. Popular name for Schubert's Quintet in A, op. 114 (1819), for violin, viola, cello, double bass, and piano, in five movements, the fourth being a set of variations on his song "The Trout" [G. *Die Forelle*].

Trouvère. Collective designation for the 12th- and 13th-century poet-musicians active in northern France, who imitated the movement initiated by the Provençal *troubadours. The development began in the late 12th century with Blondel de Nesles (b. *c.* 1155), Grace Brulé (d. 1220), Chatelain de Coucy (d. 1203), and Conon de Béthune (*c.* 1160–1219); continued with Gautier d'Epinal (fl. 1220–40), Thibaut IV (Count of Champagne and later King of Navarre, 1201–53), Colin Muset, Moniot d'Arras, Perrin d'Angicourt, and others; and closed with Jehan Bretel (d. 1272), Adam de la Hale (*c.* 1240–87), and Gillebert de Berneville (d. *c.* 1300). [For the general aspects of the movement, see Troubadour.]

Of more than 4,000 trouvère poems, about 1,400 are preserved with their melodies. The main sources are listed under Chansonnier. A large majority of the songs are love lyrics in the form of strophic poems; special literary types are the *aube* [see *Alba*], *chanson de toile, jeuparti* [see *Tenso*], and *pastourelle.* Throughcomposed stanzas, which occur in the majority of troubadour songs, are relatively rare, whereas

the form with initial repeat, a a b, is the most important form of trouvère music. It may well be called *ballade* [F.], analogous to the 14thcentury *ballade* (Machaut) with the same structure. Occasionally, other repeat structures are encountered, such as a a b b, a a b b c, a b b, etc. In addition to strophic songs, the trouvère repertory includes a considerable number of *lais. The *rondeau and *virelai, however, cannot be considered forms of trouvère music [see Lit., Apel].

The melodies of the trouvères (and troubadours) are practically all notated without clear indication of rhythm [see Monophonic notation]. The rhythmic interpretation of this notation has been widely studied and disputed. Early attempts to apply the principles of mensural notation (particularly the Franconian rules of ligatures; see *RiHM* i.2, 225) were abandoned *c.* 1890 (P. Runge) in favor of a rhythmic interpretation based on the meter of the text, a principle that was considerably modified *c.* 1905 by J.-B. Beck and P. Aubry with the introduction of modal (ternary) rhythm [see Modal theory]. The modal interpretation has been rather generally accepted for trouvère melodies, whereas its applicability to troubadour and minnesinger music is more open to question. Some of the songs in the *Chansonnier Cangé* (fac. ed., J.-B. Beck, 1927) are notated in long and short values (*longa, brevis*), clearly indicative of the first or third mode (*L B L B . . . , L B B L B B . . .*).

Lit.: P. Aubry, *Trouvères et troubadours* (1909; trans. C. Aveling, 1914); *id., La Rythmique musicale des troubadours et des trouvères* (1907); H. Zingerle, *Tonalität und Melodieführung in den Klauseln der Troubadours- und Trouvèreslieder* (1958); F. Gennrich, *Grundriss einer Formenlehre des mittelalterlichen Liedes* (1932); *id., Rondeaux, Virelais und Balladen,* 2 vols. (1921, '27); W. Apel, "Rondeaux, Virelais, and Ballades in French 13th-Century Song" (*JAMS* vii, 121ff); *ReMMA,* pp. 205ff; *AdHM* i, 188ff; *GéHM,* pp. 266ff.

Literary studies: G. Raynaud, *Bibliographie des chansonniers français* (1884); A. Jeanroy, *Bibliographie sommaire des chansoniers français du moyen âge* (1918). See also Chansonnier; Lai.

Trovatore, Il [It., The Troubadour, or The Minstrel]. Opera in four acts by Verdi (libretto by S. Cammarone, based on a play by A. Gutiérrez), produced in Rome, 1853. Setting: Spain, 15th century.

Troyens, Les [F., The Trojans]. Opera in five acts by Berlioz (to his own libretto, after Virgil), in two parts, *Le Prise de Troie* (The Taking of Troy) and *Les Troyens à Carthage* (The Trojans at Carthage), composed 1856–58. Only the first part was produced during Berlioz' lifetime (Paris, 1863); the whole work was first produced (in German) in Karlsruhe, 1890. Setting: Troy and Carthage, 1200 B.C.

Trugschluss [G.]. Deceptive cadence. See Cadence I.

Trumpet [F. *trompette;* G. *Trompete;* It. *tromba;* Sp. *trompeta*]. I. The modern orchestral trumpet is a *brass instrument with a cup-shaped mouthpiece and a narrow tube that is cylindrical for about three-fourths its length, then widening out into a moderate-sized bell. These characteristics distinguish it from the horn, which has a prevailingly conical bore and funnel-shaped mouthpiece. [For ill. see Brass instruments.] They account for the different timbres of the two instruments, the trumpet's being bright, brilliant, and penetrating, whereas the horn's is mellow and full. The horn is circular in shape and the trumpet oblong, a difference of secondary importance to the sound. The trumpet has three *valves (rotary or piston), which, singly or in combination, lower the natural pitch of the instrument by one to six semitones; hence, the name "valve trumpet" [F. *trompette-à-pistons* or *chromatique;* G. *Ventiltrompete;* It. *tromba ventile, t. a macchina, t. a pistoni*] to distinguish it from the earlier natural trumpet [see II]. How tones are produced on the trumpet is explained under Wind instruments.

The modern orchestral trumpet is pitched in B^b and has the chromatic compass shown:

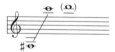

In most scores (Beethoven, Brahms) it is notated as a transposing instrument, either in B^b throughout or in different transpositions according to the crooks [see II], these being indicated in the score.

At the end of the 19th century a larger trumpet, pitched in F (or, for military bands, E^b), was popular. In length of tubing and actual pitch this instrument is closer to the horn and has a much nobler tone than the B^b trumpet. It lacks,

however, the latter's agility and has now been practically abandoned.

Bass trumpets, pitched in low E, D, or C, were demanded by Wagner for his *Ring des Nibelungen* but have proved impracticable. The instruments known by this name and used as substitutes are actually valve trombones, pitched in C.

II. *History.* The oldest ancestors of the modern trumpet are discussed under Brass instruments. Prior to *c.* 1700 the trumpet existed mainly in the form known as natural trumpet [G. *Naturtrompete*], a plain brass cylindrical bore without any such devices as side-holes, crooks, slides, or valves to bridge the gaps of the natural scale of harmonics. From the 14th century on the trumpet became associated with military and ceremonial functions. Playing it was a carefully guarded privilege of the nobility, reserved for official court trumpeters [see *Feldmusik*]. After 1600 the trumpet began to be used in art music, the *clarino* and *trombe sordine* of Monteverdi's *Orfeo* (1607; see Orchestra II) being an early though isolated instance. In 1638 Fantini's method of learning to play the trumpet appeared [see Lit.]. Toward the end of the 17th century trumpets were quite frequently used in operas, cantatas, etc., for military scenes or for expressing joyful triumph (Purcell, Buxtehude). At this time the art of playing the highest register of the trumpet, where the harmonics form a full scale, was developed; formerly only the low and middle registers, in which only fanfare-like motifs are possible, had been used [see Clarino (2)].

During the 18th century various attempts were made to overcome the limitation in the natural trumpet's compass. As early as Bach's time crooks—additional lengths of tubing— were inserted between the mouthpiece and the instrument in order to lower the pitch by several semitones or whole tones. This, of course, was only an expedient to make a single instrument useful for pieces in a variety of keys; still, in any such key only the natural tones were available. More drastic steps were taken toward the end of the 18th century with the introduction of side-holes covered with keys and a sliding mechanism. Key trumpets were invented in 1801 by the court trumpeter Anton Weidinger of Vienna, but they were soon abandoned because side-holes, though fairly satisfactory on conical instruments such as cornets and bugles (key bugle), produce a muffled sound on instruments with a cylindrical bore.

More successful was the application of the

sliding mechanism, which had always been used for trombones. In an earlier construction, documented as early as the 15th century, the slide was part of the elongated mouthpiece, which could be pulled out so that all the gaps in the natural scale could be filled. It is probably this instrument [F. *trompette à coulisse;* G. *Zugtrompete*] that Bach meant when he indicated *tromba da tirarsi* (Cantatas nos. 5, 20, 77). The terms *tromba o corno da tirarsi* (Cantata no. 46) and *corno da tirarsi* (Cantatas 67, 162) probably mean the same instrument [see *SaHMI*, p. 384f]. [See ill. under Brass instruments.] At the beginning of the 19th century another construction was made by John Hyde (1804; or by Richard Woodham, *c.* 1810?) in which the U of the upper coil was transformed into a movable slide, similar to that of the trombone, and provided with springs to bring it back to its normal position. This instrument was in constant use in England throughout the 19th century [see *GD* v, 395f; *GDB* viii, 567ff]. Although it had the fine sound of the natural trumpet, it lacked the agility demanded in modern scores and was therefore finally abandoned in favor of the valve trumpet.

The invention of valves (1813) opened the way for the permanent establishment of the trumpet in the orchestra. One of the first parts for the valve trumpet is that in Halévy's *La Juive* (1835), in which two valve trumpets are used along with two crooked natural trumpets. The modern development of a brilliant trumpet technique has enabled composers to use the trumpets as melody instruments equal and occasionally superior in importance to the woodwinds. The scores of Stravinsky, Shostakovitch, and others contain many interesting trumpet passages, frequently of a comic nature. The repertory for trumpet includes concertos by Haydn and Hummel, a sonata by Hindemith, and works by Purcell, Bach, Vivaldi, and Enesco.

Lit.: W. Worthmüller, *Die Instrumente der Nürnberger Trompeten- und Posaunenmacher* (*Mitteilungen des Vereins für Geschichte der Stadt Nürnberg,* 1955); *id., Die Nürnberger Trompeten- und Posaunenmacher des 17. und 18. Jhs.* (*Mitteilungen des Vereins für Geschichte der Stadt Nürnberg,* 1954; J. E. Altenburg, *Versuch einer Anleitung zur . . . Trompeter- und Pauker-Kunst* (1795; fac. ed., 1911); G. Fantini, *Modo per imparare a sonare di tromba* (1638; fac. ed. 1934); H. Heyde, *Trompete und Trompetenblasen im europäischen Mittelalter* (1965); C. Sachs, "Chromatic Trumpets in the Renaissance" (*MQ* xxxvi); W. F. H. Blandford, "The 'Bach

Trumpet'" (*Monthly Musical Record* lxv); E. Halfpenny, "William Shaw's 'Harmonic Trumpet'" (*GSJ* xiii); *id.,* "William Bull and the English Baroque Trumpet" (*GSJ* xv); *id.,* "Two Oxford Trumpets" (*GSJ* xvi); R. Morley-Pegge, "The Regent's Bugle" (*GSJ* ix); J. Wheeler, "New Light on the 'Regent's Bugle'; with some Notes on the Keyed-Bugle" (*GSJ* xix); *id.,* "Further Notes on the Classic Trumpet" (*GSJ* xviii); D. Smithers, "The Trumpets of J W Haas" (*GSJ* xviii); C. A. Hoover, "The Slide Trumpet of the Nineteenth Century (*Brass Quarterly* vi); F. Jahn, "Die Nürnberger Trompeten- und Posaunenmacher im 16. Jahrhundert" (*AMW* vii); W. Osthoff, "Trombe sordine" (*AMW* xiii); C. Titcomb, "Baroque Court and Military Trumpets and Kettledrums: Technique and Music" (*GSJ* ix).

Trumpet marine. *Tromba marina.

Trumscheit [G.]. *Tromba marina.

Trutruka. The most commonly used instrument of the Araucanian Indians of southern Chile and Argentina. It is a straight trumpet, ten feet long and two inches in diameter, made of bamboo or *küla* wood, with an upturned bell of horn at one end and a diagonal mouthpiece cut into the other. The player holds the instrument horizontal by resting it either on special supports or on the shoulders of a *kona* boy. The timbre is similar to the bassoon's, and twelve to thirteen overtones can be obtained by expert players.

J.O-S.

T.s. Abbr. for *tasto solo.

Tuba. (1) [L.]. Ancient Roman straight trumpet [see Brass instruments V (a)].

(2) In modern usage, generic name loosely used for any bass-pitched brass instrument other than the trombones. This group comprises instruments of many sizes and shapes, depending on where and by whom they were made, a fact partly explained by their extensive use in military and other bands. The most important of them, such as the euphonium, helicon, sousaphone, and baritone, are briefly described under Brass instruments III.

The tubas of the modern orchestra are bass instruments with an oblong shape, a conical bore, a bell pointing upward, a cupped mouthpiece, and three to five valves. There are three sizes: (a) tenor tuba [G. *Baryton*] in B-flat; (b) bass tuba, pitched either in E-flat (E-flat or EE-flat bass tuba) or in F (F bass tuba); (c) double-bass or contrabass tuba (usually called BB-flat bass tuba or BB-flat bass), pitched an octave below the tenor tuba.

Wagner tuba or Bayreuth tuba are names given to instruments designed for Wagner's *Ring*. They have a somewhat narrower bore (similar to that of the *cornet) and a funnel-shaped mouthpiece like that of the horns. Wagner used two tenor and two bass instruments of this type, together with a normal double-bass tuba for the lowest part. The Wagner tubas combine the agility of the cornet with the mellow timbre of the true tubas. They have also been used by Bruckner and R. Strauss (*Elektra*). See ill. under Brass instruments. See R. Bryant, "The Wagner Tubas" (*Monthly Musical Record* lxvii).

(3) In Gregorian chant, see under Psalm tones.

Tubaphone. A percussion instrument like the glockenspiel, but with lengths of metal pipe instead of metal bars. It has been used by A. Khatchaturian in his ballet *Gayane*.

Tucket, tuck. Elizabethan name for a trumpet flourish. The word appears to be an anglicization of toccata [see Toccata (2)]. Cf. the German *Tusch* and French *touche*.

Tudor Church Music. See Editions LI.

Tumba [Sp.]. Folk dance similar to the *tarantella* that originated in Santo Domingo *c.* 1822. It is also known as *contradanza criolla*. Although the *tumba* replaced such group dances as the Spanish *cuadrilla* and the minuet and emphasized the importance of the individual couple, the break with tradition was not complete. Many of the traditional figures were retained but were danced to a different music and to syncopated rhythmic patterns showing African influence. In the Western portion of the island (Haiti), where French influence prevailed, the dance, known as the *tumba francesa,* was rhythmically somewhat more elaborate than the *tumba dominicana,* showing predominantly Spanish influence. The former version also became popular in Cuba.   J.O-S.

Tuna. See *Tamborito*.

Tune. *Melody.

Tune book. Generic term for the many volumes of three- and four-part vocal music published in the American colonies and United States in the 18th and 19th centuries, which contain psalm tunes, hymn tunes, fuging tunes, anthems, odes, "motettos," and occasionally even a cantata. The music was written in open score with the text usually placed over the tenor (until the mid-19th century), the reason for this being that the tenor rather than the soprano had the principal melodic line. The tune books always included a theoretical introduction, those prior to 1800 being of particular importance for the study of colonial music. A few of the more important 18th-century tune books are: John Tufts, *Introduction to the Singing of Psalm Tunes* (Boston, 1721; fac. repr. of 1726 ed., 1954); James Lyon, *Urania* (Philadelphia, 1761); Oliver Holden, *The Union Harmony* (Boston, 1793); William Billings, *The Continental Harmony* (Boston, 1794; fac. repr., 1961); O. Holden, Samuel Holyoke, and Hans Gram, *The Massachusetts Compiler* (Boston, 1795).

Soon after 1800 the theoretical introductions become stereotyped music-reading manuals. Typical of this stage are Thomas Hastings, *Musica Sacra* (Utica, 1816); Lowell Mason, *The Boston Handel and Haydn Society Collection of Church Music* (Boston, 1822); *id., Carmina Sacra* (Boston, 1841); *id.* and G. J. Webb, *The Psaltery* (Boston, 1845); William Bradbury, *The Jubilee* (New York, 1858).

The tune books of the Midwest and South, which emerged after 1800, used shape notes [see Fasola]. Their introductions deal with the rudiments of music, but in terminology and content they often show more affinity to 18th-century tune books than those published in the Northeast at the same time. Among the Midwestern and Southern tune books are: Ananias Davisson, *Kentucky Harmony* (Harrisonburg, 1815?); Allen Carden, *Missouri Harmony* (St. Louis, 1820); B. F. White and E. J. King, *The Sacred Harp* (Philadelphia, 1844; repr., 1936, as *The Original Sacred Harp*); William Walker, *The Southern Harmony and Musical Companion* (New Haven, Conn., 1835; repr., 1939). Three earlier works should also be mentioned: William Little and William Smith, *The Easy Instructor* (New York, 1802), the first publication to use shape notes; Andrew Law, *The Art of Singing* (4th ed., 1803), which has shape notes without staves; and John Wyeth, *Repository of Sacred Music, Part Second* (Harrisburg, 1813), which had considerable influence on Southern tune books.

The publication on microcards of *Early American Imprints, 1639–1800* (Worcester; American Antiquarian Society, 1955ff) has made available the most valuable segment of tune-book literature. The key to that series is Charles Evans' *American Bibliography,* 14 vols. (1903–59).

Lit. *General:* G. Chase, *America's Music* (1955), ch. 2, 7, 10, 11; W. S. Pratt, "Tune Books," *GD, American Supplement* (1930); F. J. Metcalf, *American Psalmody (1721–1820)* (1917); I. Lowens, *Music and Musicians in Early America* (1964). *Specific:* A. Britton, "Theoretical Introductions in American Tune Books to 1800" (diss. Univ. of Michigan, 1950); G. P. Jackson, *White Spirituals in the Southern Uplands* (1933); E. C. Krohn, "The Missouri Harmony, A Study in Early American Psalmody" (Missouri Historical Society *Bulletin* vi, 25–33); *id.,* "A Check List of Editions of the Missouri Harmony" (*ibid.,* pp. 374–99); I. Lowens, "John Wyeth's *Repository of Sacred Music, Part Second"* (*JAMS* v, 114–31); *id.,* "John Tufts' *Introduction to the Singing of Psalm Tunes*" (*Journal of Research in Music Education* ii, 89–102); *id.* and A. Britton, "*The Easy Instructor* (1798–1831): A History and Bibliography of the First Shape Note Tune Book" (*ibid.* i, 31–55); F. J. Metcalf, " 'The Easy Instructor,' A Bibliographical Study" (*MQ* xxiii, 89–97).   L.B.S.

Tuning. Adjustment of the strings of stringed instruments (including the piano and harpsichord) or the pipes of the organ to their proper pitch. Modern piano tuning is based on the pure octave and the well-tempered fifth. The former is tuned so as to give no *beats, while the latter is obtained (in practice) by lowering the pure fifth (no beats) to the point where it gives one beat per second. In this manner, a succession of fifths (with their lower octave)—a, e, b, f♯, etc.—is tuned. As soon as a third is available (a–c♯ being the first), it is used for testing. After the middle section of the keyboard (the groundwork) has been tuned, the higher and lower registers are tuned by octaves. A later system of tuning, introduced by O. C. Faust and widely accepted (outside piano factories), begins with c′ and uses major thirds upward and fifths downward. The accompanying scheme illustrates the general procedure. Even more radical is a method

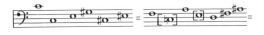

advocated by E. Neugebauer, which has pure fifths but slightly sharp fourths and octaves. See J. Redfield, *Music: A Science and an Art* (1928); A. H. Howe, *Scientific Piano Tuning and Servicing* (1947); F. Hubbard, *Harpsichord Regulating and Repairing* (1963); J. W. Link, *Theory and Tuning* (1963). Also see Temperament.

Tuning fork [F. *diapason;* G. *Stimmgabel;* It. *corista;* Sp. *diapasón*]. A two-pronged steel fork used to indicate absolute pitch. Modern tuning forks usually give the international pitch for the tone *a* (440 vibrations per second). The instrument was invented by John Shore in 1711 and improved *c.* 1850 by Rudolph König of Paris. For acoustical demonstration entire sets of tuning forks are built. They retain their pitch for long periods and produce almost pure tones, without harmonics. See E. A. Kielhauser, *Die Stimmgabel* (1907).

Tuning slide. In organ building, a movable metal clip or tube attached to the upper end of an open flue pipe. By lowering or raising it the length of the pipe, and hence its pitch, can be adjusted.

Tuning wire. In organ building, a wire whereby the length of the vibrating tongue of reed pipes is changed. Tuning only "on the wire" can seriously alter a pipe's volume and tone color; skillful tuners find the balance between tuning "on the wire" and "on the top" [see Tuning slide] of the resonator.

Tuono [It.]. *Tono.

Tupan. A cylindrical drum (also called *topan*) of the Balkans, used in combination with a shawm (*zurla*) to accompany dancing. See Y. Arbatsky, *Beating the Tupan in the Central Balkans* (1953).

Turandot. Unfinished opera in three acts by Puccini, completed by F. Alfano (libretto by G. Adami and R. Simoni, based on C. Gozzi's play), produced in Milan, 1926. Setting: China, legendary times.

Turba [L.]. In oratorios, Passions, etc., name for a choral movement representing the Jews or heathens. It is usually an allegro in fugal style, using short motifs in close imitation. There are numerous examples in Bach's St. Matthew Passion. See G. Adler, in *CP Liliencron.*

Turca, alla [It.]. In the Turkish style, i.e., in imitation of Turkish military music (*Janizary music), which became popular in Europe in the late 18th century.

Turkey. I. *Theory.* Turkish classical music as practiced at the court and the great monasteries of Constantinople (Istanbul) is based on a fundamental scale containing twenty-four notes to the octave. Earlier, octaves of seventeen and twenty-three notes were used. The tones of the scale are calculated mostly on the basis of the Pythagorean system (consecutive fifths), thus differing from those of the European *quarter-tone system [see *LavE* i.5, 3016]. From this fundamental scale about one hundred different "modes" are selected. Among them are the mode *Tchariguiah,* which is the Pythagorean scale of C, and the *Raste,* the most common mode of all, in which the E and B are those of *just intonation ($\frac{5}{4}$ and $\frac{15}{8}$), i.e., a comma lower than the corresponding tones in the Pythagorean mode. Thirty of the modes are illustrated in *LavE* i.5, 2997ff. No less elaborate is the Turkish system of rhythm, called *oussoul.* It is based on the playing of the kettledrum with two fundamental kinds of drumstroke, one in the center (called *dum,* i.e., muffled) and one at the side (called *tek,* clear). There are about fifty standard combinations of these beats, which correspond to Western meters, each combination being repeated throughout the entire composition. Rhythmic schemes involving nine or seven beats are common.

II. *Practice.* The religious music "consists of *Ilahi,* hymns for all the months of the Mohammedan calendar, *Tevchih,* hymns in praise of Mohammed, and *Ayni Cherif,* offices of the whirling dervishes. Together these make up an important body of music. Important individual works are the famous *Nat* by Itri, the magnificent *Bayram Tekbiri,* also by him, and the *Sala, Temdjid, Sabah essalati,* and *Miradjiye*" [see E. Borrel, in *GD,* Sup. vol., p. 633]. Secular art music is derived largely from *Arab practices. The most important form is the *Fasl,* a kind of suite made up of several pieces, instrumental and vocal, all in the same "key," i.e., *maqam* [see Arab music]. The instruments (tanbur, 'ud, *kanun) are also those used in Arab music. Of particular interest is the music of the *Janizary.

Modern Western music was introduced in Turkey by Joseph Marx and Paul Hindemith, who taught at Ankara from 1935 to 1937. The best-known modern Turkish composer is Ahmed Adnan Saygun (b. 1907), who wrote an oratorio *Yunus Emre* (1946) and an opera *Kerem,* the first Turkish opera performed at Ankara (1953).

Lit.: K. Reinhard, *Türkische Musik;* H. G. Farmer, *Turkish Instruments of Music in the Seventeenth Century* (1937); *LavE* i.5, 2945–

3064; A. Adnan Saygun, "La Musique turque," *Histoire de la musique* i, 573–617, in *Encyclopédie de la Pléiade,* ed. Roland-Manuel, ix (1960); V. Belaiev, "Turkish Music" (*MQ* xxi); B. Bartók, "Collecting Folk Songs in Anatolia" (*The Hungarian Quarterly* iii [1937], 337–46); E. Borrel, "La Musique turque" (*RdM* 1922, p. 149; 1923, p. 26); R. Yekta, "Musique orientale" (*RMC* vii, viii); G. Oransay, "Das Tonsystem der türkei-türkischen Kunstmusik" (*MF* x).

Turkish crescent [also *Turkish* or *Chinese pavilion* or *hat, jingling Johnny;* F. *chapeau chinois;* G. *Schellenbaum;* Turk. *chaghāna*]. A percussion instrument consisting of a wooden stick surmounted by crescent-shaped crossbars and an ornament shaped like a pavilion or Chinese hat, all hung with numerous small bells and jingles. [For ill. see under Percussion instruments.] The instrument was used in Turkish *Janizary music, whereby it was introduced into the military bands of many European nations. See H. G. Farmer, *Turkish Instruments of Music in the Seventeenth Century* (1937).

Turmsonaten [G.]. A type of 17th-century German *Gebrauchsmusik* that was played by brass instruments from the tower of the town hall or a church to signal the hours at noon, sunset, etc. It consisted of harmonized chorales, plain tunes, military signals, or "sonatas" [see Sonata B I]. Interesting collections of such pieces are Johann Christoph Pezel's (Petzold) *Hora decima* (1670) and *Fünfstimmigte blasende Musik* (1685). New ed. in *Ddt* 63; see also *SchGMB,* no. 221.

Turn. [F. *double cadence, doublé, brisé;* G. *Doppelschlag;* It. *fioritura;* Sp. *grupito*]. An ornament consisting of a group of four or five notes that turn around the principal note. The most common form of turn in the music of the 17th and 18th centuries is indicated by a curved line, contains four notes, and begins on the beat with the note above the written note [Ex. 1]. It is important to note that the melodic form of the turn is identical with that of a trill with closing notes. For this reason the turn was regarded in the 17th and 18th centuries as synonymous with the short trill; it may be substituted for the latter whenever the tempo is too fast to permit the clear execution of a greater number of notes.

The sign for the turn was originally used only for the first trill of the compound ornament known as a *double cadence. The formula, shown in Ex. 2 and occurring frequently in the works of J. S. Bach and his contemporaries, actually constitutes a single ornament; there should be no break between the turn and the ensuing trill. So closely was the sign in question associated with this formula that it was retained for the isolated turn along with its name, *double cadence.*

In Ex. 2 the sign for the turn is placed slightly to the right of the written note instead of directly above it, showing that the main note should be

sounded first. In Bach's works this occurs only when another ornament (generally a trill) is to be played immediately afterward, as in the *double cadence.* Later, however, this practice became quite common, as seen in the accompanying examples by Mozart [Ex. 3] and Beethoven [Ex. 4].

Until *c.* 1750 the turn was regularly performed as four equal notes, taking up the whole time value of the written note. J. S. Bach frequently wrote out this execution in ordinary notes [see Ex. 5, from *The Well-Tempered Clavier* ii, no. 24]. K. P. E. Bach introduced the custom of playing the first two notes of the *Doppelschlag* (as the turn was now called) more rapidly than the last, as in Ex. 6 [Mozart, Violin Sonata, G minor]. This execution does not apply, however, to a turn that is played after the written note or to a turn on a very short note.

The practice of indicating the turn with small grace notes (which became popular during the classical period) is more ambiguous than the use of the sign, since it is not always easy to determine whether a turn on a note or a turn between two notes is intended. Ex. 7 and 8 show

that the turn upon the note requires three small notes, while the turn after the note requires four.

The romantic composers often used five- or six-note turns. Their rhythm is exceedingly flexible, the only definite rule being that they are to be performed in the time value of the preceding note [Ex. 9 and 10, Chopin, Nocturnes op. 37, no. 1, and op. 48, no. 2].

Among the unusual forms of turn are: (1) The *geschnellter Doppelschlag,* a rapid five-note turn beginning with the main note [Ex. 11, K. P. E. Bach]; it was known in Italy as *gruppo* (*groppo*) or *gruppetto,* and in Germany as *Rolle.* (2) The *prallender Doppelschlag,* a turn combined with an appoggiatura and short trill [Ex. 12, K. P. E. Bach]. (3) The *inverted turn,* somtimes indicated by the ordinary sign upside down or in a vertical

position but more often represented by tiny notes as in Ex. 13 [Mozart, Rondo in A minor, K. 511].

P.A.

Turn of the Screw, The. Opera in two acts and a prologue by B. Britten (libretto by M. Piper, based on H. James' tale), produced in Venice, 1954.

Tusch [G.]. A fanfare played on brass instruments. See Tucket.

Tutti [It.]. In orchestral works, particularly concertos, indication for the parts for the whole orchestra as distinct from those for the soloist.

Tuyau [F.]. Tube, pipe. *T. à anche,* reed pipe; *t. à bouche,* flue pipe.

Tvisöngur [Icel.]. In Icelandic folk music, a type of two-part singing that represents a survival of the 9th-century organum at the fifth. As in the English *gymel,* the voice-parts often cross, so that the "organal" part (sung by a soloist) moves alternatingly a fifth above and a fifth below the "principal" part (usually sung by a small group). See A. Hammerich, in *SIM* i; H. Helgason, in *CP 1958.*

Twelve-tone technique. A 20th-century method of composition devised (*c.* 1920) by A. Schoenberg. See under Serial music. Others, e.g., Hauer, had invented similar systems prior to Schoenberg [see Trope (2)].

Twentieth-century music. Among the most important styles and trends since 1900 are *expressionism, *atonality, *serial music, *neoclassicism, and, since World War II, *electronic music, *aleatory music, and *musique concrète.

The second decade of the century, dominated by World War I, saw daring and widespread musical experimentation. Of basic importance was the work of Schoenberg, who, casting away the harmonic system and formal methods of the past, arrived at *atonality (*Drei Klavierstücke* op. 11, 1909). Simultaneously, new possibilities in rhythm were exploited, e.g., by Bartók in his *Allegro barbaro* (1911) and Stravinsky in *Petrushka* (1911) and *Sacre du printemps* (1913). The French writer Cocteau aptly expressed the spirit of this period: "After the music with the silk brush, the music with the axe." Provocative terms such as *bruitisme* (noise music), *futurism, motorism, and machine music appeared, although most of them left no lasting imprint. Experimentation with tonal material led to *quarter-tone music. Besides the leaders already mentioned, composers such as Kodály, Malipiero, Casella, Honegger, Milhaud, Berg, and Webern contributed their experiments.

The neoclassical movement, which began in the early 1920's, fostered a return to the aesthetic ideals and formal methods of the 17th and 18th centuries, recast in modern idioms. Stravinsky took the lead with such compositions as the *Octet for Wind Instruments* (1923). Bartók and Hindemith, the major composers of the movement (along with Stravinsky) began to receive international recognition. Hindemith helped develop *Gebrauchsmusik* and provided a useful theoretical explanation of the new harmonic and tonal concepts. Bartók represents another major development of the post-1920 period: the assimilation and synthesis of the experimental techniques of the second decade into a colorful, expressive musical language. Other noteworthy features of the 1920's are the development of *serial music and the influence of American jazz on serious music (e.g., in Stravinsky's *Ragtime,* 1918; Hindemith's *Suite 1922;* Krenek's jazz opera *Jonny spielt auf,* 1926).

For further developments, see Aleatory music; Electronic music; *Musique concrète;* Serial music.

Lit.: G. Abraham, *This Modern Music,* rev. ed. (1955); A. Copland, *Our New Music* (1941); W. Mellers, *Studies in Contemporary Music* (1947); R. H. Myers, *Music in the Modern World* (1939); M. Bauer, *Twentieth Century Music,* rev. ed. (1947); N. Demuth, *Musical Trends in the 20th Century* (1952); H. Hartog, *European Music in the Twentieth Century* (1957); R. H. Myers, ed., *Twentieth-century Music* [1960]; J. Machlis, *Introduction to Contemporary Music* [1961]; V. Persichetti, *Twentieth-Century Harmony* [1961]; L. Dallin, *Techniques of Twentieth-Century Composition* [1957]; H. Cowell, *New Musical Resources* (1930); D. Ewen, *The Book of Modern Composers* (1942); H. Andrews, *Modern Harmony* (1934); R. Lenormand and M. Carner, *A Study of Twentieth-Century Harmony,* 2 vols. [1940, '42]; W. Dunwell, *The Evolution of Twentieth-Century Harmony* [1960]; N. Slonimsky, *Music Since 1900,* rev. ed. (1949); H. Pleasants, *The Agony of Modern Music* (1955); H. H. Stuckenschmidt, *Neue Musik* (1951); E. Forneberg, *Der Geist der neuen Musik* (1957); A. Goléa, *Esthétique de la musique contemporaine* (1954); B. Gavoty and D. Lesur, *Pour ou contre la Musique moderne?* (1957); P. Collaer, *A History of Modern Music,* trans. S. Abeles [1961]; E. Blom, "The Truly Modern in Music" (*ML* iv, no. 3); R. W. Wood, "Modern Counterpoint" (*ML* xiii, no. 3); G. Dyson, "The Texture of Modern Music" (*ML* iv, no. 3); E. Wellesz, "Problems of Modern Music" (*MQ* x); H. Cowell, "New Terms for New Music" (*MM* v, no. 4); W. Apel, "Neue Klaviermusik" (*DM* xxiv, i, ii); W. Austin, "The Idea of Evolution in the Music of the 20th Century" (*MQ* xxxix); *Tempo* (London), various articles; *MQ* li, various articles. See also under Atonality; Electronic music; *Musique concrète;* Neoclassicism; Serial music.

Twilight of the Gods, The. Wagner's *Götterdäm-merung.* See under *Ring des Nibelungen, Der.*

Two-step. See under One-step.

Tymbalon, tymbal. An early Provençal kettle-drum.

Tympanon, tympanum [Gr., L.]. A frame drum beaten with the hand. In the Middle Ages the name meant kettledrum, although some writers (e.g., Giraldus Cambrensis) applied it to the dulcimer. In modern writings tympani occurs as a misspelling of timpani.

Tyrolienne. A Tyrolean folksong, in the rhythm of a *Ländler,* and sung with that sudden change from chest voice to falsetto known as *yodel. The name is also used for operatic ballets (e.g., Rossini, *Guillaume Tell,* Act III) and popular pieces written in the style of Tyrolean folk dance.

U

Über- [G.]. Over, above. *Überblasen,* to over-blow; *Übergang,* transition; *übergreifen,* to cross the hands (in piano playing); *Überleitung,* transi-tion; *übermässig,* augmented (for intervals); *überschlagen,* to cross the hands; *übersetzen,* to put over (in piano fingering).

Übung [G.]. Exercise, study.

U.c. *Una corda.*

'Ud, oud [Arab.]. See under Arab music; Lute II.

Uguale [It.]. Equal, uniform.

Uilleann pipes. Irish *bagpipe. The name was later corrupted into "union pipes." See A. Baines, *Bagpipes* (1960), pp. 103, 120ff.

Ukrainian Symphony. Tchaikovsky's Symphony no. 2, in C minor, op. 17 (1872), also called *Little-Russian Symphony,* "Little Russia" being the common 19th-century name for the Ukraine.

Ukulele. A Hawaiian instrument of the guitar family, with four strings and a long fingerboard, usually fretted. It probably developed from a Portuguese guitar called *machete* [see Guitar family] and became popular in the United States *c.* 1920. The notation for this instrument follows the principles used in the lute tablatures of the 16th century but was invented independently [see Tablature VI]. See ill. under Guitar family.

Umfang [G.]. Compass, range (of a voice, etc.).

Umkehrung [G.]. Inversion (of intervals, chords, melodies).

Umstimmen [G.]. To change the tuning, e.g., of kettledrums.

Una corda [It.]. In piano playing, direction (abbr. *u.c.*) to use the left pedal (soft pedal; F. *pédale douce;* G. *Verschiebung*), which, by moving the entire action, keyboard, and hammers, a little to the right, causes the hammer to strike a single string (in modern instruments usually two strings) instead of all three. The indication is canceled by *tre corde* or *tutte le corde* (*t.c.*). Bee-thoven, the first composer to use the indication *una corda,* calls for not only a gradual increase in volume (*una corda, due, e poi tre corde;* G-major Concerto op. 58, slow movt.), but a gradual execution of the shift. *Nach und nach mehrere Saiten* (Piano Sonata op. 101, slow movt.). The latter is, of course, impossible to execute literally. See Mute.

Una Cosa rara [Sp., A Rare Thing]. Opera by Vicente Martín y Soler, a Spanish composer (1754–1806). It was produced in Vienna, 1786, and is remembered today only because Mozart included a long section from it in the finale of Act II of *Don Giovanni,* as part of the music played during the Don's supper.

Un Ballo in maschera [It.]. See *Ballo in maschera, Un.*

Undezime [G.]. Eleventh.

Unequal temperament. A *temperament midway between pure intonation and equal tempera-ment, i.e., any system of tuning in which the pure intervals are retained for some keys (C, G, F) and adjustments are made for the more remote keys, with the result that the most remote keys (G-sharp, C-sharp) cannot be used. Various systems were in use prior to the general acceptance of equal temperament, e.g., the mean-tone system (which some writers do not consider an unequal temperament; see *GD* v, 301; *GDB* viii, 388), and the systems of L. Euler and J. P. Kirnberger. See Temperament.

Unequal voices. Mixture of men's and women's voices.

Unfinished Symphony. Schubert's Symphony no. 8, in B minor, so called because only the first two movements exist. They were written in 1822, six years before the composer's death. That Schubert intended to complete the work appears from the fact that he had sketched out the beginning of the Scherzo. Probably he was too busy with other compositions to finish this symphony. Schubert sent the two movements to his friend Hüttenbrenner, and not until the latter's death in 1868 was the work published, though its first performance took place in 1865.

Ungaresca [It.]. A 16th-century name for dance tunes of Hungarian derivation. Found in lute books (Wolf Heckel, 1556, '62; P. Phalèse, 1583) and collections of keyboard music (B. Schmid the elder, 1577; J. Paix, 1583; A. Nörmiger, *c.* 1590; G. Picchi, 1621), they usually consist of short repeated phrases supported by a 1–5–8 drone. See E. Haraszti, in *RdM* 1930, p. 176ff.

Ungarische Tänze. See *Hungarian Dances.*

Ungebunden [G.]. Unrestrained, free.

Ungestüm [G.]. Violent, raging.

Ungrader Takt [G.]. Uneven, i.e., triple meter.

Union of Soviet Socialist Republics. See Russia.

Union pipes. See under Uilleann pipes.

Unis [F.]. In orchestral music, unison (after **divisi*). In organ music, it means 8′ pitch (stops) only; also, without octave couplets.

Unison (1) Simultaneous performance of the same notes or melody by various instruments or by the whole orchestra, either at exactly the same pitch or in a different octave, e.g., violin and cello in unison (*all'unisono*). (2) The pseudo-interval formed by a tone and its duplication [G. *Prime*], e.g., c–c, as distinguished from second, c–d, etc.

Unisono, all' [It.]. See Unison; *A due.*

United States. The history of American music may be divided into two major periods, (1) music written before America achieved artistic and aesthetic parity with the rest of the West (*c.* 1607–*c.* 1929), and (2) the internationally important music of the recent past (1929 to present). Two factors determined the development of American music: immigration within a relatively short time to a largely empty continent and the predominance of the English settlers in the new land. The virtually unopposed tenure of the English thoroughly defined America's politics, religion, and language during the first two centuries, so that all succeeding ethnic groups had to choose between assimilation with or isolation from the Anglo-Saxon mainstream. Unequivocal evidence of English influence is found in traditional religious and folk or popular music, but there are indications of other influences, less easily traced to their origins. Although the precise process is difficult to determine, it would seem that various melodic inflections and rhythms of later ethnic groups were grafted onto the Anglo-Saxon stock. Thus, though the immigrants' native languages were abandoned for English, those elements of language, accent, and inflection that are essentially musical were integrated into the dominant Anglo-Saxon culture as music.

Also important was the importation of European art music and of professional European musicians. For example, the English version of Weber's *Der Freischütz* (Berlin, 1821), performed in London in 1824, was brought to New York in 1825. The same year, also in New York, Rossini's *Il Barbiere di Siviglia* (Rome, 1816) was produced in Italian by Manuel Garcia. Such performances by traveling companies could not help but influence musical taste. Just as significant was the influx of professional musicians, many of whom left Europe because of political upheavals ranging from the French Revolution to the present. They transmitted European standards of musical excellence and craftmanship; without them American music would have remained provincial.

The development of American music took place in four stages: 1607–1790, the period of English influence; 1790–1865, the period of European professional influence; 1865–1929, the period of the second school of New England composers; 1929 to the present, the arrival of American music on the international scene.

I. *1607–1790.* Presumably many of the early colonists at Jamestown (1607), Plymouth (1620), and Massachusetts Bay (1629) brought with them their native English music, sacred and secular, but only in the case of the northern settlements is the record clear. The Pilgrims sang psalms to thirty-nine different tunes, or a Psalter originally compiled in Holland by Henry Ainsworth in 1612. Some of these melodies came from Calvin's French Psalter, and until 1692, after annexation by the larger Massachusetts Bay Colony, the Ainsworth Psalter was used exclusively in Plymouth [see Psalter].

Massachusetts Bay settlers around Boston first used the Sternhold and Hopkins Psalter of 1562, but in 1640 the Puritan ministers made their own translation of the psalms. Popularly called the *Bay Psalm Book,* it was the first book printed in British North America and was widely use in many succeeding editions. The chief feature of these Protestant psalters was their rhymed and metered English poetry, which made the text easy to memorize and permitted a few tunes, having the same rhythms as the poetry, to be used as melodies for many psalms. In 1698, the ninth edition of the *Bay Psalm Book,* issued with thirteen traditional tunes and basses that supplied music for all the psalms, became the first book of music printed in America.

Until 1700, however, the smallness of the population, the hard pioneer life, and the Puritan attitude of disapproval toward the lively arts inhibited more active musical development. Scholes [see Lit., *The Puritans*] claims that the Puritans were not hostile to music and that the tradition of intolerance toward music in New England is fallacious. However, although there are references in contemporary records to a few musical instruments and even indications of musical scholarship, the Puritan colonists seem to have viewed secular amusements and excessive pleasures with suspicion and distrust.

As skill in reading both text and tune waned in the late 17th century, the practice of "lining out" [see Lining] became popular. A deacon would sing one line of a psalm, which the congregation would then repeat by rote. Abuses of this manner of performance, variously interpreted as improvised folk singing by some [see Lit., G. Chase], but regarded by contemporaries as an "odd noise," led in the early 18th century to a reform movement that stressed singing "by note" or sight-singing instead of "lining out." Several instruction books for sight-singing appeared: first, John Tufts' *A Very Plain and Easy Introduction to the Singing of Psalm Tunes* (earliest existing ed., 1721; 5th ed., 1726), and then

Thomas Walter's *The Grounds and Rules of Musick Explained* (1721), to which at first there was strong opposition. Gradually, the new pedagogy gained acceptance. After *c.* 1750, a considerable number of *tune books were published, among them an American edition of William Tans'ur's *The Royal Melody Compleat* (London, 1755; Boston, 1767), James Lyon's *Urania* (1761, containing six original pieces by Lyon), and Josiah Flagg's *Collection of the Best Psalm Tunes* (1764).

From these beginnings grew the singing schools, whereby generations were taught to read and sing music by itinerant singing masters. Nathaniel D. Gould (1781–1864), one of the last of his profession, claimed to have instructed 50,000 pupils between 1799 and 1843 in classes ranging from New Jersey to New Hampshire [see his *Church Music in America* (1853), p. 238]. A further indication of the popularity of singing was the large number of tune books published in the late 18th and 19th centuries. From before 1810, more than 370 tune books have survived. See Tune book.

It was in this milieu that the Yankee composers, a veritable first school of New England composers, flourished. Most famous of the tunesmiths was a Boston tanner, William Billings (1746–1800), who published six books of original vocal compositions, among which are examples of the conscious use of dissonance and a type of imitative counterpoint called *fuging* [see Fuge tune]. Another master of the fuge tune was Daniel Read (1757–1836), who, with such composers as Jacob French (b. 1754), Timothy Swan (1758–1842), Justin Morgan (1747–98), and Jeremiah Ingalls (1764–1828), formed a school bound together by such stylistic features as the use of parallel fifths, strange voice-leading, modal pentatonic melody, and cadences on chords lacking the third. Even more striking was the characteristic manner of performance: in four written parts, the soprano was doubled an octave lower, and the tenor, carrying the tune, was doubled an octave higher. The resulting six-part texture is perhaps closest to the medieval organum.

With an increasing vogue for European music *c.* 1800, the native tunes and the whole singing-school movement were driven from the urbanized East Coast to the more rural Midwest and South. There the Yankee hymn tunes, as "white spirituals," doubtless influenced the late Negro "spirituals."

Some immigrants chose isolation from the

dominant English culture and therefore had little influence on American music. Among them were the German-speaking, musically sophisticated members of the Ephrata (Pa.) Cloister under Johann Conrad Beissel (1690–1768). At Ephrata worshipers sang hymns in five, six, and seven parts, and it is said that Beissel composed more than a thousand of them. Benjamin Franklin printed an Ephrata hymn collection in 1730. Another group of isolated immigrants were the members of the United Brethren or Moravians, who settled Bethlehem (Pa.) in 1741 and later Salem (N.C.). Recent discoveries of large manuscript collections written by Moravian musicians in the then prevailing idiom of serious European music have revealed a musical tradition unequaled elsewhere in America. Among the more gifted Moravian composers were Johannes Herbst (1735–1812), John Antes (1740–1811), and Johann Friedrich Peter (1746–1813); see Collegium musicum.

Concerts in American colonial cities began to be held in the 18th century and apparently followed closely the advent of professional musicians who played for church, chamber, and theater. Organs were used in Episcopal services from an early date (King's Chapel, Boston, after 1713). According to newspaper advertisements, the first concert of record was held in Boston in 1731, followed by Charleston, S.C. (1732), New York (1736), and Philadelphia (1757). Such men as William Selby, who came to Boston (c. 1771) from London and was organist of King's Chapel, and William Tuckey, who came to New York from Bristol Cathedral in 1753 to become organist and choirmaster at Trinity Church, were active as composers and conductors of choral concerts. Tuckey directed the first American performance of excerpts from Handel's *Messiah* in 1770.

Such musical amateurs as Benjamin Franklin and Francis Hopkinson (1737–91), a signer of the Declaration of Independence and the first native-born American composer, stand out, Hopkinson for his songs in the simple and tuneful style of the contemporary London stage and Franklin for his "armonica," a species of mechanically spun musical glasses [see Glass harmonica].

II. *1790–1865.* The American Revolution interrupted musical activities, but afterward they were resumed, this time more intensively. In the last decade of the 18th century, a large-scale immigration from Europe brought musi-

cians from England and, after the French Revolution, from France. Attracted by opportunities arising from the growing urban culture of the East Coast, singing actors, instrumentalists, and dancing masters immigrated, many of them equally at home in choirloft and theater. Unlike the Moravians, they had a lasting effect on American music. They molded musical taste, and through their publishing firms and music shops they satisfied the demand for the new music, instruments, and instruction books. As teachers, they trained almost two generations of amateurs.

The most important of the newly arrived professional musicians were Raynor Taylor (c. 1747–1825), an English organist and theatrical conductor; his one-time pupil, Alexander Reinagle (1756–1809), who came to New York from London in 1786 and later settled in Philadelphia, where he was conductor at the Chestnut Street Theater (1794); Benjamin Carr (1768–1831), also of London, who established America's first music store in Philadelphia (1793), where he was active as a composer, singer, and organist as well as a founder of The Musical Fund Society (1820); James Hewitt (1770–1827), leader of the Old American Company orchestra, who wrote the opera *Tammanny* (1794) and began a publishing firm (1798); J. C. Gottlieb Graupner (1767–1836), son of a German oboist, who came to America in 1795 after having played under Haydn in London and settled in Boston, where he kept a music shop and publishing business and was active in the Handel and Haydn Society (1815); and Victor Pelissier, horn player and composer of the opera *Edwin and Angelina* (New York, 1796).

The impact of the professionals began to be felt after the War of 1812. Once exposed to the sophisticated sounds of Handel, Haydn, Grétry, and J. W. A. Stamitz, church music committees, musical societies, and even some Yankee tunesmiths turned away from the less elegant hymn tunes. Conscious of their mission to uplift cultural standards, these groups began to publish and perform only the music they considered "scientifically" correct. Although their activities may have driven away poorly trained but imaginative native composers, this was, perhaps, an inevitable result of the quest for cultural parity with Europe. Whether or not motivated by intellectual and aesthetic needs or merely by fashion, the establishment of such organizations for the performance of European master-works as the Handel and Haydn Society (Boston,

1815), The Musical Fund Society (Philadelphia, 1820), and the Philharmonic Society (New York, 1842)—all of which survive today—laid the foundation for serious American art music.

Lowell Mason (1792–1872), grandson of a Yankee singing-school teacher, was leader of this movement. In 1822 he published his first volume of sacred music, the *Boston Handel and Haydn Society Collection of Church Music,* which included melodies from Handel, Mozart, and Beethoven. Later, as president and conductor of the Society (1827), founder of the Boston Academy of Music (1832), head of music in the Boston public schools (1838–45), and organizer of music teachers' conventions, Mason spread the gospel of good (if not always inspired or original) music and himself composed more than 1,200 hymns. He also established a musical dynasty that included the founders (Lowell, Jr. and Henry) of the Mason and Hamlin Pianoforte Company; William Mason (1829–1908), a pianist and composer; and Daniel Gregory Mason (1873–1953), composer and teacher.

During the first few decades of the 19th century there emerged five highly original composers who seemed to dominate American music: Anthony Philip Heinrich (1781–1861), William Henry Fry (1813–64), George Frederick Bristow (1825–98), Louis (Moreau) Gottschalk (1829–69), and Stephen Foster (1826–64). Heinrich, born in Bohemia to wealth and position, lost his fortune in America, and then turned to his violin and to composition, working in the Kentucky wilderness. His uninhibited imagination is seen in his *The Sylviad; or Minstrelsy of Nature* [1825], published by J. C. G. Graupner and containing almost 400 pages of music for all media. As a token of affection for his adopted land, he often used national tunes like "Yankee Doodle." Some of his music has the simplicity of folksong, whereas other of his works are more grandiose in conception than Beethoven's (with whom he was compared) or Berlioz'. W. H. Fry composed the first American grand opera, *Leonora* (Philadelphia, 1845), in which the influence of Donizetti and Bellini is seen. A colleague of his in New York, George Frederick Bristow, son of an English immigrant musician, wrote the first American grand opera on an American subject, *Rip van Winkle* (New York, 1855). Louis (Moreau) Gottschalk went from his native New Orleans to Paris, where he captivated French audiences with his brilliant piano playing, especially of his own compositions. Many of his works were based on Latin American,

Negro, and American popular and folk music, thus anticipating some of the important stylistic trends of 20th-century American music. His contemporary, Stephen Foster, also capitalized on Negro and folk elements. Foster songs, such as "Old Folks at Home," "Oh, Susanna," and "Camptown Races" (parodied in Gottschalk's piano fantasia, "The Banjo"), have become American folksongs.

III. *1865–1929.* Between the end of the Civil War and the Great Depression of the 1920's, a spectacular growth took place in American music, fostered by rapid industrialization and an almost fourfold increase in population. After 1848, the arrival of German musicians with technical skills and aesthetic concepts of music far superior to any known in America influenced the quality of the development. By the 1920's American music had achieved an independence nurtured by the less dogmatic musical ideologies of France, Italy, and Russia.

By 1870, no major city was without its contingent of resident German musicians, many of whom attained key positions in musical institutions. Carl Zerrahn (1826–1909) was conductor of Boston's Handel and Haydn Society; Carl Bergmann (1821–76) led the New York Philharmonic Society; Hermann Kotzschmar (1829–1909) was the leading musician of Portland, Maine; and Theodore Thomas (1835–1905) did much for the performance of contemporary music, including compositions by Americans, as conductor of his own and later the Chicago Symphony Orchestra (1891). Their precise yet sensitive readings of romantic music had a tremendous impact on audiences accustomed to hymn tunes and oratorios, and they inspired the young generation of Americans who were to become a second school of American composers (Billings and the tunesmiths comprising the first).

Among the members of this second school were John Knowles Paine (1839–1906), Dudley Buck (1839–1909), Arthur Foote (1853–1937), George Whitefield Chadwick (1854–1931), Edward A. MacDowell (1861–1908), and Horatio W. Parker (1863–1919). All were united by ties of friendship, geographical proximity, and, with the exception of MacDowell, whose ancestry was Scottish, all were proud of their Yankee heritage. They were the first Americans trained in both the United States and Germany. Paine, Kotzschmar's most brilliant pupil, studied in Berlin with Karl August Haupt (1810–91) and Friedrich Wilhelm Wieprecht (1802–72). Some years later (1867) he conducted his Mass in D at the Berlin Singakademie. In 1875 he was appointed professor of music at Harvard, and for thirty years he occupied the first such chair established in an American university. Among his major works are two symphonies, incidental music to *Oedipus Tyrannus,* and an opera, *Azara,* published in 1901 (but never staged).

G. W. Chadwick's career followed the pattern set by Paine. He was educated by American musicians with German training and later studied at Leipzig with Salomon Jadassohn (1831–1902) and at Munich with Josef Rheinberger (1839–1901). Back home, Chadwick gained a reputation as a composer, teacher, organist, and conductor. In 1897 he became director of the New England Conservatory of Music. He wrote in every form, ranging from musical comedy (*Tabasco,* Boston, 1894) to a verismo opera dealing with Italian immigrants (*The Padrone,* 1915), and from symphonies to program music. His best-selling textbook on harmony is noteworthy for its pragmatism. Although reflecting European techniques, Chadwick's music is distinguished by originality derived from the pentatonic melodies, modal harmonies, and boisterous rhythms of his hymn-tune, folk heritage. In his later works, especially in the symphonic ballad *Tam O'Shanter* and in *The Padrone,* he broke away from German influence.

Edward A. MacDowell, the most celebrated composer of the period, was not, strictly speaking, a member of the second school (or New England group), since he worked chiefly in New York, where he was the first professor of music at Columbia University (1896). His early training was as a pianist under Maria Teresa Carreño (1853–1917) in New York, and later under Antoine-François Marmontel (1816–98) at the Paris Conservatory. The most influential of his teachers was Joseph Joachim Raff (1822–82), with whom he studied composition in Frankfurt. Less solid a craftsman than Paine and less versatile than Chadwick, MacDowell far surpassed his colleagues in melodic and harmonic originality, as can be seen in his two piano concertos and even more in his solo piano music, especially the *Sea Pieces* op. 55 (1898) and the Sonata no. 4 (Keltic), op. 59 (1901). The youngest member of the group, Horatio W. Parker, began as Chadwick's pupil. After studying also under Rheinberger, Parker returned to the United States. There he worked as an organist and composed the oratorio *Hora Novissima*

(1893), which made him nationally famous. In 1894 he was appointed professor of music at Yale, a position he retained until his death. His two operas, *Mona* (New York [Metropolitan], 1912) and *Fairyland* (Los Angeles, 1915) won prizes of $10,000 each.

With the second New England school, American composition won a position of respect. As early as the 1889 *Exposition Universelle* concert of American works in Paris, critics noted a special American flavor and the technical finesse of what Julien Tiersot called the *jeune école américaine.* As teachers of composition, heads of academic departments and institutions, and conductors, they gradually supplanted German musicians. Many of their pupils went to France for further instruction, and there was a noticeable tendency to adopt French, Russian, and Italian ideals.

Another significant force in the American search for a musical identity was Antonin Dvořák, who taught at the National Conservatory of Music in New York (1892–95). Though he was not the first composer to see artistic merit in Negro melody (Chadwick had used a "plantation song" in his Second Symphony in B♭ major), the success of Dvořák's symphony "From the New World" (1893), in which similar material was employed, served as an example to younger American composers, some of whom studied with him, among them Rubin Goldmark (1872–1936) and Harvey Worthington Loomis (1865–1930).

Generally speaking, the second school and its pupils dominated American composition until the Depression. Ethnically Anglo-American and by temperament conservative, such composers as Frederick S. Converse (1871–1940), John Alden Carpenter (1876–1951), Daniel Gregory Mason (1873–1953), Henry Hadley (1871–1937), Edward Burlingame Hill (1872–1960), Arthur Shepherd (1880–1958), Charles Wakefield Cadman (1881–1946), and Mrs. H. H. A. Beach (1867–1944), along with Paine, Chadwick, and MacDowell, continued a style of composition that amalgamated sturdy hymnic melody with a variety of late 19th-century harmonic idioms and orchestral techniques. Though many of them lived through the epochal innovations of Schoenberg and Stravinsky, they tended to reject the new ideas of sonority and rhythm and strove for what they felt was beautiful rather than attempting 20th-century musical idioms.

But there were some exceptions. Chief among them were Charles Martin Loeffler (1861–1935), an Alsatian-born violinist-composer whose *A Pagan Poem,* op. 14, is one of the most striking American works, and Charles E. Ives (1874–1954), Horatio Parker's most famous pupil. Not only did Ives anticipate such modern devices as polytonality, dissonant counterpoint, polyrhythm, and serial construction, but he evolved a musical philosophy, which he called "musical relativism," based on such variable factors as tempo and feeling. Other unconventional features of his music were the use of *tone clusters and the omission of time signatures and bar lines. Ives' importance does not rest entirely on his imaginative approach; rather, it lies in the blending of these devices with the *melos* of the hymn tune, popular song, and dance that make his music so universal and at the same time so American. Perhaps the most interesting aspect of Ives' career is the fact that he did not study in Europe or become a professional musician. Instead, he organized an insurance agency whose financial success, Ives felt, was aided by his composition, which in turn was helped by his business activities. After decades of relative obscurity, Ives has become the best-known composer of the older American school, largely through his Second Symphony (completed 1902; first perf. 1951), a symphonic piece, *Three Places in New England* (composed 1903–1914), his *A Book of 114 Songs* (pub. 1922), and the second piano sonata, or *Concord Sonata* (completed 1915).

IV. *1930—.* With this generation of composers American music arrived on the world scene. Performances of American music, which had been sporadic at best, now became quite common in Europe and, especially after World War II, trends in American composition began to influence musicians the world over.

World War I helped upset the equilibrium that balanced the leading Yankee composers, teachers, and church musicians against the largely European personnel of the opera houses and symphony orchestras. Also, first- and second-generation Americans of non-Yankee stock began to become known as composers with modernist tendencies, much to the dismay of the older conservatives. In contrast to their predecessors, after early study in the United States they went to Paris, where many were guided by Nadia Boulanger (b. 1887). French pedagogy tended to cultivate taste rather than instill dogma, and so there developed a third school of American composers, united by neither ethnic ties nor geography but by a desire to explore the advancing horizons of music while creating an uninhibited American musical idiom. This they accomplished by integrating popular and folk idioms and modern stylistic elements.

The music of Aaron Copland (b. 1900) reveals this duality. In *Music for the Theatre* (1925), *Concerto for Piano and Orchestra* (composed 1926), *Billy the Kid* (1938), and *Appalachian Spring* (1944), he consciously created an "American" sound; other of his works, such as the *Piano Variations* (composed 1930), *Sextet* (composed 1937) and *Piano Fantasy* (1957), are essays in a contemporary learned style in which nationalist features are notably absent. Similarly, the music of Virgil Thomson (b. 1896) shows a polarity between an American and a cosmopolitan style. He established a definite American style in his two operas, *Four Saints in Three Acts* (1934) and *The Mother of Us All* (1947), through scrupulous attention to the natural accent and inflection of American speech and the use of characteristic melodic lines, but in the *Missa Pro Defunctis* (1960) he used a more universal manner that explores the limits of polytonality and contrapuntal parallelism. Contemporaries such as Roy Harris (b. 1898), Walter Piston (b. 1894), Roger Sessions (b. 1896), Douglas Moore (b. 1893), Howard Hanson (b. 1896), and Randall Thompson (b. 1899) all exhibit, with due consideration for their individuality, similar tendencies. Piston and Harris became basically symphonic composers, while Moore found success in operas and Thompson carried on a tradition of choral composition with roots going back to the early tunesmiths.

The succeeding generation of 20th-century American composers, many of them pupils or followers of the above-named, pursued both musical Americanism and cosmopolitanism. It includes Samuel Barber (b. 1910), Leonard Bernstein (b. 1918), David Diamond (b. 1915), William Schuman (b. 1910), Paul Bowles (b. 1910), Morton Gould (b. 1913), Paul Creston (b. 1906), Irving Fine (1914–62), Vincent Persichetti (b. 1915), Norman Dello Joio (b. 1913), Elliott Carter (b. 1908), Lukas Foss (b. 1922), Alan Hovhaness (b. 1911), George Rochberg (b. 1918), Vittorio Giannini (b. 1903), Leon Kirchner (b. 1919), Ross Lee Finney (b. 1906), and Gunther Schuller (b. 1925).

Experimentation has been a hallmark of American music from Billings to Ives, and it is not surprising that American music today should emphasize novelty, imagination, and experimentation with new materials and media for musical construction. A leader in the quest for new sonorities was Edgard Varèse (1885–1965), who came to the United States from Paris in 1915. Chief among his works are *Ionisation* (1931), where sounds of indefinite pitch are organized musically, and *Poème Électronique* (1958), composed for 400 spatially arranged loudspeakers. Independent composers in this genre are Carl Ruggles (b. 1876), John J. Becker (1886–1961), Henry Cowell (1897–1965), George Antheil (1900–1959), John Cage (b. 1912), Henry Brant (b. 1913), and Vladimir Ussachevsky (b. 1911), who have constructed pieces out of various materials, from tone clusters and random elements to tape-recorded and synthesized sounds. Milton Babbitt (b. 1916), a most articulate theoretician, has stressed the elements of control and serialization in his compositions, which successfully combine vocal and synthesized sounds. [Also see Electronic music; Serial music; Aleatory music.]

Despite the recognized stature of contemporary American composition, it would be misleading to ignore the significance of all kinds of popular music in the United States. Actually, some of the most unique and influential American music has come from the dance hall, theater, and motion picture (*film music). Ever since the appearance of Negro-style minstrel music in the early 19th century, popular entertainment music seems to have been the most typical American musical manifestation to the world at large. Notable examples have been Foster's song-dance idiom, which joined Negro traits to the sentimental theater song, the various adaptations of Irish and Scotch vaudeville songs and dances, and the coalescence of these with other folk material from work songs, blues, and marches into *ragtime and *jazz in the bordellos and saloons of the South and West. [Also see Negro music.] Jazz is more a matter of performance than a specific form or technique, and so its recordings rather than scores are historically important. Aside from being an important idiom in itself, jazz has also influenced art music. See Jazz.

A new popular melodic idiom, developed after 1900 in numerous Yiddish-language theaters of New York City, signaled the contribution of one of the last immigrant groups to arrive in America before the gates were closed in 1924. Its features resulted from the mutual assimilation of Jewish, American, and Negro musical elements and later had an impact on the style

of Broadway musical comedies and plays. The apex of this style is reached in George Gershwin's (1898–1937) opera *Porgy and Bess* (1935). Besides Gershwin, Irving Berlin (b. 1888), Jerome Kern (1885–1945), Vincent Youmans (1898–1946), Cole Porter (1893–1964), Richard Rodgers (b. 1902), and Marc Blitzstein (1905–64) all have made important contributions to an internationally popular music that is recognizably American. [Also see Operetta.]

Lit. *General:* J. T. Howard, *Our American Music,* rev. ed. [1965]; G. Chase, *America's Music* (1955); O. Thompson, *American Music and Musicians* (1939); H. C. Lahee, *Annals of Music in America* (1922); M. H. Despard, *The Music of the United States, Its Sources and Its History* (1936); H. W. Foote, *Three Centuries of American Hymnody* (1940; repr. 1961); C. Reis, *Composers in America* (1947); W. T. Upton, *Art-Song in America* (1930); *Bio-Bibliographical Index of Musicians in the United States of America Since Colonial Times,* rev. ed. (1956); *GDB,* Am. suppl.; vi of 4th ed. (1944); H. E. Johnson, *Operas on American Subjects* (1964); W. T. Marrocco and H. Gleason, ed., ‡*Music in America, An Anthology* (1964); R. P. Phelps, "The History and Practice of Chamber Music in the United States from Earliest Times up to 1875" (diss. State Univ. of Iowa, 1951).

For I: I. Lowens, *Music and Musicians in Early America* (1964); R. H. Scott, *Music among the Moravians, 1741–1816* (1938); O. G. Sonneck, *Early Concert Life in America (1731–1800)* (1907); *id., Bibliography of Early Secular American Music,* rev. by W. T. Upton (1945); R. T. Daniel, *The Anthem in New England before 1800* (1966); *Church Music and Musical Life in Pennsylvania in the Eighteenth Century,* 3 vols. (pub. by The Pennsylvania Society of the Colonial Dames of America, 1926–47); P. A. Scholes, *The Puritans and Music in England and New England* (1934); W. S. Pratt, *The Music of the Pilgrims* (1921); H. C. MacDougall, *Early New England Psalmody, An Historical Appreciation, 1620–1820* (1940); C. Cyclone, "Religion and Music in Colonial America" (diss. Stanford Univ., 1949); G. H. Yerbury, "Styles and Schools of the Art-Song in America, 1720–1850" (diss. Indiana Univ., 1953).

For II: O. G. Sonneck, *Early Opera in America* (1915); K. S. Hackett, *The Beginning of Grand Opera in Chicago (1850–1859)* (1913); L. C. Elson, *The National Music of America and Its Sources* (1900); R. J. Wolfe, *Secular Music in America, 1801–1825; A Bibliography,* 3 vols.

(1964); R. M. Kent, "A Study of Oratorios and Sacred Cantatas Composed in America before 1900" (diss. State Univ. of Iowa, 1954); O. G. Sonneck, "Early American Operas" (*SIM* vi). *Sources from the period:* G. Hood, *A History of Music in New England* (1846).

For III. *Sources from the period:* L. C. Elson, *The History of American Music* (1904, '25); W. L. Hubbard, *The American History and Encyclopedia of Music* [1908]; H. M. Brooks, *Olden-Time Music* (1888); W. A. Fisher, *Notes on Music in Old Boston* (1918); N. D. Gould, *Church Music in America* (1853); W. S. B. Mathews, ed., *A Hundred Years of Music in America* (1889); F. L. Ritter, *Music in America* (1883); R. Hughes, *Contemporary American Composers* (1900); F. O. Jones, ed., *A Handbook of American Music and Musicians, Containing Biographies of American Musicians, and Histories of the Principal Musical Institutions, Firms and Societies* (1886); *Dwight's Journal of Music, A Paper of Art and Literature* (1852–83).

For III and IV: W. A. Fisher, *One Hundred and Fifty Years of Music Publishing in the United States . . . 1783–1933* (1933); J. Mattfeld, *A Hundred Years of Grand Opera in New York 1825–1925* (1927); D. Ewen, *American Composers Today* (1949); J. T. Howard, *Our Contemporary Composers* (1941); H. Cowell, *American Composers on American Music* (1933; repr. 1962); A. Copland, *Our New Music* (1941); L. Stringfield, *America and Her Music* (1931); V. F. Yellin, "The Life and Operatic Works of George Whitefield Chadwick" (diss. Harvard Univ., 1957); *id.*, "The Conflict of Generations in American Music" (*Arts and Sciences* i, 13–16); *id.*, "Opera's American History" (*Music Journal* xix, 60ff); D. Slepian, "Polyphonic Forms and Devices in Modern American Music" (*MQ* xxxiii); *MM, passim* (1923–46).   V.Y.

Unit organ. A type of organ in which one rank of pipes is arranged to serve for several stops through the medium of an electric coupling device. See Organ.

Unmerklich [G.]. Imperceptible.

Un peu [F.], **un poco** [It.]. See *Peu; Poco.*

Unruhig [G.]. Restless.

Unter- [G.]. Below, under. *Unterdominante,* subdominant; *Untermediante,* submediant; *unter setzen,* to put under (the thumb, in piano playing); *Unterstimme,* lower or lowest part; *Untertaste,* white key; *Unterwerk,* *choir organ.

Upbeat [G. *Auftakt*]. One or several initial notes of a melody that occur before the first bar line. The upbeat plays a central part in the theory of H. Riemann and others that every melody or phrase begins with an upbeat (real or imaginary). This is a gross exaggeration of the fact that the beginning or end of a phrase frequently does not coincide with the bar line (particularly in Bach's music). See Phrasing and articulation [G. *Auftaktigkeit*].

Before 1600 the upbeat was rarely used. Various scholars have suggested that in 13th-century music the second mode, normally a downbeat iambic pattern [see Modes, rhythmic], could also have meant an upbeat trochaic pattern—in other words, an upbeat variant of the first mode [see H. Husmann, in *AMW* xi, 14, 15, 299]. In 14th- and 15th-century music only about one composition in a hundred begins with an upbeat. Examples are Machaut's "Comment qu'a moy," B. Cordier's "Belle Bonne," and Binchois' "De plus en plus" [see *HAM,* nos. 46a, 48b, 69]. It is probably no coincidence that all these are from the secular repertory. In contrast to their scarcity in vocal music, upbeat formations in the form of a quick turn (f–e–d–e–f) are a characteristic trait of early organ music, in the Codex Faenza (*c.* 1400) as well as in 15th-century German sources (Ileborgh, C. Paumann, Buxheim Organ Book). Several of the 17th-century dance types begin with an upbeat, and the *gavotte with a doubled upbeat of two quarter notes.

Urlar. See under Pibroch.

Urlinie, Ursatz [G.]. See under Schenker system.

Uruguay. Colonial church music in Uruguay got a later start than in Mexico, Peru, Venezuela, or Brazil, not becoming clearly established until the end of the 18th century. At that time the first three- and four-part Masses with organ accompaniment written in Uruguay began to replace the older, semipopular religious hymns used in churches from the time of the Spanish Conquest. The earliest example preserved is a *Misa para día de Difuntos,* written in 1802 by Father Manuel Ubeda (1760–1823). However, the names of a number of Brazilian and Argentinian church composers were well known before this time, and their music was used extensively in Uruguayan churches. In addition to such compositions, the archives of the Church of San Francisco in Montevideo contain the manuscript of a *Misa a duo* by Father Juan José de Sostoa (*c.* 1750–1813).

From *c.* 1830 to the early 20th century, music in Uruguay was strongly influenced by Italian opera. A few native composers, together with a number of Spaniards, Brazilians, and Argentinians who settled for short periods in Montevideo, were responsible for maintaining Uruguay's distinctive musical life. To this period belong Fernando Quijano (1805–71), a talented actor, pianist, singer, choreographer, and amateur composer; Luis Preti (1826–1902), an outstanding composer and conductor, who as founder of the *Sociedad Filarmónica* in 1868 was the first to conduct Beethoven's symphonies in Uruguay; Oscar Pfeiffer (1824–1906), a composer and pianist of international repute; and Francisco José Debali (1791–1859), who composed more than 143 works, including the national anthem. Late 19th-century composers such as Luis Sambucetti (1860–1926) and León Ribeiro (1854–1931) continued to write music in the Italian tradition.

The founders of the modern school of composition in Uruguay are Carlos Pedrell (1878–1941), Alfonso Broqua (1876–1946), César Cortinas (1892–1918), a composer of much promise who produced a concerto for piano and several other compositions, and, most important, Eduardo Fabini (1883–1950). Fabini, an impressionist and a strong proponent of *nationalist music, won fame in Latin America through his *Campo* and *La Isla de los Ceibos.* Other 20th-century Uruguayan composers are Vicente Ascone (b. 1897), Luis Cluzeau Mortet (1893–1957), Carlos Estrada (b. 1909), and Guido Santórsola (b. 1904). The leading figure of the next generation is Héctor Alberto Tosar Errecart (b. 1923), composer of a Te Deum for chorus, baritone, and orchestra, *Stray Birds* for voice and chamber ensemble, and many instrumental compositions. José Serebrier (b. 1938), in addition to composing, became an outstanding conductor, while Sergio Cervetti (b. 1940) and Leon Biriotti (b. 1942) have produced works of international significance.

Musical life in Uruguay owes a great deal to the musicologist Francisco Curt Lange (b. 1903), founder of the *Instituto Interamericano de Musicologia* of Montevideo (1940) and editor of the *Boletín Latino-Americano de Música* (1935–47).

Uruguayan folk music has virtually the same characteristics as Argentine folk music. The *tango, *triste, *estilo, and many other forms are as popular in Uruguay as in Argentina, although they are sometimes known by different names. Perhaps the only form that can be considered wholly Uruguayan is the *pericón. See L. Ayestarán, *La Música en el Uruguay* (1953). Also see under Latin America.   J.O-S.

U.S.S.R. See Russia.

Ut. The first of the Guidonian syllables of solmization; see Hexachord II. In French nomenclature, name for C [see Pitch names]. *Ut-re-mi-fa-sol-la* has been used as a title for compositions based on the tones of the hexachord (by Byrd, J. Bull, Sweelinck, *et al.*).

Utility music. See *Gebrauchsmusik.*

Ut supra [L.]. As above, as before.

V

V. Abbr. for (1) *vide,* i.e., "see"; (2) violin (also V°); VV, violins; (3) *voci,* e.g., 3 v, for three voices; (4) in liturgical books, ℣ means *verse or versicle.

Va. Abbr. for viola.

Vagans [L.]. In 15th- and 16th-century Masses and motets, name for the fifth part (also called *quinta vox*). The most probable reason for the name is that this part had no specific range but could be a second *superius,* tenor, or bass, especially in a partbook containing a number of compositions.

Vaghezza, con [It.]. With grace, with charm.

Valkyrie, The. See *Ring des Nibelungen, Der.*

Valor [L.]. In mensural notation, the time value of a note, particularly as represented by its equivalent in smaller values, e.g., of a semibreve by two or three minims. For *integer valor,* see Proportions.

Valse [F.], **vals** [Sp.]. *Waltz. *Valse à deux temps,* a waltz whose melody proceeds in units of two beats instead of three, in cross-rhythm with the accompaniment. The best-known example is in Gounod's *Faust.* Others are in the works of Tchaikovsky (*Eugen Onegin;* piano suite, *The Seasons*).

Valse, La. "Poème choréographique" (dance poem) for orchestra by Ravel, composed 1920, imitating and cleverly parodying the Viennese waltz of Johann Strauss, Jr. It is often used for ballet performances.

Valses nobles et sentimentales. A set of waltzes for piano by Ravel, composed in 1911 and orchestrated by the composer to serve as music for the ballet *Adélaïde, ou le Langage des Fleurs.* The adjectives "noble" and "sentimental" (already used by Schubert) are used to distinguish between the "elegant" and the "lyrical" types of waltz.

Valse Triste. A popular waltz for orchestra by Sibelius, originally composed (1903) as part of the incidental music to the play *Kuolema.*

Valve [F. *piston;* G. *Ventil;* It. *pistone;* Sp. *pistón*]. A mechanism invented *c.* 1815 by Blühmel (Silesia) and, simultaneously, by H. Stölzel (Berlin), that makes available all the tones of the chromatic scale on brass instruments. The device alters an instrument's pitch by increasing or decreasing the tube length through which the wind must pass. Descending valves bring extra lengths of tube (loops) into play, lowering the pitch; ascending valves eliminate a portion of the main tubing, raising the pitch. Horns and trumpets usually have three valves, which lower the pitch a whole tone, semitone, and minor third respectively. By using two or all three valves together, the pitch can be lowered by six semitones, resulting in a complete chromatic scale [see Wind instruments IV (c)]. The simultaneous use of two valves produces tones that are slightly sharped, since an additional tubing calculated to lower the normal pipe by a semitone is a little too short to produce the same effect on a pipe already lengthened by another tubing. The effect is even more extreme when three valves are combined. This drawback is corrected by "compensation valves" (numerous patents; see the article in *GD; GDB*) and avoided in Adolphe Sax's "ascending valves," which shorten the original

pipe. Neither kind, however, has gained acceptance.

Two types of valve are in use, piston valves and rotary (or cylinder) valves. In the former a piston works up and down in a casing. This type is used in France, Belgium, Holland, England, and the United States. The rotary valve, preferred for the French horn in the United States and on the Continent though not in England, is a four-way stopcock turning in a cylindrical case and controlled by a metal spring. The four ways form part of the main pipe, and the other two, on being rotated 90°, admit it to the bypath. See Horn; Trumpet; Tuba; Wind instruments IV (c).

Valve instruments. Brass instruments provided with a *valve mechanism. Today all brass instruments (trumpets, horns, tubas, etc.) except the trombone are built with valves. The terms "valve horn," "valve trumpet," etc., distinguish the modern instruments from the earlier natural or keyed instruments.

Vamp. An extemporized accompaniment consisting of simple chords. *Vamping tutor,* a book of instruction in this type of accompaniment.

Vamphorn. A megaphone, 2 to 8 feet long, that was used in English churches during the 18th and 19th centuries for making announcements.

Vanessa. Opera in four acts by S. Barber (libretto by G. C. Menotti), produced in New York, 1958.

Variante [G.]. In H. Riemann's system of harmonic analysis, term for parallel key (substitution of minor for major, or vice versa).

Variation, technique of. In the most general sense, a restatement that retains some features of the original while others are discarded, altered, or replaced. One of the most fundamental techniques of composition, it takes such forms as ornamentation, transposition, inversion, retrograde motion, augmentation, rhythmic modification, *transformation, etc. Even the twelve-tone technique is a variation technique [see Serial music]. Some writers go so far as to maintain that all music is a variation of certain basic structures of pitch (scales) and duration (rhythm, meter).

Usually, however, the term refers to a specific, fairly simple practice: the immediate restatement, in varied form, of a musical theme (tune). Examples are the varied repeat, the *double,* and the musical form known as "theme with variations." The varied repeat is often used in the late 16th-century English *pavane, each of whose three sections is repeated in a varied form. The *double is a simple variation on a dance of a suite. In the theme with variations the musical idea is presented in a number of successive modifications; see Variations.

Variation canzona. See Canzona (5) I.

Variations. A musical form (variation form) resulting from the consistent application of *variation techniques so that a musical theme is followed by a varying number of modified restatements, each being a "variation." Such compositions appear as independent works (Bach, Goldberg Variations, *Clavier-Übung,* part iv; Beethoven, Diabelli Variations op. 120) or as a movement of a sonata or symphony, usually the slow movement (Beethoven, Appassionata Sonata op. 57; Ninth Symphony).

I. *Theme.* The theme is usually a simple tune in binary form, from 16 to 32 measures long and frequently borrowed from another composer (e.g., Beethoven's variations on a theme by Diabelli; Brahms' variations on a theme by Handel op. 24, for piano solo with fugue). There is, however, a special kind of variations where the theme is not a complete tune but only a four- or eight-measure scheme of harmonies or a bass line of the same length. Of this kind are the examples known as *chaconne, passacaglia,* *ground, and *basso ostinato.* The difference between these two kinds of variations might be described as "sectional variations" versus "continuous variations." In sectional variations the theme is a full-grown tune with a definite ending and hence each variation has a definite end (except in cases where the composer prescribes *segue subito,* "follow immediately," with the next variation). In continuous variations the theme is a short succession of harmonies to be repeated over and over without interruption. In sectional variations the theme always has a distinct melody, whereas in continuous variations it consists only of a scheme of harmonies, frequently (but not necessarily) represented by a reiterated bass. To distinguish between the two as "variations of a melody" and "variations of a bass" is not too helpful, since numerous chaconnes and passacaglias lack a clearly defined bass line [see Chaconne and passacaglia]. A borderline case is the *strophic bass of the 17th century, whose theme is a bass so long and so complete that a sectional structure results. The discussion below refers chiefly to the normal (sectional) "theme with variations."

II. *The fixed elements.* Those features that a variation on a theme has in common with the theme are the so-called "fixed elements." Some writers distinguish between variations in which the original melody is preserved, or "melodic" variations, and those in which the original harmonies are preserved, or "structural" or "harmonic" variations [see the article in *GD* (*GDB*), which, however, is not always consistent in the use of these terms]. This distinction is unsatisfactory, however. Stability of the harmonic scheme (at least in its main outlines) is a prerequisite for practically all variations, except the entirely free variations of modern composers (e.g., Stravinsky, *Sonata for Two Pianos,* 2nd movt. [1943–44]). Stability of the melody is an additional restriction that was traditionally observed in the early period of variation (16th, 17th cent.) but is the exception rather than the rule with composers such as Mozart, Beethoven, Schubert, and Brahms.

There are four basic kinds of variation: *A.* a variation that preserves both melody (though perhaps with new ornamentation) and harmony of the theme; *B.* one that preserves the essential harmony of the theme; *C.* one in which the harmonies deviate but the over-all structure, such as the number of measures, the structure of sections and phrases, and the cadential endings, is preserved; *D.* the entirely free variations of modern composers in which even the structural outlines of the theme are no longer recognizable.

Historically, category *A* prevails throughout the 16th and 17th centuries, category *B* throughout the classical period, category *C* is common among romantic composers, and *D* is characteristic of the most recent style (beginning with D'Indy, Reger, and R. Strauss). All continuous variations [see I above] belong to category *B* (not *A*), since in these the thematic substance does not include a melody, so that of necessity each variation will be melodically independent. This type of variation prevailed mainly during the baroque era, when, it appears, categories *A* and *B* existed side by side, *A* for sectional variations (such as Scheidt's *Passamezzo* with twelve variations) and *B* for continuous variations (passacaglias, chaconnes, grounds).

There is still a fifth kind of variation, in which the melody is retained but the harmonies are altered. In the classical period this type was used occasionally as a "trick," as, for example, variation no. 6 of Beethoven's Eroica Variations op. 35, in which the original melody is harmonized in C minor instead of E-flat major.

However, it was more important somewhat earlier, in the contrapuntal variations of the baroque, in which the melody is treated as a *cantus firmus* [see e.g., variation no. 4 of Samuel Scheidt's "Wehe, Windgen, wehe"; *DdT* 1; *HAM,* no. 196].

III. *The variable elements.* Although it is difficult to generalize, there are some standard ways in which themes are varied. In category *A* [see II above], the most common procedure is to ornament the melody (*ornamenting variation;* see Ex. 1). Another method, frequently used in the 16th and 17th centuries, is to present the theme as part—often an inner part—of a contrapuntal-imitative web (*contrapuntal variation;* see Ex. 2). In category *B* are practically all the variations of the classical period except the ornamenting variations. Among these are: (a) *melodic variations,* in which a new melody is invented to the original scheme of harmonies

[Ex. 3]; perhaps the earliest instances of full-scale melodic variations are Bach's Goldberg Variations; another striking example is the first variation in the final movement of Beethoven's Piano Sonata op. 109; (b) the *figural variation,* in which a characteristic figure is employed throughout [Ex. 4]; (c) the *canonic variation* [Ex. 5]; (d) the *harmonic variation* [Ex. 6]; (e) the *tempo variation,* involving a change of tempo; (f) the *modal variation,* involving a change from major to minor or vice versa; (g) the *character variation,* which bestows on the theme a special character, such as that of a dance, a military march, etc. The last three methods are summarily illustrated in Ex. 7. Naturally, most of these procedures may occur in any of the four categories of II; however, the ornamenting variation is restricted to category *A,* the melodic variation cannot occur in *A,* and the harmonic variation belongs to category *C.*

IV. *History.* (1) To 1600. In some books on music history, a late 14th-century composition entitled *Di molen van Pariis* (translated as "The Windmills of Paris") is given as the earliest extant example of a theme with variations [see, e.g., R. Haas, *Aufführungspraxis der Musik* (1931), p. 103f]. Actually, it is a rondeau, "Amis tous dous," of which there are two versions with differently ornamented upper parts [see F. Kammerer, *Die Musikstücke des Prager Codex XI E 9* (1931) i, 145ff; also *CP 1924*, p. 101ff]. The view that this is a "theme with two variations" is farfetched. The same applies to the different versions of "Frowe all myn hoffen" in the Ileborgh Organ Tablature of 1448, and to those of Binchois' "Je loue amours" in the Buxheim Organ Book of *c.* 1460–70.

The documented history of variations as a musical form begins in the early 16th century. Judging from the surviving examples, Spain and England have about an equal claim to precedence, England in continuous variations (H. Aston's "Hornepype," in *ApMZ* ii, 5; "My Lady Careys Dompe," both *c.* 1525; see Hornpipe; Dump; Ostinato), and Spain in both continuous variations and sectional variations based on a fully developed theme (vihuela variations by Narvaez, 1538; see *HAM*, no. 122; *ApMZ* ii, 14). The advanced style of the "Hornepype" as well as of Narvaez' variations indicates an extensive earlier development, all traces of which are lost. By 1550 the evolution of the Spanish variations, called **diferencias* [see also *Glosa*], had culminated in the works of Antonio de Cabezón (1510–66; see *HAM*, no. 134). Cabezón's variations are mostly contrapuntal, a type that continued to prevail with the later masters (Sweelinck, Scheidt, Frescobaldi). Toward the end of the 16th century the English virginalists (Byrd, Bull, J. Munday, Gibbons) established the figural variation, frequently in brilliant virtuoso style (rapid scales, broken-chord figures, figures in parallel thirds, etc.; see *HAM*, no. 177). While with Byrd the technical and musical qualities are well balanced, Bull's variations are conspicuous for their exploitation of technique, frequently at the expense of artistic quality. Another great master of the variation was Sweelinck, who used the technical achievements of the virginalists but with superior ingenuity. His variations on "Mein junges Leben hat ein End" are among the masterpieces in this form. Measured against this standard, the variation technique of Samuel Scheidt is rather elementary, but his variations on "Wehe, Windgen, wehe" [*DdT* 1; *HAM*, no. 196] charm through their very simplicity.

(2) 1600–1750. In Italy the traceable history of variations begins with the Neapolitan composers Valente, Trabaci, and A. Mayone, who, probably influenced by Cabezón, wrote **partitas* to popular bass patterns such as the **romanesca, *ruggiero, zefiro,* etc. [see also *Folia*]. Their tradition was continued, more artistically, in the numerous partitas of Frescobaldi [see *HAM*,

no. 192; also no. 199 by Marini]. Froberger's (1616–67) partitas "Auff die Meyerin" are one of the first examples of character variations, in the style of a courante or saraband. They represent a trend, quite common in the baroque era, toward merging the form of variations with that of the **suite*. Thus Wolfgang Ebner's "Trentasei Variazioni sopra un' Aria del l' Imperatore Ferdinando III" (*c.* 1660; *TaAM* vii) consist of three groups of twelve variations each, the first dozen in the style of an allemande and the second and third in the styles of the courante and saraband (regarding the absence of the gigue, see under Suite III). A remarkable specimen is Alessandro Poglietti's "Aria allemagna" (1677; *DTO* 27, pp. 13ff), which consists mainly of programmatic character variations such as "Lyra," "Böhmisch Dudlsackh," "Holländisch: Flagolett," "Bayrische Schalmay," "Alter Weiber Conduct," "Gaugler Seiltantz," "Französische Baiselemens" (French kiss-the-hand). Although not very refined, these pieces are amusing portrayals or caricatures. They were dedicated to the Austrian Empress Maddalena Theresa in 1677. Of particular importance is the German 17th-century tradition of variations based on a chorale [see Chorale variations]. For other types, see Chaconne and passacaglia; Ground; Strophic bass; Noel. At the end of the baroque period came a fitting climax, Bach's **Goldberg Variations*, in which category *B* [see II above] prevails for the first time.

(3) 1750–1900. Compared to the elaborate variation technique of the baroque, that of Mozart's piano variations is fairly simple and standardized. The first variations usually are ornamented with triplets or sixteenth notes, followed by some with special pianistic or contrapuntal devices. After these there is usually a slow variation, sometimes in a minor key, and then a final fast variation in a different meter (duple instead of triple or vice versa). Haydn's greatest contributions to the repertory are in his symphonies and, particularly, in his late quartets, notably the Emperor Quartet (op. 76, no. 3, 2nd movt.) with its variations on "Gott erhalte Franz den Kaiser." With Beethoven the variation form reached its ultimate peak. For the more conventional methods, particularly ornamentation, he substituted a wealth of individual treatments and ideas. He also was the first to organize the succession of variations into contrasting groups, a procedure particularly evident in his "continuous" variations in C minor op. 32 (sometimes described as a cha-

conne). In his Eroica Variations op. 35 the theme is preceded by a short group of "negative variations," based on the bass motif only. His Diabelli Variations op. 120 (1823) are incomparably ingenious, and in the variations of his late quartets and piano sonatas superb technique is combined with the finest artistic quality (e.g., the "ornamenting" variations of piano sonatas op. 109 and 111).

Close behind Beethoven is Franz Schubert in such great though little-known works as his variations for four hands in B minor op. 84, no. 1, and in A-flat major op. 35. Schumann's greatest contributions are the *Etudes symphoniques* op. 13, the first instance of free variations, since in some of them the theme serves as no more than a springboard.

Franz Liszt made very effective use of a brilliant virtuoso-like variation technique in many of his rhapsodies, as well as in his variations on a theme by Paganini (Paganini Études, no. 6), which was also used by Brahms for a series of extremely difficult and interesting variations. However, Brahms' fame as a master of this form rests chiefly on his Variations on a Theme by Handel (op. 24) for piano and his orchestral Variations on a Theme by Haydn (op. 56; also for two pianos). His variations belong mostly to category *C*, owing to the freedom with which he treats the harmonies while still retaining the structural outlines of the theme. Following the precedent of Beethoven's Eroica and Diabelli Variations, he climaxes the series of variations with an elaborate fugue (in the Haydn Variations a passacaglia).

(4) 1900—. Shortly before 1900 two important examples of "free variation" appeared, Vincent d'Indy's *Istar* Variations [1897] and Richard Strauss' *Don Quixote* [1898]. The former are "variations in reverse" in so far as the "theme" (properly, two thematic motifs) appears at the end, a procedure of "disrobing" that is implied by the story of Istar, the Babylonian goddess of love. Compared to these two works, Elgar's *Enigma Variations* are considerably more conventional, approximately along the lines of Schumann's *Études symphoniques*. The last composer to work in this fashion was Max Reger, who wrote numerous variations for piano, organ, and orchestra, among which the Variations and Fugue on a Theme by Bach (op. 81, 1904) for piano and the orchestral Variations and Fugue on a Theme by Mozart (op. 132, 1914) are outstanding. His Variations and Fugue on a Theme by Telemann (op. 134,

1914) for piano attempts, not very successfully, to revert to the tradition of Mozart. Later composers have shown more interest in the baroque type of the chaconne (Busoni, Krenek) than in the traditional 19th-century variation.

Lit.: R. U. Nelson, *The Technique of Variation* (1948); M. J. E. Brown, *Schubert's Variations* (1954); R. Gress, *Die Entwicklung der Klaviervariation von Andrea Gabrieli bis zu Johann Sebastian Bach* (1929); L. Neudenberger, *Die Variationstechnik der Virginalisten im Fitzwilliam Virginal Book* (1937); E. Reichert, *Die Variations Arbeit bei Haydn* (1926); A. Albrecht, *Die Klaviervariationen im 20. Jahrhundert* (1961); I. Horsley, "The Variation before 1580" (diss. Harvard Univ., 1954); W. Schwartz, *Robert Schumann und die Variation* (1932); P. Mies, in *AMF* ii (Mozart); V. Luthlen, in *StM* xiv (Brahms); K. von Fischer, in *RBM* vi (K. P. E. Bach); I. Horsley, in *JAMS* xii (16th cent.).

Variations on a Theme by Diabelli (**Handel, etc.**). See under *Diabelli Variations, Handel Variations,* etc.

Variations symphoniques [F., Symphonic Variations]. Work for piano and orchestra by Franck (composed 1885) in which the expected theme-and-variations structure is expanded by a developmental treatment more characteristic of a symphony with two themes.

Varsovienne. A Polish dance, named for the city of Warsaw, in slow mazurka rhythm, usually with an accented dotted note on the first beat of every second and fourth measure. It was popular in ballrooms from about 1850 to 1870.

Vater unser [G., Our Father]. German version of the Lord's Prayer [L. *Pater noster*]. It is sung as a hymn [G. *Chorale*] to a 16th-century melody (by Luther?), which has been used as the basis for compositions by Hans Leo Hassler ("Vater unser," in ten sections, each based on a phrase of the chorale; in *Psalmen und Christliche Gesäng*, 1607; new ed. by R. von Saalfeld, 1957), Johann Ulrich Steigleder (*Tabulatur Book Darinnen dass Vatter unser . . . viertzig mal varit würdt*, 1627), Bach (organ chorales), and others. See *HAM*, nos. 190a–d.

Vatican Edition ("Editio Vaticana"). See under Liturgical books II.

Vaudeville [F.]. In the late 16th century, a song with a short lyrical or amorous text, composed in a simple chordal style with the melody in the highest voice. The form *vaul de ville* occurs as early as 1507 in a morality play by Nicole de La Chesnaye. Some 16th-century publications include F. Layolle's *Chansons et vaudevilles à 4* (1561; no copies remain), Le Roy's *Premier Livre de chansons en forme de vau de ville* (1573), and Jehan Chardavoine's *Le Recueil des... chansons en forme de voix de ville* (1576). The preface to A. Le Roy and R. Ballard's *Livre d'airs de cour* (1571) states that the songs formerly called *voix de ville* (= vaudeville?) were now called *airs de cour.* Despite this alleged transformation, the *vaudeville* continued an independent existence as a satirical poem sung to a popular melody (usually pre-existent). The same melody or *timbre* commonly served for many different texts. The *vaudeville* was the principal type of song in the early *opéra comique* (1715–c. 1735). Large collections of *vaudevilles* are in A. R. Le Sage's *Le Théâtre de la foire* (10 vols., 1721–37), J. B. C. Ballard's *La Clef des chansonniers* (2 vols., 1717), and other contemporary publications, as well as in the numerous editions of *La Clé du caveau* by P. Capelle (2 vols., 1807). In the 19th century, *vaudeville* was the name given to short comedies interspersed with popular songs. More recently, in the U.S., the name has been used for miscellaneous popular entertainments, including songs, which are presented in cafés or variety theaters.

Lit.: A. Font, *Favart, l'operá comique et la comédie-vaudeville aux xviie et xviiie siècles* (1894); J. Tiersot, *Histoire de la chanson populaire en France* (1889); P. Coirault, *Formation de nos chansons folkloriques,* 4 vols. (1953–63); *id., Notre Chanson folklorique; étude d'information générale* (1941).   D.J.G.

Vcl. Abbr. for violoncello, i.e., cello.

Vela [Sp.]. In the Dominican Republic, name for certain semireligious celebrations in which singing plays an important role. The *vela de muerto* is a ceremony honoring the dead; when the deceased is an infant, it is similar to the *angelito.* The rural population of the Dominican Republic hold celebrations in honor of saints, known as *vela de ofrecimiento.* These usually consist of processions to roadside shrines during which religious songs such as the "Salve" and "Ave Maria" alternate with litanies and improvised verses praising the Saints or the Virgin. Accordions and the *tambora* are used to accompany the procession, but the religious vocal episodes are essentially solo songs with choral responses of a strongly modal character.
                                                        J.O-S.

Velato [It.]. Veiled, subdued.

Veloce [It.]. Fast.

Venetian school. A 16th-century school of Flemish and Italian composers working in Venice. It was inaugurated by Adrian Willaert (c. 1490–1562; appointed *maestro di cappella* at St. Mark's in 1527) and included, among others, Andrea Gabrieli (c. 1520–86), Cipriano de Rore (1516–65)—both pupils of Willaert—and Gioseffe Guami (c. 1540–1611), Giovanni Gabrieli (c. 1555–1612), Giovanni Croce (c. 1560–1609), the organ composers Jacques Buus (d. 1565), Annibale Padovano (1527–75), Vincenzo Bell'Haver (c. 1530–87), and Claudio Merulo (1533–1604), and the theorists Nicola Vicentino (1511–72) and Gioseffo Zarlino (1517–90).

Whereas the contemporary *Roman school represents the culmination of a long development of polyphonic music, the Venetian school is important mainly for its innovations and progressive tendencies, which, together with Florentine *monody, paved the way for the 17th century. Among these contributions are Willaert's chromaticism and freer use of modulation, the toccata style of A. Gabrieli and C. Merulo, Vicentino's daring speculations and experiments with microtones [see Arcicembalo], Zarlino's investigations of *just intonation, *dualism, and, to some extent, equal temperament, and finally—and most important—Giovanni Gabrieli's magnificent "Venetian style" with its broad masses of sound, *polychoral treatment, *echo effects, and progressive use of instruments, winning him the name "father of orchestration" [see Orchestra II]. The movement spread, especially to Germany, where Jacobus Gallus (Händl, 1550–91), Hieronymus Praetorius (1560–1629), Hans Leo Hassler (1564–1612), and Michael Praetorius (1571–1621) became the most important representatives of the Venetian style.

Although temporarily eclipsed by the novelty of Florentine monody (c. 1600), the Venetian school continued to exercise a lasting influence throughout the baroque, a period whose roots are as much in Florence (vocal music) as in Venice (instrumental music). See Baroque music.

Lit.: C. von Winterfeld, *Johannes Gabrieli und sein Zeitalter,* 3 vols. in 2 (1834); R. B. M. Lenaerts, "La Chapelle de Saint-Marc à Venise sous Adrian Willaert (1527–1562)" (*Bulletin de l'institut historique belge de Rome* xix).

Venetian swell. See under Swell.

Venezuela. In 1591 the *Ayuntamiento de Caracas* provided funds for the establishment of a school whose curriculum included the teaching of plainsong; two years later a further subsidy was granted to Don Juan de Arteaga to continue this program. In 1698 the services of a music master were engaged by the *Colegio Seminario.* With the founding of the *Universidad de Santiago de León* in Caracas in 1725, a chair of music was established, to which Francisco Pérez Camacho (1659–*c.* 1725), an organist, was appointed.

The most homogeneous school of composers in South America was flourishing in Venezuela by the end of the colonial period and remained active during the first decades after independence. A great deal of its success was due to Father Pedro Palacios y Sojo (1739–99), who founded the religious order of the Oratory of S. Filippo Neri in Caracas. In addition, there was added, under the leadership of Juan Manuel Olivares (1760–97), the *Academia de Música,* where the outstanding composers of the time were trained. Notable members of this school were José Francisco Velásquez (*c.* 1755–1805), José Antonio Caro de Boesi (*c.* 1760–1814), Pedro Nolasco Colón (*c.* 1750), José Cayetano Carreño (1774–1836), Juan José Landaeta (*c.* 1780–1812), José Luis Landaeta (1772–1812), Lino Gallardo (*c.* 1775–1837), who was director of the *Academia de Música* and also conductor of the first concert of the *Sociedad Filarmónica,* and Juan Francisco Meserón (d. *c.* 1850), an outstanding flutist and composer. The greatest figure of this period was José Angel Lamas (1775–1814), composer of many forms of church music, among them his well-known *Popule Meus.* Many of his compositions are preserved in the archives of the *Escuela de Música* of Caracas.

The first opera written in Venezuela was *Virginia* (1873) by José Ángel Montero (1839–81), member of a large family of musicians and an outstanding figure in 19th-century Venezuelan music. He also composed church music and *zarzuelas.* His contemporary, Felipe Larrazábal (1816–73), was a pianist of international prestige and a composer whose trio for piano, violin, and cello is one of the few of his works that were saved from shipwreck during an Atlantic crossing. The most prolific composer of this period in Caracas was Federico Villena (1835–*c.* 1900), who wrote chamber music, orchestral compositions, songs, church music, and *zarzuelas.* Another well-known Venezuelan-born musician

was Reynaldo Hahn (1875–1947), whose family moved to Paris when he was eight years old.

While the turn of the century saw little activity in composition, Venezuelan music of this period became prominent through Maria Teresa Carreño (1853–1917), a great pianist who also wrote several piano compositions, a string quartet, and other chamber music. Among her pupils was Edward MacDowell.

By the end of World War I, there emerged a group of composers who brought music beyond its amateurish prewar level. Among them were Vicente Emilio Sojo (b. 1887), director of the *Escuela de Música* and the choral society *Orfeón Lamas;* Juan Bautista Plaza (1898–1965), a musicologist who edited many of the works of colonial composers; José Antonio Calcaño (b. 1900); Juan Lecuna (1898–1964); Miguel Ángel Calcaño (1904–58); and María Luisa Escobar (b. 1903).

Many younger 20th-century Venezuelan composers continued to adhere to French impressionism as well as to Venezuelan folk traditions. The best-known composer of this generation is Antonio Estévez (b. 1916). Others are Inocente Carreño (b. 1919), Blanca Estrella, Gonzalo Castellanos (b. 1926; also an outstanding conductor), Evencio Castellanos (b. 1915), Carlos Enrique Figueredo, Antonio Lauro (b. 1917), and Ángel Sauce (b. 1911). Among those following more progressive lines are Rhazés Hernández López (b. 1918) and Alejandro Enrique Planchart (b. 1935).

Folk music of Venezuela's coastal region largely shows prevailing Negro influences. That of the inland plains has retained its early Spanish traditions, free from indigenous or other influences. The **joropo* and **guasa* are typical of the coastal forms, and the *tono llanero* and **corrido* of inland songs and dances. A third, more urban group, includes the **merengue* and **pasillo.*

Lit.: J. A. Calcaño, *La Ciudad y su Música* (1958); *id., Contribución al Estudio de la Música en Venezuela* (1939); I. Aretz, *La Etnomusicologia en Venezuela* (1965); ‡*Archivo de Música colonial venezolana,* ed. J. B. Plaza, 12 vols. (1942–43); J. B. Plaza, in *MQ* xxix, 198–213.

J.O-S.

Veni Sancte Spiritus [L.]. The sequence for Whitsunday (Pentecost). See Sequence II D.

Venite exultemus [L.]. See under Invitatory.

Vent [F.]. Wind. *Instruments à vent,* wind instruments.

Ventil [G.], **ventile** [It.]. Valve. *Ventilhorn* [G.], valve horn.

Veränderungen [G.]. Variations.

Verbunkos [Hung.]. A Hungarian soldiers' dance that was used to attract recruits for enlistment in the army. The name is a corruption of G. *Werbung,* enlistment. The dance was used from *c.* 1780 until 1849, when the Austrian government imposed conscription, and it has survived as a ceremonial dance. In its fully developed form it consisted of two or more sections, some in the character of a slow introduction (*lassu*), others very rapid and wild (*friss*). Among the numerous composers of *verbunkos* were János Bihari, A. G. Csermák, and János Lavotta (early 19th cent.). Many collections of *verbunkos* were published during the 19th century. In art music, the *verbunkos* was imitated by Liszt (Hungarian Rhapsody, no. 2), Bartók (rhapsodies for piano or violin with orchestra), and Kodály (Intermezzo from the opera *Háry János*). See E. C. Rearick, *Dances of the Hungarians* (1938); B. Szabolcsi, *A Concise History of Hungarian Music* [1964], pp. 53ff; *id.,* "Probleme der alten ungarischen Musikgeschichte" (*ZMW* vii, viii).

Verdoppeln [G.]. To double. See Double (2).

Ver[e]eniging voor [Noord-] Nederlands[che] Muziekgeschiedenis. See Editions LII.

Vergleichende Musikwissenschaft [G.]. Comparative musicology, now called *ethnomusicology.

Vergrösserung [G.]. Augmentation.

Verhallend [G.]. Fading away.

Verismo [It.]. An Italian operatic school of the late 19th century that is the musical counterpart of the literary realism of Zola, Flaubert, Ibsen, and others. Instead of the idealistic librettos of earlier operas, realistic subjects from everyday life were chosen, often embellished with violent and theatrical incidents. Coloratura arias and other features of earlier Italian opera were abandoned in favor of a melodramatic recitative that was more naturalistic. Mascagni's *Cavalleria rusticana* of 1890 (scenes from peasant life) and Leoncavallo's *Pagliacci* of 1892 (circus life) were the first products of the new movement. They were followed, in 1900, by Charpentier's more naturalistic *Louise.* Puccini's *La Bohème* (1896) represents a somewhat modified, more lyrical

veristic opera. See M. Rinaldi, *Musica e verismo* [1932].

Verkaufte Braut, Die [G.]. See *Bartered Bride, The.*

Verklärte Nacht [G., Transfigured Night]. Sextet in one movement, for two violins, two violas, and two cellos, by Schoenberg (op. 4, 1899). It was inspired by a poem of R. Dehmel describing how the happiness of two lovers, despite personal tragedy, can transfigure a bleak winter's night into a thing of great beauty. The style of this early work derives from the "love music" of Wagner and R. Strauss, and shows the first traces of *atonality. It was later arranged for full string orchestra, and finally became the music for the ballet, *Pillar of Fire.* Also see Expressionism.

Verkleinerung, Verkürzung [G.] Diminution.

Vermindert [G.]. Diminished (interval).

Vers [F., G.]. (1) See under Verse (2). (2) See under *Canzo.*

Verschiebung [G.]. Soft pedal. See *Una corda;* Mute.

Verschwindend [G.]. Disappearing, fading away.

Verse [F. *vers;* G. *Vers;* It., Sp. *verso;* L. *versus*]. (1) In poetry, a line of metrical writing or a larger unit, e.g., a stanza of a poem. In German, *Vers* always means a stanza, the single line being called *Zeile.* (2) In Gregorian chant, the term (abbreviated ℣) denotes a verse of a psalm or canticle, or a sentence from other scriptural texts. Single verses of this kind are found chiefly in Graduals, Alleluias, and Introits (where they are indicated Ps., i.e., psalm; see Psalmody II, III). They are always sung by the soloist (though usually with a short choral opening). The soloist connotation of the plainsong verse survived in the verse service and verse anthem of the Anglican Church, settings that include sections for solo voices as distinguished from the purely choral full service and full anthem. (3) For organ verse, see Verset.

Verset [F. *verset;* G. *Versett, Versetl;* It. *verso, versetto;* Sp. *versillo*]. Organ verse, i.e., a short organ piece, usually in fugal style, designed to be played in place of a plainsong *verse of a psalm, canticle, or other short items of the service (section of a Kyrie). From the 16th to 18th centuries it was customary to have alternate (usually the odd-numbered) verses of a psalm or canticle replaced by organ versets, in alternation with plainsong performance for the others [see Magnificat], in order to relieve the monotony of traditional psalm singing. Although from the liturgical point of view this practice represents an abuse, it gave great impetus to organ composition. Composers usually provided a number of versets (four to eight) for each church mode (*Versi octo tonorum*). The vast repertory of such versets includes contributions by P. Attaingnant (*Magnificat sur les huit tons,* 1530), Girolamo Cavazzoni (*Intavolatura cioè recercari canzoni himni magnificati,* 1542, '43), A. de Cabezón (*Obras de música,* 1578; see *HAM,* no. 133), A. Valente (*Versi spirituali,* 1580), C. Erbach (after 1600; see *DTB* 7), M. R. Coelho (*Flores de música,* 1620; see *HAM,* no. 200); J. E. Kindermann (*Harmonia organica,* 1645); J. Speth, (*Ars magna consoni et dissoni,* 1693); F. X. A. Murschhauser (*Octi-tonium novum organicum,* 1696; *DTB* 30); J. K. E. Fischer (*Blumen Strauss,* c. 1700; new ed. R. Walter, 1956); and Gottlieb Muffat (*Zwölf Toccaten und 72 Versetl,* 1726; *DTO* 58). In the more recent of these collections the first verset is often in freer style and therefore called "Toccata." For the versets designed especially for the Magnificat, see Magnificat.

The practice of replacing plainsong with organ music still exists, particularly in France, and is known as "supplying." While the organist plays, the clergy and choir merely repeat the words to themselves. Pope Pius X, in his *Motu Proprio of 1903, abolished much of this practice.

Versetto [It.]. *Verset.

Versetzung [G.]. Transposition. *Versetzungszeichen,* accidental.

Versicle. In the Roman Catholic and Anglican rites, a short text from the Scriptures or another source sung by the officiant, to which the choir (or the congregation) responds in like fashion, e.g., ℣. *Dominus vobiscum.* ℟. *Et cum spiritu tuo* (℣. The Lord be with you. ℟. And with thy spirit). In the Roman Catholic service, the ℣. *Deus in adjutorium* with ℟. *Domine ad adjuvandum* . . . is sung at the beginning of each Office [*LU,* pp. 221, 224, etc.]. Also, the hymns and brief responsories close with a versicle and response. See also Preces; Suffrages.

The term "versicle" is also loosely used for subdivisions of longer texts, particularly for the two parallel lines of a sequence, which are called double versicle.

Versillo [Sp.]. *Verset.

Versmass [G.]. *Poetic meter.

Vers mesuré [F.]. A late 16th-century practice of applying to French poetry the quantitative principles of classical Greek and Latin, also known as *vers mesurés à l'antique.* Attempts in this direction had been made as early as 1497 by Michel de Boteauville. However, it was not until the 1560's that the practice became established, mainly through Baïf, founder of the *Académie de poésie et musique,* who in 1567 translated the psalms into *vers mesuré* and also wrote *Chansonettes mesurées.* The method, although a failure from the literary point of view, was readily adopted by musicians, who set the texts to music so that the accented syllables received doubled values, resulting in an irregular succession of half and quarter notes (*musique mesurée*). The foremost composers of *musique mesurée* were Claude Le Jeune (1528–1600; *Le Printemps,* 1603 [see *HAM,* no. 138]; *Psaumes en vers mesurez,* 1606 [*Editions XXV, nos. 11–14]); Jacques Mauduit (1557–1627; *Chansonettes mesurées,* 1586; see *HAM,* no. 10), and François-Eustache Du Caurroy (1549–1609; *Meslanges de la musique,* 1610; *HAM,* no. 17). The practice survived in some of the *airs de cour of the 17th century.

Lit.: P.-H. Masson, "L'Humanisme musical en France" (*CP 1906*); D. P. Walker, "The Influence of *Musique mesurée* . . . on the *Airs de cour*" (*MD* ii); *id.,* "Some Aspects . . . of Musique mesurée" (*MD* iv); *id.* and F. Lesure, "Claude Le Jeune and *Musique mesurée*" (*MD* iii).

Verso [It.]. *Verse; *Verset.

Verstärken [G.]. To reinforce (the sound).

Versus [L.]. Psalm verse. *Versus alleluiaticus,* the verse added to *Alleluia. *Versus ad repetendum,* see *Repetenda.

Verwechslung, enharmonische [G.]. *Enharmonic change.

Verzierung [G.]. Ornaments indicated by signs or small notes.

Vesperal [L. *vesperale*]. See under Liturgical books I (7).

Vespers. The seventh of the canonical hours. See Office.

Via [It.]. Away. *Via sordini,* remove the mutes.

Vibraharp, vibraphone. A percussion instrument originating in the United States. It is similar to the *marimba but has metal bars and electrically driven rotating propellers under each bar, causing a vibrato sound. Other special effects can be obtained. The instrument, although mainly used in dance bands, has occasionally been used in art music (A. Berg, *Lulu;* O. Messiaen, *Trois Petites Liturgies;* K. H. Stockhausen, *Nr. 11 Refrain,* 1961; etc.). See also *GDB* viii, 763.

Vibrations. See under Acoustics I.

Vibrato. (1) In stringed instruments, a slight fluctuation of pitch produced on sustained notes by an oscillating motion of the left hand. Violinists and cellists use vibrato freely in order to increase the emotional quality of the tone. Some great violinists have strongly objected to such application, holding that vibrato should be reserved for moments of heightened expression. Sensible as such advice may be, most players consider vibrato a basic technique but usually apply it with sufficient moderation so as to produce no noticeable fluctuation of pitch.

Lute players of the 17th century distinguished between vibrato produced by a motion of the finger [E. *closed shake;* F. *langeur;* It. *ondeggiamento*] and one performed with the aid of a second finger that lightly taps the string as close as possible to the stopping finger [E. *sting;* F. **battement*]. A particularly expressive vibrato is possible on the clavichord [see *Bebung*].

(2) In singing, there is some uncertainty as to what vibrato actually means, as well as some confusion of it with *tremolo. According to some authorities, vocal vibrato is the quick reiteration (usually eight times per second) of the same pitch produced by a quickly intermittent stream of breath with fixed vocal chords. This effect corresponds to what string players call "tremolo." Most singers use the term "vibrato" for a scarcely noticeable wavering of the tone, an effect that would correspond to the violinist's moderate vibrato, since it increases the emotional effect of the sound without resulting in a noticeable fluctuation of pitch. Excessive vibrato results in a real wobble, caused by a lack of control of the vocal apparatus, extreme fatigue, or even psychological factors. This unwelcome effect in singing is called "tremolo," which hence has an altogether different meaning from that used by string players.

Lit.: C. Seashore, ed., *The Vibrato* (1932); *id., Psychology of the Vibrato in Voice and Instrument* (1936); F. C. Field-Hyde, *Vocal Vibrato, Tremolo, and Judder* (1946); A. Bonaccorsi,

"Terminologia confusa: Vibrato, Tremolo, Bebung" (*LRM* xix, 52ff).

Victimae paschali laudes [L.]. The sequence for Easter Sunday. See Sequence II D.

Vidala [Sp.]. A traditional song, also known as *vidalita,* generally performed by northern Argentine Indians during carnival. Its texts consist of alternation of refrains and couplets, with occasional additions of a kind of versified parody called *trova.* The melody is either modal (Dorian or Lydian) or pentatonic. The song is usually performed by two voices in parallel thirds accompanied by a drum and arpeggiated guitar chords.   J.O-S.

Vide [F.]. (1) Empty. *Corde à vide,* open string. (2) [L.]. See. The term is used, with its syllables *Vi–* and *–de* placed at separate places of the score, to indicate an optional omission, the player being permitted to proceed from the place marked *Vi–* immediately to the place marked *–de.*

Vielle [F.]. The most important stringed instrument of the 13th to 15th centuries, mentioned by numerous writers and described in detail, though not quite clearly, by Hieronymus de Moravia, according to whom it had a drone string and four fingered strings [*CS* i, 153]. Its prominent role is also attested in the inscription "In seculum viellatoris" found with instrumental pieces of the 13th century [see In seculum]. Later (15th cent.) the name was applied to the *hurdy-gurdy, properly called *vielle à roue* (wheel viol). See ill. under Violin.

Vielstimmig [G.]. For many voices, polyphonic.

Viennese classical school [G. *Wiener Klassiker*]. Collective name for the masters of classical music, Haydn, Mozart, and Beethoven, who worked in Vienna. See Classicism. The term "Viennese school" is sometimes used in a wider sense, including such of their predecessors as Johann A. K. G. von Reutter, Jr. (1708–72), Georg C. Wagenseil (1715–77), and Georg M. Monn (1717–50). For the latter two, see Mannheim school.

Vierhebigkeit [G.]. A term introduced by H. Riemann for musical phrases involving four accents (four measures) or multiples thereof. The great majority of all melodies and themes are of this kind, a fact strongly emphasized by Riemann, who claimed for it almost universal validity throughout the entire history of music.

Actually, it was not until the end of the 17th century that the four-measure phrase became established as a structural principle in music other than dance music and simple songs. Composers such as Cesti and Carissimi were among the first to use it with some consistency, giving their music a novel touch of "popularization." The somewhat obvious and facile regularity of music written in four-measure phrases is a pitfall of which the great masters have usually been aware but that lesser composers have not always avoided. The accompanying example from Haydn's Quartet op. 20, no. 5 (second movt.; the "trio" of Menuetto) is a striking warning against the idolization of four-measure phrases.

Riemann's attempts to use *Vierhebigkeit* as a scholarly principle in interpreting medieval monophonic music were particularly unfortunate [see his interpretations of Gregorian chants, *RiHM* i.2, 32ff, or the two-voice "Ut tuo propitiatus," *ibid.*, p. 141; cf. *ApNPM*, p. 208]. Riemann's principle was applied, with equally unfortunate results, by F. Liuzzi to the 14th-century *laude* [in *La Lauda*, 2 vols. (1924)]. See also Monophonic notation.

Viertel [G.]. Quarter. *Viertelnote,* quarter note; *Viertelton,* quarter tone.

Vietnam. Musically, Vietnam is one of the nations that shares the *Chinese tradition, along with *Japan, *Korea, and Mongolia. In these countries one finds a similar terminology, similar musical instruments, similar systems of notation, and scales of the anhemitonic pentatonic type. Their traditional music is essentially melodic. Vietnam has also come into contact with *Indian civilization, which has affected the traditional music of Vietnam in the use of the *trông cởm,* a long barrel drum with two skin-covered heads, each with a patch of tuning paste made of rice

applied to the center, like the *mridanga* of South India; in the importance of the improvised prelude, the *rao* or *zao,* comparable to the Indian *alapa;* and in the teaching of cyclical rhythmic patterns by onomatopoeia, as in the Indian system of *bols* and *theka.*

The Vietnamese have assimilated both Chinese and Indian music and have made their own contributions through original instruments, like the *đàn bâu* or *đàn độc huyền,* a monochord that produces sound exclusively by *harmonics and the variation in tension of the single metal string. Another original instrument is the *đàn đảy,* a rectangular long-necked lute with three silk strings, used to accompany singers, which combines characteristics of the moon-shaped lute (*nguyệt cầm*), pear-shaped lute (*tỳ bà*), and three-string lute (*đàn tam*). Another instrument is the *sinh tiền* (coin clappers), which unites in a single instrument the characteristics of the scraper, clappers, and bells.

The history of Vietnamese music can be divided into four main periods, beginning in the 10th century with the founding of the first Vietnamese dynasty, the Dinh (968–980). Of the music prior to that time, dating from earliest antiquity, no records remain. The first period (10th–14th cent.) is characterized by the combined influence of Indian and Chinese elements. The second period (15th–18th cent.) is characterized by the predominance of Chinese influence. The third period (1800–1940) is characterized by the affirmation of original Vietnamese music and the beginning of at least superficial Western influence. The fourth period (1945 to present) is characterized by the decline of and attempts to restore traditional music, as well as the development of a new music in the Western style.

Vietnamese music uses scales of two, three, four, or five tones with or without auxiliary degrees. Its art music has modal characteristics. There is a close relationship between melody and linguistic intonation (the Vietnamese language has six different linguistic tones). Polyrhythm and polyphony (or heterophony) are present in ritual music, theater music, and entertainment music.

There are many varieties of folk music. Vietnam's population includes more than fifty ethnic minorities. Besides Vietnamese folk music, there is the music of the Thái, Mùởng, Lolos, Kha, etc., in the north, and of the Rhadés, Mnong Maa, Mnong gar, Djorai, etc., in the high central plateaus. It includes work songs (the *hò*), songs of rural feasts (*hát hôi*), alternating songs (*cò lã, trống guân, quan họ*), songs of the blind (*hát xâm*), songs of possession (*châù văn*), healing songs (*phù thũy*), songs of the theater (*hát chèo, hát bội*), and songs accompanied by dancing (*xoe*).

Art music includes ceremonial music, both court and popular, the music of entertainment and of the theater. The court repertory is very rich: music of the "esplanade of heaven," music of the temples, music for formal audiences, banquet music, palace music, music executed by large instrumental ensembles of more than forty players (*Đại Nhạc*), with such dances as civil dance (*văn vũ*), military dance (*võ vũ*), dance of fabulous animals, and dance of the flowers. Popular ceremonial music includes funeral music, Buddhist music, and Cao Dai music. Entertainment music has three main traditions: that of the north, with the *hát ã dào* (song of the professional women singers); the central region, with the *Ca Húê* (music of Húê); and the south, with the *dàn tài-tũ* (so-called amateurs' music). Traditional theater music (*hát tuồng, hát bội*), like court music, is disappearing. But both the music of the popular theater (*hát chèo*) in the north and the so-called "renewed theater" (*hát cãi lùồng*) in the south are very popular.

The recent influence of Western music has given rise to a music called "renewed" music (*nhạc cãi-cách*) and a new music (*tân nhạc*), made up largely of songs, dance or variety music, and sometimes compositions for Western instruments, like the piano and violin, and symphonic works. But this music is of too recent an origin to be discussed with any perspective.

Lit.: Song Bân, *The Vietnamese Theatre* (1960); Trần Văn Khê, *La Musique du Viêt Nam* (1967); *id.*, *La Musique viêtnamienne traditionnelle* (1962); *id.*, "Le Théâtre viêtnamien," in *Les Théâtres d'Asie* (1961), pp. 203–19; G. de Gironcourt, *Recherches de géographie musicale en Indochine* (1943; also in *Bulletin de la Société des Études Indochinoises* xvii); Nguyễn Văn Huyên, *Les Chants alternés des garçons et des filles en Annam* (1934), pp. 27–53; G. Dumoutier, *Les Chants et les traditions populaires des Annamites* (1890); *LavE* i.5, 3100–46; Trần Văn Khê, "Place de la musique dans les classes populaires au Viêt Nam" (*Bulletin de la Société des Études Indochinoises*, nouv. sér., xxxiv, 361–77): *id.*, in *Encyclopédie de la musique* (Fasquelle) i, ii, iii [1958, '59, '61]; *id.*, "Aspects de la cantillation: techniques du Viêt Nam" (*RdM* 1961, 37–53); *id.*, "Note sur l'ornementation au Viêt Nam" (*CP 1961*, pp. 445–50); G. Knosp, "Rapport sur

une mission officielle d'études musicales en Indochine" (*Internationales Archiv für Ethnographie* xx, 123–51, 165–88, 217–44, xxi, 59–65); Nguyễn Đình Lai, "Etude sur la musique sino-viêtnamienne et les chants populaires du Viêt-Nam" (*Bulletin de la Société des Études Indochinoises*, nouv. sér., xxxi, 1–86); Thái Văn Kiêm, "Panorama de la musique classique viêtnamienne des origines à nos jours" (*Bulletin de la Société des Études Indochinoises,* nouv. sér. xxxix [1964].   T.V.K.

Vif [F.]. Lively.

Vihuela [Sp.]. Early name for various stringed instruments. (1) *Vihuela de arco,* a viol [see *GD* iii, opp. 260; *GDB* v, frontis.]. (2) *Vihuela de Flandres* (from Flanders), the lute.

(3) *Vihuela de mano,* or simply *vihuela,* a six-course guitar of the 16th century [see Guitar family]. The tuning was similar to that of the lute and the notation like Italian lute tablature, though with distinctive features, such as the use of red ciphers to indicate a singing part (e.g., in Fuenllana's tablature). An impressive repertory of music for vihuela survives in seven printed tablatures [see Spain II; also Tablature].

A repertory for the vihuela is also indicated in the titles of the two remaining books of Spanish 16th-century organ music, by L. Venegas de Henestrosa (1557) and Antonio de Cabezón (1578), which both bear the remark, "para tecla, [h]arpa y vihuela" (for keyboard, harp and vihuela). However, they contain only strictly polyphonic organ music, most of which could not be played on a harp or vihuela without considerable adaptation.

Lit.: J. B. Trend, *Luis Milan and the Vihuelistas* (1925); J. M. Ward, "The Vihuela de mano and Its Music (1536–1576)" (diss. New York Univ., 1953); G. Morphy, ‡*Les Luthistes espagnols du XVI siècle,* 2 vols. (1902; the transcriptions are unreliable); L. Schrade, *Luys Milan* [*Editions XLVI, 2]; E. Martínez Torner, ‡*Colección de vihuelistas españoles del siglo XVI* (1923); E. Pujol, editions of Luys de Narvaez and Alonso Mudarra (*MME* iii and vii); W. Apel, "Early Spanish Music for Lute and Keyboard Instruments" (*MQ* xx); G. Chase, in *BAMS* vi.

Villancico [Sp.]. In the 15th and 16th centuries, a type of Spanish poetry, idyllic or amorous in subject matter and consisting of several stanzas (*copla*) linked by a refrain (*estribillo*): E C_1 E C_2 E. . . . The *copla* consists of two sections, *mudanza* and *vuelta,* which correspond exactly to the *piedi* and *volta* of the Italian *ballata, while the *estribillo* corresponds to the Italian *ripresa*. The resulting form is:

estribillo	copla		estr.	copla	
	mudanza	vuelta		mud.	vuelta
music A	b b	a	A	b b	a
text a a	b b	b a	a a	b b	b a etc.

A characteristic trait of the *villancico* (and *ballata*) is a rhyme scheme that does not wholly correspond to the musical form; see under Virelai II.

Numerous *villancicos* composed for three or four voices are preserved in the Spanish **cancioneros,* e.g., the *Cancionero musical del palacio* (*c.* 1500; see Sources, no. 27). Some of them, presumably representing an older tradition, are in a fairly elaborate polyphonic style, and others in a simple chordal style. Juan Urreda (or Jean Wreede, a Fleming) and Francisco de la Torre are among the earliest composers, while Juan del Encina (1468–1529) is probably the most important. After 1500 the *villancico* was also composed as a solo song with vihuela accompaniment. Luis Milán, Miguel de Fuenllana, and Alonso Mudarra wrote a number of Spanish and Portuguese *villancicos* that are outstanding for their grace and refinement, and indeed might be considered the earliest examples of song in the modern sense of the word.

The earliest documented use of the term *villancico* is the title of a poem written shortly after 1400 by Iñigo López de Santillana. However, the late 13th-century MS *Cantigas de Santa María* contains numerous songs showing the metrical and musical form of the *villancico,* the only difference being the subject, which is religious.

In the 17th century the *villancico* reappeared as a religious composition comparable to the church cantata or anthem. The text consists of an introductory *estribillo* of irregular versification and a number (six, nine, or more) of *coplas,* each of four lines. The *estribillo* is composed in a rather elaborate style for four-part (sometimes eight-part) chorus with organ accompaniment, while the *coplas* are short solo songs with organ accompaniment. Instruments were also used. Usually, all the *coplas* are sung to the same melody, but sometimes three or four melodies are used in alternation. Occasionally the composition closes with a short choral movement, called *respuesta.* Possibly, the *estribillo* could also be repeated at the end. Among the com-

posers of such *villancicos* are Carlos Patiño (d. 1683) and Fray Juan Romero (fl. *c.* 1670; see *LavE* i.4, 2050ff). A number of *villancicos* are preserved in MSS at the library of Munich [see the catalog by J. J. Maier, *Die musikalischen Handschriften* (1879)]. These and other sources have not been investigated, so it is difficult to obtain an accurate idea of this phase of Spanish music. Fortunately, the gap has been filled to some extent by the publication of the *villancicos* of Joan Cererols (1618–76), a member of the school of Montserrat [see Editions XXVI, *Vocal Music,* 1–3; *HAM,* no. 227].

During the 17th and 18th centuries a considerable number of *villancicos* were produced in Latin America, all using Spanish texts. Most of them were intended for church use, and approximately one-third of the entire repertory were settings of texts dealing with Christmas. Although the Church discouraged the use of this form, mainly because of its secular origin, *villancicos* were written for every saint's day, sung at Matins, and even interpolated in the Mass. The foremost writer of *villancicos* in colonial Mexico was Sor Juana Ines de la Cruz (1651–95). Settings for her texts were composed by Joseph de Agurto y Loaysa (fl. 1690), Antonio de Salazar (fl. 1690), and others. Simultaneously the *villancico* was cultivated in Peru by Juan de Araujo, Tomáz de Torrejón, Sebastián Durón, and many others, while a prominent Colombian composer was Juan Ximenez [see Colombia].

Beginning in the first decades of the 18th century, the *villancico* in Latin America developed into a sort of cantata, with an opening chorus, interspersed arias, and a choral ending. This expanded form was cultivated by such composers as Manuel Zumaya [see Mexico] and Estaban Salas [see Cuba]. The villancico also developed into several types of traditional Latin American folksong, known variously as *adoración, alabanza, aguinaldo, esquinazo,* etc.

Lit.: I. Pope, "Musical and Metrical Form of the Villancico" (*AnnM* ii); *id.,* "The Musical Development and Form of the Spanish *Villancico*" (*PAMS* 1940); G. Chase, *The Music of Spain,* rev. ed. (1959), pp. 47ff; V. Ripollés, *El Villancico i la Cantata del Segle XVIII a València* (1935); *LavE* i.4, 2006ff; A. Geiger, "Bausteine zur Geschichte des iberischen Vulgär-Villancico" (*ZMW* iv). add. by J.O-S.

Villanella. A 16th-century type of vocal music that originated in Naples (*v. alla napoletana*) and that, in both text and music, represents a sharp contrast to—probably a reaction against —the refinements of the contemporary madrigal. M. Praetorius' description of the villanella as "eine Bäurisch Music zu einer Bäurischen Matery" is less apt than Morley's "clownish musick to a clownish matter," since the villanella, although suggested by folk music, had no more relation to the Italian peasantry than the 18th-century *style galant* did to the shepherds of France. A sophisticated parodistic device of the villanella is its frequent use of "forbidden" par-

Dol - ce mi - se - ri - a u - scir di af-fann e pe - ne

allel fifths [see Ex.]. The earliest collections of villanelle are by G. D. da Nola (1541), Tomaso Cimello (1545), A. Willaert (1545), and Baldassare Donati (1550). The villanella style spread, particularly to Germany, where it was used for drinking songs, jesting songs, etc., not without losing a good deal of its Italian flavor and becoming either more civilized (Orlando di Lasso) or simply dull.

Subspecies of the villanella are the *greghesca, giustiniana, mascherata,* and *moresca.* The *greghesca* is a *villanella alla napoletana* in three parts, the text a mixture of Venetian and Greek. Its creator was the Venetian-Levantine poet-musician Antonio Molino, to whose dialect texts many Venetian composers, from Willaert to Bell'Haver, composed music. The *giustiniana* is a type of villanella, always in three parts, whose text ridicules the ineffectual stuttering Venetian patrician. The poems have no relationship whatever to the choice lyrics, called *giustiniani,* of the early 15th-century poet Leonardo Giustiniani (1385–1446). [See, however, Rubsamen, Lit.] The *mascherata* is a type of villanella to be sung during a masked ball or procession [ex. by Da Nola in *EiBM,* no. 18]. Collections of such songs were published by G. Scotto (*Il Primo Libro delle justiniane,* 1578), A. Gabrieli (*Greghesche et justiniane,* 1571; *Mascherate,* 1601), Orazio Vecchi (*Selva di varia recreatione,* 1590), and others. The *moresca* is a type in which the singers represent Moorish girls (examples in Lasso, *Sämtliche Werke* [1894–1926], vol. x). It has no relationship to the dance called **moresca.* See also *Maggiolata; Villanesca.*

More recent composers, among them Berlioz, Chabrier, Dukas, Granados, and Loeffler, have used the term "villanelle" or "villanesca" for instrumental pieces in the style of a rustic dance, usually in quick 6/8 meter. An early example of such a piece (in 4/4) is in a suite by G. P. Telemann (no. 5 of *Ouverture 'La Putain,'* c. 1725).

Lit.: W. Scheer, *Die Frühgeschichte der italienischen Villanella* (1936); E. Gersen-Kiwi, "Studien zur Geschichte des italienischen Liedmadrigals im XVI. Jahrhundert" (diss. Heidelberg, 1937); B. M. Galanti, *Le Villanelle alla napolitana* (1954); G. M. Monti, *Le Villanelle alla napoletana* (1925); A. W. Ambros, *Geschichte der Musik,* 5 vols. (1868), iii, 510f; E. Hertzmann, *Adrian Willaert in der weltlichen Vokalmusik seiner Zeit* (1931), pp. 55ff; A. Einstein, *The Italian Madrigal,* 3 vols. (1949), i, 352ff; P. Bellasio, ‡*Villanelle,* ed. G. Vecchi (1952); G. de Antiquis, ‡*Villanelle alla Napolitana,* ed. S. A. Luciani (1941); A. Einstein, "The Gregescha and the Giustiniana of the Sixteenth Century" (*MD* i); id., "Die Parodie in der Villanella" (*ZMW* ii); F. Nicolini, "La Villanella napoletana" (*RMI* liv).

Villanesca. An earlier name for what was later called **villanella. It first appears in an anonymous collection of 1537, then in G. D. da Nola's *Canzoni villanesche* of 1541. See *ReMR,* pp. 332ff, 443ff.

Villota. A type of 16th-century Italian song of irregular structure, often including a popular or street song in its texture. Some *villote* close with a more rapid section, called *nio.* Its local character is indicated in such titles of publications as *Villote alla veneziana* (1535), *Villote padovane* (1550), *Villote alla napoletana* (1550), and *Villote mantovane* (1583). An attempt by F. Torrefranca to prove that the *villota* is a "missing link" between the Italian music of the 14th and 16th centuries rests on very weak evidence.

Lit.: K. Somborn, *Das venezianische Volkslied: die Villota* (1901); F. Azzaiolo, ‡*Villotte del Fiore,* ed. F. Vatielli (1921); id., *Il secondo libro de villotte del Fiore,* ed. G. Vecchi (1953); O. Kinkeldey, "Fausto Torrefranca's Theory of the 'Villota'" (*BAMS* vi); H. Springer, "Vilota und Nio" (*CP Liliencron*).

Vīna. The main melody instrument of India, somewhat resembling a guitar but actually a zither. See under India VIII; ill. under Zither.

Vingt-quatre Violons du Roi. A string orchestra of twenty-four players, in the service of the French Kings Louis XIII, Louis XIV, and Louis XV (c. 1650–1761), which became particularly famous under Lully. Lully first (1655) directed a smaller group of sixteen players, called "petite bande," but later became conductor of the "grande bande." Its main function was to play at court balls, at the king's levée, banquets, etc. Lully organized the band into a string orchestra that became famous all over Europe and was imitated by various sovereigns, e.g., by Britain's Charles II, whose group was called "King's Music."

Vinnula, vinola [L.]. An ornamenting neume or special vocal effect of Gregorian chant, mentioned by Aurelianus Reomensis [*GS* i, 57] and others. Its meaning is not known. See Neumes I; Vox.

Viol. I. *General.* Name for a family of stringed instruments in use mainly during the 16th and 17th centuries, replacing the various types of medieval fiddle (*rabab, *vielle) and in turn superseded by the *violin family. The viols have about the same relationship to the violins as the harpsichord to the piano and the recorder to the flute. They are very delicate and soft in timbre, lacking the brilliance and versatility of the modern instruments. Thus they are suited for the intimacy of a small room and for amateur players more than for the concert hall or for professional virtuosos. The making and playing of viols has been revived to some extent, owing chiefly to the initiative of Arnold Dolmetsch in England.

The viols differ from the violins in the following ways: (a) the shoulders slope from the neck instead of being set at right angles to it; (b) the back is usually flat instead of bulging; (c) the ribs are deeper; (d) the normal number of strings is six instead of four; (e) the fingerboard generally has frets in the form of pieces of gut tied around it; (f) the sound holes are usually in the shape of a C instead of an F [see Sound hole]; (g) the bridge is wider and less arched, facilitating the playing of full chords; (h) the strings are thinner and less tense; (i) it is played with an older type of bow whose stick curves outward from the hair [see Bow], and the hand is held palm up; (j) the instrument is held upright, resting on the player's lap or between his legs. See ill. under Violin.

II. *Standard types.* In the 17th century, the classical period of the viols, they were built in three sizes, treble viol [F. *dessus de viole*], tenor viol [*taille de viole*], and bass viol [*basse de viole*], the last also known as *viola da gamba [mod. G. *Gambe*]. According to T. Mace [*Musick's Monu-*

ment, 1676], a good set of viols (a so-called "chest of viols") consisted of "2 basses, 2 tenors, and 2 trebles: all truly, and proportionably suited." The tuning of these instruments followed that of the 16th-century lute, i.e., in fourths around a central third: bass viol, D G c e a d'; tenor viol, A d g b e' a'; treble viol, d g c' e' a' d''. Toward the end of the 17th century French musicians added a small viol tuned a fourth above the treble viol, called the *pardessus de viole.* The corresponding English term is "descant viol," a name also used for the treble viol. The French bass viol often had a seventh string, usually tuned A_1.

III. *Viol music.* Although instrumental ensemble music of the 16th century, such as the ricercars of Willaert, canzonas of Maschera, etc., were doubtless played on viols (as well as other melody instruments, such as recorders or cornetts), it was in England that viol making, viol playing, and viol composition reached its "golden age," mainly *c.* 1625–75. Preceded by the *"In nomines" and *brownings, the English *fancy of the 17th century became the chief form of English viol music [see also Consort]. About 1660 the appearance of the violin in England quickly ended this splendid development [see England V]. The bass viol had a long career as a solo instrument, from about 1550 to 1750; see Viola da gamba.

IV. *Special types.* In addition to the standard types, the viol family included several other instruments.

1. Double-bass viol [F. *contre-basse de viole;* It. *violone;* Sp. *contrabajo*]. A six-stringed instrument tuned an octave below the bass viol. It is the ancestor of the modern *double bass, which has retained some features of the viols together with the alternate name "bass viol." The *violone* frequently called for in Bach's cantatas probably was an intermediate instrument between the old six-stringed type and the modern double bass. See Violone.

2. Division viol. A slightly smaller bass viol, which was preferred for playing *divisions upon a ground and similar solo performance.

3. Lyra viol. An instrument still smaller than the division viol. Since its size was between the bass viol and tenor viols, it was also called *viola bastarda.* [See ill. under Violin.] The lyra viol, or "bass viol lyra-way," as John Playford called it (1658), was tuned in fifths and fourths, e.g., C G c e a d' or A_1 E A e a d', unlike the other viols but like the older *lira da gamba;* hence the name *lyra-way* [see *GDB* v, 453, for additional

lyra tunings]. This manner of tuning, which greatly facilitated playing chords, was also known as "harp-way tuning" (T. Mace). The music for this instrument was not written in ordinary notation but in *tablature [ex. in *WoHN* ii, 226f].

4. Viola d'amore. See separate entry.

5. Baryton. An 18th-century instrument that might be regarded as a viola da gamba provided with sympathetic strings, or as a larger *viola d'amore. The broad neck was usually carved out under the fingerboard (leaving only an oblong frame) so that the sympathetic strings could be plucked from underneath with the thumb of the left (!) hand [see ill. under Violin]. A number of late 18th-century compositions for the baryton survive. Many of them were written for Prince Nikolaus Esterhazy, who was very fond of the instrument. They include *Neun Partien auf die Viola Paradon* by J. G. Krause (*c.* 1700), 175 compositions by Haydn [see C. F. Pohl, *Joseph Haydn* i, 249ff], 24 divertimenti by Luigi Tomasini (1741–1808), and pieces by Joseph Weigl (1766–1846) and others.

Lit. *General:* N. Bessaraboff, *Ancient European Musical Instruments* (1941), pp. 255–89, 357–73; G. R. Hayes, *Musical Instruments and Their Music,* vol. ii (1930); *LavE* ii.3, 1753ff; E. van der Straeten, *History of the Violoncello, the Viol da Gamba, Their Precursors and Collateral Instruments* (1915); *id.,* "The Revival of the Viols" (*The Strad,* Feb. 1909–June, 1912); J. Pulver, "The Viols in England" (*PMA* xlvii); C. Bouvet, "Les Pièces de viole de François Couperin" (*RdM* 1922, no. 2); W. Coates, "English Two-Part Viol Music, 1590–1640" (*ML* xxxiii, 141ff).

Baryton: LavE ii.3, 1779ff; W. O. Strunk, "Haydn's Divertimenti for Baryton, Viola, and Bass" (*MQ* xviii); L. Greilsamer, in *BSIM* 1910, pp. 45ff.

Viola. (1) In modern usage, the second member of the violin family [F. *alto;* G. *Bratsche*]. It is tuned a fifth lower than the violin, c g d' a'. Nonetheless, it is only one-seventh larger than the violin, a disproportion that makes its timbre more nasal and veiled than those of the violin and cello. For modern constructions in various sizes, see Violin family (c), (d). [For ill. see under Violin.] In contrast to the violin, the viola has been used almost exclusively as an ensemble instrument, in the orchestra or in chamber music [see String quartet]. Notable exceptions are P. Hindemith's Sonatas for viola solo (op. 11, no. 5; op. 25, no. 1) and for viola and piano (op. 11, no. 4; op. 25, no. 4; without op. number, 1939).

About 1600 the viola was called *violino* (*violino ordinario*), the smaller violin being called *violino piccolo* [see Violin II]. It would seem, therefore, that at this time the viola was the normal type of the violin family. In the 17th and 18th centuries it was frequently called *violetta, the name "viola" being used for the viola da gamba [see, e.g., J. Rosenmüller's Symphoniae, in *DdT* 18].

(2) In the Renaissance and baroque periods, *viola* was the generic Italian name for all bowed stringed instruments. There were two main classes: *viole da gamba* (leg viols) and *viole da braccio* (arm viols). The former, which were held on or between the legs, are the *viols; the latter, which were held against the shoulder (at least the smaller sizes), are the immediate forerunners of the violins [see Violin II]. Later, each of these collective terms became identified with a particular member of the group, the viola da gamba [G. *Gambe*] with the bass viol [see Viol II] and the viola da braccio [viola; G. *Bratsche*] with the alto violin.

Lit.: B. Tours and B. Shore, *The Viola* (1946); R. Dolejší, *Modern Viola Technique* (1939); W. Altmann and W. Borissowsky, *Literaturverzeichnis für Bratsche und Viola d'amore* (1937); F. Zeyringer, Literatur für Viola (1963); C. Meyer, ed., ‡*Alte Meister des Violaspiels* [1958]; R. Clarke, "The History of the Viola in Quartet Writing" (*ML* iv, 6); E. van der Straeter, "The Viola" (*The Strad,* July 1912–April 1916).

Viola alta. See under Violin family (c).

Viola bastarda [It.]. Name for the lyra viol [see Viol IV, 3]. See C. Sachs, in *ZIM* xv.

Viola da gamba [It.]. Originally, name for all the viols, because they were held on or between the legs; see Viola (2). Specifically, the bass size of this family, also called bass viol [ill. under Violin]. It had six strings, normally tuned D G C e a d'. The instrument is especially important because it was often used as a solo instrument. Silvestro Ganassi's *Regola Rubertina* of 1542 contains ricercars for viola da gamba (unaccompanied) involving double stops, fourth and fifth positions, and other elements of virtuoso playing [ex. in *HAM,* no. 119]. The *Tratado de glosas* by Diego Ortiz (1553) contains a number of ricercars that can be played by "Violon con el Cymbalo," i.e., for viola da gamba and harpsichord. Famous players of the 17th century were Christopher Simpson (*c.* 1610–

69; *The Division Violist*, 1659), André Maugars (*c.* 1580–*c.* 1645), Hotman (d. 1663), and Jean Rousseau (*Traité de la viole*, 1687). Important composers were Marin Marais (1656–1728; 5 vols. of pieces for 1–3 viole da gamba, 1686–1725), his son Roland Marais (two books of *Pièces de violes*, 1735, '38), Jean Schenck (1656–*c.* 1700; *Scherzi musicali, c.* 1692; see Editions LII, 28; also *SchGMB*, no. 245), Ernst Christian Hesse (1676–1762), August Kuhnel (1645–*c.* 1700; *Sonate ô partite ad una ô due viole da gamba*, 1698; several repub. by A. Einstein, Döbereiner, Bennat), Antoine Forqueray (1672–1745; *Pièces de viole*, ed. by his son Jean Baptiste; several repub. by Karl Schröder), Louis de Caix d'Hervelois (*c.* 1670–*c.* 1760; 6 books, *Premiere* [*Seconde,* etc.] *Livre de pièces de viole*, 1725–52; several sonatas repub. by Karl Schröder), and Karl Friedrich Abel, the last of the violists (1723–87; numerous MS pieces, one sonata pub. by R. Engländer; see Lit., Einstein). Bach wrote three fine sonatas for viola da gamba (*BG* ix, 175ff), and the aria "Komm süsses Kreuz" of the St. Matthew Passion is for viola da gamba and bass. There also is an early sonata by Handel [see under Thoroughbass II].

Lit.: J. Bacher, *Die Viola da gamba* [1933]; A. Einstein, *Zur deutschen Literatur für Viola da gamba im 16. und 17. Jahrhundert* (1905); C. W. Hughes, "The Music for Unaccompanied Bass Viol" (*ML* xxv); E. Albini, "La Viola da gamba in Italia" (*RMI* xxviii).

Viola d'amore [It.; F. *viole d'amour;* G. *Liebesgeige*]. An instrument the size of a treble viol but having *sympathetic strings made of thin wire that were stretched behind the bowed strings, producing a silvery resonance. Unlike the viols proper, it had no frets and was held like a violin. Along with this type there existed viole d'amore without sympathetic strings, and with metal strings replacing the gut strings of the ordinary viols. This instrument had a metallic timbre. The name viola d'amore may refer to the instrument's scroll, which usually was fashioned like a blindfold face resembling that of the god Amor [see *SaHMI*, pp. 364ff]. The *English violet* mentioned by Leopold Mozart probably was a larger variety of viola d'amore with seven bowed and fourteen or fifteen sympathetic strings [see N. Bessaraboff, *Ancient European Musical Instruments* (1941), p. 286f]. See ill. under Violin.

The literature for the viola d'amore is quite extensive. It includes compositions by Attilio Ariosti (1666–*c.* 1740; 6 sonatas, new ed., Augener, Durand); J. S. Bach (1685–1750; St. John Passion); Michel Corrette (1709–95; sonata, new ed. Lemoine); Haydn (1732–1809; divertimento, new ed. Nagel); and Karl Stamitz (1745–1801; *DTB* 28; also new ed., Schott). In 1782 Milandre published a *Méthode facile pour la viole d'amour*. In the 19th century the instrument was used by Meyerbeer (*Les Huguenots*), Charpentier (*Louise*), Puccini (*Madama Butterfly*), R. Strauss (*Sinfonia domestica*), and C. M. Loeffler (*The Death of Tintagiles*). It was also revived for concert performance by Louis van Waefelghem (1840–1908), Carl Zoeller (1840–89), François Casadesus (1870–1954), and others. Hindemith wrote a sonata (op. 25, no. 2) and concerto (op. 46, no. 1) for viola d'amore.

Lit.: C. Zoeller, *The Viole d'amour* [n.d.]; R. Dolejší, *Modern Viola Technique* (1939), pp. 38ff, 133; K. Stumpf, *New School for Viola d'Amore* (1956); P. Shirley, *The Study of the Viola d'Amore* (1958); *LavE* ii.3, 1781ff; W. Altmann and W. Borissowsky, *Literaturverzeichnis für Bratsche und Viola d'amore* (1937); W. E. Köhler, *Beiträge zur Geschichte und Literatur der Viola d'amore* (1938); F. Scherber, in *Musikbuch aus Österreich* (1910); H. Danks, in *ML* xxxviii.

Viola da spalla [It.]. An 18th-century variety of cello that was held across the player's chest suspended by a strap over the shoulder [*spalla*, shoulder].

Viola di bordone [It.], **viola paradon** [E.]. Other names for baryton; see Viol IV, 5.

Viola pomposa. An 18th-century instrument of the violin (not viol) family, whose invention is erroneously ascribed to J. S. Bach (in unreliable sources dating from 1782 to 1792). The only works for the instrument are two compositions by Telemann, a concerto by J. G. Graun, and a *Sonata per la Pomposa col Basso* by Cristiano G. Lidarti from *c.* 1760. From these pieces it has been deduced that the viola pomposa was a larger viola held on the arm (not under the chin) and with five strings, tuned c–g–d′–a′–e″. The *violino pomposo* found in some sources denoted the same instrument. [For ill. see under Violin.] See F. W. Galpin, in *ZMW* xiv, 35ff; *id.*, in *ML* xii, 354ff; H. Engel, in *ZMW* xiv, 38; G. Kinsky, in *ZMW* xiii, xiv; F. T. Arnold, in *ZMW* xiii, xiv; *SaHMI*, pp. 367f.

Viole [F.]. *Viol. Viole d'amour,* see Viola d'amore.

Violet. A name sometimes given to the *viola d'amore.

Viole-ténor [F.]. See under Violin family (g).

Violetta. (1) A 16th-century three-stringed instrument of the violin type [see Violin II]. (2) A 17th- and 18th-century name for the viola, used by J. Rosenmüller, Bach, and other German composers; *violetta marina,* for viola d'amore; *violetta piccola,* according to M. Praetorius (*Syntagma musicum,* 1614–20), a small viol, but it may also have meant a violin.

Violin [F. *violon;* G. *Violine, Geige;* It. *violino;* Sp. *violín*]. I. *General.* The most important of the stringed instruments, in the orchestra as well as in chamber and solo music. Its main parts are: (a) the body, consisting of the table (soundboard), back, and ribs (side walls); (b) the fingerboard, ending in a pegbox and scroll; (c) the string holder (tail piece); (d) the bridge. [See the accompanying illustrations.] Inside the body is the *bass-bar, which is glued to the table, reinforcing blocks glued to the corners of the bouts and to the back, and the *sound post, fixed between the table and the back. The violin has four strings tuned in fifths, g d' a' e''.

The prominence of the violin in Western music rests on its singular qualities, among them an expressiveness ranging from soft lyricism to extreme dramatic excitement, a soulful, sensitive timbre, crescendos and diminuendos unequaled by other instruments, and vast opportunity for variety in performance, including many types of *bowing as well as *pizzicato and the use of *harmonics.

Whereas all other modern instruments (except the organ) were not perfected until the late 19th century, the great period of violin building followed soon after the instrument emerged as a definite type. From 1600 to 1750 Cremona was the center for great masters of violin making, notably Niccolò Amati (1596–1684), Antonio Stradivari (1644–1737), and Giuseppe B. Guarneri (Giuseppe del Gesù, 1698–1744). Their instruments are priceless treasures for which fabulous sums have been paid. Although the craftsmanship and beauty of these instruments are unsurpassed, modern makers have produced instruments whose sound cannot be distinguished from that of a genuine "Strad." The widespread notion that the composition of the varnish has a decisive influence on a violin's sound has been proven false. The luster of the old instruments adds greatly to their beauty but nothing tangible to their tone quality.

II. *History.* The violin, the main representative of bowed chordophones, or "fiddles" [see Instruments IV, B, 2], has a relatively short history. There is no evidence of the use of a bow prior to the 9th century, when it is mentioned in Persian and Chinese sources. There is some evidence that the fiddle originated in Central Asia, whence it spread to the Far East as well as to Europe. A Chinese fiddle called *huchyn* (*hu ch'in*) has a small cylindrical soundbox made of bamboo, wood, or coconut, with the lower end open and the upper end covered with snakeskin. A long neck, in the form of a stick, pierces the body, and over it two strings are stretched. The bow cannot be removed since it passes between the strings, rubbing some from below and others from above. A similar instrument is the Persian *kemânğe* or *kamānja* [see Persia]. In India a folk instrument called *sārangī* comes in a variety of strange shapes [see *SaHMI*]. The Arab *rabab* was imported into Europe, where it was usually called *rebec* [see Rabab].

The earliest European fiddles were shaped like a slender bottle or pear and were known by various names, among them *rebec,* *gigue,* and *lyra.* The slightly pear-shaped form was retained in the Italian *lira da braccio* and *lira da gamba.* The slender fiddle (rebec) persisted in the *klein geigen* [see below] and *kit.* The most important medieval fiddle was the *vielle* of the 13th century. The development during the next two centuries is obscure, but sometime between *c.* 1550 and 1600 the violin developed from several earlier types, each of which contributed some essential features. Bearing in mind the differences between the violin and the earlier viols [see under Viol], a number of the violin's forerunners can be singled out. The practice of leaning the instrument against the shoulder and bowing palm-downward was used with the vielle. Tuning in consecutive fifths is documented as early as 1533 (G. M. Lanfranco, *Scintille di musica*) and was consistently used with the three-stringed *klein geigen* (descendants of the slender rebec) throughout the 16th century (M. Agricola, *Musica instrumentalis deudsch,* 1528). The rectangle between the fingerboard and upper end of the body is present in a *lira designed by Rafael (*c.* 1510) as well as in the *violettas mentioned by Lanfranco and Ganassi (1543). The latter instruments, which had no frets and three strings tuned in fifths, were very similar to the classical violin. A picture by Gaudenzio Ferrari from *c.* 1535 shows violettas with shallow ribs, pointed corners, round shoulders, a depression running around the edge, F-holes, and a scroll [see *SaHMI*, p. 357]. Only the addition of a fourth string was needed to create what might be called "the first violin."

The emergence of the name "violin" did not coincide with the emergence of the instrument. Throughout the 16th century names such as *violini* and *violons* were used for viols and similar instruments. About 1600, *violino* meant *viola rather than violin, as, e.g., in G. Gabrieli's *Symphoniae sacrae* (1597). In Monteverdi's *Orfeo* (1607), *violino ordinario* means viola and *violino piccolo* probably means violin [see Violin family (a)].

The first known makers of true violins were Gasparo (Bertolotti), called after his birthplace "da Salò" (1540–1609), G. Paolo Maggini (1580–*c.* 1630), both working in Brescia, and the brothers Amati (Antonio, 1550–1638; Girolamo, 1556–1630), who made Cremona famous as the center of violin making. Girolamo's son Niccolò Amati (1596–1684) was the first of the great three violin makers. The Amatis created the classical shape of the violin, flattening the body (which is deeply bulging in instruments of Gasparo da Salò) by deepening the middle bouts, sharpening the corners, rounding the holes in a more elegant shape, and improving the varnish.

Niccolò Amati's pupil Antonio Stradivari (1644–1737) built the most famous of all violins. Working at first along the lines of his master, he created in 1690 the model that came to be known as the "Long Strad" (length 14¾₆ in., width 8 in., vs. ordinary length 14 in., width 8⅛ in.). In 1698 he returned to the shorter pattern and made violins about 14 in. long but in widths similar to those of the "Long Strad." It was in this pattern that, from 1700 on, Stradivari made his finest instruments, such as the "Betts" (1704), now in the Library of Congress, "Viotti" (1709), "Parke" (1711), "Boissier" (1713), "Dolphin" (1714), "Messie" (1716), "Cessol" (1715), "Maurin" (1718), "Rode" (1722), "Sarasate" (1724), "Wilhelmj" (1725), and "Song of the Swan" (1737). All together Stradivari is believed to have made more than 1,000 instruments between 1666 and 1737; of these, 400 violins, 16 violas, and 39 cellos are actually known to be his.

Giuseppe Guarneri (1666–*c.* 1740) worked along different lines from Stradivari's. He revived the bold and rugged outline and with it the massive build and powerful tone of the earlier Brescian masters, Gasparo da Salò and G. Paolo

Maggini. He was interested mainly in tone quality. Unlike Stradivari, he worked with no uniformity of design, size, appearance, or finish, relying only on his intuition and experience.

Other famous violin makers of Italy were the Ruggieri (Francesco, known as "il Per," Giovanni Battista, and others), whose instruments bear a general resemblance to the Amatis'; the Rogeri (Giovanni and Pietro) of Brescia; and the Testore (Carlo Giuseppe, Carlo Antonio, and Paolo Antonio) of Milan. A famous German violin maker, scarcely second to the great Italians, was Stainer of Absam, Tyrol (1621–83), whose tradition was continued by the Klotz family of Mittenwald, Bavaria (Matthias, 1653–1743; Sebastian, 1696–1768; and others). Nine-tenths of the violins that pass as "Stainers" were made by the Klotz family and their followers. In England violin making began with Thomas Urquhart (active 1648–80) and continued with Edward Pamphilon (fl. 1670–90) and Barak Norman (1688–1740). A French maker of note was Nicolas Lupot (1758–1824), known for his valuable copies of Stradivari violins.

For information concerning other instruments illustrated under Violin and Violin family, see Gusle; Hardingfele (Hardanger fiddle); Hurdy-gurdy; Lira (Lira da braccio); Tromba marina; Viol (bass viol; lyra viol; baryton); Viola da gamba; Viola d'amore; Viola pomposa.

Lit. (selected): W. Henley, *Universal Dictionary of Violin and Bow Makers,* 5 vols. (1959); F. Geminiani, *The Art of Playing on the Violin, 1751,* fac. ed., D. D. Boyden [1951?]; E. Heron-Allen, *De Fidiculis Bibliographia,* 2 vols. (1890, '94); A. Bachmann, *An Encyclopedia of the Violin* (1925); F. B. Emery, *The Violinist's Encyclopedic Dictionary* [1928]; R. Vannes, *Dictionnaire universel des Luthiers,* rev. ed. (1951; suppl. 1959); E. van der Straeten, *The History of the Violin,* 2 vols. (1933); H. Poidras, *Critical and Documentary Dictionary of Violin Makers,* 2 vols. (1928, '30); P. Stoeving, *The Story of the Violin* (1904); *id., The Violin* (1929); W. M. Morris, *British Violin Makers,* rev. ed. (1920); W. Henley, *Antonio Stradivari, Master Luthier* (1961); W. H. Hill, *The Violinmakers of the Guarneri Family* (1931); H. Petherick, *Antonio Stradivari* (1900); *id., Joseph Guarnerius* (1906); *id., The Repairing and Restoration of Violins* (1903); W. L. F. von Lütgendorff, *Die Geigen- und Lautenmacher,* 2 vols. (1922); O. Haubensak, *Ursprung und Geschichte der Geige* (1930); L. Grillet, *Les Ancêtres du violon et du violoncelle,* 2 vols. (1901); E. Heron-Allen, *De fidiculis bibliographia: Being an Attempt towards a Bibliography of the Violin,* 2 vols. (1890, '94); A. K. Tottman, *Führer durch die Violinliteratur . . . Auflage von Wilhelm Altmann* (1935); A. Seiffert, "Eine Theorie der Geige" (*AMW* iv); A. Jarosy, "The Secret of the Italian Violin Makers" (*ML* xvi, 116ff); E. Peluzzi, "Chi fu l'inventore del violino" (*RMI* xlv).

Violin concerto. See under Concerto II, III (b).

Violin family. The chief members of this family are the *violin, *viola, *cello, and *double bass. These four instruments form the string section of the orchestra, the first three also being used in chamber music (*string quartet) and the last in *jazz. For more details, see the separate entries.

A great number of in-between sizes have been constructed, none of which achieved permanent importance. Among them are (in order of size):

(a) Violino piccolo [G. *Quartgeige*]. Tuned a fourth above the violin. Bach scored for this instrument in his Cantata no. 140 and his first Brandenburg Concerto. The *violini piccoli* of

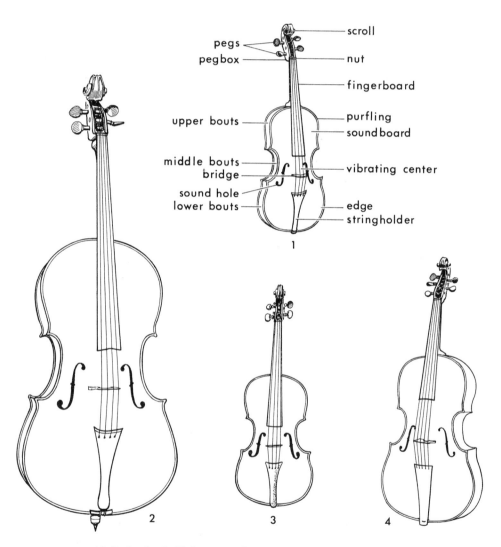

Violin family: 1. Violin. 2. Cello. 3. Viola. 4. Viola pomposa.

Violin family: 5. *Vielle (fidel).* 6. *Hardanger fiddle.* 7. *Hurdy-gurdy.* 8. *Lira da braccio.* 9. *Bass viol.* 10. *Viola da gamba.* 11. *Viola d'amore.* 12. *Lyra viol.*

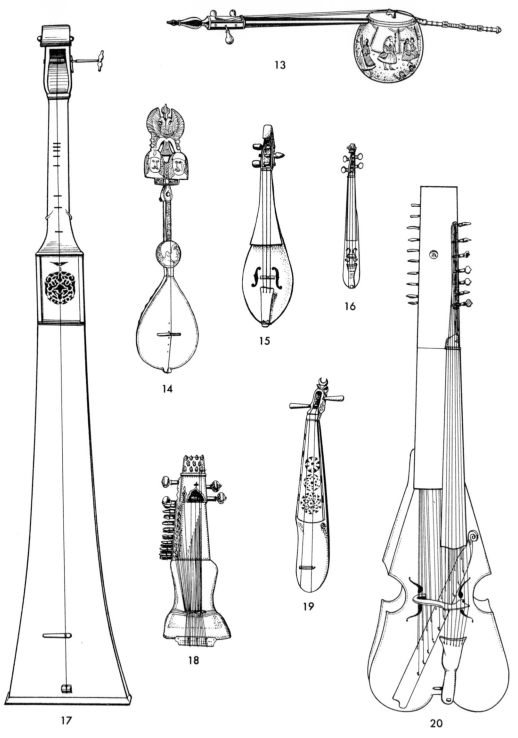

Violin family: 13. Kamānja. 14. Gusle. 15. Rebec. 16. Kit. 17. Tromba marina. 18. Sārangī.
19. Rabab. 20. Baryton.

Monteverdi's *Orfeo* (1607) have been interpreted as true violins (*SaHMI,* p. 358), as Bach's *violino piccolo* (A. Moser, in *ZMW* i), as the *pochette* or *kit* (*GD* v, opp. p. 524; *GDB* viii, opp. p. 146), and as the modern ¾-size violin, a major third above the violin (Forsyth).

(b) Contra-violin, introduced (1917) by H. Newbould, slightly bigger than the normal violin and designed to take the place of the second violin in chamber music.

(c) Viola alta, introduced by H. Ritter and used during the Bayreuth festivals 1872–75. This was a larger viola (length 19 in.) and was later provided with a fifth string tuned e''.

(d) Contralto, a larger viola with a fuller tone, constructed by J.-B. Vuillaume, 1855.

(e) Violotta, constructed by A. Stelzner in 1891, a tenor violin, measuring 28 in., tuned G d a e'. F. Draeseke, Max von Schillings (*Pfeifertag*), and others have scored for it.

(f) Tenor violin. Name for various instruments between the viola and cello in size (27½ to 29½ in. in length). They were used from the mid-16th century but became obsolete in the 18th century. The most common baroque tuning appears to have been F c g d'. Later attempts to build similar instruments include those of Vuillaume (1855), H. Ritter, A. Stelzner [see (c), (d), (e)], and others. See H. Besseler, *Zum Problem der Tenorgeige* (1949).

(g) Viole-ténor [F.], constructed by R. Farramon in 1930; it is held like a cello. Also called *alto-moderne.*

(h) Violoncello piccolo. An instrument 36 to 38 in. long that Bach frequently preferred to the cello because its smaller size facilitated the execution of solo passages. It was tuned like the cello. The *violoncello à cinque cordes,* which Bach scored for in the sixth of his Suites for cello solo, was probably only slightly smaller than the usual cello.

(i) Cellone, constructed by Stelzner [see (e)], a large cello (length 46 in.), tuned G_1 D A e (a fourth lower than the cello) and intended chiefly as a contrabass for chamber music.

(j) Octobasse, constructed by J. B. Vuillaume in 1849, a giant double bass, about 13 feet high, with three strings tuned C_2 G_2 C_1. They were stopped by a mechanical system of levers and pedals. An American model made by John Geyer in 1889 measures almost 15 feet.

See also Quinton.

Violin music. The violin first appeared in Italian polyphonic compositions of the late 16th cen-

tury, with one part marked *Violino.* In this period, however, the term was also used for the *viola, so only the range can indicate which instrument was intended. The *violino* part in Giovanni Gabrieli's celebrated *Sonata pian'e forte* (*Sacrae Symphoniae,* 1597; see *HAM,* no. 173) is obviously written for a viola (range d to a'). On the other hand, many of the canzonas in the same publication have undesignated upper parts that could hardly have been performed on any instrument other than the violin (e.g., Canzona IX, with sixteenth-note passages up and down from f♯' to a''). From similar evidence, it appears that the two *Violini* accompanying the aria "Possente spirto" of Monteverdi's *Orfeo* (1607) are probably violins. Among the first composers of solo violin music were Salomone Rossi (1587–*c.* 1630) and Giovanni Battista Fontana of Brescia (d. 1631). Rossi published four books, the first three (1607, 1608, with only 2nd ed. of third book preserved, 1623) designated for "due viole," and the fourth (1622) for "due violini" [see W. Newman, *The Sonata in the Baroque Era* (1959), p. 111]. Most probably they all contain music for two violins (and accompaniment). Fontana's compositions are preserved in a posthumous edition of 1641, containing eighteen sonatas, the first six for solo violin and accompaniment [see *HAM,* no. 198; also Wasielewski, *Instrumentalsätze*]. Two composers who treated the instrument with striking virtuosity were Biagio Marini (*c.* 1595–1665) and Carlo Farina (*c.* 1600–*c.* 1640). Their sonatas and other pieces make use of double-stops, trills, and tremolos [see *HAM,* no. 199; *SchGMB,* nos. 182, 183], and in Farina's "Capriccio stravagante" (in *Ander Theil newer Paduanen, Gagliarden,* 1627) these techniques as well as pizzicato, *col legno,* and harmonics are used to imitate the barking of dogs, caterwauling, fifes and drums, etc. [see Wasielewski, *Instrumentalsätze,* no. 11]. Double-stops and higher positions (up to the 5th) are common in the pieces of Marco Uccellini (b. *c.* 1610; see Wasielewski, Torchi). While virtuoso exploitation of the instrument continued in Germany under J. H. Schmelzer (*c.* 1623–80), Nicolaus Adam Strungk (1640–1700), Heinrich Ignaz Franz von Biber (1644–1704; see *DTO* 11 and 25; *HAM,* no. 238; *SchGMB,* no. 238; see Scordatura), and J. J. Walther (b. 1650), the Italian composers after 1650 turned to the true musical qualities of the violin and developed its "singing" style. Giovanni Legrenzi (1626–90), G. B. Vitali (*c.* 1644–92), G. Torelli (1658–1709), and others led up to the "classical" simplicity of

Arcangelo Corelli (1653–1713), who, despite somewhat academic tendencies, holds a central position in the history of violin music [see also Bologna school]. Still another type of violin music, characterized by animated flow and rhythmic precision, was inaugurated by Antonio Vivaldi (1669–1741), whose violin concertos attracted the interest of Bach. Francesco Maria Veracini (1690–c. 1750), Giuseppe Tartini (1692–1770), and Pietro Locatelli (1695–1764) represent the acme of Italian baroque violin music. Their sonatas opened new possibilities of lyric and passionate expression, while their concertos, particularly those of Tartini, are written in a highly virtuoso style. The contemporary French school is represented by J.-B. Anet (c. 1661–1755) and J. M. Leclair (1697–1764).

Bach wrote an early suite (A major) and six sonatas for violin and harpsichord. His six sonatas for violin without accompaniment (actually three sonatas and three suites, one of which includes the celebrated Chaconne) represent a peak in the extensive literature for violin solo, which includes pieces by Thomas Baltzar (c. 1630–63; see SchGMB, no. 237), J. J. Walther (Hortulus Chelicus, 1688), Nicola Matteis (fl. c. 1672), H. I. F. von Biber (1644–1704), F. Geminiani (1687–1762), G. P. Telemann (1681–1767), and Johann Georg Pisendel (1687–1755) [see A. C. Roncalio, in The Journal of Musicology ii, no. 2, 72ff]. The violin pieces of the *Mannheim group, particularly the sonatas of J. Schobert (c. 1720–67), are written in a dynamic style that foreshadows the idiom of Mozart and Beethoven [see DdT 39]. A happy amalgamation of this style with the achievements of the Italian school is represented by G. B. Viotti (1755–1824), of whose twenty-nine violin concertos no. 22 is outstanding (also eighteen violin sonatas and numerous duets). Of his predecessors, Antonio Lolli (c. 1730–1802) and Gaetano Pugnani (1731–98) merit mention.

With Mozart and Beethoven begins a new period of violin music. Throughout the 19th century the favored type of violin music was the concerto [see Concerto II]. Violin sonatas were written by Schumann (3), Brahms (3), Grieg (3), Franck (1), Reger (7; also 11 for unaccompanied violin), Debussy (1), Ives (5), Hindemith (3; also 3 for unaccompanied violin), Bartók (2), Bloch (2), Prokofiev (3), Martinu (3), and many others.

Lit.: H. Letz, Music for the Violin and Viola (1948; a checklist); A. Tottmann, Führer durch die Violin-Literatur, rev. ed. (1935); W. S. Newman, The Sonata in the Baroque Era (1959); id.,

The Sonata in the Classic Era (1963); A. Moser, Geschichte des Violinspiels (1923); W. J. von Wasielewski, Die Violine und ihre Meister, rev. ed. (1883; last ed., 1927); id., Die Violine im XVII Jahrhundert (1874; musical suppl., pub. separately as ‡Instrumentalsätze vom Ende des XVI. bis Ende des XVII. Jahrhunderts); G. Beckmann, Das Violinspiel in Deutschland vor 1700 (1918); B. Studeny, Beiträge zur Geschichte der Violin Sonate im 18. Jahrhundert (1911); H. Lungershausen, Probleme der Übergangszeit von der altklassischen zur klassischen Epoche: Stilkritische Analysen am nordeutschen Violinsolokonzert des 18. Jahrhunderts (1928); A. Pougin, Le Violon, les violinistes et la musique de violon du XVIe au XVIIIe siècle (1924); L. de La Laurencie, L'École française du violon de Lully a Viotti, 3 vols. (1922–24); D. D. Boyden, The History of Violin Playing from Its Origins to 1761 (1965); A. Bonaventura, Storia del violino, dei violinisti e della musica per violino (1925); A. Baudet-Maget, Guide du violoniste; oeuvres choisies pour violon . . . classées d'après leur degré de difficulté [n.d.]; G. Beckmann, ‡Das Violinspiel in Deutschland vor 1700, 5 vols. (1921); G. Jensen, ‡Classical Violin Music [1890?]; H. Riemann, ‡Old Chamber Music, 4 vols. (1896–98); id., ‡Collegium musicum, 70 vols.; A. Schering, ‡Alte Meister des Violinspiels; J. W. Wasielewski, ‡Instrumentalsätze . . . des XVII Jahrhunderts; L. Torchi, ‡L'Arte musicale in Italia, vol. vii [*Editions III]; D. Boyden, "The Violin and Its Technique in the 18th Century" (MQ xxxvi); M. Scott, "Solo Violin Sonatas" (ML x, 46ff); K. Gerhartz, "Die Violinschule . . . bis Leopold Mozart" (ZMW vii, 553ff); M. Pincherle, "La Technique du violon chez les premiers sonatistes français (1695–1723)" (BSIM 1911).

Violino piccolo. See Violin family (a).

Violin playing. See Bowing.

Violon [F.]. Violin. Violón [Sp.], viol, bass viol, double bass.

Violoncello. See Cello.

Violoncello piccolo. See under Violin family (h).

Violoncino. Old name for violoncello (cello), e.g., in G. B. Fontana, Sonate . . . per il violino or cornetto, fagotto, chitarone, violoncino (1641).

Violone [It.]. The largest size of the viols [see Viol IV, 1]. In Diego Ortiz' Tratado de glosas . . . en la música de violones (1553) it obviously is a synonym for viola da gamba. Praetorius, in

"Syntagma musicum," describes it as a much larger instrument, approximately of double-bass size. That the name also meant a member of the violin family, "intermediate between the violoncello and the double bass" (SaHMI, p. 363), is doubtful. See B. Disertori, in RMI xlvi.

Violotta. See under Violin family (e).

Virelai [F.]. I. An important form of medieval French poetry and music (also called *chanson balladée), consisting of a refrain (R) that usually alternates with three stanzas (S): R S₁ R S₂ R S₃ R. The stanzas begin with two rhyming versicles and close with a versicle paralleling the refrain (the term *versicle here means a section of the text; it may consist of one, two, three, or more lines of the poem). The musical structure corresponds exactly to that of the poem, the two parallel versicles being sung to the same music and the closing versicle to that of the refrain. In the following diagram, for R S₁ R and a two-line refrain, the refrain is indicated by italics in the textual structure and by capital letters in the musical structure:

	R	S₁	R
Text	*a b*	c c a b	*a b*
Music	A	b b a	A

The entire musical structure is A b b a A b b a A b b a A, but usually the virelai form is understood to comprise only the first five units. In modern scores it is represented as follows:

```
A            ‖:B        :‖
1.5. (refr.)  2. . . . . .
4. . . . . .  3. . . . . .
```

The music B usually has different endings for lines 2 and 3 (*ouvert and clos).

A few examples of the virelai have been found in 13th-century sources, one of them, "C'est la fin" (HAM, no. 19f), in a late trouvère chansonnier (Vaticana, Fond Christ.) and three or four others in tenors of motets, among them "E, dame jolie" (HAM, no. 19g). Two examples are among the monophonic songs of Jehannot de l'Escurel (d. 1304), preserved in an appendix to the Roman de Fauvel [see Sources, no. 8; see P. Aubry, ed., Le Roman de Fauvel (1907)]. It was Machaut who established the virelai as one of the *formes fixes of French poetry and music. It continued to be composed in the late 14th century, and sparingly throughout the 15th, by Dufay and Ockeghem [see HAM, nos. 74, 75] and by Busnois, who preferred the shorter *bergerette, as did others after him.

II. The virelai is not a form of *trouvère music, as was formerly assumed. More likely its origins are Spanish, and perhaps ultimately Arab [see Zejel]. The Spanish *cantigas of the second half of the 13th century (some possibly even earlier) include, among c. 400 songs, more than 100 in strict virelai form and many more showing essentially the same form with some modifications [see below]. The Italian laude of the same period also have a general virelai structure but with some variants of the musical form. The strict form appears in 14th-century Italian music, known as the *ballata, and in Spanish music of the 15th and 16th centuries as the *villancico. Unlike the French type, the Italian and Spanish forms do not always restate the refrain after each stanza, nor do they always have the strict conformity of poetic structure to musical form that is characteristic of the French virelai. This is especially evident in their rhyme structure, which in many cases is asymmetrical, e.g., a b | c c c b, instead of symmetrical, a b | c c a b. Practically all the Italian ballate (Landini) are asymmetrical. In the Spanish repertory both types are encountered, in the 13th-century cantigas as well as in the polyphonic *cancioneros of the 15th and 16th centuries, where the name villancico is reserved for the asymmetrical type, the symmetrical one being called *canción. Below are some examples of each type (a, b, etc. indicate rhymes; the designations ripresa, piedi, volta are adopted from the ballata):

		ripresa	piedi	volta
Music		A	B B	A
Symmetrical text	1.	aa	b b	aa
	2.	abba	cd cd	abba
	3.	abab	ca ca	abab
Asymmetrical text	4.	aa	b b	ba
	5.	aa	bc bc	ca
	6.	abb	cd cd	dbb

1. Cantigas, no. 86 (*Editions IV, 15).   2. Cancionero del palacio, no. 30 (*Editions XXXII, 5). 3. Machaut, Virelai, no. 3 (L. Schrade, ed.,‡ Polyphonic Music of the Fourteenth Century, vol. iii). 4. Cantigas, no. 114 (HAM, no 22c).   5. Landini, "Amor c'al tuo suggetto" (HAM, no. 53).   6. Cancionero del palacio, no. 54 (*Editions XXXII, 5).

Besides the normal virelai form, there are various modified types, particularly in the laude and cantigas, e.g.:

	ripresa	piedi	volta
Normal.	A B	c c	A B
1.	A B	a a	A B
2.	A B	b b	A B
3.	A B	a a	B A
4.	A B	c c	D B
5.	A B	c d	A B

Types 1, 2, and 3 involve more repeat than the normal form, while the others represent "weakened" modifications.

Lit.: See under Rondeau (1); F. Gennrich, *Rondeaux, Virelais, und Balladen,* 2 vols. (1921, '27); E. Heldt, *Französische Virelais aus dem 15. Jahrhundert* (1916); I. Pope, "Musical and Metrical Form of the Villancico" (*AnnM* ii); G. Reaney, in *MD* xiii; *id.,* in *CP Fellerer.*

Virga [L.]. See under Neumes I.

Virgil clavier. A practice piano, patented by the American A. K. Virgil in 1892, that has no sound-producing parts but that, by means of a slight click accompanying the depression and the release of the key, gives perfect control over legato playing.

Virginal. A type of *harpsichord with one choir of transverse strings described as early as 1511, in S. Virdung's *Musica getutscht,* a fact that clearly refutes the idea that the name refers to the "maiden Queen Elizabeth." Whether it is so called because "like a virgin, it sound with a sweet and tranquil voice" (Paulus Paulirinus, 1460; see J. Reiss, in *ZMW* vii) or because "virgins play on them" (John Minshen, 1617; see his *Ductor in Linguas*), or with reference to L. *virga* (rod, i.e., jack: see *SaHMI,* p. 335), is uncertain. The earliest virginals were in the shape of a small oblong box, to be placed on a table or even held in the player's lap. Toward the end of the 16th century the term was indiscriminately applied to all types of harpsichord, whether rectangular, wing-shaped, or trapezoidal [see Spinet]. Thus it cannot be assumed that the virginalist composers wrote for the oblong virginals. The common term was "pair of virginals," an idiom whose origin is not known.

Lit.: F. Hubbard, *Three Centuries of Harpsichord Making* (1965); D. Boalch, *Makers of the Harpsichord and Clavichord 1440–1840* (1956).

Virginal music. The earliest extant examples of virginal music are a few dances in an English MS of *c.* 1530 (Brit. Mus., *Roy. App.* 58), including a "Hornepype" by H. Aston, "My Lady Carey's Dompe" [*HAM,* no. 103], and "My Lady Wynk-

fyld's Rownde." The *Mulliner Book (*c.* 1560) also contains some dances, among them "A Pavan" by Newman in the key of C minor. A large repertory of such music exists in the so-called virginal books of the late 16th and early 17th centuries. The most important of these are (in approximate chronological order): (a) "My Ladye Nevells Booke" (1591), containing 42 compositions by William Byrd (ed. H. Andrews, 1926); (b) "Fitzwilliam Virginal Book" (also called, erroneously, "Queen Elizabeth's Virginal Book"), the most extensive and most important collection, containing 297 compositions by practically every composer of the virginalist school (2 vols., ed. J. A. Fuller-Maitland and W. Barclay Squire, 1894–99; for a detailed list of contents, see *GD* v, 545ff; *GDB* ix, 4ff); (c) "Benjamin Cosyn's Virginal Book," containing 98 pieces, chiefly by John Bull, Orlando Gibbons, and Benjamin Cosyn; (d) "Will. Forster's Virginal Book," containing 78 pieces, mostly by William Byrd. Numerous later MSS of less importance are in the libraries of London, New York, and Paris. A printed collection is the *Parthenia.

The most important composers of virginal music, arranged in three generations, are: I. William Byrd (1543–1623); II. Thomas Morley (1557–1602), Peter Philips (1561–1628), Giles Farnaby (*c.* 1560–1640), John Bull (*c.* 1562–1628); III. Thomas Weelkes (*c.* 1575–1623), Thomas Tomkins (1572–1656), Orlando Gibbons (1583–1625). The "three famous Masters William Byrd, Dr. John Bull and Orlando Gibbons," as they are called in the title of the *Parthenia,* were born twenty years apart and all of them died in the 1620's. Although Byrd seems to have been the first to concentrate on the virginal, his music qualitatively dwarfs that of all the other virginalists except Gibbons. John Bull is noted mainly for his exploitation of the technical means of the instrument (rapid passages, scales in parallel thirds, broken-chord figures, etc.), a contribution that left traces in the works of Sweelinck and Scheidt.

The repertory of the virginalist composers comprises dances (mainly *pavanes and galliards), variations, *preludes, fantasias, liturgical pieces (organ hymns; see also In nomine), and transcriptions of madrigals.

Lit.: W. Apel, *Geschichte der Klavier- und Orgelmusik bis 1700* (1967), pp. 288–318; C. van den Borren, *Les Origines de la musique de clavier en Angleterre* (1912; Eng. trans. 1914); M. H. Glyn, *About Elizabethan Virginal Music and Its*

Composers, rev. ed. (1934); W. Niemann, *Die Virginalmusik* (1919); H. Andrews, ‡*My Ladye Nevells Book* (1926); J. A. Fuller-Maitland and W. Barclay Squire, ‡*The Fitzwilliam Virginal Book,* 2 vols. (1894–99; repr. 1949); *id.,* ‡*Twenty-five Pieces for Keyed Instruments from Benjamin Cosyn's Virginal Book* (1923); William Byrd, ‡*Forty-five Pieces for Keyboard Instruments,* ed. S. D. Tuttle (1939); K. Stone, ed., ‡*Parthenia* (1951); J. M. Ward, ed., ‡*The Dublin Virginal Manuscript* (1954); Thomas Weelkes, ‡*Pieces for Keyed Instruments,* ed. M. H. Glyn (1924); *Editions XXXIV, 5, 14, 19, 20, 24; H. Andrews, "Elizabethan Keyboard Music" (*MQ* xvi); M. H. Glyn, "Famous Books on Virginal Music . . . in the New York Public Library" (*Musical Courier* lxxviii, 12); T. Dart, "New Sources of Virginal Music" (*ML* xxxv, 93); M.-L. Pereyra, "Les Livres de virginal de la Bibliothèque du Conservatoire de Paris" (*RdM* 1926–33, nos. 20, 21, 24, 28, 29, 37, 42, 45).

Virtuoso. A performer who excels in technical ability; sometimes, one who excels in this only. Perhaps the first virtuoso was Arnolt Schlick (*c.* 1460–after 1517), whose *Ascendo ad patrem meum* [see Arnolt Schlick, ‡*Hommage à l'empereur Charles-Quint,* ed. M. S. Kastner and M. Querol Gavalda (1954)], in six parts for the manuals and four parts for the pedal, indicate he was an amazingly accomplished organist. John Bull (*c.* 1562–1628) was an eminent master of the harpsichord, as was, more than a century later, Domenico Scarlatti (1685–1757). The virtuoso qualities of the violin were exploited by Carlo Farina (*c.* 1600–*c.* 1640), Heinrich Ignaz Franz von Biber (1644–1704), Giuseppe Tartini (1692–1770), and others [see Violin music]. In the 18th century, the famous *castrati* developed a vocal technique that has never been equaled. The 19th century saw the spectacular rise of virtuoso pianists (Chopin, Liszt, Anton Rubinstein, Leschetizky, Busoni), violinists (Paganini, Sarasate, Jan Kubelík), singers (Malibran, Sontag, Lind, Melba, Caruso, M. Battistini), and other performers.

Visigothic chant. See Mozarabic chant.

Visitation, The. Opera by Gunther Schuller (libretto by the composer, based on Kafka), produced in Hamburg, Germany, 1966.

Vista [It.]. Sight. *A prima vista,* at sight [see Sight-reading].

Vite, vitement [F.]. Fast, quickly.

Vivace [It.]. Quick, lively. *Vivacissimo,* very quick.

Vivement [F.]. Lively.

Vl. Abbr. for violin. *Vla.,* viola. *Vlc.,* violoncello. *Vll.,* violins.

Vocalization [F. *vocalise;* G. *Vokalise;* It. *vocalizzo;* Sp. *vocalización*]. A long melody sung on a vowel, i.e., without text. The term is used chiefly for vocal exercises (*solfège) and so has a somewhat pejorative connotation, implying technical display for its own sake. However, without a text the singer can concentrate on using pure tone in the sense of the instrumentalist, unimpeded by words, for expressive purposes. In the case of study vocalises, the added hazard of a text is eliminated until the sensation of making pure tone has been firmly established. Throughout the early history of singing (i.e., prior to 1800) composers have fully appreciated this fact. Bach's and Handel's works contain numerous highly artistic vocalizations (usually called *coloraturas), and the untexted melismas of Gregorian chant are even more remote from any inference of virtuosity for its own sake [see Neuma].

Particularly interesting is the role that vocalization played in the polyphonic music of the 13th to 15th centuries. The textless tenors of 13th-century motets, which have frequently been interpreted as "instrumental tenors," are actually vocalizations on the vowel of the *incipit [see Clausula; Motet A, I]. For an example of a long vocalization in the upper parts of a 13th-century motet, see *ApNPM,* pp. 315ff. Most of the accompanied songs (*ballades* [F.], madrigals) of the 14th century contain long passages without a text, passages that no doubt were to be sung as vocalizations. Unfortunately, some modern editors, such as H. Riemann and A. Schering, have interpreted such passages as "instrumental preludes" (or interludes, postludes), a procedure that frequently leads to an artificial interruption of a continuous melodic line [see, e.g., *RiHM* i.2, 306–34, and *SchGMB,* no. 19; for a correct rendition of Giovanni da Cascia's "Nel mezzo a sei paon," cf. *WoGM* iii, 92ff]. See also Text and music (reference to Kyrie).

There is a considerable literature of pieces to be performed in vocalization throughout. This manner of performance is indicated in various 16th-century publications inscribed "da cantare e sonare" (to sing and to play), e.g., Willaert's *Ricercari* of 1559 or C. Merulo's *Ricercari da* cantare, a quattro voci (1574). These long pieces (in three or four parts) have no text, and they probably are meant (judging from the precedence given to the word cantare) to be vocalized throughout in all the parts. This practice persisted in the numerous two-part ricercars of the 17th century, some of which are expressly designated as "vocal exercises" [see Ricercar II (d)]. Spontini, in his opera Nurmahal, chose vocalization for the "Chorus of Heavenly Spirits," and several later composers have written for vocalizing voices, e.g., Debussy ("Sirènes," movt. 3 of Nocturnes, 1899), Ravel (Vocalise en forme d'habanera, 1907), Rachmaninoff (Vocalise, op. 34, no. 14, 1912), Medtner (Sonata-Vocalise, op. 41, no. 1; Suite-Vocalise, op. 41, no. 2); and Roussel (Padmâvatî, comp. 1914, perf. 1923). See W. Apel, "Die menschliche Stimme als Instrument" (Zeitschrift: Stimmen [1949], p. 404); M. Dauge, "Essai sur la vocalise" (RM, 1935, no. 16).

Vocal music. Music written for voices, either solo or chorus [see Choral music]. Practically all music prior to 1500 is vocal, as is nine-tenths of the music of the 16th century. During the baroque period vocal and instrumental music were about equal in quality and prominence, but after 1750 instrumental music gained the upper hand [see Instrumental music]. Below is a survey of the most important types of vocal music (italics indicate accompanied vocal music):

A. Period of superior importance (to 1600). 6th–9th centuries: Gregorian chant. 9th–12th (13th) centuries: Sequence; trope; organum. 12th–13th centuries: Troubadours; trouvères; minnesingers. 13th century: Clausula; conductus; motet. 14th century: Motet; Mass items; ballade; virelai; rondeau; madrigal; ballata; caccia. 15th century: Motet (Flemish); Mass; chansons. 16th century: Motet; Mass; madrigal; polyphonic lied; chanson; frottola; lute song; villanella.

B. Period of equal importance (1600–1750): Cantata; opera; oratorio; aria; anthem; glee.

C. Period of inferior importance (1750–present): Lied; French, English, etc. song; opera.

Regarding vocal versus instrumental style in early music, see under Ensemble (3). See also S. Kagen, Music for the Voice; A Descriptive List of Concert and Teaching Material (1949); J. M. Knapp, ed., Selected List of Music for Men's Voices (1952); L. Hibberd, in MQ xxviii, no. 2, xxxii, no. 1. Also see under Choral music.

Voce, pl. **voci** [It.]. Voice. A due (tre) voci, for two (three) voices. Colla voce, see Colla. Voce di gola, throat voice, guttural voice; voce di petto, chest voice; voce di testa, head voice, *falsetto. Voci pari or eguali, equal voices.

Voces [L]. See Vox.

Vodoum. See Voodoo.

Voice. The physical process of voice production was for a long time understood only superficially. Formerly, it was thought that the larynx, containing the "vocal cords," initiates the tone much as the lips do in the mouthpiece of a brass instrument. The breath is pressed upward from the lungs through these "vocal lips," which are held close together, at varying tensions according to the pitch desired, setting the lips and breath into vibration. However, in the case of brass instruments, the player presses his lips together deliberately and learns how much to do so for a desired pitch. The muscular motion of his lips is thus a matter of conscious control. The vocal cords, on the other hand, are not among the muscles that can be controlled consciously. Thus the origin of the sound must lie elsewhere.

Observation of children reveals that sound in singing, as in speech, is originated by an impulse to produce it. A spontaneous, strong impulse of this kind starts deep in the body, moving the muscles of the lower abdomen, which in turn cause the diaphragm to push air from the lungs through the vocal apparatus. The vocal mechanism in turn has been set in position to produce a desired pitch as preconceived by the singer. The resulting tone is modified by contact with all the inner surfaces of the mouth, nose, throat, and even the lungs.

While singers generally concur on what constitutes an agreeable tone, there is a great difference of opinion as to how to achieve this ideal. Physically, singing is intensified and prolonged speech, and the same complex of muscles is used in both processes. Therefore attempts to achieve conscious control over all the muscles is futile. There are, however, initial and important points of control that involve positioning the body, jaw, larynx, and tongue, which in turn shape speech. So-called "natural singers," untutored vocally, among them such figures as F. I. Shaliapin and A. Galli-Curci, have instinctively known how to use and coordinate the proper muscles.

What, however, creates good tone quality? Almost any singer will agree that muscular tension is the main cause of bad tone. Most often, muscular tension results from undue pressure or restraint of the tone, and such forcing or holding the tone is in turn caused by self-consciousness. Self-consciousness diverts the singer's attention. If he could concentrate wholly on the expression of his song, he would relax and sing well. However, such total concentration is very difficult to attain, and the very presence of tension in a particular area (jaw, throat, etc.) tends to compound the problem.

To counteract tension, teachers use many devices to divert the singer's attention from such problems. For example, the tongue under tension thickens and draws back, partly closing the throat. The back nasal passages become too stretched, or too relaxed; the jaw becomes set and stiff, and a corresponding distortion appears in the tone. If the pupil is taught to "place the voice" or imagine the vibration of the tone gently in the front mouth surfaces and nose, his throat and tongue tend to relax and the nasal passages become free of their own accord. Unfortunately, the singer may then feel that he must push his tone into place, causing a new set of tensions. Various devices are then employed to teach the pupil to "support the breath," leading him to find the knack of avoiding this "forcing." Thinking now of his breath, the pupil tends to strain breathing, feeling that he is aiding the process. Tension returns and he finds his throat closing again.

The great problem of singing, therefore, is to coordinate all of the many areas involved, and different teachers tend to concentrate on different areas and techniques.

For a historical view of the art of singing, see Singing.

Lit.: W. T. Bartholomew, *Acoustics of Music* (1942); J. F. Cooke, *Great Singers on the Art of Singing* [1921]; S. Fucito and B. J. Beyer, *Caruso and the Art of Singing* [1922]; H. P. Greene, *Interpretation in Song* (repr. 1931); I. Franca, *Manual of Bel Canto* [1959]; W. E. Ross, *Secrets of Singing* [1959]; G. Henschel, *Articulation in Singing* [1926]; S. Kagen, *On Studying Singing* (1950); Lilly Lehmann, *How to Sing*, rev. ed. (1914); P. A. Duey, *Bel Canto in Its Golden Age* (1951); C. L. Reid, *Bel Canto: Principles and Practices* (1950); P. M. Marafioti, *Caruso's Method of Voice Production* (1922); G. O. Russell, *Causes of Good and Bad Voices* [n.d.]; W. E. Brown, *Vocal Wisdom: Maxims of G. B. Lamperti* (1931); D. Stanley, *The Science of Voice* [1929]; E. G. White, *Science and Singing* (1938);

J. C. Wilcox, *The Living Voice* [1935]; F. Martienssen-Lohmann, *Der wissende Sänger* [1956]; M. Benharoche, *L'Art vocal,* 2 vols. [1957]; M. Garcia, *Traité complet de l'art du chant* (1847). See also Pronunciation.   rev. O.A.

Voice exchange [G. *Stimmtausch*]. The restatement of a contrapuntal passage with the voice-parts exchanged, so that, e.g., the soprano part sings the alto part and vice versa (without the octave transposition found in *invertible counterpoint). The result of duple or triple exchange can be indicated as:

```
b  a              c  a  b
        or        b  c  a
a  b              a  b  c
```

This method is described by Walter Odington (*CS* i, 246f), who called it *rondellus* and gives an example of the triple form [see *OH* i, 320f].

Sporadic examples of voice exchange occur in the 12th-century sources of St. Martial and Compostela [see *NOH* ii, 302] and are common in the upper parts of the *organa tripla* and *quadrupla* of the school of Notre Dame, as well as in the conductus [see Y. Rokseth, *Polyphonies du XIIIe siècle* iv, 87ff]. The accompanying example shows a double voice exchange from the conductus "Quod promisit" [Wolfenbüttel

MS *677,* f. 130']. The conductus "Veris ad imperia" [Florence, *Plut. 29.i,* f. 228; see F. Gennrich, *Grundriss einer Formenlehre* (1932), p. 85] begins with a duple exchange over a repeated tenor, whereas a "Benedicamus Domino" [*ibid.,* f. 47ᵛ, also in Codex Huelgas, f. 25ᵛ; see Gennrich, p. 88] consists entirely of triple exchanges:

```
   "Veris"              "Benedicamus"
 c  b  c          c  a  b    c  a  b    c
 b  c  b          b  c  a    b  c  a    b
 a  a  a etc.     a  b  c    a  b  c    a etc.
```

In the late 13th century the technique of voice exchange was taken over by English composers, who used it as a structural device rather than a stylistic element. Many of the compositions of the so-called school of Worcester are, or include, *rondelli,* usually duple *rondelli* over a repeated tenor [ex. in *HAM,* no. 57a].

Voice exchange, although usually not recognized as such, is used in all *rounds. It also occurs in the two upper parts of baroque trio sonatas. See J. Handschin, in *ZMW* x, 535; *id.,* in *ZMW* xvi, 119; M. Bukofzer, in *MQ* xxvi, 35.

Voice-leading. In contrapuntal music, the principles governing the progression of the various voice-parts (particularly those other than the soprano), especially in terms of the individual lines. Among such principles are preference of step-wise motion (at least in the three upper parts), contrary motion in at least one part, and avoidance of parallel fifths and octaves.

Voices, range of. Human voices are usually divided into six ranges: three female voices, soprano, mezzo-soprano, and contralto, and three male voices, tenor, baritone, and bass. In choral singing the middle voice of each group may be omitted. The normal range of these voices is roughly an octave (or a seventh) below and above the notes d, f, a, and e′, g′, b′ [see Ex.]. The

Bass Baritone Tenor Contralto Mezzo Soprano

indication of range differs markedly in different countries, e.g., England, Italy, Germany, Russia.

Trained soloists frequently exceed these ranges. The soprano Lucrezia Agujari (1743–83) could reach c″″, and a bass part in Handel's *Aci, Galatea e Polifemo* (1708), written for Giuseppe Boschi, shifts, within one measure, from a′ to C♯, more than two and one-half octaves. Some Russian basses have reached F_1, a fifth below low C. Contemporary composers often demand such tremendous ranges.

Opera singers are further classified, mainly with regard to the character and timbre of the voice:

Dramatic soprano, with powerful voice and marked declamatory and histrionic ability; *lyric soprano,* with lighter quality and pleasant cantabile style; *coloratura soprano,* with great agility and a high range.

Dramatic contralto, with slightly lower range than the dramatic soprano (one or two tones) but capable of producing a powerful sound, as well as great dramatic expression.

Tenore robusto (robust tenor), with full voice and vigor; *lyric tenor,* corresponding to the lyric soprano; *Heldentenor* (heroic tenor), combining agility, brilliant timbre, and expressive power.

Basso profondo [F. *basse profonde*], with low range, powerful voice, and solemn character; *basso cantante* [*basse chantante*], with qualities similar to the lyric soprano; *basso buffo,* comical, agile bass.

Voicing. In organ building, adjustment of the timbre and pitch of the pipes. In piano building, the adjustment of the hammer felts to produce a pleasing timbre.

Voilé [F.]. Veiled, subdued.

Voix [F.]. Voice. *Voix de poitrine,* chest voice; *voix de tête,* head voice; *voix mixte,* the medium register. *Voix céleste,* organ stop; see Organ IX (c).

Voix de ville [F.]. See under *Vaudeville.*

Vokal [G.]. Vowel. *Vokalisieren,* to vocalize; *Vokalise,* vocalization.

Volante [It.]. Rushing.

Volkslied [G.]. Folksong.

Volkstümliches Lied [G.]. The German art song of the latter part of the 18th century, which, in reaction to the alleged artificiality of the coloratura aria [G. *Kunstlied*], reverted to a somewhat affected simplicity of expression and style approximating folk music. Representative composers of such songs include J. A. P. Schulz (1747–1800), J. F. Reichardt (1752–1814), K. F. Zelter (1758–1832), and F. Silcher (1789–1860). See Lied IV; Berlin school. Ex. in *SchGMB,* no. 309b.

Volles Werk [G.]. Full organ.

Volo di Notte, Il [It., The Night Flight]. Opera in one act by L. Dallapiccola (libretto after A. Saint-Exupéry), produced in Florence, 1940. Setting: Buenos Aires airport, about 1930.

Volta, volte [It.]. (1) A dance of the period c. 1600, usually in dotted 6/8 meter. It was extremely popular, perhaps owing to its lascivious connotations (e.g., in the dance, the woman was lifted high in the air). English writers (Shakespeare) and musicians often called it *Lavolta* or *Levalto.* (2) See under *Ballata.* (3) In modern scores, *prima* and *seconda volta* indicate the first and second ending of a section to be repeated: ⌐1a ⫶⌐2a. See also *Ouvert* and *clos.*

Volteggiando [It.]. Crossing the hands (in piano playing).

Volti [It.]. Turn over (the page); *volti subito* (abbr. *v.s.*), turn quickly.

Voluntary. Name for an English organ piece played at the church service. As suggested by the name, voluntaries originally were free, quasi-improvisatory pieces. Thus, Morley says in his *A Plaine and Easie Introduction to Practicall Musicke* (1597): "To make two parts upon a plainesong is more hard then to make three parts into voluntary." The earliest voluntaries (*Mulliner Book, c.* 1550) are short pieces in imitative counterpoint, not based on a *cantus firmus* (plainsong). Three voluntaries by Byrd are in "My Ladye Nevells Booke" [see Virginal music]; others are among keyboard works by O. Gibbons and T. Weelkes [see the editions by M. H. Glyn]. During the 17th and 18th centuries the voluntary changed along with general changes in style, incorporating elements of the prelude, toccata, operatic aria, suite, sonata, etc., and frequently far exceeding the limitations of proper church style. Among the composers of such voluntaries are Benjamin Rogers (1614–98), John Blow (1648/9–1708), Purcell (*c.* 1659–95), John Stanley (1713–86), Maurice Greene (1695–1755), Thomas Roseingrave (1690–1766), Samuel Wesley (1766–1837; see *GD* v, 700ff; *GDB* ix, 262ff), and numerous lesser composers of the 18th and 19th centuries.

The voluntary had no fixed place in the service but was most commonly played either between the reading of the psalms and the first lesson, or between the end of Morning Prayer and the beginning of Communion. During the 19th century voluntaries began to be used as preludes and postludes, those written for this use generally being called opening and concluding voluntaries. In many churches today a voluntary is played as an *offertory piece. Voluntaries were and still are frequently improvised, and during the late 19th and early 20th centuries they often degenerated into transcriptions from anthems, oratorios, and instrumental works, a practice that by now has fortunately almost vanished through the efforts of contemporary composers of voluntaries, such as H. Willan, E. Thiman, and many others.

Lit.: C. H. Trevor, ed., ‡*Old English Organ Music for Manuals,* 4 vols. (1966); G. Frotscher, *Geschichte des Orgelspiels und der Orgelkomposition,* 2 vols. [1935, '36], *passium.*   add. by B.J.O.

Voodoo, vodoum. Haitian ritual that represents a mixture of European and African traditions. It is a sort of social and religious code to which most of the songs and dances of the country are related and with which the most important native instruments are associated. Hence the term is also used for certain drums [see *Arada* drums], for various styles of dancing and singing, and for a vast system of magical practices in which music plays an important role.   J.O-S.

Vorausnahme [G.]. Anticipation.

Vorbereiten [G.]. To prepare in advance (organ stops).

Vordersatz [G.]. First subject.

Vorhalt [G.]. Suspension (*vorbereiteter Vorhalt*) or appoggiatura (*freier Vorhalt*).

Vorimitation [G.]. In organ chorales or vocal settings of chorales, the fugal treatment of a

chorale line (or its initial motif), frequently in halved or quartered note values (*diminution), in preparation for the final appearance of the chorale line in full note values. Usually each line of the chorale is preceded by such a *Vorimitation.* See Ex., from Bach's organ chorale *Ach Gott und Herr* (*BG* xl, 5).

Vorschlag [G.]. See Appoggiatura (2). *Kurzer, langer Vorschlag,* short, long appoggiatura.

Vorspiel [G.]. Prelude, overture. Also, performance (*vorspielen,* to perform before an audience).

Vortrag [G.]. Interpretation; performance.

Vortragszeichen [G.]. Expression marks.

Vorwärts [G.]. Go ahead, continue.

Vorzeichnung [G.]. Signature, both of key and of meter.

Vox, pl. *voces* [L.]. In medieval treatises, the word has the following meanings: (1) Sound, tone color. Aurelianus Reomensis (*c.* 850) enumerates, in a chapter called "De vocum nominibus" [*GS* i, 34f], a large number of types, e.g., *vox* *harmonica* (human voice), *v. organica* (organ, wind instruments), *v. spissa* (thick, low?), *v. acuta* (high), *v. aspera* (rough), *v. pinguis ut virorum* (fat, as that of men), *v. vinola...flexibilis* (charming, flexible), etc. Adhemar von Chavanne (d. 1034) speaks of *voces tremulas, vinnolas, collisibiles,* which the Franks supposedly could not master [see *ApGC,* p. 116]. (2) In the "Musica enchiriadis," *vox principalis* and *vox organalis* mean the two voice-parts of organum (*GS* i, 152ff). (3) Same as note, pitch; i.e., the seven notes of the scale (Guido, *septem discrimina vocum; GS* ii, 7). Later the term was used especially for the six notes of the hexachord, called *sex voces* or *voces musicales.* In Josquin's *Missa*

L'Homme armé super voces musicales, the *L'Homme armé* melody is used successively on the degrees of the hexachord from c to a. In Senfl's *Fortuna ad voces musicales* [*SchGMB,* no. 86], the counterpoint to the *Fortuna* melody consists of the *hexachordum naturale* as it was used in elementary instruction: c c–d c–d–e c–d–e–f, . . . c–d–e–f–g–a, and descending.

V.s. Abbr. for **volti subito.*

Vuoto [It.]. "Empty," toneless. *Corda vuota,* open string.

Vv. Abbr. for violins.

Wachsend [G.]. Growing, increasing.

Wagner tuba. See under Tuba.

Wait. Originally, an English town watchman who (like the *Nachtwächter* in Wagner's *Meistersinger*) sounded the hours of the night. In the 15th and 16th centuries the waits developed into bands of musicians, paid by the town and supplied with handsome uniforms, who played on ceremonial occasions. At Christmas they performed before the houses of notables; it is this meaning that has survived, a wait today being a street performer of Christmas music. The term wait (wayte) was also used for the waits' characteristic instrument, a shawm, as well as the tunes played by the various local guilds, e.g., London Waits, Chester Waits. Many of these tunes are preserved in 17th- and 18th-century dance books, such as J. Playford's *The English Dancing Master* (1651). See W. L. Woodfill, *Musicians in English Society from Elizabeth to Charles I* (1953); G. Hayes, *King's Music* (1937); L. Langwill, *The Waits* [1953]; A. H. Frere and F. W. Galpin, "Shawms and Waits" (*ML* iv, 170ff); J. C. Bridge, "Town Waits and Their Tunes" (*PMA* liv).

Waldhorn [G.]. The French **horn, either natural or with valves.

Waldstein Sonata. Beethoven's Piano Sonata in C, op. 53 (1803–04), dedicated to Count Ferdinand von Waldstein. It consists of three movements, the second being a relatively short Adagio in somewhat improvisory style, serving as an introduction to the Finale, a long movement in rondo form.

Wales. See under Bard. Also see P. Crossley-Holland, *Music in Wales* (1948).

Walküre, Die. See *Ring des Nibelungen, Der.*

Waltz. A dance in moderate triple time that originated *c.* 1800 and not only has retained its popularity to the present day, but has, time and again, inspired composers. The waltzes of Beethoven [sup. vol., ser. xxv of B.-H. edition; cf. also the well-known theme of the Diabelli Variations] still resemble the earlier *Ländler* or *deutsche Tanz,* as do, to some extent, Schubert's numerous waltzes [vol. xii of comp. ed.]. Weber's "Aufforderung zum Tanze" (1819) is the first example of the characteristic rhythm and accompaniment associated with the waltz. Later notable composers of waltzes include Chopin, Johann Strauss (father and son; see *DTO* 63 and 68), Berlioz (*Symphonie fantastique*), Brahms (*Liebeslieder*), Richard Strauss (in *Der Rosenkavalier*), and Ravel (*Valses nobles et sentimentales;* also *La Valse,* for orchestra).

The waltz developed from an Austrian peasant dance, the *Ländler* (the erroneous theory of its French origin and derivation from the *volta* is discussed in *GD* v, 623; *GDB,* ix, 165). As early as 1700 its characteristic idiom appeared in the ritornello of a pastoral Singspiel [see Ex.].

As a dance in which the partners embraced one another, the waltz evoked both enthusiastic response and violent protest. Burney, in Rees' *The Cyclopaedia* (*c.* 1805), speaks of the "familiar treatment" and "obliging manner in which the freedom is returned by the females" and, probably confusing *walzen* with *sich wälzen*, makes an allusion to "rolling in the dirt of mire." Although the waltz was already popular in Vienna in the time of Haydn and Mozart—the Irish singer Michael Kelly records its vogue in 1783 [*The Reminiscences of Michael Kelly,* 2 vols. (1826)]—it is misleading to assume that Haydn and Mozart wrote waltzes. Mozart's *Deutsche Tänze* (K. 509, 536, 567, etc.) are true *Ländler* in musical style. Beethoven's name has been associated with a number of waltzes ("Beethoven's Last Waltz," "The Spirit Waltz," "Jubelwalzer") so utterly trivial that such attribution is clearly false.

Lit.: E. Reeser, *The History of the Waltz* [1949]; M. Carner, *The Waltz* (1948); B. Weigl, "Die Geschichte des Walzers" (*Musikalisches Magazin* xxxiv [1910]); I. Mendelssohn, in *StM* xiii; P. Nettl, in *BUM* iii; H. J. Ullrich, in *Musicology* ii, no. 2.

Walze [G.]. (1) Crescendo pedal of the organ. (2) An 18th-century term for stereotyped undulating figures, such as an *Alberti bass.

Wanderer-Fantasie [G., Wanderer Fantasy]. Schubert's Fantasy (actually a sonata) in C for piano, op. 15 (1822), so called because the second movement is a series of variations on a theme from his song "Der Wanderer" (1816). The initial pattern of this theme is also used at the beginning of the other three movements, making this work the earliest example of a completely *cyclic sonata.

Wärme, mit [G.]. With warmth.

War of the Buffoons [F. *querelle* (*guerre*) *des bouffons;* G. *Buffonistenstreit;* It. *guerra dei buffoni*]. A famous quarrel that developed in 1752 between two parties of Parisian musicians and opera enthusiasts—those favoring the national French serious opera (exemplified by the works of Lully, Rameau, Destouches) and those preferring the Italian *opera buffa* (e.g., that of Pergolesi). Pergolesi's comic opera *La Serva padrona,* composed in 1733 as an *intermezzo, had been first given in Paris in 1746 without arousing more than moderate interest. The second performance, however, given in 1752 by a troupe of Italian comedians (*buffi*), led to a quarrel that split Paris in two. The national party consisted largely of the aristocracy (including Louis XV and Madame de Pompadour) and plutocracy, while the Italian side was taken by intellectuals and connoisseurs of music (including the Queen, Rousseau, D'Alembert, and Diderot). The latter considered Italian opera superior because it had more melody, expression, and naturalness, and had shaken off completely the "useless fetters of counterpoint." In effect, the *querelle des bouffons* was a fight between the rising rococo and the dying baroque. [For a similar movement in Spain, see *Zarzuela*.] Rousseau's famous *Lettre sur la musique française* of 1753 (repr. in part in *SSR*) was one of numerous pamphlets issued during this controversy. The efforts of French musicians to compete with the popular *opera buffa* resulted in a new kind of French comic opera known as *comédie mêlée d'ariettes* [see Comic opera II C].

Lit.: G. Cucuel, *Les Créateurs de l'opéra-comique français* (1914); L. Richebourg, *Contribution à l'histoire de la "Querelle des Bouffons"* (1937); N. Boyer, *La Guerre des bouffons et la musique française 1752-54* (1945); E. Hirschberg, *Die Encyclopädisten und die französische Oper im 18. Jahrhundert* (1903); L. de La Laurencie, in *BSIM* viii (1912); A. van der Linden, in *CP Masson* ii.

Wasserorgel [G.]. *Hydraulos.

Water Music. Orchestral suite by Handel, composed in 1715 for a celebration that took place in boats on the Thames. See W. Michael, in *ZMW* iv.

Wechsel- [G.]. Change. *Wechseldominante,* the dominant of the dominant, i.e., the (major) supertonic. *Wechselgesang,* alternating or antiphonal singing. *Wechselnote* is somewhat loosely used for *nonharmonic tones involving a change of direction, e.g., *cambiata, échappée, appoggiatura; verlassene* or *Fux'sche Wechsel-note* is always the *cambiata,* particularly in combination with a suspension:

Wedge Fugue. Popular name for Bach's great organ fugue in E minor, so called because of the increasingly wider intervals in the subject.

Wehmütig [G.]. Sad, melancholy.

Weihnachtsmusik [G.]. Christmas music.

Weihnachts Oratorium [G.]. See *Christmas Oratorio.*

Wellingtons Sieg [G., Wellington's Victory]. A "battle symphony" by Beethoven (full title: *Wellingtons Sieg oder die Schlacht bei Vittoria,* op. 91, 1813), written in celebration of Wellington's victory over Napoleon. It consists of English and French fanfares, settings of "Rule Britannia" and "Marlborough s'en va-t-en guerre," the Battle (punctuated by English and French guns), a Charge, and, in the second part, a Victory Symphony containing a quotation from "God Save the King." It was originally written for a mechanical instrument invented by Mälzel but was orchestrated by the composer.

Well-Tempered Clavier, The [G. *Das Wohltem-perierte Clavier*]. Bach's collection of 48 [see Forty-eight] preludes and fugues, published in two parts (1722, '44), each of which contains 24 preludes and fugues, one for each major and minor key (C major, C minor, C♯ major, C♯ minor, etc.). The name refers to the then novel system of equal temperament [see Temperament III], which made it possible to play equally well in all the keys and of which Bach's collection was the first complete realization [see, however, the reference to Cima (1606) under Transposition II]. The first printed edition appeared in 1799 (Kollmann, London). The pieces in the two collections date from various periods of Bach's life. The most obvious difference in style between the first and second parts lies in the preludes in aria style and binary form, which appear in the second collection but not in the first. The "proper" instrument for these pieces, i.e., harpsichord or clavichord, has long been disputed. In this problem, as in many others concerning early music, the "either-or" point

of view has proved detrimental. Some writers have gone so far as to maintain that certain preludes of the *Well-Tempered Clavier* are written for clavichord while the corresponding fugue is written for the harpsichord.

An important forerunner of Bach's work is J. K. F. Fischer's *Ariadne musica* (*c.* 1700; ed. by E. von Werra, 1901), which contains 20 preludes and fugues in 19 different keys. Particularly interesting is the unmistakable thematic similarity between some of Fischer's fugues and those of Bach in the same key, e.g., those in G minor (*Wt. Cl.* i), E major (*Wt. Cl.* ii), and F major (*Wt. Cl.* i), a similarity too striking to be coincidental [see *HAM,* no. 248]. On the other hand, a collection of 24 preludes and fugues by B. C. Weber, with the same title as Bach's first collection, is not a forerunner but an imitation of Bach's work (the date 1689, which appears on the MS of the Brussels Conservatory, is spurious; Weber lived from 1712 to 1758. See W. Tappert, in *MfM* xxxi, no. 8, 123–27 and no. 9, 129–33; ed. in *Veröffentli-chungen der Neue Bach-Gesellschaft* xxxiv (1933).

Lit.: J. A. Fuller-Maitland, *The "48," Bach's Wohltemperiertes Clavier* (1925); C. Gray, *The Forty-eight Preludes and Fugues of J. S. Bach* (1938); W. Emery, "The London Autograph of 'The Forty-Eight'" (*ML* xxxiv, 106ff). See also under Keyboard music.

Welsh music. See under Bard; Wales.

Werk principle. In organs, a rule often followed in the 16th, 17th, and 18th centuries, according to which the pipework controlled by any one keyboard of the organ is set forth in its own separate tone cabinet, separated both aurally and visually from the pipework controlled by the other keyboards. Implicit is the concept of each keyboard, including the pedal, as a separate instrument in its own right. See Organ VII.

C.B.F.

Werther. Opera in four acts by J. Massenet (libretto by E. Blau, P. Milliet, and G. Hartmann, based on Goethe's *Die Leiden des jungen Werthers*), produced (in German) in Vienna, 1892. Setting: Germany, 1772.

Western Wynde. An English tune of the 16th century, known from three Masses, by Taverner, Tye, and J. Shepherd, that use it as a *cantus firmus.* In Taverner's setting [*Editions LI, 1] the melody is stated 34 times, so that the Mass consists of 34 sections, each a "variation" of the tune [see H. B. Collins, in *PMA* xxxix, 58]. Two of the sections, "Benedictus" and "Osanna," are in *HAM,* no. 112. J. Shepherd followed this plan but reduced the number of sections to 23. The *Qui sedes* from Tye's setting is partly reproduced in *OH* ii, 326f.

Whistle. A small, simple, end-blown pipe, made of wood, cane, metal, or plastic.

Whistle flute. In the classification of instruments, generic designation for flutes blown by means of a "flue" [see Instruments III, B, 2, c]. A synonymous term is fipple flute. The upper end of the pipe is stopped by a plug or fipple [G. *Block,* hence *Blockflöte* for recorder], with a narrow slit remaining (flue). The breath is led through the flue toward the sharp edge of a small opening below the fipple. The same principle is used in organ flue pipes [see Organ VIII]. The whistle flutes include the *recorders and flageolets. The flageolets differ from the recorders mainly in that they have fewer finger holes, four in front and two thumb holes in the rear. In the 19th century the flageolet acquired keys. See N. Bessaraboff, *Ancient European Musical Instruments* (1941), pp. 60ff. For ill. see under Flute.

Whole note. See under Notes.

Whole tone. The interval of the major second. See Interval.

Whole-tone scale [G. *Ganztonleiter*]. A scale consisting of whole tones only, six to the octave. Only two such scales exist: c–d–e–f♯–g♯–b♭–c' and c♯–d♯–f–g–a–b–c♯'. The whole-tone scale lacks three fundamental intervals of traditional music, the prefect fifth, perfect fourth, and leading tone. Thus its use by Debussy represented a rebellion against the harmonic system of the 19th century. Owing to the presence of only one kind of interval, the whole-tone scale completely lacks the feeling of "centralization" and "localization" that, in the normal scales or in church modes, is indicated by the term "tonic." Its inherent indecision and vagueness make it appropriate for the impressionist style but at the same time limit its usefulness for other styles. Indeed, after a short vogue in the first decade of the 20th century, it lost most of its appeal and is seldom used today. Rebikov's (1866–1920) *Les Démons s'amusent* is written entirely in the whole-tone scale, as are sections of Debussy's "Voiles" (from *Préludes pour piano,* 1910; see Ex.). Whole-tone formations in earlier composi-

tions (Schubert, Rossini, Berlioz) are merely modulatory progressions within the conventional system of melody and harmony. An "Ut, re, mi, fa, sol, la" by John Bull [*Editions XXXIV, 14, p. 56] is based throughout on such progressions. A true whole-tone scale occurs repeatedly in Glinka's opera *Russlan and Ludmilla* (composed 1842).

Whole-tube instruments. See under Wind instruments II.

Wie aus der Ferne. See *Ferne.*

William Tell. See *Guillaume Tell.*

Winchester Troper. See under Troper.

Wind band. See Band.

Wind cap [G. *Windkapsel*]. In 16th-century double-reed instruments, a cylindrical cap (also called reed cap), with a blowhole on top, that was placed over the upper end of the pipe, enclosing the reeds from the lips of the player. Thus the reed was set in vibration by a wind pressure comparable to that of the organ. The wind cap was used mainly on the crumhorns [see Oboe family III; also see ill. of crumhorn under Oboe family].

Wind chest. In organs, an airtight box that receives the wind from the bellows and controls its passage to the pipes. See Organ I.

Wind gauge. (1) Device for indicating the pressure of air in the bellows of organs. It is usually a simple S-shaped tube partly filled with water, the pressure being measured in inches of water. It is used by organ builders to check chest pressures before *voicing. (2) In older organs, a device that indicated to the organist when sufficient pressure was available for playing.

Wind instruments. Generic name for all instruments in which the sound-generating medium is an enclosed column of air. They are also known as aerophones, although strictly speaking the aerophones also include the "free aerophones," which usually are not included in the category wind instruments [see Instruments III A, B]. The main wind instruments are the *brass instruments (*trumpets, *horns, *trombones, *tubas, etc.), and *woodwinds (*flutes, *clarinets, and *oboes); there is a separate entry for each of these [see also Reed].

I. In each wind instrument an enclosed column of air, cylindrical or conical (depending on the bore of the instrument), is set into vibration [see Acoustics V]. Neither the material (whether brass or wood) nor the shape (whether straight or bent) is important. The pitch of the sound produced depends on the length of the pipe and whether the pipe is an open or closed resonator; its timbre depends mainly on the mouthpiece (single reed in the clarinets, double reed in the oboes, mouth-hole in the flutes, cupped mouthpiece in the trumpets, funnel mouthpiece in the horns, etc.), shape of the bore, widening of the bell, etc.

II. A pipe of given length gives one tone only. However, by proper control of the breath and lips, called *overblowing,* a pipe can easily be made to sound not only its normal tone, the fundamental, but also the higher harmonics. These tones constitute the "natural tones" of a wind

1 2 3 4 5 6 7 8 9 10

instrument, e.g.: c c′ g′ c″ e″ g″ b♭″ c‴ d‴ e‴, etc. Another name for the fundamental tone is *pedal tone.* In a number of instruments the pedal tone is practically unobtainable, and a distinction is made between *whole-tube instruments,* in which the air column can be made to vibrate as a whole, thus producing the pedal tone, and *half-tube instruments,* in which even the slightest air pressure is likely to set up vibrations of the half length, thus producing the first harmonic (c′). To the former category belong all the woodwinds and the brass instruments of wide bore (tubas); to the latter, nominally, the brass instruments of narrow bore (trumpets, horns, trombones, higher saxhorns). Today, however, skilled players can obtain the pedal notes on trumpets and saxhorns, so that the French horn and the trombone in the lower positions of the slide remain, for all practical purposes, the only half-tube instruments.

III. The description above applies to the so-called *open pipes,* i.e., pipes that are open at their lower end. If a pipe of the same length is closed at the lower end (*stopped pipe*), its fundamental is an octave lower than in the open pipe [see Acoustics V], and, moreover, only the odd-numbered partials above this fundamental are obtainable. If an open pipe and a stopped pipe half its length are compared, the fundamentals will be the same but the natural series will differ as follows:

	1	2	3	4	5	6	7	8	9	10
Open 4′ pipe	c	c′	g′	c″	e″	g″	b♭″	c‴	d‴	e‴
Stopped 2′ pipe	c		g′		e″		b♭″		d‴	

Stopped pipes are frequently used in organ building to obtain lower tones from relatively short pipes [see Organ IX (b)]. Wind instruments with a cylindrical bore usually act as stopped pipes although they are not actually stopped at the lower end. The most important instrument of this type is the clarinet, which is said to "overblow at the fifth" (actually, at the twelfth), whereas the instruments with a conical bore (oboes, horns, etc.) overblow at the octave. The German name for the former is *quintierend* [F. *quintoyer*] and for the latter *oktavierend* [F. *octavier*].

IV. In a wind instrument that consists simply of a pipe, only the natural tones are available (e.g., the "natural" horn or trumpet). In order to obtain the numerous tones between the gaps of the natural series, there must be a means of temporarily shortening or lengthening the pipe. Four main kinds of device are so used: (a) slides; (b) crooks; (c) valves; (d) side holes.

(a) Slide. The instrument consists of two separate portions of tubing, one sliding inside the other so that it can be drawn out. Thus the tube can actually be lengthened, and in each position a new series of natural tones, beginning respectively with C, B, B♭, etc., becomes available. Since the largest gap in the series of overtones is the fifth (c–g′), a complete chromatic scale can be obtained by the combined tones of seven series of overtones, e.g., from c–g–c′ ... down to F♯–c♯–f♯ .... This principle is used with the *trombone.

(b) Crook or shank. An additional piece of tubing is inserted by the player when needed. Since adding a crook or shank takes time, it does not really serve to fill in the gaps of the natural scale but only gives the instrument a different (lower) tuning for different pieces or different sections of a piece. This method was used with trumpets in the 18th century [see Trumpet II; also Horn II].

(c) Valves. The name is misleading, since what is really meant are crooks attached permanently to the instrument, to be opened and closed momentarily by means of a valve. Normally the instrument is provided with three valves (I, II, III), which lower the pitch respectively by 2, 1, or 3 semitones, while their combined use yields a lowering of 5 (I + III), 4 (II + III), and 6 (I + II + III) semitones. Thus seven series of over-

926

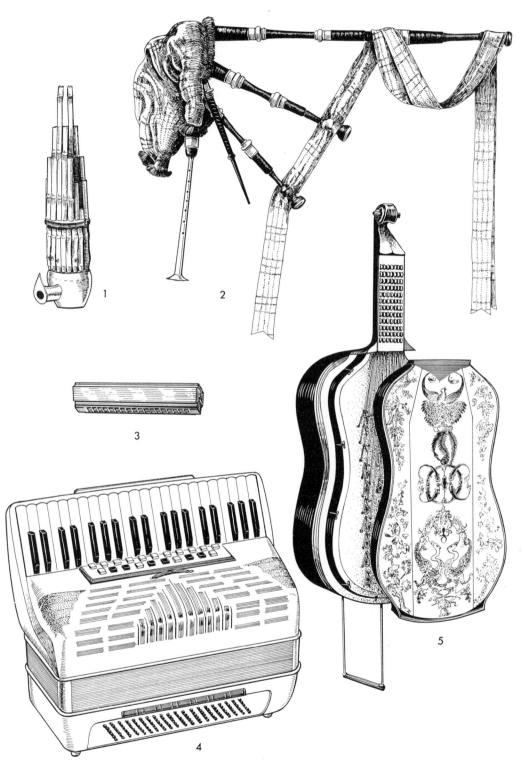

Miscellaneous wind instruments: 1. Sheng. 2. Bagpipe. 3. Harmonica (shown twice its actual size in relation to the others). 4. Accordion. 5. Mélophone.

tones become available, resulting in a complete chromatic scale, as explained under (a). Also see Valve.

(d) Side holes. These are holes bored in the side wall of the instrument (today, in woodwinds only; formerly, also in trumpets and cornets, e.g., key trumpet, key bugle) that can be opened and closed by the fingers, usually with the help of a key mechanism [see Key (1)]. If all the holes are closed, the pipe sounds its fundamental. If some of the holes are opened, the acoustical length of the air column is shortened and higher tones are produced.

In the horns pitch can also be altered by "stopping" [see Horn].

For the miscellaneous wind instruments illustrated in this article, see the separate entries for each.

For bibl. see under Brass instruments; Woodwinds.

Wind machine [F. *Éoliphone;* G. *Windmaschine*]. A device designed to imitate the sound of wind, occasionally used for descriptive purposes (R. Strauss, *Don Quixote, Eine Alpensinfonie*). It consists of a barrel framework covered with cloth, which is rotated so that the cloth rubs against cardboard or wood.

Winterreise [G,. Winter Journey]. Cycle of twenty-four songs by Schubert, in two parts, composed in 1827 to poems by Wilhelm Müller. They are romantic pictures of a rejected lover's lonely journey in wintertime.

Wirbel [G.]. (1) Peg of a violin; *Wirbelkasten,* pegbox. (2) A drum roll.

Wohltemperierte Clavier, Das [G.]. See *Well-Tempered Clavier, The.*

Wolf [G.]. Any disagreeable effect resulting from imperfect tuning in instruments, e.g., by organ pipes not quite in tune. Specifically: (1) The slight difference in pitch between G♯ and A♭ in the mean-tone system, and similar discordance in other systems of unequal temperament [see Temperament II]. (2) In violins and cellos, *Wolf-note* is a term used for certain tones that differ markedly in both intensity and quality from those in adjoining parts of the compass. This undesirable effect is particularly noticeable near the F♯ on the D-string of the cello, a tone that has a poor and somewhat wobbly sound. In the violin a similar effect occurs near the C♯ on the A-string. The wolf is found in practically all instruments, regardless of their quality. In fact,

the more sonorous the general sound of the instrument, the more obtrusive the wolf. The wolf has often been attributed to some defect in construction of the particular instrument, e.g., uneven thickness of the belly, unequal elasticity of the wood, etc. However, later investigators have shown that it is a defect inherent in the design of the violin and other instruments of the same family, the result of particularly strong vibration patterns of the belly. See C. V. Raman, in *Nature,* vol. xcvii (1916), 362f, and in *Philosophical Magazine* xxxii (1916); J. A. Kessler, "Mechanical Operation of Stringed Instruments: Wolf notes" (honors thesis Harvard Univ., 1942).

Woodwinds. See under Orchestra I; Wind instruments.

Lit.: A. Baines, *Woodwind Instruments and Their History,* rev. ed. [1962]; *id., European and American Musical Instruments* [1966]; R. Houser, *Catalogue of Chamber Music for Woodwinds,* rev. ed. (1960); L. G. Langwill, *An Index of Musical Wind-Instrument Makers,* rev. ed. [1962]; A. Carse, *Musical Wind Instruments* (1939); M. Rasmussen and D. Mattran, *A Teacher's Guide to the Literature of Woodwind Instruments* (1966); F. W. Westphal, *Guide to Teaching Woodwinds* [1962]; T. Warner, "Indications of Performance Practice in Woodwind Instruction Books of the 17th and 18th Centuries" (diss. New York Univ., 1964); *GSJ, passim*; *Brass and Woodwind Quarterly* (continuation of *Brass Quarterly* viii), *passim.*

Worcester, school of. A repertory of English compositions of *c.* 1300, many of which seem to have originated at the Cathedral of Worcester. They are preserved only in fragments, the original sources having been cut up to serve as fly-leaves. A characteristic trait of the Worcester style is the frequent use of *voice exchange. Some pieces are remarkable for their extensive employment of *sixth-chord style. Ex. in *HAM,* nos. 57a, b.

Lit.: Dom A. Hughes, ‡*Worcester Mediaeval Harmony* (1928); L. A. Dittmer, ‡*The Worcester Fragments* (1957); *id.,* "An English Discantuum Volumen" (*MD* viii); *id.,* "Binary Rhythm, Musical Theory and the Worcester Fragments" (*MD* vii); K. J. Levy, "New Material on the Early Motet in England" (*JAMS* iv).

Word painting. The expression through music of the ideas presented or suggested by the words of a song or other vocal piece. The term usually refers to the portrayal of single words or phrases that lend themselves to specific treatment, rather than the rendition of the "general mood" of the text. Modern composers usually reject word painting as naïve. In earlier music, however, particularly in the baroque period, it played a prominent role. It is hardly an exaggeration to say that, in the entire vocal literature of the baroque, it would be difficult to find the word "heaven" or "water" without an ascending or undulating motion in the music. As explained under Program music II, there are two main kinds of direct word painting: imitation of natural sounds (laughing, fanfares, birds), and imitation of physical movements (running, falling, ascending, descending). Both may, of course, occur with associated words, such as "war" (fanfare), "heaven" (ascent), "death" (fall). The accompanying examples from Bach's cantatas nos. 8, 26, and 12 illustrate the descriptive treatment of the words "Ruhstatt" (resting place), "Tropfen" (drops), and "Ich folge" (I follow). There are, of course, other associations that can

be "translated" into music. For instance, Weelkes in *As Vesta Was from Latmos Hill Descending* successively uses voices numbering two, three, six, and one for the words, "First two by two, then three by three to-gether, Leaving their goddess all alone." In Schütz's oratorio *Die sieben Worte am Kreuz*, Christ's words "Warum hast du mich verlassen" (Why hast thou forsaken me) are accompanied by two violins playing mere fragments and ending without the final notes (as if "forsaken") [see *HAM*, no. 201b]. Word painting is aptly summed up by Joachim Thuringus (*Opusculum bipartitum*, 1625; see F. Feldmann, in *AMW* xv, 130, fn. 2), who classifies it as: (1) *Verba affectuum;* (2) *Verba motus et locorum;* (3) *Adverbia temporis, numeri*. To category (1) belong "rejoicing, weeping, laughing," etc., as well as words suggestive of a sound (bird

calls, etc.); to (2), "to stand, to run, to jump, heaven, hell, mountains," etc.; to (3), "quick, slow, twice, often, rarely," etc.

Less direct and highly suggestive word painting can be achieved mainly through scoring. Some of the best examples of this technique are in the works of Josquin. For instance, in his motet "Tu pauperum refugium" the harmonic and contrapuntal treatment is orthodox up to the point where the words *via errantium* (the life of the erring ones) occur; here the ensuing aimlessness of lines and the absence of harmonic agreement between them result in a startlingly vivid portrayal of the idea of the text, a portrayal strengthened by the clear and obviously appropriate harmonic implications of the music at the words *veritas et vita* (truth and life).

Countless instances of word painting of one sort or another might be cited in every period from the time of Josquin on. Some contemporary composers, to be sure, seem little concerned with this matter, perhaps because the idiom they employ is better suited to the conveyance of abstract musical ideas expressed instrumentally. Many stimulating examples, however, may be found in the vocal works of such composers as Milhaud, Honegger, Walton, R. Thompson, Vaughan Williams, Pizzetti, and Holst.

Words and music. See Text and music.

Wozzeck. Opera in three acts by Alban Berg (to his own libretto, based on G. Büchner's drama of 1836), produced in Berlin, 1925. Setting: Germany in the 1830's. The entire score, atonal without adhering to the twelve-tone technique, is organized in abstract musical forms. The first act is a suite in five movements; the second, a symphony in five movements with the usual classical forms; the third, a series of inventions in the form of variations. The opera, revived in the mid-20th century after years of neglect, is widely admired for its musical craftsmanship and emotional appeal.

W.-T. C., Wt. Cl. Abbr. for Bach's *Well-Tempered Clavier.*

Wuchtig [G.]. Weighty, heavy.

Würdig [G.]. Stately, with dignity.

Wurstfagott [G.]. Racket bassoon; see under Oboe family III.

Wydawnictwo dawnej muzyki polskiej (*Publications de musique ancienne polonaise*). See Editions LIII.

X

Xácara [Sp.]. See *Jácara.*

Xango. Afro-Brazilian invocation to St. Jerome, employing the *macumba ritual music. The saint, who is regarded as one of the most powerful spirits guiding the people's daily life, is honored in these ceremonies, which are part of a folk heritage based on the fusion of Christian and African traditions.   J.O-S.

Xerxes or **Serse.** Opera in three acts by G. F. Handel (It.; librettist unknown), produced in London, 1738. Setting: Persia, 5th century B.C.

Xota. **Jota.*

Xylophone. A percussion instrument consisting of graduated bars of hardwood that are struck with a stick. For the modern orchestral instrument, see Percussion instruments A, 3; also Marimba. Xylophones are commonly used in non-Western cultures, particularly in Africa, and have attained a high degree of perfection in the *Javanese orchestra. About 1500 they became known in Europe as *hültze glechter* ("wooden percussion"; Arnolt Schlick, *Spiegel der Orgelmacher und Organisten,* 1511) and *Strohfiedel* (straw fiddle, so called because the bars lay on straw). Still other names are *Holzharmonika* [G.], *gigelira* [It.], and *ligneum psalterium* [L.]. About 1830 a Russian Jew, J. Gusikow, a famous Strohfiedel player, aroused the interest of Mendelssohn [see *GD* v, 765n; *GDB* ix, 379]. The instrument has been employed by Saint-Saëns in his *Danse Macabre* (1874) to describe the rattling of skeletons, and in several later works, e.g., Shostakovitch's Fifth Symphony.

Lit.: O. Boone, *Les Xylophones du Congo Belge* (1936); D. Vela, *La Marimba* (1962); A. M. Jones, *Africa and Indonesia* (1964).

Y

Yankee Doodle. A popular American tune that, in the course of 150 years, has been used for numerous humorous texts. The origin of the tune is as mysterious as that of the words "Yankee" and "Doodle." It first appeared in James Aird's *Selection of Scotch, English, Irish and Foreign Airs* (*c.* 1775), where it is given with its title but without words. It may have originated as a tune for the flute. Dvořák used it, somewhat modified, in the last movement of his *New World Symphony.* See O. G. T. Sonneck, *Report on "The Star-Spangled Banner," "Hail Columbia," "America," "Yankee Doodle,"* (1909), pp. 79–156.

Yaraví [Sp.]. A plaintive song of the Bolivian Andes, also known in Peru and Ecuador, generally in slow 3/4 meter and set to an elegiac text. Metaphors and mythological allusions are often used by the singer. The Indian name for this type of song is *llaqui-aru.*   J.O-S.

Yevgeny Onyegin. See *Eugen Onegin.*

Yodel [G. *Jodel*]. A special type of singing practiced by the mountain peoples of Switzerland and Austria (Tyrol) and characterized by frequent and rapid passing from a low chest voice to a high falsetto. A *Jodler* is a vocalization appended to a song, with low vowels (a, o) used for the low tones and high vowels (e, i) for the high ones. Possibly this type of singing in Europe originated as a vocalization, in imitation of the harmonic intervals of the *alphorn, although African Pygmies also yodel. See W. Sichardt, *Der alpenländische Jodler* (1939); W. Wiora, *Zur Frühgeschichte der Musik in den Alpenländern* (1949); E. M. von Hornbostel, in *CP 1924;* G. Kotek, in *CP 1927;* C. Brailoiu, in *CP 1949.*

Youth's Magic Horn, The. See *Knaben Wunderhorn, Des.*

Yuehchyn (yüeh ch'in). A Chinese guitar. See under Guitar family.

Yugoslavia. Since the political entity of Yugoslavia has existed only since 1918 and represents a union of several related southern Slavic peoples, it is impossible to speak of Yugoslav music as a uniform body. In western Yugoslavia the Slovenes and Croats were for centuries dominated and influenced by the culture of Austria and Italy, and as a result art music had an earlier beginning in those areas. Of Slovenian origin was the internationally famous Jacobus Gallus (1550–91), who worked chiefly in Bohemia. Under the influence of Venice a very active musical life developed in the 17th and 18th centuries on the Dalmatian coast, where the most prominent figures were Ivan Lukačić (*c.* 1574/87–1648), Vinko Jelić (1596–1636?), and the Italian composer and organist Tomaso Cecchini (*c.* 1580–1644). In the city of Dubrovnik, Luka Sorkočević-Sorgo (1734–89) wrote preclassical symphonies. J. B. Novak (*c.* 1756–1833) wrote a Singspiel, *Figaro,* in 1790. Romanticism appeared in the works of Vatroslav Lisinski (1819–54). Since the mid-19th century almost all contemporary trends in music were represented in both Slovenia and Croatia. Probably the greatest composer from that region of Yugoslavia was Josip Slavenski (1896–1955), who in his works combined modernist trends of the avant-garde with nationalist and folk elements.

In eastern Yugoslavia, the strong cultural influence of the Byzantine Empire and the long period of Turkish domination delayed the beginnings of art music. In this area is a strong tradition of epic poetry [see Gusle] among the Serbs, Montenegrins, Bosnians, and Macedonians, as well as a folk tradition of great variety and intricacy. The first important composer, Stevan Mokranjac (1856–1914), wrote choral works based on folksongs, not merely stylizing them but revealing a great artistic talent. Prominent also are the works of Stevan Hristić (1885–1958), composer of the ballet *The Legend of Ohrid,* and of Petar Konjović (b. 1882).

Among the Yugoslav composers born after 1918, internationally known is Milko Kelemen (b. 1924), one of the leaders of the avant-garde.

Lit.: *MGG* vii, cols. 306–78, with bibl.; E. Helm, "Music in Yugoslavia" (*LBCM*); J. Andreis and S. Zlatić, ed., *Yugoslav Music* (1959); A. Dobronić, "A Study of Jugoslav Music" (*MQ* xii); *AdHM* ii, 1168; P. Panóff, in *BüHM* i; E. Wellesz, "Die Struktur des serbischen Oktoechos" (*ZMW* ii); *ReMR,* pp. 757ff.

M.V.

Z

Zählzeit [G.]. Beat.

Zajal. See *Zejel.*

Zaleo. Same as **jaleo.*

Zamba [Sp.]. Argentine *danza de pañuelos* (scarf dance) in 6/8 meter, slightly slower than the **gato,* consisting of a guitar introduction followed by a vocal section based on a four-measure theme repeated twice. It came to Argentina from Peru in colonial times, when it was called *zambacueca* or *zamacueca,* and thereafter it was divided into two different dances, the *zamba* and *cueca.* J.O-S.

Zambumbia. See under *Caramba.*

Zampogna [It.]. A mouth-blown **bagpipe.

Zanfona [Sp.]. **Hurdy-gurdy.

Zapateado [Sp.]. A Spanish solo dance in triple time, the rhythm being marked by stamping of the heels, frequently in syncopation and other rhythms contrasting with the rhythm of the melody.

Zapfenstreich [G.]. A **tattoo; on special occasions the *Zapfenstreich* is a much more elaborate performance of military music, including signals as well as marches played by a large band.

Zarabanda [Sp.]. See Saraband.

Zarge [G.]. The ribs of the violin.

Zart [G.]. Tender, soft.

Zarzuela [Sp.]. The most important type of Spanish opera, distinguished from ordinary opera in that the music is intermingled with spoken dialogue, as in *comic opera. Its subjects, however, are not restricted to comedy. Its name comes from the Palace of La Zarzuela (a royal country seat near Madrid, comparable to Versailles), where festive representations called *Fiestas de Zarzuela* were given. The earliest on record is Lope Felix de Vega Carpio's *eclogue *La Selva sin amor* (The Forest without Love) of 1629. The earliest known composer of *zarzuelas* is Juan Hidalgo, whose *Los Celos hacen estrellas* (text by Velez de Guevara; produced 1644?) uses recitative [see *LavE* i.4, 2066] as well as choruses in the style of a madrigal. He also composed the music for Pedro Calderón de la Barca's *Ni amor se libra de Amor* (c. 1640; see F. Pedrell, *Teatro lírico español,* iv, v) and *Celos aun del aire matan* (1662; first act pub. by Subirá, 1933). In the latter part of the 17th century the *zarzuela* resembled the French *ballet de cour,* with its emphasis on elaborate stage production and the addition of ballets and popular dances accompanied by guitar and castanets (José Clavijo y Fajardo, 1730–1806). This type of "aristocratic opera," based largely on mythological subjects, reached its zenith with Sebastián Durón (c. 1650–c. 1716) and Antonio Literes Carrión (1670–1747). At the same time there arose a "popular" reaction against the *zarzuela* in the *tonadilla,* a development parallel to the *War of the Buffoons. The increasing influence of Italian opera—clearly present in the works of José de Nebra (c. 1688–1768)—also contributed to the decline of the *zarzuela,* a decline that went hand in hand with that of the Spanish drama.

An attempt at revival in a more popular form, made c. 1770 by the dramatist Ramón de la Cruz in collaboration with the composer Antonio Rodríguez de Hita (d. 1787), was only briefly successful. It was not until the middle of the 19th century that a forceful national movement led to a new era for the *zarzuela*. This revival began chiefly with Francisco A. Barbieri (1823–94; *Jugar con Fuego,* 1851) and Pascual Arrieta y Corera (1823–94; *Marina,* 1871). In 1865 the *Teatro de la Zarzuela* was founded, and the movement found numerous participants, e.g., Ruperto Chapí y Lorente (1851–1909), M. Fernández Caballero (1835–1906), Tomás Bretón y Hernández (1850–1923), Joaquín Valverde (1846–1910), and Amadeo Vives (1871–1932). The modern *zarzuelas* are classified as *zarzuela grande,* in three acts, and *género chico* or *zarzuelita,* in one act. The former tend to deal with serious, dramatic subjects; the latter are essentially comic. Bretón y Hernández' *La*

Dolores (1895) and *La Verbena de la paloma* (1897) are outstanding examples of each type. Later important composers of the *zarzuela grande* are Francisco Alonso (b. 1887) and Federico Moreno-Torroba (b. 1891); of the *género chico* (with features derived from Viennese operetta and even American jazz), Jacinto Guerrero (1895–1951), and others.

Lit.: G. Chase, *The Music of Spain,* rev. ed. (1959), *passim,* bibl.; E. Cotarelo y Mori, *Historia de la zarzuela,* i (1934); M. Muñoz, *Historia de la zarzuela y el género chico* (1946); *LavE* i.4, 2052ff; H. Anglés and J. Pena, *Diccionario de la música Labor,* 2 vols. (1954), s.v. *zarzuela;* A. Salazar, "Music in the Primitive Spanish Theatre" (*PAMS* 1938); G. Chase, "Origins of the Lyric Theatre in Spain" (*MQ* xxv); id., "Barbieri and the Spanish Zarzuela" (*ML* xx, 32); J. Subirá, in *AM* iv, no. 2; A. Pedrell, in *SIM* iv.

Zauberflöte, Die [G., The Magic Flute]. Opera in two acts by Mozart (libretto by E. Schikaneder), produced in Vienna, 1791. Setting: magical world. *Zauberflöte,* Mozart's last opera, is a blending of diverse operatic elements into a truly German style which transcends *Singspiel. The Italian *opera buffa* idea, which prevails in *Nozze di Figaro* and *Don Giovanni,* is replaced here by a seriousness of purpose and sincerity of feeling that presage Beethoven.

Zeitmass [G.]. Tempo.

Zeitmesser [G.]. Metronome.

Zejel [also *zajal*]. A type of medieval Arab poetry characterized by the alternation of a refrain and various stanzas. Abén Guzmán (Ibn Kuzmān, c. 1080–1160) wrote numerous *zejels,* most of them in a form such as ab ccc ab ddd ab, etc., which has been cited as the model for the *virelai or, more properly, its Spanish counterpart as found in many of the 13th-century *cantigas. However, the most characteristic trait of the virelai form, the inclusion of two lines paralleling the refrain at the end of the stanza, is not found in the *zejel.* See *ReMMA,* p. 245f; H. Spanke, in *AnM* i, 13ff.

Zeunertanz [G.]. Old term for *Zigeunertanz,* i.e., gypsy dance (in H. Newsidler, *Lautenbuch,* 1536).

Zhizn za Tsarya. See *Life for the Czar, A.*

Zibaldone [It.]. Same as *quodlibet.*

Ziehharmonika [G.]. *Accordion.

Ziemlich [G.]. Rather. *Ziemlich schnell,* rather fast.

Zigeunerbaron, Der [G., The Gypsy Baron]. Operetta in three acts by J. Strauss, Jr. (libretto by I. Schnitzer after a story by M. Jókai), produced in Vienna, 1885. Setting: Austro-Hungarian Empire, mid-18th century.

Zigeunermusik [G.]. Gypsy music.

Zimbalon. *Cimbalom.

Zingarese, alla [It.]. In the style of Gypsy music.

Zink(en) [G.]. *Cornett.

Zirkelkanon [G.]. Circular canon.

Zither (1) A folk instrument used chiefly in Bavaria and Austria, consisting of a flat wooden soundbox over which 4 or 5 melody strings and as many as 37 accompaniment strings are stretched. The melody strings, nearest to the player, are stopped on a fretted fingerboard with the fingers of the left hand and are plucked by a plectrum worn on the right thumb. The accompaniment strings are plucked by the fingers of the right hand. See T. Norlind, *Geschichte der Zither* (1936); C. Maclean, in *ZIM* x. (2) A large class of stringed instruments, also called *psalteries [see Instruments IV, A, 1, a]. Also see accompanying ill. For the instruments illustrated under Zither, see the separate entries for each; also Finland (kantele); India VIII (vīṇa). (3) Old German spelling for cittern. See Guitar family.
Lit.: J. Brandlmeier, *Handbuch der Zither* (1963).

Znamenny chant. The chant of the Russian Church, as used from the 12th through 17th centuries. The name is derived from *znamia,* sign or neume. The oldest extant musical sources date from *c.* 1200 and are notated in signs very similar to those of early Byzantine notation. Later sources (11th to 17th cent.) are written in the so-called *kriuki* (or *znamenny*) notation, a system including more than ninety different signs for single notes as well as for stereotyped melodic formulas. They have not yet been deciphered. In time the number of signs was reduced and certain auxiliary symbols were added, usually in red ink (hence the name Cinnabar letters) by I. Schaidurov (16th cent.). About the same time the simple outlines of the original chant were amplified into rich and ornamented contours, the two types being distinguished as "lesser" and "greater" chant.

Beginning in the 17th century there were abuses [see Anenaiki] that finally led to the decline of the chant. See also Russia I.
Lit.: A. J. Swan, "The Znamenny Chant of the Russian Church" (*MQ* xxvi; shortened version in *PAMS* 1938); *ReMMA*, pp. 97ff (bibl. p. 435f); P. Panóff, *Die altslavische Volks- und Kirchenmusik* (in *BüHM* i); *WoHN* i, 89ff; O. von Riesemann, *Die Notationen des altrussischen Kirchengesanges* (1909); *AdHM* i, 141.

Zopf, Zopfstil [G.]. A derogatory term for the conventional style of the period when a pigtail [G. *Zopf*] was fashionable attire, particularly the latter part of the 18th century.

Zoppa, alla [It.]. Inverted dotted rhythm [see Dotted notes III]. The term *zoppa* also was used for 17th-century dance movements in syncopated rhythm, e.g., by Vitali [see Editions III, 7].

Zortziko. A Basque folk dance in quick 5/8 time and dotted rhythm. The Castilian *rueda is also in quintuple time but without dotted notes. See the examples in *LavE* i.4, 2363.

Zuffolo [It.]. General name for a primitive shepherd pipe, whistle flute, flageolet, etc.

Zug [G.]. Slide. *Zugposaune,* slide trombone, the ordinary trombone. *Zugtrompete,* slide trumpet.

Zunge [G.]. Reed. *Zungenpfeife,* reed pipe.

Zurückhalten [G.]. To hold back, *rallentando.*

Zwerchflöte. Old name for transverse flute.

Zwischendominante [G.]. Secondary dominant.

Zwischensatz [G.]. The middle section in ternary form, also used for the development section in sonata form.

Zwischenspiel [G.]. Interlude, particularly the instrumental interludes between the stanzas of a song (*ritornello*) or the *tutti* sections in a concerto. Also, name for fugal episodes [see *Durchführung*], or the episodes in rondo form.

Zwölftonsystem [G.]. Twelve-tone technique. See Serial music.

Zyklisch [G.]. *Cyclic, always in the sense explained under Cyclic (1).

Zymbel [G.]. *Cymbal.

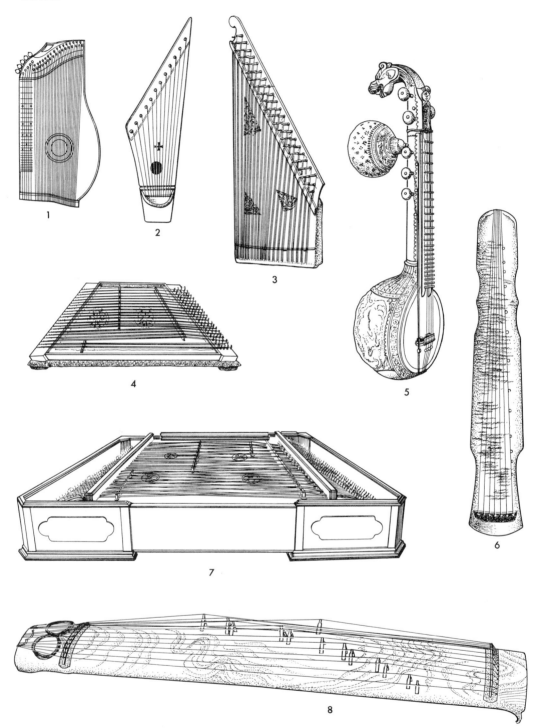

Zithers: 1. Zither. 2. Kantele. 3. Kanun. 4. Psaltery. 5. Vīṇa. 6. Chyn. 7. Cimbalom (Hungarian). 8. Koto.

Zymbelstern [G.]. A percussion stop found in many organs of the baroque period that produces a random tinkling sound of fairly high pitch. It is found in several forms, from a rotating star with bells at its points on the outside of the organ case (from which its name derives) to a pneumatically operated device inside the organ that spins suspended steel plates centrifugally against fixed bars. This device is again coming into use, although modern versions generally consist of small brass bells or telephone bells revolved electrically.   B.J.O.